AMERICAN SONG

THE COMPLETE COMPANION TO
TIN PAN ALLEY SONG

AMERICAN SONG

THE COMPLETE COMPANION TO TIN PAN ALLEY SONG

VOLUME 4: INDEXES

KEN BLOOM

Schirmer Books
an imprint of the Gale Group
New York • Detroit • San Francisco • London • Boston • Woodbridge, CT

Schirmer Books
1633 Broadway
New York, New York 10019

Gale Group
27500 Drake Road
Farmington Hills, Michigan 48331-3535

Set ISBN: 0-02-865478-1
Volume 3: 0-02-865476-5
Volume 4: 0-02-865477-3

Printed in the United States of America

Printing number
1 2 3 4 5 6 7 8 9 10

The Cataloging-in-Publication data for *American Song: The Complete Musical Theatre Companion* is reprinted below at the request of the Library of Congress. This record will be updated to incorporate volumes 3 and 4.

Library of Congress Cataloging-in-Publication Data

Bloom, Ken, 1949–
    American song: the complete musical theatre companion / Ken Bloom. — 2nd ed.
        p.   cm.
    ISBN 0-02-864573-1 (v. 1). — ISBN 0-02-864572-3 (v. 2)
    1. Musicals — United States — Bibliography. 2. Songs, English — United States — Indexes. I. Title.
ML128.M78B6 1996
782.1'4'0973 — dc20   95-49840
                                                                                CIP

This paper meets the requirements of ANSI/NISO Z39.48-1992 (Permanence of Paper).

TABLE OF CONTENTS

COLLABORATOR INDEX

Citations refer users to the songwriter(s) and year(s) of the collaboration.

A

Aarons, Alex A.   Smith, Harry B. 1901

Aarons, Alfred A.   Smith, Harry B. 1904; Smith, Robert B. 1904

Aaronson, Irving   Fain 1925; Webster 1942

Abbott, Bud   Mills 1942

Abbott, Frank   Edwards 1904; Johnson, J. Rosamond 1932, 1934; Von Tilzer 1903

Abbott, Jerry   Webster 1962

Abercrombie   Carmichael Date Unknown

Abernathy, Pat   Heyman 1943

Abicair, Shirley   Webster 1968

Abraham   Freed, Ralph 1946

Abraham, Paul   Hammerstein 1933; Parish 1929

Abrahams, Maurice   Berlin 1908, 1913; Brown, Lew 1915, 1917, 1929; Bryan 1918; Caesar 1927; Clare 1927, 1929; Clarke 1912, 1913, 1914; DeSylva 1929; Gilbert 1912; Gordon 1929; Henderson 1929; Leslie 1912, 1913, 1914, 1915, 1918; Lewis 1913, 1917, 1919, 1920, 1926, 1927, 1928; Rose 1928; Ruby 1916; Young, Joe 1913, 1915, 1917, 1919, 1920, 1927, 1928

Abreu, Zequinha   Drake 1943, 1945

Accooe, William   Smith, Harry B. 1901

Achron, Isadore   Webster 1934

Ackers, Andrew   Hoffman 1950

Ackmann, Herman   Brown, Lew 1927

Acquaviva, Nick   Harburg 1959; Sigman 1955

Actman, Irving   De Lange 1944; Loesser 1936, 1937, 1938, 1945, Date Unknown; Schwartz, Jean 1942; Styne 1940

Adair, Tom   DePaul 1953; Styne 1954

Adam, Ben   Yellen 1929

Adams, Armon   Russell 1943

Adams, Billy   Cahn 1973, 1976

Adams, Bob   Howard, Joseph E. 1908

Adams, Chick   Hoffman 1945

Adams, Ed   Waller 1924

Adams, Frank R.   Howard, Joseph E. 1904, 1905, 1906, 1907, 1908, 1909, 1910, 1915, 1940, 1942, 1946, 1947

Adams, Franklin Price   Kern 1920

Adams, India   Lawrence 1958

Adams, Stanley   Ager 1935; Alter 1956, 1958, 1959; Baer 1941, 1942, 1946; Carmichael 1935, 1936, 1937, 1939, 1940, 1945; Fain 1981; Gorney 1938; Henderson 1942; Herbert 1946; Hoffman 1932, 1934; Leslie 1942; Meyer 1941, 1947; Romberg 1943; Rose 1940; Schwartz, Arthur 1981, 1982; Stept 1933, 1944; Waller 1930, 1931; Warren 1939; Young, Victor 1955

Addinsell, Richard   David, Mack 1962; Sigman 1958

Addison, John   David, Mack 1964; Evans 1966; Livingston, Jay 1966

Addison, P.   Coslow 1920

Addy, Mickey   Johnson, Howard 1934; Sigman 1950

Adelman, Ben   Fisher 1935, 1936, 1947

Adelman, Sam   Fisher 1935, 1947

Adelson, Lenny   Duke 1963, Date Unknown; Livingston, Jerry 1959, 1960, 1961, 1962, 1963, 1970, 1973

Adelson, Peter   Livingston, Jerry 1973

Adlam, Basil G.   David, Mack 1940; Freed, Ralph 1962; Lerner, Sammy 1946; Rose 1934

Adlan, George B.   Kahn 1933

Adler, Charles   Egan 1920; Whiting 1920

Adler, Richard   Hoffman 1950; Sigman 1950

Adolfo, Antonio   Bergman 1969

Aerts, Bill   Robison 1983

Agner, Charles   Kahn 1932

Ahlert, Richard   Bryan 1950, 1961

Aide, Hamilton   Duke 1942

Aiken, S. Burrell   Whiting 1920

Akers, Howard   Blane 1957

Alan, Charles   Weill 1939

Albaniz, I.   Lawrence 1941

Albert, Carlos   McHugh 1940

Albert, Dave   Webster 1967

Albert, Harry   Caesar 1923

Albin, Jack   Razaf 1931

Albini, Felix   Atteridge 1913

Alden, John   Kahn 1921, 1924, 1927

Alden, Joseph   Egan 1925; Whiting 1925

Alekhine, V.   Rome 1943

Alexander, E.   Hoffman 1959

Alexander, Edna   Mitchell 1926

Alexander, Irene   Loewe 1935

Alexander, Jeff   Brooks 1957, 1959; David, Mack 1970; Harburg 1971

Alexander, Melville   Brown, A. Seymour 1914; Caesar 1920; Herbert 1919; Smith, Robert B. 1919

Alexander, Perry   Coots 1943

Alexander, Van   Brooks 1948; Mills 1947, 1948, 1949; Raye 1940; Ruby 1959; Spina 1957; Washington 1967

Alexandre, Josef   Dubin 1929

Alexandrov   Rome 1944

Alfred, Lou H.   Coots 1920

Alfred, Roy   Hoffman 1949, 1951, 1953; Silver 1947, 1950, 1955, 1956, 1957, 1958

Alfven, Hugo   Sigman 1954

Alguero, Augusto   Sigman 1968

Allan, Fleming   Styne 1941

Allan, John   Donaldson 1941

Allan, Lewis   Gorney 1945, 1947; Weill 1943

Allen, Barclay   Spina 1947

Allen, Bob   Kahn 1925

Allen, Bud   Johnson, James P. 1945; Waller 1927

Allen, Larry   Adams 1957

Allen, Peter   Bacharach 1981, 1982

Allen, Robert   David, Mack 1958, 1960; Freed, Ralph 1954; Gilbert 1955; Russell 1955; Sigman 1953

Allen, Steve   Burke 1958, 1959; Cahn 1958; David, Mack 1959; Ellington 1964; Heyman 1968; Leigh 1956; McHugh 1959, 1960; Russell 1958

Allen, Stuart   Mancini 1953, 1954

Allgire, Harry   Brown, Lew 1940

Allingham, William   Duke 1942

Allvine, Earl F.   Stept 1941

Almeida, Laurindo   Brooks 1955; Brown, Lew 1940; Mercer 1953, 1964, 1982

Aloma, Hal   Bryan 1945

Alper, Al   Fisher 1938

Alpert, Harry   DeSylva 1925

Alpert, Herb   Bergman 1971

Alpert, Mickey   Adamson 1939; Coots 1950, 1951, 1952, 1953, 1954; Davis 1937; De Lange 1933; Lawrence 1939

Alpert, Milton I.   Coots 1951; Egan 1951

Alstone, Alex   David, Hal 1950; David, Mack 1951, 1956; Dietz 1956; Drake 1946, 1947, 1950; Gorney 1948; Heyman 1964, 1965; Hoffman 1951, 1952, 1953; Lawrence 1945; Leigh 1955; Livingston, Jerry 1951; Parish 1954; Robison 1950, 1952, 1953; Rome 1952; Sigman 1953

Altemus, Jim   Parish 1930

Altizer, Laura   Howard, Joseph E. 1937, 1942

Altman, Arthur   Ager 1935, 1936; David, Hal 1947, 1948, 1949, 1950, 1951, 1952, 1958; David, Mack 1935, 1946; Freed, Ralph 1941, 1944; Hoffman 1940, 1941, 1944; Lawrence 1930, 1931, 1932, 1933, 1934, 1935, 1939, 1940, 1941; Loesser 1938; Young, Joe 1934, 1935

Aluli, I.F.   Hoffman 1957

Alves, Lucie   Hoffman 1955

Alvis, Hayes   Ellington 1940; Mills 1940

Alwood, Lester R.   Whiting 1918

Amaral, Nestor   Mercer 1953, 1982

Ames, Elliston   Kahn 1924

Amfitheatrof, Daniele   Brooks 1948; David, Mack 1956, 1957; Evans 1958; Livingston, Jay 1958; Washington 1965

Amsterdam, Morey   Davis 1950; Silver 1950

Andersen, Fritz   Freed, Ralph 1947

Anderson, Arthur   Akst 1918; Atteridge 1912

Anderson, Cat   Ellington 1968; Mills 1966

Anderson, Grace Burke   Adams 1957, 1958

Anderson, John Murray   Ager 1920, 1930; Caesar 1922, 1923, 1924, 1925; Conrad 1923; Gershwin, George 1923; Gorney 1924; Yellen 1920, 1930

Anderson, Leroy   Parish 1950, 1951, 1952, 1954

Anderson, Maxwell   Schwartz, Arthur 1955; Weill 1938, 1940, 1949, 1950; Wrubel 1959

Anderson, Milton H.   Webster 1967

Anderson, R.A.   Hoffman 1957

Andino, J.E.   Yellen 1922

Andree, F.   Kahn 1930

Andrieu, Harry   Sterling 1918

Angeleri, Luciano   Drake 1980

Anka, Paul   Bacharach 1979, 1980; Bergman 1979; Cahn 1973, 1975, 1977, 1978, 1979; David, Hal 1978

Anson, Bill   Livingston, Jerry 1954

Anthony, J.R.   Coots 1921

Anthony, Michael   Parish 1950

Anthony, Ron   Cahn 1968, 1969

Antonini, Alfredo   Drake 1951; Parish 1958

Antonio, Luis   Webster 1962

Apelman, Martin   Von Tilzer 1953

Applebaum, Cecelia   Leigh 1979

Applebaum, Stanley   Cahn 1968; Stept 1957, 1958

Arbelo, Fernando   Razaf 1936

Archer, Harry   Caesar 1929; Eliscu 1930; Gilbert 1926; Hanley 1929; Johnson, Howard 1922, 1924; Kahn 1930; Mercer 1933

Arcilla, J.B.   Drake 1949

Arenstein, I.B.   Gilbert 1931

Arias, Clotilde   Ahlert 1947; Leslie 1947

Arlen, Jerry   Van Heusen 1933, 1934, 1936

Armand, George   Hoffman 1959, 1960

Armenthout, Lee   Leslie 1944

Armstrong, George   Von Tilzer 1909

Armstrong, Harry   Bryan 1903, 1933; Kahn 1930; Sterling 1900

Armstrong, Lil   Raye 1939

Armstrong, Louis   Johnson, Howard 1940; Raye 1950; Razaf 1940; Robison 1940

Arnaud, Leo   Blane 1969

Arnaz, Desi   Brooks 1946; Russell 1946

Arnaz, Lucie   Coleman 1986

Arneim, Gus   Rose 1924

Arnesson, Trgvye   Lawrence 1953

Arnheim, Gus   Freed, Arthur 1922, 1939; Freed, Ralph 1931; Kahn 1924, 1932; Turk 1925

Arnold, Buddy   Davis 1950; Silver 1947, 1950; Young, Victor 1956, 1957

Arnold, Gene   Clare 1930; DeSylva 1922; Kahn 1931; Williams 1931

Arnold, Malcolm   David, Mack 1964, 1967

Arnold, Murray   Bullock 1947; Myrow 1956; Spina 1947, 1952, 1970

Arodin, Sidney   Carmichael 1931

Arthur, Art   Loesser 1942

Arthur, Bob   Hoffman 1950

Arthur, Jack   Coots 1952

Arthur, Robert   Cahn 1963

Arthurs, George   Kern 1911

Artzt, Billy   Cahn 1945; Styne 1945

Ash, Paul   Ager 1928; Akst 1927; Davis 1926, 1927; Donaldson 1926, 1927; Mills 1924; Yellen 1928

Ash, Sam   Brennan 1920

Ashe, Thomas   Duke 1942

Asher, W.   Razaf 1925

Asherman, Edward   Freed, Ralph 1952; Hoffman 1952, 1953, 1955

Ashton, Harry J.   Fisher 1913

Asso, Raymond   Rome 1950

Astaire, Fred   Mercer 1935, 1959; Parish 1930; Webster 1936

Atteberry, Duke   Coslow 1937

Attie, Paulette   Strouse 1976

Auerbach, Gustav   Coslow 1956

August, Jan   Sigman 1951

Auric, Georges   Parish 1959; Sigman 1956

Austin, Ernie   Drake 1944

Austin, Gene   Coslow 1926, 1934; Johnson, James P. 1935; Johnston 1934; Koehler 1927; McHugh 1924; Mills 1924; Rose 1928

Autrey, Herman   Waller 1945

Autry, Gene   Lawrence 1937; Styne 1941, 1944

Avola, Al   David, Hal 1951; David, Mack 1946; Hoffman 1951

Axe, Ronald   Gorney 1960

Axelrod, Herman A.   Hammerstein 1917

Axt, William   Bryan 1927; Dietz 1928; Kahn 1933, 1934, 1937
Ayer, Nat D.   Brown, A. Seymour 1909, 1910, 1911, 1912, Date Unknown; Brown, Lew 1913, 1914; Williams 1911
Ayers, Bob   Drake 1945
Ayers, Lita   Drake 1945
Ayres, Mitchell   David, Mack 1948
Aysay, Sally   Young, Victor 1952
Azevedo, Waldyr   Lawrence 1952
Aznavour, Charles   Sigman 1958, 1975

B

Bacal, Harvey   Caesar 1948
Bacalov, Luis   Cahn 1973
Bach, J.S.   Cahn 1947; Styne 1947
Bach, Johann Sebastian   Johnson, Howard 1939
Back, Will   Carroll 1950
Backy-Dello   Sigman 1968
Badale, Andy   Cahn 1968
Badtke, Hill   Sigman 1949
Baer, Bugs   Gilbert 1926
Baer, Charles E.   Whiting 1914
Bagar, Robert   Baer 1931; David, Mack 1934; Mills 1935
Bagley, E.E.   Freed, Ralph 1944
Bagoslavsky, N.   David, Hal 1946
Bailey, Bob   Brooks 1967
Bailey, Buster   Mills 1935, 1938
Bailey, Mildred   Razaf 1935
Bailey & Barnum   Razaf 1926
Bainbridge, K.   Friml 1950
Bairnsfather, Bruce   Baer 1926
Bakaldy, L.   Rome 1943
Baker, Buddy   Evans 1976; Livingston, Jay 1976
Baker, H.   Styne 1954
Baker, Paul   Heyman 1940
Baker, Phil   Atteridge 1929; Brown, Lew 1927; DeSylva 1927; Kahn 1923; Mitchell 1921
Baker, Polly   Carroll 1945, 1948, 1950
Balaban, Cherry   Drake 1943; Russell 1948
Balanchine, George   Schwartz, Arthur 1982
Balinar, A.   Drake 1943
Ball, Ernest R.   Brennan 1914, 1915, 1916, 1917, 1918, 1919, 1920, 1921, 1922, 1923, 1926, 1927; Dubin 1917, 1919, 1920; Johnson, Howard 1927; Olcott 1910, 1911, 1913, 1920; Silver 1923
Ball, Guy   Lawrence 1940
Ballard, Bob   Adamson 1963; David, Mack 1970
Ballard, Francis Drake   Hanley 1939; Johnson, Howard 1928
Ballard, Pat   Hanley 1938, 1939; Martin 1948; Meyer 1948
Ballentine, Eddie   Hoffman 1955
Bambridge, Bill   Robin 1931
Banker, Lester   Webster 1933; Young, Joe 1931
Bankhart, George   Dubin 1913
Banta, Frank C.   Mitchell 1919
Barberis, Alberto   Raye 1956
Barbosa, Harold   Hoffman 1955
Barbour, William R.   Young, Victor 1924
Barcelata, Lorenzo   Russell 1941
Barclay, Eddie   Leigh 1956
Bard, Ben   Coslow 1930; Snyder 1918
Barer, Marshall   Carmichael 1957; Duke Date Unknown; Ellington 1961, 1965, 1966; Lane Date Unknown; Martin 1962
Baretz, Phyllis   Stept 1955
Barker, Ambrose   Koehler 1942

Barker, Danny   Raye 1953
Barker, Warren   Raye 1958
Barlow, Harold   Yellen 1950, 1951, 1977
Barnes, Charles   Revel 1955
Barnes, Paul   Cobb 1906
Barnes, Wade   Blane 1961
Barnet, Charlie   Mills 1939; Parish 1938; Robison 1944, 1954; Van Heusen 1938
Barnett   Gilbert 1921
Barnett, Benjamin F.   Snyder 1909
Barnett, Jackie   Akst 1952; Davis 1952; Fain 1947, 1949, 1950, 1951, 1955, 1956, 1957, 1961, 1963, 1964, 1965
Barnett, Lillian   Friml 1945
Baro, Pete   David, Mack 1941
Baron, Paul   David, Mack 1946, 1955; Davis 1951; Mills 1940; Wrubel 1948
Baron, William Le   Herbert 1917
Barone, Anthony Dominic   Young, Joe 1943
Barouh, Pierre   Sigman 1967
Barozi, Tibor   Lewis 1936
Barr, Ray   Webster 1965
Barr, T.   Russell 1957
Barratt, Augustus   Atteridge 1918; Romberg 1916, 1918
Barrett, Hughie   Parish 1932; Van Heusen 1938
Barrie, George   Cahn 1971, 1972, 1975, 1976, 1977, 1978, 1982
Barris, Harry   Davis 1932; Freed, Arthur 1932, 1935; Freed, Ralph 1931, 1934; Johnson, Howard 1928, 1934; Koehler 1931; Loesser 1941; Mills 1925
Barron, Bernard   Edwards 1918
Barron, Malcolm   Heyman 1978
Barron, Ted B.   Jerome 1924
Barrosa, Paulo   Drake 1948
Barroso, Ary   Drake 1943, 1944; Russell 1941; Washington 1944, 1953
Barrows, Charlie   Friend 1948
Barrows, Marjorie   Carmichael 1957
Barry, Bill   Ager 1935; Pollack 1956
Barry, Billy   Spina 1932
Barry, John   Bergman 1986; David, Hal 1969, 1970, 1978; David, Mack 1966; Lawrence 1968; Leigh 1968; Lerner, Alan Jay 1971
Barry, Pat   Bryan 1927
Barry, Peter   Duke 1942
Bart, Teddy   Heyman 1965, 1966
Bartholomae, Philip   Atteridge 1917; Romberg 1917
Bartlett, Dean   Ellington 1966
Bartlett, Edith G.   Kahn 1917
Bartlett, Rev. D.J.   Ellington 1965
Barton, Ben   Razaf 1942
Barzizza, Pippo   Lawrence 1954
Barzman, Sol   Styne 1936
Basie, Count   David, Mack 1938; Johnson, James P. Date Unknown; Livingston, Jerry 1938; Razaf Date Unknown; Russell 1945
Baskette, Billy   Blake 1947; Clarke 1919; Davis 1917; Fisher 1919; Johnson, Howard 1918, 1921; Pollack 1919; Rose 1924
Bass, Sid   David, Hal 1946; Raye 1938
Bassman, George   Blane 1945, 1946; Davis 1955; Loesser 1951; Sigman 1949; Washington 1932; Young, Joe 1934
Bataille, Henri   Coslow 1926; Lewis 1928; Young, Joe 1928
Bates, Bert   Davis 1930
Bates, Charles   Ager 1924; Mercer 1935; Rose 1928; Yellen 1924

Battle, Edgar   Myrow 1942; Sissle 1945, 1946
Bauer, Fredy   Rome 1949
Bauer, Rolf   David, Hal 1960
Baum, Bernie   Hoffman 1948
Baum, Claude   Livingston, Jerry 1957
Baumgart, Gil P.   Mills 1946, 1947
Baxter, Les   David, Mack 1954; Heyman 1951; Koehler 1955; Merrill 1968; Russell 1956; Washington 1965
Baxter, Phil   Friend 1932; Kahn 1932; Rose 1934; Young, Joe 1932
Bayer Sager, Carole   Mancini 1979
Bayes, Nora   Akst 1918; Atteridge 1915; Norworth 1908, 1909, 1910, 1911, 1912, 1917; Smith, Harry B. 1911
Bayha, Charles A.   Carroll 1919; Gilbert 1920; Meyer 1914; Razaf 1936
Bayley, T.H.   Evans 1946; Livingston, Jay 1946
Beach, Bonnie   Adamson 1939
Beal, Charlie   Razaf 1937
Beal, Joe   Hoffman 1959, 1962
Beamish, Richard J.   Herbert 1918
Bean, Carl   David, Hal 1940
Beaty, Ivan   Arlen 1927
Beaumont, Charles   Merrill 1962
Becaud, Gilbert   David, Mack 1966; Lawrence 1955; Sigman 1958, 1962
Bechet, Sidney   Mills 1924; Sissle 1934
Beck, Edward   Davis 1919; Kahn 1917
Beck, Morty   Parish 1947
Beda   Caesar 1931
Beer, Morris Abel   Lane 1929
Beethoven, Ludwig   Caesar 1923; Loesser 1940; Mercer 1939; Sigman 1946
Behim, Arthur E.   Howard, Joseph E. 1919; Ruby 1919; Sterling 1910
Behl, Walter R.   Burke 1939
Behn, Harry   Coslow 1936
Behrens, Herman   Fisher 1941, 1942
Behrke, Dick   Cahn 1981
Beiderbecke, Bix   Carmichael 1962; Webster 1962
Belcher, Fred E.   Berlin 1910
Belden, Al   Stept 1917
Belidre, Johnny   Coots 1963
Bell, Aaron   Ellington 1962
Bell, L.M.   Edwards 1920
Belle, Barbara   David, Mack 1947
Belledna, Alex   Gilbert 1919
Belles, Hal   Kahal 1940
Bellin, Lewis Paul   Ager 1937; Evans 1944, 1945; Koehler 1950, 1951, 1952; Livingston, Jay 1944, 1945; Parish 1936; Silver 1948
Bellson, Louis   Stept 1957, 1958
Benatzky, Ralph   Brennan 1925; Caesar 1936; Smith, Harry B. 1923
Bender, Milton G.   Rodgers 1920
Benedict, J.   Johnson, Howard 1939
Benes, Jara   Caesar 1936; Robin 1931
Benet, Stephen Vincent   Mercer 1966; Strouse 1950
Benjamin, Herbert   Schwartz, Arthur 1922
Bennett, Emerson Dunlap   Bryan 1951
Bennett, George   Coots 1924; Sterling 1927; Warren 1925
Bennett, George J.   Carroll 1934
Bennett, Jack   Bullock 1935; Robison 1952; Whiting 1935
Bennett, Joe   Kahn 1931
Bennett, Leo   Lewis 1910, 1911, 1912
Bennett, Peter   Parish 1957

Bennett, Richard Rodney   Webster 1967, 1971
Bennett, Robert Russell   Gershwin, Ira 1924; Kern 1937
Bennett, Rube   Kahn 1923
Bennett, Tony   Ellington 1968
Benson, Aba   Fisher 1936
Benson, Ellsworth   Washington 1949
Benson, Jerry   Howard, Joseph E. 1921; Johnson, Howard 1927; McHugh 1922; Sterling 1918
Benson, John Brooks   Russell 1948
Benson, Sally   Blane 1945, 1966
Berbinger   Coslow 1924
Berchman, Henri   Bryan 1927, 1928
Berens, Norman   Brooks 1941, 1942, 1943, 1945
Bereny, Henry   Smith, Harry B. 1912; Smith, Robert B. 1912
Berg, Harold   Coslow 1924
Berg, Jimmy   Loesser 1941
Berg, S.M.   Johnson, Howard 1929
Bergen, Edgar   Kalmar 1937; Ruby 1937
Berger, August   Friml Date Unknown
Bergere, Roy   Dubin 1927
Bergersen, Baldwin   David, Mack 1945
Bergh, Arthur   Webster 1939, 1940
Bergman, Dewey   Bryan 1945; David, Mack 1945; Robison 1963; Silver 1947
Bergman, Olle   Sigman 1957
Beringer   Smith, Harry B. 1925
Berkman, Ted   Fisher 1943
Berle, Milton   Ager 1947, Date Unknown; Cahn 1940, 1949; Coots 1934; Davis 1950; Drake 1944; Gordon 1955; Hoffman 1943, 1958; Livingston, Jerry 1939, 1943; Magidson 1947; Mills 1938; Oakland 1940, 1947; Silver 1948, 1950; Stept 1953; Young, Victor 1956, 1957
Berman, Al   Whiting 1926
Berman, Arthur   David, Hal 1953, 1954
Berman, Dorothy   Henderson 1939
Berman, Irving   Drake 1948
Berman, Sidney   Hoffman 1953; Silver 1951, 1953
Bern, Roger   Lawrence 1945
Bernard, Al   Lerner, Sammy 1931; McHugh 1923; Stept 1925, 1926, 1927; Turk 1923; Woods 1923
Bernard, Billy   Henderson 1922
Bernard, Donald   Young, Victor 1929
Bernard, Felix   Bryan 1936, 1937; Coslow 1945; De Lange 1940; Fisher 1919; Gilbert 1935, 1936; Hoffman 1931; Kalmar 1945; Magidson 1930, 1931; Washington 1941; Webster 1933, 1936
Bernard, Fred   McHugh 1953
Bernard, Helen   David, Mack 1933
Bernard, Hollan   De Lange 1935
Bernard, Mike   Edwards 1903; Snyder 1911
Bernardi, Noni   David, Mack 1940
Bernhole, Michel   Sigman 1971
Bernie, Ben   Bullock 1934; Kahn 1931, 1932
Bernie, Dave   Clare 1954; Mills 1927
Bernie, Saul   Conrad 1925, 1926, 1928; Coslow 1925, 1927, 1928; Gilbert 1926; Johnson, James P. 1929; Silver 1924
Bernier, Buddy   Loesser 1935; Motzan 1935; Sigman 1940; Weill 1939; Young, Victor 1953
Bernstein, Elmer   Bergman 1976; Brooks 1952, 1955, 1957; Cahn 1958, 1961; David, Mack 1958, 1962, 1963, 1964, 1966; Leigh 1965, 1967; Mercer 1964; Webster 1961
Bernstein, Leonard   Comden and Green 1944, 1953, 1964, 1968; Lerner, Alan Jay 1976; Sondheim 1957, 1968, 1974
Berquist, Richard   Kahn 1931
Berry, Bert   Mills 1929

Berry, Leon   Razaf 1936
Bert, Max   Rome 1951
Berte, Emil   Brennan 1929
Bertino, Michael   Bullock 1952
Berton   Kern 1918
Berton, Eugene   Eliscu 1928
Bertram, Rudolph   Rose 1937
Besche, C.F.   Johnson, Howard 1920; Yellen 1920
Bessinger, Frank   Gilbert 1925; Lewis 1925; Young, Joe 1925
Besso, Claude   Hoffman 1950
Bestor, Don   Kahn 1924; Young, Joe 1932
Bestor, John   Young, Joe 1932
Bethel, B.   Russell 1957, 1958
Betti, Henri   Parish 1951; Rome 1949
Betts, Tony   Lewis 1962
Betzner, Jack   Mills 1941
Beverly, Sam   Kahn 1921
Bibo, Irving   Akst 1920; Baer 1922; Brennan 1940; Clare
   1946, 1947, 1950; Conrad 1923, 1924; Coslow 1925;
   Edwards 1925; Johnson, Howard 1921, 1923, 1924, 1925,
   1926, 1927, 1929; Motzan 1920, 1924; Pollack 1927;
   Robin 1926; Rose 1921; Snyder 1940, 1956
Biddu   Cahn 1980
Bidoli, Bruno   Rome 1951
Bierman, Emil   Kahal 1927
Biese, Paul   Kahn 1920, 1921
Bigard, Barney   Ellington 1931, 1937; Mills 1930, 1931, 1937;
   Parish 1931
Bigelow, F.E.   Freed, Ralph 1944; Leslie 1943; Yellen 1917
Bigelow, Robert   Ager 1924; Yellen 1924
Bilder, Robert   Young, Joe 1935
Billington, Moe   Blane 1969
Binder, A.W.   Brooks 1959
Bindi, Umberto   David, Hal 1960
Bingham, Bing   Davis 1974
Bingham, Julia W.   Carmichael 1945, 1952
Biondi, Remo   Loesser 1939
Bird, Bill   Howard, Joseph E. 1938
Bird, S.   Howard, Joseph E. 1942
Birken, William J.   Sterling 1923
Birkenhead, Susan   Strouse 1999; Styne 1982, 1984, 1985
Birnbrier, Ed   Coleman 1964, 1966
Bishop, Joe   Adamson 1939; Raye 1940
Bishop, Walter   Johnson, James P. 1945; Parish 1936; Styne
   1949
Bissett, Ann   Styne 1969
Bivens, Burke   Kahn 1937; Parish 1938; Sterling 1927
Bizet, Georges   Berlin 1929; Hammerstein 1943
Blaauw, Pierre   Revel 1929
Black, Ben   Kahn 1927
Black, Don   Mancini 1968, 1973, 1976; Strouse 1987, 1990;
   Styne 1978
Black, Florence   Friend 1963
Black, Frank J.   Robison 1930; Young, Joe 1932
Black, Freddie   Sigman 1940
Black, John W.   Gorney 1961
Black, Johnny   Fisher 1919, 1920; Johnson, Howard 1920
Blackman, Elaine   Blake 1946; Merrill 1946
Blackman, Leona   Blake 1958; Merrill 1946
Blade, James   Heyman 1938; Lawrence 1940
Blaha, Vaclav   Parish 1948
Blake, Bebe   David, Mack 1954; Fain 1957; Young, Victor
   1953, 1954
Blake, James   Berlin 1924
Blake, William   Strouse 1962

Blalock, Edwin   Raye 1956
Blanco, Julio   Rome 1945
Blanke-Belcher, Henrietta   Berlin 1910; Bryan 1908, 1910,
   1911, 1912
Blanter, M.   Rome 1943
Blaufus, David   Washington 1933
Blaufuss, Walter   Donaldson 1926; Kahn 1918, 1919, 1920,
   1921, 1923, 1926, 1927
Bleyer, Archie   Lawrence 1946; Mercer 1932, 1933
Blitzstein, Marc   Weill 1954
Bloch, John   Gorney 1962
Bloch, Philippe   Lawrence 1956
Bloch, Ray   Davis 1965; Friend 1936
Blondy, Claude   Sigman 1963
Bloom, Marty   Koehler 1921, 1927; Leslie 1926; Motzan
   1924, 1925; Rose 1924, 1925
Bloom, Mickey   Parish 1933; Young, Joe 1934
Bloom, Murray   Kahn 1923, 1924; Leslie 1912, 1913
Bloom, Phillip   Lawrence 1956
Blossom, Henry   Atteridge 1918; Herbert 1905, 1906, 1908,
   1914, 1915, 1916, 1917, 1919; Romberg 1918
Blue, Ralph   Hoffman 1933
Bluett, Treva   Donaldson 1938
Blum, Bob   David, Mack 1946
Blum, Celia   Kahn 1920
Blum, Harry   Cahn 1962
Blyer, Archie   Mercer 1932
Blyler, James   Clare 1921; Conrad 1921; Friend 1921
Blythe, Harry   Bryan 1928
Boasberg, Al   Davis 1933; Fain 1933; Fisher 1929; Meyer
   1930; Mitchell 1930
Bochmann, Werner   Young, Joe 1932
Bock, W.E.   Smith, Harry B. 1903
Bogle, Robert L.   Johnson, Howard 1960
Bohm, Carl   Johnson, Howard 1939
Bohr, Jose   Woods 1929
Boland, Clay   Davis 1957; De Lange 1942, 1943, 1945, 1949
Boland, Myrtle   Jerome 1924
Boling, Van   Stept 1943
Bolon, Joe   David, Hal 1947
Bolton, Guy   Hanley 1932; Schwartz, Jean 1919
Bolton, Ralph W.   Mercer 1931, 1932
Bonds, Margaret   Razaf 1939, 1941
Bonfa, Luiz   Mercer 1969; Sigman 1966, 1967, 1968
Boni, J.   Strouse 1975
Bonino, Ernest   Parish 1954
Bonx, Nat   Brown, Lew 1925
Booker, Arthur   Mills 1924
Booking, Thomas   Coots 1951
Borel-Clerc, Charles   Cahn 1937; Lawrence 1949
Borganoff, Igor   Harburg 1932
Bories, Merton   Johnson, James P. 1921, 1922
Borlini, Jeanne   Brown, Nacio Herb 1932
Borne, Hal   Cahn 1955, 1956, 1957, 1967; Coslow 1942,
   1952; Mercer 1940, 1956; Washington 1951; Webster
   1941, 1942, 1949, 1952, 1955, 1961, 1963
Bornkessell, Jack   Parish 1932
Borodin, A.   Atteridge 1913
Borreli, Bea   Silver 1955
Borrelli, Charles   Leslie 1925
Borzage, Don   Mercer 1958, 1961, 1964; Robin 1964;
   Webster 1966
Bosford, George   Kahn 1932
Bossone, Frank   Johnson, James P. 1954
Bostic, Earl   Mills 1943

Boswell, Connie   Lawrence 1957

Botkin Jr., Perry   Webster 1972

Botsford, George   Berlin 1910; Brown, A. Seymour 1912;
    Friend 1924; Gordon 1943

Botts, Walter   Robison 1948

Bouchard, Pauline   Coslow 1940

Bourdillon, F.W.   Duke 1942

Bouret, Grace   Blake 1950, 1954

Bourne, Carol   Gordon 1929

Bourne, Charles   Kahn 1955

Bourne, Val   Young, Joe 1932

Bousquet, Louis   Bryan 1918

Boutelje, Phil   Coslow 1938; Dubin 1927, 1928; Evans 1947;
    Herbert 1940; Kahn 1923; Livingston, Jay 1947; Loesser
    1939, 1940, 1941; Snyder 1952, 1953, 1954; Washington
    1938; Weill 1938; Yellen 1926; Young, Joe 1938; Young,
    Victor 1938, 1947

Boutsis, Thomas   Brown, Lew 1943

Bovet, Joseph   Rome 1951

Bovill, C.H.   Kern 1908

Bowen, John   Raye 1959

Bowers, Frederick V.   Jerome 1900; Mills 1926

Bowers, Robert Hood   Smith, Harry B. 1909, 1910, 1911;
    Smith, Robert B. 1910, 1911, 1912, 1919

Bowman, Charles   Parish 1925

Bowman, Elmer   Von Tilzer 1911

Bowman, Euday L.   Razaf 1914, 1942

Boyd, Elisse   Gorney 1964

Boyd, William   Brown, Nacio Herb 1951

Boyer, Elda A.   Mitchell 1919

Boyer, Jean   Conrad 1926

Boynton, Jean   Young, Joe 1911

Brachman, James   Sterling 1903

Braddock, Bobby   David, Hal 1976

Bradford, Perry   Blake 1960; Dubin 1929; Johnson, J.
    Rosamond 1929; Johnson, James P. 1927, 1928, 1929,
    1930; Sissle 1960; Yellen 1917

Bradley   Koehler 1923

Bradley, Grace   Burke 1932

Bradley, Will   Sigman 1940, 1941

Bradtke, Hans   Drake 1963; Mercer 1965; Sigman 1961

Braggiotti, Mario   Harburg 1930

Brahms, Johannes   Bergman 1978; Evans 1951; Leslie 1947;
    Livingston, Jay 1951; Loesser 1940

Brailowski, Jack   Caesar 1947

Braley   Kern 1918

Brandt, Augusto   Bryan 1935

Brandt, Eddie   Dietz 1930

Brandwynne, Nat   Caesar 1944; Heyman 1937

Bransen, W.   Lerner, Sammy 1931

Brant, Ira   David, Hal 1952

Brasa, G.   Johnson, Howard 1935

Braschoss, Pete   Meyer 1948

Bratton, John W.   Cahn 1940; Edwards 1905; Jerome 1900;
    Smith, Harry B. 1901; Von Tilzer 1901

Bratton, Jown W.   Brown, A. Seymour 1909

Bravard, Raymond   Duke 1955

Brean, Denis   David, Hal 1947; David, Mack 1947

Breau, Louis   Caesar 1925, 1938; Henderson 1920, 1921,
    1922, 1938; Yellen 1922

Brecht, Bertolt   Weill 1944

Breen, Harry   Fisher 1910; Howard, Joseph E. 1915

Breen, Jerry   Howard, Joseph E. 1915

Breen, May Singhi   Robison 1934

Bregman, Buddy   Bergman 1956; Young, Joe 1962

Brejean, Philippe   Sigman 1974

Brennan, Ed   Mills 1939

Brennan, James A.   Jerome 1924, 1927

Brent, Earl   Blane 1945; Brown, Nacio Herb 1945, 1948;
    Cahn 1950, 1951, 1953; Freed, Arthur 1946; Freed, Ralph
    1942; Harburg 1943; Kahn 1939, 1940; Leigh 1952;
    Warren 1946

Bresler, Jerry   Lawrence 1959

Breslow, Lou   Akst 1938

Breton, Raoul   Rome 1945

Brett, Lola   Motzan 1918

Bretton, Elise   Cahn 1967

Breuder, M. Edward   Johnson, Howard 1936

Breuer, Ernest   Bryan 1917, 1918; Clare 1924; Dixon 1923;
    Fisher 1939; Henderson 1923; Lewis 1921; Loesser 1934;
    Rose 1923, 1924; Young, Joe 1921

Brewer   Styne 1927

Brewer, Ted   Livingston, Jerry 1932

Brewster, Jimmy   Robison 1952; Stept 1952

Brice, Elizabeth   Goetz 1910

Brice, Monty C.   Ager 1942; Donaldson 1917, 1918; Fisher
    1918

Bricusse, Leslie   Mancini 1967, 1978, 1982, 1986, 1993, 1995;
    Styne 1970, Date Unknown

Bridges, Ethel   Johnson, Howard 1920; Kahn 1925

Bridgewater, Leslie   Russell 1961

Brier, E.   Parish 1957

Briers, Larry   Caesar 1920

Bright, Ronnell   Mercer 1966; Webster 1966

Brilant, Arthur   Smith, Harry B. 1923; Snyder 1923

Brill, Leighton K.   Alter 1930

Bristow, Owen   Clare 1953; Young, Victor 1953

Brito, Alfredo   Mercer 1934

Brito, Julio   Adamson 1940

Brito, Phil   Hoffman 1950

Brito, Rubens   Lewis 1941

Britt, Addy   Ahlert 1926; Berlin 1926; Bryan 1926; Coslow
    1926; Fain 1927; Johnson, Howard 1934; Kahal 1927;
    Rose 1927; Schwartz, Jean 1931; Stept 1924; Turk 1922,
    1923, 1924

Brockman, David   Lawrence 1956; Parish 1928

Brockman, James   Baer 1925; Bryan 1918; Edwards 1929;
    Gilbert 1924; Hanley 1929, 1930; Johnson, Howard 1920;
    Leslie 1927; Monaco 1930; Rose 1924; Snyder 1930,
    1931; Williams 1912

Brodsky, Roy   Mills 1950

Brodsky, Vera   Bryan 1936

Brodszky, Nicholas   Cahn 1950, 1951, 1952, 1953, 1954,
    1955, 1956, 1957, 1958; Lawrence 1954; Robin 1952,
    1953; Webster 1952, 1957

Broner, Irwin   Caesar 1955

Brooke, Rupert   Kern 1956

Brooks, Al   Fisher 1937

Brooks, Dudley   Cahn 1944; Clare 1953; Styne 1944

Brooks, Elodie   Motzan 1922

Brooks, Gene   Gordon 1958; Young, Joe 1958

Brooks, Harry   Mitchell 1921; Razaf 1929, 1930, 1936; Sissle
    1939; Waller 1929; Young, Joe 1930

Brooks, Helen Hughes   De Lange 1943

Brooks, John Benson   David, Mack 1946; De Lange 1941,
    1942, 1943, 1946; Lawrence 1947; Russell 1947, 1948,
    1954

Brooks, Marty   Fisher 1930

Brooks, Ruth   Ahlert 1924; Lewis 1924; Young, Joe 1924

Brooks, Shelton   Clarke 1919; Johnson, Howard 1917; Lewis 1923; Young, Joe 1923

Broones, Martin   Egan 1932, 1952; Fisher 1929; Freed, Arthur 1930, 1931; Warren 1926, 1927; Webster 1950, 1951, 1952, 1954, 1958, 1964

Brothers, Bowman   Snyder 1906

Broufin, Ren   Fisher 1923

Broughton, Philip   Merrill 1951

Brower, Charles S.   Razaf 1946

Brown, Al W.   Atteridge 1913; Kahn 1918, 1921; Schwartz, Jean 1913; Sterling 1918; Yellen 1923

Brown, Albert W.   Atteridge 1913

Brown, Eddy   Smith, Harry B. 1920

Brown, Forman   Friml 1950; Weill 1944

Brown, George R.   Brown, Lew 1943; Bullock 1940; Eliscu 1929, 1930; Ellington 1962; Fisher 1940; Freed, Ralph 1943; Friend 1932; Hoffman 1928, 1930; Loesser 1941; Mills 1962; Pollack 1948; Styne 1940, 1941, 1942, 1943, 1947, 1948; Von Tilzer 1952; Waller 1932; Woods 1932, 1950; Young, Joe 1932; Young, Victor 1932

Brown, George Walter   Bryan 1909, 1911

Brown, Georgia Lane   Johnson, Howard 1917

Brown, Jack   Revel 1959, 1962

Brown, K.B.   Martin 1959

Brown, Les   Mercer 1966

Brown, Louis Yule   Cahn 1954, 1956

Brown, Michael   Arlen 1954

Brown, Nacio Jan   Brown, Nacio Herb 1961

Brown, Nacio Porter   Brown, Nacio Herb 1957; Leigh 1952

Brown, Ted S.   Lewis 1906

Brown, Tom   Fisher 1920

Brown, Trego   Gorney 1966

Browne, R.A.   Edwards 1906

Browne, Sam   Stept 1953

Browning, Robert   Hanley 1932

Bruce, Gary   Cahn 1962, 1967, 1968, 1973, 1976; Hoffman 1944; Van Heusen 1959

Bruce, James   Young, Joe 1947

Bruce, Mary R.   David, Mack 1953

Brucker, B.   Bryan 1913

Bryan, Frederick   Leslie 1912

Bryan, Vincent   Berlin 1911; Carroll 1912; Cobb 1906; Edwards 1904, 1905, 1906, 1908, 1929, 1930, 1931; Goetz 1907, 1911; Herbert 1908, 1944; Howard, Joseph E. 1909, 1910; Johnson, Howard 1914; Schwartz, Jean 1911; Smith, Harry B. 1906; Snyder 1909, 1911; Sterling 1902, 1907; Von Tilzer 1901, 1902, 1906, 1907, 1908, 1909, 1910, 1911, 1913, 1914, 1915, 1917, 1918, 1919, 1937

Bryant, Willie   Raye 1936; Van Heusen 1938

Bryer, Lloyd   DeSylva 1953

Brymn, Tim   Gilbert 1921

Buchanan, Donald   Coots 1919

Buchanan, William V.   Friend 1958

Buchholz, Heinz   Drake 1963

Buck, Ram   Brown, Lew 1945

Buck, Ronald   Mitchell 1941

Buckbinder, W.   Hoffman 1957

Budd, Roy   Cahn 1975

Buddie, Bill   Kahn 1939

Buffano, Jules   Akst 1952; Davis 1952; Lewis 1924; Young, Joe 1924

Buffington, Joseph   Herbert 1944

Bulhoes, Max   Drake 1947

Bunch, Boyd   David, Mack 1937; Freed, Ralph 1934; Friend 1935, 1936; Heyman 1932, 1933; Livingston, Jerry 1936; Young, Joe 1932, 1935

Bundy, Eve   Friml 1953

Burbelo, F.   Adamson 1940

Burckhardt, John F.   Sterling 1927

Burdette, Robert   Loesser 1940

Burge, John H.   Johnson, Howard 1938

Burgess, F.A.   Brown, Lew 1924

Burgess, Kendall   Smith, Harry B. 1926

Burgoyne, Arthur G.   Herbert 1944

Burk, Robert   Livingston, Jerry 1940

Burke, Gus   Blake 1942

Burke, J.F.   Webster 1951

Burke, Joe   Brown, A. Seymour 1913; Bryan 1927, 1931; Davis 1918, 1922, 1924, 1925, 1926, 1927, 1928, 1929, 1932, 1933, 1940; De Lange 1935; Dixon 1925, 1932; Donaldson 1926, 1927; Dubin 1911, 1916, 1917, 1923, 1925, 1926, 1927, 1929, 1930, 1931, 1932, 1941; Freed, Arthur 1932; Freed, Ralph 1935; Friend 1933, 1934; Gilbert 1928; Johnson, Howard 1933; Kahal 1932; Kahn 1925, 1926, 1927, 1931; Leslie 1935, 1936, 1937, 1938, 1939, 1940, 1945, 1948; Lewis 1927, 1941; Magidson 1944; McHugh 1923; Parish 1954; Rose 1925, 1927, 1928; Washington 1934, 1935; Webster 1931, 1972; Woods 1933; Young, Joe 1927

Burke, Kevin   Burke 1953

Burke, Sonny   Brooks 1950; Cahn 1958; David, Mack 1942, 1953; De Lange 1942; Mercer 1947; Raye 1941, 1954, 1955, 1957, 1958; Russell 1950; Sigman 1968; Webster 1948, 1949, 1950, 1952, 1953, 1955, 1959, 1971

Burke, Tom   Gorney 1924

Burke Jr., Johnny   Burke 1958

Burkhardt, Addison   Bryan 1908; Edwards 1906; Fisher 1908, 1910, 1917, 1918, 1920; Hanley 1917; Howard, Joseph E. 1907, 1910, Date Unknown; Monaco 1918; Von Tilzer 1905, 1910, 1911

Burkhart, Elsie   Johnson, Howard 1921

Burnett, Ernie   Hanley 1914

Burns, Annelu   Conrad 1932; Motzan 1930; Young, Joe 1932

Burns, Bob   Coslow 1937

Burns, Jeanne   Merrill 1949

Burns, Ralph   Mercer 1952

Burns, Robert   Van Heusen 1959

Burrell, Evelyn   Brooks 1952

Burrows, Abe   Loesser 1944

Burt, Benjamin Hapgood   Leslie 1954; Motzan 1915; Norworth 1936; Williams 1908

Burtnett, Earl   Dubin 1921, 1922; Freed, Arthur 1920

Burton, Andy   Sigman 1953

Burton, Nat   Davis 1944; Van Heusen 1938; Wrubel 1944

Burton, Val   Young, Victor 1941

Burwell, Cliff   Parish 1928, 1947; Razaf 1930

Bury, Herman   Stept 1927

Busey, Bernice Bland   Blake 1956; Sissle 1956

Bushkin, Joe   Burke 1958, 1960

Busse, Henry   Gilbert 1925

Bustanoby, Jacques   Romberg 1913

Butler, Artie   Cahn 1969, 1976

Butler, Charles   Carmichael 1949

Butler, Larry   David, Mack 1976

Butterfield, Erskine   Razaf 1940, 1942, 1944

Butternuth, Bobby   Brown, Lew 1925; Caesar 1926

Buttolph, David   Gorney 1935; Washington 1956; Webster 1958

Butts, Dale   Kalmar 1951
Butts, Jimmy   Johnson, James P. 1947
Buzar, Nonato   Cahn 1969
Buzzell, Eddie   Brown, Lew 1919; Gershwin, George Date
    Unknown; Kalmar 1924; Ruby 1924; Warren 1965
Byl, Holly   Sigman 1968
Byrnes, James   Norworth 1917

C

Cabler, Dan   Heyman 1929
Caddigan, Jack   McHugh 1916, 1917
Cadman, Charles Wakefield   Eliscu 1937
Caerts, Leo   Sigman 1968
Caesar, William   Dubin 1921
Cahan, Jacques   Hoffman 1954
Cahan, Les   Coots 1948
Caignet, Felix B.   Gilbert 1931
Caine, Sid   McHugh 1949
Calame, Bob   Loesser 1939
Calderon, A.   Sherman 1957
Calderon, Juan Carlos   Evans 1974; Livingston, Jay 1974
Caldwell, Anne   Friml 1923; Harbach 1926; Kern 1919, 1920,
    1921, 1922, 1923, 1925, 1926; Ruby 1926; Schwartz, Jean
    1914; Youmans 1926
Caldwell, Charles   Kahn 1923
Cali, Vito William   Cahn 1975
Calibi   Lawrence 1953
Calkin, Philip   Atteridge 1924
Call, Audrey   Lewis 1951
Callahan, Fred B.   Carmichael 1944
Callahan, Will J.   Ager 1918; Brennan 1915
Callincos, Constantine   Webster 1953
Calloway, Cab   Ellington 1944; Mills 1931, 1934, 1935, 1937,
    1938, 1939; Parish 1932; Razaf 1938; Silver 1941
Calvert, Peggy   Parish 1932
Calvi, Gerard   Rome 1965
Calvi, P.   David, Hal 1959
Camacho, Johnnie   David, Mack 1947
Camarata, Tuttie   Russell 1944
Cameron, Al   Ager 1932; Hoffman 1932
Camoria, Frank   Kahn 1925
Camp, Shep   Smith, Harry B. 1927
Campbell, Charles J.   Edwards 1906
Campbell, David   Heyman 1956
Campbell, Ian   Baer 1929
Campbell, Jimmy   Conrad 1927, 1933, 1938; Coslow 1933,
    1954; Kahn 1932, 1933; Woods 1932, 1933, 1934
Canfora, B.   David, Hal 1966
Canfora, D'Armand   Parish 1961
Canning, Effie I.   Evans 1949; Livingston, Jay 1949; Loesser
    1940
Cansucci, Leonello   Caesar 1930
Cantor, B.   Koehler 1927
Cantor, Eddie   Ahlert 1923; Akst 1923, 1931; Brown, Lew
    1925; Caesar 1922; Clare 1923; Coslow 1923; Davis 1923,
    1931; Egan 1918; Fisher 1921, 1922; Kalmar 1932; Robin
    1930; Ruby 1932; Schwartz, Jean 1922; Stept 1924; Turk
    1923; Whiting 1918
Cantor, Harry   Lerner, Sammy 1930
Cantor, Lew   Johnson, Howard 1921
Capano, Frank   Myrow 1931
Capewell, Maria   Robison 1951
Capie, Frank   Smith, Harry B. 1922
Capman, Milford   Yellen 1923

Capote, Truman   Arlen 1954, 1968
Capp, Al   Stept 1946
Capps, Al   David, Mack 1974
Caputo, D.   Caesar 1923
Carazo, Castro   Lewis 1934
Carete, Hans   Parish 1954
Carew, Ora   Brown, Nacio Herb 1927; Clarke 1927
Carey, Bill   Mancini 1956, 1957, 1958
Carey, Bob   Razaf 1946
Carey, Morgan   Blake 1916
Cargoli, G.   Livingston, Jerry 1960
Carle, Frankie   David, Hal 1951; David, Mack 1940, 1946;
    Lawrence 1939; Merrill 1946; Parish 1931, 1933, 1943;
    Razaf 1940
Carle, Richard   Edwards 1902
Carless, Dorothy   Hoffman 1950
Carleton, Robert L.   Young, Joe 1946, 1947
Carlo, Monte   Bryan 1921, 1923, 1931, 1934, 1935, 1941,
    1942, 1943, 1944, 1950; Fisher 1921; Johnson, Howard
    1921; Yellen 1922
Carlton, Carle   Johnson, Howard 1922, 1924, 1927;
    Schwartz, Jean 1921
Carmen, Richard   Mills 1940
Carmen, Ted   Parish 1932
Carmi, Lao   Sigman 1956
Carmichael, Ralph   Evans 1956; Livingston, Jay 1956
Carney, Art   David, Hal 1954
Carney, Don   Young, Victor 1934
Carney, Harry   Ellington 1931, 1937, 1943; Mills 1937
Carosone, Renato   Hoffman 1958
Carpenter, C.   Leigh 1981
Carpenter, Edward Childs   Herbert 1916
Carpenter, Imogen   Cahn 1969; Leigh 1954
Carr, Alexander   Fisher 1907
Carr, James   Parish 1926
Carr, Jerry   David, Hal 1947
Carr, Jimmy   Friend 1923
Carr, Leon   David, Hal 1951, 1952, 1953, 1954, 1955, 1956,
    1957, 1958, 1959, 1960, 1962, 1963; Hoffman 1944, 1949,
    1950, 1951, 1952, 1954
Carr, Michael   Davis 1949; Fain 1960; Silver 1949
Carretta, Jerry   Leigh 1955; Sigman 1958
Carroll, Albert   Schwartz, Arthur 1926, 1929
Carroll, Barbara   Caesar 1956
Carroll, Ben   Coots 1954
Carroll, Earl   Atteridge 1912; Brennan 1915; Carroll 1914;
    Revel 1945, 1947; Turk 1923; Von Tilzer 1940;
    Washington 1940; Young, Victor 1940
Carroll, Gene   Coots 1940, 1951, 1953, 1954; Dixon 1940
Carroll, Irv   Livingston, Jerry 1941
Carroll, Jack   Coslow 1927; Kahal 1926; Mills 1927
Carroll, Lewis   DePaul 1951; Eliscu 1949; Fain 1951; Raye
    1951
Carroll, Pauline   Carroll 1940, 1942
Carroll, Richard   Schwartz, Jean 1907
Carroll, Roy   David, Mack 1956; Mancini 1956
Carruth, Lucy   Coots 1961
Carruthers, Ben   Ellington 1937; Mills 1937
Carson, Milton   Sigman 1957
Carter, Bennett   Waller 1927
Carter, Benny   Cahn 1965; Heyman 1939; Mills 1934, 1935,
    1942; Raye 1946, 1957; Russell 1965; Waller 1946;
    Washington 1935
Carter, Desmond   Caesar 1936; Dietz 1929; Dubin 1931;
    Duke 1927; Egan 1927; Gershwin, George 1924, 1925,

1926; Gershwin, Ira 1924; Hanley 1926; Henderson 1936; Kahn 1927; Kern 1926; Rodgers 1927; Schwartz, Arthur 1929, 1930, 1933, 1934, 1936; Weill 1935

Carter, Francis   Razaf 1955

Carter, Frank   Romberg 1917

Carter, Helen M.   Coots 1955, 1958

Carter, June   Loesser 1953

Carter, K.   Mills 1931

Carter, Ray   Baer 1945

Carter, Richard   Brooks 1970

Carus, Emma   Fisher 1909

Caruso, James A.N.   Bryan 1921

Carvarentz, George   Sigman 1975

Caryll, Ivan   Caesar 1920; Smith, Harry B. 1914, 1918

Casadei, Arturo   Hoffman 1959

Case, Russ   Robison 1961

Caserta, Charles   Sigman 1957

Casey, Charles E.   Olcott 1907

Cash, Bobby   Cahn 1967

Caslar, Dan   Gilbert 1919; Stept 1955; Sterling 1915; Washington 1933

Casman-Steinberg   Cahn 1938

Cassel, Irwin   Gilbert 1955

Cassia, Jimmy   Hoffman 1951

Castellyi, Oliveros   Johnson, Howard 1936

Castle, Nick   Clare 1938, 1940, 1953; Sigman 1960; Styne 1938, 1940

Casucci, Leonello   Caesar 1985

Cates, George   David, Mack 1965; Silver 1958; Webster 1956, 1958, 1968

Cates, Paul   Sigman 1935

Catlett, Sid   Sigman 1946, 1948

Cato, Minto   Razaf 1931; Waller 1931

Causer, Bob   Fisher 1923; Razaf 1937

Cavallaro, Carmen   Parish 1942

Cavanaugh, Dave   Warren 1961

Cavanaugh, James   Arlen 1928; Hoffman 1930, 1933, 1949; Johnson, Howard 1928, 1933, 1934, 1935, 1936; Lane 1930; Magidson 1928, 1929; Mills 1935; Parish 1934, 1936; Razaf 1937; Washington 1929

Cavanaugh, Jess   Hoffman 1955

Cavanaugh, Joseph   Johnson, Howard 1934

Cavanaugh, Page   Raye 1953

Cavi, Fred   Mills 1928; Parish 1929, 1980

Caymmi, Danilo   Evans 1970; Livingston, Jay 1954

Caymmi, Dorival   Heyman 1948; Sigman 1946

Ceballos, Larry   Johnson, Howard 1921

Cecil, Bob   Hoffman 1949

Cesana, Otto   Egan 1942

Cezar, Fernando   Stept 1956

Chait, C.   Hoffman 1954

Chambers, Eddie   Howard, Joseph E. 1944

Chaminade, C.   Johnson, Howard 1935

Chamlee, Mario   Gilbert 1935

Chandler, Jeff   Mancini 1954, 1955, 1957

Chaney, Roger   Razaf 1941; Revel 1959

Channing, Robert   Coots 1952

Chaplin, Charles   De Lange 1941; Kahn 1925; Willson 1941

Chaplin, Saul   Adamson 1955; Akst 1947; Brooks 1948, 1950; Cahn 1933, 1934, 1935, 1936, 1937, 1938, 1939, 1940, 1941, 1942, 1943, 1945, 1947, 1948, 1950, 1953, 1955, 1958, 1961, 1963, 1968; Comden and Green 1947; De Lange 1945, 1946; Fain Date Unknown; Mercer 1958; Raye 1935, 1938; Warren 1950

Chapman, Henry   Friml 1911

Chappelle, Frederic   Caesar 1922

Charig, Phil   Caesar 1924, 1927, 1929; DeSylva 1925; Dietz 1930; Gershwin, Ira 1924, 1926, 1928, 1930; Kahn 1932; Mercer 1930; Robin 1927, 1928, 1931; Smith, Robert B. 1930

Charlap, Moose   Adams 1956; Leigh 1954; Russell 1956

Charles, Dick   Carmichael 1946, 1947; De Lange 1945; Lawrence 1952, 1954

Charles, Jacques   Monaco 1924

Charles, L.   Gilbert 1931; Johnson, J. Rosamond 1931

Charles, Milton   Yellen 1924

Charles, Ray   Russell 1940

Charnin, Martin   Arlen 1964, 1965, 1966; Duke 1963; Rodgers 1970, 1979; Sondheim 1963; Strouse 1977, 1989, 1993, 1999, 2000

Chase, Charles   Sterling 1923

Chase, Newell   Caesar 1935; Coslow 1930, 1931, 1940; Davis 1929; Egan 1941, 1942; Heyman 1934, 1935, 1941; Parish 1935; Robin 1930, 1931; Robison 1944; Silver 1928; Whiting 1930, 1931

Chatau, Henri   Sigman 1954

Chatman, Bo   Parish 1932

Chayefsky, Paddy   Arlen 1958; Warren 1955

Cheiffetz, Hyman   Arlen 1924

Chekova, Josepha   Friml 1931

Chenoweth, Wilson   Lerner, Sammy 1930

Cherkose, Eddie   Coslow 1945; Mills 1947; Ruby 1945; Styne 1940, 1941, 1943, 1946, 1947, 1950

Cherniavsky, Josef   Ahlert 1929; Parish 1932; Turk 1929

Cherwin, Richard   Washington 1945

Cheskin, Dave   Friend 1944

Chevalier, Maurice   Rome 1951

Chick, Leonard   Snyder 1908, 1910, 1939

Chijo, Antonio Torroella   Norworth 1912

Childs, Reggie   Heyman 1933

Chimola, George   Stept 1922

Chitwood, Alton Brooks   Donaldson 1941

Choch, Robert   Brennan 1938

Cholly, Paul   Washington 1932

Chopin, Frederic   Johnson, Howard 1935

Christie, George   Sterling 1909

Christine, Henri   Goetz 1925

Christine, P.H.   Smith, Harry B. 1906, 1913

Christney, Etta Vivian   Carmichael 1940

Christy, Bob   Razaf 1946

Christy, Harold   Caesar 1924; Conrad 1923, 1924; Henderson 1921, 1922, 1923; Motzan 1922, 1923, 1930; Silver 1924

Christy, Howard   Conrad 1924; Henderson 1923, 1926; Motzan 1923

Church, Harden   Heyman 1934

Churchill, Frank E.   Lawrence 1952; Pollack 1945; Sherman 1963; Washington 1941; Webster 1938, 1939, 1945

Chute, Marchette Gaylord   Carmichael 1952

Cicognini, Alessandro   Cahn 1954; David, Mack 1958; Sigman 1955

Cines, Eugene   Sigman 1955

Cini   Hoffman 1954, 1958

Cirina, Joseph A.   Conrad 1925

Citorello, Paolo   Brown, Lew 1938

Ciucicini, Signor   Herbert 1908

Claire, Evelyn   Cahn 1952

Clapp, Sunny   Carmichael 1931; Mills 1929

Clar, Arden   Sigman 1965

Clare, Sidney D.   Whiting 1934

Claret, Gaston   Parish 1933
Clark, Al   Johnson, Howard 1916
Clark, Buddy   Myrow 1936
Clark, Edward   Friml 1923; Harbach 1917; Schwartz, Jean 1912; Von Tilzer 1910
Clark Jr., Charles B.   Young, Victor 1937
Clarke, Bert   Waller 1935; Young, Joe 1934
Clarke, George   Waller 1935; Young, Joe 1934
Clarke, Harry   Edwards 1932; Kern 1918
Clarke, Joseph I.C.   Herbert 1913, 1914, 1922
Clarkson, Geoffrey   Blake 1942; De Lange 1936; Mercer 1955, 1966; Razaf 1942
Clavell, Mario   David, Mack 1947
Clay, Ned   Sissle 1915
Clay, William R.   Robison 1925
Clayton, Stanley   Stept 1958
Cleary, Michael   Heyman 1943; Hoffman 1933; Magidson 1928, 1929, 1930; Mercer 1934; Washington 1928, 1929, 1930, 1933; Wrubel 1933
Cleary, Ruth   De Lange 1944; Raye 1939, 1940
Clemmons, Larry   Fain 1977
Clerc, Ch. Borel   Dubin 1924
Cliff, Laddie   Conrad 1922
Clifford, Gordon   Brown, Nacio Herb 1931; Kahn 1932; Mills 1945; Oakland 1934
Clifford, William H.   Schwartz, Jean 1926
Clint, H. O'Reilly   Parish 1930
Clinton, Larry   Sigman 1947, 1956
Coates, Carroll   Spina 1967
Coates, Eric   Caesar 1936; Lawrence 1940
Coatsworth, Elizabeth   Blane 1960
Cobb, George L.   Carroll 1915; Kahn 1916; Whiting 1916; Yellen 1913, 1914, 1915, 1916
Cobey, Louis   Caesar 1953; Clarke 1924; Leslie 1924; Mills 1924; Yellen 1953
Coburn, Richard   Brown, Nacio Herb 1921, 1927
Cochran, Dorcas   McHugh 1952
Cochran, Gifford   Weill 1933
Cogane, Nelson   Coots 1944; Fain 1937, 1938, 1939, 1946; Hanley 1941; Johnson, James P. 1936, 1962; Livingston, Jerry 1941, 1982; Romberg 1943
Cohan, Charles C.   Howard, Joseph E. 1910
Cohen, Cy   Friend 1949; Livingston, Jerry 1949; Spina 1966
Cohen, Henry R.   Caesar 1925, 1926
Cohen, Hy   Snyder 1931
Cohen, Joseph F.   Sissle 1915
Cohen, Leo   Silver 1947
Cohen, Phil   Gorney 1929; Harburg 1929
Cohn, C.   Styne 1926
Cohn, Chester   Kahn 1929
Cohpin, Frederic   Merrill 1950
Colby, Robert   David, Hal 1957
Cole, Bob   Johnson, J. Rosamond 1900, 1901, 1902, 1903, 1904, 1906, 1907, 1909, 1916, 1946, Date Unknown
Cole, Nat "King"   Burke 1961; Drake 1951; Hoffman 1958; Mills 1943, 1944
Coleman   Goetz 1915
Coleman, Arthur   Parish 1925
Coleman, G. McKinley   Johnson, James P. 1936
Coleman, Larry   Leigh 1955; Spina 1955
Collahon, Gladys   Lewis 1950
Collins, Aaron   Russell 1957, 1958
Collins, Bill   Stept 1924
Collins, Errol   Brown, Nacio Herb 1919
Collins, Kim   Warren 1960

Collins, Melville   Leslie 1908
Collins, Walter B.   Gilbert 1929
Collins, Will   Magidson 1924; McHugh 1923; Stept 1924, 1929
Colman, Emil   Fisher 1920
Colonna, Jerry   Spina 1953, 1956, 1957, 1958, 1959
Colonna, Johnny   Freed, Ralph 1964
Colpet, Max   Bacharach 1965; David, Hal 1965
Colt, Phyllis   Robison 1941
Colton, Sammy   Cahn 1935
Columbo, Russ   Conrad 1931; Dubin 1931; Robin 1931
Concina, Carlo   Sigman 1953
Condra, A.   Livingston, Jerry 1958
Confrey, Zez   Coslow 1922; Dubin 1924; Mills 1935
Conley, Larry   Davis 1925, 1929; Kahn 1924; Robison 1929, 1930, 1935
Conley, Steve   McHugh 1924
Conlin, James P.   Gilbert 1920
Conly, Charles   Parish 1948
Conn, Chester   Gordon 1957; Kahn 1930, 1932
Connelly, Marc   Gershwin, Ira 1924
Connelly, Reg   Conrad 1927, 1949; Warren 1952; Woods 1932, 1933, 1934
Conney, Nat   Stept 1958
Connor, Joseph P.   Carroll 1943
Connor, Pierre   Hanley 1927
Connor, Tommie   Waller 1938
Connors, Carol   Fain 1977
Conover, A.   Dubin 1924
Conrad, Eddie   Coots 1926, 1928
Conrad, Eugene   Carroll 1933; Edwards 1936
Conrad, John   Kahn 1921
Conrad, Lew   Heyman 1932
Conroy, Frank J.   Snyder 1908
Conselman, Jimmy   Whiting 1927
Conselman, William   Whiting 1934
Constantin, Jean   Sigman 1959
Conte, Eugene   Johnson, Howard 1929
Conte, P.   Sigman 1968
Contet, Henri   Parish 1962
Conti, Bill   Bacharach 1987
Conway, Carlton   Raye 1957
Coogan, Jack   Gilbert 1912
Cook, Charles Emerson   Herbert 1907, 1908
Cook, Hartwell   Razaf 1932
Cook, Mercer   Johnson, James P. 1942
Cook, Will Marion   Smith, Harry B. 1902, 1903; Sterling 1910; Von Tilzer 1910
Cooke, Charles L.   Blake 1940; Egan 1916; Kahn 1917, 1921; Razaf 1940, 1942, 1944, 1953; Whiting 1914, 1916, 1917, 1918; Yellen 1921
Coolidge, Edwina   Dubin 1940, 1944
Cooper, Bob   Russell 1957, 1977; Woods 1925
Cooper, Bud   Stept 1925, 1927, 1928; Warren 1926, 1931
Cooper, Edward   Hoffman 1950
Cooper, Harry   Gilbert 1919
Cooper, Joe   Brown, Lew 1914; De Lange 1941, 1946; Freed, Ralph 1954; Gilbert 1912, 1919, 1920, 1949; Johnson, Howard 1925; Kahn 1928; Kalmar 1915; Lerner, Sammy 1951; Leslie 1913; Lewis 1923, 1924; Ruby 1950; Young, Joe 1923, 1924
Cooper, Lew   Akst 1923; Leslie 1913
Cooper, Paul   Rose 1937
Copeland, Allan   Gilbert 1913; Russell 1957
Copen, Leonard   Drake 1957

Copland, Aaron   Gershwin, Ira 1943

Corbin, Cy   Hoffman 1943; Livingston, Jerry 1943

Corda, Michael   Burke 1961; Mercer 1965; Webster 1969, 1971, 1974, 1983

Corday, Leo   Hoffman 1949, 1950, 1951, 1952, 1954

Corder, Don   Kahal 1926

Cordish, Nat   Mills 1928

Cormack, Rennie   Brown, A. Seymour 1913, 1915; Dubin 1914, 1915, 1916

Cornell   Bryan 1932; Parish 1930

Cornell, C.B.   Gilbert 1944

Cornell, Howard   Van Heusen 1953

Cornett, Alice   Hoffman 1952

Cornwall, Frank   Bryan 1930

Corso, Vin   Hoffman 1952

Cort, Harry L.   Hanley 1920; Motzan 1920

Cory, George   Sigman 1948

Costa, Guy   David, Mack 1971

Costello, Bartley   Bloom 1925; Fisher 1917; Johnson, J. Rosamond 1934; Motzan 1924; Snyder 1909; Stept 1921; Sterling 1900, 1901, 1902, 1903, 1910; Von Tilzer 1903, 1910, 1924; Waller 1934

Costello, Elvis   Bacharach 1996

Costello, Lou   Mills 1942

Costen   Sterling 1900

Cotes, Sherman   Gilbert 1906

Covington, Allan H.   Kahn 1922

Cowan, Joel   Russell 1947

Cowan, Lynn Freeman   Bryan 1924

Cowan, Rubey   Brown, Lew 1917, 1918, 1919; Stept 1925, 1927

Cowan, Stan   Oakland 1973

Coward, Noel   Gershwin, Ira 1943; Kahn 1940

Cox, Eddie   Clarke 1916, 1917; Donaldson 1917; Mitchell 1918; Monaco 1916

Craig, Doug   Davis 1938

Craig, Jimmy   Silver 1956

Crane, Hal   Donaldson 1918

Crane, Paul   Coslow 1921

Crane, Richard   Strouse 1963

Crane, Vernon   Hanley 1942

Craven, Frank   Kern 1920

Craver, Al   Johnson, Howard 1927

Cravis, Irving   David, Mack 1945

Crawford, Helen   Brown, Lew 1927; DeSylva 1927; Kahn 1929

Crawford, Jesse   Burke 1930; Kahn 1922, 1923, 1924, 1931; McHugh 1923

Crawford, Stanley   Bryan 1902; Schwartz, Jean 1908; Sterling 1904; Williams 1908

Crawley, James   Johnson, James P. 1947

Creamer, Henry   Atteridge 1925; Blake 1927; Brown, Lew 1925; Conrad 1928; Hanley 1923, 1924, 1925, 1926; Johnson, James P. 1923, 1926, 1927, 1928, 1929, 1930, 1936, 1943, 1944, 1945, 1961, 1962; McHugh 1926; Motzan 1925; Pollack 1923; Warren 1924, 1925, 1926, 1927

Creatore, Luigi   David, Mack 1958; Hoffman 1957

Creston, Paul   Parish 1963

Cristearson, L.   Revel 1947

Crook, John   Kern 1912

Crooker, Earle   Loewe 1930, 1936, 1937, 1938, 1942

Crosby, Bing   Ahlert 1931; Burke 1939; Monaco 1939; Parish 1933; Turk 1931; Van Heusen 1960; Washington 1932; Young, Victor 1932

Crosby, Bob   Cahn 1951, 1956; Duke 1956

Cross, Christopher   Bacharach 1981

Cross, Douglass   Sigman 1948

Croswell, Ann   Bacharach 1959

Crothers, Kay   Pollack 1943

Crowthers, Dorothy   Rodgers 1923

Crum, Frank   Ager 1927; Yellen 1927

Crumit, Frank   Johnson, Howard 1921; Waller 1934

Csida, Joe   Stept 1952

Cugat, Xavier   Adamson 1939, 1940; De Lange 1940; Drake 1946, 1948; Freed, Ralph 1947; Mercer 1940; Stept 1946

Cullbreth, William   Mills 1935

Culley, Jack   McHugh 1926; Mills 1926

Cummings, Byron   Robison 1954

Cummings, Margery   Arlen 1942; Harburg 1942; Lane 1942

Cunningham, Paul   Baer 1939, 1940, 1945, 1946, 1947, 1950, 1951; Brennan 1918, 1919, 1921, 1926; Coots 1944, 1954; Davis 1944; Dubin 1919, 1920, 1921; Edwards 1919; Howard, Joseph E. 1918; McHugh 1958, 1959, 1960; Meyer 1947, 1950; Monaco 1918, 1919; Schwartz, Jean 1940; Silver 1926; Stept 1942, 1950; Von Tilzer 1914

Curb, Mike   David, Mack 1970, 1971, 1972, 1974, 1976, 1979

Curbelo, Fausto   Adamson 1939, 1940; David, Mack 1947

Curiel, Gonzalo   Hammerstein 1940; Russell 1941

Curtis, Alton   Johnson, James P. 1964

Curtis, Bennett   Meyer 1923

Curtis, Billy   Friend 1941; Hoffman 1930; Koehler 1930; Lane 1930; Sterling 1919; Von Tilzer 1919, 1920, 1921, 1923, 1924, 1927

Curtis, Loyal   Kahn 1926, 1927

Curtis, Mann   Akst 1953; Coots 1952; David, Hal 1957; DePaul 1955; Hoffman 1941, 1942, 1943, 1945, 1946, 1950, 1951, 1952, 1954; Livingston, Jay 1942; Livingston, Jerry 1941, 1942, 1943, 1945, 1946, 1954; Robison 1956; Silver 1947, 1950

Cushing, Catherine Chisholm   Friml 1916, 1918, 1922

Cushman, Howard B.   Brown, Lew 1925

Cuvillier, Charles   Smith, Robert B. 1914

Czibulka, A.   Johnson, Howard 1935

Czida, Joe   Hoffman 1952

D

Dabney, Ford   Brown, Lew 1924; Buck 1915; Conrad 1934; Heyman 1934; Kern 1915; Razaf 1944

D'Acosta, Leon   Young, Joe 1934

D'Acquisito, V.D.   Sigman 1977

Daissain, Marcel   Bryan 1928

Dallavo, John   Hoffman 1927

Dalton, Grace   DeSylva 1927; Young, Joe 1930

Daly, Joseph M.   Parish 1923

Daly, Lew   Bryan 1927

Daly, Tom   Edwards 1898, 1899, 1900

Daly, William   Caesar 1920, 1923, 1924; DeSylva 1922; Gershwin, George 1922; Gershwin, Ira 1922, 1923; Harbach 1923; Robin 1937; Schwartz, Jean 1919; Turk 1923, 1924

Dameron, Tadd   Sigman 1946, 1958

Dancer, Earl   Mills 1954

Dane, Bob   David, Mack 1958

Dane, Clemence   Young, Victor 1949

Dane, Constance   Carmichael 1966

Daniderff, Leo   Buck 1925

Daniels, Charles N.   Kahn 1928

Daniels, Eliot   Adamson 1951; Heyman 1932; Lawrence 1936, 1938, 1939, 1943, 1953, 1956

Daniels, Peter   Cahn 1968, 1969, 1970, 1973, 1979, 1981, 1982; Merrill 1981

Danis, Jack   Drake 1945

Danko, C.   Parish 1957

Danvers, Charles   Sigman 1957, 1961

D'Anzi, G.   Sigman 1946, 1959

Danzig, Evelyn   Sigman 1953, 1954

Dapper, Johnny   Johnson, James P. 1958

Daray, Gabriel   Buck 1923

Darby, Ken   De Lange 1937; Gordon 1950; Pollack 1949; Warren 1950; Young, Victor 1955

Darcey, Joe   Henderson 1923; Johnson, Howard 1925

Darewski, Herman   Goetz 1920, 1929

Darewski, Max   Conrad 1913

D'Artega, Alfonso   Lawrence 1940

D'Artega, Pedro   Parish 1938

Daryaux, Georges Jouvin   Hoffman 1958

Dash, Irwin   Dubin 1923, 1924; McHugh 1923, 1924; Mills 1924

Dast, Charles   Mercer 1952

Dauchy, Andre   Raye 1958

Daugherty, Dan   Warren 1926

Daulton, Ernst   Parish 1928

D'Aury, Wen   Mills 1942

Davenport, Charles   Cahn 1935

Davenport, P.   Russell 1940

David, Dwight   Evans 1958; Livingston, Jay 1958

David, Lee   Brennan 1923, 1925, 1929; Davis 1936; Dixon 1927; Dubin 1926; Friend 1944; Hanley 1928; Johnson, Howard 1932; Kahal 1931; Parish 1934; Rose 1923, 1927, 1928, 1929, 1930, 1932; Young, Joe 1932

David, Morron   Kern 1911

Davidson, Morrey   Brown, Lew 1924; Coots 1933, 1936, 1940, 1967; Davis 1936; Fain 1948; Waller 1929; Yellen 1948

Davidson, Walter   Von Tilzer 1907

Davies, Lew   Drake 1962, 1967

Davis, Beryl   Mancini 1953

Davis, Bob A.   Brown, Lew 1948

Davis, Buster   Styne 1954, 1965

Davis, Charles   Johnson, Howard 1934

Davis, Collin   Howard, Joseph E. 1906, 1908, 1910, 1911, 1913, 1918

Davis, Dohl   Davis 1928

Davis, Eddie   Akst 1926; Coslow 1921; Davis 1926; Robin 1935

Davis, Jeff   Parish 1954

Davis, Joe   Johnson, Howard 1926, 1928, 1929, 1933, 1935, 1938, 1939; Razaf 1930, 1932, 1934, 1936, 1937, 1938, 1939, 1940, 1942, 1945, Date Unknown; Waller 1937

Davis, Lou   Arlen 1929; Baer 1923; Brown, Lew 1927; Coots 1928, 1929, 1930; Fain 1928; Pollack 1929; Silver 1926

Davis, Mack   Bryan 1926; Fain 1932; Robin 1926

Davis, Maxwell   David, Hal 1953

Davis, Paul   Razaf 1940

Davis, Stanley   Oakland 1960

Dawes, Charles G.   Sigman 1951

Dawn, Marilow   Coots 1949

Dawson, Eli   Schwartz, Arthur 1923

Day, Bobby   Burke 1955

Day, Frederick   Kern 1910, 1911

Day, Lucille   Yellen 1954

de Alberich, Ralph   Woods 1930

de Alberich, Salvador   Ahlert 1930

Dean, Agnes Louise   Carmichael 1956

Dean, Buddy   David, Hal 1946

Deane, Doug   Revel 1957, 1961, 1963

Deani, C.   Raye 1957

Dearie, Blossom   Mercer 1973

Dearmer, Geoffrey   Carmichael 1937

De Armond, Robert   Young, Victor 1919, 1924

Deas, M.   Razaf 1925

De Azevedo, Alexis K.   David, Mack 1974, 1976

De Bolis, Aldo Bolito   Brooks 1950; Parish 1946

De Burgh, Chris   Bacharach 1988

Debussy, Claude   Bergman 1978

Decock, Omer   Coslow 1957

DeCosta, Harry   Ahlert 1923, 1924; Clare 1926, 1953; Dubin 1918, 1936; Johnson, Howard 1916; Lewis 1915; Monaco 1926; Norworth 1916; Silver 1926; Snyder 1952, 1953

Decrescenzi, L.   Fain 1918

de Curtis, Ernesto   Caesar 1921; Robin 1930

De Francesco, Louis E.   Bryan 1928, 1931, 1932

De Frank, Paul   Mills 1926

de Gombert, G.   Heyman 1936

De Gresac, Fred   Herbert 1913; Smith, Harry B. 1913

DeGuercho, Lucius   Coots 1953

De Halnut, Rirmin   Robison 1948

De Haven, Carter   Snyder 1909

deHollanda, C.B.   Russell 1966

DeJesus, Luchi   Russell 1977; Webster 1967

DeKoven, Reginald   Smith, Harry B. 1900, 1901, 1902, 1908, 1911, 1913

Delance, Pierre   Lawrence 1955; Sigman 1962, 1971

Delaney, J.P.   Meyer 1933

Del Barrio, George   Cahn 1969

Delbridge, Del   Kahn 1926; Koehler 1922

DeLeath, Vaughn   Berlin 1920; Gilbert 1932; Henderson 1921; Silver 1932

de Leon, Martin   Rainger 1936

De Leon, Robert   Carmichael 1940

Delettre, Jean   Harburg 1934; Parish 1934, 1935

de Leur, Joop   Rome 1952

Delibes, Leo   Johnson, Howard 1935

Dellon, Harold A.   Razaf 1923, 1924

Del Ragno, Frank   Coots 1963

Del Rio, M.   Heyman 1938

Delugg, Milton   Loesser 1950, 1953

Demao, J.   Raye 1943

de Martini, Henri   Brown, Lew 1923; Yellen 1924

De May, Joseph   Smith, Harry B. 1923

De Mejo, Oscar.   Brooks 1952; Leigh 1953

De Metruis   Russell 1955

Dempsey, Wilda   Cahn 1952

Denison, C.M.   Meyer 1909

Denniker, Paul   Conrad 1932; Johnson, Howard 1926; Razaf 1924, 1925, 1926, 1927, 1929, 1930, 1931, 1933, 1934, 1935, 1936, 1937, 1938, 1940, 1941, 1942, Date Unknown

Dennis, Matt   Cahn 1976, 1979; Raye 1956, 1957, 1958; Russell 1957, 1958, 1960

Denny, Martin   David, Mack 1959

Denza, Luigi   Johnson, Howard 1932; Sherman 1960

De Oliveira, Milton   Drake 1947; Evans 1958; Livingston, Jay 1958

De Ponti   Raye 1961

Deppen, Jessie L.   Dietz 1929

Derche, C.F.   Johnson, Howard 1921; Kahn 1921

Derickson, Charles Edwards 1925
De Rienzo, Silvio Fisher 1950
De Roe, Hopwood Johnston 1920
De Rose, Peter Adamson 1940, 1941, 1942; Ahlert 1936;
    Baer 1938, 1942; Clare 1928, 1929, 1932; Coslow 1919,
    1921, 1922; David, Mack 1934; Davis 1932, 1942; Dixon
    1929; Donaldson 1943; Freed, Ralph 1935; Harbach
    1945, 1953; Harburg 1930; Heyman 1936; Johnson,
    Howard 1934; Kahal 1929; Leslie 1943, 1954; Lewis
    1932, 1935, 1936, 1937, 1938, 1942, 1943, 1944; Parish
    1937, 1939, 1940, 1941, 1942, 1943, 1946, 1953, 1954;
    Robison 1928, 1934; Russell 1943, 1945, 1946, Date
    Unknown; Sigman 1946, 1947, 1949, 1950, 1951, 1952;
    Woods 1929; Young, Joe 1934, 1936
Desort Dubin 1921
d'Esposito, Salve Akst 1953
De Sylva, Jo Caesar 1934; Carroll 1934
Deutsch, Adolph Styne 1927; Webster 1950
Deutsch, C. Fisher 1933
Deutsch, Emory Hoffman 1952; Lawrence 1932, 1933, 1941,
    1943; Parish 1937; Webster 1934
Deutsch, Helen Livingston, Jerry 1956
DeVauney, E. Stept 1953
De Vol, Frank David, Hal 1973; David, Mack 1964, 1967,
    1968
De Vos, Herre Bryan 1938
De Waal, Anton Brown, Lew 1949, 1952; Sigman 1951
Dey, Larry Webster 1941
Diamond Gilbert 1921
Diamond, Leo David, Hal 1941; Webster 1955, 1956;
    Young, Joe 1933
Diamond, Neil Bacharach 1984, 1986; Bergman 1981
Diamond, Ora May Hoffman 1953, 1954, 1957; Silver 1953,
    1954
Di Capua, E. Dubin 1924; Goetz 1910; Johnson, Howard
    1932
Di Chiara, Vincenzo Johnson, Howard 1932
Dick, Dorothy De Lange 1937; Waller 1949
Dickens, Charles Young, Victor 1954
Dietrich, James Yellen 1930
Di Lazzaro, Bruno Adamson 1940
Di Lazzaro, Eldo Adamson 1940, 1942
Dillon, J.I. Olcott 1907
Dillon, Will Carroll 1912; Conrad 1918; Coots 1957; Friend
    1922; Lewis 1915; Von Tilzer 1909, 1910, 1911
Dilworth, George Kahn 1930
Di Minno, Danny Koehler 1950
Di Napoli, Mike Hoffman 1952
Di Novi, Gene Mercer 1965, 1966
Discepolo, E.B. Drake 1945
Diskant, Mark Silver 1951
Diston, Leo Parish 1930
Ditts, Dandy Hoffman 1950; Merrill 1950
Dixon, Fred Herbert 1895
Dixon, Harold Dubin 1927; Mills 1928, 1929; Parish 1928;
    Stept 1926, 1927
D'Joseph, Jac Gordon 1946
Dmitrenko, V. Freed, Ralph 1944
Doane, Dorothy David, Mack 1941
Dobson, Austin Duke 1942
Dodd, Jimmie David, Mack 1955; Hoffman 1955;
    Livingston, Jerry 1955
Dodge, Mamie Kahn 1920
Doe, John Raye 1939
Doelle, Franz Lerner, Sammy 1931

Doerr, Cliff Mills 1923
Doerr, Clyde McHugh 1922; Mills 1922
Doerr, Eddie Von Tilzer 1916
Dolan, Robert Emmett Coslow 1944; Harburg 1934; Mercer
    1944, 1946, 1947, 1948, 1949, 1950, 1951, 1962, 1963,
    1964; Webster 1959
Dolen, Bernie Bryan 1931
Dolezal, John D. Lawrence 1940
Dolin, Gerald Fisher 1937
Dolin, Max Mills 1924
Doll, Roy Silver 1928
Dolmatovsky, E. Rome 1943
Dominguez, Alberto. Russell 1940
Dominguez, Armando Drake 1943
Donahue, Al Van Heusen 1938
Donahue, Dick Coots 1953, 1957
Donahue, Sam David, Mack 1946
Donaldson, Will Gershwin, George 1917; Harbach 1926;
    Turk 1927
Donato, E. Johnson, Howard 1936
Donida, Carlo Drake 1962; Lawrence 1953; Sigman 1963,
    1966
Donizetti, Gaetano Brooks 1945; Johnson, Howard 1939
Donnelly, Dorothy Romberg 1921, 1924, 1927, 1928, 1954;
    Webster 1954
Donnelly, Harry Caesar 1938, 1945; Gilbert 1921
Donnelly, Leo Atteridge 1911
Donovan, Walter Kahn 1923; Yellen 1922
Dorff, Steve David, Mack 1982
Dorsey, Jimmy Van Heusen 1938
Dorsey, Tommy Davis 1939
Dorsey, William C. Sigman 1952
D'Ortega Lawrence 1947
Dosher, George Blake 1950
Dostal, Nico Johnson, Howard 1935
Doucet, Clement Young, Victor 1930
Dougall, Bernard Fields 1952; Kern 1933, 1952
Dougall, Hugh Harbach 1921
Dougherty, Dan Ager 1929; Myrow 1930; Yellen 1928, 1929,
    1930, 1931, 1932, 1933, 1934, 1935, 1937, 1938, 1941,
    1944, 1947, 1950, 1954, 1955, 1977, 1978, Date
    Unknown
Douglas, Bert Meyer 1933
Douglas, Charles Edwards 1905
Douglas, Johnny Cahn 1972
Douglas, R.H. Coslow 1934
Douglass, Louis Johnson, James P. 1938
Dowell, Edgar McHugh 1927; Mills 1927; Razaf 1923, 1925,
    1926, 1931, 1932; Sissle 1916; Waller 1932
Dowell, Saxie David, Mack 1941; Parish 1929; Revel 1951;
    Warren 1954
Dowling, Eddie Coots 1932, 1933; Hanley 1926, 1927, 1928,
    1929, 1930; Johnson, Howard 1921
Dowman, Euday L. Robison 1949
Downey, Morton Bryan 1933; Coots 1933; Hanley 1933;
    Wrubel 1931
Downing, Harry Egan 1913
Downing, Sam Kalmar 1915, 1922; Ruby 1922
Downz, George "Treby" Johnson, James P. 1968
Doyle, Alfred J. Sterling 1911; Von Tilzer 1911
Doyle, Laid Friml 1936
Draddy, Gregory Coots 1943
Draddy, Vincent Coots 1943
Dragon, Carmen Brooks 1947, 1951

Drake, Milton Alter 1951, 1952, 1953; Carroll 1932; Conrad 1932, 1934, 1937; Duke 1968; Freed, Ralph 1935, 1936; Hoffman 1942, 1943, 1944, 1945, 1946, 1963; Livingston, Jerry 1942, 1943, 1944, 1945, 1946, 1963; Magidson 1940; Meyer 1951; Oakland 1934, 1935, 1936, 1937, 1938, 1940, 1941, 1942, 1943, 1946, 1962, 1968; Silver 1932; Styne 1953

Drake, Oliver Stept 1935, 1942

Drdla, Franz Johnson, Howard 1934

Drejac Lawrence 1949

Dreyer, Dave Brown, Lew 1926; Clare 1926, 1929; Conrad 1935; David, Mack 1933; Davis 1931, 1932; DeSylva 1929; Friend 1931, 1949; Gilbert 1930; Johnston 1926, 1927, 1929, 1930; Monaco 1926; Rose 1927, 1928, 1929; Sterling 1920; Turk 1934; Webster 1936; Woods 1925; Young, Joe 1932, 1933

Dreyfus, Max Kern 1905; Sterling 1899

Driggs, Colline Hoffman 1950

Drigo, R. Johnson, Howard 1934

Dring, Perry Parish 1930

Drislane, Jack Bryan 1909, 1910; Meyer 1908, 1909, 1910, 1911, 1912, 1913

Druce, Jeanette Blake 1955

Drury, Charles Bryan 1954; Kahn 1921

Drutman, Irving Lawrence 1945, 1946, 1947, 1951; Mancini 1946

Dubin, Joe Mercer 1953

Duboff, Al Warren Date Unknown

DuBois, Gladys Conrad 1929, 1931

Dubussy, Claude Parish 1956

Duchesne, Raphael Caesar 1944, 1945

Duchin, Peter Adams 1975; Heyman 1967

Duddy, Lyn Lawrence 1959, 1960

Dudley, Bide Friml 1919; Harbach 1919; Norworth 1917

Duffy, James Kern 1912

Duffy, Jimmy Fisher 1921, 1924; Hanley 1929

Dulmage, Will Whiting 1926

Dumont, Charles David, Hal 1961

Dunbar, Paul Lawrence Blake 1957; Johnson, J. Rosamond 1917

Duncan, Harrison Johnson, James P. 1957, 1959, 1960

Duncan, Rosetta Coslow 1924, 1932

Duncan, Vivian Coslow 1924, 1932

Duncan, William Cary Caesar 1924; Friml 1922; Hammerstein 1923; Harbach 1922; Schwartz, Jean 1928; Youmans 1923

Dunham, "By" Myrow 1959

Dunham, Sunny Cahn 1937

Duning, George Bergman 1966; Brooks 1962; Styne 1961; Washington 1956, 1957, 1958, 1959, 1960, 1961

Dunkerley, Stanley Johnson, Howard 1920

Dunlap, Paul Heyman 1955

Dunn, Edward Delaney Atteridge 1921; Smith, Harry B. 1923

Dunne, Kirby Caesar 1954

Dunstedter, Eddie Coslow 1940; Loesser 1943, 1944

Dupree, Frank Smith, Harry B. 1927

Durand, Paul Drake 1956; Parish 1948, 1950, 1959, 1961, 1962; Sigman 1956

Durante, Jimmy Adamson 1934; Akst 1952; Bryan 1944, 1945; Bullock 1938; Caesar 1938, 1944; Coslow 1923; Davis 1952; Hart 1932, 1933, 1934; Johnston 1932; Rodgers 1933, 1934; Spina 1938, 1944, 1950

Durham, Billy Norworth 1916

Duromo, R. Waller 1931

Dvorak, Anton Dubin 1922; Johnson, Howard 1932; Kahn 1927

Dyrenforth, David Rodgers 1917

Dyrenforth, James Duke 1927; Rose 1931

Dyson, Hal Coslow 1927

E

Eager, Edward Coots 1946, 1950, 1959; Revel 1957

Easdale, Brian Sigman 1958

East, Ed Adamson 1940; Coots 1945

Easter, Jimmy Freed, Ralph 1965, 1966

Eastwood, Clint Cahn 1987

Eaton, Farley Revel 1947

Eaton, Jimmy Carroll 1939; Silver 1940

Ebb, Fred Strouse 1956, 1957

Ebbins, Milton Freed, Ralph 1943; Russell 1943, 1945

Eberwein Webster 1954

Eckstein, William Buck 1920

Eckstine, Billy Parish 1944; Russell 1948

Eddy, Nelson Oakland 1960; Weill 1944

Eddy, Simon David, Mack 1955

Edelheit, Harry Howard, Joseph E. 1921; Parish 1933

Edelstein, Hilly Ellington 1939; Loesser 1939

Edelstein, Walter Mercer 1971

Edens, Roger Atteridge 1954; Blane 1945, 1946, 1948, 1964; Brown, Lew 1943; Brown, Nacio Herb 1937, 1940; Comden and Green 1947, 1949, 1952, 1955; Freed, Arthur 1937, 1940, 1941, 1946; Freed, Ralph 1941, 1943, 1946; Harburg 1933, 1943; Kahn 1938; Martin 1945, 1946, 1964; Romberg 1954; Rose 1933

Edmonds, Charles Dubin 1921

Edwards, Anne Jean Coots 1943

Edwards, Ben Leslie 1910

Edwards, Clara Lawrence 1940, 1941

Edwards, Cliff Caesar 1925; Conrad 1926; Dubin 1926; Koehler 1928; Mills 1926; Turk 1924

Edwards, E.B. Mercer 1950

Edwards, Ed Brown, A. Seymour 1940, 1941, 1943

Edwards, Julian Smith, Robert B. 1909

Edwards, Leo Atteridge 1915; Brown, Lew 1913, 1923, 1950; Bryan 1903, 1905, 1915, 1916, 1929; Caesar 1924, 1925, 1928, 1938, Date Unknown; Clarke 1918, 1919; Cobb 1950, Date Unknown; Dubin 1924; Edwards 1907, 1909; Fisher 1918, 1919; Gilbert 1916; Rose 1934; Smith, Robert B. 1909

Edwards, Michael Mills 1950; Parish 1945

Edwards, Nole Johnson, Howard 1960

Edwards, Powell Razaf 1938

Edwards, Ralph Meyer 1912

Edwards, Sherman David, Hal 1958, 1959, 1960, 1961, 1962, 1963; David, Mack 1961, 1962, 1963

Effros, Bob Mills 1923

Egan, Jack Brown, Lew 1917, 1918, 1949

Egen, Austin Brown, Lew 1924

Egizi, Alfred Coots 1938

Eglash, Jack Cahn 1976

Ehrle, J.M. Heyman 1943

Ehrlich, Sam Clare 1924; Conrad 1919; Schwartz, Jean 1912

Eiger, Walter Sigman 1954, 1958

Eisler, Hans Coslow 1943

Eisler, Paul Robin 1932

Eldridge, Al Davis 1925

Elgar, Edward Johnson, Howard 1935

Elgart, Betty Sigman 1946

Elias, Al   Silver 1958

Elias, Michael   Coots 1953, 1955

Elie, Paul   Burke 1956

Eller, Harry   Johnson, Howard 1928

Ellington, Mercer   De Lange 1945; Ellington 1943

Elliott, Billy   Friend 1920

Elliott, Dean   Russell 1956, 1957, 1958

Elliott, Jack   Brown, Nacio Herb 1952; Fain 1965; Oakland 1953, 1968, 1969, 1970; Spina 1941, 1947, 1948, 1949, 1950, 1951, 1952, 1953, 1954, 1957; Young, Victor 1950, 1951

Ellis, Charles   Russell 1960

Ellis, Don   Mills 1966

Ellis, Herb   Mills 1966

Ellis, Jack   Arlen 1929; Coots 1926, 1929; Johnson, Howard 1928

Ellis, Melville   Jerome 1910

Ellis, Phil   Johnson, Howard 1928

Ellis, Steve   Hoffman 1945

Ellis, Vivian   Caesar 1936; Yellen 1930

Ellstein, Abraham   Bullock 1950; Parish 1964

Ellwood, Fred   Snyder 1909

Elman, Ziggy   David, Mack 1940; Mercer 1939

Eltinge, Julian   Snyder 1908

Elvey, Maurice   Stept 1963

Emanuel, G.A.   Warren Date Unknown

Emer, Michael   Adamson 1951; Davis 1950; Parish 1935, 1948; Rome 1948

Emerson, Howard   Sterling 1899

Emerson, Ida   Howard, Joseph E. 1899, 1902

Emery, Ruth Miller   Johnson, Howard 1928

Emmerich, Bob   Fisher 1935, 1936; Loesser 1934, 1935; Parish 1936; Razaf 1934

Emmet, Bob   Hoffman 1949

Emmett, Dan   Coslow 1936

Endor, Chick   Koehler 1929

Endrigo, Sergio   Sigman 1968

Engelberger, Willy   Caesar 1925

Englander, Ludwig   Smith, Harry B. 1896, 1900, 1901, 1902, 1903, 1904, 1905, 1906, 1908

English   Monaco 1910

English, Granville   Brennan 1928

Engvick, William   David, Mack 1952

Epstein, Don K.   Cohan 1970

Erdman, Ernie   Brown, Lew 1922; Davis 1919, 1920; Donaldson 1925; Kahn 1921, 1922, 1923, 1925; Koehler 1923; Yellen 1920

Erdman, Sid   Davis 1919

Erdody, Leo   Ager 1932; Parish 1931

Erickson, F.   Russell 1953

Erickson, Jack   Friend 1936

Erlich, Sam   Conrad 1935; Edwards 1907; Fisher 1919

Ernst, Eddy   Sigman 1959

Ervin, Fred   Bryan 1912

Ervin, Michael   David, Mack 1971

Erwin, George "Pee Wee"   Robison 1959

Erwin, Ralph   Lewis 1929; Young, Joe 1929

Eshbaugh, Ted   Coots 1953

Essary, Nettie   Woods 1933

Etting, Ruth   Baer 1927; Fisher 1930; Gilbert 1927

Europe, James Reese   Blake 1918, 1919; Buck 1915; Kern 1915; Sissle 1918, 1919, 1921

Evans, Howard   David, Mack 1945, 1957

Evans, Paul   David, Hal 1962

Evans, Redd   David, Hal 1950; Silver 1942

Evans, Tolchard   Kahn 1926

Evans, Tom   Parish 1929

Everest, John   Duke 1968

Everly, Margaret   David, Mack 1979

Eyre, Laurence   Herbert 1924

Eysler, Edmund   Atteridge 1911, 1912; Romberg 1915

Eyton, Frank   Dietz 1930; Heyman 1930; Schwartz, Arthur 1933

F

Faber, Billy   Parish 1932

Fabian, Don   David, Hal 1946

Faconi, Norbert   Coslow 1958

Fadden, Bill   Raye 1955

Fagan, Jimmy   Johnson, J. Rosamond 1935

Fagas, Leo E.   Hoffman 1957

Fain, Pearl   Dubin 1931; Meyer 1931

Fairbanks Jr., Douglas   Johnson, Howard 1930

Fairchild, Edgar   Brooks 1945, 1946, 1947

Fairman, George   Leslie 1927; Mills 1931, 1947; Mitchell 1920

Faith, Percy   David, Mack 1965; Drake 1951; Evans 1965, 1966; Livingston, Jay 1965, 1966; Mercer 1963; Russell 1949; Sigman 1950, 1951, 1952, 1953, 1954, 1955, 1957, 1958, 1959, 1960, 1967; Webster 1969

Falco, Anthony   David, Hal 1959

Falco, Ralph   David, Hal 1959

Fall, Leo   Atteridge 1922; Romberg 1922; Smith, Harry B. 1910, 1911, 1913

Fall, Richard   Caesar 1936; Gilbert 1922, 1924, 1925

Fanidi, Theo   Webster 1965

Fanta, Josef   Parish 1953

Farmer, J.   Ellington 1939

Farnsworth, P.   Russell 1952

Farrar, Redmond   Dixon 1927; Kalmar 1925; Leslie 1926, 1927; Rose 1926, 1927; Ruby 1925

Farrar, Walt   Carmichael 1948

Farras, O.   Russell 1941

Farrell, Tom   Fisher 1914

Farrell, William H.   Johnson, James P. 1916, 1917

Farres, Osvaldo   Burke 1951; Cahn 1956; De Lange 1945; Drake 1943; Spina 1948

Farrow, Johnny   Hoffman 1950, 1957

Fascinato, Jack   Kahal 1938; Spina 1966, 1967

Fay, Frank   Alter 1929

Fay, Sheldon   Brooks 1952

Faye, Alice   Lerner, Sammy 1938; Oakland 1938

Faye, Francis   Raye 1939

Faziola, Bernice   Silver 1943

Fazioli, Bernardo   Adamson 1939; Lawrence 1939

Fazioli, Billy   Fisher 1920; Monaco 1923

Fazioli, Caesar   Lawrence 1939

Feather, Leonard   Razaf 1942, 1960

Feeley, Michael   Johnson, J. Rosamond 1935

Feenburg, Barney   Hoffman 1954

Feeney, John   Coots 1946

Fein, Lupin   Ellington 1939; Mills 1938, 1939, 1940; Myrow 1939, 1940

Feingold, Michael   Weill 1977

Feist, Felix F.   Alter 1930; Edwards 1929; Johnson, Howard 1930; Kahn 1930

Felder, E.   Woods 1950

Feldkamp, Walter   Fisher 1926

Feldman, A.C.   Bryan 1913

Felix, Gerald   Mitchell 1921
Felix, Hugo   Harbach 1910
Fellavicini, V.   Sigman 1968
Feller, Sherm   Sigman 1952, 1953
Fender, Harry   Conrad 1926
Fenstock, Belle   Bryan 1934, 1952; Burke 1940; Caesar 1953, 1956; David, Mack 1941; Harbach 1942; Leslie 1935; Meyer 1934, 1941; Rose 1940; Yellen 1953; Young, Joe 1934
Ferazzano, Fred   Drake 1949
Ferera, Frank   McHugh 1923; Sterling 1926
Ferguson, Harvey   Robin 1929; Whiting 1929
Fernandes, Ivan   Drake 1943
Fernandez, A.   Johnson, Howard 1935
Fernandez, C.   Dubin 1924
Fernwood, Al   Johnson, Howard 1935
Ferrari, Louis   Lawrence 1955; Raye 1951; Sigman 1956; Yellen 1958
Ferre, Cliff   Brooks 1952, 1953, 1954
Ferreira, Djalma   Webster 1962
Ferreria, Bruno   Hoffman 1958, 1959
Fertitta, Paul   Parish 1932
Fetter, Ted   Carmichael 1936; Duke 1936, 1937, 1939, 1940; Eliscu 1931; Revel 1940; Rose 1938, 1939
Fetters, Robert   Howard, Joseph E. 1948, 1950, 1952
Feuchtwanger, Lion   Blane 1955
Feyne, Buddy   Brown, Nacio Herb 1954; Revel 1946, 1948, 1951, 1955, 1956, 1962, 1971
Fibich, Zdenko   Johnson, Howard 1935; Webster 1933, 1944
Fidanzini, Vieri   David, Mack 1947
Fidenco   David, Hal 1961
Fielding, Jerry   Evans 1968; Livingston, Jay 1968; Russell 1969; Washington 1962
Fields, Arthur   Brennan 1915; Burke 1931; Carroll 1911, 1912; Mitchell 1919; Rose 1929
Fields, Benny   Davis 1932; Young, Joe 1934
Fields, Buddy   Lerner, Sammy 1925, 1926, 1932; Rose 1925; Stept 1925; Whiting 1925, 1926
Fields, Frank   Razaf Date Unknown
Fields, George   Brooks 1955
Fields, Herbert   Hart 1922; Rodgers 1920
Fields, Irving   David, Hal 1950, 1951, 1952; Davis 1942, 1948; Drake 1947; Hoffman 1956, 1957, 1958, 1959, 1960; Leigh Date Unknown; Mills 1962
Fields, John Irving   Coots 1950
Fields, R.   Rose 1926; Whiting 1926
Fields, Sammy   Cahn 1981
Fier, Neuman   Parish 1920
Filtzch, Priscilla   McHugh 1958
Fimberg, Hal   Oakland 1970
Fina, Jack   Bullock 1947
Finch, Dick   Kalmar 1925; Lewis 1925; Ruby 1925; Stept 1924; Turk 1924; Young, Joe 1925
Finck, Herman   Goetz 1911
Fine, Sylvia   Cahn 1956
Finegan, William   Sigman 1940
Fink, E.   Rome 1943
Fink, Henry   Silver 1918, 1943
Finke, Johnny   Blake 1953; Razaf 1949, 1950, 1951, 1952, 1953, 1954, 1955, 1956, 1957
Finley, Lorraine N.   Friml 1944; Herbert 1940
Finn, Jack   Parish 1953, 1954
Finston, Nat   Robin 1933
Fiorito, Ted   Brown, Lew 1923, 1944; Bullock 1936, 1952; Coots 1936; Davis 1925, 1928, 1936; Dixon 1929; Dubin

1932, 1937; Egan 1932; Friend 1927; Heyman 1952; Johnson, Howard 1929; Kahn 1921, 1923, 1924, 1925, 1926, 1927, 1928, 1929, 1930, 1931, 1933, 1934; Kalmar 1937; Koehler 1923; Lewis 1928, 1929; Loesser 1939; Parish 1936, 1962; Pollack 1929; Rose 1928; Ruby 1937; Warren 1928, 1929; Webster 1942, 1948, 1950, 1957, 1961; Young, Joe 1928, 1929; Young, Victor 1926
Firari, Clarence   Coots 1961
Firestone, Elizabeth   Brooks 1947
Fischer, Carl   Davis 1955; Merrill 1950
Fischer, Steve   Oakland 1970
Fishback, Cliff   Heyman 1940
Fisher, Aileen   Carmichael 1957
Fisher, Dan   Drake 1946
Fisher, Doris   Bryan 1936, 1939; Fisher 1936, 1937, 1938, 1940, 1941, 1964
Fisher, Eddie   Ager 1953; Akst 1953; Davis 1953
Fisher, George   Gilbert 1941; Heyman 1940; McHugh 1941
Fisher, Harve   Carmichael 1950
Fisher, Irving   Akst 1918
Fisher, Mark   Davis 1925
Fisher, Marvin   Howard, Bart 1965
Fitzgerald   Whiting 1920
Fitzgerald, Edward   Spina 1954
Fitzgerald, Ella   Heyman 1938; Myrow 1940
Fitzgerald, Meph   Egan 1920; Whiting 1920
Fitzhugh, Ellen   Mancini 1985, 1986
Flaherty, Pat   Dubin 1928
Flanagan, Bud   Woods 1932
Flanigan, Ralph   Lawrence 1947
Flatow, Leon   Bryan 1923, 1929, 1930; Clare 1924; Gilbert 1919; Kahn 1922; Mitchell 1927
Fleming, Rhonda   David, Mack 1982
Fletcher, Archie   De Lange 1935; Leslie 1935
Fletcher, Bob   Porter 1935
Fletcher, Bruz   Conrad 1933
Fletcher, Don   David, Hal 1973
Fletcher, Tex   Baer 1955
Flick, Sid   Mills 1951, 1952, 1955
Flindt, Emil   Kahn 1930
Flippen, Jay C.   Gordon 1928, 1929
Flores, Jose Asuncion   Hoffman 1955
Floyd, Chick   Parish 1938
Flynn, Jimmy   Gilbert 1925
Flynn, John H.   Cobb 1900
Fodor, Maurice   Edwards 1937, 1938
Fogarty, Frank   Howard, Joseph E. 1916
Fogarty, J. Paul   Styne 1930
Fokine, Larry   David, Hal 1947
Folsom, Janet   Coslow 1940
Fong, Paul   Fisher 1937
Fontenoy, Marc   Lawrence 1953
Foose, Diana   Lawrence 1940
Foote, Ralph A.   Davis 1919
Forbes, Elliot   Lerner, Alan Jay 1939
Forbes, Lou   Evans 1965; Heyman 1953; Livingston, Jay 1965
Forbes, Randolph   Johnson, J. Rosamond 1944
Ford, Ernie   Blake 1947, 1954; Johnson, J. Rosamond 1944, 1947
Ford, Harry   Coots 1928
Ford, Joseph   Yellen 1928
Ford, Tom   Revel 1935
Ford, Walter   Edwards 1900
Foresythe, Reginald   Razaf 1932, 1933, 1937
Forre, Leo   Robison 1954

Forrest, Chet   Brown, Nacio Herb 1937; Donaldson 1936, 1937, 1940; Drake 1952; Friml 1937; Harbach 1937; Herbert 1946; Pollack 1940

Forricone, Jean   Robison 1946

Forsythe, Reginald   Fields 1934; McHugh 1934

Foss, Chick   Baer 1947

Foster, David   Bacharach 1982

Foster, Frank   Mills 1966

Foster, G.   DeSylva 1917

Foster, Norman   Akst 1937; Clare 1937

Foster, Stephen   Berlin 1933; Gordon 1940; Lawrence 1946; Mercer 1945

Fotine, Larry   David, Hal 1948; Ellington 1946; Washington 1946

Fountain, William   Caesar 1930

Fowler, Roger W.   Gilbert 1937

Fox, Charles   Cahn 1976

Foy, Bryan   Clarke 1921; DeSylva 1919; Hanley 1921; Jerome 1955

Framer, Walt   Coots 1952, 1953, 1955

Francis, Helen   Blake 1961

Francis, William T.   Goetz 1912; Smith, Robert B. 1902

Frank, Melvin   Cahn 1976

Frank, Sid   Styne 1953

Frankel, Abe   Rose 1927

Franklin, Arthur   Clare 1932

Franklin, Blanche   Clare 1923; Friend 1923; Von Tilzer 1924

Franklin, Dan   David, Hal 1941

Franklin, Dave   Dubin 1941, 1943, Date Unknown; Friend 1936, 1937, 1938, 1939, 1947, 1948, 1950, 1951, 1953, 1954; Hanley 1929; Monaco 1937; Parish 1934; Stept 1935, 1936; Warren 1940, 1942, Date Unknown; Washington 1936; Yellen 1923; Young, Victor 1935

Franklin, Gloria   Bryan 1939

Franklin, Jerry   Livingston, Jerry 1943

Franklin, Jimmie   Coots 1944; Johnston 1949; Livingston, Jerry 1941

Franklin, Malvin M.   Brown, Lew 1913; Bryan 1939; Gilbert 1915, 1916, 1922; Goetz 1913; Jerome 1914; Smith, Robert B. 1919

Franklyn, Arthur   Rose 1928

Fray, Jacques   Eliscu 1930; Harburg 1930

Frazzini, Al   Mills 1926

Fredericks, Marc   Cahn 1972, 1973; Parish 1957

Freeborn, Cassius   Olcott 1914

Freeburg, Stan   Young, Victor 1955

Freed, Fred   Rome 1947, 1951; Sigman 1953

Freed, Martin   Gilbert 1929

Freed, S.T.   Freed, Ralph 1957

Freed, Walter   Freed, Ralph 1976

Freedland, Beverly   Russell 1941

Freedland, Judy   Russell 1941

Freeman, L.E.   Cahn 1936

Freeman, Ned   Raye 1959

Freeman, R.   Leigh 1981

Freeman, Stan   Lawrence 1960, 1961, 1962, 1964, 1966, 1968

Freeman, Ticker   David, Mack 1946, 1949, 1953, 1954; Mills 1934

French, Alex   Sissle 1928

Frey, Fran   Young, Victor 1942

Frey, Hugo   Alter 1927; Atteridge 1907; Bryan 1926; Caesar 1919; Johnson, Howard 1930; Robison 1928, 1929

Freyberg, Mart   Drake 1941

Fried, Barbara   Coleman 1972, 1979, 1983, 1984

Fried, Gerald   Bergman 1957; Mercer 1962

Friedhofer, Hugo   Washington 1956; Webster 1957

Friedland, Anatole   Atteridge 1912; Brown, A. Seymour 1912, 1913, 1914; Bryan 1908; Dixon 1923; Gilbert 1915, 1916, 1917, 1918, 1919, 1937; Kahn 1920

Friedland, Malvin D.   Gilbert 1917

Friedlander, William B.   Conrad 1924, 1925; Howard, Joseph E. 1907, 1942, 1943, 1964

Friedman, Alan   Heyman 1963

Friedman, Allan Jay   Webster 1965

Friedman, Charles   Rome 1937

Friedman, Leo   Bryan 1907

Friedman, Max   Brown, Lew 1926; Stept 1917

Friedman, Max C.   Silver 1956

Friedman, Robert   Mercer 1973; Webster 1973

Friend, A.   Kalmar 1922; Ruby 1922

Friend, Madge   Friend 1923

Friml, Mrs. Rudolf   Friml 1911

Friml, William   Harburg 1952

Frisby, George   Norworth 1954

Frisch, Al   Burke 1958; David, Hal 1947, 1950; Sigman 1960; Silver 1947, 1948

Frisch, Billy   Caesar 1931, 1933; Davis 1929; Donaldson 1923; Jerome 1923; Johnson, Howard 1918; Loesser 1933, 1934; Motzan 1928, 1929, 1930, 1931, 1932, 1933, 1934; Schwartz, Jean 1931

Fristorp, Goran   David, Hal 1985

Frohlichstein, Harvey   Hoffman 1943; Livingston, Jerry 1943

Frontenoy, Marc   Lawrence 1953

Frost, Chester E.   Mills 1930

Frost, Frances   Young, Victor 1945

Frost, Jack   Donaldson 1922; Fisher 1922; McHugh 1922

Fryberg, Mart   Friend 1949

Fulcher, Charlie   Parish 1980

Fuller, Dee   Fain 1964

Fuller, Dolores   Cahn 1960; Van Heusen 1960, 1963

Fulton, Johnny   Young, Joe 1932

Fumiere, Francis   Sigman 1967

Funk, Franz   Rome 1953

Furber, Douglas   Caesar 1925, 1927, 1929; Gershwin, Ira 1930; Schwartz, Arthur 1929, 1933; Youmans 1925

Furin, Matt   Coots 1949, 1950, 1952, 1953, 1954, 1955, 1958, 1967

Furin, Steve   Coots 1954

Furtado, Tommy   David, Hal 1957

Furth, George   Sondheim 1971

Furth, Seymour   Bryan 1911; Cobb 1907; Jerome 1907; Kalmar 1910

Furthman, Jules   Hanley 1931

Fysher, A. Nilson   Gilbert 1915

G

Gabler, Milt   Ellington 1940

Gaboroche, Gaston   Dubin 1924

Gade, George A.   Adamson 1975

Gaines, Lee   Ellington 1941

Galassi, Frank   Mills 1928, 1929

Galdieri, M.   Raye 1956

Gale, Bill   Brown, Lew 1939

Gale, Kay Wood   Washington 1952

Galian, Geri   Clare 1954; Young, Victor 1954

Gallagher, Ed   Dubin 1924; McHugh 1924

Gallagher, S.T.   Russell 1947

Gallop, Sammy   Bacharach 1956; Bloom 1947; Coots 1947, 1956; Hoffman 1954, 1955; Livingston, Jerry 1954, 1955,

1959; Sigman 1949, 1950; Silver 1950, 1955; Van Heusen 1955; Woods 1946, 1956, 1957

Galvin, Frank   Kahn 1924

Gamble, Louis   Egan 1925; Whiting 1925

Gamble, Maynard   Razaf 1946

Gamble, William   Snyder 1909

Gannaway, Al   Carmichael 1948, 1949

Ganne, Louis   Johnson, Howard 1935

Gannon, Kim   Alter 1954, 1955; Coots 1940, 1942; Myrow 1940, 1941, 1942, 1943, 1967; Stept 1952; Styne 1941, 1943

Garber, Jan   Turk 1927

Garcia, Caridad   Rome 1945

Garcia, Russ   Russell 1956, 1958

Gardenier, Ed   Edwards 1904, 1907, 1908, 1909; Fisher 1907

Gardner, Ed "Archie"   Carmichael 1946

Gardner, Herb   Styne 1980

Gardner, Nat   Cahn 1935

Garinei   Sigman 1964

Garland, Joe   Mills 1935; Razaf 1939

Garland, Joseph   Mills 1935

Garner, Erroll   Burke 1954; Cahn 1973; Heyman 1962, 1963, 1980; Mercer 1980; Russell 1957

Garreau, Claude   Parish 1931

Garren, Joseph J.   Dubin 1922

Garrett, Joe   Dubin 1923

Garson, Henry   Brooks 1950

Garson, Milt   Russell 1965

Garson, Mort   David, Hal 1960, 1961; David, Mack 1961, 1965; Russell 1968

Gartin, Paula   Friend 1926

Gartland, Joseph   Mills 1934

Garvarentz, G.   Raye 1964

Gary, John   Fain 1964

Gaskill, Clarence   Brown, A. Seymour 1915; Brown, Lew 1925; Bryan 1932; Conrad 1927; Donaldson 1918; Dubin 1917, 1919, 1920, 1921, 1925; Ellington 1930; Fisher 1923, 1924; Leslie 1926; McHugh 1925, 1926, 1928, 1938; Mills 1925, 1926, 1930, 1931; Monaco 1919; Parish 1934; Robin 1931; Rose 1925

Gasman, Ira   Coleman 1984, 1996; Lane Date Unknown; Styne 1976

Gaso, Heine   Hoffman 1957

Gaspar, Tiberio   Bergman 1969

Gasparre, Dick   Adamson 1940; Heyman 1938

Gaste, Louis   Lawrence 1955

Gaston, Billy   Conrad 1932; Young, Joe 1932

Gay, Byron   Dubin 1917; Egan 1926; Freed, Arthur 1925; Whiting 1925, 1926, 1927, 1935

Gay, Noel   Kahn 1931

Gayle, Tim   Coots 1945, 1949, 1951

Gayten, Paul   Russell 1958

Gaze, Heino   Adamson 1957, 1966; David, Mack 1951; Howard, Bart 1959; Sigman 1953, 1958; Spina 1960

Gebest, Charles J.   Cohan 1908; Jerome 1911

Gedarro, Carlos   Drake 1954

Gehrig, Mrs. Lou   Fisher 1935, 1936

Geiger, Dorothy   Hoffman 1954

Gelbart, Larry   Martin 1958

Gelbtrunk, Adam   Caesar 1936, 1938

Geller, H.   Russell 1950

Geller, Harry   Brooks 1952, 1954; David, Mack 1954

Genet, Rosalind   Bryan 1936

Genise, Adolfo   Caesar 1921

Gensler, Lewis E.   Bryan 1958; Caesar 1923; De Lange 1958; DeSylva 1925, 1926; Gershwin, Ira 1923, 1924, 1925; Hammerstein 1922; Harburg 1932, 1958; Mercer 1932, 1933, 1935, 1958; Mitchell 1922; Robin 1928, 1934, 1935, 1936

George, Dick   Arlen 1926

George, Don   Ellington 1944, 1945, 1946, 1947, 1953, 1967, 1968; Oakland 1935; Schwartz, Jean 1948; Wrubel 1946, 1947

George, Don R.   Gilbert 1945, 1950; Spina 1967

Gerard, William F.   Edwards 1910

Gerber, Alex   Akst 1925; Brennan 1919, 1921; Johnson, Howard 1916, 1917, 1918; Meyer 1918; Romberg 1919, 1920, 1924; Schwartz, Jean 1921, 1922, 1923, 1924; Silver 1919, 1920, 1921

Gerlach, Horace   Van Heusen 1937

Gerow, Bob   Cahn 1933

Gershenson, Joseph   David, Mack 1967

Gershwin, Arthur   De Lange 1940; Heyman 1935

Gerstenberger, Emil   Johnson, Howard 1927

Gerun, Tom   Freed, Arthur 1932

Gesner, Harry   Parish 1931, 1932

Getzov, R.   Styne 1953

Ghertler, Monte   Strouse 1974

Ghossman   Silver 1918; Sterling 1918

Gianini, Vittorio   Robin 1927

Gibbons, Carroll   Rose 1931

Gibbons, Paul   Snyder 1939

Gibbs, Ruth D.   Blake 1956

Gibling, Howard   Myrow 1942

Gibson, Joe   Coslow 1920

Gibson, Sidney   Dixon 1923

Gideon, Melville   Atteridge 1911, Date Unknown; Bryan 1908; Gilbert 1911; Goetz 1908, 1909, 1910, 1911, 1919; Leslie 1909; Porter 1918

Gietz, Hans   Russell 1960

Gietz, Heinz   Adamson 1957; Caesar 1961; Sigman 1955, 1958, 1961; Washington 1957; Webster 1956

Gifford, H. Eugene   Johnson, Howard 1934; Washington 1933

Gigandet, Joseph   Stept 1955

Gigante, Marcello   Stept 1956

Gil, Chucho Martinez   Duke 1941

Gilbert, Bobby   Gilbert 1921

Gilbert, Herschel Burke   Bergman 1957; Heyman 1955; Russell 1956, 1958

Gilbert, Jean   Atteridge 1914; Duke 1926; Eliscu 1932; Gordon 1932; Revel 1932; Romberg 1914; Smith, Harry B. 1912, 1913, 1928, 1930, 1932; Smith, Robert B. 1912

Gilbert, Jerry   Young, Joe 1941

Gilbert, Joseph George   Baer 1955; Bryan 1935; Leslie 1926, 1927, 1928, 1929, 1932; McHugh 1924; Yellen 1949

Gilbert, Mercedes   Johnson, James P. 1922, 1923, 1924

Gilbert, Ray   Carmichael 1943, 1944; Johnston 1948; Oakland 1952, 1954, 1955, 1956, 1960, 1961; Pollack 1943, 1950; Russell 1948, 1949; Wrubel 1946, 1954

Gilbertson, Virginia   Stept 1953

Gill, Emerson   Kahn 1925; Whiting 1925

Gillen, Frank J.   Motzan 1919

Gillespie, Arthur   Edwards 1899, 1907; Howard, Joseph E. 1906, 1910

Gillespie, Dizzy   Russell 1957

Gillespie, Haven   Baer 1934, 1965; Carroll 1950; Coots 1934, 1935, 1936, 1937, 1938, 1950, 1956, 1957, 1958, 1964; David, Mack 1938; Egan 1956; Herbert 1935; Parish

1935, 1936; Schwartz, Jean 1955; Whiting 1926, 1927, 1928, 1929, 1956; Young, Victor 1931, 1952

Gillette, Gladys   Yellen 1922

Gillham, Art   Johnson, Howard 1931

Gilmore, Helen   Parish 1930

Gilrod, Louis   Motzan 1937

Gilroy, John   Goetz 1906

Gilson, Paul   Duke 1948

Gimbel, Norman   Bacharach 1961, 1976, 1977; Hoffman 1952, 1954, 1955, 1956; Mancini 1964

Gindhart, Thomas   Myrow 1939

Giordano, A.   Raye 1958

Giovannini   Sigman 1964

Giraud, Hubert   Lawrence 1958; Sigman 1958, 1960

Gismonti, Egberto   Evans 1970; Livingston, Jay 1970

Gittleman, Aubrey   Egan 1915

Gladstone, Jerry   Myrow 1959, 1960

Glanzberg, Norbert   Raye 1960; Sigman 1959

Glaser, C.J.M.   Smith, Harry B. 1909

Glason, Billy   Coots 1933; Johnson, Howard 1933; McHugh 1949; Pollack 1924

Glasser, Al   Bergman 1957

Gleason, Jackie   Caesar 1963; Cahn 1962; Davis 1952, 1953, 1954

Glick, Jesse G.M.   Howard, Joseph E. 1918

Glicker, Johann   Hoffman 1957

Glickman, Fred   Washington 1950

Glogau, Jack   Brown, Lew 1914, 1923, 1927; Clare 1923; Fisher 1919, 1921; Johnson, Howard 1915, 1916, 1917, 1929; Lewis 1932; Magidson 1928; Ruby 1912; Turk 1928; Yellen 1917; Young, Joe 1912

Glover, Benny   Leigh 1951

Glynn, John   Kahn 1924

Godard, Benjamin   Johnson, Howard 1934; Lawrence 1946

Godhard, Kate   Carmichael 1952

Godowsky, Leopold   Mitchell 1921

Godwin, George   Hoffman 1947; Robin 1947

Goehring, George   Caesar 1976; Webster 1963

Goell, Kermit   Donaldson 1944; Hoffman 1950; Silver 1951

Goering, Al   Bryan 1928; Bullock 1934; Kahn 1931; Mills 1928, 1929; Young, Joe 1934

Goetschius, M.   Hoffman 1952, 1954

Goetz, Coleman   Ager 1915; Carroll 1915; Donaldson 1915; Johnson, Howard 1914, 1917; Koehler 1924, 1926; Meyer 1917; Schwartz, Jean 1915; Stept 1925, 1927, 1929

Goetzl, Anselm   Cohan 1919

Gogotsky, N.   Robin 1931

Gold, Ernest   Cahn 1975; David, Mack 1964; Washington 1965; Webster 1964

Gold, Jack   David, Hal 1953, 1954

Gold, Joe   Bryan 1931; Coslow 1920; Davis 1926; Friend 1956; Parish 1927; Turk 1928; Young, Joe 1932

Gold, Lew   Davis 1924; Kahn 1923

Gold, Lou   Davis 1926; Sterling 1927

Gold, Martin   Drake 1944

Gold, Moe   Parish 1930

Gold, Ray   Razaf 1945

Goldberg, David   Dietz 1929; Edwards 1930; Schwartz, Arthur 1929

Goldberg, Phil   Davis 1920; Kahn 1920, 1922

Goldberg, Rube   Caesar 1934

Golden, Ernie   Bryan 1927; Coslow 1926; Dubin 1922; Fisher 1925; Johnson, Howard 1926; Mitchell 1921; Yellen 1921

Golden, Jack   Koehler 1931; Lewis 1931; Mills 1957; Pollack 1934; Webster 1934

Golden, John   Kern 1912, 1914, 1916

Golden, Ray   Adams 1953; Carmichael 1949; Fain 1950, 1958; Mitchell 1938; Pollack 1938; Styne 1938; Webster 1941, 1950, 1955, 1958

Goldenberg, Billy   Bergman 1978

Goldman, Edwin Franko   Bryan 1929; Rome 1949

Goldsen, Mickey   Mills 1938

Goldsmith, Jerry   Webster 1975

Goldstein, Max   Bryan 1909

Goldstein, Nat   Bryan 1909; DeSylva 1920; Dubin 1924; Kahn 1920

Goldstone, Richard   Adamson 1935; Lane 1935

Gomez, Eddie   Friend 1957

Gomez, Vincente   Parish 1947

Goncalves, Solon   Sigman 1959

Gondringer, Larry   Johnson, Howard 1945

Gonsales Jr., Aaron   Parish 1935

Gonzales, Babs   Russell 1956

Gonzalez, Aaron   Young, Victor 1957

Gonzalez, B.   Russell 1955

Goodhart, Al   Ager 1932; David, Hal 1949, 1950; David, Mack 1934; Egan 1933; Freed, Arthur 1932, 1933; Freed, Ralph 1933; Heyman 1931, 1932, 1933; Hoffman 1930, 1931, 1932, 1933, 1934, 1935, 1936, 1937, 1938, 1939, 1945; Kahn 1933, 1934; Lerner, Sammy 1932, 1934, 1937, 1939; Lewis 1931; Magidson 1932, 1933; Meyer 1947; Parish 1930, 1933, 1954; Washington 1932, 1934; Young, Joe 1934

Goodhart, Arthur J.   Fisher 1912

Goodman, Al   Adamson 1936; Atteridge 1922, 1923; Coots 1925, 1926; Coslow 1924; Friend 1921; Friml 1923; McHugh 1937; Mitchell 1921; Parish 1949; Pollack 1921; Romberg 1922; Schwartz, Jean 1923; Smith, Harry B. 1923, 1926

Goodman, Benny   De Lange 1939; Mills 1935, 1938; Parish 1938; Razaf 1936; Van Heusen 1939

Goodman, Danny   Baer 1956

Goodman, Frank   Stept 1921

Goodman, Helen Thrall   Robin 1932

Goodman, I.R.   Howard, Joseph E. 1907

Goodman, Lillian R.   Kahn 1925

Goodwin, George   David, Mack 1951; Hoffman 1944, 1950, 1951

Goodwin, J. Cheever   Kern 1904

Goodwin, Joe   Ager 1917; Alter 1929, 1930, 1931; Brown, Lew 1911, 1913, 1914; Burke 1930; Donaldson 1915; Dubin 1933; Edwards 1915, 1916, 1929, 1930, 1936; Egan 1929; Fain 1933; Fisher 1912, 1913; Freed, Arthur 1931; Goetz 1914; Hanley 1917, 1918, 1919, 1920, 1922; Henderson 1925; Leslie 1913, 1915; Meyer 1911; Monaco 1917, 1932; Pollack 1941, 1942; Snyder 1914

Goodwin, Ron   Leigh 1957

Goodwin, Theodore   Schwartz, Arthur 1926

Goold, Sam   Parish 1921; Pollack 1924; Silver 1923

Gordon, Gray   Sigman 1942

Gordon, Irving   Ellington 1938, 1939, 1943; Hoffman 1940; Lawrence 1937; Mills 1938, 1939; Silver 1942; Stept 1940

Gordon, Stubby   Kahn 1924

Gordon, Westell   Mitchell 1926

Gore, Christopher   Coleman 1975

Goreau, Lorraine   Lawrence 1953

Gorin, Igor   Adamson 1941

Gorman, Billy   Von Tilzer 1923

Gorman, Eddie   Von Tilzer 1923

Gorman, Jack   Sterling 1911; Von Tilzer 1911

Gorman, Ross   Leslie 1922; Warren 1922, 1923

Gorney, J.   Atteridge 1923

Gorrell, Stuart   Carmichael 1930

Gosch, Robert H.   Cahn 1966, 1967, 1968

Gottesfeld, Charles   Caesar 1943

Gottler, Archie   Baer 1920; Caesar 1921; Clare 1918, 1919, 1920, 1921, 1927, 1928, 1929, 1931, 1944, 1950, 1954, 1958, Date Unknown; Clarke 1918, 1922; Conrad 1928, 1929, 1930, 1932, 1933, 1934, 1935, 1938; Davis 1922, 1928; Edwards 1930; Fain 1931; Fisher 1921; Hoffman 1933; Johnson, Howard 1914, 1915, 1920, 1921; Johnston 1940; Kahal 1931, 1932; Kalmar 1916, 1917; Lerner, Sammy 1944; Leslie 1915, 1916, 1917, 1922; Lewis 1916, 1918, 1927; Meyer 1929, 1930, 1931; Mitchell 1918, 1919, 1920, 1928, 1929, 1930, 1931, 1933, 1934, 1935; Monaco 1932; Pollack 1930; Ruby 1917; Stept 1931, 1934, 1942; Young, Joe 1916, 1918, 1927

Gottlieb, E.   Mercer 1932, 1933

Gottlieb, Raymond   Parish 1937

Gottschalk, Louis F.   Smith, Harry B. 1901

Gould, Morton   Comden and Green 1945; Fields 1950; Heyman 1944, 1961; Lawrence 1955; Leigh 1976, 1977

Gould, William   Edwards 1902

Goulding, Edmund   Freed, Ralph 1956; Gordon 1948; Robin 1930

Gounod, Charles   Johnson, Howard 1935, 1939

Gouraud, Jackson   Kern 1906

Graff, George   Warren 1957

Graff Jr., George   Fisher 1938; McHugh 1923; Olcott 1910, 1911, 1913, 1914

Graham, Berkeley   Friend 1936

Graham, Harry   Kalmar 1928; Kern 1928; Ruby 1928; Smith, Harry B. 1916

Graham, Howard   Von Tilzer 1900

Graham, Irvin   Drake 1952, 1953, 1954, 1955

Graham, John   Kern 1928

Graham, Lewis   Coots 1957

Graham, Margaret   Johnson, J. Rosamond 1918

Graham, Percy   Goetz 1923

Graham, Ruth   Mills 1964

Graham, Steve   Brooks 1955; Evans 1954; Livingston, Jay 1954; Russell 1951; Warren Date Unknown

Grainger, Porter   Johnson, J. Rosamond 1931; Mills 1928

Grand, Murray   Coleman 1965, 1968

Grande, V.   Parish 1935

Grandee, George   Brennan 1949

Grandei, Jacques   Lewis 1919, 1920; Smith, Harry B. 1919, 1920; Young, Joe 1919, 1920

Granet, Eliseo   Gilbert 1931

Granichstaedten, Bruno   Smith, Robert B. 1912

Granlund, Nils T.   Brown, Lew 1923; Hanley 1923

Grant, Bert   Atteridge 1920; Brown, A. Seymour 1911, 1912, 1913; Clarke 1914, 1915; Goetz 1913, 1914, 1915, 1916; Lewis 1912, 1916, 1918, 1919, 1920, 1929; Williams 1913, 1914; Young, Joe 1911, 1912, 1913, 1914, 1915, 1916, 1918, 1919, 1920, 1929

Grant, Eddie   Brown, A. Seymour 1928

Grant, F. Bernard   McHugh 1923

Grant, Freddy   Hoffman 1956, 1957, 1958

Grant, Harold   Coslow 1957; David, Mack 1956; Drake 1941; Leigh 1955

Grant, Ian   Ahlert 1944; Howard, Bart 1938, 1944; Johnston 1938

Grant, John   Mills 1942

Grant, Teddy   Hoffman 1954

Granville, B.   Hanley 1915

Grapewin, Charles   Schwartz, Jean 1911, 1912; Williams 1909

Grass, Francis   Coots 1949

Grassi, Andre   Evans 1954; Livingston, Jay 1954

Grasso, Frank   Razaf 1946

Gravelle, Jeanne   Parish 1928, 1980

Gray, Harold   Mills 1928

Gray, Henry   Kahn 1925

Gray, Jerry   De Lange 1941, 1948; Mercer 1966; Sigman 1940

Gray, Robert   Oakland 1967

Gray, Thomas J.   Carroll 1913; Fisher 1908, 1910; Smith, Robert B. 1915

Gray, Timothy   Blane 1959; Martin 1951, 1952, 1959, 1964, 1969, 1972, 1973, 1977

Greason, Belle   Spina 1954

Greaves, R.B.   David, Mack 1972

Greco, Buddy   Coleman 1964

Greeley, George   Sigman 1954

Green, A.   Leslie 1925

Green, Bernard   Bergman 1958; Kahal 1935

Green, Bud   Baer 1938; Bloom 1928, 1946; Brown, Lew 1923, 1946; Bryan 1933; Burke 1932; Carroll 1926; DeSylva 1924, 1926; Dixon 1931; Dubin 1916, 1920; Fain 1928, 1937; Fisher 1943; Friend 1933; Gorney 1927; Hanley 1923, 1929; Henderson 1922, 1923, 1924, 1942, 1943; Hoffman 1940; Johnson, Howard 1921; Johnson, James P. 1925; Johnston 1920; Monaco 1924, 1933; Myrow 1936; Spina 1932; Stept 1919, 1920, 1925, 1928, 1929, 1930, 1931, 1933, 1934, 1935; Warren 1924, 1925, 1926, 1927, 1928, 1931, 1939, Date Unknown

Green, Dan   Davis 1972

Green, David   Davis 1981; Leigh 1957

Green, H.J.   Smith, Harry B. 1903

Green, Harry   Washington 1956

Green, Jack   Caesar 1947; DeSylva 1923; Gershwin, George 1923; Goetz 1923

Green, Joe   Brennan 1928; Parish 1931

Green, Johnny   Adamson 1940; Blane 1946; Brown, Lew 1943; David, Mack 1932, 1933; Davis 1933, 1939; Dietz 1930; Duke 1930; Eliscu 1939; Freed, Ralph 1943, 1944; Gershwin, Ira 1939; Harburg 1930, 1934, 1935, 1939, 1941, 1944, 1962; Heyman 1929, 1930, 1931, 1932, 1933, 1934, 1935, 1944, 1962; Kahn 1928, 1936; Koehler 1938, 1945; Lawrence 1943, 1945; Lerner, Sammy 1929; Loesser 1946; Mercer 1933, 1939, 1940, 1952, 1965, 1966; Raye 1942, 1959; Robin 1947; Rose 1931; Webster 1958, 1959

Green, Mac   Spina 1932

Green, Marty   Woods 1969

Green, Paul   Weill 1936

Green, Sanford   David, Hal 1947; David, Mack 1935, 1936, 1946

Greenbank, Percy   Duke 1926

Greenberg, Abner   Bryan 1913; Williams 1913; Young, Joe 1913

Greene, Alan   Spina 1946

Greene, Clay M.   Herbert 1898

Greene, George H.   Egan 1919

Greene, I.M.   Caesar 1920

Greene, Iris   Howard, Joseph E. 1951

Greene, Mort   Donaldson 1943, 1944, 1947; Oakland 1954; Pollack 1942, 1946; Revel 1940, 1941, 1942, 1944, 1947, 1952; Wrubel 1944, 1949, 1950, 1951

Greene, Schuyler   Caesar 1921; Gershwin, George 1918; Gershwin, Ira 1921, 1922; Harbach 1925; Kern 1915, 1916, 1917; Motzan 1915, 1916; Smith, Harry B. 1915; Youmans 1921, 1925

Greener, Bob   Oakland 1961

Greenfield, Mannie   Coots 1952, 1953, 1957, 1958

Greenwood, Lil   Ellington 1959

Greer, Jesse   Adamson 1932; Ager 1939; Carroll 1929; Coslow 1927; Davis 1925, 1926, 1927, 1931, 1939; Dixon 1927, 1932, 1936, 1938; Egan 1917; Gilbert 1931; Johnson, Howard 1928, 1929; Kahn 1922; Lewis 1930, 1931; Mitchell 1921; Parish 1931; Rose 1927, 1928, 1930; Sigman 1948; Stept 1933

Gregory, Dan   Friend 1925

Gregory, James   Blane 1962, 1971

Gregory, Paul   Conrad 1931

Grenet, Eliseo   Gilbert 1941

Grennard, Elliott   Conrad 1932; Spina 1937; Waller 1932; Wrubel 1934

Gress, Louis   Friend 1923; Schwartz, Jean 1923

Grever, Maria   Caesar 1945, 1950; Coslow 1930, 1931, 1932; David, Mack 1940; Drake 1946, 1948; Harburg 1934; Lawrence 1938, 1939, 1944; Rainger 1932

Grey, Alan   Parish 1933, 1934

Grey, Clifford   Adamson 1929, 1930, 1932; Atteridge 1925; Brown, Nacio Herb 1931; Caesar 1920, 1924, 1925; Coots 1924, 1925, 1926, 1928; Coslow 1924; Freed, Arthur 1930; Friml 1928; Gershwin, George 1922, 1923; Gershwin, Ira 1925; Gorney 1924; Hanley 1926; Herbert 1925; Johnson, Howard 1930; Kern 1916, 1920; Robin 1927; Romberg 1924, 1925; Schwartz, Arthur 1929; Schwartz, Jean 1924, 1928; Youmans 1925, 1927, 1929, 1930, 1932

Grey, Lanny   Myrow 1954; Parish 1983; Stept 1956

Grey, Ronnie   Oakland 1954

Grier, Jimmie   Coslow 1930, 1932, 1935; Koehler 1936; Stept 1936

Griffin, Gerald   Bryan 1940; Silver 1940

Grimes, Tiny   Sigman 1946

Griselle, Thomas   Young, Victor 1922, 1930, 1932

Grode, Howard   Mills 1930

Grofe, Ferde   Adamson 1943, 1946; Caesar 1932, 1934; Coslow 1922; Kahn 1935; McHugh 1922; Mills 1922; Silver 1924; Turk 1924

Grogan, Francis   Snyder 1930

Gross   Snyder 1924

Gross, Milt   Dubin 1925; McHugh 1925; Monaco 1936

Gross, Raymond   Howard, Bart 1938

Gross, Walter   David, Mack 1930; Dixon 1938; Lawrence 1947; Russell 1956; Sigman 1961; Washington 1934

Grossman, Bernie   Akst 1934; Blake 1927; Coslow 1924; Goetz 1910; Johnston 1946; Leslie 1916; Motzan 1916; Sterling 1917, 1918

Grossman, Julius   Parish 1950

Grossman, Larry   Cahn 1964; Comden and Green 1982; Davis 1961; Mancini 1985, 1986

Grossmith, George   Kern 1906, 1908, 1909, 1921, 1923

Grosz, Wilhelm   Dubin 1932

Grosz, Will   Brown, Lew 1941; Coslow 1939, 1940; David, Mack 1941; Dubin 1940, 1944; Gordon 1939, 1943

Grouya, Ted   Adamson 1944; Cahn 1978; De Lange 1947; DeSylva 1945; Duke 1955; Gershwin, Ira 1942; Gilbert

1945; Heyman 1943; Loesser 1944; Washington 1941, 1962; Webster 1978

Growling Tiger   DePaul 1957

Gruelle, Johnny   Mercer 1931

Grunwald, Alfred   Young, Joe 1930

Grupp, Dave   Hoffman 1945

Grusin, Dave   Bergman 1968, 1975, 1979, 1980, 1982, 1986, 1987; Russell 1968

Guanieri, John   Blake 1972

Guardia, Dilo   Lewis 1941

Guarino, Gian Mario   Livingston, Jerry 1958

Guerra, Roy   Evans 1970; Livingston, Jay 1970

Guerrero, Manuel   Hoffman 1955

Guest, Edgar A.   Loesser 1935

Guggenheim, William   Silver 1940

Guglielmi, Danny   Spina 1954

Guiffre, Jimmy   Russell 1957

Guizar, Pepe   Evans 1946, 1966; Livingston, Jay 1966

Guizar, Tito   Evans 1946, 1966; Fisher 1932; Livingston, Jay 1966

Gulon, Jack   Johnson, Howard 1916

Gumble, Albert   Brown, A. Seymour 1912, 1913, 1914, 1915, 1916; Bryan 1908, 1909, 1910, 1911, 1912, 1913, 1914, 1915, 1916, 1918, 1920, 1921, 1923, 1928, 1929, 1930, 1938, 1958; Conrad 1913; Davis 1917; DeSylva 1918, 1919; Fisher 1932; Goetz 1910; Jerome 1913; Kahn 1918; Mitchell 1917, 1921, 1927; Monaco 1929; Smith, Harry B. 1909; Sterling 1915; Williams 1911; Yellen 1915, 1916, 1917, 1918, 1920, 1922; Young, Joe 1913

Gundry, Bob   David, Mack 1970

Gusman, Meyer   Lewis 1931

Gussev, Victor   Rome 1943

Guthrie, Ruth   Sissle 1915

Gutmann, Arthur   Kahn 1939

Gwynn, Francis   Parish 1930

H

Haase, Alfred L.   Coots 1919

Hackady, Hal   David, Hal 1955

Hackett, Bobby   Drake 1959

Hadjidakis, Manos   Sondheim 1967

Haenschen, Walter Gustave   Akst 1950; Bryan 1939; Buck 1914; Caesar 1920

Hagaev, H.   Rome 1943

Hagen, Earl   Russell 1951

Hagen, Earle   Bullock 1949; Ruby 1954

Hagen, Ross   Freed, Ralph 1964

Hager, Clyde   David, Mack 1939; Livingston, Jerry 1939

Haggar, George A.   Razaf 1946

Haggart, Bob   Burke 1941; Lawrence 1941

Hague, Albert   Adams 1983; Fields 1959

Haines, H.E.   Smith, Robert B. 1905

Hajos, Karl   Brennan 1928, 1929, 1943; Harburg 1935; Rainger 1933; Robin 1930, 1933; Smith, Harry B. 1925, 1928

Hakim, Raphael   De Lange 1948

Hale, Charles   Mercer 1965

Hale, Emory   Gilbert 1945

Halfin, Bob   Parish 1954

Hall, Cliff   Henderson 1922

Hall, Fred   Rose 1929

Hall, G.   Russell 1948

Hall, Jimmy   Howard, Joseph E. 1956

Hall, Skippa   Merrill 1943

Hall, Teddy   David, Mack 1941

Hall, Wendell   Coots 1936; Davis 1936; Johnson, Howard 1934

Halletz, Erwin   Lawrence 1955; Sigman 1959

Halmy, Lou   Heyman 1942

Ham, Al   Bergman 1965, 1966

Hamilton   Fisher 1904, 1905

Hamilton, Andy   Stept 1922

Hamilton, George   Sterling 1901, 1902

Hamilton, Grace   Kahn 1929

Hamilton, Jimmy   Ellington 1964, 1968

Hamilton, Morris   Gershwin, Ira 1924

Hamilton, Nancy   Harburg 1934

Hamilton, Spike   Kahn 1927, 1928

Hamlisch, Marvin   Bacharach 1983; Bergman 1970, 1973, 1979, 1988, 1989, 1990; Leigh 1985; Mercer 1971

Hammed, Tosh   Whiting 1929

Hammerstein, Arthur   Drake 1953

Hammerstein, William   Hammerstein 1942

Hammond, Albert   David, Hal 1974, 1975, 1984

Hamnid, T.A.   Johnston 1921

Hampton, Lionel   Mercer 1947

Hampton, Paul   Bacharach 1958, 1959, 1960, 1961; David, Hal 1958, 1959, 1960, 1961, 1962, 1963, 1977, 1987; Oakland 1968

Hanaford, Maude   Young, Victor 1920

Hancock, Hank   Carroll 1914

Hancock, John   Fisher 1935

Handler, Al   Mills 1927

Handman, Lou   Ahlert 1927; Baer 1942; Bryan 1932, 1933, 1934, 1935, 1936; Caesar 1933; Clarke 1922; David, Mack 1934; Davis 1938; Kahn 1926, 1927; Kalmar 1923; Leslie 1922; Lewis 1922, 1923, 1926; Rose 1923, 1924; Ruby 1923; Turk 1923, 1925, 1926, 1927, 1928; Young, Joe 1922, 1923, 1926

Handy, Elizabeth   Razaf 1936

Handy, W.C.   Coslow 1934; David, Mack 1958; Loesser 1941; Razaf 1935, 1937, 1940, 1942, 1953

Hanford, Ernie   De Lange 1947

Hanighen, Bernard   Adamson 1940; De Lange 1944; Freed, Ralph 1935; Mercer 1933, 1934, 1935, 1937, 1938, 1939, 1940, 1941, 1947, 1979; Sigman 1941

Hanlon, Bert   Akst 1924; Bryan 1922, 1926; Conrad 1918; Donaldson 1917; Johnson, Howard 1921, 1922; Meyer 1922, 1926; Silver 1926; Sterling 1918; Von Tilzer 1917, 1918, 1919

Hanna, Jack   Parish 1925

Hanna, Phil   Oakland 1947

Hannan, Walter F.   Monaco 1941; Spina 1944

Hansen, Al   Mercer 1954, 1958

Hansen, Bill   Livingston, Jerry 1963

Hansen, Dorothy   Spina 1948

Hansen, Juul   Livingston, Jerry 1959

Hansen, Nels   Caesar 1955

Harbach, William   Harbach 1943

Harbin, Loraine C.   Drake 1948

Hare, Ernest   Coslow 1920

Harford   Heyman 1939

Hargauer, Harold   Adamson 1942

Haring, Robert C.   Parish 1980

Harley, John   Razaf 1939

Harline, Leigh   Brooks 1955, 1961; Washington 1938, 1939, 1940, 1946, 1953

Harling, W. Franke   Brennan 1933; Bryan 1928; Coslow 1930, 1931, 1932, 1936; Dubin 1939; Kahn 1934; Rainger 1930, 1932; Robin 1930, 1932; Whiting 1930

Harman, Barry   Lane 1985

Harmati, Sandor   Heyman 1934

Harnell, Joe   Heyman 1967; Parish 1969; Webster 1968

Harnick, Sheldon   Coleman 1972, 1984; Lane 1996; Martin 1959; Rodgers 1976

Harold, Charles   Fisher 1937, 1938, 1940; Lewis 1932

Harold, William   Kahn 1930

Harriman, Al   Brown, Lew 1917, 1918

Harris, Bob   Webster 1967

Harris, Charles K.   Coslow 1921, Date Unknown; Howard, Joseph E. 1915, 1921, 1924

Harris, Dave   Carroll 1923; Kalmar 1919; Leslie 1919, 1947, 1949, 1950

Harris, F. Clifford   Kern 1905, 1906, 1912

Harris, George F.   Sigman 1941

Harris, Harry   Cahn 1946; Fain 1961; Gordon 1934; Mills 1926; Pollack 1942, 1944; Styne 1933, 1946; Young, Victor 1930

Harris, Jack   Brown, Lew 1924

Harris, Johnny   Cahn 1975

Harris, Mort   Heyman 1930; Snyder 1928, 1930, 1931, 1944

Harris, Phil   Kahn 1933

Harris, Remus   Baer 1942, 1944, 1950, 1951, 1952, 1953, 1962, 1965

Harris, Will J.   Ager 1917, 1918; Hanley 1917; Snyder 1915; Young, Victor 1928, 1929

Harrison, Jean   Stept 1953

Hart, Bob   Hoffman 1951, 1954, 1955, 1956, 1957; Silver 1954

Hart, Charles C.   Johnson, J. Rosamond 1913

Hart, Maurice   Hoffman 1953

Hart, Will J.   Lewis 1915; Monaco 1914

Harte, Murray   Fisher 1937

Harting, Frank   Coots 1952

Hartley, Ray   Lawrence 1955, 1958, 1959; Stept 1953

Hartman, Don   Gorney 1933, 1934, 1935; Hoffman 1933; Rainger 1937; Robin 1937

Hartman, E.   Duke 1934; Harburg 1934

Harvey, Bob   Hoffman 1958

Harvey, J. Clarence   Edwards 1907

Harvey, Norman   Parish 1923

Harvey, Steve   David, Hal 1957

Harwell, Ernie   Mercer 1985

Haskins, Will B.   Sterling 1924

Hassen, Douglas   Van Heusen 1962

Hatch, Tony   Stept 1958

Hathaway, Charles   De Lange 1940, 1946; Fisher 1931; Raye 1957; Russell 1943, 1944

Hatley, Marvin   Bullock 1936, 1937

Hauser, Jack   Burke 1932; Fain 1926

Havel, Arthur   Coots 1945, 1946

Havez, Jean   Atteridge 1911; Cobb 1917; Edwards 1913, 1914, 1917; Von Tilzer 1910

Havez, Lou   Edwards 1914

Hawes, Norman   McHugh 1960, 1969

Hawk, Charles   Coots 1954

Hawkins, Barbara   Johnson, Howard 1966

Hawkins, Coleman   Sigman 1941

Hawkins, N.D.   Friml 1949

Hawkshaw, Alan   Bergman 1988

Hayel, Arthur   Coots 1946

Hayes, Bruce   Drake 1943

Hayes, Edgar   Koehler 1932; Mills 1932, 1934, 1935, 1936; Washington 1932, 1934

Hayes, George   Mills 1931

Hayes, Grace   Yellen 1930

Hayes, Peter Lind   Brown, Nacio Herb 1958; Loesser 1944, Date Unknown; Robison 1950, 1958, 1967

Haymes, Joe   Friend 1932; Mills 1935

Hays, Billy   Koehler 1929; Myrow 1939

Hayton, Lennie   Freed, Ralph 1942

Hazel, Rupert   Caesar 1922

Hazill, Fred J.   Snyder 1906

Hazzard, John E.   Kern 1915

Headland, I.T.   Carmichael 1944

Heale, Pat K.   Revel 1929

Healy   Snyder 1924

Healy, Dan   Kahal 1927; McHugh 1927

Healy, Vincent   Von Tilzer 1926, 1936

Heard, James   Porter 1918

Heath, Bobby   Brown, Lew 1917; Fisher 1918; McHugh 1923, 1924

Heath, Milt   Stept 1944

Heatherton, Ray   David, Mack 1938; Livingston, Jerry 1938

Hecht, Ben   Wrubel 1958

Hecht, Ken   David, Hal 1946; Raye 1938; Revel 1954

Heelan, Will A.   Edwards 1901; Sterling 1916

Hefti, Neal   Bergman 1972; Cahn 1968; David, Hal 1967; Evans 1965; Howard, Bart 1959; Livingston, Jay 1965; Mercer 1967

Heidt, Horace   Baer 1931

Heifitz, Vera   Davis 1946; Silver 1946

Heilner, Irwin   Van Heusen 1937

Hein, Silvio   Brennan 1925; Brown, A. Seymour 1910; Bryan 1902; Goetz 1910; Hammerstein 1917; Smith, Harry B. 1915; Sterling 1902, 1903

Heindorf, Ray   Blane 1949; Cahn 1949, 1950, 1951, 1955; Koehler 1944, 1945; Washington 1956; Webster 1955, 1958

Held, Anna   Bryan 1916, 1917

Held, Wilbur   Fisher 1922; Rose 1922

Helf, J. Fred   Bryan 1910; Leslie 1913; Smith, Robert B. 1905; Sterling 1909

Heller, E.H.   Revel 1947

Helm, Emery H.   Mills 1939

Henderson, Bob   De Lange 1940

Henderson, Charles E.   Adamson 1954; Gordon 1940, 1943, 1945, 1948; Heyman 1934; Robin 1931, 1942; Snyder 1942

Henderson, F.   Parish 1962

Henderson, Fletcher   Mills 1934, 1935, 1942; Razaf 1952

Henderson, Luther   Blake 1958

Hendler, Nerb   Oakland 1957

Hendrie, D.   Woods 1932

Henkel, George   Baer 1965

Henneman, Hanle   Edwards 1927

Henning, Horst-Heinz   Sigman 1974

Henriques, Dudley   Fisher 1934

Henry, Clarence   Russell 1958

Henry, S.R.   Gilbert 1915; Goetz 1910

Henshel, J.G.   Johnson, Howard 1920; Yellen 1920

Henshel, Jimmie   Kahn 1923

Herbert, Eugene   Parish 1925, 1926

Herbert, Fitz   Drake 1945

Herbert, Frederick   Mancini 1953, 1954

Herbert, Jean   Ager 1935, 1937; Caesar 1936; Coots 1929; Coslow 1926, 1927; Dubin 1927; Fain 1925, 1928; Fisher 1923; Hanley 1929, 1934, 1935, 1938; Loesser 1933; Mills 1929; Rose 1927, 1938

Herbert, Joseph W.   Herbert 1911, 1923; Smith, Harry B. 1911

Herbin, Vittorio   Parish 1954

Herman, Al   Hoffman 1945, 1946; Silver 1918, 1919

Herman, Lenny   Merrill 1949

Herman, Pinky   Caesar 1958; Coots 1944, 1963; Silver 1943

Herman, Woody   Mercer 1952

Hernandez, Chuy   Drake 1948

Hernandez, Rafael   Drake 1948

Herpin, Rome 1945

Herrand, Marc   Sigman 1950

Herrick, Paul   Wrubel 1947, 1948

Herschell, William   Carmichael 1946

Herscher, Louis   Davis 1922; Gilbert 1925, 1939; Hoffman 1931; Loesser 1935; Mills 1964; Parish 1924, 1928, 1929, 1930, 1934

Hess, Cliff   Ager 1919, 1920; Ahlert 1914; Baer 1938, 1939, 1941, 1942, 1943, 1949, 1952, 1953, 1965, 1966; Bryan 1918; Clarke 1917; Goetz 1915, 1916; Johnson, Howard 1919, 1920, 1921, 1922; Leslie 1918; Lewis 1917, 1922, 1929, 1938; Meyer 1907, 1925; Mitchell 1918, 1919; Turk 1907, 1925; Yellen 1919; Young, Joe 1917, 1922, 1929, 1930

Hess, John   Lawrence 1947

Heuberger, Richard   Burke 1948

Hewitt, Joseph F.   Brown, Lew 1943; Parish 1947

Heyman, Werner R.   Harburg 1931; Kahn 1934; Koehler 1937

Heyward, DuBose   Gershwin, George 1935; Gershwin, Ira 1935; Kern 1939

Heywood, Donald   Ellington 1962; Lewis 1929; Mills 1931; Razaf 1938, 1962, Date Unknown; Young, Joe 1929

Hibbler, Ray   Egan 1915

Hibo, R.   Mitchell 1928

Hickman, Art   Williams 1918

Hicks, Robert   Johnson, James P. 1940

Hicks, William P.   Mills 1937

Higginbotham, Irene   David, Mack 1946; Drake 1946; Johnson, Howard 1940; Razaf 1941, 1944, Date Unknown; Silver 1942

Higgins, Bob   Lawrence 1946

Hilbert, J.   Caesar 1919

Hilbert, N.   Caesar 1919

Hill, Alex   Mills 1934, 1935; Razaf 1930, 1931, 1933, 1935; Waller 1930, 1931, 1933, 1937

Hill, Billy   Brennan 1936; Bryan 1933; Davis 1944; Lewis 1932, 1933, 1934; Robison 1946; Young, Joe 1933

Hill, Dedette Lee   Ager 1939; Robison 1938

Hill, H.   Mercer 1966

Hill, Henry   Heyman 1955; Raye 1956; Washington 1956

Hill, J. Leubrie   Atteridge 1915; Johnson, J. Rosamond 1911, 1912

Hillebrand, Fred   Hanley 1938

Hilliam, B.C.   Edwards 1929

Hilliard, Bob   Arlen 1949; Bacharach 1960, 1961, 1962, 1963, 1965, 1966; Fain 1948, 1949, 1950, 1951, 1955, 1961, 1976; Russell 1947; Sigman 1947, 1948, 1949, 1950, 1952, 1953; Silver 1957; Styne 1950, 1953, 1954; Young, Victor 1950, 1952

Hillman, Roc   David, Hal 1945; Freed, Ralph 1934; Merrill 1952; Spina 1947

Hilton, James   Warren 1956

Hime, Francis   Evans 1970; Livingston, Jay 1970

Hines, Earl   Ellington 1966; Razaf 1933

Hines, Joe   Leslie 1943

Hinkle, Hart   Johnson, J. Rosamond 1942

Hinton, Frayser   Kahn 1932

Hinton, Frayzer   Kahn 1927

Hird, Russell J.   Akst 1923; Davis 1923; Koehler 1925

Hirsch, Hugo   Caesar 1922

Hirsch, Louis A.   Atteridge 1911, 1912, Date Unknown; Buck 1915, 1916, 1918, 1922; Caesar 1922, 1923, 1924; Conrad 1923, 1924; Gershwin, George 1923; Goetz 1907, 1908, 1909, 1911; Harbach 1917, 1920, 1921, 1924

Hirsch, Sandy   Sterling 1900

Hirsch, Walter   Burke 1931; Carmichael 1934; Friend 1923; Hanley 1921; Koehler 1927; Motzan 1921, 1922; Pollack 1927; Styne 1934; Warren 1926; Yellen 1923

Hirschhorn, Joel   David, Mack 1965

Hirst, George   Eliscu 1932

Hobart, George V.   Herbert 1906, 1907, 1909, 1911, 1914, 1940; Kern 1912; Schwartz, Jean 1905

Hoch, Harry   Snyder 1919

Hodel, Andree   Razaf 1953

Hodges, Johnny   Drake 1951; Ellington 1938, 1939, 1943, 1944, 1945, 1946, 1961, 1962, 1968; Mercer 1952; Mills 1938, 1939, 1940, 1941, 1942, 1966

Hodkinson, Jack   Parish 1948

Hoff, Carl   Brooks 1948

Hoff, Fred   Bryan 1927

Hoffman, A   Lerner, Sammy 1937

Hoffman, Aaron B.   Von Tilzer 1905, 1916

Hoffman, Gertrude   Smith, Harry B. 1906

Hoffman, Jack   Livingston, Jerry 1956; Warren 1959

Hoffman, John   Coslow 1921, 1958

Hoffman, Judy   McHugh 1958

Hoffman, Sherman   Coslow 1921

Hoffman, Stan   Mercer 1963

Hoffmann, Max   Atteridge 1912; Smith, Harry B. 1906, 1907; Sterling 1903; Williams 1910

Hoffstein, Gunmar   Lawrence 1953

Hogan, Inez   Carmichael 1957

Hogue, S. Mark   Willson 1950

Hohengarten, Carl   Loesser 1939

Holden, Eddie   Coslow 1933; Johnston 1933

Holden, Sidney   Conrad 1949; Coslow 1923; Fisher 1922, 1923, 1924; Johnson, Howard 1926; McHugh 1926; Motzan 1927; Parish 1925

Holiner, Mann   Brennan 1929

Holland, Brian   David, Mack 1982

Holland, Eddie   David, Mack 1982

Holland, Peanuts   Evans 1941; Livingston, Jay 1941

Hollander, Frederick   Brooks 1953; Coslow 1936, 1937; Freed, Ralph 1937, 1938, 1939, 1943, 1955; Heyman 1934; Loesser 1939, 1940, 1941, 1942, 1943; Robin 1936, 1937, 1947; Washington 1940; Whiting 1936

Hollander, Irma   Caesar 1943; Lerner, Sammy 1943

Hollander, Will   Hanley 1927; Razaf 1933

Hollyfield, Wayland   Lane 1992

Holmes, John   Waller 1924

Holmes, Leroy   Cahn 1972; Dubin 1943; Leigh 1971; Merrill 1951

Holmes, Ralph   Egan 1928; Whiting 1927, 1928

Holt, David   Cahn 1953, 1954, 1956

Holtsworth   Gilbert 1921

Holzer, Lou   Carmichael 1954

Homer, B.   Russell 1957

Honneger, Arthur   Gilbert 1937

Hooker, Brian   Burke 1956; Friml 1921, 1925, 1927, 1956; Gershwin, George 1923

Hooper, Edgar   Donaldson 1941

Hooven, Joe   Wrubel 1948

Hoover, Rosalie   Robison 1925, 1929

Hope, Maurice   Mitchell 1923

Hopkins, Kenyon   Drake 1960

Hopkins, Phil   Young, Victor 1930

Horan, Edward A.   Gershwin, Ira 1922

Hornez, Andre   Rome 1950

Horsely, Gus   Johnson, James P. 1930

Hortis, Joseph P.   Sterling 1902

Horvath, Charles   Coslow 1924

Horwitt, Arnold   Revel 1945

Horwitz, Howie   David, Mack 1959

Hoschna, Karl   Harbach 1908, 1910, 1911; Smith, Harry B. 1905

Hosedale, Lillian   Kahn 1920

Hotchner, A.E.   Coleman 1988, 1999

Hough, William M.   Howard, Joseph E. 1904, 1905, 1906, 1907, 1908, 1909, 1910, 1915, 1940, 1942, 1946, 1955

House, Judson   Brennan 1923

Houston, Dan   Howard, Joseph E. 1937, 1942

Houston, Mark   Oakland 1972

Howard, Arthur Platt   Kern 1905

Howard, Bob   Howard, Joseph E. 1938

Howard, Caroline   Silver 1951

Howard, Dick   Lewis 1915

Howard, Eddy   David, Mack 1947; Stept 1944, 1950

Howard, Eugene   Fain 1921; Silver 1920

Howard, F.E.   Friml 1949

Howard, Harold   Clare 1937

Howard, James Newton   Bergman 1989

Howard, John S.   Conrad 1923; Pollack 1923

Howard, John Tasker   Harbach 1952

Howard, Miriam S.   Howard, Joseph E. 1964

Howard, Paul Mason   McHugh 1957

Howard, Richard   Coots 1943; Lewis 1920; Woods 1926; Young, Joe 1920

Howard, Willie   Fain 1921; Silver 1920

Howe, William   Young, Victor 1939

Howell, Dan   Lawrence 1937, 1939; Raye 1939

Hubbell, Raymond   Buck 1914, 1917, 1922, 1924, 1925; Cobb 1913; DeSylva 1923; Gershwin, Ira 1923; Goetz 1911, 1918; Jerome 1912; Smith, Harry B. 1906, 1909, 1910, 1912, 1919; Smith, Robert B. 1905, 1906, 1907, 1908, 1912

Hubble, Martie   Oakland 1956

Hubert   Johnson, Howard 1939

Huddleston, Floyd   Coleman 1964, 1966; Robison 1961, 1983

Hudley, E.   Mills 1939

Hudson, Will   De Lange 1934, 1935, 1936, 1937; Duke 1941; Mills 1934, 1936, 1937, 1938, 1939, 1941; Parish 1936, 1937

Huerta, B.   David, Mack 1978

Hueston, Billy   Coots 1945; Fisher 1921, 1922; Johnson, Howard 1925; Loesser 1935

Hughes, Elmer S.   Waller 1931

Hughes, Langston   Blake 1948, 1949; Ellington 1945; Johnson, J. Rosamond 1927; Johnson, James P. 1938, 1939, 1943; Sissle 1948; Weill 1947

Hughes, Lester   David, Mack 1945, 1957

Hughes, Revella   Razaf 1932

Hugo & Luigi   David, Mack 1963

Hulbert, Claude   Gershwin, George 1925; Woods 1933

Hulbert, Lee   Bryan 1936
Humphries, Rolfe   Mercer 1955
Hunter, Charles A.   Johnson, J. Rosamond 1911
Hunter, Frank   Hart 1921; Rodgers 1921
Hunter, James   Raye 1957
Hunter, Pinkie   Coslow 1927
Huntington, E.S.S.   McHugh 1917
Hup, Irving   Friend 1921
Hupfeld, Herman   Alter 1927
Hurd, Danny   Lawrence 1947
Hurley, Edward   Hanley 1923; Lerner, Sammy 1930
Hussar, E.   Romberg 1919
Hussey, James   Atteridge 1921; Hanley 1920; Pollack 1921;
   Schwartz, Jean 1921
Hussey, Owen   Pollack 1921
Hutton, Ina Rae   Freed, Ralph 1940
Hyde, Alex   De Lange 1936

I

Iavello, Antone   Mercer 1949
Ibert, Jacques   Parish 1957
Icini   Sigman 1955
Igelhoff, Peter   Raye 1954
Ilda, Lewis   Coslow 1935
Ingraham, Herbert   Goetz 1909; Leslie 1911; Sterling 1910,
   1911
Ingraham, Roy   Brennan 1923; Brown, Lew 1919; Freed,
   Ralph 1934, 1940; Hoffman 1929, 1930; Lerner, Sammy
   1929; Styne 1940
Ingram, Allan   Parish 1936
Iona, Andy   Adamson 1940
Irvis, C.   Waller 1927
Irwin, Gene   Blake 1935; Myrow 1940, 1943
Irwin, Vic   Bryan 1934
Irwin, Wallace   Kern 1908
Irwin, Will   Dixon 1930; Harburg 1936; Rose 1930
Israel, Irving   Brennan 1938
Israel, Leo   Johnson, James P. 1944

J

Jackson, Arthur   Ager 1915; Caesar 1921; Clare Date
   Unknown; DeSylva 1918, 1919, 1924; Donaldson 1919;
   Fisher 1915; Gershwin, George 1919, 1920, 1921, 1924;
   Gershwin, Ira 1922, 1924; Gilbert 1915; Hanley 1916,
   1917; Whiting 1919
Jackson, Calvin   Freed, Ralph 1946
Jackson, Fred   Gershwin, Ira 1921; Youmans 1921
Jackson, George   Johnson, Howard 1959
Jackson, Howard   Brooks 1955; Eliscu 1933; Magidson 1932;
   Mercer 1953, 1954, 1956; Parish 1943; Robin 1930;
   Washington 1934, 1943
Jackson, Mike   Razaf 1938, 1942
Jackson, Tony   Kahn 1916, 1917
Jacobi, Victor   Smith, Harry B. 1916, 1917
Jacobs, Al   Ager 1939; Brown, Lew 1943, 1944; Oakland
   1947; Raye 1940
Jacobs, D.   Sigman 1969
Jacobs, Dick   Merrill 1955
Jacobs, Jack   Yellen 1964
Jacobs, Jacob   Cahn 1938
Jacobs, Juliette U.   Howard, Joseph E. 1946
Jacobs, Roy   Cahn 1941; DePaul 1939, 1943
Jacobsen, Sascha   Drake 1946

Jacobson, Fred   Loesser 1941
Jacobson, Harry   Heyman 1939, 1941
Jacoby, Elliott   Mills 1928, 1929, 1939; Parish 1928, 1929,
   1980
Jacquet, H. Maurice   Brennan 1927
Jacquet, Illinois   Russell 1951
Jaden, Hazel   Carroll 1931
Jaffe, Moe   Atteridge 1929; Brennan 1929; Brown, Lew 1925;
   De Lange 1943; Hoffman 1950
Jakobowski, E.   Caesar 1920
Jamblan   Rome 1945
James, Arthur   Goetz 1917
James, B.   Brown, A. Seymour 1920
James, Billy   Dubin 1926; Mills 1928, 1929; Parish 1928,
   1929, 1948
James, Dennis   Coots 1950
James, Freddy   Coots 1947
James, Harry   Brooks 1952; Ellington 1944; Lawrence 1939;
   Raye 1939, 1941
James, Kelly   Livingston, Jerry 1963, 1970, 1971, 1974
James, Lewis   Ahlert 1953
James, Paul   Youmans 1930
James, Will   Johnson, J. Rosamond 1913
Jamor, Laszlo   Lewis 1936
Janis, Elsie   Berlin 1919; Kern 1915
Janney, Russell   Friml 1954
Janssen, Werner   Brennan 1925, 1929; Buck 1925; Gilbert
   1939; Hanley 1921
Jarnigin, Jerry   Clare 1936
Jarre, Maurice   Bergman 1972; David, Hal 1980; David, Mack
   1970, 1974, 1979; Evans 1966; Livingston, Jay 1966;
   Washington 1968; Webster 1953, 1966, 1974, 1975, 1976,
   1979
Jarreau, Al   Mancini 1989
Jarry-Wilke, Michael   Sigman 1949
Jarvis, Al   Mercer 1949
Jarvis, Jane   Davis 1969
Jasmyn, Joan   Magidson 1931, 1932, 1933; Parish 1930, 1931
Jefferson, Maceo   Razaf 1924, 1957
Jeffries, Herb   Mills 1945
Jelesnik, Eugene   Harbach 1958
Jemail, Jimmy   Coots 1950
Jenkins, Gordon   Mercer 1933, 1934, 1959; Russell 1961;
   Sigman 1958
Jenkins, John   Martin 1948
Jenkins, Marshall   Stept 1952
Jenkins, Stanley S.   Revel 1947
Jenney, Jack   De Lange 1946
Jennings, H.   Davis 1944
Jenny, Jack   David, Mack 1939
Jentes, Alfred   Hanley 1921; Johnson, Howard 1917
Jentes, Harry   Ager 1918; Clarke 1918; Fisher 1936; Jerome
   1918; Johnson, Howard 1916, 1917, 1918, 1945; Leslie
   1914; Lewis 1915; Monaco 1917; Parish 1950; Silver
   1926; Young, Joe 1914
Jeremiah, Kenneth   Young, Joe 1972
Jerome, Ben   Caesar 1927; Smith, Harry B. 1903
Jerome, Henry   Drake 1949, 1950
Jerome, Jerome   Hoffman 1940
Jerome, M.K.   Ahlert 1950; Brennan 1929; Brown, Lew 1925;
   Bryan 1918, 1927, 1930; Dubin 1929; Gilbert 1962;
   Kalmar 1919, 1920, 1923, 1924, 1925; Koehler 1936,
   1944, 1945, 1946, 1947, 1948, 1949, 1954, 1955; Leslie
   1918, 1919; Lewis 1918, 1919, 1920, 1924, 1925;
   Magidson 1931, 1932, 1933, 1935; Mitchell 1918; Motzan

1920, 1921, 1925; Parish 1930, 1931; Ruby 1919, 1920, 1923, 1924, 1925, 1952, 1957, 1958; Smith, Harry B. 1919, 1920, 1921; Turk 1921; Washington 1929, 1956; Yellen 1927, 1928; Young, Joe 1918, 1919, 1920, 1924, 1925

Jessel, George   Baer 1929; Cobb 1938; Conrad 1925; De Lange 1941; Edwards 1938; Gilbert 1946; Kalmar 1940; Lerner, Sammy 1951; Magidson 1937; Oakland 1936, 1937, 1938, 1943, 1944, 1946, 1954, 1958, 1959, 1973; Parish 1934; Ruby 1919, 1940, 1950, 1951; Sterling 1951; Turk 1919, 1921; Von Tilzer 1951

Jessel, Raymond   Rodgers 1979

Jimeno, F.   Mills 1940

Jirik, V.   Hoffman 1954

Jockers, Al   Smith, Harry B. 1923

John, Graham   Caesar 1930; Kern 1930

Johns, Val   David, Hal 1976

Johnson, Arnold   Coots 1929; Davis 1919, 1921; Fields 1934; Kahal 1929; McHugh 1934; Parish 1936; Smith, Harry B. 1922

Johnson, Arthur "Jug"   Johnson, James P. 1961, 1968

Johnson, Austen-Croom   Leigh 1953

Johnson, Bill   Revel 1959

Johnson, Billy   Bryan 1902; Snyder 1911

Johnson, Buddy   Washington 1943

Johnson, Cee Pee   Carmichael 1941

Johnson, Charles L.   Bryan 1910; Yellen 1921

Johnson, Chic   Evans 1940; Livingston, Jay 1940

Johnson, Donald M.   Johnson, J. Rosamond 1954, Date Unknown

Johnson, George   Parish 1925

Johnson, Harold R.   Johnson, Howard 1941

Johnson, Henry   David, Mack 1958

Johnson, Howard   Warren 1927

Johnson, J.C.   De Lange 1934; Razaf 1926, 1927, 1928, 1929, 1930, 1931, 1932, 1938, 1939, 1941, 1942, 1961, 1965, 1966, Date Unknown; Waller 1927, 1938, 1939, 1945

Johnson, James Weldon   Johnson, J. Rosamond 1900, 1901, 1903, 1904, 1906, 1907, 1910, 1911, 1912, 1913, 1914, 1915, 1916, 1917, 1923, 1946

Johnson, Jerry   Mills 1937

Johnson, Joan   Johnson, Howard 1966

Johnson, Lonnie   Razaf 1930

Johnson, Lorenzo   Johnson, James P. 1958

Johnson, Malcolm   Brown, Lew 1943

Johnson, Margaret   Razaf 1926

Johnson, Philander   Caesar 1920; Howard, Joseph E. 1917, 1918

Johnson, William   Revel 1962

Johnson, Willie May   Johnson, James P. 1933

Johnston, Earle   Fisher 1921

Johnston, J.   Leigh 1981

Johnston, Pat   DePaul 1942, 1945; Raye 1945

Jollet, C.   Parish 1961

Jolson, Al   Ahlert 1919; Akst 1927, 1930, 1944, 1947, 1950; Atteridge 1913, 1918, 1919, 1921; Berlin 1928; Brown, Lew 1921, 1927, 1928, 1929; Bryan 1918; Caesar 1926, 1930, 1931, 1933; Clarke 1921, 1927; Conrad 1921, 1925; Davis 1919, 1923, 1944, 1947; DeSylva 1918, 1919, 1921, 1925, 1927, 1929; Freed, Ralph 1935; Friend 1920, 1921, 1933; Henderson 1929, Date Unknown; Kahn 1918, 1919, 1924, 1927; Kalmar 1944, 1947; Lewis 1918; Monaco 1921; Razaf 1933, Date Unknown; Romberg 1918, 1921; Rose 1927, 1928, 1929; Ruby 1947; Schwartz,

Jean 1918; Waller 1933; Warren 1930, 1931; Young, Joe 1918; Young, Victor 1935

Jonas, Nita   Bacharach 1960

Jones, Arthur   De Lange 1933, 1934; Loesser 1943; Mills 1938; Myrow 1934, 1938

Jones, Asbestos   Razaf 1931

Jones, B.   Russell 1946

Jones, Bobby   Atteridge 1915; Conrad 1920

Jones, Claude   Mills 1938

Jones, Dale   Mills 1936

Jones, Danny   Razaf 1939

Jones, Earle C.   Bryan 1907, 1908; Buck 1914; Meyer 1907, 1908, 1909; Norworth 1908; Whiting 1913, 1914

Jones, Freddy   Friend 1958

Jones, Gus   Rome 1950

Jones, Isham   Davis 1923; Friend 1927; Johnson, James P. 1922; Kahn 1922, 1923, 1924, 1925, 1926, 1927, 1928; Kalmar 1920; Lerner, Sammy 1952; Ruby 1920; Smith, Harry B. 1920; Yellen 1948

Jones, Jimmy   Blake 1956; Sissle 1955, 1956

Jones, Joe   Johnson, Howard 1966

Jones, Marc Edmunds   Johnson, J. Rosamond 1946, 1950

Jones, Paul   Meyer 1908

Jones, Peggy Lipton   Bergman 1983

Jones, Quincy   Bergman 1967, 1968, 1969, 1983; David, Mack 1965, 1967; Fields 1968, 1969; Russell 1965, 1967, 1968, 1977

Jones, Richard M.   DePaul 1947

Jones, Stephen   Atteridge 1924; Caesar 1923, 1927; Conrad 1928; DeSylva 1925

Jones, Tom   Sigman 1946

Jones, Willie   Yellen 1926

Joplin, Scott   Leigh 1976; Russell 1950; Styne 1950

Jordan, Archie   David, Hal 1976, 1977, 1978, 1979; David, Mack 1980, 1984

Jordan, B.   Oakland 1956

Jordan, Joe   Fisher 1908; Johnson, J. Rosamond 1930, 1931; Razaf 1941

Josefovits, Teri   Razaf 1944, 1946, 1947, 1948, 1950; Schwartz, Jean 1949

Joseloff, Stanley   Rose 1936, 1937, 1940

Joseph, Ray   David, Hal 1958; David, Mack 1941, 1956

Joseph, Vincent Redmond   Razaf 1950

Joy, George   Woods 1924

Joy, Len   Razaf 1930

Joy, Leonard   Washington 1945, 1950

Joyce, Archibald   Mitchell 1919

Joyce, Billy   Brown, Lew 1922, 1923; Hanley 1923; Warren 1920

Judell, Maxson   Carmichael 1948; Washington 1934; Young, Victor 1934

Judge, Jack   Williams 1914

Judson, Lester   Howard, Bart 1954

Julian, C.C.   Bryan 1923

Julian, Doris   Ellington 1954

Jurgens, Dick   David, Mack 1944; Freed, Ralph 1940

Jurmann, Walter   Adamson 1935; Dubin 1931; Kahn 1935, 1936, 1937, 1938; Robin 1931; Washington 1935, 1936; Webster 1942, 1943, 1946, Date Unknown

K

Kabalevsky, Dmitri   Rome 1943, 1949

Kaempfert, Bert   Sigman 1967

Kaften, George   Revel 1960

Kahn, Art   Kahn 1925; McHugh 1924; Mills 1924

Kahn, Donald   Cahn 1969; Mercer 1964

Kahn, Grace LeBoy   Kahn 1908, 1909, 1910, 1911, 1912,
1913, 1914, 1915, 1916, 1917, 1925, 1926, 1928, 1930,
1931, 1932; Norworth 1914; Van Heusen 1953; Whiting
1917

Kahn, Herman   Hanley 1922

Kahn, Mari   Gorney 1965, 1967

Kahn, Marvin   David, Hal 1954

Kahn, Roger Wolfe   Brown, Lew 1925; Caesar 1928; Dubin
1927; Silver 1926

Kailimai, Henry   Kern 1915

Kaley, C.   Styne 1927

Kaliz, Armand   Hanley 1922

Kalman, Emmerich   DeSylva 1922; Eliscu 1929;
Hammerstein 1927; Harbach 1927; Harburg 1932; Hart
1943; Mercer 1930; Romberg 1916; Smith, Harry B. 1926,
1927

Kalmanoff, Martin   David, Mack 1954; Hoffman 1950, 1951,
1952

Kalmus, Bea   Silver 1952

Kaminskeho, S.   Friml 1909

Kamnetz, Eddie   Henderson 1922

Kandilou, Jean   David, Mack 1958

Kane, Bernie   Loesser 1939

Kaper, Bronislau   Adamson 1935; Blane 1947; Brooks 1952;
Cahn 1956, 1957, 1968; David, Mack 1959, 1960, 1961,
1966, 1967; Freed, Ralph 1944; Kahn 1935, 1936, 1937,
1938, 1939, 1940; Parish 1956; Russell 1949, 1955, 1964,
1974, Date Unknown; Washington 1935, 1936, 1947;
Webster 1950, 1952, 1957, 1959, 1963

Kaplan, Bert   Heyman 1933

Kaplan, Dave   Gilbert 1920

Kaplan, Sol   Eliscu 1949, 1960, 1961, 1962; Russell 1945,
1946, 1964; Webster 1942

Kapp, David   Johnson, Howard 1928; Rome 1951; Sigman
1957; Van Heusen 1951, 1952

Kapp, Jack   Young, Victor 1932

Kardone, Bella   Hoffman 1954

Karger, Fred   Russell 1951

Karle, Ernest   Bryan 1928

Karron, Edgar T.   Snyder 1909

Kassel, Art   David, Mack 1944, 1945; Kahn 1930, 1931; Ruby
1951

Kassner, E.   Koehler 1951

Katscher, Robert   Caesar 1931; DeSylva 1926; Gilbert 1942;
Washington 1935, 1937

Katz, Bill   Ellington 1957, 1963

Katz, Dick   Cahn 1980

Katz, William   Brown, Nacio Herb 1948, 1949

Katzman, Henry   Drake 1956

Kaufman, Al   David, Hal 1950, 1960; Hoffman 1945; Mercer
1968; Silver 1942, 1953

Kaufman, George S.   Gershwin, Ira 1924

Kaufman, Irving   Mitchell 1919; Stept 1919

Kaufman, J.   Hoffman 1956

Kaufman, Murray   Hoffman 1954

Kautzman, Frank   Carmichael 1949

Kavanaugh, James   Bacharach 1976; Hoffman 1943

Kay, Al   Fisher 1925

Kay, Edward   Washington 1938

Kay, M.   Russell 1955

Kay, Mack   David, Mack 1941

Kay, Melvin   Burke 1940

Kay, Nancy   Burke 1971

Kaydan, Lee   Russell 1945; Sigman 1945

Kaye, Buddy   McHugh 1955, 1956, 1960, 1961; Styne 1951;
Van Heusen 1955, 1959

Kaye, Jean   Parish 1932

Kaye, Laurie   David, Mack 1970

Kaye, Milton   Heyman 1962

Kaye, Norman   David, Mack 1956

Kaye, Sammy   Davis 1951; Lawrence 1940; Parish 1936,
1937; Sigman 1954, 1955; Silver 1951

Kaye, Sylvia Fine   Lawrence 1953

Kazze, Louis   Burke 1949, 1951

Keane, Tom   Bacharach 1988

Keating, Tom   Cahn 1967

Keene, Kahn   David, Hal 1940

Keiler-Bean   Burke 1940

Keiler, J.   Russell 1968

Keiser, Robert A.   Hanley 1917; Sterling 1916

Keith, Marilyn   Bergman 1952, 1953, 1956

Kellem, Milton   Hoffman 1951, 1952, 1953; Silver 1952,
1953, 1955

Keller, Jack   David, Mack 1976; Freed, Ralph 1970; Russell
Date Unknown

Keller, Jerry   Heyman 1963

Keller, Sheldon   Brooks 1959, 1960, 1961; Martin 1958

Keller, Stan   Hoffman 1945, 1946; Livingston, Jerry 1945,
1946

Kellette, John William   Bryan 1919; Whiting 1919

Kelly, Billy   Kahn 1926

Kempner, Nicholas   Caesar 1923; Conrad 1928; Gershwin,
Ira 1923; Gilbert 1928

Kendis, James   Brown, Lew 1923; Bryan 1906, 1907, 1909,
1910, 1913, 1914, 1915, 1918; Goetz 1910; Johnson,
Howard 1920; Leslie 1920; McHugh 1927; Mills 1926

Kennedy, Tom   Coots 1942, 1943

Kenner, Dave   Mills 1951, 1952, 1955

Kennon, Lillian   Howard, Joseph E. 1947

Kenny, Charles   Coots 1931, 1948, 1949, 1951, 1953, 1955,
1957, 1959; Coslow 1940; Fain 1927, 1947; Leslie 1925;
Mills 1927, 1931; Robison 1954; Silver 1943, 1944, 1945,
1946; Wrubel 1940

Kenny, Gerard   Lerner, Alan Jay 1985

Kenny, Nick   Coots 1931, 1948, 1949, 1951, 1953, 1955,
1957, 1959; Coslow 1940; David, Mack 1934; Davis 1932;
Ellington 1933; Fain 1947; Parish 1941; Robison 1954;
Silver 1932, 1933, 1934, 1943, 1944, 1945, 1946; Snyder
1932; Stept 1932; Von Tilzer 1935; Wrubel 1940

Kent, Arthur   De Lange 1946; Heyman 1964; Mercer 1968;
Sigman 1957, 1963, 1971

Kent, Billy   Schwartz, Jean 1928

Kent, Carl   Drake 1941, 1943

Kent, Charlotte   Alter 1930, 1932, 1933; Kahn 1933; Rose
1930

Kent, Erwin   Parish 1947

Kent, Walter   Adamson 1966; Brown, Lew 1939; Carroll
1932; Conrad 1934; David, Mack 1932, 1942; Gilbert
1947; Hoffman 1939, 1940, 1950, 1953; Merrill 1949;
Russell 1945; Silver 1932, 1950, 1966

Keogh, Edna   Coots 1942

Keogh, Joe   Coslow 1927

Kerker, Gustave   Atteridge 1912; Smith, Harry B. 1902, 1903

Kernell, William   Gilbert 1934, 1937, 1955

Kerr, Anita   Evans 1973; Livingston, Jay 1973; Spina 1966

Kerr, Harry D.   Brown, Nacio Herb 1922, 1924, 1925;
Motzan 1917, 1918, 1919, 1920, 1925

Kerr, Jean   Gorney 1949

Kerr, Walter   Gorney 1949

Kerran, Edgar T.   Snyder 1908

Kershaw, George   Snyder 1923; Von Tilzer 1918, 1920, 1923, 1927

Kessel, Sid   Sigman 1960

Kessler, Bob   Carmichael 1968

Ketelbey, Albert   David, Mack 1944

Keto, Waeko M.   Brown, Nacio Herb 1957

Keveson, Peter   Freed, Ralph 1954; Hoffman 1954

Keyes, Bert   Cahn 1976

Kharite, Nickolas   De Lange 1945

Khrennikov, T.   Rome 1943

Kidder, Edward K.   Herbert 1897

Kilgour, Garfield   Howard, Joseph E. 1920; Von Tilzer 1916, 1917, 1918

Killen, Buddy   David, Hal 1976

Kilmer, Joyce   Herbert 1919

Kimber, Richard   Mercer 1933

King, Arthur C.   Mitchell 1926

King, Charles E.   Burke 1951; Hoffman 1957

King, Harry   Sigman 1951

King, Henry   Sigman 1946

King, Jack   Adamson 1935; Coslow 1930, 1931; Fisher 1936; Freed, Arthur 1920; Howard, Joseph E. 1920; Robin 1930

King, Pete   Webster 1956, 1962, 1964, 1965

King, Robert A.   Brown, Lew 1922, 1923, 1924, 1925; Davis 1926; DeSylva 1924, 1925; Dixon 1924; Hanley 1919, 1921, 1923, 1925; Henderson 1923, 1924, 1925, 1926, 1927; Johnson, Howard 1926, 1927, 1928, 1929; Kahn 1924, 1926; Lewis 1931, 1932; Magidson 1928; Mitchell 1925; Stept 1925; Sterling 1925, 1926, 1927, 1928, 1929; Warren 1925, 1926, 1928

King, Tempo   Meyer 1936

King, Wayne   Kahal 1940; Kahn 1930, 1933, 1937; Parish 1938; Yellen 1924; Young, Victor 1931, 1933

Kingsley, Dorothy   Adamson 1955

Kinney, Ray   Adamson 1940

Kinsley, Frederick   Gorney 1929; Harburg 1929

Kipling, Rudyard   Howard, Joseph E. 1905

Kippel, Mickey   Johnson, J. Rosamond 1932

Kirby, M.B.   Schwartz, Jean 1902

Kirk, Malcolm Ray   Hanley 1943

Kirk, William F.   Von Tilzer 1910

Kirkeby, Ed   David, Hal 1947; Waller 1939, 1941, 1942, 1944, 1946

Kirkland, Leroy   Gilbert 1952

Kisco, Charley   Coslow 1935, 1937; Freed, Ralph 1930, 1931, 1932, 1937; Hoffman 1932; Robin 1936

Kissel, Walter D.   Drake 1947

Kissen, Murray   Kalmar 1923; Ruby 1923

Kissenger, Frederick   Young, Joe 1972

Kita, Koji   David, Mack 1971

Klaer, Jimmy   Parish 1938

Klages, Raymond   Alter 1926, 1927, 1928, 1930; Baer 1934; Carroll 1929; Clare 1925; Coots 1922, 1928, 1929, 1932, 1933, 1934; Hoffman 1933; Johnston 1946, 1948; Magidson 1929; Monaco 1923, 1924, 1925, 1928, 1932, 1933, 1934, 1935, 1936; Motzan 1924; Waller 1927

Klapholz, Ernest   Smith, Harry B. 1922

Klarboly, Ernest   Snyder 1922

Klatzkin, Leon   Bergman 1956, 1980

Klein, Lou   Fisher 1934, 1936; Johnson, Howard 1917, 1925, 1926, 1935; Lewis 1915; McHugh 1927; Mills 1927; Mitchell 1922; Robison 1939; Von Tilzer 1916, 1917, 1918

Klein, Manuel   Olcott 1908; Schwartz, Jean 1905; Smith, Harry B. 1903; Williams 1905

Klein, Saul   Mills 1929

Kleinkauf, Henry   Lawrence 1940

Kleinman, Sy   Adams 1953

Klenner, John   Bryan 1926, 1927, 1928; Coots 1944; Hoffman 1931; Lewis 1930, 1931, 1932, 1933; Mills 1940; Robison 1946

Klickmann, F. Henri   Dubin 1924, 1925, 1926; Razaf 1946, 1947

Kline, Jud   Ahlert 1926; Snyder 1925

Knight, Al   Mills 1924

Knight, Percival   Kern 1909, 1910

Knight, Raymond   Baer 1942; Loewe 1942

Kniper, Lev   Rome 1943

Knisch, Gabor   Sigman 1980

Knopf, Edwin H.   Adamson 1935

Knowlton, Joe   Davis 1974

Knox, Collie   Duke 1929

Knox, Helen Boardman   Motzan 1933, 1934

Knudson, Thurston   David, Mack 1951

Kobe, Vincent   Bryan 1955

Koff, Charles   Sigman 1946

Kogen, Harry   Johnson, Howard 1935; Kahn 1931; Spina 1937

Kollo, Walter   Goetz 1928; Kern 1912, 1913; Smith, Harry B. 1913, 1930

Kooper, Irma   Caesar 1939

Kopp, C.   Olcott 1907

Kopp, Rudolph   Adamson 1936; Robin 1935; Whiting 1935

Koppell, Al   Bryan 1944, 1945, 1946, 1953, 1955; Caesar 1937, 1942, 1943, 1953, 1954, 1955, 1956; Conrad 1927; Fisher 1925; Hanley 1935; Mills 1928, 1929; Monaco 1929, 1930; Motzan 1931; Parish 1929

Koppstein, Jacques   Revel 1952

Kornblum, I.B.   Bryan 1923, 1924; Gilbert 1933, 1937, 1942, 1943, 1949; Howard, Joseph E. 1919, 1920

Korngold, Erich Wolfgang   Hammerstein 1936; Koehler 1947

Kortlander, Max   Brown, Lew 1923; Bryan 1922, 1928, 1930; Coslow 1923; Dubin 1924; Johnson, Howard 1933; Leslie 1922, 1923; McHugh 1924, 1926; Yellen 1924, 1926

Korzynski, A.   Sherman 1977

Kosma, Joseph   Mercer 1950

Koven, Reginald De   Smith, Harry B. 1891

Kraemer, Richard O.   Warren 1967, 1969, 1970, 1971, 1972, 1976, 1979, 1993, Date Unknown

Kramer, Alex   David, Mack 1943, 1944, 1945, 1966; Hoffman 1950; Robison 1963

Kramer, Arthur   Rome 1937

Kramer, Corki   Sigman 1964

Kraus, Moe   Kalmar 1925; Ruby 1925

Krausz, Michael   Young, Joe 1931

Kravchenko, F.   Rome 1943

Krechter, Joe   Conrad 1932

Kreisler, Fritz   Fields 1936; Razaf 1949

Kresa, Helmy   Young, Joe 1932

Kreuger, B.   Styne 1927

Kreusch, W.C.   Edwards 1902

Krickett, Ernie   Warren 1926

Kries, Richard   Raye 1943

Krim, Zenobia   Blake 1969; Sissle 1969

Krimsky, Jerrold   Weill 1933

Krissel, Walter D.   Drake 1948, 1949

Krone, Beatrice   Willson 1957

Krueder, Peter   Sigman 1968

Krumbein, Maurice   Leslie 1943

Krupa, Gene   Loesser 1939

Krutchinine, V.   Rome 1943

Kuhn, Richard S.   Baer 1952, 1954, 1955; Lawrence 1939; Leslie 1954

Kuller, Sid   Carmichael 1953; Duke 1963; Ellington 1941, 1959; Mitchell 1938; Pollack 1938, 1948; Styne 1938; Webster 1941

Kummer, Clare   Kern 1912; Schwartz, Jean 1929

Kummer, Frederic Arnold   Herbert 1920; Romberg 1919

Kunneke, Edward   Smith, Harry B. 1923, 1925

Kupferman, Meyer   Rome 1961

Kuppel, Al   Fisher 1926

Kur-Zhene, Massard   Robin 1930

Kurtz, Manny   Ager 1935, 1936; Blake 1935; David, Mack 1940; Edwards 1938; Ellington 1935; Hoffman 1938, 1939, 1940, 1951; Mills 1934, 1935, 1936, 1942; Silver 1940; Stept 1940; Van Heusen 1938; Waller 1942

Kusik, Larry   Bacharach 1962; Mancini 1975, 1981

Kvale, Alfred   Kahn 1923

L

Laakso, Nels   Sterling 1943

Lacey, Mary   Von Tilzer 1958

Lackenbauer, W.   Sterling 1934, 1935

Lafarge, Guy   Gordon 1958

La Freniere, E.P.   Styne 1934

Lago, Mario   Adamson 1941

Lahm, David   Fields 1969

Lai, Francis   Bergman 1968; Cahn 1967; Sigman 1967, 1969, 1974

Laine, Frankie   Carmichael 1947; Ellington 1942; Webster 1965

Lait, Jack   Conrad 1924; Coots 1922

Lake, Bonnie   David, Mack 1955; De Lange 1946, 1948; Freed, Ralph 1934; Sigman 1950

Lake, Sol   David, Mack 1966; Webster 1967

La Lucia, Vala   Coslow 1919

La Magna, Carl   De Lange 1938

Lamare, Milton   Mercer 1958

LaMarge, Jimmie   Johnston 1949; Livingston, Jerry 1943

Lamb, Arthur J.   Conrad 1924; Fisher 1910; Hanley 1920; Von Tilzer 1900, 1901, 1902, 1903, 1907, 1925

Lambert, Dennis   Mancini 1986

Lambert, Edward J.   Fisher 1937; Mills 1938

Lambert, Harold   Lerner, Sammy 1932

Lambert, L.   Loesser 1940

Lambert, Scrappy   Young, Joe 1931

Lambro, Phillip   Webster 1968, 1972

Lamm, Bobby   Russell 1974

Lampert, Diane   Fain 1962, 1968; Freed, Ralph 1959

Lampkin, Phil   Sigman 1957

Lampl, Carl G.   Hoffman 1943, 1945; Livingston, Jerry 1942, 1943

La Mure, Pierre   Adamson 1952; Lawrence 1954; McHugh 1952

Land, Eddie   David, Mack 1941

Landers, Sam   Johnson, Howard 1921

Landfield, Sid   Davis 1922

Landman, Lou   Bryan 1934

Landres, Sam   Clare 1923; Friend 1923

Lane, Ken   Cahn 1959; Coslow 1947

Lang, Albert   Snyder 1909

Lang, Harris   Cahn 1956

Lang, Morton   Johnson, Howard 1932

Lang, Phil   Mills 1942

Langdon, Dory   Arlen 1962, 1963, 1964; DePaul 1957; Van Heusen 1964

Lange, Alfred   Sterling 1917

Lange, Arthur   Brown, Lew 1934; Bryan 1913, 1925; Caesar 1929; Fisher 1930; Gilbert 1932; Gorney 1934; Motzan 1925; Smith, Harry B. 1922; Snyder 1922; Sterling 1917, 1918

Lange, Harry   Friend 1923

Lange, Johnny   Burke 1954; Donaldson 1944

Langford, Frances   Lewis 1929; Young, Joe 1929

Lanikai   Spina 1977

Lanin, Paul   Youmans 1921

Lannin, Paul   Caesar 1920, 1921; Gershwin, Ira 1921, 1922

Laparcerie, Miarka   Davis 1962; Lawrence 1950

Lara, Augustin   Lewis 1932; Washington 1938

Lardner, Ring   Kern 1915; Youmans 1930

Larimer, Bob   Cahn 1978

LaRocca, D.J.   Mercer 1950; Parish 1921; Sigman 1955

Larsen, Milt   Sherman 1984

Larsen, Ralph   Howard, Joseph E. 1926

Lartseylear, B.   McHugh 1924

Larue, Jacques   Lawrence 1956; Parish 1956

Laska, Edward   Kern 1905, 1906; Motzan 1919

Lasky, Jesse   Fisher 1908

Lasky Jr., Jessy   Young, Victor 1949

Lasry, Albert   Lawrence 1947

Last, James   Sigman 1971, 1972

Laszlo, Alexander   Gilbert 1948, 1949

Latars, The   Johnson, James P. 1960, 1968

Latouche, John   Donaldson 1942; Duke 1940, 1941, 1942; Ellington 1940, 1946, 1947; Revel 1941, 1959

Laubach, Harriet   David, Mack 1947

Lauchaume, Aime   Smith, Harry B. 1901

Lauran, Sammy   Lawrence 1972

Laurent, Evelyn T.   Dubin 1924

Lava, William   Alter 1948; Cahn 1962; De Lange 1948; Washington 1969

LaVere, Charles   Mills 1935

Lavere, F.   Russell 1941

La Voie, Elizabeth   Mills 1946, 1947

Lawlor, Charles B.   Berlin 1924

Lawnhurst, Vee   Bryan 1940; David, Mack 1931, 1940, 1941, 1943, 1945, 1946; Heyman 1936, 1937; Turk 1932, 1933; Young, Victor 1932

Lawrence, Elliott   Comden and Green 1972

Lawrence, Francis   Lerner, Alan Jay 1939

Lawrence, Harry   Russell 1960

Lawrence, Jerome   Duke 1955; Warren 1956

Lawrence, John   Razaf 1954

Lawrence, Laurie   Lerner, Sammy 1936

Lawrence, Marc   Warren Date Unknown

Lawrence, Reginald   Young, Victor 1954

Lawrence, Roy   Bryan 1918

Lawrence, Steve   Mancini 1956

Lawson, Elsie   Friml 1923

Layton, Turner   Lewis 1923; Young, Joe 1923

Lazarus, Emma   Berlin 1949

Lazarus, Sidney F.   Motzan 1921

Leader, Ed   Johnson, Howard 1927

Leahy, Joe   Livingston, Jerry 1959, 1960; Sigman 1957

Leaman, Lou   Parish 1932, 1935, 1936

Lean, Cecil   Stept 1920

LeBaron, William   Herbert 1922, 1923; Loesser 1941; Young, Victor 1941

Lebedev-Kumach, V.   Rome 1943

Leca, Henri   Lawrence 1953

Lecuona, Ernesto   De Lange 1940, 1946; Drake 1943; Dubin 1941; Gilbert 1931; Myrow 1940, 1946; Parish 1938; Ruby 1947

Lecuona, Margarita   Russell 1940, 1941

Lederer, Charles   Blane 1952; Wrubel 1959

Lee, Bert   Norworth 1911, 1917; Youmans 1927

Lee, Dave   Gilbert 1915, 1916, 1917

Lee, Dedette   Friend 1932

Lee, Fenton   Leslie 1944

Lee, Lester   Davis 1928; Rose 1927; Russell 1951, 1952, 1953, 1954, Date Unknown; Washington 1953, 1954, 1955, 1957

Lee, Peggy   Arlen 1961; Coleman 1963, 1964, 1965, 1967, 1984; Ellington 1959; Robison 1948, 1964; Young, Victor 1951, 1952, 1953, 1954

Lee, Robert E.   Duke 1955; Warren 1956

Leeds   Van Heusen 1938

Leeds, Milton   Mills 1935; Russell 1941

Leftwich, Vernon   De Lange 1951

Le Gallienne, Richard   Olcott 1906, 1908

Legget, Hazel C.   Egan 1923

Legrand, Michel   Bergman 1968, 1969, 1970, 1971, 1973, 1976, 1977, 1981, 1982, 1983, 1984, 1988, 1990; Cahn 1980; David, Hal 1973, 1974; David, Mack 1968; Howard, Bart 1963; Leigh 1956; Lerner, Alan Jay 1985; Mercer 1968

Lehac, Ned   Eliscu 1930, 1931, 1952; Rome 1939; Rose 1938

Lehar, Franz   Atteridge 1910, 1913; Caesar 1925, 1926; Dubin 1924; Eliscu 1937; Harbach 1914; Hart 1934; Johnson, Howard 1933, 1941; Kahn 1934, 1939; Leigh 1955; Mitchell 1925; Smith, Harry B. 1911; Smith, Robert B. 1911; Webster 1952

Lehman, Samuel   Egan 1922

Lehmann, John   Wrubel 1946

Lehr, Lew   Hanley 1937; Pollack 1932

Leigh, Fred W.   Kern 1905

Leigh, Mitch   Adams 1993; Cahn 1977, 1980; David, Mack 1968, 1970

Leigh, Rowland   Friml 1934; Revel 1929; Romberg 1948; Schwartz, Jean 1935, 1942

Leiken, Molly-Ann   Mancini 1978

Lekytie, Paul   David, Hal 1966

Leleiohaku   Freed, Ralph 1940

Lelievre, Leo   Baer 1927; Kahn 1927

LeMaire, Jules   Kahn 1931, 1932

Lemar, Joyce   David, Mack 1944

Lemare, Edwin   Johnson, Howard 1933

Lemare, Jules   Whiting 1928

Lembeck, Billy   Buck 1940

Lemmon, Jack   Lerner, Alan Jay 1981

Lengsfelder, Hans J.   Drake 1941, 1942, 1943, 1944, 1947, 1951, 1954, 1959

Lenn, Bernard   Parish 1932

Lennart, Aileen   McHugh 1950

Lenoir, Jean   Caesar 1931

Lenzberg, Julius   DeSylva 1919; Kahn 1919

Leonard, Harold   Bryan 1926; Dubin 1924; Friend 1926; Kahn 1924, 1927

Leonard, Jack   Kalmar 1925; Ruby 1925

Leonardi, Leon   Gilbert 1938; Webster 1936

Leoncavallo, R.   Johnson, Howard 1939; Styne 1938

Leonetti, Tommy   David, Mack 1978; Heyman 1966; Russell 1962, 1967, 1969

Leoni, R.   Sigman 1966

Leopold, J. Walter   Brennan 1914

LePon   Webster 1967

Leshay, J.   Russell 1957

Leslie, Aleen   Pollack 1945

Leslie, Nat   Mills 1931, 1945

Le Soir, Jack   Silver 1928

Lessing, Edith Maida   Monaco 1911, 1912

Lester, Harry N.   Snyder 1909

Letich, Craig   Snyder 1939

Levant, Oscar   Caesar 1930; Clare 1929, 1930, 1935; Coots 1936; Davis 1936; Dixon 1928; Fields 1935; Freed, Arthur 1932; Harburg 1931, 1932; Heyman 1933, 1936; Kahal 1936; Kahn 1933, 1934; Lawrence 1939; Lewis 1927, 1928; Parish 1935; Rose 1928; Young, Joe 1927, 1928, 1936

Leveen, Raymond   Caesar 1950; Loesser 1934; Motzan 1936

Lever, Beatrice Rae   Webster 1959, 1965

Levey, Harold   Brown, Lew 1926; Clare 1926; Parish 1932

Levey, L.   Coots 1919

Levi, Maurice   Smith, Harry B. 1901, 1908, 1909

Levine, Louis   Gilbert 1955

Levinson, Herman D.   Sigman 1946

Levinson, Leonard   Freed, Arthur 1927

Levinson, Lew   Schwartz, Arthur 1929, 1930

Levitch, Bula   Drake 1946

Levy, E.P.   Blake 1938

Levy, Hal   Bergman 1951, 1953, 1954, 1955, 1957

Levy, Newman   Duke 1930

LeWinter, David   Rome 1944, 1945

Lewis, Al   Ager 1935; Baer 1933; Conrad 1930, 1931; Coslow 1964; Hoffman 1931, 1932, 1938; Johnson, Howard 1933; Kahn 1927; Lerner, Sammy 1926; Silver 1929, 1935, 1937, 1950; Whiting 1925, 1926, 1927; Wrubel 1933

Lewis, Ben   Hoffman 1951

Lewis, Eddie   Kahn 1922

Lewis, Harold "Lefty"   Coslow 1933, 1934

Lewis, Henry   Bryan 1918; Fisher 1918; Gilbert 1918; Johnson, Howard 1918; Kalmar 1916; Silver 1920; Sterling 1917, 1920

Lewis, John   Sigman 1971

Lewis, Lester   Mitchell 1926

Lewis, Meade "Lux"   Razaf 1938

Lewis, Morgan   Eliscu 1931; Harburg 1934

Lewis, Roger   Johnson, Howard 1918; Kahn 1923; Monaco 1911, 1917; Yellen 1920

Lewis, Ted   Davis 1924, 1927; Sterling 1920; Von Tilzer 1920

Lewis, Welcome   Johnson, J. Rosamond 1934

Lewis Jr., J.C.   Kahn 1932

Ley, Benton   Davis 1923

Liberace   Webster 1955

LiCausi, Franco   Webster 1967

Lieberman   Sigman 1966

Liebling, Estelle   Blane 1958

Liebman, Joseph   Leigh 1968

Liebman, Mac   Parish 1929, 1980

Lief, Max   Alter 1930; Atteridge 1929; Fain 1967; Rainger 1929; Schwartz, Arthur 1928, 1929, 1930

Lief, Nathaniel   Alter 1930; Atteridge 1929; Duke 1940; Rainger 1929; Schwartz, Arthur 1928, 1929, 1930

Liferman, Georges   Lawrence 1955; Parish 1962

Light, Ben   Freed, Ralph 1948

Light, Betty   Coots 1931

Light, Enoch   Bryan 1936; Drake 1962, 1967; Hoffman 1939

Lilley, Joseph J.   Brooks 1953; Burke 1955; Cahn 1957; David, Mack 1946, 1954; Evans 1946; Jerome 1955; Livingston, Jay 1946; Loesser 1942; Rainger 1943; Robin 1943

Lincke, Paul   Gilbert 1930; Harbach 1914; Mercer 1952; Smith, Harry B. 1908

Lindemann, Billy   Friend 1925

Lindsay, John   Goetz 1913

Lindsey, Mort   Bergman 1963

Linick, A.   Koehler 1928

Link, Harry   Berlin 1926; Coslow 1926; Dixon 1933; Dubin 1928; Razaf 1929; Rose 1927, 1929; Turk 1926; Waller 1929, 1949

Link, Peter   Mancini 1975

Lins, Ivan   Bergman 1984

Lipet, James   Davis 1939

Lippman, Sherman   Akst 1954

Lippman, Sidney   Cahn 1955; David, Hal 1960, 1961; Heyman 1965; Sigman 1956, 1957

Lippmann, Robert K.   Hammerstein 1917, 1918; Hart Date Unknown

Lipschultz, George   Hoffman 1927

Lipshultz, Billy   McHugh 1912

Lipshultz, George   Gilbert 1932

Lipton, Dan   Norworth 1911

Lipton, James   Coleman 1965, 1972, 1984, 1988

Lisbona, Edward Maurice   Bryan 1952, 1953, 1954; Caesar 1952, 1965; David, Hal 1951

Lish, Harold E.   Blake 1938, 1941

Lish, S.   Blake 1941

Liszt, Franz   Bergman 1978; Comden and Green 1955; Freed, Ralph 1946; Johnson, Howard 1932; Kahn 1937; Robin 1936

Little, Eric   Duke 1927

Little, George A.   Burke 1929, 1930, 1931; Coots 1931; Johnson, Howard 1921; McHugh 1921; Motzan 1921; Whiting 1926

Little, Little Jack   Bryan 1926, 1935; Coots 1931, 1932, 1937; Coslow 1926; David, Mack 1936; Leslie 1936; Lewis 1924, 1927; Meyer 1935, 1936; Silver 1928; Spina 1931; Stept 1952; Warren 1929; Young, Joe 1924, 1927, 1930, 1931, 1932, 1935, 1938

Littler, Emile   Coslow 1955

Lively, Bill   Russell 1974

Lively, K.A.   Pollack 1928

Livingston, Bill   De Lange 1934

Livingston, Billy   Coots 1951

Livingston, Fud   Kahn 1931; Young, Joe 1932

Livingston, Pat   Robison 1945

Livingstone, Mabel   Young, Victor 1934, 1939, 1944

Llossas, Juan   Harburg 1932

Lloyd, Archie   Dubin 1916

Lloyd, Jack   DePaul 1968; Young, Victor 1956

Lobo, Fernando   Heyman 1948

Lobo, Harold   Evans 1958; Livingston, Jay 1958

Locke, Catherine   David, Mack 1930

Locke, Charles O.   Duke 1939

Locke, Edward   Herbert 1919

Locke, Stan   Willson 1952

Lockwood, Elizabeth   Friml 1913

Lockyer, Malcolm   Heyman 1974

Lodge, Henry   Fisher 1922, 1923; Hoffman 1929; Leslie 1925, 1927; Parish 1929, 1980

Lodge, Henry Cabot   Ager 1929; Yellen 1929

Lodge, Jack   Ager 1933

Loeb, John Jacob   Baer 1931, 1932; Brown, Lew 1944; Davis 1942; Heyman 1937; Kahal 1937; Lawrence 1942; Leslie 1940, 1942; Parish 1945; Rose 1934, 1935; Styne 1948; Webster 1931, 1932, 1933, 1934

Loeb, Paul Francis   Webster 1930

Lofthouse, Charles   Gilbert 1931, 1932

Logan, Frederick Knight   Olcott 1911, 1920; Yellen 1921

Loggins, Kenny   Bergman 1976

Lohner, Fritz   Kalmar 1927; Ruby 1927

Lojacono, Corrado   Cahn 1961

Loman, Jules   Brooks 1938, 1940; Schwartz, Jean 1937

Lombardo, Carmen   Ahlert 1935, 1936; Bryan 1931; Caesar 1932; Coots 1931, 1936; Coslow 1930, 1932, 1935; David, Mack 1940, 1941; Davis 1929, 1931, 1936; Dixon 1933; Eliscu 1931; Freed, Arthur 1932; Friend 1932, 1934, 1935, 1936, 1939; Heyman 1932, 1937; Johnson, Howard 1928; Kahn 1928, 1930, 1932, 1935; Lawrence 1939; Magidson 1933; Meyer 1932; Monaco 1931, 1934; Russell 1945; Stept 1931, 1932, 1933, 1940, 1949, 1950; Styne 1929; Whiting 1926, 1927; Young, Joe 1930, 1931, 1932, 1933, 1935, 1936

Lombardo, Guy   Bryan 1930; Donaldson 1938; Monaco 1930; Motzan 1930

Lombardo, Lebert   Friend 1936

Lonfa, Luiz   Cahn 1967

Long, Bill   Razaf 1939

Longfellow, Henry Wadsworth   McHugh 1919

Longuire, Judy   McHugh 1958

Lopez, Francis   Rome 1950; Yellen 1958

Lopez, Francisco   Rome 1951

Lopez, Freddy   Mancini 1989

Lopez, Ray   Kahn 1925

Lopez, Vincent   Bryan 1925; Clare 1925; Coots 1924; Monaco 1925; Razaf 1937

Lord, Robert   Freed, Arthur 1927; Warren 1934

Lord Radio   Raye 1957

Lorenzo, Ange   Egan 1925, 1926; Kahn 1928; Whiting 1925, 1926, 1928

Loring, Bob   Fisher 1937

Loring, Richard   Freed, Ralph 1959; Heyman 1959; Washington 1945, 1950

Lorraine, Sid   Young, Victor 1930

Loti   Mercer 1961

Lottman, George D.   Mills 1924

Louiguy   David, Mack 1948, 1951

Louise, Mildred   Johnson, J. Rosamond 1929

Lovelace, Mark   David, Mack 1944

Loveman, Robert   Young, Victor 1914

Lover, Fanny   Herbert 1915

Lover, Samuel   Herbert 1915

Lovett, Leroy C.   Johnson, James P. 1954

Loving, Walter Howard   Razaf 1952

Lowe, Fred   Dubin 1924

Lowe, Harry   Mills 1940

Lowe, Ruth   David, Mack 1943; Freed, Ralph 1940

Lowell, James R.   Herbert 1897

Lowell, Jimmy K.   Rainger 1937; Robin 1937

Lowitz, John   Johnson, Howard 1914; Snyder 1909

Lowry, Edward   Gordon 1928; Meyer 1927

Lozito, James   Parish 1946

Luber, Mildred   Robin 1931

Lubin, Harry   Gilbert 1931

Lubin, Irv   Oakland 1954

Lubitsch, Ernst   Robin 1947

Luboff, Norman   Bergman 1955, 1957, 1958, 1959, 1960, 1961, 1962, 1964, 1983, 1987; Russell 1955, 1961
Lubowirski, K.   Cahn 1948; Styne 1948
Lucas, Gene   Gilbert 1917
Lucas, Jimmy   Fisher 1920, 1924; Von Tilzer 1909
Lucas, Nick   Gilbert 1925; Stept 1925, 1926, 1928
Luce, Janice   Razaf 1945
Lueders, F. Kay   Monaco 1940
Luke, Lou Mallory   Kahn 1932
Lunceford, Jimmie   Cahn 1935; Parish 1955; Raye 1935; Razaf 1937
Lund, Eddie   Brooks 1952
Luner, Fritz   Kern 1913
Luttazzi, L.   Sigman 1955
Lyman, Abe   Davis 1928; Donaldson 1926; Freed, Arthur 1922, 1939; Hanley 1928; Johnson, Howard 1924, 1934; Kahn 1924, 1925, 1927, 1928; Rose 1924; Snyder 1931; Turk 1925, 1928
Lyman, Tommy   Stept 1925
Lyn, Ev E.   Blake 1960; Bryan 1927, 1928, 1929; Fain 1928; Snyder 1927, 1928, 1929
Lynding, George   Dubin 1917
Lynott, Billy   Von Tilzer 1917
Lynton, Everett   Bryan 1929; Leslie 1928
Lyons, George   Dubin 1917; Goetz 1910; Lewis 1925; Young, Joe 1925
Lyons, Jimmy   Pollack 1914
Lyons, Joe   Kahn 1922
Lytell, J.   Parish 1935
Lytle, Hub   Parish 1940

M

Macaway, Martin   Brooks 1959
MacBoyle, Darl   Brown, Lew 1917; Coslow 1921; Gilbert 1919, 1920; Hanley 1921, 1922, 1927; Motzan 1916, 1919
MacConnell, Harry T.   Smith, Harry B. 1900, 1901; Smith, Robert B. 1900
Macdonald, Ballard   Atteridge 1925; Carroll 1909, 1910, 1911, 1912, 1913, 1914, 1915, 1916, 1917, 1918, 1920, 1921, 1923, 1925, 1926, 1928, 1937, Date Unknown; Conrad 1921, 1931; Coslow 1926; DeSylva 1923, 1924; Donaldson 1918, 1926, 1931; Edwards 1912; Freed, Arthur 1925; Gershwin, George 1923, 1924; Goetz 1923; Hanley 1916, 1917, 1918, 1919, 1920, 1921, 1922, 1925, 1926, 1927, 1930, 1933, 1934; Henderson 1935; Johnson, J. Rosamond 1911; Johnston 1929, 1930; Monaco 1920, 1927, 1928; Romberg 1921; Rose 1925, 1927, 1928, 1930, 1932, 1934; Stept 1920; Warren 1926, 1927; Yellen 1935
MacDonough, Glen   Ager 1917; Carroll 1918; Goetz 1917, 1918; Herbert 1896, 1903, 1904, 1905, 1907, 1908, 1909, 1923
Macey, Joe   McHugh 1924
MacGinsey, Robert   Gilbert 1943
MacGregor, Chummy   Koehler 1935; Mercer 1943; Parish 1939
Mack, Al   Mercer 1958
Mack, Andrew   Goetz 1910; Jerome 1894; Williams 1908
Mack, Cecil   Blake 1937; Brown, Lew 1924; Johnson, James P. 1922, 1924, 1925, 1926, 1933, 1942; Mills 1933; Smith, Harry B. 1902; Young, Joe 1911
MacKaye, Hugh   Raye 1939
Macklin, Hal M.   Kahal 1935
MacLean, Ross   Johnson, Howard 1932
Mac Leish, Archibald   Weill 1942

MacPherson, Jeanie   Robin 1935; Whiting 1935
MacRae, Sheila   Clare 1955
Madden, Edward   Edwards 1904, 1908, 1909, 1910, 1911, 1912, 1913, 1914; Freed, Arthur 1917; Hanley 1916, 1917; Kern 1911; Meyer 1909; Schwartz, Jean 1911, 1912; Von Tilzer 1910
Madera, Bobby   Sigman 1956
Madinez   Mercer 1961
Madriguera, Enric   Friend 1932; Heyman 1935; Johnson, James P. 1933; Lewis 1932
Maduro, Charles   Bryan 1930
Maffay, Don   Mitchell 1925
Magenta, Guy   Raye 1958
Magine, Frank   Arlen 1929; Davis 1920; Kahn 1920, 1921, 1922; Koehler 1920, 1921, 1922, 1923, 1928, 1929
Magloni, G.   Sigman 1957
Magne, Michel   Blane 1971
Magnini, Frank   Bryan 1928
Maher, Brent L.   David, Mack 1989, 1990
Mahoney, Jack F.   Fisher 1919; Hanley 1919, 1922; Jerome 1918, 1924; Meyer 1911; Von Tilzer 1907, 1908, 1912, 1915, 1916, 1917, 1921, 1925, 1940
Mahoney, Will   Pollack 1924
Mahr, Curley   Van Heusen 1937
Maine, Norman   Parish 1962
Makalno, Kaji   Sigman 1973
Malevsky, Serge   Robin 1954; Whiting 1954
Malgoni, C.   Sigman 1961, 1963
Malie, Thomas   Koehler 1928; Magidson 1924; Stept 1921, 1922, 1924, 1925
Mallory, Eddie   Razaf 1937
Malneck, Matty   Cahn 1958; David, Mack 1936; Davis 1935; Dixon 1932; Friend 1936; Gilbert 1928, 1929; Gordon 1933; Heyman 1936; Johnson, Howard 1934; Kahn 1931, 1932; Loesser 1937, 1939, 1940, 1947; Magidson 1946, 1952; Mercer 1934, 1935, 1936, 1957, 1958; Mills 1929; Parish 1935, 1939, 1941; Raye 1945, 1946, 1950, 1953; Russell 1953; Sigman 1954; Wrubel 1946; Young, Joe 1932, 1933
Malotte, Albert Hay   Brennan 1944; Yellen 1923
Malsiner, Bela   Cahn 1956
Maltby, Richard   Stept 1955
Maltby Jr., Richard   Strouse 1991
Maltin, Bernard   Freed, Ralph 1935, 1936; Johnson, Howard 1951; Mills 1928; Young, Joe 1933, 1934
Malvin, Arthur   McHugh 1979
Mamdry, Ernest   Parish 1932
Mamorsky, Morris   Leigh 1955
Mancini, Chris   Mancini 1979
Mancini, Felice   Mancini 1970, 1975
Mandel, Frank   Caesar 1925; Hammerstein 1928
Mandel, Johnny   Bergman 1966, 1987, 1988, 1989; David, Hal 1970; Mercer 1965; Webster 1966, 1969
Mandell, Herbie   Parish 1929
Manilow, Barry   David, Hal 1976; Mercer 1984
Mank, Chaw   Coots 1953
Manlio, Tito   Akst 1953
Mann, Bert   Bryan 1944
Mann, Dave   David, Mack 1942
Mann, David A.   Loesser Date Unknown
Mann, Herbie   Sigman 1962
Mann, Mickey   Conrad 1935; Magidson 1935
Mann, Paul   Adamson 1941; Cahn 1939; De Lange 1940; Heyman 1939; Lewis 1938; Parish 1948
Mann, Sally   Johnson, Howard 1949

Mann, Stephen   Lawrence 1931
Mann, Steve   Drake 1955; Sigman 1952, 1954
Mann, W.L.   Bryan 1935
Manners, Gerry   Livingston, Jerry 1955
Manners, Henry   David, Mack 1933; Drake 1946, 1957;
     Lewis 1935
Manning, Charles J.   Romberg 1917
Manning, Dick   Freed, Arthur 1933; Hoffman 1931, 1938,
     1939, 1949, 1952, 1953, 1954, 1955, 1956, 1957, 1958,
     1959, 1960, 1961, 1963, 1967; Livingston, Jerry 1943,
     1944; Magidson 1954, 1956; Raye 1961
Manning, Milo   Gilbert 1931
Manone, Wingy   Mercer 1944, 1949, 1952; Mills 1935
Manson, Eddy L.   Sigman 1963; Webster 1967
Mantovani   Adamson 1959; Webster 1957
Manuel, Joe   Von Tilzer 1925
Marbot, R.   Heyman 1946
Marceau, V.   Parish 1956
Marchant, J.C.   Motzan 1934
Marcos   Sigman 1971, 1972
Marcotte, Don   Stept 1954; Wrubel 1949
Mares, Paul   Mills 1942
Marfin, Jane   Webster 1954
Margaretten, Bill   Coots 1957, 1958
Margis, Alfred   Johnson, Howard 1935; Sterling 1924
Margulis, Max   Johnson, James P. 1944
Mariani, Hugo   Brown, Lew 1941
Mariano, John   Dubin 1921
Mario, E.A.   Raye 1958
Marion Jr., George   Coslow 1935, 1937; Fain 1946, 1947;
     Rainger 1930, 1931, 1932; Revel 1953, 1960; Schwartz,
     Jean 1926; Waller 1943; Whiting 1929, 1930, 1933, 1935,
     1936, 1944
Mark, F.W.   Kern 1915
Mark, Stephen   Bullock 1949
Markes, Larry   Carmichael 1947; Stept 1947
Markham, Erwin   Carmichael 1952
Marks, Charley   Warren 1926
Marks, Clarence   Romberg 1921
Marks, Dennis   Styne 1977
Marks, Edward B.   Johnson, J. Rosamond 1935
Marks, Franklin   Mills 1938
Marks, Gerald   Bryan 1936, 1937, 1938, 1939, 1942, 1952,
     1953, 1955; Caesar 1934, 1935, 1936, 1937, 1938, 1939,
     1940, 1941, 1942, 1943, 1944, 1945, 1947, 1950, 1952,
     1953, 1958; Clare 1933, 1937; Davis 1932; Egan 1935;
     Harbach 1936; Lerner, Sammy 1926, 1932, 1933, 1934,
     1935, 1936, 1937, 1938, 1943, 1948, 1950; Whiting 1926;
     Young, Joe 1933, 1934
Marks, Johnny   Ager 1939; Robison 1936, 1950
Marks, L.R.   Cahn 1964
Marks, Larry   Bergman 1965, 1966, 1968; De Lange 1945
Marks, Leo   Fisher 1920
Marks, Sammy   Lawrence 1940
Marks, Steve   Russell 1951, 1957
Markush, Fred   Parish 1932
Markwell, Mark   Hoffman 1957, 1958, 1959
Marlow, Harry   Kern 1910
Marn, Mickey   Parish 1945
Marnay, Eddy   Blane 1971
Marquina, Pasqual   Sigman 1977
Marr, Alex   Brown, A. Seymour 1920; Dubin 1927
Marreiros, E.   Drake 1945
Marroquin, Jose Sabre   Drake 1941
Marsala, Joe   Caesar 1944; Sigman 1941; Woods 1955

Marsh, Lyle   Robison 1949
Marsh, Roy   Woods 1957
Marsh, Roy K.   Egan 1920; Kahn 1926
Marsh, Royal   De Lange 1936; Mercer 1939
Marshal, Albert Lee   Brennan 1943
Marshall, Henry I.   Brown, Lew 1942, 1943; Dietz 1925,
     1927, 1946; Egan 1920, 1923, 1926, 1927, 1938; Kahn
     1916, 1917; Norworth 1945; Stept 1942; Whiting 1923,
     1926, 1927
Marshall, Jack   Mercer 1957; Raye 1958, 1959
Marshall, Jerry   Revel 1962
Marston, Lew   Kahal 1929
Martell, John   Robison 1957
Martell, Paul   Drake 1944
Martin, Brat   Schwartz, Arthur 1922
Martin, Carroll   Kahn 1923
Martin, Charles   Fain 1968; Freed, Ralph 1946
Martin, Darrel   Brennan 1930
Martin, Diane   Parish 1957
Martin, Earl   Kahn 1932
Martin, Freddy   Bullock 1947; David, Mack 1970; Spina
     1952, 1970
Martin, Herbert   Ellington 1958
Martin, John   Young, Victor 1934
Martin, Louis   Coots 1944; Drake 1945
Martin, Paul   Wrubel 1943
Martin, T.   Johnson, Howard 1922
Martin, Tony   Cahn 1955; David, Mack 1968; Heyman 1952;
     Magidson 1950; Oakland 1950, 1951, 1963, 1965, 1968;
     Young, Victor 1952
Martinez, Gilbert   Mercer 1970; Webster 1970
Martita   David, Hal 1956; David, Mack 1953, 1956
Martorella, Robert   Young, Joe 1972
Marvin, Dick   McHugh 1947
Marx, Arthur   Johnston 1931
Marx, Chico   Davis 1951; Parish 1943
Marx, Groucho   Ruby 1952
Marx, Kay   Kalmar 1949; Ruby 1950
Maryorga, Lincoln   Russell 1965
Mascagni   Johnson, Howard 1939
Mascheroni   Adamson 1953; Rome 1948; Sigman 1958
Maschwitz, Eric   Coslow 1955
Maslof, Irving   Clarke 1922; Davis 1927; Fisher 1921; Lewis
     1923; Mitchell 1920; Silver 1918; Young, Joe 1923
Mason, Charles A.   Egan 1919; Whiting 1918, 1919
Mason, Jack   Heyman 1932
Mason, Jane   Turk 1924
Mason, Nikki   Razaf 1947
Massara, Pino   David, Hal 1960
Massenet, Jules   Johnson, Howard 1934; Rome 1948; Wrubel
     1951
Masser, Michael   Mercer 1966
Massey, Dott   Gilbert 1938
Massey, Robert   Warren 1925
Masters, Frankie   Burke 1940; David, Hal 1940; Dubin 1943;
     Heyman 1938; Parish 1938
Masters, M.D.   Friml 1949
Matanzas   Livingston, Jerry 1959
Mathias, Jack   Cahn 1943; Russell 1943
Mattes, Willy   Sigman 1955
Matthews, Edward   Razaf 1951
Matthews, Onzy   Ellington 1969
Maxwell, Charles   McHugh 1931
Maxwell, Eddie   Akst 1951; Oakland 1951, 1952, 1953, 1954,
     1960

Maxwell, Elsa   Akst 1935; Brown, Lew 1935

Maxwell, Gale   Robison 1957

Maxwell, Robert   Myrow 1939; Sigman 1953, 1954, 1966, 1973; Silver 1956; Webster 1968

May, B.   Sherman 1961

May, Billy   Russell 1958

May, Hans   Parish 1934; Young, Joe 1931

Mayer, Archie   Hanley 1915

Mayer, H.   Harburg Date Unknown

Mayer, Henry   Mercer 1965

Mayer, Natalie   Bryan 1939

Mayer, Ray   Robison 1939, 1943, 1944, 1945

Mayo, Harry   Mitchell 1925; Von Tilzer 1924

Mayorga, Lincoln   Russell 1964, 1977

Mayuzumi, Toshiro   Webster 1966

Mazziotto, R.   Dubin 1924

McCallum, David   Webster 1967

McCane, Mabel   Howard, Joseph E. 1913, 1914

McCann, John W.   Herbert 1895

McCann, Les   Mercer 1967

McCann, M.J.   Herbert 1915

McCarey, Leo   Adamson 1954, 1957, 1962; DeSylva 1926; Johnston 1934; Oakland 1955; Warren 1954, 1957, 1962

McCarron, Charles   Brown, Lew 1916, 1917; Donaldson 1916; Johnson, Howard 1915, 1918; Meyer 1918

McCarron, Earl   Mercer 1932

McCarthy, Charles   Livingston, Jerry 1941; Parish 1934

McCarthy, Joseph   Ager 1938; Ahlert 1941; Baer 1942; Bryan 1912, 1918; Carroll 1918; Clarke 1915, 1925; Coleman 1952, 1964, 1965; Donaldson 1939; Fisher 1912, 1913, 1914, 1915, 1916, 1917, 1918, 1919; Hanley 1929, 1930, 1931, 1937; Herbert 1924; Johnson, Howard 1914, 1915, 1916, 1917; Meyer 1942; Monaco 1913, 1914, 1915, 1916, 1917, 1919, 1925, 1929, 1930, 1937, 1938, 1945, 1946; Rose 1940; Schwartz, Jean 1938; Sigman 1939; Van Heusen 1940

McCarthy Jr., Joseph   Coleman 1953, 1956; Monaco 1942; Russell 1947

McCarthy, Justin Huntley   Herbert 1913

McCarthy, Lillian   Johnson, Howard 1953

McCarthy, Merrick   Young, Victor 1945

McCarthy, Patsy   Dietz 1957

McCleod, Keith   Kahn 1930

McComb, Malcolm   Rose 1930

McConnell, Alfred   Bryan 1938

McConnell, George B.   Bryan 1928, 1930, 1931, 1933, 1934, 1937, 1938, 1940, 1944, 1945, 1951; Dubin 1916, 1917, 1924, 1925, 1927; Fisher 1934, 1936, 1938; Johnson, Howard 1933; Leslie 1927; McHugh 1916, 1924; Mills 1939, 1940; Razaf 1934; Spina 1931; Sterling 1920

McCord, Harold   Carmichael 1952

McCord, Mary J.   Sigman 1958

McCormack, Josephine   Sterling 1928

McCormack, Rennie   Dubin 1917

McCoy, Bessie   Kern 1911

McCoy, Jack   Lewis 1926; Young, Joe 1926

McCune, Hank   Koehler 1955

McCurdy, Marsh   Brennan 1928

McDiarmid, Don   Adamson 1940

McEvoy, J.P.   Conrad 1906, 1925, 1926

McGavish, James   Fisher 1910

McGee, W.E.   Young, Joe 1928

McGhee, Granville   Raye 1960

McGinnis, D.   Russell 1964

McGlohon, Loonis   Martin 1977

McGowan, Jack   Coslow 1925; Silver 1925; Young, Joe 1923

McGrane, Paul   Drake 1941, 1942, 1943, 1944, 1947

McGrath, Fulton   Mercer 1942

McGuire, Joseph Desmond   Carmichael 1940; Monaco 1940

McHugh, Irving   Dubin 1924

McIntire, Lani   Brown, Lew 1940; Bryan 1938, 1940; Hanley 1938

McIntosh, Tom   Evans 1980

McKee, Kenneth   Parish 1950

McKee, Kip   Bryan 1931

McKee, Raymond   Young, Victor 1930

McKeernum, Joe   Brennan 1928

McKenkenra, William J.   Snyder 1919

McKuen, Rod   Mancini 1956, 1957, 1969

McLaughlin, John   Brennan 1928; Bryan 1929; McHugh 1927; Meyer 1929; Mills 1927

McLeod, Jessie L. Deppen   Brennan 1926

McNeely, J.B.   Ellington 1939

McPartland, Marian   Caesar 1956

McPartland, Parnell   Edwards 1912

McPhail, Lindsay   Parish 1930

McWatters, Tyson   Lewis 1911

Meachum, C.W.   Leslie 1942

Meadows, Fred   Hanley 1933

Meakor, Harry   Mitchell 1921

Meakor, Jacob   Mitchell 1921

Mears, John Henry   DeSylva 1919; Gershwin, George 1919

Meeker, Bobby   Kahn 1941

Meher, Donovan   Sissle 1928

Mehlinger, Artie   Bryan 1920; Johnson, Howard 1918; Meyer 1918, 1920

Meinardi, Helen   Carmichael 1937, 1940, 1948

Meinken, Fred   Kahn 1922

Meissner, J.J. Zep   Mills 1946, 1947

Melamed, Lou   Bacharach 1957, 1958; David, Hal 1957, 1958

Melette, Rosalie   Pollack 1923

Mellin, Robert   Stept 1952, 1954

Mellissinos, Margaret   Howard, Joseph E. 1942

Meltzer, Robert   Eliscu 1943

Memphis Five, The   Coslow Date Unknown

Menaker, Louis   Parish 1945

Mencher, Murray   Ager 1935, 1936; Baer 1934; Clare 1931, 1932, 1933; Davis 1954; Freed, Ralph 1934; Gilbert 1934; Hoffman 1938; Johnson, Howard 1933; Magidson 1932

Mendelson, D.   Russell 1948

Mendelssohn, Felix   Bergman 1983; Brooks 1945; Loesser 1941

Mendes, Sergio   Bergman 1968

Mendez, Jose Antonio   Mercer 1954

Mendoza, David   Bryan 1927; Dietz 1928

Menescal, R.   Russell 1966

Mercier, Rene   Coslow 1926

Merhoff, Benny   Coslow 1927; Gilbert 1939; Kahn 1927; Pollack 1939; Styne 1927; Van Heusen 1937, 1938

Merkur, J.L.   Clarke 1920

Merrill, Blanche   Edwards 1914, 1934; Freed, Arthur 1927; Hanley 1930; Schwartz, Jean 1918, 1920

Merrill, George   Mancini 1987

Mersey, Robert   Lawrence 1967

Merwin, Bob   Mills 1929

Meskill, Jack   Ager 1933; Baer 1923; Bloom 1935; Bryan 1928, 1931; Conrad 1925, 1927, 1930, 1931, 1932; Edwards 1932, 1937; Fain 1924, 1932; Fisher 1926; Friend 1923; Hoffman 1929; Johnson, Howard 1933, 1958; Kahal 1929; Leslie 1926, 1945; Monaco 1933, 1937;

Motzan 1924; Parish 1936; Rose 1924, 1925; Schwartz, Jean 1930; Silver 1928; Stept 1927, 1937; Waller 1932

Mesone, Jimmy   Hoffman 1950

Messenheimer, Sam   Johnson, Howard 1929, 1930; Kahn 1955

Meth, Max   David, Mack 1954; Livingston, Jerry 1954

Metzger, H.   Russell 1941

Metzl, Lothar   Caesar 1943

Meyer, Al   Fisher 1921

Meyer, Joseph   Adamson 1942; Akst 1928; Baer 1925; Brown, Lew 1943, 1944; Bryan 1927, 1933; Caesar 1922, 1923, 1924, 1925, 1926, 1927, 1928, 1929, 1931, 1932, 1934, 1954; Clare 1925; Clarke 1923, 1924; Davis 1926, 1927, 1933; De Lange 1934, 1942; DeSylva 1921, 1924, 1925; Dixon 1933, 1941; Dubin 1925, 1928; Eliscu 1929; Fields 1945; Freed, Arthur 1923, 1930, 1931; Freed, Ralph 1940; Friend 1925, 1935; Gershwin, Ira 1923, 1928, 1930; Hanley 1925; Harburg 1932, 1941, Date Unknown; Heyman 1934, 1935, 1939; Johnson, Howard 1921, 1923, 1930, 1933; Kahal 1931; Kalmar 1924; Leigh 1952; Leslie 1923, 1924, 1942; Lewis 1928, 1929; Loesser 1934, Date Unknown; Magidson 1934, 1935; Mercer 1933, 1941, 1949, 1972; Parish 1951; Robin 1927, 1931; Rose 1925, 1928; Ruby 1924; Russell 1939, 1940; Sigman 1939, 1940, 1941, 1942, 1946, 1951; Silver 1933; Turk 1925, 1932; Yellen 1935; Young, Joe 1928, 1929, 1933

Meyer, Joseph P.   Russell 1977

Meyer, Sol   Akst 1943; Styne 1940, 1941, 1942, 1943, 1944, 1950, 1956

Meyerowitz, David   Cahn 1939; Rome 1949

Meyers, Artie   Davis 1925

Meyers, Billy   Dubin 1924; Kahn 1923; Mills 1923

Meyers, C.   Fisher 1929

Meyers, Henry   Dietz 1930; Rainger 1930

Meyers, Joseph   Rose 1934

Meyers, Richard   Eliscu 1929, 1930

Meyers, Vic   Von Tilzer 1927

Meyers, Zeke   Howard, Joseph E. 1919, 1920, Date Unknown

Meyerson, H.   Sigman 1969

Michel, Leo   Woods 1923

Michel, Werner   Caesar 1943

Michelet, Michel   Heyman 1944; Russell 1950

Michelson, Lew   Fisher 1928

Middleton, J.A.   Johnson, J. Rosamond 1916

Middleton, R.   Russell 1957

Mierisch, Fred E.   Johnson, Howard 1914

Mighty Sparrow   Raye 1957

Migliacci, F.   Mancini 1964; Mercer 1963

Migliaccio, Oreste   Gilbert 1911

Mikell, F. Eugene   Sissle 1917

Miles, Dick   David, Mack 1947

Miles, Nat   Styne 1927

Miles, Vajen   Silver 1952

Miley, Bubber   Ellington 1937

Milford, Jack   Van Heusen 1938

Militin, V.   Rome 1943

Millbau, Margot   Mercer 1933

Miller, Alice Duer   Kern 1920

Miller, Bill   Parish 1938

Miller, Bob   David, Mack 1945

Miller, Ed   Fisher 1913

Miller, Eddie   Mercer 1947, 1958

Miller, Everett   Mercer 1930, 1932

Miller, Flournoy E.   Blake 1955, 1958, 1964; Johnson, James P. 1941, 1944, 1947, 1948, 1950; Sissle 1964

Miller, Fritz   Loesser 1939

Miller, Glenn   Parish 1939

Miller, Hap   Washington 1932

Miller, Irving   Baer 1944

Miller, Maury   Pollack 1932

Miller, Ned   Styne 1926, 1929, 1931

Miller, Patsy Ruth   Conrad 1924

Miller, Ray   Fisher 1920, 1925

Miller, Ron   Leigh 1985; Styne 1985

Miller, S.   Russell 1951

Miller, Sonny   Styne 1927, 1929

Miller, Sy   Fain 1963

Miller, Wilbur   Meyer 1947

Millham, Margot   Oakland 1933; Robison 1933

Millinder, Lucky   De Lange 1941; Mills 1935, 1936

Mills, Annette   Fain 1938

Mills, Carley   Atteridge 1923; Caesar 1923; Romberg 1923

Mills, F.A.   Harbach 1911; Schwartz, Jean 1911

Mills, Felix   Wrubel 1943, 1944

Mills, Gilbert   Hoffman 1945

Mills, Jay   Koehler 1925, 1927

Mills, Kerry   Brown, Lew 1915, 1917; Bryan 1904, 1908, 1909; Gilbert 1913, 1914; Goetz 1910; Leslie 1909, 1910, 1912; Lewis 1910, 1911; Smith, Harry B. 1903; Sterling 1902, 1904, 1908, 1909, 1910; Von Tilzer 1910

Mills, L.   Silver 1952

Mills, Pvt. Paul   Myrow 1943

Milne, A.A.   Brooks 1960

Milton, Jay   Wrubel 1949

Mineo, Sam   Friend 1944; Russell 1957

Miron, I.   Parish 1950

Misraki, Paul   David, Mack 1945; Drake 1946; Rome 1951, 1956; Sigman 1958

Mitchell, Mel   Mancini 1956

Mitchum, Julie   Bryan 1958

Mitchum, Robert   Raye 1958

Mittenhal, J.   Dubin 1924

Miyagawa, Hiroshi   Cahn 1971

Mizzi, Alberto   Coslow 1922

Mizzy, Vic   David, Hal 1950; Hoffman 1940; Lawrence 1960; Parish 1954, 1955, 1961, 1967; Yellen 1956, 1957, 1978

Mobett, Larry   Stept 1928

Mobley, Earle   Parish 1931

Mockridge, Cyril   Cahn 1954; Washington 1959

Modugno, Domenico   Baer 1960; David, Hal 1959; David, Mack 1958; Parish 1958, 1959; Raye 1958, 1965

Moesser, Peter   Webster 1957

Mogol   Raye 1961

Mohr, Halsey K.   Bryan 1915; Leslie 1907, 1908, 1909, 1911

Mohrens, Th.   Sigman 1959

Mokrousov, V.   Rome 1943

Molchanov, E.   Rome 1943

Mole, Miff   Parish 1944; Russell 1945

Molino, Carlos   Johnston 1932

Moll, Billy   Bryan 1930; Hanley 1926; Johnson, Howard 1927, 1929; Koehler 1931; Monaco 1932; Waller 1929, 1930; Warren 1927; Woods 1931; Wrubel 1925

Monaco, Tommy   Kahal 1926

Monahan, Jack   Carroll 1918

Monath, Norman   David, Hal 1951, 1956

Monnot, Marguerite   Cahn 1956; Lawrence 1956; Parish 1951; Rome 1950, 1956; Sigman 1959

Monod, Flavien   Gordon 1958

Monroe, George   Lawrence 1946
Montclair, Addison   Livingston, Jerry 1959
Montenegro, Hugo   Bergman 1969
Montes, Octavio Mars   Sigman 1946
Montgomery, Reggie   Fisher 1929, 1930; Johnson, Howard 1930
Montrose, Percy   Raye 1958
Mooca, M.   Revel 1930
Moody, Phil   Oakland 1950, 1952, 1954, 1956; Washington 1964
Moon   Johnson, Howard 1927
Mooney, Hazel   Fain 1928
Moore, Allie   Razaf 1924
Moore, Beth   Kahn 1924
Moore, Billy   Mills 1954
Moore, Dudley   Cahn 1967
Moore, Elizabeth Evelyn   Young, Victor 1924
Moore, Fred   Kahn 1923
Moore, Jack   Waller 1924
Moore, Leslie   Leslie 1926
Moore, Mavor   Burke 1981
Moore, McElbert   Conrad 1924; Coots 1921, 1922, 1923, 1924, 1926; Schwartz, Jean 1923
Moore, O.   Leigh 1981
Moore, Phil   Eliscu 1943; Johnson, Howard 1926; Kahn 1924
Moore, Raymond   Sterling 1900
Moore, Robert   David, Mack 1940
Moore, Wilton   Baer 1946; Meyer 1947
Morales, Noro   Adamson 1942; Caesar 1945; Sigman 1946
Morales, Obdulio   Rome 1945
Moran, Edward P.   Baer 1950; Brown, Lew 1918, 1919; Johnson, Howard 1914; Monaco 1913; Sterling 1901, 1916, 1921, 1922, 1942; Von Tilzer 1901, 1917, 1918, 1920, 1921, 1922, 1935, 1936
Morano, Jose   Drake 1946
Morbelli   Lawrence 1954
Moren, Art   Lawrence 1931
Mores, M.   Drake 1945
Moret, Neil   Bryan 1910; Egan 1925, 1929; Friend 1933, 1934, 1950, 1952; Kahn 1927, 1928, 1932; Kalmar 1925; Ruby 1925; Whiting 1925, 1928, 1929; Williams 1917, 1919, 1922
Moretti, Raoul   Caesar 1931; Harburg 1932; Washington 1931
Morgan, Agnes   Atteridge 1913; Schwartz, Arthur 1926, 1929
Morgan, Carey   Gilbert 1916, 1917; Norworth 1921; Parish 1921; Sterling 1913
Morgan, David   Adamson 1961
Morgan, Dennis   David, Mack 1982
Morgan, Duke   Howard, Joseph E. 1942
Morgan, Edward   Sterling 1916; Von Tilzer 1916
Morgan, Jimmy   Davis 1919
Morgan, Margaret   Mills 1937
Morgan, May   Carmichael 1944
Morgan, Russ   Baer 1942; David, Mack 1942, 1943; Davis 1942, 1943, 1945; De Lange 1938, 1943, 1947; Meyer 1943; Parish 1936; Stept 1943
Moriarty, George J.   Egan 1923; Whiting 1914, 1915, 1917, 1923
Moritz, Al   Razaf 1943
Moross, Jerome   Leigh 1963; Washington 1958
Morris, Hayward   Sigman 1956
Morris, Jack   Conrad 1925
Morris, John   Leigh 1976
Morris, Lee   Johnston 1946; Meyer 1947

Morris, Melville   Brown, A. Seymour 1912; Kahn 1916; Yellen 1919; Young, Joe 1913
Morris, Mike   Parish 1924, 1934
Morris, Thomas   Waller 1927, 1928
Morrissey, Will   Atteridge 1915; Blake 1930; Hanley 1929; Razaf 1930
Morrow, Buddy   Hoffman 1945
Morse, Dolly   Baer 1931; Donaldson 1927, 1928
Morse, Lee   Pollack 1925; Razaf 1930
Morse, Theodore   Ager 1919; Brennan 1918; Bryan 1903; Clarke 1913; Johnson, Howard 1915; Leslie 1913; Meyer 1919; Mitchell 1918; Sterling 1910
Morthens, Haukur   Livingston, Jerry 1960
Morton, Harry K.   Smith, Harry B. 1926
Morton, James J.   Howard, Joseph E. 1923
Morton, Lew   Mitchell 1921; Pollack 1921
Mosby, Evan   Mills 1938
Moser, James   Washington 1955; Young, Victor 1955
Mossman, Ted   Hoffman 1946
Motaggart, Jack   Oakland 1937
Motola, George   Mercer 1950
Mott, Harold   Coots 1957; Van Heusen 1940
Mottier, Jean-Pierre   McHugh 1953, 1954; Webster 1955
Mottler, J.P.   David, Hal 1960
Mottola, Tony   David, Mack 1962; Drake 1967
Mouque, Georges   Parish 1935
Mouradian, Sarky   Webster 1976
Moussorgsky, H.   Johnson, Howard 1935
Mozart, Wolfgang Amadeus   Freed, Ralph 1939, 1942; Mercer 1938; Warren 1938
Muir, Lewis F.   Brown, Lew 1915; Bryan 1914; Clarke 1912, 1913; Gilbert 1912, 1913, 1914, 1916; Goetz 1909; Leslie 1911, 1912, 1913
Mullan, Richard   Van Heusen 1955
Mullane, Frank   Johnson, Howard 1922
Mullen, Charles E.   Atteridge 1906
Mullen, J.B.   Bryan 1908
Mullen, Richard   Van Heusen 1954
Muller, Carl   McHugh 1916, 1917
Muller, Werner   Sigman 1956
Mundy, Jimmy   Lawrence 1940; Mercer 1943; Mills 1941; Raye 1958
Munro, Bill   Sterling 1920; Von Tilzer 1920
Muradelli, V.   Rome 1943
Mure, Billy   David, Hal 1955
Murfin, Jane   Webster 1964
Murphy, C.W.   Norworth 1911
Murphy, Owen   Ager 1928; Atteridge 1921; Caesar 1924; Clare 1923; Conrad 1926, 1928; Friend 1923; Gorney 1923, 1924, 1925; Jerome 1923; Kahn 1922; Koehler 1923; Pollack 1921; Schwartz, Jean 1921; Yellen 1928
Murphy, Spud   Adamson 1939; Mills 1935
Murphy, Stanley   Carroll 1911, 1917; Motzan 1915; Von Tilzer 1911, 1912, 1913
Murphy & Charles   Donaldson 1941
Murray   Silver 1919
Murray, Bill   Cahn 1967
Murray, John P.   Coots 1932; Davis 1928; Fain 1928, 1929, 1962; Hoffman 1931, 1932, 1933, 1955; Johnson, Howard 1951; Mills 1927, 1928; Oakland 1928, 1930, 1931, 1958; Rose 1934
Murray, John T.   Edwards 1929, 1930
Murray, Lyn   David, Mack 1962, 1965; Heyman 1955, 1976

Murry, Ted   Davis 1942, 1943, 1944, 1945, 1946, 1952, 1953, 1954, 1955, 1956, 1959, 1960, 1961, 1962, 1963, 1964, 1965, 1966, 1967, 1970
Murtagh, Henry   Kalmar 1925; Ruby 1925
Muse, Clarence   Johnson, J. Rosamond 1938
Muskin, Sy   David, Hal 1958
Mutile, Emmanuelle   Hoffman 1954
Myattway, Art   Livingston, Jerry 1930
Myers, Harlan   Young, Victor 1939
Myers, Henry   Coots 1926; Eliscu 1940, 1941, 1942, 1943, 1944, 1949, 1955; Gorney 1938, 1940, 1941, 1942, 1943, 1944, 1955, 1958, 1959, 1969; Schwartz, Arthur 1927, 1929
Myers, Peter   Oakland 1970
Myers, Richard   Gershwin, Ira 1923; Harburg 1932, 1934; Heyman 1931, 1932, 1933, 1934, 1935, 1952; Lawrence 1950, 1954, 1957, 1958; Mercer 1930, 1932, 1933; Robin 1926, 1927, 1928, 1929, 1931; Smith, Robert B. 1930
Myers, Sherman   Freed, Ralph 1931
Mysels, Sammy   David, Mack 1938, 1944, 1961; Davis 1950; Hanley 1938, 1940, 1941; Silver 1950
Mysler, Nat   Washington 1956

N

Nacit   Koehler 1922
Nadell, Leo   Johnston 1920
Nagle, Paul   Fisher 1936
Napoleon, Phil   Donaldson 1924; Heyman 1929; McHugh 1923
Napton, Johnny   Russell 1942, 1943
Nascimbene, Mario   Freed, Arthur 1962; Lawrence 1954; Webster 1957, 1958
Naset, C.   Kahn 1924
Nash, Ogden   Duke 1946, 1949, 1952, 1956; Weill 1943
Nathan, J. Casper   Leslie 1911; Monaco 1911
Nathan, Ted   Silver 1944
Nathansen-Borgel   Kahn 1927
Natoli, Nathan   Young, Victor 1929
Navara, Leon   Parish 1929; Washington 1950, 1952
Nazelles, Ray   Washington 1931
Neal, Joseph   Howard, Joseph E. 1915
Nedbal, Oscar   Atteridge 1915; Friml 1915
Needa, Magda   Silver 1953
Negrette, George   Adamson 1940; Ellington 1941
Negulesco, Dusky   Duke Date Unknown
Neiburg, Al J.   Ager 1937; Conrad 1931; Coots 1950, 1951, 1952, 1953, 1954, 1955, 1957, 1959, 1961, 1962, 1964; Livingston, Jerry 1932, 1933, 1934, 1935, 1936, 1937, 1939, 1941, 1954, 1955; Myrow 1930, 1931, 1932, 1934, 1948; Romberg 1943; Silver 1939; Woods 1958
Neil, Marcia   Merrill 1951
Neilan, Marshall   Kahn 1924
Neilson, Bob   Parish 1927
Nelson   Pollack 1923
Nelson, B.   Davis 1929
Nelson, Bob   McHugh 1923; Silver 1922
Nelson, David   Baer 1956
Nelson, Ed G.   Ager 1932; Baer 1927, 1933; Blake 1927; Burke 1931; Coots 1921, 1929; Donaldson 1923; Dubin 1927; Hoffman 1930, 1931, 1932, 1933; Johnson, Howard 1921, 1923, 1926, 1933, 1934, 1935; Lewis 1931; Mills 1924, 1927; Parish 1920, 1921; Sherman 1953
Nelson, Eddie   Blake 1915, 1916; Sissle 1915, 1916
Nelson, Jack   Akst 1923; Kahn 1923

Nelson, Ozzie   Coots 1931
Nelson, Rudolph   Johnson, Howard 1925
Nelson, Steve   Burke 1930, 1931; Coots 1939; Parish 1930, 1931
Nelson, William Warvelle   Kahn 1923, 1925
Nemo, Henry   De Lange 1943; Ellington 1938; Gordon 1939; Mills 1937, 1938, 1939, 1940; Woods 1943
Nesbitt, John   Willson 1937
Nesdan, Ubirajara   Brown, Lew 1940
Ness, Walter C.   Johnson, Howard 1927
Nestice, Sammy   Mercer 1971
Nestor, Johnny   Fisher 1921
Neubach, Beda   Kalmar 1927; Ruby 1927
Neubach, Ernst   Kalmar 1927; Ruby 1927; Young, Joe 1931
Neufeld, Mace   Hoffman 1950
Neuman, N.   Kahn 1930; Young, Victor 1930
Neumann, Helen   David, Mack 1948
Nevin, Arthur   Smith, Harry B. 1900
Nevins, Harry   Silver 1952
Nevins, Morty   David, Hal 1950, 1951; Merrill 1949
New, Arnold   Johnson, J. Rosamond 1934; Yellen 1930
Newley, Anthony   Bacharach 1979
Newman, Alfred   Adamson 1942; Blane 1951; Bullock 1940, 1941; Caesar 1922, 1924; Cahn 1955, 1959, 1961; David, Hal 1966; De Lange 1947; Gordon 1940, 1941, 1949, 1950, 1953; Harbach 1923; Kalmar 1937, 1949; Loesser 1937, 1946; Ruby 1937, 1951; Washington 1945; Webster 1941, 1956, 1961, 1970
Newman, Charles   Ager 1935, 1936; Burke 1931, 1932, 1933; Coots 1931, 1933, 1937, 1938, 1939, 1949, 1950, 1957, 1960; Friend 1934; Gordon 1928; Hoffman 1932, 1933, 1934; Monaco 1932, 1934, 1935, 1936, 1939, 1940, 1941, 1942; Oakland 1954; Pollack 1940, 1943, 1944, 1946; Spina 1933, 1936, 1940, 1957; Stept 1935, 1939; Styne 1929; Washington 1934; Wrubel 1940, 1941, 1942, 1944, 1945, 1946, 1947, 1949, 1952; Young, Joe 1934; Young, Victor 1930, 1931, 1939, 1954
Newman, Emil   De Lange 1947
Newman, Evan   Washington 1944
Newman, Greatrex   Dietz 1930; Schwartz, Arthur 1930
Newman, Lionel   Koehler 1943; Loesser 1940; Ruby 1947; Russell 1949, 1950, 1951, 1959, 1965; Warren 1943
Nicholls, Horatio   Bryan 1929; Leslie 1927, 1928, 1929; Parish 1936
Nichols, Alberta   Coots 1926
Nichols, E.L.   Ager 1927; Yellen 1927
Nicholson, Nick   Berlin 1907
Nicodemus   Raye 1942
Niesen, Gertrude   Coslow 1938; Loesser 1940
Nisa   Hoffman 1954, 1958; Raye 1961
Nitke, Maurice   Gershwin, Ira 1924
Nixon, Theodore Fenderson   Razaf 1925
Nizza   Lawrence 1954
Nobbs, John   Snyder 1911
Nobile, Eugenio   Drake 1945
Noble, Harry   Coots 1967
Noble, Johnny   Adamson 1939, 1940; Donaldson 1938; Freed, Ralph 1940
Noble, Leighton   Parish 1938
Noble, Ray   Cahn 1950; Kahn 1932
Noble, T. Tertius   Bullock 1944
Nocella, William   Young, Joe 1972
Noel, Art   Johnston 1938
Noel, James   Snyder 1931
Noel, Robert   Razaf Date Unknown

Noel, Rose   Gorney 1948
Nogul   Sigman 1966
Nomath, Norman   Hoffman 1955
Norbett, Larry   Stept 1929
Nordstrom, Clarence   Gilbert 1937
Noriega, Nenette   Fisher 1932
Norman, Fred   Sigman 1956
Norman, Marsha   Merrill 1993; Styne 1993
Norman, Pierre   Brennan 1925, 1938; Coslow 1935; Dubin
    1931, 1945; Duke 1930; Fain 1928, 1929, 1930, 1931,
    1932; Hanley 1929, 1931; Kahal 1928, 1929, 1930, 1931,
    1932, 1935; Parish 1945; Stept 1950; Young, Joe 1931
Normand, Claude   Parish 1950
Norris, Cal   Oakland 1929
Norris, Jimmy   Coots 1943, 1945
North, Alex   Adamson 1961; Bergman 1961, 1964; Brooks
    1955; Cahn 1957, 1958, 1959; David, Hal 1955, 1956;
    Mercer 1956, 1963; Russell 1948; Webster 1955, 1966,
    1969
North, John Ringling   Caesar 1955; Coots 1944; Goetz 1952,
    1954
Northrup, Theo. H.   Kahn 1915
Norton, George A.   Coslow 1934; Loesser 1941; Smith,
    Harry B. 1903
Norvo, Red   De Lange 1938; Mills 1935; Van Heusen 1938
Norwood, C.   Russell 1947, 1948
Norworth, Amy   Norworth 1954
Norworth, Dorothy A.   Norworth 1927, 1938
Norworth, Ned   Silver 1921
Nosals, Billy   Yellen 1923
Novello, Ivor   Kern 1916
Novy, Mischa   De Lange 1948; Washington 1952
Nugent, Maude   Jerome 1903, 1927; Schwartz, Jean 1927
Nusbar, Ernest   Kahn 1920
Nussbaum, Joseph   Bryan 1928; Hoffman 1929

O

Oakes, Clarence P.   Brown, Lew 1943
O'Brien, Bobby   Lewis 1926; Young, Joe 1926
O'Brien, Jack   Kahn 1932
O'Brien, John J.   Dubin 1916
O'Connell, Phillip   Mills 1924
O'Day, Alan   David, Mack 1973, 1975
O'Dea, James   Herbert 1912; Kern 1907
Odette, Marcelene   Russell 1941
O'Dice, S.I.   Dubin 1921
O'Farrell, Frank   Parish 1925
Offenbach, Jacques   Brooks 1960; Duke Date Unknown;
    Harburg 1961; Johnson, Howard 1934; Raye 1958
Offi   Sigman 1955; Spina 1955
O'Flynn, Charles   Coots 1931; Fisher 1926; Gordon 1930;
    Hoffman 1929, 1930; Johnson, Howard 1929; Leslie
    1925; Meyer 1932, 1933, 1934; Parish 1934; Robison
    1947; Waller 1924
Ogden, Beatrice   Silver 1950
Ogerman, Klaus   Drake 1963, 1964; Sigman 1958, 1965,
    1966
O'Gorman, W.J.   Bryan 1908
O'Hagen, Jack   Gilbert 1938
O'Hara, Emmet   Mills 1924
O'Hara, Fiske   Brennan 1916
O'Hara, Geoffrey   Gordon 1940; Smith, Harry B. 1934, 1935
Ohman, Phil   Mercer 1936; Turk 1924; Washington 1943,
    1944, 1946

O'Keefe, Lester   Coots 1953, 1961; Johnson, Howard 1929;
    Revel 1930
Olbru, Albert   Leslie 1941
Olias, Lotar   Bacharach 1965; Coslow 1954; David, Hal 1965;
    David, Mack 1955; Parish 1957; Sigman 1954, 1960;
    Webster 1957
Oliveira, Luis   Russell 1955
Oliver, Sy   Cahn 1943; Parish 1955; Raye 1939; Robison
    1963
Oliveri, Dino   Livingston, Jerry 1957
Oliviera, A.   Drake 1943
Oliviera, L.   Russell 1956, 1957
Oliviero, Nino   Parish 1954; Rome 1952, 1954
Olman, Abe   Ager 1922; Brennan 1915; Caesar 1961; Coots
    1924; Egan 1917; Friend 1922; Hanley 1915; Kahn 1923;
    Meyer 1919; Mitchell 1923; Motzan 1920; Turk 1924;
    Warren 1926; Yellen 1919, 1920, 1921, 1922, 1923
Olsen, George   Friend 1945
Olsen, Harry B.   Dubin 1920
Olsen, Ole   Dixon 1923; Evans 1940; Livingston, Jay 1940
Olshey, Alex   Raye 1940
Olson, Elmer   Howard, Joseph E. 1920
O'Malley, Victor   Bryan 1910; Meyer 1910
O'Neil, Danny   Baer 1925
Openshaw, John   Bryan 1928; Caesar 1925, 1926, 1953
Opilant, S.   Silver 1922
Opler, Alfred   Mercer 1931, 1932
Oppenheim, Dave   Baer 1931, 1932, 1956; Fisher 1932, 1934;
    Friend 1931, 1932; Meyer 1933; Mills 1940; Monaco
    1913; Robison 1930, 1934; Silver 1930, 1931; Stept 1919,
    1932; Young, Joe 1932
Oppenheimer, George   Fields 1935; McHugh 1935
Orban, Jeff   Kahn 1939
O'Reilly, Wilton   Robison 1946
Orenstein, Larry   Harburg 1971
Original Dixieland Jass Band   Sigman 1955
Original Indiana 5   Fisher 1926
Orlob, Harold   Caesar 1927; Friml 1933; Goetz 1918;
    Harbach 1907, 1936, 1950; Howard, Joseph E. 1909,
    1937; Smith, Robert B. 1915
Orosco, Efrain   Drake 1945
Orser, Murray   Webster 1949
Ortman, Will   Brennan 1927; Egan 1924, 1925, 1927; Kahn
    1925, 1927; Whiting 1924, 1925
Ortolani, Riz   David, Mack 1962; Sigman 1967; Webster
    1964, 1966
Osborn, A.H.   Brown, Lew 1943
Osborne, Nat   Brown, Lew 1911; Clarke 1914; Friend 1921;
    Goetz 1911; Johnson, Howard 1920; Leslie 1914
Osborne, Will   Bryan 1930; Hoffman 1930; Razaf 1930
Osmond, Alan   David, Mack 1972
Osterman, Jack   Buck 1925; Coslow 1929; Parish 1921;
    Young, Victor 1929
Otelio   Warren 1964
Oteo, A.E.   David, Mack 1934
Otis, Arthur   Kahn 1925
Ott, Vi   Merrill 1947, 1948
Otto, J. Frank   Fisher 1937
Otvos, A. Dorian   Dubin 1922; Johnson, Howard 1924
Ouida, Don   Fisher 1938
Owen, Larry   Young, Joe 1931
Owens, Harry   Gordon 1942; Kahn 1939
Owens, Hugh   Norworth 1911
Owens, Jack N.   Lawrence 1937
Owens, Paul   Young, Joe 1974

P

Paaluhi, John   Sterling 1926

Pack, Lorenzo   Merrill 1946

Padilla, Jose   Goetz 1922, 1923; Johnson, Howard 1934, 1936; Robin 1927

Padwe, Frank   Mills 1928

Paff, Doris   Robison 1957

Pafumy, Joe   Parish 1932

Page, Martin   David, Hal 1990

Page, Patricia   Washington 1939

Page, Patti   Merrill 1951

Page, Paul   Merrill 1945

Paich, Marty   Webster 1966

Paige, Roger   David, Hal 1956

Paley, Herman   Brown, Lew 1912, 1913; Bryan 1906, 1907, 1909, 1910, 1912, 1914, 1915, 1916, 1917, 1918, 1921, 1927, 1928, 1934; Goetz 1910; Mitchell 1917; Silver 1927; Yellen 1921

Paley, Lou   Bryan 1914; Gershwin, George 1917, 1918, 1919, 1920, 1921, 1926; Gershwin, Ira 1917, 1918, 1921

Pallavicini, V.   Sigman 1964, 1966

Palm, Emil   Brown, Lew 1939

Palmer, Bee   Akst 1926; Mitchell 1926

Palmer, Bisbell   Young, Victor 1946

Palmer, Jack   Koehler 1929; Leslie 1925; McHugh 1927; Mills 1928, 1929, 1936, 1955; Razaf 1924, 1926, 1927, 1928, 1929, 1931, 1937; Robison 1940, 1941, 1944, 1945, 1946, 1947, 1949, 1950, 1954, 1956; Silver 1928, 1941; Woods 1925

Palmer, King   Sigman 1956

Palomar, Luis   Yellen 1964

Panella, Manuel   Adamson 1959

Panico, Louis   Kahal 1938; Kahn 1923, 1924

Panzeri   Sigman 1958

Panzutti, V.   Raye 1957; Rome 1952

Paona, Nicola   Sigman 1952

Parenteau, Zoel   Atteridge 1918; Caesar 1921; Romberg 1918; Young, Victor 1951

Pares, Ph.   Lerner, Sammy 1931

Parfumy, Jose   Drake 1943

Paris Sisters, The   McHugh 1957

Parker, Dan   Fisher 1943

Parker, Dorothy   Herbert 1924; Rainger 1935

Parker, John L.   Cahn 1980

Parker, Katherine   Willson 1962

Parker, Kaye   Koehler 1932

Parker, Robert   Carmichael 1949

Parker Jr., Ray   Bacharach 1987

Parkes, Karl   Lawrence 1955

Parks, Bernie   Mancini 1954

Parks, W. Dean   David, Hal 1973

Parks, William   Kahn 1928

Parlak, Albert   Magidson 1926, 1927, 1928

Parraga, G.   Mills 1940

Parris, Herman   Parish 1947

Parsons, Donovan   Coots 1925; Schwartz, Arthur 1929

Parsons, Homer   Willson 1942, 1943

Parsons, William A.   Baer 1964

Pasano   Mercer 1961

Pascal, Milton   Styne 1955, 1957

Pascoe, Richard W.   Whiting 1915, 1926

Paskman, Dailey   Caesar 1923; Fain 1963; Friml 1923, 1924, 1945, 1948, 1952, 1956, 1959, 1960, 1963; Loesser 1945; Motzan 1922, 1924, 1925; Parish 1925; Young, Victor 1964

Passmore, Walter   Coslow 1934

Pasternacki, Stephen   Coslow 1932, 1933; Egan 1924, 1926; Rainger 1932; Robin 1936; Whiting 1924, 1926

Pasternak, Joe   Adamson 1964; Lawrence 1955

Patrick   Egan 1917

Patrick, Fred   Hoffman 1950; Sissle 1939

Patrick, John   Akst 1938; Warren 1960

Patterson, Agnes   Hoffman 1959, 1962

Patterson, Henri   Washington 1958

Paul, Charles   Coots 1951, 1953

Paul, Marcel   Rome 1947

Paul, Victor   David, Mack 1958

Paulton, Edward A.   Edwards 1908; Romberg 1917

Payne, B.   Mills 1935

Peacock, Trevor   Freed, Ralph 1965

Pearl, Jack   Monaco 1932

Pearl, Lee   Livingston, Jerry 1943

Pearson, Johnny   Sigman 1972

Pease, Harry   Baer 1927, 1933; Coots 1921; Donaldson 1923; Dubin 1927; Johnson, Howard 1917, 1918, 1921, 1922, 1923, 1926, 1933, 1934, 1945; Mills 1924, 1927, 1934, 1942; Monaco 1931; Parish 1920, 1921; Schwartz, Jean 1930

Pease, Sharon   Lawrence 1943

Peccuci, E.   Sterling 1924

Peck, Murray   Webster 1963

Peck, Raymond   Howard, Joseph E. 1903

Peckham, Ted   Evans 1938; Livingston, Jay 1938

Pecon, J.   Parish 1949

Pelham, Alfred M.   Blake 1962

Pelosi, Don   Johnston 1938

Penn, Arthur A.   Edwards 1918

Penn, Delbert O.   Johnson, Howard 1939

Penner, Joe   Conrad 1934; Oakland 1934

Peple, Edward   Herbert 1909

Pepper, Buddy   Whiting 1949

Pepper, Jack   Robison 1949, 1950, 1951, 1953

Peretti, Hugo   David, Mack 1958; Hoffman 1957

Perkins, Edward B.   Gershwin, George 1918

Perkins, Edward D.   Johnson, James P. 1961

Perkins, Frank   Koehler 1948; Lewis 1934; Mercer 1965; Mills 1929, 1931; Parish 1930, 1932, 1933, 1934, 1935, 1936, 1937, 1980

Perkins, Lindsay S.   Motzan 1917

Perkins, Ray   Akst 1930; Atteridge 1917, 1918; Blake 1923; Brennan 1929; Bryan 1921; Clarke 1930; Gilbert 1955; Lewis 1919; Magidson 1930; Parish 1931; Romberg 1920; Sissle 1923; Turk 1919; Washington 1930; Young, Joe 1919

Perkins, Sallie Porter   Razaf 1950

Perlet, Herman   Smith, Harry B. 1901

Perlman, Morris   Bryan 1936, 1961; Dubin 1943

Perrin, Pierre   Sigman 1963

Perrone, A.   Sigman 1957

Perry   Blake 1958; Sissle 1958

Perry, Alfred Kealoha   David, Hal 1963

Perry, Maurice   Brown, Lew 1944

Perry, Sam A.   Coots 1920; Johnson, Howard 1923; Magidson 1930; Parish 1929

Perry, Ward   Kahn 1928

Perschk, Max   Harbach 1914

Pestalozza, A.   Johnson, Howard 1933; Lawrence 1939

Peter, Billy   Schwartz, Jean 1949

Peterat, Louis   Rome 1951

Peters, Billy   Blake 1967

Peters, Lester Grant S.   Revel 1947

Peters, William F.   Atteridge 1915; Schwartz, Jean 1918

Petersburski, J.   Caesar 1931

Peterson, Furniss T.   Carmichael 1944, 1950; Webster 1944, 1950

Petkere, Bernice   Ager 1936; Akst 1942; David, Mack 1935; Davis 1933; Lewis 1932; Washington 1933; Young, Joe 1931, 1932, 1933, 1934

Petremont, Patricia   Ellington 1968

Pettersson, Evante   Sigman 1960

Pettis, Jack   Mills 1928, 1929, 1930; Waller 1927, 1928

Pettis, John B.   Bryan 1928

Peyton, Thomas Roy   Razaf 1952

Pfeil, J.   Parish 1945

Philippe-Gerard, M.   Mercer 1951

Phillips, Don   McHugh 1947

Phillips, E.   Sterling 1917

Phillips, Fred   Brown, A. Seymour 1929; Bryan 1926, 1928; David, Mack 1933; Fisher 1931; Hoffman 1933; Johnson, Howard 1923, 1924; Lewis 1926, 1928, 1951; Young, Joe 1926, 1928, 1932, 1951

Phillips, Howard   De Lange 1934, 1943; Myrow 1934

Phillips, John   Bacharach 1981

Phillips, Katherine   Friend 1945

Phillips, Phil   Egan 1928

Piaf, Edith   Cahn 1956; David, Mack 1948, 1951; Rome 1949; Sigman 1953

Piani, Harry   Lewis 1923; Stept 1920; Young, Joe 1923

Piantadosi, Al   Akst 1926, 1927; Berlin 1909; Brennan 1915; Brown, Lew 1914, 1921; Bryan 1909, 1910, 1914; Carroll 1940; DeSylva 1926; Gilbert 1925; Hanley 1922; Johnson, Howard 1915, 1921; Leslie 1908, 1909, 1910, 1912, 1913; Lewis 1925, 1926, 1927; Mitchell 1922; Monaco 1928; Norworth 1921, 1922; Schwartz, Jean 1948; Stept 1919, 1925; Warren 1927; Young, Joe 1925, 1926, 1927

Piantadosi, George   Turk 1928

Pickard, John Henry   Loesser Date Unknown

Pierce, Charlie   Dubin 1916, 1920; Hanley 1916; Yellen 1917

Pinchi   Lawrence 1953; Sigman 1955; Spina 1955

Pincus, Herman   Pollack 1956; Spina 1932

Pine, John P.   Herbert 1916

Pine, Lester   Brooks 1946

Pineiro, Ignacio   Gilbert 1931

Pinero, Sir Arthur Wing   Kern 1912

Pinkard, Edna Belle Alexander   Razaf 1929

Pinkard, Maceo   Brown, Lew 1925; Clare 1925, 1927, 1928; Coslow 1926; Davis 1928; Johnson, Howard 1926; Mitchell 1922, 1926; Parish 1930; Razaf 1924, 1926; Rose 1923, 1927, 1929; Silver 1927, 1928, 1929; Stept 1929; Turk 1925, 1926; Yellen 1924

Pinnella, E.G.   Hanley 1933

Pinterally, Al   Drake 1951

Piot, Paul   David, Hal 1961

Piotti, Lewis C.   Bryan 1928

Piotti, Prince   Gilbert 1926

Pippin, Donald   Cahn 1980; Leigh 1979

Pisano, John   Webster 1967

Pitkin, Maxwell I.   Herbert 1920

Pitman, George   Parish 1931

Pits, Tom   Egan 1920

Planquette, Robert   Smith, Harry B. 1911

Plante, Jacques   Merrill 1952

Plaza, Guillermo   Parish 1933

Pleis, J.   Webster 1968

Plumb, Edward H.   Drake 1944

Pockriss, Lee   David, Hal 1954, 1958, 1959, 1960, 1961; David, Mack 1966; Leigh 1964, 1973, 1974, 1976, 1977, Date Unknown

Poff, Lou   Robison 1955

Pokrass, Dan   Rome 1943

Pokrass, Dimitri   Rome 1943

Pokrass, Samuel   Baer 1934; Bullock 1939; Clare 1938; Fisher 1936; Harburg 1933, 1934, 1935; Koehler 1938; Lawrence 1937; Lewis 1934; Loesser 1934; Parish 1935, 1937; Yellen 1938

Pola, E.   Russell 1961

Pola, Eddie   Warren 1953

Pola, Edward   David, Hal 1954, 1955; Dixon 1933; Johnston 1938, 1940; Koehler 1931; Lane 1931; Livingston, Jerry 1954; Spina 1954

Pola, Ted   Dietz 1930; Lane 1930

Polla, W.C.   Bryan 1935; Dubin 1927; Friend 1925

Pollack, Frank   Egan 1915

Pollack, Jean   Schwartz, Jean 1921

Pollack, Phil   Fain 1920

Pollard, Otis   Merrill 1950

Pollia, Joseph A.   Hanley 1933

Pollock, Bert   Blane 1954

Pollock, Muriel   Atteridge 1929; Caesar 1930; Coslow 1921; Dietz 1929; Heyman 1933, 1935; Schwartz, Arthur 1928, 1929

Pollyoz   Dixon 1923

Pomerance, Maurice   Fisher 1921

Pon, Maurice   Merrill 1952

Ponce, Ethel   Dixon 1934

Ponce, Jack   Yellen 1928

Ponce, Phil   Leslie 1926; McHugh 1921; Mitchell 1917; Waller 1936

Poncher, D.   Russell 1966

Poore, Diana   Lawrence 1943

Pope, Helen   Parish 1934

Porter, Arthur   Blake 1935, 1937, 1957

Porter, Lew   Gilbert 1939; Parish 1930; Silver 1918; Sterling 1917

Pothier, Charles   Coslow 1926

Potine, Larry   Gilbert 1957

Potter, Harold   Fisher 1932; Howard, Joseph E. 1948; Parish 1980

Potter, Paul M.   Atteridge 1913

Pourman, E.J.   Sterling 1918

Powell, Edgar   McHugh 1926

Powell, Felix   Goetz 1917

Powell, Mel   Russell 1947

Powell, Teddy   Coots 1940, 1944, 1945; De Lange 1940; Friend 1948, 1949; Hoffman 1950, 1953; Johnson, Howard 1934, 1935, 1938; Merrill 1954; Pollack 1934; Stept 1944; Webster 1934

Powell, W.C.   Williams 1904

Powers, James T.   Atteridge 1912

Powers, William   Johnson, Howard 1930

Prado, Miguel   Russell 1941

Prager, Stanley   Bergman 1963

Prairie Sweethearts, The   Stept 1941

Praskins, Leonard   Gershwin, George 1913

Pratz, Rodrigo   Drake 1949

Press, Jacques   Carroll 1943; Loesser 1942; Rome 1953

Preston, Walter   Coots 1952

Prevert, Jacques   Mercer 1950

Previn, Andre   Brooks 1957; Comden and Green 1955;
    Harburg 1969; Lerner, Alan Jay 1969; Mercer 1974;
    Russell 1957, 1958; Webster 1958
Previn, Charles   Adamson 1939; Freed, Ralph 1940, 1946;
    Kahn 1940; Lerner, Sammy 1940, 1941, 1943
Pribor, Richard   Blane 1956; Martin 1956
Price, George E.   Davis 1922; Gorney 1923; Magidson 1928;
    McHugh 1922; Silver 1922, 1926, 1927, 1928; Stept 1920
Prima, Louis   Mills 1934, 1935; Parish 1938; Revel 1946
Prince, David   Sterling 1928
Prince, Hughie   DePaul 1944; Merrill 1951; Raye 1936, 1939,
    1940, 1941, 1944, 1945
Prince, Merle   Razaf 1952
Prival, Max   Bryan 1926; Coslow 1925; Lerner, Sammy 1929;
    Parish 1923; Pollack 1929; Rose 1925; Silver 1921, 1926;
    Sterling 1928
Profes, Anton   Gilbert 1927; Lerner, Sammy 1931
Proser, Sid   Carmichael 1946
Provo, Frank   Loesser Date Unknown
Prozorovsky, B.A.   Kahn 1939
Pryme, Charles Titus   Razaf 1950, 1955, 1957
Puccini, Giacomo   Dietz 1952; Lerner, Sammy 1943
Puck, Harry   Kalmar 1913, 1914; Leslie 1914
Pugsley, Estelle   Johnson, J. Rosamond 1914
Putman, Curly   David, Hal 1976
Putnam, Belinda   Ellington 1958
Putnam, Bill   Ellington 1958
Pyle, Harry   Caesar 1944

Q

Quadling, Lew   David, Mack 1942, 1944; De Lange 1951;
    Mercer 1952, 1953; Spina 1947
Quanz, Willibald   Yellen 1958
Quicksell, Howard   Razaf 1929
Quinn, Jimmy   Davis 1925
Quints, Marty   Lerner, Sammy 1929

R

Rabideau, I.   Russell 1947
Radford, Dave   Coots 1924; Egan 1922; Whiting 1914, 1915,
    1916, 1917, 1920, 1922
Radoff, Bob   Sigman 1952
Radtke, Hiller   Sigman 1950
Raif, Paul   Robison 1949
Raksin, David   Brooks 1964; Cahn 1957; David, Mack 1964,
    1965; Evans 1968; Gordon 1948; Livingston, Jay 1968;
    Mercer 1944, 1947, 1954; Webster 1950, 1964
Ram, Buck   Brown, Lew 1944; De Lange 1938, 1943; Mills
    1939, 1940; Russell 1942
Ramez, Peter   Drake 1953
Ramin, Sid   Bergman 1969; Brooks 1956, 1960, 1963
Ramsbottom, Harold   Gilbert 1925
Rand, Ellery   Young, Joe 1934
Rand, Lloyd   Edwards 1910
Randall, Carl   Loesser 1936
Randolph, Bob   Howard, Joseph E. 1937, 1938, 1939, 1942
Ranken, Frederick   Herbert 1899; Smith, Harry B. 1903
Ranmal, Alfred H.   Friml 1923
Rapee, Erno   Ahlert 1930; Heyman 1933; Mitchell 1927;
    Pollack 1926, 1927, 1928, 1929; Turk 1930
Raphael, Julian J.   Johnson, J. Rosamond 1933
Raposo, Joe   David, Hal 1982, 1985
Rapp, Barney   David, Mack 1930

Rascel, Renato   Bullock 1954; Sigman 1955
Rasch, Ray   Lawrence 1954; Russell 1954; Webster 1954
Raskin, Milton   Mercer 1955, 1959
Raskin, William   Bryan 1925, 1926, 1928, 1942; Caesar 1940;
    Clare 1924, 1926, 1927; Clarke 1926; Coslow 1924, 1925,
    1926; Dubin 1926, 1927, 1928; Eliscu 1929, 1930; Fain
    1924, 1925, 1929, 1930; Fisher 1920, 1921, 1923, 1927,
    1937, 1940; Freed, Ralph 1932; Friend 1926; Hoffman
    1929; Johnson, Howard 1935; Kahal 1929, 1930, 1931;
    McHugh 1925; Mills 1925; Monaco 1924, 1926; Pollack
    1927; Rose 1924, 1927; Silver 1925; Snyder 1927; Stept
    1937; Woods 1924
Rath, Fred   Dubin 1919, 1920, 1922, 1923
Ravasini, Nino   Merrill 1955; Sigman 1955; Spina 1955
Rawson, Ralph   Razaf 1920
Ray, Don   Oakland 1951
Ray, Floyd   Raye 1940
Ray, Joey   Wrubel 1948
Rayburn, Joseph Randolph   Razaf 1950
Rayburn, Randy   Drake 1947
Raymond, Fredy   Kalmar 1927; Lerner, Sammy 1931; Ruby
    1927
Raymond, George   Razaf 1932, 1944; Sissle 1932
Raymond, Harold   Razaf 1934
Raymond, Harry   Kahn 1917
Rayner, Bill   Leigh 1957
Read, P.   Robin 1932
Readon, Frank   Cahn 1955
Reaves, Erell   Freed, Ralph 1931
Reben, Louis A.   Razaf 1935
Reber, Harry   Ahlert 1936; Young, Joe 1936
Rebner, Arthur   Coslow 1934
Rector, Eddie   Waller 1926, 1937
Reddie, Milton   Blake 1935, 1936, 1937, 1938, 1944, 1947,
    1950, 1953, 1954, 1957, 1962, 1963, 1964; Sissle 1962,
    1964
Redding, Joseph D.   Herbert 1911
Redman, Don   Drake 1943; Johnson, James P. 1934; Razaf
    1929, 1930, 1932, 1934, 1935, 1943, 1961; Waller 1932
Redmond, John   Ellington 1938; Mills 1938; Myrow 1938
Reed, Billy   Raye 1939
Reed, Bob   Martin 1948
Reed Jr., Dave   Brennan 1915; Olcott 1910
Reeker, Cecelia   Razaf 1934
Rees, Clara H.   Whiting 1912, 1914, 1915
Reese, Della   Ellington 1962
Reese, Floyd   Dubin 1921
Regney, Noel   Heyman 1965
Rehbein, Herbert   Sigman 1967
Reichner, Bickley   De Lange 1943; Hoffman 1954, 1961;
    Howard, Bart 1965; Myrow 1940, 1943
Reid, Mike   David, Mack 1984, 1989, 1990
Reif, Paul   Eliscu 1956; Merrill 1950
Reinhardt, Heinrich   Smith, Harry B. 1910; Smith, Robert B.
    1910
Reinicke, C.   Freed, Ralph 1939
Reisch, Walter   Egan 1932; Young, Joe 1930, 1931
Reisenfeld, Hugo   Gilbert 1928; Smith, Harry B. 1920
Reisfeld, Bert   Brown, Lew 1955; Cahn 1950; Egan 1939;
    Lewis 1940; Raye 1939
Reisner, C. Francis   Davis 1917
Reisner, Charles   Alter 1929, 1930; Johnson, Howard 1929
Reitz, William R.   Leslie 1926
Relf, Paul   Lawrence 1947
Remsen, Alice   David, Mack 1944

Renard, A. Lerner, Sammy 1944

Renard, Jean Sigman 1963

Renaud, Andre Koehler 1932

Rene, Henri Drake 1946; Russell 1957; Sigman 1958

Rene, Leon Mercer 1949; Razaf 1953

Rene, Otis Webster 1941, 1942

Rene Jr., Otis Razaf 1953

Renesford, Maurice Revel 1929

Renoir, Jean Lawrence 1955

Renyi, Aladar Harbach 1914

Reser, Harry Akst 1926; Davis 1926

Reslit, Albert Sterling 1902

Resner, Arthur Coslow 1933

Reubusch, Sylvester Howard, Joseph E. 1964

Reunier, Michel Cahn 1978

Reveberi David, Hal 1961

Revel, Renny Revel 1963

Reveu, Jean Sigman 1951

Revil, Rudi Merrill 1955

Reynolds, Brad Robison 1945, 1954

Reynolds, Herbert Atteridge 1915; Coots 1926; Friml 1914, 1915; Hanley 1922, 1926; Henderson 1923; Kern 1913, 1914, 1915, 1916, 1917, 1918, 1923; Romberg 1915

Reynolds, Jack Davis 1970; Friend 1940, 1949, 1961; Johnson, J. Rosamond 1932

Rezlit, Albert Smith, Harry B. 1901

Rhines, Howard Howard, Bart 1938

Ribalto, J. Carner Gorney 1930, 1935; Rainger 1930

Ribaud, Joe Coslow 1920

Ricca, Lou David, Hal 1945, 1946, 1947; David, Mack 1946

Rice, Andy Fisher 1909, 1913, 1915, 1930

Rice, Bob Conrad 1932

Rice, Carl Loesser 1929, 1930, 1931, Date Unknown

Rice, Elmer Weill 1947

Rice, Gitz Brennan 1925, 1926; Johnson, Howard 1925

Rich, Byral Whiting 1925

Rich, Fred Coslow 1926; Gilbert 1926

Rich, Freddie Livingston, Jerry 1939

Rich, Jack Heyman 1932

Rich, Max Gordon 1929, 1930; Hoffman 1930, 1931; Schwartz, Jean 1933; Washington 1931

Rich, Penelope Howard, Joseph E. 1946

Richards, Chuck Mills 1936

Richards, Dick Caesar 1956

Richards, Johnny Leigh 1953

Richards, S. Mills 1938

Richards, Stephen Mills 1938

Richards, Tom Robison 1957

Richardson, Herb Coots 1946

Richardson, Randell Caesar 1963; Robison 1960, 1961, 1963, 1964, 1965, 1966, 1967, 1968

Richin, A. Webster 1967

Richley, Tom Bullock 1937

Richman, Harry Akst 1926, 1936; Brown, Lew 1936; Bryan 1925, 1926, 1930; Conrad 1925; Davis 1926; Fain 1926; Friend 1920, 1922; Gordon 1931; Gorney 1924; Kahal 1926, 1931; Kahn 1927; Lewis 1931; Revel 1931; Schwartz, Jean 1930; Silver 1925, 1926, 1928

Richmond, Frank Bryan 1910

Richmond, Howie Leigh 1955

Richmond, Jack Johnson, Howard 1923

Rickard, Gwen Conrad 1929

Ricos, Lou David, Hal 1941, 1946

Ricotta, J. Webster 1967

Riddle, Nelson Cahn 1959; David, Mack 1961; Raye 1952, 1957; Russell 1957, 1958, 1960; Willson 1974

Ridemus, Edward Smith, Harry B. 1923

Ridley, Walter Cahn 1974

Riese, Paul Freed, Arthur 1924

Riesenfeld, Hugo Gorney 1931; Harburg 1931; Pollack 1927; Willson 1928; Yellen 1929

Riley, James Whitcomb Carmichael 1951

Riley, Lou Mills 1927

Riley, Mike Johnson, James P. 1936

Riley, Robert Blake 1949

Rimsky-Korsakov, Nicholas Brooks 1947; Cahn 1951; Dubin 1924; Mercer 1953

Rines, Joe Baer 1941, 1942, 1943, 1944; De Lange 1942; Gilbert 1942

Ringle, Dave Coots 1923; Coslow 1921; De Lange 1932; Ellington 1937; Fain 1924; Yellen 1927

Rinker, Al Kahn 1954; Mercer 1952

Rinker, Charles DePaul 1954, 1955; Spina 1959; Warren Date Unknown

Rinker, Chuck Oakland 1961

Rio, Rosa Baer 1953, 1954, 1965

Rios, Tomas Drake 1943

Riscoe, Arthur Gershwin, Ira 1922

Riskin, Harry Gordon 1934

Ritchie, Ben Bryan 1912

Riter, N.E. DeSylva 1925

Rittman, Trude Leigh 1954

Rivera, Lillian Russell 1949

Rivera, Ray Razaf 1957

Rizzo, Marco David, Hal 1961

Roame, Kenneth A. Howard, Joseph E. 1952

Roaring Ranger Fisher 1935

Roark, Elden Robison 1961

Robbins, Andrew McHugh 1965; Razaf 1924, 1965

Robbins, Ayn Fain 1977

Robbins, John Fisher 1931

Robert, Camille Bryan 1918

Roberti, Roberto Adamson 1941

Roberts, Allan Hoffman 1943, 1945, 1947; Livingston, Jerry 1943, 1945; Myrow 1950; Oakland 1950; Sigman 1953; Van Heusen 1956, 1959

Roberts, B. Sherman 1958, 1959, 1960

Roberts, Bob Freed, Ralph 1965, 1966

Roberts, Bruce Bacharach 1989

Roberts, Fred Lawrence 1940

Roberts, Lee S. Brennan 1939; Gilbert 1915, 1916

Roberts, Luckeyth DeSylva 1921; Johnson, Howard 1917; Lewis 1922, 1924; Razaf 1937, 1942, 1944; Young, Joe 1922, 1924

Roberts, Ralph Arthur Brooks 1957

Roberts, Ruth Ellington 1957, 1963

Roberts, S.T. Freed, Ralph 1957

Roberts, W.S. Russell 1957

Robertson, Bruce Bacharach 1981, 1982, 1987

Robertson, D. Koehler 1928

Robertson, Dick Hanley 1940, 1941; Hoffman 1944

Robertson, Don Spina 1965, 1966

Robertson, Guy Edwards 1932

Robey, Joe Bryan 1921

Robinson, A. Young, Joe 1930, 1931

Robinson, C. Warren 1925

Robinson, Earl Harburg 1932, 1944, 1945, 1946, 1966, 1969, 1971

Robinson, J. Russel   Ahlert 1924, 1926; Buck 1927; Conrad 1920, 1937; Coots 1931; Coslow 1928; Davis 1920, 1921, 1931; De Lange 1932, 1934; Dubin 1928, 1929; Egan 1929, 1937; Kahal 1929, 1931; Lerner, Sammy 1946, 1953; Lewis 1920, 1924; Magidson 1933; Mills 1932; Parish 1931; Razaf 1930, 1931, 1932, 1941, 1942, 1950; Robison 1925, 1927; Sissle 1932; Snyder 1925; Turk 1921, 1922, 1923, 1924, 1927, Date Unknown; Washington 1932; Wrubel 1933; Youmans 1928, 1930; Young, Joe 1920, 1924

Robinson, Sidney   Johnson, Howard 1943

Robison, Harris   Carmichael 1940

Robledo, Julian   Baer 1922

Robuschi   David, Hal 1961

Roddie, John   Monaco 1963

Roddie, Vin   Gordon 1946; Parish 1946

Rode, Walter S.   Coots 1927; Dubin 1927

Rodemich, Gene   Kahn 1924

Roden, Robert F.   Coslow 1922; Meyer 1911, 1912; Sterling 1909; Von Tilzer 1909

Roder, Milan   Smith, Harry B. 1920

Rodgers, Gladys   Conrad 1928

Rodgers, Mary   Cahn 1958; Sondheim 1963, 1966, Date Unknown

Rodman, Mary   McHugh 1957; Russell 1958, 1960

Rodney, Don   David, Hal 1946, 1947, 1948, 1949, 1950, 1951, 1952, 1953, 1958, 1960; David, Mack 1946

Rodriguez, G.H. Matos   Johnson, Howard 1936

Roemheld, Heinz   Bergman 1957; Lawrence 1951; Parish 1953; Sigman 1953

Roger, Jeannine   McHugh 1954

Rogers, Alex   Johnson, Howard 1917; Johnson, J. Rosamond 1909; Johnson, James P. 1922

Rogers, Buddy   Clare 1932

Rogers, David   Strouse 1975, 1980

Rogers, E.W.   Kern 1914

Rogers, Eddy   Caesar 1950

Rogers, Howard E.   Ager 1918; Akst 1919, 1920; Clarke 1916, 1918, 1919; Fisher 1919; Meyer 1918, 1921; Mitchell 1918; Monaco 1914, 1917, 1919; Motzan 1919; Schwartz, Jean 1914

Rogers, Lela   David, Mack 1951; Young, Victor 1951

Rogers, Milt   Freed, Ralph 1960

Rogers, Randy   Robison 1957

Rogers, Shorty   Russell 1969, 1977

Rohde, Lester Newell   Razaf 1950

Rohlf, Earl   Coots 1967

Roig, Gonzalo   David, Mack 1949

Rolandi, Gianpiero   Lawrence 1968

Rollini, Adrian   Brown, Lew 1945; Mills 1928

Roma, J.   Hoffman 1954

Roman, Martin   Leigh 1954

Romanelli, Luigi   Parish 1931, 1932

Romano, Nick   Leigh 1953

Romano, Phil   Burke 1954

Romano, Tony   Webster 1967

Romans, Alain   Parish 1954; Sigman 1956; Webster 1957

Romay, Lina   Howard, Joseph E. 1942

Romeo, Armando   Coslow 1956

Romero, Aldemaro   Cahn 1971, 1972

Romoff, Colin   Burke 1962

Ronell, Ann   Bullock 1950; Burke 1933; Lawrence 1945; Spina 1950; Weill 1938, 1948; Young, Victor 1941

Rooney, Don   Silver 1950

Rooney, John Jerome   Herbert 1915

Rooney, John L.   Coots 1942, 1944, 1949, 1950

Rooney, Mickey   Spina 1957, 1958

Rooney Sr., Pat   Howard, Joseph E. 1955

Rosas   Johnson, Howard 1935

Rosas, Juventino   Evans 1953; Livingston, Jay 1953; Webster 1950

Rose, Bert   Parish 1932

Rose, David   Bergman 1970; Cahn 1952, 1956; Evans 1965, 1977; Livingston, Jay 1965, 1977; Mills 1935; Robin 1941, 1943, 1945, 1946, 1947; Russell 1947; Sigman 1952; Webster 1966

Rose, Ed   Fisher 1906, 1907, 1911, 1936; Lewis 1915; Meyer 1907, 1910, 1915; Pollack 1914, 1919, 1920, 1921; Snyder 1904, 1905, 1906, 1907, 1908; Whiting 1921

Rose, Frank   Davis 1924

Rose, Fred   Fisher 1935, 1936; Koehler 1926; Mills 1923; Razaf 1938; Waller 1938

Rose, Gene   Akst 1936; Brown, Nacio Herb 1922; Clare 1936

Rose, Harry   Friend 1921

Rose, Irving   Lawrence 1941

Rose, Martin   Russell Date Unknown

Rose, Milton   Brooks 1957, 1968

Rose, Peter De   Harbach 1948; Parish 1940

Rose, Sam   Bryan 1924; Koehler 1926

Rose, Stanley R.   Mancini 1989

Rose, Vincent   Brown, Nacio Herb 1921; Bryan 1930, 1931, 1932, 1943; Clare 1932; Conrad 1932; David, Mack 1933, 1934; Davis 1922; DeSylva 1921, 1922, 1924; Egan 1926, 1927; Gilbert 1925; Johnson, Howard 1933, 1958; Kahn 1924; Lerner, Sammy 1935; Leslie 1944; Lewis 1927, 1929; Mills 1935; Rose 1925, 1929; Sigman 1939; Snyder 1908; Whiting 1926, 1927; Young, Joe 1927, 1929, 1932

Rosebrook, Leon   Razaf 1929

Rosell, E.   Heyman 1938

Rosen, Milton   Brooks 1945, 1946, 1959, 1960

Rosenblatt, Cantor Josef   Silver 1928

Rosenfeld, Monroe H.   Lewis 1910; Snyder 1909; Sterling 1900

Rosenman, Leonard   Webster 1957

Rosenstein, Michel   Lawrence 1953

Rosenstock, L.   Bryan 1938

Rosenthal, Harry   Bryan 1926; Caesar 1925, 1926, 1928, 1929; Conrad 1928

Rosenthal, Laurence   Bergman 1971

Rosenus, Alan   Oakland 1963; Webster 1963

Rosey, Joe   Davis 1921

Roslyn, Morton   Kahn 1920

Rosner, Paul   Howard, Bart 1955

Rosoff, Charles   Bryan 1928, 1931; Friend 1926, 1927; Heyman 1931; Kahn 1924, 1929, 1952; Lewis 1929, 1930; Robin 1926, 1927; Turk 1924; Young, Joe 1923, 1929, 1933

Ross, Adrian   Kern 1908, 1909, 1911, 1916; Smith, Harry B. 1923

Ross, Ben   Meyer 1950

Ross, David   Gorney 1966, 1969

Ross, Hal   Cahn 1973

Ross, Harry   Ager 1939; David, Hal 1947

Ross, Jack   Duke 1938

Ross, Jerry   Hoffman 1950

Ross, Lanny   Silver 1939

Ross, Manny   Fain 1927; Kahal 1927

Ross, Marv   Bacharach 1982

Ross, Murray   Baer 1953, 1954

Rossellini, Renzo   David, Mack 1951

Rossetti, Christina G.   Carmichael 1956

Rossi, C.A.   Adamson 1953; David, Hal 1959; Howard, Bart 1961; Raye 1958

Rossini, Gioacchino   Brooks 1945; Robin 1936

Rota, Nino   Lawrence 1955; Raye 1956

Rotella, Johnny   Cahn 1961; Clare 1961, 1982; Mercer 1962; Russell 1968

Roth, A.P.   Mills 1966

Roth, Alexandro   Parish 1964

Roth, Charles   Snyder 1908, 1910, 1939

Roth, Ed   Yellen 1927

Roth, Jack   Coslow 1923

Roth, Lillian   Magidson 1928

Roth, Murray   Donaldson 1917; Dubin 1917; Gershwin, George 1916, Date Unknown; Hanley 1920, 1921, 1922; Johnson, Howard 1917, 1919; Von Tilzer 1921

Rothberg, Bob   Coots 1936; Davis 1936; Hoffman 1933; Meyer 1934

Rothenberg, Walter   Sigman 1954

Rothschild, Dorothy   Caesar 1962

Rotter, Fritz   Gilbert 1931; Lewis 1929; Young, Joe 1929, 1930

Rottman, D.R.   Young, Victor 1930

Roubanis, N.   Russell 1941

Roulette, Rene   Raye 1955

Roulien, Raul   Clare 1935

Rourke, M.E.   Gershwin, George 1919; Kern 1906, 1907, 1908, 1909, 1910, 1911, 1912, 1913

Rouvray, Fernand   Baer 1927; Kahn 1927

Rouzaud, Rene   Lawrence 1955

Rowell, Glenn   Coots 1940, 1950, 1951, 1953, 1954; Dixon 1940

Rowland, Adele   Von Tilzer 1917

Rowles, Jimmie   Mercer 1967

Roy, Eduardo   Washington 1949

Royce, James Stanley   Brennan 1927

Royce, Milton   Myrow 1937

Rozsa, Miklos   Brooks 1946, 1954; David, Mack 1945, 1963; Heyman 1943, 1946; Webster 1951, 1961

Rubens, Maurie   Atteridge 1928, 1929; Brennan 1915, 1926, 1927, 1928, 1929, 1930; Coots 1925, 1926, 1928; Coslow 1924; Eliscu 1929; Smith, Harry B. 1926, 1932

Rubens, Paul   Goetz 1922, 1923, 1925

Rubicam, Shannon   Mancini 1987

Rubin, Ada   Razaf 1936, 1938

Rubinchek, M.   Russell 1955

Rubini, Jan   Lewis 1919; Young, Joe 1919

Rubinstein, Anton   Johnson, Howard 1935

Ruby, Cyrus   Johnston 1925

Ruby, Herman   Akst 1944; Bloom 1929; Buck 1912, 1913; Clare 1942; Coots 1926; Freed, Arthur 1930; Johnston 1925, 1929; Kalmar 1921, 1923, 1944; Monaco 1923, 1950; Pollack 1941, 1942, 1943, 1944, 1945, 1952; Rose 1923, 1924; Ruby 1916, 1917, 1921, 1923, 1957; Stept 1927, 1929; Woods 1925

Ruggieri, Edmond   Robison 1934

Rugolo, Pete   Cahn 1959; McHugh 1960; Russell 1957, 1958; Washington 1960

Ruick, Walter   De Lange 1947; Whiting 1935

Ruiz, Gabriel   Washington 1945

Rule, Bert   Brennan 1918, 1919, 1920, 1921; Dubin 1920, 1921; Gordon 1929

Rule, James S.   Brennan 1921; David, Hal 1946; Johnson, Howard 1933; Washington 1965

Rumsey, Murray   Parish 1929

Rumshinsky, Joseph   Gilbert 1931

Rush, Jimmy   Mills 1929

Rusik, Adeline   Gilbert 1944

Rusincky, Paul   Johnson, Howard 1936

Ruskin, Harry   Alter 1930; Robin 1935

Russell, Al   Russell 1947

Russell, Benee   Ager 1931; Baer 1927, 1928, 1931; Conrad 1934; Fain 1922, 1926, 1928, 1933, 1935; Friend 1923, 1924; Henderson 1925; Johnson, Howard 1923, 1927; Meyer 1923, 1931, 1933; Mills 1926; Monaco 1933; Oakland 1934, 1935, 1937; Parish 1935, 1937; Rose 1924; Warren 1923; Woods 1924; Wrubel 1934; Young, Joe 1931, 1932

Russell, Bobby   Bacharach 1974

Russell, Gilbert   Willson 1952

Russell, Henry   Cahn 1957; David, Mack 1940; De Lange 1948; Raye 1957

Russell, Margaret   Drake 1959

Russell, Robert L.   Bacharach 1977

Russo, Dan   Burke 1931; Dubin 1927; Kahn 1923, 1925; Young, Victor 1930

Ruth, Barbara   Coots 1951

Ruthven, Ormond R.   Kahn 1938

Ryan, Ben   Ahlert 1950; Akst 1924, 1948, 1950; Bryan 1938, 1939; Dixon 1923; Johnson, Howard 1921; Rose 1921, 1929; Snyder 1923; Von Tilzer 1918, 1919

Ryan, Jimmy   Robison 1963

Ryskind, Morrie   Dietz 1927; Gershwin, Ira 1924; Gorney 1927; Kalmar 1940; Rodgers 1921; Schwartz, Arthur 1929, 1934

S

Sabre, Mel R.   Strouse 1947

Sacco, Tony   Ahlert 1935; Coots 1935; Stept 1958

Sadero, Gini   Evans 1951; Livingston, Jay 1951

Sadoff, Robert   Drake 1952; Leigh 1952

Sager, Carole Bayer   Bacharach 1980, 1981, 1982, 1983, 1984, 1985, 1986, 1987, 1988, 1989

Saint-Saens, Camille   Johnson, Howard 1939

Salabert, Franz   Freed, Ralph 1941

Salami, A.   Johnson, Howard 1940; Parish 1929

Sallet, Louis   Rome 1948

Salpeter, Sophie   Von Tilzer 1953, 1956

Salta, Menotti   David, Mack 1951

Salter, Hans J.   Brooks 1945, 1946, 1947, 1956, 1959; Washington 1955

Saltzborg, Herman   Robison 1949

Salvador, Henri   Howard, Bart 1961; Merrill 1952; Russell 1961; Webster 1967

Sambor, Walter   Revel 1947

Sampson, Edgar   Mills 1935, 1938; Parish 1938, 1939; Razaf 1936, Date Unknown

Samuels, Arthur   Dietz 1923

Samuels, Eddy   Freed, Ralph 1965; Mercer 1956

Samuels, H.   Pollack 1928

Samuels, Hilton   Mercer 1965

Samuels, Joe   Caesar 1919, 1920; Gilbert 1919

Samuels, Joseph Wilson   Lewis 1919; Young, Joe 1919

Samuels, Milton   De Lange 1948

Samuels, Walter G.   DeSylva 1935; Freed, Ralph 1940

Sanchez, Manuel   David, Mack 1946

Sanchez de Fuentas, Eduardo   Gilbert 1931

Sandefur, W.H.   Bryan 1922

Sandelman, Harold   Brown, Lew 1927; DeSylva 1927

Sanders   Johnson, Howard 1936

Sanders, Alma   Bryan 1921, 1923, 1931, 1934, 1935, 1941, 1942, 1943, 1944, 1950; Fisher 1921; Johnson, Howard 1921; Yellen 1922

Sanders, Irving T.   Motzan 1917

Sanders, Joe   Ager 1941; Davis 1925, 1926, 1928; Gilbert 1937; Kahn 1924, 1928, 1929, 1930

Sanders, Joseph   Kahn 1926

Sanders, Paul   Fain 1958, 1964

Sanders, Troy   Clare 1935, 1936; Evans 1949; Livingston, Jay 1949; Loesser 1939, 1942

Sandoval, Miguel   Bryan 1937; Mitchell 1936

Sands, Ben   Cahn 1963; David, Mack 1960

Sanford, Dick   Bryan 1933, 1934; David, Mack 1941, 1944, 1961; Fisher 1939

Sanford, Herb   Carmichael 1940

Sanford, William   Burke 1959; Cahn 1960

Santa, Frank   McHugh 1929

Santaella, Salvatore   Lewis 1919; Young, Joe 1919

Santell, Al   Lane 1938

Santiago, Osvaldo   David, Mack 1946

Santly, Henry W.   Baer 1923; Brown, Lew 1925; Clare 1923; Conrad 1921, 1922; Davis 1921, 1923; DeSylva 1921; Friend 1923; Johnson, Howard 1933; Kahn 1922; Lewis 1926; Motzan 1921, 1922; Pollack 1928; Razaf 1932; Stept 1925; Young, Joe 1926

Santly, Joseph H.   Bryan 1937; Burke 1954; Caesar 1929; Clare 1923, 1924; Friend 1924, 1927; Johnson, Howard 1916, 1917, 1919, 1920, 1928; Kahn 1923, 1924, 1931; Meyer 1919; Mitchell 1918

Santly, Lester   Ager 1921; Baer 1921; Davis 1921; Gilbert 1924; Johnson, Howard 1924; Razaf 1934; Waller 1929

Santos, Moacir   Evans 1970; Livingston, Jay 1970

Sarazan, Paul W.   Friend 1919

Sarno, Alberto   Adamson 1974

Sarony, Leslie   Rome 1956

Sarrendill, N.   Dubin 1924

Satterfield, Tom   Coslow 1934

Savino, Domenico   Brennan 1938; Harbach 1940; Johnson, Howard 1932; Parish 1939, 1943

Savitt, Jan   Adamson 1939; Mills 1937; Raye 1939

Sawens, Bill   Leigh 1953, 1954, 1955

Sawtell, Paul   Fain 1959; Washington 1957; Webster 1959

Saxon, Al   Russell 1962, 1977

Saxon, David   David, Hal 1954; Russell 1944

Saxon, Grace   Freed, Ralph 1958, 1959, 1960, 1961, 1962, 1963, 1964, 1966, 1969

Sayers, Henry J.   Willson 1943

Scanlan, Walter   Coots 1932

Schaeffer, Mary   Bryan 1934, 1937, 1940, 1950; Coots 1942, 1943; De Lange 1942; Hoffman 1940; Livingston, Jerry 1936, 1937

Schafer, Bob   Bryan 1925, 1926; Burke 1931, 1932; Coslow 1920, 1921, 1926; Ellington 1962; Fisher 1925, 1926; Lawrence 1941; Mills 1927, 1928, 1962; Razaf 1928, 1932

Schafer, S.   Fain 1926

Scharf, Walter   Brooks 1948, 1949, 1950, 1955, 1958, 1959, 1960; David, Mack 1968; Parish 1941; Warren 1960; Washington 1945

Scharfenberger, W.   Livingston, Jerry 1958

Scharr, Henry   Dubin 1920

Schawn, Nelson   Burke 1931

Scheiner, Harry   Parish 1980

Schenck, Joe   Ager 1930; Akst 1923; Bryan 1917; Davis 1923; Pollack 1927; Sterling 1919, 1920; Yellen 1916, 1919, 1927, 1930

Scherman, Robert   Freed, Ralph 1949

Schertzinger, Victor   Brown, Lew 1935; Bullock 1936; Burke 1940; Kahn 1934, 1935; Lewis 1920; Loesser 1940, 1941; Mercer 1942, 1953; Mitchell 1936; Robin 1929; Young, Joe 1920

Schifrin, Lalo   Bergman 1980

Schilling, Gus   Monaco 1950

Schisgal, Murray   Bacharach 1967

Schlosburg, E.   Young, Joe 1941

Schluger, Bill   Bullock 1966; Cahn 1967; Coleman 1964, 1965

Schmid, Johann C.   Brown, A. Seymour 1913

Schmidseder, Ludwig   Raye 1958

Schmidt, Irwin   Yellen 1923

Schneider, Max   Monaco 1940

Schneider, P.   Mancini 1981

Schneider, Paul   Russell 1964

Schoebel, Elmer   Dubin 1924; Kahn 1923, 1928, 1931; Mills 1923, 1924, 1936

Schoen, Vic   DePaul 1941; Raye 1939, 1940, 1941, 1942; Wrubel 1954

Schoenberg, Chris   DeSylva 1917

Schofield, Al   Merrill 1950

Scholl, Jack   Alter 1935, 1944; Baer 1934; Blake 1930; Conrad 1934, 1935; Coots 1934, 1952, 1954; Magidson 1934; Mills 1928, 1929; Motzan 1932; Parish 1928; Romberg 1945; Schwartz, Jean 1930, 1933, 1938

Scholz, Paul   Parish 1931

Schonberg, Chris   Kahn 1933

Schonberger, John   Freed, Ralph 1934; Kahn 1924, 1925, 1927; Pollack 1934

Schrag, Belle   Johnson, Howard 1945

Schraubstader, Carl   Brown, Lew 1923, 1925

Schreiber, Hans   Sigman 1952

Schreier, Rodell W.   Sigman 1950

Schroeder, Aaron   David, Mack 1954, 1957; Hoffman 1949, 1950, 1951; Merrill 1950; Silver 1954, 1955, 1956, 1957, 1964

Schroeder, John   Silver 1954, 1955, 1956

Schubert, Franz   Bergman 1983; Johnson, Howard 1933, 1939; Robin 1936

Schuffman, D.   Russell 1957

Schuger, Bill   Raye 1965

Schultz, Norbert   David, Mack 1943

Schulz-Reichel, Fritz   Sigman 1954

Schuman, William H.   Loesser 1931

Schumann, Robert   Johnson, Howard 1939

Schumann, Walter   Brooks 1947, 1948, 1951; David, Mack 1956; Webster 1957

Schuster, Ira   Ager 1921; Baer 1922, 1925, 1926, 1927, 1929, 1938, 1939, 1940; Bryan 1925, 1926, 1935, 1936; Caesar 1929; Conrad 1923; Dixon 1926; Friend 1924, 1936; Gilbert 1925, 1926; Johnson, Howard 1916, 1918, 1921, 1922, 1925, 1938; Lewis 1932; Schwartz, Jean 1935, 1940; Stept 1932; Yellen 1917; Young, Joe 1932, 1934, 1935, 1938

Schuster, Joe   Baer 1929; Bryan 1930, 1931, 1943; Coots 1926; Dixon 1926; Hoffman 1931; Von Tilzer 1927; Young, Joe 1933

Schwab, Lawrence   Hammerstein 1928

Schwandt, W.   Kahn 1930

Schwartz, Abe   Hoffman 1959

Schwartz, J.   Rome 1943

Schwartz, Phil   Atteridge 1910, 1915, 1916, Date Unknown

Schwartz, Samuel S.   Mercer 1961

Schwartz, Seymour   Cahn 1951

Schwartz, Stephen   Strouse 1986

Schwarzwald, Milton   Brooks 1946, 1947, 1948, 1950; Gershwin, Ira 1922, 1924; Gorney 1924; Kahn 1917

Schwimmer, Walter   Willson 1966

Sciapiro, Michael   Parish 1929

Scibetta, Anthony   Mercer 1967; Yellen 1962

Scibilia, Anton F.   Gordon 1925

Sciorilli, Eros   David, Hal 1959

Scott, Bobby   Russell 1969; Sigman 1967

Scott, Cyril   Parish 1956

Scott, E.H.   Young, Victor 1930

Scott, John Newell   Freed, Arthur 1932

Scott, Johnnie   Cahn 1950, 1955, 1957, 1959; Carmichael 1955; Kalmar 1950; Ruby 1949, 1950

Scott, Leo   Brown, Lew 1924

Scott, Raymond   Brown, Lew 1938; David, Mack 1951, 1955, 1956; De Lange 1944; Lawrence 1939, 1940; Mitchell 1938; Parish 1934; Pollack 1938

Scott, Winifred   Mills 1954, 1955

Scotti, John A.   Coots 1954

Scotto, Vincent   Conrad 1926; Parish 1937; Smith, Harry B. 1906

Seagrave, Malcolm R.   Ruby 1958

Seaholm, Undine   Coots 1953

Seaman, Bernie   Bloom 1929; Mills 1928

Sears, Al   Drake 1951

Sears, Jerry   Razaf 1939

Sears, Zelda   Youmans 1924

Secunda, Sholom   Cahn 1938; Yellen 1964

Seebic, Eugene   Razaf 1939; Waller 1939

Seelen, Jerry   Coslow 1950; De Lange 1945; Fain 1953; Myrow 1945; Raye 1939; Rome 1951; Young, Victor 1952

Seeley, Blossom   Goetz 1911

Segal, Al   Caesar 1926; Kahal 1930

Segal, Jack   David, Mack 1945; Hoffman 1946; Leigh 1965; Livingston, Jerry 1946; Sigman 1969

Segovia   Yellen 1964

Selden, Edward Gaines   Bryan 1910; Fisher 1910

Selinsky, Vladimir   David, Mack 1957

Selsman, Victor   Ager 1939; Livingston, Jerry 1939; Van Heusen 1938

Seltzer, David   Davis 1961

Seltzer, Sol   Friend 1937

Selvin, Ben   Mills 1924

Semprini, Alberto   Sigman 1959

Sendrey, Al   Cahn 1950; Wrubel 1944

Senna, Clarence   Davis 1920

Seracini, S.   Sigman 1960, 1977

Seress, Rezso   Lewis 1936

Serino, Del   Cahn 1960

Serwer, Sam   Fain 1932; Kahal 1932

Sewley, Harry   McHugh 1917

Sexton, Al   Hanley 1938

Seyler, Clifford   Alter 1926

Seymour, Harry   Friend 1952, 1953, 1960, 1962

Seymour, Tot   Atteridge 1924; Baer 1938; Conrad 1932; Coots 1929, 1931, 1932, 1933, 1934, 1940, 1947, 1952, 1964; Heyman 1937; Hoffman 1930, 1931, 1932; Motzan 1921; Pollack 1933, 1934; Romberg 1924; Schwartz, Jean 1924, 1936; Smith, Harry B. 1921

Shaftel, Selig   Myrow 1933; Oakland 1950; Parish 1933

Shafter, Bert   Fain 1959; Webster 1959

Shaiman, Marc   Comden and Green 1991

Shakespeare, William   Blane 1960; Rome 1969

Shand, Terry   Carroll 1939; David, Mack 1938, 1939; Davis 1937; De Lange 1934, 1935; Dixon 1933; Lawrence 1936, 1938; Lewis 1940; Livingston, Jerry 1938; Merrill 1947, 1948, 1949, 1950, 1952; Razaf 1940, 1960; Robison 1950, 1953, 1954, 1963; Sigman 1957

Shane, Craig   Freed, Ralph 1958

Shanklin, Michael T.   Mercer 1972

Shanklin, W.   Sherman 1953

Shaper, Hal   Russell 1957; Warren 1963

Shapiro, Dan   Fain 1955; Livingston, Jerry 1955, 1957, 1958, 1960, 1962, 1963, 1967; Oakland 1960, 1961, 1962, 1963, 1964, 1967, 1969; Stept 1949, 1950

Shapiro, Edward   Kahn 1931

Shapiro, Elliott   Hanley 1921

Shapiro, Joe   Mills 1950

Shapiro, Ken   Livingston, Jerry 1967

Shapiro, Phil   Arlen 1925

Shapiro, Ted   Davis 1939, 1942, 1946; Kahn 1927, 1928, 1956; Lawrence 1940; Lerner, Sammy 1928, 1936; Yellen 1929, 1930, 1944, 1978

Sharpe, Eddie   Gilbert 1925

Sharpe, John Rufus   Mercer 1950

Sharples, Winston   David, Mack 1945, 1946

Shatford, Sarah   Edwards 1913

Shauer, Mel   Hart Date Unknown; Rainger 1935; Robin 1935

Shavers, Charlie   Raye 1939

Shaw, Artie   Mercer 1940; Oakland 1941; Raye 1939

Shaw, Charles   Merrill 1949

Shaw, Sidney   Howard, Bart 1956

Shaw, Syd   Bacharach 1959, 1960

Shawn, Nelson A.   Burke 1931; Coots 1943; Styne 1941

Shay, Dorothy   Merrill 1948

Shay, Jerome   Bryan 1909, 1910, 1911

Shay, Larry   Egan 1928, 1929; Jerome 1928; Johnson, Howard 1931; Parish 1933

Shayne, Al   Stept 1961

Shayne, Gloria   Heyman 1964, 1967

Sheeny, Eleanor   Raye 1940

Shefter, Bert   Coslow 1940; Webster 1959

Sheldon, Ernie   Spina 1967

Shelley, Gladys   Henderson 1945; Silver 1941, 1954, 1955

Shelton, Chuck   Webster 1975

Shelton, James   Van Heusen 1953

Shelton, Marla   Alter 1945, 1947; De Lange 1947; Freed, Arthur 1945

Shemer, Naomi   Hoffman 1959, 1963

Sheppard, Madelyn   Koehler 1939

Sherman, Al   Ager 1935; Baer 1933; Brown, Lew 1939; Bryan 1928; Caesar 1924; Clare 1925, 1926, 1928, 1931, 1942, 1943, 1945, 1948, Date Unknown; Conrad 1924, 1927, 1928, 1930, 1931; Coslow 1921, 1922, 1923, 1925, 1958, Date Unknown; Davis 1926; DeSylva 1925, 1926; Dubin 1928; Fisher 1923; Freed, Ralph 1940; Friend 1923; Gilbert 1927, 1928, 1944; Hanley 1925; Henderson 1927; Heyman 1936; Hoffman 1939, 1943, 1950; Johnson, Howard 1926, 1927, 1928, 1933; Leslie 1928, 1937; Livingston, Jerry 1943; Mills 1922, 1926, 1965, 1966; Mitchell 1923, 1926; Monaco 1926; Parish 1933, 1934, 1936, 1937, 1938; Pollack 1942, 1948; Rose 1925; Silver 1926, 1927, 1929, 1935, 1936, 1937, 1938, 1942, 1947, 1950; Webster 1933; Woods 1926, 1927; Wrubel 1932, 1933

Sherman, Allan   Coleman 1964; Livingston, Jay 1966

Sherman, Noel   Van Heusen 1964
Sherman, Robert   Evans 1950; Livingston, Jay 1950
Shermer, Naomi   Hoffman 1959
Sherr, Norm   Parish 1943
Sherrill, Albeth   McHugh 1958
Sherrill, Pony   Oakland 1950, 1952, 1954, 1956
Sherwin, Manning   Bullock 1940; Eliscu 1930; Freed, Ralph
   1937; Loesser 1937, 1938, Date Unknown
Sherwood, Bob   Sissle 1915
Sherwood, Ray   Coots 1950; Von Tilzer 1915
Sherwood, Robby   Parish 1943
Sherwood, Rod   Freed, Ralph 1958, 1959
Sherzer, George   Blake 1935
Shevelove, Burt   Sondheim 1960, Date Unknown
Shield, Leroy   Parish 1938
Shields, Eddie   Howard, Joseph E. 1948
Shields, Larry   Mercer 1950; Sigman 1955
Shields, Ren   Bryan 1909; Cobb 1904, 1906; Snyder 1906,
   1907
Shiers, Ralph   Goetz 1910
Shilkret, Jack   Caesar 1921; Davis 1921; Smith, Harry B.
   1925
Shilkret, Nathaniel   Baer 1928; Brennan 1928; Caesar 1921;
   Coslow 1940; Freed, Ralph 1944; Gershwin, George
   1937; Gilbert 1928, 1929, 1931, 1935, 1936, 1937;
   Hoffman 1928; Johnston 1943; Kalmar 1936; Lerner,
   Sammy 1930; Mercer 1944; Pollack 1928, 1929; Robison
   1929; Ruby 1936; Washington 1929; Wrubel 1937; Yellen
   1928
Shilkret, Neil W.   Russell 1964
Shipp, J.A.   Johnson, J. Rosamond 1909
Shire, David   Bergman 1976, 1978, 1980
Shirl, Jimmy   Drake 1946, 1947, 1948, 1949, 1950, 1951,
   1952, 1953, 1954, 1955, 1956, 1957, 1958, 1960
Shirley, Gene   Egan 1920, 1925; Whiting 1920, 1925
Shisler, Charles P.   Dubin 1909
Short, Albert E.   Kahn 1923, 1926
Shostakovich, Dmitri   Harburg 1943; Rome 1943
Shoup, Don   Carroll 1951
Shrigley, Guy   Kahn 1922
Shubert, John   Friml 1934
Shuken, Leo   Loesser 1939
Shuman, Frank   David, Hal 1949
Sidney, George   Adamson 1955
Sidney, Harold   Bryan 1928
Sidney, Louis   Willson 1938, 1941
Sieczynski, Rudolf   Caesar 1923, 1951
Siegel, Al   Coslow 1937; Donaldson 1924; Freed, Ralph
   1934, 1941; Kahal 1939; Mills 1924, 1939, 1940; Rainger
   1936; Robin 1936; Silver 1924; Turk 1924
Siegel, M.   Caesar 1926
Siegel, Moe   Bryan 1927; Silver 1927
Siegel, Monty   Brown, Lew 1928; Bryan 1928; DeSylva 1928;
   Fain 1928, 1932; Henderson 1928; Hoffman 1930;
   Johnson, Howard 1927; Magidson 1932
Siegel, Paul   Hoffman 1950; Parish 1951
Siegel, Ralph Maria   Coslow 1956; Robison 1956; Sigman
   1955
Siegfried, S.   David, Mack 1968
Sievier, Bruce   Woods 1932
Sigler, Maurice   Conrad 1938; Coots 1933, 1934, 1938, 1940,
   1944, 1955, 1956; Hoffman 1933, 1934, 1935, 1936, 1937,
   1940, 1950; Johnston 1938; Magidson 1933, 1934;
   Monaco 1933, 1934; Silver 1933
Sigler, Mose   Washington 1933; Wrubel 1933

Sigman, Terry   Sigman 1958
Signorelli, Frank   Davis 1935; Dixon 1932; Donaldson 1924;
   Gilbert 1928, 1929; Gordon 1933; Heyman 1929;
   Johnson, Howard 1934; Kahn 1932; Kalmar 1956;
   McHugh 1923; Mercer 1934; Mills 1929; Parish 1935,
   1939, 1941, 1944, 1964; Russell 1945; Sigman 1963;
   Young, Joe 1933
Silbert, Sharon   Freed, Ralph 1958, 1959, 1961, 1964, 1965
Siltmitzer, Morris   Dubin 1909
Silva, Mario   Romberg 1945
Silvano, Theodore   Webster 1949
Silver, Louis   Turk 1917
Silver, Maxwell   Bryan 1908, 1910; Fisher 1936; Sterling 1904
Silver, Morris   Edwards 1928
Silver, Morris S.   Howard, Joseph E. 1947
Silvers, Frank   Coslow 1925
Silvers, Louis   Brown, Lew 1920; Bullock 1939; Caesar 1920,
   1921; Clarke 1927, 1929; DeSylva 1919, 1920, 1921;
   Edwards 1913, 1914; Fisher 1929; Freed, Arthur 1917;
   Gershwin, Ira 1921, 1922; Rose 1929; Turk 1921; Yellen
   1921
Silvers, Phil   Adamson 1944; Cahn 1967; McHugh 1944; Van
   Heusen 1944
Silvers, Sid   Akst 1935; Kalmar 1936, 1937, 1938; Koehler
   1925; Ruby 1936, 1937, 1938; Spina 1957, 1959; Yellen
   1931
Silverstein, Dave   Conrad 1931
Silvey, Matt   Leslie 1912
Simeon, Omar   Johnson, James P. 1946
Simmons, Rousseau   Ellington 1962
Simms, Alice D.   Coots 1946, 1948, 1952; Razaf 1944
Simon, Bill   Blane 1957
Simon, Carly   Bacharach 1979
Simon, George T.   Ellington 1962; Hoffman 1950
Simon, Howard   Whiting 1925, 1926
Simon, Nat   Hoffman 1933; Lawrence 1941, 1956, 1961;
   Merrill 1950; Parish 1934; Razaf 1934; Sigman 1946
Simon, Neil   Bacharach 1974
Simon, Robert A.   Oakland 1933
Simons, Moises   Gilbert 1931
Simons, Rousseau   Mills 1924, 1962
Simons, Seymour   Brown, Lew 1921; Caesar 1930; Davis
   1922, 1923, 1932; Friend 1929; Gorney 1927; Kahn 1923,
   1924, 1927, 1929, 1930; Leslie 1930; Mitchell 1921, 1922;
   Silver 1921; Whiting 1926, 1927, 1928, 1930; Young, Joe
   1930
Simonson, Sellig   Harbach 1909
Sims, Alice D.   Coots 1950
Sinatra, Frank   Stept 1950
Sinatra, Ray   Adamson 1972, 1974; Brooks 1947, 1948, 1952;
   Wrubel 1932; Young, Victor 1932
Sindelar, Andy   Dubin 1925
Sindelar, James   Dubin 1925
Singer, Dolph   Coots 1926; Stept 1928; Von Tilzer 1925,
   1926, 1927, 1928, 1929, 1938
Singer, Lou   Drake 1960; Ellington 1938; Mills 1935, 1938
Singer, Murry   Hoffman 1950
Singin' Sam   Young, Joe 1932
Siras, John   Friend 1932; Young, Joe 1931, 1932
Siravo, George   Leslie 1959
Sirmay, Albert   Buck 1921, 1924; Caesar 1925, 1927, 1930,
   1943; Coots 1943; Lewis 1936; Schwartz, Arthur 1930
Sirowy, Josef   Lawrence 1953
Sisko, Cowboy Joe   Coots 1954
Sisler, George   Razaf 1953

Sizemore, Arthur   Kahn 1921, 1922

Skalski, Andre   Duke 1944

Skiles, Marlin   Brooks 1950; Wrubel 1952

Skinner, Frank   Brooks 1946, 1948, 1949, 1951; Freed, Ralph 1939, 1940; Lerner, Sammy 1940; Mancini 1953; McHugh 1937; Robison 1929; Webster 1957

Skinner, Ralph   Edwards 1906

Sklerov, Gloria   David, Mack 1975

Skylar, Sunny   Oakland 1951; Revel 1946; Ruby 1947; Silver 1942; Stept 1944, 1946, 1952, 1954, 1962

Slack, Freddie   Mercer 1944; Raye 1946, 1948; Sigman 1944

Slanter, M.   Rome 1943

Slavitt, Alexander   Schwartz, Arthur 1922

Sloane, A. Baldwin   Berlin 1912; Goetz 1910, 1911, 1912, 1913; Smith, Harry B. 1901, 1903, 1918

Sloane, Everett   Hoffman 1954

Sloane, Mae Anwerda   Smith, Harry B. 1901

Smalle, Edward   Dubin 1924; Lewis 1915; Parish 1923

Smalls, Danny   Razaf 1932

Smay, Stephanie   Oakland 1974

Smeck, Roy   Baer 1964

Smelser, Cornell   Bryan 1936

Smith, A. Evelyn   Coots 1961

Smith, Beasley   Freed, Ralph 1957, 1958, 1959

Smith, Chick   Razaf 1930

Smith, Chris   Bryan 1909, 1914, 1920; Gilbert 1915; Leslie 1909; Mills 1927; Waller 1927

Smith, Clay   Lewis 1912

Smith, Dick   Ahlert 1935; Coots 1935

Smith, Edgar   Mitchell 1921

Smith, Edgar A.   Alter 1929; Atteridge 1916; Cobb 1907; Edwards 1904, 1907, 1923; Hanley 1916; Herbert 1906; Johnson, J. Rosamond 1903; Kern 1904; Romberg 1916; Schwartz, Jean 1904

Smith, Fredrika Shumuay   Carmichael 1957

Smith, George Porter   Whiting 1913

Smith, George Totten   Edwards 1910; Sterling 1901; Von Tilzer 1900, 1901, 1902

Smith, Grace   Blake 1938

Smith, Harl   Washington 1932

Smith, Henry Clay   Lewis 1910, 1912

Smith, Hezekiah Leroy   Razaf 1955

Smith, Howard   Goetz 1920; Mercer 1954

Smith, Jack   Raye 1956; Turk 1926

Smith, Johnny   Mills 1937

Smith, Kate   Hoffman 1931; Washington 1931

Smith, Ken   Heyman 1929, 1930

Smith, L. Raymond   Young, Joe 1936

Smith, L.O.   Sterling 1902

Smith, Lee   Sterling 1902

Smith, Margo   David, Mack 1979, 1981

Smith, Murray   Caesar 1928; Friend 1928

Smith, Paul   Raye 1950; Washington 1953

Smith, Paul Gerard   Carroll 1924; Coslow 1930; Young, Victor 1951

Smith, Richard Lee   De Lange 1943

Smith, Russell   Mills 1928; Sissle 1913

Smith, Stuff   Parish 1938

Smith, Van   Drake 1948

Smith, Walter   Egan 1917

Smith, Willie "The Lion"   Ellington 1968; Johnson, James P. 1940, 1944; Parish 1936, 1944; Razaf 1942, Date Unknown

Smith Sisters   Carroll 1944

Smolen, Johnny   Young, Joe 1953

Smolev, Marvin   Arlen 1927; Bloom 1929; Mills 1928

Smolin, Harry   Turk 1933

Snell, Dave   Dubin 1921; Edwards 1929, 1931; Egan 1930, 1933; Kahn 1933, 1940

Snow, Russell   Parish 1931

Snowhill, George   Robison 1949

Snyder, Bill   Stept 1953

Snyder, Charles A.   Coots 1919

Snyder, Eddie   Davis 1958, 1959

Soby, Walter V.   Revel 1929

Soffici, Piero   Sigman 1961

Sokole, Lucy Bender   Edwards 1930; Sigman 1933, 1936

Soler, Raul   Freed, Ralph 1946, 1947

Solman, Alfred   Bryan 1907, 1912, 1913, 1917; Caesar 1920; Gorney 1927; Kahn 1926, 1927; Motzan 1934; Parish 1924, 1925; Sterling 1917, 1918

Solomon, Harold   Harbach 1961

Solomon, Joe   David, Mack 1940; Lawrence 1940

Solomons, Roy   Parish 1954

Somers, Perrin   Gilbert 1920

Sonenscher, Dave   Sissle 1928

Sorkin, Herbert   Heyman 1940

Sosnik, Harry   Friend 1936; Lawrence 1957; Parish 1943; Washington 1934, 1943

Sour, Robert   Dietz 1930; Drake 1943; Heyman 1929, 1930; Rome 1939

Sousa, John Philip   Freed, Ralph 1939, 1940; Parish 1959; Russell 1950; Smith, Harry B. 1906; Willson 1940

Sousa, Nobrega E.   Sigman 1959

Souto, Edmundo   Evans 1970; Livingston, Jay 1954

Souvaine, Henry   Conrad 1906, 1925, 1926; Dietz 1927; Gorney 1927; Harburg 1929, 1930; Mercer 1932

Spaeth, Sigmund   Caesar 1923; Friml 1923; Parish 1945, 1947

Spear, Eric   Drake 1952

Specht, Paul L.   Razaf 1954; Yellen 1926

Special, Mike   Bryan 1924

Spence, Lew   Bergman 1952, 1953, 1955, 1956, 1957, 1958, 1959, 1960, 1961, 1962, 1983; Cahn 1957; Lane Date Unknown; Raye 1952; Russell 1951, 1952, 1954

Spence, Ralph   Conrad 1925; Rose 1925

Spencer, Herbert   De Lange 1947, 1948; Ruby 1954; Russell 1951

Spencer, Otis   Coots 1921; Dubin 1924; Fisher 1923; Smith, Robert B. 1919

Spencer, Robert E.   Razaf 1937

Spielman, Fred   Cahn 1950; Carmichael 1947; David, Mack 1956; Hoffman 1950; Lawrence 1953; Loesser 1941; Webster 1951, 1953

Spier, Larry   Ahlert 1938; Akst 1940; Conrad 1924, 1927; Coots 1929; Coslow 1926, 1927, 1929, 1930, 1939; Davis 1940; DeSylva 1924, 1925; Fain 1927; Friend 1925; Robin 1931; Silver 1926; Young, Joe 1934, 1938

Spitalny, H. Leopold   Kahn 1924

Spitalny, Maurice   Coots 1938; Coslow 1927; Fisher 1938

Spitalny, Phil   Brown, Lew 1925; Davis 1926; Friend 1925; Kahn 1924, 1926; Leslie 1943

Spoliansky, Mischa   Dixon 1930; Kahn 1931; Rose 1930

Spondis, Bob   Kahal 1926

Sprigato, Sylvester   Parish 1931

Springer, Phil   Harburg 1956, 1973, 1979; Lawrence 1957, 1960; Leigh 1956, 1957, 1958

Springer, Thomas G.   Young, Victor 1923

Springfield, Tom   Webster 1968

Squires, Frank   Parish 1944

Squires, Harry D.   Davis 1925; Edwards 1927; Parish 1921, 1922, 1923, 1925, 1926, 1949; Sterling 1925

Stacy, Jess   Robison 1974

Stadiger, Norman   Snyder 1909

Stafford, Jo   Cahn 1958; Mercer 1946

Stahl, Felix   Livingston, Jerry 1958; Rome 1949; Sigman 1965

Staley, M.V.   Whiting 1915

Stallings, Laurence   Schwartz, Arthur 1937

Stambaugh, Ken   Coots 1945, 1949, 1953, 1963; Mills 1927

Stamper, Dave   Buck 1912, 1913, 1914, 1915, 1916, 1917, 1918, 1919, 1920, 1921, 1922, 1923, 1924, 1925, 1927, 1931, 1938, 1943, Date Unknown; Caesar 1926; DeSylva 1921; Kern 1911; Norworth 1911; Rose 1927; Smith, Harry B. 1911

Stanford, Dok   Carmichael 1946, 1950, 1951; Livingston, Jerry 1954, 1956, 1957, 1959; Van Heusen 1955; Wrubel 1952

Stanford, Trevor   Parish 1959

Stange, Stanislaus   Jerome 1904; Schwartz, Jean 1904; Von Tilzer 1909

Stanley, Hal   Russell 1951, 1953

Stanley, Jack   Dubin 1923, 1938; Hanley 1922, 1923; Motzan 1921

Stanley, Ralph   Norworth 1938; Rome 1956

Stanny, A.J.   Motzan 1919

Stansbaugh, Ken   Coots 1929

Stanton, Charles   Razaf 1930

Stark, Karl   Bryan 1932; Hanley 1927, 1933, 1934, 1938; Lawrence 1938

Starr, Tony   David, Hal 1949

Staunton, Frank   Edwards 1912

Stearns, Helen   Carmichael 1957

Stedman, Al   Sterling 1924, 1941

Steel, John   Fisher 1919

Steele, Fred   Johnson, Howard 1932

Stein, Herman   Mancini 1955

Stein, Jules K.   Kahn 1927, 1930

Stein, Ronald   Bergman 1986

Stein, William   Loesser 1945

Steinberg, Bob   Parish 1938

Steiner, Herbert   Baer 1923, 1963; Bryan 1930; Coots 1928

Steiner, Howard   Davis 1957; Dubin 1943

Steiner, Max   Cahn 1953; Clare 1955; David, Mack 1939; Drake 1965; Egan 1934; Eliscu 1932, 1933; Evans 1964; Fields 1935; Kahn 1941, 1948; Koehler 1947; Livingston, Jay 1964; Sigman 1952, 1956, 1957; Smith, Harry B. 1923; Smith, Robert B. 1923; Washington 1944, 1949, 1953; Webster 1955, 1958; Young, Joe 1933

Steiner, Roslyn R.   Stept 1957

Steinert, Alexander   Kalmar 1940

Steininger, Franz   Bullock 1959; Dixon 1933; Mercer 1936

Stellar   David, Hal 1961

Stempfel Jr., Theodore   Howard, Joseph E. 1912

Stergis, Frank   Gilbert 1915

Sterling, Ray   Sterling 1934, 1935, 1943

Stern, Emil   Parish 1954

Stern, Harold   Fisher 1931; Johnson, James P. 1930

Stern, Henry R.   Bryan 1907, 1911

Stern, Jack   Bryan 1916; Leslie 1914; Romberg 1921; Yellen 1923; Young, Joe 1914, 1916

Sternberg   Harburg 1969, 1974

Sterns, Helen   Silver 1953

Stevens, Bert   David, Hal 1941

Stevens, David   Herbert 1913

Stevens, Gay   Mercer 1931

Stevens, Graham   Revel 1940

Stevens, Helen   Sissle 1939

Stevens, Jimmy   Coots 1946

Stevens, Leith   Brooks 1948; Evans 1951, 1955; Livingston, Jay 1951, 1955; Van Heusen 1938

Stevens, Morton   Drake 1971; Mercer 1967

Stevens, Sally   Bacharach 1979

Stevens, Vernon   Yellen 1922

Stevenson, Rudy   Cahn 1970

Stewart, Al   Revel 1959

Stewart, Arthur   Johnson, J. Rosamond 1942

Stewart, Carl   Snyder 1909

Stewart, Ernie   Silver 1952

Stewart, Grant   Herbert 1904, 1921

Stewart, Michael   Coleman 1977, 1980; Strouse 1955, 1956

Stewart, Pat   Ellington 1961

Stewart, Peggy   Sigman 1956

Stewart, Rex   Ellington 1938, 1939; Mills 1935, 1938, 1939

Stiebe, Paul   Yellen 1920

Stiles, Norman   Strouse 1975

Stillman, Al   Ager 1938; Ahlert 1939, 1940, 1941, 1946, 1956; Coleman 1964; Dietz 1938; Drake 1952, 1953; Duke 1940, 1941; Gershwin, George 1936; Lawrence 1942; Mancini 1963; Ruby 1947; Schwartz, Arthur 1937, 1938, 1948; Young, Victor 1952, 1960

Stilwell, Frank   Bryan 1913

Stits, Harry   Hoffman 1953

Stock, Larry   Bryan 1935, 1936, 1937, 1943, 1945, 1948, 1952, 1953, 1955, 1956, 1957, 1960; David, Mack 1933; De Lange 1956; Hoffman 1933; Lawrence 1952; Leslie 1944; Webster 1934

Stock, Roslyn   Blake 1960; Sissle 1960

Stoddard, George E.   Gorney 1926; Hanley 1920; Motzan 1920

Stoll, Georgie   Adamson 1964; Blane 1945, 1946; Freed, Ralph 1944, 1946; Friml 1954

Stoloff, Morris   Cahn 1945, 1950; Washington 1956, 1960

Stolz, Robert   Atteridge 1925; Brennan 1928; Caesar 1936; David, Hal 1950; Egan 1932; Gilbert 1931; Hammerstein 1927; Harbach 1927; Harburg 1931; Kahn 1940; Lerner, Sammy 1931; Parish 1933; Young, Joe 1930, 1931

Stone, Billy   Leslie 1926, 1927, 1928

Stone, Blaine   Sigman 1952

Stone, Eddie   Merrill 1951, 1952

Stone, Gregory   Lawrence 1938; Washington 1938

Stone, H.A.   McHugh 1927; Mills 1927

Stone, Jean   Myrow 1954

Stone, Justin   Stept 1947

Stone, Lew   Carmichael 1933

Stone, Roger   David, Hal 1958

Stone, Wilson   Bacharach 1955, 1957, 1959; David, Mack 1955; Young, Victor 1953, 1957

Stonehill, Maurice   Howard, Joseph E. 1902; Kern 1910

Stoner, M.S.   Razaf 1946, 1947

Stor, Jean   Razaf 1943

Stordahl, Axel   Cahn 1945, 1949, 1950, 1951

Storey, Rachel   Motzan 1919

Storfer, Herb   Revel 1959

Storfer, Herbert   Revel 1959

Storm, Raphael   Kern 1935

Story, Milt   Hoffman 1956

Stothart, Herbert   Atteridge 1924; Brown, Nacio Herb 1933, 1941; Caesar 1929; Fields 1931; Freed, Arthur 1930, 1933, 1934; Freed, Ralph 1934, 1942, 1944, 1947; Friml 1924, 1936, 1937, 1954; Gershwin, George 1925; Gorney

1924; Hammerstein 1920, 1922, 1923, 1924, 1925, 1926, 1927, 1940; Harbach 1920, 1923, 1924, 1925, 1926, 1927; Harburg 1943; Howard, Joseph E. 1912, 1915; Johnson, Howard 1930; Kahn 1933, 1934, 1936, 1938, 1939; Kalmar 1928; McHugh 1931; Rome 1943; Ruby 1928; Washington 1935; Webster 1954; Woods 1930; Youmans 1923, 1926

Straight, Charley   Donaldson 1926; Kahn 1919, 1923, 1924

Stransky, Otto   Gilbert 1927

Straus, Oscar   Alter 1937; Atteridge 1921; Caesar 1945; Freed, Arthur 1930, 1931; Freed, Ralph 1941; Leigh 1955; Robin 1932; Romberg 1917; Smith, Harry B. 1913, 1926; Smith, Robert B. 1913; Webster 1937

Strauss, Johann   Ager 1953; Akst 1953; Burke 1948; Comden and Green 1955; Davis 1953; Dietz 1950; Freed, Ralph 1939, 1947; Hammerstein 1948, Johnson, Howard 1932, 1935, 1941; Kahn 1940; Lerner, Sammy 1943, 1945

Strayhorn, Billy   Ellington 1939, 1940, 1941, 1942, 1953, 1954, 1955, 1957, 1965, 1966, 1971; Leslie 1939; Mercer 1953, 1954; Russell 1946

Strecker, Heinrich   Akst 1954

Street, David   Spina 1948

Streisand, Barbra   Bergman 1988

Strickland, K.   Mancini 1981

Stride, Harry   David, Mack 1932; Freed, Ralph 1935, 1936; Young, Joe 1933, 1934

Stromberg, John   Smith, Harry B. 1898, 1899; Smith, Robert B. 1902

Strong, Bob   Raye 1940

Strong, Patience   Carmichael 1956

Struble, Mabel   Hoffman 1927

Stuart, Monica   Strouse 1957

Sturges, Preston   Snyder 1936, 1937

Sturgis, Frank   Johnson, J. Rosamond 1913, 1914

Sturm, Maurice   Johnson, Howard 1927

Sturm, Murray   Brown, Lew 1923; Rose 1924

Stutz, Carl   Heyman 1964

Styne, Stanley   Styne 1958, 1959, 1961, 1963, 1964, 1965, 1967

Suarez, Humberto   David, Mack 1947

Suesse, Dana   Adamson 1939; Coslow 1939; Harburg 1934; Heyman 1931, 1932, 1933, 1934, 1935; Kahal 1936; Lerner, Sammy 1930, 1931; Robin 1931; Rose 1930, 1936, 1937, 1938, 1939, 1940, Date Unknown

Sukman, Harry   Adamson 1957, 1966; David, Mack 1958; Washington 1960; Webster 1967

Sullivan, Alex   Gilbert 1918

Sullivan, Daisy   Whiting 1914, 1916

Sullivan, Daniel J.   Dubin 1917; Olcott 1907, 1908, 1909, 1911

Sullivan, Henry   Dubin 1931; Eliscu 1929, 1931, 1932; Olcott 1938; Schwartz, Arthur 1929; Yellen 1929

Sullivan, Joe   Sigman 1951

Sullivan, Ken   Robison 1950

Sumner, George   Duke 1941

Sundgaard, Arnold   Weill 1948

Sunshine, Marion   Gilbert 1931

Sussman, Al   Robison 1954

Sutton, Michael   David, Mack 1975, 1977

Suzuki, Kunihiko   David, Mack 1971

Svigals, Phil   Brennan 1929

Swales II, Jackson   Loesser 1937

Swanson, Bob   Mercer 1959

Swanstrom, Arthur   Alter 1933, 1934, 1935; Carmichael 1948; Conrad 1928; Coots 1929, 1934; Davis 1929;

Hanley 1934, 1935, 1936; Leslie 1935; Norworth 1921, 1922; Schwartz, Arthur 1930

Swarthart, G.   Howard, Joseph E. 1907

Swayze, Edward   Mills 1934, 1935

Sweatman, Wilbur C.   Brown, Lew 1939, 1957

Swift, Kay   Freed, Ralph 1947; Gershwin, George 1933; Gershwin, Ira 1933, 1947; Heyman 1933

Swinburne, A.C.   Herbert 1907

Sylvester, B.   David, Hal 1946

Sylviano, Rene   Young, Joe 1931

Symes, Marty   Ager 1936, 1937, 1938; Bloom 1951; Coots 1945; David, Hal 1953; Freed, Ralph 1940, 1944; Hoffman 1943; Livingston, Jerry 1932, 1933, 1934, 1935, 1936, 1937, 1942, 1944; Myrow 1934; Robison 1942; Stept 1940, 1944, 1947, 1949

Symons, Arthur   Duke 1944

Szabolos, F.   Rose 1937

Szathmary, Irving   David, Mack 1937

T

Tabak, Sam   Young, Joe 1931

Tabet, W.G.   Brooks 1950

Tableporter, Mitchell   Brown, Nacio Herb 1955, 1957

Tabot, Andre   Lawrence 1945

Tackaberry, Carl   Sigman 1946

Taconuni, E.   Hoffman 1957

Talbert, Doug   Webster 1965

Talbert, Fred   Webster 1967

Talbot, Howard   Smith, Harry B. 1911

Talbot, Lee   Mercer 1985

Tana   Freed, Ralph 1939

Tanassy Jr., Cornel   Mills 1929; Parish 1929, 1980

Tannennill, F.   Snyder 1919

Tansman, Alexandre   Webster 1945

Tanzman, Joseph   Coslow 1927

Tapajos, Paulinho   Evans 1970; Livingston, Jay 1954

Tarbox, Russell   Atteridge 1918

Tarkington, Booth   Herbert 1944; Kern 1922

Taub, Allen   Hoffman 1931

Taub, Jules   Razaf 1954

Tauber, Doris   Lawrence 1954; Mercer 1961; Parish 1930

Taubman, Paul   Alter 1960

Taylor, Bernard U.   Young, Victor 1950

Taylor, Billee   Norworth 1910

Taylor, Charles H.   Kern 1905, 1906, 1913

Taylor, Charles M.   Smith, Robert B. 1905

Taylor, Irving   Hoffman 1940; Spina 1953

Taylor, J. Floyd   Young, Victor 1929

Taylor, Ken   Coslow 1947

Taylor, Russ   Hoffman 1959, 1962

Tazewell, Charles   Young, Victor 1951

Tchaikovsky, Peter   Bergman 1983; Brooks 1945; David, Mack 1939, 1940; Fain 1958; Freed, Ralph 1944; Kahn 1937, 1938; Lawrence 1941; Lerner, Sammy 1941; Loesser 1939; Parish 1945, 1954; Romberg 1938

Teasdale, Sara   Young, Victor 1913, 1914

Teener, Ed   Mills 1959

Teetor, Macy O.   David, Mack 1940; Mercer 1936

Teixeira, Humberto   Adamson 1953

Telaak, Bill   Clare 1937

Tell, Al   Leigh 1955

Temple, Nat   David, Mack 1942

Templeton, Alec   Kahn 1944

Tenco   David, Hal 1961

Tenney, Harry   Silver 1918

Tenney, Marty   Drake 1943

Tennyson, Alfred Lord   Young, Victor 1911

Tepper, Saul   Heyman 1971; Silver 1950, 1953, 1954, 1971

Tepper, Sid   Mills 1950

Terker, Arthur   Bryan 1927; Caesar 1931; David, Mack 1939; Egan 1937; Johnson, J. Rosamond 1934; Livingston, Jerry 1939; Motzan 1931

Terr, Max   Robin 1930

Terriss, Dorothy   Baer 1922

Terry, Ray   David, Mack 1942

Thal, Perry   Burke 1937

Tharp, Winston   Gilbert 1938; Waller 1935

Thayer, Pat   Coots 1925

The Lion   Raye 1957

Therrien, Henri   Stept 1928

Thiele, Bob   Ellington 1957, 1963

Thirlet, Maurice   Gilbert 1937

Thomas   Johnson, Howard 1927

Thomas, Addie   David, Mack 1961

Thomas, Augustus   Herbert 1906

Thomas, Danny   Revel 1959

Thomas, Eddie   Friend 1955, 1956

Thomas, Edith   Friml 1947

Thomas, Milton   Hart 1919

Thomas, Sir C.   Russell 1951

Thomas, Tony   Warren 1964, 1978, 1980, 1985, Date Unknown

Thomas, Vincent   Drake 1943

Thomas, Walter   Razaf 1938

Thompson, Al   Von Tilzer 1927

Thompson, Babe   Razaf 1923

Thompson, Bob   Russell 1957

Thompson, Christopher T.   Oakland 1972

Thompson, E.L.   Parish 1957

Thompson, Elsie   Kahn 1931

Thompson, Fred   Friend 1953, 1954, 1955, 1956; Oakland 1956

Thompson, Kay   Blane 1945, 1946, 1957; Mercer 1945; Warren 1945

Thompson, Noah N.   Howard, Joseph E. 1942

Thompson, Randall   Schwartz, Arthur 1926

Thomson Jr., Maj. C.E.   Washington 1955; Young, Victor 1955

Thorne, George   Waller 1953

Thornhill, Claude   Parish 1938

Thornton, Arthur   Burke 1946

Thornton, Bob   Van Heusen 1940

Thorpe, Charles   Young, Joe 1934

Thow, George   Von Tilzer 1960

Tiefenthal, Don   Carmichael 1939

Tierney, Harry   Atteridge 1916; Bryan 1916, 1917, 1918; Cohan 1919; Davis 1930; Egan 1931, 1932, 1933, 1934, 1935, 1937, 1938, 1942; Herbert 1924; Jerome 1916; Kalmar 1915; Leslie 1915

Timberg, Herman   Atteridge 1916, 1917; Fisher 1921; Motzan 1916, 1917; Romberg 1916, 1917

Timberg, Sammy   Brennan 1928; David, Mack 1947; Eliscu 1929; Fisher 1924; Heyman 1938, 1949; Lerner, Sammy 1931, 1932, 1933, 1934; Loesser 1941

Timm, Wladimir A.   Brown, Lew 1939, 1943

Tinturin, Peter   Caesar 1930; Clare 1932; Freed, Arthur 1932; Lawrence 1934, 1936, 1937, 1938, 1957; Lewis 1930; Mercer 1932, 1933, 1934, 1951; Meyer 1934; Parish 1935; Young, Joe 1930, 1931

Tiomkin, Dimitri   Coslow 1929; Egan 1930; Eliscu 1932; Johnson, Howard 1929; Kahn 1937; Lawrence 1954; Robin 1929, 1933; Washington 1947, 1952, 1953, 1954, 1955, 1956, 1957, 1958, 1960, 1961, 1964, 1967; Webster 1953, 1954, 1956, 1959, 1960, 1961, 1963, 1964, 1972

Tishman, Fay   Lawrence 1956; Sterling 1961; Von Tilzer 1961

Titheradge, Dion   Gorney 1926

Titus, Libby   Bacharach 1979, 1980

Tizol, Juan   Burke 1953; Drake 1942; Ellington 1937, 1938, 1941; Mills 1935, 1937, 1938, 1939, 1941; Russell 1957

Toang   Raye 1961

Tobani, Theo M.   Kahn 1931; Smith, Harry B. 1903

Tobias, Charles   Akst 1953, 1956, 1961; Arlen 1929; Baer 1933, 1934, 1936, 1937, 1939, 1940, 1941, 1944, 1945, 1961; Bloom 1931; Brown, Lew 1939, 1941, 1942, 1943, 1949; Bryan 1930, 1931; Clare 1928, 1929, 1931, 1932, 1933, 1936, 1937, 1948; Clarke 1929; Coots 1931, 1932, 1933; Coslow 1926; Davis 1932, 1954; Fain 1929, 1935, 1936, 1938, 1964; Freed, Ralph 1934, 1935; Friend 1928, 1935, 1936, 1940, 1941, 1943, 1944, 1945, 1950; Gilbert 1927; Henderson 1924, 1926, 1944; Jerome 1928; Johnson, Howard 1926, 1927, 1928, 1933, 1935; Johnston 1931, 1932; Kahal 1929; Lerner, Sammy 1931; Lewis 1935; Livingston, Jerry 1955, 1957, 1958, 1959; Loesser 1934; Magidson 1932; Merrill 1950; Meyer 1936, 1952; Monaco 1928, 1933; Pollack 1933; Romberg 1943, 1950, 1951; Rose 1928; Schwartz, Jean 1975; Silver 1926, 1929; Stept 1932, 1934, 1935, 1936, 1937, 1938, 1939, 1940, 1941, 1942, 1943, 1948, 1949, 1959; Turk 1927, 1928; Washington 1937; Whiting 1928, 1929; Woods 1926, 1927, 1929, 1940; Young, Joe 1933, 1934

Tobias, Fred   Bacharach 1960; Strouse 1958, 1959, 1960

Tobias, Harry   Clare 1921, 1922; Conrad 1921; Coslow 1926; Davis 1954; Friend 1922, 1933, 1934, 1950, 1952; Henderson 1924, 1926; Johnson, Howard 1927, 1929, 1937; Schwartz, Jean 1975; Young, Joe 1932

Tobias, Henry   Dubin 1927; Gilbert 1927; Johnson, Howard 1927, 1929, 1937; Lerner, Sammy 1931; Lewis 1935; Mills 1927, 1940; Parish 1941; Rose 1927, 1930; Schwartz, Jean 1975; Webster 1980; Young, Joe 1932

Tobias, Henry H.   Young, Joe 1933

Tobin, Lew   Johnson, Howard 1947, 1958

Toccati, Joseph   Hoffman 1928

Todaro, Tony   Carmichael 1966

Todd, Art   Oakland 1954

Todd, Clarence   Conrad 1928; Razaf 1928, 1938

Todd, Dottie   Oakland 1954

Todd, Peter   Robison 1957

Tolliver, James   Sissle 1934

Tomlin, Pinky   Caesar 1944; Mercer 1952

Torme, Mel   Ellington 1946; Parish 1943

Torre, Janice   Carmichael 1947; Webster 1951

Tortomas, Tony   Coots 1928

Tosti   Coslow 1935

Tour, Robert   Harburg 1930; Heyman 1930

Tours, Frank   Gorney 1930; Harbach 1911; Harburg 1929, 1930

Touzet, Rene   Drake 1947; Parish 1941

Towne, Joanne   Ellington 1956

Towner, J.   Russell 1956

Towser, C.   Raye 1940

Trace, Al   Hoffman 1943, 1949, 1950, 1951, 1953, 1954, 1955, 1956, 1958, 1959; Livingston, Jerry 1943; Silver 1955, 1958

Trace, Ben   Hoffman 1951

Tracey, Billy   Parish 1934

Tracey, William G.   Baer 1950, 1951; Brown, A. Seymour 1929; Donaldson 1916; Dubin 1922, 1923, 1938; Fisher 1910; Hanley 1919, 1920, 1921; Johnson, Howard 1917; Meyer 1917; Silver 1921

Tracy, Arthur   Kahn 1933; Young, Victor 1933

Trainor, Val   Von Tilzer 1917

Traveller, Lou   Bryan 1924

Traver, John   Brown, Lew 1923

Traynor, Chris   Hanley 1934

Trebla, Al   Smith, Harry B. 1922

Tree, Ray   Rome 1956

Trenet, Charles   Goetz 1938; Lawrence 1944, 1947; Rome 1945; Sigman 1950, 1954, 1958

Trent, Jo   Alter 1928, 1929, 1930; Carmichael 1932; Coots 1926; Ellington 1923, 1924, 1962; Johnson, James P. 1931, 1932, 1933, 1934; Mills 1962; Robison 1928, 1929, 1952; Waller 1924, 1926, 1927; Warren 1926

Tresselt, Frank   Clare 1939

Tressler, I.   Howard, Joseph E. 1907

Trevelvan, Arthur   Von Tilzer 1900

Trevor, Huntley   Norworth 1917, 1920

Trilliin, Bud   Lane Date Unknown

Trini, Anthony   Hoffman 1930

Trinkaus, George J.   Brennan 1924

Trivers, Barry   Coslow 1937; Gorney 1948; Oakland 1930, 1931, 1954, 1958, 1960

Trolli, J.   Parish 1949

Trootwyck, Arthur   Porter 1910

Trotta, Ray   David, Hal 1950

Trotter, John Scott   De Lange 1948

Troup, Bobby   David, Mack 1956; Ellington 1962; Mancini 1957; Mercer 1955

Troustine, Joe   Hart 1922

Trovajoli, Armando   Howard, Bart 1961; Sigman 1964

Troy, Harry   Waller 1926

Trumbauer, Frank   Waller 1927

Tschaikovsky, Peter   Brooks 1959

Tucci, Terig   Mills 1940

Tucker, Bobby   Blane 1945

Tucker, Johnny   Bryan 1931, 1943; Dixon 1926; Hoffman 1931; Johnson, Howard 1927; Leslie 1924, 1926; Young, Joe 1933

Tuiteleapaga, Napoleon   Evans 1954; Livingston, Jay 1954

Tuminello, Phil   Cahn 1957

Turner, Frank   Silver 1947

Turner, Jimmie   Lawrence 1940

Turner, Nancy Byrd   Carmichael 1946

Turner, Ray   Washington 1943

Tuvim, Abe   Mills 1940

Twomey, Kay   Cahn 1956; Meyer 1936, 1947; Mills 1935

Tyers, William H.   Sigman 1955

Tyle, Ted   Heyman 1967

Tyler, Clark   Yellen 1920

U

Uhl, Constance   DeSylva 1919

Uhr, Billy   Myrow 1931

Uncle Robert   Johnson, Howard 1925

Underwood, R.   Leigh 1981

Unger, Stella   Fisher 1931, 1933, 1934, 1935, 1936; Johnson, James P. 1929, 1930, 1962; Young, Victor 1953, 1955, 1960, 1963

Usera, Raymond   Sissle 1934

Utrera, Adolfo   Adamson 1930; Gilbert 1931; Gordon 1930; Revel 1929, 1930

V

Val, Jack   Friend 1931; Stept 1929

Valando, George   Sigman 1960

Valdespi, Armando   Van Heusen 1937

Valencia, C.   Drake 1943

Valentine, Buddy   Hoffman 1928, 1929; Mills 1928, 1929; Yellen 1928

Valentine, E.   Conrad 1922

Valentine, Mike   David, Mack 1941

Valerio, Frederico   Yellen 1949

Vall, Jack   Baer 1923

Valle, M.   Bergman 1971

Valle, Paulo   Bergman 1971; Sigman 1971, 1972

Vallee, Rudy   Brown, Lew 1938; Carmichael 1933; Fain 1930; Johnson, J. Rosamond 1934; Kahal 1930; Kahn 1930; Webster 1931

Valpree, Hal   Coslow 1923

Valverde, J.   Goetz 1913

Van, Freddie   Howard, Joseph E. 1947

Van, Gus   Ager 1930; Akst 1923; Bryan 1917; Davis 1923; Pollack 1927; Sterling 1919, 1920; Yellen 1916, 1919, 1927, 1930

Van Alen, Patricia   Adamson 1931

Van Alstyne, Egbert   Brown, A. Seymour 1914; Bryan 1915; Edwards 1928; Egan 1917, 1926; Kahn 1913, 1914, 1915, 1916, 1917, 1918, 1919, 1923, 1924, 1925, 1926, 1929, 1931, 1938; Williams 1903, 1904, 1905, 1906, 1907, 1908, 1909, 1910, 1911, 1912; Young, Victor 1931

Van Brunt, Walter   Von Tilzer 1915, 1917

Vance, Dave   Kahn 1925

Van Cleve, Nathan   Brooks 1956

Van Dam, Albert   Hoffman 1959

Vandersloat, G.M.   Sterling 1904

Van Eps, George   Freed, Ralph 1935

Van Eps, John   Freed, Ralph 1935

Van Eps Jr., Fred   Drake 1946

Van Eps, Robert   Adamson 1964

Van Gelder, Leon   Razaf 1939

Van Hasselt, Betty   Baer 1964

Van Horne, Randy   Raye 1961, 1962

Vanhoy, Rafe   David, Hal 1976

Vanick, Ted   Sigman 1955

Van Loan, Paul   Ahlert 1924; Brown, Lew 1925; Bryan 1925; Gilbert 1924, 1926; Rose 1928; Sterling 1926

Vann, Al   Heyman 1932; Stept 1940

Van Parys, George   Lawrence 1955; Lerner, Sammy 1931

Van Studam, H.T.   Wrubel 1951

Vargas, Don   Lewis 1944

Varna, Henri   Baer 1927; Kahn 1927

Varnick, Ted   Sigman 1955

Vars, Henry   Stept 1975

Vasilescu, Ion   Baer 1938; Lewis 1938

Vasory, Claude   Cahn 1973

Vatsures, John   Caesar 1955

Vaughn, Denny   Webster 1966

Vaughn, Robert S.   Edwards 1917

Vause, Norman J.   Howard, Joseph E. 1923

Vecsei, Armand   Akst 1938; Clare 1938; Gilbert 1932, 1934, 1943

Vecsei, D.J.   Gilbert 1933

Vejvoda, Jaromir   Brown, Lew 1939, 1943, 1952
Velazques, Ramon   Johnson, Howard 1935
Venn, Lawrence   Duke 1929
Venuti, Joe   Lerner, Sammy 1935; Robison 1956, 1957
Veo, Harold   Conrad 1925
Veran, Florence   Adamson 1951; Duke 1955
Verdi, Giuseppe   Brooks 1959; Robin 1947
Verges, Joe   Koehler 1925, 1928, 1930
Vermelho, Aloyr Pires   David, Mack 1946
Verney, L.   Smith, Harry B. 1900
VerPlanck, Billy   Drake 1995, 1998; Razaf 1957
Victor, Lou   Carmichael 1941
Vigneau, Frank   Razaf 1942
Villoldo, A.P.   Fields 1934; McHugh 1934
Vimmerstadt, Sadie   Mercer 1959
Vincent, Larry   Leslie 1925
Vincent, Nat   Ager 1917, 1918; Bryan 1903; Clare Date
     Unknown; Gilbert 1918, 1919; Hanley 1917; Johnson,
     Howard 1916; Pollack 1918; Von Tilzer 1924
Vincent, Paul   Washington 1928
Vinikov, V.   Rome 1943
Violinsky, Sol   Ager 1947; Akst 1948; Davis 1951; Dixon
     1923; Donaldson 1924; Johnson, Howard 1920, 1921;
     Leslie 1942; Monaco 1920; Rose 1924, 1928, 1929
Viorst, Judith   Strouse Date Unknown
Vivian, Thomas J.   Herbert 1898
Vodery, Will H.   Buck 1915; Lewis 1944; Sissle 1942
Vol, Frank De   David, Mack 1968
Vollstedt, R.   Johnson, Howard 1935
von Baumbach, Rudolph   Herbert 1915
Vondells, The   Johnson, James P. 1964
Von Holstein, H.   Whiting 1915
Von Platen, H.   Meyer 1928
Von Suppe, Franz   Brooks 1946; Caesar 1931
Von Tilzer, Albert   Brennan 1936; Brown, A. Seymour 1921,
     1922, 1927, 1928, 1929 1933; Brown, Lew 1911, 1912,
     1913, 1916, 1917, 1919, 1920, 1921, 1922, 1924, 1925;
     Gilbert 1934; Henderson 1924; Lewis 1915; Norworth
     1906, 1907, 1908; Robin 1926; Rose 1924
Voodin, William   Mercer 1932
Vosburgh, Dick   Oakland 1967, 1971
Voynow, Dick   Carmichael 1939; Mills 1939; Parish 1925
Vraz, Victor   Friml 1933

W

Wade, Stuart   Spina 1947
Wadsworth, Wheeler   Fisher 1921
Waggner, George   Alter 1935; Cobb 1930; Edwards 1929,
     1930; Hoffman 1932, 1933; Johnson, Howard 1930, 1933;
     Kahal 1931; Kahn 1931; Silver 1929, 1930; Youmans
     1930
Wagner, Art   Burke 1963
Wagner, F.   Smith, Harry B. 1912
Wagner, John H.   Kern 1904
Wagner, Larry   Razaf 1940
Wagner, Lenny   Drake 1944
Wagner, Richard   Brooks 1945; Johnson, Howard 1939
Waite, Jack   Johnson, Howard 1926
Wakefield, Jean   Razaf 1928
Wald, M.   Sigman 1949
Walderen, E.V.   Johnson, Howard 1936
Waldman, Eddie   Lawrence 1952
Waldteufel, Emile   Johnson, Howard 1935
Walker, Allan   Davis 1927

Walker, Bee   Cahn 1956; David, Hal 1956; Merrill 1950;
     Parish 1956
Walker, Bill   Revel 1951, 1959
Walker, Dee   Merrill 1950
Walker, Don   Lawrence 1951, 1952, 1956, 1958; Rome 1950
Walker, James J.   Hanley 1939
Walker, Lee N.   Caesar 1920
Walker, Raymond   Lewis 1915
Wall, Phil   Yellen 1926
Wallace, Oliver   Freed, Arthur 1919, 1920, 1922, 1925, 1930;
     Howard, Joseph E. 1920; Lawrence 1952; Washington
     1939, 1941; Young, Victor 1952
Wallace, Walter   Parish 1929
Wallington, George   David, Mack 1955; Parish 1955
Wallis, Ruth   Mills 1947, 1948, 1949
Walsh, Art   Young, Victor 1921, 1922
Walsh, Christy   Berlin 1926
Walsh, J. Brandon   Norworth 1919
Walter, E.E.   Robison 1958
Walter, James   Yellen 1923
Walter, Serge   Brooks 1948; Koehler 1931; Mercer 1934,
     1959; Parish 1933
Walters, Charles   Blane 1945
Walthan, Tom   Webster 1955
Walton, Bert   Hanley 1922
Walton, Lester A.   Johnson, J. Rosamond 1910
Waner, Art   David, Hal 1956; David, Mack 1951
Ward, Billy   David, Hal 1947
Ward, Charles B.   Sterling 1900
Ward, Edward   Brennan 1943; Bryan 1929, 1930; Coslow
     1947; Dubin 1930; Kahn 1936; Koehler 1929
Ward, George   Fisher 1929, 1930; Johnson, Howard 1930
Ward, Helen   Drake 1945
Ward, Joe   Johnson, Howard 1926; Silver 1928
Ward, Sam   Coots 1929; Hoffman 1955; Johnston 1920,
     1921; Stept 1922
Ward, Samuel Augustus   Spina 1958
Ward, Will J.   Fisher 1920
Warfield, Joseph   Hoffman 1950
Waring, Tom   Raye 1936, 1937, 1944, 1950
Wark, Colin   Woods 1932
Warner, Steve   David, Mack 1978
Warnick, Clay   Leigh 1955
Warren, Bob   Davis 1941
Warren, Charlie   Johnson, Howard 1928; Turk 1927
Warren, Diane   Bacharach 1987
Warren, Edgar T.   Snyder 1910
Warren, Jophe   Warren Date Unknown
Warshauer, Frank   Parish 1931, 1944
Washington, George   Mills 1936
Waters, Sanford   Snyder 1908
Waterson, Henry   Brown, Lew 1925; Bryan 1928; Snyder
     1928
Watson, Charles A.   Mills 1924
Watson, Ernie   Bryan 1934
Watson, Freddy   Leslie 1911
Watson, John   Stept 1954
Watson, Johnny   Adamson 1939
Watson, Nola   Livingston, Jerry 1940
Watson, Whitford   Edwards 1907
Watts, Clem   Freed, Ralph 1953; Hoffman 1949, 1950, 1951,
     1953, 1954, 1956, 1957, 1958, 1961; Merrill 1949, 1951;
     Silver 1954
Watts, Dick   Hoffman 1954
Watts, Grady   Cahn 1937

Waxman, Franz   Brooks 1951; David, Hal 1962; David, Mack 1954, 1962; Evans 1951; Harburg 1935, 1945; Kahn 1936, 1937; Livingston, Jay 1951; Loesser 1942, 1952; Rome 1954; Sigman 1957; Webster 1957, 1959, 1960, 1961

Wayburn, Ned   Gershwin, George 1919

Wayne, Anthony   Mills 1927, 1928

Wayne, Artie   Merrill 1946, 1947; Oakland 1952, 1954; Spina 1946, 1947

Wayne, Bernie   Leigh 1955; Mercer 1958, 1960

Wayne, Dorothy   McHugh 1962, 1964

Wayne, Jerry   David, Mack 1951

Wayne, Mabel   Baer 1925; Brown, Lew 1950; Bryan 1934; Cahn 1957; David, Mack 1934; Dubin 1941; Eliscu 1931; Gilbert 1925, 1928, 1929, 1932; Heyman 1936; Hoffman 1934, 1950; Kahn 1927, 1930; Leslie 1930, 1931; Lewis 1926, 1927; Merrill 1950; Parish 1933; Rose 1929, 1930, 1935; Sigman 1951; Webster 1934; Young, Joe 1926, 1927, 1932, 1934

Wayne, Sid   David, Hal 1955; Livingston, Jerry 1955, 1956, 1961, 1962; Silver 1958, 1960

Webb, Chick   David, Mack 1962; Heyman 1938; Livingston, Jerry 1962; Razaf 1936, 1937

Webb, Roy   De Lange 1932; Hart 1919

Weber, Fritz   Sigman 1957

Webster, Ben   Revel 1944

Weeks, Anson   Washington 1935

Weeks, Harold   Akst 1932

Weems, Ted   Davis 1938; Hoffman 1933; Razaf 1933

Wehl, Ernie   Johnson, Howard 1930

Weill, Irving   Brennan 1925; Dubin 1920; Fain 1925; Henderson 1921; McHugh 1925

Weinberg, Mortimer   Warren 1926

Weiner, Edward   Mills 1938; Myrow 1938

Weiner, Stanley F.   Baer 1932; Edwards 1936, 1938

Weinstein, Harry   Stept 1956

Weire, Audie Marie   Monaco 1940

Weirick, Paul   Young, Joe 1932

Weisman, Ben   Cahn 1968; David, Hal 1958, 1961; David, Mack 1957; Sigman 1953; Webster 1963, 1965, 1972, 1974

Weiss, George David   Ellington 1961; Gordon 1925, 1928, 1929; Styne 1960

Weiss, Larry   David, Mack 1976

Weiss, Stephan   Adamson 1941; Cahn 1939; De Lange 1940; Dietz 1946; Heyman 1939; Hoffman 1948; Lawrence 1931; Lewis 1938; Parish 1948; Sigman 1954

Welch, J.M.   McHugh 1924

Weldon, Frank   David, Hal 1954, 1958; David, Mack 1941; Hoffman 1943, 1944, 1949; Johnson, Howard 1933, 1934, 1935; Lawrence 1946; Magidson 1931; Razaf 1930, 1931; Washington 1932

Weldon, Johnson, James   Johnson, J. Rosamond 1901

Weldon, William   Razaf 1942

Welk, Lawrence   Loesser 1939; Parish 1943; Webster 1963

Wellington, Larry   Gilbert 1938

Wells, Bob   Coleman 1965, 1966, 1971, 1972, 1974, 1975

Wells, Cameron   Parish 1938

Wells, George   Adamson 1955

Wells, Gilbert   Akst 1926

Wells, Jack   Bryan 1912, 1913, 1914, 1915, 1917, 1918; Snyder 1919

Wells, R.D.   Coots 1955

Wells, Robert   Blane 1954; Ellington 1946; Mancini 1964, 1979; Myrow 1954, 1956, 1959; Revel 1951, 1959

Wells, William K.   Monaco 1932

Welmon, Harry   Bryan 1908

Welsh, Ona   Gorney 1965

Wences, Senor   Hoffman 1959

Wendall, Ola   Howard, Joseph E. 1948

Wendling, Pete   Ager 1915, 1916; Ahlert 1916, 1919; Brown, Lew 1928, 1950, 1951; Bryan 1917, 1922, 1926, 1927, 1928, 1930, 1931, 1933, 1934, 1939; Clarke 1922, 1923, 1931; Coots 1930; David, Mack 1935, 1936, 1937, 1938; Davis 1927, 1930; DeSylva 1928; Donaldson 1924; Goetz 1916; Henderson 1928; Hoffman 1928, 1929, 1930, 1931; Kahal 1929; Kalmar 1919, 1920; Leslie 1919, 1920, 1921, 1922, 1923, 1928, 1932, 1945, 1964; Lewis 1917, 1918, 1921, 1922, 1933, 1934, 1935, 1936, 1938, 1944, 1948, 1949, 1950, 1951, 1952, 1954, 1955, 1962; Meyer 1932, 1933, 1934, 1935, 1936, 1937, 1938, 1939, 1949, 1952, 1954, 1955; Monaco 1920, 1923, 1927; Motzan 1923; Parish 1936; Rose 1923; Young, Joe 1916, 1917, 1918, 1921, 1922, 1932, 1933, 1934

Wenrich, Percy   Brennan 1927; Bryan 1908; Bullock 1936; Egan 1939; Fisher 1915; Gilbert 1928; Goetz 1918; Harbach 1917; Jerome 1918; Johnson, Howard 1917, 1918, 1924; Kahn 1921, 1923; Leslie 1925; Loesser 1932; Yellen 1917

Werfel, Franz   Weill 1937

Werner, Eduard   Lewis 1925; Whiting 1927; Young, Joe 1925

Werner, Hans   Lawrence 1953

Wertheim, Arnold   Strouse 1945

Weschler, Walter   Mercer 1955

Weslyn, Louis   Olcott 1913, 1920; Romberg 1910

Wesman, H.   Leigh 1954

Wessel, Harry   Yellen 1918

West, Adam   Warren 1967

West, Alvy   Hoffman 1950

West, Bob   David, Mack 1930

West, Eugene   Bryan 1925, 1927; Conrad 1923; Coots 1921; McHugh 1923; Meyer 1934; Monaco 1922, 1925; Parish 1933; Woods 1923

West, Mae   Fisher 1938

West, Paul   Edwards 1908; Herbert 1904; Kern 1906, 1907, 1912

Weston, Paul   Bergman 1959, 1961, 1962, 1963, 1966, 1968; Brooks 1959; Cahn 1945, 1949, 1951, 1953, 1954, 1956, 1957, 1958, 1959; Evans 1968; Lawrence 1953; Livingston, Jay 1968; Mercer 1944, 1945, 1946; Raye 1946; Russell 1950; Washington 1955; Webster 1951

Weston, R.P.   Kern 1917; Norworth 1915, 1916, 1917; Youmans 1927

Weston, Willie   Bryan 1917; Snyder 1911

Westphal, Frank   Kahn 1921, 1922, 1929

Wetstein Jr., Paul   Freed, Ralph 1938

Wever, Ned   Ager 1932, 1933, 1934, 1936, 1938, 1942, 1953; Caesar 1934; Heyman 1935; Livingston, Jerry 1938; Rose 1942; Schwartz, Jean 1933, 1934

Wheatly, Tom   Cahn 1973

Wheeler, Clarence   Kahn 1927

Wheeler, D.E.   Young, Victor 1947

Wheeler, Dan   Young, Victor 1921

Wheeler, Francis   Bryan 1928; Fain 1927, 1928, 1929; Friml 1925; Kahal 1927, 1928, 1929; Robin 1942; Smith, Harry B. 1922, 1923, 1924, 1925; Snyder 1921, 1922, 1923, 1924, 1927, 1928, 1942

Wheeler, Hubert   Robison 1964

Whelan, Albert   Edwards 1923

Whidden, Jay   Conrad 1910, 1912; Young, Joe 1912

Whitcup, Leonard   David, Hal 1942, 1945, 1946, 1948, 1949, 1954; David, Mack 1942; Eliscu 1969

White, Al   Young, Joe 1930

White, Al H.   Alter 1921; Stept 1921

White, Bob   Van Heusen 1940

White, Daniel J.   Sigman 1955

White, E.   Silver 1955

White, Eddy   Lawrence 1940

White, Elmore   Johnson, James P. 1925

White, Flo   Coots 1949

White, George   Arlen 1932; Caesar 1929, 1932; Friend 1929

White, Harry   Fain 1923; Johnson, James P. 1931; Mills 1931, 1935, 1937; Parish 1931, 1934; Razaf 1931; Rose 1924; Warren 1926

White, John   Friend 1924

White, Lew   Gilbert 1952; Lewis 1929; Pollack 1929; Young, Joe 1929

White, Mildred   Johnson, Howard 1926

White, Ted   Ager 1935; Mills 1935; Razaf 1935

White, Willy   Clarke 1924; Goetz 1917; Kalmar 1920; Leslie 1924; Lewis 1920; Rose 1924; Ruby 1920; Turk 1919; Young, Joe 1920

Whiteman, Paul   Baer 1921, 1924; DeSylva 1924, 1927; Friend 1924; Merrill 1955

Whiting, George   Baer 1929; Berlin 1909; Brennan 1921; Clarke 1918; Coots 1928; De Lange 1934; Donaldson 1925, 1927; Fisher 1904, 1906, 1941; Hoffman 1929, 1930, 1932; Kalmar 1917; Livingston, Jerry 1936; Meyer 1907, 1918; Motzan 1933; Pollack 1927, 1928; Snyder 1907, 1909, 1929, 1932; Sterling 1911; Von Tilzer 1910, 1911, 1913, 1914, 1917; Yellen 1923

Whitlock, William (Billy   Sigman 1949

Whitman, Paul   Whiting 1927

Whitman, Walt   Weill 1942

Whitney, Howard   Cahn 1940

Whitney, Joan   David, Mack 1943, 1944, 1945, 1966; Robison 1963

Whittaker, Charles   Brown, Nacio Herb 1931

Whyman, Al   Spina 1932

Wicker, Irene   Styne 1940

Wicks, Virginia   Brown, Nacio Herb 1944

Wiedoft, Rudy   Robin 1926

Wienstock, J.   Gilbert 1955

Wilber, Lucky   Gilbert 1924

Wildberg, Otto   Friml Date Unknown

Wilde, Christian   McHugh 1969

Wilde, Harriet   Parish 1932

Wilder, Alec   De Lange 1939; Dietz 1930; Lawrence 1952; Mercer 1976

Wildman, Charles   Raye 1951

Wilensky, Elliot   David, Mack 1976

Wiley, Lee   Robison 1974; Washington 1932, 1933; Young, Victor 1932, 1933

Wilhite, Monte   Bryan 1929; David, Mack 1945, 1947

Wilkie, Bernett   Egan 1918

Wilkinson, Dudley   Davis 1928; Hammerstein 1922; Heyman 1932; Mitchell 1922

Willemetz, Albert   DeSylva 1922; Romberg 1933

Willemetz, Andre   Monaco 1924

Willensky, Elliot   David, Mack 1975

Willet, Chappie   Razaf 1944

Williams, Arthur   Sigman 1954

Williams, Barney   Bacharach 1961; David, Mack 1961

Williams, Bert   Buck 1914; Clarke 1911; Johnson, J. Rosamond 1909; Sterling 1910

Williams, C.   Lerner, Sammy 1926; Whiting 1926

Williams, Clarence   Johnson, James P. 1920, 1929, 1930, 1941; Razaf 1924, 1926, 1928, 1929, 1933, 1939; Waller 1923, 1924, 1925, 1926, 1928, 1929, 1936, 1937

Williams, Cootie   Ellington 1939, 1968; Merrill 1946; Mills 1952

Williams, Dick   Cahn 1968

Williams, Doyle   Fain 1957

Williams, Edna   Gilbert 1915

Williams, Flora   Young, Victor 1927

Williams, Gene   Brown, Lew 1926; Leslie 1927

Williams, Hugh   Clare 1930

Williams, J.M.   Parish 1932

Williams, John   Bergman 1966, 1967, 1982, 1988; Mercer 1967, 1973; Russell 1956

Williams, K.   Russell 1957, 1958

Williams, Leroy   Raye 1942; Razaf 1946

Williams, Mary Lou   Lawrence 1940, 1943; Styne 1943; Webster 1940

Williams, Mayo   Raye 1960

Williams, Ned   Mills 1934

Williams, Pat   Evans 1981; Livingston, Jay 1981

Williams, Patrick   Bergman 1978

Williams, Ralph   Donaldson 1925, 1926; Fisher 1919; Kahn 1924, 1925, 1926

Williams, Roger   Coslow 1959

Williams, S. Walter   Razaf 1923

Williams, Sam   DeSylva 1926

Williams, Sande   Evans 1941; Livingston, Jay 1941

Williams, Spencer   Ager 1913; Johnson, Howard 1929; Johnson, James P. 1929, 1930; Koehler 1918, 1928; Magidson 1928; Mills 1924; Razaf 1924, 1928, 1929, 1930, 1931, 1932, 1940, 1945; Stept 1932; Waller 1924, 1925, 1926, 1929, 1932, 1933, 1936, 1937, 1938, 1941, 1945, 1946

Williams, Warwick   Friml 1923

Williamson, G.   Silver 1923

Willing, Henry   Howard, Joseph E. 1923

Willow, Raymond   Carroll 1951

Wills, Jay   Koehler 1926

Wills, Ruth   Mills 1947

Willson, Dixie   Young, Victor 1921, 1923, 1924

Wilson   Young, Joe 1928

Wilson, Al   Motzan 1920

Wilson, Art   Freed, Ralph 1932

Wilson, Carolyn   Kahn 1919

Wilson, Claude   Livingston, Jerry 1943

Wilson, Dan   Razaf 1926

Wilson, Donald   Johnson, Howard 1960

Wilson, Frank   Coots 1957

Wilson, Gerald   Ellington 1966

Wilson, Jack   Revel 1952; Sigman 1979

Wilson, Jerry   Parish 1945

Wilson, Lee   Dubin 1918; Robison 1954, 1955, 1956

Wilson, Lucile   Kahn 1923

Wilson, Mort   Caesar 1928

Wilson, Norris D.   David, Mack 1979

Wilson, Teddy   Adamson 1939; Mills 1935

Wilson, Wesley   Raye 1941

Wimperis, Arthur   Coots 1920; Duke 1926, 1927; Goetz 1920, 1929; Romberg 1924, 1925; Von Tilzer 1907

Winchell, Walter   Fain 1964

Windsor, Peter   Howard, Bart 1948

Winkler, Bernard   Sigman 1953

Winslow, Horatio G.   Howard, Joseph E. 1912

X

Y

Z

Ziegler, Mano   Parish 1950
Zinman, Frances   Washington 1932; Young, Victor 1932
Zippel, David   Coleman 1989
Zirpoli, Pat   Russell 1947, 1956; Sigman 1947
Zitto, Torrie   Cahn 1976
Zoeller, Lou   Friend 1927; McHugh 1953
Zoob, Dave   Johnson, Howard 1921
Zorilla, J.A.   Drake 1941
Zucca, Mana   Gilbert 1938, 1955
Zuro, Josiah   Johnson, Howard 1929; Snyder 1930

SONG INDEX

Citations refer users to songwriter(s) and year(s).

A

(A Mother Tonight Is Rocking) A Cradle in Bethelehem   Bryan 1952

(Nothing Like) A Darn Good Cry   Cohan 1923

(Ev'ry Day Is Like) A Day in Maytime   Robin 1951; Styne 1951

(Doop Doo-De-Doop) A Doodlin' Song   Coleman 1958; Leigh 1958

(It Seems There Was) A Fellow and a Girl   Eliscu 1940; Gorney 1940

A Francesa   Johnson, Howard 1939

(You're) A Handy Thing to Have Around the House   Rome 1959

'A' Is for Aardvark   Spina 1976

A la Hockey   Atteridge 1919; Romberg 1919; Schwartz, Jean 1919

A la Lenox Avenue   Arlen 1932; Koehler 1932

(It's Gonna Be) A Long, Long Winter   Styne 1951

A-1 March   Sondheim 1964

A Most Respectable Married Woman   Cahn 1955; Styne 1955

(On My Mind and) A New Love   Caesar 1928

(I'm on the Wrong Side of) A One-Sided Love Affair   Lawrence 1952

(Love Is) A Private Affair   Livingston, Jay 1959; McHugh 1959

(Ho Hum — Ho Hum) A Quiet Little Place in the Country   Gordon 1953; Myrow 1953

(Someone They Call) A Senior Citizen   Livingston, Jerry 1982

(Build Yourself) A Sky House with a Prayer   Lewis 1955; Meyer 1955

(I'm) A Square in the Social Circle   Evans 1945; Livingston, Jay 1945

(There'll Be) A Yankee Christmas   Alter 1944; Webster 1944

Abadaba Club, The   Caesar 1929

Abbondanza   Loesser 1956

Abbul Babble Gabble   Mills 1940

A-B-C   Leigh 1967

ABC of Traffic (inst.), The   Schwartz, Arthur 1929

A-B-C's of the U.S.A., The   Cohan 1908

Abdication   Romberg 1928

Abe an' Anna   Clare 1953; Snyder 1953

Abe Lincoln Had Just One Country   Hammerstein 1938; Harbach 1938; Kern 1938

Abie and Me and the Baby   Brown, Lew 1915; Von Tilzer 1915

Abie Sings an Irish Song   Berlin 1913

Abie's Irish Rose   Hanley 1923

About a Quarter to Nine   Dubin 1935; Warren 1935

About Face   Lerner, Sammy 1948

Above and Beyond   Coleman 1963; Leigh 1963

Above the Law   Strouse 1993

Above the Stars   Merrill 1962

Above the Tears Beyond the Pain   David, Hal 1978

Abracadabra   Porter 1944

Abraham   Berlin 1942; Sterling 1904; Von Tilzer 1904

Abraham Jefferson Washington Lee (You Ain't Goin' to Pick No Fuss Out of Me)   Sterling 1906; Von Tilzer 1906

Abraham Lincoln (The White House in the Boy)   Davis 1942; Parish 1942

Abram Control Yourself   Brown, Lew 1916

Absence Makes the Heart Grow Fonder   Lewis 1930; Warren 1930; Young, Joe 1930

Absent Minded Flo   Clare 1933; Coots 1933

Absent Minded Me   Merrill 1958, 1964; Styne 1964

Absent Minded Moon   Burke 1941; Van Heusen 1941

Absentminded   Dietz 1934; Schwartz, Arthur 1934

Absent-Minded Maid   Herbert 1897; Smith, Harry B. 1897

Absinthe   Porter 1913

Absinthe Drip, The   Porter 1913

Absinthe Frappe   Herbert 1904

Absolute Don of a Juan, An   Caesar 1920

Absolutely Certain   Caesar 1920

Absotively, Posilutely, Most Emphatic'lly, Yes!   Razaf 1945

Abu Ali the Mouse and Boomalakia Wee   David, Mack 1958; Livingston, Jerry 1958

Academic Fugue   Merrill 1967

Academy Award Song   Sherman 1966

Acapulco Polka   Wrubel 1947

Accent Makes No Difference in the Language of Love, The   Harbach 1911

Ac-cent-tchu-ate the Positive   Arlen 1944; Mercer 1944

Accident, An   Herbert 1906

Accidents Will Happen   Burke 1950; Van Heusen 1950

According to Mr. Grimes   Gershwin, George 1928; Gershwin, Ira 1928

According to the Moonlight   Magidson 1935; Yellen 1935

According to the Stars   Friend 1952

Accusation   Johnson, James P. 1947

Ace in the Hole   Porter 1941; Waller 1934

Aces and Deuces   Brooks 1970

Acey Deucey   Cahn 1956; Van Heusen 1956

Ach, Du Lieber Oom-Pah-Pah   Gershwin, Ira 1953; Lane 1953

Ach Louis   Fisher 1923

Aches, Pains and Strains   Spina 1944

Acre of Heaven   Alter 1954

Acrobatic Rag, The   Buck 1918

Acrobats   Gershwin, George 1927; Gershwin, Ira 1927

Across the Bridge of My Dreams   Kahn 1925

Across the Continent   Jerome 1900; Schwartz, Jean 1900

Across the Garden Wall   Hart 1925; Rodgers 1925

Across the Hills to Georgia   Cobb 1899; Edwards 1899

Across the Meadow and Over the Hill   Drake 1950

Across the River (And Into the Trees)   Silver 1950
Across the River from Sing Sing   Martin 1951
Across the River, 'Round the Bend   Bacharach 1970; David, Hal 1970
Across the Wide Missouri (A-Roll, A-Roll, A-Ree)   Drake 1950
Act I Ensemble Observation   Gershwin, George 1922
Act I Finale   Herbert 1910
Act of Love (L'Amour de Sarah)   Lawrence 1972
Action   Loesser 1937, 1950
Actions Speak Louder than Words   Donaldson 1926
Ad   Sondheim Date Unknown
Ad Ripae Mildewensis Fluminis   Eliscu 1941; Gorney 1941
Ada   David, Mack 1961
Adagio Dan   Duke 1940
Adam and Eve Had a Wonderful Time   Brown, A. Seymour 1913
Adam Never Had Any Mammy, Got Along, Got Along, Got Along   Young, Joe 1934
Adam Was a Happy Married Man   Jerome 1902; Schwartz, Jean 1902
Adam Was the Only Lover   Romberg 1916; Smith, Robert B. 1916
Adantino (Starlight & Sunshine)   Johnson, Howard 1933
Add a Little Wiggle   Ager 1928; Yellen 1928
Add Another Line, Sweet Adeline   Gordon 1930
Addie's at It Again   Lawrence 1964
Addio   Hoffman 1954; Willson 1955
Adelaide   Loesser 1955
Adelaide's Lament   Loesser 1950
Adeste Fidelis   Johnson, Howard 1939
Adieu   Washington 1935; Young, Joe 1930
Adieu, Madame   Egan 1942
Adios   Caesar 1929
Adios Americano   Coslow 1940
Adios Amigo   Freed, Ralph 1962; Livingston, Jerry 1962
Adios Amigos   David, Mack 1941
Adios Argentina   Porter 1935
Adios for Now   Spina 1977
Adios Muchachos   Johnson, Howard 1936
Adios Panama   Parish 1938
Adios Senorita   Evans 1965; Livingston, Jay 1965
Adios-Adieu   Brooks 1948
Adirondacks   Merrill 1971; Styne 1971
Admiral Boom (inst.)   Sherman 1964
Admiration   Mills 1935
Admiration (inst.)   Schwartz, Jean 1930
Adobe   Bergman 1963
Adolescence   Duke 1944
Adolfo and Benito   Caesar 1943
Adopt a Pretty Baby   Atteridge 1917; Romberg 1917
Adorable   Whiting 1933
Adorable Dora   Clare 1928
Adorable You   Bloom 1930; Lewis 1930
Adoration   Brennan 1929
Adored One   Caesar 1930; Gershwin, George 1929; Gershwin, Ira 1929; Gordon 1940; Harbach 1930; Kahn 1929; Romberg 1930
Adrift on a Star   Harburg 1961
Adult Delinquency   Razaf 1957
Advantage of a College Education   Edwards 1905; Smith, Robert B. 1905
Advantages of Floating in the Middle of the Sea, The   Sondheim 1976

Adventure   Comden and Green 1960; Russell 1957; Styne 1960
Adventuring   Leigh 1954
Advertising   Kalmar 1923; Ruby 1923
Advertising for a Baby   Lawrence 1947
Advertising Song (I Believe), The   Rome 1947
Advice to the Lovelorn   Drake 1959
Advice to the Shepherd (Golden Ram)   Bergman 1960
Advice to the Young   Atteridge 1915
Aesop, That Able Fable Man   Berlin 1955
Aesop Was a Very Moral Man   Smith, Harry B. 1916; Smith, Robert B. 1916
Aesthetic Dancing   Harbach 1910
Affable Balding Me   Mercer 1949
Affair   Russell 1957
Affair to Remember, An   Adamson 1957; Warren 1957
Affair with a Stranger (Kiss and Run)   Coslow 1950
Affection   Bryan 1931; Monaco 1931
Affectionate Dan   Blake 1918; Sissle 1918
Affluent Society, The   Lawrence 1964
A-Flat Blues (A-flat Dream) (inst.)   Johnson, James P. 1940
Afraid   Brooks 1952; Willson 1953
Afraid to Dream   Gordon 1937; Revel 1937
Afraid to Fall in Love   Blane 1948; Warren 1948
Afraid to Go Home at All   Smith, Harry B. 1908
Africa   Hammerstein 1927; Hanley 1924; Harbach 1927; Smith, Harry B. 1912; Smith, Robert B. 1912
Africa Shrieks   Eliscu 1931
Africa Smiles No More   Akst 1930; Clarke 1930
African   Brown, Nacio Herb 1927
African Dip   Blake 1921; Sissle 1921
African Etude   Burke 1941; Van Heusen 1941
African Lament   Gilbert 1931
African Lullaby   Mills 1935
African Ripples (inst.)   Waller 1931
African Song (On that Great Civilized Morning), An   Harburg 1964
After a Million Dreams   Donaldson 1930; Leslie 1930
After a Parade (Manhattan Beach)   Bergman 1958
After a Thousand Years   Dubin 1917; Monaco 1917
After a While   Akst 1926; Davis 1926; Egan 1925; Whiting 1925
After All   Arlen 1947; Drake 1952; Koehler 1947
After All I'm in Love with You   Coots 1929; Davis 1929
After All, I'm Only a Schoolgirl   Porter 1929
After All Is Said and Done   Stept 1925
After All These Years   Koehler 1948
After All, You're All I'm After   Heyman 1933; Schwartz, Arthur 1933; Young, Victor 1930
After All You've Been a Pretty Good Pal   Johnson, Howard 1913
After Awhile   Ahlert 1932; Leslie 1932
After Business Hours   Smith, Harry B. 1903
After Business Hours (That Certain Business Begins)   Dubin 1929
After Commencement (inst.)   Blane 1974; Martin 1974
After Dark   Brown, Nacio Herb 1935; Freed, Arthur 1935; Revel 1959
After Every Party   Freed, Arthur 1920
After Every Quarrel   Rose 1925
After Every Wedding There's Always Someone Blue   Caesar 1931; Motzan 1931
After Everything I Doodle, Doodle, Doodle Do   Caesar 1967
After Ev'ry Rainstorm   Lerner, Sammy 1940

After Forty It's Patch, Patch, Patch   Coleman 1972; Fields 1972
After High School   Leigh 1985
After Hours (inst.)   Johnson, James P. 1922
After I Gave My Heart to You   Bryan 1927
(What Can I Say, Dear) After I Say I'm Sorry   Donaldson 1926
After I Took You into My Heart, You Took the Heart out of Me   Dubin 1927
After I've Spent My Best Years on You   Razaf 1940
After Looking at You   Hoffman 1938
After Midnight   Evans 1950; Livingston, Jay 1950; McHugh 1923
After Midnight (inst.)   Revel 1956
After My Blues Came a Bluebird   Gordon 1934
After My Laughter Came Tears   Turk 1928
After One Kiss   Heyman 1962; Mancini 1962
After Sundown   Brown, Nacio Herb 1933; Freed, Arthur 1933
After That I Don't Remember   Parish 1937
After That I Want a Little More   Bryan 1911; Fisher 1911
After the Battle Is Over Then You Can Come Back to Me   Gilbert 1918
After the Clouds Roll By   Clare 1929; Coots 1922
After the Curfew Rings   Kalmar 1924; Ruby 1924
After the Dance (The Bells Ding-Dong) (Der Tanz Is Aus)   Caesar 1931; Motzan 1931
After the First of July   Buck 1918
After the Fox   Bacharach 1966; David, Hal 1966
After the Honeymoon   Berlin 1911; Snyder 1911
After the Rain   Drake 1941; Freed, Ralph 1939; Kahn 1922
After the Rain Is Over   Coots 1950
After the Shadows Comes the Dawn   Davis 1927
After the Show   Fain 1946; Freed, Ralph 1946
After the Storm   Jerome 1922; Schwartz, Jean 1922
After the Sunshine   Atteridge 1915; Friml 1915
After the Tryst   Duke 1944
After the War Is Over (Will There Be Any Home Sweet Home)   Sterling 1918
After Thinking It Over   Davis 1929
After Tonight   Brooks 1946; Friend 1932; Johnson, James P. Date Unknown; Razaf Date Unknown; Yellen 1931
After Tonight Goodbye   Sterling 1915; Von Tilzer 1915
After Twelve O'Clock   Carmichael 1932; Mercer 1932
After We Say Goodnight   Davis 1939
After You   Coslow 1937; David, Mack 1963; DePaul 1958; Drake 1956; Raye 1958
After You Feed the Little Chickens They Want a Little Chicken Feed   Atteridge 1923; Schwartz, Jean 1923
After You Get What You Want You Don't Want It   Berlin 1920
After You, Who?   Porter 1932
After Your Kiss   Brown, Nacio Herb 1930; Eliscu 1930
Afterbeat, The   Mercer 1959
Afterglow, The   David, Mack 1946; Fain 1941
Afterglow, An   Young, Joe 1935
Afternoon   Friml 1913; Harbach 1913
Afternoon Delight   Duke 1968
Afternoon Dream   Lawrence 1953
Afternoon in Amsterdam, An   Heyman 1934
Afternoon Moon   De Lange 1945
Afternoon of Your Years, The   Livingston, Jerry 1973
Afternoon Tea, An   Atteridge 1914; Carroll 1914; Romberg 1914
Afterthoughts   DePaul 1965; Leigh 1965

Afterwards   Johnson, Howard 1939
Against a Crooked Sky   David, Mack 1976
Age of Innocence   Lawrence 1968
Age of Innocence (inst.), The   Schwartz, Arthur 1929
Age of Not Believing, The   Sherman 1971
Age of Rock — Rock of Ages   Styne 1964
Ages Ago   Duke 1957; Webster 1966
Aggie's Sewing Machine Song   Weill 1936
Aggravatin' Papa Don't You Try to Two-Time Me   Turk 1922
Agony   Sondheim 1987
Agreer, The   Merrill 1967
Agua Agua   David, Mack 1940
Ah! Ah! Ah!   Hanley 1922
Ah Ah Ah Ah Baby   Fain 1951
Ah, Ah, Ah (The Song that Haunts My Heart) (Je N'en Connais Pas La Fin)   Rome 1956
Ah, At Last   Smith, Harry B. 1911
Ah' Bin Rich (an' Ah'm Gwynme t'be Rich Agin')   Blane 1945
Ah, But in Dreams   Herbert 1905
Ah, But Is It Love   Gorney 1933; Harburg 1933
Ah, But I've Learned   Coots 1932; Turk 1932
Ah, Cupid, Meddlesome Boy   Herbert 1895; Smith, Harry B. 1895
Ah Fong Low   Porter 1919, 1922
Ah, Go On   Coots 1933; Young, Joe 1933
Ah How I Love Thee   Spina 1955
Ah! Jus' Like You   Gorney 1930; Harburg 1930
Ah Loo Loo   Cahn 1941
Ah Lovely Art, We Worship at Thy Shrine   Smith, Harry B. 1906
Ah Loves Ya!   Arlen 1950; Mercer 1950
Ah, Miss   Sondheim 1979
Ah, Our Germans   Merrill 1990
Ah, Paris!   Sondheim 1971
Ah Still Suits Me   Hammerstein 1936; Kern 1936
Ah! Surprise   Akst 1933; Eliscu 1933
Ah, Sweet Mystery of Life (Dream Melody)   Herbert 1910
Ah the Moon Is Here   Fain 1933; Kahal 1933
Ah to Be Home Again Barabanchik   Loesser 1965
Ah, What Wonderful Things One Little Girl Can Do   Yellen 1917
Ah! Woe Is Me   Herbert 1899
Ah Woo Ah Woo to You   Friend 1936
Ah-Ha!   Clare 1925; Monaco 1925
Ahleff Baze Gimmell Dollid   Schwartz, Jean 1948
Ah-oom   Merrill 1962
Ahoy for a Sailor   Friml 1928
Ahoy There   Drake 1954
A-Hunting We Will Go   Gershwin, George 1928; Gershwin, Ira 1928; Loesser 1937
Ai Paisano   Loesser 1942
Aida McCluskie   Kern 1908
Aimiro   Porter 1928
Ain't Broadway Grand   Adams 1993
Ain't Cha Comin' Out?   Kalmar 1939; Ruby 1939
Ain't Cha Coming Back, Mary Ann to Maryland   Blake 1921; Sissle 1921
Ain't Everything Grand!   Hammerstein 1931; Whiting 1931
Ain't God Good to Indiana   Carmichael 1946
Ain't Gonna Leave My Home   Russell 1960
Ain't Got a Dime to My Name (Ho Ho Hum)   Burke 1942; Van Heusen 1942
Ain't Got No One, Never Had   Kalmar 1924; Ruby 1924

Ain't Got No Tears Left   Comden and Green 1944

Ain't Gwine to Work No More   Johnson, J. Rosamond 1900

Ain't He Cute   Coleman 1999

Ain't He Good Lookin'   Clare 1938

Ain't I Good to You?   Razaf 1929

Ain't I Got Rosie (Ain't Rosie Got Me)   Dubin 1925; Warren 1925

Ain't It a Grand a Glorious Feeling?   Kern 1917

Ain't It a Shame About Mame   Burke 1940; Monaco 1940

Ain't It Awful   Cohan 1908

Ain't It Awful, the Heat?   Weill 1947

Ain't It Crazy to Be Nuts   Hoffman 1949

Ain't It de Truth   Arlen 1943; Harburg 1943

Ain't It Funny What a Difference (Just) a Few Drinks Make?   Buck 1916; Kern 1916

Ain't It Grand in New Orleans?   Brennan 1919

Ain't It Hard To Lose Your Husband   Bryan 1908

Ain't It Nice?   Mills 1934

Ain't It Romantic   Gershwin, George 1926; Gershwin, Ira 1926

Ain't It Sad   Coleman 1960; Leigh 1960

Ain't It the Truth   Arlen 1957; Fields 1932; Harburg 1957; McHugh 1932

Ain't It the Truth Babe   David, Mack 1968

Ain't Love Grand   Caesar 1924; Conrad 1921; DeSylva 1921; Donaldson 1921; Gorney 1924; Robin 1927

Ain't Love the Darndest Thing   Friend 1949

Ain't Love Wonderful   DeSylva 1925

Ain't Misbehavin'   Razaf 1929; Waller 1929

Ain't My Baby Grand?   Brown, Lew 1925; Henderson 1925

Ain't Nature Grand   Mercer 1952; Rome 1952; Rose 1921; Schwartz, Arthur 1952; Schwartz, Jean 1921

Ain't Nothin' but Trouble Trouble   Russell Date Unknown

Ain't She Sweet   Ager 1927; Yellen 1927

Ain't She the Dainty   Woods 1933

Ain't That a Grand and Glorious Feeling   Ager 1927; Yellen 1927

Ain't That a Kick in the Head   Cahn 1960; Van Heusen 1960

Ain't that Always the Way   Atteridge 1915; Carroll 1915; Romberg 1915

Ain't That Just Like a Man   DePaul 1943; Raye 1943

Ain't That Sumpin'   Donaldson 1934; Kahn 1934

Ain't That the Way It Goes   Ahlert 1931; Turk 1931

Ain't There Anyone Here for Love   Adamson 1953; Carmichael 1953

Ain't We Got Fun   Egan 1921; Kahn 1922; Whiting 1921

Ain't We Got Love   Blake 1937

Ain't We Like Two Millionaires — Ain't We   Livingston, Jerry 1933

Ain't Ya Gonna Swim   Gordon 1955

Ain't Ya Kinda Sorry   Davis 1953

Ain't You Ashamed?   Brown, Lew 1921; Mitchell 1921

Ain't You Baby   Ager 1930; Yellen 1930

Ain't You Comin' Back from California   Fisher 1938

Ain't You Coming Back to Dixieland   Egan 1917; Whiting 1917

Ain't You Coming Out Malinda   Sterling 1921; Von Tilzer 1921

Ain't You Glad You Found Me   Williams 1907

Ain't You Got Nothin' to Say   Jerome 1906; Schwartz, Jean 1906

Ain'tcha   Gordon 1929

Ain't-Cha Glad   Razaf 1933; Waller 1933

Aintcha Got Music?   Johnson, James P. 1932; Razaf 1932

Ain'tcha Kinda Sorry Now?   Ager 1932

Air Force Takes Command, The   Washington 1955; Young, Victor 1955

Air Minded   Brown, Lew 1930; DeSylva 1930; Henderson 1930

Air Transport Command   Washington 1943

Air-Minded Executive   Mercer 1940

Al Fresco   Arlen 1959; Herbert 1904; Mercer 1959

Alabam'   Williams 1909

Alabama Barbecue   Coots 1936; Davis 1936

Alabama Christmas   Willson 1954

Alabama Jubilee   Yellen 1915

Alabama Labor Day Parade   Razaf 1928

Alabama Man   Gordon 1933; Revel 1933

Alabama Stomp   Johnson, James P. 1926

Alabamy Beauty Shop   Ahlert 1935; Young, Joe 1935

Alabamy Bound   DeSylva 1924; Henderson 1924

Alabamy Cradle Song   Kahn 1925

Alabamy Home   Ellington 1937

Alabamy Snow   Rose 1929

Alacazam   Sterling 1915; Von Tilzer 1915

Aladdin   Atteridge 1916; Porter 1958; Romberg 1916

Aladdin's Daughter   Burke 1942; Van Heusen 1942, 1946

Alaska and a South Sea Island   Young, Victor 1924

Alaskans (Gold Fever), The   David, Mack 1959; Livingston, Jerry 1959

Albany   Jerome 1905; Schwartz, Jean 1905

Albert the Great   Gordon 1948

Albertina's Beautiful Hair   Arlen 1968

Album of My Dreams, The   Arlen 1929

Album Song   Arlen 1934; Gershwin, Ira 1934; Harburg 1934

Alcazar   Smith, Harry B. 1926

Alderberan   Coleman 1975

Al-Di-La   Drake 1962

A-L-E   Jerome 1909; Schwartz, Jean 1909

Ale, Ale, Ale   Hart 1925; Rodgers 1925

Alessandro the Wise   Gershwin, Ira 1945; Weill 1945

Alexander   Sterling 1904; Von Tilzer 1904

Alexander and His Clarinet   Berlin 1910; Snyder 1910

Alexander's Back in Town   Razaf 1938

Alexander's Bagpipe Band   Berlin 1912; Goetz 1912

Alexander's Band Is Back in Dixieland   Yellen 1918

Alexander's Blitztime Band   Hart 1943

Alexander's Got a Jazz Band Now   DeSylva 1917

Alexander's Jazz Band   Donaldson 1917

Alexander's Ragtime Band   Berlin 1911

Alfa Romeo   Styne 1964

Alfie   Bacharach 1966; David, Hal 1966

Algerian Girl   Atteridge 1917; Romberg 1917

Algy   Herbert 1909

Ali Baba   Coots 1923

Ali Baba Babies, The   Harbach 1926; Kern 1926

Ali Baba (Be My Baby)   Evans 1953; Livingston, Jay 1953

Alibi Baby   Dietz 1923; Heyman 1937

Alice   Kahal 1927; Snyder 1927

Alice in Wonderland   Berlin 1916; Fain 1951; Kern 1914; Robin 1933; Smith, Harry B. 1914

Alice Where Art Thou   Johnson, Howard 1939

Alike, Alike   Cahn 1980

Alimony Club   Conrad 1935; Mitchell 1935

Alimony Jail   Coleman 1988

Alimony Rap   Coleman 1988

Ali-Up   Hammerstein 1926; Harbach 1926; Romberg 1926

Alive and Kicking   Blane 1963; Martin 1963

Alive at Last   Duke 1963

All   Robison 1958

All a Dream   Styne 1958

All Aboard   Arlen 1932; Atteridge 1914; Eliscu 1929; Goetz 1913; Koehler 1932

All Aboard for Blanket Bay   Sterling 1910; Von Tilzer 1910

All Aboard for Broadway   Cohan 1906

All Aboard for Dixieland   Friml 1913; Harbach 1913; Yellen 1913

All Aboard for Dreamland   Sterling 1904; Von Tilzer 1904

All Aboard for Dreamland, Baby Kiss Mama and Papa Goodnight   Baer 1932; Young, Joe 1932

All Aboard for Georgia   Razaf 1939

All Aboard for Heaven, All Aboard for Home Sweet Home   Rose 1925

All Aboard for Monkey Town   Meyer 1910

All Aboard for Paris   Smith, Harry B. 1925

All Aboard for Times Square   Buck 1927

All Aboard the Mine Train   Sherman 1961

All Aboard the Navy   Dubin 1935; Warren 1935

All About Love   Evans 1952; Gordon 1956; Livingston, Jay 1952; Myrow 1956

All Across the Nation   Brooks 1958

All Alone   Berlin 1924; Von Tilzer 1911

All Alone in a City Full of Girls   Romberg 1916

All Alone in a Crowd   Conrad 1924

All Alone (inst.)   Waller 1923

All Alone Monday   Kalmar 1926, 1927, 1930; Ruby 1926, 1927, 1930

All Alone on Broadway, Blase Broadway   Gilbert 1912

All Alone Together   Dubin 1930

All Alone with You in a Little Rendezvous   Lewis 1924; Snyder 1924; Young, Joe 1924

All American   Brennan 1940; Meyer 1930; Mitchell 1930; Snyder 1940

All American Swing, The   Gordon 1938; Revel 1938

All Around the Christmas Tree   Coots 1955

All Around the Clock   Hoffman 1958

All Around the Town   Sherman 1995

All Around the World   Burke 1946; Van Heusen 1946

All at Once   Cahn 1969; Gershwin, Ira 1945; Hart 1937; Rodgers 1937; Weill 1945

All at Once You Love Her   Hammerstein 1955; Rodgers 1955

All Because of You   Stept 1928

All By My Lonesome Blues   Coslow 1921

All By My Ownsome   Dubin 1927

All By Myself   Berlin 1921

All Danced Out   David, Hal 1960

All Dark People   Hart 1937; Rodgers 1937

All Day   Burke 1956; Heyman 1937; Robin 1955; Styne 1955

All Day Singin' and Dinner on the Ground   Hoffman 1952

All Decked Out   Brown, Lew 1927; Friend 1927

All Dolled Up   Strouse 1989

All Done All Through   Cahn 1942; Styne 1942

All Dressed Up and No Place to Go   Heyman 1936

All Dressed Up in a Tailor Made   Cohan 1918

All Dressed Up in Rhythm   Bullock 1937

All Dressed Up to Go Dreamin'   Webster 1943

All Dressed Up to Go Dreaming   Revel 1943

All Dressed Up with No One to Love   Gordon 1938; Revel 1938

All Ears   Razaf 1949

All er Nothin   Hammerstein 1943; Rodgers 1943

All for a Man Whose Love Was Gold   Cobb 1900; Edwards 1900

All for Charity   Hammerstein 1923; Youmans 1923

All for Him   Lerner, Alan Jay 1951; Loewe 1951

All for Love   Coleman 1979

All for One?   DePaul 1941; Raye 1941

All for One and One for All   Cahn 1964; Friml 1928; Lawrence 1938; Van Heusen 1964

All for the Love of a Girl   Gorney 1935; Leslie 1915; Meyer 1915; Young, Joe 1915

All for the Love of Gold   Robison 1959; Woods 1959

All for the Sake of a Girl   Herbert 1914; Smith, Robert B. 1914

All for Thee   Herbert 1897; Smith, Harry B. 1897

All for You   Davis 1921; Freed, Arthur 1925; Herbert 1915; Johnston 1949; Sondheim 1954; Washington 1935

All Full of Empty   Schwartz, Jean 1948

All Full of Ginger   Smith, Robert B. 1915

All Full of Talk   Kern 1916

All Glass   Adams 1972; Strouse 1972

All God's Chillun' Got Rhythm   Kahn 1937

All Hail the Political Honeymoon   Weill 1938

All Hail to Danville High (Dan-Dan-Danville High)   Blane 1948; Warren 1948

All Hail to Midwest State   Cahn 1952; Duke 1952

All Hail to the General   Hammerstein 1926; Harbach 1926; Romberg 1926

All Hail to You, Marines!   Herbert 1918

All Hallowe'en   Herbert 1912

All Hands on Deck   Evans 1961; Livingston, Jay 1961

All He Does Is Follow Them Around   Clarke 1914

All His Children   Bergman 1971; Mancini 1971

All I Bring to You Is Love   Berlin 1977

All I Can Do Is Just Love You   Clarke 1915; Monaco 1915

All I Can See Is You   Johnson, Howard 1930

All I Crave Is More of Life   Herbert 1910

All I Do Is Beat This Gol-Durn Drum   Coslow 1945

All I Do Is Dream of You   Brown, Nacio Herb 1934, 1935; Freed, Arthur 1934

All I Do Is Follow Butterflies   Dixon 1929; Woods 1929

All I Do Is Sit and Look On   Sterling 1922; Von Tilzer 1922

All I Do Is Think of You   Brown, Nacio Herb 1936

All I Get Is Consolation   Ahlert 1919; Leslie 1919

All I Give 'em's the Air   Carroll 1920

All I Have Is a Love Song   Yellen 1957

All I Have Is You   Mills 1954

All I Know Is What I Feel   David, Hal 1976

All I Need Is a Handshake   Cahn 1980; Strouse 1980

All I Need Is a Little More Sleep   Coots 1950

All I Need Is the Girl   Sondheim 1959; Styne 1959

All I Need Is You   Davis 1942; Parish 1942

All I Need Is Your Love   Coslow 1931

All I Owe Ioway   Hammerstein 1945; Rodgers 1945

All I Remember Is You   De Lange 1939; Van Heusen 1939

All I Want from You Is You   Howard, Joseph E. 1919

All I Want in the Wide, Wide World Is You   Smith, Robert B. 1908

All I Want in the Wide, Wide, World Is You, Just You   Edwards 1907

All I Want in This World (Is You)   Robison 1957

All I Want Is a Home   Hammerstein 1933

All I Want Is a Lolli-Lollipop   Razaf 1955

All I Want Is a Lullaby   Buck 1927

All I Want Is a Seat (To See the Beatles)   Cahn 1964

All I Want Is Just One   Robin 1932; Whiting 1932

All I Want Is Just One Girl   Robin 1930; Whiting 1930

All I Want Is Just Your Love   Von Tilzer 1927

All I Want Is My Black Baby Back   Cobb 1898; Edwards 1898

All I Want Is Not to Want   Strouse Date Unknown

All I Want Is One Loving Smile from You-oo-oo   Meyer 1908

All I Want Is You   Akst 1927; Clare 1927; Davis 1927; Kern 1906; Leslie 1944; Silver 1952

All I Want Is You for Christmas   Coots 1957

All I Want to Do (Is Be with You)   Donaldson 1926

All I Want To Do Is Love You   Brown, Nacio Herb 1941; Freed, Ralph 1941

All I Want to Do Is Sing   Brooks 1945

All I Want to Do-Do-Do Is Dance   Dubin 1929

All in a Lifetime   Russell 1974

All in a Little Dance   Atteridge 1913

All in a Short Half Hour   Hanley 1920

All in Favor Say 'Aye'   Friend 1939

All in Fun   Hammerstein 1939; Kern 1939

All in God's Good Time   Robison 1968; Silver 1953

All in the Golden Afternoon   Fain 1951

All in the Wearing   Cohan 1922

All Is Forgiven (And All Is Forgotten)   Loesser 1953

All Is Forgiven Baby Come Home   Coots 1934; Parish 1934

All Is Well   Akst 1956; Gilbert 1943; Razaf 1948

All' Italiana   Lawrence 1961

All I've Got Is Me   Strouse 1989

All I've Got to Get Now Is My Man   Porter 1940

All Kinds of People   Hammerstein 1955; Rodgers 1955

All Lanes Must Reach a Turning   Dietz 1924; Kern 1924

All Men   Livingston, Jerry 1960

All Men Have Their Troubles   Herbert 1900; Smith, Harry B. 1900

All Mine   Evans 1970; Livingston, Jay 1970

All Mixed Up   Clare 1938

All Mucked Up   Mercer 1974

(They're) All My Boys   Cohan 1922

All My Girls   Harbach 1908

All My Hopes, All My Dreams, All My Prayers   David, Hal 1962

All My Life   Akst 1918, 1923, 1930; Clare 1930; Davis 1923, 1930; Evans 1952; Livingston, Jay 1952; Magidson 1936; Mitchell 1936, 1942; Robin 1927; Stept 1936, 1942

All My Life, I'll Make You Happy, Dear   Brown, Lew Date Unknown; DeSylva Date Unknown; Henderson Date Unknown

All My Life I've Been a Slave   Kalmar 1938; Ruby 1938

All My Love   Akst 1947; Caesar 1947; Parish 1950; Spina 1977

All My Saturday Nights   Cahn 1994; Coleman 1994

All My Sweeties Rolled into One   Carroll Date Unknown

All My Tomorrows   Cahn 1959; Van Heusen 1959

All My Tomorrows (For One Yesterday)   Razaf Date Unknown

All My Victories Are Losses   Razaf Date Unknown

All Night Long   Cohan 1923; Johnson, James P. 1933

All Night Long in Paris   Coleman 1959; Leigh 1959

All of a Sudden   Pollack 1937; Woods 1932; Yellen 1937

All of a Sudden My Heart Sings   Rome 1945

All of My Life   Berlin 1944; Comden and Green 1960; Oakland 1968; Styne 1960

All of No Man's Land Is Ours   Blake 1919; Sissle 1919

All of the Time   David, Mack 1966; Woods 1928

All of Them Was Friends of Mine   Gershwin, Ira 1924

All of You   Porter 1955

All on Account of a Schmoo   Robison 1949

All on Account of a Strawberry Sundae   Dixon 1934; Wrubel 1934

All on Account of the War   Hanley 1916

All One Large Family (At Christmas)   Sherman 1984

All or Nothing at All   Lawrence 1940

All Out for Freedom   Arlen 1944; Koehler 1944

All Out Moon Man   Donaldson 1941

All Over Nothing At All   Lawrence 1937

All Over the Country   Drake 1954

All Over the World   Brown, Lew 1952; Henderson 1952

All Over Town   Gershwin, George 1923

All Over You   Bryan 1913

All Pull Together   Caesar 1922

All Pulling Together (inst.)   Revel 1960

All Quiet on the Old Back Porch   Wrubel 1944

All Quiet on the Western Front   Mills 1929; Parish 1929

All Right for You   Rainger 1938; Robin 1938

All She Did Was This   Youmans 1924

All Suit, No Man   Coots 1946

All that a Girl Should Be   Livingston, Jerry 1963

All that He'd Want Me to Be   Lane 1979; Lerner, Alan Jay 1979

All That I Am   Van Heusen 1964

All That I Am I Owe to You Angel Mother of Mine   Johnson, Howard 1917; Monaco 1917

All That I Do   Livingston, Jerry 1962

All That I Dreamed He Would Be   Lane 1985

All that I Ever Get Is Sympathy, All that I Want Is Love   Fisher 1932

All That I Need Is a Hallway   Silver 1919

All That I Need Is You   Baer 1921

All that I Need to Know Is that You Come from Dixie   DeSylva 1919

All That I Want   Hammerstein 1920; Harbach 1920

All That I Want Is Somebody to Love Me   Kern 1916; Smith, Harry B. 1916

All that I Want Is You   Monaco 1917

All That I'm Asking Is Sympathy   Davis 1929

All That Is Mine Is Yours   Yellen 1933

All that Love Went to Waste   Cahn 1972

All that Meat and No Potatoes   Waller 1941

All the Boys Keep Looking Down   Von Tilzer 1926

All the Boys Love Mary   Sterling 1920

All the Colors of the Rainbow   Blane 1956; Martin 1956

All the Comforts of Home   Atteridge 1919; Carroll 1919

All the Elks and Masons   Arlen 1934; Gershwin, Ira 1934; Harburg 1934

All the Girls Think I'm Wonderful   Fisher 1925

All the Grey Haired Men   Russell Date Unknown

All the Irish   Cohan 1972

All the King's Horses   Dietz 1930

All the Knicker Knockers Wear Knickerbockers Now   Egan 1923; Kahn 1923; Whiting 1923

All the Latin I Know Is "Si Si"   Pollack 1944

All the Little Glooms Start Dancing   Atteridge 1920

All the Livelong Day (And the Livelong Night)   Gershwin, George 1964; Gershwin, Ira 1964

All the Love in the World   Adams 1959, 1962; Parish 1947; Sigman 1966; Strouse 1959, 1962

All the Luck in the World   Duke 1959

All the Quakers Are Shoulder Shakers Down in Quaker Town   Kalmar 1919; Leslie 1919

All the Sad Young Man   Livingston, Jerry 1962; Webster 1962

All the Things I've Missed   Howard, Joseph E. 1937

All the Things You Are   Hammerstein 1939; Kern 1939
All the Time   Evans 1958; Fain 1946; Fields 1939; Freed, Ralph 1946; Livingston, Jay 1958; Magidson 1958; Schwartz, Arthur 1939
All the Time and Ev'rywhere   Merrill 1952
All the Time Is Loving Time   Caesar 1927
All the Way   Cahn 1957; Styne 1943; Van Heusen 1957
All the Way for Jesus   Razaf 1952
All the Way from Oklahoma to the Land of La Paloma   Leslie 1930
All the Way Home   Leigh 1971; Styne 1963
All the Way to Paradise (And Back Again)   Bacharach 1976; David, Hal 1976
All the While   DeSylva 1919
All the World Is Dancing Mad   Jerome 1905; Schwartz, Jean 1905
All the World Is Lonely for a Little Black-Bird   Razaf 1927
All the World Is Madly Prancing   Atteridge 1912
All the World Is Swaying   Kern 1918
All the World Know's I'm in Love with You   Atteridge 1928
All the World Loves a Lover   Smith, Harry B. 1912; Smith, Robert B. 1912
All the World Will Be Jealous of Me   Dubin 1917
All the World Will Smile Again After Tomorrow   Hanley 1932
All the World's in Love   Bryan 1910
All the Wrongs You Done to Me   Blake 1924; Sissle 1924
All These People I Have Wronged   Hammerstein 1925; Harbach 1925; Kern 1925
All Things Are Not What They Seem   Cobb 1900; Edwards 1900
All Things Are Passing   Clare 1946
All Things Bright and Beautiful   Sondheim 1971
All This and Heaven Too   De Lange 1940; Van Heusen 1940
All This is Home   David, Mack 1956; Livingston, Jerry 1956
All This Is My Love   Cahn 1960; Young, Victor 1960
All This Thunder and Lightnin'   Robison 1940
All Those in Favor of Swing Say Aye   Davis 1939
All Through the Day   Hammerstein 1946; Kern 1946
All Through the Night   Mercer 1940; Porter 1934; Schwartz, Arthur 1942
All Thru the Night   Pollack 1928
All Tied Up   Carmichael 1950; Mercer 1950
All to Myself   Gershwin, George 1922; Gershwin, Ira 1922
All Together   Davis 1951
All Too Soon   Ellington 1940; Sigman 1940
All Washed Up   Dubin 1934; Warren 1934
All We Need Is Love   Cahn 1992; Lane 1992
All Wet   McHugh 1947
All with You   Friend 1960
All Woman   Adams 1960; Leigh 1973; Strouse 1960
All Work No Play   Brooks 1958
All Wrong   Kahn 1923
All Year Long   Sondheim Date Unknown
All Year Round   Davis 1964; Romberg 1924
All You Can Do Is Tell Me You Love Me   Lerner, Alan Jay 1971
All You Gotta Do Is Tell Me   Merrill 1972; Styne 1972
All You Have to Do Is Knock on Wood   Brooks 1958
All You Have to Do Is Wait   Coleman 1989
All You Need Is a Girl   Kern 1924
All You Need Is a Quarter   Comden and Green 1960; Styne 1960
All You Need to Be a Star   Hart 1920; Rodgers 1920
All You Want to Do Is Dance   Burke 1937; Johnston 1937

All Your Own Am I   Herbert 1911; Smith, Harry B. 1911
All Yours   Heyman 1963
Alla Breve Song (inst.)   Kern 1956
Allah   Ahlert 1919; Leslie 1919
Allah Jazz   Atteridge 1920
Allah's Holiday   Friml 1914; Harbach 1914
All-American Man   Fain 1946
Allan Owen Theme   Oakland 1954
All-Army Team, The   Stept 1951
Allay Up   Hanley 1921
Al-lee-o Al-lee-ay   David, Hal 1952
Allegheny Al   Hammerstein 1937; Kern 1937
Allegheny Fiddler (Fiddle-Didle-Do)   Drake 1951
Allegheny Moon   Hoffman 1956
Allegiance to the Flag   Wrubel 1943
Allegretto Grazioso (inst.)   Kern 1956
Allegro   Hammerstein 1947; Rodgers 1947
Alley Oop   Evans 1955; Livingston, Jay 1955
Alley-Up   Dixon 1923
Allez-Up   Hart 1926; Rodgers 1926
Allez-Vous-En (Go Away)   Porter 1953
Allied High Command, The   Weill 1936
Allies   Herbert 1915
Alligator and the Crocodile, The   Dubin 1943; Monaco 1943
Alligator Crawl   Razaf 1937; Waller 1937
Alligator Crawl (inst.)   Waller 1927
Allo, Allo, Allo   Cahn 1962
Allow Me to Present Myself to You   Lawrence 1938
All's Fair in Love and War   Dubin 1936; Smith, Harry B. 1930, 1932; Warren 1936
All's Well   Dietz 1932; Rainger 1939; Robin 1939; Schwartz, Arthur 1932
All's Well (In Coronado By the Sea)   Coslow 1935; Whiting 1935
All's Well that Ends Well   Conrad 1927; Coslow 1927
All's Well with the World   Harbach 1931; Kern 1931
Alma Mammy   Whiting 1929
Alma Mater   Arlen 1931; Bacharach 1967; Kalmar 1926; Oakland 1938; Ruby 1926; Styne 1941, 1956; Yellen 1931
Alma Mater, Hail to Thee (Glaudemus Igitur)   Bergman 1958
Alma Mater Song of the Catholic University of America (inst.)   Herbert 1921
Alma Mater, We're with You   Johnson, Howard 1930
Almanac Covers, The   Eliscu 1929
Almighty God   Ellington 1972
Almost   Blane 1960; Cahn 1980; Lawrence 1964; Lerner, Sammy 1939; Martin 1960; Oakland 1939
Almost a Love Song   Mancini 1995
Almost in Your Arms   Evans 1958; Livingston, Jay 1958
Almost Like Being in Love   Lerner, Alan Jay 1947; Loewe 1947
Aloha   Brennan 1930; Friml 1930; Mitchell 1919
Aloha Lowdown   DePaul 1941; Raye 1941
Aloha Oahu   Mills 1928
Aloha Oe   Johnson, Howard 1939
Aloha State March, The   Willson 1960
Aloma of the South Seas   Loesser 1941
Alomo   Brennan 1927
Alone   Brown, Nacio Herb 1935; Freed, Arthur 1935; Hoffman 1946; Livingston, Jerry 1946
Alone Again   Woods 1935
Alone at a Table for Twelve   Spina 1977
Alone at Last   Kahn 1925; Kern 1913, 1914, 1915; Smith, Harry B. 1913, 1914; Young, Victor 1952

Alone at Night   Duke 1963

Alone Beside the Lonesome River   Johnson, Howard 1933

Alone in a Corner   Yellen 1931

Alone in a Crowd   Loewe 1942

Alone in My Own Little House   Blane 1969

Alone in the Dark   Dixon 1933

Alone in the Light   Merrill 1993; Styne 1993

Alone in the World   Merrill 1962; Styne 1962

Alone in Your Class, Little Girl   Loesser Date Unknown

Alone (My Lover)   Friml 1927

Alone on a Lonesome Trail   Lawrence 1955

Alone on Life's Highway   Romberg 1925; Smith, Harry B. 1925

Alone on Saturday Night   Davis 1928; Rose 1928

Alone on the Lonesome   Lawrence 1952; Young, Victor 1952

Alone on the Range   David, Mack 1934

Alone (The Whaling Widows)   Duke 1950; Rome 1950

Alone Together   Dietz 1932; Schwartz, Arthur 1932

Alone Too Long   Fields 1954; Russell 1969; Schwartz, Arthur 1954

Alone with Love   Blake 1952; Sissle 1952

Alone with Me   Howard, Bart 1955

Alone with My Dreams   Kahn 1930

Alone with My Tears   Parish 1933

Alone with Only Dreams   Brown, Lew 1928; DeSylva 1928; Henderson 1928

Alone with You   Dietz 1946; Howard, Joseph E. 1919; Mitchell 1938; Pollack 1938; Porter 1918

Along about Evenin'   Pollack 1946

Along About Now   Sigman 1967

Along Came Georgia Lee   Parish 1943

Along Came Henry   Styne 1965

Along Came Joe   Bacharach 1961; David, Hal 1961

Along Came Pete (If It Wasn't for Pete)   Stept 1936; Washington 1936

Along Came Ruth   Berlin 1914, 1926

Along Came Sweetness   Dixon 1928; Warren 1928

Along Came You   Rose 1925

Along Fraternity Row   Lawrence 1938

Along Life's Highway   Howard, Joseph E. 1907

Along Miami Shore   Warren 1926

Along the Broadway Trail   Coslow 1937

Along the Gypsy Trail   Stept 1926

Along the Mississippi Shore   Donaldson 1915; Johnson, Howard 1915

Along the Navajo Trail   De Lange 1945

Along the Prado   Coots 1961

Along the Rialto   Fisher 1915

Along the Rio Grande   Caesar 1924; Conrad 1924; Harbach 1924

Along the Road to Love   Brennan 1927

Along the Rocky Road to Dublin   Young, Joe 1915

Along the Santa Fe Trail   Dubin 1940, 1944

Along the Trail where the Blue Grass Grows in the Hills of Old Kentucky   Friend 1919

Along the Way   Merrill 1965; Sigman 1957; Styne 1965

Along the Way that Leads to Yesterday   Bloom 1931; Clare 1931

Along the Way to Waikiki   Kahn 1917; Whiting 1917

Along the Winding Road   Hammerstein 1941; Romberg 1941

Along with Me   Rome 1946

Aloyisious I Love You   Fisher 1920

Aloysius (Al-o-wish-us)   Meyer 1924; Turk 1924

Alpha, Beta, Pi   Harbach 1933; Kern 1933

Alpha Ro Song   Loesser 1940

Alphabet of Love Begins and Ends with You, The   Mercer 1932

Alphabet Song, The   Cahn 1976; Johnson, Howard 1934; Lane 1976

Alpine Girl, The   Goetz 1913

Alpine Horn (Tyrolean Song), The   Herbert 1899; Smith, Harry B. 1899

Alpine Rose   Porter 1928

Alright Already   Parish 1954

Alt Wein   Dietz 1935; Schwartz, Arthur 1935

Alter of Love   Webster 1983

Alter of the Angels, The   Livingston, Jerry 1954; Webster 1954

Alteutscher Leibersreim   Jerome 1907; Schwartz, Jean 1907

Although I Dropped $100,000   Sherman 1962

Although I'm So Demure   Smith, Harry B. 1903

Altogether Too Fond of You   Porter 1918

Always   Berlin 1925

Always Alone   Davis 1922

Always, Always in My Dreams   Merrill 1953

Always Be a Gentleman   Hammerstein 1935; Romberg 1935

Always but All Ways   Robin 1930

Always Comb Your Hair   Styne 1940

Always Do As People Say You Should   Herbert 1898; Smith, Harry B. 1898

Always Dreaming of You   Silver 1921

Always Go in Without Knocking   Cobb 1901; Edwards 1901

Always Goodbye (Toujours Adieu)   Hanley 1931

Always Help Your Mommy   Styne 1940

Always Hold Your Umbrella High   Caesar 1943

Always in All Ways   Whiting 1930

Always in My Dreams   Yellen 1921

Always in My Heart, Forever on My Mind   Coots 1932; Turk 1932

Always in the Dark   Johnson, Howard 1930

Always Keep a Fellow Guessing, If You Want His Love   Lewis 1911

Always Keep Me in Your Heart   Egan 1931

Always Keep on Smiling (inst.)   Revel 1959

Always Leave 'em Laughing (When You Say Goodbye)   Cohan 1903

Always Leave Them Asking for More   Loesser Date Unknown

Always Leave Them Laughing   Cahn 1949

Always Look for a Rainbow   Johnson, Howard 1924

Always Mademoiselle   Lerner, Alan Jay 1969

Always Make Allowances for Love   Smith, Harry B. 1900

Always One Day More (Death of a Ballad)   Leigh 1956

Always Remember   Adamson 1944

Always Say Please   Styne 1940

Always Say Thank You   Styne 1940

(There's) Always Something There to Remind Me   Bacharach 1964; David, Hal 1964

Always Take a Girl Named Daisy ('Cause Daisies Won't Tell)   Bryan 1913; Lewis 1913; Meyer 1913

Always Take Mother's Advice   Johnson, Howard 1939

Always the Lady   Gordon 1946; Myrow 1946

Always the Same   Baer 1930; Berlin 1963; Coslow 1924; Gilbert 1930; Romberg 1924

Always Together   Atteridge 1912

Always Tomorrow   Russell 1977

Always Treat Her Like a Baby   Berlin 1914

Always True to the Navy   Adamson 1945; McHugh 1945

Always True to You in My Fashion   Porter 1948

Always You   Hammerstein 1920; Lerner, Sammy 1948

Always You Alone   Young, Joe 1947

Am an Is, A   David, Mack 1961

Am I a Wife, Widow or Maid?   Smith, Harry B. 1908

Am I a Wizard   Herbert 1895; Smith, Harry B. 1895

Am I Awake or Am I Dreaming   Razaf 1932

Am I Blue?   Akst 1929; Clarke 1929

Am I Dreaming?   Baer 1936

Am I Gonna Have Trouble with You   Fain 1936

Am I Gonna See You Some More?   Donaldson 1930

Am I in Another World?   Koehler 1938

Am I in Love   Baer 1955; Brooks 1952; Dubin 1937; Porter 1953; Warren 1937

Am I in Love Again?   Leigh 1973

Am I My Brother's Keeper   Razaf 1952

Am I On?   Razaf 1936

Am I on a Wild Goose Chase?   Ahlert 1941

Am I the Lucky One   Lane 1938; Loesser 1938

Am I the Only One Who Cares for Me?   Bryan 1936

Am I to Blame?   Baer 1934; Friml 1917; Lewis 1934

Am I to Wish Her Love   Merrill 1993; Styne 1993

Am I too Fresh?   Hanley 1932

Am I Wasting My Dreams on You   Dixon 1941

Am I Wasting My Time on You   Johnson, Howard 1926

Am I You're Once-in-a-While   Hoffman 1930; Silver 1930

Amanda   Rome 1968

Amarillo   Hart 1941; Rodgers 1941

Amarillo (inst.)   Robison 1926

Amarillys at the Piano   Willson 1957

Amaryllis   Bergman 1983

Amateur Entertainer, The   Smith, Harry B. 1900

Amazing   Ellington 1966; Razaf 1940

Amazing what Love Can Do   Carmichael 1940; Mercer 1940

Amazons, The   Razaf Date Unknown

Ambassador's Polka, The   Willson 1960

Amber Club, The   Atteridge 1914

Amber Threads Tied in Blue   Johnson, Howard 1939

Ambiguous Means I Love You   Mercer 1951

Ambition   Comden and Green 1960; Styne 1960

Amble on Alone   Egan 1910

Ambolyn   Lane 1952; Robin 1952

Ameer, The   Herbert 1899

Amen to That   Friend 1965

America   Brown, Lew 1927; Friend 1927; Smith, Harry B. 1927; Sondheim 1957

America Calling   Willson 1941

America Did It Again   Koehler 1927

America Don't Know How Any More   Coleman 1979

America, Here's Looking at You   Caesar 1951

America Here's My Boy   Sterling 1917

America, He's for You   Sterling 1918

America I Love You   Leslie 1915

America Is   David, Hal 1985

America Is Bathed in Sunlight   Coleman 1979

America Marches On   Adamson 1940

America Needs You Like a Mother, Would You Turn Your Mother Down   Clarke 1917; Schwartz, Jean 1917

America Never Took Water and America Never Will   Brennan 1919; Edwards 1919

America, Spirit of 76 (oral only)   Adams 1974; Strouse 1974

America, This Wonderland   Leigh 1976

American Barcarolle (inst.)   Warren 1940

American Beauty   Bryan 1918; Leslie 1918

American Beauty Rose   David, Hal 1950; Hart 1926; Rodgers 1926

American Beauty Rose, An   Friml 1912; Harbach 1912

American Bolero (inst.)   Brown, Nacio Herb 1935

American Boy   Dubin 1943; Monaco 1943

American Cannes   Adamson 1948; McHugh 1948

American Couple (inst)   Rodgers 1937

American Dancers   Atteridge 1923; Schwartz, Jean 1923

American Dollars   Comden and Green 1974; Styne 1974

American Dreaming   Lerner, Alan Jay 1976

American Express, The   Porter 1929

American Flag (inst.), The   Young, Victor 1955

American Girl in Paris, The   Smith, Harry B. 1906

American Heiress, The   Smith, Robert B. 1912

American Heiress, An   Herbert 1905; Smith, Harry B. 1903, 1905

American Humoresque (inst.)   Romberg 1939

American Idea, The   Cohan 1908

American in Paris Blues Ballet, An   Gershwin, George 1929; Kahn 1929

American Jazz   Atteridge 1922, 1924; Romberg 1924; Schwartz, Jean 1924

American Lullaby (inst.)   Romberg 1936

American Maxixe, The   Atteridge 1914

American Millionaire, An   Howard, Joseph E. 1910

American Monte Carlo, The   Jerome 1909; Schwartz, Jean 1909

American Music 'Tis Better than Old Parsifal to Me   Herbert 1905; Smith, Harry B. 1905

American Plan   Gorney 1940

American Primitive   Gorney 1949

American Punch, The   Porter 1922

American Ragtime, The   Cohan 1908

American Revue Girls   Conrad 1926

American Rhapsody, The   Hoffman 1958

American Serenade   Herbert 1917

American Serenade (inst.), An   Alter 1942

American Soldier   Sigman 1946

(A Real) American Tune   Brown, Lew 1928; DeSylva 1928; Henderson 1928

American Waltz, The   Parish 1940

American Way, The   Schwartz, Arthur 1981

Americana   Conrad 1936; Magidson 1936

Americana, U.S.A.   Goetz 1952

Ameri-can-can, The   Caesar 1928

Americans All Drink Coffee   Porter 1940

Americans Are Coming, The   Hammerstein 1931; Romberg 1931

Americans Are Here, The   Brown, Lew 1928; DeSylva 1928; Henderson 1928

America's Answer   Egan 1919; Whiting 1919

America's Fighting Back   Atteridge 1917; Motzan 1917; Romberg 1917

America's Popular Song (Tune)   Atteridge 1919; Romberg 1919; Schwartz, Jean 1919

Americonga   Adamson 1940

Amigo   Dietz 1936; Schwartz, Arthur 1936

Amigo Mio   Burke 1934; Spina 1934

Amigo We Go Riding Tonight   Cahn 1940

Amigos   Fain 1959; Webster 1959

Amnesia (The Inderal Song)   Bacharach 1979

Amo Amas   Porter 1944

Amo, Que Paso?   Sherman 1960

Amoeba's Lament (inst.), The   Schwartz, Arthur 1929

Among My Memories   Evans 1970; Livingston, Jay 1970

Among My Souvenirs   Leslie 1927

Among the Lillies   Johnson, Howard 1939

Among the Missing   Webster 1933

Amontillado (A Case of Amontillado) (inst.)   Young, Victor 1955

Amor Amor (Amore)   Spina 1960

Amor Mio   Cahn 1972

Amor Mio (My Love)   Friend 1930; Monaco 1930

Amor, Mon Amour, My Love   Sigman 1963

Amore Mio   Stept 1956

Amorita   Bergman 1961

Amour! Amour! I Have Love   Spina 1959

'Ampstead Way, The   Burke 1946; Van Heusen 1946

Amukirki (The Lord Willing)   Livingston, Jerry 1955; Russell 1955

Amy's Apology   Russell 1945

An' Furthermore   Warren 1928

Anaconda Copper   Willson 1953

Analyse My Baby Back to Me   Ahlert 1953

Anastasia   Webster 1956

Anatomy of a Love Song   Howard, Bart 1988

Ancestors   Akst 1936; Clare 1936

Ancestors Bold   Smith, Harry B. 1911

Ancient Minstrel, The   Atteridge 1913

And a Host of Others Too Numerous to Mention   Comden and Green 1958; Styne 1958

And a Little Bit More   Bryan 1907; Fisher 1907

And Away We Go (Aw-a-a-a-y)   Davis 1954

And Brought You Unto Myself   David, Mack 1964; Warren 1964

And Dreams Come True   Atteridge 1915; Friml 1915

And Dreams Remain   Freed, Ralph 1946

And Father Wanted Me to Learn a Trade   Berlin 1915

And He'd Say Oo La La Wee Wee   Ruby 1919

And How   Akst 1923; Kahn 1923; Magidson 1927

And I Am All Alone   Kern 1917

And I Believed in You   Lewis 1925; Young, Joe 1925

And I Broke My Mother's Heart, All Over You   Bryan 1914

And I Have You   Gershwin, George 1930; Gershwin, Ira 1930

And I Laughed   Smith, Harry B. 1906

And I Love You   Burke 1958; Evans 1954; Livingston, Jay 1954; Van Heusen 1958

And I Married Him   Bryan 1911

And I Still Do   Ahlert 1934; Leslie 1934

And I Thought He Was a Business Man   Von Tilzer 1910

And I Thought I Was Through with Love   Davis 1933; Oakland 1933

And I Was Kissing You   Spina 1951; Webster 1951

And I'll Be There   Burke 1959

And I'll Be There (inst.)   Revel 1961

And I'm So Glad   Schwartz, Jean 1935

And It Happened Last Night   Clare 1935; Johnston 1935

And It Still Goes   Stept 1949

And Love Was Born   Hammerstein 1932; Kern 1932

And Now   Akst 1923

And Now Tomorrow   Heyman 1944; Young, Victor 1944

And Points Beyond   Mercer 1974

And Russia Is Her Name   Harburg 1944; Kern 1944

And She Went Home in a Barrel   Buck 1918

And So Am I   Drake 1957

And So Do I   De Lange 1940

(A Sky of Blue, with You) And So Forth   Johnson, Howard Date Unknown

And So Goodbye   Wrubel 1933

And So Goodbye, My Love   Bacharach 1963; David, Hal 1963

And So I Sorrow   Blake 1954

And So I Walked Home   Merrill 1954

And So On   Cahn 1978

And So on Down the Line   Eliscu 1949

And So To Bed   Gordon 1932; Mercer 1946; Revel 1932

And So To Sleep (inst.)   Revel 1957

And So Will You   Loewe 1938

And Still I Came   Heyman 1932

And Still I Love Her   Bergman 1962; Cahn 1971

And Still I Love You   Caesar 1933; Friml 1933

And Still the Volga Flows   Willson 1942

And Suddenly It's Christmas   Drake 1980; Lane 1980

And That Ain't All   Stept 1919

And That Is That   Willson 1956

And That Is You   Blake 1947

And that Little Girl Is You   Herbert 1911; Smith, Harry B. 1911

And That Woman Made a Monkey Out of Me   Clare 1936

(Yo Te Amo Mucho) And That's That   Drake 1946; Stept 1946

And the Angels Sing   Mercer 1939

And the Band Played On   Fisher 1924; Rose 1927

And the Cat Came Back   Johnson, Howard 1915

And the Dream Comes True   Friml 1914

And the Great Big World Went Round and Round   Sterling 1915; Von Tilzer 1915

And the Green Grass Grew All Around   Jerome 1912; Von Tilzer 1912

And the Manager Said. . .?   Cohan 1901

And the Moonlight's Calling You   Schwartz, Jean 1926

And the People were with Her   Bacharach 1971; David, Hal 1971

And the World Keeps Rolling Along   Smith, Harry B. 1909

And Then   Bryan 1912; Mitchell 1936; Stept 1936; Young, Joe 1933

And then Came Love   Razaf 1942

And Then I Forgot   Davis 1926

And Then I Met Yvette   Hoffman 1956

And Then I Wrote   Oakland 1965; Spina 1965

And then She Walked Right Through the Door   Bacharach 1974

And then Some   Ellington 1962

And Then You Came Along   Fain 1928

And Then You Happened Along   Lerner, Sammy 1931

And Then You Kissed Me   Cahn 1944; Styne 1944

And Then You Know What He Did   Bacharach 1974

And There I Stood with My Piccolo   Willson 1950

And There You Are   Fain 1945; Gordon 1951, 1953; Koehler 1945; Myrow 1953

And There You Are Again   Burke 1933; Spina 1933; Young, Joe 1933

And Thereby Hangs a Tail   Hart 1925; Rodgers 1925

And They Call It a Popular Song   Johnson, Howard 1917

And They Lived Happily Ever After   David, Mack 1931

And They Lived Happily Ever Afterward   Herbert 1912

And They Said It Wouldn't Last   David, Mack 1952

And They Still Fall in Love   Dubin 1929

And This I Find Is Beautiful   David, Mack 1976

And This Is Life   Razaf 1933; Waller 1933

And This Is Mine   Bacharach 1961; David, Hal 1961

And to Think I Left My Happy Home for You   Kalmar 1914; Leslie 1914

And We Were in Love   Webster 1976

And We'll Fight Forever After   Clarke 1921; Monaco 1921

And Yet the World Rolls On   Harburg Date Unknown

And You Forgot About Me   Hanley 1938, 1940
And You Know Why   Friml 1952
And You'll Be Home   Burke 1950; Van Heusen 1950
And Your Mother Said   Cahn 1965; Van Heusen 1965
Andalusia Bolero   Herbert 1946
Andantino   Johnson, Howard 1939
Andiamo   Arlen 1951; Fields 1951
Andrew's Fantasy ("Yes" Ballet) (inst.)   Loesser 1960
Andy Jackson   Livingston, Jerry 1960
Andy's Mystery Tune   Evans 1965; Livingston, Jay 1965
Anema E Core   Akst 1953
Angel   Evans 1964; Freed, Arthur 1945; Livingston, Jay 1964;
     Parish 1940; Robin 1937; Warren 1945
Angel Baby   Parish 1961
Angel Bells   Ruby 1954
Angel Child   Davis 1922; Johnston 1938; Silver 1922
Angel Cries, An   David, Hal 1960
Angel Eyes   Bryan 1909; Lewis 1926; Parish 1921; Young,
     Joe 1926
Angel Face (You've Got the Devil in Your Big Blue
     Eyes)   Spina 1947
Angel in a Furnished Room   Dubin 1937
Angel in the Christmas Play, The   Merrill 1954
Angel in the Night   Evans Date Unknown; Livingston, Jay
     Date Unknown
Angel Kissed Me Last Night, An   Washington 1954; Young,
     Victor 1954
Angel May Care   Drake 1944
Angel Puss   Donaldson 1941; Parish 1941
Angel Que   Merrill 1970
Angel Without Wings   Hart 1938; Rodgers 1938
Angela   Evans 1966; Livingston, Jay 1966
Angela Mia   Pollack 1928
Angelina   Coleman 1960; Harburg 1976; Lane 1976; Leigh
     1960
Angelina Baker   Johnson, Howard 1939
Angeline   Freed, Ralph 1952; Waller 1932; Willson 1957
Angelique   Atteridge Date Unknown
Angelo   Berlin 1910
Angels   Atteridge 1916; Berlin 1910; Motzan 1916, 1917;
     Romberg 1916; Snyder 1910
Angels Are Crying, The   Livingston, Jerry 1961
Angels Are with You Tonight   Bryan 1944
Angels Came Thru, The   Dubin 1941
Angels Cried, The   Mercer 1948
Angels of Mercy   Berlin 1942
Angels Over the Fields   Herbert 1903
Angel's Tears   David, Mack 1954
Angels (We Call Them Mothers Down Here)   Kalmar 1921;
     Ruby 1921
Angels with Dirty Faces   Fisher 1938
Angeltown   Evans 1959; Livingston, Jay 1959
Angelus, The   Harbach 1910; Herbert 1897, 1913; Smith,
     Harry B. 1897; Smith, Robert B. 1913
Angelus Bells   Bergman 1963
Angie's Patriotic Rally   Bryan 1917
Angling   Harbach 1914
Angling by a Babbling Brook   Kern 1904
Angry Young Men, The   Raye 1958
Anima Anceps (Or the Negro's Heart)   Johnson, James P.
     1944; Razaf 1944
Animal Attraction   Adams 1962; Strouse 1962
Animal Ballet   Adamson 1936; Conrad 1936; Magidson 1936
Animal Crackers in My Soup   Caesar 1935; Henderson 1935;
     Koehler 1935

Animal's Christmas Song, The   Bergman 1960
Animated Objects   Hart 1933; Rodgers 1933
Anita   Clare 1928; Pollack 1928
Anita (inst.)   Waller 1939
Ankle Up the Alter with Me   Eliscu 1930
Ann and Her Little Sedan   Hanley 1923
Anna   Loesser 1976
Anna Lilla   Merrill 1957
Anna Lize's Wedding Day   Berlin 1913
Anna Maria   McHugh 1955; Sigman 1955
Anna Mary   Martin 1952
Anna of Havana   Smith, Harry B. 1916; Smith, Robert B.
     1916
Anna Rosa   David, Mack 1947; Hoffman 1947; Livingston,
     Jerry 1947
Annabella's Bustle   Pollack 1942, 1944
Annabelle   Brown, Lew 1923; Duke 1955; Henderson 1923;
     Parish 1938
Annabelle Lee   Caesar 1923
Annapolis Farewell   Coslow 1935
Anne Lee   Dubin 1928
Anne of the Indies   Lerner, Sammy 1951
Annette   Smith, Harry B. 1930; Sterling Date Unknown
Annie   Strouse 1977
Annie Ain't Annie Anymore   Strouse 1993
Annie Doesn't Live Here Anymore   Burke 1933; Spina 1933;
     Young, Joe 1933
Annie Laurie   Johnson, Howard 1939
Annie McGuinnis Pavlova   Hammerstein 1917
Annina   Friml 1934
Anniversary Rose   Evans 1955; Livingston, Jay 1955
Anniversary Song (Remembrance)   Leigh 1977
Anniversary Waltz, The   Dubin 1941
Announcement of Inheritance   Porter 1943
Announcement/Rehearsal (inst.)   Duke 1963
Anonymous Phone Call   Bacharach 1962; David, Hal 1962
Anorita   Heyman 1935
Another Autumn   Lerner, Alan Jay 1951; Loewe 1951
Another Big Strike   Willson 1960
Another Birthday, Another Year (Voice in the Night)   Revel
     1957
Another Case of the Blues   Mercer 1933
Another Day   Comden and Green 1967; Styne 1967
Another Day, Another Buck   Duke 1955
Another Day, Another Darling   Sigman 1949
Another Day Goes By   Brooks 1946
(As One Door Closes) Another Door Opens   David, Hal
     1959
Another Dream Gone Wrong   Hoffman 1932; Lerner,
     Sammy 1932; Wrubel 1936
Another Human Being of the Opposite Sex   Burke 1951;
     Van Heusen 1951
Another Hundred People   Sondheim 1970
Another Kiss   DeSylva 1945
Another Language   Silver 1933
Another Law   Weill 1938
Another Life   Lerner, Alan Jay 1983; Strouse 1983
Another Little Dream Won't Do Us Any Harm   Rainger
     1941; Robin 1941
Another Little Girl   Kern 1915
Another Love   Comden and Green 1944; Stept 1956
Another Lovely April Day   Loewe 1937
Another Melody in F   Hart 1920, 1922; Rodgers 1920
Another Mile   Kahal 1936; Rose 1936
Another Miracle of Love   Johnson, James P. 1960

Another National Anthem   Sondheim 1990
Another New Day   Hammerstein 1940; Schwartz, Arthur 1940
Another New Year   Rose 1937
Another Night   Bacharach 1966; David, Hal 1966
Another Night Alone   Arlen 1932; Koehler 1932
Another Night in Your Arms   Hanley 1933
Another Night Like This   Ruby 1947
Another Night Together   Adamson 1935, Date Unknown; Donaldson 1935, Date Unknown
Another Night Within Your Arms   Coots 1929
(You'll Be Just) Another Notch on Father's Shotgun Effen You Don't Marry Me   Wrubel 1948
Another Op'nin', Another Show   Porter 1948
Another Perfect Night Is Ending   Coots 1936; Davis 1936
Another Princely Scheme (Tarantella)   Leigh 1954
Another Season   Davis 1953
Another Sentimental Song   Porter 1919
(It's Time to Sing) Another Song   Mancini 1975
Another Song About a Woman That a Man Done Wrong   Cahn 1980; Strouse 1980
Another Spring   Webster 1964
Another Spring Will Rise (inst.)   Bacharach 1977
Another Tear Falls   Bacharach 1962; David, Hal 1962
Another Time Another Place   Evans 1958; Livingston, Jay 1958; Russell 1958; Warren 1958
Another World   Sondheim Date Unknown
Answer   Cohan 1908
Answer Is Love, The   Stept 1939
Answer Man, The   Oakland 1972
Answer Me   Berlin 1911; Motzan 1925; Sigman 1953; Willson 1956
Answer My Heart   Comden and Green 1966, 1967; Styne 1966, 1967
Answer the Call   Willson 1952
Answer to Everything, The   Bacharach 1961
Answer to Lilly the Werewolf   Caesar 1945
Answer to the Maple on the Hill   Fisher 1936
Anthem for Presentation Theme   Berlin 1952
Anthem of the Atomic Age   Willson 1950
Anthem of the Clams   Van Heusen 1960
Anthem of the Union of Soviet Socialist Republics   Rome 1944
Anthony for President   Brooks 1968
Anticipation   Cahn 1967; Romberg 1917
Anticipation and Hesitation   Ellington 1969
Anticipation Without Realization   Friend 1948
Antiques   Harbach 1923
Antoinette   Herbert 1914
Antoinette Birby   Porter 1910
Antoinette (inst.)   Schwartz, Jean 1930
Antonia   Mercer 1954
Antonio   Jerome 1905; Schwartz, Jean 1905
Antonio, You'd Better Come Home   Berlin 1912
Ants, The   Adams 1961; Strouse 1961
Anvil Chorus, The   Brown, Lew 1931; Henderson 1931
Any Bonds Today   Berlin 1941
Any Day Now   Bacharach 1962
Any Day the Sun Don't Shine   Razaf 1924; Waller 1924
Any Day's a Perfect Day for a Wedding   Strouse 1975
Any Fool Can Fall in Love   Cahn 1944; Styne 1944
Any Fool Would Have Known   David, Mack 1958
Any Friend of Yours Is a Friend of Mine   Hoffman 1943
Any Gal from Texas   Blane 1954; Myrow 1954
Any Girl Is a Wonderful Girl   Yellen 1921

Any Kind of Man   Friml 1918
Any Little Girl Can Make a Bad Man Good (And a Good Man Bad They Say)   Hanley 1917
Any Little Girl That's a Nice Little Girl Is the Right Little Girl for Me   Fisher 1910
Any Little Girl Will Fall   Atteridge 1923; Caesar 1923; Romberg 1923
Any Little Melody   Atteridge 1920
Any Little Thing   Kalmar 1927; Ruby 1927
Any Little Tune   Gershwin, George 1923; Kalmar 1926; Ruby 1926
Any Love Today   Berlin 1931
Any Man Who Loves His Mother   Cahn 1964; Van Heusen 1964
Any Minute Now   Loesser 1940
Any Moment   Sondheim 1987
Any Moment Now   Gershwin, Ira 1944; Harburg 1945; Kern 1944, 1945; Leigh 1985
Any Night on Broadway   Atteridge 1916, 1921; Motzan 1916, 1921; Romberg 1916, 1921
Any Night on Old Broadway   Atteridge 1921; Schwartz, Jean 1921
Any Ol' Woes   DePaul 1958; Raye 1958
Any Old Dream in a Storm   Blane 1939
Any Old Lane Is Lovers' Lane (As Long As I'm with You)   Johnson, Howard 1938
Any Old Night Is a Beautiful Night, If You're Out with a Beautiful Girl   Monaco 1914
Any Old Night Is a Lonesome Old Night   Young, Joe 1916
Any Old Night (Is a Wonderful Night)   Kern 1915; Motzan 1915; Smith, Harry B. 1915
Any Old Place I Can Hang My Hat Is Home Sweet Home to Me   Jerome 1901; Schwartz, Jean 1901
Any Old Place with You   Hart 1919; Rodgers 1919; Smith, Harry B. 1908
Any Old Port in a Storm   Pollack 1943
Any Old Thing   Drake 1958; Smith, Harry B. 1903
Any Old Time At All   Brown, A. Seymour 1911; Buck 1918; Jerome 1906; Schwartz, Jean 1906
Any Old Time (Mu Quarto e Luna)   Rome 1952
Any Old Time of the Day   Bacharach 1964; David, Hal 1964
Any Old Time with You   Atteridge 1915
Any One Else   Fields 1930; McHugh 1930
Any Place Down South   Razaf 1942
Any Place I Hang My Hat Is Home   Arlen 1946; Mercer 1946
Any Place Is Home Sweet Home with You   Caesar 1920
Any Place Is Paradise As Long As You Are There   Coslow 1933
Any Place the Old Flag Flies   Cohan 1911
Any Place Will Do with You   Atteridge 1921; Romberg 1921
Any Place Would Be Wonderful with You   Buck 1920
Any Questions?   Oakland Date Unknown; Russell 1953, Date Unknown
Any Similarity Is Just Coincidental   Carmichael 1950; Mercer 1950
Any Thing Can Happen in the Moonlight   McHugh 1958
Any Time, Any Day, Anywhere   Washington 1933; Young, Victor 1933
Any Time at All   Coots 1924; Friend 1923; Hoffman 1932; Van Heusen 1938
Any Time Is Dancing Time   Schwartz, Jean 1918
Any Time New York Goes Dry   Herbert 1919
Any Way the Wind Blows   Burke 1942; Friend 1933; Stept 1933; Van Heusen 1942

Any Way the Wind Blows My Sweetie Goes   Hanley 1924

Any Wednesday   Bergman 1966

Any Woman Who Is Willing Will Do   Dietz 1944; Duke 1944

Anybody but You   Brown, Nacio Herb 1931; Eliscu 1931

Anybody Can Write   Berlin 1956

Anybody for the Blues   McHugh 1959

Anybody Here Want to Try My Cabbage   Razaf 1925; Waller 1925

Anybody's Gal   Spina 1977

Anyone and Everyone   Sigman 1969

Anyone but You   Washington 1953

Anyone Can Dream   David, Mack 1946

Anyone Can Fall in Love   Cahn 1954

Anyone Can Whistle   Sondheim 1964

Anyone Else   McHugh 1931

Anyone for Love   Washington 1957

Anyone for Tennis   Drake 1954

Anyone Who Do's That, Can't Be So Dumb   Brown, A. Seymour 1927

Anyone Who Had a Heart   Bacharach 1963; David, Hal 1963

Anyone Who Loves   Lerner, Alan Jay 1983; Strouse 1983

Anyone Would Love You   Rome 1959

Anything   Caesar 1925

Anything at Any Time   Razaf 1924

Anything Can Happen   Burke 1959; Gorney 1948; Henderson 1935; Yellen 1935

Anything Can Happen in Brooklyn   Baer 1954; Leslie 1954

Anything Can Happen in New York   Harburg 1941; Lane 1941

Anything Can Happen in the Moonlight   Adamson 1950; McHugh 1950

Anything Can Happen on Halloween   Strouse 1987

Anything, Everything for Love   Livingston, Jerry 1955

Anything for a Laugh   Russell 1952

Anything for You   Gershwin, George 1921; Gershwin, Ira 1921

Anything Goes   Porter 1934

Anything Is Nice If It Comes from Dixieland   Ager 1918; Clarke 1918; Meyer 1918; Yellen Date Unknown

Anything May Happen Any Day   Kern 1930

Anything That's Near to Where You Are   Styne 1958

Anything That's Part of You   Dixon 1934; Wrubel 1934

Anything to Hold Your Baby   Conrad 1929; Mitchell 1929

Anything You Can Do   Berlin 1946

Anything You Say   Donaldson 1928; Parish 1933

Anything You Want to Do, Dear   Harbach 1920

Anytime   Porter 1912

Anytime, Anywhere, Anyhow   Hart 1925; Rodgers 1925

Anytime You Need Some Love   Sigman 1958

Anyway We've Had Fun   Youmans 1930

Anywhere   Cahn 1945, 1947; Styne 1945; Young, Victor 1952

Anywhere but Here   Evans 1958; Livingston, Jay 1958

Anywhere I Wander   Loesser 1952

Anywhere If You Are There Is a Paradise to Me   Friend 1927

Anywhere on Earth Is Heaven   Washington 1942; Young, Victor 1942

Anywhere Under the Sun   Hanley 1929

Anywhere You Go   Drake 1966

A.O.K.   Evans 1970; Livingston, Jay 1970

Apache Argentine   Caesar 1924; Conrad 1924; Harbach 1924

Apache Dance   Atteridge 1924; Romberg 1924; Schwartz, Jean 1924

Apache Dance (Inst.)   Brooks 1960

Apaches, The   Porter 1953

Apacionada   Russell 1961

Apalachicola, F.L.A.   Burke 1947; Van Heusen 1947

Apassionette   Heyman 1934

Aphrodesia   Myrow 1951

Aphrodite   Hart 1920; Rodgers 1920

Apologize   Howard, Joseph E. 1919

Appasionato   Heyman 1935

Applause   Adams 1970; Gilbert 1910; Strouse 1970

Applause! Applause!   Gershwin, Ira 1953; Lane 1953

Apple Blossoms   Youmans 1923

Apple Blossoms and Chapel Bells   Hoffman 1939

Apple Blossoms in the Rain   Pollack 1942

Apple for the Teacher, An   Burke 1939; Monaco 1939

Apple Jack   Gorney 1948; Johnson, James P. 1948; Weill 1950

Apple Mary Maguire   Smith, Harry B. 1904; Smith, Robert B. 1904

Apple of My Eye, The   Waller 1932; Young, Joe 1932

Apple on a Cherry Tree   David, Hal 1960

Apple on a Pear Tree   Hoffman 1954

Apple on a Stick   Coots 1953

Apple Pie Guy   Coots 1950

Apple Sauce   Freed, Arthur 1922

Apple Seed Love   Carmichael 1953

Apple Tree and the Bumble Tree, The   Berlin 1913

Applejack, The   Livingston, Jerry 1954; Sigman 1954

Apples   Strouse 1977; Styne 1985

Appointments   Livingston, Jerry 1973

Apprentice Seaman   Dietz 1944; Duke 1944

April Birthday Song   Caesar 1940

April Blossoms   Hammerstein 1923; Harbach 1923

April Can't Do This to Me   De Lange 1944

April Child   Evans 1970; Livingston, Jay 1970

April Face   Blane 1945, 1952

April Fool   Hart 1925; Rodgers 1925; Von Tilzer 1911

April Fool Ditty   Howard, Joseph E. 1907

April Fool Rag (inst.)   Schwartz, Jean 1911

April Fooled Me   Fields 1956; Kern 1956

April Fools, The   Bacharach 1969; David, Hal 1969

April in Harlem (inst.)   Johnson, James P. 1944

April in My Heart   Carmichael 1937

April in Paris   Duke 1932; Harburg 1932

April Love   Fain 1957; Webster 1957

April Made a Fool of Me   Parish 1946

April Played the Fiddle   Burke 1940; Monaco 1940

April Showers   DeSylva 1921

April Sings   Washington 1952

April Snow   Fields 1945; Romberg 1945

April Song   Coleman 1958; Leigh 1958

April Song, An   Cahn 1980

April Special   Oakland 1952

April Springs   Adamson 1953; Carmichael 1953

April Wants to Dance Again   Burke 1944; Van Heusen 1944

Aqua Sincopada Tango   Porter 1929

Arabella, I Wuv Awa-Bewwa   Friend 1941

Arabella's Wedding Day   Meyer 1926

Arabia   Hanley 1915

Arabian for 'Get Happy'   Fain 1951; Harburg 1951

Arabian Lover   Fields 1929

Arabian Market Place, The   Brooks 1960

Arabian Moon   Blake 1932; Sissle 1932

Arabian Mwaaah   Brooks 1960

Arabian Number   McHugh 1934

Arabiana   Davis 1922; Gordon 1937; Revel 1937

Araby   Berlin 1915

Araminta to Herself   Lawrence 1951
Aramis March (inst.)   Willson 1929
Arbor Day   Clare 1939
Arcady   DeSylva 1921
Archibald   Dixon 1924; Henderson 1924
Archie's Little Love Song   Carmichael 1946
Architect, The   Martin 1972
Ardent Night (inst.)   Revel 1949
Are We Dancing?   Sherman 1967
Are We Downhearted? No!   Davis 1928
Are We Picking Up Where We Left Off   Baer 1950; Leslie 1950
Are We Talking About the Same Thing?   Adamson 1963; Fain 1963
Are We Widows, Wives or What?   Atteridge 1912
Are You a Buffalo   Von Tilzer 1901
Are You a Dream   Parish 1932
Are You a Flop   Drake 1956
Are You Afraid of Me   Oakland 1929
Are You Angry with Me Darling   Johnson, Howard 1939
Are You Ashamed of Me?   Hoffman 1930; Lerner, Sammy 1930
Are You Asking Me to Forget   Cahn 1965; Van Heusen 1965
Are You Bucking Up Your Commander-In-Chief   Eliscu 1944; Gorney 1944
Are You Certain that You Care   Parish 1930
Are You Coming Out Tonight, Mary Ann   Sterling 1906; Von Tilzer 1906
Are You Dancing?   Gershwin, George 1930; Gershwin, Ira 1930
Are You Dreaming Too   Johnson, Howard 1927
Are You for Real   Friend 1956
Are You from Dixie Cause I'm from Dixie Too   Yellen 1915
Are You from Heaven   Gilbert 1917
Are You Gettin' On   Robison 1957
Are You Going to Be Home   Dixon 1928; Dubin 1928; Stept 1928
Are You Happy   Ager 1927; Yellen 1927
Are You Happy in Your Work   Evans 1944; Livingston, Jay 1944
Are You Havin' Any Fun   Fain 1936; Yellen 1936
Are You in Love?   Alter 1927
Are You in Love with Me?   Warren 1927
Are You in the Mood for Mischief   Gordon 1939; Revel 1939
Are You in Trouble   Loesser 1937
Are You Just a Beautiful Dream   Robin 1951; Styne 1951
Are You Kiddin'?   Rainger 1942; Robin 1942
Are You Kiddin' Bud?   Davis 1942
Are You Listenin'   Young, Victor 1932
Are You Listening Tonight Mother Dear   Leslie 1927
Are You Living Old Man   Silver 1942
Are You Lonesome?   Kahn 1909
Are You Lonesome Tonight   Turk 1926
Are You Love?   Hammerstein 1931; Romberg 1931
Are You Mine   Cahn 1956
Are You My Love?   Hart 1936; Rodgers 1936
Are You Now   Eliscu 1955; Gorney 1955
Are You Prepared for the Summer?   Kalmar 1916; Leslie 1916; Schwartz, Jean 1916
Are You Ready, Gyp Watson?   Rome 1959
Are You Really Mine   Caesar 1929
Are You Really Mine (Really)   Hoffman 1958
Are You Satisfied   Brown, Lew 1926; DeSylva 1926; Henderson 1926
Are You Sincere   Bryan 1908

Are You Smiling?   Gorney 1969
Are You Sorry?   Ager 1925; Davis 1925
Are You Steppin' Out Tonight   Atteridge 1919
Are You Stepping Out Tonight   Atteridge 1919; Carroll 1919
Are You Sure?   Willson 1960
Are You the One Who Loves Me   Mancini 1986
Are You There (with Another Girl)   Bacharach 1965; David, Hal 1965
Are You Thinking of Me Tonight   Akst 1927; Davis 1927; Gilbert 1927
Are You This Wonderful Every Day   Revel 1953
Are You with It?   Revel 1945
Are Your a Dreamer   Lawrence 1938
Area, The   Robison 1958
Area Code 213   David, Mack 1972
Aren't We All   Brown, Lew 1931; Conrad 1924; DeSylva 1931; Henderson 1931
Aren't You Glad   Loesser 1956
Aren't You Glad You're You   Burke 1945; Van Heusen 1945
Aren't You Kind of Glad We Did?   Gershwin, George 1947; Gershwin, Ira 1947
Aren't You the Girl (I Met in Sherry's)   Goetz 1907
Arfie the Doggie in the Window   Merrill 1953
Argentina   DeSylva 1922; Gershwin, George 1922; Razaf 1929
Argentina Skies   Van Heusen 1938
Argentine   Bryan 1927; Ellington 1962; Mills 1962; Parish 1962; Schwartz, Jean 1927; Smith, Harry B. 1923
Argentine Arango, The   Friml 1923
Argentine Fire Brigade   Spina 1953
Argentine Nights   Akst 1937; Clare 1937
Argentine Swing   Akst 1937; Clare 1937
Argentine Tango   Friml 1918
Arguements   Merrill 1957
Argument   Adams 1996; Loesser 1948; Strouse 1996
A-Rhythm-a-Tic   DePaul 1953; Raye 1953
Aria   Romberg 1948
Aria, An   Hammerstein 1920; Harbach 1920
Aria from Antonia   Hammerstein 1931; Romberg 1931
Ariane   Mercer 1957
Arioso   Johnson, Howard 1939
Arise (Clock Song)   Robin 1930
Arise My Love   Washington 1940
Aristocats, The   Sherman 1970
Arithmatic   Merrill 1950
Arithmetic   Edwards 1908
Arithmetic Blues   Leslie 1922
Arizona   Cobb 1907; Edwards 1907; Spina 1948; Stept 1950
Arizona Sundown   Alter 1946; De Lange 1946
Arizona Weddin', An   Stept 1949
Arkansas   Coots 1947; Willson 1953
Arkansaw Rip-Saw   Robison 1957
Arlene   Pollack 1933
Arm in Arm   Dietz 1944; Duke 1944; Washington 1932; Willson 1963; Young, Victor 1932
Arm of the Law (inst.), The   Revel 1960
Arm with a Bow in It's Hand (Yipaloo), An   Sigman 1950
Armchair with an Armful of You, An   Gordon 1930; Silver 1930
Armed Forces on Parade, The   Stept 1953
Armful of Sunshine, An   Cahn 1976; Lane 1976
Armful of Trouble   Harbach 1933; Kern 1933
Armful of You, An   Robin 1927; Youmans 1927
Armful of You (inst.), An   Waller 1954
Armorer's Song   Smith, Harry B. 1891

Arms for the Love of America   Berlin 1942

Army, The   Romberg 1916

Army Air Force, The   Gorney 1941

Army Air Patrol, The   Adamson 1943; McHugh 1943

Army Aviation Song, The   Cahn 1964; Van Heusen 1964

Army Band (Here Comes the Band), The   Adamson 1935; Lane 1935

Army Blue   Hammerstein 1938; Harbach 1938; Kern 1938

Army Brat, The   Fain 1946; Freed, Ralph 1946

Army Club, The   Atteridge 1914; Carroll 1914; Romberg 1914

Army Mule Song, The   Blane 1952

Army of Hippocrates, The   Carmichael 1942

Army Service Forces, The   Rome 1943

Army Song   Weill 1954

Army's Always There, The   Stept 1952

Army's Full of Irish   Donaldson 1917

Army's Made a Man Out of Me, The   Berlin 1942

Around the Bend   Mercer 1953

Around the Corner   Kahn 1930

Around the Corner (Come Petred Dimenticarti)   Sigman 1966

Around the Corner from the Blues   Sigman 1956

Around the House that Jack Built   DeSylva 1918

Around the Old Saskatchewan   Bryan 1950

Around the Rainbow (There Is No Color Line)   Caesar 1932

Around the Town   Atteridge 1916; Motzan 1916; Romberg 1916

Around the World in 80 Days   Adamson 1956; Young, Victor 1956

Around You   Robin 1932; Whiting 1932

Arouse, Arouse   Rome 1968

A-Rovin' I'll Go   Woods 1931

Arrah, Come In Out of the Rain, Barney McShane   Sterling 1909

Arrah Go 'Long with You, Do You See Any Green in My Eye   Sterling 1921; Von Tilzer 1921

Arrah Go on I'm Gonna Go Back to Oregon   Lewis 1916; Young, Joe 1916

Arrival   Comden and Green 1982

Arrival of Guests   Caesar 1930; Harbach 1910, 1930; Romberg 1930

Arrival of Society, The   Cohan 1923

Arrival of Steamboat   Caesar 1936

Arrival of the Plot, The   Cohan 1923

Arrival of the Princess Pat   Herbert 1915

Arrival of Tourists   Caesar 1936

Arriverderci   Coots 1952

Arroz   Mercer 1982

Arsenic and Old Waffles   Oakland 1953; Raye 1953

Art   Porter 1955

Art in the Night   Rome 1964

Art Is Calling for Me (I Want to Be a Prima Donna)   Herbert 1911; Smith, Harry B. 1911

Art of Conversation, The   Russell 1957

Art of Conversation Has Declined, The   Bergman 1955; Mercer 1955

Art of Fascination, The   Edwards 1923; Smith, Robert B. 1923

Art of Love, The   Coleman 1965; Raye 1965; Robison 1957

Art of Making Up, The   Williams 1909

Art of Self-Defense, The   Razaf Date Unknown

Art Pallen Theme   Oakland 1954

Art Song   Herbert 1917

Art with a Capital 'A'   Smith, Harry B. 1909

Arthur Murray Taught Me Dancing in a Hurray   Mercer 1942

Arthur's Theme (The Best That You Can Do)   Bacharach 1981

Artist and Model   Schwartz, Jean 1937

Artists   Duke 1963

Artists and Models   Brooks 1955; Coslow 1924; Romberg 1924; Warren 1955

Arts, The   Adams 1956; Strouse 1956

As Big As My Love for You   David, Hal 1960

As Big As Texas   David, Mack 1962

As Far As I'm Concerned   Livingston, Jerry 1934; Rodgers 1970

As Good As a Man   Coleman 1980

As I Live and Breathe (I Live and Breathe for You)   Pollack 1935; Webster 1935

As I Love You   Evans 1955, 1958; Livingston, Jay 1955, 1958; Porter 1913

As I Recall   Cahn 1945; Styne 1945

As I Remember You   Blane 1945

As I Was Remarking   Rome 1969

As I Was Say'n to the Duchess   Washington 1938

As I Was Walkin'   David, Hal 1960

As If I Didn't Know   Kahn 1940

As If You Didn't Know   Cahn 1941; Spina 1957; Stept 1944

As Long As Happiness Is There   Johnson, Howard 1924

As Long As He Loves Me   Brown, Lew 1923; Hanley 1923

As Long As He's a Regular Guy   Blake 1945; Sissle 1945

As Long As I Have You   Silver 1958; Stept 1925

As Long As I Have You (And You Have Me)   Dubin 1930

As Long As I Live   Arlen 1934; Gordon 1932; Koehler 1934; Merrill 1952; Revel 1932

As Long As I Love   Oakland 1938; Weill 1935

As Long As I'm Dreaming   Burke 1947; Van Heusen 1947

As Long As I'm with You   Akst 1930; Clarke 1930

As Long As It's Not About Love   Porter 1938

As Long As It's You, Dear, O.K.   Donaldson 1929; Leslie 1929

As Long As I've Got My Art   Martin 1946

As Long As I've Got My Mammy   DeSylva 1925; Hanley 1925

As Long As Love Lives On   Young, Joe 1932

As Long As the Band Will Play   Atteridge Date Unknown

As Long as the Wife Don't Know   Brown, A. Seymour 1923

As Long As the World Goes Round   Johnson, J. Rosamond 1909

As Long As the World Goes Round, I Will Love You   Sterling 1913; Von Tilzer 1913

As Long As There's an Apple Tree   Bacharach 1968; David, Hal 1968

As Long As There's Love   Schwartz, Jean 1935

As Long As There's Music   Cahn 1944; Styne 1944

As Long As They Keep on Making Them, I'll Keep Taking Them All the Time   Johnson, Howard 1924

As Long as We Have   Bromo Seltzer in Our Love Nest   Harburg 1932

As Long As We're in Love   Brown, Lew 1925; Clare 1925; Fields 1928; McHugh 1928

As Long As We're Together   Coslow 1930; Friend 1938

As Long As You Believe in Me   Davis 1929

As Long As You Live   Sissle 1970

As Long As You Live (You Gonna Be My Baby)   Blake 1957

As Long As You Live You'll Be Dead If You Die   Mercer 1938

As Long As You Love Me   Silver 1930

As Long As You're Happy   Strouse 1991

As Long As You're Near Me   Lane 1930; Lerner, Sammy 1930

As Long As You're There   Leslie 1931; Monaco 1931

As of Today   Fields 1939; Schwartz, Arthur 1939

As on Through the Seasons We Sail   Porter 1955

As Once I Loved You   Rodgers 1976

As Soon As They See Eileen   Robin 1955; Styne 1955

As the Case May Be   Rome 1970

As the Day Went On   Strouse Date Unknown

As the Girls Go   Adamson 1948; McHugh 1948

As the Grain Needs the Rain, So I Need You, Once Again   Howard, Joseph E. 1919

As the Parade Goes Marching By   Bergman 1958

As the Waters Flow They Softly Whisper Flo Flo Flo   Leslie 1908

As the Wind Bloweth (There I Goeth)   Webster 1946

As the Years Roll By   Hanley 1932; Herbert 1917; Mitchell 1932

As Though You Were There   Hart 1929; Rodgers 1929

As We Pass By   Von Tilzer 1916

As We Sat at the Saturday Evening Post   Kalmar 1916; Leslie 1916; Schwartz, Jean 1916

As You Are   Stept 1945

As You Come In   Edwards 1930; Johnson, Howard 1930

As You Desire Me   Wrubel 1932

As You Walk Down the Strand   Smith, Harry B. 1908

As You Were   Cahn 1945; Styne 1945

As You Were (For Mary, the Baby and Me)   Monaco 1919

As Young As We Are Tonight   Merrill 1955

As Young As You Feel   Martin 1962

Asbestos (inst.)   Waller 1945

ASCAP Song, The   Duke 1941

Ascot Gavotte   Lerner, Alan Jay 1956; Loewe 1956

Ash Can Stomp   Johnson, Howard 1927

Ashandai Aschandai   Spina 1959

Ashby de la Zooch   Hoffman 1945; Livingston, Jerry 1945

Ashley   Strouse Date Unknown

Ashley's Departure   Rome 1973

Asi Se Besa   Kern 1935

Asia   Goetz 1913

Ask   Spina 1969

Ask a Foolish Question   David, Mack 1963

Ask Anybody (Who Loves You)   Coots 1950

Ask Her in Springtime   Whiting 1917

Ask Her While the Band Is Playing   Herbert 1908

Ask Her While You're Dancing   Freed, Ralph 1941; Lane 1941

Ask Me   Spina 1953

Ask Me Again   Gershwin, George 1930, Date Unknown; Gershwin, Ira 1930, Date Unknown

Ask Me Another   Brown, Lew 1927; DeSylva 1927; Henderson 1927

Ask Me! Because I'm So in Love   Rome 1951

Ask Me No Questions   Brown, Lew 1917

Ask Me No Questions (I'll Tell You No Lies)   Bergman 1981; Mancini 1981; Russell 1947; Sigman 1947

Ask Me-Not   Cobb 1906; Edwards 1906

Ask My Mother   Kalmar 1911; Snyder 1911

Ask Not   Willson 1964

Ask the Cabby   Howard, Joseph E. 1909

Ask the Madame   Cahn 1944; Styne 1944

Ask the Man   Howard, Joseph E. 1905

Ask the Rose   Yellen 1920

Ask Your Heart   Davis 1939; Lawrence 1940

Ask Yourself Who Loves You, Tell Yourself It's Me   Davis 1932

Ask Yourself Why   Bergman 1970

Asking for Trouble   Loesser 1974

Asking for You   Comden and Green 1960; Styne 1960

Asleep or Awake   Lawrence 1939

Asparagus Is Served   Lane 1951; Lerner, Alan Jay 1951

Assembling of the Two Courts   Smith, Harry B. 1906

Assignment   Johnson, J. Rosamond 1950

Assignment Hollywood   Hoffman 1959

A-Stairable Rag   Porter 1941

Astroidiana (inst.)   Revel 1955

Astronaut of Space (Alan Shepard), The   Gilbert 1961; Oakland 1961

Asylum Chorus   Weill 1936

At 11 P.M.   Gershwin, Ira 1924

At a Carnival in Venice   Livingston, Jerry 1937

At a Dixie Roadside Diner   Leslie 1940

At a Grand Hotel   Smith, Harry B. 1916

At a Little Hot Dog Stand   Coslow 1939

At a Masquerade in Rio   Revel 1941

At a Perfume Counter on the Rue de la Paix   Leslie 1938

At a Reception   Harbach 1908

At Any Age at All   Strouse 1975

At Arrowhead Inn   Williams 1910

At Gay Raatenbad   Goetz 1912

At Half Past Nine   Lewis 1918; Young, Joe 1918

At Half Past Seven   DeSylva 1923; Gershwin, George 1923

At Home with My Range   Johnson, James P. 1947

At Last   Comden and Green 1982; Gordon 1941, 1942; Herbert 1920; Howard, Bart 1938; Lewis 1935; Smith, Harry B. 1906; Smith, Robert B. 1920; Warren 1941, 1942

At Last I'm Happy   Conrad 1930; Friend 1930

At Last in Your Arms   Porter 1930

At Last We're Alone   Blane 1955; Martin 1955

At Least I Tried   Coleman 1980

At Least I'm Happy   Clare 1930

At Least It Was Good for a Laugh   Burke 1953

At Long Last Love   Porter 1938

At Longchamps Today   Porter 1929

At Madame Regay's   Cohan 1923

At Mammy's Fireside   Carroll 1913

At Maxims   Leigh 1955

At Mrs. Simpkin's Finishing School   Gershwin, George 1929; Gershwin, Ira 1929; Kahn 1929

At My Dad and Mammy's Golden Wedding Jubilee   Stept 1919

At My Side   Coleman 1988

At Our House   Oakland 1954

At Peace with the World   Berlin 1926

At Sea   Fields 1933; McHugh 1933

At Seven, Seventeen and Seventy   Egan 1917

At Sonya's Cafe   Hoffman 1942; Livingston, Jerry 1942

At Stony Brook   Hammerstein 1932; Kern 1932

At Such a Tender Age   Leigh 1955

At Sundown   Donaldson 1927; Razaf 1926

(Some Day) At Sunrise   Parish 1928

At Ten to Ten in Tennessee   McHugh 1926

At that Bully Wooly Wild West Show   Clarke 1913; Leslie 1913

At that San Francisco Fair   Kern 1915

At that Town Hall Minstrel Show   Kahn 1914

At that Yiddish Society Ball   Lewis 1915

At the Alter   Spina 1976

At the Automat   Goetz 1912
At the Bal Masque   Herbert 1912
At the Ball   Kern 1921
At the Barber's Ball   Cohan 1908
At the Beach   Sherman 1972
At the Beach at Malibu (Hullabaloo at Malibu)   Akst 1936;
   Clare 1936
At the Beaux Arts Ball   Drake 1956
At the Bed-D-Bye Motel   Lerner, Alan Jay 1971
At the Bottom of the Hill   Coots 1933; Young, Joe 1933
At the Bow-Wow Ball   Heyman 1933
At the Button-Hole Makers' Ball   Johnson, Howard 1917
At the Cafe de la Paix (Fredo)   Raye 1958
At the Cafe Rendezvous   Cahn 1949; Styne 1949
At the Cake Walk Ball   Akst 1918; Lewis 1918; Meyer 1918;
   Young, Joe 1918
At the Candlelight Cafe   David, Mack 1948
At the Canton Tea Garden with You   Burke 1931
At the Carnival   Evans 1947; Livingston, Jay 1947
At the Carnival in Rio   Revel 1959
At the Casino (inst.)   Kern 1902
At the Check Apron Ball   Merrill 1957
At the Cinderella Ball   Baer 1941
(Did I Get Stinking) At the Club Savoy   Donaldson 1942
At the Codfish Ball   Mitchell 1936; Pollack 1936
At the Copa   Drake 1954
At the Court Around the Corner   Berlin 1921
At the Cross of God   Coots 1956
At the Crossroads   Russell 1941
At the Dawn Tea   Porter 1913
At the Devil's Ball   Berlin 1912
At the Dixie Military Ball   Carroll 1918
At the Drive-In Movie   Silver 1956
At the Eleventh Hour   Drake 1959
At the End of a Kiss   Coots 1958
At the End of a Winding Lane   Kahn 1924
At the End of an Evening (With You)   Howard, Joseph E.
   1948
At the End of the Rainbow of Love   Mills 1929; Motzan
   1925
At the End of the Road   Hanley 1922
At the End of the Sunset Trail   Edwards 1938
At the End of the Trail (I Found You)   Parish 1928
(A la Fin de la Se-Mane) At the End of the Week   Robison
   1954
At the Ex King's Club   Gershwin, George 1927; Gershwin,
   Ira 1927
At the Fair   Brooks 1960; Hammerstein 1927; Kern 1927
At the Fancy Dress Ball   Sigman 1940
At the Fireman's Ball   Adamson 1946; McHugh 1946
At the Flower Garden Ball   Atteridge 1913; Schwartz, Jean
   1913
At the Flying "W"   Wrubel 1948
At the Follies Bergere   Sterling 1911; Von Tilzer 1911
At the Foot of the Hill of Dreams   DeSylva 1926; Hanley
   1926
At the Fox Trot Ball   Atteridge 1915; Carroll 1915; Romberg
   1915
At the Garden Gate   Carmichael 1952
At the Grand Turkish Jubilee (Do a Little Turkey)   Fisher
   1920
At the High Brown Babies Ball   Davis 1919
At the Hoboe's Ball   Lewis 1915
At the Hockey Game   Leigh 1971
At the Hotel   Freed, Arthur 1925

At the Irish Jubilee   Brown, A. Seymour 1922
At the Jazz Band Ball   Mercer 1950
At the Jazz Town Novelty Ball   Pollack 1918
At the Junction of the Chenango and the Susquehana
   Rivers   Willson 1953
At the Mardi Gras   Dietz 1948; Schwartz, Arthur 1948
At the Midnight Masquerade   Brown, Lew 1913
At the Mississippi Cabaret   Brown, A. Seymour 1914
At the Moving Picture Ball   Johnson, Howard 1920
At the Music Hall   Schwartz, Jean 1904
At the Nickleodeon   Evans 1948; Livingston, Jay 1948
At the Old Barn Dance   Lawrence 1937
At the Old Plantation Ball   Ager 1915; Donaldson 1915;
   Goetz 1915
At the Old Town Pump   Von Tilzer 1917
At the Opera   Caesar 1948
At the Palace   Strouse 1975
At the Pan-American   Smith, Harry B. 1901
At the Party   DeSylva 1925; Kalmar 1926; Ruby 1926
At the Piano   Bryan 1920; Schwartz, Jean 1920
At the Picture Show   Berlin 1913; Goetz 1913
At the Prohibition Ball   Silver 1919
At the Prom   Donaldson 1926
At the Psychological Moment   Burke 1940, 1949; Van
   Heusen 1940, 1949
At the Pullman Porter's Full Dress Ball   Blake 1916; Sissle
   1916
At the Quilting Party (inst.)   Revel 1960
At the Ragtime Ball   Monaco 1911
At the Ragtime Strollers Ball   Koehler 1918
At the Rainbow   Porter 1912
At the Rainbow's End   Herbert 1924
At the Red Rose Cotillion   Loesser 1948
At the Reefer Smoker's Ball   Razaf 1935
At the Rodeo   Cahn 1948; Styne 1948
At the Round Table (Knight's Opening)   Hart 1927; Rodgers
   1927
At the Roxy Music Hall   Hart 1938; Rodgers 1938
At the Russian Cabaret   Johnson, Howard 1918
At the Saskatchewan   Hart 1926; Rodgers 1926
At the Stage Door   Atteridge 1923; Schwartz, Jean 1923
At the Sugar Shoppe   Drake 1958
At the Teddy Bear's Birthday Party   Coots 1952
At the Toy Shop   Atteridge 1915; Romberg 1915
At the Water's Edge, Just Edging Around   Lewis 1929;
   Young, Joe 1929
At the Wedding of Sammy and Me   Ruby 1917
At the Winter Garden   Romberg 1919; Schwartz, Jean 1919
At the World's Fair   Caesar 1943
At the Yankee Doodle Ball   Adamson 1945; McHugh 1945
At the Yankee Military Ball   Johnson, Howard 1917
At the Yiddish Cabaret   Gilbert 1913
At the Yiddisha Wedding Dance   Carroll 1911
At Twilight   Friml 1913; Razaf 1944; Waller 1944
At Twilight Time   Egan 1920; Whiting 1920
At Ye Olde Coffee Shoppe in Cheyenne   Porter 1936
At Your Beck and Call   De Lange 1938
At Your Service Madame   Dubin 1935; Warren 1935
A-Tangle, A-Dangle   Loesser 1960
Athena   Blane 1954; Duke 1963; Martin 1954
Athena's Dance (inst).   Duke 1963
Athletic Boy   Caesar 1924; Conrad 1924; Harbach 1924
Athletic Prancing   Harbach 1910
Atlanta   Dietz 1948; Schwartz, Arthur 1948
Atlanta Burning   Rome 1973

Atlantic Blues   Hart 1926; Rodgers 1926

Atlantic City   Coleman 1975

Atlas Did It (But He Won't Admit It)   DePaul 1942; Raye 1942

Atlas Is Itless   Brown, Lew 1929; DeSylva 1929; Henderson 1929

Atmosphere (For Love)   Robin 1955; Styne 1955

Atom Bomb Baby (Mambo)   Sondheim 1957

Atomic Lace   Razaf Date Unknown

'Atta Girl   Gershwin, Ira 1924

Attitude   Mancini 1995

Attitude of Doin' Right, The   Carmichael 1951

Attwater Prairie Chickens   Sherman 1991

Au Revoir   Cobb 1918; Drake 1947; Edwards 1918

Au Revoir but not Good-Bye   Alter 1927

Au Revoir But Not Good-Bye, Soldier Boy   Brown, Lew 1917

Au Revoir, Cher Baron   Porter 1938

Au Revoir Cherie   Spina 1957

Au Revoir (Means We'll Soon Meet Again)   Caesar 1927; Friend 1927

Au Revoir, Paree   Dietz 1942; Schwartz, Arthur 1942

Au Revoir, Pleasant Dreams   Schwartz, Jean 1930

Auction Rag   Atteridge 1919; Carroll 1919

Auctioneer's Song   Smith, Harry B. 1891

Auctions   Lerner, Alan Jay 1976

Audience, The   Adams 1961; Rome 1964; Strouse 1961

Audition   Hammerstein 1939; Kern 1939; Merrill 1993; Styne 1993

Auditions   Rainger 1932; Robin 1932

Auf Japan   Friml Date Unknown

Auf Widersehn   Porter 1931

Auf Wiedersehen   Lerner, Alan Jay 1983; Romberg 1915; Strouse 1983

Auf Wiedersehen, My Dear   Ager 1932; Hoffman 1932

August Birthday Song   Caesar 1940

Auld Lang Syne   Johnson, Howard 1939

Aunt Jemima   Egan 1925; Silver 1921; Whiting 1925

Aunt Jemima's Birthday (inst.)   Bloom 1931

Aunt Jemima's Divorce, Minutes of the Case   Blake 1930; Razaf 1930

Aunt Molly   Johnson, J. Rosamond 1944

Aunt Polly's Soliloquy   Sherman 1973

Aupres de Ma Blonde   Bergman 1958; Cahn 1952; Duke 1952

Aura Lee   Johnson, Howard 1939

Aurora   Adamson 1941; Razaf 1957

Aurora Blushing Rosily   Herbert 1913

Aurora Borealis   Schwartz, Jean 1905, 1908; Williams 1908

Auto Da Fe (What a Day)   Sondheim 1974

Auto Girls Song   Buck 1917

Auto Show Girl   Rodgers 1917

Autograph Chant (An Autograph of Hazel Flagg)   Styne 1953

Autograph Your Photograph   David, Mack 1965

Autograph Your Photograph for Me   Hoffman 1934

Automat Cabaret   Carroll 1917

Automobile Ballet   Brooks 1959

Automobile Has Two Big Eyes, An   Caesar 1937

Automobile Horn Song   Donaldson 1928; Kahn 1928

Automobiles   Fain 1957; Webster 1957

Autumn   Koehler 1950; Stept 1950

Autumn Courting (inst.), The   Loesser 1960

Autumn in Argentina   Leslie 1936

Autumn in Azusa   Spina 1957

Autumn in New York   Duke 1934

Autumn in Rome   Cahn 1954

Autumn Leaves   Mercer 1950

Autumn Leaves Are Falling   Kalmar 1931; Ruby 1931

Autumn Lullaby, An   Razaf 1944

Autumn Moon   Harbach 1911

Autumn Night   Alter 1959

Autumn Nocturne   Myrow 1941

Autumn Reverie (inst.)   Warren 1959

Autumn Rhapsody   Leigh 1955

Autumn Sings a Sad, Sad Song   Cahn 1968

Autumn Twilight   Fain 1946; Freed, Ralph 1946; Mercer 1953

Autumn's Elegy   Motzan 1933

Autumn's in the Air   Styne 1965

Aux Armes   Atteridge 1923; Romberg 1923; Schwartz, Jean 1923

Available   Cahn 1964

Avalon   DeSylva 1921; Evans 1946; Livingston, Jay 1946

Avalon By Moonlight   Lawrence 1936

Avalon Town   Brown, Nacio Herb 1927; Clarke 1927

Ave Maria   Johnson, Howard 1939; Warren Date Unknown

Ave Maria and Finale   Freed, Ralph 1946

Ave Regina   Brown, Nacio Herb 1945

Avenida De La Rosa   Russell 1951

Avenue of Trees   Oakland 1936

Average   Cahn 1971; Van Heusen 1971

Average American Guy, An   Oakland 1954

Aviation   Atteridge 1910

Aviation Ballet   Buck 1927

Aviator   Gershwin, George 1927; Gershwin, Ira 1927

Aw! C'mon, Whatta Ya Got to Lose?   Robin 1930; Whiting 1930

Aw Come On Now   Mercer 1944

Aw Gee Don't Be that Way Now   Turk 1927

Aw, What's the Use   Harburg 1930

Await Your Love (Concubine's Song)   Hart 1928; Rodgers 1928

Awake, Children, Awake   Gershwin, Ira 1929

Awake Dearest One   Smith, Harry B. 1908

Awake in a Dream   Robin 1936

Awake, Ma Chile   Smith, Harry B. 1903

Awake My Love   Parish 1954

Awake or Dreaming   Coots 1935; Parish 1935

Awakened Love   Smith, Harry B. 1911

Awakening, The   Johnson, J. Rosamond 1913

Awards   Leigh 1985

Away Down East in Maine   Donaldson 1922

Away Down South   Akst 1922; Lewis 1922; Young, Joe 1922

Away Down South in Heaven   Warren 1927

Away for a Lovely Ocean Cruise   Friml 1912; Harbach 1912

Away from It All   Porter 1950

Away from You   Ager 1925; Davis 1925; Koehler 1928; Rodgers 1976

Away Out West   Adamson 1956; Cahn 1947; Styne 1947; Young, Victor 1956

Away Up There   Drake 1954

Away, Way Out in the Sticks   Fain 1933

Away We'll Float   Herbert 1908; Smith, Harry B. 1908

A-Wearin' the Blues   Turk 1921

Awful Lot My Gal Ain't Got, An   Waller 1925

Awfully Nice to Love One Girl   Herbert 1907

Awkward Age, The   Atteridge 1917; Motzan 1917; Romberg 1917

Axe the Axis Polka   Sherman 1971

Axion Theme (inst.) Strouse 1975
Ay Ay Ay Russell 1941
Aye Aye Aye Aye O Russell 1952
Aye, Lad Mercer 1974
Ayes Have It David, Hal 1946
Azalea Ellington 1942
Azalia (inst.) Warren 1977
Azure Ellington 1937; Mills 1937
Azuri's Dance of Triumph (inst.) Romberg 1926
Azuza, Cucamonga and Anaheim Stept 1947

B

B Apostrophe K Apostrophe L-Y-N Cahn 1944; Styne 1944
B Flat Stride, The Mills 1936
Baa, Baa Black Sheep Johnson, Howard 1939
Babalu Russell 1941
Babbit the Rabbit Coots 1951
Babbitt and the Bromide, The Gershwin, George 1927; Gershwin, Ira 1927
Babbitts in Love Hart 1925; Rodgers 1925
Babbler's Exit Adams 1970; Strouse 1970
Babbling Babette Kern 1923
Babes in Arms Hart 1937; Rodgers 1937
Babes in the Wood Kern 1915
Babes in Toyland Herbert 1903
Babes on Broadway Freed, Ralph 1941; Lane 1941
Babette Coleman 1978; Comden and Green 1978
Babette of Beaujolais Herbert 1913
Babette's Military Dance Smith, Harry B. 1927
Babette's Wedding Day Smith, Harry B. 1927
Babies a la Mode (Frocks and Frills) Cobb 1930; Edwards 1930
Babs Ahlert 1935; Young, Joe 1935
Bab's Melody Spina 1977
Baby! DeSylva 1925; Fields 1928; Gershwin, George 1925; Gershwin, Ira 1925; Kahn 1919; Lerner, Alan Jay 1948; Loesser 1942; McHugh 1928, 1942; Monaco 1933; Weill 1948
Baby — Oh Where Can You Be? Koehler 1929
Baby, Ain'tcha Satisfied? Mills 1935
Baby, Baby, Baby David, Mack 1950; Livingston, Jerry 1950
Baby Be Good Caesar 1924; Conrad 1924; Harbach 1924
Baby, Be Nice to Me Revel 1959
Baby Be Smart Blake 1954
Baby Be Yourself Duke 1930; Harburg 1930
Baby Blue Donaldson 1919; Jerome 1910; Lewis 1919; Schwartz, Jean 1910; Young, Joe 1919
Baby Blue Eyes Leslie 1950
Baby Blues, The Gershwin, George 1921; Goetz 1921
Baby Bond for Baby, A Hart 1937; Rodgers 1937
Baby Buntin' Blake 1923; Sissle 1923
Baby Couldn't Dance Duke 1952
Baby, Do I Make Myself Clear Mills 1947
Baby, Does Your Maybe Mean Yes Parish 1929
Baby Doll Friml 1918; Mercer 1951; Warren 1951
Baby Dollie Walk Conrad 1921
Baby Dolls DeSylva 1919; Gershwin, George 1919
Baby, Don't Be Mad at Me David, Mack 1946
Baby, Don't Jump — Don't Jump! Freed, Ralph 1964
Baby, Don't Start Cheating on Me (Not After All These Years) Mills 1948
Baby Don't You Cry Washington 1943
Baby, Don't You Quit Now Mercer 1967
Baby, Dream Your Dream Coleman 1966; Fields 1966

Baby Dreams Hammerstein 1920; Harbach 1920
Baby Duck Young, Victor 1934
Baby Duet Smith, Harry B. 1911; Smith, Robert B. 1911
Baby Elephant Walk David, Hal 1962; Mancini 1962
Baby, Exceptional Baby Bryan 1933; Monaco 1933
Baby Face Akst 1926; Davis 1926; Howard, Joseph E. 1921; Kalmar 1924; Ruby 1924
Baby Face the Elephant Martin 1958
Baby Feet Go Pitter-Patter Kahn 1927
Baby Fix It for Me Johnson, Howard 1930; Woods 1930
Baby Follies Edwards 1929; Johnson, Howard 1929
Baby Games Porter 1941
Baby, Have You Got a Little Love to Spare Koehler 1947; Warren 1947
Baby, I Don't Like You! Howard, Bart 1984
Baby I Have to Have You Conrad 1930; Meyer 1930; Mitchell 1930
Baby, I Love Ya Up to Here Cahn 1964; Van Heusen 1964
Baby I'd Know It Was You Coots 1949
Baby, I'm Holding Out for You Raye 1944
Baby, I'm the Greatest Mills 1964
Baby It Isn't in the Cards Russell 1957
Baby, It Upsets Me So Razaf 1930
Baby, It's Cold Outside Loesser 1948
Baby It's You Bacharach 1961; David, Mack 1961
Baby June and Her Newsboys Sondheim 1959; Styne 1959
Baby Knows Best Brown, Lew 1943
Baby Let Me Hear from You Sigman 1973
Baby, Let Me Take You Dreaming Cahn 1956
Baby, Let's Dance Porter 1928
Baby Let's Face It Fain 1946
Baby Lindy Mills 1930
Baby Looks Like Me, The Kalmar 1925; Ruby 1925
Baby Lou Howard, Joseph E. 1908
Baby Love Von Tilzer 1914
Baby Me Sherman 1995
Baby Me Blues Gershwin, Ira 1923; Youmans 1923
Baby Mine Blake 1930; Razaf 1930; Washington 1941
Baby My Baby David, Mack 1979
Baby, My Little Baby Jerome 1903; Schwartz, Jean 1903
Baby o' Mine Brown, Nacio Herb 1919
Baby, Obey Me! Evans 1950; Livingston, Jay 1950
Baby Please Hurry to Me Razaf Date Unknown
Baby Please Stop and Think about Me Ellington 1943
Baby Racketeers Bryan 1931
Baby San Arlen 1966
Baby Save Your Tears (Baby Weine Nicht) Gilbert 1931
Baby Sitter (I'm Goin' to Sit with Baby) Burke 1949
B-A-B-Y Spells Baby Johnson, Howard 1925
Baby Stars Hart 1934; Rodgers 1934
Baby Stop-Stop-Stop Lewis 1927; Young, Joe 1927
Baby, Take a Bow Brown, Lew 1934; Gorney 1934
Baby Talk Williams 1910
Baby, Talk to Me Adams 1960; Strouse 1960
Baby that Should Have Been Mine, The Baer 1956
Baby That's for Me Donaldson 1942
Baby that's Me Martin 1959
Baby, the Ball Is Over Bergman 1963
Baby Vampire Atteridge 1921; Kahn 1917; Kern 1917; Pollack 1921; Schwartz, Jean 1921; Smith, Harry B. 1917
Baby Vampire Land Bryan 1919; Schwartz, Jean 1919
Baby, Wait Till It Happens to You Hammerstein 1933
'Baby Wampus' Stars, The Brown, Lew 1939; Stept 1939
Baby Wants to Dance Hart 1922; Rodgers 1922
Baby, We're Through Harburg 1932

Baby! What?   Brown, Lew 1927; DeSylva 1927; Henderson 1927

Baby, Whatcha Gonna Do Tonight?   Hoffman 1937; Lerner, Sammy 1937

Baby, When You Ain't There   Ellington 1941; Parish 1941

Baby, Won't You Say You Love Me   Gordon 1950; Myrow 1950

Baby Y'Know   Russell 1957

Baby, You Can Count on Me   Adams 1981; Strouse 1981

Baby You Haunt Me   Friend 1953

Baby You Knock Me Out   Comden and Green 1955

Baby You Love, The   Hammerstein 1953; Rodgers 1953

Baby, You'll Never Be Sorry   Robin 1951; Styne 1951

Baby, You're Right for Me   Mills 1966

Baby, You're Too Much   Ellington 1967

Baby You're Zoot   Fain 1943; Harburg 1943

Baby-Doll Dance   Brennan 1929

Babying You   Kalmar 1926; Ruby 1926

Babykins   Caesar 1930

Babylon   Williams 1922

Baby-o   Mercer 1962

Baby's a Big Girl Now   Cahn 1942; Styne 1942

Baby's Asleep   Heyman 1939; Romberg 1939

Baby's Awake Now   Hart 1928; Rodgers 1928

Baby's Best Friend, A   Hart 1928; Rodgers 1928

Baby's Bottle   Woods 1934

Baby's First Christmas   Davis 1961

Baby's Gone   Brown, A. Seymour 1909

Baccanale Dance   Johnson, Howard 1921

Baccarole   Romberg 1916

Bacchanal Rag, The   Atteridge 1912

Bacchanale (inst.)   Weill 1943

Bach & Me   Oakland 1967

Bach Invention #1   Cahn 1947; Styne 1947

Bach Up to Me (inst.)   Waller 1938

Bachanol   Coots 1926

Bachelor, The   Merrill 1966

Bachelor Belles, The   Smith, Harry B. 1910

Bachelor Days   Harbach 1911

Bachelor Dinner Song   Mercer 1951; Warren 1951

Bachelor Gal   Drake 1964

Bachelor Girl and Boy, A   Romberg 1916

Bachelor in Paradise   David, Mack 1961; Mancini 1961

Bachelor of the Art   Coslow 1934; Johnston 1934

Bachelor Party (And the Linen Shower), The   Drake 1954

Bachelor Song, The   Weill 1938

Bachelorhood   Duke 1955

Bachelors   Coleman 1988

Bachelor's Ball, The   Fain 1961; Raye 1961

Bachelor's Dream, The   Buck Date Unknown

Bachelor's Life, A   Russell 1952

Back at the Grind   Brooks 1959

Back, Back, Back to Indiana   Kahn 1914

Back Bay Beat   David, Mack 1943; Livingston, Jerry 1943

Back Bay Polka, The   Gershwin, George 1947; Gershwin, Ira 1947

Back Beats   Mills 1935

Back from Hollywood   Brown, Lew 1931; Henderson 1931

Back from the Great Beyond   Merrill 1971; Styne 1971

Back Home   Ager 1923; Evans 1954; Fain 1930; Gershwin, George 1920; Gershwin, Ira 1920; Kahal 1930; Livingston, Jay 1954; Yellen 1923

Back Home Among the Carolina Pines   Parish 1932; Snyder 1932

Back Home for Keeps   Russell 1945, Date Unknown

Back Home in Illinois   Stept 1925

Back in Business   Sondheim 1990

Back in Circulation   Dietz 1944; Duke 1944

Back in Circulation Now   Razaf 1945

Back in Mothers Day   Davis 1967

Back in My Old Home Town   Edwards 1929

Back in My Shell   Fields 1940; Kern 1940

Back in Show Biz Again   Adams 1981; Strouse 1981

Back in the Kitchen   Comden and Green 1967; Styne 1967

Back in the Quaint Little School in Caroline   Carroll 1918

Back in Tipperary Town   Yellen 1917

Back in Your Arms   De Lange 1937; Mills 1937

Back in Your Own Back Yard   DeSylva 1929; Rose 1927

Back Part of the Paper, The   Brooks 1959

Back Seat Drivers   Loesser 1935

Back the Bringin' 'Em Back   Cahn 1945; Styne 1945

Back the Red, White and Blue with Gold   Hoffman 1942; Livingston, Jerry 1942

Back to Back   Berlin 1939

Back to Baltimore   Williams 1904

Back to Dixieland   Yellen 1914

Back to Killarney   Harbach 1923

Back to My Heart   Duke 1926

Back to My Old Home Town   Norworth 1910

Back to Nature   Atteridge 1916; Hart 1926; Motzan 1916, 1917; Porter 1933; Rodgers 1926; Romberg 1916

Back to Normal   Livingston, Jerry 1960

Back to School Again   Adams 1962; Strouse 1962

Back to Sioux City   Schwartz, Jean 1905; Williams 1905

Back to the Backwoods   Lawrence 1938

Back to the Carolina You Love   Clarke 1914; Schwartz, Jean 1914

Back to the Days of Auld Lang Syne   Dubin 1913

Back to the Heather   Kern 1928

Back to the Palace   Sondheim 1987

Back to the Woods   Jerome 1902; Schwartz, Jean 1902

Back to the Woodwork!   Styne 1958

Back to Work   Rome 1937

Back Where I Come From   Arlen 1952; Blane 1953

Back Where the Daffodils Grow   Donaldson 1924

Back Where We Started   Razaf 1930

Back Yard Follies   Oakland 1931

Backlot Blues, The   Duke 1955

Backsliders   Robison 1930

Backstage Babble   Adams 1970; Strouse 1970

Backstage Music (Opening Scene) (inst.)   Kern 1938

Backward Child   Davis 1961

Backwoods Barbecue   Revel 1942

Backyard Cook Out (Stereo Patio Party)   Robison 1959

Bacon and the Egg, The   Duke 1927

Bad Baby   Lewis 1930; Warren 1930; Young, Joe 1930

Bad, Bad Baby   Egan 1917

Bad, Bad Men, The   Gershwin, George 1924; Gershwin, Ira 1924

Bad Bill Jones   Johnson, James P. 1948, 1950

Bad Boy   Leslie 1930; Monaco 1930

Bad Boys and Girls   Robison 1959

Bad Chinaman from Shanghai, A   Berlin 1917

Bad Dream Blues   Turk 1921

Bad for Each Other   Arlen 1963; Leigh 1963

Bad for My Complexion   Dietz 1959; Schwartz, Arthur 1959

Bad Girl   Parish 1928

Bad in Every Man, The   Hart 1934; Rodgers 1934

Bad Is for Other People   Coleman 1966

Bad Little Apple and the Wise Old Tree, The   Hart 1943

Bad Little Boy and Good Little Girl   Romberg 1922
Bad Little Boy with Dancing Legs   Coots 1926
Bad Little Boys Aren't Goody-Good to the Goody-Good Little Girls, The   Ager 1922; Yellen 1922
Bad Little Three Blind Mice, The   Lerner, Sammy 1942
Bad Man   Rainger 1935; Robin 1935; Whiting 1935
Bad Man Number   Friml 1927
Bad Man's Life, A   Revel 1946
Bad Men   Porter 1916
Bad News   Evans 1954; Leigh Date Unknown; Livingston, Jay 1954
Bad News Blues   Akst 1923; Davis 1923
Bad Temptation Like You, A   Leslie 1931; Meyer 1931
Bad Timing   Comden and Green 1945
Baffi Bajon   Sigman 1955; Spina 1955
Bagdad   Ager 1924; Atteridge 1918; Brooks 1949; Bryan 1930; Herbert 1912; Romberg 1918; Yellen 1924
Bagpipe Rhumba, The   Bullock 1940; Wrubel 1940
Bagpipe Serenade   Kern 1906
Bagpipes of Buckingham, The   Gordon 1943; Warren 1943
Bagpipes on Parade   Von Tilzer 1940
Bah, Bah Black Sheep   Johnston 1948
Bahama   Woods 1923
Bahama Mama (That Tropical Charmer) (That Goombay Tune)   Gilbert 1932
Bahia   De Lange 1944; Stept 1944
Baker's Boy and the Chimney-Sweep, The   Herbert 1914; Smith, Robert B. 1914
Baker's Keyboard Blues   Drake 1959
Bal Masque   Coslow 1936, 1945; Young, Victor 1936, 1945
Bal Tabarin, The   Atteridge 1924; Romberg 1924; Schwartz, Jean 1924
Balalaika Boogie Woogie   Coots 1945
Balance of Nature   Bacharach 1972; David, Hal 1972
Balboa   Blane 1956; Martin 1956; Mitchell 1936; Pollack 1936; Razaf 1936
Balboa Bay   Blane 1947; Brown, Nacio Herb 1947
Balcony Episode   Johnson, Howard 1930
Balcony Waltz, The   Johnson, Howard 1935
Bali Hai   Hammerstein 1949; Rodgers 1949
Ball and Chain Blues   Razaf 1925; Waller 1925
Ball Begins, The   Atteridge 1923; Romberg 1923
Ball Dance   Loesser 1937
Ball Is in Your Court, The   Coleman 1989
Ball Was Had By All, A   Coots 1957
Ballad for a Pencil   Bergman 1964; Fain 1964
Ballad in Blue   Carmichael 1935; Kahal 1935
Ballad of a Gun   Rome 1959
Ballad of Alvarez Kelly, The   Mercer 1966
Ballad of Baby Face McGinty, The   Duke 1936; Gershwin, Ira 1936
Ballad of Booth, The   Sondheim 1990
Ballad of Caryl Chessman (Let Him Live, Let Him Live, Let Him Live), The   Hoffman 1960
Ballad of Cat Ballou, The   David, Mack 1965; Livingston, Jerry 1965
Ballad of Czolgosz, The   Sondheim 1990
Ballad of Dependency   Weill 1954
Ballad of Guiteau, The   Sondheim 1990
Ballad of Jack and the Beanstalk, The   Livingston, Jerry 1956
Ballad of Johnny Cool, The   Cahn 1963; Van Heusen 1963
Ballad of Magna Carta   Weill 1940
Ballad of Marcia LaRue, The   Rome 1948
Ballad of Marshall Flagg, The   Washington 1969
Ballad of Mary Jane   Cahn 1981

Ballad of Millicent De Vere, The   Burke 1944; Van Heusen 1944
Ballad of Sam Older, The   Carmichael 1959
Ballad of Scatter Gun Hill, The   Livingston, Jerry 1960
Ballad of Sloppy Joe, The   Rome 1943
Ballad of Smith and Gabriel Jimmy Boy, The   Russell 1969
Ballad of Surfer Bill   Russell Date Unknown
Ballad of Sweeney Todd, The   Sondheim 1979
Ballad of the Alamo   Webster 1960
Ballad of the Easy Life   Weill 1933, 1954
Ballad of the Garment Trade   Rome 1962
Ballad of the Lily of Hell   Weill 1977
Ballad of the Mooncussers   Sherman 1962
Ballad of the Robbers   Weill 1938
Ballad of the South (Lazy, Lazy Liza)   Gordon 1933; Revel 1933
Ballad of Thunder Road   Raye 1958
Ballad of Wes Tancred   Myrow 1956
Ballad of Will Kane, The   Adamson 1966
Ballads, Boogie and Blues   Leslie 1955; Schwartz, Jean 1955
Ballerina   Revel 1953; Sigman 1947
Ballet   Friml 1925; Herbert 1905, 1911; Smith, Harry B. 1911
Ballet Dance   Atteridge 1924; Romberg 1924; Schwartz, Jean 1924
Ballet Divertissement (dance)   Herbert 1946
Ballet for a Dinosaur   Spina 1977
Ballet (inst.)   Kern 1956
Ballet Loose, The   Herbert 1916
Ballet Mignon   Razaf 1948
Ballet Modern   Youmans 1924
Ballet Moderne (inst.)   McHugh 1937
Ballet Music   Gershwin, George 1924
Ballet Music (inst.)   Schwartz, Arthur 1931
Ballet of Siam, A   Atteridge 1922
Ballet of the Book According to Gerald   Lerner, Alan Jay 1945; Loewe 1945
Ballet of the Pyramids (inst.)   Pollack 1921; Schwartz, Jean 1921
Ballet Oriental   Atteridge 1922; Romberg 1922
Ballet (Pearl of Ceylon) (inst.)   Kern 1927
Ballet Romantique (inst.)   Friml 1928
Ballet Suite, The   Herbert 1912, 1915
Ballett (inst.)   Warren Date Unknown
Ballet-Youth   Herbert 1912
Ballin' the Blues   Ellington 1953
Ballo Felicidad Amor   Brooks 1955
Balloon Ballet (Inst.)   Gershwin, George 1937
Balloon Girls, The   Cohan 1916
Balloon Song, The   Clare 1947
Balloon Underplay (inst.)   Fain 1963
Ballooning   Kern 1907
Bally Cottin   Robison 1947
Bally-Burlesk (inst.)   Herbert 1922
Ballyho Bay   Fisher 1919
Ballyhoo   Berlin 1946
Ballyhooey Lassies (Opening Act II)   Harburg 1932
Ballyhujah   Harburg 1932
Baloombala   Adamson 1953
Baloo's Blues   Sherman 1969
Baltimo'   Razaf 1913
Baltimore   Donaldson 1922; Kahal 1927; McHugh 1927
Baltimore and Ohio   Magidson 1951; Sigman 1951
Baltimore Blues, The   Blake 1919; Sissle 1919
Baltimore Buzz   Blake 1921; Sissle 1921

Baltimore, MD. — That's the Only Doctor for Me   Schwartz, Arthur 1923

Baltimore Oriole   Carmichael 1942; Webster 1942, 1944

Baltimore Sun   Merrill 1964; Styne 1964

Baltimore Todalo (inst.), The   Blake 1962

Bam Bam Bammy Shore, The   Dixon 1925; Henderson 1925

Bambalina   Hammerstein 1923; Harbach 1923; Youmans 1923

Bambalina Maid   Meyer 1926

Bambazoola   Bryan 1927; Schwartz, Jean 1927

Bambino   Coots 1950; Gershwin, Ira 1920; Leslie 1928; Youmans 1920

Bamboo Babies   Hanley 1925

Bamboo Bay   Donaldson 1922; Egan 1922; Whiting 1922

Bamboo Isle   Henderson 1922

Bamboo Lane   Jerome 1909; Schwartz, Jean 1909

Bamboo Tamboo   Bergman 1957

Bamboola   Conrad 1925

Bamboula   Evans 1948; Livingston, Jay 1948

Bamboula (El Relicario)   Goetz 1922

Bambuco   Mills 1939

Baminay (The New Orleans Chimney Sweep)   Fain 1952; Lawrence 1952

Bammy (Alabamy)   Conrad 1922

Ban the Book!   Duke 1968

Banana Boat   Evans 1954; Livingston, Jay 1954

Banana Oil   Dubin 1925; McHugh 1925

Bananas   Freed, Arthur 1945; Warren 1945

Banbury Lane   David, Mack 1941

Band, The   Willson 1959

Band, Band, Band   Brown, A. Seymour Date Unknown

Band Came Back, The   Brown, A. Seymour 1911

Band from Dixie-Land   Atteridge Date Unknown

Band of Angels   Sigman 1957

Band of Reubenville   Schwartz, Jean 1905; Williams 1905

Band of the Ne'er-Do-Wells, The   Hart 1923; Rodgers 1923

Band Played All the Time, The   Dubin 1915

Band Played On, The   Johnson, Howard 1939

Band Played Out of Tune, The   Stept 1938

Band Started Swinging a Song, The   Porter 1944

Bandage on Your Knee   Caesar 1942

Bandana Ball   Berlin 1924

Bandana Days   Blake 1921; Sissle 1921

Bandana Ways   Blake 1932; Sissle 1932

Bandanna Babies   Fields 1928; McHugh 1928

Bandanna Land   Herbert 1904

Bandido Love   Ahlert 1930; Turk 1930

Bandit Band, The   Porter 1922

Bane of Man, The   Eliscu 1937

Bang   Sondheim 1973

Bang — The Bell Rang   Loesser 1936

Bang! Bang!   Cahn 1964; Van Heusen 1964

Bang on Your Tambourine   Dixon 1923

Bang! There Goes My Heart   Schwartz, Arthur 1930

Bang Up Time   Atteridge 1924; Romberg 1924; Schwartz, Jean 1924

Bangaway Island   Akst 1927; Davis 1927

Bangin' the Bongo   Hoffman 1956

Banishment (inst.), The   Romberg 1926

Banjo Eyes   Duke 1941; Kahn 1927; Whiting 1927

Banjo King   Sherman 1978

Banjo Land   Johnson, James P. 1922

Banjo Papa, You'd Better Stop Pickin' on Me   Razaf 1928

Banjo that Man Joe Plays, The   Porter 1929

Banking on the Weather   Fain 1932; Young, Joe 1932

Banks of the Danube   Revel 1960

Banners and Bonnets   Willson 1952

Banquet at Buckingham (inst.)   Coots 1947

Banquet in Misery Hall, The   Von Tilzer 1902

Bansheela   Henderson 1922

Bantu Baby   Johnson, James P. 1930; Razaf 1930

Bar Mitzvah, The   Styne 1978

Bar Mitzvah of Eliot Green   Styne 1978

Baraboo   Edwards 1903

Barbara   Carmichael 1957; David, Mack 1977; Rose 1927; Silver 1927; Van Heusen 1977; Weill 1954

Barbara Fritchie (inst.)   Young, Victor 1955

Barbarian Dance   Herbert 1905

Barbaric (inst.)   Carmichael 1930

Barbary Coast   Adamson 1963; Gershwin, George 1930; Gershwin, Ira 1930

Barbary Coast Saloon   Adamson 1959; Young, Victor 1959

Barbecue, The   Herbert 1908; Smith, Harry B. 1908

Barbecue Song   Johnson, James P. 1943

Barber and His Wife, The   Sondheim 1979

Barber of Seville   Brooks 1945

Barber Shop Boogie, The   Drake 1952

Barber's Bear, The   Clarke 1912; Schwartz, Jean 1912

Barbie Goodnight   Livingston, Jerry 1963

Barbie Look, The   Livingston, Jerry 1963

Barbie's Fashion Parade   Livingston, Jerry 1963

Barcarole, The   Caesar 1923; Conrad 1923; Smith, Robert B. 1915

Barcarolle   Johnson, Howard 1934; Smith, Harry B. 1925

Barcarolle Blues   Friend 1923

Barcelona   Kahn 1926; Porter 1912; Sondheim 1970

Barefoot Boy   Kahn 1923

Barefoot Days   Atteridge 1921; Cobb 1916; Edwards 1916; Romberg 1921

Barefoot Girl   Caesar 1930

Barefoot in the Park   Mercer 1967

Bargain Counter Doll   Merrill 1956

Bargaining   Rodgers 1965; Sondheim 1965

Barker, The   Baer 1928; Gilbert 1928

Barking Baby Never Bites, A   Hart 1940; Rodgers 1940

Barley 'n' Beans   David, Hal 1951

Barn Dance   Herbert 1909

Barn Dance — Schottische   Herbert 1910

Barn Dance (inst.)   Bloom 1933

Barnard! Barnard!   Rodgers 1964

Barney Brontosaur   Sherman 1954

Barney Donohue   Jerome 1904; Schwartz, Jean 1904

Barney Google   Conrad 1923; Fisher 1923; Rose 1923

Barney McGuire   Herbert 1905; Smith, Harry B. 1905

Barney O'Flynn   Herbert 1903

Barney's Beanery   Spina 1977

Barnum & Bailey Rag   Cohan 1914

Barnum and Bailey Ball, The   Burke 1952; Van Heusen 1952

Barnum and Beery and Me   Johnson, Howard 1935

Barnum Had the Right Idea   Cohan 1911

Barn-Yard Harmony   Clarke 1913; Schwartz, Jean 1913

Barnyard Romeo   Alter 1931; Freed, Arthur 1931

Baron de Ragotin   Romberg 1933

Baron Is in Conference, The   Gordon 1941; Warren 1941

Baroness Bazooka   Comden and Green 1943

Barons   Sigman 1948

Barracuda   Bacharach 1961

Barrel House Bessie from Basin Street   Magidson 1942; Styne 1942

Barrel of Beads   Dietz 1944; Duke 1944

Barrel of Monkeys, A   Burke 1959; Van Heusen 1959

Barrelhouse Beguine   Kern 1942; Mercer 1942

Barrel-House Music   Robison 1935

Barrels 'n' Barrels of Roses   Merrill 1952

Barry   Strouse 1971

Barry from Ballymore   Olcott 1910

Bartered Bride As She Might Have Been (I Wanna Go),
    The   Willson 1955

Baseball   Bryan 1919; Schwartz, Jean 1919

Baseball Girl, The   Goetz 1911

Baseball Glide, The   Sterling 1911; Von Tilzer 1911

Baseball Hoedown   Drake 1957

Baseball Papa — Race Track Mama   Razaf Date Unknown;
    Waller Date Unknown

Bashful   Friend 1930; Kahn 1926; Monaco 1930

Bashful Baby   Friend 1929; Silver 1929

Bashful Chappie, The   Edwards 1909; Smith, Robert B. 1909

Basket of Buttercups (inst.)   Coots 1947

Basket of Dreams   Webster 1971

Basket of Oriental Flowers   Johnston 1926; Turk 1926

Basket Weaver Man   Donaldson 1939

Basket Weaver, The (inst.)   Spina 1977

Basketball   Leigh 1971

Bass Fiddle Boogie Woogie, The   Blake 1956; Sissle 1956

Bass Fiddle Boogie Woogie Blues, The   Sissle 1955

Bat Lady, The   Brooks 1955; Warren 1955

Bat Song   Mancini 1979

Bath and Dressmaking Sequence   Hart 1933; Rodgers 1933

Bath Scene (inst.)   Brown, Nacio Herb 1933

Bathing   Buck 1915

Bathing Beauty Ballet (inst.)   Styne 1947

Bathing Girls, The   Smith, Harry B. 1909

Bathtub Ran Over Again   Mercer 1934

Baton Rouge   Merrill 1954

Bats About You   Gershwin, Ira 1940; Weill 1940

Battalion of France   Smith, Harry B. 1900

Batten Down Her Hatches   Loesser 1948

Batter Up (inst.)   Drake 1958

Battle, The   Leigh 1954

Battle (inst.), The   Weill 1936

Battle of B Flat, The   Herbert 1914

Battle of Paris   Harburg 1929

Battle of San Juan Hill, The   Weill 1936

Battle Song   Burke 1953; Van Heusen 1953

Battle Song of Liberty, The   Yellen 1917

Battle Was Over, It Was Quiet Now, The   Spina 1944

Bauer's House   Gershwin, George 1932; Gershwin, Ira 1932

Bavarian Yodel   Johnson, Howard 1939

Bay of Angels   Fain 1960; Parish 1960

Bay of Botany   Dietz 1943; Duke 1943

Bay of Naples   Spina 1957

Bayaderes   Herbert 1909

Bayou Lullaby, The   Cahn 1950

Bayou Trouble Tree   Hammerstein 1940

Bazaar Hymn   Rome 1973

Bazaar Opening Chorus   Herbert 1905

Bazazz   Blane 1957

Be a Clown   Porter 1948

Be a Folk Singer   Rome 1950

Be a Good Scout   Adamson 1938; Carroll 1917; McHugh
    1938

Be a Good Soldier While Your Daddy's Away   Caesar 1942

Be a Good Sport   Gordon 1937; Revel 1937

Be a Jumping Jack   Washington 1952; Young, Victor 1952

Be a Little Darlin'   David, Hal 1954

Be a Little Sunbeam   Kern 1917

Be a Man   Ellington 1965

Be a Mess   Gorney 1949

Be a Mother   Coleman 1962; Leigh 1962

Be a Performer!   Coleman 1962; Leigh 1962

Be a Phony   Lawrence 1964

Be a Santa   Comden and Green 1961; Styne 1961

Be Aesthetic   Caesar 1920

Be Anything but a Girl   Blane 1960; Martin 1960

Be Aware   Bacharach 1971; David, Hal 1971

Be Brave Men   Brooks 1946

Be Calm   Rome 1942

Be Careful   Friml 1921; Livingston, Jerry 1962

Be Careful How You Handle Me   Jerome 1910; Schwartz,
    Jean 1910

Be Careful How You Wish   Adamson 1964; Fain 1964

Be Careful It's My Heart   Berlin 1942

Be Careful Song, The   Brooks 1953

Be Careful What You Do   Buck 1914

Be Careful Young Lady   Coslow 1935

Be Clever   Smith, Harry B. 1900

Be Close to Paradise   Merrill 1956

Be Cool and Groovy for Me   Ellington 1968

Be Demure   Smith, Harry B. 1906

Be Faithful   Coots 1949

Be Good   Smith, Harry B. 1908

Be Good Baby   Fisher 1936

Be Good to California, Mr. Wilson   Sterling 1916

Be Good to Me   Brooks 1956

Be Good to Me (Smiles)   Youmans 1930

Be Graceful (Something's Wrong with Me)   Kern 1957

Be Happy   Lerner, Alan Jay 1974; Loewe 1974; Meyer 1926

Be Happy Boys Tonight   Herbert 1914

Be in Style with a Smile   Turk 1925

Be Jolly Holly   Leslie 1909

Be Joyful   Cahn 1966; Van Heusen 1966

Be Kind to Poor Pierrot   Herbert 1903; Smith, Harry B. 1903

Be Kind to Your Parents   Rome 1954

Be Like a Basketball and Bounce Right Back   Adams 1978;
    Strouse 1978

Be Like Me   Cahn 1955; Styne 1955

Be Like the Bluebird   Porter 1934

Be Mine   Washington 1936

Be Modern, There's Happiness in Store for You   Waller 1930

Be My All (Or Be My Nothing)   Howard, Bart 1956

Be My Baby   Drake 1952

Be My Guest   Adams 1957; Coslow 1955; Heyman 1954;
    Mercer 1951; Strouse 1957; Young, Victor 1954

Be My Host   Rodgers 1962

Be My Love   Cahn 1950

Be Neat, Be Tidy   Styne 1940

Be Optimistic   Bullock 1938; Rainger 1933; Robin 1933;
    Spina 1938

Be Our Mother   Leigh 1954

Be Our Parents   Leigh 1954

Be Pan-American   Ager 1941; David, Mack 1941

Be Patient, My Darling   Sigman 1953

Be Prepared   Brooks 1961

Be Quiet When People Talk   Styne 1940

Be Ready   Razaf 1933

Be Satisfied   Bryan 1926

Be Smart My Heart   Dixon 1953; Henderson 1953; Rose
    1953

Be Somewhere   Merrill 1993; Styne 1993

Be Still My Sorrow   Pollack 1935; Webster 1935

Be Sure   David, Mack 1949; De Lange 1940; Sigman 1960
Be Sure Beloved   Sigman 1955
Be Sure It's Light the Musical Shore   Friml 1917; Harbach 1917
Be Sure, My Heart, Be Sure   Drake 1951
Be Sweet to Me   Warren Date Unknown
Be Sweet to Me Cherie   Bryan 1931
Be Sweet to Me Kid   Howard, Joseph E. 1908
Be that Way   Brennan 1929
Be the Life of the Crowd   DeSylva 1924; Gershwin, George 1924
Be the Secret of My Life   Caesar 1929
Be There At Twilight   Bryan 1907; Meyer 1907
Be True to Yourself   Bacharach 1963; David, Hal 1963
Be Yourself   Bergman 1960; Blake 1950; Drake 1956; Gilbert 1925; Mitchell 1917
Beach Scene   Porter 1935
Beach Time   Sherman 1959
Beachcomber, Beachcomber   Robison 1954
Beaded Bag, A   Romberg 1924; Schwartz, Jean 1924
Beale Street Blues   Bryan 1919; Schwartz, Jean 1919
Beale Street Mamma   Turk 1923
Beale Street Trolley   Brown, Lew 1943; Fain 1943; Freed, Ralph 1943
Beans   Gordon 1952; Loesser 1938
Bear Down Pelham   Whiting 1929
Bear Likes Honey, A   Brooks 1960
Beard in a Gilded Frame   Silver 1940
Beardley Ballet (inst.)   Merrill 1959
Beardsley School for Girls   Lerner, Alan Jay 1971
Beast's Song, The   Martin 1969
Beat Beat Drums   Weill 1942
Beat Me Daddy Eight to the Bar   Raye 1940
Beat of My Heart, The   Burke 1934; Spina 1934
Beat of the Blues, The   Evans 1959; Livingston, Jay 1959
Beat of the Feet in the Street, The   Carroll 1936; Parish 1936
Beat Out Dat Rhythm on a Drum   Hammerstein 1943
Beat the Band   Spina 1959
Beata Beata Drum   Merrill 1953
Beatin' Around the Bush   Akst 1931; Kahn 1931; Whiting 1931
Beatin' on the Bongos   Mancini 1957
Beatin' the Blues   Arlen 1931; Yellen 1931
Beatnik Bull Fighter (Beatnik Matador), The   Brooks 1966
Beatnik Do   Robison 1960
Beatrice Barefacts   Herbert 1903, 1904
Beatrice Fairfax, Tell Me What to Do   Clarke 1915; Monaco 1915
Beau Brummel   Edwards 1929; Gershwin, George 1924; Johnson, Howard 1929
Beau Brummel Joe (The Beau of Memphis Town)   Warren 1924
Beau Night in Hotchkiss Corners   Magidson 1941; Oakland 1941
Beaucoup D'Amour   Howard, Bart 1961
Beautiful   Sondheim 1984; Strouse 1989
Beautiful and Damned   Atteridge 1923; Romberg 1923; Schwartz, Jean 1923
Beautiful Annabell Lee   Bryan 1920; Meyer 1920
Beautiful Baby   Conrad 1925; DeSylva 1926; Hanley 1926
Beautiful, Beautiful   David, Mack 1958; Livingston, Jerry 1958
Beautiful Beautiful Girl   Jerome 1912
Beautiful Beulah (Railroad Rag)   Sherman 1963
Beautiful Bird   Gershwin, George 1917; Gershwin, Ira 1917

Beautiful Birds   Buck 1920
Beautiful Briny, The   Sherman 1971
Beautiful Buxom Barmaid   Coslow 1939
Beautiful Candy   Merrill 1961
(Beautiful Faces Need) Beautiful Clothes   Berlin 1920; Pollack 1952
Beautiful Coney Island   Rainger 1943; Robin 1943
Beautiful Dawn   Brennan 1928
Beautiful Dreamer   Johnson, Howard 1939
Beautiful Dreamtown   Herbert 1906
Beautiful Eggs   Bryan 1914
Beautiful Evening   Egan 1927; Whiting 1927
Beautiful Eyes   Snyder 1909
Beautiful Eyes (Les Beaux Yeux)   Gilbert 1915
Beautiful Face Have a Heart   Fisher 1928; Monaco 1928; Rose 1928
Beautiful Face (With a Figure to Match), A   David, Hal 1956
Beautiful Face — Have a Heart   Rose 1934
Beautiful Faces   Atteridge 1921; Pollack 1921
Beautiful Faces (Need Beautiful Clothes)   Berlin 1920; Pollack 1952
Beautiful Fairy Tales   Smith, Harry B. 1901; Von Tilzer 1901
Beautiful Fan, A   Coots 1926
Beautiful Feathers Make Beautiful Birds   Meyer 1922
Beautiful Feathers Make Beautiful Girls   Goetz 1921
Beautiful Girl   Brown, Nacio Herb 1933; Bryan 1911; Buck 1917; Freed, Arthur 1933; Razaf 1928
Beautiful Girl, Goodbye   Buck 1917
Beautiful Girls   Coots 1925; Kalmar 1922; Ruby 1922; Sondheim 1971
Beautiful Girls Are Like Opium   Atteridge 1921; Bryan 1921; Pollack 1921; Schwartz, Jean 1920, 1921
Beautiful Girls of Vienna (The Beautiful Girls of Berlin), The   Coots 1956
Beautiful Girls (You Have the World at Your Feet)   Ager 1923; Yellen 1923
Beautiful Gwend'lyn   Friend 1919
Beautiful Gypsy   Gershwin, George 1927; Gershwin, Ira 1927
(I Feel) Beautiful Inside   Howard, Bart 1965
Beautiful Island of Girls   Buck 1916
Beautiful Isle of Dreams   Herbert 1906
Beautiful Isle of Love   Bryan 1938
Beautiful Isle of Oomph (Down on the Island of Oomph)   Whiting 1935
Beautiful Isle of Oomph (Down on the Isle of Oomph), The   Coslow 1935
Beautiful Isle of the Sea   Johnson, Howard 1939
Beautiful Lady   Friend 1934
Beautiful Lady in Blue, A   Coots 1935; Lewis 1935
Beautiful Land of Love, The   Sterling 1906; Von Tilzer 1906
Beautiful Land of My Dreams   Razaf 1934
Beautiful Legs   Razaf Date Unknown; Waller Date Unknown
Beautiful Life, The   Evans 1970; Livingston, Jay 1970
Beautiful Love   Leslie 1911; Young, Victor 1931
Beautiful Madness   David, Mack 1951; Wrubel 1945
Beautiful Mohongahela   David, Mack 1959; Oakland 1959
Beautiful Mucho Chito (Muchachita)   Revel 1952
Beautiful Music to Love By   Sigman 1952
Beautiful Night   Friml 1918; Hanley 1934
Beautiful People   Coleman 1972
Beautiful People of Denver   Willson 1960
Beautiful, Primitive Indian Girls   Porter 1916
Beautiful Princess, The   David, Mack 1958; Livingston, Jerry 1958

Beautiful Romance   Ellington 1939
Beautiful Rose Marie   Bryan 1918; Fisher 1918
Beautiful Senorita   Revel 1951
Beautiful Ship from Toyland, The   Friml 1912; Harbach 1912
Beautiful Shoulders   Bryan 1920; Schwartz, Jean 1920
Beautiful Show Girls   Coots 1927; Dubin 1927
Beautiful Soup   DePaul 1951; Raye 1951
Beautiful Through and Through   Merrill 1972; Styne 1972
Beautiful Tunes   Drake 1953
Beautiful Ulalee   Bryan 1939
Beautiful Valleys   Burke 1964
Beautiful Volga Blues   Donaldson 1924
Beautiful Way to Go Crazy   Brown, Lew 1953; Henderson 1953
Beautiful Woman   Spina 1953
Beautiful Women   Howard, Bart 1956
Beautiful Word, A   Mancini 1993
Beautiful You   Carroll 1934
Beautifying the City (Life Begins at City Hall)   Arlen 1934; Gershwin, Ira 1934; Harburg 1934
Beauty Adorned   Coots 1926
Beauty and Beast   Atteridge 1918; Romberg 1918
Beauty and the Beast   Kalmar 1934; Ruby 1934
Beauty and the Beat   Drake 1958
Beauty Contest (Miss Hampstead Heath/Opening the Beauty Contest/Opening, Act I), The   Hart 1930; Rodgers 1930
Beauty Doctor, The   Herbert 1917
Beauty for Sale   De Lange 1945
Beauty in a Song   Willson 1956
Beauty in the Movies   Caesar 1928
Beauty Is Like a Rose   Bryan 1920; Schwartz, Jean 1920
Beauty Is Only Skin Deep   Raye 1957
Beauty Isn't Everything   Bacharach 1956; Heyman 1956
Beauty Must Be Loved   Fain 1934; Kahal 1934
Beauty of Another Day, The   Hart 1926; Rodgers 1926
Beauty That Drives Men Mad, The   Merrill 1972; Styne 1972
Bebe   Coslow 1923; Silver 1923
Bebe of Gay Paree   Porter 1955
Be-Bop La Rumba   Coslow 1949
Because, Because   Gershwin, George 1931; Gershwin, Ira 1931
Because Him Is a Baby   Merrill 1957
Because I Am Not Understood   Smith, Robert B. 1905
Because I Can't Tango   Buck 1914
Because I Love Him   David, Mack 1970
Because I Love Nice Things   Fields 1929; McHugh 1929
Because I Love You   Berlin 1926; Brennan 1927
Because I Love You Dear   Johnson, Howard 1921
Because I Love You So   DeSylva 1922; Herbert 1922
Because I Worship You   Freed, Arthur 1931
Because I'm Still in Love with You   Coots 1954
Because My Baby Don't Mean Maybe Now   Donaldson 1928
Because of Once Upon a Time   Young, Joe 1933
Because of You   Dubin 1931; Edwards 1930; Freed, Ralph 1944
Because She's Happy Now   Conrad 1929; Mitchell 1929
Because There's You   Rome 1973
Because We Care   Bergman 1980
Because We Love Each Other   Silver 1953
Because We're Young   Hart 1930; Rodgers 1930
Because You Believe in Me   Brennan 1918
Because You Flew Away (The Younger Generation)   Sterling 1928
Because You Love the Singer   Kern 1923

Because You're Beautiful   Brown, Lew 1928; DeSylva 1928; Henderson 1928
Because You're in Love   Brooks 1950
Because You're Irish   Kahn 1917
Because You're Mine   Cahn 1952
Because You're You   Caesar 1924; Herbert 1906
Beccha, Reecha La-ree-a-la   Hoffman 1951; Merrill 1951
Becky from Babylon   Silver 1920
Becky Green the Queen of the Screen   Von Tilzer 1920
Becky's Got a Job in a Musical Show   Berlin 1912
Bed of Roses   Brown, Lew 1932; Henderson 1932
Be-Da-Lum, Bo-Da-Lum   Clarke 1919
Bedalumbo, The   Atteridge 1918
Bedelia   Jerome 1903; Schwartz, Jean 1903
Bedouin Chief   Herbert 1907; Smith, Harry B. 1907
Bedtime on the Prairie   Harburg 1940; Lane 1940
Bee, The   Loesser 1948
Bee Bop on the Range   Revel 1955
Bee-Da-Lum, Bo-Da-Lum   Warren 1919
Beedle Booper's Song, The   Warren 1958
Beedle Um Bo   Akst 1927; Davis 1927
Beedle-Dum Boo   Young, Joe 1913
Beedy-Boo   Brown, Nacio Herb 1919
Been a Hell of an Evening   Arlen 1966
Been a Long Day   Loesser 1961
Beer Barrel Polka, The   Brown, Lew 1939; Styne 1941
Beer, Beautiful Beer   Smith, Harry B. 1900
Beer Here (Bier Her)   Webster 1954
Beer That I Left on the Bar, The   Brown, Lew 1950; Cobb 1950
Bees 'n' Flowers   Arlen 1959; Mercer 1959
Beethoven, Mendelssohn and Lizst   Coslow 1937
Beethoven's Sangwattni (inst.)   Waller 1926
Beetle Dance Theme (inst.)   Youmans 1954
Beetle Race, The   Warren 1956
Beets and Turnips   Ahlert 1914
Before and After   Herbert 1903; Hoffman 1959
Before I Gaze at You Again   Lerner, Alan Jay 1960; Loewe 1960
Before I Get Over   Gordon 1958
Before I Go and Marry (I Will Have a Talk with You)   Berlin 1910
Before I Go (Before You Go)   Eliscu 1929; Rose 1929; Youmans 1929
Before I Kiss the World Goodbye   Dietz 1963; Schwartz, Arthur 1963
Before I Met You   Kern 1918
Before Long   Sigman 1948
Before that Last Goodnight   Turk 1933
Before the Parade Passes By   Adams 1964; Strouse 1964
Before the Show   Cahn 1976
Before the World Began   Harbach 1921
Before We Leave the Air   Brooks 1960
Before We Married   Smith, Robert B. 1907
Before We Say Goodnight   Davis 1928
Before We Start   Drake 1954
Before We Were Married   Gershwin, Ira 1928
Before You Can Say Jackie Robinson   Blake 1949
Before You Go   Burke 1935; Spina 1935
Before You Know It I'll Be Home Mary   Silver 1942
Before You Leave Me   Bacharach 1976; David, Hal 1976
Before You Say Good-Bye   Akst 1931; Clarke 1931; Whiting 1931
Before You Throw the Match Away   Caesar 1940
Before Your Very Eyes   Livingston, Jerry 1973

Beg, Borrow or Steal   Freed, Ralph 1966; Livingston, Jerry 1966

Beg, Steal or Borrow   Lawrence 1951

Begat, The   Harburg 1947; Lane 1947

Beggar, The   Kahal 1927; Snyder 1927

Beggar in Love, A   Merrill 1951

Beggar Waltz, The   Dietz 1931; Schwartz, Arthur 1931

Beggars' Chorus   Smith, Harry B. 1903

Beggar's March   David, Mack 1958; Livingston, Jerry 1958

Beggars of Life   Brennan 1928

Beggars of Love   Fain 1932; Kahal 1932

Begger and the Rose, The   Webster 1949

Begging   Harbach 1911

Begin the Beguine   Porter 1935, 1939

(I've Got) Beginner's Luck   Gershwin, George 1937; Gershwin, Ira 1937; Young, Victor 1930

Beginnin' of Sinnin', The   Davis 1957

Beginning, The   Strouse 1971, 1993

Beginning of a Beautiful Love, The   Stept 1934; Washington 1934

Beginning of Loneliness, The   Bacharach 1966; David, Hal 1966

Beginning of Love, The   Brown, Lew 1931; Henderson 1931; Russell 1958

Behave Yourself   Fields 1959

Behind Milady's Fan   Atteridge 1924; Romberg 1924; Schwartz, Jean 1924

Behind My Lady's Fan   Coslow 1924

Behind the Clouds Are Crowds and Crowds of Sunbeams   Davis 1926; DeSylva 1926

Behind the Clouds There's Always Sunshine   Sterling 1922; Von Tilzer 1922

Behind the Eight Ball   Bryan 1946

Behind the Fan   Berlin 1921

Behind the Mask   Cohan 1927; Sigman 1953

Behind These Prison Walls   Silver 1956

Behold a Prima Donna   Smith, Harry B. 1934

Behold How Beautiful   Carmichael 1945

Behold My Love   Russell 1948

Behold the Governor   Cohan 1901

Bei Mir Bist du Schon (Means that You're Grand)   Cahn 1938

Being Alive   Sondheim 1970

Being Good for My Baby   Cahn 1980

Being Good Isn't Good Enough   Comden and Green 1967; Styne 1967

Being in Love   Willson 1962

Belfry Bells   Young, Joe 1932

Believe in Love   Brooks 1948; Webster 1956

Believe in Me   Davis 1922; Hanley 1930; Schwartz, Arthur 1928; Sigman 1955; Smith, Harry B. 1928

Believe It or Not I Found My Man   Baer 1930; Gilbert 1930

Believe It Or Not I Lost My Man   Baer 1930; Gilbert 1930

Believe It or Not, It's Always You   Monaco 1929

Believe Me   Bryan 1929; Edwards 1910; Johnson, J. Rosamond 1909; Kalmar 1924; Ruby 1924; Smith, Harry B. 1910

Believe Me If All those Endearing Young Charms   Johnson, Howard 1939

Believe Me, That's Love   Snyder 1929

Believe You Me   Oakland 1952

Belinda's Love Song   Rome 1970

Belinda's Rainy Day   Livingston, Jerry 1961

Bell Bottom Blues   David, Hal 1953

Bell for Adano, A   Dietz 1956; Schwartz, Arthur 1956; Styne 1967

Bell that Couldn't Jingle, The   Bacharach 1962

Bella Bella Florence   Sherman 1962

Bella Bella Mia   Hoffman 1950

Bella Bella Napoli   Revel 1955

Bella Donna   Romberg 1948

Bella Donna, Beautiful Lady   Smith, Harry B. 1923; Snyder 1923

Bella Signora   Heyman 1950; Young, Victor 1950

Bellboys   Porter 1912

Belle, a Beau and a Boutonniere, A   Schwartz, Jean 1928

Belle Baker Wop Song   Lewis 1929; Pollack 1929; Young, Joe 1929

Belle, Belle, My Liberty Belle   Merrill 1951

Belle O'Brien   Herbert 1895

Belle of Bagdad (inst.), The   Motzan 1919

Belle of Bald Head Row, The   Howard, Joseph E. 1907

Belle of Bohemia, The   Smith, Harry B. 1900

Belle of Buttercup Lane, The   David, Mack 1979

Belle of Madrid   Gordon 1956; Revel 1956

Belle of New York, The   Mitchell 1921; Pollack 1921

Belle of the Ball   Parish 1952

Belle of the Baltimore Ball   Lawrence 1941

Belle of the Barber's Ball   Berlin 1912; Cohan 1912

Belle of the Nineties   Coslow 1934; Johnston 1934

Belle of the Ring, The   Smith, Harry B. 1908

Belle of the Yukon, The   Burke 1944; Van Heusen 1944

Belles of Gay Madrid, The   Gordon 1948; Myrow 1948

Belles of Gay Paree, The   Gordon 1948; Myrow 1948

Belles of the Bronx, The   Friml 1923

Belles of the Tally-Ho Boarding School   Harbach 1911

Bellissima   Oakland 1953; Raye 1953

Bellport Will Shine Tonight   Robin 1936

Bells   Berlin 1920; Warren Date Unknown; Webster 1965

Bells Are Ringing   Comden and Green 1956; Freed, Ralph 1938; Styne 1956

Bells Bells Bells   Cahn 1981

Bells Contretemps (inst.)   Kern 1956

Bells of Christmas, The   Cahn 1969; Van Heusen 1969

Bells of Heidelberg, The   David, Mack 1959

Bells of Honolulu   Mercer 1936; Mills 1928

Bells of Monterey, The   Freed, Ralph 1940; Stept 1935, 1940; Washington 1935

Bells of San Gabriel's, The   Brennan 1927

Bells of Santa Ynez   Bergman 1963

Bells of Treasure Isle, The   Webster 1938

Belly Up to the Bar, Boys   Willson 1960

Belong to Me   Blake 1958; Sigman 1958

Belonging   Sigman 1955

Belonging To Someone   Hoffman 1957

Beloved   Kahn 1928; Webster 1952

Beloved (Aloha - Nui - Ia)   Koehler 1944; Lane 1944

Beloved Bandit   Dietz 1959; Schwartz, Arthur 1959

Beloved, Be Faithful   Drake 1950

Beloved Infidel   Webster 1959

Beloved Philippines   Razaf 1952

Beloved When I Adore   Spina 1955

Below the Equator   Dietz 1944; Duke 1944; Friend 1941

Below the Macy-Gimbel Line   Hammerstein 1920; Harbach 1920

Ben Bolt   Johnson, Howard 1939

Bench in the Park, A   Ager 1930; Gorney 1948; Yellen 1930

Bend Down Sister   Conrad 1931

Bend Your Knee and Tie My Shoe   Duke 1939

Beneath the Curtain of Night   Mercer 1934
Beneath the Eastern Moon   Gershwin, George 1923
Beneath the Moon   Jerome 1907; Schwartz, Jean 1907
Beneath the Moon of Mexico (Luna Mexicana)   Adamson 1930; Gordon 1930; Revel 1930
Beneath the Parisian Moonlight   Young, Joe 1930
Beneath the Spell of a Yellow Delta Moon   Robison 1933
Beneath the Stars   Gordon 1936; Revel 1936
Beneath the Sunshine Tree   Motzan 1916
Beneath the Winter Snows   Kahn 1938; Romberg 1938
Beneath Those Sunny Skies   Howard, Joseph E. 1915
Beneath Venetian Skies   Lewis 1927; Young, Joe 1927
Benn Gun Dance Music (inst.)   Styne 1985
Benny Sent Me   Rome 1938; Waller 1936
Benny the Bow Legged Bowler   Gilbert 1950; Oakland 1950
Benny the Magic Bunny   Hoffman 1952
Benny to Helen to Chance   Loesser 1953
Bentonville Fair, The   Fain 1957; Webster 1957
Benvenuta   Loesser 1956
Berkeley Square and Kew   Gershwin, George 1924
Bermuda   Hanley 1921; Motzan 1916
Bermuda Buggyride   David, Mack 1936
Bermuda (inst.)   Monaco 1919
Bernadine   Mercer 1957; Rome 1957
Bernard & Phillips   Lewis 1916; Meyer 1916; Young, Joe 1916
Bernie's Love Song   Gordon 1937; Revel 1937
Berries, The   Blake 1930; Razaf 1930
Bertie   Romberg 1924, 1925
Bertie and Gertie   Porter 1936
Bertram's Nonny   Strouse 1975
Beside a Babbling Brook   Donaldson 1923; Kahn 1923
Beside a Garden Wall   Kahn 1926
Beside a Lazy Stream   Stept 1928
Beside a Moonlit Stream   Coslow 1937
Beside a Wayside   Gordon 1932; Revel 1932
Beside an Indian Wigwam   Dubin 1927
Beside the Big Tonto   DePaul 1941; Raye 1941
Beside the Coral Sea   Gilbert 1932; Hanley 1932
Beside the Old Oak Gate   Lewis 1906
Beside the Rippling Stream   Kalmar 1920; Monaco 1920; Ruby 1920
Beside the Sea Beside You   Coots 1936; Davis 1936
Beside the Side of a Stream   Lerner, Sammy 1931
Beside the Sunset Trail   Hoffman 1932
Beside You   Evans 1947; Livingston, Jay 1947
Bess, You Is My Woman Now   Gershwin, George 1935; Gershwin, Ira 1935
Bessie, Bessie, Bessie   Waller 1944
Bessie Guessie   Caesar 1950
Bessie in a Bustle   Gordon 1944; Monaco 1944
Bessie My Right Hand Bower   Cobb 1899; Edwards 1899
Bessie's Blues   Merrill 1966
Bessie-Whoa Babe   Ellington 1941; Webster 1941
Best Ain't Good Enough, The   Adams 1957; Strouse 1957
Best Dance I've Had Tonight, The   Hammerstein 1923; Harbach 1923; Youmans 1923
Best Days of Our Lives, The   Howard, Joseph E. 1948
Best I Ever Get Is the Worst of It, The   Brennan 1929
Best I Get Is the Worst of It, The   Friml 1922; Harbach 1922
Best in the Trade, The   Kalmar 1924; Ruby 1924
Best Is None Too Good for Me, The   Stept 1943
Best Is Yet to Come, The   Coleman 1959; Leigh 1959
Best Little Sweetheart of All, The   Goetz 1915; Romberg 1915

Best Man Never Gets the Worst of It, The   Friml 1918
Best Night of My Life, The   Adams 1970; Strouse 1970
Best of All   Freed, Ralph 1959; Wrubel 1944
Best of Buddies, The   Sherman 1972
Best of Everything, The   Cahn 1959; DeSylva 1919, 1924; Gershwin, George 1919
Best of Friends, The   Drake 1948
Best of Friends Must Part, The   Berlin 1908
Best of Things Are Free, The   Young, Victor 1934
Best of Times (inst.), The   Bacharach 1988
Best Part College Days   Arlen 1931; Yellen 1931
Best Part of a Letter, The   Drake 1952
Best Performance, The   Cahn 1967
Best Score of a Musical   Bergman 1969; Mancini 1969
Best Seat in the House, The   Bergman 1986
Best Sort of Mother, Best Sort of Child   Kern 1915
Best Style Show   Brooks 1959
Best Sweetheart of All, The   Friend 1932
Best Thing a Waiter Does Is Wait, The   Howard, Joseph E. 1909
Best Thing for You, The   Berlin 1950
Best Things   Lerner, Alan Jay 1969
Best Things Happen While You're Dancing, The   Berlin 1954
Best Things in Life Are Free, The   Brown, Lew 1927; DeSylva 1927; Henderson 1927; Johnson, Howard 1917
Best Time of the Day, The   Sondheim Date Unknown
Best Time of Your Life, The   Sherman 1974
Best Toast of All (Kiss Her and Look in Her Eyes), The   Harbach 1914
Best Tunes of All Come from Carnegie Hall, The   Strouse 1943
Best Undressed Girl in Town   Evans 1961; Livingston, Jay 1961
Best Waltz of All, The   Atteridge 1915
Best Wishes   Cahn 1967; Ellington 1932; Koehler 1932; Van Heusen 1967
Best Years of His Life, The   Gershwin, Ira 1940; Weill 1940
Best Years of My Life, The   Bullock 1939; Spina 1939
Best Yet, The   Clare 1954
Bet Steal or Borrow (Why Oh Why)   Lawrence 1960
Bet You a Little Kiss I'll Kiss Ya   Hoffman 1931
Bet Your Bottom Dollar   De Lange 1946; Myrow 1946
Better All the Time   Bergman 1964; Fain 1964
Better Be Good to Me   Hart 1928; Rodgers 1928
Better Call Preacher Man   Rose 1925
Better Day Is Comin', A   Cahn 1944; Styne 1944
Better for Both of Us   Ager 1934; Coots 1934; Young, Joe 1934
Better Get Away from Here   Russell 1940
Better Get Off Your High Horse   Friend 1936
Better Get Out of Here   Loesser 1948
Better Loved You'll Never Be   David, Mack 1957
Better Luck Next Time   Berlin 1948; Dietz 1948; Lawrence 1937; Schwartz, Arthur 1948
Better Not Try It   Magidson 1930; Washington 1930
Better Than a Dream   Comden and Green 1956; Styne 1956
Better than Ever   Lawrence 1957
Better Things of Life   Fisher 1930
Better Think It Over   Eliscu 1931
Better Think Twice   Coots 1933
Better to Love You My Dear, The   David, Mack 1934; Hoffman 1934
Better Together   Merrill 1966
Better Wait Till You're Eighteen   Hanley 1931
Better Way, A   Blane 1969; Lane Date Unknown

Bettin' Calls   Arlen 1959; Mercer 1959
Betting on a Man   Robin 1951; Styne 1951
Betty   Ahlert 1926
Betty Behave   Smith, Harry B. 1920
Betty Boop   Heyman 1932
Betty (inst.)   Revel 1948
Betty Lee   Caesar 1924; Conrad 1924; Harbach 1924
Betty Lou   Johnson, J. Rosamond 1930
Betty of the Rosy Lips   Friml 1911
Betty Washboard's Rag (inst.)   Blake 1976
Betty, You're the One Best Bet   Edwards 1908
Between a Kiss and a Sigh   Burke 1937; Johnston 1937
Between Romances   Dubin 1940; Fain 1940
Between the Dances   Dubin 1924; McHugh 1924
Between the Devil and the Deep Blue Sea   Arlen 1931;
    Koehler 1931
Between the Divil and the Deep Blue Sea   Brennan 1919
Between the Lines   Alter 1930; Johnson, Howard 1930
Between the River and the Railroad Track   Robison 1960
Between Two Fires   Adamson 1939; Johnston 1939
Between Yesterday and Tomorrow   Bergman 1990
Between You and Me   Burke 1933; Freed, Arthur 1931;
    Porter 1939; Spina 1933
Between You and Me and the Floor Lamp   Dubin 1928
Between You and Me and the Lamp-Post   Bryan 1926; Duke
    1940; Ahlert 1941
Bevans, Dear Bevans   Gordon 1936; Revel 1936
Beverly Hillbillies   Russell Date Unknown
Beverly Hills (Anthem)   Mancini 1989
Beverly (Take Care of Your Baby)   David, Mack 1978
Bevo   Berlin 1918
Beware   Brooks 1960; David, Mack 1955; Revel 1942
Beware, I'm Beginning to Care   Burke 1940; Monaco 1940
Beware My Heart   Coslow 1947
Beware of a Girl With a Fan   Brown, Lew 1925; DeSylva
    1925; Henderson 1925
Beware of Me   Herbert 1924
Beware of Pink Pajamas   Lewis 1916; Schwartz, Jean 1916;
    Young, Joe 1916
Beware of the Boy with His Mind Made Up   Leigh 1954
Beware of the Flaterer   Bergman 1960
Beware of the Hawk My Baby (Indian Lullaby)   Herbert
    1911
Beware of the Sirens   Smith, Harry B. 1911
Beware of the Sophomore   Porter 1913
Beware of the Woman   Howard, Bart 1984
Beware of Those Who Gossip   Razaf 1937
Beware of Yale   Porter 1910
Beware the Dragon   Rome 1940
Beware the Jabberwock   DePaul 1951; Raye 1951
Beware the Safety Pirate   Caesar 1943
Bewitched, Bothered and Bewildered   Hart 1940; Rodgers
    1940
Bewitched By the Night   Gorney 1938
Beyond Glory   Evans 1948; Livingston, Jay 1948
Beyond My Fondest Dreams   Kahn 1937
Beyond My Wildest Dreams   Styne 1985
Beyond the Blue Horizon   Robin 1930; Whiting 1930
Beyond the Horizon   Brown, Nacio Herb 1930; Eliscu 1930
Beyond the Laughing Sky   Fain 1951
Beyond the Moon   Mercer 1931; Rainger 1939; Robin 1939
Beyond the Moonbeam Trail   Ager 1923; Yellen 1923
Beyond the Mountains   Bergman 1958
Beyond the Sea (Le Mer)   Lawrence 1947
Beyond the Shadow of a Doubt   Adamson 1935; Lane 1935

Beyond the Stars   Koehler 1920
Beyond Tomorrow   DePaul 1955
Beyond Words   Strouse 1991
Beyond You   Whiting 1935
B.G. Bigelow, Inc.   Fain 1951; Harburg 1951
Bharatha Natyan   Fain 1960; Webster 1960
Bi——-   Kahn 1922
Bianca   Porter 1948
Biarritz   Coots 1958
Bibbidi-Bobbidi-Boo (The Magic Song)   David, Mack 1950;
    Hoffman 1950; Livingston, Jerry 1950
B-I-Bi   Russell 1941
Bichloride of Mercury   Porter 1916
Bicycle Song, The   Blane 1945; Martin 1964
Biddle-e-um-de-dum   Fisher 1936
Biddy Deane Theme   Oakland 1954
Bide-A-Wee   Edwards 1928
Bide-a-Wee in Soho, The   Weill 1954
Bidin' My Time   Gershwin, George 1930; Gershwin, Ira 1930
Big Apple   Warren Date Unknown
Big Back Yard, The   Fields 1945; Romberg 1945
Big Bad Bill Is Sweet William Now   Ager 1924; Yellen 1924
Big Bad Moon, The   Freed, Ralph 1944; Hoffman 1944
Big Banana Man from Yucatan, The   Silver 1947
Big Banshee, The   Howard, Joseph E. 1905, 1908
Big Battle, The   Leigh 1954
Big Beat, The   Sherman 1974
Big Beautiful Ball, A   Mercer 1967
Big Ben Family, The   Alter 1930; Johnson, Howard 1930
Big Big Lie, The   Lawrence 1953
Big Black Giant, The   Hammerstein 1953; Rodgers 1953
Big Blonde Baby   Bryan 1912; Fisher 1912
Big Blonde Venus   Monaco 1923; Rose 1923
Big Blue Sky (Is the Place for Me), The   David, Mack 1952;
    Livingston, Jerry 1952
Big Bouquet for You, A   Kahn 1930
Big Boy!   Ager 1924; Razaf 1944; Yellen 1924
Big Boy Blues   Lawrence 1937
Big Brass Band from Brazil   Sigman 1947
Big Brother   Hart 1938; Rodgers 1938
Big Brown Boo Loo Eyes   Cohan 1908
Big Brown Eyes, Red Cherry Lips   Friend 1960
Big Butter and Egg Man, The   Clare 1924; Friend 1924
Big Ca-lown Balloons, The   Willson 1963
Big Cat   David, Mack 1963
Big Chief Alimony   Williams 1913; Young, Joe 1913
Big Chief Burke   Atteridge Date Unknown
Big Chief de Sota   Razaf 1936
Big Chief Hole in the Ground   Robin 1951; Styne 1951
Big Chief Kill-a-Hun   Bryan 1918; Leslie 1918
Big Chief No-Pain   De Lange 1941
Big Chief Suzique   Kalmar 1940; Ruby 1940
Big Chief "Swing It"   Mitchell 1937; Pollack 1937
Big Circus, The   Fain 1959; Webster 1959
Big City Blues   Conrad 1929; Mancini 1957; Mitchell 1929;
    Russell 1946, Date Unknown
Big Clock, The   Evans 1948; Livingston, Jay 1948
Big Cowboys and Indians Fight at Casino Royale (inst.),
    The   Bacharach 1967
Big D   Loesser 1956
Big Day   Adams 1983
Big Dig, The   DePaul 1958; Raye 1958
Big Doin's   Evans 1954; Livingston, Jay 1954
Big Dreams   Hoffman 1956
Big Fat Heart   Coleman 1973; Fields 1973

Big Game, The   Livingston, Jerry 1963
Big Hand, Little Hand   David, Hal 1957
Big Hats, The   Smith, Harry B. 1908
Big Hearted Baby   Egan 1928
Big High Mountain with Nothing on the Top, The   Sigman 1948
Big Indian Chief   Johnson, J. Rosamond 1903
Big Job, A   Adams 1993
Big Lie, The   Robison 1950
Big Mole   Weill 1949
Big Mouth Minnie   Razaf 1938
Big Movie Show in the Sky, The   Mercer 1949
Big Name Dropper, The   Robison 1954
Big Night of the Year, The   Strouse 1975
Big One, A   Rome 1965
Big Papoose Is on the Loose   Fields 1930; McHugh 1930
Big Parade, The   Porter 1944
Big People   Coleman 1979
Big Pet Peeve Society   Robison 1954
Big Polka (inst.), The   Young, Victor 1954
Big Record, The   Drake 1956
Big Red Motor and the Little Blue Limousine   Whiting 1913
Big Red Shawl, The   Johnson, J. Rosamond 1909
Big Red Theme   Sherman 1962
Big Reign, The   Robison 1958
Big Show   Brown, Nacio Herb 1948; Kern 1918
Big Sister Blues   DePaul 1957; Russell 1951, 1957
Big Spender   Coleman 1966; Fields 1966
Big Spring Drive, The   Kern 1918
Big Sunday School   Robison 1954
Big Swamp Bogie Man, The   Meyer 1907
Big Talk   Comden and Green 1967; Lewis 1974; Styne 1967; Young, Joe 1974
Big Temptation Like You, A   Leslie 1931; Meyer 1931
Big Time, The   Coleman 1991; Comden and Green 1991
Big Time Comin'   Arlen 1941; Koehler 1941
Big Town   Kalmar 1956; Porter 1944
Big Town Blues, The   Carmichael 1962; Davis 1957
Big Towns and the Small Towns, The   Cahn Date Unknown; Duke Date Unknown
Big Tree Tall   David, Hal 1959
Big Trouble   Cahn 1972; Leigh 1967; Van Heusen 1972
Big Turntable   Robison 1958
Big White Mountain   Ellington 1958
Bigger and Better than Ever   Friend 1929
Bigger and Better Things   David, Hal 1960
Bigger Isn't Better   Coleman 1980
Bigger than Both of Us   Howard, Bart 1956
Bigger than Texas   Fain 1958; Webster 1958
Bigger the Army and Navy, The   Yellen 1944
Biggest Bloomin' Bumbershoot in the World   Hoffman 1953
Biggest Change in 15 Years, The   Coleman 1964
Biggest Little Scam in Old New York   David, Hal 1991; Strouse 1991
Biggest Men Stumble, The   Rome 1965
Biggest Sin of All, The   Davis 1962
Big-Hearted Joe   Razaf Date Unknown
Bilbao Song, The   Weill 1977
Bill   DeSylva 1919; Hammerstein 1927; Kern 1918, 1919, 1927
Bill and Coo   Caesar 1920
Bill Bailey Won't You Please Come Home   Johnson, Howard 1939
Bill of Rights (Congress Shall Make No Law), The   Gorney 1940

Bill Randle Theme   Oakland 1954
Bill Robinson Walk, The   Coots 1937; Davis 1937
Bill the Buffalo   Caesar 1965
Billet-Doux, A   Smith, Harry B. 1901; Von Tilzer 1901
Billie   Cohan 1928
Billikin Man   Goetz 1909
Bill's a Liar   Kern 1907
Billy, Billy, Bounce Your Baby Doll   Bryan 1912; Fisher 1912
Billy Boy   Johnson, Howard 1939
Billy Boy — Billy Boy   Lawrence 1939
Billy Goat   Young, Victor 1923
Billy Grey, U.S.A., O.K.   Cobb 1903; Edwards 1903
Billy Symphony   Pollack 1934
Billy-A-Dik   Carmichael 1945; Webster 1945
Billy's Fight with Chuck   Russell 1946
Billy's Melody   Gilbert 1912
Bim Bam Boom   Adamson 1942
Bimbombey   David, Mack 1958
(When the Wild Wild Women Go in Swimmin' Down in) Bimini Bay   Adamson 1953; Carmichael 1953; Egan 1921; Kahn 1921; Whiting 1921
Biminy   Buck 1924
Bing, Bang   Loesser 1946
Bing Bang Bong   Evans 1958; Livingston, Jay 1958
Bing Bang Boom   David, Hal 1953
Bingen on the Rhine   Bryan 1914
Bingo Eli Yale   Porter 1910
Biography   DePaul 1958; Raye 1958
Bioscope Song, The   Ellington 1958
Birchlake Forever   Alter 1937; Webster 1937
Bird and the Cricket and the Willow Tree, The   Webster 1953
Bird Bath (inst.)   Bacharach 1966
Bird in a Gilded Cage, A   Von Tilzer 1900
Bird in the Hand Is Worth Two in the Bush, A   Razaf 1939
Bird Man, The   David, Mack 1962
Bird of Gay Bohemia, The   Bryan 1917
Bird of Paradise   Atteridge 1912
Bird of Passage, A   Weill 1949
Bird That Never Learned to Fly, A   Duke 1963
Bird Watcher's Song (We're the Ladies' Walking Society)   Cahn 1947; Styne 1947
Birdie   Berlin 1917
Birdie Out of a Cage   Hoffman 1937; Lerner, Sammy 1937
Birdie Song, The   Hoffman 1938
Birdman of Alcatraz   Webster 1963
Birds and People   Davis 1964
Birds and the Bees, The   Fields 1945; Romberg 1945
Birds Are Winging   Romberg 1924
Birds of a Feather   Burke 1941; Caesar 1932; Van Heusen 1941; Williams 1907
Birds of Plumage   Atteridge 1923; Romberg 1923; Schwartz, Jean 1923
Birds on the Wing (inst.)   Schwartz, Jean 1930
Birds Up High (Birds on High)   Hart 1926; Rodgers 1926
Birmingham Bertha   Akst 1929; Clarke 1929
Birmingham Boogie (inst.)   Revel 1947
Birmin'ham   Blane 1955; Martin 1955
Birth of a Snowbird   Webster 1939; Young, Victor 1939
Birth of Love, The   Howard, Bart 1959
Birth of Passion, The   Harbach 1910
Birth of Rumba   Rainger 1935
Birth of the Blues, The   Brown, Lew 1926; DeSylva 1926; Henderson 1926
Birth of the Butterfly   Harbach 1910

Birth of the Butterfly (inst.)   Herbert 1903
Birth of the Century Girl, The   Herbert 1916
Birthday. . .   Willson 1969
Birthday Child   Baer 1962; Leslie 1962
Birthday Kid, The   Drake 1954
Birthday of a Kiss, The   Webster 1931
Birthday of the Dauphin (inst.), The   Herbert 1921
Birthday Party   Brown, Nacio Herb 1933; Freed, Arthur
     1933; Gershwin, George 1927; Gershwin, Ira 1927; Kahn
     1933
Birthday Party (Rich Kid's Rag)   Coleman 1962; Leigh 1962
Birthday Polka, The   De Lange 1948; Revel 1948
Birthday Song   Rome 1954; Styne 1950
Birthdays   Caesar 1955
Birthdays Are Fun   Brooks 1960
Bis Bolo   Atteridge 1916; Motzan 1916, 1917; Romberg 1916
Bismark Is a Herring, Napoleon Is a Cake   Eliscu 1929; Rose
     1929; Youmans 1929
Bit By Bit You're Breaking My Heart   Kahn 1923
Bit of Gingham, A   Bryan 1928; Schwartz, Jean 1928
Bit of Green, a Blade of Grass, A   Wrubel 1932
Bit of Home, A   Styne 1985
Bit of Opera, A   Atteridge 1916, 1921; Motzan 1916, 1917;
     Romberg 1916
Bit of Ribbon Bit of Love, A   Goetz 1916
Bit Player Polka   Fain 1951; Webster 1951
Bitter and the Sweet, The   Russell 1950
Bitter Beguine, The   Oakland 1954
Bitter Sweet Memories (inst.)   Warren Date Unknown
Bitter with the Sweet, The   Freed, Ralph 1964
Bittersweet   Gershwin, Ira 1923; Mancini 1981; Mercer 1965
Bivouac Song   Smith, Harry B. 1911
Black and Blue   Akst 1923; Lewis 1922, 1923; Meyer 1923;
     Razaf 1929; Waller 1929; Young, Joe 1922
Black and Tan Fantasy   Ellington 1937
Black and White   Coleman 1980; Gershwin, George 1929;
     Gershwin, Ira 1929; Hart 1925; Kahn 1929; Rodgers
     1925
Black Beauty   Jerome 1910; Schwartz, Jean 1910
(Who Said) Black Birds Are Blue   Blake 1930; Razaf 1930
Black Bottom, The   Brown, Lew 1926; DeSylva 1926;
     Henderson 1926
Black Bottom Betty   Akst 1926
Black Butterfly   Ellington 1937; Mills 1937; Smith, Robert B.
     1909
Black Cat Rag (inst.)   Waller 1947
Black Coffee   Webster 1949
Black Diamond   Hart 1934; Rodgers 1934
Black Dog Blues   Razaf 1929
Black Eyed Susan   Motzan 1921
Black Eyed Susan Brown   Hoffman 1933; Magidson 1933
Black Hills of Dakota, The   Fain 1953; Webster 1953
Black Man, Black Woman   Strouse Date Unknown
Black Man Blues   Razaf 1929
Black Maria   Razaf 1938
Black Moonlight   Coslow 1933; Johnston 1933
Black Orchid, The   Spina 1977
Black Pearl of Tahiti (inst.)   Alter 1955
Black Raspberry Jam (inst.)   Waller 1938
Black Rhythm   Mills 1931
Black Roses   Spina 1959
Black Sheep Blues, The   Kahn 1923
Black Sheep in Our Family Is a Blue Eyed Baby, The   Clare
     1926; Monaco 1926

Black Sheep of the Family Is a Blue-Eyed Baby Blonde,
     The   Bryan 1926
Black (Sorrow) (inst.)   Young, Victor 1955
Black, the Bottomless (inst.)   Young, Victor 1956
Blackbirds on Parade   Blake 1930; Razaf 1930
Blackout Boogie   Young, Joe 1943
Blackout Over Broadway   Freed, Ralph 1941; Lane 1941
Blah, Blah, Blah   Gershwin, George 1931; Gershwin, Ira
     1931
(I May Feel) Blah! but Not too Blue   Lewis 1927; Young, Joe
     1927
Blair Rose   Cahn 1977
Blame It All on the Night   Romberg 1936
Blame It on Chichita   Lerner, Alan Jay 1939
Blame It on My Last Affair   Mills 1939
Blame It on My Youth   Heyman 1933
Blame It on Paree   Stept 1957
Blame It on Rio   Coleman 1984
Blame It on the Blues   David, Mack 1930
Blame It on the Danube   Akst 1938; Loesser 1938
Blame It on the Moonlight   Ager 1931; Yellen 1931
Blame It on the Night   Harbach 1936
Blame It on the Rhumba   Adamson 1937; McHugh 1937
Blame It on the Summer Night   Strouse 1986
Blame It on the Waltz   Kahn 1926
Blame It on the Wine (Zu Jeder Liebe Gehort ein Glaschen
     Wein)   Young, Joe 1931
Blame It on Yourself   Koehler 1950
Blame My Absent-Minded Heart   Cahn 1949; Styne 1949
Blame the Weather Man   Howard, Joseph E. 1907
Blamen Is Our Birthright   Herbert 1917
Blanket on the Beach   David, Hal 1962
Blankety Blank, I'm a Son-of-a-Gun (If I'm Not in
     Love)   De Lange 1934
Blarney   Kahn 1914; Norworth 1909
Blarney Castle-Walk, The   Atteridge 1915
Blarney Kate   Atteridge Date Unknown
Blarney Stone, The   Friml 1917
Bleeding Moon   Johnson, J. Rosamond 1909
Bless All the Beautiful Girls   Davis 1951
Bless My Swanee River Home   Donaldson 1919; Lewis 1919;
     Young, Joe 1919
Bless Our Happy Home   Davis 1935; Silver 1935
Bless Our Home   Cahn 1947; Styne 1947
Bless the Land   Strouse 1963
Bless the Land I Love   Silver 1954
Bless Ya, Honey Babe, I Love You   Magidson 1931; Wrubel
     1931
Bless You   Heyman 1933
Bless You All   Rome 1950
Bless You, Darlin' Mother   Stept 1936
Bless You, Darling   Baer 1965; Leslie 1965
Bless You, Gentle Woman   Robison 1956
Bless You, My Sweet   Revel 1955
Bless You, Sister   Dubin 1928
Bless Your Beautiful Hide   DePaul 1954; Mercer 1954
Bless Your Heart   Mercer 1951
Bless Your Little Heart, My Dear   Gilbert 1954; Oakland
     1954
Blessed Are They   Davis 1959
Blessed Event   Conrad 1932; DeSylva 1932; Evans 1972;
     Livingston, Jay 1972; Silver 1932; Whiting 1932
Blessing in Disguise, A   Fain 1957
Blessing of Love, The   Drake 1958
Blessings   Willson 1957; Young, Victor 1955

Blessings Before Reading Torah   Styne 1978
Bli-Blip   Ellington 1941
Blighty Bound   Egan 1919; Whiting 1919
Blimey   Cahn 1976
Blind Date   Dietz 1944; Duke 1944
Blind Date Opened My Eyes, A   Clare 1953; Snyder 1953
Blind Man   Arlen 1959; Mercer 1959
Blind Man Stood on the Road (And Cried)   Robison 1954
Blind Man's Bluff   Smith, Harry B. 1911
Blind Man's Buff   Ellington 1923
Blind Pew's Lament   Styne 1985
Blissful Christmas   Rome 1969
Blitzkreig Baby, You Can't Bomb Me   Fisher 1940
Blob, The   Bacharach 1958; David, Hal 1958; David, Mack
   1958; Sondheim 1981
Blond Sailor, The   Parish 1945
Blonde, Blase and Beautiful   Gordon 1933; Revel 1933
Blonde Blues   Atteridge 1921
Blonde in the Green Coupe, The   Russell 1952
Blonde Wimmen   Rose 1926
Blonde Wimmin   Fisher 1926
Blondie   Cahn 1945; Styne 1945
Blondy   Brown, Nacio Herb 1929; Freed, Arthur 1929
Blondy Let Me Have the Next Dance with You   Bryan 1907;
   Meyer 1907
Blondy (With Your Baby Blues Eyes)   Conrad 1927; Meyer
   1927
Bloody Mary   Hammerstein 1949; Rodgers 1949
Bloody Razor Blues   Waller 1924
Bloom Is Off the Rose, The   Dietz 1961; Schwartz, Arthur
   1961
Bloom Is Still on the Rose, The   Lane 1992
Bloomington, Indiana   Drake 1953
Bloop Bleep   Loesser 1947
Blossom   Ellington 1954; Mercer 1954
Blossom Time   Bryan 1922; Schwartz, Jean 1922
Blossoms in the Dust (inst.)   Brown, Nacio Herb 1941
Blossoms in the Moonlight   Washington 1938
Blossoms on Broadway   Rainger 1935, 1937, 1938; Robin
   1935, 1937, 1938; Whiting 1935
Blossoms on the Bough   Sigman 1949
Blow a Balloon Up to the Moon   Fain 1938
Blow Blow Blow   Brooks 1958; Conrad 1920
Blow de Whistle   Arlen 1959; Mercer 1959
Blow Gabriel   Eliscu 1932
Blow, Gabriel Blow   Porter 1934
Blow High, Blow Low   Hammerstein 1945; Rodgers 1945
Blow Hot — Blow Cold   Alter 1930
Blow Hot and Heavy   Robin 1927
Blow Little Lantern of Love   Fisher 1921
Blow Me Down   Rainger 1939; Robin 1939
Blow My Black Bird Home   Egan 1931
Blow, Northwind, Blow   Brooks 1958
Blow on Your Piccolo   Atteridge 1912
Blow that Horn   Donaldson 1936
Blow the Blues Away   Brennan 1929
Blow the Man Down   Duke 1959
Blow the Smoke Away   Howard, Joseph E. 1907
Blow the Whistle   Howard, Joseph E. 1918
Blow Those Trumpets   Gordon 1955
Blow Upon Your Bugles   Herbert 1908; Smith, Harry B. 1908
Blow Us a Kiss   Sherman 1995
Blow Your Horn   Berlin 1915
Blowin' Off Steam   Johnson, Howard 1926
Blowing of the Breeze Blew You into My Arms   Waller 1932

Blowing the Blues Away   Duke 1927; Gershwin, Ira 1926
Blowing Wild   Webster 1953
Blue   Clarke 1922; Leslie 1922
Blue Afternoon   Adamson 1959; McHugh 1959
Blue Again   Fields 1930; McHugh 1930
Blue Algerian Skies   Razaf 1939
Blue Am I   Martin 1959
Blue and Disillusioned   Coots 1939; Davis 1939
Blue and Sentimental   David, Mack 1938; Livingston, Jerry
   1938
Blue Baby   Razaf 1953
Blue Bay of Old San Jose, The   Spina 1948
Blue Bells of Broadway (Are Ringing Tonight), The   Fain
   1954; Webster 1954
Blue Bird of Happiness   Heyman 1934
Blue Bird Time   Brennan 1914
Blue Blazes   Robin 1931; Whiting 1931
Blue Blondes   Bryan 1921; Pollack 1921; Schwartz, Jean 1921
Blue, Blue   Kern 1906
Blue, Blue, Blue   Gershwin, George 1933; Gershwin, Ira
   1933
Blue Bluebird (inst.), The   McHugh 1956
Blue Bobby Socks   David, Hal 1959
Blue Bonnet (You Make Me Feel Blue)   Bryan 1926
Blue Book of Girls, A   Atteridge 1922; Romberg 1922
Blue Bouquet   Mills 1939
Blue Bowery (The Bowery)   Adamson 1930; Youmans 1930
Blue Boy Blues, The   Porter 1922
Blue Boy (inst.)   Oakland 1958
Blue Bulgarian Band, The   Kern 1910
Blue Butterfly   Drake 1962
Blue Candlelight and Red, Red Roses   Revel 1944; Webster
   1944
Blue Chimes   Hanley 1928; Turk 1928
Blue Classique (inst.)   Blake 1937
Blue Danube   Comden and Green 1955; Johnson, Howard
   1939
Blue Danube Ballet   Fain 1931; Kahal 1931
Blue Danube Blues   Kern 1921
Blue Danube Dream   Kahn 1940
Blue Daughter of Heaven   Egan 1930
Blue Dawn   Adamson 1939; Washington 1938
Blue Day   Bullock 1950
Blue Devils of France   Berlin 1918
Blue Drag   Myrow 1932
Blue Dream   Razaf 1940
Blue Dreams   Burke 1941; Davis 1932
Blue English (inst.)   McHugh 1936
Blue Eyes   Caesar 1936; Kahn 1927; Kern 1928
Blue Eyes Get Red Red Ready for Love   Hoffman 1929
Blue Fandango   Coslow 1956
Blue Fantasy (inst.)   Blake 1975
Blue Flame   Mills 1931
Blue for a Boy, Pink for a Girl   David, Hal 1949
Blue for Blues   Bergman 1960
Blue Gardenia   Russell 1953
Blue Grass   Brown, Lew 1928; DeSylva 1928; Dietz 1948;
   Henderson 1928; Razaf 1938; Schwartz, Arthur 1948
Blue Grass Blues   Mills 1923
Blue, Green, Grey and Gone   Bergman 1971
Blue Guitar   Bacharach 1963; David, Hal 1963
Blue Harmonica   Hoffman 1956
Blue Hawaii   Baer 1929; Caesar 1929; Johnson, Howard
   1927; Rainger 1937; Robin 1937
Blue Hoosier Blues   Baer 1923; Friend 1923

Blue Hour   Coots 1928
Blue Hours   Porter 1928
Blue Hullaballoo   Gershwin, George 1927; Gershwin, Ira 1927
Blue in Love   Young, Joe 1934
Blue Indian   Egan 1925; Whiting 1925
Blue Interlude   Mills 1935; Razaf 1954
Blue Is My Heart   Davis 1942; Silver 1942
Blue Is the Evening   Akst 1938; Clare 1938
Blue is the Night   Fisher 1929
Blue Island   Washington 1944
Blue Italian Waters   Webster 1939
Blue Jean Polka, The   Gordon 1950; Revel 1950; Warren 1949, 1950
Blue Jeans   Conrad 1935; Magidson 1935
Blue Jeans and Pink Lemonade   Fain 1954; Webster 1954
Blue Kentucky Moon   Donaldson 1931
Blue Kitten Blues   Friml 1922; Harbach 1922
Blue Kitten (Meow), The   Friml 1922; Harbach 1922
Blue Lagoon (inst.)   Schwartz, Jean 1930
Blue Land   Johnson, Howard 1928
Blue Light Waltz, The   Hoffman 1957
Blue Little You   Mills 1928
Blue Little You and Blue Little Me   Johnson, Howard 1929
Blue Lou   Mills 1935
Blue Love   Davis 1953
Blue Lovebird   Kahn 1940
Blue Matador   Cahn 1967
Blue Melody   Lerner, Sammy 1930
Blue Midnight   Davis 1935
Blue Midnight (inst.)   Warren 1959
Blue Mirage (Don't Go)   Coslow 1954
Blue Mizz (inst.)   Johnson, James P. 1945
Blue Monday   Ager 1916; Hart 1940; Razaf Date Unknown; Rodgers 1940; Waller Date Unknown
Blue Monday Blues   DeSylva 1922; Gershwin, George 1922
Blue Mood   Ellington 1962; Mills 1936; Razaf 1957
Blue Moods, 1, 2, and Sex (inst.)   Johnson, James P. 1944
Blue Moon   Hart 1934; Rodgers 1934
Blue Moon (I'm As Blue As You)   Friend 1932; Monaco 1932
Blue Moon on the Silver Sage   Freed, Ralph 1941; Stept 1941
Blue Moon Over the Redwoods   David, Mack 1941; Meyer 1941
Blue Moonlight   Ager 1941
Blue Music   Parish 1932
Blue Nevada Moon   Egan 1931
Blue Night   Webster 1936
Blue Nightfall   Lane 1939; Loesser 1939
Blue Nights   Rose 1924
Blue Nile   Friend 1935
Blue Note, A   Russell 1960
Blue Notes   Cahn 1935
Blue Oak Tree, The   Sherman 1963
Blue Ocean Blues   Hart 1928; Rodgers 1928
Blue on Blue   Bacharach 1963; David, Hal 1963
Blue on My Way to Reno   Fisher Date Unknown
Blue Orchids   Carmichael 1939
Blue Over Two Brown Eyes   Ager 1932
Blue Over You   Davis 1928
Blue Piano   Ellington 1963
Blue Pillow   Carmichael Date Unknown
Blue Plate Special   Burke 1951
Blue Print   Parish 1965
Blue Print Blues   Gorney 1926

Blue Rag in Twelve Keys (inst.)   Blake 1969
Blue Rain   Mercer 1939; Van Heusen 1939
Blue Raindrops   Leslie 1941; Meyer 1941
Blue Ramble   Ellington 1943
Blue Rendezvous   Razaf 1940
Blue Reverie   Merrill 1953
Blue Rhumba   Brown, Nacio Herb 1941; Freed, Ralph 1941
Blue Rhythm   Mills 1931
Blue Rhythm Be-Bop   Mills 1947
Blue Rhythm Blues   Mills 1947
Blue Rhythm Bounce   Mills 1949
Blue Rhythm Chant   Mills 1949
Blue Rhythm Jam   Mills 1947
Blue Rhythm Ramble   Mills 1949
Blue Rhythm Serenade   Mills 1949
Blue Rhythm Swing   Mills 1947
Blue Ribbon Girls, The   Smith, Harry B. 1900
Blue Ridge Moon   Kahn 1931
Blue Ridge Mountain Blues   DePaul 1943; Raye 1943
Blue Ridge Mountains of North Carolina   Willson 1953
Blue Ridge Mountains of South Carolina   Willson 1953
Blue Ridge Mountains (Tennessee Style)   Willson 1953
Blue River   Bryan 1927; Washington 1933; Young, Victor 1933
Blue Room, The   Hart 1926; Rodgers 1926
Blue Roses   Ahlert 1933; David, Hal 1966; Leslie 1933
Blue Sails Upon a Silver Sea   Egan 1949; Kahn 1949; Whiting 1949
Blue Seas   Bacharach 1969; David, Hal 1969
Blue September   Friend 1939; Parish 1940
Blue Serenade   Adamson 1935, Date Unknown; Lane 1935
Blue Shadows   Alter 1928
Blue Shadows and White Gardenias   Gordon 1942
Blue Skies   Berlin 1926
Blue Skies, Gray Skies   Cohan 1927
Blue Skirt Waltz, The   Parish 1948
Blue Sky Avenue   Conrad 1934; Magidson 1934; Mitchell 1934
Blue Sleep   Webster 1955
Blue Star   Heyman 1955; Young, Victor 1955
Blue Step   Carroll 1929
Blue Strain, The   Waller 1924
Blue Swanee   Egan 1923; Kahn 1923; Whiting 1923
Blue Sweetheart   Friend 1942
Blue Tahitian Moon   Gordon 1941
Blue Tango   Parish 1952
Blue Thoughts (inst.)   Blake 1936
Blue Train, The   Gorney 1926
Blue, Turning Gray Over You   Razaf 1930; Waller 1930
Blue Velvet   Waller 1941
Blue Venetian Waters   Kahn 1937
Blue Vignette   Coots 1959
Blue Violin   Razaf 1955
Blue Was My Favorite Color (I Am)   Heyman 1965
Blue Waters   Washington 1929
Blue White Moonlight   Donaldson 1934; Kahn 1934
Blue Willow Wind   Styne 1985
Blue Windows   Egan 1929
Blue (With You or Without You)   Kalmar 1949
Blue Without You   Parish 1930
Blue World   Oakland 1970
Bluebeard   Gershwin, George 1927; Gershwin, Ira 1927
Bluebeard's Beard (Inst)   Rodgers 1930
Bluebell   Livingston, Jerry 1958; Webster 1958
Blueberry Eyes (Kokemomo No Hitomi)   Rome 1969

Blueberry Lane   Bryan 1928
Blueberry Rhyme (inst.)   Johnson, James P. 1940
Bluebird Come Back and Feather Your Nest   Gilbert 1934
Bluebird in the Rain   Russell 1974
Bluebird (inst.)   Snyder 1907
Bluebird Is Singing to Me, A   Adamson 1946; McHugh 1946
Bluebird, Sing Me a Song   Davis 1928; Hanley 1928
Bluebird, Where Are You   Clarke 1922
Bluebirds in My Belfry   Burke 1944; Van Heusen 1944
Bluebirds in the Moonlight   Rainger 1939; Robin 1939
Bluebirds on a Blackboard   Burke 1947; Van Heusen 1947
Bluebirds, Robins and Meadowlarks   Hoffman 1953
Blue-Eyed, Blond-Haired, Heart-Breaking Baby
      Doll   Mitchell 1919
Bluer Than Blue   Bryan 1927; Donaldson 1937; Pollack 1933
Bluer than the Ocean Blues   Waller 1938
Blues   De Lange 1942
Blues — Why Don't You Let Me Alone   Blake 1937
Blues Ain't, The   Ellington 1971
Blues Ain't Got No Religion   Russell 1945
Blues Are Brewin', The   Alter 1947; De Lange 1947
Blues Are Mighty Pretty Music   Robison 1948
Blues, Blues, Blues (If the Blues Was Money)   Bergman 1960
Blues Boogie   Arlen 1959; Mercer 1959
Blues, Country Style, The   David, Mack 1959; Livingston,
      Jerry 1959
Blues Don't Care Who Gets Them, The   Bacharach 1962;
      David, Hal 1962
Blues for a Four String Guitar   David, Mack 1963
Blues for Fats (inst.)   Johnson, James P. 1948
Blues for Janet   Mills 1966
Blues for Jimmy (inst.)   Johnson, James P. 1945
Blues for Pete   Johnson, James P. 1946
Blues Have Got Me, The   Clarke 1924; Johnston 1924;
      Meyer 1924; Silver 1924; Turk 1924
Blues Idiom (inst.)   Waller 1945
Blues Improvisation   Mercer 1979
Blues in B-Flat   Mills 1935
Blues in My Heart   Mills 1931
Blues in New Orleans (inst.)   Blake 1961
Blues in the Morning (Inst.)   Warren Date Unknown
Blues in the Night   Arlen 1941; Mercer 1941
Blues (inst.)   Bloom 1931
Blues Is a Tale of Trouble, The   Bergman 1959
Blues Is a Travelin' Thing, The   Bergman 1959
Blues Is an Old Old Story, The   Bergman 1959
Blues Is What I Got   Hoffman 1962
Blues Never Die (inst.)   Waller 1923
Blues Nocturne (inst.)   Revel 1946
Blues Serenade, A   Parish 1935
Blues Stampede   Mills 1927
Blues Theme   Mercer 1955
Blues-Reel   Carmichael 1953
Bluest, The   Raye 1958
Bluesten Bowl   Willson 1953
Bluff   Cohan 1928
Blunderland   Buck 1922
Blush and Sing   Kahn 1937
Blushing Bride, A   Harburg 1967; Romberg 1922; Styne 1967
Blushing Bride and Groom, The   Ager 1917; Jerome 1917
Blushing Rose (inst.)   Schwartz, Jean 1930
Blushing Rose Where the Volga Flows   Fisher 1925
Bo Koo   Youmans 1924
Boa Noite (Good Night)   Gordon 1941; Warren 1941
Board of Directors of Continental Steel, The   Coslow 1955

Boarding House Blues (inst.)   Warren 1956
Boarding House Love Call   Schwartz, Jean 1926
Boardwalk Blues   Turk 1922
Boardwalk Crawl, The   Atteridge 1911
Boat Race Chorus   Smith, Harry B. 1909
Boat Sails on Wednesday, A   Kern 1909
Bob Kaye Theme   Oakland 1954
Bob Maxwell Theme   Oakland 1954
Bob Murphy Theme   Oakland 1954
Bob Richmond Theme   Oakland 1954
Bob White   Friend 1928; Kern 1920; Silver 1928
Bob White Whatcha Gonna Swing Tonight   Mercer 1937
Bobbed Hair Blues   Young, Victor 1922
Bobbed Haired Baby   Coots 1926
Bobbed-Haired Bandit Stole My Heart Away, A   Razaf 1924
Bobbin' Up and Down   Carroll Date Unknown
Bobby and Jackie and Jack   Sondheim 1981
Bobby and Me   Brown, Lew 1928; DeSylva 1928; Henderson
      1928
Bobby's Nightmare   Robin 1928
Bobo, The   Cahn 1967
Bob-O-Link   Rodgers 1923
Bobotchka   Rainger 1939; Robin 1939
Bobtail   Blane 1969
Bob-White   Johnston 1921
Body and Soul   Dietz 1930; Heyman 1930
Bogie Man, The   Schwartz, Jean 1905; Williams 1905
Bohemia   Herbert 1908; Howard, Joseph E. 1905; Kern 1912;
      Smith, Harry B. 1903; Smith, Robert B. 1912
Bohemian Lullaby   Revel 1951
Bohemian Rag   Atteridge 1914; Romberg 1914
Boin-n-n-ng   Stept 1947
Bojangles   Cahn 1980; Strouse 1980
Bojangles of Harlem   Fields 1936; Kern 1936
Bold Gendarmes, The   Cohan 1908
Bold Journey   Livingston, Jerry 1957; Russell 1957
Bold Pierre   Smith, Harry B. 1896
Bolero, The   Smith, Robert B. 1906
Bolero d'Amour   Sondheim 1971
Bolero (inst.)   Blake 1946
Boll Weevil   Gilbert 1943
Bolshevik Love   Caesar 1925; Youmans 1925
Bombardier Song   Hart 1942; Rodgers 1942
Bombashay   Howard, Joseph E. 1910
Bombay   Clare 1925; Monaco 1925
Bombay Bombashay, The   Romberg 1920
Bombo   DeSylva 1921
Bom-Bom-Beedle-Um-Bo   Caesar 1924; Gorney 1924
Bon Appetit (Menu Song)   Arlen 1959; Mercer 1959
Bon Bon   Hoffman 1957; Merrill 1957
Bon Bon Steppers Parade (inst.)   Johnson, James P. 1945
Bon Jour   Smith, Harry B. 1896
Bon Jour La Vie   Russell 1957
Bon Jour (The Language Song)   Willson 1960
Bon Nuit   Evans 1950; Livingston, Jay 1950
Bon Soir   Heyman 1953; Young, Victor 1953
Bon Soir Cherie   Fields 1928; McHugh 1928
Bon Soir (Gigi)   Adamson 1951
Bon Vivant   Mercer 1964
Bon Vivant (Bone Vi-vawn)   Livingston, Jerry 1959
Bon Voyage   Adamson 1959; Porter 1934; Sherman 1962;
      Young, Victor 1959
Bon Voyage, Mon Ami   Spina 1957
Bon Voyage Waltz   Sherman 1962

Bonanza   Comden and Green 1947; Evans 1959; Livingston, Jay 1959

Bon-Bon Buddy the Chocolate Man   Brown, A. Seymour 1909

Bond Street (inst.)   Bacharach 1967; Waller 1940

Bones   Hammerstein 1920; Harbach 1920

Bones and Tambourine   Fisher 1929

Boneyard Shuffle   Carmichael 1926; Mills 1926

Bonga-Boo   Gorney 1924

Bongo Bingo, The   David, Mack 1953; Livingston, Jerry 1953

Bongo on the Congo   Kern 1924

Bongo the Camel   Coots 1955

Bongo-Boola   Blake 1952; Sissle 1952

Bonita   Lewis 1934; Romberg 1927; Smith, Harry B. 1927; Styne 1941

Bonjour   Burke 1956; Friml 1956

Bonjour Finis   Coslow 1955

Bonjour Goodbye   Duke 1939

Bonjour Madame   Raye 1956

Bonjour Mam'selle   Gordon 1935; Revel 1935

Bonjour Tristesse (inst.)   McHugh 1957

Bonne Nuit   Mercer 1952

Bonne Nuit (Good Night)   Evans 1951; Livingston, Jay 1951

Bonnie   Johnson, Howard 1924

Bonnie and Clyde (inst.)   Strouse 1967

Bonnie Annie Laurie   Williams 1909

Bonnie Blue Flag   Hammerstein 1938; Harbach 1938; Kern 1938; Romberg 1927; Rome 1969

Bonnie Briar Bush   Howard, Joseph E. 1907

Bonnie Eloise   Johnson, Howard 1939

Bonnie Gone (Boni No Shi)   Rome 1969

Bonnie Jean   Bryan 1906; Snyder 1906

Bonnie Jean of Aberdeen   Bryan 1933

Bonnie Old Earth, The   Drake 1954

Bonsoir   Cahn 1964; Van Heusen 1964

Boo, Boo, Boo   Coslow 1933; Johnston 1933

Boo Hoo Hoo, Ha Ha Ha (I'm Between a Laugh and a Cry)   Leslie 1930; Warren 1930

Boo Kangaroo   Hoffman 1954

Booga-Da-Woog   Mancini 1955; Raye 1955

Boogey Boo Lady, The   Atteridge 1910

Boogie Barcarolle   Porter 1941

Boogie Dreams (inst.)   Johnson, James P. 1943

Boogie Man, The   Coslow 1934

Boogie on the Prairie (inst.)   Ruby 1946

Boogie Rag   Ager 1916

Boogie Woogie   Freed, Arthur 1945; Warren 1945

Boogie Woogie Bakery Man   Sherman 1962

Boogie Woogie Beguine   Blake 1945; Sissle 1945

Boogie Woogie Blues (inst.)   Waller 1945

Boogie Woogie Boogie Man   Koehler 1944; Lane 1944

Boogie Woogie Bugle Boy   Raye 1941

Boogie Woogie Bunga Boo   Blake Date Unknown; Razaf 1942

Boogie Woogie Conga   Revel 1941

Boogie Woogie Jump (inst.)   Waller 1945

Boogie Woogie Rag (inst.)   Waller 1945

Boogie Woogie Runway (inst.)   Johnson, James P. 1943

Boogie Woogie Stomp (inst.)   Waller 1945

Boogie Woogie Stride (inst.)   Johnson, James P. 1944

Boogie-Boo, The   Brown, A. Seymour 1909

Boogie-Woogie   Coots 1938; Davis 1938

Boogie-Woogie Man   Cahn 1941

Boogly Woogly Piggy   Cahn 1941

Boogy-Woogy   Duke 1940

Boo-Hoo   Heyman 1937

Boo-Hoo, Tee-Hee   Harbach 1908

Boo-Hoo-Hoo   Brown, Lew 1927; DeSylva 1927

Book at My Bedside   Robison 1944

Book I've Read, The   Pollack 1945

Bookends   Brooks 1960

Booker T. Washington Brigade, The   Loesser 1942; Styne 1942

Bookworm (inst.)   Bacharach 1965

Boola Boo   Friml 1917; Harbach 1917

Boola Boola   Howard, Joseph E. 1909

Boola-Boola   Goetz 1912

Booloo   Coslow 1937

Boom   Goetz 1938

Boom Biddy Boom Boom   Cahn 1950

Boom Boom By the Sea   Rose 1928

Boom! Boom! 's' Great to Be Crazy   Friend 1944

Boom Boom Song, The   Spina 1952

Boom Cheela Bim Bahm   Merrill 1956

Boom Chicka Boom   Coleman 1988; Strouse 1991

Boom Crunch   Sondheim 1987

Boom Song, The   Hoffman 1955

Boom-a-ladda Boom-Boom   Livingston, Jerry 1959

Boombah!   Rome 1958

Boom-Boom (Le Grand Boom-Boom)   Coleman 1962; Leigh 1962

Boom-Boom-Boomerang   Johnson, J. Rosamond 1931

Boomerang, The   Hart 1920; Rodgers 1920; Rose 1929

Boomerang Kisses   Friend 1953

Boomps-a-Daisy   Fain 1938

Boom-Ti, Boom-Ti, Boom   Howard, Bart 1961

Boop-Boop a Doopa Doo Trot   Burke 1930

Booperadoop   Cobb 1930; Edwards 1930

Boost Brooklyn   Jerome 1911; Schwartz, Jean 1911

Boost New York   Friend 1924

Boot Camp A-Go-Go   Mills 1965

Bootblack Blues   Gordon 1932; Revel 1932

Bootblack Man from Gramercy Square, The   Meyer 1947

Booth Hotel, The   Drake 1954

Bootlegger's Chantey (We're an English Ship), The   Hart 1929; Rodgers 1929

Boots and Saddles   Kahn 1933

Boots, Boots, Boots   Schwartz, Jean 1918

Boozers and Losers   Coleman 1968

Bop! Goes My Heart   Styne 1949

Bopeep   Egan 1916; Whiting 1916

Bored   Martin 1937

Born Again   Dietz 1963; Schwartz, Arthur 1963

(You'll Be) Born All Over Again   Dietz 1944; Duke 1944

Born and Bred in Brooklyn, Over the Bridge   Cohan 1923

Born and Bred in Old Kentucky   DeSylva 1925; Hanley 1925

Born at Last   Duke 1963

Born in a Briar Patch   Blane 1969

Born in April   Harbach 1947; Kern 1947

Born to Be Blue   David, Mack 1990; Hoffman 1930; Silver 1930

Born to Be Bored   Livingston, Jerry 1935

Born to Be Happy   Davis 1957

Born to Be Kissed   Dietz 1934; Schwartz, Arthur 1934

Born to Be Loved   Bullock 1959; Heyman 1937

Born to Dance   Brown, Nacio Herb 1935; Freed, Arthur 1935

Born to Love   Washington 1941; Young, Victor 1941

Born to Swing   Freed, Ralph 1938; Lane 1938; Mills 1937; Razaf Date Unknown

Born to the Bayou   Robison 1940

Born Too Late   Duke 1956; Strouse 1958
Borneo   Donaldson 1928; Jerome 1905; Schwartz, Jean 1905
Borrow from Me   Smith, Harry B. 1912
Borscht   Brooks 1948
Boss (For You I Shout Hooray)   Drake 1952
Boss Is Bringing Home a Bride, The   Gershwin, Ira 1940; Weill 1940
Boss Is Not Here (All at Once It's Sunday), The   Bacharach 1965; David, Hal 1965
Boss' Love Call, The   Brooks 1959
Boss Tweed   Fields 1945; Romberg 1945
Bossa Nova Roma   Cahn 1968
Boston   Johnson, James P. 1931
Boston Post Road   Caesar 1928
Boswell Weeps, The   Rainger 1932; Robin 1932
Botany Bay   Evans 1953; Livingston, Jay 1953
Both Ends Against the Middle   Eliscu 1962
Bottle Imp, The   Smith, Harry B. 1908
Bottle Me Up and Send Me Sailing   Stept 1953
Bottle Up a Pretty Girl   Bryan 1920; Schwartz, Jean 1920
Bottle Up the Moonlight   Alter 1955; Sigman 1955
Bottleneck   Rome 1959
Bottom of the Barrel   Robison 1953
Bottom of the Middle Class   Lawrence 1962
Bottomless Cup, A   Bacharach 1958; David, Hal 1958
Bottoms Up   Adamson 1934; Friend 1929; Hart 1942; Lane 1934; Rodgers 1942
Boudoir Dolls   Eliscu 1930
Bought and Paid For   Kern 1914; Smith, Harry B. 1914
Boule Miche, The   Herbert 1908
Boulevard Break   Porter 1928
Boulevard Glide   Goetz 1909
Boulevard of Broken Dreams, The   Dubin 1934; Warren 1934
Boulevard of Nightingales   Hoffman 1954
Boulevardier from the Bronx   Dubin 1936; Warren 1936
Bounce   Duke 1963; Evans 1940; Livingston, Jay 1940
Bounce a Little Ball at Your Baby   Conrad 1929; Mitchell 1929
Bounce Away Your Baby Blues   Caesar 1925
Bounce Me   Conrad 1926; Kahn 1926
Bounce Me Brother with a Solid Four   Raye 1941
Bounce Me, John, I've Rubber Heels On   Fisher 1915
Bounce the Berry   Merrill 1948
Bouncin'   Hoffman 1959
Bouncin' in Rhythm   Mills 1935
Bouncin' the Blues (inst.)   Warren 1949
Bouncing All Over Town   Buck 1921
(We Keep) Bouncing Back for More   Coleman 1960; Leigh 1960
Bouncing on the Bayou   Gilbert 1943
Bouncing the Baby Around   Dubin 1930
Bouncy Bouncy Bally   Hoffman 1950
Bound for the Bronx   Fain 1930
Bound with a Golden Chain   Sterling 1900
Bouquet   Mercer 1963
Bouquet of Girls   Atteridge 1922; Schwartz, Jean 1922
Bourbon Street Beat   David, Mack 1959; Livingston, Jerry 1959
Bourbon Street Blues   Fain 1958; Webster 1958
'Bout Eighty Miles Outside of Atlanta   Adamson 1945; McHugh 1945
'Bout Time   Sherman 1968
Bow Belles   Kern 1928
Bow Wow Ball, The   Sherman 1984
Bow Wow Blues   Friend 1921

Bow, Wow, Wow, Wow, Wow   Caesar 1940
Bowbells, North Dakota   Willson 1953
Bowery, The   Johnson, Howard 1939; Youmans 1930
Bowery After Dark, The   Ahlert 1930; Turk 1930
Bowery of Today, The   Atteridge 1923; Caesar 1923; Romberg 1923
Bowery Rose   Johnson, Howard 1924
Bowery Serenade (Sweet Pippy)   De Lange 1942
Bowl of Boullabaisse, A   Revel 1960
Bowl of Chop Suey and You-ey, A   Bullock 1934
Bowl of Roses, A   Olcott 1907
Bowlegged Polly   Bergman 1967
Bow-Legged Sal   Hammerstein 1941; Romberg 1941
Bowler Hat, A   Sondheim 1976
Bowler's Song, The   Strouse 1945
Bowling Alley   David, Mack 1950; Livingston, Jerry 1950
Bowser   Spina 1958
Boxing Bout According to F Sharp, A   Johnson, Howard 1924
Boy!   Hoffman 1956
Boy, a Girl and a Moon Means Love, A   Friend 1936
Boy, a Girl and the Moon, A   Brennan 1927
Boy and a Girl Were Dancing, A   Gordon 1932; Revel 1932
Boy and His Dreams, A   David, Mack 1961
Boy Climbed Up the Ladder, The   Caesar 1940
Boy Do We Look to the Monkeys   Hoffman 1956
Boy, Do We Need It Now   Strouse 1974
Boy Friend, The   Brown, Nacio Herb 1928; Freed, Arthur 1928
Boy Friend Back Home, The   Porter 1929
Boy From . . ., The   Sondheim 1966
Boy I Left Behind, The   Cahn 1945; Styne 1945
Boy I Left Behind Me, The   Hart 1942; Rodgers 1942
Boy in Buckskin and a Gal in Calico, A   Coots 1955
Boy in Khaki, a Girl in Lace, A   Wrubel 1942
Boy in Love, a Girl in Love, A   Burke 1971
Boy in the Blue Uniform   Johnson, Howard 1927
Boy in the Celluloid Collar, The   Blane 1947; Warren 1947
Boy Like That, A   Sondheim 1957
Boy Like You, A   Weill 1947
Boy Meets Girl   Fain 1936; Mercer 1938; Warren 1938; Willson 1953
Boy Meets Horn   Ellington 1939; Mills 1939
Boy Millionaire   Drake 1954
Boy Named Lem (and a Girl Named Sue)   Brown, Lew 1939; Stept 1939
Boy Next Door, The   Harbach 1925; Martin 1944; Youmans 1925
Boy of Mine   Buck 1915
Boy, Oh Boy   Loesser 1941
Boy Oh Boy Oh Boy I've Got It Bad   Leslie 1931; Monaco 1931
Boy on a Dolphin, The   Webster 1957
Boy on Page 35   David, Hal 1956
Boy Takes a Girl In His Arms, A   Revel 1946
Boy Ten Feet Tall, A   Washington 1965
Boy! That's Love   Johnson, J. Rosamond 1950
Boy Wanted   Gershwin, George 1921, 1924; Gershwin, Ira 1921, 1924; Merrill 1954
Boy! What Love Has Done to Me!   Gershwin, George 1930; Gershwin, Ira 1930
Boy with a Drum   Harbach 1938; Kern 1938
Boy with the Wistful Eyes, The   DePaul 1941; Raye 1941
Boy Without a Sweetheart, A   Cohan 1898
Boy-ee-yoing   Johnson, James P. 1957

Boys!   Smith, Harry B. 1896
Boys All Fall for Me, The   Schwartz, Jean 1914
Boys and Girls   Brooks 1958
Boys and Girls Like You and Me   Hammerstein 1943; Rodgers 1943
Boys Are Better than Girls   Fields 1952; Schwartz, Arthur 1952
Boys Are Like Wonderful Toys   Lewis 1919; Snyder 1919; Young, Joe 1919
Boys, Boys, Boys   Dietz 1943; Duke 1943; Howard, Joseph E. 1910; Lawrence 1964; Schwartz, Jean 1914
Boys in Gray   Romberg 1927
Boys in the Backroom, The   Loesser 1939
Boys in the Band   Loesser 1938
Boys' Night Out, The   Cahn 1963; Van Heusen 1963
Boys of Uncle Sam   Johnson, James P. 1917
Boys that Fight the Flames, The   Cohan 1908
Boy's Theme (inst.)   Young, Victor 1953
Boys Up on the Hill, The   Caesar 1952
Boys Will Be Boys — Girls Will Be Girls   Mercer 1935
Boys Will Be Boys and Girls Will Be Girls   Herbert 1907; Smith, Harry B. 1907
Boys with the Wistful Eyes, The   DePaul 1942; Raye 1942
Bozo's Hobby Song   Livingston, Jerry 1961
Bozo's Holiday   Livingston, Jerry 1962
Bozo's Magic Whistle   Livingston, Jerry 1961
Bozo's Marching Song   Livingston, Jerry 1962
Bozo's Pocket Rocket   Livingston, Jerry 1962
Bozo's Teach-a-rena   Livingston, Jerry 1963
B-R-A   Hart 1919
Bracelets   Brennan 1927
Bradley's Dance   Gordon 1935; Revel 1935
Braggin' in Brass   Ellington 1938; Mills 1938
Brain She Ain't, A   Evans 1964; Livingston, Jay 1964
Bramble Bush, The   David, Mack 1967
(Got a) Bran' New Daddy   Dietz 1943; Duke 1943
Brand New Boy   David, Hal 1962
Brand New Dress, A   Lerner, Alan Jay 1969
Brand New Friends   Rome 1973
Brand New Rainbow in the Sky, A   Stept 1950
Brand New Song in Town   Kahn 1938; Romberg 1937
Brand New Woman   Howard, Bart 1984
Brand New World   Strouse 1986
B-R-A-N-E Spells Brain!   Cahn 1963; Van Heusen 1963
Brasilia (Sernata Negra)   Mercer 1961
Brass Band Ephraham Jones   Meyer 1911
Brass Band March   Hammerstein 1930; Romberg 1930
Brass Band on Float   Merrill 1956
Brass Buttons and Epaulets   Bullock 1938; Spina 1938
Brass Rings and Daydreams   Sherman 1978
Brat, The   Smith, Harry B. 1919; Snyder 1919
Brave and the Free, The   Leigh 1971
Brave Heart, A   Blane 1948; Warren 1948
Brave Hussar, The   Harbach 1914
Brave Man   Evans 1954; Livingston, Jay 1954
Bravest Heart of All   Egan 1917; Whiting 1917
Bravest of the Brave   DePaul 1942; Raye 1942
Bravo, Antonio!   Norworth 1917
Bravo, Bravo   Smith, Harry B. 1927
Bravo, Bravo, Novelisto   Bergman 1964; Fain 1964
Bravo New Song in Town   Romberg 1938
Brazil   Russell 1941
Brazilian Baby   Edwards 1934
Brazilian Baion   Russell Date Unknown
Brazilian Bolero (inst.)   Coots 1945

Brazilian Boogie   Blane 1943; Martin 1944
Brazilian Boogie Woogie   Davis 1942
Brazilian Can-Can   Davis 1944
Brazilian Love Song   Coslow 1936; Young, Victor 1936
Brazilian Love Song (Andorinha Prata)   Hoffman 1959
Brazilian Nut   Smith, Robert B. 1915
Brazilian Rose   Razaf 1955
Brazilian Samba   Schwartz, Jean 1942
Brazilly Willy   Evans 1958; Livingston, Jay 1958
Bread and Butter   Harbach 1926; Kern 1926
Bread and Butter Love   Hoffman 1957
Bread and Cheese and Kisses   Howard, Joseph E. 1912
Bread and Freedom   Strouse 1986
Bread and Gravy   Carmichael 1935
Bread and Kisses   Gordon 1932; Revel 1932
Breadfruit Tree, The   Drake 1967
Break, Break, Break   Young, Victor 1911
Break It to Me Gently   Sigman 1940
Break It Up Cinderella   Carmichael 1940; Mercer 1940
Break My Heart Again   Drake 1994; Lane 1987
Break the Ice   Robison 1960
Break the Wall   Robison 1958
Breakaway   Bergman 1965; Conrad 1929; Mitchell 1929
Breakfast at Arable's   Strouse Date Unknown
Breakfast at Tiffany's   Merrill 1966
Breakfast Ball   Arlen 1933, 1934; Koehler 1933, 1934
Breakfast Dance   Arlen 1931; Eliscu 1930; Koehler 1931; Rainger 1930
Breakfast for Two   Duke 1963
Breakfast in Bed   Sigman 1953
Breakfast in Harlem   Caesar 1936; Lerner, Sammy 1936
Breakfast with Hazel   Caesar 1943
Breakfast with You   Ager 1928; Yellen 1928
Breakin' 'Em Down   Blake 1924; Sissle 1924
Breakin' 'Em In   Blake 1932; Sissle 1932
Breakin' in a Pair of Shoes   Stept 1936; Washington 1936
Breakin' My Heart   Waller 1932
Breaking Point, The   Bacharach 1961; David, Hal 1961; Webster 1964
Breath and Breaches   Razaf 1929
Breath o' Bloomin' Heather (From My Little Highland Home)   Brennan 1915
Breath of a Rose   Caesar 1920
Breath of Air, A   Blane 1945
Breath of Scandal   Robison 1949
Breath of Spring   Hart 1920; Rodgers 1920
Breath of Springtime   Hart 1922
Breathes There a Man   Lane 1936; Magidson 1936
Breathin' Heavy   Von Tilzer 1929
Breathtaking   Robison 1956
Breeze, Blow My Baby Back to Me   Hanley 1919
Breeze Is My Sweetheart, The Brook Is My Song, The   Sigman 1949
Breeze Kissed Your Hair, The   Harbach 1931; Kern 1931
Breezin' Along with the Breeze   Whiting 1926
Breezin' (inst.)   Waller 1954
Breezing Along   Robin 1926
Breezy   Sigman 1947
Breezy and Easy   Martin 1957
Breezy Young Fellow and a Gay Young Thing, A   Henderson 1943; Kahal 1943
Breezy's Song   Bergman 1973
Bremen Town Musician, The   Cahn 1977
Brian   Duke 1959
Bricky-Brackie Tootsies   Goetz 1917

Bridal Chorus   Johnson, Howard 1939

Bridal Procession   Hammerstein 1924; Harbach 1924

Bride, The   Fain 1962; Friml 1914; Harbach 1914; Webster 1962

Bride and Groom   Gershwin, George 1926; Gershwin, Ira 1926; Russell 1955

Bride and Groom Waltz, The   Hoffman 1949

Bride Bells   Brown, Lew 1928; DeSylva 1928; Henderson 1928

Bride Finding a Ball, A   Sherman 1976

Bride of the Sea   David, Hal 1962

Bride Was Dressed in White, The   Hammerstein 1928; Youmans 1928

Bride Wore Something Old, The   Fields 1951; Schwartz, Arthur 1951

Bride's Wedding Day Song, A   Mercer 1945

Bride's Wedding Day Song (Thank You Mr. Currier, Thank You Mr. Ives), A   Mercer 1951; Warren 1951

Bridesmaids   Romberg 1918

Bridesmaids Ballet   Henderson 1934; Koehler 1934

Bridge of San Luis Rey, The   Bryan 1928

Bridge of Sighs   Bergman 1966

Bridget McGuire   Porter 1910

Bridget McShane   Atteridge 1921; Pollack 1921; Schwartz, Jean 1921

Bridget O'Flynn (Where've You Been)   Sterling 1926

Brief and Breezy   Cahn 1958; Mancini 1958

Brigadoon   Lerner, Alan Jay 1947; Loewe 1947

Bright and Black   Lerner, Alan Jay 1976

Bright and Early   Arlen 1931; Yellen 1931

Bright and Shiny   Sherman 1961

Bright College Days   Rome 1952

Bright Eyes   Motzan 1920; Smith, Harry B. 1920

Bright Eyes and Bushy Tailed   Merrill 1953

Bright Eyes Goodbye   Williams 1905

Bright Lights   Dixon 1935; Kern 1917; Wrubel 1935

Bright Lights Gay (The New Mown Hay)   Sterling 1910; Von Tilzer 1910

Bright Lights (inst.)   Young, Victor 1957

Bright Square (inst.)   Kern 1938

Bright Star   Sondheim Date Unknown

Bright Stars and Soft Guitars   Coslow 1952

Brighten the Road   Bryan 1930

Brighten Up and Be a Little Sunbeam   Adamson 1948; McHugh 1948

Brighter Days   Parish 1925

Brighton   Sherman 1995

Brindle's Farm   Atteridge 1924

Bring Along Your Dancing Shoes   Kahn 1915

Bring Along Your Loving Ways   Hanley 1916; Romberg 1916

Bring Back Birdie   Adams 1981; Strouse 1981

Bring Back, Bring Back, Bring Back the Kaiser to Me   Von Tilzer 1917

Bring Back My Blushing Rose   Buck 1921; Friml 1921

Bring Back My Daddy to Me   Johnson, Howard 1917; Meyer 1917

Bring Back My Golden Dreams   Meyer 1911

Bring Back My Lena to Me   Berlin 1910; Snyder 1910

Bring Back My Love Dreams   Lewis 1920; Young, Joe 1920

Bring Back My Lovin' Man   Berlin 1911

Bring Back My Man   Wrubel 1929

Bring Back the Old Fashioned Waltz   Revel 1960

Bring Back the Roses (Kathleen Mavoureen)   Bryan 1918; Fisher 1918

Bring Back the Waltz   Fisher 1930

Bring Back Those Good Old Days (inst.)   Coleman 1975

Bring Back Those Rock-a-Bye Baby Days   Silver 1924

Bring Back Those Southern Skies   Motzan 1930

Bring Back Your Love   Atteridge 1913; Schwartz, Jean 1913

Bring 'Em Back   Kern 1920

Bring Him Back Here   Arlen 1929

Bring Him My Love Thoughts   Atteridge 1921

Bring Me a Girl   Kalmar 1917

Bring Me a Radio   Porter 1924

Bring Me a Ring in the Spring   Berlin 1911

Bring Me Back My Butterfly   Porter 1919

Bring Me Back My Lovin' Honey Boy   Yellen 1913

Bring Me My Bride   Sondheim 1962

Bring on the Ding Dong Bell   Gershwin, George 1926; Gershwin, Ira 1926

Bring on the Follies Girls   Buck 1931

Bring on the Girls   Adamson 1945; Atteridge 1918; Buck 1922; Lawrence 1957; McHugh 1945; Romberg 1918; Schwartz, Jean 1918; Smith, Harry B. 1923; Snyder 1923; Sondheim 1971

Bring on the Girls (inst.)   Herbert 1922

Bring on the Pepper   Berlin 1922

Bring Out the Cryin' Towel   David, Hal 1958

Bring Your Darling Daughter   Dietz 1961; Schwartz, Arthur 1961

Bring Your Kisses to Me   Atteridge 1916; Romberg 1916

Bring Your Rubber Around   Caesar 1943

Bring Your Smile Along   Davis 1955

Bringin' Up a Boy (To Be a Man)   Leigh 1953

Brinkley Coon, The   Cohan 1909

Britain's Own Ambassadors   Hart 1927; Rodgers 1927

British Subjec' Blues   Razaf 1945

Brittany   Porter 1924; Smith, Harry B. 1913

Brittwood Rag (inst.)   Blake 1962

Broad Highway   Romberg 1924

Broadcast a Jazz   Porter 1924

Broadcasting Medley   Gordon 1938; Revel 1938

Broads Ain't People   Evans 1961; Livingston, Jay 1961

Broadway   Brown, Lew 1913; Buck 1917; Conrad 1929; Drake 1954; Dubin 1923; Mitchell 1929

Broadway Baby   Sondheim 1971

Broadway Baby Dolls   Bryan 1929; Meyer 1929

Broadway Beauty Doctor Ain't Done Right By Our Nell   Leslie 1938

Broadway Belles   Snyder 1908

Broadway Blossom   Comden and Green 1945

Broadway, Broadway   Adams 1978; Strouse 1978

(Flutter on By, My) Broadway Butterfly   Atteridge 1919; Carroll 1925; Goetz 1917; Romberg 1919; Schwartz, Jean 1919

Broadway Caravan   Edwards 1923; Johnson, Howard 1923

Broadway Cinderella   Dubin 1935; Warren 1935

Broadway Favorites   Herbert 1905

Broadway Honeymoon, A   Howard, Joseph E. 1913

Broadway in Sahara   Atteridge 1921

Broadway Jamboree   Adamson 1938; McHugh 1938

Broadway Knitting Club, The   Atteridge 1915; Romberg 1915

Broadway Lady   Stept 1933

Broadway Love Song   Gorney 1949

Broadway Melody, The   Brown, Nacio Herb 1928; Freed, Arthur 1928

Broadway Musical, A   Adams 1978; Strouse 1978

Broadway Pirates   Atteridge 1921; Pollack 1921; Schwartz, Jean 1921

Broadway Prologue to Kokomo, Indiana   Gordon 1947;
  Myrow 1947
Broadway Reverie   Buck 1931
Broadway Rhythm   Brown, Nacio Herb 1935; Freed, Arthur
  1935
Broadway Sam   Atteridge 1915
Broadway School Days   Atteridge 1916; Motzan 1916;
  Romberg 1916
Broadway Serenade   Kahn 1939
Broadway Strut   Coots 1920; Turk 1922
Broadway Swell and Bowery Bum   Hammerstein 1920;
  Harbach 1920
Broadway (The Heart of the World)   Brown, Lew 1927;
  DeSylva 1927; Henderson 1927
Broadway Tipperary   Cohan 1914
Broadway's Gone Hawaii   Gordon 1937; Revel 1937
Broadway's Gone Hill-Billy   Brown, Lew 1934; Gorney 1934
Broadway's Still Broadway   Revel 1940
Broke but Happy   Razaf Date Unknown; Waller Date
  Unknown
Broke Down Papa   Razaf 1931
Broken Arrow   Washington 1957
Broken Butterfly   Brown, Lew 1924
Broken Dreams   Johnston 1930
Broken Dreams of You   Mills 1936
Broken Dreams to Mend   Gilbert 1943
Broken Guitar, A   Gorney 1939; Harburg 1939
Broken Hearted Baby   Stept 1928
Broken Hearted Doll   Sissle 1928
Broken Hearted Dolly   Edwards 1929
Broken Hearted in the Moonlight   Motzan 1930
Broken Hearted Melody   David, Hal 1959; Kahn 1922
Broken Hearted Troubadour   David, Mack 1946
Broken Idol, A   Williams 1909
Broken Melody, The   Akst 1919
Broken Record, The   Friend 1935
Broken Rhythm   Coots 1926
Broken Rhythm (inst.)   Robison 1926
Broken Serenade   Kalmar 1935; Ruby 1935
Broken Toy   Kahn 1922
Broken Up Tune   Clare 1929
Broken Wing, The   Carroll Date Unknown
Broken-Hearted   Whiting 1926
Broken-Hearted Boy   David, Hal 1962
Broken-Hearted Lover   Bryan 1930; Dubin 1930
Brokenhearted Troubadour   David, Mack 1935
Broker's Ensemble   Berlin 1930
Brom's Complaint   Weill 1938
Broncho Busters   Gershwin, George 1930; Gershwin, Ira
  1930
Broncho Sal   Meyer 1909
Bronco   David, Mack 1959; Livingston, Jerry 1959
Bronx, The   Livingston, Jerry 1973
Brook, The (inst.)   Warren Date Unknown
Brookfield Two-Step   Cohan 1908
Brooklyn Bridge, The   Cahn 1947; Styne 1947
Brooklyn Bridge Is Falling Down   Strouse 1947
Brookside Inn   Jerome 1911; Schwartz, Jean 1911
Broth of a Boy, A   Brennan 1914
Brother Against Brother   Livingston, Jerry 1960
Brother Ben   Waller 1925
Brother Can You Spare a Buck? (Anthem for a New
  Depression)   Gorney 1974; Harburg 1974
Brother Can You Spare a Dime?   Gorney 1932; Harburg
  1932

Brother Department, The   Rodgers 1970
Brother, Give Yourself a Shove   Weill 1977
Brother, Just Laugh It Off   Harburg 1929, 1930; Rainger
  1930; Schwartz, Arthur 1930
Brother of Mine   Smith, Harry B. 1926
Brotherhood of Man   Loesser 1961
Brotherhood of Railroad Men   Egan 1916; Whiting 1916
Brothers   Johnson, James P. 1945
Brothers and Sisters   Cohan 1908
(We Are) Brothers in Arms   Washington 1953
Brothers (inst.)   Drake 1958
Brown, Black and Yellow Blues   Johnson, Howard 1923
Brown Eyes   Friml 1926; Hammerstein 1926; Harbach 1926
Brown Eyes Looking into Eyes of Blue   Bryan 1936; Edwards
  1936
Brown Eyes (That Give Me the Blues)   Johnson, Howard
  1921
Brown Eyes Why Are You Blue   Bryan 1925; Meyer 1925
Brown Gal   Razaf 1928
Brown October Ale   Smith, Harry B. 1891
Brown Penny   Ellington 1946
Brown Sugar Mine   Mills 1935
Brown-Eyed Girl   Smith, Harry B. 1926
Brownies   Howard, Joseph E. 1905
Brown-Skin Gal in the Calico Gown, The   Ellington 1941;
  Webster 1941
Brownstone Baby (I've Got the Blues for You)   Dubin 1935;
  Warren 1935
Brownstone Front   Young, Victor 1951
Br-rrr-rr-m (Kiss)   Leigh 1955
Bruin Song, The   Livingston, Jerry 1974
Brunswick Yodel (That's All I Did)   David, Mack 1981
Brush Off, The   Arlen 1966
Brush Up Your Shakespeare   Porter 1948
Brushoff, The   Hoffman 1957
Bryan Believed in Heaven, That's Why He's in Heaven
  Tonight   Dubin 1925
Bubble, The   Friml 1913
Bubble and the Butterfly, The   Brown, A. Seymour 1909
Bubble Ballet (inst.)   Kern 1956
Bubble Dance (Pas Seul) (inst.)   Kern 1932
Bubble Song   Herbert 1924
Bubble-Loo, Bubble-Loo   Carmichael 1948; Webster 1948
Bubbles   Arlen 1962; Atteridge 1924; Harbach 1913; Harburg
  1962; Herbert 1919; Jerome 1924; Merrill 1955; Romberg
  1924; Schwartz, Jean 1924; Smith, Harry B. 1903
Bubbles in the Wine   Loesser 1939
Bubbling Over   Burke 1933; Spina 1933
Bubbling Over with Love   Ager 1931; DePaul 1958; Raye
  1958
Bublitchka   Fain 1938; Parish 1938; Silver 1938
Bucharest   Harbach 1936; Romberg 1936
Buck   Atteridge 1924; Romberg 1924; Schwartz, Jean 1924
Buck Dance Bill   Leslie 1912
Buck in the Bank   Lerner, Sammy 1948
Buck Up!   Buck 1940; Friml 1917
Buckin' for Beardsley   Lerner, Alan Jay 1971
Buckin' the Wind   Coslow 1933; Johnston 1933
Buckle Down Buck Private   Blane 1942
Buckle Down Winsocki   Blane 1941
Buckskin Beauty   Cahn 1956; Van Heusen 1956
Budda   Fisher 1930
Buddha Man   Sigman 1950
Buddie   Razaf 1932; Waller 1932
Buddie Beware   Porter 1934

Buddy Boy   Merrill 1959
Buddy, Can You Spare a Buck   Gorney 1976
Buddy Rose   Baer 1927; Lewis 1927; Young, Joe 1927
Buddy System, The   Coleman 1989
Buds Won't Bud   Arlen 1937; Harburg 1937
Buenos Noches, Buenos Aires   Brown, Nacio Herb 1949;
     Heyman 1947
Buffalo Fight Song   Willson 1960
Buffalo Gals   Johnson, Howard 1939
Buffalo Rhythm (inst.)   Arlen 1927
Buffo Dance (inst.)   Kern 1915
Buffo Terzetto   Kern 1935
Bug House   Mills 1935; Razaf 1929
Bug, The (inst.)   Arlen 1941
Bug-a-Boo   David, Hal 1947
Buggy Riding   Kern 1920
Buggy Song, The   Young, Joe 1933
Bugle, The   Willson 1963
Bugle Blow   Hart 1926; Rodgers 1926
Bugle Blues   Russell 1952
Bugle Call Blues   Turk 1922
Bugle Call Rag (inst.)   Blake 1916
Bugle Is Calling Goodnight, A   Coots 1941; Harbach 1941
Build a Little Fence Around Today   Howard, Joseph E. 1908
Build a Little Home   Dubin 1933; Warren 1933
Build Me a Home in the Gloaming   Egan 1928; Whiting
     1928
Building a Home for You   Kahn 1931
Building a Nest for Mary   Rose 1928
Bulfightin' Baby   Sherman 1957
Bull and Bear   Atteridge 1920
Bull Dog   Porter 1910
Bull Frog and the Dove, The   Williams 1910
Bull Frog Patrol, The   Kern 1919
Bulldogs of Gonzaga   Burke 1937; Monaco 1937
Bullet Wound Blues   Waller 1924
Bullfights in Madrid, The   Sherman 1985
Bulls and Bears   Parish 1933
Bully Song   Hammerstein 1927; Kern 1927
Bum Diddle-De-Um Bum, That's It   Monaco 1914
Bumble Bee   Coslow Date Unknown
Bumble Bee Bumble By   Woods 1952
Bumble Boogie Samba, The   David, Hal 1947; David, Mack
     1947
Bumblebee, The   Harbach 1910
Bump, Bump, Bump in Your Automobile   Brown, Lew 1912
Bumper Found a Grand   Hart 1933; Rodgers 1933
Bumper to Bumper   Baer 1962; Leslie 1962
Bumper's Going to Work (Kangaroo Court)   Hart 1933;
     Rodgers 1933
Bumper's Home Again (My Pal Bumper)   Hart 1933;
     Rodgers 1933
Bumpty Bump   Ellington 1930; Mills 1930
Bums   Brown, Lew 1928; DeSylva 1928; Henderson 1928
Bums' Opera   Hammerstein 1955; Rodgers 1955
Bunch of Cows, A   Rome 1940
Bunch of Sweetness   Gilbert 1912; Motzan 1912
Bundle of Joy   Gordon 1956; Myrow 1956
Bundle of Love, A   DeSylva 1921
Bundle of Nerves   Smith, Harry B. 1917
Bundle of Old Love Letters, A   Brown, Nacio Herb 1930;
     Freed, Arthur 1930
Bundle of Sweetness, A   Sigman 1954
Bundling   Hammerstein 1941; Romberg 1941

(What Would You Rather Have Boys?) Bunds or
     Bonds!   Brown, Lew 1941; Henderson 1941
(Little) Bungalow in Quogue   Kern 1917
Bungalow in the Sky   Brown, Nacio Herb 1919
Bunker Hill   Razaf 1940
Bunker Hill to Yorktown   Livingston, Jerry 1960
Bunny Bee Song, The   Sherman 1984
Bunny, Bunny, Bunny (The Bunny Song)   Rome 1942
Bunny Hug, The   Jerome 1912; Von Tilzer 1912
Bunny Song   Harburg 1969
Buon Giorno, Colombo   Cahn 1972
Buon Giorno, Signore   Weill 1947
Buona Fortuna   Mercer 1958
Burbank Bounce   Fain 1954; Webster 1954
Burden, The   Brennan 1925
Burgandy and Wine   Donaldson 1930; Leslie 1930
Burglar's Serenade   Howard, Joseph E. 1907
Burlesque at the Deli   Strouse 1999
Burlesque (inst.)   Rome 1939
Burmese Babies   Razaf 1932
Burmese Ballet, A   Atteridge 1916; Motzan 1916, 1917;
     Romberg 1916
Burn a Candle at St. Mary's for Me   Egan 1937
Burn Up   Hart 1926; Rodgers 1926
Burnin' Up   De Lange 1944
Burning!   Hart 1934; Rodgers 1934
Burning Bush of Israel, The   Razaf 1952
Burning of the Henrietta (inst.)   Fain 1963
Burning Sands   Myrow 1942
Burning Up the Boulevard   Cohan 1907
Burro Flats   Webster 1949
Bury Me Beneath the Willow   Johnson, Howard 1939
Bury Me Under the Willow   Rainger 1936; Robin 1936
Bus Ride Sequence   Fields 1933; McHugh 1933
Bus Sequence   Kahn 1938
Bus To Tuscaloosa   David, Hal 1978
Bushel and a Peck, A   Loesser 1950
Business for a Good Girl Is Bad   Berlin 1949
Business Girl   Whiting 1930
Business in Missouri   Sigman 1951
Business Is Business, Rosey Cohen   Berlin 1911
Business Is Business with Me   Friend 1918, 1930; Monaco
     1930
Business of Our Own, A   DeSylva 1919; Kern 1919
Business or Pleasure   Duke 1963
Busker Alley   Sherman 1995
Buster   Young, Victor 1957
Bustin' Out of Doors   Carmichael 1957
Bustle   Caesar 1923; Conrad 1923
Busy As a Bee, I'm Buzz, Buzz, Buzzin'   Russell 1940;
     Sigman 1939
Busy Bees of DeVere's, The   Cohan 1922
Busy Body   Brown, Nacio Herb 1935; Freed, Arthur 1935;
     Johnson, James P. 1948
Busy, Busy, Busy   Cohan 1916
Busy Doing Nothing   Burke 1949; Van Heusen 1949
Busy Evening, A   Coots 1925
Busy Keepin' Happy   Henderson 1935; Koehler 1935
Busy Little Broadway   Cohan 1907
Busy Little Bumble Bee   Mercer 1964; Warren 1964
Busy Little Center, A   Cohan 1927
Busy Night   David, Hal 1957
Busy Night at Lorraine's, A   Strouse 1991
Busybody   DePaul 1950; Raye 1950
But   Ellington 1959

But After the Ball Was Over (Then He Made Up for Lost Time)   DeSylva 1918
But Alive   Adams 1970; Strouse 1970
But Are We Worried Yes!   Revel 1942
But Beautiful   Burke 1947; Van Heusen 1947
But Call Me   Freed, Ralph 1965
But Definitely   Gordon 1936; Revel 1936
But He Never Says He Loves Me   Porter 1931
But How Soon We Forget   Gilbert 1931
But I Ain't Got a Man   Berlin 1954
But I Do — You Know I Do   Donaldson 1925; Kahn 1925
But I Love Her (Just the Way She Is)   Spina 1976
But I Love You, My Darlin'   David, Hal 1951
But I Will Never Say   Willson 1969
But in the Morning, No   Porter 1939
But It Didn't Mean a Thing   David, Mack 1939; Livingston, Jerry 1939
But Me No Buts   David, Mack 1946; Hoffman 1937; Lerner, Sammy 1937
(I Have Loved Before) But Never Like This   Silver 1953
But Never My Love for You   Hoffman 1953; Silver 1953
But Not for Me   Gershwin, George 1930; Gershwin, Ira 1930
But Not for You   Smith, Harry B. 1917
But Not Today   Conrad 1926
But She's Just a Little Bit Crazy About Her Husband - That's All   Berlin 1920
But She's My Girl Now   Brown, Lew 1925; DeSylva 1925; Henderson 1925
But Still We Smile   Smith, Robert B. 1914
But That's the Way You Are   Lerner, Alan Jay 1969
But the Wind Blew Through His Whiskers Just the Same   Conrad 1925; Rose 1925
But They Better Not Wait Too Long!   Carmichael 1950; Mercer 1950
But Think of the Fun We Had   Ager 1933
But Tom-Tom Tommy   Washington 1932
But We Say No "Buts"   Hoffman 1937; Lerner, Sammy 1937
But Where Are You?   Berlin 1936
But Where Is Love   Young, Victor 1964
But Where Young Man   Merrill 1970
But Who   Heyman 1974
But You Do It   David, Hal 1974
But You Go On   Strouse 1989
But You're Wrong   Drake 1953
But Yours   Merrill 1959
Butch, the Rocking Horse Cowboy   Coots 1950
Butcher Song, The   Livingston, Jerry 1963
Butcher, the Baker, the Candlestick Maker, The   Meyer 1926
Butler and the Cook Desire   Johnson, James P. 1947
Butler and the Handy Man   Johnson, James P. 1947
Butler in the Abbey   Harburg 1967; Styne 1967
Butler's Fox-Trot, The   Atteridge 1919; Carroll 1919
Butler's Song   Kalmar 1930; Ruby 1930
Butter and Egg Baby   Warren 1925
Butterfingers   Berlin 1934
Butterflies   Howard, Joseph E. 1904; Merrill 1953; Porter 1925
Butterflies and the Bees, The   Hammerstein 1941
Butterfly   Atteridge 1913; Schwartz, Jean 1913; Strouse 2000; Webster 1934
Butterfly and the Clover, The   Smith, Harry B. 1904, 1908; Smith, Robert B. 1904
Butterfly Ballet (inst.)   Herbert 1920
Butterfly (De Jour La)   Parish 1962
Butterfly (inst.)   Blake 1972

Butterfly Lament   Goetz 1952
Butterfly Love   Leslie 1938
Butterfly Waltz   Herbert 1903; Smith, Harry B. 1903
Butternut, Neath the Beautiful Butternut Tree   Woods 1928
Butterscotch Man, The   Merrill 1954
Button, Button, Who's Got the Button   Drake 1950; Mills 1948
Button Up with Esmond   Robin 1948; Styne 1948
Button Up Your Heart   Fields 1930; McHugh 1930
Button Up Your Overcoat   Brown, Lew 1929; DeSylva 1929; Henderson 1929
Buttons and Bows   Livingston, Jay 1948
Buttons on Her Blouse   Atteridge 1913
Buttons on Her Shoes   Atteridge 1913; Schwartz, Jean 1913
Buxom Mrs. Bascom, The   Henderson 1935; Yellen 1935
Buy a Bale of Cotton for Me   Gilbert 1914
Buy a Bar of Barry's   Gordon 1936; Revel 1936
Buy a Bond   Adamson 1945; McHugh 1945
Buy a Bond for Baby   Razaf Date Unknown
Buy a Liberty Bond for the Baby   Von Tilzer 1917
Buy a Little Button from Us   Gershwin, George 1926
Buy a Piece of the Peace   Cahn 1945; Styne 1945
Buy a Red Cross Rosie   Bryan 1917
Buy a Victory Bond   Sherman 1974
Buy Bonds for Bob   Evans 1985; Livingston, Jay 1985
Buy Buy Baby   Smith, Harry B. 1911; Smith, Robert B. 1911
Buy Her a Box at the Opera   Porter 1916
Buy Her a Hat   Brooks 1952
Buy My Violets   Johnson, Howard 1934
Buy Why   Merrill 1957
Buy Your Bonds in Brooklyn   Baer 1945
Buyers, The   Howard, Joseph E. 1910
Buying Little Things for Me   Atteridge 1914; Carroll 1914; Romberg 1914
Buzz, Buzz, Buzz   Cahn 1951
Buzz on Little Busy Bee   Atteridge 1912
Buzzard Song, The   Gershwin, George 1935
Buzz-Buzz-Buzz Lookin' for My Honey   Lawrence 1940
Buzzin' Round with the Bees   Fisher 1937
By a Lazy Country Lane   Stept 1931
By a Silvery Stream   Loesser 1935
By a Waterfall   Fain 1933; Kahal 1933
By a Wishing Well   Gordon 1938; Revel 1938
By All That's Beautiful   Brown, Nacio Herb 1935; Freed, Arthur 1935
By All That's Beautiful (Sole Lucente)   Hoffman 1958
By An Old Sun Dial   Norworth 1938
By Candlelight   Freed, Arthur 1945; Lawrence 1954; Porter 1938; Warren 1945
By Dawn's Early Light   Coleman 1988
By Golly, By Jingo   Hoffman 1960
By Heck   Gilbert 1915
By Jingo Janette   Dixon 1928; Woods 1928
By Killarney's Lakes and Falls   Johnson, Howard 1939
By Lo Baby   Styne 1941
By Love Possessed   Cahn 1961; Sigman 1957
By Madame Firelle   Blane 1954; Myrow 1954
By My Fireside   Johnson, Howard 1925
By My Mien (Greta's Waltz)   Herbert 1899; Smith, Harry B. 1899
By Myself   Dietz 1937; Schwartz, Arthur 1937
By Our Bearing So Sedate   Romberg 1924
By Pigeon Post   Buck 1919
By Quiet Firesides (inst.)   Robison 1929
By Strauss   Gershwin, George 1936; Gershwin, Ira 1936

By the Bay of Napoli   Warren 1959
By the Beautiful Sea   Atteridge 1914; Carroll 1914
By the Blue Alsatian Mountains   Johnson, Howard 1939
By the Blue Lagoon   Kern 1909
By the By   Loesser 1940
By the Country Side   Kern 1913
By the Dawn's Early Light   Heyman 1932; Hoffman 1932;
   Von Tilzer 1929
By the Great Horn Spoon (You Can Bet You're in Love)   De
   Lange 1934; Mills 1934
By the Honeysuckle Vine   DeSylva 1918
By the Kissing Rock   Cahn 1950; Styne 1950
By the Light of the Campfire Glow   Brown, Nacio Herb
   1951; Gilbert 1951
By the Light of the Silvery Moon   Edwards 1908
By the Light of Your Eyes I Read Your Heart   Drake 1943
By the Lotus Pool (inst.)   Robison 1928
By the Mississinewah   Porter 1943
By the O-Hi-O O-My-O   Yellen 1920
By the People   Hammerstein 1940; Schwartz, Arthur 1940
By the Pond Again   Bergman 1976
By the Rio Grande   Brown, A. Seymour 1913
By the Rippling Waters   Willson 1956
By the River Sainte Marie   Leslie 1931; Warren 1931
By the Riverside   Bryan 1922; Clare 1922; Friend 1922
By the Road to Dublin Town   Yellen 1915
By the Sad Luana Shore   Berlin 1916; Goetz 1916
By the Sapphire Sea   Smith, Harry B. 1922; Snyder 1922
By the Sea   Sondheim 1979
By the Shalimar   Koehler 1922
By the Side of a Mill   Herbert 1906
By the Sign of the Moon   Rose 1926; Whiting 1926
By the Sign of the Rose   Lerner, Sammy 1925; Rose 1925;
   Whiting 1925
By the Silvery Nile   Yellen 1921
By the Sweat of Your Brow   Blake 1937
By the Taj Mahal   Brown, Nacio Herb 1934; Freed, Arthur
   1934
By the Way   Gordon 1948; Lewis 1929; Myrow 1948; Pollack
   1929; Young, Joe 1929
By the Zuyder Zee   Bryan 1914
By This Sweet Token   Herbert 1900; Smith, Harry B. 1900
By this Token   Romberg 1925; Smith, Harry B. 1925
By Threes   Coleman 1977
By Welawela   Brennan 1930; Friml 1930
By Yonder Moon   Dubin 1935; Warren 1935
By Your Side   Hoffman 1950
Bye   DePaul 1952; Raye 1952
Bye and Bye   Brown, A. Seymour 1909; Hart 1925; Rodgers
   1925; Von Tilzer 1918
Bye and Bye Sweetheart   Yellen 1928
Bye and Bye You Will Miss Me   Buck 1913
Bye Bye, Alibi Baby   Drake 1947
Bye Bye Baby   Motzan 1924; Robin 1948; Styne 1948
Bye, Bye, Benito   Brown, Lew 1942
Bye Bye Birdie   Adams 1962; Strouse 1962
Bye Bye Blackbird   Dixon 1926; Henderson 1926
Bye Bye Bonnie   Warren 1942
Bye Bye Boogie   Brooks 1958
Bye Bye Butterfly   Coots 1945
Bye, Bye Dear Old Broadway   Cobb 1907; Edwards 1907
Bye Bye Dearie   Sterling 1907; Von Tilzer 1907
Bye Bye for Baby   Caesar 1928
Bye Bye My Baby   Parish 1949
Bye Bye Sal   Gilbert 1912

Bye Bye Shanghai   Johnston 1926; Turk 1926
Bye-Bye   Evans 1959; Livingston, Jay 1959; Mancini 1959
Bye-Bye, Be Seein' You-All   Drake 1952
Bye-Bye Butterfly Lover   Dietz 1937; Schwartz, Arthur 1937
Bye-Bye Land   Lewis 1912; Young, Joe 1912
Bye-Bye My Little Wife   Friml 1919; Harbach 1919
Bye-Bye Sorrow   Razaf Date Unknown
Bye-Yum Pum Pum   Sherman 1967
Bygone Days   Kern 1912
Bygone Days in Dixie   Johnson, J. Rosamond 1909
Bylo Bay, The   Atteridge 1921; Romberg 1921
Byrd, The Bird of the Air   Johnson, Howard 1927
Byrd (You're the Bird of Them All)   Johnson, Howard 1935
Bzzzzzz (The Whisper Song)   Drake 1952

C

Ca C'est L'Amour   Porter 1957
Caballero   Caesar 1930; Harbach 1930; Romberg 1930
Caballeros Number   Kalmar 1930; Ruby 1930
Cabaret Girl   Hammerstein 1920; Harbach 1920
Cabaret 'Neath the Old Egyptian Moon, A   Hanley 1915
Cabaret Song   Warren Date Unknown
Cabareting in Pumpkinville   Howard, Joseph E. 1915
Cabarets   Hart 1926; Rodgers 1926
Cabbage Patch Dreams   Sherman 1984
Cabbage Patch Parade   Sherman 1984
Cabby's Serenade, The   Dubin 1940; McHugh 1940
Caberavings   Whiting 1914
Cabin Dance   Henderson 1934
Cabin Door   Razaf 1930
Cabin in the Cotton   Arlen 1932; Caesar 1932; Parish 1932
Cabin in the Cotton & Cotton in the Cabin   Caesar 1934
Cabin in the Sky   Duke 1940; Leslie 1936
Cabin on the Hilltop   Kalmar 1936; Ruby 1936
Cabin Raising Song   Sherman 1965
Cabinet Music   Porter 1935
Cabinet Number   Coslow 1935
Cablegram   Porter 1911
Cachucha   Brennan 1936
Cackling Chickens   Friml 1959
Caddie's Ensemble   Alter 1930; Johnson, Howard 1930
Cadence Count   Lawrence 1943
Cadenza   Willson 1953
Cadets   Smith, Harry B. 1901
Cadets of Gascony   Herbert 1899; Smith, Harry B. 1899
Cadets of St. Cyr, The   Smith, Harry B. 1900
Caesar Comes   Leigh 1973
Cafe   Ellington 1971
Cafe Badna Waltz   Revel 1960
Cafe Chantant   Smith, Harry B. 1904; Smith, Robert B. 1904
Cafe de Janeiro   Drake 1947
Cafe Girl (I Met Her at the Metropole)   Edwards 1908
Cafe 'Round the Corner, A   Atteridge 1910
Cafe Scene   Harbach 1931; Kern 1931
Cafe Society Still Carries On   Porter 1944
Cafe Terrace (inst.)   Brown, Nacio Herb 1933
Cafeteria Chow   Conrad 1906
Cahoots   David, Mack 1973; Livingston, Jerry 1973
Ca—ing   Silver 1927
Cairo   Freed, Arthur 1922; Harburg 1942; Howard, Joseph E.
   1909; Schwartz, Arthur 1942
Cairo, Illinois   Sherman 1974
Cajun Dance, The   Blake 1958
Cake Song   Arlen 1959; Mercer 1959

Cake Walk Ball   Brown, A. Seymour 1909
Cake Walk Promenade   Howard, Joseph E. 1915
Cakewalk   Rome 1973
Cakewalk Turns   Arlen 1959; Mercer 1959
Cakewalk Your Lady   Arlen 1946; Mercer 1946
Calabash Pipe   Arlen 1936; Brown, Lew 1936
Calcutta   Evans 1958; Livingston, Jay 1958
Calendar Girl   Adamson 1946; McHugh 1946
Calendar of Love, The   Edwards 1908
Calendar Song, The   Drake 1955
Calico Days   Arlen 1933; Blake 1923; Koehler 1933; Sissle 1923
Calico Square Dance   Willson 1953
Califo'nia   Razaf 1949
Californee Gold   Sherman 1967
California   Atteridge 1914; Bryan 1923; Cahn 1958; Conrad 1922; Eliscu 1939; Friend 1922; Heyman 1953
California 500, The   Livingston, Jerry 1971
California   Romberg 1914; Van Heusen 1958; Whiting 1915; Willson 1974; Young, Victor 1953
California and You   Leslie 1914
California Christmas   Lawrence 1971
California, Clarmont   Howard, Joseph E. 1908
California Here I Come   DeSylva 1921
California, Here We Go   Carroll 1925; Freed, Arthur 1925
California Highway Patrol March, The   Cahn 1964; Van Heusen 1964
California Is Wonderful (If You're a Grapefruit)   David, Mack 1947; Hoffman 1947; Livingston, Jerry 1947
California Moon   Lerner, Sammy 1951
California My Homeland   Brennan 1926
California (Opening Title)   Harburg 1946
California or Bust   Harburg 1946
California Rag, The   Livingston, Jerry 1974
California Rose   Evans 1952; Livingston, Jay 1952
California Scene Dance   Porter 1946
California Skies   Kalmar 1926, 1930; Ruby 1926, 1930
California Story, The   Willson 1956
California Sunbeam   Stept 1945
California Sunshine   Bryan 1925
California Twilight   Turk 1926
Californ-i-ay   Harburg 1945; Kern 1945
Caliph, The   Howard, Joseph E. 1905
Call, The   Loesser 1960
Call a Jeannie   Coleman 1964
Call Again   Berlin 1912
Call Around Again   Herbert 1914; Smith, Robert B. 1914
Call from the Grave   Weill 1954
Call It a Day   Alter 1930; Herbert 1919; Johnson, Howard 1930; Smith, Robert B. 1919
Call It a Dream   Hammerstein 1941; Romberg 1941
Call It Anything but Love   Lawrence 1941
Call It Anything, It Wasn't Love   Fisher 1934
Call It Love   Bullock 1950
Call It Un-American!   Rome 1937
Call Me   Bacharach 1959
Call Me a Fool   Warren 1960, 1980
Call Me a Loser   Brooks 1964
Call Me a Taxi   DePaul Date Unknown; Russell Date Unknown; Sigman 1941
Call Me Andre   Hart 1920; Rodgers 1920
Call Me Baby   Williams 1913; Young, Joe 1913
Call Me Flo   Kern 1912
Call Me in the Morning   Brown, A. Seymour 1912
Call Me Irresponsible   Cahn 1956; Van Heusen 1956

Call Me Mister   Rome 1946
Call Me Oop-a-Sometime   Merrill 1953
Call Me Savage   Comden and Green 1964; Styne 1964
Call Me Thine Own   Johnson, Howard 1939
Call Me to Arms   Alter 1929; Johnson, Howard 1929
Call Me Tonight   Robin 1952; Warren 1952
Call Me Uncle   Friml 1912; Harbach 1912
Call Me Up Some Rainy Afternoon   Berlin 1910
Call Me Up When You're Lonesome   Warren 1925
Call Me Whate'er You Will   Gershwin, George 1931; Gershwin, Ira 1931
Call of a Nation, The   Ahlert 1916
Call of Home, The   Hammerstein 1928; Romberg 1928
Call of Love   Kahn 1934; Parish 1929; Smith, Harry B. 1926; Styne 1941
Call of the Brands   Styne 1958
Call of the Clans   Styne 1958
Call of the Colors, The   Atteridge 1914; Romberg 1914
Call of the Delta   Mills 1935
Call of the Far-Away Hills (Alone on a Lonesome Trail), The   David, Mack 1953; Young, Victor 1953
Call of the Great White Way, The   Coslow 1925
Call of the Road, The   Young, Joe 1934
Call of the Sea, The   Harbach 1925; Youmans 1925
Call of the Siren   Akst 1936; Clare 1936
Call of the South, The   Berlin 1924, 1930
Call of the Wild   Leigh 1956; Washington 1953
Call of the Wild Women   DeSylva 1920
Call Off the Wedding (Without a Groom there Can't Be a Bride)   Bacharach 1962; David, Hal 1962
Call on Rag Doll   Goetz 1917
Call on the Marines   Stept 1937; Washington 1937
Call on Us Again   Gershwin, Ira 1949; Warren 1949
Call on Your Neighbor   Fields 1951; Schwartz, Arthur 1951
Call Out the Marines   Revel 1942
Call the Doc   Hart 1920; Rodgers 1920
Call the Plumber In   Razaf 1924; Waller 1924
Call the Tribe   Robison 1958
Call to Arms, The   Brown, Nacio Herb 1930; Freed, Arthur 1930; Heyman 1934, 1936; Schwartz, Arthur 1936
Call to Colors   Kahn 1937
Call to the Colors, The   Carroll 1914
Call to Wander, The   Loesser 1960
Call Your Police   Strouse 1987
Calling All Cars   Monaco 1934; Raye 1945
Calling All Lovers   Kahn 1939
Calling All Stars   Akst 1934; Brown, Lew 1934
Calling Me Home   Gilbert 1926; Monaco 1926
Calling Me Over the Hill   Hanley 1931
Calling of the Sea, The   Olcott 1913
Calling Romance   Blake 1950
Calliope Jane   Carmichael 1940
Calvary   Johnson, Howard 1939
Calypso   Koehler 1936; Magidson 1941; Oakland 1941
Calypso Fever   Bergman 1983
Calypso Kitty   Harburg 1941; Sigman 1941
Calypso Rock   Strouse 1957
Calypso Song   Arlen 1950; Mercer 1950
Camaraderie   Mercer 1974
Cambridge Valley   Martin 1952
Came from Germany   Atteridge 1913
Camel Dreams   Motzan 1922
Camel with the Wrinkled Knees, The   Coots 1951
Camellia (inst.)   Warren 1977
Camelot   Lerner, Alan Jay 1960; Loewe 1960

Camera Doesn't Lie, Neither Do I, The   Leslie 1937
Camera Shoot   Hart 1926, 1928; Rodgers 1926, 1928
Camille   Mitchell 1926
Camille, Colette, Fifi   Young, Victor 1955
Camouflage   Gilbert 1917
Camouflaging   Goetz 1917
Camp, Camp, Campin' on Your Doorstep   Coots 1933;
    Johnson, Howard 1933
Camp Fire Days   Hart 1916; Rodgers 1916
Camp Karefree   Rome 1952
Camp Meetin'   Coots 1949
Camp Meetin' Friends   Robison 1959
Camp Meetin' Stomp (inst.)   Waller 1925
Camp Meeting Band   Gilbert 1914
Camp Meeting Time   Williams 1906
Camp Wigwam Hiking Song   Hart Date Unknown
Campbell Soup Kids, The   Edwards 1908
Camping on the Campus   Johnson, Howard 1927
Campmeetin' Time   Williams 1907
Camp's Daily Dozen   Atteridge 1922
Camptown Races   Mercer 1945
Campus Moon   Coots 1935
Campus Queen   Livingston, Jerry 1963
Can Can   Burke 1946; Dietz 1943; Duke 1943; Van Heusen
    1946
Can He Love Me Like Kelly Can?   Lewis 1922; Young, Joe
    1922
Can I Come in for a Second   Cahn 1950
Can I Forget (That I Love You)   Caesar 1927
Can I Forget You?   Hammerstein 1937; Kern 1937
Can I Help It?   De Lange 1939; Gershwin, Ira 1943; Van
    Heusen 1939
Can I Help It (If I'm Helpless in Your Arms)   Parish 1950
Can I Help It (If I'm in Love with You)   Friend 1930;
    Monaco 1930
Can I Leave Off Wearin' My Shoes?   Arlen 1954
Can I Rely on You   Davis 1965
Can It   Hammerstein 1919; Rodgers 1919
Can It Be?   Brennan 1915
Can It Be Love   Howard, Joseph E. 1909
Can It Be Me   Dixon 1932
Can It Be Possible   Conrad 1930; Lawrence 1964; Meyer
    1930; Mitchell 1930
Can It Be that I'm in Love   DeSylva 1922
Can It Be True   Alter 1930; Johnson, Howard 1930; Razaf
    1930
Can Love Come Back Again   Brooks 1952
Can Macy Do Without Me   Romberg 1921
Can Song   Johnson, J. Rosamond 1909
Can that Boy Fox Trot!   Sondheim 1971
Can This Be the End of the Rainbow   Cahn 1938
Can You Better Your Condition   Caesar 1952
Can You Blame Me   Sigman 1957
Can You Blame Me for Lovin' Dat Man   Sterling 1901; Von
    Tilzer 1901
Can You Explain?   Arlen 1954
Can You Forget   Johnson, J. Rosamond 1911
Can You Guess   Drake 1946
Can You Imagine   Cahn 1976; Lane 1976; Loesser 1937
Can You Read in My Eyes   Coslow 1929
Can You Say that You've Done Your Share   Silver 1918
Can You Sing?   Hammerstein 1941; Romberg 1941
Can You Spell Schenectady?   Arlen 1953; Fields 1953
Can You Tame Wild Wimmen   Sterling 1918; Von Tilzer
    1918

Can You Tell the Moment   Bergman 1990
Can You Use Any Money Today?   Berlin 1950
Canada Dry and I   Willson 1947
Canada Dry Water   Willson 1954
Canada, You're Tops!   Johnson, Howard 1958
Canadian Way, The   Schwartz, Arthur 1982
Can-Can   Porter 1953; Warren Date Unknown
Can-Canada, The   Davis 1929
Can-Canola, The   Coots 1929
Cancel that Wedding March   Kalmar 1911; Snyder 1911
Cancelling   Livingston, Jerry 1970
Cancion de Carnaval (Carnival Song)   Gilbert 1933
Cancion de Cuba (Starland)   Freed, Ralph 1939
Cancion de las Buenaventura (Fortune Telling Song)   Gilbert
    1933
Candidates, The   Brooks 1959
Candied Sweets   Waller 1928
Candle in the Wind, A   Adamson 1959; McHugh 1959
Candle in the Wind (inst.)   Alter 1948
Candle in the Window, A   Parish 1934
Candle Is Burning Low, The   Robison 1946
Candle Light   Kahn 1925
Candle Light (inst.)   Revel 1959
Candlelight   Heyman 1929; Revel 1944
Candlelight and Roses   Robison 1946
Candlelight and Wine   Adamson 1945; McHugh 1943, 1945
Candlelight Concerto (Until Eternity)   Spina 1977
Candles in the Sky   Kahn 1932
Candles in the Wind   David, Hal 1941; Webster 1968
Candy   David, Mack 1966
Candy and Cake   Merrill 1950
Candy College Boys   Atteridge Date Unknown
Candy Jag   Smith, Robert B. 1919
Candy Kisses (inst.)   Von Tilzer 1911
Candy Opening   Hart Date Unknown; Rodgers Date
    Unknown
Candy Sweets (inst.)   Johnson, James P. 1944
Cane Bottom Chair   Robison 1950
Cane Dance   Buck 1923; Caesar 1930; Gordon 1932; Revel
    1932
Cane Dance (inst.)   Kern 1923
Cane Song   Buck 1917
Cannibal Barbecue, The   Herbert 1908; Smith, Harry B. 1908
Cannibal Islands, The   Herbert 1908; Smith, Harry B. 1908
Cannibal Love   Fisher 1924
Canodlin'   Livingston, Jerry 1963
Can't Be Bothered Now   Arlen 1929
Can't Do Without You   Hoffman 1955
Can't Find a Furnished Room   Carroll 1945
Can't Find My Way (C :Myers, Richard)   Heyman 1934
Can't Get Along   Harburg 1930
Can't Get Indiana Off My Mind   Carmichael 1940
Can't Get Lovin' Blues   Turk 1921
Can't Get Out of This Mood   Loesser 1942; McHugh 1942,
    1945
Can't Get Rid of Me   Gordon 1932; Revel 1932
Can't Get Stuff in Your Cuff   Cahn 1943
Can't Get to Tucson too Soon   Robison 1953
Can't Get Used to These Clothes   Martin 1959
Can't Get You Out of My Mind   Howard, Joseph E. 1948
Can't Help Lovin' Dat Man   Hammerstein 1927; Kern 1927
Can't Help Singing   Harburg 1945; Kern 1945
Can't Make It with the Same Man Twice   Fain 1968
Can't Sleep for Dreaming   Spina 1954
Can't Stop   Silver 1955

Can't Stop Talking   Loesser 1948
Can't Take It Papa   Johnson, James P. 1932; Razaf 1932
Can't Teach My Heart New Tricks   Mercer 1938
Can't Teach My Old Heart New Tricks   Whiting 1938
Can't They Leave Us Alone for a While   Lewis 1915; Meyer 1915
Can't We Be Enemies   DePaul 1957
Can't We Be Sweethearts   Coslow 1923
Can't We Dream a Midsummer Night's Dream (Though There's Frost on the Moon)   Ahlert 1935; Young, Joe 1935
Can't We Ever Be Alone   Hoffman 1932
Can't We Fall in Love   Adamson 1936; Donaldson 1935
Can't We Get Together   Akst 1932; Razaf 1929; Waller 1929; Yellen 1932
Can't We Have a Rally?   Lerner, Alan Jay 1948; Weill 1948
Can't We Talk It Over   Washington 1931, 1949; Young, Victor 1931, 1949
Can't You Be Good   Meyer 1909
Can't You Be Mine   Turk 1921
Can't You Believe It   Bacharach 1962
Can't You Do a Friend a Favor?   Hart 1943; Rodgers 1943
Can't You Hear that Mountain Music   Coslow 1937
Can't You Hear Your Country Calling   Buck 1917; Herbert 1917
Can't You Just See Yourself   Cahn 1947; Styne 1947
Can't You Read Between the Lines   Cahn 1944; Dubin 1931; Meyer 1931; Styne 1944
Can't You See   Ahlert 1931; Bryan 1909; Turk 1931
Can't You See I Love You?   Brown, A. Seymour 1909
Can't You See I Mean You   Kern 1915
Can't You See I'm Lonely   Kahn 1930
Can't You See It?   Adams 1964; Strouse 1964
Can't You See the Rainbow in the Sky   Leslie 1910
Can't You See the Signs (That I No Longer Care)   Robison 1963
Can't You See What Troubles Me?   Arlen 1929
Can't You Tell I'm in Love with You   Mills 1929
Can't You Understand   Young, Victor 1929
Cantabile (A Song Without Words) (inst.)   Kern 1938
Cantata   Leigh 1955; Spina 1955
Cantineer of the Regiment   Smith, Harry B. 1900
Canvas, Sawdust and Dreams   Sherman 1987
Canzetta   Motzan 1927
Canzone D'Amore   Sherman 1962
Canzonetta   David, Mack 1942; Hammerstein 1937; Herbert 1913; Kern 1937
Canzonetta (I'll Share them All with You)   Harbach 1931; Kern 1931
Cap Is on the Go (The Civil Air Patrol March), The   Myrow 1959
Cap with the Strap in the Back, The   Silver 1956
Capering Coopers   Freed, Arthur 1925
Capitalize That Thing Called It   Duke 1930; Harburg 1930
Capriccio Espanol   Brooks 1947
Caprice Rag (inst.)   Johnson, James P. 1917
Capricious Harlem (inst.)   Blake 1963
Capricious (inst.)   Blake 1973
Captain   Howard, Joseph E. 1918
Captain and the Nancy Lee, The   Meyer 1950
Captain Andy's Entrance and Ballyhoo   Hammerstein 1927; Kern 1927
Captain Brown   Raye 1941
Captain Buffalo   David, Mack 1960; Livingston, Jerry 1960
Captain Custard   Burke 1940

Captain Flo   Jerome 1909; Schwartz, Jean 1909
Captain Henry St. James   Evans 1958; Livingston, Jay 1958
Captain Hook's Waltz   Comden and Green 1954; Styne 1954
Captain Kidd   Goetz 1913; Strouse 1950
Captain Kiddo   Cobb 1917; Edwards 1917
Captain Kidd's Kids   Hammerstein 1922
Captain, Mate and Crew   Blake 1937
Captain of a Ten-Day Boat   Cohan 1904
Captain of the Mineola Guards, The   Edwards 1908
Captain Valentine's Tango   Weill 1936
Captain's Daughter, The   Bryan 1934
Captains of the Clouds   Arlen 1942; Mercer 1942
Captive, The   Herbert 1915
Capturing the Boys and Wendy   Leigh 1954
Cara Mia   Freed, Ralph 1962
Caramba   Smith, Harry B. 1920
Caravan   Ellington 1937; Mills 1937
Caravan of Dreams   Ahlert 1947; Leslie 1947
Caravanna   Fisher 1922
Caravelas   Young, Victor 1953
Cardinal, The   Leigh 1963
Cardinal's Guard Are We, The   Robin 1954; Romberg 1954
Care a Little Bit More for Me   Coots 1957
Care Enough   Oakland 1972
(Love Is a) Career   Cahn 1959; Van Heusen 1959
Care-Free   Berlin 1938; Heyman 1934
Carefree and Happy   Alter 1930; Johnson, Howard 1930
Carefree Camp   Stept 1938
Carefree Careterro   Hart 1941; Rodgers 1941
Carefree Miner, The   Hammerstein 1931; Whiting 1931
Carefree Years, The   Silver 1958
Careful Kate   Caesar 1943
Careful with My Heart   Harburg 1934, 1935
Careless Hands   Sigman 1948
Careless Joe   Caesar 1943
Careless Kisses   Brown, Lew 1932; Clare 1932; Stept 1932
Careless Lips (Tango Roulette)   Raye 1955
Careless Rhapsody   Hart 1942; Rodgers 1942
Careless-Like   Ager 1934
Caress Me   David, Mack 1947; Hoffman 1947; Livingston, Jerry 1947
Caresses   Monaco 1920
Cargo Watch   Oakland 1955; Webster 1955
Caribbean Love Song   Freed, Ralph 1941
Caribbean Sea   Kahn 1926; Young, Victor 1930
Caribees, The   Mercer 1948
Carino Mio   Lerner, Alan Jay 1951; Loewe 1951
Carioca   Eliscu 1933; Kahn 1933; Youmans 1933
Carioca Capers (inst.)   Warren 1959, 1964
Carissima   Spina 1964
Carless Carrie   Caesar 1943
Carlo, The   Brown, Nacio Herb 1934; Freed, Arthur 1934
Carlo's Song   Coslow 1935
Carlotta   Cahn 1950; Porter 1944; Whiting 1927
Carlotta and the Bandit (inst.)   Spina 1974
Carlotta, Ya Gotta Be Mine   Robin 1953
Carlotti's Jimmie   Hammerstein 1920; Harbach 1920
Carlsbad Legend, The   Smith, Harry B. 1910; Smith, Robert B. 1910
Carmela   Buck 1927
Carmelina   Lane 1979; Lerner, Alan Jay 1979
Carmen   Rose 1928
Carmen, Carmela   Bergman 1958
Carmen Girl, The   Atteridge 1911

Carmen Has Nothing on Me   Buck 1917, 1927
Carmen Jones Is Goin' to Jail   Hammerstein 1943
Carmen Was (The Saga of Carmen)   Henderson 1943;
   Yellen 1943
Carmencita   Atteridge 1923; Schwartz, Jean 1923; Smith,
   Harry B. 1910
Carmenita McCoy   Lerner, Sammy 1940
Carnation Time   Washington 1951; Young, Victor 1951
Carnegie Hall Pavanne   Comden and Green 1944
Carnival   Caesar 1925; Russell 1943; Smith, Harry B. 1909;
   Warren 1943; Youmans 1925
Carnival (Al Fresco), The   Herbert 1904
Carnival at Nice   Smith, Robert B. 1914
Carnival Ballet   Friml 1934; Merrill 1961
Carnival Ballet (inst.)   Van Heusen 1953
Carnival in Caroline   Ellington 1938; Mills 1938
Carnival (inst.)   Revel 1932
Carnival Maid (inst.)   Snyder 1909
Carnival Night   Romberg 1921
Carnival of Springtime   Romberg 1924
Carnival Samba   Sherman 1961
Carnival Song, The   Comden and Green 1958; Styne 1958
Carnival Song (Czardas)   Gilbert 1934
Carnival Song (Czardas) (What a Gay Occasion)   Akst 1938;
   Clare 1938
Carnival Time   Atteridge 1919; Gershwin, George 1924;
   Gershwin, Ira 1924; Romberg 1919; Schwartz, Jean 1919
Carolina   Brown, Lew 1934; Egan 1919; Gorney 1934; Kahn
   1926; Whiting 1919
Carolina Balmoral (inst.)   Johnson, James P. Date Unknown
Carolina Cabin Days   Johnson, Howard 1934
Carolina in the Morning   Donaldson 1922; Kahn 1922
Carolina Jane   Johnson, J. Rosamond 1913
Carolina Lou   Atteridge 1913; Schwartz, Jean 1913
Carolina Mine Your Rolling Stone Is Rolling Home   Friend
   1926
Carolina Moon   Davis 1928, 1940
Carolina Pines   Parish 1932
Carolina Rolling Stone   Parish 1921
Carolina Sandman   Fain 1937
Carolina Shout, The   Johnson, James P. 1922, 1925
Carolina Shout (inst.)   Johnson, James P. 1918
Carolina Stomp   Bloom 1925
Caroline   McHugh 1916; Porter 1956; Smith, Harry B. 1918
Caroline My Caroline   Coots 1931
Caroll-ina, The   Carroll 1926
Carousel, The   Cahn 1968
Carousel in the Park   Fields 1945; Romberg 1945
Carousel of Love   Adamson 1966; Parish 1949
Carr Saltines   Baer 1944
Carriage Duet   Rainger 1936; Robin 1936
Carriage for Alida, A   Eliscu 1962
Carriages at Midnight   Styne 1978
Carribean Dream   Russell 1958
Carried Away   Comden and Green 1944
Carrier Pigeon, The   Smith, Harry B. 1906
Carry Me Back to Laramie   Cahn 1956; Van Heusen 1956
Carry Me Back to My Carolina Home   Davis 1922; Silver
   1922
Carry Me Back to Old Virginny   Johnson, Howard 1939
Carry On   Adamson 1963; Fain 1963; Porter 1936
Carry On, Keep Smiling   Adamson 1930; Youmans 1930
Cartoon Town   Ager 1922; Yellen 1922
Casa Loma Meeting, The   Cahn 1936
Casablanca   Bullock 1952

Casamagordo, New Mexico   Cahn 1970; Styne 1970
Casanasia   Mitchell 1927
Casanova   Duke 1936; Fisher 1936; Porter 1933; Rainger
   1936; Robin 1936
Casanova Cricket   Carmichael 1947
Casanova, Romeo and Don Juan   Gershwin, George 1929;
   Gershwin, Ira 1929
Casbah Blues   Raye 1940
Case of Rape, A   Mercer 1964
Casetta in Canada (El Rancho de Maria)   Sigman 1958
Casey Is a Wonderful Name   Jerome 1923; Schwartz, Jean
   1923
Casey Jones   Styne 1941
Casey Junior   Washington 1941
Cash for Your Trash   Waller 1942
Cash Register Heart   Silver 1953
Casino de Paree   Dubin 1935; Warren 1935
Casino Music Hall, The   Kern 1916
Casino Royale   Bacharach 1967; David, Hal 1967
Casino Song, The   Smith, Harry B. 1900
Casper the Friendly Ghost   David, Mack 1950; Livingston,
   Jerry 1950
Cassandra (inst.)   Warren 1977
Cassidy, Private Michael Cassidy   Norworth 1915
Castaway   Sherman 1962
Castillian Dreams   Johnston 1926; Turk 1926
Castle of Love   Blake 1963; Sissle 1963
Castle Rock   Drake 1951
Castle Walk (inst.), The   Styne 1947
Castles in the Air   Atteridge 1915; Carroll 1915; Romberg
   1915
Castles in the Clouds   Livingston, Jerry 1935
Cat, The   Kahn 1927
Cat and Canary   Evans 1945; Livingston, Jay 1945
Cat and Mouse   Mancini 1995
Cat Can Look at a Queen, A   Hart 1931; Rodgers 1931
Cat Don't Like, A   Sherman 1970
Cat from Carolina   Monaco 1963
Cat 'n' Mouse   Razaf 1955
C-A-T Spells Cat   Mercer 1955
Cat with Nine Tails   Coots 1953
Catalina   Evans 1946; Livingston, Jay 1946
Catalina Moon   Adamson 1961
Catalina Rose   Mills 1929
Catalog Day   Burke 1959; Van Heusen 1959
Catamarang   Kern 1910
Catana (Cah-Tah-Na)   De Lange 1947
Catch a Star!   Fain 1955; Webster 1955
Catch As Catch Can (inst.)   Bacharach 1965
Catch 'Em Young, Treat 'Em Rough, Tell 'Em
   Nothing   Herbert 1920; Smith, Robert B. 1920
Catch Hatch   Weill 1943
Catch Me If You Can   Livingston, Jerry 1960; Weill 1947
Catch On   Baer 1929; Gilbert 1929
Catch Our Act at the Met (Vaudeville Ain't Dead)   Comden
   and Green 1951; Styne 1951
Catch'm   Gordon 1931; Revel 1931
Caterpillar (Winged Dreams), The   Young, Victor 1924
Catfish Song, The   Weill 1950
Cathedral   Parish 1965
Cathedral 'Neath the Sky   Friend 1943
Catherine the Great   Brown, Lew 1939; Stept 1939
Cathy   Cahn 1963; Van Heusen 1963
Catland   Smith, Harry B. 1905

Cats Are Goin' to the Dogs, The   Adamson 1947; McHugh 1947

Cats at the Va-dee-gan   Johnson, James P. 1968

Cat's Away, The   Leigh 1973

Cat's Eye in the Night (inst.)   Alter 1958

Cat's Got Your Number, The   Strouse 1975

Caucus Race, The   Fain 1951

Caught   Johnson, James P. 1948

Caught in the Rain   De Lange 1951; Schwartz, Arthur 1929

'Cause I Love Ya, That's A-Why   Merrill 1952

'Cause I'm in Love   Donaldson 1928; Mills 1929

'Cause My Baby Says It's So   Dubin 1937; Warren 1937

Cause of the Situation, The   Cohan 1928

'Cause We Got Cake   Hart 1939; Rodgers 1939

'Cause You Won't Do Right by Me   Harburg 1932

'Cause You Won't Play House   Harburg 1934

Cavachok   Heyman 1934

Cavalier Rustican' Rag   Williams 1910

Cavaliers   Friml 1934

Cavalier's Song   Smith, Harry B. 1904

Cave Man, The   Atteridge 1911

Caveman, The   Friml 1918; Leslie 1928

Cazzaza   Romberg 1922

Ce Soir, Cherie   David, Mack 1947

Cecil in London Town, The   Cohan 1904

Cedar Point Parade   Mercer 1973

Cedro (My Italian Romeo)   Sterling 1913; Von Tilzer 1913

Celebratin'   Woods 1935

Celebratin' Day in Tennessee   Brown, Lew 1914

Celebration #1   David, Mack 1962

Celebration   Dietz 1932; Ellington 1973; Schwartz, Arthur 1932

Celebration of St. Joan the Good   Romberg 1925

Celebration Song, The   David, Mack 1958; Livingston, Jerry 1958

Celebrity   Oakland 1953; Raye 1953

Celery Stalks at Midnight   Sigman 1941

Celesete Aida   Johnson, Howard 1939

Celestia, Beautiful Goddess of Love   Young, Joe 1915

Celestial Nocturne   Revel 1946

Celia   Robin 1929; Whiting 1929

Celia's First Essay   Mercer 1964

Celina Couldn't Say 'No'   Dietz 1937; Schwartz, Arthur 1937

Celle Qui Refusait   Dubin Date Unknown; Warren Date Unknown

Cellini's Dream   Coots 1925

Cello Fellow, The   Howard, Joseph E. 1912

'Cello Man   Whiting 1913

Cellophane   Razaf Date Unknown

Celluloid Soliloquy   Oakland 1960

Censored Letter   Hoffman 1943; Livingston, Jerry 1943

Censored Mail   Hoffman 1943; Livingston, Jerry 1943

Censorship   Duke 1968

Centennial   Kern 1946; Robin 1946; Willson 1953

Centennial Song   Merrill 1953

Center of Attraction   Brooks 1938

Centerville Alma Mater   Young, Victor 1941

Central Give Me Back My Dime   Howard, Joseph E. 1905

Central Park   Mercer 1935

Central Park (inst.)   Ruby 1940

Central Two-Two-Oh-Oh   Rainger 1941; Robin 1941

Century Girl, The   Herbert 1916

Century Promenade, The   Bryan 1920; Schwartz, Jean 1920

Century Toddle   Bryan 1921; Pollack 1921; Schwartz, Jean 1921

Certain As the Sea Is Blue   Revel 1953, 1960

Certain Individuals   Rome 1952

Certain Smile, A   Fain 1958; Webster 1958

C'est Bien Paris   Baer 1927; Kahn 1927

C'est Comme Ca   Ellington 1966

C'est Defendu   Rome 1965

C'est la Guerre   Evans 1954; Livingston, Jay 1954; Mercer 1952; Schwartz, Arthur 1952

C'est la Vie   Arlen 1934; Coleman 1961; Gershwin, Ira 1934; Harburg 1934; Leigh 1961; Young, Victor 1955

C'est la Vie, C'est l'Amour   Coslow 1959

C'est L'Amour   Sherman 1984

C'est Magnifique   Porter 1953

C'est Merveilliux   Van Heusen 1953

C'est Moi   Lerner, Alan Jay 1960; Loewe 1960

C'est Paree   Caesar 1933; Romberg 1933

C'est Pas Comme Ca (It's Not Like That)   Washington 1931

C'est Vous (The Madonna's Secret)   Washington 1945

Ceylon Rose   Kalmar 1920; Motzan 1920; Ruby 1920

CFD and G Seventh Blues   Robison 1967

Cha Cha Cha Romance   Coots 1958

Cha-Cha-Cha for Gia   Mancini 1956

Chain Dance   Mitchell 1921; Pollack 1921

Chain Reaction   David, Hal 1954

Chain Store Daisy   Rome 1937

Chains   Spina 1966

Chair Ballet   Atteridge 1920

Cha-Lypso, The   Hoffman 1957

Chamber Music and Boy's March   Harbach 1931; Kern 1931

Chameleon   Raye 1953

Champagne   Blane 1955; Martin 1955

Champagne and Laughter   Smith, Harry B. 1916; Smith, Robert B. 1916

Champagne and Music   Silver 1950

Champagne and Orchids   Hammerstein 1935; Kern 1935

Champagne and Wedding Cake   Styne 1954

Champagne Cocktail (inst.)   Stept 1957

Champagne fo' de Lady   Arlen 1959; Mercer 1959

Champagne Safari   Robin 1936

Champagne Song   Herbert 1898, 1911; Smith, Harry B. 1898, 1911

Champagne Waltz, The   Conrad 1937; Oakland 1937; Smith, Harry B. 1900

Championship of the World (inst.), The   Herbert 1921

Chance at Love, A   Sigman 1955

Chance of a Life Time, The   Coslow 1936

Chance of a Lifetime   Lerner, Sammy 1940

Chance to Dream   Lerner, Alan Jay Date Unknown

Chances Are   David, Hal 1951; Freed, Ralph 1931

Change for a Penny   Merrill 1957

Change of Guard   Kahn 1937; Romberg 1937

Change of Heart, A   Adamson 1943; Heyman 1953; Stept 1954; Styne 1943; Young, Victor 1953

Change of Scene   Drake 1954

Change of Scenery, A   Coots 1955

Change of Seasons (Where Do You Catch the Bus for Tomorrow), A   Bergman 1980; Mancini 1979

Change of Sky   Harburg 1979

Change Partners   Berlin 1938; Herbert 1920

Change Your Step   Ager 1923; Yellen 1923

Changeable   Parish 1962

Changeable Girls   Carroll 1918

Changeable Heart   Brooks 1942

Changes   Donaldson 1927; Strouse 1993; Yellen 1948

Changing My Tune   Gershwin, George 1947; Gershwin, Ira 1947

Changing of the Guards   Oakland 1931

Changing the Key   Whiting 1923

Chanson Apache   Bryan 1919; Schwartz, Jean 1919

Chanson Des Chercheuses D—-   Hoffman Date Unknown; Warren Date Unknown

Chanson on the Prater, A   Hammerstein 1935; Romberg 1935

Chansonette   Buck 1923; Caesar 1923; Friml 1923

Chant   Cahn 1970; Styne 1970

Chant des Galleriens   Romberg 1933

Chant of the Jungle   Brown, Nacio Herb 1929; Freed, Arthur 1929

Chante Moi   David, Mack 1951

Chanty, A   Hammerstein 1928; Romberg 1928

Chanukah Time in Dublin   Drake 1997

Chapel Bells   Adamson 1938; McHugh 1938

Chapel in Apple Valley, A   Adamson 1958; McHugh 1958

Chapel of the Roses   Baer 1951

Chaperons   Porter 1913

Chaplin Walk, The   Kern 1915; Motzan 1915

Chapman Report Marching Song, The   Webster 1963

Chapman's Cheerful Cheese   Gordon 1941; Warren 1941

Chaps from Annapolis   Adamson 1956; McHugh 1956

Chapter 54, Number 1909   Coleman 1973; Fields 1973

Characteristic Waltz   Cohan 1911

Charade   Mancini 1964; Mercer 1964

Charcoal Man   Drake 1943

Charge   Coleman 1972; Fields 1972; Leigh 1971

Charge of the Footmen   Herbert 1905

Charge of the Song Brigade   Egan 1919; Whiting 1919

Charisse   Brown, Nacio Herb 1949

Charity   Brown, Nacio Herb 1932; DeSylva 1932; Porter 1912; Whiting 1932

Charity Bazaar   Drake 1954; Herbert 1905

Charity Party   Strouse 1993

Charity's Soliloquy   Coleman 1966; Fields 1966

Charity's Theme (inst.)   Coleman 1966

Charleston   Comden and Green 1945; Coots 1925; Johnson, James P. 1922

Charleston Charley   Mills 1924

Charleston Charlie   Sherman 1962

Charleston Dance, The   Johnson, James P. 1923

Charleston Hound   Waller 1926

Charleston Mad   Conrad 1925

Charleston Rag (inst.)   Blake 1917

Charleston Time   Carroll 1925; Freed, Arthur 1925

Charleston Waterfront   Razaf Date Unknown

Charley Express, The   Adams 1996; Strouse 1996

Charley My Boy   Kahn 1924

Charley the Busker   Sherman 1995

Charlie   Bacharach 1977; Strouse 1980

Charlie and Algernon   Strouse 1980

Charlie Brown's Calliope (inst.)   Sherman 1972

Charlie, Ike and Gus   Edwards 1929

Charlie McCarthy   Kalmar 1937; Ruby 1937

Charlie, My Back Door Man   Conrad 1928

Charlie (Opening Act I)   Kern 1928

Charlie Two-Step   Carmichael 1932

Charlie's Home   Coots 1933; Young, Joe 1933

Charlie's Number   Leigh 1967

Charlie's Place   Sherman 1974

Charlotte Couldn't Charleston   Cahn 1964; Van Heusen 1964

Charlotte's Letter   Lerner, Alan Jay 1971

Charlotte's Spinning Song   Strouse Date Unknown

Charlotte's Web   Sherman 1973

Charm   Coslow 1924; Romberg 1924; Schwartz, Jean 1935

Charm Against Trouble   Blane 1940

Charm of You, The   Cahn 1945; Styne 1945

Charm School, The   Bryan 1920; Schwartz, Jean 1920

Charmaine   Pollack 1926

Charming   Cohan 1927; Strouse 1982

Charming, Charming (Store Opening)   Hart 1926; Rodgers 1926

Charming Eyes   Mills 1928

Charming Ladies   Atteridge 1921

Charming Little Faker   Burke 1940

Charming Senoritas   Caesar 1930; Harbach 1930; Romberg 1930

Charming Waltz (inst.)   Duke 1963

Charming Women   Coots 1925

Charms Are Fairest When They're Hidden   Friml 1914; Harbach 1914

Charro!   Bergman 1969

Chase, The   Ellington 1946; Hammerstein 1925; Harbach 1925; Kern 1925; Lerner, Alan Jay 1947; Loewe 1947; Rodgers 1976

Chase All Your Cares (And Got to Sleep, Baby)   Berlin 1931

Chase Me, Catch Me Polka   Sigman 1950

Chase Me Charlie   Von Tilzer 1923

Chase Me, I'm Single   Williams 1913; Young, Joe 1913

Chase of the Fox, The   Caesar 1925; Youmans 1925

Chase the Cat   Arlen 1930; Koehler 1930

Chased to Be Married   Leigh 1953

Chasin' After Him   Strouse 1957

Chasing   Loesser 1937

Chasing Butterflies   Howard, Joseph E. 1918

Chasing Shadows   Davis 1935; Silver 1935

Chasing the Squirrel   Bryan 1917

Chasing You Around   Loesser 1938

Chatanooga Playboy   Parish 1933

Chateau Chantal (inst.)   Bacharach 1965

Chattachoochee   Dubin 1923; Fain 1923; Rose 1923

Chattanooga Booga Boo   Donaldson 1922; Johnson, Howard 1922

Chattanooga Choo Choo   Egan 1926; Gordon 1941; Warren 1941; Whiting 1926

Chatter, Chatter   Berlin 1914

Chatterbox   Ellington 1938; Mills 1938

Chatter-Box (inst.)   Schwartz, Jean 1930

Chauffeur   Johnson, James P. 1947; Williams 1910

Chaug-Buma-Guma-Maug Lake   Russell 1947

Chauve-Souris of Our Own, A   Caesar 1922

Cheap Cigars   Fain 1948

Cheat on Me   Mercer 1965

Cheatin' Billy   Bergman 1961

Cheatin' Child   Lewis 1923; Schwartz, Jean 1923; Young, Joe 1923

Cheatin' on Me   Pollack 1925; Yellen 1925

Cheating   Fisher 1919

Cheating Peddler, The   Smith, Harry B. 1900

Check It Out!   Coleman 1996

Checkin' My Heart   Robin 1952; Warren 1952

Chee Chee Mood   Razaf 1950

Chee-Chee's Second Entrance   Hart 1928; Rodgers 1928

Cheek to Cheek   Berlin 1935

Cheeky-Cheeky Hoopla   Hoffman 1950; Merrill 1950

Cheer, Girls, Cheer   Caesar 1924; Conrad 1924; Harbach 1924

Cheer Up   Brown, A. Seymour 1923

Cheer Up — Keep Smiling   Meyer 1927

Cheer Up and Smile   Conrad 1930

Cheer Up (Better Times Will Soon Be Here)   Leslie 1915; Young, Joe 1915

Cheer Up, Cherries Will Soon Be Ripe   Bryan 1908; Meyer 1908

Cheer Up, Eat and Grow Thin   Goetz 1917

Cheer Up Father, Cheer Up Mother   Bryan 1918

Cheer Up! Girls   Kern 1907

Cheer Up Hamlet   Strouse 1986

Cheer Up Mary   Bryan 1906

Cheer Up, My Honey   Harbach 1910

Cheer Up the Old Folks at Home   Mitchell 1924; Pollack 1924

Cheer Up, the Sun Will Soon Be Shining   Sterling 1917

Cheerful Little Earful   Gershwin, Ira 1930; Rose 1930; Warren 1930

Cheerie Beerie Be From Sunny Italy   Lewis 1927; Young, Joe 1927

Cheerio   Clare 1925; Fields 1931; Gershwin, Ira 1924; Hart 1925; McHugh 1931; Monaco 1925; Rainger 1939; Robin 1939; Rodgers 1925

Cheerio, but Not Goodbye   Razaf 1953

Cheerio Cheery Lips, Cheerio   Dixon 1928; Warren 1928

Cheerio, Old Dear   Clare 1925; Monaco 1925

Cheers for the Hero   Harburg 1961

Cheese and Crackers   Freed, Ralph 1964

Chelsea   Porter 1919

Cher Ami   Coslow 1933

Cher Ami (inst.)   Coslow 1932

Chera Bochcha (Hello, Hello, Hello)   Lewis 1921; Young, Joe 1921

Cherchez la Femme   Friml 1922

Cherchez la Femme (Get Your Woman)   Conrad 1925

Cheri-Beri   Hart 1926; Rodgers 1926

Cherie   Revel 1951

Cherie, Paree Is Mine (Paris, C'est Toi)   Hanley 1932

Cherokee Charlie   Brooks 1942

Cherokee Kid   Willson 1953

Cherries Ripe   Smith, Harry B. 1905

Cherry   Drake 1943; Russell 1941

Cherry and White Wins the Day   Davis 1938

Cherry Blossom   Bergman 1958; Kahn 1917

Cherry Blossom Lane   Bryan 1919; Schwartz, Jean 1919

Cherry Blossom Maid   Johnston 1926; Turk 1926

Cherry Blossoms on Capitol Hill   Sigman 1941

Cherry Pies Ought to Be You   Porter 1950

Cherry Pink and Apple Blossom White   David, Mack 1951

Cherry Street Cafe   Strouse 1986

Chesapeake and Ohio, The   Magidson 1951; Sigman 1951

Chess and Checkers   Merrill 1957

Chester Must Have His Siesta   Baer 1945

Chestermeyer's Chewing Gum   Ruby 1944

Chestertown   Hart 1919

Chestnut Street   Willson 1953

Chevy Chase (inst.), The   Blake 1914

Chevy Moon   Brooks 1959

Cheyanne (Shy Ann)   Williams 1906

Cheyenne   David, Mack 1959; Livingston, Jerry 1959

Cheyenne of the Cherokees   Johnson, James P. 1930

Cheyyanos   Brooks 1959

Chianti   Friml 1918

Chi-Baba, Chi-Baba (My Bambino, Go to Sleep)   David, Mack 1947; Hoffman 1947; Livingston, Jerry 1947

Chic, Chic, Chic Are We   Harburg 1961

Chic, Chic, Chic, Chic, Chicken   Buck 1913

Chic Talk   Duke 1959

Chica Chica Boom Chic   Gordon 1941; Warren 1941

Chicago   Clare Date Unknown; Pollack 1921; Schwartz, Jean 1921; Willson 1957

Chicago — That Toddling Town   Fisher 1922

Chicago (A Great Big Town)   Hart 1940; Rodgers 1940

Chicago Bears   Johnson, Howard 1956

Chicago Fair Waltz   Gordon 1959; Revel 1959

Chicago Farewell   Bacharach 1979

Chicago Fire, The   Styne 1960

Chicago, Illinois   Mancini 1982

Chicago Stomp Down   Johnson, James P. 1928

Chicago Style   Burke 1952; Van Heusen 1952

Chic-Chic Chiquita   Donaldson 1924

Chi-Chi   Friml 1913; Harbach 1913

Chi-Chi Club   Gordon 1950

Chi-Chi Face   Sherman 1968

Chick! Chick! Chick!   Kern 1920

Chick with the Band   Merrill 1946

Chickabees   Coleman 1988

Chick-a-Boom   Merrill 1953

Chick-a-pen   Willson 1960

Chicken   Jerome 1909; Schwartz, Jean 1909

Chicken Fat   Willson 1961

Chicken Feed   Ellington 1943; Russell 1943

Chicken or the Egg, The   Conrad 1929; Mitchell 1929

Chicken Pie   Young, Victor 1930

Chicken Soup (I Ain't Gonna Take It Sittin' Down)   Merrill 1949

Chicken Thief Man, The   Edwards 1910; Smith, Harry B. 1910

Chicken Walk, The   Bryan 1929; Meyer 1929

Chickens Come Home to Roost   Blake 1932; Sissle 1932

Chickens on Parade   Edwards 1914

Chickie   Mills 1924

Chick-Keeta   Friend 1926

Chico   Baer 1930; Gilbert 1930

Chico Chico (From Porto Rico)   Adamson 1945; McHugh 1945

Chico's Choo-Choo (The Choo-Choo Cha-Cha)   Cahn 1959; Van Heusen 1959

Chico's Reverie   Young, Victor 1955

Chidlins   Johnson, Howard 1930

Chief Hokum   Von Tilzer 1923

Chief of Love   Comden and Green 1958; Styne 1958

Chiffon   Russell 1976

Chiffon Fantasie (inst.)   Herbert 1920

Chihuahua Choo Choo Train   Carmichael 1968

Chihuahua Choo-Choo   Evans 1954; Livingston, Jay 1954

Child, The   Webster 1965

Child in a Man's World (A Woman in a Man's World), A   David, Hal 1978

Child Is Born, A   Johnson, Howard 1930; Livingston, Jerry 1960

Child of All Nations   Caesar 1946

Child of the Sixties (inst.)   Coleman 1983

Child of the Wild, A   Mercer 1964

Childhood   Bryan 1908

Childhood Days   Romberg 1916

Childhood Lesson   Atteridge 1915

Childhood's Happiest Moments   Edwards 1908

Children and Art   Sondheim 1984
Children and Mothers   Styne 1970
Children at Play   Caesar 1943
Children at Play (inst.)   Blake 1977
Children Belong in the Country   Robison 1950
Children of Dreams   Hammerstein 1931; Romberg 1931
Children of the Wind   Strouse 1986
Children, Walk with Me   Razaf 1931
Children Will Listen   Sondheim 1987
Children's Children's Children   Martin 1952
Children's Day, A   Razaf 1950
Children's Game   Weill 1947
Children's Music Box, The   Pollack 1945; Webster 1945
Children's Play Song   Harburg 1971
Children's Song   Freed, Ralph 1947; Washington 1945
Child's Letter, A   Willson 1953
Child's Play (inst.)   Strouse 1953
Chile   Ellington 1937; Mills 1937; Razaf 1937
Chile Con Conga   Mills 1940
Chile Moonlight   Loesser 1936; Motzan 1936
Chili Bean   Brown, Lew 1920
Chili Bom Bom   Donaldson 1924; Friend 1924
Chilimar, The   Fisher 1928
Chilli Con-Can   Howard, Joseph E. 1915
Chillicothe, Ohio   Drake 1947
Chilly Pom Pom Pee   Bryan 1928
Chim-Chim-Cher-ee   Sherman 1964
Chime of the Liberty Bell   Herbert 1908; Smith, Harry B. 1908
(Those Beautiful) Chimes   Johnson, Howard 1924
Chimes at the Meetin'   Fisher 1936
Chimes in the Chapel, The   Livingston, Jerry 1933
Chimes in the Steeple   David, Mack 1938; Meyer 1938
Chimes of Avalon   Spina 1977
Chimes of Big Ben   Parish 1941
Chimes of Indiana   Carmichael 1937
Chimes of Normandy   Bryan 1917
Chimes of Notre Dame   Bryan 1925; McHugh 1938
Chimes of Spring (Spring Beautiful Spring)   Gilbert 1930
Chimes of the Chapel   Egan 1925; Kahn 1925
Chimney Corner Dream   Mercer 1951
Chimneys Are Black, The   Blane 1961
Chin Chin Chinaman   Hanley 1917
Chin Chin Open Your Heart and Let Me In   Brown, A. Seymour 1915
Chin Up   Sherman 1973
Chin Up! Cheerio! Carry On!   Harburg 1941; Lane 1941
Chin Up, Stout Fellow   Mercer 1958
China   Hart 1920; Rodgers 1920
China Boy   Pollack 1914
China Dreams   Egan 1917; Kahn 1917
China Gate   Adamson 1956; Young, Victor 1957
China Girl   Gershwin, George 1929; Gershwin, Ira 1929
China Jumps (inst.)   Waller 1941
China Seas   Brown, Nacio Herb 1935; Freed, Arthur 1935
China Stomp (inst.)   Fisher 1937
China (Temple Bells) (inst.)   Warren Date Unknown
China, We Owe a Lot to You   Ager 1917; Johnson, Howard 1917
Chinatown   Magidson 1930; Washington 1930
Chinatown, My Chinatown   Jerome 1910; Schwartz, Jean 1910
Chin-Cha   Russell 1946
Chinchilla   Akst 1927; Davis 1927
Chin-Chin   Atteridge 1915; Romberg 1915

Chinee Lullaby Man, The   Henderson 1923
Chinese Blues   Coslow 1926; McHugh 1926; Mills 1926
Chinese Celebration   Cohan 1914; Schwartz, Jean 1914
Chinese Dance (inst.)   Rodgers 1928
Chinese Dragon Blues   Caesar 1919; Donaldson 1919
Chinese Firecrackers   Berlin 1920
Chinese Fox Trot (inst.)   Schwartz, Jean 1915
Chinese Lantern Love (inst.)   Kern 1956
Chinese Letter Song   Goetz 1917
Chinese Love Boat, The   Brennan 1929
Chinese Love Song   Friml 1944
Chinese New Year's Ballet   Mitchell 1921; Pollack 1921
Chinese Nightingale   David, Mack 1958; Livingston, Jerry 1958
Chinese One Step (inst.)   Schwartz, Jean 1915
Chinese Party   Youmans 1930
Chinese Rhythm   Mills 1937
Chinese Serenade   Loesser 1937
Chinese Waltz (inst.)   Schwartz, Jean 1915
Ching   Hanley 1941
Ching a Ling's Jazz Bazaar   Johnson, Howard 1920
Ching, Ching, Ching   Fisher 1930
Ching, Ching (Ding, Ding, Ding)   Sherman 1960
Ching Ching-a-ling (Zing-Zing-a-Ling)   Merrill 1952
Chink! Chink!   Smith, Harry B. 1900
Chink, Chink, Don't Talk to Me of Marriage   Herbert 1899; Smith, Harry B. 1899
Chink of the —-er's Gold, The   Von Tilzer 1902
Chink-Chink, Chink-Chink, Chinyman   Johnson, J. Rosamond 1909
Chinkee Chinee Charlie Chan   Coots 1937
Chinky Chinee Bogie Man   Whiting 1929
Chinky Chink   Hammerstein 1922
Chinquapin Bush   Arlen 1946; Mercer 1946
Chip o' the Old Block   Wrubel 1932
Chip-Chip-Chippewa   Hanley 1926
Chiquette   Atteridge 1924; Coots 1923; Romberg 1924; Schwartz, Jean 1923, 1924
(Here Comes) Chiquita   Dubin 1936; Gilbert 1928; Stept 1941; Warren 1936
Chiquita From Santa Anita   Adamson 1947; McHugh 1947
Chiripah, The   Porter 1935
Chiropractic Papa   Conrad 1926
Chiropractor Blues   Razaf 1930
Chirp a Little Ditty   Magidson 1937; Wrubel 1937
Chirp-Chirp   Gershwin, Ira 1928
Chisholm Trail   Brooks 1960; Revel 1946
Chita (Chee-Tah)   Myrow 1965
Chitty Chitty Bang Bang   Sherman 1968
Chivalry Reel   Rome 1948
Chivaree   Johnson, James P. 1948
Chloe   DeSylva 1918; Kahn 1927; Smith, Harry B. 1901
Chloe, Cling to Me   Hart 1922
Choc'late Bar   Razaf 1928; Waller 1928
Chocolate Candy Daddies   Blake 1923; Sissle 1923
Chocolate Dandies   Blake 1924; Sissle 1924
Chocolate Shake   Ellington 1941; Webster 1941
Chocolate Soldier   Jerome 1910; Leigh 1955; Schwartz, Jean 1910
Chocolate Sundae on a Saturday Night, A   David, Hal 1947
Choir   Harbach 1931; Kern 1931
Choir Boy Days   Wrubel 1933
Cholla Gardens (inst.)   Young, Victor 1957
Choo Choo   Razaf 1939; Waller 1939
Choo Choo Love   Conrad 1926; Kahn 1926

Choo Choo Song   David, Hal 1951
Choo Choo Train (Le Petit Train)   Lawrence 1953
Choose Your Partner   Lawrence 1951
Chop Stick Rag   Schwartz, Jean 1912
Chop Suey   Hammerstein 1958; Rodgers 1958
Chopin Ad Lib (Opening Chorus)   Kern 1921
Chop-Stick Blues   Johnston 1927; Turk 1927
Chopsticks   Carroll 1925; Freed, Arthur 1925; Lawrence 1939
Choral Russe   Burke 1946; Van Heusen 1946
Chords   Willson 1952
Choreography   Berlin 1954
Chores   Evans 1952; Livingston, Jay 1952
Choro   Washington 1953
Chorus and Entrance of Regent   Herbert 1911; Smith, Harry B. 1911
Chorus Girl, The   Atteridge 1917; Motzan 1917; Romberg 1917
Chorus Girl Blues   Hart 1921; Rodgers 1921
Chorus Girl (inst.), The   Kern 1905
Chorus Girl's Dream, The   Oakland 1953; Raye 1953
Chorus of Citizens   Ellington 1946
Chorus of Hussars   Herbert 1898; Smith, Harry B. 1898
Chorus of Soldiers   Romberg 1925; Smith, Harry B. 1925
Chorus of Villagers   Johnson, J. Rosamond 1904
Chorus Picking Time on Broadway   Hanley 1926
Chose Your Partner for the Last Dance   Drake 1952
Chosen Few, The   Leigh 1956; Livingston, Jerry 1956
Chow Mein   Merrill 1955
Choy-Choy-Hoy-Toy (Ch-Boom, Ch-Bah)   Drake 1951
Christ Has Come, The   Livingston, Jerry 1960
Christ Is Alive   Livingston, Jerry 1960
Christening, The   Johnson, J. Rosamond 1909
Christening of the Boat, The   Smith, Robert B. 1908
Christina   Adamson 1957; Conrad 1929; Mitchell 1929
Christina Swanson   Howard, Joseph E. 1908
Christine   Fain 1960; Webster 1960
Christine the Christmas Tree   Drake 1951
Christmas at Hampton Court   Rodgers 1976
Christmas Blues, The   Cahn 1953
Christmas Came in May   De Lange 1946
Christmas Carol, A   Young, Victor 1954
Christmas Chimes   Baer 1955; Clare 1950
Christmas Comes But Once a Year   Razaf 1947
Christmas Dances   Smith, Harry B. 1909
Christmas Day   Bacharach 1968; David, Hal 1968; Davis 1952
Christmas Dinner Country Style   Freed, Ralph 1958
Christmas Eve Supper   Blane 1966
Christmas Fair Waltz   Herbert 1903
Christmas Hoop-De-Do   Sherman 1984
Christmas Hop   Freed, Ralph 1958
Christmas in America   Cahn 1955
Christmas in Birdland   Mancini 1956
Christmas in Los Angeles   Sherman 1980
Christmas in New York   Drake 1993
Christmas in Rio   Oakland 1955; Webster 1955
Christmas Is a Day of Joy   Warren Date Unknown
Christmas Is a Little Doll   Sigman 1954
Christmas Is A-Comin   DePaul 1955; Raye 1955
Christmas Is Coming   Blake 1957
Christmas Is for Children   Cahn 1959; Van Heusen 1959, 1968
Christmas Is in Your Heart   Adams 1974
Christmas Is the Season of the Bells   Bergman 1963

Christmas Island at Christmas Time   Sondheim Date Unknown
Christmas Land   Merrill 1962
Christmas Love Song, A   Bergman 1989
Christmas Night in Harlem   Parish 1934
Christmas Presents   Willson 1956
Christmas Song   Fain 1951; Harburg 1951; Warren 1962
Christmas Spell, The   Robison 1947
Christmas Star   Webster 1963
Christmas Surprise   Ellington 1965
Christmas Time Is Coming   Robison 1963
Christmas Time Seems Years and Years Away   Berlin 1909; Snyder 1909
Christmas Toyland Wedding   Drake 1957
Christmas Vacation   Livingston, Jerry 1963
Christmas Valley   Razaf 1949
Christmas Waltz   Cahn 1954; Styne 1954; Webster 1956
Christmas (Where's the Family)   Mills 1955
Christmas Wish, A   Blake 1961
Christmastide Love   Goetz 1917
Christmas-y Day, A   Cahn 1976; Lane 1976
Christobel   Sondheim Date Unknown
Christopher Columbus   Razaf 1936
Christopher Street   Comden and Green 1953
Christy Girl, The   Smith, Harry B. 1909
Chromolume #7   Sondheim 1984
Chrysanthemum Tea   Sondheim 1976
Chu Chin Chow   Buck 1917
Chucha-Pacha-Poo-Poo, A   Henderson 1923
Chuck It   Hart 1926; Rodgers 1926
Chuck Wagon Gang   Willson 1953
Chuckle a Day, A   Willson 1953
Chug Chug, Choo-Choo, Chug   Gordon 1944; Monaco 1944
Chula Chihuahua   Clare 1940; Styne 1940
Church   Lane 1979; Lerner, Alan Jay 1979
Church Around the Corner   Freed, Arthur 1925
Church Bells   Coots 1932; Young, Joe 1932
Church Bells Are Ringing for Mary, The   Brown, Lew 1927; DeSylva 1927; Henderson 1927
Church Bells on Sunday Morning   Fain 1947; Yellen 1947
Church Bells Told, The   Schwartz, Jean 1935; Young, Joe 1935
Church Music   Russell 1949
Church of My Choice   Bergman 1964; Fain 1964
Ciao Always Ciao   Sigman 1975
Ciao Ciao Bambino   Parish 1959
Ciao, Compare   Merrill 1966
Cielito Lindo   Robin 1936
Cielito Lindo (Beautiful Heaven)   Dubin 1924
Cigarette   Henderson 1935; Robison 1952; Yellen 1935
Cigarette and a Silhouette, A   De Lange 1938; Van Heusen 1938
Cigarette (inst.)   Kern 1941
Cigarettes   Kalmar 1941; Ruby 1941
Cigarettes, Cigars!   Gordon 1931; Revel 1931
Cigars! Cigarettes! Nuts!   Brown, Lew 1931; Henderson 1931
Cigolette   David, Mack 1949; Sigman 1949
Cimarron   Webster 1961
Cincinnati   Evans 1948; Livingston, Jay 1948; Porter 1914
Cincinnati Tomorrow Night   Freed, Ralph 1960
(Little) Cinderelatives   DeSylva 1922; Gershwin, George 1922
Cinderella   David, Mack 1950; Gordon 1925; Hanley 1926; Hoffman 1950; Livingston, Jerry 1950; Turk 1923

Cinderella at the Grave   Sondheim 1987
Cinderella Blues   Caesar 1922
Cinderella Brown   Fields 1930; McHugh 1930
Cinderella, Darling   Loesser 1961
Cinderella Dreams   Whiting 1925
Cinderella Girl   Harbach 1926; Kern 1926
Cinderella Goes to Town   Hanley 1938
Cinderella Jones   Cahn 1946; Styne 1946
Cinderella Lost Her Slipper   Berlin 1917
Cinderella on Broadway   Atteridge 1920
Cinderella Stay a While   David, Mack 1975
Cinderella Story   Russell 1944
Cinderella Sue   Fain 1931; Harburg 1946; Kahal 1931; Kern 1946
Cinderella Waltz   Atteridge 1912; Mercer 1958
Cinderella Work Song (The Work Song)   Hoffman 1950
Cinderella's Consolation   Kahal 1929
Cinderella's Dream   Herbert 1912
Cinderella's Dreams   Egan 1925; Kahn 1925
Cinderella's Fella   Brown, Nacio Herb 1933; Freed, Arthur 1933
Cinderella's Ride   Harbach 1926; Kern 1926
Cinderelvis   Drake 1957
Cinders   Friml 1923
Cindy   Atteridge 1920; Mercer 1946; Revel 1944; Webster 1944
Cindy Kate   Jerome 1905; Schwartz, Jean 1905
Cindy Lou McWilliams   Revel 1942
Cinema Girl   Atteridge 1922
Cinema Lorelei   Eliscu 1931
Cinerama Holiday (Souvenirs of Paris)   Lawrence 1955
Cing Cing's Samisen   Howard, Joseph E. 1906
Cingalee   Whiting 1928
Cingalese Girls   Harbach 1927; Kalmar 1927; Ruby 1927
Cingalese Village   Kalmar 1927; Kern 1927; Ruby 1927
Cinnamon and Clove   Bergman 1966
Circassian Dance   Friml 1914; Harbach 1914
Circle of Your Arms, The   Leigh 1965
Circle This Day on the Calendar   Cahn 1966; Van Heusen 1966
Circulatin' 'Round   Coots 1935
Circus   Adamson 1935, 1936; Alter 1949; Lane 1935, 1936; Russell 1949
Circus Ballet (inst.), The   Herbert 1919
Circus Day   Coots 1952
Circus Day in Dixie   Yellen 1915
Circus Days   Ager 1928; Atteridge 1922; Johnson, James P. 1929; Monaco 1912; Yellen 1928
Circus Is Coming to Town, The   Berlin 1918; Mercer 1947
Circus Is on Parade, The   Hart 1935; Rodgers 1935
Circus Queen   Hammerstein 1934; Kern 1934
Circus, the Circus, The   Cahn 1964; Van Heusen 1964
Circus Theme   Brooks 1960
Circus World   Washington 1964
Ciribiribin   Johnson, Howard 1933; Lawrence 1939
Ciribiribin on the Mandolin   Hoffman 1951
Cissy & Bob   Blake 1947
Cissy, I Love You   Johnson, James P. 1962
City Called Heaven   Blake 1952; Sissle 1952
City Flat, A   Hart 1926; Rodgers 1926
City Kept Gal   Blake 1938; Sissle Date Unknown
City of Angels Theme   Coleman 1989
City of Enchantment   Drake 1955
City of Hope   Freed, Ralph 1954
City on Fire!   Sondheim 1979

City Street   Brooks 1959
City with a Caring Heart   Drake 1994
City Within a City   Washington 1959
Ciu-e, A   David, Hal 1959
Ciumachella (Tender Flower)   Sigman 1964
Civic Improvement   Fain 1951; Webster 1951
Civil Defense March   Cahn 1958
Civil War Ballet (inst.)   Arlen 1944
Civilian   Dietz 1944; Duke 1944
Civilian Mary   Yellen Date Unknown
Civilization   Johnson, Howard 1921
Civilization (Bongo Bongo Bongo)   Sigman 1947
Clang Dang the Bell   Loesser 1960
Clap Hands, Clap Hands till Daddy Comes Home   Merrill 1950
Clap Hands Here Comes Charlie   Rose 1925
Clap Hands Till Papa Comes Home   Turk 1925
Clap Yo' Hands   Dietz 1926; Gershwin, George 1926; Gershwin, Ira 1926
Clap Your Hands   Clare 1953; Young, Victor 1953
Clara, Don't You Be Downhearted   Gershwin, George 1935
Clara the Crumb of the Chorus   Raye 1945
Clara the Turtle   Strouse 1999
Clarabelle's Clarabus   Coots 1955
Claremont   Cohan 1907
Clarence, the Cross-Eyed Lion   Coots 1964
Clarinet and the Coronet   Atteridge Date Unknown
Clarinet's Love, The   Atteridge Date Unknown
Class   Adams 1993; Davis 1960; Sondheim 1954; Strouse 1991
Class of 1913 Song   Porter 1910
Class of Fifty-Nine, The   Sherman 1983
Class of Summer '32, The   Livingston, Jerry 1973
Class Room Number   Coslow 1933; Johnston 1933; Robin 1933
Class Will Tell   Leslie 1939
Classical Music   Leigh 1985
Classification Blues   Loesser 1944
Classy Clothes Chris   Gordon 1938; Revel 1938
Clean As a Whistle   Fields 1933; McHugh 1933
Clean Break   Sigman 1954
Clean Livin'   David, Hal 1960
Clean Sweep   Strouse 1993
Clean Up Chicago   Gordon 1950; Myrow 1950
Cleanin' My Rifle (And Dreamin' of You)   Wrubel 1943
Cleaning Up the Floor with Lulu   Hart 1932; Rodgers 1932
Clear Out of This World   Dubin 1940; McHugh 1940
Clementina   Harbach 1933; Kern 1933
Clementine   Brown, Nacio Herb 1924; Martin 1959
Clementine from New Orleans   Johnson, James P. 1927; Warren 1927
Clem's Drill (Dance Drill) (inst.)   Styne 1967
Cleo and Me-O   Merrill 1953
Cleo (inst.)   Brown, Nacio Herb 1923
Cleo Steps Out   Blake 1957
Cleo Zell My Creole Belle   Blake 1921; Sissle 1921
Cleopatra   Bryan 1917, 1918, 1919; Loesser 1941; Schwartz, Jean 1918, 1919; Styne 1941; Webster 1963
Cleopatra's Aria   Herbert 1895; Smith, Harry B. 1895
Cleopatricola (Cleo-Patrick-Ola)   Bryan 1920; Schwartz, Jean 1920
Cleopatterer   Kern 1917
Cleveland   Porter 1910
Clever, These Chinese   Adamson 1930; Youmans 1930
Click of Her Little Brogans, The   Brennan 1921

Clickety-clack   Weill 1938
Climb Ev'ry Mountain   Hammerstein 1959; Rodgers 1959
Climb High   Sondheim Date Unknown
Climb Those Golden Stairs   Edwards 1929
Climb Up the Mountain   Porter 1950
Climb Up the Social Ladder   Gershwin, George 1933; Gershwin, Ira 1933
Climbin' Up Dem Golden Stairs   Adamson 1944; McHugh 1944
Climbing Some Other High Hill   Von Tilzer 1956
Climbing the Rickety Stair   Bryan 1928
Climbing Up the Scale   Berlin 1923
Clinching the Sale   Oakland 1931
Cling a Little Closer   Goetz 1915; Parish 1947; Romberg 1915
Cling Cling   Herbert 1924
Cling to Me   David, Hal 1952; David, Mack 1947; Hoffman 1947; Leslie 1935; Livingston, Jerry 1947
Clinging Vine   Harbach 1911
Clink Clank Clunk   Evans 1954; Livingston, Jay 1954
Clink Your Glasses   Cahn 1949
Clip-Clop Song (Le Fiacre), The   Rome 1952
Clippity Clop and Clementine   Arlen 1973
Clock, The   Smith, Harry B. 1914
Clock (inst.), The   Kern 1946
Clock Song   Bryan 1920; Schwartz, Jean 1920
Clock without Hands, A   Livingston, Jerry 1962; Webster 1962
Clockmaker's Song   Herbert 1903; Smith, Harry B. 1903
Clop, Clop, Clop   Martin 1958
Clorinda   Brown, A. Seymour 1909
Clorinda Jackson   Howard, Joseph E. 1905
Close   Bacharach 1960; Porter 1937
Close as Pages in a Book   Fields 1945; Romberg 1945
Close Beside You   Adamson 1965; Carmichael 1955, 1965
Close Harmony   Comden and Green 1964; Styne 1964
Close Quarters   Bacharach 1959; David, Hal 1959
Close Those Eyes   Washington 1945
(It Must Be Getting) Close to Christmas   Cahn 1959; Van Heusen 1959, 1969
Close to Me   Lewis 1936; Porter 1944
Close to My Heart   Sigman 1952; Sterling 1915; Von Tilzer 1915
Close to You   Hoffman 1943; Livingston, Jerry 1942; Young, Joe 1936
Close Your Eyes   Dietz 1963; Schwartz, Arthur 1963
Close Your Eyes and Make Believe   Cahn 1954
Close Your Eyes and Make Believe It's Me   Kahal 1929; Monaco 1929
Close Your Eyes and See   Gorney 1935
Close Your Eyes, Mr. Moon   Sherman 1965
Closer and Closer   Parish 1943; Woods 1943
Closer and Closer and Closer   Lerner, Alan Jay 1974; Loewe 1974
Closer than a Kiss   Cahn 1958; Van Heusen 1958
Closer to Heaven   Brown, Nacio Herb 1930; Freed, Arthur 1930
Closer to You   Blane 1964; Gilbert 1929; Martin 1964
Closer You Are, The   Robin 1951; Styne 1951
Closing Love Duet   Merrill 1956
Clothes   Hammerstein 1920; Harbach 1920
Clothes Line Ballet (inst.)   Waller 1934
Clothes Parade   Bryan 1930
Cloud By Day, A   Livingston, Jerry 1962
Cloud Nine   Johnson, James P. 1959

Clouds   Carmichael 1956; Donaldson 1934; Kahn 1934
Clouds in My Heart   Ellington 1937; Mills 1937
Clouds Roll By Dance   Coots 1922
Clouds Will Soon Roll By   Woods 1932
Cloudy   Sigman 1951
Clover Blossom Blues   Kahn 1922
Clover in the Meadow   Fain 1957; Webster 1957
Clown, The   Comden and Green 1951; Styne 1951
Clowning   Akst 1929; Clarke 1929
Clowning at the N.V.A.   McHugh 1949
Clowns   Akst 1927; Davis 1927
Clowns in Clover   Fields 1933; McHugh 1933
Club Time   Spina 1954
Clump! Clump! Swish!   Weill 1938
Clumsy Waltz, The   Strouse 1975
Coach and Four, A   Evans 1946; Livingston, Jay 1946
Coachman's Heart, A   Hammerstein 1922
Coal Black Lady   Hammerstein 1927; Kern 1927
Coal-Black Eyes and Lily-White Hands   Sigman 1950
Coaling Up in Color Town   Egan 1916; Whiting 1916
Coast to Coast on a Bus   Baer 1942
Coax Me   Brown, Lew 1923; Hanley 1923; Sterling 1904; Von Tilzer 1904
Coax Me a Little   Webster 1956
Cobbler Cobbler   Sherman 1961
Cobbleskill School Song   Brooks 1947
Cobble-Stones   Clare 1927; Pollack 1927
Cobra   Sherman 1958
Cobra Ritual Dance (inst.)   Fain 1960
Cocabola Tree, The   Blane 1945, 1946
Cock of the Walk, The   Edwards 1910; Smith, Harry B. 1910
Cock-A-Doodle Doo   Caesar 1923; Conrad 1923; Friend 1923
Cock-a-Doodle, I'm Off My Noodle (My Baby's Back)   Johnson, Howard 1926
Cock-a-Doodle-Doo   Brennan 1929; Caesar 1922; Howard, Joseph E. 1907
Cockebur Song, The   Blane 1945
Cockeyed Optimist, A   Hammerstein 1949; Rodgers 1949
Cockney (Piccadilly Lil)   Strouse 1999
Cockney Rhyming Slang   Bergman 1961
Cocktail, The   Dietz 1937; Schwartz, Arthur 1937
Cocktail Melody   Donaldson 1926
Cocktail Party   Sondheim Date Unknown
Cocktail Time   Hoffman 1936; Porter 1922
Cocktails for Two   Coslow 1934; Johnston 1934
Coco   Lerner, Alan Jay 1969
Coco Palm Tree Island   Styne 1964
Cocoanut Oil Shampoo (TV Commercial)   Arlen 1954; Gershwin, Ira 1954
Cocoanut Sweet   Arlen 1957; Harburg 1957
Cocoanut Tree, The   Russell 1977
Cocoanut Water   Raye 1957
Cocoanuts   DePaul 1957; Russell 1957
Coconut and Banana   Bergman 1958
Cocotte, The   Porter 1933
C.O.D. (Help! I'm in Love)   Atteridge 1910
Code, The   Fain 1955
Code of the West, The   Evans 1954; Livingston, Jay 1954
Co-Ed, The   Conrad 1925
Coffee and Kisses   Freed, Ralph 1938
Coffee Bean Conga   Raye 1940
Coffee Break   Loesser 1961
Coffee Cocoa Tea   Hoffman 1951

Coffee in the Morning and Kisses at Night   Dubin 1934; Warren 1934

Coffee Mother Used to Make, The   Smith, Harry B. 1912

Coffee Time   Brown, Nacio Herb 1960; Freed, Arthur 1945; Warren 1945

Cognac   Coots 1921

Cohan's Pet Names   Cohan 1908

Cohan's Rag Babe   Cohan 1908

Cohen Is Living the Life O'Reilly   Pollack 1927; Yellen 1927

Cohen Owes Me Ninety-Seven Dollars   Berlin 1915

Cohen's Band   Atteridge 1912

Coke! The Cat! The Cook!, The   Cahn 1959; Van Heusen 1959

Cold and Dead   Loesser 1956

Cold, Cold Mammas Burn Me Up   Gilbert 1924

Cold, Cold, Room   Rome 1965

Cold Cream Jar Song   Rome 1954

(It's a) Cold, Cruel World   Russell 1946

Cold Hearted Woman   Hoffman 1951; Merrill 1951

Cold in the Morning   Coleman 1975

Coldest Gal in Town, The   Fain 1947; Yellen 1947

Colet and Company   Robin 1932

Colinette   Egan 1926; Whiting 1926

Coliseum March, The   Drake 1967

Collage November   Mercer 1953

Collective Loading-Time Song   Gershwin, Ira 1943

Colleen   Schwartz, Jean 1926

Colleen Fair with the Raven Hair   Merrill 1949

Colleen O'Killarney   Johnston 1933; Robin 1933

College Boy, A   Atteridge 1914

College Boys   Atteridge 1911

College Boy's Dream   Edwards 1907

College Days   Coots 1926; Goetz 1912; Howard, Joseph E. 1908; Rose 1927

College Education Is a Joke, A   Coots 1921

College Humor   Brown, Lew 1927; DeSylva 1927; Henderson 1927

College Hymn   Brown, Nacio Herb 1930, 1934; Freed, Arthur 1930, 1934

College Inn Rag, The   Carroll 1915

College Love   Dubin 1932

College on Broadway, A   Hart 1920; Rodgers 1920

College Rhythm   Gordon 1934; Revel 1934

College Song, The   Kalmar 1933; Ruby 1933

College Swing   Carmichael 1938; Loesser 1938

College Trot, The   Harbach 1917

College Widow   Mills 1938

Collegiana   Fields 1929; McHugh 1929

Collegiate   Brown, Lew 1925

Collegiate Sam   Coots 1929; Davis 1929

Collegiate Wedding   Fain 1934; Kahal 1934

Collette   Baer 1927; Kahn 1927

Colloque Sentimental   Parish 1965

Colombo   Weill 1947

Colonel and the Major, The   Friml 1928

Colonel Buffalo Bill   Berlin 1946

Colonel Corn   Fisher 1944

Colonel Hathi's March (The Elephant Song)   Sherman 1967

Colonel, Major and Captain   Donaldson 1934; Kahn 1934

Colonel of the Crimson Hussars, The   Smith, Harry B. 1916

Colonel's Lady, The   Ellington 1966

Colonial Ballet   Atteridge 1917; Romberg 1917

Colonial Chorus   Cohan 1906

Colonial Days   Buck 1919, 1920; Gilbert 1912

Colonna and Vague Specialty   Styne 1940

Colonna Opening   Oakland 1960

Colony Motel, The   Sherman 1983

Color and Light   Sondheim 1984

Color Blind   Rome 1964

Color Green, The   Brooks 1959

Color Music   Smith, Harry B. 1934

Color of Her Eyes, The   Hart 1928; Rodgers 1928

Color of Love   Russell 1964

Color of Your Eyes, The   Freed, Ralph 1940

Color Your Life   Oakland 1972

Colorado   Hanley 1917; Styne 1956

Colorado, My Home   Willson 1960

Colorado Night   Robison 1925

Colorado Sunset   Conrad 1938, 1939; Gilbert 1938, 1939

Colorado Sunset (inst.)   Willson 1964

Colored Romeo   Berlin 1910; Snyder 1910

Colored Soldiers on Parade (inst.)   McHugh 1925

Colorful   Adams 1964; Strouse 1964

(You Can't Lose the Blues with) Colors   Berlin 1957

Colors of Autumn   Brooks 1959

Colors of My Life, The   Coleman 1980

Colossal, Tremendous, Terrific   Rose Date Unknown

Columbia (Anthem)   Herbert 1898

Columbia's Colleen   Edwards 1909; Smith, Robert B. 1909

Columbus' Blues   Comden and Green 1972

Columbus (inst.)   Young, Victor 1955

Combat Pay   Coleman 1988

Come Across   Hammerstein 1920; Harbach 1920; Herbert 1920; Smith, Robert B. 1920

Come Across for the Red Cross   Lerner, Sammy 1954; Oakland 1954

Come Across Yankee Boy, Come Across   Bryan 1918; Fisher 1918

Come Along   Berlin 1920; Buck 1915; Johnson, Howard 1917

Come Along Children   Blake 1958; Sissle 1958

Come Along, Let's Gamble   Gershwin, George 1927; Gershwin, Ira 1927

Come Along, Ma Cherie   Smith, Harry B. 1911; Smith, Robert B. 1911

Come Along Mandy   Edwards 1910; Smith, Harry B. 1910

Come Along My Mandy   Norworth 1910

Come Along, Pretty Girl   Kern 1910

Come Along to the Circus   Coots 1952

Come Along to the County Fair   Johnson, J. Rosamond 1946

Come Along to Toy Town   Berlin 1918

Come Along with Alice   Berlin 1924

Come Along with Me   Jerome 1907; Porter 1953; Schwartz, Jean 1907

Come and Dance with Me   Atteridge 1911; Romberg 1919

Come and Get It   Waller 1944

Come and Get Me   Bacharach 1966; David, Hal 1966

Come and Get Your Happiness   Yellen 1938

Come and Kiss Your Little Baby   Brown, Lew 1912

Come and Play with Me   Ager 1917

Come and See Me Tomorrow   Rainger 1936

Come and Take a Skate with Me   Edwards 1906

Come and Take a Walk with Me   Jerome 1905; Schwartz, Jean 1905

Come and Tell Me   Hart 1926; Rodgers 1926

Come, Answer to Our Call   Romberg 1924

Come Around and Make Love to Me   Brown, A. Seymour 1913

Come Around on Our Veranda   Kern 1907

Come As a Carrier Dove   Smith, Harry B. 1911; Smith, Robert B. 1911

Come A-Wandering with Me   Dietz 1961; Schwartz, Arthur 1961

Come Away   Dietz 1961; Schwartz, Arthur 1961

Come Away Little Girl   Bryan 1910; Meyer 1910

Come Back   Drake 1954; Oakland 1954

Come Back Again Ya Hear   DePaul 1942; Raye 1942

Come Back Little Genie   Fain 1951; Harburg 1951

Come Back, Little Sheba   Freed, Ralph 1953

Come Back Marguerite   Bryan 1911; Fisher 1911

Come Back Sweet Dream   Romberg 1916

Come Back to Aaron   Von Tilzer 1911

Come Back to Arizona   Bryan 1916

Come Back to Erin   Hanley 1917; Johnson, Howard 1939

Come Back to God/Me   Harburg 1967; Styne 1967

Come Back to Jumbo Gumbo   Dubin 1920

Come Back To Little Yo San   Brown, Nacio Herb 1927; Clarke 1927

Come Back to Me   Akst 1930; Atteridge 1911, 1912, 1919; Clarke 1930; DePaul 1958; Dubin 1915; Lane 1965; Lerner, Alan Jay 1963, 1965; Raye 1958; Romberg 1919; Schwartz, Jean 1919

Come Back to Me — My Melody   Berlin 1912; Snyder 1912

Come Back to My Arms   Freed, Ralph 1954

Come Back to Old Manhattan, Dearie   Jerome 1907; Schwartz, Jean 1907

Come Back to Sorrento   Johnson, Howard 1939

Come Back to Sorrento (Torna a Sorrento)   Robin 1930

Come Be My Wife   Herbert 1919

Come Birdie Fly   Edwards 1910

Come Blow Your Horn   Cahn 1963; Van Heusen 1963

Come Boys   Romberg 1924

Come Boys, Let's All Be Gay Boys   Romberg 1954; Webster 1954

Come! Come! Come Closer!   Gershwin, George 1927; Gershwin, Ira 1927

Come, Come, Come/Convent Maids   Herbert 1910

Come Completely to Me   Bacharach 1959

Come Dance with Me   Cahn 1958; Van Heusen 1958

Come Down Ma Evening Star   Smith, Robert B. 1902

Come Down, Mister Moon Man   Brown, Lew 1912

Come Down Salomy Jane   Goetz 1907

Come Down to Argentine   Johnson, Howard 1924

Come Down to Earth, My Dearie   Jerome 1910; Schwartz, Jean 1910

Come Down to Tony Spagoni's Cabaret   Dubin 1917

Come Dream with Me   Cahn 1972; Van Heusen 1972

Come Easy Go Easy Love   Carmichael 1931

Come Farballe   Romberg 1948

Come Fly with Me   Cahn 1958, 1963; Van Heusen 1958, 1963

Come Follow the Band   Coleman 1980

Come Forward   Robison 1945

Come, Gentle Stranger   Smith, Harry B. 1900

Come, Go Bungalowing   Jerome 1915; Schwartz, Jean 1915

Come Here, You   Leigh 1952

Come Hither Eyes   Friml 1913; Harbach 1913

Come Home   Hammerstein 1947; Koehler 1932; Merrill 1993; Rodgers 1947; Styne 1993; Warren 1932

Come Home Prosperity, All Is Forgiven   Caesar 1932

Come Hot It Up with Me   Johnson, Howard 1930

Come In Mornin'   Weill 1950

Come In Out of the Rain   Russell 1946; Sigman 1946

Come Into My Arms or Get Out of My Life   Sigman 1971

Come Into My Heart   Yellen 1921

Come Josephine in My Flying Machine   Bryan 1910; Fisher 1910

Come Let in Love   Webster 1975

Come Let's Have a Good Cry   David, Mack 1945

Come Light the Lovelight   Sherman 1960

Come Little Fishes (Gold Fish Song)   Herbert 1911; Smith, Harry B. 1911

Come Little Girl and Dance with Me   Von Tilzer 1910

Come Lonely Lover   Brooks 1946

Come Love   Bergman 1965

Come, Love, and Play Peek-a-Boo   Jerome 1911; Schwartz, Jean 1911

Come Love Me   Lawrence 1958

Come My Dear   Smith, Harry B. 1906

Come O Come (Pittsburgh)   Dietz 1948; Schwartz, Arthur 1948

Come on a Dip, Dip, Dip in the Deep Deep Water   Livingston, Jerry 1934

Come On a Play Wiz Me, My Sweet Baby   Kalmar 1919; Leslie 1919; Ruby 1919

Come on Along   Conrad 1925

Come on Along with the Bluebird   Fain 1929; Kahal 1929

Come On and Baby Me   Lewis 1916; Meyer 1916; Young, Joe 1916

Come on and Pet Me   Hammerstein 1923; Youmans 1923

Come On and Play   DeSylva 1925; Hanley 1925

Come On and Play Ball with Me   Edwards 1909

Come on and Sit Beside the Sea   Ahlert 1932; Turk 1932

Come on and Stomp, Stomp, Stomp   Mills 1927; Waller 1927

Come On, Baby   Clare 1928, 1929

Come on Baby and Beg for It   Hanley 1932

Come on Boys Let's Follow the Band   Sterling 1904; Von Tilzer 1904

Come On! Come On!   Cahn 1944; Styne 1944

Come on Down to Venezuala   Comden and Green 1960; Styne 1960

Come on Down Town   Cohan 1908

Come on Home   Akst 1922; Ellington 1952; Hanley 1935; Lewis 1922; Meyer 1922; Young, Joe 1922

Come On In   Clare 1929; Porter 1939

Come On in the Dancing's Fine   Atteridge 1914

Come On in, the Water's Fine   Styne Date Unknown

Come on Leathernecks   Stept 1938; Washington 1938

Come On Let's Go   Brooks 1959; Buck 1921; Youmans 1924

Come On, Let's Two Step   Howard, Joseph E. 1907

Come On, Li'l Augie   Arlen 1946; Mercer 1946

Come On, Men   Hart 1930; Rodgers 1930

Come On, Midnight   Arlen 1966

Come on Out and Into My Arms   Dubin 1928

Come on Over Here   Brown, A. Seymour 1909; Kern 1912, 1913; Smith, Harry B. 1913

Come On Over Let's Get Acquainted   Brown, A. Seymour 1911

Come On Papa   Leslie 1918; Ruby 1918

Come on Red, You Red Hot Devil Man   Fisher 1924

Come on Slowpoke   Ahlert 1931; Turk 1931

Come On Spark Plug   Conrad 1923; Rose 1923

Come on Strong   Cahn 1962; Van Heusen 1962

Come on to Nashville, Tenn.   Donaldson 1916

Come On, You Moon   Wrubel 1933

Come Out — Come Out — Wherever You Are   Freed, Arthur 1933

Come Out, Come Out   Cahn 1945; Drake 1954; Styne 1945

Come Out, Come Out Wherever You Are   Cahn 1944; Hoffman 1933; Styne 1944
Come Out Dinah on the Green   Johnson, J. Rosamond 1901
Come Out of the Clouds   Friend 1957
Come Out of the Nursery (Come Out of the Nursery and Dance)   Hart 1930; Rodgers 1930
Come Out of the Rain   Leigh 1952
Come Over Here   Sondheim 1959; Styne 1959
Come Play Wiz Me   Sondheim 1964
Come Rain or Come Shine   Arlen 1946; Mercer 1946
Come Right Back to Me   Johnson, Howard 1914
Come Sing with Me   Cahn 1959; Van Heusen 1959
Come Sir, Will You Join Our Noble Saxton Corps   Romberg 1924
Come Spring   Cahn 1959; Van Heusen 1959
Come Sta   Bergman 1964; Fain 1964
Come Summer   Cahn 1972; Coleman 1972; Leigh 1971; Van Heusen 1972
Come, Sweet Love   Howard, Bart 1961
Come Take a Skate with Me   Edwards 1906
Come Take a Swim in My Ocean   Cobb 1909; Edwards 1909
Come Take Me   Heyman 1931
Come Tiny Goldfish to Me   Kern 1910
Come to Bohemia   Porter 1912
Come to Florence   Gershwin, Ira 1945; Weill 1945
Come to Gypsy Land   Smith, Harry B. 1917
Come to Life   Sigman 1952
Come to Loveland   Blane 1943; Martin 1943
Come to Lower Falls   Caesar 1927
Come to Me   Brown, Lew 1931; Coleman 1972; DeSylva 1931; Duke 1963; Henderson 1931; Heyman 1953; Mancini 1976; Stept 1929, 1953; Young, Victor 1953
Come to Me, Bend to Me   Lerner, Alan Jay 1947; Loewe 1947
Come to Me Chimpanzee   Atteridge 1912
Come to My Arms   Robin 1953
Come to My Heart   Motzan 1919
Come to My Party   Romberg 1924
Come to Order, Men   Wrubel 1959
Come to Paris   Gershwin, Ira 1945; Weill 1945
Come to St. Thomas's   Cohan 1928
Come to Sunny Spain   Herbert 1911; Smith, Harry B. 1911
Come to the Beach Tonight   Blane 1948; Warren 1948
Come to the Circus   Lawrence 1947
Come to the Fair   Robison 1938
Come to the Land of Bohemia   Snyder 1906
Come to the Land of the Argentine   Berlin 1914
Come to the Mardi Gras   Drake 1947
Come to the Moon   Gershwin, George 1919
Come to the Pavilion   Leigh 1955
Come to the Sea   Johnson, Howard 1939
Come to the Supermarket in Old Peking   Porter 1958
Come to Your Daddy   Gilbert 1913
Come, Toddle Along   Jerome 1909; Schwartz, Jean 1909
Come Tom   Herbert 1917
Come Tuesday   Bergman 1966
Come Up and Have a Cup of Coffee   Henderson 1943; Yellen 1943
Come Up and See Me Sometime   Alter 1933; Razaf Date Unknown
Come Up to My Place   Comden and Green 1944
Come Up Tonight   Kalmar 1913
Come Waltz with Me   Cahn 1961; Van Heusen 1961

Come West, Little Girl, Come West   Donaldson 1928; Kahn 1928
Come Where My Love Lies Dreaming   Johnson, Howard 1939
Come Where the Lillies Bloom   Johnson, Howard 1939
Come with Me   Hart 1938; Rodgers 1938
Come with Me and Be Beloved   Coots 1954
Come with Me My Honey   David, Mack 1944
Come with Me to My Bungalow (Cohan's Bungalow Song)   Cohan 1911
Come with Me to San Torino   Lane 1979; Lerner, Alan Jay 1979
Come with Me to Tennessee   Motzan 1916
Come with Me to the Tango Tea   Conrad 1913
Come Ye Heroes All (The Emperor's War Song)   Smith, Harry B. 1906
Comedy Ain't No Joke   Coleman 1988
Comedy Dance   Friml 1934
Comedy Tonight   Sondheim 1962
Come-Look-At-The-War Choral Society   Gershwin, George 1927; Gershwin, Ira 1927
Comes Another Spring   Gordon 1963; Myrow 1963
Comes Love   Brown, Lew 1939; Stept 1939
Comes Once in a Lifetime   Comden and Green 1961; Styne 1961
Comes the Revolution   Gershwin, George 1933; Gershwin, Ira 1933
Comes the Revolution Baby   Mercer 1935
Comet and the Earth (Mister Earth and His Comet Love), The   Edwards 1910; Smith, Harry B. 1910
Come-Tooly-Um-Tooly-Ay-O   Drake 1952
Comfort Me   Hart 1922; Rodgers 1922
Comforts of Home, The   Dietz 1943; Duke 1943
Comforts of Home Sweet Home   Coots 1921
Comfy and Cozy in My Baby's Arms   Ahlert 1930; Turk 1930
Comic Land   Brooks 1957
Comic Strips   Brooks 1959
Comin' Home   Kalmar 1925; Ruby 1925
Comin' Home to You   Bergman 1957, 1982
Comin' Home When the Last Bugle Blows   Coots 1944
Comin' In on a Wing and a Prayer   Adamson 1942; McHugh 1942
Comin' 'Round the Bend   Brooks 1959
Comin' Thru the Rye   Johnson, Howard 1939
Coming Attractions   Strouse 1971
Coming Down the Stairs   Johnson, James P. 1962
Coming from You   David, Mack 1964
Coming Through the Rye   Hammerstein 1928; Youmans 1928
Command Performance   Duke 1963
Commanderess-in-Chief   Herbert 1904
Comme Ca   Parish 1956
Comme Ci, Comme Ca   Caesar 1929; Friml 1921
Comme un Oiseau   Heyman 1936
Comment Allez Vous (How Are Things with You)   Blane 1954; Myrow 1954
Commerce, The   Buck 1921; Lane 1929
Commerce March   Lane 1929
Commercial   Arlen 1954; Gershwin, Ira 1954
Common Sense   Fain 1946
Como Camel Corps, The   Hammerstein 1926; Harbach 1926; Youmans 1926
Como Esta Usted?   Sherman 1960
Compact, The   Herbert 1914
Companeros   Loesser 1969

Companions, I Have Summoned You   Herbert 1913
Companions of the Blade   Herbert 1905
Company   Sondheim 1970
Company of Men, The   Merrill 1959
Company She Keeps, The   Burke 1947; Van Heusen 1947
Company Way, The   Loesser 1961
Company's Comin'   Burke 1933; Spina 1933
Company's Coming Tonight   Brown, A. Seymour 1922
Compared to You   David, Mack 1941
Comparisons   Burke 1956; Friml 1956
Compensation   Parish 1965
Compere, The   Buck 1921
Competition   Silver 1947
Complaint Fanfare (inst.)   Willson 1964
Completely   Robin 1936; Robison 1964; Silver 1943
Complexities of Radio   Willson 1953
Composers Corner   Drake 1958
Computer Song, The   Sherman 1982
Comrade Alonzo   Porter 1938
Comrade, You Have a Chance Here   Smith, Harry B. 1925
Comrades   Carmichael 1956
Comrades Fill No Glass for Me   Johnson, Howard 1939
Comrades, Try Out My Song   Smith, Harry B. 1935
Concentrate   Harbach 1923
Concentratin' on You   Razaf 1931; Waller 1931
Concentration   Porter 1911
Concert in the Park   Friend 1939
Concerto for Piano and Orchestra (inst.)   Strouse 1963
Concerto for Two   Lawrence 1941
Concerto in E-Flat Major   Dubin 1940; Fain 1940
Concerto Jazz-a-Mine (inst.)   Johnson, James P. 1947
Conchita   Brown, Lew 1932; Caesar 1923; Coslow 1936;
   Henderson 1932; Johnson, Howard 1927; Razaf 1930
Conchita Marquita Lolita Pepita Rosita Juanita
   Lopez   Magidson 1942; Styne 1942
Concrete and Steel   Ruby 1953
Coney Island   Dubin 1935, 1936; Magidson 1930; Strouse
   1989; Von Tilzer 1916; Warren 1935, 1936; Washington
   1930
Coney Island Ballet   Duke 1941
Coney Island Boat   Fields 1954; Schwartz, Arthur 1954
Coney Island (Opening, Act I)   Hart 1930; Rodgers 1930
Coney Island U.S.A.   Lawrence 1964
Conference, The   Gordon 1941; Warren 1941
Confession   Dietz 1931; Heyman 1932; Schwartz, Arthur
   1931; Sigman 1966
Confetti March   Smith, Harry B. 1911; Smith, Robert B. 1911
Confidence   Smith, Harry B. 1912; Smith, Robert B. 1912
Confidential Source   Kern 1911; Smith, Harry B. 1911
Confidentially   Dubin 1938; Mercer 1938; Warren 1938
Confidentially Yours   Gilbert 1941; Lawrence 1938; McHugh
   1941
Confirmation   Hanley 1927
Confucius Say   Friend 1939
Confusion   Razaf 1946
Conga!   Comden and Green 1953
Conga Beso   DePaul 1941, 1942; Raye 1941, 1942
Conga Tap, The   Blake Date Unknown; Razaf 1942
Congai   Hammerstein 1931; Romberg 1931
Congalero   Mills 1942
Congeroo   DePaul 1941; Raye 1941
Congo   Kahn 1931
Congo Cohen   Duke 1940
Congo Conga   Coots 1938; Davis 1938
Congo Ivory   Gorney 1958

Congo Kate   Johnson, James P. 1934
Congo Lou (inst.)   Waller 1926
Congo Love Song   Johnson, J. Rosamond 1903
Congoland Melody   Johnson, James P. 1927
Congorilla   Bryan 1932
Congratulations   Hart 1922; Oakland 1971; Rodgers 1922;
   Schwartz, Arthur 1930; Stept 1929
Congress and the Senate, The   Bryan 1936
Congress of the U.S.A.   Motzan 1934
Conjure Man   Arlen 1959; Mercer 1959
Connecticut   Blane 1943; Martin 1944; Silver 1945
Connecticut March   Dixon 1935; Wrubel 1935
Connie's Pitch   Fields 1951
Connubial Bliss   Herbert 1914
Conqueror, The   Heyman 1955; Young, Victor 1955
Conqueror (inst.), The   Young, Victor 1955
Conscience   Johnson, J. Rosamond 1946
Consequence Is Awful, The   Weill 1938
Consider Yourself in Love   Bullock 1941; Spina 1941
Consideration   Robison 1952
Consolation   Hammerstein 1927; Harbach 1927; Robin 1931;
   Whiting 1931
Consoler of Women   Brennan 1929
Conspirators' Chorus   Johnson, J. Rosamond 1904
Constantina Number   Friml 1918
Constantinople   Von Tilzer 1917
Constantly   Burke 1942; Stept 1931; Van Heusen 1942
Constantly (L'Eriera)   Sigman 1977
Consternation   Fain 1951; Harburg 1951
Construction Song   Stept 1936
Contagious Rhythm   Arlen 1930; Koehler 1930
Contented   Hanley 1931; Mills 1928
Contentment   Ruby 1953
Contest, The   Sondheim 1979
Continental Can-Can, The   Blane 1946
Continental Honeymoon   Hanley 1934
Continental Polka, The   Blane 1946
Continental Waltz, The   Hoffman 1954
Continental (You Kiss While You're Dancing), The   Conrad
   1934; Magidson 1934
Continue   Adamson 1957; Warren 1957
Contract, The   Lerner, Alan Jay 1973; Loewe 1973
Contrapunto   Hart 1941; Rodgers 1941
Contrary Mary   Hammerstein 1944; Herbert 1903; Kern 1944
Control Yourself   Coots 1948
Convent Bells Are Ringing   Romberg 1925; Smith, Harry B.
   1925
Convent Song   Smith, Harry B. 1896
Convention, The   Hart 1932; Rodgers 1932
Conversation   Adams 1954; Strouse 1954
Conversation (inst.)   Blake 1946
Conversation Piece (Nice People, Nice Talk)   Comden and
   Green 1953
Conversation Step, The   Harbach 1921
Conversation While Dancing   Mercer 1945
Conversational Song   Jerome 1905; Schwartz, Jean 1905
Convict Song, The   Spina 1957
Convict's Rosary   Fisher 1928
Convict's Song (I've Got a Number for a Name), The   Spina
   1977
Coo-Coo   Robin 1927
Coo-Coo, Coo-Coo   Kern 1910
(Jolson's) Coo-Coo Song   DeSylva 1921
Coo-ee, Australian Bush Call   Motzan 1918
Coo-ee, Coo-ee   Von Tilzer 1903

Coo-ee-doo   Hanley 1921
Cook of Company B, The   Baer 1943; Lewis 1943
Cookies and Bookies   DeSylva 1925; Hanley 1925
Cooking   Carmichael 1957
Cooking Breakfast for the One I Love   Rose 1930
Cooking Up a Show   Gordon 1945; Warren 1945
Cook's Cookin' Boogie   Razaf 1953
Cook's Song   Bryan 1930; Dubin 1930
Cool   Sondheim 1957
Cool Alaska Rock and Roll, The   Brown, Nacio Herb 1958
Cool New World   Magidson 1957; Oakland 1957
Cool Off   Kalmar 1928; Ruby 1928; Sigman 1951
Cool Tango (inst.)   Oakland 1956
Coolie Dance (inst.)   Kern 1921
Coolie's Prayer   Sondheim 1968
Coon Banshee, The   Herbert 1904
Coon College   Edwards 1907
Cooperate with Your Air Raid Warden   Magidson 1942;
     Styne 1942
Co-op-hooray-shun   De Lange 1945; Myrow 1945
Cootie Tickle   Yellen 1919
Cop Number   Edwards 1929
Cop on the Boat, the Man in the Moon and Me,
     The   Hoffman 1932
Copenhagen Polka, The   Coots 1950
Copper Canyon   Evans 1950; Livingston, Jay 1950
Copper Colored Gal   Coots 1936; Davis 1936
Coppin' a Plea   Cahn 1941
Cops   Warren Date Unknown
Cops and Robbers   Spina 1959
Cop's Lament   Lerner, Alan Jay 1948; Weill 1948
Cop's Serenade   Lerner, Alan Jay 1948; Weill 1948
Coquette   Berlin 1928; Kahn 1928; Robin 1948; Styne 1948
Cora Angelique (Musical Comedy Queen)   Mitchell 1921;
     Pollack 1921
Cora, The Fair Chorine   Porter 1911
Coral Sea   Brown, Nacio Herb 1920; Parish 1980
Cordilia Malone   Jerome 1904; Schwartz, Jean 1904
Corduroy Road   Coleman 1960; Leigh 1960
Corky the Camel (With the Knock Knock Knees)   Coots
     1950
Corn and Bunyon Blues   Razaf 1928
Corn Beef and Cabbage I Love You   Rainger 1934; Robin
     1934
Corn Beef Hash   Rainger 1933
Corn Is Green, The   Coots 1946
Corn Keeps A-Growin', The   Lerner, Sammy 1950; Oakland
     1950
Corn Pickin'   Mercer 1939; Warren 1939
Corn Shuckin' Time   Johnson, J. Rosamond 1946
Corn Silk   Kahal 1940
Corner Chestnut and Low in Baltimore (inst.)   Blake 1969
Corner in My Heart, A   Atteridge 1910
Corner in Paradise, A   Bryan 1957
Corner of Heaven with You, A   Gershwin, George 1918
Cornet Man   Merrill 1964; Styne 1964
Cornfield Capers (inst.)   Von Tilzer 1904
Cornflower Blue   David, Mack 1962
Cornie's Pitch   Warren 1951
Corny Horn Harry   Baer 1944
Corny Talk   Revel 1940
Coronation, The   Friml 1926; Hammerstein 1926; Harbach
     1926; Howard, Joseph E. 1905
Coronation of King Neptune (inst.)   Myrow 1938
Coronation Polka, The   Coots 1952

Coronation Song   Romberg 1925; Smith, Harry B. 1925
Coronation Waltz   Parish 1937
Corporation Is Our Soul, The   Gorney 1962
Corps de Ballet   Merrill 1993; Styne 1993
Corrandoli Song   Smith, Robert B. 1914
Correspondence   Goetz 1910
Corrigan Bop   Mills 1938
Corrine Corrina   Parish 1932
Corsica   Smith, Robert B. 1907
Corsican, The   Atteridge 1912
Cortez   Strouse 1989
Coryphee, The   Herbert 1911; Smith, Harry B. 1911
Cosetta   Mitchell 1928; Motzan 1928
Cosi Cosa   Washington 1935
Cosmetics By Dupree   Dixon 1934; Wrubel 1934
Cosmic Capers (inst.)   Revel 1955
Cosmics (inst.)   Carmichael 1933
Cosmo Cosmetics   Arlen 1950; Blane 1950
Cossack Love Song (Don't Forget Me)   Gershwin, George
     1925; Hammerstein 1925; Harbach 1925
Costa Del Sol   Cahn 1964; Van Heusen 1964
Costa Rica   Ruby 1947
Coster's Glide, The   Johnson, J. Rosamond Date Unknown
Cosy Corner   Bryan 1919; Schwartz, Jean 1919
Cotcha Too-ta Mee (Alma Mater)   Cahn 1942; Styne 1942
Cote D'Azur (inst.)   Coleman 1975
Cotillion, The   Atteridge 1912
Cottage By the Moon, A   Freed, Ralph 1935
Cottage By the Sea   Coleman 1999
Cottage for Sale, A   Robison 1929
Cottage I Call Je T'Aime   Schwartz, Jean 1926
Cottage in Kent, A   Kern 1923
Cottage in the Country   Smith, Harry B. 1930
Cottage in the Country, That's the Thing, A   Donaldson
     1930
Cottage in the Hills, A   Gilbert 1932; Silver 1932
Cottage in the Rain   Waller 1938
Cottage of Content   Harbach 1931; Kern 1931
Cottin' Pickin'   Johnson, James P. 1927
Cottleston Pie   Brooks 1960
Cotton   Bloom 1935; Brown, Nacio Herb 1929; Fisher 1930;
     Freed, Arthur 1929; Koehler 1935
Cotton Blossom   Hammerstein 1927; Kern 1927
Cotton Blossom Lullaby   Kahn 1924
Cotton Blossom Time   Smith, Robert B. 1915
Cotton Club   Ellington 1938; Mills 1938
Cotton Club Express   Ellington 1937; Mills 1937
Cotton Club Stomp   Ellington 1943
Cotton Hollow Harmony   Whiting 1918
Cotton Mill Blues   Fisher 1936
Cotton Pickin' Time in Dixieland Buy a Bale   Howard,
     Joseph E. 1914
Cotton Pickin' Time in Tennessee   Howard, Joseph E. 1913
Could Be   Donaldson 1938; Gorney 1969; Mercer 1938;
     Rome 1952
Could Be I Love You (Balad de Copacabana)   Hoffman 1955
Could I   Drake 1954
Could I Be in Love   Robin 1937
Could I? I Certainly Could   Ager 1926; Yellen 1926
Could I Leave You?   Sondheim 1971
Could I Love You More   Raye 1959
Could It Be You   Brown, Nacio Herb 1943; Caesar 1943;
     Porter 1943
Could She — Could She Kiss   Hoffman 1938

Could You Be True to Eyes of Blue If You Looked Into Eyes of Brown   Cobb 1902; Edwards 1902

Could You Care for Me   Rose 1924

Could You Get Along with Me?   Caesar 1924; Gorney 1924

Could You Grow Fond of a Nice Young Blond If You Love a Sweet Brunette   Snyder 1909

Could You Love a Dreamer   Robin 1948; Styne 1948

Could You Love a Girl Like Me   Smith, Robert B. 1912

Could You Pass in Love   Gordon 1938; Revel 1938

Could You Use Me?   Gershwin, George 1930; Gershwin, Ira 1930

Could'a Been Worse   Strouse 1999

Couldn't Be   Porter 1943

Couldn't Be More in Love   Adamson 1947; McHugh 1947

Couldn't Care More   Coslow 1954

Couldn't Get In   Johnson, James P. 1947

Couldn't Help It If I Tried   Burke 1931

Couldn't I   Razaf 1928

Couldn't If I Tried   De Lange 1947

Couldn't that Baby Baby Me   Gorney 1927

Couldn't You Care for That   Dubin 1929

Couldn't You (inst.)   Drake 1958

Could've Been a Ring   Loesser 1960

Count Me In   Stept 1942

Count Me Out   Alter 1947; De Lange 1947

Count on Me   Comden and Green 1949

Count the Stars   Duke 1963

Count Your Blessings   Brooks 1948; Caesar 1934; Porter 1944

Count Your Blessings Instead of Sheep   Berlin 1954

Count Your Calories   Gordon 1953; Myrow 1953

Counterfeit Bill From Louisville   Brown, Lew 1922; Henderson 1922

Countess Dubinsky   Rose 1934

Countin' Our Chickens   Arlen 1959; Mercer 1959

Counting All the Days   Adams 1996; Strouse 1996

Counting Sheep (inst.)   Revel 1957

Counting the Sheep, Counting the Hours   Alter 1930

Country Belles   Smith, Harry B. 1903

Country Boogie   Raye 1951; Spina 1951

Country Boy Blues   Robison 1945

Country Boys and Girls   Edwards 1908

Country Bumpkin   Bergman 1963

Country Cousin, The   Bryan 1920; Youmans 1920

Country Dance   Herbert 1903; Romberg 1927

Country Fair   Strouse Date Unknown

Country Gal Blues   Robison 1975

Country House   Sondheim 1987

Country Mouse   Rodgers 1927

Country Music   Drake 1954

Country Music Holiday   Bacharach 1958; David, Hal 1958

Country Needs a Man, The   Hart 1932; Rodgers 1932

Country Style   Burke 1947; Van Heusen 1947

Country Tunes   Willson 1956

Country's Going to War, The   Kalmar 1933; Ruby 1933

Country's in the Very Best of Hands, The   DePaul 1956; Mercer 1956

Countryside (This Is the Life for a Man), The   Gershwin, George 1924

Couple of Birds (With the Same Thing in Mind), A   Johnson, Howard 1930

Couple of Caballeros, A   Arlen 1942; Harburg 1942

Couple of Kids in Love, A   Oakland 1954

Couple of Senseless Censors, A   Berlin 1924

Couple of Song and Dance Men, A   Berlin 1946

Couple of Sweethearts, A   Sigman 1949

Couple of Swells, A   Berlin 1948

Couple Upstairs, The   Davis 1925

Courage   Lerner, Sammy 1948

'Course I Will   Hammerstein 1923; Harbach 1923; Youmans 1923

Course of True Love, The   Smith, Robert B. 1912

Court Dance   Friml 1934; Rome 1940

Court House Scene   Johnson, James P. 1938

Court Is Like a Chessboard, A   Smith, Harry B. 1905

Court of Last Resort   Raye 1959

Courtin' of Elma and Ella, The   Gershwin, Ira 1949; Warren 1949

Courting, The   Loesser 1960

Courtly Etiquette   Rodgers 1923

Courtroom Cantata   Coleman 1999

Courtship Dance   Kern 1915; Smith, Harry B. 1915

Cousin Victor's Elixer   Sherman 1965

Covenant, The   Rodgers 1970

Cover a Clover with Kisses   Dixon 1930, 1931; Warren 1930, 1931

Cover Girl (That Girl on the Cover)   Gershwin, Ira 1944; Kern 1944

Cover Me Up with Sunshine, and Feather My Nest with Love   Dixon 1926; Henderson 1926

Cover Me Up with the Sunshine of Virginia   Lewis 1923; Meyer 1923; Young, Joe 1923

Cover Me with Kisses   Freed, Arthur 1925

Cover My Face with Shame   Merrill 1954

Cow and a Plough and a Frau, A   Fields 1950

Cow Bells   Mitchell 1922

Cow Cow Boogie   DePaul 1943; Raye 1943

Cow Parade, The   Caesar 1947

Cow Ponies Always Weep Just a Little   Willson 1948

Cow Song   Sondheim 1959; Styne 1959

Cowbells at Eventide   Robison 1949

Cowboy and the Senorita, The   Washington 1946

Cowboy Dan   Friend 1930

Cowboy Ditty   Johnson, Howard 1930

Cowboy from Brooklyn   Mercer 1938; Warren 1938

Cowboy Hoedown   Loesser 1956

Cowboy Serenade, A   Freed, Arthur 1931

Cowboy Song (Oh, the Rio Grande)   Weill 1936

Cowboy Songs   Caesar 1924; Conrad 1924; Harbach 1924

Cowboy, Where Are Your Riding To   Dietz 1934; Schwartz, Arthur 1934

Cowboy's Gal, A   Brown, Lew 1937, 1940; Fain 1937, 1940

Cowboy's Never Lonesome, A   Brooks 1947

Cowboy's Serenade, A   Whiting 1931

Cowboy's Time of Day   Brooks 1959

Cowpoke Song, The   Sherman 1968

Cows May Come and Cows May Go but the Bull Will Go on Forever   Von Tilzer 1915

Cows Must Cow and Bull Must Bull   Schwartz, Jean 1923

Cows Must Cow and the Bull Must Bull, The   Lewis 1923; Young, Joe 1923

Cowshed Rhapsody   Caesar 1936

Coz D'Or   Brooks 1947

Cozy Corner   Russell 1956

Cposo Dance (inst.)   Young, Victor 1955

Cracker Barrel County   Loesser 1941; Styne 1941

Crackly Grain Flakes   Mitchell 1938; Pollack 1938

Cradle in Bethlehem, A   Bryan 1960

Cradle Me with a Ha Cha Lullaby   Coslow 1933; Johnston 1933

Cradle of Democracy (inst.)   Kern 1946
Cradle of Love   Gilbert 1928
Cradle of Rhythm   Razaf 1942
Cradle of the Deep   Hart 1926; Rodgers 1926
Cradle Song   Duke 1944; Freed, Ralph 1942; Rainger 1933;
   Robin 1933
Crambambuli   Webster 1954
Cranky Old Yank (In a Clanky Old Tank), The   Carmichael
   1942
Crap Game Fugue   Gershwin, George 1935
Crashing the Golden Gate   Gorney 1929; Harburg 1929
Crazy   Bergman 1959
Crazy 'Appy Tears   Sherman 1995
Crazy As a Loon   Dubin 1940; McHugh 1940
Crazy Blues   Carmichael 1953
Crazy 'Bout My Gal   Mills 1930
Crazy 'Bout that Man I Love   Waller 1926
Crazy Dream, A   Ahlert 1934; Leslie 1934
Crazy Dreams   Magidson 1937, 1940; Oakland 1937, 1940
Crazy Elbows   Hart 1928; Rodgers 1928
Crazy Feet   Conrad 1929; Mitchell 1929
Crazy for You   Kahn 1927
Crazy He Calls Me   Russell 1949; Sigman 1949
Crazy Horse   Blane 1956; Martin 1956
Crazy Kind-a-Love   Davis 1955
Crazy Language   Fisher 1936
Crazy Love   Cahn 1957
Crazy Me   Adamson 1944; McHugh 1944
Crazy Night Ballet   Leigh 1967
Crazy Old World   Harburg 1979
Crazy Otto Polka   Brown, Lew 1955
Crazy People   Leslie 1932; Monaco 1932
Crazy Quilt   Dixon 1931; Sterling 1926; Warren 1931
Crazy Quilt Sextette, The   Harburg 1931; Rose 1931; Warren
   1931
Crazy Red Lips   DePaul 1952; Raye 1952
(Where Did He Get Those) Crazy Red Shoes   DePaul 1951;
   Raye 1951
Crazy Rhythm   Caesar 1928
Crazy Street   Adamson 1931; Lane 1931
Crazy Things You Do When You're in Love, The   Hoffman
   1950
Crazy Times   Bacharach 1960
Crazy Walk   Stept 1933
Crazy with Love   Hoffman 1936
Crazy Words, Crazy Tune, Vo-Do-De-O   Ager 1927; Yellen
   1927
Crazy World   Mancini 1982
Cream of Mush Song   Rome 1937
Cream Puff   Mancini 1962; Mercer 1962
Creation   David, Mack 1958; Livingston, Jerry 1958
Creation of the World, The   Spina 1976
Creation Scene (inst.)   Herbert 1920
Creatore   Brown, A. Seymour 1911; Young, Joe 1911
Credo (Rich Is Better)   Leigh 1967
Creep, The   Sigman 1953
Cremes   Bacharach 1960
Creole   Caesar 1934; Johnson, James P. 1962; Meyer 1934
Creole Caprice (inst.)   Coots 1946
Creole Crawl   Johnson, Howard 1927
Creole Crooning Song   Hart 1926; Rodgers 1926
Creole Gal   DePaul 1958; Raye 1958
Creole Love Song, The   Hammerstein 1927; Kern 1927
Creole Lullaby   Johnson, James P. 1946
Creole Man   Gordon 1934; Revel 1934

Creole Rhapsody   Ellington 1944
Crescendo (inst.)   Romberg 1945
Crew of the Peek-a-Boo   Herbert 1905
Cricket   Henderson 1921
Cricket on the Hearth   Herbert 1913; Smith, Robert B. 1913
Cricket Song, The   Brooks 1960
Crickets Are Calling, The   Kern 1917
Crime Doesn't Pay   Sondheim Date Unknown
Crime Will Never Pay   Robison 1950
Crimson Street   Brooks 1938
Crinoline Days   Berlin 1922
Crinoline Girl, The   Atteridge 1914; Romberg 1914
Cripple Creek   Bergman 1962
Crispus Attucks   Eliscu 1943; Gorney 1943; Razaf 1942
Crispy and Crunchy   Duke 1946
Crispy, Crunchy Crackers   Harburg 1940; Lane 1940
Criss Cross   Harbach 1926; Kern 1926
Cristo Columbo   Fisher 1910
Critic, The   Strouse 1971
Critics, The   Rome 1964
Crocodile   Akst 1919; Motzan 1919
Crocodile, A Crocodile, A   Strouse 1987
Crocodile Crawl, The   Coslow 1955; Egan 1913
Crocodile Wife   Rome 1965
Crooner - A Comic, A   Berlin 1954
Crooner's Lullaby   Coslow 1935; Johnston 1935
Crooning   Dubin 1921
Crosby, Columbo and Vallee   Dubin 1931
Cross Each "T" with Your Kisses   David, Mack 1970
Cross My Heart and Hope to Die   Von Tilzer 1917
Cross of God, The   Coots 1951
'Cross the Great Divide, I'll Wait for You   Lewis 1913;
   Meyer 1913
Cross Word Puzzles   Atteridge 1929
Cross Words, Why Were They Spoken   Dubin 1925
Cross Your Fingers   Coots 1929; Davis 1929
Cross Your Heart   DeSylva 1926; Howard, Joseph E. 1905
Cross-Country   Spina 1973
Crosses Mean Kisses   Bryan 1926
Cross-Eyed Cowboy on the Cross-Eyed Horse, The   Stept
   1937
Crossover   Johnson, James P. 1940
Crossroads   David, Mack 1960
Crosstown Bus   Bacharach 1960; David, Hal 1960
Crosswinds   Evans 1951; Livingston, Jay 1951
Cross-Word Mamma You Puzzle Me (But Papa's Gonna
   Figure You Out)   Clare 1924; Monaco 1924
Crossword Puzzle, The   Romberg 1925
Crossword Puzzle Song   Rodgers 1925
Crowd of Girls   Smith, Harry B. 1918
Crucible's Toast, The   Herbert 1944
Crucifixion, The   Livingston, Jerry 1960
Cruikshank March   Comden and Green 1947
Crumbs of Your Love, The   Razaf 1931; Waller 1931
Crusade for Freedom   McHugh 1953
Cry and You Cry Alone   Cahn 1945; Styne 1945
Cry Baby   Kalmar 1923; Rome 1948; Ruby 1923
Cry Baby Blues   Lewis 1921; Meyer 1921; Young, Joe 1921
Cry, Baby, Cry   Rome 1950
Cry for the Man   David, Hal 1960
Cry from the Dungeon   Weill 1933
Cry in the Night, A   Washington 1956
Cry Like the Wind   Comden and Green 1960; Styne 1960
Cry, the Beloved Country   Weill 1949
Cry Wolf   Bergman 1960

Cryin' for the Carolines   Lewis 1930; Warren 1930; Young, Joe 1930

Cryin' for Your Kisses   Livingston, Jerry 1955

Cryin' Mood   Razaf 1937

Cryin', Sobbin', Wailin'   Bacharach 1960

Cryin' the Blues   Mills 1928

Crying for Joy   Monaco 1948; Rose 1948

Crying for Love   Bryan 1929; Meyer 1929

Crying for Love, Laughing at Love   Alter 1929; Johnson, Howard 1929

Crying for the Moon   Leslie 1921

Crying for You   Coslow 1921

Crying in My Coffee (Since Someone Else Is Taking You to Tea)   Parish 1931

Crying in My Dreams for You   Robison 1939

Crying in the Moonlight   Gordon 1933

Crying Jane   Cohan 1916

Crying Melody   Coslow 1921

Crying Polka   Loesser 1953

Crypto-Vestimenta-Cyclo-Furo-Mania   Willson 1953

Crystal   Caesar 1956

Crystal Ball   Conrad 1926; Friml 1918; Kahn 1926

Crystal Candalabra   Harbach 1931; Kern 1931

Crystal Chandelier (inst.)   Spina 1953

Crystal Girl   Bryan 1929

Crystal Lady   Youmans 1930

Crystal Moon   Gilbert 1930

Crystal Temple, The   Rose 1938

Crystal Throne, The   Edwards 1902

Crystal Waters   Akst 1930; Baer 1930; Clarke 1930; Gilbert 1930

Csardas   Lerner, Alan Jay 1948; Weill 1948

Cuacamonga   Freed, Ralph 1954

Cuando el Amor Llama (Love Calls)   Gilbert 1933

Cuba   Goetz 1912

Cuba Libra (inst.)   Stept 1957

Cuba (You Must Be a Wonderful Place)   Dubin 1919

Cuba-Duba-Doo   Bryan 1937; Caesar 1937

Cubalero, The   Young, Joe 1931

Cuban Cabaret   Heyman 1933

Cuban Eyes   Caesar 1921

Cuban Glide, The   Edwards 1910; Smith, Harry B. 1910

Cuban Holiday   Parish 1931

Cuban Love Song   Fields 1931; McHugh 1931

Cuban Serenade   Burke 1934; Spina 1934

Cuban Song   Herbert 1897; Smith, Harry B. 1897

Cubana   Motzan 1920

Cubanella   Coslow 1922

Cubano   Fisher 1921

Cubanola Glide, The   Von Tilzer 1909

Cubanola Rumbanette   Lerner, Sammy 1934

(My) Cubist Girl   Goetz 1913

Cubist Opera, The   Herbert 1914; Smith, Robert B. 1914

Cuckoo and the Canary, The   Wrubel 1949

Cuckoo Clock, The   Carroll 1925; Freed, Arthur 1925; Gorney 1958; Young, Victor 1932

Cuckoo Clock (I Know I'm Cuckoo)   Alter 1930; Johnson, Howard 1930

Cuckoo in the Clock   Donaldson 1939; Freed, Ralph 1931; Mercer 1939

Cuckoo in the Cuckoo Clock   Coots 1955

Cuckoo Song, The   Donaldson 1929; Leslie 1929

Cuckoo Town   Atteridge 1919; Carroll 1919

Cuddle and Kiss   Kalmar 1920; Ruby 1920

Cuddle Me   Coslow 1922; Sherman 1984

Cuddle Me As We Dance   Atteridge 1923; Romberg 1923

Cuddle Up   Atteridge 1923; Berlin 1911; Caesar 1923; Gershwin, George 1923; Meyer 1927

Cuddle Up a Little Closer, Lovey Mine   Harbach 1908

Cuddled in Your Arms   DePaul 1958; Raye 1958

Cuddles and Kisses   Egan 1925; Whiting 1925

(I Want to Cuddle Some) Cuddlesome Baby   Coslow 1929; Robin 1929; Whiting 1929

Cuddle-Uddle Up   Parish 1923

Cuddling Arms   Lewis 1920; Young, Joe 1920

"Cues"   Martin 1959

Cuff of My Shirt, The   Merrill 1953

Cuh-Razy for Love   Coots 1934

Cumana   Spina 1947

Cumberland County Jail   Drake 1969

Cup Full of Tears   Merrill 1966

Cup of Coffee, A   Comden and Green 1964; Styne 1964

Cup of Coffee, A Sandwich and You, A   Dubin 1925; Rose 1925

Cup of Tea, A   Smith, Harry B. 1916

Cup of Tea (Lido Lady, Opening), A   Hart 1926; Rodgers 1926

Cupid   Coslow 1934; Gershwin, George 1918; Gershwin, Ira 1918

Cupid and I   Herbert 1897; Smith, Harry B. 1897

Cupid in the Moonlight (Trip to Nowhere)   Gilbert 1933

Cupid Is the Captain   Smith, Harry B. 1902

Cupid Keeps the Love Light Buring   Smith, Robert B. 1914

Cupid Tell Me Why   Herbert 1911; Smith, Harry B. 1911

Cupid the Conqueror   Smith, Harry B. 1911

Cupid, the Cunnin' Pandeen   Herbert 1917

Cupid, the Winner   Kern 1920

Cupid Will Guide   Herbert 1899

Cupid's After Me   Styne 1940

Cupid's Auction Sale   Smith, Harry B. 1906

Cupid's Cooking School   Kahn 1910

Cupid's I.O.U.   Bryan 1910; Meyer 1910

Cupid's Lane   Atteridge Date Unknown

Cupid's Soldiers   Atteridge 1913

Cupid's Wireless Telephone   Goetz 1910

Curad (inst.)   Strouse 1976

Curbstone Blues   Whiting 1926

Cure, The   Arlen 1959; Mercer 1959; Smith, Harry B. 1910; Smith, Robert B. 1910

Cure Me with Love   Fisher 1938

Cured   Williams 1909

Curfew Bell Has Sounded, The   Smith, Harry B. 1911

Curfew Shall Not Ring Tonight, The   Heyman 1936; Robin 1927

Curfew Song   Caesar 1945

Curfew Walk, The   Bryan 1927; Schwartz, Jean 1927

Curiosity   David, Mack 1951; Harbach 1921; Hoffman 1951; Livingston, Jerry 1951

Curly Head   Ager 1922; Lewis 1913; Meyer 1913; Yellen 1922

Curly Top   Henderson 1935; Koehler 1935

Curly Top's Birthday   Mitchell 1937; Pollack 1937

Currier and Ives   Fields 1945; Romberg 1945

Curse   Arlen 1959; Mercer 1959

Curse of the Blues   Blake 1946

Curtain Calls   Strouse Date Unknown

Curtains of Night, The   Johnson, Howard 1939

Curtsey, The   Kern 1928

Cushion Dance   David, Mack 1958; Livingston, Jerry 1958

Customer Is Always Wrong, The   Adamson 1947; McHugh 1947

Customer's Always Right, The   Dubin 1940; Fain 1940

Custom-Made Maids   Caesar 1920

Cut In   Fields 1930; McHugh 1930

Cut Off My Heels and Call Me Shorty   Raye 1940

Cut Yourself a Tiny Slice of Dream Cake   Coslow 1954

Cute Little Rumba (Rum-Ti-Di-Um-Ba Bay)   Clare 1934; Gorney 1934

Cute Little Seat Behind, The   Johnson, Howard 1916

Cute Little Summery Time   Goetz 1915; Jerome 1915; Schwartz, Jean 1915

Cute Little Things You Do, The   Hanley 1931

Cute Little Two by Four   Hammerstein 1920; Harbach 1920

Cute Little Wiggle   Hoffman 1959

Cute Peekin' Knees   Adamson 1931; Lane 1931; Schwartz, Jean 1926; Whiting 1929

Cutest Kid in Town, The   Hoffman 1931; Magidson 1931; Turk Date Unknown

Cutey   Goetz 1909

Cutey Boy   Williams 1913; Young, Joe 1913

Cutey (Jou-Jou)   Motzan 1917

Cutie   Friml 1922; Harbach 1922

Cutie Come and Tie My Tie   Smith, Harry B. 1908

Cutting the Cane   Hart 1941; Rodgers 1941

Cyclone   Adamson 1935; Donaldson 1935; Kahn 1935; Lane 1935

Cynthia   Donaldson 1939

Cynthia Jones   Smith, Harry B. 1903

Czardas (Romany Life)   Herbert 1898; Smith, Harry B. 1898

D

Da Da Da   Meyer 1927

Da Da Da Dum Dum Da Dum   Turk 1925

Da, Da, Da, My Darling   Leslie 1921; Monaco 1921

Da Da Nellie Goodbye   Fisher 1924

Daddies   Coslow 1919

Daddy   Brown, A. Seymour 1912; Friml 1922; Harbach 1922; Smith, Harry B. 1912

Daddy Boy   Motzan 1927

Daddy Buy Me a Bow Wow   Atteridge 1921; Pollack 1921; Schwartz, Jean 1921

Daddy Come Home   Berlin 1913

Daddy Darling Here's Your Angel Child   Clarke 1918; Meyer 1918

Daddy Dear   Atteridge 1918; Romberg 1918

Daddy Did a Wonderful Thing   Lewis 1912; Meyer 1912

Daddy Found You Down Beside the Garden Wall   Egan 1917

Daddy Has a Sweetheart and Mother Is Her Name   Buck 1912

Daddy Long Legs   Lewis 1919; Mercer 1955; Ruby 1919; Young, Joe 1919

Daddy Long-Legs   Martin 1952

Daddy Mine   Dubin 1918

Daddy O' Mine   Fisher 1921

Daddy Treat Your Baby Right   Razaf 1923

Daddy Won't You Please Come Home   Blake 1921; Coslow 1929; Sissle 1921

Daddy You've Been a Mother to Me   Fisher 1920

Daddy-O (I'm Gonna Teach You Some Blues)   DePaul 1948; Raye 1948

Daddy's Away   Hart Date Unknown; Rodgers Date Unknown

Daddy's Not My Daddy Anymore   Razaf 1950

Daddy's on the Phone   Styne 1940

Daddy's Report Card   Drake 1953

Dad's Lullaby (inst.)   Oakland 1958

Daffodil, The   Atteridge 1921; Romberg 1921

Daffodils and Red Red Robins   De Lange 1946

Daffy Doodle   Coots 1953

Daffy-Dill, The   Conrad 1924

Daffydils   Norworth 1910

Dagger and the Rose, The   Eliscu 1928

Dagger Dance   Herbert 1911

Dagger Dance (inst.)   Brown, Nacio Herb 1948; Warren 1935

Dago and Monk, The   Smith, Harry B. 1901

Daily Bread   Dubin 1931; Hanley 1931

Daily Dozen, The   Caesar 1924; Conrad 1924; Harbach 1924; Robin 1928

Daintiness Rag (inst.)   Johnson, James P. 1917

Dainty June and Her Farmboys   Sondheim 1959; Styne 1959

Dainty, Quainty Me   Porter 1944

Dainty Wisp of Thistledown   Hammerstein 1928; Romberg 1928

Daiquiri (inst.)   Stept 1957

Daisy   Kern 1917

Daisy and Rainbows   Harburg 1969

Daisy and the Lark, The   Hart 1920; Rodgers 1920

Daisy Bell   Johnson, Howard 1939

Daisy Days   Atteridge 1921; Kahn 1921; Pollack 1921; Schwartz, Jean 1921

Daisy Time   Young, Victor 1913

Daisy Went and Told on Me   Bryan 1915; Lewis 1915; Meyer 1915

Daisy, Why Won't You Tell   Bryan 1927

Dakota   Sherman 1968; Sissle 1928

Dame Crazy   Adamson 1956; McHugh 1956

Dames   Coslow 1930; Dubin 1934; Warren 1934

Damn Clever, These Chinese   Atteridge 1924; Romberg 1924; Schwartz, Jean 1924

Damn the Torpedoes (Full Speed Ahead)   Eliscu 1943; Gorney 1943

Damn You, Sheriff Black   David, Mack 1975

Damsel, Damsel (Prithee Come Crusading with Me)   Porter 1916

Damsel Who Done All the Dirt, The   Hart 1926; Rodgers 1926

Dan Dailey's Solo   Comden and Green 1955

Dan Sing (The China Dancing Man)   Turk 1925

Dance   Egan 1931; Gordon 1931; Revel 1931; Romberg 1919; Russell 1954

Dance a Little Closer   Lerner, Alan Jay 1983; Strouse 1983

Dance a Little More   Hanley 1916; Romberg 1916; Smith, Harry B. 1916

Dance Alone with You (Why Does Everybody Have to Cut In)   Gershwin, George 1927; Gershwin, Ira 1927

Dance and Dream   Schwartz, Jean 1940

Dance and Grow Thin   Berlin 1917; Meyer 1917

Dance at the Gym, The   Sondheim 1957

Dance Away the Night   Hammerstein 1928; Kern 1928

Dance Ballerina Dance   Russell 1947

Dance Charactuertique   Friml 1934

Dance Conceptions   Atteridge 1914; Carroll 1914; Romberg 1914

Dance Coquette   Leslie 1909

Dance, Dance, Dance   Atteridge 1917; Friml 1927; Mitchell 1921; Pollack 1921; Romberg 1917

Dance de Limbo Lower the Stick   Bergman 1957

Dance de Maitre de Ballet   Smith, Harry B. 1909

Dance de Nautica Americaine   Egan 1919; Whiting 1919

Dance Eccentric   Atteridge 1914; Romberg 1919

Dance Eccentric (inst.)   Romberg 1924

Dance Eccentrique   Atteridge 1914; Carroll 1914; Herbert 1903; Romberg 1914

Dance Eccentrique (dance)   Herbert 1913

Dance Eccentrique (inst.)   Kern 1921

Dance Extraordinaire   Atteridge 1914

Dance Fantastique   Herbert 1909

Dance Finale   Fain 1955

Dance Fool Dance   Fields 1930; McHugh 1930

Dance from Down Yonder, The   DeSylva 1925; Hanley 1925

Dance Hall Doll   Yellen 1931

Dance in the Snow   Comden and Green 1947

Dance (inst.)   Kern 1921

Dance Into His Heart   Smith, Robert B. 1912

Dance It Again with Me   Freed, Arthur 1925

Dance Like a Fool   Hammerstein 1935; Kern 1935

Dance Mamma, Dance Pappa, Dance (Marriage French Style)   Bacharach 1965; David, Hal 1965

Dance Me Again Till I'm Dreamy   Howard, Joseph E. 1942

Dance Me Around   Fields 1952; Schwartz, Arthur 1952

Dance Me Away with You   Hanley 1917

Dance Me, John   Johnson, Howard 1927

Dance Me 'Till I'm Dizzy   Bryan 1908

Dance Montage, The   Bergman 1978

Dance Must Go On (inst.), The   Kern 1938

Dance, My Darlings   Hammerstein 1935; Romberg 1935

Dance o' the Dollys   Ager 1916

Dance of Beauty   Atteridge 1924; Romberg 1924; Schwartz, Jean 1924

Dance of Bewilderment   Smith, Robert B. 1915

Dance of Danger, The   Harbach 1910

Dance of Fury (inst.)   Brown, Nacio Herb 1948

Dance of Joy   Smith, Robert B. 1915

Dance of Life   Mercer 1974

Dance of Moderate Chastity (inst.)   Warren 1956

Dance of Sacrifice (inst.)   Fain 1963; Henderson 1930

Dance of the Aborigines   Weill 1938

Dance of the Blue Danube, The   Fisher 1928

Dance of the Blues   Bryan 1919; Schwartz, Jean 1919

Dance of the Camel Boys   Harbach 1926; Kern 1926

Dance of the Crinoline Ladies   Porter 1929

Dance of the Daffodills   Alter 1929, 1930; Johnson, Howard 1930

Dance of the Dolls   Goetz 1917

Dance of the Fortune Wheel, The   Atteridge 1914

Dance of the Four Leaf Clovers   Harbach 1926; Kern 1926

Dance of the Golden Calf, The   Weill 1937

Dance of the Golden Sprite   Harbach 1926; Kern 1926

Dance of the Grizzly Bear, The   Berlin 1910

Dance of the Levants   Friml 1918

Dance of the Little Dutch Doll (inst.)   Coots 1946

Dance of the Marionettes   Herbert 1910, 1935; Kahn 1935

Dance of the Midnight Sons, The   Atteridge 1915; Romberg 1915

Dance of the Mirrors   Fain 1931; Kahal 1931

Dance of the Parisian Twist, The   Smith, Harry B. 1909

Dance of the Porters   Friml 1918

Dance of the Ragamufins   Porter 1929

Dance of the Robots   Alter 1930

Dance of the Rose, The   Friml 1917

Dance of the Squareheads   Atteridge 1915; Romberg 1915

Dance of the Tumblers   Brooks 1947

Dance of the Tumblers, The (inst.)   Weill 1940

Dance of the Two Black Crows (inst.), The   Bloom 1928

Dance of the Waitresses   Duke 1939

Dance of the Waves (Inst.)   Gershwin, George 1937

Dance of the Wooden Shoes   Magidson 1930; Washington 1930

Dance of Time (Inst.)   Warren 1956

Dance of Times   Friml 1934

Dance of Victory (inst.)   Henderson 1930

Dance of Welcome (Inst.)   Warren 1956

Dance Only with Me   Comden and Green 1958; Styne 1958

Dance Orientale   Romberg 1919

Dance Rozika (inst.)   Schwartz, Jean 1915

Dance Tangerine   Johnson, Howard 1921

Dance the Wedding Waltz with Me Before We Steal Away   Conrad 1927; Gilbert 1927

Dance to the Sun God   Dietz 1944; Duke 1944

Dance Trio (inst.)   Kern 1915

Dance Vampire   Romberg 1919

Dance We All Do for Al, The   Caesar 1931

Dance with Me   Brooks 1945; Brown, A. Seymour 1923; Coslow 1935; Romberg 1925; Smith, Harry B. 1910, 1925; Smith, Robert B. 1910

Dance with Me (At the Mardi Gras)   Berlin 1940

Dance with Me (Moisson)   Yellen 1958

Dance Your Cares Away   Davis 1922

Dance Your Troubles Away   Berlin 1922

Dance Your Way to Paradise   Gorney 1924

Danceannette   Sherman 1961

Dance-O-Mania   Gilbert 1920

Dancer of the Nile, The   Hanley 1923

Dances of the Tabarin, The   Smith, Harry B. 1908

Dancin' Around   Davis 1922; Hanley 1922

Dancin' Dan   Dubin 1923

Dancin' My Blues Away   Lerner, Alan Jay 1985

Dancin' on a Dime   Conrad 1924

Dancin' to a Jungle Drum (Let's End the Beguine)   Porter 1944

Dancing   Adams 1978; Atteridge 1923; Conrad 1924; Porter 1912; Schwartz, Jean 1923; Strouse 1978

Dancing and Dreaming   Ager 1934; Coots 1934; Davis 1934; Hoffman 1955

Dancing Around (Opening Chorus Act I)   Atteridge 1914; Romberg 1914

Dancing Around the Course   Edwards 1923; Smith, Robert B. 1923

Dancing Around the Town   Atteridge 1916; Motzan 1916, 1917; Romberg 1916

Dancing Around the U.S.A.   Atteridge 1915; Romberg 1915

Dancing at the Wedding   Herbert 1919

Dancing Blues, The   Atteridge 1921; Pollack 1921

Dancing Butterfly   Young, Joe 1932

Dancing Ceremony, The   Cohan 1908

Dancing Colors   Coslow 1924

Dancing Conversation   Caesar 1936; Schwartz, Arthur 1936

Dancing Daffodils (Inst.)   Warren 1944

Dancing Dan the Ragtime Rattling Man   Leslie 1912

Dancing Debutantes   Wrubel 1931

Dancing Detective, The   Cohan 1922

Dancing Devil   Caesar Date Unknown

Dancing Family   Atteridge 1917; Motzan 1917; Romberg 1917

Dancing Feet   Mitchell 1936; Stept 1936

Dancing Festival, The   Atteridge 1915; Romberg 1915

Dancing Fool, The   Bacharach 1979; Smith, Harry B. 1922; Snyder 1922

Dancing Fools   Mitchell 1921; Pollack 1921

Dancing for Nickels and Dimes   Loesser 1940

Dancing Hour   Gershwin, George 1925, 1927; Gershwin, Ira 1925, 1927

Dancing in the Dark   Coslow 1925; Dietz 1931; Schwartz, Arthur 1931

Dancing in the Dawn   Brown, Nacio Herb 1943; Robin 1943

Dancing in the Moonlight   Donaldson 1934; Eliscu 1929; Kahn 1934; Rose 1929; Schwartz, Arthur 1928; Youmans 1929

Dancing in the Open   Clare 1936

Dancing in the Streets   Dietz 1943; Duke 1943; Gershwin, George 1932; Gershwin, Ira 1932

Dancing Into My Heart   Freed, Ralph 1937; Lane 1937

Dancing Lady   Hart 1933; Rodgers 1933

Dancing Lesson   Dietz 1944; Duke 1944; Friml 1918; Herbert 1914; Lane 1965; Smith, Robert B. 1914

Dancing Machine   David, Hal 1973

Dancing Man   Howard, Joseph E. 1912

(I'm in a) Dancing Mood   Hoffman 1936

Dancing Mountains   Spina 1955

Dancing My Heart Away   Conrad 1938; Gilbert 1938

Dancing My Worries Away   Cohan 1922

Dancing on a Dime   Lane 1941; Loesser 1941

Dancing on Daisies   Yellen 1958

Dancing on Mars   Magidson 1930

Dancing on the Ceiling   Hart 1930; Rodgers 1930

Dancing on the Levee   Bryan 1928; Schwartz, Jean 1928

Dancing on the Stars   Ellington 1939; Mills 1939

Dancing Partner   Arlen 1954; Gershwin, Ira 1954

Dancing Partners   Baer 1937; Lewis 1937

Dancing Pirates, The   Cohan 1916

Dancing Politely   Dietz 1944; Duke 1944

Dancing Princess   Merrill 1962

Dancing Romeo, A   Atteridge 1914

Dancing 'Round   Herbert 1924

Dancing 'Round the U.S.A.   Carroll 1915; Yellen 1915

Dancing School   Romberg 1918

Dancing School-Her First Lesson (inst.), The   Herbert 1920

Dancing Shoes   Atteridge 1919; Buck 1921; Carroll 1919; Davis 1922; Gershwin, George 1921; Gershwin, Ira 1921; Hanley 1922

Dancing Spanish   Friml 1918

Dancing Step Child   Caesar 1923; Conrad 1923

Dancing Sunshine   Snyder 1909

Dancing the Blues Away   Fisher 1914; Johnson, Howard 1914

Dancing the Cotillion   Smith, Harry B. 1909

Dancing the Devil Away   Harbach 1927; Johnson, Howard 1933; Kalmar 1927, 1930; Ruby 1927, 1930

Dancing the Numbers   Howard, Joseph E. 1918

Dancing the Seasons Away   Berlin 1921

Dancing the Viennese   Coslow 1935

Dancing through Life   Mercer 1955

Dancing Time   Dietz 1924; Kern 1921, 1924

Dancing to Grandmother's Waltz   Johnson, Howard 1927

Dancing to Heaven   Bryan 1929

Dancing to Our Score   Duke 1936; Gershwin, Ira 1936

Dancing to Save Your Sole   Baer 1930; Gilbert 1930

Dancing to the Music in Our Hearts   Bullock 1937

Dancing to the Rhythm of Love   Davis 1944

Dancing to the Sugar Tune, Slip the Boys Another Dime   Gilbert 1918

Dancing Town   Dietz 1930; Schwartz, Arthur 1930

Dancing Wedding   Adamson 1930; Cohan 1911; Youmans 1930

Dancing Will Keep You Young   Romberg 1917

Dancing with Lucilla   Gershwin, Ira 1945; Weill 1945

Dancing with My Darling   Parish 1934

Dancing with My Shadow   Woods 1934

Dancing with Tears in My Eyes   Dubin 1930

Dancing With Tears in Their Eyes   Dixon 1930; Rose 1930

Dancing with the Daffodils, Down at the Garden Ball   Young, Joe 1931

Dancing with the Fools   Strouse 1986

Dancing with the One You Love   Hoffman 1933

Dancing with You   Coots 1946; Lewis 1946

Dancing with You (Dance Avec Moi)   Rome 1950

Dandies on Parade (The Sports of Gay Chicago)   Hammerstein 1927; Kern 1927

Dandilova   Evans 1959; Livingston, Jay 1959

Dandy Sandy   Fain 1965

Danger   Kahn 1925

Danger — Love at Work   Gordon 1937; Revel 1937

Danger Ahead   Lawrence 1938

Danger I Love You   Eliscu 1932

Danger in the Dark   Dubin 1939; McHugh 1939

Danger Men Blasting   Raye 1939

Dangerous   David, Hal 1955

Dangerous Age, The   Comden and Green 1964; Drake 1968; Styne 1964

Dangerous Girl   Von Tilzer 1916

Dangerous (Peligrosa)   Blane 1946

Dangerous You   Schwartz, Arthur 1936

Dangling in the Air   Hoffman 1952

Daniel in the Lion's Den   Fisher 1917

Daniel the Cocker Spaniel   Hoffman 1954; Silver 1954

Daniel the Great Social Lion   Arlen Date Unknown; Harburg Date Unknown

Danny   Raye 1962

Danny Cupid at the Bat   Harbach 1911

Danny the Dragon   Styne 1960

Danny's Hideaway   Stept 1952

Danse Bohemienne (inst.)   Friml 1928

Danse de Volstead   Atteridge 1924; Romberg 1924; Schwartz, Jean 1924

Danse Diversement   Gorney 1926

Danse Eccentrique   Atteridge 1915; Romberg 1915

Danse Erotique   Porter 1939

Danse Modern   Friml 1934

Danse Poetic   Atteridge 1915; Friml 1915

Danse Tzigane   Porter 1939

Danse Victoire   Porter 1939

Danser Calenda   Bergman 1957

Dan-Sing   Johnston 1926

Dante, Petrach and Poe   Lerner, Alan Jay 1971

Daphne   Coleman 1965; Merrill 1972

Dapper Dan   Brown, Lew 1921

Darby and Joan   Herbert 1920; Smith, Robert B. 1905

Dardanella   Fisher 1919

Dardanella Blues   Fisher 1920

Dare Me Lovely Lady   Freed, Arthur 1930

Daring Gibson Girl, The   Brown, Lew 1929; DeSylva 1929; Henderson 1929

Dark Eyes   Johnson, Howard 1940; Parish 1929; Razaf 1942

Dark Glasses   Coots 1954

Dark Haired Girl, The   Duke 1944

Dark Is the Night   David, Hal 1946; Mercer 1933

Dark Is the Night (C'est Fini)   Cahn 1951

Dark Rosaleen   Bryan Date Unknown; Fisher Date
    Unknown

Dark Side of Love, The   Fain 1975; Webster 1975

Dark Song   Arlen 1968

Darkest Before the Dawn   Mercer 1974

Darkies Have Music in Their Souls   Cahn 1935

Darkie's Lament (inst.), A   Waller 1927

Darkies Never Dream   Burke 1933; Spina 1933

Darkies' Ragtime Ball, The   Meyer 1912

Darkies' Serenade   Brown, A. Seymour 1909; Johnson,
    Howard 1915

Darkness Gives Me You Again (inst.), The   Revel 1950

Darktown Dancing School   Yellen 1918

Darktown Huskin' Bee, The   Johnson, James P. 1962

Darktown Interlude   Gordon 1945

Darktown Poker Club   Buck 1914

Darky Rhythm   Lewis 1930; Young, Joe 1930

Darlene   Russell 1952

Darlin' Do   Egan 1920; Whiting 1920

Darlin' Girl   Bergman 1965

Darling   Romberg 1918; Smith, Harry B. 1901; Sondheim
    1981

Darling, He's Playing Our Song   Lawrence 1959

Darling, How Could You   David, Mack 1951; Livingston,
    Jerry 1951

Darling, I Am Growing Young   Gorney 1969

Darling, It's Been Fun, Hasn't It   Duke 1949

Darling Jane   Sterling 1903

Darling Je Vous Adore   Friml 1952

Darling Lili   Mancini 1970; Mercer 1970

Darling Nellie Gray   Johnson, Howard 1939

Darling, Not Without You   Heyman 1936; Silver 1936

Darling of My Dreams   Parish 1935

Darling of the Day, The   Harburg 1967; Styne 1967

Darling Sue   Sterling 1907; Von Tilzer 1907

Darling the Answer Is in this Song   Fisher 1938

Darling They're Playing Our Song   Coslow 1953

Darling Will Not Grow Older   Hart 1922, 1925; Rodgers
    1922, 1925

Darn Clever These Chinese   Carmichael 1940; Mercer 1940;
    Robin 1935

Darn Fool Woman Like Me   Dubin 1930

Darn Nice Campus, A   Hammerstein 1947; Rodgers 1947

Darn that Dream   De Lange 1939; Van Heusen 1939

Das Glueck Kommt Auch Zu Dir   Woods 1950

Dat Draggy Rag   Berlin 1910; Snyder 1910

Dat Friend of Mine   Williams 1905

Dat Lovin' Touch   Lewis 1911

Dat Ol' Boy   Hammerstein 1943

Dat Ol' Devil Sea   Wrubel 1932

Date Night in Hawaii   Sherman 1960

(We Had a) Date with Destiny   Revel 1962

Dat's Love   Hammerstein 1943

Dat's Our Man   Hammerstein 1943

Dat's-A My Gal   Berlin 1911

Daugherty Is My Name   Ager 1930; Yellen 1930

Daughter of Mademoiselle   Akst 1938, 1939; Clare 1938,
    1939

Daughter of Mine   Mitchell 1919

Daughter of Molly Malone, The   Evans 1965; Livingston, Jay
    1965

Daughter of Rosie O'Grady   Donaldson 1918

Daughter of Satan   Atteridge 1922

Daughter of Silence   Sigman 1962

Daughter of Sweet Adeline   Dubin 1927; Snyder 1927

Daughter of the Devil   Adams 1983

Daughter of the Latin Quarter   Dubin 1929

Daughter of the Moon Am I, A   Von Tilzer 1903

Daughter of the Regiment, The   Edwards 1909; Smith,
    Robert B. 1909

Daughter of the Regiment (Hats Off to the Queen's
    Hussars), The   Romberg 1917

Daughters   Caesar 1925; Youmans 1925

Daughters of Mademoiselle from Armentiers, The   Pollack
    1944

Daughters of Pleasure   Rodgers 1923

Daughters of the Evolution   Hart Date Unknown; Rodgers
    Date Unknown

Dave Waldman Theme   Oakland 1954

David and Lenore   Brown, Lew 1926; DeSylva 1926;
    Henderson 1926

David Crockett (Davy Crockett) (Who Kept the Wolves Away
    from the Door When Davy Crockett Went to
    War)   Hart 1926; Rodgers 1926

David's Psalm   Weill 1937

Dawgs (Are Man's Best Friends)   Sherman 1984

Dawn   Brown, Lew 1927; David, Mack 1954; DeSylva 1927;
    Hammerstein 1927; Harbach 1927; Henderson 1927;
    Kalmar 1925; Livingston, Jerry 1954; Ruby 1925;
    Sondheim Date Unknown

Dawn Music   Porter 1916

Dawn (My Dawn of Love)   Pollack 1934; Webster 1934

Dawn of a New Day   Gershwin, George 1939; Gershwin, Ira
    1939

Dawn of Love, The   Freed, Ralph 1940; Friml 1917; Goetz
    1912; Sigman 1960

Dawn of Love (L'Alba D'Amore), The   Friml 1912; Harbach
    1912

Dawn Patrol   Lawrence 1933

Dawning of Love, The   Lawrence 1958

Day   Blane 1948

Day After Day   Dietz 1932; Gershwin, Ira 1928; Schwartz,
    Arthur 1932

Day After Day After Day   Mercer 1984

Day After Forever, The   Burke 1944; Van Heusen 1944

Day at the Races, A   Kalmar 1936; Ruby 1936

Day Before Spring, The   Lerner, Alan Jay 1945; Loewe 1945

Day Borrowed from Heaven, A   Loesser 1960

Day By Day   Blake 1961; Cahn 1945; Lewis 1927; Young, Joe
    1927; Young, Victor 1954

Day By Day in Every Way I'm Getting Better Day By
    Day   Jerome 1923; Schwartz, Jean 1923

Day Dream   Ellington 1940; Rome 1945

Day Dreaming   Kahn 1941; Kern 1941

Day Dreaming (All Night Long)   Dubin 1938; Mercer 1938;
    Warren 1938

Day Dreams   Atteridge 1924; Duke 1926; Hoffman 1956;
    Johnson, James P. 1929; Kalmar 1924, 1926; Olcott 1906;
    Romberg 1924; Ruby 1924, 1926; Schwartz, Jean 1924;
    Smith, Harry B. 1906; Smith, Robert B. 1910

Day Dreams Come True at Night   Freed, Ralph 1940

Day I Do, The   Coleman 1960; Leigh 1960

Day I Rode Half Fare, The   DeSylva 1925; Hanley 1925

Day I Say I Love You, The   Spina 1967

Day In — Day Out   Bloom 1939; Mercer 1939

Day In, Day Out   Ahlert 1931; Turk 1931

Day in the Country, A   Fain 1956; Webster 1956

Day in the Life of a Fool (Manha de Carneval), A   Sigman
    1966

Day Is Here   Herbert 1940
Day Late and a Dollar Short, A   David, Mack 1971; Fain 1973; Harburg 1973
Day of Day   Cahn 1977
Day of Days   Robin 1930; Whiting 1930
Day of the Fair   Friml 1928
Day Off, The   Sondheim 1984
Day That I Lost You   Fisher 1926
Day that the Circus Left Town, The   Leigh 1954; Spina 1954
Day the Rains Came, The   Sigman 1958
Day the Snow Is Meltin', The   Burke 1961
Day with Barbie, A   Livingston, Jerry 1963
Day Without You, A   Coslow 1933, 1934
Day You Came Along, The   Coslow 1933; Johnston 1933
Day You Fall in Love, The   Magidson 1929; Washington 1929
Day You Leave Me, The   Coleman 1975
Day You Were Born, The   Heyman 1935
Daybreak   Adamson 1943; Carmichael 1932; Duke 1941
Daybreak Blues, The   Mercer 1955
Daydreams in the Moonlight   Drake 1943
(Lonesome Little) Daylight Moon   Robison 1949
Days of Love   Webster 1966
Days of Pharaoh   Atteridge 1922
Days of the Week   Brooks 1959
Days of Wine and Roses, The   Mancini 1963; Mercer 1963
De Best I Like   Bergman 1957
De Bode o' Edicashun   Johnson, J. Rosamond 1907
De Camp Town Races   Johnson, Howard 1939
De Cards Don't Lie   Hammerstein 1943
De Chain Gang   Johnson, J. Rosamond 1938
De Corazon a Corazon (Heart to Heart)   Washington 1945
De Dago, De Org and De Wonk   Von Tilzer 1901
De Goblin's Glide   Kern 1911
De Land o' Good Times   Hammerstein 1938; Harbach 1938; Kern 1938
De Lawd Looks After All His Chillun'   Washington 1946
De Lawd's Plan   Mancini 1953
De Little Pickaninny's Gone to Sleep   Johnson, J. Rosamond 1910
De Oily Boid   Dietz 1959; Schwartz, Arthur 1959
(Nobody's Lookin' but) De Owl an' De Moon   Johnson, J. Rosamond 1901
De Right Answer   Arlen 1959; Mercer 1959
De Time to Cotch a Possom   Snyder 1909
De Trop   Friml 1912; Harbach 1912
De Ye Ken John Peel   De Lange 1938
Deacon Is Speakin', The   Hoffman 1945; Livingston, Jerry 1945
Dead Fall   Silver 1955
Dead Men Tell No Tales   Gershwin, George 1928; Gershwin, Ira 1928
Deadwood Stage (Whip-Crack-Away!), The   Fain 1953; Webster 1953
Dealer Manager Song   Coleman 1964
Deanna   Adamson 1939; McHugh 1939
Dear Algerian Land   Harbach 1926; Kern 1926
Dear Bath   Friml 1917
Dear Boy (Shall We Dance)   Stept 1946
Dear Curracloe   Friml 1917
Dear Daddy Long-Legs   Martin 1951
Dear! Dear!   Hart 1930; Rodgers 1930
Dear! Dear! Dear!   Russell 1950
Dear, Dear Departed   Johnson, Howard 1927
Dear, Dear School   Drake 1955

Dear Diary   Washington 1950
Dear Doctor   Porter 1912
Dear Eyes that Haunt Me   Smith, Harry B. 1927
Dear Fatherland Farewell   Bergman 1958
Dear Friend   Hammerstein 1944; Rodgers 1944
Dear Friends and Gentle Hearts   Carmichael 1943
Dear Good Mr. Best, The   Sterling 1897; Von Tilzer 1897
Dear Heart   Evans 1965; Howard, Joseph E. 1907; Livingston, Jay 1965; Mancini 1965
Dear Hearts and Gentle People   Fain 1950
Dear Home of Mine, Goodbye   Smith, Harry B. 1926
Dear Joe   Rome 1943
Dear June   Hart 1933; Rodgers 1933
Dear Liar   Eliscu 1960
Dear Li'l Pal   Blake 1923; Sissle 1923
Dear Little Boy of Mine   Brennan 1918
Dear Little Cafe   Kahn 1940
Dear Little Cottage   Dietz 1944; Duke 1944
Dear Little Game of Guessing   Harbach 1908
Dear Little Games of Guessing   Harbach 1911
Dear Little Ghost of Your Smile   Howard, Joseph E. 1910
Dear Little Girl (I Hope You've Missed Me)   Gershwin, George 1926; Gershwin, Ira 1926
Dear Little Girl Who Is Good, The   Herbert 1905
Dear Little Girly Girly   Cohan 1899
Dear Little Mountain Sweetheart   Waller 1944
Dear Little Peter Pan   Kern 1923
Dear Little Pup   Brennan 1929
Dear Little Shadow   David, Mack 1958
Dear Little Wise Old Bowery   Jerome 1905; Schwartz, Jean 1905
Dear Lord   Drake 1961
Dear Love, My Love   Friml 1921
Dear Mayme, I Love You   Berlin 1910; Snyder 1910
Dear Me   Hart 1925; Rodgers 1925
Dear Miss Lonely Hearts   Raye 1957
Dear Mister Sinatra   Hoffman 1943; Livingston, Jerry 1943
Dear Mom and Dad   Bergman 1979; Mancini 1979
Dear Mr. Santa Claus (If Santa Claus Were Crazy)   Willson 1963
Dear, Oh Dear   Hart 1928; Rodgers 1928
Dear Old Broadway   Berlin 1911
Dear Old Bronx   Norworth 1917
Dear Old Buddy of Mine   Davis 1926; Henderson 1926
Dear Old Correspondence School   Gershwin, Ira 1924
Dear Old Daddy Long-Legs   Brennan 1914
Dear Old Dixieland   Jerome 1905; Schwartz, Jean 1905
Dear Old Dublin   Friml 1917
Dear Old East Side   Edwards 1907
Dear Old Fairyland   Herbert 1911
Dear Old Farm   Jerome 1905; Schwartz, Jean 1905
Dear Old Fashioned Irish Songs My Mother Sang to Me   Von Tilzer 1915
Dear Old Father   Norworth 1909
Dear Old Gal, Who's Your Pal Tonight   Egan 1920; Whiting 1920
Dear Old Gown   Romberg 1918
Dear Old Heidelberg   Goetz 1912
Dear Old Lady   Von Tilzer 1923
Dear Old Manhattan Island   Jerome 1904; Schwartz, Jean 1904
Dear Old Mother Dixie   Kahn 1932
Dear Old Moulin Rouge   Atteridge 1924; Romberg 1924; Schwartz, Jean 1924
Dear Old Pal   David, Mack 1947

Dear Old Pet   Schwartz, Jean 1914
Dear Old Prison Days   Kern 1918
Dear Old Rose   Meyer 1912
Dear Old South   Edwards 1905
Dear Old Syracuse   Hart 1938; Rodgers 1938
Dear Old Wigwam Days   Rodgers 1916
Dear Old Winter Time   Brown, A. Seymour 1910
Dear Old Wisconsin Days   Howard, Joseph E. 1912
Dear, on a Night Like This   Caesar 1927; Conrad 1927
Dear One   Coots 1924
Dear Sing Sing   Jerome 1901; Schwartz, Jean 1901
Dear Sir   Fain 1930; Kahal 1930
Dear Son of Mine, My Little Lad   Caesar 1943
Dear to Me   Kahn 1928; Razaf 1950
Dear Tommy   Russell 1958
Dear, When I Met You   Brown, A. Seymour 1928
Dear Wife   Evans 1949; Livingston, Jay 1949
Dearest, Darest I   Burke 1940; Van Heusen 1940
Dearest Darling   Merrill 1967
Dearest Enemy   Hart 1925; Rodgers 1925
Dearest Little Marionette   Harbach 1911
Dearest One   Kahn 1920
Dearest, You're the Nearest to My Heart   Akst 1922; Davis 1923
Dearie   Friml 1918
Dearie If You'll Marry Me   Brown, A. Seymour 1913
Dearie, You and I   Howard, Joseph E. 1910
Dearly Beloved   Kern 1942; Mercer 1942
Death Duet   Strouse 1982
Death in the Afternoon   Dietz 1935; Schwartz, Arthur 1935
Death March   Robin 1930
Death Message   Weill 1954
Death of Jesse James   Johnson, Howard 1929
Death of Me, The   Rodgers 1970
Death of Tinker Bell   Leigh 1954
Death Valley Just Half Way to My Home   Razaf 1930
Deborah   Sigman 1968
Debts   Berlin 1933
Debutante   Ager 1915; Fields 1934; McHugh 1934; Romberg 1914, 1948; Smith, Harry B. 1914
Debutante Number One   Loesser 1941; Young, Victor 1941
Debutante One-Step   Herbert 1914; Smith, Robert B. 1914
Debutante Waltz, The   Meyer 1934
Debutante Waltz (The Deb Star Waltz)   McHugh 1964
Decca Blues   Rome 1944
Deceiving Blue Bird   Coots 1927; Dubin 1927
December Birthday Song   Caesar 1940
Deck the Halls   Cahn 1972; Van Heusen 1972
Declaration   Parish 1965
Declaration Day   Henderson 1934; Koehler 1934
Decorating Eliza   Lerner, Alan Jay 1956; Loewe 1956
Decoy, The   Loesser 1937
Dedicated to You   Cahn 1936
Dedication   Drake 1954
Deduco Commercial   Robin 1947
De-Dum-Dum   Bryan 1927; Schwartz, Jean 1927
Deed I Do Do Blues   Johnson, James P. 1938
Deedle Deedle Dum   Coslow 1922; Mills 1922
Deedle, Deedle Dumpling (The Beggar Woman's Lullaby)   Sondheim 1979
Deedle-Dee-Dum Teasy Easy Tune   Razaf 1947
Deefeecult for You — Easy to Me   Hoffman 1959
Dee-lightful Is the Word   Burke 1961
Deenah, My Argentine Rose   Dubin 1920
Deep Are the Roots (Of My Love)   Razaf Date Unknown

Deep Blue   Styne 1927
Deep Blue Water   Robison 1948
Deep Down Inside   Coleman 1962; Leigh 1962
Deep Down Inside You   Dietz 1944; Duke 1944
Deep Down 'n Your Heart   Friend 1947
Deep Elm, You Tell 'Em I'm Blue   Robison 1925
Deep End   Blake 1950
Deep Forest (A Hymn to Darkness)   Razaf 1933
Deep in a Dream   De Lange 1938; Van Heusen 1938
Deep in My Dreams — Deep in the Night   Young, Joe 1932
Deep in My Heart   Youmans 1924
Deep in My Heart Dear   Romberg 1924, 1954; Webster 1954
Deep in My Soul   Razaf Date Unknown
Deep in the Blues   Parish 1940
Deep in the Dark   Sherman 1973
Deep in the Dark of the Night   Livingston, Jerry 1933
Deep in the Heart of the Rockies, Just Across the Great Divide   Freed, Ralph 1932
Deep in the Heart of the South   Lawrence 1937
Deep in the Shadows   Adamson 1939; Duke 1939
Deep in Your Eyes   Dixon 1932; Parish 1931; Warren 1932
Deep in Your Heart   Snyder 1930
Deep Purple   Parish 1939
Deep Rapture   Adamson 1964; Fain 1964
Deep River   Robison 1953
Deep River (inst.)   Johnson, James P. 1944
Deep Sea Divin' Papa   Arlen 1932; Koehler 1932
Deep Silence   Razaf Date Unknown
Deep South in My Heart   Mercer 1932
Deep Summer Music   Robison 1944
Deep Water   Bryan 1931; Schwartz, Jean 1931
Deeper   Harbach 1920
Deeper than the Sea   Fain 1929
Deeply   Bacharach 1961
Deevil, Devil, Divil, The   Russell 1945; Sigman 1945
Defense   Leigh 1971
Defiance (inst.)   Willson 1929
Defying the Storm   Smith, Harry B. 1911; Smith, Robert B. 1911
Deirdre   Mercer 1966
Del Icado   Lawrence 1952
Delaware   Dixon 1925; Henderson 1925; Rose 1925
Delectable Dream   Evans 1950; Livingston, Jay 1950
Delfy's Song   Martin 1969
Deli   Caesar 1921
Delicatessen (A Way of Life) (Gaiety)   Cahn 1965; Van Heusen 1965
Delicious Delirium   Revel 1942
Delighted, I'm Sure   Sondheim 1954
Delighted to Meet You   Coslow 1937
Delilah   Evans 1967; Fisher 1926; Leigh 1955; Livingston, Jay 1967; Rose 1927
Delilah Done Me Wrong (The No Haircut Song)   Rome 1965
Delishious   Gershwin, George 1931; Gershwin, Ira 1931
Delivery 'Mon', What Is in That Bag You Got   Brown, Lew 1948
Dell, The (inst.)   Warren 1956
Della   Edwards 1904; Smith, Robert B. 1904
Della's Entrance (Whatcha Sayin' Della?)   Arlen 1959; Mercer 1959
Delphine   Robin 1929
Delta Iota Mu   Sondheim Date Unknown
Delta Serenade   Ellington 1935; Mills 1935
Delta's Lament   Mercer 1964

Deluge   David, Mack 1966

Delusion   Bryan 1937

Deming, New Mexico, High School Wildcats' Song   Brown, Nacio Herb 1959

Democracy's Call   Weill 1936

Democratic Club Dance   Strouse 1986

Demon in the Compass   Harburg 1971

Demon of the Deep, The   Smith, Harry B. 1900

Demon Rum   Gershwin, George 1947; Gershwin, Ira 1947

Demonstrate   Edwards 1923; Smith, Robert B. 1923

Den of Iniquity   Hart 1940; Rodgers 1940

Dennis the Menace   Hoffman 1953

Dentist Song (Easy, Mister, Easy), The   Razaf 1940

D-E-N-V-E-R   Spina 1973

Denver Police, The   Willson 1960

Department Store Opening   Alter 1930; Johnson, Howard 1930

Departure   Comden and Green 1982

Depends on Beautiful Clothes   DeSylva 1919; Gershwin, George 1919

Der Deitcher's Dog (Where, O Where Has My Little Dog Gone)   Johnson, Howard 1939

Der Deutscher Rag   Lewis 1910

Derby Day Honeymoon   Goetz 1952

Derby Day in Dixie   Egan 1918; Whiting 1918

Dere's a Cafe on de Corner   Hammerstein 1943

Dere's Yellow Gold on de Trees   Cahn 1956

Derry Down Dilly   Mercer 1952

Derry-Up, Derry-Down Dey   Willson 1950

Descriptive Song   Smith, Harry B. 1900

Desdamona   Brown, Nacio Herb 1936; Freed, Arthur 1936

Desdie, My Desdemona   Jerome 1905; Schwartz, Jean 1905

Desert Flame, The   Rome 1950

Desert Gold   Lewis 1919; Young, Joe 1919

Desert Island   Schwartz, Jean 1919

Desert Lullaby, The   Hart Date Unknown; Rodgers Date Unknown

Desert of Dreams   Brennan 1949

Desert Rose   Bryan 1922; Schwartz, Jean 1922

Desert Sands   Heyman 1955

Desert Song, The   Hammerstein 1926; Harbach 1926; Romberg 1926

Designing Woman   Brooks 1957

Desire   Razaf 1926; Robin 1936; Romberg 1948

Desiree   Oakland 1953; Raye 1953

Desiree (inst.)   Warren 1976

Desperate Blues, The   Johnson, James P. 1922

Desperate Hours, The   Bacharach 1955

Dessert Finale   Gordon 1945; Warren 1945

Destination Is Love   Leigh 1965

Destination Unknown   Razaf 1944

Destiny   Bryan Date Unknown; DePaul 1944, 1958; Fisher Date Unknown; Pollack 1928; Raye 1958

Detectiveland   Strouse 1991

Determined Woman, A   Rome 1948

Detroit   Sherman 1967

Deuce Young Man, The   Herbert 1913

Deutschland   Bryan 1907

Devil and the Deep Blue Sea, The   Herbert 1917

Devil Can't Hurt Me   Razaf 1940

Devil Dance, The   Rose 1937

Devil Does a Jig, The   Oakland 1961

Devil Dogs in the Air   Martin 1943

Devil Has Bought Up All the Coal, The   Berlin 1918

Devil in Disguise   Heyman 1934; Romberg 1934

Devil in the Moon   Mills 1935

Devil in You Is Strong, The   Dietz 1944; Duke 1944

Devil Is Afraid of Music, The   Robison 1926

Devil May Care   Burke 1940; Warren 1940

Devil Me, Angel You   Bryan 1952

Devil with the Devil (The Devil Don't Frighten Me), The   Ruby 1960

Devil's Child   Adams 1957; Strouse 1957

Devil's Holiday   Mills 1935

Devil's in Your Toes, The   Caesar 1922

Devil's Serenade, The   Friend 1953; Howard, Joseph E. 1907

Devoted to You   Washington 1936; Wrubel 1936

Devotion   Brooks 1951

(What Do We Do on a) Dew, Dew, Dewy Day   Johnson, Howard 1927

Dew on the Heather, The   Smith, Harry B. 1904; Smith, Robert B. 1904

Dew Was on the Rose, The   Gershwin, Ira 1946; Schwartz, Arthur 1946

Dewey Blues   Johnson, James P. 1938

Di Quando In Quando   Drake 1982

Diabolo   Atteridge 1916

Diamond, a Pearl and an Ermine Wrap, A   Fain 1956

Diamond Earrings (inst.)   Alter 1955

Diamond for Carla, A   Fain 1959; Webster 1959

Diamond Head   David, Mack 1962

Diamond in the Rough   Duke 1968; Hammerstein 1928; Youmans 1928

Diamond Jubilee Song   Ellington 1940

Diamonds Are a Girl's Best Friend   Robin 1948; Styne 1948

Diamonds Don't Care Who Wear Them   Cobb 1900; Edwards 1900

Diamonds in the Starlight   Blane 1960; Martin 1960

Diamonds on the Moon   Kahn 1938; Romberg 1938

Diana   Atteridge 1915; Duke 1946; Romberg 1915

Diane   Pollack 1927

Diavolo   Hart 1935; Rodgers 1935

Dick Gilbert Theme   Oakland 1954

Dick Smith Theme   Oakland 1954

Dickey Bird Song, The   Dietz 1947; Fain 1947

Dickey Birds   Coots 1923

Dictation   Gorney 1926

Dicty's on 7th Avenue (inst.)   Blake 1961

Did an Angel Kiss You (The Day You Were Born)   Freed, Ralph 1938

Did Anyone Call   Sigman 1952

Did Anyone Ever Tell You?   Adamson 1937; Cahn 1941; McHugh 1937

Did He Write That?   Warren 1978

Did I Get Stinkin' at the Club Savoy   Harburg 1936

Did I Just Fall in Love?   Blane 1964; Martin 1962, 1964

Did I Remember (To Tell You I Adore You)?   Adamson 1936; Donaldson 1936

Did I Say No   Fain 1928; Kahal 1928

Did My Heart Beat, Did I Fall in Love   Meyer 1933

Did the Moon Tap on Your Window   Parish 1946

Did You Close Your Eyes?   Merrill 1957

Did You Ever Get Stung?   Hart 1938; Rodgers 1938

Did You Ever Have One of Those Days   Cahn 1950

Did You Ever Have the Feeling You're Flying   Hoffman 1934

Did You Ever Hear that in Turkey?   Williams 1910

Did You Ever Look at You   Coleman 1966; Fields 1966

Did You Ever See a Dream Walking?   Gordon 1933; Revel 1933

Did You Happen to Find a Heart   Pollack 1942

Did You Happen to Find a Heart (This Morning)   Magidson 1942; Pollack 1944

Did You Have Fun   McHugh 1952

Did You Know?   Cahn 1984; Drake 1954

Did You Know It Was Me   Bergman 1973

Did You Mean It   Bryan 1927; Dixon 1936; Schwartz, Jean 1927

Did You Mean What You Said Last Night   Lewis 1932; Young, Joe 1932

Did You Notice   Drake 1953

Did You See a Couple of WAVES (Of G.I. Guys)   Drake 1953

Did You Try the Pasta   Drake 1953

Diddle-daddle   Duke 1950; Rome 1950

Did-ee Did-ee Do Right By You?   Clare 1950

Did-Ja   Waller 1946

Didja Ever See the Like?   Hammerstein 1920; Harbach 1920

Didn't I Tell You   Monaco 1927; Rose 1927

Didn't It?   Brown, Lew 1927; Friend 1927

Didn't The Angels Sing? (Martin Luther King)   Blake 1968; Sissle 1968

Didn't You Believe?   Kern 1921

Die, Die, Die Like a Soldier   Herbert 1917

Die Glocke Toent Bim-Bam   Caesar 1931

Die Neue Art   Goetz 1912

Die Susse Pariserin   Kern 1913

Diet Song   Comden and Green 1974; Styne 1974

Different Days   Romberg 1922

Different Kinds of Weather   Herbert 1908; Smith, Harry B. 1908

Diff'rence of a Drink or Two, The   Atteridge 1910

Dig, Dig, Dig, Dig for Your Supper   Gordon 1950; Revel 1950; Warren 1950

Dig Dig Dig for Victory   Styne 1942

Dig, Sister, Dig   Hammerstein 1920; Harbach 1920

Dig You Later (A-Hubba-Hubba-Hubba)   Adamson 1945; McHugh 1945

Dig You Most   Mercer 1953

Diga Diga Do   Fields 1928; McHugh 1928

Digah's Stomp (inst.)   Waller 1928

Dignity   Pollack 1914

Dignity (We Got to Get Us Some)   Willson 1964

Dill Pickles   Bryan 1910

Dilly   Duke 1955

Dim Cafe, A   David, Mack 1952; Livingston, Jerry 1952

Dime and a Dollar, A   Evans 1954; Livingston, Jay 1954

Dimple on My Knee, The   Gershwin, George 1931; Gershwin, Ira 1931

Dimples   Coleman 1962; Leigh 1962

Dimples and Cherry Cheeks   Oakland 1951; Raye 1951

Dinah   Akst 1925; Lewis 1925; Turk Date Unknown; Young, Joe 1925

Dinah (Dianna Lee)   Blake 1930; Razaf 1930

Dinah Lou   Bloom 1935; Koehler 1935

Dinah's Daughter   Fields 1934; McHugh 1934

Ding Dong   Atteridge 1913; Berlin 1918; Smith, Harry B. 1934

Ding Dong Daddy Time   Livingston, Jerry 1961

Ding Dong Dell Spells I Love You   Brown, Lew 1927; Friend 1927

Ding Dong Ding   Hammerstein 1922; Mitchell 1922

Ding Dong, It's Kissing Time   Kern 1920

Ding Dong, Sing a Song   Styne 1943

Ding-A-Ling   Mancini 1957

Dingbat, the Singing Cat   Hoffman 1946

Ding-Dong Blues   Koehler 1951

Ding-Dong! The Witch Is Dead   Arlen 1939; Harburg 1939

Ding-Dong-Dell (The Bells of Chinatown)   Hanley 1921

Dingle, Dingle, Dingle   Conrad 1912; Smith, Harry B. 1912; Young, Joe 1912

Dingle Ling, Dingle Ling   Merrill 1965; Styne 1965

Dingle Song, The   David, Mack 1964

Dingle-Dee   Coots 1951

Dining Car   Willson 1953

Dining Out   Kern 1908

Dinner   Porter 1916

Dinner at Eight   Fields 1933; McHugh 1933

Dinner Is Served   Dietz 1963; Schwartz, Arthur 1963

Dinner Song   Gershwin, Ira 1946; Schwartz, Arthur 1946

Dinny's Serenade   Herbert 1917

Din't Cha Mother Tell You Nothin'?   Kalmar 1941; Ruby 1941

Dip in the Ocean, A   Smith, Harry B. 1901

Dip Your Bread in a Bucket of Rum   Bryan 1930

Dip Your Brush in the Sunshine and Keep on Painting Away   Razaf 1928

Dip Your Pen in Sunshine and Write a Letter to the One You Love   Coots 1955

Diplomacy   Herbert 1899; Howard, Joseph E. 1905; Smith, Harry B. 1899, 1901

Dipping in the Moonlight   Caesar 1924

Direct from Vienna   Merrill 1961

Dirge for a Soldier   Weill 1938

Dirge for Two Veterans   Weill 1942

Dirty Dingus Magee   David, Mack 1970

Dirty Dozens   Brooks 1970

Dirty Face   Martin 1962

Dirty Hands Dirty Face   Clarke 1921; Leslie 1921; Monaco 1921

Dirty Pitchers, Dirty Books   Martin 1951

Dis Flower   Hammerstein 1943

Dis Is de Day   Arlen 1959; Mercer 1959

Dis Little While   Arlen 1959; Mercer 1959

Disappointed   Freed, Arthur 1928; Friend 1928

Disappointed and Disgusted   Ahlert 1938; Young, Joe 1938

Disappointed in Love   Razaf 1934

Disappointed Moon   Brown, Nacio Herb 1930; Eliscu 1930

Disappointed Suitors   Kalmar 1928; Ruby 1928

Disco for Margo   Adams 1970; Strouse 1970

Discord in "A" Flat   Oakland 1931

Discouraged Over You   Burke 1958; Van Heusen 1958

Disenchanted Castle   Leigh 1965

Disenchanted (inst.)   Alter 1976

Disgustingly Rich   Hart 1940; Rodgers 1940

Dish Ran Away with the Spoon, The   Robin 1932

Disillusioned   Webster 1933

Dismal Mood, A   Razaf 1948

Dismissal Whistle   Caesar 1928

Disneyland '61   Sherman 1961

Disneyland Anniversary March   Sherman 1965

Disordered Dream, A   Johnson, James P. 1950

Disraeli   Martin 1972

Dissapated Kitten, The   Smith, Harry B. 1903

Dissatisfied Blues   Blake 1930; Razaf 1930

Dissertation on the State of Bliss (Love and Learn)   Arlen 1954; Gershwin, Ira 1954

Dissolves   Arlen 1959; Mercer 1959

Distance to the Moon, The   Spina 1955

Distant Melody   Comden and Green 1954; Styne 1954

Ditto (inst.)   Strouse 1949

Divali Festival, The   Fain 1960; Webster 1960

Divertissement   Atteridge 1914; Burke 1946; Romberg 1914; Van Heusen 1946

Divertissement Parisien (inst.)   Razaf 1948

Dixiana   Davis 1930

Dixiana Rose, The   Friml 1913; Harbach 1913

Dixie   Coslow 1921; Fields 1928; McHugh 1928; Revel 1942

Dixie After Dark   Mills 1934; Oakland 1934; Parish 1934

Dixie Ann in Afghanistan   Blake 1940; Razaf 1940

Dixie Anna   McHugh 1936

Dixie Bungalow   Bryan 1925; Meyer 1925; Rose 1925

Dixie Cinderella   Razaf 1929; Waller 1929

Dixie Dan   Cobb 1907

Dixie Doodle Dandy   Johnson, James P. 1929

Dixie Doorway   Parish 1932

Dixie Down Beat   Mills 1947

Dixie Dreams   Clarke 1924, 1938; Johnston 1924, 1938; Meyer 1924; Turk 1924

Dixie Highway   Donaldson 1922; Kahn 1922

Dixie, I Love You   Howard, Joseph E. 1907

Dixie Isn't Dixie Any More   Bloom 1936

Dixie Isn't Dixie Anymore   Mercer 1936

Dixie Jamboree   Johnson, Howard 1929

Dixie Love   Goetz 1912

Dixie Love Song   Goetz 1912

Dixie Moon   Blake 1924; Sissle 1924

Dixie Rose   Caesar 1918

Dixie Rose (Swanee Rose)   DeSylva 1918

Dixie, the Flag and You   Goetz 1921; Meyer 1921

Dixie Twister   Johnson, Howard 1930

Dixie Vagabond, The   Donaldson 1927; Kahn 1927

Dixie Volunteers, The   Leslie 1917; Ruby 1917

Dixie Wildflowers   Clarke 1924; Johnston 1924; Meyer 1924; Turk 1924

Dixie-Anna   Koehler 1936

Dixieland   Mercer 1959

Dixieland Band, The   Mercer 1935

Dixieland Daddy   Merrill 1950

Dixieland Echoes   Johnson, James P. 1928

Dixie's Favorite Son   Brown, Lew 1924

Dizzily, Busily   Gershwin, Ira 1945; Weill 1945

Dizzy Baby   Porter 1928

Dizzy Feet   Kalmar 1929; Ruby 1929

D.J. Ghost   Coots 1963

Djer Kiss   Ager 1918

Do a Duet   Schwartz, Jean 1926

Do a Little Rumba with Me   Rainger 1935; Robin 1935

Do As You Would Be Did By   Hoffman 1955

Do Buy Some Candy, Sir   Romberg 1917

Do, Do, Do   Gershwin, George 1926; Gershwin, Ira 1926

Do Do Do What Your Heart Says   Lawrence 1955

Do I?   Akst 1922; Lewis 1922; Young, Joe 1922

Do I Do Wrong?   Kern 1928

Do I Have to Say More   Bacharach 1962; David, Hal 1962

Do I Hear a Waltz?   Rodgers 1965; Sondheim 1965

Do I Hear You Saying "I Love You"?   Hart 1928; Rodgers 1928

Do I Know What I'm Doing?   Ager 1930; Fisher 1926; Kalmar 1929; Lawrence 1939; Pollack 1943; Rose 1926; Ruby 1929; Yellen 1929, 1930

Do I Know What I'm Doing While I'm in Love   Coslow 1929; Robin 1929, 1933; Whiting 1929

Do I Know Why   Fields 1931; McHugh 1931

Do I Love My Teacher   Dubin 1935; Warren 1935

Do I Love You   DePaul 1951; Hart 1943; Porter 1939; Rainger 1934; Raye 1951; Robin 1934

Do I Love You Because You're Beautiful?   Hammerstein 1957; Rodgers 1957

Do I Love You when There's Nothing but Yes in Your Eyes   Goetz 1925

Do I Make You Happy?   Merrill 1978

Do I Need You   Cahn 1942; Harburg 1962; Sigman 1957

Do I Really Deserve It from You   Clare 1930; Williams 1931

Do It Again   Berlin 1912; DeSylva 1922; Gershwin, George 1922

Do It for Charity   Brown, Lew 1927; Friend 1927

Do It for Me   Harbach 1917

Do It in the Dark   Lewis 1912; Meyer 1912

Do It Now   Kern 1918; Lawrence 1942; Williams 1911

Do It the Hard Way   Hart 1940; Rodgers 1940

Do It Yourself   Comden and Green 1960; Fain 1957; Styne 1960; Webster 1957

Do Me a Favor   Ellington 1966; Lawrence 1934

Do Me a Favor, Lend Me a Kiss   Razaf 1932; Waller 1932

Do Me a Favor Please   Lewis 1949; Meyer 1949

Do My Mother a Favor   Davis 1951

Do Not Be Afraid of Love   Arlen 1968

Do Nothin' Till You Hear from Me   Ellington 1943; Russell 1943

Do Puppies Go to Heaven   Merrill 1964; Styne 1964

Do, Re, Mi   Hammerstein 1920; Harbach 1920

Do Say You Do   Adamson 1932; Gordon 1932; Revel 1932

Do Something   Drake 1953; Stept 1929; Wrubel 1949

Do Something Different   Gordon 1931; Revel 1931

Do Something The Girl You Dream About   Howard, Joseph E. 1908

Do Svedanya   Merrill 1993; Styne 1993

Do that Doo-Da   Brennan 1926

Do that Thing   Akst 1927; Davis 1927

Do the Black Bottom with Me   Meyer 1927

Do the Buckaroo   Rainger 1938; Robin 1938

Do the Funny Fox Trot   Carroll 1914

Do the New Fangled Spelling Bee   Fain 1946

Do the Truck   Cahn 1935

Do These Old Eyes Deceive Me   Adamson 1943; Styne 1943

Do Unto Others   Drake 1947

Do We Have to Say Goodnight   David, Mack 1947; Hoffman 1947; Livingston, Jerry 1947

Do We Understand Each Other   Eliscu 1929; Rose 1929; Youmans 1929

Do what the Bluebirds Do   Caesar 1930

Do What You Did Last Night   Razaf 1928

Do What You Do   Gershwin, George 1929; Gershwin, Ira 1929; Kahn 1929

Do What You Like!   Robin 1931

Do What You Like With Me   Baer 1929; Gilbert 1929

Do What You Wanna Do   Duke 1940

Do What Your Heart Tells You   Parish 1953

Do Ya Wanna Little Iss-kay   Magidson 1929; Washington 1929

Do You   Dubin 1943

Do You Believe (I Do)   Davis 1958

Do You Believe in Fairy Tales?   David, Mack 1941

Do You Believe in Flirting   Atteridge 1910

Do You Believe in Love at First Sight   Kahn 1931

Do You Believe Your Eyes - Or Do You Believe Your Baby?   Berlin 1930

Do You Call That a Buddy   Raye 1941

Do You Do, Do You Do, Do You Do, Do You Don't, Do You Don't, Do You Don't   Drake 1945

Do You Don't You Love Me   Koehler 1928

Do You Ever Go to Boston?   Merrill 1967

Do You Follow Me?   Herbert 1899; Smith, Harry B. 1899

Do You Have to Go   Waller 1944

Do You Hear Music?   DePaul 1943; Raye 1943

Do You Hear What I Hear   Hoffman 1940

Do You Intend to Put an End to a Sweet Beginning Like This   Ahlert 1935; Young, Joe 1935

Do You Know?   Herbert 1913

Do You Know a Better Way to Make a Living   Rome 1950

Do You Know Any Chicks in Chicago   Silver 1947

Do You Know Dan McPherson   Fisher 1926

Do You Know the Way to San Jose   Bacharach 1968; David, Hal 1968

Do You Know What It Means to Be Lonely   Hoffman 1946; Livingston, Jerry 1946

Do You Know What It Means to Miss New Orleans?   Alter 1947; De Lange 1947

Do You Know Why?   Burke 1940; Van Heusen 1940

Do You Like Me?   Loesser 1937

Do You Love As I Love   Caesar 1923, 1924, 1927

Do You Love Me?   Hart 1925; Rodgers 1925; Ruby 1946

Do You Mind If I Fall in Love   Coots 1929

Do You Notice Anything?   Hart 1926; Rodgers 1926

Do You Play, Madame?   Whiting 1930

Do You Really Mean to Go?   Hart 1926; Rodgers 1926

Do You Recall?   Parish 1957

Do You Remember   Brown, Nacio Herb 1955; Coots 1922; Kalmar 1939; Ruby 1939

Do You Remember Jimmy Jones   Hoffman 1943; Livingston, Jerry 1944

Do You Still Love Me   Wrubel 1942

Do You Take This Woman for Your Lawful Wife   Sterling 1913; Von Tilzer 1913

Do You Tell Her the Things You Told Me   David, Mack 1938; Meyer 1938

Do You Think I Came Here for My Health   Sigman 1952

Do You Think I Could Grow on You?   Gordon 1929; Silver 1929; Snyder 1929

Do You Think It's Fair   Howard, Joseph E. 1946

Do You Think of Me?   Mills 1928

Do You Think of Me Once in a While   Friend 1929; Silver 1929

Do You Think that I Could Grow on You?   Silver 1930

Do You Wanna Jump, Children?   Van Heusen 1938

Do You Want to See Paris?   Porter 1929

Do You Want Us to Lose?   Norworth 1917

Do You Wonder   Raye 1956

Do You Wonder that I Love You?   Mills 1928

Do Your Duty, Doctor   Berlin 1909; Snyder 1909

Do Your Moonlight Shopping Early   Oakland 1951; Webster 1951

Do Your Stuff   Rainger 1935; Robin 1935

Doc   Yellen 1948

Doctor, A   Strouse 1999

Doctor and Squire's Lament   Styne 1985

Doctor Brown   Bryan 1912

Doctor Jim   Robison 1949

Doctor, Lawyer, Indian Chief   Carmichael 1945; Webster 1945

Doctor Munyon   Goetz 1907

Doctor Quackenbush   Kalmar 1936; Ruby 1936

Doctor Rhythm   Burke 1938; Monaco 1938

Doctor Song   Clare 1936

Doctor Sunshine's Almanac   Merrill 1955

Doctor Tinkle Tinker   Harbach 1911

Doctor's Soliloquy, A   Fain 1960; Webster 1960

Dodge Brothers March   Herbert 1920

Dodgers, The   Cahn 1963; Van Heusen 1963

Dodger's Song, The   Caesar 1947

Dodging the Clouds   Ahlert 1930; Turk 1930

Dodie   Freed, Ralph 1956

Dodie Ann   Sherman 1960

Dodo Bird in the Banyan Tree, The   David, Mack 1954

Do-Do-Re-Do   Comden and Green 1944

Does a Duck Love Water?   Duke 1936; Gershwin, Ira 1936

Does an Elephant Love Peanuts   Hanley 1929

Does Anybody Want a Blonde   Edwards 1907; Smith, Robert B. 1907

Does Anybody Want My Fido   Von Tilzer 1953

Does Anybody Want to Take Charlie's Place   Sterling 1911; Von Tilzer 1911

Does Baby Feel All Right?   Burke 1946; Van Heusen 1946

Does Baby Want to Be Babied Now   Alter 1930; Johnson, Howard 1930

Does He Know   Rome 1954

Does It Belong to Me?   Ruby 1951

Does It Make Any Diff'rence to You   Kahn 1927

(I Ask You) Does It Pay to Be a Lady?   Eliscu 1929; Rose 1929; Youmans 1929

Does It Really Matter?   Cahn 1970; Styne 1970

Does It Show   Strouse 1958

Does My Baby Love Nobody but Me   Ager 1930; Yellen 1930

Does Santa Claus Believe in You   Cahn 1959; Van Heusen 1959

Does She?   Dixon 1924; Henderson 1924

Does She Love Me — Positively Absolutely   Coslow 1927

Does She or Doesn't She Love Me and Only Me   Caesar 1958

Does the Moon Shine Through the Tall Pine   Loesser 1940; Young, Victor 1940

Does the Spearmint Lose It's Flavor on the Bed Post Overnight   Rose 1924

Does This Go On Forever?   Arlen 1929; Coots 1929

Does You Wanna Go to Hebben   Akst 1936; Clare 1936

Does Your Heart Beat for Me   Parish 1936

Does Your Mother Know You're Out Mademoiselle   Hanley 1919

Doesn't Anybody Love Me   Davis 1954

Doesn't that Mean Anything to You   Loesser 1934

Dog Eat Dog   Arlen 1959; Mercer 1959

Dog Face   Loesser 1944

Dog Is a Man's Best Friend, A   Mercer 1951

Dog Song, The   Brown, Nacio Herb 1949; Heyman 1947

Doggie, Take Your Time   Cahn 1941

Doggone That Chilly Man   Berlin 1911

Dog's Life, A   David, Hal 1961

Doin' All Right   Rainger 1936; Robin 1936

Doin' the 1940   Lerner, Sammy 1939; Oakland 1939

Doin' the Bob Hope Show   Coleman 1988

Doin' the Campus Crawl   Mills 1929

Doin' the Chamberlain   Dubin 1939; McHugh 1939

Doin' the Crazy Walk   Ellington 1930; Mills 1930

Doin' the Cut-In   Gilbert 1936

Doin' the Dumb-Bell   Gordon 1934; Revel 1934

Doin' the French Can-Can   Merrill 1955

Doin' the Gorilla   Robin 1927

Doin' the Mozambique   Blake 1930; Razaf 1930
Doin' the New Low-Down   Fields 1928; McHugh 1928
Doin' the New York   Oakland 1931
Doin' the Raccoon   Coots 1929; Magidson 1929; Robin 1929;
    Whiting 1929
Doin' the Reactionary   Rome 1937
Doin' the Rhumbatamba   Wrubel 1931
Doin' the Rumba   Mills 1931
Doin' the Sigma Chi   Conrad 1930
Doin' the Socialite   Akst 1939; Clare 1939
Doin' the Suzi-Q   Coots 1936; Davis 1936
Doin' the Town   Davis 1957
Doin' What Comes Natur'lly   Berlin 1946
Doin' what I Please   Johnson, James P. 1931; Razaf 1931,
    1933; Waller 1933
Doin' What You're Doin'   Kalmar 1933; Ruby 1933
Doing a Little Clog Dance (Doing a Little Waltz Clog)
    Hart 1930; Rodgers 1930
Doing Good   Adams 1966; Strouse 1966
Doing My Bit   Atteridge 1917; Romberg 1917
Doing the Apache   Atteridge 1923; Romberg 1923; Schwartz,
    Jean 1923
Doing the Boom Boom   Conrad 1929; Mitchell 1929
Doing the Derby   Conrad 1930
Doing the Dumbbell   Gordon 1931; Revel 1931
Doing the Eddie Cantor   Atteridge 1922; Schwartz, Jean
    1922
Doing the Light Fantastic Alley Style   Johnson, Howard
    1924
Doing the Saboo   De Lange 1939; Van Heusen 1939
Doing the Town   Kalmar 1924; Ruby 1924
Doing the Uptown Lowdown   Gordon 1933; Revel 1933
Doing Time   Coleman 1962; Leigh 1962
Do-It-Yourself Cha Cha, The   Evans 1956; Livingston, Jay
    1956
Dolce Far Niente   Willson 1960
Doll Dance, The   Atteridge 1915; Romberg 1915
Doll Dance (inst.), The   Gorney 1934
Doll Dance (What a Peculiar Tune) (inst.), The   Brown,
    Nacio Herb 1927
Doll Fantasy, A   Hammerstein 1935; Romberg 1935
Doll on a Music Box   Sherman 1968
Doll Song   Smith, Harry B. 1930
Dollar Bill's the Flag that Rules the World, The   Goetz 1912
Dollar for a Dime   Blake 1940; Razaf 1940
Dollar Sign, The   Smith, Harry B. 1908
Dollars and Debutantes   Goetz 1910
Dolly   Gershwin, Ira 1921; Youmans 1921
Dolly Dear   Norworth 1907
Dolly Dimple   Jerome 1901; Merrill 1959; Schwartz, Jean
    1901
Dolly Dimples (inst.)   Alter 1927
Dolly Dollars   Herbert 1905
Dolly Doolittle   Bryan 1939; Fisher 1940
Dolly Show Your Dimple   David, Hal 1951
Dollys and Their Collies, The   Porter 1924
Dolly's Seduction   Lane 1965; Lerner, Alan Jay 1965
Dolores   Alter 1941; Davis 1928; Hart 1934; Kahn 1934;
    Loesser 1941; Rodgers 1934; Silver 1928; Smith, Harry B.
    1914
Dolphin Fan Song, The   Davis 1970
Dom Pedro of Brazil (inst.)   Kern 1946
Domestic Champagne Waltz, The   Lane 1965; Lerner, Alan
    Jay 1965
Domino   Raye 1951

Don Carlos Is Riding Tonight   Rainger 1936; Robin 1936
Don Jose of Far Rockaway   Rome 1952
Don Jose of Seville   Herbert 1897; Smith, Harry B. 1897
Don Pedro Pistachio   Styne 1941
Don Quixote de la Mancha (inst.)   Spina 1977
Don' Yo' Want to See de Moon?   Hammerstein 1920;
    Harbach 1920
Donald Duck   Bryan 1936; Washington 1939
Donaldsonia   Donaldson 1922
Donaldson's New Moon Song   Donaldson 1931
Done Gone Mad (inst.)   Waller 1923
Donkey and the Hay, The   Smith, Harry B. 1911
Donkey Serenade, The   Friml 1937
Donkey Small   Bergman 1957
Donna   Spina 1947
Donna Bella Mia   Fisher 1920
Donna Maria   Wrubel 1941
Donna Marie   Coots 1953
Donna Means Heartbreak   David, Hal 1962
Donnybrook   Burke 1961
Don't   Livingston, Jerry 1961; Strouse Date Unknown
Don't Ask!   Gershwin, George 1926; Gershwin, Ira 1926
Don't Ask a Lady   Coleman 1982; Leigh 1982
Don't Ask Me Not to Sing   Harbach 1931, 1933; Kern 1931
Don't Ask Me Why   Young, Joe 1931
Don't Ask too Much of Love   Mercer 1930
Don't Be a Cry Baby   Rainger 1933; Robin 1933
Don't Be a Do Badder   Cahn 1964; Van Heusen 1964
Don't Be a Fool You Fool   Conrad 1925; Dixon 1925
Don't Be a Fool You Fool (Don't Be a Foolish Fool)   Rose
    1925
Don't Be a Foolish Fool   Conrad 1925; Dixon 1925
Don't Be a Furniture Climber   Caesar 1943
Don't Be a Geografoof   Gorney 1958
Don't Be a Meanie   Baer 1930; Gilbert 1930
Don't Be a Sailor   Atteridge 1916; Hanley 1916; Romberg
    1916
Don't Be a Snork   DePaul 1955; Raye 1955
Don't Be a Woman If You Can   Gershwin, Ira 1946;
    Schwartz, Arthur 1946
Don't Be Afraid   Fields 1951; Merrill 1972; Schwartz, Arthur
    1951; Styne 1972; Weill 1977
Don't Be Afraid of an Animal   Rodgers 1967
Don't Be Afraid of Love   Dubin 1932
Don't Be Afraid of Romance   Berlin 1962
Don't Be Afraid to Come Home   Ager 1925; Bryan 1925;
    Yellen 1925
Don't Be an Old Maid Molly   Bryan 1909
Don't Be Angry with Me   Donaldson 1926
Don't Be Anybody's Moon but Mine   Howard, Joseph E.
    1909
Don't Be Ashamed of a Teardrop   Comden and Green 1960;
    Styne 1960
Don't Be Cross with Me   Howard, Joseph E. 1909
Don't Be Far Away   Silver 1950
Don't Be Greedy   Styne 1940
Don't Be Like That   Kalmar 1928; Ruby 1928
Don't Be Mad at Me   Donaldson 1931; Young, Joe 1932
Don't Be Mean, Geraldine!   Sherman 1960
Don't Be Rash   Atteridge 1913
Don't Be Silly   Brown, A. Seymour 1928
Don't Be Silly, Sally   Brown, Lew 1922; Hanley 1922
Don't Be So Bashful   Bryan 1908; Meyer 1908
Don't Be Sorry for Me   Conrad 1925

Don't Be Subtle, Don't Be Coy   Cahn 1944, 1945; Styne 1944, 1945

Don't Be Such a Wolf, Mr. Fox   Yellen 1977

Don't Be That Way   Parish 1938

Don't Be too Big for Your Britches   Robison 1950

Don't Be Too Old Fashioned (Old Fashioned Girl)   Gordon 1945

Don't Believe   Caesar 1926

Don't Believe a Word They Say   Parish 1933

Don't Believe Everything You Dream   Adamson 1945; McHugh 1943, 1945

Don't Believe Everything You Read   Evans 1958; Livingston, Jay 1958

Don't Believe Me   Bryan 1954

Don't Believe Me (No Me Creas)   Gorney 1935

Don't Bite the Hand that Feeds You   Drake 1964

Don't Blame It All on Broadway   Williams 1913; Young, Joe 1913

Don't Blame Me   Fields 1933; McHugh 1933; Stept 1925

Don't Blame Me for What Happens in the Moonlight, Blame the Moon   Young, Joe 1915

Don't Blame Poor Elaine   Kahal 1927; Snyder 1927

Don't Blow That Horn, Gabriel   Duke 1941

Don't Bother to Cry   Merrill 1947

Don't Break My Heart   Leslie 1912

Don't Break the Heart that Loves You   Davis 1961

Don't Break the Spell   Dubin 1943

Don't Break Up That Team   Caesar 1944

Don't Bring Lulu   Brown, Lew 1925; Henderson 1925; Rose 1925

Don't Bring Me Nothing Else but Love   Fisher 1930

Don't Bring Your Heartaches to Me   David, Mack 1950; Livingston, Jerry 1950

Don't Call 'em in the Morning   Johnson, Howard 1926

Don't Call It Love   Mancini 1979; Washington 1947; Wrubel 1947

Don't Call Me Darlin' My Darlin'   David, Mack 1951; Hoffman 1951

Don't Call Me, I'll Call You   David, Mack 1963; Van Heusen 1963

Don't Call on Me   Cahn 1946; Styne 1946

Don't Care — For the Heck of It   Carmichael 1950; Mercer 1950

Don't Carry Tales Out of School   Gordon 1944; Monaco 1944

Don't Change, Be As You Are   Turk 1933

Don't Change Horses   Hoffman 1944; Livingston, Jerry 1944

Don't Change Sweethearts in the Middle of a Dream   Evans 1946; Livingston, Jay 1946

Don't Change Your Heart in the Middle of a Dream   Lawrence 1939

Don't Cheat on the Meat   Blake 1958

Don't Choose a Gibson Girl   Howard, Joseph E. 1909

Don't Come Back Until You Say You're Sorry   Stept 1946

Don't Come Crying to Me   Adamson 1936; Donaldson 1936

Don't Count the Days   Bacharach 1966; David, Hal 1966

Don't Count the Stars   Washington 1956

Don't Count Your Kisses (Before You're Kissed)   Freed, Ralph 1936

Don't Cry   Loesser 1956

Don't Cry Baby   Johnson, James P. 1929; Kahn 1928; Silver 1926

Don't Cry Bo-Peep   Herbert 1903

Don't Cry, Cherie   Brown, Lew 1941; Henderson 1941

Don't Cry, Darling   Gorney 1952

Don't Cry, Dolly Grey   Bryan 1916

Don't Cry for Rover, Fido Is Here   Brown, Lew 1924

Don't Cry Frenchy, Don't Cry   Donaldson 1919; Lewis 1919; Young, Joe 1919

Don't Cry Little Cloud   Lane 1939; Loesser 1939, 1941

Don't Cry Little Fish   Kahn 1937

Don't Cry Swanee   Conrad 1921

Don't Cry When He's Gone   Meyer 1926

Don't Cry When We Say Goodbye   Woods 1943

Don't Dally with the Devil too Long   Robison 1937

Don't Disappear   Burke 1942; Van Heusen 1942

Don't Do Anything Dangerous   Bacharach 1961; David, Hal 1961

Don't Do Anything Half Way   Merrill 1958

Don't Do Anything I Wouldn't Do   Donaldson 1933

Don't Do Anything that I Wouldn't Do   David, Hal 1954

Don't Do Anything That You'll Be Sorry For   Conrad 1913

Don't Do Anything 'Till You Hear from Me   Clare 1931; Leslie 1931; Smith, Robert B. 1919; Stept 1931

Don't Do It   Schwartz, Arthur 1929

Don't Do It Darlin'   Adamson 1962; McHugh 1962

Don't Do the Charleston   Buck 1926; Hanley 1926

Don't, Don't Stop Loving Me Now   Hanley 1922

Don't Dream of Anybody but Me   Howard, Bart 1959

Don't Eat too Much Candy   Styne 1940

Don't End Our Dance of Love Now   David, Mack 1930

Don't Envy Me   Bacharach 1961; David, Hal 1961

Don't Ever Be Afraid to Go Home   Sigman 1952

Don't Ever Be Blue   Dubin 1931

Don't Ever Break a Promise   David, Mack 1941

Don't Ever Do That to Me   Fisher 1934

Don't Ever Leave Me   Hammerstein 1929; Kern 1929

Don't Ever Let Me Be Yours   Livingston, Jerry 1977; Russell 1977

Don't Ever Run Away from Love   Webster 1946

Don't Ever Say Goodbye   Ellington 1958

Don't Ever Say Goodnight   Sigman 1942

Don't Fail Me, Dice   Stept 1926

Don't Fall Until You've Seen Them All   Harbach 1920

Don't Feel Sorry for Me   Clarke 1922; Leslie 1922

Don't Fence Me In   Porter 1935

Don't Follow the Fellow Ahead   Caesar 1943

Don't Fool Around (With My Poor Heart)   Spina 1953

Don't Fool Around with the Moon   Ager 1968

Don't Forget   DeSylva 1926; Hanley 1926

Don't Forget I Love You   Merrill 1958

Don't Forget Me   Smith, Harry B. 1908; Von Tilzer 1916

Don't Forget Me in Your Dreams   Conrad 1930; Leslie 1930

Don't Forget Me in Your Dreams Tonight   Friend 1935; Stept 1935

Don't Forget 127th Street   Adams 1964; Strouse 1964

Don't Forget the Beau You Left at Home   Goetz 1911

Don't Forget the Boys Who Fought for You and Me   Ahlert 1919; Atteridge 1919

Don't Forget the Girl from Punxsutawney   David, Mack 1943; Livingston, Jerry 1943

Don't Forget the Girl You Left Behind   Howard, Joseph E. 1909

Don't Forget the Lilac Bush   Weill 1947

Don't Forget the Number   Howard, Joseph E. 1909, 1910

Don't Forget the Number of the House   Gilbert 1912

Don't Forget the Sailor Lad   Fisher 1939

Don't Forget to Come Back, Mack   Monaco 1918

Don't Forget to Dream   Gorney 1948

Don't Forget to Drop a Line to Mother   Williams 1908

Don't Forget to Mention   Drake 1955
Don't Forget to Say "No" Baby   Carmichael 1941
Don't Forget to Say Your Prayers   Sigman 1956
Don't Forget to Write   Lawrence 1953
Don't Forget to Write a Letter Home   Parish 1923
Don't Forget To-Morrow Night   Monaco 1911
Don't Forget when the Summer Rolls By   Clare 1927;
    Pollack 1927
Don't Forget Your Don'ts   Alter 1929; Johnson, Howard
    1929
Don't Forget Your Mother   Sterling 1899
Don't Get Around Much Anymore   Ellington 1942; Russell
    1942
Don't Get Down on Your Knees to Pray Until You Have
    Forgiven Everyone   Ellington 1968
Don't Get Married   Hoffman 1958
Don't Get Your Education in the Middle of the
    Street   Caesar 1943
Don't Give a Good Gosh Darn   Gordon 1936; Revel 1936
Don't Give Me a Ring on the Telephone Until You Give Me
    a Ring on My Hand   Burke 1958; Van Heusen 1958
Don't Give Me that Jive, Come on with the Come
    On   Waller 1944
Don't Give Me the Run Around   Baer 1923; Friend 1923
Don't Give Up on Me   Webster 1983
Don't Give Up the Ship   Dubin 1935; Warren 1935
Don't Give Your Kisses to Somebody Else (Save All Your
    Kisses for Me)   Adamson 1952; McHugh 1952
Don't Go Away   Romberg 1917
Don't Go Away Monsieur   Dietz 1937; Schwartz, Arthur
    1937
Don't Go Breaking My Heart   Bacharach 1965; David, Hal
    1965
Don't Go in the Lion's Cage   Goetz 1906
Don't Go in the Water   Harbach 1917
Don't Go in the Water Daughter   Jerome 1908; Schwartz,
    Jean 1908
Don't Go Lookin' for Trouble   Spina 1974
Don't Go Near the Water   Cahn 1957
Don't Go Now (Soldier Girl)   Drake 1953
Don't Go on a Diet Baby   Fain 1935; Kahal 1935
Don't Go to Paris   Brooks 1961; Warren 1961
Don't Go to Sleep   Freed, Arthur 1932
Don't Go too Dangerously Nigh   Johnson, J. Rosamond
    1904
Don't Go Too Far Girls   Brennan 1928; Smith, Harry B. 1928
Don't Grow Any Older (My Little Boy Blue)   Loesser 1935
Don't Hang Your Dreams on a Rainbow   Kahal 1929
Don't Hate Me 'Cause Yo Own Me Money   Robison 1949
Don't Hesitate with Me   Atteridge 1914; Romberg 1914
Don't Hold Everything, Let Everything Go   Brown, Lew
    1928; DeSylva 1928; Henderson 1928
Don't Hurt this Heart   Silver 1953
Don't I Do   Whiting 1930
Don't Introduce Me to that Angel   Loesser 1948
Don't It Break Your Heart   David, Mack 1980
Don't It Mean a Thing to You?   Akst 1929; Clarke 1929
Don't Join the Navy to See the World   Adamson 1956;
    McHugh 1956
Don't Just Sit There   Freed, Ralph 1955; Livingston, Jerry
    1955
Don't Keep Calling Me Dearie   Friml 1921
Don't Keep Me in the Dark, Bright Eyes   Bryan 1928
Don't Kick a Nation when It's Down   Fisher 1923
Don't Kick My Dreams Around   Styne 1980

Don't Kill the Goose (That Lays the Golden Egg)   Fain 1947;
    Magidson 1947
Don't Kiss Me Again   De Lange 1934; Mills 1934
Don't Kiss Me Goodnight   David, Mack 1936; Meyer 1936
Don't Laugh   Sondheim 1963
Don't Laugh When I Cry   Cahn 1936
Don't Leave Banana Peels on the Street   Caesar 1943
Don't Leave Me   Freed, Ralph 1959
Don't Leave Me Mammy   Conrad 1921; Davis 1921; DeSylva
    1921
Don't Leave Me, Mother Mine   Stept 1921
Don't Leave Me Now   Adams 1996; Russell 1948, 1964;
    Strouse 1987, 1996; Von Tilzer 1911
Don't Leave Your Girl Alone   Bryan 1926; Meyer 1926
Don't Leave Your Wife Alone   Berlin 1912
Don't Let a Blackout Give You a Knockout   Caesar 1942
Don't Let a Good Thing Get Away   Leigh 1967
Don't Let a Mem'ry Speak Your Heart   Fain 1964
Don't Let Anybody Vamp Your Man   Romberg 1925
Don't Let 'em Catch You with Your Sunshine Down   Merrill
    1953
Don't Let Him Linger when His Leave Is Over   Cohan 1918
Don't Let It Bother You   Gordon 1934; Revel 1934
Don't Let It Get Away   David, Hal 1962
Don't Let It Get You Down   Gordon 1940; Harburg 1940;
    Lane 1940; Porter 1938
Don't Let It Get Your Goat   Mills 1940
Don't Let It Happen Again   Bryan 1913; Duke 1941;
    Livingston, Jerry 1934
Don't Let Me Catch You Falling in Love   Hanley 1920
Don't Let Me Down   Robison 1944; Sherman 1971
Don't Let Me Dream   Washington 1945
Don't Let Me Love You   Loesser 1936
Don't Let Our Love Die on the Vine   Freed, Ralph 1954;
    Livingston, Jerry 1954
Don't Let that Moon Get Away   Burke 1938; Monaco 1938
Don't Let the Parade Pass You By   Young, Joe 1932
Don't Let the Rhythm Go to Your Head   Cahn 1938
Don't Let This Night Get Away   Adamson 1955; Lane 1955
Don't Let Your Baby Go to Miami   Hoffman 1955; Silver
    1955
Don't Let Your Love Come Down   Razaf 1927
Don't Let's Be Beastly to the Germans   Gershwin, Ira 1943
Don't Lie to Me   Mills 1954
Don't Like Goodbyes   Arlen 1954
Don't Listen to Gossip   Stept 1953
Don't Look at Me   Sondheim 1971
Don't Look at Me that Way   Coslow 1937; Porter 1928
Don't Look Now   Cahn 1936; Kahal 1935
Don't Look Now Mr. Dewey (But Your Record's
    Showing)   Harburg 1944; Schwartz, Arthur 1944
Don't Lose Your Head (And Lose Your Gal)   Johnson,
    James P. 1947
Don't Lose Your Way   Atteridge 1918; Romberg 1918
Don't Love Me Blues   Blake 1923; Sissle 1923
Don't Love Me Like Othello   Hart 1920; Rodgers 1920
Don't Make a Move   Bergman 1964; Fain 1964
Don't Make a Plaything Out of My Heart   Blake 1958; Sissle
    1958
Don't Make Faces   Sigman 1952
Don't Make Me Cry   David, Hal 1954
Don't Make Me Love You   David, Hal 1961
Don't Make Me Over   Bacharach 1962; David, Hal 1962
Don't Marry Me   Hammerstein 1958; Rodgers 1958
Don't Marry that Girl   Stept 1946

Don't Mention Love to Me   Fields 1935
Don't Mess Around with Your Mother-in-law   Coleman 1999
Don't Misunderstand   Sigman 1950
Don't Need a Horseshoe   Brooks 1959
Don't Need Nobody to Tell Me I'm in Bad   Johnson, James P. 1922
Don't Never Do-o-o That, You Nasty Man   Conrad 1934; Oakland 1934
Don't Never Tell Nobody What Your Good Man Can Do   Johnson, James P. 1923
Don't Never Trust a Traveling Man   Goetz 1911
Don't Nobody Move   Sigman 1958
Don't Overdo It   Smith, Harry B. 1903
Don't Oversell Me, Baby   Robison 1960
Don't Pass Me By   Harburg 1947; Lane 1947
Don't Play that Song   Oakland 1951; Raye 1951
Don't Play with Fire   Bryan 1916
Don't Play with Me   Romberg 1916
Don't Pour the Thames Into the Rhine   Harburg 1967; Styne 1967
Don't Promise Me the Moon   Fain 1949
Don't Pull Up the Flowers   David, Hal 1974
Don't Put a Tax on the Beautiful Girls   Ager 1919; Yellen 1919
Don't Put Bananas on Bananas   Willson 1951
Don't Put Out the Light   Berlin 1911; Leslie 1911
Don't Rain on My Parade   Merrill 1964; Styne 1964
Don't Remind Me (I'm Trying to Forget)   Clare 1928; Pollack 1928
Don't Rock the Boat, Dear   Arlen 1950; Blane 1950
Don't Run Away from the Rain   Mercer 1953
Don't Run Mirandy   Harburg 1950; Lane 1950
Don't Run Upstairs   Robison 1960
Don't Rush Me   Livingston, Jerry 1962; Wrubel 1952
Don't Save Your Love for a Rainy Day   Bullock 1937; Spina 1937
Don't Save Your Smiles   Coots 1936; Davis 1936
Don't Say a Word — Just Dance   Burke 1935; Spina 1935
Don't Say F-A-T in Front of Conrad   Adams 1981; Strouse 1981
Don't Say Goodbye to Love   Oakland 1955
Don't Say Good-Bye to Your Summer Love   Fisher 1934
Don't Say Goodnight   Dubin 1934; Warren 1934
Don't Say Home Sweet Home Again Tonight   Leslie 1910
Don't Say I Didn't Love You   Bacharach 1965; David, Hal 1965
Don't Say I Didn't Tell You   Mitchell 1940; Pollack 1940
Don't Say It   Coslow 1954
Don't Say It If You Don't Mean It   Coots 1936; Davis 1936
Don't Say "Love" — I've Been There and Back   Arlen 1966
Don't Say Paris, Say Paree   Cahn 1964; Van Heusen 1964
Don't Say You Care Unless You Really Do   Hoffman 1950
Don't Say You Love Me If You Don't Mean It   Stept 1952
Don't Say You Will When You Know that You Won't   Coslow 1923
Don't Sell the Night Short   Blane 1941; Martin 1941
Don't Send Me Back to Petrograd   Berlin 1924
Don't Send Me Home   David, Hal 1952
Don't Send Me to Bed   Sigman 1949
Don't Send My Boy to Prison   Conrad 1928
Don't Send Out My Laundry, Baby   David, Mack 1970
Don't Send Your Wife to the Country (Keep Her Home and Love Her Yourself)   Atteridge 1921; Conrad 1921; DeSylva 1921

Don't Settle for Less (Than the Best)   Sherman 1970
Don't Shoot the Hooey to Me Louie   Sherman 1974
Don't Shut Me Out   Sigman 1957
Don't Sing — Everybody Swing   Akst 1936; Clare 1936
Don't Sit Under the Apple Tree with Anyone Else but Me   Brown, Lew 1942; Stept 1942
Don't Slam the Door   Von Tilzer 1917
Don't Smoke in Bed   Robison 1948
Don't Stampede Me   Hoffman 1955
Don't Stay Away too Long   David, Hal 1954; Hoffman 1955; Stept 1950
Don't Stay Away too Long, Baby   Johnson, Howard 1934
Don't Steal the Sweetheart of a Soldier   Brown, Lew 1942; Coots 1942
Don't Stop   David, Mack 1951; Livingston, Jerry 1951; Sterling 1914; Von Tilzer 1914
Don't Stop Loving Me   Drake 1952
Don't Stop Me If You've Heard It Before   Hoffman 1934
Don't Stop Now   Friend 1958
Don't Stop the World for Me   Yellen 1963
Don't Sweetheart Me   Friend 1944
Don't Take a Fast Ride, It May Be Your Last Ride   Caesar 1943
Don't Take a Girl Down to Coney   Cobb 1910; Edwards 1910
Don't Take a Rose from the Devil   Silver 1957
Don't Take Advantage of My Good Nature   Monaco 1919
Don't Take Away My Jesus   Friml 1950
Don't Take Me Home   Von Tilzer 1937
Don't Take Much   Coleman 1996
Don't Take My Boop-oop-a-doop Away   Lerner, Sammy 1934
Don't Take My Heart   Davis 1965; Evans 1953; Livingston, Jay 1953
Don't Take that Black Bottom Away   Coslow 1926
Don't Take the Bums from Brooklyn   Robison 1955
Don't Take the Red and the White Out of the Flag (And Leave Us the Blues)   Donaldson 1921; Lewis 1921; Young, Joe 1921
Don't Take Your Beau to the Seashore   Berlin 1911; Goetz 1911
Don't Take Your Lips Away   Hoffman 1954
Don't Take Your Meaness Out on Me   Robison 1944
Don't Talk   Fields 1950
Don't Talk . . . Just Sing!   Cahn 1964; Van Heusen 1964
Don't Talk About God   Cahn 1970; Styne 1970
Don't Talk Back to Baby   Baer 1946
Don't Talk, Don't Think   David, Hal 1974
Don't Talk to Me of Spring   Young, Victor 1927
Don't Talk to the Driver (Talking to the Driver)   Caesar 1937
Don't Tamper with My Sister   Lane 1965; Lerner, Alan Jay 1965
Don't Teach Me to Swim Alone   Howard, Joseph E. 1909
Don't Tease   Lewis 1911
Don't Tell a Blue Bell   Lewis 1927; Young, Joe 1927
Don't Tell a Man about His Woman   Robison 1944
Don't Tell a Secret to a Rose   Rainger 1938; Robin 1938
Don't Tell a Soul   Howard, Bart 1955
Don't Tell Her What's Happened To Me   Brown, Lew 1930; DeSylva 1931; Henderson 1930
Don't Tell Mama   Brown, Lew 1922; Hanley 1922
Don't Tell Me   Adams 1978; Russell 1977; Strouse 1978
Don't Tell Me I'm Flying   Cahn 1977
Don't Tell Me It's Bad   Henderson 1934; Koehler 1934
Don't Tell Me, Let Me Guess   De Lange 1932

Don't Tell Me Who You Are   Porter 1920
Don't Tell Your Folks   Hart 1930; Rodgers 1930
Don't Tempt Me   Kern 1917; Smith, Harry B. 1915, 1917, 1926
Don't Tempt Me (For When I Love, I Love)   Spina 1952
Don't Thank Me   Comden and Green 1956; Styne 1956
Don't Think that We're the Chorus of the Show   Hart 1921; Rodgers 1921
Don't Think This Ain't Been Charming   McHugh 1940; Mercer 1940
Don't Throw Kisses   Akst 1937; Clare 1937
Don't Throw Me Down   Brown, Lew 1921; Coots 1927; Dubin 1927
Don't Throw My Love Away   David, Hal 1955
Don't Touch Him   Comden and Green 1972
Don't Touch Me   Freed, Ralph 1957
Don't Trifle with a Trusting Heart   Cobb 1900; Edwards 1900
Don't Trust Anyone   Blane 1968; Martin 1968
Don't Try to Explain   Drake 1949
Don't Try to Figure It Out   Comden and Green 1960; Styne 1960
Don't Try To Steal the Sweetheart of a Soldier   Bryan 1917
Don't Turn Me Off Baby   Brooks 1967
Don't Turn My Picture to the Wall   Kern 1912; Smith, Robert B. 1912
Don't Turn the Smiles to Tears   Whiting 1916
Don't Turn Your Back on Me   Razaf 1928
Don't Unless You Love Me   Bacharach 1959; David, Hal 1959
Don't Wait   Burke 1937; Johnston 1937
Don't Wait Till the Night Before Christmas   Baer 1938; Lewis 1938
Don't Wait Too Long   Berlin 1925; Coots 1956
Don't Wait Until the Lights Are Low   Johnson, Howard 1928
Don't Wait Up for Me, Mom   Sigman 1947
Don't Wake Me Up, Let Me Dream   Baer 1925; Gilbert 1925
Don't Wake Me Up (Un Ange Comme Ca C'est du Tonnerre)   Raye 1958
Don't Wake the Baby Up   Dixon 1929; Woods 1929
Don't Wake Up My Heart   Lewis 1938; Meyer 1938
Don't Wanna Write About the South   Rome 1950
Don't Want You No More (inst.)   Waller 1923
Don't We Carry On   Clare 1923; Friend 1923
Don't Wish Your Life Away   Heyman 1959; Strouse 1943
Don't Worry   Snyder 1907; Styne 1943
Don't Worry 'Bout Me   Bloom 1939; Koehler 1939
Don't Worry, Don't Worry (I Don't Worry)   Cahn 1965; Van Heusen 1965
Don't Worry Island   Dubin 1943; Monaco 1943
Don't Write Me Letters, But Come Right Back to Me   Lewis 1916; Young, Joe 1916
Don't You Believe It   De Lange 1945; Myrow 1945
Don't You Care   Stept 1952
Don't You Care Little Girl   Lewis 1910
Don't You Care What Anyone Says — You Fall in Love with Me   Cahn 1937
Don't You Dare to Call Me Up at Home   Brown, A. Seymour 1914
Don't You Ever Cross Me Path   Duke 1959
Don't You Ever Let Me Go   Parish 1945
(I Love You and) Don't You Forget It   Mancini 1963
Don't You Go   Bryan 1913
Don't You Know   Burke 1942; Van Heusen 1942

Don't You Know I Care (Or Don't You Care to Know)   David, Mack 1944; Ellington 1944
Don't You Know or Don't You Care   Fain 1937; Kahal 1937
Don't You Love Me Anymore   David, Mack 1947; Hoffman 1947; Livingston, Jerry 1947
Don't You Make a Noise   Harbach 1911; Lewis 1911; Schwartz, Jean 1911
Don't You Remember?   Gershwin, Ira 1924; Hammerstein 1920
Don't You Remember Me   Magidson 1933; Stept 1933
Don't You Tell   Howard, Joseph E. 1907
Don't You Think It's Time to Get Married   Edwards 1906
Don't You Think She's a Pretty Baby   Silver 1926
Don't You Think We Better Dance   Burke 1940
Don't You Want a Paper, Dearie?   Kern 1906
Don't You Want to Take Me?   Kern 1920
Don't You Wish that It Was Summer   Norworth 1910
Don't You Wish You Were a Kid Again   Buck 1916
Don'tcha Hate It   Duke 1955
Doo, Dah, Deh   Eliscu 1929; Rose 1929; Youmans 1929
Doo Dat, The   Raye 1943
Doo-ah Doo-ah Know What I'm Doing   Akst 1934; Turk 1934
Doo-Dab, The   Kalmar 1925; Ruby 1925
Doodle Do'd It   Friend 1958
Doodle-Bug Rag, The   Carmichael 1952
Doodletown   Bergman 1966
Doo-Hickey Thing-Ma-Jiggy, The   Merrill 1956
Doolittle Hop, The   Lane 1945
Doomed, Damned and Delighted   Drake 1995
Door Is Open Again, The   Caesar 1937; Lerner, Sammy 1937
Door of Her Dreams (Bridal Procession)   Friml 1924; Hammerstein 1924; Harbach 1924
Door Opened, The   Howard, Bart 1952
Door Senor, The   Hoffman 1952
Door Will Be Open (A Light Will Be Burning), The   Sigman 1968
Doors of the World Swing on New Britain Hinges, The   Willson 1953
Dope Fiend, The   Jerome 1910
Dorando   Berlin 1909
Do-Re-Mi   Hammerstein 1959; Rodgers 1959
Do-Re-Mi (inst.)   Motzan 1918
Dorine   Gorney 1931; Harburg 1931
Dorioso   Howard, Joseph E. 1956
Dormi, Dormi, Dormi (Sleep, Sleep, Sleep)   Cahn 1958; Warren 1958
Dorothy Anne (inst.)   Revel 1948
Dorothy (inst.)   McHugh 1929
Dorrie's Wish   Loesser 1960
Dos Almas (My Lady of the Roses)   David, Hal 1946
Dos I Dos   Willson 1956
Do-Sol-Do   Willson 1956
Dost Thou   Rome 1948
Dot, Dot, Dot   Adams 1966; Strouse 1966
Dou Dou   Eliscu 1932
Double Check Stomp   Mills 1930
Double Cross   Spina 1957
Double Dummy Drill   Gershwin, George 1933; Gershwin, Ira 1933
Double or Nothing   Burke 1937; Duke 1940; Young, Victor 1937
Double Soliloquy   Harburg 1967; Styne 1967

Double Standard   Evans 1958; Livingston, Jay 1958;
   Schwartz, Arthur 1929

Double Talk   Coleman 1989

Double Trouble   Dietz 1937; Rainger 1935, 1937; Robin
   1935, 1937; Schwartz, Arthur 1937; Whiting 1935

Doubting Thomas   Gershwin, George 1936

Doucement   Warren Date Unknown

Doughboy's in the Dough Again, The   Ahlert 1936; Turk
   1936; Young, Joe 1936

Doughboy's Lullaby   Hanley 1930

Dougherty   Jerome 1910; Schwartz, Jean 1910

Dougherty Is My Name   Yellen 1930

Doughnut Song, The   Merrill 1950

Doughnuts   DeSylva 1919; Gershwin, George 1919;
   Sherman 1971

Doughnuts and Coffee   Fain 1938; Kahal 1938

Dove Dance   Norworth 1916, 1917

Dove of Peace, The   Von Tilzer 1914

Dove of Peace (inst.)   Motzan 1915

Dowdling   Burke 1961

Down a Carolina Lane   Parish 1933

Down a Daisy Lane (inst.)   Robison 1929

Down a Long Long Road   Mercer 1933

Down a Shady Lane   Herbert 1906

Down Alongside the Docks   Johnson, Howard 1927

Down Among the Sleepy Hills of Tennessee   Lewis 1923;
   Meyer 1923; Young, Joe 1923

Down Among the Sleepy Pines   Clare 1931

Down Among the Sugar Cane   Clarke 1929

Down Among the Sugar-Cane   Clare 1929

Down Argentina Way   Gordon 1940; Warren 1940

Down Aroun' Malibu Way   Akst 1936; Clare 1936

Down Around the River (At the Dixie Jubilee)   Yellen 1919

Down Around the 'Sip 'Sip 'Sippy Shore   Donaldson 1921;
   Lewis 1921; Young, Joe 1921

Down Around These Old New Hampshire Hills   Davis 1931

Down Around Those Indiana Hills   Davis 1932

Down at Dinty Moore's   Johnson, Howard 1927

(Ev'ryone Is Singing) Down at My House   Sigman 1947

Down at that Ole Cabin Door   Blake 1930; Razaf 1930

Down at the Bootlegger's Ball   Hanley 1921

Down at the Bottom of the Sea   Johnson, J. Rosamond 1904

Down at the Farm   Martin 1952

Down at the Hippodrome   Donaldson 1923; Friend 1923

Down at the Old Barn Dance   Johnson, Howard 1933

Down at the Old Church Bazaar   Ager 1935

Down at the Old Minstrel Show   Von Tilzer 1935

Down Back Alleys Up Side Streets Looking for Someone I
   Love   Burke 1930

Down Beat   Blake 1938

Down Beside the Cider Mill   Bryan 1920

Down Boy   Carmichael 1953

Down Boy! Down Boy!   Adamson 1955

Down By the Beautiful Nile   Bryan 1917; Meyer 1917

Down By the Congo   Mills 1928

Down By the Erie Canal   Cohan 1914

Down By the Meadow Brook   Leslie 1919

Down By the Millside Along the Hillside, You Made All My
   Dreams Come True   Brown, Lew 1918

Down By the Nile   Romberg 1919

Down By the Ocean   Fain 1943, 1946; Freed, Ralph 1943,
   1946

Down By the Old Oak Tree   Leslie 1929

Down By the Old Sea Side   Edwards 1910

Down By the Railroad Track   Blake 1940; Razaf 1940

Down by the River   Hart 1935; Rodgers 1935

Down By the Sea (Whoopie)   Hart 1928; Rodgers 1928

Down By the Shore   Johnson, James P. 1959

Down de Curtains of Night   Johnson, Howard 1939

Down de Lover's Lane   Smith, Harry B. 1900

Down de Road   Johnson, Howard 1939

Down Deep in an Irishman's Heart   Brennan 1925; McHugh
   1925

Down, Down, Down, Down   David, Mack 1965

Down Georgia Lane   Gorney 1923

Down Goes the Price of Eggs   Howard, Joseph E. 1909

(While the Sun Is Going Down) Down Home   Rainger 1934;
   Robin 1934

Down Home Rag (Deeten Datten Dooten)   Brown, Lew
   1939

Down Home Stomp   Ellington 1962

Down in a Coal Mine   Johnson, Howard 1939

Down in a Dungeon Deep   Porter 1914

Down in an Irishman's Heart   Coslow 1919

Down in Argentine   Mills 1929

Down in Arkansas   Ahlert 1930; Coslow 1937; Kalmar 1928;
   Ruby 1928; Turk 1930

Down in Bom-Bombay   Carroll 1915

Down in Cairo Town   Johnson, Howard 1917

Down in Catty Corner   Atteridge 1915; Romberg 1915

Down in Chattanooga   Berlin 1913

Down in Cherry Lane   Sterling 1898; Von Tilzer 1898

Down in Dear Old New Orleans   Conrad 1912; Young, Joe
   1912

Down in Hindustan   Egan 1917

Down in Maryland   Kalmar 1922; Ruby 1922

Down in Midnight Town   Sterling 1921; Von Tilzer 1921

Down in Monkeyville   Clarke 1913; Leslie 1913

Down in Mulberry Bend   Johnson, J. Rosamond 1904

Down in My Heart   Berlin 1912

Down in Old Havana Town   Caesar 1927; Friend 1927

Down in Our Neighborhood   Schwartz, Jean 1923

Down in Papeetee Tahiti   Warren Date Unknown

Down in Shenandoah Valley   Gordon 1930; Silver 1930

Down in Sunshine Valley   Turk 1919

Down in the Carolines   Young, Joe 1941

Down in the Depths   Porter 1936

Down in the Everglade   Williams 1909

Down in the Indies   Mills 1948

Down in the Land of Dancing Pickaninnies   Blake 1923;
   Sissle 1923

Down in the Old Cherry Orchard   Bryan 1907

Down in the Old Meadow Lane   Williams 1911

Down in the Old Neighborhood   Whiting 1915

Down in the Old Rathskeller   Goetz 1912

Down in the Philippines   Johnson, J. Rosamond 1907

Down in the Subway   Jerome 1904; Schwartz, Jean 1904

Down in the Sunshine Alley Sally   Meyer 1909

Down in the Valley   Mercer 1949; Weill 1948

Down in Waterloo   Bryan 1914

Down Louisiana Way (Cane Grinding) (inst.)   Kern 1942

Down Lovers Lane   Porter 1914

Down Mexico Way   Styne 1941

Down Moonlight Lane   Bullock 1939; Spina 1939

Down Old Harmony Way   Monaco 1913

Down Old Virginia Way   Yellen 1922

Down on a South Sea Isle   Von Tilzer 1903

Down on Ami Ami Oni Oni Island   Gordon 1942

Down on Indigo Bay   Fisher 1922

Down on MacConnachy Square   Lerner, Alan Jay 1947; Loewe 1947

Down on Old Long Island Sound   Jerome 1921; Von Tilzer 1921

Down on the Bangaway Isle   Brennan 1929

Down on the Brandy Wine   Henderson 1924; Rose 1924

Down on the Delta   Stept 1932; Waller 1932

Down on the Desert   Friend 1957

Down on the Dude Ranch   Harburg 1940; Lane 1940

Down on the Farm   Adams 1983; Drake 1954

Down on the Florida Shore   Carroll 1926

Down on the Old Kansas Farm (That Farm Out in Kansas)   Harbach 1920

Down on the Old-Time Farm   Schwartz, Arthur 1934

Down on Uncle Jasper's Farm   Monaco 1913

Down on Wabash Avenue   Gordon 1950; Myrow 1950

Down Red Rose Lane   Brown, A. Seymour 1909

Down South   DeSylva 1921; Donaldson 1921

Down South Camp Meetin'   Mills 1935

Down South Feeling   Mills 1929

Down Stream   Loesser Date Unknown; Whiting 1928

Down the Colorado Trail   Bryan 1937

Down the End of the Road   Lewis 1932

Down the Fairway   Warren 1933

Down the Glacier Trail   Stept 1941

Down the Lane   Friend 1918

Down the Lane and Home Again   Kalmar 1919; Leslie 1919

Down the Lane that Leads to Home Sweet Home   Brown, Lew 1923; Henderson 1923

Down the Lane to Yesterday   Loesser 1935

Down the Lane with Linda Jane   Meyer 1908

Down the Line with Arabella   Jerome 1905; Schwartz, Jean 1905

Down the Milky Way   David, Hal 1947

Down the Old Ox Road   Coslow 1933; Johnston 1933

(That Place) Down the Road a Piece   Raye 1942

Down the Road to Maryland   Coots 1924

Down the Stairs and Out the Door (Went My Baby)   Loesser 1948

Down the Trail to Home, Sweet Home   Dubin 1920

Down the Well   Lerner, Sammy 1948

Down Through the Ages   Brown, A. Seymour 1923; Mercer 1930

Down Through the Valley   Young, Victor 1948

Down Thru Melody Lane   Wrubel 1932

Down Time   De Lange 1944

Down to Steamboat, Tennessee   Robison 1974

Down to the Folies Bergere   Berlin 1911; Snyder 1911

Down Town Blues (inst.)   Warren 1956

Down T'Uncle Bill's   Carmichael 1934; Mercer 1934

Down Up, Left Right   Harbach 1917

Down Virginia Way   Atteridge 1916; Motzan 1916, 1917; Romberg 1916

Down Where Banjoes Were Born   Robison 1934

Down Where the Bluebells Grow   Coots 1946; Edwards 1923; Friend 1946; Smith, Robert B. 1923

Down Where the Cotton Blossoms Grow   Sterling 1901; Von Tilzer 1901

Down Where the East River Flows   Adamson 1930; Youmans 1930

Down Where the Jack O'Lanterns Grow   Berlin 1917; Cohan 1918

Down Where the Mortgages Grow   Hammerstein 1923; Youmans 1923

Down Where the South Begins   Donaldson 1932; Kahn 1932; Lewis 1924; Young, Joe 1924

Down Where the Swanee River Flows   Sterling 1903; Von Tilzer 1903

Down Where the Sweet Potatoes Grow   Von Tilzer 1917

Down Where the Wurzburger Flows   Von Tilzer 1901

Down with Everybody But Us   Porter 1929

Down with Love   Arlen 1937; Harburg 1937

Down with Sauerkraut (It Drives Me to the Dogs)   Johnson, Howard 1927

Down Yonder   Gilbert 1921

Downcast Eye, The   Kern 1904

Downhill and Shady   Bacharach 1965; David, Hal 1965

('Cause I'm Just a) Downstream Drifter   Egan 1933; Kahn 1933

Downtown   Adams 1954, 1956; Strouse 1956

Downtown Rag   Merrill 1964; Styne 1964

Downtown Saturday Night   David, Hal 1962

Dowry Song, The   Cahn 1940

Dr. Baltimore M.D.   Motzan 1915

Dr. Bernstein   Russell Date Unknown

Dr. Blotz   Herbert 1904

Dr. Crippen   Weill 1943

Dr. Freud   Lawrence 1964

Dr. Grouch Is Going Away   Friml 1913; Harbach 1913

Dr. Hackenbush   Kalmar 1939; Ruby 1939

Dr. Watson and Mr. Holmes   Mercer 1934

Dracula   Strouse 1999

Drag Race for Cockroaches   Spina 1976

Draggin' the Chain   Bryan 1928; Schwartz, Jean 1928

Draggin' the Dragon Drag   Johnston 1927; Turk 1927

Drago and the Colonel   Carmichael 1940

Dragon Dance   Rome 1940

D-R-A-G-O-N (Dee-Are-A-Gee-O-En)   Merrill 1962

Dragon Rag   Brooks 1959

Dragon's Last Ballad   Brooks 1960

Drama Quartet   Martin 1972

Dramatic Situation   Smith, Harry B. 1906

Draw the Blinds   Adams 1972; Strouse 1972

Draw Up the Pre-Nup   Drake 1997

Drawing of a Gardener's Hat (with Flowers)   Loesser 1967

Dream   Mercer 1944; Strouse 1971; Webster 1965

Dream a Dream   Hammerstein 1925; Harbach 1925; Kern 1925

Dream a Golden Day Dream   Oakland 1970

Dream a Little Dream of Me   Kahn 1930

Dream After Dream   Parish 1947

Dream Along with Bozo   Livingston, Jerry 1962

Dream Along with Me, I'm on My Way to a Star   Sigman 1955

Dream Away   Bryan 1930; Dubin 1930

Dream Awhile   Mercer 1936

Dream Baby   Caesar 1929; Friend 1929, 1949

Dream Big   Bacharach 1958

Dream Big (Work Hard, Aim High)   Robison 1963

Dream Blues   Mills 1940

Dream Boat   Adamson 1936; Kahn 1938; McHugh 1937; Romberg 1938

Dream Boy   Sherman 1960

Dream By Dream   Hoffman 1950

Dream Caravan   Fain 1951; Razaf 1938

Dream Clouds   Egan 1939

Dream Concerto, A   David, Mack 1945

Dream Dance   Schwartz, Jean 1942

Dream Dancing   Porter 1941

Dream Days of Auld Lang Syne   Leslie 1928
Dream, Dream   Romberg 1930; Smith, Harry B. 1917
Dream Dream Dream   Hoffman 1952
Dream Dream, Dream (Long, Long, Long)   McHugh 1954; Parish 1952
Dream Drummin'   Sherman 1974
Dream Dust   Coots 1938; Leigh 1957
Dream Express   Rome 1951
Dream Faces   Johnson, Howard 1939
Dream Fantasies   Atteridge 1921
Dream Fantasy   Loesser 1952; Oakland 1956
Dream for a Lovely Night, A   David, Mack 1958; Warren 1958
Dream for You, a Dream for Me, A   Woods 1937
Dream Girl   Evans 1948; Hoffman 1956; Johnson, Howard 1943; Livingston, Jay 1948
Dream Girl, Give Back My Dream to Me   Romberg 1919
Dream Girl o' Mine   Olcott 1914
Dream Harbor   Lawrence 1954
Dream House   Bryan 1958
Dream House Number   Adamson 1936; Donaldson 1936
Dream in Your Eyes   Caesar 1926
Dream Is a Wish Your Heart Makes, A   David, Mack 1950; Hoffman 1950; Livingston, Jerry 1950
Dream Kingdom   Heyman 1934
Dream Kisses   Adamson 1936; Donaldson 1936; Yellen 1927
Dream Lady   Schwartz, Jean 1933; Young, Joe 1933
Dream Love ('Twas Only Dreaming)   Herbert 1908
Dream Lovers, The   Caesar 1923; Conrad 1923
Dream Lullaby   Mills 1935
Dream Maker of Japan   Friml 1924; Lewis 1924; Young, Joe 1924
Dream Man   Kahn 1929
Dream Man, Make Me Dream Some More   Ager 1934; Young, Joe 1934
Dream Men   Friend 1957
Dream Minute   Howard, Joseph E. 1909
Dream Moon Valley   Bryan 1937
Dream of a Bum, The   Mills 1929; Parish 1929
Dream of a Girl, A   Hoffman 1958
Dream of a Ladies Cloakroom Attendant (inst.)   Kern 1935
Dream of a Soldier Boy, The   Dubin 1917; Monaco 1917
Dream of All My Dreams   Coslow 1931, 1932; Rainger 1932
Dream of Love   Bergman 1978; Kahn 1937
Dream of Me and I'll Dream of You Sweetheart   Leslie 1909
Dream of Me Darling Tonight   Johnson, Howard 1934
Dream of My Dream   Sigman 1968
Dream of My Dreams   Lewis 1912; Young, Joe 1912
Dream of My Last Waltz with You   Kahn 1921
Dream of Orange Blossoms, A   DeSylva 1922; Herbert 1922
Dream of Your Smile, A   Conrad 1921
Dream On   Clare 1933; DeSylva 1922; Herbert 1904, 1922; Smith, Harry B. 1930
Dream on a Piece of Wedding Cake   Hanley 1930
Dream On, James   David, Hal 1967
Dream On, James, You're Winning (inst.)   Bacharach 1967
Dream On, Little Soldier Boy   Berlin 1918
Dream Peddler's Serenade, The   Mercer 1950
Dream Rag (inst.)   Blake 1959
Dream River   Hoffman 1928
Dream, Safe with Me   Strouse 1980
Dream Sequence   Bullock 1939
Dream Sequence (We're from the Journal, The Wahrheit, the Telegram, The Times. . .)   Gershwin, George 1931; Gershwin, Ira 1931

Dream Serenade   Bryan 1939
Dream Shadows   Adamson 1939; Coots 1935; Parish 1935
Dream Sonata   Bullock 1947
Dream Song   Porter 1939
Dream Stars   Friend 1934
Dream Street   David, Hal 1946; Robison 1956
Dream, Sweet Dreamer   Bacharach 1967; David, Hal 1967
Dream Theme   Spina 1977
Dream Time   Coots 1936; Davis 1936
Dream Tonight   Loesser 1937
Dream Voyage, A   Young, Victor 1921
Dream Waltz   DePaul 1958; Raye 1958
Dream Waltz (Inst.)   Warren 1956, Date Unknown
Dream Was Born, A   Young, Victor 1952
Dream Was So Beautiful, The   Brown, Nacio Herb 1934; Freed, Arthur 1934
Dream Weaver   Fain 1950
Dream with Me   Comden and Green 1944; David, Mack 1960
Dream World   Gershwin, Ira 1953; Lane 1953; Leigh 1955
Dreamboat   Evans 1946; Livingston, Jay 1946
Dreamer, The   Evans 1980; Livingston, Jay 1979; Loesser 1943; Razaf Date Unknown; Schwartz, Arthur 1943
Dreamer, Dreamer   Caesar 1945
Dreamer (inst.)   Warren Date Unknown
Dreamer of Dreams   Kahn 1924
Dreamer Who Gets Things Done, The   Burke 1950; Van Heusen 1950
(Let's Drift Away On) Dreamers Bay   Spina 1931
Dreamer's Cloth   Russell 1952
Dreamer's Hill   Mills 1947
Dreamer's Holiday   Friend 1947
Dreamer's Lullaby   Freed, Ralph 1942
Dreamin' All the Time   Bacharach 1962
Dreamin' Is My Business   David, Mack 1950; Livingston, Jerry 1950
(I'm) Dreamin' Out Loud   Pollack 1946
Dreamin' Suits Me Just Fine   Arlen 1973
Dreaming   Bloom 1962; Conrad 1925, 1926; Fields 1931; Howard, Joseph E. 1909; Kahn 1926; Koehler 1962; McHugh 1931
Dreaming About You   Johnson, Howard 1959
Dreaming Alone   Hammerstein 1922; Mitchell 1922
Dreaming By the Fireside   Livingston, Jerry 1936
Dreaming, Dreaming   Herbert 1897; Smith, Harry B. 1897
Dreaming Dreams that Won't Come True   Friend 1931
Dreaming, I'm Always Dreaming You Are Mine   Bryan 1921
(Love's Dear Yearning) Dreaming in Paradise   Hammerstein 1926; Harbach 1926; Romberg 1926
Dreaming in the Gloaming   Whiting 1928
Dreaming Is Fine for Passing the Time   Razaf 1946
Dreaming of Allah   Harbach 1926; Kern 1926
Dreaming of Home Sweet Home   Hanley 1917
Dreaming of Louise   Bryan 1943
Dreaming of Love   Coots 1958
Dreaming of the Day   Turk 1928
Dreaming of Tomorrow   Davis 1925
Dreaming of You   Martin 1953; Mitchell 1936; Ruby 1954; Stept 1936
Dreaming Out Loud   Coslow 1940; Rainger 1934, 1936; Robin 1934, 1936
Dreaming Princess, The   Herbert 1911; Smith, Harry B. 1911
Dreaming to Music   Washington 1943
Dreaming True   Hart 1920; Rodgers 1920
Dreamland   Goetz 1954

Dreamland Choo-Choo to Lullaby Town, A   Gordon 1936; Revel 1936

Dreamland Rendezvous   Gilbert 1946; Oakland 1946

Dreams   Bergman 1978; Carmichael 1952; Sterling 1919; Von Tilzer 1919

Dreams Ago   Bullock 1950

Dreams and Memories (Tosellia Serenade)   Sigman 1966

Dreams Are Just a Dime a Dozen   Parish 1945

Dreams Are Made for Children   David, Mack 1954, 1958; Livingston, Jerry 1954, 1958

Dreams Come True   Comden and Green 1945

Dreams Do Come True   Robin 1947

Dreams for Sale   Friend 1960; Hanley 1922, 1926

Dreams, Just Dreams   Berlin 1910; Snyder 1910

Dreams Never Die   Robin 1926

Dreams of the Past   Atteridge 1914; Romberg 1914

Dreams Patter   Brooks 1959

Dreams Were Made for Lovers   Coots 1955

Dreamsville   Evans 1959; Hoffman 1957; Livingston, Jay 1959; Mancini 1959

Dreamy   Johnson, James P. 1942; Spina 1957

Dreamy Amazon   Gilbert 1919

Dreamy Araby   Conrad 1924

Dreamy Argentina   Friend 1925

Dreamy Day   De Lange 1948

Dreamy Delaware   Donaldson 1924

Dreamy Eyes   Friend 1927; Koehler 1948; Mills 1928; Silver 1927; Stept 1948

Dreamy Fandango Tune (The Spanish Fandango Rag)   Jerome 1910; Schwartz, Jean 1910

Dreamy Florence   Atteridge 1919; Jerome 1919; Romberg 1919; Schwartz, Jean 1919

Dreamy Hawaiian Eyes   Mills 1928

Dreamy Indiana Moonlight   Parish 1949

Dreamy Isle of Dreams   Bryan 1938

Dreamy Kalua   Parish 1939

Dreamy Melody   Koehler 1922

Dreamy Montmartre   Baer 1927; Lewis 1927; Young, Joe 1927

Dreamy Parisian Croon, The   Goetz 1917

Dreamy River   Egan 1956; Whiting 1956

Dreamy Street   Webster 1933

Dreamy Town   Meyer 1910

Dreamy Waters (inst.)   Schwartz, Jean 1930

Dresden China Soldiers   Porter 1914

Dresden Northwest Mounted, The   Gershwin, George 1932; Gershwin, Ira 1932

Dress, Dress, Dress   Atteridge 1918; Romberg 1918; Schwartz, Jean 1918

Dress Is Cool, The   Gordon 1955

Dressed Up for Your Sunday Beau   Robin 1927

Dressing Up   Leigh 1954

Drift with Me   Kern 1917; Smith, Harry B. 1917

Driftin' Down the Dreamy Ol' Ohio   Spina 1949

Drifting   Dixon 1936; Goetz 1911; Henderson 1936

Drifting Alone   Gordon 1929

Drifting Alone on Dreamy River   Johnson, Howard 1935

Drifting Along on a Blue Lagoon   Kahn 1920

Drifting Along the Delaware (inst.)   Kern 1946

Drifting Along with the Tide   Gershwin, George 1921

Drifting Apart   Ager 1921; Johnson, Howard 1921; Kahn 1926

Drifting Back to Honolulu   Hoffman 1930

Drifting Down a Little Dutch Canal   Coots 1938

Drifting Down the River of Dreams   Lawrence 1939

Drifting Down the Shalimar   Monaco 1932

Drifting On   Hammerstein 1920; Johnson, Howard 1928

Drifting on to Avalon   Hoffman 1930

Driftwood   Kahn 1923

Drill of the Seventh   Cohan 1911

Drink   Porter 1944

Drink from the Cup of Tomorrow   Bullock 1939

Drink It Down   Rainger 1936; Robin 1936

Drink Out the Old Drink   Smith, Harry B. 1918

Drink the Waters   Dietz 1961; Schwartz, Arthur 1961

Drink to Me Only with Thine Eyes   Johnson, Howard 1939; Mills 1939

(Let Us) Drink to the Girl of My Dreams   Baer 1930; Gilbert 1930

Drink to the Glorious Night   Howard, Joseph E. 1905

Drink to the Health of This Great Man   Herbert 1909

Drink with Me   Cohan 1907

Drinking Again   Mercer 1961

Drinking Song   Brooks 1959; Brown, Lew 1930; DeSylva 1930; Friml 1925; Henderson 1930; Johnson, Howard 1939; Porter 1957; Romberg 1924, 1954; Schwartz, Jean 1930; Styne 1941; Webster 1954

Drip, Drip, Drip, Went the Waterfall   Carroll 1915

Drip Drop!   Carmichael 1943

Drive Under Thirty-Five   Caesar 1943

Driver's Prayer, A   Caesar 1943

Drivin' and Dreamin'   Harburg 1979

Driving Home with Angeline   Goetz 1917

Driving on Monday or Tuesday or Sunday   Caesar 1940

Drop a Nickel in the Slot   Ahlert 1938; Young, Joe 1938

Drop a Penny in the Wishing Well   Webster Date Unknown

Drop Another Bean in the Bucket Joe   DePaul 1950; Raye 1950

Drop in on Me at Luncheon   Smith, Robert B. 1905

Drop Me Off in Harlem   Ellington 1933

Drop Out   Lawrence 1966

Drop that Name   Comden and Green 1956; Styne 1956

Drop the Old Folks a Line   Razaf Date Unknown; Waller Date Unknown

Drop Your Kerchief   Caesar 1929; Friend 1929

Drowsy Head   Berlin 1920

Drowsy Lullaby (inst.)   Kern 1946

Drug Store Song, The   Rome 1946

Drugstore Opening   Hart 1930; Rodgers 1930

Drum Beat   Washington 1954; Young, Victor 1954

Drum Brigade, The   Cahn 1935

Drum Crazy   Berlin 1948

Drum in My Heart — Gun in My Hand   Leigh 1985; Styne 1985

Drummer Boy   Strouse 1956

Drummer Song   Jerome 1905; Schwartz, Jean 1905

Drummin' Drummin' Drummin'   Sherman 1968

Drumming Out   Fields 1933; McHugh 1933

Drums and Dreams   Robin 1943; Warren 1943

Drums and Drill   Robin 1955; Youmans 1955

Drums Are the Heartbeat Passin' with the Dragon   Brooks 1959

Drums in My Heart   Heyman 1931; Youmans 1931

Drums in the Night   Loesser 1940; McHugh 1940

Drums of All Nations, The   Herbert 1912

Drums of Kane   Brennan 1930; Friml 1930

Drums of the Fore and Aft   Howard, Joseph E. 1905

Drumstick Parade, The   Coots 1951; Egan 1951

Drunk with Love   Evans 1948; Livingston, Jay 1948

Drunken Rag   Wrubel 1929

Dry Bones   Johnson, J. Rosamond 1938
Dry Martini   Mills 1929
Dry Martini (inst.)   Stept 1957
Du Barry Was a Lady   Porter 1939
Du Bist Mein Liebe   David, Mack 1959
DuBarry Was a Lady   Freed, Ralph 1943; Lane 1943
Dublin Bay   Kahn 1912
Dublin Rag, The   Atteridge 1910
Dublinola   Atteridge 1924; Romberg 1924; Schwartz, Jean 1924
Ducal Cousin   Smith, Harry B. 1906
Duchess, The   Herbert 1911; Smith, Harry B. 1911
Duchess Has a Twinkle in Her Eye, The   Washington 1935
Duchess of Devonshire, The   Atteridge 1918; Romberg 1918; Schwartz, Jean 1918
Duchess of Killarney, The   Goetz 1907
Duchess of Table d'Hote, The   Smith, Harry B. 1908
Duchess of the Long Ago, The   Romberg 1918; Schwartz, Jean 1918
Duchess's Entrance   Gershwin, Ira 1945; Weill 1945
Duck, The   Loesser Date Unknown
Duck Antics   Loesser 1937
Duck Fights, The   Loesser 1937
Duck Hunt Finale   Loesser 1937
Ducky Christmas   Sherman 1959
Dude and a Doll, A   Evans 1977; Livingston, Jay 1977
Dude Ranch Boogie   Drake 1955
Duel of Hearts, The   Bryan 1903
Duello, The   Hammerstein 1941; Romberg 1941
Duet   Adams 1957; Gorney 1931; Harburg 1931; Sigman 1950; Strouse 1957
Duet for One (The First Lady of the Land)   Lerner, Alan Jay 1976
Duettino   Kern 1957; Mercer 1957
(I'm the) Duke of Kak-I-Ak   Donaldson 1929; Leslie 1929
Duke the Spook   Burke 1943; Van Heusen 1943
Duke's Place   Ellington 1957
Dulcima   Cahn 1972
Dull and Gay   Hart 1930; Rodgers 1930
Dull Dance   Mancini 1955
Dumb Bell   Schwartz, Jean 1905; Williams 1905
Dumb Dora   Coslow 1924; Silver 1924
Dumb Luck   Blake 1924; Sissle 1924
Dumb-Dumb-Dumb   Martin 1952
Dumber They Come the Better I Like 'Em, The   Ahlert 1923
Dummy Song   Brown, Lew 1925; Henderson 1925; Rose 1925
Dump the Ump   Leigh 1971
Dumpty Deedle Dee Dum Dee   Donaldson 1918
Dunerwetter   Harbach 1910
Dunes of Doorma, The   Rainger 1939; Robin 1939
Dunk, Dunk, Dunk   Conrad 1931
Duo   Drake 1954
Duodessimalogue   Porter 1913
Duration Blues   Mercer 1944
Dusk on the Desert   Ellington 1938; Mills 1938
Dusky Dixie Rose   Edwards 1929; Johnson, Howard 1929
Dusky Dudes   Jerome 1899; Schwartz, Jean 1899
Dusky Rose (inst.)   Johnson, James P. 1945
Dusky Stevedore   Razaf 1928
Dust   Fisher 1930
Dust Off Your Knees   Johnson, Howard 1930
Dust Over the West   Lawrence 1938
Dusting Around   Blake 1932; Sissle 1932
Dusty Road   Parish 1935

Dusty Roads   Pollack 1929
Dusty Shoes   Gorney 1933; Harburg 1933
Dusty Trails   Heyman 1939
Dutch Treat   David, Mack 1958; Evans 1958; Livingston, Jay 1958; Livingston, Jerry 1958
Duty, Honor, Country   Blane 1963
Dwight D. Eisenhower   Livingston, Jerry 1960
D'Ye Love Me?   Hammerstein 1925; Harbach 1925; Kern 1925
Dying Flamingo, The   Caesar 1931
Dying Rag   Berlin 1911
Dynamic Personality   Fisher 1930
Dynamite Blasting   Willson 1953
Dynamite Joe   Henderson Date Unknown; Razaf Date Unknown

E

Each Day Till I Die   Olcott 1911
Each Morning After an Evening with You   Lerner, Sammy 1935
Each Pearl a Thought   Kern 1913; Smith, Harry B. 1913
Each Spring   DePaul 1958; Raye 1958
Each Time I Dream   David, Mack 1956; Warren 1956
Eadie Was a Lady   Brown, Nacio Herb 1932; DeSylva 1932; Whiting 1932
Eager Beaver   Rodgers 1962
Eagle and Me, The   Arlen 1944; Harburg 1944
Eagle Rock, The   Atteridge 1914; Carroll 1914
Eagle Soliloquy   Rome 1965
Earful of Music, An   Donaldson 1934; Kahn 1934
Earl Pudney Theme   Oakland 1954
Early American   Burke 1950; Van Heusen 1950
Early Autumn   Mercer 1952
Early Bird   Mitchell 1936; Pollack 1936
Early Birds   Coslow 1929; Robin 1929, 1933
Early Hours of the Morn   Atteridge 1914
Early in the Morning   Conrad 1926; Kahn 1926
Early in the Morning Down on the Farm   Kahn 1916
Early Monday Morning   Eliscu 1943; Gorney 1943
Early Mornin' Blues   Razaf 1939
Early Morning Blues   Coleman 1965
Early Morning Sequence   Kahn 1938
Early Morning Song, The   Fain 1950
Early Morning Strangers   David, Hal 1976
Early Spring   McHugh 1960; Washington 1960
Early to Bed and Early to Rise Never Made Anyone Wise   Silver 1920
Early to Bed, Early to Rise   Styne 1940
Earnin' a Livin'   Styne Date Unknown
Earth and Other Minor Things, The   Lerner, Alan Jay 1973; Loewe 1973
Easier Way, An   Comden and Green 1947
Easiest Thing in the World, The   David, Hal 1947
Easin' Right Along   Razaf 1928
East Is East and West Is West   Hanley 1919
East Is East, West Is West, But South Is Paradise   Ager 1922; Yellen 1922
East Is West   Gershwin, Ira 1929
East of Java   David, Mack 1968
East of Siam   Lawrence 1954
East of the Sun — West of the Moon, Where Can You Be   Livingston, Jerry 1933
East of the West Wind   Davis 1942; Parish 1942
East River   Yellen 1934

East River Drive   Drake 1995; Styne 1950
East Side Lil   Jerome 1902; Schwartz, Jean 1905
East Side of Heaven   Burke 1939; Monaco 1939
East Side Walk   Jerome 1902; Schwartz, Jean 1905
East Wind   Hammerstein 1931; Romberg 1931
Easter   Carmichael 1957
Easter Bunnies   Heyman 1935
Easter Dawn, An   Herbert 1907
Easter in Napoli   Gilbert 1954; Oakland 1954
Easter in Your Heart   Young, Victor 1954
Easter Nocturne (inst.)   Coots 1946
Easter Parade   Berlin 1933
Easter Sunday Morning   Drake 1951
Easter Sunday Parade   Cohan 1927
Eastern and Western Love   Hammerstein 1926; Harbach
    1926; Romberg 1926
Eastern Moon   Kern 1907
Easy Baby   Bergman 1974; Mancini 1974
Easy, Brother, Easy   Brooks 1953; Warren 1953
Easy Come, Easy Go   Atteridge 1918; Evans 1947; Heyman
    1934; Livingston, Jay 1947; Rodgers 1979; Romberg 1918
Easy Does It   David, Hal 1974; Gorney 1949; Rome 1940;
    Russell 1943
Easy for You   Strouse 1986
Easy Goin' Gal   Rainger 1934, 1935; Robin 1935; Whiting
    1934, 1935
Easy Goin' Mamma Don't Play Hard to Get with Me   Ahlert
    1924; Lewis 1924; Young, Joe 1924
Easy Going Woman   Lawrence 1933
Easy Living   Rainger 1937; Robin 1937
Easy Money   Coleman 1996
Easy on the Eyes   Coslow 1935, 1937; David, Mack 1934;
    Hoffman 1934
Easy Pickin's   Kern 1921
Easy Ridin' Papa   Bloom 1966; Koehler 1966
Easy Strain   Arlen 1925
Easy Street   Arlen 1959; Mercer 1959; Strouse 1977
Easy to Be With   Coleman 1975
Easy to Have Around   Robison 1954
Easy to Kiss   Merrill 1954
Easy to Love   Fain 1934; Kahal 1934; Porter 1936
Easy to Love Again   Bacharach 1981
Easy to Take   Ellington 1966
Eat a Big Breakfast   Robison 1954
Eat a Little Something   Rome 1962
Eat a Piece of Pie   Fisher 1926; Rose 1926
Eat and the World Eats with You   Romberg 1918
Eat, Drink and Be Healthy   Willson 1954
Eat, Drink and Be Merry   Friend 1932; Stept 1932
Eat Marlowe's Meat   Clare 1933; Gorney 1933
Eat Mush, Mush, Mush, Mush, Mushroom Soup   Styne 1946
Eating   Strouse Date Unknown
Eating Is Such Fun!   Rome 1940
Ebb Tide   Rainger 1937; Robin 1937; Sigman 1953
Ebenezer Brown   Sterling 1904; Von Tilzer 1904
Ebony Dreams (inst.)   Johnson, James P. 1927
Ebony Echoes (inst.)   Edwards 1901
Ebony Rhapsody   Coslow 1934; Johnston 1934
Eccentric Dance   Hammerstein 1924; Harbach 1924; Herbert
    1905
Eccentricity Waltz   Johnson, James P. 1926
Echo (inst.)   Schwartz, Arthur 1946
Echo of a Dream   Mercer 1959
Echo of a Love Song, An   Friend 1937
Echo of Her Smile   Howard, Joseph E. 1918

Echo of Love   Sigman 1956
Echo Song   Leigh 1954; Sondheim 1962
Echo Waltz   Howard, Bart 1938
Echoes   Caesar 1920; Mercer 1957; Mills 1935
Echoes in the Night (Lassame Sunna)   Raye 1957
Echoes of Aloha   Stept 1959
Echoes of Dixieland   Johnson, James P. 1927
Echoes of Hawaii   Mitchell 1939; Pollack 1939
Echoes of the Jungle   Mills 1952
Echoing Mountains and Whisperin' Trees   Silver 1951
Echoing Mountains and Whispering Trees   Davis 1951
Economic Situation (Aren't You Wonderful), The   Duke
    1936; Gershwin, Ira 1936
Economics   Lerner, Alan Jay 1948; Rome 1937; Weill 1948
Ecstacy (inst.)   Young, Victor 1951
Eddie Be Good   Buck 1925
Eddie Jordan Story, The   Oakland 1960
Eddie's Fifth Encore   Merrill 1964; Styne 1964
Eddie's Song   Merrill 1959
Edelaine   Harburg 1979
Edelweiss   Hammerstein 1959; Rodgers 1959; Romberg
    1925; Smith, Harry B. 1914
Edinboro Wriggle, The   Kern 1911
Edison March (inst.)   Young, Victor 1947
Edna May   Clarke 1912; Schwartz, Jean 1912
Educate Your Feet   Ager 1929; Yellen 1929
Educated Fool (It Keeps Me Guessing All the Time),
    An   Herbert 1905; Smith, Harry B. 1905
Educated Rhythm   Kalmar 1937; Ruby 1937
Edward   Merrill 1954
Edward My Son   Davis 1949; Silver 1949
Eee-o Eleven   Cahn 1960; Van Heusen 1960
Eenie Meenie Minee Chinee   Edwards 1935
Eenie, Meenie, Minee, Mo   Duke 1941
Eenie Meenie Minie Chinee   Bryan 1935
Eeny Meany Miney But What Became of Mo   Kalmar 1950
Eeny Meeny Miney Mo   Mercer 1935
Eeny Meeny Miney Pow   Evans 1953; Livingston, Jay 1953
Eeny Meeny Miny Mo   Smith, Harry B. 1910
Effervescent (inst.)   Waller 1934
Effie Klinker   Henderson 1945
Egg and I, The   Akst 1947; Kalmar 1947; Ruby 1947
Egg Has Fallen Down, The   Johnson, J. Rosamond 1904
Egghead   Hoffman 1956
Eglatine!   Sherman 1971
E-gypt   Fisher 1921; Goetz 1916; Silver 1943
Egypt, You and I   Kahn 1924
Egyptian Ballet   Duke 1940
Egyptian Butterfly   Kalmar 1919; Leslie 1919
Egyptian Dance, The   Friml 1921
Egyptian Melange   Hanley 1922
Egyptian Rag   Atteridge 1917; Romberg 1917
Egyptian Rose   Smith, Harry B. 1923; Snyder 1923
Egypt's No Place for a Lady   Freed, Arthur 1925
Eh   Cahn 1951
Eight Ball (inst.)   Robison 1927
Eight Bells   Atteridge 1915; Romberg 1915
Eight Girls in a Boat   Coslow 1934
Eight Little Darkies on a Fence   Kahn 1934
Eight Little Girls   Kern 1910
Eight Little Letters   Donaldson 1931
Eight Little Letters Make Three Little Words   Kalmar 1911;
    Snyder 1911
Eight Little Notes   Fain 1938
Eight Note Symphony, The   Oakland 1960

Eight O'Clock in Paris   Livingston, Jerry 1960
Eight Piece Band on a Nine Day Cruise, An   David, Hal 1949
Eight P.M.   Drake 1956
18 Days Ago   Brown, Lew 1929; DeSylva 1929; Henderson 1929
Eighteenth Amendment Repealed   Berlin 1933
Eighteenth Century Blues   Oakland 1952; Raye 1952
Eighth Avenue   Leigh 1976; Styne 1976
Eighty Miles Outside of Atlanta   Adamson 1944; McHugh 1944
86th! The 86th! The Fighting Men of the 86th!, The   Cahn 1955; Van Heusen 1955
Eileen, Allana Asthore   Herbert 1917
Eileen Aroon   Bergman 1987
Eileen Asthore   Olcott 1906
Eileen Christy Polka (inst.)   McHugh 1957
Eisenhower Song   Brown, Lew 1952
El Botecito (Ferry-boat Serenade)   Adamson 1940
El Brut (inst.)   Motzan 1918
El Bruta   Howard, Joseph E. 1918
El Caballero   Magidson 1930; Washington 1930
El Casino   Mercer 1972
El Choclo   Fields 1934; Johnson, Howard 1939; McHugh 1934
El Cubanito   Fain 1935; Kahal 1935
El Gaucho   Fain 1937; Kahal 1937
El Huapango   Loesser 1939
El Morocco (inst.)   Coots 1946
El Pajaro Carpintero   Adamson 1940
El Rancho   Loewe 1942
El Relicario (Rendezvous of Love)   Johnson, Howard 1936
El Rey Del Jazz   Gorney 1930
El Sombrero   Coleman 1960; Leigh 1960
El Tango de Reve   Johnson, Howard 1936
El Tango del Perroquet   Dubin 1927
El Tenorio de Broadway (The Tenor of Broadway)   Gorney 1935
Elbow Room   Harburg 1945; Kern 1945
Eleanor   Atteridge 1922; Mills 1947
Eleanor, I Adore You   Rose 1940; Van Heusen 1940
Eleanor, the Song that I Sing in My Dreams (Serenade, the Song that I Sing in My Dreams)   Hanley 1930
Election Day   Blake 1921; Caesar 1946; Sissle 1921
Election in Jungle Town, The   Brown, A. Seymour 1912
Electric Light, The   Smith, Harry B. 1901
Electrician Blues   Razaf 1931
Electricity   Coots 1922
Elegance   Merrill 1964
Elegant Captain Hook, The   Cahn 1952; Fain 1952
Elegant Elephant, The   Sherman 1991
Elegant Swelegant You   Hoffman 1932; Lerner, Sammy 1932
Elegie   Dubin 1924; Johnson, Howard 1934
Elegy   Arlen 1959; Mercer 1959
Elegy (inst.)   Motzan 1926
Elenita   Conrad 1929; Mitchell 1929
Elephant Never Forgets, An   Cahn 1963; Van Heusen 1963
Elephant Skid   Freed, Arthur Date Unknown
Elevator Man, The   Caesar 1941
Elevator Man (Going Up - Going Up - Going Up)   Berlin 1912
Elevator Papa, Switchboard Mama   Johnson, James P. 1930; Razaf 1930
Elevator Song   Mercer 1951
Eleven Levee Street   Hammerstein 1941; Romberg 1941

Eleven O'Clock Song   Fain 1955
Eleventh Commandment, The   Ellington 1966
11th Hour Melody   Sigman 1956
Elf King, The   Smith, Harry B. 1908
Eli   Porter 1910
Eliza   Kahn 1924
Elizabeth   Caesar 1931; Rodgers 1976
Ella the Elephant   Dietz 1943; Duke 1943
Ella Vino Al Valle   David, Mack 1978
Ellen Bayne   Johnson, Howard 1939
Ellen Roe   Burke 1961
Ellenville   Coleman 1983; Leigh 1983
Ellie   Styne Date Unknown
Ellie Lou, You Left Me There in Charleston   Sigman 1960
Elopement, The   Cohan 1903
Elsie   Blake 1923; Meyer 1910; Sissle 1923
(That's My) Elsie Schultz-en-heim   Friend 1926
(That's My) Elsie Shultz-En-Heim   Silver 1926
Elsie, There Isn't Anybody Else but You   Carroll 1924
Eltibadabo Pooka-Pooka   Livingston, Jerry 1958
Elusive Mr. Rassendyl, The   Duke 1963
Elvis   Adams 1958
Emaline   McHugh 1921; Parish 1934
Emancipation   Livingston, Jerry 1941
Emancipation Day   Buck 1920
Embassy Burglarious, An   Smith, Harry B. 1903
Embassy Waltz (inst.)   Loewe 1956
Emblems of Love   Mitchell 1923; Pollack 1923
Embrace Me   Hammerstein 1931; Romberg 1931
Embraceable You   Gershwin, George 1929, 1930; Gershwin, Ira 1929, 1930
Emerald Eyes (inst.)   Alter 1955
Emerald Isle   Webster 1954
Emigrants' Song   Brown, Lew 1927; Friend 1927
Emile's Reel   Sherman 1962
Emily   Mercer 1965
Emmaline   Jerome 1908; Schwartz, Jean 1908
Emmett's Lullaby   Johnson, Howard 1939
Emmy Lou   Brooks 1960
Emperor Is a Man, The   Strouse 1982
Emperor Jones   Wrubel 1933
Emperor Waltz   Burke 1948
Emperor's Bones, The   Webster 1941
Emperor's Guards, The   David, Mack 1958; Livingston, Jerry 1958
Emperor's Thumb, The   Rodgers 1967
Empire Days   Atteridge 1919; Romberg 1919; Schwartz, Jean 1919
Empire State Opening   Brown, Lew 1931; Henderson 1931
Employment Agency, The   Atteridge 1915; Romberg 1915
Empress of Crime, The   Strouse 1990
Empty Arms   Conrad 1929; Howard, Joseph E. 1931; Mitchell 1929; Young, Joe 1960
Empty Ballroom   Spina 1953
Empty House Blues   Razaf 1929, 1953
Empty Interlude   Razaf 1941
Empty Place, The   Bacharach 1976; David, Hal 1976
Empty Pockets Filled with Love   Berlin 1962
Empty Promises   Robison 1949
Empty Saddles   Brennan 1936
Empty Tables   Mercer 1974; Van Heusen 1974
En Douce   Atteridge 1924; Romberg 1924; Schwartz, Jean 1924
Enbothered   Carmichael 1952
Encanto   Hart 1941; Rodgers 1941

(Why Do I Feel So) Enchanted   David, Mack 1958;
   Livingston, Jerry 1958
Enchanted April   DePaul 1950; Egan 1941; Raye 1950
Enchanted Ballroom   Spina 1955
Enchanted Clock, The   Harburg 1979
Enchanted Land   Cahn 1951
Enchanted Mountain   Bergman 1963
Enchanted Train, The   Kern 1924
Enchanting Girls   Duke 1963
Enchantment   DePaul 1949; Fain 1951; Harburg 1951; Raye
   1949
Enchilada Man, The   David, Mack 1953; Livingston, Jerry
   1953; Washington 1944
Enclosed Are My Tears   Coots 1953
Enclosed Please Find   Robin 1932; Whiting 1932
Encore, Cherie   Coots 1946
Encore, Encore, Encore   Parish 1967
End, The   Adams 1996; Strouse 1956, 1996
End of a Beautiful Friendship, The   Adamson 1953; Duke
   1953
End of a Perfect Day, The   Brown, Lew 1919
End of a Perfect Night   Duke 1932; Harburg 1932
End of a String, The   Gershwin, George 1924; Gershwin, Ira
   1924
End Title   Cahn 1964; Loesser 1936
Endie   Alter 1947; De Lange 1947
Endless   Davis 1953
Endless Love   Myrow 1955
Endless Nights   Kalmar 1934; Ruby 1934
Endless River   Robison 1959
Engaged   Rome 1970
Engagement Ring, The   Johnson, Howard 1927
English Bow, The   Smith, Robert B. 1905
English Hedgehogs   Sherman 1991
English March   Friml 1937
English Summer Day, An   Martin 1964
English Teacher, An   Adams 1960; Strouse 1960
Englishman's Idea of Ragtime, An   Smith, Harry B. 1901
Enjoy It   Sherman 1962
Enjoy Today   Gershwin, George 1927; Gershwin, Ira 1927
Enjoy Yourself (It's Later than You Think)   Magidson 1948;
   Sigman 1948
Enlloro (Voodoo Moon)   Rome 1945
Enough   Adams 1972; Strouse 1972
Enough of This   David, Hal 1955
Enough of Work   Herbert 1906
Ensemble   Cohan 1918; Goetz 1913; Smith, Harry B. 1912;
   Smith, Robert B. 1912
Ensemble Finale   Buck 1922
Ensemble Song   Romberg 1948
Ensenada Nights   Washington 1938
Enter Juliet   Leigh 1977
Enter Laughing   David, Mack 1967
Entertaining Papa   Yellen 1978
Enthusiasm   Brooks 1962
Entire History of the World in Two Minutes and Thirty-Two
   Seconds   Strouse 1955
Entirely Surrounded by Girls   Atteridge 1919; Carroll 1919
Entr'acte (inst.)   Friml 1906
Entrance and Song of Czarina   Smith, Harry B. 1925
Entrance Chorus of the Khedive   Smith, Harry B. 1900
Entrance of Arabs   Herbert 1907; Smith, Harry B. 1907
Entrance of Babette   Herbert 1903; Smith, Harry B. 1903
Entrance of Brahmins   Herbert 1897; Smith, Harry B. 1897

Entrance of Cinderella and Princess of Far Away   Herbert
   1912
Entrance of Czarina   Smith, Harry B. 1925
Entrance of Dancers   Caesar 1930; Harbach 1921, 1930;
   Romberg 1930
Entrance of Dolly   Herbert 1905; Smith, Harry B. 1905
Entrance of Dorothy   Herbert 1905; Smith, Harry B. 1905
Entrance of Duke and Dolores (Who Can This Be?)   Herbert
   1897; Smith, Harry B. 1897
Entrance of Emigrants   Porter 1929
Entrance of Eric   Porter 1935
Entrance of Herr Bangkeyski and the Piano King   Herbert
   1911; Smith, Harry B. 1911
Entrance of Humpy Grogan   Herbert 1917
Entrance of Johnny Rocks   Smith, Robert B. 1906
Entrance of Lew Fields with Children   Herbert 1909
Entrance of Lucy James   Porter 1936
Entrance of Mary and Wintergreen   Gershwin, George 1931;
   Gershwin, Ira 1931
Entrance of Montana   Porter 1944
Entrance of Omar (Oriental March)   Herbert 1907; Smith,
   Harry B. 1907
Entrance of Prince Ivan   Herbert 1911; Smith, Harry B. 1911
Entrance of Prince Paul   Porter 1937
Entrance of Rose   Herbert 1911; Smith, Harry B. 1911
Entrance of Sailors (When the Guns Are Booming)   Kern
   1921
Entrance of Shah   Herbert 1907; Smith, Harry B. 1907
Entrance of Supreme Court Judges   Gershwin, George 1931;
   Gershwin, Ira 1931
Entrance of Sylvia   Herbert 1913; Smith, Robert B. 1913
Entrance of the Count   Herbert 1898; Smith, Harry B. 1898
Entrance of the Courtesans   Harburg 1961
Entrance of the Emperor and the Empress   Smith, Harry B.
   1925
Entrance of the French Ambassador   Gershwin, George
   1931; Gershwin, Ira 1931
Entrance of the Friendly Rivals' Club   Herbert 1905; Smith,
   Harry B. 1905
Entrance of the Hussars   Romberg 1928
Entrance of the Regent   Herbert 1911; Smith, Harry B. 1911
Entrance of the School Children   Herbert 1908; Smith, Harry
   B. 1908
Entrance of Vivien   Herbert 1911; Smith, Harry B. 1911
Entrance of Yvonne, Colombe and Gomez   Herbert 1897;
   Smith, Harry B. 1897
Entre Nous   Romberg 1948
Entre-Nous   Rome 1938
Entry of the Council   Weill 1938
Ephasafa Dill   Sterling 1903; Von Tilzer 1903
Ephraham Played Upon the Piano   Berlin 1911
Ephraham the Bunny   Coots 1950; Egan 1950
Epilogue   Duke 1936
Epiphany   Sondheim 1979
Episode in Victor's Play The Passionate Pilgrim   Harbach
   1931; Kern 1931
Episode of the Swing   Hammerstein 1932; Kern 1932
Epitaph   Weill 1936
Epitaph for a Poet   Parish 1965
Epitomy of Femininity, The   Gordon 1955
Equal Rights   Herbert 1914
Equity Star, The   Herbert 1921
Era of Jazz   Evans 1955; Livingston, Jay 1955
Erbie Fitch's Twitch   Fields 1959
Ergo Bibamus   Webster 1954

Erin Is Smiling   Ager 1916; Jerome 1916
Erin Slanthogal Go Bragh   Herbert 1917
Errand Boy   Johnson, James P. 1964
Errand of Mercy, An   Bacharach 1962; David, Hal 1962
Escapade   Burke 1940; Mercer 1970; Russell 1957; Van Heusen 1940
Escape   Spina 1976
Eskimo Bacchante   Duke 1946
Eskimo Named Moe   Donaldson 1943
Esmeralda   David, Hal 1961
Esmerelda   David, Mack 1961; Porter 1915
E.S.P.   Lane 1965
Espagnola   Herbert 1908
Ess Ess Mein Kindt   Gilbert 1966; Myrow 1966
Esta Noche (Tonight)   Young, Victor 1951
Estellita   Herbert 1915
Esther   Cahn 1952; Duke 1952
Eternal City of Dreams   Kahn 1923
Eternal Flame, The   Brennan 1922
Eternal Love   Revel 1959
Eternal Summer   Warren 1979
Eternally Yours   Gilbert 1939
Ethics Waltz, The   Adams 1957; Strouse 1957
Ethiopian Essence, An   Smith, Harry B. 1901
Etiquette   Coots 1923; Freed, Arthur 1950; Sherman 1989; Smith, Robert B. 1902; Warren 1950
Etiquette in the Zoo   Caesar 1943
Etiquette Quintette   Romberg 1927
Etta in Bolivia (inst.)   Bacharach 1969
Eubie Duebie   Blake 1972
Eubie's Boogie Woogie Rag (inst.)   Blake 1958
Eubie's Classical Rag (inst.)   Blake 1972
Eubie's E-flat Blues (inst.)   Blake 1976
Eubie's Slow Drag (inst.)   Blake 1962
Eugene O'Neill's Hairy Ape   Atteridge 1922
Eugenie Girls   Atteridge 1914; Romberg 1914
Eulalie   Kern 1909
Eureka   Harburg 1961; Strouse 1975
European Importation, A   Young, Joe 1934
Evalina Jackson's Wedding Day   Silver 1918; Sterling 1918
Evangeline   Berlin 1928; Hanley 1928; Rose 1928
Eve   Mills 1929
Evelina   Arlen 1944; Harburg 1944
Evelyn   Conrad 1924
Evelyn, What Do You Say?   Hart 1927; Rodgers 1927
Even a Soldier Can Cry   Freed, Ralph 1966
Even As You and I   Brown, Lew 1925; DeSylva 1925; Fain 1931; Henderson 1925; Kahal 1931
Even If I Say It Myself   Carmichael 1940; Mercer 1940
Even If You Don't Love Me   Dixon 1926; Henderson 1926
Even though You're Not Beside Me   Brooks 1957
Even When You Cry   Bergman 1968
Evenin'   Parish 1934; Whiting 1928
Evenin', Caroline   Stept 1926
Evening   Kahn 1932
Evening at Ciro's, An   Pollack 1943
Evening Hymn, An   Kern 1905
Evening in 32 Bars, An   Russell 1949
Evening in Manhattan   Snyder 1936
Evening Star   Akst 1930; Brooks 1945; Brown, Nacio Herb 1948; Davis 1930; Gershwin, George 1924; Gershwin, Ira 1924; Johnson, Howard 1939; Parish 1941
Evening Star, Help Me Find My Man   Ahlert 1928; Turk 1928
Evening Sun, Morning Moon   Bergman 1975

Evening with You, An   Dubin 1936; Warren 1936
Evenings We Spent at Joe's, The   Stept 1951
Eventually Comes Love   Brown, Lew 1944
Ever After   Sondheim 1987
Ever and Ever Yours   Porter 1916
Ever By Your Side   Atteridge 1918; Romberg 1918
Ever Homeward   Cahn 1948; Styne 1948
Ever Lovin' Bee   Buck 1923, 1924
Ever Near, Never Far   Bacharach 1959; David, Hal 1959
Ever Since Adam   Stept 1938; Washington 1938
Ever Since Leavin' Wichita   Warren 1970
Ever Since the Day I Found You   Heyman 1933
Ever Since the Night You Left Me   Ager 1934; Young, Joe 1934
Ever Since You Told Me that You Loved Me I'm a Nut — I'm a Nut   Clarke 1913; Leslie 1913; Schwartz, Jean 1913
Ever So Gently   Cahn 1971; Van Heusen 1971
Ever So Lightly   Cahn 1959; Van Heusen 1959
Ever So Often   Silver 1942
Everchanging Times   Bacharach 1987
Everglades   Leslie 1935
Evergreen Tree, The   Robison 1961
Everlasting   Comden and Green 1951; Styne 1951
(The) Everlasting Arms   Webster 1950
Everlasting Mountain, The   David, Mack Date Unknown; Warren Date Unknown
Ever-Lovin' Lover   Ellington 1963
Every Baby Is a Sweet Bouquet   Brown, A. Seymour 1909
Every Blossom I See Reminds Me of You   Buck 1938
Every Boy in Town's My Sweetheart   Cohan 1928
Every Child Is So Happy   Burke 1965
Every Day   Kern 1917; Willson 1949
Every Day a Little Death   Sondheim 1973
Every Day Every May   Lawrence 1960
Every Day I Love You Just a Little More   Snyder 1910
Every Day in Every Way   Kern 1922
Every Day Is Father's Day with Baby   Caesar 1934; Henderson 1934; Yellen 1934
Every Day Is Holiday in Kidland   Edwards 1929
Every Day Is Ladies Day with Me   Herbert 1906
Every Day Is Lovely   Hoffman 1945; Livingston, Jerry 1945
Every Day Is Mother's Day for Me   Edwards 1925
Every Day Is New Year's Eve   Cahn 1982
Every Day Is Sunday   Davis 1981
Every Day'll Be Sunday When the Town Goes Dry   Jerome 1918
Every Day's a Happy Day   Cahn 1955; Schwartz, Arthur 1955
Every Day's a Holiday   Coslow 1936, 1937
Every Evening (I Miss You)   McHugh 1927; Rose 1927
Every Flower Has It's Melody   Goetz 1912
Every Girl   Kern 1921
Every Girl Has a Way   Gershwin, George 1921; Gershwin, Ira 1921
Every Girl I Get, Somebody Else Takes Her Right Away from Me   Stept 1924
Every Girl I Love Is Someone's Wife   Howard, Joseph E. 1910
Every Girl I Meet   Kern 1910
Every Girl in All America   Kern 1918
Every Girl Is Doing Her Bit   Buck 1917
Every Girl Is Like a Weather Glass   DeSylva 1922; Herbert 1922
Every Girl Must Have a Little Bull   Coots 1925

(What) Every Girl Should Know   Revel 1959

Every Girlie Loves Me but the Girl I Love   Harbach 1911

Every Girl's a Soldier in the Army of Love   Herbert 1911;
      Smith, Harry B. 1911

Every Heart Has a Dream   Smith, Harry B. 1923; Smith,
      Robert B. 1923

Every Heart Must Have Its Sorrow   Williams 1910

Every Hour Away from You Is Sixty Minutes Lost   Herbert
      1920; Smith, Robert B. 1920

Every Little Dog Must Have His Day   Olcott 1902

Every Little Doggie Has His Day   Livingston, Jerry 1935

Every Little Girl He Sees   Akst 1930; Clarke 1930

Every Little Moment   Fields 1935; McHugh 1935

Every Little Movement   Harbach 1910

Every Little Object Has a History   Smith, Harry B. 1906

Every Little Thing You Do   Buck 1926; Hanley 1926

Every Living Thing   Drake 2000

Every Lover Must Meet His Fate   Herbert 1913; Smith,
      Robert B. 1913

Every Man Is a Stupid Man   Porter 1953

Every Man Should Marry   Davis 1956; Silver 1956

Every Minute of the Day   Strouse 1999

Every Moment of My Life   Adamson 1975; Davis 1951;
      Silver 1951

Every Morn' You'll Hear Them Say Good Night   Kalmar
      1915

Every Morning   Monaco 1912; Sterling 1912

Every Mother's Lullaby   Cobb 1921; Edwards 1921

Every New Tomorrow   Ager 1954; Akst 1954; Davis 1954

Every Night   Drake 1953; Rome 1954; Warren 1956

Every Night About This Time   Monaco 1942

Every Night at Eight   Fields 1935; McHugh 1935

Every Night Dear   Caesar Date Unknown

Every Night He Goes Over the Top   Johnson, Howard 1918;
      Meyer 1918

Every Night I Bring Her Frankfurter Sandwiches   Dubin
      1927

Every Night I Cry Myself to Sleep Over You   Johnson,
      Howard 1923

Every Night in the Week   Lewis 1928; Warren 1930; Young,
      Joe 1930

Every Night (inst.)   Warren Date Unknown

Every Night When You Say a Prayer   McHugh 1958

Every Number Needs a Button   Strouse 1999

Every Once in a While   Brooks 1959; Dixon 1936;
      Henderson 1936; Rome 1959; Stept 1929

Every Rose Must Have a Thorn   Brown, Lew 1927; DeSylva
      1927

Every Silken Lady   Gorney 1924

Every Silver Lining   Hammerstein 1922; Mitchell 1922

Every Small Town Girlie Has a Big Town Way   Atteridge
      1915

Every So Often   Cahn 1945; Mercer 1947; Parish 1945; Styne
      1945; Warren 1947; Woods 1945

Every Stand Up Act Is Sitting Down Today   Cahn 1963; Van
      Heusen 1963

Every Star Falls in Love with His Mate   Olcott 1907

Every Step Brings Me Closer to My Lovin' Honey
      Lamb   Pollack 1923

Every Street's a Boulevard in Old New York   Styne 1953

Every Telephone (Telephone Song)   Buck 1920

Every Time a Moment Goes By   Brooks 1942

Every Time I Hear a Band Play   Buck 1921; Friml 1921

Every Time I Meet a Lady   Harbach 1920

Every Time I Meet You   Gordon 1948; Myrow 1948

Every Time the Clock Ticks   Gorney 1924

Every Time You Danced with Me   Warren 1956

Every Wednesday Night   Friend 1922

Every Week We Get a Stack of Mail   Brooks 1959

Every Woman Is a Queen   Willson 1969

Every Woman Wants to Marry   Revel 1960

Everybody   Burke 1934; Spina 1934

Everybody Be Happy   Hoffman 1955

Everybody but Me   Meyer 1924; Rose 1924

Everybody Calls Me Little Red Riding Hood   Kern 1923

Everybody Dance   Atteridge 1924; Buck 1915; Coslow 1942;
      Gordon 1936; Revel 1936; Romberg 1924; Schwartz, Jean
      1924

Everybody Does It Now   Johnson, James P. 1928

Everybody Gives Me Good Advice   Bryan 1906

Everybody Has a Favorite Song   Drake 1953

Everybody Has a Laughing Place   Wrubel 1946

Everybody Has a Tip   Von Tilzer 1916

Everybody Hum with Me   Atteridge 1915; Romberg 1915

Everybody Is Ragtime Crazy   Jerome 1910; Schwartz, Jean
      1910

Everybody Knew but Me   Berlin 1940

Everybody Knows Everybody   Willson 1953

Everybody Knows what Jazz Is   Buck 1925

Everybody Knows You By Your First Name Baby   Russell
      1950

Everybody Likes a College Girl   Lewis 1911

Everybody Likes Music   Burke 1933; Spina 1933

Everybody Loves a Chicken   Atteridge 1912

Everybody Loves a Winner   Comden and Green 1964; Styne
      1964

Everybody Loves Everybody   Duke Date Unknown; Rome
      1952

Everybody Loves Leona   Rodgers 1965; Sondheim 1965

Everybody Loves Louis   Sondheim 1984

Everybody Loves Me   Lane 1996; Styne 1980

Everybody Loves Me but the One I Love   Edwards 1908

Everybody Loves Money   Spina 1953

Everybody Loves My Girl   Brown, Lew 1914

Everybody Loves Somebody   Coslow 1947

Everybody Loves to Take a Bow   Styne 1953

Everybody Means It When They Say Good-Bye   Atteridge
      1914

Everybody Misses You   Spina 1967

Everybody Needs a Buddy   Baer 1929; Gilbert 1929

Everybody Ought to Have a Maid   Sondheim 1962

Everybody Rag with Me   Kahn 1914

Everybody Said   Spina 1957

Everybody Says Don't   Sondheim 1964

Everybody Sing   Akst 1937; Brown, Nacio Herb 1937; Freed,
      Arthur 1937

Everybody Sings   Loesser 1937

Everybody Snap Your Fingers with Me   Kalmar 1913

Everybody Sometime Must Love Somebody   Buck 1913

Everybody Sometime Must Love Someone   Buck 1913;
      Schwartz, Jean 1914

Everybody Sometimes Must Love Someone   Cohan 1909

Everybody Step   Berlin 1921

Everybody Step with Me   Johnson, James P. 1920

Everybody Swat the Profiteer   Gershwin, George 1920

Everybody Swing   Akst 1937; Clare 1937

Everybody Tap   Ager 1929, 1930; Yellen 1929, 1930

Everybody Tells It to Sweeney and Sweeney Tells It to
      Me   Mitchell 1920

Everybody Today Is Turning On   Coleman 1977

Everybody Took a Kick at Nicholas   Lewis 1917; Young, Joe 1917

Everybody Want to Live a Long, Long Time (But Nobody Want to Grow Old)   Gilbert 1957

Everybody Wants a Key to My Cellar   Pollack 1919

Everybody Wants My Business   Fain 1948; Yellen 1948

Everybody Wants to Do a Musical   Strouse 1991

Everybody Wonders Why They Married   Howard, Joseph E. 1909

Everybody Yell Meow, Let's See if Kitty's Home   Lewis 1924; Young, Joe 1924

Everybody's Buddy   Adams 1956

Everybody's Cabareting   Jerome 1912; Schwartz, Jean 1912

Everybody's Crazy Half of the Time   Herbert 1919; Smith, Robert B. 1919

Everybody's Crazy Over Winnie   Edwards 1931

Everybody's Dancing Mad   Davis 1919

Everybody's Does the Charleston Now   Johnson, James P. 1925

Everybody's Doing It Now   Berlin 1911

Everybody's Falling in Love   Coots 1951

Everybody's Got a Price   Strouse 2000

Everybody's Got Somebody But Me   McHugh 1926

Everybody's Got the Right   Sondheim 1990

Everybody's Got to Be Somebody   David, Hal 1976

Everybody's Gotta Be Somewhere   Coleman 1989

Everybody's Happy   Drake 1953

Everybody's Happy When the Sun Shines   Cohan 1903

Everybody's Knittin' Now   Hanley 1917

Everybody's Laughing   Lerner, Sammy 1938; Oakland 1938

Everybody's Lookin' (Around for an Angel)   Howard, Bart 1961

Everybody's Out of Town   Bacharach 1970; David, Hal 1970

Everybody's Ragtime Crazy   Jerome 1909; Schwartz, Jean 1909

Everybody's Ship Comes In (Not Mine)   Loesser 1935

Everybody's Sister but Yours and Mine   Lewis 1926; Young, Joe 1926

Everybody's Struttin' Now   Blake 1923; Sissle 1923

Everybody's Sweetheart   David, Hal 1952

Everybody's Swingin' It Now   Coots 1936; Davis 1936

Everybody's Talking About My Girl   Kahal 1927; Snyder 1927

Everybody's Twisting   Bloom 1962; Koehler 1962

Everybody's Whispering   Coots 1935; Davis 1935

Everyday Is a Holiday in Florida   Alter 1930

Everyday Will Be Sunday When the Town Goes Dry   Friml 1918

Everyday's an Opening Night on Wall Street   Stept 1956

Everyone   Ellington 1972

Everyone Baby   Cahn 1953; Livingston, Jerry 1953

Everyone but You   Drake 1994

Everyone Celebrate   Robin 1926

Everyone (Everybody) Wants to Get in the Act   De Lange 1945; Myrow 1945

Everyone I Love Lives Down in Dixie   Dubin 1918

Everyone in the World (Is Doing the Charleston)   Berlin 1925

Everyone in Town Likes Mary   Schwartz, Jean 1912

Everyone in Town Loves Little Mary Brown   Davis 1931

Everyone in Town Loves My Girl   Brown, Lew 1913

Everyone Is Wanted in Wyoming   Revel 1952

Every-One Is Wanted in Wyoming (inst.)   Revel 1960

Everyone Kiss the Bride   David, Mack 1976

Everyone Knows It but You   Coslow 1932, 1939; Johnston 1932, 1939

Everyone Needs Someone (to Love)   Bacharach 1977; David, Hal 1977

Everyone Remembers But You   Oakland 1933

Everyone Wants Something   Van Heusen 1953

Everyone Who Is Anyone (Is Going to Be There)   David, Hal 1991; Strouse 1991

Everyone Who's Been in Love with You (Has Cried and Cried and Cried)   Bacharach 1962; David, Hal 1962

Everyone's Moving Up on Broadway (Everyone's Moving Up Town)   Atteridge 1915; Carroll 1915; Romberg 1915

Everyone's Wrong but Me   Cahn 1937; Fain Date Unknown

Every-Ready Freddie   Hart 1926; Rodgers 1926

Everything Beautiful   Evans 1961; Livingston, Jay 1961

Everything Can Be Lovely in the Morning   Strouse 2000

Everything Changes but Love   Friml 1934

Everything Happens to Me   Carmichael 1940; Mercer 1940

Everything Has a Useness   David, Mack 1951; Hoffman 1951; Livingston, Jerry 1951

Everything Has Been Done   Romberg 1917

Everything Has Stung Me but a Bee   Herbert 1920; Smith, Robert B. 1920

Everything I Do   Heyman 1954; Young, Victor 1954

Everything I Dreamed   Burke 1971

Everything I Have Is Yours   Adamson 1933; Lane 1933

Everything I Need   Bacharach 1974

Everything in America Is Ragtime (Ragtime Finale)   Berlin 1915

Everything Is All Right   Hammerstein 1923; Harbach 1923; Youmans 1923

Everything is Buttercups and Daisies   Woods 1932

Everything Is Coming Back Again (Won't You Come Back to Me)   Parish 1934

Everything Is Different Now-a-days   Buck 1913

Everything Is French in Dixieland   Fisher 1920

Everything Is Hotsy Totsy Now   McHugh 1925; Mills 1925

Everything Is Jake with Rosie and Everything Is Rosie with Jake   DeSylva 1923; Monaco 1923; Rose 1923

Everything Is K.O. in K.Y.   Egan 1923; Whiting 1923

Everything Is Lovely   Adams Date Unknown; Johnson, Howard 1929

Everything Is Peaches Down in Georgia   Ager 1918; Clarke 1918; Meyer 1918

Everything Is Rosy Now   Atteridge 1918; DeSylva 1918; Romberg 1918

Everything Is Rosy Now for Rosie   Berlin 1919; Clarke 1919

Everything Is Spanish Now   Dubin 1927

Everything Is Still the Same   Stept 1953

Everything Is Talent Today   Cahn 1943

Everything Is Tickety-Boo   Mercer 1958

Everything Isn't Sunshine and Roses   Davis 1950

Everything Looks Rosy and Bright   Goetz 1917

Everything Makes Music When You're in Love   Cahn 1964; Van Heusen 1964

Everything Reminds Me of You   Blake 1921; Sissle 1921

Everything that Father Did Was Right   Howard, Joseph E. 1909

Everything that Happens to You   David, Hal 1974

Everything That's Gonna Be Has Been   Rodgers 1970

Everything That's Nice Belongs to You   Stept 1931

Everything They Say About Love Is True   Blake 1962; Sissle 1962

Everything to Make Us Happy   Norworth 1938

Everything Was Irish   Young, Joe 1911

Everything Was Perfect   Strouse 1980
Everything Was Wonderful   Drake 1953
Everything We Like, We Like Alike   Fain 1928
Everything Will Happen for the Best   DeSylva 1926
Everything You Said Came True   Friend 1937
Everything's Already Alright   Robison 1963
Everything's As It Should Be   Schwartz, Jean 1933; Young, Joe 1933
Everything's Been Done Before   Adamson 1935
Everything's Bigger Down in Texas   Oakland 1953; Raye 1953
Everything's Comin' Up Roses   Sondheim 1959; Styne 1959
Everything's Ducky   Spina 1961
Everything's Easy when You Know How   Adams 1966; Strouse 1966
Everything's Going to Be All Right   Conrad 1925
Everything's Gonna Be All Right   Akst 1926; Conrad 1922; Davis 1926; Fisher 1922
Everything's Great   Adams 1964; Strouse 1964
Everything's in Rhythm in My Heart   Hoffman 1935
Everything's Lovely in the Morning   Strouse 1984
Everything's Rosey   Revel 1953
Everything's Talent Today   Cahn 1936
Everything's the Same   Brooks 1959; Koehler 1932; Myrow 1932; Young, Victor 1932
Everytime   Caesar 1923; Conrad 1923
Everytime I Dance the Polka   Romberg 1948
Everytime I Fall in Love   David, Hal 1960
Everytime I Look at You   Stept 1955
Everytime I Think of You   Bergman 1968
Everytime We Meet   Cahn 1956
Everytime You Pray   Davis 1953
Everytime You Smile   Parish 1957
Evig Evol   Lawrence 1958
Evil Eye, The   Ager 1923; Russell 1962; Yellen 1923
Evil Minded Papa Blues   Razaf 1925
Evils of Drink!, The   Arlen 1953; DePaul 1953; Fields 1953
Eviva   Romberg 1927
Ev'ning in Caroline   Donaldson 1931
Ev'ntide   Carmichael 1936
Evoe for the Dead   Sondheim 1974
Evoe! (Hymn to Dionysos)   Sondheim 1974
Evolution   Mills 1949; Stept 1936; Washington 1936
Evolution of a Rag   Goetz 1915; Romberg 1915
Evolution of Ragtime   Johnson, J. Rosamond 1903
Ev'ry Day   Fain 1935; Kahal 1935
Ev'ry Day a Holiday   Porter 1939
Ev'ry Day (Comes Something Beautiful)   Rodgers 1979
Ev'ry Day I Love You (Just a Little Bit More)   Cahn 1948; Styne 1948
Ev'ry Day Is Mother's Day   Jerome 1923; Schwartz, Jean 1923
Ev'ry Day She Wanted Something Else   Bryan 1908; Meyer 1908
Ev'ry Girl Is Diff'rent   Burke 1944; Van Heusen 1944
Ev'ry Guest Is in the Room   Hammerstein 1925; Harbach 1925; Kern 1925
Ev'ry Hour on the Hour I Fall in Love with You   Ellington 1945
Ev'ry Little Bit Helps   Fisher 1904
Ev'ry Little Bit of Me Loves Ev'ry Little Bit of You   Bryan 1928, 1932; Meyer 1932; Young, Joe 1932
Ev'ry Little Stone   Howard, Joseph E. 1952
Ev'ry Little While   Friml 1928; Harbach 1931; Kern 1931
Ev'ry Minute of the Day   Spina 1977

Ev'ry Month Is May   Brennan 1929
Ev'ry Morning She Makes Me Late   DeSylva 1918; Kahn 1918
Ev'ry Night About this Time   Koehler 1942
Ev'ry Night at Nine O'Clock They Pull in the Sidewalks   Hoffman 1958
Ev'ry Night at Seven   Lane 1951; Lerner, Alan Jay 1951
Ev'ry Night You'll Find Her Painting New York Town   Bryan 1914
Ev'ry Night's Like New Year's Eve   Stept 1949
Ev'ry Old Back Porch Is New in the Summertime   Fain 1929; Kahal 1929
Ev'ry One Home Is Asking for You   Kahn 1925
Ev'ry One of Us   Duke 1968
Ev'ry Second, Ev'ry Minute, Ev'ry Hour, Ev'ry Day   Razaf 1948
Ev'ry Second of Ev'ry Minute   Johnson, Howard 1930
Ev'ry Show Must Have a Finale   Razaf 1953
Ev'ry Sunday Afternoon   Hart 1940; Rodgers 1940
Ev'ry Time   Martin 1941
Ev'ry Time I Pick a Sweetie   Razaf 1924
Ev'ry Time My Heart Beats   Davis 1932
Ev'ry Time You're Lonely Don't Forget that I Am Lonely Too   Leslie 1912
Ev'ry Woman's Eyes   Johnson, J. Rosamond 1912
Ev'rybod-ee Who's Anybod-ee   Porter 1935
Ev'rybody but Me   Hanley 1920; Johnson, J. Rosamond 1913
Ev'rybody Clap Hands   Hoffman 1950
Ev'rybody Else   Brown, Lew 1951; Lewis 1951
Ev'rybody Else's Girl Looks Better to Me than Mine   Herbert 1908
Ev'rybody Get Hot   Razaf 1934
Ev'rybody Goes when the Wagon Comes   Razaf 1940
Ev'rybody Has the Right to Be Wrong   Cahn 1965; Van Heusen 1965
Ev'rybody Knows I Love Somebody   Gershwin, George 1927; Gershwin, Ira 1927
Ev'rybody Likes You   Merrill 1961
Ev'rybody Loves   Hart 1937; Rodgers 1937
Ev'rybody Loves a Sailor   Parish 1934
Ev'rybody Loves My Girl   Lewis 1927; Young, Joe 1927
Ev'rybody Loves My Marguerite   Woods 1933
Ev'rybody Loves You   Warren 1929
Ev'rybody Needs a Helping Hand   Robison 1958
Ev'rybody Wants to Be Loved   Howard, Bart 1959
Ev'rybody's Crazy But I'm All Right   DePaul 1951; Raye 1951
Ev'rybody's Gal   Razaf Date Unknown
Ev'rybody's Got a Home but Me   Hammerstein 1955; Rodgers 1955
Ev'ryone Home Is Asking for You   Donaldson 1925
Ev'ryone in Favor Say Aye   Norworth 1910
Ev'ryone Remembers but You   Davis 1933
Ev'ryone Says, I Love You   Kalmar 1932; Ruby 1932
Ev'ryone's a Fighting Son of that Old Gang of Mine   Caesar 1940
Ev'ryone's Out, So Let's Stay in Tonight   Caesar 1937
Ev'rything Goes when the Whistle Blows   Robison 1943
Ev'rything I Love   Porter 1941
Ev'rything I Want   Lawrence 1964
Ev'rything Is Even, Even Worse than It Was Before   Young, Joe 1930
Ev'rything Is Peaches 'neath the Old Apple Tree   Meyer 1934
Ev'rything Is Shapin' Up Fine   Hoffman 1959

Ev'rything Is Sweet 'n Pretty   Ager 1920; Yellen 1920
Ev'rything I've Got   Hart 1942; Rodgers 1942
Ev'rything You Said Came True   Friend 1934; Monaco 1934
(You Know, I Know) Ev'rything's Made for Love   Johnson, Howard 1926
Ev'rything's O.K. with Me Since I'm O.K. with You   Coots 1930
Ev'rything's the Same   Koehler 1932
Ev'rytime I Look at You   Mitchell 1936; Stept 1936
Ev'rytime We Say Goodbye   Porter 1944
Ev'rytime You Make the Ends Meet   Cahn 1971; Van Heusen 1971
Exactly Like You   Fields 1930; McHugh 1930
Examination Number   Fields 1931; McHugh 1931
(Musical Scene #2) Examination of Loo Loo   Whiting 1933
Except with You   Rainger 1942; Robin 1942
Excitement U.S.A.   Coleman 1966
Excitingly Diff'rent   Johnson, James P. 1959
Exclusive Love   Razaf Date Unknown
Excuse for a Song and Dance   Dixon 1931; Warren 1931; Young, Joe 1931
Excuse Me   Young, Joe 1934
Excuse Me Lady   Leslie 1929
Excuse Me Mister Moon   Johnson, J. Rosamond 1912
Excuse My Laughter   Harburg 1961
Excuse Us, Mister Moon   Meyer 1908
Exemption   Friend 1918
Exercise   Hart 1926; Porter 1912; Rodgers 1926
Exercise Your Perogative   DePaul 1964; Mercer 1964
Ex-Gigolo   Harburg 1930
Exhibit "A"   Sondheim 1954
Exhibition Dance (inst.)   Duke 1944
Exhortation   Conrad 1928; Johnson, James P. 1928
Exile   Caesar 1940
Exile's Haven   Herbert 1940
Exotic Melody   Freed, Arthur 1931
Exotica (inst.)   Myrow 1952
Expect Things to Happen   Willson 1963
Expectation   Parish 1965
Experience   Burke 1947; Dietz 1937; Mills 1955; Schwartz, Arthur 1937; Van Heusen 1947
Experiment   Porter 1933
Explaining   Razaf 1928
Explosive Generation, The   Webster 1961
Exquisite   Brennan 1949
Exquisite Moment   Caesar 1934; Friml 1934
Extenuatin' Circumstances   Cahn Date Unknown; Duke Date Unknown
Extra! Extra!   Berlin 1949; Willson 1960
Extra Man, The   Porter 1929
Extraordinary High Pressure   Loewe 1937
Extraordinary Is the Ordinary, The   Drake 1955
Extravagant Gestures   Bacharach 1986
Extravaganza   Mercer 1974
Extr'ordinary Rag (inst.)   Motzan 1915
Eye of a Needle, The   Bacharach 1965; David, Hal 1965
Eye That Never Sleeps, The   Atteridge 1912
Eye-Catcher   Robison 1948
Eyeful of You   Dubin 1927
Eyeful of You, An   Coots 1927; Dubin 1927; Gilbert 1929
Eyes   Young, Victor 1930
Eyes, Eyes   Atteridge 1912
Eyes Like a Stranger   Loesser 1956
Eyes Like That   Strouse 1999

Eyes of Black and Eyes of Blue   Herbert 1900; Smith, Harry B. 1900
Eyes of Blue Brought Skies of Blue   Coslow 1964
Eyes of Blue, Eyes of Brown   Sterling 1902
Eyes of Blue (Shane)   Young, Victor 1953
Eyes of Fire   Bergman 1963
Eyes of Love, The   Russell 1967; Sherman 1964
Eyes of Love (inst.)   Warren Date Unknown
Eyes of the Army   Egan 1919; Whiting 1919
Eyes of the Girl I Love   Howard, Joseph E. 1919
Eyes of the Night   David, Mack 1957; Dixon 1934; Wrubel 1934
Eyes of the Soul   Fisher 1919
Eyes of the World Are on You, The   Hoffman 1937; Lerner, Sammy 1937
Eyes of Thee I'm Fondly Dreaming   Johnson, Howard 1939
Eyes of Verdun   Whiting 1919
Eyes of Youth   Berlin 1919
Eyes of Youth See the Truth, The   Cohan 1918
Eyes (Ojos)   Brooks 1966
Eyes So Dark and Luring   DeSylva 1922
Eyes that Come from Ireland   Olcott 1906, 1908
Eyes that Haunt Me   Smith, Harry B. 1925
Eyes that Love   Romberg 1927; Smith, Harry B. 1927
Eyes that Say I Love You   Fisher 1919
Eyes (Until They Looked at Me)   Young, Victor 1921

F

Fa Deedle Dee, Fa Deedle Doo, Fa Deedle Da   Davis 1944
Fa La La, Fa, Fa La La   Willson 1963
Fa La Nana Bambin   Evans 1951; Livingston, Jay 1951
Fable of the Rose, The   Myrow 1940
Fabric of Dreams   DeSylva 1923; Gershwin, Ira 1923
Fabulous   Harburg 1952
Fabulous Mister Crow   Sigman 1940
Facade   Russell 1968
Face, The   Martin 1962
Face Behind the Mask, The   Herbert 1914; Smith, Robert B. 1914
Face in the Crowd, A   Alter 1939; Bergman 1971; Heyman 1950; Webster 1939; Young, Victor 1950
Face in the Mirror, The   Russell 1968
Face It with a Smile   Baer 1931; Gilbert 1931
Face Lifting   Smith, Harry B. 1935
Face, Not the Image, The   David, Hal 1974
Face of an Angel, The   Silver 1957
Face of My Love, The   Cahn 1967
Face of the Girl I Love, The   Schwartz, Jean 1907
Face on the Dime, The   Rome 1946
Face the Fact   Mills 1955
Face the Facts   Hart 1933; Rodgers 1933
Face the Music   Cahn 1955; Schwartz, Arthur 1955
Face to Face   Cahn 1953; Carroll 1921; Fain 1953; Lerner, Alan Jay 1960; Loewe 1960
Faces   Atteridge 1916; Motzan 1916; Romberg 1916
Faces, Voices   Drake 1966
Fact Can Be a Beautiful Thing, A   Bacharach 1968; David, Hal 1968
Factory Whistles Are Bugles Too   Caesar 1943
Facts of Life, The   Coleman 1959; Fain 1955; Leigh 1955, 1959; Mercer 1960
Facts of Life Backstage, The   Herbert 1946
Fade Out   Mills 1937
Fade Out — Fade In   Comden and Green 1964; Styne 1964

Faded Flowers   Brown, Lew 1926; Clare 1926
Faded Rose   Carroll 1924; Hammerstein 1928; Youmans 1928
Fading Away   Baer 1929; Gilbert 1929
Fading Girl   Atteridge 1914; Carroll 1914; Romberg 1914
Fading Golden Love Dream   Atteridge 1921
Faggot Dance   Mancini 1955
Fagin You'se Is a Viper   Gordon 1935; Revel 1935
Fair and Square   Razaf 1938
Fair and Warmer   Dubin 1934; Warren 1934
Fair and Warmer Cocktail, The   Cohan 1916
Fair Co-Ed, The   Bryan 1927
Fair Enough   Hammerstein 1922
Fair Honeymoon   Herbert 1919
Fair is Fair   Rodgers 1964
Fair Lady   Sondheim Date Unknown
Fair Lady (inst.)   Whiting 1937
Fair Lady (Opening Act II), A   Kern 1928
Fair Land of Dreaming   Smith, Harry B. 1925
Fair Lombardy   Mitchell 1937; Pollack 1937
Fair One   Porter 1911
Fair Rosita   Hammerstein 1928; Romberg 1928
Fair Sex, The   Rome 1948
Fair Trade   Rodgers 1979
Fair Warning   Rome 1959
Fair Weather Friend   Heyman 1959
Fair Weather Friends   Conrad 1924
Fairer on the Riviera   Warren 1934
Fairfield County   Adams 1970; Strouse 1970
Fairies' Lullaby, The   Smith, Harry B. 1900
Fairies' Revel   Herbert 1911
Fairy Dance   Atteridge 1920
Fairy Music   Herbert 1912
Fairy Song   Romberg 1916
Fairy Tale   Egan 1925; Kahn 1925
Fairy Tale Stomp   Brooks 1957
Fairy Tales   Herbert 1897; Norworth 1911; Smith, Harry B. 1897
Fairy Tales Are All Untrue, The   Rome 1940
Fairyland   Johnson, J. Rosamond 1904; Merrill 1961
Fairyland Parade   Snyder 1930
Fairylands (inst.)   Herbert 1922
Faith   Lawrence 1964
Faith Has Many Voices   Robison 1954
Faith Is a Song   Cahn 1969; Van Heusen 1969
Faith of Our Children   Willson 1960
Faith that You Have in Me, The   Silver 1954
Faithful   Rainger 1939; Robin 1939
Faithful Forever   Rainger 1939; Robin 1939
Faithful Heart, The   Cahn 1959; Van Heusen 1959
Faithful Kind, The   David, Mack 1960; Livingston, Jerry 1960
Faithful to the Homeland   Leslie 1943
Faithfully   Bacharach 1959; Cahn 1959; Van Heusen 1959
Faithfully Yours   Romberg 1943; Snyder 1931
Faithless   Comden and Green 1945
Faker, Faker   Bacharach 1959; David, Hal 1959
Falcon and the Dove (Love Theme from El Cid), The   Webster 1961
Faljandio (inst.)   Herbert 1922
Fall   Drake 1954
Fall Guy, The   Carroll 1910
Fall in Line with Joe McCarthy   Leslie 1954
Fall in Love   Gordon 1950; Revel 1950; Warren 1950
(If You) Fall in Love in Rome   Spina 1969
Fall in Love with Me   Friend 1956

Fall Into Somebody's Arms   Lawrence 1952
Fall of Love, The   Washington 1964
Fall of the Leaves, The   Coots 1926
Fallen Idols   Bryan 1919; Fisher Date Unknown; Whiting 1919
Fallen Woman   Leigh 1963
Falling Castle (inst.)   Waller 1941
Falling Down the Side of a Mountain of Love   Hanley 1919
Falling for You   Razaf 1925
Falling in Love   Blake 1932; Caesar 1927; Sissle 1932
Falling in Love Waltz, The   Burke 1954
Falling in Love with Love   Hart 1938; Rodgers 1938
Falling In Love with You   Davis 1926
Falling Leaves   Brennan 1928; Cahn 1969; David, Mack 1940
Falling Leaves Ballet (inst.)   Herbert 1917
Falling Love   Howard, Joseph E. 1964
Falling Off the Wagon   Harburg 1932
Falling Out of Love   Gordon 1932; Revel 1932
Falling Out of Love Can Be Fun   Berlin 1949
Falling Star   Ager 1928; De Lange 1941; Heyman 1932; Willson 1941; Yellen 1928
Falling Stars   Norworth 1909
False Faces   Leslie 1919
False Friends   David, Hal 1963
False Love   Davis 1953
False Opinion   Robison 1951
F-A-M-E   Cohan 1908
Fame, Fame, Fame   Bryan 1917
Fame (inst.)   Revel 1949
Fame of a Name Cannot Die   Caesar 1945
Family   Adams 1996; Strouse 1996
Family Brawl, The   Harbach 1911
Family Council, The   Smith, Harry B. 1911
Family Lovin' Folks   Caesar 1959; Robison 1959
Family Piper's Song, The   Brooks 1960
Family Reputation   Berlin 1925
Family Way, The   Rome 1962
Fam'ly Trouble   Schwartz, Arthur 1981
Fam'ly We Will Be, A   Rodgers 1979
Famous You   Hammerstein 1920; Harbach 1920
Fan Me   Russell 1960
Fan Me with a Movement Slow   Kern 1911
Fan Number   Atteridge 1924; Romberg 1924; Schwartz, Jean 1924
Fan Tan Fannie   Hammerstein 1958; Rodgers 1958
Fancies, Only Fancies   Herbert 1899
Fancy, Fancy   Duke 1936; Gershwin, Ira 1936
Fancy Free   Arlen 1950; Mercer 1950
Fancy Me Just Meeting You   Youmans 1927
Fancy Meeting You   Arlen 1936; Harburg 1936
Fancy Meeting You Here   Cahn 1958; Van Heusen 1958
Fancy Nancy Clancy   Coots 1932; Turk 1932
Fancy Nancy Doing That   Baer 1930; Gilbert 1930
Fancy Pants   Evans 1950; Livingston, Jay 1950
Fancy You Fancying Me   Norworth 1917
Fandango   Brooks 1947
Fanfare   Bergman 1966
Fanfare and Arena Sequence   Sondheim Date Unknown
Fanfare and Drums   David, Mack 1962
Fanfare for If the King Stops Here   Lane 1996
Fanmail   Willson 1953
Fanny   Rome 1954
Fanny Frankenstein   Fisher 1936
Fantabulous   David, Hal 1960
Fantana Song   Smith, Robert B. 1905

Fantasie   Hammerstein 1920, 1938; Harbach 1920, 1938; Kern 1938
Fantastic   Howard, Bart 1960
Fantastic Dance   Herbert 1909
Fantasy   Warren 1980, Date Unknown
Far Above Cayuga's Waters   Cahn 1951
Far Across the Sea (The Magic Island)   Mercer 1960
Far Apart, You're Still in My Heart   Carroll 1918
Far Away   Gershwin, George 1925; Hammerstein 1925; Harbach 1925; Porter 1938; Van Heusen 1952
Far Away and Long Ago   Brennan 1928; Smith, Harry B. 1928
Far Away Rooms and Long Ago Moments   Bergman 1968
Far, Far Away   Alter 1928; Mitchell 1928; Porter 1911
Far, Far Away from Home   Dietz 1959; Schwartz, Arthur 1959
Far Far Far Away   Loesser 1965
Far from Love   Johnson, James P. 1944; Razaf 1944
Far From the Madding Crowd   Webster 1967
Far from Wonderful   Duke 1956
Far Into the Night   David, Mack 1947; Hoffman 1947; Livingston, Jerry 1947
Far Off Village   Blane 1961
Far Out   Lawrence 1967
Far Up the Hill   Herbert 1913
Farandola   Fields 1940; Kern 1940
Faraway Boy   Loesser 1960
Faraway Home   Comden and Green 1960; Styne 1960
Far-Away Island   Davis 1946
Faraway Islands, The   Loesser 1941
Faraway Land, A   Cahn 1963; Van Heusen 1963
Far-Away Love   Johnson, James P. 1948
Fare Thee Well   Coslow 1934; Johnston 1934; Porter 1912
Fare Thee Well Annabelle   Dixon 1935; Wrubel 1935
Fare Thee Well Annie Laurie   Parish 1938
Fare Thee Well, My Love   Freed, Ralph 1964
Fare Thee Well to Eldorado   Webster 1942
Fare-Thee-Well   Robin 1929; Whiting 1929
Fare-Thee-Well, Dear Alma Mater   Gordon 1947; Myrow 1947
Fare-Thee-Well to Harlem   Mercer 1933
Farewell   Brooks 1952; Hammerstein 1926; Harbach 1926; Herbert 1919; Razaf 1933; Romberg 1926; Sondheim 1972
Farewell, Alma Mater   Drake 1956
Farewell, Amanda   Porter 1949
Farewell Covina   Fain 1934; Kahal 1934
Farewell Dear   Romberg 1924
Farewell, Dear Toys   Kern 1913
Farewell Duet   Weill 1947
Farewell, Farewell   Comden and Green 1967; Styne 1967
Farewell for a While   Dietz 1943, 1944; Duke 1943, 1944
Farewell, Goodbye   Weill 1936
Farewell, High School, Farewell   Freed, Ralph 1960
Farewell Killarny   Edwards 1908
Farewell, Kind Friends   Robison 1960
Farewell Letter   Sondheim 1994
Farewell, Little Dream, Goodbye   Lerner, Alan Jay 1971
Farewell Malihini (Hawaiian Farewell)   Gilbert 1936
Farewell, Mr. Abner Hemingway   Jerome 1905; Schwartz, Jean 1905
Farewell Music   Loewe 1947
Farewell My Country (Adios Mi Tiera)   Mitchell 1936
Farewell My Darling Farewell   Loesser Date Unknown
Farewell My Lady Love   Howard, Joseph E. 1964

Farewell My Lassie   Bergman 1959
Farewell, My Life's True Love   Rome 1970
Farewell My Love   Wrubel 1951
Farewell My Lovely   Coots 1946; Dietz 1935; Schwartz, Arthur 1935
Farewell, O Life (Finale, Act II)   Hart 1928; Rodgers 1928
Farewell, Old Friends   DePaul 1958; Raye 1958
Farewell Prosperity   Smith, Harry B. 1909
Farewell, Sweet Senorita   Woods 1935
Farewell Tango   Weill 1933
Farewell to Adrian   Romberg 1922
Farewell to Arms   Silver 1933; Webster 1957; Wrubel 1933
Farewell to Dreams   Kahn 1937; Romberg 1937
Farewell to Juanita   Webster 1958
Farewell to New York   Duke 1955
Farewell Waltz, The   Smith, Robert B. 1905; Wrubel 1949
Farewell with Love   Blake 1952; Sissle 1952
Farm Days   Young, Joe 1913
Farm Yard Jazz, The   Razaf 1920
Farmer and the Cowman, The   Hammerstein 1943; Rodgers 1943
Farmer in the Dell, The   Johnson, Howard 1939
Farmer Jacob   Romberg 1924
Farmer Takes a Wife, The   Freed, Ralph 1934
Farmer's Daughter   Arlen 1944; Harburg 1944; Johnson, Howard 1930
Farmer's Daughter's Wedding Day, The   Magidson 1933; Washington 1933; Wrubel 1933
Farmer's Life, A   Herbert 1906; Silver 1956; Smith, Harry B. 1925
Farmer's Life Is a Very Merry Life, A   Gordon 1946; Myrow 1946
Farmers Market Hoe Down   Fain 1951; Webster 1951
Farming   Porter 1941
Farming Life-Country Life   Smith, Harry B. 1911
Far-Off Land   Friend 1957
Fascinating Devil (With Those Angel Eyes)   Monaco 1930
Fascinating Eyes   Kahal 1928; Snyder 1928
Fascinating Lady   Coots 1926
Fascinating Rhythm   Gershwin, George 1924; Gershwin, Ira 1924
Fascinating Widow, The   Goetz 1910; Harbach 1911
Fascination   Atteridge 1915; Coslow 1958; Gershwin, Ira 1922; Heyman 1943; Mills 1927; Romberg 1915; Young, Victor 1935
Fascination (inst.)   Johnson, James P. 1917
Fascination Waltz, The   Hoffman 1955; Johnson, J. Rosamond 1911
Fashion   Edwards 1907
Fashion Girl, A   Arlen 1937; Harburg 1937
Fashion Parade, The   Friml 1923
Fashion Show, The   Atteridge 1917; Fields 1935; Gordon 1936; McHugh 1938; Revel 1936; Romberg 1917
Fashion Show (inst.)   Kern 1933
Fashion Slave, A   Atteridge 1914; Romberg 1914
Fashion Waltz   Atteridge 1916; Motzan 1916; Romberg 1916
Fashion's Slave, A   Carroll 1914
Fast and Furious   Gordon 1931; Revel 1931
Fast Goodnight, A   Friend 1957
Fast Steppers   Atteridge 1916, 1919; Hanley 1916; Romberg 1916, 1919; Schwartz, Jean 1919; Smith, Harry B. 1916
Fast Talk   Blake 1954
Fasten Your Seat Belts   Adams 1970; Strouse 1970
Faster and Faster   Atteridge 1917; Motzan 1917; Romberg 1917

Faster, Faster My Heart Is Breaking   Caesar 1938

Faster Than Sound   Blane 1954; Martin 1954

Fat, Fat the Water Rat   Weill 1947

Fat Man Blues (inst.)   Waller 1927

Fat Philistine Merchant, The   Young, Victor 1949

Fatal Blonde   Schwartz, Jean 1926

Fatal Fascination   Dietz 1932; Schwartz, Arthur 1932

Fatal Ring, The   Hanley 1917

Fate   Herbert 1914; Porter 1932; Smith, Robert B. 1914

Fate Is Late Again   Rainger 1931

Fate Misunderstood You   Johnson, James P. 1931

Fate Said Only You   Young, Joe 1962

Fated to Be Mated   Porter 1957

Fat-Fat-Fatima   Romberg 1921

Father and Son   Smith, Harry B. 1912; Smith, Robert B. 1912

Father Brings Home Something Every Day   Cobb 1909; Edwards 1909

Father, Brother, Uncle, Nephew   David, Mack 1961; Livingston, Jerry 1961

Father Forgive   Ellington 1968

Father in Heaven, Bless Mother o' Me   Fisher 1917

Father in That Factory   Caesar 1943

Father Keeps on Doing It   Brown, A. Seymour 1909

Father Knickerbocker   Atteridge 1917; Motzan 1917

Father Knickerbocker Fox Trot   Atteridge 1917; Romberg 1917

Father Mississippi   Akst 1929; Gilbert 1929

Father, Mother, Sister and Brother   Bryan 1933

Father Mountain   Razaf 1939

Father of Girls, The   Drake 1963

Father of Our Country, The   Livingston, Jerry 1960

Father of the Bride   Ruby 1959

Father of the Land We Love   Cohan 1931

Father of the Man   Rodgers 1971

Father Wanted to Two-Step, Mother Wanted to Waltz   Ager 1934; Schwartz, Jean 1934; Young, Joe 1934

Father William   Eliscu 1949

Fatherland, Mother of the Band   Gershwin, George 1932; Gershwin, Ira 1932

Fatherland, the Motherland, the Land of My Best Girl, The   Carroll 1914

Father's Allowed to See Us Twice a Year   Williams 1908

Father's Beard   Berlin 1912

Father's Daughter   Eliscu 1962

Father's Day   Adamson 1948; McHugh 1948; Ruby 1943

Father's Day March (inst.)   Henderson 1934

Fathers of the World   Brown, Lew 1928; DeSylva 1928; Henderson 1928

Father's Song, The   Martin 1969

Fatima Brown   Monaco 1915

Fats Waller et le Swing (inst.)   Waller 1942

Fats Waller Stomp   Waller 1927

Fault of the Nightingale, The   Spina 1955

Faust Up to Date   Goetz 1913

Fe Fi Fo Fum   Gershwin, Ira 1922

Fear   Comden and Green 1964; Fain 1933; Styne 1964; Weill 1949; Young, Joe 1933

Fearless Waltz, The   Atteridge 1912

Feast of the Lanterns   Romberg 1927; Smith, Harry B. 1927

Feather Bed Lane   Bryan 1921

Feather in a Breeze   Fain 1931; Kahal 1931

Feather Your Nest   Johnson, Howard 1920

Feathers   Coleman 1971; Leigh 1971

Feathers in the Wind   David, Mack 1934; Silver 1934

Feathery Feelin', The   Loesser 1947

Febbre Siciliana   Warren 1964

February Birthday Song   Caesar 1940

Fedelia   Willson 1952

Fee Fi Fo Fum   Livingston, Jerry 1956

Fee Fi Fo Fum (inst.)   Motzan 1920

Feed Me with Love   Schwartz, Jean 1931; Young, Joe 1931

Feed the Birds   Sherman 1964

Feeding the Chickens   Gorney 1926

Fee-Fie-Fo-Fum   Schwartz, Arthur 1937

Feel of the Land, The   Bullock 1950; Spina 1950

Feelin'   Schwartz, Jean 1973

Feelin' Blue (inst.)   Johnson, James P. 1930

Feelin' High   Dietz 1934; Donaldson 1934

Feelin' High and Happy   Bloom 1938; Koehler 1938

Feelin' Low   Parish 1936

Feelin' Mighty Perky   Drake 1955

Feelin' the Way I Do   DeSylva 1923; Donaldson 1923

(When Your Heart Is) Feeling Foolish in Brazil   Sigman 1956

Feeling I'm Falling   Gershwin, George 1928; Gershwin, Ira 1928

Feeling in Your Heart, A   Cohan 1927

(I'm) Feeling Lucky Today   Duke 1941

Feeling No Pain   Bacharach 1962; Leslie 1945

Feeling of Jazz, The   Ellington 1962

Feeling Sentimental   Gershwin, George 1929; Gershwin, Ira 1929; Kahn 1929

Feeling Zero   Revel 1944

Feeling's Mutual, My Dear, The   Hoffman 1933

Feet Do Yo' Stuff   Comden and Green 1967; Styne 1967

Feet in the Gutter, Looking Up at the Stars   Gilbert 1932; Hanley 1932

Feet on the Sidewalk (Head in the Sky)   Lerner, Sammy 1943

Feet Up (Pat Him on the Po-po)   Merrill 1952

Felicia   Russell 1941; Sherman 1960

Felicia No Capicia   Hoffman 1945; Livingston, Jerry 1945

Felix the Cat   Bryan 1928

Fella with an Umbrella, A   Berlin 1948

Feller from Indiana, A   Dietz 1948; Schwartz, Arthur 1948

Feller Who Plays in a Band   Coslow 1942

Fellow Citizens   Drake 1954

Fellow I'd Follow, The   Cahn 1953; Robin 1952

Fellow Master   Eliscu 1929

Fellow Needs a Girl, A   Hammerstein 1947; Rodgers 1947

Fellow Who's Singing This Love Song Loves You   Brown, Lew 1937; Henderson 1937

Fellow with the Yellow Carnation, The   Parish 1936

Feminine Fashions   Freed, Arthur 1945; Warren 1945

Feminine Rhythm   Gordon 1932; Revel 1932

Femininity   Evans 1958; Livingston, Jay 1958; Sherman 1963

Femme Fatale   Dietz 1963; Schwartz, Arthur 1963

Fences   Young, Victor 1934

Fencing   Buck 1923

Fencing Girl, The   Smith, Harry B. 1901

Fencing Number (inst.)   Herbert 1923

Fender Mender   Bacharach 1966; David, Hal 1966

Ferryboat Called Minerva, A   Hoffman 1957

Festive Days   Atteridge Date Unknown; Romberg Date Unknown

Festive March (inst.)   Duke 1963

Festive Nights   Atteridge 1919; Romberg 1919; Schwartz, Jean 1919

Festive Overture   Raye 1945

Fete of the Veiled Mugs   Johnson, J. Rosamond 1909

Feudin' and Fightin'   Lane 1945; Loesser 1945

Few Conversations Ago, A   Meyer 1945
Few Days   Robison 1964
Few Fast Steppers, A   Atteridge 1924; Romberg 1924;
    Schwartz, Jean 1924
Few Moments at the Piano (inst.), A   Alter 1926
Few of the Things I'd Like to Do for You, A   Friend 1934;
    Monaco 1934
Few Small Tasks, A   Adams 1957; Strouse 1957
Few Tender Words, A   David, Mack 1962
Fez, He Says, A   Russell 1958
F.F. (Forbidden Fruit)   Comden and Green 1964; Styne 1964,
    1967
Fi Fi (inst.)   Motzan 1918
Fiasco   Lerner, Alan Jay 1969
Fickle Finger of Fate, The   Lawrence 1964
Fickle Flo   Yellen 1935
Fickle Flo from Kokomo   Turk 1922
Fickle Sex (Woman's Said to Be), The   Romberg 1917
Fickle Weather Vane, The   Smith, Robert B. 1906
Fickle-Hearted Fair Weather Gal   Hoffman 1951
Fiddle, a Rifle an Axe and a Bible, A   Fain 1958; Webster
    1958
Fiddle and Gittar Band, The   Evans 1950; Livingston, Jay
    1950
Fiddle Dee Dee   Berlin 1912; Cahn 1949; Styne 1949
Fiddle 'em Up Again   Johnson, J. Rosamond 1935
Fiddle Just a Little   Spina 1932
Fiddle-Dee-Dee-Dee   Yellen 1926
Fiddle-Faddle   Parish 1950
Fiddle-Foot Fanny (On Shoo-Shoo Street)   Friend 1956
Fiddle-iddle-up   Willson 1956
Fiddler and the Fighter, The   Comden and Green 1964;
    Styne 1964
Fiddler Paul   Johnson, Howard 1922
Fiddlesticks   Henderson 1934
Fiddlin' Joe   Mills 1935
Fidelity   Leigh 1955
Fidelity Fiduciary Bank   Sherman 1964
Fidgety Feet   Freed, Arthur 1925; Gershwin, George 1926;
    Gershwin, Ira 1926; Sigman 1955
Fidgety Joe   Loesser 1939
Fido and Me   Alter 1947; Heyman 1947
Fido Simply Said Bow Wow   Leslie 1910
Fie on Goodness   Lerner, Alan Jay 1960; Loewe 1960
Field of Cloth of Gold, The   Rodgers 1976
Fields, The   Hammerstein 1937; Kern 1937
Fiesta   Atteridge 1917; Brown, Lew 1932; Goetz 1954;
    Henderson 1932; Romberg 1917, 1927; Smith, Harry B.
    1927
Fiesta in Brazil   Mills 1957
Fiesta in Spain   Adamson 1963; Young, Victor 1959
Fiesta (Inst.)   Warren 1945
Fiesta of the Bulls, The   Sigman 1977
Fifer, The   Cohan 1972
Fifi   Coslow 1937; Mercer 1952; Schwartz, Arthur 1952
Fifi's Song   Romberg 1945
Fifteen Kisses on a Gallon of Gas   David, Mack 1939;
    Livingston, Jerry 1939
Fifth Army's Where My Heart Is, The   Berlin 1944
Fifth Avenue   Atteridge 1915; De Lange 1946; Gordon 1940,
    1950; Romberg 1915; Warren 1940, 1950
Fifth Avenue — A Sidewalk in Paris   Harburg 1934
Fifth Avenue Brigade, The   Harbach 1908
Fifth Avenue Bus (inst.)   Bloom 1946
Fifth Maxixe, The   Burke 1946; Van Heusen 1946

Fifty   Yellen 1948
Fifty Cents   Merrill 1978
55 Days at Peking   Webster 1963
Fifty Friendly Nations   Caesar 1946
Fifty Gals for Every Guy in Argentina   Hoffman 1958
Fifty Million Frenchmen Can't Be Wrong   Fisher 1927; Rose
    1927
Fifty Million Sweethearts   Rainger 1936; Robin 1936
Fifty Percent   Bergman 1978
(I Wish We Were Sweethearts) Fifty Years Ago   Freed,
    Ralph 1951; Hoffman 1951
Fifty Years of Disneyland   Sherman 1973
Fifty-Second Street   Bullock 1937; Spina 1937
52nd Street   Cahn 1937; Dubin 1933; Warren 1933
Fifty-Seven Ways to Win a Man   Atteridge 1911
Fig Leaf Number   Bryan 1920; Schwartz, Jean 1920
Figaro   Mitchell 1928; Motzan 1928; Washington 1946
Figaro and Cleo   Washington 1940, 1953
Fight, The   Adams 1964; Magidson 1936; Oakland 1936;
    Strouse 1964
Fight Duet, The   Strouse Date Unknown
Fight 'Em   Brown, Nacio Herb 1930, 1934; Freed, Arthur
    1930, 1934
Fight, Fight for Southern   Bullock 1950; Spina 1950
Fight Is Made and Won, The   Herbert 1898
Fight on for Madison   Loesser 1939; Young, Victor 1939
Fight on for Tannenbaum   Ruby 1943
Fight On, Men of Westwood   Livingston, Jerry 1963
Fight Over Me   Cahn Date Unknown; Duke Date Unknown;
    Harbach 1925; Youmans 1925
Fight Song, The   Adams 1962; Strouse 1962
Fighter Waltz, The   David, Mack 1950; Livingston, Jerry 1950
Fightin' Mad 'Cause I'm a Bad Loser   Raye 1957
Fighting Kid, The   Edwards 1908
Fighting Kid from Cripple Creek, The   Raye 1957
Fightingest Bull in Spain, The   Sherman 1985
Figi Islands   Webster 1954
Fiji   Atteridge 1919; Romberg 1919; Schwartz, Jean 1919
Fill 'Er Up   Comden and Green 1947
Fill It Up   Gordon 1937; Revel 1937
Fillmargo   Willson 1953
Filomena   Adamson 1974
Filth   Adams 1981; Strouse 1981
Fin de Siecle   Hammerstein 1929; Kern 1929
Finagle   Willson 1953
Finale — First Act Naughty Marietta   Herbert 1935; Kahn
    1935
Finale Act One (Wedding)   Hammerstein 1927; Kern 1927
Finale: Can We Do Anything?   Gershwin, George 1924;
    Gershwin, Ira 1924
Finale (Can You Hear Me Now?)   Comden and Green 1982
Finale (Hail the Female Relative)   Porter 1916
Finale Love   Johnson, James P. 1947
Finale of Chorus   Bryan 1930
Finale of Movietone Follies   Conrad 1929; Mitchell 1929
Finaletto Act I: He Knows Milk   Gershwin, George 1927;
    Gershwin, Ira 1927
Finaletto Act II, Scene I: On Single Life Today   Gershwin,
    George 1926; Gershwin, Ira 1926
Finally   Fain 1955
Financial Viking, The   Romberg 1916
Find a Girl   Livingston, Jerry 1960; Mitchell 1927; Motzan
    1927
Find a Star of Your Own   Livingston, Jerry 1962

Find Another Tree to Build Your Nest   Bryan 1907; Meyer 1907

Find Love   Bacharach 1979

Find Me   Styne 1985

Find Me a Girl   Lewis 1912; Meyer 1912

Find Me a Primitive Man   Porter 1929

Find Out what They Like (And How They Like It)   Razaf 1929; Waller 1929

Find the Foot   Strouse 1975

Find the Map   Leigh 1985; Styne 1985

Find Yourself a Man   Merrill 1964; Styne 1964

Find Yourself a Melody   Loesser 1941

Finder of Lost Loves   Bacharach 1985

Finders Are Keepers   Mercer 1935; Sigman 1935

Finding the Long Way Home   Kahn 1929; Warren 1929

Finding You — Losing You   Caesar 1936; Henderson 1936

Fine and Dandy, Andy   Mills 1947

Fine Art of Treachery, The   Gorney 1969

Fine Feathers   Atteridge 1917, 1921; Coots 1926; Pollack 1921; Romberg 1917; Schwartz, Jean 1921

Fine, Fine, Fine   Cahn 1953; Robin 1952

Fine Mess, A   Mancini 1986

Fine Romance, A   Fields 1936; Kern 1936

Fine Thing!   Mercer 1947

Fine Vignettes, The   Brooks 1957

Fine Young Man, A   Rodgers 1967

Finery   Gordon 1932; Revel 1932

Finesse   Ellington 1968

Finest of the Finest, The   Gershwin, George 1927; Gershwin, Ira 1927

Finest Thing in the Country, The   Schwartz, Jean 1918

Fingerprints of Heaven   Bryan 1954

Fingers and Thumbs   Cobb 1912; Schwartz, Jean 1912

Fini for Now   Russell 1968

Finis   Razaf 1940

Finishing School   Adamson 1956; McHugh 1956

Finishing the Hat   Sondheim 1984

Finisterre (inst.)   Johnson, James P. 1967

Finnegan   Brown, A. Seymour 1912

Fire   Whiting 1926

Fire Belles   Goetz 1911

Fire Brigades, The   Bryan 1926; Snyder 1926

Fire Chief's Daughter, The   Fain 1946; Freed, Ralph 1946

Fire Cracker   Atteridge 1921

Fire Down Below   Washington 1957

Fire in the Night (Feuer der Nacht)   Raye 1958

Fire Ladies' Ball, The   Goetz 1911

Fire Music (inst.)   Duke 1930

Fire Up   Willson 1943

Firebird Two   Brooks 1959

Fireflies Shall Light You, The   Spina 1955

Firefly   Blake 1936; Coleman 1958; Leigh 1958; Leslie 1928

Fireman, Save My Child   Adamson 1937; McHugh 1937

Fireman's Ball, The   Loesser 1947

Fireman's Bride, The   Fields 1945; Romberg 1945

Fires of Faith   Lewis 1919; Young, Joe 1919

Fireside Chat, A   Hoffman 1942; Livingston, Jerry 1942

Fireworks   Comden and Green 1960; Kalmar 1929; Ruby 1929; Styne 1960; Willson 1957

First Act Finale   Oakland 1970

First and Only   Howard, Joseph E. 1907

First Auto Theme   Mercer 1955

First Baseball Game, The   DePaul 1948; Raye 1948

First Blossom, The   Gershwin, George 1925; Hammerstein 1925; Harbach 1925

First Bouquet   Romberg 1948

First Call of Love   Howard, Joseph E. 1915

First Chinese Theme   Mercer 1955

First Christmas, The   Washington 1953

First Class Number One Bum   Cahn 1970; Styne 1970

First Class Private Mary Brown   Loesser 1944

First Day of May   Kern 1919

First Day of My Life, The   Cahn 1972

First Family of Christmas, The   Webster 1971

First Finale   Weill 1933

First Hundred Years, The   Burke 1944; Van Heusen 1944

First Impressions   Leigh 1954; Rome 1937

First Kiss, The   Dubin 1928

First Kiss of Spring, The   Webster 1934

First Lady, The   Berlin 1962

First Lady and First Gent   Gershwin, George 1933; Gershwin, Ira 1933

First Lady of the Land, The   Brown, Lew 1940; DeSylva 1940; Henderson 1940

First Lady Waltz, The   Comden and Green 1960; McHugh 1961; Styne 1960; Washington 1961

First, Last and Always   Akst 1923; Atteridge 1922; Davis 1923; Mercer 1984

First Lesson, The   Atteridge 1923; Schwartz, Jean 1923

First Letter   Sondheim 1994

First Love   Coslow 1955; Dubin 1924; Hart 1921; Rodgers 1921

First Love Days   Goetz 1911

First Love Is the Best of All   Atteridge 1915

First Man I Kiss, The   Hammerstein 1928; Romberg 1928

First March   Arlen 1959; Mercer 1959

First Mate Martin   Hammerstein 1929; Kern 1929

First Midnight   Sondheim 1987

First Mrs. Frazer, The   Woods 1932

First Night   Dietz 1944; Duke 1944

First Night of the Full Moon, The   David, Hal 1963

First Nighters   Goetz 1917; Johnson, Howard 1924

First One, The   Willson 1956

First Prize at the Fair   Dietz 1948; Schwartz, Arthur 1948

First Rose of Summer   Kern 1919, 1921

First Rose of Summer (The Last Rose of My Heart), The   Caesar 1936; Lerner, Sammy 1936

First Sip of Love   Young, Joe 1962

First Six Days, The   Drake 1969

First Snowfall, The   Webster 1955

First Song of Christmas, The   Coots 1949

First Spring Day, The   Eliscu 1933

First Sunbeam   Schwartz, Arthur 1930

First Thing I Knew, The   Conrad 1933; Kahn 1933

First Thing You Know, The   Lerner, Alan Jay 1969

First Time, The   Strouse 1956

First Time I Heard a Bluebird, The   David, Hal 1974

First Time I Kissed You, The   Blane 1947, 1948; Warren 1947, 1948

First Time I Saw You, The   Wrubel 1937

First We Throw Moe Out (Finaletto, Act II, Scene I)   Hart 1926; Rodgers 1926

First Year of Love, The   Livingston, Jerry 1959

First You Get the Money, Then You Get the Flat, Then Its Time Enough to Get the Girl   Bryan 1911; Fisher 1911

First You Have Me High (Then You Have Me Low)   Arlen 1936; Brown, Lew 1936

Firstest with the Mostest, The   David, Mack 1946

Fish   Dietz 1956; Loesser Date Unknown; Porter 1928; Schwartz, Arthur 1956

Fish Don't Fly   Styne 1964
Fish Go Higher than Tigers   Arlen 1966
Fisherman's Bride, The   Coots 1952
Fisherman's Chanty   Young, Victor 1939
Fisherman's Wharf   Dietz 1944; Duke 1944
Fishin' from the Bridges (On the Florida Keys)   Robison
    1954
Fishing   Atteridge 1915; Buck 1916
Fishing Is an Art   Smith, Robert B. 1908
Fishing Song, The   Mills 1948
Fit As a Fiddle (And Ready for Love)   Freed, Arthur 1933;
    Hoffman 1933
Fit for a King   Bergman 1957
Fit to Be Tied   Donaldson 1939
Five a Four Blues   Myrow 1945
Five A.M.   Duke 1936; Gershwin, Ira 1936
Five A.M. Ballet   De Lange 1945; Myrow 1945
Five Card Stud   Washington 1968
Five Foot Two, Eyes of Blue (Has Anybody Seen My
    Girl)   Henderson 1925; Lewis 1925; Young, Joe 1925
Five-Four   Russell 1966
Five Hundred Million   Porter 1936
Five Hundred Pounds   Brooks 1960
$500 Reward   Leigh 1954
Five Little Miles from San Berdoo   Coslow 1950
Five Love Songs   Friml 1933
Five Minutes After Forever   Washington 1958
Five Minutes More   Cahn 1946; Styne 1946
Five Minutes of Spring   Gorney 1931, 1932; Harburg 1931,
    1932, 1961
Five More Minutes in Bed   Revel 1945
Five O'Clock   Dietz 1937; Schwartz, Arthur 1937
Five O'Clock Drag   Adamson 1942; Ellington 1942
Five O'Clock Sky   Fields 1969
Five O'Clock Tea   Berlin 1925; Smith, Harry B. 1906
Five O'Clock Whistle   Myrow 1940
Five Pounds Overweight   Fain 1968
Five Senses, The   Cahn 1953; Fain 1953
5-6-7-8 Nine Little Miles from Ten-Tennessee   Conrad 1930
Five Wives   Magidson 1952
Five Years Ain't So Long   Coslow 1938; Weill 1938
Five Zeros   Coleman 1978; Comden and Green 1978
Five-Four   Russell 1966
Five-Step, The   Brown, Lew 1927; DeSylva 1927; Henderson
    1927
Fix Yo'self Up   Arlen 1959; Mercer 1959
Fixin' for a Long Cold Winter   Lawrence 1951
Fizz Water (inst.)   Blake 1914
Fla De Dah   Porter 1910
Flag (inst.), The   Schwartz, Arthur 1931
Flag of Freedom, The   Freed, Ralph 1942
Flag of Our Land   Buck 1917
Flag that Flies, The   Romberg 1924
Flagenheim's Odorless Cheese   Dubin 1935; Warren 1935
Flaggin' the Train to Tuscaloosa   David, Mack 1951, 1955
Flag's Flying High, The   Bergman 1958
Flags of Freedom (Banderas de Libertad)   Mills 1940
Flag's Still There Mr. Key, The   Oakland 1943
Flahooley   Fain 1951; Harburg 1951
Flame and the Rose, The   David, Mack 1957
Flame In My Heart   Lawrence 1946
Flame Indigo   Ellington 1941; Webster 1941
Flame of Love, The   Atteridge 1915; Friml 1915, 1923
Flame Water   Blane 1968; Martin 1968
Flame Within (inst.), The   Kern 1935

Flamenco   Dietz 1934; Schwartz, Arthur 1934
Flamenco Guitar   Parish 1962
Flaming Rose, The   David, Mack 1956
Flaming Ruth   Bryan 1927
Flaming Youth   Brown, Lew 1927; DeSylva 1927; Henderson
    1927
Flamingo and the Rose, The   Burke 1944; Van Heusen 1944
Flang Dang Saturday Night   Hoffman 1959
Flannel Petticoat Gal, The   Hammerstein 1923; Youmans
    1923
Flannel Petticoat Girl, The   Youmans 1923
Flap-a-Doodle   Harbach 1926; Kern 1926
Flapper, The   Atteridge 1922; DeSylva 1922; Gershwin,
    George 1922; Schwartz, Jean 1922
Flapper and the Vamp, The   Friml 1921
Flapper Flip, The   Sherman 1961
Flapper Walk, The   Kahn 1922
Flapperette (inst.)   Henderson 1925
Flappers   Atteridge 1924; Buck 1922; Caesar 1925; Romberg
    1924; Schwartz, Jean 1924; Youmans 1925
Flappers on Parade   Coots 1929; Davis 1929
Flash of Lightning, A   Silver 1956
Flashback   Sondheim 1994
Flat in Montmartre, A   Pollack 1928
Flat Tire Papa, Mama's Gonna Give You the Air   Waller
    1924
Flatfoot's Theme (inst.)   Duke 1940
Flattery   Rome 1952
Flattery Got the Cheese   Bergman 1960
Flavia (inst.)   Duke 1963
Flea Flew in My Flute, A   Loesser 1939
Flea in Her Ear, A   Cahn 1968
Fleeting Honeymoon   Harbach 1923
Fleet's In, The   Mercer 1942
Fletcher's American Cheese Choral Society   Gershwin,
    George 1927; Gershwin, Ira 1927
Fleur D'Amour   Conrad 1930; Meyer 1930; Mitchell 1930
Fleur de Lis   Bloom 1928
Fleur-de-lis Will Bloom Again, The   Wrubel 1944
Fleurette   Fisher 1929; Rose 1929
Flex-a-tone   Coots 1925
Flick Your Troubles Off Your Thumb and Brush Your Blues
    Away   Ahlert 1930; Turk 1930
Flicker Tail, The   Whiting 1930
Flight Eight   Mills 1946
Flight of Fancy, A   Robin 1952; Warren 1952
Flight of the Birds   Loesser 1937
Flight of the Bomber B-17   Hoffman 1943; Livingston, Jerry
    1943
Flights of Fancy   Atteridge 1915; Romberg 1915
Flim Flam   Adams 1983
Flings   Merrill 1957
Flippity Flop, The   Coslow 1929; Robin 1929; Whiting 1929
Flip's Theme   Sherman 1989
Flirt, The   Brooks 1952
Flirtation   Smith, Harry B. 1911
Flirtation Dance   Harbach 1920; Smith, Harry B. 1926
Flirtation Fantasies   Smith, Robert B. 1919
Flirtation on the Beach   Cohan 1903; Smith, Harry B. 1901
Flirtation Walk   Dixon 1934; Wrubel 1934
Flirtation Waltz   Cohan 1927
Flirtations Frascita   Comden and Green 1972
Flirting   Herbert 1915
Flirting (inst.)   Kern 1956
Flirting with Danger   Sigman 1952

Flitterin'   Sherman 1963
Flittin' and A-Flirtin'   David, Hal 1960
Flo   Bryan 1928
Float Me Charlie   Jerome 1905; Schwartz, Jean 1905
Floatin' Like a Feather   Cahn 1959
Floating Along   Youmans 1926
Floating Down a Moonlight Stream   Romberg 1918
Floating Down a Stream   Johnson, Howard 1925
Floating Down the Nile   Johnson, J. Rosamond 1907
Floating Down the River on the Alabama   Brown, Lew 1912
Floating Isle of Bong Bong, The   Howard, Joseph E. 1905
Floating on a Bubble   Friend 1936
Floating Thru the Air   Schwartz, Arthur 1927
Flood, The   Eliscu 1929; Rose 1929; Youmans 1929
Floogie Walk   Bloom 1939; Koehler 1939
Floradora Girls   Blake 1920; Sissle 1920
Floradora Slide   Atteridge 1913
Floral Wedding, The   Herbert 1907; Smith, Harry B. 1907
Floretta   Herbert 1903
Florida   Brooks 1960; Coots 1945
Florida By the Sea   Berlin 1925
Florida Flo   Johnson, Howard 1939
Florida Fresh Frozen Concentrate   Willson 1954
Florida Garden   Robison 1944
Florida Low Down   Waller 1926
Florida Mammy   Atteridge 1925
Florida Oranges   Willson 1953
Florida Panthers   Sherman 1991
Florida, the Moon and You   Buck 1926; Friml 1926; Hanley 1926
Flotsom and Jetsam   DePaul 1942; Raye 1942
Flourish (inst.)   Romberg 1945
Flow Along River Tennessee, to the Home of the Girl I Love   Bryan 1913
Flow, Flow White Wine   Kahn 1939
Flow Gently Sweet Afton   Johnson, Howard 1939
Flow Gently, Sweet Rhythm (inst.)   Bloom 1946
Flow On River   Hart Date Unknown; Rodgers Date Unknown
Flow on Silvery Hudson   Bryan Date Unknown; Fisher Date Unknown
Flower Garden Ball, The   Jerome 1915; Schwartz, Jean 1913, 1914, 1915
Flower Garden of My Heart, The   Hart 1940; Rodgers 1940
Flower Girl of Bordeaux, The   Mills 1966
Flower Maidens   Porter 1913
Flower of Dawn   De Lange 1938
Flower of My Heart, My Rose   Atteridge 1915
Flower of San Antone, The   David, Mack 1956
Flower of Spain   Meyer 1927
Flower of the Snow   Smith, Harry B. 1920
Flower of the Woodland   Atteridge 1923; Schwartz, Jean 1923
Flower on My Lapel   Conrad 1935; Magidson 1935
Flower Song, The   Adamson 1946; Heyman 1950; McHugh 1946; Porter 1914; Young, Victor 1950
Flower Story, A   Young, Victor 1914
Flower to Me Thou Seemest, A   Johnson, Howard 1939
Flower Vendor   Arlen 1959; Mercer 1959
Flowerpot Blues   Lewis 1974; Young, Joe 1974
Flowers   Martin 1964
Flowers and You   Young, Victor 1920
Flowers for Madame   Dixon 1935; Wrubel 1935
Flowers Never Die   Sherman 1977
Flowers of Dixieland, The   Johnson, J. Rosamond 1903

Flowers of Happiness   Alter 1929; Johnson, Howard 1929
Flowers on the Water   Mancini 1954
Flowers That Bloom in the Spring, The   Johnson, Howard 1939
Flowers that Never Die   Sigman 1949
Flowers to Remember You (Me) By   Friml 1931
Flubbber Theme (Flubber Song)   Sherman 1961
Flubby Dub (The Cave Man)   Kern 1917
Flugel Street Rag   Ellington 1965
Flute Segue (inst.)   Willson 1964
Flutter By, Little Butterfly   Coslow 1937
Fly Away to Ioway   Hart 1934; Rodgers 1934
Fly Butterfly   Brown, Lew 1925; DeSylva 1925; Henderson 1925
Fly by Night   Dietz 1937; Schwartz, Arthur 1937
Fly in Ireland (inst.)   Oakland 1958
Fly in Israel (inst.)   Oakland 1958
Fly Me to the Moon (In Other Words)   Howard, Bart 1954
Fly Now, Pay Later   Duke 1956
Fly the Magic Carpet   Yellen 1956
Fly Up to Heaven   Bryan 1928; Schwartz, Jean 1928
Flyers' Safety Song   Caesar 1943
Flying Down to Rio   Eliscu 1933; Kahn 1933; Youmans 1933
Flying Dutchman, Ahoy, Ahoy, Ahoy, The   Drake 1950
Flying Field   Harbach 1931; Kern 1931
Flying Home   De Lange 1939; Van Heusen 1939
Flying Marines, The   Fain 1943; Freed, Ralph 1943
Flying Off the Handle   Fisher 1936
Flying Saucer — First Stop Berlin (inst.)   Bacharach 1967
Flying the Blimp   Hart 1920; Rodgers 1920
Fogarty and Mandolin Girls   Burke 1946; Van Heusen 1946
Fogarty and Nelly Bly Parade   Burke 1946; Van Heusen 1946
Fogarty the Great   Burke 1946; Van Heusen 1946
Fogg's in Yokohama   Adamson 1959; Young, Victor 1959
Foggy Day (In London Town), A   Gershwin, George 1937; Gershwin, Ira 1937
Fol de Rol Dol Dol   Schwartz, Jean 1912
Fol-De-Rol   Atteridge 1912
Fol-de-rol-rol   Ellington 1946
Folk Dance   Sondheim 1968
Folk Song   Loesser 1937
Folk Song (inst.)   Kern 1956
Folks   Arlen 1959; Mercer 1959
Folks Are Walkin' 'Round   Brooks 1959
Folks in New York City Ain't Like Folks Down South   Razaf 1926
Folks Who Live on the Hill, The   Hammerstein 1937; Kern 1937
Foller It Through   Coleman 1960; Leigh 1960
Follies Chorale Ensemble, The   Harburg 1934
Follow a Dream   Webster 1976
Follow a Star   Yellen 1930
Follow Handy Andy   Dietz 1924; Kern 1924
Follow in My Footsteps   Brown, Nacio Herb 1937; Freed, Arthur 1937
Follow in Our Footsteps   Rodgers 1967
Follow Me   Brooks 1960; Lerner, Alan Jay 1960; Loewe 1960; Smith, Harry B. 1910, 1926
Follow Me Around   Berlin 1912
Follow Me, Boys!   Sherman 1966
Follow Me (Love Song)   Webster 1963
Follow Me 'Round   Kern 1911
Follow Me to Dixie Land   Silver 1918
Follow Me to My Grave (If You Love Me)   Friend 1948
Follow Me Up the Stairs   Ellington 1966

Follow My Footsteps   Woods 1939

Follow On   Hart 1926; Mitchell 1921; Pollack 1921; Rodgers 1926

Follow that Man   Sigman 1955

Follow the Band   De Lange 1946; Myrow 1946

Follow the Boys   Davis 1965

Follow the Crowd   Berlin 1914; Gorney 1926

Follow the Drum   Gershwin, George 1927; Gershwin, Ira 1927

Follow the Flag   Smith, Harry B. 1908

Follow the Flag We Love   Smith, Harry B. 1925

Follow the Fold   Loesser 1950

Follow the Footprints   Howard, Bart 1961

Follow the Lamb   Cahn 1970; Styne 1970

Follow the Leader Jig   Berlin 1949

Follow the Man that Leads the Band   Smith, Harry B. 1901

Follow the Midnight Girl   Goetz 1913

Follow the Midnight Sun   Atteridge 1923; Schwartz, Jean 1923

Follow the Minstrel Band   Gershwin, George 1929; Gershwin, Ira 1929; Kahn 1929

Follow the Rainbow Trail   Howard, Joseph E. 1909

Follow the Rajah   Romberg 1925

Follow the River   Washington 1957

Follow the Sun to the South   Romberg 1927

Follow the Swallow   Dixon 1924; Henderson 1924; Rose 1924

Follow the Swallow to Hide-a-Way Hollow   Carmichael 1949; Webster 1949

Follow the Swallow to Old Sleepy Hollow   Carmichael 1949; Webster 1949

Follow the Way of the Lord   Cahn 1980; Strouse 1980

Follow the Yellow Brick Road   Arlen 1939; Harburg 1939

Follow Through   Brown, Lew 1927; Friend 1927

Follow Thru   Brown, Lew 1929; DeSylva 1929; Henderson 1929

Follow Your Dreams   Ahlert 1956

Follow Your Heart   Bullock 1936; Mitchell 1936

Follow Your Star   Coots 1925; Coslow 1924

Follow Your Uncle Dudley   Cohan 1907

Following Behind the Girl Behind the Smile   Goetz 1912

Following Famous Footsteps   Edwards 1929

Following in Father's Footsteps   Kalmar 1927; Ruby 1927

Following in Mother's Footsteps   Caesar 1934; Henderson 1934; Yellen 1934

Following in Your Footsteps   Stept 1935; Washington 1935

Following the Drum   Smith, Harry B. 1916

Following the Stars   Stept 1935

Following You Around   Dubin 1927

Folly Is Our King   Herbert 1904

Fond Love   Smith, Harry B. 1911

Fond Love, True Love   Herbert 1899

Fond of the Ladies   Herbert 1912

Fond of You   DeSylva 1925; Gordon 1937; Revel 1937

Fond Recollections, Mem'ries of Old   Young, Joe 1933

Food for Scandal   Hart 1938; Rodgers 1938

Food for Thought   Romberg 1948

Foof to Old Geography   Gorney 1958

Fool   Sigman 1972

Fool and His Money Are Soon Parted, A   Lawrence 1939

Fool Killer, The   Bacharach 1963; David, Hal 1963

Fool Me   Bryan 1917

Fool Me Again   Bacharach 1981

Fool Meets Fool   Hart 1942; Rodgers 1942

Fool Number One   Sigman 1984

Fool that I Am   David, Hal 1960; Mercer 1934; Mills 1940

Fool That I Was   Dietz 1944; Duke 1944

Fool There Was, A   Davis 1949; Dubin 1913; Fisher 1934; Porter 1937; Silver 1949

Fooled   Russell 1941

Fooled By the Fickle Fingers of Fate   David, Hal 1946

Foolin' Around with Love   Bloom 1953; Johnson, James P. 1931; Leslie 1953

Foolin' Myself   Lawrence 1937; Razaf 1955; Waller 1955

Foolin' Nobody But Me   Russell 1947

Foolin' with the Other Woman's Man   Akst 1934; Brown, Lew 1934

Foolish   Davis 1952

Foolish Baby   Harburg 1930; Heyman 1930

Foolish Cinderella Girl   Atteridge 1913; Schwartz, Jean 1913

Foolish Face   Dietz 1930; Schwartz, Arthur 1930

(That) Foolish Feeling   McHugh 1937

Foolish, Foolish Pride   David, Hal 1960

Foolish Gardener, The   Herbert 1908

Foolish Heart   Weill 1943

Foolish Little Maiden, I, A   Romberg 1917

Foolish Little Rumors   Mills 1951

Foolish Ones, The   Parish 1965

Foolish Waltz   Lawrence 1953

Foolishness   Atteridge 1912; Kern 1915; Smith, Harry B. 1913, 1915

Fool's Advice, A   Young, Joe 1977

Fool's Errand   Sigman 1957

Fools Fall in Love   Berlin 1940

Fools Gold   Cahn 1976

Fools' Parade, The   Young, Joe 1930

Fool's Paradise   Merrill 1949

Fools Rush In (Where Angels Fear to Tread)   Bloom 1940; Mercer 1940

Football   Brown, Nacio Herb 1930; Freed, Arthur 1930

Football Boys and Girls, The   Cohan 1903

Football Freddie My Collegiate Man   Conrad 1930; Leslie 1930

Football King, A   Porter 1910

Football Song   Magidson 1929; Washington 1929

Football Song (Opening Act II)   Kern 1917

Football Special   Drake 1954

Footloose   Mercer 1974; Russell 1946

Footloose and Fancy Free   Kahn 1935

Footprints in the Sands of Time   Russell 1944

Footsore Blues   McHugh 1965; Razaf 1965

Footwork   Brown, Lew 1928; DeSylva 1928; Henderson 1928

For 1 for 6 Forever   Willson 1954

For a Buck and a Quarter a Day   Dubin 1936; Warren 1936

For a Good Game of Marbles   Caesar 1940

For a Little While   Egan 1927; Kahn 1927

For a Moment of Your Love   Burke 1953; Van Heusen 1953

For a New America   Lawrence 1956

For a Song   Willson 1956

For Adults Only   Drake 1962

For All Time   Bacharach 1960; David, Hal 1960

For All We Know   Coots 1934; Lewis 1934

For All You Care   Davis 1932

For Alma Mater   Bullock 1950; Spina 1950

For Baby and Me   Meyer 1926

For Better, For Worse   Coslow 1954

For Better or for Worse   Herbert 1915

For Better or Worse   Dietz 1963; Razaf 1955; Schwartz, Arthur 1963

For Charity's Sake   Smith, Harry B. 1906

For Ching-a-Ling and Me   Johnston 1926; Turk 1926
For Crying Out Loud   Dixon 1923
For Dancers Only   Raye 1939
For Days and Days   Kalmar 1913
For Days and Days (I Love You, I Do)   Caesar 1927
For Dixie and Uncle Sam   Brennan 1916
For Doin' Things Like This   Freed, Arthur 1930; Woods 1930
For Ever   David, Mack 1954
For Every Boy Who's Lonely There's a Girl Who's Lonely
     Too   Harbach 1911
For Every Fish (There's a Little Bigger Fish)   Arlen 1957;
     Harburg 1957
For Every Lonely Heart   Kahn 1937
For Every Lover   Herbert 1913; Smith, Robert B. 1913
For Every Man There's a Woman   Arlen 1948; Robin 1948
For Every Smile on Broadway There's a Tear at Home Sweet
     Home   Fisher 1921
For Every Young Heart   Davis 1962
For Ev'ry Little Girl Who's Lonely, There's a Boy Who's
     Blue   Monaco 1934; Parish 1934
For Ev'ry Wave that Leaves the Shore Another Comes Rollin'
     In   Hanley 1930
For Forty-Eight Reasons We Love You   Caesar 1940
For Fun   Rome 1972
For Goodness' Sake   Duke 1927
For Heaven's Sake   Bryan 1926
For He's a Jolly Good Fellow   Brooks 1960; Johnson,
     Howard 1939
For He's the One, the Only Baby   Brown, A. Seymour 1909
For He's the Prince of Good Fellows   Clare 1929
For Honor   Robin 1930, 1931; Whiting 1930, 1931
For I'm a Jolly Postillion   Herbert 1897; Smith, Harry B. 1897
For I'm a Simple Maid   Clare 1930
For I'm in Love Again   Dixon 1930; Rose 1930
For Instance   Woods 1950
For Johnny and Me   Brown, Lew Date Unknown;
     Henderson Date Unknown
For Jupiter and Greece   Hart 1942; Rodgers 1942
For Laughing Out Loud   Rainger 1933; Robin 1933
For Losers Only   Oakland 1968
For Love I Depend on You   Hanley 1916
For Love of Ivy   Russell 1968
For Love of Thee   Olcott 1906
For Lovers   Lawrence 1954
For Lovers Only   Dubin 1935; Livingston, Jerry 1954; Mercer
     1935; Warren 1935
For Mary and Me   Rose 1927
For Mary Jane   Razaf 1930
For Mary, the Baby and Me   Monaco 1918
For Me   Hoffman 1953
For Me Alone   Sigman 1969
For Me and My Gal   Goetz 1917; Leslie 1917; Meyer 1917
For Months and Months   Norworth 1911; Smith, Harry B.
     1911
For Months and Months and Months   Norworth 1910
For My Baby   Kahal 1927; Snyder 1927
For My Mary   Strouse 1986
For My Own   Burke 1961
For My Sweetheart   Donaldson 1926; Kahn 1926
For Myself Alone   Robin 1927; Youmans 1927
For No Good Reason at All   Baer 1926; Lewis 1926; Young,
     Joe 1926
For No Reason at All   Brown, Lew 1927; Donaldson 1920;
     Gershwin, Ira 1920; Lewis 1920, 1921; Meyer 1921;
     Young, Joe 1920, 1921

For No Rhyme or Reason   Porter 1938
For Now and Always   Stept 1955
For Old Times' Sake   Brown, Lew 1927; DeSylva 1927;
     Henderson 1927; Kahn 1932
For Once in My Life   Coleman 1966
For One!   Rome 1937
For One Another   Fields 1929; McHugh 1929
For One Little Kiss from You   Johnson, Howard 1930
For One Sweet Day   Bryan 1917
For Only You   Merrill 1955
For People Like Us   Kahal 1929
For Practical Reasons   Cahn 1951
For Sentimental Reasons   Heyman 1936; Silver 1936
For Someone I Love   Davis 1929; Snyder 1929
For Squares Only   Oakland 1967
For Sweet Charity   Merrill 1959
For Sweet Charity's Sake   Brown, Lew 1928; DeSylva 1928;
     Henderson 1928
For Sweethearts Only   Lerner, Sammy 1930
For the Boys Over There   Kahn 1918
For the Common Good of Mankind   Duke 1963
For the First Time   Adamson 1938, 1955; Dietz 1961;
     McHugh 1938, 1955; Schwartz, Arthur 1961
For the First Time in My Life   Mills 1938
For the Flag, For the Home, For the Family (For the Future
     of All Mankind)   Cohan 1942
For the Flag He Loved So Well   Herbert 1944
For the Life of Me   David, Hal 1952; Gershwin, Ira 1944,
     1945, 1946; Schwartz, Arthur 1946; Warren 1944, 1945
For the Likes o' You and Me   Stept 1929
For the Longest Time   Baer 1953
For the Love of You   Fain 1959; Webster 1959
For the Man I Love   Kern 1923
For the Papa   Brennan 1929
For the People   Hammerstein 1940; Schwartz, Arthur 1940
For the Sake of Humanity   Atteridge 1917; Romberg 1917
For the Sake of Lexington   Brown, Lew 1939; Stept 1939
For the Sake of the Baby at Home   Dubin 1924
For the Sake of the Children   Cahn 1964; Van Heusen 1964
For the Thrill of a Hill Billy Waltz   Schwartz, Jean 1934;
     Young, Joe 1934
For the Two of Us   Leslie 1918; Ruby 1918
For the Very First Time   Berlin 1952
For the Want of a Nail   Webster 1950
For the Want of You   Styne 1943
For Those in Love   Davis 1946
For Those Who Think Love   David, Mack 1964; Livingston,
     Jerry 1964
For to Win a Bride   Young, Victor 1949
For Twenty Dollars Plain   Oakland 1970
For Want of a Kiss   David, Hal 1952
For Want of Your Love   David, Hal 1962
For What   Burke 1947; Van Heusen 1947
For You   Brown, Lew 1932; Dubin 1929, 1941; Gordon 1932;
     Henderson 1932; Jerome 1904; Koehler 1937; Revel
     1932; Romberg 1928; Rome 1965; Schwartz, Jean 1904;
     Styne 1980
For You a Rose   Cobb 1917; Edwards 1917
For You Alone   Snyder 1936
For You and Me Sweetheart   Silver 1929; Turk 1929
For You Baby   Gordon 1929
For You, Bright Eyes   Harbach 1910
For You For Me   Coslow 1931
For You, For Me, For Evermore   Gershwin, George 1947;
     Gershwin, Ira 1947

For You, for Me, for Love   Johnson, Howard 1958
For You, My Love, On Christmas   Bergman 1983
For Your Applause   Evans 1956; Livingston, Jay 1956
For Your Boy and My Boy   Kahn 1918
For Your Convenience   Young, Joe 1934
For Your Country and My Country   Berlin 1917
Forbidden Fruit   DeSylva 1922; Silver 1956
Forbidden Lips   Gorney 1934
Forbidden Love   Lewis 1932; Spina 1949
Forbidden Melody   Harbach 1936
Forced Rhyme   Brooks 1960
Fords Out Front   Willson 1954
Foremost Dairy   Mercer 1953
Forest Song   Smith, Harry B. 1891
Forever   Ager 1928; Conrad 1924; David, Mack 1966;
    Donaldson 1934; Ellington 1966; Kahn 1934; Merrill
    1967; Myrow 1931; Rainger 1939; Robin 1939; Rose
    1927; Yellen 1928
Forever Amber   Mercer 1947
Forever and a Day   Hammerstein 1941; Kern 1941; Martin
    1964
Forever and Ever   Ager 1928; Styne 1941; Yellen 1928
Forever and Ever with You   Davis 1925
Forever, Darling   Cahn 1956
Forever Delighting in Fighting   Smith, Harry B. 1906
Forever Faithful   Bacharach 1957; David, Mack 1957
Forever, Forever I Want You   Howard, Joseph E. 1926
Forever in Your Arms   Parish 1932
Forever June   Heyman 1953; Young, Victor 1953
Forever My Love   Bacharach 1961; David, Hal 1961
Forever Nearer to Me   Martin 1964
Forever Waltz, The   Cahn 1969
Forever with You   Alter 1929
Forever Yours   Silver 1946
Forever Yours I Remain   Bacharach 1964; David, Hal 1964
Forget All Your Books   Dietz 1930; Lane 1930; Lerner,
    Sammy 1930
Forget Her (Forget Him)   Hoffman 1956
Forget It, Baby   Freed, Ralph 1965
Forget Me   David, Hal 1953; Drake 1959; Loesser 1939
Forget Me Not   Hoffman 1928; Leslie 1928; Williams 1909
Forget My Name and Address   Davis 1955
Forget the Past   Akst 1933; Mitchell 1933
Forget-Me-Not   DeSylva 1919; Kern 1919
Forget-Me-Nots in Your Eyes   Leslie 1944; Warren 1944
Forgetting a Love Affair   Kahal 1932
Forgetting You   Brown, Lew 1928; DeSylva 1928; Henderson
    1928; Raye 1962
Forgive   Leigh 1955
Forgive and Forget   Blane 1969; Smith, Harry B. 1911
Forgive Me   Ager 1926, 1941; Robin Date Unknown; Spina
    1976; Warren Date Unknown; Yellen 1926, 1941
Forgive Me Again   Donaldson 1942
Forgive Me (for Giving You Such a Bad Time)   Bacharach
    1962; David, Hal 1962
Forgive Me for Loving You   Dubin 1933; Warren 1933
Forgotten Dreams   Parish 1954
Forgotten Melody   Kahn 1931
Form of Stimulation, A   Brooks 1960
Formula for Love   Monaco 1940
Forsaken   Johnson, Howard 1939
Forsaken Again   Heyman 1932
Forsaking All Others   Donaldson 1934; Kahn 1934; Wrubel
    1947
Fort Knox   Silver 1956

Forth and Back   Willson 1953
Fortissimo (I'm Yours to Love)   Coots 1957
Fortune Teller (inst.)   Johnson, James P. 1962
Fortune Teller (Slumber On, My Little Gypsy
    Sweetheart)   Herbert 1898; Smith, Harry B. 1898
Fortune Teller's Song   Romberg 1927; Smith, Harry B. 1927
Fortune's Darling   Leigh 1954
Fortune's Fool   Mills 1928
Fortuosity   Sherman 1967
Forty Acres and a Mule   Lerner, Alan Jay 1976
Forty and One for All   Brennan 1943
Forty Days   Sondheim 1994
Forty Golden Nuggets   Drake 1948
Forty Long Years   Livingston, Jerry 1962
Forty Minutes for Lunch (inst.)   Weill 1943
Forty Nights   Rodgers 1970
Forty Thieves Forty   Cahn 1958
Forty Winks   Dietz 1948; Schwartz, Arthur 1948
Forty-Eight Hour Leave   Coots 1943
Forty-Eight Kisses   Coots 1949
48 Letters from 48 States   David, Hal 1956
Forty-Five Minutes from Broadway   Cohan 1906
Forty-Niner and His Clementine   Hammerstein 1928;
    Youmans 1928
Forty-Second Street   Dubin 1933
Forty-Second Street Moon   Caesar 1924; Romberg 1924
Forward March   Brown, Lew 1933; Henderson 1933
Forward March Into My Arms   Gordon 1932; Revel 1932;
    Smith, Harry B. 1930
Forward (Song of the Red Army Tank Brigade)   Rome 1943
Fosca's Entrance   Sondheim 1994
Foul Owl   Bergman 1967
Found When I Found You   Davis 1937
Fountain, The   Bergman 1958
Fountain Fay Protective Institution, The   Smith, Robert B.
    1910
Fountain in the Rain   Mercer 1965
Fountain of Dreams   Fain 1959; Webster 1959
Fountain of Teardrops   Sherman 1965
Fountain of Youth   Atteridge 1924; Livingston, Jerry 1955;
    Porter 1928; Romberg 1924; Schwartz, Jean 1924;
    Webster 1955
Fountains of Versailles   Russell 1957
Four A.M.   Lawrence 1940
Four A.M. Shout (inst.)   Johnson, James P. 1922
Four Black Dragons   Sondheim 1976
Four for Texas   Cahn 1963; Van Heusen 1963
Four Freedoms, The   Eliscu 1943; Gorney 1943
Four Frightened People   Rainger 1934; Robin 1934
Four Fugitives from a Bolero Cabin Gang   Arlen 1936;
    Harburg 1936
496th Marching Song, The   Freed, Ralph 1944
Four Leading Ladies   Cahn 1956
Four Legged Friend   Brooks 1952
Four Little Angels of Peace   Rome 1937
Four Little Girls with a Future and Four Little Girls with a
    Past   DeSylva 1921; Friml 1921
Four Little Sirens   Gershwin, George 1924; Gershwin, Ira
    1924
Four Little Song Pluggers   Hart 1926; Rodgers 1926
Four Little Walls and Me   Akst 1924
Four Moon Skits (I Can't Find a Mountain for My
    Moon)   Gordon 1933; Revel 1933
Four O'Clock   Weill 1949
Four O'Clock Groove (inst.)   Johnson, James P. 1952

Four O'Clock Tea   Atteridge 1912
Four Rivers, The   Eliscu 1943; Gorney 1943
Four Seasons, The   Russell 1956; Styne 1960
Four Seasons of Love, The   Spina 1977
Four Star Napoleon (Grenadier's March)   Spina 1959
Four Walls   Rose 1927
Four Walls (And One Dirty Window Blues)   Robison 1953
Four Well Known Dames and a Guy   Buck 1922
Four Winds and the Seven Seas, The   David, Hal 1949
Four-Score and Seven Years Ago   Cahn 1935
1400 Dream Street   Wrubel 1948
Fourth, The   Willson 1956
Fourth Letter   Sondheim 1994
Fourth of July, The   Strouse 1986
4th of July Parade   Burke 1981
Fox Has Left His Lair, The   Hammerstein 1925; Harbach 1925; Kern 1925
Fox in Sevalio, The   Bacharach 1966; David, Hal 1966
Fox Trot   Atteridge 1918; Caesar 1922; Romberg 1918
Fox Trot (inst.), The   Bacharach 1966
Foxfire   Mancini 1955
Foxy   Mercer 1964
Foxy Grandpa   Ager 1915
Foxy Moon   Snyder 1909
Foxy Quiller's Entrance Chorus   Smith, Harry B. 1900
F'r Instance   Gorney 1934
Fraction of an Inch   Strouse 1999
Fractious Fingering (inst.)   Waller 1938
Fragment (inst.), A   Young, Victor 1946
Fragonard Girl   Atteridge 1922
Fragrant Night   Alter 1939; Loesser 1939
Frahngee-Pahnee   Porter 1944
'Fraidy Cat   Magidson 1934; Monaco 1934
Frame without a Picture, A   David, Hal 1961
Framed   Ellington 1962; Razaf 1962
Fran and Bill's Tune   Merrill 1957
France Is Free   Hart 1943
France (We Have Not Forgotten You)   Ager 1918; Clarke 1918
Francie   Styne 1950
Francis (The Talking Mule)   Mills 1950
Franco-American Rag   Schwartz, Jean 1909
Franco-American Ragtime   Jerome 1909; Schwartz, Jean 1909
Franco-American Step, The   Atteridge 1924; Romberg 1924; Schwartz, Jean 1924
Francophile   Adams 1977; Strouse 1977
Frangipani Blossom   Evans 1956; Livingston, Jay 1956
Frank and Johnnies   Martin 1972
Frank Merriwell Opening   Styne 1956
Frank the Bank   Caesar 1950
Frankenstein   Webster 1963
Frankie and Johnny   Brooks 1949; Cahn 1956
Frankie Laine Time   Drake 1955
Franklin D. — Winston C. — Joseph V. — Victory Jones   Rome 1942
Franklin D. Roosevelt   Caesar 1933
Franklin D. Roosevelt Jones   Rome 1938
Franklin Shepard, Inc.   Sondheim 1981
Franklin's Foods   Pollack 1936; Yellen 1936
Frantically Romantic   Merrill 1967
Frantzi   Kern 1909
Fraternal Fiesta   Leigh 1985
Fraternal Order of the Eagles, The   Fain 1973
Fraulein   Lawrence 1956

Fraulein Katrina (inst.)   Kern 1908
Frazier (The Sensuous Lion)   Mercer 1972
Freckle Face, You're Beautiful   Friend 1934
Freckles   Ager 1919; Johnson, Howard 1919
Fred   Cahn 1968
Freddie, Get Ready   Blane 1949; Warren 1949
Freddy Chant   Merrill 1966
Freddy the Freshman, the Freshest Kid in Town   Friend 1931
Free   Berlin 1950; Clare 1931; Heyman 1933; Russell 1946; Sondheim 1962
Free Am I   Adams 1963; Strouse 1963
Free and Easy, The   Ahlert 1930; Mancini 1957; Turk 1930
Free and Equal Blues   Harburg 1944
Free As the Air   Duke 1959
Free at Last   Arlen 1962; Harburg 1962
Free Fall   Bacharach 1971; David, Hal 1971
Free for All   Hammerstein 1931; Whiting 1931
Free Indeed   Carroll 1975
Free Thought in Action Class Song   Coleman 1966; Fields 1966
Free to Be Free   Friml 1954; Webster 1952
Free Trade and a Misty Moon   Herbert 1917
Free with Love   Mitchell 1935; Stept 1935
Freebootin'   Sherman 1973
Freedom   Sherman 1974
Freedom Can Be a Most Uncomf'table Thing   Fain 1960; Webster 1960
Freedom Is the Word   Harburg 1964; Lane 1964
Freedom March (inst.)   Styne 1967
Freedom Now   Strouse Date Unknown
Freedom of the C's   Bryan 1919; Schwartz, Jean 1919
Freedom (Parts 1-7)   Ellington 1968
Freedom (Sweet Fat and That)   Ellington 1968
Freedom Train, The   Berlin 1948
Freedom (Word You Heard)   Ellington 1968
Freedonia Hymn   Kalmar 1933; Ruby 1933
Freeze and Melt   Fields 1929; McHugh 1929
Freida   Kern 1908
French   Coleman 1979; Loesser 1947
French Ballet Class (Inst.)   Gershwin, George 1937
French Fling   Coots 1921
French Flip Flop   Von Tilzer 1916
French Have a Word for It, The   Rome 1939
French Heels   Evans 1957; Livingston, Jay 1957
French Lesson   Comden and Green 1947
French Line (2), The   Blane 1954
French Line, The   Myrow 1954
French Militaire   Cohan 1908
French Military Marching Song   Hammerstein 1926; Harbach 1926; Romberg 1926
French Pastry Walk   Gershwin, Ira 1922
French Soldiers on Leave Dance   Egan 1919; Whiting 1919
French Waltz   Sondheim Date Unknown
French Way, The   Strouse 1974
French with Tears   Rome 1950
French You Hear on Broadway   Harbach 1910
Frenchman Thought of It First, A   Revel 1953, 1960
Frenchman's Paree, The   Evans 1958; Livingston, Jay 1958
Frenesi   Russell 1940
Frere Jacque   Styne 1941
Frere Jacques   Brooks 1959
Fresh Air and Exercise   Weill 1943
Fresh As a Daisy   Porter 1940
Fresh from the Country   Clare 1935; Stept 1935

Freshman Hop   Mills 1929
Fresno Beauties   Loesser 1956
Freud   Webster 1963
Freud and Jung and Adler   Gershwin, George 1932; Gershwin, Ira 1932
Friars, The   Herbert 1907
Friars' Parade   Berlin 1916
Friar's Song, The   Herbert 1908
Friday Afternoon Bus   Yellen 1977
Friend of Mine, A   Merrill 1953; Rome 1940; Wrubel 1949
Friend of Mine Told a Friend of Mine, A   Bryan 1906
Friend of the Family   Carmichael 1940; Mercer 1940
Friend of Yours, A   Burke 1945; Van Heusen 1945
Friendless Blues (inst.)   Waller 1924
Friendliest Thing, The   Drake 1964
Friendly Bar, A   Dietz 1943; Duke 1943
Friendly Country   Russell 1946
Friendly Crickets, The   Robison 1961
Friendly Doctor (I Am the Friendly Doctor), The   Caesar 1947
Friendly Enemy   Lerner, Sammy 1948
Friendly Finance Company   Evans 1951; Livingston, Jay 1951
Friendly Henry Wallace   Ager 1948; Harburg 1948
Friendly Islands, The   Arlen 1950; Blane 1950
Friendly Little Farm   Hammerstein 1942
Friendly Moon   Coots 1936; Davis 1936; Young, Victor 1934
Friendly Mountains   Burke 1948
Friendly Night   Razaf 1950
Friendly Persuasion (Thee I Love)   Webster 1956
Friendly Polka   Brooks 1948
Friendly Star   Gordon 1950; Revel 1950; Warren 1950
Friends   Jerome 1906; Johnson, Howard 1919; Meyer 1919; Schwartz, Jean 1906
Friends Cause Me to Be Out in the Street   Razaf 1930
Friends that Are Staunch and True   Herbert 1904
Friends to the End   Lerner, Alan Jay 1945; Loewe 1945; Mancini 1993
Friends Who Understand   Hammerstein 1923; Harbach 1923; Youmans 1923
Friendship   DeSylva 1922; Porter 1939
Friendship Leads Us to Love   Johnson, Howard 1924
Friendship Song, The   Caesar 1947
Friendship's Sacred Touch   Smith, Harry B. 1906
Friggin New Orleans Interlude (inst.)   Styne 1971
Frisco   Smith, Harry B. 1912
Frisco Bay   Fisher 1926; Rose 1926
Frisco Flo   Coots 1936; Davis 1936
Frisco Frizz   Howard, Joseph E. 1911
Frisco Melody, The   Cohan 1916
Frisky   Norworth 1936
Fritz   Norworth 1909
Frivolette Valse   Romberg 1933
Frocks and Frills   Atteridge 1917; Friml 1918; Romberg 1917
Frog and the Girl, The   Smith, Harry B. 1905
Frogs, The   Sondheim 1974
Frolic of a Breeze   Kern 1905, 1906
Frolic of the Fairies   Herbert 1911
Frolics of Pierrot, The   Edwards 1907
From a Logical Point of View   Raye 1957
From Afar   Rodgers 1976
From Africa   Smith, Harry B. 1900
From Alpha to Omega   Porter 1938
From Another World   Hart 1940; Rodgers 1940
From Far Cohoes   Mitchell 1921; Pollack 1921
From Heavens on High   Herbert 1903

From Here on In   Cahn 1943; Styne 1943
From Here to Shanghai   Berlin 1917
From Island to Island   Arlen 1952; Blane 1953
From Me to You   Lerner, Alan Jay 1939
From Morning Till Night   Kahn 1923; Motzan 1923
From Niagara Falls to Reno Is Only a Step Away   Akst 1931; Clarke 1931; Whiting 1931
From Nikki's Garden   Carmichael 1966
From Now On   Brown, Nacio Herb 1934; Davis 1925; DeSylva 1919; Eliscu 1929; Freed, Arthur 1934; Friend 1927; Gershwin, George 1919; Pollack 1927; Porter 1938; Stept 1955
From Now On I'm Ready for Love   Johnson, Howard 1927
From Now Onward   Romberg 1948
From One Pair of Arms to Another   Dubin 1931; Fain 1931; Kahal 1931
From Rocking Horse to Rocking Chair   Bacharach 1964; David, Hal 1964
From Saturday Night Till Monday Morning   Dubin 1927
From Saturday to Monday   Kern 1904
From the Chimney to the Cellar   Lerner, Alan Jay 1943; Loewe 1943
From the Circle to the Square   Oakland 1936
From the Coast of Maine to the Rockies   Davis 1942
From the Cradle to the Grave   Dietz 1944; Duke 1944
From the First Cigarette in the Morning to the Last Cigarette at Night   Robison 1955
From the First Good-Morning to the Last Good-Night   Schwartz, Jean 1938
From the First Hello to the Last Goodbye   Burke 1956
From the Land of Dreams   Cohan 1908
From the Meadow's Fairest Flower   Atteridge 1913
From the Sidewalks to the Stand   Drake 1957
From the Top of Your Head to the Tip of Your Toes   Gordon 1935; Revel 1935
From the U.S.A. to the U.S.S.R   Porter 1938
From This Day On   Bullock 1950; Lerner, Alan Jay 1947; Loewe 1947
From This Moment On   Porter 1950
From Tomorrow Morning On   Dixon 1926; Henderson 1926
From You   Styne 1941
From You, For Me   Howard, Joseph E. 1912
From Your Heart to Mine   Hanley 1920
Fromage   Coslow 1955
Front Page News   Dietz 1937; Schwartz, Arthur 1937
Front Page Story   Bacharach 1982
Front Porch Talk (And Rocking Chair Music)   Robison 1947
Frosted Chocolate   Rose 1934; Webster 1934
Frosty Mornin'   Caesar 1950; Lerner, Sammy 1950
Frou, Frou   Sigman 1954
Frowns   Gordon 1931; Revel 1931
Fruit Pickers' Song   Hammerstein 1931; Romberg 1931
Fruitti Di Mare   Friml 1934
Frustration   Mills 1947
Fryin' that One Lonely Egg   Wrubel 1951
Fuddle-Dee-Duddle (Funny Little Tune)   Fain 1938
Fuddy Duddy Watchmaker, The   Loesser 1943; McHugh 1943
Fudge   Dietz 1959; Schwartz, Arthur 1959
Fugitive from Esquire, A   Dietz 1940; McHugh 1940
Fugue   Duke 1940
Fugue for Tinhorns   Loesser 1950
Fu-Ji   Freed, Arthur 1925
Full Moon   Russell 1941
Full Moon and an Empty Heart, A   Revel 1942

Full Moon Street   Blane 1961
Full of Love   Bergman 1957
Full of Pep   Brennan 1929
Full of Shadows   Ellington 1958
Full of the Devil   Fields 1934; McHugh 1934
Full-Blown Roses   Hart 1925; Rodgers 1925
Fum Fiddle Dee Dum   Sherman 1954
Fun and Laughter   Sherman 1989
Fun and Things and Stuff   Fisher 1937
Fun City   Cahn 1967
Fun Fair   Sherman 1968
Fun Is More Fun   Livingston, Jerry 1963
Fun 'n' Games   Spina 1977
Fun on the Beach   Parish 1938; Silver 1938
Fun on the Farm   Ahlert 1924; Lewis 1924; Young, Joe 1924
Fun to Be Fooled   Arlen 1934; Gershwin, Ira 1934; Harburg 1934
Fun to Be Free   Alter 1942; Heyman 1942
Fun with Music   David, Mack 1955; Hoffman 1955; Livingston, Jerry 1955
Functionizin'   Mills 1935; Waller 1935
Functionizin' (inst.)   Waller 1935
Fundamental Character   Lerner, Sammy 1948
Fundamental-Friend-Dependability   Sherman 1972
Funeral Dirge   Sondheim 1962
Funeral Exit (inst.)   Styne 1971
Funeral Music (inst.)   Duke 1959
Funiculi Funicula   Johnson, Howard 1932
Funnies, The   Berlin 1933
Funnies Aren't Funny When I'm Blue   Hoffman 1936
Funnies on Parade   Razaf 1936
Funniest People Fall in Love, The   David, Hal 1947
Funny   Coleman 1989
Funny Face   Coslow 1954; Gershwin, George 1927; Gershwin, Ira 1927; Sterling 1909; Von Tilzer 1909
Funny Feet   Berlin 1922
Funny Girl   Merrill 1964, 1968; Styne 1964, 1968
Funny Little Girl   McHugh 1964
Funny Little Melody, The   Berlin 1912
Funny Little Money Man   David, Hal 1947
Funny Little Old World   Gorney 1949
Funny Little Ole Bluebird   Young, Victor 1954
Funny Little Sailor Men   Hammerstein 1928; Romberg 1928
Funny Little Something   Kern 1918
Funny Little Song   Friend 1938
Funny Little Tracks in the Snow   Porter 1914
Funny Little You   Razaf 1930
Funny Money Man, The   Hoffman 1942; Livingston, Jerry 1942
Funny (Not Much)   Merrill 1951
Funny Old Hills, The   Rainger 1938; Robin 1938
Funny Old House   Hammerstein 1934; Kern 1934
Funny Old Phonograph, The   Hoffman 1940
Funny Paper Capers (In a Dream)   Gilbert 1936
Funny Papers   Sigman 1947
Funny Side of That (Although a Duke of High Degree), The   Herbert 1897; Smith, Harry B. 1897
Funny Thing   Sigman 1954; Van Heusen 1954
Funny Thing Happened (On My Way to Love), A   Rome 1962
Funny Things Happen in Dreams   Friend 1938
Funny, What a Kiss Can Do   Hoffman 1957
Funny What a Little Kiss Can Do   Hoffman 1929; Lerner, Sammy 1929
Funnybone   Sherman 1995

Funny-Paper Capers in a Dream   Oakland 1954
Funshine   Friend 1958
Furnished for Monty   DeSylva 1920; Kern 1920
Furnishing a Home for Two   Berlin 1914
Furs and Feathers   Herbert 1905
Further It Is from Tipperary, The   Norworth 1917
Fussin' Around (inst.)   Waller 1945
Fussin' with the Budget   Robison 1941
Future Is Here to Stay   Brooks 1959
Future Lies Ahead, The   Drake 1960
Future Mrs. Coleman, The   Gershwin, Ira 1946; Schwartz, Arthur 1946
Futures (inst.)   Bacharach 1977
Futurist Girl   Buck 1914
Futuristic   Razaf 1928
Futuristic Melody   Gershwin, George 1921; Goetz 1921
Futuristic Rhythm   Fields 1928; McHugh 1928
Fuzzy Wuzzy   Hoffman 1944; Livingston, Jerry 1944

G

G Minor Is My Favorite Key   Willson 1956
Gabby's Exploits   Rainger 1939; Robin 1939
Gabey's Comin'   Comden and Green 1944
Gabriel Is Blowing His Horn   Dietz 1927; Gorney 1927
Gabrielle   Lerner, Alan Jay 1969
Gaby   Cohan 1916; Parish 1956
Gaby Can Can (inst.)   Gorney 1935
Gadabout   Evans 1953; Livingston, Jay 1953
Gag Song   Baer 1929; Gilbert 1929
Ga-Ga   Eliscu 1929
Gaggle of Geese, The   Sondheim 1962
Gaiety Chorus Girls, The   Hammerstein 1934; Kern 1934
Gaily, Gaily   Bergman 1969; Mancini 1969
Gal from Baton Rouge, The   Blake 1958
Gal from Joe's   Ellington 1939; Mills 1939
Gal in Calico, A   Robin 1946; Schwartz, Arthur 1946
Gal in Malibu, The   Drake 1948
Gal Named Cinderella, A   Fain 1952; Harburg 1952
Gal that Used to Do the Hootchy Kootchy   Baer 1939; Gilbert Date Unknown; Lewis 1939
Gale's Tales   Oakland 1960
Gall with the Yaller Shoes, The   Cahn 1956
Gallagher   Sherman 1965; Sterling 1910; Von Tilzer 1910
Gallagher and Shean Parodies   Caesar 1943
Gallant Lady   Ahlert 1934; Leslie 1934
Gallavantin' Around   Hammerstein 1936; Kern 1936
Galli Curci Rag   Schwartz, Jean 1918
Galli-Curci Rag, The   Atteridge 1918; Romberg 1918
Gallop   Parish 1957
Gallop, Gallop   Harbach 1910
(You'll Have to) Gallop Some   Atteridge 1916; Romberg 1916; Smith, Harry B. 1916
Galloping Comedians, The   Rome 1949
Gamble in the Wind, A   McHugh 1959
Gamble on Me   Atteridge 1915
Gambler of the West, The   Gershwin, George 1930; Gershwin, Ira 1930
Gamblers, The   Arlen 1959
Gambler's Lullaby   Webster 1946
Gamblin' Fool, A   Oakland 1968
Gamblin' Man, The   David, Hal 1954
Gambling   Herbert 1910
Gambling Man   Jerome 1902; Rome 1969; Schwartz, Jean 1902

Game Is Over, The   Davis 1966
Game of Cards, A   Atteridge 1915
Game of Chance, A   Drake 1962
Game of Halloween   Herbert 1912
Game of Love, The   Herbert 1908, 1913; Smith, Harry B. 1901; Smith, Robert B. 1913; Warren Date Unknown
Game of Poker, A   Arlen 1959; Mercer 1959
Game of Romance   Brooks 1959
Games a la Francaise (inst.)   Coots 1946
Gang Song   Koehler 1938
Gangway   Hoffman 1937; Lerner, Sammy 1937
Garage Sale   Spina 1976
Garbage   Lerner, Alan Jay 1985
Garbo Green   Fisher 1936
Garcon, S'il Vous Plait   Gershwin, George 1931; Gershwin, Ira 1931
Garden, The   Strouse 1971
Garden — The Beauty Contest, A   Herbert 1924
Garden By the Sea in Old Hawaii, A   Parish 1931
Garden Gate Was Open (My Beautiful Rose Was Gone), The   Brennan 1914
Garden in Encino, A   Carroll 1940
Garden in Granada, A   Baer 1938; Lewis 1938
Garden in Old Kentucky   Bryan 1935
Garden in the Sky   Dietz 1944; Duke 1944
Garden in Versailles (inst.)   Coots 1946
Garden of Dreams   Smith, Robert B. 1907
Garden of Eden   Adams 1954; Hanley 1922; Porter 1953; Strouse 1954
(The Flowers of Evil) Garden of Evil   Atteridge 1923; Schwartz, Jean 1923
Garden of Flowers   Goetz 1912
Garden of Girls, The   Atteridge 1912, 1914; Carroll 1914; Romberg 1914
Garden of Liberty (I've Got a Vegetable Garden) (Vegetable Song)   Bryan 1917
Garden of Love, A   Adams 1983; Bergman 1958; DeSylva 1923; Gershwin, George 1923; Schwartz, Jean 1924
Garden of My Dreams   Buck 1918
Garden of Night   Bryan 1928
Garden of Paradise   Atteridge 1915; Romberg 1915
Garden of the Moon   Dubin 1938; Mercer 1938; Warren 1938
Garden of Used to Be, The   Gorney 1924
Garden of Yesterday, The   Goetz 1912
Garden Party   Herbert 1912
Garden Scene   Hammerstein 1938; Harbach 1938; Kern 1938
Garden Sequence   Sondheim 1994
Garden that Blooms for You, The   Cohan 1908
Garlands Bright   Romberg 1924
Garret in the Gay Montmartre, A   Meyer 1934; Young, Joe 1934
Garrison Ball, The   Howard, Joseph E. 1908
Garside the Great   Lawrence 1964
Gary, Indiana   Willson 1954, 1957
Gascony   Friml 1928
Gasoline Gypsies   Mercer 1937; Whiting 1937
Gas-Rubber Hog, The   Caesar 1943
Gaston's Soliloquy   Lerner, Alan Jay 1958; Loewe 1958
Gates of Emerald City   Arlen 1939; Harburg 1939
Gates of Gladness   Brennan 1919
Gates of Happiness, The   Parish 1957
Gates of Love   Brown, Nacio Herb 1927
Gateway of the Temple of Minerva, The   Hart 1942; Rodgers 1942

Gather All Ye Merry Carolers   Freed, Ralph 1960
Gather Lip Rouge While You May   DeSylva 1933; Robin 1933; Whiting 1933
Gather the Rose   Friml 1927
Gather Ye Autographs While Ye May   Porter 1935
Gather Ye Rosebuds   Gershwin, George 1925; Gershwin, Ira 1925
Gather Your Dreams   Howard, Bart 1963
Gathering   Cohan 1923
Gaucho, The   DeSylva 1935
Gaucho Love Song, A   Caesar 1930; Harbach 1930; Romberg 1930
Gaucho March   Caesar 1930; Harbach 1930; Romberg 1930
Gaucho with the Black Mustache, The   Davis 1941; Stept 1941
Gave of Give and Take, The   Lawrence 1953
Gavotte   Friml 1934; Hart 1925; Herbert 1903; Porter 1939; Rodgers 1925; Romberg 1924
Gavotte No. 1 (inst.)   Carroll 1914; Romberg 1914
Gavotte No. 2 (inst.)   Carroll 1914; Romberg 1914
Gay and Joyous (inst.)   Kern 1956
Gay Brazilian   Atteridge 1921; Pollack 1921; Schwartz, Jean 1921
Gay Butterfly on the Wheel   Bryan 1922; Schwartz, Jean 1922
Gay Cattin' Daddy   Razaf 1927
Gay Continental Am I, A   Brooks 1953; Warren 1953
Gay Desperado, The   Freed, Ralph 1938; Lane 1938
Gay Friends Are Essential   Willson 1956
Gay Life, The   Dietz 1961; Herbert 1914; Schwartz, Arthur 1961; Smith, Robert B. 1914
Gay Little Melody, A   Hoffman 1946; Livingston, Jerry 1946
Gay Little Wives (Six Little Wives)   Porter 1935
Gay Lothario, The   Kern 1908
Gay Love   Clare 1929, 1930
Gay Monte Carlo   Drake 1954
Gay Nineties, The   Fain 1938
Gay Paree   Mancini 1982; Strouse 1999
Gay Waltz, The   Davis 1951
Gay White Way   Magidson 1941; Oakland 1941
Gaze on This Face   Herbert 1895, 1897; Smith, Harry B. 1895, 1897
Gazooka, The   Duke 1936; Gershwin, Ira 1936
G'bye Now   Evans 1984; Livingston, Jay 1984
G'Bye Now New York   Robin 1955; Styne 1955
Gee, Ain't I Glad I'm Home!   Cohan 1907
Gee, Ain't It Tough When There's No One Around to Call You Dear   Young, Joe 1911
Gee Baby, Ain't I Good to You   Razaf 1929
Gee! But I Hate to Go Home Alone   Hanley 1922
Gee, But I Like Music with My Meals   Brown, A. Seymour 1911
Gee, but I'd Like to Be Bad   Hanley 1926
Gee, but I'm Tickled to Death, You Married Me   Johnson, Howard 1915
Gee! But It Was Hot in Chile   Young, Joe 1932
Gee, But It's Great to Be Falling in Love   McHugh 1953
Gee, But It's Great to Meet a Friend from Your Home Town   Fisher 1910
Gee but It's Sweet to Cheat Just a Little   Von Tilzer 1925
Gee But It's Tough to Be Alone on a Saturday Night   Davis 1928; Rose 1928
Gee, but You're Swell   Baer 1936
Gee How I Wish I Had You Back Again   Bryan 1926

Gee I Only Wish that I Could Make My Dreams Come True   Buck 1915

Gee, I Should Have Been Born a Boy   Brown, A. Seymour 1912

Gee! I Wish I Had a Girl Like You   Friend 1921; Pollack 1921

Gee I Wish I Had Someone to Rock Me in the Cradle of Love   Blake 1919; Sissle 1919

Gee, I Wish I Listened to My Mother   McHugh 1941; Mercer 1941

Gee, I Wish I Was Back in the Army   Berlin 1954

Gee I Wish I Was Big   Von Tilzer 1913

Gee! I'm Glad I'm Home Again   Monaco 1927; Rose 1927

Gee I'm Glad that I'm from Dixie So I Can Get a Dixie Welcome Home   Blake 1919; Sissle 1919

Gee, I'm Glad to Be the One That I Am   Lerner, Sammy 1946

Gee, It Must Be Tough to Be a Rich Man's Kid   Cobb 1912; Edwards 1912

Gee, It's Gonna Be Wonderful   Evans 1950; Livingston, Jay 1950

Gee, It's Great to Be Alive   Brown, Lew 1928; DeSylva 1928; Henderson 1928

Gee It's So Good, It's Too Bad   Arlen 1930; Koehler 1930

Gee, Officer Krupke   Sondheim 1957

Gee Whiz! Those Eyes   Howard, Joseph E. 1918

Gee Whizz, Whilikens, Golly Gee   David, Mack 1960; Livingston, Jerry 1960

Gee Willikens! (inst.)   Warren 1953

Gefrunk   Mercer 1979

Geisha Boy, The   Brooks 1958

Gelt   Gilbert 1952

Gemutlichkeit   Coleman 1960; Leigh 1960

Gendarme, The   Dietz 1937; Schwartz, Arthur 1937

Gendarme's Dance, The   Cohan 1908

Geneology   Brown, Lew 1928; DeSylva 1928; Henderson 1928

General Dance   Herbert 1917

General Douglas MacArthur's "Duty, Honor, and Country"   Blane 1969

General Hiram Johnson Jefferson Brown   Donaldson 1934; Kahn 1934

General Hooligan   Von Tilzer 1915

General Ike   Caesar 1945

General MacArthur's Army   Eliscu 1942; Gorney 1942

General Nuisance   Lewis 1915

General Orders   Loesser 1944

General Unveiled (inst.)   Rome 1937

General's Lookin'   David, Mack 1941

General's Song, The   Duke 1940

Generation Gap   Young, Joe 1974

Gene's Gem   DePaul 1953

Geneva (A Satrical Ballet) (inst.)   Rome 1938

Genie with the Light Brown Rug   Brooks 1960

Genie's Theme   Porter 1958

Genieve   Hoffman 1950

Genius   Willson 1969

Genius of Me, The   Adams 1972; Strouse 1972

Gent from Georgia, The   Spina 1957

Genteel   Eliscu 1962

Genteel Bastard   Arlen 1959; Mercer 1959

Gentle Afternoon   Merrill 1990

Gentle and Sentimental   Willson 1956

Gentle Carpenter of Bethlehem, The   Drake 1951

Gentle Is My Love   Raye 1965; Webster 1966

Gentle Love   Washington 1959, 1961

Gentle River   Goetz 1910

Gentleman in the Next Apartment, The   Van Heusen 1954

Gentleman Is a Dope, The   Hammerstein 1947; Rodgers 1947

Gentlemen of Fortune   Styne 1985

Gentleman of the Old School   Webster 1946

Gentlemanly Brigand, The   Smith, Harry B. 1911

Gentleman's Gentleman, A   Harburg 1967; Styne 1967

Gentlemen   Drake 1952

Gentlemen of the Press   Caesar 1930; Cohan 1906; Gordon 1953; Myrow 1953; Schwartz, Jean 1926

Gentlemen Prefer Blondes   Berlin 1925; Caesar 1926; DeSylva 1926; Friml 1926; Robin 1948; Styne 1948

Gentlemen Unafraid   Hammerstein 1938; Harbach 1938; Kern 1938

Gentlemen, Why Don't You Mingle   Brooks 1959

Gentlemen's Understanding   Eliscu 1962

Geography   Edwards 1908

George Cohan's Rag   Cohan 1911

George Washington Carver   Razaf 1943

George Washington, Jr.   Cohan 1904

George White's Scandals   Brown, Lew 1928; Caesar 1934; DeSylva 1928; Henderson 1928; Yellen 1934

Georgette   Brown, Lew 1922; Henderson 1922

Georgia   Bryan 1914; Donaldson 1922; Johnson, Howard 1922; Razaf 1939; Revel 1929

Georgia Bo-Bo   Waller 1926

Georgia Cabin Door   Parish 1922

Georgia Gal   Razaf 1940

Georgia Georgia   Mercer 1966

Georgia Gigolo   Johnson, Howard 1929

Georgia Grind, The   Goetz 1910

Georgia Gut   Razaf 1928

Georgia Home   Conrad 1927

Georgia Land   Carroll 1912

Georgia May   Razaf 1934

Georgia on My Mind   Carmichael 1930

Georgia Rockin' Chair   Fisher 1935

Georgia Sand   Porter 1933

Georgia Trail   Razaf 1940

Georgianna   Akst 1926; Lewis 1926; Young, Joe 1926

Georgia's Gorgeous Gal   Parish 1934

Georgie   Harbach 1923

Georgie and I   Conrad 1926

Georgy Porgy Comes to the Fair   David, Mack 1958; Livingston, Jerry 1958

Geraldine   Akst 1927; Clare 1953; Davis 1927; Young, Victor 1953

Geraniums in the Winder   Hammerstein 1945; Rodgers 1945

German Town (inst.)   Kern 1946

Gershwin Specialty   Porter 1928

Gertrude Hoffman Glide, The   Atteridge 1912

Gertrude Hoffman March   Atteridge 1912

Get a Girl to Lead the Army   Bryan 1917

Get a Girl To Love You   Bryan 1910

Get a Girlie   Atteridge 1916

Get a Horse   Fields 1951; Mancini 1965; Mercer 1965; Schwartz, Arthur 1951; Schwartz, Jean 1904

Get a Horse (For Your Horseless Carriage)   Martin 1952

Get a Horse, Get a Mule   Hammerstein 1928; Youmans 1928

Get a Job for Purple Heart Joe   Coots 1947

Get a Little Fun Out of Life   Kalmar 1932; Ruby 1932

Get a Load o' Me   Bergman 1955

Get a Load of That   Lewis 1926; Weill 1947; Young, Joe 1926
Get a Load of that Crazy Walk   DePaul 1953; Raye 1953
Get a Map   Willson 1969
Get a Model   Johnson, J. Rosamond 1950
Get Aboard the Bondwagon   Russell 1943
Get Acquainted with Yourself   Cahn 1935
Get Along Home, Cindy   Drake 1955
Get Along, Little Dream   Howard, Bart 1957
Get Along Without Me (inst.)   Kern 1938
Get Away for a Day in the Country   Cahn 1947; Styne 1947
Get Away from It All   Dietz 1935; Schwartz, Arthur 1935
Get Away from My Window   Johnson, James P. 1929
Get Away Young Man   Waller 1943
Get 'Em While They're Dancing Around   Baer 1920; Mitchell 1920
Get Goin'   Conrad 1934; Oakland 1934
Get Happy   Arlen 1930; Koehler 1930
Get Her Away from Me   Adams 1970; Strouse 1970
Get Hot Foot   Stept 1933
Get in Step   Mitchell 1936; Stept 1936
Get It Southern Style   Mills 1937
Get Me One of Those   David, Hal 1950
Get Me Out of Here   Martin 1972
Get Me Some Acres of Land   Revel 1946
Get Me to the Church on Time   Lerner, Alan Jay 1956; Loewe 1956
Get Next to the Man with a Pull   Smith, Harry B. 1901
Get Off   Johnson, James P. 1932; Razaf 1932
Get Off the Cotty, Potty (The Tide Is Coming In)   Robison 1963
Get Off the Grass Liza Jane   Johnson, James P. 1962
Get Off the Pot   Ruby 1943
Get on Board Little Children   DePaul 1942, 1944; Raye 1942, 1944
Get on Ted   Robison 1964
Get on the Merry-Go-Round   Edwards 1908
Get One for Me   Brown, Lew 1914
Get Out and Get Under the Moon   Jerome 1928
Get Out of Town   Porter 1938
Get Rhythm in Your Feet   Razaf 1941
Get Rid of Monday   Burke 1955; Van Heusen 1955
Get That Ho Do Ho in Your Soul   Mills 1935
Get that Sun into You   Harburg 1932
Get the Feel of the Wheel of a Ford   Sherman 1990
Get the Man in the Mood   Whiting 1930
Get the Money   Jerome 1905; Rainger 1943; Robin 1943; Schwartz, Jean 1905
Get Thee Behind Me, Clayton   Rainger 1941; Robin 1941
Get Thee Behind Me Satan   Berlin 1934
Get Together   Friml 1923
Get Under the Sun   Loesser 1935
Get Up, Get Out, Get Under the Sun   Arlen 1931; Koehler 1931
Get Up Off Your Knees   Razaf 1929
Get Up on a New Routine   Dietz 1929; Schwartz, Arthur 1929
Get Used to Me   Davis 1981
Get Your Man   Hart 1943; Rainger 1943; Robin 1943
Get Your Police Gazette   Gordon 1943; Warren 1943
Get Your Program for de Big Fight   Hammerstein 1943
Get Yourself a Broom and Sweep You Troubles Away   Rose 1924
Get Yourself a Geisha   Dietz 1935; Schwartz, Arthur 1935
Get Yourself a Girl   Porter 1941

Get Yourself a Girl and Fall in Love   Gordon 1932; Revel 1932
Get Yourself a Little Cup of Sunshine   Gordon 1932; Revel 1932
Get Yourself a New Broom   Arlen 1933; Koehler 1933
Get Yourself a Phonograph   Burke 1948; Van Heusen 1948; Young, Victor 1948
Gettin' a Man   Mercer 1959
Gettin' It All for Free   Adamson 1958; McHugh 1958
Gettin' It Together   Sherman 1972
Gettin' Nowhere Road   Koehler 1936
Gettin' Sentimental   Kahn 1931
Gettin' Some   Styne 1980
Getting Away with Murder   Kalmar 1936; Ruby 1936
Getting Dressed   Loesser 1950
Getting Married   Comden and Green 1961; Styne 1961
Getting Married (Living As One)   Styne 1967
Getting Married to a Person   Rodgers 1970
Getting Married Today   Sondheim 1970
Getting Myself Annoyed with Floyd   Robison 1965
(Running Around in Circles) Getting Nowhere   Berlin 1946
Getting Over You   Drake 1996
Getting Some Fun Out of Life   Leslie 1937
Getting to Know You   Hammerstein 1951; Rodgers 1951
Gettysburg Address   Livingston, Jerry 1959
Ghetto   Brennan 1925
Ghost at Gettysburg   Loesser 1950; Spina 1950
Ghost Goes West, The   Styne 1958
Ghost Music (inst.)   Duke 1959
(I Don't Stand a) Ghost of a Chance with You   Washington 1932; Young, Victor 1932
Ghost of a Love   Russell Date Unknown
Ghost of a Rag, The   Brown, Lew 1912
Ghost of an Old Romance, The   Brown, A. Seymour 1941
Ghost of Deacon Brown, The   Johnson, J. Rosamond 1907
Ghost of Dinah, The   Young, Joe 1935
Ghost of Grandfather Clock, The   Alter 1930
Ghost of Kelly, The   Jerome 1910; Schwartz, Jean 1910
Ghost of Love   Lawrence 1943; Mercer 1933; Spina 1933
Ghost of Old Black Joe   Bryan 1919; Schwartz, Jean 1919
Ghost of Smokey Joe, The   Bloom 1939; Koehler 1939
Ghost of the Goblin Man, The   Sterling 1912; Von Tilzer 1912
Ghost of the Terrible Blues, The   Von Tilzer 1916
Ghost of the Violin, The   Kalmar 1912; Snyder 1912
Ghost Quintette   Smith, Harry B. 1912; Smith, Robert B. 1912
Ghost Recitative   Johnson, James P. 1922
Ghost Routine   Styne 1940
Ghost that Never Walked, The   Jerome 1904; Schwartz, Jean 1904
Ghost Town   Coots 1951
Ghost Town Music   Spina 1965
Ghosts of Grandfather's Clock   Johnson, Howard 1930
Ghosts of the Ukulele, The   Atteridge 1916; Motzan 1916, 1917; Romberg 1916
G.I. Jive   Mercer 1943
G.I. Song   Koehler 1946
Gianina   Romberg 1919
Giannina Mia   Friml 1912; Harbach 1912
Giant   Webster 1956
Giant Step, A   Adams 1991; Strouse 1991
Giants in the Sky   Sondheim 1987
Gibbledy Gob   Hoffman 1953; Silver 1953
Gibbs and Finney   Baer 1942

Gibson Coon, The   Cohan 1908
Gibson Girl, The   Smith, Harry B. 1906
Gibson School Marm, The   Howard, Joseph E. 1908
Gid-Ap Garibaldi!   Johnson, Howard 1927; Warren 1927
Giddy-Ap! (Buggy Ride Song) (Chic a Chiquito)   Rome 1951
Giddy-Ap Joe   Lewis 1924; Young, Joe 1924
Giddy-Bug Galop (inst.), The   Ellington 1941
Gideon Briggs, I Love You   Loesser 1960
Gideon's Charm   Loesser 1960
Gift for Every Day of the Week, A   Duke 1963
Gift from Heaven, A   Young, Joe 1934
Gift Number   Gorney 1948
Gift of a Second Chance, The   Coleman 1962; Leigh 1962
Gift of Gab   Conrad 1934; Magidson 1934
Gift of Love, A   Duke 1963; Fain 1957, 1958; Freed, Ralph
    1966; Webster 1957, 1958
Gift of Time, A   Duke 1963
Gift (Recado Bossa Nova), The   Webster 1962
Gift Today (The Bar Mitzvah Song), A   Rome 1962
Giggle Bush, The   Sherman 1960
Gigi   Lerner, Alan Jay 1958; Loewe 1958
Gigolette   Caesar 1925; Sigman 1948
Gigolo   Hart 1926, 1927; Rodgers 1926, 1927; Romberg 1927
Gigolo Joe   Mills 1931
Gigoloes   Brown, Lew 1931; Henderson 1931
Gigot   Cahn 1962
Gilding the Guild   Hart 1925; Rodgers 1925
Gilly Gilly Osenfeffer Katzenellen Bogen By the
    Sea   Hoffman 1954
Gimme a Clue   Drake 1958
Gimme a Little Kiss Will Ya Huh   Turk 1926
Gimme a Man Who Makes Music   Washington 1953
Gimme a Raincheck   Coleman 1966; Fields 1966
Gimme Some   Adams 1964
Gimme Some (Beer and Whiskey)   Strouse 1964
Gimme Some More, More   Meyer 1934; Young, Joe 1934
Gimme Some Skin   DePaul 1941
Gimme Some Skin (My Friend)   Raye 1941
Gimme the Casbah   Silver 1948
Gimme the Shimmie   Clare Date Unknown
Gimme the Shimmy   Rome 1950
Gimme This — Gimme This — Gimme That   Gilbert 1918
Gimme-Gimme Take-Take   Sherman 1984
Gin and Tonic (inst.)   Stept 1957
Gin Rummy Rhapsody   Rome 1948
Gina   Myrow 1965
Gina Mia (I Love You)   Spina 1957
Ginette   Schwartz, Jean 1928
Ginger   Clarke 1915; Freed, Ralph 1935; Goetz 1912, 1917;
    Gorney 1925; Stept 1935
Ginger and Spice   Carmichael 1946
Ginger Brown   Johnson, James P. 1922
Ginger Girl   Goetz 1915; Romberg 1915
Ginger Town   Kern 1919
Gingerbread House   David, Hal 1948
Ginger's Rhumba (Inst.)   Gershwin, George 1937
Ginny   Silver 1955
Ginny Ginny Shore   Atteridge 1921; Romberg 1921
Giovanni   Monaco 1940
Gip-Gip   Cohan 1927
Gipsy Song (inst.)   Warren Date Unknown
Girl, The   Webster 1965
Girl, a Boy and Moonlight, A   Brown, A. Seymour 1913
Girl, a Drink and a Song, A   Edwards 1908
Girl and French Chauffeurs   Atteridge 1911

Girl at the End of Our Street Back Home (inst.)   Kern 1956
Girl at the Helm, The   Smith, Robert B. 1905
Girl at the Ironing Board, The   Dubin 1934; Warren 1934
Girl Begind the Gun, The   Herbert 1917
Girl Behind the Counter, The   Howard, Joseph E. 1908
Girl Behind the Man Behind the Ball, The   Drake 1955
Girl Behind the Venetian Blind, The   Friend 1939
Girl Belongs to You, The   Atteridge 1920
Girl By the Tree, A   Coslow 1934
Girl Can't Say, A   David, Hal 1954
Girl for Me, The   Atteridge 1917; Romberg 1917
Girl Friday Blues   Robison 1964
Girl Friend, The   Hart 1926; Johnston 1935; Kahn 1935;
    Rodgers 1926
Girl Friend of a Boy Friend of Mine, A   Donaldson 1928;
    Kahn 1928
Girl Friend of the Whirling Dervish, The   Dubin 1938;
    Mercer 1938; Warren 1938
Girl from Casimo   Hammerstein 1923; Harbach 1923
Girl from Casino   Youmans 1923
Girl from Havana, The   Styne 1940
Girl from Home Sweet Home, The   Atteridge 1912
Girl from My Home Town, The   Buck 1915
Girl from Noofchateau (Believe Me You Should Know My
    Girl From Noo Chateau), The   Ahlert 1929; Turk 1929
Girl from Oscaloosa, The   Silver 1930
Girl from the Golden West, A   Coots 1922
Girl Has a Sailor in Every Port, A   Atteridge 1921; Romberg
    1921
Girl Has Got to Do the Best She Can, A   Yellen 1956
Girl He Left Behind Him Has the Hardest Fight of All,
    The   Bryan 1918; Kalmar 1918; Leslie 1918; Ruby 1918
Girl Hunt Ballet (inst.)   Schwartz, Arthur 1952
Girl I Call My Sweetheart Must Look Like You, The   Olcott
    1911
Girl I Know, A   Cohan 1904
Girl I Left Before I Left the Girl I Left Behind, The   Von
    Tilzer 1912
Girl I Left Behind, The   Howard, Joseph E. 1909
Girl I Left Behind Me, The   Johnson, Howard 1939; Leslie
    1935; Meyer 1935; Rose 1935
Girl I Love, The   Gershwin, George 1927; Gershwin, Ira
    1927
Girl I Love Is Like a Will-O-The-Wisp, The   Ager 1923;
    Yellen 1923
Girl I Love to Leave Behind, The   Hart 1943; Rodgers 1943
Girl I Loved and Lost, The   Cobb 1901; Edwards 1901
Girl I Loved and Lost Long, Long Ago, The   Sterling 1898;
    Von Tilzer 1898
Girl I Loved in Old Virginia, The   Sterling 1899
Girl I Used to Know, The   Olcott 1904; Smith, Harry B. 1909
Girl I Used to Love Long Ago, The   Sterling 1899
Girl I'll Call My Sweetheart Must Look Like You,
    The   Olcott 1920
Girl in Every Port   Atteridge 1919; Romberg 1919; Schwartz,
    Jean 1919
Girl in No Man's Land, The   Mancini 1970; Mercer 1970
Girl in Nottingham Lace, The   Cahn 1945; Styne 1945
Girl in the Front Porch Swing, The   Coots 1946
Girl in the Spotlight   Herbert 1920; Smith, Robert B. 1920
Girl in Your Arms, A   Caesar 1926; Gorney 1926
Girl Is Like a Book, A   Lerner, Alan Jay 1943; Loewe 1943
Girl Is Like Sunshine, A   Turk 1924
Girl Is Nobody, A   Caesar 1924, 1930
Girl Is Out to Get a Man   Brooks 1958

Girl Is You and the Boy Is Me, The   Brown, Lew 1926
Girl Like Grandma   Romberg 1921
Girl Like I, A   Comden and Green 1974; Styne 1974
Girl Like Nina, A   Hammerstein 1933
Girl Like That, A   Dietz 1961; Schwartz, Arthur 1961
Girl Like You, A   Bacharach 1959; Blane 1961
Girl Most Likely, The   Russell 1957
Girl Most Likely to Succeed, The   Cahn 1959; Van Heusen 1959
Girl Named Gigolette, A   Oakland 1961; Webster 1961
Girl Named Mary, A   Bryan 1956
Girl Named Mary and a Boy Named Bill, A   David, Mack 1951; Livingston, Jerry 1951
Girl Named Tamiko, A   David, Mack 1963
Girl Next Door, The   Blane 1954; Hammerstein 1931; Martin 1954; Whiting 1931
Girl of All Nations   Mercer 1951
Girl of Greater New York, The   Smith, Harry B. 1901
Girl of My Dreams   Harbach 1911
Girl of My Heart (Is You Mother Dear), The   Coots 1950
Girl of the Fan, The   Atteridge 1915; Romberg 1915
Girl of the Golden West   Kahn 1938; Romberg 1938
Girl of the Great Divide, The   Smith, Robert B. 1907
Girl of the Moment   Gershwin, Ira 1940; Weill 1940
Girl of the Pi Beta Phi, A   Brown, Lew 1927; DeSylva 1927; Henderson 1927
Girl of the Year   Drake 1964
Girl of To-Day, The   Atteridge 1914; Romberg 1914
Girl of Tomorrow, The   Brown, Lew 1925; DeSylva 1925; Henderson 1925
Girl on My Mind, The   Burke 1971
Girl on My Mind (inst.)   Revel 1957
Girl on the Little Blue Plate, The   Alter 1935
Girl on the Magazine Cover, The   Berlin 1915
Girl on the Police Gazette, The   Berlin 1937
Girl on the Prow, The   Hammerstein 1928; Romberg 1928
Girl on the Square   Atteridge 1916; Motzan 1916, 1917; Romberg 1916
Girl on the Train, The   Smith, Harry B. 1910
Girl Rush, The   Blane 1955; Martin 1955
Girl Should Never Ripple When She Bends, A   Waller 1943
Girl that I Court in My Mind, The   Blane 1952
Girl that I Know   Duke 1969; Kern 1969
Girl That I Marry, The   Berlin 1946
Girl That Waits for Me, The   Rome 1943
Girl that Was, The   Harburg 1969
Girl that's Most Chased After, The   Gorney 1925
Girl to Remember, A   Comden and Green 1964; Styne 1964
Girl Trouble   Fisher 1930
(Little) Girl Up There   Harbach 1908
Girl Upstairs, The   Cahn 1955
Girl Who Broke My Heart, The   Dubin 1928
Girl Who Can Love, A   Herbert 1920; Smith, Robert B. 1920
Girl Who Cares for Me   Cobb 1904; Edwards 1904
Girl Who Drinks Champagne, The   Atteridge 1917; Motzan 1917; Romberg 1917
Girl Who Gets Her Man, The   Razaf 1932
Girl Who Is Up-to-Date, The   Smith, Harry B. 1900
Girl Who Keeps You Waiting, The   Herbert 1920; Smith, Robert B. 1920
Girl Who Knows It All, The   McHugh 1964
Girl Who Used to Be Me, The   Bergman 1989
Girl Who Works in the Laundry, The   Dubin 1940; Fain 1940
Girl Who Wouldn't Spoon, The   Harbach 1911

Girl with a Flame, A   Fields 1950
Girl with the Bells, The   David, Mack 1956; Van Heusen 1956
Girl with the Come Hither Eyes   Friml 1912; Harbach 1912
Girl with the High Button Shoes, The   Washington 1943
Girl with the Maracas, The   Adamson 1950; McHugh 1950
Girl with the Pigtails in Her Hair   Cahn 1939
Girl with the Prettiest Legs in Town, The   Cahn Date Unknown; Duke Date Unknown
Girl with the Spanish Drawl, The   David, Mack 1947
Girl with the Stardust in Her Eyes   Russell 1952
Girl with the Storybook Dream, The   Oakland 1957
Girl with the Sugar Brown Hair, The   Bullock 1941
Girl with the Yellow Hair, The   Dietz 1950
Girl Won't Forget (A Boy Who Remembers), A   David, Hal 1960
Girl You Dream About, The   Howard, Joseph E. 1907
Girl You Left Behind, The   Jerome 1915; Schwartz, Jean 1915
Girl You See in the Looking Glass, The   Meyer 1908
Girl You Used to Be, The   Dubin 1937; Warren 1937
Girlie   Kern 1918
Girlie of the Cabaret   Atteridge 1915; Romberg 1915
Girlie Was Just Made to Love, A   Meyer 1911
Girlie-Land, A   Herbert 1911; Smith, Harry B. 1911
Girlies Are Out of My Life   Atteridge 1915; Romberg 1915
Girlies You've Kissed in Your Dreams, The   Harbach 1911
Girlish Laughter   Atteridge 1912
Girls   Bryan 1919; Carroll 1919; Duke 1963; Evans 1953; Fisher Date Unknown; Kalmar 1941; Livingston, Jay 1953; Porter 1944; Ruby 1941
Girls Ahoy!   Adams 1993
Girls and Boys   Smith, Harry B. 1905
Girls and Rassendyl   Duke 1963
Girls Are at It Again, The   David, Hal 1959
Girls Are Different   Lawrence 1958
Girls Are Getting Wiser, The   Romberg 1916; Smith, Robert B. 1916
Girls Are Getting Wiser Ev'ry Day, The   Bryan 1917
Girls Are Marching, The   Comden and Green 1952; Styne 1952
Girl's Best Friend, A   Ellington 1965
Girls Do Not Tempt Me   Hart 1925; Rodgers 1925
Girls Dream of One Thing   Coots 1925
Girl's Entitled, A   Arlen 1966
Girls from DeVere's   Cohan 1922
Girls! Girls! Girls!   Brown, Lew 1945; Hart 1934; Henderson 1945; Kahn 1934; Leigh 1955; Webster 1952
Girls, Glorious Girls   Sherman 1965
Girls, Good Bye   Romberg 1927
Girls Grow More Wonderful Day by Day   Harbach 1923
Girls, I Am True to All of You (I'm True to Everyone)   Smith, Harry B. 1927
Girls I Left Behind, The   Smith, Harry B. 1908
Girls in Summertime   David, Hal 1960
Girls in the Band, The   Merrill 1972; Styne 1972
Girls in the Sea   Kern 1920
Girls Know How   Bacharach 1982
Girls Like Me   Comden and Green 1961; Styne 1961
Girls of All Nations   Akst 1934
Girls of America, We All Depend on You   Kalmar 1917; Leslie 1917; Ruby 1917
Girls of France   Bryan 1918; Leslie 1918; Ruby 1918
Girls of Long Ago   Caesar 1930
Girls of My Dreams, The   Berlin 1920

Girls of San Francisco, The   Sherman 1967
Girls of Summer, The   Sondheim 1956
Girls of the U.S.A.   Cohan 1904
Girls Prepare   Atteridge 1916; Romberg 1916
Girls School Alma Mater   Loesser 1952
Girls that Can Never Be Mine, The   Howard, Joseph E. 1909
Girls that Win My Heart, The   Smith, Harry B. 1914
Girls Want a Hero   Ellington 1946
Girls Want Everything They See   Drake 1953
Girls We Never Did Wed, The   David, Hal 1951
Girls We Remember, The   Dubin 1930
Girls Were Made to Take Care of Boys   Blane 1948
Girls Who Go Upon the Stage   Brown, A. Seymour 1909
Girls You Are Such Wonderful Thing   Smith, Harry B. 1916
Git a Horse   Schwartz, Jean 1905; Williams 1905
Git Along   Drake 1953
Git Away!   Razaf 1940
Git It, I'd Like to See You Wid It   Russell 1943
Gitka's Song, The   Rodgers 1970
Giuggiola   Cahn 1961
Give a Girl a Break   Gershwin, Ira 1953; Lane 1953
Give a Girl a Chance   Hammerstein 1923; Youmans 1923
Give a Guy a Kiss   Coslow 1930
Give a Little Credit to the Navy   DeSylva 1918; Kahn 1918
Give a Little Get a Little   Comden and Green 1951; Styne 1951
Give a Little, Get a Little Kiss   Caesar 1925; Romberg 1925
Give a Little Thought to Me   DeSylva 1919; Kern 1919
Give a Little Whistle   Washington 1940
Give a Little Whistle (And I'll Be There)   Coleman 1960; Leigh 1960
Give a Look (Looky Look)   Hoffman 1957
Give a Man a Job   Hart 1934; Rodgers 1934
Give a Man a Tree   Freed, Ralph 1965
Give a Man Enough Rope   Coleman 1991; Comden and Green 1991
Give a Thought   Baer 1956
Give a Viva!   Rome 1941
Give Every Child a Chance   Adamson 1953; McHugh 1953
Give, Give   Harbach 1921
(I Would) Give Heaven Back to the Angels   Drake 1952
Give Her a Kiss   Hart 1932; Rodgers 1932
Give Her a Pint and She'll Tell It All   Cahn 1936
Give Her My Love   Cahn 1940
Give Her Perfume   Revel 1953
Give Him a Roll on the Drum   David, Mack 1937
Give Him Back His Job   Egan 1919; Whiting 1919
Give Him the Oo-La-La   Porter 1939
Give Him Your Sympathy   Caesar 1924; Conrad 1924; Harbach 1924
Give It   Magidson 1929; Washington 1929
Give It All You've Got   Evans 1950; Livingston, Jay 1950
Give It Back to the Indians   Hart 1939; Rodgers 1939
Give Me   Merrill 1955
Give Me a Band and a Bandana   Brown, Nacio Herb 1944; Robin 1944
Give Me a Band and My Baby   Robin 1955; Styne 1955
Give Me a Bit More than You Gave Reilly   Bryan 1917
Give Me a Chance   Smith, Harry B. 1928
Give Me a Chance at Heaven   Magidson 1932
Give Me a Cigarette, Please   Livingston, Jerry 1937
Give Me a Day in June   Kahn 1927
Give Me a Gentle Girl   Fain 1957; Webster 1957
Give Me a Heart to Sing To   Washington 1934; Young, Victor 1934

Give Me a Kiss   Snyder 1918
Give Me a Kiss Sweetheart   Coslow 1930
Give Me a Look   Hoffman 1953
Give Me a Million Beautiful Girls   Parish 1920
Give Me a Moment Please   Robin 1930; Whiting 1930
Give Me a Night in June   Friend 1927
Give Me a Rod, a Reel (a Boat and a Creel)   Johnson, J. Rosamond 1947
Give Me a Roll on a Drum   Caesar 1933; Romberg 1933
Give Me a Saddle   DePaul 1942
Give Me a Sailor   Carmichael 1938; Coslow 1938; Loesser 1938
Give Me a Share in America (I Want a Share in America)   Styne 1971
Give Me a Shoulder to Cry On   David, Mack 1955
Give Me a Smile   Sterling 1927
Give Me a Song to Sing   Davis 1959
Give Me a Song with a Beautiful Melody   Cahn 1949; Styne 1949
Give Me a Tam Tam Tambourine   Cahn 1949
Give Me a Trio Ev'rytime   Cahn 1960; Van Heusen 1960
Give Me a Ukulele and a Ukulele Baby and Leave the Rest to Me   Brown, Lew 1926
Give Me an Old-Fashioned Girlie   Norworth 1917
Give Me (I Want) a Share in America   Merrill 1971
Give Me Just a Little Bit of What You've Got   Donaldson 1925
Give Me Just a Moment   Hart 1932; Rodgers 1932
Give Me Liberty or Give Me Love   Rainger 1933; Robin 1933
Give Me My Mammy   DeSylva 1921; Donaldson 1921; Gershwin, George 1923
Give Me My Saddle   Raye 1942
Give Me One Day   Caesar 1922
Give Me One Hour   Friml 1927
Give Me One of Those Old Hellos   Caesar 1950
Give Me Sincerity   Woods 1935
Give Me Something I Can Dream About   David, Hal 1955
Give Me Something in a Uniform of Blue   Goetz 1913
Give Me Something to Dream About   David, Mack 1946; Hoffman 1946; Livingston, Jerry 1946
Give Me that Rose   Herbert 1944
Give Me the Corner, Give Me the Girl   Johnson, Howard 1925
Give Me the Hudson Shore   Atteridge 1913
Give Me the Land   Porter 1955
Give Me the Man (Who Does Things)   Robin 1930
Give Me the Moonlight, Give Me the Girl (And Leave the Rest to Me)   Brown, Lew 1917
Give Me the Moonshine of My Old Kentucky Home   Atteridge 1919
Give Me the Open Air   Sondheim 1968
Give Me the Right to Be Wrong   David, Hal 1958
Give Me the Simple Life   Bloom 1946; Ruby 1946
Give Me the South All the Time   Bryan 1919; Schwartz, Jean 1919
Give Me the Sultan's Harem   Silver 1919
Give Me the Sunshine   Conrad 1928; Johnson, James P. 1928
Give Me Those Good Old Circus Days   Gordon 1932; Revel 1932
Give Me Tonight   Carmichael 1933
Give Me You   David, Hal 1956
Give Me Your Affection, Honey   Bryan 1931
Give Me Your Hands   Lawrence 1955

Give Me Your Lips   Cahn 1952; Duke 1952
Give Me Your Love   Lewis 1911; Snyder 1907
Give Me Your Love Dear   Mills 1926
Give Me Your Tired, Your Poor   Berlin 1949
Give My Best to Bessie   Wrubel 1941
Give My Lonely Heart a Break, Cherie   Baer 1955
Give My Regards to Basel   Von Tilzer 1910
Give My Regards to Broadway   Bryan Date Unknown;
    Cohan 1904; Fisher Date Unknown
Give Old Ireland to the Irish   Egan 1922; Whiting 1922
Give Out when You're Blue   Washington 1940; Young,
    Victor 1940
Give Praise! Give Praise! Give Praise!   Cahn 1964; Van
    Heusen 1964
Give the Kids a Break   Gilbert 1955; Oakland 1955
Give the Kids a Chance   Cahn 1942; Styne 1942
Give the Little Girl a Great Big Hand   Evans 1950;
    Livingston, Jay 1950
Give Them Girls   Rose 1938
Give This Little Girl a Great Big Hand   Coslow 1952
Give This Little Girl a Hand (Give That Little Girl a
    Hand)   Hart 1926; Rodgers 1926
Give Thy Love   Evans 1949; Livingston, Jay 1949
Give to the March of Dimes   Caesar 1946
Give Trouble the Air   Alter 1927; Robin 1927
(Why Don't They) Give Us a Chance   Berlin 1915
Give Us a Fleet   Herbert 1908; Smith, Harry B. 1908
Give Us a Hitch   Coslow 1929
Give Us a Ragtime Tune   Smith, Harry B. 1910
Give Us Dames   Cahn 1944; Styne 1944
Give Us Peace   Robison 1946
Give Us the Charleston   DeSylva 1925; Henderson 1925
Give Us this Day   Coots 1934
Give Us This Night   Hammerstein 1936; Lawrence 1935
Give You Greeting   Smith, Harry B. 1906
Give Your Back a Pat (When You Tuck Yourself in
    Bed)   Woods 1953
Give Your Heart a Holiday   Gilbert 1932; Hanley 1932
Give Your Heart in June-Time   Atteridge 1925; Herbert 1925
Give Yourself a Pat on the Back   Davis 1944
Givers and Takers   Merrill 1972; Styne 1972
Giving   Drake 1998
Giving It This and That   Conrad 1930; Meyer 1930; Mitchell
    1930
Glad   Davis 1922; Hanley 1922
Glad Days   Webster 1965
Glad I Have a Boy   Brennan 1930; Friml 1930
Glad Rag Doll   Ager 1929; Yellen 1929
Glad Tidings   Ager 1928; Yellen 1928
Glad Tidings in the Air   Gershwin, George 1927; Gershwin,
    Ira 1927
Glad to Be Home   Berlin 1962
Glad to Be Unhappy   Hart 1936; Rodgers 1936
Glad to Have You Aboard   Blane 1952; Warren 1952
Glad to See You Again   Johnson, James P. 1939
Glad, Triumphant Hour   Herbert 1917
Gladly   Arlen 1929; Koehler 1929
Gladyse (inst.)   Waller 1929
Glamorous   Ellington 1962; Mills 1962
Glamorous Life, The   Sondheim 1973
Glamour Girl   Rose Date Unknown
Glass Mountain, The   Evans 1966; Livingston, Jay 1966
Gleason Glide, The   Davis 1953
Glen, The (inst.)   Warren Date Unknown
Glide, The   Sherman 1961

Glide DeLuxe   Atteridge 1921; Romberg 1921
Glide, Glider, Glide   Porter 1940
Gliding Through My Memoree   Hammerstein 1958; Rodgers
    1958
Glimpse of Love   Rome 1952
Globe Trot, The   Atteridge 1921; Romberg 1921
Glockenspiel Song, The   Drake 1957
Gloom   Robin 1928
Gloomy Sunday   Lewis 1936
Gloria from Peoria   Baer 1944
Gloria, Get Busy   Johnson, J. Rosamond 1950
Gloriana   Friml 1918
Glorianna   Bryan 1928; Clare 1928; Pollack 1928; Schwartz,
    Jean 1928
Glorias, The   Atteridge 1920
Gloria's Got a Glow   Merrill 1951
Gloria's Romance (inst.)   Kern 1915
Gloria's Theme   David, Mack 1960
Glories Good Mornin' (inst.)   Waller 1932
Glorifying the American Girl   Fain 1944; Freed, Ralph 1944
Glorifying the Girls   Buck 1923
Glorious Chase, The   Romberg 1927
Glorious Day   Revel 1952
Glorious Fourth, The   Sherman 1975
Glory   Blake 1932; Harburg 1930; Koehler 1936; Razaf 1930;
    Sissle 1932; Smith, Harry B. 1903
Glory Alley   David, Mack 1952; Livingston, Jerry 1952
Glory Be (A New York Spiritual)   Revel 1943; Webster 1943
Glory Day   Rainger 1942; Robin 1942
Glory! Glory! I'm a Sap   Razaf 1931
Glory of Spring   Atteridge 1929; Brennan 1929
Glory of the Corps   Harbach 1947; Kern 1947
Glory of the Morning Sunshine, The   Atteridge 1925
Glory Shout (inst.)   Johnson, James P. 1923
Glory That Is Greece, The   Harburg 1961
Glory to the Great I Am   Carroll 1975
Glory-Land Intro   Willson 1969
Glove Dance   Young, Victor 1955
Glow Worm   Mercer 1952
Glow Worm (inst.)   Young, Victor 1954
Glow-Worm Ball   Howard, Joseph E. 1937
Glub-iddy-glub-iddy-glub   Stept 1947
Glutton for Love, A   Razaf 1930
Gnome-Mobile Song (In Me Jaunting Car), The   Sherman
    1967
Go Ahead and Dance a Little More   Atteridge 1916; Hanley
    1916
Go Ahead, Break My Heart   Freed, Ralph 1962
Go and Get the Habit   Von Tilzer 1915
Go and Get Your Old Banjo   Martin 1952
Go As Far As You Like   Smith, Harry B. 1909
Go Ask Hannah   Brown, Lew 1925; Clare 1925; Friend 1925
Go Away   Spina 1966
Go Away, Girls   Romberg 1917
Go Away Girls Go Away   Atteridge 1924
Go Away My Love   Evans 1956; Livingston, Jay 1956
Go Back   Williams 1909
Go Back Over There   Fisher 1938
Go Back to Your Doll, Little Girl   Bryan 1952
Go Blow, Joe   Kahn 1912
Go Choose Your East   Kern 1937
Go Down to Boston Harbor   Lane 1945
Go Easy on the Money   Robison 1941
Go Easy with Mama   Styne 1970
Go Easy with My Dreams   Warren Date Unknown

Go Easy with Rosa   Styne 1970
Go Find Somebody to Love   Magidson 1929; Washington 1929
Go Fly a Kite   Burke 1939; Monaco 1939
Go for Broke   Drake 1955
Go Forth   Livingston, Jerry 1960
Go Get 'em, Harry   Livingston, Jerry 1960
Go Get 'Em Soldier Boys   Howard, Joseph E. 1942
Go Get Em Yankees   Davis 1970
Go Get 'Im   Donaldson 1928; Kahn 1928
Go Get that Guy   Williams 1913; Young, Joe 1913
Go! Go! Go!   Cahn 1960; Oakland 1960; Van Heusen 1960
Go, Go, Go, Go   David, Mack 1951; Livingston, Jerry 1951
Go Go Go You Bruins   Freed, Ralph 1955; Livingston, Jerry 1955
Go Happy Bride   Herbert 1909
Go Harlem   Johnson, James P. 1930; Razaf 1930
Go Home and Tell Your Mother   Fields 1930; McHugh 1930
Go Home and Tell Your Mother that I Love You   Baer 1927
(Ev'rybody Ought to Take a Day Back Home) Go Home Ev'ry Once in a While   Cohan 1928
Go Home, Little Girl   Robison 1955
Go Home, Little Girlie, Go Home!   Razaf 1944
Go Home to Your Next Pal, Go Home   Stept 1932
Go Home Train   Comden and Green 1964; Styne 1964
Go Home, Ulysses   Spina 1957
Go In and Out the Window   Bullock 1939; Pollack 1939
Go in the Best of Health   Livingston, Jerry 1973
Go Into Your Dance   Atteridge 1923; Dubin 1935; Porter 1930; Romberg 1923; Schwartz, Jean 1923; Warren 1935
Go Into Your Trance   Martin 1964
Go Little Boat   Kern 1917, 1918
Go 'Long Sundown   Akst 1934; Turk 1934
Go Man Go   Brooks 1958
Go On Your Mission   Jerome 1910; Schwartz, Jean 1910
Go Out Big   Styne 1980
Go Places and Do Things   Kalmar 1928; Ruby 1928
Go Right Along Mr. Wilson (And We'll All Stand By You)   Brown, A. Seymour 1915
Go South Young Man   Coots 1937; Davis 1937; Heyman 1934; Romberg 1934
Go to Bed   Dubin 1929
Go to It, Old Girl!   Adams 1972; Strouse 1972
Go to Sleep   Lane 1965; Lerner, Alan Jay 1965
Go to Sleep, Go to Sleep, Go to Sleep   Cahn 1950
Go to Sleep Slumber Deep   Herbert 1903
Go 'Way Blues Ya Bother Me   Adamson 1940
Go 'Way Mister Moon   Bacharach 1959
Go West   Kahn 1940
Go West Young Girl   Atteridge 1918
Go West Young Lady   Cahn 1941
Go West, Young Man   Burke 1936; Johnston 1936; Kalmar 1947; Ruby 1947
Go While the Goin' Is Good   Herbert 1906
Go Yankee Go   Davis 1967
Gobble-De-Gook   Hoffman 1958; Silver 1958
Gobel Dreaming   Brooks 1957
Goblin Market   Mills 1935
God Be with You Tonight My Love   Coots 1955
God Bless!   Adams 1970; Strouse 1970
God Bless America   Berlin 1918
God Bless Every State in the U.S.A.   Ruby 1943
God Bless My Good Old Mother   Edwards 1900
God Bless Rockefeller   Weill 1977
God Bless the Buskers   Sherman 1995

God Bless the Glory of Rum   Styne 1985
God Bless the One I Love   Willson 1954
God Bless the Women   Porter 1940
God Bless You All the Day   Burke 1981
God Gave Me Eyes   Hart 1931; Rodgers 1931
God Gave You to Me   Berlin 1914
God Give Me Strength   Bacharach 1996
God Gives Us One Mother That's All   Brown, Lew Date Unknown; Henderson Date Unknown
God Has His Arms Around Me   Adamson 1956, 1957; Young, Victor 1956, 1957
God Has His Hands on My Shoulders   Coots 1950
God Has Those Angels   Ellington 1968
God Is Alive   Cahn 1969; Van Heusen 1969
God Is Everywhere   Coots 1953
God Is Good to Me   Hoffman 1958
God Is Good to the Irish   Cohan 1927
God Is in the Plan   Robison 1961
God Is Love   Strouse 1967
God Is My Co-Pilot   Russell 1943
God Is My Friend   Coots 1950
God Is Never too Busy   Spina 1976
God Lives   Spina 1966
God Only Knows How I Miss You   Cobb 1917; Edwards 1917
God Put the Green in the Rainbow to Remind Us of Ireland   Johnson, Howard 1927
God Shall Abade Us (inst.)   Herbert 1944
God, Spare Our Boys Over There   Jerome 1918
God Spare the Emerald Isle   Herbert 1923; Jerome 1923
God, That's Good   Sondheim 1979
Goddess of Liberty, The   Howard, Joseph E. 1909
Goddess of Mine   Herbert 1913
Goddess of Rain   Razaf 1929; Waller 1929
God-Given Goodness   Robison 1963
God's Country   Arlen 1937; Harburg 1937
God's Garden   Merrill 1971; Styne 1971
God's Green World   Lerner, Alan Jay 1945; Loewe 1945
God's Little Creatures   Mancini 1993
God's Morning   Brennan 1938
God-Why-Don't-You-Love-Me Blues, The   Sondheim 1971
Goil on the Flying Trapeze, The   Johnson, Howard 1935
Goin' Back to School   Martin 1952
Goin' Co'tin'   DePaul 1954; Mercer 1954
Goin' Crazy with the Blues   Razaf 1927
Goin' Down to the River Jordan   Fisher 1936
Goin' Home   Coleman 1975; Comden and Green 1975; Fields 1939; Schwartz, Arthur 1939
Goin' Home Train   Rome 1946
Goin' My Way   Woods 1943
Goin' on a Hayride   Blane 1952
Goin' on an Errand for Uncle Sam   Razaf 1944
Goin' Steady   Fields 1951; Schwartz, Arthur 1951
Goin' to Broadway (Disco)   Adams 1978; Strouse 1978
Goin' to Heaven on a Mule   Dubin 1934; Warren 1934
Goin' to the County Fair   Gordon 1943; Warren 1943
Goin' to the Door   Merrill 1959
Goin' to the Zoo   Livingston, Jerry 1962
Goin' to Town   Conrad 1934; Mitchell 1934
Goin' to Town Figurin' Out the Long Way Home   Meyer 1933
Goin' to Town with Me   Adamson 1931; Lane 1931
Goin' Wild   Ahlert 1930; Turk 1930
Goin' with the Birds   Fields 1952; Schwartz, Arthur 1952
Going Away Party   Drake 1954

Going Back to Old Cheyenne   Koehler 1947
Going Back to the One I Love   Friend 1932
Going, Going, Gone!   Eliscu 1931; Lerner, Alan Jay 1971
Going Great   Cahn 1968
Going Hollywood   Brown, Nacio Herb 1933; Freed, Arthur 1933
Going Home on New Year's Morning   Gershwin, George 1925; Hammerstein 1925; Harbach 1925
Going Home to Lulu   Howard, Joseph E. 1912
Going My Way   Burke 1944; Van Heusen 1944
Going Places, Seeing Faces (Looking for Someone to Love)   Woods 1928
Going Rowing   Youmans 1924
Going to the Devil with Me   Robin 1954; Romberg 1954
Going to the Opera   Herbert 1906
Going Up   Gorney 1930; Harbach 1917; Harburg 1930
Going Up (In My Aeroplane)   Williams 1910
Goitie   Rainger 1933
Gold   Freed, Ralph 1957; Weill 1949
Gold and Silver   Johnson, Howard 1941
Gold Bug March   Herbert 1896
Gold Can Buy Anything (But Love)   Sherman 1951
Gold Digger, The   Hanley 1923
Gold Diggers Are Back Again, The   Adamson 1945; McHugh 1945
Gold Digger's Blues   Coslow 1924
Gold Dollar Moon   Goetz 1952
Gold Dusters Song   Porter 1940
Gold Fever   Lerner, Alan Jay 1969
Gold Fish   Bryan 1921; Pollack 1921; Schwartz, Jean 1921
Gold, Gold, Who's Got the Gold (inst.)   Bacharach 1966
Gold Rush (Gold Discovery Montage), The   Harburg 1946
Gold Rush Towns   Willson 1953
Gold, Silver and Green   Atteridge 1924; Romberg 1924; Schwartz, Jean 1924
Golden Age, The   Herbert 1914; Smith, Robert B. 1914
Golden Anniversary   Lawrence 1957
Golden Arrow   Williams 1909
Golden Bands of Nassau   Stept 1954
Golden Bells   Adamson 1954; Warren 1954
Golden Boy   Adams 1964; Strouse 1964
Golden Broom and the Green Apple, The   Ellington 1965
Golden Butterfly, The   Smith, Harry B. 1908
Golden Calf, The   Livingston, Jerry 1962
Golden Day Dream   Oakland 1970
Golden Days   Romberg 1924, 1954; Webster 1954
Golden, Delicious Fish   Merrill 1961
Golden Dreams   Smith, Harry B. 1926
Golden Eagle March (inst.), The   Coots 1945
Golden Earrings   Evans 1947; Livingston, Jay 1947; Young, Victor 1947
Golden Gate   Leslie 1927; Rose 1928
Golden Gates of Happiness   Coots 1926
Golden Girl, The   Howard, Joseph E. 1909
Golden Guitars (inst.)   Livingston, Jerry 1957
Golden Hair   Hoffman 1952
Golden Harvest Days   Lewis 1934
Golden Long Ago, The   Herbert 1911
Golden Memories   Akst 1925; Davis 1925
Golden Moment   Lawrence 1951
Golden Moments   Kalmar 1920; Leslie 1920
Golden Moments of Perfume   Rose 1927
Golden Net, The   Smith, Harry B. 1905
Golden Oldies   Drake 1996
Golden Pheasant, The   Romberg 1917

Golden Ram, The   Rodgers 1970
Golden Sands of Waikiki   Yellen 1921
Golden Song, A   Oakland 1955; Webster 1955
Golden Stairs of Love, The   Atteridge 1913; Schwartz, Jean 1913
Golden Trail   Caesar 1923
Golden Voyage   Warren 1967
Golden Wedding Day   DePaul 1942; Raye 1942
Golden Wedding Song   Burke 1939; Monaco 1939
Golden Wedding Waltz, The   Oakland 1935
Golden West, The   Atteridge 1917; Howard, Joseph E. 1908; Motzan 1917; Romberg 1917
Golden West and You, The   Coslow 1931
Golden Years, The   Evans 1953; Livingston, Jay 1953
Goldfarb, That's I'm!   Gershwin, George 1930; Gershwin, Ira 1930
Goldfish Glide   Hanley 1927
Goldfish Song   Fain 1934; Kahal 1934
Goldie Goes with the Mine   Loesser 1947
Goldwater Fairyland   Rome 1964
Golf Song   Loesser 1937
Golfer's Glide, The   Webster 1957
Golfers (Intermezzo), The   Loesser 1937
Golfing Blues   Atteridge 1923; Schwartz, Jean 1923
Golly   Hoffman 1957
Gonda Waltzes   Smith, Harry B. 1910
Gondola and the Girl, The   Goetz 1923
Gondolier   Buck 1921; Gershwin, Ira 1920; Williams 1904; Youmans 1920
Gondolier Song   Friml 1934
Gondolier's Serenade, The   David, Mack 1954
Gone   Davis 1926; Kahn 1913, 1936; Razaf 1929; Waller 1929
Gone Again Gal   Kahn 1926
Gone Are the Days   Cahn 1947; Goetz 1952; Hart 1920; Rodgers 1920; Styne 1947
Gone Are the Love Days   Brennan 1921
Gone But Not Forgotten   Bergman 1962
Gone for the Day   Russell 1957
Gone, Gone, Gone!   Gershwin, George 1935
Gone Is the Smile   Caesar 1920
Gone to Chicago   Willson 1949
Gone with the Beat   Gorney 1964
Gone with the Dawn   Rose 1936
Gone with the Wind   Ahlert 1937; Magidson 1937; Rome 1973; Wrubel 1937; Young, Joe 1937
Gone-Again Corrigan   Mills 1938; Myrow 1938
Gong Song, The   Bullock 1936, 1937
Gonna Be a Judgement Day   Wrubel 1942
Gonna Build a Big Fence Around Texas   Friend 1945
Gonna Fall in Love with You   Blane 1946
Gonna Go Along with Lincoln   Harbach 1947; Kern 1947
Gonna Hand in My Guitar   Sigman 1957
Gonna Have Lassies in the Mornin'   Johnson, Howard 1939
Gonna Hitch My Wagon to a Star   Lewis 1936
Gonna Join the Navy   Webster 1983
Gonzaga Men   Burke 1951; Van Heusen 1951
Gonzales Gonzargo Rodrigo   Brooks 1960
Goo   Hoffman 1939
Goo Goo   Gordon 1934; Revel 1934
Goo Goo Goo   Conrad 1906
Goo Googily Goo   Lewis 1924; Young, Joe 1924
Good Advice   Smith, Harry B. 1916; Young, Victor 1934
Good and Lucky   Schwartz, Arthur 1937
Good and Welfare Polka   Russell 1950

Good at Making Friends   Cahn 1976; Lane 1976
Good Bad Woman!   Hart Date Unknown; Rodgers Date Unknown
Good Boy   Kalmar 1928; Ruby 1928
Good Boy Wedding March   Kalmar 1928; Ruby 1928
Good Bye   Romberg 1922
Good Bye Everybody   Smith, Harry B. 1913
Good Bye, Little Rose-Bud   Hammerstein 1923; Harbach 1923
Good Bye Lizzie   Baer 1927; Gilbert 1927
Good Bye Maria   Gilbert 1914
Good Bye, Mr. Ragtime   Cohan 1908
Good Bye My Lady Love   Howard, Joseph E. 1904
Good Clean Sport   Dietz 1930; Schwartz, Arthur 1930
Good Companions   Mercer 1974
Good Corn Liquor and Bad Champagne   Lawrence 1948
Good Day   Coleman 1999
Good Deed for Today   Duke 1946
Good Evenin'   Hoffman 1930
Good Evenin', Mister Nightingale   Pollack 1933
Good Evening — Good Morning   Oakland 1973
Good Evening Caroline   Norworth 1908
Good Evening, Friends   Caesar 1931
Good Evening, Madamoiselle   Adamson 1953; Duke 1953
Good Evening Once Again   Oakland 1970
Good Evening, Princess   Porter 1938
Good Fairy, The   David, Mack 1958; Livingston, Jerry 1958
Good Fellow Blues, The   Blake 1921; Sissle 1921
Good Fellow Gal   Brennan 1921
Good Fellow Mine   Hart 1926; Rodgers 1926
Good Fellows Club, The   Atteridge 1915; Romberg 1915
Good for Him — Good for Me   Spina 1957
Good for Nothin'   Johnson, James P. 1930; Razaf 1930
Good for Nothin' (But Love)   De Lange 1938; Van Heusen 1938
Good for Nothin' Joe   Bloom 1935; Koehler 1935
Good for Nothing but Love   Pollack 1946
Good for You, Bad for Me   Brown, Lew 1930; DeSylva 1930; Henderson 1930
Good Friends   Adams 1970; Strouse 1970
Good Friends Are Few (And Far Between)   Robison 1953
Good Friends Surround Me   Caesar 1933; Romberg 1933
Good Girl   Hammerstein 1944; Kern 1944
Good Good Thing, A   Rome 1959
Good Green Acres of Home, The   Fain 1935; Kahal 1935
Good Guy Always Wins, The   Livingston, Jerry 1961
Good Guys, The   Evans 1968; Livingston, Jay 1968
Good Impression, A   Coleman 1966, 1972; Fields 1966, 1972
Good in Me, The   Robison 1949
Good Intentions   Coleman 1957; Evans 1954; Friend 1930; Leigh 1957; Livingston, Jay 1954; Monaco 1930
Good King Phillip   Harburg 1971
Good Little, Bad Little Lady   Brooks 1945
Good Little Bad Little You   Stept 1928
Good Little Girls   Cahn 1952; Duke 1952
Good Little Things That We Do, The   Carroll 1918
Good Little Tune   Caesar 1918; Gershwin, George 1918
Good Lookin'   David, Hal 1991; Strouse 1991
Good Lord Never Made a Bad Day, The   Caesar 1957; Robison 1957
Good Luck, Best Wishes   Davis 1936; Hanley 1936
Good Luck, Good Health, Happiness   Magidson 1952
Good Luck Mary   Bryan 1909; Leslie 1909
Good Luck, Mr. Flyin' Man   Hammerstein 1943
Good Luck Sweetheart   Coots 1933

Good Man Bit the Dust (inst.)   Revel 1960
Good Mornin'   Coslow 1937
Good Morning   Brown, Nacio Herb 1939; Caesar 1927; Clare 1934; Egan 1928; Freed, Arthur 1939; Goetz 1912; Whiting 1934
Good Morning All   Friml 1919; Harbach 1919
Good Morning Dearie   Kern 1921
Good Morning Glory   Gordon 1933; Revel 1933
Good Morning, God   David, Mack 1970
Good Morning, Heartache   Drake 1946
Good Morning (Irish Theme) (inst.)   Young, Victor 1951
Good Morning Judge   Goetz 1911
Good Morning, Miss Standing   Porter 1935
Good Morning, Morning Glory   Adamson 1950; David, Hal 1951; McHugh 1950
Good Morning Mr. Sunshine   Mills 1966
Good Morning Mrs. Benson   Comden and Green 1964; Styne 1964
Good 'n' Plenty   Fain 1930; Kahal 1930
Good Neighbor Doctor, The   Robison 1951
Good Neighbor Song, The   Livingston, Jerry 1963
Good News   Brown, Lew 1927; DeSylva 1927; Henderson 1927
Good News, Bad News   Caesar 1943
Good News for You, Brother   Robison 1949
Good Night   Buck 1914, 1923; Conrad 1924
Good Night and God Bless You   Drake 1960
Good Night Angel   Magidson 1938; Wrubel 1938
Good Night, Angeline   Blake 1916, 1919; Sissle 1919
Good Night, Good Morning   Burke 1950; Van Heusen 1950
Good Night, Good Neighbor   Loesser 1943; Schwartz, Arthur 1943
Good Night, Good Night   Gilbert 1906
Good Night, Joe   Bryan 1955
Good Night Ladies   Johnson, Howard 1939
Good Night, Lovely Little Lady   Gordon 1934; Revel 1934
Good Night, My Beautiful   Ager 1939; Fain 1939; Yellen 1939
Good Night, My Dear   Gershwin, George 1923
Good Night My Lady Love   Young, Joe 1932
Good Night My Lucky Day   Koehler 1937; Mitchell 1937; Stept 1937
Good Night Now (My Dove)   Robison 1951
Good Night People   Howard, Joseph E. 1955
Good Night, Sleep Tight   Kahn 1924
Good Night Sweetheart   Johnson, Howard 1939
Good Night, Sweetheart, Good Night   Harbach 1908
Good Ol' Otis Lee   Sherman 1984
Good Old Atwater   Kern 1917
Good Old Burlesque Show, A   McHugh 1979
Good Old California   Cohan 1904
Good Old Circus Band   Smith, Harry B. 1912
Good Old Days   Conrad 1934; Drake 1953; Mitchell 1934
Good Old Days Back Home, The   Monaco 1916
Good Old Days Gone By, The   Von Tilzer 1909
Good Old Days in Alabam   Gilbert 1915
Good Old Days of Burlesque, The   Adamson 1956; McHugh 1956
Good Old Days of Yore   Harbach 1910
Good Old Fashioned Cocktail (With at Good Old Fashioned Girl), A   Dubin 1935; Warren 1935
Good Old Fashioned Get Together   Styne 1964
Good Old German Beer   Von Tilzer 1910
Good Old Harry   Hart 1926; Rodgers 1926
Good Old Iron Side   Alter 1929; Johnson, Howard 1929

Good Old Levee Days   Atteridge 1914; Carroll 1914

Good Old Noah   Sterling 1935

Good Old Songs, The   Cahn 1959; Van Heusen 1959

Good Old Songs of the Blue and Gray, The   Sterling 1906; Von Tilzer 1906

Good Pals   Romberg 1927; Smith, Harry B. 1927

Good People All   Dietz 1932; Schwartz, Arthur 1932

Good Place to Be, A   David, Mack 1970

Good Provider   Hart Date Unknown; Rodgers Date Unknown

Good Sauce From the Gravy Bowl   Mills 1935

Good Ship Mary Ann, The   Kahn 1914

Good Spirits   Robin 1930, 1931; Whiting 1930, 1931

Good Thing Going   Sondheim 1981

Good Things and Bad Things   Atteridge 1924; Romberg 1924

Good Things Are Happening   Bullock 1966

Good Things Come to Those Who Wait   Razaf 1929

Good Time Charlie   Burke 1945; Fields 1954; Schwartz, Arthur 1954; Van Heusen 1945

Good Time Girl (V.D. Polka), The   Sherman 1974

Good Time Polka   Friend 1945

Good Times   Coleman 1977; David, Hal 1991; Strouse 1985, 1991

Good Times Are Comin'   David, Hal 1970

Good Times Are Here, When My Baby Is Near   Ahlert 1931; Turk 1931

Good Time's Comin'   Kahn 1932

Good Times with Hoover, Better Times with Al   Berlin 1928

Gooda-Bye John   Williams 1906

Good-Bye   Atteridge 1919; Bergman 1961; Herbert 1908; Kalmar 1930; Lawrence 1951; Mercer 1974; Romberg 1919; Ruby 1930; Schwartz, Jean 1919; Sissle 1915

Goodbye Again   Adamson 1933; Coots 1933; Eliscu 1937; Lewis 1933

Good-Bye, Au Revoir, Auf Wiedersehen   Caesar 1936

Good-Bye Bargravia   Cohan 1919

Good-Bye Barney Boy   Brennan 1918

Goodbye Beckie Cohn   Fisher 1910

Good-Bye Becky Cohen   Berlin 1910

Goodbye Blues   Fields 1934; Johnston 1932; McHugh 1934

Goodbye Boogie   Brooks 1958

Goodbye Boys   Jerome 1913; Porter 1911; Sterling 1913; Von Tilzer 1913

Goodbye, Carlotta   Jerome 1908; Schwartz, Jean 1908

Goodbye Carrabian Nights   Egan 1918; Whiting 1918

Goodbye, Charlie   Ellington 1966

Goodbye Chickasaw County   Merrill 1971; Styne 1971

Goodbye Darlin'   Loesser 1956

Goodbye Darling, Hello Friend (C'est Fini)   Rome 1951

Goodbye, Dear Friend   Lawrence 1951

Goodbye, Dear Old Bachelor Days   Buck 1916

Goodbye Dinah   Edwards 1908

Goodbye Dobbin'   Johnson, Howard 1924

Goodbye Dolly Grey   Cobb 1906

Goodbye Eliza Jane   Sterling 1903; Von Tilzer 1903

Goodbye, Failure, Goodbye (Gawk, Tousle and Shucks)   Leigh 1967

Good-Bye Flo   Cohan 1904

Goodbye for Just a While   Hoffman 1951

Goodbye for Now   Sondheim 1981

Goodbye Forever   Coslow 1935; Friml 1923

Good-Bye, France   Berlin 1918

Goodbye G.I. Al   Akst 1951

Goodbye Girlie and Remember Me   Berlin 1909; Meyer 1909; Snyder 1909

Goodbye, Good Luck, Get Lost   Baer 1947

Goodbye, Good Luck, God Bless You Is All that I Can Say   Brennan 1916

Good-Bye, Good-Bye, London Town   Atteridge 1914

Goodbye Is a Lonesome Sound   Bergman 1962

Goodbye John   Herbert 1906

Goodbye Jonah   Schwartz, Arthur 1937

Goodbye Lenny   Hart 1926; Rodgers 1926

Goodbye Little Captain of My Heart (Adieu, Mein Kleiner Gardeoffizier)   Young, Joe 1931

Good-Bye, Little Dream, Good-Bye   Porter 1936

Goodbye Little Girl   Oakland 1952; Webster 1952

Good-Bye Little Girl, Good-Bye   Cobb 1901; Edwards 1901

Goodbye Little Rosebud   Youmans 1923

Goodbye Lolipops, Hello Lipstick   Hoffman 1956

Good-Bye Love   Conrad 1933; Mitchell 1933; Rome 1952

Goodbye, Maggie Doyle   Jerome 1905; Schwartz, Jean 1905

Good-Bye Main Street   Atteridge 1922; Schwartz, Jean 1922

Goodbye Mama I'm Off to Yokahama   Coots 1941

Goodbye Mary   McHugh 1917

Goodbye, Miss Liberty   Jerome 1909; Schwartz, Jean 1909

Goodbye Mother Machree   Brennan 1918

Goodbye, Mr. Ragtime   Jerome 1908; Schwartz, Jean 1908

Goodbye My Coney Island Baby   Coots 1955

Goodbye, My Dream, Goodbye (inst.)   Young, Victor 1938

Good-bye, My Dreams, Good-bye   Webster 1938

Goodbye My Emerald Land   Olcott 1911, 1920

Goodbye My Friend   Merrill 1956

Goodbye My Heart   Akst 1938; Clare 1938

Good-Bye, My Hello Baby   Bryan 1952

Goodbye My Honey   Rome 1973

Good-Bye My Honey, I'm Gone   Blake 1918; Sissle 1918

Good-Bye, My Little Lady   Hanley 1917

Goodbye, My Love   Cahn 1957; Coots 1954; Hammerstein 1930; Herbert 1904; Romberg 1930; Young, Victor 1952

Good-Bye My True Love   Porter 1913

Good-Bye, Old Gal (I'm Going Away on the 2:10 Train)   Brown, Lew 1911

Goodbye Poor Old Manhattan   Goetz 1913

Goodbye Pretty Butterfly   Yellen 1921

Good-Bye Prohibition, Good-Bye Blue Nose   Johnson, J. Rosamond 1933

Goodbye Red Man Goodbye   Kalmar 1916; Leslie 1916; Snyder 1916

Goodbye Shanghai   Bryan 1919; Fisher Date Unknown; Johnson, Howard 1921; Schwartz, Jean 1919

Goodbye, Slim   Donaldson 1918

Goodbye, So Soon   Mancini 1986

Goodbye Still Means Goodbye   Russell Date Unknown

Goodbye Sunshine Hello Moon   Buck 1919

Goodbye, Sweet Old Manhattan Isle   Jerome 1905; Schwartz, Jean 1905

Goodbye Sweetheart   Goetz 1910

Goodbye Sweetheart Goodbye   Johnson, Howard 1939

Good-Bye Teddy Roosevelt, You Were a Real American   Bryan 1919; Fisher 1919

Goodbye, That Means You   Sterling 1917

Good-Bye to All That   Gershwin, Ira 1946; Schwartz, Arthur 1946

Good-Bye to Dear Old Alaska   Caesar 1922

Goodbye to Love that Overtakes Us   Dietz 1952

Goodbye to Rome (Arrivederci Roma)   Sigman 1955

Good-Bye to the Old Love, Hello to the New   Gershwin, George 1928; Gershwin, Ira 1928
Goodbye Today! Hello Tonight   Martin 1977
Goodbye Virginia   Clarke 1915; Schwartz, Jean 1915
Goodbye Wild Women Goodbye   Ager 1919; Johnson, Howard 1919; Meyer 1919; Yellen Date Unknown
Goodbye, World   Fain 1944; Freed, Ralph 1944
Goodfellow Days   Egan 1925; Kahn 1925
Good-Lookin', It's Good Lookin' at You   Caesar 1944
Goodness Gracious   Kalmar 1929; Ruby 1929
Goodness Gracious Agnes   Donaldson 1926; Kahn 1926
Goodnight   Friml 1914; Harbach 1914
Goodnight — Molly O'Day   Bryan 1938
Goodnight Again   Magidson 1940
Good-Night Boat   Kern 1920
Goodnight Captain Curlyhead   Ahlert 1942; Lewis 1942
Goodnight, Girl of Mine, Goodnight   Cobb 1912; Edwards 1912
Goodnight Good Friends (Wherever You Are)   Coots 1952
Goodnight, Goodnight (Sweet Dreams to You)   Spina 1946
Goodnight Is Not Goodbye   Bergman 1978
Goodnight Kiss   Gorney 1934
Good-Night Kisses   Kalmar 1937; Ruby 1937
Goodnight, Ladies   Williams 1911
Goodnight Little Girl, Goodnight   Dubin 1914
Goodnight Moon   Donaldson 1931
Goodnight, Mother   Bryan 1940; David, Mack 1940
Goodnight, Mrs. Calabash   Fain 1972; Harburg 1972
Goodnight, My Darling   Willson 1955
Goodnight, My Love   Gordon 1936; Revel 1936
Goodnight, My Own True Love   Jerome 1904; Schwartz, Jean 1904
Goodnight My Someone   Willson 1957
Goodnight My Sweet   David, Mack 1945
Good-Night Owl   Bryan 1927
Goodnight Serenade   Brown, Nacio Herb 1931; Eliscu 1931
Good-Night Waltz   Conrad 1923
Goodnight Wherever You Are   Hoffman 1944
Good-Will Movement, The   Porter 1944
Goody Goody Girl   Young, Joe 1933
Goody Goody Goody Goody Goody Goody   Berlin 1912
Goody, Goody Gum Drops   Livingston, Jerry 1963
Goody-Goody   Mercer 1936
Goof Plays on the Roof, A   Caesar 1937
Goofus   Kahn 1930
Goofy Newsreel   Coslow 1952
Googilly Goo   Davis 1928
Goo-Goo Da Da (Goo Goo G'Da)   Loesser 1934
Goo-Goo Doll Song   David, Hal 1955
Goo-Goo-Good Night Dear   Friend 1924
Goombay Drum   Bergman 1957
Goona Goo, The   Ahlert 1936; Young, Joe 1936
Goona Goona   Parish 1933
Goose Girl, The   Smith, Harry B. 1906
Goose Hangs High, The   Akst 1930; Clarke 1930; Friend 1936
Goose Never Be a Peacock   Arlen 1959; Mercer 1959
Goose Pimples   Conrad 1931
Gootman Is a Hootman Now   Lewis 1916; Young, Joe 1916
Gorgeous   Akst 1927; Davis 1927
Gorgeous Alexander   Hammerstein 1928; Romberg 1928
Gorgeous to Gaze At   Schwartz, Jean 1942
Gosh Darn   Coots 1932; Young, Joe 1932
Gospel   Duke 1940
Gospel of No Name City, The   Lerner, Alan Jay 1969

Gospel Time   Eliscu 1966
Gossip   Blane 1964; Fain 1971; Lerner, Alan Jay 1958; Loewe 1958; Martin 1964; Sondheim 1984; Webster 1971; Young, Victor 1945
Gossip (inst.)   Burke 1957
Gossip Theme (Have You Heard About Phileas Fogg?)   Adamson 1959; Young, Victor 1959
Gossip Trio   Weill 1947
Gossips   Friml 1928; Loesser 1948
Gossips Song   Herbert 1906
Got a Bad Case of Loving You   Lewis 1974; Young, Joe 1974
Got a Bran' New Suit   Dietz 1935; Schwartz, Arthur 1935
Got a Cold in the Nose for Christmas   Merrill 1954
Got a Feelin'   David, Mack 1953; Livingston, Jerry 1953
Got a Gal in Californ-i-a   Rainger 1935; Robin 1935
Got a Hula Hula Honey   Baer 1950
Got a Little Brush (inst.)   Kern 1956
Got a Locket in My Pocket   David, Hal 1959
Got a Man on My Mind (Worryin' Away)   Dietz 1930; Rainger 1930; Robin 1930
Got a Million Dollars Worth of Dreams   Brooks 1945
Got a New Boy Friend   Schwartz, Jean 1942
Got a New Kind-a Rhythm   Clare 1935; Stept 1935
Got a New Lease on Life   Fields 1935
Got a Pair of New Shoes   Brown, Nacio Herb 1937; Freed, Arthur 1937
Got a Rainbow   Gershwin, George 1928; Gershwin, Ira 1928
Got a Tickle in My Toes   Woods 1935
Got a Way of Doin' Things   Rainger 1935; Robin 1935; Whiting 1935
Got an Invitation   Evans 1944; Livingston, Jay 1944
Got 'em Guessing How I Do It (And Still Keep My Good Name)   Brown, A. Seymour 1910
Got Everything (Don't Want Anything but You)   McHugh 1927; Razaf 1927
Got Her Off My Hands but Can't Get Her Off My Mind   Lewis 1951; Young, Joe 1951
Got Love   Russell 1977
Got Me Doin' Things   Gordon 1935
Got My Eye on You   Hammerstein 1936; Kern 1936
Got My Mind on Music   Gordon 1938; Revel 1938
Got My Workin' Papers   Drake 1958
Got Myself Another Jockey Now   Razaf 1928; Waller 1928
Got No Room for Mr. Gloom   Robin 1955; Styne 1955
Got No Time   Bloom 1939; Cahn 1939; Kahn 1925; Koehler 1939; Whiting 1925
Got that Good Time Feelin'   Lane 1945
Got the Feeling   Sherman 1959
Got the Jitters   Rose 1934; Webster 1933
Got the Moon in My Pocket   Burke 1942; Van Heusen 1942
Got the South in My Soul   Washington 1932; Young, Victor 1932
Got to Be Bad to Be Good   Comden and Green 1944
Got to Dance My Way to Heaven   Coslow 1936
Got to Go to Town   Dixon 1931; Warren 1931; Young, Joe 1931
Got to Have a Man of My Own   Razaf 1942
Got to Keep 'em Struttin'   Revel 1929
Got to Wear You Off My Weary Mind   Arlen 1944; Mercer 1944
Got What It Takes   Stept 1950
Got Wings on My Broncho in the Sky   Baer 1942; Meyer 1942
Got You where I Want You Right in My Arms   Yellen 1932
Gott Iss Gut   Cahn 1970; Styne 1970

Gotta Be, Gonna Be Mine   Razaf 1932; Waller 1932
Gotta Dance   Martin 1948
Gotta Feelin' for You   Alter 1929, 1930
Gotta Get a Girl   Bacharach 1961; David, Hal 1961
Gotta Get Home (The Train Song)   Hanley 1939
Gotta Get Joy   Dubin 1944; Lane 1944
Gotta Get Me Somebody to Love   Wrubel 1946
Gotta Get Myself a Brand New Gal   Turk Date Unknown
Gotta Get Some Shut-Eye   Donaldson 1939; Mercer 1939
Gotta Getta Girl   Kahn 1924
Gotta Go Now   Dixon 1931; Warren 1931; Young, Joe 1931
Gotta Have a Man, Sometime   Adamson 1956; McHugh 1956
Gotta Have Me Go with You   Arlen 1954; Gershwin, Ira 1954
Gotta Keep 'Em Humming   Sondheim 1984
Gotta Lotta Love   Hoffman 1960
Gotta Lotta Love for You   Baer 1932; Lewis 1932
Gotta Lotta Tunes in My Guitar   Hoffman 1958
Gotta See a Girl about Love   Hoffman 1945
Gotta See a Man About a Dog   Fisher 1936
Gotta See a Man About His Daughter   Hanley 1934
Gotta Settle This Tonight or Never   Robin 1931
Gotta Sing, Gotta Dance   Davis 1955
Gout (The Spasm) (inst.), The   Lane 1965
(If I Were the) Governor of Guam   Herbert 1904
Governor of the State, The   Cohan 1901
Governor's Ball Solo   Hammerstein 1937; Kern 1937
Governor's Entrance   Herbert 1910
Governor's Lady   Caesar 1924
Gown for Each Hour of the Day, A   Smith, Harry B. 1906
Gown Is Mightier than the Sword, The   Hart 1920; Rodgers 1920
Gowns Soft and Clingy   Friml 1919; Harbach 1919
Gozinto   Buck 1917
Gra Ma Chree   Olcott 1901
Grab a Girl   Dietz 1924; Kern 1924
Grab Bag, The   Gershwin, George 1922; Goetz 1922
Grab Him!   Razaf 1953
Grab Them While You Can   Rome 1962
Grace   Burke 1958; Van Heusen 1958
Grace Kelly Wedding Waltz, The   Washington 1956
Graceful and Elegant (Inst.)   Gershwin, George 1937
Gracious a Dios   David, Mack 1966
Grade "A" Treatment   Merrill 1966
Graduation Waltz, The   Livingston, Jerry 1935
Graffitti   Spina 1977
Graft   Herbert 1911; Smith, Harry B. 1905; Smith, Robert B. 1906
Grand   Ahlert 1932; Turk 1932
Grand Cafe, The   Comden and Green 1982
Grand Canal   Atteridge 1914; Carroll 1914
Grand Central Episode   Brown, Nacio Herb 1933; Freed, Arthur 1933
Grand Central Station   Coleman 1978; Comden and Green 1978
Grand Fantasy   Herbert 1911
Grand Imperial Cirque de Paris   Merrill 1961
Grand Manner, The   Duke 1968
Grand Old Acquaintance (Of Mine)   Robison 1953
Grand Old Ivy   Loesser 1961
Grand Old Life   Schwartz, Jean 1914
Grand Old Party, The   Lerner, Alan Jay 1976
Grand Opera Sequence   Robin 1932
Grand Street Boys   Blake 1958; Caesar 1960; Sissle 1958

Grand Street Presentation, A   Merrill 1978
Grand Street Tivoli Presentation, A   Merrill 1978
Grand Vacation with Pay, A   Gilbert 1941; McHugh 1941
Grandfather Clock   Carmichael 1957
Grandfather's Clock   David, Mack 1934; Johnson, Howard 1939; Silver 1934
Grandma   Bryan 1908; Snyder 1908
Grandma Dear Grandma   Romberg 1918
Grandma Said   Magidson 1939; Wrubel 1939
Grandma Teeter Totter   Carmichael 1949
Grandma's Day   Friml 1923
Grandma's Flowers   Robison 1946
Grandma's Song   Hammerstein 1937; Kern 1937
Grandmother's Clock (inst.)   Romberg 1940
Grandpa's Old But Very Happy   Brooks 1959
Grandpa's Very Old   Brooks 1958
Grandpeople   Davis 1974
Granny   Gilbert 1919; Merrill 1965; Razaf 1953; Styne 1965
Granny, (You're) My Mammy's Mammy   Akst 1921; Lewis 1921; Young, Joe 1921
Granny's Gulch   Merrill 1965; Styne 1965
Granny's Rocking Chair   Johnston 1948
Grant Avenue   Hammerstein 1958; Rodgers 1958
Grape Dance, The   Atteridge 1914; Romberg 1914
Grape Juice Bill   Sterling 1919
Grapefruit Acres   Dubin 1933; Warren 1933
Grapes of Roth (inst.)   Bacharach 1968
Grapevine   Silver 1956
Grass Grows Green (In No Man's Land), The   Sherman 1974
Grass Grows Greener Way Down Home, The   Yellen 1928
Grass Is Always Greener in the Other Fellow's Yard, The   Egan 1924; Whiting 1924
Grass Is Gettin' Greener All the Time, The   Burke 1933; Spina 1933
Grass Widows   Coslow 1924
Grasshopper (inst.)   Stept 1957
Gratification   Sherman 1973
Grauman's Chinese Sequence   Loesser 1947
Gravy Train   Carroll 1950
Grazie Per Niente   Bergman 1964; Fain 1964
Grazioso in D Major (inst.)   Kern 1938
Great Adventure   Revel 1946
Great American Broadcast, The   Gordon 1941; Warren 1941
Great American Dream   Carmichael 1964; Parish 1964
Great American Plan, The   Stept 1960
Great Big Baby, A   Blake 1940; Razaf 1940
Great Big Bear   Hammerstein 1925; Harbach 1925
Great Big Blue Eyed Baby   Brown, A. Seymour 1909
Great Big Bunch of You, A   Dixon 1932; Warren 1932
Great Big Sky, The   Weill 1947
Great Camp Meetin' Day   Sissle 1928
Great Camp Meeting Day   Sissle 1917
Great Chord Sequence, Man   Russell 1968, 1977
Great Day   Duke 1940; Eliscu 1929; Rose 1929; Youmans 1929
Great Entertainer, The   Strouse 1976
Great Expectations   Fain 1961
Great Feelin'   Evans 1947; Livingston, Jay 1947
Great, Great Choir in the Sky, The   Woods 1954
Great, Great Lover, The   Caesar 1920
Great Guns   Mercer 1949; Warren 1949
Great Guns, How the Money Rolls In   Fain 1943; Harburg 1943
Great I Am, Leader of the Band   Schwartz, Jean 1930

Great Indoors, The   Porter 1930
Great Leader, Krantz, The   Bryan 1954
Great Man Says, The   Heyman 1944; Spina 1944
Great Manitou   Herbert 1911
Great Musician, The   Razaf 1952
Great Musicians   Smith, Harry B. 1908
Great New York Police, The   Cohan 1922
Great News, The   Styne 1978
Great News Is in the Making   Adamson 1943; McHugh 1943
Great North Road, The   Mercer 1974
Great Scott   Waller 1926
Great Vino, The   Martin 1958
Great White Easiest Way, The   Herbert 1908
Great White Way, The   Gordon 1953; Myrow 1953
Great Wide Open Spaces, The   Buck 1924
Greatest, The   Hoffman 1957
Greatest Attraction in the World, The   Oakland 1938
Greatest Battle Song of All, The   Atteridge 1915; Kalmar 1915; Romberg 1915
Greatest City, The   Mancini 1985
Greatest Enemy of Love, The   Gilbert 1937
Greatest General of Them All, The   Brown, Lew 1940; Henderson 1940
Greatest Gift, The   David, Hal 1975; Mancini 1975
Greatest Little Sign in the World, The   Cahn 1957; Van Heusen 1957
Greatest Man in the World, The   Russell 1948
Greatest Man on Earth, The   Coots 1952
Greatest Miracle of All, The   Cahn 1971; Styne 1971
Greatest Mistake of My Life, The   Lawrence 1945
Greatest Navy in the World, The   Smith, Harry B. 1909
Greatest Papa in the World, The   Robin 1952
Greatest Show on Earth, The   Gershwin, Ira 1940; Rose 1939; Weill 1940
Greatest Show on Earth (Come to the Circus), The   Washington 1952; Young, Victor 1952
Greatest Story Ever Told   (inst.), The   Young, Victor 1951
Greek Dance   Sondheim 1968
Greek Goddess   Spina 1967
Greek Marine Hymn, The   Harburg 1961
Greek Scene   Porter 1935
Greek to You   Porter 1938
Greeks Had a Word for It (The Olympics), The   Harburg 1961
Greeks Have Got the Girdle, The   Hart 1942; Rodgers 1942
Greeks Have No Word for It, The   Hart 1940; Rodgers 1940
Green and Blue   Blake 1937
Green and Gray   Hart 1919
Green Apple One Step, The   Spina 1970
Green Bay, Wisconsin   Willson 1953
Green Eyes   Harburg 1934
Green Eyes (Aquallos Ojos Verdes)   Gilbert 1931
Green Fields   Bryan 1931; Schwartz, Jean 1931; Warren Date Unknown
Green Fields and Bluebirds   Bryan 1936
Green Finch and Linnet Bird   Sondheim 1979
Green Fire   Brooks 1954
Green Grass Grows All Around   Bergman 1960
Green Grass Starts to Grow   Bacharach 1970; David, Hal 1970
Green Grow the Grass   Hoffman 1956
Green Leaves of Summer   Webster 1960
Green Light   Lewis 1976; Young, Joe 1976
Green Light Ahead   Arlen 1954; Gershwin, Ira 1954

Green Love for Walter, A   Burke 1947; Van Heusen 1947
Green Pastures   Blake 1930; Razaf 1930
Green Pine Tree, The   Merrill 1952
Green, White and Red in Italy   Warren 1964
Green with Envy Blues   Sherman 1961
Green Years of Love, The   Webster 1969
Greenback Dollar   Fisher 1936
Greener Pastures   Leigh 1955
Greenhorns   Strouse 1986
Green-Up Time   Lerner, Alan Jay 1948; Weill 1948
Greenwich Village   Drake 1953; Kern 1918
Greenwich Village Belle   Atteridge 1917; Romberg 1917
Greenwich Village Nights   Caesar 1922
Greenwillow Christmas   Loesser 1960
Greenwillow Walk   Loesser 1960
Greeting Cards, The   Duke 1941
Greetings, Gates   Carmichael 1940; Mercer 1940
Greetings to the King   Gorney 1925
Grenadier's Song   Smith, Harry B. 1911
Greta the Misfit Greyhound   Sherman 1964
Gretchen   Egan 1932
Greyfriar's Bobby   Sherman 1962
Greyhound   Youmans 1926
Grievin'   Ellington 1939
Grieving for You   Coslow 1920
Grind Me a Pound   Sherman 1958
Grinding Out a Revue   Kalmar 1923; Ruby 1923
Grizzly Bear   Gordon 1943
Grotto Rose (inst.)   Bacharach 1966
Grouchy Blues   Mills 1922
Ground You Walk Upon, The   David, Hal 1958
Group Voice   Young, Victor 1950
Grovers Corner   Cahn 1955; Van Heusen 1955
Growing Away from the Crowd   Strouse 1960
Growing Pains   Fields 1951; Schwartz, Arthur 1951
Growing Up   Sondheim 1985
Growing Up Isn't Easy   Strouse 1987
Grown Ups   Harburg 1971
Grown-ups Are the Stupidest People   Cahn 1944; Styne 1944
G-String Melody   Robison 1925
Guadalajara Hop   Coslow 1949
Guadeamus (Finale)   Webster 1954
Guard Watch   Oakland 1956; Webster 1956
Guarded   Smith, Harry B. 1927
Guardian Angel   Mercer 1955; Monaco 1942
Guardin' the Garden   Blane 1969
Guatemala   Davis 1948
Guatemala Melody   Gilbert 1928
Guenevere   Lerner, Alan Jay 1960; Loewe 1960
Guerillas' Song, The   Webster 1942
Guess Again   Gordon 1934; Revel 1934
Guess I'll Be on My Way   Russell 1947
Guess I'll Go Back Home This Summer   Robison 1939
Guess My Heart Is Haunted   Parish 1943; Woods 1943
Guess We're Gonna Get Along   Razaf 1934
Guess What   Merrill 1967
Guess What Charlie   Leigh 1967
Guess Who   Freed, Ralph 1936; Gershwin, George 1926; Gershwin, Ira 1926; Lane 1936
Guess Who's Boffo   Drake 1953
Guess Who's Coming to Dinner   David, Mack 1968
Guess Who's in Town (Nobody but that Gal of Mine)   Razaf 1928
Guessing   Mitchell 1921

Guess-Yes   Schwartz, Jean 1926
Guest in the Nest   Russell 1948
Guiding Me Back Home   Revel 1928; Sissle 1928
Guilt   Strouse 1975
Guilty   Ahlert 1931; Akst 1931; Coleman 1988; Kahn 1931;
    Turk 1931; Whiting 1931
Guilty Heart   Sigman 1958
Gui-Pi-Pia   Ruby 1947
Guitar Country   Mercer 1963; Robison 1963
Guitars of Love   Brennan 1936
Gulf Crest Gasoline   Coleman 1958; Leigh 1958
Gum Shoe Man, The   Sterling 1913; Von Tilzer 1913
Gun Song   Sondheim 1990
Gunfight at the O.K. Corral, The   Washington 1957
Gunga Din   Hart 1920; Rodgers 1920
Gunner in the Navy, A   Smith, Harry B. 1901
Guns of Navarone, The   Webster 1961
Gush-Gush-Gushing   Gershwin, George 1918; Gershwin,
    Ira 1918
Gut Stomp (inst.)   Johnson, James P. 1940
Guten Morgen, Buon Giorna, Bon Jour   Herbert 1898;
    Smith, Harry B. 1898
Guy from Albuquerque, The   Akst 1943
Guy in the Next Bunk to Me, The   Brown, Lew 1943; Stept
    1943
Guy on Monday, A   Berlin 1963
Guy Sat at a Piano, A   Hoffman 1952
Guy that Can Hand You a Laugh, The   Howard, Joseph E.
    1906
Guy What Takes His Time, A   Rainger 1933
Guy Who Brought Me, The   Martin 1941
Guy Who Brought Me (Can't Send Me), The   Blane 1963
Guy with the Polka Dotted Tie, The   Styne 1941, 1956
Guys and Dolls   Loesser 1950
Guys and Dolls Preamble   Loesser 1950
Guys Were Made for Girls   Bacharach 1960; David, Hal 1960
G'wan Home, Your Mudder's Callin'   Fain 1946; Freed,
    Ralph 1946
Gypsy   Gilbert 1928; Heyman 1934; Kahn 1934; Webster
    1952
Gypsy Blues   Blake 1921; Sissle 1921; Turk 1922
Gypsy Born and Bred Am I   Smith, Harry B. 1911; Smith,
    Robert B. 1911
Gypsy Camp   David, Mack 1962
Gypsy Caravan   Dietz 1924; Kern 1924
Gypsy Charmer   Akst 1929; Clarke 1929
Gypsy Dance   Atteridge 1915
Gypsy Days   Schwartz, Arthur 1929
Gypsy Fiddles   Wrubel 1933
Gypsy Fire   Merrill 1962
Gypsy Girl   Herbert 1924
Gypsy Hearts   Bryan 1932
Gypsy, I'm Love-Tippy for You   Jerome 1922; Schwartz, Jean
    1922
Gypsy in Me, The   Porter 1934
Gypsy (inst.)   Bloom 1931
Gypsy Jan   Herbert 1898; Smith, Harry B. 1898
Gypsy Joe   Kahn 1928
Gypsy Joe (Gypsy Song)   Donaldson 1928
Gypsy Kiss   Smith, Harry B. 1911
Gypsy Life   Herbert 1924
Gypsy Love   Fields 1930; McHugh 1930; Smith, Harry B.
    1911; Smith, Robert B. 1911
Gypsy Love Song   Herbert 1898, 1924; Smith, Harry B. 1898

Gypsy Lullaby (Scak Egy Szep Lany Van E Vilagon)   Freed,
    Ralph 1940
Gypsy Madness   Coslow 1935
Gypsy Maid   Wrubel 1924
Gypsy Man, The   Atteridge 1917; Romberg 1917
Gypsy Moon   Sigman 1960; Young, Victor 1935
Gypsy of Love   Lawrence 1938
Gypsy of Song, A   Friml 1933
Gypsy Passion   Smith, Harry B. 1926
Gypsy Romance (inst.)   Young, Victor 1953
Gypsy Rose   Gorney 1925; Lewis 1923; Meyer 1923; Young,
    Joe 1923
Gypsy Serenade   Coslow 1934
Gypsy Song   Brooks 1947; Kahn 1928; Romberg 1917;
    Smith, Harry B. 1911
Gypsy Sweetheart   Parish 1930
Gypsy Told Me, A   Yellen 1938
Gypsy Trail   Caesar 1921
Gypsy Warned Me, The   Caesar 1922
Gypsy Wedding Waltz (inst.)   Coots 1946
Gypsy Without a Song   Ellington 1938

H

Ha   Styne 1964
Ha! Cha! Cha!   Harbach 1931; Kern 1931
Ha! Ha!   Herbert 1908
Ha, Ha, Ha   Atteridge 1915; Carroll 1915; Clarke 1921;
    Herbert 1911; Porter 1938; Romberg 1915
Ha Ha Ha (Chella Lla)   Hoffman 1957
Ha, Ha, I'm Laughin' at You   Conrad 1922
Ha, Ha, They Must Sail to Siberia   Porter 1912
(My Sweet) Ha Wa Ta   Clare 1921; Friend 1921
Ha Ya, Bud   Hoffman 1940
Habanera   Herbert 1911; Johnson, Howard 1939
Haberdashers Department   Gordon 1934; Revel 1934
Ha-Cha-Cha   Kahn 1934
Hadacol   Burke 1959; Van Heusen 1959
Haffner   Willson 1956
Haga-Daga-Day   David, Mack 1959
Haggis, Baggis   Drake 1958
Ha-Ha-Ha (Gang Song)   Arlen 1931; Koehler 1931
Hail, Alma Mater   Burke 1944; Stept 1936, 1937; Van
    Heusen 1944; Washington 1936; Willson 1962
Hail and Farewell   Pollack 1942
Hail and Reign   Smith, Harry B. 1935
Hail Bibinski   Porter 1955
Hail, Cape Cod   Howard, Bart 1984
Hail Celestial Potentate   Smith, Robert B. 1905
Hail Franz of Zilania   Herbert 1913; Smith, Harry B. 1913;
    Smith, Robert B. 1913
Hail, Hail, America   Wrubel 1944
Hail, Hail, Hail   Porter 1950
Hail! Hail! Hail to Ellum Dale   DeSylva 1935
Hail Majesty   Loesser 1965
Hail Mary   Livingston, Jerry 1960
Hail Number One   Rome 1940
Hail of the Friendly Songs, The   Herbert 1913
Hail Sigma Psi   Koehler 1938
Hail Stonewall Jackson   Romberg 1927
Hail the Groom   Gordon 1935; Revel 1935
Hail, The Happy Couple   Gershwin, George 1932;
    Gershwin, Ira 1932
Hail the Home of Freedom   Freed, Ralph 1944
Hail the Wedding Pair   Smith, Harry B. 1911

Hail to Bolenciecwcz   Rainger 1941; Robin 1941

Hail to Chester   Rainger 1936; Robin 1936

Hail to Christmas   Herbert 1903

Hail to Colby   Snyder 1939

Hail to Cyril   Porter 1914

Hail to MacCracken's   Mercer 1951

Hail to Monty   DeSylva 1920; Kern 1920

Hail to Our General   Atteridge 1921

Hail to the Baron Maunchausen   Fields 1933; McHugh 1933

Hail to the King   David, Mack 1958; Livingston, Jerry 1958

Hail to the School   Weill 1947

Hail to the Sphinx   Drake 1968

Hail to Thee, Peppelbrink   Drake 1954

Hail to Yale   Porter 1910

Hail U.S.A.   Atteridge 1923; Caesar 1923; Romberg 1923

Hail Yale '29   Rome 1939

Hair of the Dog that Bit You, The   Von Tilzer 1910, 1929

Ha-Ja-La-Ka   Hoffman 1958

(The Adventures of) Hajji Baba   Washington 1954

Hal Murray Theme   Oakland 1954

Half a Dozen Dreams Ago   Adamson 1957; McHugh 1957

Half a Dream to Go   De Lange 1945; Myrow 1945

Half a Kiss   Duke 1927

Half a Love   David, Hal 1963

Half a Moon Is Better than No Moon   Hanley 1926

Half a Photograph   Russell 1951, 1953

Half and Half   Rose 1940

Half As Big As Life   Bacharach 1968; David, Hal 1968

Half Moon in Three Quarter Time, A   Revel 1944; Webster 1944

Half Moon on the Hudson   Bullock 1938; Spina 1938

Half of a Couple   Adams 1981; Strouse 1981

Half of It, Dearie, Blues, The   Gershwin, George 1924; Gershwin, Ira 1924

Half of Life   Adams Date Unknown; Strouse 1973

Half of Me   David, Hal 1980

Half of Me Wants to Be Good   Lewis 1935

Half of My Heart   Washington 1956

Half Past April and a Quarter to May   Cahn 1966; Van Heusen 1966

Half Past Kissing Time   Lewis 1922; Meyer 1922; Young, Joe 1922

Half Past Love   Young, Victor 1960

Half Time   Leigh 1971

Half-Forgotten Teddy Bear   Rome 1964

Half-Past Lovin' O'Clock   Bryan 1936

Half-sies   Mercer 1959

Half-sies (Hav-Zies)   Bloom 1959

Halfway Down on Jackson Street   Mills 1945

Halfway to Heaven   Dubin 1928

Hall of Fame   Drake 1955

Hallelu   Livingston, Jerry 1960

Hallelujah   Robin 1927; Youmans 1927

Hallelujah Baby!   Comden and Green 1967; Styne 1967

Hallelujah, Bless the Peace   Caesar 1946

Hallelujah, I'm a Bum   Hart 1933; Rodgers 1933

Hallelujah Pray for Peace   Caesar 1971

Hallelujah Round-Up   Razaf 1950

Hallelujah Train Routine   Styne 1954

Hallowe'en   Arlen 1950; Blane 1950; Hanley 1926; Herbert 1905

Halloween Ballet (inst.)   Schwartz, Arthur 1951

Hallowe'en Whoopee Ball   Donaldson 1928; Kahn 1928

Hallow'eve (inst.)   Loesser 1960

Ham and Candy   Revel 1952

Ham and Eggs   Blake 1930; Razaf 1930

Ham and Eggs in the Morning   Conrad 1927; Dubin 1927; Silver 1927

Ham That I Am   Duke 1946

Ham Tree Barbecue   Jerome 1905; Schwartz, Jean 1905

Hamburg Waltz   Rome 1965

Hamlet   Loesser 1949

Hamlet Was a Melancholy Dane   Jerome 1903; Schwartz, Jean 1903

Hammacher Schlemmer, I Love You   Dietz 1929; Schwartz, Arthur 1929

Hammershine   Herbert 1914

Hammock on the Porch   Dietz 1950; Schwartz, Arthur 1950

Hammock Song (Then You Swing, Swing, Swing)   Smith, Harry B. 1911; Smith, Robert B. 1911

Hand in Hand   Hammerstein 1934; Kern 1934; Lawrence 1947; Leslie 1931; McHugh 1924; Monaco 1931; Razaf 1936; Washington 1931

Hand in Hand Again   Egan 1919; Whiting 1919

Hand in Hand in Heaven   Oakland 1936

Hand Me Down, The   Loewe 1942

Hand Me Down Love   Ellington 1955; Sigman 1955

Hand Me Down My Walking Cane   Parish 1934

Hand Me Down that Can o' Beans   Lerner, Alan Jay 1951; Loewe 1951

Hand that Rocked My Cradle Rules My Heart, The   Berlin 1919

Hand that Swept the Stars Across the Sky, The   Livingston, Jerry 1957

Handful of Dreams, A   Webster 1955

Handful of Keys   Razaf 1933; Waller 1933

Handful of Scales and a Ching-Boom, A   Willson 1955

Handful of Stars   Lawrence 1940

Handle Me with Care   Jerome 1907; Schwartz, Jean 1907

Handle My Heart with Care   Revel 1959

Handlebar Moustache, The   Rose 1938

Hand-Me-Down Blues, The   Youmans 1924

Hands   Hart 1930; Rodgers 1930; Russell 1962

Hands Across the Border   Carmichael 1943; Revel 1942; Washington 1943

Hands Across the Sea   Eliscu 1929

Hands Across the Table   Parish 1934

Hands of Time   Webster 1967

Hands Off   Harbach 1948; Sterling 1914; Von Tilzer 1914

Hands Off, That's My Gal   Razaf 1926

Hand-Shakin' Day   Robison 1950

Handsome Prince, The   David, Mack 1958; Livingston, Jerry 1958

Handwriting's on the Wall, The   Fain 1933; Young, Joe 1933

Handy Andy   Atteridge 1912; Razaf 1940

Handy Man   Johnson, James P. 1947

Handy with Your Feet   Mercer 1937; Whiting 1937

Hang a Lantern in Your Window   Sherman 1962

Hang In There   Sondheim 1968

Hang March   Herbert 1903

Hang on to Me   Gershwin, George 1924; Gershwin, Ira 1924

Hang On to Your Lids, Kids   Arlen 1941; Mercer 1941

Hang Onto a Rainbow   Stept 1930

Hang Onto Your Happiness   Fisher 1930; Johnson, Howard 1930

Hang Out the Stars   Lawrence 1952

Hang Out the Stars in Indiana   Woods 1931

Hang Up!   Fields 1954; Schwartz, Arthur 1954

Hang Up My Saddle   Bullock 1936; Whiting 1936

Hang Up Papa, You're on a Busy Line   Razaf 1924

Hang Your Hat on the Moon   Schwartz, Jean 1928
Hang Your Heart on a Hickory Limb   Burke 1939; Monaco 1939
Hang Your Teardrops in the Sunshine   Yellen 1949
Hang Your Troubles on a Rainbow   Revel 1943; Webster 1943
Hangin' Around with You   Gershwin, George 1929; Gershwin, Ira 1929
Hangin' Around Your Door   Johnson, James P. 1931
Hangin' at the End of a Rope   Hanley 1932
Hangin' on the Garden Gate, Sayin' Goodnight   Kahn 1929
Hangin' On to You   Arlen 1943; Mercer 1943
Hangin' Round   Donaldson 1930
Hanging Out a Rainbow Over the U.S.A.   Fain 1943; Freed, Ralph 1943; Harburg 1943
Hanging Throttlebottom in the Morning   Gershwin, George 1933; Gershwin, Ira 1933
Hanging Tree, The   David, Mack 1959; Livingston, Jerry 1959
Hangman, The   Bacharach 1959; David, Hal 1959
(Here Comes) Hank the Whip   Coots 1952
Hankerin'   Cahn 1948; Styne 1948
Hanky-Panky Glide, The   Goetz 1912
Hannah   Herbert 1906; Spina 1977
Hannah Will Take Care of You   Merrill 1990
Hannah Won't You Open that Door   Sterling 1904; Von Tilzer 1904
Hannah's a Hummer   Cohan 1899
Hannibal, Mo (Zour-ee)   Sherman 1973
Hannibal's Victory March   Adamson 1955; Lane 1955
Hans   Porter 1928
Hans the Man   Adams 1993; Strouse 1993
Hansel and Gretel Theme   Coots 1954
Hansom Cab Drivers   Edwards 1929; Johnson, Howard 1929
Happiest Birthday Routine   Styne 1941
Happiest Day of My Life, The   Lane 1951; Lerner, Alan Jay 1951
Happiest Girl Alive, The   Sherman 1968
Happiest Girl in the World, The   Harburg 1961
Happiest House on the Block, The   Hammerstein 1955; Rodgers 1955
Happiest Moment of My Life, When I Kissed Another Man's Wife — My Mother, The   Bryan 1913
Happily Ever After   Comden and Green 1979; Duke 1929; Rome 1940; Sondheim 1970; Styne 1954
Happily Married Wolf, A   Cahn 1977
Happiness   Brooks 1948; Fisher 1908; Jerome 1924; Johnson, Howard 1922; Parish 1946; Sondheim 1994
(There Must Be) Happiness Ahead   Dixon 1934; Revel 1943; Wrubel 1934
Happiness Ahead (Happiness Bound)   Webster 1943
Happiness Bound   Revel 1943
Happiness Calling   Schwartz, Jean 1942
Happiness, Happiness   Magidson 1949; Oakland 1949
Happiness (I Find My Happiness Dear with You):   Meyer 1921
Happiness Is a Thing Called Joe   Arlen 1943; Harburg 1943
Happiness Is Just the Other Side of Loneliness   David, Hal 1976
Happiness Is Where You Find It   Russell 1951, 1954
Happiness Now   Cahn 1970
Happiness Theme   Fain 1957
Happiness, Where Are You   Gilbert 1919
Happy   Caesar 1919; Cohan 1928; Livingston, Jerry 1934
Happy Again   Dietz 1944; Duke 1944

Happy and His One Man Band   Bacharach 1959
Happy Anniversary   Kern 1946; Robin 1946
Happy Anniversary Baby   Bergman 1969
Happy Anniversary to You   Wrubel 1943
Happy Any Day   Arlen 1966
Happy As a Lark   Webster 1938
Happy as the Day Is Long   Arlen 1933; Koehler 1933
Happy Bachelor (Or the Courtship of Miles Standish), The   DePaul 1959; Mercer 1959
Happy Barbie Birthday, A   Livingston, Jerry 1963
Happy Because I'm in Love   Eliscu 1929; Rose 1929; Youmans 1929
Happy Birthday   Gershwin, George 1929; Gershwin, Ira 1929; Kahn 1929, 1936; Strouse 1999
Happy Birthday America   Cahn 1951; Duke 1951
Happy Birthday Dear Country   Spina 1959
Happy Birthday Dear Heartache   David, Mack 1984
Happy Birthday Dear Jesus, Merry Christmas to You   McHugh 1960
Happy Birthday Erwin   Evans 1961; Livingston, Jay 1961
Happy Birthday Hoe Down   Sherman 1984
Happy Birthday, Mrs. J.J. Brown   Willson 1960
Happy Birthday to Love   Rose 1937, 1940
Happy Blues   Mills 1923
Happy Christmas, Little Friend   Hammerstein 1952; Rodgers 1952
Happy Cowboy   Brown, Nacio Herb 1929; Freed, Arthur 1930; Styne 1941
Happy Daddy   Gilbert 1937
Happy Day (inst.)   Youmans 1954
Happy Day March   Smith, Harry B. 1908
Happy Days   Brown, Lew 1927; Davis 1951; DeSylva 1927; Dietz 1927; Gorney 1927; Hanley 1930; Henderson 1927; Herbert 1940; Loesser 1940; Schwartz, Jean 1908; Smith, Harry B. 1918; Williams 1909
Happy Days and Lonely Nights   Fisher 1930; Rose 1930
Happy Days Are Here Again   Ager 1929, 1930; Yellen 1929, 1930
Happy Days in Dixie   Smith, Harry B. 1903
Happy Dogs   Styne 1964
Happy Easter   Berlin 1948
Happy End, The   Weill 1977
Happy Ending, A   Brown, A. Seymour 1928; Gershwin, Ira 1921; Mitchell 1938; Pollack 1938
Happy Ending (inst.)   Strouse 1973
Happy Endings   Atteridge 1924
Happy Face Baby   Brooks 1956
Happy Falling Said I to My Heart   Burke 1956
Happy Family, A   Caesar 1925; Harbach 1921; Smith, Robert B. 1912; Youmans 1925
Happy Feeling (inst.)   Waller 1940
Happy Feet   Ager 1930; Yellen 1930
Happy Go Lucky   Kalmar 1927; Loesser 1943; Mitchell 1953; Stept 1937; Washington 1937
Happy Go Lucky (Bird)   Ruby 1927
Happy Go Lucky Lane   Lewis 1928; Young, Joe 1928
Happy Go Lucky You and Broken Hearted Me   Friend 1928
Happy Habit   Fields 1954; Schwartz, Arthur 1954
Happy Happenstance, A   Cahn 1971; Van Heusen 1971
Happy, Happy Day   Parish 1957
Happy, Happy, Happy, Happy, Happy, Happy, Happy, Happy, Happy, Happy, Happy Wedding Day   Willson 1945
Happy, Happy New Year   Lerner, Alan Jay 1983; Strouse 1983

Happy Harvest   David, Hal 1955

Happy Heart, The   Fields 1957; Lane 1957

Happy Heaven of Harlem, The   Porter 1929

Happy Hindu Waltz   Rome 1970

Happy Hoboes   Brown, Lew 1928; DeSylva 1928; Henderson 1928

Happy Hollywood   Adams 1954; Strouse 1954

(In a) Happy Home for Two   Freed, Arthur 1925

Happy Horns and Merry Bells   Duke 1963

Happy Hottentot   Jerome 1920; Von Tilzer 1920

Happy Hottentots   Atteridge 1916; Romberg 1916

Happy Humming Bird   Dixon 1928; Woods 1928

Happy Hunting   Fain 1951; Harburg 1951

Happy Hunting Horn   Hart 1940; Rodgers 1940

Happy, I Am Happy   Kahn 1934

(Everybody's) Happy in Jimtown   Razaf 1928; Waller 1928

Happy in Love   Fain 1941

Happy in Love, Hi, Ho the Hoe-Down Way   Yellen 1941

Happy in the Rain   Johnson, Howard 1929

Happy Is the Boy   Leigh 1954

Happy Is the Word   Fain 1960; Webster 1960

Happy Journey   Koehler 1942; Monaco 1942

Happy Land of Hunzac, The   Washington 1957

Happy Land of Once-Upon-a-Time, The   Herbert 1908; Smith, Harry B. 1908

Happy Landing   Brown, Lew 1930; DeSylva 1930; Henderson 1930

Happy Little Butterfly   Dixon 1932; Fain 1932

Happy Little Country Girl   Berlin 1913

Happy Little Crook   Young, Victor 1955

Happy Little Mill   Adamson 1955; McHugh 1955

Happy Little Verse and Chorus   Arlen 1950; Blane 1950; Fain 1951; Gordon 1951

Happy Little Worries   Hoffman 1931

Happy Lot, A   Martin 1962

Happy Medium Song   Caesar 1945

Happy Melody   Caesar 1924

Happy New Year   Hoffman 1931

Happy New Year, A Wonderful New Year   Brown, Nacio Herb 1957

Happy New Year Blues, The   Berlin 1924

Happy New Year for You   Carmichael 1940; Mercer 1940

Happy New Year from Howdy Doody, A   Coots 1955

Happy New Year to You   Coleman 1967

Happy Night   Evans 1971; Livingston, Jay 1971

Happy People   Davis 1959

Happy Polka, The   Mills 1959

Happy Prince   Caesar 1925

Happy Recipe, A   Arlen 1973

Happy Rickshaw Man (Jinrikisha Song)   Romberg 1927; Smith, Harry B. 1927

Happy Song   Rome 1965

Happy Song (Eine Zwei), The   Livingston, Jerry 1958

Happy Sunday   Dubin 1917

Happy Talk   Hammerstein 1949; Rodgers 1949

Happy Thanksgiving   Lerner, Alan Jay 1985

Happy the Bride the Sun Shines Upon   Arlen 1953; Fields 1953

Happy Time, The   Leigh 1965; Warren 1970; Washington 1952

Happy Time Again   Koehler 1936

Happy Times   Fields 1932; McHugh 1932

Happy to Keep His Dinner Warm   Loesser 1961

Happy to Make Your Acquaintance   Loesser 1956

Happy Tomorrows   Sherman 1971

Happy Train, The   Koehler 1950; Stept 1950

Happy Tree   Young, Victor 1952

Happy Valley   Friend 1949

Happy Wedding Day, A   Kern 1919

Happy Week (Operetta), A   Young, Victor 1934

Happy with the Blues   Arlen 1961

Happy-Go-Lucky   Loesser 1943; McHugh 1943

Happy-Go-Lucky Guy   Howard, Bart 1938

Happy-Go-Lucky Lady   Brooks 1945

Happy-Go-Lucky You and Broken Hearted Me   Hoffman 1932

Happyland   Bryan 1916

Harbor Bells of Normandy, The   Livingston, Jerry 1958; Webster 1958

Harbor Down Deep in My Heart, The   Porter 1922

Harbor of Dreams   Gershwin, George 1925; Gershwin, Ira 1925

Harbor of Home   Harbach 1911

Harbor of Home Sweet Home, The   Ahlert 1933; Leslie 1933; Webster 1950

Harbor of Lost Dreams, The   Johnson, J. Rosamond 1909

Harbor of My Heart, The   Heyman 1942; Robin 1927; Youmans 1927

Hard Boiled Mamma   Johnson, J. Rosamond 1927

Hard Boiled Rose   McHugh 1924; Mills 1924

Hard Eights   Oakland 1960

Hard Hearted Hannah   Ager 1924; Yellen 1924

Hard Luck in Society   Atteridge 1912

Hard Problems   Robison 1928

Hard to Get Along With   Robin 1927

Hard to Get Gal   Davis 1925

Hard to Get (inst.)   Warren Date Unknown

Hard to Replace   Gershwin, Ira 1938; Kern 1938

Hard Way, The   Burke 1945; Van Heusen 1945

Hard-Boiled Herman   Hammerstein 1924; Harbach 1924

Hard-Boiled Rose   Dubin 1924

Hardest Thing in the World to Do, The   Blane 1961

Hard-to-Get Gertie   Ager 1926; Yellen 1926

Hare Pieces   Mercer 1955

Harem Dance (Inst.)   Brooks 1960

Harem Days   Rainger 1940

Harem Life   Berlin 1919

Harem Scarem   Harbach 1910

Hark Hark the Lark   Johnson, Howard 1939

Hark to the Song of the Night   Porter 1950

Hark to the Voice of Your Lover   Smith, Robert B. 1906

Harlem   Blake 1941; Razaf 1930

Harlem at Its Best   Fields 1935; McHugh 1935

Harlem Band (inst.)   Johnson, James P. 1948

Harlem Bolero   Coots 1937; Davis 1937

Harlem Bon-Bon Babies   Johnson, James P. 1962

Harlem Butterfly   Mercer 1948

Harlem Choc'late Babies   Johnson, James P. 1927

Harlem Choc'late Babies (inst.)   Johnson, James P. 1926

Harlem Flat   Burke 1933; Spina 1933

Harlem Fuss (inst.)   Waller 1930

Harlem Heaven   Alter 1930

Harlem Holiday   Arlen 1932; Koehler 1932

Harlem Hospitality   Van Heusen 1933

Harlem Hot-Cha   Johnson, James P. 1932; Razaf 1932

Harlem Lullaby   Robison 1933

Harlem Madness   Ager 1930; Mills 1934; Yellen 1930

Harlem Moon   Blake 1932; Sissle 1932

Harlem Number Man   Johnson, James P. 1938

Harlem on My Mind   Berlin 1933

Harlem on the Sand   Hart 1929; Rodgers 1929

Harlem Prance, The   Akst 1926; Mitchell 1926

Harlem Rhythm Dance   Razaf 1933

Harlem River Chanty   Gershwin, George 1925; Gershwin, Ira 1925

Harlem River Quiver   Fields 1928; McHugh 1928

Harlem Rose   Conrad 1928

Harlem Sandman   Adamson 1943; Styne 1943

Harlem Serenade   Gershwin, George 1929; Gershwin, Ira 1929; Kahn 1929

Harlem Strut (inst.)   Johnson, James P. 1921

Harlem to Hollywood   Bloom 1936; Mercer 1936

Harlem Town   Johnson, James P. 1929

Harlem Vs. Jungle (Ain't Ya Givin' in to Harlem)   Akst 1934; Brown, Lew 1934

Harlem Woogie   Johnson, James P. 1938

Harlemania   Fields 1931; McHugh 1929

Harlem's a Garden   Blake Date Unknown; Razaf 1942

Harlem's Hot As Hades   Arlen 1930; Koehler 1930

Harlequinade   Herbert 1912

Harlequin's Doll   Buck 1923

Harlow   Bacharach 1965; David, Hal 1965

Harmonica Jim   Stept 1926

Harmonize   Blane 1954; Martin 1954

Harmony   Burke 1946; Van Heusen 1946

Harmony Boys, The   Rome 1937

Harmony Hill   Smith, Harry B. 1934

Harmony in Harlem   Ellington 1938; Mills 1938

Harolds of This World, The   Styne 1978

Harp and a Fiddle and a Flute, A   Burke 1956; Friml 1956

Harp in the Wind   Woods 1955

Harp That Once Thro' Tara's Halls, The   Johnson, Howard 1939

Harp with the Broken String, The   Hanley 1930

Harriet   Baer 1946

Harrigan   Cohan 1908

Harry Is Only Physical   Webster 1946

Harry Masters, Jack Craft and Company   Caesar 1922; Coots 1922

Harry Nigocia Theme   Oakland 1954

Harry the Hat   Robison 1967

Harry Warren O Melody (Inst.)   Warren Date Unknown

Harry Who?   Warren 1980

Hartman Ballet (inst.)   Kern 1925

Harum-Scarum, The   Harbach 1911

Harvest Days   Atteridge 1915

Harvest Moon, The   Friml 1921

Harvest Moon Is Shining, Liza (For You and Me), The   Stept 1926

Harvey   Carmichael 1929; Mills 1929

Harvey Hudson Theme   Oakland 1954

Harvey, I Lost You   Martin 1972

Harvey, the Humble Bumble Bee   Burke 1942; Van Heusen 1942

Harvey, the Victory Garden Man   Mercer 1943

Harvey, The Victory-Garden Man   Arlen 1943

Harvey's Theme (inst.)   Duke 1959

Has Anybody Got a Kiss to Spare   Kahn 1910

Has Anybody Got a Place for Me in California   Leigh 1977

Has Anybody Seen My Bennie   Hammerstein 1926; Harbach 1926; Romberg 1926

Has Anybody Seen My Kitty   Hoffman 1954

Has Anybody Seen My Man   Styne 1941

Has Anybody Seen Our Nellie   Ager 1930; Yellen 1930

Has Anyone Ever Told You, You're As Pretty As a Picture   Adamson 1938; McHugh 1938

Has Anyone Seen Heine   Rose 1924

Has Anyone Seen My Crocodile   Strouse 1987

Has Anyone Seen My Joe?   DeSylva 1922; Gershwin, George 1922

Has Cupid Laid in Wait for You   Herbert 1911

Has I Let You Down?   Arlen 1954

Has to Be   Styne 1941

Hasbrook Heights   Bacharach 1970; David, Hal 1970

Hasta La Vista, Goodbye   Merrill 1958

Hasta La Vista, Senora   Livingston, Jerry 1959

Hasta Luego   Porter 1943

Hasta Manana (Toda Una Vida)   De Lange 1945

Hasten Jason!   Freed, Ralph 1944; Stept 1944

Hat Like That, A   Ager 1939; Fain 1939; Yellen 1939

Hat My Father Wore Upon St. Patrick's Day, The   Jerome 1909; Schwartz, Jean 1909

Hat that I Kissed You Under, The   Howard, Joseph E. 1946

Hatcheck Girl   Merrill 1958

Hate   Howard, Bart 1961

Hate the Lies, Love the Liar   David, Mack 1982

Hate to Talk About Myself   Rainger 1935; Robin 1935, 1936; Whiting 1935, 1936

Hats   Adams 1996; Akst 1952; Davis 1952; Strouse 1996

Hats Make the Woman   Herbert 1905

Hats Off   Magidson 1936; Oakland 1936

Hats Off — Here Comes a Lady   Young, Joe 1932

Hattie's Place   Spina 1977

Haul Away, My Lou   Evans 1951; Livingston, Jay 1951

Haunted   Razaf 1960

Haunted Ballroom   Spina 1973

Haunted Cask, The   Smith, Harry B. 1908

Haunted Heart   Dietz 1948; Schwartz, Arthur 1948

Haunted Hot Spot   Duke 1952

Haunted House   Berlin 1914

Haunted Organ, The   Young, Joe 1932; Young, Victor 1932

Haunted Pool, The   Howard, Joseph E. 1909

Haunting Chopin Strain   Johnson, Howard 1935

Haunting Eyes   Razaf 1949

Haunting Me   De Lange 1934; Myrow Date Unknown

Haunting Melody   Atteridge 1912

Haunting My Heart   Rainger 1929; Robin 1929

Haute Couture   Cahn 1965; Van Heusen 1965

Havana   Egan 1927; Goetz 1910; Lerner, Sammy 1940

Havana Anna Ann   Atteridge Date Unknown

Havana for a Night   Hammerstein 1940

Havana (Havana Opening)   Hart 1926; Rodgers 1926

Havana Heaven (Cielo de la Habana)   Johnson, Howard 1935

Havana Moon   Russell 1946

Havana Nights   Caesar 1922; Razaf 1927

Have a Cup of Tea   Gorney 1958

Have a Dream   Adams 1962; Strouse 1962

Have a Dream on Me   Mercer 1938; Warren 1938

Have a Drink on Me   Warren 1954

Have a Drink to Yankee Land   Williams 1909

Have a Good Time Everybody   Blake 1924; Sissle 1924

Have a Heart   Adamson 1931; Buck 1916; Cohan 1914; Johnson, Howard 1924; Kern 1916, 1917; Lane 1931; Mercer 1965

Have a Heart (Be My Valentine)   Brooks 1958

Have a Heart, Gigolette (Gigolette)   Rome 1952

Have a Heart, Have Mine   Baer 1931

Have a Heart Josephine   Davis 1942

Have a Heart, Taft-Hartley, Have a Heart   Lawrence 1947
Have a Hope, Have a Wish, Have a Prayer   David, Hal 1954
Have a Little Dance with Me   Friml 1922
Have a Little Dream on Me   Rose 1934
Have a Little Drinkee   Eliscu 1931
Have a Little Faith in Me   Lewis 1930; Warren 1930; Young, Joe 1930
Have a Little Faith in Uncle Sam   Adamson 1932; Coots 1932
Have a Little Lunch with Maggi McNellis and Herb Sheldon   Sigman 1947
Have a Little Sympathy Cherie   Fisher 1935
Have a Nice Day   Mercer 1971
Have a Restaurant of Your Own   Atteridge 1915; Carroll 1915; Romberg 1915
Have a Smile for Every One You Meet and They Will Have a Smile for You   Brennan 1918
Have a Smile (inst.)   Schwartz, Jean 1919
Have a Smile with Momus   Jerome 1910; Schwartz, Jean 1910
Have an Old Waltz with Me   Kern 1913; Smith, Harry B. 1913
Have an Umbrella   Martin 1964
Have Feet Will Dance   Fields 1957; Lane 1957
Have Guitar Will Travel   Silver 1958
Have I Ever Told You   DePaul 1943; Raye 1943
Have I Got a Girl for You?   Sondheim 1970
Have I Got a Piece of Boiled Beef for You   Brown, Lew 1925; Clare 1925; Friend 1925
Have I Stayed Away too Long   Loesser 1943
Have I the Right   Strouse 1980
Have I Told You   DePaul 1947; Raye 1947
Have I Told You Lately   Adamson 1946; McHugh 1946; Rome 1962
Have It Your Way Foolish Heart   Kahal 1938, Date Unknown; Warren 1938, Date Unknown
Have of Me   Heyman 1950; Young, Victor 1950
Have Pity, Sheriff   Schwartz, Arthur 1928
Have Reindeer, Will Travel   Livingston, Jerry 1963; Webster 1963
Have the Last Kiss on Me   Evans 1946; Livingston, Jay 1946
Have the Time of Your Life (With NBC)   Cahn 1965
Have You Been to Gay Paree   Gordon 1945
Have You Been True to Me?   Hart 1929; Rodgers 1929
Have You Been Waiting Long   Sondheim Date Unknown
Have You Ever Been in Heaven   Lawrence 1937
Have You Ever Been in Love   Lerner, Sammy 1934
Have You Forgotten   Ager 1926; Johnson, Howard 1927; Robin 1931; Yellen 1926
Have You Forgotten Cherie   Coots 1929; Davis 1929
Have You Forgotten Me   Monaco 1916
Have You Forgotten Me? Blues   Kern 1922
Have You Forgotten So Soon   Coslow 1938, 1939; Heyman 1939; Silver 1939; Von Tilzer 1936
Have You Forgotten the You and Me that Used to Be   Bullock 1937; Wrubel 1937
Have You Forgotten What I Can't Forget   Young, Joe 1932
Have You Found Heaven   Howard, Joseph E. 1964
Have You Got Any Castles, Baby?   Mercer 1937; Whiting 1937
Have You Got Old Clothes   Caesar 1945
Have You Got What You Came With?   Lerner, Alan Jay 1971
Have You Heard   Gershwin, George 1925; Livingston, Jerry 1973

Have You Heard about Philias Fogg?   Young, Victor 1963
Have You Heard About the Meeting?   Harburg 1945
Have You Heard? (Gossip Song)   Arlen 1959; Mercer 1959
Have You Love to Go with That   De Lange 1943
Have You Met Mandy Murphy   Cobb 1906; Edwards 1906
Have You Met Miss Fandango   Young, Victor 1960
Have You Met Miss Jones?   Hart 1937; Rodgers 1937
Have You Met My Oucho Ma Gaucho   Gordon 1940; Warren 1940
Have You No Pity on Me   Coots 1958
Have You Seen My Baby   Edwards 1908
Have You Seen My Sweetheart in His Uniform of Blue   Cobb 1902; Edwards 1902
Have You Seen the Ducks   Goetz 1917
Have You Tried a Prayer   Fain 1961; Raye 1961
Have You Written Any Good Books Lately   Mercer 1950
Have You Written Him Today   De Lange 1944
Have You Written Home to Mother   Davis 1935
Have Yourself a Merry Little Christmas   Martin 1944
Have Yourself Some Fun   Stept 1950
Haven't Got a Worry   Evans 1953; Livingston, Jay 1953
Haven't Got No Peace of Mind   Rainger 1933
Haven't We Met Before?   David, Mack 1943; Livingston, Jerry 1943
Havin' a Ball   Johnson, James P. 1936, 1938; Mercer 1951; Razaf 1936
Havin' a Birthday   Merrill 1953
Havin' a Hoedown   Drake 1958
Havin' a Time   Comden and Green 1945
Havin' a Wonderful Wish (Time You Were Here)   Evans 1949; Livingston, Jay 1949
Havin' Fun, Brop-dee-o-dee   Raye 1960
Havin' Myself a Time   Rainger 1938; Robin 1938
Having a Good Time Wish You Were Here   Dubin 1931; Fain 1931; Kahal 1931
Having a Wonderful Time (Wish You Were Here)   Dubin 1936
Having My Own Sweet Way   Eliscu 1929
Having You Is Heaven   Johnson, Howard 1934
Hav-Zies   Mercer 1962
Hawaii   David, Mack 1966; Rome 1965
Hawaii, I'm Lonesome for You   Yellen 1917
Hawaii, Pearls of the Sea   Carmichael 1966
Hawaii Sang Me to Sleep   Loesser 1939
Hawaii Swings   Hoffman 1959
Hawaiian Band on Float   Merrill 1956
Hawaiian Blues   Motzan 1921; Turk 1921
Hawaiian Eye   David, Mack 1959; Livingston, Jerry 1959
Hawaiian Eyes   Coots 1921
Hawaiian Harmony Blues   Johnson, Howard 1927
Hawaiian Love Call   Parish 1980
Hawaiian Love-Bird   Razaf 1929
Hawaiian Melody   Friml 1948
Hawaiian Memory   Caesar 1931
Hawaiian Moon   Brennan 1930; Friml 1930
Hawaiian Moonlight   Bryan 1919; Schwartz, Jean 1919
Hawaiian Night in Dixieland   Turk 1922
Hawaiian Nights in Dixieland   Coots 1923
Hawaiian Party   Mercer 1941; Schwartz, Arthur 1941
Hawaiian Prelude   Gordon 1942; Warren 1942
Hawaiian Romance   Baer 1929; Caesar 1929
Hawaiian Song of Love   Akst 1927
Hawaiian War Chant (Ta-hu-wa-hu-wai)   Freed, Ralph 1940
Hawaiian Wedding Song, The   Hoffman 1957
Hawaiiannette (Hawaiian Love Talk)   Sherman 1960

Hawaii's Shore   Brennan 1930; Friml 1930
Hawks!   Sherman 1971
Hay Foot, Straw Foot   Carroll 1925; Freed, Arthur 1925
Hay Hay Farmer Took Another Load Away (The Farmer Took Another Load Away Hay Hay)   Leslie 1925
Hay, Hay, Hazel   Whiting 1923
Hay Ride, The   Kern 1907
Hay! Straw!   Hammerstein 1928; Youmans 1928
Ha-Ya Soph   Yellen 1977
Hayfoot, Strawfoot   Drake 1942
Hay-Long   Fain 1921
Hayride   Mercer 1945; Warren 1945
Hayward's Harlem Hellions   Hammerstein 1920
Haywire   Heyman 1934
Hazel   Cahn 1962; Van Heusen 1962
H.C. Potter's Ball   DePaul 1958; Raye 1958
He   Merrill 1964; Styne 1964
He Ain't Got Rhythm   Berlin 1937
He Ain't Heavy. . . He's My Brother   Russell 1969
He Always Comes Home to Me   Lerner, Alan Jay 1983; Strouse 1983
He Always Gets His Man   Burke 1933; Spina 1933
He and I   Heyman 1931; Youmans 1931
He and She   Hart 1938; Rodgers 1938
He Blew on His Bugle-e-oo   Clarke 1913; Leslie 1913; Schwartz, Jean 1913
He Came Along   Adamson 1965; Youmans 1965
He Can Cure You of Love   Cohan 1916
He Can Dance   Fain 1938; Kahal 1938
He Can Waltz   Loesser 1947
He Certainly Kills the Women   Porter 1944
He Cha Cha'd In   Burke 1958
He Comes Up to See Me Once in a While   Meyer 1926
He Couldn't Speak a Word of English   Silver 1929
He Danced with Me (The Slipper and the Rose Waltz)   Sherman 1976
He Dangled Me on His Knee   Von Tilzer 1903
He Didn't Ask Me   Cahn 1942
He Didn't Even Say Goodbye   Hoffman 1934
He Didn't Have the Know How No-How   Mercer 1950
He Died Good   Loesser 1960
He Died Like Every Pirate Should from Rum   Styne 1985
He Died of Love   Loesser 1939
He Does Me So Much Good   Bryan 1919; Schwartz, Jean 1919
He Doesn't Know   Brooks 1961; Strouse 1977; Warren 1961
He Doesn't Know I'm Alive   Strouse 1989
He Doesn't Know What It's All About   Berlin 1925
He Doesn't Love Me Anymore   Oakland 1931
'He' for Me, The   Friml 1928
He Goes to Church on Sunday   Goetz 1907
He Goes to Work in the Night Time and She Goes to Work Ever Day   Johnson, Howard 1917
He Got a Poison Ivy Instead of a Clinging Vine   Dubin 1930
He Got Right Up on the Wagon   Williams 1910
He Had a Little Gun   Russell 1962, 1977
He Had Refinement   Fields 1951; Schwartz, Arthur 1951
He Had to Pay the Piper   Carroll 1925; Freed, Arthur 1925
He Has a Way   Sherman 1995
He Has Such Charm (Il est Charmant)   Harburg 1932
He Hasn't a Thing Except Me   Duke 1936; Gershwin, Ira 1936
He Is My Friend   Silver 1952
He Is Sweet, He Is Good   Atteridge 1914; Carroll 1914; Romberg 1914

He Is the Type   Kern 1925
He Isn't My Style At All   Smith, Harry B. 1934
He Just Beats a Tom-Tom   Akst 1934; Brown, Lew 1934
He Kept Running After the Girl   Johnson, Howard 1914
He Knew What He Wanted   Webster 1965
He Knocked at the Door of Heaven   Bryan 1954
He Knows   Robison 1958
He Knows By the Way I Live Each Day   Spina 1957
He Knows Milk   Gershwin, Ira 1929
He Left Her Behind Before   Bryan 1926; Silver 1926
He Lied and I Listened   Loesser 1941
He Lights Another Mecca   Hart 1919
He Looks at Her and Then He Goes Ha-Ha-Ha-Ha-Ha   Henderson 1924; Rose 1924
He Looks Like an Angel, but Fights Like the Devil   Hoffman 1943; Livingston, Jerry 1943
He Looks So Good To Me   Hart 1931; Rodgers 1931
He Lost   Spina 1944
He Loved Me Till the All Clear Came   Arlen 1942; Mercer 1942
He Loves and She Loves   Gershwin, George 1927; Gershwin, Ira 1927
He Loves Her (You)   Fain 1960; Webster 1960
He Loves It   Clarke 1922; Leslie 1922
He Makes Me Believe He's Mine   Ellington 1947
He Makes Me Feel I'm Lovely   Burke 1961
He May Be Old but He's Got Young Ideas   Johnson, Howard 1916
He May Say 'Yes' Today   Smith, Harry B. 1926
He Met Her on the Prairie   Rainger 1936; Robin 1936
He Must Be Nice to Mother   Kern 1912
He Needs You   Evans 1961; Livingston, Jay 1961
He Never Looked Better in His Life   Russell 1952
He Never Looks My Way   Livingston, Jerry 1956
He Never Took a Lesson in His Life   Fisher 1913
He Only Comes to See Me Once in a While   Clarke 1924; Johnston 1924; Meyer 1924; Turk 1924
He Only Had 84 Points   Cahn 1945; Styne 1945
He Outfoxed the Fox   Ellington 1958
He Passed Me By   Rainger 1933
He Played It on His Fid, Fid Fiddle-Dee-Dee   Berlin 1912; Goetz 1912
He Played on His Old Bazooka   Conrad 1936; Kahn 1936
He Plays Gin Rummy   David, Mack 1941; Silver 1941
He Plays It Cool   Washington 1958
He Pleases Me   Mancini 1979
He Promised Me   Berlin 1911
He Pulled the Temple Down   Johnson, James P. 1962
He Put the "Uh" in the Mambo   Blane 1954; Martin 1954
He Ran Upstairs, Took a Look, and Ran Right Down Again   Kalmar 1913
He Rides the Range   Webster 1949
He Said   Cahn Date Unknown; Duke Date Unknown
He Say Go I Say No   Rainger 1931
He Says Yes, She Says No!   Friml 1912; Harbach 1912
He, She and Me   Egan 1957; Whiting 1957
He Shouldn't-a, Hadn't-a, Oughtn't-a Swang on Me   Mancini 1965; Mercer 1965
He Talks with His Fingers   Bryan 1921; Pollack 1921; Schwartz, Jean 1921
He Thinks, He Thinks   Burke 1933; Spina 1933
He Took Her Up, Up, Up, 'Way Up High   Bryan 1912
He Took His Girl in Bathing in the Summer Time   Dubin 1914
He Took It Away from Me   Turk 1921

He Tried to Make a Dollar   Cahn 1947; Styne 1947

He Used to Be a Farmer but He's a Big Town Slicker Now   Sterling 1919; Von Tilzer 1919

He Walks Across the Sky   Heyman 1944; Spina 1944

He Walks with Me   Romberg 1950

He Wanted to Go and He Went   Herbert 1920; Smith, Robert B. 1920

He Wants Someone to Call Him Papa, She Wants Someone to Call Her Ma   Gilbert 1913

He Wants to Get Into My Pantry   Mills 1947

He Was a Cowboy   Williams 1909

He Was a Dandy   Koehler 1936; McHugh 1936

He Was a Friend of Mine   Howard, Joseph E. 1915

He Was a Gentleman   Gorney 1935

He Was a Married Man   Smith, Harry B. 1900

He Was a Perfect Gentleman   Burke 1945; Van Heusen 1945

He Was a Roving Romeo   Jerome 1921; Schwartz, Jean 1921

He Was a Sailor   Jerome 1903; Schwartz, Jean 1903

He Was a Soldier Too   Herbert 1908

He Was a Wonderful Man   Cohan 1906

He Was All Right Here (He'll Be All Right There)   Eliscu 1943; Gorney 1943

He Was Her Man   Dixon 1935; Wrubel 1935

He Was My Partner   Oakland 1950

He Was the Last Rose of Summer   Hart Date Unknown; Rodgers Date Unknown

He Was Too Good to Me   Hart 1930; Rodgers 1930

He Wasn't Born in Araby but He's a Sheikin' Fool   Razaf 1923

He Went A-Hunting   Von Tilzer 1907

He Went in Like a Lion and Came Out Like a Lamb   Sterling 1919; Von Tilzer 1919

He Went That-a-Way She Went This-a-Way   Hoffman 1949

He Went to Work in the Morning, She Went to Work in the Night   Gilbert 1944; Oakland 1944

He Who   Adams 1963; Strouse 1963

He Who Gets Slapped   Schwartz, Arthur 1927

He Who Has Love   Hoffman 1953

He Who Loves   Bacharach 1968; David, Hal 1968

He Who Loves and Runs Away   Friml 1937; Kahn 1937

He Who'd Thrive Must Rise at Five   Herbert 1903; Smith, Harry B. 1903

He Will Always Carry You Through   Blane 1965; Martin 1965

He Will Forgive You   Robison 1957

He Will Tonight   Fields 1950

He Will Understand   Friml 1917; Harbach 1917

He Will Walk with Thee   Harburg 1971

He Won't Be Happy Till He Gets It   Herbert 1903

He Would Never Leave Me   Russell 1977

He Would Play the Piano   Silver 1918

He Wouldn't Dare   Duke 1963

He Writes a Song   Smith, Harry B. 1925

Head in the Stars   Eliscu 1962

Head Low   Robison 1929

Head Man   Buck 1940

Head on Her Shoulders, A   Loesser 1960

Head Over Heels   Kern 1918

Head Over Heels in Love   Gordon 1936; Hanley 1926; Revel 1936

Headin' for a Weddin'   Adamson 1933; Lane 1933

Headin' for a Weddin' in the Sky   Harbach 1947; Kern 1947

Headin' for Baltimore   Conrad 1925; Coslow 1925

Headin' for Harlem   Hanley 1927

Headin' for Heaven   Parish 1933; Pollack 1933

Headin' for Louisville   DeSylva 1925

Headin' for New Orleans   Lane 1951; Lerner, Alan Jay 1951

Headin' for the Bottom   Fain 1955

Headin' Home   Kahn 1923; Meyer 1923; Rose 1923; Washington 1935

Headless Horseman, The   DePaul 1949; Raye 1949

Headlines   Cahn 1979

Heads High   Brown, Lew 1938; Pollack 1938

Heads Up   Duke 1930; Harburg 1930

Heads Up, America   Cahn 1956

Health Food Man, The   Herbert 1903

Health, Harmony and Happiness   Robison 1949

Health to Noah   Friml 1917

Healthy, Normal American Boy, A   Adams 1960; Strouse 1960

Heap Love (An Indian Serenade)   Howard, Joseph E. 1905

Heap o' Misery   Arlen 1930; Koehler 1930

Hear Me   Eliscu 1928; Herbert 1900; Smith, Harry B. 1900

Hear My Plea   Stept 1952

Hear My Shout Bubilchka   Mills 1938

Hear My Song of Love (Serenade)   Herbert 1907; Smith, Harry B. 1907

Hear No Evil, See No Evil, Speak No Evil   Washington 1953

Hear O Israel   Gilbert 1931; Livingston, Jerry 1962

Hear that Band   Evans 1965; Livingston, Jay 1965

Hear the Coachman Crack His Whip   Herbert 1903; Smith, Harry B. 1903

Hear the Gypsies Playing   Harbach 1936; Romberg 1936

Hear the Trumpet Call   Romberg 1927; Smith, Harry B. 1927

Hear Those Drums   Drake 1954

Hear What My Heart Is Saying   Adamson 1935; Lane 1935

Hear Ye! Hear Ye!   Weill 1945

Heard a Mocking Bird Singing (In California)   Robison 1947

Heart and Soul   Carmichael 1938; Loesser 1938; Parish 1937

Heart Bowed Down, The   Johnson, Howard 1939

Heart Breaking Sal   Johnson, James P. 1927

Heart for Sale, A   Kern 1920

Heart Full of Love, A   Hoffman 1946; Livingston, Jerry 1946

Heart Fund Valentine   Willson 1958

Heart in Hand   Lawrence 1951

Heart Is a Lonely Hunter, The   Fain 1957; Webster 1957

Heart Is Free, The   Johnson, Howard 1927

Heart Is Quicker than the Eye, The   Hart 1936; Rodgers 1936

Heart Like the Ocean, A   Mills 1935

Heart Must Learn to Cry, A   Webster 1964

Heart o' Mine   Rose 1929

Heart o' the Hills   Lewis 1919; Ruby 1919; Young, Joe 1919

Heart of a Drum   Evans 1958; Livingston, Jay 1958

Heart of a Fool, The   David, Hal 1954

Heart of a Girl, The   Adams 1954; Strouse 1954

Heart of a Rose   Atteridge 1915; Friml 1915

Heart of a Sailor, The   David, Mack 1957; Livingston, Jerry 1957

Heart of a Woman, The   Adams 1974; Strouse 1974

Heart of Broadway   Edwards 1929

Heart of Harlem   Ellington 1945; Loesser 1937

Heart of Heaven   Bryan 1930; Dubin 1930

Heart of Humanity   Turk 1919

Heart of Kentucky   Johnson, Howard 1927

Heart of Mine   Freed, Ralph 1939; Friml 1928; Heyman 1938; Smith, Harry B. 1908; Washington 1962

Heart of Paddy Whack, The   Brennan 1914

Heart of Paris (I Left My Heart in the Heart of Montmartre)   Parish 1955

Heart of Stone   Waller 1931

Heart of the Ghetto   Norworth 1925

Heart of the Ukraine   Gilbert 1937

Heart of Virginia   Motzan 1922

Heart O'Mine (Merry Wives of Gotham)   Herbert 1924

Heart Strings (inst.)   Schwartz, Jean 1930

Heart that Once Belonged to Me Belongs to Someone Else, The   Waller 1925

Heart to Heart   Romberg 1916

Heart to Heart Talk with My Heart   Howard, Joseph E. 1944

Heart to Let, A   Howard, Joseph E. 1906, 1907; Razaf 1926

Heart You Break May Be Your Own, The   Hoffman 1957

Heartache   Hoffman 1931

Heartache High School, U.S.A.   Freed, Ralph 1964

Heartaches   Norworth 1919

Heartaches and Dreams   Kahn 1927

Heartbreak   Brooks 1946

Heartbreak Avenue   Merrill 1952

Heartbreak of Love   Bacharach 1987

Heart-Breaker   Sigman 1952

Heart-Breakers   Bryan 1919, 1920; Schwartz, Jean 1919, 1920

Heartbroken and Lonely   Conrad 1928; Coslow 1928

Heartease   Bryan Date Unknown; Fisher Date Unknown

Heartless   Washington 1945

Heartless Heart   David, Hal 1953

Heartless Human   Robison 1961

Hearts Are Never Blue in Blue Kalua   Bryan 1938

Hearts Are Trumps   Herbert 1911

Hearts in Harmony   Rainger 1936; Robin 1936

Hearts in Tune   Blake 1923; Sissle 1923

Hearts Win, You Lose   Sterling 1904

Heart-Sickness Blues   Coslow 1919

Heat Is On, The   Leigh 1985; Washington 1953

Heat It Up   Rainger 1935; Robin 1935

Heat of a Rose   Coots 1925

Heat Wave   Berlin 1933

Heathen   Dietz 1944; Duke 1944

Heathen Lullaby   Brown, Nacio Herb 1922

Heather on the Hill, The   Lerner, Alan Jay 1947; Loewe 1947

Heave Ho! My Lads, Heave Ho!   Lawrence 1946

Heave-Ho, Let the Wind Blow   Arlen 1944; Harburg 1944

Heaven   Caesar 1940; Ellington 1968

Heaven Be Praised   Magidson 1954; Oakland 1954

Heaven Came Down to Earth (Last Night)   Stept 1958

Heaven Can Wait   De Lange 1939; Van Heusen 1939

Heaven Christened Dixie Land   Egan 1920; Whiting 1920

Heaven for Two   DePaul 1941; Raye 1941

Heaven Help a Sailor on a Night Like This   Coslow 1937

Heaven Help You (When You Fall in Love)   Fain 1951; Webster 1951

Heaven Helps Him, Who Helps Himself   Cahn 1969; Van Heusen 1969

Heaven in My Arms (Music in My Heart)   Hammerstein 1939; Kern 1939

Heaven Is a Place Called Home   Magidson 1945; Wrubel 1945

Heaven Is Where You Are   Hoffman 1950

Heaven Knows   Merrill 1958

Heaven Measured You for Me   Harbach 1914

Heaven O'Clock   Magidson 1938; Wrubel 1938

Heaven on a Hilltop   Lawrence 1940

Heaven on Earth   Akst 1934; Dietz 1926; Gershwin, George 1926; Gershwin, Ira 1926; Gorney 1948; Hoffman 1931; Turk 1934

Heaven Only Knows   Adamson 1932; Coots 1932; Revel 1959; Wrubel 1932

Heaven Sent   Lerner, Sammy 1948

Heaven Sent Wonderful You   Blake 1937

Heaven Smiles on Tepancingo   Loesser 1969

Heaven Was Never Like This   David, Mack 1954

Heaven Watch the Philipines   Berlin 1945

Heaven Will Come Down to You   Hanley 1917

Heaven-Hop, The   Porter 1928

Heavenly   Bacharach 1959

Heavenly Day   Gershwin, Ira 1946; Schwartz, Arthur 1946

Heavenly Days   Evans 1953; Livingston, Jay 1953

Heavenly Harvest   David, Hal 1951

Heavenly, Isn't It   Revel 1942

Heavenly Lover   David, Hal 1959

Heavenly Music   Coslow 1943

Heavenly Night   Brown, Nacio Herb 1931; Eliscu 1931

Heavenly Party   Fields 1938; Kern 1938

Heavens Declare!, The   Johnson, J. Rosamond 1944

Heaven's Just a Kiss Away   Revel 1959

Heavens to Betsy   Johnston 1948

Heav'n Heav'n   Johnson, Howard 1939

Heavy Bomber Song, The   Washington 1951; Young, Victor 1951

Heavy, Heavy, Mah Po'r Heart   Akst 1930; Clarke 1930

Heavy Sugar   Razaf 1929; Waller 1929

Hebrew Chant (inst.)   Young, Victor 1948

Hector   Norworth 1917

Hector the Humble Bumble Bee   Burke 1947; Van Heusen 1947

Hector, the Stowaway Pup   Sherman 1964

He'd Have to Answer the Bell   Brown, Lew 1915

He'd Have to Get Under, Get Out and Get Under (To Fix His Automobile)   Clarke 1913; Leslie 1913

He'd Kiss Her From London to Dover   Bryan 1914; Fisher 1914

He'd Push It Along   Clarke 1914; Leslie 1914

Hedge Rose   Johnson, Howard 1939

Hee-Bee Jee-Bees   Gorney 1924

Heebie Jeebie Blues   Clarke 1924; Johnston 1924; Meyer 1924; Turk 1924

Heebie Jeebie River, The   Evans 1973; Livingston, Jay 1973

Hee-Cup Song   Johnson, Howard 1928

Hee-Haw   Ager 1915

Hee-Hoo Song (Hip de Minnega Honnega Rock de Bumpty la Hee-Hoo), The   Revel 1948

Heel, The   Robison 1954

Heel and Toe   Caesar 1929

Heel and Toe Polka   Rainger 1938; Robin 1938

Heel Beat   Brown, Lew 1928; DeSylva 1928; Henderson 1928

Heffalumps and Woozles   Sherman 1968

Heidi   Cahn 1976; Lane 1976; Leigh 1955

Heidi Doody   Coots 1955

Heigh Ho — Howdy Do   Bergman 1961

Heigh Ho for Mother (Heigh Ho for a Husband)   Blane 1968; Martin 1968

Heigh Ho, the Gang's All Here   Adamson 1931; Lane 1931, 1933

Heigh-ho, Ev'rybody, Heigh-ho   Woods 1929

Heigh-Ho, Lackaday   Hart 1925; Rodgers 1925

Heigh-Ho the Merry-O   Adamson 1938; McHugh 1938

Heigh-Ho the Radio   Rainger 1936; Robin 1936

Heilige Sekele   Motzan 1937

Heinie   Ahlert 1928; Turk 1928

Heinz Is Pickled Again   Williams 1909

Heir to the Throne   Spina 1959

Helen Maria   Kahn 1924

Helen of Troy   Hoffman 1951

Helen of Troy, New York   Hanley 1922; Kalmar 1923; Ruby 1923

Helfried   Friml Date Unknown

He'll Always Be One of Those Guys   Yellen 1923

Hell and High Water   Coslow 1933, 1935; Johnston 1933

He'll Be There!   Kern 1904

Hell Hath No Fury   Cahn 1956

He'll Have to Cross the Atlantic to Get to the Pacific   Cahn 1945; Styne 1945

He'll Make Some Girl a Wonderful Husband   Russell 1946

Hell of a Hole, A   Gershwin, George 1933; Gershwin, Ira 1933

Hello   Arlen 1966; Cahn 1980; DePaul 1980; Hart 1926, 1934; Rodgers 1926, 1934; Russell 1956

Hello Again   Davis 1958; Spina 1947

Hello, Aloha, Hello!   Johnson, Howard 1917; Meyer 1917

Hello, Aloha, How Are You   Baer 1926; Gilbert 1926

Hello and Goodbye   Bergman 1976

Hello Are You There, Hello   Stept 1926

Hello Atlanta Town   Waller 1924

Hello Baby   Whiting 1926

Hello Beautiful!   Donaldson 1931

Hello, Bluebird   Friend 1926

Hello Boys, I'm Back Again   Von Tilzer 1915

Hello, Broadway   Cohan 1914

Hello Cello   Williams 1919

Hello Central, Give Me No Man's Land   Lewis 1918; Schwartz, Jean 1918; Young, Joe 1918

Hello Cupid, Send Me a Fellow   Atteridge 1912

Hello Cutie   Friend 1927

Hello Darlin'   De Lange 1943

Hello Dere   Davis 1962

Hello Dynamite   Stept 1934

Hello, Everybody   Atteridge 1919; Carroll 1919

Hello France   Davis 1917

Hello, Frisco, I Called You Up To Say Hello   Buck 1915

Hello Girlie   Bryan 1917; Howard, Joseph E. 1918

Hello, Good Morning   Gershwin, George 1931; Gershwin, Ira 1931

Hello! Goodbye   Harbach 1923

Hello Gorgeous   Donaldson 1932

Hello, Hawaii, How Are You   Kalmar 1915; Leslie 1915; Schwartz, Jean 1915

Hello, Hazel   Styne 1953

Hello Heaven! Hello Love!   Donaldson 1930

Hello, Hello   Atteridge 1913; Howard, Joseph E. 1911; Smith, Harry B. 1923

Hello, Hello, Hello   Berlin 1918; Buck 1922; Martin 1951

Hello! Hello! Hello! Chera Bochcha   Akst 1921; Lewis 1921

Hello, Hello, Sandy   Brown, Nacio Herb 1926; Freed, Arthur 1926

Hello, Hello, Telephone Girlie   Harbach 1925; Youmans 1925

Hello, Hello There   Comden and Green 1956; Styne 1956

Hello Lemonade   Kalmar 1919; Leslie 1919

Hello Little Bluebirds Have Flown, The   Atteridge 1925

Hello, Little Girl   Sondheim 1987

Hello, Little Miss U.S.A.   Atteridge 1914

Hello, Ma Baby   Howard, Joseph E. 1899; Sterling 1899

Hello, Ma! I Done It Again   Rainger 1941; Robin 1941

Hello, Ma Lulu   Johnson, J. Rosamond 1904

Hello Melody, Goodbye Jazz   Edwards 1929

Hello, Mi Amigo   Eliscu 1943; Gorney 1943

Hello, Miss Chapel Street   Porter 1911

Hello Miss Knickerbocker   Atteridge 1921

Hello! Miss Liberty   Fisher 1908

Hello, Miss Tango!   Atteridge 1917; Romberg 1917

Hello Mister Stein   Sterling 1907; Von Tilzer 1907

Hello, Mom   Leigh 1976; Loesser 1943; Styne 1976

Hello Montreal   Dixon 1928; Rose 1928; Warren 1928

Hello Moon   Buck 1920

Hello, Mr. Moon Man   Atteridge 1910

Hello, Must Do a Show, Goodbye!   Duke 1963

Hello, My Darling   Loesser 1939

Hello My Dearie   Buck 1917

Hello, My Lover, Goodbye   Heyman 1931

Hello My Ragtime Gal   Sterling 1899

Hello, New Year, Hello   Razaf 1947

Hello New York   Robin 1955; Styne 1955

Hello Out There, Hello   Mercer 1952

Hello Paris   Johnson, J. Rosamond 1911

Hello Red, You're Lookin' Blue   Sigman 1941

Hello Springtime   Martin 1958

Hello Stranger Just Stick Around   Leslie 1911

Hello Summer, Where You Been All Winter   Caesar 1953

Hello Swanee Hello   Coslow 1926

Hello, Sweetheart, Hello (I Just Called to Say Goodnight)   Sissle 1932

Hello Timmie Rogers   Carmichael 1953

Hello to the Blues   Lawrence 1956

Hello 'Tucky   DeSylva 1925; Hanley 1925

Hello Virginia   Friend 1920

Hello, Wisconsin, Won't You Find My Yonnie Yonson   Kalmar 1917; Leslie 1917; Ruby 1917

Hello Yankee Doodle   Hanley 1927

Hello, Young Lovers   Hammerstein 1951; Rodgers 1951

Hello, Yourself   Robin 1928

Hellraker's Dance (inst.), The   Lane 1965

Hell's Kitchen   Spina 1977

Hell's Loose   Freed, Arthur 1930

Helluva Group, A   Merrill 1964; Styne 1964

Hellzapoppin'   DePaul 1941; Fain 1938; Leigh 1976; Raye 1941; Styne 1976

Hellzapoppin Polka, The   Lane 1945

Help   Fain 1960

Help Help   Coslow 1930

Help, Help, Help, I'm Falling in Love   Von Tilzer 1910

Help, Help, Help, I'm Sinking in a Beautiful Ocean of Love   Von Tilzer 1917

Help Me   DePaul 1958; Raye 1958

Help Me to Help My Neighbor   Berlin 1947

Help Stamp Out Dirt   Strouse 1975

Help the Drive   Romberg 1927

Help Us Tonight   Eliscu 1929; Rose 1929; Youmans 1929

Help Wanted — Male   Bullock 1938; Spina 1938

Help Yourself to Happiness   Gordon 1931; Revel 1931; Young, Victor 1930

Helping Our Friends   Wrubel 1959

(I Feel So) Helpless   Spina 1958; Warren 1963

He-Man, The   DeSylva 1925; Gershwin, George 1925; Gershwin, Ira 1925; Robin 1928

Hen and the Cow (It's Only a Dream of the Past), The   Bryan 1920; Caesar 1920; Meyer 1920

Hen and Weather Vane, The   Herbert 1908; Smith, Harry B. 1908

Hence It Don't Make Sense   Porter 1944

Henceforth I'll Call on Friday   Stept 1927
Henny Klein   Jerome 1905; Schwartz, Jean 1905
Henry   Kern 1928; Rome 1969
Henry Leek   Harburg 1967; Styne 1967
Henry Oh Henry Your Ma Wants You   Kahn 1912
Henry Street   Merrill 1964; Styne 1964
Henry Sweet Henry   Merrill 1967
Hep Cat, The   Blake 1940; Razaf 1940
Hep Cat's Ball   Robison 1940
Hep Cats Done Gone High Hat   Blake 1958
Hep, Hep, Hep   Howard, Joseph E. 1918
Hep, Hot and Solid Sweet   Henderson 1943; Yellen 1943
Her Beaus Are Only Rainbows   Bryan 1926; Meyer 1926
Her Bodyguard   Coslow 1933, 1935; Johnston 1933
Her Easter Bonnet   Young, Victor 1934
Her Eyes Are Blue for Dear Old Yale   Howard, Joseph E. 1909
Her Face   Merrill 1961
Her First Roman   Drake 1968
Her Gentleman Friend   Cohan 1898
Her Hair Is Black as Licorice   Hart 1928; Rodgers 1928
Her Heart Was in Her Work   Porter 1953
Her Innocent Pretension Is a Veil of Invention   Dietz 1952
Her Irish Eyes of Blue   Jerome 1930; Schwartz, Jean 1930
Her Lips Were Like Velvet   Hoffman 1958
Her Love Is Always the Same   Friml 1922; Harbach 1922
Her Lover   Russell 1948, 1964
Her Majesty the Queen   David, Mack 1958; Livingston, Jerry 1958
Her Master's Voice   Robin 1936
Her Name Is Joanna   David, Hal 1962
Her Name Is Mary Donohue   Jerome 1909; Schwartz, Jean 1909
Her Name Was Nina   Davis 1948; Silver 1948
Her Petticoat Was Showing   Ruby 1967
Her Portrait   Smith, Harry B. 1906
Her Waltz   Johnston 1927
Herby the Mer-man   Freed, Ralph 1958
Here Again, Gone Again Love Affair   Magidson 1932; Washington 1932; Wrubel 1932
Here Am I   Hammerstein 1929; Kern 1929
Here Am I Broken-Hearted   Brown, Lew 1927; DeSylva 1927; Henderson 1927
Here Am I Doing It   Gordon 1938; Revel 1938
Here Am I, Where Are You   Conrad 1929
Here and There   Duke 1963
Here Are My Arms   Livingston, Jerry 1960
Here Come the Blues   DePaul 1955; Oakland 1960; Raye 1955
Here Come the British   Mercer 1934
Here Come the Clowns   Coots 1940; Egan 1940
Here Come the Dreamers   Martin 1962
Here Come the Soldiers   Cohan 1919
Here Come the Springtime (Ho-Dalee, Hi-Dalee, Hay)   Willson 1951
Here Come the Stars of Tomorrow   Coots 1956
Here Come the Waiters   Hanley 1931
Here Come the Waves   Arlen 1944; Mercer 1944
Here Come the Yanks   Buck 1918; DePaul 1958; Raye 1958
Here Come Those Lies Again   David, Mack 1976
Here Comes a Blackbird   Burke 1954
Here Comes Another Song about Texas (Pass the Cotton, Pass the Cotton)   Cahn 1958; Van Heusen 1958
Here Comes Baby Now   Russell 1948
Here Comes Company   Lawrence 1934; Young, Joe 1934

(Lookie-Lookie-Lookie) Here Comes Cookie   Gordon 1935
Here Comes Emily Brown   Conrad 1930
Here Comes Everything   Johnson, Howard 1928
Here Comes Fatima with Her Ta-Ra-Boom Dee-Ay   Brown, Lew 1926; Friend 1926
Here Comes Heaven Again   Adamson 1945; McHugh 1945
Here Comes Katrinka   Loesser 1942; Styne 1942
Here Comes Love   Stept 1936
Here Comes Love Again   Ruby 1951
Here Comes Malinda   Akst 1926; Davis 1926
Here Comes My Baby   McHugh 1927; Mills 1927
Here Comes My Ball and Chain   Coots 1928; Robin 1929; Whiting 1929
Here Comes My Blackbird   Fields 1928; McHugh 1928
Here Comes My Bride   Oakland 1981; Webster 1981
Here Comes My Daddy Now   Gilbert 1912
Here Comes My Minstrel Man   Goetz 1912
Here Comes Never   Styne 1980
Here Comes Nixon   Coots 1960
Here Comes Stanley   Styne 1977
Here Comes Talullah   Akst 1950; Davis 1950
Here Comes that Moon Again   Caesar 1942
Here Comes the Banana Man   Fain 1924
Here Comes the Bandwagon   Porter 1929
Here Comes the Birdie   Smith, Harry B. 1918
Here Comes the Bride   Goetz 1919; Gorney 1926; Meyer 1919
Here Comes the Bride (The Girl Who Stole My Lovin' Man Away)   Brown, Lew 1912
Here Comes the Cheer Parade   Parish 1932
Here Comes the Coast Guard   Brown, Lew 1943
Here Comes the Navy   Brown, Lew 1943; Cahn 1953; Fain 1953
Here Comes the Night   Loesser 1939
Here Comes the Prince of Wales   Schwartz, Arthur 1927
Here Comes the Queen   Willson 1956
Here Comes the Rain   David, Hal 1976
Here Comes the Sandman   Dubin 1937; Warren 1937
Here Comes the Show Boat   Rose 1929
Here Comes the Spring   Duke 1949
Here Comes the Summertime   Coots 1968
Here Comes the Sun   Comden and Green 1964; Freed, Arthur 1930; Woods 1930
Here Comes the Sunshine, There Goes the Rain   Kahal 1929; Snyder 1929
Here Comes Tomorrow (Gimme Another Kiss Goodnight) (Actman, Irving)   Loesser 1937
Here Ends the Rainbow (I Found My Love)   Burke 1951
Here Goes   Arlen 1934; Koehler 1934
Here Goes Nothing   Arlen 1959
Here He Is   Hart 1937; Rodgers 1937
Here I Am   Bacharach 1965; Brown, Lew 1926; David, Hal 1965; DeSylva 1926; Henderson 1926; Merrill 1967; Rose 1927
Here I Am Again   Stept 1936
Here I Am Doing It   Gordon 1938; Revel 1938
Here I Am in the Army and I Don't Look Good in Brown   Coots 1941; Egan 1941
Here I Go Again   Coleman 1966; Revel 1945
Here I'll Stay   Lerner, Alan Jay 1948; Weill 1948
Here in My Arms   Hart 1925, 1926; Rodgers 1925, 1926
Here in Pleasure's Favorite Court   Herbert 1903; Smith, Harry B. 1903
Here in Tahiti We Make Love   Freed, Arthur 1950; Warren 1950

Here in the Dark   Hammerstein 1927; Harbach 1927
Here in the Moonlight on the Fence   Edwards 1907
Here in the Playbill   Adams 1978; Strouse 1978
Here Is a Sword   Schwartz, Arthur 1930
Here Is My Heart   Rainger 1934; Robin 1934; Spina 1932
Here Is My Heart for Christmas   Baer 1964
Here Is the Tunic of a Soldier   Smith, Harry B. 1911
Here It Comes   Hammerstein 1934; Kern 1934
Here It Is   Brown, Lew 1931; Henderson 1931
Here It Is, Come and Get It   Mills 1954
Here It Is Daddy (No Hand Has Touched It but Mine)   Mills 1924
Here Lies Love   Rainger 1932, 1933; Robin 1932, 1933
Here Merrily Ride the Bandit Tribe (When Day's Honest Work Is Done)   Herbert 1897; Smith, Harry B. 1897
Here on the Fence at Doolittle College   Edwards 1907
Here or There As Long As I'm with You   Davis 1926
Here Pidgie Pidgie   Hoffman 1951
Here Pretty Kitty   Livingston, Jerry 1963
Here She Comes   Drake 1954
Here She Comes (Musical Entrance — Tilly/All Set! Let's Go)   Hart 1928; Rodgers 1928
Here She Comes Now (East River Hoedown)   Comden and Green 1951; Styne 1951
Here She Is   Burke 1961
Here, Steward   Gershwin, Ira 1921; Youmans 1921
Here They Are   Romberg 1928
Here 'Tis   Blake 1932; Sissle 1932
Here Today, Gone Tomorrow   Lewis 1934; Meyer 1934
Here We Are   Berlin 1930; Hammerstein 1930; Kahn 1929; Martin 1952; Romberg 1930; Warren 1929
Here We Are - In Heaven Alone   Ahlert 1938; Young, Joe 1938
Here We Are Again   Drake 1951; Merrill 1957; Rodgers 1965; Sondheim 1965
Here We Are Face to Face Again   Russell 1960
Here We Are in Love   Oakland 1931
Here We Are Scrubbing   Goetz 1911
Here We Are Studying History   Loesser 1941; Styne 1941
Here We Are Together Again (Opening Act I)   Hammerstein 1925; Harbach 1925; Kern 1925
Here We Come   Drake 1954
Here We Go   Brooks 1959
Here Where There Is Love   Bacharach 1965; David, Hal 1965
Here Ye! Hear Ye!   Gershwin, Ira 1945
Here You Are   Akst 1930; Clarke 1930; Ellington 1966; Evans 1954; Livingston, Jay 1954; Rainger 1934, 1942; Robin 1934, 1942
Hereafter   Porter 1944
Heredity   Oakland 1960
Here's a Bale of Cotton for You   Atteridge 1915; Carroll 1915; Romberg 1915
Here's a Cheer for Dera Old Ciro's   Porter 1944
Here's a Day to Be Happy   Adamson 1930; Youmans 1930
Here's a Hand   Hart 1942; Rodgers 1942
Here's a Heart   Loesser 1939; Young, Victor 1939
Here's a Kiss   Hart 1925; Rodgers 1925
Here's a Kiss for Cinderella   Gershwin, George 1931; Gershwin, Ira 1931
Here's a Rose for You   Dubin 1914
Here's a Salute to the Army   Cahn 1967
Here's a Song Everyone Can Sing   Willson 1956
Here's a Toast to the Coast Guard   Lawrence 1942
Here's an Invitation   Brooks 1957
Here's Charlie   Davis 1954

Here's Cheers!   Warren 1970
Here's Hopin'   Davis 1926
Here's Hoping   Adamson 1932; Coleman 1963; Coots 1932; Leigh 1963
Here's How   Herbert 1914; Romberg 1927
Here's Howe   Caesar 1928
Here's Looking at You   Arlen 1936; Davis 1934; Fain 1968; Hanley 1934; Harburg 1936; Heyman 1934; Kahal 1968; Leigh 1985
Here's Love   Willson 1963
Here's Love in Your Eye   Rainger 1936; Robin 1936
Here's Martin the Groom   Hart 1943; Rodgers 1943
Here's My Hand — You're in My Heart Until We Meet Again   Hanley 1930
Here's One Who Wouldn't   Brown, Lew 1928; DeSylva 1928; Henderson 1928
Here's that Heart Again   Bullock 1938; Pollack 1938
Here's That Party Now, In Person   Ager 1928; Yellen 1928
Here's That Rainy Day   Burke 1953; Van Heusen 1953
Here's the Key to My Heart   Clare 1934; Whiting 1934
Here's the Kind of Advice   Brooks 1958
Here's to Aunt Octavia   Coslow 1930
Here's to Dear Old Us   Fain 1955
Here's to Health, Here's to Wealth (Here Is Health)   Herbert 1914
Here's to J. Spencer Gray   Coots 1951
Here's to Love   Ahlert 1930; Evans 1949; Freed, Ralph 1939; Lane 1939; Livingston, Jay 1948; Magidson 1934; Turk 1930; Wrubel 1934
Here's to My Comrades and You   Herbert 1908
Here's to My Lady   Bloom 1951; Mercer 1951
Here's to Night   Eliscu 1932
Here's to Ninety-Nine (Birthday Toast)   Leslie 1953
Here's to Panama Hattie   Porter 1940
Here's to Romance   Conrad 1935; Magidson 1935
Here's to the Bridegroom   Drake 1954
Here's to the Builder   Loesser 1935
Here's to the Flag! Keep It Flying Over Her, Over There, Everywhere   Coots 1942
Here's to the Folks Back Home   Hanley 1930
Here's to the Girl of My Heart   Donaldson 1928; Kahn 1928
Here's to the Girls   Freed, Arthur 1946
Here's to the I.B.M.   Kalmar 1941; Ruby 1941
Here's to the Ladies   Brooks 1950; Freed, Ralph 1946; Webster 1960
Here's to the Land We Love, Boys!   Herbert 1914
Here's to the Old Folks at Home   Sterling 1902
Here's to the Two of You   Harbach 1917
Here's to Tomorrow   Pollack 1943
Here's to Us   Coleman 1962; Koehler 1950; Leigh 1962; Stept 1950
Here's to You   Heyman 1934; Romberg 1915; Turk 1933
Here's to Your Illusions   Fain 1951; Harburg 1951
Here's to Your Last Girl   Howard, Joseph E. 1909
Here's What I'm Here For   Arlen 1954; Gershwin, Ira 1954
Here's Where I Came In   Coleman 1959; Leigh 1959
Here's Where the Action Is   Leigh 1965
Here's Your Chance   Young, Joe 1932
Herman   Jerome 1907; Schwartz, Jean 1907
Herman, Let's Dance That Beautiful Waltz   Berlin 1910; Snyder 1910
Herman the Mouse   David, Hal 1952
Herman's Paree, The   Evans 1958; Livingston, Jay 1958
Hermit in the Heart of Town   Coots 1949
Hermits, The   Hart 1922, 1923; Rodgers 1922, 1925

Hero, A   Rome 1940
Hero Ballet (inst.)   Arlen 1937
Hero Is Coming, A   Sondheim 1964
Hero of Yesterday   Freed, Ralph 1940; Styne 1940
Heroes in the Fall   Rodgers 1939
Heroes of Peace   Caesar 1937
He's a Bad Man   Fain 1935; Kahal 1935
He's a Big, Big Man from the South with a Big Cigar in His
   Mouth   Bloom 1929; Woods 1929
He's a Colonel from Kentucky   Baer 1934
He's a Cute Brute (A Gentleman and a Scholar)   Revel 1933
He's a Cute Little Brute (A Gentleman and a
   Scholar)   Gordon 1933; Revel 1933
He's a Dear Old Pet   Jerome 1912; Schwartz, Jean 1912
He's a Demon, He's a Devil, He's a Doll   Raye 1950; Spina
   1950
He's a Devil in His Own Home Town   Berlin 1914; Clarke
   1914; Leslie 1914
He's a Devil on Saturday Night   Donaldson 1917
He's a Fallen Angel   Blane 1968; Martin 1968
He's a Fox Hunting Polo Playing Son of a British
   Nobleman   Fain 1935; Kahal 1935
He's a Genius   Harburg 1967; Styne 1967
He's a Good Man to Have Around   Ager 1929; Yellen 1929
He's a Hero   Cahn 1946; Styne 1946
He's a Humdinger   Hoffman 1934
He's a Jolly Good Fellow   Strouse 2000
He's a Ladies Man   Brown, Lew 1927; DeSylva 1927;
   Henderson 1927
He's a Man's Man   Brown, Lew 1929; DeSylva 1929;
   Henderson 1929
He's a Mean Man   Alter 1930
He's a No Good-a No More   Clarke 1917; Monaco 1917
He's a Panic   Akst 1921; Lewis 1921; Young, Joe 1921
He's a Rag Picker   Berlin 1914
He's a Regular Guy   Fisher 1922; Rose 1922
He's a Right Guy   Porter 1943
He's a Son of the South   Razaf 1932
He's a V.I.P.   Comden and Green 1960; Styne 1960
He's a Wild Man (When It Comes to Playing Jazz)   Friend
   1923; Schwartz, Jean 1923
He's a Winner (Sporting Life/Reporters' Opening)   Hart
   1926; Rodgers 1926
He's Always Hanging Around   Blake 1919; Sissle 1919
He's Awfully Fond of My Husband   Von Tilzer 1910
He's Back in Town   Duke 1955
He's Coming Back   Kalmar 1911; Snyder 1911
He's Coming Home   Romberg 1916
He's Dead but He Won't Lie Down   Carmichael 1950;
   Mercer 1950
He's Doing His Bit for the Girls   Von Tilzer 1917
He's Gay   Leigh 1977
He's Getting Too Darn Big for a One-Horse Town   Berlin
   1916
He's Good Enough for Me   Edwards 1930
He's Good for Me   Coleman 1973; Fields 1973
He's Good for Nothing but Me   Dietz 1944; Duke 1944
He's Got a Secret Weapon   Adamson 1943; McHugh 1943
He's Got Everything To Live For (Tiene De Todo en la
   Vida)   Brooks 1966
He's Got Larceny in His Heart   Merrill 1964; Styne 1964
He's Got Those Big Blue Eyes Like You, Daddy Mine   Dubin
   1918
He's Got Time   Merrill 1956
He's Here   Leigh 1967

He's in the Calaboose Now   Blake 1958
He's Just an Old Guy with Whiskers   Johnson, Howard 1929
He's Just Crazy for Me   Robin 1952; Warren 1952
He's Just Like You   Brown, Lew 1917
He's Just My Ideal   Brennan 1929
He's Just that Kind of a Guy   Parish 1922
He's Lyin'   David, Mack 1979
He's Mah Dancing Man   Howard, Joseph E. 1913
He's Me Pal   Edwards 1905
He's Mine   Caesar 1928; Johnson, Howard 1933
He's Mine! All Mine!   Johnson, J. Rosamond 1946
He's Mine and I Love Him   Adamson Date Unknown;
   Warren Date Unknown
He's More to Be Pitied Than Laughed At   Sterling 1899
He's My Cousin, If She's Your Niece   Bryan 1914
He's My Friend   Willson 1964
He's My Guy   Adams 1993; DePaul 1942, 1943; Raye 1942,
   1943
He's My Uncle   Pollack 1940
He's No Good   Coleman 1996
He's Not an Aristocrat   Ruby 1943
He's Not Himself   Gershwin, George 1932; Gershwin, Ira
   1932
He's not Worth Your Tears   Dixon 1930; Rose 1930; Warren
   1930
He's Off His Noodle 'bout the Cutest Little Gal   Gilbert
   1914
He's on a Boat that Sails Last Wednesday (He's Coming
   Home)   Brown, Lew 1913
He's Only Wonderful   Fain 1951; Harburg 1951
He's Oversexed   Gershwin, George 1932; Gershwin, Ira
   1932
He's Ravin', Let Him Rave   Cohan 1903
He's So Good   Buck 1913
He's So Good to Me   Berlin 1913
He's So Unusual   Silver 1929
He's Starting to Get to Me   Cahn 1959; Van Heusen 1959
He's Stuck in the Chimney Again   Coleman 1966
He's That Kind of Pal   Ager 1930; Yellen 1930
He's the Champion of Them All, Little Maxie
   Rosenthal   Howard, Joseph E. 1909
He's the Hottest Man in Town   Gorney 1924
He's the Kind of a Man that You Like (If You Like that Kind
   of a Man)   Lewis 1924; Snyder 1924; Young, Joe 1924
He's the Last Word   Donaldson 1927; Kahn 1927
He's the Wonder of Them All   Goetz 1911
He's Well Worth Waiting For   Von Tilzer 1918
He's Worth His Weight in Gold   Bryan 1928
He's Younger Than I Am   Drake 1994
Hesitate Me Around, Bill   Jerome 1914
Hesitation   Herbert 1914
Hey   Comden and Green 1967; Styne 1967
Hey Babe Hey   Porter 1936
Hey, Boy!   Cahn 1980; Strouse 1980
Hey Bub! Let's Have a Ball   Gordon 1944; Monaco 1944
Hey, Daddy - Go Home   Coleman 1996
Hey, Did You Know?   Coleman 1984
Hey, Eula   Cahn 1958
Hey Fellas Let's Talk   Comden and Green 1961; Styne 1961
Hey Feller   Hammerstein 1927; Kern 1927
Hey, Fifi!   Sherman 1959
Hey for the Merry Greenwood   Smith, Harry B. 1891
Hey for the Tartan   Warren Date Unknown
Hey, Gang   Drake 1956
Hey Georgio   Brooks 1958

Hey Girlie   Rodgers 1970

Hey, Good Lookin'   Loesser 1939; Porter 1943

Hey, Granny   Cahn 1980; Strouse 1980

Hey! Hey!   Hart 1926; Rodgers 1926

Hey! Hey! And Hee! Hee! (I'm Charleston Crazy)   Mills 1924

Hey, Hey, Fever   Gordon 1925

Hey, Hey, Hazel   Egan 1923; Kahn 1923

Hey! Hey! Hey! Hey! Your Cares Away   Johnson, James P. 1936

Hey! Hey! Let 'er Go!   DeSylva 1924; Gershwin, George 1924

Hey, Jealous Lover   Cahn 1956

Hey Jimmy, Joe, John, Jack   Evans 1961; Livingston, Jay 1961

Hey, Joe   Adams 1984; Revel 1946; Strouse 1984

Hey, Jose (Que Sera)   Evans 1946, 1966; Livingston, Jay 1946, 1966

Hey Junior   Styne 1940

Hey Little Birdie   Silver 1958

Hey, Little Girl   Young, Joe 1962

Hey Look at Me   Strouse 1980

Hey, Look Me Over   Coleman 1960; Leigh 1960

Hey Look, No Crying   Styne 1982

Hey, Madame   Evans 1958; Livingston, Jay 1958

Hey, Marty   Warren 1955

Hey Paisan   Davis 1948; Silver 1948

Hey Pop, Buy Me Another Bond!   Rome 1945

Hey, Punchinello   Evans 1954; Livingston, Jay 1954

Hey Rookie   Eliscu 1944; Gorney 1944

Hey Rube   Ager 1928; Schwartz, Jean 1908; Williams 1908; Yellen 1928

Hey Sailor   Fain 1934; Kahal 1934

Hey Sexy   Porter 1956

Hey, Sport   Raye 1959

Hey There   Coleman 1977

Hey There, May There   Cohan 1903

Hey, What Did the Bluejay Say   Koehler 1936; McHugh 1936

Hey, What's Your Name   Cahn 1945; Styne 1945

Hey, Why Not!   Merrill 1972; Styne 1972

Hey Wollyo (inst.)   Revel 1946

Hey You in the Looking Glass   Silver 1950

Hey, You with the Crazy Eyes   Cahn 1960; Van Heusen 1960

Hey Young Fella   Adamson 1933; Fields 1932; Lane 1933; McHugh 1932

Hey Young Fella Close Your Old Umbrella   Fields 1933; McHugh 1933

Hey, Yvette!   Sherman 1974

Hey Zeke! Your Country's Callin'   Hoffman 1942; Livingston, Jerry 1942

Hey-O   Blane 1969

Hi De Hi Ho in Harlem   Waller 1943

Hi, Good Lookin'   Raye 1944

Hi, Ho the Hoe-Down Way   Fain 1941

Hi, Ho, the Merrio (Inst.)   Gershwin, George 1937

Hi Lee, Hi Low   Willson 1954

Hi Nellie   Dixon 1934; Wrubel 1934

Hi There   Drake 1953

Hi There, Miss Goodthighs (inst.)   Bacharach 1967

Hi Wyoming   Revel 1952

Hi Yo Silver   Bergman 1958

Hi-A-Le-A-Lou   Baer 1927; Kahn 1927

Hiawatha   McHugh 1919

Hiawatha's Lullaby   Donaldson 1933; Young, Joe 1933

Hiawatha's Melody of Love   Bryan 1920; Meyer 1920

Hibiscus   Coleman 1958; Leigh 1958

Hickory Stick   Webster 1941

Hicky Do   Atteridge 1916; Motzan 1916, 1917; Romberg 1916

Hidden in My Heart   Young, Victor 1954

Hidden Valley   Bullock 1943; Mitchell 1936; Stept 1936; Wrubel 1943

Hide and Seek   David, Mack 1936; Harbach 1911; Monaco 1936

Hide Me in Your Arms   Sigman 1959

Hide Your Sister   Adamson 1963; Fain 1963

Hideaway Heart   Bacharach 1961; David, Hal 1961

Hi-De-Higher Education   Yellen 1937

Hi-De-Ho Miracle Man   Coots 1936; Davis 1936

Hi-De-Ho Romeo   Coots 1937; Davis 1937

Hi-De-Home Sweet Home   Dietz 1934; Schwartz, Arthur 1934

Hi-Diddle-Dee-Dee (An Actor's Life for Me)   Washington 1940

Hi-Diddle-Dee-Dem   Conrad 1935; Magidson 1935

Hiding in the Corner of Your Smile   Pollack 1928

Higgitus-Figgitus   Sherman 1963

High and Dry (inst.)   Carmichael 1930

High and Low   Dietz 1929, 1931; Schwartz, Arthur 1929, 1931

High and the Mighty, The   Washington 1954

High As a Georgia Pine   Razaf 1940

High Brown Blues   Ager 1922; Yellen 1922

High Brown (inst.)   Johnson, James P. 1934

High Class Ladies and Elegant Gentlemen   David, Mack 1973; Livingston, Jerry 1973

High Cost of Loving, The   Bryan 1914; Meyer 1914

High Flyin' Wings on My Shoes   Porter 1957

High Hat   Gershwin, George 1927; Gershwin, Ira 1927

High Hat, a Piccolo, and a Cane, A   Akst 1936; Brown, Lew 1936; Fain 1936

High Hat Hop, The   Rainger 1936; Robin 1936

High Hat (inst.)   Alter 1928

High Hats   Hart 1926; Rodgers 1926

High Heels   Adams 1954; Strouse 1954

High, High, High   Brennan 1929

High, High, High Up in the Hills   Lewis 1926

High Hopes   Cahn 1959; Fain 1954; Van Heusen 1959; Webster 1954

High Hopes and Empty Pockets (The Gambler's Lament)   Fain 1957; Webster 1957

High Is Better Than Low   Dietz 1963; Schwartz, Arthur 1963

High Jinks   Conrad 1910; Friml 1913; Harbach 1913

High Jinks Tango   Friml 1913; Harbach 1913

High Life Made a Low Life Out of Me   Stept 1928

High, Low, Jack and the Game   Arlen 1946; Mercer 1946

High Muck di Muck (inst.)   Blake 1972

High Noon   Washington 1952

High on a Hill   Hammerstein 1926; Harbach 1926; Romberg 1926

High on the List   Burke 1950; Van Heusen 1950

High Ridin' Woman   Adamson 1957

High School Cadets   Freed, Ralph 1939, 1940

High School Cadets (inst.), The   Willson 1965

High School Fool, The   Adams 1958; Strouse 1958

High Silk Hat and Walking Cane   Kahal 1929

High Society   Atteridge 1913; DePaul 1956; Mercer 1956

High Society Blues   Hanley 1930

High Society, Calypso   Porter 1956

High Speed   Fain 1932; Kahal 1932

High Temperature, Low Resistance (inst.)   Bacharach 1965; David, Hal 1965

High Tor   Sondheim Date Unknown

High Up in Harlem   Hammerstein 1939; Kern 1939

High Up in the Hills   Caesar 1936

High Up on a Hill-Top   Baer 1929; Gilbert 1928

High Water   Brennan 1928

High, Wide and Handsome   Hammerstein 1937; Kern 1937

Highbrow, Lowbrow   Gorney 1949

Higher and Higher   Adamson 1943; McHugh 1943

Higher den de Moon   Arlen 1959; Mercer 1959

Higher than a Hawk (Deeper than a Well)   Fain 1953; Webster 1953

Highest Judge of All, The   Hammerstein 1945; Rodgers 1945

High-Hat, Low-Down   Davis 1960

High-High-High Up in the Hills Watching the Clouds Roll By   Young, Joe 1927

Highland Mary   Bryan 1909; Jerome 1905; Schwartz, Jean 1905

Highland Swing   Coots 1938; Davis 1938; Johnston 1938

Highlander's Castle, A   Styne 1958

Highly Important Fly, The   Von Tilzer 1903

Highly Respectable You   Adamson 1930; Gordon 1930; Revel 1930

Highway Polka, The   Evans 1944; Livingston, Jay 1944

Highway to Heaven   Dubin 1930

Highway's Call, The   Egan 1925; Kahn 1925

Hi-Ho!   Gershwin, George 1937; Gershwin, Ira 1937

Hi-Ho, Good-Bye   Johnson, Howard 1930

Hi-Ho, Lack-a-Day, What Have We Got to Lose   Alter 1933; Kahn 1933

Hi-Ho the Merrio, As Long As She Loves Me   Brown, Lew 1926; Conrad 1926; Davis 1926

Hikin' Down the Highway   Kahal 1931

Hiking   Adamson 1935; Lane 1935

Hilda Matilda   Blane 1952; Warren 1952

(Oh How I Love My) Hildegarde   Coots 1947

Hill Billy Bride, The   Brennan 1930

Hillbilly Grand Opera   Coslow 1952

Hill-Billy-Hop, Zu-Zu-Zu-Zu   Drake 1943

Hills Are Free, The   Drake 1957

Hills of Ixopo, The   Weill 1949

Hills of Old Wyoming, The   Rainger 1936; Robin 1936

Hills of Tomorrow, The   Sondheim 1981

Hills of Yesterday, The   Mancini 1970; Webster 1970

Hilltop Heaven   Coots 1931; Eliscu 1931

Hilo Hattie   Adamson 1940

Himmlisher Vater   Cahn 1970; Styne 1970

Hindo, The   Von Tilzer 1910

Hindoo Honey   Smith, Harry B. 1909

Hindoo Hop, The   Brown, A. Seymour 1923

Hindoo Lady   Friend 1919

Hindoo Moon   Davis 1927; Hanley 1927

Hindoo Serenade   Henderson 1943; Yellen 1943

Hindoo Song of Love   (Inst.)   Henderson 1924

Hindu Dance Tag (inst.)   Fain 1963

Hindustan Maid   Silver 1943

Hinky Dinky   Dubin 1929

Hinky Dinky Parlee Voo   Johnson, Howard 1939

Hip   Dietz 1943; Duke 1943

Hip Command, The   Raye 1958

Hip Hip Hooray   Loesser 1942; Styne 1942

Hip, Hip Hooray for Andy Jackson   Porter 1944

Hip Hip Hooray for the Rainbows   Johnson, Howard 1930

Hip, Hip, Hypnotize Me   Von Tilzer 1910

Hip Hip Pooh-Ray!   Sherman 1968

Hip Trip   David, Mack 1975

Hip-Di-Dee-O-Tee   Russell 1946

Hippety-Hop the Kangaroo   Caesar 1965

Hippity Hop   Ahlert Date Unknown; Donaldson 1919; Lewis 1919; Turk Date Unknown; Young, Joe 1919

Hippodrome Folks   Cohan 1914

Hippopotamus   Fisher 1936; Kern 1910

Hiram's Band   Berlin 1912; Goetz 1912

His and Hers   Fain 1955

His and His   Cahn 1963; Van Heusen 1963

His Chances Are Not Worth a Penny   Hart 1937; Rodgers 1937

His Cute Moving Picture Machine   Bryan 1916

His Delay Is Not His Denial   Caesar 1963; Robison 1963

His Excellency Is Due   Kalmar 1933; Ruby 1933

His Eye Is On the Sparrow   Webster 1955

His Eyes — Her Eyes   Bergman 1968

His Hand Is on Your Shoulder   Coots 1963

His Highness   Herbert 1895; Smith, Harry B. 1895

His Honor, the Mayor   Burke 1933; Spina 1933

His Honor, the Mayor of New York   Cahn 1957

His Little Sister   Smith, Robert B. 1905

His Little World   Adamson 1963; Fain 1963

His Love Makes Me Beautiful   Merrill 1964; Styne 1964

His Majesty the American   Brown, Lew Date Unknown; Henderson Date Unknown

His Majesty the Clock   Revel 1959

His Majesty's Dragoons   Kern 1928

His Master's Voice   Edwards 1925; Johnson, Howard 1925

His Name Is Charlie Gordon   Strouse 1980

His Name Was Judas   Oakland 1955

His Old Man   Rome 1946

His Own Little Island   Evans 1961; Livingston, Jay 1961

His Rock Will Never Roll   Caesar 1957; Robison 1957

His Rocking Horse Ran Away   Burke 1944; Van Heusen 1944

His Royal Highness   Adams 1972; Strouse 1972

His Royal Shyness   Berlin 1923

His Songs Will Never Grow Old   Drake 1954

His Word Is As Good As His Bond   Coots 1942

Hissing Song, The   Brown, Lew 1940; Henderson 1940

History Eight to the Bar   Rome 1942

History Is Made at Night   Rome 1939

History of New York, A   Weill 1938

History of the Beat (That'll Get It), The   Mercer 1955

History of the World   Spina 1977

Hit Me with a Hot Note and Watch Me Bounce   Ellington 1944

Hit Parade Finale   Bullock 1940; Styne 1940

Hit Parade Idea   Oakland 1960

Hit the Dirt   Stept 1952

Hit the Leather (Cavalry Song)   Willson 1943

Hit the Ramp   Duke 1941

Hit the Road   Raye 1940

Hit the Road to Dreamland   Arlen 1942; Mercer 1942

Hit the Road (You Bumble Bee)   Blake 1969; Razaf 1969

Hit the Stride   Blake 1958

Hitch Up the Horses   Conrad 1925

Hitch Your Wagon to a Star   Alter 1930; Johnson, Howard 1930; Robison 1928

Hitch Your Wagon to Forty-Eight Stars   Caesar 1943

Hitchhikers (On that Highway Called Life)   Harburg 1973

Hitchy Koo   Gilbert 1912

Hitchy Koo Girl   Goetz 1918

Hitchy-Koo   Goetz 1917

Hitchy's Garden of Roses   Porter 1919

Hither Bring the Bold Intruder   Smith, Harry B. 1906

Hitler und Goering und Goebbels und Schacht   Gorney 1939; Harburg 1939

Hitler's Funeral March   Silver 1943

Hits and Misses   Baer 1944

Hitsitty Hotsitty   Hoffman 1951

Hittin' the Bottle   Arlen 1930; Koehler 1930

Hittin' the Ceiling   Conrad 1929; Mitchell 1929

Hittin' the Sky   Robin 1930

Hittin' the Trail for Hallelujah Land   Bloom 1931; Young, Joe 1931

Hitting the Deck   Johnson, Howard 1929

Hive Full of Honey   Fain 1953; Webster 1953

Hi'Ya Duchess   Burke 1933; Spina 1933

Hi-Ya Love   Rainger 1941; Robin 1941

Hi-Yum Hi-Yum Hi-Yum   Mills 1938

H'lo Baby   Magidson 1929; Washington 1929

Hm! She Is the One Girl   Smith, Harry B. 1911

Ho, Billy, O!   Lerner, Alan Jay 1948; Weill 1948

Ho! Ho! Jose   Evans 1947; Livingston, Jay 1947

Ho! (The Riff Song)   Hammerstein 1926; Harbach 1926; Romberg 1926

Ho! Ye Townsmen   Herbert 1898; Smith, Harry B. 1898

Hobbies   Herbert 1920

Hobble on the Cobbles   Blake 1958

Hobble-de-hoy and a Gallop a Trot, A   David, Hal 1949

Hobo Zobo Band   Jerome 1903; Schwartz, Jean 1903

Hobohemia   Robin 1927

Hoby Tyler Campaign Song   Lane 1952; Robin 1952

Hocking Song, The   Oakland 1960

Hoctor's Ballet (Inst.)   Gershwin, George 1937

Hocus Pocus   Brooks 1952; Brown, Lew 1925; Hanley 1925

Hodge Podge   Johnson, J. Rosamond 1909

Hoe Cake, Hominy and Sassafras Tea   Hoffman 1949

Hoe Down   Freed, Ralph 1941

Hoedown   Loesser 1956

Hoe-Polli   Evans 1955; Livingston, Jay 1955

Hog Man Stomp   Waller 1928

Hogan's Alley   Dietz 1927; Gorney 1927

Ho-Ho (Deedle-ee-di-di)   Merrill 1951

Ho-Hum   Heyman 1931; Livingston, Jerry 1963

(If I Were of the) Hoi Polloi   Conrad 1924

Hoiriger Schottische   Coslow 1939

Hokey Pokey Polka, The   Adamson 1950; Coslow 1952; McHugh 1950

Hoku Loa   Brennan 1930; Friml 1930

Hokum   Hanley 1929

Hokum March (inst.)   Hanley 1932

Hokum-Smokum-Indian-Man   Stept 1926

Hola, Fellow (Song of Greeting)   Smith, Harry B. 1926

Hola! Hola!   Smith, Harry B. 1913

Hold Back the Dawn   David, Mack 1956

Hold 'Em   De Lange 1932

Hold 'em Cowboy   Brennan 1929

Hold Ev'rything 'Til I Get Back to You   Stept 1943

Hold It!   Lerner, Sammy 1948

Hold It Down   Friend 1957

Hold Me   Atteridge 1920; Bryan 1920; Schwartz, Jean 1920

Hold Me Close (Love Beat)   Parish 1955

Hold Me Close to You   Blane 1952; Warren 1952

Hold Me in Your Arms Again   Freed, Arthur 1925

Hold Me in Your Arms for 30 Days   Russell 1953

Hold Me in Your Heart   Hoffman 1952

Hold Me in Your Loving Arms   Buck 1915

Hold Me Just a Little Longer, Daddy   Baer 1950

Hold Me Sweetheart   Coots 1951

Hold Me Thusly   Ruby 1943

Hold Me Tight   Bergman 1955

Hold Me Tight and Say How Much You Love Me   Friend 1929

Hold Me-Hold Me-Hold Me   Comden and Green 1951; Styne 1951

Hold My Hand   Caesar 1934; David, Mack 1971; Henderson 1934; Lawrence 1950; Waller 1938; Yellen 1934

Hold On   Robison 1954

Hold on To Love   Webster 1957

Hold on to Your Hats   Harburg 1940; Lane 1940; Pollack 1944

Hold On to Your Heart   Revel 1959, 1962

Hold on to Your Heart Here We Go Again   Mitchell 1938; Stept 1938

Hold Out Your Hand to an Old Friend (Who Holds Out a Heart to You)   Coots 1950

Hold that Bulldog   Mitchell 1936; Pollack 1936

Hold That Co-Ed   Gordon 1938; Revel 1938

Hold That Smile   Henderson 1943; Yellen 1943

Hold the Lanterns High   Smith, Robert B. 1905

Hold Your Hats, Here We Go Again   Loesser 1937

Hold Your Head Up High (Opening Hymn)   Hammerstein 1932; Kern 1932

Hold Your Horses   Bryan 1932; Monaco 1932; Schwartz, Jean 1905; Williams 1905

Hold Your Man   Brown, Nacio Herb 1933; Duke 1930; Freed, Arthur 1933; Harburg 1930

Holdin' Up the Parade   Merrill 1951

Holding Hands   Herbert 1897; Smith, Harry B. 1897, 1905

Holding Hands in the Moonlight   Akst 1940; Davis 1940

Holding Hands (J'ai ta Main)   Rome 1945

Holding Hands with Myself   Hoffman 1934; Washington 1934

Holding Up the Parade   Hoffman 1933

Hold-Up Ensemble   Porter 1916

Hole in the Wall, A   Young, Joe 1938

Holiday   Dixon 1934; Fain 1958; Lawrence 1958

Holiday Cruise   Evans 1950; Livingston, Jay 1950

Holiday for Cars   Brooks 1959

Holiday for Lovers   Cahn 1959; Van Heusen 1959

Holiday Forever   De Lange 1943

Holiday Greetings   Stept 1945

Holiday in Heaven   Woods 1944

Holiday in Hollywood   Duke 1955

Holiday in Mexico   Fain 1946; Freed, Ralph 1946

Holiday in the Country   Adamson 1948, 1958; McHugh 1948, 1958

Holiday Parade   Parish 1943

Holiday Sweetheart   Caesar 1936; Henderson 1936

Holidays   Atteridge 1924; Coleman 1988; Romberg 1924; Schwartz, Jean 1924

Holka-Polka   Egan 1925; Kahn 1925

Holler Blue Murder   Sigman 1947

Hollow of My Hand   Caesar 1922

Holly Golightly   Merrill 1966

Holly Gollucci   Merrill 1966

Hollyhocks of Hollywood, The   Hart 1922; Rodgers 1922

Hollywood   Atteridge 1924; Carroll 1925; Freed, Arthur 1925; Romberg 1924

Hollywood and Vine   Brown, Lew 1939; Sondheim 1971; Stept 1939

Hollywood Be Thy Name   Loesser 1933

Hollywood Boulevard   Cahn 1975

Hollywood Canteen   Koehler 1944

Hollywood Cinderella   Pollack 1941

Hollywood Holiday   Coots 1935; Parish 1935

Hollywood Jubilee (inst.)   Brown, Nacio Herb 1959

Hollywood Nights   Conrad 1929, 1930; Meyer 1930; Mitchell 1929, 1930

Hollywood or Bust   Fain 1956; Webster 1956

Hollywood, Park Avenue and Broadway   Brown, Lew 1933; Henderson 1933

Hollywood Party   Hart 1934; Rodgers 1934

Hollywood Relief, A   Freed, Arthur 1927

Hollywood Rose   Kahn 1927

Hollywood Rose (You're Out of the Picture Now)   Fisher 1923

Hollywood Story, The   Martin 1963

Holy Cow   Evans 1956; Livingston, Jay 1956

Holy Lie Production Routine   Akst 1936; Clare 1936

Holy of Holies (Prayer)   Hart 1928; Rodgers 1928

Holy Smoke   Mercer 1983; Merrill 1956

Holy Smoke, Can't You Take a Joke   Mercer 1939

Home   Merrill 1964; Strouse 1999; Styne 1964

Home Again   Bryan 1914; Buck 1925; Coleman 1979; Lerner, Alan Jay 1939; Meyer 1926; Razaf 1954; Romberg 1916; Smith, Harry B. 1908; Styne 1993

Home Again Blues   Akst 1920; Berlin 1920

Home Alone Blues   Waller 1924

Home at the End of My Dreams, The   Monaco 1929

Home Before Dark   Cahn 1958; McHugh 1958

Home Blues   Gershwin, George 1929; Gershwin, Ira 1929; Kahn 1929

Home Bound   Razaf 1939

Home Companion, A   Hart 1927; Rodgers 1927

Home Cooking   Evans 1950; Livingston, Jay 1950

Home Folks   Hanley 1932

Home for Wayward Girls   Merrill 1966

Home for You, A   Friml 1927

Home from Algeria   Smith, Harry B. 1925

Home from the Hill   David, Mack 1959

Home, Home, Home   Spina 1947

Home in Oklahoma (Way Down Thar on the Farm)   Carroll 1945

Home in Pasadena   Clarke 1923; Leslie 1923; Warren 1923

Home in the Meadow   Cahn 1962

Home in Your Arms   Hammerstein 1938; Oakland 1938

Home Is a Little Bit of Heaven   Stept 1950

Home Is Everything   Styne 1934

Home Is Heaven, Heaven Is Home   Donaldson 1930; Leslie 1930

Home Is Home   Howard, Joseph E. 1906

Home Is Mine   Leslie 1929

Home Is My Lover   David, Mack 1959

Home Is the Place   Sondheim 1959; Styne 1959

Home Is the Shepherd   Livingston, Jerry 1962

Home Is Where the Heart Is   Cahn 1953; Coots 1951; David, Hal 1962; Fain 1953; Gorney 1948

Home, James, Don't Spare the Horses (inst.)   Bacharach 1967

Home Lights I Long to See   Carroll 1923

Home Lovin' Gal   Gershwin, George 1929; Gershwin, Ira 1929; Kahn 1929

Home Lovin' Man   Gershwin, George 1929; Gershwin, Ira 1929; Kahn 1929

Home Made Heaven   Lerner, Alan Jay 1939; Rainger 1932; Robin 1932

Home o' Mine   Smith, Harry B. 1928

Home of My Heart   Egan 1925; Kahn 1925

Home of My Own, A   Woods 1946

Home of Our Own, A   Lerner, Alan Jay 1948; Rome 1946; Weill 1948

Home on the Range   Johnson, Howard 1939

Home on the Range Cha Cha   Brooks 1959

Home Pals   Lewis 1925; Young, Joe 1925

Home Road   Hanley 1937

Home Run Bill   Bryan 1911

Home Should Be Your Heaven, The   Robison 1957

Home, Sweet Heaven   Martin 1964

Home Sweet Home   Conrad 1929; Johnson, Howard 1939; Kern 1919; Mitchell 1929; Smith, Harry B. 1906

Home Sweet Home Sounds Good to Me   Sterling 1906; Von Tilzer 1906

Home Ties   Loesser 1934

Home to Harlem   Brown, Lew 1933; Henderson 1933

Home Town   Caesar 1927

Home Town Paper   DePaul 1941

Home Was Never Like This   Brown, A. Seymour 1915

Home with the Milk in the Morning   Jerome 1905; Schwartz, Jean 1905

Home Wrecker   Evans 1977; Livingston, Jay 1977

Homecoming   Brooks 1953; Donaldson 1942; Mercer 1942

Home-Cookin'   Raye 1936

Homeland   Henderson 1925; Romberg 1925

Homeless   Strouse 1987

Homeless Girl in Harlem   Cohan 1903

Homely, But Clean   Youmans 1926

Homemade Sunshine   Fain 1930; Kahal 1930

Homer, the Old Tromboner   Parish 1935

Homer's Pitch   Cahn 1970; Styne 1970

Homesick   Berlin 1922; Lerner, Alan Jay 1983; Strouse 1983

Homesick and Lonesome   Hoffman 1932; Magidson 1932

Homesick Blues   Robin 1948; Styne 1948

Homesick for New England   Sigman 1960

Homesick Hillbilly   Blane 1955; Martin 1955

Homespun   Davis 1943

Homestead Must Be Sold, The   Eliscu 1929; Rose 1929; Youmans 1929

Homestead on the Hill   Sterling 1900

Hometown Blues   Coots 1923

Hometown Paper   Raye 1941

Hometown Rag, The   Livingston, Jerry 1956

Homeward Bound   Berlin 1915; Gershwin, George 1927; Gershwin, Ira 1927; Goetz 1917; Johnson, Howard 1917; Meyer 1917; Smith, Harry B. 1906

Homeward Bound on the Old Greyhound   Bryan 1935

Homework   Berlin 1949

Homing Pigeon, Fly Away, Fly Away Back Home   Drake 1950

Homogeneous Cabinet, A   Hart 1937; Rodgers 1937

Honchi Chonch   Ellington 1940

Honduran Mahogany   Gorney 1958

Honduras   Kalmar 1924; Ruby 1924

Honest Abe   Bullock 1950; Livingston, Jerry 1960; Spina 1944

Honest and True   Cobb 1912; Schwartz, Jean 1912

Honest Injun   Sterling 1916; Von Tilzer 1916

Honest Injun' — I Love You!   Howard, Joseph E. 1910

Honest John   Washington 1940

Honest Love   Sigman 1957

Honest, Really, Truly   Ahlert 1931; Turk 1931

Honest to Goodness   Conrad 1934; Oakland 1934

Honest Work   Evans 1961; Livingston, Jay 1961

Honestly   Bryan 1931; Harburg 1961; Parish 1935

Honestly (Amore Baciami)   Adamson 1953

Honestly Sincere   Adams 1960; Strouse 1960

Honesuckle Lane   Dixon 1927; Henderson 1927; Rose 1927

Honey   Adams 1964; Johnson, James P. 1927; Smith, Harry B. 1903; Sondheim 1981; Strouse 1964; Whiting 1928

Honey, Ain't It Thrillin'   Drake 1954

Honey Babe   Blake 1950; Cohan 1907

Honey, Be Mine   Buck 1926; Hanley 1926

Honey, Be My Honey-Bee   Coots 1928

Honey Bear   Evans 1961; Livingston, Jay 1961

Honey Behave   Brown, A. Seymour 1913

Honey Boy   Norworth 1907

Honey Bun   Hammerstein 1949; Rodgers 1949

Honey Bunch   Friend 1925; Sterling 1915

Honey Chile   Clare 1935; Rainger 1936; Robin 1936

Honey Come and Love Me Some More   Johnson, J. Rosamond 1913

Honey, Come Hurry Along   Howard, Joseph E. 1918

Honey Darlin'   Merrill 1953

Honey Dear   Conrad 1934; Heyman 1934

Honey Do   Donaldson 1927; Razaf 1932

Honey Gal o' Mine   Hammerstein 1943

Honey Honeysuckle Baby, Make Those Google Eyes With Me   Bryan 1908; Fisher 1908

Honey Hula   Fisher 1921

Honey Hush   Waller 1939

Honey, I'm in Love with You   Conrad 1925

Honey in the Honeycomb   Duke 1940

Honey in the Rock   Hoffman 1955

Honey Love   Herbert 1911

Honey, Love Me All the Time   Jerome 1905; Schwartz, Jean 1905

Honey Lu   DeSylva 1922; Donaldson 1922

Honey Man Blues   Razaf 1925

Honey Moon Land   Brown, A. Seymour 1909

Honey, Oh, My Honey   Evans 1952; Livingston, Jay 1952

Honey on Our Honeymoon   Jerome 1909; Schwartz, Jean 1909

Honey, Please Don't Turn Your Back on Me   Clare 1936; Stept 1936

Honey Sal   Atteridge Date Unknown

Honey, Send Home for Money   Howard, Joseph E. 1903

Honey Town   Lewis 1911

Honey Trust Me   Eliscu 1955; Gorney 1955

Honey What a Pleasure Meetin' Up with You   Coots 1933; Turk 1933

Honey Where You Been So Long   Fisher 1938

Honey Won't You Call Me   Evans 1945; Livingston, Jay 1945

Honey, Won't You Honeymoon with Me   Hoffman 1950

Honey You Certainly Know How to Love   Sterling 1914; Von Tilzer 1914

Honey, You're a Honey   Parish 1936

Honey-Babe (The Marching Song)   Webster 1955

Honey-Bun   Youmans 1924

Honey-Bunch   Buck 1921

Honeychile   Spina 1951

Honeycomb   Merrill 1953

Honey-Love   Meyer 1911

Honeymoon   Fain 1955

Honeymoon Belle (inst.)   Motzan 1918

Honeymoon Blues   Conrad 1924

Honeymoon Cake   Stept 1952

Honeymoon Chimes   Brown, Lew 1922

Honeymoon Home   Bryan 1921

Honeymoon Hop   Brennan 1927

Honeymoon Hotel   Cahn 1964; Dubin 1933; Van Heusen 1964; Warren 1933

Honeymoon Inn   Kern 1917

Honeymoon Is Over, The   Coleman 1988

Honeymoon Island   Schwartz, Jean 1918

Honeymoon Isle   Kern 1923

Honeymoon Land   Atteridge 1918; Kern 1918; Romberg 1918, 1919

Honeymoon Lane   Hanley 1926; Kern 1913

Honeymoon Love   Brown, A. Seymour 1912

Honeymoon of Pancho Pincus, The   Caesar 1943

Honeymoon Parade   Edwards 1930; Meyer 1930; Mitchell 1930

Honeymoon Trail   Howard, Joseph E. 1908, 1909

Honeymoon Train, The   Drake 1957

Honeymoon (When Will You Shine for Me?)   Gershwin, Ira 1921

Honeymooning in Hawaii   Hanley 1938

Honeymooning in the Sky with You   Ager Date Unknown; Yellen Date Unknown

Honeypie's Dance (inst.)   Duke 1943

Honeysuckle Rose   Razaf 1929; Waller 1929

(In) Honeysuckle Time (When Emmaline Said She'd Be Mine)   Blake 1921; Sissle 1921

Hong Kong   Gershwin, George 1918; Gershwin, Ira 1918

Hong Kong Blues   Carmichael 1939, 1945

Hong Kong Ferry   Spina 1977

Hong Kong, Take a Little Rickshaw Ride   Adamson 1959; Young, Victor 1959

Hong Kong to Hoboken   Burke 1946; Van Heusen 1946

Honk Honk (Rumble Seat Song)   DePaul 1943

Honking Bird in the Willow Tree, The   Webster 1956

Honky Tonk Toddle   Brown, Nacio Herb 1926; Freed, Arthur 1926

Honky-Tonk (inst.)   Kern 1945

Honolulu   Kahn 1939; Warren 1939

Honolulu, America Loves You, We've Got to Hand It to You   Clarke 1916; Monaco 1916

Honolulu Blues, The   Clarke 1916; Monaco 1916; Von Tilzer 1916

Honolulu Eyes   Johnson, Howard 1920

Honolulu Hicki-Boola-Boo, The   Brown, Lew 1916

Honolulu Hula Boola Boo   Edwards 1913

Honolulu Lou   Egan 1915

Honolulu Lu   Cahn 1941; Hoffman 1959

Honolulu Lulu   Robin 1936

Honolulu Pa-ki-ka, The   DeSylva 1916

Honolulu Rag   Williams 1910

Honolulu Rock-A Roll-A   Hoffman 1956

Honolulu Songbird   Leslie 1927

Honolulu Stars and Hawaiian Guitars   Lawrence 1936

Honolulu-lu   Howard, Joseph E. 1905

Honor and Glory   Smith, Harry B. 1925

Honor Bright   Fisher 1918; McHugh 1941; Mercer 1941

Honor Me with This Dance   Cahn Date Unknown; Duke Date Unknown

Honor of the Family, The   Cohan 1927

Honor of Your Presence, The   Lerner, Alan Jay 1976

Honor the Brave   Herbert 1909

Honora Doolin   Snyder 1906

Honorable Bozo   Livingston, Jerry 1962

Honorable Congratulations   Evans 1957; Livingston, Jay 1957

Honorable Ladies   Drake 1954

Honorable Moon   Gershwin, Ira 1923, 1943; Harburg 1943; Schwartz, Arthur 1943

Hon'rable Profession of the Fourth Estate, The   Berlin 1949

Honya   Baer 1943

Hoodle Dee Doo Dee Doo Doo   Turk 1926

Hoodlum, The   Lewis 1919; Ruby 1919; Young, Joe 1919

Hoodoo Man, The   Brown, Nacio Herb 1924

Hoof, Hoof   Robin 1927

Hooker's Ball, The   Coleman 1996

Hook's Entrance Song   Leigh 1954

Hook's Hook   Styne 1954

Hooligans Are Hooli Hooli Mad, The   Hanley 1916

Hoo-oo I'm Waving at You   Dubin 1914

Hoop-de-Dingle   Rome 1959

Hoop-de-doo   Loesser 1950

Hoopla   Hoffman 1957

Hoop-La-La, Papa!   Kern 1912

Hoops   Dietz 1931; Schwartz, Arthur 1931

Hoop-Ti-Do   Atteridge 1919; Romberg 1919; Schwartz, Jean 1919

Hoorah for Jones   Loesser 1965

Hooray for Anywhere   Lane 1945

Hooray for Baby and Me   Meyer 1930; Mitchell 1930

Hooray for Captain Spaulding!   Kalmar 1928; Ruby 1928

Hooray for George the Third   Fields 1954; Schwartz, Arthur 1954

Hooray for Ghio   Lane 1952; Robin 1952

Hooray for Hollywood   Mercer 1938; Whiting 1938

Hooray for Looey   Drake 1953

Hooray for Love   Arlen 1948; Fields 1935; McHugh 1935; Robin 1948

Hooray for Our Side   Brooks 1945

Hooray for Spinach   Mercer 1939; Warren 1939

Hooray for the Irish   Leslie 1926; Monaco 1926

Hooray for the United States   Yellen 1949

Hooray for the U.S.A.!   DeSylva 1924; Gershwin, George 1924

Hooray for Today   Rainger 1941; Robin 1941

Hooray for What?   Arlen 1937; Harburg 1937

Hooray, Hooray for Nancy Mix   Caesar 1940

Hooray, The Land of the Midnight Sun   Fisher 1915

Hoot Mon   Burke 1952; Van Heusen 1952

Hootch Rhythm   Bryan 1922; Schwartz, Jean 1922

Hootin' Owl Trail   Mercer 1949

Hootspa   Strouse 1985

Hooty Sapperticker   Sherman 1958

Hop Hop Hop Along to Bed   Silver 1950

Hop on Your Pogo Stick   Washington 1941

Hop Skip   Caesar 1926

Hop, Skip and Jump   Bullock 1938; Hoffman 1946; Livingston, Jerry 1946; Spina 1938

Hop Up   Weill 1948

Hopalong Cassidy March   Brown, Nacio Herb 1951; Gilbert 1950

Hope   Ager 1934; Schwartz, Jean 1934; Young, Joe 1934

Hope for the Best   Gershwin, Ira 1946; Schwartz, Arthur 1946

Hopeless Love Affair, A   Razaf 1938; Waller 1938

Hopelessly   Robison 1960

Hopelessly in Love   Robin 1936

Hoping   Caesar 1923; Mercer 1954

Hoping That Some Day You'd Care   Gershwin, George 1927; Gershwin, Ira 1927

Hoppin' the Buck   Johnson, Howard 1927; Rose 1927

Hoppy   Coots 1957

Hoppy and the Hopi Indians   Brown, Nacio Herb 1951; Gilbert 1951

Hoppy, Topper and Me   Brown, Nacio Herb 1950; Gilbert 1950

Hoppy Wishes You a Happy Birthday   Brown, Nacio Herb 1951; Gilbert 1951

Hop-Scotch Polka (Scotch Hot)   Sigman 1949

Hop-Skip and Jump (inst.)   Schwartz, Jean 1930

Horatio's Narration   Adamson 1955

Horicon Hop   Hart 1919

Horizontal   David, Hal 1945

Horn in a Fiddle Shop (inst.), A   Romberg 1952

Horoscope   Brooks 1959

Horrible, Horrible Love!   Martin 1948

Horse and Buggy and Freedom   Kahal 1942; Stept 1942

Horse and Buggy Doctor, A   Razaf 1949

Horse and Buggy Ride   Kalmar 1939; Ruby 1939

Horse Finale   Loesser 1965

Horse on the Carousel, The   Cahn 1963; Stept 1953; Van Heusen 1963

Horse Sense   David, Mack 1950; Willson 1953

Horse that Knows the Way Back Home, A   Burke 1943; Van Heusen 1943

Horse Told Me, The   Burke 1950; Van Heusen 1950

Horse Trot, The   Atteridge 1921; Romberg 1921

Horse with the Dreamy Eyes, The   Donaldson 1937

Horse Won't Talk, The   Arlen 1962; Harburg 1962

Horses   Whiting 1926

Horses Number (Opening Bit for Race Track Scene)   Alter 1930; Johnson, Howard 1930

Horse-Sense   Hoffman 1950; Livingston, Jerry 1950

Horseshoes Are Lucky   Mercer 1949

Hortense   Donaldson 1921; Lewis 1921; Young, Joe 1921

Hosanna   Conrad 1929; David, Mack 1944; Mitchell 1929; Robin 1931

Hospital, Scene Commercial (Eat Mush, Mush, Mush, Mush, Mushroom Soup)   Cahn 1946

Hospitality   Coleman 1973; Fields 1973

Hostess in the U.S.O., The   Baer 1943

Hostess with the Mostes' on the Ball, The   Berlin 1950

Hot   Schwartz, Arthur 1930

Hot and Bothered   Kalmar 1929; Ruby 1929

Hot and Cold   Comden and Green 1956; Hammerstein 1928; Romberg 1928; Styne 1956

Hot and Cold Water   Caesar 1937

Hot and Happy   Yellen 1938

Hot Blues (inst)   Rodgers 1930

Hot Bolero   Conrad 1935; Magidson 1935

Hot Bread   Loesser 1937

Hot Catfish and Corn Dodgers   Alter 1940; Loesser 1940

Hot Choc'late   Bryan 1928; Schwartz, Jean 1928

Hot Choc'late Soldiers   Brown, Nacio Herb 1933; Freed, Arthur 1934

Hot Chocolate   Alter 1929; Fields 1929; McHugh 1929

Hot Curves (inst.)   Johnson, James P. 1930

Hot Diggety   Donaldson 1925; Kahn 1925

Hot Diggity   Hoffman 1956

Hot Diggity Dog   Johnson, James P. 1923

Hot Dog!   Kern 1922

Hot Dog, A Blanket and You, A   Coots 1931

Hot Dog (Ain't that Wiener Good)   Raye 1942
Hot Dog, Mustard and You   Brennan 1949
Hot Dog that Made Him (Her) Mad   Raye 1953
Hot Feet   Blake 1980; Fields 1929; Gordon 1931; McHugh 1929; Revel 1931; Sissle 1980
Hot Food   Bacharach 1968; David, Hal 1968
Hot Footin' It   Conrad 1929; Mitchell 1929
Hot Gavotte   Loewe 1942
Hot Gold (inst.)   Bacharach 1966
Hot Harlem   Johnson, James P. 1931
Hot Heels   Rose 1927
Hot Henry   Carroll 1926
Hot Hindoo   Gershwin, Ira 1923
Hot Honey   Bryan 1936
Hot, Hot Honey   Bryan 1927; Schwartz, Jean 1927
Hot Jello   Razaf Date Unknown
Hot Man   Conrad 1929; Mitchell 1929
Hot Meat Blue Plate Special   David, Mack 1942
Hot Moonlight   Gorney 1931; Harburg 1931
Hot Number   Duke 1936; Gershwin, Ira 1936
Hot Pants   Caesar 1928
Hot Rhythm   Johnson, James P. 1931
Hot Spell   Bacharach 1958; David, Hal 1958; David, Mack 1958; Mills 1936; Myrow 1936
Hot Spot   Harbach 1933; Kern 1933
Hot Steps   Carroll 1925; Freed, Arthur 1925
Hot Stuff   Sterling 1911; Von Tilzer 1911
Hot Summer Night   Russell 1957
Hot Tamale Alley   Cohan 1893
Hot Tamale Baby   Razaf 1924
Hot Tamale Man, The   David, Mack 1945; Mills 1939; Washington 1938
Hot Tamales   Kalmar 1939; Ruby 1939
Hot Tempered Fugue (inst.), The   Rome 1947
Hot Towel   Loesser 1936, 1937
Hot Turkey   Loesser 1937
Hot Voo-Doo   Coslow 1932; Rainger 1932; Robin 1932
Hot Water   David, Hal 1991; Strouse 1991
Hot Water Bottle   Fisher 1938
Hotcha Chornia Brown   Stept 1934
Hot-Cha Joe the Georgia Gigolo   Yellen 1933
Hotcha Ma Chotch   Adamson 1930; Youmans 1930
Hotcha Razz-Ma-Tazz   Mills 1934; Razaf 1934
Hot-Dog Waltz   Weill 1947
Hotel Life   DeSylva 1919; Gershwin, George 1919
Hotel Never Tell   Caesar 1925; Youmans 1925
Hotel Oasis   Arlen 1948; Robin 1948
Hot-Foot'n, We're Gonna Have Fun   Akst 1925; Lewis 1925; Young, Joe 1925
Hot-Hot-Hottentot   Fisher 1924
Hot-House Rose   Porter 1927
Hotsy Totsy Nazi   Merrill 1990
Hotsy Totsy Town   Kalmar 1923; Ruby 1923
Hotten Trot, The   Meyer 1926
Hottentot, The   Cahn 1955; Coslow 1923; Styne 1955
Hottentot Hop   David, Mack 1930
Hottentot Love Song, A   Johnson, J. Rosamond 1906
Hottentot Potentate   Dietz 1935; Schwartz, Arthur 1935
Hottentot Trot   Fields 1929; McHugh 1929
Hottest Gal in Town, The   Fisher 1937
Hour After Hour   Friend 1954
Hour Ago, An   Dietz 1944; Duke 1944
Hour Before the Dawn, The   Parish 1946
Hour of Parting, The   Kahn 1931; Parish 1965
Hours I Spent with You, The   Lewis 1927; Young, Joe 1927

House, a House (My Life for a House), A   Raye 1946
House and Garden   Loesser 1956
House and the Old Wisteria Tree, The   Silver 1951
House Is a Home, A   David, Hal 1951
House Is Haunted (By the Echo of Your Last Goodbye), The   Rose 1934
House Is Not a Home, A   Bacharach 1964; David, Hal 1964
House Jack Built for Jill, The   Robin 1936
House of 7 Joys   David, Mack 1968
House of Bamboo   Brooks 1955
House of Blue Lights, The   Raye 1946
House of David Blues   Mills 1923
House of Flowers   Arlen 1954
House of Flowers Waltz (inst.)   Arlen 1954
House of Lords (L'Earl — Le Duke)   Ellington 1966
House of Marcus Lycus, The   Sondheim 1962
House of Melody   Willson 1937
House of Singing Bamboo   Freed, Arthur 1950; Warren 1950
House on Breckenridge Lane, The   Freed, Ralph 1966
House on Chapel Row, The   David, Mack 1938; Livingston, Jerry 1938
House on Easy Street, The   Heyman 1954; Young, Victor 1954
House on Rittenhouse Square, A   Robin 1948; Styne 1948
House Party Stomp (inst.)   Waller 1925
House Rent Party Day   Mills 1935
House that Jack Built, The   Atteridge 1920; Johnson, J. Rosamond 1904
House that Monty's "Jack" Built, The   Robin 1926
House Where I Was Born, The   Caesar 1934; Carroll 1934
House with Stained Glass Windows, The   Silver 1957
Housekeeping   Freed, Arthur 1925
(When I Am) Housekeeping for You   Dietz 1929; Gorney 1929
Housewear Department   Gordon 1934; Revel 1934
Houston Trails   Brooks 1960
How   Livingston, Jerry 1962
How a Monocle Helps the Mind   Johnson, J. Rosamond 1904
How About   Bacharach 1955
How About a Cheer for the Navy?   Berlin 1942
How About a Date?   Burke 1946; Van Heusen 1946
How About a Hand for the Comic   Lane Date Unknown
How About a Little Date for Breakfast?   Harburg 1932
How About a Man Like Me?   Gershwin, George 1927; Gershwin, Ira 1927
How About It   Hart 1931; Rodgers 1931
How About Me?   Berlin 1928
How About Me Calling You My Sweetheart   Snyder 1931
How About You   Freed, Ralph 1941; Lane 1941
How About You and Me   Yellen 1932
How Actresses Are Made   Smith, Harry B. 1900
How Are Things in Glocca Morra?   Harburg 1947; Lane 1947
How Are You Fixed for Love   Cahn 1958; Van Heusen 1958
How Are You My Honey   Young, Joe 1932
How Are You Tonight in Hawaii   Leslie 1930; Warren 1930
How Beautiful   Gershwin, George 1931; Gershwin, Ira 1931
How Beautiful the Days   Loesser 1956
How Blue the Night   Adamson 1944; McHugh 1944
How Can a Girl Say No   Heyman 1931
How Can a Lady Be Certain?   Conrad 1924
How Can Any Girlie Be a Good Little Girl (When She Loves a Naughty Little Boy)   Johnson, Howard 1917
How Can Anyone Keep from Singin'   Fain 1964

How Can Anything So Wrong Be So Right   Evans 1968;
  Livingston, Jay 1968
How Can I Be a Sweet Mama to You   Clare 1923; Friend
  1923
How Can I Be Alone   Evans 1959
How Can I Be Alone Again   Livingston, Jay 1959
How Can I Be Happy with No, No, No-One to Love   Akst
  1926; Davis 1926
How Can I Believe You When You've Lied to Me So Many
  Times   Johnson, Howard 1923
How Can I Call You My Pal, After You've Stolen My
  Gal   Brown, Lew 1921; Norworth 1921
How Can I Change My Luck   Berlin 1931
How Can I Ever Be Alone?   Hammerstein 1940; Schwartz,
  Arthur 1940
How Can I Face Tomorrow?   Coleman 1972
How Can I Forget We're not Together?   Razaf 1943
How Can I Forget (When There's So Much to
  Remember)   Berlin 1917
How Can I Forget You   Washington 1945
How Can I Hold Somebody Else in My Arms   Koehler 1948
How Can I Hold You Close Enough   Harburg 1935, 1944;
  Heyman 1935, 1944
How Can I Hurt You   Bacharach 1965; David, Hal 1965
How (Can I Keep from Loving You)   Caesar 1926
How Can I Keep My Mind on Driving   Fisher 1936
How Can I Leave Thee   Johnson, Howard 1939
How Can I Make the One That I Love Love Me   Lane Date
  Unknown
How Can I Marry One Little Girl, When I'm in Love with
  Them All   Fisher 1920
How Can I Replace You?   Van Heusen 1955
How Can I Resist You   Gordon 1934; Revel 1934
How Can I Show I Love You   Wrubel 1929
How Can I Sleep at Night when My Wife Eats Crackers in
  Bed   Rose 1937; Silver 1937
How Can I Stop Loving You   De Lange 1947
How Can I Tell Her   Bergman 1978; Coots 1967; Evans
  1955; Livingston, Jay 1955
How Can I Tell You (How Much I Love You)   Coots 1955
How Can I Thank You   Bullock 1938; Spina 1938
How Can I Wait?   Lerner, Alan Jay 1951; Loewe 1951
How Can I Win You Now?   DeSylva 1922, 1925; Gershwin,
  George 1925; Gershwin, Ira 1925; Herbert 1922
How Can I, With You in My Heart   Waller 1938
How Can It Be a Beautiful Day   Kahn 1934
How Can Love Survive?   Hammerstein 1959; Rodgers 1959
How Can the Radio Know   Sigman 1968
How Can There Be So Many Moons   Caesar 1935;
  Henderson 1935; Koehler 1935
How Can They Tell I'm Irish   Goetz 1912
How Can They Tell That I'm Irish   Norworth 1910
How Can We Be Wrong   Dietz 1938; Schwartz, Arthur 1938
How Can We Help but Miss You   Hart 1925; Rodgers 1925
How Can We Part   Rainger 1936; Robin 1936
How Can We Say Goodbye   Cahn 1958
How Can You Cry with Those Beautiful Eyes   Ager 1932;
  Fisher 1932
How Can You Describe a Face   Comden and Green 1961;
  Styne 1961
How Can You Face Me   Razaf 1932; Waller 1932
How Can You Forget?   Hart 1938; Rodgers 1938
How Can You Keep Your Mind on Business?   Friml 1926;
  Hammerstein 1926; Harbach 1926
How Can You Love Such a Man?   Berlin 1910

How Can You Say Goodbye   Coslow 1922
How Can You Say No on a Beautiful Night Like
  This   Friend 1927
How Can You Say No When All the World Is Saying
  Yes   Dubin 1932; Kahal 1932
How Can You Say You Feel Rich Anymore   Coleman 1979
How Can You Say You Love Me   Ahlert 1931; Turk 1931
How Can You Tell an American?   Weill 1938
How Close He Came   Cahn 1969
How Cold, Cold, Cold (An Empty Room)   Rome 1965
How Come?   Oakland 1969; Sherman 1973
How Could a Fellow Want More   Harbach 1936; Romberg
  1936
How Could a Girl Like You Do a Thing Like That To a Boy
  Like Me on a Night Like This — Well, I Like
  That   Gordon 1933; Revel 1933
How Could Anything So Good Be So Bad   Whiting 1928
How Could I Be Blue?   Razaf 1926
How Could I Ever Be Untrue to You   Hoffman 1955
How Could I Ever Say No   Strouse 1989
How Could I Forget   Gershwin, George 1929; Gershwin, Ira
  1929; Kahn 1929
How Could I Know that You Loved Me?   Brown, A.
  Seymour 1912
How Could I Know What Was Goin' On?   Merrill 1971;
  Styne 1971
How Could We Be Wrong   Porter 1933
(Blue Eyes) How Could You!   Brooks 1952; Bryan 1906;
  Dubin 1937; Warren 1937
How Could You Believe Me When I Said I Love You When
  You Know I've Been a Liar All My Life   Lane 1951;
  Lerner, Alan Jay 1951
How Could You Do It to Me   Howard, Joseph E. 1964
How Could You Forget   Razaf 1933
How Could You Put Me Down   Johnson, James P. 1944;
  Parish 1944
How Dad   Rodgers 1962
(Home) How Dear Can It Be   Robison 1956
How Deep Is the Ocean? (How High Is the Sky?)   Berlin
  1932
How Did It Happen   Kahal 1942, Date Unknown; Warren
  1942, Date Unknown
How Did They Know I Was American   Harbach 1923
How Did Venus Make Love   Clare 1919; Mitchell 1919
How Did You Know?   Drake 1999
How Different Things Would Be   Donaldson 1926
How Do I Feel   Blane 1968; Martin 1968
How Do I Grow a Rose?   Spina 1944
How Do I Know?   Brown, Lew 1921; De Lange 1946
How Do I Know He Loves Me?   Conrad 1924
How Do I Know It's Sunday   Fain 1934; Kahal 1934
How Do I Look?   Blane 1960; DeSylva 1933; Martin 1960;
  Robin 1933; Whiting 1933
How Do I Rate with You   Coslow 1935; Whiting 1935
How Do They Do It?   Porter 1930
How Do Yo Do?   Dietz 1937; Schwartz, Arthur 1937
How Do You Account for That?   Smith, Robert B. 1906
How Do You Do?   Atteridge 1912; Brooks 1958
How Do You Do, Beautiful You   Magidson 1932
How Do You Do I Love You   Leigh 1965
How Do You Do It?   Burke 1946; Harburg 1932; Van
  Heusen 1946
How Do You Do It, Mabel, On Twenty Dollars a
  Week?   Berlin 1911
How Do You Do, Katinka?   Kern 1922

How Do You Do-Good-Bye (How'dy Do, Good-Bye)   Atteridge 1914

How Do You Doodle Do?   Coots 1925

How Do You Get that Way?   Herbert 1919; Smith, Robert B. 1919

How Do You Get to Doodletown   Bergman 1968

How Do You Keep the Music Playing?   Bergman 1982

How Do You Know?   Atteridge 1912

How Do You Know We're in Love   Evans 1957; Livingston, Jay 1957

How Do You Like My Eyes   Wrubel 1931

How Do You Marry a Man   DePaul 1958; Raye 1958

How Do You Say Auf Wiedersehn   Mercer 1967

How Do You Say It   Cahn 1941

How Do You Speak to an Angel?   Styne 1953

How Do You Spell Ambassador   Porter 1938

How Does a Man Become a Puppet   Bacharach 1969; David, Hal 1969

How Does Your Garden Grow?   Burke 1944; Van Heusen 1944

How D'Ya Like to Be Me   Coots 1928

How D'Ya Like Your Eggs in the Morning   Cahn 1951

How D'Ya Say "Baby" in Arabian   Russell 1965

How D'ya Talk to a Girl   Cahn 1966; Van Heusen 1966

How D'Ye Do   Brown, Lew 1927; Friend 1927

How Easy We Forget   Russell Date Unknown

How Far Can a Lady Go?   Burke 1953; Van Heusen 1953

How Far is It to the Next Town?   Lerner, Alan Jay 1971

How Far Will You Go with Me   Weill 1938

How Fly Times   Lerner, Alan Jay 1943; Loewe 1943

How Green Was My Valley   Davis 1941; Silver 1941; Webster 1941

How Happy Is the Bride   Heyman 1931; Youmans 1931

How Happy We'll Be If You'll Just Care Again   Burke 1962

How High Can a Little Bird Fly   Dietz 1934; Schwartz, Arthur 1934

How I Could Go for You   Alter 1930

How I Love a Pretty Face   Smith, Robert B. 1910

How I Love Flowers   Smith, Harry B. 1908

How I Love Her and She Loves Me Is Nobody's Business   Mills 1925

How I Love that Girl   Kahn 1924

(I'm Tellin' the Birds, Tellin' the Bees) How I Love You   Brown, Lew 1926; Friend 1926

How I Loved Her   Adams 1968; Strouse 1968

How I Loved You in Your Sleep   Spina 1955

How I Missed You, Mary   Coots 1922

How I React to You   Hammerstein 1931; Whiting 1931

How I Saved Roosevelt   Sondheim 1990

How I Wish I Could Sing a Love Song   Harburg 1930

How Is Everything Back Home?   Johnson, Howard 1921

How Is Your Technique?   Dubin 1940; Fain 1940

How It Lies, How It Lies, How It Lies   Webster 1949

How 'Ja Do   Donaldson 1928; Kahn 1928

How Jazz Was Born   Razaf 1928; Waller 1928

How Late Can You Stay Out Tonight   Fisher 1913

How Like Her Papa   Romberg 1916

How Little It Matters, How Little We Know   Leigh 1956

How Little We Know   Carmichael 1945; Mercer 1945

How Long   Bacharach 1986; Hammerstein 1955; Rodgers 1955

How Long Can Love Keep Laughing?   Rome 1938

How Long Can You Play Around   Merrill 1957

How Long Did I Dream   Burke 1941; Van Heusen 1941

How Long Does It Take to Get Lonesome   Woods 1953

How Long Has This Been Goin' On   Davis 1927

How Long Has This Been Going On?   Gershwin, George 1927; Gershwin, Ira 1927; Magidson 1938; Mercer 1932; Wrubel 1938

How Long Have I Loved Libby?   Sherman 1995

How Long Have You Been Married?   Brown, A. Seymour 1913

How Long Is Forever?   Evans 1967; Livingston, Jay 1967

How Long Is That Train Been Gone   Johnson, James P. 1930

How Long Will You Remember (How Soon Will You Forget)   Leslie 1959

How Long Will You Take to Get Lonely   Brown, Lew 1954; Woods 1954

How Love Speaks   Fisher 1904

How Lovely to Be a Woman   Adams 1960; Strouse 1960

How Lovely to Love a Woman   Adams 1963; Strouse 1963

How Lovely You Are   Heyman 1971; Silver 1971; Washington 1939

How Lovely You Can Be   Conrad 1930; Meyer 1930; Mitchell 1930

How Lucky   Rome 1973

How Lucky Can a Guy Get   Oakland 1968

How Lucky Can You Get?   Fain 1952; Harburg 1952

How Many Days of Sadness   Bacharach 1964; David, Hal 1964

How Many People Can Say   Hoffman 1952

How Many Rhymes Can You Get   Friend 1937

How Many Stars Are There in the Sky?   Blane 1961

How Many Times?   Berlin 1926; Turk 1921

How Many Times Do I Have to Tell You   Adamson 1944; McHugh 1944

How Many Times Have I Told You   Warren 1974

How Much Do You Love Me   Drake 1954

How Much I Care   Cahn 1987; Friml 1945

How Much I Love You   Berlin 1930; Weill 1943

How Much Is that Doggie in the Window   Merrill 1952

How Much Longer   Akst 1933; Mitchell 1933

How Much More Can You Hurt Me   Davis 1951; Silver 1951

How Much Will I Love You   Evans 1963; Livingston, Jay 1963

How My Sweetie Loves Me, She Loves Me All the Time   Coots 1924; Mitchell 1923; Pollack 1923

How Nice for Me   Carmichael 1940; Mercer 1940

How Nice of Love   Heyman 1932

How Now Dow Jones   Leigh 1964

How Now Down Jones   Leigh 1967

How Often   Rome 1973

How Old Do You Have to Be?   Hoffman 1958

How Old Do You Have to Be to Fall in Love   Davis 1981

How Peaceful Is the Evening   Rome 1948

How Proud I'll Be   Akst 1923; Davis 1923

How Quickly They Forget   Russell 1966

How Sad My Love (Je Vous Attends)   Gorney 1948

How Shall I Tell?   Lewis 1930; Warren 1930; Young, Joe 1930

How Shall We Begin   Evans 1968; Livingston, Jay 1968

How Should You Feel   Brooks 1959; Revel 1959

How Small We Are   Van Heusen 1962

How So Dear to My Heart   Coslow 1948; Johnston 1948

How Soon, Oh Moon?   Harburg 1961

How Soon You Are Forgotten When You're Gone   Fisher 1906

How Sorry You'll Be Wait'll You See   Kalmar 1919; Ruby 1919

How Strange   Kahn 1939; Young, Victor 1951

How Sweet Is the Summer (inst.)   Kern 1956
How Sweet It Is   Caesar 1963
How Sweet to Be a Cloud   Brooks 1960
How Sweet You Are   Loesser 1943; Schwartz, Arthur 1943
How Sweetly Friendship Binds   Weill 1936
How the Time Can Fly whenever I'm with You   Donaldson 1931
(My) How the Time Goes By   Coleman 1957; Leigh 1957
How They Changed the Day   Akst 1927; Davis 1927
How Thoughtful of You   Sigman 1946
How to Be a Successful Failure   Spina 1977
How to Be Happy Though Married   Smith, Harry B. 1904; Smith, Robert B. 1904
How to Be Very, Very Popular   Cahn 1955; Styne 1955
How to Behave Like a Lady (How to Dress Like a Lady/How to Faint Like a Lady)   Blane 1960; Martin 1960
How to Get in Central Park   Jerome 1905; Schwartz, Jean 1905
How to Handle a Woman   Lerner, Alan Jay 1960; Loewe 1960
How to Kill a Man 100 Ways Ballet (inst.)   Strouse 1960
How to Make a Pretty Face   Atteridge 1916; Motzan 1916; Romberg 1916
How to Make Love to an Heiress   Spina 1977
How to Pick a Man a Wife   Fain 1960; Webster 1960
How to Play an Ole Banjo   Blake 1930; Razaf 1930
How to Save Your Marriage and Ruin Your Life   David, Mack 1968
How to Spell Friendship   Caesar 1946
How to Succeed in Business without Really Trying   Loesser 1961
How to Survive   Weill 1954
How to Tell a Fairy Tale   Herbert 1905, 1911; Smith, Harry B. 1911
How to Win a Man   Hammerstein 1928; Youmans 1928
How to Win Friends and Influence People   Hart 1938; Rodgers 1938
How to Write a Popular Song   Donaldson 1942
How Warm It Is the Weather (How Cold It Is Your Heart)   Blane 1939
How Was I to Know   De Lange 1934; Hart 1928; Howard, Joseph E. 1907; Rodgers 1928
How Well I Remember (The Things You Forgot)   David, Hal 1956
How Were You to Know   Heyman 1965
How, Where, When, Why, What Made Me Start to Love You   Johnson, Howard 1926
How Will I Know   Russell 1977
How Will I Remember You   Sigman 1961
How Will He Know?   Comden and Green 1951; Styne 1951
How Wonderful   Razaf 1952
How Wonderfully Fortunate   Gershwin, Ira 1945; Weill 1945
How Would I Know   Fain 1944; Kahal 1944
How Would I Know? (I Wish Dat Dere Wasn't No War)   Hammerstein 1938; Kern 1938
How Would You Feel   Brooks 1946, 1960; Kahn 1941; Rainger 1938; Revel 1960; Robin 1938
How Would You Like to Bounce a Baby on Your Knee   Bryan 1916
How Would You Like to Take My Picture   Adamson 1945; McHugh 1945
How Y' Doin' in the Love Department   Yellen 1978
How Ya Baby   Waller 1938
How Ya Doin' in the Love Department   Russell 1944; Spina 1944

How 'Ya Gonna Keep 'Em Down on the Farm, After They've Seen Paree   Donaldson 1919; Lewis 1919; Young, Joe 1919
How Ya Gonna Keep Your Mind on Dancing (When You're Dancing with Someone You Love)?   Brown, Lew 1923; Hanley 1923
How Ya Gonna Stop Their Petting Parties   Dixon 1927; Monaco 1927
How You Played the Game   Cahn 1968
How'd Ya Like to Meet Me in the Moonlight   Coslow 1926
How'd You Get Out of My Dreams   Fain 1945; Yellen 1945
How'd You Happen to Fall for Me?   Ager 1937
How'd You Like an Apple   Meyer 1948
How'd You Like to?   Caesar 1927; Edwards 1925
How'd You Like to Be a Kid   McHugh 1922
How'd You Like to Be a Sailor?   Warren 1918
How'd You Like to Be My Daddy   Lewis 1918; Snyder 1918; Young, Joe 1918
How'd You Like to Float Me (Come on and Float Me Freddy Dear)   Goetz 1907
How'd You Like to Marry Me   Kahn 1908
How'd You Like to Put Your Head Upon My Pillow   Bryan 1921; Schwartz, Jean 1921
How'd You Like to Spoon with Me?   Kern 1905, 1906
How'd You Like to Take Me Home with You   Cobb 1907; Edwards 1907
Howdja Like to Go to Heaven with a Smile   Motzan 1930
How'dja Like to Love Me   Lane 1938; Loesser 1938
How-Dow   Drake 1958
Howdy Christmas   Lawrence 1981
Howdy Cloudy Morning   Dixon 1939; Woods 1939
Howdy Doody Polka, The   Coots 1952
Howdy Doody's Birthday   Coots 1955
Howdy Friends and Neighbors   DePaul 1956; Mercer 1956
Howdy Friends (Salud Amigo)   Coots 1961
Howdy! How D'You Do?   Kern 1909
Howdy Neighbor, Happy Harvest   Gordon 1950; Revel 1950; Warren 1950
Howdy Stranger   Mercer 1938; Revel 1946; Whiting 1938
Howdy to Broadway   Hart 1926; Rodgers 1926
Howdy-Do, Goodbye   Romberg 1915
Howdy-Do Valley   Freed, Ralph 1952; Hoffman 1952
How'm I Doin'   Strouse 1985
How'm I Doin' with You   Mitchell 1936; Stept 1936
How's About an Orchid (For Walter Winchell)   Robison 1954
How's About Tomorrow Night?   Bloom 1934; Koehler 1934
How's By You   Arlen 1936; Harburg 1936
How's Chances?   Berlin 1933
How's de Mammy?   Kalmar 1913
How's Every Little Thing in Dixie   Yellen 1916
How's the King   Gorney 1925
How's Your Health?   Hart 1940; Rodgers 1940
How's Your Little Maltese Cat   Gilbert 1913
How's Your Romance?   Porter 1932
How's Your Uncle?   Fields 1931; McHugh 1931
(On the Beach at) How've-You-Been?   DeSylva 1923; Gershwin, George 1923
Hoy, Hoy, Hoy   Cahn 1939
Hubby   Gershwin, Ira 1922, 1923
Huckleberry Duck   Lawrence 1940
Huckleberry Finn   Lane 1951; Lerner, Alan Jay 1951; Lewis 1917; Sherman 1974; Young, Joe 1917
Huckleberry Man, The   Koehler 1940; Warren 1940

Huckleberry Pie   Adamson 1950; Conrad 1918; McHugh 1950

Hud   David, Mack 1963

Huddlin'   Magidson 1929; Washington 1929

Hudson Duster   Brown, Lew 1927; DeSylva 1927; Henderson 1927

Hug Me a Hug, Kiss Me a Kiss   David, Hal 1953

Huggable and Kissable   Stept 1953

Huggin' and Muggin'   Blake 1937

Hugo   Silver 1923

Hugo, I Go Where You Go   Gilbert 1925

Hugo If You Go I'm Going Too   Snyder 1908

Hugs and Kisses   Alter 1926

Huguette Waltz   Friml 1925

Hul A Bal Loo Ba Lay   Russell 1943

Hula Ba Luau   DePaul 1941; Raye 1941

Hula Baloo   Rainger 1937; Robin 1937

Hula Boola Boo   Gilbert 1928

Hula Holiday   Rainger 1932; Robin 1932

Hula Hula Dream Girl   Kahn 1924

Hula, Hula, Sailor Man   Atteridge 1924; Romberg 1924; Schwartz, Jean 1924

Hula Lou   Yellen 1924

Hula Love Song   Sherman 1995

Hula Love Tune   Freed, Arthur 1931

Hula Serenade   Kahn 1917

Hula-Hula Love   Clarke 1915; Monaco 1915

Hullabaloo and Hoopahlah   Drake 1955

Hum a Tune   Gordon 1932; Revel 1932

Hum, Hum, Hum, Hum Your Troubles Away   Friend 1926; Woods 1926

Hum To   Hart 1926; Rodgers 1926

Human Nature   Kern 1915; Smith, Harry B. 1915

Human Night Key of New York, The   Smith, Harry B. 1908

Human of the Year, The   Drake 1956

Human Race, The   Robison 1954; Sherman 1970

Humble Hollywood Executive, A   Porter 1944

Humble Pie   Bacharach 1957; David, Hal 1957

Humble Side of the Town, The   Fain 1935; Kahal 1935

Humility (inst.)   Robison 1928

Humming   Caesar 1938; Henderson 1938; Merrill 1961

Humming a Tune   Atteridge 1922

Humming Bird Hum for Me   Henderson 1920

Humming (inst.)   Kern 1956

Humming-Bird   Adamson 1942

Humoreskimo   Bryan 1928

Humoresque   Dubin 1922; Johnson, Howard 1932

Humoresquimos   Atteridge 1922; Schwartz, Jean 1922

Humpty Dumpty   Caesar 1943; Herbert 1916; Johnson, Howard 1939; Robin 1927; Sterling 1921; Von Tilzer 1921

Humpty Dumpty Drag   Buck 1915

Humpty Dumpty Heart   Burke 1941; Van Heusen 1941

Humpty Dumpty March   Johnson, Howard 1925

Humpty Dumpty's Holiday   Coots 1936

Humpty-Dumpty   Brown, Nacio Herb 1932; DeSylva 1932; Whiting 1932

Hunder Runs Off to the Sea (inst.)   Blane 1961

Hundred Dreams from Now (Champagne Oasis), A   Burke 1958; Ellington 1958

Hundred Hills, A   Merrill 1951

Hundred Miles from Nowhere, A   Styne 1954

Hundred Million Miracles, A   Hammerstein 1958; Rodgers 1958

Hundred Women in One, A   Duke 1959

Hundred Years Ago, A   Friend 1933; Magidson 1933

Hundred Years from Now, A   DeSylva 1920

Hundred Years from Today, A   Washington 1933; Young, Joe 1933; Young, Victor 1933

Hungarian Rhapsody   Washington 1938

Hungaria's Hussars   Herbert 1898; Smith, Harry B. 1898

Hungry   Razaf 1932; Waller 1932; Young, Joe 1932

Hungry Blues   Johnson, James P. 1939

Hungry for Love   Spina 1957

Hungry Women   Ager 1928; Yellen 1928

Hunika   Fisher 1920

Hunkadola   Friend 1935

Hunky Dory   Strouse Date Unknown

Hunky Dunky Dory   Styne 1941

Hunt Dance, The (inst.)   Kern 1925

Hunted, The   Ellington 1946

Hunted Stag, The   Hart 1939; Rodgers 1939

Hunter's Chorus, The   Howard, Joseph E. 1905; Smith, Harry B. 1891

Hunter's Fox Trot Ball   Atteridge 1916; Hanley 1916; Romberg 1916; Smith, Harry B. 1916

Hunter's Holiday   Von Tilzer 1910

Hunting   Friml 1925

Hunting Chorus   Smith, Harry B. 1908

Hunting Dance, The   Romberg 1927

Hunting Days   Caesar 1930

Hunting of the Cook, The   Herbert 1905

Hunting Song   Hart 1930; Herbert 1911; Rodgers 1930; Smith, Harry B. 1911

Hunting the Fox   Hart 1930; Rodgers 1930

Huntsman's Song of Love, The   Robin 1931

Hup! Tup! Thrup! Four! (Joe, the Sleepy Jeep)   Rome 1943

Hup-Two-Three   Harburg 1961

Hurdy Gurdy   Dietz 1944; Duke 1944

Hurdy Gurdy Man, The   Cobb 1908; Dietz 1934; Edwards 1908; Gershwin, George 1923; Gershwin, Ira 1918, 1923; Schwartz, Arthur 1934

Hurdy-Gurdy   Loewe 1937

Hurdy-Gurdy Man, The   Buck 1914; Cahn 1936

Hurdy-Gurdy Song (The Black Orchid Street Melody), The   David, Mack 1958

Hurrah for the Bars and Stripes   Howard, Joseph E. 1909

Hurrah for the Summer Time   Von Tilzer 1910

Hurrah, Hurrah and Hurroo for That   Smith, Robert B. 1907

Hurray Hurray   Myrow 1956

Hurricane   Spina 1965

Hurroo, Hurray and Hurrah for That   Smith, Harry B. 1906

Hurry Back   Adams 1970; Strouse 1970

Hurry Back to My Bamboo Shack   Berlin 1916

Hurry, Hurry, Hurry (Darling, Come Home)   Robison 1952

Hurry! It's Lovely Up Here   Lane 1965; Lerner, Alan Jay 1965

Hurry, Little Children   Smith, Harry B. 1912

Hurry on Home   Leigh 1973

Hurry Sundown   Harburg 1966

Hurry Sundown, Let Tomorrow Come   Robison 1927

Hurry Up   Atteridge 1924; Romberg 1924; Schwartz, Jean 1924

Hurry Up! (Alberto's Lullaby)   Robin 1947

Hurry Up and Find Some Scrap   Caesar 1943

Hurry Up, Matilda   Kalmar 1925; Ruby 1925

Hurry Up 'n Hurry Down   Bergman 1969

Hurryin' Home   Ager 1934; Schwartz, Jean 1934; Young, Joe 1934

Hurst & Grady Theme   Oakland 1954

Hurt but Happy   Arlen 1964
Hurt They Write About, The   Merrill 1959
Hurtin' (For the Love of You)   Sherman 1959
Husband   Willson 1953
Husband Cage   Arlen 1954
Husbands! Husbands! Husbands!   Herbert 1914
Husband's Only a Husband, A   DeSylva 1922
Hush Hush   Weill 1938
Hush, Hush, Hush   Porter 1950
Hush, Hush, Sweet Charlotte   David, Mack 1964
Hush, I Think I Hear Him   Howard, Joseph E. 1909
Hush, Little Heartache   Livingston, Jerry 1955; Parish 1955
Hush Ma Mouth   Arlen 1936; Harburg 1936
Hush My Heart   Yellen 1938
Hush My Mouth If I Ain't Goin' South   Hoffman 1933
Hush Your Fuss   Brennan 1934; Snyder 1934
Hush-a-Bye   Fain 1953
Hush-a-Bye Don't Let Me Hear You Cry (The Moon Man Has His Eyes on You)   Fisher 1914
Hush-a-Bye Island   Adamson 1947; McHugh 1947
Hush-A-Bye Land   Duke 1941
Hushabye Mountain   Sherman 1968
Hush-a-Bye My Baby   Bryan 1919; Schwartz, Jean 1919
Hush-a-bye Wee Rose of Killarney   Koehler 1947
Husking Bee, The   Comden and Green 1958; Styne 1958
Hussars March   Romberg 1928
Hussars' Song, The   Smith, Harry B. 1927
Hustle Bustle   Drake 1955
Hustle, Bustle, Rustle of Spring   Hoffman 1937; Lerner, Sammy 1937
Hustlin' and Bustlin' for Baby   Woods 1933
Hut! 2-3-4 (I Love the Marching Song)   Friend 1943
Huxley   Gershwin, Ira 1940; Weill 1940
Hyacinth, The   Loesser 1948
Hyde Park on a Sunday   Burke 1946; Van Heusen 1946
Hydrophobia Blues   Harbach 1926; Kern 1926
Hymn   Duke 1946; Rainger 1937; Robin 1937
Hymn for a Sunday Evening   Adams 1960; Strouse 1960
Hymn to Him, A   Lerner, Alan Jay 1956; Loewe 1956
Hymn to Hymen   Porter 1936
Hymn to Peace   Weill 1936
Hymn to Thanksgiving   Lawrence 1971
Hymn to the Moon   Rodgers 1921
Hymn to the Sun   Brooks 1947; Friml 1927
Hypnosis (inst.)   Revel 1957
Hypnotic Kiss, The   Harbach 1908
Hypnotique   David, Mack 1959
Hypnotizing Man   Atteridge 1912

I

I Accuse You   Davis 1955; Silver 1955
I Admire You Very Much, Mr. Schmidt   Cahn 1970; Styne 1970
I Adore Eleanor   Coots 1926
I Adore New York   Cahn 1955; Styne 1955
I Adore You   Coslow 1926; Porter 1958; Rainger 1936; Robin 1936
I Ain't Afraid   Arlen 1959; Mercer 1959
I Ain't Afraid of Scarecrows (I Ain't Scared of Crows)   Eliscu 1929; Rose 1929; Youmans 1929
I Ain't A-Goin' to Weep No More   Von Tilzer 1900
I Ain't Been Right Since You Left   Hoffman 1957
I Ain't Comin' on that Tab (If You Go Barrel House)   Mills 1938

I Ain't Down Yet   Willson 1960
I Ain't Gonna Carry No Torch   Coslow 1934
I Ain't Gonna Cry No More   Donaldson 1925
I Ain't Gonna Give Nobody None of My Love   Blake 1955
I Ain't Gonna Lead This Life No More   Drake 1959
I Ain't Gonna Love Any More   Warren 1979
I Ain't Gonna Love No More   Von Tilzer 1935; Warren 1956, 1972
I Ain't Gonna Marry   Martin 1952
I Ain't Gonna Sin No More   Conrad 1934; Magidson 1934
I Ain't Got It for the Guy That's Got It for Me   Leigh 1967
I Ain't Got No Ear for Music   Jerome 1911; Schwartz, Jean 1911
I Ain't Got No Hard Luck Now   Dixon 1926
I Ain't Got Nobody and I Don't Want Nobody but You   Baer 1926; Lewis 1926; Young, Joe 1926
I Ain't Got Nobody to Love   Coslow 1924; Silver 1924
I Ain't Got Nothin' but the Blues   Ellington 1944
I Ain't Got Time to Be Your Baby   Edwards 1900
I Ain't Got Weary Yet   Johnson, Howard 1918
I Ain't Mad at Nobody   Robison 1955
I Ain't Never Been Kissed   Leslie 1929
I Ain't Never Felt So Good Before   Lane 1951; Lerner, Alan Jay 1951
I Ain't No Fool   Smith, Harry B. 1912
I Ain't Nobody's Fool   Washington 1946
I Ain't that Kind of a Baby   Fain 1927; Kahal 1927
I Ain't Your Hen, Mr. Fly Rooster   Razaf 1928
I Ain't-en Got-en No Time to Have the Blues   Sterling 1919; Von Tilzer 1919
I Almost Forgot   Clare 1943
I Always Believe Me   Lerner, Alan Jay 1971
I Always Come Back to You   Smith, Harry B. 1911
I Always Give the Wrong Impression   Caesar 1920
I Always Go to Sleep with the Blues   Brown, Lew 1927; DeSylva 1927; Henderson 1927
I Always Keep My Girl Out Late   Hammerstein 1933
I Always Knew   Porter 1943; Strouse 1993
I Always Meant to Tell You   Cahn 1946; Styne 1946
I Always Say   Sigman 1957
I Always See Them Safely Home   Johnson, Howard 1916
I Always Shake the Tree   Drake 1953
I Always Think I'm Up in Heaven, When I'm Down in Dixieland   Lewis 1919; Schwartz, Jean 1919; Young, Joe 1919
I Always Think of Sally   Duke 1941
I Always Wanted to Be a Dancin' Man   Cahn 1980; Strouse 1980
I Always Wanted to Waltz in Berlin Under the Linden Tree   Caesar 1943
I Always Wear My Derby When It Rains   Fain 1932; Young, Joe 1932
I Am   Merrill 1956
I Am a Court Coquette   Herbert 1899; Smith, Harry B. 1899
I Am a Fact (I Am an Is)   David, Mack 1961; Livingston, Jerry 1961
I Am a Living Thing   David, Hal 1978
I Am a Potentate   Smith, Harry B. 1906
I Am a Prince   Hart 1928; Rodgers 1928
I Am a Witch   Hammerstein 1955; Rodgers 1955
I Am Afraid to Waltz with You   Coslow 1930
I Am An Is   Livingston, Jerry 1961
I Am Ashamed that Women Are So Simple   Porter 1948
I Am Captured   Romberg 1927; Smith, Harry B. 1927
I Am Cleopatra   Goetz 1920

I Am Craving for that Kind of Love (Kiss Me)   Blake 1921;
    Sissle 1921
I Am Gaston   Porter 1938
I Am Getting Better All the Time   Schwartz, Arthur 1922
I Am Going to Like It Here   Hammerstein 1958; Rodgers
    1958
I Am Happy Here   Gershwin, Ira 1945; Weill 1945
I Am Hawaii   David, Mack 1966
I Am Headed for Southland   Razaf 1930
I Am in Love   Porter 1953
I Am Inkas   Sherman 1954
I Am Losing My Little Wren   Rome 1970
I Am Loved   Porter 1950
I Am Melpomene   Jerome 1910; Schwartz, Jean 1910
I Am Mrs. Stanhope Van Hepworth And   Cahn 1964; Van
    Heusen 1964
I Am Music   Revel 1951
I Am Never Alone   Cahn 1969; Van Heusen 1969
I Am Only Human After All   Duke 1930; Gershwin, Ira
    1930; Harburg 1930
I Am Only Me   Lawrence 1961
I Am Only Mimi   Dietz 1952
I Am Over 25 but You Can Trust Me   David, Mack 1976
I Am Praying Humble   Lawrence 1938
I Am So Eager   Hammerstein 1932; Kern 1932
I Am the Girl (And I Am the Boy)   DeSylva 1919
I Am the Man They Talk So Much About   Smith, Harry B.
    1906
I Am the Pasha   Romberg 1919; Smith, Harry B. 1903
I Am the Singer, You Are the Song   Caesar 1933; Romberg
    1933
I Am the Words (You Are the Melody)   Brown, Lew 1930;
    DeSylva 1930; Henderson 1930
I Am Thinking of You   Caesar 1923, 1924; Conrad 1924;
    Harbach 1924
I Am True to All   Romberg 1916; Smith, Robert B. 1916
I Am Waiting for the Summertime and You   Edwards 1908
I Am Waiting in the Desert   Spina 1955
I Am What I Am   Cahn 1970; Styne 1970
I Am Writing a Love Song for You   Styne 1980
I Am Your Dream   Webster 1958
I Am Yours   Davis 1928
I and Albert   Adams 1972; Strouse 1972
I Apologize   Hoffman 1931
I Ask No More of Thee   Brennan 1918
I Ask You   Cahn 1952; Duke 1952
I Asked My Heart   Eliscu 1937
I Ay Ay   Russell 1956
I Be Gwine Back to Dixie   Johnson, Howard 1939
I Beg Your Pardon   Berlin 1911; Coots 1941; Gordon 1941;
    Hart 1925; Rodgers 1925
I Beg Your Pardon, Dear Old Broadway   Snyder 1911
I Beg Your Pardon Mademoiselle   Magidson 1932; Stept
    1932
I Begged Her   Cahn 1945; Styne 1945
I Believe   Cahn 1947; Drake 1952; Styne 1947
I Believe Ev'ry Word I've Heard about You   Bryan 1936
I Believe in God   Bryan 1952
I Believe in Love   Bergman 1976
I Believe in Me   Blane 1961
I Believe in Miracles   Lewis 1934; Meyer 1934
I Believe in Santa Claus   Coots 1945; David, Hal 1950; Egan
    1945
I Believe in Takin' a Chance   Dietz 1963; Schwartz, Arthur
    1963

I Believe in This Country   Sherman 1967
I Believe in You   Dietz 1937; Loesser 1961; Schwartz, Arthur
    1937
I Believe You   Buck 1924
I Believed All They Said   Kern 1918
I Believed It All   Bergman 1965, 1966; Mancini 1973
I Belong   David, Hal 1985
I Belong, Belong, Belong   Drake 1956
I Belong in Alabam'   Ager 1933; Young, Joe 1933
I Belong to Everybody   Brown, Nacio Herb 1931; Eliscu 1931
I Belong to Someone   Silver 1926
I Belong to Something   David, Mack 1961; Livingston, Jerry
    1961
I Belong to the Majority   David, Mack 1961; Livingston,
    Jerry 1961
I Belong to You   Brooks 1955; Hoffman 1951; Mercer 1971
I Belong to You, You Belong to Me   Henderson 1926
I Betcha (She Won't Let-cha Get Out of Her Arms)   Wrubel
    1944
I Blush   Hart 1927; Rodgers 1927
I Boogied when I Should Have Woogied   Mercer 1941
I Bought It   Lawrence 1961
I Bow a Glad Good Day (Tavern Opening)   Hart 1928;
    Rodgers 1928
I Bring a Love Song   Hammerstein 1930; Romberg 1930
I Bring a Song   Kahn 1933; Young, Victor 1933
I Bring, You a Rose   Stept 1927
I Bring You Love   David, Hal 1960
I Brought Red Roses in December to You   Bryan 1916
I Brought Them Home to Mother   Herbert 1904
I Brought You a Gift   Rodgers 1976
I Built a Dream One Day   Hammerstein 1935; Romberg
    1935
I Cain't Say No   Hammerstein 1943; Rodgers 1943
I Call Her Virgin Mary   Johnson, Howard 1921
I Call Upon You Gentlemen   Hart 1926; Rodgers 1926
I Call You Sunshine   Caesar 1921; DeSylva 1921
I Called to Say Good-Night   Conrad 1932; Young, Joe 1932
I Called You My Sweetheart   Clarke 1916; Johnson, Howard
    1916; Monaco 1916
I Came All the Way from Texas   Adamson 1950; McHugh
    1950
I Came Back to Say I'm Sorry   David, Hal 1956
I Came Here   Gershwin, Ira 1924
I Came Here to Talk for Joe   Brown, Lew 1942; Stept 1942
I Came Home to an Empty Heart   Webster 1974
I Came! I Saw! I Fell!   Atteridge 1922
I Came, I Saw, You Conquered   Heyman 1932
I Came to Life   Harburg 1929
I Came to Life when I Found You   Gorney 1930; Harburg
    1930
I Came to Say Goodbye   Spina 1958
I Came to You   Conrad 1929; Mitchell 1929
I Can Always Find a Little Sunshine in the Y.M.C.A.   Berlin
    1918
I Can Always Find Another Partner   Hammerstein 1923;
    Harbach 1923; Youmans 1923
I Can Cook Too   Comden and Green 1944
I Can Count the Times on My Fingers   Wrubel 1947
I Can Do Without Tea in My Teapot   Porter 1943
I Can Do Without You   Fain 1953; Webster 1953
I Can Do Wonders with You   Hart 1929, 1930; Rodgers
    1929, 1930
I Can Dream, Can't I   Fain 1938; Kahal 1938

I Can Get More Lovin' from a Dum, Dum, Dummy than I've Been Getting from You   Brown, Lew 1924; Henderson 1924; Rose 1924

I Can Hardly Wait   Bergman 1980; Lane 1980

I Can Hear It Now   Rome 1950

I Can Live Without You   Buck 1913

I Can Live Without Your Kisses, but I Won't Be Happy Dear   Bryan 1916

I Can Make Most Anything but I Can't Make a Man   Bloom 1930; Young, Joe 1930

I Can Make You Laugh (But I Wish I Could Make You Cry)   Berlin 1954

I Can Make You Love Me   Russell 1943, 1945

I Can Never Keep Away from You   Clarke 1916; Monaco 1916

I Can Pull a Rabbit Out of My Hat   David, Mack 1936

I Can See It All Now   Bergman 1964; Fain 1964

I Can See You   Cahn 1951

I Can See You All Over the Place   Waller 1936

I Can See You Now   Magidson 1942; Pollack 1942

I Can Sew a Button   Lerner, Sammy 1933

I Can Spell Banana but I Never Know when to Stop   Mercer 1955

I Can Still Remember   De Lange 1944; Stept 1944

I Can Still Smile   Warren 1972, 1979

I Can Sympathize with You   Davis 1931

I Can Take It on the Chin but not on the Heart   Fisher 1937

I Can Take It or Leave It   Cahn Date Unknown; Duke Date Unknown

I Can Talk!   Sherman 1973

I Can Teach Them   Adams 1962; Strouse 1962

I Can Tell By Looking in Your Eyes   Howard, Joseph E. 1938

I Can Tell By the Way You Dance Dear   Friml 1914; Harbach 1914

I Can Wiggle My Ears   Hoffman 1935

I Cannot Be Faithful   Friml 1934

I Cannot Drink the Old Drinks   Goetz 1912

I Cannot Let You Go   Loesser 1969

I Cannot Live Forever So You'd Better Love Me Now   Brown, Lew 1913

I Cannot Live Without Your Love   Caesar 1936

I Cannot Make Him Jealous   Drake 1968

I Cannot Sing the Old Songs   Johnson, Howard 1939

I Cannot Sleep Without Dreaming of You   Herbert 1920; Smith, Robert B. 1920

I Cannot Take a Step Too Far   Smith, Harry B. 1915

I Cannot Tell You Why All I Know Is I'm in Love with You   Coots 1932; Turk 1932

I Can't Afford to Dream   Brown, Lew 1939; Henderson Date Unknown; Stept 1939

I Can't Argue with You   DeSylva 1922; Herbert 1922

I Can't Be Bothered Now   Gershwin, George 1937; Gershwin, Ira 1937

I Can't Be Happy   Youmans 1926

I Can't Be True So Far Away   Howard, Joseph E. 1909

I Can't Begin to Tell You   Gordon 1945; Monaco 1945

I Can't Believe It   Heyman 1928

I Can't Believe It Was All Make Believe (Last Night)   Coots 1947; Lewis 1947

I Can't Believe It's True   Whiting 1936

I Can't Believe My Eyes   De Lange 1945

I Can't Believe that It's You   Gilbert 1932; Silver 1932

I Can't Believe that You're in Love with Me   McHugh 1925

I Can't Believe You're Alone   Davis 1928

I Can't Blame the Boys for Lovin' You   Razaf 1926

I Can't Break the Habit of You   Razaf 1937

I Can't Complain   Rodgers 1970

I Can't Do the Sum   Herbert 1903

I Can't Do This I Can't Do That   Schwartz, Jean 1920

I Can't Do Without You   Berlin 1928; Leslie 1927

I Can't Escape from You   Coslow 1935; Robin 1936; Whiting 1936

I Can't Face the Music (Without Singin' the Blues)   Bloom 1938; Koehler 1938

I Can't Feel Too Bad   Drake 1954

I Can't Fool My Heart   Davis 1970

I Can't Forget   Cahn 1956; Dietz 1929; Kahn 1916; Schwartz, Arthur 1929; Whiting 1916

I Can't Forget (N'Oublie Jamain)   Lawrence 1955

I Can't Forget that You Forgot About Me   Kahn 1932

I Can't Forget the Melody   Sherman 1976

I Can't Forget the Minuet   Burke 1932; Hoffman 1932; Spina 1932

I Can't Forget You   Akst 1923; Conrad 1930; Lewis 1923; Mitchell 1930; Young, Joe 1923

I Can't Forget Your Eyes   Kern 1913; Smith, Harry B. 1913, 1915, 1924; Snyder 1924

I Can't Forgive You   Waller 1938

I Can't Get a Girl   Kalmar 1914; Leslie 1914; Snyder 1914

I Can't Get Along with Horses   Kahn 1940

I Can't Get Along Without My Baby   Mills 1931

I Can't Get Along Without You   Kahn 1918

I Can't Get Enough   Smith, Harry B. 1911

I Can't Get Enough of You   Adamson 1952; McHugh 1952

(I've Got Her Off My Hands, Now That She's Off My Hands) I Can't Get Her Off o' My Mind   Lewis 1926; Young, Joe 1926

I Can't Get Into the Quota   Schwartz, Arthur 1927

I Can't Get Mississippi Off My Mind   Akst 1931; Young, Joe 1931

I Can't Get Started   Duke 1936; Gershwin, Ira 1936

I Can't Get the One I Want   Rose 1924

I Can't Get to First Base with You   Fisher 1935

I Can't Get Used to Being Your Used to Be   Burke 1931

I Can't Get You Out of My Mind   Blake 1964; Brooks 1945, 1946; Sissle 1964

I Can't Give Her Up   Lewis 1915

I Can't Give You Anything but Love   Fields 1928; McHugh 1928

I Can't Go Back   Comden and Green 1964; Styne 1964

I Can't Go on Like This   Johnson, Howard 1934

I Can't Go on This Way   Rainger 1929; Robin 1929, 1931; Whiting 1931

I Can't Help It If I Love You   Stept 1944

I Can't Help It If I'm Fidgety   Leslie 1908

I Can't Help Loving You   Magidson 1953

I Can't Hold On   David, Hal 1979

I Can't Imagine   Fisher 1930; Freed, Ralph 1939; Lane 1939

I Can't Keep My Eyes from Looking at You   Atteridge 1913

I Can't Keep You Out of My Dreams   Fain 1926; Kahal 1926

I Can't Let You Down   Coleman 1966; Fields 1966

I Can't Let You Go   Coleman 1972; Fields 1972

I Can't Lose that Longing for You   Dixon 1936

I Can't Love Everybody   Howard, Joseph E. 1909

I Can't Love You Any More (Any More than I Do)   Magidson 1940; Wrubel 1940

I Can't Make My Feet Behave   Edwards 1930

I Can't Make My Heart Behave   Eliscu 1929; Rose 1929; Youmans 1929

I Can't Make My Husband Behave   Youmans 1926

I Can't Make Up My Mind   Cahn 1963; Kahn 1938;
   Romberg 1938; Van Heusen 1963
I Can't Put My Arms Around a Memory   Ellington 1944
I Can't Reach Your Heart   Davis 1962
I Can't Realize You Love Me   DeSylva 1925; Donaldson
   1925
I Can't Realize You're Gone   Kahn 1923; Meyer 1923
I Can't Remember   Berlin 1933
I Can't Remember the Words   Ager 1929; Yellen 1929
I Can't Resist a Boy in a Uniform   David, Mack 1952;
   Livingston, Jerry 1952
I Can't Resist Them When They're Beautiful   Buck 1921
I Can't Say Goodbye Nobody's Property   Sherman 1978
I Can't Say Manana   Gilbert 1955
I Can't Say You're the Only One   Kern 1908
I Can't See You All   Atteridge 1918; Romberg 1918
I Can't Sleep   Adams 1950; Strouse 1950
I Can't Spell Hippopotamus   Coots 1956
I Can't Stand It   Ahlert 1927; Freed, Ralph 1966; Kahn 1927
I Can't Stand Losing You   Myrow 1943
I Can't Stop Babying You   Kahn 1924
I Can't Stop Cryin'   Sherman 1958
I Can't Stop Crying   McHugh 1964
I Can't Stop Dancing   Strouse 1994
I Can't Stop Loving   Gordon Date Unknown; Warren Date
   Unknown
I Can't Stop Loving You Now   Kalmar 1914; Leslie 1914;
   Snyder 1914
I Can't Tell a Lie   Berlin 1942
I Can't Tell a Waltz from a Tang   Hoffman 1954
I Can't Tell My Heart   Friend 1960
I Can't Tell Where They're from When They Dance   DeSylva
   1922; Gershwin, George 1922; Goetz 1922
I Can't Tell Why I Love You But I Do   Cobb 1900; Edwards
   1900
I Can't Tell You   Strouse 1980
I Can't Throw the Old Dreams Away   Hanley 1939
I Can't Wait   Fields 1929; McHugh 1929
I Can't Wait to Take You Home to Mother   Cahn 1964; Van
   Heusen 1964
I Can't Wait Until Tomorrow 'Cause Tomorrow I Go Home
   on Leave   Drake 1942
I Can't Waltz Alone   Fields 1935
I Can't Wed Ya (But My Sister She Might)   Mills 1949
I Cantelope Tonight   Johnson, Howard 1924
I Care   Cahn 1980; DePaul 1980
I Care for Her and She Cares for Me   Stept 1925
I Care for You — You Care for Me   Caesar 1943
I Caught a Ball at the Ball Game   Hoffman 1941; Livingston,
   Jerry 1941
I Certainly Didn't Know When You First Came In   Sterling
   1900; Von Tilzer 1900
I Challenge You   Cahn 1950
I Click ze Heel and I Kees ze Hand   Arlen 1937; Harburg
   1937
I Cling to You   Duke 1939
I Close My Eyes   Styne 1940, 1941
I Close My Eyes and Dream   Brennan 1928
I Come A-Runnin'   Loesser Date Unknown
I Come from Delaware   Blane 1948
I Come from Gascony   Herbert 1899; Smith, Harry B. 1899
I Come to You   Bacharach 1973; David, Hal 1973
I Concentrate on You   Porter 1939
I Confess   Lawrence 1953
I Congratulate You, Mr. Cowboy   Hart 1941; Rodgers 1941

I Could Be a Mountain   David, Hal 1958
I Could Be Good for You   Arlen 1964
I Could Be Happy with One Little Boy If There Were No
   Others Around   Whiting 1919
I Could Be in Heaven If You'd Come Down to
   Earth   Hoffman 1936
I Could Be Wrong   Gilbert 1945
I Could Cook   Arlen 1953; Fields 1953
I Could Do a Lot for You   Friml 1922; Harbach 1922
I Could Do It for You   Conrad 1929; Mitchell 1929
I Could Do This All Night Long   Brown, Lew 1941, 1943;
   Freed, Ralph 1943; Henderson 1941, 1943
I Could Expect It from Anyone but You   Hoffman 1932
I Could Get Along with You   Burke 1949; Van Heusen 1949
I Could Get Along Without You   Burke 1941; Van Heusen
   1941
I Could Get Used to This   Strouse 1989, 1999
I Could Give Up Anything But You   Brown, Lew 1929;
   DeSylva 1929; Henderson 1929
I Could Go for You   Fields 1930; McHugh 1930
I Could Go Home to a Girlie Like You   Atteridge 1915;
   Romberg 1915
I Could Go on Forever   DePaul 1958; Raye 1958
I Could Go on Singing (Till the Cows Come Home)   Arlen
   1963; Harburg 1963
I Could Have Danced All Night   Lerner, Alan Jay 1956;
   Loewe 1956
I Could Have Told You   Loesser Date Unknown; Sigman
   1954; Van Heusen 1954
I Could Kick Myself   Bacharach 1958; David, Hal 1958;
   Porter 1957
I Could Kick Myself (For Getting a Kick Out of
   You)   Hoffman 1938
I Could Kiss You for That   McHugh 1941; Mercer 1941
I Could Love a Man Like That   Brown, Lew 1930; DeSylva
   1930; Henderson 1930
I Could Make You Care   Cahn 1940
I Could Make You Mine   Bacharach 1960; David, Hal 1960
I Could Say Goodnight to a Thousand Girls (But Only
   Dream of One)   Cobb Date Unknown
I Could Use a Dream   Bullock 1938; Spina 1938
I Could Write a Book   Hart 1940; Rodgers 1940
I Couldn't Be Annoyed   Robin 1932; Whiting 1932
I Couldn't Be True to an Angel   Brown, Lew 1953;
   Henderson 1953
I Couldn't Care Less   Cahn 1959; Van Heusen 1959
I Couldn't Get Along (Without You)   Mills 1955
I Couldn't Get to It   Woods 1924
I Couldn't Go to Ireland So Ireland Came to Me   Von Tilzer
   1918
I Couldn't Have Done It Alone   Adams 1962; Strouse 1962
I Couldn't Hold My Man   Arlen 1934; Gershwin, Ira 1934;
   Harburg 1934
I Couldn't If I Wanted To — Wouldn't If I Could   Mills 1928
I Couldn't Keep Away from You   Kahn 1914
I Couldn't Live Without the Lovin' that You Gave to
   Me   Friend 1918
I Couldn't Love You Anymore   Brooks 1946
I Couldn't Sleep a Wink Last Night   Adamson 1943;
   McHugh 1943
I Couldn't Stand to See My Baby Lose   Cobb 1899; Edwards
   1899
I Couldn't Take My Eyes Off You   Merrill 1953
I Couldn't Tell Them What to Do   Turk 1933
I Count My Blessings   Ruby 1952

I Cover the Waterfront   Heyman 1933

I Cried Enough Tears (To Float a Boat)   Drake 1952

I Cried for You (Now It's Your Turn to Cry Over
   Me)   Freed, Arthur 1939

I Cried Like a Baby   Drake 1954

I Cry Alone   Bacharach 1960; David, Hal 1960

I Cry More   Bacharach 1956; David, Hal 1956

I Dance when I Walk   Hoffman 1957

I Dare not Love You   Romberg 1925; Smith, Harry B. 1925

I Dare to Speak of Love to You   Smith, Harry B. 1927

I Dare You   Freed, Ralph 1942; Lane 1942

I Dearly Adore a Saloon   Dietz 1944; Duke 1944

I Dearly Do Love to Eat   Cahn 1971; Van Heusen 1971

I Depend on You   Evans 1967; Livingston, Jay 1967

I Did It and I'm Glad   Fields 1952; Schwartz, Arthur 1952

I Did It for Defense   Rome 1942

I Did It for the Missus   Burke 1946; Van Heusen 1946

I Did It for the Red, White and Blue   Bloom 1939; Mercer
   1939

I Did It on Roller Skates   Merrill 1964; Styne 1964

I Didn't Ask to Be Born   Ruby 1962

I Didn't Believe   Young, Joe 1962

I Didn't Come Here to Steal Anybody's Man   Brown, Lew
   1912

I Didn't Dream It Was Love   Conrad 1932; Waller 1932

I Didn't Expect It from You   Clare 1950

I Didn't Go Home at All   Berlin 1909; Leslie 1909; Snyder
   1909

I Didn't Know About You   Ellington 1944; Russell 1943

I Didn't Know How Much I'd Miss ——   Russell Date
   Unknown

I Didn't Know She Loved Me   Spina 1977

I Didn't Know what Time It Was   Hart 1939; Rodgers 1939

I Didn't Know Where My Next Dream was Comin'
   From   Russell 1947; Sigman 1947

(I'm Sorry) I Didn't Mean a Word I Said   Adamson 1946;
   McHugh 1946

I Didn't Mean It   Davis 1929; Magidson 1933; Monaco 1933;
   Silver 1929

I Didn't Mean No Harm   Smith, Robert B. 1905

I Didn't Mean to Hurt Your Feelings, I Didn't Mean to Make
   You Cry   Coots 1932; Kahn 1932

I Didn't Raise My Boy To Be a Soldier   Bryan 1914

I Didn't Think I'd Like To   Johnston 1946

I Didn't Think You Cared   Warren Date Unknown

I Didn't Wanna, But I Wanna Love You Now   Brown, Lew
   1926; Clare 1926; Monaco 1926

I Didn't Wanna Love You   Ager 1934; David, Mack 1934;
   Schwartz, Jean 1934

I Didn't Want to Love You   Russell 1956

I Didn't Want to Love You (I Don't Want to Love
   You)   Conrad 1934; Washington 1934

I Didn't Want You to Be Sorry for Me   Whiting 1925

I Do   DeSylva 1925; Porter 1953; Webster 1933

I Do Believe in Fairies, I Do, Don't You   Whiting 1925

I Do Better Up in the Mountains than I Do Down By the
   Sea   Stept 1950

I Do Business in My Hat   Weill 1938

I Do, Do, Do Like You   Wrubel 1947

I Do! He Doesn't!   Lawrence 1951

I Do! I Do! I Do!   Evans 1953; Livingston, Jay 1953; Razaf
   1950

I Do, I Don't Know Why   Friml 1952

I Do It All By Proxy   Smith, Harry B. 1906, 1935

I Do It with My Oo-La-La   Monaco 1930

I Do It with My Oo-La-La-La-La   Friend 1930; Monaco
   1930

I Do Like You   Sondheim 1962

I Do Not Choose to Swim   Gordon 1955

I Do Not Know a Day I Did Not Love Her   Rodgers 1970

I Do, So There!   Mitchell 1921; Pollack 1921

I Do You — Do You Me?   Friend 1946

I Done Caught You Blues   Mills 1928

I Don't Believe I'll Ever Be a Lady   Herbert 1906

I Don't Believe in Kissing   Johnson, Howard 1926

I Don't Believe in Signs   Mercer 1939; Warren 1939

I Don't Believe in Sometime   David, Hal 1958

I Don't Believe It but Say It Again   Silver 1926

I Don't Believe You   Von Tilzer 1910

I Don't Care for You Any More   Leslie 1921; Monaco 1921

I Don't Care If I Never Dream Again   Brooks 1945, 1946

I Don't Care If I Never Go to Bed   Hoffman 1945;
   Livingston, Jerry 1945

I Don't Care If It Rains All Night   Cahn 1948; Styne 1948

I Don't Care If She's Not Good Lookin'   Leslie 1954

I Don't Care If the Sun Don't Shine   David, Mack 1953

I Don't Care If the World Knows It   Revel 1944; Webster
   1944

I Don't Care to Be Yo' Lady Fren' No Mo'   Cobb 1904;
   Edwards 1904

I Don't Care What They Say About Me   Davis 1957

I Don't Care What You Used to Be (I Know What You Are
   To-Day)   Dubin 1924; McHugh 1924

I Don't Care Who Knows It   Adamson 1945; McHugh 1945

I Don't Dig You, Kookie (Whatcha Tryin' to Say)   Drake
   1959

I Don't Do Duets   Bergman 1990

I Don't Feel at Home on the Range   Evans 1948; Livingston,
   Jay 1948

I Don't Give a Continental   Hoffman 1936

I Don't Have to Die to Go to Heaven   Ager 1920; Johnson,
   Howard 1920

I Don't Have to Dream Again   Dubin 1936; Warren 1936

I Don't Have to Look in the Papers   Brooks 1959

I Don't Hurt Anymore   McHugh 1964

I Don't Know   Lerner, Alan Jay 1983; Strouse 1983

I Don't Know but I'd Like to Learn   Meyer 1909

I Don't Know How   Rodgers 1979

I Don't Know How I Can Do Without You   Egan 1932

I Don't Know How I Do It but I Do   Herbert 1913; Smith,
   Harry B. 1913; Smith, Robert B. 1913

I Don't Know How It Happened   Parish 1954

I Don't Know If I Want You   Oakland 1954

I Don't Know Myself Since I Know You   Akst 1936; Clare
   1936

I Don't Know What I Want   Blane 1956; Martin 1956

I Don't Know what I'd Do Without You   Buck 1922

I Don't Know What I've Got   Cahn 1952; Duke 1952

I Don't Know What Kind of Blues I've Got   Ellington 1942

I Don't Know Where I'm Going   Drake 1968

I Don't Know Where My Next Kiss Is Coming
   From   Adamson 1959; Fain 1948; McHugh 1950; Yellen
   1948

I Don't Know Where She Got It   Comden and Green 1967;
   Styne 1967

I Don't Know Whether to Laugh or to Cry Over You (The
   Hysteria Song)   Coslow 1949

I Don't Know Why   Caesar 1922

I Don't Know Why, I Just Do   Ahlert 1931; Turk 1931

I Don't Know Why I Love You, I Only Know I Do   Kahn 1924

I Don't Know Why I Love You So   Ellington 1947; Mills 1947

I Don't Know Why (When I Dance with You)   Caesar 1920; Gershwin, George 1920

I Don't Know Why You Make Me Love You   Dixon 1924; Henderson 1924; Rose 1924

I Don't Know You Well Enough for That   Hanley 1930

I Don't Know Your Name (But You're Beautiful)   Caesar 1935; Lerner, Sammy 1935

I Don't Laugh at Love Any More   Hammerstein 1920; Harbach 1920

I Don't Like Music   Oakland 1937

I Don't Like the Sea   Atteridge 1915

I Don't Like Them Too   Donaldson 1926

I Don't Like this Dame   Loesser 1956

I Don't Like Your Family   Howard, Joseph E. 1907

I Don't Love Nobody but You   Johnson, James P. 1929

I Don't Love You — Not Much   Akst 1935; Brown, Lew 1935

I Don't Love You Anymore   Strouse Date Unknown

I Don't Love You No More, No More   Cahn 1944; Styne 1944

I Don't Love You Well Enough for That   Smith, Robert B. 1908

I Don't Mean a Thing to You I Knew   Robin 1936

I Don't Mind   Ellington 1942

I Don't Mind Being All Alone, When I'm All Alone with You   McHugh 1926; Mills 1926

I Don't Mind Walking in the Rain (When I'm Walking in the Rain with You)   Hoffman 1930

I Don't Need a Psychiatrist   Johnson, J. Rosamond 1950

I Don't Need Any Dreams   Burke 1946

I Don't Need Anything but You   Strouse 1977

I Don't Need Atmosphere (to Fall in Love)   Coslow 1930

I Don't Need to Know   Robison 1952

I Don't Need You Anymore   Bacharach 1979

I Don't Repent   Schwartz, Jean 1942

I Don't See You Anymore   Warren 1953

I Don't Sleep at Night, but Oh How I Dream All Day   Caesar 1936

I Don't Suppose   Kahn 1931

I Don't Think I Love You, I Know I Do   Williams 1910

I Don't Think I'll End It All Today   Arlen 1957; Harburg 1957

I Don't Think I'll Fall in Love Today   Gershwin, George 1928; Gershwin, Ira 1928

I Don't Think I'm in Love   Cahn 1966; Van Heusen 1966

I Don't Think You Know How Much It Hurts Me   David, Hal 1961

I Don't Trust . . .   Styne Date Unknown

I Don't Wanna Be Alone Again   Mercer 1954

I Don't Wanna Be Loved (By Anyone But You)   Coslow 1927

I Don't Wanna Be Married (I Just Wanna Be Friends)   Berlin 1932

I Don't Wanna Die   Strouse 1989

I Don't Wanna Lose Ya   David, Hal 1959

I Don't Wanna Lose You   Alter 1933

I Don't Wanna Play   Coslow 1934; Johnston 1934

I Don't Wanna Say Goodnight   David, Hal 1959

I Don't Want a Girlie   DeSylva 1925; Henderson 1924; Youmans 1925

I Don't Want a Little Canoe   Jerome 1905; Schwartz, Jean 1905

I Don't Want a Million Dollars   Gordon 1944; Howard, Joseph E. 1908; Monaco 1944

I Don't Want an Auto   Jerome 1907

I Don't Want Any Labor in My Job   Johnson, James P. 1948

I Don't Want Any More   Meyer 1907

I Don't Want Any Other Sweetheart If I Can't Have You   Sterling 1911; Von Tilzer 1911

I Don't Want Any Wurzburger   Jerome 1904; Schwartz, Jean 1904

I Don't Want Anybody Around   Hanley 1919

I Don't Want Anybody At All (If I Can't Have You)   Magidson 1942; Styne 1942

I Don't Want Anyone to Love You but Me   Strouse 1993

I Don't Want Him   Conrad 1926; Kahn 1926

(If This Is Love) I Don't Want Love   Heyman 1931

I Don't Want Sympathy I Want Love   Lawrence 1957

I Don't Want That Kind of Love   Warren 1923

I Don't Want the World   Davis 1926

I Don't Want to Be a Gentleman   Robin 1957; Styne 1957

I Don't Want to Be a Soldier   Smith, Harry B. 1927

I Don't Want to Be Gay!   Rome 1940

I Don't Want to Be in Dixie   Buck 1922

I Don't Want to Be Loved a Little By a Lot of Little Boys (But By One Little Boy A Lot)   Hanley 1917

I Don't Want to Be Loved by Anyone Else but You   Livingston, Jerry 1942

I Don't Want to Be President (If It Means Losing You)   Akst 1934; Brown, Lew 1934

I Don't Want to Change the Subject (But Did You Buy a Bond Today?)   Brown, Lew 1945; Henderson 1945

I Don't Want to Fall in Love with You   Sondheim Date Unknown

I Don't Want to Get Married, I'm Having too Much Fun   Jerome 1924

I Don't Want to Get Thin   Ager 1929; Yellen 1929

I Don't Want to Get Well   Johnson, Howard 1917

I Don't Want to Go Home   Herbert 1919; Smith, Robert B. 1919

I Don't Want to Grow Old   Adams 1996; Strouse 1993, Date Unknown

I Don't Want to Know   Hoffman 1956

I Don't Want to Love No One but You   Brown, Lew Date Unknown; Henderson Date Unknown

I Don't Want to Make History (I Just Want to Make Love)   Rainger 1935; Robin 1935

I Don't Want to Marry Your Family   Howard, Joseph E. 1909

I Don't Want To (Oh, Come On)   Brown, A. Seymour 1913

I Don't Want to Play in Your Yard   Johnson, Howard 1939

I Don't Want to Walk Without You   Loesser 1942; Styne 1942

I Don't Want You to Be a Sister to Me   Kern 1910

I Don't Want You to Be Sorry for Me   Kahn 1925; Whiting 1925

I Don't Want Your Kisses If I Can't Have Your Love   Fisher 1929

I Don't Want Your Sympathy   Sigman 1953

I Dream of a Castle in Spain   Brennan 1923

I Dream of a Girl in a Shawl   Porter 1929

I Dream of a Past Love (inst.)   Revel 1950

I Dream of Hawaii and You   Mills 1929

I Dream of Indiana   Parish 1933

I Dream of You   Lerner, Alan Jay 1939

I Dream of Your Eyes   Smith, Harry B. 1927

I Dream too Much   Fields 1935; Kern 1935; McHugh 1935

I Dreamed of Foster   Silver 1956

I Dropped By to Say Hello   David, Hal 1959

I Dug a Ditch   Brown, Lew 1943; Freed, Ralph 1943; Lane 1943

I Enjoy Being a Girl   Hammerstein 1958; Rodgers 1958

I Envy the Bird   Herbert 1895, 1897; Smith, Harry B. 1895, 1897

I Envy the Moon   Ager 1933; Young, Joe 1933

I Fall in Love Too Easily   Cahn 1945; Styne 1945

I Fall in Love with You Every Day   Loesser 1938

I Fall in Love with You Ev'ry Day   Stept 1945

I Fear Nothing   Russell 1952

I Feel a Polka Coming On   Stept 1952

I Feel a Song Coming On   Fields 1935; McHugh 1935

I Feel at Home with You   Hart 1927; Rodgers 1927; Styne 1958

I Feel Humble   Drake 1964

I Feel It   Razaf 1929

I Feel Like a Feather in the Breeze   Gordon 1936; Revel 1936

I Feel Like a Million Dollars   Davis 1934; Hanley 1934

I Feel Like a Mountain   Silver 1956

I Feel Like Dancing   Robin 1951; Styne 1951

I Feel Like I'm Falling in Love with You   Coots 1954

I Feel Like I'm Gonna Live Forever   Styne 1953

I Feel Like I'm Not Out of Bed Yet   Comden and Green 1944

I Feel Like New Year's Eve   Bergman 1964

I Feel Like They Feel in Castile   Burke 1953; Van Heusen 1953

I Feel My Luck Comin' Down   Arlen 1946; Mercer 1946

I Feel Pretty   Sondheim 1957

I Feel So Jazzy   Robin 1948; Styne 1948

I Feel So Spanish Tonight   Friend 1935; Stept 1935

I Feel Sorry for You   David, Hal 1950

I Feel Sorta—   Heyman 1934

I Feel that Certain Feeling Coming On   Friend 1930; Monaco 1930

I Feel You Near Me   Hanley 1930

I Fell and Broke My Heart   Ellington 1968

I Fell in Love All By Myself   Howard, Joseph E. 1909

I Fell in Love on Monday   Howard, Joseph E. 1909

I Fell in Love with the Leader of the Band   Magidson 1941; Styne 1941

I Fell in Love with You   Lerner, Sammy 1929

I Fell in Love with Your Picture   Bacharach 1964; David, Hal 1964

I Fell in with Evil Companions   Drake 1968

I Fell Overboard (I Fall Overboard)   Loesser 1940

I Fell Up to Heaven   Rainger 1938; Robin 1938

I Find 'Em, Fool 'Em, Fondle and Forget 'Em   Schwartz, Jean 1923

I Find Fascination   Smith, Harry B. 1914

I Find I'm Lost without You   Lewis 1962

I Follow Shadows   Raye 1942

I For My Glory Land   Willson 1969

I Forget What I Started to Say   Gershwin, George 1927; Gershwin, Ira 1927

I Forgive You   Arlen 1932; Yellen 1932

I Forgot to Forget   Lewis 1954; Meyer 1954

I Forgot to Get the Lady's Name   Carroll 1937

I Forgot What It Was Like   Bacharach 1963; David, Hal 1963

I Fought Every Step of the Way   Mercer 1951

I Found a Dream   Gorney 1935

I Found a Four Leaf Clover   DeSylva 1922; Gershwin, George 1922

I Found a Friend   Brennan 1929

I Found a Friendship   Robison 1958

I Found a Horseshoe   Willson 1957

I Found a Million Dollar Baby   Fisher 1926; Rose 1926

I Found a Million Dollar Baby in a Five and Ten Cent Store   Dixon 1931; Rose 1931; Warren 1931

I Found a Peach in Orange, New Jersey   Heyman 1942; Spina 1942

I Found a Rose   Revel 1940

I Found a Rose in the Devil's Garden   Fisher 1921

I Found a Rosebud in Roseland   McHugh 1917

I Found a Round-About Way to Heaven   Silver 1926

I Found Contentment   Ruby 1957

I Found Happiness Now   Mills 1929

I Found Happiness (When I Found You)   Pollack 1929

I Found My Love   Loesser 1939

I Found My Romance for Ten Cents a Dance   Dubin 1932; Kahal 1932; Stept 1932

I Found My Sunshine in the Rain   Mills 1928

I Found My Way to You   Brown, Lew 1928; DeSylva 1928; Henderson 1928

I Found Myself a Guy   McHugh 1955

I Found Out This Morning, that I Fell in Love Last Night   Freed, Ralph 1944; McHugh 1944

I Found Out Where Annie Lives   Hoffman 1934; Washington 1934

I Found Some Body to Love   Stept 1925

I Found Sunshine in Your Smile   Leslie 1928

I Found the Fountain of Youth   Coslow 1934

I Found the Heart of You   Freed, Arthur 1917

I Found You   Gilbert 1919

I Found You at Last   Lerner, Alan Jay 1971

I Found You, I Lost You, I Found You Again   Gilbert 1933

I Found Your Purse Madam   Bryan Date Unknown; Fisher Date Unknown

I Gave Her My Heart in Acapulco   Berlin 1948

I Gave Her That   DeSylva 1918

I Gave My Heart Away   Adamson 1939; McHugh 1939

I Gave You a River   Evans 1971; Livingston, Jay 1971

I Gave You All I Could Give   Dubin 1943

I Gave You Up Just Before You Threw Me Down   Ahlert 1922; Kalmar 1922; Ruby 1922

I Get a Funny Feeling   Blane 1952; Warren 1952

I Get a Hankerin' for You   Russell 1957

I Get a Kick Out of You   Porter 1931, 1934

I Get a Kick Outa Corn   Adamson 1940

I Get a Warm Feeling   Cahn 1951

I Get Along Without You Very Well (Except Sometimes)   Carmichael 1938

I Get Embarrassed   Merrill 1959

I Get Lonely for a Plaything   Ellington 1958

I Get Married   Leigh 1977

I Get So All Fired Tired   Robison 1959

I Get that Cold Shoulder from You   Lerner, Sammy 1939; Mitchell 1939; Pollack 1939

I Get the Neck of the Chicken   Loesser 1942; McHugh 1942

I Get Tired   Coleman 1988

I Give   Lewis 1976; Young, Joe 1976

I Give My Love to You This Christmas   Warren Date Unknown

I Give Myself Away   Eliscu 1930

I Give You a Jewel   Russell 1948

I Give You the Ladies   Egan 1933

I Glow   Mills 1965
I Go for That   Loesser 1939
I Go for You   David, Hal 1955
I Go My Way   Dietz 1952; Leigh 1955
I Go Off in All Directions   Cahn 1963; Van Heusen 1963
I Go to Sicily   Burke 1963
I Got a Big Surprise for You   Friend 1952
I Got a Code in My Doze   Rose 1929
I Got a Friend   Strouse 1980
I Got a Gal Back Home   Pollack 1937; Yellen 1937
I Got a Lot of Love in My Heart   Hoffman 1957
I Got a Mama Down in New Orleans, Another Mama Up in Maine   McHugh 1926; Mills 1926
I Got a Marble and a Star   Weill 1947
I Got a New Girl   Lerner, Alan Jay 1983; Strouse 1983
I Got a Song   Arlen 1943; Harburg 1943
I Got a Woman Crazy for Me, She's Funny That Way   Whiting 1928
I Got an Aunt in Bridgeport   De Lange 1934
I Got Beauty   Porter 1950
I Got Butterflies   Cahn 1953; Fain 1953
I Got Dat Feelin'   Arlen 1941; Koehler 1941
I Got Happy Too Soon   Dixon 1953; Henderson 1953; Rose 1953
I Got It — You'll Get It   Pollack 1922
I Got It Bad and That Ain't Good   Ellington 1941; Webster 1941
I Got It Made   Evans 1961; Livingston, Jay 1961
I Got It the Fidgety Fidge   Pollack 1923
I Got It, You'll Get It (Just the Same As Me)   Brown, Lew 1921; Pollack 1921
I Got Lost in His Arms   Berlin 1946
I Got Love   Fields 1935; Kern 1935; McHugh 1935; Waller 1938
I Got Me   Strouse 1993
I Got Me a Baby   Lane 1951; Lerner, Alan Jay 1951
I Got My Eyes on You   Brown, Lew 1925; Friend 1925
I Got My Man   Coleman 1960; Leigh 1960
I Got Myself in Bad Being too Good to You   Fain 1932; Lewis 1932
I Got News   Willson 1952
I Got No Talent   Spina 1950, 1957
I Got Out of Bed on the Right Side   Mercer 1952; Schwartz, Arthur 1952
I Got Plenty o' Nuthin'   Gershwin, George 1935; Gershwin, Ira 1935
I Got Religion   DeSylva 1932; Youmans 1932
I Got Rhythm   Gershwin, George 1930; Gershwin, Ira 1930
I Got Shoes You Got Shoesies   Friend 1935; Yellen 1935
I Got Sugar, Plenty Sugar   Razaf 1942
I Got Ten Bucks and 24 Hours' Leave   Livingston, Jerry 1943
I Got the Bird on the Canary Islands   Heyman 1940
I Got the Message   Warren 1970, 1976
I Got the Mumps   Sherman 1960
I Got the Sun in the Morning   Berlin 1946
I Got Time and I Got No Place to Go   Coslow 1936
I Got to Have a Somebody   Loesser 1969
I Got to See de Minstrel Show   Von Tilzer 1907
I Got Tookin By a Good Good Lookin Man   Spina 1941, 1950
I Got What I Wanted   Friend 1930; Monaco 1930
I Got You   Coleman 1991; Comden and Green 1991
I Gotcha Where I Wantcha   Heyman 1933
I Gotta   Coleman 1979
I Gotta Back to New York   Hart 1933; Rodgers 1933

I Gotta Be Good 'Cause My Baby's in Town   Clare 1925; Monaco 1925
I Gotta Gal I Love (In North and South Dakota)   Cahn 1945, 1947; Styne 1945
I Gotta Get Myself Somebody to Love   Lewis 1926; Young, Joe 1926
I Gotta Get Outta Here   Strouse 1999
I Gotta Go Home   Freed, Ralph 1960
I Gotta Have Love — I've Gotta Have Music   Ruby 1953
I Gotta Have You   Magidson 1929; Washington 1929
I Gotta Hear that Beat   Robin 1952
I Gotta Keep My Eye on You   Smith, Harry B. 1930
I Gotta Ride   Lane 1941; Loesser 1941
I Gotta Right to Sing the Blues   Arlen 1932; Koehler 1932
I Gotta See a Man about a Girl   Oakland 1934
I Grew Up Last Night   Sigman 1960
I Grovel to Earth (Chee-Chee's First Entrance)   Hart 1928; Rodgers 1928
I Grovel to Your Cloth (Chee-Chee's Third Entrance)   Hart 1928; Rodgers 1928
I Guaran-Tootin'-Tee Ya   Hoffman 1954
I Guess I Should Be Satisfied (Finale Act I)   Hart 1926; Rodgers 1926
I Guess I Talk Too Much   Herbert 1908; Smith, Harry B. 1908
I Guess I'll Dress Up for the Blues   David, Mack 1953
I Guess I'll Hang My Tears Out to Dry   Cahn 1944; Styne 1944
I Guess I'll Have that Dream Right Now   Adamson 1947; McHugh 1947
I Guess I'll Have to Change My Plan   Dietz 1929; Schwartz, Arthur 1929
I Guess I'll Have to Telegraph My Baby   Cohan 1898
I Guess I'll Take a Ride   Howard, Joseph E. 1905
I Guess I'm More Like Mother than Like Father   Egan 1919; Whiting 1919
I Guess It Was You All the Time   Carmichael 1950, 1953; Mercer 1950, 1953
I Guess It Wasn't Meant to Be   Donaldson 1932; Kahn 1932
I Guess It's Time   Mancini 1995
I Guess I've Made a Mess of Things   Merrill 1953
I Guess the Cards Were Stacked Against Me   Blake 1947
I Guess This Is Goodbye   Sondheim 1987
I Guess We're Gonna Get Along   Razaf 1941
I Had a Ball   Lawrence 1964
I Had a Devil of a Time   Jerome 1913; Von Tilzer 1913
I Had a Dog   Romberg 1915
I Had a Dream   Alter 1968; Davis 1968
I Had a Dream Last Night   Alter 1935
I Had a Feeling (There Was Somebody Else)   Ager 1947
I Had a Gal, I Had a Pal, He Stole My Gal Away   Gilbert 1914
I Had a Love Once   Arlen 1973
I Had a Night   Livingston, Jerry 1973
I Had Just Been Pardoned   Gershwin, Ira 1945; Weill 1945
I Had Myself a True Love   Arlen 1946; Mercer 1946
I Had the Craziest Dream   Gordon 1942; Warren 1942
I Had to Come Back to You   Rose 1928
I Had to Do It   Razaf 1938; Waller 1938
I Had to Fall in Love with You   Coslow 1929
I Had to Kiss You   Robin 1953
I Had to Surrender to Virginia   Mitchell 1918
I Had too Much to Dream Last Night   Hoffman 1946; Livingston, Jerry 1946
I Had Twins (He Had Twins)   Hart 1938; Rodgers 1938

I Had You and Then I Lost You   Fisher 1932

I Had Your Number   Mills 1947

I Hail from Cairo   Atteridge 1918; Romberg 1918

I Hain't Tain't Ain't   Evans 1948; Livingston, Jay 1948

I Happen to Be in Love   Porter 1939

I Happen to Like New York   Porter 1930

I Happen to Love You   Martin 1958; Russell Date Unknown; Woods 1946

I Happened to Walk Down First Street   Robin 1946; Schwartz, Arthur 1946

I Happy New Year to You   Friml 1956

I Hate a Parade   Rome 1950

I Hate Her   Rome 1970

I Hate Him   Merrill 1961; Rome 1959

I Hate Husbands   Russell 1948

I Hate Little Boys   Burke 1981

I Hate Men   Porter 1948

I Hate Myself Ev'ry Morning   Razaf 1946

I Hate Myself for Being So Mean to You   Ager 1934; Davis 1934; Young, Joe 1934

I Hate Myself (For Falling in Love with You)   Silver 1930

I Hate to Be Alone   Adamson 1935; Lane 1935

I Hate to Leave You Now   Waller 1949

I Hate to Lose You (I'm So Used to You Now)   Clarke 1918

I Hate to Love You (But What Else Can I Do)   Parish 1922

I Hate to Love You So   Smith, Harry B. 1935

I Hate to Say Goodnight   Mills 1938

I Hate to Talk About Myself   Hart 1920; Rodgers 1920

I Hate to Tell a Lie   Livingston, Jerry 1940

I Hate to Think That You'd Grow Old Baby   Brown, Lew 1933; Henderson 1933

I Hate to Travel   Adamson 1963; Fain 1963

I Hate to Work on Monday   Howard, Joseph E. 1908

I Hate You   Berlin 1914

I Hate You Because I Love You   Gilbert 1931

I Hate You, Darling   Porter 1941

I Have a Date   Friml 1919; Harbach 1919

I Have a Dream   Adamson 1955; Lane 1955

I Have a Longing for Long Acre Square   Cohan 1907

I Have a Love   Sondheim 1957

I Have a Love in Every Port   Cahn 1946; Styne 1946

I Have a Rendezvous with Love   Parish 1935

I Have a Run in My Stocking   Eliscu 1932

I Have a Secret   Styne 1985

I Have a Single Track Mind   Parish 1957

I Have a Song   Rome 1940

I Have an Ear for Love   Mancini 1979

I Have Confidence in Me   Rodgers 1965

I Have Courted in Vain   Atteridge 1913

I Have Double-Checked   Brooks 1959

I Have Dreamed   Hammerstein 1951; Rodgers 1951

I Have Everything to Live For   David, Mack 1940

I Have Eyes   Rainger 1937, 1938; Robin 1937, 1938

I Have Faith, So Have You   Brown, Lew 1943; Stept 1943

I Have Found Them All   Smith, Harry B. 1911

I Have Given My Love   Ellington 1968

I Have Grown to Love New York   Dietz 1943; Duke 1943

I Have Just One Heart for Just One Boy   Berlin 1918

I Have Longed So Long   Norworth 1911

I Have Love   Friml 1952

I Have Loved You   Spina 1955

I Have My Arms Around the World   Burke 1939; Warren 1939, Date Unknown

I Have My Fingers Crossed   Friml 1918

I Have My Moments   Kalmar 1928; Ruby 1928

I Have My Own Way   Burke 1961

I Have Never Danced Before   Lane 1987

I Have One Gift   Russell 1953

I Have Only One Heart to Give   Brooks 1958

I Have Plenty of Men in My Life but No Life in My Men   Mills 1948

I Have Room in My Heart   Loewe 1938

I Have Said Goodbye a Thousand Times (Good-Bye Sweetheart Good-Bye)   Buck 1912

I Have Somebody's Labor Agitator   Atteridge 1920

I Have Something in My Eye and It's You   Bryan 1910

I Have the Funniest Feeling   Sondheim Date Unknown

I Have the Love   Friml 1954; Webster 1954

I Have the Room Above Her   Hammerstein 1936; Kern 1936

I Have to Cry   Sigman 1958

I Have to Have You   Robin 1929; Whiting 1929

I Have to Laugh   Herbert 1906; Rainger 1933; Robin 1933

I Have to Leave the Boys   Romberg 1917

I Have to Tell You   Rome 1954

I Have Waited for You   Herbert 1920; Smith, Robert B. 1920

I Have Written a Play   Coleman 1978; Comden and Green 1978

I Have You   Akst 1928; Davis 1928; Yellen 1931

I Have You to Thank   Robin 1957; Styne 1957

I Haven't a Bean in My Jeans   Duke Date Unknown

I Haven't a Thing to Wear   Revel 1941, 1942

I Haven't Changed a Thing   Mills 1938

I Haven't Got a Thing to Lose   Sigman 1948

I Haven't Got a Thing to Sell   Coslow 1947

I Haven't Got a Thing to Wear   Wrubel 1959

I Haven't Got a Worry in the World   Hammerstein 1946; Rodgers 1946

I Haven't Got Time for Anyone Else Till John Gets Home   Monaco 1918

I Haven't Got You   Rose 1927

I Haven't Heard a Word from You   Gordon Date Unknown; Revel Date Unknown

I Haven't Met the Right One Yet   Hoffman 1958

I Haven't the Heart   Webster 1958

I Haven't Time to Be a Millionaire   Burke 1940; Monaco 1940

I Haven't Told Her, She Hasn't Told Me   Dubin 1927; Fain 1927; Kahal 1927

I Hear a Call to Arms   Coslow 1937

I Hear a Different Drummer   Drake 1966

I Hear a Dream (Come Home Again)   Rainger 1939; Robin 1939

I Hear a Song in My Heart   Mercer 1945

(I Think) I Hear a Woodpecker Knocking at My Family Tree   Howard, Joseph E. 1909

I Hear America Singing   Parish 1941

I Hear Bells   Loesser 1965

I Hear Bluebirds   Woods 1940

I Hear Love Call Me   Smith, Harry B. 1925

I Hear Music   Lane 1941

I Hear My Heart Saying You're Mine (I Hear My Heart Saying Mm-Mm)   Coots 1933; Lewis 1933

I Hear (Oil)   Coleman 1960; Leigh 1960

I Hear the Music Now   Fain 1953

I Hear the Voice of an Angel   Burke 1932

I Hear You Calling, Pal of Mine   Dubin 1924; McHugh 1924

I Hear You, Master   Drake 1956

I Hear Your Voice   Freed, Arthur 1930

I Hear Your Voice in the Wind   Heyman 1944

I Heard   Evans 1959; Livingston, Jay 1959

I Heard a Bugle Blowing   Harbach 1947; Kern 1947
I Heard a Forest Praying   Lewis 1937
I Heard a Song   Freed, Ralph 1951
I Heard a Song in a Taxi   Caesar 1936; Henderson 1936
I Heard from a Mem'ry Last Night   Freed, Ralph 1965;
    Livingston, Jerry 1963
I Heard It on the Hit Parade   Ruby 1942
I Heard the Birdies Sing   Rainger 1942; Robin 1942
I Heard You Were Lovely (I Heard You Were
    Lonely)   Adamson 1940
I Hit a New High   Adamson 1938; McHugh 1938
I Hold Her Hand and She Holds Mine   Rose 1921
I Hope I Don't Love Him   Adams 1983
I Hope I Don't Meet Molly on the Day I Marry Flo   Brown,
    Lew 1927; DeSylva 1927; Woods 1927
I Hope She'll Be Happy   Coots 1952
I Hope the Band Keeps Playing   Blane 1945
I Hope You Settle for Me   Brown, Nacio Herb 1948
I Hope You'll Like It   Kahn 1931
I Hope You're Not in Love with Anyone   Stept 1949
I Hope You're Satisfied   Waller 1928
I Hum a Waltz   Gordon 1937; Revel 1937
I Hum to Myself   Sherman 1983
I Hunder   Blane 1961
I Hurry Home to You   Adams 1978; Strouse 1978
I Intend to End It All   Rome 1970
I Introduced   Porter 1919
I Jupiter, I Rex   Porter 1950
I Just Ain't Lucky with Men   Merrill 1957
I Just Came Back to Haunt You, Bogey, Bogey, Bogey
    Boo   Loesser 1935
I Just Came Back to Say Good-Bye   Berlin 1909; Snyder
    1909
I Just Can't Do Enough for You Baby   Fain 1951; Gordon
    1951
I Just Can't Help Loving That Man   Sterling 1902; Von
    Tilzer 1902
I Just Can't Keep from Taking Hold of Things   Cobb 1900;
    Edwards 1900
I Just Can't Make My Eyes Behave   Cobb 1906; Edwards
    1906; Smith, Harry B. 1906
I Just Can't Make My Heart Behave   Von Tilzer 1924
I Just Can't Remember the Words   Spina 1948
I Just Can't Resist You   Baer 1954
I Just Can't Wait   Comden and Green 1961; Styne 1961
I Just Can't Wait to See You with Your Clothes On   Strouse
    1976
I Just Couldn't Do Without You   Kern 1907
I Just Don't Believe in Being Lonely   Robison 1957
I Just Don't Deserve It (Long, Long, Lashes)   Loesser Date
    Unknown
I Just Don't Know what to Do with Myself   Bacharach 1962;
    David, Hal 1962
I Just Dropped In   Herbert 1897; Smith, Harry B. 1897
I Just Dropped in to Say Goodbye   Coslow 1955
I Just Found Out About Love   Adamson 1956; McHugh
    1956
I Just Got In   Brooks 1945
I Just Have to Breathe   Bacharach 1972; David, Hal 1972
I Just Kissed Your Picture Goodnight   David, Mack 1942
I Just Looked at You   Gershwin, George 1929; Gershwin, Ira
    1929; Kahn 1929
I Just Made Up with My Darling   Coots 1926
I Just Need a Lover   Cahn 1971

I Just Said Goodbye to My Troubles When I Said Hello to
    You   Davis 1926
I Just Simply Love to Carry On   Jerome 1921; Schwartz,
    Jean 1921
I Just Stepped in to Get Out of the Rain   Brown, Lew 1918
I Just Stood and Stared   Warren 1967
I Just Telephone Upstairs   Lewis 1951
I Just Wanna Be Like You   Revel 1946
I Just Wanna Cuddle Up, Cuddle Up   Baer 1954
I Just Wanna Play with You   David, Mack 1940
I Just Want to Be a Song and Dance Man   Adamson 1956;
    McHugh 1956
I Just Want to Be with You   Bergman 1954
I Just Want You to Want Me   Washington 1957
I Keep Coming Back for More   Ager 1938; David, Hal 1952;
    Yellen Date Unknown
I Keep Looking for You   Cahn 1977
I Keep My Wife in the City and Make Love To Her
    Myself   Bryan 1911; Meyer 1911
I Keep on Believing in You   Kahn 1931
I Keep on Singing   Hart 1935; Rodgers 1935
I Keep Running Away from You   Berlin 1957
I Killed Him 'Cause I Loved Him   Hanley 1935
I Killed Myself Because of You   Wrubel 1944
I Kinda Dream   Loesser 1939
I Kiss Your Hand Madame   Eliscu 1929; Lewis 1929; Young,
    Joe 1929
I Kissed Her in My Dreams   Drake 1948
I Kissed My Girl Goodbye   Dietz 1944; Duke 1944
I Kissed My Heart Goodbye   Adamson 1950; McHugh 1950
I Kissed My Heart Goodnight   Washington 1950
I Knew   Bloom 1936; Mercer 1936; Robin 1934, 1935, 1936
I Knew a Girl in Barcelona   Parish 1957
I Knew Him Before He Was Spanish   Rose 1930
I Knew Him When   Arlen 1934; Gershwin, Ira 1934;
    Harburg 1934; Herbert 1920; Smith, Robert B. 1920
I Knew Him When He Was All Right   Von Tilzer 1914
I Knew I Was Wrong   Hanley 1922
I Knew I'd Find You   Burke 1933; Spina 1933
I Knew I'd Love You   Adamson 1946
I Knew It Would Be This Way   Coslow 1942
I Knew that You were Mine   Mills 1929; Parish 1929
I Knew that You Would Come Along Someday   Cobb 1901;
    Edwards 1901
I Knew You Well   Duke 1950; Rome 1950
I Knew You When   Coots 1933; Drake 1943; Magidson 1934
I Knew You'd Pass Me By   Lawrence 1933
I Know   Carroll 1918; DePaul 1946; Martin 1952; Mills 1929;
    Raye 1946; Russell 1945; Strouse 1987
I Know a Dream When I See One   David, Mack 1952;
    Livingston, Jerry 1952
I Know a Foul Ball   Gershwin, George 1933; Gershwin, Ira
    1933
I Know a Friendly City   Caesar 1946
I Know a Girl   Drake 1954
I Know a Lazy Lane   Brennan 1930
I Know a Man   Spina 1944
I Know a Place (The Place You Hold My Heart)   Cahn 1952;
    Duke 1952
I Know a Road   Brennan 1936
I Know about Love   Comden and Green 1960; Styne 1960
I Know and She Knows   Kern 1913; Smith, Harry B. 1913
I Know How It Is   Loesser 1956
I Know I Got More than My Share   Clarke 1916; Johnson,
    Howard 1916

I Know, I Know, I Know   Russell 1949

I Know I Shall Meet Her Someday   Herbert 1920; Smith, Robert B. 1920

I Know I'm in Harlem   Loesser 1936

I Know I'm Nobody   Brown, Lew 1939; Stept 1939

I Know I'm not Your Mother   Merrill 1953

I Know It and You Know It   Willson 1953

I Know It Can Happen Again   Hammerstein 1947; Rodgers 1947

I Know It's Not Meant for Me   Porter 1937

I Know It's Wrong   DePaul 1944

I Know Now   Coots 1937; Dubin 1937; Warren 1937

I Know Somebody (Who Loves You)   Gershwin, George 1925; Gershwin, Ira 1925

I Know Someone   Brooks 1962

I Know Something I Won't Tell   Adamson 1939; Donaldson 1939

I Know that I Love You   Kalmar 1924; Ruby 1924

I Know that I'm in Love   Mitchell 1921; Pollack 1921

I Know that You Know   Youmans 1926

I Know That You Love Me   Kalmar 1926; Ruby 1926

I Know the Feeling   Bergman 1988

I Know the Kind of Girl (A Girl Like You)   Schwartz, Arthur 1933

I Know the Name of Every Flower Now   Hoffman 1944; Livingston, Jerry 1944

I Know the Way to Timbuktu   David, Hal 1978

I Know Things Now   Sondheim 1987

I Know What Aloha Means   Rainger 1937, 1939; Robin 1937, 1939

I Know what God Is   Raye 1959

I Know What It Is to Be Alone   Merrill 1978

I Know What It Means to Be Lonesome   David, Mack 1946

I Know what You Do   Mills 1942

I Know What You're Thinkin' (But You're Wrong)   Hoffman 1950

I Know Where I'm Going   Mancini 1995

I Know Where There's a Cozy Nook   Gershwin, Ira 1945; Weill 1945

I Know Why   Berlin 1920; Davis 1919

I Know Why (And So-Do-You)   Gordon 1941; Warren 1941

I Know You   Smith, Harry B. 1917; Sterling 1917

I Know You Are There   David, Hal 1974

I Know You By Heart   Martin 1941

I Know You'll Be Very Happy   Hoffman 1954

I Know Your Heart   Martin 1964

I Know Your Husband Very Well   Friml 1913; Harbach 1913

I Know Your Kind   Rome 1959

I Know Your Mother Loves You   Cahn 1955; Schwartz, Arthur 1955

I Know You're Lying but I Love It   Stept 1932

I Know You're Too Wonderful for Me   Hart 1922; Rodgers 1922

I Laughed at Love   Adams 1963; Davis 1952; Silver 1952; Strouse 1963

I Laughed at Love (Now Love Has the Laugh on Me)   Gilbert 1942

I Laughed When I Should Have Cried   Lawrence 1944

I Lay Me Down to Sleep   Wrubel 1933

I Lead a Charmed Life   Russell 1956

I Learn a Merengue Mama   Raye 1957

I Learned About Love from Her   Parish 1933

I Learned About Women from Her   Atteridge 1922; Herbert 1920; Schwartz, Jean 1922; Smith, Robert B. 1920

I Learned to Cry   Baer 1942; De Lange 1942

I Learned to Love You in Dreamland   Yellen 1916

I Learned to Love You When I Learned My A.B.C.'s   Warren 1920

I Learned to Pray   Leigh 1954

I Left a Good Deal in Mobile   Mills 1945

I Left Her in New Hampshire   Brown, Lew 1915

I Left Her on the Beach at Honolulu   Buck 1916

I Left My Door Open and My Daddy Walked Out   Berlin 1919

I Left My Hat in Haiti   Lane 1951; Lerner, Alan Jay 1951

I Left My Heart at the Stage Door Canteen   Berlin 1942

I Left My Heart with You Virginia   Parish 1923

I Left My Old Kentucky Home for You   Jerome 1912; Von Tilzer 1912

I Left My Sugar Standing in the Rain   Fain 1927; Kahal 1927

I Left the Door Wide Open   Cahn 1956; Van Heusen 1956

I Lerve You   Harburg 1932

I Let a Song Go Out of My Heart   Ellington 1938; Mills 1938

I Let a Tear Fall in the River   David, Mack 1962; Livingston, Jerry 1962

I Let My Heart Command Me   Coslow 1936

I Lie Awake and Dream   Parish 1951

I Like a Big Town, I Like a Small Town   Kalmar 1923; Ruby 1923

I Like a Little Girl Like That   Ager 1930; Yellen 1930

I Like a Man Who Makes Music   Magidson 1942; Pollack 1942

I Like a Military Tune   Gordon 1942; Warren 1942

I Like All the Girls   Atteridge 1912

I Like Being Alone   Cahn 1963; Van Heusen 1963

I Like, but You I Love   David, Hal 1956

I Like Everything About You   Brown, Lew 1940; Henderson 1940

I Like Ev'rybody   Loesser 1956

I Like Honorable Everybody   David, Mack 1958; Livingston, Jerry 1958

I Like Humped-Backed Salmon   Lane 1938; Loesser 1938

I Like Ike   Berlin 1952

I Like It Better Every Day   Williams 1912

I Like It Here   Brown, Nacio Herb 1943; Fields 1950; Robin 1943

I Like It, I Like It   David, Mack 1951; Livingston, Jerry 1951

I Like It that Way   Conrad 1934; Mitchell 1934

I Like It with Music   Henderson 1935; Yellen 1935

I Like London   Lane Date Unknown

I Like Love   Blane 1945; Martin 1940

I Like Men   Mercer 1952; Schwartz, Arthur 1952

I Like Mike   Gordon 1946; Myrow 1946

I Like My Love This Way   Burke 1959; Revel 1959

I Like Myself   Comden and Green 1955

I Like Myself for Liking You   Gorney 1934

I Like Pretty Things   Porter 1944

I Like Singing   Ellington 1958

I Like that Little One   Kahn 1925

I Like the Boys   Atteridge 1918; Romberg 1918; Smith, Harry B. 1916, 1927

I Like the Feeling   Blane 1956; Martin 1956

I Like the Hat, I Like the Dress and I Like the Girl That's In It   Bryan 1911

I Like the Ladies   Coleman 1960; Leigh 1960

I Like the Likes of You   Duke 1934; Harburg 1934

I Like the Look   Mancini 1967

I Like the Looks of You   Revel 1930

I Like This Loving You   Cahn 1945, 1947

I Like to Be Loved by You   Gordon 1942; Revel 1942; Warren 1942

I Like to Do Things for You   Ager 1930; Yellen 1930

I Like to Get Up Early in the Morning   Lawrence 1947

I Like to Go Strange Places   Loesser 1936

I Like to Go to School   Bergman 1958

I Like to Hike   Cahn 1955; Schwartz, Arthur 1955

I Like to Keep My Eyes on You   Cobb 1917; Edwards 1917

I Like to Lead when I Dance   Cahn 1964; Van Heusen 1964

I Like to Make Music for You   Pollack 1944

I Like to Recognize the Tune   Hart 1939; Rodgers 1939

I Like to Walk with a Pal Like You   Blake 1923; Sissle 1923

I Like what I Do   Adams 1981; Strouse 1981

I Like What You Like, I Wish You'd Never Grow Up at All   Eliscu 1929; Rose 1929; Youmans 1929

I Like You   Brown, Nacio Herb 1948; Gordon 1931; Revel 1931; Rome 1954; Smith, Harry B. 1930

I Like You as You Are   Hammerstein 1928; Youmans 1928

I Like You Like   Spina 1957

I Like You, Too   Howard, Joseph E. 1905; Williams 1907

I Like Your Face   Dietz 1930; Schwartz, Arthur 1930

I Like Your Style   Coleman 1980

I List the Trill in Golden Throat   Herbert 1911

I Live a Little While   Van Heusen 1937

I Live Again (Because I'm in Love Again)   Washington 1940; Young, Victor 1940

I Live for Love   Dixon 1935; Hammerstein 1933; Wrubel 1935

I Live for Only You (India)   Hoffman 1955

I Live for that Day   Weill 1947

I Live for You   Sigman 1954

I Live for You Alone   Smith, Robert B. 1912

I Live for You (Just You)   Gilbert 1955

I Live, I Die for You   Romberg 1927; Smith, Harry B. 1927

I Live in the Woods   Bacharach 1979

I Live in Turkey   Berlin 1920

I Live My Love (inst.)   Coleman 1964

I Live to Love   Cahn 1956

I Live to Love and Love to Live   Baer 1929; Gilbert 1929

I Live to Love You Only   Gordon 1929

I Live Up Town   Bryan 1911; Meyer 1911

I Lived in a House with a Piano   Dietz 1944; Duke 1944

I L-L-Love You So   Heyman 1941

I Long to Be a Melody   Gilbert 1917

I Long to Be Loved   Sigman 1959

I Long to Be with Betty but She's Living in Connecticut   Johnson, Howard 1917; Meyer 1917

I Long to Belong   Gorney 1924

I Long To Belong to Someone Who Longs to Belong to Me   Bryan 1926; Silver 1926

I Long to Linger Longer Dearie, I Love the River and You   Buck 1919

I Look Across the Table   Wrubel 1959

I Look at You and a Song Is Born   Rainger 1931

I Look at You with Love   Styne 1970

I Look 'Em Over in the Daytime So I Know what I'm Getting at Night   Fisher 1921

I Look for Love   Hammerstein 1928; Youmans 1928

I Looked for You   Bacharach 1959; David, Hal 1959

I Looked in Your Eyes   Freed, Arthur 1934

I Looked Into Your Eyes   Brown, Nacio Herb 1934

I Lost a Day   Lewis 1949; Meyer 1949

I Lost a Slice of Paradise   Norworth 1922

I Lost a Wonderful Pal When I Lost You   Dubin 1924

I Lost Another Sweetheart   Dixon 1933

I Lost My Beat   Cahn 1944; Styne 1944

I Lost My Cat Today!   Cahn 1980; DePaul 1980

I Lost My Gal Again   Lewis 1930

I Lost My Heart   Brennan 1928; Robin 1935

I Lost My Heart (And Found My Heart's Desire)   Robin 1936

I Lost My Heart At the Ball   David, Mack 1950; Hoffman 1950; Livingston, Jerry 1950

I Lost My Heart in a Drive-In Movie   Brooks 1964

I Lost My Heart in Dixieland   Berlin 1919

I Lost My Heart in Heidelberg   Kalmar 1927; Ruby 1927

I Lost My Heart in Honolulu   Cobb 1916; Edwards 1916

I Lost My Heart in June   Parish 1924

I Lost My Heart in Monterey   Egan 1926; Whiting 1926

I Lost My Heart in the Subway   Gordon 1933; Revel 1933

I Lost My Heart in the Subway (When I Gave My Seat to You)   Fisher 1935

I Lost My Heart to the Girl of My Dreams   Mills 1930

(Oh Mom, Dear Mom) I Lost My Job Again   Coots 1945; Lewis 1945

I Lost My Job on Account of You   Hoffman 1934

I Lost My Shirt   Berlin 1929

I Lost the Love of Anatol   Dietz 1961; Schwartz, Arthur 1961

I Lost the Rhythm   Strouse 1956

I Lost You   Martin 1951

I Lost You (The Moment I Found You)   Martin 1943

I Love a Fat Man   Cahn 1977

I Love a Genius   Myrow 1950

I Love a Lark   Atteridge 1924; Romberg 1924; Schwartz, Jean 1924

I Love a Little Love Now and Then   Donaldson 1924

I Love a Man in a Uniform   Monaco 1927; Rose 1927

I Love a Musical Comedy Show   Bryan 1919; Schwartz, Jean 1919

I Love a Mystery   Robin 1947

I Love a New Yorker   Arlen 1950; Blane 1950

I Love a Parade   Arlen 1931; Koehler 1931

I Love a Piano   Berlin 1915

I Love a Stranger   Heyman 1955

I Love a Ukelele   Friend 1926; Kahn 1926

I Love a Wedding   Dietz 1961; Schwartz, Arthur 1961

I Love America   Harbach 1923

I Love an Elephant (Cause an Elephant Don't Forget)   Bryan 1948

I Love an Esquire Girl   Brown, Lew 1943; Freed, Ralph 1943

I Love an Old Fashioned Song   Cahn 1945; Styne 1945

I Love Anything that Has Anything to Do with You   Fain 1929

I Love but You   Friml 1918

I Love Corny Music   DePaul 1944; Raye 1944

I Love Dixie   Brooks 1953

I Love Eggs   Cahn 1946; Styne 1946

I Love Elephants (Cause Elephants Don't Forget)   Bryan 1938

I Love 'Em All   Adams 1981; Strouse 1981

I Love 'Em All from A to Z   Howard, Joseph E. 1910

I Love 'Er   Akst 1923; Davis 1923

I Love Everyone in the Wide Wide World   Cohan 1901

I Love Gardenias   Fields 1934; McHugh 1934

I Love Gina   Stept 1956

I Love Halloween   Davis 1953

I Love Her — She Loves Me   Caesar 1922

I Love Her, Oh! Oh! Oh!   Monaco 1913

I Love Her That's Why   Hoffman 1955

I Love Him   Brown, Lew Date Unknown; Fain 1960; Friml 1924; Hammerstein 1924; Harbach 1924; Henderson Date Unknown; Loesser 1956, 1969; Webster 1960

I Love Him and He Loves Me (Tho' We Both Love the Same Sweet Girl)   Johnson, Howard 1921

I Love Him Just the Same   Rose 1924

I Love Him, the Rat   Hammerstein 1931; Whiting 1931

I Love, I Love, I Love My Wife, But Oh You Kid   Von Tilzer 1909

I Love It   Goetz 1910; Von Tilzer 1910

I Love It Rag   Von Tilzer 1910

I Love Louisa   Comden and Green 1964; Dietz 1931; Schwartz, Arthur 1931; Styne 1964

I Love Love   Brennan 1928

I Love Lucy   Adamson 1951

I Love Lydia   Evans 1950; Livingston, Jay 1950

I Love Ma Babe   Sterling 1899

I Love Morris, Lovely Morris, but I Don't Like Morris Plan   Lane 1930; Lewis 1930

I Love My Babe   Johnson, J. Rosamond Date Unknown

I Love My Baby, My Baby Loves Me   Warren 1925

I Love My Billy Sunday but Oh You Saturday Night   Clarke 1917; Leslie 1917; Meyer 1917

I Love My Little Susie   Harbach 1926; Kern 1926

I Love My Machine Gun   Gorney 1969

I Love My Mommy Best of All   Coots 1955

I Love My Mother-in-Law   Brown, A. Seymour 1914

I Love My Old Fashioned Man   Fain 1928; Kahal 1928

I Love My Wife   Bryan 1911; Coleman 1977; Lerner, Alan Jay 1976

I Love My Wife So Keep Away   Edwards 1909

I Love New York   Revel 1954; Spina 1977

I Love Not One but All   Herbert 1914

I Love Olive   Baer 1927, 1944; Kahn 1927

I Love Only One Girl, at a Time   Edwards 1936; Johnson, Howard 1936

I Love Only One Girl in the Wide, Wide World   Cobb 1903; Edwards 1903

I Love Only You   Porter 1933

I Love Only You Dear   Friend 1926

I Love Paris   Porter 1953

I Love Rosie Casey   Jerome 1923; Schwartz, Jean 1923

I Love That   Sterling 1921; Von Tilzer 1921

I Love that Rickey Tickey Tickey   Cahn 1955

I Love the Boys   Atteridge 1924; Romberg 1924; Schwartz, Jean 1924

I Love the Girls (In My Own Peculiar Way)   Harburg 1930

I Love the Ground You Walk On   Herbert 1920; Smith, Robert B. 1920

I Love the Heart of Dixie   Bryan 1918; Schwartz, Jean 1918

I Love the Horses and the Hounds   Woods 1934

I Love the Ladies   Clarke 1914; Schwartz, Jean 1914

I Love the Land of Old Black Joe   Clarke 1920; Donaldson 1920

I Love the Lassies (I Love 'em All)   Kern 1920

I Love the Moon   Goetz 1925

I Love the Moonlight   Akst 1926; Carroll 1913; Davis 1926

I Love the Name of Mary   Olcott 1910

I Love the Rain   Bryan 1930

I Love the Way We Fell in Love   Fain 1938; Kahal 1938

I Love the Way You're Breaking My Heart   Alter 1951

I Love Thee   Johnson, Howard 1939

I Love Thee, I Adore Thee   Herbert 1897; Smith, Harry B. 1897

I Love Them All   Brennan 1915; Conrad 1924; Romberg 1925; Smith, Harry B. 1925

I Love this Land   Lerner, Alan Jay 1976

I Love Those Men   Loesser 1948

I Love to Be in Love   Robin 1936

I Love To Be Loved   Buck 1915

I Love to Beat the Big Bass Drum   Mercer 1951; Warren 1951

I Love to Catch Brass Rings on a Merry-Go-Round   Conrad 1927; Dubin 1927; Silver 1927

I Love to Cry at Weddings   Coleman 1966; Fields 1966

I Love to Dance   Bergman 1978; Berlin 1915; Conrad 1926; Freed, Ralph 1946; Kahn 1926; Lane 1946

I Love to Dance a Waltz   Adams 1963; Strouse 1963

I Love to Dance When I Hear a March   Coots 1924; Coslow 1924

I Love to Dance with You   Friend 1934; Raye 1955

I Love to Do It   Meyer 1930; Mitchell 1930

I Love to Dream   Akst 1935

I Love to Go Swimmin' with Wimmin'   Romberg 1921

I Love to Go to School 'Cause I Love My Teacher   Hoffman 1932; Young, Joe 1932

I Love to Have the Boys Around Me   Berlin 1914

I Love to Hear a Banjo   Baer 1964

I Love to Hear a Choo Choo Train   DePaul 1952; Raye 1952

I Love to Hear an Irish Band Play on St. Patrick's Day   Jerome 1912; Schwartz, Jean 1912

I Love to Hear You Say I Love You   Edwards 1930

I Love to Hit Myself on the Head with a Hammer   Magidson 1929; Washington 1929

I Love to Laugh   Sherman 1964

I Love to Lie Awake in Bed   Hart Date Unknown; Schwartz, Arthur Date Unknown

I Love to Play the Palace   Oakland 1965

I Love to Quarrel with You   Berlin 1914

I Love to Raise the Dickens   Buck Date Unknown

I Love to Ramble   Leigh 1955

I Love to Read the Papers in the Morning   Herbert 1911

I Love to Rhyme   Gershwin, George 1938; Gershwin, Ira 1938

I Love to Ride on a Choo Choo Train   Baer 1939

I Love to Ride the Horses on a Merry-Go-Round   Pollack 1935; Yellen 1935

I Love to Say Hello to the Girls (But I Hate to Say Goodbye)   Romberg 1920

I Love to See a Big Parade   Bergman 1958

I Love to Sing   Davis 1962

I Love to Sing a Duet   Friend 1946

I Love to Sing the Words   Caesar 1943

I Love to Sing the Words While We're Dancing   Caesar 1938; Lerner, Sammy 1938

I Love to Sing with You   Buck 1918

I Love to Sing-a   Arlen 1936; Harburg 1936

I Love to Stay at Home   Berlin 1915

I Love to Tango with My Tea   Bryan 1915

I Love To Think of You   Brown, Nacio Herb 1922

I Love to Walk in the Rain   Bullock 1938; Spina 1938

I Love to Watch the Moonlight   Myrow 1940

I Love to Whistle   Adamson 1938; McHugh 1938

I Love Vanilla   Brown, A. Seymour 1928

I Love What I'm Doing   Robin 1948; Styne 1948

(Just One Way to Say) I Love You   Berlin 1949; Gershwin, George 1921; Hammerstein 1928; Harburg 1958; Herbert 1906; Jerome 1905; Porter 1944; Romberg 1928; Schwartz, Jean 1905; Willson 1953

I Love You - You Love Him   Berlin 1948

I Love You and I Adore You   Brennan 1928; Smith, Harry B. 1928

I Love You and I Like You   Schwartz, Arthur 1930

I Love You and You Love Me   Spina 1967

I Love You (As Much As I Am Able)   Coleman 1962; Leigh 1962

I Love You As Much As I Love Myself   Baer 1931; Gilbert 1931

I Love You Because I Love You   Hoffman 1932

I Love You but Good   De Lange 1945; Myrow 1945

I Love You but I Like You Even More   Schwartz, Arthur 1929

I Love You 'Cause I Love You   Adamson 1930; Gordon 1930; Revel 1930

I Love You Darling   Revel 1946

I Love You Dear!   Ahlert 1932; Friml 1918; Turk 1932

I Love You Dear and What's More Who Wouldn't   Meyer 1950

I Love You, Deep River   Robison 1928

I Love You Do   Young, Victor 1954

I Love You Dolly   Smith, Harry B. 1903

I Love You Florida   Davis 1972

I Love You For That   Stept 1945

I Love You, I Adore You   Herbert 1946

I Love You, I Hate You (For Making a Fool Out of Me)   Bryan 1929; Meyer 1929

I Love You, I Love You, I Love You   Hammerstein 1923; Harbach 1923; Youmans 1923

I Love You in Technicolor   Van Heusen 1938

I Love You Just Because You Love Another   Edwards 1899

I Love You Just Like Lincoln Loved the Old Red, White and Blue   Jerome 1914; Schwartz, Jean 1914; Young, Joe 1914

I Love You Just the Same   Buck 1914

I Love You Madly   Baer 1954

I Love You, Mary Darling   Eliscu 1932

I Love You Miss Annabelle   Blake 1964; Sissle 1964

I Love You More   Cahn 1941

I Love You More Each Day   Berlin 1910; Parish 1931; Snyder 1910

I Love You More in Technicolor   Blane 1946; Martin 1946

I Love You More Than Ever   Davis 1925

I Love You More than Yesterday   Hart 1928; Rodgers 1928, 1929

I Love You More Today Than Yesterday   Hart 1929

I Love You Much Too Much   Raye 1940

I Love You Much Too Much Muchacha   Gordon 1937; Revel 1937

I Love You, My Darling   DeSylva 1924; Gershwin, George 1924

I Love You Oh! Oh! Oh!   Brown, A. Seymour 1909

I Love You (Prince) Pizzicato   Gordon 1933; Revel 1933

I Love You, Samantha   Porter 1956

I Love You Sincerely   Silver 1926

I Love You So   Duke 1927; Kahn 1930; Porter 1912; Romberg 1922; Strouse 1999

I Love You So Much   Kalmar 1930; Ruby 1930

I Love You Sweetheart   Harbach 1917

I Love You, That's One Thing I Know   Gilbert 1915

I Love You, That's Why   Ahlert 1956

I Love You This Morning   Lerner, Alan Jay 1945; Loewe 1945

I Love You to Little Pieces   Sigman 1948

I Love You Too Much   Washington 1962

I Love You Truly   Evans 1946; Livingston, Jay 1946

I Love You, Whoever You Are   Cahn 1958

I Love Your Eyes   Yellen 1921

I Love Your Sunny Teeth   Comden and Green 1956; Styne 1956

I Love Your Vibrato   Blane 1968; Martin 1968

I Love Ze Parisienne   Herbert 1909

I Loved Her (A Little Bit More than He Did)   Dietz 1957

I Loved Her Best of All   Atteridge 1924; Romberg 1924; Schwartz, Jean 1924

I Loved Her, Too   Weill 1947

I Loved Him But He Didn't Love Me   Porter 1929

I Loved Him So   DePaul 1942; Raye 1942

I Loved that Man   Freed, Arthur 1930

I Loved Ya   Heyman 1932

I Loved You Before I Met You (For I Saw You in My Dreams)   Hoffman 1930

I Loved You Once in Silence   Lerner, Alan Jay 1960; Loewe 1960

I Loved You Wednesday   Silver 1932

I Loves You, Porgy   Gershwin, George 1935; Gershwin, Ira 1935

I Lulee, Lulee   David, Mack 1962

I Made a Deal   Cahn 1977

I Made a Fist   Loesser 1956

I Made My Mind Up You're Gonna Wind Up with Me   Lewis 1927; Young, Joe 1927

I Made Myself a Promise   Cahn 1953; Fain 1953

I Make a Motion   Hoffman 1936

I Make Hay While the Moon Shines   Gershwin, George 1924

I Make Up for That in Other Ways   Brown, Lew 1932; Henderson 1932

I Married an Angel   Hart 1938; Rodgers 1933, 1938

I Married for Money   Oakland 1955; Webster 1955

I May   Smith, Harry B. 1926

I May Be a Little Green, But I Ain't No Fool   Waller 1924

I May Be Dancing with Somebody Else (But I Love You)   Brown, Lew 1926; Clare 1926; Conrad 1926

I May Be Gone for a Long Long Time   Brown, Lew 1917

I May Be Small but I Have Big Ideas   Atteridge 1917; Romberg 1917

I May Be Wrong   DePaul 1958; Raye 1958

I May Believe Half-That's All   Romberg 1916

I May Fall in Love Again   Duke 1930; Harburg 1930

I May Feel Blah but Not too Blue   Baer 1927; Lewis 1927

I May Have Left Paree (But Paree Has Never Left Me)   Hoffman 1957

I May Look Green, but I Ain't Nobody's Fool   Buck 1912

I May Need You Bad but Not As Bad As All That   Friend 1923

I May Never Fall in Love with You   Willson 1960

I May Never Get Well Again   Duke 1968

I May Never Go Home Anymore   Brooks 1957

I May Never Pass Your Way Again   Kahal 1932; Warren 1932

I May Say Maybe   Cahn Date Unknown; Duke Date Unknown

I May Stay Away a Little Longer   Brown, Lew 1918; Goetz 1917

I Mean No-One-Else-But-You   Caesar 1922

I Mean to Say   Gershwin, George 1929; Gershwin, Ira 1929

I Mean to Say I Love You   Hammerstein 1936

I Meant to Tell You   Cahn 1943

I Met a Girl   Comden and Green 1956; Styne 1956

I Met a Man   Merrill 1971; Styne 1971

I Met Her on Monday   Wrubel 1942

I Met Him in Paris   Carmichael 1937

I Met Lincoln   Leslie 1962; Schwartz, Jean 1962

I Met My Waterloo   Coslow 1934; Johnston 1934, 1935

I Met My Waterloo (When I Met Lulu)   Coots 1950; Lewis 1950

I Met You   Young, Victor 1920

I Met You in a Dream   Donaldson 1942

I Met You in Pittsburgh   Atteridge 1911

I Might Be Coaxed Dear, But Not By You   Von Tilzer 1916

I Might Be Your Once-in-a-While   Herbert 1913, 1919; Smith, Robert B. 1913, 1919

I Might Drop Around in Your Dreams   Merrill 1955

I Might Fall Back on You   Hammerstein 1927; Kern 1927

I Might Frighten Her Away   Bacharach 1973; David, Hal 1973

I Might Grow Fond of You   Hammerstein 1925; Harbach 1925; Kern 1925

I Might Have Known   Fisher 1930; Stept 1926

(I'd Better not Try It) I Might Like It   Magidson 1929; Washington 1929

I Might Say 'Yes' To You   Smith, Harry B. 1917

I, Miles Gloriousus   Sondheim 1962

I Miss a Little Miss Who Kisses Me   Coots 1929

I Miss My Darling   Davis 1951; Silver 1951

I Miss My Mama, My Black Eyed Charmer Down in Yokohama Way   Brown, Lew 1922

I Miss My Swiss, My Swiss Miss Misses Me   Baer 1922; Gilbert 1922

I Miss that Feeling   Adamson 1947; McHugh 1947

I Miss that Mississippi Miss that Misses Me   Lewis 1918; Young, Joe 1918

I Miss You   Mancini 1993; Russell 1957

I Miss You and You're Not Even Gone   David, Hal 1962

I Miss You in a Thousand Different Ways   Cobb 1906; Edwards 1906

I Miss You in the Morning   Leslie 1938

I Miss You Miss America   Gilbert 1916

I Miss You Most of All   Monaco 1913

I Miss You Yes I Miss You Sweetheart Mine   Snyder 1911

I Missed You   DeSylva 1922; Herbert 1922

I Murdered Them in Chicago   Cahn 1944; Styne 1944

I Must Be Doing Something Right   Coleman 1984

I Must Be Dreaming   Dubin 1928

I Must Be Going   Hart 1926; Rodgers 1926

I Must Be Home By Twelve O'Clock   Gershwin, George 1929; Gershwin, Ira 1929; Kahn 1929

I Must be Loved By Someone (and That Someone Must Be You)   Cobb 1921; Edwards 1921

I Must Be Lucky   Donaldson 1937

I Must Be One of Those Roses   Schwartz, Arthur 1930

I Must Be Out of Your Mind   Raye 1940

I Must Go to Moscow   Dixon 1923

I Must Have an Italian Gal   Yellen 1927

I Must Have Been Crazy   Strouse 1999

I Must Have Been Madly in Love   Loesser 1947

I Must Have Company   Kahn 1924; Meyer 1924

I Must Have Her   Lane 1979; Lerner, Alan Jay 1979

I Must Have Jazz   Mitchell 1919

I Must Have One More Kiss Kiss Kiss   Hoffman 1939

I Must Have Priorities on Your Love   Clare 1942; Pollack 1942

I Must Have that Man   Fields 1928; McHugh 1928

I Must Love Someone   David, Mack 1939; Livingston, Jerry 1939

I Must Love You   Hart 1928; Rodgers 1928

I Must Marry a Handsome Man   Herbert 1899; Smith, Harry B. 1899

I Must Obey My Heart   Davis 1935; Silver 1935

I Must See Annie Tonight   Friend 1939

I Nearly Let Love Go Slipping Through My Fingers   Woods 1936

I Need a Change of Sky   Ellington 1973; Harburg 1973

I Need a Garden   DeSylva 1924; Gershwin, George 1924

I Need a Girl   Johnson, James P. 1960

I Need a Little Bit, You Need a Little Bit   DeSylva 1927; Henderson 1927

I Need a Little Bit, You Need a Little Bit, It Just Had to Happen (A Little Bit of Love)   Brown, Lew 1927; Friend 1927

I Need Affection   Herbert 1915

I Need Air   Lerner, Alan Jay 1974; Loewe 1974

I Need Lovin'   Johnson, James P. 1926

I Need Music   Cahn 1980; Strouse 1980

I Need New Words   Harburg 1934

I Need Some Cooling Off   Hart 1927, 1928; Rodgers 1927, 1928

I Need Some Pettin'   Kahn 1924

I Need Somebody to Lullaby Me   Coslow 1924, 1925; Silver 1924

I Need Someone Like You (inst.)   Waller 1929

I Need the Morning Air   Howard, Joseph E. 1908

I Need You   Bacharach 1957; Johnson, James P. 1929; Stept 1952

I Need You Like I Need a Hole in the Head   Wrubel 1948

I Need You So   Dietz 1929; Schwartz, Arthur 1929

I Never Broke Nobody's Heart when I Said Good-Bye   Bryan 1923

I Never Can Think of the Words   Yellen 1930

I Never Cried Before I Met You   Coslow 1926

I Never Danced Before   Drake 1987; Lane Date Unknown

I Never Did Imagine   Merrill 1971; Styne 1971

I Never Do Anything Twice   Sondheim 1976

I Never Dream When I'm Asleep   Martin 1952

I Never Dreamed   Akst 1954; Howard, Bart 1938; Kahn 1927

I Never Felt Better   Blane 1954; Martin 1954

I Never Felt Better in My Life   Stept 1953

I Never Felt More Like Falling in Love   Freed, Ralph 1954

I Never Felt This Way Before   Dubin 1940; Ellington 1940; Gordon 1953, 1956; Myrow 1953, 1956

I Never Felt This Way for Anyone Before   Adams 1966; Strouse 1966

I Never Go Anywhere (That I Can't Come Back From)   Johnston 1948

I Never Got Out of Paris   Silver 1956

I Never Had a Chance   Berlin 1934; De Lange 1946; Dietz 1961; Schwartz, Arthur 1961

I Never Had a Dream Like This Before   Coslow 1957

I Never Had a Dream to My Name   Webster 1942

I Never Had a Man to Cry Over   Gordon 1935; Revel 1935

I Never Had a Man to Love Me Like You   Von Tilzer 1911

I Never Had It So Good   Oakland 1950

I Never Had Waltzes Before   Howard, Bart 1938

I Never Has Seen Snow   Arlen 1954

I Never Heard of a Singer that Didn't Want to Be   Cahn 1961

I Never Heard of Anybody Dying from a Kiss Did You   Sterling 1913; Von Tilzer 1913

I Never Kissed a Baby Like You   Johnson, Howard 1928

I Never Knew   Berlin 1919; Kahn 1925; Mercer 1956;
Schwartz, Jean 1918; Williams 1913; Young, Joe 1913

I Never Knew Heaven Could Speak   Gordon 1939; Revel
1939

I Never Knew How Much God Gave to Me   Brennan 1923

I Never Knew I Could Do Anything Like That   Edwards
1929

I Never Knew (I Could Love Anybody Like I'm Loving
You)   Egan 1920

I Never Knew I Had a Wonderful Wife   Brown, Lew Date
Unknown; Henderson Date Unknown

I Never Knew I Loved You   Yellen 1950

I Never Knew Till Now   Motzan 1916

I Never Knew What Love Could Do   Arlen 1924; Brown, A.
Seymour 1912

I Never Knew What Love Was, Sweetheart Till I Met
You   Johnson, J. Rosamond 1910

I Never Knew What Love Was, Till I Fell in Love With
You   Bryan 1908; Fisher 1908

I Never Knew What Love Was (Till I Met You)   Howard,
Joseph E. 1946

I Never Knew what the Moonlight Could Do (Till the Night I
Met You)   Coslow 1926

I Never Knew Why   Coleman 1984

I Never Know How to Behave When I'm with Boys   Carroll
1909

I Never Left Home   Hoffman 1953; Silver 1953

I Never Liked, Like I Like You   Young, Joe 1932

I Never Loved a Man as Much as That   Smith, Robert B.
1902

I Never Make Love   Johnson, Howard 1933

I Never Meant to Fall in Love   Fain 1960; Webster 1960

I Never Met a Beautiful Girl Till I Met You   Jerome 1913;
Schwartz, Jean 1913

I Never Met a Girl Like You   Cohan 1923

I Never Met a Rose   Lerner, Alan Jay 1974; Loewe 1974

I Never Met a Russian I Didn't Like   David, Hal 1974

I Never Met a Texan   Cahn 1948; Styne 1948

I Never Met Before a Girl Like You   Olcott 1914

I Never Miss   Hammerstein 1920

I Never Miss the Sunshine (I'm So Used to the Rain)   Parish
1923

I Never Realized   Porter 1919

I Never Said I Love You   David, Hal 1976

I Never Saw a Bathing Suit in Russia   Fisher 1928

I Never Saw a Better Night   Mercer 1935

I Never Saw a King Before   Loewe 1938

I Never Saw Such Jealousy in All My Life   Sterling 1906;
Von Tilzer 1906

I Never Say Oui, Oui!   Brooks 1946

I Never Should Have Let You Go   Von Tilzer 1952

I Never Slept a Wink Last Night   Razaf 1934

I Never Thought   Kern 1918

I Never Thought I'd Be Along Here   Willson 1956

I Never Thought I'd Fall in Love Again   Freed, Ralph 1939;
Lane 1939

I Never Thought That You'd Do That to Me   Kahal 1926

I Never Thought You'd Say Goodbye   Bacharach 1987

I Never Took a Chance in My Life   Smith, Harry B. 1904;
Smith, Robert B. 1904

I Never Trust a Woman   Adamson 1955; Lane 1955

I Never Wanna Hear that Song Again   Davis 1956

I Never Wanna Look into Those Eyes Again   Mercer 1955

I Never Want to Go Home Again   Lerner, Alan Jay 1973;
Loewe 1973

I Never Want to See You Again   Berlin 1956; Lerner, Alan
Jay 1983; Strouse 1983

I Never Was Born   Arlen 1944; Harburg 1944

I Never Was Right in My Life   Smith, Harry B. 1906

I Never Would Do It in Society   Goetz 1912

I New Orleans   Hart 1926; Rodgers 1926

I Nominate You (To Be My Sweetheart)   David, Mack 1936

I Nominate You (To Me My Sweetheart)   Schwartz, Jean
1936

I Offer You   Oakland 1956

I Offer You My Heart   Davis 1954

I Once Had a Heart   Young, Victor 1956

I Once Was Yours, I'm Somebody Else's Now   Razaf 1927

I Only Have Eyes for You   Dubin 1934; Warren 1934

I Only Know One Way to Love   Revel 1959

I Only Know that I Love You, That's All that Matters to
Me   Magidson 1932; Stept 1932

I Only Know that You Are Beautiful   Kahn 1930

I Only Love One   Lerner, Sammy 1931

I Only Meant   Martin 1951

I Only Saw You for a Moment   Bergman 1957

I Only Want to Love You   Spina 1950, 1957

I Only Wanted to See If You Loved Me   Hoffman 1951

I Only Wish I Had You with Me Last Night Honey   Monaco
1929

I Ought to Dance   Cahn 1938, 1943

I Ought to Know More About You   Young, Victor 1950

I Oughta Hate Ya — But I Don't   Ager 1933; Young, Joe
1933

I Oughta Know More About You   Heyman 1950

I Owe It All to You   Arlen 1945; Friend 1948; Mercer 1945

I Owe It All to You (Mother O' Mine)   McHugh 1927; Mills
1927

I Owe You   Lawrence 1937; Lerner, Sammy 1929

I Owe You a Kiss   Cahn 1947; Styne 1947

I Own a Piece of a Girl   Dietz 1944; Duke 1944

I Paid for the Lie I Told You   Hoffman 1939

I Paid My Income Tax Today   Berlin 1942

I Passed By Your Window   Lawrence 1953

I Passed this Way Before   Robison 1945

I Passed Up a Wonderful Thing   Fisher 1938

I Passed Your House Tonight   Raye 1952

I Picked a Daisy   Lerner, Alan Jay 1963

I Picked a Pansy in the Garden of Love   Yellen Date
Unknown

I Picked the Wrong One to Love   Kahn 1924

I Planted a Rose (In the Garden of Your Heart)   Brown, Lew
1943; Brown, Nacio Herb 1943; Freed, Ralph 1943

I Played a Fiddle for the Czar   Gordon 1932

I Played Fiddle for the Czar   Revel 1932

I Played My Concertina   Atteridge 1915; Romberg 1915

I Plead, Dear Heart   Smith, Harry B. 1928

I Pledge Allegiance to Your Heart   Fain 1938

I Popped the Question to Her Pop   Johnson, Howard 1924

I Positively Refuse to Sing   Gordon 1934; Revel 1934

I Poured My Heart Into a Song   Berlin 1939

I Pray   Mercer 1953

I Prithee Please   Cahn 1971; Van Heusen 1971

I Promise   Freed, Ralph 1949; Wrubel 1951

I Promise You   Arlen 1944; Lerner, Sammy 1938; Mercer
1944; Oakland 1938

I Promised Their Mothers   Robin 1954; Romberg 1954

I Proved that I Knew Something When I Fell in Love with You   Bryan 1917

I Put a Four Leaf Clover in Your Pocket   Davis 1942

I Put My Money in Dreams (And Bet Them All on You)   Robison 1951

I Qual Que Tu   Gorney 1931

I Question Not   Harbach 1911

I Raised My Boy to Be a Soldier in the Army of the Lord   Bryan 1955

I Read   Sondheim 1994

I Realize   Fisher 1920

I Really Can't Make My Feet Behave   Atteridge 1918; Romberg 1918; Schwartz, Jean 1918

I Really Loved You   Strouse 1980

I Refuse to Answer on the Ground That It May Intend to Incriminate Me (Do You Love Me)   Robison 1951

I Refuse to Rock 'n Roll   Cahn 1956

I Remember   Cahn 1937; David, Hal 1961; Sondheim 1966; Webster 1975

I Remember a Dream   Caesar 1936; Schwartz, Arthur 1936

I Remember It Well   Lerner, Alan Jay 1948, 1958; Loewe 1958; Weill 1948

I Remember Mama   Rodgers 1979

(That's How) I Remember Rome   Cahn 1972; Van Heusen 1972

I Remember That   Sondheim 1954

I Remember the Darkness   Dietz 1952

I Remember You   Mercer 1942; Von Tilzer 1909

I Remember You from Somewhere, Somewhere in My Dreams   Leslie 1930; Warren 1930

I Remember You Love   Drake 1951

I Repent (inst.)   Waller 1941

I Rise Again   Coleman 1978; Comden and Green 1978

I Run to You   Stept 1943

I Said Good Morning   Comden and Green 1955

I Said Goodbye to Happiness, When I Said Goodbye to You   Ahlert 1932; Turk 1932

I Said Goodbye to My Troubles   Davis 1927

I Said Goodbye to the Sunshine When I Said Goodbye to You   Coots 1929; Davis 1929

I Said It and I'm Glad   Comden and Green 1961; Styne 1961

I Said My Prayers Last Night   Coots 1951

I Said "No"   Loesser 1942; Styne 1942

I Sailed Yesterday   Bacharach 1962

I Sang a Thousand Songs   Drake 1960

I Saw Flying Saucers   Silver 1947

I Saw Her at Eight O'Clock   Mercer 1935

I Saw My Future in Your Eyes   Hanley 1932

I Saw My Sweetie in the Newsreel   De Lange 1943

I Saw Myself in Your Eyes   David, Hal 1978

I Saw Stars   Hoffman 1934

I Saw the Light of Day Last Night   Burke Date Unknown; Van Heusen 1938

I Saw the Roses and Remembered You   Kern 1923

I Saw You Dancing   Oakland 1955

I Saw You First   Adamson 1943; David, Mack 1940; McHugh 1943

I Saw You Looking in My Dreams   Mercer 1934

I Saw You on Television   Sigman 1948

I Saw You Smile   Harbach 1950

I Saw Your Eyes   Hammerstein 1931; Romberg 1931

I Say a Little Prayer   Bacharach 1967; David, Hal 1967

I Say, Flo   Cohan 1908

I Say Hello   Rome 1959

I Say It's Spinach - And the Hell with It   Berlin 1932

I Say What I Mean, and I Mean What I Say   Herbert 1907; Smith, Harry B. 1907

I Says to Him   Duke 1946

I Scream — You Scream — We All Scream for Ice Cream   Johnson, Howard 1927

I See. . .   Adams 1983

I See a Man   Livingston, Jerry 1973

I See a Morning Star   Arlen 1944; Harburg 1944

I See a Rainbow   Arlen Date Unknown

I See By the Papers   Hoffman 1932; Washington 1932

I See By Your Smile   Herbert 1900; Smith, Harry B. 1900

I See It All Now   David, Hal 1963

I See My Mother in You   Fisher 1931

I See Something   Drake 1964

I See the Moon   Willson 1951

I See Things Differently Now   Bacharach 1976; David, Hal 1976

I See Two Lovers   Dixon 1934, 1935; Wrubel 1934, 1935

I See Vienna in Your Eyes (In Deinen Augen Liegt Das Herz von Wien)   Young, Joe 1930

I See Wheatfields in the Moonlight   Robison 1954

I See You Everywhere   Brown, Nacio Herb 1945

I See You for the First Time   Bacharach 1976; David, Hal 1976

I See Your Face Before Me   Dietz 1937; Schwartz, Arthur 1937

I See Your Face in Ev'ry Rose   Johnson, J. Rosamond 1914

I Seen Her at the Station   Loesser 1956

I Send My Love with These Roses   Davis 1932; Dubin 1932

I Sent My Wife Away for a Rest, I Needed It   Brown, Lew 1917

I Sent My Wife to the Thousand Islands   Sterling 1916; Von Tilzer 1916

I Shall Be Happy   Rome 1970

I Shall Not Let Money Get in My Way   Rome 1970

I Shall Positively Pay You Next Monday   Porter 1953

I Shall Return   Drake 1952; Parish 1945

I Should Care   Cahn 1945

I Should Hate You   Friend 1949

I Should Have Known Better   Coots 1931; Davis 1931

I Should Have Known You Years Ago   Carmichael 1940

I Should Have Met You a Long Time Ago   Brown, Lew 1913

I Should Have Quit When I Was Ahead   Evans 1950; Livingston, Jay 1950

I Should Have Told You Before   Cahn 1951

I Should Think that You Could Guess   Herbert 1905

I Should Worry   Gilbert 1911; Smith, Harry B. 1912

I Shoulda Quit When I Was Ahead   Evans 1948; Livingston, Jay 1948

I Shoulda Said   Hoffman 1952

I Should'a Stood in Pennsylvania   Harburg 1946

I Shouldn't Care   Ahlert 1932; Turk 1932

I Shouldn't Love You   Rome 1948

I Should've Said   Cahn 1966; Van Heusen 1966

I Should've Stood in Bed   Rainger 1939; Robin 1939

I Sing a Hymn to Men   Pollack 1943

I Sing All My Love Songs to You   Hoffman 1929

I Sing for You Alone   Washington 1933

I Sing of Love   Porter 1948

I Sing of Spring   Clare 1936

I Sing Tra-La   Atteridge Date Unknown

I Sleep Easier Now   Porter 1950

I Smiled Yesterday   Bacharach 1962; David, Hal 1962

I Speak English Now   Gershwin, Ira 1929

I Speak to the Stars   Fain 1954; Webster 1954

I Spent a Thousand Years Today   DePaul 1958; Raye 1958

I Start Sneezing   Coleman 1984

I Started on a Shoestring   Dietz 1930; Schwartz, Arthur 1930

I Still Believe in Love   Whiting 1936

I Still Believe in You   Akst 1929; Clarke 1929; Davis 1929; Duke 1927; Gilbert 1926; Hart 1930; Robin 1929; Rodgers 1930; Sterling 1923

I Still Belong to You   Robin 1929; Whiting 1929

I Still Call You Sweetheart   Yellen 1930

I Still Can Dream   DeSylva 1922

I Still Get a Thrill Thinking of You   Coots 1930; Davis 1930

I Still Get Jealous   Cahn 1947; Styne 1947

I Still Have My Dream   Koehler 1947; Stept 1947

I Still Have That Other Girl   Bacharach 1996

I Still Have Your Beautiful Pictures   Leslie 1927; Schwartz, Jean 1927

I Still Keep Dreaming of You   Davis 1928

I Still Like Ike   Berlin 1954

I Still Look at You That Way   Dietz 1963; Schwartz, Arthur 1963

I Still Love the Red, White and Blue   Porter 1931, 1932

I Still Love to Kiss You Good Night   Bullock 1937; Spina 1937

I Still Love You   Ager 1928; Yellen 1928

I Still Remember, Do You!   Akst 1928; Davis 1928

I Still See Elisa   Lerner, Alan Jay 1951; Loewe 1951

I Still Want You   Mills 1935

I Struck a Match in the Dark   Hoffman 1941; Livingston, Jerry 1941

I Struck Out   Coleman 1972; Fields 1972

I Stumbled Into Heaven (Falling for You)   Koehler 1932; Mitchell 1932; Pollack 1932

I Stumbled Over You and Fell in Love   Adamson 1930; Gordon 1931; Revel 1930, 1931

I Sure Hate Love   Cahn 1966; Van Heusen 1966

I Sure Have Been in Love   Duke 1955

I Surrender   Hart 1920, 1921; Rodgers 1920

I Surrender, My Darling   Coots 1957

I Take a Dim View   Willson 1952

I Take a Dim View of the West   Blane 1955; Martin 1955

I Take After Rip   Caesar 1930

I Take Just as Much Pride in My Dear Little Bride   Willson 1953

I Take My Sugar with a Grain of Salt   Robison 1965

I Take to You   Gordon 1941; Warren 1941

I Talk to the Trees   Lerner, Alan Jay 1951; Loewe 1951

I Talked with a Tree   Burke 1934; Spina 1934

I Tank I Go Home   Edwards 1932

I Taught Her Everything She Knows   Leigh 1968

I Thank You   Yellen 1922

I Thank You, Mr. Moon   Baer 1931

I Theenk   David, Mack 1947; Hoffman 1947; Livingston, Jerry 1947

I Theenk You Weenk   Fain 1947

I Think a Lot of You   Coslow 1940

I Think an Awful Lot of You   Johnson, J. Rosamond 1907

I Think I Oughtn't Auto Any More   Goetz 1907

I Think I'll Put My Blue Suit on To-Night   Schwartz, Jean 1928

I Think I'm Going to Like It Over Here   Dietz 1963; Schwartz, Arthur 1963

I Think I'm Gonna Fall in Love   Bacharach 1980

I Think I'm Gonna Like It Here   Strouse 1977

I Think I'm in Love with My Wife   Hammerstein 1933

I Think It's Here to Stay   Myrow 1959

I Think of What You Used to Think of Me   Hanley 1928; Turk 1928

I Think of You   Mancini 1954

I Think of You Every Hour of the Day   Spina 1957

I Think of You the Whole Year Round   Jerome 1907; Schwartz, Jean 1907

I Think That You and I Should Get Acquainted   Comden and Green 1964; Styne 1964

I Think the World of You   Edwards 1910

I Think Too Much of You   Donaldson 1932; Kahn 1932

I Think You Have Got Something There   Loesser 1937

I Think You'd Better Hurry Home   Friml 1914; Harbach 1914

I Think You'll Like It   Whiting 1929

I Think You're Absolutely Wonderful (What Do You Think of Me)   Carroll 1918

I Think You're Ducky   Clare 1937

I Think You're Pretty Too   Duke 1952

I Think You're Sweet As Can Be, What Do You Think of Me   Brown, Nacio Herb 1927; Friend 1927

I Think You're Swell   Johnson, James P. 1932; Razaf 1932

I Think You're Wonderful   Adamson 1934; Lane 1934; Silver 1928

I Think You're Wonderful, Say What Do You Think of Me   Friend 1925

I Think You've Got Something There   Raye 1950

I Thought About You   Mercer 1939; Van Heusen 1939

I Thought He Was a Business Man   Edwards 1910; Smith, Harry B. 1910

I Thought I Heard a Voice   Burke 1933; Spina 1933

I Thought I Knew   Harbach 1936

I Thought I Meant Something to You   DePaul Date Unknown; Russell Date Unknown

I Thought I Wanted Opera   Williams 1910

I Thought I'd Die   Henderson 1922

I Thought of You Last Night   Freed, Ralph 1952

I Thought They'd Never Leave   Comden and Green 1955

I Threw a Bean Bag at the Moon   Ager 1935

I Threw a Kiss in the Ocean   Berlin 1942

I Threw a Pebble in the Pond   Hanley 1935; Leslie 1935

I Told My Heart   Cahn 1950

I Told My Love to the Roses   Johnson, J. Rosamond 1916

I Told the Daisies   Spina 1957

I Told Them All About You   Friend 1927

I Told You (He Wasn't for You)   Mills 1952

I Told You So   Brown, Lew Date Unknown; Clare 1932; DePaul 1944; Henderson Date Unknown; Raye 1944; Stept 1932

I Took a Walk   Livingston, Jerry 1954

I Took My Strength from You   Bacharach 1976; David, Hal 1976

I Treasure You   Leslie 1928; Monaco 1928

I Tried!   Evans 1957; Livingston, Jay 1957; Merrill 1964; Styne 1964

I Tried for a Week to Speak to the Sheik   Hanley 1930

I Tried not to Love You (O Cara Diletta Del Cuore)   Mills 1951

I Turn to You   Evans 1968; Livingston, Jay 1968

I Turned White Overnight Over You   Revel 1941

I Understand   Comden and Green 1944

I Understand Tonight   Coslow 1930, 1931

I Ups to Her and She Ups to Me   Hoffman 1938

I Used to Be   Oakland 1947

I Used to Be Above Love   Duke 1936; Gershwin, Ira 1936

I Used to Be Afraid to Go Home in the Dark   Williams 1908

I Used to Be Color Blind   Berlin 1938
I Used to Be Everybody's Baby   Davis 1962
I Used to Call Her Baby (And Now She's a Mother to
    Me)   Johnson, Howard 1919
I Used to Hate Ya   Hoffman 1956
I Used to Laugh at Love   Hanley 1938
I Used to Love Her in the Moonlight, But She's in the
    Limelight Now   Lewis 1929; Young, Joe 1929
I Used to Love them All   Hart 1919
I Used to Love to Go Dancing (But Now I Go Dancing to
    Love)   Johnson, Howard 1923
I Used to Play It by Ear   Berlin 1963
I Used to Shower Her with Kisses   Henderson 1926; Lewis
    1926; Young, Joe 1926
I Waited for You   Russell 1957
I Waited So Long   Evans 1956; Livingston, Jay 1956
I Wake at Morning   Hart 1928; Rodgers 1928
I Wake Up Crying   Bacharach 1961; David, Hal 1961
I Wake Up in the Morning   Fain 1945; Yellen 1945
I Wake Up in the Morning Feeling Fine   Loesser 1949
I Wake Up Smiling   Ahlert 1933; Leslie 1933
I Walk a Little Dog   Comden and Green 1961; Styne 1961
I Walk a Little Faster   Coleman 1958; Leigh 1958
I Walk the Streets   Raye 1965
I Walk with Music   Carmichael 1940; Mercer 1940
I Walked Around   Snyder 1908
I Walked In (With My Eyes Wide Open)   Adamson 1945;
    McHugh 1945
I Walked Out when You Walked In (Somebody's Else's
    Arms)   Stept 1958
I Walked with the Angels   David, Mack 1944
I Wanna   David, Mack 1947
I Wanna Be a Buccaneer   Leigh 1953
I Wanna Be a Cowboy in the Movies   Cahn 1948; Styne
    1948
I Wanna Be a Dancin' Man   Mercer 1951; Warren 1951
I Wanna Be a Texas Cowboy   Baer 1965
I Wanna Be Around   Mercer 1959
I Wanna Be Around My Baby All the Time   Meyer 1931;
    Young, Joe 1931
I Wanna Be Bad   Ellington 1946
I Wanna Be Good 'n' Bad   Martin 1951
I Wanna Be in Love Again   Mercer 1965
I Wanna Be in Winchell's Column   Gordon 1937; Revel 1937
I Wanna Be Kissed   Brown, Nacio Herb 1931
I Wanna Be Like You (The Monkey Song)   Sherman 1967
I Wanna Be Loved   Heyman 1931; Rose 1931
I Wanna Be Loved by You   Kalmar 1928; Ruby 1928
I Wanna Be Real (Slowly Surely)   Sherman 1985
I Wanna Be with You   Stept 1927
I Wanna Be Yours   Coleman 1982; Leigh 1982
I Wanna Count Sheep Till the Cows Come Home   Young,
    Joe 1931
I Wanna Fall Asleep and Wake Up in Virginia   Young, Joe
    1930
I Wanna Go Back   Dietz 1944; Duke 1944
I Wanna Go Back to Bali   Dubin 1938; Warren 1938
I Wanna Go Back to Dear Old Mother's Knee   Hanley 1919
I Wanna Go Back to Heaven Again   Koehler 1926
I Wanna Go Home   Yellen 1922
I Wanna Go Places and Do Things   Robin 1929; Whiting
    1929
I Wanna Go to City College   Fain 1946
I Wanna Go to the Zoo   Gordon 1936; Revel 1936
I Wanna Go Voom Voom   Brown, Lew 1927; Friend 1927

I Wanna Go Where You Go — Do What You Do Then I'll Be
    Happy   Brown, Lew 1925; Clare 1925; Friend 1925
I Wanna Hum Sumpin' Pretty to a Sweet Pretty
    Thing   Ahlert 1937
I Wanna Hurt You   Freed, Ralph 1964
I Wanna Know   David, Hal 1956
I Wanna Love You, Cara Mia (Te Voglio, Bene, Tanto,
    Tanto)   Bullock 1954
I Wanna Make Love   Friend 1935
I Wanna Make with the Happy Times   Loesser 1940
I Wanna Marry a Bombardier   David, Mack 1942
I Wanna Meander with Miranda   Gordon 1933; Revel 1933
I Wanna Play House with You   Dixon 1935; Wrubel 1935
I Wanna Ride with the Man Who Blows the
    Whistle   Webster 1941
I Wanna Sing about You   Friend 1931
I Wanna Sing, I Wanna Laugh, I Wanna Love   Alter 1951;
    Eliscu 1951
I Wanna Sing Like an Angel (Dance Like a Devil)   Fain
    1954; Webster 1954
I Wanna Walk in the Rain   Spina 1957
I Wanna Wander   Gordon 1953; Myrow 1953
I Wanna Woman   Robin 1955; Styne 1955
I Want a Beautiful Baby Like You   Caesar 1919
I Want a Beautiful Doll for Christmas   Hoffman 1946;
    Livingston, Jerry 1946
I Want a Boy Who's Determined to Do What I
    Say   Harbach 1917
I Want a Daddy Like You   Brown, Lew 1917
I Want a Doll   Von Tilzer 1918
I Want a Fair and Square Man   Woods 1933
I Want a Girl from Old Kentucky (Where My Dad Got His
    Best Girl)   Sissle 1915
I Want a Girl Just Like a Girl That Married Dear Old
    Dad   Von Tilzer 1911
I Want a Girl Like You   Atteridge 1916; Howard, Joseph E.
    1905; Motzan 1916, 1917; Romberg 1916
I Want a Girl to Call My Own   Buck 1926; Friml 1926
I Want a Good Baby — Bad   Young, Joe 1922
I Want a Good Baby - Bad   Lewis 1922
I Want a Good Girl (And I Want Her Bad)   Bryan 1917
I Want a Good Man, and I Want Him Bad   Brown, A.
    Seymour 1921; Magidson 1928
I Want a Good Time Bad   Coslow 1929
I Want a Kiss   Hammerstein 1926; Harbach 1926; Romberg
    1926
I Want a Little Corner in Your Heart   Sterling 1909
I Want a Loveable Baby   Brown, Lew 1925; DeSylva 1925;
    Henderson 1925
I Want a Man   Hammerstein 1928; Hart 1922, 1926, 1931;
    Howard, Joseph E. 1910; Rodgers 1922, 1926, 1931;
    Youmans 1928
I Want a Man for All Seasons   Fain 1967
I Want a Man to Love Me   Herbert 1909
I Want a New Romance   Coslow 1938; Lane 1937
I Want a Phos Phos   Brown, Lew 1924
I Want a Postal Card from You   Fisher 1908
I Want a Pretty Girl   Harbach 1923
I Want a Ragtime Bungalow   Kalmar 1913
I Want a Red Blooded Papa to Chase My Blues
    Away   Coslow 1935
I Want a Thrill   Howard, Joseph E. 1907
I Want a Toy Soldier Man   Atteridge 1913; Schwartz, Jean
    1913

I Want a Whole Lot of Girls (I Want a Lot of Girlies, Girlies)   Jerome 1910; Schwartz, Jean 1910

I Want a Wife that Can Cook   Smith, Harry B. 1934

I Want a Yes Girl   Caesar 1928; Friend 1928

I Want a Yes Man   Caesar 1925; Gershwin, Ira 1925; Youmans 1925

I Want All the World to Know   Friml 1914; Harbach 1914

I Want Another Chance with You   Baer 1925; DeSylva 1925

I Want Another Portion of That   Brown, Lew 1932; Henderson 1932

I Want 'em Wild, Weak, Warm and Willing   Coslow 1923

I Want Everyone to Know   Davis 1944

I Want Him Back Again   Brown, Lew 1918

I Want It to Be Right   Adams 1957; Strouse 1957

I Want My Bib   Von Tilzer 1925

I Want My Husband When I Wed   Romberg 1918

I Want My Little Gob   Kern 1919

I Want My Mommy and Daddy Together for Christmas   Burke 1954

I Want My Money Back   Loesser 1947

I Want My Ragtime   Cohan 1901

I Want My Share of Love   Cahn 1939

I Want Plenty of You   Fields 1928; McHugh 1928

I Want Romance   Rome 1940

I Want Somebody to Cheer Me Up   Kahn 1926

I Want Somebody to Play With   Williams 1909

I Want Someone to Call Me Dearie   Williams 1908

I Want Someone to Flirt with Me   Sterling 1910; Von Tilzer 1910

I Want Someone Who's Lonesome   Smith, Robert B. 1915

I Want Something New To Play With   Atteridge 1911, 1912; Cobb 1911; Edwards 1911

I Want That Man   Hart 1930; Rodgers 1930

I Want that Star   Buck 1916

I Want the Best for Him   Coleman 1999

I Want the South to Win the War for Christmas   Cahn 1959; Van Heusen 1959

I Want the Strolling Good   Atteridge 1913; Schwartz, Jean 1913

I Want the Whole World To Love You   Bryan 1936

I Want the World to Know   Friml 1937; Kahn 1937; Robin 1928

I Want the World to Know I Love You   Cohan 1907

I Want to Be a Bad Little Boy   Egan 1925; Kahn 1925

I Want to Be a Ballet Dancer   Berlin 1924

I Want to Be a Drummer (In the Band)   Fain 1945; Yellen 1945

I Want to Be a Gambling Man   Herbert 1907

I Want to Be a Good Lamb   Herbert 1940

I Want to Be a Hill-billy Bride   Hanley 1939

I Want to Be a Liberty Belle   Gorney 1926

I Want to Be a Minstrel Man   Adamson 1934; Lane 1934

I Want to Be a Naughty Little Girl   Herbert 1908; Smith, Harry B. 1908

I Want to Be a Popular Millionaire   Cohan 1906

I Want to Be a Romeo   Romberg 1916

I Want to Be a War Bride   Gershwin, George 1929; Gershwin, Ira 1929

I Want to Be a Wild, Wild Rose   Herbert 1911

I Want to Be a Yale Boy   Porter 1910

I Want to Be Alone with Mary Brown   Leslie 1929

I Want to Be Bad   Brown, Lew 1929; DeSylva 1929; Henderson 1929

I Want to Be Free   Brown, Lew 1925

I Want to Be Glorified   Berlin 1927

I Want to Be Happy   Caesar 1925; Youmans 1925

I Want to Be in Dixie   Berlin 1912; Snyder 1912

I Want to Be Kissed   Fisher 1925

I Want to Be Kissed by a Matinee Idol   Smith, Harry B. 1909

I Want to Be Left Alone   Kahn 1924

I Want to Be Loved   Romberg 1924

I Want to Be Loved By a Soldier   Silver 1918

I Want to Be Married (To a Delta Kappa Epsilon Man)   Porter 1912

I Want to Be Raided By You   Porter 1929

I Want to Be Seen with You   Strouse 1964

I Want to Be Seen with You Tonight   Merrill 1964; Styne 1964

I Want to Be Talked About   Brooks 1946

I Want to Be Teacher's Pet   Gordon 1949; Myrow 1949

I Want to Be the Guy   Rainger 1941; Robin 1941

I Want to Be the Leader of the Band   Yellen 1920

I Want to Be the Leady Lady   Sterling 1901

I Want to Be There   Clarke 1915; Dietz 1924; Kern 1924; Monaco 1915; Romberg 1927; Smith, Harry B. 1927

I Want to Be Vamped in Georgia   Turk 1922

I Want to Be Wanted By You   Gershwin, George 1920; Gershwin, Ira 1920

I Want to Be Way Down Yonder in the Corn Field   Leslie 1915; Young, Joe 1915

I Want to Be with You   Adams 1964; DeSylva 1932; Donaldson 1926; Kahn 1926; Strouse 1964; Youmans 1932

I Want to Be Your Sweetheart   Revel 1929

I Want to Believe You   Sigman 1966

I Want to Dance a Little, Romance a Little   Coslow 1935

I Want to Dream By the Old Mill Stream   Bryan 1931

I Want to Follow You   Freed, Ralph 1941

I Want to Get Arrested   Comden and Green 1967; Styne 1967

I Want to Go Back to Michigan (Down on the Farm)   Berlin 1914

I Want to Go Home   Atteridge 1924; Gilbert 1913; Jerome 1924; Porter 1938; Romberg 1924; Schwartz, Jean 1924

I Want to Go to Chicago   Willson 1954

I Want to Go to Church with You   Goetz 1917; Monaco 1917

I Want to Go to Mexico   Edwards 1914

I Want to Go to Paree, Papa   Cohan 1903

I Want to Go to the Land Where Sweet Daddies Grow   Von Tilzer 1920

I Want to Go to Tokio   Fisher 1914

I Want to Hear a Yankee Doodle Tune   Cohan 1903

I Want to Hear You Say C'est Vous   Lewis 1929; Young, Joe 1929

I Want To! I Got To! I Have to Be Loved   Fisher 1929

I Want to Learn to Jazz Dance   Buck 1918

I Want to Live (As Long As You Love Me)   Fain 1940; Yellen 1940

I Want to Look Nice for You   Mills 1937

I Want to Love You   Ellington 1961

I Want to Make Sure You Love Me   Henderson Date Unknown

I Want to Make Sure You Love Me, 'Cause I've Been Fooled Before   Brown, Lew 1919; Monaco 1919

I Want to Make Up with You   Donaldson 1927; Kahn 1927

I Want to Marry   Carroll 1918; Herbert 1906

I Want to Marry a Male Quartette   Friml 1914; Harbach 1914

I Want to Marry a Marionette   Gershwin, George 1928;
   Gershwin, Ira 1928
I Want to Meander in the Meadow   Woods 1929
I Want to Play House with You   Harbach 1910
I Want to Report a Fire   Heyman 1935
I Want to Ring Bells   Coots 1933
I Want to Rock-A-Bye My Mammy   Dubin 1921
I Want to Row on the Crew   Porter 1914
I Want to See a Minstrel Show   Berlin 1919
I Want to See My Tennessee   Ager 1924; Yellen 1924
I Want to Share It with You   David, Mack 1973; Livingston,
   Jerry 1973
I Want to Shimmie   Clarke 1919
I Want to Sing in Opera   Kern 1911
I Want to Sing, Sing, Sing for You   Sigman 1954
I Want to Sleep with You Now   Strouse Date Unknown
I Want to Spoon to the Tune of the Silver Moon   Edwards
   1911
I Want to Step   Coots 1923
I Want to Talk with You   Howard, Joseph E. 1947
I Want to Thank You   Baer 1951
I Want To Watch Over You   Bryan 1915
I Want Twins   Porter 1924
I Want Two Husbands   Hammerstein 1925; Harbach 1925
I Want What I Want When I Want It   Herbert 1905
I Want You   Cohan 1907; Davis 1952; Edwards 1930; Fisher
   1930; Herbert 1920; Johnson, Howard 1925
I Want You All to Myself   Eliscu 1929
I Want You As You Are   Johnson, J. Rosamond 1950
I Want You for a Sunbeam   Merrill 1953
I Want You for Christmas   Stept 1937; Washington 1937
I Want You in the Picture   Harbach 1910
I Want You Ma' Honey   Smith, Harry B. 1906
I Want You Morning, Noon and Night   Cobb 1921
I Want You to Love Me   Blane 1945
I Want You to Marry Me   Herbert 1906
I Want You to Meet My Mother   Dubin 1914
I Want You to Want Me   Hoffman 1958
I Want You To Want Me To Want You   Bryan 1925; Fisher
   1925
I Want You To Want Me with You   Bryan 1917
I Want Your for Myself   Berlin 1931
I Want Your Kisses If You Want My Kisses   Arlen 1925
(If I Love Ya, then I Need Ya, If I Need Ya) I Wantcha
   Around   Merrill 1954
I Wanted to Change Him   Comden and Green 1967; Styne
   1967
I Wanted to Come to Broadway   Cohan 1914
I Was a Florodora Baby   Carroll 1920, 1928
I Was a Fool to Let You Go   Razaf 1940
I Was a Little Too Lonely   Evans 1956; Livingston, Jay 1956
I Was a Shoo-In   Comden and Green 1961; Styne 1961
I Was Afraid of That   Rainger 1939; Robin 1939
I Was Alone   Hammerstein 1930; Harbach 1925; Kern 1930
I Was an Incubator Baby (And She Was the Girl Next
   Door)   Ruby 1966
I Was Anything but Sentimental   Hoffman 1937; Lerner,
   Sammy 1937
I Was Aviating Around   Berlin 1913
I Was Born Happy   Sigman 1949
I Was Born in Virginia (Ethel Levey's Virginia Song)   Cohan
   1906
I Was Born on the Isle of Man   Atteridge 1914; Carroll 1914;
   Romberg 1914
I Was Born to Be Loved   Clare 1931

I Was Born to Sing   Oakland 1952; Raye 1952
I Was Born too Late   Friend 1935; Yellen 1935
I Was Born with Blues in My Heart   Arlen 1930; Koehler
   1930
I Was Doing All Right   Gershwin, George 1938; Gershwin,
   Ira 1938
I Was Glad to Let You Go, but I'm So Sorry
   Now   Donaldson 1925; Friend 1925
I Was Here When You Left Me, I'll Be There When You Get
   Back   Stept 1945
I Was Hoping You'd Ask Me   Hoffman 1958
I Was in Kalua   Baer 1937
I Was Just Supposing   Smith, Robert B. 1906
I Was Left Behind   Lawrence 1932
I Was Lonely   Kern 1918
I Was Lost   Strouse 1982
I Was Meant for Someone   Hanley 1925
I Was Naive   Gershwin, Ira 1938; Kern 1938
I Was Never Nearer Heaven in My Life   Clarke 1916; Leslie
   1916; Snyder 1916
I Was Not too Particular   Stept 1929
I Was Once in Love When (inst.)   Kern 1956
I Was Only Pretending   Adamson 1972
I Was Saying to the Moon   Burke 1936; Johnston 1936
I Was Silly, I Was Headstrong, I Was Impetuous   Cahn
   1946; Styne 1946
I Was So Happy I Cried   Burke 1935; Spina 1935
I Was So Romantic   Freed, Arthur 1923
I Was So Weak, Love Was So Strong   Johnson, James P.
   1932; Razaf 1932
I Was So Young and You Were So Beautiful   Bryan 1919;
   Caesar 1919; Gershwin, George 1919
I Was Something   David, Hal 1991; Strouse 1991
I Was Taken By Storm   Alter 1935; Heyman 1935
I Was Talking to Myself, I Was   Revel 1963
I Was the Most Beautiful Blossom   Gershwin, George 1931;
   Gershwin, Ira 1931
I Was the Power Behind the Throne   Lawrence 1938
I Was There   David, Mack 1973; Livingston, Jerry 1973
I Was Thinking of You   Kahn 1914; Whiting 1914
I Was Waiting for You   Evans 1950; Livingston, Jay 1950;
   Smith, Harry B. 1934
I Was Waltzing to a Rhumba Last Night   Revel 1944
I Was Wearin' Horseshoes   Arlen 1953; Fields 1953
I Was Wrong   Sondheim 1996
I Was Young in Budapest (inst.)   Kern 1938
I Was Yours   Russell 1960
I Wasn't Born to Be Lonesome   Brown, Lew 1917
I Wasn't Born Yesterday   Burke 1937; Johnston 1937
I Wasted My Love on You   Silver 1918
I Watch the Love Parade (Crystal Candalabra)   Harbach
   1931; Kern 1931
I Welcome You   Robin 1936
I Went Merrily Merrily on My Way   Fain 1935; Kahal 1935,
   1947
I Whistle a Happy Tune   Hammerstein 1951; Rodgers 1951
I Whoever I Am   Fain 1973; Harburg 1973
I Will   Arlen 1966
I Will Always Follow You   Clarke 1914; Young, Joe 1914
I Will Be a Soldier Bride   Kahn 1933
I Will Be Your Chanticleer   Von Tilzer 1910
I Will Give You All for Love   Smith, Harry B. 1911; Smith,
   Robert B. 1911
I Will Kill Her   Lane 1985
I Will Love You Tomorrow and Tomorrow   Parish 1931

I Will Remember, You Will Forget   Coslow 1929, 1930
I Will Say Goodbye   Bergman 1971
I Will Show You the Way   Atteridge Date Unknown
I Will Wait   Howard, Joseph E. 1919
I Wind Up Taking a Fall   Mercer 1951
I Wish I Could Be a Singing Cowboy   Cahn 1953
I Wish I Could Believe You   Smith, Harry B. 1923; Smith, Robert B. 1923
I Wish I Could Forget You   Sondheim 1994
I Wish I Could Forget Your Kisses (Like You Forgot My Tears)   Parish 1983
I Wish I Could Laugh at Love   Dixon 1931; Warren 1931; Young, Joe 1931
I Wish I Could Leave You Alone   Young, Joe 1932
I Wish I Could Move the Swanee Far from the Old Folks at Home   Jerome 1915; Schwartz, Jean 1915
I Wish I Could Stop Remembering   Coslow 1926
I Wish I Could Tell You   Bloom 1946; Ruby 1946
I Wish I Didn't Love You So   Loesser 1947
I Wish I Had a Dime for Ever Time I Missed You   Hoffman 1941; Livingston, Jerry 1941
I Wish I Had a Girl   Kahn 1908
I Wish I Had a Papa Like the Papa who Lives Next Door   Donaldson 1923
I Wish I Had a Record (Of the Promises You Made)   David, Hal 1949
I Wish I Had an Elephant   Coots 1955
I Wish I Had Died in My Cradle Before I Grew Up to Love You   Brown, Lew 1926
I Wish I Had My Old Gal Back Again   Ager 1926; Pollack 1926; Yellen 1926
I Wish I Had Someone Like You   Mercer 1958
I Wish I Had Someone to Cry Over   Parish 1923
I Wish I Had Wings   Woods 1932
I Wish I Had You Back in My Arms   Davis 1926
I Wish I Hadn't Said Hello   Young, Joe 1932
I Wish I Knew   Gordon 1945; Warren 1945; Young, Victor 1929
I Wish I Knew Her Name   Coleman 1965
I Wish I Was a Big Sky-Rocket   Goetz 1917
I Wish I Was a Boy and I Wish I Was a Girl   Norworth 1909
I Wish I Was a Bunny   Coots 1956
I Wish I Was a Hero Too   Williams 1908
I Wish I Was a Queen   Hammerstein 1920; Harbach 1920
I Wish I Was an Island in an Ocean of Girls   Herbert 1915
I Wish I Was Back in St. Louis   Revel 1952
I Wish I Was in Prison   Dubin 1926; Fain 1926
I Wish I Was in the Land of Cotton Now   Johnson, Howard 1918; Meyer 1918
I Wish I Was the Willow   Lane 1938; Loesser 1938
I Wish I Were   Strouse 1963
I Wish I Were a Clown Like Pagliacci   Leslie 1936; Monaco 1936
I Wish I Were a Fish   Adamson 1964; Brooks 1953; Fain 1964; Young, Victor 1953
I Wish I Were a Fisherman   Egan 1934
I Wish I were a Goldfish   Alter 1947; De Lange 1947
I Wish I Were Aladdin   Gordon 1935; Revel 1935
I Wish I Were Back in My Cradle   Brennan 1929
I Wish I Were Back in Your Arms Tonight   Conrad 1930
I Wish I Were in Love Again   Hart 1937; Rodgers 1937
I Wish I Were Irish   Burke 1958; Van Heusen 1958
I Wish I Were Somebody Else   Burke 1951; Van Heusen 1951
I Wish I Were Twins   De Lange 1934; Loesser 1934

I Wish, I Wish I Had a Picture of You   Merrill 1950
I Wish I Wuz a Kid Again and Knew What I Know Now   Edwards 1928
I Wish It Could Be Otherwise   DePaul 1959; Mercer 1959; Raye 1959
I Wish It Was Me   Brown, Lew 1925; Friend 1925
I Wish It Were Now   David, Hal 1960
I Wish Somebody Cared Enough to Cry   Merrill 1948
I Wish Someone Was Waiting for Me   Bryan 1931
I Wish That He Was Back in Tipperary   Brennan 1915
I Wish That I Could Be a Singing Cowboy   Cahn 1941
I Wish that I Could Love You   Revel 1946
I Wish that I Could Say the Same   David, Hal 1961
I Wish that I Could Try   David, Hal 1959
I Wish that I'd Been Born in Borneo   Clarke 1920; Donaldson 1920
I Wish that I'd Been Satisfied with Mary   Henderson 1925
I Wish that Kisses Grew on Trees   Merrill 1950
I Wish That You Was My Gal, Molly   Berlin 1909; Snyder 1909
I Wish There Were a Television to Heaven   Parish 1931; Silver 1931
I Wish We Could Dance Forever   Hoffman 1932
I Wish We Didn't Have to Say Goodnight   Adamson 1944; McHugh 1944
I Wish We Were Siamese Twins   Magidson 1930; Washington 1930
I Wish We Were Sweethearts Again   Hoffman 1954
I Wish You a Waltz   Bergman 1978
I Wish You All the Best   Stept 1955
I Wish You All the Luck in the World   Washington 1929
I Wish You Needed Me   Burke 1963, 1981
I Wish You Were Here   Raye 1941
I Wish You Were Here Tonight   Hoffman 1927
I Wish You'd Have Happened to Me   Robison 1948
I Wish You'd Keep Out of My Dreams   Clarke 1913; Leslie 1913; Schwartz, Jean 1913
I Wished   Adams 1958
I Wished on the Moon   Rainger 1935
I Wish't I Was in Peoria   Dixon 1925; Henderson 1925; Rose 1925; Woods 1925
I Wisht I Wuz a Woman with a Past   Oakland 1960
I Woke Up with a Cold   Caesar 1947
I Wonder   Berlin 1919; Burke 1930; Davis 1928; Herbert 1899; Kern 1912; Lawrence 1981; Lewis 1954; Meyer 1954; Robin 1936; Silver 1928; Smith, Harry B. 1899
I Wonder How I Ever Passed You By   Harbach 1921
I Wonder How I Look When I'm Asleep   Brown, Lew 1927; DeSylva 1927; Henderson 1927
I Wonder How It Is (To Dance with a Boy)   Merrill 1967
I Wonder How She Is Tonight   Heyman 1940
I Wonder How the Old Folks Are Tonight   Yellen 1932
I Wonder How They Get that Way   Buck 1923
I Wonder If a Certain Girl Is Listening   Drake 1954
I Wonder If It's True   Atteridge 1911
I Wonder If She Cares   Smith, Harry B. 1927
I Wonder If She Will Remember   Smith, Harry B. 1927
I Wonder If She's Waiting   Sterling 1899; Von Tilzer 1899
I Wonder If They're All True to Me   Smith, Harry B. 1908
I Wonder If You Care   Harbach 1911
I Wonder If You Miss Me (As I Miss You)   Snyder 1904
I Wonder If You Still Care for Me   Smith, Harry B. 1921; Snyder 1921
I Wonder (If You're Lonesome)   Koehler 1932
I Wonder What Became of Me?   Arlen 1946; Mercer 1946

I Wonder What He Meant By That   Duke 1963

I Wonder What He Said to Her   Drake 1953

I Wonder What He's Doing Tonight   Hanley 1917

I Wonder what Is Really on His Mind   Bryan 1929

I Wonder What It's Like to Be in Paris   Warren 1962

I Wonder what Rebecca Was Doing by the Well   Fisher 1920

I Wonder What the Folks Will Think of Me   Clarke 1917; Johnson, Howard 1917; Monaco 1917

I Wonder What the King Is Doing Tonight   Lerner, Alan Jay 1960; Loewe 1960

I Wonder What They're Doin' Back in Punxsatawney   Drake 1952

I Wonder what They're Doin' Down in Ding Dong Dell   Woods 1935

I Wonder What They're Doing To-Night   Brown, Lew 1918

I Wonder What They're Doing Tonight, Your Girl and Mine   Henderson Date Unknown

I Wonder What's Become of Joe   Turk 1926

I Wonder What's Become of Sally   Ager 1924; Yellen 1924

I Wonder What's Become of Yaaka Hickey Doola Lou   Donaldson 1934; Kahn 1934

I Wonder What's the Matter with My Eyes   Smith, Harry B. 1908; Williams 1908

I Wonder Where I'll Be Next Christmas   Warren 1970

I Wonder Where Mary Is Tonight   Parish 1929

I Wonder Where My Baby Is Tonight   Donaldson 1925; Kahn 1925

I Wonder Where My Buddies Are Tonight   Egan 1926; Rose 1926; Whiting 1926

I Wonder Where My Girl Is Now   Porter 1912

I Wonder Where My Hula Girl Has Gone   Donaldson 1938

I Wonder Where My Lovin' Man Has Gone   Whiting 1914

I Wonder Where My Old Girl Is To-Night   Kalmar 1925; Ruby 1925

I Wonder Where My Sweetie Can Be   Blake 1925; Sissle 1925

I Wonder Where Sweet Genevieve Can Be   Parish 1931

I Wonder Where They'll Go   Smith, Harry B. 1908

I Wonder Who (Has Taken My Place with You)   Davis 1920

I Wonder Who She Spoons with Now   Smith, Robert B. 1915

I Wonder Who Wished Her on Me   Sterling 1914; Von Tilzer 1914

I Wonder Who's Dancing with You Tonight   Dixon 1924; Henderson 1924; Rose 1924

I Wonder Who's Keeping Him Now   Alter 1930; Rose 1930

I Wonder Who's Kissing Her Now   Howard, Joseph E. 1909

I Wonder Who's Kissing the Girl I Left Behind   Howard, Joseph E. 1942

I Wonder Who's Under the Moon with You Tonight   Coots 1931; Davis 1931

I Wonder Who's Waltzing with the One I Love   Parish 1933

I Wonder Who's With You When I'm Not There   Dixon 1927; Monaco 1927

I Wonder Why   Coots 1922; Goetz 1916; Henderson 1925; Kern 1917; Romberg 1927; Smith, Harry B. 1917

I Wonder Why I Love No One but You   Cobb 1900; Edwards 1900

I Wonder Why (inst.)   Young, Victor 1952

I Wonder Why (Once I Had a Friend)   Sondheim Date Unknown

I Wonder Why She Kept on Saying Si-Si-Si-Si Senor   Lewis 1918; Snyder 1918; Young, Joe 1918

I Wonder Why the Glow-Worm Winks His Eye   Hammerstein 1923

I Wonder Why They're Always Pickin' on My Little Pickaninny   Mitchell 1918

I Won't Be a Nun   Duke 1944

I Won't Be Back Till August   Bryan 1910

I Won't Be Home to Dinner   Edwards 1908

I Won't Believe My Eyes   Bergman 1987, 1989

I Won't Break   Bacharach 1981

I Won't Care for You Anymore   Leslie 1921; Monaco 1921

I Won't Come Back   Atteridge Date Unknown

I Won't Cry   Lawrence 1952; Young, Victor 1952

I Won't Dance   Fields 1935; Hammerstein 1934, 1935; Kern 1934, 1935

I Won't Ever Let You Go   David, Hal 1978

I Won't Forget the Dawn   DePaul 1944; Raye 1944

I Won't Give Up Till You Give In   Robin 1931; Whiting 1931

I Won't Give Up Till You Give in to Me   Gershwin, George 1936; Gershwin, Ira 1936

I Won't Go Home   Friend 1938

I Won't Go Home Tonight   Conrad 1926; Gilbert 1926

I Won't Grow Up   Leigh 1954

I Won't Let You Get Away   Comden and Green 1974; Styne 1974

I Won't Let You Out of My Heart   Mancini 1954

I Won't Lose My Faith in Them All   Fisher 1937

I Won't Say Good-Bye Until My Heart Says Good-Bye   Bryan 1934

I Won't Say I Will, but I Won't Say I Won't   DeSylva 1923; Gershwin, George 1923; Gershwin, Ira 1923

I Won't Stand in Your Way   Duke 1963

I Won't Take No for an Answer   Baer 1937

I Won't Think about Tomorrow (As Long As You Love Me)   Gorney 1933; Lerner, Sammy 1933

I Won't Twist   Cahn 1961; Van Heusen 1961

I Work Eight Hours, Sleep Eight Hours, That Leaves Eight Hours for Love   Kalmar 1915; Leslie 1915; Snyder 1915

I Worry About You   Loesser 1961

I Worship at Your Shrine (Madame)   Parish 1980

I Worship You   Merrill 1958; Porter 1929, 1931

I Would Be True   Robison 1958

I Would Die   Merrill 1959

I Would Do Most Anything for You   David, Mack 1955

I Would Find You Dear   Brennan 1915

I Would Have Bet Against It   Cahn 1978; Schwartz, Arthur 1978

I Would If I Could But I Can't   Parish 1933

I Would Like to Know Why   Blake 1926; Sissle 1926

I Would Like to Play a Lover's Part   Hammerstein 1927; Kern 1927

I Would Like to See the Peaches   Schwartz, Jean 1912; Smith, Harry B. 1912

I Would Like to Try It, But I'm Just a Bit Afraid   Brown, Lew 1912

I Would Love to Have You Love Me   Caesar 1936; Lerner, Sammy 1936

I Would Rather Dance a Waltz   Kalmar 1924; Ruby 1924

I Would Rather Fight Like Ma   Howard, Joseph E. 1909

I Would Trade Christmas (And All that Jolly Jazz)   Cahn 1969; Van Heusen 1969

I Wouldn't Be One Bit Surprised   Donaldson 1925; Kahn 1925

I Wouldn't Be Surprised   Sterling 1921; Von Tilzer 1921

I Wouldn't Be Where I Am If You Hadn't Gone Away   Brown, Lew 1925; Henderson 1925; Rose 1925

I Wouldn't Bet One Penny   Burke 1961

I Wouldn't Care   Robin 1932

I Wouldn't Care for That   Wrubel 1929

I Wouldn't Change a Thing   Sondheim Date Unknown

I Wouldn't Change You for the World   David, Mack 1937; Meyer 1937

I Wouldn't Dream of It   Cahn 1971; Van Heusen 1971

I Wouldn't Fool a Little Girl Like You   Conrad 1926; Meyer 1926

I Wouldn't Give My Heart to Any Other Girl but You   Leslie 1910

I Wouldn't Give That for the Boy Who Couldn't Dance   Berlin 1918

I Wouldn't Have Had To   Evans 1961; Livingston, Jay 1961

I Wouldn't Know   Lawrence 1954

I Wouldn't Leave My Home If I Were You   Sterling 1899; Von Tilzer 1899

I Wouldn't Marry You   Dietz 1961; Schwartz, Arthur 1961

I Wouldn't Steal the Sweetheart of a Soldier Boy   Bryan 1916

I Wouldn't Take a Case Like That   Herbert 1908; Smith, Harry B. 1908

I Wouldn't Take a Million   Gordon 1940; Warren 1940

I Wouldn't Trade the Silver in My Mother's Hair for All the Gold in the World   Coots 1932

I Wouldn't Want Her Any Other Way   Spina 1969

I Wrestled with the Devil   Dubin Date Unknown; Warren Date Unknown

I Write My Buddies   Drake 1952

I Wrote a Play   Porter 1944

I Wrote a Song for You (Canzonne Per Te)   Sigman 1968

I Wuv a Wabbit   Drake 1944

I Yes, Me! That's Who   Cahn 1970; Styne 1970

I Yi Yi Yi Yi (I Like You Very Much)   Gordon 1941; Warren 1941

Iaydor   Johnson, Howard 1957

Ibbedy Bibbedy Sibbedy Sab   Loesser 1946

Ibbidi Bibbidi Sibbidi Sab (Finale, Act I)   Hart 1927; Rodgers 1927

Ice   Martin 1958

Ice Cold Katy   Loesser 1943; Schwartz, Arthur 1943

Ice Cold Papa, Mama's Gonna Melt You Down   Razaf 1924; Waller 1924

Ice Cream Baby   Russell 1951

Ice Cream Fantasy   Donaldson 1934; Kahn 1934

Ice Cream Sextet   Weill 1947

Ice Man Live in an Ice House, The   Waller 1931

Ice Skating Is Nice Skating   Caesar 1937

Ich Denk' Oft an Meine Jugendzeit   Lerner, Sammy 1931

Ich Liebe Dich   Fisher 1929

Ich Liebe Dich (I Love You)   Lewis 1932

Ichabod   DePaul 1949; Raye 1949

Icky Wicky Woo   Coslow 1925

Icy Switzerland   Carroll 1921

I'd Be a Fool   Hammerstein 1931; Romberg 1931

I'd Be a Fool Again   Livingston, Jerry 1936

I'd Be a Fool to Fool with You   Turk 1923

I'd Be a Wild Man   Brown, A. Seymour 1923

I'd Be Crazy If I Wasn't Crazy Over You   Bryan 1933; Meyer 1933

I'd Be Happy Anywhere with You   Romberg 1916

I'd Be Lost in Someone Else's Arms   Raye 1940

I'd Be Lost Without You   Donaldson 1936

I'd Be So Happy   Coots 1968

I'd Be So Happy with You   Freed, Arthur 1930

I'd Be Telling a Lie   Washington 1933; Young, Victor 1933

I'd Climb the Highest Mountain If I Knew I'd Find You   Brown, Lew 1926; Clare 1926

I'd Climb to Heaven   Revel 1959

I'd Do Anything for You   Friend 1929; Pollack 1929

I'd Do As Much for You   Jerome 1912; Von Tilzer 1912

I'd Do It Again   Hart 1933; Kahn 1933; Rodgers 1933

I'd Do It All Over Again   Conrad 1926; Leigh 1985; Meyer 1926; Styne 1985

I'd Do the Same   Friml 1917

I'd Fall in Love All Over Again (If You Could Just Forgive and Forget)   Fain 1930; Kahal 1930

I'd Give a Dollar for a Dime   Blake 1953; Razaf 1953

I'd Give a Lot of Love to Get a Little Love from Someone   Woods 1926

I'd Give a Lot to Know Just What Is on His Mind   Cahn 1955; Styne 1955

I'd Give a Million Tomorrows (For Just One Yesterday)   Livingston, Jerry 1939

I'd Give All the Lights on Broadway for that One Candlelight at Home   Schwartz, Jean 1921

I'd Give Anything Under the Sun to Get You Under the Moon   Friend 1934; Mitchell 1934

I'd Give Every Rose on Broadway for that Little Rose Back Home   Fisher 1924

I'd Give My Life Just to Hear Mother Say Goodnight Little Baby Good Night   Leslie 1917

I'd Give the World Could I Forget   Cobb 1901; Edwards 1901

I'd Give them All Up for You   Sigman 1949

I'd Gladly Trade   Martin 1941

I'd Hate to Tell You   Adamson 1935; Donaldson 1935

I'd Know You Anywhere   McHugh 1940; Mercer 1940

I'd Leave My Happy Home for You   Von Tilzer 1899

I'd Leave Ten Men Like Yours to Love One Man Like Mine   Leslie 1926

I'd Let You Break My Heart All Over Again   Davis 1966

I'd Like a Honeymoon with You   Herbert 1920

I'd Like a Lighthouse   Kern 1920

I'd Like a Memory   Willson 1947

I'd Like Another Situation Just Like That   Smith, Robert B. 1907

I'd Like It   Herbert 1899

I'd Like My Picture Took   Berlin 1949

I'd Like to Baby You   Evans 1952; Livingston, Jay 1952

I'd Like to Be a Bee in Your Boudoir   Whiting 1930

I'd Like to Be a Boy Again   Jerome 1922; Schwartz, Jean 1922

I'd Like to Be a Gardener in a Garden of Girls   Buck 1925

I'd Like to Be a Gypsy   Washington 1930

I'd Like To Be a Happy Bride   Bryan 1930; Dubin 1930

I'd Like to Be a Quitter, But I Find It Hard to Quit   Herbert 1915

I'd Like to Be in Your Shoes   Fisher 1936

I'd Like to Be Liked   Kalmar 1929; Ruby 1929

I'd Like To Be On an Island with You   Bryan 1914

I'd Like to Be Rip Van Winkle, in Rip Van Winkle Town   Ahlert Date Unknown; Leslie 1919; Turk Date Unknown

I'd Like to Be Your Affinity, You Certainly Look Good to Me   Von Tilzer 1907

I'd Like to Be Your Mother's Son-in-Law   Goetz 1911

I'd Like to Believe You   Henderson 1924; Motzan 1924; Rose 1924

I'd Like to Borrow a Kiss   Atteridge 1913

I'd Like to Build a Coop for a Chicken Like You   Carroll 1913

I'd Like to Corral a Cat   Buck 1925

I'd Like to Correspond with You   Jerome 1909; Schwartz, Jean 1909

I'd Like to Dance the Whole Night Thru   David, Mack 1935

I'd Like to Do Things for You   Coslow 1937

I'd Like to Do What I'd Like to Do   Friend 1942

I'd Like to Dunk You in My Coffee   Akst 1934; Brown, Lew 1934

I'd Like to Find the Guy Who Stole My Gal (And Thank Him from the Bottom of My Heart)   Freed, Ralph 1953; Hoffman 1953

I'd Like to Find You in My Stocking when I Wake Up Christmas Morn   Coots 1949

I'd Like to Get Together with You   Friend 1932; Monaco 1932

I'd Like to Go on a Honeymoon with You   Smith, Harry B. 1911; Smith, Robert B. 1911

I'd Like to Go Up in an Airship   Smith, Harry B. 1909

I'd Like to Have a Million in the Bank   Kern 1915

I'd Like to Have a Photograph of You   Fisher 1913

I'd Like to Have You Around   Herbert 1915

I'd Like to Have You Call Me Honey   Howard, Joseph E. 1908

I'd Like to Hide It   Hart 1925; Rodgers 1925

I'd Like to Hitch a Ride with Santa Claus   Burke 1950; Van Heusen 1950

I'd Like to Love Them All   Brennan 1929

I'd Like to Make a Mash Mit You   Fisher 1907; Kern 1907

I'd Like to Meet Your Father   Kern 1907

I'd Like to Pin a Medal on You   David, Mack 1958; Livingston, Jerry 1958

I'd Like to Poison Ivy   Hart 1924; Rodgers 1924

I'd Like to Poison the Cook   Baer 1971; Lewis 1971

I'd Like to Put Another R in Mary   Fisher 1910

I'd Like to Ride Away to a Little Hideaway   Bryan 1928; Hoffman 1928

I'd Like to Say a Few Words about Texas   Hoffman 1956

I'd Like to Say I Love You   Warren Date Unknown

I'd Like to See a Little More of You   Cobb 1906; Edwards 1906

I'd Like to See Some Mo' of Samoa   Spina 1937

I'd Like to See Somoa of Samoa   Bullock 1937

I'd Like to See the Kaiser with a Lily in His Hand   Johnson, Howard 1918

I'd Like to Set You to Music   Revel 1943; Webster 1943

I'd Like to Take a Flying Leap Over the Moon   Lawrence 1933

I'd Like to Take You Away   Smith, Harry B. 1920

I'd Like to Take You Home to Meet My Mother   Hart 1925; Rodgers 1925

I'd Like to Take You Out Dreaming   Fields 1951; Schwartz, Arthur 1951

I'd Like to Talk About the Weather   Duke 1941

I'd Like to Tell Your Fortune Dearie   Williams 1910

I'd Like to Tie You to My Heart Strings   Burke 1931

I'd Like to Wrap You Up and Put You in My Pocket   David, Hal 1949

I'd Like To Write a Song To End All War   Bryan 1945

I'd Like To Write a Song To Win the War   Bryan 1944; Caesar 1944

I'd Like You to Like Me to Like You   Lane 1931

I'd Like You to Love Me   Brown, Lew 1927; DeSylva 1927; Henderson 1927

I'd Love to Be a Lady   Herbert 1917

I'd Love to Be a Talking Picture Queen   Hanley 1930

I'd Love to Be a Talking-Picture Queen   Hanley 1930

I'd Love to Be Shot from a Cannon with You   Berlin 1940

I'd Love to Dance Through Life with You   Kern 1915; Smith, Harry B. 1915

I'd Love to Fall Asleep and Wake Up in My Mammy's Arms   Ahlert 1920; Lewis 1920; Young, Joe 1920

I'd Love to Go on Dreaming   Fain 1946; Freed, Ralph 1946

I'd Love to Hate You, But If I Love You, How Can I Hate You   Yellen 1964

I'd Love To Have a Million Eyes   Bryan 1937

I'd Love to Have Ya Love Me All the Same   Kahn 1922

I'd Love to Have You Love Me All the Time   Clare 1923; Kahn 1923

I'd Love to Know   Motzan 1920

I'd Love to Know You Better   Magidson 1942; Styne 1942

I'd Love to Lead a Marching Band (Hands Across the Sea)   Bergman 1958

I'd Love to Love You All the Time   Davis 1925

I'd Love to Make Love to You   Bergman 1955

I'd Love to Meet that Old Sweetheart of Mine   Davis 1926

I'd Love to Play a Love Scene (Opposite You)   Coslow 1938

I'd Love to Put My Arms Around You   Friend 1949

I'd Love to Take Orders from You   Dubin 1935; Warren 1935, 1943

I'd Love to Waltz Through Life with You   Buck 1923; Herbert 1923

I'd Much Rather Stay at Home   Kern 1908

I'd Rather Be a Lemon than Grapefruit   Williams 1905

I'd Rather Be Alone Just Thinking of You   Ager 1926; Yellen 1926

I'd Rather Be Blue (Over You Than Be Happy with Somebody Else)   Fisher 1928; Rose 1928

I'd Rather Be Blue than Green   Razaf 1924; Waller 1924

I'd Rather Be Me   Coslow 1945; David, Hal 1959; Livingston, Jerry 1959

I'd Rather Be Outside A-Lookin' In then on the Inside A-Lookin' Out   Snyder 1906

I'd Rather Be Right   Hart 1937; Rodgers 1937

I'd Rather Be with You   Akst 1935; Brown, Lew 1935

I'd Rather Be Wrong than Be Sorry   David, Hal 1948

I'd Rather Charleston   Gershwin, George 1926

I'd Rather Cry Over You (Than Smile at Somebody Else)   Yellen 1928

I'd Rather Dance   Brown, Nacio Herb 1941; Freed, Ralph 1941

I'd Rather Dance Here than Hereafter   Caesar 1928

I'd Rather Do Without You Baby   Gilbert 1945

I'd Rather Forgive You than Forget You   Bryan 1953

I'd Rather Fox Trot than Waltz   Motzan 1923

I'd Rather Have a Maybe (From You Baby)   Hoffman 1956

I'd Rather Have a Pal than a Gal Anytime   Gordon 1953; Myrow 1953

I'd Rather Lead a Band   Berlin 1936

I'd Rather Listen to Your Eyes   Dubin 1935; Warren 1935

I'd Rather Look at You   Coslow 1938; Revel 1947

I'd Rather Love an Old Rag Doll than a Bashful Boy Like You   Meyer 1909

I'd Rather Love My Old Rag Doll Than a Bashful Boy Like You   Bryan 1909

I'd Rather Love What I Can't Have   Howard, Joseph E. 1910

I'd Rather Put a Record on the Gramophone and Dance Around with the Mrs. at Home   Clarke 1921; Monaco 1921

I'd Rather Say Hello than Say Good-Bye   Bryan 1910

I'd Rather Stay Home and Be Lonely (Than Go Out with
   Somebody Else)   Davis 1942

I'd Rather Stay Home with a Memory   Drake 1947

I'd Rather Wake Up By Myself   Fields 1954; Schwartz,
   Arthur 1954

I'd Rather Write a Song   Cohan 1934

I'd Ring the Wedding Bells for You   Jerome 1910; Schwartz,
   Jean 1910

I'd Sooner Be a Has Been than a Never Was at All   Jerome
   1907; Schwartz, Jean 1907

I'd Steal a Star   Youmans 1926

I'd Still Be a Fool   Bacharach 1976; David, Hal 1976

I'd Sure Like to Give It a Shot   Cahn 1970; Styne 1970

I'd Write a Song   Caesar 1933; Romberg 1933

Ida   Atteridge 1912

Ida from Idaho   Adamson 1959; McHugh 1959

Ida, I Do   Kahn 1925

Ida, I Don't Wanna Be Blue   Leslie 1931; Meyer 1931;
   Young, Joe 1931

Iddle-Iddle-Iddle-E   Howard, Joseph E. 1910

Identification   Lawrence 1971

Identify   David, Mack 1961; Livingston, Jerry 1961

Idle Cloud Drifts By (inst.), An   Coots 1947

Idle Conversation   Burke 1958

Idle Dollars — Busy War Bonds   Johnson, J. Rosamond
   1945; Razaf 1945

Idle Dreams   Gershwin, George 1920

Idle Hours   Ahlert Date Unknown; Lewis 1919; Turk Date
   Unknown; Young, Joe 1919

Idles of the King   Hart 1926, 1927; Rodgers 1926, 1927

Idol of Eyes, The   Smith, Robert B. 1915

Idyll   Porter 1914

If   DePaul 1942; Raye 1942; Razaf 1935

If a Baby Would Never Grow Older (A Mother Would Never
   Be Sad)   Bryan 1916

If a Gal Like You Loved a Boy Like Me   Cobb 1905;
   Edwards 1905

If a Girl Isn't Pretty   Merrill 1964; Styne 1964

If a Man Answers, Hang Up   Drake 1947

If a Rooster Can Love As Many Little Chickens, Can't a Man
   Love More Than One   Bryan 1912; Meyer 1912

If a Table at Rector's Could Talk   Cobb 1913

If a Vagabond Were King   Burke 1956; Friml 1956

If a Wish Could Make It So   Hammerstein 1920; Harbach
   1920

If Aladdin Would Lend Me His Lamp   Cobb 1902; Edwards
   1902

If All Moons Were Honey Moons   Howard, Joseph E. 1909

If All My Thoughts Were Stars   Conrad 1924

If All the Girls I Knew Were Like You   Berlin 1913

If All the Girls in All the World Were Just as Nice as
   You   Fisher 1912

If All the Girls were Good Little Girls   Clarke 1920;
   Donaldson 1920

If All the Stars Were Mine   Smith, Harry B. 1899

If All the Stars Were Movie Stars   Coslow 1930

If All the Stars Were Pretty Babies   Fisher 1926; Rose 1926

If All the World Were Paper   Bullock 1938; Spina 1938

If All Who Pray Would Pray for All   Robison 1956

If an Apple Tempted Adam, What a Peach Could Do for
   Me   Silver 1920

If and When   Cahn 1962; Myrow 1962

If Anyone Had Told Me   Bergman 1978

If Anything Happened to You   Van Heusen 1938

If Bill Gilette Could Only See Me Now   Cohan 1901

If Dreams Come True   Mills 1938

If Eve Had Left the Apple on the Bough   Herbert 1917

If Ever a Heart Was in the Right Place, It's Yours   Woods
   1939

If Ever Day Were Valentine's Day   Fain 1978; Harburg 1978

If Ever I Would Leave You   Lerner, Alan Jay 1960; Loewe
   1960

If Ever Married I'm   Porter 1948

If Ever We Get Out of Jail   Porter 1955

If Every Hour Were a Day   Bryan 1911; Fisher 1911

If Everyone Got What They Wanted   David, Mack 1973;
   Livingston, Jerry 1973

If Flutterby Wins   Evans 1961; Livingston, Jay 1961

If God Can Forgive Me, Why Can't You   Bryan 1952; Caesar
   1952

If He Brings You Flowers   Brooks 1959

If He Can Fight Like He Can Love Goodnight
   Germany   Clarke 1918; Meyer 1918

If He Looks Good to Mother (Don't Look for
   Another)   Lewis 1913; Meyer 1913

If He Phones   Silver 1954

If He Really Loves Me   Arlen 1931; Yellen 1931

If He Wears a Little Golden Eagle   Coots 1945

If He'll Come Back to Me   Robin 1927; Youmans 1927

If He's Good Enough to Fight For His Country   Yellen 1950

If I   Friend 1953

If I Be Your Best Chance   Cahn 1966; Van Heusen 1966

If I Became the President   Gershwin, George 1929;
   Gershwin, Ira 1929

If I Came Back to You and Said I'm Sorry   Cobb 1913;
   Edwards 1913, 1929

If I Came to You with a Heart Bowed Down (Would You
   Remember Me)   Kahn 1914; Whiting 1914

If I Can Count on You   Ager 1933

If I Can Take You from Someone   Howard, Joseph E. 1927

If I Can't Get the Sweetie I Want I Pity the Sweetie I
   Get   Lewis 1923; Schwartz, Jean 1923; Young, Joe 1923

If I Can't Have All   Johnson, James P. 1962

If I Can't Have You   Bryan 1929; Caesar 1921; Donaldson
   1928; Meyer 1929; Monaco 1921

If I Can't Have You All for Myself (Then I Don't Want You
   At All)   Davis 1950

If I Can't Sell It I'll Keep Sittin' on It   Razaf 1935

If I Can't Sing About My Mammy, I Don't Want to Sing at
   All   Conrad 1924; Lewis 1924; Young, Joe 1924

If I Can't Sing, I've Got to Dance   Woods 1935

If I Can't Take It with Me When I Go   David, Mack 1956

If I Cared for Someone Else   Bryan 1927; Monaco 1927

If I Choose (I Can Go Home)   Brooks 1959

If I Could Be Back   Bacharach 1973; David, Hal 1973

If I Could Be the Only Child   Strouse Date Unknown

If I Could Be with You (One Hour Tonight)   Johnson, James
   P. 1926

If I Could Forget (In Dreamland Fancies)   Smith, Harry B.
   1928

If I Could Get to Paree in 10 Hours   Silver 1927

If I Could Get to Paree in 10 Hours (If I Could Get to Paris
   in 30 Hours)   Dubin 1927

If I Could Have My Way   Mercer 1934; Razaf 1926

If I Could Have You Now   Bryan 1913

If I Could Hold You in My Arms   David, Hal 1957

If I Could Live Again   Egan 1916; Whiting 1916

If I Could Live Life Over I'd Live It All for You   Snyder 1919

If I Could Live My Life All Over Again   Gordon 1931; Revel 1931

If I Could Love You   Baer 1953

If I Could Make You Cry I'd Be Happy   Davis 1949; Silver 1949

If I Could Only Borrow Something on My Dream   Koehler 1949; Stept 1949

If I Could Only Have My Way   Razaf 1931

If I Could Only Read Your Mind   Mercer 1934

If I Could Say to You in English (What I Think of You in French)   Cahn 1950

If I Could Teach My Teddy Bear to Dance   Herbert 1908; Smith, Harry B. 1908

If I Could Write a Love Song   Friend 1950

If I Dared Tell My Love for You   Cobb 1900; Edwards 1900

If I Didn't Care   Ager 1934; Schwartz, Jean 1934; Young, Joe 1934

If I Didn't Dare   Lawrence 1939

If I Didn't Have You   Ager 1931; Brown, Lew 1937; Fain 1937; Harburg 1931; Spina 1950

If I Didn't Know Your Husband and You Didn't Know My Wife   Baer 1926; Gilbert 1926

If I Do, I Ded a Whippin', I Dood It   Baer 1942

If I Don't Love You   Burke 1957

If I Ever Catch the Guy Who Taught My Wife the Twist   Fain 1962

If I Ever Fall in Love   DePaul 1955; Raye 1955

If I Ever Find Another Sweetheart   Caesar 1930

If I Ever Get a Job Again   Baer 1933; Lewis 1933

If I Ever Get Back to Hannah   Henderson 1942

If I Ever Lose My Heart   Davis 1954

If I Ever Lost You   Kalmar 1940; Ruby 1940

If I Ever Make You Cry   Bacharach 1965; David, Hal 1965

If I Ever Saw a Dream It's You   Spina 1957

If I Feel This Way Tomorrow   Brown, Lew 1939; Henderson 1939

If I Feel This Way Tomorrow Then It's Love   Arlen 1936; Brown, Lew 1933, 1936; Henderson 1933

If I Find a Bit of Heaven in Your Irish Heart of Love   Brennan 1917

If I Find Spanish Joe From Mexico (Oh O-O-O! Oh O-O-O!)   Brown, Lew 1915

If I Find the Girl   Kern 1915

If I Forgive You   Caesar 1933

If I Gave You   Martin 1964

If I Give in to You   Hart 1930; Rodgers 1930

If I Give Up the Saxophone (Will You Come Back to Me)   Fain 1929; Kahal 1929

If I Had a Baby (You're the Kind of a Baby I'd Want My Baby to Be)   Donaldson 1927; Kahn 1927

If I Had a Dozen Hearts   Revel 1945; Webster 1945

If I Had a Girl   Hammerstein 1931

If I Had a Girl Like My Mother, I'd Be a Feller Like Dad   Young, Joe 1932

If I Had a Girl Like You   Dixon 1925; Henderson 1925; Romberg 1931; Rose 1925

If I Had a Golden Umbrella   Merrill 1953

If I Had a Lover   Rose 1927

If I Had a Million Dollars   Mercer 1934

If I Had a Penny   Russell 1947; Sigman 1947

If I Had a Talking Picture of You   Brown, Lew 1929; DeSylva 1929; Henderson 1929

If I Had a Theatre on Broadway   Smith, Harry B. 1904; Smith, Robert B. 1904

If I Had a Wishing Ring   Alter 1945

If I Had an Igloo   Blane 1960; Martin 1960

If I Had Been So Sure of You   Clare 1931; Stept 1931

If I Had Married Rip Van Winkle   Howard, Joseph E. 1955

If I Had My Druthers   DePaul 1956; Mercer 1956

If I Had My Life to Live Over, I'd Do It All Over Again   Silver 1918

If I Had My Way   Gilbert 1921; Kahal 1935

If I Had Napoleon's Hat   Woods 1933

If I Had Only Known   Livingston, Jerry 1943

If I Had Some One at Home Like You, I Wouldn't Want to Go Out   Monaco 1914

If I Had Someone to Love Me the Way I Love You   Friend 1938

If I Had Three Wishes for Christmas   Styne 1959

If I Had to Do It All Over Again   Spina 1946

If I Had Waited for You   Razaf 1933; Waller 1933

If I Had You   Berlin 1914

If I Hadn't a Husband   Porter 1944

If I Hadn't Met You   Baer 1938; Lewis 1938

If I Have to Go On Without You   Dubin 1931; Woods 1931

If I Just Think of Her   Smith, Harry B. 1910

If I Knew   Rainger 1935; Willson 1960

(I'd Climb the Highest Mountain) If I Knew I'd Find You   Brown, Lew 1926

If I Knew Now   Ellington 1966

If I Knew You Then As I Know You Now   Brown, Lew 1923; Hanley 1923

If I Knew You Were Comin' I'd've Baked a Cake   Hoffman 1949; Merrill 1949

If I Knock the L Out of Kelly, It Would Still Be Kelly to Me   Lewis 1916; Young, Joe 1916

If I Look Like I Feel   Van Heusen 1937

If I Love Again   Oakland 1928

If I Love You a Mountain   Gordon 1953; Myrow 1953

If I Loved You   Hammerstein 1945; Rodgers 1945

If I Loved You More   Coots 1937

If I Meant Something to You   Waller 1938

If I Meet the Guy that Made This Country Dry   Jerome 1920; Von Tilzer 1920

If I Never Get to Love You   Bacharach 1962; David, Hal 1962

If I Never See You As Long As I Live That'll Even Be Too Soon   Baer 1925; Turk 1925

If I Only Had a Brain   Arlen 1939; Harburg 1939

If I Only Had a Five Cent Piece   Caesar 1932

If I Only Had a Heart   Arlen 1939; Harburg 1939

If I Only Had a Match   Johnston 1946; Meyer 1947

If I Only Had the Nerve   Arlen 1939; Harburg 1939

If I Only Had the Pipe That Peter Pan Used to Pipe   Fisher 1917

If I Only Had the Pipe that Peter Piper Used to Pipe   Johnson, Howard 1917

If I Only Had You Back Again   Davis 1926

If I Only Had You Back Again How Different Things Would Be   Turk 1924

If I Only Had You Now   Kahn 1927

If I Only Knew How I Stood with You   Cobb 1916; Edwards 1916

If I Only Said My Name Was Flannigan   Edwards 1908

If I Only Were a Boy   Hart 1920; Rodgers 1920

If I Put My Heart in My Song   Coslow 1937

If I Saw Much of You   Herbert 1920; Smith, Robert B. 1920

If I Should Dream of You   Herbert 1911; Smith, Harry B. 1911

If I Should Ever Get You (I'll Never Let You Go)   Woods 1969

If I Should Lose You   Rainger 1935; Robin 1935

If I Should Love Again   Coots 1952

If I Should Love You Now   Robison 1960

If I Steal a Kiss (Dear)   Brown, Nacio Herb 1948; Heyman 1948

If I Steal Your Heart   Brown, Nacio Herb 1948; Heyman 1948

If I Thought I Could Live Without You I'd Die   Brown, Lew 1931; Henderson 1931

If I Thought You Wouldn't Tell   Berlin 1909; Snyder 1909

If I Told You   Hammerstein 1923; Harbach 1923; Youmans 1923

If I Told You that I Loved You   Meyer 1908

If I Wait Till the End of the World   Von Tilzer 1920

If I Was a Dove   Lerner, Alan Jay 1976

If I Was a Millionaire   Cobb 1910; Edwards 1910

If I Was Only Twenty-One   Fisher 1941

If I Were a Bell   Loesser 1950

If I Were a Football Man   Porter 1912

If I Were a Hungry Cannibal   Fisher 1920

If I Were a Little Pond Lily   Dubin 1937; Warren 1937

If I Were a Man   Mancini 1995

If I Were a Man Like That   Herbert 1903

If I Were a Traveling Salesman   Dubin 1930

If I Were Adam and You Were Eve   Hanley 1932

If I Were Anybody Else but Me   Herbert 1910, 1935; Kahn 1935

If I Were in Love with Somebody Else, I Wouldn't Be Here with You   Howard, Joseph E. 1923

If I Were in Love with You   Edwards 1913

If I Were King   Coslow 1930; Hart 1922, 1923, 1925; Herbert 1895; Merrill 1955; Robin 1930; Rodgers 1922, 1925; Smith, Harry B. 1895

If I Were King of the Forest   Arlen 1939; Harburg 1939

If I Were on the Stage   Herbert 1908

If I Were on the Stage (Kiss Me Again)   Herbert 1905

If I Were Only Mr. Morgan   Cohan 1903

If I Were Really a King   Smith, Harry B. 1896

If I Were Santa Claus for a Day   Clare 1942; Pollack 1942

If I Were She   Lane 1985

If I Were Sure of You   Bloom 1939; Koehler 1939

If I Were the Bride of a Soldier   Smith, Harry B. 1903

If I Were the Man in the Moon   Howard, Joseph E. 1905

If I Were the Ocean and You Were the Shore, I'd Be Kissing You All the Day   Bryan 1914

If I Were You   Adams 1962; Alter 1930; Blake 1936; Brown, Nacio Herb 1949; Coots 1951; Hart 1926, 1928; Heyman 1947; Rodgers 1926, 1928; Strouse 1962

If I Were You I'd Fall in Love with Me   Fain 1929

If I Were You Love, I'd Jump Right in the Lake   Youmans 1930

If I Were Your Daddy and You Were a Mamma to Me   Turk 1921

If I Were Your Son   Styne 1985

If I Weren't King   Hammerstein 1957; Rodgers 1957

If I'd Only Believed in You   Akst 1926; Davis 1926

If I'm Blue to You   DeSylva 1932; Whiting 1932

If I'm Dreaming, Don't Wake Me Up Too Soon   Dubin 1929

If I'm Going to Die I'm Going to Have Some Fun   Cohan 1907

If I'm Lucky   De Lange 1946; Myrow 1946, 1955

If I'm Nice to You   Brown, Nacio Herb 1932; Whiting 1932

If I'm Not Back in Five Minutes (Start Without Me)   Hoffman 1942; Livingston, Jerry 1942

If in Spite of Our Attempts   Porter 1916

If It Ain't Fun   Lerner, Alan Jay 1971

If It Ain't Love   Razaf 1932; Waller 1932

If It Could Happen   Adamson 1945; McHugh 1945

If It Don't Belong to You   Robison 1954

If It Hadn't Been for You   Dietz 1961; Schwartz, Arthur 1961

If It Isn't Everything   Burke 1961

If It Isn't Pain (Then It Isn't Love)   Rainger 1937; Robin 1937

If It Pleases You   Blake 1958

If It Rains Who Cares   Leslie 1938

If It Takes a Thousand Years   Brennan 1915

If It Wasn't for an Early Bird — I'd Still Be Dreaming of You   Hoffman 1934

If It Wasn't for Dear Old Ireland   Johnson, Howard 1915

If It Wasn't for Her Tra-La-La-La-La   Lewis 1927; Young, Joe 1927

If It Wasn't for Love   Razaf 1979

If It Wasn't for Mother Love   Bryan 1913

If It Wasn't for My Dear Old Daddy   Parish 1925

If It Wasn't for the Irish   Blane 1947; Warren 1947

If It Wasn't for the Irish and the Jews   Jerome 1912; Schwartz, Jean 1912

If It Wasn't for the Wife   Atteridge 1919; Carroll 1919

If It Wasn't for You   Davis 1927; Stept 1925; Von Tilzer 1914

If It Were Easy to Do   Sigman 1947

If It Were Not for Dear Old Father   Norworth 1909

If It Were Up to Me   Stept 1952

If It's a Dream   Brooks 1942; Young, Victor 1955

If It's All Right with You, It's All Right with Me   Clare 1924; Monaco 1924; Rose 1924

If It's All the Same to You   Sigman 1947

If It's All the Same to You (Cela M'est Egal)   Burke 1953; Van Heusen 1953

If It's Any News to You   Blake 1932; Sissle 1932

If It's for Me, I'm not Home   David, Hal 1945

If It's Good Enough for Gentlemen   Hammerstein 1933

If It's Good Enough for the Birds and Bees, It's Good Enough for You and Me   Friend 1931

If It's Love   Akst 1934; Brown, Lew 1934; Cahn 1942, 1954, 1955; Styne 1942, 1954, 1955

If It's O.K. with You, It's O.K. with Me   Clare 1925; Monaco 1925

If It's the Last Thing I Do   Cahn 1937

If It's You   Oakland 1941

If Jesus Don't Love You   Merrill 1959

If Life Were All Peaches and Cream   Webster 1941

If Little If Were Not a Word (Ja, Wenn Das Wortchen Wenn Nicht War)   Young, Joe 1931

If Love Ain't There (It Ain't There)   Burke 1963

If Love Came Wrapped in Cellophane   Heyman 1935

If Love Makes You Give Up Steak and Potatoes, Then I Don't Want Love   Alter 1934; Brown, Lew 1934

If Love Remains   Gershwin, Ira 1945; Weill 1945

If Love Should Come to Me   Dietz 1927; Gorney 1927

If Love Should Die   Wrubel 1933

If Love Were King   Fain 1932; Kahal 1932

If Love Were What the Rose Is   Herbert 1907; Johnson, Howard 1939

If Me No If — But Me No But   Cahn 1966; Van Heusen 1966

If Momma Was Married   Sondheim 1959; Styne 1959

If Morgan Had Bought an Army for Me   Herbert 1904

If Mother Could Only See Us Now   Pollack 1942

If Mother Has a Radio in Heaven   Bryan 1931

If Mothers Could Live on Forever   Johnson, Howard 1937

If Mr. Boston Lawson Has His Way   Cohan 1906

If Mr. Ragtime Ever Gets Into that War   Kern 1916; Motzan 1916

If My Baby Cooks   Kahal 1926

If My Dreams Came True   Johnston 1924

If My Dreams Come True   Clarke 1924; Meyer 1924; Turk 1924

If My Friends Could See Me Now   Coleman 1966; Fields 1966

If My Friends Find You They'll Steal You From Me   Kahn 1930

If My Heart Belonged to Somebody Else   Edwards 1923

If My Heart Could Only Talk   Drake 1952

If My Prayers Are Answered   Coots 1950

If Only   Romberg 1948; Rome 1973

If Only a Little Bit Sticks   Styne 1978

If Only I Listened to You   Sigman 1955

If Only I Were Santa Claus   Smith, Harry B. 1909

If Only Someone Would Teach Me   Harbach 1911

If Only There Were Something I Could Do   Sigman 1951

If Only They Would Take a Tip from Me   Harbach 1910

If Only You Could Love Me   Porter 1953

If Only You Were Mine   Herbert 1899; Smith, Harry B. 1899

If Pennies Were Wishes   David, Mack 1958; Livingston, Jerry 1958

If Promises Were Made of Gold   David, Mack 1945

If Rip Van Winkle Had My Gal, He Would Never Have Slept at All   Fisher 1925

If Sammy Simpson Shot the Chutes Why Shouldn't He Shoot the Shots   Von Tilzer 1917

If Santa Claus Fell Asleep   Akst 1961

If Santa Claus Would Fill My Stocking with a Brother Just for Me   Von Tilzer 1953

If Santa Gets Stuck in the Chimney!   Styne 1969

If She Hadn't Dropped Her Love   Hoffman 1932; Washington 1932

If She Hums You a Waltz   Whiting 1930

If She Means What I Think She Means   Buck 1918; DeSylva 1918

If She Was What She Was When She Was Sixteen   Lewis 1923; Meyer 1923; Young, Joe 1923

If She Were Mine   Sigman 1963

If Somebody Only Would Find Me   Herbert 1924

If Someday Ever Comes Again   Mercer 1976

If Someone Ever Breaks My Heart   David, Mack 1976

If Someone Should Ask You   Cahn 1947; Styne 1947

If Someone Should Kiss Me Tonight While I'm Dreaming   Hanley 1930, 1931

If Spring Were Only Here to Stay   Burke 1946; Van Heusen 1946

If Tears Could Bring You Back to Me   Johnson, Howard 1926

If Tears Would Bring You Back   Freed, Ralph 1940

If That Doesn't Do It!   Burke 1951; Van Heusen 1951

If that Dog o' Mine Could Talk   Magidson 1933; Monaco 1933

If that Was Love   Merrill 1957

If That's Not Love What Do You Call It?   Herbert 1920; Smith, Robert B. 1920

If That's Propaganda   Arlen 1941; Gershwin, Ira 1941; Harburg 1941

If That's Society Excuse Me   Johnson, J. Rosamond 1900

If That's What You Want   Romberg 1927; Smith, Harry B. 1927

If That's Your Idea of a Wonderful Time (Take Me Home)   Berlin 1914

If the Best Things in Life Were Free   Edwards 1930; Johnson, Howard 1930

If the Girl Has Charm   Burke 1981

If the Girl Wants You (Never Mind the Color of Her Eyes)   Kern 1909

If the Girlies Could Be Soldiers   Buck 1915

If the Good Lord's Willin'   Hoffman 1956

If the King Stops Here   Lane 1996

If the Man in the Moon Was a Coon   Fisher 1906

If the Managers Only thought the Same as Mother   Berlin 1909; Snyder 1909

If the Moon Was a Great Big Banjo   Buck 1913

If the Shoe Fits   Cahn 1977

If the Shoe Fits You, Wear It   Pollack 1943

If the Wealth of This World Belonged to Me   Sissle 1949

If the World Should End To-Morrow, I'd Be To-Night with You   Fisher 1915

If There Are Stars in My Eyes   Hoffman 1959

If There Is Someone Lovelier than You   Dietz 1934; Schwartz, Arthur 1934

If There Were More People Like You   Coleman 1973; Fields 1973

If There Were No Men in the World   Willson 1953

If There Were No Women at All   Willson 1953

If There's a Lovers Lane in Heaven, I Know We'll Meet Again   Fisher 1920

If There's Anybody Here from Out of Town   Robison 1953

If (There's Anything You Want)   Kern 1918

If There's Love in Your Heart   Johnston 1935; Kahn 1935

If These Walls Could Speak   Fain 1965

If They Could See You through My Eyes   Merrill 1956

If They Could Talk (Amour, Amour)   Bergman 1971

If They Ever Had an Income Tax on Love   Monaco 1931; Washington 1931

If They Ever Put a Tax on Love   Yellen Date Unknown

If They Ever Take the Sun Out of Sunday   Jerome 1918; Von Tilzer 1918

If They Feel Like a War Let Them Keep It Over There   Johnson, Howard 1935

If They Gave Me a Million   Magidson 1940; Oakland 1937, 1940

If They'd Only Left Poor Adam's Rib Alone   Howard, Joseph E. 1909

If They'd Only Move Old Ireland Over Here   Schwartz, Jean 1914

If Things Were What They Seem   Herbert 1917

If This Be Slav'ry   Adamson 1955; Lane 1955

If This Is a Dream   Lane Date Unknown

If This Is Love   Coslow 1930

If This Isn't Dreaming   Dubin 1937; Warren 1938

If This Isn't Love   Harburg 1947; Lane 1947

If War Is What Sherman Said It Was   Sterling 1915

If Washington Needs Me I'll Answer the Call but They Better Not Call Me Collect   Caesar 1944

If Washington Should Come to Life   Cohan 1906

If We Can Be Together   Kahn 1917

If We Can't Be the Same Old Sweethearts, We'll Just Be the Same Old Friends   Monaco 1915

If We Could Live on Promises   Johnson, Howard 1924

If We Did Here What They Do on the Cannibal Isles   Johnson, Howard 1917

If We Ever Get Out of Here (inst.)   Bacharach 1980

If We Had a Little More Time   Dietz 1948; Schwartz, Arthur 1948

If We Had 'Em Here Like He's Got 'Em There   Johnson, Howard 1916

If We Had Met Before   Burke 1971; Herbert 1920

If We Hadn't Taken in Boarders   Dietz 1959; Schwartz, Arthur 1959

If We Knew What the Milkman Knows   Goetz 1907

If We Never Meet Again   Lerner, Sammy 1932

If We Never Should Meet Again   Donaldson 1929; Leslie 1929

If We Should Meet Again   Henderson 1921

If We Were in Love   Bergman 1982

If We Were on Our Honeymoon (Railway Duet)   Kern 1913; Smith, Harry B. 1913

If What You Say Is True   Gordon 1939

If Widows Are Rich   Kahn 1934

If Widows Are Rich (Widows Are Gay)   Hart 1934

If Wives Were Put on Sale   Caesar 1922

If Women Had their Way   Edwards 1909; Smith, Robert B. 1909

If Yankee Doodle Hadn't Come to Town   Bryan 1902

If You Ain't Got It Go and Get It   Bryan 1909

If You Are There   Washington 1943, 1946

If You Become Bored   Hammerstein 1956; Kern 1956

If You Believe   Berlin 1930

If You Believe in Make-Believe   Sherman 1985

If You Believe in Me   Baer 1929; Gilbert 1929; Heyman 1954; Young, Victor 1954

If You Believed in Me   Baer 1929

If You Believed in Me As I Believe in You   Davis 1926

If You Build a Better Mouse Trap   Mercer 1942

If You but Knew   Silver 1950

If You Can Dream   Cahn 1956

If You Can Learn How to Cry   Bacharach 1976; David, Hal 1976

If You Can Love, (Like) You Can Dance   Herbert 1919; Smith, Robert B. 1919

If You Can Take Her from Someone (Someone Else Can Take Her from You)   Caesar 1961

If You Can Take It   Mercer 1938; Warren 1938

If You Can't Be As Happy As You Want to Be (Just Be As Happy As You Can)   Herbert 1911; Smith, Harry B. 1911

If You Can't Be Good, Be Careful   Razaf 1953; Waller 1953

If You Can't Be Good in Hollywood, Be as Good as You Can   Hanley 1931

If You Can't Control Your Man   Razaf 1940

If You Can't Enlist, Buy a Victory Bond   Razaf 1942

If You Can't Get a Drum with a Boom-Boom-Boom (Get a Tuba with an Oom-Pah-Pah)   David, Hal 1950

If You Can't Get a Girl in the Summertime   Davis 1950; Silver 1950

If You Can't Get a Girl in the Summertime You'll Never Get a Girl at All   Kalmar 1915

If You Can't Get Five Take Two   Razaf 1934

If You Can't Get the Love You Want   Dietz 1944; Duke 1944

If You Can't Have the Girl of Your Dreams   Warren 1930; Young, Joe 1930

If You Can't Hold the Man You Love (Don't Cry When He's Gone)   Fain 1926; Kahal 1926

If You Can't Kiss Your Popper Proper, You Can Kiss Your Popper Good-Bye   Dixon 1924; Henderson 1924

If You Can't Land 'em on the Old Veranda   Silver 1926

If You Can't Say Something Nice   Sherman 1963

If You Can't Sing, Dance   Smith, Harry B. 1911; Smith, Robert B. 1911

If You Can't Sing It You'll Have to Swing It (Mr. Paganini)   Coslow 1936

If You Can't Swim or Float, Don't Change Places on a Boat   Caesar 1943

If You Can't Tell the World She's a Good Little Girl (Just Say Nothing at All)   Dubin 1926; Fain 1926; Kahal 1926

If You Care for the Boys   Cahn 1945; Styne 1945

If You Cared for Me As I Care for You   Snyder 1908

If You Come Through   Bloom 1956; Mercer 1956

If You Could Be as True to Me as I Could Be to You   Hanley 1925

If You Could Care   Goetz 1920, 1929

If You Could Love Me   Porter 1935

If You Could Read My Mind   Schwartz, Jean 1918

If You Could See Me Now   Sigman 1946

If You Could Uke a Ukelele   Coslow 1925

If You Didn't Love Me, Who Else Would   Loesser 1936

If You Do, I'll Die   Friml 1919; Harbach 1919

If You Do It Without the Army   Cahn 1975

If You Do What Your Do   Turk 1923

If You Don't Do Your Homework   Dubin Date Unknown; Warren Date Unknown

If You Don't Get Married This Summer, You Won't Get Married at All   Dubin 1916

If You Don't Like the Jokes Watch the Girl   Davis 1953

If You Don't Love   Webster 1950

If You Don't Love Me   Ager 1928; Carmichael 1949; Yellen 1928

If You Don't Love Me (O'Jin-Ja)   Brooks 1957

If You Don't Mind My Saying So   Willson 1957

If You Don't Stop Making Eyes at Me, I'm Goin' to Make Eyes at You   Brennan 1919

If You Don't Tell Me How Am I Gonna Know?   Henderson 1924

If You Don't Think I'm Leaving (Just Count the Days I'm Gone)   Cahn 1961

If You Don't Think So You're Crazy   Turk 1922

If You Don't Think You Ought to Do What You Oughtn't Do, Don't Do It at All   Sterling 1922; Von Tilzer 1922

If You Don't Want Me Now   David, Hal 1961

If You Don't Want Me Why Do You Hand Around?   Berlin 1913

If You Don't Want My Peaches You Better Stop Shaking My Tree   Berlin 1914

If You Don't Want to Be Sweehearts (I Don't Want to Be Friends)   Fain 1933; Kahal 1933

If You Don't Want to Love Me   Brown, Lew Date Unknown; Henderson Date Unknown

If You Ever Came Back   Conrad 1933; Coslow 1933

If You Ever Come Down to Virginia There'll Be Nothing Too Good for You   Brown, A. Seymour 1915

If You Ever Get Lonely   Kahn 1916

If You Ever Need Me   Warren 1964

If You Ever See Anything of Flora   Ager 1934; Schwartz, Jean 1934; Young, Joe 1934

If You Ever Should Leave   Cahn 1937

If You Ever Want a Favor Mention Me   Herbert 1909

If You Feel Like Singing, Sing   Gordon 1950; Revel 1950; Warren 1950

If You Follow the Bluebird   Coots 1954

If You Go Home to Your Husband I'll Have to Go Home to
My Wife   Leslie 1912

If You Grow Tired Little Girl   Howard, Joseph E. 1907

If You Had Only Remembered   Friend 1950

If You Hadn't Answered No   Kalmar 1917; Leslie 1917;
Ruby 1917

If You Hadn't But You Did   Comden and Green 1951; Styne
1951

If You Have a Girl Who Loves You, Leave the Other Girls
Alone   Friend 1922

If You Have Ever Loved   David, Hal 1956

If You Have Love   Gorney 1966

If You Haven't Answered No   Goetz 1917

If You Haven't Got a Girl   Davis 1930; Hoffman 1930

If You Haven't Got a Sweetheart   Fields 1951; Schwartz,
Arthur 1951

If You Haven't Got an Ear for Music   Berlin 1962

If You Haven't Got Love   Brown, Lew 1931; DeSylva 1931;
Henderson 1931

If You Haven't Got the Things It Takes to Hold Your Man,
Then You Can't Blame Me   Razaf 1924

If You Haven't Lost Your Sense of Honor (You Haven't Lost
a Gosh Darn Thing)   Davis 1953

If You Haven't Somebody to Love   Brown, A. Seymour 1929

If You Knew   Clare 1921; Conrad 1921

If You Knew Her Side of the Story   Dubin 1923; McHugh
1923

If You Knew Susie (Like I Know Susie)   DeSylva 1925

If You Knew What I Know about Men   Goetz 1911

If You Knew Would You Care   Yellen 1921

If You Knew You'd Hurt Somebody, Why Did It Have to Be
Me   Stept 1931

If You Know How to Strut   Berlin 1923

If You Know What I Mean   Schwartz, Arthur 1926

If You Know What I Think   Romberg 1927; Smith, Harry B.
1927

If You Leave London   Ahlert 1944; Howard, Bart 1944

If You Leave Paris   Howard, Bart 1938

If You Like Bananas   Caesar 1943

If You Like Me Like I Like You   Gilbert 1921; Waller 1929

If You Like to Get Around   Brooks 1959

If You Like to Learn   Cahn 1980; DePaul 1980

If You Lived Here, You'd Be Dead By Now   Lane Date
Unknown

If You Lived in the Mountains   Burke 1933; Spina 1933

If You Look in Her Eyes   Harbach 1917

If You Love a Man   Livingston, Jerry 1973

If You Love But Me   Herbert 1906

If You Love Her (Tell Her So)   Freed, Arthur 1925

If You Love Me Like I Love You   Edwards 1934

If You Love Me, Why Don't You Tell Me   Woods 1954

If You Loved Me Truly   Porter 1953

If You Miss Me As I Miss You   Davis 1926

If You Never Get the One You Want   Bryan 1950

If You Never Say Goodbye   Bacharach 1972; David, Hal
1972

If You Only Care Enough   Kern 1918

If You Only Had a Heart (To Go with That Beautiful
Face)   Livingston, Jerry 1955; Webster 1955

If You Only Knew   Gershwin, George 1917; Gershwin, Ira
1917, 1918

If You Only Knew the Ways to Pull the Wires   Smith, Harry
B. 1904; Smith, Robert B. 1904

If You Please   Burke 1943; Van Heusen 1943

If You Really Love Your Baby   Razaf 1929

If You Really Want to Know   Hoffman 1956

If You Said No   Cahn 1957

If You Saw All that I Saw in Arkansas   Ager 1917

If You Saw What I Saw in Nassau   Hoffman 1950

If You See Sally   Donaldson 1927; Egan 1927; Kahn 1927

If You See Sally Kiss Her for Me   David, Mack 1947

If You See that Gal of Mine Send Her Home   Ahlert 1925;
Lewis 1925; Young, Joe 1925

If You Should Ever Leave   Fain Date Unknown

If You Should Ever Need Me   Dubin 1931

If You Should Leave Me   Stept 1950

If You Should Say Goodbye   Hoffman 1953

If You Smile at Me   Porter 1946

If You Smile at the Sun (The Sun Will Smile at
You)   Hoffman 1950

If You Stub Your Toe on the Moon   Burke 1949; Van
Heusen 1949

If You Talk in Your Sleep Don't Mention My Name   Brown,
A. Seymour 1911

If You Think It's Love You're Right   Dietz 1924; Kern 1924

If You Turn Me Down   Sigman 1951

If You Walk Out that Door   Fain 1957

If You Wanna Be My Sugar Papa (You Gotta Be Sweet to
Me)   Mills 1927

If You Wanna See Mamie Tonight   Fain 1956; Webster 1956

If You Want Love   Mills 1955

If You Want My Love   Hoffman 1953

If You Want the Rainbow (You Must Have the Rain)   Dixon
1928; Rose 1928

If You Want to Be an Edison   Caesar 1943

If You Want to Be Successful in the Cinema   Gordon 1931;
Revel 1931

If You Want to Make a Deal with Russia   Caesar 1943

If You Want to Make a Hit with Fifi   Coslow 1947

If You Want to Make a Hit with the Ladies Tell Them
They're Beautiful   Kalmar 1919; Leslie 1919; Ruby 1919

If You Were a Traveling Salesman   Dubin 1930

If You Were As Lonely (As You Are Lovely)   Burke 1935;
Spina 1935

If You Were Here   Goetz 1917

If You Were I and I Were You   Coslow 1935; Herbert 1908

If You Were in My Place   Ellington 1938; Mills 1938

If You Were Mine   Adamson 1972; Bryan 1929; Lerner,
Sammy 1931; Mercer 1935; Merrill 1953; Meyer 1929

If You were Only Here   Meyer 1912

If You Were Someone Else   Schwartz, Arthur 1937

If You were Someone Else I Know   Goetz 1908

If You Were the Only Girl in the World and I Was the Only
Boy   Brown, Lew 1916; Meyer 1916

If You Were You   Hart 1920; Rodgers 1920

If You Will Marry Us We'll Stroll Beneath the Babbling
Brook   Kalmar 1923; Ruby 1923

If You Will Take Our Tip   Gershwin, George 1927;
Gershwin, Ira 1927

If You Won't Marry Me, then I'll Marry You   Howard,
Joseph E. 1910

If You Would Listen   Robison 1944

If You Would Love Me   Baer 1952

If You Would Only Come Away   Hammerstein 1943

If You Would Only Love Me   Kern 1912

If You'd Only Show a Little Love for Me   Monaco 1914

If You'll Be Mine   Martin 1948

If You'll Be My Eve, I'll Build an Eden for You   Johnson, J.
Rosamond 1912

If You'll Be My Lolly I Will Be Your Pop   Johnson, Howard
  1921; Rose 1921
If You'll Be My Soldier, I'll Be a Red Cross Nurse   Bryan
  1917
If You'll Believe in Me   David, Mack 1948; Hoffman 1951;
  Livingston, Jerry 1951
If You'll Let Me Be Your Husband, I'll Let You Be My
  Wife   Edwards 1913
If You'll Only Lead the Way   Harbach 1911
If You'll Only Say It with Flowers   Goetz 1920
If You'll Only Say You'll Be a Friend of Mine   Goetz 1910
If You'll Only Take a Chance   Blane 1955; Martin 1955
If Your Best Friend Won't Tell You   Dubin 1929
If Your Heart Doesn't Dance, It Isn't Love   Hoffman 1957
If Your Heart Should Skip a Beat   Caesar 1953
If Your Kisses Can't Hold the Man You Love Your Tears
  Won't Bring Him Back   Yellen 1930
If Your Name Had Been LaRotta   Hammerstein 1926;
  Harbach 1926; Youmans 1926
If Your Want to See Paree (Look in My Eyes)   Donaldson
  1929; Leslie 1929
If You're a Friend of Mine   Kern 1928
If You're Askin' Me   Bergman 1957
If You're Crazy About the Women, You're Not Crazy at
  All   Bryan 1918; Leslie 1918; Ruby 1918
If You're Ever in My Arms Again   Van Heusen 1937
If' You're Gettin' Bad Breaks Pull Up Your Stakes and Move
  On   Brown, Lew 1952; Henderson 1952
If You're Gonna Be a Witch — Be a Witch!   Cahn 1963; Van
  Heusen 1963
If You're Happy, I'll Be Glad   Johnson, Howard 1931
If You're in Love   Loesser 1941; Styne 1941, 1945;
  Washington 1952
If You're List'ning to This Record   Carmichael 1954
If You're Nice to Me   Mitchell 1953; Stept 1953
If You're Not Kissing Me   Brown, Nacio Herb 1930; Freed,
  Arthur 1930
If You're Single   Hart 1923; Rodgers 1923
If You're Spanish   Cahn 1942
If You're Waiting I'm Waiting Too   Cahn 1946; Styne 1946
If You've Been Having Trouble with the Blues   Brooks 1958
If You've Never Been in Love   Conrad 1930; Davis 1930
If You've Never Been to Vegas   Cahn 1956
If You've Never Been Vamped by a Brownskin (You've Never
  Been Vamped at All)   Blake 1921; Sissle 1921
If'n I Was God   Sherman 1973
Igloo Song   Baer 1929; Gilbert 1929
Ignatz   Evans 1963; Livingston, Jay 1963
Ignore Dior   Willson 1953
Igual Que Tu   Gorney 1931; Harburg 1931
I-Itty-Love-Itty-You-Itty   Hoffman 1949
Ike for Four More Years   Berlin 1956
Ike's Golf Game   Willson 1953
Ikky Tikky Tanbo   Hoffman 1944; Livingston, Jerry 1944
Il Est de Beaux Reves   Romberg 1933
Il Mio Mondo (You're My World)   Sigman 1964
Il Mio Muletto (My Little Mule)   Merrill 1955
Il Torrente (You Can't Keep Running)   Sigman 1956
Il Trovatore   Robin 1947
I'll Always Be an Optimist   Hart 1922; Rodgers 1922
I'll Always Be Beside You   Hoffman 1944
I'll Always Be in Love with You   Stept 1929
I'll Always Be Irish   Sherman 1967
I'll Always Be Lucky with You   Bullock 1938; Spina 1938
I'll Always Be Mother's Boy   Stept 1929

I'll Always Keep a Corner in My Heart for
  Tennessee   Clarke 1920; Donaldson 1920
I'll Always Love Old Dixie   Johnson, J. Rosamond 1907
I'll Always Love You   Loesser 1948
I'll Always Love You Dear   Brown, A. Seymour 1910; Goetz
  1910
I'll Always Love You (Querida Mia)   Evans 1950; Livingston,
  Jay 1950
I'll Always Need Someone Like You   Caesar 1922
I'll Always Need You   Loesser Date Unknown
I'll Always Practice Safety   Caesar 1943
I'll Always Remember   Schwartz, Arthur 1928, 1930
I'll Always Remember September   Hoffman 1931
I'll Always Speak Well of You   Clare 1932
I'll Answer You   Fisher 1930
I'll Applaud You with My Feet   Dubin 1940; McHugh 1940
I'll Ballyhoo You   Eliscu 1932
I'll Be a Buoyant Girl   Hammerstein 1926; Harbach 1926;
  Romberg 1926
I'll Be a College Boy's Dear   Atteridge 1917; Motzan 1917;
  Romberg 1917
I'll Be a Good Soldier Too   Razaf 1941
I'll Be a Hero Too!   Rome 1940
I'll Be a Pal to Your Boy If You'll Be a Pal to Mine   Bryan
  1928
I'll Be a Santa Claus to You   Buck 1915
I'll Be a Star   Hart 1931; Rodgers 1931
I'll Be Among Those Present   Dixon 1932
I'll Be Back   Razaf 1942
I'll Be Back in Me Low Back Car   Donaldson 1915; Lewis
  1915; Young, Joe 1915
I'll Be Busy As a Bee   Clare 1920; Mitchell 1920
I'll Be Close to You   Coslow 1940
I'll Be Easy to Find   Howard, Bart 1958
I'll Be Faithful   Washington 1933; Wrubel 1933
I'll Be Forgetting You   DePaul 1958; Oakland 1961; Raye
  1961
I'll Be Glad   Johnson, J. Rosamond 1938
I'll Be Good But I'll Be Lonesome (When You're
  Gone)   Fisher 1921
I'll Be Happy Too   Williams 1910
I'll Be Happy When the Preacher Makes You
  Mine   Donaldson 1919; Lewis 1919; Young, Joe 1919
I'll Be Hard to Handle   Fields 1952; Kern 1933, 1952
I'll Be in My Dixie Home Again Tomorrow   Turk 1922
I'll Be Lonely   Dixon 1927; Woods 1927
I'll Be Loving You   Cahn 1952; Duke 1952
I'll Be Loving You Forever   David, Mack 1930
I'll Be Marching to a Love Song   Rainger 1942; Robin 1942
I'll Be Married to the Music of a Military Band   Herbert 1908
I'll Be Over Your Way in the Mornin' Bill   Ruby 1918
I'll Be Respectable   Arlen 1959; Mercer 1959
I'll Be Seeing You   Brown, Nacio Herb 1932; Egan 1932;
  Fain 1938; Kahal 1938; Whiting 1932
I'll Be Sittin' in de Lap o' de Lord   Schwartz, Arthur 1937
I'll Be Smiling   Schwartz, Jean 1928
I'll Be So Happy   Ahlert 1929; Turk 1929
I'll Be Somewhere in France   Buck 1917
I'll Be the Meanest Man in Town (Till You're Nice to
  Me)   Stept 1932
I'll Be the Words and You'll Be the Music   Von Tilzer 1917
I'll Be the Words, You Be the Tune   Coots 1930; Magidson
  1930

I'll Be There   Coots 1929; Herbert 1920; Russell 1977;
    Schwartz, Arthur 1930; Smith, Robert B. 1920; Stept
    1944; Webster 1965

I'll Be There, I'll Be There, Mary Dear   Sterling 1902; Von
    Tilzer 1902

I'll Be There in a Public Square   Cohan 1903

I'll Be There with Bells On   Cohan 1906; Freed, Ralph 1951;
    Hoffman 1950, 1951; Rainger 1935; Robin 1935; Whiting
    1935

I'll Be Thinking of You   Hoffman 1957

I'll Be True to My Honey Boy   Cohan 1908

I'll Be True to You   Smith, Harry B. 1912; Smith, Robert B.
    1912

I'll Be Waiting Down in Rio   Warren 1975, 1977

I'll Be Waiting for You   Brooks 1960

I'll Be Waiting 'Neath Your Window   Kern 1912

I'll Be with You Again   Burke 1971

I'll Be with You when the Roses Bloom Again   Cobb 1901;
    Edwards 1901

I'll Be with You when the Roses Bloom in Spring   Von Tilzer
    1923

I'll Be Worthy of You   De Lange 1956

I'll Be Your Artist and You Be My Model   Akst 1927; Davis
    1927

I'll Be Your Chanticleer   Harbach 1910

I'll Be Your Honey when It's Moonlight   Howard, Joseph E.
    1910

I'll Be Your Jujube   Edwards 1908

I'll Bet My First Dream and Last Dream on You   Woods
    1959

I'll Bet on Anything but Girls   Romberg 1922

I'll Bet on You   Clare 1934; Whiting 1934

I'll Bet You   Howard, Joseph E. 1909

I'll Bet You Tell that to All the Girls   Stept 1936

I'll Black His Eyes   Porter 1938

I'll Blame the Waltz (Not You)   Gordon 1934; Revel 1934

I'll Bob Up with the Bob-O-Link (In the Morning)   Fain
    1930; Kahal 1930

I'll Bribe the Stars   Herbert 1903; Smith, Harry B. 1903

I'll Bring Along My Banjo   Bacharach 1961

I'll Bring the Ring   David, Hal 1960

I'll Build a Broadway for You   Bullock 1938; Spina 1938

I'll Build a Bungalow   Hammerstein 1922

I'll Build a Fence Around You   Lewis 1910

I'll Build a Home in the Jungle   Caesar 1922

I'll Build a Stairway to Paradise   DeSylva 1922; Gershwin,
    George 1922; Gershwin, Ira 1922

I'll Build a Wall Around Loveland   Lewis 1912; Meyer 1912

I'll Build for You a Little Nest   Harbach 1910

I'll Butter Him Up   Bergman 1960

I'll Buy Everybody a Beer   Loesser 1956

I'll Buy It   Fields 1957; Lane 1957

I'll Buy that Dream   Magidson 1945; Wrubel 1945

I'll Buy You a Star   Fields 1951; Schwartz, Arthur 1951

I'll Call Him "Bambi"   Sherman 1963

I'll Call It Love   Arlen 1930; Koehler 1930

I'll Capture Your Heart   Berlin 1942

I'll Cling to You   Carroll 1915

I'll Close My Eyes to the Rest of the World and Dream
    Sweet Dreams of You   Friend 1929

I'll Collaborate with You   Hammerstein 1923; Harbach 1923

I'll Come Back As Many Times As You Need Me   David,
    Hal 1976

I'll Come Back to You   Atteridge 1914; Heyman 1931;
    Youmans 1931

I'll Come Back to You When It's All Over   Brown, Lew 1917

I'll Come Sailing Home to You (A Long Way from
    Broadway)   Carroll 1917

I'll Come to the Wedding   Loesser 1938

I'll Come to You   Coots 1953

I'll Cry Tomorrow   Mercer 1956

I'll Dance at Your Wedding   Magidson 1947; Oakland 1947

I'll Dance at Your Wedding (Honey Dear)   Carmichael 1941;
    Loesser 1941

I'll Dance My Way into Your Heart   DeSylva 1922

I'll Dance Rings Around You   Berlin 1945

I'll Do Anything But —   Bryan 1910

I'll Do Anything in the World for You   Cobb 1906; Edwards
    1906

I'll Do It All Over Again   Brown, A. Seymour 1914

I'll Do It For You   Styne 1943

I'll Do More than That for You   Fisher 1913

I'll Do No Turkey Trotting   Atteridge Date Unknown

I'll Do the Strutaway (In My Cutaway)   Caesar 1938

I'll Do What My Heart Tells Me To   Stept 1935

I'll Do What My Heart Tells Me to Do   Friend 1935

I'll Do What the Rest Do   Smith, Harry B. 1915

I'll Dream of Thee   Herbert 1908

I'll Dream Tonight   Mercer 1938; Whiting 1938

I'll Eat My Hat   Evans 1944; Livingston, Jay 1944

I'll Find a Boy (Girl)   Atteridge 1912

I'll Find My Love in D-I-X-I-E   Blake 1924; Sissle 1924

I'll Fly the Skyway   Sherman 1970

I'll Follow My Baby   Coslow 1937

I'll Follow the Trail   Brennan 1930; Friml 1930

I'll Follow You   Ahlert 1932; Turk 1932

I'll Follow Your Smile   Harburg 1945; Kern 1945

I'll Fool that Sweet Senorita   Brown, Lew 1927; DeSylva
    1927; Henderson 1927

I'll Forgive Anything but a Lie   Merrill 1950

I'll Forgive You   Cahn 1955; Duke 1955

I'll Forsake You Not My Darling (inst.)   Revel 1960

I'll Get Along As Long As I Have You   Turk 1926

I'll Get Away with It   Strouse 1990

I'll Get By, As Long As I Have You   Ahlert 1928; Turk 1928

I'll Get Even   Mercer 1964

I'll Get Him Back   Russell 1948

I'll Get My Man   Brown, Lew 1930; DeSylva 1930;
    Henderson 1930

I'll Get You   Cobb 1913; Edwards 1913

I'll Get You — In the End   McHugh 1941; Mercer 1941

I'll Get You Yet Cigarette   Smith, Robert B. 1915

I'll Give a Penny for Your Thoughts   Lewis 1909; Snyder
    1909

I'll Give All My Tomorrows for Just One Yesterday   Kahn
    1931

I'll Give You One Guess   Cahn 1947; Styne 1947

I'll Give You Three Guesses   Mancini 1970; Mercer 1970

I'll Go   Sigman 1953

I'll Go Along with You   Livingston, Jerry 1956

I'll Go Home with Bonnie Jean   Lerner, Alan Jay 1947;
    Loewe 1947

I'll Go On Caring   Davis 1970

I'll Go on Loving You   Merrill 1953

I'll Go the Route for You   Cohan 1909

I'll Go to Flannigan   Yellen 1934

I'll Go with You   Robison 1958; Woods 1958

I'll Hate Myself in the Morning   Cahn 1944; Lawrence 1947;
    Styne 1944

I'll Haunt You   Sigman 1960

I'll Have Faith in You   DePaul 1958; Raye 1958

I'll Have My Opera on the East Side (When Maggie Sings the Old Songs)   Sterling 1910

I'll Have the Blues Until I Get to California   Robison 1925

I'll Have to Ask My Mother (inst.)   Revel 1959

I'll Have to Make a Safety   Caesar 1942

I'll Hold You in My Heart (Until You Hold Me in Your Arms)   Robison 1964

I'll Hold Your Hand in Mine   Dietz 1952

I'll Just Go Along   Kahn 1927

I'll Keep a Warm Spot in My Heart for You   Johnson, J. Rosamond 1906

I'll Keep It Turned to the Wall   Razaf 1940

I'll Keep Looking for the Roses Tho' the World Is Full of Thorns   Bryan 1920; Meyer 1920

(You Keep Your Eye On Me and) I'll Keep My Eye on You   Carroll 1912

I'll Keep on Dreaming   Smith, Harry B. 1926

I'll Keep on Dreaming of You   Coots 1927; Dubin 1927

I'll Keep the Roses Blooming for You   Smith, Robert B. 1915

I'll Kiss You Goodnight in the Morning   Bacharach 1957; David, Hal 1957

I'll Know   Loesser 1950

I'll Know and She'll Know   Kalmar 1929; Ruby 1929

I'll Know Better the Next Time   Berlin 1957

I'll Know Him   Brown, Lew 1930; DeSylva 1930; Henderson 1930

I'll Know It's Love   Ruby 1947

I'll Learn Ya   Evans 1961; Livingston, Jay 1961

I'll Leave My Heart with You   Davis 1942

I'll Lend You Everything   Edwards 1910; Smith, Harry B. 1910

I'll Lend You Everything I've Got Except My Wife   Von Tilzer 1910

I'll Let the World Know I Love You   Brennan 1927

I'll Love Them All to Death   Smith, Harry B. 1928

I'll Love You Always   David, Hal 1960

I'll Love You As Long As I Live   Brennan 1915

I'll Love You Honey, When Your Money's Gone, but I'll Not Be with You   Johnson, J. Rosamond 1915

I'll Love You in My Dreams   Baer 1931

I'll Love You Just the Same   Brown, Lew 1927; Friend 1927

I'll Love You Marina   Harbach 1914

I'll Love You More for Losing You   Egan 1918; Whiting 1918

I'll Love You Till the Cows Come Home   Ahlert 1930; Turk 1930

I'll Make a Happy Landing (The Lucky Day I Land You)   Fields 1931; McHugh 1931

I'll Make a Home for You in This Heart of Mine   Harburg 1931

I'll Make a Man of the Man   Cahn 1966; Van Heusen 1966

I'll Make a Man of You   Carroll 1914

I'll Make a Ring around Rosie   Jerome 1910; Schwartz, Jean 1910

I'll Make the Pies Like Mother if You'll Make the Dough Like Dad   Von Tilzer 1924

I'll Make You a Little Nest   Harbach 1910

I'll Make You Happy   Dietz 1934; Schwartz, Arthur 1934

I'll Make You Like the Town   Atteridge 1915; Romberg 1915

I'll March in April with May   Bryan 1910; Meyer 1910

I'll Marry a Soldier   Duke 1963

I'll Marry a Sunshine Girl   Goetz 1912

I'll Meet You at Sundown   Mills 1941

I'll Meet You Down by the River   Lane 1951; Lerner, Alan Jay 1951

I'll Meet You in Las Vegas   DePaul 1958; Oakland 1961; Raye 1961

I'll Miss You   Merrill 1953; Parish 1936; Rodgers 1976

I'll Miss You in the Evening   Berlin 1931

I'll Miss You in the Golden Summertime   Bryan 1902

I'll Miss You, Old Ireland   Brennan 1920

I'll Mooch Along   Brown, Lew 1922; Hanley 1922

I'll Never Ask for More   Ahlert 1928; DeSylva 1929; Turk 1928

I'll Never Be Alone Again   Alter 1967; Kahal 1967

I'll Never Be the Same   Kahn 1932

I'll Never Belong to Anyone Else If I Can't Belong to You   Drake 1947

I'll Never Care for Any Girl but You   Sterling 1909

I'll Never Change   Clare 1938; Johnston 1938

I'll Never Change Again   Brown, Lew 1943

I'll Never Ever Pass Your House Again   Johnson, Howard 1941

I'll Never Fail You   Mills 1938

I'll Never Fall in Love Again   Bacharach 1968; David, Hal 1968

I'll Never Forget   Kahn 1928

I'll Never Forgive Myself   David, Mack 1942; Davis 1942; Mercer 1968

I'll Never Get Along Any Longer Alone   Fain 1928

I'll Never Go to Heaven   Brooks 1947

I'll Never Grow Tired of You   Leslie 1932

I'll Never Kiss Her Anymore   Johnson, James P. 1927

I'll Never Know   Styne 1993

I'll Never Learn   Fields 1950

I'll Never Leave You   Schwartz, Arthur 1930; Strouse 1985

I'll Never Let a Day Pass By   Loesser 1941

I'll Never Let My Heart Get Out of Hand   Burke 1950; Van Heusen 1950

I'll Never Let You Cry   Clare 1938; Mitchell 1938; Pollack 1938

I'll Never Lose You   Duke 1937

I'll Never Love Again   Gilbert 1943

I'll Never Love Another Gal   Coslow 1952

I'll Never Love Another Love Like I Love You   Cobb 1904; Edwards 1904

I'll Never Love You   Cahn 1950

I'll Never Make a Frenchman Out of You   Martin 1951

I'll Never Make the Same Mistake Again   Coots 1942; Magidson 1947; Oakland 1947

I'll Never Make the Same Mistake Twice   Heyman 1964

I'll Never Need the Moon ('Nu Quarto 'e Luna)   Rome 1954

I'll Never, Never Forget What's Her Name   Bacharach 1960; David, Hal 1960

I'll Never Say Goodbye   Bergman 1978

I'll Never Say Goodbye to You Again   Willson 1953

I'll Never Say I Love You   Willson 1969

I'll Never Say "Never Again" Again   Woods 1935

I'll Never Say No   Willson 1960

I'll Never See You Again   Fields 1950

I'll Never Share You (If You Were My Concubine)   Hart 1928; Rodgers 1928

I'll Never Stand in Your Way   Silver 1931

I'll Never Stop Loving You   Cahn 1955

I'll Never Tell You I Love You   Mills 1937

I'll Never Waltz Again Without You   Cahn 1961; Van Heusen 1961

I'll Not Let Love Disparage Marriage   Harbach 1914

I'll Not Marry   Lane 1965; Lerner, Alan Jay 1965

I'll Only Miss Her when I Think of Her   Cahn 1965; Van Heusen 1965

I'll Open the Door, and Close the Door   Brown, Lew 1917

I'll Pay the Check   Fields 1939; Schwartz, Arthur 1939

I'll Peek-a-boo You   Romberg 1927; Smith, Harry B. 1927

I'll Pin Another Petal on the Daisy (So It'll Tell Me You Care)   Fain 1933; Kahal 1933

I'll Promise   Brown, Nacio Herb 1921

I'll Put a Tax   Smith, Harry B. 1900

I'll Put the Blue Back in Your Eyes   Bryan 1939; Meyer 1939

I'll Remember   Freed, Ralph 1939; Lane 1939

I'll Remember and Dream   Brennan 1921

I'll Remember April   DePaul 1942, 1944, 1945; Raye 1942, 1944, 1945

I'll Remember Everything that You'll Forget   Bryan 1934

I'll Remember Only You   Brown, Nacio Herb 1933; Freed, Arthur 1933

I'll Remember This Night   Baer 1964; Lewis 1964

I'll Remember Tonight   Fain 1958; Webster 1958

I'll Remember You   Freed, Arthur 1930

I'll Remember Your Eyes   Bryan 1930

I'll Ring the Bell   Herbert 1906

I'll Run in from Troy   Cohan 1903

I'll Run Out of Time (Before I Run Out of Love for You)   Warren 1971

I'll Save All My Evenings for You   Gorney 1925

I'll Save My Heart   Heyman 1934; Romberg 1934

I'll Say Good Morning where the Morning Glories Grow   Schwartz, Jean 1923

I'll Say I Do   Dubin 1927

I'll Say It with a Pretty Little Song   Stept 1926

I'll Say She Does   DeSylva 1918; Kahn 1918

I'll Say So   Hammerstein 1920

I'll See You After Church on Sunday Mornin'   Wrubel 1950

I'll See You at the "Mets"   Baer 1962

I'll See You in Church   Hoffman 1933

I'll See You in C-U-B-A   Berlin 1920

I'll See You in My Dreams   Kahn 1924

I'll See You in the Morning   Loesser 1932

I'll See You on the Radio (Laura)   Bacharach 1986

I'll See You Some-Moa in Samoa   Johnson, Howard 1926

I'll Settle for Love   Akst 1937; Clare 1937

I'll Settle for You   Rainger 1940; Robin 1940

I'll Share It All with You   Berlin 1946

I'll Show You a Wonderful World   DeSylva 1919; Gershwin, George 1919

I'll Show You Off   Hammerstein 1933

I'll Si, Si Ya in Bahia   Robin 1952; Warren 1952

I'll Sing a Hymn to You at Twilight   David, Mack 1945

I'll Sing No Duet with You   Willson 1953

I'll Sing of a Golden Age   Weill 1938

I'll Sing Thee Songs of Araby   Johnson, Howard 1939

I'll Sing You a Song   Blane 1952

I'll Sing You a Thousand Love Songs   Dubin 1936; Warren 1936

I'll Sing You Home   Sigman 1984

I'll Sit Right on the Moon   Monaco 1912

I'll Smile Away Your Sorrows, and Kiss Away Your Tears   Conrad 1931

I'll Stand Beneath Your Window Tonight and Whistle   McHugh 1922

I'll Stand By   Coots 1936; Davis 1936

I'll Still Belong To You   Brown, Nacio Herb 1928; Egan 1930; Eliscu 1928

I'll String Along with You   Dubin 1934; Warren 1934

I'll Supply the Title, You Supply the Tune   Arlen 1939; Gershwin, Ira 1939

I'll Swing for This   Cahn 1939

I'll Take a Little of You on Toast   Hart 1935; Rodgers 1935

I'll Take a Ragtime Tune   Goetz 1912

I'll Take an Option on You   Rainger 1933; Robin 1933

I'll Take Any Man   Coleman 1966; Fields 1966

I'll Take Care of You   Bryan 1908; Coslow 1930; Meyer 1908

I'll Take Care of Your Cares   Dixon 1927; Monaco 1927

I'll Take Chicago   Cahn 1952

I'll Take Her Back If She Wants to Come Back   Leslie 1924; Monaco 1924

I'll Take Love   Friend 1951

I'll Take Mah Troubles Down to the River   Washington 1946

I'll Take Manila   Arlen 1942; Harburg 1942; Lane 1942

I'll Take My Baby Back Again   Coslow 1927

I'll Take Romance   Hammerstein 1937; Oakland 1937

I'll Take Tallulah   Arlen 1942; Harburg 1942; Lane 1942

I'll Take the Blame   David, Mack 1955; Van Heusen 1955

I'll Take the City   Duke 1941

I'll Take the High Note   Adamson 1940

I'll Take You As You Are   Sigman 1953

I'll Take You Back If You Want to Come Back   Young, Joe 1932

I'll Take You Back to Ireland   Carroll 1912

I'll Take You Back to Italy   Berlin 1917

I'll Take You Dreaming   Cahn 1956

I'll Take You Home Again Kathleen   Johnson, Howard 1939

I'll Take You Home in My Heart Tonight   David, Mack 1949; Livingston, Jerry 1949

I'll Take You Home in My Old Wheel-Barrow   Burke 1934; Spina 1934

I'll Take You Home Tomorrow If You'll Take Me Home Tonight   Howard, Joseph E. 1910

I'll Take You To Paradise   Brown, Nacio Herb 1931

I'll Tell a Policeman on You   David, Mack 1950; Evans 1951; Livingston, Jay 1951; Livingston, Jerry 1950

I'll Tell the Man in the Street   Hart 1938; Rodgers 1938

I'll Tell the World   Atteridge 1918; DeSylva 1918; Loewe 1942; Mercer 1974

I'll Tell the World I Miss You   Dubin 1921

I'll Tell the World That's News   Mills 1935; Razaf 1935

I'll Tell the World You're All the World to Me   Ahlert 1929; Turk 1929

I'll Tell You   Smith, Harry B. 1930

I'll Tell You Why, Can't You See I'm in Love with You   Davis 1922; Silver 1922

I'll Thank You to Stay Out of My Dreams   Arlen 1936; Harburg 1936

I'll Think of You   Coslow 1927; Kahn 1927

I'll Treat You Just Like a Sister   Harbach 1921

I'll Try   Fields 1959

I'll Try Anything Once   Brown, A. Seymour 1911

I'll Wait   Hoffman 1958

I'll Wait for You   Kahn 1919; Revel 1929

I'll Wait for You by the River   Lane 1951; Lerner, Alan Jay 1951

I'll Wait for You Forever   Coots 1940

I'll Walk Alone   Cahn 1944; Styne 1944

I'll Walk with God   Webster 1952

Ill Wind   Arlen 1934; Koehler 1934

Illegitimate Daughter, The   Gershwin, George 1931; Gershwin, Ira 1931

Illinois   Evans 1948; Harbach 1947; Kern 1947; Livingston, Jay 1948

Illinois Republican, An   Bullock 1950; Spina 1944

Ill-Tempered Clavichord, The   Lerner, Alan Jay 1943; Loewe 1943

Illusion   Coslow 1929; Parish 1965; Russell 1946

I'm a Bachelor in the Art of Ha-Cha-Cha   Coslow 1933; Johnston 1933

I'm a Bad, Bad Man   Berlin 1946

I'm a Bad Boy Looking for a Good Girl (And Will Make a Bad Boy Good)   Stept 1926

I'm a Bear for You   Jerome 1910; Schwartz, Jean 1910

I'm a Beggar of Love   Lewis 1931

I'm a Better Man (for Having Loved You)   Bacharach 1969; David, Hal 1969

I'm a Big Girl Now   Hoffman 1945; Livingston, Jerry 1945

I'm a Black Sheep Who's Blue   Rainger 1934; Robin 1934

I'm a Brass Band   Coleman 1966; Fields 1966

I'm a Broken Hearted Blackbird   Fields 1926; McHugh 1926

I'm a Business Man   Edwards 1923

I'm a Cave Man   Stept 1919

I'm a Cheese Man Myself   Bergman 1960

I'm a Cinch to Fall in Love   Clare 1982

I'm a Collector of Moonbeams   Arlen 1934; Gershwin, Ira 1934; Harburg 1934

I'm a Cossack   Pollack 1943

I'm a Crazy Daffydill   Kern 1911

I'm a Daughter of Peru   Caesar 1930; Harbach 1930; Romberg 1930

I'm a Detective   Meyer 1909

I'm a Devil with the Ladies   Atteridge 1923; Caesar 1923; Romberg 1923

I'm a Do-Right Woman Looking for a Do-Right Man   Leslie 1912

I'm a Dreamer, Aren't We All   Brown, Lew 1929; DeSylva 1929; Henderson 1929

I'm a Dumb-Bell   Berlin 1921

I'm a Fan   Leigh 1971

I'm a Fisher Maiden   Von Tilzer 1903

I'm a Fool about My Mama   Robison 1943

I'm a Fool for Loving You   Lewis 1936

I'm a Fool Little One   Hart 1928; Rodgers 1928

I'm a Fool Who Believed in You   Clarke 1914; Leslie 1914

I'm a Fugitive from a Chain Letter Gang   Caesar 1935; Lerner, Sammy 1935

I'm a Gambler   Leslie 1935; Monaco 1935

I'm a Genius Too   Leigh 1976

I'm a Gigolo   Porter 1929

I'm a Girl with Too Much Heart   Merrill 1978

I'm a Good Girl, Dammit   Gordon 1932; Revel 1932

I'm a Grand Street Boy   Edwards 1925; Johnson, Howard 1925

I'm a Great Big Baby   Blake 1979; Razaf 1979

I'm a Gypsy   Bullock 1938; Kalmar 1930; Ruby 1930; Spina 1938

I'm a Happy Guy   Bergman 1956

I'm a Happy Married Man   Berlin 1910; Snyder 1910

I'm a Happy-Go-Lucky Fellow   Washington 1940

I'm a Highway Gentleman   Robin 1927

I'm a Hundred Percent for You   Mills 1934; Oakland 1934; Parish 1934

I'm a King   Rome 1940

I'm a Ladies Home Companion   Hanley 1921

I'm a Lawyer   Smith, Harry B. 1906; Smith, Robert B. 1907

I'm a Little Big Shot Now   Dixon 1935; Wrubel 1935

I'm a Little Bit Afraid of You Broadway   Von Tilzer 1913

I'm a Little Bit Fonder of You Than of Myself   Caesar 1925, 1927

I'm a Little Blackbird Looking for a Bluebird   Clarke 1924; Johnston 1924; Meyer 1924, 1926; Turk 1924

I'm a Little Coconut (Swingin' on a Coconut Tree)   Baer 1966

I'm a Little Jail Bird Looking for a Love Bird Like You   Gordon 1925

I'm a Little Moon Mad   Dixon 1936

I'm a Little Moon-Mad   Henderson 1936

I'm a Little Movie Queen   Schwartz, Jean 1926

I'm a Little Negative Looking for a Positive   Bryan 1929

I'm a Little Tired Baby   Coots 1955

I'm a Little Too Old to Dance   Conrad 1926; Kahn 1926

I'm a Little Wabbit in Da Sunshine   David, Mack 1941

I'm a Lonesome Little Raindrop   Hanley 1920

I'm a Lonesome Little Waltz   Fisher 1921; Schwartz, Jean 1921

I'm a Lonesome Melody   Meyer 1915; Young, Joe 1915

I'm a Lonesome Romeo   Goetz 1912

I'm a Loser in the Game of Love   Coslow 1920

I'm a Lover   Spina 1977

I'm a Lover of Paree   Rainger 1933; Robin 1933

I'm a Married Man   Carroll 1910

I'm a Member of the Midnight Crew   Jerome 1909; Schwartz, Jean 1909

I'm a Musical Magical Man   Cahn 1937

I'm a Nurse for Aching Hearts   Buck 1915

I'm a One Girl Man   Cohan 1928

I'm a One-Man Girl   Robin 1926

I'm a One-Man Mama   Coslow 1923; Donaldson 1923

I'm a Part of You   Dietz 1934; Schwartz, Arthur 1934

I'm a Person Too   Coleman 1974

I'm a Pickford that Nobody Picked   Carroll 1925; Freed, Arthur 1925

I'm a Poached Egg   Gershwin, George 1964; Gershwin, Ira 1964

I'm a Poor Unhappy Maid   Jerome 1903; Schwartz, Jean 1903

I'm a Popular Man   Cohan 1907

I'm a Prize   Kern 1923

I'm a Queen in My Own Domain   Hart 1934; Rodgers 1934

I'm a Red Hot Cradle Snatcher   Robin 1926

I'm a Red Hot Hot-House Flower   Dixon 1927; Woods 1927

I'm a Rough Man, I'm a Tough Man   Romberg 1917

I'm a Ruler of a South Sea Island   Arlen 1952; Blane 1953

I'm a Sailor   Schwartz, Jean 1942

I'm a Seeker of Beauty   Coslow 1933, 1934; Johnston 1934, 1935

I'm a Simple Hearted Man   Robin 1930; Whiting 1930

I'm a Singer   Cahn 1933

I'm a Sinner   Lewis 1955; Meyer 1955

I'm a Slave, a Slave to Love   Friend 1930; Monaco 1930

I'm a Slave to You   David, Mack 1948

I'm a Sleuth   Adamson 1963; Fain 1963

I'm a Society Bud   Kalmar 1923; Ruby 1923

I'm a Star   Merrill 1978

I'm a Star of the Cinema   Oakland 1960

I'm a Statesman   Buck 1914

I'm a Stationary Woman Lookin' for a Permanent Man   Razaf 1930

I'm a Strange Little Girl Today   Evans 1954; Livingston, Jay 1954

I'm a Stranger Here Myself   Leigh 1965; Merrill 1958; Weill 1943

I'm a Stranger in My Own Home Town   Oakland 1938;
   Silver 1919
I'm a Stranger to Myself   Bergman 1962
I'm a Swingin' Dingin' Daddy   Mills 1937
I'm a Texas Boy   Cahn 1958; Van Heusen 1958
I'm a Traveling Salesman (For the U.S.A.)   Robison 1954
I'm a Twelve O'Clock Fellow (In a Nine O'Clock
   Town)   Kalmar 1917; Von Tilzer 1917
I'm a Vamp from East Broadway   Berlin 1920; Kalmar 1920;
   Ruby 1920
I'm a Very Different Girl   Atteridge 1918; Romberg 1918
I'm a Very Good Sailor on Land   Johnson, J. Rosamond
   1904
I'm a Very Lucky Boy   Martin 1958
I'm a Woman   Lane 1979; Lerner, Alan Jay 1979
I'm a Woman of Importance   Jerome 1905; Schwartz, Jean
   1905
I'm a Wonderful Man in Yonkers   Jerome 1911
I'm a Yank Full of Thankfulness   Fain 1938
I'm a Yiddish Cowboy   Leslie 1908
I'm About to Be a Mother (Who Could Ask for Anything
   More?)   Gershwin, George 1931; Gershwin, Ira 1931
I'm About to Become a Lover   Duke 1955
I'm Above All That   Sondheim Date Unknown
I'm A-Comin' A-Courtin', Corabelle   Wrubel 1947
I'm Afraid   Caesar 1930; Hart 1940; Rodgers 1940
I'm Afraid I Can't Get Out Tonight Marie   Hanley 1930
I'm Afraid I Love You   Porter 1944
I'm Afraid I'm Beginning to Love You   Brown, Lew 1913
I'm Afraid It's Love   Comden and Green 1944; Fisher 1938
I'm Afraid of Myself   Lawrence 1941; Silver 1941
I'm Afraid of the World Without You   Kahal 1932
I'm Afraid of You   Bryan 1910; Cobb 1921; Edwards 1921;
   Egan 1930; Eliscu 1930; Freed, Ralph 1939, 1943;
   Rainger 1930; Schwartz, Arthur 1930
I'm Afraid of You Tonight   Dubin 1942; Friend 1942
I'm Afraid, Pretty Maid, I'm Afraid   Berlin 1912
I'm Afraid, Sweetheart, I Love You   Porter 1948
I'm Afraid that Ev'rything's All Right   Coots 1929
I'm Afraid the Masquerade Is Over   Magidson 1938; Wrubel
   1938
I'm Afraid to Be Alone   Howard, Joseph E. 1909
I'm Afraid to Come Home in the Dark   Williams 1907
I'm Afraid to Go Home in the Dark   Smith, Robert B. 1907
I'm Afraid to Like You too Much   Mills 1948
I'm Afraid to Love You   Coots 1953
I'm Afraid to Remember   Caesar 1948
I'm Afraid to Sleep Alone   Bryan 1909
I'm Afraid to Waltz with You   Coslow 1931, 1932
I'm Afraid to Waltz with You (Vals Ritmo)   Coslow 1930
I'm After Mme. Tetrazinni's Job   Edwards 1909
I'm Against It   Kalmar 1932; Ruby 1932
I'm Against Rhythm   Dietz 1937; Schwartz, Arthur 1937
I'm Alive and Kickin'   Rainger 1941; Robin 1941
I'm All a Twitter (And All A-Twirl)   Robin 1929; Whiting
   1929
I'm All A-Tremble Over You   Loesser 1939
I'm All A-Twitter Over You   Brown, Nacio Herb 1943; Robin
   1943
I'm All Bound 'Round with the Mason Dixon Line   Lewis
   1917; Schwartz, Jean 1917; Young, Joe 1917
I'm All Burned Up   Dubin 1929
I'm All Burned Up Over the Firemen   Johnson, Howard
   1930
I'm All Dressed Up With a Broken Heart   Fisher 1931

I'm All Excited   Harbach 1921
I'm All for You   Goetz 1911
I'm All In   Alter 1934
I'm All O.K. with K. and E.   Cohan 1909
I'm All Right   Harbach 1910
I'm All Thine   Smith, Harry B. 1911; Smith, Robert B. 1911
I'm All Upset About You   Gilbert 1925
I'm All Wrapped Up in a Bundle of Love   Fisher 1930
I'm All Wrapped Up in You   Adamson 1931; Gordon 1931;
   Revel 1931
I'm All Yours   Leigh 1976; Styne 1976
(Doctor) I'm Allergic to Love   Howard, Bart 1956
I'm Allergic to You   Drake 1954
I'm Alone   Hammerstein 1932; Kern 1932
I'm Alone Because I Love You   Young, Joe 1930
I'm Alone but Never Lonely   Hoffman 1954
I'm Alone, That's Where I Am   David, Hal 1976
I'm Always Chasing Rainbows   Carroll 1918; Johnson,
   Howard 1939
I'm Always Doing Something I Don't Want to Do   Herbert
   1906
I'm Always Falling in Love with the Other Fellow's
   Girl   Caesar 1920; Meyer 1920
I'm Always in the Mood for You   Coots 1937; Davis 1937
I'm Always Just a Little Bit Not Just Right   Donaldson 1925;
   Kahn 1925
I'm Always Misunderstood   Herbert 1905
I'm Always on the Wrong Side of the Right Girl   Lewis 1931
I'm Always Romantic (But You're Always Hungry)   Webster
   1952
I'm Always Stuttering   Mitchell 1922
I'm Always Thinking of Georgia   Monaco 1917
I'm Always Thinking of Someone Who's Never Thinking of
   Me   Donaldson 1925; Kahn 1925
I'm Amazed at You   Loesser 1942; Spina 1942
I'm an Anaesthetic Dancer   Porter 1919
I'm an Honorary Member of the Patsy Club   Sterling 1910;
   Von Tilzer 1910
I'm an Indian Assassin   Johnson, Howard 1920
I'm an Indian Too   Berlin 1946
I'm an International Sweetheart   Yellen 1930
I'm an Old Cowhand   Mercer 1936
I'm an Old Fashioned Guy   Ager 1930; Yellen 1930
I'm an Old Spanish Customer   Russell 1949
I'm an Ordinary Man   Lerner, Alan Jay 1956; Loewe 1956
I'm an Unemployed Sweetheart Looking for Somebody to
   Love   Leslie 1931; Monaco 1931; Washington 1931
I'm Arrangin' for Changin' Your Name   Baer 1926; Gilbert
   1926
I'm Arranging for Changing the Key   Egan 1923; Whiting
   1923
I'm as Lonesome as the Lonesome Pine   Bryan 1927
I'm As Ready As I'll Ever Be   Cahn 1947; Styne 1947
I'm Askin' Ye (Ain't It the Truth)   Fisher 1936
I'm Asking Ya, Ain't It de Truth   Norworth 1922
I'm at Home in Any Town but My Home Town   Caesar
   1925; Egan 1925; Whiting 1925
I'm at the Mercy of Love   Coots 1936; Davis 1936
I'm A'Tingle, I'm A'Glow   Robin 1948; Styne 1948
I'm Away from It All   Lawrence 1957
I'm Away from the World when I'm Away from You   Clare
   1927; Pollack 1927
I'm Awfully Afraid of Girls   Kahn 1910
I'm Awfully Glad I Met You   Meyer 1909
I'm Awfully Strong for You   Cohan 1908

I'm Back in Circulation   Fields 1959; Porter 1938

I'm Back in Love   Strouse 1993

I'm Back in Love Again   Friend 1927

I'm Bashful   Merrill 1950

I'm Beginning to Miss You   Berlin 1949

I'm Beginning to See the Light   Ellington 1944

I'm Betting on You   Akst 1935; Brown, Lew 1935

I'm Between Two Fires   Stept 1934; Washington 1934

I'm Betwixt and Between   Cahn 1947; Styne 1947

I'm Bidding My Buddy Good-Bye   Dixon 1931; Woods 1931

I'm Blue for My Little Gray Home   Fisher 1924

I'm Blue for You   Sherman 1962

I'm Blue for You Blonde   Fisher 1930

I'm Blue for You New Orleans   Akst 1929; Clarke 1929

I'm Blue (I Wish I Was Dead)   Comden and Green 1944

I'm Blue Too   Merrill 1967

I'm Bound for Heaven   Adamson 1935; Lane 1935

I'm Breakin' My Back (Puttin' Up a Front for You)   Wrubel 1950

I'm Brilliant   Silver 1922

I'm Bringing a Red, Red Rose   Donaldson 1928; Kahn 1928

I'm Broke   Hart 1921; Rodgers 1921

I'm Bubbling Over   Gordon 1937; Revel 1937

I'm Bugs Over You   Buck 1923

I'm Building a Sailboat of Dreams   Friend 1939

I'm Building Castles Again   Coots 1960

I'm Building Up to an Awful Let Down   Mercer 1935

I'm Burning for You   Coslow 1932; Johnston 1932

I'm Buying a Bond for My Baby   Gilbert 1942; McHugh 1942

I'm Called the King   Duke Date Unknown

I'm Calling You from Las Vegas   Brown, Nacio Herb 1959

I'm Calm   Sondheim 1962

I'm Captain Cholly Chumley of the Guards   Herbert 1897; Smith, Harry B. 1897

I'm Checking Out — Goom Bye   Ellington 1939

I'm Choosin' a Tune About June   Coots 1929

I'm Clean   Styne Date Unknown

I'm Coming at Your Call   Romberg 1924

I'm Coming Back   Brown, A. Seymour 1911

I'm Coming Back in Springtime   Yellen 1914

I'm Coming Back to California, That's Where I Belong   Brennan 1916

I'm Coming Home   Hammerstein 1932; Kern 1932

I'm Coming Home With a Skate On   Berlin 1915

I'm Cookin' with Gas   Mercer 1942

I'm Counting on You   Monaco 1931; Oakland 1934; Washington 1931

I'm Crazy About My Baby, and My Baby's Crazy 'Bout Me   Waller 1931

I'm Crazy about Somebody   Buck 1920

I'm Crazy About the Charleston   Hart 1926; Rodgers 1926

I'm Crazy 'bout Somebody   Buck 1912

I'm Crazy 'bout the Turkey Trot   Meyer 1911

I'm Crazy 'Bout You Daisy   Meyer 1908

(Oh You Fool) I'm Crazy for You   Silver 1924; Turk 1924

I'm Crazy for Your Cannibal Love   Bryan 1930

I'm Crazy Over Every Girl in France   Bryan 1917

I'm Crazy Over You   Brown, A. Seymour 1909

I'm Crazy to Be a Jazz Band Leader   Coots 1919

I'm Crazy to Go on the Stage   Cobb 1904; Edwards 1904

I'm Crazy When the Band Begins to Play   Jerome 1909; Schwartz, Jean 1909; Smith, Harry B. 1908

I'm Crooning a Love Song to Heaven   Hoffman 1932

I'm Crying Just for You   Monaco 1913

I'm Cuckoo Over You   Mitchell 1921

I'm Cuckoo-Crazy 'Bout You   Baer 1950

I'm Cured   Buck 1914; Lewis 1915; Meyer 1915

I'm Cynical   Rome 1940

I'm Dancin' on a Rainbow   Brown, Nacio Herb 1933; Freed, Arthur 1933

I'm Dancing To Be Near You   Bryan 1936

I'm Dancing with Empty Arms   Drake 1954

I'm Dancing with the Mamas with the Moolah   Fain 1941; Kahal 1941; Yellen 1941

I'm Dependable   Raye 1937

I'm Depending on You   Mills 1966

I'm Designed for Love   Schwartz, Arthur 1930

I'm Dining with Elsa   Porter 1920

I'm Doin' It for Defense   Arlen 1942

I'm Doin' Okay in My Own Way   Merrill 1971; Styne 1971

I'm Doin' that Thing   Fields 1930; McHugh 1930

I'm Doin' What I'm Doin' for Love   Ager 1929; Yellen 1929

I'm Doing It for Defense   Mercer 1942

I'm Down in Honolulu Looking Them Over   Berlin 1916

I'm Down to My Last Dream   Coots 1945

I'm Dreaming of a Bygone Day   Cobb 1929; Edwards 1929

I'm Drunk with Love   Revel 1930

I'm Dying for You   Smith, Harry B. 1910

I'm Easy to Get Along With   Baer 1946

I'm Facing the Music   Pollack 1934; Webster 1934

I'm Falling in Love   Caesar 1931

I'm Falling in Love with Someone   Herbert 1910

I'm Falling in Love with You Tonight   Davis 1961

I'm Fancy Free   Smith, Harry B. 1910

I'm Fascinating   Adams 1962; Strouse 1962

I'm Feathering a Nest (for a Little Bluebird)   Ager 1929; Yellen 1929

I'm Feelin' Blue   Fields 1931; McHugh 1931

I'm Feelin' Blue 'Cause I've Got Nobody   Fields 1930; McHugh 1930

I'm Feelin' High   Dietz 1934; Donaldson 1934; Freed, Ralph 1937; Lane 1937

I'm Feelin' Like a Million   Brown, Nacio Herb 1937; Freed, Arthur 1937

I'm Feeling Blue for Mammy Lou   Pollack 1923

I'm Feeling My Way Thru' the Fog   Johnson, Howard 1930

I'm Flirting with You   Friend 1926

I'm Flyin' High   Silver 1928

I'm Flying   Leigh 1954

I'm Flying High   Brown, Lew 1930; DeSylva 1930; Henderson 1930

I'm for You One Hundred Percent   Rose 1931

I'm for You, You're for Me   Brennan 1929

I'm Forever Falling in Love with Someone   Leslie 1932; Monaco 1924

I'm Forgetting Myself for You   Caesar 1932

I'm Fresh from the Coutnry   Hammerstein 1922

I'm from Chicago   Romberg 1915

I'm from Dalius, Texas   Carmichael 1950

I'm from Hollywood   Oakland 1960

I'm from Missouri   Lane 1951; Lerner, Alan Jay 1951

I'm from Ohio   Brennan 1918

I'm Full of Love for Her, She's Full of Love for Me   Rose 1926; Woods 1926

I'm Full of the Devil   Fields 1933; McHugh 1933

I'm Gettin' a New Deal from that Old Gal of Mine   Turk 1933

I'm Gettin' Tired of My Tired Man   Snyder 1930

I'm Getting Better!   Hart Date Unknown; Rodgers Date Unknown

I'm Getting Married in the Morning (I'm Gonna Get Married in the Morning)   Carmichael 1946

I'm Getting Mine   Coots 1926

I'm Getting Myself Ready for You   Porter 1930

I'm Getting Nowhere Fast   Blake 1954

I'm Getting Seasick   Schwartz, Jean 1905

I'm Getting Sentimental Over You   Washington 1932

I'm Getting Superstitious About Delicious You   Spina 1931

I'm Getting Tired So I Can Sleep   Berlin 1942

I'm Getting Used to a Broken Heart   Bryan 1952

I'm Getting What I Want   Robin 1932; Whiting 1932

I'm Glad for Your Sake but I'm Sorry for Mine   Lawrence 1938

I'm Glad I Said I'm Sorry   Coots 1931

I'm Glad I Took that Second Look at You (inst.)   Gordon 1959; Revel 1959

I'm Glad I Waited   Adamson 1930; Youmans 1930

I'm Glad I Waited for You   Cahn 1946; Styne 1946

I'm Glad I'm from Dixie   Bryan 1919; Schwartz, Jean 1919

I'm Glad I'm Happy   Motzan 1922

I'm Glad I'm Here   Heyman 1931

I'm Glad I'm Home Again   Carroll 1910

I'm Glad I'm Irish   Leslie 1909

I'm Glad I'm Leaving   Styne 1953

I'm Glad I'm Married   Norworth 1908

I'm Glad I'm Not a Man   Duke 1956

I'm Glad I'm Not Young Anymore   Lerner, Alan Jay 1958; Loewe 1958

I'm Glad I'm on the Bum   Mills 1929; Parish 1929

I'm Glad I'm Single   Brown, A. Seymour 1909; Dietz 1961; Schwartz, Arthur 1961

I'm Glad I'm Spanish   Atteridge 1921; Romberg 1921

I'm Glad I'm Your Woman   David, Hal 1978

I'm Glad It Was Only a Dream   Mills 1929

I'm Glad It's Me (inst.)   Stept 1936

I'm Glad It's Raining   Dietz 1934; Schwartz, Arthur 1934

I'm Glad My Wife's in Europe   Johnson, Howard 1914

I'm Glad to Get Back to New York   Smith, Harry B. 1908

I'm Glad to See You Back   Warren Date Unknown

I'm Glad You Met Me   Heyman 1932

I'm Glad You're Sorry   Whiting 1916

I'm Glad You're Sorry, Ain't You Sorry I'm Glad   Stept 1953

I'm Goin' Huntin'   Waller 1927

I'm Goin' Out If Lizzie Comes In   Brown, Lew 1925; DeSylva 1925; Henderson 1925

I'm Goin' Places   Cahn Date Unknown; Duke Date Unknown

I'm Goin' 'Round in Circles   Spina 1950

I'm Goin' Shoppin' with You   Dubin 1935; Warren 1935

I'm Goin' South   Woods 1921

I'm Goin' to Do What I Please   Bryan 1909; Snyder 1909

I'm Goin to Lose Myself when I Find Myself in My Sweetie's Arms   Akst 1924

I'm Goin' to Settle Down Outside of London Town, When I'm Dry, Dry, Dry   Monaco 1917

I'm Goin' to Stay Right Here in Town   Bryan 1913

I'm Goin' to Wait till the Right One Comes Along   Buck 1925

I'm Going Away   Kern 1913; Smith, Harry B. 1913

I'm Going Back   Comden and Green 1956; DeSylva 1924; Gershwin, George 1924; Styne 1956

I'm Going Back Again to Old Nebraska   Revel 1928; Sissle 1928

I'm Going Back to Dixie   Atteridge 1912

I'm Going Back to Dixie (I Want to Be in Dixie)   Berlin 1912; Snyder 1912

I'm Going Back to Kentucky Sue   Brown, Lew 1912

I'm Going Back to Old Virginia   Buck Date Unknown

I'm Going Back to the Farm   Berlin 1915

I'm Going Down to Dance at Clancey's   Conrad 1939; Magidson 1939

I'm Going Down to Tennessee   Carroll 1912

I'm Going in for Love   Porter 1938

I'm Going North   Loesser 1943; Schwartz, Arthur 1943

I'm Going on a Long Vacation   Berlin 1910; Snyder 1910

I'm Going Right Along   Waller 1924

I'm Going Right Back to Chicago   Williams 1906

I'm Going South   Silver 1921

I'm Going South with the Birds This Winter   DePaul 1958; Raye 1958

I'm Going Spanish Now   Egan 1930

I'm Going Steady with a Memory   Ruby 1963

I'm Going to Adopt a Little Boy   Norworth 1945

I'm Going to Dance at Your Wedding   Caesar 1924; Conrad 1924; Harbach 1924

I'm Going to Find a Girl   Kern 1917

I'm Going To Get a Girl Named Ivy, 'Cause Ivy Always Clings   Bryan 1914

I'm Going to Hang My Hat on Broadway   Howard, Joseph E. 1947

I'm Going to Leave You   Howard, Joseph E. 1905

I'm Going to Let the Whole World Know I Love You   Edwards 1914

I'm Going to Make You Love Me   Brown, A. Seymour 1914

I'm Going to Marry a Nobleman   Cohan 1908

I'm Going to Meet Minnie Tonight   Carroll 1913; Cobb 1913; Edwards 1923; Johnson, Howard 1929; Smith, Robert B. 1923

I'm Going to Scotland   Webster 1957

I'm Going to Settle Down   Schwartz, Jean 1918

I'm Going to Spend My Honeymoon in Dixie   Brown, Lew 1913

I'm Going to Steal Some Other Fellow's Girl (If I Can't Find One of My Own)   Brown, Lew 1911

I'm Going to Steal the Moon   Howard, Joseph E. 1908

I'm Going to the Ball (We're Going to the Ball)   Brooks 1960

I'm Going Up the Girl's House Tonight   Baer 1926; Dixon 1926

I'm Going Way Back Home and Have a Wonderful Time   Jerome 1916; Schwartz, Jean 1916

I'm Gone Before I Go   Carroll 1916

I'm Gonna Ask the Moon a Little Favor   Parish 1950

I'm Gonna Be Busy Dating You, Darling, Monday thru Sunday   Baer 1952

I'm Gonna Borrow a Sweet Ma-ma Because Somebody Borrowed Mine   Fisher 1922

I'm Gonna Break that Mason-Dixon Line Until I Get to that Gal of Mine   Bryan 1919; Schwartz, Jean 1919

I'm Gonna Bring a Watermelon to My Girl Tonight   Conrad 1924; Rose 1924

I'm Gonna Buy a One-Way Ticket to a Little One-Horse Town   Parish 1922

I'm Gonna Charleston Back to Charleston   Turk 1925

I'm Gonna Do It If I Like It   Akst 1921; Buck 1921

I'm Gonna Do It If I Like It (And I Like It)   Berlin 1921

I'm Gonna Fall in Love   Waller 1938

I'm Gonna Fall in Love, I Feel It in My Bones   Akst 1935; Brown, Lew 1935; Henderson 1935

I'm Gonna Get Him   Berlin 1956

I'm Gonna Getcha   Revel 1959

I'm Gonna Go Fishin'   Ellington 1959

I'm Gonna Go Go Go — To Chicago in 1933   Caesar 1933;
   Friend 1933

I'm Gonna Hang Up Mommy's Stocking Instead of Mine on
   Christmas Night   Coots 1953

I'm Gonna Hate Myself in the Morning   Adamson 1945;
   McHugh 1945

I'm Gonna Hit the Number Today   Johnson, James P. 1938

I'm Gonna Knock, Knock, Knock on the Old Front
   Door   Hanley 1922

I'm Gonna Lasso a Dream   David, Mack 1946; Hoffman
   1946; Livingston, Jerry 1946

I'm Gonna Live Till I Die   Hoffman 1950

I'm Gonna Lock Myself in Dixieland and Throw Away the
   Key   Schwartz, Jean 1921

I'm Gonna Love You More in 1933   Washington 1933

I'm Gonna Love You While I Can   Mills 1965

I'm Gonna Make a Fool Out of April   Heyman 1950; Young,
   Victor 1950

I'm Gonna Make Haste (To Where the Sun Shines in
   Virginia)   Johnston 1926; Turk 1926

I'm Gonna Make Hay While the Sun Shines in
   Virginia   Lewis 1916; Young, Joe 1916

I'm Gonna Make Things Merry for My Mary in
   Maryland   Lewis 1922; Meyer 1922; Young, Joe 1922

I'm Gonna Make You Love Me   Spina 1967

I'm Gonna March in April with May   Freed, Arthur 1930

I'm Gonna Meet My Sweetie Now   Davis 1927

I'm Gonna Move to the Outskirts of Town   Razaf 1942

I'm Gonna Pick Myself a Mary Where the Huckleberries
   Grow   Bryan 1925; Silver 1925

I'm Gonna Pin My Medal on the Girl I Left Behind
   Me   Berlin 1918

I'm Gonna Pop My Papa   Johnston 1926; Turk 1926

I'm Gonna Ring the Bell Tonight   Cahn 1952; Duke 1952

I'm Gonna Salt Away Some Sugar (For My Sugar and
   Me)   Coots 1940

I'm Gonna See My Mother   DeSylva 1922; Gershwin,
   George 1922

I'm Gonna Sit Right Down and Write Myself a
   Letter   Ahlert 1935; Young, Joe 1935

I'm Gonna Sleep with One Eye Open (So I Can See You in
   My Dreams)   Parish 1954

I'm Gonna Specialize on You   Johnson, Howard 1929

I'm Gonna Spread My Wings (And Fly a Little)   Coots 1951

I'm Gonna Stay Awake All Night   Drake 1952

I'm Gonna Steal Somebody Else's Baby Cause Somebody
   Else Stole Mine   Davis 1923

I'm Gonna Take My Love Where I Find It   Coots 1964

I'm Gonna Take Possession of You   Coslow 1932; Eliscu
   1935

I'm Gonna Take Something from You   Razaf 1965

I'm Gonna Take What's Coming   Revel 1946

I'm Gonna Take You Dancin' (on Saturday Night)   Baer
   1942

I'm Gonna Take You Home Tonight to Meet the
   Family   Gilbert 1935

I'm Gonna Tell Your Fortune   Freed, Ralph 1965

I'm Gonna Tie a String Around My Finger   Wrubel 1949

I'm Gonna Tie Myself to Dixieland with the Mason-Dixon
   Line   Coots 1924; Mitchell 1924; Pollack 1924

I'm Gonna Tramp, Tramp, Tramp   DeSylva 1924; Woods
   1924

I'm Gonna Try   Oakland 1972

I'm Gonna Vote for Santa Claus   Hoffman 1952

I'm Gonna Wash That Man Right Outa My
   Hair   Hammerstein 1949; Rodgers 1949

I'm Gonna Worry   Howard, Bart 1984

I'm Gonna Write a Letter to Jesus   Robison 1964

I'm Good for Nothing Else but You   Edwards 1915

I'm Grateful   Drake 1954

I'm Grateful to You   Coots 1936; Davis 1936

I'm Great   Robin 1955; Styne 1955

I'm Grover   Duke 1930

I'm Growing Fonder of You   Meyer 1934; Young, Joe 1934

I'm Guilty   Evans 1945; Livingston, Jay 1945

I'm Hans Christian Andersen   Loesser 1952

I'm Happy about the Whole Thing   Mercer 1939; Warren
   1939

I'm Happy 'Cause I Was Wrong   Caesar 1929; Woods 1929

I'm Happy 'Cause I'm Lucky   Parish 1951

I'm Happy Darling, Dancing with You   Ahlert 1937; Lewis
   1937; Young, Joe 1937

I'm Happy Now   Turk 1924

I'm Happy Now that You're Gone   Von Tilzer 1927

I'm Happy to Know You're Happy   Hoffman 1950

I'm Happy to Know You're Happy with Someone
   Else   Bryan 1928

I'm Happy When You're Happy   Baer 1931; Davis 1931;
   Hoffman 1937; Lerner, Sammy 1937

I'm Happy when You're Jealous   Kalmar 1932; Ruby 1932

I'm Happy, You're Happy Since We Became
   Sweethearts   Clare 1927

I'm Happy-Go-Lucky and Free   Robin 1947

I'm Hard to Please   Hart 1930; Rodgers 1930

I'm Harold, I'm Harold   Romberg 1925

I'm Harry   Bergman 1976

I'm Havin' a Party   Carmichael 1957

I'm Having More Fun Since I'm Sixty   Yellen 1978

I'm Head Over Heels in Love   Caesar 1925

I'm Headed for Big Things   Arlen 1959; Mercer 1959

I'm Headin' for a Shotgun Weddin'   Friend 1948

I'm Headin' Home   Rome 1949

I'm Healthy Cause I'm Happy   Caesar 1947

I'm Hearin' from Erin   Gilbert 1917

I'm Here   Sondheim 1966; Strouse Date Unknown

I'm Here Again   Smith, Harry B. 1915

I'm Here Lawd!   Arlen 1941; Koehler 1941

I'm Here, Little Girls, I'm Here   Kern 1917

I'm His Mother   Bryan 1954

I'm Hittin' the Hot Spots   Adamson 1937; McHugh 1937

I'm Hitting a High Spot   Raye 1943

I'm Holding Heaven in My Arms   Drake 1945

I'm Holding My Head Up High   Pollack 1929

I'm Holding the World in My Arms   Sterling 1934

I'm Home   Adams 1954, 1966; Strouse 1954, 1966

I'm Home Again   Wrubel 1940

I'm Homesick   Sterling 1915; Von Tilzer 1915

I'm Hummin' — I'm Whistlin' — I'm Singin'   Gordon 1934;
   Revel 1934

I'm Hungry for Beautiful Girls   Fisher 1922; Rose 1922

I'm Hurtin'   Fain 1955

I'm in a Fog About You   Dixon 1938

I'm in a Happy Frame of Mind   Bloom 1938; Parish 1938

I'm in a Highly Emotional State   Coleman 1973; Fields 1973

I'm in a Jam with Baby   Koehler 1944

I'm in a Lazy Mood   Leslie 1943

I'm in a Loveable Mood Tonight   Coots 1940; De Lange
   1940

I'm in a Tree   Merrill 1971; Styne 1971

I'm in Another World   Ellington 1939; Mills 1939

I'm in Another World when I'm with You   Stept 1935; Washington 1935

I'm in Another World with You   Revel 1959

I'm in Dreamland   Lane 1938; Loesser 1938

I'm in Glory   Adamson 1941; McHugh 1941

I'm in Good Shape (For the Shape I'm In)   Revel 1941

I'm in Heaven, Campin' in Caroline   Livingston, Jerry 1937

I'm in Heaven when I'm in My Mother's Arms   Ager 1920; Johnson, Howard 1920

I'm in Love   Brennan 1929; Brown, Lew 1918; Cahn 1948; Conrad 1926; Harbach 1926; Kahn 1926; Mills 1936; Myrow 1936; Porter 1929; Romberg 1918; Russell 1958; Styne 1948

I'm in Love Again   Coleman 1964; Porter 1924

I'm in Love All Over Again   Fields 1935; McHugh 1935

I'm in Love at Last   Coots 1929

I'm in Love With a Beautiful Baby   Brown, Lew Date Unknown; Henderson Date Unknown

I'm in Love with a Boy   Sondheim Date Unknown

I'm in Love with a Certain One, Guess Who   Friend 1925; Turk 1925

I'm in Love with a Dame   Dietz 1943; Duke 1943

I'm in Love with a Jitterbug   Burke 1939; Monaco 1939

I'm in Love with a Lover   Cahn 1937

I'm in Love with a Soldier Boy   Porter 1943

I'm in Love with a Song   Coslow 1952

I'm in Love with a Tattooed Man   Coslow 1934; Johnston 1934

I'm in Love with a Tune   Rainger 1932

I'm in Love with a Voice on the Radio   Kahal 1931

I'm in Love with All the Girls I Know   Howard, Joseph E. 1909

I'm in Love with an Older Man   Fain 1967

I'm in Love with Gomer Pyle   Brooks 1966

I'm in Love with My Best Friend's Sweetheart   Raye 1953; Spina 1953

I'm in Love with My Top Sergeant   Dietz 1944; Duke 1944

I'm in Love with One of the Stars   Cohan 1909

I'm in Love with Someone   Stept 1927

I'm in Love with the Beautiful Bugs   Von Tilzer 1903

I'm in Love with the Honorable Mr. So and So   Coslow 1939

I'm in Love With the Man in the Moon   Bryan 1908; Snyder 1908

I'm in Love with the Mother of My Best Girl   Kahn 1913

I'm in Love with the Prince of Wales   Conrad 1924

I'm in Love with Two Sweethearts — Mary and Mother   Fisher 1927; Rose 1927

I'm in Love with Vienna   Hammerstein 1938

I'm in Love with You   DePaul 1950; Edwards 1910; Lewis 1919; Livingston, Jerry 1973; Oakland 1960; Raye 1960; Smith, Harry B. 1910; Snyder 1919; Spina 1967; Young, Joe 1919

I'm in Love with You That's Why   Dixon 1926; Henderson 1926

I'm in My Glory   Adamson 1938; McHugh 1938

I'm in No Mood for Music   Loesser 1941

I'm in Pursuit of Happiness   Robin 1957; Styne 1957

I'm in Seventh Heaven   Brown, Lew 1929; DeSylva 1929; Henderson 1929

I'm in that Mood   Brown, Lew 1931; Henderson 1931

I'm in the Market for You   Hanley 1930

I'm in the Middle of a Muddle   David, Mack 1950; Hoffman 1950; Livingston, Jerry 1950

I'm in the Mood for Love   Fields 1935; McHugh 1935

I'm in the Mood for Solitude   Livingston, Jerry 1945

I'm in the Mood for You   Parish 1932

I'm in the Pink   Lane 1938; Loesser 1938

I'm in Training for You   Baer 1930; Gilbert 1930

I'm Innocent   Silver 1956

I'm Invited to a Wedding   Coots 1953

I'm Irish   Mitchell 1919

I'm Jealous   Akst 1923; Davis 1923; Spina 1977

I'm Jealous of Your Time   Johnson, J. Rosamond 1950

I'm Just a Bundle of Sunshine   Gershwin, George 1929; Gershwin, Ira 1929; Kahn 1929

I'm Just a Fool in Love with You   Conrad 1930; Kahn 1932; Meyer 1931; Mitchell 1931

I'm Just a Fool with a Fantasy   Robin 1964

I'm Just a Good Man   Carroll 1918

I'm Just a Jitterbug   David, Mack 1938; Livingston, Jerry 1938

I'm Just a Little Bit Confused   Warren 1956

I'm Just a Little Boy Blue   Washington 1934; Young, Victor 1934

I'm Just a Little Ol' Cowboy   Johnson, Howard 1930

I'm Just a Little Olive   Gordon 1932; Revel 1932

I'm Just a Little Sparrow   Fain 1960; Webster 1960

I'm Just a Lonely Little Kid   Norworth 1922

I'm Just a Lucky So and So   David, Mack 1944; Ellington 1944

I'm Just a Sentimental Fool   Hammerstein 1928; Romberg 1928

I'm Just a Sentimental Soul   Leslie 1932

I'm Just a Simple Girl   Blake 1955

I'm Just a Slave to Your Crave   Cahn 1935

I'm Just a Stranger in Town   Eliscu 1943; Gorney 1943

I'm Just a Weakie   Styne 1940

I'm Just an Old Jay from the U.S.A.   Von Tilzer 1918

I'm Just Drifting Along   Stept 1927

I'm Just in the Mood Tonight   Leslie 1929

I'm Just Like a Wheel that Is Turning, By the Old Mill Stream   Fisher 1919

I'm Just Nuts About You   Rome 1937

I'm Just Pinin' for You   Williams 1910

I'm Just Simply Full of Jazz   Blake 1921; Sissle 1921

I'm Just Taking My Time   Comden and Green 1961; Styne 1961

I'm Just that Way   Akst 1934; Turk 1934

I'm Just too Mean to Cry   Parish 1921

I'm Just Wild About Animal Crackers   Coslow 1926

I'm Just Wild About Harry   Blake 1921; Sissle 1921

I'm Just Wild about Horses, and Horses Are Wild About Me   Silver 1930

I'm Just Wild About You   Razaf 1929; Waller 1929

I'm Just Wonderin' Who   Mills 1929

I'm Ka Razy for You   Rose 1928

I'm Keeping Myself Available for You   McHugh 1979

I'm Keeping those Keepsakes You Gave Me   Ahlert 1935

I'm King Again   Friend 1935

I'm Kissing Her Now   Bryan 1961

I'm Kooky Over You   Blane 1964; Martin 1964

I'm Late   Fain 1951

I'm Laughin'   Brown, Lew 1934; Gorney 1934

I'm Laughin' at Love   Spina 1977

I'm Laughing at You   Conrad 1922; Kahn 1922

I'm Laughing Up My Sleeve Ha-Ha-Ha-Ha-Ha   Lawrence 1937

I'm Laying Away a Buck   Cahn 1944; Styne 1944

I'm Learning a Lot from You   Fields 1930; McHugh 1930

I'm Learning Something Every Day   Norworth 1908; Smith, Harry B. 1908

I'm Leavin' My Troubles Behind   Mills 1928

I'm Leaving the Whole Thing to You   Coots 1929

I'm Leaving You   Coleman 1996

I'm Left Out in the Cold   Gilbert 1932; Hanley 1932; Silver 1932

I'm Left with an Old Love Song   Meyer 1950

I'm Like a Bird (French Gergerette)   Adamson 1939

I'm Like a Bird with a Broken Wing   Clare 1927; Pollack 1927

I'm Like a Fish Out of Water   Mercer 1938; Revel 1943; Webster 1943; Whiting 1938

I'm Like a New Broom   Fields 1951; Schwartz, Arthur 1951

I'm Like a Sailor Home from the Sea   Dietz 1929; Schwartz, Arthur 1929

I'm Like the Bluebird   Sondheim 1964

I'm Liking This   David, Hal 1958

I'm Livin' in a Great Big Way   Fields 1935; McHugh 1935

I'm Living a Day at a Time   Davis 1949; Silver 1949

I'm Living from Kiss to Kiss   Drake 1943

I'm Living My Life for You   Washington 1932

I'm Living on Love   Young, Joe 1933

I'm Lonely   Hammerstein 1930; Romberg 1930

I'm Lonely when I'm Alone   Friml 1919; Harbach 1919

I'm Lonely (Without You)   Warren 1926

I'm Lonesome for You   Howard, Joseph E. 1905

I'm Lonesome in Your Arms   Bryan 1931

I'm Lonesome Virginia   David, Mack 1945

I'm Longing for a Girl Named Mary   Stept 1926

I'm Longing for My Carolina Home   Fisher 1939

I'm Longing for Someone to Love Me   Howard, Joseph E. 1917

I'm Lookin' for Another Handy Man   Arlen 1933; Koehler 1933

I'm Lookin' for the Guy that Stole My Gal   Freed, Ralph 1952; Hoffman 1952

I'm Lookin' Forward to Goin' Back Home   Baer 1934; Lewis 1934

I'm Looking at Tomorrow   Revel 1952

I'm Looking Down at the Moon   Schwartz, Arthur 1948

I'm Looking for a Certain Little Girl   Edwards 1910

I'm Looking for a Daddy Long Legs   Berlin 1922

I'm Looking for a Financier   Harbach 1910

I'm Looking for a Girl Like Mother   Kahn 1916

I'm Looking for a Rainbow (inst.)   Waller 1945

I'm Looking for a Warm Spot   Leslie 1915

I'm Looking for an Honest Face   Wrubel 1959

I'm Looking for an Irish Husband   Kern 1913

I'm Looking for My Love   Johnson, James P. 1958

I'm Looking for Old Broadway (I'm Looking for the Great White Way)   Buck 1917

I'm Looking for One Honey   Edwards 1913

I'm Looking for Someone to Look After Me   Parish 1925

I'm Looking for Someone's Heart   Atteridge 1915; Romberg 1915

I'm Looking for that Man of Mine   Davis 1925

I'm Looking for Tulips to Kiss My Troubles Away   Mills 1928

I'm Looking Into Heaven (When I'm Looking in Your Eyes)   Johnson, Howard 1929

I'm Looking Over a Four Leaf Clover   Dixon 1927; Woods 1927

I'm Lord Knows Who   Atteridge 1915; Carroll 1915; Romberg 1915

I'm Losing You   Lewis 1929; Young, Joe 1929

I'm Lost for Words   De Lange 1935

I'm Lost, in Dreams of You   Johnson, J. Rosamond 1953

I'm Lost without You, Sally   Ager 1932; Lewis 1932

I'm Lost Without You, Without You I'm Gone   Monaco 1920

I'm Ludwig Von Drake   Sherman 1961

I'm Mad About the Girl Next Door   Gordon 1953; Myrow 1953

I'm Mad About You   Koehler 1936; Stept 1936

I'm Mad at Me   Heyman 1931

I'm Madly in Love with a Dream Girl   Romberg 1917

I'm Madly in Love with You   Coots 1938; Davis 1938

I'm Makin' for Macon Tonight (I'm Makin' for Macon In Georgia)   Kalmar 1914

I'm Makin' Hay While the Sun Shines, By Makin' Hey Hey Under the Moon   Burke 1931

I'm Making a Bid for Popularity   Smith, Harry B. 1898

I'm Making a Play for You   Rainger 1940, 1941; Robin 1940, 1941

I'm Making Believe   Gordon 1944; Monaco 1944

I'm Marching Along with Time   Berlin 1938

I'm Marching Home to You   Silver 1929

I'm Married, I'm Single, I'm Divorced, I'm in Love   Atteridge 1918; Romberg 1918

I'm Mighty Glad I'm Living and That's All   Cohan 1904

I'm Mighty Proud of That Old Gang of Mine   Koehler 1942; Stept 1942

I'm Mighty Proud You're Mine   Alter 1921; Stept 1921

I'm Mighty Sweet on My Sweet Sweetie (She's Mighty Sweet on Me)   Johnson, Howard 1922

I'm Mighty Sweet on My Sweetie (She's Mighty Sweet on Me)   Baer 1922

I'm Missin' Mammy's Kissin'   Clare Date Unknown

I'm Missin' Mississippi   Donaldson 1941

I'm More than Satisfied   Lawrence 1931; Waller 1927

I'm Moving Away   Caesar 1925

I'm My Mama's Baby Boy   Turk 1921

I'm Myself   Burke 1981

I'm Naive   Merrill 1965; Styne 1965

I'm Needin' You   Young, Joe 1930

I'm Never Alone   Cahn 1959; Van Heusen 1959

I'm Never Blue Where the Grass Is Green   Coots 1932; Young, Joe 1932

I'm Never Gonna Kiss You (Till You Tell Me that You Love Me) (Andorinha Prata)   Hoffman 1958

I'm Never Gonna Tell   Hoffman 1957

I'm Never in Tune with You   Woods 1939

I'm Never Lonesome when I'm Alone   Fisher 1921

I'm Never too Busy for You   Hoffman 1936

I'm Nobody's Baby   Ager 1921; Davis 1921

I'm Not a Bit Superstitious   Herbert 1911

I'm Not a Well Man   Rome 1962

I'm Not Afraid Anymore   Sigman 1957

I'm Not Afraid (I Believe in America)   Berlin 1954

I'm Not Ashamed of You Molly, I Want You Just As You Are   Leslie 1914; Young, Joe 1914

I'm Not Blaming You   Davis 1952

I'm Not Complaining   Ahlert 1932; Gershwin, Ira 1938; Turk 1932; Weill 1938

I'm Not Finished Yet   Adams 1966; Strouse 1966

I'm Not Giving You Up   Wrubel 1951
I'm Not Good Enough for You   David, Mack 1942
I'm Not Having Any (This Year)   Raye 1945
I'm Not Hep to that Step (But I'll Dig It)   Mercer 1940
I'm Not His Sister Anymore   Duke 1968
I'm Not in Love Anymore (Acre Mentuer)   Webster 1967
I'm Not in Love with You   Friml 1921
I'm Not in Philadelphia   Adams 1962, 1996; Strouse 1962, 1996
I'm Not Just Anybody's Baby   Russell 1942
I'm Not Lettin' On   Monaco 1934; Young, Joe 1934
I'm Not Lonely   Bergman 1961
I'm Not Myself   Arlen 1934; Gershwin, Ira 1934; Harburg 1934
I'm Not Myself Anymore   Washington 1943
I'm Not Myself at All   Porter 1944
I'm Not Myself Today   Bullock 1938; Spina 1938
I'm Not Myself Tonight   David, Hal 1958
I'm Not Prepared   Berlin 1916
I'm Not So Bright   Martin 1948
I'm Not So Particular Now   Herbert 1907; Smith, Harry B. 1907
I'm Not So Very Sure   Stept 1953
I'm Not Sorry   Ager 1929; Yellen 1929
I'm Not Supposed to Be Blue, Blues   Russell 1957
I'm Not That Kind of Girl   Brown, Lew Date Unknown; Henderson Date Unknown; Smith, Harry B. 1908
I'm not the Girl   Merrill 1966
I'm Not the Kind of a Girl to Marry   Johnson, Howard 1966
I'm Not the Marryin' Kind   David, Mack 1962
I'm Not the Same   Oakland 1930
I'm Not too Sure of My L'Amour   Hoffman 1949
I'm Not Too Young to Dream   Davis 1959
I'm Not Worrying   Waller 1929
I'm Nothin' but a Dreamer   Merrill 1956
I'm Now Prepared to Tell the World It's You!   Razaf 1932; Waller 1932
I'm Nuts About Mutts   Dixon 1933; Woods 1933
I'm Nuts about You   Bryan 1910; Meyer 1910
I'm Nuts on You   Brennan 1930; Friml 1930
I'm Odd   Fain 1951
I'm Off of You   Harburg 1932
I'm Off the Downbeat   Arlen 1954; Gershwin, Ira 1954
I'm Off the Wagon   Carmichael 1940; Mercer 1940
I'm Oh So Lonesome Tonight   Merrill 1949
I'm Old Fashioned   Kern 1942; Mercer 1942
I'm Olga from the Volga   Gordon 1937; Revel 1937
I'm On a Diet of Love   Baer 1929; Gilbert 1929
I'm on a Green Branch Now   Coots 1944
I'm on a Long, Long Ramble Over There I'll Be Rambling with You   Lewis 1918; Young, Joe 1918
I'm on a Wild Goose Chase   Lawrence 1936
I'm on My Merry Way   Whiting 1927
I'm on My Own   Adamson 1931
I'm on My Way   Gershwin, George 1935; Lerner, Alan Jay 1951; Loewe 1951
I'm on My Way Home   Berlin 1926
I'm on My Way Special   Oakland 1952
I'm on My Way to Berlin   Coslow 1930
I'm on My Way to College   Cahn 1942; Styne 1942
I'm on My Way to Dreamland   Leslie 1925
I'm on My Way to Mandalay   Bryan 1913; Fisher 1913
I'm on My Way to Reno   Jerome 1910; Schwartz, Jean 1910
I'm on My Way to Rio   David, Mack 1947

I'm on Pins and Needles, 'Cause I'm Dead Stuck on You   Young, Joe 1932
I'm on the Crest of a Wave   Brown, Lew 1928; DeSylva 1928; Henderson 1928
I'm on the Gravy Train   Robison 1944
I'm on the Inside   Sherman 1995
I'm on the Jury   Kahn 1913
I'm on the Right Side of the Right Girl Now   Coots 1931; Davis 1931
I'm on the Road to Happiness   Coots 1929; Davis 1929
I'm on Your Side   Lerner, Alan Jay 1974; Loewe 1974
I'm One Ahead of My Shadow   Cahn 1936
I'm One Little Party   Kalmar 1927; Ruby 1927
I'm One of God's Children   Harburg 1932
I'm One of God's Children Who Hasn't Got Wings   Alter 1930; Hammerstein 1930
I'm One of the Boys   Hart 1934; Rodgers 1934
I'm One of Your Admirers   Burke 1953; Van Heusen 1953
I'm Only a Fair Sun Bather   Lewis 1911
I'm Only a Pilgrim   Smith, Harry B. 1923
I'm Only Another to You   Johnson, Howard 1926
I'm Only Dreaming   Friml 1917; Harbach 1917
I'm Only Dreaming of You   Brennan 1917
I'm Only Guessin'   Brown, Nacio Herb 1931; Egan 1931
I'm Only Happy, That's All   Carmichael 1943
I'm Only Happy when I'm Sad   Jerome 1910; Schwartz, Jean 1910
I'm Only Human   Lawrence 1957; Young, Joe 1972
I'm Only Human, That's All   Johnson, Howard 1924
I'm Only Making Believe   Coots 1929; Davis 1929
I'm Only Teasin'   Heyman 1944
I'm Oriental   Atteridge 1921; Pollack 1921
I'm Out for No Good Reason Tonight   Gershwin, George 1929; Gershwin, Ira 1929; Kahn 1929
I'm Out of My Mind   Fisher 1934
I'm Out of this World when I'm in Your Arms   Baer 1954
I'm Out on Strike for a Beautiful Girl   Johnson, Howard 1920
I'm Over Here and You're Over There   Atteridge Date Unknown
I'm Over Here, You're Over There   Brown, Lew Date Unknown; Henderson Date Unknown
I'm Painting Pictures   Leslie 1931; Monaco 1931
I'm Painting the Town Red to Hide a Heart that's Blue   Stept 1935
I'm Pally with Sally Again   Coots 1933
I'm Part of a Family   Brooks 1960
I'm Part of You   Dietz 1956; Schwartz, Arthur 1956
I'm Past My Prime   DePaul 1956; Mercer 1956
I'm Paving My Way to Your Heart   Egan 1921; Whiting 1921
I'm Payin' You (Pay Day)   Russell 1946
I'm Percy Pinchill of Harlem   Blake Date Unknown; Razaf 1942
I'm Perfectly Satisfied   Leslie 1929
I'm Pinin' for the Pines of Carolina   Johnson, Howard 1927
I'm Pixilated Over You   Heyman 1936; Spina 1936
I'm Playing with Fire   Berlin 1932
I'm Plenty That Way Too   Harburg 1930
I'm Popeye the Sailor Man   Lerner, Sammy 1934
I'm Positively in Love, and Absolutely with You   Ahlert 1932; Turk 1932
I'm Proud I'm Irish   Howard, Joseph E. 1915
I'm Proud of You   Coots 1930; Fields 1952; Magidson 1930; Schwartz, Arthur 1952
I'm Proud to Be a Platypus   Sherman 1991

I'm Proud to Be the Mother of a Boy Like You   Sterling
   1915; Von Tilzer 1915
I'm Putting All My Eggs in One Basket   Berlin 1936
I'm Putty in Your Hands   Adamson 1934
I'm Ready   Friend 1960
I'm Ready to Quit and Be Good   Harbach 1911
I'm Really Disappointed with America   Buck 1913
I'm Red, White and Blue Over You   De Lange 1942; Stept
   1942
I'm Referin' Just to Her 'n Me   Coots 1929
I'm Rhythm Crazy Now   Mills 1942
I'm Rich   Bergman 1957
I'm Riding to Glory (With a Glorious Girl)   Dixon 1927;
   Woods 1927
I'm Right   Revel 1946
I'm Rolling in Love   Mills 1929
I'm Rolling in Rainbows   Burke 1950; Van Heusen 1950
I'm Rotten I'm Rotten   Cahn 1977
I'm Ruined   Hart 1938; Rodgers 1938
I'm Satisfied   Buck 1922; Ellington 1941; Freed, Ralph 1934;
   Parish 1941
I'm Satisfied Beside that Sweetie o' Mine   Yellen 1924
I'm Satisfied to Step Aside   Donaldson 1918; Gilbert 1918
I'm Savin' Up My Pennies (inst.)   Waller 1938
I'm Saving All My Kisses for Someone   Woods 1929
I'm Saving My Kisses   Atteridge 1912
I'm Saving My Love for You   Bryan 1913
I'm Saving Up for Lost Time   Sigman 1952
I'm Saving Up the Means to Get to New Orleans   Johnson,
   Howard 1916
I'm Saving Up To Buy a Saddle   Brown, Nacio Herb 1951;
   Gilbert 1951
I'm Saying Goodbye to You While the Music Plays   Carroll
   1931
I'm Scared   Fields 1950
I'm Screwy Over Looey   Dubin 1930
I'm Seein' the World at Home   Dubin Date Unknown;
   Warren Date Unknown
I'm Seeking for Siegfried   Atteridge 1914; Carroll 1914;
   Romberg 1914
I'm Sending You Roses   Merrill 1951
I'm Serving Out a Heavy Sentence (Loving You)
   (Huddleston, Floyd)   Coleman 1966
I'm Setting a Trap   Blake 1962; Sissle 1962
I'm Setting a Trap to Catch You   Blake 1936
I'm Shadowing You   Mercer 1973
I'm Sharing My Wealth   Duke 1936; Gershwin, Ira 1936
I'm Shootin' High   Koehler 1935; McHugh 1935
I'm Simply Crazy 'Bout You Now   Monaco 1932
I'm Simply Crazy Over You   Goetz 1915; Jerome 1915;
   Schwartz, Jean 1915
I'm Simply Mad about the Man   Friml 1923
I'm Simply Mad for Bones   Harburg 1967; Styne 1967
I'm Simply Starved   Drake 1956
I'm Simply Wild about You   Brown, A. Seymour 1923
I'm Singing Your Praises   Gordon 1934; Revel 1934
I'm Sittin' on Top of a Hill Top (I'm Sittin' High on a Hill
   Top)   Johnston 1935; Kahn 1935
I'm Sittin' on Top of the World (Just Rolling Along, Just
   Rolling Along)   Lewis 1925; Young, Joe 1925
I'm Sitting on Top of the World   Brown, Lew 1928; DeSylva
   1928; Henderson 1928
I'm Sitting Pretty in a Pretty Little City   Baer 1923
I'm Skipping Rope with a Rainbow   Drake 1949

I'm Slappin' Seventh Avenue (With the Sole of My
   Shoe)   Ellington 1938; Mills 1938
I'm So Afraid of My Shadow Telling on Me   Lewis 1930
I'm So Afraid of You   Kalmar 1930; Ruby 1930
I'm So Alone with the Crowd   Young, Joe 1932
I'm So Backward and She's So Forward   Fields 1931;
   McHugh 1931
I'm So Busy   Kern 1917
I'm So Disappointed in You   Donaldson 1925; Kahn 1925
I'm So Glad   Schwartz, Jean 1942
I'm So Glad (I'm a Little Boy and You're a Little
   Girl)   Merrill 1954
I'm So Glahd to Meet You   Porter 1944
I'm So Happy   Jerome 1904; Schwartz, Jean 1904
I'm So Happy I Could Cry   Baer 1965; Heyman 1935
I'm So Humble (Inferiority Complex)   Hart 1926; Rodgers
   1926
I'm So in Love   Donaldson 1932
I'm So in Love (I Don't Know What I'm Doin')   Koehler
   1947
I'm So in Love with You   Ellington 1931; Gordon 1957; Mills
   1931; Porter 1939; Spina 1957
I'm So Sorry I Ain't Got It You Could Have It If I Had It
   Blues   Lewis 1919; Snyder 1919
I'm So Sympathetic   Atteridge 1919; Carroll 1919
I'm So Tired of Dreaming   Gilbert 1919
I'm So Tired of It All   Hanley 1929
I'm So Tired of Livin', I Don't Care When I Die   Sterling
   1902
I'm Sober   Buck 1915
I'm Somebody Nobody Loves   Akst 1923; Davis 1923
I'm Somebody's Baby Now   Gordon 1929
I'm Somebody's Somebody Now   Johnson, Howard 1927;
   Silver 1927
I'm Somethin' on Avenue A   DeSylva 1925; Gershwin,
   George 1925; Gershwin, Ira 1925
I'm Sorry   Mills 1928; Norworth 1906
I'm Sorry for Myself   Berlin 1939
I'm Sorry for Satan   Meyer 1908
I'm Sorry I Ain't Got It If I Had It You Could Have It
   Blues   Lewis 1919; Snyder 1919; Young, Joe 1919
I'm Sorry I Can't See My Old Gal Tonight   Fain 1933;
   Young, Joe 1933
I'm Sorry I Made You Cry   Spina 1957
I'm Sorry, I Want a Ferrari   Wrubel 1959
I'm Sorry My Dreams Came True   Gordon 1932; Revel 1932
I'm Sorry Now   Clare 1923; Davis 1923
I'm Sorry Sally   Kahn 1928
I'm Spending a Long Day   Donaldson 1929; Leslie 1929
I'm Spending Tonight with Mother   Washington 1933;
   Wrubel 1933
I'm Spending too Much Time By Myself   Fain 1931; Kahal
   1931
I'm Starting All Over Again   Yellen 1955
I'm Stepping Out with a Memory Tonight   Magidson 1940;
   Wrubel 1940
I'm Stepping Out with Lulu   Johnson, James P. 1927
I'm Still Crazy for You   Rainger 1942; Robin 1942
I'm Still Here   Sondheim 1971
I'm Still in Love with You   Conrad 1925; Koehler 1927;
   Snyder 1931
I'm Still Me   Adams 1970; Strouse 1970
I'm Still Sitting Under the Apple Tree   Cahn 1947; Styne
   1947

I'm Still without a Sweetheart with Summer Coming On   Ahlert 1932; Turk 1932

I'm Still Yours Tho' You're No Longer Mine   Coots 1938; Davis 1938

I'm Stuck on Molasses and Molasses Is Stuck on Me   Brown, A. Seymour 1929

I'm Such a Nervous Man   Romberg 1916

I'm Such a Romantic Girl   Herbert 1911; Smith, Harry B. 1911

I'm Sure of Everything but You   Meyer 1932

I'm Sure of Your Love   Comden and Green 1945

I'm Takin' a Shine to You   Merrill 1950

I'm Takin' My Time with You   Ahlert 1939

I'm Takin' the Dream Train (Hug-A-Chug)   Friend 1946

I'm Taking a Chance on You   Stept 1933

I'm Taking a Shine to You   Magidson 1938; Wrubel 1938

I'm Taking the Steps to Russia   Porter 1938

I'm Talking About My Wonderful Gal   Mills 1928

I'm Talking to My Pal   Hart 1940; Rodgers 1940

I'm Tall   Coleman 1972

I'm Tellin' the World about You   Friend 1930; Monaco 1930

I'm Tellin' You   Merrill 1956

I'm Tellin' You in Front, So You Won't Feel Hurt Behind   Razaf 1937

I'm Telling the Birds and Bees How I Love You   Brown, Lew 1926

I'm Telling the World About You   Friend 1930

I'm Telling You Now   Adamson 1946; McHugh 1946

I'm Thankful   Johnston 1931

I'm Thankful for the Love You Showed Me   Young, Joe 1932

I'm That Way About Broadway   Magidson 1933

I'm that Way Over You   Coots 1929; Davis 1929

I'm the Answer to a Maiden's Prayer   Monaco 1923; Rose 1923

I'm the Bluest Man in Town   Bryan 1928

I'm the Boy   Edwards 1909; Smith, Robert B. 1909

I'm the Bravest Individual   Coleman 1966; Fields 1966

I'm the Brother of the Lily of the Valley   Gilbert 1918

I'm the Captain of the Pinafore   Johnson, Howard 1939

I'm the Echo (You're the Song I Sing)   Fields 1935; Kern 1935; McHugh 1935

I'm the Extra Man   Friml 1926; Hammerstein 1926; Harbach 1926

I'm the Fellow Who Loves You   Henderson 1935; Yellen 1935

I'm the First Girl in the Second Row in the Third Scene of the Fourth Number   Martin 1948

I'm the First Man   Blane 1945

I'm the Governor's Son   Cohan 1901

I'm the Greatest Father of Them All   Jerome 1955

I'm the Greatest Individual   Fields 1966

I'm the Greatest Papa in the World   Lane 1952

I'm the Greatest Star   Merrill 1964; Styne 1964

I'm the Guy Who Can Do It   Russell 1945

I'm the Guy Who Guards the Harem   Berlin 1919

I'm the Guy Who Loves You   Kahn 1940

I'm the Head Man   Berlin 1929

I'm the Human Brush (that Paints the Crimson on Paree)   Kern 1911

I'm the Last of the Red Hot Mommas   Ager 1929; Yellen 1929

I'm the Leader of Society   Herbert 1900; Smith, Harry B. 1900

I'm the Leading Lady   Williams 1907

I'm the Lily   Jerome 1910; Schwartz, Jean 1910

I'm the Little Peanut Vendor's Little Missus   Carroll 1933

I'm the Lonesomest Gal in Town   Brown, Lew 1912

I'm the Man in Washington   Smith, Harry B. 1906

I'm the Man Who Makes the Money in the Mint   Cobb 1902; Edwards 1902

I'm the Medicine Man for the Blues   Akst 1929; Clarke 1929

I'm the Old Man in the Moon   Kern 1917

I'm the One Who's Lonely   Styne 1941

I'm the Only Mother that You Ever Knew   Goetz 1911

I'm the Only Star that Twinkles on Broadway   Sterling 1905; Von Tilzer 1905

I'm the Queen Thamar   Porter 1955

I'm the Reason   Akst 1930; Clarke 1930

I'm the Secretary to the Sultan   Robin 1943

I'm the Stupidest Girl in the Class   Loesser 1939

I'm the Villain   Porter 1912

I'm the Wealthiest Man in the World   Ahlert 1929; Turk 1929

I'm the Worryin' Kind   Mercer 1952

I'm There   Bergman 1972

I'm Thinking of My Darling   David, Mack 1944

I'm Thirsty for Kisses, Hungry for Love, Lonely with Only Just Me   Coots 1928

I'm Thirsty for Your Kisses   Coots 1929; Davis 1929

I'm Threading My Needle with Twilight   Coots 1942

I'm Thrilled   Baer 1955; DePaul 1939

I'm Through   Lawrence 1940

I'm Through with Love   Kahn 1931

I'm Through with Roaming Romeos   Friml 1913; Harbach 1913

I'm Throwin' My Love Away   Adamson 1934; Lane 1934

I'm Throwing a Ball Tonight   Porter 1940

I'm Throwing Good Love After Bad   Caesar 1939

I'm Thru (with) Saying I'm Thru   Kahn 1933; Kalmar 1933; Ruby 1933

I'm Thru' with War   Smith, Harry B. 1927

I'm Thru with You   Howard, Bart 1953

I'm Tickled Silly   Gershwin, Ira 1921; Youmans 1921

I'm Tickled to Death that You're Irish   Donaldson 1919; Lewis 1919; Young, Joe 1919

I'm Tired   Jerome 1901; Schwartz, Jean 1901

I'm Tired of Love   Harburg 1932

I'm Tired of Me   David, Hal 1974

I'm Tired of My Tired Man   Snyder 1944

I'm Tired of Running After You   Silver 1926

I'm Tired of Texas   Martin 1948

I'm to Be a Blushing Bride   Harbach 1911; Lewis 1911; Schwartz, Jean 1911

I'm Toein' the Line   Blake 1940; Razaf 1940

I'm Too Young To Be Careful (And Too Sweet To Be Good)   Bryan 1929; Meyer 1929

I'm too Young to Die   Adams 1966

I'm Too Young to Die It's a Long, Slow Climb Going Up but a Short, Fast Slide Coming Down   Strouse 1966

I'm Tracin' the Mason-Dixon Line   Stept 1919

I'm Trailing Arbutus   Alter 1930; Johnson, Howard 1930

I'm Treatin' Myself to a Birds-Eye View of Heaven   Lane 1931

I'm True to Them All, and They're Just As True to Me   Cohan 1918

I'm Twisting Loops in Pretzels to Pass the Time Away   Johnson, Howard 1933

I'm Tying the Leaves Back on the Trees   David, Mack 1979

I'm Under New Management Now   Conrad 1930; Meyer 1930; Mitchell 1930

I'm Unlucky   Jerome 1902; Schwartz, Jean 1902

I'm Unlucky at Gambling   Porter 1929

I'm Up in Heaven When You're in My Arms   Silver 1924;
   Turk 1924

I'm Upside Down   Eliscu 1949

I'm Waiting for Just One Girl   Carroll 1910

I'm Waiting for Ships that Never Come In   Yellen 1919

I'm Waiting for Winnie   Goetz 1910

I'm Waiting for You   Harbach 1925; Youmans 1925

I'm Waiting Just for You   Leigh 1951

I'm Waiting Till Somebody Grows Up   Meyer 1911

I'm Walkin' on Air   Lewis 1931

I'm Walking Around in Circles   Lewis 1926; Young, Joe 1926

I'm Walking Around on Dangerous Ground   Friend 1930

I'm Walking Between the Raindrops   Fisher 1928; Rose 1928

I'm Walking in Between the Raindrops but a Rainbow's
   Shining on Me   Friend 1930; Monaco 1930

I'm Walking in the Sunshine, Sitting in the Moonlight
   Now   Friend 1929

I'm Walking on Air   Conrad 1930; Meyer 1930; Mitchell
   1930

I'm Walking Through Clover, I'm Happy in Love   Friend
   1929; Pollack 1929

I'm Walking with the Moonbeams, Talking to the
   Stars   Gordon 1929

I'm Walter   Bergman 1976

I'm Waltzing to the Raindrops   Fisher 1928; Rose 1928

I'm Watching the World Thru My Grandmother's
   Glasses   Egan 1932

I'm Way Ahead   Coleman 1966; Fields 1966

I'm Way Ahead of the Game   Brown, Nacio Herb 1932;
   DeSylva 1932; Mercer 1964; Whiting 1932

I'm Wearing My Heart on My Sleeve   Parish 1932

I'm Weary for You Dearie   Carroll 1911

I'm Well Known   Kern 1907

I'm Whistlin' for My Honey   Monaco 1934; Young, Joe 1934

I'm Wide Awake when I Dream   Gilbert 1931

I'm Wild About a Baseball Game   Baer 1928; Gilbert 1928

I'm Wild about Wild Men   Bryan 1922; Schwartz, Jean 1922

I'm Willing to Be Your Good Man Friday   Monaco 1934

I'm Wingin' Home   Baer 1929; Gilbert 1929

I'm Wise   Williams 1907

I'm with the Right Girl Now   Bloom 1935

I'm with You   Comden and Green 1964; Donaldson 1931;
   Friend 1961; Mercer 1955; Styne 1964

I'm Wonderful   Duke 1927

I'm Wondering Why   Hoffman 1927

I'm Worried Over You   Kahn 1924

I'm Writing to You, Sammy   Brown, Lew 1917

I'm You   Loesser 1936

I'm Your Girl   Hammerstein 1953; Rodgers 1953

I'm Your Guy   Coleman 1979

I'm Your Man   Lerner, Alan Jay 1948; Weill 1948

I'm Yours   Coots 1929; Davis 1929; Harburg 1930; Porter
   1938

I'm Yours for the Asking   Kalmar 1937; Ruby 1937

I'm Yours for Tonight   Leslie 1932; Monaco 1932; Rainger
   1935

I'm-a Love You   Hoffman 1953

Image of His Papa, The   Adams 1983

Image of Me, The   Lane 1979; Lerner, Alan Jay 1979

Image of You, The   Ahlert 1937; Burke 1935; Lewis 1937;
   Spina 1935; Young, Joe 1937

Imagination   Burke 1939; Caesar 1928; Van Heusen 1939

Imagine   Blane 1954; Cahn 1967; Hart 1937; Martin 1954;
   Razaf 1930; Rodgers 1937

Imagine Me Without My You (And You Without Your
   Me)   Gershwin, Ira 1924

Imagine Me without You   Gorney 1924

Imagine My Frustration   Ellington 1966

Imagined Death Sequence (inst.)   Bacharach 1980

Imagining Things   Howard, Bart 1965

Imaginings   Cahn 1980; DePaul 1980

Imitation of Daphne, The   Smith, Harry B. 1910

Imitation of Life   Fain 1959; Webster 1959

Imitations of You   Blake 1935; Mills 1935

Imitator's Rag (inst.)   Johnson, James P. 1913

Immaturity   Cahn 1964; Van Heusen 1964

Immigration Rose   McHugh 1923

Impatient Years, The   Cahn 1955; Fain 1946; Freed, Ralph
   1946; Van Heusen 1955

Impossible   Caesar 1955; Freed, Ralph 1966; Hammerstein
   1957; Rodgers 1957; Sondheim 1962

Impossible Men   Schwartz, Arthur 1930

Impossible Things   Loesser 1947

Impresario   Merrill 1993; Styne 1993

Impressions   Atteridge 1914; Romberg 1914

Impressions (inst.)   Johnson, James P. 1928

Impromptu in E Flat (inst.)   Romberg 1940

Impromptu in Two Keys (inst)   Gershwin, George 1929

Impromptu Song (Talking Song)   Hart 1930; Rodgers 1930

Improvements   Herbert 1906

Improvisation   Akst 1937; Clare 1937

In 2010   Atteridge 1912

In 1960 You'll Find Dixie Looking Just the Same   Mitchell
   1918

In a Bamboo Garden   Donaldson 1928

In a Beer Garden Waltzing with You   Heyman 1933

In a Big Big Way   Washington 1929

In a Blue and Pensive Mood   Livingston, Jerry 1934

In a Bungalo   Jerome 1905; Schwartz, Jean 1905

In a Bungalow   Conrad 1924; Howard, Joseph E. 1910

In a Bungalow for You   Hammerstein 1930

In a Cabaret in Old Paree   Fain 1931; Kahal 1931

In a Cafe in Montmartre   Mercer 1933

In a Canoe (Beneath the Willow on the River)   Styne 1930

In a Chimney Corner   Sterling 1906; Von Tilzer 1906

In a Corner of My Heart   Parish 1929

In a Corner of the World All Our Own   Kahn 1922

In a Cosy Bungalow in Loving Town   Jerome 1914;
   Schwartz, Jean 1914

In a Cosy Corner   Livingston, Jerry 1934

In a Cozy Kitchenette Apartment   Berlin 1921

In a Cup of Tea Leaves   Coots 1957

In a Curio Shop   Atteridge 1921; Romberg 1921

In a Darktown Cabaret   Razaf 1927

In a Dixie Land with Dixie Lou   Meyer 1912

In a Dusty Caravan   Gilbert 1916

In a Fanciful Mood   Lerner, Sammy 1961

In a Garden Down in Monterey   Lewis 1915

In a Garret in Old Paree   Fain 1931; Young, Joe 1931

In a Great Big Way   Fields 1928; Hart 1928; McHugh 1928;
   Rodgers 1928

In a Hammock Built for Two   Sterling 1905; Von Tilzer 1905

In a Heart As Brave As Your Own   Kahn 1938; Romberg
   1938

In a House of Gingerbread and Sugar Candy   Coots 1954

In a Hurry   Friml 1914; Harbach 1914

In a Hut in Old Havana   Myrow 1934

In a Jocular Vein   Fain 1982; Harburg 1982

In a Jungle Bungalow   Akst 1930; Clarke 1930

In a Kingdom of Our Own   Cohan 1919

In a Kitchenette   Dubin 1929

In a Land that's Far Away   Jerome 1902; Schwartz, Jean 1902

In a Little Bamboo Bungaloo   Robin 1931

In a Little Cafe in Calais   Coots 1944; Lewis 1944

In a Little Canoe   Caesar 1927

In a Little Dutch Kindergarten (Down By the Zuider Zee)   Bryan 1938

In a Little English Inn   Coslow 1935

In a Little French Cafe   Fain 1922; Parish 1922, 1928

In a Little Front Parlor   Egan 1921; Whiting 1921

In a Little German Garden Underneath the Pretzel Vine   Coots 1932; Kahn 1932

In a Little Gypsy Tea Room   Leslie 1935

In a Little Hideaway   Dietz 1928

In a Little Hole in the Wall   Fisher 1936

In a Little Hula Heaven   Rainger 1937; Robin 1937

In a Little Italian Garden   Lane Date Unknown

In a Little Lane in Honoloo   Mills 1928; Parish 1929

In a Little Patio Down in Mexico   Coots 1931

In a Little Red Barn on a Farm Down in Indiana   Ager 1934; Schwartz, Jean 1934; Young, Joe 1934

In a Little Roadside Rendezvous   Coots 1937; Davis 1937

In a Little Sedan Chair   Johnson, J. Rosamond 1916

In a Little Soda Shop   Meyer 1947

In a Little Spanish Town, 'Twas on a Night Like This   Lewis 1926; Young, Joe 1926

In a Little Street Cafe   Conrad 1935

In a Little Stucco in the Sticks   Gordon 1932; Revel 1932

In a Little Two By Four for Two   Hoffman 1928

In a Little Waterfront Cafe   Robison 1959

In a Little Wayside Inn   Bryan 1936; Meyer 1936

In a Little While   Egan 1925

In a Little World for Two   Herbert 1915

In a Love Boat with You   Atteridge 1919; Romberg 1919; Schwartz, Jean 1919

In a Magic Garden   De Lange 1944

In a Mellow Tone (Baby, You and Me)   Ellington 1940

In a Midnight Club   Rainger 1933; Robin 1933

In a Moment of Madness   Freed, Ralph 1944; McHugh 1944

In a Moment of Madness We Found a Lifetime of Love   Coslow 1938; Silver 1938

In a Moment of Surrender   McHugh 1941; Mercer 1941

In a Moment of Weakness   Mercer 1939; Warren 1939

In a Moorish Garden   Porter 1928

In a One Room Flat (And a Two Pants Suit)   Rainger 1933; Robin 1933

In a One-Night Stand   Cohan 1903

In a Park in Paree   Robin 1932

In a Penny Arcade   DePaul 1943; Raye 1943

In a Persian Market   David, Mack 1944

In a Persian Palace   Harbach 1940

In a Poinsettia Garden (inst.)   Robison 1928

In a Sentimental Mood   Ellington 1935; Mills 1935

In a Shady Bungalow (inst.)   Kern 1903

In a Shady Little Dell in Delaware   Carroll 1914

In a Shanty in Old Shanty Town   Young, Joe 1932

In a Shower of Stars   Heyman 1944

In a Silly Little Hilly Billy Town   Dubin 1931

In a Soda Fountain Mirror   Ahlert 1935

In a Spring Parade   Kahn 1940

In a Taxi Cab   Brown, Nacio Herb 1926; Freed, Arthur 1926

In a Ten Gallon Hat   Pollack 1943

In a Tent   Koehler 1923

In a Town in Old New England   Bryan 1934

In a Very Special Way (Pour la Toute Premiere Fois)   Razaf 1953

In a Village (Where the Lazy Daisies Grow)   Fisher 1936

In a Window, In a House, In Caroline   Motzan 1930

In a Wistful Vista   Gilbert 1945

In a World of My Own   Fain 1951

In a World Such as This   Bacharach 1987

In a Year from Now   Sondheim Date Unknown

In Acapulco   Gordon 1945; Warren 1945

In Accordance with the Customs   Lawrence 1971

In After Years   Young, Joe 1912

In an Eighteenth Century Drawing Room   Lawrence 1939

In an Old Arm Chair   Johnson, Howard 1932

In an Old Cathedral Garden   Clare 1942; Pollack 1942

In an Old Cathedral Town   Baer 1937

In an Old Dutch Garden (By an Old Dutch Mill)   Gordon 1939

In an Oriental Garden   DeSylva 1920; Kahn 1920

In and Out (inst.)   Stept 1936

In and Out the Window   Hoffman 1938

In Any Language   Gordon 1938; Revel 1938

In Arabia   Atteridge 1915; Romberg 1915

In Araby with You   Hammerstein 1926; Harbach 1926; Kern 1926

In Arcady   Kern 1915

In Armenia   Smith, Harry B. 1926

In Attitudes Alert!   Herbert 1897; Smith, Harry B. 1897

In Bad Man's Land   Jerome 1905; Schwartz, Jean 1905

In Bad with Sinbad   Fisher 1938

In Bamville   Blake 1924; Sissle 1924

In Banjo Land   Clarke 1912; Schwartz, Jean 1912

In Berry Pickin' Time   Yellen 1917

(I've Got Me) In Between   Ellington 1946; Lerner, Alan Jay 1951; Loewe 1951

In Between the Heartaches   Bacharach 1965; David, Hal 1965

In Blinky, Winky, Chinky Chinatown   Jerome 1915; Schwartz, Jean 1915

In Blue Samoa   Bryan 1938

In Bohemia with You   Edwards 1908

In Bokhara, Miss O'Hara   Romberg 1921

In Brazil   Romberg 1922

In Buddy's Eyes   Sondheim 1971

In Buenos Aires   Styne 1941

In Caliente   Dixon 1935; Wrubel 1935

In California   Gorney 1924; Hart 1931; Rodgers 1931

In Central Park   Caesar 1927

In Chicago   Eliscu 1929

In Chi-chi-castinango   Gorney 1940

In China   Motzan 1919

In Cincinnati   Jerome 1903; Schwartz, Jean 1903

In Cloudland   Harbach 1908

In Copacabana   Revel 1941

In Dahomey   Hammerstein 1927; Kern 1927

In Darkest Russia   Meyer 1926

In Day Dreams   Herbert 1915

In Days of ABC   Egan 1917

In Days of Long Ago   Smith, Harry B. 1923; Snyder 1923

In Dear Old Georgia   Williams 1905

In Dear Old Kankakee   Howard, Joseph E. 1905

In Dear Old Sunny Spain   Howard, Joseph E. 1918

In Ding Dong Land   Lewis 1919; Snyder 1919; Young, Joe 1919
In Dreamland   Herbert 1895; Smith, Harry B. 1895
In Dreams So Fair   Herbert 1905
In Dreams with You   Sterling 1924
In Dutch   Caesar 1924
In Egern on the Tegern See   Hammerstein 1932; Kern 1932
In Ensenada   Bacharach 1982
In Erin's Isle   Herbert 1917
In Every Dancing Show   Atteridge 1924; Romberg 1924; Schwartz, Jean 1924
In Every Nook and Corner You Are Missing   Fain 1933; Kahal 1933
In Every Way   Revel 1947
In Fair Andalusia   Herbert 1897; Smith, Harry B. 1897
In Fair Japan   Ager 1920; Yellen 1920
In Fairyland   Herbert 1911
In Florida   Smith, Harry B. 1901
In Florida Among the Palms   Berlin 1916
In Gay Havana   Kahn 1920
In Gay Paree   Cohan 1908
In Germany   Bryan 1908; Fisher 1908
In Gingham   Hart 1925; Rodgers 1925
In Good Old Paree   Freed, Arthur 1930
In Good Old San Jose   Revel 1947
In Grandma's Day They Never Did the Fox Trot   Buck 1915
In Grandpa's Beard   Pollack 1943
In Happy Slumberland   Herbert 1908; Smith, Harry B. 1908
In Harlem   Waller 1924
In Harlem's Araby   Waller 1924
In Havana   Gordon 1932; Revel 1932
In Hennequeville   DeSylva 1922; Herbert 1922
In His Arms   Hart 1926; Rodgers 1926
In Hitler's Hat   Sterling 1943
In Idyllwild (An American Anthem)   Willson 1950
In Indiana   Caesar 1932; Friend 1932
In Italy   Atteridge 1922
In Jail   Herbert 1908
In June   Egan 1923; Kahn 1913; Whiting 1923
In June and July with August   Leslie 1911
In Kansas   Robison 1944
In Khorossan   Buck 1921; Herbert 1921
In Little Old New York   Atteridge 1921; Schwartz, Jean 1920
In Louisiana   Adamson 1934; Lane 1934; McHugh 1979
In Love   Kern 1928
In Love at Last   Dubin 1927; Wrubel 1947
In Love in Vain   Kern 1946; Robin 1946
In Love with a Memory of You   Loesser 1931
In Love with Love   Friml 1923; Kern 1923
In Love with Paree   McHugh 1956
In Love with Romance   Romberg 1948
In Loveyland   Conrad Date Unknown
In Loving Memory   Mercer 1964
In Madagascar Land   Gilbert 1920
In Mandalay with My Fair Lady   Motzan 1927
In Mattawan   Von Tilzer 1915
In Memoriam   Hart 1919
In Memory of You   Dubin 1929
In Miami Where Mammy's Waiting for Me   Mitchell 1919
In Monticello's Kingdom Grand   Smith, Harry B. 1935
In Montmartre   Alter 1929; Johnson, Howard 1929
In More Ways than One   Van Heusen 1937
In Moscow   Smith, Harry B. 1908
In My Arms   Loesser 1944

In My Arms, That's Where You Belong   Brown, A. Seymour 1914
In My Baby's Eyes   Waller 1924
In My Birch Bark Canoe   Goetz 1912; Norworth 1912
In My Birch Bark Canoe (With Emmy Lou)   Goetz 1912
In My Bouquet of Memories   Akst 1928; Lewis 1928; Young, Joe 1928
In My Canoe   Snyder 1906
In My Castle in Sorrento   Baer 1927; Lewis 1927; Young, Joe 1927
In My Country That Means Love   Burke 1934; Spina 1934
In My Dreams   Dietz 1943; Duke 1943; Herbert 1911; Hoffman 1956
In My Dreams of You   Smith, Harry B. 1910
In My Estimation of You   Coots 1936; Davis 1936
In My Garden   Caesar 1933; Romberg 1933
In My Garden of Eden for Two   Goetz 1913
In My Gondola   Warren 1926
In My Harem   Berlin 1913
In My Heart — It's You   Hoffman 1930
In My Heart on My Mind   Smith, Harry B. 1930
In My Heart, On My Mind, All Day Long   Kalmar 1921; Ruby 1921
In My Home Town   DeSylva 1919; Gershwin, George 1919; Kalmar 1922; Ruby 1922
In My Hour of Need   Sigman 1949
In My Igloo (The Snow Shoe Fox Trot)   Gilbert 1920
In My Indiana Inn   Bryan 1926; Fisher 1926
In My Little Benzine Buggy   Jerome 1908; Schwartz, Jean 1908
In My Little Blue Bonnet   Freed, Arthur 1925
In My Little Dream House on the Hill   Lewis 1927; Young, Joe 1927
In My Little Hope Chest   Coslow 1930
In My Little Hottentot Hut for Two   Goetz 1909
In My Little Red Book   Coots 1922
In My Little Runabout   Smith, Robert B. 1908
In My Lonely Little Room   Parish 1934
In My Lonely Reverie   Parish 1936
In My Looking Glass   Herbert 1920; Smith, Robert B. 1920
In My Looking Glass of Dreams   Wrubel 1931
In My Memoirs   Dubin 1939; McHugh 1939
In My Merry Oldsmobile   Edwards 1905
In My Moonlight Memories   Johnson, Howard 1940
In My Museum Now   Smith, Harry B. 1900
In My Neck o' the Woods   Hoffman 1953
In My Ohio Home To-Night   Schwartz, Jean 1931
In My Own Backyard   Donaldson 1924; Rose 1924
In My Own Irresistible Way   Coleman 1960; Leigh 1960
In My Own Little Corner   Hammerstein 1957; Rodgers 1957
In My Own Way   Spina 1969
In My Pajamas   Pollack 1924
(On a Holiday) In My Playroom   Clare 1936
In My Reality   Bacharach 1987
In My Rickshaw of Bamboo   Smith, Robert B. 1905
In My Tippy Canoe   Fisher 1921
In My Wildest Dreams   Cahn 1942; Carmichael 1935; Heyman 1935; Mercer 1952; Schwartz, Arthur 1952
In Napoli   Brown, Lew 1919
In No Time at All   Bergman 1964; Fain 1964
In November or December I Will Marry You   Conrad 1913; Young, Joe 1913
In Old Ben Franklin's Day   Herbert 1899
In Old Champlain   Friend 1941
In Old Chicago   Gordon 1938; Revel 1938

In Old Chihuahua   Donaldson 1925; Friend 1925
In Old Granada   Atteridge 1921; Romberg 1921
In Old Japan   Bryan 1920
In Old Madrid   Johnson, Howard 1939
In Old Missouri   Kahn 1915
In Old Nantucket By the Sea   Bryan 1931; Schwartz, Jean 1931
In Old New Hampshire Far Away   Motzan 1930
In Old New York   Jerome 1905; Schwartz, Jean 1905
In Old Tijuana Town   Warren 1975
In Old Versailles   Buck 1918
In Old Vienna   Fisher 1934; Leslie 1928
In Old Vienna Town   Romberg 1921
In Old Wyoming   Fisher 1938
In One Little Lifetime   Brown, Lew 1950; Lewis 1950
In Other Words — We're Through   Livingston, Jerry 1934
In Other Words I'm in Love   Clare 1935
In Other Words, Seventeen   Hammerstein 1939; Kern 1939
In Our Chateau in Brooklyn   Duke 1955
In Our Childhood's Bright Endeavor   Weill 1977
In Our Cocktail of Love   Von Tilzer 1936
In Our Cozy Little Cottage of Tomorrow   Revel 1945
In Our Hide-Away   Berlin 1962
In Our Little Heaven Down Below   Sterling 1914; Von Tilzer 1914
In Our Little Home Sweet Home   Romberg 1917
In Our Little Loveland Bungalow   Hanley 1915
In Our Little Paradise   Schwartz, Jean 1919
In Our Little Part of Town   Hanley 1939
In Our Little San Fernando Valley Home   Gershwin, Ira 1940; Weill 1940
In Our Little Wooden Shoes   Mitchell 1937; Pollack 1937
In Our Mountain Bower   Johnson, Howard 1921
In Our Orange Grove   Freed, Arthur 1927
In Our Own Orange Grove   Carroll 1925; Freed, Arthur 1925
In Our Parlor on the Third Floor Back   Hart 1926; Rodgers 1926
In Our Quiet Cloister   Herbert 1897; Smith, Harry B. 1897
In Our Time   Sigman 1973
In Our United State   Gershwin, Ira 1953; Lane 1953
In Paris   Smith, Harry B. 1908
In Paris and Brussels and Prague   Stept 1944
In Paris and In Love   Robin 1954; Romberg 1954
In Pastures Green (inst.)   Robison 1929
In Perfect Harmony   Hoffman 1931
In Philadelphia   Edwards 1907
In Pittsburgh, Pa.   Goetz 1910
In Poughkeepsie   Coots 1928; Dubin 1928
In Praise of Women   Sondheim 1973
In Pursuit of Happiness   Coleman 1957; Leigh 1957
In Rockabye Baby Land   Razaf 1936
In Romany   Washington 1928
In Rome Do As the Romans Do   David, Mack 1968; Oakland 1968
In Room 202   Kalmar 1919; Leslie 1919
In Ruritania   Romberg 1925; Smith, Harry B. 1925
In Salem   Atteridge 1919; Romberg 1919; Schwartz, Jean 1919
In San Domingo   Lewis 1917; Snyder 1917; Stept 1953; Young, Joe 1917
In San Jose   Baer 1963
In Sapphire Seas   Friml 1912; Harbach 1912
In Sardinia   DeSylva 1925; Gershwin, George 1925; Gershwin, Ira 1925

In Secret Service I Won Her Heart   Bryan Date Unknown; Fisher Date Unknown
In Shadowland   Ahlert 1924; Lewis 1924; Young, Joe 1924
In Slumberland   Blake 1930; Razaf 1930
In Society   DePaul 1956; Mercer 1956
In Someone's Eyes   Sondheim 1971
In So-So Society   Herbert 1911
In Spanish   Motzan 1930
In Spirit Land   Smith, Harry B. 1912; Smith, Robert B. 1912
In Spotless Town   Jerome 1902; Schwartz, Jean 1902
In Sunkissed Normandy   Meyer 1921
In Sunny Isles   Monaco 1937
In Sunny Italy   Bryan 1909; Fisher 1909
In Sweet Cherry Time   Lerner, Sammy 1944
In Sweet September   Leslie 1920; Monaco 1920
In Sweetheart Time   Coots 1926
In Tammany Hall   Jerome 1905; Schwartz, Jean 1905
In that Little Irish Home Sweet Home   Jerome 1921; Von Tilzer 1921
In that Old College Town   Goetz 1909
In that Southern Harem of Mine   Akst 1923; Lewis 1923; Meyer 1923; Young, Joe 1923
In that Sunny Honey Comb of Mine   Parish 1980
In that Vine Covered Chapel in the Valley   Fisher 1935
In the Absence of Monsieur   David, Mack Date Unknown; Warren Date Unknown
In the Afternoon   Drake 1994
In the Afternoon of Our Years   Livingston, Jerry 1973
In the Air   Russell 1955
In the Arms of an Army Man   Dubin 1936; Warren 1936
In the Arms of Love   Evans 1966; Livingston, Jay 1966; Mancini 1966; Revel 1971
In the Army   Loesser 1942; Spina 1942
In the Back of a Hack   Gorney 1930, 1948, 1955; Harburg 1930, 1956
In the Barrio   Leigh 1977
In the Bathroom Tra La   Dietz 1927; Gorney 1927
In the Beautiful Garden of Girls   Buck 1917
In the Beautiful Seaside Air   Donaldson 1916
In the Big Money   Porter 1939
In the Blue Velvet Night   David, Mack 1947; Hoffman 1947; Livingston, Jerry 1947
In the Boat   Loesser 1937
In the Bottom of My Glass   Meyer 1934; Young, Joe 1934
In the Broken Promise Land of Fifteen   Lerner, Alan Jay 1971
In the Candle Light   Young, Joe 1931
In the Candle-Light   Coots 1924
In the Carefree Realm of Fancy   Loewe 1938
In the Champs de Mars   Robin 1948; Styne 1948
In the Churchyard   Carmichael 1934
In the City of Brotherly Love   Brown, A. Seymour 1915
In the City of Sighs and Tears   Sterling 1902
In the City of the Angels   Adamson 1950; McHugh 1950
In the Clear Light of Dawn   Burke 1953; Van Heusen 1953
In the Clouds   Brennan 1930; Friml 1930
In the Convent They Never Taught Me That   Herbert 1913; Smith, Robert B. 1913
In the Cool, Cool, Cool of the Evening   Carmichael 1950; Mercer 1950
In the Cool of the Evenin'   Buck 1912
In the Cool of the Evening   Bullock 1940; Hart 1930; Rodgers 1930; Styne 1940
In the Corner of My Mind   Kalmar 1924; Ruby 1924

In the Cottage of My Heart   Atteridge 1923; Schwartz, Jean 1923
In the Courtroom (inst.)   Schwartz, Arthur 1946
In the Cradle of My Arms (inst.)   Revel 1959
In the Dark of an Arkansas Moon   Leigh 1956
In the Darkest Place   Bacharach 1996
In the Days Gone By   Smith, Harry B. 1926
In the Days of '49   Howard, Joseph E. 1908
In the Days of Auld Lang Syne   Von Tilzer 1917
In the Days of Splendor   Webster 1968
In the Dim Dim Dawning   Hoffman 1932
In the Doorway   Coots 1940; Dixon 1940
In the Evenin' (When the Sun Goes Down)   DePaul 1958; Raye 1958
In the Evening   Donaldson 1923; Edwards 1910; Hanley 1927, 1928; Smith, Harry B. 1910
In the Evening By the Fire   David, Hal 1951
In the Evening By the Moonlight   Waller 1946
In the Evening By the Moonlight, Dear Louise   Johnson, Howard 1939; Sterling 1906; Von Tilzer 1906
In the Evening Time   Howard, Joseph E. 1916
In the Eyes of the Girl You Love   Silver 1954
In the Eyes of Your Mother   Hoffman 1951
In the Folds of the Starry Flag   Herbert 1904
In the Front o' the Bottom of Me Middle   Blane 1969
In the Garden   Brown, Lew 1934; Gorney 1934
In the Garden of Allah   Donaldson 1936
In the Garden of Other Days   Freed, Arthur 1922
In the Garden of the Gods   Brennan 1914
In the Garden of Your Eyes   Brennan 1918
In the Garden, Under the Tree   Webster 1967
In the Gloaming   Johnson, Howard 1939
In the Gloaming of Wyoming, Back with the Girl I Love   Young, Joe 1915
In the Glow and Sighs of Texas   Sterling Date Unknown
In the Gold Fields of Nevada   Leslie 1915
In the Golden Harvest Time   Meyer 1912
In the Good Old Irish May   Von Tilzer 1918
In the Good Old Used to Be   Cobb 1912; Edwards 1912
In the Good Old Winter Time   Adamson 1934; Gordon 1934; Revel 1934
In the Great Smokies (inst.)   Young, Victor 1943
In the Green Hills of County Mayo   Porter 1944
In the Harbor of My Mother's Arms   Fisher 1918
In the Harbor of Sunshine and Love   Meyer 1909
In the Hash   Lane 1935
In the Hash in the Stew   Adamson 1934; Lane 1934
In the Heart of a Geisha   Fisher 1921; Gershwin, George 1921
In the Heart of Old Paree   Robin 1930, 1931; Whiting 1930, 1931
In the Heart of Sierra Nevada   Parish 1930
In the Heart of Spain   Robin 1927
In the Heart of the Dark   Hammerstein 1939; Kern 1939
In the Heart of the Kentucky Hills   Gilbert 1913
In the Heart of the Mighty Deep   Von Tilzer 1901
In the Heat of the Night   Bergman 1967
In the Hills of Tennessee   Lewis 1932
In the Hills of West Virginny   Ruby 1958
In the Hollow of His Hand   Warren 1956
In the Hush of the Night   Hoffman 1929; Lerner, Sammy 1929
In the Isle of Our Dreams   Herbert 1906
In the Japanese Gardens   Merrill 1971; Styne 1971
In the Land   Cahn 1945; Styne 1945

In the Land o' Yama Yama   Fisher 1917
In the Land of Beginning Again (Where Broken Dreams Come True)   Clarke 1918; Meyer 1918
In the Land of Chee-ree-bee-ree-bee (Ciribiribi)   Henderson 1922
In the Land of Elephants   Sigman 1962
In the Land of Go to Be Early   Lewis 1919; Snyder 1919; Young, Joe 1919
In the Land of Happy People   Hanley 1939
In the Land of Harmony   Kalmar 1911; Snyder 1911
In the Land of Jack and Jill   Lewis 1925; Young, Joe 1925
In the Land of Jazz   Brennan 1929
In the Land of Let's Pretend   Akst 1929; Clarke 1929
In the Land of Let's Suppose   Robin 1926
In the Land of Long Ago   Herbert 1911
In the Land of Make Believe   Bacharach 1963; Baer 1929; David, Hal 1963; Gilbert 1929
In the Land of School Days   Dubin 1920; Edwards 1920
In the Land of Spain   Herbert 1903; Smith, Harry B. 1903
In the Land of Sunny Sunflowers   Blake 1932; Sissle 1932
In the Land of Sweet Sixteen   Meyer 1922
In the Land of the Buffalo   Williams 1907
In the Land of the Free   Smith, Harry B. 1911; Smith, Robert B. 1911
In the Land of Wedding Bells   Johnson, Howard 1917; Meyer 1917
In the Land of Yesterday   Romberg 1920
In the Land Where My Heart Was Born   Porter 1913
In the Land Where the Green Shamrock Grows   Jerome 1923; Von Tilzer 1923
In the Lanes of the Seven Seas   Harbach 1952
In the Life of a Working Girl   Atteridge 1913
In the Little Red School House   Williams 1908
In the Little White Church on the Hill   Fields 1933; McHugh 1933
In the Long Run You'll Run After Me   Baer 1927; Lewis 1927; Young, Joe 1927
In the Magic of Maytime   Livingston, Jerry 1935
In the Magic of the Moonlight   Fisher 1919
In the Mandarin's Orchid Garden   Gershwin, George 1929; Gershwin, Ira 1929
In the Meantime   Brown, Lew 1927; David, Mack 1951; DeSylva 1927; Henderson 1927; Young, Joe 1930
In the Merry Month of May   Fisher 1938
In the Merry Month of Maybe   Gershwin, Ira 1931; Rose 1931; Warren 1931
In the Middle of a Dance   Yellen 1941
In the Middle of a Dark, Dark Night   Merrill 1957
In the Middle of a Kiss   Coslow 1934, 1935; Freed, Ralph 1932; Pollack 1934; Webster 1934
In the Middle of May   Ahlert 1946
In the Middle of Nowhere   Adamson 1944; McHugh 1944
In the Middle of the Night   Arlen 1958; Dietz 1934; Donaldson 1924; Rose 1924; Russell 1977; Schwartz, Arthur 1934
In the Mood   Razaf 1939
In the Mood for Solitude   Hoffman 1945; Livingston, Jerry 1945
In the Moonlight   Kalmar 1933; Ruby 1933
In the Moonmist   Lawrence 1946
In the Mornin'   Oakland 1974
In the Morning   Berlin 1929
In the Morning of My Life   David, Mack 1974
In the Mountains of the Moon   Bryan 1927
In the Movies   Smith, Harry B. 1913; Sondheim 1954

In the Musical Comedy Shows   Johnson, Howard 1924
In the Name of Art   Hart 1926; Rodgers 1926
In the Name of Love   Coleman 1988
In the Name of the King   Herbert 1917
In the Night   Fisher 1920; Motzan 1924
In the Night (inst.)   Strouse 1961; Young, Victor 1953
In the Noonday Sun   Dietz 1934; Schwartz, Arthur 1934
In the Old Kentucky Hills of Tennessee   Magidson 1932;
    Wrubel 1932
In the Old Red School   Lewis 1917; Snyder 1917; Young, Joe
    1917
In the Old Rope Swing   Coots 1952
In the Old Town Hall In the Old Town Hall   Johnson,
    Howard 1921
In the Orange Blossom Land   Howard, Joseph E. 1905
In the Pale Moonlight   Jerome 1903
In the Park   Romberg 1924
In the Park in Paree   Rainger 1933; Robin 1933
In the Parlor   Hoffman 1943; Livingston, Jerry 1943
In the Pathway of Roses and Thorns   Bryan 1903
In the Privacy of My Dreams   David, Mack 1961
In the Rain   Gershwin, George 1923
In the Rattle of the Battle   Gershwin, George 1929;
    Gershwin, Ira 1929
In the Red   Akst 1933; Eliscu 1933; Fain 1951
In the Right Kind of Light   Bacharach 1968; David, Hal 1968
In the Shacks that Little Flower Built   Howard, Joseph E.
    1908
In the Shade of a Sheltering Palm   Berlin 1924
In the Shade of My Bungalow   Howard, Joseph E. 1907
In the Shade of the Alamo   Buck 1925
In the Shade of the Lemon Tree   Goetz 1913
In the Shade of the New Apple Tree   Arlen 1937; Harburg
    1937
In the Shade of the Old Apple Tree   Williams 1905
In the Shade of the Shally-Go-Shee   Livingston, Jerry 1963;
    Webster 1963
In the Shadows   Goetz 1911; Harbach 1947; Kern 1947
In the Shadows of Dreamland Isle   Young, Joe 1946
In the Shadows of the Alamo   Stept 1949
In the Shanty Where Santy Claus Lives   Woods 1931
In the Silence of the Night   Arlen 1932; Koehler 1932;
    Washington 1933; Young, Victor 1933
In the Sing Song Sycamore Tree   Dixon 1928; Woods 1928
In the Slums (Of the Town)   Cohan 1923
In the Spell of the Night   Brennan 1942; Friml 1942
In the Spring   Donaldson 1925; Drake 1954; Kahn 1925
In the Springtime   Waller 1924
In the Springtime of Life   Adamson 1972
In the Springtime When the Roses Bloom Around the
    Cottage Door   Leslie 1908
In the Starlight   DeSylva 1922
In the Still of the Night   Carmichael 1932; Gordon 1933;
    Porter 1937; Revel 1933
In the Stores (Quartermaster Stories)   Russell 1962
In the Suburbs   Sherman 1965
In the Summer   Kalmar 1929; Ruby 1929
In the Summertime   Williams 1911
In the Sunshine of Your Love   Olcott 1910
In the Sweet Bye and Bye   Bryan 1928; Herbert 1906; Von
    Tilzer 1902
In the Sweet Cry and Cry   Meyer 1919
In the Sweet Dry and Dry   Ager 1919; Yellen Date
    Unknown

In the Sweet Long Ago   David, Mack 1952; Leslie 1935;
    Livingston, Jerry 1952
In the Swim   Gershwin, George 1927; Gershwin, Ira 1927;
    Smith, Harry B. 1901
In the Timberland of Old Wyoming   Mills 1936
In the Toymaker's Workshop   Herbert 1903
In the Twee Twee Twilight   Parish 1931
In the Valley of Montbijou   Kern 1911
In the Valley of My Dreams   Hanley 1929
In the Valley of the Moon   Hanley 1931
In the Valley of Yesterday   Johnson, Howard 1934
In the Valley (Where the Evening Sun Goes Down)   Mercer
    1945; Warren 1945
In the Village By the Sea   Sterling 1904
In the Waldorf Halls   Cohan 1909
In the War Against Men   Atteridge 1915; Romberg 1915
In the Way Off There   Atteridge 1921; Romberg 1921
In the Wee Small Hours   David, Mack 1954
In the Wilderness   Livingston, Jerry 1962
In the Winter   David, Mack 1955
In the Woodshed (She Said She Would)   Johnson, Howard
    1927
In the Year of Fifty-Fifty   Ager 1920; Yellen 1920
In This Automatical World   Johnson, Howard 1924
In This Our Last Night Together   Coslow 1940
In this Wide, Wide World   Lerner, Alan Jay 1973; Loewe
    1973
In Those Good Old Bowery Days   Berlin 1927
In Those Good Old Country Days   Bryan 1908; Meyer 1908
In Those Good Old Days of Fairies   Olcott 1914
In Three Quarter Time   Gershwin, George 1932; Gershwin,
    Ira 1932
In Time   Rodgers 1976
In Time In a Brownstone Mansion   Eliscu 1962
In Time of Peace Prepare for War   Smith, Robert B. 1915
In Times Like These   Bacharach 1959; David, Hal 1959;
    Dietz 1942; Fain 1944, 1951; Harburg 1944, 1951;
    Schwartz, Arthur 1942
In Times of War and Tumult   Weill 1936
In Toddlin' Town   Johnson, Howard 1930
In Trinidad   Cahn 1948; Schwartz, Jean 1942; Styne 1948
In Tune   Bacharach 1980; Coleman 1973; Fields 1973;
    McHugh 1957
In 2010   Atteridge 1912
In Twos   Caesar 1927
In Vacation Time   Sterling 1905; Von Tilzer 1905
In Vanity Fair   Smith, Harry B. 1910
In Variety   Hart 1926; Rodgers 1926
In Vaudeville   Herbert 1906; Howard, Joseph E. 1908
In Venice   Herbert 1920
In Vienna   Friml 1914; Harbach 1914
In Vino Veritas   Drake 1968
In Waikiki   Ager 1939; Fain 1939; Mercer 1941; Schwartz,
    Arthur 1941; Yellen 1939
In Walked Bill   Smith, Robert B. 1908
In Walked Luck   Revel 1953
In Watermelon Time   Johnson, Howard 1920
In Winter Dear I Love You   Snyder 1931
In You, All My Dreams Come True   Von Tilzer 1929
In Your Arms   Davis 1962
In Your Arms I'll Always Feel at Home   Dubin Date
    Unknown; Warren Date Unknown
In Your Cradle of Love   Brennan 1930; Friml 1930
In Your Eyes   Clarke 1918; Coots 1953; David, Mack 1973;
    Livingston, Jerry 1973; Loesser 1965

In Your Eyes, in Your Arms, in Your Heart   Koehler 1927
In Your Eyes, When I Met You   Burke 1937
In Your Forgettery   Brown, Nacio Herb 1932; Egan 1932
In Your Green Hat   Ager 1926; Yellen 1926
In Your Memory   Gilbert 1935
In Your Own Little Way   Coots 1937
In Your Own Quiet Way   Arlen 1936; Harburg 1936
In Youth's Fair Springtime   Smith, Harry B. 1930
In Zanzibar   Cobb 1904; Edwards 1904
In Zinzinnati   Brown, Lew 1952
Inamorata   Caesar 1943
Inauguration Day   Atteridge 1913
Inch Worm, The   Loesser 1952
Inchin' Up   Sherman 1953
Incidental Music   Gorney 1961
Incidental Waltz   Coleman 1965; Leigh 1965
Incidents in the Lives of Famous Men   Smith, Harry B. 1902
Incompatibility   Arlen 1957; Harburg 1957
Inconvenience   Razaf 1940
Incurably Romantic   Cahn 1960; Van Heusen 1960
Indecision   Blane 1956; Martin 1956
Indefinable Charm   Dietz 1943; Duke 1943
Indelible You   Ruby 1943
Independance   Gorney 1926
Independance Day Parade   Styne 1964
Independence   Russell 1957
Independence Day   Blane 1948; Warren 1948
Independent   Comden and Green 1956; Styne 1956
India   Razaf 1929; Stept 1919
India Countryside   Adamson 1959; Young, Victor 1959
India Rubber   Hammerstein 1920; Harbach 1920
Indian Butterfly (Naomi)   Leslie 1927
Indian Ceremonial Music   Friml 1927
Indian Chant   Schwartz, Arthur 1927
Indian Country   Spina 1950
Indian Cradle Song   Kahn 1927
Indian Fox Trot Ball, The   Buck 1916
Indian Girls Chant   Porter 1916
Indian Holiday   Fain 1946; Freed, Ralph 1946
Indian Invocation   Herbert 1911
Indian Love Call   Friml 1924; Hammerstein 1924; Harbach 1924
Indian Love Song   Howard, Joseph E. 1909
Indian Lullaby   Friml 1927
Indian Maiden's Chorus   Porter 1916
Indian Maiden's Lament, The   Coleman 1978; Comden and Green 1978
Indian Moods (inst.)   Oakland 1958
Indian Moon   Loesser 1935
Indian Music   Willson 1953
Indian on the Nickel, The   Ruby 1950
Indian Prance   Harbach 1921
Indian Prayer to the Setting Sun   DePaul 1958; Raye 1958
Indian Rag, The   Brown, A. Seymour 1912
Indian Raid (inst.)   Fain 1963
Indian Scene (inst.)   Fain 1963
Indian Serenade (inst.)   Motzan 1937
Indian Suffragette, The   Smith, Robert B. 1915
Indian Summer   Dubin 1939; Herbert 1939; Mercer 1933
Indian Talk   Baer 1950; Leslie 1950
(Back Home Again in) Indiana   Hanley 1917
Indiana County Fair (inst.)   Coots 1946
Indiana Dinner   Evans 1948; Livingston, Jay 1948
Indiana Holiday   Webster 1956

Indiana Moon   Bloom 1930; Davis 1923; Freed, Arthur 1919; Koehler 1930
Indians   Leigh 1954
Indians and Trees   Cohan 1934
Indians Are About   Leigh 1954
Indians in the Evening   Hoffman 1945; Livingston, Jerry 1945
Indians Never Say Why   Revel 1952
Indignation Meeting   Harbach 1926; Kern 1926
Indigo Echoes   Ellington 1947; Mills 1947
Indiscreet   Cahn 1958; Van Heusen 1958
Indiscretion   Cahn 1954
Individual Thing, An   Merrill 1971; Styne 1971
Individuality   Robison 1957
Indoor Girl   Arlen 1954
Indoor Sport   Bacharach 1960
Indoor Sports   Atteridge 1919; Romberg 1919; Schwartz, Jean 1919
Inebriated Acrobation   Bryan 1920; Schwartz, Jean 1920
Infantry Song, The   Wrubel 1942
Infantry, the Infantry (The Bunion Brigadiers), The   Caesar 1944
Inferiority of Your Sex (And the Superiority of Mine), The   Drake 1956
Infinity   Sigman 1972
Influenza Blues   Smith, Robert B. 1919
Information Please   Porter 1938
Ingle-Go-Jang-Go-Jay   Washington 1946
Ingratitude   Blane 1969
Inhibition Papa   Yellen 1977
Injun Gal — Heap Hep   Rainger 1943; Robin 1943
Injun Love   Williams 1911
Inn of the Sixth Happiness, The   Webster 1958
Innamorata (Sweetheart)   Brooks 1955; Warren 1955
Inner Office Scene   Fain 1951; Harburg 1951
Inner Peace   Adams 1981; Strouse 1981
Inner Thoughts   Adams 1970; Strouse 1970
Innocent Appearance   Wrubel 1959
Innocent Bessie Brown   Berlin 1910
Innocent Chorus Girls of Yesterday   Hart 1931; Rodgers 1931
Innocent Eyes   Atteridge 1924; Coots 1923; Romberg 1924; Schwartz, Jean 1923, 1924
Innocent, Innocent Maids   Porter 1914
Innocent Lonesome Blue Baby   Gershwin, George 1923
Innocent Stander-By, The   Cahn 1944, 1947; Styne 1944, 1947
Innovation (inst.)   Johnson, James P. 1917
Insanity   Norworth 1907
Inside Looking Out   Eliscu 1932
Inside Story, The   Heyman 1931
Inside This Heart of Mine   Waller 1938
Inside U.S.A.   Dietz 1948; Schwartz, Arthur 1948
Insignificant Me   Smith, Harry B. 1923; Smith, Robert B. 1923
Inspection   Arlen 1952; Blane 1953
Inspector Barnes   Comden and Green 1956; Styne 1956
Inspiration   Atteridge 1924; Comden and Green 1947; Hart 1920; Martin 1962; Rodgers 1920; Romberg 1924; Schwartz, Jean 1924
Inspiration Lane   Akst 1927; Clare 1927; Davis 1927
Instant Love   Bergman 1962
Instead of a Million Dollars   Akst 1932; Freed, Arthur 1932
Instead Of Song   Weill 1954
Instead of You   Robin 1931

Insurgents   Howard, Joseph E. 1905
Interesting Questions   Sondheim 1987
Interim   Parish 1965
Interlude   Friml 1927; Goetz 1913; Hammerstein 1932;
    Herbert 1946; Kern 1932; Russell 1957, 1958; Stept 1937;
    Washington 1937; Webster 1957
Interlude in a Barber Ship   Hammerstein 1935; Romberg
    1935
Interlude in the Dark (We Are a Band of
    Brothers)   Hammerstein 1938; Harbach 1938; Kern 1938
Interlude (inst.)   Young, Victor 1954
Intermezzo   Atteridge 1925; Harbach 1910; Herbert 1906,
    1910; Loesser 1937; Romberg 1925, 1927; Smith, Harry
    B. 1925
Intermezzo — Serenade (inst.)   Romberg 1921
Intermission Talk   Hammerstein 1953; Rodgers 1953
Intermission's Great, The   Comden and Green 1944
International, The   Livingston, Jerry 1935
International Cowboys   Styne 1938
International Melody, The   McHugh 1950
International Merry Widow, The   Smith, Harry B. 1908
International Rag, The   Berlin 1913
International Rhythm   Fields 1930; McHugh 1930
International Twist, The   Oakland 1961
International Vamp   Bryan 1927; Schwartz, Jean 1927
Interrupted Allegory   Smith, Harry B. 1910; Smith, Robert B.
    1910
Interrupted Love Song, The   Smith, Harry B. 1911
Interrupted Love Song, An   Hammerstein 1928; Romberg
    1928
Interviews   Leigh 1985
Into His Hands   Sherman 1974
Into My Arms in April (Into My Heart in May)   Rose 1928
Into My Heart   Ahlert 1930; Turk 1930
Into the Sun   Bloom 1946; Ruby 1946
Into the Woods   Sondheim 1987
Intrigue   Akst 1947; Davis 1965; Drake 1956; Lerner, Sammy
    1947
Introduce Me   Fields 1956; Kern 1956
Introduce Me to Joe   Hoffman 1958
Introducing   Fisher 1936
Introducing Mr. Rassendyl (inst.)   Duke 1963
Introducing the Futurity Debutante Chorus   Romberg 1921
Introduction   Caesar 1937
Introduction Act I (inst.)   Kern 1921
Introduction Act III   Herbert 1917
Introduction to a Scotch Medley   Merrill 1951
Introduction to Betty Jane Cooper   Gordon 1936; Revel 1936
Introduction to Foreign Carols   Freed, Ralph 1961
Introduction to Neverland   Leigh 1954
Intuition   Comden and Green 1956; Styne 1956
Invalid Entrance   Gershwin, George 1927; Gershwin, Ira
    1927
Investigation   Rome 1952
Investigator's Song, The   Rome 1947
Invisible Man   Martin 1972; Strouse 1971
Invisible Tears   Oakland 1964; Webster 1964
Invitation, The   Adams 1996; Drake 1953; Lerner, Alan Jay
    1945; Loewe 1945; Strouse 1996; Webster 1952
Invitation, An   Heyman 1931; Youmans 1931
Invitation to a Gunfighter   David, Mack 1964
Invitation to Happiness   Loesser 1939
Invitation to Love   Gordon 1938; Revel 1938
Invitation to the Mardi Gras   Drake 1953
Invocation   Sondheim 1962

Invocation to the Gods and Instructions to the
    Audience   Sondheim 1974
Invocation to Venus   Duke Date Unknown
I.O.U., An   Blake Date Unknown; Razaf Date Unknown
Iowa   Edwards 1907; Willson 1944
Iowa — A Place to Grow   Willson 1970
Iowa Fight Song   Willson 1951
Iowa Indian Song (I-o-wun), The   Willson 1948
Iowa Stubborn   Willson 1957
Ireland a Gra Ma Chree   Olcott 1901
Ireland Is Free   Brown, A. Seymour 1922
Ireland Is Ireland to Me   Brennan 1916
Ireland Isn't Ireland Any More   Von Tilzer 1909
Ireland Must Be Heaven for My Mother Came from
    There   Fisher 1916; Johnson, Howard 1916
Ireland, My Land of Dreams   Cohan 1918
Ireland My Sireland   Herbert 1917
I-R-E-L-A-N-D Spells Heaven to Me   Fisher 1921
Ireland the Footstool of God   Brennan 1916
Ireland Was Never Like This   Fain 1960; Webster 1960
Irene   Kahn 1929
Irene (Old Gypsy) (inst.)   Young, Victor 1954
Iris (inst.)   Revel 1928
Irish American   Cohan 1904
Irish and Proud of It Too   Atteridge 1914; Carroll 1914;
    Romberg 1914
Irish Blues   Johnson, Howard 1924
Irish Cakewalk   Cohan 1898
Irish Eyes   Edwards 1910; Sterling 1910
Irish Eyes of Blue   Brennan 1914
Irish Have a Great Day Tonight, The   Herbert 1917
Irish Heart, An   Carroll 1915
Irish Is in My Heart, The   Davis 1949; Silver 1949
Irish Jewish Jubilee   Kalmar 1921; Ruby 1921
Irish Jig (inst.)   Herbert 1917
Irish Love   Bryan 1916
Irish Lullaby (inst.)   Kern 1938
Irish Rag, The   Carroll 1910
Irish Recruiting Song   Brooks 1948
Irish Reel   Herbert 1917
Irish Serenade   Brown, Nacio Herb 1933; Freed, Arthur 1933
Irish Swell, The   Olcott 1901
Irish Twist   Mills 1962
Irish were Egyptians Long Ago, The   Bryan 1920
Iron Horse   Drake 1952
Iron! Iron! Iron! (Opening Chorus)   Herbert 1913; Smith,
    Robert B. 1913
Irresistible   Burke 1934; Spina 1934
Irresistible You   DePaul 1944; Dietz 1943; Duke 1943;
    Monaco 1927; Raye 1944; Rose 1927
Irving Berlin Barrett   Berlin 1957
Irvington   Revel 1953, 1960
Is a Daffydill As Crazy As a Crazy Quilt   David, Mack 1936
Is Better When You Ain't Got on the Shoes   Yellen 1957
Is He My Boy Friend   Edwards 1928
Is He Nisnardi?   Parish 1957
Is He the Only Man in the World   Berlin 1962
Is I Gotta Ma   Raye 1948
Is It a Crime?   Comden and Green 1956; Styne 1956
Is It a Crime to Be Young?   Adams 1958; Strouse 1958
Is It a Dream or Do These Things Really Happen   Webster
    1983
Is It Ah-Ha or Ugh-Hum Tonight   Rose 1927
Is It All a Dream   Dietz 1931; Schwartz, Arthur 1931
Is It All for You   Atteridge 1915

Is It Any Wonder   Fisher 1927; Gorney 1924; Rose 1926

Is It Asking too Much   Sigman 1955

Is It Better?   Freed, Ralph 1960; Livingston, Jerry 1960

Is It Hard to Guess?   Romberg 1921

Is It Him or Is It Me?   Lerner, Alan Jay 1948; Weill 1948

Is It Joy?   Porter 1957

Is It Just Another Thrill   Monaco 1932

Is It Just for Tonight   Coots 1961

Is It Love?   Caesar 1930; Smith, Harry B. 1925

Is It Love or Infatuation   Coslow 1937

Is It Me or My Uniform   Coots 1944

Is It Nothing to You   Dubin 1929

Is It Possible?   Dubin 1939; McHugh 1939

Is It Possible (That She Loves Me)   Dixon 1927; Woods 1927

Is It Possible You're Possessable?   Dubin 1937; Warren 1937

Is It Really Love (Or Just the Gypsy in Me)   Webster 1943

Is It Really Me   Blane 1955; Martin 1955

Is It Spain?   Lewis 1929; Young, Joe 1929

Is It Taboo to Fall in Love with You   Leslie 1941

Is It the Girl? (Or Is It the Gown?)   Porter 1944

Is It the Uniform?   Hart 1928; Rodgers 1928

Is It True   Baer 1929; Gilbert 1929

Is It True What They Say About Dixie   Caesar 1936; Lerner, Sammy 1936

Is It True What They Say About Safety   Caesar 1943

Is It True What They Say about Worry   Caesar 1953

Is It Warm Enough for You   Bryan 1906

Is It Worth It   De Lange 1946; Drake 1953

Is It Yes, or Is It No   Brooks 1948

Is Izzy Azzy Woz?   Caesar 1929; Friend 1929

Is Julia Home   Bryan 1909; Leslie 1909

Is Love a Beautiful Illusion   Rainger 1936; Robin 1936

Is Love a Moon Flower?   Rainger 1935; Robin 1935

Is My Face on Straight   Herbert 1908; Smith, Harry B. 1908

Is My Girl Refined?   Hart 1926; Rodgers 1926

Is Rhythm Necessary   Fain 1931; Kahal 1931

Is She My Girl Friend (How-De-Ow-Dow)   Ager 1927; Yellen 1927

Is She the Only Girl in the World   Berlin 1954

Is Something the Matter with Otto Kahn   Rose 1928

Is That Asking too Much   Fain 1954; Gilbert 1954

Is that Good?   Cahn 1965; Rainger 1941; Robin 1941; Van Heusen 1965

Is That My Prince?   Fields 1951; Schwartz, Arthur 1951

Is that Religion   Parish 1930

Is the Curtain Up?   Arlen Date Unknown

Is the Old Love Lamp Still Burning   Young, Joe 1914

Is there Another Way to Love You   Bacharach 1965; David, Hal 1965

Is There Anybody There Tango   Martin 1964

Is There Anyone Here from Texas?   Adamson 1947; McHugh 1947

Is There Anyone More Wonderful than You   Hoffman 1937; Lerner, Sammy 1937

Is There Anything Better Than Dancing?   Strouse 1991

Is There Anything Else That I Can Do for You?   Berlin 1910; Snyder 1910

Is There Anything Wrong in That   Magidson 1928

Is There Something I Should Know   Silver 1955

Is There Still Room for Me 'Neath the Old Apple Tree   Brown, Lew 1915; Leslie 1915

Is This a Private Song (Or Can Anyone Sing Along)   Hoffman 1961

Is This Gonna Be My Lonely Summer?   Bloom 1937; Davis 1937

Is This Love at Last   Friml 1913; Harbach 1913

Is This the Music of Love?   Coslow 1931; Rainger 1931

Is this the Night?   Blane 1964; Martin 1964

Is This What You Call Love?   Sondheim 1996

Is What's It's All About   Arlen 1973

Is Your Face Red   Dixon 1936

Is Zat So?   DeSylva 1925; Warren 1925

Isabella   David, Hal 1957; Lewis 1929; Young, Joe 1929

Isabella Catholica   Willson 1969

Isabella Kissed a Fella   Hoffman 1942; Livingston, Jerry 1942

Isabelle   Mercer Date Unknown; Warren Date Unknown

Isadore   Fisher 1915

Isch Ka Bibble (I Should Worry)   Lewis 1913

Isch Ka-Bibble (I Should Worry)   Meyer 1913

Island Called Love, An   Oakland 1962

Island in the Sun   Fain 1956; Webster 1956

Island in the West Indies   Duke 1936; Gershwin, Ira 1936

Island Lullaby   Howard, Bart 1961

Island of Dreams   Freed, Arthur 1932

Island of Sweet Sixteen   Herbert 1911

Island of the Moon, The   DePaul 1942, 1945; Raye 1942, 1945

Island Serenade   Adamson 1940

Island, The (Linz, Ivan)   Bergman 1980

Islands of Love   Freed, Arthur 1931

Isle d'Amour   Atteridge 1915

Isle o' Dreams   Olcott 1913

Isle of Lost Romance, The   Goetz 1917

Isle of My Love   Yellen 1921

Isle of Romance   Clarke Date Unknown; Coslow Date Unknown

Isle of Sweethearts   Caesar 1922

Isle of Tangerine   Johnson, Howard 1921

Isle of Youth   Atteridge 1918; Romberg 1918

Isle of Zanzibar   Razaf Date Unknown

Islola Bella   Spina 1957

Isn't (Ain't) She Beautiful   Razaf 1926

Isn't It   Sondheim 1954

Isn't It a Crazy World   Silver 1948

Isn't It a Pity?   Gershwin, George 1932; Gershwin, Ira 1932

Isn't It a Wonderful Night   Drake 1954

Isn't It Exasperating, Sadie   Jerome 1910; Schwartz, Jean 1910

Isn't It Great to Be Married?   Kern 1915

Isn't It Heavenly   Harburg 1932

Isn't It June?   Henderson 1934; Koehler 1934

Isn't It Kinda Fun?   Hammerstein 1945; Rodgers 1945

Isn't It Love   Mills 1945

Isn't It Lovely to Be on the Stage   Sterling 1903; Von Tilzer 1903

Isn't It Nasty of Papa?   Herbert 1911; Smith, Harry B. 1911

Isn't It Nice to Be in Love   Cohan 1897

Isn't It Romantic   Hart 1932; Rodgers 1932

Isn't It Strange   Brown, Nacio Herb 1926; Drake 1953; Freed, Arthur 1926

Isn't It Strange How the Weather Can Change Over Night   Coots 1946; Lewis 1946

Isn't It Swell to Dream   Stept 1933

Isn't It Terrible What They Did to Mary Queen of Scots   Gershwin, George 1924

Isn't It Time for the People   Strouse 1985

Isn't It Wonderful   Brown, Lew 1926; Friend 1926; Gershwin, George 1924; Gershwin, Ira 1924; Schwartz, Jean 1918

Isn't It Wonderful, Isn't It Swell   Mitchell 1938; Pollack 1938

Isn't Love a Rainbow   Heyman 1943
Isn't Love the Grandest Thing?   Alter 1935
Isn't Love the Strangest Thing   Coots 1936; Davis 1936
Isn't Love the Sweetest Thing?   Alter 1935
Isn't Nature Wonderful   Fields 1930; McHugh 1930
Isn't She the Busy Little Bee   Von Tilzer 1917
Isn't She the Sweetest Thing   Donaldson 1925; Kahn 1925
Isn't That a Pretty Picture   Drake 1952
Isn't That Just Like Love   Burke 1940; Van Heusen 1940
Isn't That Like a Man!   Smith, Harry B. 1916; Smith, Robert B. 1916
Isn't There a Crowd Everywhere?   Kern 1916
Isn't This a Cockeyed World   De Lange 1946; Dubin 1930
Isn't This a Day   Harburg 1967; Styne 1967
Isn't This a Lovely Day (To Be Caught in the Rain)   Berlin 1935
Isn't This the Night, Isn't That the Moon   Caesar 1934; Carroll 1934
Israel   Berlin 1959; Fisher 1920
Israel Is Your Name   Merrill 1958
Issue Dodger   Robison 1964
It   Hammerstein 1926; Harbach 1926; Romberg 1926
It Ain't Being Done No More   Blake 1935
It Ain't Etiquette   Porter 1939
It Ain't Far to the Bar   Merrill 1948
It Ain't Gonna Rain No Mo'   Johnson, Howard 1939
It Ain't Like It Used to Was   Clare Date Unknown
It Ain't Necessarily So   Gershwin, George 1935; Gershwin, Ira 1935
It Ain't Right   David, Hal 1960
It Ain't Right to Say Ain't   De Lange 1941
It All Adds Up   Cahn 1965; Van Heusen 1965
It All Belongs to Me   Berlin 1927
It All Belongs to You   Porter 1938
It All Depends on You   Brown, Lew 1925, 1928; DeSylva 1925, 1928; Henderson 1925, 1928
It All Goes Up in Smoke   Kahn 1910
It Always Rains But Always   David, Hal 1947
It Amazes Me   Coleman 1958; Leigh 1958
It Began in Yucatan   Robin 1951; Styne 1951
It Better Be Good   Dietz 1931; Schwartz, Arthur 1931
It Can Happen to Anyone   Hammerstein 1941; Romberg 1941
It Can Happen to You   Ahlert 1936; Turk 1936; Young, Joe 1936
It Cannot Be   Bergman 1957
It Can't Be a Sin to Love You   Coots 1945
It Can't Be Did   Berlin 1910
It Can't Be Done   Fisher 1939; Kern 1917; Smith, Harry B. 1917
It Can't Be Wrong   Friml 1919; Harbach 1919
It Can't Go on Like This   Gorney 1930; Harburg 1930
It Can't Happen Here   Rose 1940
It Changes   Sherman 1972
It Comes So Natural   Ager 1916; Donaldson 1916
It Comes Up Love   Loesser Date Unknown
It Cost Me Just a Nickel   Fain Date Unknown; Kahal Date Unknown
It Costs Just a Nickel   Kahal 1932
It Costs Me Just a Nickel   Fain 1932
It Costs Nothing to Dream   Fields 1931; McHugh 1931
It Could Be Worse   Cahn 1958
It Could Be You   Davis 1957
It Could Happen to Me   Adamson 1947; McHugh 1947
It Could Happen to You   Burke 1944; Van Heusen 1944

It Could Have Been Me   Russell 1955
It Could Only Happen in Brooklyn   Cahn 1945, 1950; Styne 1945
It Could Only Happen in the Movies   Adamson 1941; Duke 1941
It Couldn't Happen to a Nicer Guy   Coots 1951
It Couldn't Happen to Two Nicer People   Fields 1951; Schwartz, Arthur 1951
It Depends on the Hair   Smith, Harry B. 1906
It Does My Heart Good   Baer 1961
It Does Not   Duke 1963
It Doesn't Cost a Dime to Dream   Evans 1951; Livingston, Jay 1951
It Doesn't Cost You Anything to Dream   Fields 1945; Romberg 1945
It Doesn't Make Sense   Brooks 1942
It Doesn't Matter   Schwartz, Jean 1918
It Doesn't Matter Anymore   Bacharach 1966; David, Hal 1966
It Doesn't Matter Now   Rome 1973
It Doesn't Pay to Fall in Love   Young, Joe 1931
It Doesn't Take a Minute   Fields 1959
It Doesn't Take So Much to Make Me Happy   Brown, A. Seymour 1929
It Don't Make Sense   Rainger 1936, 1938; Robin 1936, 1938
It Don't Mean a Thing (If It Ain't Got that Swing)   Ellington 1932; Mills 1932
It Don't Mean a Thing Without You   Coots 1929
It Feels Good   Hammerstein 1953; Rodgers 1953
It Feels Like Forever   Loesser 1950
It Feels Like Saturday Night   Lawrence 1953
It Gets a Little Shorter Every Day   Von Tilzer 1918
It Gets Lonely Early   Cahn 1965; Van Heusen 1965
It Get's Lonely in the White House   Berlin 1962
It Gets You   Sherman 1961
It Goes Like This   Leigh 1985
It Goes Like This (That Funny Melody)   Caesar 1928; Friend 1928
It Goes on Like That for Days and Days   Brown, Lew 1925; DeSylva 1925; Henderson 1925
It Goes to Your Feet   Brown, Lew 1937; Fain 1937
It Goes to Your Toes   Brown, Nacio Herb 1944; Robin 1944
It Goes without Saying   Clare 1954
It Got to Be a Habit   Leigh 1976
It Had Better Be Tonight (Meglio Stasera)   Mancini 1964; Mercer 1963
(I Guess) It Had to Be that Way   Coslow 1933; Johnston 1933
It Had to Be You   Kahn 1924
It Happened   Burke 1954; Friml 1934
It Happened at the Fair   Mills 1939; Myrow 1939
It Happened Every Night   Dubin 1916
It Happened in 1600   Carroll 1925; Freed, Arthur 1925
It Happened in Chicago   Kahal 1936; Rose 1936
It Happened in Dreamland   Dixon 1929; Woods 1929
It Happened in Hawaii   Dubin 1941
It Happened in Kaloha   Freed, Ralph 1940
It Happened in Miami   Rose 1939
It Happened in Monterey   Rose 1930
It Happened in Sun Valley   Gordon 1941; Warren 1941
It Happened in the Dark   Hart 1943
It Happened, It's Over, Let's Forget It   Rainger 1940; Robin 1940
It Happened on a Train   Hoffman 1949

It Happened One Night   Burke 1934; DePaul 1956; Mercer 1956; Spina 1934

(It Could Have Happened to Anyone) It Happened to Happen to Me   Gershwin, Ira 1945; Weill 1945

It Happened to Me   Brooks 1953; Young, Victor 1953

It Happened When Your Eyes Met Mine   Akst 1936; Turk 1936

It Happens Every Spring   Gordon 1949; Myrow 1949; Raye 1962

It Happens Ev'ry Time   Gershwin, Ira 1953; Lane 1953

It Happens I Have a Picture   Fain 1958; Lawrence 1958

It Happens in the Best of Families   Coots 1936; Davis 1936

It Happens Only Once in a Lifetime   Schwartz, Arthur 1974

It Happens to the Best of Friends   Bloom 1934; Parish 1934

It Has All Begun   Adams 1972; Strouse 1972

It Hasn't Been Chilly in Chile (Since Lilly O'Reilly's Around)   Burke 1946; Van Heusen 1946

It Hasn't Got a Chance   Cahn 1980; Strouse 1980

It Hurts Me to See You So Happy   Freed, Ralph 1963

It Hurts too Much to Laugh   David, Hal 1961

It Is Always Music to His Ear   Caesar 1946

It Is G, It Is Minor, It's Mozart   Willson 1956

It Is I Julia Dear   Smith, Harry B. 1913

It Is Not the End of the World   Rodgers 1979

It Is the Fourteenth of July   Gershwin, George 1924

It Is the Girl and Not the Horse that Wins the Prize   Smith, Robert B. 1905

It Is the Most Unusual Weather for This Time of the Year   Cahn 1957; Styne 1957

It Is Written   DePaul 1944; Raye 1944

It Isn't Any Trouble Just to S-M-I-L-E   Hoffman 1951

It Isn't Done   Porter 1929

It Isn't Easy   Cahn 1951; Strouse 1999

It Isn't Easy Being a Star   Cahn 1980; Strouse 1980

It Isn't Hard to Do   Hammerstein 1920; Harbach 1920

It Isn't Quite the Same   Cahn 1968

It Isn't So Much That I Wouldn't   Adamson 1933; Lane 1933

It Isn't the Style   Dubin 1920

It Isn't What He Said (It's the Way He Said It)   Berlin 1914

It Isn't what She Does that Makes Me Love Her   Mitchell 1920

It Isn't What You Have   Dietz 1963; Schwartz, Arthur 1963

It Isn't Your Fault   Kern 1915

It Just Had to Happen   Brown, Lew 1927; Friend 1927

It Just Happened   Freed, Ralph 1941; McHugh 1941

It Just Happened One Day (At a Sidewalk Cafe)   Revel 1952

(How Do You Fall in Love) It Just Happens to Happen   Revel 1942

It Just Isn't Home without You   David, Mack 1954

It Just Isn't There   Cahn 1942

It Just Occurred to Me   Cahn 1952; Duke 1952

It Looked So Good in the Window   Merrill 1949

It Looks Like a Big Night Tonight   Williams 1908

It Looks Like an Early Fall   Coots 1935

It Looks Like Arabia   Drake 1953

It Looks Like It's Gonna Be You   Dixon 1929; Woods 1929

It Looks Like Liza   Gershwin, Ira 1940; Weill 1940

It Looks Like Love   Fain 1956; Freed, Arthur 1930; Webster 1956; Woods 1930

It Looks Like More People Were Agin' Him   Spina 1944

It Looks Like Old Times Again   Johnson, Howard 1933

It Looks Like Rain   Meyer 1910

It Looks Like Rain in Cherry Blossom Lane   Leslie 1937

It Looks Like Susie   Friend 1931

It Made You Happy When You Made Me Cry   Donaldson 1926

It Makes Me Happy to Worry Over You   Lane 1930; Leslie 1930

It May Be a Good Idea   Hammerstein 1947; Rodgers 1947

It May Be the Fault of Man   Fain 1930; Kahal 1930

It May Rain   Hart 1926; Rodgers 1926

It Means So Little to You   Heyman 1931

It Might As Well Be Me   David, Hal 1963

It Might as Well Be Spring   Hammerstein 1945; Rodgers 1945

It Might As Well Be You   Cahn 1966; Kahn 1918; Van Heusen 1966

It Might Be You   Bergman 1982

It Might Have Been   Porter 1943

It Might Have Been a Diff'rent Story   Monaco 1933

It Might Have Been Me   Coslow 1924

It Might Have Been You   Coslow 1920

It Moves   David, Hal 1961

It Must Add Up   Drake 1957

It Must Be Ernie   Weill 1943

It Must Be Fun to Be You   Porter 1944

It Must Be Good   Cahn 1952; Duke 1952

It Must Be Heaven   Hart 1929; Rodgers 1929

It Must Be Her (Him)   David, Mack 1966

It Must Be June   Dubin 1933; Warren 1933

It Must Be Love   Gordon 1929; Hart 1934; Kahn 1918, 1934; Koehler 1937; Meyer 1912; Mitchell 1937; Rodgers 1934; Silver 1930; Snyder 1929; Stept 1937; Youmans 1924

It Must Be Love or Something   Coslow 1935; Rainger 1935

It Must Be Spring   Blane 1945, 1952

It Must Be You   Ahlert 1930; Conrad 1920; Eliscu 1930; Turk 1930

It Must Have Been the Night   Henderson 1934; Koehler 1934

It Must Have Been the Wine   De Lange 1940

It Must Have Been Two Other People   Lawrence 1939

It Needs Work   Coleman 1989

It Never Can Happen Again   Atteridge Date Unknown

It Never Dawned on Me   Coots 1935; Lewis 1935

It Never Ends   Cahn 1971, Date Unknown; Warren Date Unknown

It Never Entered My Head   Porter 1938

It Never Entered My Mind   Hart 1940; Rodgers 1940

It Never Happened Before   Hart 1930; Rodgers 1930

It Never, Never Can Be Love   Herbert 1910

It Never Rains — But What It Pours   Gordon 1938; Revel 1938

It Never Was You   Brooks 1960; Weill 1938

It Never Would Have Worked   Lerner, Alan Jay 1983; Strouse 1983

It Not Where You Start   Fields 1954

It Only Happens Once   Cahn 1963; Webster 1967

It Only Happens when I Dance with You   Berlin 1948

It Only Happens When I'm with You   Cahn 1964

It Only Hurts for a Little While   David, Mack 1956

It Only Took a Minute   David, Hal 1961

It Pays to Advertise   Cohan 1914; DeSylva 1926; Porter 1910

It Pays to Advertise (inst.)   Waller 1942

It Pays to Have Friends   Livingston, Jerry 1973

It Puzzles Me So   Porter 1910

It Seemed So Right Last Night   Bacharach 1958; David, Hal 1958

It Seems Like Old Times   Stept 1939

It Seems Like Only Yesterday   Livingston, Jerry 1954; Webster 1954

It Seems Like Yesterday   Hoffman 1932; Stept 1945

It Seems to Be Spring   Whiting 1930

It Seems to Me (inst.)   Waller 1923

It Shouldn't Happen to a Dream   Ellington 1946

It Sort of Makes a Fellow Stop and Think   DeSylva 1919; Gershwin, George 1919

It Started with a Kiss   Bullock 1940

It Sure Is Groovy   Bergman 1967

It Take a Long Pull to Get There   Gershwin, George 1935

It Takes a Cop to Cop the Girls   Edwards 1908

It Takes a Good Woman to Keep a Good Man at Home   Ager 1926; Yellen 1926

It Takes a Guy Like I   Cahn 1942; Styne 1942

It Takes a Little Bit More   Coslow 1945

It Takes a Little Rain with the Sunshine to Make the World Go Round   Carroll 1913

It Takes a Woman to Get a Man   Adamson 1948; McHugh 1948

It Takes All Kinds   Sondheim 1996

It Takes an Irishman to Make Love   Berlin 1916

It Takes Love to Build a Home   Wrubel 1959

It Takes Love to Cure the Heart's Desire (inst.)   Johnson, James P. 1921

It Takes More Than Love to Keep a Lady Warm   Berlin 1956

It Takes Two   Sondheim 1987

It Takes Two (To Make a Dream Come True)   Lerner, Sammy 1952

It. . . That. . .   Cahn 1965; Van Heusen 1965

It Thrills! It Thrills!   Harbach 1914

It Took a Long Time to Make You Care   Brennan 1923

It Took a Lot of Blue   Washington 1929

It Took a Small Town Girl To Fool a Big Town Man   Brown, Lew 1915

It Took Dreams   Sherman 1959

It Took Her a Long Time To Learn To Say Yes and Now She Can't Say No   Brown, Lew 1925; Henderson 1925; Rose 1925

It Took Nineteen Hundred and Nineteen Years to Make a Girl Like You   Snyder 1919

It Twas Not So To Be   Johnson, Howard 1939

It Used to Be   DePaul 1952; Raye 1952

It Was a Dark and Stormy Night   Fain 1935; Kahal 1935

It Was a Frenchman Who Thought of It First   Rainger 1930

It Was a Good Time (Rosie's Theme)   David, Mack 1970

It Was a Night in June   Clare 1933; Gordon 1933; Revel 1933

It Was a Peach of a Fight   Sterling 1921; Von Tilzer 1921

It Was a Very Good Year   Drake 1961

It Was All in Fun   Freed, Ralph 1937; Lane 1937

It Was Almost Like a Song   David, Hal 1977

It Was Always You   Adams 1970; Strouse 1970

It Was Always You (Always, Always You)   Merrill 1961

It Was April   Silver 1923

It Was Fair   Friml 1926; Hammerstein 1926; Harbach 1926

It Was Good Enough for Grandma   Arlen 1944; Harburg 1944

It Was Great Fun the First Time   Porter 1948

It Was Great While It Lasted   Washington 1953

It Was in the Moonlight   Dubin 1927

It Was in the Time of Roses   Young, Joe 1916

It Was Long Ago   Arlen 1934; Gershwin, Ira 1934; Harburg 1934

It Was Love   Adamson 1959

It Was Meant to Be   Kalmar 1923; Ruby 1923

It Was Never Like This   Arlen 1934; Dietz 1932; Gershwin, Ira 1934; Harburg 1934; Schwartz, Arthur 1932

It Was Nice Knowing You   Dietz 1944; Duke 1944

It Was Only a Dream   Dixon 1924; Henderson 1924; Rose 1924

It Was Only a Dream Kiss   Robin 1932

It Was Only a Sun Shower   Kahal 1927; Snyder 1927

It Was So Beautiful   Freed, Arthur 1932

It Was So Good Once   David, Hal 1963

It Was So Nice Having You   Lerner, Sammy 1948

It Was Sweet While It Lasted   Freed, Ralph 1948

It Was the Dawn of Love   Coots 1928

It Was Worth It (That's What I'll Say)   Howard, Bart 1953

It Was Worth the Price   Cahn 1980; Strouse 1980

It Was Written in the Stars   Arlen 1948; Coots 1943; Porter 1939; Robin 1948

It Was You   Coleman 1972

It Was You Again   Lerner, Alan Jay 1985

It Wasn't Meant to Happen   Sondheim 1971

It Wasn't My Fault   Kern 1917

It Will All End Up with the Right End Up   Goetz 1918

It Will Always Be You   Oakland 1951

It Will Have to Do Until the Real Thing Comes Along   Cahn 1936

It Won't Be Fun (But It's Gotta Be Done)   Rainger 1940; Robin 1941

(How Do You Like My Baby) It Won't Be Long Before She Belongs to Me   Friend 1926; Woods 1926

It Won't Be Long Before We're Home   Howard, Joseph E. 1918

It Won't Be Long Now   Brown, Lew 1927; DeSylva 1927; Henderson 1927; Hoffman 1932; Johnson, Howard 1926; Washington 1932

It Won't Be Long Till Christmas   Sherman 1969

It Won't Be the Same Old Broadway   Atteridge 1913; Schwartz, Jean 1913

It Won't Cool Off   Cahn 1959

It Won't Mean a Thing   Hammerstein 1925; Harbach 1925; Kern 1925

It Worries Me   Sigman 1954

It Would Be No Holiday   Spina 1944

It Would Happen Anyway   Herbert 1920; Smith, Robert B. 1920

It Would Have Been Wonderful   Sondheim 1973; Strouse 1993

It Wouldn't Be You   Coleman 1988

Italian Ballet Miniature   Atteridge 1916; Motzan 1916, 1917; Romberg 1916

Italian Fuzz (inst.)   Bacharach 1966

Italian Girl   Meyer 1911

Italian Honeymoon, The   Leslie 1911

Italian Kisses   Baer 1930; Gilbert 1930

Italian Romeo   Edwards 1911

Italian Serenade (inst.)   Warren Date Unknown

Italian Street Singers   Porter 1920

Italian Street Song   Herbert 1910

Italian Village (inst.)   Ruby 1939

Italian Whirlwind, The   Cohan 1923

Italianesque Scene   Gorney 1958

Italiannette   Sherman 1960

Italy   Fain 1955; Hart Date Unknown; Meyer 1912; Rodgers Date Unknown

Italy in Technicolor   Weill 1947

It'll Always Be You   Stept 1945

It'll Be All Right in a Hundred Years   Gorney 1949

It'll Be Good for Me   Adams 1970; Strouse 1970

It'll Be Great to Get Back Home   Freed, Ralph 1946

It'll Be the First Time for Me   Henderson 1930

It'll Come to You   Berlin 1940

It'll Take a Little Time   Hoffman 1932

Its   Coleman 1958; Leigh 1958

It's 1200 Miles from Palm Springs to Texas   Cahn 1958; Van Heusen 1958

It's a Bad, Bad World   Lerner, Alan Jay 1971

It's a Beautiful Day to Be Glad   Coslow 1930, 1931

It's a Beautiful Day Today   Donaldson 1928; Kahn 1928

It's a Big, Big, Big, Big Day   Spina 1950

It's a Big Big Day for Love   Spina 1957

It's a Big Country   Revel 1946

It's a Big Night   Porter 1944

It's a Bore   Lerner, Alan Jay 1958; Loewe 1958

It's a Boy   Coleman 1991; Comden and Green 1991; Drake 1952

It's a Chemical Reaction, That's All   Porter 1955

It's a Clue   Goetz 1915; Romberg 1915

It's a Cruel, Cruel World   Davis 1949; Silver 1949

It's a Crying Shame   Drake 1981; Russell 1944; Stept 1944

It's a Cute Little Way of My Own   Bryan 1916

It's a Darn Good Thing   Cahn 1962; Van Heusen 1962

It's a Different World   Duke 1936; Gershwin, Ira 1936

It's a Dirty Shame   Livingston, Jay 1948

It's a Dog's Life   Adamson 1939; McHugh 1939

It's a Fairy Tale   Merrill 1993; Styne 1993

It's a Fake   David, Mack 1946

It's a Fine Old Institution   Burke 1953; Van Heusen 1953

It's a Funny Little Small World After All   Hanley 1930

It's a Gentleman's World   Burke 1946; Van Heusen 1946

It's a Girl Like You   Magidson 1931

It's a Glorious Fourth   Robin 1957; Styne 1957

It's a Good Night for Stayin' at Home   Drake 1953

It's a Good Thing Cows Don't Cry   Leslie 1926

It's a Good Thing I Don't Care   Burke 1940, 1957; Cahn 1957; Monaco 1940; Van Heusen 1957

It's a Good World After All   Edwards 1904

It's a Grand Night for Singing   Hammerstein 1945; Rodgers 1945

It's a Grand Old Game   Jerome 1907; Schwartz, Jean 1907

It's a Grand Old Life   Jerome 1913; Schwartz, Jean 1913

It's a Great Big Land   Kern 1917

It's a Great Big World   Mercer 1945; Warren 1945

It's a Great Country   Adamson 1955; Warren 1955

It's a Great Day in Brooklyn Tonight   Coots 1955

It's a Great Feeling   Cahn 1949; Styne 1949

It's a Great Life   Porter 1936

It's a Great Life (If You Don't Weaken)   Robin 1930; Whiting 1930

It's a Great Life If You Weaken   De Lange 1945; Myrow 1945

It's a Great Little World   Gershwin, George 1925; Gershwin, Ira 1925

It's a Great Sport   Brown, Lew 1929; DeSylva 1929; Henderson 1929

It's a Great Time of the Year   Howard, Bart 1961

It's a Great World After All   Razaf 1961

It's a Habit of Mine   Robin 1929; Whiting 1929

It's a Happening (The Happening)   Strouse 1966

It's a Happy World   Harburg 1931

It's a Hard, Hard World   Kern 1918

It's a Hit!   Sondheim 1981

It's a Hit, It's a Flop   Adams 1970; Strouse 1970

It's a Hot Night in Alaska   Robin 1951; Styne 1951

It's a Hundred to One You're From Dixie   Gilbert 1917

It's a Hundred to One You're from Washington   Hoffman 1938

It's a Hundred to One You're In Love   Von Tilzer 1916

It's a Jolly Good Thing to Be Alive   Smith, Robert B. 1905

It's a Kick   Sherman 1969

It's a Law   Weill 1938

It's a Lie (It's a Lie, It's a Lie)   Hoffman 1946; Livingston, Jerry 1946

It's a Living   Cahn 1964; Leigh 1976; Van Heusen 1964

It's a Lonely Life without a Wife   Livingston, Jerry 1946

It's a Long Dark Night   Rainger 1933; Robin 1933

It's a Long Day at Our Hotel   Caesar 1925; Youmans 1925

It's a Long, Long Day   Kern 1923

It's a Long Long Road I'm Travelin' on but I Got Good Shoes   Young, Joe 1930

It's a Long, Long Way to Broadway   Arlen 1936; Harburg 1936

It's a Long Long Way to the U.S.A. and the Girl I Left Behind   Von Tilzer 1917

It's a Long Long Way to Yesterday   Adamson 1942

It's a Long, Slow Climb Going Up but a Short, Fast Slide Coming Down   Adams 1966

It's a Long Time Between Kisses   Akst 1931; Kahn 1931; Whiting 1931

It's a Long Time Till Tomorrow   Bullock 1950

It's a Long Way from Broadway to Edinboro Town   Cohan 1916

It's a Long Way from Broadway (To Leicester Square)   Davis 1953

It's a Long Way to Tiffany's   Carroll 1918

It's a Long Way to Tipperary   Williams 1914

It's a Lot of Idle Gossip   Livingston, Jerry 1935

It's a Lovely Day Today   Berlin 1950

It's a Lovely Day Tomorrow   Berlin 1940

It's a Loving Wife for Mine   Smith, Harry B. 1909

It's a Mad, Mad, Mad, Mad World   David, Mack 1964

It's a Man Every Time, It's a Man   Dubin 1923; McHugh 1923

It's a Man's World   Gordon 1951; Hart 1929; Myrow 1951; Rodgers 1929

It's a Matter of Military Tactics   Burke 1953; Van Heusen 1953

It's a Me O Lord   Johnson, Howard 1939

It's a Mighty Fine Country We Have Here   Fain 1941; Kahal 1941; Yellen 1941

It's a Million to One You're in Love   Akst 1927; Davis 1927

It's a Miracle   Hoffman 1953

It's a Most Important Affair   Adamson 1943; McHugh 1943

It's a Most Unusual Day   Adamson 1948; McHugh 1948

It's a New Kind of Thing   Fain 1941; Kahal 1941; Yellen 1941

It's a New World   Arlen 1954; Gershwin, Ira 1954

It's a Nice Face   Coleman 1968; Fields 1968

It's a Night in a Million   Mercer 1935; Warren 1935

It's a Nuisance Having You Around   DePaul 1956; Mercer 1956

It's a Perfect Relationship   Comden and Green 1956; Styne 1956

It's a Pippin   Motzan 1917

It's a Pleasure   Ager 1928; Bryan 1928; Schwartz, Jean 1928; Yellen 1928

It's a Priv'lege to Live in Brooklyn   Evans 1951; Livingston, Jay 1951

It's a Quaint Little Custom   Duke 1963

It's a Quiet Town (Crossbone County)   Russell 1948; Spina 1948

It's a Real Real Purty   David, Hal 1950

It's a Scandal! It's an Outrage!   Hammerstein 1943; Rodgers 1943

It's a Scream How Levene Does the Rhumba   Mills 1948

It's a Serious Situation!   Blane 1961

It's a Short, Short Walk to a Long Sleep   Harburg 1974

It's a Short Way Through Mother's Doorway but It's a Long Way Back to Mother's Knee   Sterling 1917

It's a Simple Little System   Comden and Green 1956; Styne 1956

It's a Small World   Adamson 1936; Donaldson 1936; Pollack 1963; Revel 1944; Sherman 1964; Webster 1944, 1963

It's a Small World After All   Sterling 1919; Von Tilzer 1919

It's a Struggle   Donaldson 1926; Kahn 1926

It's a Sure Sign   Kern 1917

It's a Swelluva Life in the Army   Eliscu 1944; Gorney 1944

It's a Temporary Arrangement   Merrill 1964; Styne 1964

It's a Thrill   Smith, Harry B. 1923

It's a Topsy Turvy World   Adams 1957; Strouse 1957

It's a Typical Day   DePaul 1956; Mercer 1956

It's a Very Easy Thing to Put a Ring Upon a Finger, But Try to Take It Off   Young, Joe 1914

It's a Walk-In with Walker   Berlin 1925

It's a Way We Have in Spain   Herbert 1903; Smith, Harry B. 1903

It's a Whistle-in Kinda Morning   Brooks 1953; Warren 1953

It's a Whole New Thing   Monaco 1939

It's a Widow for Mine   Harbach 1920

It's a Windy Day at the Battery   Romberg 1917

It's a Wishing World   Blane 1952

It's a Woman's World   Cahn 1954; Evans 1954; Livingston, Jay 1954

It's a Wonderful Day for a Ball Game   Cahn 1947; Styne 1947

It's a Wonderful Day Today   Coots 1952

It's a Wonderful, Wonderful Feeling   Revel 1947

It's a Wonderful Wonderful World   DeSylva 1927

It's a Wonderful World   Adamson 1939; Hammerstein 1931; Romberg 1931

It's a Wonderful World After All   Davis 1926

It's a World of Color   Cahn 1952; Duke 1952

It's About Time   Livingston, Jerry 1935; Mercer 1932

It's Afro-American Day   Blake 1969; Sissle 1969

It's All a Dream   Yellen 1915

It's All a Part of Love   Davis 1959

It's All for Art's Sake   Brown, Nacio Herb 1944; Robin 1944

It's All for the Best   Lerner, Alan Jay 1981

It's All for the Best (I Loved You Yesterday)   Whiting 1933, 1934

It's All for You   Turk 1925

It's All in a Lifetime   Gordon 1941; Warren 1941

It's All in Fun   Stept 1925; Warren 1925

It's All in the Book You Know (Ollendorf Duet)   Herbert 1905; Smith, Harry B. 1905

It's All in the Game   Sigman 1951

It's All in the Hands of the Lord   Spina 1976

It's All in the Mind   Mancini 1978

It's All in Your Heart   Drake 1953

It's All Mine   Fields 1954; Schwartz, Arthur 1954

It's All My Fault   Meyer 1932

It's All Over but the Memories   Fain 1930; Kahal 1930

It's All Over but the Shouting   Porter 1937

It's All Over Now   Atteridge 1912; Lewis 1912

It's All Over Town   Livingston, Jerry 1957

It's All Right If You Love (One Another)   Leslie 1917; Ruby 1917

It's All Right Now   Smith, Harry B. 1896

It's All Right with Me   Porter 1953

It's All Right with Me Sweetheart   Coslow 1926

It's All So New to Me   Henderson 1935; Heyman 1935

It's All the Same to Me   Turk 1925

It's All There in the Papers   Brooks 1959

It's All Up to You Caroline   Friend 1928; Silver 1928

It's All Up to You (To Make North Carolina No. 1 in Good Health)   Cahn 1946; Styne 1946

It's All Your Fault   Blake 1915; Sissle 1915

It's All Yours   Fields 1939; Schwartz, Arthur 1939

It's Alright with Me (If It's Alright with You)   Robin 1926

It's Always a Beautiful Day   Robin 1947

It's Always Four A.M.   Cahn 1968

It's Always Going to Be that Way   Herbert 1911

It's Always Like the First Time   Styne 1993

It's Always Linda   Heyman 1967

It's Always Love   Merrill 1972; Styne 1972

It's Always Summer in the Winter, in the South   Monaco 1937

It's Always Summertime in the Winter Garden   Bryan 1919; Schwartz, Jean 1919

It's Always the Way   Hammerstein 1927; Harbach 1927

It's Always You   Burke 1941; Van Heusen 1941

It's an Old Fashioned World After All   Bryan 1934; Meyer 1934

It's an Old Southern Custom   Friend 1935; Yellen 1935

It's an Old Spanish Custom   Brown, Lew 1928; Burke 1953; DeSylva 1928; Henderson 1928; Van Heusen 1953

It's an Old Spanish Custom in the Moonlight   Leslie 1930; Meyer 1930

It's an Old-Fashioned World After All   Meyer 1934

It's Anybody's Spring   Burke 1945; Van Heusen 1945

It's Awful Hard to Try to Be a Lady   Kalmar 1910, 1911; Snyder 1911

It's Awful Hard When Mother's Not Along   Porter 1912

It's Awful (I Mean It's Awfully Nice)   Kahal 1928; Snyder 1928

It's Awfully Nice to Be a Regular Soldier   Cobb 1901; Edwards 1901

It's Awfully Nice to Love One Girl   Herbert 1907; Smith, Harry B. 1907

It's Bad for Me   Porter 1933

It's Bad for My Complexion   Schwartz, Arthur 1974

It's Been a Long, Long Time   Cahn 1945; Styne 1945

It's Been Done   Duke 1955

It's Been Fun   Cahn 1954

It's Been Nice   Cahn 1966; Van Heusen 1966

It's Been Pleasant, Pleasant   Duke Date Unknown

It's Been So Long   Adamson 1936; Donaldson 1936

It's Beginning to Look Like Christmas   Willson 1951

It's Better in the Dark   Cahn 1956; Van Heusen 1956

It's Better Rich   Martin 1952

It's Better than a Dream   Styne 1956

It's Better to Be a Man   DeSylva 1920; Kern 1920

It's Better to Dream than to Cry   Robin 1952

It's Better to Have Loved and Lost than Never to Have Loved at All   Stept 1919

It's Better to Wait for Someone You Love   Davis 1924; Silver 1924

(Bertha the Sewing Machine Girl) It's Better with a Union Man   Rome 1937

It's Bigger than Both of Us   Fain 1950

It's Bigger Than You and Me   Robin 1955; Styne 1955

It's Blue on the Blue Danube   Fisher 1938

It's Bologny   Rose 1927

It's Catching   Burke 1950; Van Heusen 1950, 1951

It's Christmas   Strouse 1977

It's Christmas on the Islands (inst.)   Spina 1977

It's Christmas Time   Young, Victor 1952

It's Christmas Time All Over the World   Martin 1965

It's Circus Day Again   Washington 1941

It's Crazy   Sigman 1967

It's Cruel to Take a Sweetheart   Merrill 1959

It's Dark on Observatory Hill   Burke 1934; Spina 1934

It's Deductible   Arlen 1950; Blane 1950

It's Delightful!   Kern 1970; Webster 1971

It's Delightful Down in Chile   Robin 1948; Styne 1948

It's Delightful to Be Married   Smith, Harry B. 1906

It's De-lovely   Porter 1936

It's Different with Me   Arlen 1931; Yellen 1931

It's Doom   Comden and Green 1958; Styne 1958

It's Dreamtime   Brooks 1947

It's Dynamite   Fields 1951; Warren 1951

It's Easier to Kiss than Talk   Ager 1917; Goetz 1917

It's Easter Time   Willson 1951

It's Easy as A.B.C.   Lewis 1931

It's Easy to Blame the Weather   Cahn 1939

It's Easy to Love   Carmichael 1936

It's Easy to Remember   Hart 1935; Rodgers 1935

It's Easy to Say   Mancini 1979

It's Easy to Say Hello (But So Hard to Say Goodbye)   Brown, Lew 1927; Friend 1927

It's Easy to Say Hello! It's Hard to Say Good Bye   Akst 1933; Eliscu 1933

It's Easy to Say You're Sorry   David, Hal 1958; Hoffman 1944; Livingston, Jerry 1944

It's Easy When You Know How   Mercer 1964

It's Enough to Make a Country Boy Cry   Robison 1963

It's Enough to Make a Lady Fall in Love   Harburg 1967; Styne 1967

It's Every Girl's Ambition   Heyman 1931; Youmans 1931

It's Fair Time   Johnston 1948

It's Falling in Love Weather   Davis 1964

It's Fate Baby, It's Fate   Comden and Green 1949

It's Feminine   Leigh 1965

It's Foolish — But It's Fun   Kahn 1940

It's from Hunger   Fain 1933; Young, Joe 1933

It's Fun to Be Free   Rome 1942

It's Fun to Be in London   Warren 1956

It's Fun to Be in Love   Cahn 1956

It's Fun to Do a Show   Cahn 1956

It's Fun to Take a Bubble Bath   Fain 1946; Freed, Ralph 1946

It's Fun to Think   Adams 1962; Strouse 1962

It's Funny to Everyone but Me   Lawrence 1939

It's Funny (When You Fall in Love)   Warren 1961, 1962

It's Gayer Whistling As You Go (Gaily I Whistle a Song)   Harbach 1938; Kern 1938

It's Get Together Weather   Baer 1965

It's Gettin' the Best of Me   Coots 1942; De Lange 1942

It's Gettin' too Hot for Me   Spina 1957

It's Getting Dark on Old Broadway   Buck 1922

It's Getting Hot in Tahiti   Blane 1946

It's Getting Hotter in the North   Hammerstein 1927; Kern 1927

It's Going to Be a Cold, Cold Winter But I'll Never Freeze when You're Around   Brown, Lew 1914; Leslie 1914

It's Going to Be Good to Be Gone   Rodgers 1979

It's Gonna Be a Big Hit   Cahn 1953; Fain 1953

It's Gonna Be You   Leigh 1967; Young, Joe 1932

It's Gonna Belong to Me   Strouse 1986

It's Gonna Take a Red Hot Mama   Yellen 1978

It's Gonna Take Time   Howard, Bart 1984

It's Good   Cahn 1980; Duke 1946

It's Good for a Woman's Morale   Bergman 1964; Fain 1964

It's Good for You   Willson 1953

It's Good to Be Alive   Merrill 1957; Rome 1965

It's Good to Be Back Home   Comden and Green 1964; Styne 1964

It's Good-Bye Pal   Howard, Joseph E. 1908

It's Goodnight Time (It's Time to Say Goodnight Again)   Davis 1961

It's Got to Be Love   Hart 1936; Rodgers 1936

It's Grand   Lane 1939; Loesser 1939

It's Grand to Be So Beautiful   Blake 1935

It's Great   Comden and Green 1964; Styne 1964

It's Great Not to Be Nominated   Cahn 1958; Van Heusen 1958

It's Great to Be a Yankee   Davis 1971

It's Great to Be Alive   Brown, Lew 1932, 1933; Eliscu 1944; Gorney 1944; Henderson 1932, 1933; Mercer 1949

It's Great to Be an Actor   Howard, Joseph E. 1907

It's Great to Be an Orphan   Martin 1952

It's Great to Be Back on Broadway   Merrill 1962; Styne 1962

It's Great to Be Home Again   Fain 1938; Kahal 1938

It's Great to Be in Love   DeSylva 1919; Friend 1931; Gershwin, George 1919

It's Great to Be in Love Again   Fields 1935; Koehler 1936; McHugh 1935, 1936

It's Great to Be in Uniform   Eliscu 1944

It's Great to Be Married   Friml 1919; Harbach 1919

It's Great to Be Married (And Lead a Single Life)   Johnson, Howard 1921

It's Great to Be Necked   Brown, Lew 1929; DeSylva 1929; Henderson 1929

It's Great to Be Young   Bacharach 1955

It's Great to Communicate   Cahn 1971; Styne 1971

It's Great When You Marry for Love   Sterling 1911

It's Greek to Me   Kern 1918

It's Half Past Kissin' Time and Time to Kiss Again   Willson 1952

It's Happening Here   Strouse 1999

It's Hard to Be a Hero   Herbert 1905

It's Hard to Love Somebody (When that Somebody Don't Love You)   Blake 1958

It's Hard to Sing the Old Songs All Alone   Hanley 1938

It's Hard to Tell   DeSylva 1919; Gershwin, George 1919

It's Heartbreak Time   David, Hal 1962

It's Heaven to Me   Brown, Lew 1927; Friend 1927

It's High Time   Robin 1948; Styne 1948

It's High Time I Got the Low Down on You   Heyman 1934

It's Home   Gorney 1934; Merrill 1964; Styne 1964; Yellen 1934

It's Hot in Chile   David, Mack 1940; Heyman 1940; Livingston, Jerry 1940

It's Hot Up Here   Sondheim 1984

It's in the Air   Alter 1931; Harburg 1931; Rose 1931

It's in the Cards   Coslow 1941; Rainger 1941; Robin 1941

It's Julep Time in Dixie Land   Akst 1936; Clare 1936

It's June   Blane 1955; Martin 1955

It's Just a Matter of Time   Davis 1922

It's Just a New Spanish Custom   Gordon 1934; Revel 1934

It's Just a Song and Dance   Washington 1933; Young, Joe 1933; Young, Victor 1933

It's Just a Tune Without a Name   Brown, Nacio Herb 1927; Friend 1927

It's Just About that Time Again   Bergman 1957

It's Just an Old Spanish Custom   Gordon 1932; Revel 1932

It's Just Because I'm Falling in Love with You   Turk 1927

It's Just Because It's You   Young, Victor 1928

It's Just Like Taking Candy from a Baby   Russell 1947

It's Just Like the Good Old Days   Porter 1944

It's Just that Feeling for Home   Ahlert 1923; Lewis 1923; Young, Joe 1923

It's Just Too Bad   Styne 1929

It's Just What I Wanted   Fields 1957; Lane 1957

It's Just Yours   Porter 1944

It's Kind of Lonesome Out Tonight   Ellington 1947

It's Legitimate   Comden and Green 1960; Styne 1960

It's Like Gettin' a Donkey to Gallop   Burke 1957

It's Lilac Time in Lovers' Lane   Whiting 1917

It's Lonely   Bergman 1960

It's Lonely, Life without a Wife   David, Mack 1946; Hoffman 1946

It's Lonesome Out Tonight   Clare 1953

It's Lonesome Tonight   Howard, Joseph E. 1907

It's Love   Coleman 1988; Comden and Green 1953; Kahn 1937

It's Love - Love - Lovely You   Lane 1952; Robin 1952

It's Love Again   Coslow 1936

It's Love I'm After   Mitchell 1936; Pollack 1936

It's Love Love Love   David, Mack 1943

It's Love that Really Counts (in the Long Run)   Bacharach 1962; David, Hal 1962

It's Lovely When Your Love Loves You   Goetz 1906

It's Magic   Cahn 1948; Styne 1948

It's Mating Time   Baer 1934; Coots 1934

It's Matrimonial Weather   Parish 1957

It's Me   Hammerstein 1953; Rodgers 1953

It's Me Again   Brown, Lew 1939; Henderson Date Unknown; Stept 1939

It's Me Oh Lord   Raye 1945

It's Me Remember   McHugh 1962

It's Midnight My Love   De Lange 1933

It's Mighty Sweet of You, to Be So Nice to Me   Young, Joe 1932

It's Mine, It's Yours (The Pitchman)   Arlen 1954; Gershwin, Ira 1954

It's Moonlight on the Prairie, Mary   Conrad 1931

It's More Fun than a Picnic   Adamson 1948; McHugh 1948

It's Murder   Cahn 1963

It's My Body   Coleman 1984

It's My Business to Know Them All   Leslie 1912; Meyer 1912

It's My Nature   Heyman 1931

It's My Turn Now   Alter 1974; Cahn 1939; Davis 1974

It's Natural   Oakland 1929

It's Naughty — but It's Nice   DeSylva 1920

It's Never Quite the Same   Evans 1958; Livingston, Jay 1958

It's Never Too Late   David, Mack 1933; Heyman 1933

It's Never too Late to Have a Little Fun   Yellen 1954

It's Never Too Late to Mendelssohn   Gershwin, Ira 1940; Weill 1940

It's Never too Warm to Wear Mink   Coots 1955

It's New to Us   Berlin 1941

It's Nice in Nice   Revel 1953

It's Nice to Go Trav'ling   Cahn 1958; Van Heusen 1958

It's Nice to Reminisce   Brooks 1958

It's Nicer to Be Naughty   Duke 1926

It's No Fun   Ager 1935

It's No Fun Eating Alone   Eliscu 1941; Gorney 1941

It's No Laughing Matter   Porter 1938

It's No Use Trying to Leave that Man   Coslow 1931

It's Nobody Else but You   Cahn 1980; Strouse 1980

It's Not a Secret Anymore   Freed, Ralph 1932; Hoffman 1932; Koehler 1948

It's Not Easy to Forget (I Love You)   Mancini 1954

It's Not Funny When It Happens to You   Stept 1927

It's Not in the Cards   Fields 1936; Kern 1936

It's Not Like Loving You   Brown, Lew 1918

It's Not So Bad to Be Good   Duke 1940

It's Not the Mountain Air (It's the Mountaineer)   David, Hal 1947

It's not the Principle, It's Just the Money   Gorney 1925

It's Not the Same Without You   Ruby 1952

It's Not the Trick Itself but It's the Tricky Way It's Done   Goetz 1911

It's Not the World, It's You   Smith, Harry B. 1906

It's Not Where You Start   Coleman 1973; Fields 1954, 1973; Schwartz, Arthur 1954

It's Not Wrong to Have Fun   Blake 1958

It's Not Your Nationality It's Simply You   Johnson, Howard 1916

It's Nothing   Styne 1978

It's Off Again — On Again   De Lange 1947; Warren 1947

It's Oh, It's Ah! (It's Wonderful)   Rainger 1933; Robin 1933

It's On, It's Off   Coslow 1937

It's One of Those Days   Donaldson 1941

It's Only a Hole-in-the-Wall   Young, Joe 1935

It's Only a Man   Webster 1949

It's Only a Paper Moon (If You Believed in Me)   Arlen 1932; Harburg 1932; Rose 1932

It's Only a Play   Sondheim 1974

It's Only a Song Tonight   Coslow 1930

It's Only Human   Adamson 1935; Lane 1935

It's Only Love   Robin 1947

It's Only Money   Cahn 1952; Styne 1952

It's Only Or-ee-vwor (Au Revoir)   Livingston, Jerry 1960

It's Only Your Carriage that Counts   Johnson, Howard 1921

It's Our Duty to the King   Schwartz, Arthur 1937

It's Paddy Again   Robin 1933; Whiting 1933

It's Paradise   Akst 1930; Clarke 1930

It's Patriotic and Sporty Not to Drive Over Forty   Caesar 1943

It's People Like You   DePaul 1941, 1942; Raye 1941, 1942

It's Perfectly All Right   Smith, Harry B. 1912; Smith, Robert B. 1912

It's Possible   Hammerstein 1957; Rodgers 1957

It's Pretty in the City   Hart 1940; Rodgers 1940

It's Pretty Soft for Simon   Herbert 1910

It's Probably Just as Well   Porter 1931

It's Quite Enough to Make Me Weep   Hart 1925; Rodgers 1925

It's Raining Again   Evans 1958; Livingston, Jay 1958

It's Raining Dreams   Spina 1940

It's Raining, I'll Have to Go Home in the Dark   Sterling 1922; Von Tilzer 1922

It's Raining Sunbeams   Coslow 1937

It's Raining Sundrops   Cahn 1950; Styne 1950

It's Raining Sunshine   Bryan 1938; David, Mack 1938; Meyer 1938

It's Raining Tonight in Jersey   Hanley 1931

It's Raining (Why Must It Keep Raining)   Mills 1951

(Hooray, Hooray) It's Ray-Ray-Raining   Johnson, Howard 1927

It's Round Up Time in Reno   Lawrence 1937

It's Rumor   Ellington 1955

It's Saturday   Ellington 1958

It's Shadow Time Again   Webster 1952

It's Smart to Be People   Harburg 1944; Lane 1944, 1945

It's So Easy   Drake 1958

It's So Easy to Sing (About Things in the Southland)   Harbach 1948

It's So Heartwarming   Eliscu 1962

It's So Nice to Have a Man Around the House   Spina 1950

It's So Temptin' (inst.)   Monaco 1915

It's Something New to Me   Parish 1957

It's Spring   Cahn 1980

It's Spring Again   Washington 1941

It's Spring, It's Spring   Raye 1961

It's Style That Makes the Girl   Smith, Harry B. 1910

It's Sunday Down in Caroline   Livingston, Jerry 1933

It's Super Nice   Adams 1966; Strouse 1966

It's Superman   Adams 1966; Strouse 1966

It's Swell Even Tho' It's Just a Dream   Livingston, Jerry 1934

It's Swell of You   Gordon 1937; Revel 1937

It's Takes a Lot of Raindrops (To Grow a Little Rose)   Drake 1950

It's Ten to One You're Lookin' at Lila   Davis 1930

It's Terribly, Horribly, Frightfully Nice   Robin 1957; Styne 1957

It's Terrific   Rainger 1932

It's that Kind of Neighborhood   Sondheim 1954

It's That Time Again   Cahn 1953

It's That Time of Day   Coots 1955

It's that Time of the Evening   Coots 1952

It's the Animal in Me   Gordon 1934; Revel 1934

It's the Army Everytime   Davis 1953

It's the Band   Sterling 1903

It's the Beast in Me   Russell 1952

It's the Better Me   Webster 1946

It's the Bump   Herbert 1911; Smith, Harry B. 1911

It's the Company   Burke 1981

It's the Cook Who Saves the Day   Youmans 1925

It's the Dancer You Love Who Makes You Love to Dance   Kalmar 1924; Ruby 1924

It's the Darndest Thing   Fields 1931; McHugh 1931, 1932

It's the Doctor's Orders   Brown, Lew 1930; Fain 1930

It's the Dreamer in Me   Van Heusen 1938

It's the End of My Life   Dietz 1952

It's the End of the World   Adams 1953; Strouse 1953

It's the Girl!   Baer 1931

It's the Girl Behind the Man   Von Tilzer 1912

It's the Good Little Things that We Do   Fisher 1918

It's the Goods   Loesser Date Unknown

It's the Gown that Makes the Girl   Smith, Robert B. 1915

It's the Happiest Time of Their Lives   Norworth 1938

It's the Hard-Knock Life   Strouse 1977

It's the Husband of Mother Machree   Sterling 1916

It's the Irish   Herbert 1908; Smith, Harry B. 1908; Weill 1947

It's the Irish in Me   Clare 1933; Gorney 1933; Yellen 1934

It's the Last Time I Fall in Love   Stept 1940

It's the Least I Can Do for You   David, Hal 1976

It's the Little Bit of Irish   Berlin 1918

It's the Little Things in Texas   Rodgers 1962

It's the Little Things that Count Most Ev'ry Way   Bryan 1916

It's the Little Things You Do that Count   Merrill 1948

It's the Love that I Feel for You   Parish 1943

It's the Lover's Knot   Gordon 1942; Warren 1942

It's the Music — Not the Words   Styne 1933

It's the Natural Thing to Do   Burke 1937; Johnston 1937

It's the New Generation   Donaldson 1942

It's the Nicest Sort of Feeling   Caesar 1920

It's the Old Army Game   Adamson 1944; McHugh 1944

It's the Only One for Me   Atteridge 1918; Romberg 1918

It's the Only Way to Travel   Van Heusen 1962

It's the Pretty Things You Say   Bryan 1908; Snyder 1908

It's the Principle of the Thing!   Rome 1940

It's the Rhythm in Me   Mills 1935

It's the Same Old Dream   Cahn 1947; Styne 1947

It's the Same Old Play with a New Leading Man   Burke 1931

It's the Same Old South   Eliscu 1940; Gorney 1940

It's the Second Time You Meet that Matters   Comden and Green 1958; Styne 1958

It's the Shirt   Goetz 1911

It's the Smart Little Feller Who Stocked Up His Cellar, That's Getting the Beautiful Girls   Ager 1920; Clarke 1920

It's the Smile   Edwards 1905

It's the Smile that Gets 'Em   Ahlert 1937; Lewis 1937; Young, Joe 1937

It's the Strangest Thing   Akst 1938; Clare 1938

It's the Talk of the Town   Livingston, Jerry 1933

It's the Truth   Drake 1947

It's the Tune that Counts   Raye 1939

It's the Way You Look at Me   Brown, Nacio Herb 1919

It's the Woman Who Pays   Cobb 1916; Edwards 1916

It's the Yacka Hula in Me   Stept 1931

It's the Youth in Me   Blake 1937

It's Three O'Clock   Friml 1934

It's Thrilling   Heyman 1934

It's Time for a Cheer-Up Song   Adams 1978; Strouse 1978

It's Time for a Love Song   Lane 1979; Lerner, Alan Jay 1979

It's Time for Every Boy to Be a Soldier   Bryan 1917

It's Time for Love   Adamson 1963

It's Time for the Love Scene   Loesser 1946

It's Time I Had a Break   Webster 1946

It's Time to Go   Adams 1993; Oakland 1952

It's Time to Go Home   Johnson, Howard 1933

It's Time to Keep Away from You   Brown, Lew 1925; Friend 1925

It's Time to Say 'Aloha'   Fain 1938

It's Time to Say Goodbye   Fain 1958

It's Time to Say Goodnight   Friend 1935; Yellen 1935

It's Time to Say Goodnight Again   Davis 1954; Silver 1954

It's Time to Sing Sweet Adeline Again   Davis 1933; Fain 1933

It's Tomorrow   Evans 1953; Livingston, Jay 1953

It's Too Early to Tell   Coots 1964

It's Too Late Now   Coots 1949

It's Torment   Evans 1953; Livingston, Jay 1953

It's Tough to Be a Flower Girl in Uric   Gorney 1925

It's Tough to Be a Hostess   Rose 1927

It's Tough to Be a Man   Duke 1959

It's Tough to Be a Prima Donna   Rose 1930

It's Tough to Be a Working Girl   Duke 1959

It's Tough to Be Tattooed with Tillie (When You Want to Get Married to May)   Woods 1950

It's Tough when Izzy Rosenstein Loves Genevieve Malone   Kahn 1910
It's True   Woods 1934
It's True, It's True   Cahn 1955
It's Tulip Time in Holland   Whiting 1915
It's Turkey Lurkey Time   Bacharach 1968; David, Hal 1968
It's Twelve O'Clock   Coots 1959
It's Unanimous Now   Stept 1929
It's Unbelievable   Bullock 1938; Spina 1938
It's Up to Me   Adams 1962, 1992; Strouse 1962
It's Up to the Band   Berlin 1927
It's Up to You   Conrad 1931; Fields 1954; Friend 1931; Schwartz, Arthur 1954
It's Up to You (J'en Ai Marre)   DeSylva 1922
It's Vacation Time Again   Livingston, Jerry 1936
It's Way Past My Bedtime   Heyman 1946; Spina 1946
It's What You Believe In   Leigh 1954
It's Whatcha Do with Watcha Got   DePaul 1948; Raye 1948
It's Winter Again   Freed, Arthur 1932; Hoffman 1932
It's Within Your Power   Gordon 1932; Revel 1932
It's Wonderful   Atteridge 1918; DeSylva 1918; Parish 1938; Romberg 1918
It's Wonderful to Be Married   Mills 1947
It's Worth Imagining   Adamson Date Unknown; Warren Date Unknown
It's You   Conrad 1921; Davis 1921; Motzan 1919; Willson 1957
It's You and Me   Johnson, James P. 1961
It's You I Love   Coots 1929; Davis 1929; Wrubel 1951
It's You I Want to Love Tonight   Friml 1934
It's You I'm Talking About   Gordon 1936; Revel 1936
It's You or No One   Cahn 1948; Styne 1948
It's You Who Taught It to Me   Razaf 1939
It's Young and It Doesn't Know   Dubin 1924
It's Your Birthday   Sigman 1949
It's Your Life   Burke 1946; Van Heusen 1946
It's Your Own Fault Annabelle   Whiting 1926
It's Yours   Berlin 1930
It's Yours at the Statler Hotel   Coots 1948
Itsa-Bitsa Cooka-Ritsa (Nuts, Nuts, Nuts)   Hoffman 1948
Ivan's Song   Adamson 1935; Lane 1935
I've a Cabaret at Home   Dubin 1915
I've a Feeling You'll Say Yes To-Day   Young, Joe 1931
I've a Fever   Brooks 1959
I've a Garden in Sweden   Norworth 1911; Smith, Harry B. 1911
I've a Great Big Heart with a Great Big Love for a Little Girl Like You   Leslie 1910
I've a Little Bit of Scotch in Me   Atteridge 1917; Romberg 1917
I've a Little Favor   Kern 1906
I've a Lover in My Heart   Johnson, J. Rosamond 1946
I've a Million Reasons Why I Love You   Kern 1907
I've a Rendezvous with Spring   Duke 1933; Harburg 1933
I've a Shooting-Box in Scotland   Porter 1914, 1916
I've a Strange New Rhythm in My Heart   Porter 1937
I've Always Been a Good Sport   Cohan 1909
I've Always Been Fond of Babies (That's Why I'm in Love with You)   Hanley 1920
I've Always Loved   DePaul 1944; Raye 1944
I've Always Loved You   Rome 1945
I've Always Meant to Tell You   Cahn 1952; Styne 1952
I've Appeared Before Crowned Heads   Herbert 1895; Smith, Harry B. 1895
I've A'ready Started In   Willson 1960

I've Been a Good Santa Claus to You   Williams 1910
I've Been All Over the World   Spina 1957
I've Been Alone too Long (Flavia)   Sigman 1952
I've Been Around a Bit   Kern 1915; Smith, Harry B. 1915
I've Been Decorated   Herbert 1908
I've Been Expecting You   Parish 1932
I've Been Fiddle-ing   Kahn 1917
I've Been Floating Down the Old Green River   Kalmar 1915
I've Been Fooling Around   Smith, Harry B. 1934
I've Been Had   Cahn 1963; Van Heusen 1963
I've Been Here Before   Cahn 1967; Van Heusen 1967
I've Been in a Daze for Days   Martin 1944
I've Been in Love Before   Loesser 1940
I've Been in Love with You   Howard, Bart 1984
I've Been in the Country So Long   Johnson, J. Rosamond 1943
I've Been in Those Shoes   Adams 1978; Strouse 1978
I've Been Kissed Before   Russell 1951
I've Been Longing for a Girl Like You   Johnson, Howard 1927
I've Been Looking   Drake 1954
I've Been Looking for a Perfect Man   Herbert 1911; Smith, Harry B. 1911
I've Been Loved   Cahn 1968
I've Been Married   Lerner, Alan Jay 1985
I've Been Starting Tomorrow   David, Hal 1974
I've Been There   David, Mack 1958
I've Been There and I'm Back   Evans 1958; Livingston, Jay 1958
I've Been There Before   David, Hal 1991; Russell 1946; Strouse 1991
I've Been Through the Mill   Gilbert 1913
I've Been to Hollywood   Merrill 1947
I've Been Waiting All My Life   Bergman 1978
I've Been Waiting All Winter (For a Summer Night Like This)   Mills 1935; Oakland 1935; Parish 1935
I've Been Waiting for You   Atteridge 1923; Gorney 1923
I've Been Waiting for You All the Time   Kern 1919
I've Been Waiting to Tell You I've Been Wanting You   Monaco 1930
I've Been Wanting to Tell You I've Been Wanting You   Kahn 1930
I've Been Wanting You   Atteridge 1923
I've Been Writing My Heart Out to You   Stept 1953
I've Come to California   Adamson 1957; Warren 1957
I've Come to Wive It Wealthily in Padua   Porter 1948
I've Confessed to the Breeze I Love You   Harbach 1925; Youmans 1925
I've Cried a Million Years   Davis 1961
I've Danced to Beat the Band   Herbert 1919
I've Done It All   Mancini 1993
I've Dreamed About This   Bullock 1937
I've 'Eard the Bloody 'Indoos 'As It Worse   Adams 1972; Strouse 1972
I've Fallen for Love   Johnson, James P. 1933; Razaf 1933
I've Fallen Out of Love   Gordon 1931; Revel 1931
I've Forgotten You   Brown, Lew 1943; Fain 1943; Freed, Ralph 1943
I've Found a Bud Among the Roses   Friml 1922; Harbach 1922
I've Found My Dream Girl   Johnson, Howard 1920; Yellen 1920
I've Found My Place in the Sun   Adamson 1935; Lane 1935
I've Found My Sweetheart Sally   Ager 1925; Pollack 1925; Yellen 1925

I've Found the Bluebird   Robin 1926
I've Found the Girl I Want   Dubin 1913
I've Found the Nesting Place of the Bluebird   Yellen 1919
I've Found You at Last   Howard, Joseph E. 1937
I've Going to Settle Down   Schwartz, Jean 1919
I've Gone Goofy Over Miniature Golf   Parish 1930
I've Gone Off the Deep End   Rainger 1939; Robin 1935, 1939
I've Gone Romantic on You   Arlen 1937; Harburg 1937
I've Got ???? Except My Wife   Edwards 1910; Smith, Harry B. 1910
I've Got a Bone to Pick with You   Gordon 1941; Warren 1941
I've Got a Bug in My Head   Fields 1930; McHugh 1930
I've Got a Communistic Feeling for You   Wrubel 1931
I've Got a Crush on You   Gershwin, George 1928, 1929; Gershwin, Ira 1928, 1929; Porter 1929
I've Got a Date   Drake 1954
I've Got a Date with a Dream   Gordon 1938; Hanley 1938; Revel 1938
I've Got a Date with Hate   Fields 1932; McHugh 1932
I've Got a Date with Judy   Pollack 1945
I've Got a Day Off Today   Caesar 1925; Youmans 1925
I've Got a Dream on My Hands   McHugh 1960
I've Got a Feelin' You're Foolin'   Brown, Nacio Herb 1935; Freed, Arthur 1935
I've Got a Feeling for Ophelia   Dixon 1924; Henderson 1924
I've Got a Feeling I'm Falling   Rose 1929; Waller 1929
I've Got a Funny Feeling   Blane 1947; Warren 1947
I've Got a Gal in Ev'ry Port   Gordon 1943
I've Got a Gal in Kalamazoo   Gordon 1942; Warren 1942
I've Got a Heartful of Music   Mercer 1938; Whiting 1938
I've Got a Heavy Date   Kahn 1936
I've Got a Lazy Way of Living   Freed, Arthur 1935
I've Got a Little Chalet in the Valley   Goetz 1913
I've Got a Little Confession to Make   Davis 1933
I've Got a Little Love Song   Ager 1929; Yellen 1929
I've Got a Live One Now   Brown, A. Seymour 1910
I've Got a Locket in My Pocket   David, Mack 1945
I've Got a Molly   Livingston, Jerry 1973
I've Got a Moonlight Date (At the Golden Gate)   Webster 1938
I've Got a New Lease on Love   Ahlert 1937; Young, Joe 1937
I've Got a New Sweetheart Now   Friend 1931
I've Got a One Track Mind   Dietz 1944; Duke 1944; McHugh 1940; Mercer 1940
I've Got a Pair of Swinging Doors that Lead Right into My Heart   Lewis 1919; Young, Joe 1919
I've Got a Pal in Guadalcanal   Magidson 1943; McHugh 1943
I've Got a Passport from Georgia (And I'm Going to the U.S.A.)   Webster 1941
I've Got a Passport to Heaven Since I Fell in Love with You   Coots 1929
I've Got a Penny   Merrill 1966
I've Got a Pocket Full of Sunshine   Johnston 1935; Kahn 1935
I've Got A Pocketful of Dreams   Burke 1938; Monaco 1938
I've Got a Problem   Drake 1953
I've Got a Ragtime Bee in My Bonnet   Gilbert 1911
I've Got a Rainbow Working for Me   Harburg 1967; Styne 1967
I've Got a Red Cross Rosie Going Across with Me   Kalmar 1917; Leslie 1917; Ruby 1917

I've Got a Roof Over My Head   Fields 1933; McHugh 1933
I've Got a Sneaky Feelin'   Baer 1939
I've Got a Sunday Feeling in My Heart   David, Mack 1949; Livingston, Jerry 1949
I've Got a Sweet Tooth Bothering Me   Berlin 1916
I've Got a Ten Day Pass for a Honeymoon with the Girl I Left Behind   Hanley 1918
I've Got a Thousand Plows and Cows and Chickens   Donaldson 1924
I've Got a Two Day Pass for a Honeymoon for the Girl I Left Behind   Donaldson 1918
I've Got a Warm Spot in My Heart   Burke 1933; Spina 1933
I've Got a Warm Spot in My Heart for You   Young, Joe 1933
I've Got a Watch   Coots 1934
I've Got a Wonderful Girl   Meyer 1927
I've Got a 'Yes' Girl   Dietz 1927; Gorney 1927
I've Got an Awful Lot to Learn   Porter 1916
I've Got an Invitation to a Dance   Livingston, Jerry 1934
I've Got Ants in My Pants (Bugology)   Friend 1931
I've Got Blues for Home Sweet Home   Meyer 1916
I've Got Charm   Cahn 1960; Van Heusen 1960
I've Got Class   Brooks 1962
I've Got Everything   Ager 1938; Howard, Bart 1960; Yellen Date Unknown
I've Got Everything I Want but You   Schwartz, Jean 1914
I've Got Ev'rything (As Long As I've Got You)   Johnson, Howard 1928
I've Got Ev'rything but You   Burke 1930
I've Got Five Dollars   Hart 1931; Rodgers 1931
I've Got Friends   Dubin 1922
I've Got Him Now!   Buck 1914
I've Got It All   Coleman 1978; Comden and Green 1978
I've Got It (But It Don't Do Me No Good)   Fain 1930; Kahal 1930
I've Got Manhattan on My Mind   Coslow 1937
I've Got Money in the Bank   Kern 1913
I've Got My Arms Wrapped Around a Rainbow   Coots 1953
I've Got My Captain Working for Me Now   Berlin 1919
I've Got My Eye on You   Stept 1930
I've Got My Eyes on You   Porter 1939
I've Got My Fingers Crossed   Koehler 1935; McHugh 1935
I've Got My Fingers Crossed till You Come Home   Turk 1933
I've Got My Heart Set on You   Freed, Ralph 1944; Gordon 1937; McHugh 1944; Revel 1937
I've Got My Love to Keep Me Warm   Berlin 1937
I've Got My Man Where I Want Him   Parish 1933
I've Got My Mind Made Up   Bacharach 1979
I've Got My Old Love on My Mind Tonight   Ahlert 1932; Turk 1932
I've Got No Strings   Washington 1940
I've Got Nothin' to Do   Fain 1964
I've Got Nothin', You've Got Nothin', We Ain't Got Nothin' to Lose   Davis 1927
I've Got Nothin', You've Got Nothin', We've Got Nothin' to Lose   DeSylva 1932; Whiting 1932
I've Got Nothing to Do   Bergman 1964
I've Got Nothing to Lose but the Blues   Bergman 1954, 1955
I've Got Plenty to Be Thankful For   Berlin 1942
I've Got Rain in My Eyes   Livingston, Jerry 1937
I've Got Rhumbatism   David, Mack 1934; Hoffman 1934
I've Got Rhythm   Styne 1955
I've Got Sand in My Shoes   Alter 1934
I've Got Some New Shoes   Bullock 1935; Coslow 1935; Whiting 1935

I've Got Some Unfinished Business with You   Porter 1941

I've Got Somebody Waiting   Porter 1919

I've Got Somethin'   Kalmar 1941; Ruby 1941

I've Got Something in My Eye   Bryan 1909; Clarke 1917; Leslie 1917; Meyer 1917; Monaco 1936

I've Got Something to Sing About   Oakland 1960

I've Got that Lonesome Feeling   Hoffman 1951

I've Got that Old Christmas Feeling (In My Heart Tonight)   Coots 1950

I've Got the A.B.C.D. Blues   Von Tilzer 1920

I've Got the Army Blues   Gilbert 1916

I've Got the Beer Barrel Polka Blues   Brown, Lew 1939

I've Got the Best Shoulder in Town   Cahn 1955; Styne 1955

I've Got the Blue Ridge Blues   Whiting 1918

I've Got the Blues   Fields 1930; McHugh 1930

I've Got the Blues for Home Sweet Home   Goetz 1916; Jerome 1916; Meyer 1916

I've Got the Blues for Maryland   Parish 1944

I've Got the Blues for the Wearing of the Green   Fisher 1921

I've Got the Blues for You   Kahn 1931

I've Got the Funniest Feeling   Meyer 1933

I've Got the Girl   Donaldson 1926

I've Got the Joys   Akst 1921; Lewis 1921; Young, Joe 1921

I've Got the Man   Smith, Harry B. 1927

I've Got the Nerve to Be in Love   Rome 1937

I've Got the Nicest Little Home in Dixie   Donaldson 1917

I've Got the Place for You, Baby   Howard, Bart 1961

I've Got the President's Ear   Adamson 1948; McHugh 1948

I've Got the Sweetest Girl in Maryland   Donaldson 1917

I've Got the Sweetest Little Baby   Clarke 1914; Goetz 1914

I've Got the Words, I've Got the Tune, Hummin' to Myself   Fain 1932; Magidson 1932

I've Got the World on a String   Arlen 1932; Koehler 1932

I've Got the World Right in the Palm of My Hand   Coots 1929

I've Got the World (With a Fence Around It)   Washington 1929

I've Got the Yes Sir, No Sir Blues   Rose 1925; Silver 1925

I've Got the Yes, We Have No Banana Blues   Brown, Lew 1923; Hanley 1923

I've Got Those Laughin' While My Heart Is Breaking Blues   Meyer 1923

I've Got Those Old Man River Blues   Sissle 1929

I've Got to Be a Chaste Woman   Conrad 1925

I've Got to Be a Rug Cutter   Ellington 1936

I've Got to Be Around   Berlin 1962

I've Got to Be Lovely to Harry   Johnson, James P. 1947, 1948

I've Got to Be There   Gershwin, George 1932; Gershwin, Ira 1932

I've Got to Dance   Kern 1915

I've Got to Fall in Love Again   Burke 1951; Van Heusen 1951

I've Got to Find a Reason   Merrill 1961

I've Got to Get Hot   Henderson 1935; Yellen 1935

I've Got to Get Out of the Habit   Burke 1950; Van Heusen 1950

I've Got to Get Some Money   Snyder 1908

I've Got to Get Somewhere with You   Burke 1946; Van Heusen 1946

I've Got to Give Her Her Own Way   Smith, Harry B. 1911

I've Got to Go and Get Myself a Girl Like You   Cobb 1911; Edwards 1911

I've Got to Go to Sleep My Baby Blues   Hanley 1923

I've Got to Hand It to You   Duke 1941

I've Got to Have Some Lovin' Now   Berlin 1912

I've Got to Keep Busy   Strouse 1987

I've Got to Leave You   Friml 1919; Harbach 1919

I've Got to Pass Your House to Get to My House   Brown, Lew 1933

I've Got to See My Partner   Ager 1930; Yellen 1930

I've Got to Sing a Torch Song   Dubin 1933; Warren 1933

I've Got to Stop Dreaming of You   Kalmar 1938; Ruby 1938

I've Got to Thank You for That   Davis 1949; Silver 1949

I've Got Troubles   Young, Joe 1962

I've Got Troubles of My Own   Johnson, J. Rosamond 1900

I've Got What It Takes   Turk 1922; Warren 1975

I've Got You   Loesser 1942

I've Got You All to Myself   Rainger 1941; Robin 1941

I've Got You and You've Got Me   Brown, Lew 1923; Henderson 1923

I've Got You on My Mind   Porter 1931, 1932

I've Got You on the Top of My List   Clare 1934; Gorney 1934

I've Got You to Lean On   Sondheim 1964

I've Got You Under My Skin   Porter 1936

I've Got You Where I Want You   Waller 1933

I've Got Your Future All Planned   Gorney 1935

I've Got Your Number   Bryan 1910; Coleman 1962; Leigh 1962; Meyer 1910

I've Got Your Picture Over the Telephone   McHugh 1958

I've Gotta Be On My Way (You'll Have the Blues I Know)   Mercer 1958

I've Gotta Crow   Leigh 1954

I've Gotta Go Back to Texas   Berlin 1914

I've Gotta Have You   Gordon 1943; Warren 1943

I've Gotta Hear that Beat   Cahn 1953

I've Gotta Keep My Eye on You   Gordon 1932; Revel 1932

I've Gotta See for Myself   Pollack 1943

I've Gotta Yen for You   Whiting 1930

I've Grown Accustomed to Her Face   Lerner, Alan Jay 1956; Loewe 1956

I've Had a Lovely Time, Good Night   Goetz 1911

I've Had a Terrible, Horrible, No Good, Very Bad Day   Strouse Date Unknown

I've Had about As Much As I Can Take   Bergman 1960

I've Had Enough   Evans 1954; Livingston, Jay 1954

I've Had My Moments   Donaldson 1934; Kahn 1934

I've Had This Feeling Before, But Never Like This   Stept 1943

I've Heard   Lawrence 1954

I've Heard So Much About You   Smith, Robert B. 1906

I've Heard that Before   Atteridge 1911

I've Heard that Song Before   Cahn 1942; Styne 1942

I've Hitched My Wagon to a Star   Mercer 1938; Whiting 1938

I've Just Been Waiting for You   Kern 1915; Smith, Harry B. 1915

I've Just Begun   Styne 1978

I've Just Got Eyes for Susie   Lewis 1931; Woods 1931

I've Just Had a Good Cry   Silver 1952

I've Just Lost My Teddy Bear   Johnson, J. Rosamond 1909

I've Just Seen Her   Adams 1962; Strouse 1962

I've Known You All of My Life   Sondheim Date Unknown

I've Lived, I've Loved, I'm Satisfied   Brown, Lew Date Unknown; Henderson Date Unknown

I've Looked for Trouble   Kern 1926

I've Lost All My Love for You   Akst 1927; Lewis 1927; Young, Joe 1926, 1927

I've Lost Enough Sleep Over You   Bullock 1952

I've Lost My Baby   Sterling 1899; Von Tilzer 1899

I've Lost My Gal   Williams 1909

I've Lost My Head Over You   Razaf 1925

I've Lost My Heart but I Don't Care   Howard, Joseph E. 1909

I've Loved the Same Girl for Fifty Years   Alter 1934; Brown, Lew 1934

I've Made a Habit of You   Dietz 1929; Schwartz, Arthur 1929

I've Made Up My Mind   Dietz 1937; Schwartz, Arthur 1937

I've Made Up My Mind To Mind a Maid Made Up Like You   Bryan 1919; Schwartz, Jean 1919

I've Made Up My Mind to Sail Away   Sterling Date Unknown

I've Never Been in Love Before   Loesser 1950

I've Never Been Loved By Anyone Like You   Mills 1929

I've Never Been Over There   Cohan 1906

I've Never Been So Happy   Strouse 1977

I've Never Forgotten   Cahn 1946; Styne 1946

I've Never Had a Manifestation   Martin 1964

I've Never Known a Night Like Tonight   Warren 1954

I've Never Left Your Arms   Bergman 1958

I've Never Seen Anything Like It in My Life   Adams 1962; Strouse 1962

I've No Idea Where I'm Going   Mancini 1995

I've Nothing to Offer   Akst 1934; Brown, Lew 1934

I've Only Just Started to Care   Freed, Ralph 1954; Livingston, Jerry 1954

I've Said Goodbye to Broadway   Buck 1916

I've Said It a Thousand Times   Russell Date Unknown

I've Said My Last Farewell, Toot Toot Goodbye   Fisher 1906

I've Saved All My Love for You   Buck 1916

I've Seen All Sides   Washington 1959

I've Sent My Wife to the Country   Dubin 1914

I've Shed a Hundred Tears   Brooks 1950

I've Spent Half a Moon   Burke 1935; Spina 1935

I've Still Got My Health   Porter 1940

I've Take Such a Fancy to You   Kern 1912

I've Taken a Fancy to You   Clare 1938, 1939; Mitchell 1938; Pollack 1938, 1939

I've the Lovin'es' Love for You   Blake 1918; Sissle 1918

I've Told Ev'ry Little Star   Hammerstein 1932; Kern 1932

I've Told My Love   Friml 1919; Harbach 1919

I've Tried   David, Mack 1957; Livingston, Jerry 1957

I've Tried Everything   Coleman 1966; Fields 1966

I've Turned the Corner   Gershwin, Ira 1938, 1944; Kern 1938, 1944

I've Waited for This   Egan 1926; Whiting 1926

I've Waited for You   Romberg 1927; Smith, Harry B. 1927

I've Walked Through Wonderland   Loesser 1940

Ivory Lace (inst.)   Alter 1928

Ivy   Carmichael 1947

Ivy and Oak   Romberg 1916

Ivy and the Oak, The   Herbert 1913; Smith, Robert B. 1913

Ivy (Cling to Me)   Johnson, James P. 1922

Ivy Rose   Hoffman 1957

Iyone, My Own Iyone   Bryan 1926

Izzie Get Busy Write Another Little Ragtime Tune   Brown, A. Seymour 1916

J

J. Flynn   DeSylva 1922; Herbert 1922

Ja, Ja, Ja!   Hammerstein 1930; Romberg 1930

Jack and Jill   Cohan 1908; Coslow 1929; Duke 1929; Harbach 1923; Hart 1921, 1923; Johnson, Howard 1939; Rodgers 1921, 1923

Jack and the Beanstalk   Loesser 1948; Russell 1952

Jack and the Giant   Livingston, Jerry 1956

Jack Go Back to Jill   Heyman 1966

Jack How I Envy You   Von Tilzer 1897

Jack in the Box   Kahal 1927

Jack O' Lantern Love   Herbert 1912

Jack of All Trades   Magidson 1941; Oakland 1941

Jack of Diamonds   Oakland 1952; Webster 1952

(My) Jack O'Lantern   Howard, Joseph E. 1909; Smith, Harry B. 1901

Jack O'Lantern Girl   Herbert 1904

Jack O'Rourke's Party Line   Razaf 1956

Jack Thayer Theme   Oakland 1954

Jack the Ripper Song   McHugh 1960

Jackie Coogan   Atteridge 1923; Schwartz, Jean 1923

Jackpot   Dietz 1944; Duke 1944

Jacob's Ladder   Johnson, J. Rosamond 1931; Wrubel 1931

Jacques and Jill   Bergman 1980

Jaded, Degraded Am I   Bergman 1964

Jag, a Drone and a Tank of Air, A   Smith, Harry B. 1908

Jaggy-Jazz, The   Herbert 1920

J'ai Vu Dans Ter Yeux   McHugh 1953

Jail Bird and the Tiger, The   Howard, Joseph E. 1905

Jail Blues   Ellington 1963

Jail of Jealousy   Robison 1963

Jail Song   Weill 1944

Jailbreak   David, Mack 1973

Jailer, Jailer   Comden and Green 1982

Jake - Jake   Berlin 1913

Jake the Baker   Hart Date Unknown; Rodgers Date Unknown

Jake the Sheik   Yellen Date Unknown

Jalopy Song, The   Styne 1960

Jam Session in Brazil (The Batacada)   De Lange 1946; Myrow 1946

Jamaica Rumba   DePaul 1949; Raye 1949

Jamaica (Tahiti)   Yellen 1958

Jamboree   Adamson 1937; Fisher 1944; McHugh 1937; Mills 1935; Willson 1954

Jamboree Jones   Mercer 1936

Jamboree Opening   Brooks 1958

James Van Heusen's Melody (inst.)   Van Heusen 1961

Jamie   Bullock 1977; David, Hal 1960; Spina 1977

Jamie Boy   Freed, Ralph 1970

Jamie's Responsibilities   Blane 1952

Jammin'   Coslow 1937

Jane   Herbert 1903

Jane and Jim, the Safety Twins   Caesar 1943

Jane (From a Little Town in Maine)   Gilbert 1935

Jane We'll Start Chasing Rainbows Again   Fisher 1926

Janette   Martin 1951

Janis (inst.)   Brooks 1957

Janis' Philosophy (inst.)   Brooks 1957

January Birthday Song   Caesar 1940

January, February, March   Sigman 1951

January, February (The Calendar Song)   Stept 1946

January (inst.)   Young, Victor 1956

January Through December   Stept 1944

Japan (An American Battle Song)   Razaf 1944

Japanese   Razaf 1929

Japanese Ballet   Atteridge 1915; Romberg 1915

Japanese Dream, A   Fields 1929; McHugh 1929

Japanese Evening (Japanese Hello)   Brooks 1959

Japanese Girl Like 'Merican Boy (Too Much — Too Much)   Fain 1951; Gordon 1951

Japanese Goodnight   Brooks 1959

Japanese Mammy   Donaldson 1928; Kahn 1928

Japanese Moon   Buck 1927; Fields 1929

Japanese Procession (inst.)   Styne 1971

Japanese Sandman   Egan 1920; Whiting 1920

Japanese Serenade   Romberg 1927; Smith, Harry B. 1927

Japanese Tea Rose   Hanley 1922

Japanese Thank You   Brooks 1959

Japanese Toyland   Carroll 1929

Japanese Willow   Coots 1923

Japansy   Bryan 1927

Jas Nursery's Tattle Tales   Johnson, Howard 1921

Jason   David, Mack 1982

Jassamine Lane   Blake 1924; Sissle 1924

Java   Johnston 1926; Porter 1930; Turk 1926

Java Jive   Oakland 1942

Java Junction (inst.)   Warren 1944

Javanese Flower   Pollack 1923

Javanese Temple Dance (inst.)   Coots 1945

Jawohl, Mein Liebchen, Jawohl   Ruby 1957

Jay McMaster Theme   Oakland 1954

Jaywalker, The   Caesar 1943

Jaz-o-Mine   Akst 1917

Jazz   Martin 1948

Jazz a la Carte   Ellington 1937; Mills 1937

Jazz All Your Troubles Away   Romberg 1918

Jazz Band Jamboree   Raye 1957

Jazz Chase   Washington 1958

Jazz Fugue (inst.)   Duke 1940

Jazz Heaven   Clare 1929

Jazz in a Harem   Brooks 1960

Jazz Legato   Parish 1950

Jazz Marimba   Romberg 1919; Schwartz, Jean 1919

Jazz Marimba Dance   Atteridge 1919

Jazz Patrol   Caesar 1929

Jazz Pizzicato   Parish 1950

Jazz Reception (Kindly Nullify Your Fears)   Hart 1929; Rodgers 1929

Jazz Singer, The   Dubin 1928; Monaco 1928

Jazz Sunday   Johnson, J. Rosamond 1930; Wrubel 1930

Jazz Time Came from the South   Clarke 1924; Johnston 1924; Meyer 1924, 1926; Turk 1924

Jazz Wedding   Atteridge 1923; Schwartz, Jean 1923

Jazz what Have You Done to Me   Fisher 1920

Jazz Your Troubles Away   Johnson, James P. 1922

Jazza Painted Jazzama-Remos   Bryan 1922; Schwartz, Jean 1922

Jazzabeaux   Mills 1966

Jazzadadadoo   Atteridge 1921, 1954; Romberg 1921

Jazzanova   Atteridge 1921; Pollack 1921; Schwartz, Jean 1921

Jazz — How I Love It   Romberg 1918

Jazzin' the Alphabet   Lewis 1919; Snyder 1919; Young, Joe 1919

Jazzing Thunder Storming Dance (Thunderstorm Jazz)   Blake 1923; Sissle 1923

Jazzmania   Brown, Lew 1923; Hanley 1923

Jazztime Baby   Blake 1924; Sissle 1924

Je M'len Fiche du Sex-Appeal   Hart 1930; Rodgers 1930

Je N'Ai Rien   Ellington 1966

Je Ne Comprends Pas   Bryan 1920; Schwartz, Jean 1920

Je Ne Sais Pa Pa (I Do Not Know)   Fisher 1920

Je Ne Sais Pas   Egan 1919; Whiting 1919

Je T'Adore   Akst 1934

Je T'Aime   Dietz 1930; Hoffman 1931; Schwartz, Arthur 1930

Je T'aime . . . a Travers les Ages (You Know You Belong to Somebody Else, So Why Don't You Leave Me Alone)   Monaco 1924

Je T'Aime — I Love You   Duke 1950; Rome 1950

Je T'Aime Commercial   Mercer 1954

Je Vous Adore   Coslow 1936; Young, Victor 1936

Je Vous Adore (I Love You)   Hoffman 1957

Je Vous Aime   Coslow 1924, 1947; Silver 1928

Je Vous Aimerai dans L'Ombre   Romberg 1933

Jealous Blues   Friend 1963

Jealous Moon   Buck 1917

Jealous of Me   Razaf 1938; Waller 1938

Jealousy   Gordon 1931, 1935; Harbach 1911; Howard, Joseph E. 1907; Revel 1931, 1935; Weill 1954

Jealousy Begins at Home   Eliscu 1937

Jealousy Duet   Weill 1933

Jean and Dinah (Yankee Gone)   Raye 1957

Jean the Campus Queen   Coots 1939

Jeanne with the Light Brown Rug   Brooks 1962

Jeannette and Her Little Wooden Shoes (Sabot Dance) (Clip Clop Clop) (Wooden Shoes Dance)   Herbert 1913; Smith, Robert B. 1913

Jeannie's Packin' Up   Lerner, Alan Jay 1947; Loewe 1947

Jeannine, I Dream of Lilac Time   Gilbert 1928

Jean's Magic Song   Hart 1943

Jeep (inst.)   Young, Victor 1945

Jeepers Creepers   Mercer 1938; Warren 1938

Jefferson Davis, The   Donaldson 1924

Jello Family Round   Willson 1949

Jello Pudding Sounds   Willson 1949

Jello Shimmer   Willson 1949

Jelly Donuts and Chocolate Cake   Strouse 1980

Jennie   Conrad 1922; Dietz 1963; Friend 1922; Schwartz, Arthur 1963; Sterling 1902; Von Tilzer 1902

Jennie Lee   Von Tilzer 1902

Jennie MacIntyre   Leslie 1929

Jennifer   Evans 1981; Livingston, Jay 1981

Jenny   Burke 1944; Gershwin, Ira 1940, 1944; Weill 1940, 1944

Jenny, Jenny (Save Your Dreams)   Duke Date Unknown

Jenny Kissed Me   Loesser 1974

Jenny Lind   Caesar 1922; Hammerstein 1940; Schwartz, Arthur 1940

Jenny on a Horse   Livingston, Jerry 1959

Jericho   Robin 1928, 1929

Jerome the Boogie Man   Jerome 1905; Schwartz, Jean 1905

Jerry, My Soldier Boy   Porter 1941

Jerry Nebler Theme   Oakland 1954

Jerry or Joe   Loesser 1943; McHugh 1943

Jerry Strom Theme   Oakland 1954

Jerry's Ectasy   Merrill 1972; Styne 1972

Jersey Americans, The   Alter 1967; Davis 1967

Jersey Bull Blues   Fisher 1939

Jersey City   Robison 1952

Jersey Plunk, The   Weill 1943

Jersey Sweet (inst.)   Johnson, James P. 1943

Jersey Walk (Shake 'em Up Kid)   Hanley 1926

Jerusalem   Bergman 1971; Harburg 1971; Strouse 1993

Jerusalem You're Calling Me   Motzan 1918

Jervis Bay (inst.)   Willson 1943

Jesse James   Freed, Ralph 1954; Livingston, Jerry 1954

Jesse James Glide, The   Cohan 1914

Jester's Song (Jester and Me), The   Robin 1947

Jesus Died that Man Might Live   Livingston, Jerry 1960

Jesus Loves Me   Oakland 1974

Jesusita en Chihuahua (The Cactus Polka)   Drake 1944

Jet   Revel 1949

Jet Song   Sondheim 1957

Jethro and Jezebelle   Warren 1970

Jets March Song   Caesar 1968

Jett Rink Ballad   Webster 1956

Jew-Boy Blues (inst.)   Carmichael 1925

Jewel Ballet   Atteridge 1919; Romberg 1919; Schwartz, Jean 1919

Jewel Song, The   Atteridge 1923; Romberg 1923; Schwartz, Jean 1923

Jewels in the Sky (inst.)   Livingston, Jerry 1957

Jewels of Pandora, The   Ager 1920; Yellen 1920

Jews Have Got Their Irish Up, The   Fain 1947; Yellen 1947

Jezebel   Mercer 1938; Warren 1938

Jezebel Jones   Arlen 1943; Harburg 1943

Jig   Dietz 1970; Herbert 1917; Schwartz, Arthur 1970

Jig Jig Jigaloo   Akst 1929; Clarke 1929

Jig Walk   Ellington 1924

Jigaboo Jig, The   Rose 1927

Jigaree, The   Atteridge 1915; Romberg 1915

Jiggle Your Feet   Baer 1927; Lewis 1927; Young, Joe 1927

Jig-Jig-Jigaloo   Bryan 1929; Meyer 1929

Jijibo, The   DeSylva 1924; Gershwin, George 1924

Jilted   Gershwin, George 1931; Gershwin, Ira 1931

Jim   Friml 1913; Harbach 1913; Raye 1945

Jim Ameche Time   Spina 1957

Jim Bowie   Clare 1955

Jim Corny Well Dressed Man   Styne 1940

Jim Dandy   Ellington 1924

Jim, How Could You Do Such a Thing?   Gershwin, George 1927; Gershwin, Ira 1927

Jim Jam Jems   Donaldson 1917; Goetz 1917; Hanley 1920

Jim, Jim, Don't Come Back Till You Win   Von Tilzer 1918

Jim, Jim, I Always Knew that You'd Win   Von Tilzer 1918

Jiminy Cricket Is the Name   Washington 1940

Jimmie   Coots 1922

Jimmy   Berlin 1927

(Gimme Jimmy) Jimmy Carter   Leigh 1976

Jimmy Had a Nickel   Hoffman 1933

Jimmy, I Love But You   Smith, Harry B. 1922

Jimmy Lowe Theme   Oakland 1954

Jimmy Valentine and Sherlock Holmes   Atteridge 1921; Romberg 1921

Jimmy-Da-Walk, Da Boss-a New York   Johnson, Howard 1928

Jimsy   Brennan 1930; Friml 1930

Jimtown's Fisticuffs   Blake 1921; Sissle 1921

Jing Jang   Spina 1977

Jinga-Bula-Jing-Jing   Lewis 1920; Young, Joe 1920

Jing-a-ling Jing-a-ling   Raye 1950

Jingle Bells   Ager 1922; Johnson, Howard 1939; Yellen 1922

Jingle Bells, I'm in Love   Friend 1937

Jingle Feet   Jerome 1905; Schwartz, Jean 1905

Jingle Jag   Howard, Joseph E. 1937

Jingle Jangle Jingle   Loesser 1942

Jingle of the Jungle   Hoffman 1937; Lerner, Sammy 1937; Mills 1934; Oakland 1934; Parish 1934

Jingle Step   Blake 1923; Sissle 1923

Jingles and Jokes   Howard, Joseph E. 1907

Jingles (inst.)   Johnson, James P. 1926

Jitterbug, The   Arlen 1939; Cahn 1945; Harburg 1939; Mills 1934; Styne 1945

Jitterbug Jamboree   Bloom 1939; Koehler 1939

Jitterbug, The (inst)   Styne 1942

Jitterbug Tree, The   Razaf 1938; Waller 1938

Jitterbug Waltz (inst.), The   Waller 1942

Jitterbugging with the Young Folks   Fain 1940

Jitterbug's Lullaby   Mills 1938

Jitterbug's Lullaby (Jitterbug's Death)   Loesser 1942; Spina 1942

Jitterbug's Lullaby (Jitterbug's Holiday)   Ellington 1938

Jive Drill   Blake 1952; Sissle 1952

Jive Samba   Pollack 1942

Jive Stomp   Ellington 1966

Jivey Jones   Baer 1944

J.J. Jones   Evans 1959; Livingston, Jay 1959

Jo Jo Josephine   Waller 1930

Joan of Arc   Harbach 1917; Strouse 1999

Joan of Arc (They Are Calling You)   Bryan 1917

Joan of Arkansaw   Heyman 1935

Joanie the Genie   Brooks 1957

Joanie's Forever   Bacharach 1960

Joanie's Shadow   David, Hal 1962

Joanna   Mancini 1959; Mercer 1959; Mills 1929

Joanne   Cahn 1964; Silver 1928; Van Heusen 1964

Job Application, The   Bergman 1978

Job for Me, A   Martin 1958

Job Is a Home to a Homeless Man, A   David, Hal 1974

Job Lots   Romberg 1917

Job with a Future, A   Robin 1930; Whiting 1930

Jobo (The Funny Little Clown)   Coots 1955

Jockey on the Carousel, The   Fields 1935; Kern 1935; McHugh 1935

Jockey Song   Buck 1913

Jockey's Life for Mine   Blake 1924; Sissle 1924

Joe   Conrad 1930

Joe Carioca   Heyman 1944

Joe Deane Theme   Oakland 1954

Joe Dynamite's Dentistry Song   Coleman 1960; Leigh 1960

Joe Hill   Robison 1958

Joe Is Here   Kalmar 1923; Ruby 1923

Joe, Jack, Moe and Mack   Gordon 1950; Myrow 1950

Joe Jazz   Whiting 1930

Joe Martin Calling   Lawrence 1957

Joe O'Grady   Styne 1941

Joe the Bomber   Mills 1937

Joey   Cahn 1962; Loesser 1956; Van Heusen 1962

Jogafree   Herbert 1905

Jogging Along through the Park   Hanley 1934

Johanna   Sondheim 1979

Johannesburg   Magidson 1950; Oakland 1950

John and Jim   Styne 1985

John and Mary Upright   Caesar 1947

John Barleycorn   Schwartz, Arthur 1955

John Craig March (inst.)   Johnson, Howard 1912

John Held Jr.   Atteridge 1924; Romberg 1924; Schwartz, Jean 1924

John Henry, That Superman   Razaf 1937; Waller 1937

John Johnson   Herbert 1903

John Saw the Number   Blake 1944

John Sweet Ballet (inst.), The   Styne 1971

John Wrigley Theme   Oakland 1954

John-John-John   Arlen 1965

Johnnie   Atteridge 1923; Schwartz, Jean 1923

Johnnie Get Your Hair Cut Short Like Mine   Johnson, J. Rosamond 1935
Johnnie I'll Take You   Cobb 1904; Edwards 1904
Johnnie Jones' Sister Sue   Cobb 1902; Edwards 1902
Johnnie on the Spot   Von Tilzer 1914
Johnnie's Comin' Home Tonight   Wrubel 1943
Johnny and Lucille   Blane 1948
Johnny and the Puckwudgies   Lawrence 1951
Johnny Cake   Fields 1950
Johnny Christmas   David, Mack 1955
Johnny Crewcut   David, Mack 1953
Johnny Fedora and Alice Blue Bonnet   Wrubel 1946, 1954
Johnny Fiddle   Livingston, Jerry 1960
Johnny Freedom   Styne 1960
Johnny Get Angry   David, Hal 1962
Johnny, Get Off the Corner   Cohan 1903
Johnny Get Your Gun Again   DePaul 1942; Raye 1942
Johnny Guitar   Hoffman 1953; Silver 1953; Young, Victor 1954
Johnny Has Gone for a Soldier   Lawrence 1952
Johnny Is a Hoarder   Rome 1942
Johnny Is Getting It Now, Oh Goody Goody   Clarke 1914
Johnny Is My Darling   Rome 1973
Johnny Jones   Loesser 1941
Johnny Morgan   Williams 1905
Johnny One-Note   Hart 1937; Rodgers 1937
Johnny Peddler (I Got)   Brown, Lew 1940
Johnny Q. Public of the U.S.A.   Cohan 1937
Johnny Ride the Sky   Lawrence 1951
Johnny Shiloh   Sherman 1963
Johnny Stop! Please Don't! Mon-Ma   Fisher 1923
Johnny Zero   David, Mack 1943
Johnny's Arrest and Homecoming   Weill 1936
Johnny's Bugle   Sherman 1965
Johnny's Got a To-To   Mills 1947
Johnny's in Town   Meyer 1919; Yellen 1919
Johnny's Melody   Weill 1936
Johnny's on a Journey   Lane 1956; Lawrence 1956
Johnny's Patter   Loesser 1942
Johnny's Song (Listen to My Song)   Weill 1936
Johnny's Speech   Weill 1936
Johnson Rag   Lawrence 1940
Johnston for Governor   McHugh 1958
Joie De Vivre   Sherman 1967
Join in the Dances (inst.)   Kern 1956
Join It Right Away   Porter 1940
Join the Circus   Coleman 1980
Join the Human Race   Blane 1965; Martin 1965
Join the Marines   Dietz 1944; Duke 1944
Join the Navy   Robin 1927; Youmans 1927
Join the Navy (The Navy Song)   Arlen 1944; Mercer 1944
Join the Party   Clare 1936
Joint Is Jumpin', The   Razaf 1938; Waller 1938
Jo-Jo the Cannibal Kid   Bloom 1936; Mercer 1936
Jo-Jo the Dog-Faced Boy   Sherman 1959
Joker (In the Card Game of Life), The   Parish 1954
Jokes   Adams 1978; Strouse 1978
Joke's on Me, The   Evans 1976; Livingston, Jay 1976; Mancini 1976; Strouse 1993
Joline   Robison 1922
Jolly Cuirassier   Herbert 1908
Jolly Friars March (inst.), The   Coots 1945
Jolly Good Fellow   Cohan 1901; Smith, Robert B. 1912
Jolly Holiday   Sherman 1964
Jolly Hunters, The   David, Mack 1958; Livingston, Jerry 1958

Jolly Jingle Bells   Sherman 1959
Jolly Me   Smith, Robert B. 1919
Jolly Tar and the Milkmaid, The   Gershwin, George 1937; Gershwin, Ira 1937
Jolly Troubadour (inst.), The   Schwartz, Arthur 1929
Jolly Yourself Along   Edwards 1909; Smith, Robert B. 1909
Jollyanna   Harburg 1952
Jolson Tribute, The   Oakland 1953
Jones' Family Friends, The   Cohan 1928
Jonny   Heyman 1934
Joobalai   Rainger 1938; Robin 1938
Joop Joop   Freed, Ralph 1951; Hoffman 1951
Jophe's Waltz   Warren Date Unknown
Jose   Mills 1947
Jose, Can't You See   Brown, Lew 1932; Henderson 1932
Joseph   Livingston, Jerry 1960
Joseph, Joseph   Cahn 1938
Joseph Taylor, Jr.   Hammerstein 1947; Rodgers 1947
Josephine   Ahlert 1933; Bryan 1920; Kahn 1937; Leslie 1933; Porter 1955; Schwartz, Jean 1920; Willson 1956
Josephine (inst.)   Warren Date Unknown
Josephine Waters   Dietz 1936; Schwartz, Arthur 1936
Joshua   Lerner, Alan Jay 1943; Loewe 1943
Joshua Fit de Battle   Blake 1932; Sissle 1932
Josie   Cahn 1945; Monaco 1910; Spina 1954; Styne 1945
Jourdain the Would-Be Gentleman (Epilogue)   Drake 1951
Journey into Love, A   Coots 1958
Journey to a Star, A   Robin 1943; Warren 1943
Journey to Your Lips, A   Webster 1942
Journey's End   Fields 1932; Kern 1921, 1925; McHugh 1932; Schwartz, Jean 1926
Journey's End (inst.)   Hanley 1929
Jousts, The   Lerner, Alan Jay 1960; Loewe 1960
Joy   Russell 1948
Joy and Gloom   Atteridge 1924; Romberg 1924; Schwartz, Jean 1924
Joy Bells   Friend 1927; Kern 1923; Smith, Harry B. 1927
Joy in the Morning   Fain 1965; Webster 1965
Joy Is Mine   Hart 1928; Rodgers 1928
Joy of Easter   Young, Victor 1954
Joy of Loving You, The   Howard, Bart 1960
Joy or Strife   Smith, Harry B. 1928
Joy Ride   Webster 1958
Joy Spreader, The   Hart 1925; Rodgers 1925
Joy Street   Conrad 1929; Mitchell 1929
Joyful Thing, A   Cahn 1966; Van Heusen 1966
Joy-Meetin' (inst.)   Johnson, James P. 1925
Joyous and Thankful   Willson 1956
Joyride   De Lange 1945; Myrow 1945
Joys   Akst 1921; Lewis 1921; Young, Joe 1921
Joys of Love, The   Smith, Harry B. 1911
J.P. Boogie (inst.)   Johnson, James P. 1943
J.P. Williamson   Ellington 1958
Juanita   Dubin 1924; Gershwin, George 1924; Gershwin, Ira 1924; Johnson, Howard 1939
Juanita's Place Montage   Bacharach 1966; David, Hal 1966
Juarez and Lincoln   Eliscu 1943; Gorney 1943
Juba Dance   Johnson, James P. 1922
Jubilation!   Blane 1971
Jubilation T. Cornpone   DePaul 1956; Mercer 1956
Jubilee   Carmichael 1937
Jubilee (inst.)   Robison 1927
Jubilee Presentation   Porter 1935
Jubilee Tonight   Blake 1960; Sissle 1960
Jubilee Trail   Clare 1953, 1954; Young, Victor 1953, 1954

Jubilesta   Ellington 1938; Mills 1938

Jubi-lie, Jubi-lo   Evans 1958; Livingston, Jay 1958

Jubilo   Kern 1919

Judaline   DePaul 1943, 1948; Raye 1943, 1948

Judge, Don't Send Me to Jail!   Lawrence 1959

Judgement at Nuremberg   Webster 1963

Judgement Day   Brown, A. Seymour 1929; Young, Victor 1924

Judgement of Paris, The   Duke Date Unknown; Porter 1935

Judy   Carmichael 1934; Fain 1928; Kahal 1928; Lerner, Sammy 1934; Martin 1972

Judy (inst.)   Robison 1928

Judy Says   David, Hal 1961

Judy, Who D'ya Love?   Robin 1927

Judy, You'll Never Know   Freed, Ralph 1962

Jug of Jive, a Loaf of Bread and Thou, A   Razaf 1950

Jug of Wine, A   Lerner, Alan Jay 1945; Loewe 1945; Spina 1954

Juggling a Jig-Saw   Ahlert 1933; Leslie 1933

Juke Box Hop, The   Comden and Green 1960; Styne 1960

Juke Box Jump   Mills 1942

Juke Box Millionaires   David, Mack 1944

Juke Box Serenade   Baer 1965

Jules Theme   Styne 1954

Julia   Conrad 1923; Davis 1923

Julia and Donald and Joe   Cohan 1916

Julianne   Egan 1938

Julie   De Lange 1941; Jerome 1903; Schwartz, Jean 1903

Julie Dooley   Howard, Joseph E. 1905

Julie O'Dooley   Leslie 1945

Julienne   Turk 1921

Julie's Dream (inst.)   Mercer 1955

Juliet   Kalmar 1934; Ruby 1934

Julius   Fisher 1920

Julius You Wonderful Boy   Conrad 1926; Meyer 1926

July and I   De Lange 1948

July Birthday Song   Caesar 1940

Jump de Broom   Arlen 1968

Jump for Joy   Ellington 1941; Webster 1941

Jump Jim Crow   Romberg 1917

Jump, Little Chillun   Fain 1951; Harburg 1951

Jump Steady   Blake 1924; Sissle 1924

Jump Up Carnival   Raye 1957

Jump when I Say Frog   Merrill 1958

Jumpin' at the Woodside   De Lange 1939; Van Heusen 1939

Jumpin' Frog   Duke 1968

Jumpin' Jubilee   Harburg 1950; Lane 1950

Jumpin' on Saturday Night   Brooks 1945

Jumpin' on the Moon   Friend 1958

Jumping Jack   Bloom 1928, 1929; Hart 1921; Rodgers 1921

Jumping Room Only   Ellington 1973

Jumping to the Jukebox   Rome 1943

June   Bryan 1928; Goetz 1911; Johnson, J. Rosamond 1949; Parish 1980; Schwartz, Jean 1928

June Bride   DePaul 1954; Mercer 1954

June Bug, The   Young, Victor 1934

June Comes Around Every Year   Arlen 1945; Mercer 1945

June Honeymoon   Kalmar 1911; Snyder 1911

June in Genoa   Russell 1955

June in January   Rainger 1934; Robin 1934

June Is Bustin' Out All Over   Hammerstein 1945; Rodgers 1945

June Is Living the Life of Reilly   Mills 1948

June Is Warm   Brooks 1959

June Love   Friml 1921

June My Honeymoon Girl   Fisher Date Unknown

June Night   Romberg 1927

June Night (Just Give Me a June Night, the Moonlight and You)   Baer 1924; Friend 1924

June of Long Ago   Robison 1925

June Time Is the Love Time for Everyone but Me   Clare 1931

June, Why Did July to Me   Rome 1951

Jungaleena   Arlen 1928; Magidson 1928

Jungelitis (The Monkey Song)   Carmichael 1952

Jungle Ball   Buck 1915

Jungle Bungalow (I'll Build a Home in the Jungle)   Hanley 1922

Jungle Chant   Carmichael Date Unknown

Jungle Fever   Dietz 1934; Donaldson 1934

Jungle Honeymoon   Burke 1952; Van Heusen 1952

Jungle Jamboree   Ellington 1929; Razaf 1929

Jungle Jigolo   Fisher 1936

Jungle Jingle   Berlin 1927; Loesser 1940

Jungle Joy   Conrad 1906

Jungle Land   Coslow 1923

Jungle Love   Freed, Ralph 1938; Rainger 1938; Robin 1938

Jungle Mess Around   Johnson, James P. 1958

Jungle Nights in Dixieland   Clarke 1924; Johnston 1924; Meyer 1924, 1926; Turk 1924

Jungle Nights in Harlem   Ellington 1934; Mills 1934

Jungle Nymphs (inst.)   Johnson, James P. 1922

Jungle of Love, The   Howard, Bart 1957

Jungle of Your Heart, The   Drake 1970

Jungle Red   Cahn 1956

Jungle Rhythm Roundup   Razaf 1942

Jungle Shadows   Hammerstein 1927; Harbach 1927

Jungle Town Has Moved to Dixieland   Clarke 1924; Johnston 1924; Meyer 1924; Turk 1924

Jungle Wedding Bells   Edwards 1911

Jungle Wedding March, The   Burke 1952; Van Heusen 1952

Junio   Donaldson 1929

Junior   Lane 1938, 1939; Loesser 1938, 1939

Junior Fire Marshal Song (Junior Fire Marshals Are We), The   Caesar 1957

Junior Miss   Fields 1957; Howard, Joseph E. 1907; Lane 1957

Junior Miss with a Senior Kiss, The   Hoffman 1957

Junior-Senoir Prom, The   Mills 1929

Junk Man   Loesser 1934

Junkman's Jingle, The   Gordon 1953; Myrow 1953

Junkman's Song   Carmichael 1957

Juno, My Honeymoon Girl   Bryan 1919; Schwartz, Jean 1919

Jupiter Forbid   Hart 1942; Rodgers 1942

Jupiter Jumps (inst.)   Revel 1955

Just a Baby's Prayer at Twilight   Lewis 1918; Young, Joe 1918

Just a Barefoot Boy Awhistlin' to His Dog   Hanley 1934

Just a Big Ego   Caesar 1985

Just a Big-Hearted Man   Brennan 1929

Just a Bird's Eye View (Of My Old Kentucky Home)   Donaldson 1926; Kahn 1926

Just a Bit o' Blarney   Goetz 1910

Just a Bit o' Dreaming   Kahn 1920

Just a Blue Serge Suit   Berlin 1945

Just a Blue-Eyed Blonde   Kahn 1931

Just a Boy that Girls Remember   Clare 1923; Turk 1923

Just a Bunch of Wild Flowers   Schwartz, Jean 1926

Just a Child of Manhattan   Bryan 1932; Edwards 1932

Just a Corner of Heaven to Me   Hanley 1927

Just a Corporal   Egan 1932

Just a Cottage Small by a Waterfall   DeSylva 1925; Hanley 1925

Just a Couple of Kids (Who Never Grew Up)   Schwartz, Jean 1948

Just a Cozy Hide-Away   Brown, Lew 1927; DeSylva 1927; Henderson 1927

Just a Fair Weather Friend   Mercer 1934

Just a Few Thrills Ago   Coslow 1940

Just a Friend of Mine   Schwartz, Arthur 1930

Just a Gentle Word from You Will Do   Ellington 1969

Just a Gigolo   Caesar 1930

Just a Girl of Yesterday   Meyer 1916

Just a Girl that Men Forget   Dubin 1922

Just a Golden Butterfly   Cobb 1901; Edwards 1901

Just a Good Joe   Leigh 1958

Just a Home Sweet Home Girl   Jerome 1913; Schwartz, Jean 1913

Just a Kid Named Joe   David, Mack 1938; Livingston, Jerry 1938

Just a Kiss   Atteridge 1919; Carroll 1919; Parish 1938

Just a Kiss Apart   Robin 1948; Styne 1948

Just a Kiss for Now Cherie   Hanley 1930

Just a Kiss in the Moonlight   Coslow 1930; Robin 1930

Just a Letter for a Boy Over There from a Gray Haired Mother Over Here   Sterling 1918

Just a Little ———   Conrad 1928

Just a Little Affection   Livingston, Jerry 1940

Just a Little Band of Gold   Lewis 1910

Just a Little Bit   Egan 1925; Kahn 1925

Just a Little Bit Behind the Times   Hanley 1920

Just a Little Bit More   Fields 1939; Ruby 1951; Schwartz, Arthur 1939

Just a Little Bit o' Driftwood   Davis 1928

Just a Little Bit o' Love   Carroll 1917

Just a Little Bit of Dreaming   Egan 1923; Whiting 1923

Just a Little Bit of Lingerie   Goetz 1911

Just a Little Bit of Love   Smith, Harry B. 1917, 1923; Snyder 1923

Just a Little Bit of Lovin' When You're Feeling Lonesome   Fisher 1931

Just a Little Blue for You   Hanley 1929

Just a Little Brook   Coslow Date Unknown

Just a Little Closer   Johnson, Howard 1930

Just a Little Cottage in the Country   Sterling 1917

Just a Little Daisy for Mary and Me   Von Tilzer 1929

Just a Little Extra   Schwartz, Jean 1926

Just a Little Faded Rose   Conrad 1928; Silver 1928

Just a Little Flower Shop Around the Corner   Woods 1933

Just a Little Fond Affection   Bryan 1906

Just a Little Glimpse of Paradise   Kalmar 1929; Ruby 1929; Warren 1929

Just a Little Home for the Old Folks   Ahlert 1932; Leslie 1932

Just a Little Joint with a Juke Box   Martin 1941

Just a Little Kiss at Twilight   Egan 1928

Just a Little Lane Off Main Street   Coots 1934; Magidson 1934

Just a Little Laughter   Friml 1918

Just a Little Lie   Hart 1921, 1923; Rodgers 1921, 1923

Just a Little Line   Kern 1919

Just a Little Lonely   Kahn 1926

Just a Little Longer   Berlin 1926

Just a Little Love   Sterling 1911; Von Tilzer 1911

Just a Little Love Song   Akst 1921; Lewis 1921; Young, Joe 1921

Just a Little Love Song (Mais le Son de Ta Voix)   Lewis 1923; Young, Joe 1923

Just a Little Lovin' for Baby Please   Sterling 1912; Von Tilzer 1912

Just a Little on Account   Meyer 1907

Just a Little Rose   Kahn 1926

Just a Little Smile   Howard, Joseph E. 1911

Just a Little Smile from You   Hanley 1927

Just a Little Song for You   Smith, Harry B. 1923

Just a Little Space Can Be a Growing Place   David, Hal 1974

Just a Little Sweeter than the Rest   Lerner, Sammy 1931

Just a Little Thing   Hart 1928; Rodgers 1928

Just a Little Way Away from Home   Lewis 1928; Young, Joe 1928

Just a Little While   Berlin 1930

Just a Little White House   Rome 1950

Just a Little Word (inst.)   Kern 1956

Just a Love Song at Sundown   David, Mack 1938; Livingston, Jerry 1938

Just a Melody for a Memory   Harburg 1930

Just a Melody from a Memory   Fain 1929; Gorney 1929; Kahal 1929

Just a Memory   Brown, Lew 1927; DeSylva 1927; Henderson 1927

Just a Minute (inst.)   Young, Joe 1974

Just a Minute More to Say Good-Bye   Lewis 1931

Just a Moment   Donaldson 1935

Just a Moment More   Evans 1951; Livingston, Jay 1951

Just a Moment Please   Warren Date Unknown

Just a Night for Meditation   Lewis 1928; Pollack 1928; Young, Joe 1928

Just a Paper Doll   Howard, Joseph E. 1907

Just a Pretty Little Home   Brown, A. Seymour 1923

Just a Quiet Evening   Mercer 1937; Whiting 1937

Just a Record on the Phonograph   Coots 1948

Just a Regular Girl   Romberg 1922

Just a Rose Covered Doorway   Hanley 1933

Just a Scamp   Razaf 1955

Just a Sentimental Tune   Alter 1930

Just a Shade on the Blue Side   Adamson 1948; Carmichael 1948

Just a Simple Country Maiden   Cobb 1917; Edwards 1917

Just a Simple Melody   Cahn 1937, 1938

Just a Smile   Clare 1926; Hammerstein 1920; Harbach 1920; Monaco 1926

Just a Song Without a Name   Stept 1927

Just a Sweet Old Gent and a Quaint Old Lady   Brown, Lew 1937; DeSylva 1937; Henderson 1937

Just a Tender Spot for Father Dear   Jerome 1902; Schwartz, Jean 1902

Just a Thought of You   Hanley 1919

Just a Tiny Cup of Tea   DeSylva 1922; Gershwin, George 1922

Just a Touch   Hammerstein 1922; Mitchell 1922

Just a Week Ago To-Day   Johnson, Howard 1925

Just a Week from Today   Dubin 1920

Just a Word of Sympathy   Kahn 1916

Just a Year Ago   Williams 1911

Just a Year Ago Tonight   Rose 1927

Just Across the Bridge of Gold   Sterling 1904; Von Tilzer 1904

Just Across the Mountains   Mercer 1968

Just Across the River on a Hill   Carmichael 1953

Just Across the River on the Hill   Von Tilzer 1934

Just Across the Street   Rome 1948

Just Across the Way   Lewis 1940

Just Act Natural   Cohan 1923

Just an Echo in the Valley   Woods 1932

Just an Echo of Aloha   Ahlert 1957; Young, Joe 1957

Just an Error in the News   Mills 1938

Just an Honest Mistake   Evans 1961; Livingston, Jay 1961

Just an Hour of Love   Bryan 1929

Just an Old Banjo Without Any Strings   Johnson, J. Rosamond 1934

Just an Old Lady   Fisher 1939

Just an Old Love Affair   Kahn 1929

Just an Old Manuscript   Razaf 1943

Just an Old Pressed Rose in the Old Family Album   Revel 1959

Just an Ordinary Guy   Johnson, James P. 1943

Just an Out-of-the-Way Little Love Nest   Fain 1929; Lerner, Sammy 1929

Just Another Chance   Mancini 1953

Just Another Day Wasted   Turk 1927

Just Another Day Without You   Kahn 1926

Just Another Dream Gone Wrong   Harburg 1930

Just Another Dream of You   Burke 1931; Davis 1932

Just Another Kill   Berlin 1920

Just Another Kiss   Caesar 1919; Coots 1929; Davis 1929

Just Another Love Affair   Davis 1928; Lewis 1930; Yellen 1931

Just Another Night   Conrad 1931; Donaldson 1928

Just Another Page in Your Diary   Porter 1938

Just Another Polka   Loesser 1953

Just Another Poor Man Gone Wrong   Sterling 1919; Von Tilzer 1919

Just Another Rendezvous   Lewis 1931

Just Another Rhumba   Gershwin, George 1938; Gershwin, Ira 1938

Just Another Romance, Now I Know It's Love   Conrad 1931

Just Another Waltz that Goes with the Night   Young, Joe 1932

Just Around the Corner   Dietz 1932; Kahn 1918; Schwartz, Arthur 1932; Von Tilzer 1925

Just Around the Corner from Broadway   Edwards 1914

Just Around the Corner from Easy Street   Egan 1919; Whiting 1919

Just Around the Corner from Paradise   Stept 1925

Just as Easy as Rolling Off a Log   Bryan 1936; Schwartz, Jean 1936

Just As Long As I Have You   Young, Victor 1929

Just As Long As I Know Katie's Waitin'   Brown, Lew 1943; Freed, Ralph 1943

Just As Long as the Swanee Flows   Bryan 1911

Just As Long As the World Goes 'Round and Around, and I Go Around with You   Woods 1935

Just As Long As You Belong to Me   Lewis 1929; Pollack 1929; Young, Joe 1929

Just As Long As You're Treatin' Me Right   Mills 1929

Just As Long As You're With Me   Stept 1953

Just As Soon As I Laid Eyes on You   Cobb 1916; Edwards 1916

Just As Though You Were Here   De Lange 1942

Just As We Used to Be   Von Tilzer 1920

Just As We Used to Do   Brown, Lew 1919

Just As You Are   Kahn 1927

Just As You were in My Dreams   Johnson, James P. 1961

Just As Your Mother Was   Sterling 1917; Von Tilzer 1917

Just a-Settin' and a Rockin'   Ellington 1941

Just Be a Builder of Dreams   Lewis 1929; Pollack 1929; Young, Joe 1929

Just Because I Loved You Long Ago   Sterling 1900

Just Because I'm French   Razaf 1944

Just Because You Used to Be an Old Sweetheart of Mine   Lewis 1931

Just Because You're a Poor Little Girl   Edwards 1909

Just Because You're You   Buck 1917; Friend 1932; Kern 1917; Leigh 1952

Just Because You're You. . . That's Why I Love You   Turk 1922

Just Becuz   Willson 1948

Just Before Daybreak (inst.)   Johnson, James P. 1946

Just Begging for Love   Berlin 1931

Just Beyond the Rainbow   Revel 1945

Just Blew in from the Windy City   Fain 1953; Webster 1953

Just Born to Be Lonesome   Kahn 1933; Pollack 1933

Just Bring Two Lips Alone   Meyer 1914

Just By Your Example   Woods 1935

Just Call Me Sunny   Warren Date Unknown

Just Cause the Moon Was Shinin'   Smith, Harry B. 1902

Just Come Home   Sigman 1959

Just Come Up and Take Your Presents Back   Sterling 1898; Von Tilzer 1898

Just Don't Take It Away   Merrill 1971; Styne 1971

Just Dreaming Till You Come Home   Dubin 1943; Friend 1943

Just Eighteen   Hammerstein 1931; Whiting 1931

Just Follow the Sun   Donaldson 1933; Kahn 1933

Just for a Change   Loesser 1937

Just for a Day   Oakland 1929

Just for a Moment   Meyer 1926

Just for a Thrill   Raye 1939

Just for a While   Brooks 1948

Just for Awhile   Cahn 1939

Just for Fun   Evans 1949; Livingston, Jay 1949

Just for Me and Mary   Clarke 1919

Just for Old Time's Sake   Stept 1924

Just for Once   Fields 1959

Just for Remembrance Bring Me a Red Red Rose   Parish 1923

Just for Today   Drake 1968; Herbert 1900; Smith, Harry B. 1900

Just for Tonight   Carmichael 1962; Mancini 1962; Mercer 1962

Just for You   Brown, Nacio Herb Date Unknown; Cahn 1944; Freed, Arthur Date Unknown; Friml 1936; Howard, Joseph E. 1911; Kahn 1936; Robin 1952; Styne 1944; Warren 1952

Just for You Alone   Baer 1943

Just for You from Above   Smith, Harry B. 1908

Just Friends   Bacharach 1980; Lewis 1931

Just Get Along   Styne 1965

Just Get Out and Walk   Herbert 1905; Smith, Harry B. 1905

Just Girls   Buck 1917

Just Give Me Ragtime Please   Berlin 1916

Just Give Me the Girl   Donaldson 1933

Just Give Me Time   Leigh 1952

Just Give the Southland to Me   Revel 1928; Sissle 1928

Just Good Friends   Kern 1909

Just Goofy   Mills 1929

Just Have the Band Play Home Sweet Home   Sterling 1902

Just Hello   Harbach 1936; Romberg 1936

Just Help Yourself   Sterling 1907; Von Tilzer 1907

Just Hold Her Hand (She'll Understand)   Howard, Joseph E. 1947

Just Home from College   Jerome 1907; Schwartz, Jean 1907

Just Hot   McHugh 1923

Just How Much Do I Love You   Spina 1967

Just How Much I Love You   Johnson, J. Rosamond 1907

Just Imagine   Brown, Lew 1927; DeSylva 1927; Henderson 1927

Just in Case   Gershwin, Ira 1945; Weill 1945

Just in Case We Have to Say Goodbye Again   Cahn 1950; Fain 1950; Kahal 1950

Just In Case You Change Your Mind   Freed, Ralph 1936

Just in Time   Comden and Green 1956; Styne 1956

Just Joggin' Along   Loesser 1937

Just Keen about You   Fisher 1930

Just Keep A-Dreaming   Howard, Joseph E. 1910

Just Keep Singing a Song   Revel 1928; Sissle 1928

Just Keep the Dear Boys Guessing   Harbach 1911

Just Kids   Carroll 1924; Clare 1928; Monaco 1928

Just Kiss Me and Say Good Bye   Gilbert 1906

Just Kiss Yourself Goodbye   Jerome 1902; Schwartz, Jean 1902

Just Lean on Me   Caesar 1924; Conrad 1924; Harbach 1924

Just Let Me Get Away with This One   Strouse 1989

Just Let Me Look at You   Fields 1938; Kern 1938

Just Like a Butterfly that's Caught in the Rain   Dixon 1927; Woods 1927

Just Like a Corner of Heaven to Me   Hanley 1933

Just Like a Diamond   Atteridge 1923; Schwartz, Jean 1923

Just Like a Doll   Romberg 1922

Just Like a Man   Duke 1946

Just Like a Melody Out of the Sky   Donaldson 1928

Just Like a Song   Willson 1956

Just Like a Vagabond   Magidson 1929

Just Like a Wild, Wild Rose   Buck 1927

Just Like a Woman   Willson 1956

Just Like Children   Duke 1959

Just Like Clingin' Roses on a Clingin' Vine   Davis 1951; Silver 1951

Just Like Darby and Joan   Leslie 1928

Just Like Frankie and Johnnie   Kahal 1931

Just Like in a Story Book   Hanley 1930

Just Like Jimmy and Me   Fain 1930; Kahal 1930

Just Like Last Night   Sondheim 1987

Just Like That   Brooks 1959; DeSylva 1922; Herbert 1922; Loesser 1937

Just Like the End of a Story   Pollack 1927

Just Like the Rose   Berlin 1909

Just Like This   Friml 1918

Just Like Washington Crossed the Delaware, General Pershing Will Cross the Rhine   Johnson, Howard 1917; Meyer 1917

Just Like You   Gershwin, Ira 1921

Just Like Your Shadow   Davis 1932; Stept 1932

Just Look Around   Hammerstein 1923; Youmans 1923

Just Love Me   Styne 1927

Just Love Me All the Time   Herbert 1912

Just Loving You   Brown, Lew 1943; Freed, Ralph 1943

Just Lucky, I Guess   Duke 1955

Just Married   Drake 1953

Just Mention Joe   Akst 1934; Brown, Lew 1934

Just Missed the Opening Chorus   DeSylva 1924; Gershwin, George 1924

Just My Luck   Bullock 1938; Burke 1946; Pollack 1938; Van Heusen 1946

Just My Style   Smith, Robert B. 1905

Just My Type (They're All My Type)   Atteridge 1919; Romberg 1919; Schwartz, Jean 1919

Just Once Again   Donaldson 1927

Just Once Around the Clock   Hammerstein 1935; Romberg 1935

Just Once Around the Moon (And then Home)   Merrill 1951

Just Once Too Often   Stept 1934; Young, Joe 1934

Just One Girl   Razaf 1960

Just One Good Time   Mitchell 1921; Pollack 1921

Just One Kiss   Johnston 1925; Kalmar 1926; Ruby 1926; Washington 1951, 1953; Young, Victor 1951, 1953

Just One Little Smile   Egan 1918

Just One More Chance   Coslow 1931; Johnston 1931

Just One More Dance Madame   Webster 1936

Just One More Night in Your Arms   Fisher 1924

Just One of the Boys   Styne 1950

Just One of Those Days   Monaco 1930

Just One of Those Nights   Myrow 1940

Just One of Those Things   Porter 1930, 1935

Just One Olay and a Day from the Border   Bergman 1958

Just One Sprig of Shamrock from the County Kildare   Brennan 1914

Just One — For Fun   Harbach 1907

Just Over the Hill   Razaf 1942

Just Over the Mountain   Razaf 1949

Just Picture You Lovin' Just Me   Johnston 1926; Turk 1926

Just Plain Folk   Leslie 1929

Just Plain Folks   Fisher 1938

Just Plain Lonesome   Burke 1942; Van Heusen 1942

Just Remember   Mercer 1936; Sigman 1936

Just Remember Coq d'Or   Hart 1921; Rodgers 1921

Just Reminiscing, Still in Love with You   Drake 1948

Just Right for Saturday Night   David, Hal 1961

Just Say, 'Auf Weidersehen'   Sherman 1963

Just Say Hello to Chicago   Howard, Joseph E. 1905

Just Say that You Will Miss Me   Howard, Joseph E. 1912

Just Say, "Yes I Can"   Sherman 1983

Just Say You Care   Howard, Joseph E. 1908

Just Sing a Song for Ireland   Sterling 1898; Von Tilzer 1898

Just Sociable   Razaf 1929

Just Squeeze Me   Ellington 1941

Just Strike a Match   Spina 1969

Just Suppose   De Lange 1940

Just Supposing   DeSylva 1924; Gershwin, George 1924

Just Tell Me What You Want   Adams 1979; Strouse 1978, 1979

Just Tell Me with Your Eyes   Goetz 1911

Just Tell Them That You Saw Me   Johnson, Howard 1939

Just the Crust   Cahn 1965; Van Heusen 1965

Just the Girl   Razaf 1940

Just the Kind of a Girl You'd Love to Make Your Wife   Von Tilzer 1917

Just the Letter "Q"   Mercer 1963

Just the One I'm Looking For   Goetz 1906

(I'll Love You) Just the Same   Brown, Lew 1927; Donaldson 1927; Friend 1927

Just the Sweethearts — Mother and Dad   Bryan 1919; Schwartz, Jean 1919

Just the Way You Are   Oakland 1960; Revel 1945

Just the Way You Are (I Like My Eggs Over Easy)   Freed, Ralph 1950

Just Think It Over   Davis 1924

Just Think of All the Money You Could Save   Jerome 1911; Schwartz, Jean 1911

Just to Be Near You   DePaul 1942; Raye 1958
Just to Be with You   Davis 1925
Just to Hear You Say I Love You   Robin 1930
Just To Keep Expenses Down   Bryan 1917
Just to Know You Are Mine   Gershwin, George 1921; Gershwin, Ira 1921
Just to Make a Long Story Short   Whiting 1926
Just to Make a Long Story Short, I Love You   Coots 1943
Just to Mend Mamma's Heart   Donaldson 1919; Lewis 1919; Young, Joe 1919
Just to While the Hours Away   Sterling 1908; Von Tilzer 1908
Just Try to Picture Me Back Home in Tennessee   Jerome 1915
Just Try to Picture Me Back Home in Tennessee (Just Try to Picture Me Down Home in Tennessee)   Donaldson 1915
Just Try to Think of Me   Stept 1925
Just Two Sweethearts — Mother and Dad   Bryan Date Unknown; Fisher Date Unknown
Just Use a Bit of Blarney   Howard, Joseph E. 1905
Just Wait   Strouse 1977
Just Wait and See Sweetheart   Robin 1929; Whiting 1929
Just We Two   Friml 1917; Goetz 1916; Romberg 1924
Just What I Need   Strouse 1999
Just What I Wanted   Dietz 1961; Romberg 1917; Schwartz, Arthur 1961
Just What I Wanted for Christmas   Cahn 1959; Van Heusen 1959
Just What My Heart Had in Mind   Robison 1983
Just When We're Falling in Love   Russell 1951
Just Whisper I Love You   Gorney 1929; Harburg 1929; Silver 1937
Just Wond'ring   Kahn 1926
Just Yesterday   Sigman 1965
Just You   Magidson 1924
Just You and I and the Baby   Conrad 1925
Just You and I and the Moon   Buck 1913
Just You and I in Dreamland   Herbert 1912
Just You and Me   Adams 1972; Buck 1917; Strouse 1972
Just You Wait   Lerner, Alan Jay 1956; Loewe 1956
Just You Watch My Step   Kern 1917
Justine Johnstone Rag, The   Romberg 1917

K

Ka-choo! (The Sneezing Song)   Razaf 1944
Kaddish   Strouse 1986
Kadey Song, The   Oakland 1954
Kaigoon   Burke 1940; Monaco 1940
Kaintucky   Kahn 1923
Kaintucky Colonel   Donaldson 1934
Kaiser Bill   Egan 1918; Whiting 1918
Kala Kala Polee Kala   Oakland 1954
K-A-L-A-M-A-ZOO, That's My Home Town   Monaco 1929
Kaleidescope   David, Hal 1975
Ka-Lu-A   Kern 1921
Kalua Bay   Parish 1929
Kalua Lu   Egan 1926; Whiting 1926
Kalua Lullaby   Kahn 1933
Kama's Garden   Caesar 1923
Kaminsky Rag, The (Inst.)   Styne 1977
Kanawha   Leslie 1908
Kandahar Isle   Coots 1926
Kangaroo   Johnson, James P. 1927

Kangaroo Hop, The   Atteridge 1912; Kahn 1916; Lane 1930
Kansas City   Hammerstein 1943; Rodgers 1943
Kansas City Blues   Bergman 1959; Robison 1949
Kansas City Kitty   Donaldson 1929; Leslie 1929
Kansas Was Never Like This   Ahlert 1929; Turk 1929
Kappa Sigma Girl, The   Carmichael 1949
Karabitz!   Adams 1992; Strouse 1992
Karen Lynn   Drake 1948
Karinina   Revel 1941
Kashmir   Washington 1957
Kashmiri Moon   Parish 1928
Katchen-Polka   Parish 1953
Kate (Have I Come Too Early, Too Late)   Berlin 1947
Kate O'Donoghue   Olcott 1897
Kate the Great   Cahn 1963; Porter 1934; Van Heusen 1963
Kathakali   Fain 1960; Webster 1960
Katherine Receives Advice   Lerner, Alan Jay 1945; Loewe 1945
Kathleen   Cobb 1902; Edwards 1902; Porter 1944; Smith, Harry B. 1921; Snyder 1921
Kathleen Aroon   Olcott 1913
Kathleen, Mine   Heyman 1931; Youmans 1931
Kath'rine the Great!   Razaf 1944
Kathy   Evans 1970; Livingston, Jay 1970; Washington 1949
Katie   Fain 1979
Katie Gray   Edwards 1908
Katie Keep Your Feet on the Ground   Sterling 1929
Katie Mahone   Olcott 1894
Katie of the Y.M.C.A.   Porter 1910
Katie Sweet Colleen   Snyder 1909
Katie Went to Haiti   Porter 1939
Katinka   DeSylva 1923; Friml 1914; Gershwin, George 1923; Goetz 1923; Harbach 1914
Katinkitschka   Gershwin, George 1931; Gershwin, Ira 1931
Katrina   DePaul 1949; Raye 1949
Katy Was a Business Girl   Kern 1907
Katy-Did   Kern 1913; Smith, Harry B. 1913
Katy-Did, Katy-Didn't   Carmichael 1941; Loesser 1941
Katz Is Putting on the Dog   Bryan 1925; Silver 1925
Kayo Tortoni   Buck 1923
Keeley Cure, The   Howard, Joseph E. 1964
Keeno, Screeno and You   Coslow 1937
Keep a Fox Trot for Me   Caesar 1920
Keep a Happy Thought   Cahn 1963; Van Heusen 1963
Keep a Little Dream Handy   David, Mack 1952; Livingston, Jerry 1952
Keep a Little Song Handy   Lerner, Sammy 1932
Keep a Little Sunshine in Your Heart   Von Tilzer 1926
Keep a Song in Your Heart   Coots 1955
Keep a Song in Your Soul   Waller 1930
Keep a Taxi Waiting, Dear   Berlin 1911
Keep a Twinkle in Your Eye   Bloom 1936; Mercer 1936
Keep A-Countin' Eight   Cohan 1923
Keep All Your Love for Me   Motzan 1919
Keep A-Lookin' Straight Ahead   Cahn 1952
Keep Away   Ahlert 1932; Turk 1932
Keep Away from the Fellow Who Owns an Automobile   Berlin 1912
Keep Away from the Moonlight   Hart 1934; Rodgers 1934
Keep Away from Those Swinging Doors   Mercer 1938; Warren 1938
Keep Coolidge in the White House   Motzan 1924
Keep Doing It   Hanley 1931
Keep 'em Guessing   Johnson, James P. 1948
Keep 'Em Laughing   DePaul 1942; Raye 1942

Keep 'Em Rolling   Hart 1942; Rodgers 1942

Keep 'Em Smiling   Ager 1942; Rose 1942

Keep in Tune with the Times   Henderson 1934; Koehler 1934

Keep It Dark   Romberg 1921

Keep It Gay   Hammerstein 1953; Rodgers 1953

Keep It in the Family   Coleman 1966, 1972; Fields 1966, 1972

Keep It Simple   Evans 1958; Livingston, Jay 1958

Keep It Under Your Hat   Fain 1953; Webster 1953

Keep It Up for Upton   Meyer 1930; Mitchell 1930

Keep Jazzin' It, Ras'   Sterling 1918

Keep Me Close to You   Styne 1985

Keep Me in Mind   Bacharach 1955

Keep Me in Your Dreams   Freed, Ralph 1934

Keep Movin'   Johnson, James P. 1945

Keep Moving   Johnson, James P. 1922; Motzan 1915; Porter 1928

Keep Mum Chum   Howard, Joseph E. 1942

Keep Off the Grass   DePaul 1950; Friml 1917; Harbach 1917; Raye 1950; Von Tilzer 1903

Keep Off the Grass (inst.)   Johnson, James P. 1921

Keep on A-Going   Cobb 1918; Edwards 1918

Keep on A-Loving Me   Jerome 1905; Kern 1905

Keep on Believin'   Oakland 1974

Keep on Croonin' a Tune   Fain 1925; McHugh 1925

Keep on Doin' what You're Doin'   Kalmar 1934; Ruby 1934

Keep on Smiling   Friml 1918

Keep on the Right Hand Side of Father   Bryan 1917

Keep on Treating Me Sweet   Ellington 1962

Keep on Walking   Berlin 1913

Keep Our Love on an Even Keel   Styne 1958

Keep Out of the Moon   Schwartz, Jean 1918

Keep Out of the Rain   Fisher 1930

Keep Paramount Friendly   Lane Date Unknown

Keep Passing the Buck   Gorney 1962

Keep Repeating It   Romberg 1917

Keep Romance Alive   Kalmar 1934; Ruby 1934

Keep Sakes   Egan 1920; Whiting 1920

Keep Shufflin'   Razaf 1928; Waller 1928

Keep Smiling   Hammerstein 1934; Kern 1934

Keep Smiling and Carry On   Donaldson 1930

Keep Smiling at Trouble (Troubles's a Bubble)   DeSylva 1925

Keep Sweeping the Cobwebs Off the Moon   Lewis 1927; Young, Joe 1927

Keep That Great Wheel Turning   Woods 1952

Keep that School Girl Complexion   Freed, Arthur 1925

Keep that Twinkle in Your Eye   Clare 1935; Eliscu 1935

Keep the Home Push Up for Pershing   Mitchell 1918

Keep the Light Burning Bright (In the Harbor)   Dietz 1942; Harburg 1942; Schwartz, Arthur 1942

Keep the Love Lamps Burning in the Windows of Your Eyes   Smith, Harry B. 1920

Keep the Lovelight Singing in the Window   McHugh 1917

Keep the Magic of Maytime   Kahn 1937

Keep the Party Going   Kalmar 1924; Ruby 1924

Keep the Rhythm Going   Mills 1935

Keep the Songs of Safety Ever in Your Mind   Caesar 1940

Keep the Trench Lines Going for the Boys Over There   Von Tilzer 1918

Keep Them in a Golden Cage   Bryan 1921; Pollack 1921; Schwartz, Jean 1921

Keep to the Right   Caesar 1937

Keep You Spirits High   Robison 1963

Keep Young and Beautiful   Dubin 1933; Warren 1933

Keep Your Amateur Standing   Dietz 1943; Duke 1943

Keep Your Chin Up   Blake 1932; Porter 1955; Sissle 1932

Keep Your Eye in the Sky   Hoffman 1936

Keep Your Eye on Little Mary Brown   Bryan 1917

Keep Your Eye on My Darlin'   Leigh 1953

Keep Your Eye on the Ball   Baer 1927; Friml 1921; Lewis 1927; Young, Joe 1927

Keep Your Eye on the Boy   Loesser 1947

Keep Your Eye on the Girl   Brown, Lew 1927; Friend 1927

Keep Your Eye on the Girlie You Love   Johnson, Howard 1916

Keep Your Eye on the Sky   Loesser Date Unknown

Keep Your Eyes Down Mary   Egan 1920; Whiting 1920

Keep Your Eyes Open   Livingston, Jerry 1962

Keep Your Fingers Crossed   Coslow 1935; Whiting 1935

Keep Your Foot on the Soft Pedal   Von Tilzer 1909

Keep Your Golden Gate Wide Open   Edwards 1913

Keep Your Hand on My Heart   Loewe 1938

Keep Your Last Goodnight for Me   Ahlert 1932; Turk 1932

Keep Your Love for Me   Buck 1914

Keep Your Nose Out of Mama's Business   Razaf 1932

Keep Your Powder Dry   Cahn 1944; Styne 1944

Keep Your Skirts Down Mary Ann   Henderson 1925; Sterling 1925

Keep Your Thumbs Up   Brooks 1941

Keep Your Undershirt On   Kalmar 1929; Ruby 1929

Keep Your Weight Down   Bryan 1920; Schwartz, Jean 1920

Keep-a-Hoppin'   Willson 1960

Keeper, Keeper Take the Boy Away   Brown, Lew 1927; DeSylva 1927; Henderson 1927

Keeper of My Heart, The   Mercer 1935

Keeper of the Ivory Keys, The   Heyman 1934; Romberg 1934

Keepin' a Prayer in Your Heart   Burke 1947; Van Heusen 1947

Keepin' Myself for You   Clare 1930; Youmans 1930

Keepin' Out of Mischief Now   Razaf 1932; Waller 1932

Keepin' Out of Trouble   Brown, Nacio Herb 1926; Freed, Arthur 1925, 1926; Razaf 1942

Keeping Cool with Coolidge   Robin 1948; Styne 1948

Keeping It Private (Me and Private Joe)   Donaldson 1944

Keeping the Wolf from the Door   Dubin 1929

Keeps Gettin' Better All the Time   Coleman 1986

Keepsakes   Herbert 1946

Kellerman Girlie, The   Jerome 1910; Schwartz, Jean 1910

Kelly Green (A Bit o' the Auld Sod) (inst.)   Warren 1960

Kelly Green (inst.)   Warren 1959

Kelly Is Living the Life of Reilly   Lewis 1929; Pollack 1929; Young, Joe 1929

Kelly's Are at It Again, The   Norworth 1913; Williams 1913

Kennedy Years, The   Webster 1965

Kenneth Won the Yachting Race   DeSylva 1925; Gershwin, George 1925; Gershwin, Ira 1925

Kentucky   Koehler 1955

Kentucky Colonel Song   Mills 1939

Kentucky Echoes   Gilbert 1921

Kentucky in the Moonlight   Styne 1938

Kentucky Love   Fisher 1907

Kentucky Opera   Styne 1938

Kentucky Sue   Blake 1920; Sissle 1920

Kentucky's Way of Sayin' Good Mornin'   Kahn 1925

Keokuk Culture Club, The   Herbert 1905

Kept in Suspense   Rose 1931

Kerchoo   Dixon 1923; Romberg 1927; Rose 1923

Ker-Choo (Geshundheit)   Mitchell 1926

Kermesse Dance   Romberg 1925; Smith, Harry B. 1925

Kermesse Day   Herbert 1903; Smith, Harry B. 1903

Kerryanna   Meyer 1910

Ke-tonky-i-o   Willson 1943

Kettle Song, The   Kern 1918

Kevin   Blane 1952

Kewtee Bear Song, The   Freed, Ralph 1956; Livingston, Jerry 1956

Key to My Heart, The   Alter 1931; Blake 1930; Eliscu 1928; Gershwin, Ira 1931; Merrill 1955; Razaf 1930

Key to the Gates, The   Dietz 1944; Duke 1944

Key to the Kingdom, The   Sigman 1959

Keyboard Strut, The   Coslow 1923; Mills 1923

Keys of My Heart, The   Harbach 1923

Keys to Heaven   Hart 1926; Rodgers 1926

Keys to the City, The   Drake 1953

Keys to Your Heart   Fields 1930; McHugh 1930

(It's a) Keystone Comic World   Spina 1977

Keystone Glide, The   Smith, Robert B. 1915

Khonghouse Song   Hart 1928; Rodgers 1928

Ki Yi Yippee Yi Yo What a Night!   Lane 1952; Robin 1952

Kick in the Pants, The   Berlin 1943

Kick It Around   Spina 1959

Kick Off Your Shoes   Coleman 1965

Kick the Door   Cahn 1970; Styne 1970

Kickapoo Kick, The   Robin 1957; Styne 1957

Kickapoo Trail   Egan 1926; Whiting 1926

Kickin' a Hole in the Sky   Rose 1930

Kickin' the Can   Raye 1958

Kickin' the Clouds Away   DeSylva 1925; Gershwin, George 1925; Gershwin, Ira 1925

Kickin' the Conga Around   Stept 1941

Kickin' the Gong Around   Arlen 1931; Koehler 1931

Kickin' Up a Storm   Adamson 1956; McHugh 1956

Kicking Over the Traces   Woods 1939

Kicking the Blues Away   Hanley 1929

Kicking the Kaiser Around   Johnson, Howard 1918

Kicky-Koo, You for Me-Me for You   Young, Joe 1922

Kid Days   Cohan 1903; Coots 1922

Kid, I Love You   Hart 1920; Rodgers 1920

Kid Is Clever, The   Edwards 1923; Smith, Robert B. 1923

Kid Next Door, The   Cahn 1982; Leslie 1926

Kid Shelleen   David, Mack 1965; Livingston, Jerry 1965

Kid Stuff   Russell 1946

Kid that I've Never Seen, The   Akst 1944; Kalmar 1944

Kid that Opens Up and Closes Broadway, The   Snyder 1909

Kid with the Drum, The   Cahn 1941

Kid with the Whiskers   David, Mack 1945; Meyer 1945

Kiddie Kapers   Hoffman 1928; Pollack 1928

Kiddie Polka   Friend 1952

Kidland   Cobb 1910; Edwards 1910

Kids   Adams 1960; Strouse 1960

Kids Ain't (Like Everybody Else)   Sondheim 1957

Kids in School, The   Weill 1947

Ki-I-Youdling Dog   Schwartz, Jean 1913

Kikerikee   Caesar 1920

Kiki   DeSylva 1925

Ki-Ki-Koo, You for Me-Me for You   Lewis 1922; Meyer 1922

Kill 'em with Kindness   Silver 1921

Kill Him   Styne 1978

Killarney   Brooks 1949

Killarney, the Blarney and You   Leslie 1924

Killer Love   Mancini 1989

Killers, The   Raye 1958

Killing Sequence   Arlen 1959; Mercer 1959

Killing Time   Leigh 1983; Styne 1983

Killy-Ka-Lee   Dixon 1938

Kind of a Girl I'd Like to Be, The   Blane 1968; Martin 1968

Kind of Girl a Man Likes Best, The   Edwards 1909; Smith, Harry B. 1909

Kind of Man for Me, The   Razaf 1929

Kind of Moody   Ellington 1953; Sigman 1953

Kind to Animals   Martin 1952

Kind Words   Bryan 1915

Kinda Cute   Gorney 1929; Harburg 1929

Kinda Like You   Heyman 1931; Youmans 1931

Kinda Lonesome   Carmichael 1939; Coslow 1939; Robin 1939

Kinda Peculiar Brown   Burke 1943; Van Heusen 1943

Kinder, The   Livingston, Jerry 1973

Kindergarten Blues   Hammerstein 1922

Kindergarten Conga (Ring Around the Rosie), The   Rainger 1941; Robin 1941

Kindly Pay Us   DeSylva 1919; Gershwin, George 1919

Kindly Remit the Kisses That You Borrowed in Fun   Coots 1930

King and Queen Sequence   Sondheim Date Unknown

King Can Do No Wrong, A   Coslow 1935; Kalmar 1933; Romberg 1928; Ruby 1933

King Chanticleer   Brown, A. Seymour 1910

King Cocoa   Evans 1946; Livingston, Jay 1946

King Cotton   Robison 1950

King Fit the Battle of Alabam   Ellington 1963

King for a Day   Lewis 1928; Young, Joe 1928

King Has Everything, The   Heyman 1954; Young, Victor 1954

King Has Had a Change of Heart, The   Burke 1934; Spina 1934

King Isn't King Any More, The   Leslie 1925; Monaco 1925

King Louie   Robin 1930

King Midas Birthday Song   Brooks 1960

King of a Slave, A   David, Hal 1955

King of Baby Land, The   Brown, A. Seymour 1909

King of Broadway   Berlin 1917

King of Jam (inst.)   Alter 1937

King of Jazzmania   Coslow 1929; Robin 1929; Whiting 1929

King of New Orleans   Brooks 1953

King of Swing   Gershwin, George 1936

King of Swing Is Havin' a Dream, The   Cahn 1935

King of the Air   Bryan 1929

King of the Bushongo   Rome 1964

King of the Mound   Coleman 1988

King of the Pampas, A   Hanley 1930

King of the Sword   Brennan 1928

King of the Wide, Wide World, The   Leslie 1910

King Size Kisses   David, Hal 1953

King Solomon   Brown, A. Seymour 1923

Kingdom of Dreams   Romberg 1928

Kingdom of Love   Bergman 1976; Gilbert 1914

Kingdom of My Heart   Motzan 1917

Kingdom of the Future   Bullock 1940

Kings and Cabbages   Duke 1963

King's Dilemma   Mancini 1995

King's Favorite, The   Atteridge 1919; Romberg 1919; Schwartz, Jean 1919

King's Musketeers, The   Herbert 1899; Smith, Harry B. 1899

King's New Clothes, The   Loesser 1952

Kinky Kids Parade, The   Donaldson 1925; Kahn 1925

Kip   Martin 1951

Kip's Tune   Warren 1966

Kismet   Bryan 1930; Edwards 1931

Kiss, A   Brooks 1952; Brown, Nacio Herb 1955; DePaul 1958; Friml 1919; Harbach 1919; Raye 1958

Kiss a Four Leaf Clover   Harbach 1926; Kern 1926

Kiss a Lonely Wife   Fisher 1936

Kiss a Miss from Tennessee   Fisher 1938

Kiss Across the Continent, A   Parish 1954

Kiss an Make Up with Baby   Egan 1931

Kiss and a Promise, A   Cahn 1959; Davis 1951

Kiss and Make Up Waltz, The   Freed, Ralph 1935

Kiss and Make-Up   Rainger 1934; Robin 1934

Kiss and Remember   Bryan 1939

Kiss and Run Lover   DePaul 1958; Raye 1958

Kiss at Midnight   Loesser 1945

Kiss at Twilight   Loesser 1945

Kiss Before I Go, A   Friml 1928

Kiss Burglar   Atteridge 1919; Goetz 1911; Romberg 1919; Schwartz, Jean 1919

Kiss By Kiss   Brooks 1954

Kiss Can Tell a Lie, A   David, Hal 1959

Kiss for Cinderella, A   Carroll 1918; Cobb 1917; Edwards 1917; Hart 1928; Rodgers 1928

Kiss for Consolation, A   Leslie 1937; Parish 1958

Kiss for You, A   Livingston, Jerry 1937

Kiss from a Red-Headed Miss, A   Caesar 1922

Kiss from Angelina   Heyman 1935

Kiss from the Girl You Love, A   Edwards 1907

Kiss from You   Howard, Joseph E. 1920; Mitchell 1925

Kiss Her for Me   Hoffman 1933

Kiss Her for Me (Be Sure and Say Hello)   Adamson Date Unknown; Warren Date Unknown

Kiss I Must Refuse You, A   Caesar 1930; Harbach 1930; Romberg 1930

Kiss in a Cab, A   Blake 1950

Kiss in the Dark, A   DeSylva 1922; Herbert 1922

Kiss in the Moonlight and the World Began, A   Fain 1933; Kahal 1933

Kiss in Your Eyes, The   Burke 1948

Kiss Intended for Linda, The   Robison 1954

Kiss is Forever, A   Cahn 1956

Kiss Ma Again   Waller 1925

Kiss Me   Harbach 1917; Howard, Joseph E. 1910; Sondheim 1979

Kiss Me Again   Herbert 1915; Sterling 1911

Kiss Me Again, Bebe   Atteridge 1912

Kiss Me and Kill Me with Love   Fain 1955

Kiss Me and Kiss Me and Kiss Me   Hoffman 1959

Kiss Me and 'Tis Day   Friml 1912; Harbach 1912

Kiss Me Back to Heaven   Fain 1931; Kahal 1931

Kiss Me Good Night (Out the Window You Must Go)   Brown, Lew 1913

Kiss Me Goodbye   Parish 1934

Kiss Me Goodbye with a Smile   Egan 1924

Kiss Me Good-Night All Night   Bryan 1926

Kiss Me Goodnight (Not Goodbye)   Clare 1936; Hanley 1931, 1936

Kiss Me Hello (After the War Baby)   Cahn 1946; Styne 1946

(How Would You Like to) Kiss Me in the Moonlight   Adamson 1944; McHugh 1944

Kiss Me I've Never Been Kissed Before   Kalmar 1913

Kiss Me Kate   Porter 1948

Kiss Me Like This   Edwards 1936

Kiss Me Like You Kissed Me Last Night   Magidson 1934; McHugh 1958; Stept 1934

Kiss Me, My Honey, Kiss Me   Berlin 1911; Snyder 1910

Kiss Me No Kisses   Drake 1964

Kiss Me Now   David, Hal 1954

Kiss Me Now and Love Me Later   Yellen 1964

Kiss Me or I'll Scream   Cahn 1953; Fain 1953

Kiss Me Quick and Go   David, Hal 1960

Kiss Me Right Where the Kisses Should Be   Bryan 1908

Kiss Me, That's All   Gershwin, Ira 1924

Kiss Me to Sleep   Warren Date Unknown

Kiss Me Tonight, and Forever   Caesar 1950

Kiss Me Tonight for Tomorrow   Washington 1941

Kiss Me While We're Dancing   Bryan 1936

Kiss Me with Your Eyes   Lane 1939; Loesser 1939; Silver 1950

Kiss Me Yes, Kiss Me No   Fisher 1940

Kiss of Long Ago, The   Webster 1968

Kiss or Two, A   Robin 1927; Youmans 1927

Kiss Polka, The   Gordon 1941; Warren 1941

Kiss Special   Oakland 1953; Raye 1953

Kiss That Made a Fool of Me, The   Coots 1930

Kiss the Boys Goodbye   Loesser 1941

Kiss the Bride   Romberg 1927

Kiss the Bride Now   Carroll 1934

Kiss the Girls Good Morning   Willson 1954

Kiss to Build a Dream On, A   Hammerstein 1935; Kalmar 1935; Ruby 1935

Kiss to Remember, A   Bryan 1928

Kiss to Remind You, A   Eliscu 1937

Kiss Waltz   Dubin 1930; Romberg 1916

Kiss with a Kick, A   Robin 1927

Kiss You Gave, The   Harbach 1910

Kiss You Left Behind, The   Dubin 1924

Kiss Your Baby Bye-Bye   Whiting 1914

Kiss Your Baby Goodbye   Dietz 1943; Duke 1943

Kiss Your Little Baby Goodnight   Donaldson 1926

Kiss Your Minstrel Boy Goodbye   Cohan 1908; Jerome 1908; Schwartz, Jean 1908

Kiss Your Sailor Boy Good-Bye   Berlin 1913

Kiss Ze Hand   Fisher 1920

Kissable Lips   Atteridge 1923; Schwartz, Jean 1923

Kissed on the Eyes   Merrill 1990

Kisses   Bergman 1984; DeSylva 1919; Gershwin, George 1919; Jerome 1905; Schwartz, Jean 1905

Kisses and Tears   Cahn 1952; Styne 1950

Kisses at Auction   Smith, Harry B. 1910

Kisses for Sale   Von Tilzer 1910

Kisses from My Violin to You   Bryan 1936

Kisses I'll Never Forget   Merrill 1954

Kisses in My Dreams   Bryan 1935

Kisses in the Moonlight   Dubin Date Unknown

Kisses in the Night   Warren Date Unknown

Kisses That I Have Missed   Atteridge 1913

Kissimee   Caesar 1920

Kissin' Cake Polka   Drake 1953

Kissin' Cousins   Blane 1964; Martin 1964

Kissin' Kitty   Howard, Bart 1984

Kissin' My Baby Good-Night   David, Mack 1936; Meyer 1936

Kissin' on the Red Light   David, Hal 1959

Kissing   Atteridge 1906; Caesar 1925; Conrad 1906; Youmans 1925

Kissing Eyes   Hammerstein 1927

Kissing Games   Hoffman 1934

Kissing in the Rain   Bryan 1932; Clare 1932

Kissing Rock, The   Hammerstein 1942; Harbach 1942; Kern 1942

Kissing Song, The   Duke 1955; Oakland 1951

Kissing Time   Caesar 1920; Jerome 1908; Lewis 1922; Meyer 1923; Schwartz, Jean 1908; Young, Joe 1922
Kissy Face   Oakland 1940
Kit Carson   Evans 1976; Livingston, Jay 1976
Kitchen Man   Razaf 1929
Kitchen Mechanic's Parade   Johnson, James P. 1930; Razaf 1930
Kitchen Music   Carmichael 1952
Kitchen Tom (inst.)   Blake 1962
Kitchenette   DeSylva 1919; Gershwin, Ira 1918
Kitchy-Koo   Edwards 1909
Kit's Last Fight, The   Merrill 1951
Kitten on the Keys   Coslow 1922
Kitten that Couldn't Be Good   Herbert 1907; Smith, Harry B. 1907
Kitty   Evans 1945; Livingston, Jay 1945; Sigman 1957
Kitty and the Owl, The   Howard, Joseph E. 1905
Kitty Darlin'   Friml 1917; Harbach 1917
Kitty Gray   Sterling 1910
Kitty in a Basket   Merrill 1953
Kitty MacKay   Atteridge 1914; Carroll 1914
Kitty, Pretty Kitty   Jerome 1906; Schwartz, Jean 1906
Kitty Rooney   Sterling 1910
Kitty's Kisses   Conrad 1926; Kahn 1926
Kitzel Engagement, The   Hart 1926; Rodgers 1926
Ki-Yi-Yodeling Dog, The   Berlin 1913
K-K-K-Katy   Gordon 1940
K-K-K-Kiss Me A-Ga-Ga-Gain   DePaul 1950; Raye 1950
Kling-Kling Bird on the Divi-Divi Tree, The   Porter 1935
Klondike Kate   Berlin 1956
Klown Kapers   Akst 1928; Lewis 1928; Young, Joe 1928
Knave of Hearts, The   Herbert 1905
Knee Dance   Atteridge 1921; Pollack 1921; Schwartz, Jean 1921
Knee Deep in June   Gorney 1930; Harburg 1930
Knee Deep in Rhythm   Kahn 1933
Knees   Hart 1929; Rodgers 1929
Knickerbocker Grey's March   Merrill 1967
Knife, the Fork and the Spoon, The   Young, Joe 1934
Knife-Thrower's Wife, The   Duke 1936; Gershwin, Ira 1936
Knights of the Headless Horse   Sherman 1962
Knights of the Road   Berlin 1930
Knights on White Horses   Merrill 1959
Knit, Girls, Knit!   Johnson, Howard 1918
Knit Pretty   Loesser 1961
Knitting Song   Coots 1921
Knock a Little Louder Ephraham   Von Tilzer 1911
Knock Knees   Dubin 1930
Knock Knock   Brooks 1958
Knock Me a Kiss   Razaf 1942
Knock Wood   Cahn 1936; Smith, Robert B. 1905; Sterling 1911; Von Tilzer 1911
Knockin' on Wood   Eliscu 1930
Knockin' Song (True Love Is Knockin' at My Door), The   Freed, Ralph 1953; Hoffman 1953
Knocking at Your Door   Dixon Date Unknown; Warren Date Unknown
Knocking on Your Own Front Door   Burke 1944; Van Heusen 1944
Knock-Knock Nobody Home   Friml 1915
Knock-Knock-Knock (Let Me In)   Gorney 1967
Knot of Blue, The   Herbert 1904
Knothole Scene   Brown, Lew 1927; DeSylva 1927; Henderson 1927
Know   Robison 1955

Know How   Drake 1957
Know When to Smile   Brennan 1928
Know Where You're Goin' and You'll Get There   Martin 1944
Know Ye the Sound   Herbert 1895; Smith, Harry B. 1895
Knowing You Are Going Home   Robison 1954
Kobblerrumba   Fain 1948; Yellen 1948
Kohala Welcome   Hart 1928; Rodgers 1928
Kokomo, Indiana   Gordon 1947; Myrow 1947
Kolin Kelly   Evans 1963; Livingston, Jay 1963
Kongo Kate   DeSylva 1924; Gershwin, George 1924
Koni Plenty Hu-Hu   Pollack 1943
Koo Kee Koo   Brown, Nacio Herb 1921
(You've Got to Have) Koo Wah   Blake 1932; Sissle 1932
Kook Spooks   Cahn 1964; Van Heusen 1964
Kooka Rooki Bongo   Merrill 1972; Styne 1972
Korea, a Long Way from Home   Oakland 1960
Kow Tow   Adamson 1954; Warren 1954
Kranko Waltz   Atteridge 1913
Krasilofsky for Justice of the Peace   Dietz 1957; Schwartz, Arthur 1957
Krazy   Turk 1925
K-r-a-zy for You   Gershwin, George 1928; Gershwin, Ira 1928
Kris Kringle Rides Again   Gorney 1959
Kublai Kahn's Song   Adamson 1954; Warren 1954
Kuddles and Kisses   Edwards 1912
Kulebiaka   Webster 1943
Kumquat   Russell 1977

L

La Baie Verte   Willson 1953
La Bella Fiorentina   Caesar 1931
La Belle Paree   Goetz 1912
La Belle Parisienne   Mitchell 1921; Pollack 1921
La Bomba   Rainger 1936; Robin 1936
La Brea Tar Pits   Cahn 1946; Styne 1946
La Cabeza. . .   Adams 1983
La Cancion Del Paris (Derelict Song)   Akst 1933; Gilbert 1933
La Caranga   David, Hal 1961
La Clare de la Lune   Goetz 1912
La Conchita   Coots 1953
La Cucaracha   Bullock 1934; Burke 1934; Johnson, Howard 1939; Parish 1934; Spina 1934; Washington 1934
La Cumparsita   Johnson, Howard 1936
La Dance Parisienne et La Americaine   Smith, Robert B. 1905
La Danse Parisienne   Smith, Harry B. 1906
La Favorite   Friml 1923
La Festa   Fain 1955
La Fiesta (inst.)   Blake 1917
La Franchesa (inst.)   Warren 1977
La Golondrina   Dubin 1924
La Grenouille (Mister Froggy) (Ticky, Ticky, Tick)   Merrill 1955
La Grosse Valise   Rome 1965
La Hoota-Coota-Boota Mamaseta   Friend 1929
L.A. Is My Lady   Bergman 1983
La Java   Atteridge 1924; Romberg 1924; Rome 1965; Schwartz, Jean 1924
La, La, La   Rodgers 1962
La La La La   Bergman 1963
La Lee, La Loo, La Laa   David, Hal 1950

La Locumba   Clare 1935
La Mattichiche   Smith, Harry B. 1906
La Orchidea (Orchid Lady)   De Lange 1944
La Paloma   Johnson, Howard 1939
La Parisienne   David, Mack 1956; Warren 1956
La Petite Trianon (inst.)   Warren 1953
La Pintada   De Lange 1944
La Plume de Ma Tante   Hoffman 1959
La Reina de Mi Corazon (The Queen of My Heart)   Ahlert 1930
La Rhumba   Arlen 1930; Burke 1934; Koehler 1930; Spina 1934
La Spagnola   Johnson, Howard 1932
La Tra Ma La (Latramalay)   Harburg 1971
La Veda   Bryan 1920; Schwartz, Jean 1920
La Vie Parisienne   Bryan 1921; Pollack 1921; Schwartz, Jean 1921
La Volta   Spina 1953
Label on the Bottle, The   Dietz 1961; Schwartz, Arthur 1961
Labor Day Parade   Blake 1932; Sissle 1932
Labor Is the Thing   Hart 1937; Rodgers 1937
Lace Makers' Song   Harbach 1923
Lackawanna   DeSylva 1925; Hanley 1925
Lad for Ev'ry Lass, A   Duke 1955
Laddie Boy   Cobb 1917; Edwards 1917
Laddie Daddie   Gershwin, George 1924
Laddie Daddy   Gershwin, Ira 1924
Laddy Buck of Mine   Brennan 1921
La-de-da Song, The   David, Mack 1957
La-De-De La-De-Da Says I'm in Love with You   Lewis 1936
Ladies, The   Goetz 1917; Rome 1959; Schwartz, Jean 1926
Ladies and Babies a la Mode   Edwards 1923; Smith, Robert B. 1923
Ladies and Gentlemen   Drake 1954
Ladies and Gentlemen, Good Evening   Hart Date Unknown; Rodgers Date Unknown
Ladies and Gentlemen that's Love   Brown, Lew 1931; Henderson 1931
Ladies and Gentlemen, We're Here Again (Opening Act II)   Hart 1927; Rodgers 1927
Ladies and Gents and Pals   Gordon 1955
Ladies, Beware   Friml 1934
Ladies' Choice   Atteridge 1921
Ladies Day   Smith, Robert B. 1914
Ladies Day in Dixie   McHugh 1921
Ladies Don't Have Fun   Cahn 1944, 1945; Styne 1944, 1945
Ladies Fair   Friml 1912; Harbach 1912
Ladies from Paree   Lerner, Sammy 1941
Ladies from the Cultured West, The   Atteridge 1922; Romberg 1922
Ladies in Their Sensitivities   Sondheim 1979
Ladies in Waiting, The   David, Mack 1958; Livingston, Jerry 1958; Porter 1957
Ladies, Ladies   Caesar 1945
Ladies Like Us   Cahn Date Unknown; Duke Date Unknown
Ladies' Man   Brooks 1961; Warren 1961
Ladies 'n' Gentlemen   Arlen 1959; Mercer 1959
Ladies of St. James, The   Duke 1942
Ladies of the Box Office   Hart 1925; Rodgers 1925
Ladies of the Chorus   Berlin 1942
Ladies of the Dance   Coslow 1929; Robin 1929; Whiting 1929
Ladies of the Evening   Harburg 1931; Hart 1938; Rodgers 1938; Rose 1931

Ladies of the Town   Kahn 1940
Ladies Who Lunch, The   Sondheim 1970
Ladies Who Sing with a Band, The   Waller 1943
Lady   Coots 1923; Duke 1941; Friml 1923; Schwartz, Jean 1923; Strouse 1993; Willson 1969
Lady — I Love, The   Young, Joe 1932
Lady, a Lad and a Lantern, A   Drake 1955
Lady Alice   Harburg 1967; Styne 1967
Lady and the Fan, The   Livingston, Jerry 1954; Webster 1954
Lady and the Kick, The   Herbert 1897; Smith, Harry B. 1897
Lady and the Tramp   Wrubel 1954
Lady Beautiful (inst.)   Blake 1976
Lady Bug   Webster 1951
Lady Butterfly   Caesar Date Unknown
Lady Chatterly's Lover   Webster 1963
Lady Dances, The   Arlen 1936; Brown, Lew 1936
Lady Do   Baer 1927; Lewis 1927; Young, Joe 1927
Lady, Don't Look at Me Like That   Magidson 1932; Stept 1932
Lady Fair   Brown, Lew 1926; Buck 1923; DeSylva 1926; Friml 1923; Henderson 1926
Lady Fair, Lady Fair   Porter 1916
Lady Fan   Buck 1923
Lady for a Day, A   Conrad 1933; Mitchell 1933
Lady from Hollywood   Conrad 1936; Magidson 1936
Lady from Lockheed   Revel 1942
Lady from the Bayou, The   Robin 1955
Lady from Twenty-Nine Palms, The   Wrubel 1947
Lady Has a Right (March of the Suffragettes), A   Blane 1945
Lady I Love, The   Porter 1929
Lady in Blue   Ellington 1940; Mills 1940
Lady in Lace   Bryan 1955
Lady in Red, The   Dixon 1935; Wrubel 1935
Lady in the Moon   Arlen 1936; Harburg 1936; Smith, Harry B. 1900
Lady in the Tutti-Frutti Hat, The   Robin 1943; Warren 1943
Lady in the Window   Harbach 1936; Romberg 1936
Lady Is a Tramp, The   Hart 1937; Rodgers 1937
Lady Is a WAAC, The   Rome 1942
Lady Is Indisposed, The   Coleman 1956
Lady Isn't Interested, The   Drake 1955
Lady I've Vowed to Wed, The   Porter 1916
Lady Killer   Evans 1954; Livingston, Jay 1954
Lady Known as Lulu, The   Stept 1936; Washington 1936
Lady Lizzie of Milan   Gorney 1969
Lady, Look What You've Done with Your Doggone Dangerous Eyes   Kalmar 1920; Ruby 1920
Lady Love   Edwards 1908; Russell 1951
Lady Lovely   Heyman 1944; Spina 1944
Lady Loves, A   Gordon 1953; Myrow 1953
Lady Luck   Gershwin, George 1925; Gershwin, Ira 1925; Smith, Harry B. 1928
Lady Luck Is Grinning   Hart 1928; Rodgers 1928
Lady Luck (Smile On Me)   Brown, Lew 1928; DeSylva 1928; Henderson 1928
Lady Luna   Howard, Bart 1961
Lady Mary's Song to Taberie   Friml 1954
Lady Must Live, A   Hart 1931; Rodgers 1931
Lady Needs a Change, The   Fields 1939; Schwartz, Arthur 1939
Lady Needs a Rest, A   Porter 1941
Lady O'Dreams   Kahn 1919
Lady of Guadalupe   Drake 1953
Lady of Jade (inst.)   Alter 1955
Lady of Love   Bryan 1928

Lady of Mars   Atteridge 1920

Lady of the Evening   Alter 1937; Berlin 1922; Webster 1937

Lady of the House, The   Strouse 1989

Lady of the Lake   Drake 1953; Lewis 1927; Parish 1923; Young, Joe 1927

(My) Lady of the Lamp, The   Atteridge 1921

Lady of the Lantern (inst.)   Herbert 1923

Lady of the Moon   Blake 1925, 1927; Gershwin, George 1929; Gershwin, Ira 1929; Sissle 1927

Lady of the Night   Kahn 1933

Lady of the Nile   Kahn 1925

Lady of the Rose   Friml 1926; Hammerstein 1926; Harbach 1926

Lady of the Roses, The   Livingston, Jerry 1960

Lady of the Sea   Goetz 1917

Lady of the Slipper, The   Herbert 1912

Lady of the Year   Styne 1970

Lady of Tomorrow   Rose 1939

Lady on Bedloe's Island   Coots 1945; Lewis 1945

Lady on the Cameo   Hoffman 1939

Lady on the Second Floor, The   Dixon 1937; Woods 1937

Lady on the Two-Cent Stamp, The   Dubin 1938; Mercer 1938; Warren 1938

Lady Out on a Late Evening (inst.)   Bloom 1952

Lady Play Your Mandolin   Caesar 1930

Lady Raffles Behave   Hart 1920; Rodgers 1920

Lady Romance   Goetz 1917

Lady Sleeps, The   Herbert 1909

Lady Tambourine   Koehler 1931

Lady Twinklepuss   Fisher 1936

Lady Was Made to Be Loved, The   Coslow 1955

Lady Who Couldn't Be Kissed, The   Dubin 1937; Warren 1937

Lady Who Didn't Believe in Love, The   Styne 1943

Lady Who Lives for Love, A   Smith, Harry B. 1925

Lady Who Swings the Band, The   Cahn 1937

Lady Who Walks Alone   Lawrence 1945

Lady Wine   Howard, Joseph E. 1910

Lady with a Parasol, A   Wrubel 1945

Lady with Money   Smith, Harry B. 1904; Smith, Robert B. 1904

Lady with the Auburn Hair   Sterling 1899

Lady with the Light in the Harbor   David, Hal 1942; David, Mack 1942

Lady with the Mop, The   Cahn 1946; Styne 1946

Lady with the Tap, The   Dietz 1935; Schwartz, Arthur 1935

Lady without a Name, The   Lewis 1930

Lady, You Don't Know Me   Gorney 1925, 1926

Lady's in Distress, The   Brooks 1940

Lady's in Love with You, The   Lane 1939; Loesser 1939

Lady's on the Job (on Time), The   Rome 1943

Laendler   Rodgers 1959

Lafayette   Coleman 1962; Fields 1952; Kern 1952; Leigh 1962

Lafayette We're Here   Brown, Lew 1940; Henderson 1940; Sherman 1971

L'Affaire (inst.)   Myrow 1952

Laffs and Lies   Gilbert Date Unknown; Warren Date Unknown

Lailu   Mercer 1941; Warren 1941

Lak Jeem   Friml 1924; Hammerstein 1924; Harbach 1924

Lake Saint Mary   Alter 1964; Arlen 1964; Mercer 1964

Lake Tahoe   Washington 1956; Young, Victor 1956

La-La-La-La   Hammerstein 1928; Romberg 1928

La-La-Lalapalooza   Evans 1953; Livingston, Jay 1953

Lalapaluza Lu   Hoffman 1942; Livingston, Jerry 1942

Lalita   Mercer Date Unknown; Warren Date Unknown

Lallapalooza   Comden and Green 1953

Lambs in Toyland   Herbert 1904

Lambs' March (inst.), The   Herbert 1914

Lamb's Star Gambol (inst.), The   Herbert 1912

Lame, the Halt and the Blind, The   Sondheim 1964

Lament   Brown, Nacio Herb 1945; Coslow 1930; DePaul 1954; Fain 1951; Harburg 1951; Johnson, Howard 1949; Johnson, J. Rosamond 1909; Lawrence 1964; Mercer 1954; Sondheim 1987

Lament for Lost Love   Ellington 1937; Mills 1937

Lament of Ten Men   Merrill 1966

L'Amour Toujours   Mills 1947

L'Amour Toujours (Tonight for Sure)   Cahn 1951

L'Amoureuse   Smith, Harry B. 1901

L'Amour-Toujours-L'Amour (Love Everlasting)   Friml 1916

Lamp, a Chair and a Cigarette, A   Ahlert 1929; Turk 1929

Lamp Is Low, The   Parish 1939

Lamp of Love   Bryan 1919; Schwartz, Jean 1919

Lamp of Memory   Bryan 1927; Fisher 1927

Lamp on the Corner (Farolito)   Washington 1938

Lamplight Is Moonlight   Loesser Date Unknown

Lamplight Land   Atteridge 1922; Schwartz, Jean 1922

Lamplighter's Serenade, The   Carmichael 1942; Webster 1942

Lana, Lovely Lana   Martin 1959

Lancers   Herbert 1895, 1897, 1903; Smith, Harry B. 1895, 1897, 1899

Lancers' Waltz   Herbert 1906

Lanciers   Herbert 1899, 1910

Lanciers (Finale Ultimo)   Herbert 1911

Land Around Us, The   Arlen 1954; Gershwin, Ira 1954

Land Beyond the Candle Light, The   Atteridge 1920

Land of Dreams   De Lange 1942; Herbert 1907; Smith, Harry B. 1907

Land of Dreams (inst.)   Stept 1936

Land of Enchantment (Land of Romance)   Smith, Harry B. 1923

Land of Evangeline   Young, Victor 1920

(There Is a) Land of Fancy   Smith, Harry B. 1911; Smith, Robert B. 1911

Land of Going to Be   Goetz 1928

Land of Green Ginger, The   David, Mack 1958; Livingston, Jerry 1958

Land of La La La, The   Cahn 1958; Warren 1958

Land of Lemonade and Lollipops, The   Coots 1953

Land of 'Let's Pretend', The   Kern 1914; Smith, Harry B. 1914

Land of Love, The   Smith, Robert B. 1909

Land of Lullaby (Go to Sleep My Pickanniny Babe), The   Yellen 1919

Land of Maidens   Herbert 1911; Smith, Harry B. 1911

Land of Make Believe   Friend 1938; Razaf 1950

Land of Might Have Been   Rome 1949

Land of My Heart's Desire   Whiting 1919

Land of My Own Romance   Herbert 1913; Smith, Robert B. 1913

Land of Mystery   Ahlert 1930; Turk 1930

Land of No Love, The   David, Hal 1962

Land of Nod, The   Howard, Joseph E. 1905, 1907

Land of Opportunitee, The   Gershwin, Ira 1946; Schwartz, Arthur 1946

(Down in the) Land of Pickaninnies   Blake 1924; Sissle 1924

Land of Provence   Smith, Harry B. 1928

Land of Rocky Boo   Caesar 1924
Land of the Gay Caballero   Gershwin, George 1930; Gershwin, Ira 1930
Land of the Loon   De Lange 1941
Land of the Midnight Sun, The   Smith, Harry B. 1914, 1917
Land of the Pharoahs   Washington 1955
Land of the Setting Sun   Johnson, Howard 1953
Land of the Sky (Adios Senorita), The   Howard, Joseph E. 1909
Land of the Sultan's Dreams, The   Herbert 1911; Smith, Harry B. 1911
Land of Used-to-Be, The   Howard, Joseph E. 1909
Land of Yesteryear   Goetz 1918
Land on Your Feet   Rainger 1942; Robin 1942
Land where Dreams Come True, The   Friml 1917
Land Where the Good Songs Go, The   Kern 1917
Landing of the Pilgrims (Landing of the Pilgrim Fathers) (inst.)   Young, Victor 1955
Landing the Landlord   Coslow 1922
Landler (inst.)   Kern 1932
Landlord at My Door!   Gordon 1932; Revel 1932
Landlord, Stay 'Way from My Door   Woods 1932
Landslide   Howard, Joseph E. 1909
Language of Flowers, The   Porter 1916
Language of Hawaii, The   Drake 1954
Language of Love, The   Caesar 1920; DeSylva 1919; Duke Date Unknown; Friend 1932; Kern 1919; Lawrence 1937; Razaf 1929; Smith, Harry B. 1908; Spina 1956
Language of Romance, The   Parish 1954
Language of the Eyes, The   Von Tilzer 1921
Language of the Fan, The   Atteridge 1917; Romberg 1917
Languida   Lawrence 1954
Lani's Song   Rainger 1937
Lantern Fete   Smith, Robert B. 1905
Lantern Lights   Spina 1969
Lanterns in the Sky   Fain 1946; Freed, Ralph 1946
L'Apres Midi d'Un Boeuf   Porter 1939
Laramie   Evans 1948; Livingston, Jay 1948
Larceny and Love   Mercer 1964
Large Aardvark Song, The   Coleman 1964
Large As Life   Russell 1959
Largo   Herbert 1903
Largo (inst.)   Johnson, J. Rosamond 1944
Lark, The   Romberg 1927; Smith, Harry B. 1927
Larry   Williams 1907
Larry Brownell Theme   Oakland 1954
Larry Wilson Theme   Oakland 1954
Lars, Lars   Rodgers 1979
Las Vegas   Adams 1953; Drake 1955; Norworth 1954; Spina 1967
Lash the Wheel   Willson 1969
Lass I Love, The   Olcott 1901
Lass Who Loved a Sailor, The   Hart 1929; Rodgers 1929
Last Bus Left at Midnight, The   David, Hal 1961
Last Call for Love, The   Arlen 1942; Harburg 1942; Lane 1942; Monaco 1941
Last Chance   Raye 1952
Last Dance, The   Cahn 1958; Harbach 1921; Sigman 1957; Van Heusen 1958
Last Dance (Our Last Dance), The   Hammerstein 1938; Harbach 1938; Kern 1938
Last Dance, That's Out, The   Atteridge 1921; Romberg 1921
Last Dance with You, The   Hoffman 1945
Last Frontier, The   Washington 1955
Last I Love New York Song, The   Strouse 1985

Last Kiss of the First Love, The   Fisher 1923
Last Kiss You Gave Me, The   Ruby 1940
Last Leaf on the Apple Tree, The   Spina 1969
Last Little Girl Is You, The   Herbert 1911; Smith, Harry B. 1911
Last Little Mile Is Longest, When You're Longing for Home Sweet Home, The   Donaldson 1921
Last Little Mile Is the Longest,, When You're Longing for Home Sweet Home, The   Lewis 1921; Young, Joe 1921
Last Long Flight, The   Hanley 1921
Last Long Mile, The   Dietz 1944; Duke 1944
Last Love Song, The   Olcott 1938
Last Midnight   Sondheim 1987
Last Mile Is the Longest When You're on the Way Home   Davis 1932; Silver 1932
Last Night   Adamson 1944; Sterling 1912
Last Night a Miracle Happened   Lawrence 1939
Last Night I Dreamed You Kissed Me   Kahn 1928
Last Night I Kissed a Dream   Razaf 1944
Last Night I Missed You in My Dreams   Gilbert 1937
Last Night in Dreamy Dreamland   Leslie 1929
Last Night on the Back Porch (I Loved Her Best of All)   Brown, Lew 1923
Last Night on the Radio   Motzan 1925
Last Night the World Began   Kahn 1922
Last Night Was the End of the World   Sterling 1912; Von Tilzer 1912
Last Night When We Were All Alone   Mills 1929
Last Night When We Were Young   Arlen 1935; Harburg 1935
Last Night (You Promised Me the Moon)   Spina 1977
Last Night's Gardenias   Coslow 1940
Last of the Cabbies, The   Duke 1936; Gershwin, Ira 1936
Last of the Red Hot Lovers   David, Mack 1972
Last One to Be Loved, The   Bacharach 1964; David, Hal 1964
Last Ride (Another Spring Will Rise) (inst.)   Bacharach 1979
Last Rose of Summer, The   Johnson, Howard 1939
Last Song and Dance, The   Leslie 1957
Last Star of Evening, The   Sigman 1959; Young, Victor 1959
Last Sweetheart of Mine, The   Friend 1924; Monaco 1924
Last Thing I Want Is Your Pity, The   Loesser 1947
Last Time I Felt Like This, The   Bergman 1979
Last Time I Saw My Heart, The   Bacharach 1958; David, Hal 1958
Last Time I Saw Paris, The   Hammerstein 1940, 1941; Kern 1940
Last Time We'll Say Goodnight, The   Razaf 1954
Last Train from Gun Hill, The   Webster 1959
Last Two Weeks in July, The   Baer 1939; Gilbert Date Unknown; Lewis 1939
Last Waltz, The   Atteridge 1921
Last Waltz I Had with You, The   Atteridge 1920
Last Waltz with You   Heyman 1934; Romberg 1934
Last Will and Testament   Caesar 1943
Last Word, The   Willson 1953
Last Year's Love   Bacharach 1960
Latch On (inst.)   Waller 1938
Late Bloomer   Coleman 1988
Late House   Edwards 1910; Smith, Harry B. 1910
Late, Late Show, The   Comden and Green 1960; Styne 1960
Late November   Webster 1965
Late Showdown   Russell 1977
Lately   Sigman 1958
Lately Song, The   Cahn 1953; Fain 1953

Later   Adams 1992; Sondheim 1973; Strouse 1992

Later On, Some Day   Monaco 1913

Later Tonight   Brown, Nacio Herb 1943; Robin 1943

Latest Creation in Girls, The   Brown, A. Seymour 1909

Latest Society Pet, The   Herbert 1911; Smith, Harry B. 1911

Latest Thing from Paris, The   Friml 1912; Harbach 1912

Latigo   Caesar 1930; Harbach 1930; Romberg 1930

Latin in Me, The   Fain 1940; Yellen 1940

Latin Lovers   Robin 1953

Latin Quarter, The   Dubin 1938; Smith, Harry B. 1908; Warren 1938

Latin Quarter Twist   Mills 1962

Latin Rhythm (inst.)   Young, Victor 1937

Latin Tune, A Manhattan Moon and You, A   Dubin 1940; McHugh 1940

Latins Know How   Berlin 1940

Lauder Melodies   Smith, Harry B. 1908

Lauderdale By the Sea   Howard, Joseph E. 1956

Laugh   David, Hal 1951; Friml 1919; Harbach 1919; Hart 1935; Rodgers 1935

Laugh and Call It Love   Burke 1938; Monaco 1938

Laugh and Grow Fat   Romberg 1921

Laugh and Let the Clouds Roll By   Cobb 1912; Schwartz, Jean 1912

Laugh at Life   Romberg 1948

Laugh at Love   Schwartz, Jean 1926

Laugh! Clown! Laugh!   Lewis 1928; Young, Joe 1928

Laugh It Down   Duke 1930; Harburg 1930

Laugh It Off   Caesar 1943; Hammerstein 1923; Kalmar 1924; Lerner, Sammy 1939; Oakland 1939; Ruby 1924; Youmans 1923

Laugh It Up   Berlin 1962

Laugh, Laugh, Laugh with Hey, Abbott/Hey, Costello   Mills 1942

(I Don't Know Whether To) Laugh or Cry   Coslow 1955

Laugh Parade, The   Dixon 1931; Warren 1931; Young, Joe 1931

Laugh Today and Cry Tomorrow   Kalmar 1930; Ruby 1930

Laugh While You're Dancing Around   Turk 1923

Laugh with a Tear in It, A   Olcott 1908

Laugh, You Son of a Gun   Rainger 1933; Robin 1933, 1934

Laugh Your Cares Away   DeSylva 1923; Gershwin, George 1923; Goetz 1923

Laugh Your Way Through Life   Gordon 1937; Revel 1937

Laughin' at the Weather Man   Rainger 1935; Robin 1935

Laughin' at You   Stept 1924

Laughing at Love   Evans 1950; Livingston, Jay 1950

Laughing Boy Blues   Cahn 1938

Laughing Eyes   Sterling 1926

Laughing Eyes (inst.)   Schwartz, Jean 1930

Laughing Generals (inst.)   Weill 1936

Laughing Irish Eyes   Magidson 1936; Mitchell 1936; Stept 1936

Laughing Little Almond Eyes   Smith, Robert B. 1905

Laughing Marionettes   Gilbert 1929

Laughing on the Outside Crying on the Inside   Coslow 1932

Laughing Polka, The   Heyman 1952

Laughing Song   Howard, Joseph E. 1909; Koehler 1937; Von Tilzer 1903, 1909

Laughing the Clouds Away   Coslow 1934; Robin 1934

Laughing Tony   Burke 1943; Van Heusen 1943

Laughing Water   Razaf 1929; Waller 1929

Laughing Water, Stop Your Crying   Bryan 1928

Laughing While My Heart Is Breaking   Baer 1931; Lewis 1931; Young, Joe 1931

Laughs   Evans 1953; Herbert 1911; Livingston, Jay 1953

Laughter and Love and You   Brennan 1923

Laughter and Tears   Evans 1968; Livingston, Jay 1968

Laughter Opening (inst.)   Duke 1930

Laughter Symphony (inst.)   Duke 1930

Laughter Will Lead You to Love   Johnson, Howard 1930

Laundry Scene   Porter 1953

Laura   Mercer 1944

Laura De Maupassant   Styne 1953

Laura Lee   Willson 1951

Laurie Ann   Revel 1951

Laurie, My Love   Livingston, Jerry 1961; Oakland 1961; Webster 1961

Lavender Dreams   Freed, Ralph 1964

Law   Hart 1921; Porter 1953; Rodgers 1921

Law Is Law   Loewe 1937

Law Must Be Obeyed, The   Berlin 1915

Lawd, I Give You My Children   Mercer 1934

Lawd, You Made the Night too Long   Lewis 1932; Young, Victor 1932

Lawman, The   David, Mack 1959; Livingston, Jerry 1959

Lawn Mower Waltz   Willson 1953

Lawrence of Arabia   Webster 1963

Lawyers   Adams 1978; Strouse 1978

Lay Me Down to Sleep in Carolina   Ager 1926; Yellen 1926

Lay of a Gay Young Man, The   Sondheim Date Unknown

Lay Off Big Boy You Haven't Got a Chinaman's Chance   Leslie 1930; Monaco 1930; Young, Joe 1930

Lay the Music Down   David, Hal 1974

Lay Your Head on My Shoulder   Conrad 1933; Coslow 1933

Lay-De-O   Bullock 1954

Laying the Cornerstone   Hart 1933; Rodgers 1933

Laziest Gal in Town, The   Porter 1927

Lazy   Berlin 1924

Lazy Amazon, The   Sissle 1929

Lazy Bones Gotta Job Now   Robin 1935, 1936

Lazy but Free (inst.)   Kern 1935

Lazy Day   Kahn 1932

Lazy Day in the Sun Just Readin', Fishin', and Dreamin', A   Hoffman 1934

Lazy Hour   Revel 1956

Lazy in Love   Bergman 1957

Lazy Levee Loungers   Robison 1930

Lazy Little Donkey   Stept 1954

Lazy Little Stream Ripple Along   Rose 1935

Lazy Lou'siana Moon   Donaldson 1930

Lazy, Lousy Liza   Gordon 1933; Revel 1933

Lazy Mama, Can't I Get You Up?   Lewis 1923; Young, Joe 1923

Lazy Mary (Johnny Darling Can't You Get Up)   Caesar 1942

(Love's Got Me in a) Lazy Mood   Mercer 1947

Lazy Moon   Johnson, J. Rosamond 1903

Lazy Pickaninny   Gilbert 1924

Lazy Rhapsody   Ellington 1962; Parish 1943, 1962; Washington 1934, 1943

Lazy Rhythm   Magidson 1937; Oakland 1937

Lazy River   Carmichael 1931

Lazy Step   Duke 1940

Lazy Summer Night   Spina 1958

Lazy Sunday   Mills 1966

Lazy Train   Hoffman 1958

Lazy Waters   Kahn 1924

Lazy Weather   Kahal 1936

Lazy Yellow Moon   Brown, A. Seymour Date Unknown

Lazybones   Carmichael 1933; Mercer 1933

Lazy-Lack-a-Daisy Melody   Lawrence 1940
Le Beau Sabreur   Smith, Harry B. 1911
Le Can Can   Rose 1940; Van Heusen 1940
Le Chiffre's Torture of the Mind (inst.)   Bacharach 1967
Le Dimanche Est a Nous   Brooks 1950
Le Jazz Hot   Mancini 1982
Le Marquis de Faublas   Hammerstein 1933
Le Poeme (inst.)   Romberg 1913
Le Reve D'Absinthe   Porter 1911
Le Son d'Amour (I Hear)   Drake 1959
Lead 'Em On   DeSylva 1925; Hanley 1925
Lead Me to Laughter   Johnson, Howard 1920
Lead Me to Love   Berlin 1914; Snyder 1915
Lead Me to that Beautiful Band   Berlin 1912
Lead Me to that Beautiful Land   Goetz 1912
Leader Doesn't Like Music, The   Kahn 1939; Warren 1939
Leader of a Big-Time Band, The   Porter 1943
Leader of Fashion Am I   Edwards 1907
Leader of Vanity Fair, The   Smith, Robert B. 1902
Leaders Digest   Cahn 1939
Leaders of Society   Porter 1912
Leaders of the Modern Regime   Harbach 1926; Kern 1926
Leadin' Up the Stairs   Russell 1948
Leading Girl, The   Fain 1940; Yellen 1940
Leading Man   Atteridge 1924
Leadville Johnny Brown   Willson 1960
League of Nations, The   DeSylva 1919; Gershwin, George 1919
Leap Year   Brooks 1956
Leaping Music   Raye 1953
Learn About Life   Merrill 1990
Learn How to Lose   Fields 1936
Learn to Be Lonely   Comden and Green 1982
Learn to Be Lovely   Gordon 1936; Revel 1936
Learn to Croon   Arlen 1931; Coslow 1933; Johnston 1933; Yellen 1931
Learn to Do the Strut   Berlin 1923
Learn to Sing a Love Song   Berlin 1927
Learn to Smile   Harbach 1921
Learning   Livingston, Jerry 1934
Learning to Love   Webster 1957
Learning to Love You   Akst 1926; Davis 1926
Lease in My Heart   Fain 1931; Kahal 1931
Lease Your Little Lovin' Heart to Me   Whiting 1914
Least Little Thing You Do, The   De Lange 1935
Least That's My Opinion   Arlen 1946, 1959; Mercer 1946
Least You Can Do for a Lady, The   Dubin 1937
Leave a Little Love Dream   Robin 1932
Leave a Little Love for Me   David, Mack 1932
Leave a Little Smile   Dubin 1930
Leave a Message   Harburg 1952
Leave Him Alone If He Leaves You   Brown, Lew 1911
Leave It All to Me   Bergman 1979
Leave It Alone   Adams 1972; Strouse 1972
Leave It that Way   Fisher 1930
Leave It to Jane   Kern 1917
Leave It to Katarina   Caesar 1936
Leave It to Love   Gershwin, George 1924; Gershwin, Ira 1924; Gordon 1932; Revel 1932; Smith, Harry B. 1930
Leave It to the Girls   Strouse 1993
Leave It to Your Milliner   Smith, Robert B. 1919
Leave Me a Beautiful Melody   Coslow 1929
Leave Me Alone   Von Tilzer 1914
Leave Me Just a Little Bit of You   Stept 1944
Leave Me Something to Remember   Davis 1925

Leave Me Your Love When You're Gone   Fisher 1920
Leave My Pulse Alone   Dietz 1948; Schwartz, Arthur 1948
Leave My Women Alone   Adamson 1941; Duke 1941
Leave the Atom Alone   Arlen 1957; Harburg 1957
Leave the Door Open (Walk Away)   McHugh 1964
Leave the Lovin' to Me   Kahal 1929
Leave Us Face It, We're in Love   Loesser 1944
Leave Us Root for the Dodgers, Rodgers   Fisher 1943
Leave You Cheri, Jamais   Caesar 1928
Leavin' fo' de Promis' Lan'   Gershwin, George 1935
Leavin' Time   Arlen 1946; Mercer 1946
Leaving   Meyer 1909
Leaving Me   Razaf 1955; Waller 1955
Leaving Town   Merrill 1950
Leaving Town While We May   Gershwin, George 1924
Lecon le Danse   Evans 1950; Livingston, Jay 1950
Ledger   Parish 1965
Left — Right   Styne 1943
Left All Alone Again Blues   Kern 1920
Left All Alone with the Blues   Johnson, James P. 1930; Kalmar 1923; Ruby 1923
Left, Left, My Sweetie Got Mad and She Left   Johnson, Howard 1926
(I'm) Left with Memories   Brooks 1958
Leg It   Conrad 1928
Leg of Mutton   Romberg 1954
Leg of Mutton (inst.)   Romberg 1913
Leg of Nations, The   Berlin 1920
Legacy, The   Coleman 1978; Comden and Green 1978
Legalize My Name   Arlen 1946; Mercer 1946
Legend of Echo Mountain, The   Livingston, Jerry 1962
Legend of Lobo, The   Sherman 1962
Legend of Mackie Messer   Weill 1933
Legend of Niagara, The   Gorney 1938; Harburg 1930
Legend of Old California, The   Mercer 1940; Warren 1940
Legend of Robin Hood, The   Cahn 1938; Van Heusen 1971
Legend of the Castle   Herbert 1903
Legend of the Djin, The   Herbert 1907; Smith, Harry B. 1907
Legend of the Drums   Buck 1923; Herbert 1923
Legend of the Glow Worm   DeSylva 1922; Herbert 1922
Legend of the Golden Tree (The Legend of the Cyclamen Tree), The   Buck 1921; Herbert 1921
Legend of the Lovers   Spina 1977
Legend of the Mill, The   Herbert 1906
Legend of the Pearls, The   Berlin 1921
Legend of the Sons of Samson, The   Smith, Harry B. 1906
Legend of the Sword in the Stone   Sherman 1963
Legend of the Violin, The   Blane 1958
Legend of the Woodland, A   Atteridge 1923; Schwartz, Jean 1923
Legend of Vilia, The   Leigh 1955
Legend of Wyatt Earp, The   Adamson 1955; Warren 1955
Legend Song   Romberg 1927; Smith, Harry B. 1927
Legendary Tale   Brooks 1947
Legion of the Lost   Freed, Ralph 1963; Livingston, Jerry 1963
Legionnaire's Song, The   Loesser 1939
Legs   Cahn 1963; Conrad 1929; Mitchell 1929; Van Heusen 1963
Legs, Legs, Legs   Gorney 1929; Harburg 1929
Lehua (Crimson Flower-Tree)   Friml 1933
Leila   David, Mack 1957
Leit Motif   Drake 1959
L'Elefant Skeed   Egan 1919; Whiting 1919
Lemon Drop Moon   Webster 1953
Lemon Drops and Gum Drops   David, Hal 1957

Lemon Drops, Lollipops and Sunbeams   Cahn 1976

Lemon Twist   Mills 1961

Lemons   Johnson, J. Rosamond 1907

Lena from Palestreena   Conrad 1937

Lena, I Love You   Hammerstein 1935; Romberg 1935

Lena, Lena   Kern 1910

Lena the Laughing Hyena   Caesar 1965

Lena, You're Leaning All Over Me   Lewis 1924; Young, Joe 1924

Lend Me a Kiss Until To-morrow   Cobb 1921; Edwards 1921

Lend Me Your Eyes, Pretty Baby   Bryan 1928

Lend Me Your Heart   Johnson, J. Rosamond 1940

Lend Us a Daddy   Hanley 1921

Lenora   Gilbert 1928; Silver 1928

Lenore   Johnson, Howard 1921; Johnson, James P. 1964; Kahn 1921; Sterling 1924

Lenox Avenue   Caesar 1931

Lenox Avenue Blues (inst.)   Waller 1927

Lenox Avenue Waltz   Blake 1949

Leonore   Donaldson 1926

Leopard Cannot Change His Spots, A   Hanley 1932

Les Girls   Porter 1957

Les Poupess de Paris   Cahn 1964; Van Heusen 1964

Les Trois Etroit Trottoirs   Revel 1953

Less than Eighty Days   Burke 1946; Van Heusen 1946

Lesson, The   David, Mack 1967

Lesson #8   Sondheim 1984

Lesson Book Song   Smith, Harry B. 1901

Lesson in C, A   Ellington 1938; Mills 1938

Lesson in Etiquette, A   Smith, Robert B. 1905

Lesson in Flirtation, A   Smith, Harry B. 1901

Lesson in Kissing (Kiss, Kiss, Kiss), A   Smith, Harry B. 1906

Lesson in Latin, A   Freed, Ralph 1941

Lesson in Love, A   Atteridge 1924; Romberg 1924; Schwartz, Jean 1924; Smith, Harry B. 1911

Lesson in Love (Business Rhythm), A   Oakland 1931

Lesson of the Lord, The   Coots 1952

Lesson with a Fan, A   Smith, Harry B. 1901

Lessons in Love   Arlen 1959; Mercer 1959; Smith, Harry B. 1911; Smith, Robert B. 1911

Lest You Forget   Carroll 1923

Let a Man who Knows How Show You How   Adamson 1939; Donaldson 1939

Let a Smile Be Your Umbrella   Fain 1927; Kahal 1927

Let Antipholus In   Hart 1938; Rodgers 1938

Let Bygones Be Bygones   Meyer 1921; Williams 1914; Young, Joe 1914

Let Cupid In   Atteridge 1916; Motzan 1916

Let Cutie Cut Your Cuticle   DeSylva 1919; Gershwin, George 1919

Let Doctor Schmet Vet Your Pet   Porter 1943

Let Down Your Hair   Coslow 1937

Let Down Your Hair and Sing   Bullock 1937; Spina 1937

Let 'Em Dig Way Down   Brooks 1959

Let 'Em Eat Cake   Gershwin, George 1933; Gershwin, Ira 1933

Let 'Em Eat Caviar   Gershwin, George 1933; Gershwin, Ira 1933

Let 'Em Rot   Coleman 1988

Let Ev'ry Day Be Mother's Day   Stept 1945

Let Fate Decide   Smith, Harry B. 1932

Let Freedom Ring (The Freedom Song)   Willson 1951

Let Georgie Do It   Leslie 1909

Let Go of My Heart   Robin 1951; Styne 1951

Let Go the Rope   Freed, Ralph 1959

Let Her Go   Atteridge 1917; Romberg 1917

Let Her Not Be Beautiful   Duke 1963

Let Him Live (Dejalo Vivir)   Brooks 1966

Let Him Ramble, Let Him Roam   Ager 1929; Yellen 1929

Let in the Sunshine of Love   Johnson, Howard 1914

Let It Be Gay   Davis 1942

Let It Be Me   Dixon 1935; Wrubel 1935

Let It Be Soon   Friml 1919; Harbach 1919

Let It Come Down   Comden and Green 1953

Let It Happen   Adams 1967; Strouse 1967

Let It Rain Let It Pour!   Gershwin, Ira 1939

Let It Rain, Let It Pour, I'll Be in Virginia in the Morning   Donaldson 1924; Friend 1925

Let It Ride   Evans 1961; Livingston, Jay 1961

Let It Snow, Let It Snow, Let It Snow   Cahn 1945; Styne 1945

Let It Unfold   Robison 1964

Let Love Go   Hammerstein 1926; Harbach 1926; Romberg 1926

Let Me Awake   Romberg 1921

Let Me Be   Kahn 1927

Let Me Be a Friend to You   Gershwin, George 1927; Gershwin, Ira 1927

Let Me Be a People (Plain Old Me)   Brooks 1960; Warren 1960

Let Me Be Alone with You   Mills 1929

Let Me Be Born Again   Washington 1933; Young, Joe 1933; Young, Victor 1933

Let Me Be Free   Friml 1934; Herbert 1911; Smith, Harry B. 1911

Let Me Be Lonely   Bacharach 1968; David, Hal 1968

Let Me Be Loved   Evans 1957; Livingston, Jay 1957

Let Me Be Surprised   Strouse 1989

Let Me Be the First One Dearie   Bryan 1912; Fisher 1912

Let Me Be with You   David, Mack 1961

Let Me Be Your Little Love   Russell 1964, 1977

Let Me Be Your Lover   Conrad 1934

Let Me Be Your Mama   Meyer 1910

Let Me Be Your Mirror   David, Hal 1974

Let Me Be Your Sweetheart Once Again   Fisher 1936

Let Me Build a Little Fence Around Your Heart   Howard, Joseph E. 1918

Let Me Build a Nest for You   Brown, A. Seymour 1910; Goetz 1910

Let Me Call You Mine   Johnson, Howard 1934

Let Me Cry   Davis 1955

Let Me Dance   Coots 1925

Let Me Day Dream   Donaldson 1937

Let Me Down Easy   Brown, Lew 1950; Henderson 1950

Let Me Dream Some More   Koehler 1947

Let Me Drift on the Pillow of a Cloud   Revel 1959

Let Me Drink in Your Eyes   Hart 1920, 1921; Rodgers 1920, 1921

Let Me Entertain You   Sondheim 1959; Styne 1959

Let Me Fool Myself   Brown, Lew 1939; Henderson Date Unknown; Pollack 1939

Let Me Get Away   Howard, Bart 1961

Let Me Give All My Love to Thee   Hammerstein 1928; Youmans 1928

Let Me Go to Rio   Bacharach 1969; David, Hal 1969

Let Me Go to Sleep in Dreamland (and Wake Up Dreaming of You)   Johnson, Howard 1934

Let Me Have a Rainy Sunday   Coots 1937

Let Me Have My Dreams   Akst 1929; Clarke 1929

Let Me Hear You Love Me   Styne 1980

Let Me Hear You Whisper   Evans 1954; Livingston, Jay 1954

Let Me Hum a Hymn to Her Tonight   Young, Joe 1931

Let Me In   Merrill 1951

Let Me In Out of the Rain   Bullock 1940; Wrubel 1940

Let Me Into Your World   Sigman 1974

Let Me Introduce You to My Rosie   Brown, Lew 1925

Let Me Kiss Your Tears Away   Spina 1951

Let Me Know a Day Before   Monaco 1911

Let Me Lead the Way   Drake 1968

Let Me Linger Longer in Your Arms   Baer 1924; Friend 1924

Let Me Live and Love You Just for Tonight   Stept 1926

Let Me Live Today   Hammerstein 1941; Romberg 1941

Let Me Live Today (inst.)   Romberg 1940

Let Me Look at You   Arlen 1951; Fields 1951

Let Me Look Deep into Your Eyes   Egan 1933

Let Me Love You   Howard, Bart 1952

Let Me Love You (Que Te Amo!)   Evans 1954; Livingston, Jay 1954

Let Me Love You Tonight   Parish 1941

Let Me Match My Private Life with Yours   Duke 1932; Harburg 1932

Let Me Present You With My Heart   Johnson, Howard 1935

Let Me Put It This Way   Evans 1950; Livingston, Jay 1950

Let Me Remember   Kahn 1924

Let Me Ride By Your Side in the Saddle   Howard, Joseph E. 1942

Let Me Shimmy and I'm Satisfied   Buck 1918

Let Me Show You Paris   Atteridge 1912

Let Me Sing   Berlin 1963

Let Me Sing - And I'm Happy   Berlin 1930

Let Me Sing Before Breakfast   Fields 1929; McHugh 1929

Let Me Sing My Song   Adams 1978; Strouse 1978

Let Me Sing You to Sleep with a Love Song   Gordon 1935; Revel 1935

Let Me Sleep Tonight My Aching Heart   Ahlert 1938; Young, Joe 1938

Let Me So Love   Evans 1965; Livingston, Jay 1965

Let Me Spend the Night with You   Spina 1978

Let Me Steal a Kiss from You   Lewis 1910

Let Me Tell You a Tale   Drake 1953

Let Me Tell You 'Bout Louisa   Hoffman 1950

Let Me Tell You I Won't   David, Hal 1991; Strouse 1991

Let Me Think for You   David, Hal 1974

Let Me Try Again   Cahn 1973

Let Me Walk   Hart Date Unknown; Rodgers Date Unknown

Let Me Walk on the Water, Oh Lord   David, Mack 1954

Let Me Weep on Your Shoulder   Eliscu 1929

Let Me Whirl to an Old Refrain   Buck 1921

Let Me Whisper in Your Ear   Bryan 1920; Schwartz, Jean 1920

Let Me Whisper (Murmullo)   Heyman 1938

Let Nothing Come Between Us   Bryan 1925; Fisher 1925

Let Safety Have Priority   Caesar 1943

Let That Be a Lesson to You   Mercer 1938; Whiting 1938

Let the Ball Roll   Caesar 1937

Let the Band Play   Von Tilzer 1903

Let the Flag Fly   Gilbert 1917

Let the Little Joy Bells Ring   Friend 1919

Let the Lower Lights Be Burning   Comden and Green 1958; Styne 1958

Let the Man Who Makes the Gun   Egan 1935

Let the Music Play   Smith, Robert B. 1914

Let the Notes Sing Loud and Clear   Brooks 1958

Let the Rest of the World Go By   Brennan 1919

Let the Soul Kiss Be Mine Today   Smith, Harry B. 1908

Let the Sun of Thine Eyes   Herbert 1899; Smith, Harry B. 1899

Let the Trumpets Sound   Smith, Harry B. 1905

Let the World Be Full of Sunshine   Parish 1954

Let the Worry Bird Worry for You   Robin 1951; Styne 1951

Let Them Fight It Out in Their Own Back Yard   Hoffman 1932; Washington 1932

Let Them See A Star   Strouse 1987

Let There Be Love, and There Was Love   Gorney 1933

Let There Be Music   Harburg 1943

Let There Be Peace   Lerner, Sammy 1944

Let Things Be Like They Always Was   Weill 1947

Let This Be a Warning to You   Davis 1938

Let Us All Sing Auld Lang Syne   Brown, Lew 1945; Henderson 1945

Let Us All Take Care of Tillie, While the Government Is Taking Care of Willie   Brown, Lew 1941

Let Us Be Gay   Stept 1934; Washington 1934

Let Us Be Married   Smith, Harry B. 1910

Let Us Build a Little Nest   Kern 1912

Let Us Dance Till the Dawn   Harbach 1948

Let Us Drink to the Girl of My Dreams   Baer 1929; Gilbert 1929

Let Us Gather at the Goal Line   Fain 1946

Let Us Give Thanks   Spina 1957

Let Us Greet with Joy Pretended   Smith, Harry B. 1906

Let Us Have Lettuce To-Night   Fisher 1930

Let Us Have Peace (inst.)   Motzan 1915

Let Us Keep the Shimmie   Bryan 1919; Schwartz, Jean 1919

Let Us Say Goodbye with a Waltz   Parish 1922

Let Your Heart Lead the Way   David, Mack 1947; Hoffman 1947; Livingston, Jerry 1947

Let Your Heart Make Up Your Mind   Caesar 1935; Lerner, Sammy 1935

Let Your Intuition Be Your Guide   Schwartz, Jean 1955

Let Your Lips Tell Me Once   Caesar 1961

Let Your Love Come Through   Bacharach 1967; David, Hal 1967

Let Your Way Home Be My Way Home   Monaco 1933

Let Yourself Go   Berlin 1936; Gershwin, Ira 1928

L'Etang (Live for Love)   Sigman 1958

Letitia's Song   Warren 1934

Let's   Ellington 1966

Let's All Be Americans Now   Berlin 1917; Leslie 1917; Meyer 1917

Let's All Be Good Pals Together, For When You're Gone, You're Gone Forever   Davis 1919

Let's All Be Something, Uncle Sammy Wants Us Now   Sterling 1917

Let's All Go Dancing in Our Stocking Feet   Robison 1939

Let's All Go Places   Donaldson 1933

Let's All Go to Mary's House   Conrad 1927, 1928

Let's All Henry Ford   Leslie 1926; Monaco 1926

Let's All Meet at My House   Burke 1942; Van Heusen 1942

Let's All Rally   Warren 1960

Let's Back Jack!   Coots 1961

Let's Be a Little More Friendly   Woods 1936

Let's Be Buddies   Porter 1940

Let's Be Domestic   Coslow 1930

Let's Be Dreamers in Love   Egan 1932

Let's Be Frank, Mr. Frankenstein   Cahn 1964; Van Heusen 1964

Let's Be Friendly   Fain 1956; Webster 1956

Let's Be Gay   Koehler 1936; McHugh 1936

Let's Be Happy   Webster 1957

Let's Be Happy Now   Dietz 1927; Gorney 1927
Let's Be Lonesome Together   DeSylva 1923; Gershwin, George 1923; Goetz 1923
Let's Be Thankful   Oakland 1934
Let's Be Young   Duke 1946
Let's Begin   Harbach 1933; Kern 1933
Let's Bring Back the Old Fashioned Parlor   Caesar 1955
Let's Bring New Glory to Old Glory   Gordon 1942; Warren 1942
Let's Build a Little Nest   Kern 1918
Let's Bungalow   Atteridge 1915; Carroll 1915; Romberg 1915
Let's Call a Heart a Heart   Burke 1936; Johnston 1936
Let's Call It a Day   Brown, Lew 1933; Friend 1926; Henderson 1933; Kahn 1926
Let's Call It All a Dream   Pollack 1934; Webster 1934
Let's Call the Whole Thing Off   Gershwin, George 1937; Gershwin, Ira 1937
Let's Capture This Moment   Evans 1944; Livingston, Jay 1944
Let's Celebrate   Cahn 1973, 1976
Let's Change   DePaul 1958; Raye 1958
Let's Climb (Grimpons)   Sherman 1962
Let's Compromise   Wrubel 1936
Let's Confess   Freed, Arthur 1933; Hoffman 1933
Let's Dance   Baer 1954; Cahn 1965
Let's Dance and Dream   Koehler 1936; Stept 1936
Let's Dance Mam'selle   Friml 1963
Let's Dance Till the Dawn   Harbach 1947; Kern 1947
Let's Dance to Victory   Baer 1942
Let's Disappear   Cahn 1939
Let's Do a Ballet   Martin 1948
Let's Do It Again   Washington 1953
Let's Do It All Over   Howard, Joseph E. 1942
Let's Do It, Let's Fall in Love   Porter 1928
Let's Do Something Different Tonight   Motzan 1930
Let's Do Something New   Robin 1951; Styne 1951
Let's Do the Copacabana   Coslow 1947
Let's Double Up   Gordon 1934; Revel 1934
Let's Dream   Coots 1929; Davis 1929
Let's Dream Again   Hanley 1938; Rose 1938
Let's Dream in the Moonlight   Loesser 1938
Let's Dream Together   Harbach 1947, 1953; Kern 1947
Let's Dress for Dinner Tonight   David, Mack 1934; Silver 1934
Let's Drink to a Dream   Dubin 1938, Date Unknown; Warren 1938, Date Unknown
Let's Drink to Happiness   Hoffman 1953
Let's Drink to the Isle We Love   Bryan 1930
Let's Drive Out to a Drive-In   Akst 1943; Davis 1943
Let's End the Beguine   Eliscu 1944; Gorney 1944
Let's Face It   Porter 1941
Let's Face the Music and Dance   Berlin 1936
Let's Fall in Love   Arlen 1933; Koehler 1933
Let's Fall in Love Again   Brown, Nacio Herb 1957
Let's Fill the Old Oaken Bucket With Love   Bryan 1914
Let's Finish the Dream   Stept 1937; Washington 1937
Let's Fly Away   Adams 1950, 1954; Porter 1930; Strouse 1950, 1954
Let's Forget and Be Sweethearts Again   Whiting 1926
Let's Forget To-Morrow Tonight   Harburg 1934
Let's Gather 'round the Old Piano   David, Mack 1934
Let's Gather 'Round the Parlor Piano   Adamson 1951; McHugh 1951
Let's Get Busy Too   Oakland 1955
Let's Get Friendly   Yellen 1931

Let's Get Going Baby   Clare 1936
Let's Get Lost   Loesser 1943; McHugh 1943
Let's Get Married Right Away   Blake 1926; Sissle 1926
Let's Get Over and Get It Over   Razaf 1942
Let's Get Some Pizza Pie   Hoffman 1957
Let's Get the Show on the Road   Brooks 1958; Cahn 1956
Let's Get the Umpire's Goat   Norworth 1908, 1909
Let's Get This War Over With   Blane 1946
Let's Get to the Main Event   Leigh 1955
Let's Get Together   Sherman 1961
Let's Get Together and Sing   Wrubel 1948
Let's Get Up and Do Some Dancing   Robison 1947
Let's Get with It   Stept 1963
Let's Give a Cheer   Kalmar 1928; Ruby 1928
Let's Give Every Child a Chance   McHugh 1953
Let's Give Love Another Chance   Adamson 1938; Magidson 1933; McHugh 1938; Stept 1933
Let's Give the Job to Lindsay   Arlen 1965
Let's Give Three Cheers for Love   Gordon 1934; Revel 1934
Let's Give Three Cheers (For the Three Volunteers)   Mills 1928
Let's Go!   Caesar 1920; Kern 1918; Smith, Robert B. 1919
Let's Go Americana   Brooks 1945
Let's Go A-Roaming   Howard, Joseph E. 1915
Let's Go Around the Town   Berlin 1914
Let's Go Au Go-Go   Styne 1965
Let's Go Back   Drake 1954
Let's Go Back and Kiss the Girls Goodnight Again   David, Mack 1946; Stept 1946
Let's Go Back to Baby Days   Meyer 1909
Let's Go Back to the Waltz   Berlin 1962
Let's Go Bavarian   Adamson 1933; Lane 1933
Let's Go Bowling   Coots 1961
Let's Go Down to the Beer Garden   Meyer 1933
Let's Go Fly a Kite   Sherman 1964
Let's Go Flying   Coleman 1991; Comden and Green 1991
Let's Go for a Spin on Our Bicycle   Johnson, J. Rosamond 1946
Let's Go Home   Evans 1941; Lerner, Alan Jay 1969; Livingston, Jay 1941; Strouse 1991
Let's Go Native   Sherman 1971; Whiting 1930
Let's Go On with the Show   Evans 1955; Livingston, Jay 1955
Let's Go Out and Ring Doorbells   Eliscu 1943; Gorney 1943
Let's Go Over to Charlie's   Coots 1952
Let's Go Over to My House   Caesar 1927; Friend 1927
Let's Go Places   Friend 1930; Monaco 1930
Let's Go Places and Do Things   Conrad 1927
Let's Go Romancin' in the Rain   Clare 1958
Let's Go Round with a Smile   Donaldson 1919; Lewis 1919; Young, Joe 1919
Let's Go Sailor (Shore Leave)   Mercer 1942
Let's Go See the Jets   Cahn 1964; Van Heusen 1964
Let's Go Shopping   Brooks 1959; Friend 1950
Let's Go South   Coots 1946
Let's Go to Caliacabu   Brooks 1942
Let's Go to de Market Place   Bergman 1957
Let's Go to Press   Brooks 1959
Let's Go to Savannah, Ga.   Gilbert 1912
Let's Go to the Movies   Rome 1958; Sondheim 1959; Strouse 1981; Styne 1959
Let's Go to Tokyo   Strouse 1989
Let's Go Walkin'   Wrubel 1929
Let's Go West Again   Berlin 1946
Let's Go What Do You Say?   Caesar 1920

Let's Grow Old Waltzing Together   Howard, Joseph E. 1937

Let's Have a Drink on It   Sherman 1967

Let's Have a Good Time   Romberg 1924; Schwartz, Jean 1924

Let's Have a Good Time Lolita   Atteridge 1924

Let's Have a Jubilee   Mills 1934

Let's Have a Love Affair   Hammerstein 1926; Harbach 1926; Romberg 1926

Let's Have a Meeting of the Lips   David, Hal 1953

Let's Have a Party   Bullock 1950; Drake 1952; Friend 1932

Let's Have a Rattling Good Time   Bryan 1920; Schwartz, Jean 1920

Let's Have An Old-Fashioned Christmas (And Pray for a Happy New Year)   Adamson 1945; Fields 1945; McHugh 1945

Let's Have Another   Gorney 1934; Magidson 1936; Oakland 1936; Yellen 1934

Let's Have Another Cigarette   Magidson 1937; Wrubel 1937

Let's Have Another Cop O' Coffee   Berlin 1932

Let's Have Another One Before We Say Good Night   Raye 1940

Let's Have Blue Birds   Loesser 1936

Let's Have Breakfast in Bed   Stept 1934; Washington 1934

Let's Have Breakfast in Hollywood   Johnston 1948

Let's Have Fun Tonight   Friend 1945

Let's Have Some Pretzels and Beer   Adamson 1946; McHugh 1946

Let's Help Each Other Along   Brown, A. Seymour 1915

Let's Help the Red Cross Save a White Cross   Adamson 1944; McHugh 1944

Let's Hit the Nail on the Head   Arlen 1939; Koehler 1939

Let's Hitch a Horsie to the Automobile   Hoffman 1942; Livingston, Jay 1942; Livingston, Jerry 1942

Let's Hope of Thee My Guardian Be   Herbert 1903; Smith, Harry B. 1903

Let's Incorporate   Loesser Date Unknown

Let's Keep 'Em Flying   DePaul 1941; Raye 1941

Let's Keep It a Dream   Razaf 1937

Let's Keep It That Way   Drake 1943

Let's Keep on Falling in Love Again   Mills 1952

Let's Kiss   Strouse 1999

Let's Kiss and Make Up   Gershwin, George 1927; Gershwin, Ira 1927; McHugh 1957

Let's Kiss and Tell   Leslie 1943; Stept 1943; Wrubel 1934

Let's Kiss Goodbye   Caesar 1924; Conrad 1924; Harbach 1924

Let's K'nock K'nees   Gordon 1931; Revel 1931, 1934

Let's Knock the Bull Out of the Bolsheviki   Johnson, Howard Date Unknown

Let's Laugh and Be Merry   Smith, Harry B. 1927

Let's Leave It to Love   Parish 1935

Let's Live in Sin   Comden and Green 1974; Styne 1974

Let's Live, Think, Talk America   Washington 1950; Young, Victor 1950

Let's Love Tonight   Baer 1953

Let's Make a Night of It   Rainger 1935; Robin 1935

Let's Make a Rag of the Old Oaken Bucket   Leslie 1911

Let's Make a Wish   Kalmar 1936; Ruby 1936

Let's Make America What It Used to Be   Webster 1968

Let's Make an Old Fashioned Christmas   Adamson 1960; McHugh 1960

Let's Make Believe   Gorney 1926

Let's Make Comparisons   Cahn 1951

Let's Make Hay While the Moon Shines   David, Mack 1932

Let's Make History Tonight   David, Hal 1962

Let's Make It a Night   Porter 1955

Let's Make It Christmas All Year Long   Fields 1957; Lane 1957

Let's Make Love   Cahn 1960; Van Heusen 1960

Let's Make Love Amongst the Roses   Jerome 1910; Schwartz, Jean 1910

Let's Make Love Like the Crocodiles   Gorney 1933; Harburg 1933

Let's Make Memories Tonight   Brown, Lew 1939; Coots 1953; Stept 1939

Let's Make Murgatroyd Mayor   DePaul 1942; Raye 1942

Let's Make Music Together   Strouse 1989

Let's Make the Best of It   Coots 1929; Davis 1929

Let's Make the Most of Our Dream   Berlin 1937

Let's Make the World of Tomorrow Today   Caesar 1946

Let's Make This Christmas the Greatest Xmas of All   Coots 1959

Let's Make Whoopee   Rose 1927

Let's Mambo   Raye 1954

Let's Marry   Hammerstein 1920

Let's Mend the Crack in the Liberty Bell   Cobb 1922; Edwards 1922

Let's Merge   Coots 1929; Davis 1929

Let's Misbehave   Porter 1920, 1928

Let's Not Be Sensible   Cahn 1962; Van Heusen 1962

Let's Not Behave Like People   Cahn 1971; Styne 1971

Let's Not Get Married   DeSylva 1922; Herbert 1922

Let's Not Have Another Party   Cahn 1950

Let's Not Talk About Love   Porter 1941

Let's Pay the Two Dollars   Brown, Lew 1943; Stept 1943

Let's Play Cowboys and Indians   David, Mack 1941

Let's Play Hookey   Hammerstein 1922

Let's Play Hookie   Goetz 1918

Let's Play House   Brooks 1945; David, Mack 1934, 1935

Let's Play Post Office   Merrill 1950

Let's Play We're Having Fun   Romberg 1941

Let's Play (What's My Name)   Coots 1950

Let's Pow-Wow, Not Mau Mau   Caesar 1959

Let's Pretend   Bryan 1940; Herbert 1920; Romberg 1921; Silver 1940; Smith, Harry B. 1908; Smith, Robert B. 1920

Let's Pretend that We're in Love   Baer 1955

Let's Pretend We're Grownup   Bacharach 1968; David, Hal 1968

Let's Pretend We're Kids Again   Edwards 1934

Let's Pretend You Love Me   Howard, Joseph E. 1909

Let's Put It Over with Grover   Sherman 1968

Let's Put on the Ritz   Arlen 1932; Koehler 1932

Let's Put Our Heads Together   Arlen 1936; Harburg 1936

Let's Put the Sun to Bed and Wake Up the Moon   Baer 1932

Let's Put Two and Two Together   Conrad 1934; Mitchell 1934

Let's Raise an Army of Sweethearts   Bryan 1937; Fisher 1937

Let's Rally   Motzan 1917

Let's Rock Tonight in a Satellite   Robison 1957

Let's Sail Away to Sweetheart Bay   Bryan 1938

Let's Say Good Night to the Ladies and We'll Come Right Back Again   Brown, Lew 1939

Let's Say Goodnight 'Til It's Morning   Hammerstein 1925; Harbach 1925; Kern 1925

Let's Say Goodnight with a Dance   Fain 1941; Kahal 1941; Yellen 1941

Let's Say It Never Happened   Robison 1952

Let's See, Um, Um, That's Right   Sterling 1911; Von Tilzer 1911

Let's See What Happens   Harburg 1967; Styne 1967

Let's Show 'em How This Country Goes to Town (no music)   Gershwin, Ira 1943

Let's Sing a Song about Nothing   Hart 1938; Rodgers 1938

Let's Sing a Song about Susie   Gordon 1943

Let's Sing Again   Kahn 1936; McHugh 1936

Let's Sing Like a Dixieland Band   Bergman 1961

Let's Sing the Chorus Again   Howard, Joseph E. Date Unknown

Let's Sit and Talk about You   Fields 1928; McHugh 1928

Let's Sit this One Out   Cahn 1962; Fields 1933; McHugh 1933; Van Heusen 1962

Let's Spend a Quiet Evening at Home   Spina 1946

Let's Spend an Evening at Home   Freed, Ralph 1934

Let's Spill the Beans   Gordon 1935; Revel 1935

Let's Start All Over Again   Howard, Joseph E. 1919

Let's Start the New Year Right   Berlin 1942

Let's Start Where We Left Off   Clare 1939; Styne 1939

Let's Start with a Kiss   Egan 1957; Whiting 1957

Let's Stay Home Tonight   Stept 1950

Let's Stay Over Here   Howard, Joseph E. 1939

Let's Steal a Tune from Offenbach   Gorney 1940

Let's Step Out   Porter 1929

Let's Stop Saying Goodbye   Bryan 1935; Leslie 1935; Meyer 1935

Let's Stop the Clock   Coots 1937

Let's Stroll Along and Sing a Song of Love   Brown, Lew 1927; Friend 1927

Let's Suppose   Smith, Robert B. 1930

Let's Suppose I Never Knew   Raye 1963

Let's Take a Car Ride   Rose 1923

Let's Take a Ride on a Rocket   Howard, Joseph E. 1946

Let's Take a Trolly Ride   Howard, Joseph E. 1905

Let's Take a Walk Around the Block   Arlen 1934; Gershwin, Ira 1934; Harburg 1934

Let's Take Advantage of Now   Henderson 1934; Koehler 1934

Let's Take an Old-Fashioned Walk   Berlin 1949; Cohan 1907

Let's Take the Long Way Home   Arlen 1944, 1945; Mercer 1944, 1945

Let's Talk about a Woman   Rome 1954, 1959

Let's Talk about My Sweetie   Donaldson 1926; Kahn 1926

Let's Talk About the Weather   Warren 1970

Let's Talk It Over   Coots 1929; Davis 1929

Let's Tell the Truth   Robison 1963

Let's Tie the Old Forget-Me-Not   Gorney 1938; Webster 1938

Let's Try Love Again   Adams 1957

Let's Vocalize   Porter 1956

Let's Waken the World with a Love Song   Egan 1924; Whiting 1924

Let's Walk Home the Long Way 'Round   Heyman 1944; Spina 1944

Let's Waltz and Whistle   Loewe 1942

Let's Waltz for Old Time's Sake   Koehler 1937; Stept 1937

Let's Wander Down thru Mem'ry Lane   Baer 1942

Let's Wander Down to a One Horse Town   Baer 1942

Let's Wander Off Nowhere   Edwards 1907

Let's Whistle a Waltz   Fields 1933; McHugh 1933

Let's Wreck the Joint   Blake 1955

Let's You and I Just Say Good-Bye   Cohan 1923

Letter, The   Atteridge 1912; Drake 1952; Gorney 1948

Letter Boxes   Berlin 1917

Letter (Dear John), The   Webster 1951

Letter Duet   Herbert 1897; Smith, Harry B. 1897, 1916

Letter from Dixie (inst.), A   Robison 1926

Letter from Klemnacht   Comden and Green 1982

Letter from Paris   Parish 1965

Letter Gets Better (As It Goes Along), The   Hoffman 1957

Letter of Farewell, A   Smith, Harry B. 1926

Letter of the Law   Mercer 1964

Letter Reaches Santa   Drake 1952

Letter Song, The   Atteridge 1925; Freed, Ralph 1941; Kern 1919; Leigh 1955; Smith, Harry B. 1930

Letter that Never Reached Home, The   Leslie 1916

Letter Theme, The   Loesser 1956

Letter to General MacArthur   Rome 1942

Letter to the Children   Comden and Green 1982

Letter You Shouldn't Have Sent, The   Harbach 1911

Letters from an Old Sweetheart   Conrad 1932; Young, Joe 1932

Letters from Home   Herbert 1909

Letters I Write All Day   Herbert 1903; Smith, Harry B. 1903

Letters (That I'm Waiting For)   Dubin 1919

Letters that Lighten Broadway, The   Cobb 1921; Edwards 1921

Levee Gang   Meyer 1926

Levee Land (inst.)   Waller 1926

Levee Lou   Edwards 1912; Howard, Joseph E. 1924

Levee Love   Coots 1929

Levee Lovey   Donaldson 1926; Kahn 1926

Levi Is a Grand Old Name   Goetz 1913

Levine   Warren 1927

Levine with His Flying Machine   Coslow 1927

L'Exposition Universalle   Burke 1946; Van Heusen 1946

L'heure d'or (One Golden Hour)   Friml 1926; Hammerstein 1926; Harbach 1926

L'Histoire de Madame de la Tour   Hammerstein 1939; Kern 1939

Liable to Catch on   Fain 1940

Liar   Hammerstein 1928; Romberg 1928

Liasons   Sondheim 1973

Libby   Sherman 1995

Libere Sur Parole   Russell Date Unknown

Liberty Bell, The   Willson 1940

Liberty Glide, The   Howard, Joseph E. 1918

Liberty Hall   Smith, Robert B. 1912

Liberty March (inst.)   Johnson, James P. 1926

Liberty Song   Akst 1930; Clarke 1930

Lida Rose   Willson 1957

Lido Lady   Hart 1926; Rodgers 1926

Lie, The   Evans 1950; Livingston, Jay 1950

Lie a Little   Leigh 1985

Lie Still, Beloved   Spina 1955

Lie to Me   Russell 1960

Liebchen   Spina 1977

Liebechen (inst.)   Motzan 1916

Liebelei   David, Hal 1960

Lieber Augustin   Johnson, Howard 1939

Lieberstraum   Johnson, Howard 1932

Lieberstraume   Robin 1936

Lieutenants of the Lord   Weill 1977

Life   Davis 1960; Revel 1962

Life Ain't What It Used to Was   Coleman 1958; Leigh 1958

Life and Love   Herbert 1919

Life and Times of Lady Milicant Widdicomb James   Russell 1968

Life as a Twosome   Caesar 1928

Life Begins   Gershwin, Ira 1934

Life Begins at 8:40 (or Thereabouts)   Arlen 1934; Gershwin, Ira 1934; Harburg 1934
Life Begins at Forty   Yellen 1978
Life Begins at Fourteen   Evans 1950; Livingston, Jay 1950
Life Begins at Sweet Sixteen   Henderson 1935; Yellen 1935
Life Begins when You're in Love   Brown, Lew 1935
Life Can Be a Fairy Tale   Cahn 1977
Life Can Be Beautiful   Adamson 1947; McHugh 1947
Life Can Be Oh So Sweet   Baer 1953
Life Can Be So Lonesome   Dubin 1929
Life Could Be a Cakewalk with You   Arlen 1942
Life Could Not Better Be   Cahn 1956
Life Does a Man a Favor (When It Gives Him Simple Joys)   Evans 1958; Livingston, Jay 1958
Life Has Its Funny Little Ups and Downs   Gordon 1953; Myrow 1953
Life I Lead, The   Sherman 1964
Life in a Looking Glass   Mancini 1986
Life in Venetia, Life in Vienna   Sondheim 1999
Life Insurance Song   Arlen 1936; Harburg 1936
Life Is a Beautiful Thing   Evans 1952; Livingston, Jay 1952
Life Is a Carousel   Evans 1978; Livingston, Jay 1978
Life Is a Dancing Roman Holiday   Johnson, J. Rosamond 1914
Life Is a Dirty Business   Herbert 1946
Life Is a Dream   Freed, Arthur 1931
Life Is a Gamble   Atteridge 1921; Romberg 1921
Life is a Game of Checkers   Johnson, J. Rosamond 1909
Life Is a Garden   Harbach 1914
Life Is a Merry-Go-Round   Brown, Nacio Herb 1933; Freed, Arthur 1933
Life is a Riddle   Herbert 1911; Smith, Harry B. 1911
Life Is a See-Saw   Smith, Harry B. 1906; Smith, Robert B. 1907
Life Is a Song, Let's Sing It Together   Ahlert 1935; Stept 1931; Young, Joe 1935
Life Is Fine   Blake 1949
Life Is for Livin'   Cahn 1958; Van Heusen 1958
Life Is for the Living   David, Hal 1974
Life Is Happiness Indeed   Sondheim 1974
Life Is Just a Bowl of Cherries   Brown, Lew 1931; Henderson 1931
Life Is Just a Dress Parade   Atteridge 1914
Life Is Like a Checkerboard when You're in Love   Alter 1929; Johnson, Howard 1929
Life Is Like a Train   Coleman 1978; Comden and Green 1978
Life Is Like an Old La-soo Makin' It   Cahn 1980; Strouse 1980
Life Is Love   Caesar 1929
Life Is not a Fairy Tale   Cahn 1977
Life Is One Thing After Another   Atteridge 1918; Romberg 1918
Life Is Peaches and Cream   Loesser 1937
Life Is So Peculiar   Burke 1950; Van Heusen 1950
Life Is Such a Pleasure   Cahn 1952; Duke 1952
Life Is Sweet   Strouse 1999
Life Is too Short   Bergman 1964; Fain 1964
Life Is Tough   Loewe 1937
Life Is What You Make It   Mercer 1971
Life Isn't All Roses, Rosie   Bryan 1911
Life (Just What in Hell's It All About??)   Spina 1977
Life! Liberty!   Hart 1940; Rodgers 1940
Life of a Bold Free Lance, The   Herbert 1903; Smith, Harry B. 1903

Life of a Nurse, The   Eliscu 1929
Life of a Rose, The   Atteridge 1923; DeSylva 1923; Gershwin, George 1923; Romberg 1923; Schwartz, Jean 1923
Life of a Sailor, The   Porter 1924
Life of an Elephant, The   Adamson 1955; Lane 1955
Life of Her Own, A   Webster 1950
Life of the Party, The   Brooks 1945; Brown, Nacio Herb 1932; DeSylva 1932; Drake 1956; Loewe 1942; Magidson 1937; Whiting 1932; Wrubel 1937
Life Oh Life   Merrill 1967
Life Oriental   Smith, Harry B. 1911
Life Savin' Jim   Conrad 1923
Life Time, A   Cahn 1972
Life Upon the Wicked Stage   Hammerstein 1927; Kern 1927
Life Was Monotonous   Hart 1942; Rodgers 1942
Life Was Pie for the Pioneer   Harburg 1940; Lane 1940
Life with Father   Hart 1942; Rodgers 1942
Life with Rocky, A   Comden and Green 1945
Life Without a Cigarette   Johnson, Howard 1920
Life Without Love   Friml 1913; Harbach 1913
Life Would Be a Cake-Walk with You   Koehler 1942
Lifelong Love Affair, A   Kern 1971; Webster 1971
Life's a Dance   Arlen 1937; Freed, Ralph 1963; Harburg 1937; Kern 1917; Smith, Harry B. 1917
Life's a Funny Present from Someone   Dietz 1944; Duke 1944
Life's a Funny Proposition After All   Cohan 1904
Life's a Game   Adams 1966; Strouse 1966
Life's a Game at Best   Herbert 1917
Life's a Game of Polo   Smith, Harry B. 1915
Life's a Masquerade   Herbert 1905; Smith, Harry B. 1905
Life's Darkest Moment   Mercer 1964
Life's Full of Consequence (Dat Old Debbil Consequence)   Arlen 1943; Harburg 1943
Life's Not that Simple   Comden and Green 1960; Styne 1960
Life's One Sweet Song for Me, I'm in Love with You   Alter 1926
Life's So Complete   Mercer 1933
Life's too Short to Be Blue   Gershwin, George 1925; Gershwin, Ira 1925
Life-Saver's Song, The   Schwartz, Arthur 1933
Lifetime of Loneliness, A   Bacharach 1963; David, Hal 1963
Lifetime of Love   Wrubel 1933
Lift a Glass to Friendship   Bergman 1958
Lift 'Em Up and Put 'Em Down   Hammerstein 1943
Lift Every Voice and Sing   Johnson, J. Rosamond 1923
Lift the Juleps to Your Two Lips   Akst 1929; Clarke 1929
Lift Up   Robison 1958
Lift Up Your Voice   Willson 1953
Lift Your Eyes to Mine   Smith, Harry B. 1916
Lift Your Glass   Romberg 1935
Light a Bolt from the Blue   Oakland 1934
Light Goes On, the Light Goes Off, The   David, Hal 1962
Light in the Piazza   Freed, Arthur 1962
Light of My Life, The   David, Hal 1960; Revel 1942
Light of the World Is Love   Whiting 1913
Light on a Flame, A   Coots 1943
Light that Lies in Women's Eyes, The   Howard, Joseph E. 1908
Light Up   Gordon 1932; Revel 1932; Warren 1960
Light Up a Muriel   Strouse 1975
Light Up Your Face   Rainger 1936; Robin 1936
Light Up Your Face with a Smile   Cobb 1911; Edwards 1911

Light Your Little Lamp My Love for Me   Fisher 1918
Lighthouse Keeper, The   Coots 1950
Lightnin' Bug   David, Hal 1959
Lights Are Low, the Music Is Sweet, The   Friend 1934
Lights, Camera, Action, Love   Gordon 1933; Revel 1933
Light's Diamond Jubilee (inst.)   Young, Victor 1954
Lights of Rome, The   Mercer 1952
Like a Bird in the Night   Johnson, Howard 1935
Like a Bird on the Wing   Caesar 1925; Youmans 1925
Like a Bolt from the Blue   Mills 1934; Parish 1934
Like a Breath of Springtime   Dubin 1929
Like a Falling Star   Mercer 1931
Like a God   Hammerstein 1958; Rodgers 1958
Like a Little Ladylike Lady Like You   Cohan 1927
Like a Lonely Raindrop   Fisher 1950
Like a Lover   Bergman 1968
Like a Main Theme   David, Mack 1973
Like a Melody   Revel 1929
(Love Me) Like a Real, Real Man   Herbert 1912
Like a Rose You Have Faded Away   McHugh 1916
Like a Star in the Night   Heyman 1934; Romberg 1934
Like a Story in a Magazine   Livingston, Jerry 1934
Like a Straw in the Wind   Arlen 1941; Koehler 1941
Like a Train   Ellington 1955
Like a Wandering Minstrel   Cohan 1927
Like a Woman Loves a Man   Loesser 1956
Like an Angel You Flew into Everyone's Heart   McHugh
    1927; Mills 1927
Like an Old Forgotten Refrain   Dubin 1932; Friend 1932
Like Clouds Up in the Sky   Arlen 1959; Mercer 1959
Like Everyone Else (Soliloquy)   Lawrence 1964
Like He Loves Me   Youmans 1926
Like Heaven   David, Hal 1967
Like Her   Bergman 1978
Like It Was   Sondheim 1981
Like Kelly Can   Fields 1930; Fisher 1920; McHugh 1930
Like Love   Ellington 1960; Russell 1960
Like Me a Little Bit Less (Love Me a Little Bit
    More)   Adamson 1934; Lane 1934
Like Me Less — Love Me More   Gorney 1929; Harburg
    1929
Like Ordinary People Do   Hart 1931; Rodgers 1931
Like Someone in Love   Burke 1944; Van Heusen 1944
Like Taking Candy from a Baby   Hoffman 1934
Like the Breeze Blows   Rome 1965
Like the Fella Once Said   McHugh 1940; Mercer 1940
Like the Fellow and the Girl on the Late, Late Show   David,
    Hal 1962
Like the Fjords of Scandinavia   Romberg 1916
Like Wow   Livingston, Jerry 1957
Like Ya — Honey, I Love Ya   Woods 1952
Like You   Smith, Harry B. 1927
Like You Do   Kalmar 1926; Ruby 1926
Like Young   Webster 1958
Li'l Abner   Oakland 1940
Li'l Augie Is a Natural Man   Arlen 1946; Mercer 1946
Li'l Black Sheep   Arlen 1943; Harburg 1943
Li'l Boy Love   Loesser 1940
Li'l Brown Baby   Razaf 1926
Li'l Gal   Johnson, J. Rosamond 1907, 1917
Li'l Ol' You and Li'l Ol' Me   Robin 1951; Styne 1951
Lila Tremaine   Comden and Green 1964; Styne 1964
(Tell Me) Lilac Domino   Smith, Robert B. 1914
Lilac Lane   Egan 1923
Lilac Lou   Magidson 1926

Lilac Tree   Bryan 1958; Revel 1951
Lilacs in the Rain   Parish 1939
Lilacs in the Spring   Kalmar 1951
Lila's Theme (Do You Remember Me?)   Sherman 1972
Lili Marlene   David, Mack 1943
Lilies of the Field   Caesar 1925; Youmans 1925
Lillian   Bryan 1925; Snyder 1925
Lillie, Lawrence, and Jack   Hart 1926; Rodgers 1926
Lillies of the Field   Coots 1922
Lilly   Warren 1926
Lilly and Billy   Styne 1941
Lilly the Blue Loon   Robison 1952
Lilly the Contortionist   Adamson 1935; Lane 1936
Lilly-lu (Lily Lou)   Hoffman 1959
Lily   Warren 1927
Lily and the Nightingale, The   Herbert 1898; Smith, Harry B.
    1898
Lily Garland   Coleman 1978; Comden and Green 1978
Lily Lou   Mitchell 1928
Lily of Laguna   Webster 1942
Lily of Longacre Square, The   Goetz 1918
Lily of the Valley   Gilbert 1917; Youmans 1926
Lily, Oscar   Coleman 1978; Comden and Green 1978
Lily Pond (inst.)   Schwartz, Jean 1930
Lily Pool, The   Coslow 1924; Romberg 1924
Lily the Contortionist   Lane 1934
Lily-I-Lay-De-O   Harburg 1946
Lima   Porter 1916
Limbo   Washington 1957
Limbo Dance (inst.)   Styne 1967
Limbo-Land   Friml 1919; Harbach 1919
Limehouse Nights   Coslow 1934; DeSylva 1919; Gershwin,
    George 1919
Limerick Girls   Olcott 1902
Limerick Song   Gordon 1934
Limpy Dimpy   Clare 1938; Styne 1938
Lim'ricks   Arlen 1946; Mercer 1946
Lincoln Soliloquy   Spina 1944
Linda   Arlen 1930; Koehler 1930; Lawrence 1945
Linda Mujer (You Never Say Yes)   Caesar 1945
Lindbergh, the Eagle of the U.S.A.   Johnson, Howard 1927
Lindy   Berlin 1920
Lindy, Anne 'n' the Baby   Mills 1930
Lindy Come Along   Howard, Joseph E. 1911
Lindy Lou   Johnson, James P. 1947
Lindy's   Adams 1993
Line It Out, Mr. McGinnity   Jerome 1905; Schwartz, Jean
    1905
Line of Least Resistance Is to Fall in Love with You   Fain
    1937
Lines in Mollie's Hand, The   Harbach 1910
Lines to a Writer of Sonnets   Parish 1965
Lines Written on a Tablecloth   Parish 1965
Linger a Little Longer in the Twilight   Woods 1932
Linger in My Arms   Kahn 1928
Linger in My Arms a Little Longer   Magidson 1946
Linger in the Lobby   Gershwin, George 1924; Gershwin, Ira
    1924
Linger Longer, Lingerie   Smith, Harry B. 1909
Linger Longer Love   Donaldson 1924
Lingerie   Goetz 1911
Lingering Down the Lane (Ah Le Petit Vin
    Blanc)   Lawrence 1949
Lion Dance   Sondheim 1976
Lion King, The   Hart 1930; Rodgers 1930

Lion Sort Ses Griffes   Russell Date Unknown

Lion's Roar (inst.)   Waller 1928

Li-Po-Li   Bryan 1929

Lips, Lips, Lips   Romberg 1919

Lips that Laugh at Love   Brennan 1929

Lips that Touch Another's Life (Shall Never Touch Mine)   Sigman 1949

Lipstick on Your Lips   David, Hal 1960

Liquapep   Mercer 1952; Schwartz, Arthur 1952

Liquor Dealer's Dream, The   Weill 1977

Lisa   Bacharach 1967; David, Hal 1967

Lisa (Rear Window Theme)   Rome 1954

Lisette   Duke 1939

List a While, Lady   Sondheim Date Unknown

Listen   Bryan 1921; Schwartz, Jean 1921

Listen Dear   Friml 1914

Listen In, Virginia   Mills 1924

Listen Mr. Verdi   Smith, Harry B. 1923; Smith, Robert B. 1923

Listen My Children and You Shall Hear   Freed, Ralph 1937; Lane 1937

Listen My Love   Bacharach 1959; David, Hal 1959

Listen to Buddy, Stay in Bed   Bergman 1957

Listen to Me   Johnson, Howard 1921; Lawrence 1971

Listen to My Heart   Silver 1939

Listen to My Song of Love   Gilbert 1943

Listen to Sheldon   Sigman 1951

Listen to that Dixie Band   Yellen 1914

Listen To That Jungle Band   Bryan 1910

Listen to the German Band   Gordon 1931; Johnson, J. Rosamond 1946; Revel 1931

Listen to the Knocking of the Knitting Club   Von Tilzer 1917

Listen to the Mocking Bird   Johnson, Howard 1939

Listen to the Music Box   Drake 1955

Listen to the Raindrops Fall   Young, Joe 1934

Listen to the Sound of My Love   Warren 1956

Listening   Berlin 1924; Coslow 1921

Listening to the Radio   Atteridge 1924; Romberg 1924

List'ning on Some Radio   Buck 1922

Lita   Mitchell 1936; Pollack 1936; Yellen 1936

Lites — Camera — Platitude   Drake 1964

Little Ace o' Spades   Arlen 1941; Koehler 1941

Little Action, A   Merrill 1967; Styne 1967

Little Alibis   Baer 1933

Little and Lovely   Bryan 1935

Little Angel Cake   Kern 1923

Little Angel Told Me So, A   Coslow 1934, 1935

Little Annie Rooney   Johnson, Howard 1939

Little Artists   Young, Victor 1934

Little Baby   Mitchell 1921; Pollack 1921

Little Baby Curls   Johnson, Howard 1929

Little Back-Yard Band, The   DeSylva 1919; Kern 1919

Little Bag of Tricks   Gershwin, Ira 1921; Youmans 1921

Little Band of Gold, A   Von Tilzer 1910

Little Bandbox Girl   Goetz 1916

Little Bas Bleu   Smith, Harry B. 1906

Little Beer, a Pretzel and You, A   Johnson, Howard 1933

Little Betty Falling Star   Bacharach 1962

Little Big Man   Arlen 1976; Harburg 1976

Little Big Shot   Akst 1944; Davis 1944

Little Billie (inst.)   Kern 1915

Little Bird   Lawrence 1971

Little Bird of Paradise   Herbert 1908

Little Birdie Told Me So, A   Hart 1926; Rodgers 1926

Little Birds (Les P'tits Oiseaux), The   Mancini 1970; Mercer 1970

Little Bird's Story   Olcott 1905

Little Biscuit   Arlen 1957; Harburg 1957

Little Bit Bad, A   Davis 1925

Little Bit in Love, A   Comden and Green 1953

Little Bit Independent, A   Leslie 1935

Little Bit Is a Whole Lot Better Than Nothing at All, A   Bryan 1908

Little Bit Later On, A   Livingston, Jerry 1936

Little Bit More, A   Brooks 1957; Oakland 1954; Rodgers 1979

Little Bit Now, A   Caesar 1925

Little Bit of Country   Mercer 1949

Little Bit of Every Nationality, A   Atteridge 1918; Romberg 1918

Little Bit of Everything   Berlin 1912; Lawrence 1938

Little Bit of Ev'rything, A   Akst 1925

Little Bit of Happiness (Will Go a Long Way), A   Coots 1930; Davis 1930

Little Bit of Heaven Known As Mother, A   Gordon 1934; Revel 1934

Little Bit of Heaven (Shure They Call It Ireland), A   Brennan 1914

Little Bit of Irish, A   Kahn 1911

Little Bit of Jazz, A   Kalmar 1923; Ruby 1923

Little Bit of Love, A   Brennan 1933; Brown, Lew 1927; Friend 1927

Little Bit of Love Goes a Long Way, A   Johnson, J. Rosamond 1947

Little Bit of Magic, A   Harburg 1952; Lane 1952

Little Bit of Nonsense, A   Romberg 1916; Smith, Robert B. 1916

Little Bit of Opera, A   Cobb 1930; Edwards 1930

Little Bit of Silk, A   Kern 1913

Little Bit of Sunshine (From Home), A   Hanley 1918

Little Bit Older (A Little Bit Wiser), A   Parish 1969

Little Bit's a Whole Lot Better than Nothing at All, A   Edwards 1908

Little Bits and Pieces of an Old Romance   Adamson 1939; Johnston 1939

Little Black Buddie   Egan 1924; Whiting 1924

Little Black Rain Cloud   Sherman 1966

Little Black Sheep   Baer 1929; Gilbert 1929; Herbert 1905

Little Black Train   Weill 1948

Little Blue Bonnet Girl   Fisher 1919

Little Blue Gown (Blue Jeans)   Conrad 1935; Magidson 1935

Little Blue Pig, The   Romberg 1925

Little Bluebird Told Me, A   Hoffman 1946; Livingston, Jerry 1946

Little Bo Peep   Hanley 1920

Little Boats of Barclona, The   Mercer 1951

Little Bo-Peep   Caesar 1929; Clarke 1921; Johnson, Howard 1939; Monaco 1921

Little Bottles (Sittin' on a Shelf), The   Spina 1977

Little Boy and Girl (Girl and Boy)   Herbert 1919

Little Boy Blue   Johnson, Howard 1939

Little Boy Blue Jeans   Edwards 1923, 1928; Kahn 1928; Smith, Robert B. 1923

Little Boy Blues, The   Martin 1948; Turk 1923

Little Boy in Corduroy   Russell 1941

Little Boy in the Barber Shop Chair, The   Robison 1947; Woods 1947

Little Boy Lost   DePaul 1958; Raye 1958

Little Boy with the Big Horn   Friend 1950

Little Boys   Bergman 1983; Mancini 1983
Little Boys Had a Band, The   Johnson, Howard 1936
Little Bride, The   Smith, Harry B. 1911
Little Bronze Lady in the Harbor   Gilbert 1940; Ruby 1940
Little Brown Betty   Waller 1931
Little Brown Jug   Johnson, Howard 1939; Lawrence 1940
Little Brown Suit My Uncle Brought Me, The   Rome 1943
Little Bull, A   Bryan 1919; Schwartz, Jean 1919
Little Bum   Hanley 1927
Little Bunch of Shamrocks (I Am Holding in My Hand),
     A   Jerome 1913; Sterling 1913; Von Tilzer 1913
Little Bungalow, A   Berlin 1925
Little Butterfly   Berlin 1923
Little Button, A   Merrill 1967; Styne 1967
Little By Little   Rose 1924; Woods 1924
Little Cabaret at Home, A   Atteridge 1913; Schwartz, Jean
     1913
Little Cafe in Calais, A   Coots 1957; Lewis 1957
Little Cavalier   Dubin 1929
Little Change of Atmosphere, A   Brown, Lew 1927; Friend
     1927
Little Chatterbox   Leigh Date Unknown
Little Chicken Fit for Old Broadway, A   Friml 1919; Harbach
     1919
Little Child   Sigman 1951
Little Child Like Me, A   Smith, Harry B. 1901
Little China Doll   Smith, Harry B. 1904; Smith, Robert B.
     1904; Williams 1909
Little Chin-Chin (Keep Your Chin Up)   Fain 1936
Little Choo Choo, The   Coots 1953
Little Choo Choo Gee-Gee, The   Johnson, J. Rosamond
     1907
Little Christmas Tree, The   Adamson 1963; Warren 1963
Little Church Around the Corner, The   Carroll 1913; David,
     Hal 1956; Freed, Arthur 1922; Kern 1907; Romberg 1919
Little Class of One, A   Herbert 1904
Little Cloud of Sunshine, I Need You   Snyder 1930
Little Coat of Tan, A   Coots 1929
Little Colleen (Do You Believe in Fairies)   Dubin 1917
Little Colonel   Pollack 1935; Webster 1935
Little Cooperation from You, A   Hoffman 1937; Lerner,
     Sammy 1937
Little Corporal, The   Loewe 1938
Little Cowboy Blue   Donaldson 1940; Mercer 1940
Little Crazy Quilt   David, Hal 1954
Little Crumbs of Happiness You Gave Me Long
     Ago   Brennan 1920
Little Cutey   Johnson, Howard 1962; Motzan 1916
Little Dancing Boy   Monaco 1937
Little Dead-Eye Dick   Stept 1951
Little Devil   Atteridge 1918; Johnson, Howard 1924;
     Romberg 1918
Little Did I Dream   Adamson 1934; Lane 1934
Little Did I Know   David, Mack 1952; Duke 1930; Fain 1930;
     Kahal 1930; Motzan 1924
Little Dixie Lady   Brown, Lew 1924
Little Doggie with the Big Woof-Woof, The   Hoffman 1954
Little Dolly Varden   Cobb 1902; Edwards 1902
Little Door, A Little Lock, A Little Key, A   Woods 1935
Little Dream   Sondheim 1996
Little Dream Nest   Leslie 1928
Little Dream that Lost Its Way, A   Romberg 1921
Little Dreamboat of Mine   Whiting 1914
Little Drop of Irish and a Wee Bit of Scotch, A   Bryan 1919;
     Carroll 1919; Fisher Date Unknown

Little Drops of Rain   Arlen 1962; Harburg 1962
Little Dutch Doll, The   Revel 1929
Little Emmaline   Romberg 1948
Little Eva   Kern 1907
Little Farm in Normandy, A   Herbert 1917
Little Fifi   Herbert 1911
Little Fish   Comden and Green 1947
Little Fish in a Big Pond   Berlin 1949
Little Fish that Never Saw the Sea, The   Coots 1955
Little Flat in a Great Big Town, A   Williams 1908
Little French Boy (inst.)   Bacharach 1967
Little Friend (Lullaby to a Turkey)   Evans 1961; Livingston,
     Jay 1961
Little Further Down the Road a Piece, A   DePaul 1947; Raye
     1947
Little Gamins   Caesar 1943
Little Girl, a Little Boy, a Little Moon, A   Warren 1926
Little Girl at Heart, A   Merrill 1955
Little Girl at Home   Herbert 1912
Little Girl Blue   Hart 1935; Rodgers 1935
Little Girl Don't Cry   Coleman 1965
Little Girl from Little Rock, A   Robin 1948; Styne 1948
Little Girl from Who Knows Where   Johnson, Howard 1935
Little Girl in Blue   Smith, Robert B. 1907
Little Girl, Little Boy   Hart 1920; Rodgers 1920
Little Girl Who Couldn't Care   Goetz 1912
Little Girlie You Have Caught My Eye   Atteridge 1906
Little Girls   Strouse 1977
Little Girls Beware   Smith, Harry B. 1911
Little Golden Maid   Kern 1912
Little Goldie Goldfish   Coots 1953
Little Good for Nothing's Good for Something After All,
     The   Von Tilzer 1918
Little Gray House, The   Weill 1949
Little Green Pocket of Green   Hanley 1942
Little Green Snake   Merrill 1959
Little Grey Sweetheart of Mine   Fisher 1922
Little Guy   DePaul 1958; Raye 1958
Little Half Pint in a Ten Gallon Hat   Coots 1951
Little Ham   Johnson, James P. 1938
Little Hiawatha   Silver 1951
Little High Chairman   Robison 1943
Little Hindoo Man   Hammerstein 1920; Harbach 1920
Little Home in My Heart for You   Edwards 1905
Little Homestead   Davis 1931
Little Hours Music, The   Willson 1951
Little House   Lawrence 1954
Little House in Soho, A   Hart 1928; Rodgers 1928
Little House of Love   Hoffman 1927
Little House on a Hill, A   Coots 1928
Little House on the Hill, The   Mercer 1937; Whiting 1937
Little House that Love Built, The   Dubin 1937; Warren 1937
Little House to Dream By a Mountain Stream, A   Hanley
     1930
Little Housekeeper, The   Young, Victor 1934
Little Hug, a Little Kiss, then You Fall in Love Again,
     A   Meyer 1933
Little Hunka Love   Donaldson 1931
Little Igloo for Two   Schwartz, Arthur 1926
Little Indians (Happy-In-the-Heart)   Merrill 1950
Little Investigation, A   Leigh 1967
Little Irish Rose (Abie's Irish Rose)   Bryan 1928
Little Italy   Goetz 1911
Little Jack Horner   Johnson, Howard 1939
Little Jazz Bird   Gershwin, George 1924; Gershwin, Ira 1924

Little Jazz Cantata   Rome 1961
Little Jim   Fain 1946; Freed, Ralph 1946
Little Jitterbug   Cahn 1939
Little Joe   Styne 1931
Little Joe, the Wrangler   Loesser 1939
Little Johnny Chickadee   Coots 1950
Little Johnny Jelly Beans   Coots 1955
Little Johnny Jones   Cohan 1904
Little Kiss at Twilight, A   Rainger 1938; Robin 1938
Little Kiss Each Morning, A Little Kiss Each Night,
    A   Woods 1929
Little Kiss Goodnight, A   Merrill 1952
Little Kisses   Ager 1935
Little Lady in the Moon   Brown, A. Seymour 1910; Goetz
    1910
Little Lady of the Lamp Light   Robin 1936; Whiting 1936
Little Lady on the Cameo   Arlen Date Unknown; Koehler
    Date Unknown
Little Lamb   Sondheim 1959; Styne 1959
Little Less of Moonlight (A Little More of You), A   Kahal
    1931
Little Liza Lee   Donaldson 1934; Kahn 1934
Little Locket of Long Ago, A   Woods 1933
Little Log Cabin of Dreams   Hanley 1927
Little Lost Dream   Mercer 1974
Little Lost Flower   Parish 1921
Little Love, a Little Money, A   Duke 1949, 1956
Little Love, a Little While, A   Schwartz, Arthur 1955
Little Love (But not for Me), A   Kern 1915
Little Love Can Go a Long, Long Way, A   Fain 1955;
    Webster 1955
Little Love Mill, The   Carroll 1921
Little Man   Gilbert 1932; Hanley 1932
Little Man — You've Had a Busy Day   Hoffman 1934
Little Man in the Big Sombrero, The   Coots 1954
Little Man Who Wasn't There, The   Adamson 1940
Little Man with the Hammer, The   Mercer 1935
Little Marie   Buck 1926; Hanley 1926; Rose 1926
Little Marriage Is a Dangerous Thing, A   Dietz 1944; Duke
    1944
Little Mascot (Du Bist Mein Mascottchen)   Young, Joe 1931
Little Me   Coleman 1962; Leigh 1962
Little Millionaire, The   Cohan 1911
Little Min-hee-Ha! Ha! (Be My Little Injun Squaw)   Kalmar
    1921; Ruby 1921
Little Miss Broadway   Bullock 1938; Spina 1938
Little Miss Fix-It   Norworth 1911; Smith, Harry B. 1911
Little Miss Golden Curls   Meyer 1909
Little Miss Grown-Up   Sigman 1949
Little Miss Jesse James   Brooks 1943
Little Miss Killarney   Edwards 1913
Little Miss Mischief   Loesser 1935
Little Miss No-One from No-Where   Edwards 1904; Smith,
    Robert B. 1904
Little Miss Okeechobee, Oh Be Mine   Donaldson 1928
Little Miss Small Town   Baer 1927; Lewis 1927; Young, Joe
    1927
Little Miss Tippy Toes   Adamson 1954; Warren 1954
Little Miss Up-to-Date   Harbach 1908
Little Miss Victory Jones   Rome 1942
Little Miss Vogue   Cobb 1917; Edwards 1917
Little Mistakes   Kahn 1956
Little Moments of Love   Coots 1932
Little Montague the Mouse   Coots 1951
Little More Heart, A   Styne 1953

Little More Love in Our Heart, A   Hoffman 1950
Little More Love in Our Hearts, A   Merrill 1950
Little More of Your Amor, A   Robin 1953
Little More Time, A   Styne 1958
Little Moth Keep Away from the Flame   Von Tilzer 1924
Little Mother   Pollack 1928
Little Mother o' Mine in the Mountains   Johnson, Howard
    1934
Little Mousie Brown   Carmichael 1944
Little Naked Boy, The   Gershwin, Ira 1945; Weill 1945
Little Nest for Two, A   Herbert 1920
Little Night Music, A   Martin 1962
Little Nightie Hanging on the Line, A   Leslie 1926
Little Nine to Fiver   Russell 1964
Little Odd Rhythm   Magidson 1936; Oakland 1936
Little of Rhythm (In the Best of Us)   Cahn 1935
Little Ol' State of Texas, The   Cahn 1951
Little Old America for Me   Smith, Harry B. 1906
Little Old Cabin Door Mister Washington! Uncle
    George   Fields 1950
Little Old Church in England, A   Berlin 1941
Little Old Church in the Valley, The   Kahn 1931
Little Old Clock on the Mantel, The   Kahn 1924
Little Old Cross-Road Store   Mercer 1932
Little Old Dream Waltz, A   Kahn 1910
Little Old Gehenna   Harburg 1961
Little Old Lady   Carmichael 1936
Little Old Lady of Poverty Street   Hoffman 1937; Lerner,
    Sammy 1937
Little Old Man with the Big Red Coat, The   Spina 1948
Little Old New Hampshire   Hanley 1926
Little Old New York   Brown, Lew 1932; Buck 1923; Dietz
    1929; Henderson 1932; Herbert 1923; Schwartz, Arthur
    1929; Styne 1960
Little Old Rhythm   Magidson 1938; Oakland 1938
Little Old Woman Who Lived in a Shoe, The   Coots 1956
Little Old-Fashioned Music Box   David, Mack 1937; Meyer
    1937
Little Ole Lovemaker, Me   Freed, Ralph 1963
Little One   Howard, Joseph E. 1910; Porter 1956
Little One I Love Best   Bryan 1925; Schwartz, Jean 1925
Little Orphan Annie   Kahn 1928
Little Pal   Brown, Lew 1929; DeSylva 1929; Hanley 1929;
    Henderson 1929
Little Pal (At the End of the Trail)   Pollack 1942
Little Pal (Where Are You Tonight)   Parish 1924
Little Papa Satan   Duke 1940
Little Paris Breeze   Whiting 1944
Little Partner of Mine   Cobb 1921; Edwards 1921
Little Patch o' Land   Young, Victor 1946
Little Peach   Romberg 1925
Little People, The   David, Mack 1958; Livingston, Jerry 1958
Little Pete the Pirate   Coots 1950
Little Peter Potter   Coots 1955
Little Piece of Chalk, A   Cahn 1980; DePaul 1980
Little Pig Nose   Young, Victor 1921
Little Pink Clouds in the Little Blue Sky, The   Coots 1945
Little Pitchers Have Big Ears   Cahn 1947; Styne 1947
Little Plate of Soup, A   Hammerstein 1920; Harbach 1920
Little Polly Parakeet   Coots 1955
Little Pony of Mine   Caesar 1924; Conrad 1924; Harbach
    1924
Little Pops Is Tops with Me   Razaf 1940
Little Poster Maid   Herbert 1899
Little Priest, A   Sondheim 1979

Little Prince   Lerner, Alan Jay 1974; Loewe 1974
Little Privacy, A   Duke 1930; Harburg 1930
Little Quaker (inst.), A   Kern 1946
Little Rag Baby Girl   Gilbert 1913
Little Raindrop   Freed, Arthur 1925
Little Ray of Sunshine   Brown, Nacio Herb 1934; Freed, Arthur 1934
Little Ray of Sunshine Follows Each Rain Cloud, A   Meyer 1909
Little Red Apple   Evans 1967; Livingston, Jay 1967
Little Red Caboose   David, Mack 1941
Little Red Lacquer Cage, The   Berlin 1922
Little Red Roof Tops   Loesser 1944
Little Rendezvous in Honolulu, A   Leslie 1935
Little Rhumba Numba, A   Porter 1941
Little Rhythm, Go 'Way   Gershwin, Ira 1923
Little Robber (inst.)   Kern 1938
Little Robin Told Me So, A   Coots 1936; Davis 1936
Little Rock Getaway   Sigman 1951
Little Rock Roll, The   Evans 1954; Livingston, Jay 1954
Little Romero (Chic-a-lu-cheet)   Sigman 1947
Little Rose Covered Shack   Parish 1980
Little Rose of the Rancho   Rainger 1935; Robin 1935
Little Rover, Don't Forget to Come Back Home   Donaldson 1923; Kahn 1923
Little Sailboat in the Harbor   Hoffman 1959
Little Sally One Shoe   Coots 1950
Little Scandal Dolls   DeSylva 1923; Gershwin, George 1923; Goetz 1923
Little Scrap of Paper, A   DePaul 1949; Raye 1949
Little Ships   Harburg 1971
Little Side Street in Paree, A   Hanley 1922
Little Silkworm, The   Hoffman 1935
Little Siro Told Me So   Davis 1926
Little Skipper from Heaven Above, A   Porter 1936
Little Sleepy Head   Lawrence 1947
Little Smile, A Little Kiss, A   Davis 1927
Little Smile, a Little Sigh, A   Hanley 1926
Little Snowflake   Edwards 1908
Little Soda Fountain Luncheonette, A   Baer 1951; Leslie 1951
Little Soft Music Professor, A   Hoffman 1944; Livingston, Jerry 1944
Little Song in My Heart, The   Donaldson 1926
Little Souvenir, A   Hanley 1921; Hart 1926; Rodgers 1926
Little Spanish Villa By the Sea   Conrad 1932; Young, Joe 1932
Little Street Where Old Friends Meet, A   Kahn 1932; Woods 1932
Little Streptococcus, The   Dietz 1944; Duke 1944
Little Sunbeam   Gershwin, George 1918
Little Sunshine   Gershwin, Ira 1918; Meyer 1930; Mitchell 1930
Little Surplus Me (Surplus Blues)   Rome 1946
Little Swing for Swinging, A   Weill 1947
Little Tango Maid, A   Atteridge 1914; Carroll 1914
Little Tender Things   Dubin Date Unknown; Warren Date Unknown
Little Theatre   Gershwin, George 1924; Gershwin, Ira 1924
Little Theatre of Our Own   Gershwin, George 1919; Gershwin, Ira 1919
Little Thing Called Love, A   Johnson, J. Rosamond 1944
Little Thing Like a Kiss, A   Kern 1913; Smith, Harry B. 1913
Little Things in Life, The   Berlin 1930
Little Things Meant So Much to Me   Rome 1950

Little Things that Mean So Much, The   Adamson 1939
Little Things You Do Together, The   Sondheim 1970
Little Things You Used to Do, The   Dubin 1935; Warren 1935
Little Tin God, The   Weill 1949
Little Tin Man, The   Friend 1958
Little Tin Soldier, The   Hanley 1921
Little Tin Soldier (And the Little Toy Drum) (C/L Coots, J. Fred), The   Coots 1953
Little Tingle Tangle Toes (In Her Wooden Shoes)   Webster 1942
Little Tittle Tattle Tale   Edwards 1908
Little Tommy Tattle-Tale   Coots 1964
Little Too Late, A   Kahn 1931
Little Toot   Wrubel 1948
Little Town Called Home Sweet Home, A   Donaldson 1928
Little Toy Town Parade   Friend 1950
Little Train A-Chuggin' in My Heart   Sigman 1952
Little Travel Bug   Arlen 1966
Little Travelbug   Arlen 1965
Little Travelin' Music Please, A   Styne 1980
Little Traveling Music, A   Mercer 1974; Webster 1955
Little Tune, Go Away   Kern 1918
Little Two By Four   Conrad 1906
Little Usher, A   Atteridge 1916; Motzan 1916; Romberg 1916
Little Washerwoman (Down in Rio), The   Coots 1946
Little Wendy Why-Why   Hoffman 1952
Little What-If, Little Could-Be   Coleman 1960; Leigh 1960
Little White Cross on a Little Green Hill, A   Parish 1933
Little White Diamonds   David, Hal 1961
Little White Gardenia, A   Coslow 1935, 1936
Little White House   Sondheim 1971
Little White House a Little White Lady, A   Johnson, Howard 1935
Little White House at the End of Honeymoon Lane, The   Hanley 1926
Little White Lie, The   Lerner, Alan Jay 1976
Little White Lies   Donaldson 1930
Little White Lighthouse   Leslie 1937
Little White Pill on the Little Green Hill, The   Burke 1940; Monaco 1940
Little White Stone   Robison 1953
Little Wigwam for Two   Schwartz, Jean 1920
Little Wily Miss   Hammerstein 1942; Harbach 1942; Kern 1942
Little Woman   Leslie 1942
Little Woman at My Elbow   Eliscu 1928
Little Women   Smith, Harry B. 1916; Smith, Robert B. 1916
Little Women Like You (Little Women and Little Men)   Ahlert 1933; Leslie 1933
Little Wonders (Kawaii Odoroki)   Rome 1969
Little Wooden Head   Washington 1940
Little Wooden Soldier and the Walking, Talking Doll, The   Coslow 1937
Little Wooden Whistle Wouldn't Whistle, The   Von Tilzer 1923
Little Words of Kindness   Friend 1936
Little World, Good Morning   Harburg 1971
Little World of Two   Smith, Harry B. 1915
Little Yellow Ribbon in Her Hair, A   Davis 1949; Silver 1949
Little You, a Little Me, a Little Love, A   Johnson, Howard 1930; Woods 1930
Little You Know   Ager 1933; Schwartz, Jean 1933; Young, Joe 1933
Little Zouave   Hammerstein 1938; Harbach 1938; Kern 1938

Littlest Angel, The   David, Mack 1955
Littlest Angel's Christmas, The   Young, Victor 1951
Live a Little   Leigh 1967
Live a Little, Love a Little   Coslow 1955
Live a Love-Dream   Rainger 1937; Robin 1937
Live and Learn   Mitchell 1937; Pollack 1937
Live and Let Live   Porter 1953
Live and Love   Bryan 1928; Schwartz, Jean 1928
Live and Love A Lot   Duke 1968
Live and Love Tonight   Conrad 1934; Coslow 1931, 1934;
    Dubin 1934; Johnston 1934
Live Dangerously   Washington 1958
Live for All You're Worth   Goetz 1920
Live for Today   Atteridge 1921; Goetz 1916; Herbert 1910
Live Hard, Work Hard, Love Hard   Arlen 1950, 1959; Blane
    1950; Mercer 1959
Live It Up   Bergman 1961
Live, Laugh and Love   Stept 1933
Live, Laugh, Love   Sondheim 1971
Live Oak Tree, The   Robin 1952; Warren 1952
Live To-Day   Baer 1927; Lewis 1927; Young, Joe 1927
Live While You're Here   Brown, A. Seymour 1923
Live Wire, The   Gershwin, George 1924
Lively Melody (inst.)   Kern 1956
Liver Lipped Louie   Revel 1942
Livin' Doll   David, Hal 1962
Livin' in My Own Sweet Way   Revel 1944; Webster 1944
Livin' Lovin' Doll   Evans 1954; Livingston, Jay 1954
Livin' the Life of Love   Adamson 1947; McHugh 1948
Livin' with the Blues   Bergman 1958
Living Alone   Adams 1962; Strouse 1962, Date Unknown;
    Yellen 1948
Living Buddha (Impassive Buddha)   Hart 1928; Rodgers
    1928
Living Doll   David, Hal 1991; Strouse 1991
Living End, The   Mancini 1956
Living for Tonight   Sigman 1960
Living from Day to Day   Livingston, Jerry 1936
Living High (On a Western Hill)   Rainger 1942; Robin 1942
Living Idol, The   Heyman 1956
Living in Seclusion   Mills 1937
Living in Sin   Hammerstein 1931; Whiting 1931
Living It Up   Duke 1940
Living Like a Millionaire, in Jungle Land   Johnson, J.
    Rosamond 1938
Living Old Memories Over Again   Dubin 1932; Friend 1932
Living on Love   Kahal 1928; Snyder 1928
Living on Plastic   Bacharach 1976; David, Hal 1976
Living on the Town   Akst 1937, 1938; Clare 1937, 1938
Living on Velvet (Helping Each Other Along)   Dubin 1935;
    Warren 1935
Living One Day at a Time   Schwartz, Arthur 1955
Living the Life I Love   Fain 1953
Living the Life of a Lover   David, Hal 1978
Living Together, Growing Together   Bacharach 1973; David,
    Hal 1973
Livingston and Evans' Melody   Evans 1950
Liza   Friend 1927; Johnston 1940; Williams 1909
Liza (All the Clouds'll Roll Away)   Gershwin, George 1929;
    Gershwin, Ira 1929; Kahn 1929
Liza Crossing the Ice   Arlen 1944; Harburg 1944
Liza Jane's Weddin'   Johnson, James P. 1927
Liza Lee   Stept 1930
Liza Lou   Dietz 1934; Schwartz, Arthur 1934
Liza's Eyes   Coslow 1955, 1956

Lizzette   Cahn 1968; Van Heusen 1968
Lizzie the Busy Squirrel   Coots 1955
Llewellyn   Porter 1912
Lloyds of London   Adamson 1959; Young, Victor 1963
Lo and Behold   Heyman 1931
Lo Doodle La Da Da   Robison 1927
Load Is Heavy (And I'm Ready to Go), The   Snyder 1929,
    1932
Loadin' Time   Dietz 1935; Schwartz, Arthur 1935
Loading Song   Porter 1944
Loading Time at Last Is Over (From the Baltic to the
    Pacific)   Gershwin, Ira 1943
Loads of Love   Rodgers 1962
Loafin'   Drake 1945
Loafin' on the Levee   David, Mack 1936; Meyer 1936
Loafin' Time   Ager 1935
Lobby of the Roxy, The   Livingston, Jerry 1973
Lobelia's Wedding Day   Alter 1937; Webster 1937
Lobster Crawl, The   Akst 1927; Davis 1927
Loca Illusion   Mercer 1940
(The Socially Conscious Civic Minded Iron Workers Union)
    Local 403   Cahn 1965; Van Heusen 1965
Local Boy Makes Good (inst.)   Willson 1934
Local to Cheyenne   Merrill 1945
Loch Lomond   Johnson, Howard 1939
Loch Lomond Swing   Coslow 1952
Lock and Key   Johnson, James P. 1927
Lock Me in Your Harem and Throw Away the Key   Berlin
    1914
Lock Step   Ahlert 1930; Turk 1930
Lock, Stock and Barrel   Fain 1950; Webster 1950
Lock the Barn Door   Mercer 1951
Locked in Your Arms Makes Me Safe in Your Heart   Fisher
    1930
Locker Room, The   Lerner, Alan Jay 1948; Weill 1948
Locker Room Sequence   Adamson 1937; Lane 1937
Loco Over You   Razaf 1944
Lodger   Romberg 1918
Lo-Do De-O   Fain 1926
Log Cabin Blues   Mills 1924
Log Cabin Days   Johnson, James P. 1922
Log of the Ship, The   Hammerstein 1920; Harbach 1920
Logic   Herbert 1919
Loie and Chlodo   Porter 1912
Loki and Baldur   Comden and Green 1982
Lola Cornero from the Trocadero   Caesar 1922
Lola in Love   Caesar 1922
Lola Lo   Smith, Harry B. 1922
Lola Waltz (Close in Your Arms)   Hanley 1922
Lo-La-Lo   DeSylva 1923; Gershwin, George 1923
Lola-Lola   Evans 1959; Livingston, Jay 1959
Lola's Song   Johnson, Howard 1939
Lolita   Caesar 1936; Fields 1931; Hart 1941; Lerner, Alan Jay
    1971; McHugh 1931; Rodgers 1941; Romberg 1924;
    Schwartz, Arthur 1936; Schwartz, Jean 1924
Lolita, My Love   Gershwin, George 1929; Gershwin, Ira
    1929; Kahn 1929
Lolling around with Sally   Turk 1927
Lollipop Interlude   Gordon 1949
Lollypop Ball, The   Russell Date Unknown
Lollypop Prelude   Gordon 1949
Lo-Lo   Johnson, Howard 1930
Lo-Lo-Lita   Russell 1941
Loma Linda   Livingston, Jerry 1957
Lo-Man   Stept 1925

Lon Chaney's Gonna Get You (If You Don't Watch Out)
  Edwards 1929
Lona, Partner Lona   Romberg 1916
London After Dark   Caesar 1953
London Bridge Is Falling Down   Baer 1938
London, Dear Old London   Kern 1921
London in July   Cahn 1951; Duke 1951
London Love Song   Johnston 1940
London Lullaby   De Lange 1943
London on a Rainy Night   Stept 1934; Washington 1934
London Waltz, The   Bergman 1959
Londonderry Air   Mitchell 1936
Londonderry Air (inst.)   Romberg 1952
Lone Cowboy   Rainger 1934, 1936; Robin 1934, 1936
Lone Eagle   Turk 1928
Lone Star   Kahal 1936; Rose 1936
Lone Star Girl, The   Buck 1914
Lone Star Moon   Friend 1947
Lone Wolf   Bergman 1960
Lone Wolf on the Indian Trail, A   Bryan 1936
Loneliest Man in Town, The   Adams 1970; Strouse 1970
Loneliness   Clare 1928; Pollack 1928; Washington 1948;
  Young, Victor 1948
Loneliness of Evening   Hammerstein 1949; Rodgers 1949
Loneliness or Happiness   Bacharach 1961; David, Hal 1961
Lonely   Davis 1953; Howard, Joseph E. 1909; Robison 1983
Lonely Acres   Robison 1926
Lonely Am I   Herbert 1911
Lonely Baby   Egan 1920; Whiting 1920
Lonely Ballerina (inst.)   Alter 1948
Lonely Birch Tree, The   Bergman 1958
Lonely Blues   Friend 1960
Lonely Boy   Gershwin, George 1935
Lonely Christmas   Freed, Ralph 1959
Lonely City   Oakland 1956
Lonely Co-Ed   Ellington 1939; Leslie 1939
Lonely Creatures   Merrill 1968
Lonely Eyes   Akst 1926; Davis 1926
Lonely Feet   Hammerstein 1934, 1935; Kern 1934, 1935
Lonely for Love   Livingston, Jerry 1930
Lonely for You   Kahn 1923
Lonely Girl, A   Caesar 1927; Evans 1965; Livingston, Jay
  1965
Lonely Goatherd, The   Hammerstein 1959; Rodgers 1959
Lonely Gondolier   Dubin 1935; Warren 1935
Lonely Heart   Alter 1936; Berlin 1933; Brennan 1928;
  Romberg 1921; Webster 1936
Lonely Heart and a Friendly Face, A   David, Mack 1958;
  Livingston, Jerry 1958
Lonely Hearts   Davis 1919
Lonely Hills   Styne 1941
Lonely Holiday   Sigman 1954
Lonely House   Weill 1947
Lonely in a Crowd   Rose 1927
Lonely in Paris   Duke Date Unknown
Lonely Is the Name   Sigman 1967
Lonely Lady   Hammerstein 1923; Youmans 1923
Lonely Lane   Fain 1933; Kahal 1933; Parish 1929
Lonely Lights Along the Shore   Dixon 1927; Woods 1927
Lonely Little Bluebird   Dixon 1928; Woods 1928
Lonely Little Extras   Gordon 1931; Revel 1931
Lonely Little Lighthouse   Bryan 1937
Lonely Little Melody   Buck 1924
Lonely Little Ranch-House   Brooks 1947
Lonely Little Senorita   Rainger 1933; Robin 1933

Lonely Little Wallflow'r   Kahn 1923
Lonely Lonely Winter   Johnson, James P. 1959
Lonely Lover   Cahn 1959
Lonely Man, The   Brooks 1956
Lonely Mannequin   Bloom 1936; Lerner, Sammy 1936
Lonely Me   Comden and Green 1944; Stept 1924
Lonely Melody   Coslow 1927
Lonely Moon   Goetz 1912
Lonely Mothers on Parade   Akst 1930
Lonely Nest, The   DeSylva 1922; Herbert 1922
Lonely Nights   Dietz 1963; Schwartz, Arthur 1963
Lonely Ones (Solitary Street), The   Lawrence 1956
Lonely Park   David, Mack 1932
Lonely Place, A   Webster 1969
Lonely Princess (The Sleeping Princess), The   Romberg
  1916
Lonely Rider   Bergman 1958
Lonely Road   Berlin 1936
(I Want a) Lonely Romeo   Smith, Robert B. 1919
Lonely Room   Hammerstein 1943; Rodgers 1943
Lonely Serenade, A   Lawrence 1930
Lonely Star   Davis 1955; Porter 1936
Lonely Stowaway   Burke 1930
Lonely Stranger   Rome 1969
Lonely Stranger (Passing Through) (Sabishii Tabibito)   Rome
  1969
Lonely Street   Davis 1955
Lonely Town   Comden and Green 1944
Lonely Traveling Man, A   Hart Date Unknown; Rodgers
  Date Unknown
Lonely Vagabond   Snyder 1928
Lonely Winter   Mancini 1957
Lonely Wolf Blues (The Lonesomest Wolf in the
  Town)   Rome 1945
Lonesome   Leslie 1909; Meyer 1909
Lonesome Alimony Blues   Hanley 1919
Lonesome and Low   Arlen 1941; Koehler 1941
Lonesome and Sorry   Conrad 1926; Davis 1926
Lonesome at Twilight   Koehler 1923
Lonesome Baby (I'm Coming Back to Town)   Brown, Lew
  1913
Lonesome Boy's Letter Back Home, A   Friend 1926; Woods
  1926
Lonesome Boy's Rosary, A   Johnson, Howard 1928
Lonesome Cinderella   Brown, Lew 1923; Hanley 1923
Lonesome Cowboy, The   Gershwin, George 1930; Gershwin,
  Ira 1930
Lonesome Coyote, The   David, Mack 1952; Livingston, Jerry
  1952
Lonesome Cup of Coffee, A   Russell 1956
Lonesome Cup of Coffee (inst.), A   Spina 1951
Lonesome Dove, The   Weill 1948
Lonesome Freight Train   Robison 1958
Lonesome Gal   Brooks 1951
Lonesome Ghost Blues   Razaf 1927
Lonesome Hours   Friend 1921
Lonesome in a Crowd   Dietz 1934; Schwartz, Arthur 1934
Lonesome in the Moonlight   Baer 1928
Lonesome in the Saddle   Brooks 1950
Lonesome Lover   Bryan 1930; Monaco 1930
Lonesome Lullaby   Ahlert 1936; Young, Joe 1936
Lonesome Man   Blake 1932; Sissle 1932
Lonesome Me   Conrad 1932; Razaf 1932; Waller 1932
Lonesome Melody   Young, Joe 1932
Lonesome Old Hoot Owl, The   DePaul 1955; Raye 1955

Lonesome One   Razaf 1926; Waller 1926

Lonesome Polecat   DePaul 1954; Mercer 1954

Lonesome Reverie (inst.)   Johnson, James P. 1940

Lonesome River   Magidson 1933; Stept 1937; Washington 1937

Lonesome Road   Brooks 1957

Lonesome Romeos   Kalmar 1927; Ruby 1927

Lonesome Sailor Boy   Livingston, Jerry 1960

Lonesome Serenade   Hoffman 1930

Lonesome Swallow, Gonna Follow You Home   Razaf 1928

Lonesome Thoughts (Lonesome Heart)   Brooks 1959

Lonesome Walls   Kern 1939

Lonesome Waltz   Bryan 1927

Lonesomest Girl in the World, The   Harburg 1961

Lonesomest Girl in Town, The   Dubin 1925; McHugh 1925; Mills 1925

Long about Midnight   Mills 1934

Long After Tonight   Bacharach 1962; David, Hal 1962; Drake 1947

Long Ago   Duke 1941; Warren 1956

Long Ago (And Far Away)   Gershwin, Ira 1944; Kern 1944; Lawrence 1943; Rainger 1936; Robin 1936

Long Ago in Mexico   Merrill 1951

Long Ago Last Night   David, Hal 1950; Gordon 1941; Warren 1941; Webster 1967

Long Ago Last Summer   Bacharach 1959; David, Hal 1959

Long Ago 'Mid Apple Blossoms   Kahn 1923

Long Ago Tomorrow   Bacharach 1971; David, Hal 1971

Long and I Waited (inst.)   Revel 1959

Long As I Can Take You Home   Berlin 1963

Long As You've Got Your Health   Harburg 1936

Long Before I Knew You   Cahn 1950; Comden and Green 1956; Styne 1950, 1956

Long Before You Came Along   Arlen 1942; Harburg 1942

Long Black Nylons   Raye 1958

Long Day   Donaldson 1930; Leslie 1930

Long Day, Short Night   Bacharach 1965; David, Hal 1965

Long, Deep and Wide (inst.)   Waller 1927

Long Division, The   Bacharach 1996

Long Goodbye, The   Mercer 1973

Long Green, The   Smith, Robert B. 1902, 1908

Long Green Blues   Sigman 1947

Long Horn   Donaldson 1940

Long Hot Summer, The   Cahn 1958

Long Is a Wonderful Thing   Gorney 1926

Long Island Low Down   Kalmar 1928; Ruby 1928

Long Letter Later   Robison 1964

Long Live Love   Coleman 1963; Donaldson 1934; Leigh 1963; Spina 1953

Long Live Nancy   Kern 1928

Long Live Our Free America   Kern 1946; Robin 1946

Long Live the English Scene   Adamson 1959; Young, Victor 1959

Long Live the Ladies   Goetz 1916; Meyer 1916; Young, Joe 1916

Long Live the Night   Romberg 1945

Long Live the Queen   Herbert 1904

Long Live Tonight   Henderson 1951; Kahal 1951

Long Lonely Season, The   Cahn 1975

Long, Long Ago   Buck 1917; Evans 1946; Livingston, Jay 1946

Long Long Long   McHugh 1954

Long Long Miles Between Us   Egan 1942

Long Lost Mamma (Daddy Misses You)   Woods 1923

Long May We Love   Freed, Ralph 1934

Long Night, The   Washington 1947

Long Ride Home, The   Washington 1967

Long, Strong and Consecutive   David, Mack 1945; Ellington 1945

Long Time Ago, A   Loesser 1956

Long Time Dead, A   Styne 1970

Long Time No See   Donaldson 1940; Mercer 1940

Long Time No Song   Waller 1943

(Oh, How I) Long to Belong to You   DeSylva 1932; Youmans 1932

Long Way from Home   Styne 1980

Longed to Be Loved by the Girls   Carroll Date Unknown

Longer that You Linger in Virginia, the More You Long to Stay, The   Donaldson 1931

Longest Way 'Round Is the Sweetest Way Home, The   Brennan 1927

Longing   Bryan 1958; Davis 1925; Drake 1950; Friml 1923, 1934; Mercer 1958; Monaco 1933; Schwartz, Jean 1929

Longing for Dear Old Broadway   Porter 1912

Longing for You   Freed, Arthur 1922

Longing I Have for You, The   Robison 1947

Longing (Triste Ricordo)   Caesar 1921

Longtime with a Short Girl   Fisher 1936

Look Ahead, Little Girl   Fain 1963

Look and Listen   Sigman 1946

Look Around   Bergman 1968; Coleman 1991; Comden and Green 1991; Porter 1920

Look Around (You'll Find Me)   Sigman 1969

Look at All I Belong To   David, Mack 1961; Livingston, Jerry 1961

Look at 'er   Merrill 1957

Look at Me   Brooks 1949; Duke 1955; Merrill 1978; Robin 1948; Styne 1948

Look at Me Now   Smith, Harry B. 1927

Look at Me with Love   Styne 1970

Look at that Girl   Merrill 1953

Look at the Damn Thing Now   Gershwin, George 1928; Gershwin, Ira 1928

Look at the Sun   Brooks 1959

Look at Them Doing It!   Berlin 1914

Look at Things the Way I Do   Mills 1939

Look at What the Wind Blew In   Russell 1954

Look at What You've Done to Me   Baer 1965

Look at You, Look at Me   Loesser 1941; Styne 1941

Look Before You Leap   Romberg 1917

Look Behind the Mask   Hanley 1930

Look for Me on Lookout Mountain   Conrad 1930

Look for the Happy Ending   Kalmar 1923; Ruby 1923

Look for the Silver Lining   DeSylva 1919, 1920; Kern 1919, 1920

Look Forward   Hoffman 1958

Look Her Over in Summer and See what You're Goin' to Get   Johnson, Howard 1915

Look Here Comes a Rainbow   Hanley 1932

Look in Her Eyes   Kern 1913

Look in His Eyes   Kern 1917

Look in My Eyes   Donaldson 1929; Eliscu 1929

Look in My Eyes, Maria   Bacharach 1963; David, Hal 1963

Look in the Book   Kern 1917; Smith, Harry B. 1917

Look in the Looking Glass   DeSylva 1923; Gershwin, George 1923; Goetz 1923; Heyman 1931

Look in the Mirror   Mercer 1943; Silver 1951; Wrubel 1943

Look in the Mirror and See Just Who I Love   Stept 1927

Look in Your Eyes, The   Bergman 1961; Kalmar 1949; Ruby 1950

Look, Little Girl   Willson 1963
Look Me Over   Johnson, J. Rosamond 1911
Look Me Over and Tell Me, If I Am Worth Your
    Liking   Johnson, J. Rosamond Date Unknown
Look Me Over Carefully and Tell Me Will I Do   Cobb 1910;
    Edwards 1910
Look Me Over Dearie   Kern 1911
Look Me Over Once (Laughing Song)   Dietz 1950
Look No Further   Rodgers 1962
Look No Further, Angel   Merrill 1968
Look of Love, The   Bacharach 1967; Bergman 1961; Cahn
    1963; David, Hal 1967; Drake 1962; Van Heusen 1963
Look on the Bright Side   Strouse 1987
Look Out   Hart 1939; Koehler 1963; Rodgers 1939; Stept
    1963
Look Out Below   Carmichael 1948; De Lange 1948
Look Out for Jimmy Valentine   Edwards 1910
Look Out for Mister Stork   Washington 1941
Look Out for Mr. Wu   Cohan 1914
Look Out for My Heart   Dubin 1940; McHugh 1940
Look Out for the Big Banshee   Howard, Joseph E. 1919
Look Out for the Bolsheviki Man   Berlin 1919
Look Out for the Irish Tonight   Sterling 1917
Look Out for Us, Broadway   Kalmar 1924; Ruby 1924
Look Out Here Comes My Cookie   Donaldson 1926
Look Out I'm Going to Steal You   Leslie 1910
Look Out! Look Out!   Smith, Harry B. 1911
Look Pleasant   Brown, Lew 1928; DeSylva 1928; Henderson
    1928
Look to That Old Spot   Olcott 1897
Look to the Lilies   Cahn 1970; Styne 1970
Look to the Rainbow   Harburg 1947; Lane 1947
Look to Your Heart   Cahn 1955; Van Heusen 1955
Look Up and Know I'm Loving You (Ben Je in Rotterdam
    Geboren)   Rome 1952
Look Up and Smile   Davis 1928
Look What a Hole You're In   Arlen 1959; Mercer 1959
Look What a Little Sunshower Can Do   Alter 1930;
    Johnson, Howard 1930
Look What I Found   Porter 1946
Look What I've Got   Rainger 1932; Robin 1932
Look what My Boy Got in France   Conrad 1918
Look What the Wind Blew Home Today   Kahal 1927;
    Snyder 1927
Look What the Wind Blew In   Adamson 1935; Donaldson
    1935
Look What You've Done   Johnson, J. Rosamond 1930;
    Kalmar 1933; Ruby 1933
Look What You've Done to Me   Conrad 1929, 1930;
    Mitchell 1929, 1930
Look Who Is Here   Donaldson 1925; Kahn 1925
Look Who's Alone Now   Strouse 1991
Look Who's Been Dreaming   Arlen 1953; Fields 1953
Look Who's Dancing   Fields 1951; Schwartz, Arthur 1951
Look Who's Here   Adamson 1932; Lane 1932
Look Who's Here, Ship Ahoy   Sterling 1906; Von Tilzer
    1906
Look Who's in Love   Fields 1959
Look Who's Mine (Dia de Victoria)   Bergman 1971
Look Younger, Live Longer   Coslow 1952
Looka Him   Oakland 1935; Parish 1935
Looka Me   Livingston, Jerry 1956
Look-A What I Got Now   Lewis 1924; Young, Joe 1924
Look-a-Here (inst.)   Waller 1945

Lookie Lookie Lookie Here Comes Cookie   Gordon 1936;
    Revel 1936
Lookin' Around Corners for You   Gordon 1936; Revel 1936
Lookin' fo' Somebody   Arlen 1959; Mercer 1959
Lookin' for a Sweetheart   Wrubel 1932
Lookin' for Trouble   Blane 1954; Myrow 1954
Lookin' for You (Lookin' for Someone)   Lewis 1974; Young,
    Joe 1974
Lookin' Good but Feelin' Bad   Waller 1929
Lookin' Hot and Keepin' Cool   Von Tilzer 1929
Lookin' Out the Window   Raye 1959
Lookin' with My Eyes, Seein' with My Heart   Bacharach
    1965; David, Hal 1965
Looking All Over for You   Kern 1921
Looking Around   Robin 1926
(Across the Breakfast Table) Looking at You   Berlin 1930;
    Heyman 1954; Porter 1929; Young, Victor 1954
Looking Back   Burke 1971; Comden and Green 1974; David,
    Hal 1991; Strouse 1991; Styne 1974
Looking Down at the Stars   Parish 1936
Looking for a Bachelor   Drake 1954
Looking for a Boy   Gershwin, George 1925; Gershwin, Ira
    1925
Looking for a Bully   Howard, Joseph E. 1923
Looking for a Candidate   Rome 1948
Looking for a Little Bit of Blue   Woods 1934
Looking for a Sweetheart   Magidson 1932
Looking for a Thrill   Robin 1927
Looking for Daddy   Strouse Date Unknown
Looking for Love   Fields 1929; McHugh 1929
Looking for Myself   Merrill 1961
Looking for the Lovelight in the Dark   Dubin 1930
Looking for the Sunshine   McHugh 1928
Looking for Yesterday   De Lange 1940; Van Heusen 1940
Looking for Your Heart   Sherman 1960
Looking Forward   Davis 1933; Oakland 1933
Looking Forward to Looking After You   Woods 1935
Looking Glass Waltz, The   Alter 1955
Looking in the Window, Thinking of You   Bryan 1930
Looking Thru My Dreams   Burke 1931
Looks   Sondheim Date Unknown
Looks Like a Beautiful Day   Meyer 1934
Looks Like Happy Days   Baer 1927
Looks Like I'm Off o' Ya   Harburg 1940; Lane 1940
Looks Like Old Times   Donaldson 1934; Kahn 1934
Looks Like Pappy   Johnson, Howard 1930
Looks Like the End of a Beautiful Friendship   Arlen 1976;
    Harburg 1976
Looks Like Winter   Fisher 1940
Looks Like You'd Like Some Love   Martin 1948
Looloo   Robin 1927; Youmans 1927
Loo-Low   Spina 1944
Looney Mooney Man   Harbach 1910
Lo-oo De-O   McHugh 1926; Mills 1926
Loop the Loop (inst.)   Schwartz, Jean 1901
Loose Ankles   Freed, Arthur 1927
Loose Lady   Ruby 1943
Loose Lips (Sink Ships)   Sherman 1971
Loozeyana   Leigh 1977
Looz-iana   Brooks 1955
Lopeziana (inst.)   Alter 1926
Lopsided Bus, A   Hammerstein 1955; Rodgers 1955
Lora Lee   Herbert 1922
Lord Above Is My Partner, The   Spina 1953
Lord and Lady Gate   DePaul 1942; Raye 1942

Lord and Lady Whoozis   Hoffman 1937; Lerner, Sammy 1937

Lord Come and Live with Us   Martin 1977

Lord Done Fixed Up My Soul, The   Berlin 1940

Lord Have Mercy on the Married Man   Leslie 1911

Lord, I'm Glad That I Know Thee   Burke 1956; Young, Victor 1956

Lord Is a Trav'lin' Man, The   Webster 1950

Lord Knows the Way Back Home, The   Koehler 1954

Lord Looked Down, The   Brooks 1959

Lord Made a Peanut, The   Merrill 1957

Lord Only Knows, The   Hart 1920; Rodgers 1920

Lord Provideth, The   Livingston, Jerry 1962

Lord's Been Good to Me, The   Stept 1945

Lord's Bright Blessing, The   Merrill 1962; Styne 1962

Lord's Got His Arms Around Us, The   Stept 1956

Lords of Creation   Johnson, Howard 1921; Schwartz, Jean 1921

Lordy   Hammerstein 1941; Romberg 1941

Lorelei   Comden and Green 1974; Gershwin, George 1932; Gershwin, Ira 1932; Johnson, Howard 1939; Kern 1920; Smith, Robert B. 1906; Styne 1974

Lorelei Brown   Fields 1951; Schwartz, Arthur 1951

Loretta   Davis 1946; Silver 1946

Lorna Doone   Bacharach 1959; David, Hal 1959

Lorna's Here   Adams 1964; Strouse 1964

Lorraine   Young, Joe 1932

Lorraine (My Beautiful Alsace Lorraine)   Bryan 1917; Fisher 1917

Los Angeles, Los Angeles   Oakland 1967

Lose that Long Face   Arlen 1954; Gershwin, Ira 1954

Lose the Blackout Blues   Russell 1942

Losers, The   Cahn 1968; Van Heusen 1968

Losin' Your Love   Livingston, Jerry 1937

Losing End   Friend 1959

Losing My Mind   Sondheim 1971

Losing You   Coots 1954; Friend 1927; Harburg 1933; Sigman 1963; Yellen 1951

Lost   Mercer 1936

Lost — A Man's Best Pal   Gilbert 1939

Lost a Heart   Smith, Robert B. 1912

Lost (A Wonderful Girl)   Davis 1922, 1945; Hanley 1922, 1945

Lost Again   De Lange 1936

Lost Among the Stars   Bacharach 1982

Lost and Found   Coleman 1989

Lost April   De Lange 1947

Lost Chord, The   Johnson, Howard 1939

Lost Horizon   Bacharach 1973; David, Hal 1973; Kahn 1937; Warren 1956

Lost in a Crowded Place   Caesar 1956

Lost in a Dream   Bloom 1949; Leslie 1949; Parish 1938

Lost in a Fog   Fields 1934; McHugh 1934

Lost in Loveliness   Robin 1954; Romberg 1954

Lost in Meditation   Ellington 1938; Mills 1938

Lost in My Dreams   Mitchell 1936; Stept 1936

Lost in the Crowd   Conrad 1932; Dietz 1932; Schwartz, Arthur 1932

Lost in the Stars   Weill 1949

Lost In this Town   Martin 1948

Lost in Your Arms   Lewis 1932

Lost in Your Eyes   Gordon 1937; Revel 1937

Lost Liberty Blues, The   Porter 1928

Lost Little Girl   Bacharach 1963; David, Hal 1963

Lost Love   Friend 1957; Parish 1954; Razaf 1937; Waller 1937

Lost Melody   Kahn 1923

Lost Moment, The   Brooks 1948

Lost My Rhythm, Lost My Music, Lost My Man   Akst 1935; Brown, Lew 1935

Lost on an Island of Dreams   Parish 1938

Lost One   Mills 1929

Lost Sheep The Sermon, the Sword and the Song   Harburg 1971

Lost Watch (Tick Tick Tick), The   Raye 1957

Lost without You   Coots 1931; Davis 1931

Lost Word   Coleman 1975; Comden and Green 1975

Lost World, The   Friml 1924; Smith, Harry B. 1924

Lot in Common with You, A   Arlen 1943; Mercer 1943

Lot of Livin' to Do, A   Adams 1960; Strouse 1960

Lot of You, A   Henderson 1934; Koehler 1934

Lots of Little Things Can Happen   Harbach 1911

Lots of Little Things Can Happen (In a Very Little While)   Harbach 1910

Lots of Time for Sue   Caesar 1929

Lottery Blues   Lerner, Alan Jay 1939

Lottie Gibson Specialty (Please Don't Send Me Down a Baby Brother)   Fields 1954; Schwartz, Arthur 1954

Lotus Bloom   Porter 1943

Lotus Blossom (Marahuana)   Coslow 1934; Johnston 1934

Lotus Flower   Atteridge 1923; DeSylva 1922; Oakland 1951; Raye 1951; Romberg 1923; Schwartz, Jean 1923

Lotus Land   Parish 1956

Lotus Lou   Robin 1936

Lou Barile Theme   Oakland 1954

Lou German Theme   Oakland 1954

Loud and Soft   Willson 1956

Loud Speakin' Papa, You'd Better Speak Easy to Me   Pollack 1925; Yellen 1925

Loudenhammer Bird, The   Hoffman 1958

Louella   Adamson 1957; McHugh 1953; Mills 1946

Louie Sands and Jim McGee   Brooks 1948

Louis the Lion   Caesar 1965

Louis XIII Gavotte   Youmans 1924

Louisa March   Comden and Green 1964; Styne 1964

Louisa Schmid   Sterling 1904; Von Tilzer 1904

Louise   Robin 1929; Whiting 1929

Louisiana   Coots 1926; Freed, Arthur 1922; Gilbert 1943; Razaf 1928; Romberg 1924; Smith, Harry B. 1912

Louisiana Anna   Edwards 1904

Louisiana Fairy Tale   Coots 1935; Parish 1935

Louisiana Hayride   Dietz 1932; Schwartz, Arthur 1932

Louisiana Ladscape (inst.)   Coots 1946

Louisiana Louise   Edwards 1902; Sterling 1902

Louisiana Lullaby   Meyer 1952

Louisiana Purchase   Berlin 1940

Louisville   Caesar 1922

Louisville Lodge Meeting   Drake 1951

Louisville Lou, the Vampin' Lady   Ager 1923; Yellen 1923

Lounging at the Waldorf (inst.)   Waller 1938

Lou'siana   Donaldson 1923; Kahn 1923

Lou'siana Lullaby   Burke 1933; Spina 1933

Lou'sianna Moonlight   Spina 1957

Louwanna   Schwartz, Jean 1924

Lovable   Kahn 1932; Spina 1957; Woods 1932

(Tell Me What's the Matter) Lovable Eyes   Schwartz, Jean 1922

Lovable Lips   David, Hal 1960

Lovable Moon   Atteridge 1919; Schwartz, Jean 1919

Lovable Rogue   Von Tilzer 1929
Love   Coots 1951; Herbert 1899; Johnson, James P. 1947;
     Martin 1946; Merrill 1953; Sherman 1971; Smith, Harry
     B. 1899; Strouse 1993
Love Affair, The   Howard, Bart 1955
Love Affairs   Dubin 1928
Love Ahoy!   Atteridge 1918; Romberg 1918
Love Ain't Nothin' but the Blues   Revel 1959
Love Ain't Nothing but the Blues   Alter 1930
Love All the Day   Smith, Harry B. 1903
Love Alone Lives On   Arlen Date Unknown; Bloom 1931;
     Koehler 1931
Love Among the Millionaires   Baer 1930; Gilbert 1930
Love Among the Roses   Parish 1935
Love Among the Young   Styne 1959
Love and Affection   Hoffman 1957
Love and Beauty   Smith, Harry B. 1911; Smith, Robert B.
     1911
Love and Consolation   Alter 1930
Love and Hate   Raye 1953; Spina 1952
Love and I Are Playing   Herbert 1913
Love and I Went Waltzing   Cahn 1944, 1945; Styne 1944,
     1945
Love and Kindness   Loesser 1956
Love and Kisses   David, Mack 1933; Friml 1954; Hoffman
     1933; Webster 1952
Love and Kisses Finnegan   Gordon 1934; Revel 1934
Love and Kisses 'n' Everything   Youmans 1926
Love and Laughter   Romberg 1948
Love and Learn   De Lange 1946; Heyman 1936; Schwartz,
     Arthur 1936; Yellen 1935
Love and Leave 'em Joe   Dixon 1924; Henderson 1924
Love and Let Love   Gordon 1934; Revel 1934
Love and Logic   Coleman 1972; Fields 1972
Love and Marriage   Cahn 1955; Van Heusen 1955
Love and Rhythm   Brown, Lew 1933; Henderson 1933
Love and the Moon   Kern 1922
Love and the Weather   Berlin 1947
Love at Dusk   Hanley 1932
Love at Last   Gorney 1934
Love Baby   Rose 1927
Love Bandit, The   Spina 1977
Love Bank   Bacharach 1957; David, Hal 1957
Love Before Breakfast   Lane 1979; Lerner, Alan Jay 1979
Love Behind Bars   Coleman 1988
Love Being What It Is   Fain 1982; Harburg 1978, 1982; Van
     Heusen 1978
Love Birds   Caesar 1927, 1929; Friend 1929; Merrill 1949;
     Oakland 1957; Russell 1957
Love Boat   Brown, Nacio Herb 1928; Buck 1920; Freed,
     Arthur 1928; Herbert 1920
Love Boats   Gorney 1930; Harburg 1930
Love Bug   Johnson, James P. 1922
Love but You   Herbert 1906
Love By Appointment Only   Warren 1965
Love By Telephone   Herbert 1906
Love Call (Halloo of My Heart)   Johnson, Howard 1938
Love Came   Ellington 1965
Love Came and Crowned Me   Porter 1916
Love Came and Swept Me Off My Feet   Hoffman 1937;
     Lerner, Sammy 1937
Love Came Between Us   Evans 1944; Livingston, Jay 1944
Love Came Into My Heart   Adamson 1931; Lane 1931
Love Came to Me but It Didn't Stay Long   Johnson, J.
     Rosamond 1934

Love Can Be Fun   Coslow 1935
Love Can Be Like That   Coots 1964
Love Can Change the Stars   Blane 1954; Martin 1954
Love Can Get You Crazy   Strouse Date Unknown
Love Can Happen Anytime   Myrow 1955
Love Can Settle Everything   Eliscu 1941; Gorney 1941
Love Can Sometimes Make You Cry   Strouse 1993
Love Cannot Die   Heyman 1931; Youmans 1931
Love, Can't You Hear Me Calling?   Freed, Ralph 1934
Love Casts Its Shadow   Bacharach 1967
Love Clouds   Gilbert 1935
Love C.O.D.   Caesar 1924
Love Come Back   Smith, Harry B. 1911
Love Come Back to Me   Caesar 1929
Love, Come Take Me Again   Willson 1963
Love Comes a-Stealing   Kahn 1915
Love Comes But Once in a Lifetime   Johnson, Howard 1924
Love Comes First   Adams 1970; Strouse 1970
Love Comes in Different Colors   Harburg 1979
(When) Love Comes in the Moonlight   Dubin 1930
Love Commands   Robin 1936
Love Cycle (inst.)   Oakland 1972
Love Dance, The   Harbach 1910
Love Days   Cohan 1908; Jerome 1908; Schwartz, Jean 1908
Love Didn't Know Any Better   Burke 1937; Johnston 1937
Love Divided By Two   Rainger 1934; Robin 1934
Love Does That   Friend 1959
Love Doesn't Grow Like Apples on a Tree   Cahn 1969
Love Doesn't Grow on Trees   Freed, Ralph 1938; Lane 1938
Love Don't Need a Referee   Johnson, James P. 1948
Love Dream River   Friend 1930; Schwartz, Jean 1930
Love Dreams   Cohan 1923
Love Dropped in for Tea   Burke 1935; Spina 1935
Love Duet   Weill 1933
Love 'Em and Leave 'Em   Porter 1920
Love Fell In   Blane 1939, 1942
Love Finds a Way   Blane 1949; Leigh 1954; Romberg 1922;
     Warren 1949
Love Flew in My Window   Hanley 1930
Love Flies Out the Window   Hoffman 1945; Livingston,
     Jerry 1945
Love Flower   Caesar 1920; DeSylva 1920
Love for a Day   Howard, Joseph E. 1912; Loesser 1937
Love for a Year, Love for a Day   Smith, Harry B. 1911;
     Smith, Robert B. 1911
Love for Love   Koehler 1947
Love for Sale   Friml 1925; Porter 1930
Love for Sure   Duke 1959
Love from a Heart of Gold   Loesser 1961
Love from a Stranger   Hoffman 1937; Lerner, Sammy 1937
Love from Judy   Martin 1952
Love Game, The (inst.)   Spina 1974
Love Germs   Young, Victor 1920
Love Goddesses, The   David, Mack 1965
Love Goes on Just the Same   Baer 1931; Kahal 1931
Love, Happiness and Peace of Mind   Spina 1967
Love Has Come to Our House   DePaul 1955
Love Has Found a Way   Warren 1979
Love Has Found My Heart   Smith, Harry B. 1926
Love Has Made This Such a Lovely Day   Cahn 1944; Styne
     1944
Love Has Many Faces   David, Mack 1965
Love Has Nothing to Do with Looks   Blane 1952
Love Has Passed Me By   Cahn 1935; Friend 1930; Monaco
     1930

Love Hasn't Time   Burke 1937; Spina 1937
Love Held Lightly   Arlen 1959; Mercer 1959
Love Him   Evans 1952; Livingston, Jay 1952
Love, Honor and O-Baby   Hanley 1920
(I Promise To) Love, Honor and Oh Baby   Magidson 1938;
    Wrubel 1938
Love, I Give You My All   Brennan 1930; Friml 1930
Love I Have for You, The   Hoffman 1954
Love, I Hear   Sondheim 1962
Love I Long For, The   Dietz 1944; Duke 1944
Love, I Never Knew   Gershwin, George 1925
Love I Never Met, The   Webster 1972
Love, I Will Find a Home for You   Caesar 1925
Love I'm Calling   Razaf 1932
Love in a Changing World   Eliscu 1941, 1943; Gorney 1941,
    1943
Love in a Cottage   Youmans 1924
Love in a Goldfish Bowl   Bacharach 1961; David, Hal 1961
Love in a Haystack   Atteridge 1923; Schwartz, Jean 1923
(You Can Tell When There's) Love in a Home   DePaul 1956;
    Mercer 1956
Love in a Mist   Weill 1943
Love in an Orchard   Smith, Harry B. 1903
Love in Any Language   Kahn 1940
Love in Bloom   Rainger 1934; Robin 1934
Love in Loveliness, The   David, Hal 1962
Love in Outer Space   Comden and Green 1960; Styne 1960
Love in Springtime   Kahn 1914; Mills 1938
Love in the Afternoon   Mercer 1957
Love in the Air   Van Heusen 1937
Love in the Springtime   Smith, Harry B. 1909
Love Is a Balmy Thing   Cahn 1943; Styne 1943
Love Is a Battle   Herbert 1914; Smith, Robert B. 1914
Love Is a Bluebird on the Wing   Brooks 1945
Love Is a Bore   Cahn 1964; Van Heusen 1964
Love Is a Business   Johnson, Howard 1921
Love Is a Corny Thing   Cahn 1943; Styne 1943
Love Is a Dancing Thing   Dietz 1935; Schwartz, Arthur 1935
Love Is a Dreamer   Stept 1929
Love Is a Flame   Lewis 1935
Love Is a Four Letter Word   Cahn 1958; DePaul 1958; Raye
    1958; Van Heusen 1958
Love Is a Funny Little Fellow   Revel 1946
Love Is a Gambling Thing   Davis 1950; Silver 1950
Love Is a Game   Smith, Harry B. 1903
Love Is a Garden of Roses   Edwards 1923; Smith, Robert B.
    1923
Love Is a Headache   Spina 1969
Love Is a Lady in Blue   David, Hal 1952
Love Is a Lie   Romberg 1925
Love Is a Lonely Thing   Cahn 1958; Warren 1958
Love Is a Lovely Word   Fields 1951; Warren 1951; Webster
    1962
Love Is a Many Splendored Thing   Fain 1955; Webster 1955
Love Is a Masquerade   McHugh 1950
Love Is a Melody (Short and Sweet)   Leigh 1965
Love Is a Merry-Go-Round   Bloom 1937; Cahn 1946; Mercer
    1937; Styne 1946
Love Is a Pain in the Heart   Brooks 1957
Love Is a Penny Postcard   Fain 1946; Freed, Ralph 1946
Love Is a Pow'rful Thing   Cahn 1936
Love Is a Private Affair   Warren 1980
Love Is a Race   Harbach 1911
Love Is a Random Thing   Fain 1946
Love Is a Riddle   Romberg 1921

Love Is a Ripple on the Water   Carroll 1936; Parish 1936
Love Is a Sacred Thing   Ager 1953; Akst 1953; Davis 1953
Love is a Season   Howard, Bart 1958
Love Is a Story That's Old   Herbert 1913
Love Is a Ticklish Affair   Adamson 1964
Love Is a Traveler   Spina 1977
Love Is a Two-Edged Sword   Hammerstein 1926; Harbach
    1926; Romberg 1926
Love Is a Two-Way Street   Baer 1969
Love Is a Very Light Thing   Rome 1954
Love Is a Will-O-the Wisp   Howard, Joseph E. 1907
Love Is a Wonderful Thing   Gilbert 1916; Ruby 1951
Love Is a Wonderous Thing   Freed, Ralph 1946
Love Is All   Brown, A. Seymour 1923
Love Is All that Matters   Cahn 1955; Schwartz, Arthur 1955
Love Is an Art   Smith, Harry B. 1914, 1916; Smith, Robert B.
    1916
Love Is an Idle Dream   Smith, Harry B. 1927
Love Is an Intrusion   Romberg 1917
Love Is an Old Fashioned Feeling   Schwartz, Jean 1920
Love Is an Old Maid's Dream   Coleman 1964
Love Is Back in Business   Fain 1951; Gordon 1951
Love Is Blind   Dubin 1924
Love Is Calling Me   Hanley 1932
Love Is Contagious   Howard, Joseph E. 1907
Love Is Crazy   Brooks 1961
Love Is Eternal   Myrow 1954
Love Is Fire (Love Is Ice)   Bacharach 1988
Love Is for Lovers   Spina 1977
Love Is Forever   Evans 1973; Livingston, Jay 1973
Love Is Free to Everyone   Friend 1929
Love Is Good for Anything that Ails You   Friend 1936
Love Is Hate   Cahn 1980
Love Is Heaven, Heaven in Love   Bryan 1929
Love Is Hell   Evans 1958; Livingston, Jay 1958
Love Is Here to Stay   Gershwin, George 1938; Gershwin, Ira
    1938
Love Is in Command   Pollack 1934; Young, Joe 1934
Love Is in the Air   Coots 1929; Davis 1929; DeSylva 1925;
    Gershwin, George 1925; Gershwin, Ira 1925; Sondheim
    1962
Love Is Just a Dream   Coots 1959
Love Is Just a Gamble (Take Another Chance)   Mills 1924
Love Is Just a Little Bit of Heaven   Baer 1925; Bryan 1925
Love Is Just Around the Corner   Robin 1934, 1935, 1936
Love Is Just for Lovers   Warren 1974, 1980
Love Is Just the Same Old Game in Every Land   Goetz 1913
Love Is Life   Gilbert 1933
Love Is Like a Bubble   Atteridge 1916; Romberg 1916
Love Is Like a Butterfly   Atteridge 1915; Friml 1915
Love Is Like a Candle in the Wind   Spina 1957
Love Is Like a Cigarette   Herbert 1904, 1908
Love Is Like a Firefly   Friml 1912, 1937; Harbach 1912, 1937
Love Is Like a Mushroom   Buck 1921; Carroll Date
    Unknown
Love Is Like a Pinwheel   Atteridge 1924; Romberg 1924;
    Schwartz, Jean 1924
Love Is Like a Precious Pearl   Motzan 1919
Love Is Like a Rose   Bryan 1929; Meyer 1929; Von Tilzer
    1910
Love Is Like a Rubber Band (Hoop Song)   Kern 1911
Love Is Like a Song   Youmans 1930
Love Is Like a Violin   Kern 1914; Smith, Harry B. 1914
Love Is Like a Watch   Schwartz, Jean 1929
Love Is Like an Elephant   Duke 1950; Rome 1950

Love Is Like Champagne   Sigman 1959
Love Is Like the Rose   Smith, Harry B. 1911; Smith, Robert B. 1911
Love Is Love   Loewe 1937
Love Is Love Anywhere   Arlen 1933; Koehler 1933
Love Is Love in Any Language   Edwards 1938
Love Is Love (In Any Woman's Heart)   Fain 1935; Kahal 1935
Love Is Merest Folly   Herbert 1899; Smith, Harry B. 1899
Love is My Decision   Bacharach 1988
Love Is My Enemy   Gershwin, Ira 1945; Weill 1945
Love Is My Friend   Hart 1940; Rodgers 1940
Love Is Never Out of Season   Brown, Lew 1937; Fain 1937
Love Is New   Romberg 1948
Love Is News   Mitchell 1937; Pollack 1937
Love Is Not for a Day   Smith, Harry B. 1925
Love Is Nothing but a Racket   Comden and Green 1955
Love Is Oh So Easy   Cahn 1963, 1964; Van Heusen 1963, 1964
Love Is on the Air Tonight   Mercer 1937; Whiting 1937
Love Is Only What You Make It   Friml 1934
Love Is Our Umbrella   Comden and Green 1967; Styne 1967
Love Is Queen, Love Is King   Hart 1933; Rodgers 1933
Love Is Quite a Simple Thing   Hammerstein 1928; Romberg 1928
Love Is Ridin' the Range Tonight   DeSylva 1939
Love Is Somethin' Money Can't Buy   Hoffman 1953; Silver 1953
Love Is Still for Free   Cahn 1952; Duke 1952
Love Is Still in Town   Duke 1956
Love Is Strange   Brooks 1949
Love Is Such a Cheat   Caesar 1939, 1943
Love Is Such a Little Word (Precious and Absurd)   Monaco 1963
Love Is Such an Old Fashioned Thing   Loesser 1941, 1942; Styne 1942
Love Is Sweeping the Country   Gershwin, George 1931; Gershwin, Ira 1931
Love Is the Answer   Webster 1972
Love Is the Best of All   Herbert 1915
Love Is the Darndest Thing   Burke 1946; Van Heusen 1946
Love Is the Funniest Thing   Robin 1954; Romberg 1954
Love Is the Greatest   Evans 1961; Livingston, Jay 1961
Love Is the Important Thing   Blake 1964; Sissle 1964
Love Is the Reason   Atteridge 1915; Fields 1951; Schwartz, Arthur 1951
Love Is the Same   Brooks 1953
Love Is the Sun   Friml 1928
Love Is the Thing   Washington 1933; Young, Victor 1933
Love Is the Time   Friml 1947; Heyman 1947
Love Is Tyrant, So I Bid You Behave   Herbert 1899
Love Is Tyrant, So I Bid You Beware   Smith, Harry B. 1899
Love Is Unpredictable   Drake 1958
Love Is What I Got a Heartful Of   Spina 1977
Love Is What I Never Knew   Warren 1956
Love Is What You Give to Loving   Johnson, J. Rosamond 1950
Love Is Where You Find It   Brown, Nacio Herb 1948; Dubin 1938; Mercer 1938
Love Is Where You Find It Something Tells Me   Warren 1938
Love Is Why They Invented the Blues   Cahn 1984; Coleman 1984
Love Isn't Born (It's Made)   Loesser 1943; Schwartz, Arthur 1943

Love Isn't Love Till You Give It Away   David, Hal 1974
Love, It Hurts So Good   Rome 1950
Love Just Isn't My Game   Mills 1947
Love Knows Best   Hart 1938; Rodgers 1938
Love Laid His Sleepless Head   Herbert 1907
Love Laughs at Anything   DePaul 1942; Raye 1942
Love Laughs at King   Evans 1951; Livingston, Jay 1951
Love Laughs at Kings.   Young, Victor 1952
Love Leads to Marriage   Berlin 1956
Love Lessons   Bacharach 1961; David, Hal 1961
Love Let Me Know   Evans 1961; Livingston, Jay 1961
Love Letter   Drake 1969; Loesser 1939
Love Letter Kisses   Robison 1963
Love Letter to Manhattan   Rome 1950
Love Letter Words   Porter 1922
Love Letters   Donaldson 1928; Heyman 1945; Kahn 1928; Young, Victor 1945
Love Letters in the Sand   Coots 1931
Love Letters of a Lady   Burke 1937; Johnston 1937
Love Lies   Freed, Ralph 1940; Sigman 1940
Love Life   Freed, Ralph 1940
Love Life in My Dream Life, The   David, Hal 1978
Love Life of a Dangling Participle   Spina 1976
Love Light   Bacharach 1988; Williams 1909
Love Like Ours   Bergman 1987; Blake 1954; Mitchell 1938; Sondheim 1994; Stept 1938
Love Like This, A   Washington 1943; Young, Victor 1943
Love Like Yours   Mercer 1969
Love Lingers On   Baer 1953
Love Lit Eyes   Atteridge 1923; Romberg 1923
Love Look Away   Hammerstein 1958; Rodgers 1958
Love, Look what You've Done to Me   Washington 1953
Love Looks So Well on You   Bergman 1961
Love Lost   Dietz 1933; Schwartz, Arthur 1933
Love, Love, Alone   Atteridge 1915
Love! Love! Love!   Friml 1918; Jerome 1904; Schwartz, Jean 1904; Young, Victor 1955
Love Machine   Sherman 1959
Love Made a Dreamer of Me   Coots 1951; Egan 1951
Love Made a Mess Out of Me   De Lange 1942
Love Magician   Fields 1931; McHugh 1931
Love Makes Such Fools of Us All   Coleman 1980
Love Makes the Changes   Bergman 1988
Love Makes the World Go   Rodgers 1962
Love Makes the World Go 'Round   Conrad 1929; Heyman 1935; Mitchell 1929; Romberg 1919; Smith, Harry B. 1896
Love Makes the World Go 'Round (Theme from Carnival)   Merrill 1961
Love Makes Up for Everything   Hoffman 1939
Love Makes Us Whatever We Want to Be   Cahn 1983; Styne 1983
Love Makes You Do Crazy Things   Livingston, Jerry 1938; Parish 1938; Silver 1938
Love Marches On!   Dubin 1936; Warren 1936
Love May Come, Love May Go   Herbert 1900; Smith, Harry B. 1900
Love Me   Cahn 1945; DePaul 1942; Edwards 1911; Raye 1942; Styne 1945; Washington 1934; Young, Victor 1934
Love Me a Little, Love Me Long   Howard, Joseph E. 1916
Love Me All the Time   Howard, Joseph E. 1909
Love Me and I'll Live Forever   Bryan 1925; Snyder 1925
Love Me As I Am   Alter 1941; Loesser 1941
Love Me As Though There Were No Tomorrow   Adamson 1956; McHugh 1956

Love Me at Twilight   Goetz 1916; Young, Joe 1916

Love Me Baby Mine   Johnson, J. Rosamond 1909

Love Me, Don't You?   Friml 1926; Hammerstein 1926; Harbach 1926

Love Me Ever (Leave Me Never)   Webster 1957

Love Me for a While   Webster 1934

Love Me for Myself   Lawrence 1958

Love Me Forever   Adamson 1959; Dixon 1931; Kahn 1935; Warren 1931; Young, Joe 1931

Love Me Good   David, Hal 1979

Love Me If You Love Me   Livingston, Jerry 1954; Russell 1954

Love Me in the Candlelight   Bryan 1920; Schwartz, Jean 1920

Love Me in Viennese   Johnson, Howard 1935

Love Me Just Because   Howard, Joseph E. 1909

Love Me Just Like Romeo Loved Juliet (Romeo and Miss Juliet)   Jerome 1909; Schwartz, Jean 1909

Love Me Like I Like to Be Loved   Bryan 1908; Meyer 1908

Love Me Like the Ivy Loves the Old Oak Tree   Whiting 1914

Love Me, Love Me, Love Me   Coslow 1950

Love Me, Love My Dog   Herbert 1905; Mercer 1949; Von Tilzer 1929

Love Me, Love My Pekinese   Porter 1936

(I'm Gonna Be a) Love Me Not   Merrill 1947

Love Me Now   David, Hal 1953; Duke 1955; Evans 1965; Hoffman 1953; Livingston, Jay 1965

Love Me Now (Pou de Vous)   Adamson 1951

Love Me Once More   Parish 1948

Love Me or Leave Me   Donaldson 1928; Kahn 1928

Love Me or Leave Me Alone   Johnson, Howard 1915, 1925

Love Me to a Viennese Melody   Goetz 1913

Love Me to a Yiddisha Melody   Leslie 1911; Lewis 1911; Young, Joe 1911

Love Me to that Beautiful Tune   Williams 1911

Love Me Tomorrow   Lane 1985

Love Me Tomorrow (But Leave Me Alone To-Day)   Duke 1940

Love Me Tonight   Friml 1925; Hart 1932; Rodgers 1932; Washington 1932; Wrubel 1932; Young, Victor 1932

Love Me While the Lovin' Is Good   Von Tilzer 1913

Love Means Love   Sigman 1950

Love (My Everything)   Ellington 1957

Love, My Heart Is Calling You   Lewis 1923; Young, Joe 1923

Love Ne'er Came Nigh   Herbert 1895; Smith, Harry B. 1895

Love Nest, The   Harbach 1920

Love Nests in France   Carroll 1921

Love Never Went to College   Hart 1939; Rodgers 1939

Love Night   Herbert 1908

Love Nights   Bryan 1921; Meyer 1921

Love Notes   McHugh 1922; Parish 1922

Love, Nuts and Noodles (Bring 'Em Back Alive)   Harburg 1932

Love o' Mike   Kern 1917; Smith, Harry B. 1917

Love of a Boy, The   Bacharach 1962; David, Hal 1962

Love of a Wife, The   DeSylva 1919; Gershwin, George 1919

Love of God (Is with You Where Ever You Are), The   Robison 1958

Love of Long Ago   Atteridge 1922

Love of My Life, The   Lerner, Alan Jay 1947; Loewe 1947; Mercer 1940; Merrill 1967; Porter 1948

Love of My Life (inst.)   Young, Victor 1953

Love of the Lorelei, The   Herbert 1914; Smith, Robert B. 1914

Love on a Greyhound Bus   Blane 1946

Love Opened My Eyes   Freed, Ralph 1938; McHugh 1938

Love or Infatuation   Coslow 1936

Love Plays a Game   Hoffman 1929; Lerner, Sammy 1929

Love Power   Strouse 1987

Love Race   Carroll Date Unknown

Love Remains the Same   Olcott 1896; Rome 1946

Love Revolution   Coleman 1977

Love Rose   Lewis 1911

Love Rules My Heart   Alter 1930

Love Scene in Pasadena   Coots 1936; Davis 1936

Love Sick   Merrill 1956

Love Sick Blues   Friend 1922; Mills 1922

Love Sign   Goetz 1911

Love Sings a Song   Caesar 1925

Love Sneaks Up on You   Young, Victor 1955

Love Sometimes Has to Wait   Rome 1943

Love Song   Adams 1960, 1978; Carmichael 1940; Lerner, Alan Jay 1948; Mercer 1940, 1954; Smith, Harry B. 1925; Strouse 1960, 1971, 1978; Warren 1980; Weill 1948, 1954

Love Song from Beauty and the Beast   David, Mack 1958; Livingston, Jerry 1958

Love Song (inst.)   Warren 1972

Love Song of a Thief, The   Friml 1954

Love Song of Long Ago, A   Kahn 1937; Romberg 1937

Love Song of Renaldo   Fain 1940; Kahal 1940

Love Song of Tahiti   Kahn 1935

Love Song of Tom Jones, The   David, Mack 1964

Love Song to Ruth, A   Van Heusen 1951

Love Songs   Leslie 1931; Meyer 1931

Love Songs Are Born in Paris (Tout le Sonheur du Monde)   Parish 1961

Love Songs Are Made in the Night   Henderson 1943; Yellen 1943

Love Songs Are Not for Me   Evans 1955; Livingston, Jay 1955

Love Songs of the Nile   Brown, Nacio Herb 1933; Freed, Arthur 1933

Love Spans the World   Caesar 1922

Love Story   Adams 1951; Sigman 1969; Strouse 1951; Webster 1962

Love Street   Howard, Joseph E. 1948

Love Takes a Holiday   Koehler 1938; Lawrence 1935; Young, Joe 1934

Love Takes Time (Night Waltz)   Sondheim 1977

Love Tale of Alsace Lorraine, A   Coots 1928

Love Tales   Ager 1933; Davis 1933; Stept 1933

Love Test, The   Atteridge 1922; Romberg 1922

Love That Boy   DePaul 1948; Raye 1948

Love That Cannot Be   Friml 1954

Love That Game   Rome 1969

Love that Lasts, A   Hammerstein 1928; Romberg 1928

Love that Man   Rome 1950

Love that Never Happened, The   Parish 1944; Woods 1944

Love that Will Never Die, A   Conrad Date Unknown

Love, the Marvelous Magician   Herbert 1899; Smith, Harry B. 1899

Love the Wife of Your Neighbor   DeSylva 1922

Love the World Over Is Much the Same   Smith, Harry B. 1913; Smith, Robert B. 1913

Love Theme   David, Mack 1965; Webster 1958

Love Theme for Scene #82   Spina 1977

Love Theme from The Mole People   Evans 1956; Livingston, Jay 1956

Love Theme from Torn Curtain   Evans 1966; Livingston, Jay 1966

Love Theme (inst.)   Bacharach 1988

Love Theme Reel 4 No. 1   Warren 1933

Love Thoughts   Friml 1923

Love Thrills   Bryan 1929; Meyer 1929

Love through the Ages   Smith, Harry B. 1923; Snyder 1923

Love Thy Neighbor   Gordon 1934; Revel 1934

Love Time   Brown, A. Seymour 1909; Brown, Nacio Herb 1920

Love Time, Calling All Hearts   Pollack 1934; Young, Joe 1934

Love Tiptoed through My Heart   Loewe 1935

Love to Be with You   Webster 1952

Love to Take a Lesson in Love (Love to Take a Lesson from You)   Clare 1929

Love Told a Terrible Lie   Burke 1939; Warren 1939

Love Too Good to Last, The   Bacharach 1982

Love Turn Your Head Away   Webster 1965

Love Turned the Light Out   Duke 1940

Love Up a Tree   Howard, Joseph E. 1908

Love Walked In   Gershwin, George 1938; Gershwin, Ira 1938

Love Waltz, The   Brennan 1927; Cahn 1951; Smith, Harry B. 1911

Love Was Gone   Adamson 1932; Lane 1932

Love Was in the Air   Brown, Nacio Herb 1930, 1937; Freed, Arthur 1930, 1937

Love Was Young as an April Leaf   Spina 1944

Love, What Are You Doing to My Heart?   Lewis 1936

Love While You May   Romberg 1922

Love Will Always Find a Way   Romberg 1921

Love Will Call   Hart 1920; Rodgers 1920

Love Will Come Tomorrow   Coots 1951

Love Will Find a Way   Blake 1921; Dubin 1929; Sissle 1921

Love Will Find a Way — They Say   Cahn 1966; Van Heusen 1966

Love Will Find the Way   Von Tilzer 1917

Love Will Find You   Baer 1929; Gilbert 1929

Love Will Find You Some Day   Smith, Harry B. 1925

Love Will Have to Do   Stept 1946

Love Will Keep Us Young   Leslie 1947

Love Will Last Forever If It's Love   Bryan 1929

Love Will Make or Break a Man   Cohan 1909

Love Will Say Goodbye to Tears   Young, Joe 1932

Love Will See Us Through   Sondheim 1971

Love Will Soon Be Here   Adamson 1953; Carmichael 1953

Love Will Tell   Pollack 1936; Yellen 1936

Love with a Capital "U"   Hoffman 1938

Love with a Capital "You"   Loesser 1939; Rainger 1938; Robin 1938

Love with All the Trimmings   Lane 1970; Lerner, Alan Jay 1970

Love with the Proper Stranger   Mercer 1964

Love Without Words   Cahn 1980

Love Woke Me Up this Morning   Mercer 1949; Warren 1949

Love, Wonderful Love   Cahn 1957

Love Won't Let You Get Away   Cahn 1958; Van Heusen 1958

Love Won't Wait Until Tomorrow   Raye 1956

Love Words from You   Akst 1932; Davis 1932

Love X Two (inst.)   Bacharach 1966

Love Ya Like Crazy   Silver 1954

Love You   Rome 1969

Love You Are My Inspiration   Koehler 1932

Love, You Are the Sunrise   Adamson 1933; Lane 1933

Love You Dearly   Fain 1954; Webster 1954

Love, You Didn't Do Right By Me   Berlin 1954

Love, You Funny Thing   Ahlert 1932; Turk 1932

Love You, Love You, Love You Till the Cows Come Home   Stept 1950

Love You More Than   Styne 1956

Love Your Girl in an Aeroplane   Friend 1919

Love, You're Just a Laugh   Cahn 1935

Loveable   Whiting 1928

Loveable and Sweet   Clare 1929

(Tell Me What's the Matter) Loveable Eyes   Atteridge 1922

Loveable Irish, The   Burke 1961

Loveable Lady of the Night   Mills 1941

Loveable Sort of Person   Loesser 1941; Young, Victor 1941

Loved One   Heyman 1943; Leigh 1965; Russell 1941; Snyder 1930

Love-Land   Friml 1917; Harbach 1917; Smith, Harry B. 1913; Sondheim 1971, 1987

Loveland Express, The   Atteridge 1912

Loveland in the Wintertime   Friend 1938

Loveless You and Hateful Me   Duke 1963

Lovelier than Ever   Loesser 1948

Loveliest Night of the Year   Friml 1959; Webster 1950

Loveliest of Feelings, The   Sherman 1977

Loveliest Thing in Life, The   Razaf 1948

Lovelight   Buck 1921; David, Hal 1960; Herbert 1919

Lovelight in the Starlight   Freed, Ralph 1938

Lovelight in Your Eyes, The   Smith, Harry B. 1922

Loveliness and Love   Rainger 1941; Robin 1941

Loveliness of You, The   De Lange 1944; Gordon 1937, 1938; Revel 1937; Stept 1945

Love'll Work It Out   Cahn 1976

Lovely   Ahlert 1933; Dietz 1941; Leslie 1933; Schwartz, Arthur 1941; Sondheim 1962

Lovely Daughter of Allah   Johnson, J. Rosamond 1912

Lovely Day for a Murder, A   Hart 1940; Rodgers 1940

Lovely Day to Be Out of Jail, A   Coleman 1996

Lovely Flowers   Johnson, Howard 1939

Lovely Girl, A   Comden and Green 1945

Lovely Girls of Akbarabad, The   Fain 1960; Webster 1960

Lovely Heroine, The   Porter 1912

Lovely Is the Evening   Webster 1951

Lovely Ladies   Sondheim Date Unknown

Lovely Lady   Brown, Lew 1925; Brown, Nacio Herb 1928, 1933; DeSylva 1925; Freed, Arthur 1928, 1933; Friml 1926; Hammerstein 1926; Harbach 1926; Henderson 1925; Koehler 1935; McHugh 1935; Smith, Harry B. 1896

Lovely Lady in White   Mitchell 1936; Pollack 1936

Lovely Lady of My Dreams   Brown, Lew 1931; Henderson 1931

Lovely Little Fraulein   Gordon 1932; Revel 1932

Lovely Little Silhouette   Lewis 1927; Young, Joe 1927

Lovely Liza Lee   Razaf 1935

Lovely, Lonely Man   Sherman 1968

Lovely Luana   DePaul 1942, 1945; Raye 1942, 1945

Lovely Luawana Lady   Goetz 1952

Lovely Night, A   Hammerstein 1957; Rodgers 1957

Lovely Night in Spain   Egan 1929

Lovely Night to Go Dancing   Adamson 1946; McHugh 1946

Lovely One   Coslow 1934; Johnston 1934; Lerner, Sammy 1929; Loesser 1938

Lovely Party   Adams 1957; Strouse 1957

Lovely to Look At   Fields 1935; Kern 1935

Lovely Trip, A   Atteridge 1914

Lovely Vienna   Smith, Harry B. 1927
Lovely Way to Spend an Evening, A   Adamson 1943;
     McHugh 1943
Lovely Weather for Ducks   Evans 1951, 1953; Livingston, Jay
     1951, 1953
Lovely Woman's Ever Young (La Femme a Toujours Vingt
     Ans!)   Hart 1930; Rodgers 1930
Lovely You (Only You, Only Me)   Friml 1945
Love-Nest in Kalua   Bryan 1938
Lover   Clare 1923; Conrad 1923; Hart 1932; Rodgers 1932
Lover Boy   Davis 1948; Silver 1948
Lover, Come Back   Herbert 1911; Smith, Harry B. 1911
Lover, Come Back to Me   Hammerstein 1928; Romberg 1928
Lover Doll   Silver 1958
Lover Knows, A   Sigman 1979
Lover Where Are You   Leslie 1931
Lover's A-B-C, The   Smith, Harry B. 1903
Lover's Gold   David, Mack 1958; Merrill 1949
Lovers in New York   Evans 1961; Livingston, Jay 1961;
     Mancini 1961
Lovers in the Dark   Mercer 1959
Lover's Lane Is a Lonesome Road   Fisher 1930
Lover's Luck   Fain 1931; Kahal 1931
Lover's Lullaby, A   Razaf 1940
Lovers No More   Parish 1964
Lovers of Art   DeSylva 1924; Gershwin, George 1924
Lovers on Christmas Eve   Coleman 1977
Lover's Rendezvous (inst.)   Warren Date Unknown
Lover's Waltz   Mancini 1957; Revel 1951; Yellen 1924
Lovers' Waltz (You I Adore You)   Spina 1977
Love's a Bond   Sondheim 1954
Love's a Dreamy Tune   Howard, Joseph E. 1911
Love's a Golden Day   Herbert 1905
Love's a Lovely Thing   Koehler 1951
Love's a Made Humpty Dumpty Out of Me   Razaf 1930
Love's a Necessary Thing   Arlen 1938; Koehler 1938
Love's a Pretty Thing   Davis 1981
Love's a Riddle   Burke Date Unknown; De Lange 1939; Van
     Heusen 1939
Love's a Sunbeam   Smith, Harry B. 1928
Love's a Very Funny Thing   Schwartz, Jean 1919
Love's Awakening   Atteridge 1915; Friml 1915
Love's Call   Coots 1926
Love's Charming Art   Kern 1911
Loves Crystal   Coots 1921
Love's Dear Yearning (Dreaming in Paradise)   Romberg
     1926
Love's Dream   Fain 1919
Love's Dream After the Ball   Johnson, Howard 1935
Love's Dreamy Strain   Brown, A. Seymour 1912
Love's Fairy Tales   Atteridge 1913
Love's Flower Is Always Blooming   Atteridge 1913
Love's Golden Dream   Von Tilzer 1909
Love's Got Me Down Again   Cahn 1939
Love's Happy Dream   Smith, Harry B. 1930
Love's Highway   Romberg 1922
Love's Hour   Brennan 1936; Herbert 1912
Love's in My Heart   Ellington 1940; Mills 1940
Love's Intense in Tents   Hart 1920; Rodgers 1920
Love's Last Day   Smith, Harry B. 1923
Love's Lingo   Howard, Joseph E. 1904
Love's Little Island   Merrill 1955
Love's Memories (inst.)   Von Tilzer 1914
Love's Merry Go Round   Goetz 1907
Love's No Stranger to Me   Arlen 1954

Loves of July (Les Amours de Julliet), The   Webster 1967
Loves of New Orleans   Herbert 1910, 1935; Kahn 1935
Loves of Omar Khayyam, The   Evans 1957; Livingston, Jay
     1957
Love's Oracle   Herbert 1909
Love's Own Kiss   Friml 1913; Harbach 1913
Love's Prescription   Williams 1907
Love's Sentence   Meyer 1911
Love's Serenade   Mills 1935
Love's Sorcery   Smith, Harry B. 1911; Smith, Robert B. 1911
Love's Telephone   Caesar 1920
Love's What You Make It   Drake 1945
Love's Young Dream   Smith, Harry B. 1902
Lovesick Blues   Friend 1949; Mills 1949
Love-Sick Serenade   Harburg 1961
Lovesville   Freed, Ralph 1958
Lovey   Caesar 1923; Conrad 1923; Freed, Arthur 1933;
     Hoffman 1933
Lovey Came Back   Lewis 1923; Young, Joe 1923
Lovey Dove   Atteridge 1922; Friend 1959; Romberg 1922
Lovey-Dovey   Friml 1934
Lovie   Howard, Joseph E. 1905
Lovie Lee   Razaf 1928; Waller 1928
Lovin' Ain't My Aim   Johnson, James P. 1948
Lovin' Chile   Blake 1923; Sissle 1923
Lovin' Is Livin'   Cahn 1964; Van Heusen 1964
Lovin' Joe   Donaldson 1926
Lovin' Lover   Ellington 1971
Lovin' Mama   Davis 1921
Lovin' Man   Razaf 1942
Lovin' Sam the Sheik of Alabam'   Ager 1922; Yellen 1922
Loving Cup, The   Smith, Harry B. 1910; Smith, Robert B.
     1910
Loving Daddy, A   Atteridge 1917; Romberg 1917
Loving Doving   Bryan 1909
Loving for a Living   Bryan 1936
Loving Is a Way of Living   Bacharach 1959; David, Hal 1959
Loving Moon   Johnson, J. Rosamond 1911
Loving Ways   Brown, A. Seymour 1910; Goetz 1910
Loving You   Schwartz, Jean 1926; Sondheim 1994; Stept
     1924; Yellen 1930
Loving You the Way I Do   Blake 1930; Davis 1927
Loving You to Music   Howard, Joseph E. 1940
Low   Duke 1968; Oakland 1968; Rainger 1936; Robin 1936
Low and Lazy   Duke 1946
Low Bottom Woman   David, Hal 1974
Low Down Blues   Blake 1921; Sissle 1921
Low Down Lullaby   Rainger 1934; Robin 1934
Low Down Papa Don't You Try to High Hat Me   Kahn 1925
Low Down Upon the Harlem River   Gordon 1933; Revel
     1933
Low in the Lehigh Valley   Lawrence 1952
Low Moon   Friml 1928
Low Tide   Lane 1930
Low Tide Down in My Heart   Razaf 1936
Loyal, Resourceful and Cooperative   Bacharach 1968; David,
     Hal 1968
Loyal Sons of Leighton   Cahn 1942
Loyalty   Fain 1958; Webster 1958
lsn't It June   Koehler 1934
L.T.D.   Coleman 1964
Lu Lu   Gershwin, George 1920
Lu Lu Babe   Howard, Joseph E. 1908
Lu Lu Lu, My Darlin' (Sleep, My Little One, Sleep)   Revel
     1959

Luana   Brennan 1930; Friml 1930
Luana (Flower of Love)   Spina 1947
Luana Lou   Buck 1916
Luanne   Evans 1970; Livingston, Jay 1970
Luau Cha Cha Cha (Surfin' Luau)   Sherman 1960
Lucia   Fisher 1929; Rose 1929
Lucille   Donaldson 1931; Gilbert 1924; Razaf 1939; Silver 1924
Lucinda Lee   Blake 1962; Sissle 1962
Lucio's Victorian Family   Hart 1943
Lucious   Lewis 1927; Pollack 1927; Young, Joe 1927
Lucita   Coots 1925
Luck Am I (inst.)   Youmans 1954
Luck Be a Lady   Loesser 1950
Luckiest Boy in the World, The   Gershwin, George 1932; Gershwin, Ira 1932
Luckiest Man in the World   Gershwin, George 1932; Gershwin, Ira 1932
Lucky   Coots 1925; Coslow 1925; Duke 1926; Kalmar 1927; Kern 1927; Ruby 1927; Silver 1925
Lucky Beggar   Razaf 1934
Lucky Bird   Robin 1927; Youmans 1927
Lucky Boy   Baer 1929; Berlin 1925; Clarke 1924; Gilbert 1929; Leslie 1924; Monaco 1924; Sterling 1913; Von Tilzer 1913
Lucky Cowboy   Rainger 1943; Robin 1943
(This Is My) Lucky Day   Brown, Lew 1926; DeSylva 1926; Henderson 1926
Lucky Day that I Found You, The   Cobb 1921; Edwards 1921
Lucky Duck   Fields 1934; McHugh 1934; Webster 1946
Lucky Fella   Fields 1933; McHugh 1933
Lucky Horseshoe, The   Coots 1952
Lucky in Love   Atteridge 1923; Brown, Lew 1927; Caesar 1923; DeSylva 1927; Henderson 1927; Kahn 1920; Romberg 1923; Schwartz, Jean 1920
Lucky in Romance   Drake 1954
(I Got) Lucky in the Rain   Adamson 1948; McHugh 1948
Lucky Kentucky   Dixon 1924; Henderson 1924; Rose 1924
Lucky Legs   Cahn 1945
Lucky Level, The   Carmichael 1950
Lucky Lily   Coleman 1978; Comden and Green 1978
Lucky Lindy   Baer 1927; Gilbert 1927
Lucky Little Accident   Lane 1932; Young, Joe 1932
Lucky Little Devil   Dixon 1929; Woods 1929
Lucky Little Penny   Davis 1951
Lucky Me   Burke 1958; Fain 1954; Webster 1954
Lucky Me, and Loveable You   Ager 1930; Yellen 1930
Lucky Me, Loveable You   Ager 1929; Yellen 1929
Lucky Moon   Akst 1926; Davis 1926
Lucky People   Merrill 1950
Lucky Seven   Dietz 1930; Schwartz, Arthur 1930
Lucky Song, The   Brooks 1955; Warren 1955
Lucky Star, A   Whiting 1933
Lucky Starlets   Coslow 1936
Lucky to Be Me   Comden and Green 1944
Lucky Town   Drake 1954
Lucky Us!   Evans 1949; Livingston, Jay 1949
Lucky Waltz, The   Coots 1934
Lucre, Love or Liquor   Duke 1955
Lucy   Fain 1948; Yellen 1948
Lucy Anna Lou   Edwards 1910
Lucy Brown   Johnson, James P. 1962
Lucy Is Loose Again Tonight   Dixon 1927; Woods 1927
Lucy, Ma Honey Babe   Cohan 1901
Lucy's Song   Weill 1933

Lud's Wedding   Lerner, Alan Jay 1976
Luigi   Hammerstein 1936; Whiting 1936
Luisa (inst.)   Bacharach 1980
Lula Palula   Bryan 1926
Lulamae   Merrill 1966
Lullabies My Mammy Sang to Me   Silver 1919
Lullaby   Arlen 1946; Atteridge 1913, 1920; Johnson, Howard 1934, 1939; Martin 1948, 1952; Mercer 1946; Parish 1965; Rodgers 1979; Rome 1957
Lullaby Blues   Johnston 1926
Lullaby (Bye, Bye, Baby)   Herbert 1919; Smith, Robert B. 1919
Lullaby for a Debutante   Spina 1937
Lullaby for a Grown Up Baby   Pollack 1946
Lullaby for Christmas Eve   Webster 1964
Lullaby for Junior   Ellington 1946
Lullaby in Blue   Gordon 1956; Heyman 1930; Magidson 1934; Myrow 1956; Wrubel 1934
Lullaby Lady   Donaldson 1925; Hanley 1927; Johnson, Howard 1933; Kahn 1925; Young, Joe 1932
Lullaby Lane   Caesar 1923
Lullaby Moon   David, Mack 1933; Hoffman 1933; Silver 1933
Lullaby of Broadway   Dubin 1935; Warren 1935
Lullaby of the Leaves   Young, Joe 1932
Lullaby of the Lord, The   Cahn 1953; Robin 1952
Lullaby of the Shepherd   Bergman 1958
Lullaby Ostinato (inst.)   Kern 1938
Lullaby (Satin Gown and Silver Shoe)   Arlen 1944; Harburg 1944
Lullaby (Sleep, Baby, Sleep)   Weill 1947
Lullaby (String Quartet)   Gershwin, George 1919
Lullaby to a Landlord (inst.)   Rome 1939
Lullaby to Love   Drake 1946; Webster 1958
Lullabyland   Brown, A. Seymour 1909
Lulu   Caesar 1943
Lulu and Her La-La-La   Von Tilzer 1907
Lulu Belle   De Lange 1948; Dixon 1926; Henderson 1926; Robin 1926
Lulu Had a Baby   Hoffman 1959
Lulu Is Our Darling Pride   Johnson, Howard 1939
Lulu (You're Nobody's Fool)   Parish 1934
Lulu's Back in Town   Dubin 1935; Warren 1935
Lumber-Jack   Razaf 1930
Lumberjack Joe   Baer 1944
Lummir Alla Zingen (Let's All Sing)   Lawrence 1943
Lumpin'   Arlen 1959; Mercer 1959
Luna (Crazy Light)   Robison 1953
Luna de Cuba   Ellington 1941
Lunar Rhapsody (inst.)   Revel 1946
Lunatic's Lullaby, The   Leslie 1926
Lunch   Sondheim Date Unknown
Luncheon with Buster Crabbe   Coots 1952
Lunching at the Automat   Berlin 1932
Lunette   Revel 1946
Lupita   Washington 1945
Luscious   Pollack 1928; Young, Joe 1928
Lustspiel   Atteridge 1915; Romberg 1915
Lusty Month of May, The   Lerner, Alan Jay 1960; Loewe 1960
Lute Swank Campaign Song   Sherman 1964
Luti   Jerome 1904; Schwartz, Jean 1904
"Luv" Is a Three Letter Word   Ruby 1967
Luxury Lane   Styne 1985
Lydia, the Tattooed Lady   Arlen 1939; Harburg 1939

Lygia   Webster 1951
Lyin' to Myself   Carmichael 1936
Lying in State   Harburg 1967; Styne 1967
Lylah   David, Mack 1968
Lyle and Valenti   Strouse 1987
Lyre-Bird and the Jay, The   Goetz 1912
Lysistrata's Serenade   Harburg 1961
L.Z. in Quest of His Youth   Styne 1964

M

M-11   Duke 1959
M M M M M M Boy   Davis 1952
Ma   Clare 1921; Conrad 1921
Ma Belle   Friml 1928
Ma Belle Paree   Mercer 1962
Ma Belle Petronille   Romberg 1933
Ma Ebony Belle   Smith, Harry B. 1901
Ma (He's Making Eyes at Me)   Clare 1938; Conrad 1938
Ma Mamzelle Honee   Cobb 1904; Edwards 1904
Ma Mere   Caesar 1930, 1931; Warren 1930, 1931
Ma Petite Folie   Merrill 1952
Ma Petite Ninette   Porter 1911
Ma Temme   Atteridge 1921; Pollack 1921; Schwartz, Jean 1921
Mabel, Mabel   Drake 1946
M.A.C.A.R.O.N.I   Jerome 1904; Schwartz, Jean 1904
Macaroni Joe   Dubin 1917
Machine Gun Song, The   Dubin 1943; Hoffman 1943; Livingston, Jerry 1943; Monaco 1943
Machinery   Razaf 1935
Mack the Black   Porter 1948
Mack the Knife   Weill 1954
Macushla   Olcott 1911
Macushla Asthore   Brennan 1920
Macy's Parade   Willson 1963
Mad   Cahn 1942, 1945; Lerner, Alan Jay 1983; Livingston, Jerry 1962; Strouse 1983; Styne 1942, 1945
Mad about You   Koehler 1934; Stept 1934; Washington 1949; Young, Victor 1949
Mad at the World   Oakland 1934
Mad Cause You Treat Me This Way   McHugh 1923
Mad Daggar   Schwartz, Jean 1930
Mad for Art   Harburg 1967; Styne 1967
Mad House Rag, The   Leslie 1911
Mad Madam Mim   Sherman 1963
Mad Madrid, The   Harbach 1910; Von Tilzer 1910
Mad Manhattan   Johnson, James P. 1934
Mad Moments   Gordon 1932; Revel 1932
Mad Opera House   Norworth 1909
Madam Tango's Particular Tango   Arlen 1968
Madame Butterball   DePaul 1945; Raye 1945
Madame Butterfly Jones   Russell 1946; Stept 1946
Madame Esther, Queen of Hester Street   Hart Date Unknown; Rodgers Date Unknown
Madame Has Lost Her Dress   Rainger 1932
Madame, I Love Your Crepes Suzettes   Brown, Lew 1943; Freed, Ralph 1943; Lane 1943
Madame Is at Home   Loewe 1938
Madame (Ma-dahm)   Evans 1956; Livingston, Jay 1956
Madame Pompadour   Atteridge 1923; Schwartz, Jean 1923
Madame Rose's Toreadorables   Sondheim 1959; Styne 1959
Madame Satan (inst.)   Alter 1929
Madame Tango's Tango   Arlen 1954
Madame T.N.T.   Johnson, James P. 1932; Razaf 1932

Madame Venus (Take a Tip from Venus)   Smith, Harry B. 1909
Madame You've Take My Heart   David, Mack 1930
Madame Zuzu   Lerner, Alan Jay 1948; Weill 1948
Madcap Princess, A   Smith, Harry B. 1904
Madchenlied   Jerome 1907; Schwartz, Jean 1907
Made for Each Other (Tu Felicidad)   Drake 1947
Made in Nantucket   Duke 1950; Rome 1950
Made in Nashville, Tennessee   Strouse 1985
Made in Paris   Bacharach 1965; David, Hal 1965
Made in the U.S.A.   Atteridge 1915; Carroll 1915; Freed, Arthur 1945; Leigh 1985; Warren 1945
Madeira   Kalmar 1925; Ruby 1925
Madeleine   Friml 1922; Harbach 1922
Madeline Be Mine   Baer 1924; Friend 1924
Madeline's Commercial   Comden and Green 1955
Madelon   Adamson 1930; Egan 1919; Whiting 1919; Youmans 1930
Madelon I'll Be True to the Whole Regiment   Bryan 1918
Mademazelle   Porter 1925
Mademoiselle   Russell 1951
Mademoiselle Cliche de Paris   Lerner, Alan Jay 1969
Mademoiselle de Paris   Parish 1948
Mademoiselle in New Rochelle   Gershwin, George 1929; Gershwin, Ira 1929
Mademoiselle Mimi   Lewis 1927; Young, Joe 1927
Madly in Love   Duke 1956; Fields 1936
Mad-Man Moon   Leigh 1953
Madonna, Madonna   Merrill 1954
Madonna of Donwoolie Hill   Robison 1953
Madrigal   David, Mack 1964; Gorney 1969; Harbach 1933; Herbert 1911; Kern 1933; Smith, Harry B. 1911
Maedchen in Uniform   Fisher 1933; Parish 1933
Magdalena   Heyman 1964
Magdelena (inst.)   Bacharach 1979
Maggi   Coots 1950
Maggie Maguire   Sterling 1921; Von Tilzer 1921
Maggie's Theme (For Now, For Always)   Sherman 1961
Magic Age Is Seventeen, The   Styne 1961
Magic Carpet, The   Coslow 1952; Drake 1968
Magic Eyes   Brown, Lew 1923
Magic Falute, The   Harburg 1961
Magic Garden   Bergman 1956
Magic Garden of Love, The   Coots 1925
Magic Horseshoe, The   Coots 1953
Magic In the Moonlight   Mercer 1958
Magic Is the Night   Fain 1963
Magic Island   Fain 1929; Mercer 1958; Mills 1929; Parish 1929
Magic Journeys   Sherman 1982
Magic Kiss, The   Hanley 1920
Magic Lamp   Coots 1953
Magic Little Words   Blake 1962
Magic, Magic   Merrill 1961
Magic Melody, The   Kern 1915
Magic Moment   Dietz 1961; Romberg 1948; Schwartz, Arthur 1961
Magic Moments   Bacharach 1958; Coleman 1972; David, Hal 1958
Magic Moon   Gordon 1946
Magic Mountain   Stept 1940
Magic Music   Hart 1930; Rodgers 1930
Magic Music (inst.)   Duke 1963
Magic Nights   Merrill 1972; Styne 1972
Magic of Magnolias   Loesser 1941

Magic of Maytime   Kahn 1937
Magic of Springtime, The   Romberg 1924
Magic of the Moon, The   Duke 1926
Magic of Wedding Chimes, The   Leslie 1919
Magic of You, The   Rainger 1935
Magic of Your Love, The   Kahn 1939
Magic Opera   Oakland 1960
Magic Potion   Bacharach 1963; David, Hal 1963
Magic Rabbit   Bergman 1960
Magic Spell of Love, The   Brennan 1930; Friml 1930
Magic Strings (inst.)   Young, Victor 1953
Magic Touch, The   Stept 1952
Magic Touch (I Promise), The   Evans 1958; Livingston, Jay 1955
Magic Tree   Blane 1952
Magic Valley   Willson 1953
Magic Violin, The   Leslie 1928
Magic Waltz, The   Drake 1955; Leigh 1955; Yellen 1923
Magic Window, The   Burke 1953; Van Heusen 1953
Magic Words of Honolulu Kana-Nuka-Wahyn-Iahn, The   Hoffman 1950
Magical Eyes   Lewis 1913; Meyer 1913
Magical Island, The   Howard, Bart 1961
Magician of Lublin, The   Webster 1979
Magic's Missing, The   Warren 1970
'Magine   Stept 1956
Magnin Fashion Show   Lane 1935; Washington 1935
Magnolia   Brown, Lew 1927; DeSylva 1927; Henderson 1927
Magnolia Finale   Gershwin, George 1929; Gershwin, Ira 1929
Magnolias in the Moonlight   Bullock 1936
Magnolia's Wedding Day   Fields 1928; McHugh 1928
Magoo's Blues   Washington 1959
Mah Honey Love   Herbert 1911
Ma-ha-lani Papa-Doo (Hey, Hey)   Hoffman 1947; Livingston, Jerry 1947
Maharajah, The   Hoffman 1940
Maharanee   Duke 1936; Gershwin, Ira 1936
Mahatma Gandhi   Lewis 1931
Mah-Jongg   DeSylva 1924; Gershwin, George 1924
Mah-Jongg Maid   Hart 1925; Rodgers 1925
Mahogany   David, Mack 1975
Mahoneyphone, The   Adamson 1931; Lane 1931
Mahster's Coming, The   Hart 1934; Rodgers 1934
Maid and the Valet, The   Friml 1917
Maid of Gold   Buck 1923; Friml 1923
Maid of Mesh   Berlin 1923
Maid of My Heart   Gilbert 1915
Maid of Santiago   Porter 1913
Maid of the Milky Way   Coots 1925
Maid of the Mist   Carmichael 1939
Maid of Timbuctoo   Johnson, J. Rosamond 1903
Maiden By the Brook   Rainger 1938; Robin 1938
Maiden Fair   Porter 1950
Maiden Let Me In   Herbert 1924
Maiden of Guadalupe, The   Robin 1952; Warren 1952
Maiden of the Wild and Woolly West   Edwards 1905; Smith, Robert B. 1905
Maiden with the Dreamy Eyes, The   Johnson, J. Rosamond 1901
Maiden's Heart, A   Smith, Harry B. 1903
Maiden's Prayer, The   Clarke 1925; Hanley 1917; Monaco 1925
Maidens Typical of France   Porter 1953
Mail Call March   Willson 1944

Maile Dance   Rainger 1937; Robin 1937
Mailman's Song   Strouse 1987
Mailu   Gorney 1931; Harburg 1931
Maim Frank   Styne 1956
Main Street   Brooks 1959; Comden and Green 1949
Main Street in My Old Home Town   Caesar 1921
Main Street U.S.A.   Revel 1946; Sherman 1962
Main Street Wasn't Big Enough for Mary   Davis 1924; Silver 1924
Main Title   Coslow 1949; Freed, Ralph 1946; Harburg 1943
Maine   Rodgers 1962
Maine Will Remember the Maine   Lawrence 1951
Mainly That (My Honey)   Robison 1960
Mairzy Doats   Hoffman 1943; Livingston, Jerry 1943
Mais le Son de Ta Voix (Just a Little Love Song)   Lewis 1923; Young, Joe 1923
Majarajah   Coslow 1949
Major Domo, The   Romberg 1925
Major Dundee March   Washington 1965
Major General Pumpernickel   Von Tilzer 1910
Major Is a Minor, The   Spina 1977
Major Margery   Smith, Robert B. 1906
Majorca   Merrill 1958
Make a Date with a Great Psychoanalyst   Porter 1941
(I Want Someone To) Make a Fuss Over Me   Buck 1915
Make a Hit with Mother, and You'll Make a Hit with Me   Gilbert 1913
Make a Lot of Noise   Cohan 1907
Make a Miracle   Loesser 1948
Make a Movie in Sevalio   Bacharach 1966; David, Hal 1966
Make a Note of It   Burke 1933; Spina 1933
Make a Wish   Alter 1937; Livingston, Jerry 1963; Martin 1951; Merrill 1958; Webster 1937
Make Allowance for Love   Smith, Harry B. 1901
Make Believe   Davis 1921; Hammerstein 1927; Kern 1927
Make Believe Ball Room   Razaf 1936
Make Believe Ballroom   Mercer 1949
Make Believe Danceland   Razaf 1940
Make Believe Island   Coslow 1940
Make Believe Ladies Man, A   Bryan 1930
Make Believe Land   Davis 1950; Silver 1950
Make Believe Lover   David, Hal 1961
Make Believe You're Mine   Smith, Harry B. 1926
Make Each Day a Holiday   Mills 1955
Make 'Em Laugh   Brown, Nacio Herb 1952; Freed, Arthur 1952
Make Every Day a Holiday   Porter 1924
Make Faith   Coots 1954
Make Friends   Howard, Bart 1955
Make Hey! Make Hay! (While the Moon Shines)   Hart 1927; Rodgers 1927
Make Him Feel at Home   Johnson, Howard 1926
Make Him Guess   Herbert 1915
Make Him Say Please   Yellen 1977
Make It Another Old Fashioned, Please   Porter 1940
Make It Easy on Yourself   Bacharach 1962; David, Hal 1962
Make Love in the Morning   Herbert 1924
Make Love the King (Long Live the King)   Conrad 1932; Young, Joe 1932
Make Love to Me   Blake 1956
Make Me a Child Again   Washington 1955
Make Me a Christmas Present of You   Egan 1937
Make Me an Miracle   Hoffman 1957
Make Me Happy   Johnson, Howard 1926
Make Me Laugh   Bryan 1908; Snyder 1908

Make Me Look Good Tonight   Robison 1961
Make Me Love You   Meyer 1913
Make Me Love You Like I Never Loved Before   Bryan 1911; Fisher 1911
Make Me Make You Mine   Adamson 1953; Carmichael 1953
Make Me Rainbows   Bergman 1967
Make Me Want to Be Loved By You   Brown, Nacio Herb 1921
Make Me Yours   David, Hal 1956; Freed, Arthur 1932
Make Mine Latin   Davis 1946
Make Mine Love   Adamson 1959; Warren 1959
Make Morris Mayor   Lawrence 1949
Make No Mistake about Love   Robison 1944
Make Room for the Joy   Bacharach 1959; David, Hal 1959
Make Someone Happy   Styne 1960
Make that Engine Stop at Louisville   Lewis 1914; Meyer 1914
Make the Best of It   Gershwin, Ira 1921; Youmans 1921
Make the Man Love Me   Fields 1951; Schwartz, Arthur 1951
Make the Most of Your Music   Sondheim 1987
Make the Music Play   Bacharach 1963; David, Hal 1963
Make the People Cry   Styne 1953
Make Up Your Mind   Burke 1931; Fields 1930, 1933; Gordon 1925; McHugh 1930, 1933; Meyer 1926; Smith, Harry B. 1926
Make Up Your Mind to Make Up with Someone   Bryan 1925; Schwartz, Jean 1925
Make Way   Duke 1940
Make Way for a Star   Leigh 1976; Styne 1976
Make Way for the Emperor   Porter 1958
Make Way for the Fife and Drum Corps   Bergman 1958
Make Way for the Law   Comden and Green 1972
Make Way for the Rangers (The Northwest Passage Song)   Dietz 1958; Schwartz, Arthur 1958
Make Way for Tomorrow   Coslow 1937; Gershwin, Ira 1944; Harburg 1944; Kern 1944; Robin 1937; Schwartz, Jean 1937
Make with the Feet   Adamson 1941; Duke 1941
Make with the Kisses   Mercer 1939; Van Heusen 1939
Make Your Life a Ballgame   Wrubel 1931
Make Your Own Sunshine   Brennan 1925; Howard, Joseph E. 1906
Make Your Vote Count   Rome 1948
Make Yourself at Home   Bullock 1940; Clare 1931; Gordon 1929; Hammerstein 1917; Styne 1940
Make Yourself Comfortable   Merrill 1954
Make-Believe Lover   Drake 1961
Make-Believe Stranger   Drake 1956
Makes Me Feel Good All Over   Loesser Date Unknown
Makin' Faces at the Man in the Moon   Hoffman 1931; Washington 1931
Makin' for My Georgia Caroline   Fisher 1920
Makin' Love   Hoffman 1958
Makin' Love Mountain Style   Warren Date Unknown
Makin' Memories   Sherman 1982
Makin' Whoopee   Donaldson 1928; Kahn 1928
Makin' Wicky-Wacky Down in Waikiki   Hoffman 1930; Lane 1930
Making a Play for Love   Sigman 1952
Making a Venus   Herbert 1924
Making Believe You're Here   Cahn 1958; Van Heusen 1958
Making Conversation   Hammerstein 1941; Romberg 1941
Making Eyes   Jerome 1905; Von Tilzer 1905
Making History   Washington 1933; Young, Joe 1933; Young, Victor 1933

Making Love   Bacharach 1982
Making Merry in the Month of May   Johnson, Howard 1935
Making of a Girl, The   Atteridge 1916; Gershwin, George 1916; Romberg 1916
Making the Best of Each Day   Clare 1931
Making Up a Song As I Go Along   Hoffman 1937; Lerner, Sammy 1937
Makin's of the U.S.A., The   Von Tilzer 1918
Maladjusted Jester, The   Cahn 1956
Malay Love Song   Loesser 1942; Styne 1942
Male Call (The Leap Year Song)   Raye 1952
Male Is an Animal, A   Fields 1957; Lane 1957
Malibu   Ahlert 1933; Caesar 1934; Johnson, Howard 1930; Leslie 1933
Malihini Love Call   Baer 1930; Gilbert 1930
Malinda Brown   Donaldson 1922; Johnson, Howard 1922
Malora   Webster 1957
Maluna, Malalo, Mawaena (Hawaiian Drinking Song)   Gordon 1942
Mama Always Makes It Better   Rodgers 1979
Mama Come Home   Myrow 1942
Mama Don't Allow It   Cahn 1935
Mama Don't A-Wanna Hear Her Baby Cry, A   Burke 1958
Mama Don't Want No Peas an' Rice an' Cocoanut Oil   Gilbert 1931; Johnson, J. Rosamond 1931
Mama Inez   Gilbert 1931
Mama, It's Saturday Night   Eliscu 1943; Gorney 1943
Mama Kiki — Papa Wacki   Fisher 1924
Mama Like You and a Papa Like Me, A   Rose 1924; Woods 1924
Mama Love Papa   Brown, Nacio Herb 1922; Freed, Arthur 1922
Mama Loves Papa, Papa Loves Mama   Baer 1923; Friend 1923
Mama, Mama   Loesser 1956
Mama, Mama, Mama   Merrill 1952
Mama Mama Mama Where Did You Get de Cigar   Evans 1954; Livingston, Jay 1954
Mama! Mama! Papa's Got a Lot Lovin' All Saved Up for You   Friend 1921
Ma-Ma, Ma-Ma, Put the Kettle On   Drake 1952
Mama, May I   Hoffman 1959
Mama Mia   McHugh 1962; Revel 1946
Mama Mia (Italian Mother Song)   Washington 1955
Mama Never Told Me   Lawrence 1946
Mama Nicolini   Coots 1953
Mama Rosa   Revel 1957
Mama Said No   Donaldson 1924
Mama Stayed Out the Whole Night Long, but Mama Didn't Do No Wrong   Razaf 1926
Mama Talks Calypso Now   Cahn 1957
Mama, Teach Me to Dance   Hoffman 1956
Mama, that Moon Is Here Again   Rainger 1938; Robin 1938
Mama They Wanna Mambo   DePaul 1958; Raye 1958
Mama Used to Say   Spina 1959
Mama, What Is in the Pot Today   Bergman 1963
Mama, What's Love   De Lange 1949
Mama You Don't Understand Me   Strouse Date Unknown
Mama-in-Law Blues   Lewis 1976; Young, Joe 1976
Mamalu (Boojee Bee — Boojee Boo)   Brown, Lew 1944
Mama's Blues (Papa's Blues)   Johnson, James P. 1916
Mama's Captain Curly Head   Von Tilzer 1918
Mama's Dancing   Coslow 1926
Mama's in the Doghouse Now   Coslow 1930
Mama's in the Park   Caesar 1955

Mama's Little Girl   Coleman 1962; Leigh 1962
Mama's Little Pet   Harbach 1911
Mama's Melody   Bryan 1913
Mama's Well Has Done Gone Dry   Razaf 1927
Mambo (inst.)   Mercer 1955
Mambo Italiano   Merrill 1954
Mambo on My Mind   Russell 1952
Mamie   Smith, Harry B. 1925
Mamie Is Mimi   Robin 1948; Styne 1948
Mamie Magdalin   Porter 1944
Mamie Mamie Don't You Feel Ashamie   Cobb 1901;
    Edwards 1901
Mamie McGee   Carroll 1924
Mamma Ain't Cookin' Today   Robison 1952
Mamma Goes Where Papa Goes, or Papa Don't Go Out
    Tonight   Ager 1923; Yellen 1923
Mamma Loves Papa, Does Papa Love Mamma?   Brown,
    Lew 1922
Mamma Mockingbird (inst)   Carmichael 1933
Mamma Wants to Go Bye-Bye   Akst 1927; Davis 1927
Mamma Whip Mamma Spank If Yer Daddy Don't Come
    Home   Turk 1921
Mamma's Baby Boy   Fain 1923
Mammy Don't Let Pappy Go   Conrad 1937; Magidson 1937;
    Oakland 1937
Mammy, I'll Sing about You   Dubin 1935; Warren 1935
Mammy Is Gone   Brown, Lew 1928; DeSylva 1928;
    Henderson 1928
Mammy Jazz   Johnson, J. Rosamond 1920
Mammy Jinny's Jubilee   Gilbert 1913
Mammy Land   Johnson, James P. 1930; Razaf 1930
Mammy Lou   Sterling 1921; Von Tilzer 1921
Mammy Sue   Bryan 1928; Schwartz, Jean 1928
Mammy's Birthday   Meyer 1926
Mammy's Chocolate Drop   Mitchell 1919
Mammy's Chocolate Soldier   Mitchell 1918
Mammy's Day in Dixie-Land   Akst 1923; Lewis 1923; Meyer
    1923; Young, Joe 1923
Mammy's Good Night Lullaby   Jerome 1920; Von Tilzer
    1920
Mammy's Jubilee   Brown, A. Seymour 1909
Mammy's Li'l Choc'late Cullud Chile   Blake 1917; Sissle
    1917
Mammy's Little Alabama Love   Sterling 1903; Von Tilzer
    1903
Mammy's Little Angel Child   Yellen 1914
Mammy's Little Coal Black Rose   Egan 1916; Whiting 1916
Mammy's Little Silver Lining   Hanley 1923
Mammy's Little Sugar Plum   Davis 1920
Mammy's Lullaby, A   Blake 1930; Razaf 1930
Mammy's Melody   Brown, Lew Date Unknown; Kahn 1922
Mammy's Shufflin' Dance   Gilbert 1911
Mam'selle   Friml 1950; Gordon 1948; Smith, Harry B. 1900
Mam'selle Fauchette   Cohan 1904
Mamselle Lucinda   Goetz 1911
Mam'selle Sallie   Smith, Harry B. 1906
Mamushka, The   Comden and Green 1991
Mamzelle Fifi   Brown, A. Seymour 1909
Man, A   Bergman 1957; Styne 1985
Man, a Maid, a Moon, A   Burke 1934; Rainger 1935; Robin
    1935; Spina 1934
Man About Town   Dietz 1929; Loesser 1939; Magidson
    1930; Schwartz, Arthur 1929; Smith, Harry B. 1908;
    Washington 1930
Man About Yonkers   Harburg 1932

Man and a Maid, A   Caesar 1946
Man and a Train, A   David, Hal 1973
Man and His Dream, A   Burke 1939; Monaco 1939
Man and His Music, A   Cahn 1965; Van Heusen 1965
Man and the Maid, The   Herbert 1908
Man and Wife   DePaul 1955
Man and Woman   Evans 1954; Livingston, Jay 1954
Man Around the House, A   DeSylva 1919; Kern 1919
Man Behind the Badge, The   Gilbert 1955
Man Behind the Club   Jerome 1905; Schwartz, Jean 1905
Man Behind the Hammer and the Plow, The   Von Tilzer
    1917
Man Bites Dog (inst.)   Spina 1977
Man Called Gannon, A   Bergman 1968
Man Called Noon, The   Cahn 1973
Man Chases a Girl (Until She Catches Him), A   Berlin 1949
Man for Me (The Letter Song), The   Hart 1932; Rodgers
    1932
Man for Sale   Arlen 1944; Harburg 1944
Man from Galilee   David, Mack 1956
Man from Idaho, The   Webster 1957
Man from Laramie, The   Washington 1955
Man from Music Mountain   Lawrence 1938
Man from the South   Bloom 1928
Man Has Dreams, A   Sherman 1964
Man Has Got to Wear the Pants, The   Cahn 1966; Van
    Heusen 1966
Man Has to Love, A   Fain 1968
Man I Love, The   Gershwin, George 1924; Gershwin, Ira
    1924
Man I Married, The   Adams 1993
Man I Marry Must Be a Man, The   Smith, Robert B. 1908
Man I Never Met, The   Warren 1956
Man I Used to Be, The   Hammerstein 1955; Rodgers 1955
Man in Love, A   Styne 1958
Man in My Life, The   Arlen 1959; Mercer 1959
Man in the Dark   Warren 1956
Man in the Looking Glass, The   Howard, Bart 1965
Man in the Moon, The   Smith, Harry B. 1923
Man in the Next Apartment, The   Van Heusen 1955
Man in the Sky   Harbach 1931; Kern 1931
Man Is a Man, A   Clare 1953; Young, Victor 1953
Man Is Faithful Till He's Caught   Atteridge 1913
Man Is not a Man — Until!, A   Cahn 1971; Van Heusen
    1971
Man Is Nothing   Oakland 1960
Man Is Only a Man, A   Berlin 1917
Man Is the Lord of It All   Johnson, Howard 1921; Schwartz,
    Jean 1921
Man Loves Me, The   Duke 1963
Man, Man   Johnson, J. Rosamond 1904
Man, Man, Man   Spina 1976
Man Meant Well, The   Herbert 1904
Man Must Be Something, A   David, Mack 1961; Livingston,
    Jerry 1961
Man Must Belong to a Woman, A   David, Hal 1977
Man Must His Honor Defend, A   Porter 1953
Man My Mother Married, The   Cahn Date Unknown; Duke
    Date Unknown
Man Named Moses, A   Livingston, Jerry 1962
Man Never Knows when a Woman's Gonna Change Her
    Mind, A   Friend 1923
Man Never Marries a Wife, A   Lawrence 1951
Man of High Degree, A   Gershwin, George 1929; Gershwin,
    Ira 1929

Man of Music   Robison 1957

Man of My Dreams   Johnston 1927; Turk 1927

Man of My Own, A   Ager 1930; Yellen 1930

Man of the Hour   Brooks 1960; Koehler 1950; Stept 1950

Man of the People, A   Coleman 1988

Man of the World, A   Harbach 1911

Man of the Year This Week, The   Mercer 1951

Man of Vision, A   Comden and Green 1961; Styne 1961

Man on Earth Is Worth Half a Dozen on the Moon, A   Fields 1930; McHugh 1930

Man on Fire   Fain 1957; Webster 1957

Man on the Box, The   Harbach 1910

Man on the Merry-Go-Round, The   Harburg 1979

Man Once Said, A   Livingston, Jerry 1958

Man Should Have a Double When He's Single, A   Herbert 1919; Smith, Robert B. 1919

Man Song   Cahn Date Unknown; Styne Date Unknown

Man that Can Die Like a Soldier, A   Herbert 1917

Man that Got Away, The   Arlen 1954; Gershwin, Ira 1954

Man that Leads the Band that Leads the Army, The   Edwards 1905; Smith, Robert B. 1905

Man, the Master   Gershwin, Ira 1923

Man to Cook For, A   Berlin 1963

Man Upstairs, The   Duke 1940

Man Who Came to Win 'Er, The   Dubin 1940; Fain 1940

Man Who Had Power Over Women, The   David, Hal 1970

Man Who Has Everything, The   Rodgers 1962

Man Who Has It All, The   Drake 1994

Man Who Invented Ice Cream, The   Cahn 1980; Strouse 1980

Man Who Looks Like a Fool, A   David, Hal 1978

Man Who Owns Broadway, The   Cohan 1909

Man Who Owns the Sunshine, The   Van Heusen 1956

Man Who Shot Liberty Valance, The   Bacharach 1961; David, Hal 1961

Man Who Wrote "The Vampire" (Must Have Known My Wife), The   Buck 1914

Man with a Dream, A   Young, Victor 1955

Man with a Horn   De Lange 1946

Man with a Plan, A   Comden and Green 1961; Styne 1961

Man with Golden Dreams, The   David, Mack 1964

Man with the Cigarette, The   Gorney 1945

Man with the Curly Mustache, The   David, Mack 1944

Man with the Golden Arm   Cahn 1955; Van Heusen 1955

Man with the Initials, The   Harburg 1946

Man with the Lantern of Love, The   Dixon 1931; Leslie 1931; Meyer 1931

Man with the Lollypop Song, The   Gordon 1941; Warren 1941

Man with the Tambourine, The   Smith, Harry B. 1901

Man with the Weird Beard, The   Hoffman 1945; Livingston, Jerry 1945

Man with the Whiskers (And the Apple Cheeks), The   Stept 1953

Man Without a Woman, A   Schwartz, Arthur 1942

Man Worth Fightin' For, A   Adams 1981; Strouse 1981

Man You Are, The   Duke 1968

(I've Got a) Manager in Heaven   Robison 1950

Manana   Lane 1941; Loesser 1941; Rainger 1935; Robin 1935; Whiting 1935

Manchurian Candidate, The   Webster 1963

Manda   Blake 1924; Sissle 1924

Mandalay   Mitchell 1921; Pollack 1921

Mandalay Song, The   Weill 1977

Mandarin Palace on the Grand Concourse, The   David, Mack 1973; Livingston, Jerry 1973

Mandel   Lewis 1929; Pollack 1929; Young, Joe 1929

Mandolin and the Man, The   DeSylva 1920; Kern 1920

Mandolin Serenade   Smith, Harry B. 1900

Mandolola (inst.)   Meyer 1910

Mandy   Berlin 1918; Edwards 1907; Smith, Harry B. 1901; Turk 1922

Mandy Come Along   Howard, Joseph E. 1950

Mandy, I'm Just Wild about You   Waller 1924

Mandy Is Two   Mercer 1942

Mandy Make Up Your Mind   Clarke 1924; Johnston 1924; Meyer 1924; Turk 1924

Mandy 'n' Me   Conrad 1921; Kalmar 1921; Motzan 1921

Mandy's Blessing   Johnson, James P. 1947

Manhattan   Hart 1922, 1925; Rodgers 1922, 1925

Manhattan Beach March (inst.)   Willson 1965

Manhattan Downbeat   Gershwin, Ira 1949; Warren 1949

Manhattan Holiday   Styne 1940

Manhattan in the Spring   Carmichael 1940

Manhattan Mad   Atteridge 1915; Romberg 1915

Manhattan Madness   Berlin 1932

Manhattan Mary   Brown, Lew 1927; DeSylva 1927; Henderson 1927

Manhattan Masquerade (inst.)   Alter 1932

Manhattan Melodrama   Hart 1934; Rodgers 1934

Manhattan Melody   Warren Date Unknown

Manhattan Moonlight (inst.)   Alter 1930

Manhattan News Beat   Oakland 1960

Manhattan Nights   Caesar 1922

Manhattan Rag (inst.)   Carmichael 1956

Manhattan Serenade   Adamson 1942; Alter 1930, 1942; Johnson, Howard 1930

Manhattan Showboat   Cahn 1980

Manhattan Walk   Kalmar 1928; Ruby 1928

Manhattan (What a Town)   Cahn 1963

Manhattan's the Loneliest Isle   Duke 1932; Harburg 1932

Manhunt   Brooks 1959

Manic Depressives (Don't Do Rewrites)   Merrill 1971; Styne 1971

Manicure Girl, The   Kern 1911

Manita Wanna Eat, Wanna Eat   Coslow 1923

Manners and Motions   Coslow 1924; Romberg 1924

Mannikin   Young, Joe 1932

Mannikin Dolls   Atteridge 1929

Manpower   Bacharach 1961

Man's a Man for A' That, A   Herbert 1911

Man's Delight, A   Oakland 1968

Man's Favorite Sport   Mancini 1963; Mercer 1963

Man's Got a Right, A   Leigh 1955; Spina 1955

Man's Gotta Be (What He's Born to Be), A   Sherman 1973

Man's Gotta Fight, A   Arlen 1946; Mercer 1946

Man's in the Navy, The   Loesser 1940

Man's Inhumanity to Man   Strouse 1955

Mansion of Aching Hearts, The   Von Tilzer 1902

Mansion of Roses, The   Bryan 1920; Schwartz, Jean 1920

Mansion Sin Amor (Without Love in a Palace of Dreams)   Gilbert 1933

Manuela   Porter 1948

Manuelo   Fain 1941; Kahal 1941; Yellen 1941

Manuelo Tarantel, The   Sigman 1949

Manx   Mercer 1965

Many a Lofty Mountain   Hammerstein 1938; Kern 1938

Many a New Day   Hammerstein 1943; Rodgers 1943

Many a Wonderful Moment   David, Hal 1960

Many Dreams Ago   Ahlert 1939; David, Mack 1954
Many Happy Returns   Dietz 1945
Many Happy Returns of the Day   Dubin 1931
Many Kinds of Love   Arlen 1959; Mercer 1959
Many Moons Ago   Gordon 1933; Revel 1933
Many People Live Inside My Mind   David, Hal 1974
Many Tears on Many Pillows   David, Hal 1961
Many Thanks for the Dance   David, Mack 1934
Many Ways to Skin a Cat   Mercer 1964
Many Years Ago   Olcott 1901
Many Young Men from Now   Drake 1968
Manyana   Parish 1920
Many's the Time   Fisher 1907; Freed, Ralph 1960
Manzinata (inst.)   Revel 1960
Maple Leaf Rag   Russell 1950; Styne 1950
Mapleton High Chorale   Gershwin, Ira 1940; Weill 1940
Maracas   Ruby 1947
Marahuana   Coslow 1934; Johnston 1934
Marathon Step, The   Cohan 1923
Marc Antony   Atteridge 1915; Carroll 1915; Romberg 1915
Marcelina   Stept 1934
Marceline's Meat Sauce   Smith, Robert B. 1907
Marcelle   Bryan 1920; Schwartz, Jean 1920
Marcelle Wahine Special   Oakland 1960; Raye 1960
March   Herbert 1895, 1897, 1906; Smith, Harry B. 1895, 1897
March Ahead   Weill 1977
March Birthday Song   Caesar 1940
March, Book Dance   Atteridge 1914; Romberg 1914
March Boys March   Cobb 1905; Edwards 1905
March Chorus and Entrance of the Regent   Herbert 1911; Smith, Harry B. 1911
March for Queen Kelly   Fain 1932; Kahal 1932
March Goes in Like a Lion   Spina 1957
March (inst.)   Kern 1945
March Louis XI (inst.)   Rodgers 1923
March, March   Comden and Green 1955
March, March, March the Boys Are Tramping   Kahn 1940
March of Cards, The   Fain 1951
March of the Cardinals   Cohan 1937
March of the Dogies, The   Mercer 1945; Warren 1945
March of the Dolls (inst.)   Bloom 1927
March of the Enchantress   Goetz 1917
March of the Flags   Jerome 1904; Schwartz, Jean 1904
March of the Frisco Chinks   Cohan 1904
March of the Grenadiers (inst.)   Fain 1963
March of the Hoodlums (inst.)   Carmichael 1956
March of the Ill-Assorted Guards, The   Livingston, Jerry 1956
March of the King's Amazons   Cohan 1909
March of the Musketeers   Friml 1928
March of the Mystic Shrine   Lewis 1913; Meyer 1913
March of the Owls   Heyman 1939; Romberg 1939
March of the Prince's Regiment   Herbert 1911; Smith, Harry B. 1911
March of the Sengalese (inst.)   Blake 1946
March of the Spades (inst.)   Waller 1945
March of the Toys   Herbert 1903
March of the Valentines   Herbert 1908; Smith, Harry B. 1908
March of the Yuppies   Strouse 1985
March of Time, The   Alter 1933; Arlen 1930; Koehler 1930
March On   Friml 1918; Smith, Harry B. 1925
March Out of My Life   Lerner, Alan Jay 1971
March Song   Atteridge 1915; Loesser 1937
March to Freedom (inst.)   Willson 1959
March to Zion, The   Weill 1937

Marcha Del Toros   Fields 1956; Kern 1956
Marches   Buck 1922
Marches (inst.)   Herbert 1922
Marchin' Towards Ya', Georgia   Friend 1934
Marching Along   Bergman 1958; Brown, Nacio Herb 1935; Freed, Arthur Date Unknown
Marching Along (Plymouth Welcome Song)   Gordon 1938; Revel 1938
Marching Along Together   Dixon 1933
Marching By   Edwards 1932
Marching Down the Aisle   Monaco 1923; Rose 1923
Marching Home with Rosie   Sterling 1905; Von Tilzer 1905
Marching Polka, The   Blane 1957
Marching Song, The   Gilbert 1933
Marching Thru Mexico   David, Mack 1934
Marching to the Fight   Leigh 1955
Marching to the Music of the Stars   Brennan 1936
Marching with Johnny   Eliscu 1943; Gorney 1943
Marcho Poco (inst.)   Coots 1947
Marconigram   Atteridge 1915; Romberg 1915
Marco's Rebuttal   Adamson 1954; Warren 1954
Mardi Gras   Arlen 1954; Coleman 1966; Eliscu 1929; Herbert 1909; Martin 1952; Rose 1929; Youmans 1929
Mardi Gras March, The   Fain 1958; Webster 1958
Mardi Gras Parade   Spina 1959
Mardi Gras Waltz, The   McHugh 1962; Washington 1962
Mardi Gras (While We Danced at the Mardi Gras)   Mercer 1931
Margarita   Leslie 1909
Margie   Conrad 1920; Davis 1920
Margie, Who's Watching the Baby   David, Mack 1972
Margineers, The   Fields 1930, 1933; McHugh 1930, 1933
Margo   Adams 1996; Strouse 1996
Margo's Theme   Adams 1970; Strouse 1970
Margot   Hammerstein 1926; Harbach 1926; Romberg 1926
Marguerita   Revel 1946
Marguerita's Getting Mad   Oakland 1967
Marguerite's Waltz   Willson 1952
Maria   Dietz 1934; Hammerstein 1959; Porter 1938; Rodgers 1959; Schwartz, Arthur 1934; Sondheim 1957
Maria (Annina)   Friml 1934
Maria Elena   Russell 1941
Maria Inez   Gilbert 1941
Maria Maria Maria   Raye 1954
Maria Marimba   Evans 1955; Livingston, Jay 1955
Maria Mia   Motzan 1934; Sigman 1946
Maria My Own (Intermedia, Maria La O)   Gilbert 1931
Mariachi Serenade, The   Drake 1946
(Fiesta) Mariachie   Kahn 1938; Romberg 1938
Marian   Donaldson 1926; Silver 1925
Marian the Librarian   Willson 1957
Marianina   Donaldson 1938
Marianna   Webster 1961
Marianne   Ahlert 1929; De Lange 1940; Hammerstein 1928; Myrow 1940; Romberg 1928; Turk 1929
Marianni   Bergman 1958
Marie   Berlin 1928; Motzan 1921; Smith, Harry B. 1911; Williams 1909
Marie Ann   Leslie 1910
Marie from Sunny Italy   Berlin 1907
Marie, Marie   Smith, Harry B. 1908
Marie, Marie, Marie!   Brown, Nacio Herb 1925
Marie of the High Sea   Coots 1954
Marie-Louise   Kern 1912
Marigold, Marry Me   Brooks 1960

Marilyn   David, Mack 1967; Drake 1952
Marilyn (inst.)   Alter 1926
Marina   Harbach 1914
Marinella   Parish 1937
Marine's Gun Drill   Styne 1985
Marines Have Landed, The   Drake 1952; Monaco 1942
Marines' Hymn, The   Adamson 1951; McHugh 1951
Marinka   Johnson, Howard 1920
Marion   Pollack 1928; Robison 1958
Marion Davies March (inst.), The   Herbert 1922
Marionette   Drake 1949
Marionettes   Romberg 1925; Smith, Harry B. 1916, 1925; Smith, Robert B. 1916
Marionettes (inst.)   Motzan 1928
Mariutch Make-a the Hootch and Ma Kooch Down at Coney Isle   Sterling 1907; Von Tilzer 1907
Marjorie   Atteridge 1924
Marjorie Morningstar   Adams Date Unknown; Strouse Date Unknown
Mark Anthony   Atteridge 1915; Romberg 1915
Mark of a Man, The   Lerner, Alan Jay 1976
Mark of the Gun   Freed, Ralph 1964
Mark Twain Suite (inst.)   Kern 1942
Market Day   Romberg 1925
Market Day in the Village   Caesar 1936
Market Looks Great, The   Brooks 1959
Market Square   Herbert 1900; Smith, Harry B. 1900
Marking Eyes   Sterling 1905; Von Tilzer 1905
Marlen (You Are My Song of Songs)   Heyman 1933
Marlon Mood, The   Comden and Green 1956; Styne 1956
Marmalade, Molasses and Honey   Bergman 1972
Marriage   Rome 1970
Marriage a la Mode   Lane 1965; Lerner, Alan Jay 1965
Marriage C.O.D.   Hammerstein 1922; Mitchell 1922
Marriage Contract   Lane 1965
Marriage Game   Edwards 1909; Smith, Robert B. 1909
Marriage Is a Game of Blind Man's Bluff   Smith, Harry B. 1935
Marriage Is Sublime   Bryan 1903
Marriage of Convenience, A   Russell 1948
Marriage on the Rocks   Cahn 1965; Van Heusen 1965
Marriage Type Love   Hammerstein 1953; Rodgers 1953
Marriage Waltz, The   Razaf 1950
Marriage (Wedding) Song   Coleman 1979
Marriage-Go-Round   Bergman 1961
Married Couple Seeks Married Couple   Coleman 1977
Married Life   Friml 1917; Harbach 1917; Herbert 1914; Smith, Robert B. 1914; Strouse 1991
Married Life Blues   Harbach 1923
Married Man Makes the Best Soldier   Romberg 1916
Married Men and Single Men   Brown, Lew 1929; DeSylva 1929; Henderson 1929
Married Ten Weeks   Webster 1983
Marry a Girl from the Ten Cent Store   Von Tilzer 1916
Marry a Rich Woman   Adamson 1954
Marry a Sunshine Girl   Goetz 1912
Marry a Woman Uglier Than You   DePaul 1958; Raye 1958
Marry a Yiddisher Boy   Brown, A. Seymour 1912
Marry Me and See   Herbert 1920; Smith, Harry B. 1916; Smith, Robert B. 1916, 1920
Marry Me in Laramie   Carmichael 1959
Marry Me, Marry Me   Webster 1956
Marry Me Now   Coleman 1991; Comden and Green 1991
Marry the Girl You Love   Kahn 1914; Whiting 1914
Marry the Man   David, Hal 1955

Marry the Man Today   Loesser 1950
Marry Young   Coleman 1959; Leigh 1959
Marrying for Fun   Rome 1973
Marrying for Love   Berlin 1950
Mars Meditates (inst.)   Revel 1955
Mars Sequence (inst.)   Henderson 1930
Marsa's Come Home to Stay   Evans 1947; Livingston, Jay 1947; Young, Victor 1947
Marseilles   Atteridge 1919; Romberg 1919; Schwartz, Jean 1919
Marshmallow Moon   Evans 1952; Livingston, Jay 1952
Marshmallow World, A   Sigman 1949
Marta, Rambling Rose of the Wildwood   Gilbert 1931
Martin Luther Drinking Song   Romberg 1925; Smith, Harry B. 1925
Martina   Merrill 1990
Martinique   Adamson 1940; Alter 1935; Brooks 1947; Carmichael Date Unknown; Porter 1948
Martitia   Bacharach 1956; David, Hal 1956
Marty   Strouse 1999
Marty Hogan Theme   Oakland 1954
Marvelous Fire Machine   Merrill 1959
(There Never Was a Girl Named) Mary   Bryan 1953; Caesar 1923; Donaldson 1927; Harbach 1920
Mary and Doug   Buck 1920
Mary and John   Bryan 1918; Leslie 1918
Mary Ann   Carroll 1950; Davis 1927; Howard, Joseph E. 1911; Jerome 1910; Schwartz, Jean 1910; Silver 1927
Mary Beaty's Birthday   Sondheim Date Unknown
Mary Brown   Berlin 1917
Mary Came Over to Me   Caesar 1922; Herbert 1922
Mary Christmas   Freed, Ralph 1965
Mary Dear, I Miss You Most of All   Hanley 1926
Mary Does Everything but Sing   Carroll 1916
Mary Drew   Herbert 1911
Mary Dugan I Love You   Parish 1929
Mary from Maryland   Smith, Harry B. 1903
Mary from Tipperary   Johnson, J. Rosamond 1904
Mary Gave Him the Merry Ha Ha   Bryan 1909
Mary Had a Little Lamb   Dubin 1926; Johnson, Howard 1939
M-A-R-Y, I Love Y-O-U   Gordon 1929
Mary I'm in Love with You   Coots 1931
Mary Is a Real Good Fellow but Mary Is a Real Good Girl   Akst 1922; Caesar 1922
Mary Jane   Razaf 1931
Mary Jane McKane   Hammerstein 1923; Youmans 1923
Mary Lou Wilson and Johnny Brown   Livingston, Jerry 1959
Mary Louise   Gershwin, Ira 1923
Mary Loves a Sailor   Fisher 1920
Mary, Mary   Herbert 1903; Howard, Joseph E. 1910
M-a-r-y, Mary A Double R, Mary Ann   Sterling 1910
Mary, Mary, Quite Contrary   Lane 1938; Loesser 1938
Mary McGee   Kern 1907
Mary Pickford, the Darling of Them All   Whiting 1914
Mary Pistoglione   Rome 1969
Mary, Queen of Heaven   Robin 1930
Mary Queen of Scots   Rodgers 1920
Mary Rose   Buck 1923
Mary, the Milkman's Daughter   Bryan 1938
Mary, the Mother of Eternity   Young, Joe 1958
Mary to the Market Went   Egan 1925; Kahn 1925
Mary Tracy, How Would You Like to Become a Casey   Jerome 1921; Schwartz, Jean 1921
Mary Was a Manicure   Johnson, J. Rosamond 1904

Mary Went 'Round and Around and Around (With a Bumpty Umpty Ay)   Bryan 1911; Fisher 1911

Mary Wise   Williams 1907

Maryland Scene   Porter 1922

Mary's a Grand Old Name   Cohan 1906

Mary's Coming Home   Dubin 1913

Mary's Favorite Poem   Robison 1958

Mary's Lamb   Herbert 1897; Howard, Joseph E. Date Unknown; Smith, Harry B. 1897

Mary's Prayer   Livingston, Jerry 1960

Mascot of the Moon (Mascot of the Troup)   Herbert 1905

Masculine Women! Feminine Men!   Leslie 1925; Monaco 1925

Masculinity   Lawrence 1951

Mashed Potatoes   Coslow 1935; Whiting 1935

Masher Is a Bad, Bad Boy, A   Adamson 1938; McHugh 1938

Masie McIntyre   Sterling 1905; Von Tilzer 1905

Masks   Buck 1921

Mason City, Iowa   Willson 1954

Mason Dixon Blues   Atteridge 1921; Pollack 1921; Schwartz, Jean 1921

Mason Dixon Line   Gordon 1940; Warren 1940

Masque, The   Rodgers 1976

Masquerade   Webster 1931

Masquerading Is the Name of Love   Hoffman 1933

Mass in Honor of Saint Anthony   Warren 1958

Mass Retaliation   Oakland 1963

Massachusetts   McHugh 1962; Razaf 1942

Massachusetts Mermaid   Dietz 1948; Schwartz, Arthur 1948

Massacre, The   Merrill 1972; Styne 1972

Massa's in de Cold Ground   Johnson, Howard 1939

Masstoso   Herbert 1898; Smith, Harry B. 1898

Master Is Free Again   Gershwin, Ira 1945; Weill 1945

Master of the Greatest Art of All, The   Bergman 1964; Fain 1964

Matador   Mercer 1956; Russell 1948

Matador Song   Brown, Lew 1932; Henderson 1932

Matador's Prayer, The   David, Mack 1953

Match Makers, The   Harbach 1914

Matches Burn   Merrill 1958

Mates   Sherman 1995

Matinee   Russell 1947; Sigman 1947

Matinee Girls   Smith, Harry B. 1900

Matinee Maid   Herbert 1904

Mating Game, The   Adams 1959; Strouse 1959

Mating Season, The   Evans 1951; Livingston, Jay 1951

Matrimonial Handicap, The   DeSylva 1924; Gershwin, George 1924

Matrimonial Stomp, The   DePaul 1956; Mercer 1956

Matrimony   Smith, Harry B. 1911; Smith, Robert B. 1911

Matrimony Rag   Leslie 1911

Matter of Consequence   Lerner, Alan Jay 1974; Loewe 1974

Matter of Who, A   Russell 1962

Matthew A. Henson   Razaf 1944

Maude Adams of the Screen, The   Atteridge 1914; Romberg 1914

Maudita   Conrad 1929; Mitchell 1929

Mauna Loa   Mills 1928

Maverick   Merrill 1958; Webster 1958

Maverick Queen, The   Washington 1956; Young, Victor 1956

Max Jacobs   Coleman 1978; Comden and Green 1978

Maxie, Don't Take a Taxi   Lewis 1910

Maxie Jones, King of the Saxie-Phones   Clarke 1923; Leslie 1923

Maxim's   Hart 1934; Kahn 1934; Webster 1952

May All Our Children Have Rhythm   Caesar 1943

May and January   Weill 1938

May Birthday Song   Caesar 1940

May Day   Rome 1937

May Day March   Herbert 1908; Smith, Harry B. 1908

May Fuzzy   Bryan 1907

May I?   Gordon 1933, 1934; Revel 1933, 1934

May I Come to See You, Dear, Tonight?   Romberg 1924

May I Do   Oakland 1929

May I Drop a Petal in Your Glass of Wine   Gordon 1938; Revel 1938

May I Have My Gloves?   Henderson 1935; Yellen 1935

May I Have the Next Dance with You?   Burke 1931

May I Have the Next Dream with You?   Coslow 1935, 1937

May I Have the Next Romance with You?   Gordon 1936; Revel 1936

May I Have the Next Trance with You   Coslow 1942

May I Present   Blane 1969

May I Say   David, Mack 1964

May I Say I Love You?   Coots 1929; Davis 1929

May I Sing to You   Akst 1953

May I Still Hold You   Russell 1947

May I Still Hold You (When the Dance Is Over)   Russell 1949

May I Suggest Romance   Loewe 1938

May I Take Two Giant Steps   Drake 1950

May I Tempt You with a Big Red Rosy Apple   Gordon 1950; Myrow 1950

May in Mexico   Wrubel 1943

May in Monte Carlo   Livingston, Jerry 1958

May in Monterey   Rainger 1936; Robin 1936

May Is the Month That I May   Russell 1956

May Night   Brown, Nacio Herb 1948

May Tells All   Hammerstein 1939; Kern 1939

May the Best Man Win   Burke 1946; Strouse 1991; Van Heusen 1946

May the Good Lord Bless You and Keep You   Willson 1950

May We Entertain You   Sondheim 1959; Styne 1959

May Your Blessings Be Many   Young, Victor 1953

May Your Heart Stay Young (L'Chayim)   Rome 1965

Maybe   Bacharach 1983; Davis 1920; Gershwin, George 1926; Gershwin, Ira 1926; Hart 1926; Leslie 1919; Rodgers 1926; Ruby 1919; Smith, Harry B. 1918; Spina 1937; Strouse 1977

Maybe a Day, Maybe a Year   Gilbert 1914; Monaco 1914

Maybe, Baby, Maybe   Livingston, Jerry 1960

Maybe God Is Black   Oakland 1967

Maybe He's Some Kinda Crazy   Loesser 1956

Maybe I Don't   Whiting 1926

Maybe I Love You, Cause You're Wrong, All Wrong   Johnson, Howard 1917; Monaco 1917

Maybe I Love You Too Much   Berlin 1933

Maybe I Ought to Stay   Livingston, Jerry 1973

Maybe I Should Change My Ways   Ellington 1946

Maybe I Will   Caesar 1927

Maybe I'll Baby You   Buck 1927

Maybe in a Dream   Rainger 1932; Robin 1932

Maybe It's a Bear   Edwards 1908

Maybe It's a Woman's World   Blane 1952

Maybe It's All for the Best   Lewis 1923; Meyer 1923; Rose 1928; Young, Joe 1923

Maybe It's Because   Ruby 1949

Maybe It's Love   Meyer 1930; Mitchell 1930

Maybe It's Me   Hart 1926; Rodgers 1926

Maybe It's the Mood I'm In   David, Hal 1953

Maybe It's the Moon   Donaldson 1937, 1940; Whiting 1931

Maybe It's You   Harbach 1930; Kern 1930

Maybe Land   Atteridge 1914; Carroll 1914; Romberg 1914

Maybe, Maybe, Maybe   David, Mack 1956; Rodgers 1979

Maybe, Maybe Not   Adams 1993

Maybe Means Yes   Fields 1928; McHugh 1928

Maybe September   Evans 1966; Livingston, Jay 1966

Maybe She Will Some Day   Bryan 1913

Maybe (She'll Write Me) (She'll Phone Me)   Ahlert 1924; Snyder 1924; Turk 1924

Maybe Some Other Time   Drake 1964

Maybe, Someday   Friend 1930; Monaco 1930

Maybe Sometime   Kahn 1917

Maybe that Is Why I'm Lonely   Meyer 1911

Maybe There's More.   Coleman 1972

Maybe They're Magic   Sondheim 1987

Maybe This Is Love   Brown, Lew 1928; DeSylva 1928; Henderson 1928

Maybe Tomorrow   Bergman 1969

Maybe Tomorrow but Not Today   David, Hal 1961

Maybe We'd Still Be Sweethearts (If We Hadn't Listened to Friends)   Davis 1936

Maybe Yes, Maybe No   Porter 1930

Maybe Yes, Maybe No, Who Can Tell   Dubin 1926; Fain 1926; Kahal 1926

Maybe You Know What I Mean   Carmichael 1935; Mercer 1935

Maybe You Think I'm Happy   Gilbert 1911

Maybe You Were Made for Me   Bryan 1910

Maybe You Will Love Me, Sweetheart, As I Love You   Johnson, J. Rosamond 1928

Maybe You Will, Maybe You Won't   Dixon 1924; Rose 1925; Warren 1925

Maybe You Would If You Could   Bryan 1908; Meyer 1908

Maybe You'll Be There   Bloom 1947

Maybe You're Not the Right Girl After All   Kalmar 1911

Maybe You're Not the Right Girl (One) After All   Snyder 1911

Maybells   Atteridge 1924; Romberg 1924; Schwartz, Jean 1924

Maydee (Pretty Little South Sea Island Lady)   Von Tilzer 1903

Mayer Come Back from Hawaii   Brown, Lew 1917

Mayfair (inst.)   Stept 1936

Mayflower Girl   Hanley 1916; Romberg 1916; Smith, Harry B. 1916

Mayflower I Love You   Coots 1925

Mayor   Strouse 1985

Mayor of Harlem, The   Bloom 1939; Koehler 1939

Mayor's Entrance   Young, Victor 1952

Maypole Dance (inst.)   Romberg 1945

Maytime   DeSylva 1924

Maze, The   Strouse 1980

Mazeppa (inst.)   Schwartz, Jean 1909

Mazie   Rainger 1933

Mazuma   Atteridge 1922; Herbert 1914; Romberg 1922

Mazurka   Herbert 1899; Smith, Harry B. 1899

Mazurka (inst.)   Duke 1963; Styne 1953

McElwes   Snyder 1909

McGinnis   Jerome 1908; Schwartz, Jean 1908

McGuire Esquire   Kern 1905

McHugh's Melody (inst.)   McHugh 1949

McInerney's Farm   Fain 1946

McKinley Inaugural (inst.)   Herbert 1897

Me!   Berlin 1931; Cahn 1969; David, Hal 1962; Smith, Harry B. 1926

Me & Thee   Leigh 1985; Styne 1985

Me an' My Boss   Hammerstein 1928; Kern 1928

Me an' My Bundle   Berlin 1949

Me and Anthony Adverse in the Morning   Egan 1934

Me and Him   Cahn 1977

Me and Jane in a 'Plane   Leslie 1927

Me and Mamie O'Brien   Woods 1925

Me and Mandy Lee   Gilbert 1914

Me and Marie   Porter 1935

Me and Mine Are Doin' Fine   Woods 1933

Me and My Baby   Cahn 1958; Warren 1958

Me and My Buddy   Ager 1929; Yellen 1929

Me and My Fella and a Big Umbrella   Rainger 1942; Robin 1942

Me and My Imagination   Hoffman 1950; Merrill 1950

Me and My Melinda   Berlin 1942

Me and My Old World Charm   Waller 1943

Me and My Piano   Caesar 1952; Woods 1957

Me and My Puppy Dog   Coots 1955

Me and My Shadow   Rose 1927

Me and My Teddy Bear   Coots 1950

Me and My Town   Sondheim 1964

Me and Myself   Egan 1925; Kahn 1925; Whiting 1925

Me and Pollyanna   Fields 1954; Schwartz, Arthur 1954

Me and the Blues   Koehler 1946; Warren 1946

Me and the Boy Friend   Clare 1924; Monaco 1925

Me and the Evening   Monaco 1940

Me and the Ghost Upstairs   Mercer 1940

Me and the Man in the Moon   Leslie 1928; Monaco 1928

Me and the Role and You   Hammerstein 1939; Kern 1939

Me and Thee   Styne 1985

Me and You   Akst 1918; Ellington 1940; Gorney 1924; Styne 1970

Me and Your Cigarette   David, Hal 1948

Me for You   Hart 1929; Rodgers 1929

Me for You Forever   Heyman 1933; Revel 1943; Webster 1943

Me Go Where You Go, Amigo   Razaf 1946

Me Japanese Boy, I Love You   Bacharach 1964; David, Hal 1964

Me Lord and Me Lady   Egan 1933

Me Minus You   Baer 1931; Webster 1932

Me Myself and I   Webster 1950

Me, Myself and I (I and Myself and Me)   Herbert 1905

Me 'n' You   Schwartz, Arthur 1928

Me 'n' You 'n' Him   Egan 1938

Me 'n' You 'n' the Moon   Cahn 1956; Van Heusen 1956

Me Oh My Oh Man Do I Miss Milwaukee   Strouse 1987

Me Old Bamboo   Sherman 1968

Me that I Want to Be, The   Martin 1973

Me Too   Woods 1926

Me Without You   Robin 1934, 1936

Me You See, The   Dixon 1953; Henderson 1955; Rose 1955

Meadow, The   Russell 1977

Meadow Scandal, A   Young, Victor 1923

Meadow Serenade   Gershwin, George 1927; Gershwin, Ira 1927

Meadow Serenade — Verse   Lane 1987

Meadowland   Rome 1943

Meadowland   Rome 1943

Mean and Melancholy   Robison 1954

Mean Man   Eliscu 1929; Rose 1929; Youmans 1929

Mean Mean Mean   Parish 1923

Mean Tight Woman   Razaf 1974

Mean to Me   Ahlert 1929; Turk 1929

Meana Chimes   Motzan 1924

Meanest Gal in Town, The   De Lange 1934

Meanest Man in Town, The   Bryan 1907; Fisher 1907

Meaning of Spring, The   Livingston, Jerry 1967

Meaning of the Name of Kelly, The   Alter 1930; Johnson, Howard 1930

Meant to Tell Yuh   Mercer 1952

Meanwhile   Adams 1966; Alter 1953; Sigman 1980; Strouse 1966

Meanwhile Back at the Ranch   Brooks 1959

Meany, Meany   Sigman 1951

Meany Miny Moe   Loesser 1937

Meat and Potatoes   Berlin 1962; Coleman 1972; Fields 1972

Mecca   Atteridge 1921

Mechanical Bird, The   Strouse 1982

Mechanical Lovin' Man   Ager 1913

Mechanical Man   Dubin 1929

Mechanical Soldiers   Atteridge 1915; Romberg 1915

Medfield Fight Song (Absent-Minded Professor March)   Sherman 1961

Media Luz, A   Johnson, Howard 1936

Medicine Show, The   Hart 1932; Rodgers 1932

Medicine Show Is Coming to Town   Bergman 1954

Meditation Brings Me You   Johnson, Howard 1929

Meditation (inst.)   Waller 1927

Mediterranean Love   Carmichael 1958

Mediterranean Nights   Coslow 1924

Mediterrania   Brown, Lew 1925; Cobb 1921; Edwards 1921; Stept 1925

Medium Couldn't Get Through, The   Mercer 1979

Medley   Edwards 1929

Meerahlah   Porter 1946

Meet a Happy Guy   Evans 1954; Livingston, Jay 1954

Meet Captain Kidd   Russell 1952

Meet Her with a Taximeter   Kern 1908

Meet Me After the Show   Robin 1951; Styne 1951

Meet Me at Eight in the Hall   Atteridge 1912

Meet Me at Meetin' Time   Robison 1963

Meet Me at the College Bowl   Loesser 1951

Meet Me at the Copa   Cahn 1950

Meet Me at the Fair   Schwartz, Arthur 1937

Meet Me at the Masquerade   Smith, Harry B. 1908

Meet Me at the New York World's Fair   Howard, Joseph E. 1937

Meet Me at the Stage Door   Goetz 1912

Meet Me at the Station   Smith, Harry B. 1908

Meet Me at the Station, Dear   Lewis 1917; Young, Joe 1917

Meet Me at the Station, Dear (Dearie)   Snyder 1917

Meet Me at the Tabarin   Smith, Harry B. 1908

Meet Me at Twilight   Kern 1906

Meet Me Beside the River   Porter 1913

Meet Me Down By the River   Williams 1910

Meet Me Down on Main Street   Kern 1923

Meet Me Halfway   Drake 1968

Meet Me in Las Vegas   Cahn 1956

Meet Me in Orange Blossom Time   Norworth 1917

Meet Me in Rose Time Rosie   Brown, A. Seymour 1909; Cohan 1908

Meet Me in Roseland   McHugh 1924

Meet Me in Rosetime, Rosie   Jerome 1908; Schwartz, Jean 1908

Meet Me in St. Louis, Louis   Sterling 1904

Meet Me in the Gloaming   Freed, Arthur 1933; Hoffman 1933

Meet Me in the Moonlight   Conrad 1927; Davis 1927

Meet Me in the Moonlight (With the Lovelight in Your Eyes)   Friend 1926; Kahn 1926

Meet Me in the Wisteria   Edwards 1905; Smith, Robert B. 1905

Meet Me on the Fence Tonight   Jerome 1905; Schwartz, Jean 1905

Meet Me Out on the Golf Course   DePaul 1958; Raye 1958

Meet Me To-Morrow Night   Williams 1913; Young, Joe 1913

Meet Me To-Night   Berlin 1911

Meet Me Tonight in the Cowshed   Conrad 1932

Meet Me when I Come Back Home   Whiting 1915

Meet Me when the Stars Are All Aglow   Sterling 1918

Meet Miss America   Mercer 1935

Meet Miss Blendo   Mercer 1951

Meet Miss Victory   Caesar 1943

Meet Mister Callaghan   Drake 1952

Meet Mister Hines that Piano Man   Razaf 1934

Meet My Girl   Leigh 1965

Meet My Mother   Hart Date Unknown; Rodgers Date Unknown

Meet My Seester   Cahn 1970; Styne 1970

Meet My Sister   Brennan 1929

Meet the Beat of My Heart   Gordon 1938; Revel 1938

Meet the Boy Friend — Don't Laugh   Eliscu 1929; Rose 1929; Youmans 1929

Meet the Elite   Dubin 1940; Fain 1940

Meet the King   Johnston 1934

Meet the Man About Town   Parish 1933

Meet the People   Gorney 1940

Meet the President   Cahn 1935

Meet the Press   Styne 1964

Meet the Sun Halfway   Burke 1940; Monaco 1940

Meet the Wife   Sterling 1922; Von Tilzer 1922

Meet the World   Sherman 1983

Meetcha 'Round the Corner   Livingston, Jay 1948

Meeting Time   Evans 1956; Livingston, Jay 1956

Meetin's Called to Order, The   Razaf 1936

Megatron Ballet   Coleman 1973

Me-ha-lani Papa-doo (Hoy Hoy)   David, Mack 1947; Livingston, Jerry 1947

Mei Lan-Fong (inst.)   Duke 1930

Mein Kleine Akrobat   Dietz 1932; Schwartz, Arthur 1932

Mein Shana Hadass   Bergman 1983

Melancholy   Friend 1923; Whiting 1926

Melancholy Blues   Caesar 1922

Melancholy Lullaby   Heyman 1939

Melancholy Madonna   Livingston, Jerry 1960

Melancholy Me   Henderson 1927; Johnson, Howard 1927; Loesser 1929

Melancholy Melody   Davis 1955; Donaldson 1925; Kahn 1925

Melancholy Moon   Coleman 1958; Leigh 1958

Melancholy Nights Who's Afraid of You Now   Young, Joe 1934

Melancholy Rhapsody   Cahn 1950

Melancholy Sally   Monaco 1928

Melancholy Sunbeam and the Rose   Jerome 1904; Schwartz, Jean 1904

Melancholy Trumpet (Ooh-wah), The   David, Hal 1952

Melange (inst.)   Warren 1974

Melican Man, A   Hart 1926; Rodgers 1926

'Melican Papa (Chink Song)   Kern 1921

Melinda   Lane 1965; Lerner, Alan Jay 1965

Melinda the Mousie   Myrow 1943

Mellow Music and Moonlight   Johnson, Howard 1935

Melodic Rag (inst.)   Blake 1972

Melodies of May   Hammerstein 1932; Kern 1932

Melodies Within My Heart   Brennan 1928

Melodrama   Herbert 1915

Melodrama Known As Married Life   Atteridge 1913; Schwartz, Jean 1913

Melodrame (inst.)   Henderson 1929

Melody   Caesar 1933; Evans 1949; Livingston, Jay 1949; Romberg 1933; Webster 1953

(I Must Have) Melody and Moonlight   Styne 1940

Melody Farm   Kahn 1938

Melody for Cello (inst.)   Kern 1956

Melody for Two   Dubin 1937; Warren 1937

Melody for Two Sonnets, A   Raye 1962

Melody from the Sky (Love Is Everywhere), A   Alter 1936; Mitchell 1936

Melody Has to Be Right, The   Robin 1947

Melody in F (inst.)   Kern 1956

Melody in G (inst.)   Warren 1945

Melody (inst.)   Carmichael 1934

Melody Isle   Kahn 1923

Melody Land   Atteridge 1922

Melody Lingers On, The   Silver 1935

Melody Man, The   Willson 1956

Melody of Dance   Romberg 1919

Melody of Laughter   Hart 1934; Kahn 1934

Melody of Love, The   Smith, Harry B. 1911; Smith, Robert B. 1911

Melody of Love Coo to Me   Akst 1926; Davis 1926

Melody of Mine   Coslow 1923

Melody of Paree   Friend 1949

Melody of Spring   Freed, Ralph 1947

Melody of the Mill   Lewis 1934

Melody of Youth   Goetz 1916; Jerome 1916; Schwartz, Jean 1916

(Stake Your Dreams on) Melody Ranch   Styne 1940

Melody that Made You Mine, The   Friend 1925

Melody Triste   Romberg 1921

Melos, That Lovely Smiling Isle   Porter 1938

Melt Us!   Adams 1962; Strouse 1962

Melted Rainbow   Sigman 1956

Melting Pot, The   Atteridge 1915; Blane 1968; Martin 1968; Romberg 1915

Member of the Family   Robison 1960

Member of the Yale Elizabethan Club, A   Porter 1913

'Member When   Edwards 1923; Smith, Robert B. 1923

Memories   Atteridge 1915; Brown, Lew 1927; DeSylva 1927; Henderson 1927; Kahn 1915; Kalmar 1921, 1941; Robin 1927; Romberg 1915; Ruby 1921, 1941

Memories I'll Never Forget   Willson 1949

Memories of France   Dubin 1928

Memories of Long Ago   Arlen Date Unknown; Koehler Date Unknown

Memories of Madison Square Garden   Hart 1935; Rodgers 1935

Memories of Santa Lucia   Hoffman 1950

Memories of Southern Seas   Razaf 1937

Memories of You   Blake 1930; Oakland 1974; Razaf 1930; Romberg 1910

Memory Ballet (inst.)   Sherman 1995

Memory Blues   Bryan 1925

Memory Lane   Conrad 1924; DeSylva 1924

Memory Song   Mercer 1944

Memory Train, The   David, Mack 1949; Livingston, Jerry 1949

Memory Waltz, The   Davis 1933

Memory-land   Kahn 1919

Memphis Blues   Coslow 1934; Loesser 1941

Memphis in June   Carmichael 1945; Webster 1945

Memphis Kindness   Robison 1961

Mem'rey's Garden   Smith, Harry B. 1908

Mem'ries of the Past   Baer 1953

Mem'ries of Violets   Johnson, J. Rosamond 1914

Mem'ry Island   Gordon 1950; Revel 1950; Warren 1950

Men!   Adams 1983; Brooks 1959; Comden and Green 1974; Fain 1954; Herbert 1903; Strouse 1991; Styne 1974; Webster 1954

Men and Women Are Awful   Hammerstein 1931; Whiting 1931

Men Are All Alike   Brooks 1960

Men Are All the Same   DePaul 1958; Raye 1958

Men Are Ambitious   Smith, Harry B. 1903

Men Are Little Children   Brooks 1949

Men Are Not Gods   Blake 1947

Men Are Only Boys Grown Tall   Warren 1956

Men, Awake   Rome 1936

Men Behind the Man Behind the Gun, The   Rome 1942

Men Don't Cry   Leigh 1955

Men from Milwaukee   Hart 1938; Rodgers 1938

Men in Meninak, The   Coots 1961

Men in My Life, The   David, Hal 1979; Leigh 1976

Men! Men! Men!   Smith, Harry B. 1911; Smith, Robert B. 1911

Men Move Mountains   Russell 1948

Men of Calvert (Football Song)   Fain 1933; Kahal 1933

Men of Clayton   Rainger 1941; Robin 1941

Men of the Watermark   Gorney 1949

Men O'Shanter   Egan 1921; Whiting 1921

Men Who Run the Country, The   Mercer 1959

Men with Whips   Lawrence 1959

Men with Wings   Carmichael 1938; Loesser 1938

Menagerie Song   Smith, Harry B. 1901

Mendelssohn and Liszt   Atteridge 1916; Motzan 1916, 1917; Romberg 1916

Mender of Broken Dreams, The   Lewis 1930

Mene, Mene, Tekel   Rome 1937

Men's Dance   Dietz 1944; Duke 1944

Menu Song, The   Comden and Green 1964; Styne 1964

Me-O-My   Blane 1947; Warren 1947

Meow   Cahn 1940

Meow! Meow! Meow!   Herbert 1912

Mercenary Mary   Conrad 1925

Mercer's Melody   Mercer 1950

Merchant's March   Sondheim 1968

Merci Beaucoup   David, Mack 1951; Friml 1922; Gordon 1938; Livingston, Jerry 1951; Revel 1938

Merci Beaucoups   Sherman 1962

Mercury Muses (inst.)   Revel 1955

Mercy McBee   David, Mack 1967

Mercy Percy   Porter 1910

Merely Marvelous   Fields 1959

Merengue of Love   Sigman 1956

Merle Edwards Theme   Oakland 1954

Merlin Jones   Sherman 1964

Merman Mambo, The   Styne 1955

Merrie Mending   Ellington 1953

Merrie Merrie, The   Hart 1925; Rodgers 1925

Merrily on My Way   Dubin 1940; Fain 1940

Merrily We Roll Along   Sondheim 1981
Merrily We'll Roll Along   Silver 1918; Sterling 1918
Merry and Bright   Atteridge 1918; Romberg 1918
Merry Came By   Russell 1968
Merry Christmas   Bergman 1963
Merry Christmas Eve   Livingston, Jerry 1963
Merry Christmas One and All   Bergman 1958
Merry Christmas Polka, The   Webster 1949
Merry Christmas Waltz, The   David, Hal 1949
Merry Gallows, The   Friml 1954
Merry Go Round   Fisher 1944
Merry Go Round (inst.)   McHugh 1966
Merry Go Round Polka   Friend 1948
Merry Ha Ha, The   Russell 1946
Merry Little Christmas Elf, The   Sigman 1950
Merry Merry Maids of the Old Front Row, The   Atteridge 1912
Merry Minstrel Band   Jerome 1905; Schwartz, Jean 1905
Merry Minstrel Men   Bullock 1939
Merry Old King   Howard, Joseph E. 1907
Merry Old Land of Oz (Renovation Sequence), The   Arlen 1939; Harburg 1939
Merry Wedding Bells   Harbach 1917; Herbert 1919; Schwartz, Jean 1912
Merry Widow Waltz   Hart 1934; Johnson, Howard 1939; Kahn 1934; Mitchell 1925; Webster 1952
Merry-Andrew (inst.)   Gershwin, George 1927
Merry-Go-Round, The   Brown, Nacio Herb 1930; Carmichael 1944; Freed, Arthur 1930
Merry-Go-Round Broke Down, The   Friend 1937
Merry-Go-Round (Complainte de la Butte)   Lawrence 1955
Merry-Go-Round in the Rain   Mercer 1965
Merry-Go-Runaround, The   Burke 1952; Van Heusen 1952
Merrymakers, The   Drake 1955
Merry-O Cheerio Drinking Song, A   Clare 1934
Mesdames and Messieurs   Porter 1939
Mess Call, The   Rome 1943
Mess Call March   (inst.)   Young, Victor 1951
Message from the Man in the Moon, A   Kahn 1937
Message from the U.S.A., A   Baer 1941
Message to Michael   Bacharach 1963; David, Hal 1963
Messenger   Cohan 1919
Messieurs, Mesdames   Hart 1943
Messin' Around   Blake 1926; Johnson, James P. 1929; Sissle 1926
Messin' Around with the Blues   Waller 1927
Messin' Round   Brennan 1929
Methinks   Russell 1955; Styne 1955
Methus'lah   Mills 1939
Metronome Fantasy   Loesser 1952
Metropolitan Handicap, The   Buck 1921; Carroll Date Unknown
Metropolitan (inst.)   Bloom 1931
Metropolitan Ladies   Berlin 1920
Metropolitan Nights   Berlin 1914
Metropolitan Nocturne (inst.)   Alter 1935
Metropolitan Opening   Berlin 1933
Metropolitan Squak-tette, The   Atteridge 1912
Mets Are on the Move, The   Coots 1962
Mewsette   Arlen 1962; Harburg 1962
Mexicali Brass   Ellington 1969
Mexicali Moon   Mills 1929
Mexican Divorce   Bacharach 1962
Mexican Erection! (inst.)   Styne 1971
Mexican Jumping Bean   Russell 1940

Mexican Jumping Beat   DePaul 1941; Raye 1941
Mexican Love   Buck 1913
Mexican Magic   Loesser 1940; Revel 1940
Mexican Maidens   Merrill 1952
Mexican Moon Dance (inst.)   Brown, Nacio Herb 1948
Mexican Sombrero Dance (inst.)   Coots 1945
Mexicana   Dixon 1935; Edwards 1929; Washington 1945; Wrubel 1935
Mexicano   Young, Victor 1957
Mexico   Caesar 1920; Johnson, J. Rosamond 1904; Romberg 1927
Mexico Blues   Brooks 1952
Mexico Canta   Lawrence 1944
Mexico City   Donaldson 1943; Loesser 1969
Mexico (To Hell with Mexico)   Hart 1926; Rodgers 1926
Mexiconga, The   Ager 1939; Fain 1939; Magidson 1939; Yellen 1939
Meyer Come Back from Hawaii   Donaldson 1917
Mi Amado (The Wolf Song)   Lewis 1928; Warren 1928; Young, Joe 1928
Mi Amor   Bergman 1963
Mi Caballero   Magidson 1930; Washington 1930
Mi Casa, Su Casa (My House Is Your House)   Hoffman 1957
Mi Chiquita   Robin 1927
Mi Mujer (inst.)   Warren 1956
Mi Ti Ya, A   Brown, Nacio Herb Date Unknown; Freed, Arthur Date Unknown
Mi Triste Adios   Rainger 1930
Mi Vida   Ruby 1947
Mia Bella Rosa   Koehler 1928
Mia Cara (Mia Amore)   Sherman 1960
Mia Cara (My Dear)   Fain 1930; Kahal 1930
Mia Luna   Goetz 1925
(Lead 'em on) Miami   Conrad 1925; DeSylva 1925; Rainger 1941; Robin 1941
Miami Beach   Coleman 1988; Davis 1964
Miami, the Moonlight and You   Friend 1939
Miami You Own a Lot to Me   Silver 1925
Mice Wanna Play (Mazeltov) (Tu Frappes Mon Coeur), The   Hoffman 1958
Michael Angelo   Meyer 1909
Michael McGinnity   Olcott 1907
Michael McInerny   Stept 1950
Michael on His Motorcycle   Johnson, Howard 1916
Michael the Bicycle Rider   Cahn 1945
Michi Mori San   Blake 1919; Sissle 1919
Mickey   Williams 1917
Mickey O'Neill a Brother of Peggy O'Neill   Coots 1921; Johnson, Howard 1921
Mickey the Monkey   Caesar 1965
Micromaniac, The   Rome 1943
Midas Touch, The   Comden and Green 1956; Styne 1956
Middle Age Blues   Adams 1981; Strouse 1981
Middle C   Lerner, Alan Jay 1976
Middle of a Madhouse   Freed, Ralph 1959
Midian   Livingston, Jerry 1962
Midnight   Freed, Ralph 1939
Midnight at the Masquerade   Rainger 1942; Robin 1942
Midnight at the Onyx   Parish 1937
Midnight Bells   Gershwin, George 1925; Hammerstein 1925; Harbach 1925
Midnight Blue   DePaul 1958; Leslie 1936; Raye 1958
Midnight Blues   Brown, Nacio Herb 1919; Gershwin, George 1923

Midnight Eyes   Bryan 1928
Midnight Fancies (inst.)   Schwartz, Jean 1930
Midnight Flirtation   Friml 1934
Midnight Frolic Glide, The   Buck 1915
Midnight Frolic Rag, The   Buck 1916
Midnight Girl at the Midnight Cabaret, The   Atteridge 1914; Romberg 1914
Midnight Girl (One Midnight Supper at Home), The   Hart 1920; Rodgers 1920
Midnight in Paris   Conrad 1935; Magidson 1935
Midnight Jump   David, Mack 1943; Hoffman 1943; Livingston, Jerry 1943
Midnight Kiss   Fisher 1930
Midnight Madness   Coslow 1955; Gershwin, Ira 1944; Kern 1944
Midnight Man   Mercer 1947
Midnight Mood (inst.)   Ruby 1946
Midnight Moon   Coslow 1920
Midnight Music   Coslow 1943; Gershwin, Ira 1944; Kern 1944
Midnight Oil   Sherman 1958
Midnight on Main Street   Heyman 1934
Midnight on the Stormy Deep   Fisher 1938
Midnight Riding   Strouse 1980
Midnight Rose   Mitchell 1923; Pollack 1923
Midnight Rounders   Atteridge 1921; Pollack 1921; Schwartz, Jean 1921
Midnight Stomp   Waller 1926
Midnight Waltz, The   Donaldson 1925; Kahn 1925
Midnight with the Stars and You   Woods 1934
Midnight Zeppo, The   Buck 1917
Midstream   Baer 1929; Gilbert 1929
Midsummer Madness   Coslow 1935; Whiting 1935
Midsummer Night   Porter 1950; Rodgers 1979
Midsummer Night's Dream   Gordon 1925
Midsummer Waltz   Smith, Robert B. 1915
Mid-Summer-Night's Dream, A   Young, Joe 1915
Mid-Summer's Dream   Conrad 1928; Gilbert 1928
Midway Polka, The   Drake 1955
Mightiest Matador   Coslow 1929; Robin 1929; Whiting 1929
Mighty Big Dream Footloose   Russell 1946
Mighty Blue   Egan 1925; Whiting 1925
Mighty Fine   Razaf 1940; Waller 1940
Mighty Joe   Young, Joe 1972
Mighty Like a Rosenbloom   Atteridge 1921; Fisher 1920; Pollack 1921; Schwartz, Jean 1921
Mighty Man   Lewis 1974; Young, Joe 1974
Mighty Mikado, The   Drake 1954
Mighty Nice and So Particular   Akst 1930; Davis 1930
Mighty Pretty Waltz, A   Hoffman 1952
Mighty Smith Is She, The   Fain 1961
Mighty Sweet   Akst 1932; Davis 1932
Mighty Thankful   Bloom 1934; Koehler 1934
Mignonette   Herbert 1903, 1906
Mike   Davis 1926; Hart 1926; Rodgers 1926
Mike's Took Bad   Young, Victor 1945
Milady   Burke 1934, 1950; Spina 1934; Van Heusen 1950
Milady's Toilette   Bryan 1916
Milano   Adamson Date Unknown; Warren Date Unknown
Mile After Mile   Weill 1939
(I Want to Be) Miles Away from Ev'ryone, and Just a Little Closer to You   Brown, Lew 1927; DeSylva 1927; Henderson 1927
Miles Gloriosus   Sondheim 1962
Milestones   Goetz 1913

Military Ball, The   Herbert 1903; Hoffman 1929
Military Dancing Drill   Gershwin, George 1927; Gershwin, Ira 1927
Military Decoration Dance   Bryan 1919; Schwartz, Jean 1919
Military Glide, The   Jerome 1910; Schwartz, Jean 1910
Military Life   Rome 1946
Military Life — The Jerk Song   Rome 1951
Military Love Song, The   Brown, Nacio Herb 1941; Freed, Ralph 1941
Military Maid   Atteridge 1915; Romberg 1915
Military Maids   Porter 1928
Military Man   Edwards 1904; Gordon 1936; Revel 1936
Military March   Bryan 1929
Military Men I Love   Smith, Harry B. 1925
Military Policeman, The   Evans 1952; Livingston, Jay 1952
Military Polka, The   Cahn 1950; Styne 1950
Military Review   Smith, Harry B. 1908
Military Wedding Glide, The   Atteridge 1919; Romberg 1919; Schwartz, Jean 1919
Milk, Milk, Milk   Porter 1941
Milking the Milky Way   Schwartz, Jean 1905; Williams 1905
Milkmaids' Chorus   Schwartz, Jean 1905; Williams 1905
Milkman Cometh (inst.), The   Revel 1957
Milkman Keep Those Bottles Quiet   DePaul 1944; Raye 1944
Milkman's Blues   Lawrence 1933
Milkman's Matinee, The   Razaf 1936
Milky Way (inst.)   Revel 1955
Mill on the Floss, The   David, Mack 1951; Livingston, Jerry 1951
Millefleurs   Romberg 1948
Millennium, The   Atteridge 1924; Romberg 1924; Schwartz, Jean 1924
Miller's Daughter (And the Shepherd on the Hill), The   Bryan 1936
Miller's Son, The   Sondheim 1973
Millie   Brown, Nacio Herb 1931; Motzan 1916
Million, A   Smith, Harry B. 1906, 1912
Million and Fifty Things, A   David, Mack 1961; Livingston, Jerry 1961
Million Dollar Ball   Berlin 1912; Goetz 1912
Million Dollar Gambler from the West, The   Leslie 1913
Million Dollar Hat   Coots 1945
Million Dollar Pier   Cahn 1947; Styne 1947
Million Dollar Smile   Comden and Green 1945
Million Dreams, A   Kahn 1932
Million Eyes, A   Bryan 1927; Schwartz, Jean 1927
Million Miles Away Behind the Door, A   Lerner, Alan Jay 1969
Million Miles from Manhattan, A   Revel 1942
Million Miles from You, A   Sherman 1995
Million Miles from Your Heart, A   Pollack 1937; Yellen 1937
Millionaire, The   Spina 1957
Millionaire Blues   Adams 1996; Strouse 1996
Millions of Dreams Ago   Mercer 1938; Warren 1938
Millions of Times   Stept 1921
Millions of Tunes   Bryan 1920; Schwartz, Jean 1920
Milton Berle Polka, The   Brown, Lew 1949
Mimi   Caesar 1920; Conrad 1921; Hart 1932; Rodgers 1932
Mimi Jazz   Caesar 1920
Mind If I Come Aboard Ship, Sailor   Drake 1952
Mind If I Make Love to You   Porter 1956
Mind If I Tell You I Love You   Willson 1943
Mind Over Matter   Sherman 1966
Mind the Paint   Kern 1912
Mind Your Own Business   Robison 1960; Romberg 1921

Mind Your P's and Q's   Hart 1929; Rodgers 1929
Mindin' My Business   Donaldson 1923; Kahn 1924
Mindin' the Baby   Herbert 1897; Smith, Harry B. 1897
Mine   Brown, Lew 1927; Coleman 1978; Comden and Green
   1978; DeSylva 1927; Gershwin, George 1933; Gershwin,
   Ira 1933; Hanley 1927; Romberg 1951; Turk 1926
Mine Alone   Dixon 1935; Wrubel 1935
Mine and Mine Alone   Russell 1951, 1969; Spina 1951
Mine Completely   Clare 1931; Johnston 1932
Mine for Aye   Smith, Harry B. 1928
Mine Is but to Love You   Livingston, Jerry 1960
Mine, Mine, Mine   Sigman 1958
Mine, Once Upon a Time   Gordon 1932; Revel 1932
Mine 'til Monday   Fields 1951; Schwartz, Arthur 1951
Mine to Kiss   Caesar Date Unknown
Mine to Love   Young, Victor 1953
Mine Until the End of Time   Friend 1932; Stept 1932
Mine Was a Marriage of Convenience   Buck 1918
Mineola   Bergman 1964
Minerva   Robin 1936
Ming Poo   Hammerstein 1920; Harbach 1920
Ming Toy Mischa   Oakland 1937
Ming Toy Noodle Company, The   Loesser 1948
Minha Vos Vira de Sul Da America   Sigman 1972
Miniatures   Atteridge 1920
Miniatures (inst.)   Schwartz, Jean 1930
Mink Lament, The   Gordon 1945; Warren 1945
Minneapolis Ain't Talkin' to St. Paul   Merrill 1946
Minnehaha   Goetz 1952
Minnetonka Cradle Song   Kahn 1927
Minnie   Hammerstein 1931; Romberg 1931
Minnie Hotcha   Styne 1940
Minnie McAvoy   Sterling 1897
Minnie the Mermaid   DeSylva 1923
Minnie the Moocher (The Ho Do Ho Song)   Mills 1931
Minnie the Moocher's Wedding Day   Arlen 1932; Koehler
   1932
Minnie the Queen of the Schuetzenfest   Atteridge Date
   Unknown
Minnie's Divorce   Young, Joe 1933
Minnie's in the Money   Robin 1943; Warren 1943
Minny Belle's Song   Weill 1936
Minor Drag (inst.)   Waller 1947
Minor Gaff (Blues Fantasy) (inst.)   Arlen 1926
Minor Melody for Mavis, A   David, Mack 1962
Minor Nursery   Mercer 1955
Minor Poet, The   Raye 1962
Minstrel Band, The   Atteridge 1911
Minstrel Dance   Edwards 1931
Minstrel Days   Atteridge 1916; Berlin 1925; Edwards 1929
Minstrel Dream   Gershwin, Ira 1940; Weill 1940
Minstrel Memories   Baer 1929, 1930; Gilbert 1929, 1930
Minstrel Parade   Berlin 1914; Goetz 1912; Jerome 1905;
   Lerner, Alan Jay 1948; Schwartz, Jean 1905; Weill 1948
Minstrel Show Opening   Freed, Ralph 1936; Lane 1936
Minstrels on Parade   Brown, A. Seymour 1909; Gershwin,
   Ira 1949; Turk 1922; Warren 1949
Minuet   Arlen 1959; Atteridge 1920; Friml 1934; Herbert
   1905; Mercer 1959
Minuet for Milady, A   Burke 1939; Dubin 1943; Monaco
   1939
Minuet in Boogie   Adamson 1943; McHugh 1943
Minuet (inst.)   Rodgers 1923
Minuet Modernistique (inst.)   Coots 1946
Minuet (Natoma Serenade)   Herbert 1911

Minuet of the Minute, The   Hammerstein 1924; Harbach
   1924
Minuette, A   Atteridge 1923; Schwartz, Jean 1923
Minute I Laid My Eyes on You, The   Stept 1927
Minute Maid   Burke 1946; Van Heusen 1946
Minute of Prayer   Robison 1957
(Can You Imagine That) Mira   Merrill 1961
Miracle   Parish 1965
Miracle at Midnight   Mills 1939
Miracle in the Rain (I'll Always Believe in You)   Washington
   1956
Miracle Man, The   Smith, Harry B. 1919
Miracle of Christmas   Mercer 1969
Miracle of Love, The   Livingston, Jerry 1960; Merrill 1956
Miracle of Prayer, The   Davis 1953
Miracle of Spring, The   Warren 1969
Miracle of St. Marie, The   Bacharach 1961
Miracle of the Bells   Brooks 1947
Miracle of the Rose, The   David, Mack 1953, 1957
Miracle of the Wheat, The   Drake 1951
Miracle on Main Street   Alter 1951
Miracle Song   Sondheim 1964
Miracles   Howard, Bart 1984
Miracles from Molecules   Sherman 1968
Miraculous Cure, The   Smith, Harry B. 1911
Mirage, The   Coslow 1924; Romberg 1924; Russell 1948,
   1965
Mirage (Follow Your Heart)   Fain 1958; Lawrence 1958
Miranda   Howard, Bart 1959; Sissle 1928
Mirandy (That Gal o' Mine)   Blake 1918; Sissle 1918
Mirror Finale, The   Akst 1927; Davis 1927
Mirror Mine   Atteridge 1923; Gorney 1923
Mirror, Mirror   Porter 1916
Mirror of Morning, The   Russell 1969
Mirror Song, The   Rainger 1934
Mirror Song (scene), The   Robin 1934
Misbehavin' Hips   Arlen 1930; Koehler 1930
Miscellaneous   Oakland 1960
Mischa, Jascha, Toscha, Sascha   Gershwin, George 1921;
   Gershwin, Ira 1921
Mischief in Your Eyes   Atteridge 1919; Romberg 1919;
   Schwartz, Jean 1919
Miserable Me   Rainger 1932; Robin 1932
Miserable with You   Dietz 1931; Schwartz, Arthur 1931
Miserlou   Russell 1941
Miser's Dream, The   Conrad 1934; Magidson 1934
Misery   Johnson, James P. 1931; Razaf 1931
Mis'ry's Comin' Aroun'   Hammerstein 1927; Kern 1927
Miss 1934   Conrad 1934; Mitchell 1934
Miss Andrew   Sondheim Date Unknown
Miss Annabell   Blake 1950
Miss Annabelle Lee   Clare 1927; Pollack 1927
Miss Bell of the Telephone   Edwards 1913
Miss Brown to You   Rainger 1935; Robin 1935; Whiting 1935
Miss Dolly Dollars   Herbert 1905; Smith, Harry B. 1905
Miss Dynamite   Evans 1956; Livingston, Jay 1956
Miss Fiddle-Dee-Dee   Rome 1973
Miss Gabriella Brown   Magidson 1942; Wrubel 1942
Miss Green Don't Be So Mean   Jerome 1902; Schwartz, Jean
   1902
Miss Hallelujah Brown   Coots 1938; Davis 1938
Miss Harvard of Yale   Sterling 1897; Von Tilzer 1897
Miss Hilary Bacon of Beacon Hill   Lerner, Alan Jay 1985
Miss Innovation   Atteridge 1915; Romberg 1915
Miss Jemima Walks By   Burke 1943; Van Heusen 1943

Miss Johnson Phoned Again Today   Mills 1940
Miss Julie July   Evans 1948; Livingston, Jay 1948
Miss Killarney   Jerome 1934; Schwartz, Jean 1934
Miss Langley's School for Girls   Lerner, Alan Jay 1943;
     Loewe 1943
Miss Liberty   Berlin 1949
Miss Lindy Lou   Koehler 1947
Miss Liza Jane   Coots 1932
Miss Lorelei Lee   Comden and Green 1974; Styne 1974
Miss Lulu from Louisville   Rainger 1943; Robin 1943
Miss Ma-Goof   Friend 1949
Miss Marmelstein   Rome 1962
Miss Mary   Olcott 1905
Miss Nellie Machree   Coots 1952
Miss Nightingale   Conrad 1919
Miss O'Brien   Rome Date Unknown
Miss Oklahoma   Blane 1964; Warren 1964
Miss Otis Regrets   Porter 1930
Miss Page   Merrill 1993; Styne 1993
Miss Peach of the Kelly School   Cahn 1980
Miss Platt Selects Mate   Gorney 1949
Miss Satan   Lawrence 1961
Miss Turnstiles   Comden and Green 1944
Miss Universe   Davis 1961
Miss Unruly   Atteridge 1919; Romberg 1919; Schwartz, Jean
     1919
Miss U.S.A.   Davis 1961
Miss Wallflower of '46   Spina 1976
Miss Whoozis and Mr. Whatchaname   Smith, Harry B. 1923;
     Snyder 1923
Miss Wonderful   Bryan 1929
Miss You Just Like I Do   Johnson, Howard 1927
'Miss You' Kiss, A   Young, Victor 1955
(I'm) Missin' Mammy's Kissin'   Pollack 1923
Mission Bell By the Wishin' Well, The   Bacharach 1957;
     David, Hal 1957
Mission Bells   Carroll 1925; Freed, Arthur 1925
Mission of the Rose, The   Drake 1946
Mississippi   Buck 1917; Johnson, James P. 1929
Mississippi Basin   Razaf 1933
Mississippi Belle   Porter 1944
Mississippi Blues   Fain 1921
Mississippi Cradle   Yellen 1921
Mississippi Day   Johnson, J. Rosamond 1929; Youmans 1929
Mississippi Dream Boat   Brown, Lew 1943; Fain 1943; Freed,
     Ralph 1943
Mississippi Flood Song, The   Ager 1927; Yellen 1927
Mississippi Homeland   Akst 1927; Davis 1927
Mississippi Honeymoon   Blake 1955; Donaldson 1934; Kahn
     1934
Mississippi Lullaby   Bryan 1919; Schwartz, Jean 1919
Mississippi Mania   Sterling 1904
Mississippi Marbles   Parish 1934
Mississippi Miss   Sigman 1951
Mississippi Moan   Johnson, James P. 1929
Mississippi Moon   Burke 1958; Van Heusen 1958
Mississippi Ripples   Hanley 1921, 1922
Mississippi River, Keep on Croonin'   Johnson, J. Rosamond
     1932
Mississippi Siren   Evans 1948; Livingston, Jay 1948
Mississippi Steamboat   Comden and Green 1956; Styne
     1956
Missouri Bell   Rose 1927
Missouri Joe   Goetz 1911; Von Tilzer 1911
Missouri Mazurka   Styne 1953

Missouri Misery   Harburg 1934
Missouri Moon   Parish 1929
Missouri Mule (inst.)   Kern 1956
Missouri Walking Preacher (With a Little Book in His
     Hand)   Robison 1949
Missus Aouda   Porter 1946
Missus O'Malley and Mister Malone   Webster 1950
Mist Is Over the Moon, A   Hammerstein 1938; Oakland
     1938
Mist o' the Moon (inst.)   Revel 1946
Mist on the Mirror   Heyman 1935; Romberg 1935
Mistah Jim   Johnson, James P. 1925
Mistaken in Love   Dixon 1930; Pollack 1930
Mistakes   Leslie 1928
Mistakes Are Apt to Happen   Smith, Harry B. 1904; Smith,
     Robert B. 1904
Mister Aeroplane Man, Take Me Up to Heaven   Conrad
     1927
Mister and Missus Coconut   Merrill 1954
Mister and Missus Fitch   Porter 1931
Mister Answer Man   Razaf 1948
Mister Banjo Man   Evans 1952; Livingston, Jay 1952
Mister Beebe   Cahn 1944
Mister Booze   Cahn 1964; Van Heusen 1964
Mister Broadway U.S.A.   Goetz 1913
Mister Brown, Miss Drupree   Gorney 1949
Mister C. Waters   Sherman 1964
Mister Deep Blue Sea   Johnson, James P. 1935
Mister Dodd   DePaul 1941; Raye 1941
Mister Fidgety Feet   Drake 1953
Mister Five By Five   DePaul 1942; Raye 1942
Mister Fortune Tellin' Man   Monaco 1912
Mister Harvey Pruitt   Cahn Date Unknown; Duke Date
     Unknown
Mister He Kissed Her   Carmichael 1949
Mister Interlude   Hoffman 1933; Parish 1933
Mister Jive Has Gone to War   Gilbert 1944; Oakland 1944
Mister Johnson, Goodnight   Sterling 1910
Mister Kelly (He Velly Nice Man)   Wrubel 1942
Mister Mammy Man   Razaf 1930
Mister Man   Hammerstein 1938; Harbach 1938; Kern 1938
Mister McAdoo   Bryan 1918; Fisher 1918
Mister McCue, How Do You Do (inst.)   Kern 1938
Mister Meadowlark   Donaldson 1940; Mercer 1940
Mister Midnight   Lewis 1952
Mister Miracle Man   Drake 1947
Mister Misbehave   Evans 1973; Livingston, Jay 1973
Mister Mississippi   Bryan 1928; Schwartz, Jean 1928
Mister Moon, How Is Everything on No Man's
     Land   Mitchell 1918
Mister Music Master Play that Rag Some Faster   Brown,
     Lew 1911
Mister O'Toole   Sterling 1927
Mister Pessimist   DePaul 1951; Raye 1951
Mister Philosophy   Drake 1954
Mister Piano Man   Sherman 1962
Mister Pollyanna   Carmichael 1943; Mercer 1943
Mister Rag and I   Atteridge 1917; Romberg 1917
Mister Siegal   Yellen 1977
Mister Snow   Hammerstein 1945; Rodgers 1945
Mister Whitney's Little Jitney Bus   Brown, A. Seymour 1915
Mister, You've Gone and Got the Blues   Russell 1948
Misterioso   Hammerstein 1920
Mistletoe Waltz   Clarke 1924; Leslie 1924
Mistletoe Waltz (inst.)   Warren Date Unknown

Misto Christofo Columbo   Evans 1951; Livingston, Jay 1951

Misty   Burke 1954

Misty Eyed   Loesser 1947

Misty Music (Do I Hear Music)   Spina 1977

Misty Valley   Parish 1954

Misunderstood   Comden and Green 1947

Mittel-Europa   Eliscu 1941; Gorney 1941, 1942

Mitzi   Dietz 1938; Schwartz, Arthur 1938

Mitzi's Lullaby   Kern 1918

Mix!   Sondheim 1957

Mix and Mingle   Rome 1952

(Me and My) Mixed Up Guy   Robison 1954

Mmm-mm Good   Wrubel 1948

Moanin'   Mills 1931; Parish 1931

Moanin' in the Mornin'   Arlen 1937; Harburg 1937

Moanin' Low   Dietz 1929; Rainger 1929

Moaning in the Moonlight   Conrad 1935; Magidson 1935

Mobile Mud   Robison 1926

Mocambo Mambo   Duke 1955

Mock the Mocking Bird   Stept 1926

Mocking Bird, The   Romberg 1927

Mocking Bird Song   Drake 1961

Mockingbird in the Willow   Webster 1956

Model Happy Fair, A   Smith, Harry B. 1935

Model Hasn't Changed, The   Rome 1950

Model Married Pair   Smith, Harry B. 1912; Smith, Robert B. 1912

Model Toddle   Coslow 1924

Models, The   Coslow 1924; Henderson 1935; Yellen 1935

Moderation   Magidson 1956; Oakland 1956; Warren 1956

Modern Banditti, The   Smith, Harry B. 1911

Modern Bride   Friml 1923

Modern Butterfly   Howard, Joseph E. 1919

Modern Crusaders   Atteridge 1921

Modern Design for Love   Friend 1941

Modern Duel, The   Smith, Harry B. 1915

Modern Little Red Riding Hood   Gordon 1932; Revel 1932

Modern Love   Atteridge 1912

Modern Maidens (inst.)   Brown, Nacio Herb 1930

Modern Maiden's Prayer, A   Mitchell 1923; Pollack 1923; Silver 1923

Modern Sandow Girl, The   Edwards 1907; Smith, Harry B. 1907

Modern Youth   Freed, Ralph 1964

Modernistic   Johnson, James P. 1933

Modernistic Moe   Duke 1936; Gershwin, Ira 1936; Rose 1936

Modes Made in Manhattan   Duke 1941

Modiste, The   Hart 1938; Rodgers 1938

Modulating Maude   Johnson, J. Rosamond 1911

Moke from Shamokin, The   Adamson 1943; McHugh 1943

Molasses   Russell 1940

Mollie O'Donahue   Hammerstein 1929; Kern 1929

Mollie Shannon   Smith, Harry B. 1901

Molly   Kalmar 1924; Livingston, Jerry 1973; Ruby 1924

Molly and Me   Lerner, Sammy 1932

Molly Aroon   Brennan 1918

Molly Come Out of the Kitchen   Mills 1947

Molly Maguire   Sterling 1921; Von Tilzer 1921

Molly Malone   Atteridge 1919; Cohan 1927; Norworth 1917; Romberg 1919; Schwartz, Jean 1919; Sterling 1921; Von Tilzer 1921

Molly, Molly   Mitchell 1921; Pollack 1921

Molly O! Oh, Molly   Berlin 1911

Molly O'Hallerhan (Edna May's Irish Song)   Kern 1905

Molly O'Malley   Donaldson 1947

Molly O'Mara   Lewis 1923; Young, Joe 1923

Molly on a Trolley, My Golly with You   Jerome 1921; Schwartz, Jean 1921

Molly On the Shore   Gershwin, George 1922; Gershwin, Ira 1922

Molly on the Trolley   Mitchell 1921; Pollack 1921

Molly Took the Next Train Back   Von Tilzer 1911

Molly's Composers (inst.)   Kern 1906

Mom   Comden and Green 1956; Lane 1965; Lerner, Alan Jay 1965; Styne 1956

Mom-e-le (Mother Dear)   Parish 1954

Moment   Burke 1936; Johnston 1936

Moment He Turned His Back, The   Burke 1934; Spina 1934

Moment I Laid Eyes on You, The   Arlen 1942; Koehler 1942

Moment I Saw You, The   Dietz 1930; Schwartz, Arthur 1930

Moment I Think of You, The   Hoffman 1931

Moment in the Dark, A   Freed, Arthur 1932

Moment Musical   Romberg 1921

Moment of Madness, A   Coleman 1957; Leigh 1957; Russell 1960

Moment of Truth   Parish 1965

Moment of Weakness, A   Heyman 1966

Moment of Your Love   Cahn 1972

Moment to Moment   Mancini 1965; Mercer 1965

Moment We Met, The   Freed, Arthur 1930; Hoffman 1956, 1957

Moment with You, A   Duke 1939; Gordon 1939; Revel Date Unknown; Sondheim 1954

Moments   Youmans 1926

Moments from Shakespeare   Fields 1954; Schwartz, Arthur 1954

Moment's Hesitation (inst.), A   Monaco 1914

Moments in the Woods   Sondheim 1987

Moments Like This   Lane 1938, 1941; Loesser 1938

Moments of the Dance   Kern 1918

Moments to Remember   Egan 1941

Moments with You   Yellen 1928

Momi Pele   Rainger 1937

Momma Knows Best   Arlen 1966

Momma, Momma   Rome 1962

Momma's Cooking   Rome 1949

Momma's Talkin' Soft   Sondheim 1959; Styne 1959

Mommy Cat   Merrill 1967

Mommy, Daddy   Razaf 1950

Mommy Dear, I Want My Daddy   Howard, Joseph E. 1942

Momsy   Yellen 1927

Mon Ami   Eliscu 1960

Mon Ami, My Friend   Weill 1936

Mon Amour   Adamson 1952; Magidson 1930; McHugh 1952; Washington 1930

Mon Amour, Mon Amour   Sigman 1967

Mon Amour Perdu   Sherman 1962

Mon Bijou de Montbijou   Smith, Harry B. 1911

Mon Petit   Washington 1959

Mona   Conrad 1929; Johnston 1932; Mitchell 1929; Young, Joe 1916

Mona and Her Kiddies   Porter 1930

Mona From Arizona   Fields 1954; Schwartz, Arthur 1954

Mona from Bologna   Silver 1926; Turk 1926

Mona Lisa   Evans 1950; Livingston, Jay 1950

Mona Mia (inst.)   Schwartz, Jean 1930

Monaco (inst.)   Monaco 1920

Monarch and a Maid, A   Herbert 1908

Monarch of All I Survey   Young, Victor 1952

Monastery   Atteridge 1924

Monastery Bells   Leslie 1920
Monastery Opening   Hart 1928; Rodgers 1928
Monastery Processional (inst.)   Coots 1946
Monday Morning on Saturday Night   Evans 1938;
    Livingston, Jay 1938
Monday through Sunday   Arlen 1954
Monday, Wednesday, Friday   Evans 1957; Livingston, Jay
    1957
M-O-N-E-Y   Cohan 1908
Money Burner   Smith, Harry B. 1902
Money Burns a Hole in My Pocket   Styne 1953
Money Cat, The   Arlen 1962; Harburg 1962
Money Doesn't Care Who Has It   Hoffman 1961
Money Doesn't Mean a Thing   Gershwin, Ira 1924
Money Hungry Mama   Robison 1957
Money in My Clothes   Fain 1934; Kahal 1934
Money in the Pocket   Russell 1946; Sigman 1946
Money Is a Problem   Cahn 1957
Money Isn't Everything   Mercer 1964
Money Isn't Ev'rything   Hammerstein 1947; Rodgers 1947
Money Mad Men   Sherman 1959
Money Means Nothing to Me   Adams 1983
Money, Money, Money!   DeSylva 1919; Gershwin, George
    1919; Harbach 1920; Harburg 1967; Styne 1967
Money Penny Goes for Broke (inst.)   Bacharach 1967
Money Rings Out Like Freedom, The   Lerner, Alan Jay 1969
Money Song, The   Rome 1948
Money Talks   Smith, Robert B. 1912
Monica   Coleman 1977
Monique   Cahn 1958
Monk and the Maid, The   Herbert 1897; Smith, Harry B.
    1897
Monkey Bunch, The   Johnson, James P. 1917
Monkey Business   Dixon 1923
Monkey Dance (inst.)   Henderson 1930
Monkey Doodle   Goetz 1913
Monkey Doodle Doo   Berlin 1913, 1925
Monkey in the Mango Tree   Arlen 1957; Harburg 1957
Monkey on a String, The   David, Mack 1941; Hanley 1931
Monkey Sat in the Cocoanut Tree, The   Arlen 1948; Robin
    1948
Monkey See, Monkey Do   Coots 1957
Monkey Song   Carmichael 1951
Monkey Talk (inst.)   Waller 1928
Monkeys Have No Tails in Pago Pago   Raye 1939
Monkey's Uncle, The   Sherman 1965
Monk's Chorus, Act II   Herbert 1897; Smith, Harry B. 1897
Monks' Quartette, The   Herbert 1913; Smith, Robert B. 1913
Monna Vanna Sweetheart Sublime   Dubin 1928
Monongaheela   Fisher 1931
Monotonous Ain't It   Brooks 1951
Mons. France and Miss America   Buck 1917
Monsieur   Brooks 1950
Monsieur Baby   Rainger 1932; Robin 1932
Monsoon (inst.)   Drake 1964
Monstro the Whale   Washington 1940
Mont Marte   Berlin 1922
Montage Poster (inst.)   Duke 1963
Montage Theme   Mercer 1955
Montana   Howard, Joseph E. 1910
Montana Chem   Sondheim 1999
Monte Carlo   Fisher 1938; Rose 1925; Sigman 1963
Monte Carlo Calling   Coots 1958
Monte Carlo (inst.)   Monaco 1911
Monte Christo   Clare 1934; Whiting 1934

Monte Cristo   Atteridge 1919; Romberg 1919; Schwartz, Jean
    1919
Monterey   Caesar 1924; Conrad 1924; Harbach 1924
Monterey Peninsula (inst.)   Bacharach 1974
Montezuma   Robin 1926
Month of June   Donaldson 1915
Month of June Is a Song of Love, The   Kahn 1912
Month of Sundays, A   Mercer 1949
Montmart'   Porter 1953
Montmartre   Adamson 1952; Buck 1924; McHugh 1952;
    Revel 1931
Montreal, The   Silver 1937
Mooching Along   Romberg 1924; Schwartz, Jean 1924
Mood I'm In, The   Webster 1964
Mood Indigo   Ellington 1931; Mills 1931; Parish 1931
Mood You Are In, The   Harbach 1910
Mooda's Song   Akst 1930; Clarke 1930
Moods (inst.)   Bloom 1934; Warren 1959, 1961
Moods of Harlem (inst.)   Blake 1937
Moody   Gordon 1945; Warren 1945
Moody and Blue   Lerner, Sammy 1933
Moody's Mood   Fields Date Unknown; McHugh 1981
Moon, The   Gilbert 1955
Moon About Town   Harburg 1934
Moon and Music, A   Rainger 1936; Robin 1936
Moon and the Willow Tree, The   Burke 1940
Moon and You, The   Rodgers 1921
Moon Bird   Edwards 1908
Moon Came Up with a Great Idea, The   Burke 1952; Van
    Heusen 1952
Moon Country Is Home to Me   Carmichael 1934; Mercer
    1934
Moon Crazy   Alter 1935
Moon Dear   Egan 1925; Whiting 1925
Moon Dreams   Mercer 1943; Schwartz, Arthur 1922
Moon Face   Heyman 1936; Schwartz, Arthur 1936
Moon Fell in the River, The   Parish 1941
Moon Flower   Romberg 1925
Moon Got In My Eyes, The   Burke 1937; Johnston 1937
Moon Guitar   Bacharach 1961; David, Hal 1961
Moon Hangs High, The   Stept 1935
Moon in My Window   Rodgers 1965; Sondheim 1965
Moon in the Mulberry Tree   Mercer 1950
Moon Is a Silver Dollar, The   Fain 1939; Parish 1939
Moon Is Blue, The   Baer 1953
Moon Is Grinning at Me, The   Mills 1936
Moon Is in the Sky, The   Kalmar 1935; Ruby 1935
Moon Is Low, The   Brown, Nacio Herb 1930; Freed, Arthur
    1930; Merrill 1958
Moon Is on Fire, The   Merrill 1954
Moon Is on the Sea, The   Gershwin, George 1926;
    Gershwin, Ira 1926
Moon Is Shining   David, Mack 1958; Livingston, Jerry 1958
Moon June Spoon   Hoffman 1951
Moon Kissed Maid   Russell 1949
Moon Kissed the Mississippi, The   Pollack 1943
Moon Looks Down and Laughs, The   Kalmar 1938; Ruby
    1938
Moon Love   David, Mack 1939; Kern 1923
Moon, Lovely Moon   Smith, Robert B. 1912
Moon Mad   Rainger 1932, 1935; Robin 1932, 1935
Moon Maiden   Ellington 1969
Moon Man   Bacharach 1959; David, Hal 1959; Porter 1913
Moon Mist   Dubin 1936; Warren 1936
Moon Mist (inst.)   Warren 1958

Moon Moods   Revel 1946
Moon, Moon   Willson 1946
Moon Music   Magidson 1931
Moon of Asia Land   Livingston, Jerry 1933
Moon of Desire   Webster 1934
Moon of Jade (inst.)   Myrow 1947
Moon of Love   Kern 1920
Moon of Mannakoora   Loesser 1937
Moon of My Delight   Hart 1928; Rodgers 1928
Moon of Shanghai   Fain 1920
Moon of the Orient   Turk 1924
Moon or No Moon   Hoffman 1937; Lerner, Sammy 1937
Moon Over America   Hoffman 1940
Moon Over Burma   Loesser 1940
Moon Over Dixie   Ellington 1932; Koehler 1932
Moon Over Miami   Leslie 1935
Moon Over Monte Carlo   Clare 1934; Whiting 1934
Moon Over Monte Cristo   Whiting 1935
Moon Over Mulberry Street   Egan 1935
Moon Over Napoli   Berlin 1934
Moon Over Nowhere   Lawrence 1946
Moon River   Mancini 1961; Mercer 1961
Moon Rose   Fisher 1936
Moon Sails   Donaldson 1937
Moon Shines Down, The   Mercer 1930
Moon Song   Kern 1918
Moon Song (That Wasn't Meant for Me)   Coslow 1933;
     Johnston 1933
Moon Suite, The   Ellington 1969
Moon Talk   Hoffman 1958; Kahn 1910
Moon Trail, The   Robin 1946
Moon Was Yellow (And the Night Was Blue), The   Ahlert
     1934; Leslie 1934
Moon Was Yellow (El Amor Llamo), The   Ahlert 1947;
     Leslie 1947
Moon Will Help You Out, Maybe, The   Herbert 1903
Moon Will Ride Away, The   Hammerstein 1933
Moonbeam, Kiss Her for Me   Dixon 1927; Woods 1927
Moonbeams   Caesar 1920; Herbert 1906; Stept 1920
Moonbeams, Soft Lights and Music   Stept 1957
Moonburn   Carmichael 1936; Heyman 1936
Moondreams (You, Love and Me)   Evans 1970; Livingston,
     Jay 1970
Moondrift   Cahn 1956
Moondust   Parish 1937; Sigman 1968
Moon-Faced, Starry-Eyed   Weill 1947
Moonflower Lane   Brown, Nacio Herb 1949; Heyman 1947
Moonflowers   Burke 1952; Van Heusen 1952
Moonglow   De Lange 1934; Mills 1934; Motzan 1923
Mooning   Hoffman 1944
Moonland   De Lange 1939; Van Heusen 1939
Moonlight   Conrad 1921
Moonlight, a Love Song and You   Koehler 1929
Moonlight, a Waltz and You, The   Koehler 1925
Moonlight and Honeysuckle   Hanley 1921
Moonlight and Love and All   Brennan 1927
Moonlight and Melody   Kahn 1933
Moonlight and Music   Lewis 1937
Moonlight and Pretzels   Gorney 1933; Harburg 1933
Moonlight and Roses   DeSylva 1923; Donaldson 1923
Moonlight and Shadows   Robin 1936
Moonlight and Violins   Harbach 1936; Romberg 1936
Moonlight and You   Hart 1920; Rodgers 1920
Moonlight and You (inst.)   Warren 1935
Moonlight Ballet (inst.)   Herbert 1923

Moonlight Becomes You   Burke 1942; Van Heusen 1942
Moonlight Brought Me the Sunshine   Ahlert 1932; Turk
     1932
Moonlight Buggy Ride, A   Jerome 1905; Schwartz, Jean 1905
Moonlight Dreams   Sterling 1927
Moonlight Fiesta   Mills 1937; Washington 1944
Moonlight for Two   Kahal 1932
Moonlight in Hawaii   DePaul 1941; Raye 1941
Moonlight in Heaven   Alter 1935
Moonlight in Mandalay   Yellen 1920
Moonlight in Maryland   Whiting 1920
Moonlight in Normandy   Bryan 1926
Moonlight in Rio   Friend 1936
Moonlight in Versailles   Gershwin, George 1923
Moonlight in Waikiki   Friend 1938
Moonlight in Your Eyes   Parish 1933
Moonlight Kisses   Caesar 1923; Conrad 1923
Moonlight Love   Parish 1956; Stept 1919
Moonlight Madness   David, Hal 1960
Moonlight Madness (Then You Were Gone)   Coots 1928
Moonlight Mama   Hart 1924; Rodgers 1924
Moonlight Maneuvers   Berlin 1935
Moonlight Masquerade   Drake 1944; Lawrence 1941
Moonlight Matador   Brooks 1966
Moonlight Melody   Lawrence 1932
Moonlight Memory   Heyman 1933; Kahn 1931
Moonlight Millionaires   Hanley 1932; Kahal 1932; Meyer
     1932; Rose 1932
Moonlight Mississippi   Robison 1944
Moonlight Mood   Adamson 1942; Waller 1938
Moonlight Music   Robison 1947; Spina 1961
Moonlight Nights in Nassau   Gilbert 1931
Moonlight on Broadway   Dubin Date Unknown; Warren
     Date Unknown
Moonlight on the Campus   Mercer 1937; Whiting 1937
Moonlight on the Highway   Leslie 1937
Moonlight on the Lagoon   Parish 1980
Moonlight on the Meadow   Ruby 1935
Moonlight on the Mississippi   Kahn 1913
Moonlight on the Nile   DeSylva 1919; Kahn 1919
Moonlight on the Ocean   Loesser Date Unknown
Moonlight on the Rhine   Kalmar 1914; Leslie 1914; Snyder
     1914
Moonlight on the River Danube   Freed, Ralph 1934; Pollack
     1934
Moonlight on the Riviera   Fields 1934; McHugh 1934
Moonlight on the Sunset Trail   Freed, Ralph 1937; Lane
     1937
Moonlight on the Waters   Friml 1923
Moonlight Over Molokai   Lawrence 1943
Moonlight Over the Islands   Pollack 1946
Moonlight Parade, The   Baer 1934; Coots 1934
Moonlight Propaganda   Magidson 1946
Moonlight Reminds Me of You, The   Kahn 1929
(There Ought to Be a) Moonlight Saving Time   Kahal 1931
Moonlight Serenade   Parish 1939
Moonlight Silhouette   Coslow 1949
Moonlight Sonata   Caesar 1923
Moonlight Souvenirs   Cahn 1957
Moonlight, Starlight, Lovelight and You   Johnson, J.
     Rosamond 1946
Moonlight Sweetheart   Coots 1931; Davis 1931
Moonlight Trail   Egan 1926
Moonlight Troubadour, The   David, Hal 1950
Moonlight Valse (inst.), The   Romberg 1950

Moonlight Walk   Fain 1918
Moonlight Waltz, The   Washington 1934
Moonlighter Song, The   Sigman 1953
Moonlit Waltz, The   Mitchell 1936; Pollack 1936
Moonlit Waters   Brown, Nacio Herb 1927; Friend 1927
Moon-Mad Mama from Memphis   Wrubel 1948
Moon-Path   Edwards 1913
Moonraker   David, Hal 1978
Moonrise   Adamson 1939; Alter 1947, 1948; De Lange 1948
Moonrise and Violins   Webster 1940
Moonrise on the Lowlands   Livingston, Jerry 1936
Moon's on the Nile, The   Brown, Nacio Herb 1933; Whiting 1933
Moon's Our Home, The   Coslow 1936
Moonshine and Ballet   DeSylva 1922; Herbert 1922
Moonshine Lullaby   Berlin 1946
(Give Me the) Moonshine of My Old Kentucky Home   Carroll 1919
Moonshine Over Kentucky   Mitchell 1938; Pollack 1938
Moonshine Sally   Johnson, Howard 1916
Moonshine Valley   Fisher 1916
Moonstruck   Coslow 1933; Johnston 1933
Moon-tide   Robison 1941
Moontime   Hoffman 1934
Mootchin' Along at the Cotton Ball   Gilbert 1914
Mophams, The   Gershwin, George 1924
Moppin' and Boppin'   Waller 1946
Morale   Gershwin, Ira 1945; Weill 1945
Morality's a Matter of Geography   Smith, Harry B. 1902
More   Coslow 1923; Mitchell 1923; Pollack 1923; Silver 1923; Sondheim 1990
More and More   Bacharach 1960; Freed, Ralph 1976; Harburg 1945; Kern 1945
More and More Amore   Webster 1967
More and More I'm Caring for You   Monaco 1932
More Beautiful than Ever   Washington 1932; Young, Victor 1932
(The Birth of the Copa) More Coffee   Davis 1948; Silver 1948
More Hearts Are Broken that Way   Davis 1962
More I Cannot Wish You   Loesser 1950
More I Know of Love, The   Brooks 1946
More I Know You the More I Love You, The   Coots 1936; Davis 1936
More I See Hawaii the Better I Like New York, The   Kalmar 1917
More I See of Other Girls (Elephant Song), The   Hart 1935; Rodgers 1935
More I See of Others the Better I Love (Like) You, The   Herbert 1914
More I See You, The   Gordon 1945; Warren 1945
More I See You the More I Love You, The   Hoffman 1939; Lerner, Sammy 1939
More I Think About You, The   Heyman 1959
More Love   Merrill 1951
More Love than Your Love   Fields 1954; Schwartz, Arthur 1954
More Mittel-Europa   Eliscu 1941; Gorney 1941
More, More and More (Un Grand Amour)   Cahn 1956
More More More   Oakland 1954; Raye 1961; Sigman 1961
More Music   Van Heusen 1934
More Now than Ever   Koehler 1943; Monaco 1943
More of the Moonlight   Leslie 1925
More of the Same   Bergman 1978
More or Less   David, Hal 1952

More People   Cahn 1959; Van Heusen 1959
More People Like You   Fields 1973
More Power to You   Adamson 1938; McHugh 1938
More Powerful Than Voodoo   Drake 1954
More Than a Sweet Romance   Rainger 1936; Robin 1936
More Than Anyone   DePaul 1954; Raye 1954
More than Anything in the World   Drake 1949
More than Ever   Adamson 1930; Fain 1943, 1946; Freed, Ralph 1943, 1946; Mancini 1957; Youmans 1930
More than I Can Tell You   Donaldson 1938
More than Likely   Cahn 1962; Van Heusen 1962
More than One More Day   Eliscu 1962
More than One Way   Cahn 1965; Van Heusen 1965
More than You Know   Eliscu 1929; Rose 1929; Youmans 1929
More than Just a Friend   Rodgers 1962
More the Less, The   Leigh 1955
More the Merrier (The More We Are the Merrier We Be), The   Martin 1958
More Time to Be with You   Bacharach 1966
More We Are Together (The Less We Are Apart), The   Hoffman 1949
More We Dance, The   Coots 1926
More We See of People, the Better We Like Horses, The   Arlen 1936; Harburg 1936
More You Get It the More You Want It, The   Razaf 1924
More You Hurt Me, the More You Make Me Care, The   Dixon 1931; Warren 1931; Young, Joe 1931
More You See of It, The   Arlen 1966
Morenita   Ahlert 1930
Morgan the Pirate   McHugh 1961
Mormon Life, A   Dietz 1924; Kern 1924
Morning   Weill 1947
Morning After, The   Arlen 1962; Coslow 1934, 1935; DeSylva 1920; Johnston 1934
Morning After the Night Before, The   Pollack 1927; Rose 1927
Morning Anthem   Weill 1954
Morning Dew   David, Mack 1955
Morning Exercise   Berlin 1914
Morning Glories in the Moonlight   Magidson 1938; Wrubel 1938
Morning Glory   Carmichael 1942; Kern 1922; Webster 1942; Young, Joe 1933
Morning Glory Lane   Dixon 1925; Friend 1926; Henderson 1925; Rose 1925
Morning Is Midnight   Hart 1926, 1928; Rodgers 1926, 1928
Morning Mail, The   Bacharach 1956; David, Hal 1956
Morning Music of Montmartre, The   Evans 1958; Livingston, Jay 1958
Morning, Noon and Night   Alter 1933; Edwards 1921; Johnson, J. Rosamond 1916
Morning Serenade   Loesser 1937
Morning Star   David, Mack 1958; Martin 1962
Morning Will Come   Conrad 1921; DeSylva 1921
Morning Won't You Ever Come 'Round   Silver 1924; Turk 1924
Morning You Were Born, The   Duke 1963
Morning's at Seven   Hart 1940; Rodgers 1940
Morocco   De Lange 1938
Morocco Dance of Marriage (inst.)   Romberg 1926
Morris Kaplan of Hampstead Gardens   Styne 1978
Mose   Coslow 1923; Mitchell 1923
Moses   Comden and Green 1952
Moses Andrew Jackson Goodbye   Snyder 1906

Mosha from Nova Scotia   Gilbert 1915
Moskowitz, Gogeloch, Babblekroit and Svonk   Dietz 1927
Moskowitz, Gogeloch, Babblekroit and Svonk (The Lawyer
    Song)   Gorney 1927
Mosquito   Fain 1938
Mosquito Ballet (inst.)   Herbert 1922
Mosquito Song   Smith, Harry B. 1908
Most, The   Berlin 1955
Most Beautiful Girl in the World, The   Hart 1935; Rodgers
    1935
Most Beautiful Girls in the World, The   Arlen 1932; Koehler
    1932
Most Beautiful Time of the Year, The   Freed, Ralph 1947
Most Befuddling Thing, A   Sherman 1963
Most Difficult Man, A   Cahn 1980; Strouse 1980
Most Disagreeable Man, A   Rodgers 1979
Most Emphatically Yes   Razaf 1946
Most Exciting Night, The   Fields 1952; Harbach 1952; Kern
    1952
Most Expensive Statue in the World, The   Berlin 1949
Most Gentlemen Don't Like Love   Porter 1938
Most Gentlemen Don't Prefer a Lady   Cahn 1941
Most Girls   Cahn 1966; Van Heusen 1966
Most Happy Fella, The   Loesser 1956
Most Important Job   Loesser 1944
Most Important Man in the U.S.A., The   Drake 1952
Most Majestic Domestic Officials, The   Hart 1928; Rodgers
    1928
Most of All You   Bergman 1989
Most Unusual Weather (For This Time of Year)   Cahn 1944;
    Styne 1944
Most Unusual Weather (It's Such Unusual Weather)   Arlen
    1942; Harburg 1942
Moth and the Flame   Atteridge 1921; Pollack 1921;
    Schwartz, Jean 1921
Moth and the Moon, The   Herbert 1905; Smith, Harry B.
    1905
Moth for My Flame   DeSylva 1922; Gershwin, George 1922;
    Goetz 1922
Mother   Johnson, Howard 1939; Romberg 1916, 1927
M-O-T-H-E-R (A Word that Means the World to
    Me)   Johnson, Howard 1915
Mother Always Waits at Home   McHugh 1917
Mother and Child   Bergman 1990
Mother and Father   Kern 1910
Mother Brown   Evans 1965; Livingston, Jay 1965
Mother Darling   Willson 1953
Mother, Dixie and You   Johnson, Howard 1917
Mother, Dixie, the Flag and You   Goetz 1922; Meyer 1922
Mother Doesn't Know   Smith, Harry B. 1912
Mother Doesn't Matter Anymore, A   Adams 1991; Strouse
    1991
Mother Earth and Father Time   Sherman 1973
Mother Eve   Hanley 1921
Mother Goose   Herbert 1913; Smith, Robert B. 1913
Mother Goose Has Come to the Fair   David, Mack 1958;
    Livingston, Jerry 1958
Mother Grows Younger (Daughter Grows Older)   Hart 1929;
    Rodgers 1929
Mother Hasn't Spoke to Paris Since   Jerome 1908; Schwartz,
    Jean 1908
Mother Here's Your Boy   Mitchell 1918
Mother Hubbard Was a Wise Old Dame   Bryan 1914;
    Edwards 1914
Mother, I Didn't Understand   Johnson, Howard 1921

Mother Indiana   Bryan 1931; Schwartz, Jean 1931
Mother, Look, I'm an Acrobat   Hart 1943
Mother Machree   Olcott 1910, 1913
Mother Machree's Lullaby (My Machree's Lullaby)   Johnson,
    Howard 1922
Mother May I Go In to Swim   Carroll 1915
Mother Me, Tennessee   DeSylva 1925
Mother Mississippi   Lane 1945; Meyer 1933; Young, Joe
    1933
Mother Mississippi, There's No Rest for the Weary No
    Time   Bryan 1932; Fisher 1932
Mother, Mother, Mother, Pin a Rose on Me   David, Hal
    1949
Mother Nature and Me   Livingston, Jay 1974
Mother Nature, Father Time   Ahlert 1942; Russell 1942
Mother Nature's Cabaret   Razaf 1956
Mother Needs a Boyfriend   Lerner, Alan Jay 1971
Mother Never Told Me Why   Cahn 1941
Mother o' Mine   Dubin 1915
Mother of All the Blues   Drake 2000
Mother of Mine   Bergman 1959
Mother of Mine, I Still Have You   Clarke 1927
Mother of the Regiment, The   Friml 1917
Mother Phi   Porter 1911
Mother Sir   Brooks 1956
Mother Told Me So   Dietz 1932; Schwartz, Arthur 1932
Mother Told Me There'd Be Moments Like This   Baer 1965;
    Leslie 1965
Mother Who's Really a Mother, A   Dietz 1963; Schwartz,
    Arthur 1963
Motherhood   Merrill 1964; Strouse 1956; Webster 1953
Mother-in-Laws   Coleman 1988
(Sometimes I Feel Like a) Motherless Child   Robison 1953
Motherless Child (Recitative)   Gershwin, George 1935;
    Gershwin, Ira 1935
Mothers   Livingston, Jerry 1973
Mother's Blues   Merrill 1971; Styne 1971
Mother's Crazy Quilt   Conrad 1934; Oakland 1934
Mother's Getting Nervous   Lerner, Alan Jay 1948; Weill
    1948
Mother's Hands   Ager 1920; Clarke 1920
Mother's Kiss at Praying Time, A   Lewis 1923; Schwartz,
    Jean 1923; Young, Joe 1923
Mother's Little Man   Razaf 1932; Sissle 1932
Mother's Little Northern Rose   Johnson, Howard 1930
Mother's Lullaby   Gilbert 1954; Oakland 1954; Silver 1928
Mothers of Men   Cobb 1917; Edwards 1917
Mothers of the World   Brennan 1929; Romberg 1925
Mothers Ought to Tell Their Daughters   Brown, Lew 1930;
    DeSylva 1930; Henderson 1930
Mother's Prayer, A   Gilbert 1931; Heyman 1944; Spina 1944
Mother's Prayer for Her Boy Out There, A   Sterling 1918
Mother's Quilting Party   Robison 1934
Mothers Shouldn't Have Daughters   Cahn 1965; Van
    Heusen 1965
Mother's Tears   Lewis 1919, 1920; Young, Joe 1919
Motor Boat Song (Put-Put-Put Your Arms Around Me),
    The   Hoffman 1942; Livingston, Jerry 1942
Motor Car, The   Porter 1910
Motor Girl, The   Buck 1918
Motor Girls   Atteridge 1910
Motoraa Rahi   David, Mack 1951
Moulin Rouge Girls, The   Romberg 1927
Moulin Rouge Roulette   Atteridge 1912
Moulin-Rouge   Duke 1944

Mound Bayou   Johnson, James P. 1945; Razaf 1942

Mound City Blue Boys from Ol' St. Lou   Robison 1950

Mount Harissa   Ellington 1966

Mountain, The   David, Mack 1956

Mountain Dew   Coslow 1952

Mountain Girl's Lament   Young, Victor 1919

Mountain Greenery   Hart 1926; Rodgers 1926

Mountain High, Valley Low   David, Hal 1952

Mountain Maid   Fisher 1919

Mountain Song   Brown, Nacio Herb 1930; Eliscu 1930

Mountain Whippoorwill   Kahn 1944

Mountains Ain't No Place for Bad Men   Kahal 1929

Mountains Beyond the Moon, The   Sigman 1957

Mountains of Gold   Styne 1985

Mountains of Nebraska Ballet, The   Dietz 1944; Duke 1944

Mounted Messenger, The   Weill 1954

Mountie Gets His Man, The   Dietz 1970; Schwartz, Arthur 1970

Mounties, The   Friml 1924, 1954; Hammerstein 1924, 1954; Harbach 1924, 1954; Webster 1954

Mouse, The   Loesser Date Unknown

Mousie   Coots 1944

Mouth Full of Kisses, A   Bryan 1920; Schwartz, Jean 1920

Mouthful of Jam   Mercer 1932

Mouthful of Kisses, A   Bryan 1919; Schwartz, Jean 1919

Move   Bergman 1970

Move 'Em Out   Mancini 1978

Move Into My Heart   Atteridge 1919; Carroll 1919

Move Me on the Back Beat   Bacharach 1961; David, Mack 1961

Move On   Sondheim 1984

Move on Higher   Lewis 1974; Young, Joe 1974

Move on Mr. Moon   Snyder 1908

Move Over   Berlin 1914; Hanley 1927

Move Over and Make Room for Me   Bacharach 1962; David, Hal 1962

Move Over, Jehovah (I'm Moverin' In)   Robison 1942

Move Over Juanita   David, Mack 1979

Mover's Life, A   Coleman 1977

Movie Ads, The   Comden and Green 1943

Movie Ball, The   Kalmar 1926; Ruby 1926

Movie Magic   David, Hal 1975

Movie Star   Russell 1958, 1960

Movie Theme (inst.)   Henderson 1968

Movies Gonna Get Ya (If Ya Don't Watch Out), The   Harburg 1940; Lane 1940

Movietonia   Hanley 1930

Movin'   Lerner, Alan Jay 1951; Loewe 1951

Movin' Day   Johnson, James P. 1931

Movin' Man Don't Take My Baby Grand   Kalmar 1911; Snyder 1911

Movin' Out   Adams 1981; Strouse 1981

Moving Away   Sigman 1952

Moving Day   Sterling 1906; Von Tilzer 1906

Moving Day in Jungle Town   Brown, A. Seymour 1909

Moving Into a New House   Strouse 1987

Moving Man, The   Atteridge 1913

Moving Picture Actors on Parade   Fisher 1926; Rose 1926

Moving Picture Glide, The   Atteridge 1914; Carroll 1914

Moving Pictures   Bacharach 1981

Mr. and Mrs.   Conrad 1926; Gershwin, Ira 1920, 1921; Kahn 1922, 1926; Romberg 1922; Youmans 1920, 1921

Mr. and Mrs. America   Henderson 1939; Webster 1939

Mr. and Mrs. and Company   Gorney 1926

Mr. and Mrs. Doakes   Dubin 1937; Warren 1937

Mr. and Mrs. Is the Name   Dixon 1934; Wrubel 1934

Mr. and Mrs. Nobody   Burke 1951; Van Heusen 1951

Mr. and Mrs. Rover   Kern 1924

Mr. and Mrs. Sipkin   DeSylva 1925; Gershwin, George 1925; Gershwin, Ira 1925

Mr. and Mrs. Smith   Porter 1935

Mr. and Mrs. Wright   Bryan 1944

Mr. Bach and Mr. Boogie #2   Brooks 1946

Mr. Banjo Man   Evans 1953; Livingston, Jay 1953

Mr. Beebe   Styne 1944

Mr. Berle Theme (inst.)   Young, Victor 1955

Mr. Bingham   Cohan 1907

Mr. Bluebird   Carmichael 1935

Mr. Broadway   Coslow 1949

Mr. Burns of New Rochelle   Cohan 1907

Mr. Chamberlain   Kern 1906

Mr. Chamberlin and Mr. Levine   Mills 1927

Mr. Chucklehead   Rome 1942

Mr. Cosy Corner Man   Freed, Arthur 1925

Mr. Cupid   Romberg 1927

Mr. Director   Hart 1921; Rodgers 1921

Mr. Disk Jockey (Play Our Love Song Again)   Robison 1949

Mr. Dodd   DePaul 1941; Raye 1941

Mr. Doland Is Passing Through   Hart 1931; Rodgers 1931

Mr. Dooley   Jerome 1902; Schwartz, Jean 1902

Mr. Dumbell and Mr. Tough   Johnson, James P. 1948

Mr. Ed   Evans 1960; Livingston, Jay 1960

Mr. Esquire   Koehler 1937; Young, Victor 1937

Mr. Finkelstein, The Jewish Mister Dooley   Hanley 1917

Mr. Five By Five   DePaul 1943; Raye 1943

Mr. Flynn   Burke 1961

Mr. Ghost Goes to Town   Mills 1936; Parish 1936

Mr. Goldstone, I Love You   Sondheim 1959; Styne 1959

Mr. Good-for-Nothing Heart   Burke 1954

Mr. Gravvins — Mr. Gripps   Kern 1921

Mr. Greed   Coleman 1996

Mr. Hamlet Man   Meyer 1909

Mr. Hoover & Mr. Smith   Magidson 1928

Mr. Izzy Always Busy Rosentstein   Jerome 1909; Schwartz, Jean 1909

Mr. Jazz Himself   Berlin 1917

Mr. Johnson, Good Night   Harbach 1910

Mr. Lawson the Man from Boston   Jerome 1905; Schwartz, Jean 1905

Mr. Limpet March, The   Fain 1964

Mr. Lucky Goes Latin   Evans 1960; Livingston, Jay 1960

Mr. Masterson, Mr. Gun   Brooks 1959

Mr. Monkey   Cobb 1906; Edwards 1906

Mr. Monotony   Berlin 1948

Mr. Moon Man   Monaco 1950

Mr. Music   Burke 1950; Van Heusen 1950

Mr. Nevin I'm in Heaven when I Hear Your Rosary   Clarke 1919; Meyer 1919

Mr. Pagliacci   Atteridge 1912

Mr. Pagliatch   Edwards 1912

(Hey) Mr. Postman   Raye 1946

Mr. Prairie (inst.)   Revel 1960

Mr. President   Berlin 1962

Mr. President, Please Admit Me to the U.S.A.   Sigman 1948

Mr. Publisher (Have I Got a Song for You)   Gilbert 1954; Oakland 1954

Mr. Rhythm for President   Cahn 1937

Mr. Right   Lerner, Alan Jay 1948; Weill 1948

Mr. Right and Mrs. Dream   Lerner, Alan Jay 1948; Weill 1948

Mr. Roosevelt and Mr. Churchill   Eliscu 1943; Gorney 1943

Mr. Roosevelt Won't You Please Run Again   Gorney 1938

Mr. Sun Man Roll the Clouds Away   Kalmar 1919; Ruby 1919

Mr. Sweeney's Learned to Swing   Mills 1938

Mr. Swing for President   Razaf 1936

Mr. T. from Tennessee   Mercer 1936

Mr. Thrumm's Chase   Webster 1967

Mr. Tosti Goodbye   Atteridge 1915; Carroll 1915; Romberg 1915

Mr. Voodoo   Herbert 1910

Mr. Yankee Doodle   Atteridge 1912

Mr. Yankee Doodle Do the Do Do   Schwartz, Jean 1912

Mr. Yesterday   Robison 1963

Mrs. Chisolm   Cahn Date Unknown; Styne Date Unknown

Mrs. Cockatoo   Kern 1908

M.R.S. for Me   Leigh 1965

Mrs. Grundy   Herbert 1909

Mrs. James, I'm Mrs. Brown's Daughter   Freed, Ralph 1965

Mrs. Kelly's Table d'Hote   Buck 1914

Mrs. Krause's Blue Eyed Baby Boy   Brown, Lew 1930; DeSylva 1930; Henderson 1930

Mrs. Kwakk-Kwakk   Evans 1963; Livingston, Jay 1963

Mrs. Maloney   Jerome 1905; Schwartz, Jean 1905

Mrs. Meltzer Wants the Money Now   Coleman 1988

Mrs. Murphy's Chowder   Clarke 1924; Leslie 1924

Mrs. Oho   Smith, Robert B. 1907

Mrs. Sally Adams   Berlin 1950

Mrs. Santa Claus   Livingston, Jerry 1956; Sherman 1984

Mrs. Winchell's Boy   Gilbert 1932; Silver 1932

Much Too Much   Cahn 1936

Mu-Cha-Cha   Comden and Green 1956; Dubin 1935; Duke 1931; Gorney 1931; Harburg 1931; Styne 1956; Warren 1935

Muchacha (Little Dolores)   Hart 1934; Kahn 1934; Rodgers 1934

Mucho Gusto (Oye Needa)   Caesar 1945

Muezzins and Bayaderres   Herbert 1907; Smith, Harry B. 1907

Muffled Drums   Hanley 1922

Muggin' Lightly   Arlen 1933; Koehler 1933

Muggin' the Pillow   Cahn 1935

Mulberry   Fisher 1921

Mulberry Street   Davis 1952; Silver 1952

Mulberry Tree, The   Duke 1944

Mule   Willson 1953

Mule Walk (inst.)   Johnson, James P. 1939

Mule, You Lazy Mule   Livingston, Jerry 1955

Mulligatawney   Brown, Nacio Herb 1948

Multiplied by Eight   Johnson, Howard 1921

Multitudes of Amys   Sondheim 1970

Mulunghu Thabu   Hammerstein 1927; Harbach 1927

Mumbles Blues   Gilbert 1952

Mumbo Jumbo King of the Congo   Freed, Ralph 1934

Mum's the Word   Cobb 1904; Edwards 1904; Johnson, J. Rosamond 1909

Mumsey   Gilbert 1920

Mumuring   Davis 1922; Silver 1922

Munch Theme   Comden and Green 1982

Munchkinland   Arlen 1939; Harburg 1939

Murder   Harbach 1921

Murder at the Vanities (Opening)   Coslow 1934; Johnston 1934

"Murder" He Says   Loesser 1943; McHugh 1943

Murder in Parkwold   Weill 1949

Murder in the Moonlight (It's Love in the First Degree)   Lewis 1935

Murderous Monty (And Light-Fingered Jane)   Gershwin, George 1925

Murdoch, My Son (Start Haunting Around)   Styne 1958

Muriel   Freed, Ralph 1954; Hoffman 1954

Murrayisms   Romberg 1921

Museum Song   Coleman 1980

Musgrove Military Prep   Evans 1952; Livingston, Jay 1952

Mush   Hanley 1931

Mush You Haulers   Coslow 1935; Whiting 1935

Music Across the Waters   Willson 1953

Music, Always Music   Carmichael 1957

Music and Moonlight   Freed, Arthur 1932; Meyer 1932

Music and the Emotions   Hart Date Unknown; Rodgers Date Unknown

Music Box   Martin 1952; Oakland 1958

Music Box Fantasy (inst.), A   Coots 1945

Music Box (inst.), The   Young, Victor 1952

Music Box Twist   Sigman 1962

Music Box You Gave Me, The   Spina 1947

Music Call, The   Brennan 1928

Music Caressing of Violins   Smith, Harry B. 1911

Music for Lovers   Howard, Bart 1956

Music for Madame   Lawrence 1957; Magidson 1937; Wrubel 1937

Music for the Feet   Yellen 1957

Music from Across the Bay   Sigman 1971

Music from Across the Sea   Mercer 1933

Music from Another World   Lawrence 1959

Music from Beyond the Moon   Lawrence 1947

Music from Paradise   Loesser 1940, 1943; McHugh 1940, 1943

Music Grew Softer and Softer, The   David, Mack 1947; Hoffman 1947; Livingston, Jerry 1947

Music Hall Rag   Mills 1935

Music Hath Charms   Ager 1930; Oakland 1931; Yellen 1930

Music Hath Charms (My Heart Is Yours)   Friml 1934

Music in My Dreams   Coslow 1937

Music in My Fingers   Heyman 1931

Music in My Heart   Alter 1937; Fields 1935; McHugh 1935; Mills 1950; Webster 1937

Music in the Barn   Carmichael 1940; Mercer 1940

Music in the Moonlight   Coslow 1930

Music in the Night   Hammerstein 1936

Music Is Better Than Words   Comden and Green 1955

Music Is Magic   Clare 1935; Johnston 1935

Music Lesson, The   Berlin 1916

Music Lessons (C'est Chouette La)   Rome 1956

Music, Maestro, Please   Magidson 1938; Wrubel 1938

Music Makers   Raye 1941

Music Makes Me   Eliscu 1933; Kahn 1933; Youmans 1933

Music Makes Me Sentimental (Blame the Music Don't Blame Me)   Bryan 1908

Music Makin' Man, The   Coots 1937

Music, Music, Everywhere   Arlen 1932; Koehler 1932

Music of a Little Rippling Stream, The   Brown, Lew 1927; Friend 1927

Music of a Mountain Stream, The   Robison 1925

Music of Being Free, The   Bergman 1990

Music of Goodbye, The   Bergman 1986

Music of Home, The   Loesser 1960

Music of Love, The   Leigh 1979

Music of Moonlight and Love, The   Smith, Harry B. 1925

Music of My Lord   Robison 1957

Music of the Gypsies (inst.)   Brown, Nacio Herb 1930
Music of the Stricken Redeemer   Weill 1936
Music on the Shore   Loesser 1939
Music on the Water   Freed, Arthur 1950; Warren 1950
Music, Romance and 'Specially Love   Stept 1958
Music Stopped, The   Adamson 1943; McHugh 1943
Music that Makes Me Dance, The   Merrill 1964; Styne 1964
Music Thrills Me, The   Smith, Harry B. 1926
Music to a Dancing Bird   Russell 1946
Music to My Ears   Coslow 1933; Evans 1944; Fisher 1937;
    Johnston 1933; Livingston, Jay 1944
Music to Their Ears   Leigh 1967
Music Vot's Music Must Come from Berlin   Kahn 1911
Music, Wind, an Old Bouquet   Gilbert 1943
Music with Meals   Porter 1910
Musica de Roma   Mercer 1970
Musical Bill of Fare   Gershwin, George 1922
Musical Chairs   Eliscu 1941; Gorney 1941; Mercer 1953
Musical Comedy Blues   Stept 1919
Musical Comedy Maid, The   Cohan 1907
Musical Culture   Smith, Harry B. 1934
Musical Moon   Cohan 1911
Musical Opening   Fields 1933; McHugh 1933
Musical Prince, A   Oakland 1952
Musical Romance of Tom Thumb and Tiny Teena,
    The   Magidson 1930
Musical Scene No. 1: Opening   DeSylva 1933; Robin 1933;
    Whiting 1933
Musical Scene No. 2: Examination of Loo Loo   DeSylva
    1933; Robin 1933
Musical Shoes   Atteridge 1924; Romberg 1924; Schwartz,
    Jean 1924
Musical Snore, The   Friml 1917
Musical Station Breaks   Bergman 1955
Musical Tour of the City   Gorney 1948
Musical Wedding   Brooks 1945
(We're Three of the Four) Musketeers   Kalmar 1928; Ruby
    1928
Must Have a Chorus   Johnston 1938
Must I Say Adios (Amor Querido)   Bryan 1930
Must It Be Good-Bye?   DeSylva 1924
Must It Be Platonic Forever?   Ahlert 1934; Leslie 1934
Must It Be the End   Kalmar 1931; Ruby 1931
Must You Be an Elite Driver   Caesar 1943
Must You Go   Cahn 1966; Van Heusen 1966
Must You Wear a Mustache?   Silver 1928
Mustafa (The Sheik of Chicago)   Merrill 1959
Mustang   Washington 1955
Mustang Ramble   Coleman 1964
Mutiny in the Nursery   Mercer 1938
Mutiny in the Parlor   Heyman 1936
Mutiny on the Bandstand   Cahn 1936
Mutton Song   Fisher 1934
My Absent Lover   Gilbert 1943
My Adventure   Mercer 1938; Warren 1938
My Affinity   Smith, Harry B. 1908
My All   Gershwin, Ira 1923; Russell 1957
My Alsace Lorraine   Gilbert 1914
My American Beauty   Coslow 1934; Johnston 1934
My American Beauty Girl (The Melting Pot)   Buck 1916
My American Creed   Revel 1944; Webster 1944
My Angel   Adamson Date Unknown; Pollack 1927; Warren
    Date Unknown
My Angel Mother's Serenade   Johnson, Howard 1935
My Angelina   Gilbert 1929

My Angeline   Herbert 1895; Smith, Harry B. 1895
My Anna   Merrill 1956
My Apple Pie Guy   Coots 1957
My Arab Complex   Hanley 1934
My Arabian Maid   Buck 1917
My Arms   Ellington 1958
My Arms Are Open   Washington 1928
My Arms Are Waiting   Gorney 1927; Whiting 1927
My Averne Rose   Goetz 1913
My Babe from Boston Town   Cohan 1899
My Baby   Donaldson 1922
My Baby Has It   Magidson 1928
My Baby Is Driving Me Wild   Coslow 1927
My Baby Just Cares for Me   Donaldson 1928; Kahn 1928
My Baby Knows   Meyer 1907; Turk 1907
My Baby Knows How   Akst 1926; David, Mack 1940; Davis
    1926; Stept 1940
My Baby Loves to Swing   Cahn 1962; Van Heusen 1962
My Baby Made a Cry Baby of Me   Coots 1933; Johnson,
    Howard 1933
My Baby Said Yes   Rose 1929
My Baby Said Yes, Yes   Friend 1931
My Baby Sure Knows How to Love   Razaf 1929
My Baby Talk Lady   Romberg 1918
My Baby Talk Lady (My Baby Talking Girl)   Atteridge 1918
My Baby Talking Girl (My Baby Talk Lady)   Schwartz, Jean
    1918
My Baby Walked Out on Me   Revel 1959
My Baby's Baby Blue Eyes   Akst 1950; Davis 1950
My Baby's Come Back to Me   Berlin 1926
My Baby's Comin' Back Home   Waller 1924
My Baby's Gone   Johnston 1926; Turk 1926
My Baby's Got Such Lovin' Ways   David, Hal 1955
My Baby's on Strike   Hoffman 1934
My Bajadere   DeSylva 1922
My Bambazoo   Snyder 1909
My Bambino   Fisher 1920; Hoffman 1954
My Bamboo Cane   Revel 1944; Webster 1944
My Bamboo Queen   Sterling 1902; Von Tilzer 1902
My Barney Lies Over the Ocean, Just the Way He Lied to
    Me   Lewis 1919; Young, Joe 1919
My Bathing Suit   Heyman 1931
My Beautiful   Loesser 1940; Young, Victor 1940
My Beautiful Circus Girl   Hammerstein 1934; Kern 1934
My Beautiful Egypt   Bryan 1917
My Beautiful Fragonard Girl   Bryan 1922; Schwartz, Jean
    1922
My Beautiful Irish Maid   Olcott 1925
My Beautiful Mexican Rose   Mills 1924
My Beautiful Queen of Hearts   Cobb 1904; Edwards 1904
My Beautiful Rhinestone Girl   Berlin 1932
My Beautiful Senorita   Revel 1946
My Beautiful Tiger Girl   Bryan 1919; Schwartz, Jean 1919
My Beauty   Loesser 1960
My Beauty Shop   Akst 1929; Clarke 1929
My Bedouin Girl   Atteridge 1917; Romberg 1917
My Bel Ami   Lawrence 1947
My Belle Zabelle   Cobb 1907; Edwards 1907
My Beloved   Evans 1952; Livingston, Jay 1952
My Ben Ali Haggin Girl   Berlin 1921
My Best Beau   Gordon 1963; Myrow 1963
My Best Gal   Blake 1930; Razaf 1930
My Best Girl   Donaldson 1924
My Best Love   Hammerstein 1958; Rodgers 1958
My Best Wishes   Koehler 1938

My Bicycle Girl   Hammerstein 1940; Schwartz, Arthur 1940
My Big Mistake   Coleman 1991; Comden and Green 1991
My Big Moment   Cahn 1980
My Bill from Louisville   Snyder 1911
My Billboard Girl   Johnston 1938
My Bird of Paradise   Berlin 1915; Brennan 1930; Friml 1930
My Black Bess   Sterling 1899; Von Tilzer 1899
My Blackbirds Are Bluebirds Now   Caesar 1929; Friend 1929
My Blue Bird's Singing the Blues   Rainger 1933; Robin 1933
My Blue Danube   Johnson, Howard 1932
My Blue Eyed Madonna   Davis 1949; Silver 1949
My Blue Heaven   Donaldson 1927
My Blue Lagoon   Johnson, J. Rosamond 1929
My Blue Print of Dreams   DeSylva 1953
My Bluebird's Back Again   Friend 1931
My Blue-Bird's Home Again   Brown, Lew 1927; DeSylva
    1927; Henderson 1927
My Blushing Rose   Buck 1913
My Body   Coleman 1996
My Bohemian Fashion Girl   Bryan 1916
My Book of Animal Songs   Coots 1953
My Book of Memory   Heyman 1948
My Boy   Conrad 1924; Coots 1924; Harbach 1909; Kern 1918
My Boy and I   Hammerstein 1923; Youmans 1923
My Boy Friend   Hammerstein 1922
My Boy Joe   Hanley 1921
My Boy, My Boy   Loesser 1941
My Boy, You're in Society!   Smith, Harry B. 1896
My Bridal Gown   Schwartz, Arthur 1937
My Bridal Veil   Ager 1920, 1930; Yellen 1920, 1930
My British Buddy   Berlin 1943
My Broadway   Kahn 1922
My Broadway Chorus Girl   Conrad 1920
My Broadway Racketeer   Leslie 1928; Monaco 1928
My Broadway Romeo   Buck 1912
My Broken Dream   Sigman 1956
My Broker Told Me So   Duke 1946
My Broth of a Boy   Porter 1944
My Brother Bill   Atteridge 1915
My Brother's Coming with Pineapples   Mitchell 1923;
    Pollack 1923
My Brudda Sylvest   Fisher 1908
My Budapest   Cahn 1957
My Budding Rose   Gilbert 1920
My Buddy   Donaldson 1922; Kahn 1922
My Buick, My Love and I   Brooks 1951
My Bunco Queen   Smith, Harry B. 1901
My Bundle of Love   Silver 1926
My Busy Day   Hammerstein 1922; Mitchell 1922 *
My Bwana   Hammerstein 1927; Harbach 1927
My Cadill-liddle-ol-lac   Carmichael 1950; Mercer 1950
My Cairo Maid   DeSylva 1917
My Campfire Dreams   Alter 1937; Webster 1937
My Canary Has Circles Under His Eyes   Koehler 1931
My Caramel Gal   Cohan 1909
My Caravan   Gorney 1926
My Caravan of Love   Bryan 1936
My Carolina Cutey   Sterling 1911; Von Tilzer 1911
My Carolina Hide-Away   Coots 1934
My Carolina Lady   Sterling 1901
My Castillian Girl   Atteridge 1922; Schwartz, Jean 1922
My Castle in Maine   Heyman 1933
(Our) My Castle in Spain   Herbert 1903
My Castle in Spain Is a Shack in the Lane   Caesar 1929;
    Friend 1929

My Castle in the Air   Kern 1916
My Castle in the Sand   Blane 1951
My Castle on Riverside Drive   Evans 1947; Livingston, Jay
    1947
My Castle on the Nile   Johnson, J. Rosamond 1901
My Catamaran   Herbert 1904
My Cavalier   Caesar 1923; Conrad 1923; Willson 1928
My Celia   Kern 1905
My Charcoal Charmer   Cobb 1900; Edwards 1900
My Cherokee Rose   Harbach 1923
My Cherry Blossom   Smith, Harry B. 1921; Snyder 1921
My Child   Livingston, Jerry 1949
My Child Wants to Know   Leigh 1968
My Chocolate Soldier Boy   Bryan 1919; Schwartz, Jean 1919
My Christmas Song for You   Carmichael 1944, 1950;
    Webster 1944, 1950
My Christmas Wish   Parish 1945
My Cinderella   Howard, Joseph E. 1907
My City   Coleman 1973; Fields 1973; Strouse 1985
My Cleopatra Girl   Atteridge 1914
My Coal Black Mammy   Atteridge 1922
My Coca-Cola Belle   Atteridge 1913; Schwartz, Jean 1913
My Colleen from Killarney   Mills 1940
My Compliments to the Chef   Evans 1973; Livingston, Jay
    1973
My Concerto to You   Mills 1947
My Confession of Love   Strouse 1960
My Connecticut Gal   Donaldson 1927
My Consolation   Washington 1960
My Conversation   Adamson 1953; Carmichael 1953
My Conversational Man   Lerner, Sammy 1928
My Counterfeit Bill   Sterling 1911; Von Tilzer 1911
My Country   Brennan 1940; Snyder 1940
My Country Cousin   Bryan Date Unknown; Youmans Date
    Unknown
My Cousin Beauregard   Leigh 1971
My Cousin Caruso   Edwards 1908
My Cousin in Milwaukee   Gershwin, George 1932;
    Gershwin, Ira 1932
My Cozy Little Corner of the Ritz   Porter 1919
My Cradle Melody Keeps Bringing Me Back to Old
    Virginia   Meyer 1922; Young, Joe 1922
My Cradle Melody Keeps Swinging Me Back to Old
    Virginia   Lewis 1922
My Crazy Little Mixed Up Heart   Coslow 1955
My Crazy Little Mixed-Up Heart   Coslow 1956
My Creed   Robison 1958
My Crinoline Girl   Blake 1923; Sissle 1923
My Croony Melody   Goetz 1914
My Crown for Thee   Young, Victor 1914
My Crystal Ball   Johnson, J. Rosamond 1946
My Curley Headed Baby   Bryan 1919; Schwartz, Jean 1919
My Cutey's Due at Two to Two   Robin 1926
My Cymbalum   Brown, Nacio Herb 1931
My Daddies   Hart Date Unknown; Rodgers Date Unknown
My Daddy   Norworth 1921
My Daddy Don't Do Nothin' Bad   Razaf 1928
My Daddy Knows   Lewis 1920; Young, Joe 1920
My Daddy Long Legs   Goetz 1914
My Daddy's Growin' Old, So I'll Have to Look
    Aroun'   Razaf 1924
My Dad's Violin   Howard, Joseph E. 1950
My Dancing Lady   Fields 1933; McHugh 1933
My Darlin' Eileen   Comden and Green 1953
My Darlin' Has a Cordial Eye   David, Hal 1953

My Darlin' Man   Merrill 1951

My Darling   Heyman 1932; Kahn 1926; Mills 1929; Parish 1929

My Darling Is Never Late   Porter 1957

My Darling, My Darling   Loesser 1948

My Darling, My Sweetheart, My Love   Hoffman 1952

My Darling Said Yes   Coslow 1927

My Daughter Fanny the Star   Merrill 1964; Styne 1964

My Daughter Is Wed to a Friend of Mine   Cohan 1909

My Day Begins and Ends with You   Coots 1936; Davis 1936

My Day Dreams Came True Over Night   Hoffman 1929; Silver 1929

My Day Has Come   Caesar 1920; Herbert 1920

My Dear   Kahn 1929

My Dear Benvenuto   Gershwin, Ira 1945; Weill 1945

My Dear Little Home (By the Sea)   Mills 1928

My Dear Public   Caesar 1943

My Dearest, My Darling, My Sweetheart   Livingston, Jerry 1955

My Dearest One   David, Mack 1962

My DeeTees   Dubin 1940; Fain 1940

My Defenses Are Down   Berlin 1946

My Desert Rose   David, Mack 1945

My Design for Living   Gordon 1933; Revel 1933

My Destiny   Cahn 1956; David, Mack 1950; Livingston, Jerry 1950

My Destiny Is You (inst.)   Revel 1959

My Diabalo Beau   Smith, Harry B. 1908

My Diamond Girls   Atteridge 1922

My Diamond Horseshoe of Girls   Berlin 1922

My Dixie   Mitchell 1922

My Dixie Rosary   Hanley 1920

My Doctor   Harbach 1925; Youmans 1925

My Dog and Me   Merrill 1952

My Dog Loves Your Dog   Caesar 1934; Henderson 1934; Yellen 1934

My Dolly and Me   Coots 1953

My Downfall   Russell 1951; Spina 1951

My Dream   Hoffman 1959; Yellen 1977

My Dream Affair   Cahn 1951

My Dream and I   Oakland 1939

My Dream Comes True   Smith, Harry B. 1928

My Dream Concerto   David, Mack 1946

My Dream Feathered Nest   Stept 1941

My Dream for Tomorrow   Sherman 1974

My Dream Girl (I Loved You Long Ago)   Herbert 1924

My Dream Girl of Honolulu   Monaco 1927

My Dream Is Yours   Blane 1949; Warren 1949

My Dream Memory   Clare 1929

My Dream of Love Is You   DeSylva 1919; Gershwin, George 1919

My Dream of My Paree   Donaldson 1941

My Dream of Paradise   Brown, A. Seymour 1911

My Dream of the Big Parade   Dubin 1926; McHugh 1926

My Dream of the South of France   Kalmar 1966; Ruby 1966

My Dream of the Union Jack   Snyder 1910

My Dream of the U.S.A.   Snyder 1908

My Dream Sonata   David, Mack 1955; Van Heusen 1955

My Dream Song   Coots 1946

My Dreamboat Is Drifting (Down the River of Doubt)   Bacharach 1956

My Dreams   Friml 1928

My Dreams and I   Lerner, Sammy 1939

My Dreams Have Gone with the Wind   Oakland 1937

My Dreamy China Lady   Kahn 1916

My Dreamy Lou   Jerome 1903; Schwartz, Jean 1903

My Dutch Lady   Atteridge 1923; Schwartz, Jean 1923

My Dynamo   Schwartz, Arthur 1929

My Egotism Is Hurtin' Me   Robison 1951

My Empty Arms   Egan 1912; Whiting 1912

My English Into French Dictionary   Burke 1953; Van Heusen 1953

My Ever-Lovin'   Sigman 1952

My Fair Lady   DeSylva 1925; Gershwin, George 1925; Gershwin, Ira 1925; Johnston 1948; Sigman 1947

My Fair Unknown   Herbert 1905; Smith, Harry B. 1905

My Faith   Razaf 1950

My Fannie   DeSylva 1919; Gershwin, George 1919

My Farm in Normandie   Bryan 1930

My Fate Is In Your Hands   Razaf 1929; Waller 1929

My Father Said   Dietz 1934; Schwartz, Arthur 1934

My Father's Love Is All   Bryan 1930

My Favorite Brunette   Evans 1947; Livingston, Jay 1947

My Favorite Chair   Evans 1958; Livingston, Jay 1958

My Favorite Girl   David, Mack 1936; Meyer 1936

My Favorite Memory   Lawrence 1954

My Favorite Person   Fields 1933; McHugh 1933

My Favorite Song   Magidson 1944

My Favorite Things   Hammerstein 1959; Rodgers 1959

My Feelin's Are Hurt (inst.)   Waller 1931

My Feet Takes Me Away   Russell 1947, 1948

My Fellow Entertainers   Drake 1958

My Fellow Guests   Drake 1954

My Fence Around Your Heart   Johnson, J. Rosamond 1950

My Fiddle and Me   Young, Joe 1933

My Fifty Golden Years   Yellen 1954

My Filipino Pet   Smith, Harry B. 1901

My Fine Feathered Friend   Adamson 1938; McHugh 1938

My First Alphabet Song   Bergman 1958

My First and Only Love   Friend 1930; Schwartz, Jean 1930

My First Counting Song   Bergman 1958

My First Impression of You   Stept 1938

My First Long Pants   Cobb 1917; Edwards 1917

My First Love   David, Mack 1943; Lewis 1928; Young, Joe 1928

My First Love Letter   Caesar 1925; Davis 1950; Romberg 1925; Silver 1950

My First Love (Mujer)   Washington 1938

My First Love, My Last Love   Caesar 1930; Harbach 1930; Romberg 1930

My First Love to Last   Whiting 1933

My First, My Last, My Only   Caesar 1945

My First Promise   Blane 1941

My First Smoke   Jerome 1905; Schwartz, Jean 1905

My First Sweetheart   Ahlert 1928; Turk 1928

My First Waltz   Herbert 1946

My Flag   Cohan 1914

My Flame Is Just a Match for Me   Fain 1928

My Flame of Love   Bryan 1929

My Flaming Heart   Cahn 1953; Robin 1952

My Flower of Japan   Rainger 1932

My Follies Girl   Akst 1944

My Foolish Heart   Bullock 1935; Washington 1949; Whiting 1935; Young, Victor 1949

My Fortune Is Love   Harburg 1931

My Fortune Is My Face   Comden and Green 1964; Styne 1964

My Fraulein   Evans 1958; Livingston, Jay 1958

My Friend   Coleman 1996; Comden and Green 1972; Drake 1953

My Friend Franklin   Rome 1944

My Friend Irma   Evans 1949; Livingston, Jay 1948

My Friend the Night   Hart 1934; Rodgers 1934

My Friends   Sondheim 1979

My Friends Morris and Max   Kalmar 1918; Leslie 1918; Ruby 1918

My Friends, the Stars   Hoffman 1937

My Funny Valentine   Hart 1937; Rodgers 1937

My Future Just Passed   Whiting 1930

My Future Star   Clare 1934; Whiting 1934

My Future Wife   Rainger 1933; Robin 1933

My Gaby Doll   Atteridge 1923; Romberg 1923; Schwartz, Jean 1923

My Gal Alice   Revel 1942

My Gal and I   Loesser 1944

My Gal Don't Love Me Anymore   Friend 1924

My Gal Is Mine Once More   Dietz 1948; Schwartz, Arthur 1948

My Gal! My Gal!   Smith, Harry B. 1901

My Gal! My Sal!   Smith, Harry B. 1901; Sterling 1902

My Gal, Won't You Come Back to Me? (My Gal, My Pal)   Arlen 1924

My Gal's a Mule   Fields 1959

My Gal's Working at Lockheed   Loesser 1944

My Gang   Cohan 1923

My Garden of Prayer   Webster 1966

My Garret Became a Heaven When You Came Through the Door   Brennan 1925

My Gaucho   Cahn 1953; Robin 1952

My Geisha (You Are Sympathy to Me)   David, Hal 1962

My Georgia Caroline   Fisher 1920

My Georgia Gal   Porter 1913

My Georgia Lady Love   Sterling 1899

My Gift of Dreams   Razaf 1932; Waller 1932

My Gigolo   Coslow 1934; Johnston 1934

My Gink   Schwartz, Jean 1935

My Girl   Gilbert 1921; Hammerstein 1927; Kern 1927

My Girl and I   Hammerstein 1941; Romberg 1941

My Girl Back Home   Hammerstein 1949; Rodgers 1949

My Girl Don't Love Me   Caesar 1933; Motzan 1933

My Girl Friend's Boy Friend   Hoffman 1955; Merrill 1955

My Girl Has Eye Trouble   Kahn 1926

My Girl Has Halitosis   Brown, Lew 1925

My Girl (inst.)   Meyer 1910

My Girl Is Just Enough Woman for Me   Fields 1959

My Girl Is Named Yvonne   Rainger 1932

My Girls   Drake 1952

My God Is On High   Robison 1964

My God Is So High   Robison 1953

My Golden Girl   Herbert 1920

My Golden Prairie   Gilbert 1917

My Golden West   Kahn 1938; Romberg 1938

My Good Friends of Erin's Isle   Herbert 1917

My Goodbye to You   Kahn 1931

My Grandfather's Clock in the Hallway   Gordon 1936; Revel 1936

My Grandmother's Grandfather's Clock   Willson 1953

My Great Desire   Von Tilzer 1933

My Great Waltz   Johnson, Howard 1935

My Greatest Day!   Sondheim 1957

My Greatest Sin   David, Mack 1979

My Guardian Angel   Stept 1952

My Guiding Star   Comden and Green 1956; David, Mack 1970; Styne 1956

My Guy and I   Brooks 1953; Young, Victor 1953

My Gypsy Heart   DePaul 1950; Raye 1950

My Gypsy Maid   Howard, Joseph E. 1905

My Gypsy Rhapsody   Lawrence 1933

My Gypsy Sweetheart   Herbert 1909

My Hands Are Tied   Stept 1939

My Handsome   Dietz 1944; Duke 1944

My Handy Man Ain't Handy No More   Blake 1930; Razaf 1930

My Hannah Lady   Jerome 1900

My Happiness Is You   De Lange 1932

My Harlem Wench   Porter 1929

My Hat's in the Ring   Williams 1912

My Hat's on the Side of My Head   Woods 1933

My Hawaiian Dream Girl   Mills 1928

My Hawaiian Heaven   Parish 1928

My Hawaiian Paradise   Fain 1922

My Hawaiian Song of Love   Akst 1927; Davis 1927

My Hawaiian Sunshine   Gilbert 1916

My Hawaiian Sweetheart   Mills 1929; Parish 1929

My Haytian Queen   Jerome 1909; Schwartz, Jean 1909

My Head Upon Your Shoulder   Washington 1945

My Headache   Johnson, James P. 1932; Razaf 1932

My Heart   Burke 1971

My Heart and I   Rainger 1936; Robin 1936

My Heart and I Decided   Donaldson 1942

My Heart at Thy Sweet Voice   Johnson, Howard 1939

My Heart Beats Faster   Loesser 1948

My Heart Became of Age   Sherman 1959

My Heart Belongs to America   Stept 1942

My Heart Belongs to Daddy   Porter 1938

My Heart Belongs to You   Washington 1959

My Heart Cries for You   Sigman 1950

My Heart Cries Out I Love You   Friend 1929; Silver 1929

My Heart Decided   Duke 1950; Rome 1950

My Heart Does a Rumba   Rainger 1934; Robin 1934

My Heart Doesn't Know   Friend 1955

My Heart Follows My Eyes   Carroll 1950

My Heart for You Pines Away   Sissle 1913

My Heart Goes Crazy   Burke 1946; Van Heusen 1946

My Heart Goes Out to You   David, Hal 1960

My Heart Has Come a Tumbling Down   Duke 1963

My Heart Has Many Dreams   Sigman 1953

My Heart I Cannot Give to You   Kern 1911

My Heart Is a Ball of String   Bacharach 1961; David, Hal 1961

My Heart Is a Chapel   David, Mack 1956

My Heart Is a Gypsy   Kahn 1938, 1939

My Heart Is a Hobo   Burke 1940, 1947; Monaco 1940; Van Heusen 1947

My Heart Is a Singing Heart   Cahn 1953; Fain 1953

My Heart Is a Stranger   Ellington 1965

My Heart Is a Violin   De Lange 1936; Pollack 1935; Webster 1935

My Heart Is Always in Waltz Time (Until I Meet You)   Brown, Lew 1970; Henderson 1970

My Heart Is an Open Book   David, Hal 1958; Gordon 1934, 1935; Revel 1934

My Heart Is At Your Command   Johnson, Howard 1940

My Heart Is Back Again   Ager 1936

My Heart Is Bluer than Your Eyes, Cherie   Bryan 1929

My Heart Is Calling   Atteridge 1922; Romberg 1922

My Heart Is Calling You   Friend 1926

My Heart Is Dancing   Schwartz, Arthur 1937

My Heart Is Filled with You   Coots 1945

My Heart Is Home   Dixon 1932; Evans 1953; Livingston, Jay 1953

My Heart Is in the Roses   Bryan 1927; Fisher 1927

My Heart Is Like a Little Canoe   Bryan 1958

My Heart Is Like a Violin   Comden and Green 1964; Styne 1964

My Heart Is Like Missouri   Drake 1958

My Heart Is Like the Willow   Harburg 1969

My Heart Is My Master   Heyman 1938

My Heart Is Part of You   Dietz 1932; Schwartz, Arthur 1932

My Heart Is Sheba Bound   Hart 1926; Rodgers 1926

(Don't Look Now but) My Heart Is Showing   Weill 1948

My Heart Is Singing   Kahn 1936

My Heart Is So Full of You   Loesser 1956

My Heart Is Still Among the Hills of Ireland   Johnson, Howard 1935

My Heart Is Taking Lessons   Burke 1938; Monaco 1938

My Heart is the Garden and You Are My Beautiful Rose   Fisher 1917

My Heart Is Unemployed   Rome 1938

My Heart Is Waking   Atteridge 1921

My Heart Is Young   Heyman 1931; Youmans 1931

My Heart Is Yours   Gershwin, Ira 1924; Silver 1954

My Heart Is Yours (Mi Amor e Tuo)   Johnson, James P. 1954

My Heart Isn't In It   Lawrence 1942

My Heart Jumped Over the Moon   Kahal 1935; Mills 1941

My Heart Keeps on Speaking of Love   Kahn 1928

My Heart Keeps Right on Beating (But It's Beating for Another Girl)   Kahn 1911

My Heart Knows a Love Song   Cahn 1956

My Heart Left Me   Brown, Nacio Herb 1948

My Heart, My Mind, My Everything   Ellington 1958

My Heart of Hearts   David, Hal 1959

My Heart Says Yes   Coslow 1955

My Heart Sings   Rainger 1936; Robin 1936

My Heart Skips a Beat   Donaldson 1937; Drake 1952

My Heart Song   Sigman 1955

My Heart Still Belongs to You   Cahn 1937

My Heart Still Remembers   Webster 1958

My Heart Stood Still   Hart 1927; Rodgers 1927

My Heart Tells Me It's You   Johnson, Howard 1945

My Heart Tells Me (Should I Believe My Heart?)   Gordon 1943; Warren 1943

My Heart Wants to Dance   Kalmar 1936; Ruby 1936

My Heart Wants To Kiss You, Cherie   Bryan 1929

My Heart Was Doing a Bolero   Coslow 1947

My Heart Was in My Mouth   Bryan 1936

My Heart Whispers Beware   Mills 1947

My Heart Will Belong to You   Baer 1954

My Heart Will Miss You   Baer 1954

My Heart Will Sail (Across the Sea)   DeSylva 1922; Gershwin, George 1922; Goetz 1922

My Heart Will Sing   Donaldson 1934; Kahn 1934

My Heart Will Still Be Young   Bacharach 1987

My Heart Will Tell Me So   Kahn 1926

My Heart Will Tell You So   Lawrence 1960

My Heart Won't Say Goodbye   Robin 1954; Romberg 1954

My Heart's a Banjo   Gorney 1931; Harburg 1931

My Heart's Achin' for Macon   Howard, Joseph E. 1915

My Heart's an Open Book   Heyman 1934

My Heart's at Ease   Waller 1932; Young, Joe 1932

My Heart's Darlin'   Blane 1952

My Heart's Desire   David, Mack 1953; Heyman 1952; Sterling 1924; Whiting 1933; Young, Victor 1952, 1956

My Heart's in the Heart of the West   Coslow 1936; Young, Victor 1936

My Heart's in the Right Place   Monaco 1934

My Heart's Love Call   Akst 1930; Clarke 1930

My Heart's Popping   Evans 1940; Livingston, Jay 1940

My Heart's Tonight in Old New Hampshire with My Lady Jane   Sterling 1917

My Heart's Wrapped Up in Gingham   Burke 1944; Van Heusen 1944

My Heather Belle   Goetz 1912

My Heaven and Earth   Merrill 1954

My Heaven in the Pines   Conrad 1938

My Heaven of Love   Bryan 1929

My Heaven on Earth   Gilbert 1932

My Heaven with You   Friml 1927

My Hero   Ahlert 1930; Herbert 1924; Turk 1930

My Hero (Parody)   Goetz 1912

My Hidden Treasure   Kalmar 1913

My Highbrow Fling   Hammerstein 1922; Mitchell 1922

My Hills of Home   Brennan 1930; Friml 1930

My Hindoo Man   Williams 1905

My Holiday Girl   Atteridge 1918

My Home   Cahn 1958; Coslow 1925; Dubin 1925; Mills 1925; Van Heusen 1958

My Home Among the Hills   Sterling Date Unknown

My Home Is in My Shoes   Mercer 1951

My Home Lies Quiet   Ellington 1958

My Home Town   Cahn 1956; Oakland 1935, 1937

My Home Town Girl   Porter 1911

My Home Town Is a One Horse Town   Silver 1920

My Home's a Highway   Blane 1952

My Hometown   Drake 1964

My Hondloo   Parish 1928

My Honey   Warren 1925

My Honey Bunch   Smith, Harry B. 1903

My Honey Lou   DeSylva 1922; Donaldson 1922

My Honey of My Heart   Atteridge Date Unknown

My Honey's Coming Home   Kahn 1927

My Honey's Eyes   Baer 1922

My Honor and My Sword (Borrow Trouble)   Herbert 1903; Smith, Harry B. 1903

My Hour Has Come   Rainger 1932

My Houseboat on the Hudson   Dietz 1924; Kern 1924

My Houseboat on the Thames   Porter 1912

My How the Time Goes By   Adamson 1947; Brooks 1957; McHugh 1948

My, How This Country Has Changed   Arlen 1936; Harburg 1936

My Hula Hula Girl   Jerome 1903; Schwartz, Jean 1903

My Hula Maid   Atteridge 1915

My Human Magazine   Schwartz, Jean 1908; Williams 1908

My Humble Heart   Drake 1951

My Hungarian Irish Girl   Kern 1906

My Husband the Pig   Sondheim 1973

My Husband's First Wife   Hammerstein 1929; Kern 1929

My I.B.M. and I   Rome Date Unknown

My Idea of a Girl   Edwards 1913

My Idea of a Wife   Harbach 1930

My Idea of a Wife (My Idea of a Man)   Caesar 1930; Romberg 1930

My Idea of Heaven   Johnson, Howard 1927

My Idea of Love   Johnson, James P. 1930

My Idea of Paradise   Smith, Harry B. 1911

My Idea of Something to Go Home To   Herbert 1919; Smith, Robert B. 1919

My Ideal   Kalmar 1923; Leslie 1929; Robin 1930; Ruby 1923;
   Smith, Harry B. 1903; Stept 1928; Whiting 1930
My Illinois   Howard, Joseph E. 1905
My Imaginary Love   Coslow 1938; David, Hal 1952;
   Lawrence 1944
My Imaginary Sweetheart   Akst 1933; Eliscu 1933
My Impression of You   Magidson 1930; Washington 1930
My Inamorata   Mercer 1967
My Indian Family   Fain 1960; Webster 1960
My Indiana Anna   Schwartz, Jean 1905; Williams 1905
My Inspiration Is You   Leslie 1928
My International Girl   Lerner, Sammy 1933
My Introduction to Love   Caesar 1935; Carmichael 1935
My Intuition   Dietz 1930; Freed, Ralph 1965; Mercer 1945;
   Schwartz, Arthur 1930; Warren 1945
My Irish American Rose   Sterling 1918
My Irish Daisy   Jerome 1905; Schwartz, Jean 1905
My Irish Gibson Girl   Jerome 1907; Schwartz, Jean 1907
My Irish Girl   Bryan 1912; Williams 1907, 1910
My Irish Indian, Mary Ann McCue   Jerome 1905; Schwartz,
   Jean 1905
My Irish Molly O'   Jerome 1905; Schwartz, Jean 1905
My Irish Romeo   Atteridge 1913; Schwartz, Jean 1913
My Irish Rosary   Fisher 1921
My Irish Rosie   Jerome 1906; Schwartz, Jean 1906
My Irish Song of Songs   Dubin 1917
My Isle of Golden Dreams   Kahn 1918
My Isle of Hilo Bay   Gilbert 1932
My Isle of Sweethearts   Caesar 1923; Conrad 1923
My Italian Rose   Dubin 1917
My Jamaica Love   Razaf 1924; Waller 1924
My Jealous Eyes (That Turn from Blue to Green)   David,
   Mack 1953
My Jersey Lily   Von Tilzer 1900
My Jewels   Brown, Lew 1926; DeSylva 1926; Henderson
   1926
My Joe   Hammerstein 1943
My Joe Louis of Love   Razaf Date Unknown
My Journey's End   Fain 1934, 1944; Kahal 1934, 1944
My Kalua Rose   Bryan 1930
My Kid   Dubin 1924; McHugh 1924
My Kid Sister   Oakland 1937
My Kid's a Crooner   Dixon 1935; Wrubel 1935
My Kind o' Day   Evans 1953; Livingston, Jay 1953
My Kind of Country   Loesser 1940, 1941; McHugh 1940,
   1941
My Kind of Night   Lerner, Alan Jay 1948; Weill 1948
My Kind of Person   Merrill 1967
My Kind of Town   Cahn 1964; Van Heusen 1964
My Kinda Love   Alter 1928; Cahn 1941
My Kinda Music   Cahn 1941
My Kingdom for a Kiss   Dubin 1936; Rainger 1935; Robin
   1935; Warren 1936; Whiting 1935
My Kingdom for a Queen Like You   Gorney 1925
My Kisses Are Your Kisses, If Your Kisses Are
   Mine   Schwartz, Jean 1930
My Laddie   Akst Date Unknown
My Lady   Bullock 1939; Gershwin, George 1920; Johnson,
   Howard 1939; Weill 1948
My Lady and Me   Motzan 1922
My Lady Fair   Arlen 1966
My Lady Love   Coslow 1929; Robin 1929; Russell 1952
My Lady Nicotine   Howard, Joseph E. 1909
My Lady of Japan   Jerome 1905; Schwartz, Jean 1905
My Lady of the Cameo   Bryan 1920; Schwartz, Jean 1920

My Lady of the Lake   Brown, Nacio Herb 1948; Carroll 1915
My Lady of the Lamp   Pollack 1921; Schwartz, Jean 1920
My Lady of the Manor   Herbert 1903; Smith, Harry B. 1903
My Lady of the Nile   Buck 1916; Kern 1916
My Lady of the Telephone   Atteridge 1914; Romberg 1914
My Lady 'Tis for Thee   Herbert 1903; Smith, Harry B. 1903
My Lady's Clothes   Norworth 1917
My Lady's Dress   Atteridge 1919; Kern 1915, 1921; Romberg
   1919; Schwartz, Jean 1919; Smith, Harry B. 1915
My Lahaina Rose   Mills 1929
My Land   Olcott 1910
My Land and Your Land   Friend 1938
My Land of Nod   Howard, Joseph E. 1909
My Last Frontier   Coleman 1957; Leigh 1957
My Last Love   Lerner, Alan Jay 1943; Loewe 1943
My Last Night in Rome   Freed, Ralph 1956; Livingston, Jerry
   1956
My Last Romance   DePaul 1958; Raye 1958
My Last Strike   Styne 1985
My Last Year's Girl   Alter 1934
My Leader Man   Gilbert 1912; Motzan 1912
My Liebchen and Me (Mein Liebchen und Mich)   Young,
   Joe 1932
My Life Is in Your Hands   Lewis 1928; Warren 1928; Young,
   Joe 1928
My Linda   Razaf 1929
My Lips Tell the World It's All Over but My Heart Says 'I
   Love You'   Friend 1931
My Lips Want Kisses, My Heart Wants Love   Baer 1932;
   Fisher 1932
My Little Address Book   Whiting 1919
My Little Angel   Lewis 1929; Pollack 1929; Young, Joe 1929
My Little Belgian Maid   Buck 1917
My Little Bimbo Down on the Bamboo Isle   Clarke 1920;
   Donaldson 1920
My Little Bird   Willson 1953
(Within the Bound'ries of) My Little Bitty Ever Lovin'
   Heart   David, Hal 1961
My Little Blue Eyed Sue   Edwards 1899
My Little Book of Poetry   Berlin 1921
My Little Bunch of Happiness   Akst 1926; Davis 1926
My Little Canoe   Harbach 1921
My Little Castagnette   Hammerstein 1926; Harbach 1926;
   Romberg 1926
My Little China Doll   Yellen 1916
My Little Coney Isle   Sterling 1903; Von Tilzer 1903
My Little Cuckoo Out in Kokomo   Donaldson 1922
My Little Dancing Heart   Schwartz, Jean 1920
My Little Dream Boat   Coots 1928; Donaldson 1924
My Little Dream Girl   Gilbert 1915
My Little Dream Toy Shop   Blake 1954
(You're Mighty Lucky) My Little Ducky   DeSylva 1924;
   Gershwin, George 1924
My Little Friend   Cahn 1975; Smith, Harry B. 1913; Smith,
   Robert B. 1913
My Little Garden of Dreams   Woods 1936
My Little Girl   Cohan 1934; Lewis 1915
My Little Guy   Coslow 1971
My Little Gypsy Maid   Smith, Harry B. 1902
My Little Gypsy Sweetheart   Kahal 1927
My Little Hush-A-Bye Lady in Hush-A-Bye Land   Lewis
   1922; Young, Joe 1922
My Little Irish Rose   Herbert 1917
My Little Lady Bug   Smith, Harry B. 1912
My Little Lassoo   Smith, Harry B. 1905

My Little Lost Girl   Fain 1960; Webster 1960
My Little Mademoiselle   Cohan 1908
My Little Man   Dixon 1929; Woods 1929
My Little Mule Wagon   Dietz 1936; Schwartz, Arthur 1936
My Little Pansy   Smith, Harry B. 1902
My Little Pet Chicken   Buck 1914
My Little Piece o' Pie   Porter 1957
My Little Prayer   Gorney 1931, 1942; Harburg 1931, 1942
My Little Racket   Koehler 1950; Stept 1950
My Little Red Book (All I Do Is Talk about You)   Bacharach 1965; David, Hal 1965
My Little Redskin   Hammerstein 1922
My Little Road   Woods 1938
My Little Room   Robison 1960
My Little Sea Shell Told Me So   Hanley 1921
My Little Submarine   Buck 1915
My Little Sunshine   Conrad Date Unknown
My Little Swanee Sue   Coots 1932
My Little Sweetheart Mine   Sterling 1902; Von Tilzer 1902
My Little Tailor Maid   Edwards 1908
My Little Yellow Dress   Comden and Green 1958; Styne 1958
My Log Cabin Home   Caesar 1921; DeSylva 1921; Gershwin, George 1921
My Lolo Maid   Howard, Joseph E. 1908
My Lonely Love   Ellington 1968
My Lonely Rose   Edwards 1912
My Lonely Wood   Mills 1940
My Lonesome Heart Is Crying for You   Johnson, J. Rosamond 1954
My Lonesome Little Louisiana Lady   Cobb 1902; Edwards 1902
My Long Ago   Rome 1964
My Long Ago Girl   Porter 1924
My Long Gone Baby Came Home   Dixon 1936; Wrubel 1936
My Long Lost Love   Sissle 1915
My Long Lost Man Is Back Again   Brown, Lew 1927; DeSylva 1927; Henderson 1927
My Lord and Ladies   Gershwin, Ira 1945; Weill 1945
My Lord and Master   Hammerstein 1951; Rodgers 1951
My Lost Melody   Rome 1950
My Lou   Atteridge 1911
My Louisa   Porter 1929, 1930, 1933
My Loulou   Porter 1935
My Love   Bergman 1961; Brooks 1950; Warren 1952; Washington 1933; Young, Victor 1933
My Love Affair Is Falling Down (London Bridge)   Mills 1938
My Love an' My Mule   Arlen 1951; Fields 1951
My Love and I   Hammerstein 1936
My Love Bouquet   Atteridge 1923; Caesar 1923; Romberg 1923
My Love for You   David, Hal 1959; Davis 1925; Gordon 1953; Heyman 1939; Mercer 1963; Snyder 1911
My Love Gets Hungry Too   Waller 1946
My Love Has Two Faces   Lawrence 1968
My Love Is a Little Kitten   Hoffman 1956
My Love Is a Married Man   Lerner, Alan Jay 1945; Loewe 1945
My Love Is a Wanderer   Howard, Bart 1953
My Love Is Forever   Freed, Ralph 1958
My Love Is Like a Red, Red Rose   Van Heusen 1959
My Love Is Waiting   Kalmar 1964; Ruby 1964
My Love Is Yours Forever   Adamson 1941
My Love Loves Me   Evans 1948; Livingston, Jay 1948

My Love My Life   Evans 1952; Livingston, Jay 1952
My Love Song   Burke 1930; Stept 1958
My Love Will Find a Way   Norworth 1910
My Love Will Never Grow Old   Razaf 1931
My Love Will Outlive It All   Kahn 1923
My Love You Haven't Gone Away   Brown, Lew 1944
My Loveable Girl   Donaldson 1917
My Loved One   Fain 1932; Kahal 1932
My Lover   Ager 1930; Coslow 1930; DeSylva 1932; Yellen 1930; Youmans 1932
My Lover Is a Scoundrel   Loesser 1965
My Lover, Master of My Heart   Bryan 1929
My Lovin' Baby and Me   Ellington 1944
My Loving Baby   Blake 1916; Sissle 1916
My Lucky Charm   Cahn 1956
My Lucky Star   Brown, Lew 1929; DeSylva 1929; Hart 1927, 1928; Henderson 1929; Rodgers 1927, 1928; Smith, Harry B. 1904; Smith, Robert B. 1904
My Mad Moment   Whiting 1930
My Madonna   Donaldson 1921; Fisher 1929; Lewis 1921; Rose 1929; Young, Joe 1921
My Main Title and Yours   Brooks 1959
My Mama Thinks I'm a Star   Arlen 1944; Mercer 1944
My Mamie Rose   Goetz 1910
My Mammy   Donaldson 1918; Lewis 1918; Pollack 1921; Schwartz, Jean 1921; Young, Joe 1918
My Mammy's Tears   Coslow 1921
My Man   Buck 1920; Conrad 1912; Hanley 1920; Young, Joe 1912
My Man Cures the Blues   Waller 1924
My Man Friday   Lawrence 1951
My Man from Caroline   Donaldson 1930
My Man Is Good for Nothing but Love   Razaf 1929; Waller 1929
My Man Is on the Make   Hart 1929; Rodgers 1929
My Man Must Dance   Arlen 1930; Koehler 1930
My Man o' War   Razaf 1930
My Man Pete   Hoffman 1957
My Man Sends Me   Ellington 1964
My Man's Done Done Me Dirty   Razaf 1926
My Man's Gone Now   Gershwin, George 1935
My Mansion Way Down in the Lane   Bryan 1928; Fisher 1928
My Marine   Egan 1930; Whiting 1930
My Mary   Fisher 1907
My Masterpiece   Magidson 1963; McHugh 1963
My Medicine Man   Coslow 1935
My Melody   Buck 1922
My Melody Dream   Berlin 1911
My Melody Man   Clare 1929
My Melody of Memory   Johnson, Howard Date Unknown
My Memories of You   Revel 1930
My Mexicana Rose (inst.)   Warren 1928
My Middle Name Is Love   Coots 1934
My Midnight Rose   Von Tilzer 1902
My Midnight Sweetheart   Howard, Joseph E. 1919
My Mignonette   Dubin 1913
My Million Dollar Man   Clare 1925
My Mimosa   Romberg 1927
My Mind Says Don't   Harburg 1961
My Mind's Made Up to Marry Caroline   Brown, Lew 1917
My Miracle Man   Cohan 1914
My Missus   Hart 1926; Rodgers 1926
My Mistake   Coslow 1936, 1937; DePaul 1958; Raye 1958
My Mobile Gal   Smith, Robert B. 1900

My Model Girl   Atteridge 1915; Romberg 1915
My Modest Quaker Girl   Bryan 1917; Pollack 1917
My Mom   Donaldson 1932
My Moonlight Madonna   Webster 1933, 1944
My Moonlight Rosary   Stept 1931; Young, Joe 1931
My Most Delectable Dream   Evans 1950; Livingston, Jay 1950
My Most Embarrassing Moment   Dubin 1940; Fain 1940
My Most Intimate Friend   Porter 1935
My Mother in the Fatherland   Conrad 1934; Young, Joe 1933
My Mother, My Dad and My Girl   Dubin 1916
My Mother, My Father and Love   Ellington 1964
My Mother Told Me   Freed, Ralph 1944; McHugh 1944
My Mother Told Me Not to Trust a Soldier   Hammerstein 1928; Youmans 1928
My Mother Would Love You   Porter 1940
My Mother-in-Law   Strouse 1999
My Mother's Evening Prayer   Dubin 1920
My Mother's Eyes   Baer 1929; Bryan 1917; Gilbert 1929
My Mother's Garden   Hanley 1933
My Mother's Rosary   Lewis 1915; Meyer 1915
My Mother's Sabbath Candles   Yellen 1950
My Mother's Wedding Day   Lerner, Alan Jay 1947; Loewe 1947
My Mother's Wedding Dress   Bryan 1951
My Motto Is You   Sigman 1963
My Moving Picture Man   Smith, Harry B. 1915
My Music Teacher   Lewis 1912; Meyer 1912
My Musical Comedy Maiden   Cohan 1916
My! My!   Loesser 1940; McHugh 1940
My, My, My   Carroll 1950
My Name Is Love   Parish 1954
My Name Is Rumpelstiltskin   Cahn 1977
My Name Is Samuel Cooper   Lerner, Alan Jay 1948; Weill 1948
My Name's Marie, Who Wants to Be My Peanut Vendor   Brown, Lew 1931; Henderson 1931
My Nanky Panky Poo   Donaldson 1919; Lewis 1919; Young, Joe 1919
My Navajo (An Indian Lament)   Bryan 1950
My Neck of the Woods   Robison 1944
My Nelly's Blue Eyes   Johnson, Howard 1939
My Nephew from Nice   Heyman 1936; Schwartz, Arthur 1936
My New Celebrity Is You   Mercer 1977
My New Homeland   Caesar 1938
My New York   Berlin 1927; Cahn 1967; Smith, Harry B. 1900; Van Heusen 1967
My Newest Excitement   Mills 1936
My Next Romance   Freed, Ralph 1940
My Nice Ways   Merrill 1966, 1972; Styne 1972
(This Is) My Night to Howl   Mercer 1964
My Ninette   Goetz 1916
My North Dakota Home   David, Mack 1965
My Northern Home   Johnson, Howard 1930
My Northern Light (Bride 66)   Brennan 1930; Friml 1930
My Number One Dream Came True   Brown, Lew 1946
My! Oh, My!   Gordon 1933; Revel 1933
My Ohio Home   Donaldson 1927; Kahn 1927
My Old Dutch   Johnson, Howard 1939
My Old Fashioned Garden Flower   Harbach 1910
My Old Flame   Coslow 1934; Johnston 1934
My Old Girl's My New Girl Now   Caesar 1928; Friend 1928
My Old Home Town   Blane 1945; Freed, Arthur 1924; Martin 1964

My Old Hoss   Akst 1934; Brown, Lew 1934
My Old Lady   Edwards 1908
My Old Love Is My New Love   Gershwin, George 1920
My Old Man   Dixon 1928; Johnson, J. Rosamond 1909; Mercer 1933; Woods 1929
My Old Man Was an Army Man   Rainger 1940; Robin 1940
My Old Mare   Hammerstein 1935; Romberg 1935
My Old New Hampshire Home   Sterling 1898; Von Tilzer 1898
My Old Ramshackle Shack Where the Rambler Roses Ramble 'Round (Where the Rambler Roses Ramble 'Round My Old Ramshackle Shack)   Ager 1923; Yellen 1923
My Old Sweetheart Is Coming Back   Silver 1918
My Old Time Swing Rhythm Is a Racket   Blake 1937
My Old Town   Howard, Joseph E. 1908
My Old Virginia Home (On the River Nile)   Duke 1940
My One and Only Girl   Webster 1960
My One and Only Highland Fling   Gershwin, Ira 1949; Warren 1949
My One and Only (What Am I Gonna Do)   Gershwin, George 1927; Gershwin, Ira 1927
My One Big Moment   Kahn 1930; Pollack 1935; Webster 1935
My One Big Moment Is You   Johnson, Howard 1930
My One Desire   Alter 1930
(You Are) My One Love   Washington 1951
My One, My Only, My All   Evans 1949; Livingston, Jay 1948
My Only Friend   Howard, Joseph E. 1937
My Only Love (Ich Liebe Dich)   Bergman 1983
My Only One   Razaf 1930
My Only Pal Is My Radio   Leslie 1930; Monaco 1930
My Only Romance   Mitchell 1937; Pollack 1937
My Only Rose   Brennan 1921
My Oomday Oombay Down in Boom Boom Bay   Brown, Lew 1924; Dixon 1924; Henderson 1924
My Operatic Samson   Jerome 1910; Schwartz, Jean 1910
My Oriental Home   Johnston 1926; Turk 1926
My Oriental Rose   Atteridge 1912
My Oriental Symphony   Freed, Arthur 1925
My Osh-Kosh Gal   Coots 1954
My Otaheitee Lady   Kern 1913
My Other Me   Harburg 1935
My Own   Adamson 1938; McHugh 1938
My Own Academy Awards   Drake 1954
My Own America   Wrubel 1941; Young, Victor 1941
My Own Brass Bed   Willson 1960
My Own Dear Irish Queen   Olcott 1904
My Own Drum   Sherman 1986
My Own Home (Jungle Book Theme)   Sherman 1967
My Own Individual Star   Cahn 1958
My Own Iona (Not One Ionas)   Gilbert 1916
My Own Morning   Comden and Green 1967; Styne 1967
My Own True Love   David, Mack 1939; Evans 1947; Livingston, Jay 1947
My Own Wild Western Rose   Sterling 1900
My Own Willow Tree   Romberg 1927; Smith, Harry B. 1927
My Palace of Dreams   Friml 1934
My Palace Where Love Is King   Johnson, J. Rosamond 1932
My Palm Tree Rendezvous   Bryan 1938
My Pals   Coslow 1930; Robin 1930
My Papa Doesn't Two-Time No Time   Donaldson 1924
My Papa from Panama   Adamson 1956; McHugh 1956
My Paradise   Friml 1914; Harbach 1914; Magidson 1929; Washington 1929

My Paramount-Publix-Roxy Rose   Arlen 1934; Gershwin, Ira 1934; Harburg 1934
My Parcel Post Man   Kalmar 1913
My Part of Somewhere   Leigh 1985; Styne 1985
My Passion Flower   Romberg 1927
My Pathway of Love   Razaf 1930
My Peaceful Valley Home   Young, Joe 1947
My Peaches and Cream   Kern 1912
My Pearl Is a Bowery Girl   Jerome 1894
My Personal Property   Coleman 1968; Fields 1968
My Personal Rainbow   Hanley 1934
My Pet   Ager 1928; Yellen 1928
My Photograph of You   Alter 1930
My Piano Won't Play   Mercer 1958
My Picture Puzzle of You   Washington 1933; Wrubel 1933
My Piggy Bank Is Jing-a-Ling Again   Livingston, Jerry 1940
My Pillow   Gilbert 1938
My Pin-Up Girl   Rome 1943
My Pipe of Peace   Brennan 1927
My Pirate Lady   Atteridge 1916; Romberg 1916
My Pledge, I Shall Stand By Our Land to Eternity   Brennan 1918
My Poor Heart Is Full of Scars   Revel 1942
My Potential   Merrill 1978
My Pousse-Cafe   Hammerstein 1920
My Prairie Home   Robison 1960
My Prairie Song-Oifo   Meyer 1909
My Prayer for Today   Carmichael 1957
My Prayer of Love   Davis 1959
My Pretty Little Kickapoo   Sterling 1904; Von Tilzer 1904
My Pretty Little Southern Girl   Sterling 1899
My Pretty Shoo-Gah   Drake 1954
My Prince (What a Prince!)   Hart 1939; Rodgers 1939
My Private Personal Pal   Kahn 1930
My Private World   Lawrence 1947
My Problem   Livingston, Jerry 1959
My Promise to You   Drake 1947
My Puppy Bud   Stept 1925
My Queen of Lullaby Land   Coslow 1933; Johnston 1933
My Racket Is You   Hanley 1931
My Radio Man (Tell My Mammy to Come Back Home)   Friend 1924
My Radium Girl   Buck 1915
My Rag Doll Girl   Herbert 1903
My Raggydore   Atteridge 1913; Schwartz, Jean 1913
My Rainbow   Atteridge 1923; Romberg 1923; Schwartz, Jean 1923
My Rainbow Beau   Atteridge 1914; Carroll 1914; Romberg 1914
My Rainbow from Little Green Isle   Johnson, Howard 1940
My Rainbow Girl   Atteridge 1917; Romberg 1917
My Rainbow Ribbon Girl   Edwards 1918
My Rainbow Song   Parish 1941
My Rambler Rose   Buck 1922
My Real Ideal   Lane 1930; Lerner, Sammy 1930
My Rebel Heart   Washington 1958
My Red Letter Day   Duke 1936; Gershwin, Ira 1936
My Red Riding Hood   Merrill 1965; Styne 1965
My Red Roses Are Blue (inst.)   McHugh 1966
My Reg'lar Man Is Back in Town   Razaf 1930
My Regular Gal   Warren 1927
My Religion Is You   Webster 1930
My Reputation   Merrill 1957
My Resistance Is Low   Adamson 1951; Carmichael 1951
My Reuben Girlie   Atteridge 1912

My Rifle, My Pony and Me   Webster 1959
My Right Hand Doesn't Know   Gorney 1946
My Right Hand Man   Razaf 1935
My River   Johnston 1938
My River Home   Young, Joe 1932
My Rock-a-Bye Baby   Leslie 1928
My Romance   Hart 1935; Rodgers 1935; Washington 1932; Young, Victor 1932
My Room   David, Mack 1960; Heyman 1937
My Rosa   Hoffman 1951
My Rosanna   Parish 1944
My Rosary of Broken Dreams   Friend 1937
My Rosary of Melodies   Buck 1920
My Rose   Atteridge 1924; Coots 1923; Romberg 1924; Schwartz, Jean 1923, 1924
My Rose of Arizona   Cobb 1903; Edwards 1903
My Rose of Normandie   Dubin 1914
My Rose of Spain   Bryan 1927; Schwartz, Jean 1927
My Rose of the Rancho   Coslow 1936
My Rose of Tipperary   Hanley 1915
My Rose Town   Lawrence 1933
My Rosemarie   Eliscu 1929
My Rosie Rambler   Williams 1908
My Royal Majesty   Duke 1963
My Runaway Girl   Gershwin, George 1916
My Runaway Heart   Coots 1956
My Russian Girlski   Herbert 1912
My Sacrifice   David, Mack 1932; Heyman 1932
My Saddle Is My Throne   Caesar 1936; Schwartz, Arthur 1936
My Sahara Rose   Clarke 1920; Donaldson 1920
My Salvation Army Queen   Porter 1912
My Salvation Nell   Norworth 1919
My Sam   Gordon 1943; Warren 1943
My Scandinavian Baby   Merrill 1950
My Schoolday Sweetheart   Yellen 1949
My Screen Maid   Atteridge 1921; Pollack 1921; Schwartz, Jean 1921
My Second Love   Heyman 1951
My Secret Love   Coots 1931; Friml 1947; Parish 1943
My Secret Love Affair   Mitchell 1937; Pollack 1937
My Secret Song   Coslow 1937
My Senorita   Edwards 1909; Romberg 1916; Smith, Robert B. 1909
My Sentimental Heart   Parish 1942
My Sentimental Nature   Loesser 1946
My Serenade   Bergman 1983
My Sergeant and I   Berlin 1942
My Shining Hour   Arlen 1943; Mercer 1943
My Ship   Gershwin, Ira 1940; Weill 1940
My Sighing Siamese   Lewis 1927; Young, Joe 1927
My Signature   Willson 1953
My Silent Love   Heyman 1932
My Silent Love Song   Lewis 1930
My Silent Merry Xmas to You   Wrubel 1950
My Silent Symphony   Egan 1942
My Silhouette Sweetheart   Coots 1950
My Silver Dollar Man   Dubin 1937; Warren 1937
My Silver Maid   Sterling 1902
My Silver Rose   Leslie 1932; Monaco 1932
My Sin   Brown, Lew 1929; DeSylva 1929; Henderson 1929
My Six Loves   Cahn 1962; Van Heusen 1962
My Sky Without a Star   Duke 1959
My Social Hot Dog (from the Ivy League)   Livingston, Jerry 1955

My Soldier Boy   Von Tilzer 1910
My Soldier (Watashi No Heishi)   Rome 1969
My Son   Livingston, Jerry 1960
My Son in Law the King   Duke 1963
My Son John   Fain 1955; Leigh 1955; Webster 1955
My Son, My Son   Gilbert 1939; Pollack 1939
My Son the Producer   Drake 1964
My Song   Blane 1955, 1956; Brown, Lew 1931, 1944;
    Henderson 1931, 1944; Martin 1955, 1956
My Song of Hate   Razaf 1942; Waller 1942
My Song of the Nile   Bryan 1929; Meyer 1929
My Song Without Words   Duke 1941
My Son-In-Law   Gershwin, Ira 1946; Schwartz, Arthur 1946
My Sonny Boy   Olcott 1904
My Sons My Sons   Evans 1962; Livingston, Jay 1962
My Soul Mate   Washington 1933; Wrubel 1933
My South Sea Heart's Desire   Bryan 1938
My Southern Belle   Kern 1905
My Spanish Rose   Silver 1918
My Spanish Tambourine   Johnson, Howard 1930
My Sparkling Wine   Romberg 1915
My Special Friend Is Back in Town   Razaf 1927
My Spies Tell Me (You Love Nobody but Me)   Caesar 1937,
    1943; Lerner, Sammy 1937, 1943
My Spooky Girl   Buck 1915
My Springtime Thou Art   Romberg 1921
My Star   Adams 1993; Strouse 1993, 1999
(That's How I Got) My Start   Loesser 1941
My State, My Kansas, My Home   Willson 1961
My Story   Lewis 1930; Warren 1930
My Story of Love   Lawrence 1946
My Strongest Weakness Is You   Akst 1929; Clarke 1929
My Studebaker Girl   Leslie 1923
My Sugar and Me   Koehler 1929
My Sugar Plum   Hanley 1925
My Sugar's Plenty Sweet Enough for Me   Davis 1942
My Sunburnt Salome   Cobb 1906; Edwards 1906
My Sunday Fella   Gershwin, George 1929; Gershwin, Ira
    1929; Kahn 1929
My Sunday Gal   Parish 1933
My Sunday Girl   Stept 1927
My Sunny South   Silver 1929
My Sunny Sue   Sterling 1902
My Sunny Tennessee   Kalmar 1921; Ruby 1921
My Sunshine Came on a Rainy Day   Dubin 1915
My Sunshine Jane (Down Beside the Weeping Willow
    Tree)   Brennan 1917
My Sweet   Friend 1935; Hart 1931; Jerome 1905; Rodgers
    1931; Schwartz, Jean 1905
My Sweet Adair   Gilbert 1915
My Sweet Baby Irene   Razaf 1924; Waller 1924
My Sweet Bambina   Friml 1937; Kahn 1937
My Sweet (Ha Way-Yo)   Clare 1922; Friend 1922
My Sweet Helene   Bryan 1929; Meyer 1929
My Sweet Hunk o' Trash   Johnson, James P. 1948
My Sweet Italian Man   Berlin 1912
My Sweet One   Von Tilzer 1909
My Sweet Patoot with the Bumbershoot   Mills 1947
My Sweet Queen   Olcott 1901
My Sweet Tooth Says I Wanna, but My Wisdom Tooth Says
    No   Clare 1927; Stept 1927; Young, Joe 1927
My Sweet Yvette   Akst 1927; Davis 1927
My Sweeter than Sweet   Whiting 1929
My Sweetheart   Kahn 1924
My Sweetheart Is Connecticut   Merrill 1959

My Sweetheart Mamie   Kalmar 1941; Ruby 1941
My Sweetheart Serenade   Revel 1930
My Sweetheart 'Tis of Thee   Heyman 1931
My Sweetheart's a Soldier in the Army   Johnson, J.
    Rosamond 1907
My Sweetie   Berlin 1917
My Sweetie Went Away She Didin't Say Where or When or
    Why   Turk 1923
My Sweetie's Sweeter than That   Koehler 1923
My Swiss Hill Billy   Mitchell 1937; Pollack 1937
My Sword and I   Friml 1928
My Syndi-Kate   Jerome 1905; Schwartz, Jean 1905
My Tambourine Girl   Berlin 1919
My Tango Girl   Buck 1915
My Temptation   Dubin 1931
My Ten Ton Baby and Me   Willson 1942
My Tennessee   Johnson, Howard 1930
My Texas Man   Razaf 1926
My Thief   Bacharach 1996
My Time of Day   Loesser 1950
My Toast to You   Herbert 1907, 1911
My Tom Tom Man   Kahn 1915
My Tonia   Brown, Lew 1928; DeSylva 1928; Henderson 1928
My Topic of Conversation   Myrow 1937
My Topic of Conversation Is You   Coots 1936; Parish 1936
My Town   Hoffman 1950; Robison 1957
My Treasure   Herbert 1946
My Treasure Island   Styne 1985
My Trilby Maid   Atteridge 1915
My Troubles Are Over   Leslie 1928; Monaco 1928
My Troubles Float Away Like Falling Leaves (inst.)   Revel
    1950
My True Love   Martin 1952
My True Lover   Rainger 1936; Robin 1936
My Truly, Truly Fair   Merrill 1951
My 'Tucky Home   Lewis 1923; Meyer 1923; Young, Joe 1923
My Tumble-Down Cottage of Dreams   Leslie 1927
My Twilight Reflections   Mercer 1972
My Twilight Rose   Romberg 1924
My Tzatskele (Little Darling)   Ager 1955; Davis 1955
My Uncle Sam   Howard, Joseph E. 1905
My Unfinished Symphony of Love   Coslow 1935
My Unkissed Man   Jerome 1904; Schwartz, Jean 1904
My Unknown Someone   Coleman 1991; Comden and Green
    1991
My Up to Date Baby   Johnson, Howard 1927
My Used to Be Is Like She Used to Be   Monaco 1934;
    Young, Joe 1934
My Vampire Girl   Atteridge 1918
My Varsity Girl I'll Cling to You   Bryan 1928
My Very Fav'rite Christmas Card   Cahn 1959; Van Heusen
    1959
My Very First Kiss   David, Hal 1959
My Very Good Friend the Milkman   Burke 1935; Spina 1935
My Very Own   Davis 1954
My Victory (Was Conquering Your Heart)   Styne 1929
My Violet   Brennan 1925
My Violin   Romberg 1920
My Vision Girl   Blake 1920, 1921; Sissle 1920, 1921
My Vision in Vermillion   Bryan 1922; Schwartz, Jean 1922
My Voice Is Like a Flute of Gold   Brennan 1936
My Voodoo Maiden   Atteridge 1916; Romberg 1916
My Wag-a-long, Tag-a-long Too   Woods 1950
My Walking Stick   Berlin 1938
My Waltz Divine   Razaf 1923

My Warm Heart, Your Cold Shoulder   Gorney 1938
My Way or the Highway   Coleman 1996
My Wayward Heart   Leigh 1955
My Wedding   Eliscu 1929
My Wedding Day   Smith, Harry B. 1911
My Week   Weill 1948
My Weeping Heart   Coots 1953
My Weeping Willow's Smiling Just for Me   Pollack 1935;
      Webster 1935
My Weight in Gold   Mercer 1964
My, What a Diff'rent Night   Gordon 1936; Revel 1936
My White Haired Boy   Brown, Lew 1940; Henderson 1940
My White Knight   Willson 1957
My Who! My What! My Why!   Fisher 1931
My Whole Day Is Spoiled   Monaco 1934; Young, Joe 1934
My Wife   Atteridge 1921; Hammerstein 1947
My Wife Ain't Coming Back   Sterling 1909; Von Tilzer 1909
My Wife Is Dancing Mad   Johnson, Howard 1914
My Wife Is Out on Strike   Hanley 1919
My Wife! My Wife!   Harbach 1911
My Wife Sleeps with One Eye Open   Bryan 1936
My Wife's a W.A.A.C.   Styne 1943
My Wife's Gone to the Country (Hurrah! Hurrah!)   Berlin
      1909; Snyder 1909
My Wife's in Europe Today   Stept 1927
My Wigwam Lady   Jerome 1905; Schwartz, Jean 1905
My Wild Days Are Over   Brown, Lew 1918
My Wild Deer   Bryan 1908
My Wild Deer (Dear)   Snyder 1908
My Wild Imagination   Styne 1953
My Wild Irish Rose   Olcott 1901
My Wild Oat   Woods 1933
My Wild Party Girl   Robin 1929; Whiting 1929
My Window   Conrad 1929; Mitchell 1929
My Window Faces the South   Livingston, Jerry 1937; Parish
      1937; Silver 1937
My Window Faces the Street   David, Hal 1962
My Window Full of Stars   Sherman 1971
My Window of Dreams   Bryan 1928
My Wish   Willson 1963
My Wishing Doll   David, Mack 1966
My Wishing Song   Kahal 1932
My Wonder Girl   Koehler 1921
My Wonderful Love for Thee   Brennan 1916
My Wonderful One, Let's Dance   Brown, Nacio Herb 1940;
      Freed, Arthur 1940
My Word   Smith, Robert B. 1905
My Word! It Surely Was a Treat   Herbert 1905; Smith, Harry
      B. 1905
My World   Drake 1968
My World Begins and Ends with You   Hanley 1932
My World of Romance   Hart 1920; Rodgers 1920
My Yakahula Lady Love   Bryan 1938
My Yankee Doodle Boy   Clare 1928
My Yellow Jacket Girl   Atteridge 1913; Schwartz, Jean 1913
My Yiddish Colleen   Edwards 1910; Von Tilzer 1916
My Yiddisha Butterfly   Dubin 1917
My Yiddishe Mammy   Schwartz, Jean 1922
My Yiddishe Momme   Pollack 1925; Yellen 1925
My Yiddisher Romeo   Lewis 1915; Meyer 1915
My Yokohama Girl   Bryan 1917
My Yokohoma Girl   Atteridge 1917; Motzan 1917; Romberg
      1917
My Ziegfeld Midnight Girl   Buck 1915
Mynah Bird, The   Heyman 1944

Myrella   Smith, Harry B. 1912; Smith, Robert B. 1912
Myrtle's March   Leigh Date Unknown
Mysterious   Friend 1960
Mysterious Eyes   Ahlert 1925; Smith, Harry B. 1925
Mysterious Lady   Comden and Green 1954; Styne 1954
Mysterious Maid, The   Cohan 1901
Mysterious Melody   Herbert 1910
Mysterious Moon   Brown, A. Seymour 1911
Mysterious Mr. Zilch, The   Parish 1933
Mysterious Scene   Gorney 1958
Mysteriously   Porter 1931
Mystery of Clothes   Dubin 1930
Mystery of History, The   Smith, Harry B. 1906
Mystery Play, The   Cohan 1922
Mystery Song, The   Ellington 1932; Mills 1932
Mystic Magic Mastermind   Sherman 1986

N

'N' Everything   DeSylva 1918; Kahn 1918
Na Ville D'Amour Op 22   Friml 1909
Nacio Herb Brown's Blue Train (inst.)   Brown, Nacio Herb
      1956
Nacio Herb Brown's Dance of Fury (inst.)   Brown, Nacio
      Herb 1948
Nacio Herb Brown's Hymn to the Moon (inst.)   Brown,
      Nacio Herb 1956
Nacio Herb Brown's Mexican Moon Dance (inst.)   Brown,
      Nacio Herb 1956
Nacio Herb Brown's New Mexico March (inst.)   Brown,
      Nacio Herb 1948
N.A.G., The   Razaf 1953
Naga Saki   Rose 1927
Nagasaki   Dixon 1928; Warren 1928
Nagasaki Butterfly   Rose 1927
Nairobi   Merrill 1958
Naked City   Washington 1958
Naked Sea   Brooks 1955
Naked Truth, The   Robison 1960
Name It and It's Yours   Cahn 1961; Fain 1939; Parish 1939;
      Silver 1939; Van Heusen 1961
Name It and It's Yours (inst.)   Revel 1959
Name of Kelly, The   Cohan 1922
Name of the Game Is Love, The   David, Hal 1962
Name Song, The   Caesar 1940; Cahn 1977
Name the Day   Herbert 1920
Name the Lady   Rome 1970
Namely You   DePaul 1956; Mercer 1956
Na-Mi   Gilbert 1944
Nami-Nami-Nam Inamorata (Sweetheart)   Mills 1938;
      Myrow 1938
Nan   Webster 1967
Nan O'Shanter   Egan 1921; Whiting 1921
Nancy   Schwartz, Jean 1926
Nancy Clancy   Drake 1946
Nancy Hanks (inst.)   Young, Victor 1955
Nancy, I Fancy You   Herbert 1906
Nancy Lee   Davis 1958
Nancy with the Laughing Face   Van Heusen 1944
Nanette   Dietz 1931; Schwartz, Arthur 1931
Nanette and Rin Tin Tin   Atteridge 1919; Romberg 1919;
      Schwartz, Jean 1919
Nango, The   Gordon 1941; Warren 1941
Nani Oni Pua   Rainger 1937
Naomi   Howard, Joseph E. Date Unknown

Napoleon   Arlen 1957; Brown, A. Seymour 1909; Harburg
     1957; Kern 1917
Napoleon Said to Josephine Not Tonight   Revel 1929
Napoleon's a Pastry   Arlen 1937; Harburg 1937
Napoleon's Exile   Johnston 1935; Kahn 1935
Narrative for Orchestra (inst.)   Strouse 1950
Nashville (Music City USA)   Spina 1977
Nashville Nightingale   Caesar 1923; Gershwin, George 1923
Nashville Sings   Sigman 1986
Nasty Man   Caesar 1934; Henderson 1934; Yellen 1934
Natalie   Mancini 1969
Natasha   Webster 1963
Natchez and Robert E. Lee   Gilbert 1921
Natchez and the Robert E. Lee   Koehler 1947
Natchez on the Mississip'   Gershwin, Ira 1949; Warren 1949
Natchez Trace   Ellington 1966
Natchul Man   Arlen 1959; Mercer 1959
Natiesha (Bright Eyes)   Razaf 1926
Nation of Nations, A   Weill 1947
Nation of the People (By the People, For the People),
     The   Bryan 1950
Nation that Wasn't There, The   Lerner, Alan Jay 1976
National Anthem   Duke 1963
National Emblem   Freed, Ralph 1944
National Love Song (Sweethearts Are We), A   Blake 1950;
     Sissle 1950
Native Dancer   Hoffman 1953; Silver 1953
Native Son, A   Blake Date Unknown; Fain 1951; Razaf 1942;
     Webster 1951
Native Women   Atteridge 1915
Natives Are Restless, The   Sondheim 1964
Natives Are Restless Tonight, The   Drake 1956; Hoffman
     1958
Natural African Man   Strouse 2000
Natural History Class, The   Brown, A. Seymour 1909
Nature   Atteridge 1924
Nature and I   Cahn 1935
Nature Class   Herbert 1905
Nature of Things, The   Leigh 1956
Naughty Baby   Gershwin, George 1924; Gershwin, Ira 1924
Naughty Boy   Hammerstein 1929; Kern 1929; Robin 1927
Naughty but Nice   Alter 1929; Johnson, Howard 1929;
     Mercer 1951; Warren 1951
Naughty Eyes   Atteridge 1920; Friend 1920
Naughty Girl   Dubin 1924
Naughty Hula Eyes   Adamson 1940
Naughty Kiss   Clare 1924; Conrad 1924
Naughty Little Clock, The   Smith, Harry B. 1902
Naughty Little Raindrop   Freed, Arthur 1925
Naughty Little Red Cross Nurses   Friend 1918
Naughty Little Step   Coots 1925
Naughty Marietta   Herbert 1910
Naughty Maurette   Fain 1927; Pollack 1927
Naughty Naughty   Oakland 1938; Porter 1914
Naughty, Naughty, I'm Surprised at You   Oakland 1937
Naughty, Naughty, Naughty   Williams 1911
Naughty Riquette   Smith, Harry B. 1926
Naughty Waltz Blues   Yellen 1921
Naughty with Your Eyes   Dixon 1926; Henderson 1926
Navajo   Williams 1903
Navy Blue Blues   Lawrence 1952
Navy Blue (Make Way for Navy Blue), The   David, Mack
     1951; Livingston, Jerry 1951
Navy Blues   Ahlert 1929; Mercer 1941; Schwartz, Arthur
     1941; Turk 1929

Navy Gets the Gravy, but the Army Gets the Beans,
     The   David, Mack 1950; Livingston, Jerry 1950
Navy Song, The   Arlen 1944; Mercer 1944
Navy Swings, The   McHugh 1958
Navy Waltz, The   Blane 1952; Warren 1952
Navy Will Bring Them Back, The   Johnson, Howard 1918
Navy's in Town, The   Silver 1956
Nay Nay Neighbor   Coslow 1926
Naztrov'eych   Bergman 1983
NBC Jingle (inst.)   Willson 1966
Ne Monus You   Fain 1981
Neapolitan Jazz   Romberg 1919; Schwartz, Jean 1919
Neapolitan Love Song (Sweet One How My Heart Is
     Yearning) (T'Amo)   Herbert 1915
Neapolitan Lullaby (inst.)   Schwartz, Jean 1930
Near but Never Too Near   Willson 1969
Near Future, The   Berlin 1919
Near Me   Fisher 1921
Near to You   Sigman 1946
Near You   Bryan 1910; Coots 1937; Davis 1937
Nearer and Dearer   Friml 1947; Heyman 1947
Nearer My Heart to Thee   Heyman 1934
Nearer My Love to Me   Drake 1954
Nearer to Heaven (Song of the Trapeze)   Fain 1959; Webster
     1959
Nearly   Cahn 1968
Nearness of You, The   Carmichael 1937, 1939; Washington
     1937
'Neath a New Moon   Hammerstein 1928; Romberg 1928
'Neath Egyptian Skies   Yellen 1923
'Neath Italian Skies   Atteridge 1921; Romberg 1921
'Neath the Blue Neapolitan Skies   Herbert 1900; Smith,
     Harry B. 1900
'Neath the Cherry Blossom Moon   Brennan 1927; Romberg
     1927; Smith, Harry B. 1927
Neath the Eucalyptus Tree   Silver 1954
'Neath the Mississippi Moon   Meyer 1912
'Neath the Moon at Saskatoon   Akst 1937; Gilbert 1937
'Neath the Old Cherry Tree Sweet Marie   Williams 1907
'Neath the Pale Cuban Moon   Arlen 1931; Koehler 1931
'Neath the Shadow of the Pyramids   Carroll 1914
'Neath the Silv'ry Moon   Friend 1932
'Neath the South Sea Moon   Buck 1922
'Neath the Southern Moon   Herbert 1910, 1935; Kahn 1935
Neauville Sur Mer   Porter 1933
Necessity   Harburg 1947; Lane 1947
Neck Bones and Beans   Johnson, Howard 1927
Need a Friend   Lewis 1976; Young, Joe 1976
Need for Love, The   Washington 1960
Need I Speak?   Loesser 1942; Spina 1942
Need of You, The   Cahn 1967
Need to Be Loved, The   Fain 1977; Webster 1977
Needle in a Haystack, A   Conrad 1934; Magidson 1934
Needles   Conrad 1926; Kahn 1926
Needles and Pins   Lawrence 1947
Needy, The   Fain 1962
Ne'er Do Well   Revel 1959
Neighborhood Song, The   Lawrence 1964
Neighbor's Song, The   David, Mack 1973; Livingston, Jerry
     1973
Neither the Time Nor the Place   Loesser 1965
Nell Brinkley Girl, The   Smith, Harry B. 1908
Nellie Bly   Burke 1946; Van Heusen 1946
Nellie Bly Song   Brooks 1960
Nellie Kelly, I Love You   Cohan 1922

Nellie Martin   Fain 1946; Freed, Ralph 1946
Nellie, Take the Whole Darn Farm   Kahn 1923
Nelly Was a Lady   Johnson, Howard 1939
Nemo's Dream of Fourth of July   Herbert 1908; Smith, Harry B. 1908
Nenette and Rin-Tin-Tin   Friml 1918
Nenita   Gordon 1940; Warren 1940
Neopolitan Jazz   Atteridge 1919
Neptune's Daughter   Buck 1914; Clarke 1914; Loesser 1948; Schwartz, Jean 1914
Nero   Razaf 1936
Nero, Caesar, Napoleon   Eliscu 1962
Nerves   Herbert 1917; Kern 1921; Schwartz, Jean 1918
Nervous   Merrill 1967
Nesting in a New York Tree (Nesting Time in New York Town)   Cohan 1904
Nesting Time   Dixon 1927; Hanley 1921; Monaco 1927
Nesting Time in Flatbush   Kern 1917
Net, The   Bacharach 1959; David, Hal 1959
Nevada   Donaldson 1943; Gershwin, Ira 1923
Nevada Moonlight   Hammerstein 1931; Whiting 1931
Nevada Smith   David, Hal 1966
Never   Coleman 1978; Comden and Green 1978
Never a Day Goes By   Coslow 1956; Donaldson 1943; Parish 1943
Never a Dull Moment   Adamson 1940; Fields 1939; Schwartz, Arthur 1939
Never Again   Blane 1948; Kahn 1924; Kern 1970; Sigman 1953; Smith, Harry B. 1900; Warren 1948; Webster 1970
Never Be Afraid   Bergman 1957
Never Be Afraid of Anything   Caesar 1937
Never Be-Devil the Devil   Harburg 1961
Never Been in Love Before   Caesar 1930
Never Before   Brown, Nacio Herb 1943; David, Mack 1951; Davis 1933; Livingston, Jerry 1951; Robin 1943
Never Bite Off More than Your Mate Can Chew   Drake 1956
Never Brag About Your Man   Razaf 1940
Never Breathe a Word of This to Mother   Cohan 1901
Never Climb Fences, Never Climb Walls (Johnny Climbs Fences, Johnny Climbs Walls)   Caesar 1937
Never Come Sunday   Washington 1955; Young, Victor 1955
Never Feel Too Weary to Pray   Willson 1941
Never Felt Better, Never Had Less   Baer 1938; Hoffman 1934
Never for You   Hammerstein 1928; Romberg 1928
Never Forget to Write Home   Hanley 1917
Never Give Anything Away   Porter 1953
Never Give Up (inst.)   Stept 1936
Never Go to Argentina   Hart 1941; Rodgers 1941
Never Gonna Dance   Fields 1936; Kern 1936
Never Got to the Dance   Freed, Ralph 1959
Never Had an Education   Caesar 1933; Romberg 1933
Never Had It So Good   Davis 1957
Never in a Million Years   Gordon 1937; Revel 1937
Never in My Wildest Dreams   Gordon 1950; Warren 1950, 1980
Never Kiss   Howard, Bart 1956
Never Land   Leigh 1954
Never Let Me Go (Ceux Qui M'ont Quitte)   Evans 1957; Livingston, Jay 1956
Never Let the Blues Go to Your Feet   Razaf 1934
Never Let the Same Dog Bite You Twice   Fain 1948; Yellen 1948
Never Let Them Know What's Going On   Duke 1963

Never Let Yourself Forget That You Are Irish Too   Brennan 1915
Never Make Eyes (at the Gals with the Guys Who Are Bigger than You)   Fain 1947; Yellen 1947
Never Marry   Young, Joe 1916
Never Marry a Dancer   Dietz 1934; Schwartz, Arthur 1934
Never Marry a Girl with Cold Feet   Kern 1907
Never Mention Love when We're Alone   Herbert 1914; Smith, Robert B. 1914
Never Met a Man I Didn't Like   Coleman 1991; Comden and Green 1991
Never Mind   Johnson, James P. 1930; Stept 1925
Never Mind Bo-Peep   Herbert 1903
Never Mind How   Schwartz, Arthur 1930
Never, Never Again   Comden and Green 1955
Never, Never Be an Artist   Porter 1953
Never Never Knew   Friend 1957
Never Never Land   Comden and Green 1954; Herbert 1907; Smith, Harry B. 1907; Styne 1954
Never Never Never   Styne 1941
Never Never Wed   Brown, Lew 1930; DeSylva 1930; Henderson 1930
Never Once Did I Cry   David, Hal 1962
Never Play Hookey   Styne 1940
Never Point at People   Styne 1940
Never Say Die   Robin 1930
Never Say Goodbye   Friml 1952; Webster 1952
Never Say Love   Freed, Ralph 1940
Never Say Never   Schwartz, Jean 1926
Never Say Never Again   Bergman 1983
Never Say No   Porter 1933
Never Say No to a Man   Rodgers 1962
Never Should Have Told You   Friend 1936
Never Smile at a Crocodile   Lawrence 1952
Never So Beautiful   Evans 1953; Livingston, Jay 1953
Never Speak Directly to an Emperor   Strouse 1982
Never Steal Anything Small   Wrubel 1959
Never Strike Anything (Striking Things)   Caesar 1937
Never Such a Loving Two   Brown, A. Seymour 1911
Never Swat a Fly   Brown, Lew 1930; DeSylva 1930; Henderson 1930
Never Take No for an Answer   Dubin 1940; Fain 1940
Never Tell a Lie   Styne 1940
Never the Twain Shall Meet   Freed, Ralph 1958
Never Till Now   Webster 1958
Never Too Late   Evans 1965; Livingston, Jay 1965
Never Too Late for Love   Rome 1954
Never Too Late to Pray   Robison 1945
Never Took a Lesson in My Life   Lawrence 1940
Never Trust a Dream   McHugh 1964
Never Trust a Soldier   Atteridge 1914; Romberg 1914
Never Trust a Soldier Man   Carroll 1914
Never Trust a Virgin   Harburg 1961
Never Underestimate the Power of a Woman   Spina 1977
Never Was There a Girl So Fair   Gershwin, George 1931; Gershwin, Ira 1931
Never Was There Such a Perfect Day   Kahn 1938
Never Will I Marry   Loesser 1960
Never Without You   Davis 1926
Never You Mind (inst.)   Kern 1938
Nevermore   Lerner, Sammy 1948
Never's Here   Cahn 1978
Nevertheless I Can Dream   Johnston 1946
Nevertheless I'm in Love with You   Kalmar 1931; Ruby 1931
New Art Is True Art   Weill 1943

New Ashmolean Marching Society and Students Conservatory Band, The   Loesser 1948
New Boy, A   Drake 1964
New Casanova, A   Koehler 1950; Stept 1950
New Clothes   Bergman 1957
New Dawn — A New Day, A   Robin 1946
New Day, A   Brooks 1945, 1946
New Day Prayer, A   Razaf 1946
New Deal for Christmas, A   Strouse 1977
New Deal Rhythm   Harburg 1933; Rose 1933
New England Bound   Akst 1928; Gilbert 1928
New England in the Rain   Webster 1934
New Fangled Moon   Howard, Bart 1957
New Frontiers   Lawrence 1960
New Game, The   DeSylva 1925
New Hampshire   Schwartz, Jean 1922; Sterling 1928
New Hollywood Plots   Fain 1955; Webster 1955
New Ireland, The   Herbert 1914
New Irish Eyes of Blue   Schwartz, Jean 1930
New Kind of Broadway, A   Strouse 1999
New Kind of Girl   Strouse 1975
New Kind of Man (With a New Kind of Love for Me), A   Clare 1924
New Kind of Rhythm   Arlen 1932; Koehler 1932
New Kind of Show Business, A   Drake 1954
New Look, The   Martin 1948
New Love   DeSylva 1925; McHugh 1958; Schwartz, Jean 1937
New Love Is Old, A   Harbach 1931; Kern 1931
New Love, New Lips   Dixon 1938; Woods 1938
New Love Song, A   Freed, Arthur 1930; Woods 1930
New Mexico Alma Mater Hymn, The   Brown, Nacio Herb 1961; Freed, Arthur 1961
New Mexico (inst.)   Brown, Nacio Herb 1948
New Moon, The   Berlin 1919; Donaldson 1924; Koehler 1944; Lane 1944
New Moon and an Old Serenade   Coslow 1939; Silver 1939
New Moon Is Over My Shoulder, A   Brown, Nacio Herb 1934; Freed, Arthur 1934
New Mown Hay   Kahn 1934
New New York   Dietz 1930; Schwartz, Arthur 1930
New O'leans   Johnston 1935; Kahn 1935
New Orleans   Carmichael 1932; Styne 1970
New Orleans Cha-Cha   Spina 1959
New Orleans Jeunesse Doree   Herbert 1910
New Orleans Masquerade   Mills 1947
New Orleans Poon   Merrill 1971; Styne 1971
New Orleans Street Crime   Lawrence 1953
New Orleans the Cradle of Love   Revel 1959
New Orleans, the Mardi Gras and You   Goetz 1952
New Orleans Woman   Lewis 1976; Young, Joe 1976
New Pair of Shoes, A   Drake 1964
New Pan-Ameri-Can-Can   Rainger 1935; Robin 1935; Whiting 1935
New Parade, The   Arlen 1936; Harburg 1936
New Pilgrims' Prayer, The   Duke 1968
New Revue for Rue de la Paix   Meyer 1925; Turk 1925
(There Are) New Roses Every Summer   Yellen 1943
New Sensation in Sound   David, Mack 1956
New Shoes   Ellington 1958
New Stars and Stripes Forever, The   Parish 1959
New Sun in the Sky   Dietz 1931; Schwartz, Arthur 1931
New Sun Ridin' in the Sky, A   Stept 1949
New Trail   Freed, Ralph 1938
New Universal Signature (inst.)   McHugh 1937

New Vienna Woods, The   Evans 1965; Livingston, Jay 1965
New World, The   Donaldson 1941; Kahn 1941
New World Will Soon Be Here, A   Leslie 1943
New Year Filled with Love, A   Duke 1968
New Year Song, The   Brown, Nacio Herb 1957
New Year's Eve   Comden and Green 1982
New Year's Eve 1953   Drake 1953, 1954
New York   Blane 1968; Rainger 1936; Robin 1936; Strouse 1985
New York After Dark   Duke 1937
New York Ain't New York Anymore   Brown, Lew 1924; Henderson 1924; Rose 1924
New York City Ghost   Young, Victor 1953
New York Follies, The   Sondheim Date Unknown
New York Football Giants   Davis 1964
New York Is a Nice Place to Visit   McHugh 1946
New York Is Go Go Going for the Mets, The Mets Are Go Go Going for New York   Davis 1966
New York Is the Same Old Place   DeSylva 1922; Herbert 1922
New York Isn't Such a Bad Old Town   Jerome 1912; Schwartz, Jean 1912
New York Lady (211) (inst.)   Bacharach 1979
New York (Let Me Sing)   Robin 1951; Styne 1951
New York, My New York!   Alter 1960
New York, New York   Comden and Green 1944; Ellington 1972
New York Number   Hart 1943
New York on Parade   Rose 1938
New York Rhapsody   Gershwin, George 1931; Gershwin, Ira 1931
New York Serenade   Gershwin, George 1927; Gershwin, Ira 1927
New York Sketches (inst.)   Coleman 1950
New York Town   Wrubel 1931
New York Town (Is Wearing Its Bandannas on Broadway)   Dietz 1927; Gorney 1927
New York Two-Step, The   Cohan 1907
New York, What's Become of You?   Goetz 1917
New York When I Join the Circus   Martin 1968
New York Women   Cahn 1980; Strouse 1980
New Yorker, The   Ager 1929; Yellen 1929
New Yorkers   Cohan 1911
New York's a Nice Place to Visit   Adamson 1946
New York's Good Morning Song   Blane 1968; Martin 1968
Newlyweds' Song, The   Rome 1969
Newport Dip, The   Johnson, J. Rosamond 1904
Newport Glide, The   Coots 1926; Jerome 1910; Schwartz, Jean 1910
Newport Is Waiting for Me   Smith, Harry B. 1909
News   Kalmar 1928; Ruby 1928
(Manhattan) News Beat (inst.)   Oakland 1958
News Chant   Arlen 1959; Mercer 1959
News Is Always Happening   Brooks 1959
News Is Good, the News Is Bad, The   Caesar 1942
Newspaper Girl   Goetz 1918
Newspaperman's Blues, The   Razaf 1953
Newsreel   Rome 1948
Newsy Bluesies   Carmichael 1940; Mercer 1940
Next   Sondheim 1976
Next Dance, The   Ager 1915
Next Day Hill   Bacharach 1965
Next Door to Heaven   Bryan 1919; Schwartz, Jean 1919
Next May Be the Right, The   Smith, Robert B. 1910

Next Sunday Morning, He'll Get His Where I Got Mine   Sterling 1923
Next Time   Cahn 1964; Strouse 1956; Van Heusen 1964
Next Time Around, The   Livingston, Jerry 1957
Next Time I Care (I'll Be Careful), The   Gilbert 1949; Oakland 1949
Next Time I Fall in Love   Stept 1948
Next Time It Happens, The   Hammerstein 1955; Rodgers 1955
Next to Texas, I Love You   Cahn 1947; Styne 1947
Next to You, I Like Me, Next to You   Johnson, Howard 1925
Next to Your Mother, Who Do You Love?   Berlin 1909; Snyder 1909; Young, Joe 1930
Next Train Out, The   Russell 1965
Next Tuesday   Carroll 1925; Freed, Arthur 1925
Next Voice You Hear, The   Webster 1951
Next Year   Leigh 1985
Niagara Falls   Baer 1954; Drake 1954; Kern 1921; Leslie 1954
Niagara Moon   Heyman 1933
Niccolina   Harbach 1951; Kern 1951
Nice Baby   Gershwin, George 1925; Gershwin, Ira 1925
Nice Doggy-Nice Kitty   Carmichael 1952
Nice Goin'   Rainger 1939; Robin 1939
Nice Going   Donaldson 1940
Nice Goings On   Schwartz, Arthur 1933
Nice Little Plot for a Play   Cohan 1909
Nice 'n' Easy   Bergman 1960
Nice Old Fashioned Girl, A   David, Mack 1968
Nice Pizza Pie   Leslie 1959
Nice She Ain't   Sondheim 1959; Styne 1959
Nice Small Town Girls   Gorney 1926
Nice to Be Near   Fields 1956; Kern 1956
Nice to See You   Caesar 1953; Strouse Date Unknown; Yellen 1953
Nice Town   Sondheim Date Unknown
Nice Work If You Can Get It   Gershwin, George 1937; Gershwin, Ira 1937
Nicest Gift of Them All, The   Livingston, Jerry 1963
Nicest Sort of Feeling   Caesar 1924
Nicest Thing, The   Evans 1961; Livingston, Jay 1961
Nicest Thing about Saying Goodbye (Is Sayin' Hello Again), The   Davis 1953
Nicest Thing (That Ever Happened to Me), The   Hoffman 1960
Nicest Time of the Year   Comden and Green 1944
Nicest Time to Say Goodnight, The   Cahn 1970; Styne 1970
Nichevo Means Yes   Robin 1931
Nicholini   Howard, Joseph E. 1905
Nickel for a Dime, A   Blake 1940; Razaf 1940
Nickel in the Slot   Mills 1935
Nickel Machine Samba   David, Mack 1954
Nickel Man, The   Adamson 1940
Nickel to My Name, A   Duke 1941
Nickel's Worth of Jive, A   Gordon 1945; Warren 1945
Nickel's Worth of Sunshine, A   Burke 1944; Van Heusen 1944
Nickle and Dime Man   Merrill 1952
Nicknames   Hoffman 1939
Nicky Arnstein   Merrill 1964; Styne 1964
Nicodemus   Youmans 1926
Nicol in the Picolo   Razaf Date Unknown
Nicole, You Is My Woman Now   Comden and Green 1972
Nicotina   Schwartz, Arthur 1936
Niente da Fare   Strouse 1999

Night   Ager 1932; Bacharach 1976; Davis 1922; Gilbert 1933; Harburg 1932; Parish 1928; Webster 1952
Night After Night   Arlen 1964; Cahn 1949; Dietz 1930; Hoffman 1952; Lewis 1923, 1927; Meyer 1923; Rainger 1934; Schwartz, Arthur 1930; Sigman 1955; Whiting 1934; Young, Joe 1923, 1927
Night Again   Koehler 1932
Night and Day   Porter 1932
Night and You   Robin 1953
Night Before the Morning After, The   Dietz 1937; Schwartz, Arthur 1937
Night Blooming Jasmine   Loesser 1947
Night Brigade, The   Goetz 1912
Night Camp   Young, Victor 1955
Night Club Nights   Eliscu 1932
Night Club Opening   Porter 1929
Night Club Stomp   Mills 1929
Night Flies By   Hammerstein 1932; Kern 1932
Night Flight   Leigh 1955; Spina 1955
Night Flight (inst.)   Young, Victor 1955
Night Has a Thousand Eyes, The   Duke 1942
Night Has Eyes, The   Coots 1963
Night Has Lost the Moon, The   Caesar 1936; Schwartz, Arthur 1936
Night Has Many Eyes, The   Cahn 1972
Night Hawk   Gilbert 1924
Night, Hold Back the Dawn   Brown, Nacio Herb 1932; DeSylva 1932; Whiting 1932
Night in Las Vegas, A   Blane 1969
Night in Manhattan   Rainger 1936; Robin 1936
Night in Paradise   Brooks 1946
Night in the Orient, A   Atteridge 1918; Romberg 1918
Night Is Beginning, The   Kahn 1936
Night Is Blue   Mills 1935
Night Is Darkest Before the Dawn   Fisher 1930
Night Is Filled With Music, The   Berlin 1938
Night Is Filled with Music (Auf Flugeln des Gesanges), The   Bergman 1983
Night Is Filled with Wonderful Sounds, The   Duke 1963
Night Is Young, The   Hammerstein 1935; Romberg 1935
Night Is Young and You're So Beautiful, The   Kahal 1936; Rose 1936
Night Life   Schwartz, Arthur 1928
Night Life in Old Manhattan   Buck 1914
Night Life in Santa Rosa   Leigh 1985
Night May Be Dark, The   Dietz 1963; Schwartz, Arthur 1963
Night of Happiness, A   Conrad 1929; Mitchell 1929
Night of Love, A   DeSylva 1925; Romberg 1919
Night of Masquerade, A   Cohan 1927
Night of Memories, A   Yellen 1928
Night of Nights   Adamson 1935; Donaldson 1935
Night of Stars   Brooks 1959; Hoffman 1954
Night of the Quarter Moon   Cahn 1959; Van Heusen 1959
Night Our Love Song Was Born, The   Freed, Arthur 1931; Woods 1931
Night Over Shanghai   Mercer 1937; Warren 1937
Night Remembers, The   Lawrence 1934
Night Rock and Roll Died (Almost), The   Cahn 1959; Van Heusen 1959
Night Shall Be Filled with Love, The   Rainger 1934; Robin 1934
Night Shift   Bacharach 1982
Night Song   Adams 1964; Brooks 1948; Mercer 1956; Mills 1941; Strouse 1964

Night that Heaven Fell, The   Bacharach 1958; David, Hal 1958

Night that She Cried in Her Beer, The   Stept 1934; Washington 1934

Night that We Remember, A   Robin 1952

Night the Kissing Booth Burned Down, The   Spina 1976

Night, the Moon and You, The   Lewis 1920; Young, Joe 1920

Night the Old Cow Died, The   Goetz 1912

Night the Rabbi Didn't Show, The   Drake 1967

Night, the Stars, the Wind, the Sea, The   Merrill 1950

Night, the Wind, and Me, The   Razaf 1935

Night They Invented Champagne, The   Lerner, Alan Jay 1958; Loewe 1958

Night They Raided Minsky's, The   Adams 1968; Strouse 1968, 1999

Night Time   Cohan 1901; Ellington 1954; Herbert 1920; Kern 1920; Smith, Robert B. 1920

Night Time in Araby   DeSylva 1924; Gershwin, George 1924

Night Time in New York   Davis 1961

Night Time on the Danube   Fisher 1933

Night Train to Memphis   Ellington 1968

Night Waltz   Sondheim 1973

Night Was Designed for Music, The   Drake 1951

Night Was Made for Dancing, The   Hart 1934; Rodgers 1934

Night Was Made for Love, The   Harbach 1931; Kern 1931

Night We Didn't Care, The   Mills 1928

Night when Love Was Born, The   Baer 1932; Young, Joe 1932

Night Wind   Heyman 1934

Night Wind (The Sunbeam and the Rose), The   Brennan 1918

Night Winds   Clare 1930

Night You Name the Day, The   Heyman 1938; Romberg 1938

Night You Name the Day (inst.), The   Brown, Nacio Herb 1941

Night You Said Goodbye, The   Stept 1938

Night You Stole My Kisses, The   Lewis 1932; Schwartz, Jean 1932; Young, Joe 1932

Nightcap Song, The   Donaldson 1940; Mercer 1940

Nightfall   Brooks 1950; Lewis 1932; Washington 1950; Young, Victor 1950

Nightfall in Louisiana   Coots 1937; Davis 1937

Nightie Parade   Harbach 1917

Nightie-Night   Gershwin, George 1925; Gershwin, Ira 1925

Nightingale   Meyer 1910; Strouse 1982

Nightingale and the Rose, The   Herbert 1905; Young, Victor 1949

Nightingale, Bring Me a Rose   Caesar 1922

Nightingale (Samarkand), The   Kern 1917

Nightingale Song, The   Ager 1929; Yellen 1929

Nightingale's Dream (inst.)   Bloom 1946

Nightlife   Adams 1962; Strouse 1962

Nightmare and Goblin March, The   Howard, Joseph E. 1907

Nightmare Ballet (inst.), The   Lane 1976

Nights Are Six Months Long, The   Hanley 1917

Nights of Memory   Bryan 1938

Nighttime Brings Dreams of You   Davis 1929

Nighttime in Dixieland   Johnson, James P. 1914

Nighttime in Rio   Friend 1936

Night-Time Is Love-Time (When I'm with You)   Johnson, Howard 1926

Nighttime Is No Time for Thinking, The   Gershwin, Ira 1945; Weill 1945

Night-Time's the Right Time (To Spoon with the Girl You Love)   Meyer 1911

Nighty Girl   Harbach 1911

Nighty Night   Adamson 1935; Donaldson 1935; Friend 1930; Monaco 1930; Parish 1962; Stept 1938

Nighty Night Until Tomorrow   Magidson 1931

Nighty-Night, Little Sailor Boy   Hoffman 1942; Livingston, Jerry 1942

Nijigo Novgo   Kalmar 1923; Ruby 1923

Nijinski   Buck 1916

Nikki   Bacharach 1967; Coleman 1965; David, Hal 1967

Nile   Howard, Joseph E. 1937; Mercer 1963

Nina   Brennan 1929; Kalmar 1928; Porter 1948; Razaf 1931; Robin 1927; Ruby 1928

Nina Never Knew   Alter 1952

Nina Rosa   Caesar 1930; Harbach 1930; Romberg 1930

Nina the Ballerina   Coots 1955

Nina, the Pinta, the Santa Maria (Columbus), The   Gershwin, Ira 1945; Weill 1945

Nine O'Clock   Merrill 1959

Nine Out of Ten   Merrill 1958

Nine Out of Ten Girls   Alter 1968; Davis 1968

Nine Thorny Thickets   Mercer 1955

Nine to Five   Brooks 1959

Nineteen Hundred and Fifty   Coots 1950

1908 Life, The   Brown, Lew 1929; DeSylva 1929; Henderson 1929

Nineteen Princess Song   Herbert 1905

Nineteen Sixty Five   Warren Date Unknown

1934 Hot Chocolate Jazz Babies Revue, The   Adams 1978; Strouse 1978

Nineteen Twenty-Seven   Caesar 1927

Nineteenth Hole   Drake 1955; Styne 1965

Ninetta   Warren Date Unknown

Ninety Again!   Rodgers 1970

99 Miles from L.A.   David, Hal 1974

99 Percent   Ellington 1971

99% Pure   Schwartz, Arthur 1927

Ninon   Adamson 1935

Nip Ups to McCarthy   Donaldson 1941

Nita   Atteridge 1921; Raye 1943; Romberg 1921

Nita, I Need You   Gorney 1923

Nix on the Concertina Lena   Edwards 1910; Smith, Harry B. 1910

Nix on the Glow Worm, Lena   Carroll 1910

Nixon and Lodge (inst.)   Blake 1960

Nize Baby   Hanley 1926

N.M.S.U. Aggie Alma Mater   Brown, Nacio Herb 1961

No   Whiting 1926

No Account Noah   Robin 1936

No and Yes   Duke 1942

No Big Deal   Strouse 2000

No Bottom (Mississippi Opening/The Leadsman's Song)   Hart 1935; Rodgers 1935

No Callin' Card   Mills 1935

No Can Do   Rainger 1935; Robin 1935; Whiting 1935

No Comprenez, No Capish, No Versteh!   Gershwin, George 1933; Gershwin, Ira 1933

No Croissants   Coleman 1988

No, Dammit, I Don't Hafta!!!!   Spina 1977

No Doggone Business   Carmichael 1935

No Dogs Allowed   Sherman 1972

No Faceless People   David, Hal 1974

No Foolin'   Buck 1926; Hanley 1926

No Further Questions Please   Coleman 1999

No Give, No Take   Merrill 1990

No Go   Donaldson 1939

No Going Back   Sigman 1967

No Good Man (Will Make a Good Good Woman Bad),
    A   Blake 1958

No Goodbyes   Sherman 1974

No Hard Feelings   Davis 1942

No Hard Times   Robison 1960

No, He Can't Be the One for Me   Spina 1977

No Home, No Job   Loesser 1956

No Hope for the Human Race   Dietz 1963; Schwartz, Arthur
    1963

No Horse, No Wife, No Mustache   Dixon 1934; Wrubel
    1934

No Ifs! No Ands! No Buts!   Duke 1963

No Journey's Too Far for a Lover   Smith, Harry B. 1913;
    Smith, Robert B. 1913

No Letter in the Morning Mail   Leslie 1935

No Letter Today   Raye 1957

No Life   Sondheim 1984

No Lookin' Back   Eliscu 1940; Gorney 1940

No Love Blues   De Lange 1940

No Love Daboodle, The   Merrill 1955

No Love, No Nothin'   Robin 1943; Warren 1943

No Lover   Porter 1950

No Lovers Allowed   De Lange 1934

No Man   Fisher 1925

No Man Is Worth It   Lerner, Alan Jay 1983; Strouse 1983

No Man Left for Me   Coleman 1991; Comden and Green
    1991

No Man's Mama   Pollack 1925; Yellen 1925

No, Mary Ann   Sondheim Date Unknown

No Matter How You Slice It It's Bologney   Monaco 1927;
    Rose 1927

No Matter Under What Star You're Born   Gershwin, Ira
    1940; Weill 1940

No Matter What Happens   Bergman 1983

No Matter What or Where   Atteridge 1918; Romberg 1918

No Matter Where You Are   Brooks 1945

No Matter Where You Go (Sole Lucenta)   Hoffman 1954

No Me Creas   Gorney 1931; Harburg 1931

No Mind of Your Own   Comden and Green 1947

No Monkey Business   Brown, A. Seymour 1928

No More   Adams 1964; Russell 1944; Sondheim 1987;
    Strouse 1964

No More Dancing   Coots 1926

No More Flahooleys!   Fain 1951; Harburg 1951

No More Girls for Me   Romberg 1917

No More Goodbyes   Hoffman 1953

No More Ladies   Washington 1935

No More Love   Dubin 1933; Duke 1963; Warren 1933

No More Love 'Cause There's No More You   Friend 1932

No More Mornings   Comden and Green 1982

No More Mr. Nice (People Who Are Nice)   Cahn 1966

No More, No Less   David, Mack 1947; Hoffman 1947;
    Livingston, Jerry 1947

No More Shadows   Heyman 1980

No More Staying Out Late   Norworth 1911

No More Tears   Freed, Ralph 1937; Lane 1937

No More than Always   David, Hal 1960

No More Thrills   Razaf 1934

No More Toujours L'Amour (Hoya, Hoya)   Carmichael 1945;
    Webster 1945

No More Waiting   Rodgers 1967

No More Women   Brooks 1960; De Lange 1945; Gordon
    1934; Revel 1934

No More Worryin'   Donaldson 1926; Kahn 1926

No More You   Brown, Lew 1929; DeSylva 1929; Henderson
    1929

No, Mother, No   Hart 1942; Rodgers 1942

No News Blues   Clare 1961

No News Today   Burke 1946; Van Heusen 1946

No Night to Fear   Warren 1956

No, No and Moi   Spina 1948

No, No, Nanette   Bryan 1929; Caesar 1925; Harbach 1925;
    Youmans 1925

No! No! No!   Lewis 1941

No, No, No, Not That   David, Hal 1948

No, No, Nora   Kahn 1923

No No War   Akst 1933; Eliscu 1933

No Olive in My Martini, Please   Loewe 1942

No One   Adams 1953; Oakland 1968; Strouse 1953; Yellen
    1925

No One but the Right Man Can Do Me Wrong   Rainger
    1929

No One but You   Brown, Lew 1920; David, Mack 1954; De
    Lange 1942; Friml 1918; Harbach 1911; Lawrence 1954;
    Sigman 1950

No One Can Keep Me Away from You   Bryan 1917

No One Can Like the Drummer Man   Hoffman 1937;
    Lerner, Sammy 1937

No One Can Take Your Place   Gilbert 1929

No One Can Toddle Like My Cousin Sue   Razaf 1923

No One Could Do It Like My Father   Berlin 1909; Snyder
    1909

No One Could Love You, As Much As I Do   Young, Joe
    1932

No One Else   Hoffman 1954; Silver 1954

No One Else but that Girl of Mine   Caesar 1921; Gershwin,
    George 1921

No One Else but You   Kern 1928

No One Else Can Love Me Like You, Baby   Carroll 1932

No One Ever Died from Lovin'   Fisher 1911

No One Ever Fell in Love at All   Duke 1927

No One Ever Loved Like Me   Schwartz, Jean 1918

No One Ever Sends Me Roses   Davis 1962

No One Has Ever Loved Me   Sondheim 1994

No One Is Alone   Sondheim 1987

No One Is Perfect   Duke Date Unknown

No One Knows but the Red, Red Rose   Mitchell 1926

No One Knows (How Much I'm in Love)   Kern 1925

No One Knows, No One Cares   Brooks 1948

No One Knows What It's All About   Rose 1924; Woods
    1924

No One Knows Where Kelly Went   Bryan 1913

No One Loves a Clown   Atteridge 1921; Romberg 1921

No One Loves Me Like My Wilhemina   Brown, Lew 1925

No One Man Is Ever Goin' to Marry Me   Yellen 1978

No One Owns Tomorrow   Duke 1963

No One Remembers My Name   Bacharach 1976; David, Hal
    1976

No One Seems to Care   De Lange 1946

No One Thanks the Go-Between   Leigh 1955

No One to Blame but Myself   Donaldson 1939; Parish 1939

No One to Blame but You   Schwartz, Arthur 1930

No One to Call Me Victoria   Adams 1972; Strouse 1972

No One to Love   Ager 1925; Yellen 1925

No One Will Steal Him   Herbert 1905; Smith, Harry B. 1905

No One Woman Can Satisfy Any One Man All the
Time   Yellen 1947

No One's As Lucky As Me   Coots 1928

No One's Heart   Romberg 1948

No One's Here   Lawrence 1981

No One's Loved No One So Much   Merrill 1949

No One's to Blame but You   Smith, Harry B. 1915

No Other Girl   Kalmar 1924; Ruby 1924

No Other Love   Hammerstein 1953; Rodgers 1953; Russell
1950

No Other Love Was Meant for Me   Brennan 1929

No Other, No One but You   Davis 1925

No Place but Home (If We're in China)   Hart 1930; Rodgers
1930

No Place Like Home   Caesar 1928

No Place Like London   Sondheim 1979

No Place to Go, but Only Home Sweet Home   Fisher 1920

No Pretty Rich Girl   Adams 1996; Strouse 1996

No Question in My Mind (You're in My Heart)   Gershwin,
Ira 1938; Kern 1938

No Questions   Bergman 1964; Fain 1964

No Range to Ride Anymore   Sigman 1949

No Regrets   David, Hal 1961

No Rest for the Weary   Russell 1947

No Restricted Signs Up in Heaven   Drake 1946

No Ring on Her Finger   Loesser 1937

No Ross Dixon Lincoln Plaza Saloon   Russell 1946

No Sad Songs for Me   Akst 1950; Sondheim Date Unknown

No Show This Evening   Porter 1910

No Show Tonight   Herbert 1905

No Show without You   Gorney 1964

No Smoking   Ellington 1944

No Song More Pleasing   Rodgers 1976

No Star Is Lost   Fisher 1939

No Star of Night   Sondheim Date Unknown

No Strings   Rodgers 1962

No Strings (I'm Fancy Free)   Berlin 1935

No Substitute for Love   Lawrence 1960

No Surprises   Strouse 1980

No Surrender   Coslow 1943

No Swallerin' Place   Loesser 1953

No Talent Joe   DePaul 1958; Raye 1958; Robin 1951; Styne
1951

No Tax on Love!   Rome 1938

No Tickee, No Shirtee   Conrad 1923

No Tickee, No Washee   Gershwin, George 1932; Gershwin,
Ira 1932

No Time to Argue   Kahn 1939; Romberg 1939

No Trespassing   Johnson, Howard 1960

No Two People   Loesser 1952

No Two Ways About Love   Duke 1963

No Understand   Rodgers 1965; Sondheim 1965

No Use Living with No One to Love   Kahn 1930

No Use Pretending   Harbach 1936; Romberg 1936

No Used Actin' Coy with a Boy from Illinois   Harbach 1948

No Village Like Mine   Gershwin, Ira 1943

No Waiting Time   Robison 1956

No Walls Are High Enough   Bergman 1988

No Walls, No Ceilings, No Floors   David, Hal 1977

No Way to Stop It   Hammerstein 1959; Rodgers 1959

No Way to Treat a Lady   Strouse 1999

No Wings on My Angel   David, Hal 1960

No Wonder   Bergman 1983; Waller 1929

No Wonder I'm Blue   Ahlert 1920; Alter 1930; Hammerstein
1930; Lewis 1920; Young, Joe 1920

No Wonder I'm Happy, My Baby's in Love with Me   Akst
1927; Davis 1927

No Wonder I'm in Love with You   Snyder 1930

No Wonder I'm Lonesome   Lewis 1922; Meyer 1922; Young,
Joe 1922

No Wonder I'm So Crazy for You   Coots 1927

No Wonder I'm So Crazy Over You   Davis 1927

No Wonder She's a Blushing Bride   Dubin 1926; Mills 1926

No Wonder Taxes Are High   Porter 1958

No Wonder that I Love You   Davis 1924

No Wonder the Danube Is Blue   Brown, A. Seymour 1940

No Words Can Tell   Sterling 1900

No (You Can't Have Him)   Russell 1977

No You No Me   Loesser 1943; Schwartz, Arthur 1943

Noah Was His Name   Livingston, Jerry 1960

Noah's Ark   Livingston, Jerry 1960

Noah's Wife Lived a Wonderful Life   Yellen 1920

Noble Cause of Art, The   Atteridge 1914

Noble Duchess, The   Hammerstein 1935; Romberg 1935

Nobody   Egan 1925; Kahn 1925

Nobody Asked Me to Dance   Merrill 1953

Nobody but Fanny   Conrad 1925; DeSylva 1925

Nobody But My Baby Is Getting My Love   Razaf 1926

Nobody But Nobody   Lawrence 1961

Nobody but Tess   Duke 1959

Nobody but the Lord (Ever Heard Him Pray)   Robison 1958

Nobody but You   Buck 1922; DeSylva 1919; Drake 1998;
Edwards 1929; Gershwin, George 1919; Jerome 1905;
Johnson, J. Rosamond 1904; Kalmar 1925; Loesser 1937;
Ruby 1925; Schwartz, Jean 1905

Nobody Can Change My Mind   Styne 1929

Nobody Cares   Evans 1954; Livingston, Jay 1954

Nobody Cares for You   Sterling 1897; Von Tilzer 1897

Nobody Cares If I'm Blue   Akst 1930; Clarke 1929

Nobody Does It Like Me   Coleman 1973; Fields 1973

Nobody Else but Elsie   Kahal 1932; Monaco 1932

Nobody Else but Me   Hammerstein 1946; Kern 1946;
Sterling 1901

Nobody Else but You   Fisher 1905

Nobody Else Can Do the Things You Do   Bryan 1924

Nobody Ever   Caesar 1919

Nobody Ever Brings Me Violets   Hanley 1932

Nobody Ever Cried Over Me   Dixon 1923

Nobody Ever Died for Dear Old Rutgers   Cahn 1947; Styne
1947

Nobody Ever Pins Me Up   Dietz 1944; Duke 1944

Nobody Ever Said No to Nora   Ruby 1950

Nobody Home   Burke 1930; Williams 1914; Young, Joe 1914

Nobody Home Cakewalk (inst.)   Motzan 1915

Nobody in Particular   Lawrence 1947

Nobody Know Where Tosti Goes, When Tosti Says
Goodbye   Lewis 1922; Meyer 1922; Young, Joe 1922

Nobody Knows   Bergman 1970; Burke 1929; Razaf 1949;
Styne 1942; Waller 1927

Nobody Knows (And Nobody Seems to Care)   Berlin 1919

Nobody Knows but Rosie, But Oh! What Rosie
Knows!   Hanley 1929

Nobody Knows but the Lord   Kalmar 1930; Ruby 1930

Nobody Knows but the Posies   Livingston, Jerry 1936

Nobody Knows de Trouble I've Seen   Johnson, James P.
1962

Nobody Knows How Much I Love You   Howard, Bart 1959

Nobody Knows (Just What It Is But Me)   Burke 1931

Nobody Knows the Trouble I've Had   Johnson, Howard
1939

Nobody Knows What a Red Head Mama Can Do   Dubin 1925; Fain 1925; Mills 1925

Nobody Listens — Nobody Cares   Evans 1975; Livingston, Jay 1975

Nobody Looks at the Man   Hart 1930; Rodgers 1930

Nobody Loves a Bugler   Lawrence 1943

Nobody Loves a Riveter   Hart 1931; Rodgers 1931

Nobody Loves an Old Carousel   David, Mack 1966

Nobody Loves Little Me   Cobb 1904; Edwards 1904

Nobody Loves Me   Herbert 1907; Smith, Harry B. 1907

Nobody Loves Me and I Wonder Why   Brown, Lew 1925

Nobody Loves Me Now   Davis 1927

Nobody Loves No Baby Like My Baby Loves Me   Donaldson 1931

Nobody Loves You Like I Do   Akst 1924; Cahn 1947; Davis 1924; Lewis 1923; Meyer 1923; Strouse 1987; Young, Joe 1923

Nobody Makes a Pass at Me   Rome 1937

Nobody Reads Books   Sondheim Date Unknown

Nobody Rings the Telephone   Romberg 1927

Nobody Seems To Know   Buck 1914

Nobody Shows What My Baby Shows   Razaf 1928

Nobody Steps on Kafritz   Merrill 1967

Nobody Takes Me Bye-Bye   Ahlert 1924; Lewis 1924; Young, Joe 1924

Nobody Thought It Would Last   Gilbert 1947

Nobody to Love   Kahn 1920; Meyer 1920

Nobody Told Me   Rodgers 1962

Nobody Understands Me   Mercer 1951

Nobody Wants Me   Caesar 1929

Nobody Wants to Go Home   Spina 1954

Nobody Was in Love with Me   Atteridge 1914

Nobody Will Know but Me   Ahlert 1925; Lewis 1925; Young, Joe 1925

Nobody Worries 'Bout Me   Lerner, Sammy 1926; Whiting 1926

Nobody's Baby   Bullock 1937

Nobody's Baby Is Somebody's Baby Now   Kahn 1931

Nobody's Chasing Me   Porter 1950

Nobody's Ever Gonna Love You   Loesser 1956

Nobody's Fool   Fields 1931; McHugh 1931

Nobody's Gal   Lewis 1919; Young, Joe 1919

Nobody's Gonna Keep Me Away from My Girl   Kahn 1926

Nobody's Gonna Take You From Me   Kalmar 1938; Ruby 1938

Nobody's Heart   Hart 1942; Rodgers 1942

Nobody's Heart but Mine   Adamson 1948; McHugh 1948

Nobody's Lost on the Lonesome Trail   Gilbert 1949

Nobody's Perfect   Bergman 1976; Cahn 1960; Van Heusen 1960

Nobody's Sweetheart   Kahn 1923

Noche de Amor (Night of Love)   David, Mack 1957

Nocturne, The   Bryan 1927; Friml 1925; Schwartz, Jean 1927

Nocturne (inst.)   Young, Victor 1951

Nod, Nod, Nod, Little Golden Rod   Fain 1931; Kahal 1931

Nodding Away   Brennan 1929

Nodding Roses   Kern 1915

Noisy Neighbors   Johnson, James P. 1931

Non Vedo L'Ora   Drake 2000

Nona from Bologna   Silver 1926; Turk 1926

Nona (Sweetest Girl in Barcelona)   Kahn 1920

Nonchalant   Cahn 1950; Von Tilzer 1929

None but the Brave   Robison 1952

None but the Brave Deserve the Fair   Howard, Joseph E. 1909

None but the Lonely Heart   David, Mack 1947; Hoffman 1947; Johnson, Howard 1939; Livingston, Jerry 1947

None but the Lonely Heart (Nur Wer Die Sensucht Kennt)   Bergman 1983

None of Them's Got Anything on Me   Jerome 1908; Schwartz, Jean 1908

Nonsense   Brown, A. Seymour 1910; Goetz 1910, 1917; Howard, Joseph E. 1907

Non-Stop Dancing   Kern 1923

Non-Stop Lovin' Man   Ager 1923; Yellen 1923

Nora   Coots 1946; Ruby 1948

Nordland   Herbert 1904

Noreen Mavoureen   Olcott 1902

Norma   Mitchell 1919

Normal Thing to Do, The   Lane 1965; Lerner, Alan Jay 1965

Normandy   Silver 1927

Normandy Eyes   Bryan 1933

North America Meets South America   Hart 1941; Rodgers 1941

North and South   Bryan 1919; Schwartz, Jean 1919

North and South Dakota Moon   Conrad 1939; Magidson 1939

North of 53   Norworth 1917

North of Nowhere   Russell 1952

North Pole Sketch   Gordon 1937; Revel 1937

North, South, East or West   Smith, Robert B. 1905

North Wind   Brooks 1958

Norworth's College Medley   Norworth 1910

Nosensical Nonsense   Brown, A. Seymour 1909

Nostalgia   Ellington 1941; Evans 1954; Livingston, Jay 1954; Parish 1965; Webster 1941

Nostalgia (inst.)   Myrow 1945

Not a Care in the World   Duke 1940

Not a Chance in the World   Brown, Lew 1923; Clare 1923; Hanley 1923

Not a Day Goes By   Sondheim 1981

Not a Penny in My Pocket, But I'm a Millionaire   Wrubel 1932

Not Again   Cahn 1978

Not All but Nearly   Smith, Robert B. 1908

Not Another Day Like This   Strouse 1980

Not As a Stranger   Van Heusen 1955

Not As Good As Last Year   Brown, Lew 1928; DeSylva 1928; Henderson 1928

Not As Much As I Need You   David, Mack 1956

Not Cricket to Picket   Rome 1937

Not Dancing this Evening   Atteridge 1915

Not Enough Faith in the Lord   Robison 1959

Not Enough Faith (In the Word)   Robison 1962

Not Enough Love, Baby   Von Tilzer 1929

Not Even You   Schwartz, Arthur 1928

Not for All the Rice in China   Berlin 1933

Not for Children   Sondheim Date Unknown

Not for Him   Hammerstein 1926; Harbach 1926; Romberg 1926

Not Goin' Home Anymore (inst.)   Bacharach 1969

Not Guilty   Rome 1959

Not Here! Not Here!   Kern 1909

Not Here, Not There, It's Fifty Miles from Nowhere   Dixon 1923

Not in a Month of Sundays   De Lange 1934; Myrow 1934

Not in Business Hours   Hammerstein 1923; Youmans 1923

Not Love   Woods 1956

Not Me   Livingston, Jerry 1970; Raye 1957; Strouse 1991

Not Mine   Comden and Green 1967; Mercer 1942; Styne 1967

Not My Baby   David, Mack 1989

Not Now   Razaf 1946; Russell 1942

Not Now, but Later   Friml 1913; Harbach 1913

Not on Your Nellie   Harburg 1967; Styne 1967

Not One   Young, Victor 1934

Not Quite a Waltz   Evans 1959; Livingston, Jay 1959

Not Quite Night (Crickets)   Sondheim 1973

Not So Deep As a Well   De Lange 1942

Not So Good, Not So Bad   Von Tilzer 1921

Not So Innocent Fun (Nine Young Girls and Nine Old Men)   Hart 1937; Rodgers 1937

Not So Long Ago   Brown, A. Seymour 1920; Gershwin, Ira 1924

Not So Warm (inst.)   Kern 1938

Not that I Care   David, Mack 1956; Hammerstein 1931; Whiting 1931

Not that She Was Prettier   Smith, Harry B. 1915

Not There, Right Here   Waller 1938

Not too Lovely to Love (inst.)   Kern 1941

Not Until Now   Razaf 1953

Not While I'm Around   Sondheim 1979

Not with My Wife, You Don't   Mercer 1967

Not Yet   Kern 1918; Warren 1940, Date Unknown

Not Yet Suzette   Coots 1923; Coslow 1923

Not You   Kern 1918

No-Tell Motel, The   Merrill 1971; Styne 1971

Notes on an Instrumental Theme   Spina 1977

'Nother Little Kiss   Fisher 1924

Nothin'   Ahlert 1927; Russell 1946; Sherman 1968

Nothin' Does-Does Like It Used to Do-Do-Do   Fain 1927; Kahal 1927

Nothin' for Nothin'   Fields 1950

Nothin' from Nothin' Leaves You   Snyder 1905

Nothin', Nothin', Baby (Without You)   Ellington 1953

Nothin' on My Mind   Kahn 1928

Nothing   Loesser 1937

Nothing at All   Fain 1955; Kern 1908

Nothing but a Bubble   Smith, Harry B. 1909

Nothing but Love   Brown, Lew 1927; Bryan 1930; DeSylva 1927; Henderson 1927

Nothing but the Best   Leigh 1985

Nothing but You   Hart 1940; Rodgers 1940

Nothing Can Change My Mind   Revel 1942

Nothing Can Ever Happen in New York   Hanley 1927

Nothing Can Get to Me Now   Adams 1970; Strouse 1970

Nothing Can Replace a Man   Fain 1955

Nothing Can Stop Me Now   Bullock 1937; Spina 1937

Nothing Could Be Sweeter   Robin 1927; Youmans 1927

Nothing Else Matters Any More   Koehler 1925

Nothing Else Matters but Love   Friend 1926; Kahn 1926

Nothing Ever Ever Ever Hardly Ever Troubles Me   Norworth 1908

Nothing Ever Happens   Duke 1949

Nothing Ever Happens in London   Martin 1964

Nothing Ever Happens to Me   David, Mack 1940

Nothing Has Changed   Freed, Ralph 1965

Nothing Has Changed but You   Sissle 1928

Nothing in Common   Cahn 1958; Van Heusen 1958; Willson 1963

Nothing in the World   Bergman 1963

Nothing Is Forever   Leigh 1977

Nothing Is Impossible   Gershwin, Ira 1953; Lane 1953

Nothing Is New in New York   Merrill 1966

Nothing Is Too Good   Duke 1950; Rome 1950

Nothing Lasts Forever (Not Even Forever)   David, Hal 1976

Nothing Less than Beautiful   Wrubel 1933

Nothing Lives Longer than Love   Lewis 1935

Nothing More or Nothing Less   Stept 1934

Nothing Much to Do   Warren 1956

Nothing Naughtie in a Nightie   Atteridge 1924; Romberg 1924; Schwartz, Jean 1924

Nothing New Beneath the Sun   Cohan 1901, 1904, 1907, 1908

Nothing, Nothing, Nothing (inst.)   Revel 1960

Nothing on My Mind but You   Koehler 1942

Nothing On To-Day   Atteridge 1917; Romberg 1917

Nothing Personal   Bergman 1960

Nothing Seems the Same without You   Davis 1926

Nothing Stays the Same   Friend 1960

Nothing to Do   Livingston, Jerry 1963

Nothing to Do (And All Day to Do It)   Hoffman 1940

Nothing to Do but Nothing   Howard, Joseph E. 1908

Nothing to Do but Pass the Time of Day   Ruby 1959

Nothing to Do But Work   Porter 1953

Nothing to Do Until Tomorrow   Meyer 1911

Nothing to Lose   Mancini 1968

Nothing To Wear   Buck 1914

Nothing Too Good for You Dear   Howard, Joseph E. 1910

Nothing Was Ever Like This   Heyman 1934

Nothing Will Hurt Us Again   Strouse 1986

Nothing Will Keep Me Away   Evans 1959; Livingston, Jay 1959

Nothing's All Good and Nothing's All Bad   Livingston, Jerry 1973

Nothing's Blue but the Sky   Spina 1936

Nothing's Going to Hold Us Down   Friend 1930; Monaco 1930

Nothing's Good Enough for a Good Little Girl   Atteridge 1916; Motzan 1916; Romberg 1916

Nothing's Good Enough for a Good Little Girl If She's Good Enough for You   Bryan 1917

Nothing's Right When Your Love's All Wrong   Dietz 1929; Gorney 1929; Harburg 1929

Nothing's Wrong   Hart 1927; Rodgers 1927

Notice Me   Comden and Green 1964; Styne 1964

Notorious Colonel Blake, The   Hart 1935; Rodgers 1935

Notorious Landlady, The   David, Mack 1962; Fain 1962

Notre Dame Marie   Bryan 1931

Nottingham Fair, The   Cahn 1971; Van Heusen 1971

Nouveau Favori (inst.)   Kern 1956

Nova Scotia Moonlight   Coslow 1933; Johnston 1933

Novelette   Kern 1945; Robin 1946

Novelty Dance   Youmans 1924

Novelty Rag (inst.)   Blake 1972

November 22, 1963   Sondheim 1990

November Birthday Song   Caesar 1940

November Song   Merrill 1972; Styne 1972

November Twilight   Webster 1956

Now   Burke 1954; Duke 1936; Livingston, Jerry 1966; Sondheim 1973; Strouse 1980

Now and Again   Van Heusen 1964

Now and Forever   Evans 1949; Hoffman 1951; Livingston, Jay 1949; Pollack 1934; Young, Joe 1934; Young, Victor 1949

Now and Then   Pollack 1942; Smith, Harry B. 1913

Now and Then but Not All the Time   Bryan 1919; Schwartz, Jean 1919

Now! Baby! Now!   Cahn 1956

'Now' Dance (inst.), The   Styne 1980
Now Go to Your Cabin   Hart 1929; Rodgers 1929
Now He's All Stuck Up, Cause He Owns a Ford   Johnson, Howard 1916
Now He's Got a Beautiful Girl   Clarke 1916; Leslie 1916; Snyder 1916
Now He's Got a Girl   Atteridge 1916; Hanley 1916; Romberg 1916; Smith, Harry B. 1916
Now His Choice We See   Smith, Robert B. 1912
Now I Ask You   Hanley 1930
Now I Ask You Is that Nice   Clare 1920; Mitchell 1920; Pollack 1921
Now I Ask You What Would You Do   Robin 1931; Whiting 1931
Now I Believe   Hart 1931; Rodgers 1931
Now I Have Someone   Comden and Green 1961; Styne 1961
Now I Know   Arlen 1944; Brooks 1950; Clarke 1921; Koehler 1944; Monaco 1921; Stept 1958
Now I Know what Love Is   Howard, Bart 1966
Now I Lay Me Down to Sin   Loesser 1934
Now I Lay Me Down to Sleep   Coleman 1958; Hanley 1932; Heyman 1968; Leigh 1958; Meyer 1920; Mitchell 1920
Now I Understand   Coslow 1934
Now I Won't Be Lonely Anymore   David, Hal 1958
Now I'm a Lady   Coslow 1935; Fain 1935; Kahal 1935
Now I'm in Love   Yellen 1929
Now I'm Ready for a Frau   Dietz 1961; Schwartz, Arthur 1961
Now Is Forever   Cahn 1978
Now (Is the Moment)   Comden and Green 1963; Styne 1963
Now Is the Only Time Ever   Wrubel 1959
Now Is the South Wind Blowing   Herbert 1913
Now Is the Time for All Good Men   Duke 1955
Now Is Wonderful   Fields 1952; Schwartz, Arthur 1952
Now It Can Be Told   Berlin 1938
Now It's Her and Him   Adams 1975
Now It's Hook or Me   Leigh 1954
Now I've Got Some Dreaming to Do   Burke 1936; Johnston 1936
Now I've Heard Everything   Drake 1953
Now Kiss Me   Carmichael 1940; Mercer 1940
Now, Now, Now   David, Hal 1953
Now or Never   Lewis 1936
Now, Right Now   Johnson, James P. 1944
Now She Is Anybody's Girlie   Williams 1910
Now She Knows How to Parle Voo   Leslie 1914; Young, Joe 1914
Now That I Have Everything   Drake 1982
Now that I Have Springtime   Hammerstein 1934; Kern 1934
Now That I Know You   Hart 1940; Rodgers 1940
(Where Are You) Now that I Need You   Loesser 1949
Now that I Need You You're Gone   Clarke 1923; Leslie 1923
Now that I'm Free   Caesar 1943; Lerner, Sammy 1943
Now that I'm in Love   Burke 1953
Now that It's All Over   Fisher 1930
Now That I've Got My Strength   Hart 1942; Rodgers 1942
Now that I've Known Your Love   Cahn 1969
Now that I've Lost You   Johnson, James P. 1962
Now that I've Told You My Story   Revel 1952
Now that Papa's Back   Strouse 1986
Now That She's Off My Hands I Can't Get Her Off My Mind   Lewis 1928; Young, Joe 1928
Now That the Dance Is Near   Gershwin, George 1927; Gershwin, Ira 1927

Now that the Lights Are Low   Norworth 1916
Now That We Are One   Gershwin, Ira 1938; Kern 1938
Now That We're in Love   Cahn 1975
Now that We're Married   Howard, Joseph E. 1918
Now that We're Sweethearts Again (Tell Me What You Told Me)   Fisher 1934
Now That You Are Here   Dietz 1930; Rainger 1930
Now that You Know (Our Song, Mi Cancion)   Caesar 1950
Now that You Mention It   Livingston, Jerry 1970
Now That You're Gone   Kahn 1931
Now that You've Got Me, What Are You Going to Do   Williams 1913; Young, Joe 1913
Now that You've Had All the Love that You Want You Don't Want Me Around Any More   Monaco 1925
Now the Day Is Over   Johnson, Howard 1939
Now the Madame Swings   Raye 1945
Now the Wedding Day Is Here   Smith, Harry B. 1934
Now the World Begins Again   Duke 1963
Now, Vote Republican   Razaf 1952
Now We Know   Robison 1943
Now We Sing   Willson 1956
Now We're Getting Somewhere   Burke 1945; Van Heusen 1945
Now What Do We Do?   Brooks 1942
Now While I Still Remember How   David, Hal 1979
Now You Has Jazz   Porter 1956
Now You Know   Freed, Ralph 1959; Sondheim 1981
Now You Leave   Hammerstein 1951; Rodgers 1951
Now You Say You Care   Lawrence 1956
Now You See It Now You Don't   Coleman 1980; Loesser 1942
Now You See It (Now You Don't) (inst.)   Drake 1958
Now You're in My Arms   Wrubel 1931
Now You're Talking My Language   Koehler 1937; Mitchell 1937; Stept 1937
Now You've Got Me Doing It   Burke 1935; Spina 1935
Now You've Got Me Worryin' for You   Fain 1932; Young, Joe 1932
Nowhere   David, Mack 1968; Hoffman 1953; Silver 1954
Nowhere Guy   Gordon 1953; Myrow 1953
Now's the Time   Comden and Green 1967; Styne 1967
Now's the Time (When They're Young)   Friend 1958
N.R.A. March   Woods 1933
N.R.A. Song   Cohan 1933
Nudge Me Every Morning   Cahn 1972
Nudist Colony   Berlin 1931
'Nuff Said   Sherman 1958
Nuggets   Brennan 1949
Numb, Dumb and Glum   Evans 1946; Livingston, Jay 1946
Numb Fumblin'   Waller 1935
Number Four   Willson 1956
Number Six   Coslow 1924
Nurse Girls and Doctors   Williams 1907
Nursery Clock (inst.), The   Kern 1923
Nursery Fanfare (My Own Light Infantry)   Kern 1918
Nursery Land   Kalmar 1915
Nursery Rhymes   Jerome 1901, 1902; Kahn 1933; Schwartz, Jean 1901, 1902
Nurses Are We   Kern 1912
Nursie, Nursie   Gershwin, George 1927; Gershwin, Ira 1927
Nut Sundae, A   Buck 1914
Nutcracker Suite   Brooks 1945
Nutmeg Insurance   Revel 1945
Nuts, He Travels with Us Nuts   Hart 1928; Rodgers 1928
Nuts to You   Adams 1992; Strouse 1992

Nutsey Fagan   Dixon 1923; Rose 1923
Nutty Nursery Rhymes   Cahn 1938; Raye 1938
N.Y. City Opera Jingle   Comden and Green 1982
N.Y.C.   Strouse 1977
Nylons   Willson 1953
Nymph Errant   Porter 1933

O

O Baby, I Go for You   Snyder 1931
O Captain, My Captain   Weill 1942
O Charlie Is My Darling   Johnson, Howard 1939
O Come My Love   Williams 1907
O, Heart of Love   Weill 1936
O Israel, Do Not Despair   Gorney 1947
O, Katharina!   Gilbert 1922
O Land of Mine, America   Gershwin, George 1919
O Leo!   Dietz 1935; Schwartz, Arthur 1935
O! Mia Speranza   Herbert 1908
O! Mister Carpenter   Akst 1931; Eliscu 1931
O' O' O'Brien   Schwartz, Jean 1902
O Oio Mio   Hoffman 1959
O Pedro (Song of the Jealous Caballero)   Spina 1947
O Prehistoric Raiment   Dietz 1952
O Pretty Maids of France   Hammerstein 1926; Harbach 1926; Romberg 1926
O Queen of Victory   Spina 1950
O Sola Mi Whose Sole Are You   Baer 1927; Lewis 1927; Young, Joe 1927
O Sole Mio (Just Like the Sunrise)   Dubin 1924
O Southland   Johnson, J. Rosamond Date Unknown
O Spirit of the Summertime   Duke 1942
O Tixo, Tixo, Help Me   Weill 1949
O! Weather-Man!   Howard, Joseph E. 1910
O What a Wonderful World   Dietz 1935; Schwartz, Arthur 1935
O You Heavenly Body   Bryan 1920; Schwartz, Jean 1920
Oak Leaf Memorial Park, The   Livingston, Jerry 1973
Oakaloosa   Hoffman 1956
Oasis   Mercer 1961
Oath, The   Harburg 1961
Oatmeal and Farina   Leslie 1949
O'Brien Has Gone Hawaiian   Gordon 1942
O'Brien Is Tryin' to Learn to Talk Hawaiian   Dubin 1916
O'Brien to Ryan to Goldberg   Comden and Green 1949
Obviously the Gentleman Prefers to Dance   Cahn 1941
Occasional Flight of Fancy, An   Cahn 1965; Van Heusen 1965
Occasional Man, An   Blane 1955; Martin 1955
Occupancy of This Building is Limited to 382 Persons By Order of the New York Fire Department   Willson 1953
Ocean Breeze   Robin 1952; Styne 1952
Ocean, The Ocean, The   Harbach 1914
Ocean Will Never Run Dry, The   Heyman 1934
Oceans of Love   Sigman 1961
Och Louisa   Edwards 1904
O'Conner   Dietz 1963; Schwartz, Arthur 1963
Octavians   Spina 1958
Octet   Porter 1944
October Birthday Song   Caesar 1940
October Mist   Webster 1957
October Night (inst.)   Myrow 1971
October Twilight (Those Days Before the War)   Mercer 1972; Myrow 1972
October's Melody (inst.)   Robison 1929

Octopus Song, The   Freed, Ralph 1956; Livingston, Jerry 1956; Rome 1954
Octoroon   Warren 1935
Odd Ball   Coleman 1964
Odd Couple, The   Cahn 1968
Odd Lots   Romberg 1917
Odds and Ends (Of a Beautiful Love Affair)   Bacharach 1969; David, Hal 1969
Odds and Ends of an Old Love Affair   Livingston, Jerry 1933
Ode to a Key   Bergman 1964; Fain 1964
Ode to a List   Oakland 1972
Ode to a Marine (What Makes a Marine)   Myrow 1943
Ode to a Rat   Cahn 1976; Lane 1976
Ode to a Southern Woman   Drake 1953
Ode to Dorie Miller   Johnson, James P. 1945; Razaf 1945
Ode to Joy (Siwash Spring Song)   Loesser 1940
Ode to Victory   Johnston 1943
O'Donnell Ahoo! (The Clanconnel War Song)   Herbert 1915
Oedipus Rex a la Jazz   Atteridge 1923; Schwartz, Jean 1923
Of a Mornin'   Brennan 1925
Of All My Wife's Relations, I Love Myself the Best   Sterling 1924
Of All the People   Cahn 1957
Of Course It's Crazy   David, Mack 1954, 1989
Of Maestro and Men   Raye 1940
Of the People   Hammerstein 1940; Schwartz, Arthur 1940
Of the People Stomp   Rome 1940, 1942
Of Thee I Sing (Baby)   Gershwin, George 1931; Gershwin, Ira 1931
Off Again — On Again   Hoffman 1932
Off Again, On Again   Bergman 1959; Duke 1932; Harburg 1932
Off Again, On Again Blues   David, Hal 1952
Off Again-On Again   Mills 1938
Off for a Sail   Harbach 1910
Off the Record   Hart 1937; Rodgers 1937
Off the Shores of Somewhere   Romberg 1943
Off to Russia   Smith, Harry B. 1908
Off to See the World   DePaul 1941; Raye 1941
Off to the Derby   Cohan 1904
Off to Turkey   Smith, Harry B. 1903
Off to Wonderland   Lane 1952; Robin 1952
Off We Go   Brooks 1959; Caesar 1922
Off with the Old Love, On with the New, Easier to Say than Do   Carroll 1914
Offering Ballet (inst.), The   Blane 1961
Office Blues, The   Atteridge 1919; Carroll 1919
Office Hours   Berlin 1914
Officer O'Mahoney   Merrill 1955
Officers of the 125th   Romberg 1917
Official Resume   Gershwin, George 1929; Gershwin, Ira 1929
Offissa Pup   Evans 1963; Livingston, Jay 1963
Off-Time   Razaf 1929; Waller 1929
Oft in the Stilly Night   Johnson, Howard 1939
Ogalalia   Snyder 1909
Oh — What a Crazy Song   Webster 1961
Oh, Agnes   DeSylva 1919
Oh, Allah   Atteridge 1914
Oh! Argentine   Friml 1918
Oh Auntie   Fain 1941; Kahal 1941; Yellen 1941
Oh, Babe, Maybe Someday   Ellington 1936
Oh, Baby!   Blake 1942; Davis 1922; Razaf 1942
Oh Baby, Do That Little Thing for Me   Parish 1930

Oh Baby! (Don't Say No Say Maybe)   DeSylva 1924; Donaldson 1924

Oh Baby, Don't We Get Along   Brown, Lew 1927; DeSylva 1927; Henderson 1927

Oh Baby (I Know that You Wouldn't But Gosh How I Wish That You Would)   Brown, Lew 1927; Friend 1927

Oh Baby I'm on the Moon   Leslie 1959

Oh Baby, Obey   Rainger 1932, 1935, 1938; Robin 1932, 1935, 1938

Oh Baby what A Night   Brown, A. Seymour 1929

Oh Baby! What Do You Do   Friend 1930; Monaco 1930

Oh Bess, Where's My Bess   Gershwin, George 1935; Gershwin, Ira 1935

Oh Boy!   Russell 1977

Oh Boy! Couldn't You Care for That   Kahal 1927; Snyder 1927

Oh Boy! How It Was Raining   Silver 1926

Oh, Bright Fair Dream   Porter 1916

Oh Brother   Wrubel 1946

Oh Bury Me Not on the Lone Prairie   Johnson, Howard 1939

Oh, But I Do   Robin 1946; Schwartz, Arthur 1946

Oh! by Jingo!, Oh! by Gee!   Brown, Lew 1919

Oh, Carmenita   Warren 1928

Oh Christmas Tree   Brooks 1952

Oh Come to the Ball   Lerner, Alan Jay 1956; Loewe 1956

Oh, Comrades   Romberg 1925; Smith, Harry B. 1925

Oh, Couldn't I Love that Girl   Hammerstein 1931; Romberg 1931

Oh Dad, Poor Dad, Mamma's Hung You in the Closet and I'm Feelin' So Sad   David, Hal 1967

Oh Daddy   Coleman 1996

Oh Day in June!   Herbert 1920

Oh de Lawd Shake de Heaven   Gershwin, George 1935

Oh! Dear!   Friend 1921; Hart 1925; Rodgers 1925; Von Tilzer 1920

Oh! Didn't He Ramble   Johnson, J. Rosamond 1902

Oh, Diogenes   Hart 1938; Rodgers 1938

Oh Do Step the Two-Step   Smith, Harry B. 1911

Oh, Doctor   Smith, Harry B. 1912; Smith, Robert B. 1912

Oh Doctor, Doctor   Romberg 1918

Oh, Doctor Jesus   Gershwin, George 1935; Gershwin, Ira 1935

Oh Donna Clara   Caesar 1931

Oh, Don't You Love It?   Johnson, Howard 1926

Oh Doris, Where Do You Live   Kahn 1927

Oh Dream of Love   Kahn 1938

Oh Eva Ain't You Coming Out Tonight   Clarke 1924; Leslie 1924; Warren 1924

Oh, Fabulous One in Your Ivory Tower   Gershwin, Ira 1940; Weill 1940

Oh, Fascinating Night   Harbach 1914

Oh! Flo, On a Midnight Choo Choo Honeymoon   Lewis 1924

Oh Flo! On a Midnight Choo-Choo Honeymoon   Donaldson 1924; Lewis 1924; Young, Joe 1924

Oh for a Singer (inst.)   Kern 1936

Oh, for the Life of a Bootlegger's Wife   Edwards 1923; Smith, Robert B. 1923

Oh, for the Life of a Cowboy   Hanley 1927

Oh Frenchy   Conrad 1929

Oh! Frenchy (Come to Yankee Land)   Conrad 1918, 1935

Oh, Gala Day, Red-Letter Day   Hart 1928; Rodgers 1928

Oh Galatea!   Romberg 1917

Oh, Gee   Ellington 1947

Oh Gee Jennie   Donaldson 1927; Kahn 1927

Oh Gee! Oh Joy!   Gershwin, George 1927; Gershwin, Ira 1927

Oh! Georgie Look what You've Done to Me   Johnson, James P. 1927

Oh, Give Me the Good Old Days   Rome 1937

Oh God, Give Us Rain   Atteridge 1936; Hanley 1936

Oh Golly Ain't She Cute   Turk 1927

Oh, Gosh   Brown, Lew 1928; DeSylva 1928; Henderson 1928

Oh Happy Bride   Ager 1930; Yellen 1930

Oh, Happy Day   DePaul 1956; Mercer 1956

Oh, Harold   Hart 1921; Rodgers 1921

Oh Have I Got a Way with the Girls   Hanley 1930

Oh, He Looked Like He Might Buy Wine   Cahn 1951

Oh He Loves Me   Cahn 1941

Oh Henry   Burke 1934; Cahn 1946; Kahn 1925; Spina 1934; Styne 1946

Oh, Honey   Porter 1910

Oh, Honorka   Atteridge 1912

Oh How Can I Ever Forget Him   Leslie 1908

Oh How He Can Salute   Hanley 1941

Oh How He Can Sing an Irish Song   Kahn 1914; Norworth 1914

Oh How He Could Plink-A-Plunk   Howard, Joseph E. 1919

Oh How He Plays His Ukulele   Brennan 1929

Oh, How I Adore You   Turk 1933

Oh, How I Could Go for You   Porter 1943

Oh, How I Hate Bulgarians   Dixon 1926; Henderson 1926

Oh How I Hate that Fellow Nathan   Brown, Lew 1922

Oh! How I Hate to Get Up in the Morning   Berlin 1918

Oh, How I Hate to Go Home By Myself   Lawrence 1942

Oh! How I Hate Women   DeSylva 1925

Oh How I Laugh when I Think How I Cried About You   Turk 1919

Oh, How I Love a Wedding   Loesser 1942

Oh, How I Love Fannie   Warren 1925

Oh, How I Love My Boatman   Gilbert 1927

Oh How I Love My Darling   Leslie 1924; Woods 1924

Oh How I Love My Teacher   Williams 1908

Oh How I Love that Man   Coots 1945; Magidson 1945

Oh How I Love to Look at You   Henderson 1927; Johnson, Howard 1927

Oh How I Love You   Sterling 1920

Oh, How I Miss You Tonight   Davis 1925

Oh How I Pine for Carolina   Davis 1922

Oh! How I Wish I Could Sleep Until My Daddy Comes Home   Lewis 1918; Young, Joe 1918

Oh, How I Wish It were More   Woods 1952

Oh How It Hurts   Comden and Green 1956; Styne 1956

Oh, How She Can Dance   Bryan 1919; Friend 1921; Schwartz, Jean 1919

Oh How She Can Love   Davis 1925; Woods 1925

Oh How She Can Poo Poo Po Do Po   Fain 1930; Kahal 1930

Oh, How She Can Sing   Yellen 1919

Oh How She Could Dance the Ballyho   Fisher 1919

Oh! How She Could Play a Ukelele   Akst 1926; Davis 1926

Oh! How She Loves Me Now   Johnson, Howard 1927

Oh, How that Baby Could Baby Me   Gorney 1926

Oh! How That German Could Love   Berlin 1909; Snyder 1909

Oh, How that Man Can Love   Magidson 1928

Oh How That Taxi Got on My Nerves   Atteridge 1913

Oh How that Woman Could Cook   Kahn 1914
Oh, How the Girls Adore Me   Smith, Harry B. 1928
Oh How We Danced   Coots 1954
Oh, How We Enjoy   Dixon 1924; Henderson 1924
Oh How We Love Our Alma Mater   Kalmar 1930; Ruby 1930
Oh How Weary   Kahn 1934
Oh, I Can't Sit Down   Gershwin, George 1935; Gershwin, Ira 1935
Oh I Didn't Know (You'd Get that Way)   Friend 1935; Yellen 1935
Oh, I Heard, Yes I Heard   Dubin 1934; Warren 1934
Oh I Love No One But'er My Oleomargerine   Leslie 1926
Oh, I Wanna Go   Willson 1947
Oh, I Want To Be Good but My Eyes Won't Let Me   Bryan 1916
Oh, I Want to Be the Mayor   Strouse 1985
Oh, I Want to Go Home   Adams 1970; Strouse 1969
Oh! I'd Love to Be a Sailor (When a Sailor's Making Love)   Clare 1931
Oh! I'm So Busy Dreaming   Lewis 1948
Oh, I'm the Man They Talk So Much About   Smith, Harry B. 1906
Oh, Is She Dumb   Clarke 1922; Leslie 1922
Oh Is She Mad at Me   Caesar 1928; Friend 1928
Oh, Isabella   Gilbert 1926
Oh! It Looked Like He Might Buy Wine   Cahn 1955
Oh, It Looks Like Rain   Ager 1931; Harburg 1931
Oh, It Must Be Fun   Porter 1950
Oh Jack, When Are You Coming Back   Sterling 1917
Oh, Joe!   Smith, Harry B. 1923; Snyder 1923; Stept 1924
Oh Joe, with Your Fiddle and Bow You Stole My Heart Away   Donaldson 1916
Oh John   Monaco 1912; Sterling 1912
Oh, Joyful Day   Lerner, Sammy 1941
Oh! Judge He Treats Me Mean   Hanley 1920
Oh, Justine   Romberg 1917
Oh, Katherina   Gilbert 1924
Oh Kay!   Dietz 1926; Gershwin, George 1926; Gershwin, Ira 1926
Oh, King — Oh, Queen!   Ahlert 1930; Turk 1930
Oh, Lady   Akst 1927; Coleman 1972; Davis 1927; Magidson 1932; Stept 1932
Oh, Lady, Be Good!   Gershwin, George 1924; Gershwin, Ira 1924
Oh Lady! Lady!!   Kern 1918
Oh, Leo, It's Love   Clare 1934; Whiting 1934
Oh Listen to the Anvil Chorus   Von Tilzer 1929
Oh, Liza   Edwards 1902
Oh, Look!   Carroll 1918
Oh, Look (Finale, Act I)   Hart 1928; Rodgers 1928
Oh, Lord, Pour Down Your Waters and Baptize Me   Baer 1929; Gilbert 1929
Oh Lovey, Be Mine   Donaldson 1925
Oh Ma Ma   McHugh 1953
Oh Ma, What a Man   Bryan 1929
Oh Mabel   Kahn 1924
Oh! Mabel Behave   Friend 1921
Oh Malinda   Johnson, James P. 1927; Razaf 1927
Oh Mama   Johnston 1925
Oh! Ma-Ma! The Butcher Boy   Brown, Lew 1938
Oh Maria   Johnson, Howard 1932
Oh Marie   Clarke 1915; Goetz 1910; Jerome 1905; Monaco 1915; Schwartz, Jean 1905
Oh, Marjorie   Von Tilzer 1903

Oh, Mary   Porter 1922
Oh! Mary You're Contrary   Herbert 1911
Oh Me Oh My Oh Me-O   Cahn 1952; Duke 1952
Oh Me! Oh My! Oh You!   Adamson 1934; Gershwin, Ira 1921; Lane 1934; Youmans 1921
Oh, Mein Liebchen   Dietz 1961; Schwartz, Arthur 1961
Oh Melinda   Sterling 1901; Von Tilzer 1901
Oh! Min   Conrad 1923
Oh, Miss Flanagan (Heh, Heh, Heh, Heh, Miss Flanagan)   Brown, Lew 1942; Stept 1942
Oh, Miss Jaxson   Ellington 1942
Oh! Mississippi, I Miss You   Ager 1917
Oh Mister Brown   Sterling 1907; Von Tilzer 1907
Oh Mister Dream Man   Atteridge 1912
Oh Mister Man Up in the Moon   Koehler 1936; McHugh 1936
Oh Mister Straus! Nix Komm Heraus   Goetz 1910
Oh, Molly   Brown, Lew 1925
Oh Mother, I'm Wild   Johnson, Howard Date Unknown
Oh Mother, Mother (Please Speak to Willie)   Parish 1980
Oh, Mr. Chamberlain   Kern 1905
Oh, Mr. Dream Man, Please Let Me Dream Some More   Monaco 1911
Oh! Mr. Moon   Cohan 1901
Oh! Mrs. Fortune Teller, Please Find My Lovin' Man   Brown, Lew 1913
Oh, Murphy   Brown, Lew 1926; DeSylva 1926; Henderson 1926
Oh, My!   Herbert 1917
Oh, My Darlin' — Keep Rememberin'   Brown, Lew 1950; Lewis 1950
Oh, My Dear   Hammerstein 1944; Kern 1944
Oh, My Goodness   Gordon 1936; Revel 1936
Oh! My Love   Monaco 1914, 1946
Oh, My Maria (Pia Maria)   Cahn 1956
Oh My Stock Is Going Up with Susie   Lewis 1929; Young, Joe 1929
Oh, My Sweet Hortense   Donaldson 1921; Lewis 1921; Young, Joe 1921
Oh, My, What a Wonderful World   Gorney 1930; Harburg 1930
Oh, My Yes   Adamson 1931; Lane 1931
Oh! Nina   Gershwin, George 1923
Oh, No, John   Lawrence 1946
Oh! Obadiah   Donaldson 1924
Oh, Oh, Columbus   Atteridge 1921; Romberg 1921
Oh Oh, I'm Falling in Love Again   Hoffman 1958
Oh Oh Lady   Snyder 1917; Young, Joe 1917
Oh, Oh Miss Lucy Ella   Sterling 1907; Von Tilzer 1907
Oh, Oh Miss Phoebe   Sterling 1900; Von Tilzer 1900
Oh! Oh! Oh!   Herbert 1908
Oh! Oh! Oh! What a Night   Davis 1926
Oh! Oh! Oklahoma   Adamson 1938; McHugh 1938
Oh, Oh, Rosie   Merrill 1959
Oh, Oh, What Do You Know about Love   David, Mack 1938; Livingston, Jerry 1938
Oh! Omar Khayam   Donaldson 1921; Lewis 1921; Young, Joe 1921
Oh! Papa, Oh Papa (Won't You Be a Pretty Mama to Me?)   Hanley 1917
Oh, Peggy   Akst 1927; Davis 1927
Oh Play that Umpah, Umpah, Umpah   Von Tilzer 1913
Oh, Please   Merrill 1959
Oh, Please Tell Me, Darling   Hoffman 1943; Livingston, Jerry 1943

(I Won't Be There to Hear) Oh Promise Me   Myrow 1933;
    Parish 1933
Oh Promise Me that You'll Come Back to Alabam   Leslie
    1916; Meyer 1916
Oh Promise Me You'll Write to Him Today   Kern 1918
Oh Reuben Tell Your Mandy   Schwartz, Jean 1905
Oh Santa Claus, Send Daddy Back to Me   Mitchell 1917
Oh! Say Can You See   Fields 1948; Romberg 1948
Oh Say, Can You See Me?   Burke 1937; Johnston 1937
Oh Say, Oh Sue!   Caesar 1922
Oh Shush   Gilbert 1912
Oh! Silvery Moon   Smith, Robert B. 1905
Oh Sing Sweet Nightingale   David, Mack 1950; Hoffman
    1950; Livingston, Jerry 1950
Oh Sing the Praise of the Lord   Herbert 1901; Smith, Harry
    B. 1901
Oh Sing-A-Loo Whad' Ya Do with You Que?   Brown, Lew
    1922; Mitchell 1922; Pollack 1922
Oh So Lovely   Donaldson 1936; Hart 1930; Rodgers 1930
Oh, So Nice   Gershwin, George 1928; Gershwin, Ira 1928
Oh So Sweet   Silver 1929
Oh, Stop Jollyin' Me   Brown, Lew 1925; Clare 1925
Oh Susanna   Johnson, Howard 1939
Oh Susanna, Dust Off that Old Pianna   Caesar 1934;
    Lerner, Sammy 1934
Oh Sweet Amelia   Fisher 1921
Oh, Sweetheart Where Are You Tonight   Coots 1929; Davis
    1929
Oh, Tell Me If with Your Heart   Romberg 1924
Oh Tell, Oh Tell Me Honey   Caesar 1931; Motzan 1931
Oh! Tennessee, You've Won the Heart of Me   Brown, Lew
    Date Unknown; Henderson Date Unknown
Oh, That Beautiful Rag   Berlin 1910; Snyder 1910
Oh! That Hindu Skindu Dance   Conrad Date Unknown
Oh! That Mitzi   Robin 1932
Oh that Navajo Rag   Williams 1911
Oh that Strain   Gilbert 1912
Oh that Teasing Man   Meyer 1911
Oh that Yankiana Rag   Goetz 1908
Oh, the Big Red Letter   Willson 1954
Oh the Deuce, What's the Use   Howard, Joseph E. 1905
Oh the Girls, the Lonely Girls   Sterling 1902; Von Tilzer
    1902
Oh, the Heat and the Skeet!   Herbert 1906
Oh! The Pity of It All   Burke 1934; Rainger 1942; Robin
    1942; Spina 1934
Oh, the Things They Put in the Papers
    Now-a-Days   Herbert 1911
Oh! The Woman in Room 13   Donaldson 1919; Lewis 1919;
    Young, Joe 1919
Oh, Them Dudes   Loesser 1948
Oh, There You Are   Livingston, Jerry 1973
Oh, There's a Mouse   Dixon 1929; Woods 1929
Oh, This Is Such a Lovely War   Gershwin, George 1927;
    Gershwin, Ira 1927
Oh, This Love!   Smith, Harry B. 1914
Oh! Those Arabian Nights   Atteridge 1913; Schwartz, Jean
    1913
Oh, Those Boys!   Herbert 1911
Oh, Those Days   Atteridge 1915; Romberg 1915
Oh! Those Eyes   Kalmar 1925; Lane 1996; Ruby 1925
Oh, Those Sunday Drivers   Conrad 1923; Donaldson 1923;
    Johnson, Howard 1923
Oh Those Thirties   Comden and Green 1964; Styne 1964

(My Vampire Girl) Oh, Those Vampire Girls   Romberg 1918;
    Schwartz, Jean 1918
Oh, Thou Art Fair   Smith, Harry B. 1903
Oh, To Be Home Again   Berlin 1945
Oh to Be in Paris (inst.)   Oakland 1958
Oh, Up! It's Up!   Herbert 1913
Oh, Vera   Brown, Nacio Herb 1925
Oh Wendy, Wendy   Bacharach 1958; David, Hal 1958
Oh What a Beautiful Baby   Brown, A. Seymour 1915
Oh What a Beautiful Baby You Turned Out to Be   Coots
    1934; Loesser 1934
Oh, What a Beautiful Mornin'   Hammerstein 1943; Rodgers
    1943
Oh What a Beautiful World   Burke 1957
Oh, What A Day that Will Be   Caesar 1938
Oh, What a Difference You Made   DePaul 1960
Oh, What a Diff'rence You Made   DePaul 1956; Raye 1956
Oh, What a Dream   Smith, Harry B. 1901; Von Tilzer 1901
Oh, What a Horse Was Charlie   Dubin 1938; Mercer 1938;
    Warren 1938
Oh What a Hummer of a Summer   Mitchell 1919
Oh! What a Little Whopper   Friml 1919; Harbach 1919
Oh, What a Lovely Day   DeSylva 1926
Oh What a Lovely Dream   Oakland 1946; Sterling 1901;
    Von Tilzer 1901
Oh, What a Lovely Princess   Porter 1914
Oh What a Lovin' the Girls Will Get (When the Boys Come
    Home)   Johnson, Howard 1945
Oh, What a Man   Kalmar 1928; Mitchell 1937; Pollack 1937;
    Ruby 1928; Schwartz, Arthur 1928
Oh What a Memory We Made   Mercer 1956
Oh, What a Mother I Had   Ager 1922; Yellen 1922
Oh What a Night   Gilbert 1912
Oh What a Night for Love   Whiting 1926
Oh What a Pal Was Mary   Kalmar 1919; Leslie 1919
Oh What a Pal Was Whoozis   Kahn 1927
Oh, What a Pretty Pair of Lovers   Porter 1913
Oh, What a Silly Little Song (C'est Chouette la
    Musique)   Rome 1951
Oh! What a Thrill to Hear It from You   Hoffman 1931
Oh! What a Time for the Girlies when the Boys Come
    Marching Home   Lewis 1918; Ruby 1918; Young, Joe
    1918
Oh, What a Time I Had with Minnie the Mermaid   DeSylva
    1916
Oh What a Wonderful Night   Stept 1961
Oh, What a Wonderful Song   Willson 1956
Oh What Big Eyes You Have, Oh What Sweet Life You
    Have, Oh If I Only Had You   Friend 1926; Kahn 1926
Oh! What I Know About You   Berlin 1909; Wrubel 1945
Oh What I'd Do for a Girl Like You   Snyder 1909
Oh What I'm Going to Do to You   Clarke 1912; Leslie 1912
Oh, What She Hangs Out (She Hangs Out in Our
    Alley)   DeSylva 1922; Gershwin, George 1922; Goetz
    1922
Oh, What Was That Noise?   Gershwin, George 1925;
    Gershwin, Ira 1925
Oh What'll I Do with You   Conrad 1913
Oh, What's the Use?   Smith, Harry B. 1903
Oh When I'm Thinking of You Sonya   Fisher 1925
Oh, Where Are You?   Blake 1967
Oh, Where Can There Be   Willson 1956
Oh! Where Is My Wife To-Night?   Berlin 1909; Snyder 1909
Oh Where, Oh Where   Willson 1956
Oh, Why   Freed, Arthur 1930; Woods 1930

Oh Why Did I   Cahn 1951

Oh Yeah! Oh Yeah! Oh Yeah!   Cahn 1978

Oh Yeedle Ay (That Yodelin' Tune)   Fisher 1921

Oh, You Beautiful Baby   Akst 1921; Lewis 1921; Young, Joe 1921

Oh, You Beautiful Blonde   Dubin 1915

Oh, You Beautiful Coon   Cohan 1911

Oh You Beautiful Doll   Brown, A. Seymour 1911; Smith, Harry B. 1911; Smith, Robert B. 1911

Oh, You Beautiful Person   Kern 1919

Oh You Beautiful Spring   Kern 1912

Oh You Beauty   Leslie 1912

Oh You Can't Fool an Old Hoss Fly   Von Tilzer 1924

Oh! You Chicago Cubs   Dixon 1929; Woods 1929

Oh You Chicken   Fisher 1910; Goetz 1910

Oh! You Coon   Cohan 1908

Oh You Could Set Up for a Gentleman   Styne 1985

Oh! You Crazy Moon   Burke 1939; Van Heusen 1939

Oh You Cute Little Chicken   Brown, A. Seymour 1914

Oh You Delicious Little Devil   Bryan 1919; DeSylva 1919

Oh, You Dream   Jerome 1910; Schwartz, Jean 1910

Oh, You John   Atteridge 1914; Carroll 1914; Romberg 1914

Oh, You Kid   Mercer 1945; Warren 1945

Oh! You La La   Brown, Lew Date Unknown; Henderson Date Unknown

Oh You Little Bo-Peep Won't You Let Me Be One of Your Sheep   Leslie 1912

Oh You Little Bunch o' Sweetness   Yellen 1920

Oh You Little Indian River   Johnson, Howard 1927

Oh You Little Rascal   Leslie 1912; Meyer 1912

Oh, You Lovely Ladies   Romberg 1916

Oh, You Loving Gal   Meyer 1909

Oh, You Major Scales   Friml 1919; Harbach 1919

Oh You May   Williams 1907

Oh, You Merry Widow   Clare 1948; Pollack 1948

Oh, You Million Dollar Doll   Clarke 1913; Leslie 1913

Oh, You Mississippi   Lane 1939; Loesser 1939

Oh, You Mister Moon   Dubin 1911

Oh You South   Caesar 1927

Oh You Spearmint Kiddo with the Wrigley Eyes   Jerome 1910; Schwartz, Jean 1910

Oh, You Sweet Old Whatcha May Call It   Ahlert 1928; Turk 1928

Oh, You Sweet, Sweet Boy   Johnson, J. Rosamond 1913

Oh! You Sweet Thing   Razaf 1932; Waller 1932

Oh, You Sweetie   Atteridge 1917; Romberg 1917

Oh You Wedding Belle   Howard, Joseph E. 1913

Oh, You Women   Stept 1919

Oh, You Wonderful Girl   Cohan 1911

O'Hara   Rome 1969

Ohhh! Ahhh!   Heyman 1931

Ohio   Adamson 1944; Comden and Green 1953; McHugh 1944; Mercer 1953

Oh-Oh-Lady   Lewis 1917

O'Hooley   Smith, Harry B. 1903

Ohrbach's, Bloomingdale's, Best and Saks   Lerner, Alan Jay 1969

Oisgetzaichnet (Out of This World)   Rome 1965

O.K. California   Gilbert 1932; Silver 1932

(You're) O.K. for TV   Mercer 1951

O.K. Means Old Kentucky   Bryan 1930

Oka Saka Circus   Porter 1946

Okay for Sound   Fields 1939; Schwartz, Arthur 1939

Okay G-A!   Ager 1933; Schwartz, Jean 1933; Young, Joe 1933

Okay, Mister Major   Dietz 1956; Schwartz, Arthur 1956

Okay Toots   Donaldson 1934; Kahn 1934

Oklahoma   Hammerstein 1943; Rodgers 1943

Oklahoma Joe   Bryan 1930

Okolehao   Rainger 1937; Robin 1937

Oky Doky Tokyo   Leslie 1964

Ol' Benjamin Harrison   Sherman 1968

Ol' Circuit Rider, The   Robison 1960

Ol' Debbil Microphone   Robison 1933

Ol' King Cotton   Fain 1932; Kahal 1932

Ol' Kris Kringle   Adamson 1959; McHugh 1950

Ol MacDonald   Bergman 1960

Ol Man Rip   Webster 1937

Ol' Man River   Hammerstein 1927; Kern 1927

Ol' Man Spider Fingers   DePaul 1949; Raye 1949

Ol' Pappy   Livingston, Jerry 1933

Ol' Shank's Mare   DePaul 1952; Raye 1952

Olaf, You Ought-A-Hear Olaf Laff   Baer 1922; Gilbert 1922

Olcott's Fly Song   Olcott 1897

Olcott's Home Song   Olcott 1896

Olcott's Irish Serenade   Olcott 1925

Olcott's Love Song   Olcott 1906

Olcott's Lullaby   Olcott 1901

Old Actor's Dream, The   Oakland 1953; Raye 1953

Old and the New Prelude, The   Gordon 1945; Warren 1945

Old Are Getting Younger Every Day, The   Smith, Robert B. 1915

Old Army Game, The   Fain Date Unknown; Rose Date Unknown

Old Aunt Kate   Mercer 1933

Old Bachelor Bill   Robison 1958

Old Ballet Days, The   Smith, Harry B. 1911; Smith, Robert B. 1911

Old Bar 20 Quartet, The   Brown, Nacio Herb 1951; Gilbert 1951

Old Bill Baker (Undertaker)   Kern 1915

Old Biological Urge, the   Dubin Date Unknown; Warren Date Unknown

Old Black Joe   Gilbert 1930; Johnson, Howard 1939; Turk 1922

Old Blue Paradise   Romberg 1915

Old Boy Neutral   Kern 1915

Old Brant Lake   Hart 1919

Old Brass Rail, The   Dubin 1924; Silver 1924

Old Broadway   Howard, Joseph E. 1906

Old Brownstone in Brooklyn   Robison 1963

Old Buck and Wing, The   Howard, Joseph E. 1908

Old Buddy o' Mine   Donaldson 1927; Kahn 1927

Old Calliope, The   David, Mack 1951; Livingston, Jerry 1951

Old Cathay (China) (inst.)   Kern 1956

Old City Boy at Heart, An   Rodgers 1979

Old Clarinet, The   Kern 1913; Smith, Harry B. 1913

Old Country Doctor, The   Robison 1960; Schwartz, Jean 1936; Young, Joe 1936

Old Curiosity Shop   Coslow 1938; Silver 1938

Old Dan Tucker   Coslow 1936

Old Demon Rum   Rainger 1943; Robin 1943

Old Devil Moon   Harburg 1947; Lane 1947

Old Devil Sea   Duke 1930; Harburg 1930

Old Doc Flirtingrinder   Oakland 1961

Old Enough to Love   Fields 1954; Hart 1922; Rodgers 1922, 1925; Schwartz, Arthur 1954

Old Eva   Clarke 1924; Leslie 1924; Warren 1924

Old Familiar Faces   Edwards 1924; Rose 1924

Old Family Bible, The   Spina 1976; Webster 1951

Old Family Reunion   Robison 1944
Old Fashined Christmas   Merrill 1949
Old Fashioned   Arlen 1930; Koehler 1930
Old Fashioned Cake Walk   Hanley 1922
Old Fashioned Christmas, An   Freed, Ralph 1958
Old Fashioned Fourth, An   Willson 1966
(There's Something About An) Old Fashioned Girl   Brown,
    Lew 1930; DeSylva 1930; Henderson 1930
Old Fashioned Girl, An   Brown, Lew 1928; Carroll 1918;
    DeSylva 1928; Henderson 1928
Old Fashioned Gown   Coots 1922
Old Fashioned Home in New Hampshire, An   Lewis 1931
Old Fashioned (inst.)   Stept 1957
Old Fashioned Locket of Gold   Brennan 1928
Old Fashioned Love   Lawrence 1959; Loesser 1939
Old Fashioned Mother   Brown, Lew 1928; DeSylva 1928;
    Henderson 1928; Olcott 1897
Old Fashioned Mothers   Fain 1955
Old Fashioned Political Rally (Invitation)   Wrubel 1959
Old Fashioned Rag   Bryan 1919; Schwartz, Jean 1919
Old Fashioned Rose   Cobb 1921; Edwards 1921
Old Fashioned Rose, An   Herbert 1903; Kahn 1925
Old Fashioned Song, An   Kahn 1938; Romberg 1938
Old Fashioned Song for an Old Fashioned Girl, An   David,
    Mack 1952; Livingston, Jerry 1952
Old Fashioned Susie's Blues   Razaf 1924; Waller 1924
Old Fashioned Sweetheart   Atteridge 1921; Pollack 1921;
    Schwartz, Jean 1921
Old Fashioned Tin Types   Coslow 1924; Romberg 1924
Old Fashioned Tune   Duke 1946
Old Fashioned Tune Always Is New, An   Berlin 1939
Old Fashioned Waltz   Willson 1953
Old Fashioned Waltz and the Old Fashioned Girl,
    The   Stept 1934; Washington 1934
Old Fashioned Wedding   Harburg 1932
Old Fashioned Wedding, An   Berlin 1966
Old Fashioned Wife, An   Kern 1917
Old Fashioned Xmas, An   Webster 1972
Old Fireplace   Coots 1935; Davis 1935
Old Flag Never Touched the Ground, The   Johnson, J.
    Rosamond 1907
Old Flame Never Dies, An   Schwartz, Arthur 1937
Old Folks   Robison 1938
Old Folks at Home, The   Egan 1923; Gordon 1940; Kahn
    1923; Whiting 1923
Old Folks Shuffle   Waller 1926
Old Forgotten Lullaby, An   Meyer 1936
Old Forgotten Waltz, An   Myrow 1932
Old Friend   Duke 1963; Lewis 1926; Robison 1964; Young,
    Joe 1926
Old Friend Is Sweet in September, An   Egan 1932; Whiting
    1932
Old Friends   Bergman 1968; Edwards 1907; Sondheim 1981
Old Friends (inst.)   Oakland 1958
Old Friends, Old Wines, Old Love Songs   Webster 1933
Old Fun City (inst.), The   Bacharach 1969
Old Gal's Got that New Look, The   Fain 1948; Yellen 1948
Old Glory   Arlen 1942; Mercer 1942; Smith, Harry B. 1898
Old Grand Dad (inst.)   Waller 1940
Old Gray Mare, The   Johnson, Howard 1939
Old Guitar and a Old Refrain, An   Kahn 1927
Old Guitaron   Mercer 1964
Old Gypsy Man   Evans 1971; Livingston, Jay 1971
Old Heads Upon Young Shoulders   Bryan 1944
Old Hoagy   Carmichael 1953

Old Holler Family, The   Robison 1954
Old Home Guard, The   Sherman 1971
Old Home Town   Goetz 1916
Old Home Week in Alabama   Jerome 1905; Schwartz, Jean
    1905
Old Home Week in My Home Town   Gilbert 1913
Old Homestead   Loesser 1936
Old Honolulu (inst.)   Schwartz, Arthur 1941
Old Hundred   Johnson, Howard 1939
Old Immigration and Naturalization Rag, The   Adams 1962;
    Strouse 1962
Old Ireland Shall Be Free!   Herbert 1915
Old Iron Horse, The   Webster 1953
Old Ironsides (We're Mighty Proud of You)   Mills 1926
Old Jello Theme   Willson 1949
Old Jitterbug   Dubin 1940; McHugh 1940
Old Joe Blues   Gilbert 1919
Old John Barleycorn   Romberg 1927
Old Kentucky Blues   Kahn 1923
Old King Cole   Atteridge 1920; Mercer 1937; Whiting 1937
Old King Tut (In King Tutenkhamen's Day)   Jerome 1923;
    Von Tilzer 1923
Old Kitchen Kettle   Woods 1932
Old Kitchen Sink, The   Coleman 1972; Fields 1972
Old Ladies Home (One Friend), The   Caesar 1932
Old Lamb and New Lamb, An   Stept 1956
Old Left Hander, The   Robison 1955
Old Limerick Town   Olcott 1902
Old Love   Davis 1952; Van Heusen 1953
Old Love for New   Caesar 1945
Old Love Letters   Davis 1932; Silver 1932
Old Maid Jim   Silver 1924; Turk 1924
Old Maids Are Willing to Please   Herbert 1899
Old Maid's Ball, The   Berlin 1913
Old Man, The   Berlin 1954
Old Man, An   Rodgers 1970
Old Man Blues   Ellington 1930; Mills 1930; Oakland 1931
Old Man Hard Times Make Way for Kid Prosperity   Coslow
    1930
Old Man Harlem   Carmichael 1933
Old Man Jingle   Stept 1934
Old Man Moon   Carmichael 1937
Old Man Mose Ain't Dead   Cahn 1939
Old Man of the Mountain, The   Young, Victor 1932
Old Man Rhythm   Mercer 1935
Old Man Rip   Alter 1937
Old Man Sunshine, Little Boy Blue Bird   Dixon 1928; Rose
    1928; Warren 1928
Old Man Time   Friend 1961
Old Man Weaver of Dreams   Washington 1929
Old Man Winter   Bergman 1956
Old Man with the Whiskers, The   Coots 1935; Parish 1935
Old Man's Darling, Young Man's Slave   Berlin 1940
Old Man's Whiskers, The   Friend 1922
Old Melodies   Johnson, Howard 1921
Old Milano   Coleman 1965
Old Mill Wheel   Ager 1939; Davis 1939; Yellen 1939
Old Mother Earth   Robison 1944
Old Mother Nature   Brown, Lew 1933; Henderson 1933
Old Mother Oak   Young, Victor 1934
Old Music Master   Carmichael 1943; Mercer 1943
Old Music Masters   Atteridge 1920
Old Names of Old Flames   Johnson, Howard 1925
Old Neighbor   Robison 1959
Old Neighborhood   Coots 1933

Old New England Lady   Johnson, Howard 1927
Old New England March   Fisher 1936
Old New Hampshire Valley   Robison 1944
Old New York   Dubin 1935; Warren 1935
(Al-Le-Lu) Old Noah's Ark   Blake 1925; Sissle 1925
Old Noblesse, The   Herbert 1911; Smith, Harry B. 1911
Old Oak Tree, The   Loesser 1934
Old Oaken Bucket, The   Drake 1960; Johnson, Howard 1939
Old Oaken Bucket with Love   Bryan 1919; Schwartz, Jean 1919
Old Old Castle in Scotland, An   Magidson 1939; Oakland 1939
Old, Old Man, with an Old, Old Pipe and an Old, Old Lady Beside Him, An   Gordon 1933; Revel 1933
Old Old Tunes, The   Adams 1959; Strouse 1959
Old Overcoat   Carroll 1950
Old Pal   Kahn 1924
Old Pal, Why Did You Leave Me?   Brown, Nacio Herb 1930; Freed, Arthur 1930
Old Pal, Why Didn't You Answer Me   Lewis 1920; Young, Joe 1920
Old Pals Are the Best Pals After All   Rose 1928
Old Pardner   Brown, Lew 1941; Stept 1941
Old Park Bench, The   Dietz 1940; McHugh 1940
Old People   Loesser 1956
Old Pete Is in the City   Weill 1938
Old Piano Copy, An   Robison 1951
Old Pied Piper, The   Harburg 1961
Old Pigeon-Toed Joad   Robison 1940
Old Pizza Maker, The   Adams 1958; Strouse 1958
Old Prospector, The   Carmichael 1957
Old Rainmaker, The   Drake 1946
Old Rat Mort, The   Porter 1911
Old Red Rooster, The   Johnson, Howard 1934
Old Reporters Never Die   DePaul 1956; Mercer 1956
Old Rob Roy   Mercer 1944
Old Sad Eyes   Fain 1943; Kahal 1943
Old School Bell, The   Loesser 1938
Old Shanghai   Brown, Lew 1925; Friend 1925
Old Skipper   Carmichael 1934; Mercer 1934
Old Soldiers Never Die   Conrad 1929, 1932, 1938; Mitchell 1929; Spina 1951
Old Sombrero (And an Old Spanish Shawl), An   Brown, Lew 1947; Henderson 1947
Old Songs, The   Davis 1963; Herbert 1924
Old Story Teller, The   Hoffman 1949
Old Straw Hat, An   Gordon 1938; Revel 1938
Old Stuff   Young, Victor 1923
Old Time Get-Together, An   Stept 1945
Old Timer   Harburg 1940; Lane 1940; Revel 1943; Rose 1929; Webster 1943
Old Timer, An   Howard, Joseph E. 1905
Old Timer's Rosary, An   Dixon 1925; Henderson 1925
Old Timer's Tune   Raye 1957
Old Tin Can, The   Baer 1939; Lewis 1939
Old Town (Old New York), The   Kern 1920
Old Toymaker, The   David, Mack 1947; Hoffman 1947; Livingston, Jerry 1947
Old Tunes   Adams 1984
Old Village Barn, The   Silver 1948
Old Village Doctor, The   Schwartz, Jean 1934; Young, Joe 1934
Old Village Square, The   Robison 1935
Old Virginia Moon   Kahn 1924
Old Virginia Reel, The   Smith, Harry B. 1923

Old Woman Who Lived in a Shoe, The   Bryan 1903
Old World Charm   Ellington 1966
Old World Folk Song (inst.)   Kern 1956
Old Yazoo (inst.)   Waller 1932
Old Yeller Dog of Mine   Clarke 1923; Leslie 1923
Older and Wiser   Adams 1960, 1978; Strouse 1960, 1978
Older They Are the Harder They Fall, The   Smith, Harry B. 1918
Older They Are, the Younger They Want 'Em   Dubin 1920
Older They Get the Younger They Want 'em, The   Silver 1920; Yellen 1947
Oldest Established, The   Loesser 1950
Oldest Profession, The   Coleman 1996
Old-Fashioned Christmas, An   Cahn 1959; Van Heusen 1959
Old-Fashioned Garden   Porter 1919
Old-Fashioned Girl, An   Porter 1928
Old-Fashioned Girls   Atteridge 1917; Romberg 1917
Old-Fashioned Glimmer in Your Eye, An   Lawrence 1951
Old-Fashioned Groom and an Up-To-Date Bride, An   Smith, Robert B. 1915
Old-Fashioned Love   Johnson, James P. 1922
(Give Me an) Old-Fashioned Waltz   Ellington 1941; Porter 1922
Oldies   Sigman 1951
Old-Time Ball, The   Goetz 1912
Ole   Robin 1952
Ole Aunt Mariar   Hanley 1932
Ole Buttermilk Sky   Brooks 1946; Carmichael 1946
Ole Friend   Freed, Ralph 1965
Ole Jim Crow   Razaf 1928
Ole Mammy Ain't Gonna Sing No More   Magidson 1933; Monaco 1933
Ole Man River Is Lonely Now   Blake 1955
Ole South   Bryan 1937
Ole Spring Fever, The   Warren 1952
Ole Virginny's Lullaby   Mitchell 1927; Pollack 1927
O-lee-ay-ee-o   Drake 1954
Ole-O the Gigilo   Hanley 1933
Oley's Melody   Fain 1949; Yellen 1949
Olga   Johnson, Howard 1935
Olga (Come Back to the Volga)   Porter 1922
Olga from the Volga   Atteridge 1911
Oli, Oli, Oli   Hammerstein 1930; Romberg 1930
Oliphant the Elephant   Caesar 1965
Olivia from Olvera Street   Evans 1948; Livingston, Jay 1948
Olympian Dance, The   Herbert 1908; Smith, Harry B. 1908
Olympian Glide, The   Atteridge 1915; Carroll 1915; Romberg 1915
Olympian Gods (Tale of the Olympian Gods) (inst.)   Young, Victor 1955
Olympic Water Daughters of White Rock   Jerome 1920; Von Tilzer 1920
Om Mani Padme Hum   Warren 1956
Omaha (Me-Oh-Ma)   Meyer 1922
Omaha-Ha and Idaho-Ho   Bryan 1936
Omar and the Princess   Blane 1948; Warren 1948
Omar Khayam, Come On   Howard, Joseph E. 1937
Omar Khayyam   Atteridge 1914, 1919; Herbert 1907; Romberg 1914; Smith, Harry B. 1907
Omar Khayyam of Love   Carroll 1919
Omar Khyam, Where Did You Hide that Jug of Wine   Bryan 1924
Omnibus   Porter 1928
On a Beautiful Distant Island   Von Tilzer 1903

On a Beautiful Evening   Atteridge 1922; Schwartz, Jean 1922

On a Beautiful Night with a Beautiful Girl   Cobb 1912; Edwards 1912

On a Bicycle Built for Joy   Bacharach 1969

On a Bicycle Built for Two (inst.)   Bacharach 1969

On a Blue and Moonless Night   Hoffman 1930

On a Blue Lagoon (With You)   Friml 1924

On a Certain Saturday Night   Stept 1937; Washington 1937

On a Certain Sunday   Gordon 1931; Revel 1931

On a Chill-Chill-Chilly Night   Coots 1932

On a Clear Day You Can See Forever   Lane 1965; Lerner, Alan Jay 1965

On a Cold Winter Night   Fisher 1936

On a Day Like This   Merrill 1950

On a Desert Island with Thee   Hart 1927; Rodgers 1927

On a Desert Island with You   Kern 1924

On a Far Along Isle   Brennan 1921

On a Gettysburg Farm   Robison 1956

On a Golden Wedding Honeymoon   Edwards 1914

On a Holiday   Cohan 1923

On a Honolulu Honeymoon   Johnson, Howard 1934

On a Hundred Different Ships   Cohan 1909

On a Junetime Honeymoon   Goetz 1911

On a Lightless Night with You   Cobb 1918; Edwards 1918

On a Little Journey in Springtime with You   Robin 1931

On a Little Side Street   Akst 1934; Howard, Joseph E. 1921

On a Little Street in Napoli   Coots 1963

On a Little Street in Venice   Davis 1962

(Rolling Down Bowling Green) On a Little Two Seat Tandem   Myrow 1947

On a Modern Wedding Day   Atteridge 1914; Romberg 1914

On a Moonlight Night   Gilbert 1921

On a Night Like This   Kahn 1925; Koehler 1939

On a Pearly Pebble Beach in Catalina   Ahlert 1936; Young, Joe 1936

On a Pony for Two   Buck 1927; Hanley 1927

On a Pretty Picture Postal Card   Burke 1934; Spina 1934

On a Quiet Evening at Home   Baer 1926; Turk 1926

On a Roof in Manhattan   Berlin 1932

On a Saturday Night   Howard, Joseph E. 1902; Sterling 1902

On a Side Street in Gotham (inst.)   Alter 1940

On a Slow Boat to China   Fain 1946; Freed, Ralph 1946; Loesser 1947

On a Snowy, Blowy Day   Baer 1965

On a South Sea Isle   Von Tilzer 1938

On a Summer Night   Edwards 1916

On a Sunday Afternoon   Brown, Nacio Herb 1935; Freed, Arthur 1935; Sterling 1902; Von Tilzer 1902

On a Sunday by the Sea   Cahn 1947; Styne 1947

On a Sunday Morning   Harbach 1911

On a Sunny Afternoon   Herbert 1914; Smith, Robert B. 1914

On a Sunny Summer Day   Turk 1919

On a Three Party Line   David, Hal 1950

On a Tropic Night (Noche de Vera Cruz)   Washington 1938

On a Typical Tropical Night   Burke 1936; Johnston 1936

On a Wonderful Day Like Today   Herbert 1946

On Account Of   Coslow 1935

On Accounta I Love You   Stept 1934

On an Automobile Honeymoon   Jerome 1905; Schwartz, Jean 1905

On an Empty Stage   Oakland 1954

On an Irish Honeymoon   Jerome 1911; Schwartz, Jean 1911

On an Island with You   Brown, Nacio Herb 1949; DeSylva 1920; Heyman 1947

On an Old Fashioned Buggy Ride   Williams 1907

On and On   Spina 1954

On and On and On   Gershwin, George 1933; Gershwin, Ira 1933

On Any Street   Brown, Lew 1933; Henderson 1933

On Behalf of the Visiting Fireman   Donaldson 1940; Mercer 1940

On Blue Hawaiian Waters   Livingston, Jerry 1934

On Broadway and Off Broadway   Drake 1957

On Bubbling-Well Road, in Old Shanghai   Hanley 1939

On Candle Light Lane   Lewis 1928; Young, Joe 1928

(Plough, Plough Tra Tra La) On Chante Dans Mon Quartier   Heyman 1946

On Cleveland On   Willson 1970

On Cupid's Green   Atteridge 1918; Romberg 1918

On Double Fifth Avenue   Baer 1927; Lewis 1927; Young, Joe 1927

On Earth As It Is   Robison 1956

On Green Dolphin Street   Washington 1947

On Guard   Rome 1949

On Hawaiian Shores   Friml 1923

On Her Majesty's Secret Service   David, Hal 1969

On His First Day Home on Leave   Norworth 1916

On Honolulu Bay   Caesar 1955

On King's Solomon's Farm   Von Tilzer 1920

On Lake Champlain   Bryan 1916

On Lake Louise   Adamson 1941

On Lalawana's Shore   Johnson, J. Rosamond 1904

On Lookout Mountain   Lewis 1940

On Lover's Bay   Brown, Nacio Herb 1919

On Miami Shore   Loesser 1941; Young, Victor 1941

On My Calendar of Love   Gilbert 1933; Hanley 1933

On My Chicken Farm   Von Tilzer 1913

On My Mind the Whole Night Long   Gershwin, George 1920

On My Nuptial Day   Herbert 1900; Smith, Harry B. 1900

On My Own   Bacharach 1986; Comden and Green 1956; Duke 1963; Styne 1956

On My Private Telephone   Bryan 1919; Schwartz, Jean 1919

On My Ukelele Tra La La La La   Parish 1924

On My Way   Evans 1964; Livingston, Jay 1964; Mercer 1974

On My Word of Honor   Hoffman 1931

On or About the First of June   Kalmar 1937; Ruby 1937

On Oublie Tout   Gilbert 1937

On Our Houseboat in the Hudson (Happy Houseboat)   Comden and Green 1964; Styne 1964

On Our Little Merry-Go-Round   Atteridge 1918; Romberg 1918

On Parade   Herbert 1913; Smith, Robert B. 1913

On Parchment This with Grey Goose Quill   Smith, Harry B. 1906

On Patrol in No Man's Land   Blake 1919; Sissle 1919, 1921

On Rainy Afternoons   Bergman 1980

On Rainy Days   Razaf 1938; Waller 1938

On Repentin' Day   Razaf 1940

On Revival Day   Razaf 1930

On Robinson Crusoe Isle   Razaf Date Unknown

On Saturday Night   Clare 1923; Conrad 1923

On Second Thought   Coleman 1961; Leigh 1961

On Stage Interlude   Evans 1952; Livingston, Jay 1952

On Such a Beautiful Night   Caesar 1925

On Such a Night   Conrad 1924

On Such a Night As This   Martin 1962

On Sunday, When We Gathered 'Round the Organ   Razaf 1933; Waller 1933

On Sweetheart Bay   Johnson, Howard 1933

On Ten Square Miles by the Potomac River   Lerner, Alan Jay 1976

On that Carpet of Cotton   Livingston, Jerry 1934

On that Day of Days   Cahn 1970; Styne 1970

On that Old Beaten Track   Stept 1925

On that Old Production Line   Rome 1943

On the Alamo   Kahn 1922

On the Atchison Topeka and the Santa Fe   Blane 1945; Mercer 1945; Warren 1945

On the Avenue   Berlin 1937; Rome 1947

On the Bahamas   Hart Date Unknown; Rodgers Date Unknown

On the Banks of Bango Bay   Dixon 1926; Henderson 1926

On the Banks of the Mildew River   Eliscu 1941; Gorney 1941

On the Banks of the Old Raritan   Cahn 1947; Styne 1947

On the Banks of the Rhine with a Stein   Sterling 1905

On the Beach at Malibu   Clare 1936

On the Beach at Wai-ki-ki Blues   Meyer 1927

On the Beach (inst.)   Bacharach 1980

On the Beaches   Conrad 1906

On the Beam   Kern 1942; Mercer 1942

On the Beat   Arlen 1930; Koehler 1930

On the Boardwalk (In Atlantic City)   Gordon 1946; Myrow 1946

On the Border Line   Kalmar 1929; Ruby 1929

On the Bosom of the Sleepy Nile   Goetz 1920

On the Bosphorus   Hammerstein 1933

On the Boulevard   Atteridge 1923; Caesar 1923; Cahn 1980; Howard, Joseph E. 1897; Romberg 1923; Smith, Harry B. 1908; Von Tilzer 1910

On the Boulevard (inst.)   Schwartz, Jean 1930

On the Bridge of Avignon   Mercer 1958

On the Brim of Her Old-Fashioned Bonnet   Gershwin, George 1921; Goetz 1921

On the Bumpy Road to Love   Hoffman 1938

On the Campus   Brown, Lew 1927; DeSylva 1927; Henderson 1927

On the Congo   Atteridge 1911

On the Corner of Dream Street and Main   Dixon 1944; Henderson 1944

On the Corner of Sunshine and Main   Styne 1943

On the Corner of the Rue Cambon   Lerner, Alan Jay 1969

On the Day that Comes Before Monday   Jerome 1920; Von Tilzer 1920

On the Downtown Side of an Uptown Street   Livingston, Jerry 1967

On the Erie Canal   Arlen 1953; Fields 1953

On the Farm   Merrill 1957; Smith, Harry B. 1911

On the Fence Together   Brown, Nacio Herb 1932; Egan 1932

On the First Dark Night Next Week   Leslie 1911

On the First Warm Day   Howard, Bart 1951

On the Friendly Side   Mercer 1942

On the Front Porch   Sherman 1963

On the Gay White Way   Rainger 1942; Robin 1942

On the 'Gin 'Gin 'Ginny Shore   Donaldson 1921; Leslie 1921

On the Golden Trail   Hammerstein 1928; Youmans 1928

On the Good Ship B.V.D.   Donaldson 1916

On the Good Ship Honeymoon   Dubin 1914

On the Good Ship Lollipop   Clare 1934; Whiting 1934

On the Good Ship Whippoorwill   Donaldson 1915

On the Grand Old Band   Edwards 1907

On the Grand Old Sands   Cobb 1907; Edwards 1907

On the Green (inst.)   Bloom 1934

On the Hoko Moko Isle   Von Tilzer 1916

On the Island of Pines (On the Isle of Pines)   Carroll 1914

On the Isle of May   David, Mack 1940

On the Isle of Pines   Bryan 1914

(Love for Two) On the Isle of Taboo   Mills 1939

On the Isle of Wicki Wacki Woo   Donaldson 1923; Kahn 1923

On the Isle of Yap   Jerome 1921; Schwartz, Jean 1921

On the Levee   Johnson, James P. 1928

On the Levee Before the War   Atteridge Date Unknown

On the Level It's You   Schwartz, Jean 1948

On the Level with You   Johnson, James P. 1930; Razaf 1930

On the Level You're a Little Devil, but I'll Soon Make an Angel of You   Schwartz, Jean 1918; Young, Joe 1918

On the Level, You're a Little Devil, But I'll Soon Make an Angel Out of You   Lewis 1918

On the Lonely Lagoon   Edwards 1913

On the Lonely Mission Trail   Baer 1955

On the Mediterranean Sea   Silver 1937

On the Mercury   Drake 1957

On the Mississippi   Carroll 1912

On the Night We Did the Boom Boom By the Sea   Monaco 1928; Rose 1928

On the Nodaway Road   Mercer 1935

On the Old Assembly Line   Henderson 1943

On the Old East Side   Yellen 1978

On the Old Fall River Line   Jerome 1913; Sterling 1913; Von Tilzer 1913

On the Old See Saw   Edwards 1908

On the Other End of a Kiss   Evans 1946; Livingston, Jay 1946

On the Other Hand   Dietz 1963; Schwartz, Arthur 1963

On the Other Side of the Jordan   David, Mack 1935

On the Other Side of the Moon   Monaco 1931; Washington 1931

On the Other Side of the Wall   Herbert 1903; Smith, Harry B. 1903

On the Outgoing Tide   Brown, Lew 1950

On the Outside Looking In   Merrill 1956

On the Phone   Herbert 1906

On the Pillow Next to Mine   Howard, Joseph E. 1952

On the Promenade (inst.)   Kern 1956

On the Proper Side of Broadway on a Saturday P.M.   Cobb 1902; Edwards 1902

On the Radio   Conrad 1906

On the Rancho with My Pancho   Akst 1939; Clare 1939

On the River   Schwartz, Jean 1929; Sondheim Date Unknown

On the Riviera   DeSylva 1922; Gilbert 1926; Herbert 1922; Robin 1926

On the Road Back Home   Meyer 1924; Rose 1924

On the Road to Bal-Na-Pogue   Brennan 1924

On the Road to Calais   Bryan 1918; Schwartz, Jean 1918

On the Road to Home Sweet Home   Kahn 1917

On the Road to Monterey   Johnson, J. Rosamond 1909

On the Road to Old Killarney   Leslie 1915

On the Road to Paradise   Brennan 1916

On the Road to Rainbow Bay   Dixon 1929; Woods 1929

On the Road to Romance   Loesser Date Unknown

On the Roadway to the Moon   Johnson, J. Rosamond 1944, 1946

On the Rue de la Paix   Heyman 1953; Young, Victor 1953

On the Rue de la Paix in Paree   Stept 1950

On the Sands of Wa-ki-ki   Kern 1915

On the Sandwich Isles   Von Tilzer 1917
On the Screen   Coots 1923
On the Second Floor   Brooks 1959
On the Sentimental Side   Burke 1938; Monaco 1938
On the Seventh Day He Rested   Fain 1951; Webster 1951
On the Shore at Le Lei Wi   Kern 1915
On the Shores of Napoli   Brennan 1924
On the Shores of Rockaway   Johnson, Howard 1922
On the Showboat   Styne 1960
On the Sleepy Shores   Sigman 1972
On the South Sea Isle   Von Tilzer 1916
On the S.S. Bernard Cohn   Lane 1965; Lerner, Alan Jay 1965
On the Stage   Goetz 1912; Herbert 1903; Smith, Harry B. 1903
On the Steps of Grant's Tomb   Berlin 1937
On the Steps of the Great White Capitol   Clarke 1914; Leslie 1914
On the Steps of the Palace   Sondheim 1987
On the Street   Adams 1993
On the Street Where You Live   Lerner, Alan Jay 1956; Loewe 1956
On the Strict QT   Sterling 1905; Von Tilzer 1905
On the Sunny Side of the Street   Fields 1930; Kahn 1919; McHugh 1930
On the Sunset Trail   Mitchell 1936; Stept 1936
On the Swing Shift   Arlen 1942; Mercer 1942
On the Ten o' Ten for Ten-Ten-Tennessee   Coots 1953
On the Ten-Ten from Ten-Ten-Tennessee   Robin 1952; Warren 1952
On the 20th Century   Coleman 1978; Comden and Green 1978
On the Thomas J. Muldoon   Dietz 1963; Schwartz, Arthur 1963
On the Town   Comden and Green 1949
On the Trail   Adamson 1946; Kahn 1935
On the Trail of the Honeymoon   Dubin 1914
On the Trail to Santa Fe   Kahn 1915
On the Train of a Wedding Gown   Berlin 1916
On the Umpah Isle   Sterling 1922; Von Tilzer 1922
On the Up and Up   Eliscu 1929
On the Way   Robison 1959
On the Winding Santa Fe   Baer 1930; Gilbert 1930
On the Wings of a Breeze   Washington 1938
On the Wings of a Waltz   Rainger 1935; Robin 1935
On the Wings of Romance   Cahn 1964; Gershwin, Ira 1923; Van Heusen 1964
On the Wrong Side of the Fence   Wrubel 1934
On the Z-R-3   Donaldson 1924; Lewis 1924; Young, Joe 1924
On This Merry Christmas Eve   Strouse 1990
On This Show   Evans 1958; Livingston, Jay 1958
On Through the Night   Gordon 1932; Revel 1932
On Time   Rome 1943
On to Africa   Caesar 1933; Romberg 1933
On to Conquer   Atteridge 1915
On to Frisco   Leslie 1909
On to Hollywood   Hanley 1926
On to Victory   Smith, Harry B. 1906, 1918, 1935
On Top   Brennan 1929
On Top of a Tennessee Hill   Sissle 1928
On Top of Old Dumkopf   Drake 1953
On Top of the World   Lerner, Alan Jay 1983; Strouse 1983
On Top of the World Alone   Robin 1929; Whiting 1929
On Treasure Island   Leslie 1935

On Very Slowly with the Dance   Revel 1953
On Wiener Schnitzel Bay   Fisher 1928; Rose 1928
On Wings of Song   Loesser 1941
On with the Dance   Caesar 1929; Dubin 1929; Hart 1925; Kern 1920; Leslie 1929; Mercer 1937; Monaco 1929; Rodgers 1925, 1930; Whiting 1937
On with the Rehearsal   Harbach 1910
On with the Show   Akst 1929; Clarke 1929
On Your Mark   Waller 1943
On Your Toes   Hart 1936; Rodgers 1936
Once   Coots 1955; David, Hal 1960; DeSylva 1925; Gershwin, George 1925, 1927; Gershwin, Ira 1925, 1927; Russell 1951, 1954; Spina 1954
Once a Gypsy Told Me (You Were Mine)   Fain 1930; Kahal 1930
Once a Teacher   Revel 1953, 1960
Once Again   Rome 1949
Once and for Always   Burke 1949; Van Heusen 1949
Once Around the Moon   Sigman 1947
Once Around the Park (inst.)   Strouse 1957
Once Around the Rainbow   Brooks 1959
Once Every Year   Webster 1983
Once Ev'ry Four Years   Berlin 1962
Once I Fall   Cahn Date Unknown; Duke Date Unknown
Once I Was Loved   Sherman 1976
Once I Was Young   Hart 1938; Rodgers 1938
Once I Wondered   Adamson 1963; Fain 1963
Once I Wore Ribbons Here   Arlen 1966
Once in a Blue Moon   Bacharach 1956; David, Hal 1956; Gordon 1934; Kahn 1934; Kern 1923; Motzan 1929; Revel 1934
Once in a Dream   Gordon 1961; Revel 1946
Once in a Lifetime   Caesar 1920; Dietz 1959; Kahn 1934; Russell 1957
Once in a Lifetime (Once in a Blue Moon)   Donaldson 1934
Once in a Lovetime   Akst 1940; Davis 1940
Once in a Million Moons   Harburg 1945; Kern 1945
Once in a Million Years   Russell 1957
Once in a Thousand Years   Whiting 1914
Once in a While   Atteridge 1925; Conrad 1924; Fisher 1906; Lerner, Sammy 1933; Lewis 1919; Snyder 1919; Young, Joe 1919
Once in Love with Amy   Loesser 1948
Once in May   Berlin 1915; Goetz 1915; Kahn 1931
Once in the Highlands   Lerner, Alan Jay 1947; Loewe 1947
Once in Your Life   Sondheim 1957
Once Is Not Enough   Mancini 1975
Once Knew a Fella   Rome 1959
Once More   Brennan 1939; Sigman 1958
Once More, My Love, Once More   Coslow 1958
Once More the Blue and White   Burke 1950; Van Heusen 1950
Once More to Dream   Howard, Joseph E. 1907
Once There Was a Farmer's Daughter   Hammerstein 1930; Romberg 1930
Once There Were Two of Us   Gershwin, Ira 1938; Kern 1938
Once to Each Man   Webster 1975
Once to Every Heart   Kahn 1938; Koehler 1945; Lane 1944; Romberg 1938
Once to Ev'ry Heart   Mills 1935
Once Too Often   Gordon 1944; Monaco 1944
Once Upon a Dream   Brooks 1945, 1946; Cahn 1940; Fain 1958; Lawrence 1952
Once Upon a Garden   Mills 1955
Once Upon a Horse   Evans 1958; Livingston, Jay 1958

Once Upon a Long Ago   Schwartz, Arthur 1955
Once Upon a Midnight   Burke 1935; Spina 1935
Once Upon a Moonlight Night   Clare 1946
Once Upon a Song   Heyman 1944
Once Upon a Summertime   Brooks 1941
Once Upon a Time   Adams 1954, 1956, 1962; Brown, Lew
    1927; Brown, Nacio Herb 1921; Cobb 1906; Comden
    and Green 1955; Dubin 1917; Mills 1942; Strouse 1956
Once Upon a Time Is Always   Cahn 1977
Once Upon a Time (The Magic Melody)   Romberg 1919
Once Upon a Time Today   Berlin 1950
Once Upon a Yesterday   Cahn 1968
Once Word from You   Johnson, Howard 1927
Once You Say Hello to Miami Beach You Never Want to Say
    Goodbye   Davis 1964
Once You're in Love   Adamson 1937; McHugh 1937
Once You're Mine   Egan 1934
Once-in-a-While   Dietz 1934; Schwartz, Arthur 1934
Once-T Around the Park   Lawrence 1945
One   Silver 1955
One a Day   Hart 1922; Rodgers 1922
One Alone   Hammerstein 1926; Harbach 1926; Romberg
    1926
One and One Are Two   Styne 1993
One and One Makes One   Howard, Joseph E. 1906
One and Only   Atteridge 1915; Bergman 1978
One and Only, Genuine, Original Family Band,
    The   Sherman 1968
One at a Time   Bergman 1970
One Baby   Robin 1927
(It Takes a Lot of Little Likes to Make) One Big
    Love   Brooks 1953; Warren 1953
One Big Union for Two   Rome 1937
One Boy (One Girl)   Adams 1960; Strouse 1960
One Boy's Enough for Me   Caesar 1927
One Brick at a Time   Coleman 1980
One Brief Moment   Fields 1939; Schwartz, Arthur 1939
One By One   Bergman 1978
One Chocolate Soda with Two Straws   David, Mack 1958
One Chord in Two Flats   Gordon 1944; Monaco 1944
One Dam Thing After Another   Hart 1927; Rodgers 1927
One Day   Bergman 1968; Coleman 1956; Hammerstein
    1928; Leigh 1956; Romberg 1928; Spina 1953
One Day at a Time   Russell 1968; Willson 1960
One Day in June (It Might Have Been You)   Hanley 1917
One Day in May   Lewis 1932
One Day of Love   Willson 1931
One Day We Dance   Coleman 1960; Leigh 1960
One Day When We Were Young   Hammerstein 1938
One Desire   Hoffman 1951
One Diamond Morning   Wrubel 1952
One Does Not Smile   Willson 1969
One Down and Two More to Go, Boys   Brown, Lew 1943;
    Henderson 1943
One Dream for Two   Livingston, Jerry 1930
One Evening in September   Washington 1932
One Fellow's Joy Is Another Fellow's Woe   Herbert 1900;
    Smith, Harry B. 1900
One Finger Joe   Bloom 1931; Koehler 1931
One Finger Lament (inst.)   Robison 1926
One Finger Melody, The   Hoffman 1950
One Flower Grows Alone in Your Garden   Hammerstein
    1926; Harbach 1926; Romberg 1926
One Flower That Blooms for You   Hammerstein 1922
One Foot, Other Foot   Hammerstein 1947; Rodgers 1947

One for All   Schwartz, Arthur 1930
One for All, All for One   Alter 1929
One for Another   Herbert 1896
One for My Baby (And One More for the Road)   Arlen
    1943; Mercer 1943
One Girl   Berlin 1923; Davis 1952; Hammerstein 1928;
    Youmans 1928
One Girl and Two Boys   Brown, Lew 1943; Brown, Nacio
    Herb 1943; Freed, Ralph 1943
One Glourie   Styne 1958
One God   Drake 1954
One Golden Hour with You   Pollack 1927
One Good Boy Gone Wrong   Hammerstein 1974; Harbach
    1974
One Good Friend's Enough   Blane 1968; Martin 1968
One Good Man Gone Wrong   Hammerstein 1926; Harbach
    1926; Romberg 1926
One Good Time   Friml 1923
One Hallowe'en   Strouse 1970
One Hallowe'en (Remember That Hallowe'en)   Adams 1970
One Hand, One Heart   Sondheim 1957
One Hand Tied Behind My Back   Evans 1959; Livingston,
    Jay 1959
One Happy Family   Ruby 1961
One Heart   Stept 1933
One Hot Dog to a Customer   Blake 1953
One Hour with You   Robin 1932; Whiting 1932
One Hundred and One Dalmatians   Sherman 1961
One Hundred Easy Ways   Comden and Green 1953
One Hundred Women in One   Duke 1959
One I Love, The   Kahn 1938
One I Love Belongs to Somebody Else, The   Kahn 1924
One I Love Just Can't Be Bothered with Me, The   Kahn
    1929
One I Love, Two I Love   Smith, Robert B. 1919
One I Need, The   Martin 1951
One I'm Looking For, The   Gershwin, Ira 1928; Smith,
    Harry B. 1926
One in a Million   Alter 1935; Gordon 1931; Hammerstein
    1940; Mitchell 1936; Pollack 1936; Revel 1931; Schwartz,
    Arthur 1940
One in a Million Like You   Smith, Harry B. 1912
One in Love   Heyman 1934
One Indispensable Man, The   Weill 1938
One Is a Lonely Number   Webster 1957
One Is a Wanderer   Martin 1951
One Kiss   Friml 1928
One Kiss Away from Heaven (Malatia)   Coslow 1956
One Kiss (Il Bacio)   Raye 1942
One Kiss in a Million   Lewis 1936
One Kiss (Is Waiting for One Man)   Hammerstein 1928;
    Romberg 1928
One Kiss, Sweetheart, Then Goodbye   Bryan 1930; Dubin
    1930
One Last Cigarette   Sigman 1952
One Last Fling   Evans 1950; Livingston, Jay 1950
One Last Kiss   Adams 1960; Strouse 1960
One Last Kiss (inst.)   Henderson 1924
One Last Waltz (One More Waltz)   Smith, Harry B. 1923;
    Snyder 1923
One Leg Is Better Than Two   Styne 1985
One Less Bell to Answer   Bacharach 1968; David, Hal 1968
One Life   David, Hal 1974
One Life One Love   Bryan 1930; Dubin 1930

One Life, One Love, I Give Them Both to You   Clarke 1916;
   Monaco 1916, 1917
One Life to Live   Gershwin, Ira 1940; Weill 1940
One Lip Tillie   Silver 1918
One Little Boy Had Money   Atteridge 1920; Howard, Joseph
   E. 1908
One Little Brick at a Time   Cahn 1970; Styne 1970
One Little Dream   David, Mack 1945
One Little Drink   Akst 1930; Clarke 1930
One Little Drink to You   Kahn 1939
One Little Drink-o I Go Boom   Coots 1934
One Little Girl   Caesar 1920
One Little Girl at a Time   David, Hal 1967
One Little Girl I Prize, The   Brennan 1920
One Little Hour with You   Buck 1931
One Little Keepsake   Lewis 1932
One Little Kiss   Kalmar 1934; Ruby 1934
One Little Kiss from You   Yellen 1921; Young, Joe 1931
One Little Kiss in the Moonlight   Dixon 1928; Rose 1928;
   Warren 1928
One Little Lie Too Many   Hoffman 1943; Livingston, Jerry
   1943
One Little Quarrel   Hoffman 1931
One Little Raindrop   Schwartz, Jean 1930
One Little Spark   Sherman 1982
One Little Sweet Little Girl   Dubin 1913; Olcott 1907
One Little Tear Is an Ocean   Merrill 1947; Spina 1947
One Little Thing at a Time   Schwartz, Jean 1934; Young, Joe
   1934
One Little W.A.C.   Loesser 1944
One Little Waltz   Coslow 1925
One Little Word from You   Kalmar 1931; Ruby 1931
One Long Last Look   Bergman 1964; Fain 1964
One Look at You   Howard, Bart 1956; Washington 1940;
   Young, Victor 1940
One Look, One Word   Smith, Harry B. 1917
One Love   Arlen 1930; Caesar 1927; Cahn 1957; Eliscu 1929;
   Freed, Arthur 1931; Koehler 1930; Robin 1941; Rose
   1929; Youmans 1929
One Love for Two   David, Hal 1947
One Love too Many   Sigman 1952
One Loves at Sight   Smith, Harry B. 1930
One Man   Alter 1968; Davis 1968; Gershwin, George 1929;
   Gershwin, Ira 1929; Kahn 1929
One Man Ain't Quite Enough   Arlen 1954
One Man Is Like Another   Romberg 1924
One Man Is Not Enough (inst.)   Revel 1960
One Man Mary   Baer 1928; Bryan 1928
One Man that I Loved Said Goodbye, The   Myrow 1948
One Man Woman   Berlin 1963; Brooks 1947, 1948, 1950;
   Hammerstein 1924; Harbach 1924
One Man's Death Is Another Man's Living   Gershwin, Ira
   1945; Weill 1945
One Man's Love Song Is Another Man's Blues   Van Heusen
   1959
One Million Times a Day   Lewis 1924; Young, Joe 1924
One Minute of Heaven   Magidson 1929; Washington 1929
One Minute to One   Coots 1933; Lewis 1933
One Misty Moisty Morning   Hoffman 1953
One Moment Alone   Harbach 1931; Kern 1931
One Moment More   David, Mack 1953
One Moment More with You   Egan 1929; Whiting 1929
One Moment of Paradise   Johnson, Howard 1924
One Moment Please   Robin 1930; Whiting 1930
One More Dance   Hammerstein 1932; Kern 1932

One More Day   Brennan 1918; Eliscu 1962
One More Day of Sunshine   Merrill 1967
One More Dream   Coots 1938
One More Dream 'Til Christmas   Sherman 1984
One More Hill to Climb   Woods 1942
One More Kiss   De Lange 1946; Magidson 1931; Myrow
   1946; Sigman 1957; Silver 1947; Sondheim 1971
One More Love   Heyman 1953
One More Mile and We're There   Russell 1944
One More Mile to Go   Friml 1947; Heyman 1947
One More Night   Rose 1927
One More River   Razaf 1948
One More River to Cross   Styne 1954
One More Smile   Cahn 1944; Styne 1944
One More Tear Over You   Coots 1945
One More Time   Brown, Lew 1931; David, Mack 1949;
   DeSylva 1931; Henderson 1931; Livingston, Jerry 1949
One More Time Around   Bacharach 1988
One More Tomorrow   De Lange 1946; Myrow 1946
One More Vote   De Lange 1946; Myrow 1946
One More Walk Around the Garden   Lane 1979; Lerner,
   Alan Jay 1979
One More Waltz   Fields 1930; McHugh 1930
One More You   Fields 1951; Schwartz, Arthur 1951
One Morning in May   Carmichael 1933; Parish 1933
One My Yacht   Porter 1913
One Never Knows   Cahn 1966
One Never Knows, Does One?   Gordon 1936; Revel 1936
One Night Ago   Duke 1963
One Night in Acapulco (Mexico)   Magidson 1942; Pollack
   1942
One Night in Havana (inst.)   Carmichael 1928
One Night in June   Smith, Harry B. 1922; Snyder 1922
One Night in Rome   Egan 1920; Whiting 1920
One Night, Madame!   Brown, Nacio Herb 1930; Egan 1930
One Night of Love   Brennan 1929; Kahn 1934; Turk 1928
One Night Stand   Heyman 1964
One Note   Conrad 1924
One Note Trumpet Player, The   Hoffman 1933
One O'Clock Baby   Brown, Lew 1927; DeSylva 1927
One O'Clock in the Morning I Get Lonesome   Berlin 1911;
   Snyder 1911
One of a Kind   Adams 1970; Strouse 1970
One of the Beautiful People   Lawrence 1971
One of the Best Dressed Women   Russell 1965
One of the Boys   Smith, Harry B. 1912; Smith, Robert B.
   1912
One of These Days Pow   Davis 1954
One of These Days the Two of Us Are Gonna Be
   Blue   Coots 1933; Lewis 1933
One of These Fine Days   Rome 1938
One of Those Days   Leigh 1954
One of Those Goldarn UFO's   Robison 1966
One of Those Moments (Just for the Moment)   Leigh 1967
One of Those Things   Kahn 1927
One of Those Windows   Brown, Lew 1927; Friend 1927
One of Us Has Got to Go   Leigh 1974
One of Us Is a Thief   Cahn 1958
One of Us Should Be Two   Hart 1926; Rodgers 1926
One of Us Was Wrong   Kahn 1931
One on the Left, The   Sondheim 1984
One Pair of Pants for You   Caesar 1943
One Part Dog, Nine Parts Cat   Bacharach 1961
One Pip Wonder   Loesser 1944
One Potater, Two Potater   Silver 1956

One Really Big Chance   Bacharach 1960
One Rich Brother   Cahn 1958
One Rising Star   Eliscu 1937
One Robin Doesn't Make a Spring   Loewe 1930, 1937
One Romance   Loesser Date Unknown
One Second of Sex   Heyman 1931
One Sided Love Affair   Davis 1953
One Small Voice   Strouse 1957
One Smile   Johnson, Howard 1925
One Song   Bergman 1990
One Starry Moment   Cahn 1966; Van Heusen 1966
One Starry Night   Spina 1957
One Step   Caesar 1930; Romberg 1930
One Step Ahead of Everybody   Sigman 1953
One Step Ahead of Love   Porter 1938
One Step Ahead of My Shadow   Fain 1932; Kahal 1932
One Step at a Time   Strouse 1980
One Step Into Love   Romberg 1915
One Step, Two Step   Arlen 1959; Mercer 1959
One Summer Night   Coslow 1927
One Sunday Afternoon   Blane 1948; Coslow 1933; Johnston 1933
One Sunny Day   Schwartz, Jean 1928
One Sweet Day   Harburg 1969
One Sweet Letter from You   Brown, Lew 1927; Clare 1927; Warren 1927
One Sweet Little Yes   Akst 1929; Clarke 1929
One Sweet Morning   Harburg 1971
One Sweetheart   Baer 1929; Gilbert 1929
One Tender Smile   Friml 1934
One that Got Away, The   DePaul 1954; Raye 1954
One that I Love Loves Me, The   Ahlert 1929; Turk 1929
One Tiny Tear   Woods 1933
One Touch of Alchemy   Weill 1938
One Touch of Venus   Weill 1943
(I Got a) One Track Mind   Comden and Green 1945
One, Two, Button Your Shoe   Burke 1936; Johnston 1936
One, Two, Three   Gershwin, George 1947; Gershwin, Ira 1947; Kern 1918; Mercer 1930; Webster 1950
One Two Three Four   Akst 1927; Davis 1927
One Two Three Four Five   Schwartz, Arthur 1976
One, Two, Three, Make a Box   David, Mack 1951
One, Two, Three O'Leary   David, Hal 1949
One, Two, Three, Pause (The Dancing Lesson)   Burke 1956; Friml 1956
One Two Three Waltz   Spina 1959
One Umbrella Would Be Big Enough to You   Smith, Harry B. 1904; Smith, Robert B. 1904
One Way of Doing It   Smith, Harry B. 1914, 1916; Smith, Robert B. 1916
One Way Street   Caesar 1935; Donaldson 1926; Henderson 1935; Koehler 1935
One Way Street to You   Eliscu 1930
One Way to Love   Oakland 1960
One Who Will Understand   Friml 1914; Harbach 1914
One Who Yells the Loudest Is the Captain, The   Hart 1943
One Who's Always There, The   Burke 1964
One Woman Man   Fain 1963
One Wonderful Day   Sondheim 1954
One Wonderful Night   Friml 1952; Gorney 1925
One Word from You   Herbert 1911; Smith, Harry B. 1911
One World   Webster 1983
One You're Looking For   Herbert 1908
One-Sided Love   Parish 1950
One-Two-Three   Drake 1955

One-Two-Three-Four Hey   Mitchell 1936; Pollack 1936
One-Woman Man   Adamson 1963
Ongsay and Anceday   Hart 1929; Rodgers 1929
Onion Time (inst.)   Waller 1945
Onions Bring Mem'ries of You   Donaldson 1923; Friend 1923
Onions, Garlic and Fish   Fisher 1924
Only   Akst 1919; Caesar 1919
Only a Broken Toy   Cobb 1913; Edwards 1913
Only a Bunch of Violets   Sterling 1904
Only a Dream   Pollack 1927; Smith, Harry B. 1925
Only a Gypsy Knows   Burke 1938; Monaco 1938
Only a Jewel in Pawn   Bryan 1902
Only a Kiss   Atteridge 1910; Hammerstein 1924; Harbach 1924
Only a Man   Kahn 1910
Only a Midnight Adventure   Leslie 1930
Only a Moment Ago   Ager 1942; Rose 1942
Only a Mother Could Love You   Sigman 1950
Only a Rose   Friml 1925
Only a Smile   Smith, Harry B. 1928
Only a Voice on the Air   Dubin 1931
Only Another Boy and Girl   Porter 1944
Only Because I Love You   Ahlert 1936; Young, Joe 1936
Only Boy, The   Caesar 1927
Only Dance I Know (Song for Belly Dancer), The   Berlin 1962
Only for Americans   Berlin 1949
Only for Me   De Lange 1946
Only for Men   Burke 1946; Van Heusen 1946
Only for Thee   Herbert 1897; Smith, Harry B. 1897
(It Is All for You) Only for You   Atteridge 1915; Romberg 1915
Only Forever   Burke 1940; Monaco 1940; Stept 1955
Only Girl, The   Herbert 1914; Romberg 1924; Smith, Harry B. 1901
Only If You're in Love   Mercer 1951
Only in America   Gilbert 1962
Only in Dreams   Caesar 1924; Lerner, Sammy 1943, 1945; Robin 1927; Smith, Harry B. 1918
Only in the Movies   Bergman 1966
Only in the Play   Herbert 1898; Smith, Harry B. 1898
Only Kind of a Ring to Give a Girl is Upon the Telephone, The   Clarke 1919
Only Lonely   Whiting 1912
Only Lonely Little Me   Snyder 1909
Only Love Can Break a Heart   Bacharach 1962; David, Hal 1962
Only Love Can Lead the Way   Woods 1934
Only Love Is Real   Brown, Nacio Herb 1930; Freed, Arthur 1930
Only Love Me   Sigman 1953
Only Me   Brown, Lew Date Unknown; Henderson Date Unknown
Only Memories of You   Burke 1971
Only Once   Cahn 1952; Duke 1952; Woods 1939
Only One, The   Herbert 1905; Romberg 1925; Smith, Harry B. 1925
Only One for Me, The   Akst 1927; Davis 1927; DeSylva 1925
Only One Girl for Me   Romberg 1917
Only One Horse Shay   Egan 1915
Only One Love Ever Fills the Heart   Romberg 1921
Only One Man   Styne 1970
Only One of Anything   Herbert 1908
Only One Revival   Robison 1953

Only One to a Customer   Leigh 1976; Styne 1976
Only One Waltz   Smith, Robert B. 1912
Only, Only One, The   Monaco 1924; Warren 1924
Only Only One for Me, The   Monaco 1924; Warren 1924
Only, Only, Only in My Dreams   Brown, Lew 1931;
    Henderson 1931
Only Pair I've Got, The   Merrill 1959
Only Sometimes   Waller 1932; Young, Joe 1932
Only Song I Know, The   Brennan 1929
Only the Beautiful Stars   Sterling 1903
Only the Lonely   Cahn 1958; Van Heusen 1958
Only the Skies Are Blue in Kalua   Bryan 1930
Only the Strong, Only the Brave   Bacharach 1965; David,
    Hal 1965
Only Thing Green about the Girl of Today Is the Green
    Upon Her Hat, The   Buck 1926; Friml 1926
Only Those in Love   Hoffman 1958
Only Time Will Tell   Rome 1959
Only Time You're Out of Luck, The   Razaf 1935
Only Trust Your Heart   Cahn 1957, 1965
Only Way to Get 'Em, The   Fisher 1920
Only Way to Go Is Up, The   Cahn 1977
Only Way to Travel, The   Cahn 1962
Only When You're in My Arms   Conrad 1939; Kalmar 1939;
    Ruby 1939
Only with You (Io Sono Te)   Raye 1958
Only Yesterday   Donaldson 1933; Ellington 1958; Lawrence
    1933
Only You   Hammerstein 1938; Herbert 1920; Smith, Robert
    B. 1920
Only You — Only Me   Davis 1959
Only You Will Do   Burke 1971
Only Your Heart Can Tell   Gilbert 1931
Onward, America   Johnson, Howard Date Unknown
Onward Chicago: World's Fair March   Johnson, Howard
    1930
Oo   Ellington 1955
Oo, How I Love to Be Loved By You   Gershwin, George
    1919, 1920
Oo, How I Love You   Caesar 1927
Oo La La   Coslow 1924; Herbert 1920; Romberg 1924;
    Smith, Robert B. 1920
Oo-Day Oo-Yay   Magidson 1929; Washington 1929
Oogie Oogie Wa Wa   Clarke 1922; Leslie 1922
Oogie-Woogie-Shoogie   Comden and Green 1956; Styne
    1956
Ooh Bang Jiggilly Jang (But My Guy)   Merrill 1955
Ooh, But I'm Happy   Gordon 1937; Revel 1937
Ooh, Do You Love You   Adams 1966; Strouse 1966
Ooh, Gee, What You Do to Me   Burke 1933; Spina 1933
Ooh He's a Tiger   Raye 1956
Ooh Hoo, You-hoo, Don't Cha Know the Moon Is
    New-hoo   Woods 1931
Ooh, I'm Thinking   Brown, Lew 1933; Henderson 1933
Ooh! La! La!   Wrubel 1937
Ooh La La Boom Boom   Coslow 1955
Ooh! (Maybe It's a Robber)   Harbach 1911
Ooh! Maybe It's You   Berlin 1927
Ooh, My Feet   Loesser 1956
Ooh that Kiss   Dixon 1931; Warren 1931; Young, Joe 1931
Ooh!, What a Terrible Man   Kahn 1937
Ooh! What I Could Do to You!   Friend 1933; Magidson
    1933; Stept 1933
Ooh! What I'll Do (To that Wild Hungarian)   Robin 1947
Ooh, What You Can Do!   Rainger 1943; Robin 1943

Ooh, What You Did (Eterno Ritornello)   Rome 1951
Ooh! What You Do to Me   Brooks 1945
Ooh, What You Just Said   Clare 1948; Stept 1948
Ooh! What You Said   Carmichael 1940; Mercer 1940
Ooh! You Miser You!   Lewis 1934
Oo-La-La   Atteridge 1921
Oo-La-La-La-La (Joli Fifi)   Ahlert 1929; Turk 1929
Oo-Long's in Wrong in Hong Kong Now   Stept 1926
Oompa, Oompa   Smith, Harry B. 1934
Oom-Pah Papa   Evans 1956; Livingston, Jay 1956
O-oo Ernest, Are You Earnest with Me   Clare 1922; Friend
    1922
Ooo, Ooo, Lena   Kern 1912
Oooh! I Like You!!!   Cahn 1955; Styne 1955
Oooh, My Love   Bacharach 1957; David, Hal 1957
Oo-ooh I Wanna Have a Little Dance with You   Ahlert
    1936; Young, Joe 1936
Oo-oo-oo a Jula Hula Moonlight   Snyder 1940
Oo-oo-ooh! Honey! What You Do to Me   Friend 1933
Oop Sah-sah   Brown, Lew 1950; Lewis 1950
Oops!   Mercer 1951; Warren 1951
Oo-Solo-Mi (I Give My Soul to You)   Clarke 1919; Monaco
    1919
Oo-Wah-Oh   Evans 1957; Livingston, Jay 1957
'Op on Me 'Ansom   Cohan 1904
Opalisque (inst.)   Willson 1929
Opaltine   Raye 1945
Open and Shut Idea   Brennan 1929
Open Book, An   Eliscu 1929
Open Sesame   Cahn 1958
Open the Window in Your Heart (And Let the Lovelight
    Come In)   Coots 1950
Open the Window of Your Heart (And Let the Sunshine
    In)   Hoffman 1954
Open Up that Door and Let Me In   Stept 1944
Open Up the Golden Gates to Dixieland and Let Me Into
    Paradise   Yellen 1919
Open Up Those Eyes   Heyman 1931
Open Up Your Heart, Let Me In   Gilbert 1915
Open Up Your Heart, Play the Game   Eliscu 1929; Rose
    1929; Youmans 1929
Open Your Arms   Evans 1954
Open Your Arms (And Close Your Eyes)   Gorney 1926
Open Your Arms (Let Me Walk Right In)   Evans 1970;
    Livingston, Jay 1954
Open Your Arms My Alabam'   Lewis 1922; Meyer 1922;
    Young, Joe 1922
Open Your Eyes   Duke 1929; Hammerstein 1931; Lane 1951;
    Lerner, Alan Jay 1951; Strouse 1986; Whiting 1931
Open Your Heart   Drake 1948; Johnson, James P. 1922
Open Your Heart to Me   Parish 1959
Open Your Window   Brennan 1929
Opened Up Again   Rose 1927
Opening — Crazy Quilt   Gershwin, Ira 1924
Opening — First Act Naughty Marietta   Herbert 1935; Kahn
    1935
Opening — 2nd Minstrel Show   Burke 1943; Van Heusen
    1943
Opening Act One (Street Vendors)   Kern 1931
Opening Act Two (In Society)   Kern 1920
Opening Act Two (Russian Dance) (inst.)   Kern 1913
Opening (After Saga 1)   Russell 1946
Opening Cantata Act II   Schwartz, Jean 1918
Opening Carnival Scene   Von Tilzer 1916

Our Song   Fields 1937; Kern 1937
Our State Fair   Hammerstein 1945; Rodgers 1945
Our Team Is on the Warpath   Mitchell 1937; Pollack 1937
Our Theme   Cahn 1946; Styne 1946
Our Time   Sondheim 1981
Our Town   Cahn 1955; Strouse 1974; Van Heusen 1955
Our Usual Place   Duke 1963
Our Very Own   Young, Victor 1950
Our Wedding Day   Berlin 1933; Hanley 1917
Our Wedding Song   Webster 1959
Our World   Razaf 1953
Ours   Porter 1936
Out at the Prairie's End   Schwartz, Jean 1930
Out Comes Oom-Pa-Pa   Leigh 1955
Out for No Good   Dubin 1934; Warren 1934
Out in All that Rain   Evans 1964; Livingston, Jay 1964
Out in Frisco Town   Atteridge 1914; Carroll 1914
Out in the Apple Orchard (With the Apple of My
    Eye)   Burke 1933; Spina 1933; Young, Joe 1933
Out in the Cold   Conrad 1929, 1930; Meyer 1930; Mitchell
    1929, 1930
Out in the Cold Again   Bloom 1934; Koehler 1934
Out in the Cow Country   Stept 1937; Washington 1937
Out in the Great Open Spaces   Coslow 1933; Johnston 1933
Out in the Open Air   Cahn 1971; Dietz 1930; Lane 1930;
    Van Heusen 1971
Out in the Sun   Eliscu 1937
Out o' Town Gal   Donaldson 1928
Out of a Blue Sky   Conrad 1949
Out of a Clear Blue Sky   Arlen 1930; Carroll 1929; Edwards
    1925; Koehler 1930; Lewis 1919; Von Tilzer 1928; Young,
    Joe 1919
Out of a Dream   Mills 1934; Washington 1934
Out of a Million You're the Only One   Clarke 1924; Leslie
    1924
Out of Breath and Scared to Death   Mercer 1930
Out of Doors   Blane 1955; Martin 1955
Out of His Heart He Builds a Home   Herbert 1916
Out of Love   Fain 1949
Out of My Arms, But I Can't Keep You Out of My
    Heart   Hanley 1922
Out of My Dreams   Hammerstein 1943; Rodgers 1943
Out of My Dreams Into My Heart   Arlen Date Unknown;
    Koehler Date Unknown
(I Was) Out of My Mind   De Lange 1943, 1945; Fain 1947;
    Myrow 1945
Out of My Sentimental Mind   Bacharach 1960
Out of My Way   Sigman 1946
(You Came Along From) Out of Nowhere   Heyman 1931
Out of Reach   Myrow 1943
Out of Sight   De Lange 1945
Out of Sight, Out of My Mind   Fields 1935
Out of Step March (Picadore March)   Bergman 1958
Out of the Blue   Eliscu 1932; Hammerstein 1929; Kalmar
    1928; Kern 1929; Ruby 1928
Out of the Clear Blue Sky   Duke 1952
Out of the Corner of My Eye   Parish 1948
Out of the Cradle, Into My Heart   Gilbert 1916
Out of the Dark   Howard, Joseph E. 1947
Out of the Darkness (You Have Come to Me)   Turk 1932;
    Young, Victor 1932
Out of the Dawn   Donaldson 1928
Out of the Deep   Kahn 1933
Out of the Frying Pan Into the Fire   Lawrence 1953; Monaco
    1935

Out of the Goodness of Your Great Big Heart   Brennan 1936
Out of the Heart of the Sunrise   Brennan 1928
Out of the Mist   Webster 1965
Out of the Night   Brennan 1925; Bryan 1921; Johnson,
    Howard 1936
Out of the Nowhere Into the Here   Lane 1930
Out of the Past   Dubin 1924
Out of the Shadow (And Into the Light)   Koehler 1952
Out of the Shadows   Kahn 1921
Out of the Sound   Webster 1965
Out of the South (inst.)   Robison 1926
Out of the Sun   Brennan 1926
Out of the Way   Robin 1954; Romberg 1954
Out of This World   Arlen 1945; Mercer 1945; Styne 1943
Out of This World Into My Arms   Berlin 1955
Out on a Limb   Webster 1946
Out on the Broad Prairie (Broad Western
    Prairie)   Hammerstein 1935; Kern 1935
Out There   Coleman 1980
Out There in an Orchard   Hammerstein 1927; Kern 1927
Out There in the Sunshine with You   Brennan 1923
(Trouble Ends) Out Where the Blue Begins   Friend 1936;
    McHugh 1923
Out Where the Blues Begin   Fields 1928; McHugh 1928
Out Where the Moonbeams Are Born   Coots 1929
Out Where the North Begins   Gilbert 1931
Out with Somebody Else   Van Heusen 1959
Out with the Owl   Harbach 1910
Out with Your Chest and Up with Your Chin   Loesser 1940
Outa My Mind   Bergman 1958
Out-A-Town   Adams 1978; Strouse 1978
Outdoor Life   DeSylva 1925
Outdoor Man (For My Indoor Sports)   Brown, Lew 1928;
    DeSylva 1928; Henderson 1928
Out-Fox the Fox   Cahn 1956
Outlaw Song, The   Friend 1930
Outline of Jitterbug History   Coslow 1952
Outside Looking In   Eliscu 1930
Outside My Window   David, Hal 1960
Outside of Loving You, I Like You   Berlin 1963
Outside of Paradise   Lawrence 1938
Outside of that I Love You   Berlin 1940
Outside of That Why He's All Right   Sterling 1915; Von
    Tilzer 1915
Outside of You   Dubin 1935; Warren 1935
Ouzo   Leigh 1965
Over   Brooks 1959
Over a Bottle of Wine   Stept 1949
Over a Chocolate Sundae on Saturday Night   Fisher 1935
Over a Cup of Coffee   Akst 1936; Clare 1936
Over a Garden Wall   Conrad 1925
Over a Mountain   Robison 1953
Over and Over   Martin 1951
Over and Over Again   Hart 1935; Hoffman 1954; Kalmar
    1929; Rodgers 1935; Ruby 1929
Over and Under   Goetz 1916; Young, Joe 1916
Over Here   Akst 1942; Coots 1929; Davis 1929; Sherman
    1974
Over in Europe   Weill 1936
Over My Shoulder   Woods 1935
Over Night   Mitchell 1937; Pollack 1937
Over on the Jersey Side   Fields 1934; McHugh 1934;
    Norworth 1908
Over the Alpine Mountains   Bryan 1914; Fisher 1914
Over the Bars (inst.)   Johnson, James P. 1917

Over the Garden Wall Herbert 1920; Hoffman 1950; Kalmar 1913; Smith, Robert B. 1920
Over the Heather Kahn 1910
Over the Hill and Far Away Jerome 1908; Schwartz, Jean 1908
Over the Hill (inst.) Warren Date Unknown
Over the Hills (And Through the Woods) David, Hal 1940
Over the Hills To Mary Bryan 1915
Over the Lincoln Trail Bryan 1930
Over the Lowlands Hart 1921; Rodgers 1921
Over the Mountain Herbert 1899; Smith, Harry B. 1899
Over the Ocean Goetz 1913
Over the Phone Cohan 1922
Over the Plains Baer 1930; Gilbert 1930
Over the Rainbow Arlen 1939; Harburg 1939
Over the Rhine Yellen 1918
Over the River to Jersey Bryan 1926; Fisher 1926
Over the Sea, Boys Berlin 1918
Over the Sea of Dreams Robin 1930
Over the Top Bryan 1917
Over the Top of the Hill Brown, A. Seymour 1928
Over the Waves to the Port of Your Heart Johnson, Howard 1935
Over the Weekend I Fell in Love Monaco 1932; Washington 1932
Over There Cohan 1917; Harbach 1908
Over There I'll Be Rambling with You Lewis 1918; Schwartz, Jean 1918
Over You Bacharach 1987
Overalls and Calico Kahn 1920; Schwartz, Jean 1920
Overflow Gershwin, George 1935
Overheard in a Cocktail Lounge (inst.) Myrow 1937
Overnight Alter 1930; Henderson 1921; Lawrence 1955; Rose 1930
Overnight in a Warehouse of Naked Mannequines Spina 1976
Overnight Success Bacharach 1988
Overture (inst.) Herbert 1923
Overture to Love Davis 1946
Overture to Love, An Ahlert 1942; Lewis 1942
Overture to the Blues Howard, Bart 1961
'Ow Are You Feelin', 'Arry Boy Mancini 1953
Owatonna Williams 1906
Owen Roe Blane 1952
Owl and the Thrush, The Herbert 1896
Owl and the Turtle Doves, The Atteridge 1919; Carroll 1919
Owl Song (Song of the Owl) Hart 1928; Rodgers 1928
Oyaneetah (Seminole Love Song) Herbert 1904
Oysters, Cockles and Mussels (Fish Market) Rome 1954
Oysters in July Fields 1951; Schwartz, Arthur 1951
Ozarks Are Callin' Me Home, The Porter 1936
Ozzie the Ostrich Coots 1953

P

Pa Don't 'Low No Strangers Here Razaf 1952
Pa Is Rich, So Ma Don't Care Jerome 1905; Schwartz, Jean 1905
Pablo Caesar 1930; Harbach 1930; Romberg 1930
Pablo, You Are My Heart Hart 1935; Rodgers 1935
Pachenza Pachenza (Patience Patience) Hoffman 1953
Pacific Arlen 1966
Pacific Coast Highway Bacharach 1969; David, Hal 1969
Pacing the Wailing Wall Gilbert 1934
Pack Home Evans 1954; Livingston, Jay 1954

Pack of Cards, A Hammerstein 1927; Kern 1927
Pack Up Your Heart Harbach 1911
Pack Up Your Sins (And Go to the Devil) Berlin 1922
Package of Seeds, A Kern 1915, 1917
(I Still Love You All) Padam. . . .Padam Raye 1960
Paddle-Addle in Your Little Canoe Lewis 1917; Snyder 1917; Young, Joe 1917
Paddlin' Madelin' Home Woods 1925
Paddy's Cat Olcott 1901
Padre Webster 1957
Padre and the Bride, The Rainger 1936; Robin 1936
Padre, I Have Sinned Loesser 1969
Padre of San Jose Silver 1950
Paducah Robin 1943; Warren 1943
Pagan In Paris, A DePaul 1953
Pagan Love Song Brown, Nacio Herb 1929; Freed, Arthur 1929; Johnson, Howard 1939
Pagan Lullaby Loesser 1942; Styne 1942
Pagan Moon Bryan 1931; Dubin 1931
Pagan Paradise Koehler 1932
Pagan Star Carmichael 1935
Page Miss Glory Dubin 1935; Warren 1935
Page Mr. Cupid Schwartz, Jean 1920
Page Mr. Handy Robison 1925
Page Nine Yellen 1929
Pages Friml 1928
Paging Mr. Greenback Brown, Lew 1943; Fain 1943; Harburg 1943
Pagliacci Cobb 1917; Edwards 1917; Porter 1919
Pagliacci — Prologue Styne 1938
Pagnnin Paris, A Raye 1953
Pah, Pah, Pah Cobb 1901; Edwards 1901
Paid in Full Sigman 1953; Turk 1934
Pain in the Heart Caesar 1953; Yellen 1953
Paint a Rainbow Drake 1964
Paint Me a Picture Howard, Bart 1960
Paint Yourself a Rainbow Sigman 1950
Painted Butterfly Carroll 1921
Painted from Memory Bacharach 1996
Painted Mem'ries Drake 1994
Painted Rose Hanley 1930
Painting Myself Into a Corner David, Hal 1977
Painting Pictures Fisher 1964
Painting That Mother of Mine Gilbert 1915
Painting the Clouds with Sunshine Dubin 1929
Painting the Roses Red Fain 1951
Pair of Dimples and a Picture Hat, A Ager 1935
Pair of Ordinary Coons, A Berlin 1915
Pais Ideal (The Islands Are Calling Me) Akst 1933; Gilbert 1933
Paisley Shawl Ager 1923; Yellen 1923
Pajama and the Nightie, The Howard, Joseph E. 1908
Pajama Blues Dubin 1920
Pajama Dance Martin 1948
Pajama Girlies Atteridge 1916; Motzan 1916, 1917
Pakistan Burke 1954; Van Heusen 1954
Pal Is a Pal, A Coleman 1988
Pal Joey (What Do I Care for a Dame?) Hart 1940; Rodgers 1940
Pal Like You, A Kern 1917
Pal of My Dreams Friend 1923
Pal of My Sweetheart Days Coots 1929; Davis 1929
Palace Dance (inst.) Kern 1923
Palace of Dreams Schwartz, Arthur 1930
Palace of Silver and Gold Sterling 1904; Von Tilzer 1904

Pale Golden Star   Howard, Joseph E. 1909
Pale Venetian Moon, The   Kern 1922
Palermo in the Moonlight   Parish 1963
Palesteena   Conrad 1920
Palestine   Bryan 1918
Palm Beach   Dietz 1944; Duke 1944; Strouse Date Unknown
Palm Garden (inst.)   Waller 1941
(In Old) Palm Springs   Rainger 1936; Robin 1936
Palma de Majora (inst.)   Spina 1977
Palms, The   Johnson, Howard 1939
Palms of Paradise   Loesser 1940
Palmy Pinellas Peninsula   Willson 1953
Palooka (It's a Grand Old American Name)   Burke 1933
Pals   Baer 1953; Coots 1922; DeSylva 1925
Pals Forever   Yellen 1929
Pals of the Pentagon   Rome 1950
Palsie Walsie   Fields 1935; McHugh 1935
Pal-Sie-Walsie   Stept 1934
Palsy Walsy   Arlen 1943; Mercer 1943
Palula Moon   Schwartz, Arthur 1923
Paminay   Lawrence 1952
Pampas Moon   Whiting 1935
Pampas Rose   Whiting 1930
Pan American Conference   Russell 1943
Pan American Jubilee   Gordon 1942; Warren 1942
Pan Pan Pan   Loesser 1969
Panache   Harburg 1967; Styne 1967
Panama   Gordon 1942; Sigman 1955; Styne 1954; Warren 1942
Panamala   Edwards 1914
Panamania   Coslow 1937
Panama-Pacific Drag   Atteridge 1915
Panamericana   Robin 1936; Whiting 1936
Pancho   Davis 1946; Rainger 1934; Robin 1934; Silver 1946
Pancho Gonzales Etcetra the Gaucho   Freed, Ralph 1939
Pancho's Widow   Stept 1937; Washington 1937
Pancito, She Would Call Me   Loesser 1969
Pandemonium   Arlen 1959; Mercer 1959; Sigman 1939
Pange Rosebud   Bryan 1938
Pango Pango   Atteridge 1923; Caesar 1923; Gershwin, George 1923
Panhandle Pete   Fain 1944; Freed, Ralph 1944
Panhandler   Carroll 1933
Panic   Leigh 1967
Panic in Panama   Kalmar 1941; Ruby 1941
Panic Is On, The   Mills 1935; Mitchell 1922; Pollack 1922; Waller 1935
Panic's On, The   Schwartz, Arthur 1930
Panisse and Son   Rome 1954
Pank Upstairs, The   Robison 1951
Panorama   Brooks 1959
Panorama Bay   Clarke 1922; Monaco 1922
Pansies   Leslie 1928
Panther Woman, The   Coslow 1932
Pantomime   Herbert 1946
Pantomime Baseball   Bryan 1919; Schwartz, Jean 1919
Pantomime (inst.)   Hanley 1921; Youmans 1954
Pantry Scene   Hammerstein 1927; Kern 1927
Pants Song, The   Hoffman 1928
Panuelo   Herbert 1911
Paoli Local   De Lange 1942
Papa   Smith, Harry B. 1913
Papa Ain't No Santa Claus, Mama Ain't No Christmas Tree   Razaf 1930
Papa, At Last I Met You   Smith, Harry B. 1934

Papa Blues   Leslie 1923
Papa, Can You Hear Me   Bergman 1983
Papa, Come Home   Loesser 1969
Papa Don't Love Mama Any More   Rome 1937
Papa Good Time   Mercer 1967
Papa Got Hot   Kalmar 1928; Ruby 1928
Papa Lewis, Mama Green   Rome 1937
Papa Likes a Hot Papoose   Gorney 1929; Harburg 1929
Papa Loves Mambo   Hoffman 1954
Papa Loves Twistin'   Hoffman 1961
Papa Mustn't Do That   Turk 1926
Papa Tree-Top Tall   Carmichael 1936
Papa We've Got to Move Uptown   Caesar 1921
Papa, Won't You Dance with Me?   Cahn 1947; Styne 1947
Papa-Mama-Cha-Cha   Hoffman 1956
Papa's Advice   Spina 1976
Papa's Got a Brand New Pig Bag   Leigh 1981
Papa's Got a Job   Rome 1939
Papa's Rocking Baby on the Dance Floor   Fisher 1938
Papaya Man, The   Bullock 1952
Papeechee La Maar   Brown, Lew 1943; Fain 1943
Paper Hat Brigade, The   Edwards 1908
Paper Heart   Russell 1962
Paper Mache   Bacharach 1969; David, Hal 1969
Papers, The   Kalmar 1929; Ruby 1929
Pappy   Fain 1922
Pappy's Little Jug   Kahal 1939
Paprica   Smith, Robert B. 1915
Paprika   Schwartz, Jean 1930
Parable, A   Cahn 1971; Styne 1971
Parable of the Monkey, The   Drake 1968
Parachute Jump, The   David, Mack 1952; Livingston, Jerry 1952
Parade, The   Leigh 1954; Merrill 1959; Parish 1957; Russell 1966
Parade Fantastique (inst.)   Willson 1928
Parade in Town, A   Sondheim 1964
Parade (inst.)   Loewe 1960; Willson 1963
Parade of Broken Hearts   Merrill 1955
Parade of Clowns   Robison 1953
Parade of the Blues   Conrad 1929, 1930; Meyer 1930; Mitchell 1929, 1930
Parade of the Chocolate Dolls   Coots 1937; Davis 1937
Parade of the Little White Mice   Lawrence 1939
Parade of the Teddy-Bears   Cahn 1940
Paradise   Coslow 1930; Johnson, Howard 1924
Paradise Alley   Atteridge 1921; Johnson, Howard 1924; Romberg 1921
Paradise Bound   Livingston, Jerry 1962; Young, Joe 1932
Paradise Harbour Coconut Beach Hotel   Howard, Bart 1961
Paradise in Waltz Time   Coslow 1936
Paradise Island   Bacharach 1958; David, Hal 1958
Paradise Lost   Martin 1972
Paradise Stolen   Romberg 1948
Paradise Waltz   Stept 1933
Paramount Don't Want Me Blues, The   Evans 1950; Livingston, Jay 1950
Paranoia   Porter 1914
Paraphernalia (inst.)   Waller 1945
Paraphrase   Loesser 1937
Parcel Post Man   Atteridge 1913; Schwartz, Jean 1913
Pardners   Cahn 1956; Van Heusen 1956
Pardon Me for Dreaming   Conrad 1936, Date Unknown; Magidson 1936, Date Unknown
Pardon Me, I've Got Some Crying to Do   McHugh 1964

Pardon Me, Madame   Kahn 1936

Pardon Me My Dear Alphonse, After You My Dear
    Gaston   Von Tilzer 1902

Pardon My Dust   Rainger 1935; Robin 1935; Whiting 1935

Pardon My English   Gershwin, George 1932; Gershwin, Ira
    1932

Pardon My Head   Drake 1953

Pardon My Sarong   DePaul 1958; Raye 1958

Pardon My Southern Accent   Mercer 1934

Paree   Ahlert 1924; Dietz 1935; Edwards 1907; Hammerstein
    1928; Robin 1927; Romberg 1928; Schwartz, Arthur 1935

Paree, Gay Paree   Atteridge 1911

Paree (I Want to Be there Again)   Fisher 1921

Paree, What Did You Do to Me?   Porter 1929

Par-ee, You're Mine, All Mine   Hanley 1932

Paree's a Branch of Broadway   Atteridge 1912

Parent Trap, The   Sherman 1961

Paris   Akst 1933; Alter 1928; Bryan 1929; Cahn 1951;
    Comden and Green 1974; Coots 1944; Eliscu 1933;
    Goetz 1928; Styne 1974

Paris After Dark   Duke Date Unknown

Paris Aller et Retour   Duke 1948

Paris By Night   Mancini 1995

Paris Carnival   Smith, Harry B. 1906

Paris, France   Martin 1951

Paris Gown (inst.)   Styne 1953

Paris Holiday   Cahn 1958; Van Heusen 1958

Paris in New York   Duke 1959

Paris in Spring   Schwartz, Jean 1935

Paris in Swing   Coslow 1937

Paris in the Evening   Snyder 1937

Paris in the Spring   Gordon 1935; Revel 1935

Paris Is a Lonely Town   Arlen 1962; Harburg 1962

Paris Is a Paradise for Coons   Coots 1926; Kern 1911

Paris Is Paris Again   Lerner, Alan Jay 1973; Loewe 1973

Paris Is Really Divine   Hart 1926, 1927; Rodgers 1926, 1927

Paris Loves Lovers   Porter 1955

Paris Lullaby   Fain 1966; Webster 1966

Paris Makes Me Horny   Mancini 1995

Paris, Oh Festive Land   Atteridge 1913

Paris Original   Loesser 1961

Paris Police   Schwartz, Jean 1935

Paris Smiles   Evans 1966; Livingston, Jay 1966

Paris Taught Me Zis   Baer 1927; Lewis 1927; Young, Joe
    1927

Paris, The Return   Smith, Harry B. 1912; Smith, Robert B.
    1912

Paris Today   Howard, Joseph E. 1910

Paris Valentine, A   Webster 1959

Paris Wakes Up and Smiles   Berlin 1949

Parisian Babies   Coots 1926

Parisian Ball, The   Brown, Lew 1912

Parisian Glide   Williams 1910

Parisian Heiress (inst.)   Drake 1959

Parisian Lover   Coslow 1931; Johnston 1931

Parisian Model, A   Smith, Harry B. 1906

Parisian Moonlight, Many the Night   Young, Joe 1930

Parisian Nights   Caesar 1922

Parisian Pretties   Fain 1954; Webster 1954

Parisian Rag, The   Smith, Harry B. 1915

Parisian Tango (inst.)   Revel 1932

Parisiana Anna   Goetz 1907

Parisians, The   Lerner, Alan Jay 1958; Loewe 1958

Parisienne   Brown, Lew 1912; Lewis 1923; Smith, Harry B.
    1906; Young, Joe 1923

Parisienne Passionettes   Atteridge 1921

Parisola   Silver 1920

Park Avenue   Dietz 1927; Gorney 1927

Park Avenue Gimp   Loesser 1939

Park Avenue Strut   Atteridge 1929

Parkin' in the Park with You   Conrad 1932

Parks of Paris, The   Arlen 1959; Mercer 1959

Parlor, a Sofa and Someone Like You, A   Coslow 1926;
    Dubin 1926; Mills 1926

Parlor Games   Norworth 1911

Parlor Songs   Sondheim 1979

Parrot from San Domingo, The   Drake 1944

Parrot on the Fortune Teller's Hat, The   Drake 1945

Parsons   Meyer 1930; Mitchell 1930

Part Two Opening   Kalmar 1933; Ruby 1933

Particular Funicular   Russell 1962

Parties   Cahn Date Unknown; Duke Date Unknown

Parting   Schwartz, Jean 1930

Parting Is Such Sweet Sorrow   Mercer 1949

Parting Kiss from Your Sweetheart Puts the Good in
    Goodbye, The   Johnson, Howard 1918; Meyer 1918

Parting Song   Mercer 1944

Partners   Harbach 1921; Styne 1943

Party, The   Mancini 1968

Party Dance   Russell 1946

Party Gets Going, The   Hammerstein 1955; Rodgers 1955

Party Girl   Cahn 1958

Party Is Over, The   Webster 1950

Party Line   Fields 1928; McHugh 1928

Party Parlando   Gershwin, Ira 1940; Weill 1940

Party, Party   Sondheim Date Unknown

Party Polka (inst.)   Young, Victor 1954

Party Talk   Bergman 1964; Fain 1964

Party That We're Gonna Have Tomorrow Night,
    The   Hammerstein 1955; Rodgers 1955

Party Waltz (inst.), The   Rodgers 1934

Party's Getting Rough, The   Rose 1926

Party's on Me, The   Coleman 1973; Fields 1973

Party's Over, The   Comden and Green 1956; Conrad 1934;
    Oakland 1934; Styne 1956

Party's Over Now, The   Martin 1972

Pas de Deux   Kern 1921

Pas de Deux (inst.)   Romberg 1954; Styne 1954

Pas de Nuit   Herbert 1906

Pas de Quarto (inst.)   Kern 1956

Pas D'Equestrienne (inst.)   Kern 1925

Pa's Not Home, He's Upstairs   Wrubel 1951

Pas Seul (inst.)   Hanley 1921

Paseo, The   Loesser 1969

Pasha Bay   Donaldson 1922

Pass Dat Possum   Bryan 1909

Pass It Along   Woods 1954

Pass It Along to Father   Von Tilzer 1908

Pass Me By   Coleman 1965; Leigh 1965

Pass Me the Nutcracker, Sweet   Wrubel 1945

Pass That Peace Pipe   Blane 1945, 1946; Martin 1945, 1946

Pass the Basket   Cahn 1956

Pass the Contribution Box   Howard, Joseph E. 1915

Pass the Football   Comden and Green 1953

Pass the Pickles Henry   Bryan 1925

Pass the Word Around   Hoffman 1934

Passe   De Lange 1942; Egan 1933; Sigman 1942

Passe Qui   Robison 1945

Passengers Will Kindly Step Back in the Sub   Willson 1953

Passers By   Smith, Harry B. 1923; Smith, Robert B. 1923

Passing By   Johnson, Howard 1939; Lawrence 1947
Passing Fancies   Smith, Harry B. 1923; Snyder 1923
Passing Fancy   Akst 1930; Clarke 1930
Passing of the Night, The   Conrad 1924
Passing Show, The   Atteridge 1917, 1922; Motzan 1917; Romberg 1917
Passing Show Cakewalk   Schwartz, Jean 1913
Passing the Buck   Rome 1943
Passing Through   Hammerstein 1920
Passion   De Lange 1942
Passion Flower, The   Berlin 1921
Passionata   Brooks 1952
Passionetta   Dixon 1923
Passionette   Magidson 1928
Passionettes   Bryan 1921; Pollack 1921; Schwartz, Jean 1921
Pasta Cheech   Warren 1954
Pastel for Piano (inst.)   Coots 1945
Pastoral   David, Mack 1962; Martin 1952
Pastry Cooks, The   Mitchell 1921; Pollack 1921
Paswonky (inst.)   Waller 1938
Pat   Herbert 1915
Pat Boone Blues, The   Evans 1958; Livingston, Jay 1958
Pat Chamers Theme   Oakland 1954
Patchland   Atteridge 1920
Path of Pride, The   Bacharach 1960
Path to Honeymoonland, The   Atteridge 1914
Pathfinder   Sigman 1966
Pathway of Love, The   Johnson, J. Rosamond 1909
Pathway to Your Heart   Motzan 1918
Pathways   Akst 1920
Patience of a Saint, The   Merrill 1959
Patisserie, The   Martin 1951
Patricia   Davis 1950
Patricia Donahue   Davis 1945
Patriotic Coon   Cohan 1898
Patriotic Family Are We, A   Caesar 1943
Patriotic Rally (Three Cheers for the Union!)   Gershwin, Ira 1929
Patriotic Rhythm   Baer 1942
Patroness of Art   Duke 1963
Patsy's Pizza Beat   DePaul 1949; Raye 1949
Patter   Koehler 1943; Romberg 1922
Patter 42nd Street   Dubin 1933; Warren 1933
Patter of the Raindrops   Sigman 1951
Patty Cake, Patty Cake (Baker Man)   Razaf 1938; Waller 1938
Paul Bartell Theme   Oakland 1954
Paul Flanagan Theme   Oakland 1954
Paul Lawrence Dunbar   Razaf 1941
Paul Revere's Ride (inst.)   Young, Victor 1955
Pauline   Atteridge 1913; Schwartz, Jean 1913
Paul's Address   Herbert 1911
Pause in the Day's Recreation (Wassail and Skoll), The   Gorney 1961
Pavanne   Bergman 1978; Herbert 1903; Smith, Harry B. 1903
Pavilion of Love, The   Smith, Harry B. 1900
Pavlova Gavotte, The   Atteridge 1914
Pay As You Go   Merrill 1957
Pay Attention to the Girls   Davis 1946
Pay Day   Caesar 1930; Harbach 1930; Loesser 1942; Romberg 1930; Russell 1946; Styne 1942
Pay Day on Levee   Johnson, James P. 1922
Pay Day Pauline   Harbach 1925; Youmans 1925
Pay Heed   Duke 1940

Pay Some Attention to Me   Gershwin, George 1930, 1937; Gershwin, Ira 1930, 1937
Pay the Lawyer   Coleman 1988
Payador   Caesar 1930; Harbach 1930; Romberg 1930
Payday   Fields 1951; Schwartz, Arthur 1951
Payday Today (Ole! It's Payday Today)   Sherman 1960
Paying for It Now   Caesar 1934; Friend 1934
Peace   Bergman 1964
Peace, Brother!   De Lange 1939; Van Heusen 1939
Peace for Our Children (inst.)   Oakland 1972
Peace of Mind   Coleman 1988
Peace on Earth   Freed, Ralph 1959
Peace, Sister, Peace   Johnson, James P. 1948
Peace to My Lonely Heart   Romberg 1921
Peaceful Ends the Day   Brooks 1942
Peaceful Rafferty   Brennan 1915
Peaceful Valley   Robison 1925, 1941
Peaceful Warriors   Leigh 1976
Peaceful Waters   Robison 1949
Peach Girl   Kern 1922
Peach of a Life, A   Kern 1917
Peach of a Pair, A   Whiting 1930
Peach on the Beach   Harbach 1925; Youmans 1925
Peach that Tastes the Sweetest Hangs the Highest on the Tree, The   Cobb 1907; Edwards 1907
Peach Tree Street   Razaf 1939
Peaches   Conrad 1921; Kalmar 1921; Ruby 1921
(Cookie's Song) Peaches an' Cream   Spina 1953
Peaches Don't Grow on a Cherry Tree   Bacharach 1974
Peaches (Poppa would Persist in Picking)   Kern 1917
Peachie   Bryan 1919; Schwartz, Jean 1919; Yellen 1920
Peacock Alley   Coots 1922; Gershwin, Ira 1921; Kalmar 1928; Ruby 1928; Whiting 1919
Peacock Rock   Brooks 1957
Peacock Strut   Atteridge 1924; Romberg 1924; Schwartz, Jean 1924
Peacock Today — Tomorrow a Feather Duster, A   Drake 1956
Peanut Butter Sandwiches and Hard Boiled Eggs   Cahn 1947; Styne 1947
Peanut Vendor   Gilbert 1931
Peanuts and Kisses   Alter 1933
Pearl Ballet   Fisher 1930
Pearl Harbor   DePaul 1958; Raye 1958
Pearl of Broadway   Kalmar 1927; Kern 1927; Ruby 1927
Pearl of Hawaii   Parish 1925
Pearl of Old Japan   Conrad 1929; Mitchell 1929
Pearl of the Orient (inst.)   Alter 1955
Pearl of the Persian Sea   Comden and Green 1949
Pearl We Called Prague, The   Merrill 1990
Pearls (inst.)   Schwartz, Jean 1930
Pearls on Velvet (inst.)   Young, Victor 1937
Pears of Anjou, The   Rodgers 1976
Peasant Girl   Atteridge 1915; Friml 1915
Peasant King, The   Adams 1954; Strouse 1956
Peck-A-Doodle-Doo   Mills 1938
Peckin'   Ellington 1937; Mills 1937
Peck's Bad Boy   Leslie 1912
Peck's Theme Song (Where There's Life There's Soap)   Gordon 1936; Revel 1936
Peculiar   David, Hal 1952
Peddler Man (Then I Loved)   Lawrence 1954
Peddler's Song   Herbert 1903; Smith, Harry B. 1903
Pedestrian Song   Brown, Lew 1927; DeSylva 1927; Henderson 1927

Pedro Mio (inst.)   Kern 1942
Pee Wee the Bunny with the Big Blue Eyes   Coots 1952
Peek-a-boo   David, Hal 1948
Peekaboo to You   Mercer 1941; Sigman 1941
Peekin' in Seek (inst.)   Waller 1945
Peek-in Pekin   Hart 1920; Rodgers 1920
Peering Left, and Peering Right (For We Are the Duke's
   Bodyguard)   Herbert 1897; Smith, Harry B. 1897
Peg o' My Heart   Bryan 1912; Fisher 1912
Peggy   Williams 1918, 1919
Peggy, Dear   Freed, Arthur 1922
Peggy Is a New Yorker Now   Johnson, J. Rosamond 1904
Peggy Jean   Whiting 1927
Peggy McCann   Hoffman 1927
Peggy, Peggy (Oh, You Peggy/The Race)   Hart 1926;
   Rodgers 1926
Peggy's a Creature of Moods   Herbert 1914; Smith, Robert
   B. 1914
Peggy's in the Pantry   Bacharach 1956; David, Hal 1953
Peggy's Leg   Friml 1917
Pekin   Fisher 1917; Johnson, Howard 1917
Pele   David, Mack 1940; Livingston, Jerry 1940
Pelican Falls High   Robin 1951; Styne 1951
Pell Street Blues   Fisher 1931
Pen of Stephen Foster, The   Johnston 1941; Robison 1941
Pendulum Song, The   Hoffman 1955
Pendulum Swings Both Ways, The   David, Mack 1968
Penetone   Revel 1959
Penguin Parade   Whiting 1935
Penguins   Brennan 1949
Penguins on Parade   Razaf 1950
Pennies From Heaven   Burke 1936; Johnston 1936
Penniless Bums   Merrill 1972; Styne 1972
Pennington Pep   Dubin 1929
Pennsylvania 6-5000   Sigman 1940
Penny   Ahlert 1951; David, Mack 1951; Drake 1949
Penny a Tune   Strouse 1986
Penny Arcade (inst.)   Strouse 1968
Penny By Penny   Oakland 1954
Penny for Your Dreams, A   Freed, Ralph 1937, 1938
Penny for Your Thoughts, A   Duke 1932; Harburg 1932;
   Hart 1920, 1923; Rodgers 1920, 1923
Penny for Your Thoughts, Junior Miss   Howard, Joseph E.
   1942
Penny in My Pocket, A   Rainger 1935; Robin 1935
Penny Polka   Revel 1963
Penny-Ante Polka   Brown, Lew 1943; Stept 1943
Penthouse in the Moon   Bryan 1935
Penthouse Promenade (inst.)   Rome 1939
Penthouse Romance (inst.)   Bloom 1934
Peony Bush, The   Willson 1949
People   Merrill 1964; Styne 1964
People Are Funny   DePaul 1951; Raye 1951
People from Missouri   Gershwin, Ira 1938; Kern 1938, 1944
People Get Hurt   Strouse 1991
People in My Life, The   Merrill 1972; Styne 1972
People Like Us   Norworth 1922
People Like You and Me   Gordon 1942; Warren 1942
People Magazine   Coleman 1996
People Should Listen to Me   Livingston, Jerry 1956
People Talk Too Much   Blane 1952
People Watchers, The   Merrill 1967
People Who Are Nice (No More Mr. Nice)   Van Heusen
   1966

People Will Say We're in Love   Hammerstein 1943; Rodgers
   1943
People Will Talk You Know   Herbert 1911
People's Choice, The   Livingston, Jerry 1960
Pep   Romberg 1925
Pep It Up   Buck 1922
Pep Step, The   Brown, Nacio Herb Date Unknown; Freed,
   Arthur Date Unknown
Pep Up, Step Up   Schwartz, Arthur 1928
Pep! Zip! and Punch!   Gershwin, George 1924
Pepita   Bergman 1958; DeSylva 1924; Gershwin, George
   1924
Pepita (inst.)   Motzan 1926
Pepola   Whiting 1930
Pepper Pot   Kern 1946; Robin 1946
Pequita   Howard, Joseph E. 1905
Per Favore   Porter 1957
Percy   Jerome 1906; Schwartz, Jean 1906
Percy Have Mercy on Me   Koehler 1924
Perdido   Drake 1942
Perdido Cha Cha Cha   Ellington 1971
Perennial Debutantes   Porter 1936
Perfect Chaperone, The   Duke 1968
Perfect Example, The   Bergman 1980
Perfect Fool, A   Monaco 1963
Perfect Gentleman   Adams 1968; Caesar 1925; Strouse 1968;
   Youmans 1925
Perfect Harmony   Strouse 1982
Perfect Jewels   Atteridge 1917; Romberg 1917
Perfect Lady, A   Atteridge 1907; Strouse 1999
Perfect Love, A   Cahn 1956
Perfect Lover, A   Bryan Date Unknown; Fisher Date
   Unknown; Hammerstein 1920; Harbach 1920; Smith,
   Harry B. 1919
Perfect Married Life, A   Cahn 1955; Van Heusen 1955
Perfect Model for Your Arms, A   Caesar 1922
Perfect Nanny, The   Sherman 1964
Perfect Paris Night, A   Carmichael 1963; Mercer 1964
Perfect Picnic, The   Sherman 1970
Perfect Stranger   Howard, Bart 1957
Perfect Symphony, The   Harbach 1958
Perfect World, A   Strouse 1990
Perfectly in Love   Snyder 1930
Perfectly Lovely Couple   Rodgers 1965; Sondheim 1965
Perfectly Terrible   Porter 1910
Perfectly Terrible, Dear   Smith, Harry B. 1908
Perfume   Russell 1958
Perfume and Passion   Bryan 1921; Pollack 1921; Schwartz,
   Jean 1921
Perfume, Candy and Flowers   Merrill 1955
Perfume of Love, The   Porter 1955
Perfume of Paradise, The   Caesar 1920
Perfume Waltz   Atteridge 1924; Romberg 1924; Schwartz,
   Jean 1924
Pergola Patrol, The   Kern 1921
Perhaps   Friml 1922; Razaf 1929; Rodgers 1965; Sondheim
   1965; Young, Joe 1938
Periwinkle Blue   Livingston, Jerry 1958; Webster 1958
Pernambuco   Loesser 1948
Perpetual Anticipation   Sondheim 1973
Perpetual Motion (inst.)   Young, Victor 1948
Perserverance   Spina 1957
Persia   Davis 1920
Persian Nights   Brown, Nacio Herb 1922
Persian Room-Ba   Duke 1959

Persian Rosebud   Leslie 1927

Persian Rug   Kahn 1927

Persian Women   Harburg 1961

Persiana   Romberg 1921

Person to Person   Coleman 1977; Comden and Green 1977

Personality   Burke 1945; Cohan 1928; Dixon 1932; Herbert 1914; Stept 1932; Van Heusen 1945

Persuasion, The   Lerner, Alan Jay 1960; Loewe 1960

Perusing in Peru   Caesar 1930; Harbach 1930; Romberg 1930

Peruvian Fire Brigade   Spina 1953

Pessimistic Character (With the Crab Apple Face), The   Burke 1940; Monaco 1940

Pet Me, Poppa   Loesser 1955

Pete Kelly's Blues   Cahn 1955

Peter Had a Wife and Couldn't Keep Her   Brooks 1945

Peter Pan   Atteridge 1919; Carroll 1919; Hart 1930; Kern 1915; Lawrence 1952; Rodgers 1930; Rose 1931; Smith, Harry B. 1915; Young, Victor 1952

Peter Pan, I Love You   Henderson 1924

Peter Pan of Tin Pan Alley, The   Arlen 1937; Harburg 1937

Peter, Peter   Woods 1933

Peter Piper   Mercer 1936; Porter 1919; Whiting 1936

Peter Please   Caesar 1950

Peter Rabbit   Livingston, Jerry 1973

Petrograd   Akst 1930; Clarke 1930

Petrushka   Fisher 1926; Rose 1926

Pets   Porter 1941

Petticoat High   Arlen 1959; Mercer 1959

Pettin' in the Park   Dubin 1933; Warren 1933

Petting   Whiting 1926

Petty Girl, The   Arlen 1950; Mercer 1950

Petty Girl Is Like a Melody, A   Martin 1946

Petty Girl Routine   Loesser 1939

Petulia   Leigh 1968

Petunia   Brown, Lew 1941; Brown, Nacio Herb 1941

Petunia's Prayer   Arlen 1943; Harburg 1943

Pevullia   Hoffman 1944; Livingston, Jerry 1944

Phantom Blues   Mills 1927

Phantom Loves   Atteridge 1920

Phantom of Pigalle, The   Oakland 1967

Phantom of Your Smile, The   Atteridge 1917; Romberg 1917

Phantom Penthouse, The   Gordon Date Unknown; Revel Date Unknown

Phantom Violin, A   Snyder 1953

Phantom Waltz (inst.), The   Romberg 1920

Pharaoh Had a Daughter and Her Name Was Cleopatra   Coslow 1930

Pharaoh's Daughter   Buck Date Unknown

Phenomena (inst.)   Willson 1929

Phi Beta Conga   Freed, Ralph 1941

Phi Phi Phi   Clare 1934

Philadelphia   Bergman 1957; Lerner, Alan Jay 1976; Rodgers 1965; Sondheim 1965

Philadelphia (America's Home Town)   Harburg 1979

Philadelphia Feeling   Fain 1946

Philadelphia, Pa.   Brown, A. Seymour 1943

Philbert   Fain 1963

Philosophy   Oakland 1960

Phi-Phi-Phi   Whiting 1934

Phoebe   Gershwin, George 1921; Gershwin, Ira 1921

Phoebe Snow the Anthracite Mama   Fisher 1925

Phoenix   Drake 1960

Phoenix City Blues   Spina 1955

Phone Call to the Past   Mancini 1969; Mercer 1969

Phone Calls   Bacharach 1968; David, Hal 1968

Phoney Phil   Fain 1925; Kahal 1925; Mills 1925

Phoning Mary Feeney   Strouse 1999

Phony King of England, The   Mercer 1973

Phos-Phos, Phis-Phos, Phos-Phos   Brown, Lew 1923

Photograph of the Sweeter Half of My Love Affair, A   Kahal 1929

Photograph of You   Atteridge 1916; Motzan 1916, 1917; Romberg 1916

Physical Fitness   Adams 1962; Strouse 1962

Physically Fit   Dubin 1930

Physician, The   Porter 1933

Physician Heal Thyself   Robison 1953

Pi Phi Sweetheart   Willson 1946

Pianissimo   Parish 1965

Piano Lesson   Willson 1957

Piano Man   Berlin 1910; Snyder 1910

Piano Phun (inst.)   Alter 1925

Piano Talk   Gorney 1958

Piano Tuner Man   Duke 1938

Pianola   Monaco 1950

Pianologue   Atteridge 1913, 1924; Romberg 1924; Schwartz, Jean 1913, 1924

Piazza San Marco (inst.)   Livingston, Jerry 1957

Pic, Click, Look and Life   Gordon 1942; Warren 1942

Piccadilly, The   Johnston 1938

Piccadilly Band, The   Atteridge Date Unknown

Piccadilly Circus   Mancini 1970; Mercer 1970

Piccadilly Schleppers   Dietz 1959; Schwartz, Arthur 1959

Piccadilly Tilly   Evans 1947; Livingston, Jay 1947

Piccadilly Walk, The   Gershwin, Ira 1922

Piccadilly's Not a Bit Like Broadway   Gershwin, Ira 1920; Youmans 1920

Piccolino, The   Berlin 1935

Piccolo Polka   Willson 1953

Pick a Pickaninny   Bryan 1928; Schwartz, Jean 1928

Pick a Rib   De Lange 1939; Van Heusen 1939

Pick a Rose in Picardy   Motzan 1927

Pick 'em Up and Lay 'em Down   Brennan 1929

Pick Me Up and Lay Me Down   Porter 1931

Pick Me Up and Lay Me Down in Dear Old Dixieland   Kalmar 1922; Ruby 1922

Pick, Pick, Pick on the Mandolin, Antonio   Berlin 1912

Pick, Pick, Pickaninny (Pick Dat Cotton)   Akst 1936; Clare 1936

Pick Up, The   Whiting 1930

Pick Up and Go   Russell 1948

Pick Up the Phone   Revel 1946

Pick Up the Pieces   Bacharach 1962; Coleman 1973; David, Hal 1961; Fields 1973

Pick Yo' Partner! (Get Ready for the Raggy Blues)   Gershwin, Ira 1920; Youmans 1920

Pick Your Hero   Leigh 1955

Pick Yourself a Star   Leigh 1955

Pick Yourself Up   Fields 1936; Kern 1936

Pick Yourself Up, Brush Yourself Off   Hanley 1930

Pick-a-Little Talk-a-Little   Willson 1957

Pickaninnies' Heaven   Coslow 1933; Johnston 1933

Pickaninny Dreams   Coslow 1919

Pickaninny Paradise   Oakland 1938

Pickaninny Shoes   Blake 1921; Sissle 1921

Pickaninny's Cryin'   Mills 1929; Parish 1929

Pickanniny Mose   Berlin 1921

Picket Fence   Bryan 1921; Pollack 1921; Schwartz, Jean 1921

Picketing the Old Plantation   Coots 1938; Davis 1938

Pickin' Cotton   Brown, Lew 1928; DeSylva 1928; Henderson 1928

Pickin' 'Em Up and Layin' 'Em Down   Kahn 1924

Pickin' Moss   Livingston, Jay 1974

Pickin' on Your Mama   Robin 1943; Warren 1943

Picking Peaches   Friml 1918

Pickle in the Middle (And the Mustard on Top)   Sigman 1946

Pickle Packer Polka   Oakland 1955

Pickle Puss   Coslow 1942

Pickles   Akst 1937; Clare 1937; Young, Joe 1923

Picnic for Two, A   Hoffman 1932

Picnic May Not Be a Picnic, A   Drake 1955

Picnic Song II and Girls Walk By   Merrill 1959

Pico and Sepulveda   Styne 1947

Picture, The   Heyman 1965

Picture Dance   Brooks 1958

Picture Framed in My Heart   Whiting 1919

Picture I Want to See, The   Kern 1917, 1918

Picture Me in a Picture Hat   Bullock 1938; Spina 1938

Picture Me Without You   Koehler 1936; McHugh 1936

Picture Medley 1 & 2   Oakland 1960; Raye 1960

Picture No Artist Can Paint, A   Friend 1930; Monaco 1930

Picture of Mary, A   Bryan 1934

Picture of Me Without You, A   Porter 1935

Picture of You, A   Warren 1966

Picture Without a Frame, A   Sterling 1922; Von Tilzer 1922

Picture You in Your Little White Apron and Me in My Blue Overalls   Coots 1951

Picyumi Gazette   Merrill 1971; Styne 1971

Piddle 'n' a Now   Hoffman 1958

Pidgee Woo   Gershwin, George 1921; Gershwin, Ira 1921

Pidgy   Dixon 1924; Henderson 1924

Pie   Kern 1923

Pie Eyed Piper   Fain 1931; Kahal 1931

Piece of a Girl, A   Dietz 1944; Duke 1944

Piece of Cake, A   Coleman 1988

Piece of Sky, A   Bergman 1983

Piece of the Action   Coleman 1996

Piece of the Rainbow, A   David, Mack 1973; Livingston, Jerry 1973

Pieces of Dreams (Little Boy Lost)   Bergman 1970

Pied Piper of Hamlin Town, The   David, Mack 1938; Livingston, Jerry 1938

Pied Piper of Harlem   Henderson 1935; Yellen 1935

Pied Piper (Pied Piper of Hamlin) (inst.)   Young, Victor 1955

Pied Pipers from Swingtown U.S.A.   Brooks 1945

Piel's Beer   Loesser 1958

Pierotte and Pierette   Ager 1928; Yellen 1928

Pierre, Please Don't Move   Smith, Harry B. 1903

Pierrot   Atteridge 1917; Motzan 1917; Romberg 1917

Pierrot Land   Atteridge 1920

Pierrot Patrole and Dance   Smith, Harry B. 1908

Pietro   Atteridge Date Unknown

Pie-Wock-A-Jilly-Wook   Drake 1952

Piff Paff   Herbert 1946

Pig and the Cow and the Dog and the Cat, The   Dubin 1935; Warren 1935

Pig Foot Pete   DePaul 1941; Raye 1941

Pig Latin Love   Gilbert 1919

Pigalle Saint Germain de Pres   Rome 1956

Pigeon Song, The   Spina 1959

Pigeon Talk   Lawrence 1946; Mancini 1946

Pigeon Walk   Lewis 1915; Monaco 1915

Pigeon Walk (inst.)   Monaco 1914

Piggy Wiggy Woo   Baer 1939

Pigtails and Freckles   Berlin 1962

Pilgrims of Love   Herbert 1913; Smith, Robert B. 1913

Pill Box Revue, The   Goetz 1917

Pillar to Post   Merrill 1967

Pillow Magic   Eliscu 1961

Pills and Booze   Strouse 1993

Pilly Pom Pom Plee   Bryan 1929; Meyer 1929

Pilot Me   Porter 1928

Pimento   Dubin 1935; Warren 1935

Pin a Bluebonnet on Your New Bonnet   Fain 1937; Kahal 1937

Pin a Rose on the Christmas Tree   Baer 1950; Leslie 1950

Pin Holes in de Sky   Atteridge 1916; Motzan 1916

Pin Striped Pants   Russell 1949

Pincus et Cie   Duke 1950; Rome 1950

Pindy-Fendy   Loesser 1948

Pine Cones and Holly Berries   Willson 1963

Pine Country   Styne 1960

Pine Point   Adams 1996; Strouse 1996

Pine Top Boogie   Mercer 1948

Pineapple Princess   Sherman 1960

Pineapple Swing   Fisher 1937

Piney Woods (Biarn's Song), The   Mercer 1957

Ping Pong   Smith, Robert B. 1902, 1909

Pingo-Pongo   Dubin 1929

Pining   Conrad 1928

Pining for You   Kahn 1926

Pink and Blue   Adamson 1954; Warren 1954

Pink Cocktail for a Blue Lady, A   Magidson 1941; Oakland 1941

Pink Elephants   Dixon 1932; Woods 1932

Pink Elephants on Parade   Washington 1941

Pink Jungle, The   Duke 1959

Pink Lady (inst.)   Stept 1957

Pink Lemonade   Livingston, Jerry 1963

Pink of Perfection, The   Sherman 1963

Pink Polemoniums   Hoffman 1959

Pink, Purple and Plaid   Livingston, Jerry 1963

Pink Pussy Cat, The   Livingston, Jerry 1960

Pink Taffeta Sample Size 10   Coleman 1966; Fields 1966

Pink, the Powder Puff (inst.)   Young, Victor 1956

Pink Tights   Cahn 1955; Styne 1955

(Locked in a) Pink Velvet Jail   Merrill 1968; Styne 1968

Pinkerton Detective Moon   Norworth 1912

Pinones   Bergman 1953

Pins and Needles, Needles and Pins   Caesar 1937

Pinto   Egan 1942

Pioneer Stock   Martin 1952

Pipe and Slippers   David, Mack 1961; Livingston, Jerry 1961

Pipe Dreaming   Porter 1946

Piper You Must Pay (Pay the Piper), The   Smith, Harry B. 1923

Pipes of Pan, The   Mercer 1958

Pipes of Pan Americana   Caesar 1943

Pipes of Pansy, The   Hart 1925, 1926, 1928; Rodgers 1925, 1926, 1928

Pippi's Lullaby   Brooks 1960

Piquant Love Song   Gorney 1934

Pirate Band, The   Brennan 1929

Pirate Jenny   Weill 1933

Pirate Rag   Romberg 1915

Pirate Song   Johnson, Howard 1930; Leigh 1954; Wrubel 1929

Pirates and Quaker Girl   Atteridge 1912

Pirate's Gold   Hammerstein 1922

Pirates of Love   Edwards 1930

Pirate's Rag   Clarke 1915; Goetz 1915; Young, Joe 1915

Pirelli's Miracle Elixer   Sondheim 1979

Pit Solo   Romberg 1927; Smith, Harry B. 1927

Pitter Patter   Gordon 1930

Pitter Patter Serenade (Lazzarella), The   David, Mack 1958

Pitter-Patter   Porter 1922

Pittsburgh Blue   Lane 1951; Lerner, Alan Jay 1951

(There's a Pawn Shop on a Corner In) Pittsburgh,
    Pennsylvania   Merrill 1952

Pity de Sunset   Arlen 1957; Harburg 1957

Pity Is Akin to Love (Won't You Have a Little Pity on
    Me)   Brown, A. Seymour 1911

Pity Me Please   Porter 1916

Pity Sakes   Mills 1937

Pity the Fond Endeavor   Willson 1973

Pity the Poor   Lerner, Alan Jay 1976

Pixie from Paree, The   Livingston, Jerry 1959

Pixies Entrance   Jerome 1904; Schwartz, Jean 1904

Pizarro Was a Very Narrow Man   Caesar 1930; Harbach
    1930; Romberg 1930

Pizza Song, The   Friend 1956

Pizzicato (inst.)   Kern 1956

P.J.'s Theme   Cahn 1968

Place in the Country   Gershwin, George 1928; Gershwin, Ira
    1928

Place in the Sun, A   Evans 1951; Livingston, Jay 1951;
    Schwartz, Arthur 1933

Place in the World, A   Merrill 1978

Place in Your Heart, A   Coslow 1934

Place Like This, A   Cahn 1971; Styne 1971

Place with No Name   Bacharach 1974

Places, Everybody   Fields 1939; Schwartz, Arthur 1939

Plain Ev'ry-Day Blues, The   Howard, Bart 1984

Plain Jane   Hammerstein 1923; Sherman 1995; Youmans
    1923

Plain Jane Doe   Cahn 1943; Styne 1943

Plain Mamie   Smith, Harry B. 1903

Plain Old Alice   Brooks 1957

Plain Old Blues, The   Burke 1937; Johnston 1937

Plain Rustic Ride ('Neath the Silv'ry Moon), A   Kern 1906

Plam Beach   Strouse 1993

Plane Balle   Burke 1946; Van Heusen 1946

Planet Claire   Mancini 1981

Planning   Cobb 1910; Edwards 1910

Plant a Little Love in Your Heart   Adams 1956; Strouse 1956

Plant a Little Seed of Kindness   Fisher 1922

Plant a Little Smile in the Garden in Your Heart   Coots
    1936; Davis 1936

Plant a Packet of Seeds   Brooks 1958

Plant Plenty of Potatoes   Kalmar 1917; Leslie 1917

Plant Roses in Memory's Garden   Smith, Harry B. 1926

Plant You Now, Dig You Later   Hart 1940; Rodgers 1940

Plantation Days   Bryan 1928; Schwartz, Jean 1928

Plantation in Philadelphia   Fields 1950

Plantation Portrait (inst.)   Coots 1946

Planting Flowers of Happiness   Alter 1930; Johnson,
    Howard 1930

Plastered in Paris   Mills 1938

Plastic Alligator, The   Willson 1963

Plastic City   Bacharach 1974

Plastic Dreams   Sigman 1971

Plate Dance   Atteridge 1919; Romberg 1919; Schwartz, Jean
    1919

Play a Simple Melody   Berlin 1914

Play Ball   Coslow 1933; Johnston 1933

Play Fiddle Play   Lawrence 1941

Play, Fiddle, Play (Sumna Violino)   Lawrence 1932

Play Gypsies, Dance Gypsies   Smith, Harry B. 1926

Play Half a Chorus   Fields 1933; McHugh 1933

Play It Slow and Easy — I'll Dance All Night   Akst 1930;
    Clarke 1930; Robin 1930; Whiting 1930

Play Mates — School Mates — Soul Mates   Schwartz, Jean
    1935; Young, Joe 1935

Play Me a Blue Song   Johnston 1930

Play Me a New Tune   Coots 1925

Play Me a Tune   Porter 1922

Play Me an Old Fashioned Melody   Gordon 1945; Warren
    1945

Play Me Something I Can Dance To   Herbert 1920; Smith,
    Robert B. 1920

Play Me that Tune   Caesar 1919; Donaldson 1919

Play My Melody   Atteridge 1916; Motzan 1916; Romberg
    1916

Play My Request   Coslow 1937

Play that Fandango Rag   Goetz 1909

Play that Hula Waltz for Me   Kahn 1917

Play That Lovey Dovey Waltz Some More   Leslie 1910

Play that Wedding March Backwards   Williams 1910

Play the Game   Eliscu 1949; Herbert 1911; Smith, Harry B.
    1911

Play the Magic Carpet   Yellen 1978

Play the Playera   Drake 1948

Play Us a Polka Dot   Hammerstein 1929; Kern 1929

Play with Fire   Romberg 1922

Playboy   Hart 1929; Rodgers 1929

Playboy Girl   Friend 1962

Playboy of Paree   Dixon 1935; Wrubel 1935

Playboy-Pussycat   Coleman 1975; Leigh 1975

Playful Melody (inst.)   Kern 1956

Play-Ground in the Sky   Hanley 1927

Playground Songs   Adams 1964; Strouse 1964

Playhouse Rock   Adams 1961; Strouse 1961

Playin' Around   Stept 1930

Playin' Hookey with Cookie   De Lange 1949

Playin' Round   Dubin 1924

Playin' the Game   Strouse Date Unknown

Playin' with the Devil (And Raisin' Cain)   Myrow 1933

Playing Around (inst.)   Kern 1945

Playing Bingo   Blake 1938

Playing Hookey   Leslie 1908

Playing Politics   Cahn 1960; Van Heusen 1960

Playing the Game   Strouse 2000

Playmates   Yellen 1917

Playmates — I Wish I Were a Boy Again   Fisher 1920

Playthings of Love   Johnson, Howard 1927

PLaza 6-9423   Rome 1938

Plaza Music   Duke 1959

Plea for Understanding, A   Martin 1959

Pleading   Yellen 1921

Pleasant Dreams   Coslow 1932

Pleasant Greeting, A   Kalmar 1924; Ruby 1924

Pleasant Little Kingdom   Sondheim 1971

Please   Lewis 1924; Rainger 1932; Robin 1932; Young, Joe
    1924

Please Be an Angel, Angel   Spina 1967

Please Be Good to Me   Hanley 1916; Silver 1930

Please Be Good to My Old Girl   Dixon 1924; Henderson
    1924; Rose 1924

Please Be Kind   Cahn 1938
Please Be My Sweetheart, Sweetheart   Spina 1952
Please Be Patient with Me   Duke 1968
Please Believe Me   Merrill 1950
Please Come Again, Summer Days   Jerome 1923; Schwartz, Jean 1923
Please Come Back to Me   Brown, A. Seymour 1910
Please Come Back to Me and Brighten My Days   Bloom 1926
Please Come Out of Your Dreams   Sigman 1938
Please Disarm My Wife   Schwartz, Jean 1921
Please Do My Family a Favor and Love Me   Clarke 1914
Please Don't Go   Sigman 1959
Please Don't Go So Soon   Sigman 1955
Please Don't Make Me Be Good   Porter 1929
Please Don't Make Me Hear that Song Again   Strouse 1982
Please Don't Monkey with Broadway   Porter 1939
Please Don't Paint a Mustache on the Girl in the Cigarette Ad   Sigman 1948
Please Don't Play that Old Song   Lawrence 1947
Please Don't Save a Place at Supper (For I'm not Coming Home)   Spina 1947
Please Don't Say No   Fain 1945; Freed, Ralph 1945
Please Don't Take Away the Girls   Bryan 1919; Schwartz, Jean 1919
Please Don't Take My Lovin' Man Away   Brown, Lew 1912
Please Don't Talk About Me when I'm Gone   Clare 1927; Stept 1930
Please Don't Talk about My Man   Razaf 1933
Please Don't Touch   Merrill 1955
Please Don't Touch My Plums   Cahn 1976
Please Don't Turn My Picture to the Wall   Clare 1982
Please Forgive Me   Ellington 1938; Mills 1938
Please Go Find My Billy Boy   Norworth 1911; Smith, Harry B. 1911
Please Go Way and Let Me Sleep   Von Tilzer 1902
Please God   Coots 1951
Please Hello   Sondheim 1976
Please Help Us Find Our Way Home   Coots 1954
Please Keep Me Young in Your Heart   Howard, Joseph E. 1909
Please Let Go   Bacharach 1976; David, Hal 1976
Please Let Me Come Back to You   Berlin 1955
Please Let Me Tell You   Loesser 1956
Please Louise   DePaul 1943; Raye 1943
Please Love Me Too   Johnson, James P. 1959
Please Make Him Love Me   Bacharach 1963; David, Hal 1963
Please Make Me Be Good   Hart 1935; Rodgers 1935
Please Make Me Care   Brown, Nacio Herb 1934; Freed, Arthur 1934
Please Mama, Buy Me a Baby   Cobb 1903; Edwards 1903
Please Mr. President   Wrubel 1933
Please, My Nerves   Ager 1928; Yellen 1928
Please Pardon Us — We're in Love   Gordon 1937; Revel 1937
Please, Please Louise   Davis 1924; Silver 1924
Please, Please Signore   Sherman 1960
Please Put Out the Light   Evans 1948; Livingston, Jay 1948
Please Send My Daddy Back Home   Duke 1936; Gershwin, Ira 1936
(Don't Go) Please Stay   Bacharach 1961
Please Take Back Your Introduction   Caesar 1956
Please Take Me   Waller 1924
Please Take Me Out of Jail   Waller 1928

Please Take My Heart   Razaf 1935
Please, Teacher   Coots 1925
Please Tell Me   Styne 1927
Please Tell Me Now   Ruby 1954
Please Tell Me what They Mean   Smith, Harry B. 1908
Please Tell Me When   Brown, Nacio Herb 1954
(We Are the Girls of the Chorus) Please Tell Me Who Looks Good to You   Ager 1922; Yellen 1922
Please Tell Me Why   Waller 1924
Please Think of Me   Davis 1942
Please Wait for Me   Sigman 1955
Please Won't You Leave My Girl Alone   Loesser 1942, 1944; McHugh 1942, 1944
Pleasure Him   Drake 1968; Friend 1963
Pleasure of His Company, The   Cahn 1961
Pleasure of Your Company   Mercer 1974
Pleasure Seekers, The   Van Heusen 1964
Pleasure Seekers Bossa Nova, The   Cahn 1964; Van Heusen 1964
Pleasure Was All Mine, The   Mills 1935
Pleasure Was Mine, The   Van Heusen 1934
Pleasure's About to Be Mine, The   Leigh 1965
Pleasures and Palaces   Loesser 1965
Pledge of Allegiance to the Flag   Caesar 1955
Plenty Bambini   Loesser 1956
Plenty of Sunshine   Brown, Lew 1927; DeSylva 1927; Henderson 1927
Plink Plank Plunk   Evans 1962; Livingston, Jay 1962
Ploddin' Along   Robison 1928
Plot, The   Buck 1924
Plot Again, The   Cohan 1923
Plow Boy   Brennan 1935; Snyder 1935
Plowboy Wants to Go Home, A   David, Mack 1950; Livingston, Jerry 1950
Plum Pudding   Cahn 1959; Van Heusen 1959
Plumbing   Porter 1933
Plundering of the Town (inst.), The   Van Heusen 1953
Plunk! Plunk! Plunk! On Your Little Guitar   Brown, A. Seymour 1912
Plymouth Farewell Song (Alma Mater)   Gordon 1938; Revel 1938
Plymouth Rock   David, Mack 1940; Drake 1946; Gordon 1938; Revel 1938
Plymouth Rock Rock!   Lawrence 1971
Po Ling Ming Toy Chinese Love Story   Friml 1953
Po Po Pocohantas   Brooks 1960
Po' Tired Chillun   Robison 1932
Pocahontas   Bryan 1905
(I've Got a) Pocketful of Dreams   Rome 1950
Pocketful of Miracles   Cahn 1961; Van Heusen 1961
Poco a Poco   Fain 1946; Freed, Ralph 1946
Poco Loco   De Lange 1944; Stept 1944
Poco Loco in the Coco   Hoffman 1950
Pocohantas   Edwards 1905
Poem, The   Livingston, Jerry 1963
Poem of Love (inst.)   Johnson, James P. 1948
Poem of Mine   Parish 1930
Poem Set to Music, A   Gordon 1942; Warren 1942
Poems   Sondheim 1976
Poetry of Motion, The   DeSylva 1925; Gershwin, George 1925; Gershwin, Ira 1925, 1949; Warren 1949
Poi   DePaul 1941; Raye 1941
Poison Ivories   Akst 1950
Poison Ivy   Whiting 1926
Poison Kiss of That Spaniard   Dubin 1929

Poisoning Peter's Medicine   Leigh 1954

Poker   Porter 1911

Poker Game   Romberg 1927; Smith, Harry B. 1927

Poker Love (Card Duet)   Kern 1906

Poker-Polka, The   Heyman 1950; Young, Victor 1950

Pokey Little Puppy   Friend 1950

Pola Espagnole (inst.)   Coots 1946

Polar Bear Strut, The   Schwartz, Arthur 1926

Polaris (North Star) (inst.)   Revel 1955

Pole Cat Polka   Friend 1949

Police, The   Caesar 1925; Youmans 1925

Police Line Up (Grand Finale in Police Station)   Loesser
   1937

Police Number   Robin 1932

Police of New York   Berlin 1931

Policeman's Ball, The   Berlin 1949

Policeman's Lot Is a Happy One, A   Atteridge 1912

Policeman's Whistle, A   Cahn 1966; Van Heusen 1966

Policemen's Hymn   Merrill 1971; Styne 1971

Policeology   Herbert 1919

Polish Up Your Funny Bone   Hanley 1930

Polite Rhumba from Havana   Loesser 1955

Politely   Willson 1953

Political Lady   Rome 1948

Political Satire   Washington 1943

Political Satire March   Washington 1946

Politics   Harburg 1961; Johnson, J. Rosamond 1946; Mercer
   1949

Polka   Friml 1934; Herbert 1895; Romberg 1948; Smith,
   Harry B. 1895

Polka Dot Polka, The   Robin 1943; Warren 1943

Polka Dot Stomp   Sissle 1934

Polka Dots and Moonbeams   Burke 1939; Van Heusen 1939

Polka Is Good Fun, The   Smith, Harry B. 1911

Polka Me   Leigh 1958

Polka Tina   Rainger 1937; Robin 1937

Polla   Herbert 1911; Smith, Harry B. 1911

Polly   Caesar 1929

Polly Believed in Preparedness   Kern 1917

Polly of Hollywood   DeSylva 1925; Hanley 1925

Polly Pigtails   David, Mack 1947; Hoffman 1947; Livingston,
   Jerry 1947

Polly Polite   Caesar 1950

Polly, Pretty Polly (Polly with a Past)   Berlin 1917; Cohan
   1917

Polly Wants a Cracker   Burke 1933; Smith, Harry B. 1900;
   Spina 1933

Polly Wolly Doodle   Johnson, Howard 1939

Polly-olly-o   Dixon 1923; Henderson 1923; Rose 1923

Polly's Entrance   Gordon 1956; Myrow 1956

Polly's Song   Weill 1954

Pollywogg Wiggle   Bryan 1910; Fisher 1910

Polly-Wolly-Doodle   Clare 1935; DeSylva 1935

Polo Rag   Atteridge 1915; Romberg 1915

Pom Pidi Pom   Hoffman 1954

Pom Tiddley Om Pom   Coslow 1934

Pomegranate   Ellington 1957

Pompadour   Caesar 1933; Romberg 1933

Pompanola   Brown, Lew 1928; DeSylva 1928; Henderson
   1928

Pompeii Club (inst.), The   Coleman 1968

Pomponette   Gilbert 1937

Pompous Circumstance   Spina 1977

Poncho and Pepita   Romberg 1916

Poncho de Panther from Brazil   Hammerstein 1943

Pony Ballet (inst.)   Schwartz, Jean 1903

Pony Galop   Jerome 1906; Schwartz, Jean 1906

Pony on the Merry-Go-Round, The   Coots 1953

Poochinella's Band   Coots 1946

Poodle Cut   DePaul 1958; Raye 1958

Poodle Walk, The   Silver 1956, 1958

Pool Hall Blues   Brooks 1953

Pools, The   Mercer 1974

Poo-Poo   Clare Date Unknown; Coslow Date Unknown

Poor Andre   Blane 1954; Myrow 1954

Poor Apache, The   Hart 1932; Rodgers 1932

Poor Archie (inst.)   Blake 1960

Poor As a Church Mouse   Dietz 1944; Duke 1944

Poor Baby   Sondheim 1970

Poor Ballerina   Coots 1940; Egan 1940

Poor Blind Men   Akst 1930; Clarke 1930

Poor but Honest   Edwards 1930

Poor Butterfings   Howard, Bart 1938

Poor Cinderella   Robin 1927

Poor Cleopatra   Strouse 1999

Poor Everybody Else   Coleman 1966; Fields 1966

Poor Fellow   Oakland 1934

Poor Fish   Hart 1920; Rodgers 1920

Poor Flo   Hanley 1921

Poor Girl   Young, Joe 1934

Poor J'en-Ai-Marre   Atteridge 1922

Poor Jimmy Green (inst.)   Blake 1969

Poor Joe   Berlin 1962; Hammerstein 1947; Rodgers 1947

Poor Katie Red (inst.)   Blake 1960

Poor Kid   Gilbert 1931

Poor Lenore   Drake 1945

Poor Little Butterfly Is a Fly Gal Now   Lewis 1919; Young,
   Joe 1919

Poor Little Cinderella   Berlin 1917

Poor Little Doll   Pollack 1956

Poor Little Doll from Japan   Johnston 1926; Turk 1917, 1926

Poor Little Fly on the Wall   Fisher 1942

Poor Little Foolish Man   Jerome 1907; Schwartz, Jean 1907

Poor Little G String   Ahlert 1930; Turk 1930

Poor Little Hollywood Star   Coleman 1962; Leigh 1962

Poor Little Marie   Caesar 1926; Hanley 1926

Poor Little Mary Dugan   Bryan 1930; Edwards 1930

Poor Little Me   Buck 1918; Davis 1922; Gordon 1936; Revel
   1936, 1945

Poor Little Me - I'm on KP (Kitchen Police)   Berlin 1918

Poor Little Model   Hart 1921; Rodgers 1921

Poor Little Mother of France   Johnson, Howard 1927

Poor Little Orphans (Sixteen of 'Em)   Eliscu 1929; Rose
   1929; Youmans 1929

Poor Little Person   Merrill 1967

Poor Little Rhode Island   Cahn 1944; Styne 1944

Poor Little Rich Girl, The   Brown, Lew 1913

Poor Little Rich Girl's Dog   Berlin 1917

Poor Little Rich Little Me   Hanley 1920

Poor Little Ritz Girl   Hart 1920; Rodgers 1920; Romberg
   1920

Poor Little Rose   Donaldson 1923; Kahn 1923

Poor Little, Shy Little, Demure Little Me   Gordon 1932;
   Revel 1932

Poor Little Side Street Girl   Robison 1954

Poor Little Tigger   Brooks 1960

Poor Little Wallflower   Johnson, Howard 1923

Poor Lizzie, What'll Become of You Now?   Silver 1928

Poor Lonesome Maiden   Brooks 1946

Poor Loulie Jean   Robison 1938

Poor Man's Polka   Brown, Lew 1969; Henderson 1969
Poor Marionette   Kahn 1931
Poor Michael! Poor Golo!   Gershwin, George 1932; Gershwin, Ira 1932
Poor Miriam   Mercer 1946
Poor Mister Chisholm   Mercer 1940
Poor Mouse (inst.)   Styne 1965
Poor Mouth Papa   Robison 1954
Poor Mrs. Peachum   Weill 1933
Poor Mrs. Tracy (The Mother of Dick)   Coots 1946
Poor Old Dad's in New York for the Summer   Williams 1909
Poor Old Florodora Girl   Hanley 1920
Poor Old Joe   Carmichael 1932
Poor Old World   Cohan 1923
Poor Papa He's Got Nothin' at All   Rose 1926; Woods 1926
Poor People   Livingston, Jerry 1934
Poor People of Paris, The   Lawrence 1956
Poor Pierrot   Harbach 1931; Kern 1931
Poor Prune   Kern 1917
Poor Punchinello   Lewis 1929; Pollack 1929; Young, Joe 1929
Poor Rich, The   Porter 1930
Poor Soul, The   Davis 1954
Poor Thing   Sondheim 1979
Poor Unlucky Me   Dixon 1929; Warren 1929
Poor Whippoorwill   Arlen 1942; Harburg 1942
Poor Willie   Mills 1952
Poor You   Arlen 1942; Harburg 1942; Lane 1942
Poor Young Millionaire   Porter 1920
Poorest Man in Town, The   Alter 1936; Mitchell 1936
Pop Corn Man   Jerome 1910; Schwartz, Jean 1910
Pop Goes the Bottle   Oakland 1937
Pop Goes the Bubble (And Soap Gets in My Eyes)   Koehler 1937; Lane 1937
Pop Goes Your Heart   Dixon 1934; Wrubel 1934
Pop Pom Pom-a-Diddle   Livingston, Jerry 1954
Pop Step Melody   Howard, Joseph E. 1907
Popcorn Machine Broke Down, The   Sherman 1960
Pop-Guns and Rifles   Caesar 1937
Popolena   Friend 1948
Poppa   Adams 1964; Strouse 1964
Poppa, Don't Preach To Me   Loesser 1947
Poppa Is Home   Styne 1970
Poppa Knows Best   Rodgers 1970
Poppa Pappadopolis   Silver 1955
Poppin' the Cork   Davis 1934; Hanley 1934
Poppin' the Corn   Styne 1940
Poppy   Coslow 1936
Poppy Blossom   Yellen 1919
Poppy Dreams   Howard, Joseph E. 1937
Poppy (inst.)   Von Tilzer 1914
Poppyland   DeSylva 1919; Gershwin, George 1919
Popsey Wopsey   Smith, Harry B. 1912; Smith, Robert B. 1912
Popular Girl, A   Smith, Harry B. 1910
Popular March   Cohan 1907
Popular Pauline   Herbert 1905
Popular Pests, The   Buck 1919
Popular Rag   Goetz 1915
Popular Song, The   Berlin 1962
Popularity   Atteridge 1924; Cohan 1906
Por Que   Freed, Arthur 1930; Woods 1930
Porcelain Maid   Berlin 1922
Pore Jud Is Daid   Hammerstein 1943; Rodgers 1943

Porgy (Blues for Porgy)   Fields 1928; McHugh 1928
Pork Chop Charlie   Merrill 1959
Porky the Porcupine   Cahn 1940
Port of Missing Men   Oakland 1950; Russell 1950
Portango (inst.)   Motzan 1923
Porter's Love Song to a Chambermaid, A   Johnson, James P. 1930; Razaf 1930
Portion of Caviar, A   Carroll 1925; Freed, Arthur 1925
Portland Fancy   Gordon 1950; Warren 1950
Portobello Road   Sherman 1971
Portobello Street Dance   Sherman 1971
Portofino   Bergman 1964; Fain 1964; Sigman 1961
Portrait, A   Young, Victor 1952
Portrait Parade, The   Harbach 1926; Kern 1926
Portraits (inst.)   Warren 1959
Portugee Fisherman (Ho Ho Bim Bahle Bahm), The   Merrill 1954
Posh!   Sherman 1968
Posin'   Cahn 1937
Position and Positioning   Sherman 1976
Positively Love You   Fields 1933; McHugh 1933
Positively No Dancing   Leigh 1954
Possession (inst.)   Revel 1949
Possibility's There, The   Burke 1955; Van Heusen 1955
Possibly, Possibly   Livingston, Jerry 1959
Post Card Beau, A   Goetz 1911
Posterity Is Just Around the Corner   Gershwin, George 1931; Gershwin, Ira 1931
Posterland   Atteridge 1917; Romberg 1917
Postillion, The   Smith, Harry B. 1911
Postman's March (Hurray for the Postman)   Gorney 1959
Postmark Vienna   David, Mack 1956
Post-Mortem   Parish 1965
Post-Office (I've Got to Be Kissed)   Adamson 1937; McHugh 1937
Posty and a Maid, A   Atteridge 1921; Pollack 1921; Schwartz, Jean 1921
Pot and Pan Parade, The   Mercer 1953
Pot Luck   Hoffman 1952
Pot, Pan and Skillet   Ellington 1941; Webster 1941
Potash and Perlmutter Ball, The   Cohan 1918
Potato, The   Buck 1917
Potatoes (inst.)   McHugh 1921
Pots, The   Hart 1934; Rodgers 1934
Pots and Pans   Schwartz, Jean 1911
Pottawatomie   Hart 1939; Rodgers 1939
Pound in Your Pocket, A   Adams 1957; Strouse 1957
Pound Your Table Polka   Drake 1941
Pour Faire le Tournedos   Romberg 1933
Pour Le Sport   Sondheim Date Unknown
Pour se Faire Adorer   Romberg 1933
Pour the Corn John   Mills 1954
Pour Vivre Aupres de Vous   Romberg 1933
Pouring Out My Heart   Razaf 1942
Pourquoi   Herbert 1909, 1911
Pousse Cafe   Smith, Harry B. 1919
Poverty Row or Luxury Lane   Edwards 1936; Johnson, Howard 1936
Pow! Bam! Zonk!   Adams 1966; Strouse 1966
Pow Wow, The   Leigh 1954
Powder, Lipstick and Rouge   Gordon 1934; Revel 1934
Powder My Back   Adams 1968; Dixon 1935; Strouse 1968; Wrubel 1935
Powder Puff   Coots 1926

Powder Your Nose   Atteridge 1924; Romberg 1924; Schwartz, Jean 1924

Power   Comden and Green 1982

Power of Love, The   Heyman 1954; Mercer 1964; Young, Victor 1954

Power of Prayer, The   Livingston, Jerry 1959

Power of the Human Eye, The   Herbert 1898; Smith, Harry B. 1898

Pow-Wow Papa   Heyman 1928

Pow-Wow Polka (inst.), The   Styne 1954

Practical Pete   Razaf 1950

Practice, The   Robin 1948; Styne 1948

Practice Makes Perfect   Willson 1953

Practising the Piano   Silver 1933; Wrubel 1933

Practising Up on You   Dietz 1930

Prairie Belle   Duke 1941

Prairie Fairy Tale, A   Stept 1940

Prairie Mary   Baer 1940, 1945

Prairie Rose   Dubin 1909; Mitchell 1937; Stept 1937

Prairie Serenade   Styne 1941

Prairieland Lullaby   Loesser 1941; Young, Victor 1941

Praise Him with Joyful Song   Willson 1980

Praise the Day   Kern 1928

Praise the Lord and Pass the Ammunition   Loesser 1942

Praise Ye   Robison 1952

Prancing Pickaninnies   Sterling 1899

Pray, And He Will Answer You   Washington 1965

Pray for Me   Cahn 1960

Pray for Me I'm in Love   Cahn 1972

Pray for Sunshine but Always Be Prepared for Rain   Lewis 1917; Young, Joe 1917

Pray Jezebel   David, Mack 1965; Livingston, Jerry 1965

Prayer, A   Blane 1955; Bryan 1953; Cahn 1970; Hart 1934; Rodgers 1934; Romberg 1948; Styne 1970

Prayer (Child of All Nations, Mother to All)   Caesar 1940

Prayer for Elaine, A   Russell 1958

Prayer for Mother and Dad, A   Razaf 1936

Prayer of a Nation, The   Davis 1944, 1951; Silver 1951

Prayer of Saint Francis of Assisi, A   Stept 1950

Prayer (Our Journey May Be Long)   Hammerstein 1932; Kern 1932

Prayers   Sondheim 1976

Prayers of Tears and Laughter   Hart 1930; Rodgers 1930

Prayin' in Rhythm   Stept 1935; Washington 1935

Preacher's Sermon, The   Loesser 1937

Precious   Egan 1926; Whiting 1926

Precious Jewels   Atteridge 1920

Precious Little Thing Called Love, A   Coots 1928

Precious Rosary   Razaf 1952

Precipevolissimevolmentge (That's Me Falling for You)   Willson 1956

Pregunta   Cahn 1956

Prehistoric Man   Comden and Green 1949

Preliminary Skirmish   Egan 1919; Whiting 1919

Prelude   Duke 1959; Herbert 1911, 1923; Lerner, Alan Jay 1976

Prelude Act Two (inst.)   Kern 1921

Prelude (inst.)   Kern 1923

Prelude to a Kiss   Ellington 1938; Mills 1938

Prelude to America (inst.)   Willson 1966

Prelude to Champagne and Orchids (inst.)   Kern 1935

Prelude to Live for Today   Herbert 1910

Prelude to Love   Friend 1961

Prelude to the Dawn (inst.)   Myrow 1948

Prelude to We're Out of the Red   Brown, Lew 1934; Gorney 1934

Preludium   Hammerstein 1959; Rodgers 1959

Premiere Danseuse (inst.)   Coots 1946

Prep School Widow, The   Porter 1914

Prep Step, The   Whiting 1929

Preparation, The   Lerner, Alan Jay 1969

Presents for Mrs. Rogers   Coleman 1991; Comden and Green 1991

Presents from Home   Bryan 1931; Hoffman 1931

Presents from the Past   Bacharach 1957; David, Hal 1957

President, The   Livingston, Jerry 1960

President Is Going to Be a Daddy, The   Gershwin, George 1952; Gershwin, Ira 1952

President Jefferson Sunday Luncheon Party March, The   Lerner, Alan Jay 1976

President's Birthday Ball, The   Berlin 1942

Presidents on Parade   Fisher 1933

Press Your Lips to Mine   Freed, Ralph 1934; Styne 1934

Pretending   Herbert 1909; Lawrence 1930

Prettier Than a Picture   Revel 1961

Prettiest Girl in Town, The   David, Hal 1958

Pretty Ankle   Atteridge 1924; Romberg 1924; Schwartz, Jean 1924

Pretty As a Picture   Arlen 1944; Harburg 1944; Herbert 1913; Smith, Robert B. 1913

Pretty Baby   Kahn 1916; Schwartz, Jean 1919

Pretty Betsy Brown   Smith, Harry B. 1901

Pretty Birdie   Berlin 1917

Pretty City Girl   Harbach 1923

Pretty Dimples   Ager 1922; Yellen 1922

Pretty Face   Buck 1921; Donaldson 1921; Lewis 1921; Young, Joe 1921

Pretty Girl   Willson 1969

Pretty Girl Is Like a Melody, A   Berlin 1919

Pretty Gypsy   Hammerstein 1930; Romberg 1930

Pretty Isabella and Her Umbrella   Herbert 1897; Smith, Harry B. 1897

Pretty Lady   Dubin 1933; Sondheim 1976; Warren 1933

Pretty Lips   Donaldson 1926

Pretty Lips of Velvet   Friml 1917

Pretty Little Bom Bom from Bombay   Johnson, Howard 1927

Pretty Little Girl in the Yellow Dress   Washington 1961

Pretty Little Girl Inside, The   Jerome 1910; Schwartz, Jean 1910

Pretty Little Hindoo   Bryan 1926

Pretty Little Lady   Hart 1927; Rodgers 1927

Pretty Little Maid of Old Madrid   Coots 1929

Pretty Little Mayflower Girl   Atteridge 1916; Hanley 1916

Pretty Little Missus Bell   Porter 1944

Pretty Little Petticoat   Lawrence 1940

Pretty Little Picture   Sondheim 1962

Pretty Little Stranger   Robin 1927

Pretty Little Thing   Akst 1923; Davis 1923; Dubin 1927; Rose 1927

Pretty Little Words   Harburg 1932

Pretty Mandolin (Tic a Tic a Tic)   Evans 1954; Livingston, Jay 1954

Pretty Mary Ann McCann   Bryan 1943

Pretty Mathilda   Johnston 1948

Pretty Ming Toy   Romberg 1920

Pretty Moon   Adamson 1954; Warren 1954

Pretty Night (The Humming Waltz)   Hoffman 1956

Pretty One (Finale)   Herbert 1913; Smith, Robert B. 1913

Pretty Please   Donaldson 1940; Mercer 1940; Von Tilzer 1916
Pretty Polly   Romberg 1922
Pretty Puppy   Conrad 1925
Pretty Soft for Me   Kahn 1909
Pretty Soft for You   Ellington 1924
Pretty Thing   Merrill 1967, 1990
Pretty Things   Friml 1924; Hammerstein 1924; Harbach 1924
Pretty to Walk With   Arlen 1957; Harburg 1957
Pretty Up, Pretty Up, Pretty Baby   Bryan 1919
Pretty Woman   Ellington 1946
Pretty Women   Sondheim 1979
Pretty World   Bergman 1969
Pretty Your Face   Merrill 1951
Prettybelle   Merrill 1971; Styne 1971
Pretzel Man, The   Myrow 1939
Pretzels   Turk 1933
Prevalent Condition of the Mind, The   Romberg 1921
Priam Faril   Harburg 1967; Styne 1967
Pride of the Mountainside   Fields 1933; McHugh 1933
Prima Donnas, The   Goetz 1912
Prima Vera (inst.)   Warren 1977
Primavera   Russell 1956, 1957
Primitive (inst.)   Bloom 1931
Primitive Island   Davis 1960
Primitive Prima Donna   Arlen 1934; Koehler 1934
Primrose Way, The   Atteridge 1915, 1920
Prince and the Princess Waltz, The   Washington 1956
Prince Charming   Dubin 1943; Hammerstein 1922; Heyman 1934; Romberg 1927; Smith, Harry B. 1930
Prince Is Giving a Ball, The   Hammerstein 1957; Rodgers 1957
Prince of Bohemia   Goetz 1910
Prince of Grand Street, The   Merrill 1978
Prince of Humbug, The   Coleman 1980
Prince of Peace, The   Russell 1951, 1954
Prince of Wales   Atteridge 1922
Princely Scheme (Hook's Tango), A   Leigh 1954
Prince's Farewell (Goodbye), The   Coleman 1962; Leigh 1962
Princess for the Prince, A   Strouse 1975
Princess of Far-Away   Herbert 1912
Princess of My Dreams, The   Buck 1921; Herbert 1921
Princess of Pure Delight, The   Gershwin, Ira 1940; Weill 1940
Princess of the Willow Tree   Rodgers 1920
Princess Procession   Spina 1957
Princess Waltz (Once Upon a Time), The (inst.)   Warren 1960
Principle of Love, The   Robison 1956
Printemps   Gordon 1935; Revel 1935
Printemps A la Rumba   Gordon 1936; Revel 1936
Printer's Lament   Styne 1941
Pripoz Diva Se   Adams 1962; Strouse 1962
Priscilla   Hart 1921; Rodgers 1921
Prison College Song   Hanley 1931
Prison Glide   Gorney 1925
Prisoner of Love   Razaf 1929; Robin 1931; Waller 1929
Prisoner of the Stocks, The   Drake 1954
Prisoner's Barcarolle, The   Spina 1959
Prisoner's Up to Date   Clarke 1924; Johnston 1924; Meyer 1924; Turk 1924
(Love Is a) Private Affair, A   Evans 1959
Private Buckaroo   Wrubel 1942
Private Confidential Secretaries   Gordon 1932; Revel 1932

Private Eye   Oakland 1960
Private Jones of the U.S.A.   Gordon 1959; Revel 1943; Webster 1943
Private Line to Heaven   Robison 1967
Private Mike M'Gee   Cobb 1918; Edwards 1918
Private Miss Jones   Harburg 1943
Private Property   Brown, Lew 1915; Silver 1957
Private Schwartz   Merrill 1964; Styne 1964
Prize Fighters' Number   Edwards 1929; Johnson, Howard 1929
Prize of Gold   Washington 1954
Prize Song   Fisher 1927
Prize Waltz, The   Hoffman 1934
Problem Child   Leigh 1955
Processional   Friml 1934
Producers   DeSylva 1920; Kern 1920
Producer's Office   Lawrence 1957
Production Lines Are Battle Lines   Caesar 1943
Professor Cupid   Herbert 1914; Smith, Robert B. 1914
Professor, Play Those Blues   Magidson 1952
Professor, Professor   Cahn 1959; DePaul 1959
Professors   Bryan 1925
Profezzor, The   Fields 1952; Schwartz, Arthur 1952
Profile in Courage, A   Webster 1965
Profit and the Loss, The   Gorney 1961
Progress   Adams 1983; Lerner, Alan Jay 1948; Weill 1948
Progress Is the Root of All Evil   DePaul 1956; Mercer 1956
Progress Report   Leigh 1973
Prohibition   Berlin 1919
Prohibition Blues   Howard, Joseph E. 1918; Smith, Harry B. 1918
Prologue   Atteridge 1923; Comden and Green 1982; David, Mack 1965; Dietz 1936; Fields 1933; Johnson, James P. 1938; Livingston, Jerry 1965; McHugh 1933; Mercer 1964; Porter 1950; Romberg 1923; Schwartz, Arthur 1936; Schwartz, Jean 1923; Strouse 1977; Weill 1936
Prologue and Interlude   Oakland 1953
Prologue March   Sondheim 1968
Prologue to Vaudeville Act   Gordon 1947; Myrow 1947
Prom Waltz, The   Rainger 1936, 1938; Robin 1936, 1938
Promenade   Burke 1946; Evans 1959; Livingston, Jay 1959; Loewe 1938; Parish 1950; Van Heusen 1946
Promenade (Street Cries)   Arlen 1959; Mercer 1959
Promenade the Esplanade   Bryan 1927; Schwartz, Jean 1927
Promenade Walk, The   Coots 1925
Promise   Hanley 1939; Weill 1937
Promise Her Anything   Bacharach 1966; David, Hal 1965
Promise in Your Eyes, The   DeSylva 1926; Hanley 1926
Promise Me a Rose (A Slight Detail)   Merrill 1959
Promise Me Not to Love Me   Arlen 1976; Harburg 1976
Promise Me You'll Be Lonely   David, Hal 1954
Promise with a Kiss   Robin 1936
Promise You'll Remember Me (For I'll Remember You)   Brown, Nacio Herb 1931
Promise Your Kisses   Conrad 1926; Kahn 1926
Promised Land, The   Livingston, Jerry 1960
Promises   Freed, Ralph 1957; Hoffman 1945; Johnson, Howard 1924; Livingston, Jerry 1945
Promises, Promises   Bacharach 1968; David, Hal 1968
Propaganda   Loesser 1965; Mercer 1943
Proper Way to Kiss, The   Smith, Harry B. 1903
Propinquity   Webster 1950
Propos De Rien, A   Burke 1953; Van Heusen 1953
Proposal, The   Bergman 1957
Proposal Waltz, The   Livingston, Jerry 1936

Proposals   Williams 1910
Prosperity Wanda   Atteridge 1915
Pross-Tchai   Cahn 1938
Protect Me   Dietz 1948; Schwartz, Arthur 1948
Protest   Gershwin, George 1925; Hammerstein 1925; Harbach 1925
Protocoligorically Correct   Sherman 1976
Proud   Coots 1936; Davis 1936; Lerner, Alan Jay 1976
Prove It   Styne 1958
Providing   Bryan 1914
Prunella   Atteridge 1914; Carroll 1914
Prunella Mine   Buck 1914
Prunes   Friml 1918
Prunes, Prisms, Potatoes   Smith, Harry B. 1934
P's and Q's   Dietz 1950
P.S. Forty-Three   Burke 1938; Monaco 1938
P.S. I Got the Job   McHugh 1941; Mercer 1941
P.S. I Love You   Mercer 1934
P.S. Mr. Johnson Sends His Regards   Cohan 1899
Psychadelic Sally   Livingston, Jerry 1967
Psychiatry Song, The   Weill 1936
Psychoanalyst Me   Hammerstein 1931; Whiting 1931
Psychological Moment   Brennan 1929
Psychology   Harbach 1947; Johnson, James P. 1962; Kern 1947
P.T. Barnum   Romberg 1917
P.T. Boat Song (Steady As You Go), The   Hammerstein 1943; Rodgers 1943
Public Enemy No. 1   Rome 1937
Public Enemy Number One   Porter 1934
Public Is Always Right, The   Cahn 1960; Van Heusen 1960
Public Jitterbug No. 1   Cahn 1940
Public Melody Number One   Arlen 1937; Koehler 1937
Publicity   De Lange 1945, 1946; Myrow 1945, 1946
Puce and the Green, The   Gilbert 1932; Hanley 1932
Puddin' Head   Styne 1940
Puddin' Head Jones   Bryan 1933
Puddle Duck, The   Merrill 1958
Pudgy the Whistling Piggy   Drake 1950
Puerto Rico   Loesser 1942; McHugh 1942
Puff, Puff, Puff   Buck 1921
Puff-A-Puff   Gordon 1938; Revel 1938
Puffed Up Proud   Eliscu 1961
Puh-leeze Mister Brown   DePaul 1957
Pull a Rabbit Out of the Hat   Duke 1963
Pull the Cork Out of Erin and Let the River Shannon Flow   Fisher 1917
Pull the Trigger   Revel 1942
Pull Your String   Coslow 1924; Romberg 1924
Pull Yourself Together   Robin 1927
Pullman Porter and the Travelin' Man, The   Stept 1950
Pullman Porters' Parade   Berlin 1913
Pulse of My Heart   Brennan 1920
Pump Song, The   Lerner, Sammy 1926; Whiting 1926
Pumpernickel   Coslow 1950
Punch and Judy   Evans 1959, 1965; Livingston, Jay 1959; Livingston, Jerry 1955; Mancini 1959
Punch and Judy Love   Merrill 1954
Punch and Judy Man   Dixon 1931; Warren 1931; Young, Joe 1931
Punchbowl Glide, The   Herbert 1912
Punchinello   Herbert 1935; Kahn 1935
Punchinello (inst.)   Herbert 1916
Punxatawney Rose   David, Hal 1962
Puppchen   Kalmar 1934; Ruby 1934

Puppet Love Song   Whiting 1934
Puppets on Parade   Friml 1959
Puppets on the Strings of Love   Cahn 1935
Puppy Love   Oakland 1952; Raye 1952
Puppy Love Is Here to Stay   Sherman 1962
Pure and White As the Lotus   Herbert 1895; Smith, Harry B. 1895
Pure White Robe   Robison 1957
Purity Brigadiers, The   Mitchell 1921; Pollack 1921
Purple Cow, A   Webster 1953
Purple Hills, The   Washington 1957
Purple Hills (1), The   Young, Victor 1957
Purple Hills of Hawaii   Kahn 1939
Purple Moonlight   De Lange 1946
Purple Reef, The   Mancini 1958
Purple Rose   Duke 1952
Purple Sage in the Twilight   Styne 1941, 1944
Purpose in Life   Schwartz, Jean 1920
Purt' Nigh' but Not Plumb   Evans 1952; Livingston, Jay 1952
Push a Button in a Hutton   Gorney 1948
Push Around   Hart 1926; Rodgers 1926
Push de Button   Arlen 1957; Harburg 1957
Push Me Along in My Pushcart   Cohan 1901
Push the Clouds Out of Heaven   Snyder 1930
Pusha Pusha Baby Cart   Fisher 1920
Pussy and the Bow-Wow   Johnson, J. Rosamond 1904
Pussy Cat   Coleman 1964
Pussy Cat Agony Five   Russell 1941
Pussy Cat Love   Bryan 1934
Pussy Cats on Parde (inst.)   Bacharach 1965
Pussy Willow (inst.)   Monaco 1917
Pussy-Footin' Around   Rainger 1939; Robin 1939
Put - Put - Put (Your Arms Around Me)   Hoffman 1945; Livingston, Jerry 1945
Put a Bonnet with a Red Cross on It (And I'll Meet You Somewhere Over There)   Johnson, Howard 1917
Put a Four-Cent Stamp on My Heart   Drake 1954
Put a Little Bet Down for Me   Cohan 1907
Put a Little Letter in My Letter Box   Berlin 1917
Put a Little Rhythm in Every Little Thing You Do   Gordon 1934; Revel 1934
Put a Little Salt on the Bluebird's Tail Before It Flies Away   Hanley 1930
Put a Sack Over Their Heads   Porter 1944
Put a Tax on Love   Gilbert 1933; Silver 1932; Warren 1933
Put a Three Cent Stamp on Me and Send Me Back to Tennessee   David, Mack 1944
Put Away a Little Ray of Golden Sunshine for a Rainy Day   Ahlert 1924; Lewis 1924; Young, Joe 1924
Put Down an Empty Blues   Parish 1936
Put Down Your Glass (Pick Up Your Girl and Dance)   Gordon 1937; Revel 1937
Put 'Em Back   DePaul 1956; Mercer 1956
Put 'Em in a Box, Tie 'Em with a Ribbon and Throw 'Em in the Deep Blue Sea   Cahn 1948; Styne 1948
Put Him Away   Rodgers 1970
Put It in Reverse   Akst 1943; Davis 1943
Put It in the Bank   Brown, Lew 1927; DeSylva 1927
Put It On, Take It Off   Leslie 1914; Young, Joe 1914
Put It Over   Smith, Robert B. 1915
Put It There, Pal   Burke 1945; Van Heusen 1945
Put Me Among the Girls   Edwards 1907
Put Me in Your Heart   Friend 1959
Put Me to Sleep in Your Heart and Wake Up with Your Love   Lewis 1919; Young, Joe 1919

Put Me to Sleep with an Old Fashioned Melody, Wake Me Up with a Rag   Lewis 1915
Put Me to the Test   Gershwin, George 1937; Gershwin, Ira 1937, 1944; Kern 1944
Put Music in the Barn   Carmichael 1940; Mercer 1940
Put on a Happy Face   Adams 1960; Strouse 1960
Put on a Uniform   Dubin 1936; Warren 1936
Put on the Dog   Donaldson 1928
Put on the Ritz   Johnson, Howard 1924
Put on Your Glasses   Ahlert 1934; Leslie 1934
Put on Your Old Brown Bowler (Take Off Your High, High Hat)   Leslie 1927
Put on Your Old High Hat   Jerome 1912; Von Tilzer 1912
Put on Your Rubbers   Howard, Joseph E. 1964
Put on Your Sunday Face   Dixon 1929
Put That Down in Writing   Dubin 1938; Warren 1938
Put that Kiss Back Where You Found It   Sigman 1946
Put the Old Man Away   Robison 1951
Put the Swanee Up in Bottles, and Send It Up To Me   Bryan 1937; Caesar 1937
Put Your Arms Around Me   Harbach 1911; Schwartz, Jean 1911
Put Your Arms Around Me Honey   Lewis 1911
Put Your Best Foot Forward Little Girl   Herbert 1912
Put Your Hands in Your Pockets and Give, Give, Give   Kahn 1918
Put Your Head Upon My Shoulder   Bryan 1910
Put Your Heart in a Song   Coots 1936; Henderson 1934; Koehler 1934; Lewis 1936
Put Your Heart Into a Song   Webster 1938
Put Your Lovin' Arms Around Me Dearie   Buck 1914
Put Your Mind Right on It   Johnson, James P. 1929
Put Your Old Bandana On   Clarke 1924; Johnston 1924; Meyer 1924; Turk 1924
Put Your Rocks in a Box   Hoffman 1959
Put Your Shoulder to the Wheel (inst.)   Young, Victor 1942
Put Your Troubles in a Candy Box   Coots 1925
Put Your Trust in Me   Oakland 1974
Put Yourself in My Place, Baby   Carmichael 1947
Putney on the Thames   Harburg 1967; Styne 1967
Puttin' It On for Baby   Bloom 1930; Koehler 1930
Puttin' on Airs   Blane 1945, 1947; Warren 1945, 1947
Puttin' on the Dog   DePaul 1941; Raye 1941
Puttin' on the Ritz   Berlin 1929; Brown, Lew 1928; DeSylva 1928; Henderson 1928
Putting It Together   Sondheim 1984
Putting Our Lives Together   Lawrence 1971
Putty in Your Hands   Spina 1954
Puzzle, The   Spina 1966
Puzzlement, A   Hammerstein 1951; Rodgers 1951
P.X., The   Berlin 1963
Pygmalion Roses   Cohan 1914
Pyramid   Ellington 1938; Mills 1938

Q

Quack, Quack   Freed, Arthur 1925
Quadrille, The   Duke 1968; Porter 1953; Rome 1973
Quainty, Dainty Me   Kalmar 1938; Ruby 1938
Quaker Maids, The   Smith, Harry B. 1901
Quaker Talk   Harbach 1911
Quakertown Cadets, The   Cohan 1901
Quality   David, Hal 1948
Quand les Soldats Vont au Pas   Romberg 1933

Quando te Digo te Amo No Me Creas   Gorney 1931; Harburg 1931
Quans, The   Raye 1971
Quarrel for Three   Ellington 1946
Quarrelling Song (You're a Cad, You're a Bounder), The   Coslow 1955
Quarterback, The   Howard, Joseph E. 1905
Quartet   Sondheim 1979
Quartet Erotica (We're Not What We Used to Be)   Arlen 1934; Gershwin, Ira 1934; Harburg 1934
Que Chica   Burke 1941; Van Heusen 1941
Queen   Willson 1956
Queen and the Sailor, The   Willson 1969
Queen Elizabeth   Hart 1926; Rodgers 1926
Queen Is Always on Display, A   Duke Date Unknown
Queen Isabella   Gershwin, George 1920
Queen Mother's Crossover (inst.)   Duke 1963
Queen of Charcoal Alley   Sterling 1899
Queen of Manhattan Isle   Harbach 1910
Queen of Musical Comedy, The   Mitchell 1921
Queen of My Dreams   Smith, Harry B. 1908
Queen of My Heart   Friml 1928
Queen of New Orleans, The   Washington 1953
Queen of Terre Haute, The   Porter 1929
Queen of the Gas House Gang   Ager 1923; Yellen 1923
Queen of the Hollywood Islands, The   Loesser 1947
Queen of the Jungle   Adamson 1936; Donaldson 1936
Queen of the Opera, The   Duke 1941
Queen of the Ring   Herbert 1905; Smith, Harry B. 1905, 1908
Queen of the South Sea Isles   Gilbert 1915
Queen of the Yale Dramat   Porter 1911
Queen of Vanity Fair, The   Smith, Harry B. 1911; Smith, Robert B. 1911
Queen Was in the Parlor, The   Freed, Arthur 1931
Queenie   Conrad 1933
Queenie (My Own)   Berlin 1908
Queenie, the Quick Change Artist   Carmichael 1950; Mercer 1950
Queenie's Ballyhoo (C'mon Folks)   Hammerstein 1927; Kern 1927
Queens   Caesar 1925; Youmans 1925
Queen's Aria   Friml 1928
Queen's Mules, The   Friend 1931; Monaco 1931
Queens of Long Ago   Atteridge 1923; Schwartz, Jean 1923
Queens of Terpsichore   Porter 1912
Quelque-Chose   Porter 1928
Querida Mia (My Sweetheart)   Pollack 1935; Webster 1935
Querido   Styne 1940
Question Me an Answer   Bacharach 1973; David, Hal 1973
Question of Love, A   Bacharach 1965
Questions   Sherman 1986
Questions and Answers   Cahn 1975
Quiche (inst.)   Youmans 1933
Quick! Cupid Shoot that Arrow   Mills 1939
Quick Henry, the Flit!   Gordon 1932; Revel 1932
Quick Like a Bunny   Silver 1954, 1956
Quick Sands   Dubin 1943; Monaco 1943
Quicker than You Can Say Jack Robinson   David, Mack 1935; Meyer 1935
Quien Sabe   Bullock 1937; Spina 1937
Quierme Y Veras   Mercer 1954
Quiero   Revel 1929
Quiet Girl, A   Comden and Green 1953
Quiet Hill, The   Raye 1952; Spina 1952

Quiet Life, A   Burke 1961
Quiet Little Rendezvous   Coslow 1955
Quiet Night   Hart 1936; Rodgers 1936
Quiet Song (inst.), A   Kern 1956
Quiet Sunday in 1920, A   Smith, Harry B. 1908
Quiet Voice, A   Leigh 1955
Quiller Has the Brain   Smith, Harry B. 1900
Quillow Plants the Blue Men   Blane 1961
Quilting Song   Revel 1952
Quincannon, Frontier Scout   Cahn 1956
Quintet   Strouse 1993
Quit While You're Ahead   Merrill 1950
Quite a Nifty and Effective Detective Am I   DeSylva 1922;
    Herbert 1922
Quite a Party   DeSylva 1924; Gershwin, George 1924
Quite the Thing   Robin 1927; Youmans 1927
Quizas, Quizas, Quizas   Burke 1951
Quoth the Raven   Revel 1944; Webster 1944

R

R and H Robin Hood Jingle (Robin Hood Beer Song)   Baer
    1950
"R" Is for Ringo   Freed, Ralph 1964
Rabbit's Foot   Mercer 1964
Rabbit's Racing Song   Bergman 1983
Race   Arlen 1959; Mercer 1959
Race Horse and the Flea, The   Berlin 1945
Race Is Over, The   DeSylva 1925; Hanley 1925
Race Through the Desert (I Have Got to Get There in Seven
    Days Flat)   Sondheim 1968
Race Track Blues, The   Leslie 1920
Race Track Finale   Alter 1930; Johnson, Howard 1930
Rachel (inst.)   Revel 1948
Rachel Rubenstein's Rag   Lewis 1912; Meyer 1912
Racin' Form   Arlen 1946; Mercer 1946
Racing Form Lullaby   Merrill 1964; Styne 1964
Rack and Ruin   Young, Victor 1934
Racket Song, The   Von Tilzer 1929
Racketeer Rose   Fisher 1931
Rackety Koo   Friml 1914; Harbach 1914
Rackety Rax   Gilbert 1932; Hanley 1932
Radar Blues   Revel 1946
Radi-adi-o   Johnson, Howard 1923
Radiance   Atteridge 1922
Radiant Diamonds   Atteridge 1923; Romberg 1923
Radio Ball Room, The   Razaf 1939
Radio City Overture   Caesar 1932
Radio Dance (inst.)   Merrill 1990
Radio in Heaven so Mother Can Listen In   Fisher 1937
Radio Joe   Clare 1924; Conrad 1924; Rose 1924
Radio Lady of Mine   Coslow 1924
Radio Papa, Broadcastin' Mama   Razaf 1932; Waller 1932
Radio Voices   Romberg 1924
Radium Dance   Jerome 1904; Schwartz, Jean 1904
Raffles   Carmichael 1957; Dubin 1940; Duke 1940
Rag, The   Merrill 1993; Styne 1993
Rag, a Bone and a Hank of Hair, A   Razaf 1953
Rag de Paree   Lewis 1910
Rag Doll, The   Bryan 1920; Schwartz, Jean 1920
Rag Doll (inst.)   Brown, Nacio Herb 1928
Rag Lad of Bagdad, The   Romberg 1918
Rag Me Around   Goetz 1912
Rag Me that Mendlessohn March   Sondheim 1955
Rag Modern (inst.)   Blake 1969

Rag Offen the Bush   DePaul 1956; Mercer 1956
Rag Picker's Dance, The   Caesar 1925; Youmans 1925
Rag Pipe Bag Pipe Band, The   Goetz 1911
Rag Time Eyes   Clarke 1912; Schwartz, Jean 1912
Rag Time Quadrille (inst.)   Cohan 1908
Rag-a-Bye Baby (inst.)   Motzan 1918
Raga-Daga-Day   David, Mack 1950; Hoffman 1950;
    Livingston, Jerry 1950
Ragadora   Yellen 1920
Ragamuffin Jane   Burke 1933; Spina 1933
Ragamuffin Rag (inst.)   Drake 1957
Raggedy Ann   Hanley 1920; Kern 1923
Raggedy Ann and Raggedy Andy   Bergman 1968
Raggedy Rag   Buck 1921
Ragging the Apache   Atteridge 1916; Motzan 1916; Romberg
    1916
Ragging the Baby to Sleep   Gilbert 1912
Ragging the Nursery Rhymes   Atteridge 1913
Ragging the Old Vienna Roll   Schwartz, Jean 1911
Ragging the Traumerei   Gershwin, George 1913
Raggity Man   Williams 1911
Rag-Lad of Bagdad, The   Atteridge 1918
Rags   Fain 1926; Kahal 1926; Silver 1926; Strouse 1986
Rags and Tatters   Hart 1930; Rodgers 1930
Rags Is Royal Raiments   Friml 1923
Rag-Tag Musketeers   Motzan 1930
Ragtime Alphabet   Goetz 1917
Ragtime Arabian Nights   Atteridge 1914
Ragtime Argument   Atteridge 1915; Romberg 1915
Rag-Time Banjo Serenade, The   Goetz 1907
Ragtime Barn Dance   Goetz 1910
Ragtime Boxing Match   Atteridge 1912
Ragtime Calisthenics   Atteridge 1916; Motzan 1916;
    Romberg 1916
Ragtime Carnival   Atteridge 1915; Romberg 1915
Ragtime College Girl, The   Harbach 1911; Lewis 1911;
    Schwartz, Jean 1911
Ragtime Cowboy Joe   Clarke 1912
Ragtime Dinner Order, The   Atteridge 1915; Carroll 1915;
    Romberg 1915
Ragtime Dream, The   Brown, Lew 1913, 1914
Ragtime Engineer, The   Lewis 1912
Ragtime Express, The   Atteridge 1913; Schwartz, Jean 1913
Ragtime Eyes   Schwartz, Jean 1912
Ragtime Fight   Romberg 1916
Ragtime Geography   Conrad Date Unknown
Ragtime Goblin Man, The   Sterling 1911; Von Tilzer 1911
Ragtime Honeymoon   Jerome 1913; Schwartz, Jean 1913
Ragtime Jockey Man   Berlin 1912
Ragtime Land   Goetz 1909
Ragtime Love   Atteridge Date Unknown
Ragtime Mocking Bird   Berlin 1912
Ragtime Piano Tricks (inst.)   Blake 1961
Ragtime Pipes of Pan   Atteridge 1915; Porter 1922; Romberg
    1915
Ragtime Polish Dance (inst.)   Blake 1960
Ragtime Rag (inst.)   Blake 1959
Ragtime Razor Brigade   Berlin 1918
Ragtime Restaurant, The   Kern 1912
Ragtime Sextette   Berlin 1912
Ragtime Soldier Man   Berlin 1912
Ragtime Terpsichore   Herbert 1920
Ragtime Violin, The   Berlin 1911
Ragtime Volunteers Are Off to War, The   Hanley 1917
Ragtime Wagon of Love, The   Jerome 1912; Von Tilzer 1912

Ragtime Wedding Bells   Lewis 1913; Meyer 1913
Ragtime Yodeling Man, The   Goetz 1913
Ragueneau's Cafe   Herbert 1899; Smith, Harry B. 1899
Rah Rah Cholly   Snyder 1925
Rah, Rah, Rah   Caesar 1932; Magidson 1932; Stept 1932
Railroad Man's Goodbye Sometimes Ain't Gone, A   Razaf 1924
Railroad Number   Smith, Harry B. 1908
Railroad Soliloquy (inst.)   Revel 1960
Railroad Song   Kern 1946; Robin 1946
Railroad that Ran through Our Land, The   Loesser 1937
Railroad Woman, A   Cahn Date Unknown; Duke Date Unknown
Rain   Fisher 1924
Rain Drops   Bryan 1928
Rain Falls Anywhere It Wants To   Bergman 1971
Rain Falls on Ev'rybody, The   Alter 1958
Rain Finale   Caesar 1936
Rain from the Skies   Bacharach 1962; David, Hal 1962
Rain in My Heart   Alter 1934; Caesar 1953; Yellen 1953
Rain in Spain, The   Lerner, Alan Jay 1956; Loewe 1956
Rain on the Pane   Woods 1938
Rain on the Range   Mills 1935
Rain on the Roof   Sondheim 1971
Rain on the Sea   Caesar 1943; Lerner, Sammy 1943
Rain or Shine   Ager 1928, 1930; Yellen 1928
Rain or Shine Pal of Mine   Leslie 1925
Rain Rain Go Away   David, Mack 1932; Heyman 1932
Rain Song   Fisher 1934
Rainbow   Bryan 1908; Conrad 1929; Mitchell 1929
Rainbow Ball   Bryan 1919; Schwartz, Jean 1919
Rainbow Blues   Brown, Lew 1922; Clare 1922; Pollack 1922
Rainbow Bridge   Russell 1941
Rainbow Filled with Music, A   Mills 1935
Rainbow from the U.S.A., A   Jerome 1918
Rainbow Gold   Smith, Harry B. 1923
Rainbow in the Flame of an Old Log Fire   Monaco 1934; Young, Joe 1934
Rainbow in the Night   Styne 1942
Rainbow Island   Coots 1944
Rainbow Land   Razaf 1942
Rainbow Man   Hanley 1929
Rainbow of Girls   Berlin 1927
Rainbow of My Dreams   Brown, Nacio Herb Date Unknown; Freed, Arthur Date Unknown
Rainbow on the River   Alter 1936; Webster 1936
Rainbow on the Way   Davis 1929
Rainbow Over Chicago   Howard, Joseph E. 1947
Rainbow People   Heyman 1968
Rainbow Rhapsody   Magidson 1930; Washington 1930
Rainbow Rider, The   Cahn 1969; Van Heusen 1969
Rainbow Round the Moon   Donaldson 1938; Rose 1938
Rainbow Round the World   Caesar 1955
Rainbow Trail, The   Coots 1947
Rainbow Valley   Leslie 1939; Pollack 1942
Rainbow Where Have You Been   Leslie 1927; Meyer 1927
Rainbows   Sondheim Date Unknown
Rainbow's End   Drake 1946; Heyman 1928; Martin 1951; Styne 1985
Raindrops   Brown, Lew 1939
Raindrops (inst.)   Blake 1946
Raindrops Keep Falling on My Head   Bacharach 1969; David, Hal 1969
Raindrops on a Drum   Friml 1947; Heyman 1947
Rain-Flower   Robin 1930

Raining   Kern 1905
Rainmaker, The   David, Hal 1956
Rains Came, The   Gordon 1939
Raintree Country   Webster 1958
Rainy Afternoon, A   Lane Date Unknown; Spina 1976
Rainy Afternoon Girls   Gershwin, George 1924; Gershwin, Ira 1924
Rainy Afternoons   Conrad 1920
Rainy Day, A   Dietz 1932; Goetz 1913; Schwartz, Arthur 1932; Young, Victor 1934
Rainy Day (inst.), The   Young, Victor 1955
Rainy Day Rose   Dixon 1927; Woods 1927
Rainy Day Sue   Berlin 1922; Lewis 1921; Young, Joe 1921
Rainy Days   Johnson, Howard 1921; Schwartz, Jean 1912
Rainy Night   Mercer 1957
Rainy Night in Rio, A   Robin 1946; Schwartz, Arthur 1946
Rainy Nights   Ellington 1973
Raise a Rukus Tonight   Mercer 1962
(Shah!) Raise the Dust!   Eliscu 1929
Raisin' the Racket   Adamson 1930; Gordon 1930; Revel 1930
Raisin' the Rent   Arlen 1933; Koehler 1933
Raisin' the Roof   Caesar 1923; Conrad 1923; Fields 1929; McHugh 1929
Rajah of Broadway, The   Smith, Harry B. 1908
Rajah's Glide, The   Jerome 1905; Schwartz, Jean 1905
Rakin' in the Hay   Baer 1925
Rakish Young Man with the Whiskers, The   Arlen 1944; Harburg 1944
Rally Around   Schwartz, Jean 1918
Rally 'Round Me   Youmans 1930
Ramble On   Leslie 1921; Monaco 1921
Rambler Rose   Smith, Harry B. 1917
Ramblin' Ever, Ramblin' Heart   Coots 1957
Ramblin' Papa Blues   Waller 1924
Rambling Sam   Schwartz, Jean 1905; Williams 1905
Ramona   Gilbert 1928
Rampage   David, Mack 1963
Rampart Street Blues   Razaf 1936
Rams Are Rollin', The   Evans 1974; Livingston, Jay 1974; Mancini 1974
Ram's Song   Cahn 1951; Styne 1951
Ramshackle Rag (inst.)   Snyder 1911
Ramshackle Shack, The   Drake 1952
Ran Tin Tin   Atteridge 1923; Schwartz, Jean 1923
Ranch House Saturday Night (inst.)   Bloom 1946
Ranch House Square Dance   Drake 1953
Ranch Up in Heaven   Fisher 1942
Rancho Pillow   Wrubel 1942
Rancho Santa Fe   Donaldson 1940; Kahn 1940
Randi's Rag (inst.)   Blake 1974
Ranger's Song, The   Romberg 1927; Smith, Harry B. 1927
Rap, Rap, Rap, On Your Minstrel Bones   Brown, Lew 1912
Rap Tap on Wood   Porter 1936
Rape and Resurrection   Merrill 1971; Styne 1971
Rap-Tap-a-Tap   Ager 1920; Yellen 1920
Rap-Up, The   Coleman 1988
Rare Wines   Comden and Green 1982
Rarin' to Go   Baer 1930; Edwards 1930; Gilbert 1930
Rascal with the Twinkle in His Eye, The   Stept 1946
Rasmussin's Law   Willson 1957
R-a-s-p-b-e-r-r-y — The New Letter Song   Friend 1928
Rasputin (That Highfalutin' Lovin' Man)   Wrubel 1933
Rather   Hoffman 1953
Rather Blustery Day, A   Sherman 1968

Rather Than See You Once in a While   Clarke 1920; Donaldson 1920

Rathskeller Trio, The   Atteridge 1915; Carroll 1915; Romberg 1915

Rats and Mice and Fish   Comden and Green 1982

Rat-Tat-Tat-Tat   Merrill 1964; Styne 1964

Rattle Rattle   Bryan 1920; Schwartz, Jean 1920

Rattling Along   Freed, Arthur 1930

Raus Mit der Kaiser   Sterling 1917

Ravenous Rooster, The   Herbert 1906

Raving Beauty, A   Blane 1960; Martin 1960, 1963

Rawhide   Russell 1965; Washington 1958

Ray Bolger Specialty Number   Kahn 1937; Romberg 1937

Raz-Ma-Taz   Atteridge 1918

Razz-Berries   Mitchell 1919

Razzle Dazzle   Cahn 1964; Merrill 1952; Van Heusen 1964

R.C.A. Theme   Young, Victor 1956

Reach for a Sweetie   Whiting 1929

Reach for Me   Howard, Bart 1984

Reach for the Stars   Evans 1953; Livingston, Jay 1953

Reach for Tomorrow   McHugh 1960; Washington 1960

Reach Out for a Rainbow   Conrad 1929, 1930; Meyer 1930; Mitchell 1929, 1930

Reach Out for Me   Bacharach 1963; David, Hal 1963

Reaching for Someone and Not Finding Anyone There   Donaldson 1929; Leslie 1929

Reaching for the Cotton Moon   Stept 1934

Reaching for the Moon   Berlin 1931; Davis 1926; Freed, Arthur 1930; Kalmar 1929; Ruby 1929

Read All About It   Rome 1948

Read Between the Lines   Friml 1922

Read the Answers in the Stars   Bryan 1903

Read the Label on the Bottle (Don't Take My Word for It Neighbor) (Get Away Boys You Bother Me)   Willson 1960

Read the Papers Every Day   Herbert 1908; Smith, Harry B. 1908

Read What the Papers Say   Brown, Lew 1925; DeSylva 1925; Henderson 1925

Reader's Digest, The   Comden and Green 1943

Readin' for a Weddin'   Bullock 1950

Readin' Rittin' and Rhythm   Blake 1936

Reading   Strouse 1980

Reading the News   Arlen 1959; Mercer 1959

Reading, Writing and a Little Bit of Rhythm   Dubin 1939; McHugh 1939

Ready Cash   Fain 1955

Ready for Action   Drake 1952

Ready for the River   Kahn 1928

Ready for the Woods   Sondheim 1987

Ready for You   Strouse 1975

Ready Made Sandwich, The   Atteridge 1917; Motzan 1917; Romberg 1917

Ready-Aim-Kiss   Pollack 1942

Real American Folk Song (Is a Rag), The   Gershwin, George 1918; Gershwin, Ira 1918

Real Girl   Berlin 1911

Real Girls, The   Cohan 1901

Real Live Girl   Coleman 1962; Leigh 1962

Real Love   Raye 1958

Real McCoys, The   Ruby 1958

Real Me, The   Adams 1962; Strouse 1962

Real Nice Clambake, A   Hammerstein 1945; Rodgers 1945

Real Thing, The   Hoffman 1959

Real True Pal, A   Loesser 1935

Reality   Herbert 1946; Lerner, Alan Jay 1948; Weill 1948

Really and Truly   Schwartz, Jean 1928

Really O'Reilly   Robison 1946

Really, Would You Believe It?   Caesar 1925; Youmans 1925

Reap the Harvest   Arlen 1959; Mercer 1959

Reap the Wild Wind   Pollack 1941; Washington 1941

Reason I Call You Sweetheart   David, Mack 1936

Reason I Love You, Because I Do, The   Smith, Harry B. 1925; Snyder 1924

Reba   Fisher 1926; Schwartz, Jean 1926

Rebecca   Oakland 1970; Williams 1907

Rebecca of Sunnybrook Farm   Brown, A. Seymour 1913

Rebirth (inst.)   Coleman 1969

Recall Goodhue   Porter 1938

Reception of the Court   Schwartz, Arthur 1930

Recipe, A   Kern 1906, 1907

Recipe for Falling in Love (Quando Vien Labera)   Raye 1960

Reckless   Hammerstein 1935; Kern 1935

Reckless Dormitory Sequence (inst.)   Kern 1935

Reckless Rooster March   Merrill 1967

Reckon I'm in Love   David, Mack 1949; Hoffman 1949; Livingston, Jerry 1950

Recognized Man of the Hour   Smith, Harry B. 1908

Recollections   Pollack 1929

Record Room, The   Parish 1957

Record Shop, The   Stept 1958

Rector Rhythm   Razaf Date Unknown

Red, A   Blake Date Unknown; Razaf 1942

Red and White of Santa Clara, The   Adamson 1937; McHugh 1937

Red Ball, The   Drake 1954

Red Ball Express   Rome 1946

Red Blues, The   Porter 1955

Red Cap Cappers   Johnson, James P. 1922

Red Cheeks and White Whiskers   Hoffman 1950; Merrill 1950

Red Confetti, Pink Balloons and Tambourines   David, Mack 1955; Livingston, Jerry 1955

Red Cross Needs You Now, The   Cobb 1918; Edwards 1918

Red Dale Theme   Oakland 1954

Red Devil   Mills 1931

Red Dust   McHugh 1957

Red Eye Back to L.A.   David, Hal 1978

Red Fox Trot, The   Smith, Robert B. 1915

Red Garters   Evans 1954; Livingston, Jay 1954

Red Hair   Bryan 1928; Snyder 1928

Red Hair and Freckles   Dietz 1929

Red Head   Johnson, Howard 1928

Red Head Blues   Brown, Lew 1927; Friend 1927

Red Head (With Those Mean Green Eyes)   Hanley 1932

Red Headed Woman, The   Egan 1932; Gershwin, George 1935; Gershwin, Ira 1935; Whiting 1932

Red Heads   Rome 1940

Red Hot   Koehler 1923

Red, Hot and Beautiful   Adamson 1945; McHugh 1945

Red, Hot and Blue   Porter 1936

Red Hot and Blue Rhythm   Coots 1929; Davis 1929

Red Hot Anna   Meyer 1927

Red Hot Chicago   Brown, Lew 1930; DeSylva 1930; Henderson 1930

(Turn On That) Red Hot Heat (Burn Your Blues Away)   Alter 1937; Webster 1937

Red Hot Mama Is a Hep Cat Jitterbug Now   Yellen 1944

Red Hot Tomatoes   Coleman 1972; Fields 1972

Red Is for Roses   Fain 1952; Lawrence 1952

Red Lantern   Fisher 1919
Red Leaves and Blue Skies   Sigman 1947
Red Letter Day   Bergman 1957; Hoffman 1936
Red Light   Ahlert 1948; Leslie 1948
Red Light Annie   Buck 1923
Red Light Ballet   Merrill 1957
Red Light Rosie   Lewis 1923; Meyer 1923; Young, Joe 1923
Red Lips - Kiss My Blues Away   Bryan 1927
Red Lips and Green Eyes   Freed, Ralph 1957
Red Lips, Kiss My Blues Away   Monaco 1927
Red Mikado   Rome 1937
Red Moon   Brown, Lew 1923
Red Moon of the Caribees (Cancion Del Mar)   Drake 1941
Red Moon Rays (inst.)   Johnson, J. Rosamond 1918
Red Nose, Where Did You Get that Nose?   Brown, Lew 1924
Red Pepper   Atteridge Date Unknown
Red, Red Roses and Pale White Moonlight   Coslow 1931
Red Riding Hood   Atteridge 1919; Carroll 1919
Red Riding Hood Improvisation (inst.)   Styne 1965
Red Riding Hood on Broadway   Coots 1923
Red River Blues   Blake 1963
Red River Valley   Johnson, Howard 1939
Red Robins, Bob Whites and Bluebirds   Gordon 1944; Monaco 1944
Red Rose of Spain, Coralito Mine   Caesar 1923
Red Roses and Pale White Moonlight   Akst 1930; Clarke 1930
Red Rosey Bush (inst.)   Young, Victor 1940
Red Seal Malt (Drink Red Seal Malt When You Are Blue)   Gordon 1937; Revel 1937
Red Shoes (inst.), The   Styne 1993
Red Slippers   Friend 1963
Red Tape Blues   Leigh 1976
Red, White and Blue   Buck 1915; Kern 1909
Red, White and Blue Can't Live on Your IOU, The   Caesar 1956
Red, White and Blue of Hawaii, The   Adamson 1960; Fain 1960
Red, White and Blues, The   Lerner, Alan Jay 1976
Red-Blooded American Boy   Lawrence 1964
Redecorate   Bullock 1950
Redemption   Parish 1929
Redheaded Baby   Coots 1931; Davis 1931
Redheads on Parade   Gorney 1935
Red-Hot Trumpet   Hart 1928; Rodgers 1928
Rednow Lipstick   Coslow 1945
Redskinland   Razaf 1929; Waller 1929
Reefer Man (Have You Ever Met That Funny Reefer Man)   Razaf 1932
Refer Them to Me   Burke 1981
Reflection   David, Hal 1972
Reflections   Bacharach 1973; Burke 1959; David, Hal 1973
Reflections in the Water   Webster 1933
Reflections (inst.)   Schwartz, Jean 1930; Warren 1959
Reflections of You   Gilbert 1931; Pollack 1931
Refrain (inst.)   Arlen Date Unknown
Refugee Song   Fisher 1964
Refugee's Lullaby   Fain 1947; Yellen 1947
Regal Sadness Sits on Me   Herbert 1895; Smith, Harry B. 1895
Regardez-moi   Hammerstein 1931; Romberg 1931
Regards   Myrow 1930
Regatta   Styne 1956
Reggie Van Gleason the Third   Davis 1954

Regimental Band   Romberg 1925
Regimental March   Hammerstein 1930; Romberg 1930
Regimental Roly Poly Girl, The   Goetz 1912
Regimental Song   Friml 1927; Kahn 1938; Romberg 1938
Regret   Friend 1923
Regretful Blues   Clarke 1917
Regular Girl, A   Kalmar Date Unknown; Ruby Date Unknown
Regular Guy, A   Blake 1923; Kern 1915; Sissle 1923; Smith, Harry B. 1915
Regular William Gilette (A Regular Mr. Gilette), A   Cohan 1901
Rehearsal, The   Johnson, J. Rosamond 1904; Leigh 1985
Rehearsal Number   Hammerstein 1935; Kern 1935
Rehearse!   Lerner, Alan Jay 1976
Re-Incarnation   Goetz 1907; Hart 1934; Mills 1942; Rodgers 1934
Relationship, The   Russell 1977
Relatives   Berlin 1920
Relatives of the Bride, The   Drake 1952
Relax   Rome 1952; Silver 1952
Relax! Enjoy a Cigar   Drake 1985
Relaxation (Je T'Aime) (inst.)   Revel 1957
Relax-ay-voo   Cahn 1955; Schwartz, Arthur 1955
Release that Man   Smith, Harry B. 1906
Religion Is Like a River   Robison 1957
Religion of Love, The   Robison 1956
Remarkable Fellow   Young, Victor 1955
Remember?   Sondheim 1973
Remember Cherie   Coslow 1935
Remember Dad   Mercer 1939
Remember Dad on Mother's Day   Mercer 1956; Warren 1956
Remember December   DePaul 1958; Raye 1958
Remember for Old Times Sake   Egan 1921; Whiting 1921
Remember Hawaii   Willson 1942
Remember Him   Warren 1956
Remember I Still Love You   Sigman 1963
Remember I'm Your Pal   Clare 1925; Monaco 1925
Remember Last Night   Coslow 1935
Remember Me   Adams 1996; Dubin 1937; Freed, Arthur 1925; Kahn 1932; Leigh 1954; Strouse 1996; Warren 1937
Remember Me in Your Dreams   David, Hal 1950
Remember Me (Love Song)   Smith, Harry B. 1925
Remember Me to Carolina   Revel 1944; Webster 1944
Remember Me to Mary If She Still Remembers Me   Stept 1928
Remember Me to You   Woods 1956
Remember Mother's Day   Akst 1948
Remember My Forgotten Man   Dubin 1933; Warren 1933
Remember or Forget   Duke 1942
Remember Our Romance   Woods 1932
(We'll Always) Remember Pearl Harbor   Bryan 1942; Howard, Joseph E. 1941; Wrubel 1942
Remember that I Care   Weill 1947
Remember the Alamo   Livingston, Jerry 1960
Remember the Girl You Left Behind   Revel 1947, 1952
Remember the Old Continentals   Herbert 1908; Smith, Harry B. 1908
Remember the Rose   Mitchell 1921
Remember the Waltz   Mitchell 1923
Remember Thomas Jefferson   Rome 1943
Remember When   De Lange 1934; Mills 1934
Remember You Belong to Me   Monaco 1923

Remember Your Name and Address   Caesar 1937
Remember Your Promise (Say the Bells of St. Thomas)   David, Hal 1952
Remembering   Sigman 1955
Remembering Time   Yellen 1950
Remembering When   Webster 1956
Remembering You   Coots 1925
Remembering Your Lips (inst.)   Revel 1950
Remembrance   Herbert 1915
Remi Ram Jam   Conrad Date Unknown
Remind Me   Fields 1940; Kern 1940
Remind Me to Tell You   David, Mack 1947; Hoffman 1947; Livingston, Jerry 1947
Remington Rollamatic March (inst.)   Willson 1959
Reminiscence   Atteridge 1921; Romberg 1917, 1918; Smith, Harry B. 1925
Reminiscences (inst.)   Kern 1917
Reminiscent of Rosy Posy   Romberg 1915
Reminiscing   Blake 1932; Donaldson 1929; Leslie 1929; Sigman 1960; Sissle 1932; Warren 1930
Renco   Brooks 1966
Rendezvous   Caesar 1933; Coots 1952; Egan 1933; Evans 1951; Livingston, Jay 1951; Mitchell 1921; Romberg 1933
Rendezvous in Rio   Kahn 1938
Rendezvous in Rose Time, A   Rainger 1939; Robin 1939
Rendezvous Time in Paree   Dubin 1939; McHugh 1939
Rendezvous with a Dream, A   Rainger 1936; Robin 1936
Rendezvous with Spring   Duke 1942; Harburg 1942
Renita Reinette   Johnson, Howard 1927
Reno   Silver 1934
Reno Blues   Hanley 1930
Reno, the Land of the Free   Gordon 1930; Silver 1930
Renunion in Vienna   Turk 1933
Repello Wine   Young, Victor 1951
Repent   Coleman 1978; Comden and Green 1978
Reporter Scene   Gordon 1945
Reprise Love   Johnson, James P. 1947
Reputation   DeSylva 1919; Gershwin, George 1919
Requiem   Warren 1956
Rescue, The   Bryan 1917
Rescue Aid Society, The   Fain 1977
Reserved for Lovers   Livingston, Jerry 1968; Webster 1968
Respectability   Mercer 1964; Rome 1959
Rest   Razaf 1938
Rest Is History, The   Stept 1933
Rest of My Life Is Yours, The   Hoffman 1931
Rest of Your Life, The   Bergman 1977
Rest Room Rose   Hart 1931; Rodgers 1931
Restful   Adamson 1936; McHugh 1936
Restless   Brown, Lew 1933; Coslow 1934; Henderson 1933
Restless Heart   Bergman 1953; Rome 1954
Restless Love   Adamson 1961
Restless River   Spina 1965
Resurrection Rag   Goetz 1918
Retiring from the Stage   Cohan 1906
Return to Dora Flora   Eliscu 1941; Gorney 1941
Return to Paradise   Washington 1953
Return to Peyton Place Theme   Webster 1961
Return to the Land of Oz March   Cahn 1963; Van Heusen 1963
Reuben Glue   Fisher 1920
Reuben, Reuben I've Been Swingin'   Mitchell 1938; Pollack 1938
Reuben Tell Your Mandy   Schwartz, Jean 1905; Williams 1905

Reubens on Parade, The   Cohan 1903
Reunion   Bergman 1958
Reveille   Smith, Harry B. 1925; Smith, Robert B. 1909
Reveille in Harlem   Raye 1952
Reveille on Vine Street   Raye 1952
Revel No. 5 (inst.)   Revel 1948
Revel No. 6 (inst.)   Revel 1948
Revel No. 7 (inst.)   Revel 1948
Revel No. 8 (inst.)   Revel 1948
Revelation Ensemble   Porter 1916
Revel's Nocturne (inst.)   Revel 1957
Revenge   Adams 1966; Akst 1928; Bergman 1957; Lewis 1928; Porter 1941; Strouse 1966; Young, Joe 1928
Reverend Johnson's Dream   Arlen 1941; Koehler 1941
Reverie   Edwards 1913; Parish 1965
Reverie in Blue   Leigh 1956
Reverie in the Rain   Lawrence 1954
Reverie (inst.)   Oakland 1958
Reveries   Herbert 1917
Review of Athletes   Herbert 1908; Smith, Harry B. 1908
Revival Day   Berlin 1914
Revolt in Cuba   Berlin 1933
Revolutionary Man   Jerome 1909; Schwartz, Jean 1909
Revolutionary March   Hammerstein 1938
Revolutionary Rhythm   Coots 1929
Revolvin' Jones   Robison 1949
Reward (For Love)   Clare 1928; Pollack 1928
Rex   Rodgers 1976
Rhapsody in Ragtime (inst.)   Blake 1973
Rhapsody in Red, White and Blue   Duke 1942
Rheims Cathedral, The   Akst 1927; Davis 1927
Rhett, Scarlet, Ashley   Dubin 1940; McHugh 1940
Rhinestones   Rose 1927
Rhode Island Is Famous for You   Dietz 1948; Schwartz, Arthur 1948
Rhodopa's Tavern   Harburg 1961
Rhumba   Loewe 1937
Rhumba Cristobal   Cahn 1948
Rhumba Goes Collegiate, The   Mitchell 1937; Pollack 1937
Rhumba Jake   Caesar 1943
Rhumba on the Right   Rome 1938
Rhumbatism   Gordon 1931
Rhumboogie   Raye 1940
Rhyme for Angela, A   Gershwin, Ira 1945; Weill 1945
Rhyme for Love, A   Rainger 1936; Robin 1936
Rhyme-Around   Sherman 1965
Rhyming Song, The   Lerner, Sammy 1931
Rhythm   Hart 1933; Rodgers 1933
Rhythm for Sale   Razaf 1931
Rhythm Holiday   Cahn 1935
(If I Had) Rhythm in My Nursery Rhymes   Cahn 1935; Raye 1935
Rhythm in the Rockies   Rainger 1943; Robin 1943
Rhythm Is Our Business   Cahn 1935
Rhythm Lullaby, A   Razaf 1934
Rhythm Makes the World Go Round   Cahn 1935
Rhythm of America   Blake 1952; Sissle 1952
Rhythm of Joy   Brennan 1929
Rhythm of Life, The   Coleman 1966; Fields 1966
Rhythm of Love, Stop Playing with My Heart   Young, Joe 1932
Rhythm of Romance, The   Heyman 1934; Romberg 1934
Rhythm of Romany   Bryan 1939
Rhythm of the Day   Oakland 1931

Rhythm of the Moon, The   Rainger 1934, 1937; Robin 1934, 1937

Rhythm of the Rain   Gordon 1935; Revel 1935

Rhythm of the Raindrops   Hanley 1933; Kahn 1933

Rhythm of the Rumba, The   Rainger 1935

Rhythm on the Brain   Revel 1929

Rhythm on the Range   Bullock 1936; Whiting 1936

Rhythm on the River   Burke 1940; Monaco 1940

Rhythm Racketeers   Hoffman 1937; Lerner, Sammy 1937

Rhythm Rag   Robison 1925

Rhythm, Rhythm   Fisher 1937

Rhythm River   Bloom 1935; Koehler 1935

Rhythm Saved the World   Cahn 1936

Rhythmania   Conrad 1937; Coslow 1937

Rhythmatic   Gordon 1936; Revel 1936

Rhythmettes   Akst 1938

Rhythmic Moments (inst.)   Arlen 1928

Rhythmical Song (inst.)   Kern 1956

Rhythmitis   Burke 1958; Van Heusen 1958

Rialto Ripples (inst.)   Donaldson 1917; Gershwin, George 1917

Ribbity Rabbity Run   Sherman 1985

Ribbon, a Ring and a Rose, A   David, Mack 1940; Oakland 1943

Ribbons and Bows   Berlin 1927

Ribbons and Roses   Lewis 1938; Meyer 1938

Rice   David, Mack 1955

Rice and Shoes   Gershwin, Ira 1921; Youmans 1921

Rich, The   Merrill 1961

Rich and Happy   Sondheim 1981

Rich in Love   Lewis 1954; Meyer 1954

Rich Kid, The   Cahn 1967

Rich Livin' Woman   Freed, Ralph 1963; Livingston, Jerry 1963

Rich Man! Poor Man!   Hart 1928; Rodgers 1928

Rich Man, Poor Man, Beggar Man, Thief   Herbert 1909

Rich Man's Frug   Coleman 1966

Rich Old Woman, Poor Young Man   Razaf 1957

Richard the Third   Gilbert 1913

Rick-Chick-A-Chick   Porter 1913

Rickety Crickety   Hammerstein 1920; Harbach 1920

Rickety Rickshaw Man   Drake 1943

Ricksha   Brooks 1960

Rickshaw (inst.)   Monaco 1920

Riddle, The   Bullock 1950

Riddle Diddle Me This   Porter 1943

Riddle Me This   Harburg 1932

Riddles   Smith, Harry B. 1906

Riddleweed   Loesser 1960

Ride 'Em Cowboy   DePaul 1941; Mercer 1949; Raye 1941

Ride 'Em Cowboys   Schwartz, Arthur 1929

Ride Me Around with You, Dearie   Atteridge 1912

Ride of Fury   Brown, Nacio Herb 1955

Ride on a Rainbow, A   Robin 1957; Styne 1957

Ride On Vaquero   Baer 1929; Gilbert 1929

Ride Out the Storm   Coleman 1973; Fields 1973

Ride, Red, Ride   Mills 1935

Ride Tenderfoot Ride   Mercer 1938; Whiting 1938

Ride the Carousel   Revel 1959

Ride Through the Night   Comden and Green 1961; Styne 1961

Ride-Ride-Ride   Blane 1947; Warren 1947

Riders of Every Nation   Smith, Robert B. 1912

Riders of the Night   Schwartz, Jean 1930

Ridgeville Fight Song   Evans 1951; Livingston, Jay 1951

Ridin' but Walkin' (inst.)   Waller 1931

(I'm) Ridin' for a Fall   Loesser 1943; Schwartz, Arthur 1943

Ridin' High   Porter 1936

Ridin' Home   Adamson 1939; McHugh 1939

Ridin' Home (When the Round-Up Is Over)   Coots 1947

Ridin' Into Tulsa   Blane 1957

Ridin' on a Blue Note   Ellington 1938

Ridin' on a Rocky Road   Styne 1941

Ridin' on the Crest of a Cloud   Brooks 1945

Ridin' on the Moon   Arlen 1946; Mercer 1946

Ridin' on the Ninety-Nine   Johnston 1948

Ridin' the Rails   Heyman 1936; Spina 1936

Ridin' the Range   Styne 1941

Ridin' Through the Park in a Hansom Cab   Arlen 1973

Ridin' Up the River Road   Woods 1935

Ridin' Up to Heaven   Clare 1953

Riding Habit   Dietz 1932; Schwartz, Arthur 1932

Riding High   Gordon 1932; Revel 1932

Riding Hobby Horses in the Park   Fisher 1937

Riding on a Blue Note   Mills 1938

Riding on a Moonbeam   Burke 1930

Rid'n   Young, Victor 1937

Riff Van Winkle   Raye 1938

Riff-Raff-Rafferty   Smith, Robert B. 1915

Riffs (inst.)   Johnson, James P. 1930

Rififi   Lawrence 1956

Rig My Gallant Ship   Styne 1985

Riga Rose   Dixon 1923

Right About Now   Myrow 1950

Right Across the Way   Ahlert 1931; Turk 1931

Right Approach, The   Bergman 1960

Right As the Rain   Arlen 1944; Harburg 1944

Right at the Start of It   Dietz 1930; Schwartz, Arthur 1930

Right Beside You   Johnson, Howard 1930; Woods 1930

Right Boy Comes Along   Coots 1922

Right Brazilian Girl, The   Romberg 1916

Right Down the Middle of the Road   Woods 1943

Right Finger of My Left Hand, The   Fields 1959

Right Girl, The   Smith, Harry B. 1916; Smith, Robert B. 1916; Sondheim 1971

Right Girl for Me, The   Comden and Green 1949

Right Girl on the Left Hand, The   David, Hal 1960

Right Guy for Me, The   Coslow 1938; Weill 1938

Right Kind of Love (From the Wrong Kind of Guy), The   Adams 1954; Strouse 1954

Right Kind of Man, The   Baer 1929; Gilbert 1929

Right Kind of Man (The Wrong Kind of Man), The   Strouse 1990

Right Now   Fisher 1907; Kern 1907; Sigman 1962

Right Off the Board   Eliscu 1929; Rose 1929; Youmans 1929

Right or Wrong   Evans 1952; Koehler 1936; Livingston, Jay 1952; Spina 1957; Stept 1936

Right or Wrong I Love You   Akst 1928; Davis 1928; Rose 1928

Right Place for a Girl, The   Friml 1952; Webster 1952

Right Romance, The   Kern 1946; Robin 1946

Right Side, The   Sherman 1983

Right Somebody to Love, The   Pollack 1936; Yellen 1936

Right to Happiness, The   Bryan Date Unknown; Fisher Date Unknown

Right to Love, The   Drake 1965

Right to the End   Coots 1958

Right Way to Love, The   Freed, Arthur 1930

Right Way Wins the Right of Way, The   Robison 1956

Rilly Rilly   Gilbert 1921

Ring a Dang Ding   Sherman 1958
Ring a Ding a Ding Dong Dell   Gershwin, George 1929; Gershwin, Ira 1929
Ring and the Ding Dong   Friend 1958
Ring Around a Romance   Dubin 1937; Warren 1937
Ring Around the Bathtub   Styne 1940
Ring Around the Moon   Ellington 1943; Russell 1943
Ring de Banjo   Johnson, Howard 1939
Ring Dem Bells   Ellington 1930; Mills 1930
Ring Fell Under the Sofa   Fain 1951
Ring for Rosy   Smith, Harry B. 1923; Smith, Robert B. 1923
Ring Me Up in the Morning   Williams 1910
Ring on the Finger   Rome 1959
Ring on the Finger Is Worth Two on the Phone, A   Meyer 1911
Ring Out Liberty Bell   Romberg 1917
Ring Out the Bells   Lane 1965; Lerner, Alan Jay 1965
Ring Out the Blues   Gorney 1930; Harburg 1930
Ring Out the Liberty Bell   Atteridge 1917
Ring the Bell   Burke 1953; Van Heusen 1953
Ring the Door Bell, and Ask for Alice   Hanley 1939
Ring Those Bells   David, Mack 1941; Silver 1941
Ring Ting Tong   Merrill 1958
Ring to the Name of Rosie, A   Cohan 1923
Ring Up the Curtain   Rome 1942
Ring-a-Ding Ding   Cahn 1961; Van Heusen 1961
Ring-a-Ding-Dong   Von Tilzer 1910
Ring-a-Ting-a-ling on the Telephone   Jerome 1912; Schwartz, Jean 1912
Ringin' the New Year In (Ringin' the Old Year Out)   Gilbert 1949
Ringle, Ringle   Merrill 1962; Styne 1962
Ringside Blues   Mills 1924
Rinso White Song   Rome 1943
Rin-Tin-Tin   Atteridge 1924; Romberg 1924, 1925; Schwartz, Jean 1924
Rio   Coleman 1999; David, Mack 1946
Rio (A Tribute to the World's Most Beautiful City)   Wrubel 1951
Rio at Your Feet   Drake 1953
Rio Bravo   Webster 1959
Rio Cristal   Duke 1941
Rio De Janeiro, The   Cahn 1941; Eliscu 1932; Spina 1958; Washington 1944
Rio de Janeiro (In Copacabana)   Sigman 1967
Rio De Janeiro (inst.)   Robison 1926
Rio Grande   Caesar 1925
Rio Janeiro   Cobb 1917; Edwards 1917
Rip the Blues from the Blue Skies   Fisher 1931
Rip Van Winkle   Fields 1945; Romberg 1945
Rip Van Winkle and His Little Men   Kern 1920
Rip Van Winkle Junior Never Slept a Wink for Twenty Years   Bryan 1944
Rip Van Winkle Slept with One Eye Open   Bryan 1918; Fisher 1918
Rip Van Winkle Was a Lucky Man   Jerome 1901; Schwartz, Jean 1901
Rippling Brook (inst.)   Schwartz, Jean 1930
Rippling Waters   Pollack 1927
Riptide   Donaldson 1934; Kahn 1934
Rise and Shine   Martin 1969
Rise 'N' Shine   DeSylva 1932; Youmans 1932
Rise Up to Heaven   Livingston, Jerry 1960
Rise Ye Shepherds   David, Mack 1962
Rising Hour, The   Robison 1955

Rising Moon   Arlen 1929
Rising Moon (inst.), A   Revel 1961
Rising Sun (O! Lead Me to My Love)   Bryan 1925; Motzan 1925
Rita   Johnson, James P. 1968
Rita, Rio   David, Hal 1953
Rita's Request   Styne 1978
Rites of Love, The   Caesar 1962
Ritual of Knighthood   Cahn 1956
Ritz Roll and Rock, The   Porter 1957
Ritzi Mitzi   Conrad 1923; Johnson, Howard 1923
River, The   Conrad 1928; Mitchell 1928
River and I, The   Myrow 1960
River and Me, The   Dubin 1930; Warren 1930
River Boat (Comes In) (inst.)   Bacharach 1979
River Chanty   Weill 1950
River God   Porter 1938
River Is Blue, The   Weill 1938
River of His Pleasure, The   Robison 1960
River of Silver (And a Meadow of Gold), A   Robison 1953
River of Smoke   Sigman 1950
River, River   David, Hal 1960; Oakland 1950; Russell 1950
River Road   David, Hal 1960
River Song   Eliscu 1929; Herbert 1940; Rose 1929; Sherman 1973; Willson 1969; Youmans 1929
River, Stay 'Way from My Door   Dixon 1929; Woods 1929
Riverboat Jamboree   DePaul 1942; Raye 1942
Riverboat Shuffle   Carmichael 1939; Mills 1939; Parish 1925
Riverboat Shuffle (inst.)   Carmichael 1924
Rivers Are for Boats   David, Hal 1974
Rivers Cannot Flow Upwards   Strouse 1982
Rivers of Tears   Rome 1965
Riverside Bus   Conrad 1926
Riviera, The   Coleman 1953; Evans 1950; Friml 1926; Hammerstein 1926; Harbach 1926; Livingston, Jay 1950
Riviera Moon   Davis 1937
Road I Didn't Take, The   Webster 1978
Road Is Open Again, The   Fain 1933; Kahal 1933
Road of Dreams, The   Coots 1925
Road of Romance   Lerner, Sammy 1930
Road of the Phoebe Snow   Ellington 1971
Road that Leads to Love, The   Berlin 1917
Road that Lies Before, The   Kern 1917
Road to Bali, The   Burke 1952; Van Heusen 1952
Road to Destiny, The (The Roads of Destiny)   Romberg 1919
Road to God Knows Where (inst.)   Revel 1960
Road to Home, The   Heyman 1931; Youmans 1931
Road to Hong Kong, The   Cahn 1962; Van Heusen 1962
Road to Morocco, The   Burke 1942; Van Heusen 1942
Road to Paradise, The   Romberg 1917
Road to Utopia   Burke 1945; Van Heusen 1945
Road to Victory, The   Loesser 1944
Road Tour, The   Adams 1964; Strouse 2000
Road Tour (The Road Town), The   Strouse 1964
Road You Didn't Take, The   Sondheim 1971
Roads   Rome 1943
Roads of Destiny, The   Atteridge 1919; Schwartz, Jean 1919
Roam On, My Gypsy Sweetheart   Kahal 1927; Snyder 1927
Roamin' Into the Sunset, Thinkin' of You, Just You   Hanley 1927
Roamin' to Wyomin'   Clare 1923; Donaldson 1923
Roaming Around   Von Tilzer 1915
Roaming Around the Town   Johnson, J. Rosamond 1904
Roaring Twenties, The   David, Mack 1960; Livingston, Jerry 1960; Merrill 1952

Roaring Twenties Strike Up, The   Rome 1950

Roaving and Dreaming   Willson 1954

Robber-Baron Minstrel Parade, The   Lerner, Alan Jay 1976

Robbers' Dance, The   Whiting 1926

Robbers Song   Loesser 1937

Robert E. Lee   Turk 1922

Robert Schuman   Willson 1956

Robert the Roue (From Reading, Pa.)   Dubin 1939; McHugh 1939

Robin and the Rose, The   Herbert 1900; Smith, Harry B. 1900

Robin Hood   Hart Date Unknown; Rodgers Date Unknown; Sigman 1955

Robin Hood's Arrest   Smith, Robert B. 1905

Robin in the Redwood Tree, The   Adamson 1952; McHugh 1952

Robin Randall Song, The   Evans 1954; Livingston, Jay 1954

Robins and Roses   Leslie 1936

Robin's Song (inst.), The   Monaco 1920

Robinson Crusoe   Atteridge 1916; Johnston 1932; Romberg 1916

Robot Ballet (inst.)   Young, Victor 1943

Rock and Ree-Ah-Zole (The Teen-Age Talk)   Sigman 1958

Rock and Roll   Clare 1934; Whiting 1934

Rock and Roll Boogie   Silver 1956

Rock and Roll Bump   Adamson 1956; McHugh 1956

Rock and Roll Funeral   DePaul 1958; Raye 1958

Rock and Roll Tumbleweed, The   Cahn 1956

Rock and Rollin' on a Saturday Night   Blake 1961

Rock Baby Rock (inst.)   Oakland 1958

Rock Church Rock   Blake 1936

Rock City Rock   Ellington 1957

Rock Gently   Raye 1958

Rock Island Rock   Willson 1957

Rock, Little Children   Fain 1976; Harburg 1976

Rock Me in a Cradle of Kalua   Bryan 1931

Rock Me in a Rocky Mountain Cradle   Bryan 1931

Rock Me in My Swanee Cradle   Parish 1922

Rock Me in the Cradle of the Blues   Donaldson 1922

Rock Me in Your Loving Arms   Atteridge 1920

Rock Me Just Like a Sweet Daddy Should   Razaf 1924; Waller 1924

Rock Me, Lord   Robison 1961

Rock Me to Sleep with My Virginia Melody   Henderson 1923

Rock 'n' Roll Kisses   David, Mack 1958

Rock 'n Roll Lover (Come Back to Me)   Cahn 1957

Rock, Rock, Rock   Adamson 1948; McHugh 1948

Rock, Rock, Rock, Keep on a-Rocking   Clarke 1913; Leslie 1913; Schwartz, Jean 1913

Rock, Rumble and Roar   Sherman 1962

Rock Was in the Snowball, A   Caesar 1940

Rockabilly Party   Hoffman 1957

Rock-A-Bye Baby   Berlin 1924; Cahn 1958; Herbert 1903; Loesser 1940; Schwartz, Jean 1919; Warren 1958

Rock-a-Bye Baby Dear (Lullaby)   Kern 1918

Rock-a-bye Bangtail   Evans 1949; Livingston, Jay 1949

Rockabye Bay   Revel 1941

Rock-a-Bye Bluebird   Adamson 1957; McHugh 1957

Rock-A-Bye Land   Kahn 1917

Rock-a-Bye Moon   Johnson, Howard 1932

Rockabye Ranch   Sigman 1949

Rock-a-Bye River   Parish 1933

Rock-a-bye the Boogie   Raye 1941

Rock-a-Bye Time   Egan 1925; Whiting 1925

Rock-a-bye Town   Hanley 1939; Meyer 1923; Sterling 1923

Rock-A-Bye Your Baby with a Dixie Melody   Lewis 1918; Schwartz, Jean 1918; Young, Joe 1918

Rock-a-Bye-Baby   Bryan 1919

Rock-A-Bye-Lullaby Mammy   Clarke 1920; Donaldson 1920

Rock-a-Cha   Sherman 1961

Rockalypso   Mills 1957

Rock-a-Polka   Sherman 1961

Rockaway   Johnson, Howard 1917

Rockaway Hunt   Ager 1915

Rockaway Mary   Stept 1920

Rocket Ship   Carmichael 1956

Rocket to the Moon   Goetz 1954

Rockin' and Reelin'   DePaul 1941; Raye 1942

Rockin' and Rollin' in Loch Lomond   Davis 1960

Rockin' and Yodelin'   Sigman 1955

Rockin' Chair   Carmichael 1930

Rockin' Chair Doctor, The   Robison 1951

Rockin' in Rhythm   Arlen 1932; Ellington 1931, 1937; Koehler 1932; Mills 1937

Rockin' the Town   Koehler 1938

Rocking in a Ragtime Beat   Sterling 1913

Rocks in My Bed   Ellington 1941

Rock's Song for Victory   Blake 1958; Sissle 1958

Rocky Mountain Lullaby, A   Meyer 1947

Rocky Mountain Moon   Egan 1923; Mercer 1951; Whiting 1923

Rocky Mountain Rose   Hoffman 1956; Turk 1923

Rocky Road to Dublin   Williams 1914; Young, Joe 1914

Rocky Road to Dublin, Isn't Rocky Any More, The   Lewis 1925; Young, Joe 1925

Rodeo Rose (Giddyap Gal)   Wrubel 1952

Rodger Young   Loesser 1945

Rodgers and Hammerstein   Sondheim Date Unknown

Roger Clark Theme   Oakland 1954

Rogue River Valley   Carmichael 1946

Roll Along Missouri   Kalmar 1923; Ruby 1923

Roll Along Sadie   Duke 1952

Roll Around   Smith, Harry B. 1907

Roll Call   Blane 1961

Roll 'Em   Lerner, Sammy 1948; Styne 1943

Roll, Jordan, Roll   Blake 1930; Johnson, Howard 1939; Razaf 1930

Roll Me Around Like a Hoop My Dear   Bryan 1912; Fisher 1912

Roll, Mississippi   Hart 1935; Rodgers 1935

Roll of the Drums   Smith, Harry B. 1928

Roll On Missouri   Carroll 1913; Goetz 1912

Roll on Rolling Road   Hammerstein 1934; Kern 1934

Roll On Silvery Moon   Fisher 1922

Roll Out of Bed with a Smile   Ager 1933; Young, Joe 1933

Roll Out the Crimson Carpet   Sherman 1952

Roll Out the Hose, Boys   Robin 1954; Romberg 1954

Roll Pony, Roll   Brennan 1949

Roll them Cotton Bales   Johnson, J. Rosamond 1913

Roll Up the Carpets, Push Back the Chairs   Hoffman 1933

Roll Up the Score   Adamson 1934; Lane 1934

Roll Up Your Sleeves   Brown, Lew 1943; Stept 1943

Roll Yer Socks Up   Merrill 1957

Roll Your Bones   Akst 1933; Mitchell 1933

Roll Your Hoop   Atteridge 1916; Motzan 1916, 1917; Romberg 1916, 1917

Roll Your Yiddishe Eyes for Me   Lewis 1915; Meyer 1915

Rolland from Holland   Johnson, Howard 1924

Rolled Into One   Kern 1917

Roller Rinkers   Atteridge 1912
Roller Skate Rag   Merrill 1968; Styne 1968
Roller Skating on a Rainbow   Kahal 1939; Rose 1939;
    Warren 1939
Roller Skating Waltz   Bryan 1919; Schwartz, Jean 1919
Rollin' Down the River   Brooks 1945; Waller 1930
Rollin' Home   Clare 1922; Pollack 1922
Rollin' in Gold   Mercer 1964
Rollin' On (inst.)   Revel 1960
Rollin' on Our Roller Skates   Washington 1933; Wrubel 1933
Rollin' Stone, A   Russell 1951, 1959
Rolling Along   Akst 1935, 1936; Brown, Lew 1935, 1936;
    Revel 1947
Rolling Around in Roses   Dubin 1927
Rolling Chair Song   Williams 1905
Rolling Down Bowling Green on a Little Two-Seat
    Tandem   Gordon 1947
Rolling Exercise   Romberg 1918
Rolling Home   Porter 1936
Rolling in Rainbows   Burke 1949; Van Heusen 1949
Rolling in the Snow   Fain 1935
Rolling, Rolling   Porter 1911
Rolling Stone   Fisher 1930
Rolling Stone Blues   Kalmar 1921; Meyer 1921
Rolling Stone Gathers No Love, A   Livingston, Jerry 1955
Rolling Stones All Come Rolling Home Again   Leslie 1916
Rolling Up the Barcarolle   Atteridge 1920
Roly Poly Eyes   Lewis 1910
Roly Poly Platypus   Friend 1950
Roma Rocka-Bolla   Stept 1957
Romance   Atteridge 1923; Cobb 1917; Donaldson 1960;
    Edwards 1917; Friml 1934; Hammerstein 1926; Harbach
    1926; Leslie 1960; Romberg 1923, 1926, 1927, 1948;
    Smith, Harry B. 1927
Romance and Musketeer   Weill 1938
Romance and Rhumba   Gordon 1941; Monaco 1941
Romance in Candlelight   Coslow 1955
Romance in the Dark   Coslow 1938; Washington 1938;
    Young, Joe 1938; Young, Victor 1938
Romance (inst.)   Bloom 1933
Romance Is a Silken Affair   Sigman 1956
Romance Land   Akst 1918; Atteridge 1913; Schwartz, Jean
    1913
Romance of Elmer Stremingway, The   Brown, Lew 1930;
    DeSylva 1930; Henderson 1930
Romance of Love Is a Waltz, The   Hanley 1938
Romance of Our People, The   Hoffman 1933; Silver 1933
Romance on the Cerebellum   Drake 1957
Romance Runs in the Family   Hoffman 1939
Romance with Music   Romberg 1948
Romancing Around   Kahn 1930
Romantic Blues   Atteridge 1920; Bryan 1920; Schwartz, Jean
    1920
Romantic Girl   Smith, Harry B. 1912
Romantic Night   Adams 1954; Strouse 1954
Romantically Inclined   Drake 1955
Romany   Kahn 1921; Meyer 1921; Schwartz, Arthur 1927
Romany Days   Kahn 1924
Romany Eyes of Love   Bryan 1961
Romany Life   Herbert 1898; Smith, Harry B. 1898
Romany Love-Spell   Caesar 1926
Romany Romance, A   Johnson, Howard 1930
Romany Rover   Coots 1927; Dubin 1927
Rome   Drake 1968
Rome Wasn't Built in a Day   Dubin 1933; Warren 1933

Rome Will Never Leave You   Bacharach 1964; David, Hal
    1964
Romeo   Caesar 1923
Romeo and Juliet   Atteridge 1916; Brooks 1945; Edwards
    1905; Kern 1928; Motzan 1916; Romberg 1916; Smith,
    Robert B. 1905
Romeo, Juliet, Johnny and Jane   Herbert 1924
Romeo, My Only Romeo   Buck 1912
Romeo Smith and Juliet Jones   Burke 1941; Van Heusen
    1941
Romp in the Hay   Schwartz, Jean 1942
Romping Red Heads, The   Herbert 1916
Rondolet   Hammerstein 1940; Romberg 1940
Roo Te Too Toot   Williams 1909
Roodle Doodle   David, Mack 1965; Livingston, Jerry 1965
Roodle-Ee-Doo   Adamson 1943; McHugh 1943
Rooftop Rendezvous   DePaul 1958; Raye 1958
Rooftop Serenade   Styne 1940
Rook in a Weary Land, A   Mercer 1972
Rookie and His Rhythm, A   Dubin 1943; Monaco 1943
Rookies on Parade   Styne 1941
Room Enough for Me   Brown, Lew 1925; DeSylva 1925;
    Henderson 1925
Room for One   Rome 1937
Room for One More   David, Mack 1963; Livingston, Jerry
    1963
Room for Two   Bryan 1927; Schwartz, Jean 1927
Room Full of People, A   Strouse 1958
Room in My Heart   Fain 1960; Webster 1960
Room Without Windows, A   Drake 1964
Rooneyisms   Romberg 1921
Roosevelt, Bryan and Hughes   Atteridge 1916; Motzan 1916;
    Romberg 1916
Roosevelt of Germany   Smith, Harry B. 1909
Roosevelt, Wilson and Hughes   Atteridge 1916; Motzan
    1916; Romberg 1916
Rooster Man   Ellington 1946
Rooster's Crowin'   Caesar 1936
Root for Riley   Cohan 1903
Roots   Comden and Green 1967; Styne 1967
Roots of Heaven, The   Washington 1958
Rosa   Brown, Lew 1949; Russell 1955
Rosa Dolores   Hanley 1930
Rosa Linda   Sigman 1961
Rosa Mia   Fisher 1932
Rosa Rigoletto   Edwards 1910
Rosa Rosetta   Norworth 1908
Rosabella   Loesser 1956
Rosalie   Cobb 1903; Edwards 1903, 1910; Fields 1930;
    Gershwin, George 1927; Gershwin, Ira 1927; Kern 1906;
    McHugh 1930; Porter 1937; Smith, Harry B. 1910;
    Willson 1953
Rosalie, I Don't Want Your Sympathy   Fisher 1926
Rosalie My Royal Rosie   Cobb 1902; Edwards 1902
Rosalilla of Sevilla   Smith, Harry B. 1913
(There's None So Sweet As) Rosalind   Herbert 1911
Rosalinda   Gilbert 1931
Rosalyn   Hoffman 1959
Rosario   Styne 1970
Rosary of Love   Pollack 1920
Rosary of the Rose, The   David, Mack 1949; Livingston, Jerry
    1949
Rosary You Gave to Me, The   Sterling 1921; Von Tilzer 1921
Rose, The   Merrill 1966
Rose, a Child, a Butterfly, A   Atteridge 1919; Carroll 1919

Rose and the Butterfly, The   Young, Victor 1963
Rose and the Heather, The   Webster 1957
Rose and the Star, The   David, Mack 1946
Rose Aria, The   Johnson, Howard 1927
Rose Briar   Kern 1922
Rose de France   Romberg 1933
Rose Duet, The   Martin 1969
Rose I Call Sweetheart, The   Johnson, Howard 1921
Rose in a Bible, A   Sherman 1974
Rose in Her Hair, The   Dubin 1935; Warren 1935
Rose in the Heather   Eliscu 1937
Rose in Your Hair (A Rose in My Hair)   Schwartz, Arthur 1930
Rose Is a Rose, A   Rome 1950
Rose Is a Song   Cahn 1977
Rose Is not a Rose (Without the Thorns), A   Sherman 1978
Rose Loved Roses   Cahn 1967; Van Heusen 1967
Rose Lovejoy of Paradise Alley   Rome 1959
Rose Lucky Rose   Herbert 1911; Smith, Harry B. 1911
Rose Marie   Brown, Lew 1924; DeSylva 1924; Friml 1954; Hammerstein 1954; Harbach 1954; Henderson 1924; Kern 1921; Webster 1954
Rose, My Heart's Rosary   Donaldson 1923; Jerome 1923
Rose, My Rose   Blane 1945
Rose of Algiers   Yellen 1929
Rose of Araby (inst.)   Blake 1970
Rose of Babylon   Yellen 1920
Rose of Bagdad I Love You So   Kahn 1920
Rose of Delight   Harbach 1926; Kern 1926
Rose of Killarney   Young, Joe 1947
Rose of Madrid   DeSylva 1924; Gershwin, George 1924
Rose of Mandalay   Koehler 1928
Rose of My Heart   Buck 1921, 1924; Kahn 1925; Whiting 1925
Rose of Old Derry, A   Olcott 1907
Rose of Old Seville   Conrad 1920
Rose of Pyramid Land   Goetz 1912
Rose of Santa Rosa   Hoffman 1943, 1947; Livingston, Jerry 1943
Rose of Spain   Atteridge 1921; Fisher 1920; Romberg 1921
Rose of St. Martin's Lane   Johnston 1938
Rose of St. Mary's   Bryan 1925; Snyder 1925
Rose of Stamboul, The   Atteridge 1922
Rose of the Lane   Bryan 1927
Rose of the Morning   Romberg 1923
Rose of the Orient, The   Smith, Harry B. 1911
Rose of the Rancho   Coslow 1931
Rose of the Rio Grande   Leslie 1922; Warren 1922
Rose of the Rockies   Wrubel 1940
Rose of the Rotisserie   Atteridge 1921; Hanley 1920; Pollack 1921; Schwartz, Jean 1921
Rose of the Snowlands   Young, Joe 1932
Rose of the Stingaree   Kahn 1934
Rose of the Studios   Rose 1927
Rose of the Volga   Kahn 1927
Rose of the World   Herbert 1908
Rose of Tralee, The   Johnson, Howard 1939
Rose of Verdun   Egan 1919; Whiting 1919
Rose of Yesterday   Atteridge 1913; Gilbert 1925
Rose Petals (inst.)   Schwartz, Jean 1930
Rose Room   Williams 1918
Rose Tattoo, The   Brooks 1955; Warren 1955
Rose You Gave Back to Me, The   Clare 1926; Friend 1926
Roseanna   Loesser 1950
Rosebud   Porter 1911

Rose-Marie   Friml 1924; Hammerstein 1924; Harbach 1924
Rosemary   Bryan 1928; DeSylva 1921; Herbert 1916; Loesser 1961
Rosenbaum   Bryan 1909; Fisher 1909
Roses   Atteridge 1917; Romberg 1917
Roses Always Remember   David, Hal 1962
Roses and Butterflies   Smith, Harry B. 1910
Roses and Champagne   Duke 1951
Roses and Memories   Snyder 1909
Roses and Revolvers   Raye 1955; Webster 1955
Roses Are Blooming, The   Spina 1946
Roses Are Forget-Me-Nots Reminding Me Of You   Hoffman 1930
Roses Are Red, the Violets Are Blue, The   Clare 1932
Roses at Dawning   Kahn 1932
Roses Bloom for Lovers   Smith, Robert B. 1912
Roses for Rememberance   Kahn 1926
Roses for the Girl I Love   Von Tilzer 1903
Roses from the South   Conrad 1922; Kahn 1922
Rose's Goodbye to Easter   Weill 1947
Roses in December   Magidson 1937; Oakland 1937
Roses in the Garden   Friml 1921
Roses in the Rain   Cahn 1972; Duke 1955; Whiting 1934
Roses in the Snow   Spina 1957
Roses (inst.)   Motzan 1927
Roses, Lovely Roses   DeSylva 1922
Roses Make Me Cry   Parish 1934
Roses of Arcadie   Motzan 1919
Roses of France   Gershwin, George 1924
Roses of Picardy   Bryan 1919; Schwartz, Jean 1919
Roses of Rio   Sigman 1958
Roses of Success, The   Sherman 1968
Roses of Yesterday   Berlin 1928
Roses Out of Reach   Atteridge 1921
Roses Red, Violets Blue   Arlen 1962; Harburg 1962
Roses Remind Me of You   Davis 1926
Roses, Roses, Roses   David, Mack 1956
Roses 'Round My Room   Loesser 1940; McHugh 1940
Rose's Turn   Sondheim 1959; Styne 1959
Roses Understand   Cohan 1927
Rose-Time   Brown, Lew 1925; DeSylva 1925; Henderson 1925
(Reminiscent of) Rosey Posey   Atteridge 1915; Edwards 1910; Smith, Harry B. 1910; Sterling 1899
Rosie   Adams 1960; Cohan 1901; Goetz 1912; Mercer 1967; Rome 1969; Strouse 1960; Warren 1967
Rosie, Make It Rosey for Me   Clarke 1920
Rosie, My Heart's Rosary   Jerome 1923
Rosie Posies   Carroll 1925; Freed, Arthur 1925
Rosie Rosenblatt, Don't Make No Theater with Me   Lewis 1915; Young, Joe 1915
Rosie Rosenblott   Atteridge 1915
Rosie Rosenblott Don't Make No Theater with Me   Meyer 1915
Rosie Rosinsky   Jerome 1904; Schwartz, Jean 1904
Rosita   Johnson, James P. 1961
Rosita and Joe   Brooks 1949
Ross Miller Theme   Oakland 1954
Rosy and Bright   Goetz 1917
Rosy Cheeks   Parish 1921; Whiting 1927
Rosy Morn, The   Smith, Harry B. 1911; Smith, Robert B. 1911
Rosy Posy   Romberg 1922
Rotisserie, The   Coots 1925
Rotten Luck   Sherman 1974

Rottenest Job   Friml 1918
Rough Riders, The   Livingston, Jerry 1960
Roulette Dance   Atteridge 1920
Rouli-Rouli   Clarke 1914; Schwartz, Jean 1914
Round, A   Herbert 1917
Round and Round and Round   Webster 1954
Round and Round the Romance Tree   Evans 1965;
      Livingston, Jay 1965
'Round Evening   Coots 1928
'Round My Heart   Young, Joe 1932
'Round My Kingdom's Door   Hanley 1931
'Round My Old Deserted Farm   Robison 1935
Round on the End and High in the Middle, O-Hi-O   Bryan
      1922
'Round the Bend of the Road   Lewis 1932
'Round the Christmas Tree   Young, Victor 1934
'Round the Corner   Friml 1919; Harbach 1919
Round Up, The   Bryan 1909
Roundabout   Duke 1946
Round-Up, The   Howard, Joseph E. 1908
Round-Up Is Over, The   Spina 1947
Roustabouts   Johnson, James P. 1922, 1929
Roustabouts' Song (We Follow the Trail)   Ager 1928; Yellen
      1928
Routine Exercise, The   Bryan 1917
Row Row   Caesar 1920
Row! Row! Rosie   Bryan 1925; Meyer 1925
Row, Row, Row   Jerome 1912; Monaco 1912
Row, Row, Row with Roosevelt on the Good Ship
      U.S.A.   Coots 1932
Rowing Song, The   Williams 1910
Royal Bangkok Academy, The   Hammerstein 1951; Rodgers
      1951
Royal Confession, A   Duke 1963
Royal Danish   Loesser 1952
Royal Nonesuch, The   Sherman 1974
Royal Procession, The   David, Mack 1958; Livingston, Jerry
      1958
Royal Wedding   Atteridge 1923; Johnston 1934; Romberg
      1923; Schwartz, Jean 1923
Royalty   Cohan 1919; Sherman 1974
Rozita   Friml 1922
Rruff (Ruv) Song   Evans 1953
Rruff Song   Livingston, Jay 1953
Rub Pub Rub   Brooks 1957
Rub Your Lamp   Porter 1941
Rubadub Dub   Egan 1933
Rub-A-Dub-Dub (I've Had a Good Rub)   Caesar 1947
Rubaiyats from the Rubaiyat   Atteridge 1921
Rubber Around and Find It   Caesar 1943
Rubberneckin' Around   Akst 1930; Clarke 1930; Magidson
      1930; Washington 1930
Rubbin' Elbows with an Angel   Russell 1943
Rube Song   Cohan 1903
Ruble a Rhumba, A   Bryan 1939
Ruby   Davis 1921; Parish 1953
Ruby and the Pearl, The   Evans 1951; Livingston, Jay 1951
Ruby and the Rose, The   Alter 1955
Ruby Red (inst.)   Alter 1955
Rue de la Paix   Donaldson 1926; Koehler 1937
Ruffian Ballet, The   Hanley 1926
Ruins   Porter 1933
Ruisenor   Schwartz, Jean 1942
Rulers of the Earth   Smith, Harry B. 1909
Rules and Regulations   Ellington 1966

Rules of the Road, The   Coleman 1960; Leigh 1960
Rum   Leigh 1985; Styne 1985
Rum, Tum Fidele   Atteridge 1912
Rum Tum Tiddle   Berlin 1913; Schwartz, Jean 1911
Rumba Fan Dance (inst.)   Henderson 1934
Rumba Jumps!, The   Carmichael 1940; Mercer 1940
Rumba Made a Hot Number of Me, The   Meyer 1931;
      Mitchell 1931
Rumba Maria (inst.)   Young, Victor 1947
Rumba Rhythm   Johnson, James P. 1930
Rumba-bomba   Ruby 1947
Rumbalero   Fisher 1934; Lane Date Unknown
Rumbatism   Revel 1931
Rumble, The   Sondheim 1957
Rumble of the Subway (Subway Chant), The   Hammerstein
      1923; Youmans 1923
Rumble, Rumble, Rumble   Friml 1926; Hammerstein 1926;
      Harbach 1926; Loesser 1947
Rumbly in My Tumbly   Sherman 1966
Rumbola   Johnson, James P. 1931
Rum-Dum-Dum-Dum   Schwartz, Jean 1926
Rump Steak Serenade   Waller 1944
Rumplestiltskin   David, Mack 1958; Livingston, Jerry 1958
Rumpus on the Campus   Hoffman 1933
Rumson   Lerner, Alan Jay 1951; Loewe 1951
Run and Games   Livingston, Jerry 1963
Run Away   David, Hal 1953; Leigh 1955; Schwartz, Jean
      1918
Run, Brother Rabbit, Run   Bergman 1970
Run, Brudder Rabbit, Run!   Johnson, J. Rosamond 1907
Run for Cover   Brooks 1955
Run for It, A   Loesser 1937
Run for the Hills, Cowboy   Warren Date Unknown
Run for the Roundhouse, Nelly   Robison 1949
Run for Your Life   Cahn 1955, 1965; Styne 1955; Van
      Heusen 1965
Run for Your Lives   Loesser 1937
Run Girl Run (inst.)   Coleman 1966
Run Home and Tell Your Mother   Berlin 1911
Run, Little Raindrop, Run   Gordon 1941, 1942; Warren 1941,
      1942
Run on the Bank   Blake 1924; Sissle 1924
Run Run Run   Cahn 1948; Evans 1961; Livingston, Jay 1961;
      Styne 1948
Run, Run, Run Cinderella   Mercer 1964
Run, Run, Run, for I'm a Yankee   Razaf 1918
Run! Run! Run! Run!   Sherman 1954
Runaway Blues   Eliscu 1933
Runaway Heart   Woods 1957
Runaway Little Girl   Friml 1921
Runaway Lovers (Of Cathay), The (inst.)   Spina 1977
Runaway Train, The   Warren 1925
Runnin' Around   Fisher 1928
Runnin' Scared   Friend 1960
Runnin' Wild   Johnson, James P. 1924
Running After You   Johnson, Howard 1925
Running Around the Raindrops   Styne Date Unknown
Running Around with Chorus Girls   Cohan 1916
Running Around with Rosie   Bryan 1945
Running Patter   David, Mack 1965; Livingston, Jerry 1965
Running Water   Willson 1953
Rural Melody (inst.)   Kern 1956
Rush In Blues   Mills 1929
Russ Coglin Theme   Oakland 1954
Russian Art   Buck 1923

Russian Dance   Friml 1914; Harbach 1914; Smith, Harry B. 1913
Russian Doll   Styne 1927
Russian Duo and Dance   Herbert 1909
Russian Fantasy (inst.)   Waller 1935
Russian Folk Song   Dubin 1934; Parish 1934
Russian Love   Caesar 1922
Russian Lullaby   Berlin 1927; Fields 1935; Kern 1935
Russian Rhapsody   Webster 1943
Russian Rhumba   Fisher 1936
Russian Rose   Johnston 1927; Turk 1927
Russian Roulette (inst.)   Coleman 1969
Russian Song   Hammerstein 1931; Whiting 1931
Russian Wedding March   Friml 1914; Harbach 1914
Rusted Strings   Spina 1977
Rustic Patrol   Herbert 1906
Rusty Old Halo, A   Merrill 1954
Rusty Pail Blues (inst.)   Waller 1927
Rusty's Up in the Air   Brown, Lew 1930; DeSylva 1930; Henderson 1930
Rutabaga Rag   Sherman 1962
Ruth St. Denis   Atteridge 1917; Motzan 1917; Romberg 1917
Rutland Bounce (inst.), The   Styne 1953
Ruv Song No. 1   Livingston, Jay 1953
Ruv Song No. 2   Evans 1953; Livingston, Jay 1953

S

'S All Over but the Shouting   Brown, Lew 1928; DeSylva 1928; Henderson 1928
'S Been a Long Time in Between Time   Monaco 1929
'S Nice Like This   Friend 1929
'S Too High   Monaco 1914
'S Wonderful   Gershwin, George 1927; Gershwin, Ira 1927
Sabers   Gorney 1935
Sabot Dance (inst.)   Friml 1928
Sabre Song, The   Hammerstein 1926; Harbach 1926; Harburg 1961; Romberg 1926
Sackbut, the Psaltar and the Dulcimer, The   Hoffman 1954
Sacramento   Russell 1947; Sterling 1907
Sacred Bodies   Coleman 1972
Sacred Flame, The   Akst 1929; Clarke 1929
Sacremento   Von Tilzer 1907
Sad Am I   Cahn 1971
Sad and Sorry   Coots 1964
Sad Bombadier, The   Loesser 1944
Sad Cowboy, The   Carmichael 1948
Sad Eyes   Davis 1926
Sad Horns, Don't Blow Your Horns at Me   Robison 1932
Sad is the Life of a Sailor's Wife   Schwartz, Arthur 1955
Sad Little Rain of China   Mercer 1951
Sad 'n Blue   Davis 1927
Sad Parisianne   Gordon 1953; Revel 1953
Sad Parisienne   Warren 1943
Sad Sack   Bacharach 1957; David, Hal 1957
Sad Sapsucker   Waller 1944
Sad Was the Day   Burke 1961
Sad Winds   Robison 1926
Sadder-but-Wiser Girl, The   Willson 1957
Saddest Tale   Ellington 1935; Mills 1935
Saddle and Go (inst.)   Revel 1960
Saddle Song   Gilbert 1943
Saddle the Wind   Evans 1958; Livingston, Jay 1958
Saddle Up the Horse   Coleman 1978; Comden and Green 1978

Saddle Up the Palomino   Drake 1949
Saddled Bridled Harnessed and Tamed   Hoffman 1956
Sad-Eyed Baby   Van Heusen 1963
Sadie   Parish 1921
Sadie Brady   Norworth 1910
Sadie Fats   Cahn 1964; Van Heusen 1964
Sadie Hawkins Ballet   DePaul 1956
Sadie Hawkins Day   Raye 1940
Sadie, Sadie (Married Lady)   Merrill 1964; Styne 1964
Sadie Salome Go Home   Berlin 1910; Leslie 1910
Sadie the Seal   Caesar 1965
Sad'n' Blue   Akst 1927
Safe in the Arms of Bill Hart   Hammerstein 1920; Harbach 1920
Safe in Your Arms   Russell 1960
Safe in Your Heart   Gorney 1924
Safe Little World   Duke 1968
Safe-T-Party   Caesar 1943
Safety Alphabet Song   Caesar 1943
Safety Begins in Your Home   Caesar 1943
Safety First   Fisher 1915
Safety First Love   Atteridge 1915; Goetz 1915; Romberg 1915
Safety for You and for Me   Caesar 1940
Safety in Numbers   Coots 1925
Safety Patrol   Caesar 1937
Safety Symphony   Caesar 1943
Safety Waltz   Caesar 1943
Saga of Billy the Kid   Russell 1946
Saga of Carmen (Carmen Was), The   Yellen 1943
Saga of Goldie Or, The   Brooks 1958
Saga of Lenny   Sondheim Date Unknown
Saga of Sadie Thompson   Evans 1964; Livingston, Jay 1964
Saga of the Presidents, The   Livingston, Jerry 1960
Sahara   Williams 1908
Sahara Butterfly   Kahn 1923
Sahara (Now We're as Dry as You) (We'll Soon Be Dry Like You)   Schwartz, Jean 1919
Said I to My Heart, Said I   Harburg 1946
Said My Right Eye to My Left Eye   Hoffman 1954
Sail Away for Lullaby Bay   Donaldson 1919; Lewis 1919; Young, Joe 1919
Sail On   Willson 1969
Sail on the Tail of a Whale, A   Von Tilzer 1903
Sailin' Away on the Henry Clay   Kahn 1917
Sailin' On   Kahn 1927
Sailing Along   Johnston 1938
Sailing at Midnight   Dietz 1944; Duke 1944; Leslie 1938
Sailing Away   Smith, Harry B. 1905
Sailing Home to England   Adamson 1959; Young, Victor 1959
Sailing on the Night Boat where the Hudson Flows   Caesar 1935; Lerner, Sammy 1935
Sailing the Sea of Romance   Pollack 1928
Sailing with My Dreamboat   Hoffman 1957
Sailor Beware   Evans 1985; Hammerstein 1940; Kern 1940; Livingston, Jay 1985; Rainger 1936; Robin 1935, 1936; Whiting 1935, 1936
Sailor Boy   Cahn 1941
Sailor on a Night Like This, A   Dubin 1927
Sailor Routine   Gordon 1945; Loesser 1941; Styne 1941
Sailor Safety Song, The   Caesar 1943
Sailor Sails the Sea, A   Brooks 1950
Sailor Song   Berlin 1915; Clare 1930
Sailor Takes a Wife, The   Blane 1945

Sailor Talk   Styne 1985

Sailor Who Never Came Home, The   Bryan 1940

Sailor with the Navy Blue Eyes, The   Hoffman 1940

Sailor's Bride, A   Romberg 1922

Sailor's Chanty (It's a Lie)   Gordon 1934; Revel 1934

Sailor's Fling   Atteridge 1916; Hanley 1916; Romberg 1916; Smith, Harry B. 1916

Sailor's Hornpipe   Akst 1930; Davis 1930; Gordon 1949

Sailor's Life, A   Herbert 1900; Merrill 1957; Smith, Harry B. 1900

Sailor's Life for Me, A   DePaul 1941; Raye 1941

Sailor's Not a Sailor ('Til a Sailor's Been Tattooed), A   Berlin 1954

Sailors of the Sky   Porter 1940

Sailors of the St. Hurrah   Cohan 1904

Sailor's Polka, The   David, Mack 1951; Livingston, Jerry 1951

Sailor's Song   Adamson 1963; Fain 1963

Sailor's Tango, The   Weill 1977

Saint and Sinner   Coots 1945

Saint of Broadway, The   Silver 1955

Saint Patrick's Prayer   Blane 1952

Saint She Ain't, A   Merrill 1956

Saint Vitus Rag, The   Johnson, J. Rosamond 1912

Saints and Sinners Theme   David, Mack 1962

Sakura   Bergman 1978

Sale (inst.), The   Martin 1951

Salem Town   Bryan 1931

Salesmanship   Leigh 1957

'S-All Right   Hoffman 1959

Sally   Herbert 1911; Kern 1920; McHugh 1979; Smith, Harry B. 1911

Sally and Irene and Mary   Johnson, Howard 1921

Sally Down Our Alley   Atteridge 1917; Romberg 1917

Sally Ensalada   David, Hal 1974

Sally Green (the Village Vamp)   Kalmar 1920; Ruby 1920

Sally in Our Alley   Johnson, Howard 1939

Sally Long   Bryan 1925; Schwartz, Jean 1925

Sally McRally   Fain 1926

Sally, My Dear Old Sally   Revel 1942

Sally Rose   Friend 1927

Sally Slide, The   Buck 1921

Sally, Won't You Come Back (Come Back to Our Alley, Sally)   Buck 1921

Sally's Got the Blues   Kahn 1925

Sally's Not the Same Old Rally   Stept 1925

Sally's Sunday Hat   Cobb 1899; Edwards 1899

Salome   Harburg 1943

Salomee (With Her Seven Veils)   Styne 1953

Salt   Coleman 1973; Fields 1973

Salt Air   Porter 1932

Salt Lake City   Bryan 1908; Meyer 1908

Salt o' the Sea   Lerner, Sammy 1941

Salt of the Earth, Salt of the Sea   Brennan 1936

Salt Water Tears   David, Hal 1951

Salud   Mercer 1958

Saludos Amigos   Washington 1941

Sa-lu-ta   Donaldson 1927; Kahn 1927

Salute   Coots 1921; Loesser 1965

Salute to Spring   Loewe 1937

Salute to the Army Service Forces   Loesser 1944

Salvage   Parish 1965

Salvation   Ellington 1965

Salvation Glide, The   Howard, Joseph E. 1913

Salvation Nell   Clarke 1913; Leslie 1913

Salvation Sal   Egan 1919; Whiting 1919

Salvo   Cahn 1946; Styne 1946

Salzburg   Comden and Green 1956; Styne 1956

Sam and Delilah   Gershwin, George 1930; Gershwin, Ira 1930

Sam Jones' Blues (You Ain't Talkin' to Mrs. Jones)   Turk 1923

Sam, Sam (The Man What Am)   Berlin 1960

Sam Spug Routine   Oakland 1960

Sam the College Leader Man   Donaldson 1938

Sam the Old Accordian Man   Donaldson 1927

Sam the Slam   Caesar 1950

Sam, You Made the Pants Too Long   Lewis 1940; Young, Joe 1940; Young, Victor 1940

Samantha   Oakland 1968

Samba Lady   Drake 1948

Samba-Boogie   Adamson 1944; McHugh 1944

Sambo   Johnson, J. Rosamond 1909

Sambo's Syncopated Russian Dance   Johnson, James P. 1930; Razaf 1930

Same As a Man   Cahn Date Unknown; Duke Date Unknown

Same As You Did to Me, The   Brown, A. Seymour Date Unknown

Same Boat Brother, The   Harburg 1945

Same Little Chapel, The   Willson 1945

Same Little Girl   Carroll 1915

Same Mistakes   Merrill 1966

Same of You (Igual Que Tu), The   Gorney 1935

Same Ol' Cry   Russell 1948

Same Ol' Me   Russell 1951

Same Old Army, The   Evans 1959; Livingston, Jay 1959; McHugh 1959

Same Old Blues   Bloom 1946

Same Old Crowd, The   Smith, Harry B. 1903

Same Old Girl, The   Howard, Joseph E. 1915

Same Old Love   Duke 1959

Same Old Love Song   Smith, Harry B. 1927

Same Old Moon   Buck 1917; Harbach 1927; Howard, Joseph E. 1907; Kalmar 1927; Ruby 1927

Same Old Moon, Same Old June, but Not the Same Old You   Friend 1929

Same Old Places   Hammerstein 1920

Same Old Routine, The   Brooks 1946

Same Old Saturday Night   Cahn 1955

Same Old Silv'ry Moon Is Shining, The   Johnson, J. Rosamond 1909

Same Old Song   Atteridge 1917; Lerner, Alan Jay 1971; Motzan 1917; Romberg 1917

Same Old Song and Dance   Cahn 1958; Van Heusen 1958

Same Old Stars, Same Old Moon   Smith, Harry B. 1920

Same Old Story, The   Brooks 1950; DeSylva 1924; Gershwin, George 1924; Howard, Joseph E. 1906, 1908

Same Old Summer Moon   Kahn 1915

(It's the) Same Old Town   Gilbert 1915

Same Old Two, The   Herbert 1908

Same Old Welcome at the Door   Carroll 1911

Same One They Picked for Me, The   Atteridge 1913; Schwartz, Jean 1913

Same Silver Moon, The   Romberg 1927

Same Sort of Girl, The   Kern 1914; Smith, Harry B. 1914

Same Time Next Year   Bergman 1979

Same Time Same Place   Weill 1943

Same Time, The Same Place, Tomorrow Night, The   David, Mack 1933; Davis 1933

Samoa   Akst 1929; Bullock 1940; Clarke 1929; Spina 1940

San Anita Waltz   Jerome 1901; Schwartz, Jean 1901
San Anton'   Razaf 1936
San Antone Story   Russell 1947
San Antonio   Williams 1907
San Diego   Edwards 1913; Raye 1959
(Hey! I'm on My Way to) San Diego Bay   Spina 1974
San Diego Waltz   Willson 1958
San Domingo   David, Mack 1953; Livingston, Jerry 1953
San Francisco   Adamson 1936; Donaldson 1936; Kahn 1936
San Francisco (At that San-Fran Pan American Fair)   Lewis
   1914; Meyer 1914
San Francisco Bound   Berlin 1913
San Francisco Fran   Styne 1960
San Francisco Sadie   Cohan 1899
San Gabriel   Willson 1948
San Jose   Bryan 1915
San Sebastian's Shores   Carroll 1918; Goetz 1918
Sanctuary (Don't Know Where I'm Goin')   Bergman 1961
Sand   Sondheim Date Unknown
Sand and Sea   David, Mack 1966
Sand Flowers   Blake 1923; Sissle 1923
Sand in My Shoes   Loesser 1941
Sand Man   Comden and Green 1949
Sand Witches   Bryan 1921; Pollack 1921; Schwartz, Jean
   1921
Sandman   Adamson 1932; Freed, Ralph 1934; Hart 1919;
   Lane 1932
Sandman Wrap Me Up in a Silver Cloud   Kahal 1929
Sandman's House on Hush-A-Bye Hill, The   Burke 1947;
   Van Heusen 1947
Sandman's Serenade, The   Woods 1936
Sands Hotel Song   Cahn 1958; Van Heusen 1958
Sands of San Jose, The   David, Hal 1946; David, Mack 1946
Sands of Time   Sherman 1967
Sandwich for Two   Rome 1965
Sandwich Man, The   Martin 1964
Sandwich Men, The   Hart 1927; Rodgers 1927
Sandy   Edwards 1930
Sandy and Me   Clare 1935; Stept 1935
Sandy and Suzie Squirrel   Coots 1950
Sandy (Dumb Dog)   Strouse 1981
Sandy McPherson (The Tightest Man in Town)   Fisher 1926
Sandy-O   Jerome 1908; Schwartz, Jean 1908
Sangaree   Evans 1953; Livingston, Jay 1953
Sanka Commercial #2   Rome 1968
Sans Souci   Mercer 1951
Santa   Lewis 1932
Santa Barbara   Bryan 1924
Santa, Bring My Daddy Home for Xmas   Freed, Ralph 1966
Santa, Bring My Daddy (Mommy) Back to Me   Lewis 1943
Santa Catalina (Island of Romance)   Spina 1946
Santa Claus   Harbach 1925; Youmans 1925
Santa Claus Blues   Kahn 1924; Merrill 1954
Santa Claus Bring My Man Back Home   Mills 1928
Santa Claus Came in the Spring   Mercer 1935
Santa Claus Is Comin' to Town   Coots 1934
Santa Claus Parade   Coots 1955
Santa Claus Valley   Revel 1959
Santa Fe   Williams 1910
Santa Fe Sketches   Spina 1946
Santa Has His Eye on You   Razaf 1950
Santa Lucia   Johnson, Howard 1932
Santa Marta   Drake 1945
Santa, Please Repair My Toys for Xmas   Freed, Ralph 1969
Santa Rosa Rose   Brown, A. Seymour 1909

Santa's Little Helper   Coots 1964
Santa's Lullaby   Comden and Green 1956; Styne 1956
Santa's Theme   Mancini 1986
Santiago   David, Mack 1966
Santo Natale   Hoffman 1954
Sapphire (inst.)   Bloom 1927
Sarafina   Styne 1970
Sarah, Come Over Here   Conrad Date Unknown
Sarah from Syracuse   Kalmar 1923; Ruby 1923
Sarah Jane   Leslie 1929
Sarah, My Sarah   Robison 1949
Sarah Rosenstein   Fisher 1904
Sarah Sitting in the Shoe Shine Shop   McHugh 1924
Sarah, the Sunshine Girl   Rose 1934
Sarah's Hat   Jerome 1911; Schwartz, Jean 1911
Saratoga   Arlen 1959; Donaldson 1937; Mercer 1959
Sardinia   Sterling 1921; Von Tilzer 1921
Sari Dance, The   Atteridge 1914; Romberg 1914
Sarong   De Lange 1948
Saroyan   Harburg 1956
Sasha Pasha Sasha   Koehler 1937
Sasha (The Passion of the Pascha)   Rose 1930
Sas-Katch-A Widja-Go-Way-Go-On!   Hanley 1930
Saskatchewan   Caesar 1936; Freed, Ralph 1942; Lerner,
   Sammy 1936; Leslie 1928
Sas'parilla, Women and Song   Bryan 1919; Schwartz, Jean
   1919
Sassy (inst.)   Schwartz, Jean 1930
Satan   Loesser 1931
Satan Leads the Band   Arlen 1931; Koehler 1931
Satan Never Sleeps   Adamson 1962; Warren 1962
Satan's Holiday   Duke 1930; Fain 1930; Kahal 1930
Satan's Li'l Lamb   Arlen 1932; Harburg 1932; Mercer 1932
Satellite City   Styne 1960
Satin and Silk   Porter 1955
Satin Doll   Ellington 1953; Mercer 1953
Satins and Spurs   Evans 1954; Livingston, Jay 1954
Satisfied   Caesar 1929; Friend 1929
Satisfied with You   Stept 1926
Saturday   Lerner, Alan Jay 1971; Mitchell 1921
Saturday Afternoon   Blake 1932; Sissle 1932
Saturday Afternoon Before the Game   Gordon 1953; Myrow
   1953
Saturday Date   Brooks 1947
Saturday Night   Cahn 1977; Kern 1916; Porter 1911;
   Schwartz, Jean 1926; Sondheim 1954; Styne 1977
Saturday Night at the Old Barn Dance   Gilbert 1938
Saturday Night CBS T.V. Special   Cahn 1977
Saturday Night Excursion Boat   Friend 1950
Saturday Night Girl   Strouse 1999
Saturday Night in Davenport, Ioway   Merrill 1951
Saturday Night in Punkin Crick   Evans 1952; Livingston, Jay
   1952
Saturday Night in Tia Juana   Bacharach 1958; David, Hal
   1958
Saturday Night Is the Loneliest Night in the Week   Cahn
   1944; Styne 1944
Saturday Night Polka   Leigh 1954
Saturday Night Satellite   Robison 1957
Saturday Night till Monday Morning   Goetz 1920
Saturday Sadies   Herbert 1904
Saturday Sunshine   Bacharach 1963; David, Hal 1963
Saturday Sweethearts   David, Hal 1961
Saturday Till Monday   Kern 1904
Saturday's Children   Russell 1958

Saturday's Kiss   David, Hal 1957

Saturn Soliloquizes (inst.)   Revel 1955

Sauce for the Goose Is Sauce Is Sauce for the Gander   Harbach 1911

Saunter Away   Loesser 1948

Savage I Remain, A   Herbert 1920; Smith, Robert B. 1920

Savage in My Soul   Bloom 1934; Parish 1934

Savage Rhythm   Coots 1937; Davis 1937

Savannah   Arlen 1957; Donaldson 1923; Duke 1940; Harburg 1957; Kahn 1923

Savannah Blues   Waller 1927

Savannah, That Georgiana Blues   Fisher 1924

Savannah's Wedding Day   Arlen 1957; Harburg 1957

Save a Dime Out of Ev'ry Dollar   Spina 1947

Save a Kiss for Rainy Weather   Egan 1924; Whiting 1924

Save a Little Daylight for Me   Smith, Robert B. 1919

Save a Little Money for a Rainy Day   Snyder 1906

Save a Place for Me   Brooks 1960

Save It for Me   De Lange 1948; Howard, Joseph E. 1919; Johnson, J. Rosamond 1903

Save Me   David, Mack 1975; Drake 1959

Save Me from Being Lonesome   Baer 1933

Save Me from Caesar   Drake 1968

Save Me Sister   Arlen 1936; Harburg 1936

Save Me the Dance (Where the Lights Go Down Low)   Drake 1980

Save That Last Grave for Me   Brown, Nacio Herb 1937

Save the Daylight for Somebody Else, But Save the Moonlight for Me   Von Tilzer 1921

Save the Last Waltz for Me   Johnson, Howard 1922

Save the World   Hoffman 1951

Save Your Kisses for a Rainy Day   Parish 1927

Save Your Love for Me   Warren 1959

Save Your Money, John   Blake 1918; Sissle 1918

Save Your Sorrow for Tomorrow   DeSylva 1925

Save Your Yesses   Duke 1936; Gershwin, Ira 1936

Saving My Kisses   Sherman 1959

(I've Been) Saving Myself for You   Cahn 1938

Saving Up for Sunday   Parish 1964

Savoy (Home of Happy Feet)   Razaf 1940

Saxophone Man   Atteridge 1924; Jerome 1924; Romberg 1924; Schwartz, Jean 1924

Say a Little Prayer for Home Sweet Home   Johnson, Howard Date Unknown

Say a Prayer   Spina 1976

Say a Prayer for Me Tonight   Lerner, Alan Jay 1956; Loewe 1956

Say a Prayer for Palestine   Johnson, Howard 1929

Say a Prayer for the Boys Over There   Magidson 1943; McHugh 1943

Say Ah!   Brown, Nacio Herb 1936; Fisher 1939; Freed, Arthur 1937

Say, Arabella (What's a Fella to Do)   Kahn 1925

Say Au Revoir but Not Goodbye   Johnson, Howard 1939

Say Boys, I've Found a Girl   Kahn 1910

Say 'Bye-Bye' to the Things you Buy, Buy!   Caesar 1944

Say! Can't You See, What You're Doin' to Me   Young, Joe 1932

Say, Darling   Comden and Green 1958; Styne 1958

Say Farewell   Cahn 1949

Say Goodbye   Bacharach 1965; David, Hal 1965

Say Goodbye to Gay Paree   Brown, Lew 1913

Say Goodbye to Sally for Me   Parish 1980

Say Goodbye to Your Traveling Man   Brown, Lew 1913

Say Goodbye (Turn Around Walk Away)   Sigman 1967

Say Goodnight but Not Goodbye   Johnson, Howard 1935

Say Hello   Bryan 1927; Cahn 1981

Say Hello to the Folks Back Home   Blake 1940; Davis 1931; Razaf 1940

Say Hey, Willie Mays   Robison 1954

Say How D'Ye Do-a to Kalua   Fields 1934; McHugh 1934

Say It!   Harburg 1931; McHugh 1922; Mills 1922

Say It After Me, I Love You   Parish 1929

Say It Again   Conrad 1924

Say It All Over Again   Hoffman 1939

Say It in a Nutshell   Hanley 1930

Say It Isn't So   Berlin 1932

Say It Once Again   Caesar 1920

Say It Over   Spina 1952

Say It (Over and Over Again)   Loesser 1940; McHugh 1940

Say It Soft, Say It Low   Parish 1950

Say It While Dancing (Ca S'Fait en Dansant)   Davis 1922; Silver 1922

Say It with a Big Brass Band   Edwards 1929

Say It with a Kiss   Dubin 1938; Mercer 1938; Robin 1926; Warren 1938

Say It with a Red Red Rose   Rose 1927

Say It with a Sable   Brown, Lew 1925; DeSylva 1925; Henderson 1925

Say It with a Solitaire   Monaco 1927; Rose 1927

Say It with a Ukelele   Atteridge 1923; Schwartz, Jean 1923

Say It with Dancing   DePaul 1942; Raye 1942

Say It with Firecrackers (inst.)   Berlin 1942

Say It with Gin   Porter 1930

Say It with Love   Evans 1944, 1945; Livingston, Jay 1944, 1945

Say It with Music   Berlin 1921

Say It with Your Eyes   Russell 1957

Say It with Your Feet   Coslow 1930; Razaf 1929; Waller 1929

Say It's Not the Last Time   Johnson, Howard 1933

Say Kid, Let's Become a Pair   Ager 1910

Say Nice Things About People   Hoffman 1951; Merrill 1951

Say No More   Akst 1947; Davis 1947; Eliscu 1962; Leigh 1964

Say No, That's All   Snyder 1908

Say One for Me   Cahn 1959; Van Heusen 1959

Say Oui Cherie   Youmans 1930

Say! Say! Sadie   Conrad 1924; Coslow 1924

Say So!   Gershwin, George 1927; Gershwin, Ira 1927

Say Something   Coots 1929

Say Something Nice About Me   Stept 1947

Say Something Sentimental   Van Heusen 1938

Say Something Sweet Sweetheart   David, Mack 1934

Say That You Have Forgiven Me   Oakland 1929

Say that You Love Me   Robin 1928

Say That You Love Me Once More   Heyman 1962

Say That You Were Teasing Me   Ahlert 1932; Turk 1932

Say the Word   Adamson 1931; Baer 1929; Friend 1932; Gilbert 1929; Lane 1931; Stept 1955

Say the Word and It's Yours   Hoffman 1935

Say (What I Wanna Hear You Say)   Brown, Lew 1932; Henderson 1932

Say What You Mean and Mean What You Say   David, Mack 1946; Hoffman 1946; Livingston, Jerry 1946

Say What You Mean, and Mean What You're Saying   Young, Joe 1933

Say What You Will   Heyman 1953; Young, Victor 1953

Say When   Carroll 1942; Comden and Green 1944; Henderson 1934; Herbert 1919; Koehler 1934; Smith, Robert B. 1919

Say When — Stand Up — Drink Down   Hart 1930; Rodgers 1930

Say Who Is that Baby Doll   Turk 1925

Say Yes   Caesar 1919; Razaf 1939; Waller 1939

Say Yes, Sweetheart, Say Yes   Smith, Harry B. 1926

Say Yes to Me   Meyer 1933

Say Yes Today   Donaldson 1928

Say You Intend to See Old Tennessee and Me   Egan 1918

Say You Intend to See Ole Tennessee and Me   Whiting 1918

Say You Love Me   Parish 1930

Say You'll Be Good to Me   Hanley 1932

Say, Young Lady   Gordon 1932; Revel 1932

Say Young Man of Manhattan   Adamson 1929; Youmans 1929

Say Your Prayers   Styne 1940

Saying My Say   Gershwin, George Date Unknown; Gershwin, Ira Date Unknown

Saying No   Clare 1953; Young, Victor 1953

Sayonara   Egan 1923; Whiting 1923

Sayonara G.I.   Revel 1955

Sayonara, Sayonara   Berlin 1953

Says I to Myself, Says I   Von Tilzer 1917

Says My Heart   Lane 1938; Loesser 1938

Says So Here   Gordon 1950; Myrow 1950

Says Who, Says You, Says I!   Arlen 1941; Mercer 1941

Scales and Arpeggios   Sherman 1970

Scalin' the Blues (inst.)   Johnson, James P. 1926

Scampi, The   Porter 1920

Scandal   Herbert 1919; Johnson, J. Rosamond 1904; Porter 1912

Scandal in Toyland   Bryan 1950

Scandal Number   Friml 1934

Scandal of Little Lizzie Ford, The   Von Tilzer 1920

Scandal of the Flowers   Edwards 1912

Scandal Walk   Gershwin, George 1920

Scandalize My Name   Robison 1964

Scandinavia (Sing Dose Song and Make Dose Music)   Bryan 1921

Scandinavian Glide, The   Johnson, J. Rosamond 1913

Scandinavian Polka (Polka Scandinavieene) (inst.)   Kern 1941

Scare Crow Maidie   Howard, Joseph E. 1910

Scarecrow in the Cornfield (inst.)   Coots 1946

Scared   Friend 1936

Scareecrow, The   Loesser 1937

Scarlet Bird in a Yellow Tree   Livingston, Jerry 1963; Webster 1963

Scarlett O'Hara   Coots 1938; Davis 1938

Scarlett (Skarettu)   Rome 1969

Scars (2), The   Weill 1938

Scat Mr. Crow!   Razaf 1950

Scat Song, The   Parish 1932

Scatterbrain   Burke 1940

Scatterbrain Finale   Styne 1940

Scattin' at the Kit Kat   Ellington 1937; Mills 1937

Scattin' the Cat   Conrad 1929; Mitchell 1929

Scena (Tingle Tangle)   Hammerstein 1932; Kern 1932

Scene and Pas de Seul   Harbach 1933; Kern 1933

Scene at Slave Market   Lane 1951

Scene Is Spain, The   Drake 1953

Scene on the Dock   Fields 1931; McHugh 1931

Scent of the Orient   Merrill 1959

Scharline   Blake 1954

Scheherazade's Interlude   Fain 1951; Harburg 1951

Scherazade   Brooks 1947

Scherzetto (inst.)   Young, Victor 1942

Scherzo, The   Willson 1956

Scherzo (inst.)   Blake 1946; Strouse 1962; Styne 1948

Scherzo No. 1 (inst.)   Blake 1964

Schlaf Mein Kind   Cahn 1977

Schlissel's Retort   Merrill 1961

Schlitz   Fisher 1910

Schmaltzy Waltz, The   Howard, Bart 1960

Schnapps   Fields 1951; Warren 1951

Schnitza Komisski, The   Kern 1920

Schnozzola   Hart 1932; Johnston 1932

Schoe Plattler Tanz   Romberg 1925

Schoene Maedel (Pretty Girl)   David, Hal 1948

Schonbrun Waltz   Revel 1960

School Day Blues   Fisher 1924

School Days Are Over   Edwards 1923; Smith, Robert B. 1923

School Days (We Were a Couple of Kids)   Edwards 1908

School Days (When We Were a Couple of Kids)   Cobb 1906; Edwards 1906

School for Anatomy (inst.)   Bacharach 1965

School for Waiters   Dietz 1948; Schwartz, Arthur 1948

School Mates   Edwards 1908

School of Hard Knocks   Sondheim Date Unknown

School Room (inst.)   Kern 1956

School, School, Heaven-Blessed School   Porter 1944

School Time   Von Tilzer 1923

Schoolday Sweetheart   Bryan 1925; McHugh 1925

Schoolhouse Blues, The   Berlin 1921

School's Out, Watch Out   Caesar 1943

Schooner Land   Goetz 1909

Schottische   Herbert 1895; Romberg 1927; Smith, Harry B. 1895

Schottische with Me   Clare 1944; Lerner, Sammy 1944

Schrafft's University   Eliscu 1929

Schuetzen Corps, The   Von Tilzer 1910

S-chut-ya Ding   Merrill 1955

Scientific Classes   Von Tilzer 1906

Scotch Air   Loesser 1937

Scotch Archer's Song   Friml 1925

Scotch Bagpipe Dance (inst.)   Coots 1946

Scotch Mist (inst.)   Stept 1957

Scotch Plaid   Turk 1949

Scotch Song   Edwards 1930; Johnson, Howard 1930

Scotch Twins   Porter 1922

Scoutin' Around (inst.)   Johnson, James P. 1927

Scouting in the U.S.A.   Kahn 1917

Scram Scoundrel Scram   Waller 1943; Washington 1943

Scrambled Egg-Head, The   Sherman 1964

Scratch a Wife and Find a Doll   Harburg 1961

Scratch My Back   Freed, Ralph 1953; Livingston, Jerry 1953

Scratchin' the Gravel   Yellen 1917

Scratchin' Up a Batch   De Lange 1946

Scream   Coleman 1977

Screen Writer's Guild Song   Ruby 1951

Screw Driver (inst.)   Stept 1957

Scrimmage of Life, The   Ellington 1946

Scrub Me Mama with a Boogie Beat   Raye 1940

Scrubbing Song   Weill 1938

Scruples! Scruples!   Gorney 1962

Scum-Dee-Dum   Merrill 1966

Scusami   Sigman 1957

Scuttlebutt Walk (inst.), The   Spina 1961

Sea, The   Leigh 1985; Styne 1985

Sea Breeze   Hoffman 1957

Sea Chantey   Porter 1946
Sea Chanty   Leigh 1967; Loesser 1942; Young, Victor 1942
Sea Gulls   Webster 1965
Sea Is Calling, The   Porter 1919
Sea Legs   DeSylva 1925
Sea of Heartbreak   David, Hal 1960, 1987
Sea of the Moon, The   Freed, Arthur 1950; Warren 1950
Sea of the Tropics Dance   Johnson, Howard 1921
Sea Shell, The   Styne 1985
Sea Song (By the Beautiful Sea), The   Fields 1954; Schwartz, Arthur 1954
Sea Symphony (inst.)   Young, Victor 1957
Seal It with a Kiss   Heyman 1936; Schwartz, Arthur 1936
Sealed Orders   Herbert 1897; Smith, Harry B. 1897
Seaman's Home   Merrill 1958
Search, The   Blane 1952; Weill 1949; Styne 1985
Search for Beauty   Rainger 1934; Robin 1934
Search for Paradise   Washington 1957
Search Is Through, The   Arlen 1954; Gershwin, Ira 1954
Search Your Soul   Sigman 1972
Searchin'   Ellington 1964
Searching   Cahn 1983; Styne 1983
Searching Wind, The   Heyman 1946; Young, Victor 1946
Seashell Telephone, The   Smith, Harry B. 1911
Seasick Sailor, The   Adamson 1943; McHugh 1943
Season, The   Martin 1964
Season for Love, The   Adams 1963; Strouse 1963
Season in the Sun   David, Mack 1971
Seasons of Youth   Drake 1961
Seattle   Fain 1943, 1946; Freed, Ralph 1943, 1946
Secluded   Donaldson 1941
Second Auto Theme   Mercer 1955
Second Avenue and 12th Street Rag   Duke 1956
Second Best Secret Agent in the Whole Wide World, The   Cahn 1965; Van Heusen 1965
Second Childhood   Brown, Lew 1928; DeSylva 1928; Henderson 1928
Second Fiddle   Friend 1954
Second Fiddle to a Harp   Gershwin, Ira 1949; Warren 1949
Second Finale   Weill 1933
Second Greatest Sex, The   Evans 1955; Livingston, Jay 1955
Second Hand Romance   Spina 1950
Second Hand Rose   Clarke 1921; Hanley 1921
Second Letter   Sondheim 1994
Second Love Gets By, The   Ahlert 1969; Cahn 1969; Turk 1969; Van Heusen 1969
Second March   Arlen 1959; Mercer 1959
Second Midnight   Sondheim 1987
Second Portrait of the Lion, The   Ellington 1966
Second Star to the Right, The   Cahn 1952; Fain 1952
Second Sunday in June, The   Friend 1950
Second Time Around, The   Cahn 1960; Van Heusen 1960
Second Time in Love   Warren 1956
Second to None   Heyman 1954; Young, Victor 1954
Second Wind   Arlen 1959; Mercer 1959
Second-Hand Turban and a Crystal Ball, A   Cahn 1956; Van Heusen 1956
Seconds   Bacharach 1974
Secret, A   Styne 1985
Secret (1), The   Herbert 1897
Secret (Gossip Song), The   Smith, Robert B. 1905
Secret Kingdom   Sherman 1976
Secret Love   Fain 1953; Webster 1953
Secret Love Affair, The   Mitchell 1937; Pollack 1937
Secret of Christmas, The   Cahn 1959; Van Heusen 1959

Secret of Love, The   Bacharach 1987
Secret of My Life, The   Caesar 1930; Harbach 1930; Romberg 1930
Secret of Staying Young, The   Bacharach 1962; David, Hal 1962
Secret Place   Lerner, Alan Jay 1985
Secret Service, The   Berlin 1962
Secret Service Club, The   Atteridge 1919; Carroll 1919
Secret Society   Von Tilzer 1903
Secret Word Is 'Escargots', The   Spina 1977
Secretary Bird   Leigh 1976
Secretary Is Not a Toy, A   Loesser 1961
Secretary Song (Bidibi Bot Bot), The   Fain 1947
Secretly   Hoffman 1958
Secretly Mine   Alter 1953; Eliscu 1953
Secrets   Harbach 1914; Lawrence 1946
Secrets in the Moonlight   Gordon 1940
Secrets of the Household   Cohan 1909
Security   Cahn 1956; Strouse 1990
Seduction, The   Harbach 1910
See America First   Blake 1916; Porter 1916; Sissle 1916
See If I Care   Stept 1935; Washington 1935
See If I Care (Eso Eres Tu)   David, Mack 1947
See Mexico   Washington 1945
See Saw Margery Daw   Johnson, Howard 1939
See Seattle   Dietz 1963; Schwartz, Arthur 1963
See that You're Born in Texas   Porter 1943
See the Circus   Evans 1953; Livingston, Jay 1953
See This Golden Rooster   Hart 1921; Rodgers 1921
See What It Gets You   Sondheim 1964
See You Around   Coslow 1949; Evans 1965; Livingston, Jay 1965; Merrill 1972; Sigman 1958; Styne 1972
See You Later Girls   Schwartz, Jean 1919
See You Later Shimmy   Schwartz, Jean 1919
See You Tomorrow — So Long for Now   Wrubel 1955
See Your Dentist Once a Day   Adamson 1937; Lane 1937
Seed, The   Webster 1965
Seeds of Brotherhood   Razaf 1953
Seein' Is Believin'   Ager 1935
Seeing Dickie Home   Gershwin, George 1924; Gershwin, Ira 1924
Seeing Red and Singing Blue (The Color Song)   Bloom 1949; Leslie 1949
Seeing Stars   Caesar 1923; Conrad 1923
Seeing Things the Way They Really Are   David, Hal 1977
Seeing You Again (Did Me No Good)   David, Hal 1959
Seeing You Tell a Lie   David, Hal 1959
Seeing You with Somebody Else   Coots 1961
Seeing's Believing   Mercer 1951; Warren 1951
Seek the Spy   Leigh 1955
Seems I've Done Something Wrong Again   De Lange 1936
Seems Like When It Comes in the Morning   Bergman 1959
Seems Like Yesterday   Stept 1950
(It) Seems to Me   Dietz 1930; Rainger 1930
Seen One, You've Seen 'Em All   Leigh 1973
Seena   Lerner, Alan Jay 1976
See-No-Evil Eye, The   Ager 1923; Yellen 1923
Seesaw   Coleman 1973; Fields 1973
Segue   Brooks 1957
Segue to Palace (inst.)   Duke 1963
Self-Expression   Comden and Green 1953; Schwartz, Arthur 1927
Selfish Love   Friend 1949
Self-Made Family (She's a Lady with Money), The   Herbert 1905; Smith, Harry B. 1905

Self-Made Man   Fields 1939; Schwartz, Arthur 1939
Self-Pity Tears   Robison 1954
Sell It   Howard, Bart 1955
Sell Me   Howard, Bart 1957
Sell Your Cares for a Song   Young, Victor 1939
Selling Blue Skies   David, Hal 1978
Selling Gowns   Romberg 1917
Selzer Theme Song   Fain 1935; Kahal 1935
Seminary Girl   Bryan 1917
Seminola   Warren 1925
Seminole   Williams 1904
Senate in Session   Gorney 1940
Senatorial Roll Call, The   Gershwin, George 1931; Gershwin, Ira 1931
Senators' Song   Rome 1946
Send a Little Love My Way   David, Hal 1973; Mancini 1973
Send a Lot of Jazz Bands Over There   Berlin 1918
Send a Melody Around the World   Donaldson 1933
Send for Me   Hart 1930; Leslie 1911; Meyer 1911; Rodgers 1930
Send for Me, When You Come to the End and Need One True Friend   Johnson, Howard 1927
Send Her Some Flowers   Coots 1951
Send in the Clowns   Sondheim 1973
Send Me   Mills 1935
Send Me a Bluebird with Beautiful Blue Eyes   Fisher 1922
Send Me a Man   Razaf Date Unknown
Send Me a Picture of the Baby   Brown, Lew 1944
Send Me a Piece of Your Wedding Cake   Bryan 1955
Send Me Back My Husband   Bryan 1917
Send Me Jackson   Friend 1940
Send Me Letters Filled with Kisses   Bacharach 1959
Send Me No Flowers   Bacharach 1964; David, Hal 1964
Send Me Your Love (Er und Seine Schwester)   Robin 1931
Send My Mail to Tennessee   Wrubel 1933
Send My Mail to the County Jail   Lawrence 1938
Send My Picture to Scranton, Pa.   Bacharach 1970; David, Hal 1970
Send One Angel Down   Schwartz, Arthur 1937
Send Us Back to the Kitchen   Revel 1945
Sender   Johnson, James P. 1948
(Kalu) Senor   Adamson 1953
Senor Jose Durante   Evans 1955; Livingston, Jay 1955
Senor Sam   Blake 1947
Senor Turista   Drake 1955
(I Offer You the Moon) Senorita   Brown, Nacio Herb 1948; Goetz 1912; Heyman 1948; Kahn 1938; Revel 1952; Romberg 1938; Stept 1954
Senorita Diaz   Mercer 1951
Senorita Mine   Waller 1926
Senorita Pepita   Parish 1959
Senorita What's Her Name   Mills 1948
Senorita's Bouquet, A   Sigman 1948
Sensation   Sigman 1955
Sensational Stomp   Bryan 1928; Schwartz, Jean 1928
Sense of Humor   Hoffman 1950
Sensible Thing to Do, The   Lawrence 1951
Sentimental   Hoffman 1954
Sentimental and Melancholy   Mercer 1937; Whiting 1937
Sentimental Baby   Bergman 1961
Sentimental Dreamer   David, Hal 1962
Sentimental Folks   Loesser 1941; Styne 1941
Sentimental Fool   Rose 1929
Sentimental Gentleman from Georgia   Parish 1932
Sentimental Me   Hart 1925; Lawrence 1931; Rodgers 1925

Sentimental Melody   Coots 1929; Davis 1929
Sentimental Moments   Freed, Ralph 1955
Sentimental Nights   Atteridge 1919; Romberg 1919; Schwartz, Jean 1919
Sentimental Rhapsody   Adamson 1942
Sentimental Sailor   David, Hal 1960
Sentimental Sally   Rose 1925
Sentimental Silly   Dietz 1927; Gorney 1927
Sentimental Song (inst.)   Kern 1956
Sentimental Sunday   Sherman 1962
Sentimental Swanee   Bryan 1928
Sentimental Things You Do, The   Merrill 1953
Sentimental Tommy   Edwards 1902; Goetz 1910, 1911
Sentimental Waltz   Carroll 1925; Freed, Arthur 1925
Sentimental Weather   Duke 1936; Gershwin, Ira 1936
Sentinel Asleep, The   Von Tilzer 1900
Separate Tables   Adamson 1958; Warren 1958
Sepia Fashion Show   Johnson, James P. 1948
September Birthday Song   Caesar 1940
September in Caroline   Bryan 1925
September in the Rain   Dubin 1935; Warren 1935, 1937
September Morning   Howard, Bart 1959
September Night   Brown, A. Seymour 1927
September of My Years, The   Cahn 1965; Van Heusen 1965
September Song   Weill 1938
September's Comin' (inst.)   Coleman 1969
Sepulveda   Evans 1946; Livingston, Jay 1946
Sequence   Willson 1956
Sequoia   Brown, Nacio Herb 1934; Freed, Arthur 1934; Kahn 1934
Serafina   Goetz 1913
Serenade   Atteridge 1918; Cahn 1956; Friml 1925; Herbert 1897; Johnson, Howard 1933, 1934, 1939; Porter 1916; Robin 1936; Romberg 1918, 1924, 1954; Schwartz, Jean 1918; Smith, Harry B. 1896, 1897, 1912, 1913; Smith, Robert B. 1912; Webster 1954
Serenade Blues   Blake 1921; Sissle 1921
Serenade for a Tin Horn (inst.)   Stept 1952
Serenade for a Wealthy Widow   Fields 1934; McHugh 1934
Serenade for Savan   Bergman 1981
Serenade for Two   Washington 1938
Serenade in Blue   Gordon 1942; Warren 1942
Serenade in F (inst.)   Blake 1962
Serenade (inst.)   Blake 1946; Kern 1956; Warren Date Unknown
Serenade Me, Sadie   Young, Joe 1912
Serenade (Napoli) (inst.)   Warren 1956
Serenade of All Nations   Herbert 1898; Smith, Harry B. 1898
Serenade of Love   Romberg 1930
Serenade of Love Tango   Caesar 1930; Harbach 1930
Serenade to a Chambermaid   Dubin 1940; Fain 1940
Serenade to a Presidential Candidate   Lawrence 1948
Serenade to a Pullman Porter   Hammerstein 1941; Ruby 1941
Serenade to a Sponsor's Ugly Daughter (inst.)   Strouse 1945
Serenade to a Tony   Gorney 1953
Serenade to a Traffic Light (inst.)   Rome 1939
Serenade to a Veal Cutlet   Spina 1976
Serenade to an Old-Fashioned Girl, A   Berlin 1946
Serenade to Love   David, Mack 1946; Stept 1946
Serenade to Santa Fe   Spina 1977
Serenade to the Emperor   Caesar 1936
Serenade to the Stars, A   Adamson 1938; McHugh 1938
Serenade to the Sun, The   Friend 1942
Serenade to Whom It May Concern, A   Revel 1953

Serenade with Asides   Loesser 1948
Serenading the Moon   Styne 1929
Serenading You   Leslie 1944
Serenata   Parish 1950
Serenata Bufa (Serenade)   Gilbert 1933
Serenata (inst.)   Bloom 1928; Kern 1956
Serendipity   Sherman 1961
Sergeant Housewife   Fields 1945
Sergeant Philip of the Dancers   Kern 1912
Sergeant's Chant   Weill 1936
Sermon, The   Loesser 1960
Serpent, The   Webster 1967
Serpentin   Caesar 1936; Schwartz, Arthur 1936
Serpentine Dance, The   Goetz 1913
Servants Chorus   Herbert 1905
Servants' Frolic Dance, The   Cohan 1923
Serve My Time   Lewis 1974; Young, Joe 1974
Serves Me Right for Treating Him Wrong   Hoffman 1934
Session at Pete's Pad   Evans 1959; Livingston, Jay 1959;
     Mancini 1959
Set Aside Your Tears Til the Boys Come Marching
     Home   Gilbert 1917
Set 'em Sadie   Johnson, James P. 1922
Set 'Em Up Joe   Brooks 1946
Setting Up Exercise   Romberg 1928
Settle Down in a Little Town   Buck 1925
Settle Down in a One-Horse Town   Berlin 1914
Settle for Less   Ellington 1966
Settling Down   DeSylva 1920
Seulement Toi   Drake 1997
Seven Ages of Women   Atteridge 1919; Romberg 1919;
     Schwartz, Jean 1919
Seven Best Years   Davis 1959
Seven Days   Dietz 1924; Kern 1924
Seven Days a Week   David, Hal 1946
Seven Deadly Virtues, The   Drake 1968; Lerner, Alan Jay
     1960; Loewe 1960
Seven Different Sweeties a Week   Hoffman 1937; Lerner,
     Sammy 1937
Seven Hills of Rome, The   Adamson 1958; Young, Victor
     1957
Seven Kinds of Lonesome   David, Mack 1961
Seven Little Steps to Heaven   Mercer 1932
Seven Long Years   Robison 1954
Seven Miles   Spina 1944
Seven Million Crumbs   Loesser 1956
Seven Moons (Moon Pilot Melody)   Sherman 1962
Seven Nights a Week   Cahn 1957; Van Heusen 1957
Seven O'Clock in the Morning   Magidson 1945; Wrubel
     1945
Seven or Eleven, My Dixie Pair o' Dice   Brown, Lew 1922;
     Donaldson 1922
Seven Plagues   Livingston, Jerry 1962
Seven Pounds of Heaven   David, Mack 1946
Seven Pretty Dreams   David, Hal 1955
Seven Sweet Ages of Love, The   Lewis 1917; Schwartz, Jean
     1917; Young, Joe 1917
Seven Thousand Islands   Styne 1985
720 in the Books   Adamson 1939
Seven Veils   Brown, Lew 1927; DeSylva 1927; Henderson
     1927
Seven Wonders of the World, The   Spina 1957
Seven Year Itch, The   Cahn 1955; Styne 1955
Seven Years Bad Luck   Razaf 1926

(When You and I Were) Seventeen   Kahn 1924; Loesser
     1940
Seventeen and Twenty-One   Gershwin, George 1927;
     Gershwin, Ira 1927
Seventeen Gun Salute, A   Burke 1953; Van Heusen 1953
1776 to 1901   Smith, Harry B. 1901
Seventeen Summers   Leigh 1955; Spina 1955
Seventh Air Force, The   Burke 1944; Van Heusen 1944
Seventh Dawn   Webster 1964
Seventh Heaven   Mitchell 1937; Pollack 1937
77 Sunset Strip (Swingin' on the Strip) (Blue Nite on the
     Strip)   David, Mack 1959; Livingston, Jerry 1959
Seventy Six Trombones   Willson 1957
Sevilla   Brown, Lew 1926; DeSylva 1926; Eliscu 1931;
     Henderson 1926; Kahal 1926
Sew a Button   Merrill 1978, 1990
Sewing   Martin 1952
Sewing Ballet (Inst.)   Brooks 1960
Sewing Department Dance   Harbach 1933; Kern 1933
Sewing Machine, The   Loesser 1947
Sex Appeal   Caesar 1927; Porter 1920
Sex Marches On   Berlin 1940
Sextette   Atteridge 1924; Herbert 1914; Johnson, Howard
     1939; Rodgers 1923; Romberg 1916, 1924; Schwartz,
     Jean 1924; Smith, Harry B. 1909; Smith, Robert B. 1914,
     1916
Sextette from Lucia   Brooks 1945
Sextette Number   Kalmar 1920; Ruby 1920
Sexually Free   Coleman 1977
Sexy Saddle   Evans 1954; Livingston, Jay 1954
Seymour   Bergman 1957
Seymour (I Wanna See More of You)   Coots 1926
Sez I   Burke 1961
Shack in the Back of the Hills, A   Ahlert 1938; Young, Joe
     1938
Shack Town   Blake 1958
Shade Went Up, The   David, Hal 1949
Shades of Night   Gilbert 1916
Shades of Old Blarney   Stept 1953
Shadow Dance   Brooks 1958
Shadow Lane   De Lange 1943; Gilbert 1921
Shadow of Love   Duke 1939
Shadow of the Moon   Kern 1924; Revel 1946
Shadow of Your Smile, The   Webster 1966
Shadow Sweetheart   Parish 1938; Van Heusen 1938
Shadow Time   Webster 1950
Shadow Waltz   Dubin 1933; Warren 1933
Shadowland   Edwards 1914
Shadows   Conrad 1929; Heyman 1962; Mills 1935; Mitchell
     1929
Shadows Always Make Me Blue   Lewis 1919; Snyder 1919;
     Young, Joe 1919
Shadows in My Heart   Coots 1961
Shadows of Midnight Blue   Evans 1939; Livingston, Jay 1939
Shadows of Paris, The   Mancini 1964
Shadows of Yesterday's Stars, The   Dubin 1934, 1935;
     Warren 1934
Shadows on the Moon   Kahn 1938; Romberg 1938
Shadows on the Sand   Brennan 1925
Shadows on the Swanee   Burke 1933; Spina 1933; Young,
     Joe 1933
Shadows on the Wall   Carroll 1934; Fisher 1931; Gordon
     1931; Revel 1931
Shadows on the Window   Washington 1932; Young, Victor
     1932

Shadows that Walk in the Night   Harbach 1936; Romberg 1936

Shadows Will Fade Away   Brennan 1919

Shadowy Glass, The   Weill 1949

Shady Dame from Seville, The   Mancini 1982

Shady Lady   Johnson, Howard 1929

Shady Lady Bird   Blane 1941

Shady Tree, A   Donaldson 1927

Shag, The   Ager 1937; Livingston, Jerry 1937

Shaganola   Fain 1938

Shake, Brother!   Robin 1927

Shake Down the Stars   De Lange 1938; Van Heusen 1938

Shake 'em but Don't Break 'em!   Strouse 1999

Shake 'Em Up at Lucinda's Honolulu Ball   Sterling 1922; Von Tilzer 1922

Shake Hands, Dear Mrs. Cow   Rome 1964

Shake Hands with a Fool   Livingston, Jerry 1957

Shake Hands with Your Air Raid Warden   Caesar 1942

Shake Hands with Your Neighbor   Loesser 1940, 1944; Young, Victor 1940, 1944

Shake High, Shake Low   Brennan 1929

Shake His Hand and Call Him Brother   Gilbert 1944

Shake It, but Don't Break It   Mercer 1980

Shake It Off and Smile   Clare 1930

Shake It Off (with Rhythm)   Arlen 1936; Brown, Lew 1936

Shake Me and Wake Me   Robin 1926

Shake that Tree   David, Mack 1947; Livingston, Jerry 1947

Shake Well Before Using   Heyman 1931

Shake Your Duster   Johnson, James P. 1930; Razaf 1930

Shake Your Feet   Buck 1923; Mills 1927; Waller 1927

Shake Your Head from Side to Side   Cahn 1933

Shake Your Salt on the Bluebird's Tail   Blane 1945

Shakespeare Lied (You'll Get Over It)   Leigh 1967

Shakespeare of 1921   Hart 1921; Rodgers 1921

Shakespeare's Garden of Love   Atteridge 1921; Pollack 1921; Schwartz, Jean 1921

Shakespearian Rag, The   Atteridge 1915

Shakesperian Blues   Ager 1923; Yellen 1923

Shakin' Hands with the Sun   Revel 1944; Webster 1944

Shakin' It All Night Long   Waller 1936

Shakin' Like a Leaf   Johnson, Howard 1930

Shakin' the African   Arlen 1930; Koehler 1930

Shakin' the Shakespeare   Gordon 1932; Revel 1932

Shakin' Up the Folks Below   Blake 1940; Razaf 1940

Shaking Hands with the South   Young, Joe 1932

Shaking the Blues Away   Berlin 1927; Coots 1926

Shaky Little Baby   David, Hal 1958

Shalimar   Leslie 1927; Washington 1957

Shall I Go, Shall I Tarry (inst.)   Revel 1960

Shall I Tell Him?   Smith, Harry B. 1925

Shall I Tell You What I Think of You?   Hammerstein 1951; Rodgers 1951

Shall They Plead in Vain   Lewis 1919; Young, Joe 1919

Shall We Dance   Burke 1934; Gershwin, George 1937; Gershwin, Ira 1937; Hammerstein 1951; Rodgers 1951; Spina 1934

Shall We Love   Sigman 1933

Shall We Say Farewell?   Harburg 1961

Shall We Sing   Drake 1953

Sham   Herbert 1911; Smith, Harry B. 1911

Shama (inst.)   Warren 1977

Shame in Two Voices (inst.)   Johnson, James P. 1944

Shame on Me   Donaldson 1944

Shame on You   Arlen 1933; Heyman 1933

Shameen Dhu   Olcott 1914

Shamrock Waltz   Revel 1959

Shanghai   Buck 1919

Shanghai Dee Ho   Robin 1936; Whiting 1936

Shanghai Dream Man   Akst 1927; Davis 1927

Shanghai Lil   Dubin 1933; Warren 1933

Shanghai Lullaby   Kahn 1923

Shango   Loesser 1950

Shangri-La   Sigman 1954; Warren 1956

Shannon Belles   Goetz 1910

Shantung   Gilbert 1919

Shanty Boat on the Mississippi   Carroll 1939

Shape Up   Adams 1981; Strouse 1981

Share a Little   Harburg 1941; Lane 1941

Share and Share Alike   Mercer 1964

Share Croppin' Blues   Robison 1943

Share the Joy   Bacharach 1973; David, Hal 1973

Share the Luck   Willson 1956

Share Your Heart   Styne 1929

Sharing   Blake 1956; Coots 1930; Davis 1930; Sissle 1956

Sharing My Love with You   Stept 1932; Young, Joe 1932

Shark in the Bathtub   Drake 1958

Sharp as a Tack   Arlen 1942; Mercer 1942

Sharp Easter   Ellington 1941

Sha-Sha   Van Heusen 1938

Sha-Sha-Nay (Walk in Peace)   David, Mack 1971

Shattuck on Parade   Davis 1935; Silver 1935

Shauny O'Shae   Martin 1948

Shauny O'Shea   Martin 1946

Shavian Shivers   Duke 1930; Harburg 1930

Shaving Song (A Man Must Shave)   Dixon 1935; Wrubel 1935

She   Cahn 1980; Ellington 1955; Strouse 1993, Date Unknown

She Ain't Your Sweetie   Dixon 1926; Woods 1926

She Alone Could Understand   Hammerstein 1920; Harbach 1920

She Believed a Gypsy   Brown, Lew 1940; Henderson 1940

She Believes I'm in Brooklyn Tonight   Norworth 1912

She Believes in Brooklyn Tonight   Goetz 1912

She Belongs to Me   Johnson, Howard 1926; Razaf 1926

She Broke My Heart In Three Places   Hoffman 1944; Livingston, Jerry 1944

She Came, She Saw, She Can Canned   Harburg 1940; Lane 1940

She Came to the Valley   David, Mack 1978

She Can Be So Nice, But She Don't Wanna   Fisher 1924

She Can Do Little Who Can't Do This   Smith, Robert B. 1905

She Can't Be Bothered with Me   Kahn 1929

She Can't Make Coffee   Schwartz, Jean 1942

She Can't Say No   Bryan 1925; Meyer 1925

She Changed Her Hi-De-Hi-De for His Yodal-O-De-Ay   Schwartz, Jean 1933

She Could Shake the Maracas   Hart 1939; Rodgers 1939

She Couldn't Say No   Bryan 1924; Schwartz, Jean 1924

She Couldn't Say No to a Sailor Named Joe   Johnson, J. Rosamond 1942

She Didn't Have the Heart to Say "No"   Freed, Ralph 1944

She Didn't Hear the Curfew Bell   Burke 1934; Spina 1934

She Didn't Say   Burke 1934; Spina 1934

She Didn't Say Yes   Harbach 1931; Kern 1931

She Didn't Seem to Care About Me   Jerome 1904; Schwartz, Jean 1904

She Does a Little Business on the Side   Silver 1950

She Doesn't Understand Me   Comden and Green 1960;
   Styne 1960
She Don't Wanna   Ager 1927; Yellen 1927
She Fell Down on Her Cadenza   Von Tilzer 1924
She Gave Her Heart to a Soldier Boy   Bryan 1941
She Gets Me All Fussed Up   Brown, Lew 1916; Hanley 1916
She Goes Out A-Fishin' with Her Hook and Her
   Line   Leslie 1915
She Got Even With Stephen   Bryan 1914; Lewis 1914; Meyer
   1914
She Got Him   Hammerstein 1941; Romberg 1941
She Had the Face of an Angel   Revel 1952
She Had to Go and Lose It at the Astor   Raye 1939
She Hadda Go Back   Willson 1963
She Has a Way   Sherman 1995
She Has to Be the Right Girl   Duke 1968
She Has Trouble with Her Eyes   Howard, Joseph E. 1908
She Is Not Thinking of Me   Lerner, Alan Jay 1958; Loewe
   1958
She Is So Lovely   Davis 1928
She Is the Sunshine of Virginia   Carroll 1916
(I Met Her in the Moonlight, But) She Keeps Me in the
   Dark   Bryan 1926
She Killed Them   Adams 1996; Strouse 1996
She Knew More than Any Girl Should Know   Ager 1918
She Knows Her Onions   Ager 1926; Pollack 1926; Yellen
   1926
She Learned About Sailors   Clare 1934; Whiting 1934
She Likes Basketball   Bacharach 1968; David, Hal 1968
She Looks Like Helen Brown   Fisher 1936; Rose 1936
She Loves Me   Brown, Lew 1924
She Loves Me Not   Heyman 1933; Jerome 1913; Schwartz,
   Arthur 1933; Schwartz, Jean 1913
She Made Me Promise   Freed, Ralph 1954; Livingston, Jerry
   1954
She Makes Me Laugh   Coleman 1999
She May Have Seen Better Days   Johnson, Howard 1939
She Needs Me   Sondheim 1967
She Never Felt Alone   Sherman 1970
She Never Loved a Man as Much as That   Smith, Robert B.
   1900
She of the Black Coffee Eyes   Spina 1945
She Parted with Her Lover   Duke 1944
She Picked It Up in Mexico   Yellen 1948
(She Walks Like You, She Talks Like You) She Reminds Me
   of You   Gordon 1933; Revel 1933
She Said 'Uh Huh' to Me   Johnson, Howard 1929
She Says No   Rose 1925
She Sees Who I Am   Strouse 1999
She Sells Seashells By the Seashore   Alter 1959; Heyman
   1959
She Shook Him in Chicago   Harbach 1910
She Still Loves You   Fain 1953; Webster 1953
She Trimmed Them All So Neatly   Smith, Harry B. 1910
She Waits By the Lookout Mountain on the Lookout for
   Me   Brown, Lew 1924
She Walks in Beauty   Oakland 1970
She Walks in Her Husband's Sleep   Sterling 1920; Von
   Tilzer 1920
She Walks Like This   Smith, Harry B. 1903
She Wants a Man   Yellen 1977
She Was a China Tea Cup   Rainger 1933; Robin 1933
She Was a Dairy Maid   Carroll 1916
She Was a Dear Little Girl   Berlin 1908; Snyder 1909
She Was a Fair Young Mermaid   Porter 1912

She Was a Girl I Used to Know   Hanley 1916
She Was a Hayseed Maid (inst.)   Herbert 1908
She Was a Wonderful Queen   Youmans 1926
She Was an Acrobat's Daughter   Kalmar 1935; Ruby 1935
She Was Happy Till She Met You   Johnson, Howard 1939
She Was in Last Night   Coots 1943
She Was It   Silver 1927; Turk 1927
She Was Just a Good Fellow Who Couldn't Say No   Clarke
   1926; Monaco 1926
She Was Kicked in the Head by a Butterfly   Magidson 1929;
   Washington 1929
She Was Made for Love   Bryan 1915
She Was My First Love   Coleman 1984
She Was Not So Bad for a Country Girl   DeSylva 1918
She Was Wearing a Big Sombrero   Lane 1939; Loesser 1939
She Wasn't You   Lane 1965; Lerner, Alan Jay 1965
She Wears Red Feathers (And a Huly-Huly Skirt)   Merrill
   1952
She Went Out to Mail a Letter   Hoffman 1946; Livingston,
   Jerry 1946
She Went to Old St. Mary's and I Went to Notre
   Dame   Bryan 1932; Meyer 1932
She Who Walks in Beauty   Oakland 1947
She Won't Charleston   Kalmar 1927; Ruby 1927
She Wore a Little Jacket of Blue   Bryan 1934; Fisher 1934
Sheba of Georgia, The   Pollack 1923
Sheeksa, The Queen of Araby   Brown, Lew 1922; Conrad
   1922
Sheep Were in the Meadow, The   Hoffman 1937; Lerner,
   Sammy 1937
Sheep's Song   Sondheim 1974
Sheik of Alabam Weds a Brown Skin Vamp, The   Johnson,
   James P. 1922
Sheik of Araby, The   Robin 1942; Smith, Harry B. 1922;
   Snyder 1922, 1942
Sheik of Avenue B, The   Kalmar 1922
She'll Be Coming 'Round the Catskill Mountains   Harburg
   1932
She'll Be Coming Round the Mountain   Johnson, Howard
   1939
She'll Be There   David, Mack 1968
She'll Love Me and Like It   Robin 1930; Whiting 1930
She'll Say Bye Bye to You   Blake 1955
Shelter in the Time of Storm   Robison 1953
Shelter of My Baby's Arms, The   Donaldson 1929; Leslie
   1929
Sheltered By the Stars, Cradled By the Moon   Waller 1932;
   Young, Joe 1932
Shema Lo-ed (What Does It Mean?)   Styne 1978
Shenandoah Rose   Livingston, Jerry 1957; Webster 1957
Shenanigans   Lawrence 1938
Shennigans (Two of Irish)   Sigman 1949
Shepherd, The   Freed, Ralph 1939
Shepherd Gavotte, The   Carroll 1914
Shepherd Gavotte No. 1, The   Atteridge 1914; Romberg
   1914
Shepherd Lullaby   Freed, Ralph 1939
Shepherd of the Hills   Leslie 1927
Shepherd's Duet   Smith, Harry B. 1900
Shepherd's Holiday, The   Duke 1944
Sheridan's Ride (inst.)   Young, Victor 1955
Sheriff Honest John Baile   David, Mack 1958
Sherman   Wrubel 1933
Sherrif's Song   Smith, Harry B. 1902

She's a Bombshell from Brooklyn (And Not from Brazil)   Dubin 1943; Monaco 1943

She's a Daughter of the Sunny South   Cobb 1899; Edwards 1899

She's a Flower from the Fields of Old Ireland   Olcott 1909

She's a Follies Girl   Adamson 1936; Donaldson 1936

She's a Girl Scout at Heart (Park Number)   Coslow 1937

She's a Good Dame   Rainger 1934; Robin 1934

She's a Good Girl   Fain 1929

She's a Good Kid   Cahn 1947; Styne 1947

She's a Good Neighbor   Rainger 1940; Robin 1940

She's a Gorgeous Thing   Coots 1930; Davis 1930

She's a Great, Great Girl   Woods 1928

She's a Gypsy from Brooklyn   Gilbert 1945; Oakland 1945

She's a Home Girl   Brown, Lew 1928; Conrad 1928; Davis 1949; DeSylva 1928; Henderson 1928; Silver 1949

She's a Latin from Manhattan   Dubin 1935; Warren 1935

She's a New Kind of Old Fashioned Girl   Rose 1929

She's a Nothing   Cahn 1976; Lane 1976

She's a Nut   Coleman 1978; Comden and Green 1978

She's a Very Dear Friend of Mine   Herbert 1904

She's a Wonderful Cook   Fisher 1936

She's a Yankee Doodle Girl   Sterling 1904; Von Tilzer 1904

She's an Alright Girl   Cobb 1900; Edwards 1900

She's an Awful Nice Gal   Meyer 1909

She's an Old Fashioned Girl from an Old Fashioned Town   Johnson, Howard 1934

She's Another Sweet Mother Machree   Jerome 1927

She's Beautiful but Dumb   Fisher 1922; Rose 1922

She's Been a Comfort to Me   Schwartz, Arthur 1929

She's Crazy Over Me   Dubin 1927

She's Dancing Her Heart Away   Gilbert 1914

She's Dixie All the Time   Bryan 1916

She's Dixie Through and Through   Bryan 1907

She's Everybody's Sweetheart but Nobody's Gal   Conrad 1924; Rose 1924

She's Everyone Else's Girl but Mine   Carroll 1918

She's Everything a Sweetie Ought to Be   Stept 1919

She's Exciting   Fields 1950

She's From Missouri   Burke 1943; Van Heusen 1943

She's Going Mad   Bryan 1914; Lewis 1914; Meyer 1914

She's Gone Away   Bacharach 1969; David, Hal 1969

She's Gonna Come Home with Me   Loesser 1956

She's Gonna Love Me   Strouse 1993, Date Unknown

She's Good Enough To Be Your Baby's Mother and She's Good Enough to Vote with You   Bryan 1916

She's Got an Awful Lot of What I Need a Lot of Now   Ahlert 1928; Turk 1928

She's Got Everything It Takes to Make a Wonderful Girl   Friend 1919

She's Got It   Akst 1927; Davis 1927; Gilbert 1927

She's Got the Biggest Parakeets in Town   Oakland 1960

She's Got To Be Good If She Comes from Hollywood   Bryan 1924; Schwartz, Jean 1924

She's Got to Be Some Woman to Steal My Man Away   Akst 1930; Clarke 1930

She's Innocent   Gershwin, Ira 1921; Youmans 1921

She's Just a Baby   Gershwin, George 1921

She's Just a Junior   Adams 1958

She's Just My Size   Cobb 1900; Edwards 1900

She's Mine, All Mine   Kalmar 1921; Ruby 1921

She's Mine to Have and to Hold   Edwards 1901

She's My Kind of People   Silver 1964

She's My Love   Merrill 1961

She's My Runabout   Gilbert 1927

She's No Longer a Gypsy   Adams 1970; Strouse 1970

She's Not Enough Woman for Me   Fields 1959

She's Not in a Class with You   Martin 1951

She's Not Made for You   Strouse 1993, Date Unknown

She's Not the Type   Arlen 1933; Koehler 1933

She's Nuts About Me   Brown, Nacio Herb 1932; DeSylva 1932; Whiting 1932

She's on Her Way   Harbach 1926; Kern 1926

She's Right (Security)   Cahn 1947; Styne 1947

She's Saving It All for Me   Johnson, Howard 1917

She's Sick   Brooks 1959

She's So Beautiful   Howard, Bart 1961

She's So Different Now   Stept 1922

She's So I Don't Know   Robin 1929; Whiting 1929

She's So Nice   Coots 1931; Davis 1931

She's Somebody's Baby   Burke 1931

She's Something Else   Cahn 1969

She's Something Spanish   David, Hal 1953

She's Still My Baby   Coslow 1926

She's Such a Comfort to Me   Schwartz, Arthur 1929

She's Tall, She's Tan, She's Terrific   Coots 1937; Davis 1937

She's the Darling of the Boys (Darling of the Guards)   Parish 1936

She's the Girl   Brown, A. Seymour 1913

She's the Greatest   Cohan 1972

She's the Hottest Gal in Tennessee   Johnson, James P. 1926

She's the Kind of a Girl that Any Fellow Could Like   Bryan 1918

She's the Reason   Akst 1930; Clarke 1930

She's the Same Old Sunbonnet Sue   Edwards 1923; Smith, Robert B. 1923

She's the Sister of Annabelle Lee   Clare 1931; Pollack 1931

She's the Sweetest Gal in Kankakee   Warren 1925

She's the Sweetheart of Six Other Guys   Johnson, Howard 1928

She's the Sweetheart of the Navy and He's True to the Red, White and Blue   Fisher 1938

She's Too Hip to Be Happy   Coleman 1967

She's Waiting for You to Love Her All the Time   Monaco 1913

She's Way Up Thar (I'm Way Down 'Yar)   Brown, Lew 1934

She's Wonderful   Donaldson 1928; Kahn 1928

Sh-h-h-h (The Shush Song)   Henderson 1922

Shhhhh! He's on the Beat!   Ellington 1941

Shicklegruber   Fain 1944; Harburg 1944

Shiek of Avenue B, The   Ruby 1922

Shika, Shika   Rome 1954

Shim Sham   Alter 1934

Shim Sham Rhumba   Loesser Date Unknown

Shim Sham Shimmy Dance, The   Razaf 1933

Shimmee Baby   Whiting 1919

Shimmee Town   Buck 1919

Shimmy a la Egyptian   Atteridge 1919; Romberg 1919; Schwartz, Jean 1919

Shimmy Nods from Chaminade   Bryan 1920; Schwartz, Jean 1920

Shimmy on Your Own Side   Edwards 1923; Smith, Robert B. 1923

Shimmy Special   Oakland 1953; Raye 1953

Shimmy Valentine   Bryan 1920; Schwartz, Jean 1920

Shimmy with Me   Kern 1921

Shimmying Everywhere   Bryan 1919; Schwartz, Jean 1919

Shimmy-Shaking Love   Atteridge 1919; Carroll 1919

(That's Why They Call Me) S-H-I-N-E   Brown, Lew 1924

Shine Boy   Hoffman 1934

Shine On   Herbert 1919

Shine On Harvest Moon   Norworth 1908

Shine On, Little Son   Bryan 1920; Schwartz, Jean 1920

Shine on Your Shoes, A   Dietz 1932; Schwartz, Arthur 1932

Shine Out All You Little Stars   Kern 1909

Shine Yo' Shoes   Gordon 1948; Myrow 1948

Shine Your Lantern   Merrill 1971; Styne 1971

Shining Shoes   Bryan 1928; Schwartz, Jean 1928

Shining World   Drake 1954

Ship Building Song (We're Busy Building Boats)   Buck 1918

Ship Has Sailed, The   Brown, Lew 1939; Stept 1939

Ship in the Bottle, The   DePaul 1957; Raye 1957

Ship (inst.), The   Revel 1959

Ship o' Dreams   Davis 1941; Stept 1941

Ship of Dreams   Howard, Joseph E. 1909

Ship of Fools   Washington 1965

Ship of My Dreams   Bryan 1929; Meyer 1929

Ship Sailed, The   David, Mack 1959

Ship without a Sail, A   Hart 1929; Rodgers 1929

Shipoopi   Willson 1957

Ship's Concert   Brooks 1960

Shipwrecked (On a Desert Island)   Spina 1954

Shirley   Johnson, Howard 1934; Mills 1939

Shirley and the Black Dots (inst.)   McHugh 1936

Shirley Early, Early Shirley   Caesar 1950

Shirley Take a Chance   Brooks 1958

Shirl's Theme   Cahn 1959

Shirt Waist Man, The   Cobb 1900; Edwards 1900

Shirts By the Millions   Gershwin, George 1933; Gershwin, Ira 1933

Shivaree   Mercer 1964

Shivk-a-ree   Robison 1950

Shloop, The   Strouse 1993

Shmoo Song, The   Styne 1948

Shoe Shine Boy   Cahn 1935

Shoe Shine Song   Hammerstein 1940; Romberg 1940

Shoe Song, The   Loesser 1952

Shoein' the Mare   Arlen 1934; Gershwin, Ira 1934; Harburg 1934

Shoemaker's Holiday   Raye 1939

Shoes   Hanley 1931

Shoes and Socks Shook Susan   Williams 1910

Shoes of Husband No. 1 Are Worn By Number Two, The   Herbert 1915

Shoes with Wings On   Gershwin, Ira 1949; Warren 1949

Shoestring (inst.)   Schwartz, Jean 1930

Sholom Aleichem   Gilbert 1931

Shoo Shoo Boogie Boo   Coslow 1929; Robin 1929, 1933; Whiting 1929

Shoo the Hoodoo Away   Silver 1930; Snyder 1930

Shooby-Dooia   Mercer 1966

Shoot the Moon (Patio Song)   Gordon 1953; Myrow 1953

Shoot the Rhythm to the One that Wants It   Mills 1938

Shoot the Works   Mills 1935

Shootin' at the Moon   Baer 1926; Gilbert 1926

Shootin' the Works for Uncle Sam   Porter 1941

Shooting   Loesser 1937

Shooting Show   Atteridge 1911

Shooting Star   Herbert 1920

Shooting Stars   Carmichael 1957

Shooting the Bull Around the Bulletin Boards   Jerome 1915; Schwartz, Jean 1915

Shop   Kern 1917

Shop Girls and Mannikins   DeSylva 1925; Gershwin, George 1925; Gershwin, Ira 1925

Shop of Santa Claus   Egan 1931

Shopping   Atteridge 1915

Shopping Around   Rome 1952

Shopping Chorus   Smith, Harry B. 1901

Shore Leave   Brennan 1930; Freed, Ralph 1942; Friml 1930; Lane 1942; Robin 1927; Youmans 1927

Shore Leave (Let's Go Sailor)   Arlen 1942

Shores of Minnetonka   Kahn 1921

Short and Sweet   De Lange 1945; Fain 1935; Lewis 1948; Myrow 1945

Short, Fat and 4F   DePaul 1943; Raye 1943

Short Time to Get There   Robison 1963

Short Trail Became a Long Trail (Since You Left Me to Walk Alone), The   Razaf 1924; Waller 1924

Shorter Than Me Routine   DePaul 1942; Raye 1942

Shortest Day of the Year, The   Hart 1938; Rodgers 1938

Shortnin' Bread Special   Oakland 1960

Shorty George, The   Kern 1942; Mercer 1942

Shorty the Gunner   Hart Date Unknown; Rodgers Date Unknown

Shot in the Dark, A   Mancini 1964

Shotgun Papa   Razaf 1932

Should I   Brown, Nacio Herb 1929, 1930; Freed, Arthur 1929, 1930; Loesser 1937

Should I Be Sorry   Johnson, Howard 1928

Should I Be Sweet   Brown, Lew 1935; DeSylva 1932; Youmans 1932, 1935

Should I Believe My Heart   Hoffman 1945

Should I Believe You   Silver 1956

Should I Reveal   Brown, Nacio Herb 1943; Freed, Arthur 1943

Should I Tell You I Love You   Porter 1946

Should We Kiss 'Em or Kill 'Em, Yes or No   Johnson, Howard 1927

Shoulda Stood in Bed   Arlen 1965

Shoulder Arms   Smith, Harry B. 1923

Shoulder Shakin' Blues, The   Brown, Lew Date Unknown; Henderson Date Unknown

Shout 'em Aunt Tillie   Ellington 1943; Mills 1943

Shout Hooray!   Baer 1942

Shout On!   Johnson, James P. 1929

Shoutin' in that Amen Corner   Razaf 1932

(There's No Business Like) Show Business   Berlin 1946

Show 'Em You Got Class   Ellington 1959

Show Girl   Martin 1972

Show Girls   Adams 1981; Strouse 1981

Show Him the Way   Hart 1921; Rodgers 1921

Show Is On, The   Carmichael 1936

Show Is Over   Conrad 1934; Coslow 1928, 1934; Dubin 1928, 1934; Friend 1958

Show Me   Lerner, Alan Jay 1956; Loewe 1956

Show Me a Happy Woman (And I'll Show You a Miserable Man)   Cahn 1953; Fain 1953

Show Me a Rose (Or Leave Me Alone)   Kalmar 1936; Ruby 1936

Show Me How to Do the Fox Trot   Berlin 1914

Show Me How to Make Love   Caesar 1925; Hart 1926; Rodgers 1926

Show Me That Kind of Girl   Dubin 1927

Show Me that You Love Me   Hoffman 1955, 1958

Show Me the Town   Gershwin, George 1926; Gershwin, Ira 1926; Hanley 1920

Show Me the Way   Berlin 1917; Davis 1924

Show Me the Way to Love   Donaldson 1930

Show Me the Way to the Kerry Fair   Koehler 1947

Show Me Your Qualifications   Razaf 1934

Show Must Go On, The   Ager 1950; Davis 1950; Gershwin, Ira 1944; Kahn 1938; Kern 1944; Spina 1959

Show Starts Right Away, The   Evans 1953; Livingston, Jay 1953

Show Stoppers   Styne 1955

Show Train   Comden and Green 1951; Styne 1951

Show Us the Way, Blue Eagle   Willson 1933

Show You What Love Can Do   Cahn 1940

Show Your Linen Miss Richardson   Mercer 1939

Shower of Stars   Spina 1957

Showing the Yankees London Town   Cohan 1908

Showmanship   Cahn 1960; Van Heusen 1960

Shows How Wrong a Gal Can Be   Cahn 1941

Showstopper Theme   Styne 1957

Shrine of Saint Anne De-Beaupre, The   Spina 1952

Shrine of St. Anne the Beaupre, The   Webster 1952

Shriner's Ballet   Strouse 1960

Shrug, The   Akst 1938; Clare 1938

Shuffle   Hart 1926, 1927; Rodgers 1926, 1927

Shuffle Along   Blake 1921; Kahn 1923; Meyer 1923; Sissle 1921

Shuffle Off to Buffalo   Dubin 1933; Warren 1933

Shuffle Song, The   David, Mack 1979

Shuffle Your Feet (And Just Roll Along)   Fields 1928; McHugh 1928

Shuffle Your Troubles Away   Hanley 1924

Shufflin' Home   Meyer 1926

Shufflin' on Saturday Night   Johnson, Howard 1930

Shufflin' Sam   Kern 1924

Shuffling Shiveree, The   Atteridge 1914; Carroll 1914; Romberg 1914

Shut Yo' Mouf   Razaf 1924; Waller 1924

Shut Your Eyes and Make Believe   Von Tilzer 1911

Shut-Eye   Eliscu 1956

Shy   Rome 1964

Shy Little, My Little Girl   Howard, Joseph E. 1919

Shy Old Billionaire, The   Robison 1967

Shy Suburban Maid, A   Herbert 1906

Shy Sweetheart, The   Rome 1943

Shy Violet   Akst 1937; Clare 1937

Si Petite   Parish 1933

Si, Si, Senor   Eliscu 1929; Rose 1929; Youmans 1929

Si, Si, Senorita   Romberg 1922

Si, Si, Si   Baer 1960

Si Vous Aimez les Poitrines   Porter 1933

Siam   Fisher 1915; Johnson, Howard 1915

Siam Soo   Motzan 1921

Siberia   Porter 1955

Siberian Dip (inst.), The   Johnson, J. Rosamond 1911

Siberian Whirl, The   Johnson, J. Rosamond 1911

Siciliana   Johnson, Howard 1939

Sick   Hart 1932

Sick, Sick, Sick   Harburg 1961

Sick Song, The   Sherman 1960

Sid, Ol' Kid   Merrill 1959

Side By Each   Donaldson 1922; Kahn 1922

Side By Side   Kahn 1922; Meyer 1930; Mitchell 1930; Woods 1927

Side by Side by Side   Sondheim 1970

Side By Side By the Beautiful Seaside   Coots 1954

Side By Side By the Zuyder Zee   Edwards 1928

Side Car, The   Porter 1935

Side Car (inst.)   Stept 1957

Side Saddle   Parish 1959

Side Street Serenade   Loesser Date Unknown

Side Street Troubadour   Ager 1940; Akst 1940; Davis 1940

Sidewalk   Atteridge 1921; Pollack 1921; Schwartz, Jean 1921

Sidewalk Cafe, A   Drake 1955

Sidewalk Shufflers, The   DePaul 1951; Raye 1951

Sidewalk Waltz, The   Coots 1933; Young, Joe 1933

Sidewalks of Cuba   Mills 1934; Oakland 1934; Parish 1934

Sidewalks of Paris   Adamson 1963; Fain 1963; Young, Victor 1959

Sidi-El-Abbes   Lawrence 1955

Sidioso   Adamson 1934; Lane 1934

Sidonie   Kern 1913; Smith, Harry B. 1913

Siege at Loha   Willson 1969

Siege (inst.), The   Willson 1929

Siempre (Till the End of Time)   Akst 1933; Gilbert 1933

Sierra   Russell 1943

Siesta   Brown, Nacio Herb 1948

Siesta, Fiesta and Amor   David, Hal 1954

Sighing Bands   Koehler 1923

Sighted Dame — Loved Same   De Lange 1943

Sights and Sounds of the Monterrey Peninsula (inst.)   Warren Date Unknown

Sights of London   Herbert 1924

Sight-Seeing Tour, A   Porter 1944

Sign   Strouse 1981

Sign, Lily, Sign   Coleman 1978; Comden and Green 1978

Sign of a Honeymoon, The   Williams 1909

Sign of the Rose, The   Brown, Lew 1923

Sign of the "V", The   DePaul 1942; Raye 1942

Sign on the Dotted Line   Duke 1963

Sign Up for Happy Days   Styne 1941

Signal, The   Gershwin, George 1925; Hammerstein 1925; Harbach 1925

Signor Mons. Muldoni   Herbert 1898; Smith, Harry B. 1898

Signora   Mercer 1966

Signora Campbell   Lane 1979; Lerner, Alan Jay 1979

Signs   Jerome 1907; Mercer 1953; Schwartz, Jean 1907; Smith, Harry B. 1903

Siguiendote   David, Mack 1947

Silas   Smith, Harry B. 1901

Silence   Howard, Bart 1938

Silence Is Golden   Martin 1972

Silencers, The   David, Mack 1966

Silent Love   Johnson, Howard 1930

Silent Movie Rag, The   Sigman 1950

Silent Movies   Brooks 1959

Silent Partner   Robison 1952

Silent Senorita   Robin 1943; Warren 1943

Silent Serenade   Rome 1952

Silent Spring, The   Arlen 1963; Harburg 1963

Silent Stranger, The   Johnson, James P. 1959; Russell 1959

Silent Treatment   Hoffman 1967

Silently   Coots 1967

Silhouette   Smith, Harry B. 1927

Silhouette Ballet   Atteridge 1914; Carroll 1914; Romberg 1914

Silhouette (inst.)   Bloom 1927

Silhouetted in the Moonlight   Mercer 1938; Whiting 1938

Silhouettes (In the Snow) (Mojave Dusk in the Desert) (inst.)   Warren 1957

Silk Stocking Sally   Rose 1927

Silk Stocking Trail, The   Atteridge 1920

Silk Stockings   Porter 1955

Silken Song, The   Willson 1969

Silks and Satins   Atteridge 1920

Silly Boy   Ruby 1945
Silly Little Sally   Freed, Ralph 1938
Silly People   Sondheim 1973
Silly Season, The   Gershwin, Ira 1921; Youmans 1921
Silly Signs Song, The   Drake 1956
Silly Song, The   David, Mack 1955
Silly Thoughts   Hanley 1921
Silvana Mangano Mambo, The   David, Mack 1955
Silver Bands of Love   Yellen 1922
Silver Bells   Evans 1951; Livingston, Jay 1951; Loesser 1975
Silver Canoe, A   DeSylva 1922
Silver Cobwebs   Ellington 1953
Silver Dollar Boys   Robison 1960
Silver Dollars Tinkling Down   DePaul 1949; Raye 1949
Silver Haired Mammy   Leslie 1926
Silver Horseshoe   Coots 1953
Silver in Your Hair   Howard, Joseph E. 1946
Silver Moon   Porter 1912
Silver Nights in Honolulu   Hanley 1931
Silver on the Sage   Rainger 1938, 1939; Robin 1938, 1939
Silver Platter   Berlin 1957
Silver Rose   Meyer 1926
Silver Saddle   Carmichael 1946
Silver Sails   Heyman 1934
Silver Shadows and Golden Dreams   Pollack 1944
Silver Shield   Dietz 1944; Duke 1944
Silver Skates   Martin 1958
Silver Song Bird   Bryan 1927
Silver Spoon   Alter 1956
Silver Star, The   Smith, Harry B. 1909
Silver Stars of Hawaii   Parish 1927
Silver Swanee   Schwartz, Jean 1922
Silver Threads Among the Gold   Johnson, Howard 1939
Silver Threads and Golden Dreams   David, Mack 1940; Stept 1940
Silver Waltz, The   Young, Victor 1956
Silver Water   Von Tilzer 1920
Silver Wedding, The   Romberg 1922
Silver Wing   Friml 1927
Silver Wings   David, Mack 1959; Dixon 1935; Livingston, Jerry 1959; Wrubel 1935
Silver Wings in the Moonlight Over the China Sea   Blake 1955
Silvery Moon   Goetz 1917
Silvery Moonlight (Only a Moonbeam Dream)   Coslow 1929; Robin 1929, 1933
Simchas (Joyous Occasions)   Styne 1978
Simon Legree   Arlen 1944; Harburg 1944; Robison 1939
Simonetta   Caesar 1953
Simon's Song   Livingston, Jerry 1973
Simpatica   DePaul 1943; Hart 1941; Raye 1943; Rodgers 1941
Simpatico   Cahn 1955; Schwartz, Arthur 1955
Simple   Sondheim 1964
Simple and Sweet   Baer 1938; Fain 1934; Gilbert Date Unknown; Kahal 1934
Simple Girl, A   Adams 1957; Strouse 1957
Simple Joys of Maidenhood, The   Lerner, Alan Jay 1960; Loewe 1960
Simple Life   Atteridge 1916; Gershwin, George 1921; Gershwin, Ira 1921; Hart 1926; Rodgers 1926; Romberg 1916
Simple Little Susie Simpkins   Sterling 1903
Simple Little Things, The   Brown, Lew 1944
Simple Little Tune   Kern 1917; Smith, Harry B. 1917

Simple Me   Hammerstein 1920; Harbach 1920
Simple Serenade   Harburg 1961
Simple Simon   Edwards 1905; Razaf 1939; Smith, Robert B. 1905
Simple Simon and Simple Sue   Bryan 1934
Simple Simon Instep, The   Hart 1930; Rodgers 1930
Simple Spanish Maid   Bryan 1927; Schwartz, Jean 1927
Simple Things in Life, The   Henderson 1935; Koehler 1935
Simplicity   Carmichael 1955
Simplified Language   Coleman 1975; Comden and Green 1975
Simply Because You're Away   Egan 1942
Simply Grand   Koehler 1935
Simply Meant to Be   Mancini 1987
Simpson Sisters, The   Fields 1959
Sin   Evans 1959; Livingston, Jay 1959
Sinatra Theme (inst.)   Young, Victor 1950
Sinbad Was in Bad All the Time   Carroll 1917
Since an Angel Like Mary Loves a Devil Like Me   Leslie 1931; Meyer 1931; Young, Joe 1931
Since Becky Became a Conductor   Silver 1918
Since Becky Put on a Smock   Johnson, Howard 1926
Since Dolly Dimple Made a Hit (Dolly Dimples)   Jerome 1904; Schwartz, Jean 1904
Since Hannah from Savannah Came to Harlem   Blake 1930; Razaf 1930
Since Henry Ford Apologized to Me   Rose 1927
Since Hiram Went to Yale   Williams 1910
Since I Am Not for Thee   Herbert 1899; Smith, Harry B. 1899
Since I Am Queen of the Carnival   Herbert 1900; Smith, Harry B. 1900
Since I Found You   Clare 1926; Gershwin, George 1913; Woods 1926
Since I Gave My Heart to You   Bryan 1929; Snyder 1929
Since I Gave Up the Old Gang for a Little Gang of My Own   Hoffman 1932; Washington 1932
Since I Kissed My Baby Goodbye   Porter 1941
Since I Kissed the Blarney Stone   Young, Joe 1953
Since I Met You   Oakland 1952
Since I Remember You   Hart 1922; Rodgers 1922
Since It Started to Rain in Lover's Lane   Hoffman 1930
Since I've Been Knowin' You   Brown, Nacio Herb 1930; Egan 1930
Since Johnny Got His Gun   Brown, Lew 1917
Since Katy the Waitress Became an Aviatress   Berlin 1919
Since Ma Got the Craze Espagnole   Porter 1919
Since Ma Is Playing Mah Jongg   Conrad 1924; Rose 1924
Since Maggie Became Marguerite   Leslie 1930
Since Maggie Dooley Learned the Hooley Hooley   Kalmar 1916; Leslie 1916; Meyer 1916
Since Mariella Learned the Dardenella   Von Tilzer 1920
Since Mary Ann McCue Came Back from Honolulu   Von Tilzer 1916
Since Mother Was a Girl   Norworth 1908
Since Mrs. McNott Learned to Do the Turkey Trot   Jerome 1913; Sterling 1913; Von Tilzer 1913
Since My Gal Is Gone I've Got the Blues   Silver 1918
Since My Margarette Became A-Da-Suffragette   Cobb 1913; Edwards 1913
Since My Wife Took Up Miniature Golf   Schwartz, Jean 1930
Since O'Keefe Is on Relief   Johnson, Howard 1935
Since Papa Becomes a Billionaire   Herbert 1911

Since Rebecca, Came Back from Mecca (Rebecca, Come Back from Mecca)   Kalmar 1921; Ruby 1921

Since Sister Nell Heard Paderewski Play   Jerome 1902; Schwartz, Jean 1902; Smith, Harry B. 1901

Since the Ballet Came to Shubert Alley   Dietz 1944; Duke 1944

Since the Boys Came Home from France   Carroll 1919

Since the Days of Grandmama   Kern 1912

Since the Farmer in the Dell Learned to Swing   Brooks 1942

Since They Turned Loch Lomond into Swing   Berlin 1938

Since We Became Sweethearts   Clare 1929

Since We Fell Out of Love   De Lange 1935

Since We've Met   Porter 1912

Since When   Loesser 1937

Since Won Long Hop Took One Long Hop to China   Waller 1932

Since Yesterday   Duke 1955

Since You   Loesser 1941; Styne 1941

Since You Gave Those Kisses to Me   Monaco 1914

Since You Gave Your Heart to Mother You Took the Heart Out of Me   Coslow 1923

Since You Have Chosen Me   Young, Joe 1933

Since You Have Left Me   Revel 1928; Sissle 1928

Since You Said Goodbye   Norworth 1938

Since You Told Me You Love Me, I Know   Clarke 1921

Since You Went Away   Caesar Date Unknown; Gershwin, George Date Unknown; Hoffman 1944; Johnson, J. Rosamond 1916; Merrill 1952

Since You Went Away Dear Old Pal   Egan 1923; Kahn 1923; Whiting 1923

Since You Whispered I Love You   Coslow 1927; Mills 1927

Since You're Not Around   Sherman 1974

Sincere   Willson 1957

Sincerely   Hoffman 1953

Sincerely I Do   Davis 1928

Sincerely I'm Yours   David, Mack 1984

Sincerely Yours   Webster 1955 .

Sincerest Form of Flattery, The   Brown, Lew 1926; Clare 1926

Sinful   Davis 1957

Sing   Hart 1926; Rodgers 1926

Sing a Happy Little Thing   Johnson, Howard 1930

Sing a Kris Kringle Jingle   Coots 1957

Sing a Little Jingle   Dixon 1931; Warren 1931

Sing a Little Love Song   Bryan 1928; Conrad 1929; Meyer 1927; Mitchell 1929; Pollack 1928

Sing a Little Song   Friend 1930; Gershwin, George 1927; Gershwin, Ira 1927; Romberg 1924; Schwartz, Jean 1930

Sing a Little Song Every Morning   Edwards 1930

Sing a Little Song of Christmas   Leigh 1979

Sing a Little Theme Song   Dubin 1930

Sing a New Song   Ager 1932

Sing a Song (Croon a Tune)   Pollack 1924

Sing a Song in the Rain   Caesar 1925, 1929

Sing a Song of Friendship   Caesar 1953

Sing a Song of Harvest   Mitchell 1938; Pollack 1938

Sing a Song of Hollywood   Warren 1964

Sing a Song of Laughter   Styne 1941

Sing a Song of Old Montana   Brown, Nacio Herb 1929, 1930; Freed, Arthur 1930

Sing a Song of Romance and You'll Wake Up the Love in My Soul   Young, Joe 1932

Sing a Song of Santa Claus   Coots 1952

Sing a Song of Sixpence (Four and Twenty Hot Blackbirds)   Rome 1940

Sing a Song of Sunbeams   Burke 1939; Monaco 1939

Sing a Song of Sunshine   Buck 1922

Sing a Tropical Song   Loesser 1943; McHugh 1943

Sing About Something   DePaul 1948; Raye 1948

Sing All Day   Sherman 1970

Sing Along with God   Webster 1963

Sing American Tunes   Akst 1933; Eliscu 1933

Sing an Old Fashioned Song   Adamson 1949; McHugh 1949

Sing an Old Fashioned Song to a Young, Sophisticated Lady   Ahlert 1935; Young, Joe 1935

Sing and Be Happy   Akst 1937; Clare 1937

Sing and Dance Your Troubles Away   Blake 1932; Sissle 1932

"Sing Another Song" (And Then We'll All Go Home)   Burke 1962

Sing, Baby, Sing   Pollack 1936; Yellen 1936

Sing Before Breakfast   Brown, Nacio Herb 1935; Freed, Arthur 1935

Sing, College Boy   Young, Joe 1934

Sing, Dance and Smile   Caesar 1927

Sing de Lawd's Music   Freed, Ralph 1941

Sing Every Song   Mercer 1985

Sing Fiddle Sing   Willson 1956

Sing for Your Special   Oakland 1953; Raye 1953

Sing for Your Supper   Hart 1938; Rodgers 1938

Sing Glory Hallelujah   Hart 1930; Rodgers 1930

Sing High, Sing Low   Adamson 1933; Gordon 1940; Lane 1933; Revel 1940

Sing Ho for the Life of a Bear   Brooks 1960

Sing It Lightly and Tenderly (inst.)   Kern 1956

Sing It Way Down Low   Carmichael 1932

Sing Jubilee   Porter 1935

Sing, Love, Sing   Jerome 1908; Schwartz, Jean 1908

Sing Mammy, Sing, Sweet and Low   Johnson, Howard 1923

Sing Me a Baby Song   Donaldson 1927; Kahn 1927

Sing Me a Come-All-Ye   Norworth 1908

Sing Me a Hill-Billy Song   Heyman 1931

Sing Me a Riddle   Carmichael 1955

Sing Me a Song   Carroll 1925; Davis 1928; Freed, Arthur 1925; Hanley 1928

Sing Me a Song of Araby   Fisher 1927

Sing Me a Song of Love   Atteridge 1915; Romberg 1915

Sing Me a Song of Nonsense (Pocketful of Love)   Carmichael 1936

Sing Me a Song of Texas   Revel 1946

Sing Me a Song of the Islands   Gordon 1942; Stept 1953

Sing Me a Song of the Sun   Johnson, Howard 1932

Sing Me a Song with Social Significance   Rome 1937

Sing Me a Swing Song and Let Me Dance   Carmichael 1936

Sing Me an Irish Come-All-Ye   Atteridge Date Unknown

Sing Me an Old Fashioned Song   Spina 1950

Sing Me Another Riddle   Carmichael 1957

Sing Me No April Songs   Cahn 1980

Sing Me Not a Ballad   Gershwin, Ira 1945; Weill 1945

Sing Me 'O Sole Mio'   Kahn 1924

Sing Me to Sleep Dear Mammy (With a Hushabye Pickaninny Tune)   Blake 1921; Sissle 1921

Sing Me to Sleep with a Twilight Song   Leslie 1928

Sing Me to Sleep with an Old-Fashioned Melody   Atteridge 1915

Sing My Heart   Arlen 1939; Koehler 1939

Sing No More   Friend 1932

Sing of Spring   Clare 1935; Gershwin, George 1937; Gershwin, Ira 1937

Sing One Song Mrs. Brown   DePaul 1958; Raye 1958

Sing Out   Waller 1942

Sing Out the Answer (Join the C.I.O.)   Eliscu 1941; Gorney 1941

Sing Out when You're Blue   Washington 1940; Young, Victor 1940

Sing Sing Again of an Old Shady Lane   Fain 1931; Kahal 1931

Sing Sing for Sing-Sing   Porter 1930

Sing Sing Sammy Sen   Howard, Joseph E. 1906

Sing, Sing, Sing, Singapore   Donaldson 1942

Sing Sing Tango Tea   Atteridge 1915; Romberg 1915

Sing, Sister, Sing   Johnson, Howard 1928

Sing Song Girl   Atteridge 1919; Gershwin, George 1929; Gershwin, Ira 1929; Kern 1921; Romberg 1919

Sing Song Girl (Little Yella Cinderella)   Hanley 1930

Sing Song Man   Conrad 1922; Friend 1922

Sing, Sorrow, Tomorrow or Joy   Gorney 1969

Sing the Merry   Fain 1951; Harburg 1951

Sing the Song of the Hammer   Baer 1943; Lewis 1943

Sing to Me   Akst 1933; Eliscu 1933

Sing to Me Guitar   Porter 1944

Sing to Me Gypsy   Herbert 1898; Smith, Harry B. 1898

Sing to Me of Love (Parlate Me d'Amor)   Caesar 1921

Sing to Your Senorita   Gordon 1940; Warren 1940

Sing Trovatore   Kern 1911

Sing You a Couple of Choruses   Fields 1934; McHugh 1934

Sing You Sinners   Coslow 1930

Sing You Son-of-a-Gun   Mercer 1938; Whiting 1938

Sing Your Little Folk Song (Sing Me a Little Folk Song)   Donaldson 1929; Leslie 1929

Sing Your Way Home   Leslie 1930; Monaco 1930; Young, Joe 1930

Sing Your Worries Away!   Revel 1942

Sing-a Loo   Brown, Lew 1921; Mitchell 1921; Pollack 1921

Singapore   Gilbert 1918

Singapore Sal   Stept 1936

Singer - A Dancer, A   Berlin 1954

Singer and the Song, The   Cobb 1899; Edwards 1899; Goetz 1912

Singer Must Be Free, A   Strouse 1982

Singin' a Song to My Man   Wrubel 1929

Singin' in the Bathtub   Magidson 1929; Washington 1929

Singin' in the Rain   Brown, Nacio Herb 1927, 1929; Freed, Arthur 1927

Singin' Pete   Gershwin, George 1924; Gershwin, Ira 1924

Singin' the Blues   Fields 1931; McHugh 1931

Singin' the Blues, Till My Daddy Comes Home   Conrad 1920; Lewis 1920; Young, Joe 1920

Singin' Your Praises   Coots 1936; Davis 1936

Singing a Love Song   Hart 1928; Rodgers 1928

Singing a Song in Your Arms   Hammerstein 1935; Kern 1935

Singing a Song to the Stars   Johnson, Howard 1930

Singing Between Kisses   Caesar 1934; Friend 1934

Singing Bone   Merrill 1962

Singing Commercial   Duke 1946

Singing Girl, The   Herbert 1899; Smith, Harry B. 1899

Singing Heart   Friend 1934

Singing Hills, The   David, Mack 1944

Singing in a Garden (inst.)   Kern 1956

Singing in the Moonlight   Mercer 1954

Singing in the Rain   Dubin 1926; Gershwin, Ira 1923

Singing in the Saddle   Porter 1935

Singing in the Sun   Freed, Arthur 1950; Warren 1950

Singing Lesson, The   Coslow 1952; Herbert 1897; Smith, Harry B. 1897, 1908

Singing Myself to Sleep   Fisher 1932

Singing on the Old Grape Vine   Von Tilzer 1909

Singing Out Loud   Sondheim Date Unknown

Singing the News   Caesar 1943

Singing to the Stars (inst.)   Kern 1956

Singing to You   Oakland 1933

Singing Wind   Webster 1969

Single   Brown, A. Seymour 1912; Coleman 1988; Young, Joe 1912

Single Girl   Bacharach 1979

Single Saddle   David, Hal 1949

Single-o   Mercer 1964

Sings of Love, The   Sigman 1965

Sing-Sing   Brown, A. Seymour 1923

Sing-Song Girl of Old Shanghai   Leslie 1928

Sing-Time Boogie-Boo Man   Sterling 1941; Von Tilzer 1941

Singy Kind of Song, A   Cahn 1980; DePaul 1980

Sink All Your Ships in the Ocean and Sail on the Ocean of Love   Fisher 1921

Sinner, The   Parish 1964

Sinner Kissed an Angel, A   David, Mack 1941

Sinner's Devotion, A   Bacharach 1962

Sins of Sura, The   Loesser 1965

Sioux City Sue   Donaldson 1924; Pollack 1942

'Sippi   Conrad 1928; Johnson, James P. 1928

'Sippi Shore   Lewis 1921

Sippin' Cider with My Ida (Down Beside the Zuyder Zee)   Coots 1944

'Sippy   Adamson 1936; McHugh 1936

Sir, Don't Go Away   Romberg 1917

Sir Galahad   Kern 1917

Sir James' Trip to Find Mata (inst.)   Bacharach 1967

Sir Pumphrey Mildew   Eliscu 1941; Gorney 1941

Siren Dream, A   Hoffman 1927; Pollack 1927

Siren of the Ballet, The   Herbert 1899; Smith, Harry B. 1899

Siren of the Nile   Parish 1980

Siren of the Sea   Coots 1924

Siren of the Tropics   Dietz 1944; Duke 1944

Sirens, The   Gershwin, George 1921; Gershwin, Ira 1921

Sirens of the Sea   Coslow 1924; Romberg 1924

Sirens So Fair   Smith, Harry B. 1911

Siren's Song, The   Kern 1917

Si's Been Drinking Cider   Berlin 1915

Sissiphus   Strouse 1971

Sissy   Kahal 1938

Sister Anne   Stept 1955

Sister, Brother   Rome 1969

Sister Hasn't Got a Chance Since Mother Burned Her Hair   Von Tilzer 1924

Sister Mine   Smith, Harry B. 1926

Sister of Tokio Rose   Styne 1954

Sister Suffragette   Sherman 1964

Sister Susie Glide   Norworth 1917

Sister Susie's Started Syncopation   Atteridge 1915; Romberg 1915

Sisters   Berlin 1954

Sisters Under the Skin   Loewe 1938

Sit Down and Tell Me How I Stand   Gordon 1933; Revel 1933

Sit Down, You're Rockin' the Boat   Clarke 1913; Jerome 1913; Loesser 1950; Schwartz, Jean 1913; Williams 1913

Sit Tight   Mills 1946

Sit Yourself Down   Freed, Ralph 1965

Sittin' Around   Kahn 1926
Sittin' Around on Sunday   Ahlert 1935; Young, Joe 1935
Sittin' By the Fire with You   Meyer 1932
Sittin' in a Corner   Kahn 1923; Meyer 1923
Sittin' in a Swing   Livingston, Jerry 1932
Sittin' in a Tree House   Bacharach 1958; David, Hal 1958
Sittin' in the Dark   Adamson 1932
Sittin' in the Jail-House   Kahn 1937; Romberg 1937
Sittin' in the Sand A-Sunnin'   Lerner, Sammy 1936
Sittin' in the Sun (Countin' My Money)   Berlin 1953
Sittin' on a Backyard Fence   Fain 1933; Kahal 1933
Sittin' on a Doorstep   Lewis 1929; Pollack 1929; Young, Joe 1929
Sittin' on a Rainbow   Yellen 1930
Sittin' on a Rubbish Can   Burke 1931
Sittin' on the Bridge at Midnight   Kalmar 1934; Ruby 1934
Sittin' on the Curbstone   Whiting 1928
Sittin' on the Fence   Gilbert 1932; Hanley 1932
Sittin' on the Inside   Brooks 1946
Sittin' Pretty   Coots 1921
Sittin' Up Waitin' for You   Razaf 1933; Waller 1933
Sitting Around Thinking of My Baby   Coslow 1929
Sitting By the Window   Conrad 1929; Mitchell 1929
Sitting in a Corner   Atteridge 1921; Buck 1922; Romberg 1921
Sitting in the Gaol   Weill 1938
Sitting in the Sun   Coots 1927; Dubin 1927
Sitting in the Sun (Just Wearing a Smile)   Caesar 1929; Friend 1929
Sitting on the Back Porch   Hammerstein 1955; Rodgers 1955
Sitting on the Fence   Ruby 1958
Sitting on the Moon   Mitchell 1936; Stept 1936
Sitting on Your Status Quo   Rome 1937
Sitting Pretty   Kern 1924
Situation   Smith, Robert B. 1907
Situation Wanted   Brown, Nacio Herb 1949
Situation Wise   Comden and Green 1955
Situation's Well in Hand, The   Merrill 1945
Siwash Alma Mater   Loesser 1940
Six   Strouse 1971
Six Bells   Styne 1985
Six Boys and Seven Boys   Sigman 1959
Six Bridges to Cross   Mancini 1954
Six Foot of Hickory   Spina 1950
Six Lessons from Madame La Zonga   Monaco 1941
Six Little Cinderellas   Robin 1927
Six Little Kitzels   Hart 1926; Rodgers 1926
Six Little Plays (Requiescat in Pace)   Hart 1926; Rodgers 1926
Six Little Squirrels   Revel 1946
Six Little Wives of the King   Buck 1916
Six O'Clock   Caesar 1927
Six O'Clock News   Leigh 1985
Six of a Kind   Rainger 1934; Robin 1934
Six of One and Half a Dozen of the Other   Adamson 1938; McHugh 1938
Six or Seven Times   Mills 1929; Waller 1929
(We Are) Six Poor Mortals   Freed, Arthur 1930
Six Shades of Blue (inst.)   Blake 1946
Six Women (Me and Henry the Eighth)   Caesar 1934; Henderson 1934; Yellen 1934
Sixes and Sevens   Brennan 1918
Sixteen Going on Seventeen   Hammerstein 1959; Rodgers 1959
Sixteen, Sweet Sixteen   Berlin 1924

16th Century Blues   Oakland 1952; Raye 1952
Sixth Finger Theme (Sixth Finger Tune) (inst.)   Strouse 1956
Sixth Sense, The   Spina 1977
Sixty Percent of the Accidents   Coleman 1972; Fields 1972
Sixty Seconds Apart   DePaul 1955
Sixty Seconds Every Minute I Think of You   Caesar 1922
Sixty Seconds Got Together   David, Mack 1938; Livingston, Jerry 1938
Sizing Up the Girls   Hammerstein 1922; Mitchell 1922
Ska-dut-ee-ut-tut-tut   Gordon 1928
Skal (Let's Have Another on Me)   Mancini 1970; Mercer 1970
Skate with Me   Berlin 1933; Silver 1918
Skating Our Way Into Love   Johnson, Howard 1935
Skeets Song, The   Robison 1949
Skeleton Ghost   Johnson, Howard 1927
Skeleton in the Closet, The   Burke 1936; Johnston 1936
Skeletons in the Closet   Harbach 1911
Skiddad Dad Daddlin' Daddy   Lewis 1923; Meyer 1923; Young, Joe 1923
Skiddle Diddle Dee-Skiddle Diddle Dey   David, Hal 1952
Skiddle-de-Skow   Johnson, James P. 1929
Skidikischatch   Friml 1914; Harbach 1914
Skies Are Blue   Cahn 1937
Ski-ing   Romberg 1916
Skin-a-Ma-Rink-a-Rink-a-Ree   Dubin 1924; McHugh 1924; Mills 1924
Skinny   Snyder 1909
Skip It, Baby, Skip It   Gordon 1934; Revel 1934
Skip the Build-Up   Fain 1955
Skip to My Lou   Martin 1944
Skipper   Livingston, Jerry 1963
Skipper, Skooter and Ricky   Livingston, Jerry 1963
Skipping Rope Hornpipe   Martin 1952
Skippy   Conrad 1930; Davis 1930
Skirts   Loesser 1944
Skirts Ahoy!   Blane 1952; Warren 1952
Skrontch   Ellington 1938; Mills 1938
Skull and Bones   Gershwin, George 1928; Gershwin, Ira 1928
Sky Blue Pink   De Lange 1946
Sky City   Hart 1929; Rodgers 1929
Sky Fell Down, The   Alter 1940; Ellington 1956; Heyman 1940
Sky Girl, The   Bryan 1927; Schwartz, Jean 1927
Sky High   Atteridge 1925; Burke 1946; Oakland 1938; Van Heusen 1946
Sky High Bungalow   Goetz 1921; Meyer 1921
Sky Ran Out of Stars, The   De Lange 1944
Sky Symphony   Adamson 1959; Young, Victor 1959
Skylark   Carmichael 1941; Mercer 1941
Skyline (inst.)   Willson 1928
Sky's the Limit   Coleman 1964
Slacks from Coma   Pollack 1948
Slap Happy   Davis 1944
Slap Polka, The   Revel 1943; Webster 1943
Slap That Bass   Gershwin, George 1937; Gershwin, Ira 1937
Slapstick   Gershwin, Ira 1921
Slav Annie   Carmichael 1940
Slave Auction   Porter 1946
Slave Dealers' Song   Smith, Harry B. 1900
Slave Girl   Drake 1956
Slave of Love, The   Blake 1924; Sissle 1924; Spina 1955
Slave to Love, A   Friend 1930; Monaco 1930
Slaving   Waller 1924

Slavlova   Atteridge 1916; Motzan 1916, 1917; Romberg 1916, 1917

Sleep and Dream   Gordon 1935; Revel 1935

Sleep, Baby, Sleep   Coslow 1935; Johnson, Howard 1939; Kalmar 1930; Ruby 1930

Sleep Baby Sleep (In Your Jeep)   Dubin 1943; Monaco 1943

Sleep Come On and Take Me   Young, Joe 1932

Sleep in Your Baby's Arms   Comden and Green 1944

Sleep It Off   Drake 1952

Sleep Me Darling Sleep Within My Arms   Lawrence 1933

Sleep My Love   Coslow 1947

Sleep, My Sweet   Brown, Nacio Herb 1932

Sleep Now, Baby Bunting   Merrill 1964; Styne 1964

Sleep, O Sleep   Eliscu 1962

Sleep Peaceful, Mr. Used-to-Be   Arlen 1946; Mercer 1946

Sleep Sublime and Perfect Poet   Herbert 1907; Smith, Harry B. 1907

Sleep Warm   Bergman 1958

Sleep, Weary Head   Hart 1928; Rodgers 1928

Sleep Well, Little Children (A Christmas Lullaby)   Bergman 1956

Sleep with Me Tonight   Bacharach 1984

Sleepin' Bee, A   Arlen 1954

Sleeping Beauty   Hammerstein 1931; Hart 1933; Rodgers 1933; Romberg 1931

Sleeping Beauty and the Beast   Jerome 1902; Schwartz, Jean 1902

Sleeping Beauty Song   Lawrence 1958; Young, Victor 1957

Sleeping Chair, The   Smith, Harry B. 1912; Smith, Robert B. 1912

Sleeping Dreams, Waking Dreams   Adams 1957; Strouse 1957

Sleeping on a Sealy   Razaf 1949

Sleeping on the Benches   Woods 1932

Sleepless Nights   Livingston, Jerry 1960

Sleepy   Loesser 1937

Sleepy Babe   Webster 1954

Sleepy Baby   Kahn 1928; Webster 1964

Sleepy Baby (Dream of Me)   Spina 1945

Sleepy Head   Davis 1926; Donaldson 1934; Kahn 1934

Sleepy Hollow   David, Mack 1958; DePaul 1949; Livingston, Jerry 1958; Norworth 1904; Raye 1949

Sleepy Hollow Days   Whiting 1920

Sleepy Hollow Home   Carmichael 1953

Sleepy Honolulu Town   Warren 1928

Sleepy House, The   Young, Victor 1939

Sleepy Lagoon   Lawrence 1940

Sleepy Little Village Where the Dixie Cotton Grows   Leslie 1922

Sleepy Moon   Robin 1943; Von Tilzer 1915; Warren 1943

Sleepy Time Gal   Egan 1925; Whiting 1925

Sleepy Time in Sleepy Hollow   Hoffman 1934

Sleepy Time in Topsy-Turvy Town   Ager 1935

Sleepy Town   Styne 1929

Sleepy Valley   Hanley 1929; Sterling 1929

Sleepy Village   Atteridge 1921; Romberg 1921

Sleepyhead   Hart 1926; Mercer 1958; Rodgers 1926

Sleepyland   Brown, A. Seymour 1909; Davis 1962

Sleepytime Soldier Boy   Coots 1939

Sleigh Bell Serenade   Webster 1952

Sleigh Bells   Caesar 1936; Dietz 1936; Schwartz, Arthur 1936

Sleigh Bells May Be Wedding Bells   Smith, Harry B. 1909

Sleigh Ride   Parish 1950

Sleigh Ride in July   Burke 1944; Van Heusen 1944

Slender Thread, The   David, Mack 1965

Slice, The   Comden and Green 1967; Styne 1967

Slide, Boy, Slide   Arlen 1954

Slidin' Down a Rainbow   Fain 1943; Freed, Ralph 1943

Sliding Down a Silver Cloud   Brennan 1929

Sliding Through the Old Stage Door   Jerome 1912; Von Tilzer 1912

Slight Case of Ecstasy, A   Fain 1946

Slightly Less than Wonderful   Waller 1943

Slightly Perfect   Revel 1945

Slightly Slightly   Revel 1945

Sligo   Brennan 1920

Slippery Hips   Johnson, James P. 1930; Razaf 1930

Slippery James the Woman in the Case   Herbert 1904

Slippin' Around the Corner   Mercer 1974

Slipping Thru My Fingers   Mills 1935

Slippy Sloppy Shoes   Rome 1965

Sloe Gin Fizz   Mills 1938

Slogan Song   Mercer 1951

Sloping Path, The   Atteridge 1914; Romberg 1914

Sloppy Water Blues (inst.)   Waller 1927

Slow, The   Spina 1976; Willson 1954

Slow & Funny   Carmichael 1953

Slow and Easy   Spina 1970; Williams 1919

Slow and Easy Goin' Man   Johnson, James P. 1922

Slow and Easy Man   Razaf 1928

Slow and Easy Melody   Bullock 1947

Slow but Sure   Bergman 1960

Slow Caravan   Hoffman 1929; Lerner, Sammy 1929

Slow Down   Eliscu 1929

Slow Down and Live   Caesar 1958

Slow Down, Slow Down, Slow Down   Silver 1956

Slow Freight   Mills 1940

Slow Hot Wind   Mancini 1964

Slow Me Down, Lord   Robison 1957

Slow Movies   Caesar 1922

Slow Poke   Coslow 1923; Silver 1923

Slow Sinks the Sun   Porter 1914, 1916

Slow Song   Kern 1957; Robin 1957

Slow Up, Papa   Razaf 1927

Slower than Molasses   Razaf 1933; Waller 1933

Slowly   Harbach 1961

Slowly but Surely   Heyman 1935, 1953; Young, Victor 1953

Slowly but Surely (Quanto te Voglio)   Parish 1954

Slue Foot Nelson (inst.)   Blake 1973

Sluefoot   Mercer 1955

Slum and Gravy   Friml 1949

Slumber Music   Smith, Robert B. 1919

Slumber Song (Goodnight)   Hammerstein 1931; Whiting 1931

Slumber Valley   Motzan 1930

Slumberland   Gilbert 1921; Herbert 1908; Sherman 1989; Smith, Harry B. 1908

Slumbertime   Friend 1937; Magidson 1929

Slumming on Park Avenue   Berlin 1937

Smack in the Middle of Maine   Burke 1947; Van Heusen 1947

Small Fry   Carmichael 1938; Loesser 1938

Small Mama — Big Mama   Razaf Date Unknown

Small One (inst.), The   Young, Victor 1955

Small Petrushka   Alter 1969; Mercer 1969

Small Potatoes   Robison 1957

Small Talk   Duke 1955

Small Things, The   Burke 1953; Van Heusen 1953

Small Town Boy   Washington 1959

Small Town Boy with Big Town Dreams, A   David, Hal 1950

Small Town Gal, The   Cohan 1908

Small Town Girl   Kahn 1936; Lewis 1916; Meyer 1916; Young, Joe 1916

Small Town Gossip   Robison 1949

Small Town Kind of Love, A   Davis 1981

Small Town Sweetheart of a Small Town Girl, The   Kahn 1914; Whiting 1914

Small Towns Are Smile Towns   Cahn 1953; Robin 1952

Small World   Duke 1955; Rome 1947; Sondheim 1959; Styne 1959

Smart as Paint   Styne 1985

Smart Little Girls   Ager 1939; Fain 1939; Yellen 1939

Smart People   Hart 1928; Rodgers 1928

Smart People Stay Single   Coleman 1962; Leigh 1962

Smart Set   Gordon 1932; Revel 1932

(It's) Smart to Be Smart   Duke 1934; Harburg 1934

(You Know It All) Smarty   Freed, Ralph 1937; Howard, Joseph E. 1907; Lane 1937; Norworth 1908

Smarty Pants   Donaldson 1939; Mercer 1939

Smashing, New York Times   Adams 1970; Strouse 1970

Smashing Thirds (inst.)   Waller 1936

Smellin' of Vanilla (Bamboo Cage)   Arlen 1954

Smile   Adamson 1930; Leigh 1985; Youmans 1930

Smile, a Kiss, Sweet Fool, A   Friml 1934

Smile a Little Bit   Davis 1934; Hanley 1934

Smile a Little Smile for Me   Smith, Harry B. 1917

Smile, A Mem'ry and an Extra Shirt, A   Bergman 1968

Smile, a Tear, a Kiss Dear, A   Howard, Joseph E. 1954

Smile Again, Kathleen Mavoureen   Jerome 1923

Smile All the While   Ager 1925; Davis 1925; Yellen 1925

Smile and Show Your Dimple   Berlin 1917

Smile Away Each Rainy Day   Mancini 1970; Mercer 1970

Smile Awhile   Lawrence 1951

Smile Comrades   Turk 1925

Smile, Comrades (Smile While We May)   Ahlert 1930; Turk 1930

Smile, Darn You, Smile   Friml 1927

Smile for the Camera   Strouse 1999

Smile for the Press   Carmichael 1940; Mercer 1940

Smile Girls   Sondheim 1959; Styne 1959

Smile Looks Good on Any Face, A   Fain 1964

Smile On Dearie   Bryan 1933

Smile on Her Lips, The   Drake 1954

Smile Right Back at the Sun   Burke 1947; Van Heusen 1947

Smile She Means for You, The   Harbach 1910

Smile, Smile, Smile   Comden and Green 1967; Coots 1954; Romberg 1916; Styne 1967

Smile, Sonya Smile   Hoffman 1943; Livingston, Jerry 1943

Smile Will Do the Trick, A   Gordon 1936; Revel 1936

Smile Will Go a Long, Long Way, A   Akst 1944; Davis 1923

Smile with Me   Willson 1936

Smile Your Blues Away   Davis 1927

Smiles   Friml 1918

Smiles for Sale   Baer 1944

Smilin' Joe   Meyer 1926

Smilin' Through My Tears   Johnson, James P. 1948

Smiling Eyes   Motzan 1927

Smiling Geisha   Berlin 1956

Smiling Joe   Akst 1927; Davis 1927

Smiling Sam   Atteridge 1921

Smiling Skies   Robin 1930; Whiting 1930

Smoke and Fire   Adams 1978; Strouse 1978

Smoke Another Cigarette (inst.)   Revel 1957

Smoke Ascending, The   Dietz 1952

Smoke Dreams   Brown, Nacio Herb 1936; Freed, Arthur 1936

Smoke Dreams (The Cigarette Song)   Coots 1921

Smoke 'Em Up, Smoke 'Em Up, Smoke 'Em Up!   Sherman 1971

(When Your Heart's on Fire) Smoke Gets in Your Eyes   Harbach 1933; Kern 1933

Smoke Rings   Friml 1922; Harbach 1922; Washington 1933

(Remember) Smoke Tree Mountain   Spina 1966

Smokey the Bear Is a Wise Bear   Willson 1957

Smokin' Reefers   Dietz 1932; Schwartz, Arthur 1932

Smoking in the Dark   Dixon 1934; Wrubel 1934

Smoky Valley   Ruby 1958

Smooth Sailing   Russell 1949

Smother Me With Kisses and Kill Me with Love   Bryan 1914; Carroll 1914

Smother Me with Your Love (inst.)   Waller 1939

S.N.A.F.U.   Adamson 1944; McHugh 1944

Snagtooth Gertie   Porter 1946

Snake Charmer's Dance   Herbert 1907; Smith, Harry B. 1907

Snake Dance, The   Brown, Nacio Herb 1934; Freed, Arthur 1934

Snake Eyes   Arlen 1959; Mercer 1959

Snake Hip Dance   Ellington 1929; Razaf 1929; Waller 1929

Snake Hips   Mitchell 1930

Snake Hips, Do the Wiggle Waggle Woo   Conrad 1929; Mitchell 1929

Snake Hips (inst.)   McHugh 1931

Snake in the Grass   Lerner, Alan Jay 1974; Loewe 1974; Razaf 1934

Snake in the Grass (inst.), The   Porter 1929

Snap a Wishbone with Me   Atteridge 1921; Bryan 1920, 1921; Pollack 1920, 1921; Schwartz, Jean 1920, 1921

Snap Into It   Baer 1927; Lewis 1927; Young, Joe 1927

Snap Out of It   Akst 1927; Davis 1927; Rainger 1933; Robin 1933

Snap Out of the Blues   Robin 1926

Snap Your Fingers   Friml 1919; Gordon 1925; Harbach 1919

Snap Your Fingers and Away You Go   Jerome 1912; Von Tilzer 1912

Snap Your Fingers at Care   Brown, Lew 1920; DeSylva 1920

Snap Your Fingers at the Blues   Ahlert 1930; Turk 1930

Snappy Show in Town   Youmans 1926

Snatched from the Cradle   Friml 1917

Sneak, The   Brown, Nacio Herb 1922

Sneakin' Home (inst.)   Waller 1941

Sneaky Steps   Cohan 1914

Sneeze   Gershwin, George 1924; Gershwin, Ira 1924

Sneeze Song, The   Lerner, Sammy 1926; Whiting 1926

Snerling Through the Flowers   Hoffman 1953

'Sno Use Talking I've Got to Be Good   Schwartz, Jean 1928

S'No Wonder They Fell in Love   Fain 1947; Freed, Ralph 1947

Snookey Ookums   Berlin 1913

Snooky-Cookie   Gilbert 1938

Snoops the Lawyer   Kalmar 1920; Ruby 1920

Snooty, The   Blake Date Unknown; Razaf 1942

S'Nora, How She Can Snora   Coslow 1923; Fisher 1923

Snow   Berlin 1954

Snow Dreams   Webster 1954

Snow Drift's in My Heart   Carmichael 1940

Snow Flakes   Gershwin, George 1920; Loesser 1935

Snow Flower   Merrill 1950

Snow in Central Park   Spina 1951

Snow Leopards   Sherman 1991

Snow Man   Oakland 1961

Snow, Snow, Beautiful Snow   Sigman 1953

Snowball   Carmichael 1933; Kahn 1924

Snowball Man, The   Hanley 1929; Monaco 1930

Snowballs   Bacharach 1957; David, Hal 1957

Snowdrops and the Spring   Atteridge 1912

Snowflakes   David, Mack 1933

Snowman, The   Burke 1950; Sigman 1948; Van Heusen 1950

Snows of Yesteryear   Robison 1952; Webster 1965

Snowtime   Johnson, James P. 1922

Snowy Morning Blues (inst.)   Johnson, James P. 1927

Snubbed   Merrill 1965; Styne 1965

Snug As a Bug in a Rug   Harbach 1923; Loesser 1937, 1939

Snuggle and Dream   Friml 1919; Harbach 1919

Snuggle Song, The   Young, Victor 1934

Snuggled on Your Shoulder, Cuddled in Your Arms   Young, Joe 1931

So   Howard, Joseph E. 1906; Russell 1957

So Am I   Gershwin, George 1924; Gershwin, Ira 1924

So Apart   Brooks 1959

So Are You!   Gershwin, George 1929; Gershwin, Ira 1929; Kahn 1929

So Ashamed!   Ager 1932; Davis 1932

So Away with Sorrow   Atteridge 1912

So Beautiful Is the Glow   Merrill 1956

So Belongs My Heart to You   Friend 1948

So Big   Donaldson 1938; Washington 1953

So Big and Strong   Wrubel 1929

So Blue   Brown, Lew 1927; DeSylva 1927; Henderson 1927

So Close to the Forest   Young, Joe 1934

So Dear   Caesar 1928; Friend 1928

So Dear to Me   Conrad 1929; Mitchell 1929

So Deep My Love   Drake 1950

So Do I   Burke 1936; Davis 1961; DeSylva 1932; Johnston 1936; Schwartz, Jean 1928; Youmans 1932

So Does an Automobile   Heyman 1938

So Does Mahatma Ghandi   Hanley 1932

So Does Your Old Mandarin   Henderson 1926; Lewis 1926; Young, Joe 1926

So Dress Up Your Dollars in Khaki and Help Win Democracy's Fight   Whiting 1918

So Far   Hammerstein 1947; Rodgers 1947

So Far Away, So Long Ago   Smith, Harry B. 1924; Snyder 1924

So Far, So Good   Comden and Green 1951; David, Mack Date Unknown; Lawrence 1940; Styne 1951; Warren Date Unknown

So Far So Good, So Good So Far, but Whatcha Gonna Do Do Now   Friend 1928

So Far So Wonderful   Revel 1946

So Few Words   Bryan 1954

So Goes My Love   Brooks 1946

So Good to See You   Merrill 1990

So Grateful   Kalmar 1932; Ruby 1932

So Happy   Sondheim 1987

So Happy I Could Cry   Alter 1948; De Lange 1948

So Help Me   Berlin 1934

So Help Me If I Don't Love You   De Lange 1938; Van Heusen 1938

So Here We Are Again   Merrill 1966

So I Bid You Beware   Herbert 1899; Smith, Harry B. 1899

(And) So I Married the Girl   Magidson 1932; Stept 1932

So I Picks Up My Ukelele (And I Sings Her a Little Song)   Burke 1930; Parish 1930

So I Said Si, Si   Russell 1955

So I'll Never Be a Millionaire   Coots 1937; Davis 1937

So I'll Tell Him   David, Mack 1973; Livingston, Jerry 1973

So in Love   Porter 1948

So Is Your Old Lady   Dubin 1926

So It's Bridge Again Tonight   Ahlert 1933; Leslie 1933

So Let Us Hail   Porter 1912

So Little Time   Evans 1956; Livingston, Jay 1956

So Little Time (The Peking Theme)   Webster 1963

So Lonesome   Johnson, J. Rosamond 1931

So Long   Conrad 1929; Friend 1960; Mitchell 1929; Porter 1944; Young, Joe 1931

So Long As He Loves You   Howard, Bart 1961

So Long as the World Goes Round   Caesar 1920

So Long Baby   Coleman 1965; Comden and Green 1944

So Long, Big Guy   Adams 1966; Strouse 1966

So Long, Big Time!   Arlen 1963

So Long but Not for Long, Aloha   Bryan 1940

So Long Cowboys   Coslow 1930

So Long, Farewell   Hammerstein 1959; Rodgers 1959

So Long for Ever So Long   Henderson 1934; Koehler 1934

So Long for Now   David, Hal 1951

So Long, Hong Kong   Hanley 1917

So Long, I'll See You Again   Brennan 1925; McHugh 1925

So Long Lily   Leigh 1976

So Long Ma (Headin' for New Orleans)   Styne 1960

So Long, Mary   Cohan 1906

So Long, Mother   Egan 1917; Kahn 1917

So Long, My Love   Cahn 1957

So Long Oolong   Kalmar 1920; Ruby 1920

So Long Pa   Coleman 1991; Comden and Green 1991

So Long Sadness   Drake 1995

So Long Sal the Best of Friends Must Part   Sterling 1918

So Long Sally   Merrill 1950

So Long Sammy   Davis 1917; Yellen 1917

So Long, Samoa   Porter 1940

So Long, San Antonio   Porter 1943

So Long Sarah Jane   Brown, Lew 1943; Fain 1943; Freed, Ralph 1943

So Long Sing Song   Atteridge Date Unknown; Cohan 1904

So Long Sue   Cobb 1912; Edwards 1912

So Long Tony So Long   Lewis 1910

So Long-No Longer   Brennan 1949

So Many Memories   Woods 1937

So Many People   Sondheim 1954

So Many Stars   Bergman 1968

So Many Things to Remember   Sigman 1958

(So Well, So What) So Maybe I'm Wrong   Kahn 1927

So Much to Do, So Little Time in the Morning   Strouse Date Unknown

So Much You Loved Me   Rodgers 1976

So Near and Yet So Far   Friml 1918; Porter 1941; Strouse 1959

So Near, So Dear, So Sweet   Freed, Arthur 1930; Woods 1930

So Near, So Far   Evans 1981; Livingston, Jay 1981

So Near Yet So Far   Donaldson 1926

So Nice   Caesar 1934; Henderson 1934; Yellen 1934

So Nice Seeing You Again   Dixon 1935; Wrubel 1935

So Nonchalant   Duke 1932; Harburg 1932

So Old So Young   Drake 1971

So Pretty   Comden and Green 1968

So Red the Rose   Lawrence 1935

So Right for Me   Blane 1955; Martin 1955

So Sentimental   Koehler 1929

So Shy   Magidson 1941

So Soon   Razaf 1945
So Sorry   Johnson, James P. 1930
(If I Hadn't Been) So Sure of You   Stept 1931
So Sympathetic   Kahn 1930
So Tender   Coots 1932; Young, Joe 1932
So That's the Kind of a Girl You Are   Dixon 1925; Dubin 1925; Rose 1925
So That's What Love Is   Leigh 1955; Spina 1955
So They Say   Herbert 1900; Smith, Harry B. 1900
So This Is Bagdad   Brooks 1957
So This Is Dixie   Yellen 1917
So This Is Heaven   Burke 1935; Magidson 1934; Spina 1935
So This Is Italy   Cahn 1944; Styne 1944
So This Is Kissing   Caesar 1925; Youmans 1925
So This Is Love   David, Mack 1950; Goetz 1923; Hoffman 1950; Livingston, Jerry 1950
So This Is Mexico   Brown, Lew 1932; Henderson 1932
So This Is Paris   Akst 1919; Atteridge 1916; Motzan 1919
So This Is Susie   Coots 1933; Lewis 1933
So This Is the Copa   Cahn 1951
So This Is the States   DeSylva 1925
So This Is the World   Styne 1985
So This Is Venice   Brown, Lew 1927; Buck 1923; Clarke 1923; Friend 1927; Leslie 1923; Warren 1923
So This Is You   Akst 1943; Cahn 1943
So Tired of It All   Rainger 1939; Robin 1939
So Undulating, So Fascinating   Friml 1918
So Warm, My Love   Webster 1965
(You're) So Well Remembered   Stept 1947
So What?   Akst 1935; Gershwin, George 1932; Gershwin, Ira 1932; Porter 1956; Rainger 1936; Robin 1936
So What Goes?   Ahlert 1941
So What Now?   Coleman 1972; Fields 1972
So What's New   Oakland 1960
So Will I   Brown, Lew 1926; Friend 1926
So Would I   Ager 1928; Burke 1946; Van Heusen 1946; Yellen 1928
So You Did It Your Way   Oakland 1970
So You Fell for Him Too   Mills 1947
So You Wanna Fall in Love   Mills 1939
So You Won't Sing   Magidson 1937; Wrubel 1937
So, You're Not Gonna Kiss Me   Oakland 1934
Soap and Water Are My Friends   Caesar 1967
Soap Bubble Days   Kahn 1910
Sob Song   Rainger 1932; Robin 1932
Sobbin' Women   DePaul 1954; Mercer 1954
Sobs   Howard, Joseph E. 1918
Social, The   Rome 1959
Social Climbers   Smith, Harry B. 1914
Social Coach of All the Fashionable Future Debutantes, The   Porter 1916
Social Dancing (inst.)   Sondheim 1987
Social Director   Rome 1952
Social Season, The   Drake 1954
Social Work   Hart 1926; Rodgers 1926
Society   Coots 1922; Goetz 1912; Kern 1915; Martin 1964
Society Blues   Atteridge 1924; Romberg 1924; Schwartz, Jean 1924
Society Circus Parade   Buck 1912
Society Farmerettes, The   Herbert 1917
Society Ladder   Kalmar 1927; Ruby 1927
Society Twist   Mills 1962
Society Wedding   Berlin 1933
Soda I, Soda You, Sodas Ev'rybody   Johnson, Howard 1929
Soda Jerk at Walgreens   Mills 1947

Soda Shop   Evans 1952; Livingston, Jay 1952
Soda Water Cowboys   Johnson, Howard 1928; Lewis 1928; Pollack 1928
Sodom and Gomorrah   Webster 1963
Soft and Low   Kahn 1921; Parish 1947
Soft and New   Myrow 1945
Soft and Warm   De Lange 1945; Myrow 1945
Soft Green Seas   Dixon 1934; Wrubel 1934
Soft Hearted   Lewis 1929; Loesser 1942; McHugh 1942; Young, Joe 1929
Soft Lights and Sweet Music   Berlin 1932
Soft Music   Sherman 1974
Soft Music Professor   Parish 1953
Soft of a Hand, The   Rome 1968
Soft Shoe (inst.)   Kern 1956
Soft Shoulders and Dangerous Curves   David, Hal 1954; Hoffman 1954
Soft Sounds   Cahn 1958; Mancini 1958
Softer Than a Kitten (That's My Feeling for You)   Hart 1930; Rodgers 1930
Softly, As in a Morning Sunrise   Hammerstein 1928; Romberg 1928
Softly My Heart Is Singing   Heyman 1944; Spina 1944
Softly Now the Light of Day   Johnson, Howard 1939
Soft-Shoe, Sword Dance   Arlen 1959; Mercer 1959
Sogni D'Oro   Bergman 1958
Solar Siesta (inst.)   Revel 1955
Sold Food Solitude and You   Washington 1958
Sold to the Man with the Broken Heart   Cahn 1957; Van Heusen 1957
Soldara Song   Bryan 1930
Soldier Boy   Berlin 1918; Smith, Harry B. 1927; Von Tilzer 1909
Soldier Dreams of You Tonight   Dubin 1942; Friend 1942
Soldier Like You, A   Harbach 1947; Kern 1947
Soldier Men   Herbert 1917
Soldier of Bohemia, A   Smith, Robert B. 1912
Soldier of Fortune, A   Smith, Harry B. 1928
Soldier of Love   Caesar 1935; Lerner, Sammy 1935
Soldier of the Czar   Kahn 1938; Romberg 1938
Soldier of the Home Defense   Caesar 1942
Soldiers All   Herbert 1899
Soldiers and Girls   Sondheim 1984
Soldier's Dream, A   Berlin 1942; Johnson, Howard 1947
Soldier's Goodbye, A   Rome 1973
Soldiers' Gossip   Sondheim 1994
Soldier's Life   Caesar 1920
Soldier's Life Is Never Long   Herbert 1908
Soldier's Love, A   Herbert 1908
Soldier's Love Song, A   Young, Joe 1958
Soldier's March   Gershwin, George 1929; Gershwin, Ira 1929
Soldiers of Fortune (Are We)   Kahn 1938; Romberg 1938
Soldiers of the King   Cohan 1908
Soldiers of the Stage, The   Cohan 1901
Soldier's Safety Song   Caesar 1942
Soldier's Song   Smith, Harry B. 1911; Weill 1933, 1938
Soldier's Story, The   Smith, Harry B. 1902
Soldier's Wife   Weill 1944
Sole to Sole   David, Mack 1959; Livingston, Jerry 1959
Solfeggio (The Do-Re-Mi Song)   Sigman 1954
Soliciting Subscriptions   Hart 1925; Rodgers 1925
Solicitor's Song   Lane 1965; Lerner, Alan Jay 1965
Solid Citizen of the Solid South, A   Robin 1946; Schwartz, Arthur 1946
Solid Eclipse   Waller 1938

Solid Potato Salad   DePaul 1944; Raye 1944

Soliloquy   Hammerstein 1928, 1933, 1945; Parish 1965; Rainger 1932, 1936; Robin 1932, 1936; Rodgers 1945; Weill 1949; Youmans 1928

Soliloquy and Song   Leigh 1954

Soliloquy (inst.)   Bloom 1926

Solita   Mills 1928; Parish 1928

Solitary Seminole (Seminole Legend)   Rainger 1941; Robin 1941

Solitude   De Lange 1934; Ellington 1934; Mills 1934

Solo   Hoffman 1956; Russell 1955

Solomon   Bryan 1919; Fisher 1936; Porter 1933; Schwartz, Jean 1919

Solomon Gundy   Styne 1985

Solomon Song   Weill 1954

Solution   Johnson, James P. 1947

Sombrero   Brown, Lew 1940; Henderson 1940

Sombrero Dance   Rainger 1936; Robin 1936

Sombrero Land   Atteridge 1911; Berlin 1911; Goetz 1911; Snyder 1911

Some Ambitious Mama's Hangin' 'Round My Papa   Stept 1925

Some Beautiful Morning I'll Find You in My Arms   Friend 1921

Some Beer, Some Bowlin'   Merrill 1971; Styne 1971

Some Big Something   Hammerstein 1920

Some Body Else   Blake 1977; Razaf 1977

Some Boy   Buck 1912

Some Bright Morning   Strouse 1980

Some Crummy Season   Lawrence 1964

Some Day   Baer 1942; Friml 1925; Herbert 1917; Romberg 1916, 1927; Ruby 1949; Smith, Harry B. 1923, 1927

Some Day Down in Caroline   Egan 1919

Some Day I'll Steal You   Motzan 1918

Some Day in Somewhere Wedding Bells Will Ring   Conrad 1918

Some Day (inst.)   Youmans 1954

Some Day Soon   Myrow 1956; Styne 1980

Some Day Sweetheart   Coots 1944

Some Day We'll Meet Again   Conrad 1936; Magidson 1936

Some Day when Dreams Come True   Williams 1907

Some Day You'll Be Sorry Pal o' Mine   Egan 1926; Whiting 1926

Some Day You'll Be Sorry that You're Glad   Conrad Date Unknown

Some Day You'll Know   Coslow 1927

Some Day (You'll Miss Me When You're Lonesome)   Brown, Lew 1911

Some Day You'll Realize   Rose 1929

Some Day You'll Say "O.K."   Donaldson 1927

Some Days Everything Goes Wrong   Drake 1964

Some Days You Are Lonely (Czardas)   Dietz 1950

Some Don't Believe in Miracles, I Do — Don't You   Hanley 1932

Some Early Morning   Monaco 1923

Some Enchanted Evening   Hammerstein 1949; Rodgers 1949

Some Far-Away Someone   DeSylva 1924; Gershwin, George 1924; Gershwin, Ira 1924

Some Fine Day   Ager 1942; Hammerstein 1922; Kern 1920; Mitchell 1922; Rose 1942

Some Folks Work (Is You Man or Mule?)   Arlen 1943; Harburg 1943

Some Girl Is on Your Mind   Hammerstein 1929; Kern 1929

Some Girls Can Bake a Pie   Gershwin, George 1931; Gershwin, Ira 1931

Some Girls Do and Some Girls Don't   Johnson, Howard 1916

Some Golden Day   Kahn 1924

Some Happy Day   Yellen 1932

Some Hearts   Cahn 1969

Some How   Schwartz, Jean 1923

Some Kind of Man   Cahn 1970; Styne 1970

Some Kind of Music   Coleman 1975; Leigh 1975

Some Like It Hot   Loesser 1939

Some Like to Hunt   Hammerstein 1923; Harbach 1923

Some Little Girl   Von Tilzer 1929

Some Little Girl (Waiting Around the Corner)   Kern 1918

Some Little Something About You   Berlin 1909; Snyder 1909

Some Little Squirrel Is Going to Get Some Little Nut   Von Tilzer 1917

Some Little World   Merrill 1967

Some Lonesome Night   Clarke 1918; Meyer 1918

Some More   Atteridge 1923; Schwartz, Jean 1923

Some Night When You're Lonely   Davis 1928

Some Nonsense   Bryan 1920; Schwartz, Jean 1920

Some of the Blues   Coleman 1964

Some of These Nights   Howard, Joseph E. 1915

Some One   Kahn 1919; Kern 1916

Some Other Bird Whistled a Tune   Bryan 1925; Fisher 1925

Some Other Day   Coots 1927; Dubin 1927

Some Other Girl   Kahn 1924

Some Other Time   Cahn 1944; Comden and Green 1944; Coslow 1935; Davis 1925; Styne 1944

Some Party   Kern 1919

Some People   Lerner, Alan Jay 1985; Sondheim 1959; Styne 1959

Some People Make Me Sick   Hammerstein 1920; Harbach 1920

Some People Take a Walk   Brooks 1959

Some Pig   Strouse Date Unknown

Some Pretty Day   Ahlert 1920; Lewis 1920; Young, Joe 1920

Some Rain Must Fall   Gershwin, George 1921; Gershwin, Ira 1921

Some Rainy Night   Parish 1921

Some Say Somewhere Wedding Bells Will Ring   Conrad 1918; Sterling 1918

Some Says There Just Ain't No Fish   Russell 1950; Sigman 1950

Some Smart, Some Smart   Cahn 1965; Van Heusen 1965

Some Smoke (inst.)   Romberg 1913

Some Sort of Somebody (All of the Time)   Kern 1915

Some Sort of Something   Duke 1927

Some Sunday   Edwards 1930; Johnson, Howard 1930

Some Sunday Morning   Egan 1917; Kahn 1917; Koehler 1945; Whiting 1917

Some Sunny Day   Berlin 1922; Donaldson 1919

Some Sweet Afternoon   Kahn 1919

Some Sweet Day   Buck 1922; Cahn 1956; Howard, Joseph E. 1937; Mitchell 1921; Pollack 1929; Van Heusen 1956

Some Sweet Morning   Hanley 1927

Some Sweet Someone   Kalmar 1928; Ruby 1928

Some Sweet Tomorrow   Dubin 1926

Some Things   Rome 1965

Some Things a Man Must Have   Rome 1940

Some Time   Jerome 1916; Parish 1934

Some Time in Springtime   Coslow 1930

Some Wonderful Sort of Someone   Gershwin, George 1918

Somebody   Ahlert 1930; Brooks 1960; Coleman 1983; Hanley 1919; Turk 1930; Warren 1960

Somebody Cares for You   Coslow 1921

Somebody Did All Right for Herself   Bergman 1978
Somebody Else   Dubin 1920; Rome 1962
Somebody Else Is Gettin' It   Sterling 1912; Von Tilzer 1912
Somebody Else, It's Always Somebody Else   Meyer 1910
Somebody Else, Not Me   Hanley 1920
Somebody Else Took You Out of My Arms, but They Can't Take You Out of My Heart   Conrad 1923; Rose 1923
Somebody Else Will If You Don't   Bryan 1912
Somebody Else's Sweetheart   Bacharach 1961; David, Hal 1961
Somebody Else's Sweetie   Lerner, Sammy 1953
Somebody from Somewhere   Gershwin, George 1931; Gershwin, Ira 1931
Somebody Goofed   Hoffman 1954
Somebody Has to Help Somebody (All the Time)   Robison 1956
Somebody Just Like You   Silver 1929
Somebody Knows   Von Tilzer 1915
Somebody Knows Somebody Who Knows Just Who You Are   Bryan 1908
Somebody Laid a Hand on My Shoulder   Robison 1953
Somebody Like You   Donaldson 1924; Friend 1924; Friml 1921
Somebody Loves Me   Cahn 1954; DeSylva 1924; Gershwin, George 1924; Styne 1954
Somebody Loves You   Brown, A. Seymour 1913; Hanley 1922
Somebody Loves You Too   Meyer 1909
Somebody Mighty Like You   Bryan 1929
Somebody New   Strouse 1980
Somebody Nobody Knows   Warren 1939
Somebody Nobody Loves   Kahn 1929
Somebody Ought to Be Told   Hammerstein 1935; Romberg 1935
Somebody Ought to Wave a Flag   Hart 1932; Rodgers 1932
(What Do I Care What) Somebody Said   Clare 1927; Hart 1926; Rodgers 1926; Woods 1927
Somebody Said That Somebody Said   Bryan 1908
Somebody Some Place   Merrill 1967
Somebody Stole My Heart Away   Gershwin, George 1929; Gershwin, Ira 1929; Kahn 1929
Somebody Stole My Kazoo   Styne 1980
Somebody Stole My Muchacha   Hoffman 1956
Somebody Sweet Is Sweet on Me   Donaldson 1928; Kahn 1928
Somebody Told Me   Gordon 1939; Howard, Joseph E. 1915
Somebody Up There Likes Me   Cahn 1956
Somebody Wants to Go to Sleep   Hammerstein 1934; Kern 1934
Somebody Was a Wonderful Pal when Somebody Won My Pal   Gilbert 1925
Somebody's Coming to My House   Berlin 1913
Somebody's Crazy About You   Gorney 1925
Somebody's Dancing with My Girl   Atteridge 1914; Carroll 1914; Romberg 1914
Somebody's Eyes   Kahn 1925
Somebody's Garden   Brennan 1925
Somebody's Going to Throw a Big Party   Porter 1929
Somebody's Gotta Do Somethin'   Strouse 1993
Somebody's Happiness   David, Hal 1974
Somebody's Heart Is So Lonely   Motzan 1919
Somebody's Keeping Score   Fain 1957; Webster 1957
Somebody's Lonely   Davis 1926
Somebody's Mother   Sterling 1921; Von Tilzer 1921
Somebody's Silver Jubilee   Burke 1959

Somebody's Sunday   Duke 1927
Somebody's Sweetheart I Want to Be   Cobb 1905; Edwards 1905
Somebody's Waiting for Me   Sterling 1902; Von Tilzer 1902
Somebody's Waiting for Someone   Sterling 1919; Von Tilzer 1919
Somebody's Walkin' in My Dreams   Adamson 1945; McHugh 1945
Somebody's Wrong   Egan 1923; Whiting 1923
Someday   Blane 1948; Merrill 1990
Someday, Honey Darlin'   Sherman 1974
Someday I'll Grow Up   Caesar 1967
Someday I'll Meet You Again   Washington 1944
Someday, Somebody's Goin' to Get You   Gilbert 1917
Someday, Sometime, Somewhere   Hanley 1933
Someday, Someway, You'll Pay   Howard, Joseph E. 1929
Someday Somewhere   Pollack 1928
Someday Soon   Carmichael 1962; Gordon 1956
Someday Soon (In a Mist)   Webster 1962
Someday, Sweetheart, Someday   Edwards 1908
Someday the Sun Will Shine   Clarke 1921; Hanley 1921; Monaco 1921
Someday Today Will Be the Good Old Times   Goetz 1952
Someday, We Will Remember   Brooks 1945
Someday We'll Meet Again   Ager 1932; Hoffman 1932
Someday when Love Finds a Way   Yellen 1922
Someday You May Change Your Mind   Coots 1928
Someday You'll Be Sorry   Evans 1965; Howard, Joseph E. 1948; Livingston, Jay 1965
Someday You'll Find Your Bluebird   Gordon 1940; Revel Date Unknown
Someday You'll Realize   Gershwin, Ira 1923
Somehow   Cahn 1968; Loewe 1937, 1942
Somehow I Knew   Gershwin, Ira 1920; Youmans 1920
Somehow I Never Could Believe   Weill 1947
Somehow I'd Rather Be Good   Smith, Harry B. 1926
Somehow It Seldom Comes True   DeSylva 1919; Gershwin, George 1919
Somehow (Somehow I Remember)   Spina 1977
Somehow You're Just My Style   Howard, Joseph E. 1919
Someone   Ager Date Unknown; Bryan 1929; Cahn 1972; Clare 1929, 1930; Gershwin, Ira 1922; Kern 1928; Meyer 1929; Smith, Harry B. 1926; Yellen Date Unknown
Someone at Last   Arlen 1954; Gershwin, Ira 1954
Someone Believes in You   Gershwin, George 1924
Someone Called Manon   Russell 1949
Someone Cares   Drake 1947
(I'm Unhappy 'Cause) Someone Else Is on Your Mind   Parish 1930
Someone Else   Mancini 1995
Someone Else May Be There While I'm Gone   Berlin 1916
Someone Else Was There   Sigman 1935
Someone Else's Sweetheart (Is the Girl of My Dreams)   Hoffman 1943; Livingston, Jerry 1943
Someone I Love   Herbert 1935
Someone I Used to Know   Atteridge 1912
Someone in a Tree   Sondheim 1976
Someone in April   Lane 1965; Lerner, Alan Jay 1965
Someone in Love   Bergman 1956
Someone in the Dark   Bergman 1982
Someone Is Coming from Dixie   Goetz 1912
Someone Is Goin' to Be Lonesome   Donaldson 1917
Someone Is Losin' Susan   Meyer 1926; Turk 1926
Someone Is Waiting   Sondheim 1970
Someone Just Like You, Dear   Berlin 1910; Snyder 1910

Someone Like You   Blane 1947, 1949; Herbert 1919; Rodgers 1965; Smith, Robert B. 1919; Sondheim 1965; Warren 1947, 1949

Someone Loves You   Parish 1931

Someone Must Be Getting Married Somewhere   Hart 1930; Rodgers 1930

Someone on Your Side   Lerner, Alan Jay 1969

Someone Should Tell Them   Hart 1927; Rodgers 1927

Someone, Someday, Somewhere   Buck 1924; Friml 1924

Someone Stole Gabriel's Horn   Mills 1932

Someone to Care For   Ellington 1966; Kahn 1932; Warren 1932

Someone to Care for Me   Kahn 1936

Someone to Love   Freed, Ralph 1946; Hanley 1929; Kahn 1925

Someone to Talk To   Martin 1962

Someone to Tell It To   Cahn 1960; Van Heusen 1960

Someone to Watch Over Me   Gershwin, George 1926; Gershwin, Ira 1926

Someone, Tra La La   Gershwin, George 1922

Someone Turned the Moon Up Side Down   Burke 1953

Someone Waiting for Me   Howard, Joseph E. 1907

Someone Who Believes in You   DeSylva 1924; Gershwin, George 1924

Someone Who Cares   Adams 1957; Strouse 1957

Someone Will Make You Smile (Vienna Dreams)   Caesar 1923

Someone Woke Up   Rodgers 1965; Sondheim 1965

Someone Wonderful I Missed   Coleman 1977

Someone's Always Calling a Rehearsal   Gershwin, George 1929; Gershwin, Ira 1929; Kahn 1929

Someone's Been Opening My Mail   Spina 1977

Someone's Been Readin' My Mail   Sigman 1953

Someone's Calling Me   Atteridge 1914; Carroll 1914; Romberg 1914

Someone's Gonna Get Kissed   Friend 1950

Someone's in Love with You   Edwards 1927

Someone's Stole Gabriel's Horn   Washington 1932

Someone's Stolen My Sweet Sweet Baby   Brown, Lew 1925; Clare 1925

Someone's Waiting for Me   Berlin 1909; Leslie 1909; Snyder 1909

Someone's Waiting for You   Fain 1977

Someplace on Anywhere Road   Burke 1950; Van Heusen 1950

Somethin' Cold to Drink   Arlen 1968

Somethin' Real Special   Arlen 1953; Fields 1953

Somethin' Ya Gotta Find Out Yo'self   Mercer 1959

Somethin' You Gotta Find Out for Yourself   Arlen 1946; Mercer 1946

Something   Friml 1912; Harbach 1912; Howard, Joseph E. 1909

Something About a War   Sondheim 1962

Something About Love   Gershwin, George 1919, 1926

Something About Me   Merrill 1964; Styne 1964

Something About Romance   Coslow 1934; Johnston 1934

Something Always Happens When It Shouldn't   Herbert 1908

Something Bad   Bacharach 1970; David, Hal 1970

Something Better than Being in Love   Burke 1953; Van Heusen 1953

Something Big   Bacharach 1965; David, Hal 1965

Something Borrowed — Something Blue   Sherman 1964

Something 'Bout Believing   Ellington 1968

Something Came and Got Me in the Spring   Schwartz, Jean 1933

Something Doesn't Happen   Rodgers 1970

Something Doing Around My Heart   Howard, Joseph E. 1906

Something Extra   Adams 1967; Strouse 1967

Something for Everybody   Bergman 1969

Something for Nothing   DeSylva 1925; Hanley 1925; Robison 1947

Something for Somebody Else   Livingston, Jerry 1963

Something for the Books   Fain 1951; Webster 1951

Something for the Browns   Revel 1953

Something Good   Rodgers 1965

Something Greater   Adams 1970; Strouse 1970

Something Had to Happen   Harbach 1933

Something Happens   Cahn 1973

Something Has Happened   Myrow 1937

Something I Can't Explain   Jerome 1912

Something I Dreamed Last Night   Ager 1939; Fain 1939; Magidson 1939; Yellen 1939

Something I Dreamed No Doubt   Burke 1940

Something I Never Told You   Howard, Joseph E. 1946

Something in Common   Burke 1949; Van Heusen 1949

Something in Here   Coots 1922

Something in My Heart   Harburg 1935, 1945

Something in the Air   David, Hal 1959; Drake 1954

Something in the Air of May   Hammerstein 1935; Romberg 1935

Something in the Night   Young, Joe 1932

Something in the Wind   Robin 1947; Styne 1953

Something Inside of Me Singing   Russell 1956

Something Is Coming to Tea   Martin 1964

Something Is Going On   Myrow 1959

Something Just Broke   Sondheim 1992

Something Like Me   Hart 1921; Rodgers 1921

Something Like This   Smith, Harry B. 1912; Smith, Robert B. 1912

Something More   Bergman 1964; Fain 1964

Something New   Duke 1963

Something New in My Life   Bergman 1984

Something New Is in My Heart   Hammerstein 1935; Romberg 1935

Something Old, Something New   Romberg 1927

Something on My Mind (inst.)   Kern 1956

Something on Your Mind   Lewis 1974; Young, Joe 1974

Something Peculiar   Gershwin, George 1920, 1921; Gershwin, Ira 1920, 1921

Something Seems Tingle-ingle-ing   Friml 1913; Harbach 1913

Something Seems to Call Me Back to You   Carmichael 1940

Something Seems to Tell Me   Caesar 1931

Something So Delightful   Leigh 1955

Something, Somewhere   Rodgers 1970

Something Sort of Grandish   Harburg 1947; Lane 1947

Something Sort of Silly   Kalmar Date Unknown; Ruby Date Unknown

Something Spanish in Your Eyes   Caesar 1929

Something Special   Cahn 1962, 1984; Coleman 1984; Van Heusen 1962

Something Tells Me   Dietz 1927; Gorney 1927; Martin 1964; Mercer 1938; Razaf 1946

Something Tells Me I Am Going to Love You   Goetz 1911

Something Tells Me I'm in Love   Williams 1906

Something Tells Me that One Is You   Turk 1925

Something Tells Me You Will Break My Heart   Brown, Lew 1912

Something that I Can't Explain   Schwartz, Jean 1912

Something to Call Our Own   Kalmar 1928; Ruby 1928

Something to Dance About   Berlin 1950

Something to Do   Leigh 1976

Something to Dream About   Sigman 1958

Something to Live For   Drake 1964; Eliscu 1929; Ellington 1939

Something to Remember   Kahn 1921

Something to Remember Him By   Mills 1947

Something to Remember You By   Dietz 1930; Schwartz, Arthur 1930

Something to Say (No One to Say It To)   Johnston 1946

Something to Shout About   Porter 1943

Something to Sing About   Adamson 1930; Youmans 1930

Something to Tell   Coots 1928

Something to Think About   Cahn 1964; Gordon 1932; Revel 1932; Van Heusen 1964

Something Turns Up to Make It Right!   Styne 1985

Something Very Mysterious   Harbach 1911

Something Warm for Christmas   Coleman 1963; Leigh 1963

Something Was Missing   Strouse 1977

Something Wonderful   Hammerstein 1951; Rodgers 1951

Something Wrong with Me   Coots 1925

Something You Never Had Before   Dietz 1961; Schwartz, Arthur 1961

Something's Always Happening on the River   Comden and Green 1958; Styne 1958

Something's Coming   Sondheim 1957

Something's Gonna to Happen to Me and You   Johnson, James P. 1931

Something's Got to Be Done   Cohan 1922; Porter 1916

Something's Got to Happen   Harbach 1933; Kern 1933

Something's Gotta Be Done   Koehler 1932

Something's Gotta Be Done About That   Johnston 1929

Something's Gotta Give   Mercer 1955

Something's Gotta Happen Soon   Brown, Nacio Herb 1935, 1936; Freed, Arthur 1935

Something's Happened to Rosie   Cohan 1923

Something's in the Air   David, Mack 1933

Something's Wrong   Gershwin, Ira 1938; Kern 1938

Something's Wrong! How Can You Ask Me to Smile?   Lewis 1924; Young, Joe 1924

Somethin's Gotta Happen Soon   Freed, Arthur 1936

Sometime   Brown, A. Seymour 1914; Friml 1918; Kahn 1925; Parish 1939; Von Tilzer 1917

Sometime in Spring   Donaldson 1936

Sometime in Springtime   Bryan 1909; Meyer 1909

Sometime in Summertime   Donaldson 1932

Sometime in the Summertime   Donaldson 1928

Sometime Promises   Cahn 1959; Van Heusen 1959

Sometime, Somewhere   Williams 1908

Sometime Tomorrow   Russell 1946

Sometime when Lights Are Low   Kahn 1920

Sometime When You're Lonely (inst.)   Coleman 1965

Sometimes   Mancini 1970

Sometimes (I Just Can't Stand You)   Spina 1967

Sometimes I'm Happy   Caesar 1925; Robin 1927; Youmans 1925, 1927

Sometimes in Dreams   Kahn 1915

Sometimes Is Forever   Warren Date Unknown

Sometimes Late at Night   Bacharach 1981

Sometimes There's a Moment   Evans 1973; Livingston, Jay 1973

Sometimes You Get a Good One and Sometimes You Don't   Sterling 1916; Von Tilzer 1916

Sometimes You Will, Sometimes You Won't   Hanley 1924

Somewhere   Bryan 1958; Sondheim 1957; Warren 1956

Somewhere a Boy Lies Dreaming   Revel 1944; Webster 1944

Somewhere Across the Sea   Baer 1954

Somewhere Alone with You   Davis 1926

(Lost My Baby) Somewhere Along the Line   Stept 1949

Somewhere Along the Trail   Cahn 1941

Somewhere (Always Somewhere Just Beyond)   Raye 1940

Somewhere Beyond the Shadow of Today   McHugh 1969

Somewhere Down the Line   Robison 1964

Somewhere East of Sunrise   Coots 1932

Somewhere I Know There's a Girl for Me   Herbert 1920; Smith, Robert B. 1920

Somewhere In a Corner of Your Heart   Burke 1950; Van Heusen 1950

Somewhere in Dixie   Von Tilzer 1917

Somewhere in Dreamland   Bryan 1930

Somewhere in France Is the Lily   Howard, Joseph E. 1917

Somewhere in Georgia Underneath the Sunny Southern Skies   McHugh 1917

Somewhere in Ireland   Brennan 1917

Somewhere in Lovers' Land   Atteridge 1925

Somewhere in Love's Garden   Romberg 1922

Somewhere in My Heart   Friml 1960

Somewhere in Paradise   Henderson 1939

Somewhere in Somebody's Arms   Carroll 1923; Kalmar 1923; Ruby 1923

Somewhere in Sonora   Parish 1933

Somewhere in the Night   Gordon 1946; Myrow 1946

Somewhere in the Used to Be   David, Mack 1962

Somewhere in the West   Freed, Arthur 1932

Somewhere My Love   Webster 1966

Somewhere Near Someplace   Davis 1962

Somewhere on Broadway   Carroll 1917

Somewhere on the Island of Somewhere   Silver 1950

Somewhere on Via Roma   Carmichael 1945

Somewhere Over the Moon (Gitarren-Serenade)   Rome 1953

Somewhere Somebody's Waiting for You   Akst 1926; Davis 1926

Somewhere, Someday   Baer 1965

Somewhere, Somehow, Someday   Carroll 1923

Somewhere Someone Is Waiting for Me   Razaf 1924

Somewhere There's a Home   Evans 1961; Livingston, Jay 1961

Somewhere There's a Rainbow   Washington 1945

Somewhere There's a Silver Lining   Norworth 1938

Somewhere Wisconsin   Washington 1958

Somewhere with Somebody Else   Leslie 1938

Son of a Billionaire   Cohan 1927

Son of a Gun Is Nothing but a Tailor, The   Hart 1932; Rodgers 1932

Son of a Gun Who Picks on Uncle Sam, The   Harburg 1942, 1945; Lane 1942, 1945

Son of a Sailor, The   David, Hal 1951

Son of God's Country, A   Coots 1935

Son of the Emperor, The   Drake 1954

Son of the Sun, A   Brennan 1930; Friml 1930

Sonambula   Bryan 1919; Schwartz, Jean 1919

Sonambulistic Tune   Buck 1916

Sonata   Drake 1946

Sonata (inst.)   Strouse 1962

Sonatina   Lerner, Alan Jay 1976

Song a Child Could Sing, A   Lane Date Unknown
Song About Love   Mancini 1963
Song Allegretto (inst.)   Youmans 1954
Song and Dance   Smith, Harry B. 1927
Song and Dance Man   Rome 1969
Song Bird   Brennan 1936
Song Bird of Melody Lane   Bryan 1927; Cobb 1902; Edwards 1902
Song Birds Quartette   Johnson, James P. 1922
Song for a Merry-Go-Round   Parish 1965
Song for American Union   Rome 1945
Song for an Anniversay   Parish 1965
Song for an Autumn Afternoon   Wrubel 1950
Song for Christmas, A   Ellington 1966
Song for Dancing, A   Bergman 1978
Song for Elizabeth Esther Barrett   Berlin 1957
Song for Humming, A   Sondheim Date Unknown
Song for Muted Strings   Parish 1965
Song for Reri   Gorney 1931
Song for Sweethearts (Come Close)   Sigman 1954
Song for the World to Sing, A   McHugh 1964
Song from Meantown   Brooks 1960
Song from the Fountain   Herbert 1910
Song I Heard Last Night, The   Parish 1955
Song I Love, The   Brown, Lew 1928; Conrad 1928; DeSylva 1928; Henderson 1928
Song in C (inst.)   Kern 1956
Song in Four Languages   Lane 1965
Song in My Heart Is a Rhumba, The   Lane 1939; Loesser 1939
Song Is Born, A   Donaldson 1942
Song Is You, The   Hammerstein 1932; Kern 1932
Song Magician, The   Oakland 1960
Song My Mother Loved, The   Hoffman 1958
Song o' My Heart   Hanley 1930
Song of a Dreamer   Gorney 1934
Song of a Fool, The   Lewis 1930
Song of a Lonesome Guitar, The   Parish 1931
Song of a Lost Love   Young, Victor 1954
Song of a Summer Night   Akst 1923; Kahn 1923; Loesser 1956
Song of Assisi, The   Harburg 1971
Song of Delilah, The   Evans 1949; Livingston, Jay 1949; Young, Victor 1950
Song of Farewell   Rome 1943
Song of Freedom   Berlin 1942; Hanley 1943
Song of Gold, The   Leslie 1929; Monaco 1929
Song of Green Mansions   Webster 1959
Song of India, A   Brooks 1947; Dubin 1924; Johnson, Howard 1939; Mercer 1953
Song of Indiana, A   Kahn 1928
Song of Italy   Webster 1939
Song of Long Ago, The   Carmichael 1968; Mercer 1968
Song of Love   Atteridge 1924; Romberg 1921, 1924; Schwartz, Arthur 1927
Song of Love Is Singing in My Heart, A   Friend 1930; Monaco 1930
Song of Margharita, A   Baer 1929; Gilbert 1929
Song of Mojave   Donaldson 1940; Gilbert 1940
Song of My Heart   Baer 1929; Gilbert 1929
Song of Old Mexico, A   Coots 1945
Song of Omar Khyyam, The   Evans 1955; Livingston, Jay 1955
Song of Our Love   Duke 1950; Rome 1950
Song of Persia   Egan 1922; Whiting 1922

Song of Provincetown   Drake 1955
Song of Reverie   Rome 1943
Song of Rockwell   Akst 1938; Clare 1938
Song of Ruth, The   Webster 1960; Weill 1937
Song of Safari   Stept 1927
Song of Shanghai   Egan 1926; Whiting 1926
Song of Sicily   Bryan 1926
Song of Song   Robison 1956
Song of Songs, The   Smith, Harry B. 1908
Song of Sorrow   Lawrence 1930
Song of Spring   Carmichael 1935
Song of Stalingrad   Rome 1943
Song of Steel, The   Edwards 1929; Johnson, Howard 1929; Willson 1934
Song of Surrender   Dubin 1934; Evans 1949; Livingston, Jay 1949; Warren 1934; Young, Victor 1949
Song of the Ads (The Pluto Boys) (The Pluto Boys, We're the Ads)   Rome 1940
Song of the Aimlessness of Life   Weill 1933
Song of the Autumn and You   Johnson, Howard 1935
Song of the Baltic Fleet   Rome 1943
Song of the Barefoot Contessa   Lawrence 1954
Song of the Bayou   Bloom 1929; Johnson, Howard 1929
Song of the Bible   Webster 1966
Song of the Big Shot   Weill 1977
Song of The Big Trail (Old Fashioned Song of Love)   Hanley 1930
Song of the Blue Lagoon   Kahn 1930
Song of the Boomps   Sherman 1989
Song of the Brass Key   Hammerstein 1926; Harbach 1926; Romberg 1926
Song of the Butterfly, The   Howard, Joseph E. 1909
Song of the Camels   Blane 1960
Song of the Cannon   Brown, Lew 1943
Song of the Carbine   Herbert 1897; Smith, Harry B. 1897
Song of the Casbah   Freed, Ralph 1943
Song of the Cash Register   Coslow 1938; Weill 1938
Song of the Chimes   Smith, Robert B. 1914
Song of the Cocktail   Goetz 1912
Song of the Comb, The   Hoffman 1953
Song of the Congo   Magidson 1930; Washington 1930
Song of the Cotton Fields   Razaf 1929; Waller 1929
Song of the Cowboys   Heyman 1928
Song of the Coyotes   Akst 1936; Clare 1936
Song of the Crusades   Robin 1935; Whiting 1935
Song of the Danube, The   Herbert 1899; Smith, Harry B. 1899
Song of the Dawn, The   Ager 1930; Yellen 1930
Song of the Desert   Brooks 1949
Song of the Dice   Smith, Harry B. 1906
Song of the Dove   Drake 1975
Song of the Drum Major   Smith, Harry B. 1900
Song of the Enchanted Rope   Fain 1951; Harburg 1951
Song of the Evening   Henderson 1934; Koehler 1934
Song of the Fashions   Smith, Harry B. 1910
Song of the Fatherland   Gershwin, Ira 1943
Song of the Fisherman (Ay Ay Ay), The   Washington 1938
Song of the Flame   Gershwin, George 1925; Hammerstein 1925; Harbach 1925
Song of the Flea   Johnson, Howard 1935
Song of the Foreign Legion (Foreign Legion Number)   Brown, Lew 1931; Henderson 1931
Song of the Free   Weill 1942
Song of the Free Lance (I Am a Salaried Warrior)   Smith, Harry B. 1906

Song of the Future (inst.)   Young, Victor 1955
Song of the Gigolo   Arlen 1930; Dubin 1935; Koehler 1930; Warren 1935
Song of the Goddess   Weill 1936
Song of the Gold Diggers   Dubin 1929
Song of the Gondolier   Adamson 1954; Warren 1954
Song of the Good Neighbor   Caesar 1946
Song of the Great Alone   Hoffman 1929
Song of the Guerrillas   Gershwin, Ira 1943
Song of the Guns   Weill 1936
Song of the Gypsy Band   Akst 1938; Clare 1938
Song of the Hangman   Gershwin, Ira 1945; Weill 1945
Song of the Harp   Livingston, Jerry 1956
Song of the Heart, A   Johnson, J. Rosamond 1918; Smith, Robert B. 1909
Song of the Hoofer   Henderson 1934; Koehler 1934
Song of the Humming Birds   Loesser 1937
Song of the King   Cohan 1908; Hammerstein 1951; Rodgers 1951
Song of the Ladies Man   Brooks 1947
Song of the Land I Love   Cahn 1968
Song of the Lark   Schwartz, Jean 1930
Song of the Lie (What Are You Doing), The   Burke 1938; Weill 1938
Song of the Marines, The   Dubin 1937; Warren 1937
Song of the Mermaid (The Mermaid and the Rainbow)   Howard, Joseph E. 1905
Song of the Metronome, The   Berlin 1939
Song of the Molly Maguires, The   Adams 1970; Strouse 1969
Song of the Moose   Snyder 1977
Song of the Musketeers   Bullock 1939
Song of the Napkin Rings   Harbach 1947; Kern 1947
Song of the Newlyweds   Burke 1939; Monaco 1939
Song of the Nose   Herbert 1899; Smith, Harry B. 1899
Song of the Owl and the Duck, The   Friend 1950
Song of the Pipe   Smith, Robert B. 1905
Song of the Poet   Herbert 1903
Song of the Priestess   Herbert 1897; Smith, Harry B. 1897
Song of the Rabbit   Gilbert 1937
Song of the Rag-Time Boy   Sterling 1906; Von Tilzer 1906
Song of the Rain   Parish 1961
Song of the Red Headed Woman   Egan 1932; Whiting 1932
Song of the Refugee   Harbach 1942
Song of the Rhineland (Trenton Bieretuse)   Gershwin, Ira 1945; Weill 1945
Song of the Riveter   Schwartz, Arthur 1929
Song of the Robin   Russell 1952
Song of the Roustabouts   Hart 1935; Rodgers 1935; Washington 1941
Song of the Samovar   Myrow 1937
Song of the Sap   Brown, Lew 1928; DeSylva 1928; Henderson 1928
Song of the Sea   Rome 1943
Song of the Seabees, The   Lewis 1944
Song of the Setting Sun   Donaldson 1928; Kahn 1928
Song of the Sewing Machine   Rose 1928
Song of the Sirens   Smith, Harry B. 1911
Song of the Ski-Troops   Coslow 1944
Song of the South   Coslow 1946; Johnson, Howard 1930; Johnston 1946; Silver 1928
Song of the Sparrow   Loesser 1937
Song of the Spirits, The   David, Mack 1958; Livingston, Jerry 1958
Song of the Subway   Oakland 1958
Song of the Teamsters Union   Caesar 1961

Song of the Tule   Brennan 1936
Song of the Vagabonds   Friml 1925
Song of the Valley, The   David, Hal 1941
Song of the Waiters   Williams 1909
Song of the Waters   Coslow 1930
Song of the Wheel   Evans 1958; Livingston, Jay 1958
Song of the Windshield Wiper   Loesser Date Unknown
Song of the Women's Army Corps   Spina 1952
Song of the Woodman   Arlen 1936; Harburg 1936
Song of the Wounded Frenchman   Weill 1936
Song of the Zodiac   Gershwin, Ira 1940; Weill 1940
Song of Troy   Freed, Ralph 1930
Song of Unity   Revel 1959
Song of Victory   Romberg 1927
Song of Vienna   Eliscu 1929
Song of Vienna (In Wien, Wo der Wein und der Walzer Bluht), The   Young, Joe 1930
Song of Virtue   Weill 1937
Song That Is Locked in My Heart, The   Johnson, Howard 1926
Song that Makes Me Blue, The   Arlen 1932; Yellen 1932
Song that Stole My Heart Away, The   Sterling 1913; Von Tilzer 1913
Song that Was Born in My Heart, The   Howard, Joseph E. 1946
Song That's Got a Beat, A   Blake 1956; Sissle 1956
Song the Angels Sing, The   Webster 1942
Song the Minstrel Sang (Old Black Joe), The   Cobb 1903; Edwards 1903
Song to Forget, A   Dietz 1948; Schwartz, Arthur 1948
Song to Remember, A   Cahn 1945
Song Was Born, A   DePaul 1948; Raye 1948
Song Without a Mountain, A   Washington 1933; Wrubel 1933
Song Without a Name   Webster 1968
Song Without End   Washington 1960
Song Without (Many) Words, A   Herbert 1920
Song Without You   Howard, Bart 1938
Songbird of Melody Lane (1), The   Bryan 1903; Edwards 1903
Song's for Free, The   Ager 1939; Fain 1939; Yellen 1939
Songs for Sale   Young, Joe 1932
Song's Gotta Come from the Heart, The   Cahn 1947; Styne 1947
Songs I Can't Forget   Buck 1922
Songs I Love, The   Cahn 1963; Van Heusen 1963
Songs My Mother Used to Sing to Who, The   Brown, Lew 1927
Songs of Long Ago, The   Gershwin, George 1920
Songs that Maggie Sings, The   Cohan 1897
Songs That Mother Taught   Johnson, Howard 1939
Songwriter   Parish 1965
Sonnet   Blane 1966
Sonny Boy   Brown, Lew 1928; DeSylva 1928; Fisher 1920; Henderson 1928
Sons and Daughters of the Sea   Blake 1937
Sons of Old Black Joe, The   Blake 1924; Sissle 1924
Sons of Sierra   Robin 1936
Sons of the Desert   Fain 1944; Freed, Ralph 1944
Sons of the Legion   Freed, Ralph 1938
Sons of Westwood   Livingston, Jerry 1963
Sonya (inst.)   Schwartz, Jean 1930
Sonya (Yup Alay Yup)   Fisher 1925
Soon   Gershwin, George 1929; Gershwin, Ira 1929; Hart 1935; Rodgers 1935; Sondheim 1973

Soon You Gonna Leave Me, Joe   Loesser 1956

Soon You'll See Me in the Movies   Cahn 1980; Strouse 1980

Sooner or Later   David, Hal 1960; Leigh Date Unknown; Sondheim 1990

Sooner or Later (Mark My Words)   Livingston, Jerry 1936

So-o-o in Love   Robin 1945

Soothin' Syrup Stomp   Waller 1927

Sophia   Gershwin, George 1964; Gershwin, Ira 1964

Sophie   Silver 1922

Sophie Tucker School for Red Hot Mamas   Yellen 1977

Sophisticated Lady   Ellington 1933; Mills 1933; Parish 1933

Sophisticated Swing   Parish 1937

Sore Foot Blues   Blake 1932; Sissle 1932

Sorority Stomp, The   Mills 1929

Sorrows   Kahn 1929; Warren 1929

Sorry   Akst 1923; Davis 1923; DePaul 1956; Mercer 1956; Whiting 1949

Sorry About That   Drake 1967

Sorry As I Am   Lane 1985

Sorry 'Bout That   Livingston, Jay 1966

Sorry 'Bout the Whole Darned Thing   Robison 1951

Sorry for Me   Brown, Lew 1928; DeSylva 1928; Henderson 1928

Sorry, Sorry, Sorry   Hoffman 1958

Sorry that I Strayed Away from You   Johnson, James P. 1929

Sorry Wrong Valley   Martin 1972

Sorry-Grateful   Sondheim 1970

Sort o' Lonesome, Kind o' Blue   Fain 1928; Kahal 1928

Sorta Blue   Cahn 1958; Mancini 1958

S.O.S. Stay on the Sidewalk   Johnson, Howard 1925

So's Your Old Man   Hammerstein 1925; Harbach 1925; Kern 1925

Soul Kiss, The   Smith, Harry B. 1908

Soul Mate   Razaf 1934

Soul Savin' Sara   Robison 1967

Soul Saving Sadie   Rose 1934

Sound and the Fury, The   Cahn 1959

Sound of Love, The   Strouse 1986

Sound of Money, The   Rome 1962

Sound of Music, The   Hammerstein 1959; Rodgers 1959

Sound of Poets, The   Sondheim 1974

Sound of the Gourd, The   Akst 1930; Baer 1930; Clarke 1930; Gilbert 1930

Sound of Your Voice, The   Parish 1936; Silver 1936

Sounds around the House, The   Mercer 1976

Sounds Exciting to Me   Burke 1954

Sounds in the Night   Cahn 1958; Dietz 1956; Russell 1958

Sounds Like October's Here   Spina 1957

Sounds of Christmas, The   Livingston, Jerry 1963; Webster 1963

Sounds of the Night, The   Mercer 1962

Soup Wouldn't Be Soup   Parish 1945

Sour Serenade, The   Hoffman 1940; Stept 1940

Sourwood Mountain   Weill 1948

Sousa's Marches, The   Atteridge 1911

South America, Take It Away   Rome 1946

South American Joe   Caesar 1934; Friend 1934

South American Way   Dubin 1939; McHugh 1939, 1940

South American Way (inst.)   Bacharach 1969

South Boy Wants to Go Home, A   Livingston, Jerry 1936

South Breeze   Carmichael 1930

South of Pago Pago   Pollack 1940

South Sea Eyes   Akst 1923

South Sea Island Baby   Kahn 1925; Whiting 1925

South Sea Island Blues   Johnson, Howard 1921

South Sea Island Rhapsody   Sherman 1971

South Sea Isles   Porter 1922

South Sea Isles (Sunny South Sea Islands)   Gershwin, George 1921

South Sea Rose   Baer 1929; Gilbert 1929

South Sea Serenade   Coslow 1923

South Sea Sweetheart   Bryan 1938

South Sea Sweethearts   Caesar 1922

South Wind   Bloom 1936; Brown, Lew 1927; DeSylva 1926; Henderson 1926; Mercer 1936

Southern Charms   Bloom 1931; Koehler 1931

Southern Comfort   Coleman 1988

Southern Gals   Yellen 1917

Southern Heart of Mine   Atteridge 1913; Schwartz, Jean 1913

Southern Hobby, A   Turk 1922

Southern Lady, A   Rome 1973

Southern Memories   Kahn 1922

Southern Memories (inst.)   Bloom 1933

Southern Queen   Johnson, J. Rosamond 1900

Southland   Adamson 1944; Johnson, J. Rosamond 1907; McHugh 1944; Turk 1922

Southland Serenade   Coots 1937

Southwest Is Calling   Johnson, Howard 1927

Southwind   Mercer 1984

Souvenir   Johnson, Howard 1934; Romberg 1948

Souvenir de Montmartre   Drake 1959

Souvenir D'Italie   Sigman 1955

Souvenir (Fair As a Day in May)   Dubin 1924

Souvenir of Love   Hanley 1932; Johnston 1938

Souvenir of Madeira   Drake 1954

Souvenir of Suzanne (inst.)   Coots 1946

Souvenirs   Caesar 1922; Gershwin, Ira 1945; Hart 1920; Rodgers 1920; Weill 1945

Sow the Seed and Reap the Harvest   Arlen 1946; Mercer 1946

Sow Your Wild Oats Early   Herbert 1919; Smith, Robert B. 1919

Space   Gilbert 1955

Space Man   Heyman 1962

Space Race   Coleman 1966

Spacious and Gracious   Ellington 1966

Spade Ballet   Caesar 1936

Spades Is Trumps   Coots 1937; Davis 1937

Spaghetti   Bryan 1909; Fisher 1909; Loesser 1933; Motzan 1933

Spagoni's Wedding Jubilee   Fisher 1918

Spain   Adamson 1959; Dubin 1935; Fields 1930; Hart 1920; Kahn 1924; McHugh 1930; Rodgers 1920; Warren 1935

Spain, Beautiful Spain   Jerome 1903; Schwartz, Jean 1903

Spangles on My Tights   Loesser 1942; Spina 1942

Spanglish   Coleman 1973; Fields 1973

Spanish   Cohan 1918; Harbach 1917

Spanish Allegretto (inst.)   Youmans 1954

Spanish Allegro (inst.)   Youmans 1954

Spanish Ballet   Atteridge 1916; Hanley 1916; Romberg 1916; Smith, Harry B. 1916

Spanish Basque Carol   Herbert 1903

Spanish Blonde, A   Burke 1935; Spina 1935

Spanish Butterfly   Bryan 1935

Spanish Dance   Atteridge 1923, 1924; Caesar 1923; Romberg 1917, 1923, 1924; Rome 1965; Schwartz, Jean 1924; Smith, Harry B. 1908

Spanish Dancer, The   Hart Date Unknown

Spanish Dancer, The (inst.)   Warren 1958

Spanish Dreams   Fisher 1981; Mills 1928
Spanish Eyes   Edwards 1929; Gilbert 1925
Spanish Fado   Atteridge 1929
Spanish Fandango, The   Atteridge 1915
Spanish in My Eyes, The   Johnson, James P. 1933
Spanish Jake   Caesar 1936; Lerner, Sammy 1936
Spanish Juanita   Coslow 1924
Spanish Lou   Mitchell 1921; Pollack 1921
Spanish Love   Berlin 1911; Caesar 1920, 1923; Gershwin,
   George 1920, 1923; Hoffman 1954; Romberg 1927; Silver
   1920; Smith, Harry B. 1911, 1927; Smith, Robert B. 1911;
   Snyder 1911
Spanish Love Song: Chiquita Senorita   Young, Joe 1933
Spanish Maid (Nina Espagnola)   Friml 1918
Spanish Moderato (Lotta's Song) (inst.)   Youmans 1954
Spanish Of Course   David, Mack 1953; Livingston, Jerry
   1953
Spanish Rose   Adams 1960; Strouse 1960
Spanish Serenade, The   Herbert 1907
Spanish Shawl, A   Bryan 1927; Schwartz, Jean 1927
Spanish Sweetheart   Caesar 1933
Spanish Villa (inst.)   Fain 1963
Spanita, a Gigolo Here, a Gigolo There   Fisher 1931
Spanking Brand New Doll   Ellington 1966
Spare Me   Sigman 1957
Spare Me Your Kindess   Coleman 1960; Leigh 1960
Spare that Building   Cahn 1965; Van Heusen 1965
Spark of Life Dance, The   Atteridge 1912
Spark of Your Love Lit the Torch in My Heart, A   Bryan
   1952
Sparklets in the Sky   Livingston, Jerry 1934
Sparkling and Refreshing (inst.)   Schwartz, Jean 1930
Sparkling Burgandy   Spina 1957
Sparkling Drink   Johnson, James P. 1950
Sparkling Moselle, The   Smith, Harry B. 1914
Sparrow in the Tree Top   Merrill 1950
Sparrows in the Rain   Egan 1932
Spats-s-s Palazzo   Merrill 1972; Styne 1972
Speak for Yourself   Styne 1956
Speak for Yourself John   Friml 1918
Speak Low   Weill 1943
Speak My Heart   Cahn 1951; Revel 1947
Speak Not a Word   Adamson 1963; Fain 1963
Speak to Me of the Tall Pine   Russell 1952
Speak to Me with Your Eyes   Parish 1934
Speak Your Heart   Magidson 1938; Wrubel 1938
Speak Your Love   Raye 1951; Spina 1951
Speakeasy, The   Merrill 1972; Styne 1972
Speaker of the House   Robison 1954
Speakin' of the Devil Here Comes an Angel   Coots 1929
Speakin' of the Devil Here She Is   David, Mack 1933
Speaking Confidentially   Fields 1935; McHugh 1935
Speaking of Dreams   Adamson 1966; Oakland 1966
Speaking of Heaven   Gordon 1939; Revel Date Unknown;
   Van Heusen 1939
Speaking of Love   Duke 1932; Freed, Ralph 1937; Harburg
   1932; Lane 1937
Speaking of Pals   Comden and Green 1945
Speaking of the Weather   Arlen 1936; Harburg 1936, 1937
Special Delivery   Loesser 1956
"Special Material"   Arlen 1936; Harburg 1936
Special Train, The   Smith, Harry B. 1900
Specialist, The   Fain 1975; Webster 1975
Specialist Am I   Harbach 1908
Specialization   Cahn 1960; Van Heusen 1960

Spectrum Song   Sherman 1961
Speech!   Clare 1925; Friend 1925
Speed   Hammerstein 1923; Magidson 1930; Washington
   1930; Youmans 1923
Speedy   Bryan 1928
Spell Me a Riddle   Styne 1958
Spell o' the Moon, The   Kahn 1927
Spell of the Blues, The   Johnston 1929
Spell You Spin, the Web You Weave, The   Russell 1968
Spellbound   David, Mack 1945
Spelling Bee, The   Fain 1937
Spend the Afternoon with Me   Cahn 1960; Van Heusen
   1960
Spend Your Vacation on Broadway   Dubin 1940; Fain 1940
Spending My Time, Saving My Love   Adamson 1933; Coots
   1933
Spending Your Vacation in Maine   Livingston, Jerry 1936
'Spesh'lly You   DePaul 1950; Raye 1950
Sphinx, The   Bryan 1920; Schwartz, Jean 1920
Sphinx (Just Sits and Thinks and Thinks and Thinks and
   Thinks), The   Warren 1926
Sphinx Won't Tell, The   Adams 1954; Strouse 1954
Spic and Spanish   Hart 1939; Rodgers 1939
Spider and Fly, The   Ellington 1966
Spider and the Fly, The   Evans 1952; Koehler 1950;
   Livingston, Jay 1952; Stept 1950
Spider and the Fly (Poor Fly, Bye-Bye), The   Razaf 1938;
   Waller 1938
Spider Man   Webster 1967
Spiders Den   Herbert 1903
Spider's Web, The   Friml 1921
Spiked Fist of War, The   Spina 1944
Spin a Little Web of Dreams   Fain 1934; Kahal 1934
Spin Around   Drake 1955
Spin I'm In, The   Sherman 1961
Spin the Records   Raye 1958
Spindletop   Willson 1953
Spin-Drift   Robison 1963
Spinning, Spinning, Spinning   Hoffman 1956
Spin-Off, The   Cahn 1977
Spin-Off Blues, The   Cahn 1977; Styne 1977
Spirit of Capsulanti   Fain 1951; Harburg 1951
Spirit of Java   Bryan 1921; Pollack 1921; Schwartz, Jean 1921
Spirit of the A.B.C.   Heyman 1943
Spirit of the Chinese Vase, The   Mitchell 1921; Pollack 1921
Spirit of the Tom Tom, The   Cahn 1935
Spirit of Yankee Doodle, The   Baer 1942; Lewis 1942
Spiritual   Coslow 1934; Johnston 1934
Spiritual Melody   Lewis 1928; Young, Joe 1928
Spirituelle (inst.)   Bloom 1928
Spite Bride, The   Lewis 1919; Ruby 1919; Young, Joe 1919
Splendor in the Grass   Webster 1963
Split Decision   Bacharach 1987
Sponge, The   Porter 1922
Spongecake and Wine   Alter 1969; Davis 1967
Spooky Wooky Polka   Hoffman 1945; Livingston, Jerry 1945
Spooky-Ookum   Herbert 1919
Spoon Bill from Louisville   Von Tilzer 1925
Spoonful of Sugar, A   Sherman 1964
Spoony Croony Tune   Atteridge 1924; Romberg 1924;
   Schwartz, Jean 1924
Sport a Sport   Gordon 1932, 1936; Revel 1932, 1936
Sport Car   Bergman 1957
Sport of Kings, The   Duke 1939
Sport Star of T.V. Today, The   Leigh 1971

S'Posin   Razaf 1929
Spozalizio   Loesser 1956
Spread a Little Sunshine As You Go   Woods 1925
Spread It Around   Cahn 1980; Strouse 1980
Spread the News   Friml 1917
Spread the Word   Russell 1956
Spread Your Wings   Washington 1941
Spreadin' Rhythm Around   Koehler 1935; McHugh 1935
Spreadin' the Jam   Blane 1945
Spreading Love Around   Henderson 1935; Heyman 1935
Spring   Caesar 1925; Comden and Green 1947; Kern 1918
Spring Again   Duke 1938; Gershwin, Ira 1938; Weill 1938
Spring and Fall   Berlin 1912
Spring Appears   Raye 1962
Spring Came Early This Year   McHugh 1954; Russell 1951, 1954
Spring Cleaning   Johnson, James P. 1947; Parish 1965
Spring Doth Let Her Colors Fly   Adams 1956; Strouse 1956
Spring Drive, The   Buck 1918
Spring Fever   Arlen 1934; Fields 1930; Gershwin, Ira 1934; Harburg 1934; McHugh 1930; Silver 1933; Wrubel 1933
Spring Fever (inst.)   Bloom 1926
Spring Has Me Out on a Limb   Arlen 1966
Spring Has Sprung   Fields 1951; Schwartz, Arthur 1951
Spring Hat   Smith, Harry B. 1901
Spring Holiday   Bloom 1931; Koehler 1931
Spring in Autumn   Egan 1925; Kahn 1925
Spring in Central Park   Gorney 1960
Spring in December, Winter in May (Passano Gli Anni)   Rome 1948
Spring in Maine   Leigh 1956
Spring in My Heart   Freed, Ralph 1939
Spring in My Room   Blane 1947; Warren 1947
Spring in Vienna   Revel 1960
Spring in Vienna (Spring in Milwaukee)   Hart 1937; Rodgers 1937
Spring Is At My Window, The   Parish 1934
Spring Is Getting On   Drake 1955
Spring Is Here   Hammerstein 1926, 1929; Harbach 1926; Hart 1938; Kern 1929; Rodgers 1938; Turk 1927; Youmans 1926
Spring Is Here in Person   Hart 1928; Rodgers 1928
Spring Is in My Heart Again   Mercer 1932
Spring Is In the Air   Dietz 1927; Edwards 1936; Freed, Ralph 1937; Gorney 1927
Spring Is in the Summer and She'll Fall   Hoffman 1929
Spring Is Spring   Brooks 1960
Spring Is the Season for Remembering   Oakland 1959
Spring Isn't Everything   Blane 1948; Warren 1948
Spring Love Is in the Air   Porter 1937
Spring Made a Fool of Me   Stept 1949
Spring Never Came Around This Year   David, Mack 1953
Spring Prelude   Kalmar 1936; Ruby 1936
Spring Reunion   Mercer 1957; Warren 1957
Spring Song   De Lange 1939; Van Heusen 1939
Spring Spring Spring   DePaul 1954; Mercer 1954
Spring Will Be a Little Late This Year   Loesser 1944
Spring Will Come   Bryan 1928
Spring Will Come Again   Comden and Green 1964
Spring Will Miss You and So Will I   Fain 1946; Freed, Ralph 1946
Spring Will Never Come Again   Adams 1963; Strouse 1963
Springtide   Herbert 1946
Springtime   Buck 1918, 1923; Kahn 1920; Livingston, Jerry 1962

Springtime Cometh, The   Fain 1951; Harburg 1951
Springtime Dance   Herbert 1920; Smith, Robert B. 1920
Springtime in Avalon   Friend 1952
Springtime in Milano (inst.)   Warren Date Unknown
Springtime in Old Granada   Hanley 1933
Springtime in the Country   Atteridge 1915
Springtime Is the Time for Loving   Romberg 1922
Springtime of Long Ago   Hanley 1927
Springtime of Love Is Fairest   Herbert 1914; Smith, Robert B. 1914
Springtime on the Avenue   Romberg 1927
Springtime Wagon of Love, The   Jerome 1915; Von Tilzer 1915
Sprinkle Me with Diamonds   Atteridge 1921; Bryan 1921; Pollack 1921; Schwartz, Jean 1921
Spy Menace   Styne 1954
Squab Farm, The   Atteridge 1918; Romberg 1918; Schwartz, Jean 1918
Square Dance   Blane 1948; Dietz 1934; Mercer 1949; Schwartz, Arthur 1934
Square Dance (inst.)   Kern 1946
Square Dance on the Mall   Drake 1954
Square Jungle, The   Bergman 1960
Square of the Hypotenuse, The   Mercer 1958
Squeaky Shoes   Fields 1929; McHugh 1929
Squee Jee (The Happy Little Clown)   Coots 1953
Squeeze Me   Waller 1925
Squeeze Me Tight   Edwards 1908
Squire and the Deacon, The   Kahal 1929
Squirrel Cage, The   Spina 1977
S.S. Commodore Ebenezer McAffee the Third   Mercer 1964
Ssh! You'll Waken Mister Doyle   Kern 1914
St. Anthony's Alma Mater Hymn   Cahn 1953
St. George Is Comin'   Brooks 1960
St. Joe, Mo.   Webster 1948
St. Louis Shuffle   Waller 1927
St. Paul   Bacharach 1974
St. Peter's Square   Adamson 1959; Warren 1959
St. Tropez   Warren 1961
Sta Di Va   Cahn 1950
Staccato Theme (inst.)   Kern 1956
Stacey Cheer   Gordon 1934; Revel 1934
Stacey Closets   Gordon 1934; Revel 1934
Stacko Lee   Fisher 1923
Stage, The   Drake 1955
Stage Door John   Mercer 1974
Stage Door Johnnies   Coots 1922
Stage Door Number   Smith, Harry B. 1912
Stage Door Scene   Gershwin, George 1929; Gershwin, Ira 1929
Stage Managers' Chorus (Walk Upon Your Toes)   Hart 1925; Rodgers 1925
Stage Society   Cohan 1923
Stage Struck   Mercer 1974
Stagecoach to Mars   David, Hal 1960
Stairway to the Stars   Parish 1939
Stamboul   Friml 1914; Harbach 1914
Stan' Up and Fight   Hammerstein 1943
Stand By Blues   Ellington 1962
Stand By for Further Announcements   Brown, Lew 1939; Stept 1939
Stand Up and Cheer!   Akst 1934; Brown, Lew 1934
Stand Up and Fight   Gershwin, Ira 1947
Stand Up and Fight like H—-   Bryan Date Unknown; Fisher Date Unknown

Stand Up and Fight Like Hell   Cohan 1906
Standard Oil Theme   Young, Victor 1956
Standin' on the Corner   Loesser 1956
Standing on the Corner   Von Tilzer 1929
Standing Pat   Edwards 1909; Smith, Robert B. 1909
Stanley Jones, Meet Amelia Furst   David, Mack 1968
Stanley Steamer, The   Blane 1948; Warren 1948
Star!   Cahn 1968; Van Heusen 1968
Star and the Rose, The   Bergman 1963; Schwartz, Jean 1935;
    Young, Joe 1935
Star Beyond the Star, The   Cahn 1971; Van Heusen 1971
Star Bright (Mara)   Coslow 1956
Star Dust   Carmichael 1929; Parish 1929
Star Eyes   DePaul 1942; Johnson, Howard 1920; Raye 1942
Star Fell Out of Heaven, A   Gordon 1936; Revel 1936
Star Gazing   Livingston, Jerry 1935
Star in the East, A   Livingston, Jerry 1960
Star in the Twilight   Brennan 1928
Star (inst.)   Youmans 1954
Star Light, Star Bright (Starlight Waltz)   Herbert 1895;
    Smith, Harry B. 1895
Star of Bethlehem   David, Mack 1949
Star of Glory, The   Smith, Harry B. 1925
Star of Hitchy Koo, The   Kern 1920
Star of Love   Atteridge 1921; Caesar 1920; Herbert 1913;
    Pollack 1921; Schwartz, Jean 1921; Webster 1980
Star of Stars   Coots 1923; Robin 1927
Star of the West   Smith, Harry B. 1920
Star Sapphire (inst.)   Alter 1953
Star Showers (inst.)   Schwartz, Jean 1930
Star Sounds   Mercer 1965
Star Spangled Night, A   Gordon Date Unknown; Revel Date
    Unknown
Star Spangled Susan Brown   Razaf Date Unknown
Star, the Rose and the Drama, The   Snyder 1909
Star Was Born, A   Ager 1953; Rose 1953
Star You Wished Upon Last Night, The   McHugh 1955
Stardust   Gorney 1924
Stardust Waltz, The   Bergman 1978
Stares that Lead to Love   Schwartz, Jean 1926
Star-Gazing   Stept 1951
Starlight   Buck 1918; Smith, Harry B. 1915
Starlight and Music   Hoffman 1939
Starlight and Tulips   Bryan 1928
Starlight Bay   Donaldson 1922; Kahn 1922
Starlight Enchantment (inst.)   Coots 1946
Starlight, Help Me Find the One I Love   Young, Joe 1931
Starlight of Hope   Romberg 1922
Starlight of Your Eyes   Smith, Harry B. 1920
Starlight on the Trail   Coslow 1934
Starlight, Starbright   DePaul 1941; Raye 1941
Starlight Waltz   Adamson 1935, Date Unknown; Lane 1935
Starlit Hour, The   Parish 1940
Starry Eyes   Loesser 1939
Starry Sky   Eliscu 1932
Starry Summer Night   Blane 1945
Stars   Koehler 1932
Stars and Rosebuds   Herbert 1917
Stars and Shadows   Bergman 1958
Stars and Shadows (Beau Soir)   Bergman 1978
Stars and Stripes, The   Bergman 1958
Stars and Stripes Forever   Russell 1950
Stars Fells on Alabama   Parish 1934
Stars Give Light   Sondheim Date Unknown
Stars in My Eyes   Fields 1936

Stars of the Stage   DeSylva 1922
Stars of the Summer Night   Johnson, Howard 1939
Stars on the Highway   Loesser Date Unknown
Stars Over Broadway   Dubin 1935; Warren 1935
Stars Over the Pacific   Webster 1959
Stars Remain, The   Gorney 1940; Leigh 1955; Livingston,
    Jerry 1955
Stars, Stars Shining Bright You May See Future Stars
    Tonight   Brown, Lew 1928; DeSylva 1928; Henderson
    1928
Stars, the Sea and I, The   Drake 1957
Stars We Know   Atteridge 1920
Star-Spangled Hill of Home   Robison 1951
Start, The   Johnson, J. Rosamond 1909
Start Cheering   Oakland 1938
Start Dancing   Burke 1946; Van Heusen 1946
Start My Heart Again   Coslow 1935
Start of an Affair, The   Strouse 1993, Date Unknown
Start Stompin'   Robin 1927
Start the Band   Akst 1927; Brennan 1929; Davis 1927
Starting Out to Live Alone Again   Wrubel 1959
Starting with You (I'm Through)   Ellington 1961
Stasha   Lerner, Sammy 1931
State of My Heart, The   Heyman 1936; Spina 1936
Stately Mansion (inst.), A   Bloom 1933
States Song (I Love the Panorama of Alabama), The   Drake
    1952
Static Strut   Yellen 1926
Station Dance (inst.)   Styne 1961
Station Rush   Styne 1961
Station Wagon Polka   Coleman 1964
Statues   Brown, Nacio Herb 1936; Freed, Arthur 1936
Status   Loesser 1961
Status Quo   Leigh 1967
Stay   Razaf 1936; Rodgers 1965; Sondheim 1965
Stay As Sweet As You Are   Gordon 1934, 1935; Revel 1934
Stay As We Are   Gershwin, Ira 1946; Schwartz, Arthur 1946
Stay at Home   Freed, Arthur 1925
Stay Awake   Sherman 1964
Stay Away from My Man   Stept 1926
Stay Away from San Antone   Coots 1932; Turk 1932
Stay Away from the Railroad Tracks   Caesar 1937
(If You Don't Like Living in a Land That's Free) Stay Away
    from the U.S.A.   Mills 1947; Styne 1947
Stay Awhile   David, Hal 1951
Stay Devoted   Bacharach 1986
Stay Down Here Where You Belong   Berlin 1914
Stay Home, Little Girl, Stay Home   Brown, Lew 1923;
    Hanley 1923
Stay in Accord (With the Lord)   Robison 1959
Stay in Love   Oakland 1960
Stay on the Right Side of the Road   Bloom 1933; Koehler
    1933
Stay on the Right Side Sister   Bloom 1955
Stay Out of My Dreams   Arlen 1956; Harburg 1956; Razaf
    1957; Washington 1933
Stay Out of the Kitchen   Johnson, James P. 1948
Stay Out of the Moonlight   Alter 1934
Stay Out, Sammy   Rome 1937
Stay Til Morning   Russell 1968
Stay Up Stan, the All Right Record Man   Robison 1939
Stay Well   Weill 1949
Stay with Me   Leigh 1963; Martin 1969; Merrill 1966, 1978;
    Sondheim 1987
Stay with Me, Nora   Comden and Green 1982

Stay with the Happy People   Styne 1950

Stayin' at Home (Happy to Be By Myself)   Razaf 1940;
     Waller 1940

Staying Away   Sigman 1955

Staying Young   Merrill 1959

Stayin'-in Woman   Dietz 1944; Duke 1944

Steady   Hoffman 1958

Steady Eddie   Buck 1923

Steal Away   Dietz 1956; Schwartz, Arthur 1956

Steal Two Eggs   Mancini 1970; Mercer 1970

Stealin' Apples   Razaf 1932; Waller 1932

Stealin' My Thunder   Razaf Date Unknown

Stealing the Star of Asia (inst.)   Brown, Nacio Herb 1941

Stealing to Virginia   Donaldson 1923; Kahn 1923

Steam Pipe Melody   Donaldson 1915; Johnson, Howard
     1915

Steam Up That Choo Choo 'Till We Land in
     Jacksonville   Johnson, Howard 1917

Steamboat Blues   Donaldson 1923; Kahn 1923

Steamboat Round the Bend   Clare 1935

Steamboat Sal   Fisher 1923

Steamboat Song   Leigh 1953

Steamboat Whistle, The   Dietz 1935; Schwartz, Arthur 1935

Steamin' Home   Brown, Lew 1925; DeSylva 1925;
     Henderson 1925

Steam-Pipe Melody, The   Clarke 1915

Steely Glint in My Eye, The   Hart 1935; Rodgers 1935

Steeple-Chase   Ager 1915

Steeplechase Rag (inst.)   Johnson, James P. 1917

Steeplejack   Schwartz, Arthur 1930

Steinland   Goetz 1912

Steins   Brown, Lew 1933; Henderson 1933

Steins on the Table   Kahn 1933

Stella   Akst 1927; Davis 1923

Stella By Starlight   Washington 1944; Young, Victor 1944

Stella, the Belle o' the Town   Coots 1936; Davis 1936

Step Down Off the Minus (Climb Aboard the Plus)   Drake
     1955

Step Henrietta   DeSylva 1924

Step In   Fields 1934; McHugh 1934

Step in the Right Direction, A   Robison 1963; Sherman 1971

Step in Time   Sherman 1964

Step Into My Parlor   Oakland 1968

Step Lightly Lady   Harburg 1959

Step Montage, A   Porter 1956

Step on It   Atteridge 1923; Caesar 1926; Romberg 1923;
     Schwartz, Jean 1923

Step Right Up   Brooks 1959; Evans 1952; Livingston, Jay
     1952

Step That'll Stop the Show, A   Cahn 1963; Van Heusen
     1963

Step This Way   Berlin 1916; Goetz 1916; Whiting 1919

Step Through a Moon Gate   Blane 1962

Step to the Rear   Leigh 1965, 1967

Step to the Rear of the Car Please   Mercer 1951

Step Up and Shake   Cahn Date Unknown; Duke Date
     Unknown

Step Up and Shake My Hand   David, Mack 1939;
     Livingston, Jerry 1939

Step Up and Take a Bow   Arlen 1939; Harburg 1939

Step Up Closer   Brooks 1959

Step We Grandly   Porter 1916

Stephanie   Sigman 1956

Steppe Sisters, The   Romberg 1927

Steppin' in Society   Akst 1925

Steppin' Into Swing Society   Ellington 1938; Mills 1938

Steppin' on the Blues   Conrad 1926; Donaldson 1926;
     Harbach 1926

Steppin' Out   Conrad 1923; Johnson, Howard 1923

Steppin' Out Tonight   Romberg 1919; Schwartz, Jean 1919

Steppin' Out with My Baby   Berlin 1948; Brooks 1958

Steppin' School   Ager 1922; Yellen 1922

Stepping   Smith, Harry B. 1923; Snyder 1923

Stepping All the Way Home   Robin 1926

Stepping Into Love   Arlen 1932; Koehler 1932

Stepping Out of the Picture   Akst 1934; Brown, Lew 1934

Stepping Stones   Kern 1923

Stepping with Baby   Gershwin, George 1926; Gershwin, Ira
     1926

Steps   Arlen 1930; Hart Date Unknown; Koehler 1930;
     Rodgers Date Unknown

Steps of the Capitol, The   Lane 1945

Stepsisters' Lament   Hammerstein 1957; Rodgers 1957

Sterling Silver Moon   Berlin 1918

Sterophonic Sound   Porter 1955

Stetson   Donaldson 1928; Kahn 1928

Steve   Snyder 1923; Von Tilzer 1910

Stevedore Stomp   Ellington 1939; Mills 1939

Stevedore's Serenade   Ellington 1939

Steven Got Even   Von Tilzer 1919

Stevenson the Man Who Takes Orders from None   Caesar
     1952

Stick Around   Adams 1964; Strouse 1964

Stick to Your Arithmetic   Rainger 1939; Robin 1939

Stick to Your Knitting   Hammerstein 1923

Stick with Me, Baby   Drake 1954

Sticks and Stones   Hoffman 1939

Sticks and Stones Will Break My Bones   Razaf 1937

Stickum   David, Hal 1961

Stiff Upper Lip   Gershwin, George 1937; Gershwin, Ira 1937

Stiffen Up that Upper Lip   Cahn 1966; Van Heusen 1966

Still As the Night   Johnson, Howard 1939

Still Doing the Same Thing   Styne 1984

Still I'd Love You   Brown, Lew 1929; DeSylva 1929;
     Henderson 1929

Still It Might Be Nice   Styne 1985

Still, Still, Still   Bergman 1958

Still the Bluebird Sings   Burke 1939; Monaco 1939

Still Water   Evans 1952; Livingston, Jay 1952

Still You'd Break My Heart   Friend 1954

Stillman's Gym   Comden and Green 1955

Stingaree   Mills 1935

Stinger (inst.)   Stept 1957

Stingo-Stungo   Brown, Lew 1923; Hanley 1923

Stingy   Razaf 1946

Stingy Blues   Merrill 1946

Stingy Kid   Bryan 1909

Stockings   Johnson, J. Rosamond 1904

Stolen Dreams (Who Steals All My Dreams?)   Harbach
     1931; Kern 1931

Stolen Harmony   Lawrence 1935; Young, Joe 1935

Stolen Heaven   Freed, Ralph 1938

Stolen Holiday   Dubin 1936, 1937; Warren 1936, 1937

Stolen Hours, The   Bergman 1963

Stolen Kisses   Romberg 1916; Snyder 1921

Stolen Melody, The   Atteridge 1915

Stolen Sweets (inst.)   Von Tilzer 1917

Stompin' at the Savoy   Razaf 1936

Stompin' on the Dime   Friend 1923

Stone Age (scene) (inst.), The   Herbert 1916

Stone Bridge at Eight, The   Hanley 1926
Stone Cutter's Song   Herbert 1895; Smith, Harry B. 1895
Stone Is Rolled Away, The   Brennan 1943; Friml 1943
Stone Walls   Loesser Date Unknown
Stonewall Jackson   Fain 1958; Webster 1958
Stonewall Moskowitz March   Caesar 1926; Hart 1926; Rodgers 1926
Stop and Go   Buck 1916
Stop and Make Love   Brooks 1945
Stop Being So Beautiful   Bullock 1938; Spina 1938
Stop Close to Me   Webster 1966
Stop Criticizin'   Robison 1960
Stop Cryin'   Gordon 1932; Revel 1932
Stop! Go!   Coots 1928
Stop, I'm Beginning to Care   Kahn 1925
Stop It   Johnson, James P. 1917; Smith, Harry B. 1906
Stop, Look and Kiss   Hammerstein 1922; Mitchell 1922
Stop, Look, and Listen   Freed, Ralph 1935; Herbert 1924
Stop! Look! Listen!   Berlin 1915; Norworth 1925
Stop Making Faces at Me   Sterling 1908
Stop, Put That Stick Down (Entr'acte)   Gershwin, George 1930; Gershwin, Ira 1930
Stop, Rest a While   Gilbert 1921
Stop Rocking the Boat   Goetz 1913
Stop, Sit Down, Relax, Think   Magidson 1953
Stop! Stop! Stop! (Love Me Some More)   Berlin 1910
Stop Stutterin', Sam   Warren 1924
Stop that Boy   Berlin 1909; Snyder 1909
Stop that Clock   Duke 1934; Harburg 1934
Stop that Dancing   Lane 1945
Stop that Dog   Johnson, James P. 1932; Razaf 1932
Stop That Rag (Keep on Playing, Honey)   Berlin 1910
Stop the Flahooleys   Fain 1951; Harburg 1951
Stop the Hubbub Bub   Evans 1944; Livingston, Jay 1944
Stop the Music   Coslow 1951
Stop the World (I Wanna Get Off)   Oakland 1956
Stop Tickling Me   Romberg 1916; Smith, Robert B. 1916
Stop Waltzing Around in My Mind   Rome 1964
Stop Your Blushing, Rosie   Lewis 1910
Stop Your Camouflaging with Me   Goetz 1917; Schwartz, Jean 1917
Stop Your Gamlin'   Robison 1950
Stop Your Kiddin'   Coslow 1922; McHugh 1922; Mills 1922
Stop! You're Breakin' My Heart   Koehler 1937; Lane 1937
Stop, You're Killing Me   Sigman 1952
Stories Adam Told to Eve   Jerome 1903; Schwartz, Jean 1903
Stories Morning Glories Tell, The   Coots 1932; Kahn 1932
Stories of a Summer Night   Howard, Joseph E. 1905
Stories that Mother Told Me, The   Sterling 1898; Von Tilzer 1898
Stork Song   Hanley 1934
Stork, Stork   Smith, Robert B. 1912
Storm, The   Leigh 1954; Mercer 1959
Storm Fear   Brooks 1955
Storm of Life   Williams 1906
Stormy   Robison 1964
Stormy Love   Eliscu 1937
Stormy Sea of Love, The   Carroll 1916
Stormy Weather   Arlen 1933; Koehler 1933
Stormy Weather Pal   Egan 1923; Whiting 1923
Story Behind My Tears, The   Bacharach 1961; David, Hal 1961
Story Conference, The   Duke 1955
Story in Variety, The   Burke 1950; Van Heusen 1950

Story of a Butterfly, The   Atteridge 1923; Caesar 1923; Romberg 1923
Story of a Marionette   Harbach 1911
Story of a Starry Night, The   Hoffman 1941; Livingston, Jerry 1941
Story of an Inventory   Weill 1943
Story of Annie Laurie, The   Lewis 1949; Meyer 1949
Story of Babette   Herbert 1903; Smith, Harry B. 1903
Story of Christmas, The   Freed, Ralph 1958
Story of Every Day Life, A   Fisher 1916; Johnson, Howard 1916
Story of Fung Toy   Atteridge 1923; Caesar 1923; Romberg 1923
Story of Jazz   Bergman 1957
Story of Kitty, The   Bullock 1950
Story of Lucy and Jessie, The   Sondheim 1971
Story of My Life, The   Bacharach 1957; Comden and Green 1953, 1964; David, Hal 1957; Russell 1948, 1949; Sigman 1949; Styne 1964
Story of My Love for You, The   Johnson, Howard 1931
Story of Sinbad, The   Brooks 1958
Story of Sorrento, The   Russell 1947
Story of the Blues   Burke 1958
Story of the Lovebird   Sigman 1949
Story of the One Man Band   Cahn 1939
Story of the Very Merry Widow, The   Gordon 1944; Monaco 1944
Story of the Wedding March, The   Cohan 1901, 1907
Story You're About to Hear Is True, The   Hoffman 1956
Stouthearted Men (Liberty Song)   Hammerstein 1928; Romberg 1928
Stowaway, The   Leigh 1955; Livingston, Jerry 1954; Sigman 1950
Straddlin' the Fence   Friend 1950
Stradivarius   David, Mack 1955; Warren 1955
Straight Down the Middle   Cahn 1958; Van Heusen 1958
Straight from the Shoulder   Silver 1955
Straight from the Shoulder (Right from the Heart)   Gordon 1934; Revel 1934
Straight Road Is a Great Road After All, The   Lewis 1911
Straight to Baby   Evans 1959; Livingston, Jay 1959; Mancini 1959
Straight to the Heart   Evans 1959; Livingston, Jay 1959; Mancini 1959
Straighten Up and Fly Right   Mills 1944
Stranded Again   Coleman 1978; Comden and Green 1978
Strange and Wonderful (Fushigisa to Subarashisa de Ippai)   Rome 1969
Strange Are the Ways of Love   Fain 1973; Washington 1958; Webster 1973
Strange As It Seems   Duke 1931; Harburg 1931; Razaf 1932; Waller 1932; Wrubel 1944
Strange Blues   Mills 1935
Strange Case of Adam Standish, The   Hammerstein 1939; Kern 1939
Strange Case of Hennessy, The   Burke 1933; Spina 1933
Strange Duet (When You Help a Friend Out)   Comden and Green 1961; Styne 1961
Strange Enchantment   Loesser 1939
Strange Faces   Coots 1952
Strange Interlude   Bryan 1932
Strange Lady in Town   Washington 1955
Strange Love   Heyman 1946
Strange Melody   Russell 1955, 1956
Strange What a Song Can Do   Alter 1947; De Lange 1947

Strange What Love Will Do   Blake 1955, 1958, 1964; Sissle 1964

Stranger, The   Parish 1965

Stranger at the Waterfall   Robison 1954

Stranger Don't Go   Lawrence 1968

Stranger in a Dream (Stranger in the Night)   Caesar 1956

Stranger in Paree, A   Dubin 1938; Warren 1938

Stranger in the City   Alter 1950

Stranger in the Mirror   Dubin 1940; Fain 1940; Kahal 1950

Stranger in the Night   Gordon 1950

Stranger or Lover (Quat Tro Chitarre)   Sigman 1964

Stranger Said, The   Webster 1957

Stranger than Fiction   Parish 1939

Stranger Things Have Happened   Coslow 1947; Davis 1939

Strangers   Coots 1931; Fisher 1925; Rodgers 1967

Strangers in the Dark   Rose 1940

Strangers in the Street   Parish 1934; Wrubel 1934

Strangers May Kiss   De Lange 1932; Wrubel 1932

Strangers When We Meet   Bergman 1957

Strategy   Harburg 1961

Stra-va-na-da   Clare 1923; Friend 1923

Straw Hat   Evans 1954; Livingston, Jay 1954

Straw Hat in the Rain   Akst 1934; Brown, Lew 1934

Straw That Broke the Camel's Back, The   Bergman 1964; Fain 1964

Strawberries   Norworth 1911; Smith, Harry B. 1911

Strawberry Jam   Romberg 1927

Strawberry Lane   McHugh 1941; Mercer 1941

Strawberry Roan, A   Merrill 1952

Strawberry Tears   Spina 1951

Straws in the Wind   Baer 1946; Herbert 1946

Strays   Sherman 1995

Streak o' Lightnin'   Arlen 1959; Mercer 1959

Streak of Blues, A   Berlin 1920

Streamline the Gordon Place   Johnson, J. Rosamond 1946

Streamlined Sheik   Eliscu 1944

Street Car Conductor Song, The   Livingston, Jerry 1963

Street Cleaner Song (Nobody Litters Anymore)   Livingston, Jerry 1963

Street Cries (Strawberry Woman, Crab Man)   Gershwin, George 1935

Street in the Rain (Strada 'Nfosa)   Raye 1958

Street Light Is My Moonlight   Weill 1947

Street of Dreams   Lewis 1932; Young, Victor 1932

Street Scene   Eliscu 1933; Kahn 1933; Youmans 1933

Street Scene in Budapest (inst.)   Coots 1946

Street Scene in Dublin (inst.)   Coots 1946

Street Scene in London (inst.)   Coots 1946

Street Scene in Paris (inst.)   Coots 1946

Street Song   Loesser 1939; Styne 1946

Street Songs   Adams 1960; Strouse 1960

Street Talk (inst.)   Bacharach 1983

Street Voices   Loesser 1952

Street Was Crowded, The   Fisher 1941

Streets of Laredo   Evans 1949; Livingston, Jay 1949

Streets of New York (In Old New York), The   Herbert 1906

Streets of Paris, The   Dubin 1939; McHugh 1939

Stremlined Sheik   Gorney 1944

Strength Is My Weakness   Rodgers 1967

Strengthen the Dwelling   Sherman 1967

Strictly Business   Adams 1983; DeSylva 1925

Strictly Formal   Mills 1938

Strike   Ager 1920; Coots 1925; Lerner, Alan Jay 1951; Loewe 1951; Yellen 1920

Strike a Happy Medium   David, Hal 1950

Strike a Match   Spina 1953

Strike Me Pink (If I Don't Think I'm Falling in Love)   Brown, Lew 1933; Henderson 1933

Strike, Strike, Strike   DeSylva 1924; Gershwin, George 1924

Strike the Loud-Resounding Zither   Gershwin, George 1931; Gershwin, Ira 1931

Strike Up a Bag Pipe Tune   Edwards 1910

Strike Up the Band   Brown, Nacio Herb 1931; Fisher 1929; Freed, Arthur 1931; Gershwin, George 1927; Gershwin, Ira 1927

Strike Up the Band for U.C.L.A.   Gershwin, George 1936; Gershwin, Ira 1936

Strike Up the Band (Here Comes a Sailor)   Sterling 1900

Strike While the Iron Is Hot   Stept 1937; Washington 1937

String a Ring of Roses 'Round Your Rosie   Jerome 1912; Schwartz, Jean 1912

String Along with Texas   Rose 1927

String Bean Anne from San Antone   Coots 1932; Turk 1932

String of Broken Hearts, A   Hoffman 1953; Silver 1953

String of Girls, A   Hammerstein 1920

String of Pearls, A   De Lange 1941

String Save in a Spaghetti Factory   Spina 1976

Stringbean Boy   DePaul 1953; Raye 1953

Stringin' Along (inst.)   Young, Victor 1951

Stringin' Along on a Shoestring   Adamson 1933; Lane 1933

Strip Calypso   Evans 1957; Livingston, Jay 1957

Strip for Action   Adamson 1956; McHugh 1956

Strip Polka   Mercer 1942

Stripping Really Isn't Sexy, Is It (inst.)   Bacharach 1965

Striver's Row   Waller 1924

Strivers' Row to Sugar Hill   Loesser Date Unknown

Stroll on the Plaza Sant'Ana, A   Porter 1940

Stroller in Dreamland, A   Atteridge 1919; Carroll 1919

Strollers, The   Smith, Harry B. 1900

Strollin' Roun' the Town   Waller 1924

Strollin' thru the Park   Bergman 1961

Strolling   Porter 1912

Strolling and Patrolling (inst.)   Kern 1946

Strolling Eyes   Atteridge 1916; Hanley 1916

Strolling on the Lido   Brennan 1929

Strolling, or What Have You?   Hammerstein 1925; Harbach 1925; Kern 1925

Strolling Quite Fancy Free   Porter 1916

Strolling Thru the Park   Fain 1938

Strolling Thru the Park One Day   Motzan 1933

Strolling thru the River   Smith, Harry B. 1900

Strolling with the One I Love the Best   Romberg 1927

Strong Heart   Atteridge 1913

Strong Silent Type   Sigman 1949

Stronger Sex, The   Burke 1953; Van Heusen 1953

Stronger than Before   Bacharach 1981

Strongest Man in the World, The   Adams 1966; Strouse 1966

Struggles   Razaf Date Unknown

Strum Strum Boogie   Brooks 1959

Strummin' on the Old Banjo   David, Hal 1949

Strummin' Song   Sherman 1961

Strumming, I Just Keep Strumming Along   Woods 1923

Strumming on an Old Guitar   Hanley 1930

Strut Lady with Me   Gershwin, George 1923

Struttin' Hound   Bryan 1928; Schwartz, Jean 1928

Struttin' School   Ager 1923; Yellen 1923

Struttin' Tut from Dixieland   Schwartz, Jean 1923

(Rachael) Struttin' with Clayton (inst.)   Revel 1951

Struttin' with Some Barbecue   Raye 1950

Struttin' Yo' Stuff   Koehler 1918
Stubborn Mule   Davis 1952; Silver 1952
Stuck for an Answer   Cahn 1965; Van Heusen 1965
Student's Ball (We're Havin' a Ball)   Martin 1951
Students' Chorus   Smith, Harry B. 1908
Student's Demonstration Song   Lane 1965
Students' Glide (Turkey Wing)   Smith, Harry B. 1911; Smith, Robert B. 1911
Students' Life   Romberg 1924
Studio Stamp   Schwartz, Jean 1926
Study in Black and White, A   Atteridge 1916, 1922; Motzan 1916, 1917; Romberg 1916, 1917
Study in Legs, A   Atteridge 1925
Study in Porcelain, A   Atteridge 1924; Romberg 1924; Schwartz, Jean 1924
Stuff Like That There   Evans 1945; Lawrence 1957; Livingston, Jay 1945
Stuff that Dreams Are Made Of, The   Cahn 1952; Duke 1952
Stumble (inst.), A   Kern 1956
Stumbling Blocks (inst.)   Warren 1956
Stumbling Over Words   Dubin 1937; Warren 1937
Stupid Melody   Rose 1932
Stuttering in the Starlight   Hoffman 1939
Style   Cahn 1964; Coots 1938; Davis 1938; Martin 1959; Van Heusen 1964
Style Show Ballet (inst.)   Arlen 1944
Su L'Boul'vard   Atteridge 1924; Schwartz, Jean 1924
Suavacito (Sweet and Tender)   Gilbert 1931
Submarine   Porter 1912
Substitiary Locomotion   Sherman 1971
Subtle Slough   Ellington 1941
Subway Directions   Comden and Green 1961; Styne 1961
Subway Express, The   Kern 1907
Subway Incident (inst.)   Styne 1961
Subway (inst.)   Schwartz, Jean 1930
Subway Love   Smith, Robert B. 1915
Subways Are for Sleeping   Comden and Green 1961; Styne 1961
Success   Comden and Green 1960; Johnson, Howard 1924; Styne 1960
Success Is Work (inst.)   Herbert 1903
Successame Street   Comden and Green 1972
Such a Beautiful World   Eliscu 1962
Such a Funny Feeling   Duke 1929
Such a Good Time   Freed, Ralph 1965
Such a Happy Family   Herbert 1920; Smith, Robert B. 1920
Such a Noble Lover   Leigh 1955
Such a Sociable Sort   Cahn 1966; Van Heusen 1966
Such Good Fun   Rodgers 1979
Such Is Life, Such Is Love   Gordon 1931; Revel 1931
Such Is My Love for You   Brennan 1918
Such Stuff as Dreams Are Made Of   Fain 1940; Kahal 1940
Such Unlikely Lovers   Bacharach 1996
Suck Up   Friml 1917; Harbach 1917
Sudan   Pollack 1920
Sudden Thrill, The   Burke 1953; Van Heusen 1953
Suddenly   Duke 1934; Harburg 1934; Rose 1934
Suddenly, It Happens   Sherman 1976
Suddenly It's Spring   Burke 1944; Lawrence 1945; Van Heusen 1944
Suddenly It's You   Cahn 1979
Suddenly the Sunrise   Arlen 1966
Suddenly You   Freed, Arthur 1934
Suddenly You Were Mine   Sigman 1961

Sudsy Suds Theme Song   Carmichael 1943; Mercer 1943
Sue   Meyer 1921
Sue Me   Fisher 1936; Loesser 1950
Sue! Sue!   Comden and Green 1956; Styne 1956
Suez Dance   Porter 1946
Sugar   Ager 1927; Merrill 1972; Meyer 1931; Mitchell 1926; Styne 1972; Yellen 1927; Young, Joe 1931
Sugar Babe   Blake 1932; Sissle 1932
Sugar Baby   Atteridge 1919; Romberg 1919; Schwartz, Jean 1919
Sugar Baby Bounce, The   Evans 1979; Livingston, Jay 1979
Sugar Beat   Rainger 1931
Sugar Cane   Coots 1946
Sugar City   Ellington 1966
Sugar Cookie Mountain   Rose 1935
Sugar in the Rain   Bergman 1969
Sugar Is Sweet and So Are You   Mills 1935
Sugar Lips   DePaul 1958; Raye 1958
Sugar Me Sweet   Russell 1948
Sugar Plum   Johnston 1935; Kahn 1935
Sugar Rose   Waller 1936
Sugar Throat Burns   Ruby 1950
Sugarfoot   Dietz 1944; Duke 1944; Webster 1958
Sugaring Off   Martin 1952
(My) Sugar-Plum   DeSylva 1925
Suicide Part II   Gordon 1935; Revel 1935
Suicide Song   Rainger 1932; Robin 1932
Suitcase on the Railroad Track   Coots 1949
Suitor Scene   Bergman 1976
Suits Me Fine   Martin 1951
Suki San (Where the Cherry Blossoms Fall)   Brennan 1917; Donaldson 1917
Sullivan   Cohan 1908
Sullivan's Got a Job   Livingston, Jerry 1973
Sultan   Caesar 1920
Summer   Strouse Date Unknown
Summer '77 (inst.)   Bacharach 1979
Summer Afternoon   Rome 1952
Summer Breeze (inst.)   Schwartz, Jean 1930
Summer Breeze Song   Willson 1956
Summer Dresses   Rome 1950
Summer Girl, The   Smith, Harry B. 1910
Summer Green — Autumn Gold   Webster 1953
Summer Holiday   Drake 1954
Summer in Brooklyn   Arlen 1965
Summer in the Snow   Comden and Green 1947
Summer in Tyrol   Revel 1960
Summer in Your Eyes   Webster 1959
Summer Incident   Cahn 1947; Styne 1947
Summer Interlude   Koehler 1955
Summer Is A-Comin' In   Duke 1941
Summer Is Here   Oakland 1954
Summer Is Over and So Is My Dream of Love   Friend 1933
Summer Knows, The   Bergman 1971
Summer Love   Mancini 1957; Myrow 1967; Young, Victor 1956
Summer Magic   Sherman 1963
Summer Me, Winter Me   Bergman 1969
Summer Met September   Russell 1949
Summer Night   Dubin 1935, 1936; Warren 1935, 1936
Summer Night (Cielito Lindo)   Bergman 1961
Summer Nights   Johnson, Howard 1924
Summer Pasttimes   Harbach 1908
Summer Rain   Livingston, Jerry 1954; Webster 1954
Summer Reminds Me of You   Bryan 1908; Meyer 1908

Summer School   Brooks 1960
Summer Souvenirs   Coots 1938
Summer Sports   Atteridge 1915
Summer Starlight   De Lange 1948
Summer Storm   Burke 1955; Van Heusen 1955
Summer Vacation   Oakland 1953
Summer Was Made for Lovers (Why Let It Go Rolling
    By)   Johnson, James P. 1932; Razaf 1932
Summer Wind   Mercer 1965; Young, Victor 1934
Summertime   Buck 1921; Friml 1928; Gershwin, George
    1935; Gershwin, Ira 1921; Rose 1927; Von Tilzer 1908;
    Young, Victor 1934
(It's Always) Summertime at the Winter Garden   Atteridge
    1919; Romberg 1919
Summertime in Heidelberg   Webster 1952
Summertime in Venice   Sigman 1955
Summertime Love   Loesser 1960
Summertime Pal Have You Forgotten Me   Coots 1933;
    Johnson, Howard 1933
Summertime Promises   Cahn 1963; Van Heusen 1963
Summertime Sweethearts Shine As They Do in the
    Fall   Kahal 1927; Snyder 1927
Summertime U.S.A.   Drake 1953
Summery Time   Goetz 1915; Romberg 1915
Summery Winter Cruise   Drake 1955
Sump'n 'bout Rhythm   Ellington 1935; Mills 1935
Sun About to Rise, The   Hammerstein 1929; Kern 1929
Sun at My Window, Love at My Door   Young, Victor 1955
Sun Is At My Window Throwing Kisses at Me, The   Lewis
    1928; Meyer 1928; Young, Joe 1928
Sun Is Blue, The   Sondheim Date Unknown
Sun Is Nigh, The   Hammerstein 1920; Harbach 1920
Sun Is on the Sea, The   Gershwin, George 1926; Gershwin,
    Ira 1926
Sun Kist Rose   Johnson, James P. 1922
Sun on My Face   Merrill 1972; Styne 1972
Sun Rises, The   Eliscu 1962
Sun Shines Brighter, The   Kern 1917
Sun Shines Out of Your Eyes, The   Styne 1978
Sun Showers   Brown, Nacio Herb 1937; Freed, Arthur 1937
Sun Starts to Shine Again, The   Kern 1918
Sun that Shines on Dixieland, The   Howard, Joseph E. 1905
Sun Will Be Shinin' for You   Johnson, James P. 1942
Sun Will Shine, The   Schwartz, Arthur 1929
Sun Will Shine Again, The   Sterling 1921; Von Tilzer 1921
Sun Will Shine Tonight, The   Rose 1938
Sun Will Soon Be Setting, The   Lerner, Sammy 1941
Sun Won't Set, The   Sondheim 1973
Sunbeam   Williams 1909
Sunbeam Serenade, The   Revel 1943; Webster 1943
Sunbeams   Kahn 1920
Sunbeams (Bestowal of Gifts)   Fain 1958; Lawrence 1958
Sunbeams (Bring Dreams of You)   Brennan 1928
Sunbeams in the Moonlight   Rainger 1939; Robin 1939
Sunbeams in Your Pocket   Fain 1958; Lawrence 1958
Sunbeams, Snowflakes and Raindrops   Herbert 1908; Smith,
    Harry B. 1908
Sunbonnet Blue and a Yellow Straw Hat, A   Fain 1935;
    Kahal 1935
Sunbonnet Sue   Cobb 1908, 1923; Edwards 1908, 1923
Sundance Kid (inst.), The   Bacharach 1969
Sunday   Coots 1926; Hammerstein 1958; Rodgers 1958;
    Sondheim 1984; Styne 1926
Sunday Afternoon   Schwartz, Arthur 1930
Sunday at Sundown   Loesser 1935; Motzan 1935

Sunday Beau   Robin 1927
Sunday Dress   Razaf Date Unknown
Sunday Girl   Livingston, Jerry 1930
Sunday in Cicero Falls   Arlen 1944; Harburg 1944
Sunday in London Town   Gershwin, George 1923
Sunday in Sorrento   Lewis 1943; Meyer 1943
Sunday in the City (inst.)   Warren 1954
Sunday in the Park   Rome 1937
Sunday in the Park with George   Sondheim 1984
Sunday in the Valley   Davis 1950; Silver 1950
Sunday Jumps (inst.)   Lane 1951
Sunday, Monday or Always   Burke 1943, 1945; Van Heusen
    1943
Sunday, Monday, Tuesday   Hoffman 1953
Sunday Morning   Burke 1961; Henderson 1934; Koehler
    1934
Sunday Morning, Breakfast Time   Porter 1935
Sunday Night Supper   Blane 1945
Sunday People   Sigman 1948
Sunday Poipers   Conrad 1906
Sunday Tan   Duke 1936; Gershwin, Ira 1936
Sundown Brings Back Memories of You   Dubin 1921
Sundown Deacon   Robison 1964
Sunflower   Cahn 1945; David, Mack 1948
Sunflower and the Sun, The   Smith, Harry B. 1903
Sunflower Song   Styne 1945
Sunflower Sue   Cobb 1908; Edwards 1908; Razaf Date
    Unknown
Sunkissed Days and Moonkissed Nights   Hoffman 1943;
    Livingston, Jerry 1943
Sun-Kissed Isle   Kahn 1927
Sunkissed Land   Carroll 1918
Sun'll Be Up in the Morning, The   Fain 1940; Yellen 1940
Sunny   Hammerstein 1925; Harbach 1925; Kern 1925;
    Sigman 1951
Sunny California   Johnson, Howard 1921; Lane 1945
Sunny Day   Loewe 1942
Sunny Days   Brennan 1928; Oakland 1974
Sunny Disposish   Caesar 1928; Gershwin, Ira 1926
Sunny Hawaii   Stept 1926
Sunny May Afternoon, A   DeSylva 1920
Sunny Rag, The   Jerome 1912; Von Tilzer 1912
Sunny River   Hammerstein 1941; Romberg 1941
Sunny Riviera, The   Smith, Robert B. 1914
Sunny Riviera Bay   Gilbert 1915
Sunny Side   Johnson, James P. 1929
Sunny Side of Things, The   Webster 1938
Sunny Side Up   Brown, Lew 1929; DeSylva 1929;
    Henderson 1929
Sunny South   Buck 1922
Sunny Southern Smiles   Gilbert 1920
Sunny Sue   Donaldson 1921; Lewis 1921; Silver 1950;
    Young, Joe 1921
Sunny Summertime   Whiting 1914
Sunny Sunbeam   Hanley 1922
Sunny Tennessee   Coots 1929
Sunray   Dubin 1909
Sunrise   Hammerstein 1928; Youmans 1928
Sunrise Bells and Alabado   Bergman 1963
Sunrise Dance, The   Caesar 1930
Sunrise Letter   Sondheim 1994
Sunrise Serenade   Lawrence 1939
Sunrise (Will Bring Another Day for You), The   Friend 1927
Sun's in My Heart, The   Baer 1932; Freed, Arthur 1932
Sunset   Razaf 1949

Sunset and Moonrise Bergman 1958
Sunset Bay Johnson, Howard 1958
Sunset Boulevard Davis 1950; Evans 1950; Livingston, Jay 1950; Martin 1972; Silver 1950
Sunset Harbor Spina 1977
Sunset in Vienna Hoffman 1937; Lerner, Sammy 1937
Sunset Land Kahn 1921
Sunset on the Bayou Spina 1957
Sunset on the Moon Fisher 1937
Sunset Strip Brooks 1955
Sunshine Berlin 1928; Clarke 1915; Hammerstein 1925; Harbach 1925; Kern 1925; Monaco 1915; Motzan 1921; Robin 1948; Styne 1948; Young, Joe 1934
Sunshine Ahead Conrad 1933; Coslow 1933
Sunshine and Poinsiettas Burke 1934; Spina 1934
Sunshine and Rain Davis 1922
Sunshine and Roses Kahn 1913
Sunshine and Shadow Buck 1920
Sunshine at Midnight Heyman 1936
Sunshine Cake Burke 1950; Van Heusen 1950
Sunshine Companions Merrill 1958
Sunshine Followed By Sunshine Drake 1953
Sunshine for Sale Styne 1936
Sunshine Girl Merrill 1957
Sunshine Hurts My Eyes, The Sigman 1953
Sunshine Is Bright Smith, Harry B. 1908
Sunshine of Paradise Alley, The Johnson, Howard 1939
Sunshine of Your Song Brennan 1927
Sunshine Sis Egan 1919; Whiting 1919
Sunshine Song, The Rome 1959
Sunshine Song (inst.), The Revel 1959
Sunshine Trail, The Gershwin, George 1923; Gershwin, Ira 1923
Sunshiny California Livingston, Jerry 1973
Sunshowers Hoffman 1951
Suntan Charlie Monaco 1934
Sun-Up to Sundown Kahn 1938; Romberg 1938
Super Doodle Dandy (Mr. Limpet March) Adamson 1964; Fain 1964
Super Type o' Hypochondriac Oakland 1960
Supercalifragilisticexpialidocious Sherman 1964
Superland Coleman 1979
Superlative Love Herbert 1917
Superman March (inst.), The Strouse 1966
Supernote, The Adams 1966; Strouse 1966
Super-Shiek Atteridge 1924; Romberg 1924
Superstition Alter 1928
Superstition Song, The Fain 1954; Webster 1954
Superstitious Blues Turk 1924
Supper Chorus Smith, Harry B. 1901
Supper Club (inst.), The Carroll 1917
Supper Out of Doors Brown, A. Seymour 1909
Supper Song Kalmar 1934; Ruby 1934
Supper Time Berlin 1933
Supple Couple Waller 1943
Supplication Revel 1959
Suppose Davis 1921; Howard, Joseph E. 1919
Suppose I Came Home at Nine Brown, Lew 1927
Supposing Caesar 1923
Supposing I Make You Wait 'Till We Get Married Bryan 1912
Sur la Mer Immense Romberg 1933
Sur L'Boul'vard Romberg 1924
Sur les Quais Lerner, Alan Jay 1971
Surabaya Johnny Weill 1977

Sure An' It's Me that Knows Von Tilzer 1919
Sure An' It's the Luck of the Irish David, Mack 1943
Sure As You're Born Bergman 1966
Sure I Are, Ev'rybody Do Hoffman 1950; Merrill 1950
Sure I Could Livingston, Jerry 1957
Sure of Me Hoffman 1933
(We've Got a) Sure Thing Burke 1950; Gershwin, Ira 1944; Kern 1944; Van Heusen 1950
Surely Snyder 1930
Surfin' Santa Robison 1963
Surfside 6 David, Mack 1960; Livingston, Jerry 1960
Surprise Evans 1958; Hoffman 1933; Livingston, Jay 1958
Surprise Package Cahn 1960; Van Heusen 1960
Surprise, Surprise, I'm Giving Me to You Von Tilzer 1935
Surrealism (inst.) Myrow 1937
Surrender Donaldson 1935
Surrender to Me Sigman 1956
Surrey with the Fringe on Top, The Hammerstein 1943; Rodgers 1943
Surrounded by Dixieland Dubin 1920
Surrounded By Roses Davis 1951
Surrounded by the Girls Atteridge 1924; Romberg 1924; Schwartz, Jean 1924
Susan Egan 1925; Kern 1904; Mancini 1957; Whiting 1925
Susan Belle, The Blake 1937
Susan Slept Here Lawrence 1954
Susan's Dream Lerner, Alan Jay 1948; Weill 1948
Susie Hart 1926; Kahn 1924; Kalmar 1922; Rodgers 1926; Ruby 1922
Susie Anna Jerome 1902; Schwartz, Jean 1902
Susie (Camel Song) Kern 1926
Susie for Everybody Mercer 1974
Susie on the Sewing Machine Drake 1943
(Dear) Susie Sapple Rainger 1937; Robin 1937
Susie 'Scuse Me Caesar 1950
(I Just Want to Be Known as) Susie's Feller Brown, Lew 1926
Suspicion Revel 1942
Suspicion Song Sondheim 1968
Susquehanna Shore Parish 1921
Susquehanna Sue Cobb 1917; Edwards 1917
Susquehanna Transfer Russell 1951, 1954; Silver 1942
Su-Tan-Tan Stept 1954
Suttee Procession Porter 1946
Suzanna Davis 1922
Suzannah Akst 1935; Brown, Lew 1935
Suzanne Carroll 1916; Donaldson 1925; Heyman 1932; Hoffman 1932; Kahn 1925; Ruby 1950
Suzanne Marie (inst.) Revel 1948
Suzanne, Suzanne Smith, Harry B. 1912; Smith, Robert B. 1912
Suzette Harbach 1931; Kern 1931
Suzette and Her Pet Kern 1909
Suzi Ann Atteridge 1915; Carroll 1915; Romberg 1915
Suzi of the Islands Lawrence 1939
Suzie Wong (The Cloud Song) Cahn 1960; Van Heusen 1960
Suzy Is a Good Thing Hammerstein 1955; Rodgers 1955
Suzzetta (inst.) Warren 1977
Swag Man, The Brooks 1948
Swahili Serenade David, Mack 1967
Swallow, The Johnson, Howard 1939
Swallows, The Hart 1928; Rodgers 1928
Swami Song (Use Swami Salts) Lane 1938
Swamp Blues Sterling 1927

Swamp Volunteers March (inst.)   Fain 1977

Swan, The   Merrill 1968; Styne 1968

Swanee   Caesar 1918; Gershwin, George 1918

Swanee Bluebird   Conrad 1922; Friend 1922

Swanee Bound   Lewis 1923; Meyer 1923; Young, Joe 1923

Swanee Butterfly   Donaldson 1925; Rose 1925

Swanee Fashion Plate   Johnson, James P. 1930; Razaf 1930

Swanee Glide   Bryan 1919; Schwartz, Jean 1919

Swanee Jubilee   Razaf 1928

Swanee Lullaby   Ellington 1962; Mills 1962; Parish 1962

Swanee Melody   Alter 1927

Swanee Melody Man   Mills 1934

Swanee Moon   Blake 1952; Sissle 1952

Swanee River   Johnson, James P. 1922; Turk 1922

Swanee River Blues   Buck 1923

Swanee River Dream Man   Friend 1934

Swanee River Rhapsody   Ellington 1930; Mills 1930

Swanee River Sandman   Rose 1927

Swanee River Trail (Indian River Trail)   Caesar 1926

Swanee Rose   DeSylva 1921

Swanee Rose (Dixie Rose)   Caesar 1921; Gershwin, George 1921

Swanee Shore   Gilbert 1912; Mitchell 1919

Swanee Shuffle   Berlin 1929

Swanee Sway, The   Hanley 1922

Swanislavsky   Martin 1972

Swank, The   Conrad 1935, Date Unknown; Magidson 1935, Date Unknown

Swap Her for a Mule   Rome 1959

Swap Shop   Bullock 1940; Styne 1940

Swattin' the Fly   Dietz 1943; Duke 1943

Sway Brittania   Duke 1936

Sway Me   Hoffman 1957

Sway, Sway, Sway   Gilbert 1913

Swearing Skipper, The   Smith, Harry B. 1900

Sweater, a Sarong, and a Peek-a-boo Bang, A   Arlen 1942; Mercer 1942

Sweater Girl   Loesser 1942; Styne 1942

Swedish Pastorale   Johnson, Howard 1930

Swedish Rhapsody   Sigman 1954

Sweep No More My Lady   Blake Date Unknown; Razaf 1942

Sweeping the Clouds Away   Coslow 1930

Sweet Anastasia Brady   Jerome 1906; Schwartz, Jean 1906

Sweet and Hot   Arlen 1931; Yellen 1931

Sweet and Low   Johnson, Howard 1939

Sweet and Low Down   Gershwin, George 1925; Gershwin, Ira 1925

Sweet and Low-Down   Gordon 1944; Monaco 1944

Sweet and Pretty   Atteridge 1916; Motzan 1916

Sweet and Simple   Caesar 1934; Henderson 1934; Yellen 1934

Sweet and Slow   Dubin 1935; Warren 1935

Sweet and Tender   Razaf 1938

Sweet and Twenty   Egan 1928; Whiting 1928

Sweet Angeline   Brown, Lew 1911; Lawrence 1940

Sweet Anita   Warren 1923

Sweet Arabian Dreams   Caesar 1924; Conrad 1924; Harbach 1924

Sweet as a Bunch of Roses   Burke 1953

Sweet as a Rose   Hammerstein 1938; Harbach 1938; Kern 1938

Sweet As a Song   Gordon 1938; Revel 1938

Sweet As a Song from Heaven   Bryan 1934

Sweet as Can Be, The Bamboola   Fisher 1924

Sweet As Sugar Cane   Eliscu 1929; Rose 1929; Youmans 1929

Sweet As You Can Be   Friml 1922; Harbach 1922

Sweet Babette She Always Did the Minuet   Sterling 1916; Von Tilzer 1916

Sweet Baby   Waller 1924

Sweet Betty   Lerner, Sammy 1933

Sweet Bonita   Motzan 1920

Sweet Brotherly Love   Oakland 1974

Sweet Bye and Bye   Duke 1946; Herbert 1910

Sweet Cactus Rose   Caesar 1924; Conrad 1924; Harbach 1924

Sweet Chariot   Ellington 1932; Mills 1932

Sweet Charity   Coleman 1966, 1968; Fields 1966, 1968

Sweet Cherie   Johnson, J. Rosamond Date Unknown

Sweet Child   Whiting 1925

Sweet Clarissa (Darky Love Song)   Herbert 1899

Sweet Cookie   Ager 1916; Jerome 1916

Sweet Corner Girl   Blane 1948

Sweet Cuban Love   Coots 1920

Sweet Dreams   Ager 1928; Coots 1924; Freed, Ralph 1938; Friml 1919; Harbach 1919; Lane 1938; Whiting 1927; Yellen 1928

Sweet Dreams of Love   Ellington 1962; Mills 1962

Sweet Dreams of You   Baer 1953

Sweet Dreams, Pretty Lady   Hanley 1933

Sweet Dreams, Sweetheart   Ager 1939; Davis 1939; Koehler 1944

Sweet Elizabeth   Blake 1947

Sweet Eloise   David, Mack 1942

Sweet Emmalina   Razaf 1928

Sweet Emmy Lou   Eliscu 1929; Rose 1929; Youmans 1929

Sweet Engagement   Bryan 1958

Sweet Evangeline of Old Arcady   Fisher 1917

Sweet Evening Breeze   Donaldson 1943; Egan 1952; Webster 1952

Sweet Flossie Farmer   Dixon 1935; Wrubel 1935

Sweet Forget-Me-Not   Kahn 1928; Robison 1930; Whiting 1928

Sweet Georgianna and Me   Whiting 1929

Sweet Geraldine   Hart 1931; Rodgers 1931

Sweet Get-Together, A   Stept 1944

Sweet Gingerbread Man   Bergman 1970

Sweet Girl Graduate, The   Smith, Harry B. 1906; Smith, Robert B. 1907

Sweet Girl of My Dreams   Olcott 1908

Sweet Harp of the Days that Are Gone   Herbert 1915

Sweet Hawaiian Dreams   Parish 1925

Sweet Hawaiian Sweetheart of Mine   Mills 1929

Sweet Heartache   Stept 1936; Washington 1936

Sweet Henry, the Pride of Tennessee   Akst 1923; Davis 1923

Sweet Hoodoo   Heyman 1935

Sweet Indiana Home   Donaldson 1922

Sweet Inniscarra   Olcott 1897

Sweet Irish Sweetheart of Mine   Lawrence 1938

Sweet Is the Blush of May   Lerner, Sammy 1941

Sweet Is the Word for You   Rainger 1937; Robin 1937

Sweet Italian Love   Berlin 1910; Snyder 1910

Sweet I've Gotten on You   Robison 1945

Sweet Ivy Green   Edwards 1907

Sweet Jennie Lee   Donaldson 1930

Sweet Kisses   Brown, Lew 1919; Henderson Date Unknown

Sweet Kitty Bellairs   Edwards 1905; Smith, Robert B. 1905

Sweet Lady   Johnson, Howard 1921

Sweet Land of Liberty   Razaf 1939

Sweet Liar   Caesar 1929, 1932
Sweet Little Buttercup   Bryan 1917
Sweet Little Devil   DeSylva 1924; Gershwin, George 1924
Sweet Little Girl Next Door   Mercer 1932
Sweet Little Mary Ann   Howard, Joseph E. 1920
Sweet Little Nora Riley   Bryan 1909
Sweet Little Stranger   Gordon 1932; Hanley 1920; Revel 1932
Sweet Little Sweetheart   Brown, Lew 1940; Wrubel 1933
Sweet Little You   Parish 1922
Sweet Lorraine   Parish 1928
Sweet Love   Sigman 1966
Sweet Madness   Washington 1933; Young, Victor 1933
Sweet Magnolia Rose   Blake 1940; Razaf 1940
Sweet Mama   Clarke 1917; Donaldson 1917
Sweet Mama of Mine   Snyder 1924
Sweet Man   Evans 1961; Livingston, Jay 1961; Parish 1924; Turk 1925
Sweet Man o' Mine   Turk 1922
Sweet Marie   Johnson, Howard 1939; Rose 1927
Sweet Marie - Make a Rag-A-Time Dance with Me   Berlin 1910
Sweet Marie, Make-a-Rag-a-Time Dance Wid Me   Snyder 1910
Sweet Matilda, June, O My, Isn't It Charming   Jerome 1903
Sweet Melody Brown   Hoffman 1944; Livingston, Jerry 1944
Sweet Melody of Night   Hammerstein 1936
Sweet Memories   Revel 1947
Sweet Mistreater   Johnson, James P. 1927
Sweet Mouth   Cahn 1967
Sweet Muchacha   Ager 1932; Hoffman 1932
Sweet Music   Dietz 1931; Dubin 1934; Schwartz, Arthur 1931; Warren 1934
Sweet Nellie Brown   Caesar 1931; Motzan 1931
Sweet Nevada   Gershwin, Ira 1946; Schwartz, Arthur 1946
Sweet Nothings Always Mean Something to Me   Henderson 1926
Sweet Nothings of Love   Donaldson 1929; Leslie 1929
Sweet Nudity   Porter 1933
(It Was) Sweet of You   Clare 1934; Whiting 1934
Sweet Old Chesapeake Bay   Donaldson 1923
Sweet Old-Fashioned Girl Skoob-el-ee Doo-bee-dum, A   Merrill 1956
Sweet One   Atteridge 1921; Romberg 1921; Schwartz, Arthur 1933
Sweet Onion Time   Coslow 1924
Sweet Packard   Gershwin, George 1947; Gershwin, Ira 1947
Sweet Patootie Kitty   Styne 1941
Sweet Peaches   Donaldson 1918
Sweet Peter   Hart 1925; Rodgers 1925
Sweet Pickings   Carroll 1925; Freed, Arthur 1925
Sweet Popularity   Cohan 1903
Sweet Potato Piper, The   Burke 1940; Monaco 1940
Sweet Pussycat   Coleman 1965
Sweet Rain   Johnson, J. Rosamond Date Unknown
Sweet Revenge   Strouse 1999
Sweet Rice Cake   Merrill 1949
Sweet Romance   Donaldson 1930; Leslie 1930
Sweet Rose Marie   Sterling 1917
Sweet Savannah Sue   Razaf 1929; Waller 1929
Sweet Seventeen: That's What I Call My Baby   Donaldson 1929; Leslie 1929
Sweet Simplicity   Porter 1916
Sweet Sixteen   Bryan 1908; Buck 1919; Eliscu 1929; Rose 1929; Smith, Harry B. 1911; Youmans 1929

Sweet Sixty-Five   Hart 1937; Rodgers 1937
Sweet So-And-So   Gershwin, Ira 1928, 1930
Sweet Solitude   Robison 1930
Sweet Somebody of Mine   Koehler 1928
Sweet Someone   Gordon 1937; Revel 1937
Sweet Someone to Love, A   Sigman 1957
Sweet Southern Breeze   Kahn 1926
Sweet Southern Love   Johnson, Howard 1925
Sweet Stranger   Ager 1938; Kahal 1927; Livingston, Jerry 1938; Snyder 1927
Sweet Stuff   Von Tilzer 1926
Sweet Sue, Just You   Young, Victor 1928
Sweet Summer Sweetheart of Mine   Coots 1948
Sweet Surrender   Heyman 1935
Sweet Suzanne   Leslie 1928
Sweet Sweet Ma-Ma   Evans 1970; Livingston, Jay 1970
Sweet Sylvia   Howard, Joseph E. 1919
Sweet Talk   Blake 1947; Coleman 1964; Razaf 1941
Sweet Thing   Ahlert 1935; Baer 1935; Coots 1932; Young, Joe 1935
Sweet Things in Life, The   Lawrence 1933
Sweet Thursday   Hammerstein 1955; Livingston, Jerry 1961; Rodgers 1955; Webster 1961
Sweet Tooth   Russell 1958
Sweet Violets   Sigman 1961
Sweet Virginia Blues   Razaf 1926
Sweet Virginia Dare   Friend 1920
Sweet Virginia Lee   Adamson 1935; Donaldson 1935
Sweet William   Loewe 1938
Sweet Wind Blowin' My Way   Arlen 1957; Harburg 1957
Sweet Wireless Whispers   Herbert 1909
Sweet Woman, How I'd Love to Sweet Papa You   Dixon 1923; Henderson 1923; Rose 1923
Sweet World   Livingston, Jerry 1956
Sweet You Know Who   Razaf 1926
Sweet Yvette   Davis 1927
Sweetenheart   Hart 1930; Rodgers 1930
Sweeter 'n All   Leslie 1920
Sweeter Than Ever   Freed, Ralph 1938
Sweeter than Sugar (Is My Sweetie)   Berlin 1919
Sweeter than Sweet   Davis 1957
Sweeter than You   Kalmar 1926, 1929; Ruby 1926, 1929
Sweetest Day, The   Gilbert 1950
Sweetest Girl from Dixie Lives Next Door, The   Hanley 1917
Sweetest Girl in Monterey   Bryan 1915
Sweetest Girl in Paris, The   Howard, Joseph E. 1910
Sweetest Girl, Silly Boy, I Love You   Kern 1908
Sweetest Kid I Ever Met, The   Blane 1948; Warren 1948
Sweetest Kiss of All, The   Robin 1926
Sweetest Little Girl in Tennessee, The   Carroll 1917
Sweetest Melody   Atteridge 1920; Mills 1929; Silver 1921
Sweetest Melody of All, The   Clarke 1916; Monaco 1916
Sweetest Music this Side of Heaven, The   Friend 1934
Sweetest Punch, The   Bacharach 1996
Sweetest Sight that I Have Seen, The   Hammerstein 1939; Kern 1939
Sweetest Sounds, The   Rodgers 1962
Sweetest Thing in Life, The   DeSylva 1924; Kern 1924
Sweetest Word of All Is Sweetheart, The   Hoffman 1949
Sweetheart   Brown, Nacio Herb 1930; Davis 1921; Freed, Arthur 1930; Raye 1953; Smith, Harry B. 1923; Spina 1953
Sweetheart Darlin'   Kahn 1933
Sweetheart Days   Clare 1928
Sweetheart from the Emerald Isle   Atteridge 1910

Sweetheart Hour   Monaco 1932; Washington 1932

Sweetheart, I Love Only You   Lewis 1925; Young, Joe 1925

Sweetheart I'm Lonely   Magidson 1926

Sweetheart (I'm So Glad that I Met You)   Gershwin, George 1923

Sweetheart Lane   Caesar 1922

Sweetheart Memories   Davis 1926

Sweetheart Moon   Conrad 1934; Magidson 1934

Sweetheart, My Sweetheart   Kalmar 1911; Snyder 1911

Sweetheart o' Mine, How I Miss You   Lewis 1920; Young, Joe 1920

Sweetheart of Auld Lang Syne   Johnson, Howard 1934

Sweetheart of Baby Talk Days   Clare 1944; Lerner, Sammy 1944

Sweetheart of Long Ago   Kahn 1926

Sweetheart of Mine   Romberg 1925

Sweetheart of My Student Days   Kahn 1930

Sweetheart of Mystery   Brown, A. Seymour 1923

Sweetheart of Our Student Corps   Brennan 1929

Sweetheart of Red River Valley   Johnson, Howard 1934

Sweetheart of Sweet Sixteen   Coots 1933; Kahn 1933

Sweetheart of the A.E.F.   Hoffman 1942; Livingston, Jerry 1942

Sweetheart of the Flowers   Johnson, Howard 1935

Sweetheart of the Ivy League   Silver 1957

Sweetheart of the Moon   Egan 1931

Sweetheart of the Nation   Cahn 1980; Strouse 1980

Sweetheart of Yesterday   Conrad 1928; Johnson, Howard 1929; Sigman 1951

Sweetheart on the Rhine (Du Blonde Lindenwirtin Vom Rhein)   Young, Joe 1931

Sweetheart Rose   Davis 1925

Sweetheart Roses   Heyman 1963

Sweetheart Semicolon   Heyman 1950; Young, Victor 1950

Sweetheart Song, The   Magidson 1933; Wrubel 1933

Sweetheart Special   Atteridge 1919; Romberg 1919; Schwartz, Jean 1919

Sweetheart, Sweetheart, Pronounced Darling   Lawrence 1936

Sweetheart Ties   Howard, Joseph E. 1908

Sweetheart Time   Caesar 1926; Coslow 1937; Smith, Harry B. 1926

Sweetheart Tree, The   Mancini 1965; Mercer 1965

Sweetheart Waltz, The   Freed, Ralph 1936; Lane 1936; Parish 1943

Sweetheart, You Make Me Laugh   Hart 1929; Rodgers 1929

Sweethearts   Gershwin, George 1922; Kahn 1916

Sweetheart's a Pretty Name when It Is Y-O-U   Leslie 1909

Sweethearts Again   Magidson 1938; Wrubel 1938

Sweetheart's Cotillion, The   Spina 1944

Sweethearts Forever   Caesar 1932; Friend 1932

Sweethearts Holiday   Kahal 1929

Sweethearts (If You Ask Where Love Is Found)   Herbert 1913; Smith, Robert B. 1913

Sweethearts in Every Town   Jerome 1905; Schwartz, Jean 1905

Sweetheart's Lullaby   David, Mack 1932

Sweethearts of America (Women of the Army Corps)   Freed, Ralph 1942; Lane 1943

Sweethearts of Boyhood Days   Howard, Joseph E. 1905

Sweethearts of the Team, The   Hart 1939; Rodgers 1939

Sweethearts of the U.S.A., The   Pollack 1942

Sweetheart's Prayer, A   Motzan 1927

Sweethearts Waltzes   Herbert 1913

Sweethearts, Wives and Goodfellows   Smith, Robert B. 1912

Sweethearts's Parade, The   Johnson, Howard 1927

Sweetie!   Drake 1964; Kern 1920

Sweetie Bear   Coots 1956

Sweetie Don't Grow Sour on Me   Waller 1924

Sweetie Mine   Buck 1917

Sweetie Pie   Akst 1926; Davis 1926

Sweetie Sweet   Leslie 1912; Meyer 1912

Sweeties   Sterling 1919; Von Tilzer 1919

Sweetly and Completely   David, Mack 1965

Sweetly and Tenderly   Coots 1936; Davis 1936

Sweetness   Akst Date Unknown; Freed, Arthur 1932; Kahn 1920

Sweetness of Your Song, The   Brennan 1928

Sweets   Clare 1933; Egan 1920; Magidson 1933; Stept 1933; Whiting 1920

Sweets for Sweet   Cahn 1977

Sweets to the Sweet   Smith, Robert B. 1919

Swell   Strouse 1991

Swifty the Thrifty Squirrel   Coots 1952

Swim, Swim, Swim   Gordon 1955

Swimmin' Suit   Merrill 1958

Swimming Master, The   Smith, Harry B. 1901

Swindle, The   Webster 1967

Swing, The   Bryan 1920; Comden and Green 1953; Schwartz, Jean 1920

Swing for Sale   Cahn 1936

Swing Gate Swing   Fisher 1936

Swing High   Carmichael 1956

Swing High, Swing Low   Freed, Ralph 1937; Lane 1937

Swing in Line   Loesser 1942

Swing into Spring   Mercer 1959

Swing Is Here to Sway   Gordon 1937; Revel 1937

Swing Is in the Air   Hoffman 1937; Lerner, Sammy 1937

Swing Is the Thing, The   Bloom 1936; Mercer 1936

Swing It, Mister Chumbly   Brooks 1945

Swing It Mr. Wu   David, Mack 1937

Swing It Sister   Adamson 1934; Lane 1934

Swing Left, Sweet Chariot   Fields 1939; Henderson 1939

Swing Low, Sweet Chariot   Brooks 1959; Johnson, Howard 1939

Swing Low Sweet Rhythm   Bullock 1940; Styne 1940

Swing Low, Swing High   Fields 1936; Kern 1936

Swing Me a Lullaby   Raye 1936

Swing Me an Old Fashioned Song   Bullock 1938; Spina 1938

Swing Me in a Hammock of Dreams   Parish 1930

Swing Me with Rhythm   Mills 1935

Swing, Mister Mendelssohn   Kahn 1938

Swing on Mississippi   Waller 1934; Washington 1934

Swing Out to Victory   Waller 1944

Swing Sister   Berlin 1937

Swing Song   Friml 1917; Herbert 1911

Swing, Swing, Swing   Von Tilzer 1913

Swing Tap, The   Rainger 1936; Robin 1936

Swing That Dear Old Alma Mater   Warren Date Unknown

Swing that Swing   Porter 1935

Swing Trot   Gershwin, Ira 1949; Warren 1949

Swing Your Calico   Harburg 1940; Lane 1940

Swing Your Lady, Mrs. Hemingway   Henderson 1943; Yellen 1943

Swing Your Partner Round and Round   Mercer 1945; Warren 1945

Swing Your Projects   Comden and Green 1961; Styne 1961

Swing Your Sweetheart   Harburg 1945; Kern 1945

Swing Your Tails   Dietz 1930; Schwartz, Arthur 1930

Swing-A-Bye My Baby   Brooks 1942

Swinga-Dilla Street   Johnson, James P. 1940; Razaf 1940; Silver 1940

Swingali   Arlen 1939; Harburg 1939

Swing-a-roo   Koehler 1936; McHugh 1936

Swingin' a Dream   De Lange 1939; Van Heusen 1939

Swingin' Along   Arlen 1932; Koehler 1932

Swingin' at the Golden Gate   Razaf 1939

Swingin' at the Lido (inst.)   Johnson, James P. 1940

Swingin' Down the Lane   Kahn 1923

Swingin' Hound   Waller 1937

Swingin' in the Corn   Magidson 1938; Wrubel 1938

Swingin' on the Moon   Carmichael 1935; Young, Joe 1935

Swingin' on the Strings Like Nobody's Business   Fisher 1935

Swingin' Sam the Cowboy Man   Styne 1941

Swingin' the Jinx Away   Porter 1936

Swingin' thru the Park   Bergman 1961

Swingin' Uptown   Parish 1955

Swinging Along   Buck 1918

Swinging Along the Blue Ridge Trail   Motzan 1930

Swinging Along the Highway   Revel 1959

Swinging Along with Lindy   Kahn 1918

Swinging Heart   Friend 1948

Swinging on a Star (Would You Like to Swing on a Star?)   Burke 1944; Van Heusen 1944

Swinging Sweethearts   Leigh 1957

Swing-Time at the Savoy   Blake 1948; Sissle 1948

Swingtime in Honolulu   Ellington 1938; Mills 1938

Swingy Little Thingy   Stept 1933

Swiss Bellringer, The   Freed, Ralph 1940

Swiss Family Calypso   Sherman 1960

Swiss Family Limbo   Sherman 1960

Swiss Miss   Gershwin, George 1924; Gershwin, Ira 1924

Swiss Yodeler Waltz (inst.)   Coots 1946

Switch, The   Johnson, Howard 1960

Switch It Miss Mitchell   Razaf Date Unknown

Switzerland   Goetz 1913

Swivel   Ellington 1966

Sword Is My Sweetheart True, The   Williams 1910

Sword of My Father, The   Friml 1917

Sword, the Rose and the Cape, The   Merrill 1961

Swords and Roses (inst.)   Spina 1977

Sylvia   Blake 1975; Sissle 1975; Webster 1964

Sympathetic Eyes   Drake 1952

Sympathetic Little Star   Razaf 1951

Sympathetic Someone   Kern 1925

Sympathizin' with Me   Coslow 1933, 1934; Johnston 1933, 1934

Sympathy   De Lange 1940; Friml 1912, 1937; Hanley 1921; Harbach 1912; Kahn 1937; Leigh 1955; Van Heusen 1940

Sympatica   Oakland 1960

Sympatico   McHugh 1964

Symphony   Lawrence 1945

Symphony in Brown (inst.)   Johnson, James P. 1935

Symphony in Dress, The   Bryan 1920

Symphony in Dress (inst.), The   Schwartz, Jean 1920

Symphony in Green, A   Loesser 1935

Symphony in Riffs   Mills 1935

Symphony of Love   Lawrence 1942

Symphony of the Clocks   Stept 1955

Symphony Special   Gilbert 1954; Oakland 1954

Symphony Under the Stars   Donaldson 1937

Symptoms   Howard, Joseph E. 1906

Syncopate Your Sins Away   Magidson 1932

Syncopated Clock, The   Parish 1951

Syncopated Cocktail   Berlin 1919

Syncopated Frolic, A   Buck 1918

Syncopated Heart   Hammerstein 1920

Syncopated Lady (inst.)   Strouse 1973

Syncopated Minuet, The   Caesar 1922

Syncopated Pipes of Pan   Porter 1924

Syncopated Vamp, The   Berlin 1920

Syncopated Walk   Berlin 1914

Syncopated Wedding   Howard, Joseph E. 1919

Syncopatia Land   Atteridge 1913; Schwartz, Jean 1913

Syncopating Sadie   Buck 1925

Syncopation   Atteridge 1915; Romberg 1915

Syncopation Stenos   Blake 1921; Sissle 1921

Syncopation's Scintillating Star   Stept 1919

Synthetic Love   Mills 1935; Washington 1935

System   DeSylva 1924; Gershwin, George 1924; Hammerstein 1922; Mitchell 1922

T

Ta, Luv   Mercer 1974

Ta Ra Ra Boom Der E   Willson 1943

Ta Rah Ta Rah   Smith, Harry B. 1934

Ta, Ta, My Dainty Little Darling   Herbert 1906

Ta Ta Old Bean   Eliscu 1930

Ta Voo   Atteridge 1920; Schwartz, Jean 1920

Table, a Tavern and You, A   Gordon 1934; Revel 1934

Table D'Hote Cabaret, The   Herbert 1920; Smith, Robert B. 1920

Table for Two, A   Atteridge 1917; Hanley 1927; Lawrence 1954; Porter 1910

Table in a Corner   Coslow 1939

Table Manners   Leigh 1955

Table Under a Tree   Lawrence 1936

Tabloid Papers   Conrad 1926

Taboo   De Lange 1934; Mills 1934; Russell 1940

Tabu   Coslow 1931

Tackin' 'Em Down   DeSylva 1918

Tact   Friml 1922; Harbach 1922

Taffetas   David, Mack 1962

Taffy   DePaul 1942; Raye 1942; Von Tilzer 1908

Tag   Comden and Green 1954; Styne 1954

Tag, You're It   Loesser Date Unknown

Taggin' Along with You   Mills 1935

Tahiti   Blake 1924; Coots 1950; Freed, Arthur 1950; Sissle 1924, 1926; Warren 1950

Tahiti Honey   Styne 1940, 1942, 1943

Tahiti, My Island   David, Mack 1951; Young, Victor 1951

Tahiti Sweetie   Donaldson 1926

Tahitian Lullaby   Gilbert 1937

Tahlequah   David, Hal 1962

Tahm Boom Bah   Adamson 1943; Styne 1943

Tailgate Ramble, The   Mercer 1944

Tailor's Dummy   Smith, Robert B. 1905

'Tain't a Fit Night Out for Man or Beast   Cahn 1936

T'ain't Gold   Mills 1925

Tain't No One but You   Silver 1928

Tain't No Sin   Brown, Lew 1930; DeSylva 1930; Henderson 1930

'Tain't No Sin to Dance Around in Your Bones   Donaldson 1930; Leslie 1930

Tain't No Use   Lane 1936; Magidson 1936

Tain't So, Honey, Tain't So   Robison 1928

'Tain't What Money Itself Can Do   Robison 1960

Tainted Rose   Henderson 1923

Taisez-Vous   Herbert 1910

Tait Song   Brown, Lew 1927; DeSylva 1927; Henderson 1927

Take 10 Terrific Girls (But Only 9 Costumes)   Adams 1968; Strouse 1968

Take a Bow   Davis 1944; Livingston, Jerry 1967

Take a Broken Heart   Bacharach 1966; David, Hal 1966

Take a Car   Snyder 1905

Take a Chance (Little Girl and Learn to Dance)   Kern 1918; Smith, Harry B. 1918

Take a Chance with Me   Bryan 1921; Meyer 1910; Pollack 1921; Schwartz, Jean 1921

Take a Crank Letter   Mercer 1949

Take a Dip in the Sea   Clare 1938; Mitchell 1938; Pollack 1938

Take a Giant Step   Evans 1959; Livingston, Jay 1959

Take a Job   Comden and Green 1960; Styne 1960

Take a Lesson from the Lark   Rainger 1934; Robin 1934

Take a Letter to the King   Schwartz, Arthur 1930

Take a Little Baby Home with You   Coots 1925

Take a Little Care   Caesar 1940

Take a Little Flower from the Winter Garden   Carroll 1918

Take a Little One Step   Youmans 1924

Take a Little Stroll with Me   Coots 1925

Take a Little Tip from Father   Berlin 1912; Snyder 1912

Take a Little Walk   Coleman 1964

Take a Little Wife   Berlin 1922

Take a Longer Look   Sherman 1970

Take a Look at Her Now   Clare 1929

Take a Look at Me Now   Sterling 1911; Von Tilzer 1910, 1911

Take a Look at This, Take a Look at That, What-Ta You Think of Me Now?   Brown, Lew 1923; Hanley 1923

Take a Memo to the Moon   Fain 1954; Webster 1954

Take a Number from One to Ten   Gordon 1934; Revel 1934

Take a Step with Me   Kern 1914; Smith, Harry B. 1914

Take a Tip from a Gypsy   Akst 1938; Clare 1938

Take a Tip from the Tulip   Magidson 1938; Wrubel 1938

Take a Trip to Harlem   Blake 1930

Take a Vacation, Mr. Moon   Kalmar 1911; Snyder 1911

Take a Walk with Me   Smith, Harry B. 1925

Take Along a Little Love   Whiting 1930

Take and Take and Take   Hart 1937; Rodgers 1937

Take Apart My Broken Heart (inst.)   Revel 1961

Take Back Your Kisses (And Give Me Back My Heart)   Coots 1955

Take Back Your Mink   Loesser 1950

Take Back Your Paper Heart   Schwartz, Jean 1949

Take Break Blues   Sondheim 1968

Take Care   Kern 1908

Take Care of My Little Girl   Ruby 1951

Take Care of This House   Lerner, Alan Jay 1976

Take Care of You for Me   DePaul 1944; Raye 1944

Take Care of Yourself   Howard, Bart 1952

Take Care Senor   Smith, Robert B. 1906

Take Comfort   Blane 1952

Take Courage   Oakland 1974

Take Down Dis Letter   Blake 1924; Sissle 1924

Take 'em to the Door Blues   Coots 1925

Take 'em to the Door (That's All There Is, There Ain't No More Blues)   Davis 1925; Henderson 1925; Rose 1925

Take Everything, But Leave Me You   Romberg 1943

Take Everything But You   Brown, Lew 1929; DeSylva 1929; Henderson 1929

Take Five   David, Mack 1946

Take Her Back If You Love Her   Bryan 1915; Fisher 1915

Take Her Down to Coney and Give Her the Air   Pollack 1921; Whiting 1921

Take Her My Boy   Eliscu 1941; Gorney 1941

Take Him   Hart 1940; Rodgers 1940

Take in the Sun — Hang Out the Moon   Lewis 1926; Woods 1926; Young, Joe 1926

Take It Easy   Blake 1953; DePaul 1958; Fields 1935; McHugh 1935; Porter 1943; Raye 1958; Razaf 1953

Take It from a Lady   Mercer 1964

Take It From Me   Lawrence 1940; Smith, Robert B. 1915

Take It from Me, I'm Takin' to You   Waller 1931

Take It from One Who Knows   Heyman 1963

Take It from the Top   Coleman 1981; Leigh 1981

Take It from There   Rainger 1943; Robin 1943; Russell 1942

Take It in Your Stride   Berlin 1946

Take It Like a Soldier   Heyman 1939; Pollack 1939

Take It Off the E String (Put It on the G String)   Akst 1943; Cahn 1943

Take It on the Chin   Dubin 1930

Take It Slow, Joe   Arlen 1957; Harburg 1957

Take Love Easy   Ellington 1946

Take Love While You May   Schwartz, Jean 1935

Take Me   Atteridge 1924; Bloom 1942; David, Mack 1942; Dixon 1924; Henderson 1924; Lane Date Unknown; Romberg 1924; Rose 1924; Schwartz, Jean 1924

Take Me Along   Merrill 1959

Take Me Along with You Dearie   Goetz 1911

Take Me Away   Clare 1932

Take Me Back   Berlin 1913; Goetz 1913; Hoffman 1955

Take Me Back to Germany   Bryan 1913

Take Me Back to Manhattan   Porter 1930

Take Me Back to My Louisiana Home   Cobb 1904; Edwards 1904

Take Me Back to New York Town   Sterling 1907; Von Tilzer 1907

Take Me Back to Old Broadway   Smith, Harry B. 1908

Take Me Back to Old New Hampshire   Young, Joe 1947

Take Me Back to Samoa Some More   Schwartz, Jean 1923

Take Me Back to Sunshine Land   Baer 1925; Bryan 1925; Jerome 1909; Schwartz, Jean 1909

Take Me Back to Texas with You   Martin 1951

Take Me Back to that Rose Covered Shack   Ager 1918; Jerome 1918

Take Me Back to the Garden of Love   Goetz 1911

Take Me Back to Town   Atteridge 1913

Take Me Back to Your Arms   Henderson 1924; Rose 1924

Take Me Back to Your Heart   Meyer 1924; Rose 1924

Take Me Dear   Smith, Harry B. 1910; Smith, Robert B. 1910

Take Me Down to Lover's Row   DePaul 1957

Take Me for a Honeymoon Ride   Hammerstein 1929; Kern 1929

Take Me Home   Sigman 1951

Take Me Home for New Years   Livingston, Jerry 1963

Take Me Home in Your Heart Tonight   David, Mack 1943; Meyer 1943

Take Me Home to the Mountains   Loesser 1935

Take Me Home with You   Atteridge 1915; Herbert 1914; Romberg 1915; Smith, Robert B. 1914

Take Me in Your Arms   Brown, Nacio Herb 1921; Freed, Arthur 1921; Parish 1932

Take Me in Your Arms Again (Mother Darling)   Sterling 1927

Take Me in Your Arms and Say You Love Me   Johnson, J. Rosamond 1912

Take Me on a Honeymoon   Meyer 1909

Take Me on the Merry-Go-Round   Kern 1905
Take Me Out to the Ball Game   Norworth 1908
Take Me There   Leigh 1967
Take Me to Broadway   Cahn 1953; Robin 1952
Take Me to that Ball, Phil   Lewis 1910
Take Me to that Swanee Shore   Gilbert 1912
Take Me to that Tango Tea   Brown, A. Seymour 1909
Take Me to the Land of Jazz   Kalmar 1919; Leslie 1919
Take Me to the Masquerade   Williams 1910
Take Me to the World   Sondheim 1966
Take Me to You Ladder   Bacharach 1960
Take Me to Your Heart Again   Carmichael 1948
Take Me Up to the Roller Rink   Von Tilzer 1909
Take Me Up with You Lord   Spina 1976
Take Me Where I Can Be Happy   Merrill 1953
Take Me with You   David, Hal 1955; Freed, Ralph 1953
Take Me With You Into Loveland   Bryan 1910
Take Mine   David, Hal 1955
Take My Advice (She Likes the Blues and Barbecue)   Lewis 1976; Young, Joe 1976
Take My Baby   Howard, Bart 1984
Take My Breath Away   David, Hal 1991; Strouse 1991
Take My Hand Paree   Arlen 1962; Harburg 1962
Take My Heart   David, Mack 1956; Parish 1944; Styne 1941; Young, Victor 1957
Take My Heart and Do with It what You Please   Ahlert 1936; Young, Joe 1936
Take My Kiss to Dreamland with You   Coots 1935; Parish 1935
Take My Love   Oakland 1960
Take My Place   Leigh 1973
Take My Song   Harburg 1932
Take My Word   Mills 1934
Take Off a Little Bit   Berlin 1915
Take Off the Coat   Rome 1948, 1950
Take Over   Robison 1959
Take Over Chicago   Lewis 1974; Young, Joe 1974
Take Teena Too   Sigman 1950
Take the Ache from My Heart   Johnson, Howard 1935
Take the Air   Buck 1927
Take the High Ground   Washington 1953
Take the Moment   Rodgers 1965; Sondheim 1965
Take the Money   Duke 1955
Take the Moonlight Express, Find Two New Lips to Press, You Don't Belong in My Dreams   Young, Joe 1932
Take the Night Boat to Albany   Atteridge 1918; Romberg 1918
Take the Note the Bluebird Wrote   David, Hal 1953
Take the Time to Fall in Love   Comden and Green 1964; Styne 1964
Take the Word of a Gentleman   Burke 1953; Van Heusen 1953
Take the World Off Your Shoulders   Brown, Lew 1937, 1939; Fain 1937, 1939
Take Things Easy   Herbert 1907; Smith, Harry B. 1907
Take This Little Rose   Mills 1935
Take This Ring   Heyman 1935
Take This Rose   Donaldson 1925; Kahn 1925
Take Us to the Forest   Strouse 1982
Take Your Brother's Hand   Robison 1946
Take Your Girl to the Ball Game   Cohan 1908; Jerome 1908; Schwartz, Jean 1908
Take Your Girl to the Boardwalk   Jerome 1923; Schwartz, Jean 1923

Take Your Girlie to the Movies If You Can't Make Love at Home   Ahlert Date Unknown; Kalmar 1919; Leslie 1919; Turk Date Unknown
Take Your Time   Burke 1933; Spina 1933; Young, Joe 1936
Take Your Time (inst.)   Oakland 1958
Take Your To-Morrow, and Give Me To-Day   Razaf 1928
Takes Money   Lewis 1976; Young, Joe 1976
Takes Time   Davis 1981
Takes Two to Make a Bargain (What's the Answer — What's the Verdict — How's About It Baby)   Gordon 1935; Revel 1935
Takes Two to Tango   Hoffman 1952
Takes You   Davis 1929
Takin' a Slow Burn   Washington 1953
Takin' Miss Mary to the Ball   Brown, Nacio Herb 1949; Heyman 1947
Takin' Time Out for Dreamin'   Woods 1960
Taking a Chance on Love   Duke 1940
Taking a Wife   Romberg 1925
Taking Care of You   Akst 1935; Brown, Lew 1935
Taking It Easy   Fisher 1930
Taking My Lessons in Rhythm   Johnson, James P. 1932
Taking My Mind Off You   Monaco 1942
Taking No Chances   Lerner, Alan Jay 1948; Weill 1948
Taking No Chances on You   Gershwin, Ira 1949; Warren 1949
Tal Hood Theme   Oakland 1954
Tale Ain't a Tale, A   Blane 1969
Tale of a Cassowary   Cobb 1904; Edwards 1904
Tale of a Shirt, The   Berlin 1925
Tale of a Song Box Shop   Herbert 1905
Tale of an Oyster, The   Porter 1929
Tale of Manhattan, A   Webster 1942
Tale of Nevada   Brooks 1948
Tale of the Jealous Cat   Atteridge 1913
Tale of the Samovar (inst.)   Bloom 1937
Tale of the Wedding Bell, The   Smith, Harry B. 1904; Smith, Robert B. 1904
Tale of Two Cities, A   Lewis 1941
Tale that the Sweet Roses Told, A   Meyer 1911
Tale the Church Bell Told, The   Lewis 1918; Young, Joe 1918
Tale the Church Bells Tolled, The   Williams 1907
Talent   Leigh 1985
Talent Is what the Public Wants   Brown, Lew 1926; DeSylva 1926; Henderson 1926
Tales from the Vienna Woods   Hammerstein 1938; Johnson, Howard 1941
Tales of Hoffman, The   Caesar 1926
Taliami Moon   David, Mack 1945
Talisman (inst.)   Youmans 1927
Talk about a Busy Little Housewife   Cohan 1927
Talk about Girls   Caesar 1927
Talk about This — Talk about That   Herbert 1913; Smith, Robert B. 1913
Talk About Yo' Luck   Herbert 1897; Smith, Harry B. 1897
Talk Fast My Heart Talk Fast   DePaul 1950; Raye 1950
Talk It Out   Robison 1959
Talk of the Town, The   Kahn 1929
Talk Talk Talk   Oakland 1954; Smith, Harry B. 1915
Talk to Me   Leigh 1953
Talk to Me, Baby   Mercer 1964
Talk to Me 'Bout the Hard Times   Lawrence 1976
Talk to Me Tomorrow   Robin 1948, 1952, 1955; Styne 1948, 1952, 1955
Talk with My Heel and Your Toes   Caesar 1930

Talkative Toes   Dietz 1930; Duke 1930

Talkin' a Blue Streak   Russell 1965

Talkin' Glory   Arlen 1946; Mercer 1946

Talkin' to Myself   Brown, Lew 1928; Conrad 1934; Magidson 1934

Talkin' to the River   David, Hal 1950

Talkin' with Your Feet   Warren 1956

Talking Chorus, The   Drake 1953

Talking in My Sleep   Mercer 1933

Talking Is a Woman   Russell 1946; Sigman 1946

Talking Piano   Oakland 1960

Talking Tango (inst.)   Warren 1957

Talking Through My Heart   Rainger 1936; Robin 1936

Talking to My Shadow on the Wall   Coots 1931; Davis 1931

Talking to Myself About You   Friend 1945

Talking to You   Martin 1964

Talking to Your Picture on the Wall   Coots 1953

Talking to Yourself   Comden and Green 1967; Styne 1967

Talking Tree, The   Drake 1950

Tall Buildings   Johnson, Howard 1934

Tall Dames and Low Comedy   Adams 1993

Tall, Dark and Handsome   Livingston, Jerry 1960

Tall, Dark, Lonesome Gentleman, A   Coslow 1937

Tall Grows the Timber   Loesser 1942

Tall Hope   Coleman 1960; Leigh 1960

Tall in the Saddle   Adamson 1950; McHugh 1950

Tall Paul   Sherman 1958

Tall Pines of Oregon   Carroll 1950

Tall Slender Weaver   Brooks 1950

Tall the Sky   Styne 1961

Tall Timber   Razaf 1933; Waller 1933

Tallahassee   Coots 1921; DeSylva 1921; Dietz 1943; Duke 1943; Loesser 1947; Mills 1935

Tallulah — Tallulah   Freed, Ralph 1964

Tamara Tango   Dubin 1924

Tambourine   Arlen 1959; Mercer 1959; Sigman 1947

Tambourine Jamboree   Oakland 1936

Tambourine Tune   Hanley 1929

Tambourine Waltz, The   Carmichael 1955; Webster 1955

Tame Me   Adams 1950, 1954; Strouse 1950, 1954

Tammany   Edwards 1905

Tammany Ball, The   Jerome 1905; Schwartz, Jean 1905

Tammy   Evans 1957; Livingston, Jay 1957

Tampa   Dietz 1927; Gorney 1927

Tampa Bay   Bryan 1919; Schwartz, Jean 1919

Tan Manhattan   Blake 1940; Razaf 1940

Tan Town Divorce   Blake 1941; Razaf 1941

Tan Town Rhythm   Razaf 1929

Tandy   Adamson 1964

Tangerine   Mercer 1942

Tangier   Spina 1948

Tangiers   Leigh 1967

Tangissimo   Arlen 1959; Mercer 1959

Tanglefeet   Brown, Lew 1919, 1922

Tango   Duke 1941; Hammerstein 1928; Leigh 1963; Romberg 1928

Tango — Ballad   Weill 1954

Tango Ballad   Weill 1933

Tango Brazilian Dreams   Buck 1914

Tango Contest, The   Bergman 1978

Tango d'Amor, The   Mills 1966

Tango D'Amour   Hammerstein 1931; Romberg 1931

Tango Diablo   Rome 1964

Tango Dip   Atteridge 1914; Carroll 1914

Tango Dreams (inst.)   Johnson, J. Rosamond 1914

Tango Espagnol   Buck 1927

Tango Il Bacio (The Kiss Tango)   Lewis 1913; Meyer 1913

Tango in the Rain   Parish 1957

Tango (inst.)   Gershwin, George 1914; Mercer 1955; Styne 1947; Youmans 1954

Tango Melody   Berlin 1925

Tango of Love   David, Mack 1951

Tango Town   Bryan 1913

Tango, What Have You Done to Me   Kalmar 1914

Tangoland Tap   Schwartz, Jean 1912

Tangolango Tap   Clarke 1912

Tangorilla   Buck 1914

Tanned Legs   Clare 1929

Tantalizing Ida   Norworth 1911; Smith, Harry B. 1911

Tanz Mit Mir (Blue Bird Girls)   Merrill 1961

Tap 'Appy Feet   Sherman 1995

(Origin of the) Tap Dance   Brown, Lew 1928; DeSylva 1928; Henderson 1928

Tap Happy   Rainger 1935; Robin 1935

Tap It Out   Freed, Ralph 1941; Lane 1941

Tap on the Shoulder and a Guilty Conscience, A   Sigman 1952

Tap Tap, The   Rose 1927

Tap the Toe   DeSylva 1925; Hanley 1925

Tap Your Feet   Rainger 1936; Robin 1936

Tapatina, The   Hoffman 1950

Tapeteers (inst.), The   Coleman 1964

(Tap-Tap-) Tapioca, The   Cahn 1967; Van Heusen 1967

Tapioca Polka   Willson 1949

Tappin' the Barrel   Washington 1933; Young, Joe 1933; Young, Victor 1933

Tappin' the Toe   Coots 1927; Dubin 1927

Taps   Donaldson 1928; Johnson, Howard 1920; Kahn 1928

Taps Is Tops   Razaf 1937

Taps Miller   Russell 1945

Tara   Rome 1973

Tarentella   Friml 1934

Target for Tonight   Oakland 1968

Tarnished Virtue   David, Mack 1965; Livingston, Jerry 1965

Tartar   Gershwin, George 1925; Hammerstein 1922, 1925; Harbach 1925

Tartar Song, The   Hart 1928; Rodgers 1928

Tarts and Flowers   Heyman 1934

Tarzan   Fisher 1938

Tarzan of Harlem   Mills 1940

Tasty Freeze   Merrill 1971; Styne 1971

Ta-Ta   Clare 1921; Fisher 1921

Ta-Ta, Little Girl   Kern 1911

Tattered Tom   Blane 1968; Martin 1968

Tattle Tale   Coots 1945; Oakland 1952

Tattle Tale Heart   Bullock 1952

Tattle Tales   Johnson, Howard 1920

Tattletale   Lawrence 1941

Tattle-Tale Duck   Merrill 1953

Tattooed Man, The   Herbert 1897; Smith, Harry B. 1897

Taurus and Virgo   Spina 1959

Tavern Song (Red Wine)   Hammerstein 1928; Romberg 1928

Taxi Taxi   Howard, Joseph E. 1909

T.C. Roundup Time   Evans 1950; Livingston, Jay 1950

Tchaikowsky   Fain 1940

Te Deum   Rodgers 1976

Te Deum Laudamus!   Friml 1925

Te Guiero   Sigman 1959

Te Traigo Flores   Coslow 1932; Rainger 1932

Tea   Sondheim Date Unknown

Tea Cup (inst.)   Rainger 1934
Tea for Two   Caesar 1925; Youmans 1925
Tea Leaves   Egan 1921; Whiting 1921
Tea on the Terrace   Coslow 1936
Tea Party, The   Smith, Harry B. 1918
Tea Song, The   Weill 1936
Tea Time   Parish 1938
Tea Time in Timbuctoo   Comden and Green 1964; Styne 1964
Tea Time Tango Tune   Gilbert 1914
Tea Time Tap   Kalmar 1927; Ruby 1927
Teach Me Dear Lord   Oakland 1974
Teach Me How to Kiss   Mitchell 1921; Pollack 1921
Teach Me How to Love   Berlin 1915
Teach Me the Dance of Love   Sigman 1958
Teach Me to Forget   Herbert 1911; Smith, Harry B. 1911
Teach Me to Pray   Webster 1965
Teach Me Tonight   Cahn 1954; DePaul 1954
Teach Them What to Say   Herbert 1906
Teacher, The   Fain 1976; Webster 1976
Teacher, Teacher   Kern 1919
Teakettle's Song, The   Young, Victor 1944
Team Work   Cahn 1962; Van Heusen 1962
Teapot Dome Blues   Mills 1924
Tear, a Kiss, a Smile, A   Motzan 1916
Tear the Town Apart (inst.)   Styne 1972
Teardrop Avenue   Leigh 1954
Teardrops from the Sky   Gorney 1965
Teardrops in the Rain   Coots 1954
Tears   Sigman 1965; Spina 1952
Tears at the Birthday Party   Bacharach 1996
Tears Come Easy, The   David, Hal 1955
Tears from My Inkwell   Dixon 1939; Warren 1939
Tears, I Shed a Million Tears   Blake 1947
Tears in Her Letter Where the Perfume Used to Be   Fain 1976
Tears in My Eyes   Burke 1958; Van Heusen 1958
Tears in Tennessee   Robison 1941
Tears in Your Eyes   Silver 1952
Tears of Joy   Loesser 1965; Webster 1967
Tears of Love   Hammerstein 1920; Harbach 1920
Tease Me Some More   Fain 1918
Teasin' Tessie Brown   Razaf 1937
Teasing the Blues   Lewis 1977; Young, Joe 1977
Technique   Martin 1962; Mercer 1957; Merrill 1956; Rome 1957
Teddy   Blake 1927; Snyder 1919
Teddy Bird, The   Edwards 1908
Teddy Girl   Jerome 1907; Schwartz, Jean 1907
Tee Hee Hee, You Can't Scare Me   David, Mack 1950; Hoffman 1950; Livingston, Jerry 1950
Tee Ta Tee   Hart 1919
Tee Total   Egan 1931
Tee-ka Tee-ka Tah   David, Hal 1950
Teen Age, The   Henderson 1944
Teen-Age Favorite   Drake 1957
Teen-age Rag   Razaf 1954
Teen-Age Special, The   Drake 1957
Teenie Weenie Bikini   Hoffman 1959
Teenie-Eenie-Weenie   Harbach 1914
Tee-Oodle-Um-Bum-Bo   DeSylva 1919; Gershwin, George 1919
Teepee (I Will Knit of Suit o' Dreams)   Kern 1918
Teeter Totter Love   Hoffman 1956
Tee-Um-Tee-Um Tee-I Tahiti   Johnson, Howard 1938

Tegucigalpa   David, Mack 1953
Tel Aviv   Evans 1957; Livingston, Jay 1957
Telegram, The   Freed, Ralph 1962
Telephone Girl, The   Atteridge 1917; Motzan 1917; Romberg 1917
Telephone Girls   DeSylva 1919; Kern 1919
Telephone Hour, The   Adams 1960; Strouse 1960
Telephone Me, Baby   Cohan 1899
Telephone Passage   Gershwin, Ira 1945; Weill 1945
Telephone Song   Brooks 1959; Sigman 1951; Smith, Robert B. 1912
Telephone Switchboard Scene   Fain 1951; Harburg 1951
Telephone Your Mother   Parish 1934
Telephone Your Riffky Issey   Edwards 1910; Smith, Harry B. 1910
Television U.S.A.   Cahn 1959; Van Heusen 1959
Tell All the Folks in Kentucky (I'm Comin' Home)   Berlin 1923
Tell 'Em Nothing   Herbert 1920
Tell Her in the Golden Summer   Howard, Joseph E. 1909
Tell Her in the Moonlight   Davis 1928; Silver 1928
Tell Her in the Springtime   Berlin 1924
Tell Him Anything (But Not That I Love Him)   Sherman 1976
Tell It All   Herbert 1904
Tell It All Over Again   Herbert 1914
Tell It on Your Piano   Bryan 1958; Schwartz, Jean Date Unknown
Tell It to Me Dad   Coleman 1979
Tell It to Sweeney   Von Tilzer 1910
Tell It to the Marines (A Bunch of Nuts)   Hart 1928; Rodgers 1928
Tell Me   Bryan 1919, 1935; Fields 1934; McHugh 1934; Meyer 1935; Oakland 1950; Schwartz, Jean 1919; Smith, Harry B. 1918
Tell Me a Bedtime Story   Berlin 1923
Tell Me Again   Schwartz, Arthur 1922; Turk 1925
Tell Me Again (inst.)   Warren 1935
Tell Me Again, Sweetheart   Smith, Harry B. 1902
Tell Me All Your Troubles, Cutie   Kern 1917
Tell Me, Am I Shooting at the Moon   Conrad 1924
Tell Me an Old Fashioned Story   Caesar 1934; Friend 1934
Tell Me Bright Eyes   Motzan 1925
Tell Me, Cigarette (Cigarette Song)   Romberg 1927; Smith, Harry B. 1927
Tell Me Crystal Ball   Friml 1918
Tell Me Daisy   Romberg 1921; Smith, Harry B. 1920
Tell Me, Dear Jane   Rodgers 1976
Tell Me, Dreamy Eyes   Kahn 1924
Tell Me Dusky Maiden   Johnson, J. Rosamond 1901
Tell Me, Gypsy   Cahn 1979
Tell Me How I Can Forget   Brennan 1925
Tell Me I Know How to Love   Hart 1933; Rodgers 1933
Tell Me I'm Wrong   Bryan 1934
Tell Me in the Gloaming   Caesar 1923; Gershwin, Ira 1923
Tell Me in Your Own Sweet Way   Arlen 1949
Tell Me It's the Truth   Ellington 1966
Tell Me Little Dream Girl   Coots 1936; Davis 1936
Tell Me, Little Gypsy   Berlin 1920
Tell Me More   Coslow 1955; DeSylva 1925; Gershwin, George 1925; Gershwin, Ira 1925; Lawrence 1956
Tell Me More, Tell Me More   Spina 1957
Tell Me No Tall, Tall Tale   Loesser Date Unknown
Tell Me Not that You Are Forgetting   Smith, Harry B. 1925
Tell Me Now   Russell 1966

Tell Me Once Again   Smith, Harry B. 1908
Tell Me Oriole   Ahlert 1933; Leslie 1933
Tell Me Pray   Herbert 1899
Tell Me Radio   Mitchell 1924; Silver 1924
Tell Me Some More   Sterling 1915; Von Tilzer 1915
Tell Me, Tain't True   Sigman 1953
Tell Me, Tell Me   Lerner, Alan Jay 1971; Merrill 1954
Tell Me, Tell Me, Dream Face   Ellington 1946
Tell Me, Tell Me Evening Star   Arlen 1944; Harburg 1944
Tell Me that Story Again   Monaco 1938
Tell Me that You Care   Johnson, Howard 1928
Tell Me That You Care (inst.)   Warren 1935
Tell Me that You Love Me   Brown, Nacio Herb 1926; Freed,
   Arthur 1926
Tell Me There's Hope for Me   Johnson, Howard 1929
Tell Me To-Night   Clare 1925
Tell Me Truly   Johnson, Howard 1924
Tell Me what Are You Fishing For   Monaco 1913
Tell Me, What Does He See in Me?   Cahn 1980; Strouse
   1980
Tell Me, What Has Happened?   Gershwin, George 1929;
   Gershwin, Ira 1929
Tell Me when I Shall Find Him   Smith, Harry B. 1900
Tell Me Where Mister Moon Spends Every
   Afternoon   Johnson, Howard 1917; Meyer 1917
Tell Me, Who's the Girl?   Sherman 1960
Tell Me Why   Comden and Green 1947; Parish 1945; Smith,
   Harry B. 1934
Tell Me Why You and I Should Be Strangers After We Used
   to Be Such Good Friends?   Fisher 1922
Tell Me Why You Smile, Mona Lisa   Egan 1932
Tell Me with a Kiss You're Mine   Adamson 1932; Coots
   1932
Tell Me with a Love Song   Arlen 1931; Koehler 1931
Tell Me with a Melody   Berlin 1923
Tell Me with Smiles   Friend 1923
Tell Me with Tulips that You'll Forget Me Not   Coots 1932
Tell Me with Your Eyes   Friml 1947; Heyman 1947; Yellen
   Date Unknown
Tell Me with Your Kisses   David, Mack 1936; Friend 1938;
   Meyer 1936
Tell Me You Are Happy   Brennan 1929
Tell Me You Love Me   Coots 1952; Pollack 1928
Tell Me Your Daydreams   Dubin 1921
Tell Me Your Troubles   Dixon 1936; Henderson 1936
Tell Me You're Sorry   Davis 1928
Tell My Love   Evans 1957; Livingston, Jay 1955; Young,
   Victor 1957
Tell that to the Marines   Atteridge 1918; Edwards 1918;
   Lewis 1918; Schwartz, Jean 1918; Young, Joe 1918
Tell the Doc   Gershwin, George 1927; Gershwin, Ira 1927
Tell the Folks in Dixie I'll Be Back There Some Day   Kahn
   1918
Tell the Town, Hello, To-Night   Atteridge 1915; Romberg
   1915
Tell the Truth   Ager 1936; Henderson 1935; Yellen 1935
Tell the Truth and Shame the Devil   Bacharach 1956; David,
   Hal 1956
Tell the World   Bryan 1958
Tell the World I'm Through   Kalmar 1927; Ruby 1927
Tell Tony and Rosabella Goodbye for Me   Loesser 1956
Tell Us a Story   Bergman 1960
Tell Us More   Gordon 1944; Monaco 1944
Tell Us Where the Good Times Are   Merrill 1953
Tell Us Which One Do You Love   Dubin 1930

Tell Ya What I'm Gonna Do   Blane 1946
Tell You What I'm Gonna Do   Stept 1948
Tell Your Friends   Adams 1970; Strouse 1970
Tell Your Troubles All Goodbye   Dubin 1927; Leslie 1927
Tellin' It to the Daisies (But It Never Gets Back to
   You)   Young, Joe 1930
Tellin' My Troubles to a Mule   Webster 1938; Young, Victor
   1938
Telling Eyes   Pollack 1925
Telling Fortunes (Your Fortune)   Smith, Harry B. 1923
Telling It to the Daisies (But It Never Gets Back to
   You)   Warren 1930
Telling Lies   Berlin 1910
Telltale Eyes   Hart Date Unknown; Rodgers Date Unknown
Temperament   Smith, Harry B. 1912; Smith, Robert B. 1912
Temperance Blues   Brooks 1952
Tempest   Loesser 1937
Temple Houston   Washington 1965
Temple of an Understanding Heart   Evans 1954; Livingston,
   Jay 1954
Temple of the Tall Trees, The   Russell 1967
Temples   Arlen 1966
Temples of Eternity, The   Williams 1905
Tempo Di Gavotte   Atteridge 1913
Tempo Fugit   Gordon 1956; Myrow 1956
Tempo of the Times, The   Coleman 1960; Leigh 1960
Temporarily   DePaul 1956; Mercer 1956
Temporarily Blue   Arlen 1932; Fain 1931; Kahal 1931;
   Koehler 1932
Temporary Arrangement, A   Styne 1964
Temporary Jones   Russell 1974
Temporary Widow, The   Atteridge 1913
Temporary Wives   Caesar 1920
Tempt Me Not   Hart 1939; Rodgers 1939
Temptation   Brown, Nacio Herb 1933; Freed, Arthur 1933;
   Hammerstein 1920; Harbach 1920; Smith, Harry B. 1908
Temptation Waltz   Gilbert 1937
Tempting   Monaco 1922
Tempus Do Fugit   DePaul 1943; Raye 1943
Ten Best Undressed Women in the World, The   Berlin 1963
Ten Cents a Dance   Hart 1930; Rodgers 1930
Ten Commandments   Leslie 1948; Livingston, Jerry 1960
Ten Commandments of Love, The   Cahn 1957; DeSylva
   1919; Fisher 1924; Gershwin, George 1918, 1919
Ten Days of Romance on a Ten-Day Cruise   Wrubel 1934
Ten Days with Baby   Gordon 1944; Monaco 1944
Ten Easy Lessons   Lane 1938; Loesser 1938
Ten Feet Off the Ground   Sherman 1968
Ten Fingers of Syncopation   Buck 1921
Ten Girls Ago   Fain 1962
Ten Little Bottles   Monaco 1920
Ten Little Bridesmaids   Norworth 1938
Ten Little Men with Feathers   Stept 1943
Ten Little Miles   Lawrence 1937
Ten Little Miles from Town   Kahn 1928; Stept 1935
Ten Little Motorists   Caesar 1943
Ten Minutes Ago   Hammerstein 1957; Rodgers 1957
Ten O'Clock Friday Night   Oakland 1972
Ten Percent Off   Fain 1947; Freed, Ralph 1947
Ten Pins in the Sky   Ager 1938
Ten Strokes Under Par   Leigh 1971
Ten Sweet Mamas   Ager 1930; Yellen 1930
Ten Thousand Bedrooms   Cahn 1957
10,400 and 32 Sheep   Cahn 1950; Styne 1950
10,000 Years Ago   Bacharach 1960

Ten Thousand Years from Now   Brennan 1923
Ten Years Old   Sondheim 1960, Date Unknown
Tender and Loving Care   Mercer 1966
Tender and True   Adamson 1957, 1958; Warren 1958
Tender Are the Ties   Sherman 1959
Tender Child   Young, Joe 1932
Tender Is the Night   Adamson 1935; Donaldson 1935; Fain 1961; Webster 1961
Tender Shepherd   Leigh 1954
Tender Spot, A   Drake 1964
Tenderfoot, The   Sherman 1965
Tenderfoot Stomp   Johnston 1927
Tenderly   David, Hal 1946; Lawrence 1947
Tenderly Special   Oakland 1953; Raye 1953
Tenderly Think of Me   Whiting 1926
Tenement Lullaby, The   Strouse 1989
Tenement Rose   Mitchell 1922
Tennessee   Williams 1904
Tennessee Babe   Webster 1960
Tennessee Dan   Hart 1931; Rodgers 1931
Tennessee Fish Fry   Hammerstein 1940; Schwartz, Arthur 1940
Tennessee Rose   Spina 1967
Tennessee Sandman   David, Mack 1979
Tennessee, That's the Place for Me   Jerome 1905; Schwartz, Jean 1904
Tennis   Goetz 1912
Tennis Champs (Helen! Susanne! and Bill!)   Hart 1926; Rodgers 1926
Tennis Terpsichorean   Atteridge 1921; Pollack 1921; Schwartz, Jean 1921
Tennis Tournament   Atteridge 1913; Schwartz, Jean 1913
Tentacion de Amor   Adamson 1940
Tenth Interval Rag (inst.)   Ruby 1924
Tentin' Down in Tennessee   Woods 1926
Tequila   Porter 1944; Styne 1940
Terence   Olcott 1904
Teresa   David, Mack 1950; Livingston, Jerry 1950
Terminus   Parish 1965
Terpsichore and Troubadour   Hart 1925; Rodgers 1925
Terrible Toreador, The   Edwards 1929
Terribly Attractive   Fields 1939; Schwartz, Arthur 1939
Terrific   Bryan 1936; Schwartz, Jean 1936
Terrific Band and a Real Nice Crowd, A   Bergman 1978
Terrific (Just a Bum)   Cahn 1937
Terzetto   Hammerstein 1932; Kern 1932
Terzetto Buffo   Harbach 1910
Tess   Turk 1921
Tess Mambo   Duke 1959
Tess's Torch Song   Arlen 1944; Koehler 1944
Test of Time, The   Cahn 1956; David, Mack 1961; Van Heusen 1956
Testament   Weill 1933
Tete A Tete   Warren 1993
Tete a Tete at Tea Time   DePaul 1943; Raye 1943
Tete-a-Tete (Kraemer, Richard O.)   Warren 1970
Tete-a-Tete with You, A   Romberg 1916; Smith, Robert B. 1916
Tetrazzini   Smith, Harry B. 1909
Texaco Opening   Cahn 1950; Styne 1950
Texas   Rose 1927
Texas Across the River   Cahn 1966; Van Heusen 1966
Texas Blues   Strouse Date Unknown
Texas Born   David, Hal 1949
Texas Boys, The   Raye 1954

Texas, Brooklyn and Heaven   Drake 1948
Texas, Brooklyn and Love   Duke 1946
Texas Dan   Jerome 1905; Schwartz, Jean 1905
Texas Is Tops with Me   Blane 1945
Texas Kindness   Robison 1956
Texas Li'l Darlin'   Mercer 1949
Texas Moon   Sigman 1946
Texas Oil Man's Ball   Gilbert 1956; Oakland 1956
Texas Panhandle   Robison 1944
Texas Pranca   Gilbert 1911
Texas Ranger Song   Coslow 1936
Texas Romp and Square Dance   Mercer 1955
Texas Tommy Jubilee, The   Clarke 1913; Leslie 1913
Texas Tommy's Dance   Leslie 1911
Texas Tornado, The   Mitchell 1936; Pollack 1936
Texas Trail   Styne 1941
Texas Waltz   Mercer 1955
Texas Will Make You a Man   Porter 1943
Texatina   Fain 1937; Kahal 1937
T.G.T.T.   Ellington 1968
10th Anniversary of Israel   Oakland 1958
10th Avenue Waltz   Davis 1946
Thaddeus Stevens   Razaf 1944
Thank Dixie for Me   Burke 1944; Van Heusen 1944
Thank God for People Like Me   Lane 1970; Lerner, Alan Jay 1970
Thank God I'm Old   Coleman 1980
Thank God You're Here, Mother Mine   Ager Date Unknown; Johnson, Howard Date Unknown; Yellen Date Unknown
Thank Heaven for Little Girls   Lerner, Alan Jay 1958; Loewe 1958
Thank Heaven for You   Rainger 1933; Robin 1933
Thank My Stars   Harburg 1932, 1958
Thank the Lawd for Small Favors   DePaul 1945; Raye 1945
Thank the Lord for This Thanksgiving Day   McHugh 1959
Thank the Man Upstairs   Robison 1939
Thank You   Drake 1948; Kahn 1923; McHugh 1923
Thank You All   Livingston, Jay 1955
Thank You Columbus   Harburg 1942, 1945; Lane 1942, 1945
Thank You for a Lovely Evening   Fields 1934; McHugh 1934
Thank You for a Lovely Time   Conrad 1932; Young, Joe 1932
Thank You for Coming   Sondheim 1981
Thank You for the Bitter Truth I'm Learning   Razaf 1944
Thank You for the Lovely Summer   Howard, Bart 1952
Thank You for the Use of Heaven   Kahal 1932
Thank You in Advance   Hart 1928; Rodgers 1928
Thank You, Joe   Dubin 1945
Thank You Kind Sir, Said She   Berlin 1910; Snyder 1910
Thank You Lord   David, Hal 1979
Thank You Ma'am   Ellington 1966
Thank You Mr. Judge   Drake 1954
Thank You, Mrs. Butterfield   Bullock 1950
Thank You So Much   Rodgers 1965; Sondheim 1965
Thank You So Much Mrs. Lowsborough—Goodby   Porter 1930
Thank You, South America   Fain 1941; Kahal 1941; Yellen 1941
Thank You, Thomas Cook   Lawrence 1961
Thank You, You're Welcome, Don't Mention It   Gordon 1932; Revel 1932
Thank Your Father (Thank Your Mother)   Brown, Lew 1930; DeSylva 1930; Henderson 1930

Thank Your Lucky Stars   Loesser 1943; Schwartz, Arthur 1943

Thank Your Lucky Stars and Stripes   Burke 1941; Van Heusen 1941

Thank Your Stars   Adamson 1966; Silver 1966

Thank Your Stars We're Under the Moon Tonight   Bryan 1935; Meyer 1935; Young, Joe 1935

Thank Zeus!!!!   Spina 1977

Thankful   Cahn 1968

Thanks   Bryan 1925; Coslow 1933; Dubin 1927; Fisher 1925; Johnston 1933

Thanks A Lot   Cahn 1944; Styne 1944

Thanks a Lot but No Thanks   Comden and Green 1955

Thanks a Million   Johnston 1935; Kahn 1935

Thanks Awful   Lewis 1926; Young, Joe 1926

Thanks! Don't Mention It   Coleman 1962; Leigh 1962

Thanks for Ev'rything   Gordon 1938; Revel 1938

Thanks for Thanksgiving   Rome 1948

Thanks for the Boogie Ride   Mitchell 1941

Thanks for the Franc   Dubin 1939; McHugh 1939

Thanks for the Kind Words, Lady   Drake 1952

Thanks for the Loan of Your Heart   Revel 1945; Webster 1945

Thanks for the Memory   Rainger 1938; Robin 1938

Thanks for the Use of Your Heart   Fain 1982; Harburg 1977

Thanks for Your Kisses but Where Is Your Heart   Merrill 1950

Thanks, Professor   Drake 1958

Thanks to Love   Duke 1963

Thanks to Mom   Coleman 1999

Thanks to You   Adams 1992; Clarke 1931; Evans 1952; Gershwin, George 1931; Gershwin, Ira 1931; Johnson, Howard 1921; Livingston, Jay 1952; Strouse 1992; Webster 1963; Whiting 1926

Thanks to You I'm a Brand New Woman   Howard, Bart 1960

Thanks to You Mr. Handy   Coots 1938; Davis 1938

Thanksgivin'   Carmichael 1932; Mercer 1932

Thanksgiving   Blane 1964; Bryan 1908; Herbert 1908; Martin 1964

Thanksgiving Day   Livingston, Jerry 1963

Thanksgiving Prayer   Sherman 1978

Thar She Comes (Hill Billy Wedding Song)   Coslow 1937

That Aeroplane Rag   Johnson, J. Rosamond 1911

That Ain't Hay (That's the U.S.A.)   Loesser 1941; Styne 1941

That Ain't Love, Baby   David, Mack 1965

That Ain't Right   Evans 1958; Livingston, Jay 1958; Mills 1943

That Airship of Mine   Atteridge 1917; Romberg 1917

That American Boy of Mine   Caesar 1923; Gershwin, George 1923

That American Look   De Lange 1946; Myrow 1946

That and a Nickel Will Get You a Cup of Coffee   Conrad 1927

That Barber in Seville   Atteridge 1921; Conrad 1921

That Big Blonde Mamma   Monaco 1923; Rose 1923

That Black and White Baby of Mine   Porter 1919

That Bohemian Rag   Edwards 1914

That Boy of Mine   Hammerstein 1920; Rodgers 1920

That Bran' New Gal o' Mine   Akst 1923; Davis 1923

That Brand New Model of Mine   Whiting 1928

That Broadway Chicken Walk   Berlin 1916

That Broadway Glide   Brown, A. Seymour 1912

That Broadway Indian of Mine   Buck 1923

That Cat Step   Henderson 1920

That Certain Age   Adamson 1938; McHugh 1938

That Certain Feeling   Gershwin, George 1925; Gershwin, Ira 1925

That Certain Party   Donaldson 1925; Kahn 1925

(She Has) That Certain Something   Cahn 1966

That Certain Woman   Dubin 1937; Warren 1936, 1937

That Chaplin Man   Leigh 1976; Styne 1976

That Charleston Dance   Blake 1924; Sissle 1924

That Chinatown Rag   Meyer 1910

That Chop Stick Rag   Brown, A. Seymour 1909

That Chopstick Rag   Clarke 1912; Schwartz, Jean 1912

That Christmas Feeling   Burke 1950; Van Heusen 1950

That Clutching Hand   Schwartz, Jean 1915

That Come Hither Look   Kern 1916

That Coontown Quartette   Clarke 1912; Schwartz, Jean 1912

That Cuddlin' Rag   Goetz 1909

That Daddy and Mother of Mine   Bryan 1932

That Dame from Rio   Rainger 1933

That Damn Blue Suit   Strouse 1999

That Dancing Big Banshee   Brown, A. Seymour 1910; Goetz 1910

That Darn Cat   Sherman 1965

That Day   Kalmar 1945; Ruby 1945

That Day in June   Mills 1927

That Dirty Old Man   Sondheim 1962

That Does It   Baer 1965; De Lange 1945; Myrow 1945

That Doesn't Mean a Thing   Yellen 1921

That Don't Do Me No Good   Mills 1954

That Dramatic Rag   Ruby 1912; Young, Joe 1912

That Dream-Waltz Melody   Howard, Joseph E. 1918

That Dreamy Barcarole Tune   Goetz 1910

That Dum Ta Rum Tum Tune   Johnson, Howard 1917; Meyer 1917

That Element of Doubt   Dietz 1948, 1957; Fain 1948

That Every Loving Love   Goetz 1910

That Face   Bergman 1957; Martin 1951

That Face (Like a Jig-Saw Puzzle)   Spina 1977

That Faraway Look   Bergman 1964; Fain 1964

That Fascinating Rag Time Glide   Leslie 1910

That Feeling for Home   Cahn 1963; Van Heusen 1963

That Feeling of Belonging   Baer 1962

That Fellow Manuelo   Dietz 1934; Schwartz, Arthur 1934

That Five O'Clock Feeling   Meyer 1947

That Florida Low Down   Coots 1926; Waller 1926

That Foolish Feeling   Adamson 1937; McHugh 1937

That Forgotten Melody   Youmans 1925

That Fortunate Feeling   Fain 1956; Webster 1956

That Frank   Sondheim 1985

That Friendly Feeling   Loesser 1940; McHugh 1940

That Frisco Bear   Edwards 1911

That Funny Jas Band from Dixieland   Kahn 1916

That Funny Little Movement   Hanley 1920

That Funny Little Something   Gilbert 1916

That Funny Oo-la-la   Bryan 1912; Fisher 1912

That Futuristic Rag (inst.)   Bloom 1923

That Gal of Mine   Atteridge 1913

That Gal Salome   Coslow 1937

That Girl Belongs to Me   Atteridge 1920

That Girl of Mine   Atteridge 1913; Schwartz, Jean 1913

That Goes for You   Adamson 1935, Date Unknown; Donaldson 1935, Date Unknown

That Golondrina Melody   Parish 1923

That Good for Nothin' Man of Mine   Freed, Ralph 1942

That Good Old Fashioned Cake Walk   Schwartz, Jean 1913

That Good Old Fashioned Cake Walk (Passing Show Cakewalk)   Atteridge 1913

That Good Old Fashioned Cakewalk (Passing Show Cakewalk)   Atteridge 1913

That Good-for-Nothin' Man o' Mine   Freed, Ralph 1942

That Goody Melody   Berlin 1917

That Grand Old Gentleman, Uncle Sam   Cobb 1918; Edwards 1918

That Grand Terrace Trot   Razaf 1934

That Great American Home   Wrubel 1933

That Great Come and Get It Day   Harburg 1947; Lane 1947

That Great Getting Up Morning   Carmichael 1953

That Great Rodeo in the Sky   Stept 1950

That Happy American Dream   Coleman 1979

That Happy Feeling   Russell 1957

That Hate-to-Face-the-Night Feeling   Evans 1957; Livingston, Jay 1957

That Haunting Melody   Cohan 1911

That Hometown Feeling   Sherman 1978

That Honky Tonk Melody   Spina 1950

That Horrible Hobble Skirt   Edwards 1910; Smith, Harry B. 1910

That House/This Time   Lerner, Alan Jay 1976

That Hula Hula   Berlin 1915

That Hypnotizing Man   Brown, Lew 1911

That International Melody   Edwards 1928; Rose 1928

That Is Art   Herbert 1913

That Is How It's Done on the Stage   Alter 1929

That Is Love   Herbert 1909

That Is the Life for Me   Atteridge 1913; Schwartz, Jean 1913

That Is the Moment of Truth (Esa es la Hora de la Verdad)   Brooks 1966

That Is what a Little Birdie Told Me   Fisher 1923

That Italian Rag   Leslie 1910

That Jungle Jamboree   Razaf 1929; Waller 1929

That Kazzatsky Dance   Berlin 1911

That Kind of Woman   Bacharach 1959; David, Hal 1959

That Kinda Night   Merrill 1957

That Lazy Drag   Von Tilzer 1910

That Lindy Hop   Blake 1930; Razaf 1930

That Lingering Longing   David, Hal 1954

That Little Dream Got Nowhere   Burke 1946; Van Heusen 1946

That Little German Band   Fisher 1913

That Little Grey House without Any Key   Brennan 1922

That Little Old Bar at the Ritz   Porter 1920

That Little Photograph of You   Koehler 1930

That Little Something   Harbach 1926; Kalmar 1926, 1927; Kern 1926, 1927; Ruby 1926, 1927

That Little Spanish Hacienda   Edwards 1936

That Little Thatched Cottage All Covered with Vine   Olcott 1910

That Little World Is Mine   Brennan 1926

That Lost Barbershop Chord   Gershwin, George 1926; Gershwin, Ira 1926

That Lovable Baby of Mine   Motzan 1928

That Lovely Night in Budapest   Lewis 1936

That Lucky Fellow   Hammerstein 1939; Kern 1939

That Lucky Lady   Kern 1939

That Lullaby of Long Ago (Sweet and Low)   DeSylva 1919; Egan 1919; Kahn 1919; Whiting 1919

That Man!   Cahn 1960; Smith, Harry B. 1904; Smith, Robert B. 1904; Spina 1977; Van Heusen 1960

That Man Could Sell Me the Brooklyn Bridge   Fain 1958; Webster 1958

That Man Is Doing His Worst to Make Good   Burke 1953; Van Heusen 1953

That Man Loves Me   Duke 1963

That Man Over There   Willson 1963

That Man's Wife   Merrill 1959

That Mellow Melody   Lewis 1912; Meyer 1912

That Melodious Melody   Howard, Joseph E. 1915

That Melody of Love   Adamson 1927; Dietz 1927; Donaldson 1927

That Mesmerizing Mendelssohn Tune   Berlin 1909

That Mexican Look   De Lange 1946; Myrow 1946

That Meyer Chickerman!   Coleman 1988

That Midnight Frolic of Mine   Brown, A. Seymour 1916

That Might Have Satisfied Grandma   Harbach 1920

That Mittel-Europa Europe Man   Eliscu 1943; Gorney 1943

That Mittel-Europa Mine   Eliscu 1955; Gorney 1955

That Moment of Moments   Duke 1936; Gershwin, Ira 1936

That Monkey Tune   Berlin 1911

That Moonlight Serenade   Lewis 1914; Meyer 1914

That Musical Tonical Dance   Razaf 1920

That Mysterious Lady Called Love   Coots 1958; Harburg 1942, 1958; Lane 1942, Date Unknown

That Mysterious Rag   Berlin 1911; Snyder 1911

That Naughty Melody   Lewis 1913; Meyer 1913

That Naughty Show from Gay Paree   Robin 1954; Romberg 1954

That Never to Be Forgotten Night   Fain 1936

That New-Fangled Mother of Mine   Gershwin, George 1924

That Night   Magidson 1932

That Night Among the Roses   Koehler 1929

That Night in Araby   Rose 1926; Snyder 1926

That Night in Avalon   Kalmar 1938; Ruby 1938

That Night in Montmartre   Heyman 1931

That Night in Paris   Loesser Date Unknown

That Night of the Embassy Ball   Arlen 1937; Harburg 1937

That O'Brien Girl   Harbach 1921

That Ol' Judge   Drake 1954

That Old Black Magic   Arlen 1942; Mercer 1942

That Old Church Bell   Schwartz, Jean 1918

That Old Enchanted Feeling   Burke 1959

That Old Fashioned Cake Walk   Cohan 1914

That Old Fashioned Garden of Mine   Buck 1923; Herbert 1923

That Old Feeling   Brown, Lew 1938; Fain 1938

That Old Gang of Mine   Dixon 1923; Henderson 1923; Rose 1923

That Old Ghost Train   Revel 1940

That Old Irish Mother of Mine   Jerome 1920; Von Tilzer 1920

That Old New England Town   Ager 1916; Jerome 1916

That Old Piano Roll   Sondheim 1971

That Old Quartette on the Corner   Dietz 1927

That Old Song and Dance   Bergman 1962

That Old-Time Gal of Mine   Lewis 1929; Young, Joe 1929

That Opera Rag   Berlin 1910; Snyder 1910

That Paradise Rag   Meyer 1911

That Parisian Trot   Smith, Harry B. 1915

That Peach-A-Reeno, Phil-I-Peeno Dance   Atteridge 1917; Motzan 1917; Romberg 1917

That Peculiar Tune   Kern 1915

That Pierrot Dance   Williams 1911

That Possum Rag   Atteridge Date Unknown

That Pretty Kittie So and So of Mine   Friend 1927

That Pretty Little Song   Herbert 1911; Smith, Harry B. 1911

That Promise in Your Eyes   Loesser Date Unknown

That Ragtime Regimental Band   Brown, A. Seymour 1912
That Rainbow Rag   Porter 1912
That Rare Romance   Hammerstein 1931; Romberg 1931
That Real Sunday Feeling   Harburg 1950; Lane 1950
That Redhead Gal   Fisher 1922
That Reminds Me   Pollack 1944
That Reminiscent Melody   Ager 1920; Yellen 1920
That Reuben Glide   Young, Joe 1911
That Rhythm Man   Razaf 1929; Waller 1929
That Rhythm Parade   Razaf 1935
That Romance of Mine   Atteridge 1923; Caesar 1923; Romberg 1923
That Russian Winter   Berlin 1942
That Saturday Night Feelin'   Russell 1951
That Sentimental Sandwich   Loesser 1939
That Shakesperian Rag   Buck 1912
That Shufflin' Tune   Razaf 1955
That Slippery Slide Trombone   Williams 1907
That Sly Old Gentleman from Featherbed Lane   Burke 1939; Monaco 1939
That Small Still Voice   Johnson, J. Rosamond 1907
That Society Bear   Berlin 1912
That Society Bud (I'm a Society Bud)   Kalmar 1923; Ruby 1923
That Something Extra Special   Harburg 1967; Styne 1967
That Soothing Symphony   Snyder 1915
(With) That Sophisticated Twist   Coleman 1961; Leigh 1961
That Soul Inspiring Sneeze   Harbach 1911
That Sounds Exciting   Burke 1957
That South Car'lina Jazz Dance   Blake 1925; Sissle 1925
That Spanish Rum Tee Ay   Fisher 1922
That Spooky Tune   Goetz 1911
That Spooney Dance (The Cooney-Spooney Dance)   Jerome 1909; Schwartz, Jean 1909
That Stolen Melody   Fisher 1928
That Stranger in Your Eyes   Harburg 1967; Styne 1967
That Street Corner Quartet   Caesar 1921; Monaco 1921
That Strictly Neutral Jag   Howard, Joseph E. 1915
That Struttin' Eddie of Mine   Waller 1926
That Stupid Melody   Rose 1927
That Swaying Tango   Brown, A. Seymour 1912
That Sweet Somebody of Mine   Snyder 1923
That Syncopated Boogie-Boo   Lewis 1912; Meyer 1912
That Syncopated Charleston Dance   Blake 1923; Sissle 1923
That Tangalo Tap   Schwartz, Jean 1912
That Tango Tokio   Bryan 1913
That Tantalizing Nod   Howard, Joseph E. 1910
That Tea Time Tango Tune   Gilbert 1913
That Terrific Rainbow   Hart 1940; Rodgers 1940
That Ticklish Feeling   Mills 1952
That Tinkling Tango Tune   Brown, A. Seymour 1913
That Tired Feeling   Friml 1930; Hammerstein 1930; Harbach 1930
That Travelin' Two-Beat   Evans 1965; Livingston, Jay 1965
That Volga Boatman Song   Silver 1927
That Was a Big Fat Lie   Cahn 1949; Styne 1949
That Was Before I Met You   Bryan 1911; Meyer 1911
That Was Destiny   Kahn 1930
That Was My Love I Gave You   Loesser 1974
That Was My Own Idea   Waller 1929
That Was the End of Jack   Johnson, Howard 1927
That Was the Love that Was   Arlen 1964
That Was Then   Johnson, James P. 1944, 1948
That Was Then and Now Is Now   Coleman 1965
That Was Then, Mr. Rassendyl   Duke 1963

That Was Yesterday   Razaf 1929
That Way Over You   Donaldson 1934; Kahn 1934
(Be Hap-Hap-Happy My Love) That We Is Me and You   Merrill 1950
That Week in Paris   Hammerstein 1938; Oakland 1938
That Well-Known Smile   Gershwin, George 1930; Gershwin, Ira 1930
That Where You Come In   Kahal 1929
That Will Keep Him True to You   Harbach 1911
That Wonderful Game Called Love   Clare 1924
That Wonderful Something Is Love   Alter 1929
That Wonderful Tune   Clarke 1912; Schwartz, Jean 1912
That Wonderful Worrisome Feeling   Hoffman 1943; Livingston, Jerry 1943
That Would Make You Homesick Too   Fisher 1909
That Yodeling Rag   Von Tilzer 1910
That Zip Cornwall Cooch   Porter 1912
Thata Old-Time Gal of Mine   Lewis 1929
That'll Be All   Hoffman 1932
That'll Be the Day   Harburg 1961
That'll Show Him   Sondheim 1962
That's a Fine, Fine, Fine Howdy Ya Do   David, Hal 1951
That's a Fine Kind of Freedom   Arlen 1965
That's a Good Girl   Berlin 1926
That's a Lovely Evening   Kahn 1914
That's a Man Everytime   Bullock 1950
That's a Miracle   Heyman 1967
That's a Plenty   Johnson, J. Rosamond 1909
That's a Real Moving Picture from Life   Sterling 1914; Von Tilzer 1914
That's a Woman   Coleman 1988
That's All   Drake 1953; Smith, Harry B. 1908
That's All, Brother   David, Mack 1939; Livingston, Jerry 1939
That's All I Ask of the World   Dubin 1928; Silver 1928
That's All I Need to Know   David, Hal 1959
That's All I Want to Know   Coots 1932; Kahn 1932
That's All (inst.)   Revel 1959; Waller 1931
That's All Right for McGilligan   Kern 1911
That's All There Is   Burke 1934; Spina 1934
That's All There Is Folks   Comden and Green 1949
That's All There Is, There Ain't No More   Woods 1925
That's Amore   Brooks 1953; Warren 1953
That's Anna   Cahn 1958
That's Annabelle   Kahn 1926
That's A-Plenty   Pollack 1950
That's Art   Smith, Robert B. 1905
That's As Far As I Can Go   Hammerstein 1920; Harbach 1920
That's As Far As It Goes   Buck 1926; Friml 1926
That's Boys Your Boys   Herbert 1911
That's Burlesque   Strouse 1999
That's Called Walking the Dog   Romberg 1916
That's Class   Burke 1946; Van Heusen 1946
That's Dancing   Mancini 1985
That's Dolly   Kahn 1927; Styne 1927
That's Enough for Tonight!   Whiting 1930
That's Entertainment   Dietz 1952; Schwartz, Arthur 1952
That's Everything   Kahn 1923
That's Falling in Love   Leigh 1954
That's for Children   Fields 1951; Schwartz, Arthur 1951
That's for Me   Burke 1940; Hammerstein 1945; Monaco 1940; Rainger 1938; Robin 1938; Rodgers 1945
That's for Sure   Mercer 1951
That's Getting First Class Yiddisha Love   Von Tilzer 1910
That's Going Some for You   Bryan 1911; Fisher 1911

That's Good   Williams 1910

That's Good Enough for Me   Leigh 1967

That's Good, That's Bad   Drake 1951; Fain 1931; Kahal 1931;
Sondheim 1963

That's Happiness   Gorney 1926

That's Harmony   Clarke 1911

That's Her Now   Ager 1929; Yellen 1929

That's Her! That's Her! What Did I Tell Ya!   DeSylva 1925;
Donaldson 1925

That's Her (That's Him)   Leigh 1973

That's Him   Weill 1943

That's Him Over There   Bergman 1952

That's Hollywood (If You Ever Need Me)   Warren 1985

That's How   DePaul 1958; Raye 1958

That's How Dreams Are Made   Gilbert 1949

That's How I Am (Asi es Que Soy Yo)   Brooks 1966

That's How I Believe in You   Dubin 1921

That's How I Feel About You, Sweetheart   Davis 1928

That's How I Know I Love You   Kahal 1927; Snyder 1927

That's How I Love the Blues   Martin 1941

That's How I Love You   Berlin 1912

That's How Imitations Look to Me   Howard, Joseph E. 1910

That's How It Goes   Fields 1951; Schwartz, Arthur 1951

That's How It Is   Evans 1956; Gershwin, Ira 1945;
Livingston, Jay 1956; Weill 1945

That's How It Looks from Here   Oakland 1969

That's How It Starts   Merrill 1959

That's How Little Dreams Are Born   Parish 1935

That's How Love Should Be (La-le-lu)   David, Mack 1951

That's How Our Love Will Grow   Sigman 1951

That's How the Ragtime Dance Is Done   Sterling 1898; Von
Tilzer 1898

That's How the Shannon Flows   Brennan 1915, 1920

That's How to Write a Song   Adamson 1943; Styne 1943

That's How Virginia Began   Kahal 1936

That's How We Met the Girl   Goetz 1907

That's Jazz   Bergman 1957

That's Jelly Roll (inst.)   Blake 1962

That's Just for Kids   David, Mack 1944

That's Just My Way of Forgeting You   Brown, Lew 1929;
DeSylva 1929; Henderson 1929

That's Life   Duke 1932; Evans 1954; Harburg 1932;
Livingston, Jay 1954

That's Life, I Guess   Lewis 1936

That's Living   Ahlert 1932; DePaul 1943; Raye 1943; Turk
1932

That's Love   Hart 1934; Rodgers 1934

That's Love with a Capital 'L'   Smith, Harry B. 1913

That's Loyalty   Loesser 1949

That's Me   Adams 1983

That's Me without You   Coots 1933; Johnson, Howard 1933

That's Music   Leigh 1967

That's Music to My Ears   Coots 1929

That's My Baby   Clare 1923; Friend 1923

That's My Boy   Brennan 1940; Fain 1950; Sterling Date
Unknown

That's My Business   Bryan 1929

That's My Doll   Revel 1959

That's My Fella   Fields 1950

That's My Girl   Davis 1926

That's My Hap-Hap-Happiness   Johnson, Howard 1926

That's My Idea of a Hero   Edwards 1905

That's My Idea of Love   Herbert 1900; Smith, Harry B. 1900

That's My Idea of Paradise   Berlin 1914

That's My Kind of Christmas   Livingston, Jerry 1961;
Webster 1961

That's My L.A.   Fain 1951; Webster 1951

That's My Mammy   Baer 1927

That's My Man   Caesar 1927; Waller 1924

That's My Middle Name   Burke 1944; Van Heusen 1944

That's My Opinion of You   Bryan 1931; Schwartz, Jean 1931

That's My Personality   Brown, Lew 1912

That's My Pop   Rome 1943

That's My Style   Coleman 1963

That's My Sweetheart   Motzan 1930

That's My Virginia   Bryan 1928

That's My Weakness Now   Stept 1928

That's Nice   Davis 1919

That's No Dream   Sterling 1898; Von Tilzer 1898

That's Not Cricket   Dietz 1935; Schwartz, Arthur 1935

That's Not the Answer   Bacharach 1962; David, Hal 1962

That's Not the Knot   Evans 1947; Livingston, Jay 1947

That's Our Annie   Strouse 1977

That's Plenty (inst.)   Pollack 1914

That's Politics   Williams 1909

That's Pollyanna   Sherman 1964

That's Right — I'm Wrong   Carmichael 1939

That's Sabotage   Gordon 1942; Warren 1942

That's Some Love   Cohan 1907, 1908

That's Southern Hospitality   Coslow 1937, 1941

That's the Best of All   Gershwin, Ira 1944; Kern 1944

That's the Fellow I Want to Get   Bryan 1910; Meyer 1910

That's the Good Old Sunny South   Ager 1929; Yellen 1929

That's the Hollywood Low-Down   Fields 1935; McHugh
1935

That's the Kind of Dame I Am   Styne 1955

That's the Kind of Fellow That I Could Love   Brown, A.
Seymour 1912

That's the Kind of Love I Crave   Sissle 1916

That's the Kind of Man for Me   Razaf 1929

That's the Kind of Woman   Strouse 1993

That's the Kind of Work I Do   Cahn 1941; Raye 1945

That's the Law   Rome Date Unknown

That's the Life of a Stable Boy   Harbach 1910

That's the Low-Down on the Low-Down   Stept 1930

That's the Meaning of Ireland   Von Tilzer 1916

That's the Meaning of Love Dear to Me   Coots 1920

That's the News I'm Waiting to Hear   Porter 1936

That's the Only Place Where Our Flag Shall Fly   Friml 1917

That's the Reason I Want You   Bryan 1913

That's the Rhythm of the Day (Go, Go, Go)   Hart 1933;
Rodgers 1933

That's the Song of Paree   Hart 1932; Rodgers 1932

That's the Stuff You Got to Watch   Johnson, James P. 1945

That's the Stuff You Gotta Watch   Sissle 1945

That's the Time   Livingston, Jerry 1970

That's the Time a Fellow Needs a Girl   Clare 1931; Stept
1931; Young, Joe 1931

That's the Time to Go   Leigh 1985; Styne 1985

That's the Time You'll Think of Me   Brown, Lew 1912

That's the Tune   Robin 1951; Styne 1951

That's the Very Spot   Drake 1953

That's the Way I Like to Hear You Talk   Hoffman 1934

That's the Way I'll Come to You   Bacharach 1963; David,
Hal 1963

That's the Way It Goes   Duke 1963; Friend 1944; Parish
1948; Romberg 1922; Spina 1977; Strouse 1977

That's the Way It Happens   Hammerstein 1953; Rodgers
1953

That's the Way I've Missed You   Kahn 1919

That's the Way My Honey Boy Makes Love   Young, Joe 1913

That's the Way the Ball Bounces   Fain 1965

That's the Way to Go   Evans 1973; Livingston, Jay 1973

That's the Way to Make Love   Meyer 1908

That's the Way to Treat a Little Doggie   Harbach 1911

That's The Way with Love   Sigman 1961

That's What a Child Can Do   Baer 1929; Gilbert 1929

That's What a Fellow Does When He's in Love   Howard, Joseph E. 1908

That's What a Sweetheart Was Made For   Coots 1964

That's What a Woman Can Do   Sherman 1953

That's What a Woman Is For   Bloom 1954; Cahn 1954

That's What Christmas Means to Me   Revel 1947

That's What Elvis Means to Me   Adams 1958; Strouse 1958

That's What Every Young Girl Should Know   David, Mack 1946

That's What Friends Are For   Bacharach 1982; Cahn 1976; Comden and Green 1974; Lane 1976; Styne 1974

That's What Friends Are For (Vulture Song)   Sherman 1967

That's What He Did   Gershwin, George 1933; Gershwin, Ira 1933

That's What Heaven Means to Me   Akst 1932; Yellen 1932

That's What I Call a Pal   Donaldson 1922; Johnson, Howard 1926

That's What I Call Heaven   Howard, Joseph E. 1938

That's What I Call Keen   Kahn 1928

That's What I Call Love   Arlen 1929; Dubin 1927; Snyder 1927

That's What I Call Spreading Joy   Johnson, Howard 1917

That's What I Call Sweet Music   Hoffman 1929

That's What I Get for Wearing My Heart on My Sleeve   Stept 1935; Washington 1935

That's What I Hate about Love   Arlen 1932; Koehler 1932

That's What I Like   Styne 1954

That's What I Like about the North   Razaf 1957

That's What I Like about You   Donaldson 1931; Friend 1930; Monaco 1930

That's What I Like 'Bout the South   Razaf 1933

That's What I Mean When I Call You Machree   Brennan 1915

That's What I See in You   Mills 1929

That's What I Think of You   Fisher 1926; Rose 1926

That's What I Told Him Last Night   Fields 1950

That's What I Want for Christmas   Caesar 1936; Cahn 1959; Van Heusen 1959

That's What I Want for Jamie   Coleman 1960; Leigh 1960

That's What I'd Do   Gilbert 1924

That's What I'd Like to Be   Mills 1952

That's What I'm Talking About   Friend 1936

That's What Ireland Means to Me   Hanley 1917

That's What It Takes   Coleman 1965

That's What It's Like   Drake 1954

That's What Keeps Me Broke   Clare 1922; Monaco 1922

That's What Love Did for Me   Brennan 1943

That's What Love Did to Me   Cahn 1934

That's What Love Is All About   David, Mack 1977

That's What Love Is For   Revel 1959

That's What Makes Paris, Paree   Cahn 1952; Duke 1952

That's What Makes the World Go 'Round   Sherman 1963; Spina 1957; Stept 1934

That's What Puts the Sweet in Home Sweet Home   Gordon 1928

That's What the Crystal Shows   Johnston 1920

That's What the Man Said   Robison 1948

That's What the Papers Say   Edwards 1909; Smith, Robert B. 1909

That's What the Poor Woman Is   Coleman 1980

That's What They Like About Autumn   Drake 1953

That's What You Jolly Well Get   Loesser 1943; Schwartz, Arthur 1943

That's What You Mean to Me   Coots 1936; Davis 1936; Evans 1956; Livingston, Jay 1956; Porter 1944

That's What's Wrong with Jimmy   David, Hal 1955

That's When a Fellow Needs a Friend   Conrad 1925

That's When I'll Marry You   Dubin 1915

That's when My Love Will End   Meyer 1927

That's When the Panic Is On   Fisher 1915; Johnson, Howard 1915

That's When Your Heartaches Begin   Fisher 1940

That's Where I Meet My Girl   Von Tilzer 1926

That's Where I'm So Different   Adamson 1953; Carmichael 1953

That's Where Our Horoscopes Lie (She's a Gemini Girl)   Weill 1947

That's Where the South Begins   Waller 1932; Yellen 1930

That's Where We Come In   Harburg 1934

That's Where You'll Find Me   Coslow 1931

That's Why Darkies Were Born   Brown, Lew 1931; Henderson 1931

That's Why I Buy Bonds   Johnson, J. Rosamond 1944; Razaf 1944

That's Why I Love You   Donaldson 1926; Friml 1926; Hammerstein 1926; Harbach 1926; Porter 1929

That's Why I Never Go Home   Kalmar 1913

That's Why I'm Crying Just for You   Monaco 1913

That's Why I'm Happy   Magidson 1929

That's Why I'm Jealous of You   Fain 1931; Kahal 1931

That's Why Lots of People Marry   Smith, Harry B. 1910

That's Why My Heart Is Calling You   Motzan 1917

That's Why She Is What She Is Now   Whiting 1925

That's Why They Say I'm Crazy   Herbert 1905

That's Why We Make Him Leader   David, Mack 1940

That's Why We're Dancing   Fields 1930; McHugh 1930

That's Why You're Called United States   Fisher 1917; Johnson, Howard 1917

That's Why You're Mary Mine   Mitchell 1925

That's Worth Waiting For   Young, Joe 1919

That's Worth While Waiting For   Baer 1930; Gilbert 1930; Lewis 1919; Ruby 1919

That's You   Evans 1974; Livingston, Jay 1974

That's You Baby   Conrad 1929; Mitchell 1929

That's You, That's Me, That's All   Coots 1932; Turk 1932

That's Your Umbrella When It Rains   Brown, Lew 1940; Henderson 1940

(The Tale of) The Bachelor and the Maid   Atteridge 1910

(Ting a Ling) The Bad Humor Man   McHugh 1940; Mercer 1940

(We're) The Berries   Razaf 1930

(Who Needs) The Birds and Bees   Berlin 1966

(The Same Thing Happens with) The Birds and the Bees   David, Mack 1956; Warren 1956

(Sadie Thompson's Song) The Blue Pacific Blues   Washington 1953

(We're Looking for) The Bobbed Hair Bandit   Johnson, Howard 1924

(The Girl Is You and) The Boy Is Me   DeSylva 1926; Henderson 1926

(The Flow'rs, the Trees) The Butterflies and Bees   Romberg 1941

The Color of Love   Russell 1964

(I've Got) The Cutest Little Red-Headed Doll   Sigman 1947

(Which Came First) The Egg or the Chicken   Davis 1950; Silver 1950

(On) The Erie Canal   Arlen 1953; Fields 1953

(There Goes) The Forgotten Man   Bacharach 1962; David, Hal 1962

The Four Seasons   Russell 1956, 1958

(At) The General Store   Evans 1952; Livingston, Jay 1952

(Gorillas Are) The Gentlest Creatures   Sherman 1991

(Better Beware of) The Grizzly Bear   Sherman 1991

(When You Do) The Hinky Dee   Cohan 1922

(I Fell in Love with) The Leader of the Band   Magidson 1942, 1945; Styne 1942, 1945

(That's) The Least You Can Do for the Lady   Warren 1937

(On) The Levee Along Broadway   Goetz 1915; Romberg 1915

(Like) The Love Birds in a Tree   Merrill 1958

(I Couldn't Get the Hang of) The Merengue   Livingston, Jerry 1955

(Don't Be Ashamed of) The Name of Abraham   Johnson, Howard 1925

The Next Time   Strouse 1956

(Dance to the Music of) The Ocarina   Berlin 1950

(I Love) The Old Tunes   Adams 1973

(The Love Story of) The Packard and the Ford   Atteridge 1915; Carroll 1915

(On) The Red Ball Line   Sissle 1946

(Love Is) The Tender Trap   Cahn 1955; Van Heusen 1955

(You Can't Take Away) The Things That Were Made for Love   Kahal 1929

(I Wish You) The Very Best Luck in the World   Livingston, Jerry 1956

(I Love) The Way You Say It   Hoffman 1959

(New In) The Ways of Love   David, Hal 1959

(Under) The Willow Tree   Atteridge 1917; Romberg 1917

Theater, the Theater, The   Adams 1993

Theatre Is a Lady, The   Duke 1952

Theatre Marquis   Brown, Lew 1933; Henderson 1933

Theatrical Blues, The   Ager 1920; Yellen 1920

Theda Bara   Atteridge 1920

Their Hearts Are Over Here   Cohan 1918

Them   Hoffman 1954

Them and They   Cahn 1970; Styne 1970

Them Contrapuntal Eyes of Blue   Drake 1959

Them Was Happy Days   Smith, Harry B. 1915

Them Was the Childhood Days   Herbert 1912

Them Who Has, Gets   DePaul 1946; Raye 1946

Theme   Koehler 1950; Stept 1950

Theme for Gina (inst.)   Spina 1977

Theme for Love (inst.)   Young, Victor 1951

Theme from The Courtship of Eddie's Father   Young, Victor 1960

Theme from The Wonderful World of the Brothers Grimm (inst.)   Merrill 1962

Theme in Two Voices (inst.)   Johnson, James P. 1944

Theme of Life   Motzan 1929

Theme Song, The   Dietz 1929; Schwartz, Arthur 1929

Then and Now   Merrill 1955

Then Came the Dawn   Dubin 1928; Warren 1928

Then Comes the Dawning   DeSylva 1922; Herbert 1922

Then He'd Give 'er Gas   Brown, Lew 1923; Hanley 1923

Then I Could Forget You   Friend 1936

Then I Had to Go and Fall in Love   Mills 1952

Then I Met You   Coslow 1925; Motzan 1925; Silver 1925

Then I Want to Settle Down   Atteridge 1913; Schwartz, Jean 1913

Then I Wouldn't Have To Worry Any More   Bryan 1913

Then I Wrote the Minuet in G   Loesser 1939

Then I'd Be Satisfied   Cohan 1901

Then I'd Be Satisfied with Life   Cohan 1903

Then I'll Be Closer to You   Brown, Nacio Herb 1948

Then I'll Be Reminded of You   Heyman 1929

Then I'll Be Tired of You   Harburg 1934; Schwartz, Arthur 1934

(When Coffee Goes Back to a Nickel a Cup) Then I'll Go Back to You   Bryan 1954

Then I'll Have Time for You   Brown, Lew 1929; DeSylva 1929; Henderson 1929

Then I'll Know   Johnson, James P. 1964

Then It All Came True (inst.)   Revel 1960

(If It Isn't Pain) Then It Isn't Love   Rainger 1935; Robin 1935

Then Love Again   Hammerstein 1920; Harbach 1920

Then Love Will Come   Romberg 1916

Then My Castle Came Tumbling Down   Koehler 1929

Then Someone's in Love   Pollack 1929

Then Suddenly   Arlen 1959; Mercer 1959

Then Things Blow Up Like a Toy Balloon   Robison 1929

Then We Canoe-dle-oodle Along   Woods 1929

Then We'll All Go Home   Williams 1909

Then You Know That You're in Love   Gorney 1924

Then You May Take Me to the Fair   Lerner, Alan Jay 1960; Loewe 1960

Then You Walked in the Room   Akst 1935; Brown, Lew 1935

Then You Went and Changed Your Mind   Fields 1932; McHugh 1932

Then You Will Know   Hammerstein 1926; Harbach 1926; Romberg 1926

Then You'll Remember Me   Fisher 1907; Johnson, Howard 1939

Then You've Never Been Blue   Lewis 1929; Young, Joe 1929

Theophilus   Harbach 1910

There   Silver 1950

There Ain't a Better Buy in the Land   Styne 1945

There Ain't Any Chorus to This Song   Livingston, Jerry 1941

There Ain't Goin-a-Be No Rhine   Young, Victor 1918

There Ain't No Baby (Can Baby Me Like Mine)   Turk 1927

There Ain't No Better Buy in the Land   Cahn 1945

There Ain't No Color Line Around the Rainbow   Caesar 1943; Lerner, Sammy 1943

There Ain't No Flies on Me   Merrill 1957

There Ain't No Guy   Mills 1947

There Ain't No Land Like Dixieland to Me   Donaldson 1927

There Ain't No Maybe in My Baby's Eyes   Donaldson 1926; Egan 1926; Kahn 1926

There Ain't No Santa Claus   Dixon 1923

There Ain't Nothin' Bigger than My Love for You   Oakland 1961; Webster 1961

There Ain't Nothin' Love Can't Do   Strouse 1958

There Are Girls   Duke 1963

There Are New Roses Every Summer   Henderson 1943; Yellen 1943

There Are No Bad Times for Wifey, and My Good Times Are Here   Young, Joe 1931

There Are No Girls Quite Like Showgirls   Cahn 1980

There Are No Heroes   Styne 1985

There Are No Lips So Sweet As Yours   Romberg 1919
There Are No Tomorrows   Brennan 1930; Friml 1930
There Are No Wings on a Foxhole   Berlin 1944
There Are No Words   Burke 1934; Spina 1934
There Are Not Enough People in Love   Gordon 1952; Revel 1952
There Are Other Things a Girl Can Do   Adamson 1948; McHugh 1948
There Are Rivers to Cross (Before We Meet Again)   Henderson 1942
There Are Some Things (You Just Can't Tell About)   Blake 1958
There Are Such Things   Baer 1941; Meyer 1941
There Are They   Webster 1966
There Are Those   Sherman 1967
There Are Too Many Girls (In the World)   Howard, Joseph E. 1909
There Are Tricks in All Trades   Smith, Harry B. 1902
There Are Two Eyes in Dixie   Berlin 1917
There Are Two Eyes in Hawaii   Hoffman 1957
There Are Two Sides to Ev'ry Girl   Fain 1946; Freed, Ralph 1946
There Are Yanks (From the Banks of the Wabash)   Dietz 1944; Duke 1944
There but for You Go I   Lerner, Alan Jay 1947; Loewe 1947
There Can Only Be One for Me   Harbach 1930
There Can Only Be Only One for Me   Caesar 1930; Romberg 1930
There Can't Be Any Harm in Saying Just Goodbye   Harbach 1921
There Comes a Time   Adams 1960, 1964; Cahn 1970, Date Unknown; Drake 1957; Duke Date Unknown; Strouse 1960, 1964; Styne 1970
There Goes a Time to Do a Little Good   Cahn 1970
There Goes Another Pal of Mine   Carmichael 1963
There Goes My Dream   Loesser 1940, 1943
There Goes My Heart   Davis 1934; Silver 1934
There Goes My Runaway Heart (Running After You)   Coots 1947
There Goes Taps   Eliscu 1944; Gorney 1944
There Goes that Feeling Again   Stept 1936; Washington 1936
There Goes that Guitar   Eliscu 1943; Gorney 1943
There Goes that Song Again   Cahn 1944; Styne 1944; Wrubel 1943
There Goes the Bride   Bloom 1962; Burke 1962
There Goes the Girl for Me   Kahn 1931
There Had to Be the Waltz   Loewe 1938
There He Goes, Mr. Phileas Fogg   Porter 1946
There He Is — Theodore K. Blair   Hart 1932; Rodgers 1932
There I Go Again   Akst 1936; Clare 1936
There I Go Dreaming Again   Brown, Lew 1932; Henderson 1932
There I Was   Duke 1959
There I'd Be   Comden and Green 1945
There I'd Settle Down   Gershwin, Ira 1928
There Is a Ball at the Savoy   Hammerstein 1933
There Is a City   Robison 1929
There Is a Garden in Loveland   Smith, Harry B. 1925
There Is a Garden in My Dreams   Fisher 1929
There Is a Happy Land   Smith, Harry B. 1911
There Is a Happy Land Far Far Away   Akst 1929; Lewis 1928; Young, Joe 1929
There is a Happy Land (Tale of Woe)   Kern 1911; Norworth 1911

There Is a Place for Lovers   Spina 1967
There Is a Way   Davis 1952
There Is Life in the Old Boy Yet   Schwartz, Jean 1920
There Is Magic in a Smile   Herbert 1913; Smith, Robert B. 1913
There Is Music in an Irish Song   Gorney 1924
There Is My Love   Rainger 1935; Robin 1935
There Is No Affair Like a Country Fair   Drake 1954
There Is No Breeze (Bea Lillie Ballad)   Kern 1938
There Is No Christmas Like a Home Christmas   Sigman 1950
There Is No Cure for L'Amour   Hoffman 1956
There Is No Land of Oz   Cahn 1963; Van Heusen 1963
There Is No Music   Gershwin, Ira 1949; Warren 1949
There Is No One Like You   Clare 1931
There Is No Other Way   Sondheim 1976
There Is No Place Like Home   Howard, Joseph E. 1908
There Is Nothin' Like a Dame   Hammerstein 1949; Rodgers 1949
There Is Nothing Dear, I Wouldn't Do for You   Buck 1913
There Is Nothing Like a Wedding   Duke 1963
There Is Nothing Too Good for You   DeSylva 1923; Gershwin, George 1923; Goetz 1923
There Is One Born Every Minute   Atteridge Date Unknown
There Is One Heart in Loveland for Me   Ager 1915
There Is Somebody for Everybody but Me   Coslow 1924
There is Something About a Kitchen (inst.)   Kern 1938
There Is Time   Bacharach 1979
There Isn't Any Harm in That   Brooks 1945
There Isn't Any Limit to My Love   Hoffman 1936
There Isn't Anybody Like You   Russell 1956, 1957
There It Is Again (When Your Favorite Girl's Not There)   Kern 1917
There May Bloom a Rose for Me   Romberg 1921; Smith, Harry B. 1921
There Must Be a Better Way   Lane Date Unknown
There Must Be a First Time   Egan 1933
There Must Be a Heaven for that Little Dog of Mine   Bryan 1936; Caesar 1936
There Must Be a Million Ways (To Say I Love You)   Cahn 1955; Styne 1955
There Must Be a Reason   Cahn 1953; Davis 1954; Fain 1953
There Must Be a Silver Lining   Donaldson 1928
There Must Be a U.N. of Love   Spina 1959
There Must Be a Way to Love You   Snyder 1919
There Must Be an Easier Way to Make a Living   Stept 1940; Woods 1940
There Must Be Little Cupids in the Briny   Willson 1946
There Must Be Paint in the Sky   Fisher 1937
There Must Be Somebody Else   Clare 1927
There Must Be Somebody for Me   Coots 1950
There Must Be Somebody Waiting for Me in Loveland   Donaldson 1929
There Must Be Someone for Me   Porter 1944
There Must Be Somethin' Better than Love   Fields 1950
There Must Be Something More   Sherman 1973
There Never Was a Baby Like My Baby   Comden and Green 1951; Styne 1951
There Never Was a Gal Like You   Williams 1907
There Never Was a Girl Like You   Friend 1932; Magidson 1932
There Never Was a Girl Like You (Wonderful Girl of Mine)   Razaf 1923
There Never Was a Night Like This   Rainger 1934; Robin 1934

There Never Was a Pal Like Aunt Jemima   Motzan 1927

There Never Was a Town Like Paree   Coots 1926

There Once Was a Princess   Herbert 1911

There Once Was an Owl   Herbert 1903; Smith, Harry B. 1903

There Ought to Be a Law Against That   Caesar 1927; Friend 1927

There Ought to Be Music   Silver 1919

There She Goes   David, Hal 1951

There She Is   Comden and Green 1982

There She Was   Carmichael 1943; Sherman 1951

There Was a Crooked Man   Adams 1970; Strouse 1970

There Was a Goose   Young, Victor 1934

There Was a Little Frog   Johnson, James P. 1962

There Was a Time   Atteridge 1915; Bryan 1913; Carroll 1913, 1915; Revel 1947; Sigman 1967; Styne 1980

There Was Moonlight in Her Hair   David, Mack 1948; Hoffman 1947; Livingston, Jerry 1947

There Was Never Such a Charming War   Gershwin, George 1929; Gershwin, Ira 1929

There Was No Room at the Inn   Fain 1968

There Was Nothing Else to Do   Kalmar 1929; Ruby 1929; Warren 1929

There Were a Lot o' People for 'Im   Spina 1944

There Were Others Passing By   Blane 1945

There Will Be a Girl (There Will Be a Boy)   Gordon 1931; Revel 1931

There Will Be No Blackout of Democracy   Pollack 1942

There Will Never Be Another Night Like This   Stept 1958

There Will Never Be Another You   Gordon 1942; Warren 1942

There Won't Be Trumpets   Sondheim 1964

There You Are   Van Heusen 1953

There You Are Again   Duke 1950; Rome 1950

There You Go, Doing It Over Again   Adamson 1932; Lane 1932

There You Have New York Town   Atteridge 1912

There You Were   Revel 1943; Webster 1943

There'll Always Be a Lady Fair   Porter 1934

There'll Always Be a Lindy's   Ruby 1943

There'll Be a Great Day in the Mornin'   Mills 1935

There'll Be a Hot Time for the Old Men While the Young Men Are Away   Clarke 1918; Meyer 1918

There'll Be a Hot Time in the Old Town Tonight   Brooks 1959

There'll Be a Yankee Christmas   Webster 1945

There'll Be Life, Love, and Laughter   Gershwin, Ira 1945; Weill 1945

There'll Be More than Sleighbells Ringing when the Snow Falls   Lewis 1912

There'll Be Mournin' in the Mornin'   Spina 1951

There'll Be No South   Brown, Lew 1935

There'll Be Other Friday Nights   Sherman 1978

There'll Be Other Nights   Brown, Lew 1939; Pollack 1939

There'll Be Some Blues Tomorrow   Bergman 1964

There'll Be Something Doing when the War's Over   Silver 1918

There'll Be Sunshine for You and For Someone You Are Waiting For   Dubin 1918; Monaco 1918

There'll Be the Devil to Pay   Hoffman 1937; Lerner, Sammy 1937

There'll Be Time   Bergman 1976

There'll Be Trouble   Weill 1947

There'll Be You and I   Stept 1929

There'll Come a Day   Bryan 1908; Harburg 1945; Kern 1945; Snyder 1908

There'll Come a Time   Hammerstein 1938; Kahn 1926

There'll Come a Time When You'll Need Me   Mills 1953; Waller 1953

There'll Never Be Another Girl Like Mary This Side of Paradise   Rose 1930

There'll Never Be Another Girl Like You   Friend 1933; Magidson 1933

There'll Never Be Another Mary   Ager 1930; Yellen 1930

There's a Barber in the Harbor of Palermo   David, Mack 1947; Hoffman 1947; Livingston, Jay 1948; Livingston, Jerry 1947

There's a Bell that Rings in My Heart, Ding, Ding   Adams 1953; Strouse 1953

There's a Big Blue Cloud Next to Heaven   Drake 1943

There's a Bit of Paree in You   Gorney 1934, 1935

There's a Bit of Silver Lining Under Every Cloud of Grey   Yellen 1920

There's a Bluebird at My Window (And a Landlord at My Door)   Gordon 1933; Revel 1933

There's a Bluebird in the Weeping Willow   Wrubel 1944

There's a Boat dat's Leavin' Soon for New York   Gershwin, George 1935; Gershwin, Ira 1935

There's a Boatman on the Volga   Egan 1926; Whiting 1926

There's a Boy in Harlem   Hart 1938; Rodgers 1938

There's a Brand New Beat in Heaven   Adams 1981; Strouse 1981

There's a Brand New Hero   Harbach 1917

There's a Brand New Picture in My Picture Frame   Friend 1938

There's a Brighter Day on the Way   Davis 1950; Silver 1950

There's a Broken Heart for Every Light on Broadway   Fisher 1915; Johnson, Howard 1915

There's a Building Boom   Rainger 1938; Robin 1938

There's a Building Going Up   Fain 1950; Webster 1950

There's a Bunch of Klucks in the Ku Klux Klan   Coslow 1921

There's a Change in Me   Coleman 1964; Leigh 1984

There's a Chicken Dinner Waiting for Me   Williams 1905

There's a Chill in the Air   Lane 1935; Washington 1935

There's a City on a Hill By the Sea   Merrill 1950

There's a Coach Comin' In   Lerner, Alan Jay 1951; Loewe 1951

There's a Convent by the Beautiful Sea   Clarke 1915; Fisher 1915

There's a Corner Up in Heaven   Berlin 1921

There's a Corny Little Corner in the Corner of My Heart   Dixon 1953; Henderson 1955; Rose 1953

There's a Cottage in Killarney   Dixon 1934; Wrubel 1934

There's a Country   Gorney 1958

There's a Cozy Little Cottage Down the Lane   Spina 1932

There's a Cradle in Caroline   Ahlert 1927; Lewis 1927; Young, Joe 1927

There's a Cross in the Argonne   Pollack 1934; Webster 1934

There's a Diff'rent You in Your Heart   Fain 1935; Kahal 1935

There's a Dixie Girl Who's Longing for a Yankee Doodle Boy   Meyer 1911

There's a Fan   Porter 1938

There's a Feeling in the Air   Mancini 1975

There's a Fella Waitin' in Poughkeepsie   Arlen 1944; Mercer 1944

There's a Flaw in My Flue   Burke 1958; Van Heusen 1958

There's a Fly on My Music   Brown, Lew 1943; Fain 1943; Freed, Ralph 1943

There's a Fool Born Every Day   Dubin 1916
There's a Four Star Moon Tonight   Coots 1935; Parish 1935
There's a Friendly Feeling in the Air   Davis 1961
There's a Friendly House   Davis 1936; Hanley 1936
There's a Girl in Arizona   Berlin 1913; Clarke 1913; Leslie 1913
There's a Girl in Chateau Thierry   Goetz 1919
There's a Girl in Havana   Berlin 1911; Goetz 1911; Snyder 1911
There's a Girl in the Heart of Maryland (With a Heart that Belongs to Me)   Carroll 1913
There's a Girl in the Heart of Wheeling, West Virginia (With a Watch that Belongs to Me)   Ruby 1966
There's a Girl in the World for Every Boy   Edwards 1939
There's a Girl in the World for Ev'ry Boy   Cobb 1942
There's a Girl Up in the Moon   Jerome 1910; Schwartz, Jean 1910
There's a Good Time Comin'   Yellen 1932
There's a Grace in Each Leaf of the Shamrock   Fisher 1920
There's a Great Big Beautiful Tomorrow   Sherman 1964
There's a Great Big Welcome in a Little Home Sweet Home   Henderson 1923
There's a Great Day Coming Manana   Harburg 1940; Lane 1940
There's a Green Pasture in the Blue Heaven   Hoffman 1939
There's a Happy Heart in Maryland and a Broken Heart in Brittany   Bryan 1919; Fisher Date Unknown; Schwartz, Jean 1919
There's a Happy Hunting Ground   Coslow 1938, 1941
There's a Happy Land in the Sky   Porter 1943
There's a Heart in Virginia for You   Sterling 1917
There's a Hill Beyond a Hill   Hammerstein 1932; Kern 1932
There's a Hollywood that's Good   Porter 1955
There's a Home in the Mountain   Adamson 1936
There's a House in Harlem for Sale   Van Heusen 1934
There's a Hundred Million Stars in the Star Spangled Banner   Davis 1945
There's a Joy that Steals Upon You   Hammerstein 1934; Kern 1934
There's a Kick in the Old Girl Yet   Fields 1930; McHugh 1930
There's a Kiss in Your Eyes   Howard, Joseph E. 1955
There's a Little Bit of Bad in Every Good Little Girl   Clarke 1916; Fisher 1916
There's a Little Bit of Devil in Your Angel Eyes   Coots 1932
There's a Little Bit of Everything on Broadway   Atteridge 1915
There's a Little Bit of Heaven in Hawaii   Edwards 1937
There's a Little Bit of Irish in Sadie Cohn   Bryan 1916
There's a Little Bit of Irish in the Rainbow   Hanley 1930
There's a Little Bit of Scotch in Me   Razaf 1941
There's a Little Bit of Something   Kahn 1923
There's a Little Bit of Spain in California   Freed, Arthur 1925
There's a Little Bit of Yes in Ev'ry Little Girl's No   Lewis 1922; Meyer 1922; Young, Joe 1922
There's a Little Bit of You (In Every Love Song)   Fain 1933; Harburg 1933
There's a Little Lane Without a Turning on the Way to Home Sweet Home   Meyer 1915; Young, Joe 1915
There's a Little Lane without a Turning the Way to Home Sweet Home   Lewis 1915
There's a Little Lost Dream   Warren Date Unknown
There's a Little Picture Playhouse in My Heart   Leslie 1935
There's a Little Side Door to Heaven   Lewis 1932
There's a Little Spark of Love Still Burning   Fisher 1914

There's a Little White House and a Little White Lady   Donaldson 1923; Johnson, Howard 1923
There's a Little White House (Where the Red Red Roses Grow)   Akst 1926; Rose 1926
There's a Lonesome Little Girl in the Lone Star State of Texas   Fisher 1921
There's a Lot of Blue-Eyed Mary's Down in Maryland   Ager 1919; Meyer 1919; Yellen 1919
There's a Lot of Little Boy in Every Grown Up Man   Yellen 1978
There's a Lot of Pretty Little Things in Paris   Goetz 1913
There's a Lot of Things that Noah Never Knew   Goetz 1907
There's a Lovely Crop of Girlies This Year   Norworth 1917
There's a Lovely Crop of Girls This Year   Norworth 1916
There's a Lucky Guy   Rainger 1933; Robin 1933
There's a Lull in My Life   Gordon 1937; Revel 1937
There's a Lump of Sugar Down in Dixie   Bryan 1918; Yellen 1918
There's a Man in My Life   Waller 1943
There's a Meeting in the Old Town Hall   Sterling 1901
There's a Message of Love in Your Eyes   Herbert 1915
There's a Method in My Madness   Adamson 1935; Donaldson 1935
There's a Method to My Madness (And My Madness Is You)   Pollack 1934; Webster 1934
There's a Mile Between the Ess-Es in Smiles   Sigman 1949
There's a Million Girlies Lonesome Tonight (And Still I'm All Alone)   Hanley 1921
There's a Million Heroes in Each Corner of the U.S.A.   Lewis 1917; Young, Joe 1917
There's a Million Little Cupids in the Sky   Blake 1924; Sissle 1924
There's a Million Reasons Why I Shouldn't Kiss You, but I Can't Think of One   Sterling 1917; Von Tilzer 1917
There's a Million Ways to Say I Love You   Ager 1932; Lewis 1932
There's a Miss I Want To Kiss On the O-Hi-O   Bryan 1926; Fisher 1926
There's a Mist on the Mountains This Morning   Dixon 1938; Woods 1938
There's a Mist Upon the Meadow   David, Mack 1947
There's a New Bird this Year in Last Year's Nest   Stept 1952
There's a New Day Comin'   Ager 1933; Young, Joe 1933
There's a New Deal on the Way   David, Mack 1973; Livingston, Jerry 1973
There's a New Flag on Iwo Jima   Adamson 1945; McHugh 1945
There's a New Gang on the Corner Where the Old Gang Used to Be   Motzan 1932
There's a New Gang on the Way   Rose 1940; Van Heusen 1940
There's a New Moon Over My Shoulder   Dubin 1933; Fain 1933
There's a New Moon Over the Old Corral   Kahn 1940
There's a New Moon (Over the Old Mill)   Magidson 1938; Wrubel 1938
There's a New Moon Shining Through the Old Apple Tree   Egan 1931; Kahn 1931; Whiting 1931
There's a New Star in Heaven Tonight   Brennan 1926; McHugh 1926; Mills 1926
There's a New World A-Comin'   Coots 1946
There's a Party Going On Somewhere   Adams 1964; Strouse 1964
There's a Place Called Omaha, Nebraska   Ruby 1952
There's a Place in the Sun for You   Fain 1928

There's a Quaint Little Country Garden   Norworth 1927

There's a Raft of Money in Graft! Graft! Graft!   Herbert 1911

There's a Rainbow on the Moon   Washington 1956

There's a Rainbow on the River   Stept 1932; Young, Joe 1932

There's a Rainbow on the Way   Coots 1929; Davis 1929

There's a Rainbow 'Round My Shoulder   Rose 1928

There's a Reason for Me Being in Love with You   Akst 1927; Davis 1927

There's a Reason (inst.)   Warren Date Unknown

There's a Reason It's Because I Love You   Coslow 1921

There's a Resting Place for Every Girl (Sun Chair Song)   Kern 1911

There's a Right Time   Robison 1960

There's a Ring Around My Rainbow   Dixon 1933

There's a Ring Around the Moon   Bryan 1911; Lewis 1931; Mercer 1933

There's a Riot in Havana   Hammerstein 1935; Romberg 1935

There's a Rising Moon (For Every Falling Star)   Fain 1955; Revel 1959; Webster 1948, 1955, 1959

There's a Robin 'Round the Corner Singin' La-Da-Da-Da-Dee   Coots 1939

There's a Romeo for Every Girl I Know   Stept 1920

There's a Shadow Between Us   Livingston, Jerry 1955; Parish 1955

There's a Shadow in the Sunshine of Your Smile   Ahlert 1935; Young, Joe 1935

There's a Small Hotel   Hart 1936; Rodgers 1936

There's a Smile in Your Eyes (Va Sonrie el Amor)   Sigman 1946

There's a Smile on My Face   Berlin 1935

There's a Soul Mate Somewhere   Herbert 1911; Smith, Harry B. 1911

There's a Spot 'Neath the Sun for Everyone   Edwards 1935; Johnson, Howard 1935

There's a Sucker Born Every Minute   Coleman 1980

There's a Sunbeam for Every Drop of Rain   Johnson, Howard 1921

There's a Sunny Side to Every Situation   Mercer 1938; Warren 1938

There's a Sunny Side to Everything   Coots 1938; Davis 1938

There's a Sweet Wind Blowin' My Way   Arlen 1957

There's a Tear for Every Smile in Hollywood   Stept 1930

There's a Tender Look in Your Eyes   Herbert 1920; Smith, Robert B. 1920

There's a Time   Warren 1960

There's a Time and Place for Everything   Ahlert 1931; Turk 1931

There's a Twinkle in Your Eye, Madame   Stept 1936; Washington 1936

There's a Typical Tipperary Over Here   Silver 1920

There's a Vacant Chair at Home Sweet Home (When the World Goes Back on You)   Hanley 1920

There's a Vacant Chair for Will Rogers in Every Home Tonight   Parish 1935

There's a Vacant Chair in Every Home Tonight   Bryan 1917

There's a Village in a Valley   Parish 1938; Silver 1938

There's a Wah Wah Gal in Agua Caliente   Donaldson 1930

There's a Wee Bit of Blarney in Killarney   Ager 1915; Gilbert 1915

There's a Whistle in the Thistle   Freed, Ralph 1935; Washington 1935

There's a Wireless Station Down in My Heart   Monaco 1913

There's a Wise Old Moon that Shines in Loveland and He Knows the Old Love Game   Meyer 1916

There's a World of Beauty in You   Lewis 1919; Schwartz, Jean 1919; Young, Joe 1919

There's a World Out There   Sigman 1968

There's Ain't No Sweet Man That's Worth the Salt of My Tears   Fisher 1929

There's Always a Girl Who Is Waiting   Atteridge 1913

There's Always a Happy Ending   Hoffman 1936

There's Always a Rain Check for a Lovely Day   Brown, Lew 1951; Henderson 1951

There's Always a Song in an Irish Heart   Brennan 1921

There's Always a Way to Remember (But I Can't Find a Way to Forget)   Fain 1927; Pollack 1927

There's Always a Woman   Sondheim 1964

There's Always My Heart   Sigman 1951

There's Always One Day More   Leigh 1956

There's Always One You Can't Forget   Atteridge 1918; Lerner, Alan Jay 1983; Romberg 1918; Strouse 1983

There's Always Room at Our House   Merrill 1951

There's Always Room for a Smile   Gorney 1924

There's Always Room for One More   Hammerstein 1919, 1920; Rodgers 1919

There's Always Somebody Else   Davis 1932

There's Always Something Wrong   Johnson, J. Rosamond 1907

There's Always the Blues   Burke 1958

There's Always Tomorrow   Cahn 1976; Hoffman 1933; Silver 1933

There's an Awful Lot of Yes in the Way You Say No   Adams 1963; Strouse 1963

There's an Empty Stool at the End of the Bar   Robison 1949

There's an Old Corral in Heaven   Coots 1945

There's an Old Oaken Bucket in Old Nantucket   Bryan 1922

There's Another Little Wrinkle on Her Brow   Ahlert 1935; Young, Joe 1935

There's April in My Heart   Carmichael 1937

There's Beauty Everywhere   Freed, Arthur 1946; Warren 1946

There's Been Some Changes Made (Since You've Been Gone)   Razaf 1928

There's Champagne in Your Eyes   Stept 1935; Washington 1935

There's Comp'ny in the Parlor   Fisher 1910; Goetz 1910

There's Danger in a Dance   Rainger 1943; Robin 1943

There's Danger in Dancing   Robin 1946

There's Dust on the Trail   Cahn 1937

There's Enough to Go Around   Bergman 1969; Mancini 1969

There's Frost on the Moon, Spring in My Heart   Ahlert 1936; Young, Joe 1936

There's Gold in Monterey   Rainger 1936; Robin 1936

There's Gold in the Sky   Snyder 1930

There's Gold in Them Thar Hills   Cahn 1964; Van Heusen 1964

There's Gold on the Trees   David, Mack 1973; Livingston, Jerry 1973

There's Gotta Be a Wedding   De Lange 1939; Van Heusen 1939

There's Gotta Be Something Better than This   Coleman 1966; Fields 1966

There's Happiness   Snyder 1929

There's Happiness Over the Hill   Silver 1930

There's Honey on the Moon Tonight   Coots 1938; David, Mack 1938

There's Just a Little Bit of Monkey Still Left in You and Me   Clarke 1916; Monaco 1916

There's Just One Girl I'd Like to Marry   Herbert 1907; Smith, Harry B. 1907

There's Just One Thing to Say   Drake 1954

There's Laughter After Tears (There's Laughter After the Blues)   Evans 1946; Livingston, Jay 1946

There's Life in the Old Dog Yet   Atteridge 1925

There's Life in Your Eyes Tonight   Friend 1936

There's Lots More Where This Came From   David, Hal 1962

There's Lots of Room for You   Dietz 1924; Kern 1924

There's Love and There's Love and There's Love   Cahn 1965; Van Heusen 1965

There's Love in My Heart for You   Coots 1936; Davis 1936

There's Love in the Air   Fields 1931; McHugh 1931

There's Love in the Heart I Hold   Brennan 1929

There's Love in Your Eyes   Johnson, Howard 1929

There's Magic in the Air   Gershwin, George 1918; Gershwin, Ira 1918

There's Magic in the Cup (A Cup of Tea)   Hart 1928; Rodgers 1928

There's Magic in the Name of the Palace   Davis 1967

There's More to Dreams Than Just Dreaming   Lane Date Unknown

There's More to Life   Cahn 1965; Van Heusen 1965

There's More to the Kiss than the Sound   Caesar 1919; Gershwin, George 1919

There's Music in a Kiss   Silver 1935

There's Music in My Heart, Cherie   Hanley 1937

There's Music in that Boy   Adams 1964; Strouse 1964

There's Music in the Air   Sterling 1902

There's Music in the Air (inst.)   Motzan 1916

There's Music in the Land   Cahn 1948; Styne 1948

There's Music in the Metro   Martin 1951

There's Music in You   Hammerstein 1953; Rodgers 1953

There's Mutiny in Baby's Eyes Tonight   Stept 1950

There's Never Been Anyone Else but You   Webster 1956

There's Never Been Anything Like Us   Lerner, Alan Jay 1983; Strouse 1983

There's No Better Use for Time than Kissing   Kern 1918

There's No Cure Like Travel   Porter 1934

There's No Depression in Love   Yellen 1931

There's No End to My Love for You   Dubin 1918; Monaco 1918

There's No Forgetting You   Loesser 1941

There's No Getting Away from You   Adamson 1948; McHugh 1948

There's No Greater Fan than a Met Fan   Davis 1969

There's No Greater Sound than Da, Da, Da, Da, Da, Da   Cahn 1980; Strouse 1980

There's No Harm in Hoping   Woods 1933

There's No Holding Me   Gershwin, Ira 1946; Schwartz, Arthur 1946

There's No Hotel Like the Algonquin   Strouse 1987

There's No Light in the Window of the House on the Hill   Young, Victor 1932

There's No Love Like   Cahn 1966; Van Heusen 1966

There's No Man Like a Snowman   Heyman 1950; Young, Victor 1950

There's No More Harmony at Home Sweet Home   Lewis 1917; Snyder 1917; Young, Joe 1917

There's No More Regular Kids   Cobb 1917; Edwards 1917

There's No One As Sweet As Trilby   Brennan 1927

There's No One Like You   Evans 1961; Livingston, Jay 1961

There's No One Livin' Gonna Break My Heart   Young, Joe 1932

There's No Other Girl, After Loving You   Davis 1931

There's No Place As Grand As Bandanaland   Blake 1924; Sissle 1924

There's No Place Like Home   Cahn 1968

There's No Place Like the Lambs   Stept 1953

There's No Song Like an Old Song   Akst 1948; Gilbert 1948

There's No Substitute for a Man   Arlen 1954; Dietz 1954

There's No Such Word as "Can't"   Blane 1961

There's No Tomorrow   Hoffman 1951

There's No Two Ways About It   Adamson 1937; Conrad 1936; McHugh 1937

There's No Two Ways About Love   Johnson, James P. 1943; Koehler 1943; Mills 1943

There's Nobody Else but Elsie   Wrubel 1948

There's Nobody Else but You   Gilbert 1923

There's Nobody Home but Me   Conrad 1918

There's Nobody Richer than Me   Davis 1953

There's Not a Chance in the World   Kahn 1927

There's Not a Girl, In All This World That Won't Have Me   Edwards 1908

There's Not a Rock on the Road to California   Johnson, Howard 1930

There's Not Another Girlie in the World Like You   Jerome 1907; Schwartz, Jean 1907

There's Not Enough Gold to Buy Him   Bryan 1906

There's Nothin' Like Love   Robin 1955; Styne 1955

There's Nothin' Papa's Doin' that Mama Ain't Did   Razaf 1946

There's Nothin' Rougher than Love   Cahn 1949; Styne 1949

There's Nothin' So Bad for a Woman   Hammerstein 1945; Rodgers 1945

There's Nothin' That Love Won't Cure   Hoffman 1930

There's Nothing Doing in the Old, Old Town   Jerome 1905; Schwartz, Jean 1905

There's Nothing Else to Do in Ma-La-Ka-Mo-Ka-Lu   Friend 1934; Mitchell 1934

There's Nothing Left for Daddy (But the Rhumba)   Lerner, Alan Jay 1948; Weill 1948

There's Nothing Left to Do   Cahn 1959; Van Heusen 1959

There's Nothing Like a College Education   Mercer 1935

There's Nothing Like a Good Old Song   Howard, Joseph E. 1937

There's Nothing Like a Hoedown   Styne 1941

There's Nothing Like a Marching Band   Bergman 1958

There's Nothing Like a Model T   Cahn 1947; Styne 1947

There's Nothing Like a Song   Gordon 1947; Myrow 1947

There's Nothing Like an Old Fashioned Waltz   Stept 1934; Washington 1934

There's Nothing Like It   Bullock 1950

There's Nothing Like Marriage for People   Gershwin, Ira 1946; Schwartz, Arthur 1946

There's Nothing Like Staying Alive   Caesar 1954

There's Nothing Like Swimming   Porter 1935

There's Nothing Like This Old Fashioned   Duke 1955

There's Nothing Like Travel   Burke 1946; Van Heusen 1946

There's Nothing Lovelier than You   Spina 1947

There's Nothing New in I Love You   Davis 1933; Oakland 1933

There's Nothing New in Old New York   Akst 1927; Davis 1927

There's Nothing Nicer than People   Rome 1952

There's Nothing Sweeter than a Girl from Dixieland   Clarke 1917; Monaco 1917

There's Nothing the Matter With Me   Brown, Lew 1932; Henderson 1932

There's Nothing the Matter with Me (You)   Herbert 1908; Smith, Harry B. 1908

There's Nothing too Fine for the Finest   Herbert 1919

There's Nothing Too Good for My Baby   Akst 1931; Davis 1931

There's Nothing Wrong in a Kiss   Caesar 1930

There's Nothing Wrong with Marriage   Duke 1963

There's Nowhere to Go but Up   Weill 1938

There's Oceans of Love By the Beautiful Sea   Coots 1932

There's One California for Mine   Bryan 1915

There's One in a Million Like You   Clarke 1912; Schwartz, Jean 1912

There's One Lane that Has No Turning   Blake 1926; Sissle 1926

There's One Little Girl Who Loves Me   Kahn 1927; Whiting 1927

There's One Thing a Wizard Can Do   Herbert 1895; Smith, Harry B. 1895

There's Only a Few of Us Left   Davis 1962

There's Only One Little Girl   Cohan 1916

There's Only One Little Old New York   Schwartz, Jean 1905

There's Only One Mary in Maryland   Whiting 1915

There's Only One that I Would Loose My Sleep for, and That's for Daddy   Monaco 1919

There's Only One Thing to Do   Friml 1919; Harbach 1919

There's Only One (Who Matters to Me)   Baer 1930; Gilbert 1930

There's Only One Who Rules My House   Romberg 1915

There's Plenty of Fish in the Ocean   Brooks 1953

There's Ragtime in the Air   Buck 1916

There's Rain in My Eyes   Ager 1938; Schwartz, Jean 1938; Yellen Date Unknown

There's Religion in Rhythm   Robison 1930

There's Rhythm in the River   Webster 1931

There's Rhythm in Them Thar Hills   Freed, Ralph 1937

There's Romance in the Air   Meyer 1932; Young, Joe 1932

There's Room Enough for Us   DePaul 1956; Mercer 1956

There's Room for Her   Duke 1963

There's Room in My Heart for Them All   Koehler 1947

There's So Much More   Hart 1931; Rodgers 1931

There's Somebody Else on Your Mind   Whiting 1928

There's Somebody for Ev'rybody (But Me)   Coslow 1926; Silver 1926

There's Somebody New   Kahn 1928

There's Someone Dreaming Tonight   Donaldson 1934; Kahn 1934

There's Someone in Your Family I'm Crazy About   Fain 1934; Kahal 1934

There's Someone Missing in the Picture   Woods 1960

There's Someone More Lonesome than You   Von Tilzer 1916

There's Someone You've Forgotten who Has not Forgotten You   Yellen 1916

There's Somethin' Mighty Peculiar Goin' On   DePaul 1956; Mercer 1956

There's Something About a Horse   Evans 1961; Livingston, Jay 1961

There's Something about a Rose   Fain 1928; Kahal 1928; Kahn 1919

There's Something About a Uniform   Cohan 1909

There's Something About a Uniform that Makes the Ladies Fall   Silver 1918

There's Something about America   Caesar 1946

There's Something about an Old Love   Mills 1938

There's Something About Me They Like   Gershwin, Ira 1921; Youmans 1921

There's Something About Midnight   Robin 1947

There's Something About Paree   Davis 1949; Silver 1949

There's Something About the Climate   Akst 1934

There's Something About You   Atteridge 1914, 1918; Carroll 1914; Romberg 1914, 1918; Smith, Harry B. 1927

There's Something About You that Appeals to Me   Smith, Harry B. 1911

There's Something Funny Going On   Bergman 1979

There's Something in a Big Parade   Washington 1935

There's Something in My Eye and I Can't Get It Out   Howard, Joseph E. 1942

There's Something in My Heart   Hoffman 1943; Livingston, Jerry 1943

There's Something in Sympathy   Coots 1926

There's Something in That   Eliscu 1929

There's Something in the Air   Adamson 1936; McHugh 1936

There's Something in the Air in Springtime   Buck 1914

There's Something in the Name of Ireland (That the Whole World Seems to Love)   Ager 1917; Johnson, Howard 1917

There's Something Magic Saying "Nitchevo"   Freed, Ralph 1939

There's Something Missing in the Movies   Atteridge 1915

There's Something Missing in Your Eyes   Gilbert 1930

There's Something New 'bout the Old Moon Tonight   Hoffman 1928; Mills 1928

There's Something Nice About Everyone, but There's Everything Nice About You   Bryan 1927

There's Something Nice About the South   Berlin 1917

There's Something Rather Odd about Augustus   Kern 1908

There's Something Spanish in Your Eyes   Caesar 1926, 1929; Friend 1926, 1929

There's Something to Be Thankful For   Young, Joe 1932

There's Still a Boy in Every Man   Styne 1985

There's that Look in Your Eyes Again   Gordon 1936; Revel 1936

(I Says to Myself Says I) There's the One for Me   Akst 1929; Yellen 1929

There's Too Many Eyes   Coots 1929; Davis 1929

There's Trouble Brewin'   Spina 1944

There's Two Sides to Ev'ry Story   Ahlert 1936; Young, Joe 1936

There's Yes in the Air   Waller 1943

There's Yes, Yes in Your Eyes   Friend 1924

There's "Yoo Hoo" in Your Eyes   Baer 1936

These Are My United States   Livingston, Jerry 1963

These Are the Good Old Days   Ellington 1966

These Are the Things I Remember   Washington 1953

These Are the Times   Eliscu 1943; Gorney 1943

These Charming People   Gershwin, George 1925; Gershwin, Ira 1925

These Colors Will Not Run   Carroll 1918

These Days   Gershwin, Ira 1949; Warren 1949

These Eyes Have Seen Too Much   Merrill 1972; Styne 1972

These Hands   Spina 1976

These Little Mem'ries   Livingston, Jerry 1963

These Lush Moments   Burke 1958; Van Heusen 1958

These Orchids   Kern 1942; Mercer 1942

These Patient Years   Fain 1946; Freed, Ralph 1946

These Precious Moments   Ager 1938; Yellen Date Unknown

These Things Are Mine   Coots 1955

These Things I Know Are True   Adams 1960; Strouse 1956, 1960

These Thousand Hills   Warren 1959; Washington 1959

These Tropics   Hammerstein 1931; Romberg 1931

Thessaly   Smith, Harry B. 1906

They   Russell 1962

They Ain't Done Right By Our Nell   Porter 1940

They All Fall in Love   Porter 1929

They All Follow Me   Cohan 1908

They All Had a Finger in the Pie   Von Tilzer 1914

They All Had a Photograph of You   Brown, Lew 1915

They All Kept Time with Their Feet   Edwards 1912

They All Kissed the Bride   David, Hal 1951

They All Laughed   Gershwin, George 1937; Gershwin, Ira 1937

They All Lived Happily Ever After   Cahn 1958

They All Look Alike   Kern 1917

They All Look Good to Me   Goetz 1916

They All Look Good when They're Far Away   Herbert 1911; Smith, Harry B. 1911

They All Miss You Just Like I Do   Johnson, Howard 1926

They All Need a Little Hot-Cha   Brown, Lew 1932; Henderson 1932

They All Remind Me of You   Friend 1925

They All Took a Lesson from Me   Evans 1955; Livingston, Jay 1955

They All Want to Goo-Goo Again   Fisher 1917

They Always Blame the Caddy   Edwards 1923; Smith, Robert B. 1923

They Always Follow Me   Jerome 1908; Schwartz, Jean 1908

They Always Follow Me Around   Berlin 1914

They Always Pick on Me   Von Tilzer 1911

They Always Run a Little Faster   Caesar 1924; Conrad 1924; Harbach 1924

They Are Angels Without Wings   Smith, Harry B. 1903

They Are Hypnotized   Cohan 1903

They Are Nothing but Girls   Smith, Harry B. 1900

They Ask Me Why I Believe in You   Sondheim Date Unknown

They Begged Me   Drake 1957

They Blew Themselves Out of Breath   Clare 1937

They Call It Dancing   Berlin 1921

They Call Me Carpenter   Motzan 1922

They Call the Wind Maria   Lerner, Alan Jay 1951; Loewe 1951

They Came to Cordura   Cahn 1959; Van Heusen 1959

They Can See Your Name in My Eyes   Carmichael 1958

(They May Change the Name of Ireland, But) They Can't Change Those Irish Eyes   Bryan 1945

They Can't Fool Me   DeSylva 1918

They Can't Get You Down   Eliscu 1941; Gorney 1941

They Can't Keep You Down   DePaul 1944; Raye 1944

They Can't Make Her Cry   David, Mack 1965; Livingston, Jerry 1965

They Can't Ration Love   Howard, Joseph E. 1964

They Can't Repeal My Love for You   Johnson, Howard 1933

They Can't Take That Away from Me   Gershwin, George 1937; Gershwin, Ira 1937

They Come, They Come   Dietz 1927; Gorney 1927

They Couldn't Compare to You   Porter 1950

They Couldn't Have Picked a Better Night   Drake 1952

They Cut Down the Old Pine Tree   Eliscu 1929

They Dance All Night (Sleep All Day)   Raye 1957

They Didn't Believe Me   Kern 1914

They Didn't Think We'd Do It, But We Did   Dubin 1920

They Died with Their Boots Laced   DePaul 1943; Raye 1943

They Don't Give Medals (To Yesterday's Heroes)   Bacharach 1966; David, Hal 1966

They Don't Grow Them Anymore Like You   Edwards 1937

They Don't Hesitate Any More   Kalmar 1914; Leslie 1914

They Don't Look the Same in the Morning   Freed, Arthur 1925

They Don't Make 'em Like That Anymore   Martin 1964, 1972

They Don't Make 'Em Like They Used To   Bacharach 1986

They Don't Make 'Em That Way Any More   Gershwin, Ira 1924

They Don't Make Them Like That Any More   Leigh 1965

They Don't Make Them That Way Any More   Yellen 1919

They Don't Play the Piano Anymore   Hoffman 1954

They Dream of Each Other All Night   Clarke 1915; Johnson, Howard 1915

They Fall in Love   Cohan 1928

They Follow Me Around   Smith, Harry B. 1934

They Follow Me Everywhere   Herbert 1911

They Get Me All Fussed Up   Brown, Lew 1917

They Go Wild Simply Wild Over Me   Fisher 1917

They Got This Little Secret   Sondheim 1968

They Had to Get the Rhythm Out of Their Souls   Blake 1958; Sissle 1958

They Had to Swim Back to the Shore   Monaco 1914

They Handed Me You   Comden and Green 1972

They Hear Drums   Sondheim 1994

They Just Chopped Down the Old Apple Tree   Adamson 1943; McHugh 1943

They Laughed at Him in His Home Town   Brown, Lew 1942; Stept 1942

They Learn About Woman from Me   Arlen 1931; Yellen 1931

They Like Ike   Berlin 1950

They Long to Be Close to You   Bacharach 1963; David, Hal 1963

They Look to Us   Adams 1996; Strouse 1996

They Looked So Pretty on the Envelope   Eliscu 1943; Gorney 1943

They Love Me   Berlin 1962

They Made It Twice As Nice As Paradise and Called It Dixieland   Egan 1916; Whiting 1916

They May Be Old, But They want to Be Loved   Silver 1919

They Met in Rio (A Midnight Serenade)   Gordon 1941; Warren 1941

They Never Told Me   Duke 1950; Rome 1950

They Obviously Want Me to Sing   Evans 1951; Livingston, Jay 1951

They Ought to Write a Book about You   Burke 1939; Van Heusen 1939

They Pass By Singing   Gershwin, George 1935

They Really Don't You Know   McHugh 1960

They Satisfy   Kahn 1930

They Say   David, Mack 1962; Ellington 1958; Heyman 1939

They Say I Oughta Dance   Cahn 1938

They Say It's Wonderful   Berlin 1946

They Say They're Not Living Together   Brown, A. Seymour 1913

They Say You're Laughing at Me (While I'm Crying for You)   Livingston, Jerry 1954

They Sing! They Dance! They Speak!   Hart 1929; Rodgers 1929

They Start in to Battle Again   Brown, Lew 1914; Leslie 1914

They Still Look Good to Me   Conrad 1925

They Talk a Different Language (The Yodel Blues)   Mercer 1949

They Told Me   Cahn 1981

They Went That-a-Way   Cahn 1958; Van Heusen 1958

They Went to Get Married   Brooks 1945

They Were Actors Then   Smith, Harry B. 1908

They Were All Out of Step but Jim   Berlin 1918

They Were Doin' the Mambo   Raye 1954

They Were Irish   Herbert 1908; Smith, Harry B. 1908

They Weren't Any Better in the Good Old Days   Ager 1923; Yellen 1923

They Won't Know Me   Rome 1952

They Would Wind Him Up and He Would Whistle   Kalmar 1939; Ruby 1939

They'll All Be There but Me   Fain 1931; Kahal 1931

They'll Be Mighty Proud in Dixie of Their Old Black Joe   Carroll 1918

They'll Be Waiting for You at the Train   Williams 1908

They'll Be Whispering It All Over Town   Goetz 1917; Schwartz, Jean 1917

They'll Be Whistling It All Over Town   Goetz 1917

They'll Never Carry Me Back to Old Virginia   Pollack 1923

They'll Never Miss the Wine in Dixieland   Bryan 1920; Meyer 1920

They'll Never Split Us Apart   Adams 1966; Strouse 1966

They'll Never Take Us Alive   Adams 1993

They'll Soon Be Gone   Livingston, Jerry 1963

They'll Still Keep Dancing (Der Tanz Geht Waiter)   Ahlert 1930; Turk 1930

They're All Congratulatin' Me   Meyer 1933

They're All Good American Names   Jerome 1911; Schwartz, Jean 1911

They're All My Friends   Cohan 1904

They're All My Type (Just My Type)   Romberg 1919

They're All Sweeties   Sterling 1919; Von Tilzer 1919

They're Always Entertaining   Porter 1933

They're at the Post   Comden and Green 1964; Styne 1964

They're Blaming the Charleston   Berlin 1925

They're Coming Home   Carroll 1944

They're Countin' in the Mountains   Pollack 1943

They're Doin' the Square Dance in the Finest Circles   Stept 1949

They're Either Too Young or Too Old   Loesser 1943; Schwartz, Arthur 1943

They're Getting Shorter All the Time   Buck 1917

They're Gonna Love It   Bacharach 1966; David, Hal 1966

They're in the Junk Pile Now   Buck 1915

They're Making Them Wonderful   Hanley 1916, 1920

They're Not Doing that This Season   Smith, Harry B. 1909

They're Off and Runnin'   Spina 1957

They're on Their Honeymoon   Goetz 1913

They're on Their Way to Mexico   Berlin 1914

They're Playing Our Song   Drake 1949; Spina 1957

They're Smiling All Over and All Over Me   Dixon 1927; Woods 1927

They've All Got Tails but Me   Brooks 1960

They've Got Me Doin' It Now   Berlin 1913

They've Got the Loopiest Loop in Chicago   Drake 1953

They've Got Their Indian Habits on in Dixieland   Akst 1923; Lewis 1923; Meyer 1923; Young, Joe 1923

They've Got to Be Dreams to Start   Merrill 1953

They've Never Figured Out a Woman   Brooks 1949

Thief, The   Fisher 1922

Thief in the Night   Dietz 1935; Schwartz, Arthur 1935

Thief of Bagdad, The   Ager 1924; Freed, Ralph 1934; Yellen 1924

Thieves   Cahn 1976

Thieves Song, The   Brooks 1960

Thieving Stranger   Drake 1960

Thin   Yellen 1948

Thin Man, The   Cahn 1959

Thine Alone   Herbert 1917

Thine Eyes So Blue and Tender   Johnson, Howard 1939

Thing Operetta   Oakland 1960

Thing to Do, The   Robin 1927; Youmans 1927

Thingamabobs (inst.)   Willson 1934

Thing-A-Ma-Jig, The   Hoffman 1959

Things!   Arlen 1934; Gershwin, Ira 1934; Harburg 1934; Merrill 1959

Things a Girl Should Be, The   Styne 1970

Things Are Changing   Cahn Date Unknown; Styne Date Unknown

Things Are Coming My Way   Adamson 1938; McHugh 1936

Things Are Getting Better All the Day   Bryan 1915

Things Are Looking Up   Gershwin, George 1937; Gershwin, Ira 1937

Things Are So Different Now-A-Days   Howard, Joseph E. 1915

Things Go Bump in the Night   Harburg 1969

Things Have Changed   Carmichael 1946; Webster 1946

Things I Am Going to Do, The   Von Tilzer 1909

Things I Might Have Been   Sherman 1952

Things I Should Have Said, The   Alter 1940; Lawrence 1940, 1968

Things I Thought I'd Hate About You (Turned Out to Be the Things I Love), The   Robison 1960

Things I Want, The   Hammerstein 1937; Kern 1937

Things I Will Not Miss, The   Bacharach 1973; David, Hal 1973

Things Look Brighter Again   Coots 1933; Lewis 1933

Things Look So Diff'rent in the Moonlight   Heyman 1963

Things Look Wonderful Now   Davis 1929

Things Might Have Been So Diff'rent   Coots 1935; Lewis 1935

Things Money Cannot Buy (Things That Money Cannot Buy), The   Cahn 1958; Van Heusen 1958

Things That Cannot Be Explained   Friml 1923

Things That Happen Every Day   Williams 1907

Things that Money Can't Buy   Caesar 1930

Things That Most Appeal to Me (inst.), The   Kern 1946

Things They Don't Teach You in School   Freed, Ralph 1958

Things to Remember   Livingston, Jerry 1963

Things We Are Not Supposed to Know   Herbert 1907; Smith, Harry B. 1907

Things We Did Last Summer, The   Cahn 1946; Styne 1946

Things We Think We Are, The   Drake 1968

Things We Want the Most Are Hard To Get, The   Bryan 1929; Meyer 1929

Things with Strings   Friend 1960

Things You Must Not Do   Friml 1917

Think a Little Kindly of Me   Johnson, Howard 1931; Woods 1931

Think About Love   Bergman 1982

Think Beautiful   Lawrence 1964

Think Ginger Rogers   Leigh 1965

Think How It's Gonna Be   Adams 1970; Strouse 1970

Think How Many People Never Find Love   Styne 1953

Think It Over   Bryan 1914; David, Mack 1955; Dietz 1934; Herbert 1920; Schwartz, Arthur 1934

Think It Over Carefully   Cohan 1908
Think Love   Coleman 1972; Livingston, Jerry 1959
Think Lunch   Strouse 1999
Think of All the Nice Things He's Done   Hoffman 1957
Think of Me   Sigman 1940
Think of Me, I'll Be Thinking of You   Kahn 1931
Think of Me Kindly   Cahn 1954; Robison 1954
Think of Me Only With a Smile   Egan 1922
Think of Me When I Am Near Not When I'm Far
    Away   Bryan 1913
Think of My Reputation   Gordon 1932; Revel 1932
Think of Something Else   Cahn 1966; Van Heusen 1966
Think of You Think of Me in the Moonlight   Fields 1929;
    McHugh 1929
Think, Think, Think   Robison 1955
Think Twice   Bullock 1938; Hoffman 1952; Spina 1938
Think Well of Me   Robison 1941
Thinkability   Coleman 1960; Leigh 1960
Thinkin'   Hammerstein 1955; Rodgers 1955
Thinkin' About the Wabash   Bullock 1943; Cahn 1943; Styne
    1943
Thinkin' Bout Home (inst.)   Johnson, James P. 1943
Thinkin' Chair   Robison 1965
Thinkin' of You   Conrad 1926; Kahn 1926
Thinkin' Things   Merrill 1959
Thinking   Rodgers 1965; Sondheim 1965
Thinking It Over   Merrill 1959
Thinking of Me   Blake 1924; Sissle 1924
Thinking of You   Donaldson 1926; Kalmar 1927; Ruby 1927
Thinking of You All Night Long   Bryan 1934
Thinking Out Loud   Akst 1934; Brown, Lew 1934
Third Day Rag   Mercer 1955
Third Degree of Love, The   Hart 1920; Rodgers 1920
Third Finale   Weill 1933
Third from the Left   Bacharach 1958; David, Hal 1958
Third Letter   Sondheim 1994
Third March   Arlen 1959; Mercer 1959
Third Window from the Right, The   Bacharach 1961; David,
    Mack 1961
Thirteen Collar   Kern 1915
Thirteen Dola' on Fourteen   Hoffman 1956
Thirteen Is a Lucky Number   Rome 1973
13th Street Ray   Mercer 1949
Thirty Days Hath September   Carmichael 1957
Thirty Miles of Railroad Track   Bacharach 1961
Thirty One Flavors   David, Mack 1964
36-24-36   Evans 1959; Jerome 1910; Livingston, Jay 1959;
    McHugh 1959; Romberg 1948; Schwartz, Jean 1910;
    Strouse 1989
Thirty Two Bars of I Love You   Willson 1953
Thirty Weeks of Heaven   Fields 1954; Schwartz, Arthur 1954
Thirty-Five Summers Ago   Henderson 1943; Yellen 1943
Thirty-three Years   Livingston, Jerry 1960
This and No More   Bullock 1949; Spina 1953
This Angel of Old Devil's Inn   Bryan 1940
This Book   Robison 1964
This Can't Be Love   Hart 1938; Rodgers 1938
This Changes Everything   Wrubel 1945
This Changing World   Adamson 1939
This Christmas   Cahn 1944; Stept 1953; Styne 1944
This Concerto Has It   Willson 1956
This Could Be Forever   Ruby 1950
This Could Be Love   Coots 1951; Egan 1951
This Could Be the Night   Cahn 1957

This Could Go On for Years   Gershwin, George 1927;
    Gershwin, Ira 1927, 1929
This Could Have Been Mine   Evans 1967; Livingston, Jay
    1967
This Dreaming   Harbach 1943
This Earth Is Mine   Cahn 1959; Van Heusen 1959
This Empty Place   Bacharach 1963; David, Hal 1963
This Funny World   Hart 1926; Rodgers 1926
This Gentle Land   Adams 1972; Strouse 1972
This Gets Better Ev'ry Minute   Pollack 1943
This Goodbye   Webster 1983
This Great Big World Owed Me a Loving   Sterling 1916;
    Von Tilzer 1916
This Guy's in Love with You   Bacharach 1968; David, Hal
    1968
This Had Better Be Love   Gorney 1949
This Happy Feeling   Evans 1958; Livingston, Jay 1958
This Harry I'm Planning to Marry   Webster 1973
This Heart of Mine   Freed, Arthur 1946; Kalmar 1939; Ruby
    1939; Warren 1946
This House is Empty Now   Bacharach 1996
This I Love Above All   Ager 1944
This I Promise You   David, Hal 1954
This Is a Great Country   Berlin 1962
This Is a Happy Little Ditty   Bullock 1938; Spina 1938
This Is a Musical   Cahn 1963; Van Heusen 1963
This Is a Song   Cahn 1963; Van Heusen 1963
This Is a Tree   Burke 1950; Van Heusen 1950
This Is Always   Gordon 1946; Myrow 1946; Warren 1946
This Is America   Davis 1960
This Is an Unexpected Pleasure   Johnson, J. Rosamond 1934
This Is As Far As I Go   Lane 1945
This Is Caplan's   Styne 1978
This Is Forever (Theme for Love)   Young, Victor 1955
This Is Greater than I Thought   Evans 1954; Livingston, Jay
    1954
This Is Greece   Drake 1953
This Is Heaven   Akst 1929; Yellen 1929
This Is Home   David, Mack 1956; Evans 1973; Livingston,
    Jay 1973; Livingston, Jerry 1956
This Is How It Feels   Rodgers 1949
This Is It   Coslow 1957; David, Mack 1961; DePaul 1942;
    Fields 1939; Gordon 1944; Henderson 1943; Livingston,
    Jerry 1961; Monaco 1944; Raye 1942; Razaf 1949;
    Schwartz, Arthur 1939; Willson 1950; Yellen 1943
This Is June   Kahn 1927
This Is Laurie (inst.)   Young, Victor 1956
This is Love   Akst 1935; Brown, Lew 1935; Coots 1957;
    Freed, Ralph 1944
This Is Madness to Love Like This   De Lange 1938; Van
    Heusen 1938
This Is Magic   De Lange 1951
This Is Miami   Davis 1946
This Is My Beloved   Revel 1945
This Is My Country   Raye 1940
This Is My Dance   Egan 1925; Kahn 1925
This Is My Favorite City   Gordon 1947; Myrow 1947
This Is My Happiest Moment   Davis 1964
This Is My Holiday   Lerner, Alan Jay 1945; Loewe 1945
This Is My Love Song   Dubin 1932
This Is My Night to Dream   Burke 1938; Monaco 1938
This Is My Night to Howl   Hart 1943; Rodgers 1943
This Is My Night with Trixie   Gilbert 1949
This Is My Pray'r for Christmas   Cahn 1962
This Is My Show   Coots 1952

This Is My Song   Howard, Bart 1938; Kahn 1938
This Is My Story   Sigman 1935
This Is My Town   Brooks 1959
This Is My Wedding Day   Baer 1927; Lewis 1927; Young, Joe 1927
This Is My Year   Fisher 1935
This Is New   Gershwin, Ira 1940; Weill 1940
This Is New York   Davis 1942
This Is No Dream   Davis 1939
This Is No Place for Me   Brown, A. Seymour 1914
This Is not a Song   Duke 1934; Harburg 1934
This Is Not Going to Change My Life   Mancini 1995
This Is Not Goodbye   Cahn 1949
This Is Not Long Island (Opening, Act II)   Hart 1928; Rodgers 1928
This Is One of Those Moments   Bergman 1983; Dubin Date Unknown
This Is Only the Beginning   Arlen 1933; Koehler 1933
This Is Our Last Chance for Peace   Caesar 1946
This Is Our Last Night Together   Brown, Lew 1934; Gorney 1934
This Is Our Lucky Day   Brown, Nacio Herb 1944
This Is Our Private Love Song   Caesar 1943; Lerner, Sammy 1943
This Is Our Secret Star   Webster 1965
This Is Our Side of the Ocean   Cohan 1940
This Is Our War!   Rome 1942
This Is Romance   Duke 1932; Heyman 1932
This Is Show Biz   Sondheim Date Unknown
This Is So Nice   Waller 1943
This Is Spring, This Is Winter   Dubin 1940; McHugh 1940
This Is the Army, Mister Jones   Berlin 1942
This Is the Beginning of the End   Gordon 1940
This Is the Dance   Drake 1955
This Is the Day   Bryan 1919; Coleman 1978; Comden and Green 1978; Howard, Bart 1952; Schwartz, Jean 1919
This Is the Day for Love   Freed, Arthur 1945; Warren 1945
This Is the Day of Days   Dixon 1929; Woods 1929
This Is the End of Me Now   Egan 1920
This Is the Finale   Cahn 1950; Styne 1950
This Is the Haffner   Willson 1956
This Is the House that Love Built   De Lange 1941
This Is the Kiss   Bloom 1951
This Is the Kiss of Romance   Parish 1934
This Is the Life   Adams 1964; Berlin 1914; Lerner, Alan Jay 1948; Strouse 1964; Weill 1948
This Is the Missus   Brown, Lew 1931; Henderson 1931
This Is the Moment   Robin 1929, 1930, 1947; Whiting 1929, 1930
This Is the Moment (Russian Gypsy Song)   Robin 1954; Whiting 1954
This Is the Naked City   Washington 1958
This Is the Night   Brown, Nacio Herb 1934, 1935; Coots 1958; Coslow 1932, 1933; Freed, Arthur 1934; Lawrence 1938; Rainger 1932
This Is the Night of My Dreams   McHugh 1941; Mercer 1941
This Is the One   Livingston, Jerry 1956
This Is the Place (inst.)   Myrow 1966
This Is the Real Thing Now   Young, Joe 1932
This Is the Same Cafe   Wrubel 1958
This Is the Song   Willson 1956
This Is the Time (To Fall in Love)   Washington 1950; Young, Victor 1950
This Is the Year   Drake 1957

This Is What I Love   Adamson 1955; Lane 1955
This Is What I Want   Coleman 1972
This Is Where I Came In   Bullock 1938; Duke 1941; Spina 1938
This Is Wonderful, Just As It Is   Livingston, Jerry 1935
This Is Worth Fighting For   De Lange 1942; Stept 1942
This Is Your Chance   Gilbert 1942
This Is Your Life   Gilbert 1948
This Isn't Heaven   Rodgers 1962
This Kind of a Girl   Dietz 1961; Schwartz, Arthur 1961
This Land Is a Big Land   David, Hal 1973
This Life   Sigman 1951
This Life Alone   Oakland 1974
This Little Doll   Kalmar 1928; Ruby 1928
This Little Dream Was a Good Little Dream   David, Hal 1950
This Little Piggie Went to Market   Coslow 1933
This Little Ripple Had Rhythm (Mr. Ripple's Animation)   Rainger 1938; Robin 1938
This Little Song Went to Battle   Fain 1944; Freed, Ralph 1944
This Love   Brown, Lew 1957; Russell 1949
This Lovely Lassie   Drake 1954
This Lovely Night   Hammerstein 1933
This Man   Ellington 1958
This May Be the Night   Gordon 1938; Revel 1938
This May Be the Place   Hoffman 1956
This Much I Understand   Lawrence 1961
This Must Be Heaven   Kalmar 1937; Ruby 1937
This Must Be Illegal (It's So Nice)   Rainger 1930
This Nearly Was Mine   Hammerstein 1949; Rodgers 1949
This Never Happened Before   Adamson 1938; McHugh 1938
This Night   Rainger 1934, 1937; Robin 1934, 1937
This Night in Florence   Gershwin, Ira 1945; Weill 1945
This Night of Stars   Sigman 1958
This Night (Will Be My Souvenir)   Kahn 1939; Warren 1939
This Night Will Seem Long Ago   Romberg 1941
This Noble Land   Adams 1972; Strouse 1972
This Ol' World   Arlen 1965
This Old Love (inst.)   Young, Victor 1955
This Old World   Sigman 1974
This One Today and That One Tomorrow Means No One at All in the End   Coslow 1925; Silver 1925
This Particular Party   Dietz 1943; Duke 1943; Gershwin, George 1928; Gershwin, Ira 1928
This Program Comes to You from My Heart   Hoffman 1933
This Rescue Is a Terrible Calamity   Hart 1928; Rodgers 1928
This Room Is My Castle of Quiet (inst.)   Revel 1950
This Same Heart   Burke 1956; Friml 1956
This Song Is Not About Lindbergh   Brown, Lew 1927; DeSylva 1927; Henderson 1927
This Strange Affair   Young, Victor 1964
This, That, and the Other Thing   Burke 1951
This They Call Love   Cahn 1950
This Thing Called Love   Lewis 1929; Young, Joe 1929
This Time   Coots 1953
This Time for Keeps   Fain 1947; Freed, Ralph 1947
This Time (Is the Last Time)   Berlin 1942
This Time It's Hook or Me   Leigh 1954
This Time It's Love   Coots 1933; DeSylva 1922; Herbert 1922; Koehler 1932; Lewis 1933
This Time Next Year   Weill 1950
This Time of the Year   Harburg 1947; Koehler 1948; Lane 1947; Stept 1948; Washington 1938

This Time of Year   David, Mack 1962; Livingston, Jerry 1959; Van Heusen 1962

This Time the Dream's on Me   Arlen 1941; Mercer 1941

This Time Tomorrow   Stept 1948; Styne 1978

This Too Shall Pass   Washington 1955

This Too Shall Pass Away   Drake 1953

This Turf Is Ours   Sondheim 1957

This Was Meant to Be   Comden and Green 1947

This Was My Sin   Sherman 1958

This Way or No Way at All   Arlen 1973

This Way Please   Coslow 1937

This Week Americans   Rodgers 1965; Sondheim 1965

(It'll) This Will Be the First Time for Me   Brown, Lew 1930; DeSylva 1930; Henderson 1930

This Woman at the Altar   Gershwin, Ira 1940; Weill 1940

This Wonderful Land of Ours   Drake 1954

This World   Sondheim 1974

This World Is a Toy Shop   Smith, Harry B. 1906

This World We Love In (Il Cielo in una Stanza)   Raye 1961

This Year's Kisses   Berlin 1937

This'll Make You Whistle   Hoffman 1936

Thistledown   Hammerstein 1923

Thistles and Thumbs   Burke 1952; Van Heusen 1952

Tho' I Had Never Meant to Tell You   Parish 1957

Tho' We've No Authentic Reason   Hart 1925; Rodgers 1925

Thomas A. Edison, Miracle Man   Cohan 1928

Thomas Jefferski   Caesar 1946

Thomas Jefferson Witherspoon   Coleman 1979

Thompson's Ragtime Cake Walk   Sterling 1899; Von Tilzer 1899

Thorny, Thorny Rose   Leigh 1956

Thoroughly Modern Millie   Cahn 1967; Van Heusen 1967

Those Blue Eyes Blues   Fisher 1922

Those Bootblack Blues   Rainger 1936

Those College Yells   Smith, Harry B. 1908

Those Come Hither Eyes   Kern 1915

Those Days Are Gone Forever   Kern 1921

Those Days Are Over   Sterling 1921; Von Tilzer 1921

Those Dear Old Wedding Bells   Williams 1910

Those Dixie Melodies   Bryan 1919; Schwartz, Jean 1919

Those Eddie Cantor Eyes   Akst 1933; Gilbert 1933

Those Evenings Spent at Joe's   Stept 1956

Those Eyes   Smith, Harry B. 1911

Those Eyes (Your Eyes, Your Smile)   Gershwin, George 1927; Gershwin, Ira 1927

Those Eyes You're Wearing   Lane 1938; Loesser 1938

Those Flippity Floppety Flappers   Johnson, Howard 1922

Those Good Old Days Back Home (inst.)   Monaco 1916

Those Good Old Days Can Never Come Again (Those Were the Happy Days)   Smith, Harry B. 1910

Those Good Old Fluffy Ruffle Days   Baer 1941

Those Irving Berlin Melodies   Cohan 1914

Those Knowing Nurses   Brown, Lew 1926; Clare 1926

Those Lips Those Eyes Those Nose   Turk 1925

Those Lonesome Nights   Akst 1931; Kahn 1931; Whiting 1931

Those Mason-Dixon Blues   Johnson, Howard 1920

Those Musical Eyes   Sterling 1915; Von Tilzer 1915

Those Panama Mammas   Johnson, Howard 1924

Those Royal Princesses   Leigh 1985

Those Since-I-Met-You Days   Herbert 1919; Smith, Robert B. 1919

Those Things That Happen Everyday   Williams 1908

(Don't You Ever Be 'Fraid to Wade) Those Troubled Waters   Robison 1929

Those Were the Days   Adams 1971; Strouse 1971; Webster 1949

Those Were the Good Old Days   Brown, Lew 1931; Henderson 1931

Those Were the Good Old Times   Herbert 1899; Smith, Harry B. 1899

Those Were the Happy Days Long, Long Ago   Koehler 1928

Those Who Believe in Forever   Adamson 1954; Warren 1954

Those Who Dance   Arlen 1934; Koehler 1934

Those Wonderful Days of Used-to-Be   Sterling 1918

Those Wonderful Eyes   Howard, Joseph E. 1909, 1912

Those Wonderful Friends   Cohan 1928

Thou Art Mine   Carroll 1915

Thou Shalt Not   Styne 1978

Thou Shalt Not Love   Drake 1959

Thou Swell   Hart 1927; Rodgers 1927

Though   Drake 1959

Though Half My Life (Is Spent)   Brooks 1959

Though I Said No to You Yesterday   Duke 1955

Though She Can't Add Up   Brooks 1959

Though Tongues May Wag   Loewe 1938

Though Your Love Is Gone   Dietz 1952

Though You're not the First One   Dubin 1931

Thought of Losing You, The   Johnson, J. Rosamond 1944

Thought of You, A   Kahn 1926; Rome 1954; Young, Victor 1926

Thoughtless   David, Mack 1943; Livingston, Jerry 1939, 1943

Thoughts   Robison 1954

Thoughts that I Wrote on the Leaves of My Heart, The   Friml 1919; Harbach 1919

Thoughts While Strolling (inst.)   Willson 1934

Thoughts Will Come to Me   Romberg 1924

Thousand and One Arabian Nights, A   Atteridge 1918; Romberg 1918

Thousand Blue Bubbles, A   Howard, Bart 1961

Thousand Burning Bridges, A   Fain 1955

Thousand Dreams of You, A   Alter 1936; Webster 1936

Thousand Good Nights, A   Donaldson 1934

Thousand Islands Song, The   Sigman 1947

Thousand Miles Away, A   Rose 1929

Thousand Times, A   Smith, Harry B. 1927

Thousand Violins, A   Evans 1949; Livingston, Jay 1949

Thousands of Miles   Weill 1949

Threads of Love   Fisher 1920

Three at a Table for Two   Johnston 1940

Three Bears, The   Hart 1929; Kalmar 1928; Rodgers 1929; Ruby 1928

Three Black Crows   Loesser 1937

Three B's, The   Bergman 1958; Martin 1941

Three B's (Questions and Answers), The   Hart 1936; Rodgers 1936

Three Cheers for Anything   Washington 1940

Three Cheers for Henry Smith   Gordon 1938; Revel 1938

Three Cheers for Holidays   Caesar 1955

Three Cheers for Love   Rainger 1936; Robin 1936

Three Cheers for Our President   Razaf 1942

Three Cheers for the Customer   Revel 1944; Webster 1944

Three Cheers for the Red, White and Blue   Alter 1930; Berlin 1922; Edwards 1930

Three Cheers for the Union!   Gershwin, George 1927; Gershwin, Ira 1927

Three Cheers for the Yanks (We've Done It Before, We Can Do It Again)   Martin 1942

Three Chimes of Silver   Willson 1951

Three Coins in the Fountain   Cahn 1954; Styne 1954

Three Cornered Moon   David, Mack 1933; Hoffman 1933; Silver 1933

Three Cornered Tune   Loesser 1950

Three Dames Ziegfeld Failed to Glorify, The   Johnson, J. Rosamond 1931

Three Day Pass   Hammerstein 1944; Meyer 1944

Three Dollars and Ninety-Eight Cents   Drake 1950

Three Dreams   Styne 1943

Three Faces East   Johnson, Howard Date Unknown

Three Favorite Airs   Herbert 1913

Three Feet Two of Rhythm   Cahn 1935

Three Friends (Two Lovers)   Bacharach 1961; David, Hal 1961

Three Girls in a Boat   Lerner, Alan Jay 1943; Loewe 1943

Three Greeks, The   Eliscu 1933; Kahn 1933; Youmans 1933

Three Guesses   Mercer 1930

Three Guesses — Who Do I Love?   Akst 1932; Davis 1932

Three Hot Tamales, The   Merrill 1972; Styne 1972

Three Hundred and Sixty-Five Days   Sherman 1959

Three Hundred Sixty-Five Days   Kern 1916

Three Important Things   Bacharach 1970; David, Hal 1970

Three Letters in the Mail Box   Webster 1943

Three Little Angels   Livingston, Jerry 1963

Three Little Bunnies   Hoffman 1954

Three Little Fishes   Kalmar 1966; Ruby 1966

Three Little Girls in Blue   Johnston 1931; Myrow 1946

Three Little Girls in Blue — Prayer Sequence   Gordon 1946; Myrow 1946

Three Little Hollywood Wolves   Coslow 1951

Three Little Maids   Dubin 1939; Edwards 1930; Johnson, Howard 1930; McHugh 1939; Romberg 1921

Three Little Maids from Damascus   Washington 1959

Three Little Maids from School   Fields 1928; McHugh 1928

Three Little Marys   Bryan 1920; Schwartz, Jean 1920

Three Little Models from an Agency   Johnson, J. Rosamond 1950

Three Little Mosquitos   Pollack 1943

Three Little Pigs Are Pork Chops Now, The   Davis 1934; Hanley 1934

Three Little Puppies   Hoffman 1952

Three Little Rooms and You   Ager 1929; Yellen 1929

Three Little Ships   Carmichael 1945

Three Little Topical Debutantes   Dubin 1940; McHugh 1940

Three Little Vampires   Atteridge 1921; Romberg 1921

Three Little Wishes   Styne 1941

Three Little Witches   Carmichael 1957

Three Little Words   Kalmar 1930; Ruby 1930

Three Love Stories   Smith, Harry B. 1906

Three Loves   Bacharach 1959; David, Hal 1959; Strouse 1955

Three Men on a Date   Blane 1941; Martin 1941

Three Mile Limit Cafe   Whiting 1919

Three Musketeers, The   Hart 1922, 1925; Kahn 1934; Rodgers 1922, 1925

Three Musketeers of Broadway   Atteridge 1920

Three O'Clock in the Morning   Baer 1922

Three on a Match   Egan 1932

Three Paradises   Evans 1958; Livingston, Jay 1958

3 Pieces (For Jazz Violin) (inst.)   Strouse 1962

Three Pullman Porters   Meyer 1926

Three Quarter Blues (inst.)   Gershwin, George 1920; Myrow 1945

Three Questions   Johnson, J. Rosamond 1917

Three Rivers (The Allegheny, Susquehanna and the Monongahela), The   Carmichael 1949; Webster 1949

Three Roads   Lawrence 1956

Three Rousing Cheers   Duke 1941

Three Sheets to the Wind   David, Mack 1957; Livingston, Jerry 1957

Three Sisters Opening (Act Two)   Hammerstein 1934; Kern 1934

Three Songs on Poems of William Blake   Strouse 1962

Three Strange Men   Adams 1957

Three Sunny Rooms   Strouse 1986

Three Sweethearts Have I   Rainger 1935; Robin 1935

3:10 to Yuma, The   Washington 1957

Three Things a Man Should Do   Drake 1952

Three Thousand Years Ago   Friml 1923

Three Times a Day   DeSylva 1925; Gershwin, George 1925; Gershwin, Ira 1925; Robin 1932; Whiting 1932

Three Trees   Smith, Harry B. 1910; Smith, Robert B. 1910

Three Twins   Harbach 1908

Three Ways   Willson 1953

Three Weeks with You   Smith, Harry B. 1908

Three Wheels on My Wagon   Bacharach 1961

Three Wise Monkeys, The   Blake 1925; Sissle 1925

(If I Had) Three Wishes for Christmas   Sondheim 1959; Styne 1959

Three Wonderful Letters from Home   Hanley 1918

Three-a Poppa, Don't Your Four-Five   Yellen Date Unknown

Three's a Crowd   Dubin 1932; Kahal 1932; Romberg 1919; Warren 1932

Threshold   Webster 1970

Thrill in Spain   Blake 1955

Thrill Is Gone, The   Brown, Lew 1931; Henderson 1931

Thrill Me   Harburg 1932

Thrill Me Again   Parish 1937

Thrill of a Hill Billy Waltz, The   Schwartz, Jean 1934; Young, Joe 1934

Thrill of a Kiss, The   Smith, Harry B. 1928

Thrill of a Lifetime   Coslow 1937; Styne 1965

Thrill of a New Romance   Adamson 1939

Thrill that Comes Once in a Lifetime, The   Stept 1932

Throckmorton's Permanent Pleasure   Leigh 1976

Throttle Throttlebottom   Gershwin, George 1933; Gershwin, Ira 1933

Through   Revel 1962

Through a Long and Sleepless Night   Gordon 1949

Through a Thousand Dreams   Robin 1946; Schwartz, Arthur 1946

Through a Window in Japan   Bryan 1936

Through! How Can You Say We're Through?   Monaco 1929

Through My Venetian Blind   Heyman 1936

Through the Courtesy of Love   Gordon 1936; Revel 1936

Through the Doorway of Dreams (I Saw You)   Rainger 1935; Robin 1935; Whiting 1935

Through the Eyes of Love   Lerner, Sammy 1930

Through the Forest   Sherman 1963

Through the Miracle of Love   Bryan 1930; Dubin 1930

Through the Mist   Atteridge 1921; Romberg 1921

Through the Moonlit Fog   Wrubel 1943

Through the Wonderful Eyes of Love   Cobb 1920; Edwards 1920

Through the Years   Heyman 1931; Youmans 1931

Through These Wonderful Glasses of Mine   Von Tilzer 1916

Through Thick and Thin   Porter 1943

Throw a Curve   Revel 1953

Throw a Kiss to Me, My Minstrel Man   Goetz 1911

Throw a Little Party   Rose 1938

Throw a Little Salt on the Bluebird's Tail   Robin 1932; Whiting 1932

Throw 'Er in High!   DeSylva 1923; Goetz 1923

Throw Her in High!   Gershwin, George 1923; Goetz 1923

Throw It Out of Your Mind   Razaf 1945

Throw It Out the Window   Alter 1930

Throw Me a Kiss from Over the Sea   Egan 1917; Whiting 1917

Throw Me Up and Catch Me and Don't Let Me Fall   Monaco 1911

Throw Out Your Chest, Keep Up Your Chin   Razaf 1934

Throw the Anchor Away   Fields 1954; Schwartz, Arthur 1954

Throw Up Your Hands   Jerome 1910; Schwartz, Jean 1910

Throwing a Party   Eliscu 1932

Throwing the Bull   Herbert 1919

Thru the Night (inst.)   Motzan 1929

Thru Your Eyes to Your Heart   Heyman 1944

Thumbelina   Loesser 1952

Thumbin' a Ride   DePaul 1956; Mercer 1956

Thumbs Up   Schwartz, Jean 1926

Thumbs Up and "V" for Victory   Webster 1942

Thumpin' 'n' Bumpin'   Johnson, James P. 1931; Razaf 1931

Thunder   Lewis 1935

Thunder and Bells   Loesser 1965

Thunder and Lightning   Loesser 1965; Russell 1961

Thunder Dance   Friml 1927

Thunder in My Dreams   Heyman 1929

Thunder in My Heart   Drake 1950

Thunder in the Sun   Washington 1959

Thunder Over Paradise   Rainger 1935; Robin 1935

Thursday Is My Jonah Day   Howard, Joseph E. 1907

Thursday Night   Blane 1945

Thursday Would Have Been a Year   Webster 1949

Tia Juana   Edwards 1929

Tia Juana (inst.)   Gorney 1935

Tia-Da-Tia-Da-Dee   Stept 1920

Tick, Tack, Toe   Olcott 1904

Tick, Tick, Tick   Blane 1949; Friml 1917; Warren 1949

Tick, Tick, Tick of the Ticker, The   Romberg 1922

Tick, Tock   Sondheim 1970

Tick Tock — I'm a Cuckoo Clock (inst.)   Revel 1959

Tick Tock Goes the Clock   Bacharach 1968; David, Hal 1968

Tick-Dee   Brooks 1960

Ticker Tape Talk   Loesser 1930

Ticket Speculator, The   Jerome 1910; Schwartz, Jean 1910

Ticket to Tomahawk (On the Colorado Trail), A   Gordon 1950; Warren 1950

(Suzi I'm) Ticking Love Taps (Tick-A-Tock)   Harbach 1914

Tickle Me   Hammerstein 1920; Harbach 1920; Smith, Harry B. 1922; Snyder 1922

Tickle the Ivories (inst.)   Blake 1969

(Do the) Tickle Toe   Harbach 1917

Tickle Toe (inst.)   Schwartz, Jean 1930

Tickled Pink   Brown, Nacio Herb 1932; DeSylva 1932; Whiting 1932

Tickling the Ivories   Berlin 1927

Tick-Tock   Hart 1933; Razaf 1950; Rodgers 1933

Tick-Tock, the Dresden Clock   Ager 1923; Yellen 1923

Tico-Tico   Drake 1943

Tiddle de Winka and Blinken and Kinky Koo   Schwartz, Jean 1931

Tiddle de Winks and Blinken and Kinky Koo   Bryan 1931

Tiddley Pom   Brooks 1960

Tiddley Winks   Coots 1950

Tide Pool, The   Hammerstein 1955; Rodgers 1955

Tie a Knot in the Rainbow   Lewis 1930

Tie a String Around Your Finger   Conrad 1929; Mitchell 1929; Youmans 1924

Tie All Your Troubles to the Tail of a Kite   Monaco 1927; Rose 1927

Tie Your Troubles to a Toy Balloon   Adamson 1936; Donaldson 1936

Tie Your Troubles to a Toy Baloon   Adamson 1935; Donaldson 1935

Ties that Bind, The   Sigman 1953

Tiffany Girl   Goetz 1915; Romberg 1915

Tiffin, Tiffin   Mitchell 1921; Pollack 1921

Tiger Baby   Warren 1926

Tiger By the Tail, The   Gorney 1961; Leigh 1956

Tiger Eyes   Bryan 1926

Tiger Lily (inst.)   Schwartz, Arthur 1948

Tiger Roar   Gordon 1934; Revel 1934

Tiger Rose   Buck 1917

Tightwad   Caesar 1955

Tiki Tiki Room, The   Sherman 1963

'Til Good Luck Comes My Way   Hammerstein 1927; Kern 1927

'Til Now   Hoffman 1952

'Til You Return   Dietz 1942; Schwartz, Arthur 1942

'Til You're Back   Drake 1954

Till   Sigman 1957

Till All the Stars Fall in the Ocean   Spina 1951

Till Doomsday   Lerner, Sammy 1933

Till Dreams Come True   Smith, Harry B. 1923

Till I Meet Someone Like You   Gershwin, George 1924

Till I Met You   Burke 1930

Till I Return to You   Baer 1942

Till It Goes Outta Style   Mercer 1964

Till My Love Comes to Me   Webster 1955

Till the Clouds Roll By   Kern 1917

Till the Last Beat of the Drum (I'll Be There)   Ahlert 1945; Bryan 1945

Till the Ocean Freezes Over   Hoffman 1956

'Till the Real Thing Comes My Way   Akst 1932; Egan 1932; Eliscu 1932

Till Then   Gershwin, George 1933; Gershwin, Ira 1933

Till There Was You   Willson 1957

'Till We All Belong   Arlen 1976; Harburg 1976

Till We Dream Together Again   Henderson 1942

Till We Meet Again   Egan 1918; Whiting 1918, 1932

Tiller Girls at Home (inst.), The   Schwartz, Arthur 1929

Tiller Girls Dance (inst.)   Herbert 1924

Tillie   Brown, Lew Date Unknown; Henderson Date Unknown

Tillie of Longacre Square   Atteridge 1925; Hanley 1925

Tillie the Tight Rope Walker   Washington 1935

Tillie the Toiler   Coots 1931

Tillie Titwillow   Atteridge 1916

Tim and Jim   Oakland 1960

Timberjack   Washington 1955; Young, Victor 1955

Timberland Brown   Sherman 1991

Timbuctoo   Kalmar 1920; Ruby 1920

Time   Friend 1949; Rodgers 1979; Snyder 1954; Strouse 1958

Time After Time   Adamson 1939; Brennan 1921; Cahn 1947; Duke 1939; Egan 1942; Styne 1947

Time Ain't Long   Robison 1953

Time Alone (Can Heal a Broken Heart)   Robison 1950

Time Alone Will Tell   Gordon 1944; Monaco 1944

Time and a Half for Overtime   Youmans 1924

Time and Again   Sigman 1960
Time and Tenderness   Bacharach 1976
Time and Tide   Duke 1932; Harburg 1932
Time and Time Again   Gershwin, George 1935
Time and Time and Time Again   Oakland 1961
Time Changes Everything but Love   Donaldson 1939; Kahn 1939
Time Drags On   Blake 1947
Time Flies   Livingston, Jerry 1957
Time for Glory   Webster 1965
Time for Jookin'   Brown, Lew 1939; Stept 1939
Time for Love   Coots 1926; Webster 1966
Time for Love (Imakoso Koi No Toki), A   Rome 1969
Time for Parting   Comden and Green 1955
Time Goes By   Styne 1970; Webster 1974
Time Is a Gypsy   Harburg 1934
Time Is On Our Side (Mary Kaye's Theme)   Evans 1973; Livingston, Jay 1973
Time Is Standing Still   Hammerstein 1941; Romberg 1941
Time Marches On!   Duke 1936; Gershwin, Ira 1936
Time Never Erases   Drake 1958
Time o' Day, The   Bergman 1965
Time of Decision, A   Webster 1965
Time of Roses, The   Styne 1970
Time of Your Life, The   Brooks 1947
Time Off for Love   Loewe 1937
Time on My Hands, You in My Arms   Adamson 1930; Gordon 1930; Youmans 1930
Time, Only Time Dear   Atteridge 1922; Romberg 1922
Time Out   Leigh 1971
Time Out for Dreaming   Washington 1945
Time Out for Love   Coots 1935; Lewis 1935; Parish 1935
Time Out for Rhythm   Cahn 1941
Time Out for Thinking   Razaf 1955
Time Remembered   Duke 1957
Time Step, The   Martin 1951
Time Stood Still   Pollack 1948; Styne 1948
Time, the Place and the Girl, The   Herbert 1905
Time: The Present   Gershwin, Ira 1944; Kern 1944
Time to Be Happy Is Now, The   Oakland 1952
Time to Go to Bed   Akst 1923; Kahn 1923
Time to Laugh, a Time to Cry, A   David, Hal 1962
Time to Love Is Now, The   Davis 1960
Time to Ride   David, Mack 1976
Time to Sing, The   Kalmar 1941; Ruby 1941
Time to Smile   Mercer 1966
Time Waits for No One   Friend 1944
Time Was   Russell 1941
Time Will Come   Herbert 1895
Time Will Tell   Baer 1929; Brooks 1946; Coots 1922; Gilbert 1929
Time You Old Gypsy Man   Harburg 1979
Time-Clock Slaves   Hammerstein 1923; Youmans 1923
Timeless Tide, The   Bacharach 1959; David, Hal 1959
Times Change   Bergman 1959
Times Have Changed   Mitchell 1927; Motzan 1927
Times May Change   Schwartz, Jean 1935
Times Square   David, Hal 1991; Strouse 1991
Times Square Arguments, The   Atteridge 1915; Carroll 1915; Romberg 1915
Times Square Dance   Fain 1940; Yellen 1940
Times Will Change, The   Sigman 1967
Timpanogos Glacier   Willson 1953
Tin Horn   Bullock 1950
Tin Horn (inst.)   Spina 1942

Tin Pan Alley   Coleman 1953
Tin Pan Alley Rag, The   Rome 1950
Tin Pan Parade   Whiting 1927
Tin Soldiers on Parade   Edwards 1929
Tin Star, The   Brooks 1957
Tin Whistle Tune   Sherman 1995
Tina   Cahn 1961; Ellington 1972; Van Heusen 1961
Tina Marie   Merrill 1954
Tina-Lina, The   Cahn 1950
Tina's Opening   Brooks 1962
Ting a Ling a Ling   Gorney 1935
Ting a Ling Ling   Smith, Robert B. 1909
Ting-A-Ling   Atteridge 1922; Goetz 1915; Romberg 1915, 1922
Ting-A-Ling (The Bell's Ring)   Berlin 1925
Ting-A-Ling-A-Ling   Gorney 1934; Howard, Joseph E. 1951
Ting-a-Ling-a-Ling on the Mason-Dixon Line   Dixon 1923
Ting-a-Ling-a-Ling Ping Pong   Edwards 1909
Tinge of the West (inst.), A   Bloom 1946
Tingle Tangle (inst.)   Von Tilzer 1914
Tinker Tailor   Hanley 1926
Tinker's Song   Smith, Harry B. 1891
Tinkle Song, The   Woods 1931
Tinkle! Tinkle!   Ager 1929; Yellen 1929
Tinkle, Tinkle, Tinkle   Woods 1935
Tiny Bit of Faith, A   Cahn 1966; Van Heusen 1966
Tiny Blue Shoe   Fisher 1940
Tiny Chinee Little Girl   Gershwin, George Date Unknown
Tiny Flat Near Soho, A   Hart 1926; Rodgers 1926
Tiny Little Fingerprints   Stept 1935
Tiny Room   Martin 1948
Tiny Scout, The   Adamson 1957; Warren 1957
Tiny Toys   Evans 1957; Livingston, Jay 1957
Tio Paco   Willson 1969
Tip, Tip, Toe Up a Tuck, Tuck, Tucky Lane   Rose 1928; Warren 1928
Tip Toe Through the Tulips (With Me)   Dubin 1929
Tip Top (inst.)   Schwartz, Jean 1930
Tip Top Toreador   Atteridge 1920
Tip Your Hat to Hattie   Herbert 1919; Smith, Robert B. 1919
Tippecanoe and Tyler Too   Livingston, Jerry 1960
Tipperary Mary   Buck 1918, 1919
Tipperary Nora   Snyder 1907
Tipperary Twirl, The   Meyer 1911
Tippety Witchet   Rainger 1937; Robin 1937
Tippicanoe   Williams 1904
Tippin' Out Tonight   Razaf Date Unknown
(Dancin' on My) Tippy Tippy Toes   Coleman 1960; Leigh 1960
Tip-Tip Tippy Canoe   Johnson, Howard 1920
Tip-Tip-Tippy Dance   Hanley 1920
Tip-Toes   Gershwin, George 1925; Gershwin, Ira 1925
Tip-Top Tipperary Mary   Carroll 1914
Tira, La La   Leigh 1955
Tired Business Man, The   Hammerstein 1920
Tired of Dreaming   Kalmar 1924; Ruby 1924; Snyder 1924
Tired of Explaining   Razaf 1966
Tired of It All   Kalmar 1934; Robin 1928; Ruby 1934
Tired of Living Alone   Porter 1910
Tired of Me   Clarke 1920; Donaldson 1920
Tirolian Woodchoppers March (inst.)   Romberg 1952
Tis a Glorious Day   Smith, Harry B. 1923
'Tis a Wonderful Thing in Nature   Blane 1952
'Tis an Irish Girl I Love and She's Just Like You   Brennan 1920; Dubin 1920

'Tis Harry I'm Plannin' to Marry   Fain 1953; Webster 1953
'Tis Love   Romberg 1927; Smith, Harry B. 1927
'Tis Summer   Coots 1964
Tis the End, So Farewell   Friml 1914; Harbach 1914
'Tisn't Easy to Say Goodbye Broadway   Cohan 1924
Tit Willow   Johnson, Howard 1939
Titina   Buck 1925; Coslow 1924
Titina's Tavern   Brown, Lew 1943
Titles   Smith, Harry B. 1908
Titusville Square and Shanty Boat (Jenny
     Dear)   Hammerstein 1937; Kern 1937
Tivolini   Herbert 1900; Smith, Harry B. 1900
Tjilerham   Russell 1964
Tkambuza (Zulu Hunting Song)   Rome 1965
T'morra', T'morra'   Arlen 1944; Harburg 1944
TNT   Ellington 1946
To a Painting (Auf Ein Altee Bild)   Bergman 1983
To a Small Degree   Merrill 1971; Styne 1971
(I Wanna Hum Sumpin' Pretty) To a Sweet Pretty
     Thing   Young, Joe 1937
To a Tango Melody   Berlin 1930
To All the Girls I've Loved Before   David, Hal 1974, 1984
To America — With Love   Webster 1968
To Any Girl (Pass This to Someone Who's Not As Lucky As
     You)   Brown, Lew 1917
To Arms   Magidson 1932
To Arms (Dear One, Divine)   Razaf 1942
To Be a Little Singing Girl   Herbert 1899; Smith, Harry B.
     1899
To Be a Performer   Coleman 1958; Leigh 1958
To Be Artistic   Merrill 1967
To Be Continued   Brooks 1965; Oakland 1961
To Be Forgotten   Berlin 1928
To Be in Love   Burke 1954; Howard, Bart 1957
To Be In Love Espesh'lly with You   Ahlert 1929; Turk 1929
To Be in Paree   Merrill 1957
To Be Loved by the One I Love   Alter 1925; Mitchell 1925
To Be Near Him   Coslow 1936
To Be or Not to Be   Berlin 1933
To Be or Not to Be in Love   Coslow 1951; Dixon 1934;
     Wrubel 1934
To Be Truly Refined   Smith, Harry B. 1902
To Be with You   Coots 1929; Davis 1929; Yellen 1926
To Be Worthy of You   Coots 1931; Davis 1931
To Be Young   De Lange 1945; Myrow 1945
To Beat the Band   Sterling 1900
To Become a Man   Leigh 1985; Styne 1985
To Boston on Business   Cohan 1899
To Call You My Own   Dixon 1935; Wrubel 1935
To Catch a Thief   Heyman 1976
To Comfort Me   Leigh 1953
To Dad with Love   Sherman 1959
To Dance with You   Razaf 1955
To Deride You   Bacharach 1986
To Do a Little Good   Styne 1970
To Do What We Like   Johnson, James P. 1938
To Each His Own   Evans 1946, 1948; Livingston, Jay 1946,
     1948
To Fall in Love in Venice   Coslow 1930
To Fly a Kite Is Lots of Fun   Caesar 1940
To Follow Every Fancy   Porter 1916
To Get Away   Porter 1935
To Get Out of this World Alive   Harburg 1967; Styne 1967
To Get Us All Together   Adams 1950, 1954; Strouse 1950,
     1954

To Give Myself to You (Is More than Giving)   David, Hal
     1973; Mancini 1973
To Have and Hold You in My Arms   Dubin 1931
To Have and to Hold   Hammerstein 1947; Rodgers 1947
To Have, to Hold, to Love   Smith, Harry B. 1930
To Have You To Hold You   Gordon 1945; Revel 1945
To Heaven on the Bronx Express   Cohan 1927
To Hell with Everyone but Us   Porter 1950
To Hold You   Baer 1930; Gilbert 1930
To Keep My Love Alive   Hart 1943; Rodgers 1943
To Keep the Chill Off the Bones   Cahn 1966; Van Heusen
     1966
To Keep You in Your Seats   Harbach 1921
To Kill a Mockingbird   David, Mack 1962
To Know You Is to Like You   Brennan 1949
To Know You Is to Love You   Brown, Lew 1928; DeSylva
     1928; Henderson 1928; Mancini 1957
To Know You Is to Want You   Lewis 1936
To Like to Love One Girl   Caesar 1920
To Live Again   Coleman 1988
To Live, to Love Again   Caesar 1920
To Lola   Robin 1929; Whiting 1929
To London   Atteridge 1913
To Love a Child   David, Hal 1982
To Love Again   Washington 1956
To Love and Be Loved   Cahn 1958; Van Heusen 1958
To Love and to Lose   Comden and Green 1960; Styne 1960
To Love or Not to Love   Porter 1937
(I Only Live) To Love You   Gordon 1955; Young, Victor
     1955, 1956
To Love You and To Lose You   Heyman 1936; Weill 1936
To Make a Mistake Is Human   Drake 1947
To Make It Short and Sweet, I Love You   Ager 1938; Davis
     1938; Silver 1938; Yellen Date Unknown
To Make Them Beautiful Ladies   Atteridge 1922; Schwartz,
     Jean 1922
To Marry   Loesser 1965
To Marry a Millionaire   Smith, Harry B. 1901
To Mary — With Love   Gordon 1936; Revel 1936
To Me   David, Mack 1984; Davis 1959; Wrubel 1946
To Me You're a Song   Merrill 1950
To Mother with Love   Sherman 1959
To My Love   Evans 1959; Livingston, Jay 1959; Mancini
     1959; Webster 1957
To My Love (Je Ne Sais Pas)   Lawrence 1955
To My Mammy   Berlin 1930
To My Wife   Rome 1954
To Paris   Herbert 1913
To Pass the Time Away   Brooks 1957
To Remind Me of You   Kahn 1931
To Rome with Love   Evans 1970; Livingston, Jay 1970;
     Livingston, Jerry 1970
To See Her   Loesser 1969
To See You   Burke 1952; Van Heusen 1952
To Smell the Flowers   Sherman 1985
To Swing or Not to Swing   Davis 1938
To Take a Dip in the Ocean   Lewis 1911
To the Banquet We Go   Brooks 1946
To the Beat of My Heart   Harburg 1934
To the Dance   Robin 1928
To the End of the World Together   Kern 1904
To the Ends of the Earth   Adamson 1954; Warren 1954
To the Fair   Dietz 1924; Kern 1924
To the Hum of My Heart   Carmichael 1937

To the Inn We're Marching   Romberg 1924, 1954; Webster 1954

To the Ladies   Oakland 1952; Webster 1952

To the Lambs   Herbert 1906

To the Land of My Own Romance   Herbert 1911; Smith, Harry B. 1911

To the Lass We Love (A Toast)   Brennan 1915

To the Lilt of a Gay Mandolin   Kahal 1956; Stept 1956

To the Music of Windchimes   Spina 1955

To the Only One   Youmans 1930

To the Pyramid   Herbert 1895; Smith, Harry B. 1895

To the Resuce   Bergman 1960

To the Rhythm of the River Rhine in Tulip Time   Bryan 1932; Fisher 1932

To the Sound of the Pipe and the Roll of the Drum   Herbert 1903; Smith, Harry B. 1903

To the Strain of that Wedding March   Kahn 1910

To the Sweetest Girl in the World   Davis 1932

To the Victor Belongs the Spoils   Gordon 1932; Revel 1932

To Think that Once We Were Sweethearts (And Now We're Not Even Friends)   Leslie 1931; Monaco 1931; Rose 1931

To Think that This Could Happen to Me   Porter 1953

To Think That You Should Care for Me   Parish 1933

To Think that You're Mine Again   Davis 1935; Silver 1935

To Think You Could Care for Me   Kahn 1937; Romberg 1937

To Those Who Wait   Leigh 1955

To Wait for Love (Is to Waste Your Life Away)   Bacharach 1963; David, Hal 1963

To War!   Weill 1938

To Whom It May Concern   Loewe 1938; Meyer 1930; Mitchell 1930

To You   Davis 1939; Myrow 1954

To You and Yours, Merry Christmas   Koehler 1949

To You, Mio Rio de Janeiro   Gorney 1937

To You Mio Rio de Jeneiro   Gilbert 1937

To Your Health   Loesser 1965

To Your Hearts Content   Russell 1941

Toast, A   Conrad 1930; Martin 1948, 1951; Meyer 1930; Mitchell 1930

Toast of New Orleans, The   Cahn 1950

Toast of the Boys at the Post, The   Duke 1941

Toast Song   Smith, Harry B. 1902

Toast the Pirate King   Brooks 1946

Toast to Prohibition   Berlin 1930

Toast to the Bride, A   Burke 1961

Toast to the Girl I Love, A   Hanley 1930

Toast to Volstead, A   Porter 1929

Toast to Women's Eyes, A   Romberg 1915

Toastin' Sequence   Arlen 1959; Mercer 1959

Toasts, The   Brooks 1958

Tobacco, The Red Man's Revenge   Rome 1964

Tobacco's but an Indian Weed   Spina 1976

Today and Tomorrow   Ahlert 1929; Turk 1929

Today at Your House, Tomorrow at Mine   Lawrence 1951

Today Didn't Pay to Get Up   Merrill 1948

Today I Am a Glamor Girl   Carmichael 1940; Mercer 1940

Today I Love Ev'rybody   Arlen 1953; Fields 1953

Today I Went Adventuring   Leigh 1954

Today I'm a Debutante   Adamson 1943; McHugh 1943

Today Is Saturday   Mills 1935

To-Day Is the Day (inst.)   Schwartz, Jean 1930

Today Is Your Birthday   Martin 1958

Today, Tomorrow, Forever   Ager 1931; David, Mack 1951; Leslie 1928; Livingston, Jerry 1951

Today, Tonight and Tomorrow   Coots 1954

Today's a Wonderful Day   Adams 1966; Strouse 1966

Today's the Day   Brown, Lew 1927; DeSylva 1927; Henderson 1927; Leigh 1977

Today's the Day (He Loves Me)   Rome 1973

Today's Your Anniversary   Mills 1939

Toddle All Over the Town   Smith, Harry B. 1915

Toddle Along   Buck 1925

Toddle Along Toward the Land of Better Days   Egan 1921; Whiting 1921

Toddle (The Teddy Toddle)   Kern 1921

Toddle Trot   Atteridge 1925

Toddle-Dee-Doo   Mitchell 1921

Toddlin' Along   Gershwin, George 1930; Gershwin, Ira 1930

Toddlin' Along with You   Dixon 1935; Wrubel 1935

Toddlin' (inst.)   Johnson, James P. 1927

Toddling the Todalo   Goetz 1911

Toe Tangling Tune   Harbach 1923

Together   Adams 1978; Brown, Lew 1927; Coleman 1978; Comden and Green 1978; Conrad 1928; DePaul 1941; DeSylva 1927, 1928; Henderson 1927; Raye 1941; Strouse 1978

Together Again   Freed, Ralph 1932; Hanley 1932

Together at Last   Gershwin, George 1932; Gershwin, Ira 1932

Together in Central Park   Duke 1959

Together, We Two   Berlin 1927

Together, Wherever We Go   Sondheim 1959; Styne 1959

Tojo, Benito and Adolph   Stept 1941

Tokens of Love   Coslow 1930

Tokio Rag   Goetz 1913

Tokyo   Ellington 1968

Tokyo Blues   Berlin 1924

Toledo   Bacharach 1996

Tom and Jack   Herbert 1897; Smith, Harry B. 1897

Tom Boy, Tom Boy   Harbach 1910

Tom, Dick and Harry and Jack (Hurry Back)   Ager 1917; Johnson, Howard 1917

Tom, Dick or Harry   Adamson 1932; Porter 1948; Youmans 1932

Tom Sawyer!   Sherman 1973

Tom Tom the Piper's Son   Harburg 1943; Lane 1943

Tomale (I'm Hot for You)   Caesar 1921; DeSylva 1921; Gershwin, George 1921

Tomatoes   Cahn 1968

Tomboy   Van Heusen 1940; Young, Joe 1931

Tomboy Sue   Razaf 1926

Tommy Atkins   Friml 1912; Harbach 1912

Tommy Atkins on Parade   Brown, Nacio Herb 1929; Freed, Arthur 1929

Tommy Atkins, You're All Right   Cohan 1908

Tommy Edwards Theme   Oakland 1954

Tommy Hawk   Johnson, Howard 1926; Warren 1926

Tommy Rot   Harbach 1911

Tommy Tax   Caesar 1946

Tommy Thank You   Caesar 1950

Tommy Tom Tom   Stept 1952

Tomorrow   Conrad 1925; Coslow 1924; Friml 1925; Kahn 1921; Koehler 1944; Lane 1944; Motzan 1921; Porter 1938; Smith, Harry B. 1921; Strouse 1977; Turk Date Unknown; Willson 1957, 1960

Tomorrow I'll Be Gone   Oakland 1972

Tomorrow Is Another Day   Kahn 1937; Rome 1973; Stept 1930

Tomorrow Is My Friend   Bergman 1969; Mancini 1969

Tomorrow Is Only a Moment   Livingston, Jerry 1973

Tomorrow Is the Time   Gershwin, Ira 1946; Schwartz, Arthur 1946

Tomorrow Land   Adamson 1957; Warren 1957

Tomorrow Means Romance   Brown, Nacio Herb 1948

Tomorrow Morning   Parish 1922; Rome 1959

Tomorrow Mountain   Ellington 1946

Tomorrow My Honey's Comin' Home   Turk 1933

Tomorrow Never Comes   Mercer 1967

Tomorrow Night   Bergman 1983; Coslow 1939

Tomorrow Song, The   Howard, Bart 1955

Tomorrow Valley   Sherman 1968

Tomorrow World   Merrill 1981

Tomorrow You Belong to Uncle Sammy   Mercer 1942

Tomorrow You Go to the Dentist   Eliscu 1952; Gorney 1952

Tomorrow's Another Day   Coots 1924; Coslow 1924

Tomorrow's Mother's Day   Sondheim 1959; Styne 1959

Tomorrow's My Lucky Day   Burke 1949; Van Heusen 1949

Tomorrow's Sunrise   Leslie 1942

Tomorrow's Violets   Egan 1928

Tom-Tom   Hammerstein 1922; Mitchell 1922; Rose 1927

Tom-Tom-Toddle   Harbach 1920

Tonda Wanda Hoy   David, Mack 1950; Livingston, Jerry 1950

Tondelayo   Dietz 1942; Duke 1942

Tondeleo   Buck 1925

Tondra   Mills 1954

Tongue-Tied   Bloom 1943; Woods 1943

Toni Caponi   Atteridge 1911

Tonight   Coots 1950; Donaldson 1944; Evans 1947; Gershwin, George 1932; Gershwin, Ira 1932; Hammerstein 1931; Johnston 1932; Livingston, Jay 1947; Mitchell 1921; Robin 1955; Schwartz, Arthur 1934; Sondheim 1957; Styne 1955; Whiting 1931

Tonight and Every Night   Cahn 1945; Styne 1945

Tonight at Sundown   Duke 1941

Tonight at the Mardi Gras   Berlin 1940

To-Night I Am Thinking of You   Parish 1929

Tonight I Love You More   Porter 1950

Tonight I Shall Sleep (With a Smile on My Face)   Ellington 1943

Tonight I'll Dream of You   Coots 1957

Tonight I'll Kiss Hello Again (The One I Kissed Goodbye)   Coots 1957

Tonight In Dreamtime   Coslow 1942

Tonight Is a Night for Romance   Brown, Nacio Herb 1948

Tonight Is All a Dream   Coslow 1932; Rainger 1932

Tonight Is Mine   Kahn 1934

Tonight Is Opening Night   Brown, Nacio Herb 1932; DeSylva 1932; Fields 1952; Kern 1952; Whiting 1932

Tonight Is Ours (Estrana Vida)   Drake 1943

Tonight Is Ours (inst.)   Warren Date Unknown

Tonight Is the Last Night   Howard, Joseph E. 1947

Tonight Is the Night   Adamson 1939; DePaul 1958; McHugh 1939; Raye 1958

Tonight May Have to Last All My Life   Mercer 1964

Tonight May Never Come Again   Caesar 1933; Davis 1928; Romberg 1933

Tonight, My Darling, Tonight (Kinderoogjes)   Coslow 1957

Tonight My Love   Evans 1951; Livingston, Jay 1951

Tonight or Never   Hart 1931; Oakland 1952; Rodgers 1931; Webster 1952

Tonight Quintet   Sondheim 1957

Tonight There's a Spell on the Moon   Gorney 1935

Tonight We Dance (inst.)   Revel 1960

Tonight We Love   Rainger 1937, 1938; Robin 1937, 1938

Tonight We Ride   Rainger 1936; Robin 1936

Tonight Will Live   Gordon 1940

Tonight Will Live (Oracion Caribe)   Washington 1938

Tonight Will Never Come Again   Howard, Joseph E. 1909; Kahn 1937

Tonight You Are in Paree   Martin 1951

Tonight You Belong to Me   Rose 1927

Tonight You're Mine   Washington 1944

Tonight's My Night   Davis 1965

Tonight's My Night with Baby   Caesar 1926

Tonight's the Night   Egan 1932; Fisher 1916; Gershwin, George 1929; Gershwin, Ira 1929; Goetz 1911; Herbert 1919; Johnson, Howard 1916; Kahn 1929; Silver 1954; Whiting 1932

Tony   Goetz 1910

Tony Pastor's   Blane 1968; Martin 1968

Tony Spagoni   Parish 1932

Tony the Monkey   Martin 1958

Tony the Peddler   Herbert 1903; Smith, Harry B. 1903

Tony, Tony, Tony   Romberg 1927; Smith, Harry B. 1927

Tony's in Town   Woods 1936

Tony's Thoughts   Loesser 1956

Tony's Wife   Adamson 1933; Lane 1933

Too Bad   Porter 1955

Too Bad I Can't Be Good   Dubin 1930

Too Bad I'm Good!   Whiting 1930

Too Bad, Jim   Razaf 1925

Too Bad, Too Sad   Donaldson 1944

Too Bad We Couldn't Fall in Love   Adams 1954; Strouse 1956

Too Beautiful to Last   Webster 1971

Too Beautiful Tonight   Duke 1963

Too Blue   Lewis 1927; Young, Joe 1927

Too Coo-Coo Birds   Rainger 1929; Robin 1929

Too Darn Hot   Porter 1948

Too Early for the Blues   David, Hal 1958

Too Good for the Average Man   Hart 1936; Rodgers 1936

Too Good to Be Meant for Me   Howard, Bart 1984

Too Good to Be True   Brown, Lew 1928; DeSylva 1928; Henderson 1928

Too Good To Talk About   Coleman 1957; Leigh 1957

Too Happy to Fall in Love   Evans 1954; Livingston, Jay 1954

Too Heavenly for This World   Drake 1948

Too Late   Akst 1930; Clarke 1930; Lewis 1931; Young, Victor 1931

Too Late for Conversation   Merrill 1946

Too Late for Tears   Cahn 1967

Too Late (inst.)   Revel 1959

Too Late, My Love (inst.)   McHugh 1963

Too Late Now   Lane 1951; Lerner, Alan Jay 1951

Too Late to Be Sorry (Too Early to Cry)   David, Hal 1952

Too Late to Worry   Bacharach 1961

Too Little Time   Evans 1956; Livingston, Jay 1956; Mancini 1953, 1964; Raye 1953, 1964

Too Long from Long Acre Square   Cohan 1908

Too Many!   Kern 1970; Webster 1970

Too Many Chiefs and Not Enough Injuns   David, Hal 1955

Too Many Faces   Kern 1971; Webster 1971

Too Many Girls   Berlin 1922; Hart 1939; Rodgers 1939

Too Many Hearts   Webster 1950

Too Many Kisses   Dubin 1926

Too Many Kisses in the Summer Bring Too Many Tears in the Fall   Dubin 1925; Rose 1925; Warren 1925
Too Many Kisses Mean Too Many Tears   Bryan 1922
Too Many Miles from Broadway   Cohan 1901
Too Many Mornings   Sondheim 1971
Too Many Nights   Howard, Joseph E. 1955
Too Many on Your Mind, Nobody in Your Heart   Kahn 1932
Too Many Parties and Too Many Pals   Dixon 1923; Henderson 1925; Rose 1925
Too Many People   Coleman 1972
Too Many Rings Around Rosie   Caesar 1925; Youmans 1925
Too Many Sweethearts   Berlin 1923, 1925; Bryan 1923; Egan 1923; Whiting 1923
Too Many Teardrops   Silver 1956
Too Many Tears   Dubin 1932; Warren 1932
Too Many Times   Friend 1962
Too Many Tomorrows   Coleman 1966; Fields 1966
Too Marvelous for Words   Mercer 1937; Whiting 1937
Too Much   David, Hal 1956
Too Much, Baby, Baby   Sigman 1955
Too Much Imagination   Burke 1935; Spina 1935
Too Much Love   Blane 1949; Stept 1940
Too Much Lovin'   Magidson 1929
Too Much Time Between Kisses   Kalmar 1937; Ruby 1937
Too Much Trouble   Lawrence 1951
Too Much-a Manana   Carmichael 1948
Too Neat to Be a Beatnik, Too Proud to Be a Square   Cahn 1959; Van Heusen 1959
Too Old to Be So Young   Styne 1980
Too Romantic   Burke 1940; Monaco 1940
Too Soon   Cahn 1947; Rome 1962; Styne 1947; Weill 1943
Too, Too Divine   Duke 1929, 1930; Harburg 1930
Too Toy   Styne 1940
Too Young to Be Old   David, Hal 1991; Strouse 1991
Too Young to Bop   Sherman 1958
Too Young to Go Steady   Adamson 1956; McHugh 1956
Toodeloo   Willson 1956
Toodle Oo   Kern 1916
Toodle Oodle Um   Hammerstein 1920; Harbach 1920
Toodle-oo!   Friml 1918; Hammerstein 1923; Youmans 1923
Toodle-oodle-oo   Coots 1954
Toodles Imitation   Loesser 1941
Took Me a Little Time   Merrill 1964; Styne 1964
Toom Balalaika (Play Balalaika)   Hoffman 1959
Too-Ra-Loo-Re (A French Pavanne)   Herbert 1917
Toot Sweets   Sherman 1968
Toot Toot Tootsie (Goodbye)   Kahn 1921
Toot-a-Loor   Willson 1953
Tooth and Claw   Ellington 1946
Toothache Blues   Arlen 1930; Koehler 1930
Tootsie   Bergman 1973, 1982
Tootsie Tripper   Edwards 1907
Tootsie-Wootsie   Atteridge 1913
Toot-Toot!   Kern 1918
Top Banana   Mercer 1951
Top Gallants (Legionaires)   Akst 1936; Clare 1936
Top Hat and Cane Dance   Brooks 1958
Top Hat, White Tie, and Tails   Berlin 1935
Top Hole   Gorney 1924
Top o' the Morning   Burke 1949; Van Heusen 1949
Top o' the Morning, Bridget McCue   Sterling 1907; Von Tilzer 1907
Top of the Mornin'   Styne 1940
Top of the Sky   Merrill 1993; Styne 1993
Top of the Tower   Washington 1958

Top of the Town   Adamson 1937; McHugh 1937
Top That If You Can   Leigh 1976; Styne 1976
Topaz Tango (inst.)   Alter 1955
Topaz Waltz (inst.)   Warren Date Unknown
Topic of the Tropics, The   Livingston, Jerry 1935
Topics of the Day   Atteridge 1920; Friend 1922
Topsy and Eva   Fields 1930; McHugh 1930
Torch Burns at Midnight, The   Parish 1961
Torch of Victory   Johnson, Howard 1946
Torch Parade   Henderson 1934; Koehler 1934
Torch Singer, The   Rainger 1933; Robin 1933
Torch Song   Berlin 1932; Dixon 1931; Warren 1931; Young, Joe 1931
Torch Songs   Brown, Lew 1933; Henderson 1933
Torchy   Sigman 1951
Toreodor Song   Johnson, Howard 1939
Torere   Hoffman 1958
Tornado (inst.), The   Willson 1929
Torpedo Jim   Monaco 1917
Torpedo Joe   Styne 1940
Torture   Freed, Ralph 1959
Tortured   Burke 1958; Van Heusen 1958
Toscanini, Stokowski and Me   Bullock 1938; Dubin 1940; McHugh 1940; Spina 1938, 1944
Toscanini, Tschaikowsky and Me   Spina 1950
Tosy and Cosh   Lane 1965; Lerner, Alan Jay 1965
Totem Dance   Comden and Green 1947
Totem Tom-Tom   Friml 1924; Hammerstein 1924; Harbach 1924
Touch, The   David, Hal 1959; Spina 1976
Touch a Hair of His Head   Cahn 1966; Van Heusen 1966
Touch and Go   Leigh 1967
Touch (inst.)   Bacharach 1981
Touch Me Not   Egan 1929
Touch of Class, A   Cahn 1972
Touch of Love, The   Cahn 1976; Silver 1955
Touch of Texas, A   Loesser 1942; McHugh 1942
Touch of the Blues, A   Livingston, Jerry 1960
Touch of the Woman's Hand, The   Harbach 1917
Touch of Voodoo, A   Martin 1952
Touch of You, A   De Lange 1944; Myrow 1944
Touch of Your Hand, The   Harbach 1933; Kern 1933
Touchdown (inst.)   Waller 1929
Touche (You Have Hit the Target at Last)   Parish 1956
Touching   Lawrence 1971
Touchstone   Oakland 1961
Tough Truckin'   Ellington 1947; Mills 1947
Toujours, A   Lerner, Alan Jay 1958; Loewe 1958
Toujours L'Amour on the Cote D'Azur   Coslow 1955
Toujours Moi (Always Me) (inst.)   Revel 1949
Tour de Force   Duke 1963
Tour Must Go On, The   Martin 1951
Tour of the Town   Gershwin, George 1947; Gershwin, Ira 1947
Touring San Francisco   Adamson 1945; McHugh 1945
Tourist in Mexico   Spina 1977
Tourist Trade, The   Cahn 1948; Styne 1948
Tourist Trap (inst.)   Bacharach 1966
Tournament of Roses Parade, The   Russell 1957
Toussaint L'Overture   Blake 1944; Johnson, James P. 1944; Razaf 1944
Tout Suite   Egan 1919; Whiting 1919
Tower of Strength   Bacharach 1961
Towers to the Sky Town   Drake 1955
Town Called Might-Have-Been   Howard, Joseph E. 1919

Town Hall Tonight   Hart 1926; Rodgers 1926

Town Topics   Smith, Robert B. 1915

Town Without Pity   Washington 1961

Townsend Harris March, The   Drake 1984

Toy Ballerina (inst.)   Alter 1948

Toy Balloon (Edie's Library)   Spina 1977

Toy Carousel, The   Myrow 1960

Toy Dance   Atteridge 1919, 1920; Romberg 1919; Schwartz, Jean 1919

Toy Doll Goodbye   Egan 1924; Whiting 1924

Toy March (inst.)   Young, Victor 1954

Toy Meets Girl   Heyman 1941

Toy of Destiny   Porter 1924

Toy Piper (inst.), The   Johnson, James P. 1945

Toy Soldiers (inst.), The   Herbert 1916

Toy Store   Comden and Green 1982

Toy Tiger   Mancini 1955

Toy Town Tune Parade   Coots 1955

Toy Trumpet   Brown, Lew 1938; Mitchell 1938; Pollack 1938

Toyland   Herbert 1903

Toyland Today (A Fantasy)   Herbert 1923

Toymakers Shop, The   Herbert 1903

Toys   Merrill 1953

Toys for Tots   Fain 1957; Webster 1957

Toys Gave a Party for Poppa Santa Claus, The   Burke 1950; Van Heusen 1950

Toys in the Closet   Spina 1966

Toys, Toys, Toys   Cobb 1917; Edwards 1917

Tra La La   Gershwin, Ira 1944

Tra La La and the Oom Pah Pah, The   Rainger 1939; Robin 1939

Tra, La! La! La!   Berlin 1913; Sterling 1920; Von Tilzer 1920

Tracey   Styne 1965

Trade Winds   Friend 1940

Tradewinds Aloha   Drake 1963

Trading Post of the Air   Bullock 1940; Styne 1940

Traffic Jam   Brooks 1959

Traffic that Roars in the Spring, The   Caesar 1942

Traffic Was Terrific, The   Loesser 1935; Motzan 1935

Tragedian Ballet (inst.)   Duke 1936

Tragedy and Comedy   Hammerstein 1920; Harbach 1920

Trail of Dreams   Johnson, Howard 1939

Trail of Glory, The   Kalmar 1932; Ruby 1932

Trail of the Lonesome Pine, The   Carroll 1913

Trail of the Tamarind Tree, The   Leslie 1928

Trail Through Lonesome Valley Is the Trail of Long Lost Dreams, The   Burke 1931

Trail to Sunset Valley, The   Gilbert 1916

Trailer Song (Roamin' in a Home on Wheels), The   Ahlert 1936; Young, Joe 1936

Trailing a Shooting Star   Schwartz, Arthur 1930

Trail's End   Brooks 1940

Train, The   Berlin 1949

Train in the Night, A   Adams 1996; Strouse 1996

Train Music (inst.)   Duke 1963

Train Must Be Fed, The   Mercer 1945; Warren 1945

Train of Sin   Webster 1983

Train that Brought You to Town, The   Loesser 1948

Train that Leaves for Town   Schwartz, Jean 1919

Train to Johannesburg   Weill 1949

Train Wheels Sang a Song, The   Friend 1945

Train Whistles   Razaf 1942

Trains and Boats and Planes   Bacharach 1964; David, Hal 1964

Train's Gonna Be Dere Tonight, The   Robison 1961

Trains in the Night   Russell 1942

Tra-La-La   Gershwin, Ira 1922; Gordon 1940; Warren 1940

Tra-La-La-La   Gordon 1947; Warren 1947

Tra-La-La-La-La   Lewis 1927; Young, Joe 1927

Tra-La-Li   Atteridge 1911

Tramp! Tramp! Tramp!   Herbert 1910, 1935; Kahn 1935

Tramp Tramp Tramp the Boys Are Marching   Kahal 1933

Trampin' Along   Hart 1926; Rodgers 1926

Trample Your Troubles   Schwartz, Jean 1928

Tramps at Sea   Fields 1931; McHugh 1931

Transatlantic Rhythm   Caesar 1936; Henderson 1936

Transformation   Hart 1926; Rodgers 1926

Transformation Lullaby   Howard, Joseph E. 1909

Trapeze   Burke 1956

Trastamara Rose, The   Willson 1969

Travelin' Light   Akst 1937; Clare 1937; Loesser 1950

Travelin' Light (inst.)   Young, Victor 1947

Travelin' Man   Coleman 1988; Howard, Joseph E. 1907

Travelin' on My Thumb   Coleman 1972

Traveling   Carmichael 1957; Johnson, Howard 1927

Traveling Around the World   Brooks 1961

Traveling Down a Lonely Road   Raye 1956

Traveling Men Are Traveling Again, The   Fain 1949; Yellen 1949

Traveling Salesman and the Farmer's Daughter, The   David, Mack 1958; Livingston, Jerry 1958

Traveling Together   Coleman 1979

Travellin'   Merrill 1966

Travellin' Down the Trail Back Home   Mills 1938

Travellin' Music   Sherman 1978

Travelogue   Blane 1956; Harbach 1926; Kern 1926; Martin 1956

Trav'lin'   Robison 1960

Trav'lin' Free   Evans 1951; Livingston, Jay 1951

Trav'lin' Light   Mercer 1943

Trav'lin' Man   Robison 1957

Trav'lling the Road   Lerner, Sammy 1934

Treasure Island   Egan 1925; Gershwin, George 1928; Gershwin, Ira 1928; Kern 1920; Styne 1985; Whiting 1925

Treat 'Em Rough   Baer 1923

Treat for the Eyes, A   Friend 1937; Stept 1937

Treat Me Like a Baby   Razaf 1931

Treat Me Like a Baby Doll   Johnson, J. Rosamond 1914

Treat Me Rough   Gershwin, George 1930; Gershwin, Ira 1930

Treaty, My Sweetie, With You, A   Hart 1937; Rodgers 1937

Tree in the Park, A   Hart 1926; Rodgers 1926

Tree in Tipperary, A   Loesser 1936

Tree of Love, The   Brennan 1929

Tree Was a Tree, A   Gordon 1933; Revel 1933

Tree-Top of Love   Brennan 1927

Trembling of a Leaf   Lawrence 1943

Tremont Avenue Cruisewear Fashion Show, The   Livingston, Jerry 1973

Tres Bien   Styne 1941

Trial, The   Sondheim 1968

Trial By Jury   Bacharach 1966; David, Hal 1966

Trial (Ladies of the Jury), The   Hammerstein 1928; Romberg 1928

Trials of a Simple Maid, The   Smith, Harry B. 1903

Triangle (inst.), The   Kern 1915; Styne 1951

Tribute   Oakland 1960

Tribute (inst.)   Alter 1938

Tribute to Ted   Oakland 1960

Trick, The   David, Hal 1960

Trick in Arithmetic, A   Drake 1955

Trick or Treat   Coots 1951

Trick or Treat (For Halloween)   David, Mack 1952; Hoffman 1951; Livingston, Jerry 1952

Trickeration   Arlen 1931; Koehler 1931

Tricky Fingers (inst.)   Blake 1959

Tried and True   Raye 1956

Trilby   Buck 1915

Trimmin' the Women   Robin 1930; Whiting 1930

Trini   Atteridge 1914, 1923; Caesar 1923; Carroll 1914; Romberg 1914

Trinidad   Cahn 1942; DePaul 1958; McHugh 1954; Raye 1958

Trinidad Daddee   Adams 1957

Trinidad Lady   Russell 1951

Trinidad Rhumba   Cahn 1955

Trinity Blue   Herbert 1944

Trinka Brinker   Martin 1958

Trio   Dietz 1944; Duke 1944; Lerner, Alan Jay 1951; Loewe 1951

Trio in Rio (Saudade)   Heyman 1948

Trip   Strouse 1971

Trip to Bermuda, A   Friml 1912; Harbach 1912

Trip to the Hole in the Wall   David, Mack 1965; Livingston, Jerry 1965

Triplets   Dietz 1937; Schwartz, Arthur 1937

Tripoli   Dubin 1920

Tripping Along in Tripoli   Johnson, Howard 1928

Tripping the Light Fantastic   Rome 1952

Tripping, Tripping   Goetz 1916

Triskaidekaphobia   Drake 1953

Triumph of His Airship, The   Ahlert 1910

Triumphant (inst.)   Schwartz, Jean 1930

Trivers Livers   Conrad 1934; Magidson 1934

Trocadero, The   Lane 1934

Trocadero Opening Chorus   Hammerstein 1927; Kern 1927

Trolley Car Swing, The   Young, Joe 1912

Trolley Song, The   Martin 1944

Trolleys of Old Broadway, The   Howard, Joseph E. 1950

Trombone Jazz   Atteridge 1918; Romberg 1918; Schwartz, Jean 1918

Troo-le-oo-le-ay   Stept 1926

Tropic Mood (inst.)   Myrow 1957

Tropic Vamps   Johnson, Howard 1921

Tropical, The   Coslow 1937

Tropical Magic   Gordon 1941; Warren 1941

Tropical Moon   Blake 1930

Tropical Night   Gershwin, Ira 1944; Kern 1944

Tropicana   DePaul 1942; Raye 1942; Schwartz, Jean 1942

Trottin' to the Fair   Blane 1952

Trottin' to the Land of Cotton Melodies   Clarke 1924; Johnston 1924; Meyer 1924; Turk 1924

Troubadour   Gorney 1930; Harburg 1930

Trouble About the Drama   Kern 1928

Trouble Doesn't Like Music — Everybody Sing   Cahn 1936

Trouble in Paradise   Ager 1933; Robin 1932; Schwartz, Jean 1933

Trouble (inst.)   Waller 1929

Trouble Man   Weill 1949

Trouble Seems to Follow Me Around   Blake 1954

Trouble with Harry, The   David, Hal 1955; Loesser 1955

Trouble with Women, The   Weill 1943

Trouble with Women Is Men, The   Fain 1951; Webster 1951

Trouble with You, The   Coleman 1988

Troubled Waters   Coslow 1934; Johnston 1934

Troubles Are Bubbles   Brooks 1960

Troublesome Ivories (inst.)   Blake 1971

Trousers   Johnson, J. Rosamond 1950

Trousseau Ball, The   Friml 1919; Harbach 1919

Trousseau for Trudy   Alter 1953

Trousseau Incomplete, The   Romberg 1921

Trousseau Song   Fain 1959; Webster 1959

Trout, The   Freed, Ralph 1941

Truck Driver's Lament   Brooks 1960

Truckin'   Bloom 1935; Koehler 1935

Truckin' in My Tails   Henderson 1935; Yellen 1935

Truckin' on Down   Blake 1935

True and Sincere Love   Gilbert 1931

True Blue   Robin 1928; Styne 1956

True Blue Gal   Silver 1919

True Blue Pals   Lawrence 1964

True Blue Sam, the Traveling Man   Brown, Lew 1922; Donaldson 1922

True Blue You   Coslow 1929; Robin 1929; Whiting 1929

True Born Soldier Man   Berlin 1912

True Confession   Coslow 1936

True Hearts   Romberg 1925

True Love   David, Hal 1951; Davis 1928; DeSylva 1925; Donaldson 1940; Gershwin, George 1921; Gershwin, Ira 1921; Hanley 1925; Kahn 1940; Porter 1956; Robin 1933; Whiting 1933

True Love at Last   Stept 1975

True Love Is an Apricot   Sherman 1962

True Love Is Not for a Day   Smith, Harry B. 1902

True Love Never Runs Smooth   Bacharach 1962; Conrad 1932; David, Hal 1962

True Love Will Find a Way   Smith, Robert B. 1914

True Love Will Never Grow Cold   Hammerstein 1923; Harbach 1923; Youmans 1923

True or False   Sigman 1953

True to the Navy   Adamson 1945; McHugh 1945

True to Them All   Gershwin, George 1927; Gershwin, Ira 1927

True to Two   Robin 1926

True to You   Parish 1931

Truly   Davis 1922; Mercer 1949

Truly Content   Sondheim 1962

Truly Loved   Loesser 1965

Truly Scrumptious   Sherman 1968

Trumpet in Stringtime   Drake 1945

Trumpet Man   DePaul 1950; Raye 1950

Trumpet Player's Lament, The   Burke 1938; Monaco 1938

Trumpeter and the Lover, The   Heyman 1931; Youmans 1931

Trumpeter, Blow Your Horn   Gershwin, George 1931; Gershwin, Ira 1931

Trust in Him   Davis 1957

Trust in Me   Ager 1936; Duke 1963; Schwartz, Jean 1934

Trust in Me (Python's Song)   Sherman 1967

Trust Me   Evans 1961; Livingston, Jay 1961; Styne 1978

Trust Your Destiny to Your Star   Porter 1958

Trusting My Luck   Johnston 1938

Truth, The   Coleman 1962; Ellington 1965; Leigh 1962

Truth About Cinderella, The   Strouse 1975

Truth About Youth, The   Sherman 1962

Truth in a Conrecte Nutshell, The   Spina 1977

Truthful Parson Brown   Robison 1928

Truthfully   Livingston, Jerry 1937

Try   Bergman 1986

Try a Little Forgiveness   Baer 1965
Try a Little Kiss   Duke 1926
Try a Little Prayer   Magidson 1956
Try a Little Something New   Sherman 1983
Try a Little Tenderness   Woods 1932
Try a Ring Dear!   Buck 1918
Try Again Tomorrow   Hart 1926, 1928; Rodgers 1926, 1928
Try an Experiment (inst.)   Kern 1938
Try and Get a Kiss from Fifi   Conrad 1927
Try and Get It   Von Tilzer 1920
Try Dancing   Kalmar 1929; Revel 1929; Ruby 1929
Try Her Out at Dances   Hammerstein 1928; Romberg 1928
Try It Over Again (If You Don't Like It)   Brown, Lew 1914
Try Love   Davis 1941, 1950
Try Loving Me   Brown, Lew 1927; DeSylva 1927; Henderson 1927
Try Me   Hammerstein 1920; Harbach 1920
Try Not to Be Lonely   Robison 1943
Try Not to Forget   Drake 1941
Try This for That Tired Feeling   Alter 1930
Try This on Your Pianna, Anna   Goetz 1911
(I've Already Started In to) Try to Figure Out a Way to Go to Work to Try to Get You   Willson 1957
Try to Forget   Harbach 1931; Kern 1931
Try to Forget Me   Cahn 1980
Try to Love Me Just As I Am   Comden and Green 1958; Styne 1958
Try to See It My Way   Bacharach 1966; David, Hal 1966
Try to See It My Way (Baby)   Dixon 1934; Wrubel 1934
Try Your Luck   Arlen 1950; Mercer 1950
Trying   Kahn 1923; Kalmar 1921; Ruby 1921; Smith, Harry B. 1925
Trying It On   Smith, Harry B. 1910
Trying on Dresses   Smith, Harry B. 1906
Trying to Forget   Yellen 1923
Trying to Forget (Where the Sweet Forget-Me-Nots Grow)   Coots 1931; Davis 1931
Trylon Song   Mills 1943
Tryst of Love (inst.)   Carmichael 1925
Tschaikowsky (And Other Russians)   Gershwin, Ira 1940; Weill 1940
Tsk, Tsk, That's Love (The Click Click Song)   Gordon 1944; Monaco 1944
T.S.U. (Alma Mater)   Mitchell 1936; Pollack 1936, 1949
T.T. on Toast   Ellington 1947; Mills 1947
Tu Carrismo   Hammerstein 1920; Harbach 1920
Tuck Me to Sleep in My Old Kentucky Home   Lewis 1921; Meyer 1921; Young, Joe 1921
Tularosa   Livingston, Jerry 1954
Tulip Time   Buck 1919; Freed, Ralph 1942; Goetz 1913; Lane 1942
Tulip Time in Sing-Sing (Dear Old Fashioned Prison of Mine)   Kern 1924
Tulip Told a Tale, A   Kalmar 1936; Ruby 1936
Tulips and Apple Strudel   Bryan 1934
Tulips and Pansies   Atteridge 1915; Romberg 1915
Tulips Are Talking Tonight, The   Magidson 1942; McHugh 1942
Tulips (Two Lips)   Kern 1905
Tuli-Tulip Time   Lawrence 1938
Tulsa   Wrubel 1949
Tum on and Tiss Me   Gershwin, George 1920
Tumble Down Shack in Havana   Styne 1941
Tumble in a Rumble Seat   Coots 1933
Tumble in Time   Whiting 1926

Tumble Inn   Atteridge 1919; Romberg 1919; Schwartz, Jean 1919
Tumbleweed   Robison 1927
Tummy-Tummy-Tum   Howard, Joseph E. 1909
Tum-Tiddly-Tum-Tum   Hammerstein 1920; Harbach 1920
Tune #6 Sept. 14 (inst.)   Youmans 1954
Tune for Humming, A   Loesser 1950
Tune In   Robison 1958
Tune in on My Heart   Gilbert 1937
Tune In (To Station J.O.Y)   DeSylva 1924; Gershwin, George 1924
Tune on the Tip of My Heart, The   Drake 1947
Tune to Tap My Toe To, A   Hoffman 1956
Tune You Can't Forget, The   Friml 1918
Tunes (inst.)   Strouse 1986
Tunnel of Love, The   Loesser 1947, 1948
Turandot — 3rd Act   Lerner, Sammy 1943
Turf Routine   Oakland 1960
Turkey Dinner   Loesser 1937
Turkey Giblets   Loesser 1937
Turkey in the Straw   Hart 1926; Johnson, Howard 1939; Rodgers 1926
Turkey Trot   Loesser 1937; Norworth 1911; Smith, Harry B. 1911
Turkey Trot (inst.)   Kern 1911
Turkey Trotting Boy (Oh! You Turkey Trotter)   Atteridge 1914; Carroll 1914
Turkish Delight (inst.)   Loesser 1965
Turkish Folk Song   Evans 1952; Livingston, Jay 1952; Young, Victor 1952
Turkish Jerk, The   Coslow 1952
Turkish Towel   Fain 1926; Mills 1926
Turlututu   Duke 1963
Turn Around   Bacharach 1984
Turn Around and Go Back Home   Hoffman 1957
Turn Back the Clock   David, Hal 1961; Parish 1933
Turn Back the Universe and Give Me Yesterday   Brennan 1916
Turn Down the Light   Kahn 1912
Turn It into a Musical   Cahn 1963; Van Heusen 1963
Turn It On   Brooks 1960; Warren 1960
Turn Me Loose on Broadway   Duke 1952
Turn Off the Moon   Coslow 1937
Turn Off the Rain (Turn on a Rainbow)   Brown, Lew 1944; Henderson 1944
Turn Off Your Light Mr. Moon Man (Turn Off the Light Mr. Moon Man)   Norworth 1911; Smith, Harry B. 1911
Turn on the Heat   Brown, Lew 1929; DeSylva 1929; Henderson 1929
Turn on the Lights   Lerner, Alan Jay 1969
Turn on the Moon   Adamson 1934; Lane 1934
Turn on the Old Music Box   Washington 1940
Turn on the Popular Moon   Conrad 1924
Turn on the Tap   Oakland 1937
Turn Out the Light   Brown, Nacio Herb 1932; DeSylva 1932; Whiting 1932
Turn Over   Jerome 1905; Schwartz, Jean 1905
Turn That Frown Upside Down   Rainger 1933; Robin 1933
Turn that Frown Upside Down, Smile at the Cockeyed World   Stept 1931; Young, Joe 1931
Turn to Me   Eliscu 1929
Turn to the Dream Ahead   Gershwin, Ira 1924
Turn to the Right   Ager 1916; Jerome 1916
Turn Yo' Damper Down   Robison 1928
(Don't Let Temptation) Turn You 'Round   Friend 1953

Turning the Town Upside Down (O.H.M.S.)   Hoffman 1937

Turntable Song (Round an' Round an' Round), The   Robin 1947

Turquoise Blue (inst.)   Alter 1953

Turtle Dove River   Robison 1951

Turtle Song   Arlen 1954

Turtle Theme (inst.), The   Young, Victor 1954

Turtle's Racing Song   Bergman 1983

Tuscaloosa   Fields 1951; Schwartz, Arthur 1951, 1954

Tuscarora, The   Willson 1942

Tutti for Cootie   Ellington 1964

Tut-Tut-Tut-Tilly   Carroll 1926

Tutu and Tights   Coleman 1973; Fields 1973

T.V. Magic   Drake 1955

Twang, Twang, Twang   Cahn 1959; Van Heusen 1959

'Twas a Balmy Summer's Evening   Friend 1933; Magidson 1933; Stept 1933

'Twas a Kiss in the Moonlight   Conrad 1928

'Twas Awfully Nice of You   Caesar 1933; Friend 1933

'Twas Brillig   DePaul 1951; Raye 1951

'Twas Different Years Ago   Herbert 1908

'Twas in a Garden   Harbach 1914

Twas in the Month of June   Herbert 1920; Smith, Robert B. 1920

'Twas Not So Long Ago   Hammerstein 1929; Kern 1929

'Twas Only a Summer Night's Dream   Kahn 1932

'Twas Only an Irishman's Dream   Dubin 1916

Tweedledee for President   Gershwin, George 1933; Gershwin, Ira 1933

Tweedledum and Tweedledee   Herbert 1913

Tweet Tweet   Brown, Lew 1926; DeSylva 1926; Henderson 1926

Tweet, Tweet, Tweedle in the Trees, The   Dixon 1936; Henderson 1936

Tweet Tweet Tweet   Washington 1949

"Tweets" Says: I've Got Nine Lives — Do You?   Sissle 1960

Tweets Says, I've Got Nine Lives, Do You?   Blake 1960

Twelfth Avenue (inst.)   Johnson, James P. 1943

Twelfth of Never, The   Livingston, Jerry 1956; Webster 1956

Twelfth Street Rag   Razaf 1914

Twelve Days of Christmas, The   Cahn 1969; Van Heusen 1969

Twelve Feet Tall   Livingston, Jerry 1956

Twelve Little Cuties   Kalmar 1938; Ruby 1938

Twelve O'Clock and All's Not Well   Oakland 1938

Twelve O'Clock at Night   Rose 1923

Twelve O'Clock Girl in a Nine O'Clock Town, A   Friml 1922; Harbach 1922

Twelve O'Clock Kiss   Friend 1951

Twelve O'Clock Rock   Raye 1957

Twelve O'Clock Waltz   Dixon 1928; Rose 1928; Warren 1928

Twelve Pretty Wives from Turkey   Smith, Harry B. 1903

Twentieth Century Love   Cohan 1927

20th Century Maiden's Prayer, The   Hanley 1917

20th Century Man, The   Leslie 1914

20th Century Rag, The   Clarke 1914

20th Century Rhapsody (inst.)   Ravel 1937

Twentieth Century Squaw   Yellen 1916

Twenty Five Years from Now   McHugh 1923

Twenty Four Hours a Day   Ager 1933; Young, Joe 1933

Twenty Four Hours from Tulsa   Bacharach 1963; David, Hal 1963

Twenty Four Little Hours Ago   Von Tilzer 1960

Twenty Happy Years   Adams 1981; Strouse 1981

Twenty Million People   Coslow 1933; Johnston 1933

27 Elm Street   Arlen 1952; Blane 1953

26 Miles of Barbed Wire   Freed, Ralph 1961

Twenty Swedes Ran Through the Weeds, Chasing One Norwegian   Bryan 1930

Twenty Third Psalm   Johnston 1948

23 Skidoo   Bullock 1937; Spina 1937

Twenty Years Ago   Atteridge 1911; Brown, Lew 1926; DeSylva 1926; Henderson 1926; Herbert 1908

Twenty-Five Bucks a Week   Gorney 1941

Twenty-Five Minutes Away   Von Tilzer 1914

Twenty-Four Hours a Day   Hanley 1935

Twenty-four Hours in Georgia   Livingston, Jerry 1934

Twenty-four Hours of Love   Brown, Lew Date Unknown; Henderson Date Unknown

Twenty-One Bucks a Week   Eliscu 1941; Gorney 1941

Twenty-Six Toots   Willson 1955

Twice a Year   Arlen 1934; Koehler 1934

Twice as Tall   Cahn 1959; Van Heusen 1959

Twickenham Ferry   Johnson, Howard 1939

Twiddle-Dee the Clown   Coots 1950

Twiddlin' My Thumbs   Cahn 1941; Livingston, Jerry 1936

Twilight   DeSylva 1925; Gorney 1925; Porter 1912; Razaf 1934; Spina 1977

Twilight at Noon   Kahal 1935

Twilight Caresses (inst.)   Gorney 1935

Twilight in Barakeesh   Herbert 1908

Twilight in Sweetheart Lane   Johnson, Howard 1935

Twilight in Tennessee   Hoffman 1957

Twilight Melodies   Young, Victor 1929

Twilight Nocturne (Beverly Hills, Blue Nocturne) (inst.)   Young, Victor 1951

Twilight on the Trail   Alter 1936; Mitchell 1936

Twilight Rag (inst.)   Johnson, James P. 1917

Twilight Rhythms   Schwartz, Jean 1935

Twilight Serenade   Caesar 1924

Twilight Song   Evans 1951; Lawrence 1946; Livingston, Jay 1951

Twilight, the Stars, and You   Brown, Nacio Herb 1925

Twilight Time   Ellington 1955

Twilight Town   Goetz 1909

Twilight Troubadour   David, Mack 1940; Silver 1940

Twilight Voices   Brennan 1929; Romberg 1925; Smith, Harry B. 1925

Twilight Waltz, The   Ruby 1958

Twilly of Fifth Avenue   Romberg 1924

Twin Sisters   Porter 1922

Twin Soliloquies   Hammerstein 1949; Rodgers 1949

Twine for Mayor   Brooks 1942

Twinkle in Your Eye, A   Hart 1938; Rodgers 1938

Twinkle, Little Lucky Star   Dubin 1924

Twinkle Little Star   Friml 1919; Harbach 1919

Twinkle Little Stars   Kalmar 1928; Ruby 1928

Twinkle Twinkle   Howard, Bart 1965

Twinkle, Twinkle, Little Star   Ager 1923; Johnson, Howard 1939; Magidson 1936; Oakland 1936; Yellen 1923

Twinkle Twinkle My Little Star   Edwards 1908

Twirly Little Girlies at the End of the Line, The   Herbert 1912

Twist My Arm   Fain 1951, 1955; Webster 1951, 1955

Twistin' in the Old Town   David, Mack 1962

Twistin' Time   Ellington 1962

Twist-o-Flex   Carmichael 1965

Twit Twit Twit   Schwartz, Jean 1918

'Twixt Love and Duty   Herbert 1917

'Twixt Myself and Me   Burke 1949; Van Heusen 1949

Twixt the Devil and the Deep Blue Sea   Schwartz, Arthur 1933

Twizzle, The   David, Mack 1962; Livingston, Jerry 1962

Two a Day for Keith (Twice a Night)   Hart 1936; Rodgers 1936

Two Against One   Gilbert 1939; Pollack 1939

Two Against the World   Bacharach 1957; David, Hal 1957

Two Alone   Burke 1934; Friend 1917; Mitchell 1917; Spina 1934

Two Are Company   Smith, Harry B. 1926

Two Aristocrats   Coslow 1933; Johnston 1933

Two Arms   Russell 1958, 1960

Two Behind the Eight-Ball!   Bryan Date Unknown; Fisher Date Unknown

Two Big Brown Eyes (inst.)   Motzan 1919

Two Big Eyes   Porter 1915

Two Birdies Up a Tree   Freed, Ralph 1937; Lane 1937

Two Black Crows Blues   Dubin 1928; Robison 1928

Two Blind Loves   Arlen 1939; Harburg 1939

Two Blue Eyes, One Little Green Isle   Bryan 1931

Two Boys   Brown, Lew 1928; DeSylva 1928; Henderson 1928

Two Brothers   Washington 1950

Two Buck Tim from Timbuctoo   Heyman 1933; Hoffman 1933

Two By Four   Caesar 1926

Two by Two   Rodgers 1965, 1970; Sondheim 1965

Two Can Go to Helen   Caesar 1976

Two Can Play that Game   Smith, Harry B. 1916

Two Castanets   Hoffman 1955; Merrill 1955

Two Cent Encyclopedia, A   Drake 1964

Two Chairs and a Table   Lewis 1934; Meyer 1934; Parish 1937

Two Characters   Drake 1955

Two Cheers Instead of Three   Berlin 1931

Two Cigarettes in the Dark   Pollack 1934; Webster 1934

Two Clean Hands   Caesar 1967

Two Dachshunds (inst.)   Kern 1946

Two Dandy Darkies   Cohan 1914

Two Days Out of Delaware   Russell 1958

Two Dirty Little Hands   Cobb 1906; Edwards 1906

Two Dreams Got Together   Friend 1938

Two Dreams Met   Gordon 1940; Warren 1940

Two Empty Arms, One Little Empty Heart   Young, Joe 1932

Two Eyes   Johnson, Howard 1925; Johnson, J. Rosamond 1903

Two Eyes in Hawaii   Parish 1926

Two Faces in the Dark   Fields 1959

Two Fairy Tales   Sondheim 1973

Two Feet in Two Four Time   Arlen 1932; Caesar 1932

Two Fellows and a Girl   Conrad 1926; Kahn 1926

Two Figures on a Wedding Cake   Bacharach 1960

Two for the Road   Mancini 1967

Two for Tonight   Coslow 1935; Gordon 1935; Revel 1935

2/4 Girl Number (inst.)   Arlen 1936

Two Friends, The   Rome 1943; Strouse 1968

Two Girls from the Chorus   Cohan 1923

Two Great Minds   Strouse 1999

Two Guitars   Johnson, Howard 1932

Two Guitars in Jive   Coslow 1952

Two Happy Tadpoles   Romberg 1916; Smith, Robert B. 1916

Two Heads Against the Moon   Ager 1935

Two Heads Are Better than One   Goetz 1912; Kern 1915

Two Heads in the Moonlight   Adamson 1935; Donaldson 1935

Two Heads in the Moonlight Are Better than One   Freed, Arthur 1931

Two Hearts   Weill 1935

Two Hearts Are Better than One (Duettino)   Kern 1946; Mercer 1946

Two Hearts Blend As One   Gershwin, George 1927; Gershwin, Ira 1927

Two Hearts Carved on a Lonesome Pine   Ahlert 1935; Young, Joe 1935

Two Hearts Divided   Dubin 1936; Warren 1936

Two Hearts in Tune   Blake 1923; Sissle 1923

Two Hearts in Wintertime   Bryan 1942

Two Hearts Swing in Three-Quarter Time (Zwei Herzen Im Dreivierteltakt)   Young, Joe 1930

Two Hearts Together   Freed, Ralph 1946

Two Horse Fellow in a One Horse Town   Edwards 1908

Two Hour Honeymoon   Bacharach 1960

Two Hugs (With a Kiss in the Middle)   Hoffman 1960

Two in a Taxi   Dietz 1940; McHugh 1940

Two in Love   Myrow 1936; Willson 1941

Two in One (inst.)   Johnson, Howard 1914

2 Is Company   Blane 1968; Martin 1968

Two Key Rag   Von Tilzer 1916

Two Ladies and a Man   Harbach 1936; Romberg 1936

Two Ladies in de Shade of de Banana Tree   Arlen 1954

Two Laughing Irish Eyes   Herbert 1915

(Cindy with the) Two Left Feet   Webster 1941

Two Lips   Dixon 1928

Two Lips Are Roses   Bryan 1923

Two Lips in Georgia   Bryan 1919; Schwartz, Jean 1919

Two Lips Like Cherries   Kahn 1933

Two Lips (To Kiss My Cares Away)   Rose 1928; Warren 1928

Two Little — New Little — Blue Little Eyes   Friend 1949

Two Little Babes in the Wood   Porter 1924, 1928

Two Little Baby Arms   Baer 1929; Gilbert 1929

Two Little Blue Little Eyes   Webster 1931

Two Little Bluebirds   Hammerstein 1925; Harbach 1925; Kern 1925

Two Little Candles on One Little Cake   Stept 1935

Two Little Doodle Bugs   Friend 1940

Two Little Ex-WACS   Johnson, J. Rosamond 1950

Two Little Eyes of Blue   Olcott 1909

Two Little Eyes, Two Little Lips, One Little Nose (Deux Jolis Yeux, Une Nez Charmant, Deux Levres Roses)   Motzan 1931

Two Little Eyes, Two Little Lips, One Little Rose   Caesar 1931

Two Little Flies on a Lump of Sugar   Fain 1934; Kahal 1934

Two Little Girls in Blue   Gershwin, Ira 1921; Youmans 1921

Two Little Kittens   Rome 1970; Smith, Robert B. 1907

Two Little Lonesome Birds Love Birds   Brown, Lew 1912

Two Little Love Bees   Smith, Robert B. 1910

Two Little Love Birds   Romberg 1921

Two Little Magic Words   Hoffman 1954

Two Little Peas in a Pod   Gordon 1934; Revel 1934

Two Little Ruby Rings   Hammerstein 1922

Two Little Shnooks, Still in Love   Rome 1954

Two Little Squirrels, The   David, Mack 1941

Two Little Windows and One Little Door   Lewis 1933

Two Little Wooden Shoes   Hanley 1922

Two Lonely Hearts   Sigman 1951

Two Lovely Lying Eyes   Buck 1921; Friml 1921

Two Lovers and Two Lives   Russell 1955

Two Lovers Met in the Night   Cahn 1948; Styne 1948

Two Loves and Two Lives   Russell 1957

Two Loving Arms   Robin 1927

2:02 Choo Choo Bound for Caroline, The   Brown, Lew 1925; DeSylva 1925; Henderson 1925

Two of a Kind   Ahlert 1941; Hart 1926; Mercer 1960; Rodgers 1926

Two of a Kind (Nitamono Doshi)   Rome 1969

Two of Us, The   Caesar 1927; Cohan 1928; Coleman 1988; David, Hal 1958; Martin 1948

Two of You   Carmichael 1937; Sondheim 1956

Two on a Bike   Raye 1943

Two on an Island   Lane 1945

Two Pals but Only One Sweetie   Baer 1929; Gilbert 1929

Two People   Bergman 1988

Two People Who Love   Comden and Green 1982

Two Perfect Lovers   Lane 1930; Lerner, Sammy 1930

Two Playhouses, The   Cohan 1914

Two Roses, The   Johnson, Howard 1939

Two Roses of Tapolorambo   Stept 1948

Two Silhouettes (In the Setting Sun)   Coslow 1938

Two Sleepy People   Carmichael 1938; Loesser 1938

Two Sparkling Eyes   Duke 1942

Two Strangers   Razaf 1930

Two Sweethearts of Mine   Fisher 1927; Rose 1927

Two Tickets to Broadway   Robin 1951; Styne 1951

Two Tickets to Georgia   Coots 1933; Young, Joe 1933

Two Tickets to Heaven   Silver 1941

Two Time Dan   Turk 1924

Two Times a Day   Caesar 1947

Two to Eleven   Hart 1926; Rodgers 1926

Two Together   Johnston 1935; Kahn 1925, 1935; Whiting 1925

Two Ton Tessie   Turk 1926

Two Tone Poems (Suite)   Johnson, James P. 1944

Two Unfortunate Orphans   Hart 1931; Rodgers 1931

Two Whippoorwills (inst.)   Robison 1928

Two Who Love As One   Alter 1952

Two Wonderful Girls in Blue   Youmans 1921

Two Wrongs Never Make a Right   Cahn 1952

Twobly's Thingamajig   Leigh 1976

Two-Cent Stamp (Brought Me Back a Million Dollar Love), A   Ager 1935

Two-Faced Woman   Dietz 1932; Schwartz, Arthur 1932

Two-Gun Cowboy   Fisher 1935

Two-Lip Salve   Kalmar 1913

Two's Company   Martin 1968; Romberg 1919

Two-Step   Herbert 1895, 1897; Smith, Harry B. 1895, 1897

Two-Time, Hot-Time, Ragtime Daddy   Evans 1948; Livingston, Jay 1948

2X a Loser   Strouse 1999

Twould Take a Gypsy Rose Lee to Find Out   Blake 1945; Sissle 1945

Ty Cobb (The Georgia Peach)   Coots 1963

Tying Up the Loose Ends   Robison 1965

Typical Opening Chorus, The   Atteridge 1915; Carroll 1915; Romberg 1915

Typical Self-Made American, A   Gershwin, George 1927; Gershwin, Ira 1927

Typical Topical Tunes   Carroll 1918

Tze Tze (inst.)   Spina 1977

Tzena, Tzena, Tzena, Tzena   Parish 1950

Tzigane (Gypsy) (inst.)   Revel 1949

Tzin-Tzun-Tzan   Lawrence 1950; Sigman 1950

U

U Dearie   Herbert 1909

Ubangi Man   Mills 1935

U.C.L.A.   Livingston, Jerry 1963

U.C.L.A. Rally Song   Coslow 1931

Ufty - Mufty and Gufty   Leslie 1935; Monaco 1935

Ugg-a-Wugg   Comden and Green 1954; Styne 1954

Ugly American, The   Webster 1963

Ugly Bug Ball, The   Sherman 1963

Ugly Dachshund, The   Sherman 1965

Ugly Duckling, The   Loesser 1952

Ugly Identical Twins   Drake 1990

Ugly, Ugly Gal   Comden and Green 1967; Styne 1967

U-Gotta-Soda   Spina 1958

Uh-Uh!   Gershwin, Ira 1924

Uh-Uh in the Moonlight   Conrad 1929

Ukalou (Pretty South Sea Island Lady)   Von Tilzer 1917

Ukeatalia (inst.)   Bacharach 1966

Ukelele Baby   Rose 1925

Ukelele Daly   Jerome 1915; Schwartz, Jean 1915

Ukelele Lady   Williams 1915

Ukelele Sweetheart   Mills 1927

Ukelele Talk   Drake 1966

Ukulele Blues   Johnson, James P. 1922

Ukulele Lady   Donaldson 1925; Kahn 1925; Whiting 1925

Ukulele Lorelei   DeSylva 1925; Gershwin, George 1925; Gershwin, Ira 1925

Ukulele Lou   Sterling 1924

Ukulele Moon   Conrad 1930; Davis 1930

Um Pom Toodle I-Ay   Jerome 1913; Schwartz, Jean 1913

Umbrella Weather   David, Hal 1948

Umbriago   Caesar 1944

Umpire Is a Most Unhappy Man, The   Howard, Joseph E. 1905

Ump-Pah-Pah   Donaldson 1920; Lewis 1920; Young, Joe 1920

Um-Um in the Moonlight   Conrad 1929; Meyer 1929; Mitchell 1929

Um-Um-Da-Da   Berlin 1923

U.N.   Goetz 1954

Un Peu D'Amour   DeSylva 1919; Gershwin, George 1919

Un Poquito de Amor   Freed, Ralph 1947

Un Sourire   Harbach 1921

Un Sueno   Coslow 1931

Una a Dieci   Styne 1970

Una Momento   David, Mack 1956

Unaccustomed As I Am   Burke 1953; Duke 1930, 1932; Harburg 1930, 1932; Van Heusen 1953

Unaccustomed As I Am to Falling in Love   Magidson 1930; Washington 1930

Unapproachable   Drake 1978

Unbirthday Song   David, Mack 1951; Hoffman 1951; Livingston, Jerry 1951

Uncertain   Warren Date Unknown

Uncle Chris   Rodgers 1979

Uncle Dan the Hockshop Man   Fisher 1936

Uncle Don's Song   Young, Victor 1934

Uncle Luke Had a Beard   Styne 1941

Uncle Sam Gets Around   Rainger 1940; Robin 1940

Uncle Sam Is Santa Claus to the World   Buck 1917

Uncle Sam Needs a "Man Who Can Take It"   Harburg 1932

Uncle Sam Rag, The   Fields 1959

Uncle Sammy Here I Am   Johnson, James P. 1941

Uncle Sammy Hit Miami   Adamson 1945; McHugh 1945

Uncle Sam's Best Girl   Howard, Joseph E. 1907

Uncle Sam's Children (inst.)   Herbert 1916
Uncle Sam's Lullaby   Brown, Lew 1939; Stept 1939
Uncle Says I Mustn't, So I Won't   Harbach 1910
Uncle Tom   Lerner, Alan Jay 1976
Uncle Tom and Old Black Joe   Blake 1921; Sissle 1921
Uncle Tom's Cabin   Brooks 1945; Schwartz, Arthur 1926
Uncle Tom's Cabin Is a Cabaret   Akst 1936; Clare 1936
Uncle Tom's Cabin Is a Drive-In Now   Webster 1941
Uncle Tom's Cabin Is a Roadhouse Now   Fisher 1936
Under a Banana Tree   Silver 1937
Under a Blanket in a Folding Bed   Cohan 1904
Under a Blanket of Blue   Livingston, Jerry 1933
Under a One-Man Top   DeSylva 1924; Gershwin, George 1924
Under a Parasol   Coslow 1924; Romberg 1924
Under a Roof in Paree (Sous les Toits de Paris)   Caesar 1931
Under a Shady Tree with You   Coots 1932
Under a Spanish Moon (inst.)   Young, Victor 1926
Under a Wurzburger Tree   Von Tilzer 1926
Under American Skies   Henderson 1921
Under an April Moon   Coots 1945
Under Any Old Flag at All   Cohan 1907
'Under Fire' Dance, The   Cohan 1916
Under Fourteen   Merrill 1958
Under Grecian Skies   Goetz 1920
Under My Umbrella   Dietz 1943, 1946; Duke 1943; Meyer 1933; Schwartz, Arthur 1946
Under Our Lovely Umbrellas   Jerome 1904; Schwartz, Jean 1904
Under Persian Skies   Edwards 1930
Under Starry Skies of Old Hawaii   Mills 1928
Under the American Flag   Sterling 1915; Von Tilzer 1915
Under the Anhauser Bush   Sterling 1903; Von Tilzer 1903
Under the Bamboo Tree   Johnson, J. Rosamond 1902
Under the Big Top   Drake 1954
Under the China Moon   Goetz 1913
Under the Cinnamon Tree   Gershwin, George 1929; Gershwin, Ira 1929
Under the Clover Moon   Bryan 1927; Schwartz, Jean 1927
Under the Coconut Tree   Razaf 1943
Under the Dream Tree   Hanley 1939
Under the Dreamy Creole Moon   Sissle 1934
Under the Dress   Porter 1955
Under the Furlough Moon   Gershwin, George 1927; Gershwin, Ira 1927
Under the Goo Goo Tree   Jerome 1904; Schwartz, Jean 1904
Under the Honeymoon   Atteridge 1918; Hanley 1919; Romberg 1918
Under the Irish Moon   Meyer 1909
Under the Jungle Moon   Blake 1930; Razaf 1930
Under the Lamp of Love   Fain 1933; Kahal 1933
Under the Lamp Post   Merrill 1952
Under the Linden Tree   Kern 1906
Under the Love Tree   Brown, A. Seymour 1912
Under the Matzos Tree   Fisher 1907
Under the Midnight   Dubin 1913
Under the Midnight Sun   Coslow 1938; Lane 1938
Under the Midsummer Moon   Smith, Harry B. 1927
Under the Mistletoe   Hart 1921; Rodgers 1921
Under the Monkey Moon   Johnson, Howard 1930; Woods 1930
Under the Moon   Snyder 1927
Under the Moon of Waikiki   Bryan 1938
Under the Moon Talking to You About Me   Snyder 1932
Under the Mulberry Tree   Von Tilzer 1903

Under the Oriental Moon   Williams 1910
Under the Palms   Coots 1924; Rose 1924
Under the Pinewood Trees   Razaf 1950
Under the Pretzel Bough   Williams 1911
Under the Ragtime Flag   Goetz 1912
Under the Ropes (inst.)   Styne 1967
Under the Rosenbloom   Bryan 1907; Meyer 1907
Under the Sea   Herbert 1916
Under the Sleeping Volcano   Gorney 1949
Under the Snookyookum Moon   Johnson, J. Rosamond 1934
Under the Spreading Chestnut Tree   Mitchell 1919
Under the Sunset Tree   Harburg 1967; Styne 1967
Under the Sweetheart Moon   Friend 1952
Under the Sweetheart Tree   Fisher 1930; Stept 1930
Under the Sycamore Tree   Von Tilzer 1958
Under the Ukelele Tree   Dixon 1926; Henderson 1926
Under the Water   Brown, Lew 1924; Henderson 1924
Under the Yum Yum Tree   Sterling 1910; Von Tilzer 1910
Under the Yum Yum Tree Cha Cha   Sterling 1961; Von Tilzer 1961
Under the Yum-Yum Tree   Cahn 1963; Van Heusen 1963
Under Vesuvian Skies   Lane 1930; Leslie 1930
Under Your Skies of Blue   Bryan 1928; Snyder 1928
Under Your Spell   Brown, Nacio Herb 1936; Dietz 1934, 1936; Freed, Arthur 1936; Schwartz, Arthur 1934, 1936
Under Your Thumb and Close to Your Heart   Bryan 1935; Schwartz, Jean 1935
(Let Me Walk) Under Your Umbrella   Adams 1950; Strouse 1950
Under Your Window   Coots 1941; Harbach 1941
Under Your Window Tonight   Clare 1931
Undercover Story, The   Coleman 1964
Undercurrent   Freed, Ralph 1947
Undercurrent (inst.)   Waller 1938
Underneath a Big Umbrella   Smith, Robert B. 1919
Underneath a Pretty Hat   Atteridge 1922
Underneath the Big Magnolia Tree   Bryan 1909
Underneath the Cotton Moon   Lewis 1913; Meyer 1913
Underneath the Harlem Moon   Gordon 1932; Revel 1932
Underneath the Honey Moon   Meyer 1910
Underneath the Japanese Moon   Buck 1914
Underneath the Kiss'l-Toe   Coots 1963
Underneath the Marquee   Adams 1964; Strouse 1964
Underneath the Overpass   Bacharach 1957; David, Hal 1957
Underneath the Palms   Atteridge 1922
Underneath the 'Sip 'Sip 'Sippi Moon   Henderson 1923
Underneath the Southern Cross   Meyer 1951
Underneath the Southern Skies   Ruby 1919
Underneath the Stars with You   Stept 1925
Underneath the Swanee Moon   Blake 1965; Sissle 1965
Underneath the Tango Moon   Carroll 1913
Underneath the Wabash Moon   Rose 1927
Underneath the Weeping Willow   Brennan 1925; McHugh 1925
Underneath the Wishing Tree   Lewis 1910
Underneath the Yum Yum Tree   Kalmar 1925; Ruby 1925
Undersea Ballet   Rose 1927
Understudies   Porter 1924
Understudy Dance Specialty, The   Hanley 1926
Undertow   Spina 1946
Underwater   Brooks 1955
Une Nuit in Paris   Goetz 1913
Unemployed Papa, Charity Workin' Mama, You Can't Take Advantage of Me   Razaf 1931
Unexpectedly   Eliscu 1962; Heyman 1955

Unfair to Love   Lerner, Sammy 1940
Unforgettable   Evans 1960; Livingston, Jay 1960; Sigman 1939; Van Heusen 1936; Weill 1940
Unforgivable   Evans 1957; Livingston, Jay 1957
Ungrateful Heart   Warren 1981
Unhappy   Dubin 1923
UNICEF Marching Song, The   Fain 1960; Webster 1960
Uniform, The   Dietz 1937; Schwartz, Arthur 1937
Uninvited Dream   Bacharach 1956
Uninvited Love   Leigh 1955; Livingston, Jerry 1955
Union Label   Eliscu 1940; Gorney 1940
Union Square   Gershwin, George 1933; Gershwin, Ira 1933
Unique Eunuch, The   Adamson 1954; Warren 1954
United Nations   Caesar 1946
United Nations (On the March)   Harburg 1943; Rome 1943
United States Moon   Heyman 1957; Spina 1957
United States Submariners, The   Wrubel 1943
United Way Song, The   Sherman 1971
United We Stand   Smith, Robert B. 1906
Unity Is Diversity   Washington 1965
Universal Peace Song (God Save Us All), The   Bryan 1917
Unkind Word, An   Cahn 1976; Lane 1976
Unknown   David, Hal 1961; David, Mack 1938; Fain 1929; Hammerstein 1918; Johnson, Howard 1921; Kahal 1929; Martin 1977; McHugh 1927; Ruby 1962; Russell 1961; Schwartz, Arthur Date Unknown; Strouse Date Unknown; Young, Victor 1950
Unknown River   Eliscu 1969
Unknown Soldier Lives Again, The   Sissle 1942
Unkw-in-it   Spina 1958
Unloved   David, Hal 1960
Unlucky in Love   Berlin 1924
Unlucky Pierre   Duke 1950; Rome 1950
Unnecessary Town   DePaul 1956; Mercer 1956
Uno, Dos, Tres, Quattro, Cinco, Seis! (The Mexican Dancing Teacher)   Brown, Nacio Herb 1949
Unofficial Spokesman, The   Gershwin, George 1927; Gershwin, Ira 1927
Unrequited Love   Adamson 1954; Warren 1954
Unsophisticated Sue   Razaf 1934
Unter der Linden, in Germany   Jerome 1907; Schwartz, Jean 1907
Until a Moment Ago   Hoffman 1957
Until Eternity   Spina 1944
Until He Gets a Girl   Merrill 1958
Until I Am No More   Johnson, James P. 1959
Until I Fell in Love with You   Berlin 1915
Until I Get You in My Arms   David, Hal 1961
Until I Live Again   Revel 1942
Until Love Comes Along   Clare 1930
Until My Heart Says Goodbye   Bryan 1950
Until My Luck Comes Rolling Alone   Cohan 1922
Until the End   Fisher 1929; Young, Victor 1931
Until the Stars Fall Down   Donaldson 1941
Until They Sail   Cahn 1957
Until Today   Coots 1936; Davis 1936
Until Today I Had No Tomorrow   Duke 1930; Harburg 1930
Until Tonight   Heyman 1950; Young, Victor 1950
Until We Kiss   Mercer 1930
Until We Kiss Again   Duke 1939; Parish 1939
Until We Meet Again   Herbert 1905
(I Never Missed Your Sweet Hello) Until We Said Goodbye   Ager 1953; Akst 1953; Davis 1953
Until Yesterday   Davis 1928
Until You Are Caught   Johnson, James P. 1948

Until You Fall in Love   Cahn 1954
Until You Get Somebody Else   Donaldson 1928; Kahn 1928
Until You Love Me   Mancini 1976
Until You Say Goodbye   Hammerstein 1920; Harbach 1920
Until You Say Yes   Coots 1922
Unto My Heart   Brennan 1929
Unusual Weather   Arlen 1962; Harburg 1962, 1980
Unworthy of Your Love   Sondheim 1990
Unzer Amerika   Eliscu 1941; Gorney 1941
Up Above the World So High   Hoffman 1957
Up an' at 'Em   Magidson 1930; Washington 1930
Up and at 'Em   Gershwin, George 1933; Gershwin, Ira 1933
Up and Down   Hammerstein 1933; Heyman 1964
Up and Down in China (inst.)   Robison 1926
Up and Down the 8 Mile Road   Donaldson 1926; Kahn 1926
Up and Down the Boardwalk   Edwards 1905, 1909; Smith, Robert B. 1905, 1909
Up and Down the Line   Sterling 1903
Up Chickamauga Hill   Weill 1936
Up Comes Love   Brooks 1945
Up, Down, and Touch the Ground   Sherman 1966
Up from the Gutter   Fields 1945; Romberg 1945
Up in a Balloon   Williams 1909
Up in a Tree   Akst 1933; Gilbert 1933
Up in Mabel's Room   Silver 1919
Up in My Aeroplane   Edwards 1909
Up in Smoke   Comden and Green 1947; Leigh 1967
Up in the Air   Bryan 1919; Schwartz, Jean 1919
Up in the Clouds   Kalmar 1927; Ruby 1927
Up in the Elevated Railway   Robin 1954; Romberg 1954
Up in the Ozark Mountains   Fisher 1940
Up Is a Long, Long Climb   Hammerstein 1920; Harbach 1920
Up Jumped the Devil with the Jive   Silver 1941
Up Jumped You with Love   Waller 1944
"Up" Number, The   Martin 1962
Up on Your Toes   Gilbert 1922; Kalmar 1923; Ruby 1923
Up the Chimney Go My Dreams   Henderson 1939; Webster 1939
Up the Creek   Dietz 1935; Schwartz, Arthur 1935
Up the Delaware Down the Delaware Bay   Johnson, Howard 1951
Up the River   Donaldson 1929; Leslie 1929; Merrill 1947
Up to Date   Clarke 1924; Johnston 1924; Meyer 1924
Up to His Old Tricks Again   Porter 1941
Up to Maggie Jones   Russell 1969
Up to My Elbows   Blane 1968; Martin 1968
Up to Now They Haven't Reached the Moon   Brooks 1959
Up to the Moon   Sondheim 1957
Up! Up! Up! in My Aeroplane   Edwards 1909
Up Where the Joke's Goin' Up   Willson 1960
Up Where the People Are (inst.)   Willson 1960
Up with the Lark   Kern 1946; Robin 1946
Up Your Ante   Ellington 1965
Up Your Bustle   Sherman 1951
Upa-Upa   Drake 1943
Upbeat   Freed, Arthur 1945; Warren 1945
Upper Park Avenue, The   Porter 1930
Ups and Down   Smith, Harry B. 1925
Upsala   Duke 1941
Upsi-Daisy   Herbert 1911; Smith, Harry B. 1911
Upside Down Parade   Fain 1949
Upstairs   Bacharach 1968; David, Hal 1968
Upstairs and Down   Donaldson 1919; Lewis 1919; Young, Joe 1919

Upstairs at the Downstairs Waltz, The   Howard, Bart 1957
Uptown   Strouse 1986
Uptown, Downtown   Sondheim 1971
Uranus Unmasked (inst.)   Revel 1955
Urga   Sondheim 1968
Us   Bacharach 1974
Us and Company   Burke 1930
U.S. Grant   Livingston, Jerry 1960
U.S.A. and You, The   Rainger 1938; Robin 1938
U.S.A. Canteen   Drake 1952
Use a Handkerchief   Styne 1940
Use Me, Lawd   Robison 1940
Use What You Got   Coleman 1996
Use Your Imagination   Porter 1950
Use Your Noggin   Cahn 1966; Van Heusen 1966
Used to You   Brown, Lew 1929; DeSylva 1929; Henderson 1929
Useless Song   Weill 1954
Usen't You Used To Be My Sweetie   Bryan 1926
Usher from the Mezzanine, The   Comden and Green 1964; Styne 1964
Using Things and Loving People   David, Hal 1977
Utilize   Robison 1958
Utopia   Gershwin, Ira 1921; Spina 1977; Youmans 1921
Utt Day Zay   Mills 1939
Utterly Lovely   Blake 1950

V

Va De Dum   Spina 1957
Va Va Va Voom (Song of the Bassoon and the Piccolo)   David, Hal 1954
Vagabond   Dubin 1928
Vagabond Dreams   Carmichael 1939; Coslow 1930; Lawrence 1939
Vagabond King   Friml 1925
Vagabond King Opening Chorus   Robin 1930
Vagabonds   Burke 1953
Vale of Dreaming, The   Atteridge 1913
Valencinita   Bergman 1958
Valentine Candy   Sherman 1967
Valentine Stomp (inst.)   Waller 1929
Valentino   Johnson, James P. 1964
Valentino Tango   Lawrence 1951
Valerie   David, Hal 1961
Valeska (My Russian Rose)   Mills 1925
Valley of a Hundred Hills   David, Hal 1959
Valley of Beautiful Dreams (The Shannon, the Shamrocks and You), The   David, Mack 1951
Valley of Dreams, The   Ager 1920; Yellen 1920
Valley of Dreams-Come-True   Lawrence 1947
Valley of Roses   Robison 1957
Valley of Tears, The   Freed, Ralph 1964
Valley of the Giants, The   Lewis 1919; Young, Joe 1919
Valley Song   Bergman 1963
Valparaiso   Bryan 1919; Schwartz, Jean 1919
Vals Song (The Lady of the Amazon)   Gilbert 1932
Valse Amelia (inst.)   Blake 1972
Valse Au L'Air   Friml 1919; Harbach 1919
Valse Brilliant (inst.)   Schwartz, Jean 1930
Valse Delma (inst.)   Blake 1976
Valse des Fleurs   Loesser 1939
Valse Duet   Caesar 1930; Harbach 1930; Romberg 1930
Valse Eileen (inst.)   Blake 1972
Valse Erda (inst.)   Blake 1968

Valse Eth-el (inst.)   Blake 1972
Valse Futuristique (inst.)   Revel 1930
Valse Hesitation   Herbert 1914
Valse Imogene (inst.)   Schwartz, Jean 1930
Valse Julian   Harbach 1911; Schwartz, Jean 1911
Valse Lente (inst.)   Kern 1956
Valse Louise   Johnson, Howard 1959
Valse Marie (inst.)   Schwartz, Jean 1930
Valse Marion (inst.)   Blake 1972
Valse Moderne (inst.)   Oakland 1935
Valse Parfumee (inst.)   Romberg 1913
Valse Petite (inst.)   Bloom 1931
Valse Vera (inst.)   Blake 1972
Value of Dreaming, The   Atteridge 1913
Value of Love, The   Sigman 1956
Vamp a Little Lady   Carroll 1918
Vamp Dolce   Bacharach 1996
Vamp of the Pampas, The   Robin 1935; Whiting 1935
Vamp Your Man   Romberg 1925
Vampire, The   Bergman 1957
Vampire Dance   Atteridge 1919; Howard, Joseph E. 1909; Romberg 1919; Schwartz, Jean 1919
Vampire Love Song, The   Leslie 1910
Vampire Maid, The   Norworth 1917
Vampires in the Dusk   Johnson, James P. 1934
Vanessa   Fisher 1934; Revel 1953
Vaniity Box, The   Caesar 1922
Vanishing American, The   Silver 1956
Vanity   Friml 1917
Vaquero!   Evans 1954; Livingston, Jay 1954; Livingston, Jerry 1936
Vaquero Song   Washington 1944
Vaquero's Song (Who Dares the Bronco Wild Defy)   Herbert 1911
Variations (The Carnival of Venice) (inst.)   Magidson 1957; Stept 1957
Variety   Caesar 1943; Coleman 1964; Herbert 1920; Smith, Harry B. 1900
Variety Reel   Oakland 1962
Varsity Bug, The   Caesar 1922
Varsity Dance (inst.)   Coslow 1935
Varsity Drag, The   Brown, Lew 1927; DeSylva 1927; Henderson 1927
Varsity Walk (inst.)   Hanley 1930
Vas Is Los Mit Loois   Cobb 1910; Edwards 1910
Vas Villst Du Haben?   Bryan 1932; Monaco 1932
Vass You There, Sharlie   Monaco 1932
Vaudeville   Coleman 1988
Va-Va-Va-Vee (For Victory)   Sherman 1971
Ve Don't Like It   Berlin 1943
Ve Grow Too Old Und Too Late Shmart   Drake 1954
Ve Vas Germans   Smith, Harry B. 1900
Ve Vodelum Voo   Rose 1923
Ve Vouldn't Gonto Do It   Weill 1938
Veil of Years   Sigman 1957
Vein of Gold, The   Comden and Green 1947
Veleska (My Russian Rose)   Fain 1925; Kahal 1925
Velvet Foot   Brown, A. Seymour 1909
Velvet Glove, The   Spina 1953
Velvet Lady   Herbert 1919
Velvet Moon   De Lange 1942, 1957; Myrow 1942, 1957
Velvet Night   Mercer 1968
Velvet Paws   Rodgers 1967
Velvo Suds Commercial   Fain 1953
Ven I Valse   Merrill 1957

Ven Papa Vould Cut a Figure Eight   Bergman 1956
Vendors' Calls   Lerner, Alan Jay 1947; Loewe 1947
Vendor's Song   Hart 1943
Venerable Mr. James Bond (inst.), The   Bacharach 1967
Venetia   Atteridge 1914; Carroll 1914; Comden and Green
     1967; Styne 1967
Venetian   Atteridge 1923; Caesar 1923; Romberg 1923
Venetian Carnival, The   Atteridge 1914; Carroll 1914;
     Romberg 1914
Venetian Isles   Berlin 1925
Venetian Love Rose   Coslow 1922
Venetian Loveboat   Koehler 1921
Venetian Moon   Kahn 1920
Venetian Nights   Atteridge 1925
Venetian Wedding Moon   Coots 1925
Venezia   Blane 1954; Martin 1954
Venezia and Her Three Lovers   Heyman 1950; Young, Victor
     1950
Venezuela   Cahn 1971; Washington 1935
Venezuela, The (Ven-ez-wee-la)   Lane 1935
Vengeance   Atteridge 1913
Veni, Vidi, Vici   Livingston, Jerry 1954; Webster 1954
Venice   Porter 1930
Venus and I Are Pals   Harbach 1914
Venus Calls and I'll Obey   Harbach 1914
Venus in Ozone Heights (inst.)   Weill 1943
Venus, My Shining Love   Cohan 1892
Venus of Milo   Porter 1910
Venus Was a Modest Goddess   Weill 1943
Ver Giacoso   Willson 1956
Vera Do Minho   Yellen 1949
Vera Violetta   Atteridge 1911
Verboten   David, Mack 1958
Verdi Duo (inst.)   Duke 1963
Verdict Is, Life with You   Razaf 1930
Vergeblichen Standchen (Come and Dance with
     Me)   Bergman 1978
Veritable Smorgasbord, A   Sherman 1973
Vernon Duccini (inst.)   Duke 1963
Veronique   Coleman 1978; Comden and Green 1978
Versailles   Atteridge 1923; Caesar 1923; Romberg 1923
Versatile DaVincis, The   Comden and Green 1947
Vertigo   Evans 1958; Livingston, Jay 1958
Very Ambitious Girl, A   Brown, A. Seymour 1911
Very Bad   Young, Victor 1954
Very Bozo Birthday, A   Livingston, Jerry 1963
Very Charming Spot, A   Loewe 1937
(He Is) Very Close to Wonderful   Cahn 1964, 1966; Van
     Heusen 1964, 1966
Very First Person I Met (in California), The   Bacharach 1970;
     David, Hal 1970
Very Good Advice   Fain 1951
Very Good Sense   Blane 1969
Very Necessary You, The   Burke 1953; Van Heusen 1953
Very Next Girl I See, The   Atteridge 1921; Romberg 1921
Very Nice Man, A   Merrill 1961
Very Nice Prince, A   Sondheim 1987
Very Precious Love, A   Fain 1958; Webster 1958
Very Proper Town, A   Evans 1958; Livingston, Jay 1958
Very Silly Story, A   Burke 1946; Van Heusen 1946
Very Special Day, A   Hammerstein 1953; Rodgers 1953
Very, Very   Weill 1943
Very, Very Young, The   Drake 1958
Very Warm for Christmas   Coleman 1964; Leigh 1964
Very Well Then   Smith, Harry B. 1908

Vesper Bell   Friml 1928
Vespers   Brooks 1960
Vesuvius   Razaf 1935
Veterans of Future Wars   Cahn 1936
Vets   Leigh 1985
Via de Paradiso   Sherman 1959
Via Veneto (inst.), The   Bacharach 1966
Vibrations   Sherman 1956
Vibrations from Venus (inst.)   Revel 1955
Vicar's Song (Finale Act II)   Kern 1921
Viceroy   Herbert 1900; Smith, Harry B. 1900
Victim of the Talkies   Oakland 1931
Victims of the Voodoo Drums   Washington 1933; Young,
     Joe 1933; Young, Victor 1933
Victor/Victoria   Mancini 1995
Victor Vitamin Brown   Burke 1947; Van Heusen 1947
Victoria   Adams 1972; Martin 1972; Strouse 1972
Victoria and Albert Waltz, The   Adams 1972; Strouse 1972
Victor's Request   Styne 1978
Victory   Buck 1918
Victory Canteen   Sherman 1971
Victory Caravan   Cahn 1942; Styne 1942
Victory Garden   Leslie 1942
Victory March, The   Friml 1925
Victory Parade, The   Pollack 1945
Victory Pie   Caesar 1943
Victory Polka   Cahn 1943; Johnson, James P. 1945
Victory Song   Oakland 1938
Victory Stride   Johnson, James P. 1944
Victory Symphony, Eight to the Bar   Rome 1943
Vict'ry Polka   Cahn 1944; Styne 1944
Viddle-de Vop   David, Mack 1947; Livingston, Jerry 1947
Vienna   Kern 1908
Vienna (Waltz Ballet) (inst.)   Styne 1944
Vienna Dreams   Caesar 1951
Vienna Garden — Waltz No. 10 (inst.)   Warren Date
     Unknown
Vienna Girls   Friml 1914; Harbach 1914
Vienna, Home of Songs (Wien, Du Stadt der
     Lieder)   Young, Joe 1931
Vienna in May   Kahn 1933
Vienna Morning (inst.)   Schwartz, Jean 1930
Vienna Roll   Smith, Harry B. 1912; Smith, Robert B. 1912
Vienna Will Sing   Hammerstein 1935; Romberg 1935
Viennese Refrain   Johnson, Howard 1933
Vigilante Song   Rainger 1935; Robin 1935
Vignette   Oakland 1953; Raye 1953
Vignettes   Dietz 1961; Schwartz, Arthur 1961
Vigolin   Bergman 1958
Vigoroso in D Flat (inst.)   Kern 1938
Vilia   Hart 1934; Johnson, Howard 1933; Kahn 1934;
     Webster 1952
Villa in the Valley, A   Adamson 1942
Village Ballroom Polka, The   Clare 1945
Village Called Hollywood, A   Duke 1955
Village Choir!   Baer 1930; Bryan 1930
Village in Peru, A   Russell 1951
Village Scene Jingles   Gershwin, Ira 1943
Villain Always Gets It, The   Fain 1955
Villain Dance (inst.)   Kern 1927
Villain Still Pursued Her, The   Jerome 1912; Von Tilzer 1912
Villains in the Play   Cohan 1908
Vilma   Coots 1929; Davis 1929
Vincennes   Spina 1966
Vineyards of Manhattan, The   Schwartz, Arthur 1929

Vingo   Raye 1942

Vingo Jingo   DePaul 1942; Raye 1942, 1944

Vino D'Amore   Cahn 1967

Vino, Vino   David, Hal 1955

Vintage Chorus   Smith, Harry B. 1925

Violate Me in Violet Time   Wrubel 1944

Violet Eyes   Bryan 1924

Violet in Broadway's Garden, A   Smith, Harry B. 1923; Snyder 1923

Violet (inst.)   Schwartz, Jean 1930

Violet of N.Y.U.   Parish 1950

Violet Ray   Buck 1921

Vi-O-Lets   Baer 1926; Smith, Harry B. 1925

Violets and Violins (Mon Coeur Et unm Violon)   Lawrence 1950

Violin Solo   Martin 1952

Violin Song, The   Romberg 1916; Smith, Robert B. 1916

Violins Are Saying "Wanting You", The   Bryan 1944

Violins from Nowhere   Fain 1950; Magidson 1950

Violins in My Heart   Davis 1962

Violins in Virginia   Robison 1952

(He's a) V.I.P.   Styne 1960

Vipers Drag (inst.)   Waller 1934

(There's a Blue Ridge in My Heart) Virginia   Bryan 1926; Hammerstein 1928; Schwartz, Arthur 1937; Youmans 1928

Virginia and Truckee Line, The   Brooks 1954

Virginia Brown   Howard, Joseph E. 1923

Virginia (Don't Go Too Far)   DeSylva 1924; Gershwin, George 1924

Virginia Hoe Down   Hammerstein 1938; Harbach 1938; Kern 1938

Virginia Lou   Berlin 1911

Virginia Reel   Rome 1973

Virginia's Calling Me   Friend 1924

Virgins Wrapped in Cellophane   Webster 1933

Virtue Is It's Own Reward   Smith, Harry B. 1912; Smith, Robert B. 1912

Virtue Wins the Day   Hart 1921; Rodgers 1921

Vision, The   Romberg 1948

Vision Ballet (inst.)   Duke 1940

Vision in Vermillion, A   Atteridge 1922; Schwartz, Jean 1922

Vision of Bernadette, The   Hoffman 1950

Vision of Hassan, A   Atteridge 1925

Vision of the Future, A   Gilbert 1931

Visit, The   Atteridge 1914

Visit Looney Park   Atteridge 1911

Visit Panama   Porter 1940

Visit Panama (inst.)   Styne 1954

Visit with Me, Lord   Robison 1955

Visiting Day   Bacharach 1966; David, Hal 1966

Visiting Firemen Opening   Oakland 1960; Raye 1960

Visitors   Coleman 1973; Fields 1973

Vitabelle   Coleman 1962; Leigh 1962

Vitamins Hormones and Pills   Yellen 1977

Vite, Vite, Vite   Porter 1938

Viva America   Rome 1945

Viva Amigos   Davis 1944

Viva el Amor   Sigman 1968

Viva for Geneva   Arlen 1937

Viva Italia   Gorney 1958; Hart 1926; Rodgers 1926

Viva la Buck   Evans 1950; Livingston, Jay 1950

Viva la Duel   Evans 1950; Livingston, Jay 1950

Viva La France   Warren 1934

Viva the Women!   Lerner, Alan Jay 1948; Weill 1948

Viva . . .Vem-Vem (The Cuban Kissing Song)   Drake 1946

Vivat Regina   Adams 1972; Strouse 1972

Vive for Geneva   Harburg 1937

Vive la Canadienne   Hammerstein 1924; Harbach 1924

Vive la Difference   Weill 1943

Vive la France   Dubin 1934; Herbert 1917

Vive la Virture   Harburg 1961

Vive La You!   Burke 1956; Friml 1956

Vive L'Amour   Blane 1945

Vive L'Amour (Love Rules Us Ever)   Smith, Harry B. 1928

Vive Le Jourdain (Prologue)   Drake 1951

Vive the U.S.A.   Martin 1951

Vivianne the Vivandiere   Herbert 1903; Smith, Harry B. 1903

Vivian's Reverie   Revel 1945

Vivienne   Porter 1928

(We Met Over a Bottle of) Vivo   Cahn 1946; Styne 1946

Vocal Overture   Sondheim 1973

Vocalize   Blane 1954; Martin 1954

Vo-de-o-do-do   Rose 1927

Vodka (Don't Give Me Vodka)   Gershwin, George 1925; Hammerstein 1925; Harbach 1925

Vo-Do-Do-De-O Blues   Ager 1927; Yellen 1927

Voice for It, The   Herbert 1905

Voice in My Heart, The   Cohan 1922

Voice in the Dark, A   Hammerstein 1928; Romberg 1928

Voice in the Night (inst.)   Revel 1957

Voice in the Old Village Choir, The   Kahn 1932; Woods 1932

Voice in the Wind   De Lange 1945; Henderson 1945; Webster 1965

Voice Inside Me, A   Baer 1965

Voice of a Rose   Leslie 1943

Voice of Bagdad, The   Hammerstein 1920

Voice of Belgium   Berlin 1915

Voice of Love, A   Gershwin, George Date Unknown; Gershwin, Ira 1924; Smith, Harry B. 1914, 1916; Smith, Robert B. 1916

Voice of Love (The Sound of Love), The   Heyman 1967

Voice of P.O.W. (inst.), The   Young, Victor 1953

Voice of Romance, The   Coslow 1937

Voice of the City   Kalmar 1928; Lawrence 1933; Ruby 1928

Voice of the Southland Keeps Calling Me Home, The   Koehler 1927

Voice of the Violet, The   Olcott 1902

Voice of the World, The   Akst 1927; Davis 1927

Voice with a Smile Wins, The   Norworth 1917

Voices from Home   Goetz 1910

Void, The   Sherman 1962

Voila   Bullock 1939; Drake 1953

Vola, Columba   Sigman 1953

Volare   Parish 1958

Volga Boat Song   Donaldson 1929; Johnson, Howard 1939; Leslie 1929

Volunteer Fireman, The   Herbert 1906

Von Drake Quake, The   Sherman 1962

Voo Doo Pageant (inst.)   Washington 1933; Young, Victor 1933

Voodle-Doodle-Yodel-Indian-Man   Stept 1925

Voodoo   Porter 1948

Voodoo Man   Blake 1960; Harbach 1923

Voodoo of the Zulu Isle   Coots 1926

Voom Voom   Coslow 1936, 1937

Vot Makes Zanta Run?   Drake 1993

Vote for Adlai   Caesar 1952

Vote for Honest Abe   Gordon 1937; Revel 1937

Vote for Mr. Rhythm   Rainger 1936; Robin 1936
Voting Blues   Rome 1950
Voulez Vous   Duke 1955
Voulez Vous, May I Have the Next Waltz, Mrs. Yiffnif   Gorney 1940
Voulez-Vous Cha Cha Ma'm'selle?   Hoffman 1960
Vous Etes Jolie   Atteridge 1913
V-Room   Livingston, Jerry 1963
Vulgar Boatman, The   Clare 1926; Monaco 1926
Vulgarian March   Sherman 1968

W

Wa Wa Watermelon   Styne 1941
Wabash   Johnson, Howard 1921; Schwartz, Jean 1921
WAC Hymn, The   Loesser 1944
Wacki for Khaki   Loesser 1942; Spina 1942
Wada Mas (Tango) (inst.)   Revel 1959
Waddya Say We Steal Away   Hanley 1926
Wade in the Water   Duke 1940
Wading We Go   Smith, Harry B. 1901
Waffles   Fisher 1926
Wagner Couldn't Write a Ragtime Song   Jerome 1913; Schwartz, Jean 1913
Wagon Song   Gershwin, Ira 1943
Wagon Tracks (inst.)   Robison 1929
(Roll Along) Wagon Train   Brooks 1958; Fain 1958; Russell 1957
Wah Hoo   Friend 1936
Wah-Dee-Dah   Mills 1932; Washington 1932
Waika Kiki Blues   Meyer 1926
Waikiki   Fain 1929; Parish 1929
Waikiki, I Hear You Calling Me   Kalmar 1922; Ruby 1922
Waikiki Is Calling Me   Sterling 1924
Waiki-Ki-Ki-Lou   Friend 1920
Wail of the Congo Trail, The   Johnson, Howard 1930; Woods 1930
Wail of the Reefer Man, The   Arlen 1932; Koehler 1932
Wail of the Winds (inst.)   Warren 1939, Date Unknown
Wait   Sondheim 1979
Wait a Bit   Smith, Harry B. 1926
Wait a Bit, Susie   Gershwin, George 1924; Gershwin, Ira 1924
Wait a Little Longer Love Bird   Dixon 1927
Wait a Little While Sweetheart   Davis 1928
Wait a Minute   Livingston, Jerry 1963
Wait and See   Mercer 1945; Razaf 1936; Romberg 1927; Smith, Harry B. 1927; Waller 1936; Warren 1945
Wait By the Marne for Me   Bryan 1926
Wait for Love   Washington 1956
Wait for Me   Adams 1968; Akst 1929; Lewis 1928; Smith, Robert B. 1919; Strouse 1968; Young, Joe 1929
Wait for Me Marlena   Sherman 1974
Wait for the Bus to Stop   Caesar 1943
Wait for the Happy Ending   Ager 1929; Yellen 1929
Wait for the Moon   Porter 1924
Wait for the Wagon   Johnson, Howard 1939; Mercer 1962
Wait 'Til I Get You in My Dreams Tonight   Spina 1946
Wait 'Til We're Sixty-Five   Lane 1965; Lerner, Alan Jay 1965
Wait 'Til You See My Twist and Twirl   Ager 1942
Wait Til' You See Paris   Blane 1954; Myrow 1954
Wait Till I Catch You in My Dream   Brown, Lew 1940; Coots 1940
Wait Till It Happens to You   Arlen 1941; Mercer 1941
Wait Till She Sees You in Your Uniform   Leslie 1940

Wait Till the Clouds Roll By   Johnson, Howard 1939
Wait Till the Morning After   Egan 1925; Whiting 1925
Wait Till the Sun Shines Nellie   Sterling 1905; Von Tilzer 1905
Wait Till the Sun Shines Nellie Blues   Sterling 1951; Von Tilzer 1951
Wait 'Till Tomorrow   DePaul 1968; Kern 1917
Wait Till Tomorrow Night   Leslie 1925; Woods 1925
Wait 'till We Gather in the Golden Corn   Lewis 1910
Wait Till You See Her   Hart 1942; Rodgers 1942
Wait Till You See Ma Cherie   Robin 1929; Whiting 1929
Wait Till You See Me in the Morning   Carmichael 1940; Mercer 1940
Wait Till You See My Baby and Me   Bryan 1925
Wait Till You See New York   Cahn Date Unknown; Duke Date Unknown
Wait Till You're Blue Mary   Caesar 1928; Friend 1928
Wait Until Dark   Evans 1967; Livingston, Jay 1967; Mancini 1967
Wait Until It's Bedtime   Porter 1929
Wait Until My Heart Finds Out   Cahn 1938
Wait Until My Ship Comes In   Atteridge 1921; Romberg 1921
Wait Until We Get Alone   Johnson, James P. 1930
Wait Until We're Married   Lewis 1913; Meyer 1913
Wait Until You Meet Her   McHugh 1964
Wait Until You See My Girl's   Sissle 1928
Wait Until Your Daddy Comes Home   Berlin 1912
Wait Until You're Married   Berlin 1963
Waiter and the Porter and the Upstairs Maid, The   Mercer 1941
Waiters   Smith, Harry B. 1927
Waiter's Dance   Atteridge 1921; Pollack 1921; Schwartz, Jean 1921
Waiter's Melody, The   Conrad 1939; Gilbert 1939
Waiter's Song   Eliscu 1933; Kahn 1933; Youmans 1933
Waiters v. Waitresses   Porter 1933
Waitin'   Arlen 1954
Waitin' Around   Davis 1924; Hanley 1924
Waitin' at the Gate for Katy   Kahn 1934; Whiting 1934
Waitin' at the Station   Spina 1950
Waitin' for Ann   Sherman 1995
Waitin' for Charlie to Come Home   Bacharach 1962
Waitin' for Katie   Kahn 1928; Snyder 1928
Waitin' for My Dearie   Lerner, Alan Jay 1947; Loewe 1947
Waitin' for the Day   Razaf 1950
Waitin' for the Evening Train   Dietz 1963; Schwartz, Arthur 1963
Waiting   Comden and Green 1974; Conrad 1929; Hammerstein 1930, 1951; Harbach 1920; Kalmar 1928; Mitchell 1929; Rodgers 1951; Romberg 1930; Ruby 1928; Styne 1974
Waiting at the End of the Road   Berlin 1929
Waiting for Billy   Davis 1965
Waiting for Me   Atteridge 1912
Waiting for Something   Caesar 1925; Youmans 1925
Waiting for the Bride   Herbert 1913; Smith, Robert B. 1913
Waiting for the Evening Whistle   Parish 1944
Waiting for the Girls Upstairs   Sondheim 1971
Waiting for the Lawn and You   Caesar 1924
Waiting for the Leaves to Fall (She Was Poor)   Hart 1930; Rodgers 1930
Waiting for the Rainbow   Akst 1927; Davis 1927; Rose 1927
Waiting for the Robert E. Lee   Gilbert 1912

Waiting for the Sun to Come Out   Gershwin, George 1920; Gershwin, Ira 1920

Waiting for the Tide to Turn   Von Tilzer 1935

Waiting for the Train   Gershwin, George 1925; Gershwin, Ira 1925

Waiting for the Whistle to Blow   Blake 1932; Sissle 1932

Waiting for This   Akst 1918

Waiting for You   DePaul 1942; Harbach 1971; Kern 1904; Raye 1942; Youmans 1971

Waiting for You to Begin   Waller 1932; Young, Joe 1932

Waiting for Your Return (Nostalgia)   Caesar 1921

Waiting in a Dream   Washington 1932

Waiting in the Garden   Bloom 1935; Koehler 1935

Waiting in the Wings   Adams 1993; Evans 1981; Livingston, Jay 1981

Waiting, Waiting   Comden and Green 1960; Styne 1960

Wait'll My Ship Comes In   Parish 1933

Wait'll We're Married   Clare 1926; Monaco 1926

Wait'll You Meet My Darlin'   Hoffman 1953

Wait'll You See Cecilia   Lerner, Sammy 1926; Whiting 1926

Wake, The   Blane 1952

Wake Island   Young, Victor 1942

Wake, Love, Wake   Porter 1916

Wake Me Up   Howard, Bart 1984

Wake Me When It's Over   Cahn 1960; Van Heusen 1960

Wake the Town and Tell the People   Livingston, Jerry 1954

Wake Up   Edwards 1929; Hammerstein 1930; Harburg 1971; Hart 1921; Rodgers 1921; Romberg 1930

Wake Up! America   Johnson, J. Rosamond 1942

Wake Up and Dream   Porter 1929

Wake Up and Live   Gordon 1937; Revel 1937

Wake Up and Sing   Friend 1936

Wake Up and Smile   Evans 1970; Livingston, Jay 1970

Wake Up, Brother, and Dance   Gershwin, George 1937; Gershwin, Ira 1937

Wake Up, Chill'un, Wake Up   Robison 1929

Wake Up Dream Girl   Fain 1928

Wake Up Every Morning with a Smile   DeSylva 1926

Wake Up, It's Cake Walk Day   Smith, Robert B. 1915

Wake Up, Jacob   DePaul 1942; Raye 1942

Wake Up! Little Rip Van Winkle   Bryan 1930, 1940

Wake Up, Malinda   Jerome 1903

Wake Up Song   Burke 1946; Van Heusen 1946

Wake Up the Gypsy in Me   Pollack 1932

Wake Up to Music   Hoffman 1956

(Adios Mi Amor) Wake Up, Wake Up Your Heart   Lewis 1944

Wake Up Your Feet   Gordon 1929

Wakin' Up the Folks Down Stairs   Blake 1930; Razaf 1930

Walk Along with Kings   Merrill 1955

Walk Among the Leaves, A   Warren 1971, 1979

Walk Away   Leigh 1967

Walk Away with a Smile   David, Hal 1952

Walk Down the Avenue with Me   Goetz 1917

Walk in the Country   Howard, Bart 1956

Walk Into My Heart   Snyder 1918

Walk Like a Sailor   Fain 1955

Walk, Little Dolly   Bacharach 1967; David, Hal 1967

Walk on Air   Leigh 1973

Walk on By   Bacharach 1964; David, Hal 1964

Walk on the Wild Side   David, Mack 1962

Walk on the Wild Wharf, A (inst.)   Bacharach 1965

Walk Sweet   Warren 1956

Walk the Plank   Carroll 1934

Walk the Way You Talk   Bacharach 1970; David, Hal 1970

Walk This Way   Schwartz, Jean 1912

Walk to de Grave   Arlen 1968

Walk to the Exit Near You   Caesar 1943

Walk Up   Howard, Bart 1956

Walk with a Wiggle   David, Hal 1953

Walk with Love   Russell 1969

Walk with Uncle Sam (Walk to Work)   Caesar 1942

Walkin' Along Mindin' My Business   Harburg 1940; Lane 1940

Walkin' and a Talkin' Doll, A   Gilbert 1945

Walkin' and Singin' the Blues   Ellington 1959

Walkin' and Wond'rin' (My Heart Cried Out in Vain)   Merrill 1953

Walkin' Backwards Down the Road   Bacharach 1968; David, Hal 1968

Walkin' Home with the Blues   Washington 1956

Walkin' My Baby Back Home   Ahlert 1930; Turk 1930

Walkin' on Air   Gordon 1931; Revel 1931

Walkin' the Bass (inst.)   Johnson, James P. 1943

Walkin' the Floor   Razaf 1932; Waller 1932

Walkin' the Streets   Wrubel 1929

Walkin' the Track   Conrad 1926; Kahn 1926

Walkin' the Zep   Alter 1929; Johnson, Howard 1929

Walkin' to Missouri   Merrill 1952

Walkin' to Paradise   Friend 1960

Walkin' with My Shadow   Mercer 1934

Walkin' with Susie   Conrad 1929; Mitchell 1929

Walking   Jerome 1905; Schwartz, Jean 1905

Walking Alone in the Dark   De Lange 1947

(When I'm) Walking Arm in Arm with Jim   Pollack 1942

Walking Away Whistling   Loesser 1960

Walking Dogs Around   Brown, Lew 1926; DeSylva 1926; Henderson 1926

Walking Happy   Cahn 1956, 1966; Van Heusen 1956

Walking Home with Josie   Kern 1925

Walking in the Sunshine   Leigh 1985; Merrill 1951

Walking Music   Sigman 1951

Walking Music Store, The   Friml 1914; Harbach 1914

Walking My Baby Back Home   Johnson, James P. 1938

Walking Off Those Balken Blues   Dubin 1929

Walking on the Ceiling   Adamson 1937; Lane 1937

Walking on the Lake   Smith, Robert B. 1915

Walking on the Sea (inst.)   Kern 1938

Walking Papers   Merrill 1955

(That's Called) Walking the Dog   Atteridge 1916; Blake 1916; Motzan 1916; Sissle 1916

Walking the Dog (Promenade) (inst.)   Gershwin, George 1937

Walking the Floor   Rainger 1935; Robin 1935

(Fifi's) Walking the Poodle   David, Hal 1958

Walking the Streets   Mills 1935

Walking Tune, A   David, Hal 1953

Walking with Susie   Conrad 1929; Mitchell 1929

Walks   Herbert 1905; Smith, Harry B. 1905

Wall Between Us, The   David, Hal 1951

Wall of Fire   David, Hal 1990

Wall Street   Magidson 1930; Washington 1930

Wall Street Hoedown   Leigh 1967

Waller-ing Around (inst.)   Waller 1925

Waller's Original E Flat Blues   Waller 1944

Wallflower Sweet   Smith, Harry B. 1911

Wallpaper Roses   Spina 1965

Wally Nelskog Theme   Oakland 1954

Walrus and the Carpenter, The   Fain 1951

Walter Walter Wall-Flower   Coots 1934, 1950; Lewis 1934

Walter Walter Wildflower   Coslow 1924
Walter Winchell Rhumba   Sigman 1946
Waltz   Bullock 1950; Herbert 1895; Smith, Harry B. 1895;
    Sondheim Date Unknown
Waltz Away the Night   Egan 1933
Waltz Caprice   Smith, Harry B. 1911
Waltz Divine   Razaf 1929; Waller 1929
Waltz, Dixieland   Arlen 1959; Mercer 1959
Waltz Down the Aisle   Porter 1934, 1935
Waltz Duet, The   Smith, Robert B. 1905
Waltz Ensemble   Romberg 1924
Waltz Fantasies   Harbach 1936; Romberg 1936
Waltz Fantasy (inst.)   Duke 1963
Waltz I Can't Forget, The   Kahn 1928
Waltz I Love, The   Washington 1935
Waltz in Blue (inst.)   Revel 1939
Waltz in Swing Time (inst.), The   Kern 1936
Waltz in the Moonlight, A   Parish 1925
Waltz (inst.)   Rodgers 1923
Waltz Interlude   Romberg 1948
Waltz Is King   Gordon 1940
Waltz Is Made for Love, The   DeSylva 1922
Waltz Is On, The   Bloom 1933; Koehler 1933
Waltz Is Over, The   Harburg 1942; Schwartz, Arthur 1942
Waltz It Should Be, A   Atteridge 1922; Romberg 1922
Waltz Lives On, The   Rainger 1938; Robin 1938
Waltz Martinique   Johnson, James P. 1962
Waltz Me Again with Your Heart   Fisher 1931
Waltz Me Around Again Willie   Cobb 1904, 1906
Waltz Me Around and Around in the Old Ball
    Room   Howard, Joseph E. 1912
Waltz Me 'Till I'm Dreamy   Howard, Joseph E. 1908
Waltz Me to Sleep in Your Arms   Monaco 1931
Waltz Moderne (inst.)   Warren Date Unknown
Waltz No. 16 (inst.)   Warren Date Unknown
Waltz No. 3 (inst.)   Warren Date Unknown
Waltz No. 4 (inst.)   Warren Date Unknown
Waltz No. 5 (inst.)   Warren Date Unknown
Waltz No. 6 (inst.)   Warren Date Unknown
Waltz No. 8 (inst.)   Warren Date Unknown
Waltz No. 9 (inst.)   Warren Date Unknown
Waltz No. I (inst.)   Warren Date Unknown
Waltz No. II (inst.)   Warren Date Unknown
Waltz of India   McHugh 1922; Mills 1922; Parish 1922
Waltz of Long Ago, The   Berlin 1923
Waltz of Love, The   Caesar 1936; Koehler 1925
Waltz of the Bells   David, Mack 1952
Waltz of the Dreamers   Myrow 1931
Waltz of the Flowers   Dubin 1936; Mercer 1938; Warren
    1936, 1938
Waltz of the Mission Bells, The   Webster 1949
Waltz of the South   Gilbert 1943
Waltz Song   Atteridge 1922; Friml 1950; Romberg 1922
Waltz that Broke My Heart, The   David, Mack 1953
Waltz that Brought You Back to Me, The   Caesar 1932
Waltz Time in Vienna   Caesar 1945
Waltz Was Born in Vienna, A   Loewe 1936, 1937
Waltz with Me   Cohan 1908; Gordon 1933; Revel 1933;
    Smith, Harry B. 1930
Waltz with Me (inst.)   Warren Date Unknown
Waltz With Me Lena at Luna   Bryan 1908
Waltz You Saved for Me, The   Kahn 1930
Waltz-Duet   Atteridge 1922; Romberg 1922
Waltzing   Von Tilzer 1910
Waltzing and Waiting   David, Mack 1954

Waltzing Around the Maypole (inst.)   Kern 1946
Waltzing Cat, The   Parish 1951
Waltzing Down the Aisle   Hoffman 1955
Waltzing in a Dream   Washington 1932; Young, Victor 1932
Waltzing in the Carolines   Young, Joe 1933
Waltzing in the Clouds   Kahn 1940
Waltzing in the Moonlight   Kalmar 1941; Ruby 1941
Waltzing Into Love   Koehler 1955
Waltzing Is Better Sitting Down   Gershwin, George 1947;
    Gershwin, Ira 1947
Waltzing Lieutenant, The   Edwards 1910; Smith, Harry B.
    1910
Waltzing on the Kalamazoo   Drake 1941
Waltzing with an Angel   Bryan 1936
Wana, When I Wana, You No Wanna   Friend 1921
Wanapoo Bay   Brennan 1930; Friml 1930
Wanda   Egan 1925; Friml 1914; Whiting 1925
Wander Away   Hammerstein 1925; Harbach 1925
Wander Off Nowhere   Edwards 1907
Wanderer, The   Gorney 1924
Wanderers (My Lop-Eared Mule, My Broken Down Horse 'n
    Me)   Webster 1936
Wandering   Dietz 1946; Johnson, James P. 1942
Wandering Heart, The   Johnson, James P. 1959
Wandering Home   Kahn 1929; Styne 1929
Wandering Minstrel, The   Hart Date Unknown; Rodgers
    Date Unknown; Smith, Harry B. 1908; Spina 1957
Wandering One   Von Tilzer 1924
Wanderlust   Sigman 1947
Wand'rin Star   Lerner, Alan Jay 1951; Loewe 1951
Wand'ring Heart   Dietz 1934; Schwartz, Arthur 1934
Wand'ring Lover   Dietz 1937; Schwartz, Arthur 1937
Waning Honeymoon, The   Howard, Joseph E. 1907
Wanna Buy a Duke?   Akst 1934; Brown, Lew 1934
Wanna Lotta Love   DeSylva 1925
Wanna Trade   Bergman 1964; Fain 1964
Wan'rin Aroun' (inst.)   Waller 1941
Want a Good Time Bad   Coslow 1930
Want a Little Lovin'?   Davis 1925; Warren 1925
Want Me   Razaf 1952; Sigman 1963
Wanted   Brooks 1970; Lawrence 1937
Wanted — Someone   Akst 1934; Clare 1934
Wanted: A Fly   Smith, Harry B. 1903
Wanted: A Wonderful Dancer   Howard, Joseph E. 1937
Wanted Someone to Love   McHugh 1924; Mills 1924
Wanting   Strouse 1986
Wanting Things   Bacharach 1968; David, Hal 1968
Wanting You   Caesar 1921; Gershwin, George 1921;
    Hammerstein 1928; Romberg 1928
War Babies   Hanley 1916
War Bond Man, The   Razaf 1944
War for Justice   Warren 1964
War in Snider's Grocery Store, The   Carroll 1914
War Is Over, The   Leigh 1955
War Is War   Hart 1925; Rodgers 1925
War of 1812, The   Livingston, Jerry 1960
War Song   Hanley 1939; Harburg Date Unknown; Porter
    1910
War Song (Title Unknown)   Gershwin, George Date
    Unknown
War That Ended War, The   Gershwin, George 1927;
    Gershwin, Ira 1927
War Wagon Theme Song   Washington 1967
Warm   Bergman 1962; Russell 1956
Warm All Over   Loesser 1956

Warm and Tender   Bacharach 1956; David, Hal 1956

Warm and Willing   Evans 1959; Livingston, Jay 1959; Loesser 1958; McHugh 1959

Warm As Wine   Evans 1946; Livingston, Jay 1946

Warm in December   Russell 1956

(She/He Keeps Me) Warm in the Winter   David, Hal 1954

Warm Lips and Cold Kisses   Coots 1957

Warm Spot in My Heart, A   Drake 1964

Warm Summer Kisses for a Cold Winter's Night   McHugh 1964; Washington 1965

Warm Summer Love   McHugh 1964; Washington 1964

Warm Sun Cold Moon   Evans 1956; Livingston, Jay 1956

Warm Valley   Ellington 1941; Russell 1941, 1943

Warmed Over Kisses (Left Over Love)   Livingston, Jerry 1954

Warmed Over Kisses, Leftover Love   David, Mack 1957

Warmer than a Whisper   Cahn 1962; Van Heusen 1962

(She's the) Warmest Baby in the Bunch   Cohan 1894

Wartime Wedding   Sherman 1974

Was Friday a Woman or Was Friday a Man   Brown, Lew 1916

Was I Just Another Love Affair to You   Conrad 1930

Was I to Blame (For Falling in Love with You)   Kahn 1930; Young, Victor 1930

Was It a Dream?   DeSylva 1924

Was It Loneliness or Love   David, Hal 1978

Was It Love   Caesar 1928; Conrad 1928

Was It Love or Wine   Whiting 1934

Was It Really Love?   Webster 1969

Was It Worth It   David, Mack 1966

Was Last Night the Last Night with You?   Davis 1928

Was My Face Red   Akst 1933; Freed, Ralph 1933

Was She Prettier than I?   Martin 1964

Was That All I Meant to You?   Davis 1932

Was That the Human Thing to Do   Fain 1931; Young, Joe 1931

Was There Ever a Pal Like You   Berlin 1919

Was There Ever a Voice?   Hammerstein 1936

Was Your Heart in Your Song   Egan 1931

Wash Behind Your Ears   Styne 1940

Washboard Blues   Carmichael 1944; Mills 1925

Washboard Blues (inst.)   Carmichael 1925

Washin' the Blues from My Soul   Robison 1930

Washington   Carmichael 1946

Washington, D.C.   Porter 1943

Washington Irving's Song   Weill 1938

Washington Square   Carroll 1934; Drake 1994; Porter 1920

Washington Square Dance   Berlin 1950

Washington Twist, The   Berlin 1962

Wasn't I There?   Burke 1950; Van Heusen 1950

Wasn't It a Wonderful Wedding   Cahn 1955; Van Heusen 1955

Wasn't It Beautiful While It Lasted   Brown, Lew 1930; DeSylva 1930; Henderson 1930

Wasn't It Fate?   Coots 1929; Davis 1929

Wasn't It Fun   Coots 1929; Davis 1929

Wasn't It Great? (It's All Over Now)   Hart 1928; Rodgers 1928

Wasn't It Nice?   Caesar 1926; Friml 1926; Young, Joe 1930

Wasn't It Romantic?   Martin 1962

Wasn't It Wonderful   DePaul 1942; Raye 1942

Wasn't It Yesterday   Berlin 1917

Wassa Matter, No Ice Today, Marie   Gordon 1932; Revel 1932

Wassa Matter with You   Lewis 1929; Young, Joe 1929

Waste a Little Time with Me   Coots 1932

Wasted Years   Dubin 1925

Wastin' Away for You   Bacharach 1961; David, Hal 1961

Wastin' Our Talents   Razaf Date Unknown

Wasting Away   Razaf 1929

Wasting My Love on You   Leslie 1930; Warren 1930

Watch, Hope and Wait Little Girl, Till I Come Back to You   Brown, Lew 1918

Watch My Dust   Comden and Green 1967; Styne 1967

Watch Out, Angel!   De Lange 1945; Myrow 1945

Watch Out for the Devil   Burke 1956; Friml 1956

Watch Out, New York!   Warren 1960

Watch Out, Wake Up   Warren 1960

Watch Over Daddy   Silver 1953

Watch Sputnik when She Crosses the Sky   Burke 1957

Watch the Birdie   DePaul 1941; Raye 1941

Watch the Birdies   Johnson, Howard 1927

Watch the Professor   Herbert 1907; Smith, Harry B. 1907

Watch Your Footwork   Sherman 1967

Watch Your Head   Gershwin, George 1932; Gershwin, Ira 1932

Watch Your Hornin' (inst.)   Carmichael 1926

Watch Your Language   David, Hal 1954

Watch Your Step   Berlin 1914

Watch Yourself   Hart 1921; Rodgers 1921

Watchin' the Clock   Kahn 1924

Watchin' the Moon Rise   Egan 1923; Kahn 1923

Watching   Mills 1938

Watching Dreams Go By (Solitary)   Sigman 1959

Watching for the Boogie Man   Johnson, Howard 1928

Watching Little Alice (inst.)   Kern 1942

Watching My Dreams Go By   Dubin 1930

Watching the Blue Smoke Curl   Howard, Joseph E. 1908

Watching the Clock   Russell 1939; Sigman 1939

Watching the Clouds Roll By   Kalmar 1928; Ruby 1928

Watching the Door   Robison 1956

Watching the Moon Rise   Whiting 1923

Watching the Moon Through the Trees   Cahn 1934

Watching the Ships Go By   David, Mack 1938

Watching the Stars   Hoffman 1934; Lerner, Sammy 1934

Watching the World Go By   Brennan 1927; Porter 1929

Watching You   Clarke 1920; Donaldson 1920

Water   Bergman 1957; DePaul 1941; Raye 1941

Water Front Pastime Dance   Cohan 1923

Water Lily   Atteridge 1919; David, Mack 1951; Livingston, Jerry 1951; Romberg 1919; Schwartz, Jean 1919

Water Melon Moon   Sterling 1941

Water Never Did That   Williams 1908

Water Pitcher Episode   Kern 1937

Water Under the Bridge   Duke 1934; Harburg 1934; Pollack 1934; Sondheim Date Unknown; Webster 1934

Water Wears Down the Stone, The   Rome 1965

Water Wonderland   Sherman 1979

Waterfall Melody   Donaldson 1933

Waterfall Serenade (inst.)   Bloom 1946

Waterfront Blues   Spina 1959

Waterloo Bridge   Lawrence 1941; Silver 1941

Watermelon Man   Ellington 1939

Watermelon Party   Smith, Harry B. 1901

Watermelon Time   Atteridge 1921; Pollack 1921; Schwartz, Jean 1921

Watermelon Weather   Carmichael 1952; Webster 1952

Waters of the Perkiomen   Dubin 1925

Waukegan Was a Thriving and Prosperous City Before Jack Benny Came Along   Willson 1953

Wave to Me, My Lady   Loesser 1945

Wax Works, The   David, Mack 1951; Livingston, Jerry 1951

Way Back in 1939 A.D.   Carmichael 1940; Mercer 1940

Way Back West   Oakland 1960; Raye 1960

Way Back When   David, Hal 1949

Way Down East   Atteridge 1914; Romberg 1914; Sterling 1897; Von Tilzer 1897

Way Down Home   Donaldson 1922

'Way Down in Arkansas   Fain 1957

Way Down in Barbizon   Brennan 1927

Way Down in Cotton Town   Leslie 1909

Way Down in C-U-B-A   Norworth 1912

Way Down in Georgia   Mills 1924

Way Down in Iowa I'm Going to Hide Anyway   Lewis 1916; Meyer 1916; Young, Joe 1916

Way Down in Jersey   Howard, Joseph E. 1906

Way Down in Mexico   Von Tilzer 1911

Way Down in Pago Pago   Atteridge 1923; Caesar 1923; Romberg 1923

'Way Down in Vo-de-o-de-o Town   Warren 1927

Way Down in Yucatan   Herbert 1919

Way Down on Honolulu Bay   Goetz 1915; Romberg 1915

Way Down on Sunny Tampa Bay   Goetz 1911

Way Down on Tampa Bay   Brown, A. Seymour 1914

Way Down on the Farm   Williams 1907

Way Down South   Berlin 1917; Johnson, James P. 1932; Razaf 1932; Smith, Harry B. 1903, 1923

'Way Down South in Chicago (By the Old Pacific Shore)   Warren 1925

Way Down South in North Carolina   Freed, Ralph 1934; Styne 1934

Way Down South of Dixie   Robin 1951; Styne 1951

Way Down Town   Hanley 1927; Kern 1921

Way Down Yonder By Myself, Can't Hear Nobody Pray   Brennan 1943

Way Down Yonder in the Cornfield   Cobb 1901; Edwards 1901

Way He Makes Me Feel, The   Bergman 1983

Way I Feel About You, The   Bacharach 1976; David, Hal 1976

Way I Feel To-Day, The   Razaf 1929

Way I Feel Tonight, The   Parish 1932

Way I Love You, The   Lawrence 1958

Way I See It, The   Coleman 1979

Way It Might Have Been, The   Martin 1948

Way It Was, The   Warren 1970

Way of Life, A   Fain 1964

Way Out in Kentucky   Mitchell 1923

Way Out West   Hart 1937; Rodgers 1937

Way Out West in Elizabeth New Jersey   Fisher 1921

Way Out West in Idaho   Fisher 1940

Way Out West in Jersey   DeSylva 1922; Herbert 1922; Weill 1943

Way Out West Where the East Begins   Harburg 1940; Lane 1940

Way Over in Jordan   Johnson, James P. 1962

Way She Walks, The   Merrill 1959

Way That I Want You, The   De Lange 1944; Myrow 1944

Way That Lovers Use, The   Kern 1956

Way that Walker Walked Away, The   Smith, Harry B. 1901

Way Things Are, The   Rome 1962; Sherman 1983

Way to a Family's Heart, The   Robin 1957; Styne 1957

Way to a Girlie's Heart, The   Smith, Robert B. 1909

Way to a Man's Heart, The   DePaul 1956; Mercer 1956

Way to Love, The   Coslow 1933; Johnston 1933; Rainger 1933; Robin 1933

Way to Win a Girl, The   Lewis 1919; Snyder 1919; Young, Joe 1919

Way Up North   Loesser 1943; Schwartz, Arthur 1943

Way Up the Hudson   Stept 1949

Way We Are, The   Lane 1952; Robin 1952

Way We Were, The   Bergman 1973

Way We Weren't, The   Bergman 1973

Way West, The   David, Mack 1967

Way with a Woman, A   Livingston, Jerry 1962; Webster 1962

Way You Look Tonight, The   Fields 1936; Kern 1936

Way You Manoeuvre, The   Robin 1927; Youmans 1927

Wayne Cody Theme   Oakland 1954

Ways of Love, The   Bergman 1961; Mancini 1958; Raye 1958

Ways of the World Are Mine, The   Brennan 1928

Wayside Flower   Romberg 1925

We   Duke 1963; Gershwin, George 1925; Gershwin, Ira 1925; Mancini 1969

We — All Together   Alter 1942; Cahn 1942

We Address Him as Mister President   Caesar 1946

We Agree Perfectly   Coots 1935; David, Mack 1935

We All Can Write   Baer 1928

We All Fall   Meyer 1911

We All Gotta Live in His House   Merrill 1958

We All Need Love   Sigman 1956

We Always Disagree   Duke 1926

We Always Get Our Girl   Brown, Nacio Herb 1943; Robin 1943

We Americans   Dubin 1927

We Are Americans Too   Blake 1940; Razaf 1940

We Are China   Strouse 1982

We Are Cut in Twain   Weill 1938

We Are Free   Atteridge 1913; Coots 1954

We Are Going on Our Honeymoon   Buck 1917

We Are Here to Sing a Chorus   Leigh 1955

We Are in Society   Rose 1928

We Are Only Poor Weak Mortals After All   Harbach 1910

We Are Only Poor Week Mortals After All   Harbach 1910

We Are Prom Girls   Porter 1913

We Are Puritans   Atteridge 1924; Romberg 1924; Schwartz, Jean 1924

We Are So Aesthetic   Porter 1912

We Are the Bright Lights of Broadway   Buck 1917, 1918

We Are the Chorus of the Show   Porter 1912

We Are the Dreamers   Webster 1974

We Are the Fixers   Romberg 1919

We Are the Follies   Buck 1918

We Are the Girls in the Chorus   Coots 1927; Dubin 1927

We Are the Heiresses   Smith, Harry B. 1900

We Are the Horrors of Deadliest Woe (Chorus of Torments)   Hart 1928; Rodgers 1928

We Are the Maids of the Merry Merry   Buck 1920

We Are the Roman Soldiers   Brown, Lew 1934

We are the Royal Canadian Mounties   Comden and Green 1972

We Are Very Highly Polished at the Court Don't You Know   Herbert 1903; Smith, Harry B. 1903

We Are Visitors   Gershwin, George 1929; Gershwin, Ira 1929

We Are Waiting   Coots 1922

We Are Yankee Doodle Winners   Cohan 1970

We Arrested the Moon   Drake 1994

We Belong to Old Broadway   Harbach 1908

We Belong to You (Watashi Mo Kokoro Mo Anatano Monoyo)   Rome 1969

We Belong Together   Fain 1943; Freed, Ralph 1943; Hammerstein 1932; Kern 1932

We Better Get Together Again   Conrad 1932; Friend 1932

We Came, We Saw, We Made 'Em!   Hart 1922; Rodgers 1922

We Can Live on Love   Coslow 1952

We Can Live on Love (We Haven't a Pot to Cook In)   Dubin 1939; McHugh 1939

We Can Make It   Robin 1955; Styne 1955

We Can Never Light that Old Flame Again   David, Mack 1982

We Cannot Let You Go   Smith, Harry B. 1900

We Can't Be as Good as Last Year   Hart 1926; Rodgers 1926

We Can't Can All the Peaches We Pick, but We Can All the Peaches We Can   Bryan 1925; Schwartz, Jean 1925

We Can't Make a Monkey of the Moon   Rainger 1934; Robin 1934

We Could Be Close   Merrill 1972; Styne 1972

We Couldn't Do Better than That   Akst 1933; Eliscu 1933

We Couldn't Have Heroes Over There If It Wasn't for the Heroes Over Here   Clarke 1918

We Couldn't Have Heroes Over There, If It Wasn't for Those Heroes Over Here   Johnson, Howard 1918

We Dance   Merrill 1990

We Deserve Each Other   Hammerstein 1953; Rodgers 1953

We Detest a Fiesta   Porter 1940

We Did It Before (We'll Do It Again)   Friend 1941

We Do Not Belong Together   Sondheim 1984

We Do the Best We Can   Bryan 1917

We Do the Dirty Work   Cohan 1911

We Don't Know Why — But   Freed, Arthur 1927

We Don't Matter at All   Adams 1966; Strouse 1966

We Don't Want Liquor   Fisher 1922

We Drink a Toast to You   Young, Joe 1928

We Drink to You, J.H. Brody   Porter 1938

We Float   Sondheim 1976

We Forgot the Number of the House   Atteridge 1914

We French Get So Excited   Loesser 1947

We Girls of the Chorus   Gordon 1953; Myrow 1953

We Go to Find the Ring   Johnson, J. Rosamond 1904

We Got Annie   Strouse 1977

We Got It!   Sherman 1974

We Got to Put Shoes on Willie   Fain 1948; Yellen 1948

We Gotta Find a New Kentucky Home   Hanley 1921

We Gotta Get Hitched Baby   Blake 1958

We Gotta Go   Coleman 1996

We Gotta Keep Up with the Joneses   Blane 1956; Martin 1956

We Had a Date with Destiny   Revel 1959

We Had a Little Rain Today   Drake 1955

We Had a Show   Comden and Green 1943

We Had to Rehearse   Schwartz, Arthur 1937

We Happen to Be in the Army   Koehler 1937; Mitchell 1937; Stept 1937

We Hate Paree!   Drake 1996

We Hate to Leave   Cahn 1945; Styne 1945

We Have a Date   Hoffman 1959

We Have a Law   Caesar 1946

We Have All the Time in the World   David, Hal 1970

We Have Been Around   Gordon 1945

We Have Each Other   Ager 1929; Yellen 1929

We Have Met Before   Coslow 1936

We Have Much to Be Thankful For   Berlin 1913

We Have Never Met As Yet   Gordon 1951, 1953; Myrow 1951, 1953

We Have Nothing to Fear   Livingston, Jerry 1960

We Have Sandwiches   Gorney 1940

We Have So Little Time   Koehler 1944; Lane 1944

We Have So Much in Common   Coleman 1960; Leigh 1960

We Have with Us Tonight   David, Hal 1951

We Haven't a Moment to Lose   Burke 1937; Johnston 1937

We Just Couldn't Say Goodbye   Woods 1932

We Just Might   Duke 1963

We Just Sing and Dance   Hart 1937; Rodgers 1937

We Kiss in a Shadow   Hammerstein 1951; Rodgers 1951

We Knew It All the Time   Styne 1947

We Know   Merrill 1952

We Know Reno   Heyman 1931

We Know Where You're Goin'   Baer 1940

We Laughed at Love   Kahn 1955

We Like It Over Here   Hammerstein 1940; Schwartz, Arthur 1940

We Like Working Together (We Like Working with Each Other)   Cahn 1956; Van Heusen 1956

We Like Working with Each Other   Van Heusen 1956

We Live on Park   Willson 1963

We Love Dear Old Appleton   Kalmar 1937; Ruby 1937

We Love the Place, O God   Bullock 1944

We Love the South   Bullock 1937; Spina 1937

We Love to Go to Work   Atteridge 1929

We Love to Live   Cohan 1901

We Love Us   Duke 1946

We Love You, Beatles   Adams 1964; Strouse 1964

We Love You, Conrad!   Adams 1960; Strouse 1960

We Loves Ya, Jimey   Fields 1959

We Made the Doughnuts Over There   Berlin 1919

We Made Up Again   Stept 1935

We Make the Show   Atteridge 1925

We May Be Happy Yet   Smith, Harry B. 1910

We Meet Again   Bergman 1961

We Meet in the Funniest Places   Dubin 1943; Monaco 1943

We Met Over a Bottle of Vivo   Styne 1946

We Might Play Tiddle De Winks   Robin 1928

We Musn't Say Goodbye   Dubin 1943; Monaco 1943

We Must Be Vigilant — American Patrol   Leslie 1942

We Must Have a Ball   Lerner, Alan Jay 1976

We Must Have a Song to Remember   Stept 1919

We Must Have Music   Brown, Nacio Herb 1941; Kahn 1941

We Mustn't Part   Sigman 1958

We Need a Little Love, That's All   Waller 1944

We Need a Man   Cohan 1932; Weill 1936

We Need Affection   Kahn 1930

We Need Him   Adams 1966; Strouse 1966

We Never, Never Lost a War, and Never Never Will   Howard, Joseph E. 1943

We Never Sleep   Caesar 1930

We Never Talk Too Much   Cahn 1951

We, Oh We Are in Society   Dixon 1928; Warren 1928

We Only Love Once   Coots 1937; Parish 1937

We Open in Venice   Porter 1948

We Ought to Dance Don't You Think?   DePaul 1942; Raye 1942

We Pirates from Weehawken   Hart 1926; Rodgers 1926

We Prize Most the Things We Miss   Caesar 1936

We Ran Away from School   Gorney 1924

We Reached a Perfect Understanding   Parish 1933

We Really Ought to Be Married   Jerome 1904; Schwartz, Jean 1904

We Rich, Rich, Rich   Howard, Bart 1961

We Rule the Waves   Rose 1940

We Said Our Goodbyes Too Soon   Coots 1950; Egan 1950

We Sail Tonight   Russell 1952, 1954

We Salute You Admiral Byrd   Baer 1931; Gilbert 1931

We Saw the Sea   Berlin 1936

We Say We'll Do a Thing   Smith, Harry B. 1903

We Shall Meet to Part, No Never   Arlen 1946; Mercer 1946

We Shall Never Be Younger   Porter 1948

We Should Be Together   Bullock 1938; Spina 1938

We Should Care   Berlin 1925

We Sing America   Rome 1937

We Speak the Same Language   Adams 1962; David, Hal 1991; Strouse 1962, 1991

We Still Have Us   David, Hal 1978

We Take It, Just Take It from You   Romberg 1919

We Take Only the Bets   Hart 1921; Rodgers 1921

We Talk, We Speak   Cahn 1973

We, the People   Razaf 1938

We Toddled Up the Hill   Leslie 1929

We Took a Chance   McHugh 1958

We Traveled Around   Brooks 1960

We Two   Friml 1923; Hammerstein 1927; Harbach 1927

We Two in an Aeroplane   Smith, Harry B. 1908; Williams 1908

We Two Shall Meet Again   Smith, Harry B. 1927

We Two (Someday)   Sherman 1971

We Used to Talk Once   Styne 1980

We Walked in the Garden   Lawrence 1941

We Walked Right in Turned Around and Walked Right Out Again   Fisher 1936

We Want Sweetheart Security   Baer 1938; Lewis 1938

We Want Teddy for Four Years More   Edwards 1904

We Want the Charleston   Brown, Lew 1925; Henderson 1925

We Want to Make the Laws   Weill 1938

We Want Wilkie   Kalmar 1940

We Want You   Kalmar 1927, 1929; Ruby 1927, 1929

We Watch the Skyways   Kahn 1941, 1948

We Were Always to be Married   Arlen 1966

We Were Married in Nevada Many, Many Years Ago   Woods 1951

We Were Meant to Meet Again   Woods 1935

We Were Only Walking in the Moonlight   Burke 1932; Spina 1932

We Were So Young   Hammerstein 1935; Kern 1935

We Were the Best of Friends   Lewis 1933; Meyer 1933; Young, Joe 1933

We Who Are About to Die   David, Mack 1964

We Will Always Be Sweethearts   Robin 1932

We Will Fight   Blane 1952; Warren 1952

We Will Find a Way   Adams 1967; Strouse 1967

We Will Find Your Sheep   Herbert 1903

We Will Live for Love and Love Alone   Carroll 1918

We Will Meet Again in Honolulu   Brown, Nacio Herb 1945; Freed, Arthur 1945

We Will Never Say   Fisher 1919

We Will Rally to the Racket   Motzan 1917

We Will Take the Road Together   Kern 1923

We Wish the World a Happy Yule   Merrill 1965; Styne 1965

We Wish We Could Turn Back the Clock   Merrill 1972; Styne 1972

We Wish You a Merry Christmas   Cahn 1972; Van Heusen 1972

We Won't Charleston   Kalmar 1926; Ruby 1926

We Won't Forget   DePaul 1958; Raye 1958

We Won't Get Home Until A.M. If We Ever Get Home at All   Donaldson 1916

We Won't Have to See the Place   Bryan 1933; Wrubel 1933

We Won't Have to Sell the Farm   Bryan 1933; Wrubel 1933

We Won't Live in a Castle   Merrill 1951

We Won't Take It Back   Dietz 1948; Schwartz, Arthur 1948

We Work Away   Smith, Harry B. 1935

We Wouldn't Take a Million for Our Baby   Fisher 1935

We Wrote Our Love Song Together   Fisher 1936

Weaken a Bit   Gershwin, George 1925; Gershwin, Ira 1925

Weaker Is the Stronger After All, The   Caesar 1922

Weaker Sex, The   DeSylva 1926

Weakness   Mills 1934

Weaknesses   Hammerstein 1919, 1920; Rodgers 1919

Wealthiest Girl in the Country   Comden and Green 1972

Wealthy, Shmelthy As Long As You're Healthy   Fain 1935; Parish 1935

Wear a Bouquet of Smiles   Blake Date Unknown; Sissle Date Unknown

Wear a Hat with a Silver Lining   Bryan 1928

Wear a Little Grin   Merrill 1990

Wear a Straw Hat in the Rain   Johnston 1940

Wear This Ring   Russell 1957

Wear Your Rubbers When It Rains   Styne 1940

Wear Your Sunday Smile   Robin 1927

Wearers of the Green   Olcott 1906

Wearin' Off the Green   Fields 1931; McHugh 1931

Wearin' the Grin   Loewe 1942

Weary   Blake 1947; Dixon 1935; Friml 1947; Heyman 1947; Razaf 1947; Wrubel 1935

Weary Blues   Blane 1948; Warren 1948

Weary Near to Dyin'   Merrill 1967

Weary of Me   Parish 1932

Weary of Waiting for You   Kahn 1925; Whiting 1925

Weary River   Clarke 1929

Weather Factory in Cloudland, The   Herbert 1908; Smith, Harry B. 1908

Weather Man   Caesar 1935; Gershwin, George 1924; Gershwin, Ira 1924

Weather Medley   Brooks 1958

Weatherman   Ellington 1955

Weather's in Your Eyes, The   Martin 1951

Weaver of Dreams   Young, Victor 1951

Weaver Specialty   Styne 1940

Weaver's Song   Bergman 1957

Weaving My Dreams   Buck 1922; Herbert 1922

Web of Dreams   Harbach 1923

Web of Lies   Lawrence 1954

Webbing (inst.)   Herbert 1923

Webson's Meat Jingle   Blane 1954; Martin 1954

We'd Better Stop Kiss-Kiss-Kissin'   Bryan 1945

We'd Like to Thank You   Strouse 1977

We'd Rather Be Right   Rome 1937

We'd Rather Dance than Eat   Buck 1927

Weddin' of Mister and Missus Swing, The   Coots 1936; Davis 1936

Wedding, The   Ellington 1966; Rome 1973

Wedding Ballet   Ellington 1946

Wedding Bells   Atteridge 1916; Friml 1923; Herbert 1906; Motzan 1916, 1917; Smith, Harry B. 1911; Smith, Robert B. 1911

Wedding Bells Are Breaking Up that Old Gang of Mine   Fain 1929; Kahal 1929

Wedding Bells Are Calling Me   Kern 1915; Smith, Harry B. 1915

Wedding Bells Polka   Drake 1946

Wedding Bells Ring On   Eliscu 1929; Rose 1929; Youmans 1929

Wedding Bells Were Ringing, The   Carroll 1925; Freed, Arthur 1925

Wedding Bells, Will You Ever Ring for Me   Lewis 1918; Schwartz, Jean 1918; Young, Joe 1918

Wedding Blues, The   Friml 1919; Harbach 1919

Wedding By Proxy   Romberg 1918

Wedding By the Sea   Atteridge 1916; Motzan 1916, 1917; Romberg 1916

Wedding Cake   Davis 1962

Wedding Cake Walk, The   Porter 1941

Wedding Chorus   Smith, Harry B. 1934

Wedding Country Style   Brooks 1959

Wedding Dance   Rome 1953, 1954

Wedding Day in Flowerland   Bryan 1931

Wedding Day Song, The   Martin 1969

Wedding Ensemble   Romberg 1927

Wedding Fete, The   Smith, Robert B. 1909

Wedding Glide, The   Atteridge 1912

Wedding Gown, Bridal Veil (For Sale)   Spina 1966

Wedding Guests   Smith, Harry B. 1911; Smith, Robert B. 1911

Wedding in the Park   Gorney 1948

Wedding in the Spring   Kern 1942; Mercer 1942

Wedding Is Off!, The   Sondheim 1970

Wedding Knell, The   Hammerstein 1925; Harbach 1925; Kern 1925

Wedding March, The   Atteridge 1922; Blane 1952; Romberg 1922

Wedding March (inst.)   Duke 1963

Wedding Music (inst.)   Herbert 1908

Wedding Night Waltz   Bergman 1983

Wedding of Dan McCann to Molly McGee, The   Baer 1951

Wedding of the Big Baboon, The   Buck 1913

Wedding of the Blue and Grey   Williams 1907

Wedding of the Blue and the Gray, The   Cohan 1906

Wedding of the Chafing Dish and the Alcohol Lamp, The   Howard, Joseph E. 1907

Wedding of the Chocolate Soldier and the Coffee Colored Doll, The   Razaf 1936

Wedding of the Lily and the Rose   Herbert 1907; Smith, Harry B. 1907

Wedding of the Painted Doll, The   Brown, Nacio Herb 1928; Freed, Arthur 1928

Wedding of the Reuben and the Maid, The   Smith, Harry B. 1901

Wedding of the Valley and the Hills, The   Eliscu 1930

Wedding of the Wooden Soldier and the Painted Doll   Raye 1939

Wedding of the Year   Drake 1964

Wedding of Words and Music   Berlin 1917

Wedding Procession (Finale Act I)   Hart 1926; Rodgers 1926

Wedding Ring   Fisher 1922

Wedding Ring Don't Mean a Thing When You're Married, The   Fisher 1922

Wedding Scene   Buck 1923; Herbert 1923

Wedding Scene (Finale Act I)   Hammerstein 1925; Harbach 1925; Kern 1925

Wedding Song   Carmichael 1935; DePaul 1956; Mercer 1956; Revel 1946; Weill 1933, 1938, 1954

Wedding Time   Coots 1922

Wedding Trip, A   Hart Date Unknown; Rodgers Date Unknown

Wedding Waltz   Carroll 1934; Conrad 1928; Gilbert 1928; Robison 1952; Spina 1957; Young, Victor 1956

Wedding, Wedding   Strouse 1993

Wedgewood Maid   Coots 1925

Wednesday's Child   David, Mack 1966

Wee Bit o' Scotch, A   Rome 1970

Wee Bit of Lace, A   Cohan 1919

Wee Gee (Ouija) (Tell Me Do)   Jerome 1920; Von Tilzer 1920

Wee Golden Warrior, The   Rodgers 1976

Wee Willie Winkle   Coots 1933

Week End   Gershwin, Ira 1928

Week End of a Private Secretary, The   Mercer 1938

Weekend Affair, A   Porter 1932

Weekend at the Waldorf   Blane 1945; Koehler 1945

Weekend Cruise (Will You Love Me Monday Morning as You Did on Friday Night?)   Arlen 1934

Weekend in Havana, A   Gordon 1941; Warren 1941

Week-end in July, A   Youmans 1926

Weekend in the Country   Gershwin, Ira 1949; Sondheim 1973; Warren 1949

Weekly Wedding, The   Friml 1914; Harbach 1914

W.E.E.P.   Bacharach 1967; David, Hal 1967

Weep and You Dance Alone   Johnston 1938

Weep No More, My Baby   Heyman 1933

Weep No More My Bonnie Lassie   Revel 1959

Weep No More My Lady (Because I Won't Take Your Loving Man Away)   Brown, Lew 1913

Weep No More My Lady, Let Me See Your Smile   Gilbert 1914

Weep No More My Mammy   Atteridge 1921; Clare 1921; Mitchell 1921; Pollack 1921

Weepin' and a Wailin' Song (I'm Happy When I'm Singin'), A   Gilbert 1955; Myrow 1956

Weepin' Blues (inst.)   Johnson, James P. 1923

Weepin' Willow Weep No More   Davis 1928; Warren 1928

Weeping   Johnson, James P. 1922

Weeping Sky, The   Dietz 1944; Duke 1944

Weeping Widow, The   Cohan 1901

Weeping Willow Tree   Dietz 1924; Kern 1924

Welch's Grape Juice   Baer 1951

Welcome   Comden and Green 1964; Dietz 1963; Razaf 1929; Schwartz, Arthur 1963; Sigman 1955; Styne 1964; Warren 1980, Date Unknown

Welcome America   Atteridge 1923; Romberg 1923; Schwartz, Jean 1923

Welcome Burleigh   Cahn 1945; Styne 1945

Welcome Egghead   Mercer 1955

Welcome Hinges   Arlen 1944; Harburg 1944

Welcome Home   Akst 1929; Berlin 1913; Clarke 1929; DeSylva 1925; Drake 1954; Hanley 1925, 1929, 1930; Motzan 1934; Robin 1957; Rome 1954; Styne 1957

Welcome Home, Angelina   Howard, Bart 1964

Welcome Home Boys   Razaf 1919

Welcome Home Laddie Boy, Welcome Home   Cobb 1918; Edwards 1918

Welcome Home Miz Adams   Lerner, Alan Jay 1976

Welcome Honey to Your Old Plantation Home   Yellen 1916

Welcome Love   Razaf 1944

Welcome Mat   Russell 1960

Welcome on the Mat Ain't Meant for Me, The   Cobb 1907; Edwards 1907

Welcome Song   Gershwin, George 1947; Gershwin, Ira 1947

Welcome Song (Your Indian Family), The   Fain 1960; Webster 1960

Welcome Stranger   Mercer 1936

Welcome to Being Dead   Strouse 1989

Welcome to Holiday Inn   Coleman 1973; Fields 1973

Welcome to Hollywood   Drake 1953

Welcome to Jerry   Porter 1940

Welcome to Kanagawa   Sondheim 1976

Welcome to Lichtenburg   Berlin 1950

Welcome to Milan   Gorney 1969

Welcome to My Dream   Burke 1945; Van Heusen 1945

Welcome to My Heart   Duke 1949

Welcome to My Love   Cahn 1967

Welcome to Napoleon   Johnston 1935; Kahn 1935

Welcome to Prince   Romberg 1924

Welcome to the Bride   Hammerstein 1934; Kern 1934

Welcome to the Club   Coleman 1988

Welcome to the Diamond Horseshoe   Gordon 1945; Warren 1945

Welcome to the Landing Stage   Caesar 1936

Welcome to the Party   Warren Date Unknown

Welcome to the Queen   Friml 1928

Welcome to the Royal American   DePaul 1958; Raye 1958

Welcome to the Theater   Adams 1970; Strouse 1970

Welcome to Union City   Adamson 1956; McHugh 1956

Welcome to Victory Ranch   Akst 1943

Welcome to Washington   Strouse 1993, Date Unknown

Welcome Welcome   Coleman 1984

Welcome Yule   Johnson, Howard 1939

Welcoming Song   Styne 1958

Welcoming the Bride   Herbert 1913; Smith, Robert B. 1913

We'll All Be in Heaven When the Dollar Goes to Hell   Berlin 1933

We'll All Go Voting for Al   Berlin 1924

Well All Right, Tonight's the Night   Raye 1939

We'll Always Be Sweethearts   Friend 1930

We'll Barricade Her   Friml 1912; Harbach 1912

We'll Be Alone at Last   Cohan 1916

We'll Be Comin' Down the Chimney   Silver 1956

We'll Be Cutting Paper Dolls Together   Egan 1929

We'll Be Dancing on the Sidewalk   Silver 1944

We'll Be the Same   Hart 1931; Rodgers 1931

We'll Be There   Coots 1929; Davis 1929; Edwards 1907

We'll Be there Little One We'll Be There   Bryan 1907; Meyer 1907

We'll Be There (On the Land, on the Sea, in the Air)   Hanley 1917

Well Beloved   Herbert 1899; Smith, Harry B. 1899

We'll Build a Cute Little Nest   Friml 1919; Harbach 1919

We'll Build a Little World of Our Own   Hanley 1930

We'll Build a Rainbow in the Sky   Egan 1918; Whiting 1918

We'll Catch You at Last   Herbert 1900; Smith, Harry B. 1900

We'll Dance Until the Dawn   Fields 1931; McHugh 1931

Well, Did You Evah!   Porter 1939, 1956

We'll Do Our Share (While You're Over There)   Brown, Lew 1918

Well Done My Lad, Well Done   Burke 1932; Monaco 1932

We'll Drift Along   Friml 1917; Harbach 1917

We'll Drink Every Drop in the Shop   Evans 1946; Livingston, Jay 1946

We'll Drown It in the Bowl   Olcott 1901

We'll Find a Way   Kahn 1932

We'll Get Along   Atteridge 1929

We'll Go Away Together   Weill 1947

We'll Go Out and Find Another Rainbow   Ager 1932

We'll Go Up in Dose Mountains   Stept 1927

We'll Greet Each Tomorrow Together   Caesar 1922

We'll Have a Bushel of Fun   Schwartz, Jean 1936

We'll Have a Honeymoon Someday   Woods 1933

We'll Have a Jubilee in My Old Kentucky Home   Donaldson 1915

We'll Have a Kingdom   Friml 1926; Hammerstein 1926; Harbach 1926

We'll Have A Lot of Fun   DePaul 1941; Raye 1941

We'll Have a New Home in the Morning   Buck 1927; Robison 1927

We'll Have a Wonderful Party   Harbach 1920

Well, I Just Wouldn't Know   Porter 1943

Well! I'll Be Switched   Blane 1954; Myrow 1954

Well, I'm Not!   Adams 1981; Strouse 1981

We'll Keep Things Going Till the Boys Come Home, Won't We Girlie   Sterling 1917

We'll Knock the Japs Right in the Laps of the Nazis   Pollack 1941; Washington 1941

Well Known Skies of Blue, The   Gershwin, Ira 1949; Warren 1949

We'll Link His Name with Lincoln   Jerome 1924

We'll Live All Over Again   Duke 1940

We'll Love Again   Evans 1956; Livingston, Jay 1956

We'll Make Hay While the Sun Shines   Brown, Nacio Herb 1933; Freed, Arthur 1933

We'll Make Love When It Rains   Brown, Nacio Herb 1933

We'll March to Hell and Back Again   Razaf 1942

We'll Meet Again in Honolulu   Freed, Arthur 1946

We'll Meet Again in Normandy   Kahn 1925

Well Minnie   Lawrence 1981

Well, Natch   David, Hal 1945

We'll Never Grow Old   Johnson, Howard 1921

We'll Never Know   Berlin 1926

We'll Never Run Short of Love   Hoffman 1937; Lerner, Sammy 1937

We'll Only Be Lonely Apart   Merrill 1950

We'll Paddle Our Own Canoe   Sterling 1904; Von Tilzer 1904

We'll See   Kern 1917; Smith, Harry B. 1917

We'll See It Through   Friend 1932

We'll Soon Be One World   Caesar 1946

We'll Stand and Cheer   Leigh 1967

We'll Stay Over Here   Monaco 1934; Young, Joe 1934

We'll Take Care of You All (Refugee Song) (The Little Refugees)   Kern 1914

We'll Take Care of You All (The Refugee Song) (The Little Refugees)   Smith, Harry B. 1914

Well Thank You   Bergman 1960

Well the Irish and the Germans Got Together   Ahlert 1928; Turk 1928

Well, This Is Jolly   Kern 1913; Smith, Harry B. 1913

We'll Tramp, Tramp Along Together   Brennan 1926

We'll Wait, Wait, Wait   Berlin 1909; Leslie 1909

Well, Well   Loesser 1941; Styne 1941

Well, Well, Well   Donaldson 1932

Well Wishers, The   Adams 1970; Strouse 1970

Well, You See, I, Oh, You Know   Heyman 1931

Wells Fargo Theme (Inst.)   Warren Date Unknown

Wells Fargo Wagon, The   Willson 1957

Wendy   Comden and Green 1954; Drake 1963; Styne 1954

Wer Hat Die Schonsten Schafchen   Freed, Ralph 1939

We're a Couple of Salesmen   Blake 1932; Sissle 1932

We're a Couple of Soldiers, My Baby and Me   Woods 1931

We're a Group of Nonentities   Porter 1913

We're About to Start Big-Rehearsin'   Porter 1936

We're All a Happy Lot   Brooks 1946

We're All A-Worry, All Agog   Gershwin, George 1927;
    Gershwin, Ira 1927

We're All Comrades Now   Bryan 1918; Fisher 1918

We're All Friends Together   Adamson 1942

We're All Going on a Honeymoon   Duke 1968

We're All Here at Siwash   Loesser 1940

We're All in the Bread Line Together   Smith, Harry B. 1935

We're All in the Same Boat   Robin 1954; Romberg 1954

We're All in the Same Boat Now   Hoffman 1942;
    Livingston, Jerry 1942

We're All Together Now   Rainger 1939; Robin 1939

We're Alone   Freed, Arthur 1932

We're Alone in the World   Cahn Date Unknown; Duke
    Date Unknown

We're Americans   Livingston, Jerry 1962

We're Back Again   Raye 1939

We're Back in Circulation Again   Mitchell 1936; Pollack 1936

We're Back Together Again, My Baby and Me   Clare 1925;
    Monaco 1925

We're Breaking Up a Lovely Affair   Mills 1939

We're Building Men   Loesser 1942; Spina 1942

We're Calling on Mr. Brooks   Brown, Lew 1928; DeSylva
    1928; Henderson 1928

We're Cleaning Up Broadway   Caesar 1926; Friml 1926

We're Coming Back to You when the Fighting Days are
    Through   Donaldson 1918

We're Coming from Cody   Yellen 1918

We're Coming, Leo   Evans 1951; Livingston, Jay 1951

We're Coming Over   Howard, Joseph E. 1942

We're Crooks   Kern 1917

We're Dancers on Parade   Razaf 1954

We're Despicable (Plunderers' March)   Merrill 1962; Styne
    1962

We're Doin' It for the Natives in Jamaica   Arlen 1953; Fields
    1953

We're for Love   Blane 1952

We're for You, Ed Wynn!   Rome 1957

We're Friends Again   Ahlert 1930; Turk 1930

We're Getting Too Old for This Jazz   Cahn 1963; Van
    Heusen 1963

We're Goin' Home   Brooks 1947

We're Goin' to Blitz the Ritzes   Johnson, James P. 1948

We're Goin' to Have a Ragtime Wedding   Leslie 1912

We're Goin' Together Once More   Ahlert 1931; Turk 1931

We're Going Back   Rome 1948

We're Going Over the Top, and We'll Be Marching Thro'
    Berlin in the Morning   Sterling 1917

We're Going to Balance the Budget (Tune Up,
    Bluebird)   Hart 1937; Rodgers 1937

We're Going to Be Dramatic   Heyman 1933

We're Going to Be Pals   Kern 1917

We're Going to Fight the Indians   Edwards 1908

We're Going to Make a Man of You   Friml 1912; Harbach
    1912

We're Going to Make Boom-Boom   Brennan 1929

We're Going to Schnectady   Willson 1954

We're Gonna Be All Right   Rodgers 1965; Sondheim 1965

We're Gonna Be Photographed   Drake 1952

We're Gonna Do It 'Till We Get It Right   Leigh 1977

We're Gonna Have a Happy New Year All Year
    Round   Hoffman 1931

We're Gonna Have Smooth Sailing   Ager 1935

We're Gonna Howl Tonight   Merrill 1965; Styne 1965

We're Gonna Make Love Tonight   Magidson 1932; Stept
    1932

We're Gonna Raise Hell (Finaletto, Scene I)   Hart 1928;
    Rodgers 1928

We're Gymnastic   Hammerstein 1925; Harbach 1925; Kern
    1925

We're Hangin' Out a Star   Brooks 1959

We're Happy   Brooks 1957

We're Happy Again   Revel 1942

We're Having a Baby, My Baby and Me   Adamson 1941;
    Duke 1941

We're Having Our Fling   David, Mack 1943; Livingston,
    Jerry 1943

We're Heading for a Wedding   Coleman 1991; Comden and
    Green 1991

We're Healthy Like Anything   Fain 1936

We're Here Because   Gershwin, George 1924; Gershwin, Ira
    1924

We're Here Because We're Here   Hoffman 1944; Livingston,
    Jerry 1944

We're Here to State   Gordon 1934; Revel 1934

We're Home   Merrill 1959

We're in Business   Arlen 1953; Fields 1953

(Gold Diggers Song) We're in the Money   Dubin 1933;
    Warren 1933

We're in the Navy   DePaul 1941, 1942, 1943; Raye 1941,
    1943

We're Jolly Good Fellows All   Johnson, Howard 1935

We're Just Poor Folks Rolling in Love   Gordon 1934; Revel
    1934

We're Just Simple Folk   Woods 1934

We're Keeping It Private   Donaldson 1947

We're Living in a Wonderful County, I Wouldn't Worry
    about a Thing If I Were You   Koehler 1941; Monaco
    1941

We're L-Losing Our L-Little Girl   Cahn 1964; Van Heusen
    1964

We're Lonesome for Someone Like You   Burke 1929

We're Looking for the Big Bad Wolf   Styne 1943

We're Looking for the Treasure (Finale Act I)   Gershwin,
    George 1928; Gershwin, Ira 1928

We're Men of Brains   Hart 1928; Rodgers 1928

We're Mr. and Mrs. Now   Johnson, Howard 1926

We're Not As Bad As We're Painted   Ager 1923; Yellen 1923

We're Not Children   Evans 1958; Livingston, Jay 1958

We're Not Getting Any Younger Baby   Magidson 1948;
    Oakland 1948

We're Not Too Poor for That   Caesar 1933; Motzan 1933

We're Nuts About Midget Auto Races   Cahn 1936

We're Off   Porter 1911

We're Off for a Hayride in Mexico   Porter 1944

We're Off on a Wonderful Trip   Gershwin, Ira 1921;
    Youmans 1921

We're Off the Wagon   Carmichael 1940; Mercer 1940

We're Off to a Wonderful Start   Freed, Ralph 1936; Oakland
    1935; Woods 1958

We're Off to Feathermore   Porter 1935

We're Off to India   Gershwin, Ira 1921; Youmans 1921

We're Off to Paris   Romberg 1924

We're Off to See the Wizard   Arlen 1939; Harburg 1939

We're Off to the Races   De Lange 1944; Harburg 1961; Stept
    1944

We're Old Enough to Cry   David, Mack 1957

We're On Our Way   Brown, Nacio Herb 1948; Hammerstein
    1944; Kern 1915; Rodgers 1944

We're On Our Way to France   Berlin 1918
We're on Our Way to Hell   Gordon 1932; Revel 1932
We're on the Map   Kalmar 1926; Ruby 1926
We're On the Road to Athens   Porter 1950
We're on the Track   Hart 1941; Rodgers 1941; Smith, Robert B. 1910
We're on the Verge of a Murder   Robin 1930
We're Only Little Extras Looking for an Opportunity   Gordon 1933; Revel 1933
We're Out of the Red   Brown, Lew 1934; Gorney 1934
We're Pals   Caesar 1920; Gershwin, George 1920
We're Pirates Bold   Adamson 1935; Lane 1935
We're Secret Society Members   Von Tilzer 1903
We're Selling Sunshine   Lerner, Alan Jay 1948; Weill 1948
We're Six Little Nieces of Uncle Sam   Gershwin, George 1917
We're Spending Our Honeymoon in Escrow   Willson 1948
We're Staying Home Tonight (My Baby and Me)   Loesser 1943; Schwartz, Arthur 1943
We're Still Friends   Coleman 1977
We're Still Holding Hands   Hoffman 1956
We're Supposed to Be   Cohan 1908
We're Taking Over Now   Lerner, Alan Jay 1948; Weill 1948
We're the Berries   Blake 1930
We're the Blondes Who Are Preferred   Johnston 1926; Turk 1926
We're the Couple in the Castle   Carmichael 1941; Loesser 1941
We're the Gentlemen of the Press   Davis 1954
We're the Girls You Can't Forget   Hanley 1927
We're the Guys Who Shoot Supplies   Buck 1943
We're the Kind of People Who Sing Lullabies   Burke 1938; Weill 1938
We're the Ones   Pollack 1944
We're the Statesmen Great   Smith, Harry B. 1935
We're the Sun Tan Tenth of the Nation   Webster 1941
We're the Sunday Drivers   Fain 1927; Mills 1927
We're the Two Greatest Lovers in the World   Magidson 1960; Oakland 1960
Were Thine That Special Face   Porter 1948
We're Through   Raye 1951; Spina 1951
We're Together Again   Brown, Nacio Herb 1933; Freed, Arthur 1933
We're Trimmin' the Old Grey Bonnet   Egan 1939
We're Two Together   Coots 1938
We're Waiting for the Weather   Brown, Lew 1928; DeSylva 1928; Henderson 1928
We're Working Our Way through College   Mercer 1937; Whiting 1937
Were You Foolin'?   Ahlert 1934; Leslie 1934
Were Your Ears Burning   Coslow 1934; Gordon 1934; Johnston 1934; Revel 1934
Were Your Ears Burning Last Night   Baer 1951; Leslie 1951
Weren't We a Couple of Fools?   Ahlert 1935; Young, Joe 1935
Weren't We Fools   Porter 1927
West Ain't Wild and Wooly Anymore, The   Bullock 1937
West Ain't Wild Any More, The   Kahn 1938; Romberg 1938
West Indies on a Banana Boat, The   Spina 1977
West Is Best, The   Loewe 1942
West of the Wide Missouri   Sherman 1968
West Point Bugle   Romberg 1928
West Point Hop, The   Myrow 1938
West Point March   Romberg 1928
West Point Song   Romberg 1928

West Pointers, The   Weill 1936
West Virginia   Blane 1948
West Wind   Ager 1936; Weill 1943; Youmans 1928
West Wind Blow in the Windmill's Face   Egan 1933; Hoffman 1933
Westchester Limited   Myrow 1942
Western Opener   Brooks 1959
Western People Funny   Hammerstein 1951; Rodgers 1951
Western Style   Baer 1952; Leslie 1952
Western Theme   Bergman 1956
Westminster Funeral   Harburg 1967; Styne 1967
Westport!   Leigh 1957
Westward   Whiting 1926
Westward Bound   Revel 1928; Sissle 1928
Wet Yo' Thumb   Akst 1923
Wetona   Atteridge 1921; Romberg 1921
We've Been Married Just One Year   Gilbert 1914
We've Been So Long Together, Why Leave Each Other Now   Bryan 1932; Clare 1932
We've Been Spending the Summer with Our Families   Porter 1930
We've Been Through the Mill Together   Dietz 1943; Duke 1943
We've Been to Boston Town   Johnson, J. Rosamond 1907
We've Been to Europe   Atteridge 1912
We've Come a Long, Long Way   Leigh 1955
We've Come a Long Way Together   Koehler 1940; Stept 1940
We've Come to the Copa   Coslow 1947
We've Decided to Stay   Warren 1956
We've Done All Right   Styne 1978
We've Got a Lot of Catching Up to Do   Harburg 1979
We've Got a Lot to Learn   Smith, Robert B. 1906
We've Got a Parrot in Our House, Pretty Poll, Pretty Poll   Gilbert 1913
We've Got a Style of Our Own   Cahn 1936
We've Got a Wonder Down Under   Hoffman 1942; Livingston, Jerry 1942
We've Got Another Bond to Buy   Adamson 1945; McHugh 1945
We've Got Forever   David, Mack 1976
We've Got Him   Cohan 1927
We've Got It   Coleman 1973; Fields 1973
We've Got Lots in Common   Sherman 1973
We've Got Something   Hammerstein 1920; Harbach 1920
We've Got the Grandest Ice Man   Fisher 1923
We've Got the Lord on Our Side   Magidson 1943; McHugh 1943
We've Got the Song   Rome 1938
We've Got the Stage Door Blues   Kalmar 1920; Ruby 1920
We've Got to Do a Job on the Japs, Baby   Baer 1941; Leslie 1941; Meyer 1941
We've Got to Get On   Schwartz, Arthur 1933
We've Got to Move Today   Williams 1903
We've Got to Put that Sun Back in the Sky   Kahal 1931
We've Got to Put Up with It   Norworth 1917
We've Had a Grand Old Time   Cohan 1927
We've Hunted the Wolf in the Forest   Herbert 1910
We've Just Begun   Rome 1937
We've Looked Around   Brooks 1959
We've Loved Before   Evans 1966; Livingston, Jay 1966; Mancini 1966
We've Met Somewhere Before   Loesser 1941
We've Rabbits of Our Own (Keep Your Rabbits, Rabbi)   Kern 1920

Wha' D'Ya Do When It Rains?   Styne 1943

Wha'd Ja Do to Me?   Ager 1931

Whadda Ya Say to Saying We Do   Baer 1932; Egan 1932

Whadda You Say We Get Together   Turk 1926

Whad'dya Gonna Do Now   Baer 1942

Whale of a Tale   Hoffman 1955

Whale Song, The   Carmichael 1937

Whaler's Life, A   Duke 1950; Rome 1950

Whaler's Return, The   Duke 1950; Rome 1950

Whaler's Song, The   Bryan 1930

Wham   Blane 1951; Martin 1941

What — No Dixie?   Washington 1933; Young, Joe 1933; Young, Victor 1933

What a Baby   Whiting 1927

What a Ball   Porter 1955

What a Ball We Had   Oakland 1964

What a Beautiful Baby You Are   Smith, Robert B. 1915

What a Beautiful Beginning   Akst 1937; Clare 1937

What a Beautiful Face Will Do   Coslow 1924; Romberg 1924

What a Beautiful Night   Kalmar 1935; Ruby 1935

What a Beautiful World This Would Be   Sterling 1903; Von Tilzer 1903

What a Blessing   Loesser 1960

What a Blue-Eyed Baby You Are   Parish 1925

What a Case I've Got on You   Dietz 1930; Schwartz, Arthur 1930

What a Charming Afternoon   Porter 1912

What a Charming Couple   Dietz 1961; Schwartz, Arthur 1961

What a Comforting Thing to Know   Sherman 1976

What a Country!   Adams 1962; Strouse 1962

What a Crazy Way to Spend Sunday   Porter 1944

What a Crisis   Robin 1947

What a Day!   Bullock 1950; David, Mack 1964; Koehler 1944; Lane 1944; Woods 1929

What a Day for a Miracle   Harburg 1971

What a Deal   Evans 1945; Livingston, Jay 1945

What a Delightful   Fain 1950; Webster 1950

What a Difference a Uniform Will Make (Ever Since I Put on A Uniform)   Berlin 1918

What a Dirty Shame   Evans 1952; Livingston, Jay 1952

What a Dream to Dream About   Alter 1930; Johnson, Howard 1930

What a Face, What a Beauty   Gordon 1955

What a Fair Thing Is a Woman   Porter 1953

What a Fool I Have Been   Monaco 1947; Washington 1947

What a Fool I Was   Freed, Arthur 1945

What a Fool I'd Be   Jerome 1913; Sterling 1913; Von Tilzer 1913

What a Girl!   Brennan 1929; Hart 1928; Rodgers 1928

What a Girl Can Do   Kalmar 1918; Ruby 1918

What a Great Pair We'll Be   Porter 1936

What a Heavenly Night   Kalmar 1937; Ruby 1937

What a Joy to Be Young   Porter 1934

What a Life! Trying to Live Without You!   Alter 1932

What a Little Bit of Love Will Do   Fisher 1931

What a Little Moonlight Can Do   Woods 1934

What a Little Thing Like a Wedding Can Do   Robin 1932

What a Lot of Loving   Brennan 1930; Friml 1930

What a Lovely Day for a Wedding   Gershwin, Ira 1940; Hammerstein 1947; Lane 1951; Lerner, Alan Jay 1951; Rodgers 1947; Weill 1940

What a Lucky Break for Me   Berlin 1930

What a Man!   Arlen 1950; Blane 1950; Cohan 1934; Coots 1933; Donaldson 1926; Razaf 1940

What a Man Won't Do for a Woman   Arlen 1954

What a Mornin'   Strouse Date Unknown

What a Nice Municipal Park   Porter 1935

What a Night   Bacharach 1959; David, Hal 1959; Friend 1934; Sissle 1939

What a Night, What a Night, What a Night   David, Hal 1953

What a Perfect Combination   Akst 1933; Caesar 1933; Kalmar 1933; Ruby 1933

What a Pleasant Surprise   Heyman 1933

What a Pleasure to Work with You   Freed, Ralph 1936; Lane 1936; Robin 1936

What a Position for Me   Hanley 1921; Herbert 1919

What a Pretty End to a Pretty Dream   Friend 1928

What a Pretty Miss   Waller 1938

What a Priceless Pleasure   Porter 1938

What a Rumba Does to Romance   Loesser 1938

What a Village Girl Should Know   Coslow 1924

What a Waste   Comden and Green 1953

What a Way to Go   Comden and Green 1964; Drake 1958; Styne 1964

What a Whale of a Difference a Woman Can Make   Robin 1927

What a Whalen of a Difference Just a Few Lights Make   Fields 1929; McHugh 1929

What a Woman   Adams 1983

What a Wonderful Life   Livingston, Jerry 1961

What a Wonderful Way to Die   Merrill 1955

What a Wonderful Way to Go Crazy   Adamson 1950; McHugh 1950

What a Wonderful Way to Spend a Summer Sunday   Drake 1955

What a Wonderful Wedding that Will Be   Fain 1927; Kahal 1927

What a Wonderful Wish That Would Be   Brennan 1917

What a World This Would Be   Brown, Lew 1925; DeSylva 1921, 1925; Henderson 1925

What a Young Girl Ought to Know   Schwartz, Arthur 1933

What About It?   Atteridge 1912

What About Me   Dietz 1934; Schwartz, Arthur 1934

What Aloha Means   Rainger 1937; Robin 1937

What Am I?   Rome 1970; Sigman 1959; Young, Victor 1959

What Am I Bid for My Apple   Robin 1930

What Am I Doin' in Kansas City (When You're in New Orleans)   Merrill 1954

What Am I Doing Here   Bacharach 1968; David, Hal 1968

What Am I Doing Here in Your Arms?   Revel 1942

What Am I Doing Wrong?   Leigh 1973

What Am I Gettin' Frettin' Over You   Brown, Lew 1926; Clare 1926; Friend 1926

What Am I Gonna Do?   Berlin 1911

What Am I Gonna Do About You?   Cahn 1947; Styne 1947

What Am I Gonna Do for Lovin'   Hoffman 1931; Magidson 1931

What Am I Gonna Do Without You?   Strouse 2000

What Am I Gonna Give My Girl for Xmas   Drake 1953

What Am I Here For?   Ellington 1942

What Am I Saying   Evans 1945; Livingston, Jay 1945

What Am I Supposed to Do   David, Hal 1979; Kahn 1926

What Am I to Do   Porter 1939

What an Awful Hullabaloo   Porter 1912

What an Existence   Young, Joe 1932

What Are Cowboys Made Of   Styne 1940

What Are Heavy (inst.)   Coleman 1972

What Are Little Girls Made Of   De Lange 1932

What Are Little Husbands Made Of   Porter 1941

What Are New Yorkers Made Of   Fain 1953

What Are the Odds Today   Adamson 1959; Young, Victor 1959

What Are the Wild Waves Saying?   Adamson 1939

What Are They Doing to Us Now?   Rome 1962

What Are We Doing in Egypt?   Drake 1968

What Are We Going to Do?   Bryan 1919; Schwartz, Jean 1919

What Are We Going to Do with All the Jeeps?   Berlin 1944

What Are We Here For?   Gershwin, George 1928; Gershwin, Ira 1928

What Are We Waiting For   David, Mack 1933; Donaldson 1925; Kahn 1925; Revel 1935

What Are Ya' Going to Do About It?   Lerner, Alan Jay 1983; Strouse 1983

What Are You Doin' the Rest of Your Life   Koehler 1944; Lane 1944

What Are You Doing in Here?   Hart 1935; Rodgers 1935

What Are You Doing New Year's Eve   Loesser 1947

What Are You Doing the Rest of Your Life?   Bergman 1969

What Are You Doing Tonight Blondy?   Dixon 1925; Henderson 1925; Rose 1925

What Are You Going to Do to Help the Boys   Kahn 1918

What Are You Going to Do with Me?   Atteridge 1914; Carroll 1914; Romberg 1914

What Are You Going to Do with Me Now   Johnson, Howard 1914

What Are You Gonna Do? (inst.)   Coleman Date Unknown

What Are You Gonna Do When You Ain't Got Nothin' to Do   Donaldson 1925; Kahn 1925

What Are You Gonna Do with All Your Money   Coots 1944

What Are You Gonna See   Drake 1953

What Are You Waitin' For, Mary?   Donaldson 1928

What Are Your Intentions?   Dubin 1934; Warren 1934

What Beautiful Is   Leigh 1977

What Became of Me?   Adams 1968; Strouse 1968

What Can Be Sweeter   Caesar 1929

What Can Be Wrong with Me   Waller 1924

What Can I Do?   Gershwin, Ira 1922

What Can I Do for You   Heyman 1938

What Can I Do for You, Baby   Howard, Bart 1984

What Can I Do, I Love that Man   Freed, Arthur 1931

What Can I Do? (Qu'est-ce Que J'ai?)   Rome 1949

What Can I Give Him   Webster 1963

What Can I Say?   Youmans 1930

What Can You Do with a General   Berlin 1948

What Can You Do with a Man?   Hart 1938; Rodgers 1938

What Can You Lose   Sondheim 1990

What Can You Say in a Love Song?   Gershwin, Ira 1934

What Can You Say in a Love Song? (That Hasn't Been Said Before?)   Arlen 1934; Harburg 1934

What Causes That?   Gershwin, George 1928; Gershwin, Ira 1928

What Cha Gonna Do When There Ain't No Jazz   Leslie 1920

What Chance Have I with Love   Berlin 1940

What Color Is Virtue?   Ellington 1963

What Could Be Fairer than That   Smith, Harry B. 1918

What Could Be Sweeter   Kahn 1923; Motzan 1936; Sterling 1919; Von Tilzer 1919; Wrubel 1946

What Could Be Sweeter Than You?   Brown, Lew 1925; Friend 1925

What Could I Do?   Brennan 1929

What Could I Do with a Man Like That   Johnson, James P. 1929

What Did Della Wear When Georgie Came Across   Schwartz, Arthur 1929

What Did Dottie Do?   Baer 1965; Gilbert 1965

What Did I Do   Cahn 1944, 1945; Gordon 1947, 1948; Myrow 1947, 1948, 1955; Styne 1944, 1945

What Did I Do that Was Wrong   Hoffman 1957

What Did I Ever Do to You   Bryan 1917; Johnson, Howard 1917; Meyer 1917

What Did I Ever Do to You that You Should Want to Do to Me   Berlin 1917; Leslie 1917; Meyer 1917

What Did I Ever See in Him?   Adams 1960; Strouse 1960

What Did I Get for Loving You   Conrad 1931

What Did I Get in Return   Young, Joe 1932

What Did I Have that I Don't Have   Lane 1965; Lerner, Alan Jay 1965

What Did Napoleon Mean   Fisher 1923

What Did Noah Do (When the Big Wind Came)?   Arlen 1957; Harburg 1957

What Did Romeo Say to Juliet   Lane 1938; Loesser 1938

What Did Romeo Say to Juliette   Fisher 1920

What Did We Do Last Night   Evans 1958; Livingston, Jay 1958

What Did William Tell?   Robin 1927

What Did You Do?   Leigh 1976; Styne 1976

What Did You Do with All the Love I Gave You   Fisher 1917

What Did You Do with It?   Kalmar 1931; Ruby 1931

What Didja Wanna Make Me Love You For   Dixon 1929; Warren 1929

What D'ja Do Sunday Junior   Caesar 1942

What Do I Care   Carroll 1929; Romberg 1925; Smith, Harry B. 1925

What Do I Care about Anything If You Don't Care about Me   Akst 1932; Yellen 1932

What Do I Care It's Home   Turk 1933

What Do I Care, What Do I Care, My Sweetie Turned Me Down   Donaldson 1925; Kahn 1925

What Do I Care What Somebody Said   Clare 1927

What Do I Do?   Coleman 1972; Fields 1972

What Do I Do for an Encore   McHugh 1964

What Do I Do Now?   Merrill 1978

What Do I Do with My New Tattoo of You   Livingston, Jerry 1962

What Do I Have to Do   DePaul 1949; Raye 1949; Russell 1946

What Do I Have to Do (To Make You Do What I Want You To)?   Ahlert 1931; Turk 1931

What Do I Have to Do to Make You Love Me   Coots 1934

What Do I Hear   Howard, Bart 1959

What Do I Know?   Blane 1952

What Do I See in You?   Martin 1952

What Do I Want with Love?   Blake 1937

What Do I Want with Money   Adamson 1947; McHugh 1948

What Do the Dickey-Birds Say   Akst 1931; Kahn 1931; Whiting 1931

What Do the Simple Folk Do?   Lerner, Alan Jay 1960; Loewe 1960

What Do They Mean By Love   Yellen 1923

What Do We Care?   Arlen 1931; Mancini 1993; Revel 1928; Sissle 1928; Yellen 1931

What Do We Do? We Fly!   Rodgers 1965; Sondheim 1965

What Do We Do with the World   Mancini 1967; Russell 1967

What Do Yo Do with a Broken Heart   McHugh 1952

What Do You Do?   Adams 1996; Strouse 1996; Warren 1956

What Do You Do in the Infantry   Loesser 1943

What Do You Do with a Broken Heart   Adamson 1952

What Do You Feel in Your Heart   Howard, Bart 1956

What Do You Give to a Man Who's Had Everything?   Merrill 1972; Styne 1972

What Do You Have to Do?   Friml 1918

What Do You Hear from the Mob in Scotland   Cahn 1938

What Do You Hear from Your Dreams   Wrubel 1942

What Do You Know about Love?   Gordon 1938; Revel 1938

What Do You Mean By Loving Somebody Else when Your Love Belongs to Me   Clare 1918; Mitchell 1918

What Do You Say   Ager 1928; Atteridge 1924; Yellen 1928

What Do You Say, Dolly Dear?   Smith, Harry B. 1913

What Do You See   Robin 1947

What Do You See in Him/Her   David, Hal 1954

What Do You Think About Me?   Evans 1966; Livingston, Jay 1966

What Do You Think About Men?   Porter 1950

What Do You Think I Am   Martin 1941

What Do You Think My Heart Is Made Of   Parish 1945

What Do You Think Those Ruby Lips Were Made For (If They Weren't Made To Kiss?)   Bryan 1943

What Do You Use for a Heart   Coslow 1954; Fain 1939

What Do You Wanna Get Married For?   Duke 1968

What Do You Want for Christmas Dear Santa   Hoffman 1954

What Do You Want from Me   Brooks 1964

What Do You Want from Somebody Else that You Didn't Get from Me   Conrad 1930; Leslie 1930

What Do You Want to Make Those Eyes at Me For   Johnson, Howard 1916; Monaco 1916

What Do You Want with Money   Hart 1933; Rodgers 1933

What Does a Queen Have?   Willson 1969

What Does a Soldier Want for Christmas   Berlin 1953

What Does a Woman Do   Wrubel 1959

What Does an English Girl Think of a Yank   Cahn 1945; Styne 1945

What Does He Mean I Can't Love?   Adams 1996; Strouse 1996

What Does He See in Me?   Strouse 1980

What Does It Matter?   Berlin 1927

What Does It Matter Who Was Wrong   Gilbert 1922

What Does It Mean?   Robin 1927

What Does It Take?   Burke 1951; DePaul 1943, 1944; Raye 1944; Van Heusen 1951

What Does Little Sweetie Want   Von Tilzer 1925

What Does One Do?   Duke 1963

What Does Your Servant Dream About   Porter 1948

What D'Ya Say   Brown, Lew 1928; DeSylva 1928; Dietz 1927; Gorney 1927; Henderson 1928

What D'Ya Say, Let's Get Married (What D'Ya Say)   Gordon 1930; Silver 1930

What D'Ya Say U.C.L.A.   Adamson 1947; McHugh 1947

What D'ya Think of That, Boys   Woods 1936

What Else Is There to Do   Livingston, Jerry 1973

What Eve Said to Adam   Smith, Harry B. 1900

What Ever Woman Knows (Frocks and Frills)   Smith, Robert B. 1914

What Every Little Girl Should Know   Schwartz, Arthur 1929

What Every Old Girl Should Know   Warren 1956

What Every Woman Knows   Smith, Harry B. 1909

What Every Young Man Should Know   Duke 1941

What Ev'ry Young Girl Should Know   Burke 1939; Carmichael 1955; Webster 1955

What Fools These Mortals Be   Styne 1940

What Fools We Mortals Be   Herbert 1908; Smith, Harry B. 1908; Smith, Robert B. 1907

What France Needs   Robin 1930

What Fun   Porter 1957

What Gives Out Now   Loesser 1942; Styne 1942

What Goes on Here (In My Heart)   Rainger 1938; Robin 1938

What Goes Up Must Come Down (And Baby, You've Been Flyin' Too High)   Bloom 1939; Koehler 1939

What Good?   Razaf 1951

What Good Am I Without You?   Ager 1930

What Good Are Words?   Hammerstein 1934; Kern 1934

What Good Does It Do?   Arlen 1957; Harburg 1957

What Good Is a Gal (Without a Guy?)   Blane 1952; Warren 1952

What Good Is Good-Morning, There's More Good in Good-Night   Lewis 1926; Young, Joe 1926

What Good Is Love?   Rome 1937

What Good Is Money?   Robin 1926

What Good Is the Good in Goodbye   David, Mack 1934; Hoffman 1934

What Good Is the Lane, If You Can't Have the Girl of Your Dreams?   Dixon 1930; Warren 1930; Young, Joe 1930

What Good Is the Moon Without You   Johnson, Howard 1940

What Good Is Water when You're Dry   Goetz 1910

What Good Would Be Tomorrow Without You Dear?   Freed, Ralph 1931

What Good Would the Moon Be?   Weill 1947

What Great Big Eyes You Have   Eliscu 1932

What Happened?   Dietz 1944; Duke 1944

What Happened Nobody Knows   Hart 1920; Rodgers 1920

What Happened to Mammy?   Johnson, Howard 1927

What Happened to Mary   Goetz 1912

What Happened to Muffin   Spina 1974

What Happened to the Conga   Robin 1955; Styne 1955

What Happened to the Couple Next Door   Fain 1931; Kahal 1931

What Happened to the Music   Leigh 1952

What Happened to the Original Six Floradora Boys?   Kalmar 1920; Ruby 1920

What Happens Now   Sigman 1954

What Harlem Is to Me   Razaf 1935

What Harm Can It Do   Styne 1978

What Has Become of Hinky Dinky Parlay Voo   McHugh 1924; Mills 1924

What Has Become of Hinky-Dinky-Parlay Vous   Dubin 1924

What Has Become of Marie   Edwards 1930

What Has Become of the Girl I Used to Know   Smith, Harry B. 1910

What Has Become of the Girls I Used to Know   Edwards 1910; Smith, Harry B. 1910

What Has He Got?   Duke 1936

What Has Love Got to Do With Getting Married?   Sherman 1976

What Has the Night Time to Do with the Girl   Jerome 1905; Schwartz, Jean 1905

What Have I?   Porter 1939

What Have I Done?   Brown, Lew 1966; DeSylva 1966; Henderson 1966; Johnson, James P. 1931

What Have I Done to Make You Stop Loving Me   DeSylva 1918; Kahn 1918

What Have We Got to Do Tonight but Dance   Kahn 1931

What Have We Lost (We Found Each Other)   Schwartz, Jean 1930

What Have You Done for Me Lately   David, Mack 1952, 1953; Livingston, Jerry 1952, 1953

What Have You Done to Make Me Feel This Way   Razaf 1927

What Have You Got for Tonight   Drake 1953

What Have You Got in Those Eyes   DePaul 1949; Raye 1949

What Have You Got That Gets Me   Rainger 1938; Robin 1938

What Have You Got to Have?   Harburg 1932, 1958

What Have You Got to Lose????   Spina 1977

What Have You Got to Lose but Your Heart   Drake 1943

What Have You to Declare?   Atteridge 1923; Caesar 1923; Romberg 1923

What I Care   Donaldson 1918; Turk 1918; Youmans 1922

What I Don't Know Will Never Hurt Me   McHugh 1964

What I Love to Hear   Gershwin, Ira 1944; Kern 1944

What I Want to Be   Cahn Date Unknown; Styne Date Unknown

What I Want to Doodle-Doo for You   Brown, Lew 1921

What I Was Warned About   Martin 1951

What If?   Drake 1994; Strouse 1971

What If Geo. Washington's Mother Had Said, I Didn't Raise My Boy to Be a Soldier   Clarke 1915; Monaco 1915

What If We Do   Johnson, James P. 1930

What If You're Not   Duke 1955

What I'm Longing to Say   Kern 1917

What in the World Did You Want   Martin 1964

What in the World Do They Want?   Blane 1964; Martin 1964

What Is a Friend For?   Arlen 1954

What Is a Girl   Merrill 1956

What Is a Heart For   Johnson, Howard 1930

What Is a Man?   Hart 1940; Rodgers 1940

What Is a Street Man   Adams 1983

What Is Done You Can Never Undo   Smith, Robert B. 1914

What Is It?   David, Hal 1974; Hart 1926; Rodgers 1926; Spina 1957

What Is It Going to Be Boys   DePaul 1958; Raye 1958

What Is Life?   Loesser 1965

What Is Life without You, Dear   Gilbert 1911

What Is Love?   Berlin 1914; Brooks 1946; Herbert 1895, 1908; Leigh Date Unknown; Rainger 1937; Robin 1937; Rome 1969; Smith, Harry B. 1895; Young, Victor 1937

What Is Love? (Canzonetta)   Herbert 1903; Smith, Harry B. 1903

What Is Love If It's Not Magic   Lewis Date Unknown; Young, Joe Date Unknown

What Is My Destiny   Sigman 1957

What Is That Tune?   Porter 1938

What Is the Use   Dubin 1924

What Is There About You   Fields 1933; McHugh 1933

What Is There to Say?   Duke 1934; Harburg 1934

What Is There to Sing About?   Strouse 1971

What Is This Feeling in the Air   Comden and Green 1961; Styne 1961

What Is This Generation Coming To   Raye 1957

What Is This Magic That's Yours   Washington 1941

What Is This Power   Johnston 1935; Kahn 1935

What Is this Power I Have?   Coslow 1930

What Is This That I Feel (Is This Really Love)   Blane 1954; Myrow 1954

What Is This Thing Called Love?   Porter 1929

What Is This Thing I've Got   Comden and Green 1964; Styne 1964

What Is Wrong with Me   Blake 1950

What Is Your Price, Madam?   Johnson, Howard 1930

What I've Always Wanted   Adams 1966; Strouse 1966

What Kind o' Love Is That   Razaf 1927

What Kind o' Man Is You   Carmichael 1929

What Kind o' Tune Did Old Nero Play   Johnson, James P. 1948

What Kind of a Wife to Choose   Edwards 1908

What Kind of an American Are You?   Brown, Lew 1917

What Kind of Boy   Caesar 1927

What Kind of Crime   Strouse 1990

What Kind of Fool   Loesser 1947

What Kind of Love Is This?   DePaul 1941, 1942; Raye 1941, 1942

What Kind of People Are You?   Hoffman 1930

What Kind of Soldier Are You?   Hammerstein 1938; Harbach 1938; Kern 1938

What Love Is   Porter 1914

What Made the Boys Like Rosie?   Brown, A. Seymour 1912

What Made the Red Man Red?   Cahn 1952; Fain 1952

What Make de Difference?   Arlen 1952; Blane 1953

What Makes a Business Man Tired?   Kalmar 1923; Ruby 1923

What Makes a Marriage Merry   Harburg 1967; Styne 1967

What Makes a WAVE?   Blane 1952; Warren 1952

What Makes It Happen   Cahn 1966; Van Heusen 1966

What Makes Me Love You   Berlin 1927

What Makes My Baby Blue   Dietz 1929; Gorney 1929

What Makes the Sunset   Cahn 1945; Styne 1945

What Makes the World Go 'Round   Kahn 1939; Warren 1939; Williams 1909

What Makes You Beautiful, Beautiful   Cahn 1946; Styne 1946

What Makes You So Sweet   Oakland 1937

What Makes You So Wonderful?   Kalmar 1928; Ruby 1928

What Matters Most   Bergman 1980

What Memories   Romberg 1924

What Men and Women Will Wear   Brennan 1929

What Men Can Do   Smith, Harry B. 1918

What More Can I Do   David, Mack 1951

What More Can I Give You?   Bryan 1920; David, Mack 1939

What More Do I Need?   Sondheim 1954

What More Do I Want   Lerner, Alan Jay 1948; Weill 1948

What More Do You Want   Cahn 1941

What More Is There   Davis 1953

What, No Mickey Mouse, What Kind of a Party Is This   Caesar 1932

What Now My Love (Et Maintenant)   Sigman 1962

What of It   Gershwin, Ira 1924

What of It, We Love It   Dixon 1928; Rose 1928; Warren 1928

What Price Love!   Akst 1931; Davis 1931; Hart 1928; Rodgers 1928

What Shall I Do?   Porter 1938

What Shall Remain   Fields 1936

What Shall We Do for an Encore Baby   Leslie 1936

What Shall We Do If the Moon Goes Out   Herbert 1920

What Shall We Do with the Drunken Sailor   Evans 1951; Livingston, Jay 1951

What She Says Goes   Kalmar 1929; Ruby 1929

What She Wanted and What She Got   Herbert 1913; Smith, Harry B. 1913; Smith, Robert B. 1913

What Should a Teen Heart Do   David, Hal 1956

What Sort of Wedding Is This?   Gershwin, George 1932; Gershwin, Ira 1932

What Takes My Fancy   Coleman 1960; Leigh 1960

What the Country Needs   Coslow 1942, 1955

What the Day Brings Forth   Robison 1957

What the Doctor Ordered   DeSylva 1920

What the Future Holds for Me   Johnson, Howard 1924

What the Girls Will Wear   Kalmar 1923; Ruby 1923

What the Well-Dressed Man in Harlem Will Wear   Berlin 1942

What the Well-Dressed Man Will Wear   Berlin 1937

What the World Needs Now Is Love   Bacharach 1965; David, Hal 1965

What This Country Needs   Burke 1936; Johnston 1936; Warren 1959; Washington 1959

What This Country Needs Is a Song   Cohan 1938

What This Party Needs   Rome 1937

What 'Tis, What 'Tis — 'Tis Spring   Woods 1954

What to Do With 'Er   Sherman 1995

What Us Poor Girls Go Through   Howard, Joseph E. 1910

What Used to Was Used to Was Now It Ain't   Cahn 1939

What Was   Warren Date Unknown

What Was Your Name in the States   Mercer 1962

What We Do in the Moonlight (We're Not Telling You)   Johnson, Howard 1928

What Wealth Is Here   Smith, Robert B. 1909

What Will Be Will Be   Hoffman 1950

What Will Become of Me   Akst 1926; Freed, Arthur 1930; Kalmar 1936; Lewis 1923, 1926; Ruby 1936; Woods 1930; Young, Joe 1923, 1926

What Will Become of Our England?   Porter 1932

What Will I Do   Coslow 1924

What Will I Do in the Morning   Waller 1938

What Will I Do when It's Spring?   Burke 1935; Spina 1935

What Will I Do Without You   Dubin 1929; Mercer 1933

What Will I Tell My Heart   Lawrence 1937

What Will Tomorrow Bring   Kahn 1932

What Will We Do on a Saturday Night when the Town Goes Dry?   Ruby 1918

What Will We Name the Baby   De Lange 1949

What Will Ya Do When There Ain't No Wimmin   Fisher 1927; Rose 1927

What Women and Men Will Wear   Akst 1927; Davis 1927

What Would $50,000 Make You Do?   Bryan 1917

What Would Happen?   Bergman 1964; Fain 1964

What Would Happen to Me If Something Happened to You   Woods 1932

What Would I Care?   Kalmar 1929; Ruby 1929

What Would I Do Without You   Gilbert 1914

What Would It Mean Without You   Ellington 1962; Mills 1962

What Would Mrs. Grundy Say   Smith, Robert B. 1905

What Would People Say   Lawrence 1956

What Would Shakespeare Have Said   Burke 1940; Monaco 1940

What Would We Do Without the Girls?   Koehler 1921

What Would We Do Without You?   Sondheim 1970

What Would You Be Doing Today   Fisher 1936

What Would You Call It   DePaul 1958; Raye 1958

What Would You Do?   Robin 1932; Whiting 1932

What Would You Do for Fifty Thousand Dollars   Bryan 1915

What Would You Do in a Case Like This?   Mills 1928

What Would You Do Mr. Moon   Oakland 1935

What Would You Give in Exchange for Your Soul   Fisher 1937

What Would You Say   De Lange 1932

What Would You Take For Me, Mama   Cobb 1920; Edwards 1920

What Would You Want to Be   Friend 1978

What Wouldcha Do Without Me?   Brooks 1953; Warren 1953

What Wouldn't I Do for that Man   Gorney 1929; Harburg 1929

What You Are and What You Want to Be   Smith, Robert B. 1915

What You Could Be If You Had Me   Johnson, Howard 1924

What You Don't Know About Women   Coleman 1989

What You Go Through   Adams 1978; Strouse 1978

What You Goin' to Do when the Rent Comes Round   Sterling 1905; Von Tilzer 1905

What You See Is What You Get   Strouse 1985

What You Want with Bess?   Gershwin, George 1935

Whatagot   Oakland 1968

Whatcha Gonna Do When I'm Gone   Razaf 1926

Whatcha Gonna Do When There Ain't No Swing   Livingston, Jerry 1936; Styne 1940

Whatcha Say   Koehler 1945; Lane 1945

What-Cha-Ma-Call-Em   Cobb 1913; Edwards 1913

Whatcha-Ma-Call-It   DePaul 1956; Mercer 1956

What'd We Come to College For?   Arlen 1931; Yellen 1931

What'd You' Do Wid de Letter, Mr. Johnson?   Smith, Harry B. 1901

Whatd'ya Feel Like Doing?   Strouse 1999

Whatever Became of Jenny?   Styne 1985

Whatever Goes Swoop Lilting Lofting   Eliscu 1955; Gorney 1955

Whatever Happened to Baby Jane   Webster 1963

Whatever Happened to Love (inst.)   McHugh 1966

Whatever Happened to Ol' Jack   Russell 1949; Sigman 1949

Whatever Happened to You?   De Lange 1940

Whatever It Is, I'm Against It   Kalmar 1933

Whatever It Is It's Grand   Robin 1930; Whiting 1930

Whatever May Be Tide   Evans 1958; Livingston, Jay 1958

Whatever May Betide   David, Mack 1958; Livingston, Jerry 1958

Whatever That May Be   Harburg 1961

Whatever Time There Is   Strouse 1980

Whatever Will Be, Will Be (Que, Sera, Sera)   Evans 1956; Livingston, Jay 1956

Whatever You Do   Schwartz, Arthur 1933

Whatever You Say, Will Be Held Against You   Adamson 1939; Coots 1939

What'll   Atteridge 1914

What'll Become of Me   Dubin 1929; Stept 1933

What'll I Do   Berlin 1924

What'll I Do If I Marry a Soldier Tush-Doo-Woggle-Oh-Toog-In-Da-Shin   Lawrence 1940

What'll I Do with My Nights the Rest of My Days   Leslie 1936; Meyer 1936

What'll I Use for Money   Washington 1944

What'll It Take   Coleman 1979

What'll they Think of Next   Carmichael 1940; Mercer 1940

What'll We Buy   Livingston, Jerry 1963

What'll We Do with Him, Boys   Sterling 1918

What'll You Do   Lewis 1915; Meyer 1915; Parish 1932

What's a Feller Gonna Do   Woods 1925

What's a Kiss Among Friends?   Robin 1927; Youmans 1927

What's 'a Matter Baby   Merrill 1958

What's a Nice Kid Like You Doing in a Place Like This   Adams 1966; Strouse 1966

What's a Parade Without a Drum and Bugle Corps   Bergman 1958

What's a Poor Soldier Going to Do?   Hanley 1919

What's All the Shoutin' For   Pollack 1941

What's All the Shouting For   Kalmar 1937; Ruby 1937

What's an Isn't   David, Mack 1961; Livingston, Jerry 1961

What's Become of Josephine   Stept 1925

What's Become of Spring   Harbach 1931; Kern 1931

What's Become of Sweet Madelon   Parish 1929

What's Become of the Night   Hammerstein 1942; Harbach 1942; Kern 1942

What's Buzzin' Cousin?   Gordon 1942

What's Come Over Me?   Burke 1971

What's Cookin'   Razaf 1940

What's Cookin' Cookie   Wrubel 1940

What's Goin' on Here?   Lerner, Alan Jay 1951; Loewe 1951

What's Going On Over My Shoulder   Brown, Lew 1945; Henderson 1945

What's Gonna Be the Outcome If the Income Don't Come In   Von Tilzer 1935

What's Gonna Be with You and Me   Coots 1934

What's Gonna Become of Me (Now that I'm in Love)   Kalmar 1951; Ruby 1951

What's Gonna Happen?   Harburg 1952; Lane 1952

What's Good about Goodbye   Arlen 1948; Robin 1948

What's Good about Good-Night?   Fields 1938; Kern 1938

What's Good Enough for Washington Is Good Enough for Me   Von Tilzer 1926

What's Good for General Bullmoose (Is Good for the U.S.A.)   DePaul 1956; Mercer 1956

What's Good for the Goose Is Good for the Gander   Friend 1933

What's Good for You (Is Bad for Me)   Lawrence 1955

What's Happened?   Robin 1926; Stept 1941

What's Happened to Me   Van Heusen 1936

What's He Got?   Cahn 1945; Styne 1945

What's Her Name Today?   Bacharach 1996

What's His Name   Blane 1968; Martin 1972

What's in a Name? (Love Is Always Love)   Ager 1920; Yellen 1920

What's in It for Harry   Merrill 1968

What's in It for Me   Rome 1962

What's in the Air Tonight?   Hammerstein 1934; Kern 1934

What's in the Pocketbook   Howard, Bart 1954

What's in Your Heart   Friend 1961

What's It Gonna Be   Mancini 1956

What's It Like in Paree   Sigman 1956

What's Mine is Yours   Dietz 1944; Duke 1944

What's Mine Is Yours (The Sharing Song)   Strouse 1989

What's My Man Gonna Be Like   Porter 1930

What's My Name?   Evans 1970; Livingston, Jay 1970

What's New   Burke 1941

What's New at the Zoo?   Comden and Green 1960; Styne 1960

What's New in New York   De Lange 1945; Myrow 1945

What's New Pussycat   Bacharach 1965; David, Hal 1965

What's on the Penny   Ahlert 1941

What's On Your Mind   Cahn 1935

What's Right   Adams 1996; Strouse 1996

What's Right for Me?   Strouse 1999

What's Right? What's Wrong?   Sherman 1974

What's She Really Like   Silver 1960

What's So Good about Good Morning   Gordon 1956; Myrow 1956

What's So Great About Beethoven   Willson 1955

What's That   Hoffman 1957

What's the Big Idea   Davis 1927; Gershwin, George 1920; Gershwin, Ira 1920; Lewis 1930; Warren 1930; Young, Joe 1930

What's the Difference   Heyman 1931

What's the Good   Cobb 1907; Edwards 1907

What's the Good of Being Good   Von Tilzer 1913

What's the Good of Good Morning, When You Have No One to Love and to Kiss You Goodnight   Fisher 1930

What's the Good of Just a Song at Twilight   Johnson, Howard Date Unknown

What's the Good Word   Oakland 1937

What's the Good Word, Mr. Bluebird   Hoffman 1943; Livingston, Jerry 1943

What's the Matter with Father   Williams 1910

What's the Matter with Harry   Heyman 1931

What's the Matter with Him   Drake 1952

What's the Matter with Me?   Lewis 1940

What's the Matter with Our City?   Gorney 1948

What's the Matter with Our Team   Von Tilzer 1906

What's the Matter with That Girl   Johnson, Howard 1924; Motzan 1924

What's the Matter with the Irish (They're Getting Better Every Day)   Johnson, Howard 1916

What's the Name of that Tune   Atteridge 1915; Romberg 1915

What's the Reason   Atteridge 1928

What's the Rush   Adams 1954; Strouse 1954

What's the Use   Dietz 1924; Edwards 1907; Gershwin, George 1926; Gershwin, Ira 1926; Harbach 1908, 1910; Hart 1926; Howard, Joseph E. 1909; Kern 1924; Rodgers 1926; Smith, Harry B. 1935; Woods 1923

What's the Use of Anything   Williams 1908

What's the Use of Being Lonesome   Friml 1917; Harbach 1917

What's the Use of Crying   Evans 1965; Livingston, Jay 1965

What's the Use of Dreaming?   Howard, Joseph E. 1906, 1908

What's the Use of Going Home   Clarke 1915

What's the Use of Kicking, Let's Go 'Round with a Smile   Donaldson 1919; Lewis 1919; Young, Joe 1919

What's the Use of Knockin'   Edwards 1906

What's the Use of Living when You've Got Nobody to Love (What's the Use of Living without Love)   Hanley 1930

What's the Use of Lovin' (Without Love)   Johnson, James P. 1929

What's the Use of Lovin' You when the Whole World Loves You Too   Caesar 1951; Howard, Joseph E. 1951

What's the Use of Loving   Mills 1939

What's the Use of Loving when You Haven't Anyone to Love   Johnson, Howard 1929

What's the Use of Moonlight?   Herbert 1911; Smith, Harry B. 1911

What's the Use of Moonlight When There's No One 'Round to Love   Kahn 1909

What's the Use of Saving Money   Meyer 1910

What's the Use of Saying No   Harbach 1911

What's the Use of Talking   Cobb 1900; Edwards 1900; Hart 1926; Rodgers 1926

What's the Use of Washing Your Face   Fisher 1936

What's the Use of Wishing It Won't Come True   Edwards 1905

What's the Use of Wond'rin'   Hammerstein 1945; Rodgers 1945

What's the Use Without a Girl   Howard, Joseph E. 1920

What's the Weather Like in Paris   Parish 1954

What's This?   Monaco 1936

What's This World A-Comin' To   Robison 1963

What's Today Got to Do with Tomorrow?   Donaldson 1924

What's Under Your Mask, Madame?   Evans 1948; Livingston, Jay 1948

What's Weak About the Weaker Sex   DeSylva 1920

What's What   Burke 1940

What's with Me   Cahn 1937

What's Wrong with Me?   Brown, Nacio Herb 1948; Heyman 1948

What's Wrong with That?   Sherman 1967

What's Wrong with the Song   Hoffman 1956

What's Your Favorite Holiday   Styne 1941

What's Your Hurry, Beatrice   Oakland 1963

What's Your Name   Turk 1926; Waller 1938

What's Your Price   Razaf 1928

What's Your Story, Morning Glory   Lawrence 1940; Webster 1940

What's Yours   Evans 1964; Livingston, Jay 1964

What'sa Matter with Angelo (inst.)   Spina 1977

What's-His-Name   Blane 1960; Martin 1960

Whatsoever   Robison 1952

What-You-May Call, A   Young, Victor 1915

Wheatless Day   Kern 1918

Wheel 'Em and Deal 'Em   Arlen 1959; Mercer 1959

Wheel Has Been Spun, The   Evans 1958; Livingston, Jay 1958

Wheel of Fate   Atteridge 1920

Wheeler Dealer (inst.)   Bacharach 1966

Wheeler Dealers, The   Cahn 1963; Van Heusen 1963

Wheels   Evans 1958; Livingston, Jay 1958

Wheels Through the Night   Weill 1939

When   Brown, Lew 1927; Coots 1926; Davis 1941; Friend 1927; Razaf 1926, 1928; Rodgers 1979; Rome 1950; Silver 1951; Stept 1941

When a Black Sheep Is Blue for Home   Razaf 1930

When a Blond Makes Up Her Mind to Do You Good   Fain 1925

When a Blonde Makes Up Her Mind to Do You Good   Mills 1925

When a Body's in Love   Porter 1916

When a Boy without a Girl Meets a Girl without a Boy   Meyer 1912

When a Carnation Meets a Red Red Rose   Blake 1955

When a Cowboy Sings a Song   Lawrence 1938

When a Dainty Peeping Ankle Peeps at You   Bryan 1917

When a Fella's Got a Girl   Styne 1940

When a Fellow Gets to Thinking   Burke 1946; Van Heusen 1946

When a Fellow Meets a Flapper on Broadway   Caesar 1929

When a Fellow's on the Level with a Girl that's on the Square   Cohan 1907

When a Gal from Alabama Meets a Boy from Tennessee   Akst 1937; Clare 1937

When a Girl   Friml 1918

When a Girl Doesn't Know Where She Is   Smith, Harry B. 1900

When a Girl Forgets to Scream   Harbach 1936; Romberg 1936

When a Girl Is Beautiful   Cahn 1961

When a Girl Needs a Friend   Johnson, J. Rosamond 1946

When a Girl Whose Heart You Long for Has a Heart that Longs for You   Meyer 1911

When a Girl's About to Marry   Herbert 1915

When a Glow Worm Gets a Gleam in His Eye   Hanley 1938

When a Good Man Takes to Drink   Revel 1945

When a Great Love Comes Along   Leslie 1935

When a Hound Dog Man Has a Good Hound Dog   Sherman 1964

When a Kid Who Came from the East Side (Found a Sweet Society Rose)   Dubin 1926; McHugh 1926

When a Lady Leads the Band   Sterling 1902

When a Lark Learns to Fly   Romberg 1941

When a Maid Comes Knocking at Your Heart   Friml 1912, 1937; Harbach 1912, 1937

When a Man Has a Daughter   Sherman 1967

When a Man Is Free   Freed, Ralph 1944

When a New Star   Hammerstein 1943; Harbach 1942; Kern 1942

When a One Star General's Daughter Meets a Four Star General's Son   Berlin 1956

When a Pal Bids a Pal Goodbye   Leslie 1932; Stept 1932

When a Pal of Mine Steals a Gal of Mine   Bryan 1909

When a Pansy Was a Flower   Rose 1930

When a Prince of a Fella Meets a Cinderella   Van Heusen 1938

When a Rambling Rose Goes Rambling Home Again   Coslow 1921

When a Regular Girl Loves a Regular Boy   Coots 1922

When a Sailor Goes Ashore   Loesser 1941; Styne 1941

When a Servant Learns a Secret   Cohan 1909

When a St. Louis Woman Comes Down to New Orleans   Coslow 1934; Johnston 1934

When a Wandering Boy Comes Wandering Back to Home Sweet Home   Egan 1926; Whiting 1926

When a Woman Exits Laughing   Harbach 1920

When a Woman Has a Baby   Weill 1947

When a Woman Loves a Man   Mercer 1934; Rainger 1930; Robin 1930; Rose 1930; Young, Victor 1960

When a Woman's in Love   Porter 1944

When Alexander Takes His Ragtime Band to France   Bryan 1918; Leslie 1918

When All Hope Was Gone I Found You, Joan   Lewis 1929

When All Hope Was Lost, I Found You Joan   Akst 1929; Young, Joe 1929

When All My Wishes Were Your Dreams   Mancini 1978

When All Our Dreams Come True   Fain 1919

When All the Streets Are Dark   Merrill 1955

When All the World Is Fast Asleep   Hoffman 1927

When All the World Is Old   Lawrence 1952

When All Your Castles Come Tumbling Down   Gershwin, Ira 1922

When Am I Getting the Mink, Mister Fink   Yellen 1955

When Am I Gonna Kiss You Good Morning   De Lange 1947

When an Englishman Marries a Parisian   Atteridge 1914; Carroll 1914; Romberg 1914

When and Where Will I Find Someone to Care   Coots 1936; Davis 1936

When April Climbs the Hill   Coots 1949

When April Comes Again   Livingston, Jerry 1935

When April Sings   Kahn 1940

When Are We Going to Land Abroad   Mercer 1941; Schwartz, Arthur 1941

When Are You Coming Back   Sterling 1917

When Are You Coming Home, My Baby   Robison 1946

When Athena Dances (inst.)   Duke 1963

When Autumn Leaves Are Falling   Coslow 1925; Silver 1925

When Banana Blossoms Bloom   Lerner, Sammy 1940, 1943

When Banana Skins Are Falling I'll Come Sliding Back to You   Mills 1926

When Beau Brummel Meets Fluffy Ruffles   Edwards 1930; Johnson, Howard 1930

When Birds of a Feather Flock Together, They're Bound to Come Across   Mills 1928; Parish 1928

When Black Sallie Sings Pagliacci   Porter 1919

When Brother Percy Sings   Jerome 1902; Schwartz, Jean 1902

When Buddha Smiles   Brown, Nacio Herb 1921; Freed, Arthur 1921

When Bugles Are Calling   Herbert 1895; Smith, Harry B. 1895

When Business Interferes with Pleasure   Parish 1936

When Cadets Parade   Gershwin, George 1927; Gershwin, Ira 1927

When Caruso Comes to Town   Silver 1920

When Cupid Calls   Smith, Harry B. 1916

When Cupid Is the Postman   Herbert 1908; Smith, Harry B. 1908

When Dad and Mother Danced to the Scarf Dance   Johnson, Howard 1935

When Daddy Came Home   Merrill 1966

When Daddy Goes A-Hunting   Youmans 1926

When Danny Brought Annie Home from Ireland   David, Mack 1945; Hoffman 1945; Livingston, Jerry 1945

When Day Is Done   DeSylva 1926

When Dear Old Santa Claus Comes to Town   Jerome 1912; Von Tilzer 1912

When Desire Dances for Me   Merrill 1952

When Did I Hear You Tell Me You Love Me   Akst 1937; Clare 1937

When Did You Know?   Coleman 1966, 1972; Fields 1966

When Did You Leave Heaven?   Bullock 1936; Whiting 1936

When Do I Get Mine?   Sherman 1995

When Do We Dance?   Gershwin, George 1925; Gershwin, Ira 1925

When Do We Eat   Coslow 1923; Dixon 1934; Wrubel 1934

When Do You Suppose   Dubin 1924

When Do You Walk Away?   Cahn 1980; Strouse 1980

When Does It Get to Be My Time   Lawrence 1961

When Does This Feeling Go Away?   Martin 1951

When East Meets West in Panama   Gershwin, George 1921

When Eden Was a Garden   Lewis 1944

When Eden Was a Garden (A Sermon in Music)   Meyer 1955

When Eden Was a Rock (A Sermon in Music)   Lewis 1955

When Eliza Rolls Her Eyes   Kahn 1928; Warren 1928

When Ella Bops   Mills 1955

When Erastus Plays His Old Kazoo   Coslow 1927; Fain 1927

When Evening Shadows Fall   Caesar 1924; Gorney 1924

When Eyes Like Yours Look into Eyes Like Mine   Howard, Joseph E. 1908

When Eyes Meet Eyes   Cobb 1901; Edwards 1901

When Eyes Meet Eyes (When Lips Meet Lips)   Cobb 1922; Edwards 1922

When Eyes of Blue Are Fooling You   Clare 1925; Monaco 1925

When Ezra Plays the Fiddle (In the Old Town Hall)   Gordon 1934; Revel 1934

When Father Carves the Bird (Turkey Day)   DePaul 1958; Raye 1958

When Father Was a Boy   Fisher 1938

When Flowers Bloom in Springtime, Molly Dear   Sterling 1906; Von Tilzer 1906

When Fortune Smiles   Smith, Harry B. 1914, 1916; Smith, Robert B. 1916

When Gabriel Blows His Horn   Razaf 1932; Waller 1932

When Gaby Did the Gaby Glide   Atteridge 1913; Schwartz, Jean 1913

When Gemini Meets Capricorn   Rome 1962

When Gentlemen Grew Whiskers and Ladies Grew Old   Robin 1927

When Girls Command the Army   Herbert 1908

When God Gave Me You   Leslie 1913

When Grand Circus Was Uptown   Egan 1921; Whiting 1921

When Grandma Was a Girl   Atteridge 1915; Carroll 1915; Goetz 1908; Romberg 1915

When Grandpa Was a Boy   Buck 1920

When Greek Meets Greek   Youmans 1924

When Grimble Hits the Cymbal   Gordon 1932, 1936; Revel 1936

When He Comes Back to Me   Buck 1916

When He Comes Home   Loesser 1944

When He Comes Home to Me   Coslow 1934; Robin 1934

When He Gets Back to New York Town   Snyder 1914

When He Waltzed in the Dark   Meyer 1931

When He Wanted to Love Her He Would Put Up the Cover   Lewis 1915; Meyer 1915

When Hearts Are Young (in Springtime)   Romberg 1922

When He's All Dolled Up He's the Best Dressed Rube in Town   Donaldson 1917

When He's Away   Norworth 1916

When He's Near   Schwartz, Arthur 1928

When Highland Mary Did the Highland Fling   Von Tilzer 1908

When His Eyes Look into Mine   Smith, Harry B. 1911

When His Lips Met Mine   Brown, Nacio Herb 1948

When I am Chief of Police   Johnson, J. Rosamond 1904

When I Am Free to Love   Robin 1954; Romberg 1954

When I Am Queen   Gorney 1926

When I Am Twenty-One   Leslie 1915; Schwartz, Jean 1915

When I Build a Home   Akst 1918

When I Can't Be with You   Johnson, James P. 1931; Razaf 1931

When I Catch Con Carney   Fisher 1938

When I Close My Door   Arlen 1953; Fields 1953

When I Close My Eyes   Hammerstein 1928; Romberg 1928

When I Come Around Again   Lane 1965; Lerner, Alan Jay 1965

When I Come Back   Stept 1935

When I Come Back to You   Woods 1923

When I Come Home   Caesar 1932

When I Crack My Whip   Hammerstein 1927; Harbach 1927

When I Dance with You   Clare 1933; Coslow 1924; Monaco 1933

When I Dance with You in Paradise   Dubin 1921

When I Discover My Man   Kern 1920

When I Discovered Sweet You   Hoffman 1931

When I Discovered You   Berlin 1914; Goetz 1914

When I Dream   Gordon 1929

When I Dream, I Dream About Hawaii   Hoffman 1945

When I Dream of the Last Waltz with You   Kahn 1925

When I Dream of the Sweethearts I've Had   Parish 1930

When I Dream of You   Livingston, Jerry 1958

When I Enter Paree   Gorney 1969

When I Fall in Love   Brooks 1946; Heyman 1952; Young, Victor 1952

When I Feel Like Loving   Howard, Joseph E. 1908

When I Fell in Love with You   Kern 1925; Sterling 1916; Von Tilzer 1916; Williams 1910

When I Find My Romeo   Herbert 1920; Smith, Robert B. 1920

When I First Met You   Lewis 1913; Meyer 1913

When I Found You   Romberg 1920

When I Gave My Love to You   Kahn 1939

When I Get Back to Caroline   Coots 1954

When I Get Back to Old Virginia   Dubin 1915

When I Get Back to the U.S.A.   Berlin 1915

When I Get Famous   Sondheim Date Unknown

When I Get in the Movies   Jerome 1923; Schwartz, Jean 1923

When I Get Out of School   Brown, Nacio Herb 1948

When I Get Time   Burke 1944; Van Heusen 1944

When I Get to Town   Cahn 1945, 1946; Styne 1945, 1946

When I Get You Alone Tonight   Fisher 1912

When I Go, I Go All the Way   Russell 1956

When I Go on the Stage   Hart 1921, 1928; Rodgers 1921, 1928

When I Grow Too Old to Dream   Hammerstein 1935; Romberg 1935

When I Grow Up   Friend 1950; Henderson 1935; Heyman 1935

When I Grow Up and Want to Be a Soldier   Cobb 1917

When I Grow Up I'm Going to Be a Soldier   Edwards 1917

When I Grow Up (The G-Man Song)   Rome 1937

When I Had a Uniform On   Porter 1919

When I Have Become a Social Butterfly   Kalmar 1923; Ruby 1923

When I Hear a Band Play Dixieland, It's Home Sweet Home to Me   Ager 1916; Johnson, Howard 1916

When I Hear a Dreamy Waltz Melody   Clarke 1919; Monaco 1919

When I Hear a Syncopated Tune   Buck 1918

When I Hear an Irishman Sing   Dubin 1922

When I Hear an Old Fashioned Melody   Friml 1926

When I Hear an Old Fashioned Waltz   Buck 1926; Friml 1926

When I Hear that Jazz Band Play   Buck 1917

When I Hear You Calling Me I'll Answer You   Fisher 1919

When I Hear You Play that Piano, Bill   Berlin 1910; Snyder 1910

When I Hear You Tell Me You Love Me   Akst 1937; Clare 1937

When I Hear Your Voice   Schwartz, Arthur 1934

When I Hit Broadway   Kalmar 1928; Ruby 1928

When I Join the Circus   Blane 1965, 1968; Martin 1968

(I Feel Like a Bee, Stealing Honey from a Rose) When I Kiss You   Mills 1928

When I Kiss You Goodnight in the Morning   Lawrence 1933

When I Knelt at the Alter and You Sang in the Choir   Coots 1932

When I Leave the World Behind   Berlin 1915

When I Look at Myself in the Mirror   Woods 1934

When I Look at You   Atteridge 1923; Friend 1927; Kalmar 1934; Ruby 1934; Schwartz, Jean 1923; Webster 1943

When I Look in the Book of My Memory   Lerner, Sammy 1931

When I Look into Those Lovey Dovey Eyes   Smith, Harry B. 1903

When I Look into Your Eyes, Mavoureen   Cohan 1918

When I Look Thru My Book of Dreams   Bryan 1928

When I Lost You   Berlin 1912

When I Love — I Love   Clare 1927; Monaco 1927

When I Love, I Love   Brown, Lew 1928; DeSylva 1928; Gordon 1941; Henderson 1928; Warren 1941

When I Made the Grade with O'Grady   Johnson, Howard 1924

When I March in April with May   David, Mack 1936

When I Marry   Carroll 1918

When I Marry Alice   Harburg 1967; Styne 1967

When I Marry You   Bryan 1908, 1958

When I Met You   Brown, Nacio Herb 1930; Freed, Arthur 1930

When I Open the Gate   Parish 1947

When I Play on My Spanish Guitar   Dubin 1927

When I Played Carmen   Herbert 1914; Smith, Robert B. 1914

When I Played Peek-a-Boo with Daddy and He Played Peek-a-Boo with Me   Bryan 1933

When I Plot a Plan   Adams 1957; Strouse 1957

When I Ring Your Front Door Bell   Snyder 1927

When I Sat on Your Doorstep and You Sat on My Knee   Conrad 1931

When I Saw Him Last (Finale, Act I)   Hart 1928; Rodgers 1928

When I Say It's So, It's So   Smith, Harry B. 1923

When I See All the Loving They Waste on Babies I Long for the Cradle Again   Johnston 1920

When I See an Elephant Fly   Washington 1941

When I See My Sugar (I Get a Lump in My Throat)   Ahlert 1929; Turk 1929

When I See Roses   Donaldson 1932; Kahn 1932

When I Sing   Lerner, Sammy 1941

When I Smoked My First Cigarette   Gilbert 1928

When I Speak of You   Ruby 1947

When I Start Comparin' Auld Erin with You   Lewis 1921; Young, Joe 1921

When I Take My Sugar to Tea   Fain 1931; Kahal 1931

When I Take You All to London   Romberg 1927; Smith, Harry B. 1927

When I Talk about You   Merrill 1964; Styne 1964

When I Teach You How to Swim   Goetz 1915; Romberg 1915

When I Think of Heaven   Brooks 1945

When I Think of the Sweethearts   Fisher 1930

When I Think of the Sweethearts that I Might Have Had   Carroll 1918

When I Tip Tip Toe Up a Tuck Tuck Tucky Lane   Dixon 1928; Rose 1928; Warren 1928

When I Told the Village Belle   Gilbert 1934

When I Trilly with My Filly   Ellington 1959

When I Truck on Down   Oakland 1938

When I Turned Over That Apple Turnover   Bryan 1936; Fisher 1936

When I Used to Lead the Ballet   Porter 1912, 1916

When I Walk My Baby   DePaul 1958; Raye 1958

When I Walk with You   Ellington 1946

When I Waltz With You   Bryan 1912; Friml 1922; Harbach 1922

When I Was 21 and You Were Sweet 16   Williams 1911

When I Was a Girl Like You   Romberg 1927

When I Was a Guy from the Mountains (And You Were a Girl from the Hills)   Young, Victor 1932

When I Was a Kid Like You   Cobb 1912; Edwards 1912

When I Was a Little Boy   Duke 1968
When I Was a Little Cuckoo   Porter 1944
When I Was a Little Girl   Drake 1954
When I Was Hikin' with You   Johnson, Howard 1927
When I Was in the Chorus of the Gaiety   Von Tilzer 1907
When I Was One and Twenty   Bergman 1960
When I Was the Village Jim Dandy, Mirandy, and You Were the Belle of the Town   Lewis 1920; Young, Joe 1920
When I Was Young   Cahn 1970; Smith, Harry B. 1913; Smith, Robert B. 1913; Styne 1970
When I Was Young (Yes, Very Young)   Merrill 1953
When I Wave My Flag   Norworth 1916
When I Went Home   Leigh 1954
When I Went to School with You   Cobb 1917; Edwards 1917
When I Woke Up this Morning   Monaco 1911; Myrow 1959
When I Wonder   Egan 1923; Whiting 1923
When I Write a Song   Styne 1930
When I'm Alone I'm Lonesome   Berlin 1911
When I'm an American Citizen   Edwards 1908
When I'm Being Born Again   Lane 1965; Lerner, Alan Jay 1965
When I'm Dancing   Eliscu 1961
When I'm Dreaming of Your Spanish Eyes   Bryan 1930
When I'm Drunk I'm Beautiful   Merrill 1971; Styne 1971
When I'm Eating Around with You   Porter 1910
When I'm in Your Arms   Davis 1926
When I'm Looking at You   Buck 1918
When I'm Loving You   Snyder 1956
When I'm Not Near the Girl I Love   Harburg 1947; Lane 1947
When I'm Out with the Belle of New York   Mercer 1951; Warren 1951
When I'm Out with You   Berlin 1915
When I'm Sippin' a Soda with Susie   Gordon 1932; Revel 1932
When I'm Thinking of You   Berlin 1912
When I'm Walking with My Sweetness, Down Among the Sugar Cane   Clare 1928
When I'm Waltzing   Goetz 1912
When I'm Waltzing with You   Smith, Harry B. 1911; Smith, Robert B. 1911
When I'm with the Girls   Gershwin, Ira 1921; Youmans 1921
When I'm With You   Brown, Lew 1944; Davis 1953; Edwards 1930; Gordon 1936; Revel 1936
When I'm with You I'm Lonesome   Donaldson 1924; Gilbert 1926
When in Rome   Coleman 1963; Leigh 1963
When Ireland Stands Among the Nations of the World   Herbert 1917
When Irish Eyes Are Smiling   Olcott 1913
When is a Kiss Not a Kiss   Freed, Ralph 1937; Lane 1937
When Is Sometime   Burke 1949; Van Heusen 1949
When It Comes to Loving   Coleman 1979
When It Dries   Rodgers 1970
When It Happens to You   Merrill 1993; Styne 1993
When It Rains, Sweetheart, When It Rains   Berlin 1911
When It Rains You Are My Rainbow   Bryan 1932
When It's All Over   Brown, Lew 1915
When It's All Said and Done   Porter 1938
When It's Blossom Time in Yakima Valley   Lawrence 1938
When It's Cactus Time in Arizona   Gershwin, George 1930; Gershwin, Ira 1930
When It's Celery Time in Kalamazoo   Sterling 1942
When It's Chilly Down in Chile   Styne 1942

When It's Christmas Time in Toyland   Baer 1949
When It's Circus Time Back Home   Yellen 1917
When It's Cotton Blossom Time, Sweet Rosalie   Sterling 1913; Von Tilzer 1913
When It's Darkness on the Delta   Livingston, Jerry 1932
When It's Daylight Saving Time in Oshkosh   Robin 1930; Whiting 1930
When It's Halloween in Aberdeen, I'll Be Coming Through the Rye   Monaco 1918
When It's Hog Callin' Time in the Valley   Magidson 1938; Wrubel 1938
When It's Honeysuckle Time Way Down in Georgia   Freed, Arthur 1920; Howard, Joseph E. 1920
When It's Lilac Time in Tokio   Coots 1919
When It's Love   Cahn 1953; De Lange 1945; Duke 1950; Rome 1950
When It's Moonlight in Brooklyn   Dubin 1927
When It's Moonlight on the Alamo   Bryan 1914; Fisher 1914; Meyer 1914
When It's Moonlight on the Blue Pacific   Davis 1942
When It's Moonlight on the Swanee Shore   Egan 1920; Whiting 1920
When It's Necking Time in Great Neck   Von Tilzer 1927
When It's Night Time Down in Burgandy   Bryan 1914
When It's Night Time in Italy, It's Wednesday Over Here   Brown, Lew 1923
When It's Night Time in Little Italy   Fisher 1917
When It's Night-Time in Dixieland   Berlin 1914
When It's Peach Blossom Time in Lichtenburg   Berlin 1954
When It's Summer   Burke 1961
When It's Summertime Down by the Seaside   Dubin 1917
When It's Sweet Patootie Time   Leslie 1919
When I've Got the Moon (Banjo Song)   Hammerstein 1935; Kern 1935
When Jack Comes Sailing Home Again   Kahn 1912
When Jeremiah Can Be with Me   Leigh 1974
When John McCormick Sings a Song   Goetz 1915; Jerome 1915; Schwartz, Jean 1915
When Johnny Comes Marching Home Again   Goetz 1908
When Johnson's Quartette Harmonize   Berlin 1912
When June Comes Along with a Song   Cohan 1923
When Kate and I Were Comin' Thru the Rye   Sterling 1902; Von Tilzer 1902
When Kentucky Bids the World Good Morning   Leslie 1930
When Knighthood Was in Flower   Atteridge 1924; Bergman 1961; Herbert 1922; Romberg 1924; Schwartz, Jean 1924
When Knott's Not Tying Knots   Gorney 1926
When Leaves Begin to Fade   Sterling 1902
When Leaves Begin to Fall   Sterling 1903; Von Tilzer 1903
When Lights Are Low   Kahn 1923; Koehler 1923
When Lindy Comes Back   Cohan 1927
When Little Bo-Peep Saw Her Little Beau Peep   Bryan 1935
When Little Children Smile   Leslie 1929
When Little Red Roses Get the Blues for You   Dubin 1930
When Louis from St. Louis Plays the St. Louis Blues   Fisher 1936
When Love Awakens   Coslow 1930
When Love Awakes (Love's Awakening)   Herbert 1917
When Love Beckoned   Porter 1939
When Love Comes Calling   Young, Victor 1914
When Love Comes Knocking at Your Heart   Brennan 1920; Brown, A. Seymour 1913
When Love Comes Marching Along   Kahn 1936; Romberg 1936
When Love Comes Stealing   Pollack 1927

When Love Comes Stealing into My Heart   Snyder 1930

When Love Comes Swingin' Along   Henderson 1934;
	Koehler 1934

When Love Comes to Call   Porter 1953

When Love Comes Your Way   Porter 1935

When Love Goes Wrong (Nothin' Goes Right)   Adamson
	1953; Carmichael 1953

When Love Is Dawning   Donaldson 1929; Leslie 1929

When Love Is Free   Smith, Harry B. 1910

When Love Is Kind   Johnson, Howard 1939

When Love Is Near   Egan 1925; Kahn 1925

When Love Is Near You   Fain 1932; Kahal 1932

When Love Is Waiting 'Round the Corner   Howard, Joseph
	E. 1909

When Love Is Young   Adamson 1937; McHugh 1937

When Love Walks By   Arlen 1944; Carmichael 1943; Mercer
	1943

When Love Was All   Berlin 1957

(In that Moment) When Love Was There   Robison 1942

When Lovers Meet   Coots 1957

When Love's in Your Heart   Martin 1969

When Lula Does the Hula-Hula Dance   Razaf 1924

When Madame Reaches Her High C   Heyman 1934

When Magnolias Bloom Again in Old Virginia   DePaul
	1943; Raye 1943

When Mama Calls   Merrill 1953

When Mariola Do the Cubanola   Von Tilzer 1910

When Mariutch Shake a Da Shimmie Sha Wot   Sterling
	1919; Von Tilzer 1919

When McGregor Sings Off Key   Fain 1938

When McKinley Marches On   Porter 1944

When Me, Mowgli, Love   Porter 1935

When Michael Dooley Heard the Booley Booley   Jerome
	1913; Von Tilzer 1913

When Miss Patricia Salome Did Her Funny Little Oo La
	Palome Von Tilzer 1907

When Morning Comes   Heyman 1935; Washington 1937

When Morning Glories Wake Up in the Morning   Fisher
	1927; Rose 1927

When Mother Sings Sweet and Low   Johnson, Howard 1923

When Mother Wields the Shingle   Young, Victor 1924

When Mr. Shakespeare Comes to Town   Jerome 1901;
	Schwartz, Jean 1901

When Mr. Yankee-Doodle Comes to Town   Meyer 1910

When My Baby Goes to Town   Porter 1943

When My Baby Smiles at Me   Sterling 1920; Von Tilzer 1920

When My Baby Talks that Double-Talk to Me   Coots 1938

When My Back Is to the Wall   Drake 1968

When My Boy Comes Home   Brennan 1944

When My Caravan Comes Home   Porter 1922

When My Darling Calls Me Darling   David, Mack 1951

When My Dixie Dreams Go Drifting Along   Johnson, J.
	Rosamond 1934

When My Dream Boat Comes Home   Friend 1936

When My Dreams Come True   Berlin 1929

When My Love Comes Back to Me   Stept 1952

When My Love Smiles   Webster 1955

When My Prince Charming Comes Along   Akst 1930; Clarke
	1930; Coslow 1935

When My Ship Comes In   Donaldson 1934; Kahn 1934;
	Smith, Harry B. 1906; Von Tilzer 1915

When My Ship Turns Around and Come In Again   Ruby
	1951

When My Sugar Walks Down the Street   McHugh 1924;
	Mills 1924

When My Sweetie Comes Back to Me   Buck 1918

When My Toreador Starts to Snore   Baer 1929; Gilbert 1929

When My Violin Is Calling   Smith, Harry B. 1925

When Nancy Brown Kissed Hirem Green Good
	Bye Howard, Joseph E. 1910

When Nathan Was Married to Rose of Washington
	Square Buck 1925

When New York Was New York, New York Was a
	Wonderful Town Cohan 1937

When Niccolo Plays the Piccolo   Woods 1929

When Night Comes On   Coots 1935; Lewis 1935

When Night Is Near   Egan 1922; Gorney 1922; Whiting
	1922

When No One Cares   Cahn 1959; Van Heusen 1959

When Nobody Wants You, and Nobody Cares, Come to
	Me Stept 1924

When Noses Are Red and Eyelids Are Blue   Caesar 1943

When October Goes   Mercer 1984

When Old Friends Are Drifting Apart   Woods 1933

When Old New York Was Young   Cobb 1921; Edwards
	1921; Johnson, Howard 1929

When Old Vienna Was New   Egan 1932

When One You Love   Atteridge 1915; Friml 1915

When Other Hearts Have Closed their Doors   Snyder 1909

When Our Hearts Go Waltzing Along (Mein Herz Hat Leise
	Dein Herz Gegrusst) Young, Joe 1931

When Our Love Was New   Parish 1931

When Our Mothers Rule the World   Bryan 1915

When Our Ship Comes Sailing In   Gershwin, George 1926;
	Gershwin, Ira 1926

When Paris Smiles   Webster 1963

When Pavlova Starts Buck and Winging   Atteridge 1916;
	Motzan 1916, 1917; Romberg 1916

When Perrico Plays   Herbert 1905

When Polly Walks Through the Hollyhocks   Woods 1928

When Priscilla Tries to Reach High C   Von Tilzer 1916

When Private Brown Becomes a Captain   Raye 1941

When Ragtime Rosie Ragged the Rosary   Leslie 1911

When Romance Comes Along   Magidson 1942; Pollack
	1942

When Rosalie Sings Chiribiribi   Goetz 1910

When Roses Bloom No More   Webster 1939

When Rosie Riccoola Do the Hoola Ma Boola She's a Hit in
	Little Italy Sterling 1917

When Sally Walks Along Peacock Alley   Mercer 1949;
	Warren 1949

When Sammy Sang the Marseillaise   Friml 1913; Harbach
	1913

When Shadows Fall I Hear You Calling California   Kalmar
	1920; Ruby 1920

When Shall I Again See Ireland   Herbert 1917

When Shall We Meet Again   Egan 1920; Whiting 1920

When She Gives Him a Shamrock Bloom   Friml 1917;
	Harbach 1917

When She Sings the Songs My Mother Sang to Me   Snyder
	1909

When She Walks in the Room   Fields 1945; Romberg 1945

When Sherman Went Marching Through Georgia   Ruby
	1916

When She's Getting Cold on You, She's Warming Up to
	Somebody Else Bryan 1925; Schwartz, Jean 1925

When She's Old Enough to Marry   Meyer 1911

When Sist' Tetrazin' Met Cousin Carus   Jerome 1910;
	Schwartz, Jean 1910

When Somebody Cares   Howard, Bart 1984

When Somebody Else Means the World to You   Sterling 1925

When Somebody Thinks You're Wonderful   Woods 1935

When Someone Wonderful Thinks You're Wonderful   David, Mack 1953; Livingston, Jerry 1953

When Songs Were Sung   Caesar 1922

When Sousa Leads the Band   Jerome 1900

When Spring Breaks Through   Bloom 1931; Koehler 1931

When Spring Comes Peeping Thru   Stept 1927

When Spring Comes 'Round   Washington 1934

When Spring Comes Springin' Along   Johnson, Howard 1940

When Stanislaus Got Married   Burke 1944; Van Heusen 1944

When Stella Did the Rhumba   Johnson, James P. 1962

When Summer Comes   Webster 1968

When Summer Days Are Come   Silver 1937

When Summer Turns to Snow   Bergman 1968

When Sunday Comes Around   Carroll 1921

When Sunday Comes to Town   Von Tilzer 1915

When Swallows Return to the Spring   Smith, Harry B. 1908

(The Angels Cry) When Sweethearts Tell a Lie   Merrill 1950

When Taft Says Yes, Then Ike Says Yes   Caesar 1952

When Tallulah Does the Hula Out of Brooklyn   Mills 1947

When Tender Love You Are Confessing   Harbach 1911

When That Band Plays   Eliscu 1932

When That Dixie Sun Goes Down   Razaf Date Unknown

When that Man Is Dead and Gone   Berlin 1942

When the Angelus Is Ringing   Young, Joe 1914

When the Apple Blossoms Fall   Cobb 1903; Edwards 1903

When the Armies Disband   Caesar 1918; Gershwin, George 1918

When the Autumn Leaves Are Falling   Buck 1917

When the Autumn Leaves of Life Begin to Fall   Brown, Lew 1931; DeSylva 1931; Henderson 1931

When the Band Begins to Play   Von Tilzer 1901

When the Band Comes Marching In (When the Band Comes Swingin' In)   Russell 1957

When the Band Plays Ragtime   Smith, Harry B. 1903

When the Banners Lead   Smith, Harry B. 1928

When the Bees Are in the Hive   Bryan 1904

When the Bees Make Honey Down in Sunny Alabam'   Donaldson 1919; Lewis 1919; Young, Joe 1919

When the Bells of St. Mary's Answer the Bells of St. James   Mills 1938

When the Bells Ting-a-ling (For Ching-a-ling)   Bryan 1944

When the Berry Blossoms Bloom   Brown, Lew 1939; Stept 1939

When the Black Sheep Returns to the Fold   Berlin 1916

When the Bo-Tree Blossoms Again   Kalmar 1927; Kern 1927; Ruby 1927

When the Boys Come Home   Arlen 1944; Harburg 1944

When the Boys Come Marching Home   Howard, Joseph E. 1917

When the Boys from Dixie Eat the Melon on the Rhine   Bryan 1918

When the Boys Get Together   David, Hal 1962

When the Boys Talk About the Girls   Merrill 1958

When the Campfire Is Low on the Prairie   Mitchell 1937; Stept 1936, 1937

When the Cat Comes Back   Smith, Harry B. 1911

When the Cat's Away   Hanley 1938; Jerome 1905; Magidson 1942; Romberg 1921; Schwartz, Jean 1905; Styne 1942

When the Cat's Away the Mice Will Play   Herbert 1905

When the Chapel Bells Tolled on the Hill   Johnson, Howard 1933

When the Children Are Asleep   Hammerstein 1945; Rodgers 1945

When the Chimes on Chapel Hill Ring Ave Maria   Coots 1944

When the Circus Wagon Came to Town   Willson 1956

When the Clock Is Striking Twelve   Eliscu 1931

When the Clouds Have Drifted By   Sterling 1900

When the Clover Moon Is Shining Down   Lewis 1910

When the Colored Band Comes Marching Down the Street   Johnson, J. Rosamond 1903

When the Colored Regiment Goes Off to War   Atteridge 1915; Romberg 1915

When the Congressman from Tennessee Meets the Senator from Maine   Fisher 1940

When the Corn Is Waving, Annie Dear   Johnson, Howard 1939

When the Crime Waves Roll   Hart 1921; Rodgers 1921

When the Crimson Snow of Russia Is White Again   Robison 1942

When the Curtain Falls   Berlin 1918

When the Dance Is Over (Let Me Linger in Your Arms)   De Lange 1934

When the Dark Becomes Dawn   Myrow 1939

When the Day Is Ended   Freed, Arthur 1925

When the Debbies Go By   DeSylva 1925; Gershwin, George 1925; Gershwin, Ira 1925

When the Devil Played the Fiddle   Duke 1950; Rome 1950

When the Dodo Bird Is Singing in the Coca-Cola Tree   Edwards 1909

When the Duchess Is Away   Gershwin, Ira 1945; Weill 1945

When the Fiddlers Fiddled on Fiddler's Green   Yellen 1962

When the Folks High-Up Do that Mean Low-Down   Berlin 1931

When the Frost Is on the Daisy   Bryan 1930

When the Frost Is on the Pumpkin Maggie Dear   Sterling 1903; Von Tilzer 1903

When the Frost Is on the Punkin   Carmichael 1951

When the Funny Paper Folks Were on Parade   Fisher 1924

When the Girl You Love Is Loving You   Jerome 1908; Schwartz, Jean 1908

When the Girls Get Wise   Goetz 1918

When the Girl's Got Your Heart and You Haven't Got the Girl   Bryan 1912; Fisher 1912

When the Girls Grow Older They Grow a Little Bolder   Lewis 1917; Schwartz, Jean 1917; Young, Joe 1917

When the Glories of Ireland Are Told   Brennan 1917

When the Going Gets Tough   Coleman 1979

When the Golden Gate Was Silver   Rainger 1934; Robin 1934

When the Golden Rod Is Waving Again Dear in the Eternal City   Von Tilzer 1925

When the Good Lord Troubles the Waters (Be Ready)   Robison 1958

When the Great Even-Upper Comes to Supper   Robison 1952

When the Green Leaves Come Again   David, Hal 1960

When the Grown Up Ladies Act Like Babies, I've Got to Love 'Em That's All   Lewis 1913; Young, Joe 1913

When the Harbor Lights Are Burning Low   Bryan 1907

When the Harvest Days Are Over and Gone   Von Tilzer 1900

When the Harvest Is Over   Conrad 1929; Mitchell 1929

When the Harvest Moon Is Shining   Sterling 1920; Von Tilzer 1920

When the Hen Stops Laying   Porter 1938

When the Henry Clay Comes Steaming into Mobile Bay   Clarke 1912; Jerome 1912; Schwartz, Jean 1912

When the Honey Moon Stops Shining   Atteridge 1913; Schwartz, Jean 1913

When the Honey-Moon Was Over   Fisher 1921

When the Hudson Flows Out to the Sea   Jerome 1927; Schwartz, Jean 1927

When the Humming Birds Return Sweet Irene   Snyder 1909

When the Idle Poor Become the Idle Rich   Harburg 1947; Lane 1947

When the Ivy Climbs Over the Wall   Sterling 1909

When the Jailbirds Come to Town   Eliscu 1944; Gorney 1944

When the Judges Doff the Ermine   Gershwin, George 1933; Gershwin, Ira 1933

When the Last Rose of Summer Whispers Goodbye   Livingston, Jerry 1933

When the Last Year Rolls Around   Clare 1934; Whiting 1934

When the Lights Are Low   Buck 1916; Johnson, Howard 1939; Kern 1916

When the Lights Are Soft and Low   Freed, Arthur 1932

When the Lights Go Out on Broadway   Stept 1917

When the Lights of the Chapter Are Low, The   Carmichael 1949

When the Logs Come Rolling Down the River   Coots 1944; Davis 1944

When the Lord Created Adam   Blake 1931; Razaf 1931

When the Love You Love Loves You   Howard, Joseph E. 1913

When the Midnight Choo-Choo Leaves for Alabam'   Berlin 1912

When the Moon Bids the Night Good-Bye   Ahlert 1939; Young, Joe 1939

When the Moon Comes Over Madison Square (The Love Lament of a Western Gent)   Burke 1940; Monaco 1940

When the Moon Comes Over the Hill   Johnson, J. Rosamond 1903

When the Moon Comes Over the Mountain   Johnson, Howard 1930; Woods 1930

When the Moon Comes Up on County Down   David, Hal 1949

When the Moon Hangs High (And the Prairie Stars Hang Low)   Bullock 1936

When the Moon Is Gone   Hoffman 1946

When the Moon Plays Peek-a-boo with You   Fisher 1907

When the Moon Swings Low Along the Ohio   Johnson, Howard 1933

When the Moonlight's Bright in Brighton   Sherman 1995

When the Morning Rolls Around   Woods 1932

When the Music Starts to Play   Edwards 1908

When the New Moon Shines on the New Moon Bay   Woods 1934

When the Nightingale Sings   David, Mack 1947; Hoffman 1947; Livingston, Jerry 1947

When the Nylons Bloom Again   Waller 1943

When the Old Gang's Back on the Corner   Hoffman 1945

When the Old Oaken Bucket Was New   Meyer 1931; Young, Joe 1931

When the Old Top Hummed (The Humming Top)   Harbach 1911

When the One You Care For   Robin 1927

When the One You Love Is Gone   Pollack 1933

When the One You Love Loves You   Baer 1924; Friend 1924

When the One You Love Simply Won't Love Back   Cahn 1946; Styne 1946

When the Organ Played Ave Maria   Davis 1949; Silver 1949

(What Does It Mean) When the Owl Says Whoo   Alter 1929

When the Party Gives a Party   Fields 1945; Romberg 1945

When the Ragtime Army Goes Away to War   Brown, A. Seymour 1914

When the Rain Comes Rollin' Down   Fisher 1935

When the Rain Goes Pitter Patter (inst.)   Schwartz, Arthur 1931

When the Rain Rain Rain Came Down   Sherman 1968

When the Rainbow of Love Appears   Lewis 1919; Young, Joe 1919

When the Red, Red Robin Comes Bob, Bob, Bobbin' Along   Woods 1926

When the Rest of the Crowd Goes Home I Always Go Home Alone   Dubin 1931

When the Rest of the World Don't Want You, Go Back to the Folks at Home   Dubin 1916

When the Right Boy Meets the Right Girl (That's the Right Time to Love)   Gorney 1925

When the Right Little Boy Rolls Around   Cobb 1917; Edwards 1917

When the Right Little Girl Comes Along   Hanley 1920

When the Right Man Sings Tra-La-La   Herbert 1911; Smith, Harry B. 1911

When the Right One Comes Along   Buck 1920; Davis 1932; Gershwin, George 1927; Gershwin, Ira 1927; Gilbert 1928

When the Right One Comes Along   (When the Right Girl Comes Along)   Herbert 1920

When the River Don Runs Dry   Razaf 1944

When the Robert E. Lee Arrives in Old Tennessee, All the Way from Gay Paree   Monaco 1919

When the Robin Sings After the Rain   Hanley 1930

When the Robin Sings His Song Again   Coots 1935; Parish 1935

When the Robins Nest Again   Johnson, Howard 1939

When the Robins Return in the Spring   Livingston, Jerry 1933

When the Roll Is Called Alma Mater   Fain 1934; Kahal 1934

When the Roses Bloom Again   Edwards 1901; Mills 1928

When the Roses Bloom Again in Normandy   Bryan 1931

When the Roses Bloom in Avalon   Bryan 1914

When the Sails Are Set for Home   Mills 1940

When the Saints Go Marchin' By   Parish 1959

When the Sandman's on His Way   Atteridge 1923; Romberg 1923

When the Shadows Grow Longer   Parish 1936

When the Shaker Plays a Cocktail Tune   Buck 1926; Hanley 1926

When the Sheets Come Back from the Laundry   Bullock 1950

When the Shepherd Leads His Flock Back Home   Warren 1931

When the Shepherd Leads His Flock (The Sheep) Back Home   Leslie 1931

When the Ships Come Home   Kern 1918

When the Sixty-Ninth Comes Back   Herbert 1919

When the Snow Is on the Ground   Sterling Date Unknown; Von Tilzer 1898

When the Spirit Moves Me   Rose 1940; Van Heusen 1940

When the Spring Is in the Air   Hammerstein 1932; Kern 1932

When the Stars Are Shinging Bright   Jerome 1903; Schwartz, Jean 1903

When the Stars Go to Sleep   Adamson 1938; McHugh 1938

When the Statues Come to Life   Atteridge 1921; Johnson, Howard 1920; Pollack 1921; Schwartz, Jean 1921

When the Storm Clouds Form   Brooks 1958

When the Summer Bids the Rose Goodbye   Dubin 1922

When the Summer Moon Comes 'Long   Porter 1910

When the Sun Comes Out   Arlen 1941; Koehler 1941

When the Sun Goes Down   Sterling 1902

When the Sun Goes Down in Romany   Goetz 1916

When the Sun Goes Down in Romany My Heart Goes Roaming Back to You   Lewis 1916; Young, Joe 1916

When the Sun Goes Down in Sleepy Hollow, That's the Time I Think of Home Sweet Home   Davis 1918

When the Sun Goes Down in Switzerland   McHugh 1916

When the Sun Goes Down on a Little Prairie Town   Kahn 1932

When the Sun Sets Down South   Blake Date Unknown; Sissle 1938

When the Swallows Homeward Fly   Johnson, Howard 1939

When the Sweet Magnolias Bloom Again   Young, Joe 1933

When the Teddy Bears Go Marching on Parade   Coots 1952

When the Troupe Comes Back to Town   Von Tilzer 1902

When the Weather's Better   Comden and Green 1967; Styne 1967

When the Wedding Chimes Are Ringing   Atteridge 1922; Schwartz, Jean 1922

When the Weekend Comes Round   Caesar 1924

When the White Roses Bloom (Down in Red River Valley)   Wrubel 1947

When the Whole World Has Gone Back on You   Edwards 1913

When the Wind Blows South   Arlen 1937; Harburg 1937

When the World Comes to an End   Cobb 1911; Edwards 1911

When the World Is at Rest   Fain 1928

When the World Was New   Kahn 1932

When the World Was Young (Ah the Apple Tree)   Mercer 1951

When the World Was Young (Quand Notre Vieux Monde Etait Tout Neuf)   Hart 1930; Rodgers 1930

When the Years Go Drifting By   Kahn 1926

When There's a Breeze on Lake Louise   Revel 1942

When There's a Chance to Dance   Gershwin, George 1917; Gershwin, Ira 1917, 1919

When There's a Heartache (There Must Be a Heart)   Bacharach 1969

When There's No One to Love   Atteridge 1921; Schwartz, Jean 1920

When They Ask About You   Stept 1943

When They Call the Roll at West Point   Harbach 1947; Kern 1947

When They Do the Hula Hula on the Boulevard   Bryan 1918

When They Go Through a Tunnel   Kalmar 1916

When They Grow Older, They Grow a Little Bolder   Meyer 1916; Young, Joe 1916

When They Handed Out Hearts   Strouse 1958

When They Name You   Stept 1924

When They Sing the Wearin' of the Green (In Syncopated Time)   Stept 1929

When They Went Driving   Caesar 1940

When They're Beautiful, They're Bound to Get By   Ager 1919; Clarke 1919; Meyer 1919; Yellen 1919

When They're Old Enough to Know Better It's Better to Leave Them Alone   Lewis 1919; Ruby 1919; Young, Joe 1919

When Things Are Bright and Rosy   Kalmar 1928; Ruby 1928

When Things Were Rotten   Adams 1975; Strouse 1975

When This Crazy World Is Sane Again   Berlin 1942

When Those Mason-Dixon Minstrels Hit the Town   Bryan 1919; Schwartz, Jean 1919

When Those Roly Poly Babies Roll Their Eyes   Kahn 1923; Meyer 1923

When Those Sweet Hawaiian Babies Roll Their Eyes   Leslie 1917; Ruby 1917

When Three Is Company (Cupid Song)   Kern 1913

When Times Get Better   Fain 1932; Kahal 1932

When Toby Is Out of Town   Gershwin, George 1924

When Tommy Atkins Marries Dolly Gray   Cobb 1906; Edwards 1906

When Tommy Atkins Smiles at All the Girls   Atteridge 1914; Carroll 1914; Romberg 1914

When Tomorrow Comes   Fain 1933; Kahal 1933

When Tonight Dies   Herbert 1911

When Tony La Board Played the Barber Shop Chord!   Young, Joe 1911

When Two Hearts Are True Hearts   Coots 1929; Davis 1929

When Two Hearts Beat Together   Smith, Robert B. 1912

When Two Lips Call   Parish 1980

When Two Love Dearly   Atteridge 1910

When Two Loving Arms Are Around You   Ager 1910

When Uncle Sam Rules the Wave   Herbert 1916

When Uncle Sammy Leads the Band   Von Tilzer 1916

When Vagabond Dreams Come True   Parish 1930

When Verdi Plays the Hurdy Gurdy   Donaldson 1916

When Was the Last Time   Oakland 1962

When Was there Ever a Night Like This   Atteridge 1912

When We Are Born Again   Warren 1956

When We Are M-A Double R-I-E-D   Cohan 1907

When We Are Married   Goetz 1916; Mitchell 1921; Pollack 1921; Rodgers 1920; Youmans 1924

When We Are One   Hoffman 1959

When We Get Our Divorce   Hammerstein 1925; Harbach 1925; Kern 1925

When We Got Together in the Moonlight   Rose 1929

When We Heard the Music Play 'Home Sweet Home'   Gilbert 1939

When We Meet Again   Rome 1946

When We Put Two and Two Together We Found Ourselves in Love   Burke 1931; Monaco 1931

When We Ride on the Merry-Go-Round   Mercer 1932

When We See One   Drake 1954

When We Waltzed in the Dark   Bryan 1928, 1931; Lewis 1931; Meyer 1931; Young, Joe 1931

When We Went to Sunday School   Kahn 1918

When We Were Both in Kindergarten   Cahn 1945; Styne 1945

When We Were Boys   Von Tilzer 1903

When We Were Married   Smith, Harry B. 1910

When We Were Twenty-One   Goetz 1916

When We Were Very Young (Terzettino)   Fields 1952; Kern 1952

When We're Alone (Rita) (inst.)   Young, Victor 1955

When We're Dancing   Drake 1990

When We're Home on the Range   Porter 1943

When We're Married   Smith, Harry B. 1906

When, When   Merrill 1956

When When When   Hoffman 1955; Silver 1955

When Will Grown-Ups Grow Up? Adams 1981; Strouse 1981

When Will I Know Silver 1956

When Will the Sun Shine for Me Davis 1923; Silver 1923

When Will We Meet Again Kahn 1927

When Willie Waltzes with Me Cahn 1966; Van Heusen 1966

When Winter Comes Berlin 1939; Carroll 1922; Freed, Arthur 1922

When Woman, Lovely Woman, Gets Her Rights Harbach 1908

When Worlds Collide Evans 1951; Livingston, Jay 1951

When Yankee Doodle Marches Thro' Berlin There'll Be a Hot Time in the U.S.A. Sterling 1917

When Yankee Doodle Sails Upon the Good Ship Home Sweet Home Fisher 1918

When You Add Religion to Love Bryan 1956

When You Ain't Got No One to Love Fisher 1927; Rose 1927

When You and I Were Strangers Porter 1944

When You and I Were Tadpoles Herbert 1920; Smith, Robert B. 1920

When You and I Were Young Maggie Johnson, Howard 1939

When You and I Were Young Maggie Blues McHugh 1922

When You Are in My Arms Mercer 1935

When You Are Mine Conrad 1934; Mitchell 1934

When You Are Near Smith, Harry B. 1901

When You Are Seventeen Bergman 1956

When You Are Young Hammerstein 1931; Romberg 1931

When You Break an Irishman's Heart Brown, Lew 1949; Stept 1949

When You Broke the Seventh Commandment David, Mack 1946; Hoffman 1946; Livingston, Jerry 1946

When You Call the Roll Alma Mater Fain 1936; Kahal 1936

When You Care a Lot for Someone Who Cares So Little for You Davis 1967

When You Carry the Torch Warren 1929

When You Climb the Stairs in School Caesar 1943

(When You Come Back, and You Will Come Back) When You Come Back, If You Do Come Back Cohan 1918

When You Come Back to Me Myrow 1965

When You Come Home Parish 1951

When You Come to the End of a Lollipop Hoffman 1960

When You Come to the End of the Day Kahn 1929; Sigman 1951

When You Dance for a King Merrill 1993; Styne 1993

When You Dance (For the Love of the Dance) Leigh 1955

When You Dance in Paris, France Robin 1957; Styne 1957

When You Do What You Do Parish 1925

When You Don't Know What to Do with It Hanley 1930

When You Dream About Hawaii Kalmar 1937; Ruby 1937

When You Drop Off at Cairo, Illinois Berlin 1916; Goetz 1916

When You Fall Freed, Ralph 1958

When You Fall in the Fall of the Year David, Hal 1962

When You Find Her Remind Her of Me Johnson, Howard 1925

When You Find Me Dreaming, Wake Me Up with a Kiss Fisher 1929

When You Find the One You Love Friend 1931

When You Find the Right Baby Mills 1948

When You First Ate an Olive Coots 1934

When You First Kiss the Last Girl You Love Howard, Joseph E. 1909

When You Gamble in the Game of Love Fisher 1917; Johnson, Howard 1917

When You Get It Tuned Up Play Us Something Leslie 1912

When You Go Blane 1939

When You Go Down by Miss Jenny's Ellington 1946

When You Go Down to London Town Von Tilzer 1903

When You Go Out to Dine Howard, Joseph E. 1906

When You Got Love Hanley 1938

When You Gotta Sing You Gotta Sing Hoffman 1937; Lerner, Sammy 1937

When You Grow Tired Just Let Me Know Howard, Joseph E. 1907

When You Grow to Be Twenty One (When I Was Twenty-One) Jerome 1916

When You Grow to Be Twenty-One (When I Was Twenty-One) Leslie 1916; Schwartz, Jean 1916

When You Grow Up Adams 1954; Strouse 1954

When You Grown Up You'll Know Lane 1951; Lerner, Alan Jay 1951

When You Have a Son Livingston, Jerry 1973

When You Have Forgotten My Kisses (And I Have Forgotten Your Name) Harburg 1971

When You Have No Man to Love Hammerstein 1930; Romberg 1930

When You Haven't a Beautiful Girl Clarke 1913; Leslie 1913

When You Hear Love's Hello Atteridge 1911; Goetz 1911

When You Hear that Humming Harbach 1938; Kern 1938

When You Hear the Sirens Blow Caesar 1940

When You Hear the Time Signal Mercer 1942

When You Hear this Song, Remember Me Freed, Ralph 1932; Hanley 1932

When You Kiss an Italian Girl Berlin 1911

When You Kiss Me Hoffman 1957; Mitchell 1927; Motzan 1927

When You Kiss Me Va-Room Hoffman 1954

When You Kiss the One You Love Von Tilzer 1910

When You Kissed Me Clare 1933

When You Know Edwards 1909

When You Know Me Better Herbert 1920; Smith, Robert B. 1920

When You Know Your Man Is Comin' Home DePaul 1958; Raye 1958

When You Learned How to Cry Motzan 1923

When You Least Expect It Stept 1960

When You Leave Your Little Old New York Jerome 1913; Schwartz, Jean 1913

When You Live in a Furnished Flat DeSylva 1919; Gershwin, George 1919

When You Live on an Island Dietz 1944; Duke 1944

When You Look at Me Bergman 1954

When You Look at Me (Nostalgia di Mandolini) Brooks 1958; Raye 1958

When You Look at the World Howard, Bart 1961

When You Look in Her Eyes Herbert 1911; Smith, Harry B. 1911

When You Look in Your Looking Glass Lewis 1938

When You Love Atteridge 1923

When You Love a Certain Girl Goetz 1909

When You Love a Summer Girl Meyer 1908

When You Love More than One You'll Have No One in Love with You Bryan 1925

When You Love Only One Dietz 1934; Schwartz, Arthur 1934

When You Love Someone Evans 1953; Livingston, Jay 1953

When You Made Me Love You Johnson, Howard 1920

When You March Back in My Arms   De Lange 1949
When You Meet a Man in Chicago   Merrill 1972; Styne 1972
When You Meet Them on Broadway   Smith, Harry B. 1912
When You Picked Your Basket of Peaches   Goetz 1917
When You Play with Fire   Hoffman 1947; Robin 1947
When You Played the Organ and I Sang the Rosary   Leslie 1927
When You Press Your Lips to Mine   Razaf 1930
When You Pretend   Brooks 1955; Warren 1955
When You Ride a Bicycle   Caesar 1937
When You Roll Your Eyes   Friend 1925
When You Said Goodbye   Sterling 1913; Von Tilzer 1913
When You Said Goodnight, Did You Really Mean Goodbye   Donaldson 1928
When You Said How Do You Do   Goetz 1912
When You See Another Sweetie Hanging Around That's the Time You'll Want to Be Coming Back to Me   Donaldson 1919; Lewis 1919; Young, Joe 1919
When You See Me with Another Beau   Williams 1907
When You See That Aunt of Mine   Johnson, Howard 1925
When You See the Snow Flakes Falling   Young, Joe 1911
When You Sign Off My Heart   Fisher 1941
When You Smile   Gershwin, George 1927; Gershwin, Ira 1927; Strouse 1989
When You Speak of Love   Sterling 1913; Von Tilzer 1913
When You Speak with a Lady   Adams 1972; Strouse 1972
When You Stop and Think   Duke 1963
When You Swim   Caesar 1937
When You Take the Road with Me   Kern 1923
When You Tell Me that You Dare   Lawrence 1933
When You Tend Baby   Caesar 1940
When You Wake Up Dancing   Kern 1918
When You Walked By   Burke 1960
When You Walked Out Someone Else Walked Right In   Berlin 1923
When You Waltz with the Girl You Love   Von Tilzer 1917
When You Want a Little Lovin' Go Out and Get It   Hanley 1914
When You Want 'Em, You Can't Get 'Em (When You Got 'Em, You Don't Want 'Em)   Gershwin, George 1916
When You Want Someone Who Don't Want You Perhaps You'll Think of Me   Leslie 1926
When You Were a Baby and I Was the Kid Next Door   Leslie 1915
When You Were a Child   Gilbert 1914
When You Were a Freshie (And I Was a Sophomore)   Parish 1934
When You Were a Smile on Your Mother's Lips and a Twinkle in Your Daddy's Eye   Fain 1934; Kahal 1934
When You Were in Love with No One but Me (And I Was in Love with You)   Ahlert 1929; Turk 1929
When You Were the Blossom of Butter Cup Lane and I Was Your Little Boy Blue   Bryan 1931; Dubin 1931; Meyer 1931
When You Were the Blossom of Buttercup Land and I Was Your Little Boy Blue   Baer 1927; Bryan 1927; Gilbert 1927
When You Were the Girl on a Scooter and I Was a Boy on the Bike   Gordon 1933; Revel 1933
When You Wish Upon a Star   Washington 1940
When You Wore a Crown of Shamrocks   Sterling Date Unknown
When Your Ankle Wears the Ball and Chain   Herbert 1914; Smith, Harry B. 1914
When Your Birthday Rolls Around   Baer 1955

When Your Bluebird Flies Away   Von Tilzer 1923
When Your Boy Becomes a Man   Hammerstein 1931; Whiting 1931
When Your College Days Are Gone   Mercer 1937; Whiting 1937
When Your Dimples Turn to Wrinkles   Fisher 1910; Goetz 1910
When Your Door Closed Another Door Opened   Razaf 1925
When Your Fair Weather Friends Leave You Out in the Blue   Fisher 1928
When Your Hand First Touched Me   Freed, Arthur 1930
When Your Heart Is Too Young   Harburg 1961
When Your Heart's on Easy Street   Washington 1943
When Your Lips Are Close to Mine   Livingston, Jerry 1960
When Your Love Comes Your Way   Porter 1933
When Your Lover Says Goodbye   Lerner, Alan Jay 1969
When Your Man Is Coming Home   DePaul 1943; Raye 1943
When Your Sweetheart Comes Home   Wrubel 1948
When Your Troubles Have Started   Porter 1936
When You're a Long, Long Way from Home   Lewis 1914; Meyer 1914
When You're Alone   Revel 1942
When You're Away   Brown, A. Seymour 1912; Dietz 1935; Herbert 1914; Schwartz, Arthur 1935; Young, Joe 1912
When You're Away (inst.)   Warren 1938
When You're Broke   Jerome 1904; Schwartz, Jean 1904
When You're Crying on My Shoulder   Oakland 1950
When You're Dancing in Your Nightie on the Lawn   Goetz 1920
When You're Dancing the Waltz   Hart 1936; Rodgers 1936
When You're Down in Louisville (Call on Me)   Berlin 1915
When You're Dressed in Blue   Loesser Date Unknown
When You're Driving Through the Moonlight   Hammerstein 1957; Rodgers 1957
When You're Falling in Love with the Irish   Hart 1933; Rodgers 1933
When You're Far Away from New York Town   Dietz 1963; Schwartz, Arthur 1963
When You're Gettin' Along with Your Gal   Fain 1932; Kahal 1932
When You're Home   Donaldson 1926; Kahn 1926
When You're in Love   Arlen 1952; Blane 1953; Burke 1929; Caesar 1928; DePaul 1954; Dixon 1924; Donaldson 1926; Gorney 1924; Henderson 1924; Jerome 1905; Mercer 1954; Meyer 1928; Rose 1924; Schwartz, Arthur 1955; Schwartz, Jean 1905
When You're in Love with More than One   Stept 1927
When You're in Love With More than One, You're Not in Love at All   Bryan 1911
When You're in Love You'll Know   Kern 1916
When You're in Right with the Right Little Girl   Romberg 1919
When You're in the Arms of the One You Love   Edwards 1925; Johnson, Howard 1925
When You're in the Room   Hammerstein 1938; Oakland 1938
When You're in Town   Berlin 1911
When You're in Wrong with the Right Girl   Kahn 1910
When You're in Wrong with the Right Little Girl (The World's All Wrong to You)   Johnson, Howard 1928
When You're In, You're In Indiana   Jerome 1921; Schwartz, Jean 1921
When You're Lonesome, You're Lonesome That's All   Brown, Lew 1922
When You're Loved   Sherman 1978

When You're Married   Bryan 1912
When You're Mine, When I'm Yours   Norworth 1916
When You're Near   Coslow 1922
When You're Not at Your Best   Gershwin, George 1924
When You're on My Mind   Blane 1943
When You're on the Stage   Smith, Harry B. 1913
When You're Only Seventeen   Hammerstein 1922; Hanley 1922; Mitchell 1922
When You're Pretty and the World Is Fair   Herbert 1906
When You're Seeing Sweetie Home   Lewis 1929; Warren 1929; Young, Joe 1929
When You're Single   Gershwin, George 1927; Gershwin, Ira 1927
When You're Smiling (What a Smile Can Do)   DeSylva 1920; Kern 1920
When You're Starring for the Movies   Atteridge 1916; Romberg 1916
When You're Tired of Me, Just Let Me Down   Razaf 1924; Waller 1924
When You're Traveling   Atteridge 1913
When You're Watching the Parade   Caesar 1937
When You're with Somebody Else   Baer 1927; Gilbert 1927
When You've Been Mothered By a Mother   Jerome 1927
When You've Been to the Beach   Brooks 1959
When You've Got a Little Springtime in Your Heart   Woods 1935
When You've Had It All   Ellington 1968
When Za-za Does the Can-Can   Freed, Ralph 1938
When Ziegfeld's Follies Hit the Town   Cohan 1918
Whenever Bing Begins to Sing   Dubin 1934; Warren 1934
Whenever I Dream   Conrad 1926; Kahn 1926
Whenever I Dream of You   Sherman 1965
Whenever I Think of You   Woods 1935
Whenever I'm with You   Blane 1968; Martin 1968
Whenever Night Falls   Friml 1950; Harbach 1950
Whenever You Are Near   Stept 1926
Whenever You Walk Along the Road at Night   Caesar 1940
When's Your Birthday Baby   Merrill 1958
Where   Livingston, Jerry 1958; McHugh 1955; Porter 1936; Sondheim 1966
Where a Water Wheel Keeps Turning On   Stept 1942
Where Am I?   Dubin 1935; Warren 1935
Where Am I Going?   Coleman 1966; Fields 1966
Where Am I Without You   DePaul 1948; Raye 1948
Where Am I Without You (Baby)   DePaul 1943; Raye 1943
Where Are the Faces?   Sherman 1995
Where Are the Girls   Silver 1926
Where Are the Men?   Porter 1934
Where Are the Plays of Yesterday   Buck 1920
Where Are the White Birds Flying   Livingston, Jerry 1956
Where Are They Now   Howard, Joseph E. 1909
Where Are You?   Adamson 1937; Bacharach 1977; Gorney 1932; Harburg 1932; Kahn 1954; McHugh 1937; Pollack 1929; Warren 1941
Where Are You, Blue Eyes   Drake 1949
Where Are You Dream Girl?   Davis 1929; Motzan 1929
Where Are You Girl of My Dreams   Rose 1925
Where Are You Little Boy Blue   Edwards 1938
Where Are You Tonight?   Caesar 1924; Conrad 1924
Where Can He Be?   Dietz 1931; Schwartz, Arthur 1931
Where Can I Find a Cherry   Razaf 1934
Where Can I Go (To Find that Gallop Man)   Clare 1982
Where Can I Go Without You   Young, Victor 1954
Where Can I Meet You Next Summer   Gilbert 1912

Where Can I Run from You   Fields 1951; Schwartz, Arthur 1951
Where Can that Somebody Be   Mills 1923
Where Can the Baby Be?   Hart 1928; Rodgers 1928
Where Can You Be   Evans 1944; Livingston, Jay 1944
Where Can You Take a Girl   Bacharach 1968; David, Hal 1968
Where Did Ev'ryone Go?   David, Mack 1963; Van Heusen 1963
Where Did He Go   Washington 1953
Where Did I Go Wrong   Webster 1972
Where Did Robinson Crusoe Go with Friday on Saturday Night   Lewis 1916; Meyer 1916; Young, Joe 1916
Where Did the Good Times Go?   Sherman 1974
Where Did the Night Go?   Rome 1952
Where Did the Time Go   Bacharach 1980
Where Did To-Day Go   Oakland 1970
Where Did You Get that Girl   Kalmar 1913
Where Did You Get that Pair of Big Bright Eyes   Motzan 1932
Where Did You Get Those Irish Eyes?   Norworth 1917
Where Did You Learn to Dance   Gordon 1953; Myrow 1953
Where Did You Learn to Love   Cahn 1946; Styne 1946
Where Do I Belong?   Lerner, Alan Jay 1948; Sondheim Date Unknown; Weill 1948
Where Do I Go from Here (Sandy's Theme)   Evans 1973; Livingston, Jay 1973
Where Do I Go from You?   Bullock 1940; Fields 1952; Schwartz, Arthur 1952; Wrubel 1940
Where Do Lonely People Go   Leigh 1953
Where Do They Come From   Goetz 1918
Where Do They Come From (And Where Do They Go)   Coslow 1934; Johnston 1934
Where Do They Get Those Guys?   Atteridge 1918; Bryan 1918; Romberg 1918; Yellen 1918
Where Do They Go   Drake 1954
Where Do We Dream from Here   Styne 1941
Where Do We Go from Here?   Gershwin, Ira 1945; Johnson, Howard 1917; Porter 1944; Russell 1957; Webster 1946; Weill 1945
Where Do We Go from Here Bill   Snyder 1909
Where Do You Catch the Bus for Tomorrow   Mancini 1981
Where Do You Go When You Arrive   Duke 1959
Where Do You Go When You're on Top?   Duke 1959
Where Do You Keep Your Heart?   Ahlert 1940
Where Do You Start?   Bergman 1988
Where Do You Think You're Going   Howard, Bart 1954
Where Do You Travel?   Blane 1941
Where Do You Work-a John? (Push-a Push-a Push)   Warren 1926
Where Does a Dream Go to Die   Livingston, Jerry 1960
Where Does Love Begin (And Where Does Friendship End)   Cahn 1944; Styne 1944
Where Does Love Go?   Merrill 1978
Where E'er I Go   Smith, Robert B. 1906
Where Else but Here?   Heyman 1939; Romberg 1939
Where Else but the U.S.A.   Cahn 1960; Van Heusen 1960
Where Ever You Go   Warren Date Unknown
Where First?   Styne 1985
Where Has My Lima Bean?   Brown, Lew 1925
Where Has the Rainbow Gone?   Fain 1978; Harburg 1978
Where Have I Heard that Melody   Coslow 1933; Johnston 1933
Where Have I Heard that Song Before?   Harburg 1961

Where Have I Seen Your Face Before   Harburg 1980; Lane 1980

Where Have Those Old Timers Gone   Johnson, Howard 1924

Where Have We Met Before?   Duke 1932; Harburg 1932; Parish 1938

Where Have You Been?   Porter 1930

Where Have You Been All My Life   Kahn 1922; Magidson 1936; Oakland 1936; Schwartz, Jean 1923

Where Have You Been Hiding All These Years   Mitchell 1918

Where Have You Been Hiding Dear   Alter 1929

Where Have You Been, You Beautiful Thing?   Gorney 1934

Where I Ain't Been Before   Brown, Nacio Herb 1937; Freed, Arthur 1937; Freed, Ralph 1937; Lane 1937

Where in the World   Comden and Green 1960; Fain 1958; Gordon 1938; Lawrence 1958; Revel 1938; Styne 1960; Webster 1972

Where in the World Could I Ever Find Another You   Freed, Ralph 1952

Where in the World Is the Moon To-Night   Fain 1931; Young, Joe 1931

Where Is Bundy?   Duke 1946

Where Is Central Park?   Burke 1938; Monaco 1938

Where Is Cinderella?   Hammerstein 1957; Rodgers 1957

Where Is Dis Road A-Leadin' Me To?   Arlen 1941; Koehler 1941

Where Is It Written   Bergman 1983

Where Is My Boy   Caesar 1923; Conrad 1923

Where Is My Heart   Rainger 1936; Robin 1936

Where Is My Little Old New York?   Berlin 1924

Where Is My Love   Rainger 1935; Robin 1935; Turk 1924

Where Is My Meyer, Where's Himalaya (Was Nacht Der Maler An Himalaya)   Gilbert 1927

Where Is My Old Girl Tonight   Dixon 1925; Rose 1925; Woods 1925

Where Is My Old Pal Tonight   Conrad 1925

Where Is My Rainbow   Edwards 1936

Where Is My Rose of Waikiki   Egan 1925; Whiting 1925

Where Is My Soldier Boy?   Rome 1973

Where Is My Son?   Rodgers 1976

Where Is My Wandering Boy Tonight?   Buck 1914

Where Is She?   DeSylva 1923; Gershwin, George 1923

Where Is She Now   Sterling 1913; Von Tilzer 1913

Where Is That Old Girl of Mine   Kahn 1924

Where Is That Old Sweetheart of Mine?   Brown, Lew 1919

Where Is That Someone for Me   Davis 1926; Young, Victor 1955

Where Is the Boss   De Lange 1945; Myrow 1945

Where Is the Dear Man   Robison 1965

Where Is the Girl I Left Behind   Cohan 1919

Where Is the Handy Man   Johnson, James P. 1947

Where Is the Language to Tell?   Atteridge 1917; Romberg 1917

Where Is the Life That Late I Led?   Porter 1948

Where Is the Man I Married?   Martin 1964

Where Is the Man of My Dreams?   DeSylva 1922; Goetz 1922

Where Is the Right Prayer for Me?   Lane Date Unknown

Where Is the Rooster (Meow-Wa, Ba Ba Ko-Goo-Ta)   Mills 1955

Where Is the Song of Songs for Me?   Berlin 1928

Where Is the Sunshine That's Supposed to Follow the Rain   Koehler 1926

Where Is Your Girl, Where Is My Girl   Howard, Joseph E. 1923

Where Is Your Heart To-Night   Bryan 1929

Where Jesus Is   Robison 1956

Where Knowledge Ends (Trust Me)   Bacharach 1973; David, Hal 1973

Where Love Grows   Smith, Harry B. 1928

Where Love Has Gone   Cahn 1964; Van Heusen 1964

Where Love Is King   Leslie 1911

Where Love Is Waiting   Smith, Robert B. 1914

Where My Caravan Rests   Atteridge 1915; Carroll 1915; Romberg 1915

Where, Oh Where?   Porter 1950

Where, Oh Where Has Johnny Gone   Friml 1911

Where, Oh Where (Is the Groom?)   Gordon 1943; Warren 1943

Where Oh Where Were You   Coots 1932; Young, Joe 1932

Where on Earth   Sigman 1959; Young, Victor 1959

Where or When   Hart 1937; Rodgers 1937

Where Rainbows End   Ahlert 1950

Where Shall We Go for Our Honeymoon   Smith, Harry B. 1914

Where the Bamboo Babies Grow   Brown, Lew 1923; Donaldson 1922

Where the Black-Eyed Susans Grow   Whiting 1917

Where the Blue of the Night Meets the Gold of the Day   Ahlert 1931; Turk 1931

Where the Coosa River Flows   Johnson, Howard 1927

Where the Dew Drops Kiss the Morning   Waller 1932

Where the Dog Sits on the Tucker Box Five Miles from Gundagei   Gilbert 1938

Where the Dreamy Wabash Flows   Baer 1924; Friend 1924

Where the Eidelweiss Is Blooming   Goetz 1912

Where the 'Ell Is 'Ome?   Sherman 1995

Where the Fairest Flowers Blooming   Herbert 1908

Where the Fairest Flow'rs Are Blooming   Herbert 1903; Smith, Harry B. 1903

Where the Flag Is Waving   Smith, Harry B. 1905

Where the Four Leaf Clovers Grow   Egan 1925; Parish 1931; Whiting 1925

Where the Four Winds Blow   Webster 1961

Where the Ganges Flow   Brown, A. Seymour 1923

Where the Heck is Mulligan?   Conrad 1925; Rose 1925

Where the Honeymoon Alone Can See   Friml 1922; Harbach 1922

Where the Honeysuckle Grows   Waller 1953

Where the Hot Wind Blows   McHugh 1960

Where the Huckleberries Grow   Bryan 1925

Where the Hudson Meets the Sea   Silver 1944

Where the Hudson River Flows   Edwards 1925; Hart 1925; Rodgers 1925

Where the Jack O'Lanterns Glow   Parish 1920

Where the Lazy Daisies Grow   Friend 1924

Where the Lazy River Goes By   Adamson 1936; McHugh 1936

Where the Lilies of the Valley Grow   Kahn 1931

Where the Little Bridge Crosses the Stream   Hanley 1930

Where the Macaroni Grows   Fisher 1910

Where the Mississippi Flows   Cobb 1901; Edwards 1901

Where the Morning Glories Grow   Egan 1917; Kahn 1917; Whiting 1917

Where the Morning Glories Twine Around the Door   Sterling 1904; Von Tilzer 1904

Where the Mountains Reach the Moon   Bryan 1936

Where the Mountains Touch the Sky   Cahn 1933

Where the Red, Red, Roses Grow   Jerome 1913; Schwartz, Jean 1913

Where the River Meets the Range   Styne 1941

Where the Shy Little Violets Grow   Kahn 1928; Warren 1928

Where the Southern Roses Grow   Norworth 1916

Where the Sun God Walks   Dietz 1944; Duke 1944

Where the Sweet Forget-Me-Nots Remember   Dixon 1929; Warren 1929

Where the Sweet Magnolias Bloom   Sterling 1899; Von Tilzer 1899

Where the Sweet, Sweet Cactus Grows   Dubin 1935; Warren 1935

Where the Trade Winds Blow   Mills 1929

Where the Turf Meets the Surf   Burke 1939; Monaco 1939

Where the Water Lillies Grow   Egan 1919; Kahn 1919; Whiting 1919

Where the Wild, Wild Flowers Grow   Dixon 1927; Woods 1927

Where There Is Love   Fields 1968

Where There Is Love There Is Hope   Fields 1969

Where There's a Heartache there Must Be a Heart   Bacharach 1969; David, Hal 1969

Where There's a Will, There's a Way   Dubin 1921

Where There's Love There's a Way   David, Hal 1957

Where There's Smoke — There's Fire   Livingston, Jerry 1934

Where There's Smoke There's Fire   Spina 1952

Where To, My Love   David, Hal 1951

Where Walks My True Love   Cahn 1956

Where Was I   Cahn 1966; Dubin 1939; Van Heusen 1966

Where Was I When the Parade Went By   David, Mack 1979

Where Was Moses when the Lights Went Out   Leslie 1913

Where We Came From   Rodgers 1979

Where Were You   David, Hal 1991; Dubin 1921; Herbert 1920; Heyman 1929; Sigman 1971; Smith, Robert B. 1920; Strouse 1991

Where Were You — Where Was I?   Cohan 1928

Where Were You Last Night   Akst 1939; Bryan 1909; Davis 1939; Dubin 1931; Woods 1931

Where Were You on the Night of June the Third   Stept 1935

Where Will I Be   Coots 1928

Where Will the Dimple Be   Hoffman 1955; Merrill 1955

Where Would I Be If I Never Met You and You Never Met Me   Gilbert 1925

Where Would I Go   Bacharach 1968; David, Hal 1968

Where Would You Be?   Styne 1985

Where Would You Get Your Coat?   Porter 1929

Where Ya Goin', What's Your Hurry, Where's the Fire   Hoffman 1949

(With You) Where You Are   Bloom 1929; Cahn 1952; Dietz 1963; Dixon 1929; Gordon 1941; Lane Date Unknown; Leigh 1965, 1967; Schwartz, Arthur 1963; Warren 1941

Where You Go I Go   Gershwin, George 1932; Gershwin, Ira 1932

Where You Lead   Brennan 1930; Friml 1930

Where Your Ears Burning?   Revel 1934

(I Love to Be 'Neath the Old Apple Tree) Where Your Name Is Carved with Mine   Brown, Lew 1928; DeSylva 1928; Henderson 1928

Whereas   Merrill 1967

Where'd dat Money Go   Robison 1944

Where'd You Get Those Eyes   Donaldson 1926

Where'er in Thick of Fight   Herbert 1898; Smith, Harry B. 1898

Where-Is-My-Daddy-Now Blues   Motzan 1920; Yellen 1920

Wherer Is the Man of My Dreams?   Gershwin, George 1922

Where're You Going? (I'm Going to Join That Minstrel Band)   Brown, Lew 1911

Where's Charley   Loesser 1948

Where's Louie?   Porter 1939

Where's My Happy Ending?   Adamson 1931; Gordon 1931; Revel 1931

Where's My Wife?   Lerner, Alan Jay 1945; Loewe 1945

Where's That Rainbow?   Hart 1926; Rodgers 1926

Where's the Baby for Me   Baer 1924; Friend 1924

Where's the Boy for Me?   Smith, Harry B. 1915

Where's the Boy? Here's the Girl!   Gershwin, George 1928; Gershwin, Ira 1928

Where's the Girl?   Kahn 1938; Romberg 1938

Where's the Girl for Me   Kern 1915, 1919; Smith, Harry B. 1915, 1919

Where's the Little Darlin'   Brooks 1950

Where's the Mate for Me?   Hammerstein 1927; Kern 1927

Where's the Music Coming From?   Styne 1978

Where's the Mustard   Spina 1977

Where's the Third One   Willson 1956

Wherever There's Music and Beautiful Girls   Carroll 1918

Wherever they Fly the Flag of Old England   Porter 1946

Wherever You Are   Hanley 1927; Kalmar 1930; Revel 1941; Ruby 1930

Wherever You Are I'll Come to You   Kahn 1932

Whether It Rains, Whether It Shines   Von Tilzer 1927

Which   Leigh 1952; Porter 1928, 1929

Which Do You Prefer?   Coslow 1924

Which Hazel?   Silver 1921

Which Is Which   Clare 1935

Which Is Which and Who Is Who   Brown, Nacio Herb 1927

Which Little Boy Wants to Play with Me   Edwards 1936

Which One   Washington 1954

Which Shall I Choose   Atteridge 1912

Which Way?   Adams 1962; Strouse 1962

Which Way Is Home   Rome 1964

Which Way Is Home? (Ie Wa Doko)   Rome 1969

Whichway'd They Go   Mercer 1949

Whiddle-Dee Wee and Whaddle-Dee Woo   Johnson, J. Rosamond 1946

While Canoeing Along with You   Lawrence 1931

While Dancing (I Know, I Know, I Know) (Kookie's Love Song)   David, Mack 1959

While I Lie Here Dreaming   Brooks 1957

While I'm Here   Drake 1999

While I'm Swinging   Coots 1923

While Miami Dreams   Egan 1922; Whiting 1922

While Others Are Building Castles in the Air I'll Build a Cottage for You   Fisher 1919

While Strolling Thru the Park One Day   Johnson, Howard 1939

While the Band Played an American Rag   Berlin 1915

While the Big Old World Rolls Round   Herbert 1911

While the City Sleeps   Adams 1964; DeSylva 1920; Strouse 1964

While the City Sleeps (inst.)   Revel 1957

While the Men Are All Drinking   Blane 1948; Warren 1948

While the Moon Shines Bright   Howard, Joseph E. 1902

While the Music Plays On   Mills 1939

While the Night Is Young   Rainger 1934, 1935; Robin 1935; Whiting 1934, 1935

While the Others Are Dancing   Fain 1928; Kahal 1928

While the Years Roll By   Lewis 1922; Young, Joe 1922

While There's Life There's Hope, You Put Hope in This Heart of Mine   Clarke 1921; Monaco 1921

While They Were Dancing Around   Monaco 1913
While We Dance the Waltz of Spain   Johnson, Howard 1935
While We Tell Them About It All (Opening Act II)   Hammerstein 1927; Kern 1927
While We Waltz   Schwartz, Jean 1930
While We're in the Mood   Adamson 1939
While We're Sitting in the Dark   Stept 1932
While We're Waiting for the Baby   Gershwin, George 1931; Gershwin, Ira 1931
While You Are Young   Arlen 1931; Yellen 1931
While You're Away   Gilbert 1918
While You're Crying in My Face, You Laugh Behind My Back   Fisher 1931
While You're Gone   Akst 1923; Davis 1923
Whiling My Time Away   Eliscu 1932
Whimsically (inst.)   Kern 1957
Whip Dance, The   Cohan 1923
Whip Hand, The   Atteridge 1921
Whip of the Wind, The   Livingston, Jerry 1960
Whipoorwill in the Weeping Willow Tree, The   Arlen 1936; Harburg 1936
Whippoorwill   Arlen 1957; Bryan 1912; DeSylva 1919; Friml 1925; Harburg 1957; Kern 1919, 1920; Raye 1958; Smith, Harry B. 1925
Whippoorwill Bill   Hoffman 1945; Livingston, Jerry 1945
Whippoorwill in a Willow Tree, A   Ahlert 1937; Lewis 1937; Young, Joe 1937
Whippoorwill Warble Away   Coots 1933; Dixon 1933
Whippoorwill's a Singin'   Evans 1947; Livingston, Jay 1947; Young, Victor 1947
Whirl of the Opera, The   Atteridge 1914
Whirl of the World, The   Atteridge 1914
Whirled Into Happiness   Atteridge 1925
Whiskers   Johnson, James P. 1927
Whisper   David, Mack 1942, 1953; Donaldson 1953
Whisper a Word of Love (Meditation de Thais)   Rome 1948
Whisper Confidentially   Heyman 1940
Whisper in the Moonlight   Fields 1932; McHugh 1932
Whisper in the Night   Caesar 1944
Whisper It   Berlin 1963
Whisper on the Wind   Coleman 1972; Fields 1972
Whisper Song, The   Friend 1927; Pollack 1927
Whisper Sweet   Johnson, James P. 1934
Whisper Sweet and Whisper Low   Bryan 1927
Whisper Sweet Nothing's to Me   Baer 1925; Kahn 1925
Whisper That You Love Me Only   Parish 1935
Whisper to Me   Romberg 1924
Whisper to the Rose   Smith, Harry B. 1924; Snyder 1924
Whisper to the Whisp'ring Pines   Hanley 1930, 1931
Whisper Waltz, The   Adamson 1951; McHugh 1951; Webster 1931
Whisper You Love Me   Friend 1925; Turk 1925
Whisper You Love Me and Make My Dreams Come True   Friend 1930; Monaco 1930
Whispering Campaign   Bacharach 1956; Heyman 1956
Whispering Grass (Don't Tell the Trees)   Fisher 1940
Whispering Grass (inst.)   Warren Date Unknown
Whispering Hope   Johnson, Howard 1939
Whispering Pine   Lawrence 1944
Whispering Pines of Nevada, The   Leslie 1927
Whispering Through the Pines   Freed, Arthur 1930
Whispering Trees   Coots 1926
Whispering Waters   David, Mack 1949; Hoffman 1948; Livingston, Jay 1948; Livingston, Jerry 1948
Whispers   Kahal 1926

Whispers in the Dark   Robin 1936
Whispers in the Night   Sigman 1974
Whispers in the Wind   Lawrence 1958
Whisper-Sh   Bryan 1926
Whist-a-lin' Dixie   Merrill 1955
Whistle   Kalmar 1926; Ruby 1926; Young, Victor 1934
Whistle a Song   Howard, Joseph E. 1920
Whistle and Blow Your Blues Away   Young, Joe 1932
Whistle and I'll Be There   Whiting 1928
Whistle and I'll Come to Meet You   Atteridge 1920
Whistle and I'll Wait for You   Meyer 1908
Whistle and Walk Away   Fain 1951; Gordon 1951
Whistle As You Walk Out   Smith, Robert B. 1907
Whistle in the Rain   Coots 1924
Whistle It   Bryan 1912; Clarke 1912; Herbert 1906; Schwartz, Jean 1912
Whistle Stop   Martin 1952
Whistle the Blues (Pretty! Pretty! Blues!)   Spina 1956
Whistle When You Walk Out   Smith, Harry B. 1906
Whistle when You're Lonely   Kern 1910
Whistle While You Work   Burke 1934; Spina 1934
Whistle While You Work, Boys   Smith, Harry B. 1930
Whistle'n Jim   Coots 1953
Whistler's Ditties (inst.)   Loesser 1940
Whistler's Holiday, The (inst.)   Warren 1969
Whistles 'n' Trestles 'n' Trains   Merrill 1949
Whistles of the Hills, The   Merrill 1953
Whistlin' Cowboy, The   Webster 1933
Whistlin' Dixie   Sherman 1959
Whistlin' Kind of Tune, A   Adamson 1957
Whistlin' Tune, A   David, Hal 1962
Whistlin' Wind, The   Merrill 1950
Whistling   Mitchell 1921; Pollack 1921
Whistling at Dawn (inst.)   Revel 1957
Whistling at the Boys   Sherman 1961
Whistling Away the Dark   Mancini 1970; Mercer 1970
Whistling Boy, The   Fields 1937; Kern 1937
Whistling Cowboy Joe   Atteridge 1913
Whistling Dan   Jerome 1903; Kern 1915; Schwartz, Jean 1903; Smith, Harry B. 1915
Whistling for a Kiss   Harburg 1932; Mercer 1932
Whistling in the Dark   Harburg 1929
Whistling in the Light   Rainger 1943; Robin 1943
Whistling in Wyoming   Davis 1944
Whistling Kettle and a Dancing Cat, A   Merrill 1952
Whistling Rag   Berlin 1911
Whistling Song, The   Leslie 1950; Schwartz, Jean 1950
Whistling Train, The   Eliscu 1952
Whistling Waltz, The   Woods 1935
Whistling Yankee Girl, The   Smith, Harry B. 1906
White and Gold Ballet   Young, Victor 1955
White Bird and the Sycamore, The   Robison 1964
White Blossoms of Tah-ni   Loesser 1941
White Buffalo, The   Bergman 1955
White Camelias   Washington 1946
White Christmas   Berlin 1942
White Clouds   Blake 1938
White Flags   Styne 1970
White Folks Calls It Chantecleer, but It's Just Plain Chicken to Me   Sterling 1910
White Heat   Dietz 1931; Schwartz, Arthur 1931
White Heather, The   Coots 1919
White Horse Inn, The   Caesar 1936
White House in Washington and the White House in the Lane, The   Bryan 1922; Howard, Joseph E. 1922

White House Is the Lighthouse of the World, The   Bryan 1918; Caesar 1918

White House of Our Own, A   Freed, Arthur 1932

White Keys and the Black Keys, The   Eliscu 1943; Gorney 1943

White Lies and Red Roses   Magidson 1939; Wrubel 1939

White Light Alley   Goetz 1911

White Lights   Coots 1927; Dubin 1927

White Lilacs   Brennan 1928

White Sails   Caesar 1936

White Shadowland   Johnson, Howard 1935

White Shadows of the Moon   Loesser 1940

White, the Young at Heart (inst.)   Young, Victor 1956

White Virgin of the Nile, The   Cahn 1958; Warren 1958

White Wash Girl   Jerome 1908; Schwartz, Jean 1908

White Way Blues   Coslow Date Unknown; Gordon 1929

White Were the Lilacs   Sigman 1959

White Wings   Edwards 1929; Johnson, Howard 1929

White Wings Carry Me Home   Johnson, Howard 1927; Silver 1927; Sterling 1927

White World of Winter, The   Carmichael 1965; Parish 1965

Whiteman Stomp   Waller 1928

Whittlin' My Wood   Dubin 1934, 1935; Warren 1934, 1935

Whizzin' Away Along de Track   Hammerstein 1943

Who   Berlin 1924; Hammerstein 1925; Harbach 1925; Kern 1925

Who Am I?   Adams 1978; Bullock 1940; Gordon 1936; Martin 1951; Mitchell 1936; Revel 1936; Smith, Harry B. 1926; Stept 1936; Strouse 1978; Styne 1940; Weill 1943

Who Am I (That You Should Care for Me)?   Kahn 1928; Youmans 1928

Who Am I to Love You?   Adamson 1972

Who Am I to Say No   Howard, Bart 1965

Who Are the British   Cahn 1943; Styne 1943

Who Are These People?   Strouse 1982

Who Are They to Say   Cahn 1958

Who Are We   David, Hal 1956; Howard, Bart 1984; Livingston, Jerry 1955; Webster 1955

Who Are We to Say (Obey Your Heart)   Kahn 1938; Romberg 1938

Who Are We Today   Romberg 1938

Who Are You?   Hart 1940; Leigh 1954; Rodgers 1940

Who Are You Now?   Merrill 1964; Styne 1964

Who Are You (To Say Adieu)?   Bryan 1931; Pollack 1931

Who Are You with Tonight?   Williams 1910

Who Ate Napoleons with Josephine when Bonaparte Was Away   Bryan 1920; Goetz 1920

Who Believes in Santa Claus?   Brooks 1948

Who Believes You   Howard, Bart 1984

Who, Besides Me, Sits Beside You   Burke 1932

Who Blew Out the Flame   Fain 1938; Parish 1938

Who but You?   Akst 1934; Brown, Nacio Herb 1947; De Lange 1948; Dixon 1935; Heyman 1947; Porter 1936; Turk 1934; Wrubel 1935

Who Calls You Baby Now   Davis 1925

Who Can Explain   Silver 1956

Who Can Forget a First Love   Spina 1969

Who Can Say   Russell 1961

Who Can Tell?   Cahn 1952; Duke 1952

Who Can Tell (Not I)   Brooks 1948

Who Can Tell Us Why   Cahn 1976

Who Can? You Can!   Dietz 1961; Schwartz, Arthur 1961

Who Cares?   Ager 1921; Gershwin, George 1931; Gershwin, Ira 1931; Kern 1917; Smith, Harry B. 1914, 1917, 1927; Yellen 1921

Who Cares — Who Cares   Heyman 1949

Who Cares About Tomorrow?   Dubin 1933; Warren 1933

Who Cares for a Name   Smith, Harry B. 1923

Who Cares What You Have Been   Gilbert 1929

Who Committed the Murder?   Heyman 1933

Who Could Be Blue?   Sondheim 1971

Who Could Be More Wonderful Than You   Davis 1926; Silver 1926

Who Could Eat Now   Rome 1952

Who Could Forget You   Loesser 1946

Who Could Help but Fall in Love with You   McHugh 1928

Who Could Love Me   David, Hal 1966

Who Could Say No?   Arlen 1929; Koehler 1929

Who Dat Up Dere?   Russell 1945

Who Dealt?   Weill 1943

Who Did? I Did — Yes, I Did   Cahn 1943; Styne 1943

Who Did It   Wrubel 1952

Who Did It — You Did It   Magidson 1938, 1952; Wrubel 1938

Who Did You Think Of   Cahn 1959; Van Heusen 1959

Who Discovered Dixie   Silver 1919

Who Do We Thank   Adams 1960; Strouse 1960

Who Do You Have to Know   Washington 1952

Who Do You Love   Buck 1918; Hanley 1918; Johnson, J. Rosamond 1907

Who Do You Love, Baby   Davis 1932

Who Do You Love, I Hope?   Berlin 1946

Who Do You Love, I Hope It's Me   Friend 1924

Who Do You Love, My Baby   Johnson, J. Rosamond 1914

Who Do You Say Good Evening to when You Say Good Night to Me   Caesar 1934

Who Do You Suppose Went and Married My Sister   Norworth 1910

Who Do You Think I Saw Last Night   Friend 1938

Who Do You Think I'm Doing It For   Silver 1926

Who Do You Think Is Thinking of You   Dixon 1929; Woods 1929

Who Do You Think We Are?   Gorney 1925

Who Do You Think You Are   Heyman 1933

Who Do You Think You're Fooling with that Million Dollar Talk   Lewis 1918; Snyder 1918; Young, Joe 1918

Who Does My Sweetie Love   Mills 1926

Who Done It?   Bullock 1950; Hoffman 1954; Lawrence 1938

Who Dreamed You Up?   Bullock 1940; Wrubel 1940

Who Else   Davis 1957

Who Else but God   Warren 1957

Who Else Can I Tell It but You   Clare 1954

Who Ever Heard of an Angel?   Freed, Ralph 1962

Who Fills the Bill   Bergman 1964

Who Forgets   Heyman 1978

Who Forgot Who   Cahn 1962

Who Gave You Permission   Bergman 1978

Who Gets the Girl (Who Gets the Guy)   Bacharach 1970; David, Hal 1970

Who Gives a Sou   Martin 1951

Who Hit You with a Horseshoe   Leslie 1928

Who Is Gonna Love Me   Bacharach 1968; David, Hal 1968

Who Is Hannah?   Merrill 1990

Who Is It?   Davis 1934; Hanley 1934

Who Is Mr. Big?   Comden and Green 1960; Styne 1960

Who Is Samuel Cooper?   Lerner, Alan Jay 1948; Weill 1948

Who Is She?   Ellington 1962; Mills 1962

Who Is Sylvia?   Blane 1964; Johnson, Howard 1939; Martin 1964

Who Is the Beau of the Belle of New York   Gordon 1940

Who Is the Bravest?   Styne 1953

Who Is the Lucky Girl to Be?   Gershwin, George 1931; Gershwin, Ira 1931

Who Is the One That You're Fooling Now   Lewis 1924; Young, Joe 1924

Who Is the Who   Friend 1927

Who Is There Among Us Who Knows?   Lane 1970; Lerner, Alan Jay 1963, 1970

Who Killed 'Er? Who Killed the Black Widder?   Carmichael 1947

Who Killed Maggie?   Adamson 1938; McHugh 1938

Who Killed Vaudeville   Fain 1941, 1945; Yellen 1941, 1945

Who Killed Who   Oakland 1931

Who Knows   Bergman 1957; Brennan 1914; DePaul 1944; Dixon 1927; Lawrence 1937; Porter 1937; Raye 1944; Revel 1942; Rome 1962; Woods 1927

Who Knows the Answers   Cahn 1975

Who Knows What Might Have Been   Comden and Green 1961; Styne 1961

Who Knows Why April Dances   Webster 1945

Who Loves You   Coots 1936; Davis 1936

Who Loves You as I Do   Caesar 1926

Who Loves You Like I Do   Merrill 1955

Who Loves You Now   Johnson, James P. 1936

Who Made Bluebeard Blue?   Razaf 1934

Who Made Little Boy Blue? (inst.)   Kern 1934

Who Me, I'm not the Man   Snyder 1907

Who Might You Do?   Herbert 1895; Smith, Harry B. 1895

Who Minds 'bout Me   Bullock 1936

Who Misses Who?   Ager 1939; David, Mack 1949; Livingston, Jerry 1949

Who Needed You   Leigh 1977

Who Needs a Woman?   Harburg 1961

Who Needs an Opening Song   Oakland 1955

Who Needs Another Song about New York?   Drake 1994

Who Needs Her?   Merrill 1966

Who Needs Him?   Sondheim 1959; Styne 1959

Who Needs It   Brooks 1960; Cahn 1952; Duke 1952

Who Needs What Moonlight   Willson 1952

Who Needs Who?   Cahn 1966

Who Needs You   Styne 1970

Who Paid the Rent for Mrs. Rip Van Winkle (When Rip Van Winkle Went Away)   Bryan 1914; Fisher 1914

Who Played Poker with Pocahontas when John Smith went Away   Ahlert 1919; Lewis 1919; Young, Joe 1919

Who Put that Moon in the Sky?   Kalmar 1937; Ruby 1937

Who Put the B on Maloney and Made Baloney Out of Him   Sterling 1928

Who Said Dixie   Sterling 1918

Who Said Dreams Don't Come True   Akst 1944; Davis 1944

Who Said Gay Paree?   Porter 1953

Who Said I Said I Don't Love You   Coots 1946; Lewis 1946

Who Said I Was a Bum?   Johnson, Howard 1932

Who Said that Dreams Don't Come True   Fields 1934; McHugh 1934

Who Said There Ain't No Santa Claus?   Fain 1951; Harburg 1951

Who Says a Coon Can't Love   Cohan 1899

Who Says Crime Doesn't Pay?   Lawrence 1948

Who Says I Wronged Thee   Spina 1955

Who Says We Can't Be Friends?   Strouse Date Unknown

Who Says You Always Have to Be Happy?   Adams 1978; Strouse 1978

Who Should Come Along but You   Parish 1941

Who Sir, Me Sir?   Evans 1953; Livingston, Jay 1953

Who Started the Rhumba? (Who Made the Rhumba)   Duke 1941

Who Stole My Leg   Styne 1985

Who Stole the Jam?   Bullock 1938, 1950; Spina 1938, 1950

Who Taught Her Everything   Merrill 1964; Styne 1964

Who Taught You How to Kiss Like That   Adamson 1959; McHugh 1959

Who Threw the Whiskey in the Well   De Lange 1941

Who Told You   Kahn 1925; Lewis 1948

Who Took Me Home Last Night   Adamson 1943; Styne 1943

Who Walked Out when I Walked In?   Lewis 1948

Who Walks in When I Walk Out   Freed, Ralph 1933; Hoffman 1933

Who Wants a Baby   Yellen 1919

Who Wants a Girl Like Me   Robin 1930

Who Wants Love   Caesar 1958; Kahn 1937

Who Wants them Tall, Dark and Handsome   Yellen 1947

Who Wants to Be a Millionaire?   Porter 1956

Who Wants to Fall in Love   Howard, Bart 1953

Who Wants to Love Spanish Ladies?   Hammerstein 1928; Youmans 1928

Who Wants to Meet Me After School Lets Out   Cobb 1912; Edwards 1912

Who Was Chasing Paul Revere?   DeSylva 1925; Hanley 1925

Who Was Made for Who   Coslow 1932

Who Was that Lady   Cahn 1960; Van Heusen 1960

Who Was That Lady I Saw You With?   Bergman 1958

Who Was the First to Make Love?   Brown, Lew 1945; Henderson 1945

Who Was the Fool   Davis 1981

Who Was the Kiddo that Captain Kidd Was Saving His Treasure For?   Johnson, Howard Date Unknown

Who? Where? When?   Evans 1946; Livingston, Jay 1946

Who, Who, Who Do You Think Of   Cahn 1956; Van Heusen 1956

Who, Who, Who, Hoolaman   Jerome 1903; Schwartz, Jean 1903

Who Will Be the First One?   Sherman 1959

Who Will I Call Mamma When She's Gone   Hanley 1915

Who Will It Be   Johnson, Howard 1923; Pollack 1923

Who Will It Be After Me?   Hoffman 1957

Who Will It Be When the Time Comes?   Arlen 1952; Blane 1953

Who Will Walk with Me?   Harburg 1971

Who Will Want Me   Baer 1931

Who Would Believe   Revel 1929

Who Would Ever Dream?   Adamson 1939; Duke 1939

Who Would Have Dreamed   Porter 1940

Who Would Have Thought   Berlin 1962

Who Would Refuse?   Hammerstein 1951; Rodgers 1951

Who Wouldn't   Donaldson 1926; Kahn 1926

Who Wouldn't Be Blue   Davis 1928

Who Wouldn't Be Thrilled   Coots 1936; Davis 1936

Who Wouldn't Love You   Davis 1925

Who Writes the Plot for Your Dreams?   Hanley 1939

Whoa, Emma   Fields 1951; Warren 1951

Whoa, Ida How, Whoa   Sterling 1905; Von Tilzer 1905

Whoa January You're Going to Be Worse than July   Sterling 1919; Von Tilzer 1919

Whoa Pagliacci   Young, Joe 1923

Whoa Whoopee — Whoa Whippee (Yippy-I-O-I-Ay)   Akst 1937; Clare 1937

Whoa! Ya Got Me   Friend 1936

Who'd Be Blue   Woods 1926
Who'd Believe   Baer 1931; Davis 1931
Who'd Believe You're in Love with Me   Davis 1932
Whodunit?   Carmichael 1939; Loesser 1939
Whoever You Are   Sherman 1967
Whoever You Are, I Love You   Bacharach 1968; David, Hal 1968
Whoever You Are (Whoever You May Be)   Hanley 1917
Whole Darned Thing's For You, The   Ahlert 1930; Turk 1930
Whole Long Year from Today, A   Leigh 1954
Whole Lot of Happy, A   Duke 1963
Whole Lotta Woman, A   McHugh 1964
Whole Word Comes from Dixie (When They Play that Dixie Tune), The   Hanley 1916
Whole World Is Dreaming of Love, The   Kahn 1924
Whole World Knows I Love You, The   Clare 1928; Kahn 1925
Whole World Loves, The   Caesar 1933; Romberg 1933
Whole World Loves a Lover and the Lover that I Love Is You, The   Whiting 1916
Whole World's Turning Blue   Gershwin, Ira 1924
Wholesale Love   Gilbert 1911
Who'll Be the Boy This Summer   David, Mack 1962; Livingston, Jerry 1962
Who'll Be the First!   Styne 1985
Who'll Be the One this Summer   Heyman 1937
Who'll Bid   Porter 1944
Who'll Buy?   Weill 1949
Who'll Buy a Rose from Margareeta   Brown, Lew 1942; Henderson 1942
Who'll Buy My Dream?   Van Heusen 1940
Who'll Buy My Flowers?   Clare 1939; Styne 1939
Who'll Buy My Song of Love   Caesar 1936; Henderson 1936
Who'll Buy My Violets   Goetz 1923
Who'll Drink Bottoms-Up with Me   Donaldson 1929; Leslie 1929
Who'll Dry Your Tears when You Cry   Akst 1921; Lewis 1921; Young, Joe 1921
Who'll Mend a Broken Heart   DeSylva 1926
Who'll Take the Place of Mary   Dubin 1919
Who'll Tie the Bell on the Old Cat's Tail   Coots 1938
Whoo-ee Loo-ee-Siana   Bergman 1951
Who-oo Is with You Tonight   Meyer 1923
Who-oo, You-oo, That's Who   Ager 1927; Yellen 1927
Whoop 'Er Up   Sterling 1910; Von Tilzer 1910
Whoop-A-Daisy   Kahn 1911
Whoop-De-Oodle-Do!   Kern 1921
Whoopee   Brown, Lew 1925; Conrad 1925; DeSylva 1925; Gershwin, Ira 1928
Whoopin' and A-Hollerin'   Mercer 1949
Whoop-La-La   Cohan 1908
Whoops My Dear   Brooks 1947; Schwartz, Jean 1935
Whoops-A-Daisy   Hoffman 1958
Whoops-A-Daisy Day   Burke 1954
Whoops-A-Daisy There I Go! Fallin' in Love Again   Monaco 1933; Parish 1933
Whoopsie   Hart 1928; Rodgers 1928
Whoop-Ti-Ay   Lerner, Alan Jay 1951; Loewe 1951
Whop-Diddy-Ay   Evans 1954; Livingston, Jay 1954
Who's Afraid   Webster 1966
Who's Afraid (Not I, Not I, Not I)   Lawrence 1954
Who's Afraid of Love!   Mitchell 1936; Pollack 1936
Who's Afraid of the Bogey Man?   Razaf 1936
Who's Afraid of the Kaiser   Gilbert 1918

Who's Afraid of Who   Cahn Date Unknown; Styne Date Unknown
Who's Afraid of You   Brown, Lew 1912
Who's Babying My Baby Tonight   Fisher 1931
Who's Beatin' My Time with You?   Ahlert 1940; David, Mack 1940
Who's Been List'ning to My Heart   Kalmar 1928; Ruby 1928
Who's Been Sleeping in My Bed   Bacharach 1963; David, Hal 1963
Who's Blue Now   Caesar 1929
Who's Complaining?   Gershwin, Ira 1944; Kern 1944
Who's Doing What to Erwin?   Evans 1961; Livingston, Jay 1961
Who's Excited   Duke 1955; Mercer 1952
Who's Gettin' Your Goodnight Kisses Now   Davis 1932
Who's Girl Is That   Henderson 1926
Who's Gonna Be Next   Yellen 1927
Who's Gonna Be the Winner?   Comden and Green 1945
Who's Gonna Get You?   Ager 1928; Yellen 1928
Who's Gonna Have the Young Goils While the Young Boys Are Away   Friend 1918
Who's Gonna Keep Your Wigwam Warm   Lerner, Sammy 1939; Oakland 1939
Who's Gonna Love You After I'm Gone   Rose 1928
Who's Gonna Teach Me (To Forget)   David, Hal 1963
Who's Gonna Win a Prize   Brooks 1959
Who's Got a Match?   De Lange 1944
Who's Got the Action   Bacharach 1963; Brooks 1962
Who's Helping Who?   Van Heusen 1945
Who's in Love   Baer 1933; Young, Joe 1933
Who's in Love with Who   Howard, Joseph E. 1937
Who's in Your Arms Tonight?   Revel 1962; Stept 1927; Warren 1926, 1931
Who's in Your Arms Tonight (inst.)   Revel 1961
Who's Kidding Who?   Burke 1944; Van Heusen 1944
Who's Little Baby Is Oo   Hanley 1930
Who's Lovin' My Sweetie Now   Stept 1925
Who's Loving You Now?   Baer 1925
Who's Loving You Tonight   Rose 1927
Who's My Baby's Baby Tonight   Donaldson 1943
Who's Sorry Now?   Kalmar 1923; Ruby 1923; Snyder 1923
Who's That Calling   Johnson, Howard 1939
Who's that Girl?   Adams 1970; Strouse 1970
Who's That Knockin' at My Door   Kahn 1927
Who's That Knockin' at My Heart   Freed, Ralph 1936; Lane 1936
Who's That Little Girl?   Hart 1926; Rodgers 1926
Who's That Woman?   Sondheim 1971
Who's the Gal   Drake 1953
Who's the Greatest —?   Gershwin, George 1933; Gershwin, Ira 1933
Who's the Lucky Fellow   Coots 1924; Coslow 1924
Who's the Who   Caesar 1926
Who's the Who (Where Has My Hubby Gones Blues)   Caesar 1925; Youmans 1925
Who's This Girl Named Whoopee, That the Boys All Want to Make   Gordon 1929
Who's to Blame   Duke 1941
Who's to Say?   Adams 1996; Freed, Ralph 1958; Strouse 1996
Who's Who   DePaul 1943, 1944; Raye 1943, 1944
Who's Who with You   Freed, Arthur 1925; Gershwin, Ira 1920, 1921; Youmans 1920, 1921
Who's Who's?   Donaldson 1926
Who's with You Tonight?   Motzan 1925

Who's Yer Hoosier Friend   Edwards 1910
Who's Your Lady Friend   Gilbert 1914
Whose Baby Are You   Cahn 1947; Kern 1920; Styne 1947
Whose Big Baby Are You   Koehler 1935; McHugh 1935
Whose Dream Are You   Willson 1945
Whose Girl Is That   Dixon 1923
Whose Hat Is That in the Hall   DePaul 1958; Raye 1961
Whose Heart Are You Breaking Tonight   Davis 1963
Whose Izzy Is He, Is He Yours or Is He Mine?   Brown, Lew 1923
Whose Little Angel Are You   Silver 1922
Whose Little Baby Boy Are You   Young, Joe 1912
Whose Little Dear Little Girlie Is Oo?   Sterling 1903; Von Tilzer 1903
Whose Little Girl Are You?   Howard, Joseph E. 1908
Whose Little Girl Are You Now   Brown, Lew 1912
Whose Little Heart Are You Breaking Now?   Berlin 1917
Whose Little Heart Are You Tearin' Apart   Stept 1954
Whose Little Sunshine Are You   Parish 1926
Whose Pretty Baby Are You   Kahn 1916
Whose Who Are You   Lerner, Sammy 1946
Whosis Whatsis, The   Brown, Lew 1925; DeSylva 1925; Henderson 1925
Why   Adams 1963; Atteridge 1923; Coots 1929; Davis 1929; Kern 1917; Razaf 1952; Rodgers 1976; Romberg 1923, 1948; Strouse 1963; Styne 1978
Why Ain't I Home   Youmans 1930
Why Ain'tcha   David, Hal 1958
Why Am I a Hit with the Ladies?   Berlin 1925
Why Am I Alone with No One to Love   Razaf 1929; Waller 1929
Why Am I Crying   David, Hal 1958
Why Am I Happy?   Arlen 1953; Fields 1953
Why Am I in Love?   Burke 1934; Evans 1954; Livingston, Jay 1954; Spina 1934
Why Am I So Gone About that Gal   Porter 1957
Why Am I So Happy?   Strouse 1982
Why Am I So Romantic   Kalmar 1930; Ruby 1928
Why Am I So Sad?   Atteridge 1923; Caesar 1923; Gershwin, George 1923
Why Am I So Sensitive to You   Robin 1930; Whiting 1930
Why Am I So Wonderful   Kalmar 1927; Ruby 1927
Why Are Chickens So High?   Bryan 1919; Schwartz, Jean 1919
Why Are the Wheels of My Bicycle Round?   Schwartz, Jean 1948
Why Are We Invited Here?   Romberg 1915
Why Are Your Eyes So Red   Cahn 1957
Why Aren't Yez Eatin' More Oranges (From Cal-i-for-ni-ay)   Brown, Lew 1925
Why Be Afraid to Dance?   Rome 1954
Why Be Good?   Gershwin, Ira 1928
Why? Because!   Kalmar 1938; Ruby 1938
Why Begin Again   Raye 1939
Why Can't He Care for Me   Cahn 1958; Warren 1958
Why Can't He Like Me?   Styne 1978
Why Can't He See?   Cahn 1970; Styne 1970
Why Can't I?   Cahn 1980; Hart 1928; Rodgers 1928; Strouse 1980
Why Can't I Agree   Gershwin, George 1922
Why Can't I Be Like You   Conrad 1929; Mitchell 1929
Why Can't I Be Two People?   Sherman 1976
Why Can't I Find Somebody to Love?   Ahlert 1932; Turk 1932
Why Can't I Have You   Davis 1924; Woods 1924

Why Can't I Remember Your Name?   Arlen 1936; Harburg 1936
Why Can't I Sing a Love Song   Akst 1943
Why Can't I Smell Like the Other Fellas Smell   Dietz 1959; Schwartz, Arthur 1959
Why Can't It Be Me?   Bloom 1936; Mercer 1936
Why Can't the English   Lerner, Alan Jay 1956; Loewe 1956
Why Can't the World Go and Leave Us Alone?   Lerner, Alan Jay 1983; Strouse 1983
Why Can't This Go on Forever   Ahlert 1932; Turk 1932
Why Can't This Night Last Forever?   Loewe 1938
Why Can't We Be Sweethearts   Turk 1927
Why Can't We Be Together   Bacharach 1989
Why Can't We Have a Little Bit of Green (In the Old Red, White and Blue)   Goetz 1917; Johnson, Howard 1917
(Birdies Sing in Cages Too) Why Can't You   Brown, Lew 1929; DeSylva 1929; Henderson 1929
Why Can't You Behave   Porter 1948
Why Can't You Care   Gilbert 1928
Why Can't You Find Time for Me   Styne 1927
Why Come Crying to Me   Sigman 1953
Why Couldn't It Be Poor Little Me   Kahn 1924
Why Dance?   Ahlert 1931; Turk 1931
Why Did Bluebeard's Beard Turn Blue   Von Tilzer 1935
Why Did Dr. Jekyll Hyde?   Johnson, Howard 1926
Why Did I Buy that Morris Chair for Morris?   Kalmar 1923; Ruby 1923
Why Did I Ever Kiss You, Tell Me Why   Bryan 1928
Why Did I Fall in Love with You   Magidson 1931; Wrubel 1931
Why Did I Go Wrong?   Razaf 1926
Why Did I Kiss that Girl?   Brown, Lew 1924; Henderson 1924
Why Did I Leave My Home   Young, Victor 1947
Why Did I Leave Wisconsin — Kenosha, Wisconsin   Dietz 1925
Why Did I Let Her Go   Monaco 1924; Motzan 1924
Why Did I Send You Roses   DePaul 1950; Raye 1950
Why Did It Have to Be You   Cahn 1974
Why Did Minnie Ha-Ha   Johnson, James P. 1926
Why Did She Have to Cry   David, Hal 1963
Why Did They Die?   Rome 1973
Why Did We Marry Soldiers?   Hammerstein 1926; Harbach 1926; Romberg 1926
Why Did You Come Into My Life   Johnson, Howard 1924
Why Did You Do It?   Dietz 1937; Schwartz, Arthur 1937
Why Did You Do It to Me Babe   Sterling 1920; Von Tilzer 1920
Why Did You Have to Be a Lawyer   Coleman 1999
Why Did You Have to Kiss Me   Russell 1955
Why Did You Kiss My Heart Awake   Eliscu 1937
Why Did You Leave Me?   Dubin 1913
Why Did You Make Me Care?   Blake 1925; Sissle 1925
Why Did You Make Me Cry   Magidson 1930
Why Did You Make Me Leave St. Louis, Mo?   Johnson, Howard 1917
Why Didn't I Meet You Long Ago   Schwartz, Jean 1920
Why Didn't I Sleep Last Night   Oakland 1940
Why Didn't We Meet Before   Porter 1920
Why Didn't You Leave Me Years Ago Instead of Leaving Me Now   Clare 1920; Mitchell 1920
Why Didn't You Tell Me   Lawrence 1943
Why Do Hawaiians Sing Aloha   Stept 1937
Why Do I?   Hart 1926; Rodgers 1926; Sigman 1955
Why Do I Always Have to Be a Dame   Stept 1956

Why Do I Care   Young, Victor 1956
Why Do I Care for You   Yellen 1923
Why Do I Cry for Joey?   Freed, Ralph 1959
Why Do I Cry in My Sleep?   Sherman 1952
Why Do I Dream Those Dreams?   Dubin 1934; Warren 1934
Why Do I Fall in Love   DePaul 1951; Raye 1951
Why Do I Feel So Enchanted   David, Mack 1958; Livingston, Jerry 1958
Why Do I Lie to Myself About You   Coots 1936; Davis 1936
Why Do I Like You   Burke 1946; Van Heusen 1946
Why Do I Love You?   DeSylva 1925; Gershwin, George 1925; Gershwin, Ira 1925; Hammerstein 1927; Kern 1927
Why Do I Miss Mississippi   Caesar 1955
Why Do Men Bring Out the Mother in Me   Ruby 1947
Why Do the Bees Hum   Heyman 1935
Why Do the Boys Love the Married Women   Fisher 1938
Why Do They All Take the Night Boat to Albany   Lewis 1918; Schwartz, Jean 1918; Young, Joe 1918
Why Do They Call a Private a Private?   Loesser 1944
Why Do They Call It Gay Paree?   Gordon 1935; Revel 1935
Why Do They Call It Greenland   Brooks 1955
Why Do They Call Them Show Girls   Fisher 1922
Why Do They Call Us Johns?   Johnson, Howard 1924
Why Do They Die at the End of a Classical Dance   Jerome 1921; Schwartz, Jean 1921
Why Do They Die at the End of Classical Dance?   Atteridge 1922; Romberg 1922
Why Do They Make Them So Beautiful   Herbert 1919; Smith, Robert B. 1919
Why Do they Play Here Comes the Bride when They Ought to Play There Goes the Groom   Sterling 1919; Von Tilzer 1919
Why Do We Follow the Big Brass Band?   Carroll 1910
Why Do We Have to Fight to Fly Old Glory   Robison 1967
Why Do We Hurt the Ones We Love?   Razaf 1933; Waller 1933
Why Do We Love Them?   DeSylva 1922; Herbert 1922
Why Do We Say Good Morning   Robin 1946
Why Do You Keep Us Guessing?   Hammerstein 1922; Mitchell 1922
Why Do You Look So Happy   Drake 1954
Why Do You Make Me Like You?   Arlen 1966
Why Do You Make Me Love You   Donaldson 1938
Why Do You Push Me Around!   Adams 1962; Strouse 1962
Why Do You Roll Those Eyes?   Harburg 1932
Why Do You Sit on Your Patio   DeSylva 1926
Why Do You Suppose?   Hart 1929; Rodgers 1929
Why Do You Tease Me?   Atteridge 1929
Why Do You Want to Hurt Me So?   Porter 1950
Why Do You Want to Know Why?'   Berlin 1926
Why Do Your Kisses Taste So Sweet   Von Tilzer 1914
Why Does It Get So Late So Early   Wrubel 1946
Why Does It Have to Be Funny?   Adams 1978; Strouse 1978
Why Does It Have to Be Me   Sigman 1953
Why Does It Have to Rain on Sunday   Merrill 1947
Why Don't I Hear from You?   Johnson, Howard 1927
Why Don't the Band Play?   Johnson, J. Rosamond 1900
Why Don't They Dance the Polka Anymore   Kern 1914; Smith, Harry B. 1914
Why Don't They Do It Now   Monaco 1914
Why Don't They Leave Us Alone   Coleman 1996; Mills 1955
Why Don't They Let Me Sing a Love Song   Akst 1944; Davis 1944
Why Don't They Play the Old Songs on a New Piano   Oakland 1960

Why Don't We Do This More Often   Wrubel 1941
Why Don't We Try Staying Home   Porter 1929
Why Don't You   Friml 1918
Why Don't You Answer My Letter   Heyman 1939
Why Don't You Be Nice to Some Nice Fellow?   Smith, Harry B. 1910
Why Don't You Believe Me   Revel 1929
Why Don't You Do It Now   Stept 1925
Why Don't You Get a Girl Like Me   Atteridge 1914
Why Don't You Get a Sweetie?   Atteridge 1920
Why Don't You Give In   Spina 1957
Why Don't You Go, Go, Go   Jerome 1903; Schwartz, Jean 1903
Why Don't You Join the Air Force Reserve   David, Hal 1953
Why Don't You Let Me Be   Ruby 1952
Why Don't You Marry the Girl   DeSylva 1926
Why Don't You Practice What You Preach   Hoffman 1934
Why Don't You Smile   Schwartz, Jean 1921
Why Don't You Speak for Yourself, John   Brooks 1953
Why Don't You Tell Me   Burke 1953; Van Heusen 1953
Why Don't You Tell Me What You Want   Monaco 1917
Why Don't You Try   Williams 1905
Why Don'tcha Kiss Me Like You Kissed Me Last Night   Wrubel 1944
Why Dream   Rainger 1935; Robin 1935; Whiting 1935
Why Fight the Feeling   Loesser 1948
Why Fight This   Mercer 1959
Why Go Anywhere at All?   Dietz 1961; Schwartz, Arthur 1961
Why Go to Havana   Yellen 1947
Why Have a Falling Out Just When We're Falling in Love   Johnson, Howard 1935
Why Have You Eyes?   Hart 1933; Rodgers 1933
Why Have You Forgotten Waikiki   Kahn 1930
Why Haven't I Found Love?   Sherman 1986
Why Him?   Lane 1979; Lerner, Alan Jay 1979
Why I Love My Baby   Berlin 1927
Why I Love You   Caesar 1922
Why Is Cecil Selling Sea Shells by the Seaside   Dubin 1917
Why Is It Night in My Heart?   Lewis 1933
Why Is It So   Cahn 1941
Why Is Love?   Coots 1925
Why Is Love So Crazy?   Freed, Arthur 1950; Warren 1950
Why Is My Heart Such a Fool   Fain 1964
Why Is Romany So Many Miles Away   Egan 1920; Whiting 1920
Why Is the Desert?   Lerner, Alan Jay 1974; Loewe 1974
Why Is the World So Changed Today?   Smith, Harry B. 1926
Why Let a Lie Break Your Heart   Coots 1953
Why Let It Go?   Bergman 1988
Why Live a Lie   Gilbert 1924; Koehler 1923
Why Marry Them   Porter 1932
Why Me?   Bergman 1960; Rodgers 1970
Why Must I Always Be Without You   Mitchell 1930; Pollack 1930
Why Must I Live Alone   Johnson, J. Rosamond 1946
Why Must I Love You   Magidson 1938; Wrubel 1938
Why Must I Say Goodbye to My Summer Love   Young, Joe 1932
Why Must There Be an Op'ning Song   Cahn 1944; Styne 1944
Why Must We Always Be Dreaming   Romberg 1928
Why Must We Fight?   Sherman 1985

Why Must We Say Goodbye   Brennan 1920; Howard, Joseph E. 1937

Why Not?   Conrad 1934; Duke 1963; Heyman 1934; Razaf 1944; Sigman 1946; Strouse 1999; Willson 1969

Why Not Have a Little Party?   Schwartz, Arthur 1930

Why Not Sing Wearin' of the Green   Johnson, Howard 1915

Why Not String Along with Me   Brown, Lew 1938; Pollack 1938

Why Not Surrender   Dietz 1956; Schwartz, Arthur 1956

Why Oh Why   Robin 1927; Snyder 1952; Youmans 1927

Why Pretend   Meyer 1936

Why Save for that Rainy Day?   Duke 1936; Gershwin, Ira 1936

Why Say Goodbye   Bryan 1953

Why Should He Fly at So Much a Week (When He Could Be the Shiek of Paree)?   Berlin 1927

Why Should I Be Sorry   Sigman 1954

Why Should I Believe in Love?   Evans 1952; Livingston, Jay 1952

Why Should I Care?   Porter 1937

Why Should I Change a Thing?   Strouse 2000

Why Should I Give My Love to You?   Conrad 1923

Why Should I Go Home   Merrill 1952

Why Should I Let You?   Atteridge 1923; Schwartz, Jean 1923

Why Should I Pine for the World to Be Mine   Donaldson 1925; Friend 1925

Why Should I Trust You?   Porter 1955

Why Should I Weep about One Sweetie (Two, Three or Four Sweeties)?   Hanley 1923

Why Should I Worry   Cahn 1958

Why Should There Be a Bridge of Sighs Across the River of Love   Brennan 1919

Why Should We Be Wasting Time   Coots 1926, 1928

Why Should We Marry When We Can Be Good Friends   Fisher 1926; Rose 1926

Why Should We Say Goodbye and Cry Tomorrow?   Lewis 1951

Why Should We Stay Home and Sew   Herbert 1914

Why Shouldn't I   Freed, Arthur 1931; Porter 1935

Why Shouldn't I Be Somebody's Baby   Koehler 1926

Why Shouldn't I Have You?   Porter 1929

Why Shouldn't We?   Hammerstein 1924; Harbach 1924

Why So Gloomy, Why So Sad   Freed, Ralph Date Unknown

Why Talk About Love?   Mitchell 1937; Pollack 1937

Why Talk About Sex?   Porter 1930

Why Tell a Lie (A Song of Alabama)   Caesar 1953

Why They Made Him King   Cohan 1909

Why Try   Brooks 1947

Why Try to Change Me Now   Coleman 1952

Why Wake Up the Echoes (Of Yesterday)   Robison 1957

Why Was I Born?   Hammerstein 1929; Kern 1929

Why Waste Your Love   Williams 1914; Young, Joe 1914

Why Wonder Why   David, Mack 1958

Why Won't He Answer Me   David, Mack 1962

Why Work and Slave All Day   Smith, Harry B. 1926

Why You No Knock   Davis 1942

Why'dya Make Me Fall in Love   Donaldson 1938

Wichita   Washington 1955

Wichita Town   Brooks 1959

Wicked Witch, The   David, Mack 1958; Livingston, Jerry 1958

Wide Open Spaces, The   Webster 1962; Whiting 1927

Wide Pants Willie   Atteridge 1925; Hanley 1925

Wide Place in the Road   Mercer 1967

Wide, Wide Countryside (Of Home)   Robison 1959

Wide Wide World   Lawrence 1956

Widow Fascinating, The   Harbach 1917

Widow Has Ways, A   Herbert 1906

Widow in Lace, The   Bullock 1937; Spina 1937

Widow Is a Lady, A   Hart 1934; Kahn 1934; Rodgers 1934

Widow of Windsor, The   Adams 1972; Strouse 1972

Widow's Cruise   Porter 1910

Widow's Daughter, The   Hanley 1936

Widow's Wile, A   Cohan 1901

Wiegenlied   Johnson, Howard 1932

Wiener Schnitzel   Hammerstein 1935; Romberg 1935

Wife Never Understand   Arlen 1968

Wife of the Life of the Party, The   Evans 1946; Livingston, Jay 1946

Wifie of Your Own, A   Kern 1913; Smith, Harry B. 1913

Wiggle-Wagg   Lewis 1913; Meyer 1913

Wigwammin'   Mills 1938

Wilbur   Strouse Date Unknown

Wild About Jazz (inst.)   Blake 1978

Wild About You   Berlin 1934

Wild and Woolly (inst.)   Schwartz, Jean 1930

Wild and Woolly West, The   Fain 1956; Webster 1956

Wild and Wooly West, The   Buck 1927; Koehler 1936; Livingston, Jerry 1962; Stept 1936

Wild Bill   Leigh 1955

Wild Cat   Donaldson 1922

Wild Cat Blues   Waller 1923

Wild Cherries   Berlin 1908; Snyder 1908

Wild Geese   Oakland 1972

Wild Honey   Bacharach 1957; David, Hal 1957

Wild Horses   Burke 1953

Wild Indians   Leigh 1954

Wild Is the Wind   Washington 1957

Wild Justice, The   Weill 1949

Wild Oat Joe   Caesar 1928

Wild Party Girl (inst.)   Whiting 1929

Wild Red Cherry River   Harburg 1979

Wild Romantic Blues   Bryan 1920; Schwartz, Jean 1920

Wild Rose   Friml 1926; Hammerstein 1926; Harbach 1926; Herbert 1911; Kern 1920; Olcott 1910

Wild Rose of Old Cheyenne   Friend 1945

Wild Rover, The   David, Mack 1978

Wild Trumpets and Crazy Piano (Got a Gal to Forget)   Loesser 1936

Wild Wedding Bells   Porter 1938

Wild, Wild River   Davis 1966

Wild, Wild West, The   Mercer 1945; Warren 1945

Wild Willie   Sherman 1959

Wildcat   Coleman 1960; Leigh 1960

Wildcat Smathers   Evans 1954; Livingston, Jay 1954

Wildcats   Berlin 1924; Hammerstein 1947; Rodgers 1947

Wilderness Man, The   Harburg 1969

Wildest Gal in Town, The   Fain 1947; Yellen 1947

Wildflower   Goetz 1908; Hammerstein 1923; Harbach 1923; Youmans 1923

Wildflower, I Love You   Harbach 1926

Wilhelm Der Grosser   Brown, A. Seymour 1909

Wilhelm, the Grocer   Lewis 1913; Meyer 1913

Wilhelmina   Berlin 1945; Gordon 1950; Myrow 1950

Wilhelmina's Concertina   Goetz 1911

Will, The   Coleman 1971; Sigman 1963

Will He Ever Smile Again?   Johnson, J. Rosamond 1904

Will I Ever Know   Gordon 1936; Revel 1936

Will I Ever Tell You   Willson 1957

Will It All End in Smoke?   Kern 1913; Smith, Harry B. 1913

Will It Always Be Me   David, Mack 1933

Will It Be Yes or No?   Brown, Lew 1919

Will o' the Wisp   Freed, Ralph 1956; Livingston, Jerry 1956; Silver 1929; Smith, Harry B. 1908; Smith, Robert B. 1919; Spina 1952

Will Rogers American   Robison 1945

Will She Come from the East (North, West, or South)?   Berlin 1922

Will Someone Ever Look at Me that Way   Bergman 1983

Will the Next Kiss Always Be Mine   Bryan 1945

Will To-Morrow Ever Come   Friml 1936

Will Will Will   Brown, Nacio Herb 1919

Will Wonders Never Cease   Freed, Ralph 1935; Oakland 1935

Will Ye Marry Me   Bergman 1959

Will You   Edwards 1905

Will You Be at Home in Heaven?   Evans 1952; Livingston, Jay 1952

Will You Be Mine   Revel 1959

Will You Be My Hero?   Smith, Harry B. 1903

Will You Be My Valentine   Spina 1957

Will You Be Sorry   Kahn 1928

Will You Forgive Me   Hart 1920, 1921, 1923; Rodgers 1920, 1921, 1923

Will You Love Me Monday Morning As You Did on Friday Night? (A Weekend Cruise)   Harburg 1934

Will You Love Me Monday Morning As You Did on Friday Night? (Weekend Cruise)   Gershwin, Ira 1934

Will You Love Me on Monday Morning   Arlen 1940; Harburg 1940

Will You Love Me Then As Now   Johnson, Howard 1939

Will You Love Me Tomorrow, As You Love Me Today   Davis 1933; Hanley 1933; Oakland 1933

Will You Love Me Tomorrow (Will You Always Remember)   Caesar 1945

Will You Love Me When My Flivver Is a Wreck?   Porter 1916

Will You Love Me When the Honeymooon Is Over   Bryan 1910; Fisher 1910

Will You Marry Me?   Freed, Arthur 1945; Hammerstein 1955; Rodgers 1955; Warren 1945

Will You Marry Me Tomorrow, Maria?   Hammerstein 1937; Kern 1937

Will You Remember Me?   Gershwin, George 1924; Gershwin, Ira 1924; Webster 1978; Weill 1938

Will You Remember (Sweetheart)   Romberg 1917

Will You Remember Tomorrow Night (All That You Told Me Tonight)   Hoffman 1953

Will You Remember Tonight Tomorrow   Friend 1938

Will You Wait in the Valley for Me   Burke 1931

Will You Waltz on the Ice with Me   Johnson, J. Rosamond 1914

Will You Write the Melody if I Write the Words to Our Little Song of Love   Dubin 1917

Willamania   Coleman 1991; Comden and Green 1991

William Tell   Razaf 1936

William Tell It to Me (William Tell Me)   Bryan 1920; Schwartz, Jean 1920

William Tell Overture   Robin 1936

William Tell Routine   Styne 1942

William the Conqueror   Eliscu 1949

Williamsburg, Virgin-ee-ya   Drake 1954

Willie of the Valley   Oakland 1940

Willie or Will He Not   Lewis 1919; Young, Joe 1919

Willie the Whipperwill   Robin 1952

Willie the Wolf of the West   Robin 1943

Willing and Eager   Rodgers 1962

Willingly   Cahn 1959; Sigman 1958; Van Heusen 1959

Will-of-the-Wisp   Buck 1916

Will-O-the-Wisp   Herbert 1908, 1914; Smith, Harry B. 1908, 1923; Smith, Robert B. 1914

Willow, The   David, Mack 1963

Willow in the Wind   Arlen 1944; Harburg 1944

Willow Tree   Razaf 1928; Waller 1928

Willow, Will Me   Webster 1963

Willson Tag   Willson 1949

Wilma (inst.)   Motzan 1915

Wimmin (I Got to Have 'Em All That's All)   Fisher 1921

Wimmin — Aaah   Warren 1926

Win   Willson 1974

Win the Big "E" with John V. Lindsay   Robison 1965

(We're Gonna) Win This War in 44   Friend 1944

Wind at My Window, The   Rainger 1939; Robin 1939

Wind Blew Through His Whiskers   Rose 1925

Wind in My Sails   Drake 1948

Wind in the Night, The   Leigh 1977

Wind in the Trees, The   Kahn 1938; Romberg 1938

Wind in the Willows, The   Livingston, Jerry 1963

Wind Me Up and Run Me Down   Johnson, J. Rosamond 1946

Wind Quillow Up (inst.)   Blane 1961

Wind Song   Howard, Bart 1961; Webster 1967

Wind that Shakes the Barley, The   Webster 1950

Wind, the Wind, The   Cahn 1956; Van Heusen 1956

Windchimes   Spina 1977

Winding Road   Ager 1953

Winding the Trail   Stept 1935

Winding, Winding   Smith, Harry B. 1900

Windmill Song, The   Brown, Nacio Herb 1951; Gilbert 1951; Parish 1951

Windmill Under the Stars   Kern 1942; Mercer 1942

Windmills of Your Mind, The   Bergman 1968

Window Across the Way   Sondheim 1962

Window Cleaners, The   Kalmar 1925; Ruby 1925

Window of Dreams, The   Evans 1958; Friend 1955; Livingston, Jay 1958

Window of Heaven, The   Bacharach 1959; David, Hal 1959

Window Shade Dance   Brooks 1958

Window Where God Looks In, A   Bryan 1958

Window Wiper Song   Evans 1940; Livingston, Jay 1940

Window Wishing   Bacharach 1965; David, Hal 1965

Windows of the World, The   Bacharach 1967; David, Hal 1967

Wind's in the West, The   Woods 1933

Winds of Chance   Webster 1970

Winds of Change, The   David, Mack 1968

Windy City   Coleman 1984

Windy City Marmalade   Merrill 1972; Styne 1972

Windy City Special   Sherman 1960

Wine   Alter 1929; Johnson, Howard 1929

Wine Ballet   Atteridge 1919; Romberg 1919; Schwartz, Jean 1919

Wine Divine   Cohan 1901

Wine Is Mine, The   Duke 1963

Wine Is Young (Our Dreams Are Old), The   Bacharach 1969; David, Hal 1969

Wine Maid Divine   Goetz 1911

Wine of Marie Dellamore, The   Russell 1977

Wine of Old Giuseppe, The   Evans 1949; Livingston, Jay 1949

Wine Song   Kahn 1934

Wine, Wine! (Champagne Song)   Kern 1904

Wine, Woman and Song   Ahlert 1929; Atteridge 1916; Romberg 1916; Turk 1929

Wine, Women and Song   Conrad 1934; Mitchell 1934

Wine, Women, Song, Women and Women, Women   Brooks 1960

Wing-Ding Tonight   Evans 1952; Livingston, Jay 1952

Winged Love   Herbert 1913

(Silver) Wings   Buck 1927; Merrill 1952

Wings in the Morning   Schwartz, Arthur 1930

Wings of Eagles, The   Brooks 1957

Wings of England, The   Adamson 1941; Revel 1941

Wings of Romance   Smith, Harry B. 1928

Wings of the Morning   Koehler 1936; McHugh 1936

Wings on High   Willson 1938

(If I Had) Wings on My Wishes   Webster 1951

Wings Over the Navy   Mercer 1939; Warren 1939

Winko   Drake 1954

Winners   Adams 1984; Strouse 1984, 2000

Winning Combination   David, Hal 1961

Winning the West   Evans Date Unknown; Livingston, Jay 1973

Winona   Ahlert 1926; Friml 1927

Winsome Widow   Edwards 1912

Winter   Bryan 1910

Winter and Spring   Eliscu 1930; Friml 1930

Winter Beaches, The   Buck 1920

Winter Blossoms   Gilbert 1939; Woods 1946

Winter Garden Hop   Atteridge 1916; Motzan 1916, 1917; Romberg 1916

Winter Headquarters   Fain 1959; Webster 1959

Winter Holiday   Davis 1944

Winter in California   Davis 1946

Winter in Central Park   Hammerstein 1929; Kern 1929

Winter in Havana   Fisher 1947

Winter in Hoosick Falls   Martin 1952

Winter in My Heart   Mercer 1944

Winter Interlude   Hoffman 1933; Parish 1933; Russell 1957, 1958

Winter Is in My Heart   Lewis 1932

Winter Moon   Adamson 1957; Carmichael 1957

Winter Nights   Clarke 1914; Schwartz, Jean 1915

Winter Rain   Coleman 1979

Winter Romance, A   Cahn 1959

Winter Rose, A   Young, Victor 1910

Winter Scene, A   Carroll 1950; Johnson, J. Rosamond 1946

Winter Song   Herbert 1903; Parish 1965

Winter Sun   Oakland 1963; Webster 1963

Winter Waltz, The   Ager 1935

Winter Warm   Bacharach 1957; David, Hal 1957

Winter Was Warm   Merrill 1962; Styne 1962

Winter Wedding Bells   Bryan 1938

Wintergreen for President   Gershwin, George 1931; Gershwin, Ira 1931

Winters Go By   Hammerstein 1947; Rodgers 1947

Wintertime   Brown, Nacio Herb 1943; Coleman 1966; Robin 1943

Wintertime and Christmastime   Fain 1964

Wintertime Dreams   Bryan 1936

Wintertime of Love (After You)   Heyman 1952

Wint's Song (Pleasant Beach House)   Merrill 1959

Wipe 'Em Off   Johnson, James P. 1930

Wipe that Frown Right Off Your Face   Gordon 1931; Revel 1931

Wipin' the Pan   Baer 1928; Robison 1929

Wisconsin Cheese   Willson 1954

Wisdom   Parish 1965

Wisdom of a Fool, The   Silver 1956

Wisdom of the Heart, The   Loesser 1969

Wise Guy   De Lange 1943

Wise Man or a Fool, A   Merrill 1952

Wise Old Owl (Caw-Caw-Caw), The   Robison 1950

Wise Resolution, A   Young, Victor 1934

Wish, The   Evans 1959; Livingston, Jay 1959

Wish I Had a Braver Heart   Blane 1948; Warren 1948

Wish I May   Martin 1943

Wish I Only Knew Which Way the Wind Was Gonna Blow   Young, Joe 1932; Young, Victor 1932

Wish Me a Rainbow   Evans 1966; Livingston, Jay 1966

Wish Me Good Luck — Kiss Me Good-Bye   Ager 1934; Davis 1934

Wish Me Good Luck (As You Wish Me Goodbye)   David, Hal 1953

Wish Me Luck   Gorney 1949

Wish Them Well   Hammerstein 1947; Rodgers 1947

Wish You Merry Christmas   Hoffman 1959

Wish You Were Here   Rome 1952

Wish You Were Special   Oakland 1952

Wish You Were Waiting for Me   Russell 1944

Wisha Wurra   Burke 1961

Wishbone Song, The   Lawrence 1951

Wishful Thinking   Rainger 1941; Robin 1941; Robison 1957

Wishin' and Hopin'   Bacharach 1963; David, Hal 1963

Wishing   Berlin 1910; Snyder 1910

Wishing and Waiting for Love   Akst 1929; Clarke 1929

Wishing Cup, The   Smith, Harry B. 1900

Wishing Star   David, Mack 1944, 1962

Wishing Tree of Harlem   Duke 1936; Gershwin, Ira 1936

Wishing Waltz, The   Gordon 1943; Warren 1943

Wishing (Will Make It So)   DeSylva 1939

Wis-s-s-con-sin   Brown, Lew 1945; Henderson 1945

Witch Ballet   Herbert 1912

Witch of Salem, The   Bryan 1952; Caesar 1952

Witch Song   Coots 1959

Witchcraft   Coleman 1957; Leigh 1957

Witchee Kitchee Koo   Parish 1928

Witches' Brew   Comden and Green 1967; Styne 1967

With a Banjo on My Knee   Adamson 1936; Alter 1940; Loesser 1940; McHugh 1936

With a Bing Bang Banjo on Your Knee   Sigman 1948

With a Bit of a Smile (I'll Find a Way to Your Heart)   Fisher 1916; Johnson, Howard 1916

With a Dream   Blake 1940; Razaf 1940

With a Feather in Your Cap   Fields 1932; McHugh 1932

With a Flair   Sherman 1971

With a Forty Dollar Buggy and a Twenty Dollar Horse   Bryan 1942

(The Frenchman Always Says It) With a Kiss   Blane 1954; Myrow 1954

With a Little Bit of Cider Inside of Ida, Ida Was Full of Ideas   Lewis 1919; Snyder 1919; Young, Joe 1919

With a Little Bit of Luck   Lerner, Alan Jay 1956; Loewe 1956

With a Man on First   Cahn Date Unknown; Duke Date Unknown

With a Nimble Little Thimble on Her Finger   Bryan 1952

With a Song in My Heart   Hart 1928; Rodgers 1928

With a Woman You Can Never Tell   Friml 1921

With All My Broken Heart   Merrill 1949
With All My Heart   Adamson 1930; Bergman 1956; Burke 1933; Carroll 1951; Evans 1955; Gordon 1930; Kahn 1936; Livingston, Jay 1955; McHugh 1936; Revel 1930; Spina 1933
With All My Heart and Soul   Brennan 1917; De Lange 1934; Mills 1934
With All My Love   Heyman 1955; Revel 1959
With an Angel Like You in My Arms   Leslie 1927
With Apparent Ebullation   Smith, Harry B. 1906
With Benjamin   Bergman 1976
With Downcast Eye   Herbert 1903
With Downcast Eye (Wedding Song)   Harbach 1911
With Every Breath I Take   Rainger 1934; Robin 1934
With Ev'ry Breath I Take   Coleman 1989
With Feeling   Howard, Bart 1965
With Frame Two Forty Nine   Herbert 1905
With God's Hand in Mine   Coots 1951
With Hearts Ablaze   Lane 1996
With His Great Love   Coots 1959
With His Little Cane and Satchel in His Hand   Jerome 1911; Von Tilzer 1911
With His Wonderful Irish Brogue   Norworth 1917
With Lance in Best   Herbert 1898; Smith, Harry B. 1898
With Louise on Lake Louise   Bryan 1935
With Love   Davis 1958; Evans 1968; Livingston, Jay 1968; Razaf 1949; Willson 1969
With Me   Robison 1957
With Military Pomp   Herbert 1900; Smith, Harry B. 1900
With Music   Berlin 1946
With My Eyes Wide Open I'm Dreaming   Gordon 1934, 1935; Revel 1934
With My Guitar and You   Heyman 1930; Silver 1930; Snyder 1930
With My Old Sweetheart in a New World   Brown, Lew 1944; Henderson 1944
With My Rub-Rub-Rubbers   Caesar 1947
With My Song   Coots 1954
With My Strings   Coots 1954
With My Sweetie in the Moonlight (Under Dreamy Southern Skies)   Clare 1932; Freed, Arthur 1932
With No One Playing the Organ   Merrill 1955
With One Side of Your Heart (The Other Side of Your Heart)   Merrill 1958
With Open Arms   Bacharach 1959; Bergman 1965; David, Hal 1959
With Papers Duly Signed   Atteridge 1922; Romberg 1922
With Pleasure   Clare 1926; Monaco 1926
With Plenty of Money and You   Dubin 1936; Warren 1936
With Red Wine   Friml 1928
With So Little to Be Sure Of   Sondheim 1964
With the Curls Hanging Down Your Back   Young, Joe 1934
With the Dawn   Caesar 1930; Harbach 1930; Romberg 1930
With the Roses in Her Hair   Spina 1947
With the Sun Warm Upon Me   Arlen 1953; Fields 1953
With the Twinkle in Her Eye   Olcott 1920
With the Whole World Listening In   Coslow 1935
With the Wind and the Rain in Your Hair   Lawrence 1940
With These Hands   Davis 1950; Leigh 1976; Silver 1950
With You   Berlin 1929; Blake 1923; Ellington 1924; Sissle 1923
With You — With Me   Clare 1929
With You Beside Me   Ahlert 1929; Kahn 1933; Turk 1929; Young, Victor 1933
With You Here and Me Here   Schwartz, Arthur 1933

With You in My Arms   Coots 1929; Egan 1927; Whiting 1927
With You on My Mind   Brown, Lew 1938; Pollack 1938
With You or Without You   Livingston, Jerry 1955; Parish 1955
With You or Without You, I Will Get Along   Razaf 1932
With You Where You Are   Dixon 1929
With You with Me   Mercer 1940
With Your Looks and My Brain   Leslie 1929; Monaco 1929
With Your Looks and My Brains   Freed, Ralph 1942; Lane 1942
With Your Looks and My Disposition   Clare 1932
With Your Permission   Silver 1947
Withdraw   Herbert 1917
Within the Land of Geishas   Romberg 1927; Smith, Harry B. 1927
Within the Law   Dubin 1913
Without a Friend   De Lange 1948
Without a Shirt   Young, Joe 1934
Without a Song   Eliscu 1929; Rose 1929; Youmans 1929
Without a Sweetheart   Fain 1932
Without a Word of Complaint   Ellington 1961
Without a Word of Warning   Gordon 1935; Revel 1935
Without Him   Evans 1954; Leigh 1977; Livingston, Jay 1954
Without Kissing, Love Isn't Love   Ager 1920; Yellen 1920
Without Love   Brown, Lew 1930; DeSylva 1930; Henderson 1930; Porter 1955
Without Magic   De Lange 1947
Without Me   Adams 1983
Without Music   Alter 1947; De Lange 1947
Without My Money   Rodgers 1970
Without Rhythm   Arlen 1931; Hoffman 1936; Koehler 1931; Yellen 1935
Without that Gal   Donaldson 1931
Without the Girl — Inside   Kern 1907
Without Warning You Kissed Me Goodbye   Hoffman 1931
Without You   Adams 1996; Coleman 1991; Comden and Green 1991; Conrad 1925, 1926; Davis 1926; Lerner, Alan Jay 1956; Loewe 1956; Mitchell 1921; Strouse 1996
Without You, Sweetheart   Brown, Lew 1927; DeSylva 1927; Henderson 1927
Witness, The   Cahn 1958
Wives and Lovers   Bacharach 1963; David, Hal 1963
Wizard, The   David, Mack 1958
Wizard of Magic Town, The   Leigh 1985
Wizard of Wall Street, The   Smith, Robert B. 1906
Wo! Ho! That's Love!   Rainger 1936; Robin 1936
Wob-a-ly Walk   Warren 1928
Woe Is Me   Caesar 1927; Lawrence 1943; Willson 1931
Woggle Bird Song, The   Cahn 1966; Van Heusen 1966
Wolf, The   Egan 1926; Rose 1926; Whiting 1926
Wolf City   David, Mack 1965; Livingston, Jerry 1965
Wolf of Gubbio, The   Harburg 1971
Wolf Song, The   David, Mack 1944; Robin 1929; Whiting 1929
Wolf that Swallowed Red Riding Hood, The   Rome 1964
Wolf Time   Fain 1946
Woman   Ellington 1968; Hammerstein 1920; Willson 1969
Woman Alone, A   Adams 1966; Comden and Green 1982; Coots 1964; Strouse 1966
Woman Alone with the Blues, A   Robison 1947
Woman and Song   Motzan 1916
Woman and the Bottle, The   Duke 1949
Woman Are Here to Stay   Blane 1968; Martin 1968

Woman for the Man (Who Has Everything), The   Adams 1966; Strouse 1966

Woman Hasn't Got Enough Eyes for a Man that Flies   Ahlert 1936; Young, Joe 1936

Woman I Love, The   Heyman 1937; Spina 1937

Woman I Was Before, The   Fain 1960; Webster 1960

Woman in His Room, A   Loesser 1948

Woman in Love, A   Loesser 1955

Woman in Love Ain't Got No Sense, A   Razaf 1937

(You Look Like a) Woman in Love (To Me)   Merrill 1967

Woman in the Case   Goetz 1907

Woman in the Shoe, The   Brown, Nacio Herb 1930; Freed, Arthur 1930; Koehler 1950; Stept 1950

Woman Is a Fickle Thing, A   Webster 1952

Woman Is a Sometime Thing, A   Gershwin, George 1935

Woman Is a Tangle, A   Johnson, J. Rosamond 1946

Woman Is Fickle   Johnson, Howard 1939

Woman Is How She Loves, A   Lerner, Alan Jay 1969

Woman Is Only a Woman but a Good Cigar Is a Joke, Puff, Puff, Puff, A   Smith, Harry B. 1905

Woman Is Only a Woman but a Good Cigar Is a Smoke, Puff, Puff, Puff, A   Herbert 1905

Woman Likes to Be Told, A   Adamson 1950; Carmichael 1950

Woman, Lovely, Woman   Herbert 1897; Smith, Harry B. 1897

Woman Needs So Little, A   Spina 1950

Woman Needs Something Like That, A   Hart 1932; Rodgers 1932

Woman Sweet   Bergman 1958

Woman that Wasn't Mine, The   Bacharach 1959

Woman, There Is No Living with You   Gershwin, Ira 1953; Lane 1953

Woman to Lady   Gershwin, George 1935

Woman Who Lived Up There, The   Weill 1947

Woman Who Thinks I'm Wonderful, A   Lerner, Alan Jay 1983; Strouse 1983

Woman Without a Man, A (A Man Without a Woman)   Harburg 1942; Schwartz, Arthur 1942

Woman Without Feelings, A   David, Hal 1976

Woman's Career, A   Porter 1948

Woman's Dream, A   Edwards 1910; Smith, Harry B. 1910

Woman's First Thought Is a Man, A   Herbert 1905

Woman's Heart, A   Kern 1913; Smith, Harry B. 1913

Woman's Intuition, A   Washington 1951; Young, Victor 1951

Woman's Kiss, A   Friml 1937

Woman's No, A   Romberg 1922

Woman's No Means Yes, A   Smith, Harry B. 1903

Woman's Perogative, A   Arlen 1946; Mercer 1946

Woman's Place   Styne 1964

Woman's Rights   Brooks 1960

Woman's Smile, A   Friml 1912; Harbach 1912

Woman's Touch, A   Fain 1953; Gershwin, George 1926; Gershwin, Ira 1926; Webster 1953

Woman's Work, A   Blane 1952

Woman's Work Is Never Done, A   Arlen 1944; Blane 1945; Gershwin, George 1925; Hammerstein 1925; Harbach 1925; Mercer 1944

Women   Hammerstein 1930; Hart 1935; Johnson, J. Rosamond 1904; Rodgers 1935; Romberg 1930

Women Are All Perfect Fools   Smith, Harry B. 1906

Women Are Here to Stay   Blane 1968; Martin 1968

Women Are Women   Hart 1938; Rodgers 1938

Women Get the Best of Us, The   Smith, Harry B. 1910

Women in the Case, The   Herbert 1904

Women in Uniform, The   Rome 1943

Women in White   Kalmar 1936; Ruby 1936

Women of America   Gershwin, Ira 1942

Women of Temperment   Atteridge 1913

Women, Wine and Jazz   Atteridge 1918; Romberg 1918

Women, Women, Women   Ellington 1946; Hammerstein 1928; Romberg 1928

Women's Club Blues   Lerner, Alan Jay 1948; Weill 1948

Women's Emancipation Proclamation   Coleman 1972; Fields 1972

Wompum-Pompum   Razaf 1926

Wonder   Bergman 1959; Razaf 1930

Wonder Bar   Dubin 1934; Warren 1934

Wonder Boy from Peru   Brooks 1952

Wonder If You Ever Think of Me   Kahn 1925

Wonder of It All, The   Cahn 1949

Wonder of Moods   Bacharach 1961; David, Hal 1961

Wonder of You, The   Ellington 1945

Wonder of You (The Lincoln Theme), The   Heyman 1955; Young, Victor 1955

Wonder What Became of You   Coleman 1975

Wonder Why   Cahn 1951, 1953

Wonderful   Blake 1942

Wonderful As Love   Bryan 1958

Wonderful Copenhagen   Loesser 1952

Wonderful Dad   Kern 1923

Wonderful Dreams   Herbert 1940; Loesser 1940

Wonderful Fall for You   Goetz 1917; Monaco 1917

Wonderful Garden of Love   Buck 1914

Wonderful Girl   Buck 1920; Coots 1925; Goetz 1916; Youmans 1926

Wonderful Girl, Goodnight   Von Tilzer 1917

Wonderful Guy, A   Hammerstein 1949; Rodgers 1949

Wonderful Husband, A   Russell 1946

Wonderful Party, A   Gershwin, George 1924; Gershwin, Ira 1924

Wonderful Plan   Willson 1954, 1969

Wonderful Season of Love, The   Webster 1957

Wonderful Show, A   Drake 1954

Wonderful Thing About Tiggers, The   Sherman 1968

Wonderful Thing Happened Today, A   Adamson 1955; McHugh 1955

Wonderful Things   Rome 1957

Wonderful Time Was Had By All, A   Hanley 1921

Wonderful to Be Young   Bacharach 1962; David, Hal 1962

Wonderful War, A   Hammerstein 1920

Wonderful Wasn't It   David, Hal 1952

Wonderful Wonderful   Washington 1961

Wonderful Wonderful Day   DePaul 1954; Mercer 1954

Wonderful Wonderful Fellow   Washington 1959

Wonderful World of Beverly Hills, The   McHugh 1964; Washington 1964

Wonderful World of Color, The   Sherman 1961

Wonderful World of Las Vegas   Styne 1965

Wonderful World of Love   Brooks 1963

Wonderful Years, The   Fain 1958; Leigh 1958

Wonderful You   Cobb 1922; Edwards 1922; Gershwin, George 1922

Wondering   Kalmar 1925; Ruby 1925

Wondering When   Razaf 1926

Wondering Who   Evans 1950; Livingston, Jay 1950

Wonderland   Williams 1907

Wonders of a Barrel, The   Arlen 1968

(The Wonder of It All) Wonderworld   Styne 1964

Wondrin' When   Evans 1948; Livingston, Jay 1948

Wond'ring   Friend 1944
Wond'ring Night and Day   Porter 1922
Won't Be Long Now   Blake 1944; Sissle 1944
Won't dat Be de Blessed Day   Arlen 1959; Mercer 1959
Won't Someone Find Me a Sweetheart?   Smith, Robert B. 1914
Won't Someone Take Me Home   Harbach 1910
Won't You Be My Baby Boy   Edwards 1907
Won't You Be My Daddy?   Atteridge 1917; Romberg 1917
Won't You Be My Girlie?   Howard, Joseph E. 1906
Won't You Be My Playmate?   Herbert 1908; Smith, Harry B. 1908
Won't You Be My Valentine?   Herbert 1908; Smith, Harry B. 1908
Won't You Buy a Flower?   Atteridge 1922; Schwartz, Jean 1922
Won't You Buy a War Stamp (War Stamps)   Atteridge 1918
Won't You Buy My Dreams   Duke 1929
Won't You Come Across?   Friml 1926; Hammerstein 1926; Harbach 1926
Won't You Come and Float Me   Smith, Harry B. 1901
Won't You Come Back to Me   Cohan 1922
Won't You Come Back to My Arms   Dixon 1924; Henderson 1924; Rose 1924
Won't You Come Crusading with Me   Porter 1914
Won't You Come Over to Dover, Jerry   Fisher 1941
Won't You Come Over to My House   Williams 1906
Won't You Come Under My Merry Widow Hat   Edwards 1908
Won't You Even Say Hello   Leslie 1908
Won't You Get Off It, Please (inst.)   Waller 1930
Won't You Give Me a Chance to Love You   Monaco 1917
Won't You Have a Little Feather?   Kern 1907
Won't You Help Me Out   Friml 1919; Harbach 1919
Won't You Kiss Me Once Before You Go?   Kern 1905
Won't You Let Me Carry Your Parcel?   Kern 1908
Won't You Marry Me?   Romberg 1927
Won't You Park Your Heart in My Little Garage of Love   Egan 1919; Whiting 1919
Won't You Play the Game?   Buck 1918
Won't You Please Have a Heart   Sterling 1913; Von Tilzer 1913
Won't You Please Help Me Find My Little Heinie   Coots 1930; Davis 1930
Won't You Say Hello   Bryan 1933; Meyer 1933
Won't You Send a Letter to Me   Atteridge 1917; Romberg 1917
Won't You Stay for Tea   Gordon 1932; Revel 1932
Won't You Take Me to Paris   Romberg 1922
Won't You Tell Me Hon, When We're Gonna Be One   Lewis 1928; Warren 1928; Young, Joe 1928
Won't You Tell Me that You'll Miss Me When You Kiss Me Goodnight   Donaldson 1925; Kahn 1925
Won't You Write Your Autograph in My Album   Goetz 1910
Won't Your Mamma Let You Come Out and Play   Johnson, J. Rosamond 1906
Won'tcha   Razaf 1929
Woo, Woo, Woo, Woo, Manhattan   Gershwin, Ira 1945; Weill 1945
Wood Words, The   Robison 1959
Wooden Shoe Polka, The   Revel 1948
Wooden Shoes   Razaf 1957
Wooden Wedding   Weill 1943
Woodland Dance   Porter 1916
Woodland Reverie   Baer 1945

Woodland Symphony   David, Hal 1941
Woodman Spare that Tree   Johnson, Howard 1939
Woodman, Woodman, Spare That Tree   Berlin 1911
Woodman's Serenade   Merrill 1965; Styne 1965
Woodpecker Song, The   Adamson 1940
Woods Are Full of Cuckoos and My Heart Is Full of Love, The   Coots 1937
Woodstock's Samba (Inst.)   Sherman 1972
Woof!   Bryan 1913
Wooing of the Violin, The   Herbert 1920; Smith, Robert B. 1920
Woolworth of Japan, The   Romberg 1927; Smith, Harry B. 1927
Wop Blues   Lewis 1924; Young, Joe 1924
Wop Song   Brown, Lew 1928; DeSylva 1928; Henderson 1928
Wops My Dear   Leslie 1912
Word a Day, A   Mercer 1951
Word in Edgeways, A   Hart 1928; Rodgers 1928
Word Is Love, The   Harburg 1971
Word of Kindness   Robison 1952
Word of Praise   Robison 1961
Word of the Heart, The   Mercer 1965
Word Portrait   Oakland 1960
Word to Remind You, A   Eliscu 1937
Words   Dubin 1924; Lawrence 1971; Strouse 1999
Words and Music   Brown, Nacio Herb 1936, 1937; Freed, Arthur 1936, 1937
Words Are in My Heart, The   Dubin 1935; Warren 1935
Words Can't Express   Razaf 1930
Words Fail Me   Coots 1936; Davis 1936
Words Have So Many Meanings   David, Mack 1958; Meyer 1958
Words, Music, Cash   Brennan 1928
Words of Uncle Jim, The   Robison 1961
Words Without Music   Duke 1936; Gershwin, Ira 1936
Words, Words, Words   Duke 1963
Work in the Morning   Robin 1946
Work of Art, A   Strouse 1999
Work Song, The   Drake 1964
Work Song (Cinderella Work Song), The   David, Mack 1950; Livingston, Jerry 1950
Work Songs   Arlen 1959; Mercer 1959
Work While You May (Bulgarian Rose Song)   Rainger 1938; Robin 1939
Workers of All Nations   Gershwin, Ira 1943
Workin' for the Yankee Dollar (Hooray for de Yankee Dollar)   Harburg 1957
Workin' Hot   Strouse 1999
Workin' Woman Blues   Waller 1925
Working for the Government   Hart 1920; Rodgers 1920
Working for the Institute   Hart 1921; Rodgers 1921
Working for the Pictures   Atteridge 1914; Romberg 1914
Working Girl   Razaf 1944
Workman's Song   Arlen 1959; Mercer 1959
Workmen's Chorus   Hammerstein 1937; Kern 1937
Workout   Adams 1964; Strouse 1964
Workout for Strings   Friml 1959
Workout Song   Strouse 2000
World and I, The   Herbert 1946
World at Large, The   Adams 1960; Strouse 1960
World Beauty Fair, The   Livingston, Jerry 1963
World Began with You, The   Washington 1938; Young, Joe 1938; Young, Victor 1938
World Belongs to the Young, The   Lerner, Alan Jay 1969

World Doesn't Want My Song, the   Warren 1970

World Famous Horseshoe Curve, The   Willson 1953

World Goes Bobbing Up and Down, The   Buck 1921

World Goes On, The   Bergman 1968

World Goes Spinning Around, The   Sigman 1949

World Has Gone Shimmee Mad, The   Buck 1919

World I Live In, The   Lawrence 1960

World in My Corner, The   Mancini 1956

World Is a Circle, The   Bacharach 1973; David, Hal 1973

World Is Beautiful Today, The   Styne 1953

World Is Full of Villains, The   Gershwin, Ira 1945; Weill 1945

World Is Going Shimmy Mad, The   Buck 1920

World Is in My Arms, The   Harburg 1940; Lane 1940

World Is Longing for the Sunshine, The   David, Mack 1947

World Is Mean, The   Weill 1954

World Is Mine, The   Cahn 1957; Gershwin, George 1927; Gershwin, Ira 1927; Harburg 1934; Young, Victor 1955

World Is My Apple, The   Mercer 1937; Whiting 1937

World Is My Oyster, The   Hart 1937; Rodgers 1937

World Is Ours Tonight, The   Kahn 1938; Romberg 1938

World Is Sick and Weary, The   Warren 1975

World Is Such a Beautiful Place, The   Cahn 1970

World Is Turning Fast, The   Schwartz, Arthur 1982

World Is Waiting to Waltz Again, The   Gordon 1941; Warren 1941

World Is Your Balloon, The   Fain 1951; Harburg 1951

World Is Yours and Mine, The   Hanley 1929; Stept 1929

World Keeps Turning 'Round To Look at You, The   Bryan 1944

World of Barbie, The   Livingston, Jerry 1963

World of Beautiful Girls, The   Sherman 1995

World of Dreamland, The   Smith, Harry B. 1935

World of Dreams   David, Hal 1962; Eliscu 1930; Herbert 1930

World of Make Believe   Bacharach 1966; David, Hal 1966

World of Make-Believe, The   Livingston, Jerry 1963; Webster 1963

World of Melody, A   Brennan 1930; Friml 1930

World of Miracles, A   Livingston, Jerry 1960

World of No Goodbyes, A   Carmichael 1944; Fain 1961; Webster 1961

World of Strangers, A   Fain 1950, 1958; Webster 1950, 1958

World of the Heart, The   Mercer 1965

World of Tomorrow, The   Heyman 1961

World of Whispers, A   Webster 1969

World of Your Arms, The   David, Hal 1958; Livingston, Jerry 1958

World of Your Embrace, The   Drake 1967

World Outside, The   Sigman 1958; Warren 1956

World Owes Me a Loving, The   Conrad 1932; Young, Joe 1932

World Owes Nothing to Me, The   Leslie 1927

World Peace   Loesser 1969

World Showcase March   Sherman 1982

World that Never Was, A   Fain 1967, 1975; Webster 1967, 1975

World Was in My Heart, The   Donaldson 1930; Leslie 1930

World We Love Will Live Again (Things We Love Will Live Again), The   Gilbert 1942

World Weary (Gotta Get Back to You)   Parish 1980

World Will Blow Up, The   Brooks 1959

Worlds   Bergman 1970

World's a Midway   Brooks 1959

World's a Stage for Every Girl, The   Atteridge 1914; Carroll 1914; Romberg 1914

Worlds Apart   Russell 1954

World's Full o' Suckers, The   Lane 1951; Lerner, Alan Jay 1951

World's Full of Girls (Boys), The   Sondheim 1971

World's Greatest Criminal Mind, The   Mancini 1986

World's Greatest Sweetheart Is You, The   Razaf 1929

World's Not Ready, The   Washington 1964

World's Worst Woman, The   Hammerstein 1923; Harbach 1923

World's Your Oyster, The   Willson 1953

World-Wide Romeo, A   Atteridge 1913

Worm Song, The   Heyman 1946; Spina 1946

Worried   Howard, Joseph E. 1908

Worried and Lonesome Blues (inst.)   Johnson, James P. 1922

Worries   Kern 1924

Worry   Blake 1940; Razaf 1940

Worry About Tomorrow, Tomorrow   Gordon 1956; Myrow 1956

Worry Is a Rockin' Chair   Hoffman 1957

Worry Not a Whit Not   Burke 1981

Worry Song, The   Fain 1945; Freed, Ralph 1945

Worryin' All Night Long   Kahn 1931

Worryin' Blues   Kahn 1924

Worryin' the Life Out of Me   Russell 1945

Worst Is Yet to Come, The   Lewis 1918; Young, Joe 1918

Worst Pies in London, The   Sondheim 1979

Worth Remembering   Cahn 1969

Wotcha-Ma-Callit, The   Carroll 1936; Parish 1936

Would He Do the Same for Me   Parish 1930

Would I   Stept 1956

Would I Love to Love You (I'd Love To)   Clare 1929

Would I Love You (Love You Love You)   Russell 1949; Spina 1949

Would I Say I Love You If I Didn't?   Lewis 1951

Would There Be Love?   Gordon 1935; Revel 1935

Would You?   Brown, Nacio Herb 1936; Burke 1945; Freed, Arthur 1936; Sterling 1920; Van Heusen 1945

Would You Ask?   Smith, Harry B. 1896

Would You Be Happy   Mills 1929

Would You Be Satisfied Sally (Sally Don't Live in Our Alley Anymore)   Fisher 1909

Would You Be So Kindly   Harburg 1940; Lane 1940

Would You Believe   Coleman 1972

Would You Believe It   Howard, Bart 1952

Would You Believe Me Sweetheart   Conrad 1933; Coslow 1933

Would You Come Back to Me?   Brown, Lew 1925; Friend 1925

Would You for a Big Red Apple?   Lerner, Sammy 1944; Myrow 1944

Would You Leave Your Happy Home for Me   Sterling 1906; Von Tilzer 1906

Would You Let Me   Blane 1960, 1961; Martin 1960

Would You Like to Buy a Dream   Cahn 1937

Would You Like to Make a Fuss Over Me   Norworth 1917

Would You Like To Sleep Upon My Pillow   Bryan 1921; Pollack 1921; Schwartz, Jean 1921

Would You Like to Take a Walk (Sump'n Good'll Come from That)   Dixon 1930; Rose 1930; Warren 1930

Would You Mind   Revel 1960

Would You Rather Be a Colonel with an Eagle on Your Arm than a Private with a Chicken on Your Knee   Fisher 1918

Would You Rather Be a Colonel with an Eagle on Your Shoulder or a Private with a Chicken on You Knee   Mitchell 1918

Would You Take Back the Love You Gave Me   Dubin 1917

Wouldja for a Big Red Apple   Mercer 1932

Would'ja Have a Cup o' Java with Me   Caesar 1936; Lerner, Sammy 1936

Wouldn't Hurt You for the World   Russell 1955

Wouldn't I Be a Wonder   Woods 1935

Wouldn't I Like to Have Someone Like You to Like Me   Johnson, Howard 1929

Wouldn't It Be Crazy   Porter 1943

Wouldn't It Be Fun   Porter 1958

Wouldn't It Be Funny?   Burke 1950; Van Heusen 1950

Wouldn't It Be Heaven   Coots 1929; Davis 1929

Wouldn't It Be Loverly?   Lerner, Alan Jay 1956; Loewe 1956

Wouldn't It Be Nice   Adamson 1944; Cahn 1956; McHugh 1944; Van Heusen 1956

Wouldn't It Be Wonderful?   Akst 1929; Clarke 1929

Wouldn't It Break Your Heart   Cahn 1966; Van Heusen 1966

Wouldn't It Make You Hungry   Von Tilzer 1903

Wouldn't that Be a Stroke of Luck   Bacharach 1968; David, Hal 1968

Wouldn't that Be Something Now (Je Ne Me Souviens de Rien)   Sigman 1971

Wouldn't You Know I'd Fall   Revel 1946

Wouldn't You Like to Be on Broadway?   Weill 1947

Wouldn't You Like to Have Me Tell Your Fortune   Bryan 1920; Schwartz, Jean 1920

Wouldn't You Like to Taste My Pear?   McHugh 1979

Wouldn't You Rather Make Love   David, Hal 1952

Woulds't   David, Mack 1958; Livingston, Jerry 1958

Wove Me, Willian (Love Me, Lillian)   Robison 1948

Wowee   Livingston, Jerry 1961

Wow-Ooh-Wolf   Porter 1944

Wrap Me in a Bundle and Take Me Home with You   Kahn 1914

Wrap Me in a Spanish Shawl   Edwards 1929

Wrap Me Up and Send Me C.O.D. to Tennessee   Johnson, Howard 1923

Wrap Me Up in a Blanket of Love   Schwartz, Jean 1914

Wrap Your Arms Around Me, I'll Never Be Cold   Bryan 1934

Wrap Your Cares in Rhythm   Cahn 1938

Wrap Your Dreams in the Red, White and Blue   Coots 1940

Wrap Your Troubles in Dreams (And Dream Your Troubles Away)   Koehler 1931

Wrap Yourself in Cellophane   Carmichael 1935; Mercer 1935

Wrapped Up in a Blanket   Brennan 1927

Wrapped Up in a Ribbon (And Tied in a Bow)   Weill 1947

Wrapped Up in Red, Red Rose   Hanley 1930

(I'm) Wrapped Up in You   Oakland 1931

Wren (La Capinera), The   Johnson, Howard 1939

Wriggly Rag   Goetz 1913

Wringin' and Twistin'   Waller 1927

Write a Letter to Me at the Old Folks Home   Caesar 1976

Write About What You Know   Martin 1962

Writer Writes at Night, A   Rodgers 1979

Writing on the Wall, The   Drake 1963

Written in Your Hand   Romberg 1948

Written on the Wind   Cahn 1956; Young, Victor 1956

Wrong!   Cahn 1965; Schwartz, Jean 1933; Van Heusen 1965; Young, Joe 1933

Wrong Girl, The   Strouse 1999

Wrong Man, The   Drake 1968

Wrong Neighborhood   Merrill 1943

Wrong Note Rag   Comden and Green 1953

Wrong Number   Parish 1931; Robison 1964; Silver 1931

Wrong Side of the Railroad Tracks, The   Ellington 1946

Wrong Song, A   Adams 1978; Strouse 1978

Wrong Thing at the Right Time, The   Gershwin, Ira 1924

Wunderbar   Porter 1948

Wunderhorn   Cahn 1976; Lane 1976

Wuzza Matter Baby, Wuzza Matter with You   Gordon 1929

Wy-Lets (Violets)   Johnson, Howard 1927

Wynken, and Blynken and Nod   David, Mack 1934

Wyoming   Fisher 1920

X

Xanadu   Rome 1945

Xanadu (Les Elephants Roses) (La Marijuana)   Rome 1965

Xylophone   Rainger 1929; Robin 1929

Y

Y' Got Me, Baby   Arlen 1932; Yellen 1932

Y' Had It Comin' to You   Lerner, Sammy 1938

Ya Darn Tootin' Gabriel   Webster 1942

Ya Getta Get Up Early in the Morning (inst.)   Revel 1960

Ya Gonna Be Home Tonight (Oh Yeh, Then I'll Be Over)   Dubin 1927; Stept 1927

Ya Got Class   Evans 1953; Livingston, Jay 1953

Ya' Got Love   Hoffman 1931

Ya Got Me   Comden and Green 1944

Ya Got Trouble   Willson 1957

Ya Gotta Be Versatile   Johnson, James P. 1930; Razaf 1930

Ya Gotta Get Up Early in the Morning   Gordon 1952; Revel 1952

Ya Gotta Give the People Hoke   Cahn 1956; Van Heusen 1956

Ya Gotta Have Music   David, Mack 1946

Ya Gotta Know How to Love   Warren 1926

Ya Gotta Lot to Learn   Ager 1939

'Ya Never Know Just 'Oo Yer Gonna Meet   Brooks 1948

Ya Pushin' Ya Luck   Arlen 1959; Mercer 1959

Ya Should a Seen Pete   Styne 1941

Ya Ya Alma   Fisher 1925

Yaaka Hula Hickey Dula   Goetz 1916; Young, Joe 1916

Yacht Club Swing   Waller 1945

Yaddie Kaddie Kiddie Kaddie Doo   Lewis 1916; Meyer 1916; Young, Joe 1916

Ya-Ha-Ha   Fain 1925

Yah-ta-ta, Yah-ta-ta (Talk, Talk, Talk)   Burke 1945; Van Heusen 1945

Yalaloo (The Song of a Bum)   Hoffman 1959

Yam, The   Berlin 1938

Y.A.M. Survival Manual, The   Leigh 1985

Yama Hula   Fisher 1921

Yamekraw (inst.)   Johnson, James P. 1927

Yamo Yamo   Oakland 1960

Yancey Special   Razaf 1938

Yank, Yank, Yank   Loesser 1944

Yan-Kee   Caesar 1920; Gershwin, George 1920

Yankee Bohemia   Goetz 1910

Yankee Boy   Strouse 1986

(Workin' for the) Yankee Dollar   Arlen 1957

Yankee Doodle   Lane 1965; Lerner, Alan Jay 1965; Porter 1929

Yankee Doodle Band   Magidson 1937; Wrubel 1937

Yankee Doodle Blues   Caesar 1922; DeSylva 1922;
    Gershwin, George 1922; Henderson 1922
Yankee Doodle Boodle   Jerome 1905; Schwartz, Jean 1905
Yankee Doodle Boy   Cohan 1904
Yankee Doodle Bunny   Friend 1951
Yankee Doodle Doll   Hoffman 1931
Yankee Doodle Doo   Spina 1957
Yankee Doodle Girl   Willson 1943
Yankee Doodle Hayride   Gordon 1944; Monaco 1944
Yankee Doodle Never Went to Town   Freed, Ralph 1935
Yankee Doodle on the Line   Kern 1918
Yankee Doodle Oo-La-La, The   Atteridge 1923; Schwartz,
    Jean 1923
Yankee Doodle Patriotic Tune   Buck 1915
Yankee Doodle Polka, The   Duke 1941; Parish 1941
Yankee Doodle Rhythm   Gershwin, Ira 1927
Yankee Doodle Tan (The "Double V" Song), A   Razaf 1942
Yankee Doodles Are Coming to Town   Lane 1979; Lerner,
    Alan Jay 1979
Yankee Doodle's Come to Town   Cohan 1908
Yankee Doodle's Gonna Go to Town Again   Rose 1939
Yankee Enterprise, The   Spina 1977
Yankee Father in a Yankee Home, The   Cohan 1927
Yankee Girl, The   Smith, Harry B. 1903
Yankee, Go Home   Rodgers 1962
Yankee Land   Herbert 1907; Williams 1909
Yankee Love   Berlin 1911; Goetz 1911
Yankee Prince March (inst.)   Cohan 1908
Yankee Prince Waltzes (inst.)   Cohan 1908
Yankee Romeo   Goetz 1910
Yankee Rose   Leslie 1907
Yankee Son of a Gun   Smith, Harry B. 1908
Yankee Strut   Atteridge 1924; Romberg 1924; Schwartz, Jean
    1924
Yankee Tar, A   Smith, Harry B. 1901
Yankee Tourist Girl, The   Schwartz, Jean 1903
Yankiana Rag   Smith, Harry B. 1908
Yanks Are at It Again, The   Brown, Lew 1918
Yanks Are Coming, The   Pollack 1942
Yanks Are on the March Again, The   Adamson 1941
Yanks Aren't Coming!, The   Rome 1940
Yankyula   Brennan 1930; Friml 1930
——-yanna   Fisher 1924
Yascha and Sascha   Adamson 1935; Lane 1935
Yascha Michaeloffsky's Melody   Berlin 1928
Yasso Rag   Schwartz, Jean 1919
Yassu (Wedding Song)   Washington 1961
Yatata, Yatata, Yatata   Hammerstein 1947; Rodgers 1947
Yazoo Rag   Bryan 1919
Ye Lunchtime Follies   Hart 1943; Rodgers 1943
Ye Olde Antique Sale   Drake 1955
Ye Shall Be Free   Robison 1946
Yea Boys, Let's Have a Time   Atteridge Date Unknown
Yeah Man   Sissle 1932
Year After Year   Howard, Bart 1955
Year After Year (We're Together)   DeSylva 1924; Gershwin,
    George 1924
Year Ago Today   Parish 1932
Year and a Day, A   Smith, Harry B. 1905
Year from Today, A   Kern 1924
Year In, Year Out   Cahn 1958
Year Is a Long Time, A   Friml 1917; Harbach 1917
Year Isn't Such a Long, Long Time, A   Brown, A. Seymour
    1941
Year of the Tear, The   Russell 1965

Yearning for Love   Ellington 1936; Mills 1936; Parish 1936
Yearning (Just for You)   Davis 1925
Years Before Us, The   Loesser 1948
Years of Love   Friml 1923
Ye'll Be Returnin' Again   Styne 1958
Yellow and Green Make Blue   Freed, Ralph 1964
Yellow Bird   Bergman 1957
Yellow Melodrama   Porter 1910
Yellow Rain   Arlen 1966
Yellow Rose of Texas   Leslie 1954
Yellow Sailboat from Hawaii   Hoffman 1962
Yenta Power   Adams 1978; Strouse 1978
Yep! The 'Zep' Came Over   Mills 1928; Parish 1928
Yes!   Arlen 1953; Fields 1953; Loesser 1960; Sondheim Date
    Unknown
Yes, He Is   Drake 1954
Yes, I Can   Adams 1964; Strouse 1964
Yes I Do   Caesar 1926
Yes I Know It Was Long Ago   Spina 1944
Yes, I Love You Honey   David, Mack 1943; Johnson, James
    P. 1931, 1943
Yes, Indeedy   Comden and Green 1949
Yes, Lord   Robison 1952
Yes, Ma'am (You're from the Show Boat)   Hammerstein
    1927; Kern 1927
Yes Me   Hart 1933; Rodgers 1933
Yes Mister Cosgrove   Lane 1952; Robin 1952
Yes My Darling Daughter   Lawrence 1941; Warren 1939
Yes, My Dear   Gordon 1933; Revel 1933
Yes, My Heart   Merrill 1961
Yes, My Love   Kern 1956; Robin 1956
Yes or No   Romberg 1925; Smith, Harry B. 1925
Yes She Did   Bryan 1909
Yes, Sir   Hammerstein 1931; Romberg 1931
Yes Sir, I Love Your Daughter   Conrad 1934; Magidson 1934
Yes Sir! That's My Baby   Donaldson 1925; Kahn 1925
Yes Sir There's People Like That   Young, Joe 1932
Yes, Sorority   Johnson, Howard 1928
Yes to You   Clare 1934; Whiting 1934
Yes! We Have No Bananas Parody   Berlin 1923
Yes, Yes   Duke 1946
Yes, Yes, My, My   Cahn 1936
Yes, Yes, Yes   Porter 1938; Strouse 2000
Yes! Yes! Yes! Yes! I'm Falling in Love with You   Mills 1936
Yes, Yes, Yvette   Caesar 1927
Yes You Are   Merrill 1951
Ye'sm Lord   Evans 1950; Livingston, Jay 1950
Yes-Suh   Razaf 1932
Yesterday   Atteridge 1924; Kahn 1927; Ruby 1940; Schwartz,
    Jean 1923
Yesterdays   Harbach 1933; Kahn 1919; Kern 1933
Yesterday's Forgotten   Duke 1963
Yesterday's Kisses   Ager 1932; Bryan 1932; Fisher 1932
Yesterday's Love   Loesser Date Unknown
Yesterthoughts   Herbert 1935; Kahn 1935
Yesterthoughts (inst.)   Herbert 1916
Yet I Know   Raye 1964
Yi, Yi, Yi (Aye, Aye, Aye)   Rome 1965
Yiddish Wedding Jubilee   Smith, Harry B. 1908
Yiddisha Charleston   Fisher 1926; Rose 1926
Yiddisha Eyes   Berlin 1910
Yiddisha Luck and Irisha Love (Kelly and Rosenbaum, That
    Mazeltoff)   Bryan 1911; Fisher 1911
Yiddisha Nightingale   Berlin 1911
Yiddisha Professor   Berlin 1912

Yiddishe Turkey Trot Carroll 1912

Yiddishkeit Oakland 1969

Yiddle on Your Fiddle (Play Some Ragtime) Berlin 1910

Yiddle-de Vop David, Mack 1947; Livingston, Jerry 1947

Yi-I-Add-I-Ay Get in Good Humor Today Young, Joe 1932

Yip! Ahoy! (Adrift on the Lo-one Prairie!) Rome 1938

Yip! Yip! Bryan 1919; Schwartz, Jean 1919

Yip-I-Addy-I-Aye Cobb 1904; Edwards 1904

Y.M.D. Smith, Harry B. 1911

Yo Ho and Off We Go David, Hal 1952

Yo Te Amo Means I Love You Bryan 1928; Whiting 1929

Yock-A-Hilo Town Donaldson 1917

Yodalo Evans 1955; Livingston, Jay 1955

Yodel O DeSylva 1919

Yodel Song Leigh 1955; Smith, Harry B. 1912

Yodelin' Cowboy Joe Stept 1927

Yodelin' Jive Raye 1939

Yogi Eyes Lewis 1920; Young, Joe 1920

Yogi (Who Lost His Will Power), The McHugh 1941; Mercer 1941

Yo-Ho! Heave Ho! Yo-Ho! Baer 1965

Yokohama Lullaby Clarke 1921; Monaco 1921

Yolanda Freed, Arthur 1945; Warren 1945

Yo-Lay-ee-oo Means I Love You Motzan 1921; Smith, Harry B. 1921

Yonkele and Rifkelel Gilbert 1931

Yonkle Doodle Goes Steppin' Mills 1937

Yonny and His Oompah Yellen 1938

Yoo Hoo Brown, Lew 1921

Yoo Hoo, Hi, There! Sondheim Date Unknown

Yoo-Hoo DeSylva 1921; Livingston, Jerry 1973; Sondheim 1984

Yoo-oo Just You Gershwin, George 1918

Yosheke, Yosheke Bergman 1983

You Adamson 1936; Brennan 1928; Cahn 1939, 1977; Donaldson 1936; Gordon 1953; Hoffman 1929; Koehler 1951; Mercer 1933; Mills 1929; Myrow 1953; Rodgers 1970; Schwartz, Arthur 1930

You 21 and You 53, You Both Stand for Liberty Sterling 1917

You Above All Webster 1950

You After All These Years Duke 1950; Rome 1950

You Ain't Gonna Shake Them Feathers No More Comden and Green 1967; Styne 1967

You Ain't Got No Savoir-Fair Hart 1931; Rodgers 1931

You Ain't Got the Girl Till the Ring Is on Her Finger Bryan 1910

You Ain't Got Time for Love Johnston 1938

You Ain't Heard Nothing Yet DeSylva 1919; Kahn 1919

You Ain't Hurtin' Your Ole Lady None Merrill 1971; Styne 1971

You Ain't Livin' If You Ain't Lovin' Caesar 1954

You Ain't Seen the Last of Me Strouse 1989

You All Got to Be Born and Bed in Kentucky Kahn 1917

You Alone Eliscu 1928

You Alone (Tu Sola) Caesar 1921

You Always Can Come Back to Me Razaf 1935

You Always Love the Same Girl Hart 1943; Rodgers 1943

You and I Brown, Nacio Herb 1944; Dietz 1950; Freed, Arthur 1944; Friml 1923; Johnson, Howard 1921, 1922; Willson 1941

You and I and Cupid Kahn 1910

You and I Are Passers By Smith, Harry B. 1928

You and I Could Be Just Like That Eliscu 1932

You and I (In Old Versailles) DeSylva 1923; Gershwin, George 1923; Goetz 1923

You and I in the Moonlight Washington 1929

You and I Know Schwartz, Arthur 1937

You and Me Comden and Green 1967; Coslow 1938; Freed, Ralph 1938; Hanley 1921; Mancini 1982; Porter 1928; Raye 1962; Styne 1967, 1985; Weill 1938

You and Me for Always Bacharach 1988

You and Me Together (The Marine's Drill) Evans 1952; Livingston, Jay 1952

You and the Moon and Me Baer 1933

You and the Night and the Music Dietz 1934; Schwartz, Arthur 1934

You and the Waltz and I Webster 1942

You and Who Else Coslow 1940; Hoffman 1934; Washington 1934

You and You and Me Hammerstein 1925; Harbach 1925

You and Your Beautiful Eyes David, Mack 1950; Livingston, Jerry 1950

You and Your Broken Heart Eliscu 1943; Gorney 1943

You and Your Flourescent Eyes Gorney 1953

You and Your Kiss Fields 1940; Kern 1940

You and Your Love Mercer 1939

You Angel Schwartz, Jean 1936; Young, Joe 1936

You Appeal to Me Bullock 1938, 1950; Romberg 1927; Smith, Harry B. 1927; Spina 1938; Whiting 1930

You Are Hart 1934; Rodgers 1934; Stept 1962

You Are a Song Robin 1930

You Are a Wonderful Girl Freed, Arthur 1920; Howard, Joseph E. 1920

You Are All I've Wanted Harbach 1936; Romberg 1936

You Are All That's Beautiful Duke 1963

You Are All the World to Me Gilbert 1949

You Are Beautiful Hammerstein 1958; Herbert 1940; Loesser 1940; Rodgers 1958

You Are Both Agreed (Finaletto, Scene 1) Hart 1928; Rodgers 1928

You Are Doing Very Well Hammerstein 1934; Kern 1934

You Are Everything to Me David, Mack 1946; Sigman 1959

You Are for Loving Blane 1960; Martin 1960

You Are Full of the Bull from Ze Boulevard Johnson, Howard 1919; Meyer 1919

You Are in Love Howard, Bart 1959

You Are Like a Song By Victor Herbert (That Is My Impression of You) Bryan 1943

You Are Lonely Ellington 1958

You Are Love Hammerstein 1927; Kern 1927

You Are Mine Motzan 1917

You Are Mine Evermore Smith, Harry B. 1927

You Are Mine 'Til the End of the Waltz Razaf 1931

You Are My Day Dream Caesar 1929; Friend 1929

You Are My Destiny Johnson, Howard 1933; Silver 1933

You Are My Downfall Fain 1946

You Are My Dream Washington 1959

You Are My Fire Bug Cobb 1906; Edwards 1906

You Are My Heart Blane 1947

You Are My Heaven Magidson 1928

You Are My Ideal Freed, Arthur 1932

You Are My Love Friend 1950; Webster 1953

You Are My Lucky Star Brown, Nacio Herb 1935; Freed, Arthur 1935

You Are My Melody Johnston 1938

You Are My Rain Beau, Under a Cry Baby Sky Lewis 1929; Young, Joe 1929

You Are My Rain-Beau Caesar 1922

You Are My Star in the Night   Caesar 1926

You Are My Sweetheart (Du Bist Mein Liebchen)   Motzan 1931

You Are My Woman   Hammerstein 1931; Romberg 1931

You Are Never Away   Hammerstein 1947; Rodgers 1947

You Are Not My First Love   Howard, Bart 1948

You Are Not the Girl   Gershwin, George 1917; Gershwin, Ira 1917

You Are So Dear to Me   Davis 1952

You Are So Fair   Hart 1937; Rodgers 1937

You Are So Lovely and I'm So Lonely   Hart 1935; Rodgers 1935

You Are So Near (So Near and Yet So Far)   Gorney 1948

You Are So Sweet to Me   Johnson, James P. 1958

You Are So Tempting   De Lange 1958

You Are Springtime   Caesar 1945

You Are the Bravest   Styne 1954

You Are the First Love   Harburg 1932

You Are the Jewel of My Heart   Fisher 1930

You Are the Light of My Life   Leigh 1952

You Are the Music to the Words in My Heart   Yellen 1938

You Are the One for Me   Pollack 1932

You Are the Rose that Will Never Die   Kalmar 1914; Leslie 1914; Snyder 1914

You Are the Someone   Atteridge 1913; Schwartz, Jean 1913

You Are the Song in My Heart   Livingston, Jerry 1932

You Are the Tree   Rome 1970

You Are There   Drake 1953; Webster 1967

You Are Tomorrow   Arlen 1966

You Are Too Beautiful   Hart 1933; Rodgers 1933

You Are Unforgettable   Gershwin, Ira 1940

You Are Woman   Merrill 1964; Styne 1964

You Are You   Gershwin, George 1925; Hammerstein 1925; Harbach 1925

You Are Your Own Best Friend   Cahn 1980; DePaul 1980

You Are Youth   Duke 1968

You Ask Me Why   David, Hal 1977

You Asked for It, You Got It   Baer 1939

You Baby Me, I'll Baby You   Bryan 1929; Meyer 1929

You Beautiful So and So   Rose 1929; Snyder 1929

You Beautiful You   Bryan 1926

You Belong in Someone Else's Arms   Bacharach 1960

You Belong to Me   David, Hal 1951; Friend 1935; Herbert 1916; Smith, Harry B. 1916; Yellen 1935

You Belong to the Night   Duke 1949

You Bet I Do   Coots 1928

You Bet I'm Glad to Be Just where I Am   Meyer 1908

You Better Keep Babying Baby   Dubin 1938

You Better Keep the Home Fires Burning Cause Your Mama's Getting Cold   Leslie 1925

You Blew It   Coslow 1971

You Blew Out the Flame in My Heart   Drake 1951

You Bother Me   Heyman 1950; Spina 1950

You Bother Me an Awful Lot   Fain 1935; Kahal 1935

You Bring Out the Lover in Me   Leigh 1956

You Bring Out the Savage in Me   Coslow 1934

You Bring Out the Worst in Me   Duke 1949

You Bring the Scotch and I'll Bring the Soda   Davis 1944

You Broke It Up (When You Said Dixie)   Razaf 1935

You Broke It Up when You Said "Georgia!"   Razaf 1940

You Brought a New Kind of Love to Me   Fain 1930; Kahal 1930

You Brought Ireland Right Over to Me   Brennan 1917

You Brought Me Love   Blake 1956; Sissle 1956

You Brought Me to My Senses   Davis 1939

You Bug Me Ann-Arlene   Sherman 1965

You Built a Fire Down in My Heart   Berlin 1911; Goetz 1911

You Burn Me Up when You Turn Me Down   Smith, Harry B. 1932

You Call It Madness, but I Call It Love   Conrad 1931

You Called It Love   Hanley 1931

You Came a Long Way from St. Louis   Russell 1948

You Came Along   Cahn 1945; Robin 1927

You Came to My Rescue   Rainger 1936; Robin 1936

You Can Always Come Back to Me   Johnson, James P. 1934; Razaf 1934

You Can Always Count on Me   Coleman 1989

You Can Always Have Me   Clarke 1920; Monaco 1920

You Can Always Judge a Gal (By the Songs She Keeps)   Cahn 1958; Van Heusen 1958

You Can Always Tell a Yank   Harburg 1944; Lane 1944

You Can Be a New Yorker Too   Strouse 1985

You Can Be Had (Be Careful)   DeSylva 1933; Robin 1933; Whiting 1933

You Can Be Kissed   Dubin 1935; Warren 1935

You Can Be My Cave Man   Berlin 1938

You Can Bet Your Life It's Love   Coots 1931

You Can Bounce Right Back   Cahn 1956; Van Heusen 1956

You Can Buy the Sun for a Song   Rainger 1939; Robin 1939

You Can Call It Swing   Cahn 1936

You Can Call Me Peter   Schwartz, Arthur 1948

You Can Close the New York Stock Exchange   Sondheim 1990

You Can Count on Me   Myrow 1939

You Can Dance with Any Girl at All   Caesar 1925; Youmans 1925

You Can Dance Your Way into Her Heart   Caesar 1920

You Can Depend on Us   Drake 1953

You Can Do It   Sigman 1952

You Can Do It, Kid   Sigman 1949

You Can Do No Wrong   Porter 1948

You Can Find a Little Bit of Dixieland No Matter where You Go   Donaldson 1918

You Can Find It in the Papers Every Day   Williams 1910

You Can Fly! You Can Fly! You Can Fly!   Cahn 1952; Fain 1952

You Can Go As Far As You Like with Me   Smith, Harry B. 1911; Smith, Robert B. 1911

You Can Have Broadway   Cohan 1906

You Can Have Every Light on Broadway   Davis 1922

You Can Have Him   Berlin 1949

You Can Have It — I Don't Want It, Daylight Savings Time   Friend 1930; Monaco 1930

You Can Have It Baby   Johnston 1934

You Can Have Paris   Russell 1961

You Can Have Your Song and Wine, Give Me the Women for Mine   Donaldson 1917; Dubin 1917

You Can in Yucatan   Drake 1948

You Can Just Tell Christmas Is in the Air   Stept 1952

You Can Kiss These Goodnight Kisses Goodbye   Freed, Ralph 1941; Hoffman 1941

You Can Make My Life a Bed of Roses   Brown, Lew 1932; Henderson 1932

You Can Never Go Back (I'll Never Go Back)   Adams 1981; Strouse 1981

You Can Only Wear One Pair of Pants at a Time   Friend 1930; Monaco 1930

You Can Put It in the Papers   Stept 1934; Washington 1934

You Can Read Me Like a Book   Van Heusen 1938

You Can Sail in My Boat   Olcott 1905

You Can Say That Again   DePaul 1958; Mercer 1944; Raye 1958; Sigman 1944

You Can See with Your Heart   David, Mack 1945

You Can Shake 'em   Merrill 1959

You Can Take Music Away   Lawrence 1981

You Can Take the Boy Out of the Country   Russell 1948, 1958

You Can Tango, You Can Trot, Dear but Be Sure and Hesitate   Sterling 1914; Von Tilzer 1914

You Can Tell Her Anything Under the Sun (When You Get Her Under the Moon)   Silver 1927

You Can Tell She Comes from Dixie   Ager 1936

You Can Tell that He's an American   Johnson, Howard Date Unknown

You Can Tell That I'm Irish   Cohan 1916

You Can Trust Me   Drake 1964

You Can Walk Under Ladders   Brooks 1958

You Cannot Make Your Shimmy Shake on Tea   Berlin 1919

You Cannot Turn Against Her   Sterling 1900

You Can't Always Have what You Want   Mercer 1958

You Can't Argue   Harbach 1910

You Can't Argue with Love   Kahn 1940

You Can't Be a Friend to Everybody   Howard, Joseph E. 1908

You Can't Be Here and Can't Be There   Harbach 1945

You Can't Be Too Choosy   Hoffman 1954

You Can't Be True to Two   Hoffman 1956

You Can't Beat My Bill   Porter 1941

You Can't Beat Us (For We've Never Lost a War)   Brennan 1918

You Can't Believe My Eyes   Bryan 1929; Meyer 1929

You Can't Blackout Romance   Bryan 1941; Schwartz, Jean 1941

You Can't Blame Me   Edwards 1917

You Can't Blame the Girlies at All   Silver 1919

You Can't Blame Your Uncle Sammy   Dubin 1924; McHugh 1924

You Can't Brush Me Off   Berlin 1940

You Can't Brush Off a Russian   Pollack 1944

You Can't Buy Everything   Freed, Ralph 1934

You Can't Can Like Girls Can   Johnson, Howard 1925

You Can't Cash in on an Alibi   Blake 1958

You Can't Change My Dream   Caesar 1944

You Can't Cook Hugs and Kisses   Yellen Date Unknown

You Can't Deep Freeze a Red Hot Mama   Yellen 1978

You Can't Deny You're Irish   Cohan 1918

You Can't Do a Waltz to a Cha Cha   Hoffman 1959

You Can't Eat Peas with a Knife   Von Tilzer 1927

You Can't Eye a Shy Baby   Baer 1927; Lewis 1927; Young, Joe 1927

You Can't Fool a Hula Hula Girl   Meyer 1931; Mitchell 1931

You Can't Fool a New York Kid   Goetz 1915; Romberg 1915

You Can't Fool Your Dreams   Hart 1920; Rodgers 1920

You Can't Get a Man with a Gun   Berlin 1946

You Can't Get Along with 'em Or Without 'em   Clarke 1916; Fisher 1916

You Can't Get Arrested for Thinking   Sterling 1915; Von Tilzer 1915

You Can't Get Away from It   Clarke 1913; Jerome 1913; Schwartz, Jean 1913

You Can't Get Away from Love   Razaf 1954

You Can't Get Away from the Lawd   Razaf 1953

You Can't Get Away from Tipperary   Atteridge 1915; Carroll 1915; Jerome 1915; Romberg 1915; Snyder 1915; Williams 1915

You Can't Get Far Without a Guitar in Texas   Woods 1951

You Can't Get Far Without a Railroad   Washington 1957

You Can't Get Over the Wall   Fields 1945; Romberg 1945

You Can't Get Something for Nothing   Coslow 1938; Weill 1938

You Can't Get to Heaven   Coleman 1996

You Can't Get to Heaven in an Aeroplane   Bryan 1927; Fisher 1927

You Can't Get to Heaven that Way   Caesar 1930

You Can't Go Home Again   Cahn 1979

You Can't Go Wrong By Going Along with Me   Turk 1927

You Can't Go Wrong with a Love Song   Coslow 1925; Johnson, Howard 1925

You Can't Go Wrong with Us   Atteridge 1914; Romberg 1914

You Can't Hang Out with Annie   Rose 1926; Woods 1926

You Can't Hate Me for That   Davis 1922

You Can't Have a Show Without Durante   Cahn 1951; Willson 1951

You Can't Have Everything   Gordon 1937; Revel 1937

You Can't Have It Unless I Give It To You   Razaf 1927

You Can't Have My Sugar for Tea   Kalmar 1928; Ruby 1928

You Can't Have Your Cake and Eat It   Waller 1945

You Can't Hurt Me Any More   Freed, Ralph 1951; Hoffman 1951

You Can't (Just) Have No One Man By Yourself   Johnson, James P. 1923

You Can't Keep a Good Dog Down   Strouse 1989

You Can't Keep a Good Dreamer Down   Burke 1946; Van Heusen 1946

You Can't Keep a Good Man Down   Howard, Joseph E. 1904, 1907

You Can't Keep a Squirrel on the Ground   Cobb 1916; Edwards 1916

You Can't Keep Me Away from You   Smith, Harry B. 1935

You Can't Keep the Old Green Down   Johnson, Howard 1914

You Can't Knock It to Me   Fain 1949; Yellen 1949

You Can't Lose a Broken Heart   Johnson, James P. 1944, 1948

You Can't Lose 'em All   Coleman 1966; Fields 1966

You Can't Lose Me   Hammerstein 1922

You Can't Love 'em All   Cahn 1959; Van Heusen 1959

You Can't Make a Monkey Out of Me   Rose 1925

You Can't Make It Anywhere   Cahn 1964; Van Heusen 1964

You Can't Make Love By Wireless   Kern 1923

You Can't Make Me Believe that It Was All Make Believe   Coots 1946; Lewis 1946

You Can't Make Me Stop Loving You   Leslie 1910

You Can't Mean Maybe with Those Eyes   Donaldson 1931

You Can't Pick Berries in Wintertime   Henderson 1951; Yellen 1951

You Can't Play My Ukelele   Hoffman 1933

You Can't Pull the Wool Over My Eyes   Ager 1936

You Can't Put Catsup on the Moon   Fain 1940; Kahal 1940

You Can't Put the Petals Back on a Rose   Freed, Ralph Date Unknown

You Can't Run Around with a Lot of Little Girls (If You Want to Run Around with Me)   Hanley 1918

You Can't Run Away from It   DePaul 1956; Mercer 1956

You Can't Run Away from Love   Gordon 1948

You Can't Run Away from Love Tonight   Dubin 1937; Warren 1937

You Can't Say No to a Soldier   Gordon 1942; Warren 1942

You Can't Say You Feel Rich Anymore   Coleman 1979
You Can't Sew a Button on a Heart   Yellen 1947
You Can't Shush Katie (The Gabbiest Gal in Town)   Warren 1926
You Can't Spell Victory with an Absent "T"   Carroll 1943
You Can't Stop Me from Dreaming   Friend 1937
You Can't Stop Me from Falling in Love with You   Coots 1930; Davis 1930
You Can't Stop Me from Loving You   Hoffman 1929
You Can't Stop Now   Brown, Lew 1945
You Can't Take It with You When You Go   Gilbert 1954; Oakland 1954
You Can't Tee Off My Fairway   Fisher 1936
You Can't Tell a Man By His Hat   Loesser 1937
You Can't Tell Love What to Do   Friend 1932; Monaco 1932
You Can't Tell the Mothers from the Daughters   Yellen 1917
You Can't Turn Back the Clock   Young, Victor 1952
You Can't Unscramble Scrambled Eggs   Gershwin, George 1930; Gershwin, Ira 1930
You Carry My Heart   Hart Date Unknown; Rodgers Date Unknown
You Catch on Quick   Stept 1940
You Could   Stept 1949
You Could Drive a Person Crazy   Sondheim 1970
You Could Have Been the One, Baby   Brown, Lew 1931; DeSylva 1931; Henderson 1931
You Could Have Knocked Me Over with a Feather   Davis 1943
You Could Hear a Pin Drop   Pollack 1943; Russell 1955
You Could Not Please Me More   Rodgers 1979
You Could Sell Me the Brooklyn Bridge   David, Hal 1945
You Could'a Knocked Me Down with a Feather   Akst 1943
You Couldn't Be Cuter   Fields 1938; Kern 1938
You Couldn't Blame Me for That   Kalmar 1929; Ruby 1929
You Couldn't Do Enough for Me (He Couldn't Do Enough for Me)   Revel 1952
You Couldn't Hardly Notice It At All   Von Tilzer 1902
You Couldn't Help but Be Wonderful   Woods 1956
You Crazy Little Things (Fall in Love)   Hart 1943
You Danced with Dynamite   Burke 1940; Van Heusen 1940
You Dare Not Meet Her Eyes   Johnson, J. Rosamond 1946
You Darlin'   Woods 1929
You Dear   Akst 1927; Davis 1927; Fain 1944; Freed, Ralph 1944
You Deserve Me   Lawrence 1964
You Did   Ahlert 1931; Kalmar 1927; Ruby 1927; Turk 1931
You Did It   Lerner, Alan Jay 1956; Loewe 1956
You Did, You Know You Did   Gilbert 1913
You Did Your Best to Break My Heart   Carmichael 1946
You Didn't Care when You Broke My Heart   Johnson, Howard 1923
You Didn't Come Back (When You Said You'd Come Back)   Sigman 1946
You Didn't Have the Heart To Tell Me   Brown, Nacio Herb 1952
You Didn't Have to Tell Me, I Knew It All the Time   Donaldson 1931
You Didn't Know the Music, I Didn't Know the Words   Coslow 1931
You Didn't Live to Love   Brown, Lew 1931; Henderson 1931
You Didn't Want Me when I Wanted You, I'm Somebody Else's Now   Yellen 1923
You Discover You're in New York   Robin 1943; Warren 1943
You Do   Gordon 1947; Myrow 1947
You Do, Don't You   Hanley 1930

You Do, I Don't   Duke 1927
You Do My Eyes a Favor   Cahn 1942; Styne 1942
You Do Something to Me   Porter 1929
You Do the Darndest Things, Baby   Mitchell 1936; Pollack 1936
You Done Me Dirty   Johnson, James P. 1933; Mills 1933
You Don't Belong in My Dreams   Young, Joe 1932
You Don't Bring Me Flowers   Bergman 1981
You Don't Even Know that I'm Alive   Burke 1935; Spina 1935
You Don't Have a Leg to Stand On   Robison 1951
You Don't Have to Be a Baby to Cry   Merrill 1950
You Don't Have to Be a Sherlock Holmes   Ahlert 1931; Turk 1931
You Don't Have to Be a Toreador   Hart 1920; Rodgers 1920
You Don't Have to Be a Tower of Strength   Bacharach 1961
You Don't Have to Come from Ireland (To Love an Irish Song)   Coots 1946
You Don't Have to Drop a Heart to Break It   Coots 1950
You Don't Have to Kiss Me Goodnight   Willson 1957
You Don't Have to Know the Language   Brooks 1959; Burke 1947; Van Heusen 1947
You Don't Have to Prove It If You Sing It   Willson 1963
You Don't Have to Tell Me   Gordon Date Unknown; Revel Date Unknown; Stept 1958
You Don't Have to Tickle Me with a Feather   Woods 1956
You Don't Know   Willson 1963
You Don't Know Him   Evans 1958; Livingston, Jay 1958
You Don't Know How Big Your Heart Is Till It Starts Breaking   David, Mack 1950; Meyer 1950
You Don't Know How Much You Can Suffer Until You Fall in Love   Friend 1939
You Don't Know Me   Bacharach 1982
You Don't Know Paree   Porter 1929
You Don't Know What I Know About You   Bryan 1918, 1920; Schwartz, Jean 1920
You Don't Know What Love Is   DePaul 1941; Raye 1941
You Don't Know What You're Doin'   Meyer 1931; Young, Joe 1931
You Don't Know What You're Doin' to Me   Gordon 1934; Revel 1934
You Don't Know what You're Missing If You've Never Had a Kiss   Von Tilzer 1918
You Don't Look for Love   Blake 1932; Sissle 1932
You Don't Love Me As I Do   Goetz 1922
You Don't Love Me As Much As I Love You   Von Tilzer 1911
You Don't Love Me No More   Ellington 1946
You Don't Need the Wine to Have a Wonderful Time (While They Still Make Those Beautiful Girls)   Akst 1919
You Don't Remind Me   Porter 1950
You Don't Tell Me   Rodgers 1962
You Don't Understand Song   Johnson, James P. 1929
You Don't Want Me Then   David, Mack 1974
You Drive Me to Dream   Coots 1947
You Dropped Me Like a Red Hot Penny   Ahlert 1936; Young, Joe 1936
You Excite Me   Cahn 1945; Lane 1945; Parish 1933; Styne 1945
You Fascinate Me   Clare 1932; Livingston, Jerry 1939; Mills 1954
You Fascinate Me So   Coleman 1958; Leigh 1958
You Find the Time and I'll Find the Place   Brown, Lew 1929; DeSylva 1929; Henderson 1929
You Flew Away from the Nest   Kalmar 1924; Ruby 1924

You Fool You   Hoffman 1950
You Fooled Me   Davis 1953
You for Me   Arlen 1959; Dubin 1940; Fain 1940; Mercer 1959
You for Me — Me for You   Stept 1925
You for Me and Me for You   Edwards 1931
You for Me, Me for You   Sterling 1903
You for Me, Me for You From Now On   Johnson, James P. 1925
You for Me when You're Sweet Sixteen   Sterling 1909; Von Tilzer 1909
You Forgot to Remember   Berlin 1925
You Forgot Your Gloves   Eliscu 1931
You Forgotcha Guitar   Monaco 1945
You Found Me and I Found You   Kern 1918
You Gambled with Love   Freed, Ralph 1937; Lane 1937
You Gave All Your Kisses to Somebody Else (So Why Bring Your Tears to Me)   Parish 1924
You Gave Me a Rose but I Gave You My Heart   Parish 1932
You Gave Me Everything but Love   Coleman 1959; David, Hal 1959
You Gave Me Ev'rything but Love   Arlen 1932; Kahn 1931; Koehler 1932
You Gave Me the Gate and I'm Swinging   Ellington 1939
You Gave Me Wings to Fly (Then Took Away My Sky)   Livingston, Jerry 1957
You Gave Me Your Heart   Smith, Harry B. 1922; Snyder 1922
You Gave Me Your Word   Adamson 1952; McHugh 1952
You Get a Lot of Help when You're in Love   Akst 1935; Brown, Lew 1935; Henderson 1935
You Get in My Way   Rome 1969
You Get Me All A-Dither With Your Zither   Baer 1950
You Get Me So Excited   Stept 1952
You Get Me So Excited when You Come Near Me   Monaco 1918
You Get on the Fence   Egan 1942
You Go Into Your Dance   Bergman 1960
You Go to My Head   Coots 1938
You Go to Your Church and I'll Go to Mine   Drake 1955
You Go Your Way   Adams 1983; Russell 1964
You Go Your Way (And I'll Go Crazy)   Revel 1941
You Go Your Way and I'll Go Mine   Johnson, J. Rosamond 1915
You Good Boy, You Get Cookie   David, Mack 1958
You Got Looks   Cahn 1956
You Got No Time for Me   Wrubel 1940
You Got to Git the Gittin' (While the Gittin' Is Good)   Blake 1958
You Got to Keep A-Goin'   Bryan 1912; Schwartz, Jean 1912
You Got to Stop a Pickin' on My L'il Pickaninny   Edwards 1912
You Got to Study Buddy   Cahn 1942; Styne 1942
You Got What Gets 'Em   Friml 1923
You Gotta Be Different   Evans 1955; Livingston, Jay 1955
You Gotta Be Good to Me   Lewis 1927; Young, Joe 1927
You Gotta Be Modernistic   Friend 1930; Monaco 1930
You Gotta Crawl Before You Walk   Ellington 1946
You Gotta Eat Your Spinach, Baby   Gordon 1936; Revel 1936
You Gotta Get a Gimmick   Sondheim 1959; Styne 1959
You Gotta Get Lucky Sometime   Burke 1958
You Gotta Get Out and Vote   Harburg 1944
You Gotta Give Credit to Love   Hoffman 1934
You Gotta Go East to Go West   De Lange 1944; Stept 1944

You Gotta Have a Slogan   Mercer 1951
You Gotta Have Dancing   Adams 1978; Strouse 1978
You Gotta Have IT   Berlin 1927
You Gotta Keep Movin' and Dance (You Gotta Keep a' Going)   Smith, Harry B. 1912
You Gotta Keep Saying 'No'   Revel 1945
You Gotta Know How   Donaldson 1925
You Gotta Know How to Dance   Dubin 1936; Warren 1936
You Gotta Live Today   Gorney 1931; Harburg 1931
You Gotta Pay the Freight   Bergman 1965
You Gotta Pull Strings   Adamson 1936; Donaldson 1936, 1941
You Gotta Sing   Revel 1952
You Gotta Stay Happy   Brooks 1948
You Gotta Swing It (inst.)   Waller 1942
You Gotta Talk Me Into It, Baby   Brown, Nacio Herb 1944
You Gotta Taste All the Fruit   Bergman 1964; Fain 1964
You Gotta Too Much-a-de Stock   Lewis 1929; Pollack 1929; Young, Joe 1929
You Gotta Toodle-oo on a Saxophone, If You Wanna Keep Your Sweet Sweet Mama Home   Lewis 1923; Young, Joe 1923
You Gotta Wanta Once in a While   Gorney 1929; Harburg 1929
You Great Big Dancing Doll   Monaco 1914
You Grow Sweeter As the Years Go By   Mercer 1939
You Grow Sweeter Every Day   Stept 1937; Washington 1937
You Had a Wonderful Time   Drake 1953
You Had It Comin' to You   Oakland 1940
You Had That Everlasting Appeal   Loesser Date Unknown
You Happened to Me   Coots 1956
You Have a Way with You   Coslow 1955; Drake 1962
You Have Cast Your Shadow on the Sea   Hart 1938; Rodgers 1938
You Have Everything   Dietz 1937; Schwartz, Arthur 1937
You Have Got to Have a Rudder on the Ark   Rodgers 1970
You Have Me   Edwards 1908; Smith, Robert B. 1907
You Have Only You   Cahn 1963; Van Heusen 1963
You Have Taken My Heart   Mercer 1933
You Have to Do What You Do Do   Gershwin, Ira 1945; Weill 1945
You Have to Have a Party to Make a Hit   Herbert 1914
You Haven't Changed at All   Lerner, Alan Jay 1945; Loewe 1945
You Haven't Lived   Fain 1951
You Haven't Lived If You Haven't Lived Way Down in Dixieland   Henderson 1922
You Haven't Lived Until You've Died in L.A.   Fain 1952; Webster 1951
You Haven't Missed a Thing   David, Hal 1952
You Heart Just Can't Go Wrong   Robin 1946; Whiting 1946
You Help Me   Drake 1964
You Hit a New High   Gordon 1934; Revel 1934
You Hit the Nail on the Head   Ager 1937
You Hit the Spot   Gordon 1936; Revel 1936
You Hold My Heart in the Hollow of Your Hand   Brennan 1938
You, I Adore You   Burke 1935; Spina 1935
You I Love   Cahn 1957; Revel 1946
You Inspire a Mad Desire   Harbach 1933; Kern 1933
You Interest Me   Comden and Green 1982
You Irritate Me So   Porter 1941
You Just Can't Copa with a Copacabana Baby   Davis 1942
You Just Can't Have No One Man By Yourself   Johnson, James P. 1924

You Keep Coming Back Like a Song   Berlin 1946

You Keep Sending 'em Over and We'll Keep Knockin' 'em Down   Mitchell 1918; Ruby 1918

You Kill Me   Robin 1948, 1952; Styne 1948, 1952

You Killed All My Love for You   Akst 1926; Lewis 1925; Young, Joe 1925

You Kissed Me   Fields 1950

You Kissed the Words Right Out of My Mouth   Mills 1948

You Know   Caesar 1920

You Know — I Know   Johnson, James P. 1962

You Know and I Know   Romberg 1919

You Know and I Know (And We Both Understand)   Kern 1915

You Know and I Know the Way   Brennan 1927

You Know How It Is   Gershwin, George 1927; Gershwin, Ira 1927

You Know How to Hurt a Guy   David, Hal 1978

You Know I Know what Makes the Grass Grow   Fisher 1936

You Know It (inst.)   Kern 1956

You Know Me, Al   Caesar 1924

You Know Me Al, You Know Me Ed   Dubin 1924; McHugh 1924

You Know Me, Alabam'   Ager 1924; Yellen 1924

You Know That It's All Worth While, The   Kahn 1931

You Know What I Mean   Buck 1920; Dubin 1919

You Know Why I Love You   Johnson, Howard 1915

You Know You Belong to Somebody Else, So Why Don't You Leave Me Alone   Monaco 1922

You Know You Don't Want Me (So Why Don't You Leave Me Alone)   Mercer 1963

You Know You Love It   Russell 1958

You Know You Won't   Brown, A. Seymour 1913

You Learn About Love Every Day   Stept 1930

You Leave Me Breathless   Freed, Ralph 1938

You Leave Me Limp   Brown, Lew 1931; DeSylva 1931; Henderson 1931

You Left Me Everything but You   David, Mack 1942; Ellington 1944

You Left Me Out in the Rain   Rose 1924

You Left Me So Blue   Young, Victor 1930

You Let Me Down   Dubin 1935; Warren 1935

You Let Me Go for Somebody Else   Clare Date Unknown

You Little Blue Devil   Atteridge 1919; Carroll 1919

You Little Heartbreaker You   Hoffman 1940

You Little Mischief Maker   Freed, Ralph 1935; Young, Victor 1935

You Little Rascal (inst.)   Warren 1938

You Little So-and-So   Coslow 1932; Robin 1932

You Live in a House   David, Mack 1961; Livingston, Jerry 1961

You Look Awful Good to Father   Howard, Joseph E. 1905

You Look Good to Me   Donaldson 1938; Rose 1938

You Look Like Someone I Used to Know   Oakland 1970; Spina 1950, 1957

You Look So Familiar   Brooks 1955; Warren 1955

You Look So Much Better When You Smile   Davis 1952; Silver 1952

You Love Me   Cahn 1950; Smith, Harry B. 1934; Styne 1950

You Love Me Only in My Dreams   Brown, Lew 1945

You Lucky People, You   Burke 1941; Van Heusen 1941

You Made a Jig-Saw Puzzle Out of My Heart   Coots 1933; Young, Joe 1933

You Made a Woman, You Made a Man   Revel 1952

You Made Me Forget How to Cry   Donaldson 1921; Lewis 1920, 1921; Young, Joe 1920, 1921

You Made Me Give Up Everyone Else and Now You Throw Me Down   Gilbert 1925

You Made Me Love You, I Didn't Want to Do It   Monaco 1913

You Made Up My Mind   Parish 1930

You Made Up My Mind for Me   Fisher 1931

You Make Heaven So Beautiful   Johnson, Howard 1935

You Make It Easy to Be True   Adamson 1957; Warren 1957

You Make Me Dream Too Much   Cahn 1944; Styne 1944

You Make Me Feel at Home   Russell 1960

You Make Me Feel So Foolish, When I'm Making Love to You   Bryan 1918; Fisher 1918

You Make Me Feel So Loved   David, Hal 1961

You Make Me Feel So Young   Gordon 1946; Myrow 1946

You Make Me That Way   Akst 1938; Clare 1938

You Make Nice   Hoffman 1956

You Make That Hat Look Pretty   Ellington 1968

You Make Up   Porter 1910

You Marry a Marionette   Herbert 1910

You Matthew Dear   Romberg 1917

You May Be a Bad Man   Atteridge 1921

You May Be a Doggone Dangerous Girl but I'm a Desperate Guy   Freed, Arthur 1917

You May Be Far Away from Me   Dietz 1935; Schwartz, Arthur 1935

You May Be Irish Murphy, But I Think That You're In Dutch   Bryan 1912; Fisher 1912

You May Be the World to Your Mother but You're Only an Oil Can to Me   Jerome 1920; Von Tilzer 1920

You May Hold a Million Girlies in Your Arms   Fisher 1916; Johnson, Howard 1916

You May Not Love Me   Burke 1946; Van Heusen 1946

You May Not Remember   Oakland 1944

You, Me and Company   Coslow 1935

You Mean Everything to Me   Evans 1961; Livingston, Jay 1961

You Mean Something Special to Me   Burke 1971

You Meet the Nicest People at the Race Track   Coots 1964

You Meet the Nicest People in Your Dreams   Hoffman 1939

You Meet the Strangest People   Oakland 1960

You Might As Well Pretend   Eliscu 1931

You Might As Well Stay on Broadway   Smith, Harry B. 1912

You Might Get to Like Me   Merrill 1967

You Missed the Boat   Friend 1950

You Misunderstood   Snyder 1931

You Moved Right In   Adamson 1945; McHugh 1945

You Must Ask Our Dear Mama   Edwards 1902

You Must Be Born with It   Berlin 1932

You Must Be Good Girls   Smith, Harry B. 1920

You Must Be Losin' Your Mind   Waller 1944

You Must Be Mine Dear   Smith, Harry B. 1910

You Must Come Over   DeSylva 1921; Kern 1921

You Must Come Over Blues   DeSylva 1925; Gershwin, Ira 1924, 1925

You Must Come Over Eyes   Gorney 1924

You Must Go Down Again   De Lange 1943

You Must Have Been a Beautiful Baby   Mercer 1938; Warren 1938

You Must Have Been a Cute Little Baby   Monaco 1914

You Must Have Known   Parish 1934

You Must Love Some One   Lewis 1913; Meyer 1913

You Must Meet My Wife   Sondheim 1973

You Mustn't Be Discouraged   Comden and Green 1964;
    Styne 1964
You Mustn't Believe a Word She Says   Cahn 1956; Duke
    1956
You Mustn't Kick It Around   Hart 1940; Rodgers 1940
You My Love   Gordon 1955; Van Heusen 1955
You Name It   Livingston, Jerry 1957
You Nasty Clarinet   Gilbert 1960; Oakland 1960
You Need a Hobby   Berlin 1962
You Need a Little Magic   Fain 1951; Harburg 1951
You Need a Man, Suzanne   DeSylva 1925
You Need No Crown of Gold to Make You a
    Queen   Harbach 1908
You Need Someone   Hammerstein 1922; Mitchell 1922
You Never Can Be Too Sure About the Girls   Brown, Lew
    1917
You Never Can Blame a Girl for Dreaming   Hammerstein
    1923; Harbach 1923; Youmans 1923
You Never Can Tell   Brown, Lew 1919; Kern 1914; Smith,
    Harry B. 1914; Smith, Robert B. 1919
You Never Can Tell About a Woman   Herbert 1906
You Never Can Tell about Love   Coots 1930; Davis 1930
You Never Can Tell By the Left Eye, What the Right Eye
    Means to Do   Johnson, Howard 1914
You Never Can Tell How a Marriage Will Take   Herbert
    1917
You Never Could Tell We Were Married   Atteridge 1912
You Never Did that Before   Ahlert 1930; Turk 1930
You Never Fall in Love Again   Oakland 1951; Webster 1951
You Never Get Nowhere Holding Hands   Johnson, Howard
    1927
You Never Had It So Good!   Cahn 1964; Van Heusen 1964
You Never Knew about Me   Kern 1917
You Never Know   Porter 1938; Razaf 1953
You Never Know What a Kiss Can Mean   Hammerstein
    1920; Harbach 1920
You Never Know What Hit You — When It's Love   Rome
    1948
You Never Know Where You're Going Till You Get
    There   Cahn 1946; Styne 1946
You Never Leave Me   Parish 1948
You Never Leave Me When You Go   Hoffman 1959
You Never Looked Better   Merrill 1971; Styne 1971
You Never Looked So Beautiful   Adamson 1936; Donaldson
    1936
You Never Looked So Beautiful to Me   Dubin 1918; Monaco
    1918
You Never Lose what You Never Had   Lerner, Sammy 1963
You Never Need Latin or Greek   Caesar 1933; Romberg
    1933
You Never Saw a Bigger Little Man   Livingston, Jerry 1941
You Never Saw That Before   Burke 1946; Van Heusen 1946
You Never Say Yes   Hart 1928; Rodgers 1928
You Never Say Yes, You Never Say No   Caesar 1944
You Never Spoke a Word   Kern 1970; Webster 1970
You Never Told Me That Before We Married   Smith, Harry
    B. 1906
You on My Mind   Sigman 1936
You Only Get One Chance   Adams 1978; Strouse 1978
You Only See What You Want to See   David, Hal 1961
You Only Want Me, When No One Else Wants You   Fisher
    1930
You Only Want Me when Nobody Else Is Around   Burke
    1931; Monaco 1931

You Opened My Eyes   Brooks 1953; Gilbert 1935; Heyman
    1932
You or No One (Here Goes Nothing)   Arlen 1959; Mercer
    1959
You or Nobody   Caesar 1927
You Ought to Be Arrested for Breaking My Heart   Alter
    1934
You Ought to Go to Paris   Berlin 1916; Goetz 1916
You Ought to Know   Blake 1924; Sissle 1924
You Ought to See Sally on Sunday   Woods 1933
You Ought to See Suzy Now   Fisher 1938
You Ought to See the Horse   Dubin 1930
You Oughta Be in Pictures   Heyman 1934
You Oughta Go an' See the Wimmin Swimmin'   Conrad
    Date Unknown
You Oughta Know   Coots 1930; Davis 1930
You Oughta See My Baby   Ahlert 1920; Turk 1920
You Out-Smarted Yourself   Razaf 1939
You Picked a Bad Day Out to Say Good-Bye   Berlin 1913
You Put a Song in My Heart   Friend 1946
You Put Music in My Heart   Spina 1959
You Put that Bug in My Ear   Fisher 1936
You Rang the Bell with Me, Ting-A-Ling, Ting-A-Ling   Baer
    1953
You Rat, You   Adams 1968; Strouse 1968
You Really Do Get Around   Magidson 1949; Oakland 1949
You Really Started Something   Freed, Ralph 1931
You Remember   Livingston, Jerry 1973
You Remember Me   Romberg 1918
You Remind Me   Warren 1975
You Remind Me of My Mother   Cohan 1922; Yellen 1917
You Remind Me of Someone   Friml 1923
You Remind Me of Someone I Want to Forget   Brown, Lew
    1911
You Remind Me So Much of My Mother   Dubin 1915
You Rocked When You Should-a Rolled   Raye 1958
You Said a Baddy   Adamson 1947; McHugh 1947
You Said Goodnight but You Meant Goodbye   Gorney 1927;
    Kahn 1927
You Said It   Arlen 1931; Porter 1940; Yellen 1931
You Said No Yesterday, Won't You Say Yes Today?   Akst
    1950
You Said Something   Kern 1917
You Said Something when You Said Dixie   Clare 1923;
    Friend 1923
You Said the Same Thing to Me   Ager 1917; Johnson,
    Howard 1917
You Said You Wouldn't, But You Done It   Johnson, James P.
    1923
You Said You Wouldn't Do It (But You Did)   Gordon 1958;
    Monaco 1958
You Satisfy   Harburg 1932
You Satisfy My Soul   David, Mack 1964
You Saved My Life   Freed, Ralph 1935; Young, Victor 1935
You Say That to All the Girls   Gordon 1934; Revel 1934
You Say the Nicest Things, Baby   Adamson 1948; McHugh
    1948
You Say the Sweetest Things Baby   Gordon 1940; Warren
    1940
You Say You Care   Robin 1948; Styne 1948
You Say You're Sorry   Lane Date Unknown
You Send Me   Adamson 1944; Caesar 1955; McHugh 1944
You Set Me Free   Kahn 1952
You Should Have Most Everything   Smith, Harry B. 1912
You Should Have Told Me   Ager Date Unknown

You Should Have Told Me You Were Only Fooling   Kahn 1924

You Should See Me Tootsie   Ager 1927; Yellen 1927

You Should See Yourself   Coleman 1966; Fields 1966

You Shouldn't Have Said What You Said   Hoffman 1963; Livingston, Jerry 1963

You Shouldn't Never Have Lied   David, Hal 1991; Strouse 1991

You Slipped Right thru My Fingers   Freed, Ralph 1944; McHugh 1944

You Smiled at Me   Kalmar 1926, 1927; Ruby 1926, 1927

You Smoke too Much (inst.)   Bacharach 1980

You, So It's You!   Brown, Nacio Herb 1945

You Speak My Language   Loesser 1942; McHugh 1942

You Spoke, I Never Heard a Word   Blake 1950

You Stand Accused   Parish 1954

You Stand Awfully Good to Me   Edwards 1909

You Started It   Gershwin, George 1931; Gershwin, Ira 1931

You Started Me Dreaming   Coots 1936; Davis 1936

You Started Something   Coslow 1955; Gorney 1931; Harburg 1931; Rainger 1940, 1941; Robin 1940

You Started Something When You Came Along   Gershwin, Ira 1921; Youmans 1921

You Stepped Out of a Dream   Brown, Nacio Herb 1941; Kahn 1941; Lane 1935; Washington 1935

You Still Belong to Me   Conrad 1926; Meyer 1926

You Still Do Those Things to My Heart   Merrill 1952

You Still Retain Your Girlish Figure   Bryan 1930; Dubin 1930

You Struck the Right Note   Hoffman 1937; Lerner, Sammy 1937

You Sure Don't Know How to Shake that Thing   Arlen 1934; Koehler 1934

You Take a Girl Like Me (inst.)   Revel 1960

You Take My Breath Away   David, Hal 1991; Strouse 1991

You Talk Just Like My Maw   Hammerstein 1943

You Taught Me How To Love, Now Teach Me To Forget   Bryan 1909; Meyer 1909

You Teach Me   Hanley 1922

You Tell 'Em   DeSylva 1919; Kern 1919

You Tell Her I Stutter   Friend 1922; Rose 1922

You Tell Her I Stutter Introduction   Loesser 1941

You Tell Me Your Dream, I'll Tell You Mine   Kahn 1928

You Tempt Me   Drake 1943

You the Fondest Thing I Am Of   Washington 1943

You There in the Back Row   Coleman 1983

You Think of Everything   Rose 1940; Van Heusen 1940

You Threw Me Overboard   Coslow 1932

You Tickle Me   Bryan 1921; Clare Date Unknown; Pollack 1921; Schwartz, Jean 1921

You Told Me to Tell You   Ruby 1949

You Told Me with Your Eyes, Now Prove It with Your Kisses   Burke 1931

You Too (Auch du Wirst Mich Einmal Betrugen)   Young, Joe 1930

You Too Can Be a Dreamer   Livingston, Jerry 1954; Parish 1954

You Too Can Be a Puppet   Fain 1951; Harburg 1951, 1952

You, Too, Can Be a Red Hot Mama   Yellen 1978

You Took Advantage of Me   Hart 1928; Rodgers 1928

You Took Me by Surprise   Duke 1941

You Took Me from the Gutter   Clare 1936

You Took My Breath Away   Coslow 1935; Duke 1963; Whiting 1935

You Took My Heart Walking   David, Mack 1936; Meyer 1936

You Took Possession of Me   Lerner, Sammy 1948

You Took the Heart Out of Me   Lewis 1927; Young, Joe 1927

You Took the Sunshine With You Mary Mine   Bryan 1907; Meyer 1907

You Took the Words Right Out of My Heart   Rainger 1938; Robin 1938

You Took the Words Right Out of My Mouth   Adamson 1935; Lane 1933

You Try Somebody Else, and I'll Try Somebody Else   Brown, Lew 1931; DeSylva 1931; Henderson 1931

You Turn on My Music   Drake 1994

You Turned the Tables on Me   Alter 1936; Mitchell 1936

You Twisted My Arm   Martin 1946

You Two   Sherman 1968

You Understand Me   Hoffman 1958; Loesser 1969

You Understand Me So   Lerner, Alan Jay 1948; Weill 1948

You U.S.A.   Dietz 1944; Duke 1944

You Wait and Wait and Wait   Hammerstein 1935; Romberg 1935

You Waited Too Long   Coots 1950

You Wake Up in the Morning in Chicago   Carroll 1915

You Walked By   Friml 1928

You Walkin' My Dreams   Ellington 1958

You Wanna Bet   Coleman 1966; Fields 1966

You Wanna Keep Your Baby Lookin' Right   Robin 1947

You Want Lovin' but I Want Love   Coslow 1929

You Want Lovin', I Want Love   Coslow 1929

You Want the Best Seats, We Have 'Em   Kern 1921

You Wanted Me, I Wanted You   Arlen 1930; Koehler 1930

You Wanted Someone to Play with, I Wanted Someone to Love   Fisher 1923

You Was   Webster 1948

You Wash and I'll Dry   Lerner, Alan Jay 1943; Loewe 1943

You Went Away Once Too Often   Bryan 1929

You Went Away Too Far, and Stayed Away Too Long   Bryan 1926; Monaco 1926

You Went Over with a Bang   Gordon 1934; Revel 1934

You Were Born to Be Loved   Blake 1947

You Were Made for Love   Freed, Ralph 1958; Russell 1948

You Were Made Just for Me (To Make Love to You)   Spina 1957

You Were Made to Order for Me   Von Tilzer 1916

You Were Meant for Me   Blake 1924; Brown, Nacio Herb 1928; Freed, Arthur 1928; Sissle 1924

You Were Never Lovelier   Kern 1942; Mercer 1942

You Were Only Romancing   Coslow 1937

You Were Somebody Else's Sweetheart   Spina 1946

You Were Talking in Your Sleep Last Night   David, Mack 1976

You Were There   DePaul 1941; Hoffman 1959; Oakland 1956; Raye 1941

You Who Go Driving for Pleasure   Caesar 1943

You Will Be Sorry Someday   Davis 1919

You Will Find Your Love in Paris   Gordon 1958

You Will Have to Sing an Irish Song   Norworth 1908

You Will Hear It Soon   Willson 1953

You Will Lose Your Heart in Honolulu   Brown, Nacio Herb 1938; Freed, Arthur 1938

You Will Never Be Lonely   Dietz 1961; Schwartz, Arthur 1961

You Will Never Know   Youmans 1930

You Will Remember Vienna   Hammerstein 1930; Romberg 1930

You Will, Won't You   Harbach 1926; Kern 1926

You Win   Romberg 1918

You Wish I'll Wash   Russell 1961

You Wonderful Thing   Parish 1932

You, Wonderful You   Brooks 1950; Revel 1947; Warren 1950

You Won't Be an Orphan for Long   Strouse 1977

You Won't Be Happy   Baer 1954

You Won't Be Sorry   David, Hal 1961; Davis 1952

You Won't Have to Cry Over Me   David, Hal 1954

You Won't Know Anybody There   Howard, Joseph E. 1909

You Won't Like Margie   Dubin 1928

You Won't See Me If I See You With Anybody Else at All   Brown, Lew 1927; DeSylva 1927; Henderson 1927

You Wouldn't Be You   Styne 1978

You Wouldn't Fool Me, Would You?   Brown, Lew 1929; DeSylva 1929; Henderson 1929

You Wouldn't Give a Pal/Gal a Break   Monaco 1940

You Wouldn't Know My Old Girl Now   Brown, Lew 1915

You Wouldn't Know the Old Town Now   Donaldson 1915; Jerome 1915

You Wouldn't, Would You   Russell 1944

You Wrote Your Name in My Heart   Parish 1935

You, You Darlin'   David, Hal 1958

You, You, You   Friml 1922; Johnson, James P. 1938; Strouse 1989

You'd Be Hard to Replace   Gershwin, Ira 1949; Warren 1949

You'd Be So Nice to Come Home To   Porter 1943

You'd Be So Nice to Have Around   Robison 1944

You'd Be Surprised   Berlin 1919; Bryan 1919; Herbert 1908; Schwartz, Jean 1919

You'd Better Dance   David, Mack 1943; Livingston, Jerry 1943

You'd Better Get a Girl Before the Boys Come Home or You'll Never Get a Girl at All   Mitchell 1918

You'd Better Love Me   Martin 1964

You'd Better See America First   Atteridge 1915

You'd Do for Me — I'd Do for You   Duke 1929

You'd Make a Wonderful Dream   Brown, Lew 1943; Freed, Ralph 1943

You'd Make a Wonderful Model for Me   Monaco 1913

You'd Never Know that Old Home Town of Mine   Donaldson, Walte   Johnson, Howard 1915

You'd Rather Forget than Forgive   Johnson, Howard 1928

You'd Think You Were in Paris   Cohan 1909

You'll Always Be My Lifetime Sweetheart   Burke 1955

You'll Always Be the Girl in My Heart   Howard, Joseph E. 1947

You'll Always Be the Same Sweet Baby   Brown, A. Seymour 1916

You'll Always Be the Same Sweet Girl   Sterling 1915; Von Tilzer 1915

You'll Always Find a Lot of Sunshine in My Old Kentucky Home   Brown, Lew 1918

You'll Answer to Me   David, Hal 1960

You'll Be Dancing with Someone Tonight (The Fortune Teller Song)   Warren 1954

You'll Be Glad to Have Your Old Sweetheart Again   Bryan 1917

You'll Be Her Baby As Long As You Live   Clarke 1916; Johnson, Howard 1916; Monaco 1916

You'll Be Regimented   Johnson, J. Rosamond 1946

You'll Be Sorry   Ager Date Unknown; Friend 1943; Leigh 1952; Yellen Date Unknown

You'll Be Sorry in the Morning   Fisher 1930

You'll Be Sorry in the Morning that You Made Me Cry Tonight   Rose 1926

You'll Be Sorry when We Say Goodbye   Howard, Joseph E. 1914

You'll Be Sorry When You're Sober   Fisher 1910

You'll Be the Prettiest Girl at the Party   Bergman 1964

You'll Be There   Brennan 1915; Coots 1945

You'll Be Welcome As Flowers in May   Egan 1918; Whiting 1918

You'll Call the Next Love the First   Atteridge 1913; Schwartz, Jean 1913

You'll Change Your Mind   Stept 1922

You'll Come Back   Meyer 1909

You'll Come Back Someday   Dubin Date Unknown; Warren Date Unknown

You'll Come Back to Me   Razaf 1928

You'll Come Running Back to Me   Baer 1954

You'll Do   Arlen 1931; DeSylva 1932; Whiting 1932; Yellen 1931

You'll Do It All Over Again   Friml 1919; Harbach 1919

You'll Do the Same Thing All Over Again   Bryan 1911

You'll Do the Same Thing Over for the Old Red, White and Blue   Cobb 1908; Edwards 1908

You'll Do the Same Thing to Someone Else   Hanley 1922

You'll Dream and I'll Dream — Then Wake to Find Your Dreams All Come True   Friml 1919

You'll Fall in Love with Venice   Coslow 1931, 1932

You'll Feel Better Then   Herbert 1908

You'll Find It on the Bill   Weill 1943

You'll Find Me Playing Mah-Jongg   Kern 1923

You'll Find Me Waiting for You   Stept 1925

You'll Find Old Dixie Land in France   Clarke 1918; Meyer 1918

You'll Find the End of the Rainbow in Your Own Back Yard   Rose 1927

You'll Find Your Answer in My Eyes   Baer 1929; Gilbert 1929

You'll Get a Cold in Your Toes   Ahlert 1937; Lewis 1937; Young, Joe 1937

You'll Get All Dat's A'Comin' to You   Sterling 1898; Von Tilzer 1898

You'll Get By with a Twinkle in Your Eye   Coots 1932; Turk 1932

You'll Get Over It   Leigh 1965

You'll Get Over It, She'll Get Over It   Parish 1937; Silver 1937

You'll Get Your Picture in the Paper   Drake 1952

You'll Get Yours   Van Heusen 1955

You'll Give In   Hanley 1930, 1931

You'll Grow Sweeter As the Years Roll By   Coots 1934

You'll Have to Do the Turkey Trot to Captivate the Men   Buck 1912

You'll Have to Guess   Smith, Harry B. 1925

You'll Have to Put a Nightie on Aphrodite   Donaldson 1920; Lewis 1920; Young, Joe 1920

You'll Have to Put Him for Sleep with the Marseillaise and Wake Him Up with an Oo-La-La   Sterling 1918; Von Tilzer 1918

You'll Know   Adamson 1951; McHugh 1951

You'll Know It   Lane Date Unknown

You'll Leave Me Blue   Whiting 1926

You'll Love Me in Paris   Leigh 1955

You'll Love Me Someday, So Why Not Now   Wrubel 1925

You'll Love the Singing   Willson 1956

You'll Never Be Forgotten   Silver 1929

You'll Never Be Missed a Hundred Years from Now   Dixon 1927; Rose 1927

You'll Never Be Poor New York   Styne 1976

You'll Never Be Sorry   Rainger 1935; Robin 1935; Whiting 1935

You'll Never Forget Me   Styne 1985

You'll Never Get Anyone to Love You (The Way that I'm Loving You Tonight)   Coots 1950

You'll Never Get Away from Me   Sondheim 1959; Styne 1959

You'll Never Get Rich   Cahn 1941

You'll Never Get Rid of Me Now   Davis 1934; Oakland 1934

You'll Never Get to Heaven (If You Break My Heart)   Bacharach 1964; David, Hal 1964

You'll Never Get to Heaven with Those Eyes   Clarke 1924; Leslie 1924; Monaco 1924

You'll Never Get Up to Heaven that Way   Baer 1933; Lerner, Sammy 1933

You'll Never Go Panhandling with a Banjo on Your Knee   Caesar 1952

You'll Never Go To Heaven (If You Break My Heart)   Bryan 1937

You'll Never Know   DeSylva 1926; Donaldson 1934; Gordon 1943; Hart 1921; Rodgers 1921; Rose 1928; Warren 1943

You'll Never Know that Old Home Town of Mine   Donaldson 1915; Johnson, Howard 1915

You'll Never Know What Hit You (When It's Love)   Rome 1950

You'll Never Know What Love Is Till I Say I Love You   Cobb 1907; Edwards 1907

You'll Never Lose Me   Harburg 1932; Spina 1957

You'll Never 'Mount to Nothin' If You Stick to Me   Cobb 1904; Edwards 1904

You'll Never Walk Alone   Hammerstein 1945; Rodgers 1945

You'll Not Be Forgotten Lady Lou   Bryan 1907; Meyer 1907

You'll Pardon Me If I Reveal   Gershwin, George 1931; Gershwin, Ira 1931

You'll See   Friml 1917

You'll Think of Someone   Bacharach 1968; David, Hal 1968

You'll Walk in the Sun   Sherman 1965

Young   Adams 1981; Strouse 1981

Young, Alive and in Love   Cahn 1962; Van Heusen 1962

Young America   Norworth 1910

Young Americans, The   Webster 1965

Young and Foolish (And in Love)   Spina 1969

Young and Healthy   Dubin 1933; Warren 1933

Young and Wild   Bacharach 1959; David, Hal 1959

Young and Wild and Free   Sigman 1969

Young at Heart   Leigh 1953

Young Black Joe   Caesar 1928

Young Emotions   David, Mack 1960; Livingston, Jerry 1960

Young Folks Should Get Married   Fields 1951; Warren 1951

Young Forever   Kahn 1936

Young Girls Are a Problem   Blane 1945

Young Grow Every Day, The   Bacharach 1976

Young Just Once   Howard, Bart 1988

Young Lady a la Mode   Herbert 1946

Young Lions, The   DePaul 1958; Raye 1958

Young Love Swings the World   Raye 1959

Young Lovers   Russell 1964

Young Man   Schwartz, Jean 1919

Young Man in Love   Hammerstein 1931; Romberg 1931

Young Man of Manhattan   Livingston, Jerry 1939

Young Man Sings, A   Raye 1939

Young Man with a Horn, The   Freed, Ralph 1944

Young Man's Fancy, A   Ager 1920; Yellen 1920

Young People   Gordon 1940; Warren 1940

Young People Think about Love   Weill 1938

Young, Pretty Girl Like You, A   Bacharach 1968; David, Hal 1968

Young Willie Wilkins   David, Hal 1962

Younger Generation   Gershwin, Ira 1943

Younger Man, A   Strouse 1989

Younger Set, The   Coots 1929; Davis 1929; Hanley 1927

Younger than Springtime   Hammerstein 1949; Rodgers 1949

Youngest Person I Know, The   Merrill 1978

You-oo Just You   Caesar 1918

Your America   Cohan 1916

Your Auto Ought to Get Girls   Atteridge 1916; Motzan 1916; Romberg 1916

Your Beautiful Eyes   Kahal 1927; Snyder 1927

Your Birthday   Robison 1959

Your Blind Date   Pollack 1942

Your Book of Life   Drake 1957

Your Broadway and My Broadway   Brown, Nacio Herb 1937; Freed, Arthur 1937

Your Captain   Styne 1985

Your Conscience Tells You   Raye 1946

Your Country Needs You   Smith, Harry B. 1925

Your Country Needs You Now   Dubin 1917

Your Dad and My Dad Were Buddies, Buddy   Kalmar 1942; Ruby 1942

Your Daddy Was a Soldier, Your Mommy Was a WAC   Mills 1948

Your Disposition Is Mine   Fields 1928; McHugh 1928

Your Dream and I   Smith, Harry B. 1920

Your Dream Is a Flying Carpet   Cahn 1958

Your Dream (Is the Same as My Dream)   Hammerstein 1938; Harbach 1938; Kern 1938

Your Ever Lovin' Arms   Spina 1955

Your Eyes   Blane 1941; DePaul 1949; Friml 1928; Kahn 1923; Martin 1941; Motzan 1929; Parish 1946; Rainger 1934, 1935; Raye 1949; Robin 1935; Whiting 1934, 1935

Your Eyes Are Blue (Once Upon a Time) (Love Story)   Sondheim 1962

Your Eyes Are Like a Million Stars   Monaco 1940'

Your Eyes Have Said   Rainger 1935

Your Eyes Have Said Remember Tho' Your Lips Have Said Forget   Kahn 1920

Your Eyes Have Told Me So   Kahn 1919

Your Eyes Have Told Me that You Love Me   Buck 1923

Your Eyes Shall Speak to Me   Caesar 1922

Your Face Is My Fortune   Caesar 1953

Your Face Is Your Fortune   David, Mack 1943; Livingston, Jerry 1943

Your Face Looks Familiar   Revel 1942

Your Family   Russell 1957, 1958

Your Father Must Have Loved Your Mother   Brown, Lew 1943, 1944; Fain 1944; Freed, Ralph 1944

Your Father Was a Soldier Too   Williams 1905

Your Fault   Sondheim 1987

Your Favorite Fool   David, Hal 1961

Your Feet's Too Big   Fisher 1936

Your Flag and Mine   Akst 1940; Davis 1940

Your Flag and My Flag   Woods 1925

Your Good-Will Ambassador   Mancini 1970; Mercer 1970

Your Guess Is Just As Good As Mine   Hoffman 1934

Your Hand in Mine   Eliscu 1961

Your Hat and My Hat   Berlin 1923

Your Head on My Shoulder   Adamson 1934; Lane 1934

Your Heart Alone Must Tell   Olcott 1905

Your Heart and Mine   Bloom 1936; Mercer 1936

Your Heart Calling Mine   Loesser 1947
Your Heart, If You Please   Herbert 1905
Your Heart Just Can't Go Wrong   Robin 1930; Whiting 1930
Your Heart, My Heart   Sigman 1954
Your Heart Skips a Beat   Johnston 1938
Your Heart Will Tell You So (Cinderella Waltz)   Mercer 1947
Your Home Is in My Arms (Swedish Rhapsody)   Raye 1951
Your Homeland and My Homeland   Coots 1940; Lewis 1940
Your Honor   Spina 1950
Your Isle   Styne 1964
Your Kind of Man   Comden and Green 1967; Styne 1967
Your Kiss   Bergman 1958; Loesser 1940, 1946
Your Kiss Told Me   Caesar 1925
Your Kisses Are Still on My Lips   David, Hal 1960
Your Land and My Land   Romberg 1927
Your Last Adios   Young, Victor 1954
Your Life, My Life (Woman) (inst.)   Bacharach 1979
Your Lips Are Warmer   Bacharach 1956; David, Hal 1956
Your Love   Washington 1934
Your Love Has Faded   Ellington 1939
Your Love I Crave   Johnson, James P. 1929
Your Love Is All That I Crave   Dubin 1929; Johnson, J. Rosamond 1929; Johnson, James P. 1929
Your Love Is Like a Sweetheart Rose   Baer 1952
Your Love Means the World to Me   Lewis 1911
Your Lullaby   Hart 1921; Rodgers 1921
Your Majesty   Burke 1958
Your Minstrel Man   Rainger 1936; Robin 1936
Your Mom's Like Mine   Merrill 1949
Your Mother   Turk 1934
Your Mother and Mine   Cahn 1952; Edwards 1929; Fain 1952
Your Mother and My Mother   Donaldson 1926
Your Mother Must Have Loved Your Father   Fain 1943; Freed, Ralph 1943
Your Name Is Love   DePaul 1954
Your Need Is Greater than Mine   Ahlert 1936; Young, Joe 1936
Your Other Side   Atteridge 1923; Romberg 1923; Schwartz, Jean 1923
Your Own College Band   Loesser 1948
Your Own Little House   Evans 1951; Livingston, Jay 1951
Your Photo   Friml 1914; Harbach 1914
Your Prayers Are Always Answered   Drake 1956
Your Prince Was Not So Charming   Heyman 1934
Your Red Wagon   DePaul 1947, 1949; Raye 1949
Your Rose   Caesar 1930; Harbach 1930; Romberg 1930
Your Smile   Parish 1965
Your Smiles, Your Tears   Caesar 1930; Harbach 1930; Romberg 1930
Your Soft Hand on My Brow (inst.)   Revel 1950
Your Song Was a Long Song (That You Never Meant)   Myrow 1930
Your Spell   Styne 1953
Your Sunny Southern Smile (I'm All Wrapped Up in You)   Gordon 1931; Revel 1931
Your Top's Too Tall   Evans 1945; Livingston, Jay 1945
Your Type Is Coming Back   Stept 1933
Your Understanding Heart   Robison 1955
Your Way or My Way   Johnson, Howard 1924
Your Wonderful U.S.A.   Gershwin, Ira 1921
Your Words and My Music   Freed, Arthur 1941
Your Worries Ain't Like Mine   Razaf 1928
You're a Bad Influence on Me   Porter 1936

You're a Beautiful Brown Eyed Burglar   Egan 1914; Whiting 1914
You're a Big Piece of Cheese   Friend 1918
You're a Blessing   Freed, Ralph 1935
You're a Blessing to Me   Rainger 1934, 1935, 1937, 1938; Robin 1934, 1935, 1937, 1938
You're a Boy After My Heart   Robison 1964
You're a Breeze in the Desert   Rainger 1936; Robin 1936
You're a Builder-Upper   Arlen 1934; Gershwin, Ira 1934; Harburg 1934
You're a Child   Lerner, Alan Jay 1974; Loewe 1974
You're a Dan-Dan-Dandy   Davis 1954
You're a Dangerous Girl   Clarke 1916; Monaco 1916
(It Is) You're a Dear Old World After All   Howard, Joseph E. 1909
You're a Different You   Alter 1929
You're a Dream Set to Music   Sissle 1939
You're a Four Star Picture to Me   Rainger 1936; Robin 1936
You're a Friend, You're a Pal, You're a Sweetheart   Hoffman 1953
You're a Glamour Girl   Silver 1940
You're a Good Little Devil   Leslie 1913
You're a Good Old Car but You Can't Climb Hills   Sterling 1921; Von Tilzer 1921
You're a Grand Old Flag   Cohan 1906
You're a Great Big Blue Eyed Baby Boy   Brown, A. Seymour 1912
You're a Great Big Lonesome Baby   Kahn 1917; Whiting 1917
You're a Heavenly Thing   Young, Joe 1935
You're a Joy to the World (But a Tear in My Heart)   Fain 1949
You're a Knockout   Akst 1936; Clare 1936
You're a Liar   Coleman 1960; Leigh 1960
You're a Little Bit of Ev'rything (That I Like)   Baer 1965
You're a Little Black Sheep   Ellington 1968
You're a Lovable Lunatic   Coleman 1973; Fields 1970
You're a Lucky Fellow Mr. Smith   Raye 1941
You're a Lucky Guy   Cahn 1939
You're a Million Miles from Nowhere (When You're One Little Mile from Home)   Donaldson 1919; Lewis 1919; Young, Joe 1919
You're a Myst'ry to Me   Coots 1943
You're a Natural   Loesser 1938; Mercer 1941; Schwartz, Arthur 1941
You're a Nice Man   Davis 1954
You're a Pain in the Heart to Me   Hoffman 1929
You're a Part of Me   Gilbert 1936
You're a Perfect Jewel to Me Dearest   Buck 1919
You're a Queer One, Julie Jordan   Hammerstein 1945; Rodgers 1945
You're a Real Sweetheart   Caesar 1927; Friend 1927
You're a Regular Girl   Brown, A. Seymour 1912
You're a Rock   Cahn 1970; Styne 1970
You're a Sentimental Guy   Berlin 1956
You're a Shot in the Arm   Coslow 1942
You're a Sucker for a Dame   Berlin 1956
You're a Sweet Little Headache   Rainger 1938; Robin 1938
You're a Sweet Patootie   Cahn 1947; Styne 1947
You're a Sweetheart   Adamson 1938; McHugh 1938
You're a Symphony of Love   Gordon 1932; Revel 1932
You're a Vision to Behold   Young, Joe 1935
You're a Woman   Lane 1985
You're a Wonderful Girl   Smith, Harry B. 1927
You're About to Be Beautiful   Martin 1962

You're Acting Strange   Caesar 1954
You're All I Know of Love   Webster 1973
You're All I Need   Adamson 1935; Kahn 1935
You're All Right Eddie   Williams 1905
You're All that I Need   DeSylva 1920
You're All that I'm Living For   Donaldson 1932
You're All the Candy with Me   Schwartz, Jean 1905;
    Williams 1905
You're All the Women in the World to Me   Spina 1977
You're All the World to Me   Lane 1951; Lerner, Alan Jay
    1951; Smith, Harry B. 1906; Smith, Robert B. 1908
You're All There Is   Freed, Arthur 1932
You're Always Breaking Something and Now You're
    Breaking My Heart   Dubin 1919
You're Always in My Heart but You're Never By My
    Side   Bryan 1913
You're Always Sure of My Love for You   Kahn 1930
You're an Angel   Brennan 1930; DePaul 1944; Fields 1935;
    Friml 1930; McHugh 1935; Raye 1944
You're an Angel Playing Hookey from Heaven   Hoffman
    1934
You're an Education   Dubin 1937, 1938; Warren 1938
You're an Eyeful of Heaven   Dixon 1935; Wrubel 1935
You're an Old Smoothie   Brown, Nacio Herb 1932; DeSylva
    1932; Whiting 1932
You're Asking for It   Robin 1952
You're at the Music Hall   Cahn 1980
You're Awful   Comden and Green 1949
You're Baby Minded Now   Dubin 1931
You're Bad for Me   Revel 1942
You're Beautiful   Spina 1959
You're Beautiful Tonight, My Dear   Young, Joe 1933
You're Bound to Meet a Party   Drake 1952
You're Breaking in a New Heart (While You're Breaking
    Mine)   Drake 1947
You're Bringing Out the Dreamer in Me   Burke 1958
You're Building a Wall Between Us   Fain 1949
You're but Oh So Right   Cahn 1953; Fain 1953
You're Calling Me, Georgia   Blake 1927
You're Charming   Turk 1932
You're Cheatin' Yourself If You're Cheatin' Me   Hoffman
    1957
You're Cuter than the Devil (Maria Belen Chacon)   Drake
    1949
You're Dancing on My Heart   Bryan 1932; Meyer 1932
You're Dangerous   Burke 1941; Van Heusen 1941
You're Dead!   Burke 1953; Van Heusen 1953
You're Deeper in My Heart   Livingston, Jerry 1954
You're Devastating   Fields 1952; Harbach 1933, 1952; Kern
    1933, 1952
You're Doin' All Right   Gordon 1953; Myrow 1953
You're Dreamlike   Dietz 1943, 1944, 1946; Duke 1943;
    Schwartz, Arthur 1946
You're Driving Me Crazy   Donaldson 1930
You're Easy on the Eyes   Coots 1933; Johnson, Howard 1933
You're Easy to Dance With   Berlin 1942
You're Easy to Remember   Dixon 1927
You're Everything Beautiful   Coots 1936; Davis 1936
You're Everything I Love   Friend 1960
You're Everything to Me   Parish 1962
You're Everywhere   Caesar 1934; Heyman 1931; Revel 1947;
    Webster 1947; Youmans 1931
You're Ev'rything Sweet   Razaf 1936
You're Famous   Hoffman 1931
You're Far Away from Home   Coleman 1960; Leigh 1960

You're Far Too Near Me   Gershwin, Ira 1945; Weill 1945
You're Fired   David, Hal 1991; Strouse 1991
You're Following Me   Bacharach 1961
You're Foolin' Yourself When You Try to Fool Me   Ager
    1932; Hoffman 1932
You're Gettin' Warm   Hoffman 1957
You're Getting a Good Girl   Friend 1950
You're Getting to Be a Habit with Me   Dubin 1933; Warren
    1933
You're Giving Me a Song and a Dance   Ager 1936
You're Goin' to Fall in Love with California, Like I Fell in
    Love with You   Monaco 1918
You're Going Far   Coleman 1972
You're Gonna Be Surprised Tonight   Dixon 1933
You're Gonna Break Somebody's Heart When You Grow
    Older   Davis 1952
You're Gonna Dance with Me, Baby   Styne 1954
You're Gonna Dance with Me, Willie   Styne 1953
You're Gonna Get My Letter (In the Morning)   Merrill 1947
You're Gonna Lose Your Gal   Monaco 1933; Young, Joe
    1933
You're Gonna Love Tomorrow   Sondheim 1971
You're Gonna Make a Wonderful Sweetheart (For Somebody
    Else)   Drake 1946
You're Gonna See a Lot of Ma   Hoffman 1938
You're Gonna Wake Up Some Day   Ager 1937
You're Good for Me   Clare 1982; Coleman 1999
You're Good for My Morale   Eliscu 1943, 1944; Gorney 1943
You're Gorgeous, But Dangerous, You're Much too Much for
    Me   Koehler 1934; Stept 1934
You're Growing On Me   Robison 1958
You're Guilty   Robin 1936
You're Gwine to Get Something what You Don't Have   Von
    Tilzer 1910
You're Haunting Me Again   Drake 1944
You're Here and I'm Here   Kern 1913, 1914; Smith, Harry B.
    1913
You're Here My Love   Burke 1955
You're Here, You're There, You're Everywhere   Kahal 1937
You're Hitting a Thousand in the Game of Love   Brennan
    1915
You're Impossible   Arlen 1963
You're in a Class By Yourself   Brown, Nacio Herb 1930;
    Freed, Arthur 1930
You're in Every One's Arms (But in Nobody's
    Heart)   Hoffman 1931
You're in Heidelberg   Romberg 1924
You're in Kentucky   Atteridge 1921; Romberg 1921
You're in Love   Friml 1917; Harbach 1917; Heyman 1931;
    Porter 1932; Youmans 1931
You're in Love and I'm in Love   Donaldson 1928
You're in Love with Every One but the One Who's in Love
    with You   Dixon 1924; Henderson 1924
You're in Love with Someone   Burke 1949; Van Heusen
    1949
You're In Love with Someone Else (But I'm in Love with
    You)   Loesser 1942; Styne 1942
You're in My Heart   Revel 1947
You're in My Heart Again   Adamson 1937; McHugh 1937
You're in My Power Ha! Ha! Ha! Ha! Ha!   Hoffman 1933
You're in Style when You're Wearing a Smile   Kahn 1918
You're in the Army Now (inst.)   Stept 1957
You're Invited to a Party   Coleman 1988
You're It   Cahn 1963, 1964; Van Heusen 1963, 1964

You're Just a Little Better (Than the One I Thought Was Best)   Atteridge 1914; Carroll 1914

You're Just a Little Bit of Everything I Love   Gordon 1928

You're Just a Little Pansy, But You're Sweeter than a Song   Silver 1918

You're Just a Little Too Late   Mitchell 1920

You're Just a Lover   Brown, Nacio Herb 1930; Egan 1930

You're Just a No Account   Cahn 1939

You're Just a Perfect Peach Beyond My Reach   Kern 1911; Smith, Harry B. 1911

You're Just a Show-Off   Dubin 1925

You're Just About Right for Me   Ahlert 1931; Turk 1931

You're Just an Old Antidisestablishmentarianismist   Ellington 1947

You're Just Another Memory   Coots 1929

(I Wonder Why) You're Just in Love   Berlin 1950

You're Just Made to Order for Me   Von Tilzer 1916

You're Just the Boy for Me   Edwards 1908

You're Just the Girlie, that I Adore   Brown, A. Seymour 1910

You're Just the Kind of a Girl I'd Like to —-   Friend 1925

You're Just the Kind of Girl I'd Like My Girl to Be   Cobb 1909; Goetz 1909

You're Just the One I've Been Looking For   Silver 1928

You're Just the Same to Me   Howard, Joseph E. 1905

You're Just the Sort of Girl that I Could Love   Buck 1913

You're Just the Type for a Bungalow   Donaldson 1921; Lewis 1921; Young, Joe 1921

You're Just Too, Too   Porter 1957

You're Kinda Grandish   Arlen 1936; Harburg 1936

You're Laughin', I'm Cryin'   Alter 1968; Davis 1968

You're Laughing at Me   Berlin 1937

You're Lettin' the Grass Grow Under Your Feet   Ager 1939; Livingston, Jerry 1939

You're Like a Beautiful Song   Dubin 1916

You're Like a Song   Adamson 1938; McHugh 1938

You're Like a Toy Balloon   Kahal 1936; Rose 1936

You're Like the Roses, Rosie   Meyer 1908

You're Living Right Next Door to Heaven when You Live in Dixieland   Bryan 1919; Schwartz, Jean 1919

You're Locked in My Heart   Kalmar 1914; Leslie 1914; Snyder 1914

You're Lonely and I'm Lonely   Berlin 1940

You're Looking for Romance, I'm Looking for Love   Lawrence 1957; Livingston, Jerry 1937

You're Loveable, So Loveable   Ahlert 1924

You're Lovely   Clare 1927; Pollack 1927

You're Lovely Love   Martin 1951

You're Lovely, Madame   Rainger 1938; Robin 1938

You're Lucky to Me   Blake 1930; Razaf 1930

You're Making a Miser of Me   Dubin 1919

You're Mama's Baby Boy   Lewis 1917; Young, Joe 1917

You're Married Under False Pretenses   Smith, Harry B. 1935

You're Marvelous (To Me She's Marvelous)   Clare 1929

You're Meant for Me to Love   Baer Date Unknown; Gilbert Date Unknown

You're Merely Wonderful   DePaul 1943, 1958; Raye 1943, 1958

You're Mine   Fisher 1931; Lewis 1917; Snyder 1917; Young, Joe 1917

You're Mine Forever   Baer 1955

You're Mine in My Memories   Coots 1943

You're Mine You   Heyman 1933

You're More Like a Pal Than a Sweetheart   Dixon 1927; Rose 1927

You're More Like Your Mommy Ev'ry Day   Drake 1952

You're My Baby   Brown, A. Seymour 1912; Goetz 1912

You're My Boy   Cahn 1947; Schwartz, Jean 1914

You're My Boy (Girl)   Styne 1947

You're My Captain Kidd   Stept 1930

You're My Desire   Mills 1937

You're My Dish   Adamson 1938; McHugh 1938

You're My Dream Girl   Baer 1943

You're My Everything   Dixon 1931; Warren 1931; Young, Joe 1931

You're My Extra Cup of Coffee in the Morning   Bryan 1943

You're My Favorite One   Clare 1936; Pollack 1936

You're My Fourth of July   Coots 1934

You're My Friend Ain'tcha   Merrill 1957

You're My Girl   Cahn 1947

You're My Happy Ending   Buck 1924; Hanley 1924

You're My Heart   Loesser 1937

You're My Ideal   Waller 1938

You're My Kissin' Girl   DePaul 1958; Raye 1958

You're My Little Baby Girl   McHugh 1912

You're My Little Pin-Up Girl   Gordon 1944; Monaco 1944

You're My Little Theme Song   Von Tilzer 1929

You're My May Day   Warren 1960

You're My Past, Present and Future   Gordon 1933; Revel 1933

You're My Poem of Love   Johnson, Howard 1935

You're My Rose   Johnson, James P. 1947, 1948

You're My Silvery Symphony   Blake 1950

You're My Star   Adams 1993

You're My Thrill   Clare 1933; Gorney 1933; Lane 1935; Washington 1935

(Eyes of Blue) You're My Waterloo   Parish 1980

You're Near and Yet So Far   Romberg 1948

You're Near but Yet So Far   Akst 1923; Davis 1923

You're Nearer   Hart 1940; Rodgers 1940

You're Never Fully Dressed without a Smile   Strouse 1977

You're Never More than Sweet Sixteen   Bryan 1932; Fisher 1932

You're Never too Old   Hammerstein 1923; Youmans 1923

You're Never Too Old to Be Kissed   Schwartz, Jean 1975

You're Never Too Old To Love   Bryan 1913; Jerome 1913

You're Never Too Young (Face the Music)   Cahn 1955; Schwartz, Arthur 1955

(T' Me Baby) You're News   Gershwin, Ira 1939; Harburg 1939, 1941

You're Next   Blane 1948; Warren 1948

You're No Brother, No Brother of Mine   Adams 1965; Strouse 1965

You're No Go   Drake 1964

You're Not Asking Me, I'm Telling You   Lewis 1929; Young, Joe 1929

You're Not At All Like You   Duke 1963

You're Not Fully Dressed Without a Smile   Arlen 1966

You're Not Giving — You're Lending   Cahn 1945; Styne 1945

You're Not in My Arms Tonight   Washington 1950; Young, Victor 1950

You're Not Living in Vain   Hoffman 1954; Silver 1954

You're Not Old Enough   Duke 1963

You're Not Pretty but You're Mine   Harburg 1932; Lane 1932

You're Not So Easy to Forget   Magidson 1947; Oakland 1947

You're Not the Kind   Mills 1936

You're Not the Mayor   Strouse 1985

You're not the One and Only (Lonely One)   Woods 1955

You're Not the Only Oyster in the Stew   Burke 1934; Spina 1934

You're not the Same   Kalmar 1931; Ruby 1931

You're Not the Same Old Sweetheart   Koehler 1929

You're Not the Type   Dietz 1961; Schwartz, Arthur 1961

You're Nothin' Without Me   Coleman 1989

You're Nowhere Until You're Home   Raye 1950

You're Number One on My Hit Parade   Robison 1936

You're OK   Parish 1933

You're Old Enough to Know   Dubin Date Unknown; Warren Date Unknown

You're on My Mind   Kalmar 1941; Ruby 1941

You're on the Lido Now   Hart 1926; Rodgers 1926

You're on the Right Road   Smith, Harry B. 1912

You're on Your Own   Adamson 1943; McHugh 1943

You're One in a Million   Heyman 1934

You're Only a Baby   Kahn 1922

You're Only a Barefoot Boy   Eliscu 1941; Gorney 1941

You're Only As Good As Your Last Kiss   Yellen 1978

You're Only Fooling You   Mills 1952

You're Only Saying It Because It's True   Stept 1949

You're Out of This World to Me   De Lange 1937

You're Over the Hill   Leslie 1947

You're Part of Me   Sigman 1958

You're Perfect   Eliscu 1929

You're Pretty As a Picture   Brown, Nacio Herb 1936; Freed, Arthur 1936

You're Pretty Terrific Yourself   Dubin 1943; Monaco 1943

You're Probably in Love   Cahn 1980

You're Responsible   Clare 1929; Monaco 1934

You're Right I'm Wrong   Davis 1951; Silver 1951

You're Right, You're Right   Cahn 1966; Van Heusen 1966

You're Sailing Away with My Heart   David, Mack 1948; Hoffman 1948; Livingston, Jerry 1948

You're Sensational   Porter 1956; Stept 1939; Webster 1934

You're Setting Me on Fire   Donaldson 1937

You're Simply Delish   Freed, Arthur 1930

You're Sixteen   Sherman 1960

You're Slightly Terrific   Mitchell 1936; Pollack 1936

You're So Beautiful — That   Mercer 1951

You're So Danceable With   Hoffman 1958

You're So Darn Charming   Burke 1935; Spina 1935

You're So Different from the Rest   Smith, Harry B. 1911

You're So Divine   Dubin 1934; Warren 1934

You're So Easy to Remember, I'm So Easy to Forget   Dixon 1927; Woods 1927

You're So Fascinating   Smith, Harry B. 1913

You're So Good to Me   Cahn 1942, 1943, 1946; Styne 1942, 1946

You're So Good to Me (And I'm So Tired of It All)   Robison 1963

You're So Happy   Donaldson 1934; Kahn 1934

You're So Indifferent   Fain 1935; Parish 1935

You're So Lovely   Magidson 1935

You're So Nice to Me   Caesar 1927

You're So Nice to Remember   Robin 1943

You're So Reliable   Loesser 1946

You're So Right   Drake 1952; Evans 1954; Livingston, Jay 1954

You're So Right for Me   Evans 1954; Livingston, Jay 1954

You're So Simpatico   Coots 1953

You're So Worth the Waiting For   Drake 1945

You're Some Girl   Brown, A. Seymour 1912

You're Someone Special   Evans 1961; Livingston, Jay 1961

You're Something New Under the Sun   Raye 1938

You're Starting to Get to Me   Cahn 1959; Van Heusen 1959

You're Stepping on My Toes   Hoffman 1938

You're Still an Old Sweetheart of Mine   Egan 1918; Whiting 1918

You're Still in My Heart   Yellen 1932

You're Still Mine in My Dreams   Leslie 1936

You're Such a Character   Stept 1944

You're Such a Comfort to Me   Gordon 1933; Revel 1933

You're Such an Angel   Razaf 1940

You're Tellin' I   Styne 1940

You're Telling Me   Donaldson 1932; Kahn 1932

You're Telling Our Secrets   Bacharach 1961; David, Hal 1961

You're That Girl   Young, Joe 1934

You're the Acme of Perfection (inst.)   Revel 1961

You're the Apple of My Eye (And I Love Apples)   Ruby 1967

You're the Apple of My Eye (You Little Peach)   Magidson 1938; Wrubel 1938

You're the Best Little Mother that God Ever Made   Brennan 1916

You're the Best Thing That's Happened to Me   Adamson 1954; McHugh 1954

You're the Better Half of Me   Fields 1930; McHugh 1930

You're the Bride and I'm the Groom   Brown, Nacio Herb 1930; Freed, Arthur 1930

You're the Cats   Hart 1931; Rodgers 1931

You're the Cause of It All   Cahn 1945; Styne 1945

You're the Certain Someone   Kahn 1924

You're the Cream in My Coffee   Brown, Lew 1928; DeSylva 1928; Henderson 1928

You're the Cure for What Ails Me   Arlen 1936; Harburg 1936

You're the Cure for what Ails Me, Baby You're Doin' Me Good   Gorney 1930; Harburg 1930

You're the Dream   Bacharach 1959; David, Hal 1959

You're the Dream, I'm the Dreamer   Davis 1944

You're the Fairest Little Daisy that Grows in the Garden   Gilbert 1913

You're the First Cup of Coffee   Gorney 1948

You're the First Thing I Pray for Each Morning (Du Bist Mein Morgen - Und Mein Nachtgebetchen)   Young, Joe 1931

You're the Girl   Clarke 1912; Leslie 1912; Schwartz, Jean 1912

You're the Girl for Me   Blane 1964; Martin 1964; Warren 1964

You're the Goddess of Beautiful Girls   Friend 1918

You're the Greatest   Davis 1953

You're the Greatest Discovery   David, Mack 1939

You're the Greatest Little Mother in the World   Lewis 1918; Young, Joe 1918

You're the Greatest (The Complimentary Song)   Baer 1967

You're the Heart that Loves Me   Merrill 1954

You're the Jewel in My Heart (Tableaux of Jewels)   Fisher 1929

You're the Keeper of My Heart   Stept 1943

You're the Last of My Past   Oakland 1936

You're the Love of My Life   Spina 1957

You're the Most Wonderful Girl   Clarke 1913; Leslie 1913

You're the Mother Type   Hart 1926; Rodgers 1926

You're the Nicest Little Girl I Ever Knew   Johnson, J. Rosamond 1911

You're the One   Harbach 1928; Schwartz, Arthur 1928; Washington 1951; Youmans 1930; Young, Victor 1951

You're the One and Only One   Mills 1928

You're the One for Me   Donaldson 1927; McHugh 1941; Mercer 1941; Merrill 1946
You're the One Girl for Me   Herbert 1914
You're the One Who Knows   Young, Victor 1960
You're the Only Girl He Loves   Kern 1912
You're the Only One Can Hurt Us   Davis 1962
You're the Only You   Sherman 1983
You're the Prize Guy of Guys   Porter 1957
You're the Rainbow   Rainger 1943; Robin 1943
You're the Reason   De Lange 1946
You're the Right One   Brooks 1953; Warren 1953
You're the Same Old Girl   Williams 1913; Young, Joe 1913
You're the Song   David, Mack 1979; Sigman 1968
You're the Sunrise   Dietz 1930; Schwartz, Arthur 1930
You're the Surest Cure for the Blues   Lerner, Sammy 1931
You're the Sweetest Girl I Know   Howard, Joseph E. 1906
You're the Sweetest Girl This Side of Heaven   Kahn 1930
You're the Top   Porter 1934
You're the Type   Hammerstein 1920; Harbach 1920
You're the Very Last Word in Love   Leslie 1938
You're the World's Fairest   Gordon 1938; Revel 1938
You're the World's Sweetest Girl   Kahn 1932
You're There, Little Girl, You're There   Edwards 1920
You're Through   Mills 1940
You're Tired of Me (Mi Vudi Lasciar)   Raye 1961
You're Too Careless with Your Kisses   Dixon 1932; Woods 1932
You're too Dangerous, Cherie (La Vie en Rose)   David, Mack 1948
You're Too Far Away   Porter 1930, 1933
You're Too Good for Me   Adamson 1935; Lane 1935
You're Too Good to Be True   Rose 1939
You're Too Intense   Cahn 1949
You're Too Sure of Me   David, Mack 1936; Meyer 1936
You're Trapped   Cahn 1951
You're Trying to Throw Me Down   Turk 1923
You're Unfair to Me   Coslow 1952
You're Walking in My Sleep   Oakland 1935
You're Waltzing on My Heart   Akst 1935; Brown, Lew 1935
You're Wasting Your Time   Burke 1971
You're Welcome   Comden and Green 1967; Styne 1967
You're What I Need   Hart 1927, 1928; Rodgers 1927, 1928
You're Wonderful   Evans 1950; Livingston, Jay 1950; Young, Victor 1950
You're Working for Me Now   Strouse Date Unknown
You're Worth While Waiting For   Gilbert 1932; Hanley 1932
You're You   Rome 1940; Strouse Date Unknown
You're Young, But You Believe   Livingston, Jerry 1956; Raye 1956
You're Your Highness to Me   Rome 1940
You're Your Mama's Little Daddy Now   Cobb 1918; Edwards 1918
Yours   Porter 1935
Yours, All Yours   Johnson, James P. 1932; Mitchell 1938; Razaf 1932; Stept 1938
Yours Alone   Drake 1953
Yours and Mine   Brown, Nacio Herb 1935; Burke 1930; Freed, Arthur 1935
Yours and Yours Alone   Brown, Nacio Herb 1930; Eliscu 1930
Yours Could Be the Love   Coots 1964
Yours for a Song   Carroll 1948; Porter 1944; Rose 1939
Yours for the Asking   Friend 1931
Yours for the Dreaming   Magidson 1954
Yours Is My Heart Alone   Smith, Harry B. 1929

Yours Sincerely   Hart 1928; Rodgers 1928
Yours Sincerely U.S.A.   Atteridge 1916; Motzan 1916; Romberg 1916
Yours the Power   Warren Date Unknown
Yours Truly Is Truly Yours   Coots 1936; Davis 1936
Yours with Love and Kisses   Silver 1926
You's Sweet to Yo' Mammy Jes the Same   Johnson, J. Rosamond 1911
Youth   Raye 1962
Youth and Spring   Romberg 1922
Youth, Joy and Freedom   Styne 1954
Youth Must Have It's Fling   Cahn 1957; Smith, Harry B. 1906
Youth Will Be Served   Alter 1940; Loesser 1940
You've Been a Good Little Mammy to Me   Blake 1919; Sissle 1919
You've Been Kissing the Blarney Stone   Smith, Harry B. 1910
You've Been Looking Through My Dreams   Burke 1952; Van Heusen 1952
You've Been So Nice and Sweet to Me   Fain 1932; Young, Joe 1932
You've Been the Sunshine of My Life   Berlin 1918
You've Been Your Mother's Baby Long Enough   Gilbert 1918
You've Built a Fire Down in My Heart   Berlin 1911
You've Changed   Heyman 1952; Young, Victor 1952
You've Come Home   Coleman 1960; Leigh 1960
You've Got a Certain Something   Donaldson 1937
You've Got a Face Full of Wonderful Things   Fields 1951; Warren 1951
You've Got a Future with Me   Coots 1934; Magidson 1934
You've Got a Hold on Me   Lerner, Alan Jay 1943; Loewe 1943
You've Got a Lease on My Heart   Fain 1931; Kahal 1931
You've Got a Lot to Learn about Love   Kalmar 1945
You've Got a Right to Be Wrong   Fain 1933; Kahal 1933
You've Got a Sweetness All Your Own   Adamson 1935; Lane 1935
You've Got a Way with You   Robin 1928
You've Got a Wonderful Sense of Humor   Fain 1949
You've Got Everything   Donaldson 1933; Kahn 1933
You've Got Me Doing It Too   Berlin 1916
You've Got Me Guessin' Again   Livingston, Jerry 1936
You've Got Me Hypnotized   Berlin 1911
You've Got Me in the Palm of Your Hand   Friend 1932; Leslie 1932; Monaco 1932
You've Got Me on a Merry-Go-Round   Pollack 1934
You've Got Me Pickin' Petals Off o' Daisies   Brown, Lew 1929; DeSylva 1929; Henderson 1929
You've Got Me Singin'   Davis 1951
You've Got Me Sittin' on the Fence   Arlen 1939; Koehler 1939
You've Got Me This Way   McHugh 1940; Mercer 1940
You've Got Me Where You Want Me   Mercer 1944; Warren 1944
You've Got Me Worrying for You   Kahal 1932
You've Got Me Wrapped Around Your Little Finger   Coslow 1950
You've Got Possibilities   Adams 1966; Strouse 1966
You've Got Something   Porter 1936
You've Got Something There   Mercer 1937; Whiting 1937
You've Got That   Hart 1934, 1935; Rodgers 1934, 1935
You've Got that Look (That Leaves Me Weak)   Loesser 1939
You've Got That Thing   Porter 1929

You've Got the Best of Me   Hart 1941; Rodgers 1941
You've Got the Indian Sign on Me   Burke 1958; Fain 1951; Hoffman 1949; Stept 1949
You've Got the Love I Love   Ellington 1962
You've Got the Wrong Rhumba   Hoffman 1936
You've Got Those Wanna Go Back Again Blues   Turk 1926
You've Got to Be a Little Crazy   Robin 1954; Romberg 1954
You've Got to Be an Acrobat   Smith, Harry B. 1926
You've Got to Be Carefully Taught   Hammerstein 1949; Rodgers 1949
You've Got to Be Fast   Schwartz, Jean 1942
You've Got to Be Good   Donaldson 1917
You've Got to Be Hard-Boiled   Porter 1930
You've Got to Be in Khaki   Cobb 1918; Edwards 1918
You've Got to Be Loved to Be Healthy   Yellen 1947
You've Got to Be Modernistic   Johnson, James P. 1929
You've Got to Be Way Out to Be In   Berlin 1967
You've Got to Come to Paris   Adamson 1959; Young, Victor 1959
You've Got to Dance to Win the Prince of Wales   Freed, Arthur 1925
You've Got to Do It   Comden and Green 1956; Styne 1956
You've Got to Give Them What They Want   Cahn 1952; Duke 1952
You've Got to Keep on Moving   Johnson, Howard 1920
You've Got to Let Me Love You   Spina 1954
You've Got to Meet Marguerite   Harbach 1931; Kern 1931
You've Got to Pay   Schwartz, Jean 1942
You've Got to See Mama Ever Night   Conrad 1922
You've Got to Sell Yourself   Eliscu 1932
You've Got to Surrender   Hart 1929; Rodgers 1929
You've Got to Take Me Home Tonight   Goetz 1911
You've Got to Take the Bad with the Good   Sterling 1917
You've Got What Gets Me   Gershwin, George 1932; Gershwin, Ira 1932
You've Got What I Need   Adams 1966; Strouse 1966
You've Got What It Takes   DePaul 1941; Raye 1941; Warren 1975
You've Got What I've Been Looking For   Johnson, James P. 1921
You've Got Your Daddy's Fighting Heart   Bryan 1943
You've Got Your Mother's Big Blue Eyes   Berlin 1913
You've Gotta Eat Your Spinach, Baby   Gordon 1933; Revel 1933
You've Gotta Have "Oomph" in the Infantry   Baer 1944
You've Gotta Have Personality   Raye 1943
You've Gotta Make Up Your Mind   Monaco 1950; Ruby 1954
You've Gotta See Mamma Ev'ry Night (Or You Can't See Mamma at All)   Rose 1923
You've Gotta S-M-I-L-E to be H-A-Double-P-Y   Gordon 1936; Revel 1936
You've Had Him Long Enough   Bryan 1917
You've Lost Your Lovin' Baby Now   Johnson, James P. 1927
You've Married a Man (Who's Been Married Before)   Leigh 1973
You've Never Been in Love   Brooks 1956
You've Never Been Loved   Stept 1950
You've Never Kissed Her   Merrill 1966
You've Only Got One Mammy to Love   Fisher 1926; Rose 1926
You've Ruined Me for Anybody's Love but Yours   Merrill 1954
You've Set Your Watch   Cahn 1968
Yow Sah   Waller 1933; Young, Joe 1933

Ypsilenti   Bryan 1915
Yubla   Brennan 1930; Friml 1930
Yu-Hy-Day Yu-Hy-Dee   Webster 1954
Yuka and Fun   Willson 1956
Yuletide, Park Avenue   Rome 1946
Yuletide Tango   Sherman 1958
Yum, Tiki, Tiki, Tum, Tum   Merrill 1961
Yum Tum Tum   Fisher 1923
Yum! Yum!   Carmichael 1940
Yum! Yum! Yum! Yum!   Brown, A. Seymour 1914
Yum, Yummy, Yummy, Yum-Yum (The Jelly Apple Song)   David, Mack 1949; Livingston, Jerry 1949
Yum-Yum-Kiss-Kiss   David, Hal 1948
Yvette   Dubin 1922
Yvonne   Caesar 1923, 1928; Duke 1926
Yvonne's Song   Robin 1930, 1931; Whiting 1930, 1931

Z

Zamar Moded   Hoffman 1963
Zana Zaranda   Revel 1942
Zaparozhti   David, Mack 1962
Zap-a-zoo   David, Mack 1955
Zarape (Antoinette's Dance) (inst.)   Duke 1963
Zaza   Loesser 1939
Zazu Zazu Tree, The   Merrill 1960
Ze English Language   Herbert 1905
Ze Repartee   Robison 1954
Zebra Girl   Buck 1915
Zel, Zel   Johnson, J. Rosamond 1904
Zenda   Duke 1963
Ziegfeld Dollies   Buck 1921
Ziegfeld Follies Rag   Buck 1917
Ziegfeld Rag   Cohan 1916
Ziegfeld Walk, The   Conrad 1934
Ziegfeld's Paper Dollies   Carroll 1921
Ziguyner Melody   Lawrence 1932
Zig-Zag   Ager 1922; Yellen 1922
Zimba, Limba, Lay   Gorney 1966
Zing a Little Zong   Robin 1952; Warren 1952
Zing Boom Bah   Smith, Harry B. 1918
Zing! Went the Strings of My Heart   Hanley 1934
Zing, Zing Go the Tambourines   Burke 1938; Monaco 1938
Zing Zing-Zoom Zoom   Romberg 1950
Zingara Vagabundo (Song of the Romany Band)   Gilbert 1933
Zingaras, The   Goetz 1912
Zinzinnati Polka   Brown, Lew 1949
Zip   Hart 1940; Rodgers 1940
Zip Your Lip!   Pollack 1942
Zip-a-dee Doo-dah   Wrubel 1946
Zis for You, Zat for You   Fisher 1913
Zis Leetle Girl   DeSylva 1920
Zol Zein Mit Mazel   Yellen 1964
Zonky   Razaf 1929; Waller 1929
Zoo-Lou   Williams 1906
Zoompa Polka, The   Brown, Lew 1941
Zoup   Silver 1928; Turk 1928
Zuckerman's Famous Pig   Sherman 1973
Zula-Boola   Motzan 1919
Zulu Lou   Gorney 1924
Zulu Love Song (Wait for Me)   Rome 1965
Zum Galli Galli   Freed, Ralph 1951
Zuyder Zee   Alter 1944; Cahn 1944; Styne 1944

CHRONOLOGICAL INDEX

Citations refer users to songwriter(s). Songs are listed by date for each individual usage of music: a song used in three separate shows could be listed under three separate years.

1891

Armorer's Song   Smith, Harry B.
Auctioneer's Song   Smith, Harry B.
Brown October Ale   Smith, Harry B.
Forest Song   Smith, Harry B.
Hey for the Merry Greenwood   Smith, Harry B.
Hunters' Chorus   Smith, Harry B.
Tinker's Song   Smith, Harry B.

1892

Venus, My Shining Love   Cohan

1893

Hot Tamale Alley   Cohan

1894

Katie Mahone   Olcott
My Pearl Is a Bowery Girl   Jerome
(She's the) Warmest Baby in the Bunch   Cohan

1895

Ah, Cupid, Meddlesome Boy   Herbert; Smith, Harry B.
Am I a Wizard   Herbert; Smith, Harry B.
Belle O'Brien   Herbert
Cleopatra's Aria   Herbert; Smith, Harry B.
Gaze on This Face   Herbert; Smith, Harry B.
His Highness   Herbert; Smith, Harry B.
I Envy the Bird   Herbert; Smith, Harry B.
If I Were King   Herbert; Smith, Harry B.
In Dreamland   Herbert; Smith, Harry B.
I've Appeared Before Crowned Heads   Herbert; Smith, Harry B.
Know Ye the Sound   Herbert; Smith, Harry B.
Lancers   Herbert; Smith, Harry B.
Love Ne'er Came Nigh   Herbert; Smith, Harry B.
March   Herbert; Smith, Harry B.
My Angeline   Herbert; Smith, Harry B.
Oriental March   Herbert; Smith, Harry B.
Polka   Herbert; Smith, Harry B.
Pure and White As the Lotus   Herbert; Smith, Harry B.
Regal Sadness Sits on Me   Herbert; Smith, Harry B.
Schottische   Herbert; Smith, Harry B.
Star Light, Star Bright (Starlight Waltz)   Herbert; Smith, Harry B.
Stone Cutter's Song   Herbert; Smith, Harry B.
There's One Thing a Wizard Can Do   Herbert; Smith, Harry B.

Time Will Come   Herbert
To the Pyramid   Herbert; Smith, Harry B.
Two-Step   Herbert; Smith, Harry B.
Waltz   Herbert; Smith, Harry B.
What Is Love   Herbert; Smith, Harry B.
When Bugles Are Calling   Herbert; Smith, Harry B.
Who Might You Do?   Herbert; Smith, Harry B.

1896

Bold Pierre   Smith, Harry B.
Bon Jour   Smith, Harry B.
Boys!   Smith, Harry B.
Convent Song   Smith, Harry B.
Gold Bug March   Herbert
If I Were Really a King   Smith, Harry B.
It's All Right Now   Smith, Harry B.
Love Makes the World Go Round   Smith, Harry B.
Love Remains the Same   Olcott
Lovely Lady   Smith, Harry B.
My Boy, You're in Society!   Smith, Harry B.
Olcott's Home Song   Olcott
One for Another   Herbert
Owl and the Thrush, The   Herbert
Serenade   Smith, Harry B.
Would You Ask?   Smith, Harry B.

1897

Absent-Minded Maid   Herbert; Smith, Harry B.
All for Thee   Herbert; Smith, Harry B.
Angelus, The   Herbert; Smith, Harry B.
Cuban Song   Herbert; Smith, Harry B.
Cupid and I   Herbert; Smith, Harry B.
Dear Good Mr. Best, The   Sterling; Von Tilzer
Don Jose of Seville   Herbert; Smith, Harry B.
Dreaming, Dreaming   Herbert; Smith, Harry B.
Entrance of Brahmins   Herbert; Smith, Harry B.
Entrance of Duke and Dolores (Who Can This Be?)   Herbert; Smith, Harry B.
Entrance of Yvonne, Colombe and Gomez   Herbert; Smith, Harry B.
Fairy Tales   Herbert; Smith, Harry B.
For I'm a Jolly Postillion   Herbert; Smith, Harry B.
Funny Side of That (Although a Duke of High Degree), The   Herbert; Smith, Harry B.
Gaze on This Face   Herbert; Smith, Harry B.
Here Merrily Ride the Bandit Tribe (When Day's Honest Work Is Done)   Herbert; Smith, Harry B.
Holding Hands   Herbert; Smith, Harry B.
I Envy the Bird   Herbert; Smith, Harry B.
I Just Dropped In   Herbert; Smith, Harry B.

I Love Thee, I Adore Thee   Herbert; Smith, Harry B.
I'm Captain Cholly Chumley of the Guards   Herbert; Smith, Harry B.
In Attitudes Alert!   Herbert; Smith, Harry B.
In Fair Andalusia   Herbert; Smith, Harry B.
In Our Quiet Cloister   Herbert; Smith, Harry B.
Isn't It Nice to Be in Love   Cohan
Jack How I Envy You   Von Tilzer
Kate O'Donoghue   Olcott
Lady and the Kick, The   Herbert; Smith, Harry B.
Lancers   Herbert; Smith, Harry B.
Letter Duet   Herbert; Smith, Harry B.
Look to That Old Spot   Olcott
March   Herbert; Smith, Harry B.
Mary's Lamb   Herbert; Smith, Harry B.
McKinley Inaugural (inst.)   Herbert
Mindin' the Baby   Herbert; Smith, Harry B.
Minnie McAvoy   Sterling
Miss Harvard of Yale   Sterling; Von Tilzer
Monk and the Maid, The   Herbert; Smith, Harry B.
Monk's Chorus, Act II   Herbert; Smith, Harry B.
Nobody Cares for You   Sterling; Von Tilzer
Olcott's Fly Song   Olcott
Old Fashioned Mother, The   Olcott
On the Boulevard   Howard, Joseph E.
Only for Thee   Herbert; Smith, Harry B.
Peering Left, and Peering Right (For We Are the Duke's Bodyguard)   Herbert; Smith, Harry B.
Pretty Isabella and Her Umbrella   Herbert; Smith, Harry B.
Sealed Orders   Herbert; Smith, Harry B.
Secret (2), The   Herbert
Serenade   Herbert; Smith, Harry B.
Singing Lesson, The   Herbert; Smith, Harry B.
Song of the Carbine   Herbert; Smith, Harry B.
Song of the Priestess   Herbert; Smith, Harry B.
Songs that Maggie Sings, The   Cohan
Sweet Inniscarra   Olcott
Talk About Yo' Luck   Herbert; Smith, Harry B.
Tattooed Man, The   Herbert; Smith, Harry B.
Tom and Jack   Herbert; Smith, Harry B.
Two-Step   Herbert; Smith, Harry B.
Way Down East   Sterling; Von Tilzer
Woman, Lovely, Woman   Herbert; Smith, Harry B.

1898

All I Want Is My Black Baby Back   Cobb; Edwards
Always Do As People Say You Should   Herbert; Smith, Harry B.
Boy Without a Sweetheart, A   Cohan
Champagne Song   Herbert; Smith, Harry B.
Chorus of Hussars   Herbert; Smith, Harry B.
Columbia (Anthem)   Herbert
Czardas (Romany Life)   Herbert; Smith, Harry B.
Down in Cherry Lane   Sterling; Von Tilzer
Entrance of the Count   Herbert; Smith, Harry B.
Fight Is Made and Won, The   Herbert
Fortune Teller (Slumber On, My Little Gypsy Sweetheart)   Herbert; Smith, Harry B.
Girl I Loved and Lost Long, Long Ago, The   Sterling; Von Tilzer
Guten Morgen, Buon Giorna, Bon Jour   Herbert; Smith, Harry B.
Gypsy Jan   Herbert; Smith, Harry B.
Gypsy Love Song   Herbert; Smith, Harry B.

Her Gentleman Friend   Cohan
Ho! Ye Townsmen   Herbert; Smith, Harry B.
Hungaria's Hussars   Herbert; Smith, Harry B.
I Guess I'll Have to Telegraph My Baby   Cohan
I'm Making a Bid for Popularity   Smith, Harry B.
Irish Cakewalk   Cohan
Just Come Up and Take Your Presents Back   Sterling; Von Tilzer
Just Sing a Song for Ireland   Sterling; Von Tilzer
Lily and the Nightingale, The   Herbert; Smith, Harry B.
Masstoso   Herbert; Smith, Harry B.
My Old New Hampshire Home   Sterling; Von Tilzer
Old Glory   Smith, Harry B.
Only in the Play   Herbert; Smith, Harry B.
Patriotic Coon   Cohan
Power of the Human Eye, The   Herbert; Smith, Harry B.
Romany Life   Herbert; Smith, Harry B.
Serenade of All Nations   Herbert; Smith, Harry B.
Signor Mons. Muldoni   Herbert; Smith, Harry B.
Sing to Me Gypsy   Herbert; Smith, Harry B.
Stories that Mother Told Me, The   Sterling; Von Tilzer
That's How the Ragtime Dance Is Done   Sterling; Von Tilzer
That's No Dream   Sterling; Von Tilzer
When the Snow Is on the Ground   Von Tilzer
Where'er in Thick of Fight   Herbert; Smith, Harry B.
With Lance in Best   Herbert; Smith, Harry B.
You'll Get All Dat's A'Comin' to You   Sterling; Von Tilzer

1899

Across the Hills to Georgia   Cobb; Edwards
Ah! Woe Is Me   Herbert
Alpine Horn (Tyrolean Song), The   Herbert; Smith, Harry B.
Ameer, The   Herbert
Bessie My Right Hand Bower   Cobb; Edwards
By My Mien (Greta's Waltz)   Herbert; Smith, Harry B.
Cadets of Gascony   Herbert; Smith, Harry B.
Chink, Chink, Don't Talk to Me of Marriage   Herbert; Smith, Harry B.
Cupid Will Guide   Herbert
Dear Little Girly Girly   Cohan
Diplomacy   Herbert; Smith, Harry B.
Do You Follow Me?   Herbert; Smith, Harry B.
Don't Forget Your Mother   Sterling
Dusky Dudes   Jerome; Schwartz, Jean
Fancies, Only Fancies   Herbert
Fond Love, True Love   Herbert
Girl I Loved in Old Virginia, The   Sterling
Girl I Used to Love Long Ago, The   Sterling
Hannah's a Hummer   Cohan
Hello, Ma Baby   Howard, Joseph E.; Sterling
Hello My Ragtime Gal   Sterling
He's More to Be Pitied than Laughed At   Sterling
I Am a Court Coquette   Herbert; Smith, Harry B.
I Come from Gascony   Herbert; Smith, Harry B.
I Couldn't Stand to See My Baby Lose   Cobb; Edwards
I Love Ma Babe   Sterling
I Love You Just Because You Love Another   Edwards
I Must Marry a Handsome Man   Herbert; Smith, Harry B.
I Wonder   Herbert; Smith, Harry B.
I Wonder If She's Waiting   Sterling; Von Tilzer
I Wouldn't Leave My Home If I Were You   Sterling; Von Tilzer
I'd Leave My Happy Home for You   Von Tilzer
I'd Like It   Herbert

If All the Stars Were Mine   Smith, Harry B.
If Only You Were Mine   Herbert; Smith, Harry B.
In Old Ben Franklin's Day   Herbert
I've Lost My Baby   Sterling; Von Tilzer
King's Musketeers, The   Herbert; Smith, Harry B.
Lady with the Auburn Hair   Sterling
Lancers   Smith, Harry B.
Lanciers   Herbert
Let the Sun of Thine Eyes   Herbert; Smith, Harry B.
Little Poster Maid   Herbert
Love   Herbert; Smith, Harry B.
Love Is Merest Folly   Herbert; Smith, Harry B.
Love Is Tyrant, So I Bid You Behave   Herbert
Love Is Tyrant, So I Bid You Beware   Smith, Harry B.
Love, the Marvelous Magician   Herbert; Smith, Harry B.
Mazurka   Herbert; Smith, Harry B.
My Babe from Boston Town   Cohan
My Black Bess   Sterling; Von Tilzer
My Georgia Lady Love   Sterling
My Little Blue Eyed Sue   Edwards
My Pretty Little Southern Girl   Sterling
Old Maids Are Willing to Please   Herbert
Our Native Land   Herbert; Smith, Harry B.
Over the Mountain   Herbert; Smith, Harry B.
Prancing Pickaninnies   Sterling
P.S. Mr. Johnson Sends His Regards   Cohan
Queen of Charcoal Alley   Sterling
Ragueneau's Cafe   Herbert; Smith, Harry B.
Rosey Posey   Sterling
Sally's Sunday Hat   Cobb; Edwards
San Francisco Sadie   Cohan
She's a Daughter of the Sunny South   Cobb; Edwards
Since I Am Not for Thee   Herbert; Smith, Harry B.
Singer and the Song, The   Cobb; Edwards
Singing Girl, The   Herbert; Smith, Harry B.
Siren of the Ballet, The   Herbert; Smith, Harry B.
So I Bid You Beware   Herbert; Smith, Harry B.
Soldiers All   Herbert
Song of the Danube, The   Herbert; Smith, Harry B.
Song of the Nose   Herbert; Smith, Harry B.
Sweet Clarissa (Darky Love Song)   Herbert
Telephone Me, Baby   Cohan
Tell Me Pray   Herbert
Thompson's Ragtime Cake Walk   Sterling; Von Tilzer
Those Were the Good Old Times   Herbert; Smith, Harry B.
To Be a Little Singing Girl   Herbert; Smith, Harry B.
To Boston on Business   Cohan
Well Beloved   Herbert; Smith, Harry B.
Where the Sweet Magnolias Bloom   Sterling; Von Tilzer
Who Says a Coon Can't Love   Cohan

1900

Across the Continent   Jerome; Schwartz, Jean
Ain't Gwine to Work No More   Johnson, J. Rosamond
All for a Man Whose Love Was Gold   Cobb; Edwards
All Men Have Their Troubles   Herbert; Smith, Harry B.
All Things Are Not What They Seem   Cobb; Edwards
Always Make Allowances for Love   Smith, Harry B.
Amateur Entertainer, The   Smith, Harry B.
Battalion of France   Smith, Harry B.
Be Clever   Smith, Harry B.
Beer, Beautiful Beer   Smith, Harry B.
Belle of Bohemia, The   Smith, Harry B.
Bird in a Gilded Cage, A   Von Tilzer

Blue Ribbon Girls, The   Smith, Harry B.
Bound with a Golden Chain   Sterling
By This Sweet Token   Herbert; Smith, Harry B.
Cadets of St. Cyr, The   Smith, Harry B.
Cantineer of the Regiment   Smith, Harry B.
Casino Song, The   Smith, Harry B.
Champagne Waltz   Smith, Harry B.
Cheating Peddler, The   Smith, Harry B.
Chink! Chink!   Smith, Harry B.
Come, Gentle Stranger   Smith, Harry B.
Demon of the Deep, The   Smith, Harry B.
Descriptive Song   Smith, Harry B.
Diamonds Don't Care Who Wear Them   Cobb; Edwards
Don't Trifle with a Trusting Heart   Cobb; Edwards
Down de Lover's Lane   Smith, Harry B.
Entrance Chorus of the Khedive   Smith, Harry B.
Eyes of Black and Eyes of Blue   Herbert; Smith, Harry B.
Fairies' Lullaby, The   Smith, Harry B.
Foxy Quiller's Entrance Chorus   Smith, Harry B.
From Africa   Smith, Harry B.
Girl Who Is Up-to-Date, The   Smith, Harry B.
God Bless My Good Old Mother   Edwards
He Was a Married Man   Smith, Harry B.
Hear Me   Herbert; Smith, Harry B.
Homestead on the Hill   Sterling
How Actresses Are Made   Smith, Harry B.
I Ain't A-Goin' to Weep No More   Von Tilzer
I Ain't Got Time to Be Your Baby   Edwards
I Can't Tell Why I Love You But I Do   Cobb; Edwards
I Certainly Didn't Know When You First Came In   Sterling;
   Von Tilzer
I Just Can't Keep from Taking Hold of Things   Cobb;
   Edwards
I See By Your Smile   Herbert; Smith, Harry B.
I Wonder Why I Love No One But You   Cobb; Edwards
If I Dared Tell My Love for You   Cobb; Edwards
If That's Society Excuse Me   Johnson, J. Rosamond
I'll Put a Tax   Smith, Harry B.
I'm the Leader of Society   Herbert; Smith, Harry B.
In My Museum Now   Smith, Harry B.
I've Got Troubles of My Own   Johnson, J. Rosamond
Just Because I Loved You Long Ago   Sterling
Just for Today   Herbert; Smith, Harry B.
Lady in the Moon, The   Smith, Harry B.
Love May Come, Love May Go   Herbert; Smith, Harry B.
Mam'selle   Smith, Harry B.
Mandolin Serenade   Smith, Harry B.
Market Square   Herbert; Smith, Harry B.
Matinee Girls   Smith, Harry B.
My Charcoal Charmer   Cobb; Edwards
My Hannah Lady   Jerome
My Jersey Lily   Von Tilzer
My Mobile Gal   Smith, Robert B.
My New York   Smith, Harry B.
My Own Wild Western Rose   Sterling
'Neath the Blue Neapolitan Skies   Herbert; Smith, Harry B.
Never Again   Smith, Harry B.
No Words Can Tell   Sterling
Oh, Oh Miss Phoebe   Sterling; Von Tilzer
On My Nuptial Day   Herbert; Smith, Harry B.
One Fellow's Joy Is Another Fellow's Woe   Herbert; Smith,
   Harry B.
Pavilion of Love, The   Smith, Harry B.
Polly Wants a Cracker   Smith, Harry B.
Quiller Has the Brain   Smith, Harry B.

Robin and the Rose, The   Herbert; Smith, Harry B.
Sailor's Life, A   Herbert; Smith, Harry B.
Sentinel Asleep, The   Von Tilzer
She Never Loved a Man as Much as That   Smith, Robert B.
Shepherd's Duet   Smith, Harry B.
She's an Alright Girl   Cobb; Edwards
She's Just My Size   Cobb; Edwards
Shirt Waist Man, The   Cobb; Edwards
Since I Am Queen of the Carnival   Herbert; Smith, Harry B.
Slave Dealers' Song   Smith, Harry B.
So They Say   Herbert; Smith, Harry B.
Song of the Drum Major   Smith, Harry B.
Southern Queen   Johnson, J. Rosamond
Special Train, The   Smith, Harry B.
Strike Up the Band (Here Comes a Sailor)   Sterling
Strollers, The   Smith, Harry B.
Strolling thru the River   Smith, Harry B.
Swearing Skipper, The   Smith, Harry B.
Tell Me when I Shall Find Him   Smith, Harry B.
That's My Idea of Love   Herbert; Smith, Harry B.
They Are Nothing but Girls   Smith, Harry B.
Tivolini   Herbert; Smith, Harry B.
To Beat the Band   Sterling
Variety   Smith, Harry B.
Ve Vas Germans   Smith, Harry B.
Viceroy   Herbert; Smith, Harry B.
We Are the Heiresses   Smith, Harry B.
We Cannot Let You Go   Smith, Harry B.
We'll Catch You at Last   Herbert; Smith, Harry B.
What Eve Said to Adam   Smith, Harry B.
What's the Use of Talking   Cobb; Edwards
When a Girl Doesn't Know Where She Is   Smith, Harry B.
When Sousa Leads the Band   Jerome
When the Clouds Have Drifted By   Sterling
When the Harvest Days Are Over and Gone   Von Tilzer
Why Don't the Band Play?   Johnson, J. Rosamond
Winding, Winding   Smith, Harry B.
Wishing Cup, The   Smith, Harry B.
With Military Pomp   Herbert; Smith, Harry B.
You Cannot Turn Against Her   Sterling

1901

Always Go in Without Knocking   Cobb; Edwards
And the Manager Said. . .?   Cohan
Any Old Place I Can Hang My Hat Is Home Sweet Home to Me   Jerome; Schwartz, Jean
Are You a Buffalo   Von Tilzer
At the Pan-American   Smith, Harry B.
Beautiful Fairy Tales   Smith, Harry B.; Von Tilzer
Behold the Governor   Cohan
Billet-Doux, A   Smith, Harry B.; Von Tilzer
Cadets   Smith, Harry B.
Can You Blame Me for Lovin' Dat Man   Sterling; Von Tilzer
Chloe   Smith, Harry B.
Come Out Dinah on the Green   Johnson, J. Rosamond
Dago and Monk, The   Smith, Harry B.
Darling   Smith, Harry B.
De Dago, De Org and De Wonk   Von Tilzer
(Nobody's Lookin' but) De Owl an' De Moon   Johnson, J. Rosamond
Dear Sing Sing   Jerome; Schwartz, Jean
Dip in the Ocean, A   Smith, Harry B.
Diplomacy   Smith, Harry B.
Dolly Dimple   Jerome; Schwartz, Jean

Down Where the Cotton Blossoms Grow   Sterling; Von Tilzer
Down Where the Wurzburger Flows   Von Tilzer
Ebony Echoes (inst.)   Edwards
Electric Light, The   Smith, Harry B.
Englishman's Idea of Ragtime, An   Smith, Harry B.
Ethiopian Essence, An   Smith, Harry B.
Fencing Girl, The   Smith, Harry B.
Flirtation on the Beach   Smith, Harry B.
Follow the Man that Leads the Band   Smith, Harry B.
Game of Love, The   Smith, Harry B.
Get Next to the Man with a Pull   Smith, Harry B.
Girl I Loved and Lost, The   Cobb; Edwards
Girl of Greater New York, The   Smith, Harry B.
Good-Bye Little Girl, Good-Bye   Cobb; Edwards
Governor of the State, The   Cohan
Gra Ma Chree   Olcott
Gunner in the Navy, A   Smith, Harry B.
I Knew that You Would Come Along Someday   Cobb; Edwards
I Love Everyone in the Wide Wide World   Cohan
I Want My Ragtime   Cohan
I Want to Be the Leady Lady   Sterling
I'd Give the World Could I Forget   Cobb; Edwards
If Bill Gilette Could Only See Me Now   Cohan
I'll Be with You when the Roses Bloom Again   Cobb; Edwards
I'm the Governor's Son   Cohan
I'm Tired   Jerome; Schwartz, Jean
In Florida   Smith, Harry B.
In the Heart of the Mighty Deep   Von Tilzer
In the Swim   Smith, Harry B.
Ireland a Gra Ma Chree   Olcott
Irish Swell, The   Olcott
It's Awfully Nice to Be a Regular Soldier   Cobb; Edwards
Jack O'Lantern   Smith, Harry B.
Jolly Good Fellow   Cohan
Just a Golden Butterfly   Cobb; Edwards
L'Amoureuse   Smith, Harry B.
Lass I Love, The   Olcott
Lesson Book Song   Smith, Harry B.
Lesson in Flirtation, A   Smith, Harry B.
Lesson with a Fan, A   Smith, Harry B.
Little Child Like Me, A   Smith, Harry B.
Loop the Loop (inst.)   Schwartz, Jean
Lucy, Ma Honey Babe   Cohan
Ma Ebony Belle   Smith, Harry B.
Maiden with the Dreamy Eyes, The   Johnson, J. Rosamond
Make Allowance for Love   Smith, Harry B.
Mamie Mamie Don't You Feel Ashamie   Cobb; Edwards
Man with the Tambourine, The   Smith, Harry B.
Mandy   Smith, Harry B.
Many Years Ago   Olcott
Menagerie Song   Smith, Harry B.
Mollie Shannon   Smith, Harry B.
My Bunco Queen   Smith, Harry B.
My Carolina Lady   Sterling
My Castle on the Nile   Johnson, J. Rosamond
My Filipino Pet   Smith, Harry B.
My Gal! My Gal!   Smith, Harry B.
My Gal! My Sal!   Smith, Harry B.
My Sweet Queen   Olcott
My Wild Irish Rose   Olcott
Mysterious Maid, The   Cohan
Never Breathe a Word of This to Mother   Cohan

Night Time   Cohan
Nobody Else but Me   Sterling
Nothing New Beneath the Sun   Cohan
Nursery Rhymes   Jerome; Schwartz, Jean
Oh Melinda   Sterling; Von Tilzer
Oh! Mr. Moon   Cohan
Oh Sing the Praise of the Lord   Herbert; Smith, Harry B.
Oh, What a Dream   Smith, Harry B.; Von Tilzer
Oh What a Lovely Dream   Sterling; Von Tilzer
Olcott's Lullaby   Olcott
Only Girl, The   Smith, Harry B.
Ostend   Smith, Harry B.
Paddy's Cat   Olcott
Pah, Pah, Pah   Cobb; Edwards
Pretty Betsy Brown   Smith, Harry B.
Push Me Along in My Pushcart   Cohan
Quaker Maids, The   Smith, Harry B.
Quakertown Cadets, The   Cohan
Real Girls, The   Cohan
Regular William Gilette (A Regular Mr. Gilette), A   Cohan
Rip Van Winkle Was a Lucky Man   Jerome; Schwartz, Jean
Rosie   Cohan
San Anita Waltz   Jerome; Schwartz, Jean
1776 to 1901   Smith, Harry B.
She's Mine to Have and to Hold   Edwards
Shopping Chorus   Smith, Harry B.
Silas   Smith, Harry B.
Since Sister Nell Heard Paderewski Play   Smith, Harry B.
Soldiers of the Stage, The   Cohan
Spring Hat   Smith, Harry B.
Story of the Wedding March, The   Cohan
Supper Chorus   Smith, Harry B.
Swimming Master, The   Smith, Harry B.
Tell Me Dusky Maiden   Johnson, J. Rosamond
Then I'd Be Satisfied   Cohan
There's a Meeting in the Old Town Hall   Sterling
To Marry a Millionaire   Smith, Harry B.
Too Many Miles from Broadway   Cohan
Wading We Go   Smith, Harry B.
Watermelon Party   Smith, Harry B.
Way Down Yonder in the Cornfield   Cobb; Edwards
Way that Walker Walked Away, The   Smith, Harry B.
We Love to Live   Cohan
Wedding of the Reuben and the Maid, The   Smith, Harry B.
Weeping Widow, The   Cohan
We'll Drown It in the Bowl   Olcott
What'd You' Do Wid de Letter, Mr. Johnson?   Smith, Harry B.
When Eyes Meet Eyes   Cobb; Edwards
When Mr. Shakespeare Comes to Town   Jerome; Schwartz, Jean
When the Band Begins to Play   Von Tilzer
When the Roses Bloom Again   Edwards
When You Are Near   Smith, Harry B.
Where the Mississippi Flows   Cobb; Edwards
Widow's Wile, A   Cohan
Wine Divine   Cohan
Won't You Come and Float Me   Smith, Harry B.
Yankee Tar, A   Smith, Harry B.

1902

Adam Was a Happy Married Man   Jerome; Schwartz, Jean
At the Casino (inst.)   Kern
Back to the Woods   Jerome; Schwartz, Jean

Banquet in Misery Hall, The   Von Tilzer
Chink of the —-er's Gold, The   Von Tilzer
Come Down Ma Evening Star   Smith, Robert B.
Could You Be True to Eyes of Blue If You Looked Into Eyes of Brown   Cobb; Edwards
Crystal Throne, The   Edwards
Cupid Is the Captain   Smith, Harry B.
East Side Lil   Jerome
East Side Walk   Jerome
Etiquette   Smith, Robert B.
Every Little Dog Must Have His Day   Olcott
Eyes of Blue, Eyes of Brown   Sterling
Gambling Man   Jerome; Schwartz, Jean
Have You Seen My Sweetheart in His Uniform of Blue   Cobb; Edwards
Here's to the Old Folks at Home   Sterling
I Just Can't Help Loving That Man   Sterling; Von Tilzer
I Never Loved a Man as Much as That   Smith, Robert B.
If Aladdin Would Lend Me His Lamp   Cobb; Edwards
If Yankee Doodle Hadn't Come to Town   Bryan
I'll Be There, I'll Be There, Mary Dear   Sterling; Von Tilzer
I'll Miss You in the Golden Summertime   Bryan
I'm So Tired of Livin', I Don't Care When I Die   Sterling
I'm the Man Who Makes the Money in the Mint   Cobb; Edwards
I'm Unlucky   Jerome; Schwartz, Jean
In a Land that's Far Away   Jerome; Schwartz, Jean
In Spotless Town   Jerome; Schwartz, Jean
In the City of Sighs and Tears   Sterling
In the Sweet Bye and Bye   Von Tilzer
Incidents in the Lives of Famous Men   Smith, Harry B.
Jennie   Sterling; Von Tilzer
Jennie Lee   Von Tilzer
Johnnie Jones' Sister Sue   Cobb; Edwards
Just a Tender Spot for Father Dear   Jerome; Schwartz, Jean
Just Cause the Moon Was Shinin'   Smith, Harry B.
Just Have the Band Play Home Sweet Home   Sterling
Just Kiss Yourself Goodbye   Jerome; Schwartz, Jean
Kathleen   Cobb; Edwards
Leader of Vanity Fair, The   Smith, Robert B.
Limerick Girls   Olcott
Little Dolly Varden   Cobb; Edwards
Long Green, The   Smith, Robert B.
Louisiana Louise   Edwards; Sterling
Love's Young Dream   Smith, Harry B.
Mansion of Aching Hearts, The   Von Tilzer
Miss Green Don't Be So Mean   Jerome; Schwartz, Jean
Money Burner   Smith, Harry B.
Morality's a Matter of Geography   Smith, Harry B.
Mr. Dooley   Jerome; Schwartz, Jean
My Bamboo Queen   Sterling; Von Tilzer
My Gal My Sal   Sterling
My Little Gypsy Maid   Smith, Harry B.
My Little Pansy   Smith, Harry B.
My Little Sweetheart Mine   Sterling; Von Tilzer
My Lonesome Little Louisiana Lady   Cobb; Edwards
My Midnight Rose   Von Tilzer
My Silver Maid   Sterling
My Sunny Sue   Sterling
Naughty Little Clock, The   Smith, Harry B.
Noreen Mavoureen   Olcott
Nursery Rhymes   Jerome; Schwartz, Jean
O' O' O'Brien   Schwartz, Jean
Oh! Didn't He Ramble   Johnson, J. Rosamond
Oh, Liza   Edwards

Oh the Girls, the Lonely Girls   Sterling; Von Tilzer
Old Limerick Town   Olcott
On a Saturday Night   Howard, Joseph E.; Sterling
On a Sunday Afternoon   Sterling; Von Tilzer
On the Proper Side of Broadway on a Saturday P.M.   Cobb; Edwards
Only a Jewel in Pawn   Bryan
Pardon Me My Dear Alphonse, After You My Dear Gaston   Von Tilzer
Ping Pong   Smith, Robert B.
Please Go Way and Let Me Sleep   Von Tilzer
Rosalie My Royal Rosie   Cobb; Edwards
Sentimental Tommy   Edwards
Sherrif's Song   Smith, Harry B.
Since Sister Nell Heard Paderewski Play   Jerome; Schwartz, Jean
Sleeping Beauty and the Beast   Jerome; Schwartz, Jean
Soldier's Story, The   Smith, Harry B.
Somebody's Waiting for Me   Sterling; Von Tilzer
Song Bird of Melody Lane, The   Cobb; Edwards
Susie Anna   Jerome; Schwartz, Jean
Tell Me Again, Sweetheart   Smith, Harry B.
There Are Tricks in All Trades   Smith, Harry B.
There's Music in the Air   Sterling
To Be Truly Refined   Smith, Harry B.
Toast Song   Smith, Harry B.
True Love Is Not for a Day   Smith, Harry B.
Under the Bamboo Tree   Johnson, J. Rosamond
Voice of the Violet, The   Olcott
When a Lady Leads the Band   Sterling
When Brother Percy Sings   Jerome; Schwartz, Jean
When Kate and I Were Comin' Thru the Rye   Sterling; Von Tilzer
When Leaves Begin to Fade   Sterling
When the Sun Goes Down   Sterling
When the Troupe Comes Back to Town   Von Tilzer
While the Moon Shines Bright   Howard, Joseph E.
You Couldn't Hardly Notice It At All   Von Tilzer
You Must Ask Our Dear Mama   Edwards

1903

After Business Hours   Smith, Harry B.
Although I'm So Demure   Smith, Harry B.
Always Leave 'em Laughing (When You Say Goodbye)   Cohan
American Heiress, An   Smith, Harry B.
Angels Over the Fields   Herbert
Any Old Thing   Smith, Harry B.
Awake, Ma Chile   Smith, Harry B.
Babes in Toyland   Herbert
Baby, My Little Baby   Jerome; Schwartz, Jean
Baraboo   Edwards
Barney O'Flynn   Herbert
Be Kind to Poor Pierrot   Herbert; Smith, Harry B.
Beatrice Barefacts   Herbert
Bedelia   Jerome; Schwartz, Jean
Before and After   Herbert
Beggars' Chorus   Smith, Harry B.
Big Indian Chief   Johnson, J. Rosamond
Billy Grey, U.S.A., O.K.   Cobb; Edwards
Birth of the Butterfly (inst.)   Herbert
Bohemia   Smith, Harry B.
Bubbles   Smith, Harry B.
Butterfly Waltz   Herbert; Smith, Harry B.

Christmas Fair Waltz   Herbert
Clockmaker's Song   Herbert; Smith, Harry B.
Congo Love Song   Johnson, J. Rosamond
Contrary Mary   Herbert
Coo-ee, Coo-ee   Von Tilzer
Country Belles   Smith, Harry B.
Country Dance   Herbert
Cynthia Jones   Smith, Harry B.
Dance Eccentrique   Herbert
Darling Jane   Sterling
Daughter of the Moon Am I, A   Von Tilzer
Dissapated Kitten, The   Smith, Harry B.
Don't Cry Bo-Peep   Herbert
Don't Overdo It   Smith, Harry B.
Down on a South Sea Isle   Von Tilzer
Down Where the Swanee River Flows   Sterling; Von Tilzer
Duel of Hearts, The   Bryan
Elopement, The   Cohan
Embassy Burglarious, An   Smith, Harry B.
Entrance of Babette   Herbert; Smith, Harry B.
Ephasafa Dill   Sterling; Von Tilzer
Everybody's Happy When the Sun Shines   Cohan
Evolution of Ragtime   Johnson, J. Rosamond
Flirtation on the Beach   Cohan
Floretta   Herbert
Flowers of Dixieland, The   Johnson, J. Rosamond
Football Boys and Girls, The   Cohan
From Heavens on High   Herbert
Gavotte   Herbert
Glory   Smith, Harry B.
Go to Sleep Slumber Deep   Herbert
Goodbye Eliza Jane   Sterling; Von Tilzer
Hail to Christmas   Herbert
Hamlet Was a Melancholy Dane   Jerome; Schwartz, Jean
Hang March   Herbert
Happy Days in Dixie   Smith, Harry B.
He Dangled Me on His Knee   Von Tilzer
He Was a Sailor   Jerome; Schwartz, Jean
He Who'd Thrive Must Rise at Five   Herbert; Smith, Harry B.
He Won't Be Happy Till He Gets It   Herbert
Health Food Man, The   Herbert
Hear the Coachman Crack His Whip   Herbert; Smith, Harry B.
Here in Pleasure's Favorite Court   Herbert; Smith, Harry B.
He's Ravin', Let Him Rave   Cohan
Hey There, May There   Cohan
Highly Important Fly, The   Von Tilzer
Hobo Zobo Band   Jerome; Schwartz, Jean
Homeless Girl in Harlem   Cohan
Honey   Smith, Harry B.
Honey, Send Home for Money   Howard, Joseph E.
I Am the Pasha   Smith, Harry B.
I Can't Do the Sum   Herbert
I Love Only One Girl in the Wide, Wide World   Cobb; Edwards
I Love You Dolly   Smith, Harry B.
I Want to Go to Paree, Papa   Cohan
I Want to Hear a Yankee Doodle Tune   Cohan
If I Were a Man Like That   Herbert
If I Were Only Mr. Morgan   Cohan
If I Were the Bride of a Soldier   Smith, Harry B.
I'll Be There in a Public Square   Cohan
I'll Bribe the Stars   Herbert; Smith, Harry B.
I'll Run in from Troy   Cohan

I'm a Fisher Maiden   Von Tilzer
I'm a Poor Unhappy Maid   Jerome; Schwartz, Jean
I'm in Love with the Beautiful Bugs   Von Tilzer
In a One-Night Stand   Cohan
In a Shady Bungalow (inst.)   Kern
In Cincinnati   Jerome; Schwartz, Jean
In the Land of Spain   Herbert; Smith, Harry B.
In the Pale Moonlight   Jerome
In the Pathway of Roses and Thorns   Bryan
In the Toymaker's Workshop   Herbert
Isn't It Lovely to Be on the Stage   Sterling; Von Tilzer
It's a Way We Have in Spain   Herbert; Smith, Harry B.
It's the Band   Sterling
Jane   Herbert
John Johnson   Herbert
Johnny, Get Off the Corner   Cohan
Julie   Jerome; Schwartz, Jean
Keep Off the Grass   Von Tilzer
Kermesse Day   Herbert; Smith, Harry B.
Kid Days   Cohan
Lancers   Herbert
Largo   Herbert
Laughing Song   Von Tilzer
Lazy Moon   Johnson, J. Rosamond
Legend of the Castle   Herbert
Let the Band Play   Von Tilzer
Let's Hope of Thee My Guardian Be   Herbert; Smith, Harry B.
Letters I Write All Day   Herbert; Smith, Harry B.
Life of a Bold Free Lance, The   Herbert; Smith, Harry B.
Love All the Day   Smith, Harry B.
Love in an Orchard   Smith, Harry B.
Love Is a Game   Smith, Harry B.
Lover's A-B-C, The   Smith, Harry B.
Maid of Timbuctoo   Johnson, J. Rosamond
Maiden's Heart, A   Smith, Harry B.
Mammy's Little Alabama Love   Sterling; Von Tilzer
March of the Toys   Herbert
Marriage Is Sublime   Bryan
Mary from Maryland   Smith, Harry B.
Mary, Mary   Herbert
Maydee (Pretty Little South Sea Island Lady)   Von Tilzer
Men   Herbert
Men Are Ambitious   Smith, Harry B.
Mignonette   Herbert
Military Ball, The   Herbert
Moon Will Help You Out, Maybe, The   Herbert
(Our) My Castle in Spain   Herbert
My Dreamy Lou   Jerome; Schwartz, Jean
My Honey Bunch   Smith, Harry B.
My Honor and My Sword (Borrow Trouble)   Herbert; Smith, Harry B.
My Hula Hula Girl   Jerome; Schwartz, Jean
My Ideal   Smith, Harry B.
My Lady of the Manor   Herbert; Smith, Harry B.
My Lady 'Tis for Thee   Herbert; Smith, Harry B.
My Little Coney Isle   Sterling; Von Tilzer
My Rag Doll Girl   Herbert
My Rose of Arizona   Cobb; Edwards
Navajo   Williams
Never Mind Bo-Peep   Herbert
Off to Turkey   Smith, Harry B.
Oh, Marjorie   Von Tilzer
Oh, Thou Art Fair   Smith, Harry B.
Oh, What's the Use?   Smith, Harry B.

O'Hooley   Smith, Harry B.
Old Fashioned Rose, An   Herbert
Old Woman Who Lived in a Shoe, The   Bryan
On a Beautiful Distant Island   Von Tilzer
On the Other Side of the Wall   Herbert; Smith, Harry B.
On the Stage   Herbert; Smith, Harry B.
Only the Beautiful Stars   Sterling
Pavanne   Herbert; Smith, Harry B.
Peddler's Song   Herbert; Smith, Harry B.
Pierre, Please Don't Move   Smith, Harry B.
Plain Mamie   Smith, Harry B.
Please Mama, Buy Me a Baby   Cobb; Edwards
Pony Ballet (inst.)   Schwartz, Jean
Proper Way to Kiss, The   Smith, Harry B.
Read the Answers in the Stars   Bryan
Reubens on Parade, The   Cohan
Rock-a-Bye Baby   Herbert
Root for Riley   Cohan
Rosalie   Cobb; Edwards
Roses for the Girl I Love   Von Tilzer
Rube Song   Cohan
Sail on the Tail of a Whale, A   Von Tilzer
Same Old Crowd, The   Smith, Harry B.
Save It for Me   Johnson, J. Rosamond
Secret Society   Von Tilzer
She Walks Like This   Smith, Harry B.
Signs   Smith, Harry B.
Simple Little Susie Simpkins   Sterling
Song of the Poet   Herbert
Song the Minstrel Sang (Old Black Joe), The   Cobb; Edwards
Songbird of Melody Lane (1), The   Bryan; Edwards
Spain, Beautiful Spain   Jerome; Schwartz, Jean
Spanish Basque Carol   Herbert
Spiders Den   Herbert
Stories Adam Told to Eve   Jerome; Schwartz, Jean
Story of Babette   Herbert; Smith, Harry B.
Success Is Work (inst.)   Herbert
Sunflower and the Sun, The   Smith, Harry B.
Sweet Matilda, June, O My, Isn't It Charming   Jerome
Sweet Popularity   Cohan
Then I'd Be Satisfied with Life   Cohan
There Once Was an Owl   Herbert; Smith, Harry B.
They Are Angels Without Wings   Smith, Harry B.
They Are Hypnotized   Cohan
To the Sound of the Pipe and the Roll of the Drum   Herbert; Smith, Harry B.
Tony the Peddler   Herbert; Smith, Harry B.
Toyland   Herbert
Toymakers Shop, The   Herbert
Trials of a Simple Maid, The   Smith, Harry B.
Twelve Pretty Wives from Turkey   Smith, Harry B.
Two Eyes   Johnson, J. Rosamond
Under the Anhauser Bush   Sterling; Von Tilzer
Under the Mulberry Tree   Von Tilzer
Up and Down the Line   Sterling
Vivianne the Vivandiere   Herbert; Smith, Harry B.
Wake Up, Malinda   Jerome
Wanted: A Fly   Smith, Harry B.
Way Down South   Smith, Harry B.
We Are Very Highly Polished at the Court Don't You Know   Herbert; Smith, Harry B.
We Say We'll Do a Thing   Smith, Harry B.
We Will Find Your Sheep   Herbert
We're Secret Society Members   Von Tilzer

We've Got to Move Today   Williams
What a Beautiful World This Would Be   Sterling; Von Tilzer
What Is Love? (Canzonetta)   Herbert; Smith, Harry B.
When I Look into Those Lovey Dovey Eyes   Smith, Harry B.
When Leaves Begin to Fall   Sterling; Von Tilzer
When the Apple Blossoms Fall   Cobb; Edwards
When the Band Plays Ragtime   Smith, Harry B.
When the Colored Band Comes Marching Down the
   Street   Johnson, J. Rosamond
When the Frost Is on the Pumpkin Maggie Dear   Sterling;
   Von Tilzer
When the Moon Comes Over the Hill   Johnson, J.
   Rosamond
When the Stars Are Shinging Bright   Jerome; Schwartz, Jean
When We Were Boys   Von Tilzer
When You Go Down to London Town   Von Tilzer
Where the Fairest Flow'rs Are Blooming   Herbert; Smith,
   Harry B.
Whistling Dan   Jerome; Schwartz, Jean
Who, Who, Who, Hoolaman   Jerome; Schwartz, Jean
Whose Little Dear Little Girlie Is Oo?   Sterling; Von Tilzer
Why Don't You Go, Go, Go   Jerome; Schwartz, Jean
Will You Be My Hero?   Smith, Harry B.
Winter Song   Herbert
With Downcast Eye   Herbert
Woman's No Means Yes, A   Smith, Harry B.
Wouldn't It Make You Hungry   Von Tilzer
Yankee Girl, The   Smith, Harry B.
Yankee Tourist Girl, The   Schwartz, Jean
You for Me, Me for You   Sterling

1904

Abraham   Sterling; Von Tilzer
Absinthe Frappe   Herbert
Al Fresco   Herbert
Alexander   Sterling; Von Tilzer
All Aboard for Dreamland   Sterling; Von Tilzer
Angling by a Babbling Brook   Kern
Apple Mary Maguire   Smith, Harry B.; Smith, Robert B.
At the Music Hall   Schwartz, Jean
Back to Baltimore   Williams
Bandanna Land   Herbert
Barney Donohue   Jerome; Schwartz, Jean
Beatrice Barefacts   Herbert
Butterflies   Howard, Joseph E.
Butterfly and the Clover, The   Smith, Harry B.; Smith,
   Robert B.
Cafe Chantant   Smith, Harry B.; Smith, Robert B.
Captain of a Ten-Day Boat   Cohan
Carnival (Al Fresco), The   Herbert
Cavalier's Song   Smith, Harry B.
Cecil in London Town, The   Cohan
Chorus of Villagers   Johnson, J. Rosamond
Coax Me   Sterling; Von Tilzer
Come on Boys Let's Follow the Band   Sterling; Von Tilzer
Commanderess-in-Chief   Herbert
Conspirators' Chorus   Johnson, J. Rosamond
Coon Banshee, The   Herbert
Cordilia Malone   Jerome; Schwartz, Jean
Cornfield Capers (inst.)   Von Tilzer
Dear Old Manhattan Island   Jerome; Schwartz, Jean
Della   Edwards; Smith, Robert B.
Dew on the Heather, The   Smith, Harry B.; Smith, Robert
   B.

Don't Go too Dangerously Nigh   Johnson, J. Rosamond
Down at the Bottom of the Sea   Johnson, J. Rosamond
Down in Mulberry Bend   Johnson, J. Rosamond
Down in the Subway   Jerome; Schwartz, Jean
Downcast Eye, The   Kern
Dr. Blotz   Herbert
Dream On   Herbert
Ebenezer Brown   Sterling; Von Tilzer
Egg Has Fallen Down, The   Johnson, J. Rosamond
Ev'ry Little Bit Helps   Fisher
Fairyland   Johnson, J. Rosamond
Folly Is Our King   Herbert
For You   Jerome; Schwartz, Jean
Friends that Are Staunch and True   Herbert
From Saturday to Monday   Kern
George Washington, Jr.   Cohan
Get a Horse   Schwartz, Jean
Ghost that Never Walked, The   Jerome; Schwartz, Jean
Girl I Know, A   Cohan
Girl I Used to Know, The   Olcott
Girl Who Cares for Me   Cobb; Edwards
Girls of the U.S.A.   Cohan
Give My Regards to Broadway   Cohan
Gondolier, The   Williams
Good Bye My Lady Love   Howard, Joseph E.
Good Old California   Cohan
Good-Bye Flo   Cohan
Goodbye My Love   Herbert
Goodnight, My Own True Love   Jerome; Schwartz, Jean
(If I Were the) Governor of Guam   Herbert
Hannah Won't You Open that Door   Sterling; Von Tilzer
Hearts Win, You Lose   Sterling
He'll Be There!   Kern
Hello, Ma Lulu   Johnson, J. Rosamond
House that Jack Built, The   Johnson, J. Rosamond
How a Monocle Helps the Mind   Johnson, J. Rosamond
How Love Speaks   Fisher
How to Be Happy Though Married   Smith, Harry B.; Smith,
   Robert B.
I Brought Them Home to Mother   Herbert
I Don't Care to Be Yo' Lady Fren' No Mo'   Cobb; Edwards
I Don't Want Any Wurzburger   Jerome; Schwartz, Jean
I Never Took a Chance in My Life   Smith, Harry B.; Smith,
   Robert B.
I Wonder If You Miss Me (As I Miss You)   Snyder
If I Had a Theatre on Broadway   Smith, Harry B.; Smith,
   Robert B.
If Morgan Had Bought an Army for Me   Herbert
If You Only Knew the Ways to Pull the Wires   Smith, Harry
   B.; Smith, Robert B.
I'll Never Love Another Love Like I Love You   Cobb;
   Edwards
I'm a Very Good Sailor on Land   Johnson, J. Rosamond
I'm Crazy to Go on the Stage   Cobb; Edwards
I'm Mighty Glad I'm Living and That's All   Cohan
I'm So Happy   Jerome; Schwartz, Jean
In the Folds of the Starry Flag   Herbert
In the Village By the Sea   Sterling
In Zanzibar   Cobb; Edwards
Irish American   Cohan
It's a Good World After All   Edwards
Jack O'Lantern Girl   Herbert
Johnnie I'll Take You   Cobb; Edwards
Just Across the Bridge of Gold   Sterling; Von Tilzer
Knot of Blue, The   Herbert

Lady with Money   Smith, Harry B.; Smith, Robert B.
Lambs in Toyland   Herbert
Life's a Funny Proposition After All   Cohan
Little China Doll   Smith, Harry B.; Smith, Robert B.
Little Class of One, A   Herbert
Little Johnny Jones   Cohan
Little Miss No-One from No-Where   Edwards; Smith, Robert B.
Long Live the Queen   Herbert
Louisa Schmid   Sterling; Von Tilzer
Louisiana Anna   Edwards
Love Is Like a Cigarette   Herbert
Love, Love, Love   Jerome; Schwartz, Jean
Love's Lingo   Howard, Joseph E.
Luti   Jerome; Schwartz, Jean
Ma Mamzelle Honee   Cobb; Edwards
M.A.C.A.R.O.N.I   Jerome; Schwartz, Jean
Madcap Princess, A   Smith, Harry B.
Mam'selle Fauchette   Cohan
Man, Man   Johnson, J. Rosamond
Man Meant Well, The   Herbert
March of the Flags   Jerome; Schwartz, Jean
March of the Frisco Chinks   Cohan
Mary from Tipperary   Johnson, J. Rosamond
Mary Was a Manicure   Johnson, J. Rosamond
Matinee Maid   Herbert
Meet Me in St. Louis, Louis   Sterling
Melancholy Sunbeam and the Rose   Jerome; Schwartz, Jean
Mexico   Johnson, J. Rosamond
Military Man   Edwards
Mississippi Mania   Sterling
Mistakes Are Apt to Happen   Smith, Harry B.; Smith, Robert B.
Mum's the Word   Cobb; Edwards
My Beautiful Queen of Hearts   Cobb; Edwards
My Catamaran   Herbert
My Lucky Star   Smith, Harry B.; Smith, Robert B.
My Own Dear Irish Queen   Olcott
My Pretty Little Kickapoo   Sterling; Von Tilzer
My Sonny Boy   Olcott
My Unkissed Man   Jerome; Schwartz, Jean
Nesting in a New York Tree (Nesting Time in New York Town)   Cohan
Newport Dip, The   Johnson, J. Rosamond
Nobody but You   Johnson, J. Rosamond
Nobody Loves Little Me   Cobb; Edwards
Nordland   Herbert
Nothing New Beneath the Sun   Cohan
Och Louisa   Edwards
Off to the Derby   Cohan
On Lalawana's Shore   Johnson, J. Rosamond
One Umbrella Would Be Big Enough to You   Smith, Harry B.; Smith, Robert B.
Only a Bunch of Violets   Sterling
'Op on Me 'Ansom   Cohan
Oyaneetah (Seminole Love Song)   Herbert
Palace of Silver and Gold   Sterling; Von Tilzer
Peggy Is a New Yorker Now   Johnson, J. Rosamond
Pixies Entrance   Jerome; Schwartz, Jean
Pussy and the Bow-Wow   Johnson, J. Rosamond
Radium Dance   Jerome; Schwartz, Jean
Rehearsal, The   Johnson, J. Rosamond
Roaming Around the Town   Johnson, J. Rosamond
Rosie Rosinsky   Jerome; Schwartz, Jean
Sailors of the St. Hurrah   Cohan

Sarah Rosenstein   Fisher
Saturday Sadies   Herbert
Saturday Till Monday   Kern
Scandal   Johnson, J. Rosamond
Seminole   Williams
She Didn't Seem to Care About Me   Jerome; Schwartz, Jean
She's a Very Dear Friend of Mine   Herbert
She's a Yankee Doodle Girl   Sterling; Von Tilzer
Since Dolly Dimple Made a Hit (Dolly Dimples)   Jerome; Schwartz, Jean
Sleepy Hollow   Norworth
Slippery James the Woman in the Case   Herbert
So Long, Sing Song   Cohan
Stockings   Johnson, J. Rosamond
Susan   Kern
Take Me Back to My Louisiana Home   Cobb; Edwards
Tale of a Cassowary   Cobb; Edwards
Tale of the Wedding Bell, The   Smith, Harry B.; Smith, Robert B.
Tell It All   Herbert
Tennessee   Williams
Tennessee, That's the Place for Me   Schwartz, Jean
Terence   Olcott
That Man   Smith, Harry B.; Smith, Robert B.
They're All My Friends   Cohan
Tick, Tack, Toe   Olcott
Tippicanoe   Williams
To the End of the World Together   Kern
Under a Blanket in a Folding Bed   Cohan
Under Our Lovely Umbrellas   Jerome; Schwartz, Jean
Under the Goo Goo Tree   Jerome; Schwartz, Jean
Waiting for You   Kern
Waltz Me Around Again Willie   Cobb
We Go to Find the Ring   Johnson, J. Rosamond
We Really Ought to Be Married   Jerome; Schwartz, Jean
We Want Teddy for Four Years More   Edwards
We'll Paddle Our Own Canoe   Sterling; Von Tilzer
When I am Chief of Police   Johnson, J. Rosamond
When the Bees Are in the Hive   Bryan
When You're Broke   Jerome; Schwartz, Jean
Where the Morning Glories Twine Around the Door   Sterling; Von Tilzer
Will He Ever Smile Again?   Johnson, J. Rosamond
Wine, Wine! (Champagne Song)   Kern
Women   Johnson, J. Rosamond
Women in the Case, The   Herbert
Yankee Doodle Boy   Cohan
Yip-I-Addy-I-Aye   Cobb; Edwards
You Can't Keep a Good Man Down   Howard, Joseph E.
You'll Never 'Mount to Nothin' If You Stick to Me   Cobb; Edwards
Zel, Zel   Johnson, J. Rosamond

1905

Advantage of a College Education   Edwards; Smith, Robert B.
Ah, But in Dreams   Herbert
Albany   Jerome; Schwartz, Jean
All the World Is Dancing Mad   Jerome; Schwartz, Jean
American Heiress, An   Herbert; Smith, Harry B.
American Music 'Tis Better than Old Parsifal to Me   Herbert; Smith, Harry B.
Antonio   Jerome; Schwartz, Jean
Ask the Man   Howard, Joseph E.

Aurora Borealis   Schwartz, Jean
Back to Sioux City   Schwartz, Jean; Williams
Ballet   Herbert
Band of Reubenville   Schwartz, Jean; Williams
Barbarian Dance   Herbert
Barney McGuire   Herbert; Smith, Harry B.
Bazaar Opening Chorus   Herbert
Because I Am Not Understood   Smith, Robert B.
Big Banshee, The   Howard, Joseph E.
Bogie Man, The   Schwartz, Jean; Williams
Bohemia   Howard, Joseph E.
Borneo   Jerome; Schwartz, Jean
Bright Eyes Goodbye   Williams
Broadway Favorites   Herbert
Brownies   Howard, Joseph E.
Caliph, The   Howard, Joseph E.
Catland   Smith, Harry B.
Central Give Me Back My Dime   Howard, Joseph E.
Charge of the Footmen   Herbert
Charity Bazaar   Herbert
Cherries Ripe   Smith, Harry B.
Chorus Girl (inst.), The   Kern
Cindy Kate   Jerome; Schwartz, Jean
Clorinda Jackson   Howard, Joseph E.
Come and Take a Walk with Me   Jerome; Schwartz, Jean
Companions of the Blade   Herbert
Conversational Song   Jerome; Schwartz, Jean
Coronation   Howard, Joseph E.
Court Is Like a Chessboard, A   Smith, Harry B.
Crew of the Peek-a-Boo   Herbert
Cross Your Heart   Howard, Joseph E.
Darby and Joan   Smith, Robert B.
Dat Friend of Mine   Williams
Dear Little Girl Who Is Good, The   Herbert
Dear Little Wise Old Bowery   Jerome; Schwartz, Jean
Dear Old Dixieland   Jerome; Schwartz, Jean
Dear Old Farm   Jerome; Schwartz, Jean
Dear Old South   Edwards
Desdie, My Desdemona   Jerome; Schwartz, Jean
Diplomacy   Howard, Joseph E.
Dolly Dollars   Herbert
Down the Line with Arabella   Jerome; Schwartz, Jean
Drink to the Glorious Night   Howard, Joseph E.
Drop in on Me at Luncheon   Smith, Robert B.
Drummer Song   Jerome; Schwartz, Jean
Drums of the Fore and Aft   Howard, Joseph E.
Dumb Bell   Schwartz, Jean; Williams
East Side Lil   Schwartz, Jean
East Side Walk   Schwartz, Jean
Eccentric Dance   Herbert
Educated Fool (It Keeps Me Guessing All the Time), An   Herbert; Smith, Harry B.
English Bow, The   Smith, Robert B.
Entrance of Dolly   Herbert; Smith, Harry B.
Entrance of Dorothy   Herbert; Smith, Harry B.
Entrance of the Friendly Rivals' Club   Herbert; Smith, Harry B.
Evening Hymn, An   Kern
Fantana Song   Smith, Robert B.
Farewell, Mr. Abner Hemingway   Jerome; Schwartz, Jean
Farewell Waltz, The   Smith, Robert B.
Float Me Charlie   Jerome; Schwartz, Jean
Floating Isle of Bong Bong, The   Howard, Joseph E.
Frog and the Girl, The   Smith, Harry B.
Frolic of a Breeze   Kern

Furs and Feathers   Herbert
Get the Money   Jerome; Schwartz, Jean
Girl at the Helm, The   Smith, Robert B.
Girls and Boys   Smith, Harry B.
Git a Horse   Schwartz, Jean; Williams
Golden Net, The   Smith, Harry B.
Goodbye, Maggie Doyle   Jerome; Schwartz, Jean
Goodbye, Sweet Old Manhattan Isle   Jerome; Schwartz, Jean
Graft   Smith, Harry B.
Hail Celestial Potentate   Smith, Robert B.
Hallowe'en   Herbert
Ham Tree Barbecue   Jerome; Schwartz, Jean
Hats Make the Woman   Herbert
Heap Love (An Indian Serenade)   Howard, Joseph E.
Henny Klein   Jerome; Schwartz, Jean
He's Me Pal   Edwards
Highland Mary   Jerome; Schwartz, Jean
His Little Sister   Smith, Robert B.
Hold the Lanterns High   Smith, Robert B.
Hold Your Horses   Schwartz, Jean; Williams
Holding Hands   Smith, Harry B.
Home with the Milk in the Morning   Jerome; Schwartz, Jean
Honey, Love Me All the Time   Jerome; Schwartz, Jean
Honolulu-lu   Howard, Joseph E.
How to Get in Central Park   Jerome; Schwartz, Jean
How to Tell a Fairy Tale   Herbert
How'd You Like to Spoon with Me?   Kern
Hunter's Chorus, The   Howard, Joseph E.
Hunting of the Cook, The   Herbert
I Didn't Mean No Harm   Smith, Robert B.
I Don't Want a Little Canoe   Jerome; Schwartz, Jean
I Guess I'll Take a Ride   Howard, Joseph E.
I Like You, Too   Howard, Joseph E.
I Love You   Jerome; Schwartz, Jean
I Should Think that You Could Guess   Herbert
I Want a Girl Like You   Howard, Joseph E.
I Want What I Want When I Want It   Herbert
I'd Rather Be a Lemon than Grapefruit   Williams
If a Gal Like You Loved a Boy Like Me   Cobb; Edwards
If I Were on the Stage (Kiss Me Again)   Herbert
If I Were the Man in the Moon   Howard, Joseph E.
I'm a Woman of Importance   Jerome; Schwartz, Jean
I'm Always Misunderstood   Herbert
I'm Getting Seasick   Schwartz, Jean
I'm Going to Leave You   Howard, Joseph E.
I'm Lonesome for You   Howard, Joseph E.
I'm the Only Star that Twinkles on Broadway   Sterling; Von Tilzer
In a Bungalo   Jerome; Schwartz, Jean
In a Hammock Built for Two   Sterling; Von Tilzer
In Bad Man's Land   Jerome; Schwartz, Jean
In Dear Old Georgia   Williams
In Dear Old Kankakee   Howard, Joseph E.
In Dreams So Fair   Herbert
In My Merry Oldsmobile   Edwards
In My Rickshaw of Bamboo   Smith, Robert B.
In Old New York   Jerome; Schwartz, Jean
In Tammany Hall   Jerome; Schwartz, Jean
In the Orange Blossom Land   Howard, Joseph E.
In the Shade of the Old Apple Tree   Williams
In Vacation Time   Sterling; Von Tilzer
Insurgents   Howard, Joseph E.
It Is the Girl and Not the Horse that Wins the Prize   Smith, Robert B.

It's a Jolly Good Thing to Be Alive   Smith, Robert B.
It's All in the Book You Know (Ollendorf Duet)   Herbert;
    Smith, Harry B.
It's Hard to Be a Hero   Herbert
It's the Smile   Edwards
Jail Bird and the Tiger, The   Howard, Joseph E.
Jerome the Boogie Man   Jerome; Schwartz, Jean
Jingle Feet   Jerome; Schwartz, Jean
Jogafree   Herbert
Johnny Morgan   Williams
Julie Dooley   Howard, Joseph E.
Just Get Out and Walk   Herbert; Smith, Harry B.
Just My Style   Smith, Robert B.
Just Say Hello to Chicago   Howard, Joseph E.
Just Use a Bit of Blarney   Howard, Joseph E.
Keep on A-Loving Me   Jerome; Kern
Keokuk Culture Club, The   Herbert
Kisses   Jerome; Schwartz, Jean
Kitty and the Owl, The   Howard, Joseph E.
Knave of Hearts, The   Herbert
Knock Wood   Smith, Robert B.
La Dance Parisienne et La Americaine   Smith, Robert B.
Land of Nod, The   Howard, Joseph E.
Lantern Fete   Smith, Robert B.
Laughing Little Almond Eyes   Smith, Robert B.
Lesson in Etiquette, A   Smith, Robert B.
Let the Trumpets Sound   Smith, Harry B.
Let's Take a Trolly Ride   Howard, Joseph E.
Life's a Masquerade   Herbert; Smith, Harry B.
Line It Out, Mr. McGinnity   Jerome; Schwartz, Jean
Little Bird's Story   Olcott
Little Black Sheep   Herbert
Little Home in My Heart for You   Edwards
Love Me, Love My Dog   Herbert
Love's a Golden Day   Herbert
Lovie   Howard, Joseph E.
Maiden of the Wild and Woolly West   Edwards; Smith,
    Robert B.
Making Eyes   Jerome; Von Tilzer
Man Behind the Club   Jerome; Schwartz, Jean
Man that Leads the Band that Leads the Army,
    The   Edwards; Smith, Robert B.
March Boys March   Cobb; Edwards
Marching Home with Rosie   Sterling; Von Tilzer
Marking Eyes   Sterling; Von Tilzer
Mascot of the Moon (Mascot of the Troup)   Herbert
Masie McIntyre   Sterling; Von Tilzer
McGuire Esquire   Kern
Me, Myself and I (I and Myself and Me)   Herbert
Meet Me in the Wisteria   Edwards; Smith, Robert B.
Meet Me on the Fence Tonight   Jerome; Schwartz, Jean
Merry Minstrel Band   Jerome; Schwartz, Jean
Milking the Milky Way   Schwartz, Jean; Williams
Milkmaids' Chorus   Schwartz, Jean; Williams
Minstrel Parade, The   Jerome; Schwartz, Jean
Minuet   Herbert
Miss Dolly Dollars   Herbert; Smith, Harry B.
Miss Mary   Olcott
Molly O'Hallerhan (Edna May's Irish Song)   Kern
Moonlight Buggy Ride, A   Jerome; Schwartz, Jean
Moth and the Moon, The   Herbert; Smith, Harry B.
Mr. Lawson the Man from Boston   Jerome; Schwartz, Jean
Mrs. Maloney   Jerome; Schwartz, Jean
My Celia   Kern
My Fair Unknown   Herbert; Smith, Harry B.

My First Smoke   Jerome; Schwartz, Jean
My Gypsy Maid   Howard, Joseph E.
My Hindoo Man   Williams
My Illinois   Howard, Joseph E.
My Indiana Anna   Schwartz, Jean; Williams
My Irish Daisy   Jerome; Schwartz, Jean
My Irish Indian, Mary Ann McCue   Jerome; Schwartz, Jean
My Irish Molly O'   Jerome; Schwartz, Jean
My Lady of Japan   Jerome; Schwartz, Jean
My Little Lassoo   Smith, Harry B.
My Southern Belle   Kern
My Sweet   Jerome; Schwartz, Jean
My Syndi-Kate   Jerome; Schwartz, Jean
My Uncle Sam   Howard, Joseph E.
My Wigwam Lady   Jerome; Schwartz, Jean
My Word   Smith, Robert B.
My Word! It Surely Was a Treat   Herbert; Smith, Harry B.
Nature Class   Herbert
Nicholini   Howard, Joseph E.
Nightingale and the Rose, The   Herbert
Nineteen Princess Song   Herbert
No One Will Steal Him   Herbert; Smith, Harry B.
No Show Tonight   Herbert
Nobody But You   Jerome; Schwartz, Jean
Nobody Else but You   Fisher
North, South, East or West   Smith, Robert B.
Nothin' from Nothin' Leaves You   Snyder
Oh, Marie!   Jerome; Schwartz, Jean
Oh, Mr. Chamberlain   Kern
Oh Reuben Tell Your Mandy   Schwartz, Jean
Oh! Silvery Moon   Smith, Robert B.
Oh the Deuce, What's the Use   Howard, Joseph E.
Old Home Week in Alabama   Jerome; Schwartz, Jean
Old Timer, An   Howard, Joseph E.
On an Automobile Honeymoon   Jerome; Schwartz, Jean
On the Banks of the Rhine with a Stein   Sterling
On the Strict QT   Sterling; Von Tilzer
Only One, The   Herbert
Oriental Dance   Herbert
Ossified Man, The   Herbert
Pa Is Rich, So Ma Don't Care   Jerome; Schwartz, Jean
Pequita   Howard, Joseph E.
Pocahontas   Bryan
Pocohantas   Edwards
Popular Pauline   Herbert
Quarterback, The   Howard, Joseph E.
Queen of the Ring   Herbert; Smith, Harry B.
Raining   Kern
Rajah's Glide, The   Jerome; Schwartz, Jean
Rambling Sam   Schwartz, Jean; Williams
Reuben Tell Your Mandy   Schwartz, Jean; Williams
Robin Hood's Arrest   Smith, Robert B.
Rolling Chair Song   Williams
Romeo and Juliet   Edwards; Smith, Robert B.
Sailing Away   Smith, Harry B.
Secret (Gossip Song), The   Smith, Robert B.
Self-Made Family (She's a Lady with Money), The   Herbert;
    Smith, Harry B.
Servants Chorus   Herbert
She Can Do Little Who Can't Do This   Smith, Robert B.
Simple Simon   Edwards; Smith, Robert B.
Somebody's Sweetheart I Want to Be   Cobb; Edwards
Song of the Mermaid (The Mermaid and the
    Rainbow)   Howard, Joseph E.
Song of the Pipe   Smith, Robert B.

Stories of a Summer Night   Howard, Joseph E.
Sun that Shines on Dixieland, The   Howard, Joseph E.
Sweet Kitty Bellairs   Edwards; Smith, Robert B.
Sweethearts in Every Town   Jerome; Schwartz, Jean
Sweethearts of Boyhood Days   Howard, Joseph E.
Tailor's Dummy   Smith, Robert B.
Take a Car   Snyder
Take Me on the Merry-Go-Round   Kern
Tale of a Song Box Shop   Herbert
Tammany   Edwards
Tammany Ball, The   Jerome; Schwartz, Jean
Temples of Eternity, The   Williams
Tennessee, That's the Place for Me   Jerome
Texas Dan   Jerome; Schwartz, Jean
That's Art   Smith, Robert B.
That's My Idea of a Hero   Edwards
That's Why They Say I'm Crazy   Herbert
There's a Chicken Dinner Waiting for Me   Williams
There's Nothing Doing in the Old, Old Town   Jerome;
    Schwartz, Jean
There's Only One Little Old New York   Schwartz, Jean
Time, the Place and the Girl, The   Herbert
Tulips (Two Lips)   Kern
Turn Over   Jerome; Schwartz, Jean
Umpire Is a Most Unhappy Man, The   Howard, Joseph E.
Until We Meet Again   Herbert
Up and Down the Boardwalk   Edwards; Smith, Robert B.
Voice for It, The   Herbert
Wait Till the Sun Shines Nellie   Sterling; Von Tilzer
Walking   Jerome; Schwartz, Jean
Walks   Herbert; Smith, Harry B.
Waltz Duet, The   Smith, Robert B.
What Has the Night Time to Do with the Girl   Jerome;
    Schwartz, Jean
What Would Mrs. Grundy Say   Smith, Robert B.
What You Goin' to Do when the Rent Comes
    Round   Sterling; Von Tilzer
What's the Use of Wishing It Won't Come True   Edwards
When Perrico Plays   Herbert
When the Cat's Away   Jerome; Schwartz, Jean
When the Cat's Away the Mice Will Play   Herbert
When You're in Love   Jerome; Schwartz, Jean
Where the Flag Is Waving   Smith, Harry B.
Whoa, Ida How, Whoa   Sterling; Von Tilzer
Why Don't You Try   Williams
Will You   Edwards
With Frame Two Forty Nine   Herbert
Woman Is Only a Woman but a Good Cigar Is a Joke, Puff,
    Puff, Puff, A   Smith, Harry B.
Woman Is Only a Woman but a Good Cigar Is a Smoke,
    Puff, Puff, Puff, A   Herbert
Woman's First Thought Is a Man, A   Herbert
Won't You Kiss Me Once Before You Go?   Kern
Yankee Doodle Boodle   Jerome; Schwartz, Jean
Year and a Day, A   Smith, Harry B.
You Can Sail in My Boat   Olcott
You Look Awful Good to Father   Howard, Joseph E.
Your Father Was a Soldier Too   Williams
Your Heart Alone Must Tell   Olcott
Your Heart, If You Please   Herbert
You're All Right Eddie   Williams
You're All the Candy with Me   Schwartz, Jean; Williams
You're Just the Same to Me   Howard, Joseph E.
Ze English Language   Herbert

1906

Abraham Jefferson Washington Lee (You Ain't Goin' to Pick
    No Fuss Out of Me)   Sterling; Von Tilzer
Accident, An   Herbert
Ah Lovely Art, We Worship at Thy Shrine   Smith, Harry B.
Ain't You Got Nothin' to Say   Jerome; Schwartz, Jean
All Aboard for Broadway   Cohan
All I Want Is You   Kern
American Girl in Paris, The   Smith, Harry B.
And I Laughed   Smith, Harry B.
Any Old Time at All   Jerome; Schwartz, Jean
Are You Coming Out Tonight, Mary Ann   Sterling; Von
    Tilzer
Ask Me-Not   Cobb; Edwards
Assembling of the Two Courts   Smith, Harry B.
At Last   Smith, Harry B.
Bagpipe Serenade   Kern
Be Demure   Smith, Harry B.
Beautiful Dreamtown   Herbert
Beautiful Isle of Dreams   Herbert
Beautiful Land of Love, The   Sterling; Von Tilzer
Because You're You   Herbert
Beside the Old Oak Gate   Lewis
Blue, Blue   Kern
Bolero, The   Smith, Robert B.
Bonnie Jean   Bryan; Snyder
By the Side of a Mill   Herbert
Cafeteria Chow   Conrad
Camp Meeting Time   Williams
Carrier Pigeon, The   Smith, Harry B.
Cheer Up Mary   Bryan
Cheyanne (Shy Ann)   Williams
Cing Cing's Samisen   Howard, Joseph E.
Colonial Chorus   Cohan
Come and Take a Skate with Me   Edwards
Come My Dear   Smith, Harry B.
Come Take a Skate with Me   Edwards
Come to the Land of Bohemia   Snyder
Come Ye Heroes All (The Emperor's War Song)   Smith,
    Harry B.
Cupid's Auction Sale   Smith, Harry B.
Day Dreams   Olcott; Smith, Harry B.
Don't Go in the Lion's Cage   Goetz
Don't You Think It's Time to Get Married   Edwards
Don't You Want a Paper, Dearie?   Kern
Down a Shady Lane   Herbert
Dramatic Situation   Smith, Harry B.
Ducal Cousin   Smith, Harry B.
Eileen Asthore   Olcott
Enough of Work   Herbert
Entr'acte (inst.)   Friml
Entrance of Johnny Rocks   Smith, Robert B.
Every Day Is Ladies Day with Me   Herbert
Every Little Object Has a History   Smith, Harry B.
Everybody Gives Me Good Advice   Bryan
Eyes that Come from Ireland   Olcott
Farmer's Life, A   Herbert
Fickle Weather Vane, The   Smith, Robert B.
Five O'Clock Tea   Smith, Harry B.
For Charity's Sake   Smith, Harry B.
For Love of Thee   Olcott
Forever Delighting in Fighting   Smith, Harry B.
Forty-Five Minutes from Broadway   Cohan
Friend of Mine Told a Friend of Mine, A   Bryan
Friends   Jerome; Schwartz, Jean

Friendship's Sacred Touch   Smith, Harry B.
Frolic of a Breeze   Kern
Gentlemen of the Press   Cohan
Gibson Girl, The   Smith, Harry B.
Give You Greeting   Smith, Harry B.
Go While the Goin' Is Good   Herbert
Going to the Opera   Herbert
Goo Goo Goo   Conrad
Good Night, Good Night   Gilbert
Good Old Songs of the Blue and Gray, The   Sterling; Von Tilzer
Gooda-Bye John   Williams
Goodbye Dolly Grey   Cobb
Goodbye John   Herbert
Goose Girl, The   Smith, Harry B.
Gossips Song   Herbert
Gown for Each Hour of the Day, A   Smith, Harry B.
Graft   Smith, Robert B.
Guy that Can Hand You a Laugh, The   Howard, Joseph E.
Hannah   Herbert
Hark to the Voice of Your Lover   Smith, Robert B.
Have You Met Mandy Murphy   Cobb; Edwards
He Was a Wonderful Man   Cohan
Heart to Let, A   Howard, Joseph E.
Her Portrait   Smith, Harry B.
Hither Bring the Bold Intruder   Smith, Harry B.
Home Is Home   Howard, Joseph E.
Home, Sweet Home   Smith, Harry B.
Home Sweet Home Sounds Good to Me   Sterling; Von Tilzer
Homeward Bound   Smith, Harry B.
Honora Doolin   Snyder
Hottentot Love Song, A   Johnson, J. Rosamond
How Could You   Bryan
How Do You Account for That?   Smith, Robert B.
How Soon You Are Forgotten When You're Gone   Fisher
How'd You Like to Spoon with Me?   Kern
Hurroo, Hurray and Hurrah for That   Smith, Harry B.
I Am a Potentate   Smith, Harry B.
I Am the Man They Talk So Much About   Smith, Harry B.
I Do It All By Proxy   Smith, Harry B.
I Don't Believe I'll Ever Be a Lady   Herbert
I Have to Laugh   Herbert
I Just Can't Make My Eyes Behave   Cobb; Edwards; Smith, Harry B.
I Love You   Herbert
I Miss You in a Thousand Different Ways   Cobb; Edwards
I Never Saw Such Jealousy in All My Life   Sterling; Von Tilzer
I Never Was Right in My Life   Smith, Harry B.
I Want to Be a Popular Millionaire   Cohan
I Want to Marry   Herbert
I Want You Ma' Honey   Smith, Harry B.
I Want You to Marry Me   Herbert
I Was Born in Virginia (Ethel Levey's Virginia Song)   Cohan
I Was Just Supposing   Smith, Robert B.
I'd Like to See a Little More of You   Cobb; Edwards
I'd Rather Be Outside A-Lookin' In then on the Inside A-Lookin' Out   Snyder
If Mr. Boston Lawson Has His Way   Cohan
If the Man in the Moon Was a Coon   Fisher
If Washington Should Come to Life   Cohan
If You Love But Me   Herbert
I'll Be There with Bells On   Cohan
I'll Do Anything in the World for You   Cobb; Edwards

I'll Keep a Warm Spot in My Heart for You   Johnson, J. Rosamond
I'll Ring the Bell   Herbert
I'm a Lawyer   Smith, Harry B.
I'm Always Doing Something I Don't Want to Do   Herbert
I'm Going Right Back to Chicago   Williams
I'm Sorry   Norworth
I'm the Man in Washington   Smith, Harry B.
Improvements   Herbert
In a Chimney Corner   Sterling; Von Tilzer
In My Canoe   Snyder
In the Evening by the Moonlight, Dear Louise   Sterling; Von Tilzer
In the Isle of Our Dreams   Herbert
In the Sweet Bye and Bye   Herbert
In Vaudeville   Herbert
Intermezzo   Herbert
Is It Warm Enough for You   Bryan
It Depends on the Hair   Smith, Harry B.
It's Delightful to Be Married   Smith, Harry B.
It's Lovely When Your Love Loves You   Goetz
It's Not the World, It's You   Smith, Harry B.
I've a Little Favor   Kern
I've Heard So Much About You   Smith, Robert B.
I've Never Been Over There   Cohan
I've Said My Last Farewell, Toot Toot Goodbye   Fisher
Jungle Joy   Conrad
Just a Little Fond Affection   Bryan
Just Kiss Me and Say Good Bye   Gilbert
Just the One I'm Looking For   Goetz
Kissing   Atteridge; Conrad
Kitty, Pretty Kitty   Jerome; Schwartz, Jean
La Danse Parisienne   Smith, Harry B.
La Mattichiche   Smith, Harry B.
Lancers' Waltz   Herbert
Legend of the Mill, The   Herbert
Legend of the Sons of Samson, The   Smith, Harry B.
Lesson in Kissing (Kiss, Kiss, Kiss), A   Smith, Harry B.
Let Us Greet with Joy Pretended   Smith, Harry B.
Life Is a See-Saw   Smith, Harry B.
Little Bas Bleu   Smith, Harry B.
Little Girlie You Have Caught My Eye   Atteridge
Little Old America for Me   Smith, Harry B.
Little Two By Four   Conrad
Look Who's Here, Ship Ahoy   Sterling; Von Tilzer
Lorelei   Smith, Robert B.
Love but You   Herbert
Love By Telephone   Herbert
Major Margery   Smith, Robert B.
Make Your Own Sunshine   Howard, Joseph E.
Mam'selle Sallie   Smith, Harry B.
March   Herbert
Mary's a Grand Old Name   Cohan
Meet Me at Twilight   Kern
Mignonette   Herbert
Million, A   Smith, Harry B.
Molly's Composers (inst.)   Kern
Moonbeams   Herbert
Moses Andrew Jackson Goodbye   Snyder
Moving Day   Sterling; Von Tilzer
Mr. Chamberlain   Kern
Mr. Monkey   Cobb; Edwards
My Hungarian Irish Girl   Kern
My Irish Rosie   Jerome; Schwartz, Jean
My Sunburnt Salome   Cobb; Edwards

Mystery of History, The   Smith, Harry B.
Nancy, I Fancy You   Herbert
Oh, I'm the Man They Talk So Much About   Smith, Harry B.
Oh, the Heat and the Skeet!   Herbert
Olcott's Love Song   Olcott
Old Broadway   Howard, Joseph E.
On Parchment This with Grey Goose Quill   Smith, Harry B.
On the Beaches   Conrad
On the Phone   Herbert
On the Radio   Conrad
On to Victory   Smith, Harry B.
Once in a While   Fisher
Once Upon a Time   Cobb
One and One Makes One   Howard, Joseph E.
Operatic Maiden, An   Herbert
Owatonna   Williams
Paris Carnival   Smith, Harry B.
Parisian Model, A   Smith, Harry B.
Parisienne   Smith, Harry B.
Pas de Nuit   Herbert
Percy   Jerome; Schwartz, Jean
Plain Rustic Ride ('Neath the Silv'ry Moon), A   Kern
Poker Love (Card Duet)   Kern
Pony Galop   Jerome; Schwartz, Jean
Popularity   Cohan
Ravenous Rooster, The   Herbert
Recipe, A   Kern
Release that Man   Smith, Harry B.
Retiring from the Stage   Cohan
Riddles   Smith, Harry B.
Rosalie   Kern
Rustic Patrol   Herbert
Same Old Story   Howard, Joseph E.
Save a Little Money for a Rainy Day   Snyder
School Days (When We Were a Couple of Kids)   Cobb; Edwards
Scientific Classes   Von Tilzer
Shy Suburban Maid, A   Herbert
Sing Sing Sammy Sen   Howard, Joseph E.
So   Howard, Joseph E.
So Long, Mary   Cohan
Something Doing Around My Heart   Howard, Joseph E.
Something Tells Me I'm in Love   Williams
Song of the Dice   Smith, Harry B.
Song of the Free Lance (I Am a Salaried Warrior)   Smith, Harry B.
Song of the Rag-Time Boy   Sterling; Von Tilzer
Stand Up and Fight Like Hell   Cohan
Stop It   Smith, Harry B.
Storm of Life   Williams
Streets of New York (In Old New York), The   Herbert
Sunday Poipers   Conrad
Sweet Anastasia Brady   Jerome; Schwartz, Jean
Sweet Girl Graduate, The   Smith, Harry B.
Symptoms   Howard, Joseph E.
Ta, Ta, My Dainty Little Darling   Herbert
Take Care Senor   Smith, Robert B.
Teach Them What to Say   Herbert
There's Not Enough Gold to Buy Him   Bryan
Thessaly   Smith, Harry B.
This World Is a Toy Shop   Smith, Harry B.
Three Love Stories   Smith, Harry B.
To the Lambs   Herbert
Trying on Dresses   Smith, Harry B.

Two Dirty Little Hands   Cobb; Edwards
Under the Linden Tree   Kern
United We Stand   Smith, Robert B.
Volunteer Fireman, The   Herbert
Waltz Me Around Again Willie   Cobb
Way Down in Jersey   Howard, Joseph E.
Wearers of the Green   Olcott
Wedding Bells   Herbert
Wedding of the Blue and the Gray, The   Cohan
We've Got a Lot to Learn   Smith, Robert B.
What's the Matter with Our Team   Von Tilzer
What's the Use of Dreaming?   Howard, Joseph E.
What's the Use of Knockin'   Edwards
When Flowers Bloom in Springtime, Molly Dear   Sterling; Von Tilzer
When My Ship Comes In   Smith, Harry B.
When Tommy Atkins Marries Dolly Gray   Cobb; Edwards
When We're Married   Smith, Harry B.
When You Go Out to Dine   Howard, Joseph E.
When You're Pretty and the World Is Fair   Herbert
Where E'er I Go   Smith, Robert B.
Whistle It   Herbert
Whistle When You Walk Out   Smith, Harry B.
Whistling Yankee Girl, The   Smith, Harry B.
Widow Has Ways, A   Herbert
With Apparent Ebullition   Smith, Harry B.
Wizard of Wall Street, The   Smith, Robert B.
Women Are All Perfect Fools   Smith, Harry B.
Won't You Be My Girlie?   Howard, Joseph E.
Won't You Come Over to My House   Williams
Won't Your Mamma Let You Come Out and Play   Johnson, J. Rosamond
Would You Leave Your Happy Home for Me   Sterling; Von Tilzer
You Are My Fire Bug   Cobb; Edwards
You Can Have Broadway   Cohan
You Never Can Tell About a Woman   Herbert
You Never Told Me That Before We Married   Smith, Harry B.
You're a Grand Old Flag   Cohan
You're All the World to Me   Smith, Harry B.
You're the Sweetest Girl I Know   Howard, Joseph E.
Youth Must Have It's Fling   Smith, Harry B.
Zoo-Lou   Williams

1907

Ain't You Glad You Found Me   Williams
All I Want in the Wide, Wide, World Is You, Just You   Edwards
Along Life's Highway   Howard, Joseph E.
Alteutscher Leibersreim   Jerome; Schwartz, Jean
And a Little Bit More   Bryan; Fisher
April Fool Ditty   Howard, Joseph E.
Aren't You the Girl (I Met in Sherry's)   Goetz
Arizona   Cobb; Edwards
Awfully Nice to Love One Girl   Herbert
Ballooning   Kern
Be There At Twilight   Bryan; Meyer
Bedouin Chief   Herbert; Smith, Harry B.
Before We Married   Smith, Robert B.
Belle of Bald Head Row, The   Howard, Joseph E.
Beneath the Moon   Jerome; Schwartz, Jean
Big Swamp Bogie Man, The   Meyer
Bill's a Liar   Kern

Birds of a Feather   Williams
Blame the Weather Man   Howard, Joseph E.
Blondy Let Me Have the Next Dance with You   Bryan;
   Meyer
Blow the Smoke Away   Howard, Joseph E.
Bluebird (inst.)   Snyder
Bonnie Briar Bush   Howard, Joseph E.
Bowl of Roses, A   Olcott
Boys Will Be Boys and Girls Will Be Girls   Herbert; Smith,
   Harry B.
Burglar's Serenade   Howard, Joseph E.
Burning Up the Boulevard   Cohan
Busy Little Broadway   Cohan
Bye, Bye Dear Old Broadway   Cobb; Edwards
Bye Bye Dearie   Sterling; Von Tilzer
Campmeetin' Time   Williams
Cheer Up! Girls   Kern
Claremont   Cohan
Cock-a-Doodle-Doo   Howard, Joseph E.
College Boy's Dream   Edwards
Come Along with Me   Jerome; Schwartz, Jean
Come Around on Our Veranda   Kern
Come Back to Old Manhattan, Dearie   Jerome; Schwartz,
   Jean
Come Down Salomy Jane   Goetz
Come On, Let's Two Step   Howard, Joseph E.
Coon College   Edwards
Corsica   Smith, Robert B.
Darling Sue   Sterling; Von Tilzer
De Bode o' Edicashun   Johnson, J. Rosamond
Dear Heart   Howard, Joseph E.
Dear Old East Side   Edwards
Deutschland   Bryan
Devil's Serenade, The   Howard, Joseph E.
Dixie Dan   Cobb
Dixie, I Love You   Howard, Joseph E.
Doctor Munyon   Goetz
Does Anybody Want a Blonde   Edwards; Smith, Robert B.
Dolly Dear   Norworth
Don't Worry   Snyder
Don't You Tell   Howard, Joseph E.
Down in the Old Cherry Orchard   Bryan
Down in the Philippines   Johnson, J. Rosamond
Drink with Me   Cohan
Duchess of Killarney, The   Goetz
Easter Dawn, An   Herbert
Eastern Moon   Kern
Entrance of Arabs   Herbert; Smith, Harry B.
Entrance of Omar (Oriental March)   Herbert; Smith, Harry
   B.
Entrance of Shah   Herbert; Smith, Harry B.
Every Star Falls in Love with His Mate   Olcott
Face of the Girl I Love, The   Schwartz, Jean
Fashion   Edwards
Find Another Tree to Build Your Nest   Bryan; Meyer
First and Only   Howard, Joseph E.
Floating Down the Nile   Johnson, J. Rosamond
Floral Wedding, The   Herbert; Smith, Harry B.
Follow Your Uncle Dudley   Cohan
Friars, The   Herbert
Frolics of Pierrot, The   Edwards
Garden of Dreams   Smith, Robert B.
Gee, Ain't I Glad I'm Home!   Cohan
Ghost of Deacon Brown, The   Johnson, J. Rosamond
Girl of the Great Divide, The   Smith, Robert B.

Girl You Dream About, The   Howard, Joseph E.
Give Me Your Love   Snyder
Handle Me with Care   Jerome; Schwartz, Jean
Hay Ride, The   Kern
He Goes to Church on Sunday   Goetz
He Went A-Hunting   Von Tilzer
Hear My Song of Love (Serenade)   Herbert; Smith, Harry B.
Heart to Let, A   Howard, Joseph E.
Hello Mister Stein   Sterling; Von Tilzer
Here in the Moonlight on the Fence   Edwards
Here on the Fence at Doolittle College   Edwards
Herman   Jerome; Schwartz, Jean
Honey Babe   Cohan
Honey Boy   Norworth
How Was I to Know   Howard, Joseph E.
How'd You Like to Float Me (Come on and Float Me Freddy
   Dear)   Goetz
How'd You Like to Take Me Home with You   Cobb;
   Edwards
Hurrah, Hurrah and Hurroo for That   Smith, Robert B.
I Don't Like Your Family   Howard, Joseph E.
I Don't Want an Auto   Jerome
I Don't Want Any More   Meyer
I Got to See de Minstrel Show   Von Tilzer
I Have a Longing for Long Acre Square   Cohan
I Just Couldn't Do Without You   Kern
I Like You Too   Williams
I Say What I Mean, and I Mean What I Say   Herbert; Smith,
   Harry B.
I Think an Awful Lot of You   Johnson, J. Rosamond
I Think I Oughtn't Auto Any More   Goetz
I Think of You the Whole Year Round   Jerome; Schwartz,
   Jean
I Want a Thrill   Howard, Joseph E.
I Want the World to Know I Love You   Cohan
I Want to Be a Gambling Man   Herbert
I Want You   Cohan
I'd Like Another Situation Just Like That   Smith, Robert B.
I'd Like to Be Your Affinity, You Certainly Look Good to
   Me   Von Tilzer
I'd Like to Make a Mash Mit You   Fisher; Kern
I'd Like to Meet Your Father   Kern
I'd Sooner Be a Has Been than a Never Was at All   Jerome;
   Schwartz, Jean
If I'm Going to Die I'm Going to Have Some Fun   Cohan
If Love Were What the Rose Is   Herbert
If We Knew What the Milkman Knows   Goetz
If You Grow Tired Little Girl   Howard, Joseph E.
I'll Always Love Old Dixie   Johnson, J. Rosamond
I'm a Lawyer   Smith, Robert B.
I'm a Popular Man   Cohan
I'm Afraid to Come Home in the Dark   Williams
I'm Afraid to Go Home in the Dark   Smith, Robert B.
I'm Not So Particular Now   Herbert; Smith, Harry B.
I'm the Leading Lady   Williams
I'm Well Known   Kern
I'm Wise   Williams
In Philadelphia   Edwards
In the Land of the Buffalo   Williams
In the Shade of My Bungalow   Howard, Joseph E.
Insanity   Norworth
Iowa   Edwards
It's a Grand Old Game   Jerome; Schwartz, Jean
It's Awfully Nice to Love One Girl   Herbert; Smith, Harry B.
It's Great to Be an Actor   Howard, Joseph E.

It's Lonesome Tonight   Howard, Joseph E.
I've a Million Reasons Why I Love You   Kern
Jealousy   Howard, Joseph E.
Jingles and Jokes   Howard, Joseph E.
Junior Miss   Howard, Joseph E.
Just a Little on Account   Meyer
Just a Paper Doll   Howard, Joseph E.
Just Help Yourself   Sterling; Von Tilzer
Just Home from College   Jerome; Schwartz, Jean
Just How Much I Love You   Johnson, J. Rosamond
Just One — For Fun   Harbach
Katy Was a Business Girl   Kern
Kentucky Love   Fisher
Kiss from the Girl You Love, A   Edwards
Kitten that Couldn't Be Good   Herbert; Smith, Harry B.
Land of Dreams, The   Herbert; Smith, Harry B.
Land of Nod, The   Howard, Joseph E.
Larry   Williams
Leader of Fashion Am I   Edwards
Legend of the Djin, The   Herbert; Smith, Harry B.
Lemons   Johnson, J. Rosamond
Let's Take an Old-Fashioned Walk   Cohan
Let's Wander Off Nowhere   Edwards
Life Is a See-Saw   Smith, Robert B.
Li'l Gal   Johnson, J. Rosamond
Little Choo Choo Gee-Gee, The   Johnson, J. Rosamond
Little Church Around the Corner, The   Kern
Little Eva   Kern
Little Girl in Blue   Smith, Robert B.
Love Is a Will-O-the Wisp   Howard, Joseph E.
Love Is Contagious   Howard, Joseph E.
Love Laid His Sleepless Head   Herbert
Love's Merry Go Round   Goetz
Love's Prescription   Williams
Lulu and Her La-La-La   Von Tilzer
Madchenlied   Jerome; Schwartz, Jean
Make a Lot of Noise   Cohan
Mandy   Edwards
Many's the Time   Fisher
Marceline's Meat Sauce   Smith, Robert B.
Marie from Sunny Italy   Berlin
Mariutch Make-a the Hootch and Ma Kooch Down at Coney
    Isle   Sterling; Von Tilzer
Mary McGee   Kern
Mary Wise   Williams
May Fuzzy   Bryan
Meanest Man in Town, The   Bryan; Fisher
Merry Old King   Howard, Joseph E.
Michael McGinnity   Olcott
Modern Sandow Girl, The   Edwards; Smith, Harry B.
Mr. Bingham   Cohan
Mr. Burns of New Rochelle   Cohan
Mrs. Oho   Smith, Robert B.
Muezzins and Bayaderres   Herbert; Smith, Harry B.
Musical Comedy Maid, The   Cohan
My Baby Knows   Meyer; Turk
My Belle Zabelle   Cobb; Edwards
My Cinderella   Howard, Joseph E.
My Irish Gibson Girl   Jerome; Schwartz, Jean
My Irish Girl   Williams
My Mary   Fisher
My Sweetheart's a Soldier in the Army   Johnson, J.
    Rosamond
My Toast to You   Herbert
'Neath the Old Cherry Tree Sweet Marie   Williams

Never Marry a Girl with Cold Feet   Kern
Never, Never Land   Herbert; Smith, Harry B.
New York Two-Step, The   Cohan
Nightmare and Goblin March, The   Howard, Joseph E.
Nobody Loves Me   Herbert; Smith, Harry B.
Nonsense   Howard, Joseph E.
Nothing New Beneath the Sun   Cohan
Nurse Girls and Doctors   Williams
O Come My Love   Williams
Oh Mister Brown   Sterling; Von Tilzer
Oh, Oh Miss Lucy Ella   Sterling; Von Tilzer
Oh You May   Williams
Old Flag Never Touched the Ground, The   Johnson, J.
    Rosamond
Old Friends   Edwards
Omar Khayyam   Herbert; Smith, Harry B.
On an Old Fashioned Buggy Ride   Williams
On the Grand Old Band   Edwards
On the Grand Old Sands   Cobb; Edwards
Once More to Dream   Howard, Joseph E.
One Little, Sweet Little Girl   Olcott
Oriental March   Herbert; Smith, Harry B.
Paree   Edwards
Parisiana Anna   Goetz
Peach that Tastes the Sweetest Hangs the Highest on the
    Tree, The   Cobb; Edwards
Perfect Lady, A   Atteridge
Poor Little Foolish Man   Jerome; Schwartz, Jean
Pop Step Melody   Howard, Joseph E.
Popular March   Cohan
Put a Little Bet Down for Me   Cohan
Put Me Among the Girls   Edwards
Rag-Time Banjo Serenade, The   Goetz
Rebecca   Williams
Recipe, A   Kern
Re-Incarnation   Goetz
Right Now   Fisher; Kern
Roll Around   Smith, Harry B.
Rose of Old Derry, A   Olcott
Run, Brudder Rabbit, Run!   Johnson, J. Rosamond
Sacramento   Sterling
Sacremento   Von Tilzer
Same Old Moon, The   Howard, Joseph E.
San Antonio   Williams
She's Dixie Through and Through   Bryan
Signs   Jerome; Schwartz, Jean
Situation   Smith, Robert B.
Sleep Sublime and Perfect Poet   Herbert; Smith, Harry B.
Smarty   Howard, Joseph E.
Snake Charmer's Dance   Herbert; Smith, Harry B.
Some Day when Dreams Come True   Williams
Someone Waiting for Me   Howard, Joseph E.
Southland   Johnson, J. Rosamond
Spanish Serenade, The   Herbert
Story of the Wedding March, The   Cohan
Subway Express, The   Kern
Sweet Girl Graduate, The   Smith, Robert B.
Sweet Ivy Green   Edwards
Take Me Back to New York Town   Sterling; Von Tilzer
Take Things Easy   Herbert; Smith, Harry B.
Tale the Church Bells Tolled, The   Williams
Teddy Girl   Jerome; Schwartz, Jean
That Slippery Slide Trombone   Williams
That Small Still Voice   Johnson, J. Rosamond
That's How We Met the Girl   Goetz

That's Some Love   Cohan
Then You'll Remember Me   Fisher
There Never Was a Gal Like You   Williams
There's a Lot of Things that Noah Never Knew   Goetz
There's Always Something Wrong   Johnson, J. Rosamond
There's Just One Girl I'd Like to Marry   Herbert; Smith, Harry B.
There's Not Another Girlie in the World Like You   Jerome; Schwartz, Jean
Things That Happen Every Day   Williams
Things We Are Not Supposed to Know   Herbert; Smith, Harry B.
Thursday Is My Jonah Day   Howard, Joseph E.
Tipperary Nora   Snyder
Tootsie Tripper   Edwards
Top o' the Morning, Bridget McCue   Sterling; Von Tilzer
Travelin' Man   Howard, Joseph E.
Two Little Kittens   Smith, Robert B.
Uncle Sam's Best Girl   Howard, Joseph E.
Under Any Old Flag at All   Cohan
Under the Matzos Tree   Fisher
Under the Rosenbloom   Bryan; Meyer
Unter der Linden, in Germany   Jerome; Schwartz, Jean
Wander Off Nowhere   Edwards
Waning Honeymoon, The   Howard, Joseph E.
Watch the Professor   Herbert; Smith, Harry B.
Way Down on the Farm   Williams
Wedding of the Blue and Grey   Williams
Wedding of the Chafing Dish and the Alcohol Lamp, The   Howard, Joseph E.
Wedding of the Lily and the Rose   Herbert; Smith, Harry B.
Welcome on the Mat Ain't Meant for Me, The   Cobb; Edwards
We'll Be There   Edwards
We'll Be there Little One We'll Be There   Bryan; Meyer
We've Been to Boston Town   Johnson, J. Rosamond
What Fools We Mortals Be   Smith, Robert B.
What's the Good   Cobb; Edwards
What's the Use?   Edwards
When a Fellow's on the Level with a Girl that's on the Square   Cohan
When I Was in the Chorus of the Gaiety   Von Tilzer
When Miss Patricia Salome Did Her Funny Little Oo La Palome   Von Tilzer
When the Harbor Lights Are Burning Low   Bryan
When the Moon Plays Peek-a-boo with You   Fisher
When We Are M-A Double R-I-E-D   Cohan
When You Grow Tired Just Let Me Know   Howard, Joseph E.
When You See Me with Another Beau   Williams
Whistle As You Walk Out   Smith, Robert B.
Who Do You Love?   Johnson, J. Rosamond
Who Me, I'm not the Man   Snyder
Without the Girl — Inside   Kern
Woman in the Case   Goetz
Wonderland   Williams
Won't You Be My Baby Boy   Edwards
Won't You Have a Little Feather?   Kern
Yankee Land   Herbert
Yankee Rose   Leslie
You Can't Keep a Good Man Down   Howard, Joseph E.
You Have Me   Smith, Robert B.
You Took the Sunshine With You Mary Mine   Bryan; Meyer
You'll Never Know What Love Is Till I Say I Love You   Cobb; Edwards

You'll Not Be Forgotten Lady Lou   Bryan; Meyer

1908

A-B-C's of the U.S.A., The   Cohan
Afraid to Go Home at All   Smith, Harry B.
Aida McCluskie   Kern
Ain't It Awful   Cohan
Ain't It Hard To Lose Your Husband   Bryan
All I Want in the Wide, Wide World Is You   Smith, Robert B.
All I Want Is One Loving Smile from You-oo-oo   Meyer
All My Girls   Harbach
Am I a Wife, Widow or Maid?   Smith, Harry B.
American Idea, The   Cohan
American Ragtime, The   Cohan
Answer   Cohan
Any Old Place with You   Smith, Harry B.
Are You Sincere   Bryan
Arithmetic   Edwards
As the Waters Flow They Softly Whisper Flo Flo Flo   Leslie
As You Walk Down the Strand   Smith, Harry B.
Ask Her While the Band Is Playing   Herbert
At a Reception   Harbach
At the Barber's Ball   Cohan
Aurora Borealis   Schwartz, Jean; Williams
Awake Dearest One   Smith, Harry B.
Away We'll Float   Herbert; Smith, Harry B.
Baby Lou   Howard, Joseph E.
Barbecue, The   Herbert; Smith, Harry B.
Be Good   Smith, Harry B.
Be Sweet to Me Kid   Howard, Joseph E.
Belle of the Ring, The   Smith, Harry B.
Best of Friends Must Part, The   Berlin
Betty, You're the One Best Bet   Edwards
Big Banshee, The   Howard, Joseph E.
Big Brown Boo Loo Eyes   Cohan
Big Hats, The   Smith, Harry B.
Blow Upon Your Bugles   Herbert; Smith, Harry B.
Bohemia   Herbert
Bold Gendarmes, The   Cohan
Boo-Hoo, Tee-Hee   Harbach
Bottle Imp, The   Smith, Harry B.
Boule Miche, The   Herbert
Boys that Fight the Flames, The   Cohan
Broadway Belles   Snyder
Brookfield Two-Step   Cohan
Brothers and Sisters   Cohan
Build a Little Fence Around Today   Howard, Joseph E.
Butterfly and the Clover   Smith, Harry B.
By the Light of the Silvery Moon   Edwards
Cafe Girl (I Met Her at the Metropole)   Edwards
Calendar of Love, The   Edwards
California, Clarmont   Howard, Joseph E.
Campbell Soup Kids, The   Edwards
Cannibal Barbecue, The   Herbert; Smith, Harry B.
Cannibal Islands, The   Herbert; Smith, Harry B.
Captain of the Mineola Guards, The   Edwards
Cheer Up, Cherries Will Soon Be Ripe   Bryan; Meyer
Childhood   Bryan
Childhood's Happiest Moments   Edwards
Chime of the Liberty Bell   Herbert; Smith, Harry B.
Christening of the Boat, The   Smith, Robert B.
Christina Swanson   Howard, Joseph E.
Cohan's Pet Names   Cohan

Cohan's Rag Babe   Cohan
College Days   Howard, Joseph E.
Come on Down Town   Cohan
Country Boys and Girls   Edwards
Cuddle Up a Little Closer, Lovey Mine   Harbach
Cutie Come and Tie My Tie   Smith, Harry B.
Dance Me 'Till I'm Dizzy   Bryan
Dances of the Tabarin, The   Smith, Harry B.
Dancing Ceremony, The   Cohan
Dear Little Game of Guessing   Harbach
Different Kinds of Weather   Herbert; Smith, Harry B.
Dining Out   Kern
Do Something The Girl You Dream About   Howard, Joseph E.
Dollar Sign, The   Smith, Harry B.
Don't Be So Bashful   Bryan; Meyer
Don't Forget Me   Smith, Harry B.
Don't Forget to Drop a Line to Mother   Williams
Don't Go in the Water Daughter   Jerome; Schwartz, Jean
Down the Lane with Linda Jane   Meyer
Dream Love ('Twas Only Dreaming)   Herbert
Duchess of Table d'Hote, The   Smith, Harry B.
Elf King, The   Smith, Harry B.
Emmaline   Jerome; Schwartz, Jean
Entrance of the School Children   Herbert; Smith, Harry B.
Espagnola   Herbert
Everybody Loves Me but the One I Love   Edwards
Ev'ry Day She Wanted Something Else   Bryan; Meyer
Ev'rybody Else's Girl Looks Better to Me than Mine   Herbert
Excuse Us, Mister Moon   Meyer
Eyes that Come from Ireland   Olcott
F-A-M-E   Cohan
Farewell Killarny   Edwards
Father's Allowed to See Us Twice a Year   Williams
Fifth Avenue Brigade, The   Harbach
Fighting Kid, The   Edwards
Fishing Is an Art   Smith, Robert B.
Follow the Flag   Smith, Harry B.
Foolish Gardener, The   Herbert
Fraulein Katrina (inst.)   Kern
Freida   Kern
French Militaire   Cohan
Friar's Song, The   Herbert
From the Land of Dreams   Cohan
Game of Love, The   Herbert
Garden that Blooms for You, The   Cohan
Garrison Ball, The   Howard, Joseph E.
Gay Lothario, The   Kern
Gendarme's Dance, The   Cohan
Geography   Edwards
Get on the Merry-Go-Round   Edwards
Gibson Coon, The   Cohan
Gibson School Marm, The   Howard, Joseph E.
Girl, a Drink and a Song, A   Edwards
Girl Behind the Counter, The   Howard, Joseph E.
(Little) Girl Up There   Harbach
Girl You See in the Looking Glass, The   Meyer
Girls I Left Behind, The   Smith, Harry B.
Give Us a Fleet   Herbert; Smith, Harry B.
Golden Butterfly, The   Smith, Harry B.
Golden West, The   Howard, Joseph E.
Good Bye, Mr. Ragtime   Cohan
Good Evening Caroline   Norworth
Good Night, Sweetheart, Good Night   Harbach
Good-Bye   Herbert

Goodbye, Carlotta   Jerome; Schwartz, Jean
Goodbye Dinah   Edwards
Goodbye, Mr. Ragtime   Jerome; Schwartz, Jean
Grandma   Bryan; Snyder
Great Musicians   Smith, Harry B.
Great White Easiest Way, The   Herbert
Ha! Ha!   Herbert
Happiness   Fisher
Happy Day March   Smith, Harry B.
Happy Days   Schwartz, Jean
Happy Land of Once-Upon-a-Time, The   Herbert; Smith, Harry B.
Harrigan   Cohan
Haunted Cask, The   Smith, Harry B.
Have You Seen My Baby   Edwards
He Was a Soldier Too   Herbert
Heart of Mine   Smith, Harry B.
Hello! Miss Liberty   Fisher
Hen and Weather Vane, The   Herbert; Smith, Harry B.
Here's to My Comrades and You   Herbert
Hey Rube   Schwartz, Jean; Williams
Home Again   Smith, Harry B.
Honey Honeysuckle Baby, Make Those Google Eyes With Me   Bryan; Fisher
Honeymoon Trail   Howard, Joseph E.
How I Love Flowers   Smith, Harry B.
How'd You Like to Marry Me   Kahn
Hugo If You Go I'm Going Too   Snyder
Human Night Key of New York, The   Smith, Harry B.
Hunting Chorus   Smith, Harry B.
Hurdy Gurdy Man, The   Cobb; Edwards
Hypnotic Kiss, The   Harbach
I Am Waiting for the Summertime and You   Edwards
I Can't Help It If I'm Fidgety   Leslie
I Can't Say You're the Only One   Kern
I Don't Love You Well Enough for That   Smith, Robert B.
I Don't Want a Million Dollars   Howard, Joseph E.
I Guess I Talk Too Much   Herbert; Smith, Harry B.
I Hate to Work on Monday   Howard, Joseph E.
I Need the Morning Air   Howard, Joseph E.
I Never Knew What Love Was, Till I Fell in Love With You   Bryan; Fisher
I Say, Flo   Cohan
I Used to Be Afraid to Go Home in the Dark   Williams
I Walked Around   Snyder
I Want a Postal Card from You   Fisher
I Want Someone to Call Me Dearie   Williams
I Want to Be a Naughty Little Girl   Herbert; Smith, Harry B.
I Wish I Had a Girl   Kahn
I Wish I Was a Hero Too   Williams
I Wonder If They're All True to Me   Smith, Harry B.
I Wonder What's the Matter with My Eyes   Smith, Harry B.; Williams
I Wonder Where They'll Go   Smith, Harry B.
I Won't Be Home to Dinner   Edwards
I Wouldn't Take a Case Like That   Herbert; Smith, Harry B.
I'd Like to Have You Call Me Honey   Howard, Joseph E.
I'd Much Rather Stay at Home   Kern
If I Could Teach My Teddy Bear to Dance   Herbert; Smith, Harry B.
If I Only Said My Name Was Flannigan   Edwards
If I Told You that I Loved You   Meyer
If I Were on the Stage   Herbert
If You Cared for Me As I Care for You   Snyder
If You Were I and I Were You   Herbert

If You were Someone Else I Know   Goetz
I'll Be Married to the Music of a Military Band   Herbert
I'll Be True to My Honey Boy   Cohan
I'll Be Your Jujube   Edwards
I'll Dream of Thee   Herbert
I'll Take Care of You   Bryan; Meyer
I'm a Yiddish Cowboy   Leslie
I'm Awfully Strong for You   Cohan
I'm Crazy 'Bout You Daisy   Meyer
I'm Crazy When the Band Begins to Play   Smith, Harry B.
I'm Glad I'm Married   Norworth
I'm Glad to Get Back to New York   Smith, Harry B.
I'm Going to Marry a Nobleman   Cohan
I'm Going to Steal the Moon   Howard, Joseph E.
I'm in Love With the Man in the Moon   Bryan; Snyder
I'm Learning Something Every Day   Norworth; Smith, Harry B.
I'm not That Kind of Girl   Smith, Harry B.
I'm Sorry for Satan   Meyer
In Bohemia with You   Edwards
In Cloudland   Harbach
In Gay Paree   Cohan
In Germany   Bryan; Fisher
In Happy Slumberland   Herbert; Smith, Harry B.
In Jail   Herbert
In Moscow   Smith, Harry B.
In My Little Benzine Buggy   Jerome; Schwartz, Jean
In My Little Runabout   Smith, Robert B.
In Paris   Smith, Harry B.
In the Days of '49   Howard, Joseph E.
In the Little Red School House   Williams
In the Shacks that Little Flower Built   Howard, Joseph E.
In the Springtime When the Roses Bloom Around the Cottage Door   Leslie
In Those Good Old Country Days   Bryan; Meyer
In Vaudeville   Howard, Joseph E.
In Walked Bill   Smith, Robert B.
International Merry Widow, The   Smith, Harry B.
Is My Face on Straight   Herbert; Smith, Harry B.
It Looks Like a Big Night Tonight   Williams
It Takes a Cop to Cop the Girls   Edwards
It's Good-Bye Pal   Howard, Joseph E.
It's the Irish   Herbert; Smith, Harry B.
It's the Pretty Things You Say   Bryan; Snyder
I've Been Decorated   Herbert
I've Got to Get Some Money   Snyder
Jack and Jill   Cohan
Jag, a Drone and a Tank of Air, A   Smith, Harry B.
Jolly Cuirassier   Herbert
Just for You from Above   Smith, Harry B.
Just Say You Care   Howard, Joseph E.
Just to While the Hours Away   Sterling; Von Tilzer
Kanawha   Leslie
Katie Gray   Edwards
Kiss Me Right Where the Kisses Should Be   Bryan
Kiss Your Minstrel Boy Goodbye   Cohan; Jerome; Schwartz, Jean
Kissing Time   Jerome; Schwartz, Jean
Lady Love   Edwards
Language of Love   Smith, Harry B.
Latin Quarter, The   Smith, Harry B.
Lauder Melodies   Smith, Harry B.
Laugh with a Tear in It, A   Olcott
Let the Soul Kiss Be Mine Today   Smith, Harry B.
Let's Get the Umpire's Goat   Norworth

Let's Pretend   Smith, Harry B.
Light that Lies in Women's Eyes, The   Howard, Joseph E.
Little Bird of Paradise   Herbert
Little Bit Is a Whole Lot Better Than Nothing at All, A   Bryan
Little Bit's a Whole Lot Better than Nothing at All, A   Edwards
Little Flat in a Great Big Town, A   Williams
Little Miss Up-to-Date   Harbach
Little Snowflake   Edwards
Little Tittle Tattle Tale   Edwards
Long Green, The   Smith, Robert B.
Love Days   Cohan; Jerome; Schwartz, Jean
Love Is Like a Cigarette   Herbert
Love Me Like I Like to Be Loved   Bryan; Meyer
Love Night   Herbert
Love Up a Tree   Howard, Joseph E.
Lu Lu Babe   Howard, Joseph E.
Make Me Laugh   Bryan; Snyder
Man About Town, The   Smith, Harry B.
Man and the Maid, The   Herbert
Man I Marry Must Be a Man, The   Smith, Robert B.
March of the Valentines   Herbert; Smith, Harry B.
Marie, Marie   Smith, Harry B.
May Day March   Herbert; Smith, Harry B.
Maybe It's a Bear   Edwards
Maybe You Would If You Could   Bryan; Meyer
McGinnis   Jerome; Schwartz, Jean
Meet Her with a Taximeter   Kern
Meet Me at the Masquerade   Smith, Harry B.
Meet Me at the Station   Smith, Harry B.
Meet Me at the Tabarin   Smith, Harry B.
Meet Me in Rose Time Rosie   Cohan
Meet Me in Rosetime, Rosie   Jerome; Schwartz, Jean
Mem'rey's Garden   Smith, Harry B.
Military Review   Smith, Harry B.
Monarch and a Maid, A   Herbert
M-O-N-E-Y   Cohan
Moon Bird   Edwards
Mosquito Song   Smith, Harry B.
Mother Hasn't Spoke to Paris Since   Jerome; Schwartz, Jean
Move on Mr. Moon   Snyder
Mrs. Cockatoo   Kern
Music Makes Me Sentimental (Blame the Music Don't Blame Me)   Bryan
My Affinity   Smith, Harry B.
My Brudda Sylvest   Fisher
My Cousin Caruso   Edwards
My Diabalo Beau   Smith, Harry B.
My Dream of the U.S.A.   Snyder
My Human Magazine   Schwartz, Jean; Williams
My Little Mademoiselle   Cohan
My Little Tailor Maid   Edwards
My Lolo Maid   Howard, Joseph E.
My Old Lady   Edwards
My Old Town   Howard, Joseph E.
My Rosie Rambler   Williams
My Wild Deer   Bryan
My Wild Deer (Dear)   Snyder
Nell Brinkley Girl, The   Smith, Harry B.
Nemo's Dream of Fourth of July   Herbert; Smith, Harry B.
None of Them's Got Anything on Me   Jerome; Schwartz, Jean
Not All but Nearly   Smith, Robert B.
Nothing at All   Kern

Nothing Ever Ever Ever Hardly Ever Troubles Me   Norworth
Nothing New Beneath the Sun   Cohan
Nothing to Do but Nothing   Howard, Joseph E.
O! Mia Speranza   Herbert
Off to Russia   Smith, Harry B.
Oh How Can I Ever Forget Him   Leslie
Oh How I Love My Teacher   Williams
Oh! Oh! Oh!   Herbert
Oh that Yankiana Rag   Goetz
Oh! You Coon   Cohan
Old Buck and Wing, The   Howard, Joseph E.
Olympian Dance, The   Herbert; Smith, Harry B.
On the Boulevard   Smith, Harry B.
On the Old See Saw   Edwards
One Little Boy Had Money   Howard, Joseph E.
One You're Looking For   Herbert
Only One of Anything   Herbert
Orchids of the Opera   Edwards
Order Wedding Bells for Two   Jerome; Schwartz, Jean
Originality   Smith, Harry B.
Over on the Jersey Side   Norworth
Over the Hill and Far Away   Jerome; Schwartz, Jean
Over There   Harbach
Pajama and the Nightie, The   Howard, Joseph E.
Paper Hat Brigade, The   Edwards
Pass It Along to Father   Von Tilzer
Perfectly Terrible, Dear   Smith, Harry B.
Pierrot Patrole and Dance   Smith, Harry B.
Playing Hookey   Leslie
Please Tell Me what They Mean   Smith, Harry B.
Queen of My Dreams   Smith, Harry B.
Queen of the Ring   Smith, Harry B.
Queenie (My Own)   Berlin
Quiet Sunday in 1920, A   Smith, Harry B.
Rag Time Quadrille (inst.)   Cohan
Railroad Number   Smith, Harry B.
Rainbow   Bryan
Rajah of Broadway, The   Smith, Harry B.
Read the Papers Every Day   Herbert; Smith, Harry B.
Recognized Man of the Hour   Smith, Harry B.
Remember the Old Continentals   Herbert; Smith, Harry B.
Review of Athletes   Herbert; Smith, Harry B.
Rosa Rosetta   Norworth
Rose of the World   Herbert
Round-Up, The   Howard, Joseph E.
Sahara   Williams
Salt Lake City   Bryan; Meyer
Same Old Story, The   Howard, Joseph E.
Same Old Two, The   Herbert
Sandy-O   Jerome; Schwartz, Jean
Say No, That's All   Snyder
School Days (We Were a Couple of Kids)   Edwards
School Mates   Edwards
She Has Trouble with Her Eyes   Howard, Joseph E.
She Was a Dear Little Girl   Berlin
She Was a Hayseed Maid (inst.)   Herbert
Shine on Harvest Moon   Norworth
Showing the Yankees London Town   Cohan
Since Mother Was a Girl   Norworth
Sing, Love, Sing   Jerome; Schwartz, Jean
Sing Me a Come-All-Ye   Norworth
Singing Lesson   Smith, Harry B.
Slumberland   Herbert; Smith, Harry B.
Small Town Gal, The   Cohan
Smarty   Norworth

Soldier's Life Is Never Long   Herbert
Soldier's Love, A   Herbert
Soldiers of the King   Cohan
Somebody Knows Somebody Who Knows Just Who You
    Are   Bryan
Somebody Said That Somebody Said   Bryan
Someday, Sweetheart, Someday   Edwards
Something Always Happens When It Shouldn't   Herbert
Sometime, Somewhere   Williams
Song of Songs, The   Smith, Harry B.
Song of the King   Cohan
Soul Kiss, The   Smith, Harry B.
Spanish Dance   Smith, Harry B.
Specialist Am I   Harbach
Squeeze Me Tight   Edwards
Stop Making Faces at Me   Sterling
Students' Chorus   Smith, Harry B.
Sullivan   Cohan
Summer Pasttimes   Harbach
Summer Reminds Me of You   Bryan; Meyer
Summertime   Von Tilzer
Sunbeams, Snowflakes and Raindrops   Herbert; Smith,
    Harry B.
Sunbonnet Sue   Cobb; Edwards
Sunflower Sue   Cobb; Edwards
Sunshine Is Bright   Smith, Harry B.
Sweet Girl of My Dreams   Olcott
Sweet Sixteen   Bryan
Sweetest Girl, Silly Boy, I Love You   Kern
Sweetheart Ties   Howard, Joseph E.
Taffy   Von Tilzer
Take Care   Kern
Take Me Back to Old Broadway   Smith, Harry B.
Take Me Out to the Ball Game   Norworth
Take Your Girl to the Ball Game   Cohan; Jerome; Schwartz,
    Jean
Teddy Bird, The   Edwards
Tell Me Once Again   Smith, Harry B.
Temptation   Smith, Harry B.
Thanksgiving   Bryan; Herbert
That's All   Smith, Harry B.
That's Some Love   Cohan
That's the Way to Make Love   Meyer
That's What a Fellow Does When He's in Love   Howard,
    Joseph E.
There Is No Place Like Home   Howard, Joseph E.
There'll Come a Day   Bryan; Snyder
There's Not a Girl, In All This World That Won't Have
    Me   Edwards
There's Nothing the Matter with Me (You)   Herbert; Smith,
    Harry B.
There's Something Rather Odd about Augustus   Kern
They All Follow Me   Cohan
They Always Follow Me   Jerome; Schwartz, Jean
They Were Actors Then   Smith, Harry B.
They Were Irish   Herbert; Smith, Harry B.
They'll Be Waiting for You at the Train   Williams
Think It Over Carefully   Cohan
Those College Yells   Smith, Harry B.
Those Things That Happen Everyday   Williams
Three Twins   Harbach
Three Weeks with You   Smith, Harry B.
Titles   Smith, Harry B.
Tommy Atkins, You're All Right   Cohan
Too Long from Long Acre Square   Cohan

'Twas Different Years Ago   Herbert
Twenty Years Ago!   Herbert
Twilight in Barakeesh   Herbert
Twinkle Twinkle My Little Star   Edwards
Two Horse Fellow in a One Horse Town   Edwards
Very Well Then   Smith, Harry B.
Vienna   Kern
Villains in the Play   Cohan
Waltz Me 'Till I'm Dreamy   Howard, Joseph E.
Waltz with Me   Cohan
Waltz With Me Lena at Luna   Bryan
Wandering Minstrel   Smith, Harry B.
Watching the Blue Smoke Curl   Howard, Joseph E.
Water Never Did That   Williams
We Belong to Old Broadway   Harbach
We Two in an Aeroplane   Smith, Harry B.; Williams
Weather Factory in Cloudland, The   Herbert; Smith, Harry B.
Wedding Music (inst.)   Herbert
We're Going to Fight the Indians   Edwards
We're Supposed to Be   Cohan
What Fools We Mortals Be   Herbert; Smith, Harry B.
What Is Love   Herbert
What Kind of a Wife to Choose   Edwards
What's the Use   Harbach
What's the Use of Anything   Williams
What's the Use of Dreaming   Howard, Joseph E.
When Cupid Is the Postman   Herbert; Smith, Harry B.
When Eyes Like Yours Look into Eyes Like Mine   Howard, Joseph E.
When Girls Command the Army   Herbert
When Grandma Was a Girl   Goetz
When Highland Mary Did the Highland Fling   Von Tilzer
When I Feel Like Loving   Howard, Joseph E.
When I Marry You   Bryan
When I'm an American Citizen   Edwards
When Johnny Comes Marching Home Again   Goetz
When Swallows Return to the Spring   Smith, Harry B.
When the Girl You Love Is Loving You   Jerome; Schwartz, Jean
When the Music Starts to Play   Edwards
When Woman, Lovely Woman, Gets Her Rights   Harbach
When You Love a Summer Girl   Meyer
Where the Fairest Flowers Blooming   Herbert
Whistle and I'll Wait for You   Meyer
White Wash Girl   Jerome; Schwartz, Jean
Whoop-La-La   Cohan
Whose Little Girl Are You?   Howard, Joseph E.
Wild Cherries   Berlin; Snyder
Wildflower   Goetz
Will o' the Wisp   Smith, Harry B.
Will-O-the-Wisp   Herbert; Smith, Harry B.
Won't You Be My Playmate?   Herbert; Smith, Harry B.
Won't You Be My Valentine?   Herbert; Smith, Harry B.
Won't You Come Under My Merry Widow Hat   Edwards
Won't You Even Say Hello   Leslie
Won't You Let Me Carry Your Parcel?   Kern
Worried   Howard, Joseph E.
Yankee Doodle's Come to Town   Cohan
Yankee Prince March (inst.)   Cohan
Yankee Prince Waltzes (inst.)   Cohan
Yankee Son of a Gun   Smith, Harry B.
Yankiana Rag   Smith, Harry B.
Yiddish Wedding Jubilee   Smith, Harry B.
You Bet I'm Glad to Be Just where I Am   Meyer

You Can't Be a Friend to Everybody   Howard, Joseph E.
You Have Me   Edwards
You Need No Crown of Gold to Make You a Queen   Harbach
You Will Have to Sing an Irish Song   Norworth
You'd Be Surprised   Herbert
You'll Do the Same Thing Over for the Old Red, White and Blue   Cobb; Edwards
You'll Feel Better Then   Herbert
You're All the World to Me   Smith, Robert B.
You're Just the Boy for Me   Edwards
You're Like the Roses, Rosie   Meyer

1909

Alabam'   Williams
A-L-E   Jerome; Schwartz, Jean
Algy   Herbert
American Monte Carlo, The   Jerome; Schwartz, Jean
And the World Keeps Rolling Along   Smith, Harry B.
Angel Eyes   Bryan
Are You Lonesome?   Kahn
Arrah, Come In Out of the Rain, Barney McShane   Sterling
Art of Making Up, The   Williams
Art with a Capital 'A'   Smith, Harry B.
As Long As the World Goes Round   Johnson, J. Rosamond
Ask the Cabby   Howard, Joseph E.
Baby's Gone   Brown, A. Seymour
Bamboo Lane   Jerome; Schwartz, Jean
Barn Dance   Herbert
Bashful Chappie, The   Edwards; Smith, Robert B.
Bathing Girls, The   Smith, Harry B.
Bayaderes   Herbert
Be Jolly Holly   Leslie
Beautiful Eyes   Snyder
Believe Me   Johnson, J. Rosamond
Best Thing a Waiter Does Is Wait, The   Howard, Joseph E.
Big Red Shawl, The   Johnson, J. Rosamond
Billikin Man   Goetz
Black Butterfly, The   Smith, Robert B.
Blarney   Norworth
Bleeding Moon   Johnson, J. Rosamond
Boat Race Chorus   Smith, Harry B.
Boat Sails on Wednesday, A   Kern
Bon-Bon Buddy the Chocolate Man   Brown, A. Seymour
Bonnie Annie Laurie   Williams
Boogie-Boo, The   Brown, A. Seymour
Boola Boola   Howard, Joseph E.
Boulevard Glide   Goetz
Brinkley Coon, The   Cohan
Broken Idol, A   Williams
Broncho Sal   Meyer
Bubble and the Butterfly, The   Brown, A. Seymour
By the Blue Lagoon   Kern
Bye and Bye   Brown, A. Seymour
Bygone Days in Dixie   Johnson, J. Rosamond
Cairo   Howard, Joseph E.
Cake Walk Ball   Brown, A. Seymour
Can It Be Love   Howard, Joseph E.
Can Song   Johnson, J. Rosamond
Can't You Be Good   Meyer
Can't You See   Bryan
Can't You See I Love You?   Brown, A. Seymour
Captain Flo   Jerome; Schwartz, Jean
Carnival   Smith, Harry B.

Carnival Maid (inst.)   Snyder
Chicken   Jerome; Schwartz, Jean
Chink-Chink, Chink-Chink, Chinyman   Johnson, J. Rosamond
Christening, The   Johnson, J. Rosamond
Christmas Dances   Smith, Harry B.
Christmas Time Seems Years and Years Away   Berlin; Snyder
Christy Girl, The   Smith, Harry B.
Clorinda   Brown, A. Seymour
Columbia's Colleen   Edwards; Smith, Robert B.
Come On and Play Ball with Me   Edwards
Come on Over Here   Brown, A. Seymour
Come Take a Swim in My Ocean   Cobb; Edwards
Come, Toddle Along   Jerome; Schwartz, Jean
Could You Grow Fond of a Nice Young Blond If You Love a Sweet Brunette   Snyder
Cubanola Glide, The   Von Tilzer
Cured   Williams
Cutey   Goetz
Dance Coquette   Leslie
Dance de Maitre de Ballet   Smith, Harry B.
Dance Fantastique   Herbert
Dance of the Parisian Twist, The   Smith, Harry B.
Dancing Sunshine   Snyder
Dancing the Cotillion   Smith, Harry B.
Darkies' Serenade   Brown, A. Seymour
Daughter of the Regiment, The   Edwards; Smith, Robert B.
De Time to Cotch a Possom   Snyder
Dear Old Father   Norworth
Do Your Duty, Doctor   Berlin; Snyder
Don't Be an Old Maid Molly   Bryan
Don't Be Anybody's Moon but Mine   Howard, Joseph E.
Don't Be Cross with Me   Howard, Joseph E.
Don't Choose a Gibson Girl   Howard, Joseph E.
Don't Forget the Girl You Left Behind   Howard, Joseph E.
Don't Forget the Number   Howard, Joseph E.
Don't Teach Me to Swim Alone   Howard, Joseph E.
Dorando   Berlin
Down Goes the Price of Eggs   Howard, Joseph E.
Down in the Everglade   Williams
Down in the Sunshine Alley Sally   Meyer
Down Red Rose Lane   Brown, A. Seymour
Dream Minute   Howard, Joseph E.
Dream of Me and I'll Dream of You Sweetheart   Leslie
Dreaming   Howard, Joseph E.
Drink to the Health of This Great Man   Herbert
Entrance of Lew Fields with Children   Herbert
Eulalie   Kern
Every Baby Is a Sweet Bouquet   Brown, A. Seymour
Everybody Sometimes Must Love Someone   Cohan
Everybody Wonders Why They Married   Howard, Joseph E.
Everybody's Ragtime Crazy   Jerome; Schwartz, Jean
Everything that Father Did Was Right   Howard, Joseph E.
Falling Stars   Norworth
Fantastic Dance   Herbert
Farewell Prosperity   Smith, Harry B.
Father Brings Home Something Every Day   Cobb; Edwards
Father Keeps on Doing It   Brown, A. Seymour
Fete of the Veiled Mugs   Johnson, J. Rosamond
Follow the Rainbow Trail   Howard, Joseph E.
For He's the One, the Only Baby   Brown, A. Seymour
Forget Me Not   Williams
Foxy Moon   Snyder
Franco-American Rag   Schwartz, Jean

Franco-American Ragtime   Jerome; Schwartz, Jean
Frantzi   Kern
Fritz   Norworth
Funny Face   Sterling; Von Tilzer
Girl I Left Behind, The   Howard, Joseph E.
Girl I Used to Know, The   Smith, Harry B.
Girls that Can Never Be Mine, The   Howard, Joseph E.
Girls Who Go Upon the Stage   Brown, A. Seymour
Go As Far As You Like   Smith, Harry B.
Go Back   Williams
Go Happy Bride   Herbert
Goddess of Liberty, The   Howard, Joseph E.
Golden Arrow   Williams
Golden Girl, The   Howard, Joseph E.
Good Luck Mary   Bryan; Leslie
Good Old Days Gone By, The   Von Tilzer
Goodbye Girlie and Remember Me   Berlin; Meyer; Snyder
Goodbye, Miss Liberty   Jerome; Schwartz, Jean
Great Big Blue Eyed Baby   Brown, A. Seymour
Greatest Navy in the World, The   Smith, Harry B.
Happy Days   Williams
Harbor of Lost Dreams, The   Johnson, J. Rosamond
Hat My Father Wore Upon St. Patrick's Day, The   Jerome; Schwartz, Jean
Haunted Pool, The   Howard, Joseph E.
Have a Drink to Yankee Land   Williams
He Was a Cowboy   Williams
Heinz Is Pickled Again   Williams
Her Eyes Are Blue for Dear Old Yale   Howard, Joseph E.
Her Name Is Mary Donohue   Jerome; Schwartz, Jean
Here's to Your Last Girl   Howard, Joseph E.
He's the Champion of Them All, Little Maxie Rosenthal   Howard, Joseph E.
Highland Mary   Bryan
Hindoo Honey   Smith, Harry B.
Hodge Podge   Johnson, J. Rosamond
Honey Moon Land   Brown, A. Seymour
Honey on Our Honeymoon   Jerome; Schwartz, Jean
Honeymoon Trail   Howard, Joseph E.
Honor the Brave   Herbert
Howdy! How D'You Do?   Kern
Hurrah for the Bars and Stripes   Howard, Joseph E.
Hush, I Think I Hear Him   Howard, Joseph E.
I Can't Be True So Far Away   Howard, Joseph E.
I Can't Love Everybody   Howard, Joseph E.
I Didn't Go Home at All   Berlin; Leslie; Snyder
I Don't Know but I'd Like to Learn   Meyer
I Don't Want to Marry Your Family   Howard, Joseph E.
I Fell in Love All By Myself   Howard, Joseph E.
I Fell in Love on Monday   Howard, Joseph E.
(I Think) I Hear a Woodpecker Knocking at My Family Tree   Howard, Joseph E.
I Just Came Back to Say Good-Bye   Berlin; Snyder
I Love, I Love, I Love My Wife, But Oh You Kid   Von Tilzer
I Love My Wife So Keep Away   Edwards
I Love You Oh! Oh! Oh!   Brown, A. Seymour
I Love Ze Parisienne   Herbert
I Never Know How to Behave When I'm with Boys   Carroll
I Remember You   Von Tilzer
I Want a Little Corner in Your Heart   Sterling
I Want a Man to Love Me   Herbert
I Want Somebody to Play With   Williams
I Want to Be Kissed by a Matinee Idol   Smith, Harry B.
I Wish I Was a Boy and I Wish I Was a Girl   Norworth
I Wish That You Was My Gal, Molly   Berlin; Snyder

I Wonder Who's Kissing Her Now   Howard, Joseph E.

I Would Rather Fight Like Ma   Howard, Joseph E.

I'd Like to Correspond with You   Jerome; Schwartz, Jean

I'd Like to Go Up in an Airship   Smith, Harry B.

I'd Rather Love an Old Rag Doll than a Bashful Boy Like You   Meyer

I'd Rather Love My Old Rag Doll Than a Bashful Boy Like You   Bryan

If All Moons Were Honey Moons   Howard, Joseph E.

If I Thought You Wouldn't Tell   Berlin; Snyder

If It Were Not for Dear Old Father   Norworth

If Only I Were Santa Claus   Smith, Harry B.

If the Girl Wants You (Never Mind the Color of Her Eyes)   Kern

If the Managers Only thought the Same as Mother   Berlin; Snyder

If They'd Only Left Poor Adam's Rib Alone   Howard, Joseph E.

If Women Had their Way   Edwards; Smith, Robert B.

If You Ain't Got It Go and Get It   Bryan

If You Ever Want a Favor Mention Me   Herbert

I'll Bet You   Howard, Joseph E.

I'll Give a Penny for Your Thoughts   Lewis; Snyder

I'll Go the Route for You   Cohan

I'll Never Care for Any Girl but You   Sterling

I'm a Detective   Meyer

I'm a Member of the Midnight Crew   Jerome; Schwartz, Jean

I'm Afraid to Be Alone   Howard, Joseph E.

I'm Afraid to Sleep Alone   Bryan

I'm After Mme. Tetrazinni's Job   Edwards

I'm All O.K. with K. and E.   Cohan

I'm Awfully Glad I Met You   Meyer

I'm Crazy Over You   Brown, A. Seymour

I'm Crazy When the Band Begins to Play   Jerome; Schwartz, Jean

I'm Glad I'm Irish   Leslie

I'm Glad I'm Single   Brown, A. Seymour

I'm Goin' to Do What I Please   Bryan; Snyder

I'm in Love with All the Girls I Know   Howard, Joseph E.

I'm in Love with One of the Stars   Cohan

I'm the Boy   Edwards; Smith, Robert B.

In My Little Hottentot Hut for Two   Goetz

In Sunny Italy   Bryan; Fisher

In that Old College Town   Goetz

In the Harbor of Sunshine and Love   Meyer

In the Waldorf Halls   Cohan

Indian Love Song   Howard, Joseph E.

Ireland Isn't Ireland Any More   Von Tilzer

Is Julia Home   Bryan; Leslie

It's a Loving Wife for Mine   Smith, Harry B.

I've Always Been a Good Sport   Cohan

I've Got Something in My Eye   Bryan

I've Just Lost My Teddy Bear   Johnson, J. Rosamond

I've Lost My Gal   Williams

I've Lost My Heart but I Don't Care   Howard, Joseph E.

(My) Jack O'Lantern   Howard, Joseph E.

Jolly Yourself Along   Edwards; Smith, Robert B.

Just Because You're a Poor Little Girl   Edwards

Just Good Friends   Kern

Just Like the Rose   Berlin

Katie Sweet Colleen   Snyder

Keep Your Foot on the Soft Pedal   Von Tilzer

Kid that Opens Up and Closes Broadway, The   Snyder

Kind of Girl a Man Likes Best, The   Edwards; Smith, Harry B.

King of Baby Land, The   Brown, A. Seymour

Kitchy-Koo   Edwards

Lady Sleeps, The   Herbert

Lament   Johnson, J. Rosamond

Land of Love, The   Smith, Robert B.

Land of the Sky (Adios Senorita), The   Howard, Joseph E.

Land of Used-to-Be, The   Howard, Joseph E.

Landslide   Howard, Joseph E.

Latest Creation in Girls, The   Brown, A. Seymour

Laughing Song   Howard, Joseph E.; Von Tilzer

Leaving   Meyer

Let Georgie Do It   Leslie

Let's Get the Umpire's Goat   Norworth

Let's Go Back to Baby Days   Meyer

Let's Pretend You Love Me   Howard, Joseph E.

Letters from Home   Herbert

Life is a Game of Checkers   Johnson, J. Rosamond

Linger Longer, Lingerie   Smith, Harry B.

Little China Doll, A   Williams

Little Miss Golden Curls   Meyer

Little Ray of Sunshine Follows Each Rain Cloud, A   Meyer

Liza   Williams

Lonely   Howard, Joseph E.

Lonesome   Leslie; Meyer

Love in the Springtime   Smith, Harry B.

Love Light   Williams

Love Me All the Time   Howard, Joseph E.

Love Me Baby Mine   Johnson, J. Rosamond

Love Me Just Because   Howard, Joseph E.

Love Me Just Like Romeo Loved Juliet (Romeo and Miss Juliet)   Jerome; Schwartz, Jean

Love Time   Brown, A. Seymour

Love Will Make or Break a Man   Cohan

Love's Golden Dream   Von Tilzer

Love's Oracle   Herbert

Loving Doving   Bryan

Lullabyland   Brown, A. Seymour

Mad Opera House   Norworth

Madame Venus (Take a Tip from Venus)   Smith, Harry B.

Mammy's Jubilee   Brown, A. Seymour

Mamzelle Fifi   Brown, A. Seymour

Man Who Owns Broadway, The   Cohan

March of the King's Amazons   Cohan

Mardi Gras, The   Herbert

Margarita   Leslie

Marie   Williams

Marriage Game   Edwards; Smith, Robert B.

Mary Gave Him the Merry Ha Ha   Bryan

Mazeppa (inst.)   Schwartz, Jean

McElwes   Snyder

Meet Me in Rose Time Rosie   Brown, A. Seymour

Michael Angelo   Meyer

Minstrels on Parade   Brown, A. Seymour

Moving Day in Jungle Town   Brown, A. Seymour

Mr. Hamlet Man   Meyer

Mr. Izzy Always Busy Rosentstein   Jerome; Schwartz, Jean

Mrs. Grundy   Herbert

Mum's the Word   Johnson, J. Rosamond

My Bambazoo   Snyder

My Boy   Harbach

My Caramel Gal   Cohan

My Daughter Is Wed to a Friend of Mine   Cohan

My Gypsy Sweetheart   Herbert

My Haytian Queen   Jerome; Schwartz, Jean
My Lady Nicotine   Howard, Joseph E.
My Land of Nod   Howard, Joseph E.
My Old Man   Johnson, J. Rosamond
My Prairie Song-Oifo   Meyer
My Senorita   Edwards; Smith, Robert B.
My Sweet One   Von Tilzer
My Wife Ain't Coming Back   Sterling; Von Tilzer
My Wife's Gone to the Country (Hurrah! Hurrah!)   Berlin; Snyder
Na Ville D'Amour Op 22   Friml
Napoleon   Brown, A. Seymour
Natural History Class, The   Brown, A. Seymour
Newport Is Waiting for Me   Smith, Harry B.
Next to Your Mother, Who Do You Love?   Berlin; Snyder
Nice Little Plot for a Play   Cohan
No One Could Do It Like My Father   Berlin; Snyder
None but the Brave Deserve the Fair   Howard, Joseph E.
Nosensical Nonsense   Brown, A. Seymour
Not Here! Not Here!   Kern
Nothing but a Bubble   Smith, Harry B.
Ogalalia   Snyder
Oh! How That German Could Love   Berlin; Snyder
Oh! What I Know About You   Berlin
Oh What I'd Do for a Girl Like You   Snyder
Oh! Where Is My Wife To-Night?   Berlin; Snyder
Oh You Loving Gal   Meyer
On a Hundred Different Ships   Cohan
On the Road to Monterey   Johnson, J. Rosamond
On to Frisco   Leslie
Only Lonely Little Me   Snyder
Operatic Solution, An   Brown, A. Seymour
Oskee Wow Wow   Howard, Joseph E.
Pale Golden Star   Howard, Joseph E.
Pass Dat Possum   Bryan
Pathway of Love, The   Johnson, J. Rosamond
Ping Pong   Smith, Robert B.
Play that Fandango Rag   Goetz
Please Keep Me Young in Your Heart   Howard, Joseph E.
Poor Old Dad's in New York for the Summer   Williams
Pourquoi   Herbert
Prairie Rose   Dubin
Pretending   Herbert
Pretty Soft for Me   Kahn
Ragtime Land   Goetz
Red White and Blue   Kern
Reveille   Smith, Robert B.
Revolutionary Man   Jerome; Schwartz, Jean
Rich Man, Poor Man, Beggar Man, Thief   Herbert
Roo Te Too Toot   Williams
Roosevelt of Germany   Smith, Harry B.
Rosenbaum   Bryan; Fisher
Roses and Memories   Snyder
Round Up, The   Bryan
Rulers of the Earth   Smith, Harry B.
Russian Duo and Dance   Herbert
Sambo   Johnson, J. Rosamond
Same Old Silv'ry Moon Is Shining, The   Johnson, J. Rosamond
Santa Rosa Rose   Brown, A. Seymour
Schooner Land   Goetz
Secrets of the Household   Cohan
Sextette   Smith, Harry B.
She Was a Dear Little Girl   Snyder
She's a Flower from the Fields of Old Ireland   Olcott

She's an Awful Nice Gal   Meyer
Shine Out All You Little Stars   Kern
Ship of Dreams   Howard, Joseph E.
Sign of a Honeymoon, The   Williams
Silver Star, The   Smith, Harry B.
Singing on the Old Grape Vine   Von Tilzer
Skinny   Snyder
Sleepyland   Brown, A. Seymour
Sleigh Bells May Be Wedding Bells   Smith, Harry B.
Soldier Boy   Von Tilzer
Some Little Something About You   Berlin; Snyder
Somebody Loves You Too   Meyer
Someone's Waiting for Me   Berlin; Leslie; Snyder
Something   Howard, Joseph E.
Sometime in Springtime   Bryan; Meyer
Song of the Butterfly, The   Howard, Joseph E.
Song of the Heart   Smith, Robert B.
Song of the Waiters   Williams
Spaghetti   Bryan; Fisher
Standing Pat   Edwards; Smith, Robert B.
Star, the Rose and the Drama, The   Snyder
Start, The   Johnson, J. Rosamond
Stingy Kid   Bryan
Stop that Boy   Berlin; Snyder
Sunbeam   Williams
Sunray   Dubin
Supper Out of Doors   Brown, A. Seymour
Suzette and Her Pet   Kern
Sweet Little Nora Riley   Bryan
Sweet Wireless Whispers   Herbert
Sweetheart's a Pretty Name when It Is Y-O-U   Leslie
Take Me Back to Sunshine Land   Jerome; Schwartz, Jean
Take Me on a Honeymoon   Meyer
Take Me to that Tango Tea   Brown, A. Seymour
Take Me Up to the Roller Rink   Von Tilzer
Taxi Taxi   Howard, Joseph E.
Tell Her in the Golden Summer   Howard, Joseph E.
Tetrazzini   Smith, Harry B.
That Chop Stick Rag   Brown, A. Seymour
That Cuddlin' Rag   Goetz
That Is Love   Herbert
That Mesmerizing Mendelssohn Tune   Berlin
That Spooney Dance (The Cooney-Spooney Dance)   Jerome; Schwartz, Jean
That Would Make You Homesick Too   Fisher
That's a Plenty   Johnson, J. Rosamond
That's Politics   Williams
That's What the Papers Say   Edwards; Smith, Robert B.
Then We'll All Go Home   Williams
There Are Too Many Girls (In the World)   Howard, Joseph E.
There's Something About a Uniform   Cohan
They're Not Doing that This Season   Smith, Harry B.
Things I Am Going to Do, The   Von Tilzer
Those Wonderful Eyes   Howard, Joseph E.
Ting a Ling Ling   Smith, Robert B.
Ting-a-Ling-a-Ling Ping Pong   Edwards
Tonight Will Never Come Again   Howard, Joseph E.
Transformation Lullaby   Howard, Joseph E.
Tummy-Tummy-Tum   Howard, Joseph E.
Twilight Town   Goetz
Two Little Eyes of Blue   Olcott
U Dearie   Herbert
Under the Irish Moon   Meyer
Underneath the Big Magnolia Tree   Bryan

Up and Down the Boardwalk   Edwards; Smith, Robert B.
Up in a Balloon   Williams
Up in My Aeroplane   Edwards
Up! Up! Up! in My Aeroplane   Edwards
Vampire Dance   Howard, Joseph E.
Velvet Foot   Brown, A. Seymour
Way Down in Cotton Town   Leslie
Way to a Girlie's Heart, The   Smith, Robert B.
Wedding Fete, The   Smith, Robert B.
We'll Wait, Wait, Wait   Berlin; Leslie
What Every Woman Knows   Smith, Harry B.
What Makes the World Go Round   Williams
What Wealth Is Here   Smith, Robert B.
What's the Use   Howard, Joseph E.
What's the Use of Moonlight When There's No One 'Round
    to Love   Kahn
When a Pal of Mine Steals a Gal of Mine   Bryan
When a Servant Learns a Secret   Cohan
When Love Is Waiting 'Round the Corner   Howard, Joseph
    E.
When Other Hearts Have Closed their Doors   Snyder
When She Sings the Songs My Mother Sang to Me   Snyder
When the Dodo Bird Is Singing in the Coca-Cola
    Tree   Edwards
When the Humming Birds Return Sweet Irene   Snyder
When the Ivy Climbs Over the Wall   Sterling
When You First Kiss the Last Girl You Love   Howard,
    Joseph E.
When You Know   Edwards
When You Love a Certain Girl   Goetz
Where Are They Now   Howard, Joseph E.
Where Do We Go from Here Bill   Snyder
Where Were You Last Night   Bryan
Why They Made Him King   Cohan
Wilhelm Der Grosser   Brown, A. Seymour
Would You Be Satisfied Sally (Sally Don't Live in Our Alley
    Anymore)   Fisher
Yankee Land   Williams
Yes She Did   Bryan
You for Me when You're Sweet Sixteen   Sterling; Von Tilzer
You Stand Awfully Good to Me   Edwards
You Taught Me How To Love, Now Teach Me To
    Forget   Bryan; Meyer
You Won't Know Anybody There   Howard, Joseph E.
You'd Think You Were in Paris   Cohan
You'll Come Back   Meyer
(It Is) You're a Dear Old World After All   Howard, Joseph E.
You're Just the Kind of Girl I'd Like My Girl to Be   Cobb;
    Goetz

1910

Aesthetic Dancing   Harbach
Ah, Sweet Mystery of Life (Dream Melody)   Herbert
Alexander and His Clarinet   Berlin; Snyder
All Aboard for Blanket Bay   Sterling; Von Tilzer
All Aboard for Monkey Town   Meyer
All I Crave Is More of Life   Herbert
All the World's in Love   Bryan
Amble on Alone   Egan
American Millionaire, An   Howard, Joseph E.
And I Thought He Was a Business Man   Von Tilzer
Angelo   Berlin
Angels   Berlin; Snyder
Angelus, The   Harbach

Antoinette Birby   Porter
Any Little Girl That's a Nice Little Girl Is the Right Little Girl
    for Me   Fisher
Applause   Gilbert
Arrival of Guests   Harbach
At Arrowhead Inn   Williams
Athletic Prancing   Harbach
Aviation   Atteridge
Baby Blue   Jerome; Schwartz, Jean
Baby Talk   Williams
Bachelor Belles, The   Smith, Harry B.
Back to My Old Home Town   Norworth
Barn Dance — Schottische   Herbert
Barry from Ballymore   Olcott
Be Careful How You Handle Me   Jerome; Schwartz, Jean
Before I Go and Marry (I Will Have a Talk with You)   Berlin
Believe Me   Edwards; Smith, Harry B.
Beware of Yale   Porter
Bingo Eli Yale   Porter
Birth of Passion, The   Harbach
Birth of the Butterfly   Harbach
Black Beauty   Jerome; Schwartz, Jean
Blue Bulgarian Band, The   Kern
Bombashay   Howard, Joseph E.
Boogey Boo Lady, The   Atteridge
Boys! Boys! Boys!   Howard, Joseph E.
Bridget McGuire   Porter
Bright Lights Gay (The New Mown Hay)   Sterling; Von
    Tilzer
Bring Back My Lena to Me   Berlin; Snyder
Bull Dog   Porter
Bull Frog and the Dove, The   Williams
Bumblebee, The   Harbach
Buyers, The   Howard, Joseph E.
Cafe 'Round the Corner, A   Atteridge
Call Me Up Some Rainy Afternoon   Berlin
Can't You See the Rainbow in the Sky   Leslie
Carlsbad Legend, The   Smith, Harry B.; Smith, Robert B.
Carmencita   Smith, Harry B.
Catamarang   Kern
Cavalier Rustican' Rag   Williams
Chauffeur, The   Williams
Cheer Up, My Honey   Harbach
Chicken Thief Man, The   Edwards; Smith, Harry B.
Chinatown, My Chinatown   Jerome; Schwartz, Jean
Chocolate Soldier   Jerome; Schwartz, Jean
Class of 1913 Song   Porter
Cleveland   Porter
Cock of the Walk, The   Edwards; Smith, Harry B.
C.O.D. (Help! I'm in Love)   Atteridge
Colored Romeo   Berlin; Snyder
Come Along Mandy   Edwards; Smith, Harry B.
Come Along My Mandy   Norworth
Come Along, Pretty Girl   Kern
Come Away Little Girl   Bryan; Meyer
Come Birdie Fly   Edwards
Come, Come, Come/Convent Maids   Herbert
Come Down to Earth, My Dearie   Jerome; Schwartz, Jean
Come Josephine in My Flying Machine   Bryan; Fisher
Come Little Girl and Dance with Me   Von Tilzer
Come Tiny Goldfish to Me   Kern
Comet and the Earth (Mister Earth and His Comet Love),
    The   Edwards; Smith, Harry B.
Coo-Coo, Coo-Coo   Kern
Corner in My Heart, A   Atteridge

I Will Be Your Chanticleer   Von Tilzer
I Won't Be Back Till August   Bryan
I Wouldn't Give My Heart to Any Other Girl but
      You   Leslie
I'd Like to Put Another R in Mary   Fisher
I'd Like to Tell Your Fortune Dearie   Williams
I'd Rather Love What I Can't Have   Howard, Joseph E.
I'd Rather Say Hello than Say Good-Bye   Bryan
I'd Ring the Wedding Bells for You   Jerome; Schwartz, Jean
Iddle-Iddle-Iddle-E   Howard, Joseph E.
If I Just Think of Her   Smith, Harry B.
If I Was a Millionaire   Cobb; Edwards
If I Were Anybody Else but Me   Herbert
If Only They Would Take a Tip from Me   Harbach
If You Won't Marry Me, then I'll Marry You   Howard,
      Joseph E.
If You'll Only Say You'll Be a Friend of Mine   Goetz
I'll Always Love You Dear   Brown, A. Seymour; Goetz
I'll Be Happy Too   Williams
I'll Be Your Chanticleer   Harbach
I'll Be Your Honey when It's Moonlight   Howard, Joseph E.
I'll Build a Fence Around You   Lewis
I'll Build for You a Little Nest   Harbach
I'll Do Anything But —   Bryan
I'll Have My Opera on the East Side (When Maggie Sings
      the Old Songs)   Sterling
I'll Lend You Everything   Edwards; Smith, Harry B.
I'll Lend You Everything I've Got Except My Wife   Von
      Tilzer
I'll Make a Ring around Rosie   Jerome; Schwartz, Jean
I'll Make You a Little Nest   Harbach
I'll March in April with May   Bryan; Meyer
I'll Take You Home Tomorrow If You'll Take Me Home
      Tonight   Howard, Joseph E.
I'm a Bear for You   Jerome; Schwartz, Jean
I'm a Happy Married Man   Berlin; Snyder
I'm a Married Man   Carroll
I'm Afraid of You   Bryan
I'm All Right   Harbach
I'm an Honorary Member of the Patsy Club   Sterling; Von
      Tilzer
I'm Awfully Afraid of Girls   Kahn
I'm Dying for You   Smith, Harry B.
I'm Falling in Love with Someone   Herbert
I'm Fancy Free   Smith, Harry B.
I'm Glad I'm Home Again   Carroll
I'm Going on a Long Vacation   Berlin; Snyder
I'm in Love with You   Edwards; Smith, Harry B.
I'm Just Pinin' for You   Williams
I'm Looking for a Certain Little Girl   Edwards
I'm Looking for a Financier   Harbach
I'm Nuts about You   Bryan; Meyer
I'm on My Way to Reno   Jerome; Schwartz, Jean
I'm Only Happy when I'm Sad   Jerome; Schwartz, Jean
I'm the Lily   Jerome; Schwartz, Jean
I'm Waiting for Just One Girl   Carroll
I'm Waiting for Winnie   Goetz
Imitation of Daphne, The   Smith, Harry B.
In a Bungalow   Howard, Joseph E.
In My Dreams of You   Smith, Harry B.
In Pittsburgh, Pa.   Goetz
In the Evening   Edwards; Smith, Harry B.
In the Sunshine of Your Love   Olcott
In Vanity Fair   Smith, Harry B.
Innocent Bessie Brown   Berlin

Intermezzo, The   Harbach; Herbert
Interrupted Allegory   Smith, Harry B.; Smith, Robert B.
Irish Eyes   Edwards; Sterling
Irish Rag, The   Carroll
Is There Anything Else That I Can Do for You?   Berlin;
      Snyder
Isn't It Exasperating, Sadie   Jerome; Schwartz, Jean
It All Goes Up in Smoke   Kahn
It Can't Be Did   Berlin
It Looks Like Rain   Meyer
It Never, Never Can Be Love   Herbert
It Pays to Advertise   Porter
It Puzzles Me So   Porter
Italian Street Song   Herbert
It's Awful Hard to Try to Be a Lady   Kalmar
It's Pretty Soft for Simon   Herbert
It's Style That Makes the Girl   Smith, Harry B.
It's Tough when Izzy Rosenstein Loves Genevieve
      Malone   Kahn
I've a Great Big Heart with a Great Big Love for a Little Girl
      Like You   Leslie
I've Been a Good Santa Claus to You   Williams
I've Got ???? Except My Wife   Edwards; Smith, Harry B.
I've Got a Live One Now   Brown, A. Seymour
I've Got Your Number   Bryan; Meyer
Josie   Monaco
Just a Bit o' Blarney   Goetz
Just a Little Band of Gold   Lewis
Just Keep A-Dreaming   Howard, Joseph E.
Katie of the Y.M.C.A.   Porter
Kellerman Girlie, The   Jerome; Schwartz, Jean
Kerryanna   Meyer
Kidland   Cobb; Edwards
King Chanticleer   Brown, A. Seymour
King of the Wide, Wide World, The   Leslie
Kiss Me   Howard, Joseph E.
Kiss Me, My Honey, Kiss Me   Snyder
Kiss You Gave, The   Harbach
Kisses at Auction   Smith, Harry B.
Kisses for Sale   Von Tilzer
Kitty Gray   Sterling
Kitty Rooney   Sterling
Lady Wine   Howard, Joseph E.
Lanciers   Herbert
Late House   Edwards; Smith, Harry B.
Lena, Lena   Kern
Let Me Be Your Mama   Meyer
Let Me Build a Nest for You   Brown, A. Seymour; Goetz
Let Me Steal a Kiss from You   Lewis
Let Us Be Married   Smith, Harry B.
Let's Make Love Amongst the Roses   Jerome; Schwartz,
      Jean
Lines in Mollie's Hand, The   Harbach
Listen To That Jungle Band   Bryan
Little Band of Gold, A   Von Tilzer
Little Lady in the Moon   Brown, A. Seymour; Goetz
Little Old Dream Waltz, A   Kahn
Little One   Howard, Joseph E.
Live for Today   Herbert
Look Me Over Carefully and Tell Me Will I Do   Cobb;
      Edwards
Look Out for Jimmy Valentine   Edwards
Look Out I'm Going to Steal You   Leslie
Looney Mooney Man   Harbach

Lots of Little Things Can Happen (In a Very Little While)   Harbach
Love Dance, The   Harbach
Love Is Like a Rose   Von Tilzer
Loves of New Orleans   Herbert
Loving Cup, The   Smith, Harry B.; Smith, Robert B.
Loving Ways   Brown, A. Seymour; Goetz
Lucy Anna Lou   Edwards
Mad Madrid, The   Harbach; Von Tilzer
Major General Pumpernickel   Von Tilzer
Man on the Box, The   Harbach
Mandolola (inst.)   Meyer
Marie Ann   Leslie
Mary Ann   Jerome; Schwartz, Jean
Mary! Mary!   Howard, Joseph E.
M-a-r-y, Mary A Double R, Mary Ann   Sterling
Maxie, Don't Take a Taxi   Lewis
Maybe You Were Made for Me   Bryan
Meet Me Down By the River   Williams
Memories of You   Romberg
Mercy Percy   Porter
Military Glide, The   Jerome; Schwartz, Jean
Mister Johnson, Goodnight   Sterling
Montana   Howard, Joseph E.
Mood You Are In, The   Harbach
Moon Talk   Kahn
Mother and Father   Kern
Mother Machree   Olcott
Motor Car, The   Porter
Motor Girls   Atteridge
Mr. Johnson, Good Night   Harbach
Mr. Voodoo   Herbert
Music with Meals   Porter
My Dream of the Union Jack   Snyder
My Girl (inst.)   Meyer
My Irish Girl   Williams
My Land   Olcott
My Love Will Find a Way   Norworth
My Mamie Rose   Goetz
My Old Fashioned Garden Flower   Harbach
My Operatic Samson   Jerome; Schwartz, Jean
My Soldier Boy   Von Tilzer
My Yiddish Colleen   Edwards
Mysterious Melody   Herbert
Naughty Marietta   Herbert
Near You   Bryan
'Neath the Southern Moon   Herbert
New Orleans Jeunesse Doree   Herbert
Newport Glide   Jerome; Schwartz, Jean
Next May Be the Right, The   Smith, Robert B.
Nightingale   Meyer
Nix on the Concertina Lena   Edwards; Smith, Harry B.
Nix on the Glow Worm, Lena   Carroll
No Show This Evening   Porter
Nonsense   Brown, A. Seymour; Goetz
Norworth's College Medley   Norworth
Nothing Too Good for You Dear   Howard, Joseph E.
Now She Is Anybody's Girlie   Williams
O! Weather-Man!   Howard, Joseph E.
Off for a Sail   Harbach
Oh, Honey   Porter
Oh! Marie   Goetz
Oh Mister Straus! Nix Komm Heraus   Goetz
Oh, That Beautiful Rag   Berlin; Snyder
Oh You Chicken   Fisher; Goetz

Oh, You Dream   Jerome; Schwartz, Jean
Oh You Spearmint Kiddo with the Wrigley Eyes   Jerome; Schwartz, Jean
(On the B, on the Bou) On the Boulevard   Von Tilzer
On with the Rehearsal   Harbach
Only a Kiss   Atteridge
Only a Man   Kahn
Opening of the Ball   Herbert
Oraibi (inst.)   Snyder
Oriental Moon   Williams
Other Fellow, The   Harbach
Our American Colleges   Edwards; Smith, Harry B.
Out with the Owl   Harbach
Over the Heather   Kahn
Paris Today   Howard, Joseph E.
Parisian Glide   Williams
Perfectly Terrible   Porter
Piano Man   Berlin; Snyder
Planning   Cobb; Edwards
Play That Lovey Dovey Waltz Some More   Leslie
Play that Wedding March Backwards   Williams
Please Come Back to Me   Brown, A. Seymour
Pollywogg Wiggle   Bryan; Fisher
Pop Corn Man   Jerome; Schwartz, Jean
Popular Girl, A   Smith, Harry B.
Prelude to Live for Today   Herbert
Pretty Little Girl Inside, The   Jerome; Schwartz, Jean
Prince of Bohemia   Goetz
Proposals   Williams
Put Your Head Upon My Shoulder   Bryan
Queen of Manhattan Isle   Harbach
Rag de Paree   Lewis
Ragtime Barn Dance   Goetz
Ring Me Up in the Morning   Williams
Ring-a-Ding-Dong   Von Tilzer
Roly Poly Eyes   Lewis
Rosa Rigoletto   Edwards
Rosalie   Edwards; Smith, Harry B.
Roses and Butterflies   Smith, Harry B.
Rosey Posey   Edwards; Smith, Harry B.
Rowing Song, The   Williams
Sadie Brady   Norworth
Sadie Salome Go Home   Berlin; Leslie
Santa Fe   Williams
Say Boys, I've Found a Girl   Kahn
Say Kid, Let's Become a Pair   Ager
Scare Crow Maidie   Howard, Joseph E.
Schlitz   Fisher
Schuetzen Corps, The   Von Tilzer
Seduction, The   Harbach
Sentimental Tommy   Goetz
Shannon Belles   Goetz
She Shook Him in Chicago   Harbach
She Trimmed Them All So Neatly   Smith, Harry B.
Shoes and Socks Shook Susan   Williams
Since Hiram Went to Yale   Williams
Smile She Means for You, The   Harbach
So Long Tony So Long   Lewis
Soap Bubble Days   Kahn
Somebody Else, It's Always Somebody Else   Meyer
Someone Just Like You, Dear   Berlin; Snyder
Song from the Fountain   Herbert
Song of the Fashions   Smith, Harry B.
Steve   Von Tilzer
Stop! Stop! Stop! (Love Me Some More)   Berlin

Stop That Rag (Keep on Playing, Honey)   Berlin
Stop Your Blushing, Rosie   Lewis
Strike Up a Bag Pipe Tune   Edwards
Summer Girl, The   Smith, Harry B.
Sweet Bye and Bye, The   Herbert
Sweet Italian Love   Berlin; Snyder
Sweet Marie - Make a Rag-A-Time Dance with Me   Berlin
Sweet Marie, Make-a-Rag-a-Time Dance Wid Me   Snyder
Sweetest Girl in Paris, The   Howard, Joseph E.
Sweetheart from the Emerald Isle   Atteridge
Sword Is My Sweetheart True, The   Williams
Table for Two, A   Porter
Taisez-Vous   Herbert
Take a Chance with Me   Meyer
Take a Look at Me Now   Von Tilzer
Take Me Dear   Smith, Harry B.; Smith, Robert B.
Take Me to that Ball, Phil   Lewis
Take Me to the Masquerade   Williams
Take Me With You Into Loveland   Bryan
Telephone Your Riffky Issey   Edwards; Smith, Harry B.
Tell It to Sweeney   Von Tilzer
Telling Lies   Berlin
Terzetto Buffo   Harbach
Thank You Kind Sir, Said She   Berlin; Snyder
That Chinatown Rag   Meyer
That Dancing Big Banshee   Brown, A. Seymour; Goetz
That Dreamy Barcarole Tune   Goetz
That Every Loving Love   Goetz
That Fascinating Rag Time Glide   Leslie
That Horrible Hobble Skirt   Edwards; Smith, Harry B.
That Italian Rag   Leslie
That Lazy Drag   Von Tilzer
That Little Thatched Cottage All Covered with Vine   Olcott
That Opera Rag   Berlin; Snyder
That Tantalizing Nod   Howard, Joseph E.
That Yodeling Rag   Von Tilzer
That's Getting First Class Yiddisha Love   Von Tilzer
That's Good   Williams
That's How Imitations Look to Me   Howard, Joseph E.
That's the Fellow I Want to Get   Bryan; Meyer
That's the Life of a Stable Boy   Harbach
That's Why Lots of People Marry   Smith, Harry B.
(The Tale of) The Bachelor and the Maid   Atteridge
Theophilus   Harbach
There's a Girl Up in the Moon   Jerome; Schwartz, Jean
There's Comp'ny in the Parlor   Fisher; Goetz
Those Dear Old Wedding Bells   Williams
Those Good Old Days Can Never Come Again (Those Were
    the Happy Days)   Smith, Harry B.
Three Trees   Smith, Harry B.; Smith, Robert B.
Throw Up Your Hands   Jerome; Schwartz, Jean
Ticket Speculator, The   Jerome; Schwartz, Jean
Tired of Living Alone   Porter
To the Strain of that Wedding March   Kahn
Tom Boy, Tom Boy   Harbach
Tony   Goetz
Tramp! Tramp! Tramp!   Herbert
Triumph of His Airship, The   Ahlert
Trying It On   Smith, Harry B.
Two Little Love Bees   Smith, Robert B.
Uncle Says I Mustn't, So I Won't   Harbach
Under the Oriental Moon   Williams
Under the Yum Yum Tree   Sterling; Von Tilzer
Underneath the Honey Moon   Meyer
Underneath the Wishing Tree   Lewis

Vampire Love Song, The   Leslie
Vas Is Los Mit Loois   Cobb; Edwards
Venus of Milo   Porter
Voices from Home   Goetz
Wait 'till We Gather in the Golden Corn   Lewis
Waltzing   Von Tilzer
Waltzing Lieutenant, The   Edwards; Smith, Harry B.
War Song   Porter
We Are Only Poor Weak Mortals After All   Harbach
We Are Only Poor Week Mortals After All   Harbach
We May Be Happy Yet   Smith, Harry B.
We're on the Track   Smith, Robert B.
We've Hunted the Wolf in the Forest   Herbert
What Good Is Water when You're Dry   Goetz
What Has Become of the Girl I Used to Know   Smith, Harry
    B.
What Has Become of the Girls I Used to Know   Edwards;
    Smith, Harry B.
What Us Poor Girls Go Through   Howard, Joseph E.
What's the Matter with Father   Williams
What's the Use   Harbach
What's the Use of Saving Money   Meyer
When I Fell in Love with You   Williams
When I Hear You Play that Piano, Bill   Berlin; Snyder
When I'm Eating Around with You   Porter
When Love Is Free   Smith, Harry B.
When Mariola Do the Cubanola   Von Tilzer
When Mr. Yankee-Doodle Comes to Town   Meyer
When Nancy Brown Kissed Hirem Green Good
    Bye   Howard, Joseph E.
When Rosalie Sings Chiribiribi   Goetz
When Sist' Tetrazin' Met Cousin Carus   Jerome; Schwartz,
    Jean
When the Clover Moon Is Shining Down   Lewis
When the Summer Moon Comes 'Long   Porter
When Two Love Dearly   Atteridge
When Two Loving Arms Are Around You   Ager
When We Were Married   Smith, Harry B.
When You Kiss the One You Love   Von Tilzer
When Your Dimples Turn to Wrinkles   Fisher; Goetz
When You're in Wrong with the Right Girl   Kahn
Where the Macaroni Grows   Fisher
Whistle when You're Lonely   Kern
White Folks Calls It Chantecleer, but It's Just Plain Chicken
    to Me   Sterling
Who Are You with Tonight?   Williams
Who Do You Suppose Went and Married My
    Sister   Norworth
Whoop 'Er Up   Sterling; Von Tilzer
Who's Yer Hoosier Friend   Edwards
Why Do We Follow the Big Brass Band?   Carroll
Why Don't You Be Nice to Some Nice Fellow?   Smith,
    Harry B.
Widow's Cruise   Porter
Wild Rose   Olcott
Will You Love Me When the Honeymooon Is Over   Bryan;
    Fisher
Winter   Bryan
Winter Rose, A   Young, Victor
Wishing   Berlin; Snyder
Woman's Dream, A   Edwards; Smith, Harry B.
Women Get the Best of Us, The   Smith, Harry B.
Won't Someone Take Me Home   Harbach
Won't You Write Your Autograph in My Album   Goetz
Yankee Bohemia   Goetz

Yankee Romeo   Goetz
Yellow Melodrama   Porter
Yiddisha Eyes   Berlin
Yiddle on Your Fiddle (Play Some Ragtime)   Berlin
You Ain't Got the Girl Till the Ring Is on Her Finger   Bryan
You and I and Cupid   Kahn
You Can Find It in the Papers Every Day   Williams
You Can't Argue   Harbach
You Can't Make Me Stop Loving You   Leslie
You Make Up   Porter
You Marry a Marionette   Herbert
You Must Be Mine Dear   Smith, Harry B.
You'll Be Sorry When You're Sober   Fisher
Young America   Norworth
You're Gwine to Get Something what You Don't Have   Von Tilzer
You're Just the Girlie, that I Adore   Brown, A. Seymour
You've Been Kissing the Blarney Stone   Smith, Harry B.

1911

Accent Makes No Difference in the Language of Love, The   Harbach
After That I Want a Little More   Bryan; Fisher
After the Honeymoon   Berlin; Snyder
Ah, At Last   Smith, Harry B.
Alexander's Ragtime Band   Berlin
All Alone   Von Tilzer
All Your Own Am I   Herbert; Smith, Harry B.
Always Keep a Fellow Guessing, If You Want His Love   Lewis
Ancestors Bold   Smith, Harry B.
And I Married Him   Bryan
And that Little Girl Is You   Herbert; Smith, Harry B.
Answer Me   Berlin
Any Old Time At All   Brown, A. Seymour
Any Place the Old Flag Flies   Cohan
April Fool   Von Tilzer
April Fool Rag (inst.)   Schwartz, Jean
Art Is Calling for Me (I Want to Be a Prima Donna)   Herbert; Smith, Harry B.
Ask My Mother   Kalmar; Snyder
At the Follies Bergere   Sterling; Von Tilzer
At the Ragtime Ball   Monaco
At the Yiddisha Wedding Dance   Carroll
Autumn Moon   Harbach
Awakened Love   Smith, Harry B.
Baby Duet   Smith, Harry B.; Smith, Robert B.
Bachelor Days   Harbach
Ballet   Herbert; Smith, Harry B.
Band Came Back, The   Brown, A. Seymour
Barnum Had the Right Idea   Cohan
Baseball Girl, The   Goetz
Baseball Glide, The   Sterling; Von Tilzer
Beautiful Girl   Bryan
Beautiful Love   Leslie
Begging   Harbach
Belles of the Tally-Ho Boarding School   Harbach
Betty of the Rosy Lips   Friml
Beware of the Hawk My Baby (Indian Lullaby)   Herbert
Beware of the Sirens   Smith, Harry B.
Bivouac Song   Smith, Harry B.
Blind Man's Bluff   Smith, Harry B.
Boardwalk Crawl, The   Atteridge
Boost Brooklyn   Jerome; Schwartz, Jean

Brass Band Ephraham Jones   Meyer
Break, Break, Break   Young, Victor
Bring Back My Golden Dreams   Meyer
Bring Back My Lovin' Man   Berlin
Bring Me a Ring in the Spring   Berlin
Brookside Inn   Jerome; Schwartz, Jean
Business Is Business, Rosey Cohen   Berlin
Buy Buy Baby   Smith, Harry B.; Smith, Robert B.
Cablegram   Porter
Can You Forget   Johnson, J. Rosamond
Cancel that Wedding March   Kalmar; Snyder
Candy Kisses (inst.)   Von Tilzer
Carmen Girl, The   Atteridge
Cave Man, The   Atteridge
Champagne Song   Herbert; Smith, Harry B.
Characteristic Waltz   Cohan
Chorus and Entrance of Regent   Herbert; Smith, Harry B.
Clinging Vine   Harbach
College Boys   Atteridge
Come Along, Ma Cherie   Smith, Harry B.; Smith, Robert B.
Come and Dance with Me   Atteridge
Come As a Carrier Dove   Smith, Harry B.; Smith, Robert B.
Come Back Marguerite   Bryan; Fisher
Come Back to Aaron   Von Tilzer
Come Back to Me   Atteridge
Come Little Fishes (Gold Fish Song)   Herbert; Smith, Harry B.
Come, Love, and Play Peek-a-Boo   Jerome; Schwartz, Jean
Come On Over Let's Get Acquainted   Brown, A. Seymour
Come to Sunny Spain   Herbert; Smith, Harry B.
Come with Me to My Bungalow (Cohan's Bungalow Song)   Cohan
Concentration   Porter
Confetti March   Smith, Harry B.; Smith, Robert B.
Confidential Source   Kern; Smith, Harry B.
Cora, The Fair Chorine   Porter
Coryphee, The   Herbert; Smith, Harry B.
Creatore   Brown, A. Seymour; Young, Joseph
Cuddle Up   Berlin
Cupid Tell Me Why   Herbert; Smith, Harry B.
Cupid the Conqueror   Smith, Harry B.
Curfew Bell Has Sounded, The   Smith, Harry B.
Dagger Dance   Herbert
Dancing Wedding, The   Cohan
Danny Cupid at the Bat   Harbach
Dat Lovin' Touch   Lewis
Dat's-A My Gal   Berlin
De Goblin's Glide   Kern
Dear Little Games of Guessing   Harbach
Dear Old Broadway   Berlin
Dear Old Fairyland   Herbert
Dearest Little Marionette   Harbach
Defying the Storm   Smith, Harry B.; Smith, Robert B.
Do It Now   Williams
Doctor Tinkle Tinker   Harbach
Does Anybody Want to Take Charlie's Place   Sterling; Von Tilzer
Doggone That Chilly Man   Berlin
Donkey and the Hay, The   Smith, Harry B.
Don't Forget the Beau You Left at Home   Goetz
Don't Forget To-Morrow Night   Monaco
Don't Leave Me Now   Von Tilzer
Don't Never Trust a Traveling Man   Goetz
Don't Put Out the Light   Berlin; Leslie
Don't Take Your Beau to the Seashore   Berlin; Goetz

Don't Tease   Lewis
Don't You Make a Noise   Harbach; Lewis; Schwartz, Jean
Down in the Old Meadow Lane   Williams
Down to the Folies Bergere   Berlin; Snyder
Dreaming Princess, The   Herbert; Smith, Harry B.
Drifting   Goetz
Drill of the Seventh   Cohan
Duchess, The   Herbert; Smith, Harry B.
Dying Rag   Berlin
Each Day Till I Die   Olcott
Edinboro Wriggle, The   Kern
Eight Little Letters Make Three Little Words   Kalmar; Snyder
Entrance of Herr Bangkeyski and the Piano King   Herbert; Smith, Harry B.
Entrance of Prince Ivan   Herbert; Smith, Harry B.
Entrance of Rose   Herbert; Smith, Harry B.
Entrance of the Regent   Herbert; Smith, Harry B.
Entrance of Vivien   Herbert; Smith, Harry B.
Ephraham Played Upon the Piano   Berlin
Every Girlie Loves Me but the Girl I Love   Harbach
Every Girl's a Soldier in the Army of Love   Herbert; Smith, Harry B.
Everybody Likes a College Girl   Lewis
Everybody's Doing It Now   Berlin
Everything Was Irish   Young, Joseph
Fair One   Porter
Fairies' Revel   Herbert
Fairy Tales   Norworth
Family Brawl, The   Harbach
Family Council, The   Smith, Harry B.
Fan Me with a Movement Slow   Kern
Far, Far Away   Porter
Farming Life-Country Life   Smith, Harry B.
Fascinating Widow, The   Harbach
Fascination Waltz   Johnson, J. Rosamond
Fifty-Seven Ways to Win a Man   Atteridge
Fire Belles   Goetz
Fire Ladies' Ball, The   Goetz
First Love Days   Goetz
First You Get the Money, Then You Get the Flat, Then Its Time Enough to Get the Girl   Bryan; Fisher
Flirtation   Smith, Harry B.
Follow Me 'Round   Kern
Fond Love   Smith, Harry B.
For Every Boy Who's Lonely There's a Girl Who's Lonely Too   Harbach
For Months and Months   Norworth; Smith, Harry B.
Forgive and Forget   Smith, Harry B.
Frisco Frizz   Howard, Joseph E.
Frolic of the Fairies   Herbert
Gee, Ain't It Tough When There's No One Around to Call You Dear   Young, Joseph
Gee, But I Like Music with My Meals   Brown, A. Seymour
Gentlemanly Brigand, The   Smith, Harry B.
George Cohan's Rag   Cohan
Girl and French Chauffeurs   Atteridge
Girl I Call My Sweetheart Must Look Like You, The   Olcott
Girl of My Dreams   Harbach
Girl Who Wouldn't Spoon, The   Harbach
Girlie Was Just Made to Love, A   Meyer
Girlie-Land, A   Herbert; Smith, Harry B.
Girlies You've Kissed in Your Dreams, The   Harbach
Give Me Your Love   Lewis
Golden Long Ago, The   Herbert

Good Morning Judge   Goetz
Goodbye Boys   Porter
Goodbye My Emerald Land   Olcott
Good-Bye, Old Gal (I'm Going Away on the 2:10 Train)   Brown, Lew
Goodnight, Ladies   Williams
Graft   Herbert
Grand Fantasy   Herbert
Great Manitou   Herbert
Grenadier's Song   Smith, Harry B.
Gypsy Born and Bred Am I   Smith, Harry B.; Smith, Robert B.
Gypsy Kiss   Smith, Harry B.
Gypsy Love   Smith, Harry B.; Smith, Robert B.
Gypsy Song   Smith, Harry B.
Ha! Ha! Ha!   Herbert
Habanera   Herbert
Hail the Wedding Pair   Smith, Harry B.
Hammock Song (Then You Swing, Swing, Swing)   Smith, Harry B.; Smith, Robert B.
Harbor of Home   Harbach
Harum-Scarum, The   Harbach
Has Cupid Laid in Wait for You   Herbert
He Promised Me   Berlin
Hearts Are Trumps   Herbert
Hello Hello   Howard, Joseph E.
Hello, Miss Chapel Street   Porter
Hello Paris   Johnson, J. Rosamond
Hello Stranger Just Stick Around   Leslie
Here Is the Tunic of a Soldier   Smith, Harry B.
Here We Are Scrubbing   Goetz
He's Coming Back   Kalmar; Snyder
He's the Wonder of Them All   Goetz
Hide and Seek   Harbach
Hm! She Is the One Girl   Smith, Harry B.
Home Run Bill   Bryan
Honey Love   Herbert
Honey Town   Lewis
Honey-Love   Meyer
Hot Stuff   Sterling; Von Tilzer
How Do You Do It, Mabel, On Twenty Dollars a Week?   Berlin
How to Tell a Fairy Tale   Herbert; Smith, Harry B.
Hunting Song   Herbert; Smith, Harry B.
I Ain't Got No Ear for Music   Jerome; Schwartz, Jean
I Always Come Back to You   Smith, Harry B.
I Beg Your Pardon   Berlin
I Beg Your Pardon, Dear Old Broadway   Snyder
I Can't Get Enough   Smith, Harry B.
I Don't Want Any Other Sweetheart If I Can't Have You   Sterling; Von Tilzer
I Have Found Them All   Smith, Harry B.
I Have Longed So Long   Norworth
I Keep My Wife in the City and Make Love To Her Myself   Bryan; Meyer
I Like the Hat, I Like the Dress and I Like the Girl That's In It   Bryan
I List the Trill in Golden Throat   Herbert
I Live Up Town   Bryan; Meyer
I Love My Wife   Bryan
I Love to Read the Papers in the Morning   Herbert
I Met You in Pittsburgh   Atteridge
I Miss You Yes I Miss You Sweetheart Mine   Snyder
I Never Had a Man to Love Me Like You   Von Tilzer
I Question Not   Harbach

I Should Worry   Gilbert

I Want a Girl Just Like a Girl That Married Dear Old Dad   Von Tilzer

I Want Something New To Play With   Atteridge; Cobb; Edwards

I Want to Be a Wild, Wild Rose   Herbert

I Want to Sing in Opera   Kern

I Want to Spoon to the Tune of the Silver Moon   Edwards

I Will Give You All for Love   Smith, Harry B.; Smith, Robert B.

I Wonder If It's True   Atteridge

I Wonder If You Care   Harbach

I'd Like to Be Your Mother's Son-in-Law   Goetz

I'd Like to Go on a Honeymoon with You   Smith, Harry B.; Smith, Robert B.

If Every Hour Were a Day   Bryan; Fisher

If I Should Dream of You   Herbert; Smith, Harry B.

If Only Someone Would Teach Me   Harbach

If You Can't Be As Happy As You Want to Be (Just Be As Happy As You Can)   Herbert; Smith, Harry B.

If You Can't Sing, Dance   Smith, Harry B.; Smith, Robert B.

If You Knew What I Know about Men   Goetz

If You Talk in Your Sleep Don't Mention My Name   Brown, A. Seymour

If You'll Only Lead the Way   Harbach

I'll Try Anything Once   Brown, A. Seymour

I'm a Crazy Daffydill   Kern

I'm a Wonderful Man in Yonkers   Jerome

I'm All for You   Goetz

I'm All Thine   Smith, Harry B.; Smith, Robert B.

I'm Coming Back   Brown, A. Seymour

I'm Crazy 'bout the Turkey Trot   Meyer

I'm Going to Steal Some Other Fellow's Girl (If I Can't Find One of My Own)   Brown, Lew

I'm Not a Bit Superstitious   Herbert

I'm Only a Fair Sun Bather   Lewis

I'm Ready to Quit and Be Good   Harbach

I'm Such a Romantic Girl   Herbert; Smith, Harry B.

I'm the Human Brush (that Paints the Crimson on Paree)   Kern

I'm the Only Mother that You Ever Knew   Goetz

I'm to Be a Blushing Bride   Harbach; Lewis; Schwartz, Jean

I'm Waiting Till Somebody Grows Up   Meyer

I'm Weary for You Dearie   Carroll

In Fairyland   Herbert

In June and July with August   Leslie

In My Dreams   Herbert

In So-So Society   Herbert

In the Land of Harmony   Kalmar; Snyder

In the Land of Long Ago   Herbert

In the Land of the Free   Smith, Harry B.; Smith, Robert B.

In the Shadows   Goetz

In the Summertime   Williams

In the Valley of Montbijou   Kern

Indian Invocation   Herbert

Injun Love   Williams

Interrupted Love Song, The   Smith, Harry B.

Island of Sweet Sixteen   Herbert

Isn't It Nasty of Papa?   Herbert; Smith, Harry B.

Italian Girl   Meyer

Italian Honeymoon, The   Leslie

Italian Romeo   Edwards

It's Always Going to Be that Way   Herbert

It's Awful Hard to Try to Be a Lady   Kalmar; Snyder

It's Great When You Marry for Love   Sterling

It's Not the Trick Itself but It's the Tricky Way It's Done   Goetz

It's the Bump   Herbert; Smith, Harry B.

It's the Shirt   Goetz

I've a Garden in Sweden   Norworth; Smith, Harry B.

I've Been Looking for a Perfect Man   Herbert; Smith, Harry B.

I've Got a Ragtime Bee in My Bonnet   Gilbert

I've Got to Give Her Her Own Way   Smith, Harry B.

I've Got to Go and Get Myself a Girl Like You   Cobb; Edwards

I've Had a Lovely Time, Good Night   Goetz

I've Heard that Before   Atteridge

(War Is Hell, but Oh You) Jealousy   Harbach

Joys of Love, The   Smith, Harry B.

June   Goetz

June Honeymoon   Kalmar; Snyder

Jungle Wedding Bells   Edwards

Just a Little Bit of Lingerie   Goetz

Just a Little Love   Sterling; Von Tilzer

Just a Little Smile   Howard, Joseph E.

Just a Year Ago   Williams

Just As Long as the Swanee Flows   Bryan

Just for You   Howard, Joseph E.

Just Keep the Dear Boys Guessing   Harbach

Just Tell Me with Your Eyes   Goetz

Just Think of All the Money You Could Save   Jerome; Schwartz, Jean

Keep a Taxi Waiting, Dear   Berlin

Kiss Burglar, The   Goetz

Kiss Me Again   Sterling

Kiss Me, My Honey, Kiss Me   Berlin

Knock a Little Louder Ephraham   Von Tilzer

Knock Wood   Sterling; Von Tilzer

Lanciers (Finale Ultimo)   Herbert

(There Is a) Land of Fancy   Smith, Harry B.; Smith, Robert B.

Land of Maidens   Herbert; Smith, Harry B.

Land of the Sultan's Dreams, The   Herbert; Smith, Harry B.

Last Little Girl Is You, The   Herbert; Smith, Harry B.

Latest Society Pet, The   Herbert; Smith, Harry B.

Laughs   Herbert

Le Beau Sabreur   Smith, Harry B.

Le Reve D'Absinthe   Porter

Leave Him Alone If He Leaves You   Brown, Lew

Lesson in Love, A   Smith, Harry B.

Lessons in Love   Smith, Harry B.; Smith, Robert B.

Let Me Be Free   Herbert; Smith, Harry B.

Let Me Know a Day Before   Monaco

Let's Make a Rag of the Old Oaken Bucket   Leslie

Let's See, Um, Um, That's Right   Sterling; Von Tilzer

Letter You Shouldn't Have Sent, The   Harbach

Life is a Riddle   Herbert; Smith, Harry B.

Life Isn't All Roses, Rosie   Bryan

Life Oriental   Smith, Harry B.

Light Up Your Face with a Smile   Cobb; Edwards

Lindy Come Along   Howard, Joseph E.

Lingerie   Goetz

Little Bit of Irish, A   Kahn

Little Bride, The   Smith, Harry B.

Little Fifi   Herbert

Little Girls Beware   Smith, Harry B.

Little Italy   Goetz

Little Millionaire, The   Cohan

Little Miss Fix-It   Norworth; Smith, Harry B.

Lonely Am I   Herbert
Look Me Over   Johnson, J. Rosamond
Look Me Over Dearie   Kern
Look Out! Look Out!   Smith, Harry B.
Lord Have Mercy on the Married Man   Leslie
Lots of Little Things Can Happen   Harbach
Love and Beauty   Smith, Harry B.; Smith, Robert B.
Love Come Back   Smith, Harry B.
Love for a Year, Love for a Day   Smith, Harry B.; Smith, Robert B.
Love Is a Race   Harbach
Love Is Like a Rubber Band (Hoop Song)   Kern
Love Is Like the Rose   Smith, Harry B.; Smith, Robert B.
Love Me   Edwards
Love Me to a Yiddisha Melody   Leslie; Lewis; Young, Joseph
Love Me to that Beautiful Tune   Williams
Love Rose   Lewis
Love Sign   Goetz
Love Waltz   Smith, Harry B.
Lover, Come Back   Herbert; Smith, Harry B.
Love's a Dreamy Tune   Howard, Joseph E.
Love's Charming Art   Kern
Love's Sentence   Meyer
Love's Sorcery   Smith, Harry B.; Smith, Robert B.
Loving Moon   Johnson, J. Rosamond
Ma Petite Ninette   Porter
Macushla   Olcott
Mad House Rag, The   Leslie
Madrigal   Herbert; Smith, Harry B.
Mah Honey Love   Herbert
Make Me Love You Like I Never Loved Before   Bryan; Fisher
Mama's Little Pet   Harbach
Mammy's Shufflin' Dance   Gilbert
Mamselle Lucinda   Goetz
Man of the World, A   Harbach
Manicure Girl, The   Kern
Man's a Man for A' That, A   Herbert
March Chorus and Entrance of the Regent   Herbert; Smith, Harry B.
March of the Prince's Regiment   Herbert; Smith, Harry B.
Marie   Smith, Harry B.
Mary Ann   Howard, Joseph E.
Mary Drew   Herbert
Mary Went 'Round and Around and Around (With a Bumpty Umpty Ay)   Bryan; Fisher
Matrimony   Smith, Harry B.; Smith, Robert B.
Matrimony Rag   Leslie
Maybe that Is Why I'm Lonely   Meyer
Maybe You Think I'm Happy   Gilbert
Maybe You're Not the Right Girl After All   Kalmar
Maybe You're Not the Right Girl (One) After All   Snyder
Meet Me To-Night   Berlin
Melody of Love, The   Smith, Harry B.; Smith, Robert B.
Men! Men! Men!   Smith, Harry B.; Smith, Robert B.
Minstrel Band, The   Atteridge
Minuet (Natoma Serenade)   Herbert
Miraculous Cure, The   Smith, Harry B.
Missouri Joe   Goetz; Von Tilzer
Mister Music Master Play that Rag Some Faster   Brown, Lew
Modern Banditti, The   Smith, Harry B.
Modulating Maude   Johnson, J. Rosamond
Molly O! Oh, Molly   Berlin
Molly Took the Next Train Back   Von Tilzer

Mon Bijou de Montbijou   Smith, Harry B.
Monte Carlo (inst.)   Monaco
Mother Phi   Porter
Movin' Man Don't Take My Baby Grand   Kalmar; Snyder
Music Caressing of Violins   Smith, Harry B.
Music Vot's Music Must Come from Berlin   Kahn
Musical Moon   Cohan
My Bill from Louisville   Snyder
My Carolina Cutey   Sterling; Von Tilzer
My Counterfeit Bill   Sterling; Von Tilzer
My Dream of Paradise   Brown, A. Seymour
My Heart I Cannot Give to You   Kern
My Heart Keeps Right on Beating (But It's Beating for Another Girl)   Kahn
My Home Town Girl   Porter
My Idea of Paradise   Smith, Harry B.
My Lou   Atteridge
My Love for You   Snyder
My Melody Dream   Berlin
My Toast to You   Herbert
My Wedding Day   Smith, Harry B.
My Wife! My Wife!   Harbach
Mysterious Moon   Brown, A. Seymour
Naughty, Naughty, Naughty   Williams
Never Such a Loving Two   Brown, A. Seymour
New Yorkers   Cohan
Night-Time's the Right Time (To Spoon with the Girl You Love)   Meyer
Nighty Girl   Harbach
No More Staying Out Late   Norworth
No One but You   Harbach
No One Ever Died from Lovin'   Fisher
Nothing to Do Until Tomorrow   Meyer
Oh Do Step the Two-Step   Smith, Harry B.
Oh! Mary You're Contrary   Herbert
Oh, Mr. Dream Man, Please Let Me Dream Some More   Monaco
Oh that Navajo Rag   Williams
Oh that Teasing Man   Meyer
Oh, the Things They Put in the Papers Now-a-Days   Herbert
Oh, Those Boys!   Herbert
Oh, You Beautiful Coon   Cohan
Oh You Beautiful Doll   Brown, A. Seymour; Smith, Harry B.; Smith, Robert B.
Oh, You Mister Moon   Dubin
Oh, You Wonderful Girl   Cohan
Old Ballet Days, The   Smith, Harry B.; Smith, Robert B.
Old Noblesse, The   Herbert; Smith, Harry B.
Old Rat Mort, The   Porter
Olga from the Volga   Atteridge
On a Junetime Honeymoon   Goetz
On a Sunday Morning   Harbach
On an Irish Honeymoon   Jerome; Schwartz, Jean
On the Congo   Atteridge
On the Farm   Smith, Harry B.
On the First Dark Night Next Week   Leslie
One O'Clock in the Morning I Get Lonesome   Berlin; Snyder
One Word from You   Herbert; Smith, Harry B.
Ooh! (Maybe It's a Robber)   Harbach
Or Know the Reason Why   Herbert; Smith, Harry B.
Oriental Eyes   Atteridge
Pack Up Your Heart   Harbach
Panuelo   Herbert

Paree, Gay Paree   Atteridge
Paris Is a Paradise for Coons   Kern
Parlor Games   Norworth
Paul's Address   Herbert
People Will Talk You Know   Herbert
Pity Is Akin to Love (Won't You Have a Little Pity on
    Me)   Brown, A. Seymour
Play the Game   Herbert; Smith, Harry B.
Please Go Find My Billy Boy   Norworth; Smith, Harry B.
Poker   Porter
Polka Is Good Fun, The   Smith, Harry B.
Polla   Herbert; Smith, Harry B.
Post Card Beau, A   Goetz
Postillion, The   Smith, Harry B.
Pots and Pans   Schwartz, Jean
Pourquoi   Herbert
Prelude   Herbert
Put Your Arms Around Me   Harbach; Schwartz, Jean
Put Your Arms Around Me Honey   Lewis
Quaker Talk   Harbach
Queen of the Yale Dramat   Porter
Queen of Vanity Fair, The   Smith, Harry B.; Smith, Robert B.
Rag Pipe Bag Pipe Band, The   Goetz
Ragging the Old Vienna Roll   Schwartz, Jean
Raggity Man   Williams
Ragtime College Girl, The   Harbach; Lewis; Schwartz, Jean
Ragtime Goblin Man, The   Sterling; Von Tilzer
Ragtime Violin, The   Berlin
Ramshackle Rag (inst.)   Snyder
Real Girl   Berlin
Ring on the Finger Is Worth Two on the Phone, A   Meyer
Rolling, Rolling   Porter
(There's None So Sweet As) Rosalind   Herbert
Rose Lucky Rose   Herbert; Smith, Harry B.
Rose of the Orient, The   Smith, Harry B.
Rosebud   Porter
Rosy Morn, The   Smith, Harry B.; Smith, Robert B.
Rum Tum Tiddle   Schwartz, Jean
Run Home and Tell Your Mother   Berlin
Sally   Herbert; Smith, Harry B.
Same Old Welcome at the Door   Carroll
Sarah's Hat   Jerome; Schwartz, Jean
Saturday Night   Porter
Sauce for the Goose Is Sauce Is Sauce for the
    Gander   Harbach
Seashell Telephone, The   Smith, Harry B.
Send for Me   Leslie; Meyer
Sentimental Tommy   Goetz
Sham   Herbert; Smith, Harry B.
Shooting Show   Atteridge
Shut Your Eyes and Make Believe   Von Tilzer
Siberian Dip (inst.), The   Johnson, J. Rosamond
Siberian Whirl, The   Johnson, J. Rosamond
Since Papa Becomes a Billionaire   Herbert
Sing Trovatore   Kern
Sirens So Fair   Smith, Harry B.
Skeletons in the Closet   Harbach
Soldier's Song   Smith, Harry B.
Sombrero Land   Atteridge; Berlin; Goetz; Snyder
Some Day (You'll Miss Me When You're
    Lonesome)   Brown, Lew
Something Tells Me I Am Going to Love You   Goetz
Something Very Mysterious   Harbach
Song of the Sirens   Smith, Harry B.
Sousa's Marches, The   Atteridge

Spanish Love   Berlin; Smith, Harry B.; Smith, Robert B.;
    Snyder
Story of a Marionette   Harbach
Straight Road Is a Great Road After All, The   Lewis
Strawberries   Norworth; Smith, Harry B.
Students' Glide (Turkey Wing)   Smith, Harry B.; Smith,
    Robert B.
Sweet Angeline   Brown, Lew
Sweet Sixteen   Smith, Harry B.
Sweetheart, My Sweetheart   Kalmar; Snyder
Swing Song   Herbert
Take a Look at Me Now   Sterling; Von Tilzer
Take a Vacation, Mr. Moon   Kalmar; Snyder
Take Me Along with You Dearie   Goetz
Take Me Back to the Garden of Love   Goetz
Tale that the Sweet Roses Told, A   Meyer
Tantalizing Ida   Norworth; Smith, Harry B.
Ta-Ta, Little Girl   Kern
Teach Me to Forget   Herbert; Smith, Harry B.
Texas Pranca   Gilbert
Texas Tommy's Dance   Leslie
That Aeroplane Rag   Johnson, J. Rosamond
That Frisco Bear   Edwards
That Haunting Melody   Cohan
That Hypnotizing Man   Brown, Lew
That Kazzatsky Dance   Berlin
That Monkey Tune   Berlin
That Mysterious Rag   Berlin; Snyder
That Paradise Rag   Meyer
That Pierrot Dance   Williams
That Pretty Little Song   Herbert; Smith, Harry B.
That Reuben Glide   Young, Joseph
That Soul Inspiring Sneeze   Harbach
That Spooky Tune   Goetz
That Was Before I Met You   Bryan; Meyer
That Will Keep Him True to You   Harbach
That's All Right for McGilligan   Kern
That's Boys Your Boys   Herbert
That's Going Some for You   Bryan; Fisher
That's Harmony   Clarke
That's the Way to Treat a Little Doggie   Harbach
There Is a Happy Land   Smith, Harry B.
There is a Happy Land (Tale of Woe)   Kern; Norworth
There Once Was a Princess   Herbert
There's a Dixie Girl Who's Longing for a Yankee Doodle
    Boy   Meyer
There's a Girl in Havana   Berlin; Goetz; Snyder
There's a Raft of Money in Graft! Graft! Graft!   Herbert
There's a Resting Place for Every Girl (Sun Chair
    Song)   Kern
There's a Ring Around the Moon   Bryan
There's a Soul Mate Somewhere   Herbert; Smith, Harry B.
There's Something About You that Appeals to Me   Smith,
    Harry B.
They All Look Good when They're Far Away   Herbert;
    Smith, Harry B.
They Always Pick on Me   Von Tilzer
They Follow Me Everywhere   Herbert
They're All Good American Names   Jerome; Schwartz, Jean
Those Eyes   Smith, Harry B.
Throw a Kiss to Me, My Minstrel Man   Goetz
Throw Me Up and Catch Me and Don't Let Me
    Fall   Monaco
Tipperary Twirl, The   Meyer
To Take a Dip in the Ocean   Lewis

To the Land of My Own Romance Herbert; Smith, Harry B.
Toddling the Todalo Goetz
Tommy Rot Harbach
Toni Caponi Atteridge
Tonight's the Night Goetz
Tra-La-Li Atteridge
Try This on Your Pianna, Anna Goetz
Turkey Trot Norworth; Smith, Harry B.
Turkey Trot (inst.) Kern
Turn Off Your Light Mr. Moon Man (Turn Off the Light Mr. Moon Man) Norworth; Smith, Harry B.
Twenty Years Ago Atteridge
Under the Pretzel Bough Williams
Upsi-Daisy Herbert; Smith, Harry B.
Valse Julian Harbach; Schwartz, Jean
Vaquero's Song (Who Dares the Bronco Wild Defy) Herbert
Vera Violetta Atteridge
Very Ambitious Girl, A Brown, A. Seymour
Virginia Lou Berlin
Visit Looney Park Atteridge
Wallflower Sweet Smith, Harry B.
Waltz Caprice Smith, Harry B.
Way Down in Mexico Von Tilzer
Way Down on Sunny Tampa Bay Goetz
We All Fall Meyer
We Do the Dirty Work Cohan
Wedding Bells Smith, Harry B.; Smith, Robert B.
Wedding Guests Smith, Harry B.; Smith, Robert B.
We're Off Porter
What Am I Gonna Do? Berlin
What Is Life without You, Dear Gilbert
What's the Use of Moonlight? Herbert; Smith, Harry B.
What's the Use of Saying No Harbach
When a Girl Whose Heart You Long for Has a Heart that Longs for You Meyer
When His Eyes Look into Mine Smith, Harry B.
When I Was 21 and You Were Sweet 16 Williams
When I Woke Up this Morning Monaco
When I'm Alone I'm Lonesome Berlin
When I'm Waltzing with You Smith, Harry B.; Smith, Robert B.
When It Rains, Sweetheart, When It Rains Berlin
When Ragtime Rosie Ragged the Rosary Leslie
When She's Old Enough to Marry Meyer
When Tender Love You Are Confessing Harbach
When the Cat Comes Back Smith, Harry B.
When the Old Top Hummed (The Humming Top) Harbach
When the Right Man Sings Tra-La-La Herbert; Smith, Harry B.
When the World Comes to an End Cobb; Edwards
When Tonight Dies Herbert
When Tony La Board Played the Barber Shop Chord! Young, Joseph
When You Hear Love's Hello Atteridge; Goetz
When You Kiss an Italian Girl Berlin
When You Look in Her Eyes Herbert; Smith, Harry B.
When You See the Snow Flakes Falling Young, Joseph
When You're in Love With More than One, You're Not in Love at All Bryan
When You're in Town Berlin
Where Love Is King Leslie
Where, Oh Where Has Johnny Gone Friml
Where're You Going? (I'm Going to Join That Minstrel Band) Brown, Lew
While the Big Old World Rolls Round Herbert

Whistling Rag Berlin
White Light Alley Goetz
Wholesale Love Gilbert
Whoop-A-Daisy Kahn
Wild Rose, The Herbert
Wilhelmina's Concertina Goetz
Wine Maid Divine Goetz
With Downcast Eye (Wedding Song) Harbach
With His Little Cane and Satchel in His Hand Jerome; Von Tilzer
Woodman, Woodman, Spare That Tree Berlin
Yankee Love Berlin; Goetz
Yiddisha Luck and Irisha Love (Kelly and Rosenbaum, That Mazeltoff) Bryan; Fisher
Yiddisha Nightingale Berlin
Y.M.D. Smith, Harry B.
You Built a Fire Down in My Heart Berlin; Goetz
You Can Go As Far As You Like with Me Smith, Harry B.; Smith, Robert B.
You Don't Love Me As Much As I Love You Von Tilzer
You Remind Me of Someone I Want to Forget Brown, Lew
You'll Do the Same Thing All Over Again Bryan
Your Love Means the World to Me Lewis
You're Just a Perfect Peach Beyond My Reach Kern; Smith, Harry B.
You're So Different from the Rest Smith, Harry B.
You're the Nicest Little Girl I Ever Knew Johnson, J. Rosamond
You's Sweet to Yo' Mammy Jes the Same Johnson, J. Rosamond
You've Built a Fire Down in My Heart Berlin
You've Got Me Hypnotized Berlin
You've Got to Take Me Home Tonight Goetz

1912

Africa Smith, Harry B.; Smith, Robert B.
Alexander's Bagpipe Band Berlin; Goetz
All Alone on Broadway, Blase Broadway Gilbert
All Hallowe'en Herbert
All the World Is Madly Prancing Atteridge
All the World Loves a Lover Smith, Harry B.; Smith, Robert B.
Always Together Atteridge
American Beauty Rose, An Friml; Harbach
American Heiress, The Smith, Robert B.
And the Green Grass Grew All Around Jerome; Von Tilzer
And Then Bryan
And They Lived Happily Ever Afterward Herbert
Antonio, You'd Better Come Home Berlin
Anytime Porter
Are We Widows, Wives or What? Atteridge
At Gay Raatenbad Goetz
At the Automat Goetz
At the Bal Masque Herbert
At the Devil's Ball Berlin
At the Rainbow Porter
Away for a Lovely Ocean Cruise Friml; Harbach
Bacchanal Rag, The Atteridge
Bagdad Herbert
Ballet Suite, The Herbert
Ballet-Youth Herbert
Barber's Bear, The Clarke; Schwartz, Jean
Barcelona Porter
Beautiful Beautiful Girl Jerome

Beautiful Ship from Toyland, The   Friml; Harbach
Becky's Got a Job in a Musical Show   Berlin
Bellboys   Porter
Belle of the Barber's Ball   Berlin; Cohan
Big Blonde Baby   Bryan; Fisher
Billy, Billy, Bounce Your Baby Doll   Bryan; Fisher
Billy's Melody   Gilbert
Bird of Paradise   Atteridge
Blow on Your Piccolo   Atteridge
Bohemia   Kern; Smith, Robert B.
Boola-Boola   Goetz
Borrow from Me   Smith, Harry B.
Bread and Cheese and Kisses   Howard, Joseph E.
Buck Dance Bill   Leslie
Bump, Bump, Bump in Your Automobile   Brown, Lew
Bunch of Sweetness   Gilbert; Motzan
Bunny Hug, The   Jerome; Von Tilzer
Buzz on Little Busy Bee   Atteridge
Bye Bye Sal   Gilbert
Bye-Bye Land   Lewis; Young, Joseph
Bygone Days   Kern
Call Again   Berlin
Call Me Flo   Kern
Call Me in the Morning   Brown, A. Seymour
Call Me Uncle   Friml; Harbach
Cello Fellow, The   Howard, Joseph E.
Charity   Porter
Chop Stick Rag   Schwartz, Jean
Cinderella Waltz   Atteridge
Cinderella's Dream   Herbert
(Oh! You) Circus Days   Monaco
Coffee Mother Used to Make, The   Smith, Harry B.
Cohen's Band   Atteridge
College Days   Goetz
Colonial Days   Gilbert
Come and Kiss Your Little Baby   Brown, Lew
Come Back to Me   Atteridge
Come Back to Me — My Melody   Berlin; Snyder
Come Down, Mister Moon Man   Brown, Lew
Come on Over Here   Kern
Come to Bohemia   Porter
Come to Me Chimpanzee   Atteridge
Confidence   Smith, Harry B.; Smith, Robert B.
Corsican, The   Atteridge
Cotillion, The   Atteridge
Could You Love a Girl Like Me   Smith, Robert B.
Course of True Love, The   Smith, Robert B.
Cuba   Goetz
Daddy   Brown, A. Seymour; Smith, Harry B.
Daddy Did a Wonderful Thing   Lewis; Meyer
Daddy Has a Sweetheart and Mother Is Her Name   Buck
Dance Into His Heart   Smith, Robert B.
Dancing   Porter
Dancing Dan the Ragtime Rattling Man   Leslie
Dancing Man   Howard, Joseph E.
Darkies' Ragtime Ball, The   Meyer
Dawn of Love, The   Goetz
Dawn of Love (L'Alba D'Amore), The   Friml; Harbach
De Trop   Friml; Harbach
Dear Doctor   Porter
Dear Old Heidelberg   Goetz
Dear Old Rose   Meyer
Dear Old Wisconsin Days   Howard, Joseph E.
Die Neue Art   Goetz

Dingle, Dingle, Dingle   Conrad; Smith, Harry B.; Young, Joseph
Dixie Love   Goetz
Dixie Love Song   Goetz
Do It Again   Berlin
Do It in the Dark   Lewis; Meyer
Doctor Brown   Bryan
Dollar Bill's the Flag that Rules the World, The   Goetz
Don't Break My Heart   Leslie
Don't Forget the Number of the House   Gilbert
Don't Leave Your Wife Alone   Berlin
Don't Turn My Picture to the Wall   Kern; Smith, Robert B.
Down in Dear Old New Orleans   Conrad; Young, Joseph
Down in My Heart   Berlin
Down in the Old Rathskeller   Goetz
Dream of My Dreams   Lewis; Young, Joseph
Drums of All Nations, The   Herbert
Dublin Bay   Kahn
Edna May   Clarke; Schwartz, Jean
Election in Jungle Town, The   Brown, A. Seymour
Elevator Man (Going Up - Going Up - Going Up)   Berlin
Ensemble   Smith, Harry B.; Smith, Robert B.
Entrance of Cinderella and Princess of Far Away   Herbert
Every Flower Has It's Melody   Goetz
Every Morning   Monaco; Sterling
Everybody Loves a Chicken   Atteridge
Everybody's Cabareting   Jerome; Schwartz, Jean
Everyone in Town Likes Mary   Schwartz, Jean
Ev'ry Time You're Lonely Don't Forget that I Am Lonely Too   Leslie
Ev'ry Woman's Eyes   Johnson, J. Rosamond
Excuse Me Mister Moon   Johnson, J. Rosamond
Exercise   Porter
Eye That Never Sleeps, The   Atteridge
Eyes, Eyes   Atteridge
Fairy Music   Herbert
Fare Thee Well   Porter
Father and Son   Smith, Harry B.; Smith, Robert B.
Father's Beard   Berlin
Fearless Waltz, The   Atteridge
Fiddle Dee Dee   Berlin
Find Me a Girl   Lewis; Meyer
Fingers and Thumbs   Cobb; Schwartz, Jean
Finnegan   Brown, A. Seymour
Floating Down the River on the Alabama   Brown, Lew
Fol de Rol Dol Dol   Schwartz, Jean
Fol-De-Rol   Atteridge
Follow Me Around   Berlin
Following Behind the Girl Behind the Smile   Goetz
Fond of the Ladies   Herbert
Foolishness   Atteridge
Four O'Clock Tea   Atteridge
Frisco   Smith, Harry B.
From You, For Me   Howard, Joseph E.
Funny Little Melody, The   Berlin
Game of Halloween   Herbert
Garden of Flowers   Goetz
Garden of Girls, The   Atteridge
Garden of Yesterday, The   Goetz
Garden Party   Herbert
Gee, I Should Have Been Born a Boy   Brown, A. Seymour
Gee, It Must Be Tough to Be a Rich Man's Kid   Cobb; Edwards
Georgia Land   Carroll
Gertrude Hoffman Glide, The   Atteridge

Gertrude Hoffman March   Atteridge
Ghost of a Rag, The   Brown, Lew
Ghost of the Goblin Man, The   Sterling; Von Tilzer
Ghost of the Violin, The   Kalmar; Snyder
Ghost Quintette   Smith, Harry B.; Smith, Robert B.
Giannina Mia   Friml; Harbach
Ginger   Goetz
Girl from Home Sweet Home, The   Atteridge
Girl I Left Before I Left the Girl I Left Behind, The   Von
    Tilzer
Girl with the Come Hither Eyes   Friml; Harbach
Girlish Laughter   Atteridge
Go Blow, Joe   Kahn
Going Home to Lulu   Howard, Joseph E.
Good Morning   Goetz
Good Old Circus Band   Smith, Harry B.
Goodnight, Girl of Mine, Goodnight   Cobb; Edwards
Goody Goody Goody Goody Goody Goody   Berlin
Ha, Ha, They Must Sail to Siberia   Porter
Handy Andy   Atteridge
Hanky-Panky Glide, The   Goetz
Happy Family, The   Smith, Robert B.
Hard Luck in Society   Atteridge
Harlequinade   Herbert
Haunting Melody   Atteridge
He Must Be Nice to Mother   Kern
He Played It on His Fid, Fid Fiddle-Dee-Dee   Berlin; Goetz
He Says Yes, She Says No!   Friml; Harbach
He Took Her Up, Up, Up, 'Way Up High   Bryan
Hello Cupid, Send Me a Fellow   Atteridge
Henry Oh Henry Your Ma Wants You   Kahn
Here Comes My Daddy Now   Gilbert
Here Comes My Minstrel Man   Goetz
Here Comes the Bride (The Girl Who Stole My Lovin' Man
    Away)   Brown, Lew
He's a Dear Old Pet   Jerome; Schwartz, Jean
Hiram's Band   Berlin; Goetz
Hitchy Koo   Gilbert
Honest and True   Cobb; Schwartz, Jean
Honeymoon Love   Brown, A. Seymour
Hoop-La-La, Papa!   Kern
How Can They Tell I'm Irish   Goetz
How Could I Know that You Loved Me?   Brown, A.
    Seymour
How Do You Do?   Atteridge
How Do You Know?   Atteridge
Hurry, Little Children   Smith, Harry B.
Hypnotizing Man   Atteridge
I Ain't No Fool   Smith, Harry B.
I Cannot Drink the Old Drinks   Goetz
I Didn't Come Here to Steal Anybody's Man   Brown, Lew
I Have Said Goodbye a Thousand Times (Good-Bye
    Sweetheart Good-Bye)   Buck
I Left My Old Kentucky Home for You   Jerome; Von Tilzer
I Like All the Girls   Atteridge
I Like It Better Every Day   Williams
I Live for You Alone   Smith, Robert B.
I Love to Hear an Irish Band Play on St. Patrick's
    Day   Jerome; Schwartz, Jean
I Love You So   Porter
I May Look Green, but I Ain't Nobody's Fool   Buck
I Never Knew What Love Could Do   Brown, A. Seymour
I Never Would Do It in Society   Goetz
I Should Worry   Smith, Harry B.
I Want Something New to Play With   Atteridge

I Want to Be in Dixie   Berlin; Snyder
I Want to Be Married (To a Delta Kappa Epsilon
    Man)   Porter
I Wonder   Kern
I Wonder Where My Girl Is Now   Porter
I Would Like to See the Peaches   Schwartz, Jean; Smith,
    Harry B.
I Would Like to Try It, But I'm Just a Bit Afraid   Brown, Lew
I'd Do As Much for You   Jerome; Von Tilzer
Ida   Atteridge
If a Rooster Can Love As Many Little Chickens, Can't a Man
    Love More Than One   Bryan; Meyer
If All the Girls in All the World Were Just as Nice as
    You   Fisher
If I Were a Football Man   Porter
If It Wasn't for the Irish and the Jews   Jerome; Schwartz,
    Jean
If You Go Home to Your Husband I'll Have to Go Home to
    My Wife   Leslie
If You were Only Here   Meyer
If You Would Only Love Me   Kern
If You'll Be My Eve, I'll Build an Eden for You   Johnson, J.
    Rosamond
I'll Be True to You   Smith, Harry B.; Smith, Robert B.
I'll Be Waiting 'Neath Your Window   Kern
I'll Build a Wall Around Loveland   Lewis; Meyer
I'll Find a Boy (Girl)   Atteridge
(You Keep Your Eye On Me and) I'll Keep My Eye on
    You   Carroll
I'll Marry a Sunshine Girl   Goetz
I'll Sit Right on the Moon   Monaco
I'll Take a Ragtime Tune   Goetz
I'll Take You Back to Ireland   Carroll
I'm a Do-Right Woman Looking for a Do-Right Man   Leslie
I'm a Lonesome Romeo   Goetz
I'm Afraid, Pretty Maid, I'm Afraid   Berlin
I'm Crazy 'bout Somebody   Buck
I'm Going Back to Dixie   Atteridge
I'm Going Back to Dixie (I Want to Be in Dixie)   Berlin;
    Snyder
I'm Going Back to Kentucky Sue   Brown, Lew
I'm Going Down to Tennessee   Carroll
I'm Saving My Kisses   Atteridge
I'm the Lonesomest Gal in Town   Brown, Lew
I'm the Villain   Porter
In 2010   Atteridge
In a Dixie Land with Dixie Lou   Meyer
In After Years   Young, Joseph
In Banjo Land   Clarke; Schwartz, Jean
In My Birch Bark Canoe   Goetz; Norworth
In My Birch Bark Canoe (With Emmy Lou)   Goetz
In Sapphire Seas   Friml; Harbach
In Spirit Land   Smith, Harry B.; Smith, Robert B.
In the Cool of the Evenin'   Buck
In the Golden Harvest Time   Meyer
In the Good Old Used to Be   Cobb; Edwards
Indian Rag, The   Brown, A. Seymour
It Must Be Love   Meyer
Italy   Meyer
It's All Over Now   Atteridge; Lewis
It's Awful Hard When Mother's Not Along   Porter
It's My Business to Know Them All   Leslie; Meyer
It's Perfectly All Right   Smith, Harry B.; Smith, Robert B.
It's the Girl Behind the Man   Von Tilzer
I've Got to Have Some Lovin' Now   Berlin

I've Take Such a Fancy to You   Kern
Jack O' Lantern Love   Herbert
Jolly Good Fellow   Smith, Robert B.
Just a Little Lovin' for Baby Please   Sterling; Von Tilzer
Just Love Me All the Time   Herbert
Just Say that You Will Miss Me   Howard, Joseph E.
Just You and I in Dreamland   Herbert
Kangaroo Hop, The   Atteridge
Keep Away from the Fellow Who Owns an
      Automobile   Berlin
Kiss Me Again, Bebe   Atteridge
Kiss Me and 'Tis Day   Friml; Harbach
Kuddles and Kisses   Edwards
La Belle Paree   Goetz
La Clare de la Lune   Goetz
Ladies Fair   Friml; Harbach
Lady of the Slipper, The   Herbert
Lamb's Star Gambol (inst.), The   Herbert
Last Night   Sterling
Last Night Was the End of the World   Sterling; Von Tilzer
Latest Thing from Paris, The   Friml; Harbach
Laugh and Let the Clouds Roll By   Cobb; Schwartz, Jean
Lead Me to that Beautiful Band   Berlin
Lead Me to that Beautiful Land   Goetz
Leaders of Society   Porter
Let Me Be the First One Dearie   Bryan; Fisher
Let Me Show You Paris   Atteridge
Let Us Build a Little Nest   Kern
Let's Go to Savannah, Ga.   Gilbert
Letter, The   Atteridge
Levee Lou   Edwards
Liberty Hall   Smith, Robert B.
(Love Me) Like a Real, Real Man   Herbert
Little Bit of Everything   Berlin
Little Girl at Home   Herbert
Little Girl Who Couldn't Care   Goetz
Little Golden Maid   Kern
Llewellyn   Porter
Loie and Chlodo   Porter
Lonely Moon   Goetz
Longing for Dear Old Broadway   Porter
Lost a Heart   Smith, Robert B.
Louisiana   Smith, Harry B.
Love for a Day   Howard, Joseph E.
Love Is Like a Firefly   Friml; Harbach
Loveland Express, The   Atteridge
Lovely Daughter of Allah   Johnson, J. Rosamond
Lovely Heroine, The   Porter
Love's Dreamy Strain   Brown, A. Seymour
Love's Hour   Herbert
Lyre-Bird and the Jay, The   Goetz
Marie-Louise   Kern
Marry a Sunshine Girl   Goetz
Marry a Yiddisher Boy   Brown, A. Seymour
Meet Me at Eight in the Hall   Atteridge
Meet Me at the Stage Door   Goetz
Meow! Meow! Meow!   Herbert
Merry Merry Maids of the Old Front Row, The   Atteridge
Merry Wedding Bells   Schwartz, Jean
Metropolitan Squak-tette, The   Atteridge
Million, The   Smith, Harry B.
Million Dollar Ball   Berlin; Goetz
Mind the Paint   Kern
Minstrel Parade, The   Goetz

Mister Fortune Tellin' Man   Monaco
Model Married Pair   Smith, Harry B.; Smith, Robert B.
Modern Love   Atteridge
Money Talks   Smith, Robert B.
Month of June Is a Song of Love, The   Kahn
Moon, Lovely Moon   Smith, Robert B.
Mother Doesn't Know   Smith, Harry B.
Moulin Rouge Roulette   Atteridge
Mr. Pagliacci   Atteridge
Mr. Pagliatch   Edwards
Mr. Yankee Doodle   Atteridge
Mr. Yankee Doodle Do the Do Do   Schwartz, Jean
My Broadway Romeo   Buck
My Empty Arms   Egan; Whiting
My Hat's in the Ring   Williams
My Heather Belle   Goetz
My Hero (Parody)   Goetz
My Houseboat on the Thames   Porter
My Irish Girl   Bryan
My Leader Man   Gilbert; Motzan
My Little Lady Bug   Smith, Harry B.
My Lonely Rose   Edwards
My Man   Conrad; Young, Joseph
My Music Teacher   Lewis; Meyer
My Oriental Rose   Atteridge
My Peaches and Cream   Kern
My Reuben Girlie   Atteridge
My Russian Girlski   Herbert
My Salvation Army Queen   Porter
My Sweet Italian Man   Berlin
Myrella   Smith, Harry B.; Smith, Robert B.
'Neath the Mississippi Moon   Meyer
New York Isn't Such a Bad Old Town   Jerome; Schwartz, Jean
Night Brigade, The   Goetz
Night the Old Cow Died, The   Goetz
Now His Choice We See   Smith, Robert B.
Nurses Are We   Kern
Oh, Doctor   Smith, Harry B.; Smith, Robert B.
Oh, Honorka   Atteridge
Oh John   Monaco; Sterling
Oh Mister Dream Man   Atteridge
Oh Shush   Gilbert
Oh that Strain   Gilbert
Oh What a Night   Gilbert
Oh What I'm Going to Do to You   Clarke; Leslie
Oh You Beautiful Spring   Kern
Oh You Beauty   Leslie
Oh You Little Bo-Peep Won't You Let Me Be One of Your
      Sheep   Leslie
Oh You Little Rascal   Leslie; Meyer
Old-Time Ball, The   Goetz
On a Beautiful Night with a Beautiful Girl   Cobb; Edwards
On the Mississippi   Carroll
On the Stage   Goetz
One in a Million Like You   Smith, Harry B.
One of the Boys   Smith, Harry B.; Smith, Robert B.
Only Lonely   Whiting
Only One Waltz   Smith, Robert B.
Ooo, Ooo, Lena   Kern
Paree's a Branch of Broadway   Atteridge
Paris, The Return   Smith, Harry B.; Smith, Robert B.
Parisian Ball, The   Brown, Lew
Parisienne   Brown, Lew
Peck's Bad Boy   Leslie

Peg o' My Heart   Bryan; Fisher
Pick, Pick, Pick on the Mandolin, Antonio   Berlin
Pinkerton Detective Moon   Norworth
Pirates and Quaker Girl   Atteridge
Please Don't Take My Lovin' Man Away   Brown, Lew
Plunk! Plunk! Plunk! On Your Little Guitar   Brown, A. Seymour
Policeman's Lot Is a Happy One, A   Atteridge
Popsey Wopsey   Smith, Harry B.; Smith, Robert B.
Prima Donnas, The   Goetz
Princess of Far-Away   Herbert
Punchbowl Glide, The   Herbert
Put on Your Old High Hat   Jerome; Von Tilzer
Put Your Best Foot Forward Little Girl   Herbert
Queens of Terpsichore   Porter
Rachel Rubenstein's Rag   Lewis; Meyer
Rag Me Around   Goetz
Rag Time Eyes   Clarke; Schwartz, Jean
Ragging the Baby to Sleep   Gilbert
Ragtime Boxing Match   Atteridge
Ragtime Cowboy Joe   Clarke
Ragtime Engineer, The   Lewis
Ragtime Eyes   Schwartz, Jean
Ragtime Jockey Man   Berlin
Ragtime Mocking Bird   Berlin
Ragtime Restaurant, The   Kern
Ragtime Sextette   Berlin
Ragtime Soldier Man   Berlin
Ragtime Wagon of Love, The   Jerome; Von Tilzer
Rainy Days   Schwartz, Jean
Rap, Rap, Rap, On Your Minstrel Bones   Brown, Lew
Regimental Roly Poly Girl, The   Goetz
Ride Me Around with You, Dearie   Atteridge
Riders of Every Nation   Smith, Robert B.
Ring-a-Ting-a-ling on the Telephone   Jerome; Schwartz, Jean
Roll Me Around Like a Hoop My Dear   Bryan; Fisher
Roll on Missouri   Goetz
Roller Rinkers   Atteridge
Romantic Girl   Smith, Harry B.
Romeo, My Only Romeo   Buck
Rose of Pyramid Land   Goetz
Roses Bloom for Lovers   Smith, Robert B.
Rosie   Goetz
Row, Row, Row   Jerome; Monaco
Rum, Tum Fidele   Atteridge
Saint Vitus Rag, The   Johnson, J. Rosamond
Scandal   Porter
Scandal of the Flowers   Edwards
Senorita   Goetz
Serenade   Smith, Harry B.; Smith, Robert B.
Serenade Me, Sadie   Young, Joseph
Sergeant Philip of the Dancers   Kern
She Believes I'm in Brooklyn Tonight   Norworth
She Believes in Brooklyn Tonight   Goetz
She Was a Fair Young Mermaid   Porter
Silver Moon   Porter
Since the Days of Grandmama   Kern
Since We've Met   Porter
Singer and the Song, The   Goetz
Single   Brown, A. Seymour; Young, Joseph
Sleeping Chair, The   Smith, Harry B.; Smith, Robert B.
Sliding Through the Old Stage Door   Jerome; Von Tilzer
Snap Your Fingers and Away You Go   Jerome; Von Tilzer
Snowdrops and the Spring   Atteridge

So Away with Sorrow   Atteridge
So Let Us Hail   Porter
So Long Sue   Cobb; Edwards
Society   Goetz
Society Circus Parade   Buck
Soldier of Bohemia, A   Smith, Robert B.
Some Boy   Buck
Somebody Else Is Gettin' It   Sterling; Von Tilzer
Somebody Else Will If You Don't   Bryan
Someone I Used to Know   Atteridge
Someone Is Coming from Dixie   Goetz
Something   Friml; Harbach
Something I Can't Explain   Jerome
Something Like This   Smith, Harry B.; Smith, Robert B.
Something Tells Me You Will Break My Heart   Brown, Lew
Something that I Can't Explain   Schwartz, Jean
Song of the Cocktail   Goetz
Spark of Life Dance, The   Atteridge
Spring and Fall   Berlin
Stage Door Number   Smith, Harry B.
Steinland   Goetz
Stork, Stork   Smith, Robert B.
String a Ring of Roses 'Round Your Rosie   Jerome; Schwartz, Jean
Strolling   Porter
Submarine   Porter
Sunny Rag, The   Jerome; Von Tilzer
Supposing I Make You Wait 'Till We Get Married   Bryan
Suzanne, Suzanne   Smith, Harry B.; Smith, Robert B.
Swanee Shore   Gilbert
Sweethearts, Wives and Goodfellows   Smith, Robert B.
Sweetie Sweet   Leslie; Meyer
Sympathy   Friml; Harbach
Take a Little Tip from Father   Berlin; Snyder
Take Me in Your Arms and Say You Love Me   Johnson, J. Rosamond
Take Me to that Swanee Shore   Gilbert
Tangoland Tap   Schwartz, Jean
Tangolango Tap   Clarke
Telephone Song   Smith, Robert B.
Temperament   Smith, Harry B.; Smith, Robert B.
Tennis   Goetz
That Broadway Glide   Brown, A. Seymour
That Chopstick Rag   Clarke; Schwartz, Jean
That Coontown Quartette   Clarke; Schwartz, Jean
That Dramatic Rag   Ruby; Young, Joseph
That Funny Oo-la-la   Bryan; Fisher
That Mellow Melody   Lewis; Meyer
That Ragtime Regimental Band   Brown, A. Seymour
That Rainbow Rag   Porter
That Shakesperian Rag   Buck
That Society Bear   Berlin
That Swaying Tango   Brown, A. Seymour
That Syncopated Boogie-Boo   Lewis; Meyer
That Tangalo Tap   Schwartz, Jean
That Wonderful Tune   Clarke; Schwartz, Jean
That Zip Cornwall Cooch   Porter
That's How I Love You   Berlin
That's My Personality   Brown, Lew
That's the Kind of Fellow That I Could Love   Brown, A. Seymour
That's the Time You'll Think of Me   Brown, Lew
Them Was the Childhood Days   Herbert
There You Have New York Town   Atteridge

There'll Be More than Sleighbells Ringing when the Snow Falls   Lewis

There's One in a Million Like You   Clarke; Schwartz, Jean

They All Kept Time with Their Feet   Edwards

Those Wonderful Eyes   Howard, Joseph E.

Tommy Atkins   Friml; Harbach

Trip to Bermuda, A   Friml; Harbach

Trolley Car Swing, The   Young, Joseph

True Born Soldier Man   Berlin

Turn Down the Light   Kahn

Twilight   Porter

Twirly Little Girlies at the End of the Line, The   Herbert

Two Heads Are Better than One   Goetz

Two Little Lonesome Birds Love Birds   Brown, Lew

Under the Love Tree   Brown, A. Seymour

Under the Ragtime Flag   Goetz

Vienna Roll   Smith, Harry B.; Smith, Robert B.

Villain Still Pursued Her, The   Jerome; Von Tilzer

Virtue Is It's Own Reward   Smith, Harry B.; Smith, Robert B.

Wait Until Your Daddy Comes Home   Berlin

Waiting for Me   Atteridge

Waiting for the Robert E. Lee   Gilbert

Walk This Way   Schwartz, Jean

Waltz Me Around and Around in the Old Ball Room   Howard, Joseph E.

Way Down in C-U-B-A   Norworth

We Are So Aesthetic   Porter

We Are the Chorus of the Show   Porter

Wedding Glide, The   Atteridge

We'll Barricade Her   Friml; Harbach

We're Goin' to Have a Ragtime Wedding   Leslie

We're Going to Make a Man of You   Friml; Harbach

We've Been to Europe   Atteridge

What a Charming Afternoon   Porter

What About It?   Atteridge

What an Awful Hullabaloo   Porter

What Happened to Mary   Goetz

What Made the Boys Like Rosie?   Brown, A. Seymour

When a Boy without a Girl Meets a Girl without a Boy   Meyer

When a Maid Comes Knocking at Your Heart   Friml; Harbach

When Dear Old Santa Claus Comes to Town   Jerome; Von Tilzer

When I Get You Alone Tonight   Fisher

When I Lost You   Berlin

When I Used to Lead the Ballet   Porter

When I Waltz With You   Bryan

When I Was a Kid Like You   Cobb; Edwards

When I'm Thinking of You   Berlin

When I'm Waltzing   Goetz

When Jack Comes Sailing Home Again   Kahn

When Johnson's Quartette Harmonize   Berlin

When the Girl's Got Your Heart and You Haven't Got the Girl   Bryan; Fisher

When the Henry Clay Comes Steaming into Mobile Bay   Clarke; Jerome; Schwartz, Jean

When the Midnight Choo-Choo Leaves for Alabam'   Berlin

When Two Hearts Beat Together   Smith, Robert B.

When Was there Ever a Night Like This   Atteridge

When You Get It Tuned Up Play Us Something   Leslie

When You Meet Them on Broadway   Smith, Harry B.

When You Said How Do You Do   Goetz

When You're Away   Brown, A. Seymour; Young, Joseph

When You're Married   Bryan

Where Can I Meet You Next Summer   Gilbert

Where the Eidelweiss Is Blooming   Goetz

Which Shall I Choose   Atteridge

Whippoorwill   Bryan

Whistle It   Bryan; Clarke; Schwartz, Jean

Who Wants to Meet Me After School Lets Out   Cobb; Edwards

Who's Afraid of You   Brown, Lew

Whose Little Baby Boy Are You   Young, Joseph

Whose Little Girl Are You Now   Brown, Lew

Winsome Widow   Edwards

Witch Ballet   Herbert

Woman's Smile, A   Friml; Harbach

Wops My Dear   Leslie

Yiddisha Professor   Berlin

Yiddishe Turkey Trot   Carroll

Yodel Song   Smith, Harry B.

You Got to Keep A-Goin'   Bryan; Schwartz, Jean

You Got to Stop a Pickin' on My L'il Pickaninny   Edwards

You Gotta Keep Movin' and Dance (You Gotta Keep a' Going)   Smith, Harry B.

You May Be Irish Murphy, But I Think That You're In Dutch   Bryan; Fisher

You Might As Well Stay on Broadway   Smith, Harry B.

You Never Could Tell We Were Married   Atteridge

You Should Have Most Everything   Smith, Harry B.

You'll Have to Do the Turkey Trot to Captivate the Men   Buck

You're a Great Big Blue Eyed Baby Boy   Brown, A. Seymour

You're a Regular Girl   Brown, A. Seymour

You're My Baby   Brown, A. Seymour; Goetz

You're My Little Baby Girl   McHugh

You're on the Right Road   Smith, Harry B.

You're Some Girl   Brown, A. Seymour

You're the Girl   Clarke; Leslie; Schwartz, Jean

You're the Only Girl He Loves   Kern

Zingaras, The   Goetz

1913

Abie Sings an Irish Song   Berlin

Absinthe   Porter

Absinthe Drip, The   Porter

Adam and Eve Had a Wonderful Time   Brown, A. Seymour

After All You've Been a Pretty Good Pal   Johnson, Howard

Afternoon   Friml; Harbach

All Aboard   Goetz

All Aboard for Dixieland   Friml; Harbach; Yellen

All in a Little Dance   Atteridge

All Over You   Bryan

Alone at Last   Kern; Smith, Harry B.

Alpine Girl, The   Goetz

Always Take a Girl Named Daisy ('Cause Daisies Won't Tell)   Bryan; Lewis; Meyer

Ancient Minstrel, The   Atteridge

Angelus, The   Herbert; Smith, Robert B.

Anna 'Lize's Wedding Day   Berlin

Apple Tree and the Bumble Tree, The   Berlin

As I Love You   Porter

As Long As the World Goes Round, I Will Love You   Sterling; Von Tilzer

Asia   Goetz

At Mammy's Fireside   Carroll

At that Bully Wooly Wild West Show   Clarke; Leslie

At the Dawn Tea   Porter
At the Flower Garden Ball   Atteridge; Schwartz, Jean
At the Midnight Masquerade   Brown, Lew
At the Picture Show   Berlin; Goetz
At the Yiddish Cabaret   Gilbert
At Twilight   Friml
Aurora Blushing Rosily   Herbert
Awakening, The   Johnson, J. Rosamond
Babette of Beaujolais   Herbert
Back to the Days of Auld Lang Syne   Dubin
Baltimo'   Razaf
Barn-Yard Harmony   Clarke; Schwartz, Jean
Beedle-Dum Boo   Young, Joseph
Beware of the Sophomore   Porter
Big Chief Alimony   Williams; Young, Joseph
Big Red Motor and the Little Blue Limousine   Whiting
Bring Back Your Love   Atteridge; Schwartz, Jean
Bring Me Back My Lovin' Honey Boy   Yellen
Brittany   Smith, Harry B.
Broadway   Brown, Lew
Broadway Honeymoon, A   Howard, Joseph E.
Bubble, The   Friml
Bubbles, The   Harbach
Butterfly   Atteridge; Schwartz, Jean
Buttons on Her Blouse   Atteridge
Buttons on Her Shoes   Atteridge; Schwartz, Jean
By the Country Side   Kern
By the Rio Grande   Brown, A. Seymour
Bye and Bye You Will Miss Me   Buck
Call Me Baby   Williams; Young, Joseph
Calling of the Sea, The   Olcott
Came from Germany   Atteridge
Canzonetta   Herbert
Captain Kidd   Goetz
Carolina Jane   Johnson, J. Rosamond
Carolina Lou   Atteridge; Schwartz, Jean
Cedro (My Italian Romeo)   Sterling; Von Tilzer
'Cello Man   Whiting
Chaperons   Porter
Chase Me, I'm Single   Williams; Young, Joseph
Chic, Chic, Chic, Chic, Chicken   Buck
Chi-Chi   Friml; Harbach
Come Around and Make Love to Me   Brown, A. Seymour
Come Hither Eyes   Friml; Harbach
Come On Over Here   Kern; Smith, Harry B.
Come to Your Daddy   Gilbert
Come Up Tonight   Kalmar
Come with Me to the Tango Tea   Conrad
Companions, I Have Summoned You   Herbert
Cotton Pickin' Time in Tennessee   Howard, Joseph E.
Cricket on the Hearth   Herbert; Smith, Robert B.
Crocodile Crawl   Egan
'Cross the Great Divide, I'll Wait for You   Lewis; Meyer
(My) Cubist Girl   Goetz
Cupid's Soldiers   Atteridge
Curly Head   Lewis; Meyer
Cutey Boy   Williams; Young, Joseph
Daddy Come Home   Berlin
Daisy Time   Young, Victor
Dance Eccentrique (dance)   Herbert
Dearie If You'll Marry Me   Brown, A. Seymour
Deuce Young Man, The   Herbert
Die Susse Pariserin   Kern
Ding Dong   Atteridge
Dixiana Rose, The   Friml; Harbach

Do You Know?   Herbert
Do You Take This Woman for Your Lawful Wife   Sterling; Von Tilzer
Don't Be Rash   Atteridge
Don't Blame It All on Broadway   Williams; Young, Joseph
Don't Do Anything That You'll Be Sorry For   Conrad
Don't Let It Happen Again   Bryan
Don't You Go   Bryan
Down in Chattanooga   Berlin
Down in Monkeyville   Clarke; Leslie
Down Old Harmony Way   Monaco
Down on Uncle Jasper's Farm   Monaco
Dr. Grouch Is Going Away   Friml; Harbach
Duodessimalogue   Porter
Each Pearl a Thought   Kern; Smith, Harry B.
Ensemble   Goetz
Entrance of Sylvia   Herbert; Smith, Robert B.
Ever Since You Told Me that You Loved Me I'm a Nut — I'm a Nut   Clarke; Leslie; Schwartz, Jean
Every Lover Must Meet His Fate   Herbert; Smith, Robert B.
Everybody Snap Your Fingers with Me   Kalmar
Everybody Sometime Must Love Somebody   Buck
Everybody Sometime Must Love Someone   Buck
Everyone in Town Loves My Girl   Brown, Lew
Everything Is Different Now-a-days   Buck
Ev'rybody but Me   Johnson, J. Rosamond
Far Up the Hill   Herbert
Farewell, Dear Toys   Kern
Farm Days   Young, Joseph
Faust Up to Date   Goetz
Floradora Slide   Atteridge
Flow Along River Tennessee, to the Home of the Girl I Love   Bryan
Flower Garden Ball   Schwartz, Jean
Flower Maidens   Porter
Follow the Midnight Girl   Goetz
Fool There Was, A   Dubin
Foolish Cinderella Girl   Atteridge; Schwartz, Jean
Foolishness   Smith, Harry B.
For Days and Days   Kalmar
For Every Lover   Herbert; Smith, Robert B.
From the Meadow's Fairest Flower   Atteridge
Game of Love   Herbert; Smith, Robert B.
Gee I Wish I Was Big   Von Tilzer
Girl, a Boy and Moonlight, A   Brown, A. Seymour
Give Me Something in a Uniform of Blue   Goetz
Give Me the Hudson Shore   Atteridge
Go Get that Guy   Williams; Young, Joseph
Goddess of Mine   Herbert
Golden Stairs of Love, The   Atteridge; Schwartz, Jean
Gone   Kahn
Good Bye Everybody   Smith, Harry B.
Goodbye Boys   Jerome; Sterling; Von Tilzer
Good-Bye My True Love   Porter
Goodbye Poor Old Manhattan   Goetz
Gum Shoe Man, The   Sterling; Von Tilzer
Hail, Franz of Zilania   Herbert; Smith, Harry B.; Smith, Robert B.
Hail of the Friendly Songs, The   Herbert
Happiest Moment of My Life, When I Kissed Another Man's Wife — My Mother, The   Bryan
Happy Little Country Girl   Berlin
Have an Old Waltz with Me   Kern; Smith, Harry B.
He Blew on His Bugle-e-oo   Clarke; Leslie; Schwartz, Jean
He Never Took a Lesson in His Life   Fisher

He Ran Upstairs, Took a Look, and Ran Right Down
Again Kalmar

He Wants Someone to Call Him Papa, She Wants Someone
to Call Her Ma Gilbert

He'd Have to Get Under, Get Out and Get Under (To Fix
His Automobile) Clarke; Leslie

Hello, Hello Atteridge

He's Mah Dancing Man Howard, Joseph E.

He's on a Boat that Sails Last Wednesday (He's Coming
Home) Brown, Lew

He's So Good Buck

He's So Good to Me Berlin

High Jinks Friml; Harbach

High Jinks Tango Friml; Harbach

High Society Atteridge

Hola! Hola! Smith, Harry B.

Honey Behave Brown, A. Seymour

Honey Come and Love Me Some More Johnson, J.
Rosamond

Honeymoon Lane Kern

Honolulu Hula Boola Boo Edwards

How Late Can You Stay Out Tonight Fisher

How Long Have You Been Married? Brown, A. Seymour

How's de Mammy? Kalmar

How's Your Little Maltese Cat Gilbert

I Can Live Without You Buck

I Cannot Live Forever So You'd Better Love Me
Now Brown, Lew

I Can't Forget Your Eyes Kern; Smith, Harry B.

I Can't Keep My Eyes from Looking at You Atteridge

I Don't Know How I Do It but I Do Herbert; Smith, Harry
B.; Smith, Robert B.

I Don't Want To (Oh, Come On) Brown, A. Seymour

I Had a Devil of a Time Jerome; Von Tilzer

I Have Courted in Vain Atteridge

I Know and She Knows Kern; Smith, Harry B.

I Know Your Husband Very Well Friml; Harbach

I Love Her, Oh! Oh! Oh! Monaco

I Love the Moonlight Carroll

I Might Be Your Once-in-a-While Herbert; Smith, Robert B.

I Miss You Most of All Monaco

I Never Heard of Anybody Dying from a Kiss Did You
Sterling; Von Tilzer

I Never Knew Williams; Young, Joseph

I Never Met a Beautiful Girl Till I Met You Jerome;
Schwartz, Jean

I Should Have Met You a Long Time Ago Brown, Lew

I Want a Ragtime Bungalow Kalmar

I Want a Toy Soldier Man Atteridge; Schwartz, Jean

I Want the Strolling Good Atteridge; Schwartz, Jean

I Want to Go Home Gilbert

I Was Aviating Around Berlin

I Wish You'd Keep Out of My Dreams Clarke; Leslie;
Schwartz, Jean

I'd Like to Borrow a Kiss Atteridge

I'd Like to Build a Coop for a Chicken Like You Carroll

I'd Like to Have a Photograph of You Fisher

If a Table at Rector's Could Talk Cobb

If All the Girls I Knew Were Like You Berlin

If He Looks Good to Mother (Don't Look for
Another) Lewis; Meyer

If I Came Back to You and Said I'm Sorry Cobb; Edwards

If I Could Have You Now Bryan

If I Were in Love with You Edwards

If It Wasn't for Mother Love Bryan

If the Moon Was a Great Big Banjo Buck

If We Were on Our Honeymoon (Railway Duet) Kern;
Smith, Harry B.

If You Don't Want Me Why Do You Hand Around? Berlin

If You'll Let Me Be Your Husband, I'll Let You Be My
Wife Edwards

I'll Do More than That for You Fisher

I'll Get You Cobb; Edwards

I'm a Little Bit Afraid of You Broadway Von Tilzer

I'm Afraid I'm Beginning to Love You Brown, Lew

I'm Crying Just for You Monaco

I'm Goin' to Stay Right Here in Town Bryan

I'm Going Away Kern; Smith, Harry B.

I'm Going to Meet Minnie Tonight Carroll; Cobb

I'm Going to Spend My Honeymoon in Dixie Brown, Lew

I'm in Love with the Mother of My Best Girl Kahn

I'm Looking for an Irish Husband Kern

I'm Looking for One Honey Edwards

I'm on My Way to Mandalay Bryan; Fisher

I'm on the Jury Kahn

I'm Really Disappointed with America Buck

I'm Saving My Love for You Bryan

I'm Through with Roaming Romeos Friml; Harbach

Imitator's Rag (inst.) Johnson, James P.

In June Kahn

In My Garden of Eden for Two Goetz

In My Harem Berlin

In November or December I Will Marry You Conrad;
Young, Joseph

In the Convent They Never Taught Me That Herbert;
Smith, Robert B.

In the Heart of the Kentucky Hills Gilbert

In the Land Where My Heart Was Born Porter

In the Life of a Working Girl Atteridge

In the Movies Smith, Harry B.

In the Shade of the Lemon Tree Goetz

Inauguration Day Atteridge

Interlude Goetz

International Rag, The Berlin

Iron! Iron! Iron! (Opening Chorus) Herbert; Smith, Robert
B.

Is This Love at Last Friml; Harbach

Isch Ka Bibble (I Should Worry) Lewis

Isch Ka-Bibble (I Should Worry) Meyer

Isle o' Dreams Olcott

It Is I Julia Dear Smith, Harry B.

It Takes a Little Rain with the Sunshine to Make the World
Go Round Carroll

It Won't Be the Same Old Broadway Atteridge; Schwartz,
Jean

It's a Grand Old Life Jerome; Schwartz, Jean

I've Been Through the Mill Gilbert

I've Found the Girl I Want Dubin

I've Got a Little Chalet in the Valley Goetz

I've Got Money in the Bank Kern

Ivy and the Oak, The Herbert; Smith, Robert B.

Jake - Jake Berlin

Jeannette and Her Little Wooden Shoes (Sabot Dance) (Clip
Clop Clop) (Wooden Shoes Dance) Herbert; Smith,
Robert B.

Jim Friml; Harbach

Jockey Song Buck

Just a Home Sweet Home Girl Jerome; Schwartz, Jean

Just You and I and the Moon Buck

Kathleen Aroon Olcott

Katy-Did   Kern; Smith, Harry B.
Keep on Walking   Berlin
Keep Your Golden Gate Wide Open   Edwards
Kelly's Are at It Again, The   Norworth; Williams
Ki-I-Youdling Dog   Schwartz, Jean
Kiss Me Good Night (Out the Window You Must
      Go)   Brown, Lew
Kiss Me I've Never Been Kissed Before   Kalmar
Kiss Your Sailor Boy Good-Bye   Berlin
Kisses That I Have Missed   Atteridge
Ki-Yi-Yodeling Dog, The   Berlin
Kranko Waltz   Atteridge
Land of My Own Romance   Herbert; Smith, Robert B.
Later On, Some Day   Monaco
Le Poeme (inst.)   Romberg
Leg of Mutton (inst.)   Romberg
Levi Is a Grand Old Name   Goetz
Life Without Love   Friml; Harbach
Light of the World Is Love   Whiting
Little Bit of Silk, A   Kern
Little Bunch of Shamrocks (I Am Holding in My Hand),
      A   Jerome; Sterling; Von Tilzer
Little Cabaret at Home, A   Atteridge; Schwartz, Jean
Little Church Around the Corner, The   Carroll
Little Miss Killarney   Edwards
Little Rag Baby Girl   Gilbert
Little Thing Like a Kiss, A   Kern; Smith, Harry B.
Lonesome Baby (I'm Coming Back to Town)   Brown, Lew
Look in Her Eyes   Kern
Love and I Are Playing   Herbert
Love Is a Story That's Old   Herbert
Love Is Just the Same Old Game in Every Land   Goetz
Love Me to a Viennese Melody   Goetz
Love Me While the Lovin' Is Good   Von Tilzer
Love the World Over Is Much the Same   Smith, Harry B.;
      Smith, Robert B.
Loveland   Smith, Harry B.
Love's Fairy Tales   Atteridge
Love's Flower Is Always Blooming   Atteridge
Love's Own Kiss   Friml; Harbach
Lucky Boy   Sterling; Von Tilzer
Lullaby   Atteridge
Magical Eyes   Lewis; Meyer
Maid of Santiago   Porter
Make a Hit with Mother, and You'll Make a Hit with
      Me   Gilbert
Make Me Love You   Meyer
Mama's Melody   Bryan
Mammy Jinny's Jubilee   Gilbert
Man Is Faithful Till He's Caught   Atteridge
March of the Mystic Shrine   Lewis; Meyer
Mary's Coming Home   Dubin
Maybe She Will Some Day   Bryan
Mechanical Lovin' Man   Ager
Meet Me Beside the River   Porter
Meet Me To-Morrow Night   Williams; Young, Joseph
Melodrama Known As Married Life   Atteridge; Schwartz,
      Jean
Member of the Yale Elizabethan Club, A   Porter
Mexican Love   Buck
Milestones   Goetz
Million Dollar Gambler from the West, The   Leslie
Miss Bell of the Telephone   Edwards
Mister Broadway U.S.A.   Goetz
Monkey Doodle   Goetz

Monkey Doodle Doo   Berlin
Monks' Quartette, The   Herbert; Smith, Robert B.
Moon Man   Porter
Moonlight on the Mississippi   Kahn
Moon-Path   Edwards
Mother Goose   Herbert; Smith, Robert B.
Mother Machree   Olcott
Moving Man, The   Atteridge
My Averne Rose   Goetz
My Blushing Rose   Buck
My Coca-Cola Belle   Atteridge; Schwartz, Jean
My Georgia Gal   Porter
My Heart for You Pines Away   Sissle
My Hidden Treasure   Kalmar
My Idea of a Girl   Edwards
My Irish Romeo   Atteridge; Schwartz, Jean
My Little Friend   Smith, Harry B.; Smith, Robert B.
My Mignonette   Dubin
My Otaheitee Lady   Kern
My Parcel Post Man   Kalmar
My Raggydore   Atteridge; Schwartz, Jean
My Yellow Jacket Girl   Atteridge; Schwartz, Jean
No Journey's Too Far for a Lover   Smith, Harry B.; Smith,
      Robert B.
No One Knows Where Kelly Went   Bryan
Not Now, but Later   Friml; Harbach
Now and Then   Smith, Harry B.
Now Is the South Wind Blowing   Herbert
Now that You've Got Me, What Are You Going to
      Do   Williams; Young, Joseph
Oh How That Taxi Got on My Nerves   Atteridge
Oh! Mrs. Fortune Teller, Please Find My Lovin'
      Man   Brown, Lew
Oh Play that Umpah, Umpah, Umpah   Von Tilzer
Oh! Those Arabian Nights   Atteridge; Schwartz, Jean
Oh, Up! It's Up!   Herbert
Oh, What a Pretty Pair of Lovers   Porter
Oh What'll I Do with You   Conrad
Oh, You Million Dollar Doll   Clarke; Leslie
Oh, You Sweet, Sweet Boy   Johnson, J. Rosamond
Oh You Wedding Belle   Howard, Joseph E.
Old Clarinet, The   Kern; Smith, Harry B.
Old Home Week in My Home Town   Gilbert
Old Maid's Ball, The   Berlin
On My Chicken Farm   Von Tilzer
On Parade   Herbert; Smith, Robert B.
On the Lonely Lagoon   Edwards
On the Old Fall River Line   Jerome; Sterling; Von Tilzer
One Little Sweet Little Girl   Dubin
One My Yacht   Porter
Only a Broken Toy   Cobb; Edwards
Opening Act Two (Russian Dance) (inst.)   Kern
Oriental Bacchanale, The   Atteridge
Oui, Oui, Marie, Oui, Oui   Brown, Lew
Our Little Cabaret Up Home   Clarke; Schwartz, Jean
Our Little Man at Home Sweet Home   Leslie
Over the Garden Wall   Kalmar
Over the Ocean   Goetz
Papa   Smith, Harry B.
Parcel Post Man   Atteridge; Schwartz, Jean
Paris, Oh Festive Land   Atteridge
Passing Show Cakewalk   Schwartz, Jean
Pauline   Atteridge; Schwartz, Jean
Pianologue   Atteridge; Schwartz, Jean
Pilgrims of Love   Herbert; Smith, Robert B.

Poor Little Rich Girl, The   Brown, Lew
Pretty As a Picture   Herbert; Smith, Robert B.
Pretty One (Finale)   Herbert; Smith, Robert B.
Pullman Porters' Parade   Berlin
Ragging the Nursery Rhymes   Atteridge
Ragging the Traumerei   Gershwin, George
Ragtime Dream, The   Brown, Lew
Ragtime Express, The   Atteridge; Schwartz, Jean
Ragtime Honeymoon   Jerome; Schwartz, Jean
Ragtime Wedding Bells   Lewis; Meyer
Ragtime Yodeling Man, The   Goetz
Rainy Day, A   Goetz
Rebecca of Sunnybrook Farm   Brown, A. Seymour
Reverie   Edwards
Richard the Third   Gilbert
Rick-Chick-A-Chick   Porter
Rock, Rock, Rock, Keep on a-Rocking   Clarke; Leslie;
    Schwartz, Jean
Rocking in a Ragtime Beat   Sterling
Roll On Missouri   Carroll
Roll them Cotton Bales   Johnson, J. Rosamond
Romance Land   Atteridge; Schwartz, Jean
Rosalilla of Sevilla   Smith, Harry B.
Rose of Yesterday   Atteridge
Rum Tum Tiddle   Berlin
Russian Dance   Smith, Harry B.
Salvation Glide, The   Howard, Joseph E.
Salvation Nell   Clarke; Leslie
Same One They Picked for Me, The   Atteridge; Schwartz,
    Jean
San Diego   Edwards
San Francisco Bound   Berlin
Say Goodbye to Gay Paree   Brown, Lew
Say Goodbye to Your Traveling Man   Brown, Lew
Scandinavian Glide, The   Johnson, J. Rosamond
Serafina   Goetz
Serenade   Smith, Harry B.
Serpentine Dance, The   Goetz
She Loves Me Not   Jerome; Schwartz, Jean
She's the Girl   Brown, A. Seymour
She's Waiting for You to Love Her All the Time   Monaco
Sidonie   Kern; Smith, Harry B.
Since I Found You   Gershwin, George
Since Mrs. McNott Learned to Do the Turkey Trot   Jerome;
    Sterling; Von Tilzer
Since My Margarette Became A-Da-Suffragette   Cobb;
    Edwards
Sit Down, You're Rockin' the Boat   Clarke; Jerome;
    Schwartz, Jean; Williams
Snookey Ookums   Berlin
Some Smoke (inst.)   Romberg
Somebody Loves You   Brown, A. Seymour
Somebody's Coming to My House   Berlin
Something Seems Tingle-ingle-ing   Friml; Harbach
Song that Stole My Heart Away, The   Sterling; Von Tilzer
Southern Heart of Mine   Atteridge; Schwartz, Jean
Star of Love   Herbert
Stop Rocking the Boat   Goetz
Strong Heart   Atteridge
Sunshine and Roses   Kahn
Sway, Sway, Sway   Gilbert
Sweethearts (If You Ask Where Love Is Found)   Herbert;
    Smith, Robert B.
Sweethearts Waltzes   Herbert
Swing, Swing, Swing   Von Tilzer

Switzerland   Goetz
Syncopatia Land   Atteridge; Schwartz, Jean
Take Me Back   Berlin; Goetz
Take Me Back to Germany   Bryan
Take Me Back to Town   Atteridge
Tale of the Jealous Cat   Atteridge
Talk about This — Talk about That   Herbert; Smith, Robert
    B.
Tango Il Bacio (The Kiss Tango)   Lewis; Meyer
Tango Town   Bryan
Tell Me what Are You Fishing For   Monaco
Tempo Di Gavotte   Atteridge
Temporary Widow, The   Atteridge
Tennis Tournament   Atteridge; Schwartz, Jean
Texas Tommy Jubilee, The   Clarke; Leslie
That Gal of Mine   Atteridge
That Girl of Mine   Atteridge; Schwartz, Jean
That Good Old Fashioned Cake Walk   Schwartz, Jean
That Good Old Fashioned Cake Walk (Passing Show
    Cakewalk)   Atteridge
That Good Old Fashioned Cakewalk (Passing Show
    Cakewalk)   Atteridge
That Is Art   Herbert
That Is the Life for Me   Atteridge; Schwartz, Jean
That Little German Band   Fisher
That Naughty Melody   Lewis; Meyer
That Tango Tokio   Bryan
That Tea Time Tango Tune   Gilbert
That Tinkling Tango Tune   Brown, A. Seymour
That's Love with a Capital 'L'   Smith, Harry B.
That's the Reason I Want You   Bryan
That's the Way My Honey Boy Makes Love   Young, Joseph
That's Why I Never Go Home   Kalmar
That's Why I'm Crying Just for You   Monaco
Then I Want to Settle Down   Atteridge; Schwartz, Jean
Then I Wouldn't Have To Worry Any More   Bryan
There Is Magic in a Smile   Herbert; Smith, Robert B.
There Is Nothing Dear, I Wouldn't Do for You   Buck
There Was a Time   Bryan; Carroll
There's a Girl in Arizona   Berlin; Clarke; Leslie
There's a Girl in the Heart of Maryland (With a Heart that
    Belongs to Me)   Carroll
There's a Lot of Pretty Little Things in Paris   Goetz
There's a Wireless Station Down in My Heart   Monaco
There's Always a Girl Who Is Waiting   Atteridge
They Say They're Not Living Together   Brown, A. Seymour
They're on Their Honeymoon   Goetz
They've Got Me Doin' It Now   Berlin
Think of Me When I Am Near Not When I'm Far
    Away   Bryan
Three Favorite Airs   Herbert
To London   Atteridge
To Paris   Herbert
Tokio Rag   Goetz
Tootsie-Wootsie   Atteridge
Tra, La! La! La!   Berlin
Trail of the Lonesome Pine, The   Carroll
Tulip Time   Goetz
Tweedledum and Tweedledee   Herbert
Two-Lip Salve   Kalmar
Um Pom Toodle I-Ay   Jerome; Schwartz, Jean
Under the China Moon   Goetz
Under the Midnight   Dubin
Underneath the Cotton Moon   Lewis; Meyer
Underneath the Tango Moon   Carroll

Une Nuit in Paris   Goetz
Vale of Dreaming, The   Atteridge
Valse Parfumee (inst.)   Romberg
Value of Dreaming, The   Atteridge
Vengeance   Atteridge
Vous Etes Jolie   Atteridge
Wagner Couldn't Write a Ragtime Song   Jerome; Schwartz, Jean
Wait Until We're Married   Lewis; Meyer
Waiting for the Bride   Herbert; Smith, Robert B.
We Are Free   Atteridge
We Are Prom Girls   Porter
We Have Much to Be Thankful For   Berlin
Wedding of the Big Baboon, The   Buck
Weep No More My Lady (Because I Won't Take Your Loving Man Away)   Brown, Lew
Welcome Home   Berlin
Welcoming the Bride   Herbert; Smith, Robert B.
Well, This Is Jolly   Kern; Smith, Harry B.
We're a Group of Nonentities   Porter
We've Got a Parrot in Our House, Pretty Poll, Pretty Poll   Gilbert
What a Fool I'd Be   Jerome; Sterling; Von Tilzer
What Do You Say, Dolly Dear?   Smith, Harry B.
What She Wanted and What She Got   Herbert; Smith, Harry B.; Smith, Robert B.
What-Cha-Ma-Call-Em   Cobb; Edwards
What's the Good of Being Good   Von Tilzer
When Gaby Did the Gaby Glide   Atteridge; Schwartz, Jean
When God Gave Me You   Leslie
When I First Met You   Lewis; Meyer
When I Was Young   Smith, Harry B.; Smith, Robert B.
When Irish Eyes Are Smiling   Olcott
When It's Cotton Blossom Time, Sweet Rosalie   Sterling; Von Tilzer
When Love Comes Knocking at Your Heart   Brown, A. Seymour
When Michael Dooley Heard the Booley Booley   Jerome; Von Tilzer
When Sammy Sang the Marseillaise   Friml; Harbach
When the Grown Up Ladies Act Like Babies, I've Got to Love 'Em That's All   Lewis; Young, Joseph
When the Honey Moon Stops Shining   Atteridge; Schwartz, Jean
When the Love You Love Loves You   Howard, Joseph E.
When the Whole World Has Gone Back on You   Edwards
When Three Is Company (Cupid Song)   Kern
When You Haven't a Beautiful Girl   Clarke; Leslie
When You Leave Your Little Old New York   Jerome; Schwartz, Jean
When You Said Goodbye   Sterling; Von Tilzer
When You Speak of Love   Sterling; Von Tilzer
When You're on the Stage   Smith, Harry B.
When You're Traveling   Atteridge
Where Did You Get that Girl   Kalmar
Where Is She Now   Sterling; Von Tilzer
Where the Red, Red, Roses Grow   Jerome; Schwartz, Jean
Where Was Moses when the Lights Went Out   Leslie
While They Were Dancing Around   Monaco
Whistling Cowboy Joe   Atteridge
Why Did You Leave Me?   Dubin
Wifie of Your Own, A   Kern; Smith, Harry B.
Wiggle-Wagg   Lewis; Meyer
Wilhelm, the Grocer   Lewis; Meyer
Will It All End in Smoke?   Kern; Smith, Harry B.

Winged Love   Herbert
Within the Law   Dubin
Woman's Heart, A   Kern; Smith, Harry B.
Women of Temperment   Atteridge
Won't You Please Have a Heart   Sterling; Von Tilzer
Woof!   Bryan
World-Wide Romeo, A   Atteridge
Wriggly Rag   Goetz
You Are the Someone   Atteridge; Schwartz, Jean
You Can't Get Away from It   Clarke; Jerome; Schwartz, Jean
You Did, You Know You Did   Gilbert
You Know You Won't   Brown, A. Seymour
You Made Me Love You, I Didn't Want to Do It   Monaco
You Must Love Some One   Lewis; Meyer
You Picked a Bad Day Out to Say Good-Bye   Berlin
You'd Make a Wonderful Model for Me   Monaco
You'll Call the Next Love the First   Atteridge; Schwartz, Jean
You're a Good Little Devil   Leslie
You're Always in My Heart but You're Never By My Side   Bryan
You're Here and I'm Here   Kern; Smith, Harry B.
You're Just the Sort of Girl that I Could Love   Buck
You're Never Too Old To Love   Bryan; Jerome
You're So Fascinating   Smith, Harry B.
You're the Fairest Little Daisy that Grows in the Garden   Gilbert
You're the Most Wonderful Girl   Clarke; Leslie
You're the Same Old Girl   Williams; Young, Joseph
You've Got Your Mother's Big Blue Eyes   Berlin
Zis for You, Zat for You   Fisher

1914

Afternoon Tea, An   Atteridge; Carroll; Romberg
(I'd Like to Wander with) Alice in Wonderland   Kern; Smith, Harry B.
All Aboard   Atteridge
All for the Sake of a Girl   Herbert; Smith, Robert B.
All He Does Is Follow Them Around   Clarke
Allah's Holiday   Friml; Harbach
Alone at Last   Kern; Smith, Harry B.
Along Came Ruth   Berlin
Always Treat Her Like a Baby   Berlin
Amber Club, The   Atteridge
American Maxixe, The   Atteridge
And I Broke My Mother's Heart, All Over You   Bryan
And the Dream Comes True   Friml
And to Think I Left My Happy Home for You   Kalmar; Leslie
Angling   Harbach
Antoinette   Herbert
Any Old Night Is a Beautiful Night, If You're Out with a Beautiful Girl   Monaco
Army Club, The   Atteridge; Carroll; Romberg
At that Town Hall Minstrel Show   Kahn
At the Mississippi Cabaret   Brown, A. Seymour
Baby Love   Von Tilzer
Back, Back, Back to Indiana   Kahn
Back to Dixieland   Yellen
Back to the Carolina You Love   Clarke; Schwartz, Jean
Baker's Boy and the Chimney-Sweep, The   Herbert; Smith, Robert B.
Barnum & Bailey Rag   Cohan
Battle of B Flat, The   Herbert
Be Careful What You Do   Buck

Be Happy Boys Tonight   Herbert
Beautiful Eggs   Bryan
Because I Can't Tango   Buck
Beets and Turnips   Ahlert
Best Toast of All (Kiss Her and Look in Her Eyes),
    The   Harbach
Bingen on the Rhine   Bryan
Blarney   Kahn
Blue Bird Time   Brennan
Bohemian Rag   Atteridge; Romberg
Bought and Paid For   Kern; Smith, Harry B.
Boys All Fall for Me, The   Schwartz, Jean
Boys, Boys, Boys   Schwartz, Jean
Brave Hussar, The   Harbach
Bride   Friml; Harbach
Broadway Tipperary   Cohan
Broth of a Boy, A   Brennan
Bum Diddle-De-Um Bum, That's It   Monaco
But Still We Smile   Smith, Robert B.
Buy a Bale of Cotton for Me   Gilbert
Buying Little Things for Me   Atteridge; Carroll; Romberg
By the Beautiful Sea   Atteridge; Carroll
By the Zuyder Zee   Bryan
Caberavings   Whiting
California   Atteridge; Romberg
California and You   Leslie
Call Around Again   Herbert; Smith, Robert B.
Call of the Colors, The   Atteridge; Romberg
Call to the Colors, The   Carroll
Camp Meeting Band   Gilbert
Carnival at Nice   Smith, Robert B.
Celebratin' Day in Tennessee   Brown, Lew
Charms Are Fairest When They're Hidden   Friml; Harbach
Chatter, Chatter   Berlin
Chevy Chase (inst.), The   Blake
Chickens on Parade   Edwards
China Boy   Pollack
Chinese Celebration   Cohan; Schwartz, Jean
Cincinnati   Porter
Circassian Dance   Friml; Harbach
Clock, The   Smith, Harry B.
College Boy, A   Atteridge
Come On in the Dancing's Fine   Atteridge
Come Right Back to Me   Johnson, Howard
Come to the Land of the Argentine   Berlin
Compact, The   Herbert
Connubial Bliss   Herbert
Corrandoli Song   Smith, Robert B.
Cotton Pickin' Time in Dixieland Buy a Bale   Howard,
    Joseph E.
Crinoline Girl, The   Atteridge; Romberg
Cubist Opera, The   Herbert; Smith, Robert B.
Cupid Keeps the Love Light Buring   Smith, Robert B.
Dance Conceptions   Atteridge; Carroll; Romberg
Dance Eccentric   Atteridge
Dance Eccentrique   Atteridge; Carroll; Romberg
Dance Extraordinaire   Atteridge
Dance of the Fortune Wheel, The   Atteridge
Dancing Around (Opening Chorus Act I)   Atteridge;
    Romberg
Dancing Lesson, The   Herbert; Smith, Robert B.
Dancing Romeo, A   Atteridge
Dancing the Blues Away   Fisher; Johnson, Howard
Darktown Poker Club   Buck
Dear Old Daddy Long-Legs   Brennan

Dear Old Pet   Schwartz, Jean
Debutante   Romberg; Smith, Harry B.
Debutante One-Step   Herbert; Smith, Robert B.
Dignity   Pollack
Divertissement   Atteridge; Romberg
Do the Funny Fox Trot   Carroll
Dolores   Smith, Harry B.
Don't Hesitate with Me   Atteridge; Romberg
Don't Stop   Sterling; Von Tilzer
Don't You Dare to Call Me Up at Home   Brown, A.
    Seymour
Dove of Peace, The   Von Tilzer
Down By the Erie Canal   Cohan
Down in a Dungeon Deep   Porter
Down in Waterloo   Bryan
Down Lovers Lane   Porter
Dream Girl o' Mine   Olcott
Dreams of the Past   Atteridge; Romberg
Dresden China Soldiers   Porter
Eagle Rock, The   Atteridge; Carroll
Early Hours of the Morn   Atteridge
Edelweiss   Smith, Harry B.
Equal Rights   Herbert
Eugenie Girls   Atteridge; Romberg
Everybody Loves My Girl   Brown, Lew
Everybody Means It When They Say Good-Bye   Atteridge
Everybody Rag with Me   Kahn
Everybody Sometime Must Love Someone   Schwartz, Jean
Ev'ry Night You'll Find Her Painting New York Town   Bryan
Face Behind the Mask, The   Herbert; Smith, Robert B.
Fading Girl   Atteridge; Carroll; Romberg
Fashion Slave, A   Atteridge; Romberg
Fashion's Slave, A   Carroll
Fate   Herbert; Smith, Robert B.
Fatherland, the Motherland, the Land of My Best Girl, The
    Carroll
Fizz Water (inst.)   Blake
Flower Garden Ball, The   Schwartz, Jean
Flower Song   Porter
Flower Story, A   Young, Victor
Follow the Crowd   Berlin
Funny Little Tracks in the Snow   Porter
Furnishing a Home for Two   Berlin
Futurist Girl   Buck
Garden Gate Was Open (My Beautiful Rose Was Gone),
    The   Brennan
Garden of Girls   Atteridge; Carroll; Romberg
Gavotte No. 1 (inst.)   Carroll; Romberg
Gavotte No. 2 (inst.)   Carroll; Romberg
Gay Life, The   Herbert; Smith, Robert B.
Georgia   Bryan
Get One for Me   Brown, Lew
Girl of To-Day, The   Atteridge; Romberg
Girls that Win My Heart, The   Smith, Harry B.
God Gave You to Me   Berlin
Golden Age, The   Herbert; Smith, Robert B.
Good Bye Maria   Gilbert
Good Night   Buck
Good Old Levee Days   Atteridge; Carroll
Good Ship Mary Ann, The   Kahn
Good-Bye, Good-Bye, London Town   Atteridge
Goodnight   Friml; Harbach
Goodnight Little Girl, Goodnight   Dubin
Grand Canal   Atteridge; Carroll
Grand Old Life   Schwartz, Jean

Grape Dance, The   Atteridge; Romberg
Hail to Cyril   Porter
Hammershine   Herbert
Hands Off   Sterling; Von Tilzer
Haunted House   Berlin
Have a Heart   Cohan
He Is Sweet, He Is Good   Atteridge; Carroll; Romberg
He Kept Running After the Girl   Johnson, Howard
He Took His Girl in Bathing in the Summer Time   Dubin
Heart of Paddy Whack, The   Brennan
Heaven Measured You for Me   Harbach
He'd Kiss Her From London to Dover   Bryan; Fisher
He'd Push It Along   Clarke; Leslie
Hello, Broadway   Cohan
Hello, Little Miss U.S.A.   Atteridge
Here's a Rose for You   Dubin
Here's How   Herbert
Here's to Health, Here's to Wealth (Here Is
      Health)   Herbert
Here's to the Land We Love, Boys!   Herbert
He's a Devil in His Own Home Town   Berlin; Clarke; Leslie
He's a Rag Picker   Berlin
He's My Cousin, If She's Your Niece   Bryan
He's Off His Noodle 'bout the Cutest Little Gal   Gilbert
Hesitate Me Around, Bill   Jerome
Hesitation   Herbert
High Cost of Loving, The   Bryan; Meyer
Hippodrome Folks   Cohan
Home Again   Bryan
Honey You Certainly Know How to Love   Sterling; Von
      Tilzer
Hoo-oo I'm Waving at You   Dubin
How Do You Do-Good-Bye (How'dy Do, Good-Bye)
      Atteridge
Hurdy-Gurdy Man, The   Buck
Husbands! Husbands! Husbands!   Herbert
Hush-a-Bye Don't Let Me Hear You Cry (The Moon Man
      Has His Eyes on You)   Fisher
I Can Tell By the Way You Dance Dear   Friml; Harbach
I Can't Get a Girl   Kalmar; Leslie; Snyder
I Can't Stop Loving You Now   Kalmar; Leslie; Snyder
I Couldn't Keep Away from You   Kahn
I Didn't Raise My Boy To Be a Soldier   Bryan
I Find Fascination   Smith, Harry B.
I Had a Gal, I Had a Pal, He Stole My Gal Away   Gilbert
I Hate You   Berlin
I Knew Him When He Was All Right   Von Tilzer
I Love My Mother-in-Law   Brown, A. Seymour
I Love Not One but All   Herbert
I Love the Ladies   Clarke; Schwartz, Jean
I Love to Have the Boys Around Me   Berlin
I Love to Quarrel with You   Berlin
I Love You Just Like Lincoln Loved the Old Red, White and
      Blue   Jerome; Schwartz, Jean; Young, Joseph
I Love You Just the Same   Buck
I Never Met Before a Girl Like You   Olcott
I See Your Face in Ev'ry Rose   Johnson, J. Rosamond
I Think You'd Better Hurry Home   Friml; Harbach
I Want All the World to Know   Friml; Harbach
I Want to Go Back to Michigan (Down on the Farm)   Berlin
I Want to Go to Mexico   Edwards
I Want to Go to Tokio   Fisher
I Want to Marry a Male Quartette   Friml; Harbach
I Want to Row on the Crew   Porter
I Want You to Meet My Mother   Dubin

I Wanted to Come to Broadway   Cohan
I Was Born on the Isle of Man   Atteridge; Carroll; Romberg
I Was Thinking of You   Kahn; Whiting
I Will Always Follow You   Clarke; Young, Joseph
I Wonder Where My Lovin' Man Has Gone   Whiting
I Wonder Who Wished Her on Me   Sterling; Von Tilzer
I'd Like To Be On an Island with You   Bryan
Idyll   Porter
If I Came to You with a Heart Bowed Down (Would You
      Remember Me)   Kahn; Whiting
If I Had Some One at Home Like You, I Wouldn't Want to
      Go Out   Monaco
If I Had You   Berlin
If I Were the Ocean and You Were the Shore, I'd Be Kissing
      You All the Day   Bryan
If It Wasn't for You   Von Tilzer
If That's Your Idea of a Wonderful Time (Take Me
      Home)   Berlin
If They'd Only Move Old Ireland Over Here   Schwartz, Jean
If You Don't Want My Peaches You Better Stop Shaking My
      Tree   Berlin
If You'd Only Show a Little Love for Me   Monaco
I'll Come Back to You   Atteridge
I'll Do It All Over Again   Brown, A. Seymour
I'll Love You Marina   Harbach
I'll Make a Man of You   Carroll
I'll Not Let Love Disparage Marriage   Harbach
I'm a Fool Who Believed in You   Clarke; Leslie
I'm a Statesman   Buck
I'm Coming Back in Springtime   Yellen
I'm Cured   Buck
I'm Glad My Wife's in Europe   Johnson, Howard
I'm Going To Get a Girl Named Ivy, 'Cause Ivy Always
      Clings   Bryan
I'm Going to Let the Whole World Know I Love
      You   Edwards
I'm Going to Make You Love Me   Brown, A. Seymour
I'm Makin' for Macon Tonight (I'm Makin' for Macon In
      Georgia)   Kalmar
I'm Not Ashamed of You Molly, I Want You Just As You
      Are   Leslie; Young, Joseph
I'm Seeking for Siegfried   Atteridge; Carroll; Romberg
Impressions   Atteridge; Romberg
In a Cosy Bungalow in Loving Town   Jerome; Schwartz,
      Jean
In a Hurry   Friml; Harbach
In a Shady Little Dell in Delaware   Carroll
In My Arms, That's Where You Belong   Brown, A. Seymour
In Our Little Heaven Down Below   Sterling; Von Tilzer
In the Garden of the Gods   Brennan
In Those Good Old Days of Fairies   Olcott
In Vienna   Friml; Harbach
Innocent, Innocent Maids   Porter
Irish and Proud of It Too   Atteridge; Carroll; Romberg
Irish Eyes of Blue   Brennan
Is the Old Love Lamp Still Burning   Young, Joseph
It Isn't What He Said (It's the Way He Said It)   Berlin
It Pays to Advertise   Cohan
It Thrills! It Thrills!   Harbach
It's a Long Way to Tipperary   Williams
It's a Very Easy Thing to Put a Ring Upon a Finger, But Try
      to Take It Off   Young, Joseph
It's Going to Be a Cold, Cold Winter But I'll Never Freeze
      when You're Around   Brown, Lew; Leslie
I've a Shooting-Box in Scotland   Porter

I've Got Everything I Want but You   Schwartz, Jean
I've Got Him Now!   Buck
I've Got the Sweetest Little Baby   Clarke; Goetz
I've Gotta Go Back to Texas   Berlin
I've Sent My Wife to the Country   Dubin
Jesse James Glide, The   Cohan
Johnnie on the Spot   Von Tilzer
Johnny Is Getting It Now, Oh Goody Goody   Clarke
Just Around the Corner from Broadway   Edwards
Just Bring Two Lips Alone   Meyer
Just One Sprig of Shamrock from the County
    Kildare   Brennan
Katinka   Friml; Harbach
Keep Your Love for Me   Buck
Kingdom of Love   Gilbert
Kiss Your Baby Bye-Bye   Whiting
Kitty MacKay   Atteridge; Carroll
Ladies Day   Smith, Robert B.
Lambs' March (inst.), The   Herbert
Land of 'Let's Pretend', The   Kern; Smith, Harry B.
Land of the Midnight Sun, The   Smith, Harry B.
Lead Me to Love   Berlin
Lease Your Little Lovin' Heart to Me   Whiting
Leave Me Alone   Von Tilzer
Let By-Gones Be By-Gones   Williams; Young, Joseph
Let in the Sunshine of Love   Johnson, Howard
Let the Music Play   Smith, Robert B.
Let's Fill the Old Oaken Bucket With Love   Bryan
Let's Go Around the Town   Berlin
Life Is a Dancing Roman Holiday   Johnson, J. Rosamond
Life Is a Garden   Harbach
Life Is Just a Dress Parade   Atteridge
(Tell Me) Lilac Domino   Smith, Robert B.
Listen Dear   Friml
Listen to that Dixie Band   Yellen
Little Bit of Heaven (Shure They Call It Ireland), A   Brennan
Little Dreamboat of Mine   Whiting
Little Tango Maid, A   Atteridge; Carroll
Lock Me in Your Harem and Throw Away the Key   Berlin
Lone Star Girl, The   Buck
Look at Them Doing It!   Berlin
Look Out for Mr. Wu   Cohan
Love in Springtime   Kahn
Love Is a Battle   Herbert; Smith, Robert B.
Love Is an Art   Smith, Harry B.
Love Is Like a Violin   Kern; Smith, Harry B.
Love Me Like the Ivy Loves the Old Oak Tree   Whiting
Love of the Lorelei, The   Herbert; Smith, Robert B.
Lovely Trip, A   Atteridge
Love's Memories (inst.)   Von Tilzer
Make that Engine Stop at Louisville   Lewis; Meyer
Mammy's Little Angel Child   Yellen
Man Who Wrote "The Vampire" (Must Have Known My
    Wife), The   Buck
March, Book Dance   Atteridge; Romberg
Marina   Harbach
Married Life   Herbert; Smith, Robert B.
Marry the Girl You Love   Kahn; Whiting
Mary Pickford, the Darling of Them All   Whiting
Match Makers, The   Harbach
Maude Adams of the Screen, The   Atteridge; Romberg
Maybe a Day, Maybe a Year   Gilbert; Monaco
Maybe Land   Atteridge; Carroll; Romberg
Mazuma   Herbert
Me and Mandy Lee   Gilbert

Mem'ries of Violets   Johnson, J. Rosamond
Metropolitan Nights   Berlin
Midnight Girl at the Midnight Cabaret, The   Atteridge;
    Romberg
Minstrel Parade   Berlin
Moment's Hesitation (inst.), A   Monaco
Moonlight on the Rhine   Kalmar; Leslie; Snyder
Mootchin' Along at the Cotton Ball   Gilbert
More I See of Others the Better I Love (Like) You,
    The   Herbert
Morning Exercise   Berlin
Mother Hubbard Was a Wise Old Dame   Bryan; Edwards
Move Over   Berlin
Moving Picture Glide, The   Atteridge; Carroll
Mrs. Kelly's Table d'Hote   Buck
My Alsace Lorraine   Gilbert
My Cleopatra Girl   Atteridge
My Croony Melody   Goetz
My Crown for Thee   Young, Victor
My Daddy Long Legs   Goetz
My Flag   Cohan
My Lady of the Telephone   Atteridge; Romberg
My Little Pet Chicken   Buck
My Miracle Man   Cohan
My Paradise   Friml; Harbach
My Rainbow Beau   Atteridge; Carroll; Romberg
My Rose of Normandie   Dubin
My Wife Is Dancing Mad   Johnson, Howard
Naughty, Naughty   Porter
'Neath the Shadow of the Pyramids   Carroll
Neptune's Daughter   Buck; Clarke; Schwartz, Jean
Never Mention Love when We're Alone   Herbert; Smith,
    Robert B.
Never Trust a Soldier   Atteridge; Romberg
Never Trust a Soldier Man   Carroll
New Ireland, The   Herbert
Night Life in Old Manhattan   Buck
Nighttime in Dixieland   Johnson, James P.
Noble Cause of Art, The   Atteridge
Nobody Home   Williams; Young, Joseph
Nobody Seems To Know   Buck
Nobody Was in Love with Me   Atteridge
Nothing To Wear   Buck
Now She Knows How to Parle Voo   Leslie; Young, Joseph
Nut Sundae, A   Buck
Ocean, The Ocean, The   Harbach
Off with the Old Love, On with the New, Easier to Say than
    Do   Carroll
Office Hours   Berlin
Oh, Allah   Atteridge
Oh, Fascinating Night   Harbach
Oh How He Can Sing an Irish Song   Kahn; Norworth
Oh How that Woman Could Cook   Kahn
Oh! My Love   Monaco
Oh, This Love!   Smith, Harry B.
Oh, What a Lovely Princess   Porter
Oh You Cute Little Chicken   Brown, A. Seymour
Oh, You John   Atteridge; Carroll; Romberg
Omar Khayyam   Atteridge; Romberg
On a Golden Wedding Honeymoon   Edwards
On a Modern Wedding Day   Atteridge; Romberg
On a Sunny Afternoon   Herbert; Smith, Robert B.
On the Good Ship Honeymoon   Dubin
On the Island of Pines (On the Isle of Pines)   Carroll
On the Isle of Pines   Bryan

On the Steps of the Great White Capitol   Clarke; Leslie
On the Trail of the Honeymoon   Dubin
Once in a Thousand Years   Whiting
One Way of Doing It   Smith, Harry B.
One Who Will Understand   Friml; Harbach
Only Girl, The   Herbert
Opera Burlesque   Berlin
Out in Frisco Town   Atteridge; Carroll
Over the Alpine Mountains   Bryan; Fisher
Panamala   Edwards
Paranoia   Porter
Path to Honeymoonland, The   Atteridge
Pavlova Gavotte, The   Atteridge
Peggy's a Creature of Moods   Herbert; Smith, Robert B.
Personality   Herbert
Pigeon Walk (inst.)   Monaco
Play a Simple Melody   Berlin
Please Do My Family a Favor and Love Me   Clarke
Poppy (inst.)   Von Tilzer
Prep School Widow, The   Porter
Professor Cupid   Herbert; Smith, Robert B.
Providing   Bryan
Prunella   Atteridge; Carroll
Prunella Mine   Buck
Put It On, Take It Off   Leslie; Young, Joseph
Put Your Lovin' Arms Around Me Dearie   Buck
Pygmalion Roses   Cohan
Rackety Koo   Friml; Harbach
Ragtime Arabian Nights   Atteridge
Ragtime Dream, The   Brown, Lew
Revival Day   Berlin
Rocky Road to Dublin   Williams; Young, Joseph
Rouli-Rouli   Clarke; Schwartz, Jean
Russian Dance   Friml; Harbach
Russian Wedding March   Friml; Harbach
'S Too High   Monaco
Same Sort of Girl, The   Kern; Smith, Harry B.
San Francisco (At that San-Fran Pan American Fair)   Lewis;
   Meyer
Sari Dance, The   Atteridge; Romberg
Secrets   Harbach
Settle Down in a One-Horse Town   Berlin
Sextette   Herbert; Smith, Robert B.
Shadowland   Edwards
Shameen Dhu   Olcott
She Got Even With Stephen   Bryan; Lewis; Meyer
Shepherd Gavotte, The   Carroll
Shepherd Gavotte No. 1, The   Atteridge; Romberg
She's Dancing Her Heart Away   Gilbert
She's Going Mad   Bryan; Lewis; Meyer
Show Me How to Do the Fox Trot   Berlin
Shuffling Shiveree, The   Atteridge; Carroll; Romberg
Silhouette Ballet   Atteridge; Carroll; Romberg
Since You Gave Those Kisses to Me   Monaco
Skidikischatch   Friml; Harbach
Sloping Path, The   Atteridge; Romberg
Slow Sinks the Sun   Porter
Small Town Sweetheart of a Small Town Girl, The   Kahn;
   Whiting
Smother Me With Kisses and Kill Me with Love   Bryan;
   Carroll
Sneaky Steps   Cohan
Social Climbers   Smith, Harry B.
Somebody's Dancing with My Girl   Atteridge; Carroll;
   Romberg

Someone's Calling Me   Atteridge; Carroll; Romberg
Sometime   Brown, A. Seymour
Song of the Chimes   Smith, Robert B.
Sparkling Moselle, The   Smith, Harry B.
Springtime of Love Is Fairest   Herbert; Smith, Robert B.
Ssh! You'll Waken Mister Doyle   Kern
Stamboul   Friml; Harbach
Stay Down Here Where You Belong   Berlin
Sunny Riviera, The   Smith, Robert B.
Sunny Summertime   Whiting
Syncopated Walk   Berlin
Take a Step with Me   Kern; Smith, Harry B.
Take Me Home with You   Herbert; Smith, Robert B.
Tango Brazilian Dreams   Buck
Tango Dip   Atteridge; Carroll
Tango Dreams (inst.)   Johnson, J. Rosamond
Tango (inst.)   Gershwin, George
Tango, What Have You Done to Me   Kalmar
Tangorilla   Buck
Tea Time Tango Tune   Gilbert
Teenie-Eenie-Weenie   Harbach
Tell It All Over Again   Herbert
20th Century Man, The   Leslie
20th Century Rag, The   Clarke
That Bohemian Rag   Edwards
That Moonlight Serenade   Lewis; Meyer
That Old Fashioned Cake Walk   Cohan
That's a Lovely Evening   Kahn
That's a Real Moving Picture from Life   Sterling; Von Tilzer
That's My Idea of Paradise   Berlin
That's Plenty (inst.)   Pollack
There's a Little Spark of Love Still Burning   Fisher
There's Something About You   Atteridge; Carroll; Romberg
There's Something in the Air in Springtime   Buck
They All Had a Finger in the Pie   Von Tilzer
They Always Follow Me Around   Berlin
They Didn't Believe Me   Kern
They Don't Hesitate Any More   Kalmar; Leslie
They Had to Swim Back to the Shore   Monaco
They Start in to Battle Again   Brown, Lew; Leslie
They're on Their Way to Mexico   Berlin
Think It Over   Bryan
This Is No Place for Me   Brown, A. Seymour
This Is the Life   Berlin
Those Irving Berlin Melodies   Cohan
(Suzi I'm) Ticking Love Taps (Tick-A-Tock)   Harbach
Tingle Tangle (inst.)   Von Tilzer
Tip-Top Tipperary Mary   Carroll
Tis the End, So Farewell   Friml; Harbach
Treat Me Like a Baby Doll   Johnson, J. Rosamond
Trini   Atteridge; Carroll; Romberg
True Love Will Find a Way   Smith, Robert B.
Try It Over Again (If You Don't Like It)   Brown, Lew
Turkey Trotting Boy (Oh! You Turkey Trotter)   Atteridge;
   Carroll
'Twas in a Garden   Harbach
Twelfth Street Rag   Razaf
Twenty-Five Minutes Away   Von Tilzer
Two Dandy Darkies   Cohan
Two in One (inst.)   Johnson, Howard
Two Playhouses, The   Cohan
Underneath the Japanese Moon   Buck
Valse Hesitation   Herbert
Venetia   Atteridge; Carroll
Venetian Carnival, The   Atteridge; Carroll; Romberg

Venus and I Are Pals   Harbach
Venus Calls and I'll Obey   Harbach
Vienna Girls   Friml; Harbach
Visit, The   Atteridge
Voice of Love, The   Smith, Harry B.
Walking Music Store, The   Friml; Harbach
Wanda   Friml
War in Snider's Grocery Store, The   Carroll
Watch Your Step   Berlin
Way Down East   Atteridge; Romberg
Way Down on Tampa Bay   Brown, A. Seymour
We Forgot the Number of the House   Atteridge
Weekly Wedding, The   Friml; Harbach
Weep No More My Lady, Let Me See Your Smile   Gilbert
We'll Take Care of You All (Refugee Song) (The Little
    Refugees)   Kern
We'll Take Care of You All (The Refugee Song) (The Little
    Refugees)   Smith, Harry B.
We've Been Married Just One Year   Gilbert
What Are You Going to Do with Me?   Atteridge; Carroll;
    Romberg
What Are You Going to Do with Me Now   Johnson,
    Howard
What Ever Woman Knows (Frocks and Frills)   Smith, Robert
    B.
What Is Done You Can Never Undo   Smith, Robert B.
What Is Love?   Berlin
What Love Is   Porter
What Would I Do Without You   Gilbert
What'll   Atteridge
When an Englishman Marries a Parisian   Atteridge; Carroll;
    Romberg
When Fortune Smiles   Smith, Harry B.
When He Gets Back to New York Town   Snyder
When I Discovered You   Berlin; Goetz
When I Played Carmen   Herbert; Smith, Robert B.
When It's Moonlight on the Alamo   Bryan; Fisher; Meyer
When It's Night Time Down in Burgandy   Bryan
When It's Night-Time in Dixieland   Berlin
When Love Comes Calling   Young, Victor
When the Angelus Is Ringing   Young, Joseph
When the Ragtime Army Goes Away to War   Brown, A.
    Seymour
When the Roses Bloom in Avalon   Bryan
When Tommy Atkins Smiles at All the Girls   Atteridge;
    Carroll; Romberg
When You Want a Little Lovin' Go Out and Get It   Hanley
When You Were a Child   Gilbert
When Your Ankle Wears the Ball and Chain   Herbert;
    Smith, Harry B.
When You're a Long, Long Way from Home   Lewis; Meyer
When You're Away   Herbert
Where Is My Wandering Boy Tonight?   Buck
Where Love Is Waiting   Smith, Robert B.
Where Shall We Go for Our Honeymoon   Smith, Harry B.
Whirl of the Opera, The   Atteridge
Whirl of the World, The   Atteridge
Who Cares!   Smith, Harry B.
Who Do You Love, My Baby   Johnson, J. Rosamond
Who Knows   Brennan
Who Paid the Rent for Mrs. Rip Van Winkle (When Rip Van
    Winkle Went Away)   Bryan; Fisher
Who's Your Lady Friend   Gilbert
Why Do Your Kisses Taste So Sweet   Von Tilzer

Why Don't They Dance the Polka Anymore   Kern; Smith,
    Harry B.
Why Don't They Do It Now   Monaco
Why Don't You Get a Girl Like Me   Atteridge
Why Should We Stay Home and Sew   Herbert
Why Waste Your Love   Williams; Young, Joseph
Will You Waltz on the Ice with Me   Johnson, J. Rosamond
Will-O-the-Wisp, The   Herbert; Smith, Robert B.
Winter Nights   Clarke
Wonderful Garden of Love   Buck
Won't Someone Find Me a Sweetheart?   Smith, Robert B.
Won't You Come Crusading with Me   Porter
Working for the Pictures   Atteridge; Romberg
World's a Stage for Every Girl, The   Atteridge; Carroll;
    Romberg
Wrap Me in a Bundle and Take Me Home with You   Kahn
Wrap Me Up in a Blanket of Love   Schwartz, Jean
You Are the Rose that Will Never Die   Kalmar; Leslie;
    Snyder
You Can Tango, You Can Trot, Dear but Be Sure and
    Hesitate   Sterling; Von Tilzer
You Can't Go Wrong with Us   Atteridge; Romberg
You Can't Keep the Old Green Down   Johnson, Howard
You Great Big Dancing Doll   Monaco
You Have to Have a Party to Make a Hit   Herbert
You Must Have Been a Cute Little Baby   Monaco
You Never Can Tell   Kern; Smith, Harry B.
You Never Can Tell By the Left Eye, What the Right Eye
    Means to Do   Johnson, Howard
You'll Be Sorry when We Say Goodbye   Howard, Joseph E.
Your Photo   Friml; Harbach
You're a Beautiful Brown Eyed Burglar   Egan; Whiting
You're Here and I'm Here   Kern
You're Just a Little Better (Than the One I Thought Was
    Best)   Atteridge; Carroll
You're Locked in My Heart   Kalmar; Leslie; Snyder
You're My Boy   Schwartz, Jean
You're the One Girl for Me   Herbert
Yum! Yum! Yum! Yum!   Brown, A. Seymour

1915

Abie and Me and the Baby   Brown, Lew; Von Tilzer
Advice to the Young   Atteridge
After the Sunshine   Atteridge; Friml
After Tonight Goodbye   Sterling; Von Tilzer
Ain't that Always the Way   Atteridge; Carroll; Romberg
Alabama Jubilee   Yellen
Alacazam   Sterling; Von Tilzer
All for the Love of a Girl   Leslie; Meyer; Young, Joseph
All for You   Herbert
All Full of Ginger   Smith, Robert B.
All I Can Do Is Just Love You   Clarke; Monaco
Allies   Herbert
Alone at Last   Kern
Along the Mississippi Shore   Donaldson; Johnson, Howard
Along the Rialto   Fisher
Along the Rocky Road to Dublin   Young, Joseph
America I Love You   Leslie
And Dreams Come True   Atteridge; Friml
And Father Wanted Me to Learn a Trade   Berlin
And the Cat Came Back   Johnson, Howard
And the Great Big World Went Round and Round   Sterling;
    Von Tilzer
Another Little Girl   Kern

Any Old Night (Is a Wonderful Night)   Kern; Motzan; Smith, Harry B.
Any Old Time with You   Atteridge
Arabia   Hanley
Araby   Berlin
Are You from Dixie Cause I'm from Dixie Too   Yellen
Arrival of the Princess Pat   Herbert
At that San Francisco Fair   Kern
At that Yiddish Society Ball   Lewis
At the Fox Trot Ball   Atteridge; Carroll; Romberg
At the Hoboe's Ball   Lewis
At the Old Plantation Ball   Ager; Donaldson; Goetz
At the Toy Shop   Atteridge; Romberg
Auf Wiedersehen   Romberg
Babes in the Wood   Kern
Ballet Suite   Herbert
Band Played All the Time, The   Dubin
Barcarole   Smith, Robert B.
Bathing   Buck
Beatrice Fairfax, Tell Me What to Do   Clarke; Monaco
Beautiful Eyes (Les Beaux Yeux)   Gilbert
Beneath Those Sunny Skies   Howard, Joseph E.
Best Little Sweetheart of All, The   Goetz; Romberg
Best Sort of Mother, Best Sort of Child   Kern
Best Waltz of All, The   Atteridge
Blarney Castle-Walk, The   Atteridge
Blow Your Horn   Berlin
Bounce Me, John, I've Rubber Heels On   Fisher
Boy of Mine   Buck
Brazilian Nut   Smith, Robert B.
Breath o' Bloomin' Heather (From My Little Highland Home)   Brennan
Bring Along Your Dancing Shoes   Kahn
Broadway Knitting Club, The   Atteridge; Romberg
Broadway Sam   Atteridge
Buffo Dance (inst.)   Kern
By Heck   Gilbert
By the Road to Dublin Town   Yellen
Cabaret 'Neath the Old Egyptian Moon, A   Hanley
Cabareting in Pumpkinville   Howard, Joseph E.
Cake Walk Promenade   Howard, Joseph E.
California   Whiting
Can It Be?   Brennan
Can't They Leave Us Alone for a While   Lewis; Meyer
Can't You See I Mean You   Kern
Captive, The   Herbert
Cassidy, Private Michael Cassidy   Norworth
Castles in the Air   Atteridge; Carroll; Romberg
Celestia, Beautiful Goddess of Love   Young, Joseph
Chaplin Walk, The   Kern; Motzan
Cheer Up (Better Times Will Soon Be Here)   Leslie; Young, Joseph
Childhood Lesson   Atteridge
Chilli Con-Can   Howard, Joseph E.
Chin Chin Open Your Heart and Let Me In   Brown, A. Seymour
Chin-Chin   Atteridge; Romberg
Chinese Fox Trot (inst.)   Schwartz, Jean
Chinese One Step (inst.)   Schwartz, Jean
Chinese Waltz (inst.)   Schwartz, Jean
Circus Day in Dixie   Yellen
Cling a Little Closer   Goetz; Romberg
Close to My Heart   Sterling; Von Tilzer
Cohen Owes Me Ninety-Seven Dollars   Berlin
College Inn Rag, The   Carroll

Come Along   Buck
Come Back to Me   Dubin
Come, Go Bungalowing   Jerome; Schwartz, Jean
Cotton Blossom Time   Smith, Robert B.
Courtship Dance   Kern; Smith, Harry B.
Cows May Come and Cows May Go but the Bull Will Go on Forever   Von Tilzer
Cute Little Summery Time   Goetz; Jerome; Schwartz, Jean
Daisy Went and Told on Me   Bryan; Lewis; Meyer
Dance of Bewilderment   Smith, Robert B.
Dance of Joy   Smith, Robert B.
Dance of the Midnight Sons, The   Atteridge; Romberg
Dance of the Squareheads   Atteridge; Romberg
Dance Rozika (inst.)   Schwartz, Jean
Dance Trio (inst.)   Kern
Dancing Around the U.S.A.   Atteridge; Romberg
Dancing Festival, The   Atteridge; Romberg
Dancing 'Round the U.S.A.   Carroll; Yellen
Danse Eccentrique   Atteridge; Romberg
Danse Poetic   Atteridge; Friml
Darkies' Serenade   Johnson, Howard
Dear Old Fashioned Irish Songs My Mother Sang to Me   Von Tilzer
Debutante   Ager
Diana   Atteridge; Romberg
Doll Dance, The   Atteridge; Romberg
Don't Blame Me for What Happens in the Moonlight, Blame the Moon   Young, Joseph
Don't Tempt Me   Smith, Harry B.
Dove of Peace (inst.)   Motzan
Down in Bom-Bombay   Carroll
Down in Catty Corner   Atteridge; Romberg
Down in the Old Neighborhood   Whiting
Dr. Baltimore M.D.   Motzan
Drip, Drip, Drip, Went the Waterfall   Carroll
Eight Bells   Atteridge; Romberg
Employment Agency, The   Atteridge; Romberg
Esmerelda   Porter
Estellita   Herbert
Every Morn' You'll Hear Them Say Good Night   Kalmar
Every Small Town Girlie Has a Big Town Way   Atteridge
Everybody Dance   Buck
Everybody Hum with Me   Atteridge; Romberg
Everyone's Moving Up on Broadway (Everyone's Moving Up Town)   Atteridge; Carroll; Romberg
Everything in America Is Ragtime (Ragtime Finale)   Berlin
Evolution of a Rag   Goetz; Romberg
Extr'ordinary Rag (inst.)   Motzan
Fascination   Atteridge; Romberg
Fatima Brown   Monaco
Fifth Avenue   Atteridge; Romberg
First Call of Love   Howard, Joseph E.
First Love Is the Best of All   Atteridge
Fishing   Atteridge
Flame of Love, The   Atteridge; Friml
Flights of Fancy   Atteridge; Romberg
Flirting   Herbert
Flower Garden Ball, The   Jerome; Schwartz, Jean
Flower of My Heart, My Rose   Atteridge
Foolishness   Kern; Smith, Harry B.
For Better or for Worse   Herbert
Foxy Grandpa   Ager
Gamble on Me   Atteridge
Game of Cards, A   Atteridge
Garden of Paradise   Atteridge; Romberg

Gee, but I'm Tickled to Death, You Married Me   Johnson, Howard
Gee I Only Wish that I Could Make My Dreams Come True   Buck
General Hooligan   Von Tilzer
General Nuisance   Lewis
Ginger   Clarke
Ginger Girl   Goetz; Romberg
Girl from My Home Town, The   Buck
Girl of the Fan, The   Atteridge; Romberg
Girl on the Magazine Cover, The   Berlin
Girl You Left Behind, The   Jerome; Schwartz, Jean
Girlie of the Cabaret   Atteridge; Romberg
Girlies Are Out of My Life   Atteridge; Romberg
(Why Don't They) Give Us a Chance   Berlin
Gloria's Romance (inst.)   Kern
Go and Get the Habit   Von Tilzer
Go Right Along Mr. Wilson (And We'll All Stand By You)   Brown, A. Seymour
Good Fellows Club, The   Atteridge; Romberg
Good Old Days in Alabam   Gilbert
Good-Bye   Sissle
Goodbye Virginia   Clarke; Schwartz, Jean
Greatest Battle Song of All, The   Atteridge; Kalmar; Romberg
Gypsy Dance   Atteridge
Ha, Ha, Ha   Atteridge; Carroll; Romberg
Harvest Days   Atteridge
Have a Restaurant of Your Own   Atteridge; Carroll; Romberg
He Was a Friend of Mine   Howard, Joseph E.
Heart of a Rose   Atteridge; Friml
He'd Have to Answer the Bell   Brown, Lew
Hee-Haw   Ager
Hello Boys, I'm Back Again   Von Tilzer
Hello, Frisco, I Called You Up To Say Hello   Buck
Hello, Hawaii, How Are You   Kalmar; Leslie; Schwartz, Jean
Here's a Bale of Cotton for You   Atteridge; Carroll; Romberg
Here's to You   Romberg
Hold Me in Your Loving Arms   Buck
Home Was Never Like This   Brown, A. Seymour
Homeward Bound   Berlin
Honey Bunch   Sterling
Honolulu Lou   Egan
Hooray, The Land of the Midnight Sun   Fisher
Howdy-Do, Goodbye   Romberg
Hula-Hula Love   Clarke; Monaco
Human Nature   Kern; Smith, Harry B.
Humpty Dumpty Drag   Buck
I Cannot Take a Step Too Far   Smith, Harry B.
I Can't Forget Your Eyes   Smith, Harry B.
I Can't Give Her Up   Lewis
I Could Go Home to a Girlie Like You   Atteridge; Romberg
I Don't Like the Sea   Atteridge
I Had a Dog   Romberg
I Left Her in New Hampshire   Brown, Lew
I Love a Piano   Berlin
I Love Them All   Brennan
I Love To Be Loved   Buck
I Love to Dance   Berlin
I Love to Stay at Home   Berlin
I Love to Tango with My Tea   Bryan
I Love You, That's One Thing I Know   Gilbert
I Need Affection   Herbert
I Played My Concertina   Atteridge; Romberg

I Want a Girl from Old Kentucky (Where My Dad Got His Best Girl)   Sissle
I Want Someone Who's Lonesome   Smith, Robert B.
I Want to Be There   Clarke; Monaco
I Want to Be Way Down Yonder in the Corn Field   Leslie; Young, Joseph
I Want To Watch Over You   Bryan
I Wish I Could Move the Swanee Far from the Old Folks at Home   Jerome; Schwartz, Jean
I Wish I Was an Island in an Ocean of Girls   Herbert
I Wish That He Was Back in Tipperary   Brennan
I Wonder Who She Spoons with Now   Smith, Robert B.
I Work Eight Hours, Sleep Eight Hours, That Leaves Eight Hours for Love   Kalmar; Leslie; Snyder
I Would Find You Dear   Brennan
I'd Like to Be a Quitter, But I Find It Hard to Quit   Herbert
I'd Like to Have a Million in the Bank   Kern
I'd Like to Have You Around   Herbert
I'd Love to Dance Through Life with You   Kern; Smith, Harry B.
Idol of Eyes, The   Smith, Robert B.
If I Find Spanish Joe From Mexico (Oh O-O-O! Oh O-O-O!)   Brown, Lew
If I Find the Girl   Kern
If It Takes a Thousand Years   Brennan
If It Wasn't for Dear Old Ireland   Johnson, Howard
If the Girlies Could Be Soldiers   Buck
If the World Should End To-Morrow, I'd Be To-Night with You   Fisher
If War Is What Sherman Said It Was   Sterling
If We Can't Be the Same Old Sweethearts, We'll Just Be the Same Old Friends   Monaco
If You Can't Get a Girl in the Summertime You'll Never Get a Girl at All   Kalmar
If You Ever Come Down to Virginia There'll Be Nothing Too Good for You   Brown, A. Seymour
I'll Be a Santa Claus to You   Buck
I'll Be Back in Me Low Back Car   Donaldson; Lewis; Young, Joseph
I'll Cling to You   Carroll
I'll Do What the Rest Do   Smith, Harry B.
I'll Get You Yet Cigarette   Smith, Robert B.
I'll Keep the Roses Blooming for You   Smith, Robert B.
I'll Love You As Long As I Live   Brennan
I'll Love You Honey, When Your Money's Gone, but I'll Not Be with You   Johnson, J. Rosamond
I'll Make You Like the Town   Atteridge; Romberg
I'm a Lonesome Melody   Meyer; Young, Joseph
I'm a Nurse for Aching Hearts   Buck
I'm Coming Home With a Skate On   Berlin
I'm Cured   Lewis; Meyer
I'm from Chicago   Romberg
I'm Going Back to the Farm   Berlin
I'm Good for Nothing Else but You   Edwards
I'm Here Again   Smith, Harry B.
I'm Homesick   Sterling; Von Tilzer
I'm Looking for a Warm Spot   Leslie
I'm Looking for Someone's Heart   Atteridge; Romberg
I'm Lord Knows Who   Atteridge; Carroll; Romberg
I'm Proud I'm Irish   Howard, Joseph E.
I'm Proud to Be the Mother of a Boy Like You   Sterling; Von Tilzer
I'm Simply Crazy Over You   Goetz; Jerome; Schwartz, Jean
I'm Sober   Buck
In a Garden Down in Monterey   Lewis

In a Little World for Two   Herbert

In Arabia   Atteridge; Romberg

In Arcady   Kern

In Blinky, Winky, Chinky Chinatown   Jerome; Schwartz, Jean

In Day Dreams   Herbert

In Grandma's Day They Never Did the Fox Trot   Buck

In Mattawan   Von Tilzer

In Old Missouri   Kahn

In Our Little Loveland Bungalow   Hanley

In the City of Brotherly Love   Brown, A. Seymour

In the Gloaming of Wyoming, Back with the Girl I Love   Young, Joseph

In the Gold Fields of Nevada   Leslie

In the War Against Men   Atteridge; Romberg

In Time of Peace Prepare for War   Smith, Robert B.

Indian Suffragette, The   Smith, Robert B.

Irish Heart, An   Carroll

Is It All for You   Atteridge

Is There Still Room for Me 'Neath the Old Apple Tree   Brown, Lew; Leslie

Isadore   Fisher

Isle d'Amour   Atteridge

Isn't It Great to Be Married?   Kern

It Isn't Your Fault   Kern

It Took a Small Town Girl To Fool a Big Town Man   Brown, Lew

It's a Clue   Goetz; Romberg

It's All a Dream   Yellen

It's All Your Fault   Blake; Sissle

It's So Temptin' (inst.)   Monaco

It's the Gown that Makes the Girl   Smith, Robert B.

It's Tulip Time in Holland   Whiting

I've a Cabaret at Home   Dubin

I've Been Around a Bit   Kern; Smith, Harry B.

I've Been Floating Down the Old Green River   Kalmar

I've Got to Dance   Kern

I've Just Been Waiting for You   Kern; Smith, Harry B.

Japanese Ballet   Atteridge; Romberg

Jigaree, The   Atteridge; Romberg

Jungle Ball   Buck

Just Try to Picture Me Back Home in Tennessee   Jerome

Just Try to Picture Me Back Home in Tennessee (Just Try to Picture Me Down Home in Tennessee)   Donaldson

Keep Moving   Motzan

Keystone Glide, The   Smith, Robert B.

Kind Words   Bryan

Kiss Me Again   Herbert

Knock-Knock Nobody Home   Friml

Law Must Be Obeyed, The   Berlin

Lead Me to Love   Snyder

Let Us Have Peace (inst.)   Motzan

Let's Bungalow   Atteridge; Carroll; Romberg

Let's Go A-Roaming   Howard, Joseph E.

Let's Help Each Other Along   Brown, A. Seymour

Life's a Game of Polo   Smith, Harry B.

Little Billie (inst.)   Kern

Little Love (But not for Me), A   Kern

Little World of Two   Smith, Harry B.

Look Her Over in Summer and See what You're Goin' to Get   Johnson, Howard

Love Comes a-Stealing   Kahn

Love Is Like a Butterfly   Atteridge; Friml

Love Is the Best of All   Herbert

Love Is the Reason   Atteridge

Love, Love, Alone   Atteridge

Love Me or Leave Me Alone   Johnson, Howard

Love's Awakening   Atteridge; Friml

Lustspiel   Atteridge; Romberg

Made in the U.S.A.   Atteridge; Carroll

Magic Melody, The   Kern

Maid of My Heart   Gilbert

(I Want Someone To) Make a Fuss Over Me   Buck

Make Him Guess   Herbert

Manhattan Mad   Atteridge; Romberg

Marc Antony   Atteridge; Carroll; Romberg

March Song   Atteridge

Marconigram   Atteridge; Romberg

Mark Anthony   Atteridge; Romberg

Mechanical Soldiers   Atteridge; Romberg

Meet Me when I Come Back Home   Whiting

Melodrama   Herbert

Melting Pot, The   Atteridge; Romberg

Memories   Atteridge; Kahn; Romberg

Midnight Frolic Glide, The   Buck

Midsummer Waltz   Smith, Robert B.

Mid-Summer-Night's Dream, A   Young, Joseph

Military Maid   Atteridge; Romberg

Miss Innovation   Atteridge; Romberg

Mister Whitney's Little Jitney Bus   Brown, A. Seymour

Modern Duel, The   Smith, Harry B.

Month of June   Donaldson

Mosha from Nova Scotia   Gilbert

M-O-T-H-E-R (A Word that Means the World to Me)   Johnson, Howard

Mother May I Go In to Swim   Carroll

Mother o' Mine   Dubin

Mr. Tosti Goodbye   Atteridge; Carroll; Romberg

My Bird of Paradise   Berlin

My Brother Bill   Atteridge

My Heart's Achin' for Macon   Howard, Joseph E.

My Hula Maid   Atteridge

My Lady of the Lake   Carroll

My Lady's Dress   Kern; Smith, Harry B.

My Little Dream Girl   Gilbert

My Little Girl   Lewis

My Little Submarine   Buck

My Long Lost Love   Sissle

My Model Girl   Atteridge; Romberg

My Mother's Rosary   Lewis; Meyer

My Moving Picture Man   Smith, Harry B.

My Radium Girl   Buck

My Rose of Tipperary   Hanley

My Sparkling Wine   Romberg

My Spooky Girl   Buck

My Sunshine Came on a Rainy Day   Dubin

My Sweet Adair   Gilbert

My Tango Girl   Buck

My Tom Tom Man   Kahn

My Trilby Maid   Atteridge

My Yiddisher Romeo   Lewis; Meyer

My Ziegfeld Midnight Girl   Buck

Native Women   Atteridge

Neapolitan Love Song (Sweet One How My Heart Is Yearning) (T'Amo)   Herbert

Never Let Yourself Forget That You Are Irish Too   Brennan

Next Dance, The   Ager

No One's to Blame but You   Smith, Harry B.

Nobody Home Cakewalk (inst.)   Motzan

Nodding Roses   Kern

Not Dancing this Evening   Atteridge
Not that She Was Prettier   Smith, Harry B.
Nursery Land   Kalmar
O'Donnell Ahoo! (The Clanconnel War Song)   Herbert
Oh Marie   Clarke; Monaco
Oh, Those Days   Atteridge; Romberg
Oh What a Beautiful Baby   Brown, A. Seymour
Oh, You Beautiful Blonde   Dubin
Old Are Getting Younger Every Day, The   Smith, Robert B.
Old Bill Baker (Undertaker)   Kern
Old Blue Paradise   Romberg
Old Boy Neutral   Kern
Old Ireland Shall Be Free!   Herbert
Old-Fashioned Groom and an Up-To-Date Bride,
    An   Smith, Robert B.
Olympian Glide, The   Atteridge; Carroll; Romberg
On the Good Ship Whippoorwill   Donaldson
On the Road to Old Killarney   Leslie
On the Sands of Wa-ki-ki   Kern
On the Shore at Le Lei Wi   Kern
On the Trail to Santa Fe   Kahn
On to Conquer   Atteridge
Once in May   Berlin; Goetz
One and Only   Atteridge
One Step Into Love   Romberg
(It Is All for You) Only for You   Atteridge; Romberg
Only One Horse Shay   Egan
Open Up Your Heart, Let Me In   Gilbert
Opening of Atlantic City   Goetz; Romberg
Orange Blossom Time in San Jose   Goetz; Romberg
Orange Girl   Goetz; Romberg
Oskaloosa Pets, The   Smith, Robert B.
Our Hearts Go Out to You Canada, Hats Off to
    You   Brennan
Outside of That Why He's All Right   Sterling; Von Tilzer
Over the Hills To Mary   Bryan
Package of Seeds, A   Kern
Painting That Mother of Mine   Gilbert
Pair of Ordinary Coons, A   Berlin
Panama-Pacific Drag   Atteridge
Paprica   Smith, Robert B.
Parisian Rag, The   Smith, Harry B.
Pass the Contribution Box   Howard, Joseph E.
Pat   Herbert
Peaceful Rafferty   Brennan
Peasant Girl, The   Atteridge; Friml
Peter Pan   Kern; Smith, Harry B.
Pigeon Walk   Lewis; Monaco
Pirate Rag   Romberg
Pirate's Rag   Clarke; Goetz; Young, Joseph
Polo Rag   Atteridge; Romberg
Popular Rag   Goetz
Primrose Way, The   Atteridge
Private Property   Brown, Lew
Prosperity Wanda   Atteridge
Put It Over   Smith, Robert B.
Put Me to Sleep with an Old Fashioned Melody, Wake Me
    Up with a Rag   Lewis
Queen of the South Sea Isles   Gilbert
Ragtime Argument   Atteridge; Romberg
Ragtime Carnival   Atteridge; Romberg
Ragtime Dinner Order, The   Atteridge; Carroll; Romberg
Ragtime Pipes of Pan   Atteridge; Romberg
Rathskeller Trio, The   Atteridge; Carroll; Romberg
Red Fox Trot, The   Smith, Robert B.

Red, White and Blue   Buck
Regular Guy, A   Kern; Smith, Harry B.
Remembrance   Herbert
Reminiscent of Rosy Posy   Romberg
Riff-Raff-Rafferty   Smith, Robert B.
Roaming Around   Von Tilzer
Rockaway Hunt   Ager
Roll Your Yiddishe Eyes for Me   Lewis; Meyer
(Reminiscent of) Rosey Posey   Atteridge
Rosie Rosenblatt, Don't Make No Theater with Me   Lewis;
    Young, Joseph
Rosie Rosenblott   Atteridge
Rosie Rosenblott Don't Make No Theater with Me   Meyer
Safety First   Fisher
Safety First Love   Atteridge; Goetz; Romberg
Sailor Song   Berlin
Same Little Girl   Carroll
Same Old Girl, The   Howard, Joseph E.
Same Old Summer Moon   Kahn
(It's the) Same Old Town   Gilbert
San Jose   Bryan
Shakespearian Rag, The   Atteridge
She Goes Out A-Fishin' with Her Hook and Her
    Line   Leslie
She Was Made for Love   Bryan
Shoes of Husband No. 1 Are Worn By Number Two, The
    Herbert
Shooting the Bull Around the Bulletin Boards   Jerome;
    Schwartz, Jean
Shopping   Atteridge
Siam   Fisher; Johnson, Howard
Sing Me a Song of Love   Atteridge; Romberg
Sing Me to Sleep with an Old-Fashioned Melody   Atteridge
Sing Sing Tango Tea   Atteridge; Romberg
Si's Been Drinking Cider   Berlin
Sister Susie's Started Syncopation   Atteridge; Romberg
Sleepy Moon   Von Tilzer
Society   Kern
Some of These Nights   Howard, Joseph E.
Some Sort of Somebody (All of the Time)   Kern
Somebody Knows   Von Tilzer
Somebody Told Me   Howard, Joseph E.
Sometimes in Dreams   Kahn
Spanish Fandango, The   Atteridge
Springtime in the Country   Atteridge
Springtime Wagon of Love, The   Jerome; Von Tilzer
Starlight   Smith, Harry B.
Steam Pipe Melody   Donaldson; Johnson, Howard
Steam-Pipe Melody, The   Clarke
Steeple-Chase   Ager
Stolen Melody, The   Atteridge
Stop! Look! Listen!   Berlin
Subway Love   Smith, Robert B.
Summer Sports   Atteridge
Summery Time   Goetz; Romberg
Sunny Riviera Bay   Gilbert
Sunshine   Clarke; Monaco
Suzi Ann   Atteridge; Carroll; Romberg
Sweet Harp of the Days that Are Gone   Herbert
Sweetest Girl in Monterey   Bryan
Syncopation   Atteridge; Romberg
Take Her Back If You Love Her   Bryan; Fisher
Take It from Me   Smith, Robert B.
Take Me Home with You   Atteridge; Romberg
Take Off a Little Bit   Berlin

Talk, Talk, Talk   Smith, Harry B.
Teach Me How to Love   Berlin
Tell Me Some More   Sterling; Von Tilzer
Tell the Town, Hello, To-Night   Atteridge; Romberg
That Clutching Hand   Schwartz, Jean
That Hula Hula   Berlin
That Melodious Melody   Howard, Joseph E.
That Parisian Trot   Smith, Harry B.
That Peculiar Tune   Kern
That Soothing Symphony   Snyder
That Strictly Neutral Jag   Howard, Joseph E.
That's How the Shannon Flows   Brennan
That's What I Mean When I Call You Machree   Brennan
That's When I'll Marry You   Dubin
That's When the Panic Is On   Fisher; Johnson, Howard
(On) The Levee Along Broadway   Goetz; Romberg
(The Love Story of) The Packard and the Ford   Atteridge;
    Carroll
Them Was Happy Days   Smith, Harry B.
There Is One Heart in Loveland for Me   Ager
There Was a Time   Atteridge; Carroll
There's a Broken Heart for Every Light on Broadway   Fisher;
    Johnson, Howard
There's a Convent by the Beautiful Sea   Clarke; Fisher
There's a Little Bit of Everything on Broadway   Atteridge
There's a Little Lane Without a Turning on the Way to
    Home Sweet Home   Meyer; Young, Joseph
There's a Little Lane without a Turning the Way to Home
    Sweet Home   Lewis
There's a Message of Love in Your Eyes   Herbert
There's a Wee Bit of Blarney in Killarney   Ager; Gilbert
There's One California for Mine   Bryan
There's Only One Mary in Maryland   Whiting
There's Only One Who Rules My House   Romberg
There's Something Missing in the Movies   Atteridge
They All Had a Photograph of You   Brown, Lew
They Dream of Each Other All Night   Clarke; Johnson,
    Howard
They're in the Junk Pile Now   Buck
Things Are Getting Better All the Day   Bryan
Things Are So Different Now-A-Days   Howard, Joseph E.
Thirteen Collar   Kern
Those Come Hither Eyes   Kern
Those Musical Eyes   Sterling; Von Tilzer
Thou Art Mine   Carroll
Tiffany Girl   Goetz; Romberg
Times Square Arguments, The   Atteridge; Carroll; Romberg
Ting-A-Ling   Goetz; Romberg
To the Lass We Love (A Toast)   Brennan
Toast to Women's Eyes, A   Romberg
Toddle All Over the Town   Smith, Harry B.
Town Topics   Smith, Robert B.
Triangle (inst.), The   Kern
Trilby   Buck
Tulips and Pansies   Atteridge; Romberg
Two Big Eyes   Porter
Two Heads Are Better than One   Kern
Two Laughing Irish Eyes   Herbert
Typical Opening Chorus, The   Atteridge; Carroll; Romberg
Ukelele Daly   Jerome; Schwartz, Jean
Ukelele Lady   Williams
Under the American Flag   Sterling; Von Tilzer
Until I Fell in Love with You   Berlin
Voice of Belgium   Berlin
Wake Up, It's Cake Walk Day   Smith, Robert B.

Walking on the Lake   Smith, Robert B.
Way Down on Honolulu Bay   Goetz; Romberg
Wedding Bells Are Calling Me   Kern; Smith, Harry B.
We'll Have a Jubilee in My Old Kentucky Home   Donaldson
We're on Our Way   Kern
What a Beautiful Baby You Are   Smith, Robert B.
What If Geo. Washington's Mother Had Said, I Didn't Raise
    My Boy to Be a Soldier   Clarke; Monaco
What Would You Do for Fifty Thousand Dollars   Bryan
What You Are and What You Want to Be   Smith, Robert B.
What'll You Do   Lewis; Meyer
What's the Name of that Tune   Atteridge; Romberg
What's the Use of Going Home   Clarke
What-You-May Call, A   Young, Victor
When a Girl's About to Marry   Herbert
When Grandma Was a Girl   Atteridge; Carroll; Romberg
When He Wanted to Love Her He Would Put Up the
    Cover   Lewis; Meyer
When I Am Twenty-One   Leslie; Schwartz, Jean
When I Get Back to Old Virginia   Dubin
When I Get Back to the U.S.A.   Berlin
When I Leave the World Behind   Berlin
When I Teach You How to Swim   Goetz; Romberg
When I'm Out with You   Berlin
When It's All Over   Brown, Lew
When John McCormick Sings a Song   Goetz; Jerome;
    Schwartz, Jean
When My Ship Comes In   Von Tilzer
When One You Love   Atteridge; Friml
When Our Mothers Rule the World   Bryan
When Sunday Comes to Town   Von Tilzer
When the Colored Regiment Goes Off to War   Atteridge;
    Romberg
When You Were a Baby and I Was the Kid Next
    Door   Leslie
When You're Down in Louisville (Call on Me)   Berlin
Where My Caravan Rests   Atteridge; Carroll; Romberg
Where's the Boy for Me?   Smith, Harry B.
Where's the Girl for Me   Kern; Smith, Harry B.
While the Band Played an American Rag   Berlin
Whistling Dan   Kern; Smith, Harry B.
Who Will I Call Mamma When She's Gone   Hanley
Why Are We Invited Here?   Romberg
Why Not Sing Wearin' of the Green   Johnson, Howard
Wilma (inst.)   Motzan
Winter Nights   Schwartz, Jean
Yankee Doodle Patriotic Tune   Buck
You Can't Fool a New York Kid   Goetz; Romberg
You Can't Get Arrested for Thinking   Sterling; Von Tilzer
You Can't Get Away from Tipperary   Atteridge; Carroll;
    Jerome; Romberg; Snyder; Williams
You Go Your Way and I'll Go Mine   Johnson, J. Rosamond
You Know and I Know (And We Both Understand)   Kern
You Know Why I Love You   Johnson, Howard
You Remind Me So Much of My Mother   Dubin
You Wake Up in the Morning in Chicago   Carroll
You Wouldn't Know My Old Girl Now   Brown, Lew
You Wouldn't Know the Old Town Now   Donaldson;
    Jerome
You'd Better See America First   Atteridge
You'd Never Know that Old Home Town of Mine
    Donaldson, Walte   Johnson, Howard
You'll Always Be the Same Sweet Girl   Sterling; Von Tilzer
You'll Be There   Brennan

You'll Never Know that Old Home Town of Mine   Donaldson; Johnson, Howard
You're Hitting a Thousand in the Game of Love   Brennan
Ypsilenti   Bryan
Zebra Girl   Buck

1916

Abram Control Yourself   Brown, Lew
Adam Was the Only Lover   Romberg; Smith, Robert B.
Aesop Was a Very Moral Man   Smith, Harry B.; Smith, Robert B.
Ain't It Funny What a Difference (Just) a Few Drinks Make?   Buck; Kern
Aladdin   Atteridge; Romberg
Alice in Wonderland   Berlin
All Alone in a City Full of Girls   Romberg
All Full of Talk   Kern
All on Account of the War   Hanley
All That I Want Is Somebody to Love Me   Kern; Smith, Harry B.
Angels   Atteridge; Motzan; Romberg
Anna of Havana   Smith, Harry B.; Smith, Robert B.
Any Night on Broadway   Atteridge; Motzan; Romberg
Any Old Night Is a Lonesome Old Night   Young, Joseph
Are You Prepared for the Summer?   Kalmar; Leslie; Schwartz, Jean
Army, The   Romberg
Around the Town   Atteridge; Motzan; Romberg
Arrah Go on I'm Gonna Go Back to Oregon   Lewis; Young, Joseph
As We Pass By   Von Tilzer
As We Sat at the Saturday Evening Post   Kalmar; Leslie; Schwartz, Jean
At a Grand Hotel   Smith, Harry B.
At the Pullman Porter's Full Dress Ball   Blake; Sissle
Baccarole   Romberg
Bachelor Girl and Boy, A   Romberg
Back to Nature   Atteridge; Motzan; Romberg
Bad Men   Porter
Ballet Loose, The   Herbert
Balloon Girls, The   Cohan
Barefoot Days   Cobb; Edwards
Be Good to California, Mr. Wilson   Sterling
Beautiful Island of Girls   Buck
Beautiful, Primitive Indian Girls   Porter
Beneath the Sunshine Tree   Motzan
Bermuda   Motzan
Bernard & Phillips   Lewis; Meyer; Young, Joseph
Beware of Pink Pajamas   Lewis; Schwartz, Jean; Young, Joseph
Bichloride of Mercury   Porter
Birth of the Century Girl, The   Herbert
Bis Bolo   Atteridge; Motzan; Romberg
Bit of Opera, A   Atteridge; Motzan; Romberg
Bit of Ribbon Bit of Love, A   Goetz
Blue Monday   Ager
Boogie Rag   Ager
Bopeep   Egan; Whiting
Bring Along Your Loving Ways   Hanley; Romberg
Bring Your Kisses to Me   Atteridge; Romberg
Broadway School Days   Atteridge; Motzan; Romberg
Brotherhood of Railroad Men   Egan; Whiting
Bugle Call Rag (inst.)   Blake
Burmese Ballet, A   Atteridge; Motzan; Romberg

Busy, Busy, Busy   Cohan
Buy Her a Box at the Opera   Porter
By the Sad Luana Shore   Berlin; Goetz
Call of a Nation, The   Ahlert
Camp Fire Days   Hart; Rodgers
Caroline   McHugh
Casino Music Hall, The   Kern
Century Girl, The   Herbert
Champagne and Laughter   Smith, Harry B.; Smith, Robert B.
Childhood Days   Romberg
Coaling Up in Color Town   Egan; Whiting
Colonel of the Crimson Hussars, The   Smith, Harry B.
Come Back Sweet Dream   Romberg
Come Back to Arizona   Bryan
Come On and Baby Me   Lewis; Meyer; Young, Joseph
Come on to Nashville, Tenn.   Donaldson
Come with Me to Tennessee   Motzan
Coney Island   Von Tilzer
Crying Jane   Cohan
Cup of Tea, A   Smith, Harry B.
Cute Little Seat Behind, The   Johnson, Howard
Damsel, Damsel (Prithee Come Crusading with Me)   Porter
Dance a Little More   Hanley; Romberg; Smith, Harry B.
Dance o' the Dollys   Ager
Dancing Around the Town   Atteridge; Motzan; Romberg
Dancing Pirates, The   Cohan
Dangerous Girl   Von Tilzer
Dawn Music   Porter
Dear Old Wigwam Days   Rodgers
Diabolo   Atteridge
Dinner   Porter
Don't Be a Sailor   Atteridge; Hanley; Romberg
Don't Cry, Dolly Grey   Bryan
Don't Forget Me   Von Tilzer
Don't Play with Fire   Bryan
Don't Play with Me   Romberg
Don't Turn the Smiles to Tears   Whiting
Don't Write Me Letters, But Come Right Back to Me   Lewis; Young, Joseph
Don't You Wish You Were a Kid Again   Buck
Dove Dance   Norworth
Down Virginia Way   Atteridge; Motzan; Romberg
Early in the Morning Down on the Farm   Kahn
Egypt   Goetz
Erin Is Smiling   Ager; Jerome
Ever and Ever Yours   Porter
Everybody Has a Tip   Von Tilzer
Faces   Atteridge; Motzan; Romberg
Fair and Warmer Cocktail, The   Cohan
Fairy Song   Romberg
Fashion Waltz   Atteridge; Motzan; Romberg
Fast Steppers   Atteridge; Hanley; Romberg; Smith, Harry B.
Finale (Hail the Female Relative)   Porter
Financial Viking, The   Romberg
(Every Girl Is) Fishing   Buck
Following the Drum   Smith, Harry B.
For Dixie and Uncle Sam   Brennan
For Love I Depend on You   Hanley
French Flip Flop   Von Tilzer
Friars' Parade   Berlin
Frisco Melody, The   Cohan
Gaby   Cohan
(You'll Have to) Gallop Some   Atteridge; Romberg; Smith, Harry B.

Get a Girlie   Atteridge

Ghost of the Terrible Blues, The   Von Tilzer

Ghosts of the Ukulele, The   Atteridge; Motzan; Romberg

Girl on the Square   Atteridge; Motzan; Romberg

Girls Are Getting Wiser, The   Romberg; Smith, Robert B.

Girls Prepare   Atteridge; Romberg

Girls You Are Such Wonderful Thing   Smith, Harry B.

Go Ahead and Dance a Little More   Atteridge; Hanley

Good Advice   Smith, Harry B.

Good Night, Angeline   Blake

Good Old Days Back Home, The   Monaco

Goodbye, Dear Old Bachelor Days   Buck

Goodbye, Good Luck, God Bless You Is All that I Can
   Say   Brennan

Goodbye Red Man Goodbye   Kalmar; Leslie; Snyder

Gootman Is a Hootman Now   Lewis; Young, Joseph

Happy Hottentots   Atteridge; Romberg

Happyland   Bryan

Have a Heart   Buck; Kern

Have You Forgotten Me   Monaco

He Can Cure You of Love   Cohan

He May Be Old but He's Got Young Ideas   Johnson,
   Howard

Heart to Heart   Romberg

He's Coming Home   Romberg

He's Getting Too Darn Big for a One-Horse Town   Berlin

Hicky Do   Atteridge; Motzan; Romberg

His Cute Moving Picture Machine   Bryan

Hold-Up Ensemble   Porter

Home Again   Romberg

Honest Injun   Sterling; Von Tilzer

Honolulu, America Loves You, We've Got to Hand It to
   You   Clarke; Monaco

Honolulu Blues, The   Clarke; Monaco; Von Tilzer

Honolulu Hicki-Boola-Boo, The   Brown, Lew

Honolulu Pa-ki-ka, The   DeSylva

Hooligans Are Hooli Hooli Mad, The   Hanley

How Like Her Papa   Romberg

How to Make a Pretty Face   Atteridge; Motzan; Romberg

How Would You Like to Bounce a Baby on Your
   Knee   Bryan

How's Every Little Thing in Dixie   Yellen

Humpty Dumpty   Herbert

Hunter's Fox Trot Ball   Atteridge; Hanley; Romberg; Smith,
   Harry B.

Hurry Back to My Bamboo Shack   Berlin

I Always See Them Safely Home   Johnson, Howard

I Am True to All   Romberg; Smith, Robert B.

I Brought Red Roses in December to You   Bryan

I Called You My Sweetheart   Clarke; Johnson, Howard;
   Monaco

I Can Live Without Your Kisses, but I Won't Be Happy
   Dear   Bryan

I Can Never Keep Away from You   Clarke; Monaco

I Can't Forget   Kahn; Whiting

I Know I Got More than My Share   Clarke; Johnson,
   Howard

I Learned to Love You in Dreamland   Yellen

I Left Her on the Beach at Honolulu   Buck

I Like the Boys   Smith, Harry B.

I Lost My Heart in Honolulu   Cobb; Edwards

I May Believe Half-That's All   Romberg

I Might Be Coaxed Dear, But Not By You   Von Tilzer

I Miss You Miss America   Gilbert

I Never Knew Till Now   Motzan

I Sent My Wife to the Thousand Islands   Sterling; Von Tilzer

I Told My Love to the Roses   Johnson, J. Rosamond

I Want a Girl Like You   Atteridge; Motzan; Romberg

I Want that Star   Buck

I Want to Be a Romeo   Romberg

I Was Never Nearer Heaven in My Life   Clarke; Leslie;
   Snyder

I Wonder Why   Goetz

I Wouldn't Steal the Sweetheart of a Soldier Boy   Bryan

I'd Be Happy Anywhere with You   Romberg

If a Baby Would Never Grow Older (A Mother Would Never
   Be Sad)   Bryan

If I Could Live Again   Egan; Whiting

If I Knock the L Out of Kelly, It Would Still Be Kelly to
   Me   Lewis; Young, Joseph

If I Only Knew How I Stood with You   Cobb; Edwards

If in Spite of Our Attempts   Porter

If Mr. Ragtime Ever Gets Into that War   Kern; Motzan

If We Had 'Em Here Like He's Got 'Em There   Johnson,
   Howard

If You Don't Get Married This Summer, You Won't Get
   Married at All   Dubin

If You Ever Get Lonely   Kahn

If You Were the Only Girl in the World and I Was the Only
   Boy   Brown, Lew; Meyer

I'm Coming Back to California, That's Where I
   Belong   Brennan

I'm Down in Honolulu Looking Them Over   Berlin

I'm Glad You're Sorry   Whiting

I'm Going Way Back Home and Have a Wonderful
   Time   Jerome; Schwartz, Jean

I'm Gone Before I Go   Carroll

I'm Gonna Make Hay While the Sun Shines in
   Virginia   Lewis; Young, Joseph

I'm Looking for a Girl Like Mother   Kahn

I'm Not Prepared   Berlin

I'm Saving Up the Means to Get to New Orleans   Johnson,
   Howard

I'm Such a Nervous Man   Romberg

In a Dusty Caravan   Gilbert

In a Little Sedan Chair   Johnson, J. Rosamond

In Florida Among the Palms   Berlin

In the Beautiful Seaside Air   Donaldson

In the Evening Time   Howard, Joseph E.

Indian Fox Trot Ball, The   Buck

Indian Girls Chant   Porter

Indian Maiden's Chorus   Porter

Ireland Is Ireland to Me   Brennan

Ireland Must Be Heaven for My Mother Came from
   There   Fisher; Johnson, Howard

Ireland the Footstool of God   Brennan

Irish Love   Bryan

Isn't That Like a Man!   Smith, Harry B.; Smith, Robert B.

Isn't There a Crowd Everywhere?   Kern

It Comes So Natural   Ager; Donaldson

It Happened Every Night   Dubin

It Takes an Irishman to Make Love   Berlin

It Was in the Time of Roses   Young, Joseph

Italian Ballet Miniature   Atteridge; Motzan; Romberg

It's a Cute Little Way of My Own   Bryan

It's a Hundred to One You're In Love   Von Tilzer

It's a Long Way from Broadway to Edinboro Town   Cohan

It's Not Your Nationality It's Simply You   Johnson, Howard

It's the Husband of Mother Machree   Sterling

It's the Little Things that Count Most Ev'ry Way   Bryan

It's the Woman Who Pays   Cobb; Edwards
I've a Shooting-Box in Scotland   Porter
I've Got a Sweet Tooth Bothering Me   Berlin
I've Got an Awful Lot to Learn   Porter
I've Got Blues for Home Sweet Home   Meyer
I've Got the Army Blues   Gilbert
I've Got the Blues for Home Sweet Home   Goetz; Jerome; Meyer
I've Said Goodbye to Broadway   Buck
I've Saved All My Love for You   Buck
Ivy and Oak   Romberg
Izzie Get Busy Write Another Little Ragtime Tune   Brown, A. Seymour
Julia and Donald and Joe   Cohan
Just a Girl of Yesterday   Meyer
Just a Word of Sympathy   Kahn
Just As Soon As I Laid Eyes on You   Cobb; Edwards
Just Give Me Ragtime Please   Berlin
Just We Two   Goetz
Kangaroo Hop   Kahn
Keep Your Eye on the Girlie You Love   Johnson, Howard
Kiss Waltz, The   Romberg
Lady Fair, Lady Fair   Porter
Lady I've Vowed to Wed, The   Porter
L'Amour-Toujours-L'Amour (Love Everlasting)   Friml
Language of Flowers, The   Porter
Let Cupid In   Atteridge; Motzan
Letter Duet   Smith, Harry B.
Letter that Never Reached Home, The   Leslie
Liebechen (inst.)   Motzan
Lift Your Eyes to Mine   Smith, Harry B.
Like a Rose You Have Faded Away   McHugh
Like the Fjords of Scandinavia   Romberg
Lima   Porter
Little Bandbox Girl   Goetz
Little Bit of Nonsense, A   Romberg; Smith, Robert B.
Little Cutey   Motzan
Little Usher, A   Atteridge; Motzan; Romberg
Little Women   Smith, Harry B.; Smith, Robert B.
Live for Today   Goetz
Lona, Partner Lona   Romberg
Lonely Princess (The Sleeping Princess), The   Romberg
Long Live the Ladies   Goetz; Meyer; Young, Joseph
Love Came and Crowned Me   Porter
Love Is a Wonderful Thing   Gilbert
Love Is an Art   Smith, Harry B.; Smith, Robert B.
Love Is Like a Bubble   Atteridge; Romberg
Love Me a Little, Love Me Long   Howard, Joseph E.
Love Me at Twilight   Goetz; Young, Joseph
Luana Lou   Buck
Making of a Girl, The   Atteridge; Gershwin, George; Romberg
Mama's Blues (Papa's Blues)   Johnson, James P.
Mammy's Little Coal Black Rose   Egan; Whiting
Marionettes   Smith, Harry B.; Smith, Robert B.
Married Man Makes the Best Soldier   Romberg
Marry a Girl from the Ten Cent Store   Von Tilzer
Marry Me and See   Smith, Harry B.; Smith, Robert B.
Mary Does Everything but Sing   Carroll
Mayflower Girl   Hanley; Romberg; Smith, Harry B.
Melody of Youth   Goetz; Jerome; Schwartz, Jean
Mendelssohn and Liszt   Atteridge; Motzan; Romberg
Michael on His Motorcycle   Johnson, Howard
Midnight Frolic Rag, The   Buck
Milady's Toilette   Bryan

Millie   Motzan
Minstrel Days   Atteridge
Mirror, Mirror   Porter
Mona   Young, Joseph
Moonshine Sally   Johnson, Howard
Moonshine Valley   Fisher
Morning, Noon and Night   Johnson, J. Rosamond
Mother   Romberg
Music Lesson, The   Berlin
My American Beauty Girl (The Melting Pot)   Buck
My Bohemian Fashion Girl   Bryan
My Castle in the Air   Kern
My Dreamy China Lady   Kahn
My Hawaiian Sunshine   Gilbert
My Lady of the Nile   Buck; Kern
My Little China Doll   Yellen
My Loving Baby   Blake; Sissle
My Mother, My Dad and My Girl   Dubin
My Musical Comedy Maiden   Cohan
My Ninette   Goetz
My Own Iona (Not One Ionas)   Gilbert
My Pirate Lady   Atteridge; Romberg
My Runaway Girl   Gershwin, George
My Senorita   Romberg
My Voodoo Maiden   Atteridge; Romberg
My Wonderful Love for Thee   Brennan
My Yiddish Colleen   Von Tilzer
Never Marry   Young, Joseph
Nijinski   Buck
Nothing's Good Enough for a Good Little Girl   Atteridge; Motzan; Romberg
Now He's All Stuck Up, Cause He Owns a Ford   Johnson, Howard
Now He's Got a Beautiful Girl   Clarke; Leslie; Snyder
Now He's Got a Girl   Atteridge; Hanley; Romberg; Smith, Harry B.
Now that the Lights Are Low   Norworth
O'Brien Is Tryin' to Learn to Talk Hawaiian   Dubin
Oh, Bright Fair Dream   Porter
Oh, I Want To Be Good but My Eyes Won't Let Me   Bryan
Oh Joe, with Your Fiddle and Bow You Stole My Heart Away   Donaldson
Oh Promise Me that You'll Come Back to Alabam   Leslie; Meyer
Oh, What a Time I Had with Minnie the Mermaid   DeSylva
Oh, You Lovely Ladies   Romberg
Old Home Town   Goetz
On a Summer Night   Edwards
On His First Day Home on Leave   Norworth
On Lake Champlain   Bryan
On the Good Ship B.V.D.   Donaldson
On the Hoko Moko Isle   Von Tilzer
On the Road to Paradise   Brennan
On the South Sea Isle   Von Tilzer
On the Train of a Wedding Gown   Berlin
One Life, One Love, I Give Them Both to You   Clarke; Monaco
One Way of Doing It   Smith, Harry B.; Smith, Robert B.
Opening Carnival Scene   Von Tilzer
Orange, White and Blue, The   Herbert
Other Side, The   Goetz
Our Military Home   Johnson, Howard
Out of His Heart He Builds a Home   Herbert
Out of the Cradle, Into My Heart   Gilbert
Over and Under   Goetz; Young, Joseph

Pajama Girlies   Atteridge; Motzan
Photograph of You   Atteridge; Motzan; Romberg
Pin Holes in de Sky   Atteridge; Motzan
Pity Me Please   Porter
Play My Melody   Atteridge; Motzan; Romberg
Please Be Good to Me   Hanley
Poncho and Pepita   Romberg
Pretty Baby   Kahn
Pretty Little Mayflower Girl   Atteridge; Hanley
Pretty Please   Von Tilzer
Punchinello (inst.)   Herbert
Ragging the Apache   Atteridge; Motzan; Romberg
Ragtime Calisthenics   Atteridge; Motzan; Romberg
Ragtime Fight   Romberg
Revelation Ensemble   Porter
Right Brazilian Girl, The   Romberg
Right Girl, The   Smith, Harry B.; Smith, Robert B.
Robinson Crusoe   Atteridge; Romberg
Roll Your Hoop   Atteridge; Motzan; Romberg
Rolling Stones All Come Rolling Home Again   Leslie
Romeo and Juliet   Atteridge; Motzan; Romberg
Romping Red Heads, The   Herbert
Roosevelt, Bryan and Hughes   Atteridge; Motzan; Romberg
Roosevelt, Wilson and Hughes   Atteridge; Motzan; Romberg
Rosemary   Herbert
Running Around with Chorus Girls   Cohan
Sailor's Fling   Atteridge; Hanley; Romberg; Smith, Harry B.
Saturday Night   Kern
See America First   Blake; Porter; Sissle
Serenade   Porter
Sextette   Romberg; Smith, Robert B.
Shades of Night   Gilbert
She Gets Me All Fussed Up   Brown, Lew; Hanley
She Is the Sunshine of Virginia   Carroll
She Was a Dairy Maid   Carroll
She Was a Girl I Used to Know   Hanley
She's Dixie All the Time   Bryan
She's Good Enough To Be Your Baby's Mother and She's
   Good Enough to Vote with You   Bryan
Simple Life   Atteridge; Romberg
Since Maggie Dooley Learned the Hooley Hooley   Kalmar;
   Leslie; Meyer
Since Mary Ann McCue Came Back from Honolulu   Von
   Tilzer
Since You Went Away   Johnson, J. Rosamond
Six Little Wives of the King   Buck
Ski-ing   Romberg
Slavlova   Atteridge; Motzan; Romberg
Slow Sinks the Sun   Porter
Small Town Girl   Lewis; Meyer; Young, Joseph
Smile, Smile, Smile   Romberg
So This is Paris!   Atteridge
Social Coach of All the Fashionable Future Debutantes,
   The   Porter
Some Day   Romberg
Some Girls Do and Some Girls Don't   Johnson, Howard
Some One   Kern
Some Time   Jerome
Someone Else May Be There While I'm Gone   Berlin
Something's Got to Be Done   Porter
Sometimes You Get a Good One and Sometimes You
   Don't   Sterling; Von Tilzer
Sonambulistic Tune   Buck
Spanish Ballet   Atteridge; Hanley; Romberg; Smith, Harry B.
Step This Way   Berlin; Goetz

Step We Grandly   Porter
Stolen Kisses   Romberg
Stone Age (scene) (inst.), The   Herbert
Stop and Go   Buck
Stop Tickling Me   Romberg; Smith, Robert B.
Stormy Sea of Love, The   Carroll
Story of Every Day Life, A   Fisher; Johnson, Howard
Strolling Eyes   Atteridge; Hanley
Strolling Quite Fancy Free   Porter
Study in Black and White, A   Atteridge; Motzan; Romberg
Suzanne   Carroll
Sweet and Pretty   Atteridge; Motzan
Sweet Babette She Always Did the Minuet   Sterling; Von
   Tilzer
Sweet Cookie   Ager; Jerome
Sweet Simplicity   Porter
Sweetest Melody of All, The   Clarke; Monaco
Sweethearts   Kahn
Tear, a Kiss, a Smile, A   Motzan
Tete-a-Tete with You, A   Romberg; Smith, Robert B.
That Broadway Chicken Walk   Berlin
That Come Hither Look   Kern
That Funny Jas Band from Dixieland   Kahn
That Funny Little Something   Gilbert
That Midnight Frolic of Mine   Brown, A. Seymour
That Old New England Town   Ager; Jerome
That's Called Walking the Dog   Romberg
That's the Kind of Love I Crave   Sissle
That's the Meaning of Ireland   Von Tilzer
Then Love Will Come   Romberg
There's a Fool Born Every Day   Dubin
There's a Little Bit of Bad in Every Good Little Girl   Clarke;
   Fisher
There's a Little Bit of Irish in Sadie Cohn   Bryan
There's a Lovely Crop of Girls This Year   Norworth
There's a Wise Old Moon that Shines in Loveland and He
   Knows the Old Love Game   Meyer
There's Just a Little Bit of Monkey Still Left in You and
   Me   Clarke; Monaco
There's Music in the Air (inst.)   Motzan
There's Only One Little Girl   Cohan
There's Ragtime in the Air   Buck
There's Someone More Lonesome than You   Von Tilzer
There's Someone You've Forgotten who Has not Forgotten
   You   Yellen
They All Look Good to Me   Goetz
They Made It Twice As Nice As Paradise and Called It
   Dixieland   Egan; Whiting
They're Making Them Wonderful   Hanley
This Great Big World Owed Me a Loving   Sterling; Von
   Tilzer
Those Good Old Days Back Home (inst.)   Monaco
Three Hundred Sixty-Five Days   Kern
Through These Wonderful Glasses of Mine   Von Tilzer
Tillie Titwillow   Atteridge
To Follow Every Fancy   Porter
Tonight's the Night   Fisher; Johnson, Howard
Toodle Oo   Kern
Toy Soldiers (inst.), The   Herbert
Trail to Sunset Valley, The   Gilbert
Tripping, Tripping   Goetz
Turn Back the Universe and Give Me Yesterday   Brennan
Turn to the Right   Ager; Jerome
'Twas Only an Irishman's Dream   Dubin
Twentieth Century Squaw   Yellen

Two Can Play that Game   Smith, Harry B.
Two Happy Tadpoles   Romberg; Smith, Robert B.
Two Key Rag   Von Tilzer
Uncle Sam's Children (inst.)   Herbert
'Under Fire' Dance, The   Cohan
Under the Sea   Herbert
Violin Song, The   Romberg; Smith, Robert B.
Voice of Love, The   Smith, Harry B.; Smith, Robert B.
Wake, Love, Wake   Porter
(That's Called) Walking the Dog   Atteridge; Blake; Motzan;
   Sissle
War Babies   Hanley
Was Friday a Woman or Was Friday a Man   Brown, Lew
Way Down in Iowa I'm Going to Hide Anyway   Lewis;
   Meyer; Young, Joseph
We Won't Get Home Until A.M. If We Ever Get Home at
   All   Donaldson
Wedding Bells   Atteridge; Motzan
Wedding By the Sea   Atteridge; Motzan; Romberg
Welcome Honey to Your Old Plantation Home   Yellen
We'll Be Alone at Last   Cohan
What Do You Want to Make Those Eyes at Me
   For   Johnson, Howard; Monaco
What's the Matter with the Irish (They're Getting Better
   Every Day)   Johnson, Howard
When a Body's in Love   Porter
When Cupid Calls   Smith, Harry B.
When Fortune Smiles   Smith, Harry B.; Smith, Robert B.
When He Comes Back to Me   Buck
When He's Away   Norworth
When I Fell in Love with You   Sterling; Von Tilzer
When I Hear a Band Play Dixieland, It's Home Sweet Home
   to Me   Ager; Johnson, Howard
When I Used to Lead the Ballet   Porter
When I Wave My Flag   Norworth
When Pavlova Starts Buck and Winging   Atteridge; Motzan;
   Romberg
When Priscilla Tries to Reach High C   Von Tilzer
When Sherman Went Marching Through Georgia   Ruby
When the Black Sheep Returns to the Fold   Berlin
When the Lights Are Low   Buck; Kern
When the Rest of the World Don't Want You, Go Back to
   the Folks at Home   Dubin
When the Sun Goes Down in Romany   Goetz
When the Sun Goes Down in Romany My Heart Goes
   Roaming Back to You   Lewis; Young, Joseph
When the Sun Goes Down in Switzerland   McHugh
When They Go Through a Tunnel   Kalmar
When They Grow Older, They Grow a Little Bolder   Meyer;
   Young, Joseph
When Uncle Sam Rules the Wave   Herbert
When Uncle Sammy Leads the Band   Von Tilzer
When Verdi Plays the Hurdy Gurdy   Donaldson
When We Are Married   Goetz
When We Were Twenty-One   Goetz
When You Drop Off at Cairo, Illinois   Berlin; Goetz
When You Grow to Be Twenty One (When I Was
   Twenty-One)   Jerome
When You Grow to Be Twenty-One (When I Was
   Twenty-One)   Leslie; Schwartz, Jean
When You Want 'Em, You Can't Get 'Em (When You Got
   'Em, You Don't Want 'Em)   Gershwin, George
When You're in Love You'll Know   Kern
When You're Mine, When I'm Yours   Norworth
When You're Starring for the Movies   Atteridge; Romberg

Where Did Robinson Crusoe Go with Friday on Saturday
   Night   Lewis; Meyer; Young, Joseph
Where the Southern Roses Grow   Norworth
Whole Word Comes from Dixie (When They Play that Dixie
   Tune), The   Hanley
Whole World Loves a Lover and the Lover that I Love Is
   You, The   Whiting
Whose Pretty Baby Are You   Kahn
Will You Love Me When My Flivver Is a Wreck?   Porter
Will-of-the-Wisp   Buck
Wine, Woman and Song   Atteridge; Romberg
Winter Garden Hop   Atteridge; Motzan; Romberg
With a Bit of a Smile (I'll Find a Way to Your Heart)   Fisher;
   Johnson, Howard
Woman and Song   Motzan
Wonderful Girl   Goetz
Woodland Dance   Porter
Yaaka Hula Hickey Dula   Goetz; Young, Joseph
Yaddie Kaddie Kiddie Kaddie Doo   Lewis; Meyer; Young,
   Joseph
Yesterthoughts (inst.)   Herbert
You Belong to Me   Herbert; Smith, Harry B.
You Can Tell That I'm Irish   Cohan
You Can't Get Along with 'em Or Without 'em   Clarke;
   Fisher
You Can't Keep a Squirrel on the Ground   Cobb; Edwards
You May Hold a Million Girlies in Your Arms   Fisher;
   Johnson, Howard
You Ought to Go to Paris   Berlin; Goetz
You Were Made to Order for Me   Von Tilzer
You'll Always Be the Same Sweet Baby   Brown, A. Seymour
You'll Be Her Baby As Long As You Live   Clarke; Johnson,
   Howard; Monaco
Your America   Cohan
Your Auto Ought to Get Girls   Atteridge; Motzan; Romberg
You're a Dangerous Girl   Clarke; Monaco
You're Just Made to Order for Me   Von Tilzer
You're Like a Beautiful Song   Dubin
You're the Best Little Mother that God Ever Made   Brennan
Yours Sincerely U.S.A.   Atteridge; Motzan; Romberg
You've Got Me Doing It Too   Berlin
Ziegfeld Rag   Cohan

1917

Adopt a Pretty Baby   Atteridge; Romberg
After a Thousand Years   Dubin; Monaco
Ah, What Wonderful Things One Little Girl Can Do   Yellen
Ain't It a Grand a Glorious Feeling?   Kern
Ain't You Coming Back to Dixieland   Egan; Whiting
Alexander's Got a Jazz Band Now   DeSylva
Alexander's Jazz Band   Donaldson
Algerian Girl   Atteridge; Romberg
All That I Am I Owe to You Angel Mother of
   Mine   Johnson, Howard; Monaco
All that I Want Is You   Monaco
All the World Will Be Jealous of Me   Dubin
Along the Way to Waikiki   Kahn; Whiting
Am I to Blame?   Friml
America Here's My Boy   Sterling
America Needs You Like a Mother, Would You Turn Your
   Mother Down   Clarke; Schwartz, Jean
American Serenade   Herbert
America's Fighting Back   Atteridge; Motzan; Romberg
And I Am All Alone   Kern

And They Call It a Popular Song   Johnson, Howard
Angels   Motzan
Angie's Patriotic Rally   Bryan
Annie McGuinnis Pavlova   Hammerstein
An-ti-ci-pa-tion   Romberg
Any Little Girl Can Make a Bad Man Good (And a Good
   Man Bad They Say)   Hanley
Are You from Heaven   Gilbert
Army's Full of Irish   Donaldson
Art Song   Herbert
As the Years Roll By   Herbert
Ask Her in Springtime   Whiting
Ask Me No Questions   Brown, Lew
At Seven, Seventeen and Seventy   Egan
At the Button-Hole Makers' Ball   Johnson, Howard
At the Old Town Pump   Von Tilzer
At the Wedding of Sammy and Me   Ruby
At the Yankee Military Ball   Johnson, Howard
Au Revoir But Not Good-Bye, Soldier Boy   Brown, Lew
Auto Girls Song   Buck
Auto Show Girl   Rodgers
Automat Cabaret   Carroll
Awkward Age, The   Atteridge; Motzan; Romberg
Baby Vampire   Kahn; Kern; Smith, Harry B.
Back in Tipperary Town   Yellen
Back to Nature   Motzan
Bad, Bad Baby   Egan
Bad Chinaman from Shanghai, A   Berlin
Battle Song of Liberty, The   Yellen
Be a Good Scout   Carroll
Be a Little Sunbeam   Kern
Be Sure It's Light the Musical Shore   Friml; Harbach
Be Yourself   Mitchell
Beautiful Bird   Gershwin, George; Gershwin, Ira
Beautiful Girl   Buck
Beautiful Girl, Goodbye   Buck
Beauty Doctor, The   Herbert
Because You're Irish   Kahn
Best Things in Life Are Free, The   Johnson, Howard
Bird of Gay Bohemia, The   Bryan
Birdie   Berlin
Bis Bolo   Motzan
Bit of Opera, A   Motzan
Blamen Is Our Birthright   Herbert
Blarney Stone, The   Friml
Blushing Bride and Groom, The   Ager; Jerome
Boola Boo   Friml; Harbach
Boys of Uncle Sam   Johnson, James P.
Bravest Heart of All   Egan; Whiting
Bravo, Antonio!   Norworth
Bricky-Brackie Tootsies   Goetz
Bright Lights   Kern
Bring Back, Bring Back, Bring Back the Kaiser to Me   Von
   Tilzer
Bring Back My Daddy to Me   Johnson, Howard; Meyer
Bring Me a Girl   Kalmar
B-R-O-A-D-W-A-Y   Buck
Broadway Butterfly   Goetz
Buck Up   Friml
Bundle of Nerves   Smith, Harry B.
(Little) Bungalow in Quogue   Kern
Burmese Ballet, A   Motzan
But Not for You   Smith, Harry B.
Buy a Liberty Bond for the Baby   Von Tilzer
Buy a Red Cross Rosie   Bryan

Call on Rag Doll   Goetz
Camouflage   Gilbert
Camouflaging   Goetz
Cane Song   Buck
Can't You Hear Your Country Calling   Buck; Herbert
Caprice Rag (inst.)   Johnson, James P.
Captain Kiddo   Cobb; Edwards
Carmen Has Nothing on Me   Buck
Charleston Rag (inst.)   Blake
Chasing the Squirrel   Bryan
Cheer Up, Eat and Grow Thin   Goetz
Cheer Up, the Sun Will Soon Be Shining   Sterling
Cherry Blossom   Kahn
Chimes of Normandy   Bryan
Chin Chin Chinaman   Hanley
China Dreams   Egan; Kahn
China, We Owe a Lot to You   Ager; Johnson, Howard
Chinese Letter Song   Goetz
Chorus Girl, The   Atteridge; Motzan; Romberg
Christmastide Love   Goetz
Chu Chin Chow   Buck
Cinderella Lost Her Slipper   Berlin
Cleopatra   Bryan
Cleopatterer   Kern
College Trot, The   Harbach
Colonial Ballet   Atteridge; Romberg
Colorado   Hanley
Come Along   Johnson, Howard
Come and Play with Me   Ager
Come Back to Erin   Hanley
Come Down to Tony Spagoni's Cabaret   Dubin
Come to Gypsy Land   Smith, Harry B.
Come Tom   Herbert
Constantinople   Von Tilzer
Crickets Are Calling, The   Kern
Cross My Heart and Hope to Die   Von Tilzer
Cupid, the Cunnin' Pandeen   Herbert
Cutey (Jou-Jou)   Motzan
Daddy Found You Down Beside the Garden Wall   Egan
Daintiness Rag (inst.)   Johnson, James P.
Daisy   Kern
Dance and Grow Thin   Berlin; Meyer
Dance, Dance, Dance   Atteridge; Romberg
Dance Me Away with You   Hanley
Dance of the Dolls   Goetz
Dance of the Rose, The   Friml
Dancing Around the Town   Motzan
Dancing Family   Atteridge; Motzan; Romberg
Dancing Will Keep You Young   Romberg
Daniel in the Lion's Den   Fisher
Daughter of the Regiment (Hats Off to the Queen's
   Hussars), The   Romberg
Dawn of Love, The   Friml
Dear Bath   Friml
Dear Curracloe   Friml
Dear Old Bronx   Norworth
Dear Old Dublin   Friml
Devil and the Deep Blue Sea, The   Herbert
Die, Die, Die Like a Soldier   Herbert
Dinny's Serenade   Herbert
Dixie Volunteers, The   Leslie; Ruby
Do Buy Some Candy, Sir   Romberg
Do It for Me   Harbach
Do You Want Us to Lose?   Norworth
Doing My Bit   Atteridge; Romberg

Don't Go Away   Romberg
Don't Go in the Water   Harbach
Don't Slam the Door   Von Tilzer
Don't Tempt Me   Kern; Smith, Harry B.
Don't Try To Steal the Sweetheart of a Soldier   Bryan
Dove Dance, The   Norworth
Down By the Beautiful Nile   Bryan; Meyer
Down in Cairo Town   Johnson, Howard
Down in Hindustan   Egan
Down Up, Left Right   Harbach
Down Virginia Way   Motzan
Down Where the Jack O'Lanterns Grow   Berlin
Down Where the Sweet Potatoes Grow   Von Tilzer
Dream! Dream!   Smith, Harry B.
Dream of a Soldier Boy, The   Dubin; Monaco
Dreaming of Home Sweet Home   Hanley
Dreamy Parisian Croon, The   Goetz
Drift with Me   Kern; Smith, Harry B.
Driving Home with Angeline   Goetz
Egyptian Rag   Atteridge; Romberg
Eileen, Allana Asthore   Herbert
Entrance of Humpy Grogan   Herbert
Erin Slanthogal Go Bragh   Herbert
Every Day   Kern
Every Girl Is Doing Her Bit   Buck
Everybody Took a Kick at Nicholas   Lewis; Young, Joseph
Everybody's Knittin' Now   Hanley
Everything Has Been Done   Romberg
Everything Looks Rosy and Bright   Goetz
Falling Leaves Ballet (inst.)   Herbert
Fame, Fame, Fame   Bryan
Fancy You Fancying Me   Norworth
Fascination (inst.)   Johnson, James P.
Fashion Show, The   Atteridge; Romberg
Faster and Faster   Atteridge; Motzan; Romberg
Fatal Ring, The   Hanley
Father in Heaven, Bless Mother o' Me   Fisher
Father Knickerbocker   Atteridge; Motzan
Father Knickerbocker Fox Trot   Atteridge; Romberg
Fickle Sex (Woman's Said to Be), The   Romberg
Fiesta   Atteridge; Romberg
Fine Feathers   Atteridge; Romberg
First Nighters   Goetz
Flag of Our Land   Buck
Flubby Dub (The Cave Man)   Kern
Fool Me   Bryan
Foolish Little Maiden, I, A   Romberg
Football Song (Opening Act II)   Kern
For Me and My Gal   Goetz; Leslie; Meyer
For One Sweet Day   Bryan
For the Sake of Humanity   Atteridge; Romberg
For You a Rose   Cobb; Edwards
For Your Country and My Country   Berlin
Free Trade and a Misty Moon   Herbert
Frocks and Frills   Atteridge; Romberg
From Here to Shanghai   Berlin
Further It Is from Tipperary, The   Norworth
Garden of Liberty (I've Got a Vegetable Garden) (Vegetable Song)   Bryan
General Dance   Herbert
Get a Girl to Lead the Army   Bryan
Ghosts of the Ukulele, The   Motzan
Ginger   Goetz
Girl Begind the Gun, The   Herbert
Girl for Me, The   Atteridge; Romberg

Girl on the Square   Motzan
Girl Who Drinks Champagne, The   Atteridge; Motzan; Romberg
Girls Are Getting Wiser Ev'ry Day, The   Bryan
Girls of America, We All Depend on You   Kalmar; Leslie; Ruby
Give Me a Bit More than You Gave Reilly   Bryan
Give Me an Old-Fashioned Girlie   Norworth
Give Me the Moonlight, Give Me the Girl (And Leave the Rest to Me)   Brown, Lew
Glad, Triumphant Hour   Herbert
Go Away, Girls   Romberg
Go Little Boat   Kern
God Only Knows How I Miss You   Cobb; Edwards
Going Up   Harbach
Golden Pheasant, The   Romberg
Golden West, The   Atteridge; Motzan; Romberg
Good Old Atwater   Kern
Goodbye Mary   McHugh
Good-Bye, My Little Lady   Hanley
Goodbye, That Means You   Sterling
Gozinto   Buck
Great Camp Meeting Day   Sissle
Greenwich Village Belle   Atteridge; Romberg
Gypsy Man, The   Atteridge; Romberg
Gypsy Song   Romberg
Happy Sunday   Dubin
Have a Heart   Kern
Have You Seen the Ducks   Goetz
Hawaii, I'm Lonesome for You   Yellen
He Goes to Work in the Night Time and She Goes to Work Ever Day   Johnson, Howard
He Will Understand   Friml; Harbach
Health to Noah   Friml
Heaven Will Come Down to You   Hanley
Hector   Norworth
Hello, Aloha, Hello!   Johnson, Howard; Meyer
Hello France   Davis
Hello Girlie   Bryan
Hello, Miss Tango!   Atteridge; Romberg
Hello My Dearie   Buck
Hello, Wisconsin, Won't You Find My Yonnie Yonson   Kalmar; Leslie; Ruby
Help, Help, Help, I'm Sinking in a Beautiful Ocean of Love   Von Tilzer
Here's to the Two of You   Harbach
He's a Devil on Saturday Night   Donaldson
He's a No Good-a No More   Clarke; Monaco
He's Doing His Bit for the Girls   Von Tilzer
He's Just Like You   Brown, Lew
Hicky Do   Motzan
Hitchy-Koo   Goetz
Homeward Bound   Goetz; Johnson, Howard; Meyer
Honeymoon Inn   Kern
How Can Any Girlie Be a Good Little Girl (When She Loves a Naughty Little Boy)   Johnson, Howard
How Can I Forget (When There's So Much to Remember)   Berlin
Huckleberry Finn   Lewis; Young, Joseph
Hula Serenade   Kahn
I Don't Want to Be Loved a Little By a Lot of Little Boys (But By One Little Boy A Lot)   Hanley
I Don't Want to Get Well   Johnson, Howard
I Found a Rosebud in Roseland   McHugh
I Found the Heart of You   Freed, Arthur

I Have to Leave the Boys   Romberg
I Know You   Smith, Harry B.; Sterling
I Like to Keep My Eyes on You   Cobb; Edwards
I Long to Be a Melody   Gilbert
I Long to Be with Betty but She's Living in
      Connecticut   Johnson, Howard; Meyer
I Love My Billy Sunday but Oh You Saturday Night   Clarke;
      Leslie; Meyer
I Love You Sweetheart   Harbach
I May Be Gone for a Long Long Time   Brown, Lew
I May Be Small but I Have Big Ideas   Atteridge; Romberg
I May Stay Away a Little Longer   Goetz
I Might Say 'Yes' To You   Smith, Harry B.
I Proved that I Knew Something When I Fell in Love with
      You   Bryan
I Sent My Wife Away for a Rest, I Needed It   Brown, Lew
I Want a Boy Who's Determined to Do What I
      Say   Harbach
I Want a Daddy Like You   Brown, Lew
I Want a Girl Like You   Motzan
I Want a Good Girl (And I Want Her Bad)   Bryan
I Want to Go to Church with You   Goetz; Monaco
I Want You To Want Me with You   Bryan
I Wasn't Born to Be Lonesome   Brown, Lew
I Wish I Was a Big Sky-Rocket   Goetz
I Wonder What He's Doing Tonight   Hanley
I Wonder What the Folks Will Think of Me   Clarke;
      Johnson, Howard; Monaco
I Wonder Why   Kern; Smith, Harry B.
I'd Do the Same   Friml
I'd Give My Life Just to Hear Mother Say Goodnight Little
      Baby Good Night   Leslie
I'd Love to Be a Lady   Herbert
If Eve Had Left the Apple on the Bough   Herbert
If I Find a Bit of Heaven in Your Irish Heart of
      Love   Brennan
If I Only Had the Pipe That Peter Pan Used to Pipe   Fisher
If I Only Had the Pipe that Peter Piper Used to
      Pipe   Johnson, Howard
If Sammy Simpson Shot the Chutes Why Shouldn't He
      Shoot the Shots   Von Tilzer
If Things Were What They Seem   Herbert
If We Can Be Together   Kahn
If We Did Here What They Do on the Cannibal
      Isles   Johnson, Howard
If You Hadn't Answered No   Kalmar; Leslie; Ruby
If You Haven't Answered No   Goetz
If You Look in Her Eyes   Harbach
If You Only Knew   Gershwin, George; Gershwin, Ira
If You Saw All that I Saw in Arkansas   Ager
If You Were Here   Goetz
If You'll Be My Soldier, I'll Be a Red Cross Nurse   Bryan
I'll Be a College Boy's Dear   Atteridge; Motzan; Romberg
I'll Be Somewhere in France   Buck
I'll Be the Words and You'll Be the Music   Von Tilzer
I'll Come Back to You When It's All Over   Brown, Lew
I'll Come Sailing Home to You (A Long Way from
      Broadway)   Carroll
I'll Open the Door, and Close the Door   Brown, Lew
I'll Take You Back to Italy   Berlin
I'm a Rough Man, I'm a Tough Man   Romberg
I'm a Twelve O'Clock Fellow (In a Nine O'Clock
      Town)   Kalmar; Von Tilzer
I'm All Bound 'Round with the Mason Dixon Line   Lewis;
      Schwartz, Jean; Young, Joseph

I'm Always Thinking of Georgia   Monaco
I'm Crazy Over Every Girl in France   Bryan
I'm Goin' to Settle Down Outside of London Town, When
      I'm Dry, Dry, Dry   Monaco
I'm Going to Find a Girl   Kern
I'm Hearin' from Erin   Gilbert
I'm Here, Little Girls, I'm Here   Kern
I'm Longing for Someone to Love Me   Howard, Joseph E.
I'm Looking for Old Broadway (I'm Looking for the Great
      White Way)   Buck
I'm Madly in Love with a Dream Girl   Romberg
I'm Only Dreaming   Friml; Harbach
I'm Only Dreaming of You   Brennan
I'm So Busy   Kern
I'm the Old Man in the Moon   Kern
I'm Writing to You, Sammy   Brown, Lew
In Berry Pickin' Time   Yellen
In Days of ABC   Egan
In Erin's Isle   Herbert
In Our Little Home Sweet Home   Romberg
In San Domingo   Lewis; Snyder; Young, Joseph
In the Beautiful Garden of Girls   Buck
In the Days of Auld Lang Syne   Von Tilzer
In the Land o' Yama Yama   Fisher
In the Land of Wedding Bells   Johnson, Howard; Meyer
In the Name of the King   Herbert
In the Old Red School   Lewis; Snyder; Young, Joseph
(Back Home Again in) Indiana   Hanley
Innovation (inst.)   Johnson, James P.
Introduction Act III   Herbert
Ireland My Sireland   Herbert
Irish Have a Great Day Tonight, The   Herbert
Irish Jig (inst.)   Herbert
Irish Reel   Herbert
Isle of Lost Romance, The   Goetz
Isn't She the Busy Little Bee   Von Tilzer
It Can't Be Done   Kern; Smith, Harry B.
It Wasn't My Fault   Kern
Italian Ballet Miniature   Motzan
It's a Great Big Land   Kern
It's a Hundred to One You're From Dixie   Gilbert
It's a Long Long Way to the U.S.A. and the Girl I Left
      Behind   Von Tilzer
It's a Pippin   Motzan
It's a Short Way Through Mother's Doorway but It's a Long
      Way Back to Mother's Knee   Sterling
It's a Sure Sign   Kern
It's a Windy Day at the Battery   Romberg
It's All Right If You Love (One Another)   Leslie; Ruby
It's Easier to Kiss than Talk   Ager; Goetz
It's Lilac Time in Lovers' Lane   Whiting
It's Time for Every Boy to Be a Soldier   Bryan
I've a Little Bit of Scotch in Me   Atteridge; Romberg
I've Been Fiddle-ing   Kahn
I've Got a Red Cross Rosie Going Across with Me   Kalmar;
      Leslie; Ruby
I've Got Something in My Eye   Clarke; Leslie; Meyer
I've Got the Nicest Little Home in Dixie   Donaldson
I've Got the Sweetest Girl in Maryland   Donaldson
Jaz-o-Mine   Akst
Jealous Moon   Buck
Jig   Herbert
Jim Jam Jems   Donaldson; Goetz
Joan of Arc   Harbach
Joan of Arc (They Are Calling You)   Bryan

Job Lots   Romberg
Jump Jim Crow   Romberg
Just a Little Bit o' Love   Carroll
Just a Little Bit of Love   Smith, Harry B.
Just a Little Cottage in the Country   Sterling
Just a Simple Country Maiden   Cobb; Edwards
Just As Your Mother Was   Sterling; Von Tilzer
Just Because You're You   Buck; Kern
Just Girls   Buck
Just Like Washington Crossed the Delaware, General
    Pershing Will Cross the Rhine   Johnson, Howard;
    Meyer
Just the Kind of a Girl You'd Love to Make Your Wife   Von
    Tilzer
Just To Keep Expenses Down   Bryan
Just We Two   Friml
Just What I Wanted   Romberg
Just You and Me   Buck
Just You Watch My Step   Kern
Justine Johnstone Rag, The   Romberg
Keep Off the Grass   Friml; Harbach
Keep on the Right Hand Side of Father   Bryan
Keep Repeating It   Romberg
Keep the Lovelight Singing in the Window   McHugh
Keep Your Eye on Little Mary Brown   Bryan
King of Broadway   Berlin
Kingdom of My Heart   Motzan
Kiss for Cinderella   Cobb; Edwards
Kiss Me   Harbach
Kitty Darlin'   Friml; Harbach
La Fiesta (inst.)   Blake
Laddie Boy   Cobb; Edwards
Ladies, The   Goetz
Lady of the Sea   Goetz
Lady Romance   Goetz
Land of the Midnight Sun, The   Smith, Harry B.
Land where Dreams Come True, The   Friml
Land Where the Good Songs Go, The   Kern
Language of the Fan, The   Atteridge; Romberg
Leave It to Jane   Kern
Let Her Go   Atteridge; Romberg
Let the Flag Fly   Gilbert
Let's All Be Americans Now   Berlin; Leslie; Meyer
Let's All Be Something, Uncle Sammy Wants Us
    Now   Sterling
Let's Rally   Motzan
Letter Boxes   Berlin
Life's a Dance   Kern; Smith, Harry B.
Life's a Game at Best   Herbert
Li'l Gal   Johnson, J. Rosamond
Lily of the Valley   Gilbert
Listen to the Knocking of the Knitting Club   Von Tilzer
Little Colleen (Do You Believe in Fairies)   Dubin
Little Farm in Normandy, A   Herbert
Little Miss Vogue   Cobb; Edwards
Long, Long Ago   Buck
Look Before You Leap   Romberg
Look in His Eyes   Kern
Look in the Book   Kern; Smith, Harry B.
Look Out for the Irish Tonight   Sterling
Lorraine (My Beautiful Alsace Lorraine)   Bryan; Fisher
Love Is an Intrusion   Romberg
Love o' Mike   Kern; Smith, Harry B.
Love Will Find the Way   Von Tilzer
Love-Land   Friml; Harbach

Loving Daddy, A   Atteridge; Romberg
Macaroni Joe   Dubin
Maid and the Valet, The   Friml
Maiden's Prayer   Hanley
Make Yourself at Home   Hammerstein
Mammy's Li'l Choc'late Cullud Chile   Blake; Sissle
Man Behind the Hammer and the Plow, The   Von Tilzer
Man Is Only a Man, A   Berlin
Man that Can Die Like a Soldier, A   Herbert
March of the Enchantress   Goetz
Married Life   Friml; Harbach
Mary Brown   Berlin
Maybe I Love You, Cause You're Wrong, All
    Wrong   Johnson, Howard; Monaco
Maybe Sometime   Kahn
Mayer Come Back from Hawaii   Brown, Lew
Meet Me at the Station, Dear   Lewis; Young, Joseph
Meet Me at the Station, Dear (Dearie)   Snyder
Meet Me in Orange Blossom Time   Norworth
Mendelssohn and Liszt   Motzan
Merry Wedding Bells   Harbach
Meyer Come Back from Hawaii   Donaldson
Mickey   Williams
Midnight Zeppo, The   Buck
Mississippi   Buck
Mister Rag and I   Atteridge; Romberg
Molly Malone   Norworth
Monkey Bunch, The   Johnson, James P.
Mons. France and Miss America   Buck
More I See Hawaii the Better I Like New York, The   Kalmar
Mother Always Waits at Home   McHugh
Mother, Dixie and You   Johnson, Howard
Mother of the Regiment, The   Friml
Mothers of Men   Cobb; Edwards
Mr. Finkelstein, The Jewish Mister Dooley   Hanley
Mr. Jazz Himself   Berlin
Musical Snore, The   Friml
My Arabian Maid   Buck
My Beautiful Egypt   Bryan
My Bedouin Girl   Atteridge; Romberg
My Cairo Maid   DeSylva
My First Long Pants   Cobb; Edwards
My Golden Prairie   Gilbert
My Good Friends of Erin's Isle   Herbert
My Heart is the Garden and You Are My Beautiful
    Rose   Fisher
My Heart's Tonight in Old New Hampshire with My Lady
    Jane   Sterling
My Irish Song of Songs   Dubin
My Italian Rose   Dubin
My Lady's Clothes   Norworth
My Little Belgian Maid   Buck
My Little Irish Rose   Herbert
My Loveable Girl   Donaldson
My Mind's Made Up to Marry Caroline   Brown, Lew
My Modest Quaker Girl   Bryan; Pollack
My Mother's Eyes   Bryan
My Rainbow Girl   Atteridge; Romberg
My Sunshine Jane (Down Beside the Weeping Willow
    Tree)   Brennan
My Sweetie   Berlin
My Yiddisha Butterfly   Dubin
My Yokohama Girl   Bryan
My Yokohoma Girl   Atteridge; Motzan; Romberg
Napoleon   Kern

Nerves   Herbert
Nesting Time in Flatbush   Kern
Never Forget to Write Home   Hanley
New York, What's Become of You?   Goetz
Nightie Parade   Harbach
Nightingale (Samarkand), The   Kern
Nights Are Six Months Long, The   Hanley
No More Girls for Me   Romberg
No One Can Keep Me Away from You   Bryan
Nonsense   Goetz
North of 53   Norworth
Nothing On To-Day   Atteridge; Romberg
Nothing's Good Enough for a Good Little Girl If She's Good
      Enough for You   Bryan
Odd Lots   Romberg
Officers of the 125th   Romberg
Oh Galatea!   Romberg
Oh Jack, When Are You Coming Back   Sterling
Oh, Justine   Romberg
Oh! Mississippi, I Miss You   Ager
Oh, My!   Herbert
Oh Oh Lady   Snyder; Young, Joseph
Oh! Papa, Oh Papa (Won't You Be a Pretty Mama to
      Me?)   Hanley
Oh Santa Claus, Send Daddy Back to Me   Mitchell
Oh, You Sweetie   Atteridge; Romberg
Oh-Oh-Lady   Lewis
Old Fashioned Wife, An   Kern
Old-Fashioned Girls   Atteridge; Romberg
On the Road to Home Sweet Home   Kahn
On the Sandwich Isles   Von Tilzer
Once Upon a Time   Dubin
One Day in June (It Might Have Been You)   Hanley
One Life, One Love, I Give Them Both to You   Monaco
One Look, One Word   Smith, Harry B.
Only One Girl for Me   Romberg
Opening Act I (Let's Make a Night of It)   Kern
Orange Blossoms   Atteridge; Romberg
Orgy   Atteridge; Motzan; Romberg
Oriental Nights   Gilbert
Oriental Prelude   Goetz
Our Little Mountain Home in Switzerland   Bryan
Our Wedding Day   Hanley
Over the Bars (inst.)   Johnson, James P.
Over the Top   Bryan
Over There   Cohan
Package of Seeds, A   Kern
Paddle-Addle in Your Little Canoe   Lewis; Snyder; Young,
      Joseph
Pagliacci   Cobb; Edwards
Pajama Girlies   Motzan
Pal Like You, A   Kern
Passing Show, The   Atteridge; Motzan; Romberg
Peach of a Life, A   Kern
Peaches (Poppa would Persist in Picking)   Kern
Peggy's Leg   Friml
Pekin   Fisher; Johnson, Howard
Perfect Jewels   Atteridge; Romberg
Phantom of Your Smile, The   Atteridge; Romberg
Photograph of You   Motzan
Picture I Want to See, The   Kern
Pierrot   Atteridge; Motzan; Romberg
Pill Box Revue, The   Goetz
Plant Plenty of Potatoes   Kalmar; Leslie
Play that Hula Waltz for Me   Kahn

Playmates   Yellen
Polly Believed in Preparedness   Kern
Polly, Pretty Polly (Polly with a Past)   Berlin; Cohan
Poor Little Cinderella   Berlin
Poor Little Doll from Japan   Turk
Poor Little Rich Girl's Dog   Berlin
Poor Prune   Kern
Posterland   Atteridge; Romberg
Potato, The   Buck
Pray for Sunshine but Always Be Prepared for Rain   Lewis;
      Young, Joseph
Pretty Birdie   Berlin
Pretty Lips of Velvet   Friml
P.T. Barnum   Romberg
Pull the Cork Out of Erin and Let the River Shannon
      Flow   Fisher
Pussy Willow (inst.)   Monaco
Put a Bonnet with a Red Cross on It (And I'll Meet You
      Somewhere Over There)   Johnson, Howard
Put a Little Letter in My Letter Box   Berlin
Ragtime Alphabet   Goetz
Ragtime Volunteers Are Off to War, The   Hanley
Rambler Rose   Smith, Harry B.
Raus Mit der Kaiser   Sterling
Ready Made Sandwich, The   Atteridge; Motzan; Romberg
Regretful Blues   Clarke
Reminiscence   Romberg
Reminiscences (inst.)   Kern
Rescue, The   Bryan
Reveries   Herbert
Rialto Ripples (inst.)   Donaldson; Gershwin, George
Ring Out Liberty Bell   Romberg
Ring Out the Liberty Bell   Atteridge
Rio Janeiro   Cobb; Edwards
Road that Leads to Love, The   Berlin
Road that Lies Before, The   Kern
Road to Paradise, The   Romberg
Rock-A-Bye Land   Kahn
Rockaway   Johnson, Howard
Roll Your Hoop   Motzan; Romberg
Rolled Into One   Kern
Romance   Cobb; Edwards
Roses   Atteridge; Romberg
Rosy and Bright   Goetz
Round, A   Herbert
Routine Exercise, The   Bryan
Ruth St. Denis   Atteridge; Motzan; Romberg
Sailin' Away on the Henry Clay   Kahn
Sally Down Our Alley   Atteridge; Romberg
Same Old Moon   Buck
Same Old Song   Atteridge; Motzan; Romberg
Says I to Myself, Says I   Von Tilzer
Scouting in the U.S.A.   Kahn
Scratchin' the Gravel   Yellen
Selling Gowns   Romberg
Seminary Girl   Bryan
Send Me Back My Husband   Bryan
Set Aside Your Tears Til the Boys Come Marching
      Home   Gilbert
Seven Sweet Ages of Love, The   Lewis; Schwartz, Jean;
      Young, Joseph
She's Saving It All for Me   Johnson, Howard
Shop   Kern
Show Me the Way   Berlin
Silvery Moon   Goetz

Simple Little Tune   Kern; Smith, Harry B.
Sinbad Was in Bad All the Time   Carroll
Since Johnny Got His Gun   Brown, Lew
Sir, Don't Go Away   Romberg
Sir Galahad   Kern
Siren's Song, The   Kern
Sister Susie Glide   Norworth
Slavlova   Motzan; Romberg
Smile a Little Smile for Me   Smith, Harry B.
Smile and Show Your Dimple   Berlin
Snatched from the Cradle   Friml
So Long, Hong Kong   Hanley
So Long, Mother   Egan; Kahn
So Long Sammy   Davis; Yellen
So This Is Dixie   Yellen
Society Farmerettes, The   Herbert
Soldier Men   Herbert
Some Day   Herbert
Some Little Squirrel Is Going to Get Some Little Nut   Von
      Tilzer
Some Sunday Morning   Egan; Kahn; Whiting
Someday, Somebody's Goin' to Get You   Gilbert
Someone Is Goin' to Be Lonesome   Donaldson
Sometime   Von Tilzer
Somewhere in Dixie   Von Tilzer
Somewhere in France Is the Lily   Howard, Joseph E.
Somewhere in Georgia Underneath the Sunny Southern
      Skies   McHugh
Somewhere in Ireland   Brennan
Somewhere on Broadway   Carroll
Southern Gals   Yellen
Spanish   Harbach
Spanish Dance   Romberg
Spread the News   Friml
Stars and Rosebuds   Herbert
Steam Up That Choo Choo 'Till We Land in
      Jacksonville   Johnson, Howard
Steeplechase Rag (inst.)   Johnson, James P.
Stolen Sweets (inst.)   Von Tilzer
Stop It   Johnson, James P.
Stop Your Camouflaging with Me   Goetz; Schwartz, Jean
Study in Black and White, A   Motzan; Romberg
Suck Up   Friml; Harbach
Suki San (Where the Cherry Blossoms Fall)   Brennan;
      Donaldson
Sun Shines Brighter, The   Kern
Superlative Love   Herbert
Supper Club (inst.), The   Carroll
Susquehanna Sue   Cobb; Edwards
Sweet Evangeline of Old Arcady   Fisher
Sweet Little Buttercup   Bryan
Sweet Mama   Clarke; Donaldson
Sweet Rose Marie   Sterling
Sweetest Girl from Dixie Lives Next Door, The   Hanley
Sweetest Little Girl in Tennessee, The   Carroll
Sweetie Mine   Buck
Swing Song   Friml
Sword of My Father, The   Friml
Table for Two, A   Atteridge
Telephone Girl, The   Atteridge; Motzan; Romberg
Tell Me All Your Troubles, Cutie   Kern
Tell Me Where Mister Moon Spends Every
      Afternoon   Johnson, Howard; Meyer
20th Century Maiden's Prayer, The   Hanley
That Airship of Mine   Atteridge; Romberg

That Dum Ta Rum Tum Tune   Johnson, Howard; Meyer
That Goody Melody   Berlin
That Peach-A-Reeno, Phil-I-Peeno Dance   Atteridge;
      Motzan; Romberg
That's the Only Place Where Our Flag Shall Fly   Friml
That's What I Call Spreading Joy   Johnson, Howard
That's What Ireland Means to Me   Hanley
That's Why My Heart Is Calling You   Motzan
That's Why You're Called United States   Fisher; Johnson,
      Howard
(Under) The Willow Tree   Atteridge; Romberg
There Are Two Eyes in Dixie   Berlin
There It Is Again (When Your Favorite Girl's Not
      There)   Kern
There's a Brand New Hero   Harbach
There's a Heart in Virginia for You   Sterling
There's a Lovely Crop of Girlies This Year   Norworth
There's a Million Heroes in Each Corner of the
      U.S.A.   Lewis; Young, Joseph
There's a Million Reasons Why I Shouldn't Kiss You, but I
      Can't Think of One   Sterling; Von Tilzer
There's a Vacant Chair in Every Home Tonight   Bryan
There's No More Harmony at Home Sweet Home   Lewis;
      Snyder; Young, Joseph
There's No More Regular Kids   Cobb; Edwards
There's Nothing Sweeter than a Girl from Dixieland   Clarke;
      Monaco
There's Something in the Name of Ireland (That the Whole
      World Seems to Love)   Ager; Johnson, Howard
There's Something Nice About the South   Berlin
They All Look Alike   Kern
They All Want to Goo-Goo Again   Fisher
They Get Me All Fussed Up   Brown, Lew
They Go Wild Simply Wild Over Me   Fisher
They'll Be Whispering It All Over Town   Goetz; Schwartz,
      Jean
They'll Be Whistling It All Over Town   Goetz
They're Getting Shorter All the Time   Buck
Thine Alone   Herbert
Things You Must Not Do   Friml
Three Questions   Johnson, J. Rosamond
Throw Me a Kiss from Over the Sea   Egan; Whiting
Tick, Tick, Tick   Friml
(Do the) Tickle Toe   Harbach
Tiger Rose   Buck
Till the Clouds Roll By   Kern
To Any Girl (Pass This to Someone Who's Not As Lucky As
      You)   Brown, Lew
Tom, Dick and Harry and Jack (Hurry Back)   Ager; Johnson,
      Howard
Too-Ra-Loo-Re (A French Pavanne)   Herbert
Torpedo Jim   Monaco
Touch of the Woman's Hand, The   Harbach
Toys, Toys, Toys   Cobb; Edwards
Twilight Rag (inst.)   Johnson, James P.
'Twixt Love and Duty   Herbert
Two Alone   Friend; Mitchell
Ukalou (Pretty South Sea Island Lady)   Von Tilzer
Uncle Sam Is Santa Claus to the World   Buck
Universal Peace Song (God Save Us All), The   Bryan
Vampire Maid, The   Norworth
Vanity   Friml
Vive la France   Herbert
Voice with a Smile Wins, The   Norworth
Wait 'Till Tomorrow   Kern

Walk Down the Avenue with Me   Goetz

Wasn't It Yesterday   Berlin

Way Down South   Berlin

We Are Going on Our Honeymoon   Buck

We Are the Bright Lights of Broadway   Buck

We Do the Best We Can   Bryan

We Will Rally to the Racket   Motzan

Wedding Bells   Motzan

Wedding By the Sea   Motzan

Wedding of Words and Music   Berlin

We'll Be There (On the Land, on the Sea, in the Air)   Hanley

We'll Drift Along   Friml; Harbach

We'll Keep Things Going Till the Boys Come Home, Won't We Girlie   Sterling

We'll See   Kern; Smith, Harry B.

We're Crooks   Kern

We're Going Over the Top, and We'll Be Marching Thro' Berlin in the Morning   Sterling

We're Going to Be Pals   Kern

We're Six Little Nieces of Uncle Sam   Gershwin, George

We've Got to Put Up with It   Norworth

What a Wonderful Wish That Would Be   Brennan

What Did I Ever Do to You   Bryan; Johnson, Howard; Meyer

What Did I Ever Do to You that You Should Want to Do to Me   Berlin; Leslie; Meyer

What Did You Do with All the Love I Gave You   Fisher

What I'm Longing to Say   Kern

What Kind of an American Are You?   Brown, Lew

What Would $50,000 Make You Do?   Bryan

What's the Use of Being Lonesome   Friml; Harbach

When a Dainty Peeping Ankle Peeps at You   Bryan

When Are You Coming Back   Sterling

When He's All Dolled Up He's the Best Dressed Rube in Town   Donaldson

When I Grow Up and Want to Be a Soldier   Cobb

When I Grow Up I'm Going to Be a Soldier   Edwards

When I Hear that Jazz Band Play   Buck

When I Went to School with You   Cobb; Edwards

When Ireland Stands Among the Nations of the World   Herbert

When It's Circus Time Back Home   Yellen

When It's Night Time in Little Italy   Fisher

When It's Summertime Down by the Seaside   Dubin

When Love Awakes (Love's Awakening)   Herbert

When Pavlova Starts Buck and Winging   Motzan

When Rosie Riccoola Do the Hoola Ma Boola She's a Hit in Little Italy   Sterling

When Shall I Again See Ireland   Herbert

When She Gives Him a Shamrock Bloom   Friml; Harbach

When the Autumn Leaves Are Falling   Buck

When the Boys Come Marching Home   Howard, Joseph E.

When the Girls Grow Older They Grow a Little Bolder   Lewis; Schwartz, Jean; Young, Joseph

When the Glories of Ireland Are Told   Brennan

When the Lights Go Out on Broadway   Stept

When the Right Little Boy Rolls Around   Cobb; Edwards

When There's a Chance to Dance   Gershwin, George; Gershwin, Ira

When Those Sweet Hawaiian Babies Roll Their Eyes   Leslie; Ruby

When Yankee Doodle Marches Thro' Berlin There'll Be a Hot Time in the U.S.A.   Sterling

When You Gamble in the Game of Love   Fisher; Johnson, Howard

When You Picked Your Basket of Peaches   Goetz

When You Waltz with the Girl You Love   Von Tilzer

Where Did You Get Those Irish Eyes?   Norworth

Where Do We Go from Here?   Johnson, Howard

Where Is the Language to Tell?   Atteridge; Romberg

Where the Black-Eyed Susans Grow   Whiting

Where the Morning Glories Grow   Egan; Kahn; Whiting

Who Cares?   Kern; Smith, Harry B.

Whoever You Are (Whoever You May Be)   Hanley

Whose Little Heart Are You Breaking Now?   Berlin

Why?   Kern

Why Can't We Have a Little Bit of Green (In the Old Red, White and Blue)   Goetz; Johnson, Howard

Why Did You Make Me Leave St. Louis, Mo?   Johnson, Howard

Why Don't You Tell Me What You Want   Monaco

Why Is Cecil Selling Sea Shells by the Seaside   Dubin

Widow Fascinating, The   Harbach

Will You Remember (Sweetheart)   Romberg

Will You Write the Melody if I Write the Words to Our Little Song of Love   Dubin

Winter Garden Hop   Motzan

With All My Heart and Soul   Brennan

With His Wonderful Irish Brogue   Norworth

Withdraw   Herbert

Wonderful Fall for You   Goetz; Monaco

Wonderful Girl, Goodnight   Von Tilzer

Won't You Be My Daddy?   Atteridge; Romberg

Won't You Give Me a Chance to Love You   Monaco

Won't You Send a Letter to Me   Atteridge; Romberg

Would You Like to Make a Fuss Over Me   Norworth

Would You Take Back the Love You Gave Me   Dubin

Year Is a Long Time, A   Friml; Harbach

Yock-A-Hilo Town   Donaldson

You 21 and You 53, You Both Stand for Liberty   Sterling

You All Got to Be Born and Bed in Kentucky   Kahn

You Are Mine   Motzan

You Are Not the Girl   Gershwin, George; Gershwin, Ira

You Brought Ireland Right Over to Me   Brennan

You Can Have Your Song and Wine, Give Me the Women for Mine   Donaldson; Dubin

You Can't Blame Me   Edwards

You Can't Tell the Mothers from the Daughters   Yellen

You Matthew Dear   Romberg

You May Be a Doggone Dangerous Girl but I'm a Desperate Guy   Freed, Arthur

You Never Can Be Too Sure About the Girls   Brown, Lew

You Never Can Tell How a Marriage Will Take   Herbert

You Never Knew about Me   Kern

You Remind Me of My Mother   Yellen

You Said Something   Kern

You Said the Same Thing to Me   Ager; Johnson, Howard

You'll Be Glad to Have Your Old Sweetheart Again   Bryan

You'll See   Friml

Your Country Needs You Now   Dubin

You're a Great Big Lonesome Baby   Kahn; Whiting

You're in Love   Friml; Harbach

You're Mama's Baby Boy   Lewis; Young, Joseph

You're Mine   Lewis; Snyder; Young, Joseph

You've Got to Be Good   Donaldson

You've Got to Take the Bad with the Good   Sterling

You've Had Him Long Enough   Bryan

Ziegfeld Follies Rag   Buck

1918

Acrobatic Rag, The   Buck
Affectionate Dan   Blake; Sissle
After the Battle Is Over Then You Can Come Back to
   Me   Gilbert
After the First of July   Buck
After the War Is Over (Will There Be Any Home Sweet
   Home)   Sterling
Alexander's Band Is Back in Dixieland   Yellen
All Dressed Up in a Tailor Made   Cohan
All Hail to You, Marines!   Herbert
All My Life   Akst
All the World Is Swaying   Kern
Alone with You   Porter
Altogether Too Fond of You   Porter
America, He's for You   Sterling
American Beauty   Bryan; Leslie
And She Went Home in a Barrel   Buck
Any Kind of Man   Friml
Any Old Time at All   Buck
Any Time Is Dancing Time   Schwartz, Jean
Anything Is Nice If It Comes from Dixieland   Ager; Clarke;
   Meyer
Argentine Tango   Friml
Around the House that Jack Built   DeSylva
At Half Past Nine   Lewis; Young, Joseph
At the Cake Walk Ball   Akst; Lewis; Meyer; Young, Joseph
At the Dixie Military Ball   Carroll
At the Jazz Town Novelty Ball   Pollack
At the Ragtime Strollers Ball   Koehler
At the Russian Cabaret   Johnson, Howard
Au Revoir   Cobb; Edwards
Baby Doll   Friml
Back in the Quaint Little School in Caroline   Carroll
Bagdad   Atteridge; Romberg
Beautiful Night   Friml
Beautiful Rose Marie   Bryan; Fisher
Beauty and Beast   Atteridge; Romberg
Because You Believe in Me   Brennan
Bedalumbo, The   Atteridge
Before I Met You   Kern
Best Man Never Gets the Worst of It, The   Friml
Bevo   Berlin
Big Chief Kill-a-Hun   Bryan; Leslie
Big Show, The   Kern
Big Spring Drive, The   Kern
Bill   Kern
Blow the Whistle   Howard, Joseph E.
Blue Devils of France   Berlin
Boots, Boots, Boots   Schwartz, Jean
Bridesmaids   Romberg
Bring Back the Roses (Kathleen Mavoureen)   Bryan; Fisher
Bring on the Girls   Atteridge; Romberg; Schwartz, Jean
Business Is Business with Me   Friend
But After the Ball Was Over (Then He Made Up for Lost
   Time)   DeSylva
By the Honeysuckle Vine   DeSylva
Bye and Bye   Von Tilzer
Can You Say that You've Done Your Share   Silver
Can You Tame Wild Wimmen   Sterling; Von Tilzer
Captain   Howard, Joseph E.
Carolina Shout (inst.)   Johnson, James P.
Caroline   Smith, Harry B.
Caveman, The   Friml
Changeable Girls   Carroll

Chasing Butterflies   Howard, Joseph E.
Cheer Up Father, Cheer Up Mother   Bryan
Chianti   Friml
Chloe   DeSylva
Circus Is Coming to Town, The   Berlin
Cleopatra   Bryan; Schwartz, Jean
Come Across Yankee Boy, Come Across   Bryan; Fisher
Come Along to Toy Town   Berlin
Come On Papa   Leslie; Ruby
Constantina Number   Friml
Coo-ee, Australian Bush Call   Motzan
Corner of Heaven with You, A   Gershwin, George
Cotton Hollow Harmony   Whiting
Crowd of Girls   Smith, Harry B.
Crystal Ball   Friml
Cupid   Gershwin, George; Gershwin, Ira
Daddy Darling Here's Your Angel Child   Clarke; Meyer
Daddy Dear   Atteridge; Romberg
Daddy Mine   Dubin
Dance of the Levants   Friml
Dance of the Porters   Friml
Dancing Lesson, The   Friml
Dancing School   Romberg
Dancing Spanish   Friml
Dancing the Numbers   Howard, Joseph E.
Dancing to the Sugar Tune, Slip the Boys Another
   Dime   Gilbert
Darktown Dancing School   Yellen
Darling   Romberg
Daughter of Rosie O'Grady   Donaldson
Dear Little Boy of Mine   Brennan
Dear Old Gown   Romberg
Dear Old Prison Days   Kern
Dearie   Friml
Derby Day in Dixie   Egan; Whiting
Devil Has Bought Up All the Coal, The   Berlin
Ding Dong   Berlin
Dixie Rose   Caesar
Dixie Rose (Swanee Rose)   DeSylva
Djer Kiss   Ager
Do It Now   Kern
Don't Forget to Come Back, Mack   Monaco
Don't Let Him Linger when His Leave Is Over   Cohan
Don't Lose Your Way   Atteridge; Romberg
Do-Re-Mi (inst.)   Motzan
Down By the Millside Along the Hillside, You Made All My
   Dreams Come True   Brown, Lew
Down the Lane   Friend
Down Where the Jack O'Lanterns Grow   Cohan
Dream On, Little Soldier Boy   Berlin
Dress, Dress, Dress   Atteridge; Romberg; Schwartz, Jean
Drink Out the Old Drink   Smith, Harry B.
Duchess of Devonshire, The   Atteridge; Romberg; Schwartz,
   Jean
Duchess of the Long Ago, The   Romberg; Schwartz, Jean
Dumpty Deedle Dee Dum Dee   Donaldson
Easy Come, Easy Go   Atteridge; Romberg
Eat and the World Eats with You   Romberg
Echo of Her Smile   Howard, Joseph E.
El Brut (inst.)   Motzan
El Bruta   Howard, Joseph E.
Ensemble   Cohan
Evalina Jackson's Wedding Day   Silver; Sterling
Ever By Your Side   Atteridge; Romberg
Every Day'll Be Sunday When the Town Goes Dry   Jerome

Every Girl in All America   Kern

Every Night He Goes Over the Top   Johnson, Howard; Meyer

Everyday Will Be Sunday When the Town Goes Dry   Friml

Everyone I Love Lives Down in Dixie   Dubin

Everything Is Peaches Down in Georgia   Ager; Clarke; Meyer

Everything Is Rosy Now   Atteridge; DeSylva; Romberg

Ev'ry Morning She Makes Me Late   DeSylva; Kahn

Exemption   Friend

Eyes of Youth See the Truth, The   Cohan

Far Apart, You're Still in My Heart   Carroll

Fi Fi (inst.)   Motzan

Finest Thing in the Country, The   Schwartz, Jean

Floating Down a Moonlight Stream   Romberg

Follow Me to Dixie Land   Silver

For Mary, the Baby and Me   Monaco

For the Boys Over There   Kahn

For the Two of Us   Leslie; Ruby

For Your Boy and My Boy   Kahn

Fox Trot   Atteridge; Romberg

France (We Have Not Forgotten You)   Ager; Clarke

Frocks and Frills   Friml

Funny Little Something   Kern

Galli Curci Rag   Schwartz, Jean

Galli-Curci Rag, The   Atteridge; Romberg

Garden of My Dreams   Buck

Gee Whiz! Those Eyes   Howard, Joseph E.

Gimme This — Gimme This — Gimme That   Gilbert

Girl He Left Behind Him Has the Hardest Fight of All, The   Bryan; Kalmar; Leslie; Ruby

Girlie   Kern

Girls of France   Bryan; Leslie; Ruby

Give a Little Credit to the Navy   DeSylva; Kahn

Give Me a Kiss   Snyder

Gloriana   Friml

Go Little Boat   Kern

Go West Young Girl   Atteridge

God Bless America   Berlin

God, Spare Our Boys Over There   Jerome

Good Little Things That We Do, The   Carroll

Good Little Tune   Caesar; Gershwin, George

Good-Bye Barney Boy   Brennan

Goodbye Carrabian Nights   Egan; Whiting

Good-Bye, France   Berlin

Goodbye Mother Machree   Brennan

Good-Bye My Honey, I'm Gone   Blake; Sissle

Goodbye, Slim   Donaldson

Grandma Dear Grandma   Romberg

Greenwich Village   Kern

Gush-Gush-Gushing   Gershwin, George; Gershwin, Ira

Happy Days   Smith, Harry B.

Have a Smile for Every One You Meet and They Will Have a Smile for You   Brennan

He Would Play the Piano   Silver

Head Over Heels   Kern

Hello Central, Give Me No Man's Land   Lewis; Schwartz, Jean; Young, Joseph

Hello, Girlie   Howard, Joseph E.

Hello, Hello, Hello   Berlin

Hep, Hep, Hep   Howard, Joseph E.

Here Come the Yanks   Buck

Here Comes the Birdie   Smith, Harry B.

He's Got Those Big Blue Eyes Like You, Daddy Mine   Dubin

He's Well Worth Waiting For   Von Tilzer

Hitchy Koo Girl   Goetz

Honey, Come Hurry Along   Howard, Joseph E.

Honeymoon Belle (inst.)   Motzan

Honeymoon Island   Schwartz, Jean

Honeymoon Land   Atteridge; Kern; Romberg

Hong Kong   Gershwin, George; Gershwin, Ira

Honor Bright   Fisher

How'd You Like to Be a Sailor?   Warren

How'd You Like to Be My Daddy   Lewis; Snyder; Young, Joseph

Huckleberry Pie   Conrad

Hurdy Gurdy Man, The   Gershwin, Ira

I Ain't Got Weary Yet   Johnson, Howard

I Ask No More of Thee   Brennan

I Believed All They Said   Kern

I Can Always Find a Little Sunshine in the Y.M.C.A.   Berlin

I Can't Get Along Without You   Kahn

I Can't See You All   Atteridge; Romberg

I Couldn't Go to Ireland So Ireland Came to Me   Von Tilzer

I Couldn't Live Without the Lovin' that You Gave to Me   Friend

I Gave Her That   DeSylva

I Had to Surrender to Virginia   Mitchell

I Hail from Cairo   Atteridge; Romberg

I Hate to Lose You (I'm So Used to You Now)   Clarke

I Have Just One Heart for Just One Boy   Berlin

I Have My Fingers Crossed   Friml

I Haven't Got Time for Anyone Else Till John Gets Home   Monaco

I Just Stepped in to Get Out of the Rain   Brown, Lew

I Know   Carroll

I Like the Boys   Atteridge; Romberg

I Love but You   Friml

I Love the Heart of Dixie   Bryan; Schwartz, Jean

I Love to Sing with You   Buck

I Love You Dear   Friml

I May Stay Away a Little Longer   Brown, Lew

I Miss that Mississippi Miss that Misses Me   Lewis; Young, Joseph

I Never Knew   Schwartz, Jean

I Never Thought   Kern

I Really Can't Make My Feet Behave   Atteridge; Romberg; Schwartz, Jean

I Think You're Absolutely Wonderful (What Do You Think of Me)   Carroll

I Want a Doll   Von Tilzer

I Want Him Back Again   Brown, Lew

I Want My Husband When I Wed   Romberg

I Want to Be Loved By a Soldier   Silver

I Want to Learn to Jazz Dance   Buck

I Want to Marry   Carroll

I Was Lonely   Kern

I Wasted My Love on You   Silver

I Wish I Was in the Land of Cotton Now   Johnson, Howard; Meyer

I Wonder What They're Doing To-Night   Brown, Lew

I Wonder Why She Kept on Saying Si-Si-Si-Si Senor   Lewis; Snyder; Young, Joseph

I Wonder Why They're Always Pickin' on My Little Pickaninny   Mitchell

I Wouldn't Give That for the Boy Who Couldn't Dance   Berlin

I'd Like to See the Kaiser with a Lily in His Hand   Johnson, Howard

If He Can Fight Like He Can Love Goodnight
Germany   Clarke; Meyer

If I Had My Life to Live Over, I'd Do It All Over
Again   Silver

If She Means What I Think She Means   Buck; DeSylva

If (There's Anything You Want)   Kern

If They Ever Take the Sun Out of Sunday   Jerome; Von
Tilzer

If You Could Read My Mind   Schwartz, Jean

If You Only Care Enough   Kern

If You Only Knew   Gershwin, Ira

If You're Crazy About the Women, You're Not Crazy at
All   Bryan; Leslie; Ruby

I'll Be Over Your Way in the Mornin' Bill   Ruby

I'll Love You More for Losing You   Egan; Whiting

I'll Say She Does   DeSylva; Kahn

I'll Tell the World   Atteridge; DeSylva

I'm a Very Different Girl   Atteridge; Romberg

I'm Always Chasing Rainbows   Carroll

I'm from Ohio   Brennan

I'm Going to Settle Down   Schwartz, Jean

I'm Gonna Pin My Medal on the Girl I Left Behind
Me   Berlin

I'm in Love   Brown, Lew; Romberg

I'm Just a Good Man   Carroll

I'm Just an Old Jay from the U.S.A.   Von Tilzer

I'm Married, I'm Single, I'm Divorced, I'm in
Love   Atteridge; Romberg

I'm on a Long, Long Ramble Over There I'll Be Rambling
with You   Lewis; Young, Joseph

I'm Satisfied to Step Aside   Donaldson; Gilbert

I'm the Brother of the Lily of the Valley   Gilbert

I'm True to Them All, and They're Just As True to
Me   Cohan

In 1960 You'll Find Dixie Looking Just the Same   Mitchell

In Dear Old Sunny Spain   Howard, Joseph E.

In Old Versailles   Buck

In the Garden of Your Eyes   Brennan

In the Good Old Irish May   Von Tilzer

In the Harbor of My Mother's Arms   Fisher

In the Land of Beginning Again (Where Broken Dreams
Come True)   Clarke; Meyer

In Your Eyes   Clarke

Ireland, My Land of Dreams   Cohan

Isle of Youth   Atteridge; Romberg

Isn't It Wonderful   Schwartz, Jean

It Doesn't Matter   Schwartz, Jean

It Gets a Little Shorter Every Day   Von Tilzer

It Might As Well Be You   Kahn

It Must Be Love   Kahn

It Will All End Up with the Right End Up   Goetz

It Won't Be Long Before We're Home   Howard, Joseph E.

It's a Hard, Hard World   Kern

It's a Long Way to Tiffany's   Carroll

It's Greek to Me   Kern

It's Not Like Loving You   Brown, Lew

It's the Good Little Things that We Do   Fisher

It's the Little Bit of Irish   Berlin

It's the Only One for Me   Atteridge; Romberg

It's Wonderful   Atteridge; DeSylva; Romberg

I've Got a Ten Day Pass for a Honeymoon with the Girl I
Left Behind   Hanley

I've Got a Two Day Pass for a Honeymoon for the Girl I Left
Behind   Donaldson

I've Got the Blue Ridge Blues   Whiting

I've the Lovin'es' Love for You   Blake; Sissle

Jazz All Your Troubles Away   Romberg

Jazz — How I Love It   Romberg

Jerusalem You're Calling Me   Motzan

Jim, Jim, Don't Come Back Till You Win   Von Tilzer

Jim, Jim, I Always Knew that You'd Win   Von Tilzer

Just a Baby's Prayer at Twilight   Lewis; Young, Joseph

Just a Letter for a Boy Over There from a Gray Haired
Mother Over Here   Sterling

Just a Little Laughter   Friml

Just Around the Corner   Kahn

Just Like This   Friml

Just One Little Smile   Egan

Kaiser Bill   Egan; Whiting

Keep Jazzin' It, Ras'   Sterling

Keep on A-Going   Cobb; Edwards

Keep on Smiling   Friml

Keep Out of the Moon   Schwartz, Jean

Keep the Home Push Up for Pershing   Mitchell

Keep the Trench Lines Going for the Boys Over There   Von
Tilzer

Kettle Song, The   Kern

Kicking the Kaiser Around   Johnson, Howard

Kiss for Cinderella, A   Carroll

Kitchenette   Gershwin, Ira

Knit, Girls, Knit!   Johnson, Howard

Land of Yesteryear   Goetz

Let Me Build a Little Fence Around Your Heart   Howard,
Joseph E.

Let Me Shimmy and I'm Satisfied   Buck

Let's Build a Little Nest   Kern

Let's Go   Kern

Let's Play Hookie   Goetz

Liberty Glide, The   Howard, Joseph E.

Life Is One Thing After Another   Atteridge; Romberg

Light Your Little Lamp My Love for Me   Fisher

Lily of Longacre Square, The   Goetz

Little Bit of Every Nationality, A   Atteridge; Romberg

Little Bit of Sunshine (From Home), A   Hanley

Little Devil   Atteridge; Romberg

Little Good for Nothing's Good for Something After All,
The   Von Tilzer

Little Sunbeam   Gershwin, George

Little Sunshine   Gershwin, Ira

Little Tune, Go Away   Kern

Lodger   Romberg

Look what My Boy Got in France   Conrad

Love Ahoy!   Atteridge; Romberg

Love! Love! Love!   Friml

Madelon I'll Be True to the Whole Regiment   Bryan

Makin's of the U.S.A., The   Von Tilzer

Mama's Captain Curly Head   Von Tilzer

Mammy's Chocolate Soldier   Mitchell

Mandy   Berlin

March On   Friml

Mary and John   Bryan; Leslie

Maybe   Smith, Harry B.

Me and You   Akst

Meet Me when the Stars Are All Aglow   Sterling

Merrily We'll Roll Along   Silver; Sterling

Merry and Bright   Atteridge; Romberg

Mine Was a Marriage of Convenience   Buck

Mirandy (That Gal o' Mine)   Blake; Sissle

Mister McAdoo   Bryan; Fisher

Mister Moon, How Is Everything on No Man's Land   Mitchell
Mitzi's Lullaby   Kern
Molly Aroon   Brennan
Moments of the Dance   Kern
Moon Song   Kern
Moonlight Walk   Fain
Mother Here's Your Boy   Mitchell
Mother's Prayer for Her Boy Out There, A   Sterling
Motor Girl, The   Buck
My Baby Talk Lady   Romberg
My Baby Talk Lady (My Baby Talking Girl)   Atteridge
My Baby Talking Girl (My Baby Talk Lady)   Schwartz, Jean
My Boy   Kern
My Friends Morris and Max   Kalmar; Leslie; Ruby
My Holiday Girl   Atteridge
My Irish American Rose   Sterling
My Isle of Golden Dreams   Kahn
My Mammy   Donaldson; Lewis; Young, Joseph
My Old Sweetheart Is Coming Back   Silver
My Pledge, I Shall Stand By Our Land to Eternity   Brennan
My Rainbow Ribbon Girl   Edwards
My Spanish Rose   Silver
My Vampire Girl   Atteridge
My Wild Days Are Over   Brown, Lew
'N' Everything   DeSylva; Kahn
Naughty Little Red Cross Nurses   Friend
Navy Will Bring Them Back, The   Johnson, Howard
Nenette and Rin-Tin-Tin   Friml
Nerves   Schwartz, Jean
Newspaper Girl   Goetz
Night in the Orient, A   Atteridge; Romberg
Night Wind (The Sunbeam and the Rose), The   Brennan
No Matter What or Where   Atteridge; Romberg
No One but You   Friml
No One Ever Loved Like Me   Schwartz, Jean
Not Yet   Kern
Not You   Kern
Now that We're Married   Howard, Joseph E.
Nursery Fanfare (My Own Light Infantry)   Kern
Oh! Argentine   Friml
Oh Doctor, Doctor   Romberg
Oh! Frenchy (Come to Yankee Land)   Conrad
Oh! How I Hate to Get Up in the Morning   Berlin
Oh! How I Wish I Could Sleep Until My Daddy Comes Home   Lewis; Young, Joseph
Oh Lady! Lady!!   Kern
Oh, Look!   Carroll
Oh Promise Me You'll Write to Him Today   Kern
(My Vampire Girl) Oh, Those Vampire Girls   Romberg; Schwartz, Jean
Oh! What a Time for the Girlies when the Boys Come Marching Home   Lewis; Ruby; Young, Joseph
Old Fashioned Girl, An   Carroll
Older They Are the Harder They Fall, The   Smith, Harry B.
On a Lightless Night with You   Cobb; Edwards
On Cupid's Green   Atteridge; Romberg
On Our Little Merry-Go-Round   Atteridge; Romberg
On the Level You're a Little Devil, but I'll Soon Make an Angel of You   Schwartz, Jean; Young, Joseph
On the Level, You're a Little Devil, But I'll Soon Make an Angel Out of You   Lewis
On the Road to Calais   Bryan; Schwartz, Jean
On to Victory   Smith, Harry B.
One Lip Tillie   Silver

One More Day   Brennan
One, Two, Three   Kern
Only in Dreams   Smith, Harry B.
Opening Chorus Act One (I'm to Be Married Today)   Kern
Oriental Song   Friml
Oui Oui Marie (Wee Wee Marie)   Bryan; Fisher
Our Acrobatic Melodramatic Home   Cohan
Our Ancestors   Atteridge; Romberg
Our Little Desert Isle   Schwartz, Jean
Our Little Nest   Kern
Over the Rhine   Yellen
Over the Sea, Boys   Berlin
Over There I'll Be Rambling with You   Lewis; Schwartz, Jean
Palestine   Bryan
Parting Kiss from Your Sweetheart Puts the Good in Goodbye, The   Johnson, Howard; Meyer
Pathway to Your Heart   Motzan
Peggy   Williams
Picking Peaches   Friml
Picture I Want to See, The   Kern
Poor Little Me   Buck
Poor Little Me - I'm on KP (Kitchen Police)   Berlin
Potash and Perlmutter Ball, The   Cohan
Private Mike M'Gee   Cobb; Edwards
Prohibition Blues   Howard, Joseph E.; Smith, Harry B.
Prunes   Friml
Put Your Hands in Your Pockets and Give, Give, Give   Kahn
Rag Lad of Bagdad, The   Romberg
Rag-a-Bye Baby (inst.)   Motzan
Rag-Lad of Bagdad, The   Atteridge
Ragtime Razor Brigade   Berlin
Rainbow from the U.S.A., A   Jerome
Rally Around   Schwartz, Jean
Raz-Ma-Taz   Atteridge
Real American Folk Song (Is a Rag), The   Gershwin, George; Gershwin, Ira
Red Cross Needs You Now, The   Cobb; Edwards
Red Moon Rays (inst.)   Johnson, J. Rosamond
Reminiscence   Romberg
Resurrection Rag   Goetz
Rip Van Winkle Slept with One Eye Open   Bryan; Fisher
Rock-a-Bye Baby Dear (Lullaby)   Kern
Rock-A-Bye Your Baby with a Dixie Melody   Lewis; Schwartz, Jean; Young, Joseph
Rolling Exercise   Romberg
Romance Land   Akst
Rose Room   Williams
Rottenest Job   Friml
Run Away   Schwartz, Jean
Run, Run, Run, for I'm a Yankee   Razaf
San Sebastian's Shores   Carroll; Goetz
Save Your Money, John   Blake; Sissle
Say You Intend to See Old Tennessee and Me   Egan
Say You Intend to See Ole Tennessee and Me   Whiting
Send a Lot of Jazz Bands Over There   Berlin
Serenade   Atteridge; Romberg; Schwartz, Jean
She Knew More than Any Girl Should Know   Ager
She Was Not So Bad for a Country Girl   DeSylva
She's Everyone Else's Girl but Mine   Carroll
She's the Kind of a Girl that Any Fellow Could Like   Bryan
Ship Building Song (We're Busy Building Boats)   Buck
Since Becky Became a Conductor   Silver
Since My Gal Is Gone I've Got the Blues   Silver

Singapore   Gilbert
Sixes and Sevens   Brennan
Skate with Me   Silver
Smiles   Friml
So Dress Up Your Dollars in Khaki and Help Win
    Democracy's Fight   Whiting
So Long Sal the Best of Friends Must Part   Sterling
So Near and Yet So Far   Friml
So Undulating, So Fascinating   Friml
Sobs   Howard, Joseph E.
Soldier Boy   Berlin
Some Day I'll Steal You   Motzan
Some Day in Somewhere Wedding Bells Will Ring   Conrad
Some Little Girl (Waiting Around the Corner)   Kern
Some Lonesome Night   Clarke; Meyer
Some Say Somewhere Wedding Bells Will Ring   Conrad;
    Sterling
Some Wonderful Sort of Someone   Gershwin, George
Sometime   Friml
Song of the Heart, A   Johnson, J. Rosamond
Spagoni's Wedding Jubilee   Fisher
Spanish   Cohan
Spanish Maid (Nina Espagnola)   Friml
Speak for Yourself John   Friml
Spring   Kern
Spring Drive, The   Buck
Springtime   Buck
Squab Farm, The   Atteridge; Romberg; Schwartz, Jean
Starlight   Buck
Sterling Silver Moon   Berlin
Struttin' Yo' Stuff   Koehler
Such Is My Love for You   Brennan
Sun Starts to Shine Again, The   Kern
Sunkissed Land   Carroll
Swanee   Caesar; Gershwin, George
Sweet Peaches   Donaldson
Swinging Along   Buck
Swinging Along with Lindy   Kahn
Syncopated Frolic, A   Buck
Tackin' 'Em Down   DeSylva
Take a Chance (Little Girl and Learn to Dance)   Kern;
    Smith, Harry B.
Take a Little Flower from the Winter Garden   Carroll
Take Me Back to that Rose Covered Shack   Ager; Jerome
Take the Night Boat to Albany   Atteridge; Romberg
Tale the Church Bell Told, The   Lewis; Young, Joseph
Tea Party, The   Smith, Harry B.
Tease Me Some More   Fain
Teepee (I Will Knit of Suit o' Dreams)   Kern
Tell Me   Smith, Harry B.
Tell Me Crystal Ball   Friml
Tell that to the Marines   Atteridge; Edwards; Lewis;
    Schwartz, Jean; Young, Joseph
Tell the Folks in Dixie I'll Be Back There Some Day   Kahn
Ten Commandments of Love, The   Gershwin, George
That Dream-Waltz Melody   Howard, Joseph E.
That Grand Old Gentleman, Uncle Sam   Cobb; Edwards
That Old Church Bell   Schwartz, Jean
Their Hearts Are Over Here   Cohan
There Ain't Goin-a-Be No Rhine   Young, Victor
There'll Be a Hot Time for the Old Men While the Young
    Men Are Away   Clarke; Meyer
There'll Be Something Doing when the War's Over   Silver
There'll Be Sunshine for You and For Someone You Are
    Waiting For   Dubin; Monaco

There's a Lump of Sugar Down in Dixie   Bryan; Yellen
There's Always One You Can't Forget   Atteridge; Romberg
There's Magic in the Air   Gershwin, George; Gershwin, Ira
There's No Better Use for Time than Kissing   Kern
There's No End to My Love for You   Dubin; Monaco
There's Nobody Home but Me   Conrad
There's Something About a Uniform that Makes the Ladies
    Fall   Silver
There's Something About You   Atteridge; Romberg
These Colors Will Not Run   Carroll
They Can't Fool Me   DeSylva
They Were All Out of Step but Jim   Berlin
They'll Be Mighty Proud in Dixie of Their Old Black
    Joe   Carroll
Those Wonderful Days of Used-to-Be   Sterling
Thousand and One Arabian Nights, A   Atteridge; Romberg
Three Wonderful Letters from Home   Hanley
Till We Meet Again   Egan; Whiting
Tipperary Mary   Buck
Toodle-oo!   Friml
Toot-Toot!   Kern
Trombone Jazz   Atteridge; Romberg; Schwartz, Jean
Try a Ring Dear!   Buck
Tune You Can't Forget, The   Friml
Twit Twit Twit   Schwartz, Jean
Typical Topical Tunes   Carroll
Under the Honeymoon   Atteridge; Romberg
Unknown   Hammerstein
Vamp a Little Lady   Carroll
Victory   Buck
Waiting for This   Akst
Walk Into My Heart   Snyder
Watch, Hope and Wait Little Girl, Till I Come Back to
    You   Brown, Lew
We Are the Bright Lights of Broadway   Buck
We Are the Follies   Buck
We Couldn't Have Heroes Over There If It Wasn't for the
    Heroes Over Here   Clarke
We Couldn't Have Heroes Over There, If It Wasn't for Those
    Heroes Over Here   Johnson, Howard
We Will Live for Love and Love Alone   Carroll
Wedding Bells, Will You Ever Ring for Me   Lewis; Schwartz,
    Jean; Young, Joseph
Wedding By Proxy   Romberg
Welcome Home Laddie Boy, Welcome Home   Cobb;
    Edwards
We'll Build a Rainbow in the Sky   Egan; Whiting
We'll Do Our Share (While You're Over There)   Brown, Lew
We're All Comrades Now   Bryan; Fisher
We're Coming Back to You when the Fighting Days are
    Through   Donaldson
We're Coming from Cody   Yellen
We're On Our Way to France   Berlin
What a Difference a Uniform Will Make (Ever Since I Put on
    A Uniform)   Berlin
What a Girl Can Do   Kalmar; Ruby
What Are You Going to Do to Help the Boys   Kahn
What Could Be Fairer than That   Smith, Harry B.
What Do You Have to Do?   Friml
What Do You Mean By Loving Somebody Else when Your
    Love Belongs to Me   Clare; Mitchell
What Have I Done to Make You Stop Loving Me   DeSylva;
    Kahn
What I Care   Donaldson; Turk
What Men Can Do   Smith, Harry B.

What Will We Do on a Saturday Night when the Town Goes Dry?   Ruby

What'll We Do with Him, Boys   Sterling

Wheatless Day   Kern

When a Girl   Friml

When Alexander Takes His Ragtime Band to France   Bryan; Leslie

When I Build a Home   Akst

When I Hear a Syncopated Tune   Buck

When I Look into Your Eyes, Mavoureen   Cohan

When I Marry   Carroll

When I Think of the Sweethearts that I Might Have Had   Carroll

When I'm Looking at You   Buck

When It's Halloween in Aberdeen, I'll Be Coming Through the Rye   Monaco

When My Sweetie Comes Back to Me   Buck

When the Armies Disband   Caesar; Gershwin, George

When the Boys from Dixie Eat the Melon on the Rhine   Bryan

When the Curtain Falls   Berlin

When the Girls Get Wise   Goetz

When the Ships Come Home   Kern

When the Sun Goes Down in Sleepy Hollow, That's the Time I Think of Home Sweet Home   Davis

When They Do the Hula Hula on the Boulevard   Bryan

When We Went to Sunday School   Kahn

When Yankee Doodle Sails Upon the Good Ship Home Sweet Home   Fisher

(When You Come Back, and You Will Come Back) When You Come Back, If You Do Come Back   Cohan

When You Wake Up Dancing   Kern

When Ziegfeld's Follies Hit the Town   Cohan

Where Do They Come From   Goetz

Where Do They Get Those Guys?   Atteridge; Bryan; Romberg; Yellen

Where Have You Been Hiding All These Years   Mitchell

Wherever There's Music and Beautiful Girls   Carroll

While You're Away   Gilbert

White House Is the Lighthouse of the World, The   Bryan; Caesar

Who Do You Love   Buck; Hanley

Who Do You Think You're Fooling with that Million Dollar Talk   Lewis; Snyder; Young, Joseph

Who Said Dixie   Sterling

Who's Afraid of the Kaiser   Gilbert

Who's Gonna Have the Young Goils While the Young Boys Are Away   Friend

Why Do They All Take the Night Boat to Albany   Lewis; Schwartz, Jean; Young, Joseph

Why Don't You   Friml

Women, Wine and Jazz   Atteridge; Romberg

Won't You Buy a War Stamp (War Stamps)   Atteridge

Won't You Play the Game?   Buck

Worst Is Yet to Come, The   Lewis; Young, Joseph

Would You Rather Be a Colonel with an Eagle on Your Arm than a Private with a Chicken on Your Knee   Fisher

Would You Rather Be a Colonel with an Eagle on Your Shoulder or a Private with a Chicken on You Knee   Mitchell

Yankee Doodle on the Line   Kern

Yanks Are at It Again, The   Brown, Lew

Yoo-oo Just You   Gershwin, George

You Can Find a Little Bit of Dixieland No Matter where You Go   Donaldson

You Can't Beat Us (For We've Never Lost a War)   Brennan

You Can't Deny You're Irish   Cohan

You Can't Run Around with a Lot of Little Girls (If You Want to Run Around with Me)   Hanley

You Don't Know What I Know About You   Bryan

You Don't Know what You're Missing If You've Never Had a Kiss   Von Tilzer

You Found Me and I Found You   Kern

You Get Me So Excited when You Come Near Me   Monaco

You Keep Sending 'em Over and We'll Keep Knockin' 'em Down   Mitchell; Ruby

You Make Me Feel So Foolish, When I'm Making Love to You   Bryan; Fisher

You Never Looked So Beautiful to Me   Dubin; Monaco

You Remember Me   Romberg

You Win   Romberg

You'd Better Get a Girl Before the Boys Come Home or You'll Never Get a Girl at All   Mitchell

You'll Always Find a Lot of Sunshine in My Old Kentucky Home   Brown, Lew

You'll Be Welcome As Flowers in May   Egan; Whiting

You'll Find Old Dixie Land in France   Clarke; Meyer

You'll Have to Put Him for Sleep with the Marseillaise and Wake Him Up with an Oo-La-La   Sterling; Von Tilzer

You-oo Just You   Caesar

You're a Big Piece of Cheese   Friend

You're Goin' to Fall in Love with California, Like I Fell in Love with You   Monaco

You're in Style when You're Wearing a Smile   Kahn

You're Just a Little Pansy, But You're Sweeter than a Song   Silver

You're Still an Old Sweetheart of Mine   Egan; Whiting

You're the Goddess of Beautiful Girls   Friend

You're the Greatest Little Mother in the World   Lewis; Young, Joseph

You're Your Mama's Little Daddy Now   Cobb; Edwards

You've Been the Sunshine of My Life   Berlin

You've Been Your Mother's Baby Long Enough   Gilbert

You've Got to Be in Khaki   Cobb; Edwards

Zing Boom Bah   Smith, Harry B.

1919

A la Hockey   Atteridge; Romberg; Schwartz, Jean

Ah Fong Low   Porter

Ain't It Grand in New Orleans?   Brennan

All I Get Is Consolation   Ahlert; Leslie

All I Want from You Is You   Howard, Joseph E.

All of No Man's Land Is Ours   Blake; Sissle

All that I Need Is a Hallway   Silver

All that I Need to Know Is that You Come from Dixie   DeSylva

All the Comforts of Home   Atteridge; Carroll

All the Quakers Are Shoulder Shakers Down in Quaker Town   Kalmar; Leslie

All the While   DeSylva

Allah   Ahlert; Leslie

Aloha   Mitchell

Alone with You   Howard, Joseph E.

Along the Trail where the Blue Grass Grows in the Hills of Old Kentucky   Friend

America Never Took Water and America Never Will   Brennan; Edwards

America's Answer   Egan; Whiting

America's Popular Song (Tune)   Atteridge; Romberg;
    Schwartz, Jean
And He'd Say Oo La La Wee Wee   Ruby
And That Ain't All   Stept
Another Sentimental Song   Porter
Any Old Place with You   Hart; Rodgers
Any Time New York Goes Dry   Herbert
Apologize   Howard, Joseph E.
Are You Steppin' Out Tonight   Atteridge
Are You Stepping Out Tonight   Atteridge; Carroll
As the Grain Needs the Rain, So I Need You, Once
    Again   Howard, Joseph E.
As You Were (For Mary, the Baby and Me)   Monaco
At My Dad and Mammy's Golden Wedding Jubilee   Stept
At the High Brown Babies Ball   Davis
At the Prohibition Ball   Silver
At the Winter Garden   Romberg; Schwartz, Jean
Auction Rag   Atteridge; Carroll
Baby   Kahn
Baby Blue   Donaldson; Lewis; Young, Joseph
Baby Dolls   DeSylva; Gershwin, George
Baby o' Mine   Brown, Nacio Herb
Baby Vampire Land   Bryan; Schwartz, Jean
Ballyho Bay   Fisher
Baltimore Blues, The   Blake; Sissle
Baseball   Bryan; Schwartz, Jean
Beale Street Blues   Bryan; Schwartz, Jean
Beautiful Gwend'lyn   Friend
Be-Da-Lum, Bo-Da-Lum   Clarke
Bee-Da-Lum, Bo-Da-Lum   Warren
Beedy-Boo   Brown, Nacio Herb
Belle of Bagdad (inst.), The   Motzan
Bermuda (inst.)   Monaco
Best of Everything, The   DeSylva; Gershwin, George
Between the Devil and the Deep Blue Sea   Brennan
Bill   DeSylva; Kern
Bless My Swanee River Home   Donaldson; Lewis; Young,
    Joseph
Blighty Bound   Egan; Whiting
Blue-Eyed, Blond-Haired, Heart-Breaking Baby
    Doll   Mitchell
Boys Are Like Wonderful Toys   Lewis; Snyder; Young,
    Joseph
B-R-A   Hart
Brat, The   Smith, Harry B.; Snyder
Breeze, Blow My Baby Back to Me   Hanley
Bring Me Back My Butterfly   Porter
(Flutter on By, My) Broadway Butterfly   Atteridge; Romberg;
    Schwartz, Jean
Broken Melody, The   Akst
Bubbles   Herbert
Bull Frog Patrol, The   Kern
Bungalow in the Sky   Brown, Nacio Herb
Business of Our Own, A   DeSylva; Kern
Butler's Fox-Trot, The   Atteridge; Carroll
By Pigeon Post   Buck
Bye-Bye My Little Wife   Friml; Harbach
Call It a Day   Herbert; Smith, Robert B.
Can It   Hammerstein; Rodgers
Candy Jag   Smith, Robert B.
Carnival Time   Atteridge; Romberg; Schwartz, Jean
Carolina   Egan; Whiting
Chanson Apache   Bryan; Schwartz, Jean
Charge of the Song Brigade   Egan; Whiting
Cheating   Fisher

Chelsea   Porter
Cherry Blossom Lane   Bryan; Schwartz, Jean
Chestertown   Hart
Chinese Dragon Blues   Caesar; Donaldson
Circus Ballet (inst.), The   Herbert
Cleopatra   Bryan; Schwartz, Jean
Colonial Days   Buck
Come and Dance with Me   Romberg
Come Back to Me   Atteridge; Romberg; Schwartz, Jean
Come Be My Wife   Herbert
Come On a Play Wiz Me, My Sweet Baby   Kalmar; Leslie;
    Ruby
Come to My Heart   Motzan
Come to the Moon   Gershwin, George
Cootie Tickle   Yellen
Cosy Corner   Bryan; Schwartz, Jean
Crocodile   Akst; Motzan
Cuba (You Must Be a Wonderful Place)   Dubin
Cuckoo Town   Atteridge; Carroll
Daddies   Coslow
Daddy Long Legs   Lewis; Ruby; Young, Joseph
Dance   Romberg
Dance de Nautica Americaine   Egan; Whiting
Dance Eccentric   Romberg
Dance of the Blues   Bryan; Schwartz, Jean
Dance Orientale   Romberg
Dance Vampire   Romberg
Dancing at the Wedding   Herbert
Dancing Shoes   Atteridge; Carroll
Dardanella   Fisher
Daughter of Mine   Mitchell
Depends on Beautiful Clothes   DeSylva; Gershwin, George
Desert Gold   Lewis; Young, Joseph
Desert Island   Schwartz, Jean
Does Your Mother Know You're Out Mademoiselle   Hanley
Don't Cry Frenchy, Don't Cry   Donaldson; Lewis; Young,
    Joseph
Don't Do Anything Till You Hear from Me   Smith, Robert B.
Don't Forget the Boys Who Fought for You and Me   Ahlert;
    Atteridge
Don't Put a Tax on the Beautiful Girls   Ager; Yellen
Don't Take Advantage of My Good Nature   Monaco
Doughnuts   DeSylva; Gershwin, George
Down Around the River (At the Dixie Jubilee)   Yellen
Down By the Meadow Brook   Leslie
Down By the Nile   Romberg
Down in an Irishman's Heart   Coslow
Down in Sunshine Valley   Turk
Down the Lane and Home Again   Kalmar; Leslie
Dream Girl, Give Back My Dream to Me   Romberg
Dreams   Sterling; Von Tilzer
Dreamy Amazon   Gilbert
Dreamy Florence   Atteridge; Jerome; Romberg; Schwartz,
    Jean
East Is East and West Is West   Hanley
Egyptian Butterfly   Kalmar; Leslie
Empire Days   Atteridge; Romberg; Schwartz, Jean
End of a Perfect Day, The   Brown, Lew
Entirely Surrounded by Girls   Atteridge; Carroll
Everybody Wants a Key to My Cellar   Pollack
Everybody's Crazy Half of the Time   Herbert; Smith, Robert
    B.
Everybody's Dancing Mad   Davis
Everything Is Rosy Now for Rosie   Berlin; Clarke
Eyes of the Army   Egan; Whiting

Eyes of the Girl I Love   Howard, Joseph E.
Eyes of the Soul   Fisher
Eyes of Verdun   Whiting
Eyes of Youth   Berlin
Eyes that Say I Love You   Fisher
Fair Honeymoon   Herbert
Fallen Idols   Bryan; Whiting
Falling Down the Side of a Mountain of Love   Hanley
False Faces   Leslie
Farewell   Herbert
Fast Steppers   Atteridge; Romberg; Schwartz, Jean
Festive Nights   Atteridge; Romberg; Schwartz, Jean
Fiji   Atteridge; Romberg; Schwartz, Jean
Fires of Faith   Lewis; Young, Joseph
First Day of May   Kern
First Rose of Summer   Kern
Flirtation Fantasies   Smith, Robert B.
Forget-Me-Not   DeSylva; Kern
Freckles   Ager; Johnson, Howard
Freedom of the C's   Bryan; Schwartz, Jean
French Soldiers on Leave Dance   Egan; Whiting
Friends   Johnson, Howard; Meyer
From Now On   DeSylva; Gershwin, George
Gates of Gladness   Brennan
Gee I Wish I Had Someone to Rock Me in the Cradle of
    Love   Blake; Sissle
Gee I'm Glad that I'm from Dixie So I Can Get a Dixie
    Welcome Home   Blake; Sissle
Ghost of Old Black Joe   Bryan; Schwartz, Jean
Gianina   Romberg
Ginger Town   Kern
Girl in Every Port   Atteridge; Romberg; Schwartz, Jean
Girls   Bryan; Carroll
Give a Little Thought to Me   DeSylva; Kern
Give Him Back His Job   Egan; Whiting
Give Me the Moonshine of My Old Kentucky
    Home   Atteridge
Give Me the South All the Time   Bryan; Schwartz, Jean
Give Me the Sultan's Harem   Silver
Good Morning All   Friml; Harbach
Good Night Angeline   Blake; Sissle
Good-Bye   Atteridge; Romberg; Schwartz, Jean
Good-Bye Bargravia   Cohan
Goodbye Shanghai   Bryan; Schwartz, Jean
Goodbye Sunshine Hello Moon   Buck
Good-Bye Teddy Roosevelt, You Were a Real
    American   Bryan; Fisher
Goodbye Wild Women Goodbye   Ager; Johnson, Howard;
    Meyer
Gowns Soft and Clingy   Friml; Harbach
Granny   Gilbert
Grape Juice Bill   Sterling
Green and Gray   Hart
Hand in Hand Again   Egan; Whiting
Hand that Rocked My Cradle Rules My Heart, The   Berlin
Happiness, Where Are You   Gilbert
Happy   Caesar
Happy Wedding Day, A   Kern
Harem Life   Berlin
Have a Smile (inst.)   Schwartz, Jean
Hawaiian Moonlight   Bryan; Schwartz, Jean
He Does Me So Much Good   Bryan; Schwartz, Jean
He Lights Another Mecca   Hart
He Used to Be a Farmer but He's a Big Town Slicker
    Now   Sterling; Von Tilzer

He Went in Like a Lion and Came Out Like a
    Lamb   Sterling; Von Tilzer
Heart o' the Hills   Lewis; Ruby; Young, Joseph
Heart of Humanity   Turk
Heartaches   Norworth
Heart-Breakers   Bryan; Schwartz, Jean
Heart-Sickness Blues   Coslow
Hello Cello   Williams
Hello, Everybody   Atteridge; Carroll
Hello Lemonade   Kalmar; Leslie
Here Come the Soldiers   Cohan
Here Comes the Bride   Goetz; Meyer
He's Always Hanging Around   Blake; Sissle
Hiawatha   McHugh
Hindoo Lady   Friend
Hippity Hop   Donaldson; Lewis; Young, Joseph
Hitchy's Garden of Roses   Porter
Home Sweet Home   Kern
Honeymoon Land   Romberg
Hoodlum, The   Lewis; Ruby; Young, Joseph
Hoop-Ti-Do   Atteridge; Romberg; Schwartz, Jean
Horicon Hop   Hart
Hotel Life   DeSylva; Gershwin, George
How Did Venus Make Love   Clare; Mitchell
How Do You Get that Way?   Herbert; Smith, Robert B.
How Sorry You'll Be Wait'll You See   Kalmar; Ruby
How 'Ya Gonna Keep 'Em Down on the Farm, After They've
    Seen Paree   Donaldson; Lewis; Young, Joseph
Hush-a-Bye My Baby   Bryan; Schwartz, Jean
I Ain't-en Got-en No Time to Have the Blues   Sterling; Von
    Tilzer
I Always Think I'm Up in Heaven, When I'm Down in
    Dixieland   Lewis; Schwartz, Jean; Young, Joseph
I Am the Girl (And I Am the Boy)   DeSylva
I Am the Pasha   Romberg
I Could Be Happy with One Little Boy If There Were No
    Others Around   Whiting
I Don't Want Anybody Around   Hanley
I Don't Want to Go Home   Herbert; Smith, Robert B.
I Found You   Gilbert
I Guess I'm More Like Mother than Like Father   Egan;
    Whiting
I Have a Date   Friml; Harbach
I Introduced   Porter
I Know Why   Davis
I Left My Door Open and My Daddy Walked Out   Berlin
I Long to Linger Longer Dearie, I Love the River and
    You   Buck
I Lost My Heart in Dixieland   Berlin
I Love a Musical Comedy Show   Bryan; Schwartz, Jean
I Might Be Your Once-in-a-While   Herbert; Smith, Robert B.
I Must Have Jazz   Mitchell
I Never Knew   Berlin
I Never Realized   Porter
I Used to Call Her Baby (And Now She's a Mother to
    Me)   Johnson, Howard
I Used to Love them All   Hart
I Wanna Go Back to Dear Old Mother's Knee   Hanley
I Want a Beautiful Baby Like You   Caesar
I Want My Little Gob   Kern
I Want to Make Sure You Love Me, 'Cause I've Been Fooled
    Before   Brown, Lew; Monaco
I Want to See a Minstrel Show   Berlin
I Want to Shimmie   Clarke

I Was So Young and You Were So Beautiful   Bryan; Caesar;
    Gershwin, George
I Will Wait   Howard, Joseph E.
I Wonder   Berlin
I'd Like to Be Rip Van Winkle in Rip Van Winkle
    Town   Leslie
Idle Hours   Lewis; Young, Joseph
If I Could Live Life Over I'd Live It All for You   Snyder
If It Wasn't for the Wife   Atteridge; Carroll
If You Can Love, (Like) You Can Dance   Herbert; Smith,
    Robert B.
If You Do, I'll Die   Friml; Harbach
If You Don't Stop Making Eyes at Me, I'm Goin' to Make
    Eyes at You   Brennan
If You Want to Make a Hit with the Ladies Tell Them
    They're Beautiful   Kalmar; Leslie; Ruby
I'll Be Happy When the Preacher Makes You
    Mine   Donaldson; Lewis; Young, Joseph
I'll Show You a Wonderful World   DeSylva; Gershwin,
    George
I'll Wait for You   Kahn
I'm a Cave Man   Stept
I'm a Stranger in My Own Home Town   Silver
I'm an Anaesthetic Dancer   Porter
I'm Crazy to Be a Jazz Band Leader   Coots
I'm Glad I'm from Dixie   Bryan; Schwartz, Jean
I'm Gonna Break that Mason-Dixon Line Until I Get to that
    Gal of Mine   Bryan; Schwartz, Jean
I'm in Love with You   Lewis; Snyder; Young, Joseph
I'm Irish   Mitchell
I'm Just Like a Wheel that Is Turning, By the Old Mill
    Stream   Fisher
I'm Lonely when I'm Alone   Friml; Harbach
I'm So Sorry I Ain't Got It You Could Have It If I Had It
    Blues   Lewis; Snyder
I'm So Sympathetic   Atteridge; Carroll
I'm So Tired of Dreaming   Gilbert
I'm Sorry I Ain't Got It If I Had It You Could Have It
    Blues   Lewis; Snyder; Young, Joseph
I'm the Guy Who Guards the Harem   Berlin
I'm Tickled to Death that You're Irish   Donaldson; Lewis;
    Young, Joseph
I'm Tracin' the Mason-Dixon Line   Stept
I'm Waiting for Ships that Never Come In   Yellen
In a Kingdom of Our Own   Cohan
In a Love Boat with You   Atteridge; Romberg; Schwartz,
    Jean
In China   Motzan
In Ding Dong Land   Lewis; Snyder; Young, Joseph
In Memoriam   Hart
In Miami Where Mammy's Waiting for Me   Mitchell
In My Home Town   DeSylva; Gershwin, George
In Napoli   Brown, Lew
In Our Little Paradise   Schwartz, Jean
In Room 202   Kalmar; Leslie
In Salem   Atteridge; Romberg; Schwartz, Jean
In the Land of Go to Be Early   Lewis; Snyder; Young,
    Joseph
In the Magic of the Moonlight   Fisher
In the Sweet Cry and Cry   Meyer
In the Sweet Dry and Dry   Ager
India   Stept
Indiana Moon   Freed, Arthur
Indoor Sports   Atteridge; Romberg; Schwartz, Jean
Influenza Blues   Smith, Robert B.

It Can't Be Wrong   Friml; Harbach
It Sort of Makes a Fellow Stop and Think   DeSylva;
    Gershwin, George
It Took Nineteen Hundred and Nineteen Years to Make a
    Girl Like You   Snyder
It's a Small World After All   Sterling; Von Tilzer
It's Always Summertime in the Winter Garden   Bryan;
    Schwartz, Jean
It's Better to Have Loved and Lost than Never to Have
    Loved at All   Stept
It's Great to Be in Love   DeSylva; Gershwin, George
It's Great to Be Married   Friml; Harbach
It's Hard to Tell   DeSylva; Gershwin, George
It's the Way You Look at Me   Brown, Nacio Herb
It's You   Motzan
I've Been Waiting for You All the Time   Kern
I've Danced to Beat the Band   Herbert
I've Found the Nesting Place of the Bluebird   Yellen
I've Going to Settle Down   Schwartz, Jean
I've Got a Pair of Swinging Doors that Lead Right into My
    Heart   Lewis; Young, Joseph
I've Got My Captain Working for Me Now   Berlin
I've Got Somebody Waiting   Porter
I've Got to Leave You   Friml; Harbach
I've Made Up My Mind To Mind a Maid Made Up Like
    You   Bryan; Schwartz, Jean
I've Told My Love   Friml; Harbach
Jazz Marimba   Romberg; Schwartz, Jean
Jazz Marimba Dance   Atteridge
Jazzin' the Alphabet   Lewis; Snyder; Young, Joseph
Je Ne Sais Pas   Egan; Whiting
Jewel Ballet   Atteridge; Romberg; Schwartz, Jean
Johnny's in Town   Meyer; Yellen
Jolly Me   Smith, Robert B.
Jubilo   Kern
Juno, My Honeymoon Girl   Bryan; Schwartz, Jean
Just a Kiss   Atteridge; Carroll
Just a Little Line   Kern
Just a Thought of You   Hanley
Just Another Kiss   Caesar
Just Another Poor Man Gone Wrong   Sterling; Von Tilzer
Just Around the Corner from Easy Street   Egan; Whiting
Just As We Used to Do   Brown, Lew
Just for Me and Mary   Clarke
Just My Type (They're All My Type)   Atteridge; Romberg;
    Schwartz, Jean
Just the Sweethearts — Mother and Dad   Bryan; Schwartz,
    Jean
Just to Mend Mamma's Heart   Donaldson; Lewis; Young,
    Joseph
Keep All Your Love for Me   Motzan
Kindly Pay Us   DeSylva; Gershwin, George
King's Favorite, The   Atteridge; Romberg; Schwartz, Jean
Kiss, The   Friml; Harbach
Kiss Burglar   Atteridge; Romberg; Schwartz, Jean
Kisses   DeSylva; Gershwin, George
Kitchenette   DeSylva
Lady O'Dreams   Kahn
Lamp of Love   Bryan; Schwartz, Jean
Land of Lullaby (Go to Sleep My Pickanniny Babe),
    The   Yellen
Land of My Heart's Desire   Whiting
Language of Love, The   DeSylva; Kern
Laugh, The   Friml; Harbach
League of Nations, The   DeSylva; Gershwin, George

Leave It to Your Milliner   Smith, Robert B.

L'Elefant Skeed   Egan; Whiting

Let Cutie Cut Your Cuticle   DeSylva; Gershwin, George

Let It Be Soon   Friml; Harbach

Let the Little Joy Bells Ring   Friend

Let the Rest of the World Go By   Brennan

Let Us Keep the Shimmie   Bryan; Schwartz, Jean

Let's All Be Good Pals Together, For When You're Gone, You're Gone Forever   Davis

Let's Go   Smith, Robert B.

Let's Go Round with a Smile   Donaldson; Lewis; Young, Joseph

Let's Start All Over Again   Howard, Joseph E.

Letter Song   Kern

Letters (That I'm Waiting For)   Dubin

Life and Love   Herbert

Limbo-Land   Friml; Harbach

Limehouse Nights   DeSylva; Gershwin, George

Lips, Lips, Lips   Romberg

Little Back-Yard Band, The   DeSylva; Kern

Little Blue Bonnet Girl   Fisher

Little Boy and Girl (Girl and Boy)   Herbert

Little Bull, A   Bryan; Schwartz, Jean

Little Chicken Fit for Old Broadway, A   Friml; Harbach

Little Church Around the Corner, The   Romberg

Little Drop of Irish and a Wee Bit of Scotch, A   Bryan; Carroll

Little Theatre of Our Own   Gershwin, George; Gershwin, Ira

Logic   Herbert

Lonely Hearts   Davis

(I Want a) Lonely Romeo   Smith, Robert B.

Lonesome Alimony Blues   Hanley

Look for the Silver Lining   DeSylva; Kern

Look Out for the Big Banshee   Howard, Joseph E.

Look Out for the Bolsheviki Man   Berlin

Lovable Moon   Atteridge; Schwartz, Jean

Love Is Like a Precious Pearl   Motzan

Love Makes the World Go 'Round   Romberg

Love of a Wife, The   DeSylva; Gershwin, George

Love Your Girl in an Aeroplane   Friend

Lovelight   Herbert

Love's a Very Funny Thing   Schwartz, Jean

Love's Dream   Fain

Lullabies My Mammy Sang to Me   Silver

Lullaby (Bye, Bye, Baby)   Herbert; Smith, Robert B.

Lullaby (String Quartet)   Gershwin, George

Madelon   Egan; Whiting

Magic of Wedding Chimes, The   Leslie

Mammy's Chocolate Drop   Mitchell

Man Around the House, A   DeSylva; Kern

Man Should Have a Double When He's Single, A   Herbert; Smith, Robert B.

Marseilles   Atteridge; Romberg; Schwartz, Jean

M-A-Y-B-E   Leslie; Ruby

Melody of Dance   Romberg

Memory-land   Kahn

Merry Wedding Bells   Herbert

Messenger   Cohan

Michi Mori San   Blake; Sissle

Midnight Blues   Brown, Nacio Herb

Military Decoration Dance   Bryan; Schwartz, Jean

Military Wedding Glide, The   Atteridge; Romberg; Schwartz, Jean

Miracle Man, The   Smith, Harry B.

Mischief in Your Eyes   Atteridge; Romberg; Schwartz, Jean

Miss Nightingale   Conrad

Miss Unruly   Atteridge; Romberg; Schwartz, Jean

Mississippi Lullaby   Bryan; Schwartz, Jean

Modern Butterfly   Howard, Joseph E.

Molly Malone   Atteridge; Romberg; Schwartz, Jean

Money, Money, Money!   DeSylva; Gershwin, George

Monte Cristo   Atteridge; Romberg; Schwartz, Jean

Moonlight Love   Stept

Moonlight on the Nile   DeSylva; Kahn

(Give Me the) Moonshine of My Old Kentucky Home   Carroll

Mother's Tears   Lewis; Young, Joseph

Mountain Girl's Lament   Young, Victor

Mountain Maid   Fisher

Mouthful of Kisses, A   Bryan; Schwartz, Jean

Move Into My Heart   Atteridge; Carroll

Mr. Nevin I'm in Heaven when I Hear Your Rosary   Clarke; Meyer

Mr. Sun Man Roll the Clouds Away   Kalmar; Ruby

Musical Comedy Blues   Stept

My Barney Lies Over the Ocean, Just the Way He Lied to Me   Lewis; Young, Joseph

My Beautiful Tiger Girl   Bryan; Schwartz, Jean

My Chocolate Soldier Boy   Bryan; Schwartz, Jean

My Cozy Little Corner of the Ritz   Porter

My Curley Headed Baby   Bryan; Schwartz, Jean

My Dream of Love Is You   DeSylva; Gershwin, George

My Fannie   DeSylva; Gershwin, George

My Idea of Something to Go Home To   Herbert; Smith, Robert B.

My Lady's Dress   Atteridge; Romberg; Schwartz, Jean

My Little Address Book   Whiting

My Midnight Sweetheart   Howard, Joseph E.

My Nanky Panky Poo   Donaldson; Lewis; Young, Joseph

My Salvation Nell   Norworth

My Tambourine Girl   Berlin

My Wife Is Out on Strike   Hanley

Nanette and Rin Tin Tin   Atteridge; Romberg; Schwartz, Jean

Neapolitan Jazz   Romberg; Schwartz, Jean

Near Future, The   Berlin

Neopolitan Jazz   Atteridge

New Moon, The   Berlin

Next Door to Heaven   Bryan; Schwartz, Jean

Night of Love   Romberg

Nobody but You   DeSylva; Gershwin, George

Nobody Ever   Caesar

Nobody Knows (And Nobody Seems to Care)   Berlin

Nobody's Gal   Lewis; Young, Joseph

Norma   Mitchell

North and South   Bryan; Schwartz, Jean

Now and Then but Not All the Time   Bryan; Schwartz, Jean

O Land of Mine, America   Gershwin, George

Office Blues, The   Atteridge; Carroll

Oh, Agnes   DeSylva

Oh! by Jingo!, Oh! by Gee!   Brown, Lew

Oh How He Could Plink-A-Plunk   Howard, Joseph E.

Oh How I Laugh when I Think How I Cried About You   Turk

Oh, How She Can Dance   Bryan; Schwartz, Jean

Oh, How She Can Sing   Yellen

Oh How She Could Dance the Ballyho   Fisher

Oh! The Woman in Room 13   Donaldson; Lewis; Young, Joseph

Oh What a Hummer of a Summer   Mitchell
Oh! What a Little Whopper   Friml; Harbach
Oh What a Pal Was Mary   Kalmar; Leslie
Oh, You Beautiful Person   Kern
Oh You Delicious Little Devil   Bryan; DeSylva
Oh, You Major Scales   Friml; Harbach
Oh, You Women   Stept
Old Brant Lake   Hart
Old Fashioned Rag   Bryan; Schwartz, Jean
Old Joe Blues   Gilbert
Old Oaken Bucket with Love   Bryan; Schwartz, Jean
Old-Fashioned Garden   Porter
Omar Khayyam   Atteridge
Omar Khayyam of Love   Carroll
On a Sunny Summer Day   Turk
On Lover's Bay   Brown, Nacio Herb
On My Private Telephone   Bryan; Schwartz, Jean
On Patrol in No Man's Land   Blake; Sissle
On the Sunny Side of the Street   Kahn
Once in a While   Lewis; Snyder; Young, Joseph
Once Upon a Time (The Magic Melody)   Romberg
One I Love, Two I Love   Smith, Robert B.
Only   Akst; Caesar
Only Kind of a Ring to Give a Girl is Upon the Telephone,
    The   Clarke
Oo, How I Love to Be Loved By You   Gershwin, George
Oo-Solo-Mi (I Give My Soul to You)   Clarke; Monaco
Open Up the Golden Gates to Dixieland and Let Me Into
    Paradise   Yellen
Opening of Hat Store   Smith, Robert B.
Opera, Comic Opera   Cohan
Orient   Atteridge; Bryan; Romberg; Schwartz, Jean
Our Cheerleader   Hart
Our Little Kitchenette   DeSylva; Gershwin, George
Our Quarrels, Dear   Gilbert
Out of a Clear Blue Sky   Lewis; Young, Joseph
Owl and the Turtle Doves, The   Atteridge; Carroll
Pagliacci   Porter
Pantomime Baseball   Bryan; Schwartz, Jean
Peachie   Bryan; Schwartz, Jean
Peacock Alley   Whiting
Peggy   Williams
Perfect Lover, The   Smith, Harry B.
Peter Pan   Atteridge; Carroll
Peter Piper   Porter
Pickaninny Dreams   Coslow
Picture Framed in My Heart   Whiting
Pig Latin Love   Gilbert
Plate Dance   Atteridge; Romberg; Schwartz, Jean
Play Me that Tune   Caesar; Donaldson
Please Don't Take Away the Girls   Bryan; Schwartz, Jean
Policeology   Herbert
Poor Little Butterfly Is a Fly Gal Now   Lewis; Young, Joseph
Poppy Blossom   Yellen
Poppyland   DeSylva; Gershwin, George
Popular Pests, The   Buck
Pousse Cafe   Smith, Harry B.
Preliminary Skirmish   Egan; Whiting
(Pretty Up, Pretty Up) Pretty Baby   Schwartz, Jean
Pretty Girl Is Like a Melody, A   Berlin
Pretty Up, Pretty Up, Pretty Baby   Bryan
Prohibition   Berlin
Put Me to Sleep in Your Heart and Wake Up with Your
    Love   Lewis; Young, Joseph
Rainbow Ball   Bryan; Schwartz, Jean

Razz-Berries   Mitchell
Red Lantern   Fisher
Red Riding Hood   Atteridge; Carroll
Reputation   DeSylva; Gershwin, George
Road to Destiny, The (The Roads of Destiny)   Romberg
Roads of Destiny, The   Atteridge; Schwartz, Jean
Rock-a-Bye Baby   Schwartz, Jean
Rock-a-Bye-Baby   Bryan
Roller Skating Waltz   Bryan; Schwartz, Jean
Rose, a Child, a Butterfly, A   Atteridge; Carroll
Rose of Verdun   Egan; Whiting
Roses of Arcadie   Motzan
Roses of Picardy   Bryan; Schwartz, Jean
'Round the Corner   Friml; Harbach
Royalty   Cohan
Sahara (Now We're as Dry as You) (We'll Soon Be Dry Like
    You)   Schwartz, Jean
Sail Away for Lullaby Bay   Donaldson; Lewis; Young, Joseph
Salvation Sal   Egan; Whiting
Sandman, The   Hart
Sas'parilla, Women and Song   Bryan; Schwartz, Jean
Save a Little Daylight for Me   Smith, Robert B.
Save It for Me   Howard, Joseph E.
Say When   Herbert; Smith, Robert B.
Say Yes   Caesar
Scandal   Herbert
Sea Is Calling, The   Porter
Secret Service Club, The   Atteridge; Carroll
See You Later Girls   Schwartz, Jean
See You Later Shimmy   Schwartz, Jean
Sentimental Nights   Atteridge; Romberg; Schwartz, Jean
Seven Ages of Women   Atteridge; Romberg; Schwartz, Jean
Shadows Always Make Me Blue   Lewis; Snyder; Young,
    Joseph
Shadows Will Fade Away   Brennan
Shall They Plead in Vain   Lewis; Young, Joseph
Shanghai   Buck
Shantung   Gilbert
She's Everything a Sweetie Ought to Be   Stept
She's Got Everything It Takes to Make a Wonderful
    Girl   Friend
Shimmee Baby   Whiting
Shimmee Town   Buck
Shimmy a la Egyptian   Atteridge; Romberg; Schwartz, Jean
Shimmying Everywhere   Bryan; Schwartz, Jean
Shimmy-Shaking Love   Atteridge; Carroll
Shine On   Herbert
Shy Little, My Little Girl   Howard, Joseph E.
Since Katy the Waitress Became an Aviatress   Berlin
Since Ma Got the Craze Espagnole   Porter
Since the Boys Came Home from France   Carroll
Sing Song Girl   Atteridge; Romberg
Slow and Easy   Williams
Slumber Music   Smith, Robert B.
Snap Your Fingers   Friml; Harbach
Snuggle and Dream   Friml; Harbach
So This Is Paris   Akst; Motzan
Solomon   Bryan; Schwartz, Jean
Some Day Down in Caroline   Egan
Some One   Kahn
Some Party   Kern
Some Sunny Day   Donaldson
Some Sweet Afternoon   Kahn
Somebody   Hanley
Somebody's Heart Is So Lonely   Motzan

Somebody's Waiting for Someone   Sterling; Von Tilzer
Somehow It Seldom Comes True   DeSylva; Gershwin, George
Somehow You're Just My Style   Howard, Joseph E.
Someone Like You   Herbert; Smith, Robert B.
Something About Love   Gershwin, George
Sonambula   Bryan; Schwartz, Jean
Sow Your Wild Oats Early   Herbert; Smith, Robert B.
Spite Bride, The   Lewis; Ruby; Young, Joseph
Spooky-Ookum   Herbert
Step This Way   Whiting
Steppin' Out Tonight   Romberg; Schwartz, Jean
Steven Got Even   Von Tilzer
Stroller in Dreamland, A   Atteridge; Carroll
Sugar Baby   Atteridge; Romberg; Schwartz, Jean
(It's Always) Summertime at the Winter Garden   Atteridge; Romberg
Sunshine Sis   Egan; Whiting
Suppose   Howard, Joseph E.
Sure An' It's Me that Knows   Von Tilzer
Swanee Glide   Bryan; Schwartz, Jean
Swanee Shore   Mitchell
Sweet Dreams   Friml; Harbach
Sweet Kisses   Brown, Lew
Sweet Sixteen   Buck
Sweet Sylvia   Howard, Joseph E.
Sweeter than Sugar (Is My Sweetie)   Berlin
Sweetheart Special   Atteridge; Romberg; Schwartz, Jean
Sweeties   Sterling; Von Tilzer
Sweets to the Sweet   Smith, Robert B.
Syncopated Cocktail   Berlin
Syncopated Wedding   Howard, Joseph E.
Syncopation's Scintillating Star   Stept
Take Me to the Land of Jazz   Kalmar; Leslie
Take Your Girlie to the Movies If You Can't Make Love at Home   Kalmar; Leslie
Tampa Bay   Bryan; Schwartz, Jean
Tanglefeet   Brown, Lew
Teacher, Teacher   Kern
Teddy   Snyder
Tee Ta Tee   Hart
Tee-Oodle-Um-Bum-Bo   DeSylva; Gershwin, George
Telephone Girls   DeSylva; Kern
Tell Me   Bryan; Schwartz, Jean
Ten Commandments of Love, The   DeSylva; Gershwin, George
That Black and White Baby of Mine   Porter
That Lullaby of Long Ago (Sweet and Low)   DeSylva; Egan; Kahn; Whiting
That's Nice   Davis
That's the Way I've Missed You   Kahn
That's Worth Waiting For   Young, Joseph
That's Worth While Waiting For   Lewis; Ruby
There Are No Lips So Sweet As Yours   Romberg
There Must Be a Way to Love You   Snyder
There Ought to Be Music   Silver
There's a Girl in Chateau Thierry   Goetz
There's a Happy Heart in Maryland and a Broken Heart in Brittany   Bryan; Schwartz, Jean
There's a Lot of Blue-Eyed Mary's Down in Maryland   Ager; Meyer; Yellen
There's a World of Beauty in You   Lewis; Schwartz, Jean; Young, Joseph
There's Always Room for One More   Hammerstein; Rodgers

There's More to the Kiss than the Sound   Caesar; Gershwin, George
There's Nothing too Fine for the Finest   Herbert
There's Only One that I Would Loose My Sleep for, and That's for Daddy   Monaco
There's Only One Thing to Do   Friml; Harbach
There's Something About a Rose   Kahn
They Don't Make Them That Way Any More   Yellen
They May Be Old, But They want to Be Loved   Silver
They're All My Type (Just My Type)   Romberg
They're All Sweeties   Sterling; Von Tilzer
This Is the Day   Bryan; Schwartz, Jean
Those Dixie Melodies   Bryan; Schwartz, Jean
Those Since-I-Met-You Days   Herbert; Smith, Robert B.
Thoughts that I Wrote on the Leaves of My Heart, The   Friml; Harbach
Three Mile Limit Cafe   Whiting
Three's a Crowd   Romberg
Throwing the Bull   Herbert
Tip Your Hat to Hattie   Herbert; Smith, Robert B.
Tipperary Mary   Buck
Tonight's the Night   Herbert
Tout Suite   Egan; Whiting
Town Called Might-Have-Been   Howard, Joseph E.
Toy Dance   Atteridge; Romberg; Schwartz, Jean
Train that Leaves for Town   Schwartz, Jean
Trousseau Ball, The   Friml; Harbach
True Blue Gal   Silver
Tulip Time   Buck
Tumble Inn   Atteridge; Romberg; Schwartz, Jean
Twinkle Little Star   Friml; Harbach
Two Big Brown Eyes (inst.)   Motzan
Two Lips in Georgia   Bryan; Schwartz, Jean
Two's Company   Romberg
Un Peu D'Amour   DeSylva; Gershwin, George
Under the Honeymoon   Hanley
Under the Spreading Chestnut Tree   Mitchell
Underneath a Big Umbrella   Smith, Robert B.
Underneath the Southern Skies   Ruby
Up in Mabel's Room   Silver
Up in the Air   Bryan; Schwartz, Jean
Upstairs and Down   Donaldson; Lewis; Young, Joseph
Valley of the Giants, The   Lewis; Young, Joseph
Valparaiso   Bryan; Schwartz, Jean
Valse Au L'Air   Friml; Harbach
Vampire Dance   Atteridge; Romberg; Schwartz, Jean
Velvet Lady   Herbert
Wait for Me   Smith, Robert B.
Was There Ever a Pal Like You   Berlin
Water Lily   Atteridge; Romberg; Schwartz, Jean
Way Down in Yucatan   Herbert
Way to Win a Girl, The   Lewis; Snyder; Young, Joseph
We Are the Fixers   Romberg
We Made the Doughnuts Over There   Berlin
We Must Have a Song to Remember   Stept
We Take It, Just Take It from You   Romberg
We Will Never Say   Fisher
Weaknesses   Hammerstein; Rodgers
Wedding Blues, The   Friml; Harbach
Wee Bit of Lace, A   Cohan
Welcome Home Boys   Razaf
We'll Build a Cute Little Nest   Friml; Harbach
What a Position for Me   Herbert
What Are We Going to Do?   Bryan; Schwartz, Jean
What Could Be Sweeter   Sterling; Von Tilzer

What's a Poor Soldier Going to Do? Hanley
What's the Use of Kicking, Let's Go 'Round with a
    Smile Donaldson; Lewis; Young, Joseph
When All Our Dreams Come True Fain
When Black Sallie Sings Pagliacci Porter
When I Had a Uniform On Porter
When I Hear a Dreamy Waltz Melody Clarke; Monaco
When I Hear You Calling Me I'll Answer You Fisher
When It's Lilac Time in Tokio Coots
When It's Sweet Patootie Time Leslie
When Mariutch Shake a Da Shimmie Sha Wot Sterling;
    Von Tilzer
When the Bees Make Honey Down in Sunny
    Alabam' Donaldson; Lewis; Young, Joseph
When the Rainbow of Love Appears Lewis; Young, Joseph
When the Robert E. Lee Arrives in Old Tennessee, All the
    Way from Gay Paree Monaco
When the Sixty-Ninth Comes Back Herbert
When There's a Chance to Dance Gershwin, Ira
When They're Beautiful, They're Bound to Get By Ager;
    Clarke; Meyer; Yellen
When They're Old Enough to Know Better It's Better to
    Leave Them Alone Lewis; Ruby; Young, Joseph
When Those Mason-Dixon Minstrels Hit the Town Bryan;
    Schwartz, Jean
When You Live in a Furnished Flat DeSylva; Gershwin,
    George
When You See Another Sweetie Hanging Around That's the
    Time You'll Want to Be Coming Back to
    Me Donaldson; Lewis; Young, Joseph
When You're in Right with the Right Little Girl Romberg
Where Is That Old Sweetheart of Mine? Brown, Lew
Where Is the Girl I Left Behind Cohan
Where the Water Lillies Grow Egan; Kahn; Whiting
Where's the Girl for Me? Kern; Smith, Harry B.
While Others Are Building Castles in the Air I'll Build a
    Cottage for You Fisher
Whip-Poor-Will DeSylva; Kern
White Heather, The Coots
Who Discovered Dixie Silver
Who Played Poker with Pocahontas when John Smith went
    Away Ahlert; Lewis; Young, Joseph
Who Wants a Baby Yellen
Whoa January You're Going to Be Worse than July Sterling;
    Von Tilzer
Who'll Take the Place of Mary Dubin
Why Are Chickens So High? Bryan; Schwartz, Jean
Why Do They Make Them So Beautiful Herbert; Smith,
    Robert B.
Why Do they Play Here Comes the Bride when They Ought
    to Play There Goes the Groom Sterling; Von Tilzer
Why Should There Be a Bridge of Sighs Across the River of
    Love Brennan
Will It Be Yes or No? Brown, Lew
Will o' the Wisp Smith, Robert B.
Will Will Will Brown, Nacio Herb
Willie or Will He Not Lewis; Young, Joseph
Wine Ballet Atteridge; Romberg; Schwartz, Jean
With a Little Bit of Cider Inside of Ida, Ida Was Full of
    Ideas Lewis; Snyder; Young, Joseph
Won't You Help Me Out Friml; Harbach
Won't You Park Your Heart in My Little Garage of
    Love Egan; Whiting
World Has Gone Shimmee Mad, The Buck
Yasso Rag Schwartz, Jean

Yazoo Rag Bryan
Yesterdays Kahn
Yip! Yip! Bryan; Schwartz, Jean
Yodel O DeSylva
You Ain't Heard Nothing Yet DeSylva; Kahn
You Are Full of the Bull from Ze Boulevard Johnson,
    Howard; Meyer
You Cannot Make Your Shimmy Shake on Tea Berlin
You Can't Blame the Girlies at All Silver
You Don't Need the Wine to Have a Wonderful Time (While
    They Still Make Those Beautiful Girls) Akst
You Know and I Know Romberg
You Know What I Mean Dubin
You Little Blue Devil Atteridge; Carroll
You Never Can Tell Brown, Lew; Smith, Robert B.
You Tell 'Em DeSylva; Kern
You Will Be Sorry Someday Davis
You'd Be Surprised Berlin; Bryan; Schwartz, Jean
You'll Do It All Over Again Friml; Harbach
You'll Dream and I'll Dream — Then Wake to Find Your
    Dreams All Come True Friml
Young Man Schwartz, Jean
Your Eyes Have Told Me So Kahn
You're a Million Miles from Nowhere (When You're One
    Little Mile from Home) Donaldson; Lewis; Young,
    Joseph
You're a Perfect Jewel to Me Dearest Buck
You're Always Breaking Something and Now You're
    Breaking My Heart Dubin
You're Living Right Next Door to Heaven when You Live in
    Dixieland Bryan; Schwartz, Jean
You're Making a Miser of Me Dubin
You've Been a Good Little Mammy to Me Blake; Sissle
Zula-Boola Motzan

1920

Absolute Don of a Juan, An Caesar
Absolutely Certain Caesar
After Every Party Freed, Arthur
After You Get What You Want You Don't Want It Berlin
All I Give 'em's the Air Carroll
All in a Short Half Hour Hanley
All That I Want Hammerstein; Harbach
All the Boys Love Mary Sterling
All the Little Glooms Start Dancing Atteridge
All You Need to Be a Star Hart; Rodgers
Allah Jazz Atteridge
Aloyisious I Love You Fisher
Always You Hammerstein
Another Melody in F Hart; Rodgers
Any Little Melody Atteridge
Any Place Is Home Sweet Home with You Caesar
Any Place Would Be Wonderful with You Buck
Anything You Want to Do, Dear Harbach
Aphrodite Hart; Rodgers
Aria, An Hammerstein; Harbach
Ask the Rose Yellen
At Last Herbert; Smith, Robert B.
At the Grand Turkish Jubilee (Do a Little Turkey) Fisher
At the Moving Picture Ball Johnson, Howard
At the Piano Bryan; Schwartz, Jean
At Twilight Time Egan; Whiting
Baby Dreams Hammerstein; Harbach
Back Home Gershwin, George; Gershwin, Ira

Bambino   Gershwin, Ira; Youmans
Be Aesthetic   Caesar
Beautiful Annabell Lee   Bryan; Meyer
Beautiful Birds   Buck
Beautiful Faces (Need Beautiful Clothes)   Berlin
Beautiful Girls Are Like Opium   Schwartz, Jean
Beautiful Shoulders   Bryan; Schwartz, Jean
Beauty Is Like a Rose   Bryan; Schwartz, Jean
Becky from Babylon   Silver
Becky Green the Queen of the Screen   Von Tilzer
Bells   Berlin
Below the Macy-Gimbel Line   Hammerstein; Harbach
Beside the Rippling Stream   Kalmar; Monaco; Ruby
Betty Behave   Smith, Harry B.
Beyond the Stars   Koehler
Bill and Coo   Caesar
Blow, Blow, Blow   Conrad
Bob White   Kern
Bombay Bombashay, The   Romberg
Bones   Hammerstein; Harbach
Boomerang, The   Hart; Rodgers
Bottle Up a Pretty Girl   Bryan; Schwartz, Jean
Breath of a Rose   Caesar
Breath of Spring   Hart; Rodgers
Bright Eyes   Motzan; Smith, Harry B.
Bring Back My Love Dreams   Lewis; Young, Joseph
Bring 'Em Back   Kern
Broadway Strut   Coots
Broadway Swell and Bowery Bum   Hammerstein; Harbach
Buggy Riding   Kern
Bull and Bear   Atteridge
But She's Just a Little Bit Crazy About Her Husband - That's
    All   Berlin
Butterfly Ballet (inst.)   Herbert
By the O-Hi-O O-My-O   Yellen
Cabaret Girl   Hammerstein; Harbach
Call Me Andre   Hart; Rodgers
Call of the Wild Women   DeSylva
Call the Doc   Hart; Rodgers
Caramba   Smith, Harry B.
Caresses   Monaco
Carlotti's Jimmie   Hammerstein; Harbach
Catch 'Em Young, Treat 'Em Rough, Tell 'Em Nothing
    Herbert; Smith, Robert B.
Century Promenade, The   Bryan; Schwartz, Jean
Ceylon Rose   Kalmar; Motzan; Ruby
Chair Ballet   Atteridge
Change Partners   Herbert
Charm School, The   Bryan; Schwartz, Jean
Chick! Chick! Chick!   Kern
Chiffon Fantasie (inst.)   Herbert
Chili Bean   Brown, Lew
China   Hart; Rodgers
Chinese Firecrackers   Berlin
Ching a Ling's Jazz Bazaar   Johnson, Howard
Cinderella on Broadway   Atteridge
Cindy   Atteridge
Cleopatricola (Cleo-Patrick-Ola)   Bryan; Schwartz, Jean
Clock Song   Bryan; Schwartz, Jean
Clothes   Hammerstein; Harbach
College on Broadway, A   Hart; Rodgers
Colonial Days   Buck
Come Across   Hammerstein; Harbach; Herbert; Smith,
    Robert B.
Come Along   Berlin

Come Back to Jumbo Gumbo   Dubin
Coral Sea   Brown, Nacio Herb
Country Cousin, The   Bryan; Youmans
Creation Scene (inst.)   Herbert
Cubana   Motzan
Cuddle and Kiss   Kalmar; Ruby
Cuddling Arms   Lewis; Young, Joseph
Cupid, the Winner   Kern
Custom-Made Maids   Caesar
Cute Little Two by Four   Hammerstein; Harbach
Daddy You've Been a Mother to Me   Fisher
Daisy and the Lark, The   Hart; Rodgers
Dance-O-Mania   Gilbert
Dancing School-Her First Lesson (inst.), The   Herbert
Darby and Joan   Herbert
Dardanella Blues   Fisher
Darlin' Do   Egan; Whiting
Dear Old Gal, Who's Your Pal Tonight   Egan; Whiting
Dearest One   Kahn
Deenah, My Argentine Rose   Dubin
Deeper   Harbach
Didja Ever See the Like?   Hammerstein; Harbach
Dig, Sister, Dig   Hammerstein; Harbach
Ding Dong, It's Kissing Time   Kern
Do, Re, Mi   Hammerstein; Harbach
Dodge Brothers March   Herbert
Don' Yo' Want to See de Moon?   Hammerstein; Harbach
Donna Bella Mia   Fisher
Don't Fall Until You've Seen Them All   Harbach
Don't Let Me Catch You Falling in Love   Hanley
Don't Love Me Like Othello   Hart; Rodgers
Don't Tell Me Who You Are   Porter
Don't You Remember   Hammerstein
Don't You Want to Take Me?   Kern
Down Beside the Cider Mill   Bryan
Down on the Old Kansas Farm (That Farm Out in
    Kansas)   Harbach
Down the Trail to Home, Sweet Home   Dubin
Dreaming True   Hart; Rodgers
Drifting Along on a Blue Lagoon   Kahn
Drifting On   Hammerstein
Drowsy Head   Berlin
Early to Bed and Early to Rise Never Made Anyone
    Wise   Silver
Echoes   Caesar
Emancipation Day   Buck
Every Hour Away from You Is Sixty Minutes Lost   Herbert;
    Smith, Robert B.
Every Telephone (Telephone Song)   Buck
Every Time I Meet a Lady   Harbach
Everybody Step with Me   Johnson, James P.
Everybody Swat the Profiteer   Gershwin, George
Everybody Tells It to Sweeney and Sweeney Tells It to
    Me   Mitchell
Everything Has Stung Me but a Bee   Herbert; Smith, Robert
    B.
Everything Is French in Dixieland   Fisher
Ev'rybody but Me   Hanley
Ev'rything Is Sweet 'n Pretty   Ager; Yellen
Fairy Dance   Atteridge
Famous You   Hammerstein; Harbach
Fantasie   Hammerstein; Harbach
Farm Yard Jazz, The   Razaf
Feather Your Nest   Johnson, Howard
Fee Fi Fo Fum (inst.)   Motzan

Fig Leaf Number   Bryan; Schwartz, Jean
Flirtation Dance   Harbach
Floradora Girls   Blake; Sissle
Flower of the Snow   Smith, Harry B.
Flowers and You   Young, Victor
Flying the Blimp   Hart; Rodgers
For No Reason at All   Donaldson; Gershwin, Ira; Lewis;
    Young, Joseph
From Your Heart to Mine   Hanley
Furnished for Monty   DeSylva; Kern
Get 'Em While They're Dancing Around   Baer; Mitchell
Girl Belongs to You, The   Atteridge
Girl I'll Call My Sweetheart Must Look Like You,
    The   Olcott
Girl in the Spotlight   Herbert; Smith, Robert B.
Girl Who Can Love, A   Herbert; Smith, Robert B.
Girl Who Keeps You Waiting, The   Herbert; Smith, Robert
    B.
Girls in the Sea   Kern
Girls of My Dreams, The   Berlin
Give Me a Million Beautiful Girls   Parish
Glorias, The   Atteridge
Golden Moments   Kalmar; Leslie
Gondolier   Gershwin, Ira; Youmans
Gone Are the Days   Hart; Rodgers
Gone Is the Smile   Caesar
Good-Bye My Emerald Land   Olcott
Good-Night Boat   Kern
Gown Is Mightier than the Sword, The   Hart; Rodgers
Great, Great Lover, The   Caesar
Grieving for You   Coslow
Gunga Din   Hart; Rodgers
Hail to Monty   DeSylva; Kern
Happy Hottentot   Jerome; Von Tilzer
Hayward's Harlem Hellions   Hammerstein
He Wanted to Go and He Went   Herbert; Smith, Robert B.
Heart for Sale, A   Kern
Heartbreakers   Bryan; Schwartz, Jean
Heaven Christened Dixie Land   Egan; Whiting
Hello Moon   Buck
Hello Virginia   Friend
Hen and the Cow (It's Only a Dream of the Past),
    The   Bryan; Caesar; Meyer
Hiawatha's Melody of Love   Bryan; Meyer
Hobbies   Herbert
Hold Me   Atteridge; Bryan; Schwartz, Jean
Home Again Blues   Akst; Berlin
Honolulu Eyes   Johnson, Howard
House that Jack Built, The   Atteridge
How Can I Marry One Little Girl, When I'm in Love with
    Them All   Fisher
Humming Bird Hum for Me   Henderson
Hundred Years from Now, A   DeSylva
Hunika   Fisher
I Always Give the Wrong Impression   Caesar
I Am Cleopatra   Goetz
I Cannot Sleep Without Dreaming of You   Herbert; Smith,
    Robert B.
I Can't Do This I Can't Do That   Schwartz, Jean
I Don't Have to Die to Go to Heaven   Ager; Johnson,
    Howard
I Don't Know Why (When I Dance with You)   Caesar;
    Gershwin, George
I Don't Laugh at Love Any More   Hammerstein; Harbach
I Hate to Talk About Myself   Hart; Rodgers

I Have Somebody's Labor Agitator   Atteridge
I Have Waited for You   Herbert; Smith, Robert B.
I Knew Him When   Herbert; Smith, Robert B.
I Know I Shall Meet Her Someday   Herbert; Smith, Robert
    B.
I Know Why   Berlin
I Learned About Women (from Her)   Herbert; Smith, Robert
    B.
I Learned to Love You When I Learned My
    A.B.C.'s   Warren
I Live in Turkey   Berlin
I Love the Ground You Walk On   Herbert; Smith, Robert B.
I Love the Land of Old Black Joe   Clarke; Donaldson
I Love the Lassies (I Love 'em All)   Kern
I Love to Say Hello to the Girls (But I Hate to Say
    Goodbye)   Romberg
I Met You   Young, Victor
I Never Knew (I Could Love Anybody Like I'm Loving
    You)   Egan
I Never Miss   Hammerstein
I Realize   Fisher
I Surrender   Hart; Rodgers
I Want to Be the Leader of the Band   Yellen
I Want to Be Wanted By You   Gershwin, George; Gershwin,
    Ira
I Want to Go to the Land Where Sweet Daddies Grow   Von
    Tilzer
I Want You   Herbert
I Was a Florodora Baby   Carroll
I Wish I Was a Queen   Hammerstein; Harbach
I Wish that I'd Been Born in Borneo   Clarke; Donaldson
I Wonder what Rebecca Was Doing by the Well   Fisher
I Wonder Who (Has Taken My Place with You)   Davis
I'd Like a Honeymoon with You   Herbert
I'd Like a Lighthouse   Kern
I'd Like to Take You Away   Smith, Harry B.
I'd Love to Fall Asleep and Wake Up in My Mammy's
    Arms   Ahlert; Lewis; Young, Joseph
I'd Love to Know   Motzan
Idle Dreams   Gershwin, George
If a Wish Could Make It So   Hammerstein; Harbach
If All the Girls were Good Little Girls   Clarke; Donaldson
If an Apple Tempted Adam, What a Peach Could Do for
    Me   Silver
If I Meet the Guy that Made This Country Dry   Jerome; Von
    Tilzer
If I Only Were a Boy   Hart; Rodgers
If I Saw Much of You   Herbert; Smith, Robert B.
If I Wait Till the End of the World   Von Tilzer
If I Were a Hungry Cannibal   Fisher
If That's Not Love What Do You Call It?   Herbert; Smith,
    Robert B.
If There's a Lovers Lane in Heaven, I Know We'll Meet
    Again   Fisher
If We Had Met Before   Herbert
If You Could Care   Goetz
If You Were You   Hart; Rodgers
If You'll Only Say It with Flowers   Goetz
I'll Always Keep a Corner in My Heart for
    Tennessee   Clarke; Donaldson
I'll Be Busy As a Bee   Clare; Mitchell
I'll Be There   Herbert; Smith, Robert B.
I'll Keep Looking for the Roses Tho' the World Is Full of
    Thorns   Bryan; Meyer
I'll Miss You, Old Ireland   Brennan

I'll Say So   Hammerstein
I'll See You in C-U-B-A   Berlin
I'm a Lonesome Little Raindrop   Hanley
I'm a Loser in the Game of Love   Coslow
I'm a Vamp from East Broadway   Berlin; Kalmar; Ruby
I'm Always Falling in Love with the Other Fellow's
   Girl   Caesar; Meyer
I'm an Indian Assassin   Johnson, Howard
I'm Crazy about Somebody   Buck
I'm Dining with Elsa   Porter
I'm in Heaven when I'm in My Mother's Arms   Ager;
   Johnson, Howard
I'm Lost Without You, Without You I'm Gone   Monaco
I'm Out on Strike for a Beautiful Girl   Johnson, Howard
In an Oriental Garden   DeSylva; Kahn
In Fair Japan   Ager; Yellen
In Gay Havana   Kahn
In Little Old New York   Schwartz, Jean
In Madagascar Land   Gilbert
In My Igloo (The Snow Shoe Fox Trot)   Gilbert
In My Looking Glass   Herbert; Smith, Robert B.
In Old Japan   Bryan
In Sweet September   Leslie; Monaco
In the Land of School Days   Dubin; Edwards
In the Land of Yesterday   Romberg
In the Night   Fisher
In the Year of Fifty-Fifty   Ager; Yellen
In Venice   Herbert
In Watermelon Time   Johnson, Howard
India Rubber   Hammerstein; Harbach
Inebriated Acrobation   Bryan; Schwartz, Jean
Inspiration   Hart; Rodgers
Irish were Egyptians Long Ago, The   Bryan
Israel   Fisher
It Isn't Hard to Do   Hammerstein; Harbach
It Isn't the Style   Dubin
It Isn't what She Does that Makes Me Love Her   Mitchell
It Might Have Been You   Coslow
It Must Be You   Conrad
It Would Happen Anyway   Herbert; Smith, Robert B.
Italian Street Singers   Porter
It's a Widow for Mine   Harbach
It's Better to Be a Man   DeSylva; Kern
It's Naughty — but It's Nice   DeSylva
It's the Nicest Sort of Feeling   Caesar
It's the Smart Little Feller Who Stocked Up His Cellar, That's
   Getting the Beautiful Girls   Ager; Clarke
I've Always Been Fond of Babies (That's Why I'm in Love
   with You)   Hanley
I've Found My Dream Girl   Johnson, Howard; Yellen
I've Got the A.B.C.D. Blues   Von Tilzer
Jaggy-Jazz, The   Herbert
Japanese Sandman   Egan; Whiting
Jazz what Have You Done to Me   Fisher
Je Ne Comprends Pas   Bryan; Schwartz, Jean
Je Ne Sais Pa Pa (I Do Not Know)   Fisher
Jewels of Pandora, The   Ager; Yellen
Jim Jam Jems   Hanley
Jinga-Bula-Jing-Jing   Lewis; Young, Joseph
Josephine   Bryan; Schwartz, Jean
Julius   Fisher
Just a Bit o' Dreaming   Kahn
Just a Little Bit Behind the Times   Hanley
Just a Smile   Hammerstein; Harbach
Just a Week from Today   Dubin

Just Another Kill   Berlin
Just As We Used to Be   Von Tilzer
Keep a Fox Trot for Me   Caesar
Keep Sakes   Egan; Whiting
Keep the Love Lamps Burning in the Windows of Your
   Eyes   Smith, Harry B.
Keep Your Eyes Down Mary   Egan; Whiting
Keep Your Weight Down   Bryan; Schwartz, Jean
Kentucky Sue   Blake; Sissle
Kid, I Love You   Hart; Rodgers
Kikerikee   Caesar
Kiss from You   Howard, Joseph E.
Kiss Ze Hand   Fisher
Kissimee   Caesar
Kissing Time   Caesar
La Veda   Bryan; Schwartz, Jean
Lady, Look What You've Done with Your Doggone
   Dangerous Eyes   Kalmar; Ruby
Lady of Mars   Atteridge
Lady Raffles Behave   Hart; Rodgers
Land Beyond the Candle Light, The   Atteridge
Land of Evangeline   Young, Victor
Language of Love, The   Caesar
Last Waltz I Had with You, The   Atteridge
Lead Me to Laughter   Johnson, Howard
Leave Me Your Love When You're Gone   Fisher
Left All Alone Again Blues   Kern
Leg of Nations, The   Berlin
Let Me Drink in Your Eyes   Hart; Rodgers
Let Me Whisper in Your Ear   Bryan; Schwartz, Jean
Let's Go!   Caesar
Let's Go What Do You Say?   Caesar
Let's Have a Rattling Good Time   Bryan; Schwartz, Jean
Let's Marry   Hammerstein
Let's Misbehave   Porter
Let's Pretend   Herbert; Smith, Robert B.
Life Without a Cigarette   Johnson, Howard
Like Kelly Can   Fisher
Lindy   Berlin
Little Bo Peep   Hanley
Little Crumbs of Happiness You Gave Me Long
   Ago   Brennan
Little Girl, Little Boy   Hart; Rodgers
Little Hindoo Man   Hammerstein; Harbach
Little Nest for Two, A   Herbert
Little Plate of Soup, A   Hammerstein; Harbach
Little Wigwam for Two   Schwartz, Jean
Live for All You're Worth   Goetz
Log of the Ship, The   Hammerstein; Harbach
Lonely Baby   Egan; Whiting
Look Around   Porter
Look for the Silver Lining   DeSylva; Kern
Lord Only Knows, The   Hart; Rodgers
Lorelei, The   Kern
Love Boat, The   Buck; Herbert
Love 'Em and Leave 'Em   Porter
Love Flower   Caesar; DeSylva
Love Germs   Young, Victor
Love, Honor and O-Baby   Hanley
Love Is an Old Fashioned Feeling   Schwartz, Jean
Love Me in the Candlelight   Bryan; Schwartz, Jean
Love Nest, The   Harbach
Love Time   Brown, Nacio Herb
Love Will Call   Hart; Rodgers
Love's Intense in Tents   Hart; Rodgers

Love's Telephone   Caesar
Lu Lu   Gershwin, George
Lucky in Love   Kahn; Schwartz, Jean
Lullaby, A   Atteridge
Macushla Asthore   Brennan
Magic Kiss, The   Hanley
Makin' for My Georgia Caroline   Fisher
Mammy Jazz   Johnson, J. Rosamond
Mammy's Good Night Lullaby   Jerome; Von Tilzer
Mammy's Little Sugar Plum   Davis
Mandolin and the Man, The   DeSylva; Kern
Mansion of Roses, The   Bryan; Schwartz, Jean
Manyana   Parish
Marcelle   Bryan; Schwartz, Jean
Margie   Conrad; Davis
Marinka   Johnson, Howard
Marry Me and See   Herbert; Smith, Robert B.
Mary   Harbach
Mary and Doug   Buck
Mary Loves a Sailor   Fisher
Mary Queen of Scots   Rodgers
Maybe   Davis
Metropolitan Ladies   Berlin
Mexico   Caesar
Midnight Girl (One Midnight Supper at Home), The   Hart;
      Rodgers
Midnight Moon   Coslow
Mighty Like a Rosenbloom   Fisher
Millions of Tunes   Bryan; Schwartz, Jean
Mimi   Caesar
Mimi Jazz   Caesar
Ming Poo   Hammerstein; Harbach
Miniatures   Atteridge
Minuet   Atteridge
Misterioso   Hammerstein
Monaco (inst.)   Monaco
Monastery Bells   Leslie
Money, Money, Money   Harbach
Moon of Love   Kern
Moon of Shanghai   Fain
Moonbeams   Caesar; Stept
Moonlight and You   Hart; Rodgers
Moonlight in Mandalay   Yellen
Moonlight in Maryland   Whiting
Morning After, The   DeSylva
Mother's Hands   Ager; Clarke
Mother's Tears   Lewis
Mouth Full of Kisses, A   Bryan; Schwartz, Jean
Mr. and Mrs.   Gershwin, Ira; Youmans
Mumsey   Gilbert
My Bambino   Fisher
My Bridal Veil   Ager; Yellen
My Broadway Chorus Girl   Conrad
My Budding Rose   Gilbert
My Daddy Knows   Lewis; Young, Joseph
My Day Has Come   Caesar; Herbert
My Dixie Rosary   Hanley
My Georgia Caroline   Fisher
My Golden Girl   Herbert
My Home Town Is a One Horse Town   Silver
My Lady   Gershwin, George
My Lady of the Cameo   Bryan; Schwartz, Jean
My Lady of the Lamp   Schwartz, Jean
My Little Bimbo Down on the Bamboo Isle   Clarke;
      Donaldson

My Little Dancing Heart   Schwartz, Jean
My Man   Buck; Hanley
My Mother's Evening Prayer   Dubin
My Old Love Is My New Love   Gershwin, George
My Pousse-Cafe   Hammerstein
My Rosary of Melodies   Buck
My Sahara Rose   Clarke; Donaldson
My Violin   Romberg
My Vision Girl   Blake; Sissle
My World of Romance   Hart; Rodgers
Name the Day   Herbert
Naughty Eyes   Atteridge; Friend
Night, the Moon and You, The   Lewis; Young, Joseph
Night Time, The   Herbert; Kern; Smith, Robert B.
No One but You   Brown, Lew
No Place to Go, but Only Home Sweet Home   Fisher
No Wonder I'm Blue   Ahlert; Lewis; Young, Joseph
Noah's Wife Lived a Wonderful Life   Yellen
Nobody to Love   Kahn; Meyer
Nona (Sweetest Girl in Barcelona)   Kahn
Not So Long Ago   Brown, A. Seymour
Now I Ask You Is that Nice   Clare; Mitchell
Now I Lay Me Down to Sleep   Meyer; Mitchell
O You Heavenly Body   Bryan; Schwartz, Jean
Oh Day in June!   Herbert
Oh Dear   Von Tilzer
Oh How I Love You   Sterling
Oh! Judge He Treats Me Mean   Hanley
Oh You Little Bunch o' Sweetness   Yellen
Old King Cole   Atteridge
Old Music Masters   Atteridge
Old Pal, Why Didn't You Answer Me   Lewis; Young, Joseph
Old Town (Old New York), The   Kern
Older They Are, the Younger They Want 'Em   Dubin
Older They Get the Younger They Want 'em, The   Silver
Olympic Water Daughters of White Rock   Jerome; Von
      Tilzer
On an Island with You   DeSylva
On King's Solomon's Farm   Von Tilzer
On My Mind the Whole Night Long   Gershwin, George
On the Bosom of the Sleepy Nile   Goetz
On the Day that Comes Before Monday   Jerome; Von Tilzer
On with the Dance   Kern
Once in a Lifetime   Caesar
One Little Boy Had Money   Atteridge
One Little Girl   Caesar
One Little Girl I Prize, The   Brennan
One Night in Rome   Egan; Whiting
Only Way to Get 'Em, The   Fisher
Only You   Herbert; Smith, Robert B.
Oo, How I Love to Be Loved By You   Gershwin, George
Oo La La   Herbert; Smith, Robert B.
Opening Act Two (In Society)   Kern
Orange Blossom Time   Norworth
Oriental Stars   Monaco
Original Oklahoma Blues   Robison
(Oui) Oui Madame   Herbert; Smith, Robert B.
Ouija Mine   Lewis; Young, Joseph
Our Hotel   Porter
Over the Garden Wall   Herbert; Smith, Robert B.
Overalls and Calico   Kahn; Schwartz, Jean
Page Mr. Cupid   Schwartz, Jean
Pajama Blues   Dubin
Palesteena   Conrad
Parisola   Silver

Passing Through   Hammerstein
Patchland   Atteridge
Pathways   Akst
Peachie   Yellen
Peek-in Pekin   Hart; Rodgers
Penny for Your Thoughts, A   Hart; Rodgers
Perfect Lover, A   Hammerstein; Harbach·
Perfume of Paradise, The   Caesar
Persia   Davis
Phantom Loves   Atteridge
Phantom Waltz (inst.), The   Romberg
Piccadilly's Not a Bit Like Broadway   Gershwin, Ira;
      Youmans
Pick Yo' Partner! (Get Ready for the Raggy
      Blues)   Gershwin, Ira; Youmans
Pierrot Land   Atteridge
Play Me Something I Can Dance To   Herbert; Smith, Robert
      B.
Playmates — I Wish I Were a Boy Again   Fisher
Poor Fish   Hart; Rodgers
Poor Little Rich Little Me   Hanley
Poor Little Ritz Girl   Hart; Rodgers; Romberg
Poor Old Florodora Girl   Hanley
Poor Young Millionaire   Porter
Precious Jewels   Atteridge
Pretty Ming Toy   Romberg
Primrose Way   Atteridge
Princess of the Willow Tree   Rodgers
Producers   DeSylva; Kern
Pulse of My Heart   Brennan
Purpose in Life   Schwartz, Jean
Pusha Pusha Baby Cart   Fisher
Queen Isabella   Gershwin, George
Race Track Blues, The   Leslie
Rag Doll, The   Bryan; Schwartz, Jean
Ragadora   Yellen
Raggedy Ann   Hanley
Ragtime Terpsichore   Herbert
Rainy Afternoons   Conrad
Rap-Tap-a-Tap   Ager; Yellen
Rather Than See You Once in a While   Clarke; Donaldson
Rattle Rattle   Bryan; Schwartz, Jean
Relatives   Berlin
Reuben Glue   Fisher
Rickety Crickety   Hammerstein; Harbach
Rickshaw (inst.)   Monaco
Rip Van Winkle and His Little Men   Kern
Robin's Song (inst.), The   Monaco
Rock Me in Your Loving Arms   Atteridge
Rock-A-Bye-Lullaby Mammy   Clarke; Donaldson
Rockaway Mary   Stept
Rolling Up the Barcarolle   Atteridge
Romantic Blues   Atteridge; Bryan; Schwartz, Jean
Rosary of Love   Pollack
Rose of Babylon   Yellen
Rose of Bagdad I Love You So   Kahn
Rose of Old Seville   Conrad
Rose of Spain   Fisher
Rose of the Rotisserie   Hanley
Rosie, Make It Rosey for Me   Clarke
Roulette Dance   Atteridge
Row Row   Caesar
Safe in the Arms of Bill Hart   Hammerstein; Harbach
Sally   Kern
Sally Green (the Village Vamp)   Kalmar; Ruby

Same Old Places   Hammerstein
Same Old Stars, Same Old Moon   Smith, Harry B.
Saturday Night till Monday Morning   Goetz
Savage I Remain, A   Herbert; Smith, Robert B.
Say It Once Again   Caesar
Scampi, The   Porter
Scandal of Little Lizzie Ford, The   Von Tilzer
Scandal Walk   Gershwin, George
Schnitza Komisski, The   Kern
Settling Down   DeSylva
Sex Appeal   Porter
Sextette Number   Kalmar; Ruby
She Alone Could Understand   Hammerstein; Harbach
She Walks in Her Husband's Sleep   Sterling; Von Tilzer
Shimmy Nods from Chaminade   Bryan; Schwartz, Jean
Shimmy Valentine   Bryan; Schwartz, Jean
Shine On, Little Son   Bryan; Schwartz, Jean
Shooting Star   Herbert
Show Me the Town   Hanley
Silk Stocking Trail, The   Atteridge
Silks and Satins   Atteridge
Silver Water   Von Tilzer
Simple Me   Hammerstein; Harbach
Since Mariella Learned the Dardenella   Von Tilzer
Singin' the Blues, Till My Daddy Comes Home   Conrad;
      Lewis; Young, Joseph
Sleepy Hollow Days   Whiting
Sligo   Brennan
Snap a Wishbone with Me   Bryan; Pollack; Schwartz, Jean
Snap Your Fingers at Care   Brown, Lew; DeSylva
Snoops the Lawyer   Kalmar; Ruby
Snow Flakes   Gershwin, George
So Long as the World Goes Round   Caesar
So Long Oolong   Kalmar; Ruby
Soldier's Life   Caesar
Some Big Something   Hammerstein
Some Fine Day   Kern
Some Nonsense   Bryan; Schwartz, Jean
Some People Make Me Sick   Hammerstein; Harbach
Some Pretty Day   Ahlert; Lewis; Young, Joseph
Somebody Else   Dubin
Somebody Else, Not Me   Hanley
Somehow I Knew   Gershwin, Ira; Youmans
Something Peculiar   Gershwin, George; Gershwin, Ira
Sometime when Lights Are Low   Kahn
Somewhere I Know There's a Girl for Me   Herbert; Smith,
      Robert B.
Song Without (Many) Words, A   Herbert
Songs of Long Ago, The   Gershwin, George
Sonny Boy   Fisher
Souvenirs   Hart; Rodgers
Spain   Hart; Rodgers
Spanish Love   Caesar; Gershwin, George; Silver
Sphinx, The   Bryan; Schwartz, Jean
Springtime   Kahn
Springtime Dance   Herbert; Smith, Robert B.
Star Eyes   Johnson, Howard
Star of Hitchy Koo, The   Kern
Star of Love, The   Caesar
Star of the West   Smith, Harry B.
Starlight of Your Eyes   Smith, Harry B.
Stars We Know   Atteridge
Streak of Blues, A   Berlin
Strike   Ager; Yellen
String of Girls, A   Hammerstein

Such a Happy Family   Herbert; Smith, Robert B.
Sudan   Pollack
Sultan   Caesar
Sun Is Nigh, The   Hammerstein; Harbach
Sunbeams   Kahn
Sunny May Afternoon, A   DeSylva
Sunny Southern Smiles   Gilbert
Sunshine and Shadow   Buck
Surrounded by Dixieland   Dubin
Sweet Bonita   Motzan
Sweet Cuban Love   Coots
Sweet Little Mary Ann   Howard, Joseph E.
Sweet Little Stranger   Hanley
Sweet Virginia Dare   Friend
Sweeter 'n All   Leslie
Sweetest Melody   Atteridge
Sweetheart o' Mine, How I Miss You   Lewis; Young, Joseph
Sweetie   Kern
Sweetness   Kahn
Sweets   Egan; Whiting
Swing, The   Bryan; Schwartz, Jean
Symphony in Dress, The   Bryan
Symphony in Dress (inst.), The   Schwartz, Jean
Syncopated Heart   Hammerstein
Syncopated Vamp, The   Berlin
Ta Voo   Atteridge; Schwartz, Jean
Table D'Hote Cabaret, The   Herbert; Smith, Robert B.
Taps   Johnson, Howard
Tattle Tales   Johnson, Howard
Tears of Love   Hammerstein; Harbach
Tell 'Em Nothing   Herbert
Tell Me, Daisy   Smith, Harry B.
Tell Me, Little Gypsy   Berlin
Temporary Wives   Caesar
Temptation   Hammerstein; Harbach
Ten Little Bottles   Monaco
That Boy of Mine   Hammerstein; Rodgers
That Cat Step   Henderson
That Funny Little Movement   Hanley
That Girl Belongs to Me   Atteridge
That Little Old Bar at the Ritz   Porter
That Might Have Satisfied Grandma   Harbach
That Musical Tonical Dance   Razaf
That Old Irish Mother of Mine   Jerome; Von Tilzer
That Reminiscent Melody   Ager; Yellen
That's As Far As I Can Go   Hammerstein; Harbach
That's How the Shannon Flows   Brennan
That's the Meaning of Love Dear to Me   Coots
That's What the Crystal Shows   Johnston
Theatrical Blues, The   Ager; Yellen
Theda Bara   Atteridge
Then Love Again   Hammerstein; Harbach
There Is Life in the Old Boy Yet   Schwartz, Jean
There's a Bit of Silver Lining Under Every Cloud of
   Grey   Yellen
There's a Grace in Each Leaf of the Shamrock   Fisher
There's a Romeo for Every Girl I Know   Stept
There's a Tender Look in Your Eyes   Herbert; Smith, Robert
   B.
There's a Typical Tipperary Over Here   Silver
There's a Vacant Chair at Home Sweet Home (When the
   World Goes Back on You)   Hanley
There's Always Room for One More   Hammerstein
They Didn't Think We'd Do It, But We Did   Dubin
They'll Never Miss the Wine in Dixieland   Bryan; Meyer

They're Making Them Wonderful   Hanley
Think It Over   Herbert
Third Degree of Love, The   Hart; Rodgers
This Is the End of Me Now   Egan
Those Mason-Dixon Blues   Johnson, Howard
Threads of Love   Fisher
Three Little Marys   Bryan; Schwartz, Jean
Three Musketeers of Broadway   Atteridge
Three Quarter Blues (inst.)   Gershwin, George
Through the Wonderful Eyes of Love   Cobb; Edwards
Tia-Da-Tia-Da-Dee   Stept
Tickle Me   Hammerstein; Harbach
Timbuctoo   Kalmar; Ruby
Tip Top Toreador   Atteridge
Tip-Tip Tippy Canoe   Johnson, Howard
Tip-Tip-Tippy Dance   Hanley
Tired Business Man, The   Hammerstein
Tired of Me   Clarke; Donaldson
'Tis an Irish Girl I Love and She's Just Like You   Brennan;
   Dubin
To Like to Love One Girl   Caesar
To Live, to Love Again   Caesar
Tom-Tom-Toddle   Harbach
Toodle Oodle Um   Hammerstein; Harbach
Topics of the Day   Atteridge
Toy Dance   Atteridge
Tra La La La   Sterling; Von Tilzer
Tragedy and Comedy   Hammerstein; Harbach
Treasure Island   Kern
Tripoli   Dubin
Try and Get It   Von Tilzer
Try Me   Hammerstein; Harbach
Tu Carrismo   Hammerstein; Harbach
Tum on and Tiss Me   Gershwin, George
Tum-Tiddly-Tum-Tum   Hammerstein; Harbach
Twas in the Month of June   Herbert; Smith, Robert B.
Ump-Pah-Pah   Donaldson; Lewis; Young, Joseph
Under Grecian Skies   Goetz
Until You Say Goodbye   Hammerstein; Harbach
Up Is a Long, Long Climb   Hammerstein; Harbach
Valley of Dreams, The   Ager; Yellen
Variety   Herbert
Venetian Moon   Kahn
Voice of Bagdad, The   Hammerstein
Waiki-Ki-Ki-Lou   Friend
Waiting   Harbach
Waiting for the Sun to Come Out   Gershwin, George;
   Gershwin, Ira
Washington Square   Porter
Watching You   Clarke; Donaldson
We Are the Maids of the Merry Merry   Buck
Weaknesses   Hammerstein
Wee Gee (Ouija) (Tell Me Do)   Jerome; Von Tilzer
We'll Have a Wonderful Party   Harbach
We're Pals   Caesar; Gershwin, George
We've Got Something   Hammerstein; Harbach
We've Got the Stage Door Blues   Kalmar; Ruby
We've Rabbits of Our Own (Keep Your Rabbits,
   Rabbi)   Kern
What Cha Gonna Do When There Ain't No Jazz   Leslie
What Did Romeo Say to Juliette   Fisher
What Happened Nobody Knows   Hart; Rodgers
What Happened to the Original Six Floradora
   Boys?   Kalmar; Ruby
What More Can I Give You?   Bryan

What Shall We Do If the Moon Goes Out   Herbert
What the Doctor Ordered   DeSylva
What Would You Take For Me, Mama   Cobb; Edwards
What's in a Name? (Love Is Always Love)   Ager; Yellen
What's the Big Idea   Gershwin, George; Gershwin, Ira
What's the Use Without a Girl   Howard, Joseph E.
What's Weak About the Weaker Sex   DeSylva
Wheel of Fate   Atteridge
When a Woman Exits Laughing   Harbach
When Caruso Comes to Town   Silver
When Grandpa Was a Boy   Buck
When I Discover My Man   Kern
When I Find My Romeo   Herbert; Smith, Robert B.
When I Found You   Romberg
When I See All the Loving They Waste on Babies I Long for
   the Cradle Again   Johnston
When I Was the Village Jim Dandy, Mirandy, and You Were
   the Belle of the Town   Lewis; Young, Joseph
When It's Honeysuckle Time Way Down in Georgia   Freed,
   Arthur; Howard, Joseph E.
When It's Moonlight on the Swanee Shore   Egan; Whiting
When Love Comes Knocking at Your Heart   Brennan
When My Baby Smiles at Me   Sterling; Von Tilzer
When Shadows Fall I Hear You Calling California   Kalmar;
   Ruby
When Shall We Meet Again   Egan; Whiting
When the Harvest Moon Is Shining   Sterling; Von Tilzer
When the Right Little Girl Comes Along   Hanley
When the Right One Comes Along   Buck
When the Right One Comes Along   (When the Right Girl
   Comes Along)   Herbert
When the Statues Come to Life   Johnson, Howard
When There's No One to Love   Schwartz, Jean
When We Are Married   Rodgers
When You and I Were Tadpoles   Herbert; Smith, Robert B.
When You Know Me Better   Herbert; Smith, Robert B.
When You Made Me Love You   Johnson, Howard
When You're Dancing in Your Nightie on the Lawn   Goetz
When You're Smiling (What a Smile Can Do)   DeSylva;
   Kern
Where Are the Plays of Yesterday   Buck
Where the Jack O'Lanterns Glow   Parish
Where Were You   Herbert; Smith, Robert B.
Where-Is-My-Daddy-Now Blues   Motzan; Yellen
While the City Sleeps   DeSylva
Whip-Poor-Will   Kern
Whistle a Song   Howard, Joseph E.
Whistle and I'll Come to Meet You   Atteridge
Who Ate Napoleons with Josephine when Bonaparte Was
   Away   Bryan; Goetz
Who's Who With You   Gershwin, Ira; Youmans
Whose Baby Are You?   Kern
Why Did You Do It to Me Babe   Sterling; Von Tilzer
Why Didn't I Meet You Long Ago   Schwartz, Jean
Why Didn't We Meet Before   Porter
Why Didn't You Leave Me Years Ago Instead of Leaving Me
   Now   Clare; Mitchell
Why Don't You Get a Sweetie?   Atteridge
Why Is Romany So Many Miles Away   Egan; Whiting
Why Must We Say Goodbye   Brennan
Wild Romantic Blues   Bryan; Schwartz, Jean
Wild Rose   Kern
Will You Forgive Me   Hart; Rodgers
William Tell It to Me (William Tell Me)   Bryan; Schwartz,
   Jean

Winter Beaches, The   Buck
With the Twinkle in Her Eye   Olcott
Without Kissing, Love Isn't Love   Ager; Yellen
Woman   Hammerstein
Wonderful Girl   Buck
Wonderful War, A   Hammerstein
Wooing of the Violin, The   Herbert; Smith, Robert B.
Working for the Government   Hart; Rodgers
World Is Going Shimmy Mad, The   Buck
Would You   Sterling
Wouldn't You Like to Have Me Tell Your Fortune   Bryan;
   Schwartz, Jean
Wyoming   Fisher
Yan-Kee   Caesar; Gershwin, George
Yogi Eyes   Lewis; Young, Joseph
You Are a Wonderful Girl   Freed, Arthur; Howard, Joseph E.
You Can Always Have Me   Clarke; Monaco
You Can Dance Your Way into Her Heart   Caesar
You Can't Fool Your Dreams   Hart; Rodgers
You Don't Have to Be a Toreador   Hart; Rodgers
You Don't Know What I Know About You   Bryan; Schwartz,
   Jean
You Know   Caesar
You Know What I Mean   Buck
You Made Me Forget How to Cry   Lewis; Young, Joseph
You May Be the World to Your Mother but You're Only an
   Oil Can to Me   Jerome; Von Tilzer
You Must Be Good Girls   Smith, Harry B.
You Never Know What a Kiss Can Mean   Hammerstein;
   Harbach
You Oughta See My Baby   Ahlert; Turk
You'll Have to Put a Nightie on Aphrodite   Donaldson;
   Lewis; Young, Joseph
Young Man's Fancy, A   Ager; Yellen
Your Dream and I   Smith, Harry B.
Your Eyes Have Said Remember Tho' Your Lips Have Said
   Forget   Kahn
You're All that I Need   DeSylva
You're Just a Little Too Late   Mitchell
You're the Type   Hammerstein; Harbach
You're There, Little Girl, You're There   Edwards
You've Got to Keep on Moving   Johnson, Howard
Zis Leetle Girl   DeSylva

1921

African Dip   Blake; Sissle
Ain't Cha Coming Back, Mary Ann to Maryland   Blake;
   Sissle
Ain't Love Grand   Conrad; DeSylva; Donaldson
Ain't Nature Grand?   Rose; Schwartz, Jean
Ain't We Got Fun   Egan; Whiting
Ain't You Ashamed?   Brown, Lew; Mitchell
Ain't You Coming Out Malinda   Sterling; Von Tilzer
All By My Lonesome Blues   Coslow
All By Myself   Berlin
All for You   Davis
All That I Need Is You   Baer
Allay Up   Hanley
Alma Mater Song of the Catholic University of America
   (inst.)   Herbert
Always Dreaming of You   Silver
Always in My Dreams   Yellen
And We'll Fight Forever After   Clarke; Monaco
Angel Eyes   Parish

Angels (We Call Them Mothers Down Here)   Kalmar; Ruby
Any Girl Is a Wonderful Girl   Yellen
Any Night on Broadway   Atteridge; Motzan; Romberg
Any Night on Old Broadway   Atteridge; Schwartz, Jean
Any Place Will Do with You   Atteridge; Romberg
Anything for You   Gershwin, George; Gershwin, Ira
April Showers   DeSylva
Arcady   DeSylva
Arrah Go 'Long with You, Do You See Any Green in My Eye   Sterling; Von Tilzer
At the Ball   Kern
At the Court Around the Corner   Berlin
Aunt Jemima   Silver
Avalon   DeSylva
A-Wearin' the Blues   Turk
Baby Blues, The   Gershwin, George; Goetz
Baby Dollie Walk   Conrad
Baby Face   Howard, Joseph E.
Baby Vampire   Atteridge; Pollack; Schwartz, Jean
Baccanale Dance   Johnson, Howard
Bad Dream Blues   Turk
Ballet of the Pyramids (inst.)   Pollack; Schwartz, Jean
Baltimore Buzz   Blake; Sissle
Bandana Days   Blake; Sissle
Barefoot Days   Atteridge; Romberg
Be Careful   Friml
Beautiful Faces   Atteridge; Pollack
Beautiful Feathers Make Beautiful Girls   Goetz
Beautiful Girls Are Like Opium   Atteridge; Bryan; Pollack; Schwartz, Jean
Because I Love You Dear   Johnson, Howard
Before the World Began   Harbach
Behind the Fan   Berlin
Belle of New York, The   Mitchell; Pollack
Bermuda   Hanley
Bimini Bay   Egan; Kahn; Whiting
Birthday of the Dauphin (inst.), The   Herbert
Bit of Opera, A   Atteridge
Black Eyed Susan   Motzan
Blonde Blues   Atteridge
Blow Little Lantern of Love   Fisher
Blue Blondes   Bryan; Pollack; Schwartz, Jean
Blue Danube Blues   Kern
Bob-White   Johnston
Bombo   DeSylva
Bouncing All Over Town   Buck
Bow Wow Blues   Friend
Boy Wanted   Gershwin, George; Gershwin, Ira
Bridget McShane   Atteridge; Pollack; Schwartz, Jean
Bring Back My Blushing Rose   Buck; Friml
Bring Him My Love Thoughts   Atteridge
Broadway in Sahara   Atteridge
Broadway Pirates   Atteridge; Pollack; Schwartz, Jean
Brown Eyes (That Give Me the Blues)   Johnson, Howard
Bundle of Love, A   DeSylva
By the Silvery Nile   Yellen
Bylo Bay, The   Atteridge; Romberg
California Here I Come   DeSylva
Can Macy Do Without Me   Romberg
Can't Get Lovin' Blues   Turk
Can't You Be Mine   Turk
Carnival Night   Romberg
Carolina Rolling Stone   Parish
Century Toddle   Bryan; Pollack; Schwartz, Jean
Chain Dance   Mitchell; Pollack

Championship of the World (inst.), The   Herbert
Charming Ladies   Atteridge
Chera Bochcha (Hello, Hello, Hello)   Lewis; Young, Joseph
Chicago   Pollack; Schwartz, Jean
Chinese New Year's Ballet   Mitchell; Pollack
Chopin Ad Lib (Opening Chorus)   Kern
Chorus Girl Blues   Hart; Rodgers
Civilization   Johnson, Howard
Cleo Zell My Creole Belle   Blake; Sissle
Click of Her Little Brogans, The   Brennan
Cognac   Coots
College Education Is a Joke, A   Coots
Come Into My Heart   Yellen
Come On, Let's Go   Buck
Comforts of Home Sweet Home   Coots
Comme Ci, Comme Ca   Friml
Commerce, The   Buck
Compere, The   Buck
Conversation Step, The   Harbach
(Jolson's) Coo-Coo Song   DeSylva
Coo-ee-doo   Hanley
Coolie Dance (inst.)   Kern
Cora Angelique (Musical Comedy Queen)   Mitchell; Pollack
Cricket   Henderson
Crooning   Dubin
Cry Baby Blues   Lewis; Meyer; Young, Joseph
Crying for the Moon   Leslie
Crying for You   Coslow
Crying Melody   Coslow
Cuban Eyes   Caesar
Cubano   Fisher
Curiosity   Harbach
Da, Da, Da, My Darling   Leslie; Monaco
Daddy Buy Me a Bow Wow   Atteridge; Pollack; Schwartz, Jean
Daddy O' Mine   Fisher
Daddy Won't You Please Come Home   Blake; Sissle
Daffodil, The   Atteridge; Romberg
Daisy Days   Atteridge; Kahn; Pollack; Schwartz, Jean
Dance, Dance, Dance   Mitchell; Pollack
Dance Eccentrique (inst.)   Kern
Dance (inst.)   Kern
Dance Tangerine   Johnson, Howard
Dancing Blues, The   Atteridge; Pollack
Dancing Fools   Mitchell; Pollack
Dancing Shoes   Buck; Gershwin, George; Gershwin, Ira
Dancing the Seasons Away   Berlin
Dancing Time   Kern
Dapper Dan   Brown, Lew
Dear Love, My Love   Friml
Deli   Caesar
Didn't You Believe?   Kern
Ding-Dong-Dell (The Bells of Chinatown)   Hanley
Dirty Hands Dirty Face   Clarke; Leslie; Monaco
Dixie   Coslow
Dixie, the Flag and You   Goetz; Meyer
Dolly   Gershwin, Ira; Youmans
Don't Cry Swanee   Conrad
Don't Keep Calling Me Dearie   Friml
Don't Leave Me Mammy   Conrad; Davis; DeSylva
Don't Leave Me, Mother Mine   Stept
Don't Send Your Wife to the Country (Keep Her Home and Love Her Yourself)   Atteridge; Conrad; DeSylva
Don't Take the Red and the White Out of the Flag (And Leave Us the Blues)   Donaldson; Lewis; Young, Joseph

Don't Think that We're the Chorus of the Show   Hart;
    Rodgers
Don't Throw Me Down   Brown, Lew
Down Around the 'Sip 'Sip 'Sippy Shore   Donaldson; Lewis;
    Young, Joseph
Down at the Bootlegger's Ball   Hanley
Down in Midnight Town   Sterling; Von Tilzer
Down on Old Long Island Sound   Jerome; Von Tilzer
Down South   DeSylva; Donaldson
Down Yonder   Gilbert
Dream Fantasies   Atteridge
Dream of My Last Waltz with You   Kahn
Dream of Your Smile, A   Conrad
Dream Voyage, A   Young, Victor
Dreaming, I'm Always Dreaming You Are Mine   Bryan
Drifting Along with the Tide   Gershwin, George
Drifting Apart   Ager; Johnson, Howard
Easy Pickin's   Kern
E-gypt   Fisher
Egyptian Dance, The   Friml
Election Day   Blake; Sissle
Emaline   McHugh
Entrance of Dancers   Harbach
Entrance of Sailors (When the Guns Are Booming)   Kern
Equity Star, The   Herbert
Every Girl   Kern
Every Girl Has a Way   Gershwin, George; Gershwin, Ira
Every Mother's Lullaby   Cobb; Edwards
Every Time I Hear a Band Play   Buck; Friml
Everybody Step   Berlin
Everything Reminds Me of You   Blake; Sissle
Eyes (Until They Looked at Me)   Young, Victor
Face to Face   Carroll
Fading Golden Love Dream   Atteridge
Fat-Fat-Fatima   Romberg
Feather Bed Lane   Bryan
Fine Feathers   Atteridge; Pollack; Schwartz, Jean
Fire Cracker   Atteridge
First Love   Hart; Rodgers
First Rose of Summer   Kern
Flapper and the Vamp, The   Friml
Follow On   Mitchell; Pollack
For Every Smile on Broadway There's a Tear at Home Sweet
    Home   Fisher
For No Reason at All   Lewis; Meyer; Young, Joseph
Four Little Girls with a Future and Four Little Girls with a
    Past   DeSylva; Friml
French Fling   Coots
From Far Cohoes   Mitchell; Pollack
Futuristic Melody   Gershwin, George; Goetz
Gay Brazilian   Atteridge; Pollack; Schwartz, Jean
Gee! I Wish I Had a Girl Like You   Friend; Pollack
Ginny Ginny Shore   Atteridge; Romberg
Girl Has a Sailor in Every Port, A   Atteridge; Romberg
Girl Like Grandma   Romberg
Give, Give   Harbach
Give Me My Mammy   DeSylva; Donaldson
Glide DeLuxe   Atteridge; Romberg
Globe Trot, The   Atteridge; Romberg
Gold Fish   Bryan; Pollack; Schwartz, Jean
Golden Sands of Waikiki   Yellen
Gondolier   Buck
Gone Are the Love Days   Brennan
Good Fellow Blues, The   Blake; Sissle
Good Fellow Gal   Brennan

Good Morning Dearie   Kern
Goodbye Pretty Butterfly   Yellen
Goodbye Shanghai   Johnson, Howard
Granny, (You're) My Mammy's Mammy   Akst; Lewis;
    Young, Joseph
Guessing   Mitchell
Gypsy Blues   Blake; Sissle
Gypsy Trail   Caesar
Ha, Ha, Ha   Clarke
(My Sweet) Ha Wa Ta   Clare; Friend
Hail to Our General   Atteridge
Happiness (I Find My Happiness Dear with You)   Meyer
Happy Ending   Gershwin, Ira
Happy Family   Harbach
Harlem Strut (inst.)   Johnson, James P.
Harvest Moon, The   Friml
Hawaiian Blues   Motzan; Turk
Hawaiian Eyes   Coots
Hay-Long   Fain
He Talks with His Fingers   Bryan; Pollack; Schwartz, Jean
He Took It Away from Me   Turk
He Was a Roving Romeo   Jerome; Schwartz, Jean
Hello! Hello! Hello! Chera Bochcha   Akst; Lewis
Hello Miss Knickerbocker   Atteridge
Here, Steward   Gershwin, Ira; Youmans
He's a Panic   Akst; Lewis; Young, Joseph
Honey Hula   Fisher
Honey-Bunch   Buck
Honeymoon Home   Bryan
Honeymoon (When Will You Shine for Me?)   Gershwin, Ira
(In) Honeysuckle Time (When Emmaline Said She'd Be
    Mine)   Blake; Sissle
Horse Trot, The   Atteridge; Romberg
Hortense   Donaldson; Lewis; Young, Joseph
How Can I Call You My Pal, After You've Stolen My
    Gal   Brown, Lew; Norworth
How Do I Know?   Brown, Lew
How Is Everything Back Home?   Johnson, Howard
How Many Times   Turk
How'd You Like to Put Your Head Upon My Pillow   Bryan;
    Schwartz, Jean
Humpty Dumpty   Sterling; Von Tilzer
Hymn to the Moon   Rodgers
I Am Craving for that Kind of Love (Kiss Me)   Blake; Sissle
I Call Her Virgin Mary   Johnson, Howard
I Call You Sunshine   Caesar; DeSylva
I Can't Resist Them When They're Beautiful   Buck
I Do, So There!   Mitchell; Pollack
I Don't Care for You Any More   Leslie; Monaco
I Found a Rose in the Devil's Garden   Fisher
I Got It, You'll Get It (Just the Same As Me)   Brown, Lew;
    Pollack
I Hold Her Hand and She Holds Mine   Rose
I Just Simply Love to Carry On   Jerome; Schwartz, Jean
I Know that I'm in Love   Mitchell; Pollack
I Look 'Em Over in the Daytime So I Know what I'm
    Getting at Night   Fisher
I Love Him and He Loves Me (Tho' We Both Love the Same
    Sweet Girl)   Johnson, Howard
I Love That   Sterling; Von Tilzer
I Love to Go Swimmin' with Wimmin'   Romberg
I Love You   Gershwin, George
I Love Your Eyes   Yellen
I Must be Loved By Someone (and That Someone Must Be
    You)   Cobb; Edwards

Last Little Mile Is Longest, When You're Longing for Home
    Sweet Home, The   Donaldson
Last Little Mile Is the Longest,, When You're Longing for
    Home Sweet Home, The   Lewis; Young, Joseph
Last Long Flight, The   Hanley
Last Waltz, The   Atteridge
Laugh and Grow Fat   Romberg
Law   Hart; Rodgers
Learn to Smile   Harbach
Legend of the Golden Tree (The Legend of the Cyclamen
    Tree), The   Buck; Herbert
Legend of the Pearls, The   Berlin
Lend Me a Kiss Until To-morrow   Cobb; Edwards
Lend Us a Daddy   Hanley
Lenore   Johnson, Howard; Kahn
Let Bygones Be Bygones   Meyer
Let Me Awake   Romberg
Let Me Drink in Your Eyes   Hart; Rodgers
Let Me Whirl to an Old Refrain   Buck
Let's Pretend   Romberg
Letters that Lighten Broadway, The   Cobb; Edwards
Life Is a Gamble   Atteridge; Romberg
Listen   Bryan; Schwartz, Jean
Listen to Me   Johnson, Howard
Listening   Coslow
Little Baby   Mitchell; Pollack
Little Bag of Tricks   Gershwin, Ira; Youmans
Little Bo-Peep   Clarke; Monaco
Little Dream that Lost Its Way, A   Romberg
Little Lost Flower   Parish
Little Love Mill, The   Carroll
Little Min-hee-Ha! Ha! (Be My Little Injun Squaw)   Kalmar;
    Ruby
Little Partner of Mine   Cobb; Edwards
Little Pig Nose   Young, Victor
Little Souvenir, A   Hanley
Little Tin Soldier, The   Hanley
Live for Today   Atteridge
London, Dear Old London   Kern
Lonely Heart   Romberg
Lonesome Hours   Friend
Longing (Triste Ricordo)   Caesar
Looking All Over for You   Kern
Lords of Creation   Johnson, Howard; Schwartz, Jean
Love Is a Business   Johnson, Howard
Love Is a Riddle   Romberg
Love Is Like a Mushroom   Buck
Love Nests in France   Carroll
Love Nights   Bryan; Meyer
Love Will Always Find a Way   Romberg
Love Will Find a Way   Blake; Sissle
Lovelight   Buck
Loves Crystal   Coots
Lovin' Mama   Davis
Low Down Blues   Blake; Sissle
Lucky Day that I Found You, The   Cobb; Edwards
Ma   Clare; Conrad
Ma Temme   Atteridge; Pollack; Schwartz, Jean
Maggie Maguire   Sterling; Von Tilzer
Main Street in My Old Home Town   Caesar
Make Believe   Davis
Make Me Want to Be Loved By You   Brown, Nacio Herb
Make the Best of It   Gershwin, Ira; Youmans
Mama! Mama! Papa's Got a Lot Lovin' All Saved Up for
    You   Friend

Mamma Whip Mamma Spank If Yer Daddy Don't Come
    Home   Turk
Mammy Lou   Sterling; Von Tilzer
Man Is the Lord of It All   Johnson, Howard; Schwartz, Jean
Mandalay   Mitchell; Pollack
Mandy 'n' Me   Conrad; Kalmar; Motzan
Marie   Motzan
Mary Tracy, How Would You Like to Become a
    Casey   Jerome; Schwartz, Jean
Masks   Buck
Mason Dixon Blues   Atteridge; Pollack; Schwartz, Jean
Mecca   Atteridge
Mediterrania   Cobb; Edwards
'Melican Papa (Chink Song)   Kern
Melody Triste   Romberg
Memories   Kalmar; Ruby
Men O'Shanter   Egan; Whiting
Metropolitan Handicap, The   Buck
Mickey O'Neill a Brother of Peggy O'Neill   Coots; Johnson,
    Howard
Midnight Rounders   Atteridge; Pollack; Schwartz, Jean
Mighty Like a Rosenbloom   Atteridge; Pollack; Schwartz,
    Jean
Millions of Times   Stept
Mimi   Conrad
Mind Your Own Business   Romberg
Mischa, Jascha, Toscha, Sascha   Gershwin, George;
    Gershwin, Ira
Mississippi Blues   Fain
Mississippi Cradle   Yellen
Mississippi Ripples   Hanley
Modern Crusaders   Atteridge
Molly Maguire   Sterling; Von Tilzer
Molly Malone   Sterling; Von Tilzer
Molly, Molly   Mitchell; Pollack
Molly on a Trolley, My Golly with You   Jerome; Schwartz,
    Jean
Molly on the Trolley   Mitchell; Pollack
Moment Musical   Romberg
Moon and You, The   Rodgers
Moonlight   Conrad
Moonlight and Honeysuckle   Hanley
(I Want You) Morning, Noon and Night   Edwards
Morning Will Come   Conrad; DeSylva
Moth and the Flame   Atteridge; Pollack; Schwartz, Jean
Mother Eve   Hanley
Mother, I Didn't Understand   Johnson, Howard
Mr. and Mrs.   Gershwin, Ira; Youmans
Mr. Director   Hart; Rodgers
Mr. Gravvins — Mr. Gripps   Kern
Mulberry   Fisher
Multiplied by Eight   Johnson, Howard
Murder   Harbach
Murrayisms   Romberg
My Ben Ali Haggin Girl   Berlin
My Boy Joe   Hanley
My Cherry Blossom   Smith, Harry B.; Snyder
My Daddy   Norworth
My Girl   Gilbert
My Heart Is Waking   Atteridge
My Irish Rosary   Fisher
My Lady of the Lamp   Pollack
My Lady's Dress   Kern
My Little Book of Poetry   Berlin
My Little Canoe   Harbach

My Little Sea Shell Told Me So   Hanley
My Log Cabin Home   Caesar; DeSylva; Gershwin, George
My Madonna   Donaldson; Lewis; Young, Joseph
My Mammy   Pollack; Schwartz, Jean
My Mammy's Tears   Coslow
My Only Rose   Brennan
My Screen Maid   Atteridge; Pollack; Schwartz, Jean
My Springtime Thou Art   Romberg
My Sunny Tennessee   Kalmar; Ruby
My Vision Girl   Blake; Sissle
My Wife   Atteridge
My Wonder Girl   Koehler
Nan O'Shanter   Egan; Whiting
Natchez and Robert E. Lee   Gilbert
Naughty Waltz Blues   Yellen
Near Me   Fisher
'Neath Italian Skies   Atteridge; Romberg
Nerves   Kern
Nesting Time   Hanley
Niagara Falls   Kern
Nita   Atteridge; Romberg
No One Else but that Girl of Mine   Caesar; Gershwin,
   George
No One Loves a Clown   Atteridge; Romberg
Not So Good, Not So Bad   Von Tilzer
Now I Ask You Is that Nice   Pollack
Now I Know   Clarke; Monaco
Oh! Dear!   Friend
Oh, Harold   Hart; Rodgers
Oh, How She Can Dance   Friend
Oh! Mabel Behave   Friend
Oh Me! Oh My! (Oh You!)   Gershwin, Ira; Youmans
Oh, My Sweet Hortense   Donaldson; Lewis; Young, Joseph
Oh, Oh, Columbus   Atteridge; Romberg
Oh! Omar Khayam   Donaldson; Lewis; Young, Joseph
Oh Sweet Amelia   Fisher
Oh Yeedle Ay (That Yodelin' Tune)   Fisher
Oh, You Beautiful Baby   Akst; Lewis; Young, Joseph
Old Fashioned Rose   Cobb; Edwards
Old Fashioned Sweetheart   Atteridge; Pollack; Schwartz,
   Jean
Old Melodies   Johnson, Howard
On a Far Along Isle   Brennan
On a Little Side Street   Howard, Joseph E.
On a Moonlight Night   Gilbert
On Patrol in No Man's Land   Sissle
On the Brim of Her Old-Fashioned Bonnet   Gershwin,
   George; Goetz
On the 'Gin 'Gin 'Ginny Shore   Donaldson; Leslie
On the Isle of Yap   Jerome; Schwartz, Jean
Once Upon a Time   Brown, Nacio Herb
One Little Kiss from You   Yellen
Only One Love Ever Fills the Heart   Romberg
Oo-La-La   Atteridge
Opening of Dance Hall Scene (Ring Those Bells)   Kern
or, Hello, Hello, Hello   Lewis
Orienta   Caesar; Youmans
Oriental Blues   Blake; Sissle
Oriental Dreams   Kern
Oriental Table Bells   Kahn
Our Home Town   Carroll
Out of the Night   Bryan
Out of the Shadows   Kahn
Over the Lowlands   Hart; Rodgers
Overnight   Henderson

Painted Butterfly   Carroll
Pantomime (inst.)   Hanley
Papa We've Got to Move Uptown   Caesar
Paradise Alley   Atteridge; Romberg
Paree (I Want to Be there Again)   Fisher
Parisienne Passionettes   Atteridge
Partners   Harbach
Pas de Deux   Kern
Pas Seul (inst.)   Hanley
Passion Flower, The   Berlin
Passionettes   Bryan; Pollack; Schwartz, Jean
Pastry Cooks, The   Mitchell; Pollack
Peace to My Lonely Heart   Romberg
Peaches   Conrad; Kalmar; Ruby
Peacock Alley   Gershwin, Ira
Perfume and Passion   Bryan; Pollack; Schwartz, Jean
Pergola Patrol, The   Kern
Persiana   Romberg
Phoebe   Gershwin, George; Gershwin, Ira
Pickaninny Shoes   Blake; Sissle
Pickanniny Mose   Berlin
Picket Fence   Bryan; Pollack; Schwartz, Jean
Pidgee Woo   Gershwin, George; Gershwin, Ira
Pleading   Yellen
Please Disarm My Wife   Schwartz, Jean
Poor Flo   Hanley
Poor Little Model   Hart; Rodgers
Posty and a Maid, A   Atteridge; Pollack; Schwartz, Jean
Potatoes (inst.)   McHugh
Prelude Act Two (inst.)   Kern
Pretty Face   Buck; Donaldson; Lewis; Young, Joseph
Prevalent Condition of the Mind, The   Romberg
Princess of My Dreams, The   Buck; Herbert
Priscilla   Hart; Rodgers
Puff, Puff, Puff   Buck
Purity Brigadiers, The   Mitchell; Pollack
Queen of Musical Comedy, The   Mitchell
Raggedy Rag   Buck
Rainy Day Sue   Lewis; Young, Joseph
Rainy Days   Johnson, Howard
Ramble On   Leslie; Monaco
Remember for Old Times Sake   Egan; Whiting
Remember the Rose   Mitchell
Reminiscence   Atteridge
Rendezvous   Mitchell
Rice and Shoes   Gershwin, Ira; Youmans
Rilly Rilly   Gilbert
Rolling Stone Blues   Kalmar; Meyer
Romany   Kahn; Meyer
Rooneyisms   Romberg
Rosary You Gave to Me, The   Sterling; Von Tilzer
Rose I Call Sweetheart, The   Johnson, Howard
Rose Marie   Kern
Rose of My Heart   Buck
Rose of Spain   Atteridge; Romberg
Rose of the Rotisserie   Atteridge; Pollack; Schwartz, Jean
Rosemary   DeSylva
Roses in the Garden   Friml
Roses Out of Reach   Atteridge
Rosy Cheeks   Parish
Rubaiyats from the Rubaiyat   Atteridge
Ruby   Davis
Runaway Little Girl   Friml
Sadie   Parish
Sally and Irene and Mary   Johnson, Howard

Sally Slide, The   Buck
Sally, Won't You Come Back (Come Back to Our Alley, Sally)   Buck
Salute   Coots
Sand Witches   Bryan; Pollack; Schwartz, Jean
Sardinia   Sterling; Von Tilzer
Saturday   Mitchell
Save the Daylight for Somebody Else, But Save the Moonlight for Me   Von Tilzer
Say It with Music   Berlin
Scandinavia (Sing Dose Song and Make Dose Music)   Bryan
Schoolhouse Blues, The   Berlin
Sea of the Tropics Dance   Johnson, Howard
Second Hand Rose   Clarke; Hanley
See This Golden Rooster   Hart; Rodgers
Serenade Blues   Blake; Sissle
Shadow Lane   Gilbert
Shakespeare of 1921   Hart; Rodgers
Shakespeare's Garden of Love   Atteridge; Pollack; Schwartz, Jean
She's Innocent   Gershwin, Ira; Youmans
She's Just a Baby   Gershwin, George
She's Mine, All Mine   Kalmar; Ruby
Shimmy with Me   Kern
Shores of Minnetonka   Kahn
Show Him the Way   Hart; Rodgers
Shuffle Along   Blake; Sissle
Siam Soo   Motzan
Sidewalk   Atteridge; Pollack; Schwartz, Jean
Silly Season, The   Gershwin, Ira; Youmans
Silly Thoughts   Hanley
Simple Life, The   Gershwin, George; Gershwin, Ira
Since Rebecca, Came Back from Mecca (Rebecca, Come Back from Mecca)   Kalmar; Ruby
Since You Told Me You Love Me, I Know   Clarke
Sing Me to Sleep Dear Mammy (With a Hushabye Pickaninny Tune)   Blake; Sissle
Sing Song Girl   Kern
Sing to Me of Love (Parlate Me d'Amor)   Caesar
Sing-a Loo   Brown, Lew; Mitchell; Pollack
Sink All Your Ships in the Ocean and Sail on the Ocean of Love   Fisher
'Sippi Shore   Lewis
Sirens, The   Gershwin, George; Gershwin, Ira
Sittin' Pretty   Coots
Sitting in a Corner   Atteridge; Romberg
Sky High Bungalow   Goetz; Meyer
Slapstick   Gershwin, Ira
Sleepy Village   Atteridge; Romberg
Slumberland   Gilbert
Smiling Sam   Atteridge
Smoke Dreams (The Cigarette Song)   Coots
Snap a Wishbone with Me   Atteridge; Bryan; Pollack; Schwartz, Jean
Soft and Low   Kahn
Some Beautiful Morning I'll Find You in My Arms   Friend
Some Rain Must Fall   Gershwin, George; Gershwin, Ira
Some Rainy Night   Parish
Some Sweet Day   Mitchell
Somebody Cares for You   Coslow
Somebody Like You   Friml
Somebody's Mother   Sterling; Von Tilzer
Someday the Sun Will Shine   Clarke; Hanley; Monaco
Something Like Me   Hart; Rodgers
Something Peculiar   Gershwin, George; Gershwin, Ira

Something to Remember   Kahn
Song of Love   Romberg
South Sea Island Blues   Johnson, Howard
South Sea Isles (Sunny South Sea Islands)   Gershwin, George
Spanish Lou   Mitchell; Pollack
Spider's Web, The   Friml
Spirit of Java   Bryan; Pollack; Schwartz, Jean
Spirit of the Chinese Vase, The   Mitchell; Pollack
Sprinkle Me with Diamonds   Atteridge; Bryan; Pollack; Schwartz, Jean
Star of Love   Atteridge; Pollack; Schwartz, Jean
Stolen Kisses   Snyder
Stop, Rest a While   Gilbert
Sue   Meyer
Summertime   Buck; Gershwin, Ira
Sun Will Shine Again, The   Sterling; Von Tilzer
Sundown Brings Back Memories of You   Dubin
Sunny California   Johnson, Howard
Sunny Sue   Donaldson; Lewis; Young, Joseph
Sunset Land   Kahn
Sunshine   Motzan
Suppose   Davis
Susquehanna Shore   Parish
Swanee Rose   DeSylva
Swanee Rose (Dixie Rose)   Caesar; Gershwin, George
Sweet Lady   Johnson, Howard
Sweet One   Atteridge; Romberg
Sweetest Melody   Silver
Sweetheart   Davis
Sympathy   Hanley
Syncopation Stenos   Blake; Sissle
Take a Chance with Me   Bryan; Pollack; Schwartz, Jean
Take Her Down to Coney and Give Her the Air   Pollack; Whiting
Take Me in Your Arms   Brown, Nacio Herb; Freed, Arthur
Tallahassee   Coots; DeSylva
Ta-Ta   Clare; Fisher
Tea Leaves   Egan; Whiting
Teach Me How to Kiss   Mitchell; Pollack
Tell Me Daisy   Romberg
Tell Me Your Daydreams   Dubin
Ten Fingers of Syncopation   Buck
Tennis Terpsichorean   Atteridge; Pollack; Schwartz, Jean
Tess   Turk
Thanks to You   Johnson, Howard
That Barber in Seville   Atteridge; Conrad
That Doesn't Mean a Thing   Yellen
That O'Brien Girl   Harbach
That Street Corner Quartet   Caesar; Monaco
That's How I Believe in You   Dubin
There Can't Be Any Harm in Saying Just Goodbye   Harbach
There May Bloom a Rose for Me   Romberg; Smith, Harry B.
There's a Bunch of Klucks in the Ku Klux Klan   Coslow
There's a Corner Up in Heaven   Berlin
There's a Lonesome Little Girl in the Lone Star State of Texas   Fisher
There's a Million Girlies Lonesome Tonight (And Still I'm All Alone)   Hanley
There's a Reason It's Because I Love You   Coslow
There's a Sunbeam for Every Drop of Rain   Johnson, Howard
There's Always a Song in an Irish Heart   Brennan
There's Something About Me They Like   Gershwin, Ira; Youmans

They Call It Dancing   Berlin
Those Days Are Gone Forever   Kern
Those Days Are Over   Sterling; Von Tilzer
Three Little Maids   Romberg
Three Little Vampires   Atteridge; Romberg
Through the Mist   Atteridge; Romberg
Tiffin, Tiffin   Mitchell; Pollack
Time After Time   Brennan
To Keep You in Your Seats   Harbach
Toddle Along Toward the Land of Better Days   Egan; Whiting
Toddle (The Teddy Toddle)   Kern
Toddle-Dee-Doo   Mitchell
Tomale (I'm Hot for You)   Caesar; DeSylva; Gershwin, George
Tomorrow   Kahn; Motzan; Smith, Harry B.
Tonight   Mitchell
Toot Toot Tootsie (Goodbye)   Kahn
Tropic Vamps   Johnson, Howard
Trousseau Incomplete, The   Romberg
True Love   Gershwin, George; Gershwin, Ira
Trying   Kalmar; Ruby
Tuck Me to Sleep in My Old Kentucky Home   Lewis; Meyer; Young, Joseph
Two Little Girls in Blue   Gershwin, Ira; Youmans
Two Little Love Birds   Romberg
Two Lovely Lying Eyes   Buck; Friml
Two Wonderful Girls in Blue   Youmans
Un Sourire   Harbach
Uncle Tom and Old Black Joe   Blake; Sissle
Under American Skies   Henderson
Under the Mistletoe   Hart; Rodgers
Unknown   Johnson, Howard
Utopia   Gershwin, Ira; Youmans
Venetian Loveboat   Koehler
Very Next Girl I See, The   Atteridge; Romberg
Vicar's Song (Finale Act II)   Kern
Violet Ray   Buck
Virtue Wins the Day   Hart; Rodgers
Wabash   Johnson, Howard; Schwartz, Jean
Wait Until My Ship Comes In   Atteridge; Romberg
Waiter's Dance   Atteridge; Pollack; Schwartz, Jean
Waiting for Your Return (Nostalgia)   Caesar
Wake Up   Hart; Rodgers
Wana, When I Wana, You No Wanna   Friend
Wanting You   Caesar; Gershwin, George
Watch Yourself   Hart; Rodgers
Watermelon Time   Atteridge; Pollack; Schwartz, Jean
Way Down Town   Kern
Way Out West in Elizabeth New Jersey   Fisher
We Gotta Find a New Kentucky Home   Hanley
We Take Only the Bets   Hart; Rodgers
Weep No More My Mammy   Atteridge; Clare; Mitchell; Pollack
We'll Never Grow Old   Johnson, Howard
We're Off on a Wonderful Trip   Gershwin, Ira; Youmans
We're Off to India   Gershwin, Ira; Youmans
Wetona   Atteridge; Romberg
What a Position for Me   Hanley
What a World This Would Be   DeSylva
What I Want to Doodle-Doo for You   Brown, Lew
What Would We Do Without the Girls?   Koehler
When a Rambling Rose Goes Rambling Home Again   Coslow
When Buddha Smiles   Brown, Nacio Herb; Freed, Arthur

When East Meets West in Panama   Gershwin, George
When Grand Circus Was Uptown   Egan; Whiting
When I Dance with You in Paradise   Dubin
When I Go on the Stage   Hart; Rodgers
When I Start Comparin' Auld Erin with You   Lewis; Young, Joseph
When I'm with the Girls   Gershwin, Ira; Youmans
When Old New York Was Young   Cobb; Edwards
When Sunday Comes Around   Carroll
When the Cat's Away   Romberg
When the Crime Waves Roll   Hart; Rodgers
When the Honey-Moon Was Over   Fisher
When the Statues Come to Life   Atteridge; Pollack; Schwartz, Jean
When There's No One to Love   Atteridge
When We Are Married   Mitchell; Pollack
When You're In, You're In Indiana   Jerome; Schwartz, Jean
Where There's a Will, There's a Way   Dubin
Where Were You   Dubin
Which Hazel?   Silver
While There's Life There's Hope, You Put Hope in This Heart of Mine   Clarke; Monaco
Whip Hand, The   Atteridge
Whistling   Mitchell; Pollack
Who Cares?   Ager; Yellen
Who'll Dry Your Tears when You Cry   Akst; Lewis; Young, Joseph
Whoop-De-Oodle-Do!   Kern
Who's Who with You   Gershwin, Ira; Youmans
Why Do They Die at the End of a Classical Dance   Jerome; Schwartz, Jean
Why Don't You Smile   Schwartz, Jean
Will You Forgive Me   Hart; Rodgers
Wimmin (I Got to Have 'Em All That's All)   Fisher
With a Woman You Can Never Tell   Friml
Without You   Mitchell
Wonderful Time Was Had By All, A   Hanley
Working for the Institute   Hart; Rodgers
World Goes Bobbing Up and Down, The   Buck
Would You Like To Sleep Upon My Pillow   Bryan; Pollack; Schwartz, Jean
Yama Hula   Fisher
Yokohama Lullaby   Clarke; Monaco
Yo-Lay-ee-oo Means I Love You   Motzan; Smith, Harry B.
Yoo Hoo   Brown, Lew
Yoo-Hoo   DeSylva
You Alone (Tu Sola)   Caesar
You and I   Johnson, Howard
You and Me   Hanley
You Made Me Forget How to Cry   Donaldson; Lewis; Young, Joseph
You May Be a Bad Man   Atteridge
You Must Come Over   DeSylva; Kern
You Started Something When You Came Along   Gershwin, Ira; Youmans
You Tickle Me   Bryan; Pollack; Schwartz, Jean
You Want the Best Seats, We Have 'Em   Kern
You'll Never Know   Hart; Rodgers
Your Lullaby   Hart; Rodgers
Your Wonderful U.S.A.   Gershwin, Ira
You're a Good Old Car but You Can't Climb Hills   Sterling; Von Tilzer
You're in Kentucky   Atteridge; Romberg
You're Just the Type for a Bungalow   Donaldson; Lewis; Young, Joseph

You've Got What I've Been Looking For Johnson, James P.
Ziegfeld Dollies Buck
Ziegfeld's Paper Dollies Carroll

1922

Act I Ensemble: Observation Gershwin, George
After Hours (inst.) Johnson, James P.
After the Clouds Roll By Coots
After the Rain Kahn
After the Storm Jerome; Schwartz, Jean
Aggravatin' Papa Don't You Try to Two-Time Me Turk
Ah! Ah! Ah! Hanley
Ah Fong Low Porter
Ain't We Got Fun Kahn
All I Do Is Sit and Look On Sterling; Von Tilzer
All in the Wearing Cohan
(They're) All My Boys Cohan
All Pull Together Caesar
All to Myself Gershwin, George; Gershwin, Ira
Always Alone Davis
American Jazz Atteridge
American Punch, The Porter
Angel Child Davis; Silver
Another Melody in F Hart
Apple Sauce Freed, Arthur
Arabiana Davis
Argentina DeSylva; Gershwin, George
Arithmetic Blues Leslie
At the End of the Road Hanley
At the Irish Jubilee Brown, A. Seymour
Away Down East in Maine Donaldson
Away Down South Akst; Lewis; Young, Joseph
Baby Wants to Dance Hart; Rodgers
Babylon Williams
Bad Little Boy and Good Little Girl Romberg
Bad Little Boys Aren't Goody-Good to the Goody-Good
    Little Girls, The Ager; Yellen
Ballet of Siam, A Atteridge
Ballet Oriental Atteridge; Romberg
Bally-Burlesk (inst.) Herbert
Baltimore Donaldson
Bamboo Bay Donaldson; Egan; Whiting
Bamboo Isle Henderson
Bamboula (El Relicario) Goetz
Bammy (Alabamy) Conrad
Bandit Band, The Porter
Banjo Land Johnson, James P.
Bansheela Henderson
Beautiful Feathers Make Beautiful Birds Meyer
Beautiful Girls Kalmar; Ruby
Because I Love You So DeSylva; Herbert
Behind the Clouds There's Always Sunshine Sterling; Von
    Tilzer
Believe in Me Davis
Best I Get Is the Worst of It, The Friml; Harbach
Bi——- Kahn
Black and Blue Lewis; Young, Joseph
Blossom Time Bryan; Schwartz, Jean
Blue Clarke; Leslie
Blue Book of Girls, A Atteridge; Romberg
Blue Boy Blues, The Porter
Blue Kitten Blues Friml; Harbach
Blue Kitten (Meow), The Friml; Harbach
Blue Monday Blues DeSylva; Gershwin, George

Bluebird, Where Are You Clarke
Blunderland Buck
Blushing Bride, The Romberg
Boardwalk Blues Turk
Bobbed Hair Blues Young, Victor
Bouquet of Girls Atteridge; Schwartz, Jean
Breath of Springtime Hart
Bring on the Girls Buck
Bring on the Girls (inst.) Herbert
Bring on the Pepper Berlin
Broadway Strut, The Turk
Broken Hearted Melody Kahn
Broken Toy Kahn
Bugle Call Blues Turk
Busy Bees of DeVere's, The Cohan
By the Riverside Bryan; Clare; Friend
By the Sapphire Sea Smith, Harry B.; Snyder
By the Shalimar Koehler
Cairo Freed, Arthur
California Conrad; Friend
Camel Dreams Motzan
Camp's Daily Dozen Atteridge
Can He Love Me Like Kelly Can? Lewis; Young, Joseph
Can It Be that I'm in Love DeSylva
Captain Kidd's Kids Hammerstein
Caravanna Fisher
Carolina in the Morning Donaldson; Kahn
Carolina Shout, The Johnson, James P.
Carry Me Back to My Carolina Home Davis; Silver
Cartoon Town Ager; Yellen
Cazzaza Romberg
Charleston Johnson, James P.
Chattanooga Booga Boo Donaldson; Johnson, Howard
Chauve-Souris of Our Own, A Caesar
Cherchez la Femme Friml
Chicago — That Toddling Town Fisher
Chinky Chink Hammerstein
Chloe, Cling to Me Hart
(Little) Cinderelatives DeSylva; Gershwin, George
Cinderella Blues Caesar
Cinema Girl Atteridge
Circus Days Atteridge
Clouds Roll By Dance Coots
Clover Blossom Blues Kahn
Coachman's Heart, A Hammerstein
Cock-a-Doodle-Doo Caesar
Cocktail Time Porter
Come on Home Akst; Lewis; Meyer; Young, Joseph
Comfort Me Hart; Rodgers
Company's Coming Tonight Brown, A. Seymour
Congratulations Hart; Rodgers
Counterfeit Bill From Louisville Brown, Lew; Henderson
Cow Bells Mitchell
Crinoline Days Berlin
Cubanella Coslow
Cuddle Me Coslow
Curly Head Ager; Yellen
Cutie Friml; Harbach
Daddy Friml; Harbach
Dance Your Cares Away Davis
Dance Your Troubles Away Berlin
Dancin' Around Davis; Hanley
Dancing Detective, The Cohan
Dancing Fool Smith, Harry B.; Snyder
Dancing My Worries Away Cohan

Dancing Shoes   Davis; Hanley
Darling Will Not Grow Older   Hart; Rodgers
Daughter of Satan   Atteridge
Days of Pharaoh   Atteridge
Dearest, You're the Nearest to My Heart   Akst
Deedle Deedle Dum   Coslow; Mills
Desert Rose   Bryan; Schwartz, Jean
Desperate Blues, The   Johnson, James P.
Devil's in Your Toes, The   Caesar
Different Days   Romberg
Ding Dong Ding   Hammerstein; Mitchell
Dixie Highway   Donaldson; Kahn
Do I?   Akst; Lewis; Young, Joseph
Do It Again   DeSylva; Gershwin, George
Do You Remember?   Coots
Doing the Eddie Cantor   Atteridge; Schwartz, Jean
Donaldsonia   Donaldson
Don't Be Silly, Sally   Brown, Lew; Hanley
Don't, Don't Stop Loving Me Now   Hanley
Don't Feel Sorry for Me   Clarke; Leslie
Don't Need Nobody to Tell Me I'm in Bad   Johnson, James P.
Don't Tell Mama   Brown, Lew; Hanley
Down in Maryland   Kalmar; Ruby
Down Old Virginia Way   Yellen
Down on Indigo Bay   Fisher
Dream of Orange Blossoms, A   DeSylva; Herbert
Dream On   DeSylva; Herbert
Dreaming Alone   Hammerstein; Mitchell
Dreams for Sale   Hanley
Dreamy Melody   Koehler
East Is East, West Is West, But South Is Paradise   Ager; Yellen
Egyptian Melange   Hanley
Eleanor   Atteridge
Electricity   Coots
Ensemble Finale   Buck
Eternal Flame, The   Brennan
Eugene O'Neill's Hairy Ape   Atteridge
Every Day in Every Way   Kern
Every Girl Is Like a Weather Glass   DeSylva; Herbert
Every Silver Lining   Hammerstein; Mitchell
Every Wednesday Night   Friend
Everything's Gonna Be All Right   Conrad; Fisher
Eyes So Dark and Luring   DeSylva
Fair Enough   Hammerstein
Fairylands (inst.)   Herbert
Faljandio (inst.)   Herbert
Farewell to Adrian   Romberg
Fascination   Gershwin, Ira
Fe Fi Fo Fum   Gershwin, Ira
Fickle Flo from Kokomo   Turk
Fiddler Paul   Johnson, Howard
First, Last and Always   Atteridge
Flapper, The   Atteridge; DeSylva; Gershwin, George; Schwartz, Jean
Flapper Walk, The   Kahn
Flappers   Buck
Forbidden Fruit   DeSylva
Four A.M. Shout (inst.)   Johnson, James P.
Four Well Known Dames and a Guy   Buck
Fox Trot   Caesar
Fragonard Girl   Atteridge
French Pastry Walk   Gershwin, Ira
Friendship   DeSylva

Funny Feet   Berlin
Garden of Eden   Hanley
Gay Butterfly on the Wheel   Bryan; Schwartz, Jean
Gee! But I Hate to Go Home Alone   Hanley
Georgette   Brown, Lew; Henderson
Georgia   Donaldson; Johnson, Howard
Georgia Cabin Door   Parish
Ghost Recitative   Johnson, James P.
Ginger Brown   Johnson, James P.
Girl from the Golden West, A   Coots
Girls from DeVere's   Cohan
Give Me One Day   Caesar
Give Old Ireland to the Irish   Egan; Whiting
Glad   Davis; Hanley
Good Bye   Romberg
Good-Bye Main Street   Atteridge; Schwartz, Jean
Good-Bye to Dear Old Alaska   Caesar
Grab Bag, The   Gershwin, George; Goetz
Great New York Police, The   Cohan
Greenwich Village Nights   Caesar
Grouchy Blues   Mills
Gypsy Blues   Turk
Gypsy, I'm Love-Tippy for You   Jerome; Schwartz, Jean
Gypsy Warned Me, The   Caesar
Ha, Ha, I'm Laughin' at You   Conrad
Half Past Kissing Time   Lewis; Meyer; Young, Joseph
Happiness   Johnson, Howard
Harbor Down Deep in My Heart, The   Porter
Harry Masters, Jack Craft and Company   Caesar; Coots
Has Anyone Seen My Joe?   DeSylva; Gershwin, George
Havana Nights   Caesar
Have a Little Dance with Me   Friml
Have You Forgotten Me? Blues   Kern
Hawaiian Night in Dixieland   Turk
He Loves It   Clarke; Leslie
Heart of Virginia   Motzan
Heathen Lullaby   Brown, Nacio Herb
Helen of Troy, New York   Hanley
Hello, Hello, Hello   Buck
Her Love Is Always the Same   Friml; Harbach
Hermits, The   Hart; Rodgers
He's a Regular Guy   Fisher; Rose
He's Just that Kind of a Guy   Parish
High Brown Blues   Ager; Yellen
Hollow of My Hand   Caesar
Hollyhocks of Hollywood, The   Hart; Rodgers
Homesick   Berlin
Honey Lu   DeSylva; Donaldson
Honeymoon Chimes   Brown, Lew
Hootch Rhythm   Bryan; Schwartz, Jean
Hot Dog!   Kern
How Can I Win You Now?   DeSylva; Herbert
How Can You Say Goodbye   Coslow
How Do You Do, Katinka?   Kern
How I Missed You, Mary   Coots
How'd You Like to Be a Kid   McHugh
Hubby   Gershwin, Ira
Humming a Tune   Atteridge
Humoresque   Dubin
Humoresquimos   Atteridge; Schwartz, Jean
Husband's Only a Husband, A   DeSylva
I Am Getting Better All the Time   Schwartz, Arthur
I Came! I Saw! I Fell!   Atteridge
I Can't Argue with You   DeSylva; Herbert

I Can't Tell Where They're from When They
　　Dance　DeSylva; Gershwin, George; Goetz
I Could Do a Lot for You　Friml; Harbach
I Don't Know what I'd Do Without You　Buck
I Don't Know Why　Caesar
I Don't Want to Be in Dixie　Buck
I Found a Four Leaf Clover　DeSylva; Gershwin, George
I Gave You Up Just Before You Threw Me Down　Ahlert;
　　Kalmar; Ruby
I Got It — You'll Get It　Pollack
I Hate to Love You (But What Else Can I Do)　Parish
I Knew I Was Wrong　Hanley
I Know You're Too Wonderful for Me　Hart; Rodgers
I Learned About Women from Her　Atteridge; Schwartz,
　　Jean
I Lost a Slice of Paradise　Norworth
I Love Her — She Loves Me　Caesar
I Love To Think of You　Brown, Nacio Herb
I Love You So　Romberg
I Mean No-One-Else-But-You　Caesar
I Miss My Mama, My Black Eyed Charmer Down in
　　Yokohama Way　Brown, Lew
I Miss My Swiss, My Swiss Miss Misses Me　Baer; Gilbert
I Missed You　DeSylva; Herbert
I Still Can Dream　DeSylva
I Thank You　Yellen
I Thought I'd Die　Henderson
I Wanna Go Home　Yellen
I Want a Good Baby — Bad　Young, Joseph
I Want a Good Baby - Bad　Lewis
I Want a Man　Hart; Rodgers
I Want to Be Vamped in Georgia　Turk
I Wonder Why　Coots
I'd Like to Be a Boy Again　Jerome; Schwartz, Jean
I'd Love to Have Ya Love Me All the Same　Kahn
If I Were King　Hart; Rodgers
If Wives Were Put on Sale　Caesar
If You Don't Think So You're Crazy　Turk
If You Don't Think You Ought to Do What You Oughtn't
　　Do, Don't Do It at All　Sterling; Von Tilzer
If You Have a Girl Who Loves You, Leave the Other Girls
　　Alone　Friend
I'll Always Be an Optimist　Hart; Rodgers
I'll Always Need Someone Like You　Caesar
I'll Be in My Dixie Home Again Tomorrow　Turk
I'll Bet on Anything but Girls　Romberg
I'll Build a Bungalow　Hammerstein
I'll Build a Home in the Jungle　Caesar
I'll Build a Stairway to Paradise　DeSylva; Gershwin,
　　George; Gershwin, Ira
I'll Dance My Way into Your Heart　DeSylva
I'll Mooch Along　Brown, Lew; Hanley
I'll Stand Beneath Your Window Tonight and
　　Whistle　McHugh
I'll Tell You Why, Can't You See I'm in Love with
　　You　Davis; Silver
I'm Always Stuttering　Mitchell
I'm Asking Ya, Ain't It de Truth　Norworth
I'm Brilliant　Silver
I'm Fresh from the Coutnry　Hammerstein
I'm Glad I'm Happy　Motzan
I'm Gonna Borrow a Sweet Ma-ma Because Somebody
　　Borrowed Mine　Fisher
I'm Gonna Buy a One-Way Ticket to a Little One-Horse
　　Town　Parish

I'm Gonna Knock, Knock, Knock on the Old Front
　　Door　Hanley
I'm Gonna Make Things Merry for My Mary in
　　Maryland　Lewis; Meyer; Young, Joseph
I'm Gonna See My Mother　DeSylva; Gershwin, George
I'm Hungry for Beautiful Girls　Fisher; Rose
I'm Just a Lonely Little Kid　Norworth
I'm Laughing at You　Conrad; Kahn
I'm Looking for a Daddy Long Legs　Berlin
I'm Mighty Sweet on My Sweet Sweetie (She's Mighty Sweet
　　on Me)　Johnson, Howard
I'm Mighty Sweet on My Sweetie (She's Mighty Sweet on
　　Me)　Baer
I'm Satisfied　Buck
I'm Wild about Wild Men　Bryan; Schwartz, Jean
In a Corner of the World All Our Own　Kahn
In a Little French Cafe　Fain; Parish
In Brazil　Romberg
In Hennequeville　DeSylva; Herbert
In Italy　Atteridge
In My Home Town　Kalmar; Ruby
In My Little Red Book　Coots
In the Garden of Other Days　Freed, Arthur
In the Land of Chee-ree-bee-ree-bee (Ciribiribi)　Henderson
In the Land of Sweet Sixteen　Meyer
In the Starlight　DeSylva
Ireland Is Free　Brown, A. Seymour
Isle of Sweethearts　Caesar
It's Getting Dark on Old Broadway　Buck
It's Just a Matter of Time　Davis
It's Raining, I'll Have to Go Home in the Dark　Sterling;
　　Von Tilzer
It's Up to You (J'en Ai Marre)　DeSylva
I've Found a Bud Among the Roses　Friml; Harbach
I've Got Friends　Dubin
I've Got What It Takes　Turk
Ivy (Cling to Me)　Johnson, James P.
J. Flynn　DeSylva; Herbert
Japanese Tea Rose　Hanley
Jazz Your Troubles Away　Johnson, James P.
Jazza Painted Jazzama-Remos　Bryan; Schwartz, Jean
Jennie　Conrad; Friend
Jenny Lind　Caesar
Jimmie　Coots
Jimmy, I Love But You　Smith, Harry B.
Jingle Bells　Ager; Yellen
Joline　Robison
Juba Dance　Johnson, James P.
Jungle Bungalow (I'll Build a Home in the Jungle)　Hanley
Jungle Nymphs (inst.)　Johnson, James P.
Just a Girl that Men Forget　Dubin
Just a Regular Girl　Romberg
Just a Tiny Cup of Tea　DeSylva; Gershwin, George
Just a Touch　Hammerstein; Mitchell
Just Because You're You. . . That's Why I Love You　Turk
Just Like a Doll　Romberg
Just Like That　DeSylva; Herbert
Keep Moving　Johnson, James P.
Kicky-Koo, You for Me-Me for You　Young, Joseph
Kid Days　Coots
Ki-Ki-Koo, You for Me-Me for You　Lewis; Meyer
Kindergarten Blues　Hammerstein
Kiss from a Red-Headed Miss, A　Caesar
Kiss in the Dark, A　DeSylva; Herbert
Kissing Time　Lewis; Young, Joseph

Kitten on the Keys   Coslow
Ladies from the Cultured West, The   Atteridge; Romberg
Lady of the Evening   Berlin
Lamplight Land   Atteridge; Schwartz, Jean
Landing the Landlord   Coslow
Last Night the World Began   Kahn
Legend of the Glow Worm   DeSylva; Herbert
Let Us Say Goodbye with a Waltz   Parish
Let's Mend the Crack in the Liberty Bell   Cobb; Edwards
Let's Not Get Married   DeSylva; Herbert
Let's Play Hookey   Hammerstein
Lillies of the Field   Coots
List'ning on Some Radio   Buck
Little Church Around the Corner   Freed, Arthur
Little Grey Sweetheart of Mine   Fisher
Little Red Lacquer Cage, The   Berlin
Little Side Street in Paree, A   Hanley
Log Cabin Days   Johnson, James P.
Lola Cornero from the Trocadero   Caesar
Lola in Love   Caesar
Lola Lo   Smith, Harry B.
Lola Waltz (Close in Your Arms)   Hanley
Lonely Nest, The   DeSylva; Herbert
Longing for You   Freed, Arthur
Lora Lee   Herbert
Lost (A Wonderful Girl)   Davis; Hanley
Lotus Flower   DeSylva
Louisiana   Freed, Arthur
Louisville   Caesar
(Tell Me What's the Matter) Lovable Eyes   Schwartz, Jean
Love and the Moon   Kern
Love Bug   Johnson, James P.
Love Finds a Way   Romberg
Love Letter Words   Porter
Love Notes   McHugh; Parish
Love of Long Ago   Atteridge
Love Sick Blues   Friend; Mills
Love Spans the World   Caesar
Love Test, The   Atteridge; Romberg
Love the Wife of Your Neighbor   DeSylva
Love While You May   Romberg
(Tell Me What's the Matter) Loveable Eyes   Atteridge
Lovelight in Your Eyes, The   Smith, Harry B.
Love's Highway   Romberg
Lovey Dove   Atteridge; Romberg
Lovin' Sam the Sheik of Alabam'   Ager; Yellen
Madeleine   Friml; Harbach
Malinda Brown   Donaldson; Johnson, Howard
Mama Love Papa   Brown, Nacio Herb; Freed, Arthur
Mamma Loves Papa, Does Papa Love Mamma?   Brown, Lew
Mammy's Melody   Kahn
Mandy   Turk
Manhattan   Hart; Rodgers
Manhattan Nights   Caesar
Marches   Buck
Marches (inst.)   Herbert
Marion Davies March (inst.), The   Herbert
Marriage C.O.D.   Hammerstein; Mitchell
Mary Came Over to Me   Caesar; Herbert
Mary Is a Real Good Fellow but Mary Is a Real Good Girl   Akst; Caesar
Maryland Scene   Porter
Mazuma   Atteridge; Romberg
Meet the Wife   Sterling; Von Tilzer

Melancholy Blues   Caesar
Melody Land   Atteridge
Merci Beaucoup   Friml
Minstrels on Parade   Turk
Mississippi Ripples   Hanley
Molly On the Shore   Gershwin, George; Gershwin, Ira
Mont Marte   Berlin
Moon Dreams   Schwartz, Arthur
Moonshine and Ballet   DeSylva; Herbert
Morning Glory   Kern
Mosquito Ballet (inst.)   Herbert
Moth for My Flame   DeSylva; Gershwin, George; Goetz
Mother, Dixie, the Flag and You   Goetz; Meyer
Mother Machree's Lullaby (My Machree's Lullaby)   Johnson, Howard
Mr. and Mrs.   Kahn; Romberg
Muffled Drums   Hanley
Mumuring   Davis; Silver
Musical Bill of Fare   Gershwin, George
My Baby   Donaldson
My Bajadere   DeSylva
My Beautiful Fragonard Girl   Bryan; Schwartz, Jean
My Boy Friend   Hammerstein
My Broadway   Kahn
My Buddy   Donaldson; Kahn
My Busy Day   Hammerstein; Mitchell
My Castillian Girl   Atteridge; Schwartz, Jean
My Coal Black Mammy   Atteridge
My Cradle Melody Keeps Bringing Me Back to Old Virginia   Meyer; Young, Joseph
My Cradle Melody Keeps Swinging Me Back to Old Virginia   Lewis
My Diamond Girls   Atteridge
My Diamond Horseshoe of Girls   Berlin
My Dixie   Mitchell
My Hawaiian Paradise   Fain
My Heart Is Calling   Atteridge; Romberg
My Heart Will Sail (Across the Sea)   DeSylva; Gershwin, George; Goetz
My Highbrow Fling   Hammerstein; Mitchell
My Honey Lou   DeSylva; Donaldson
My Honey's Eyes   Baer
My Lady and Me   Motzan
My Little Cuckoo Out in Kokomo   Donaldson
My Little Hush-A-Bye Lady in Hush-A-Bye Land   Lewis; Young, Joseph
My Little Redskin   Hammerstein
My Melody   Buck
My Rambler Rose   Buck
My Sweet (Ha Way-Yo)   Clare; Friend
My Vision in Vermillion   Bryan; Schwartz, Jean
My Yiddishe Mammy   Schwartz, Jean
Mystery Play, The   Cohan
Name of Kelly, The   Cohan
'Neath the South Sea Moon   Buck
Nellie Kelly, I Love You   Cohan
New Hampshire   Schwartz, Jean
New York Is the Same Old Place   DeSylva; Herbert
Night   Davis
Nightingale, Bring Me a Rose   Caesar
No Wonder I'm Lonesome   Lewis; Meyer; Young, Joseph
Nobody but You   Buck
Nobody Know Where Tosti Goes, When Tosti Says Goodbye   Lewis; Meyer; Young, Joseph
O, Katharina!   Gilbert

Off We Go   Caesar
Oh Baby   Davis
Oh How I Hate that Fellow Nathan   Brown, Lew
Oh How I Pine for Carolina   Davis
Oh, Is She Dumb   Clarke; Leslie
Oh, Mary   Porter
Oh Say, Oh Sue!   Caesar
Oh Sing-A-Loo Whad' Ya Do with You Que?   Brown, Lew;
    Mitchell; Pollack
Oh, What a Mother I Had   Ager; Yellen
Oh, What She Hangs Out (She Hangs Out in Our
    Alley)   DeSylva; Gershwin, George; Goetz
Olaf, You Ought-A-Hear Olaf Laff   Baer; Gilbert
Old Black Joe   Turk
Old Enough to Love   Hart; Rodgers
Old Fashioned Cake Walk   Hanley
Old Fashioned Gown   Coots
Old Man's Whiskers, The   Friend
Old-Fashioned Love   Johnson, James P.
Old-Fashioned Waltz, The   Porter
Olga (Come Back to the Volga)   Porter
Omaha (Me-Oh-Ma)   Meyer
On a Beautiful Evening   Atteridge; Schwartz, Jean
On the Alamo   Kahn
On the Riviera   DeSylva; Herbert
On the Shores of Rockaway   Johnson, Howard
On the Umpah Isle   Sterling; Von Tilzer
One a Day   Hart; Rodgers
One Flower That Blooms for You   Hammerstein
One Night in June   Smith, Harry B.; Snyder
Oogie Oogie Wa Wa   Clarke; Leslie
O-oo Ernest, Are You Earnest with Me   Clare; Friend
Open Your Arms My Alabam'   Lewis; Meyer; Young, Joseph
Open Your Heart   Johnson, James P.
Opportunity   Coots
Orange Blossoms   DeSylva; Herbert
Orphans of the Storm   Atteridge
Our Busy Needles Fly   Romberg
Our Home Sweet Home   Coots
Out of My Arms, But I Can't Keep You Out of My
    Heart   Hanley
Over the Phone   Cohan
Pack Up Your Sins (And Go to the Devil)   Berlin
Pale Venetian Moon, The   Kern
Pals   Coots
Panic Is On, The   Mitchell; Pollack
Panorama Bay   Clarke; Monaco
Pappy   Fain
Parisian Nights   Caesar
Pasha Bay   Donaldson
Passing Show, The   Atteridge
Patter   Romberg
Pay Day on Levee   Johnson, James P.
Peach Girl   Kern
Peacock Alley   Coots
Peggy, Dear   Freed, Arthur
People Like Us   Norworth
Pep It Up   Buck
Perfect Model for Your Arms, A   Caesar
Perhaps   Friml
Persian Nights   Brown, Nacio Herb
Piccadilly Walk, The   Gershwin, Ira
Pick Me Up and Lay Me Down in Dear Old
    Dixieland   Kalmar; Ruby
Picture Without a Frame, A   Sterling; Von Tilzer

Pirate's Gold   Hammerstein
Pitter-Patter   Porter
Plant a Little Seed of Kindness   Fisher
Play Me a Tune   Porter
Play with Fire   Romberg
(We Are the Girls of the Chorus) Please Tell Me Who Looks
    Good to You   Ager; Yellen
Poor J'en-Ai-Marre   Atteridge
Poor Little Me   Davis
Porcelain Maid   Berlin
Pretty Dimples   Ager; Yellen
Pretty Polly   Romberg
Prince Charming   Hammerstein
Prince of Wales   Atteridge
Quite a Nifty and Effective Detective Am I   DeSylva;
    Herbert
Radiance   Atteridge
Ragtime Pipes of Pan   Porter
Rainbow Blues   Brown, Lew; Clare; Pollack
Rainy Day Sue   Berlin
Read Between the Lines   Friml
Red Cap Cappers   Johnson, James P.
Right Boy Comes Along   Coots
Robert E. Lee   Turk
Rock Me in My Swanee Cradle   Parish
Rock Me in the Cradle of the Blues   Donaldson
Roll On Silvery Moon   Fisher
Rollin' Home   Clare; Pollack
Rose Briar   Kern
Rose of Stamboul, The   Atteridge
Rose of the Rio Grande   Leslie; Warren
Roses from the South   Conrad; Kahn
Roses, Lovely Roses   DeSylva
Rosy Posy   Romberg
Round on the End and High in the Middle, O-Hi-O   Bryan
Roustabouts   Johnson, James P.
Rozita   Friml
Russian Love   Caesar
Sailor's Bride, A   Romberg
Save the Last Waltz for Me   Johnson, Howard
Say It   McHugh; Mills
Say It While Dancing (Ca S'Fait en Dansant)   Davis; Silver
Scotch Twins   Porter
Send Me a Bluebird with Beautiful Blue Eyes   Fisher
Set 'em Sadie   Johnson, James P.
Seven or Eleven, My Dixie Pair o' Dice   Brown, Lew;
    Donaldson
Shake 'Em Up at Lucinda's Honolulu Ball   Sterling; Von
    Tilzer
Sheeksa, The Queen of Araby   Brown, Lew; Conrad
Sheik of Alabam Weds a Brown Skin Vamp, The   Johnson,
    James P.
Sheik of Araby, The   Smith, Harry B.; Snyder
Sheik of Avenue B, The   Kalmar
She's Beautiful but Dumb   Fisher; Rose
She's So Different Now   Stept
Sh-h-h-h (The Shush Song)   Henderson
Shiek of Avenue B, The   Ruby
Si, Si, Senorita   Romberg
Side By Each   Donaldson; Kahn
Side By Side   Kahn
Silver Bands of Love   Yellen
Silver Canoe, A   DeSylva
Silver Swanee   Schwartz, Jean
Silver Wedding, The   Romberg

Since I Remember You Hart; Rodgers
Sing a Song of Sunshine Buck
Sing Song Man Conrad; Friend
Sitting in a Corner Buck
Sixty Seconds Every Minute I Think of You Caesar
Sizing Up the Girls Hammerstein; Mitchell
Sleepy Little Village Where the Dixie Cotton Grows Leslie
Slow and Easy Goin' Man Johnson, James P.
Slow Movies Caesar
Smoke Rings Friml; Harbach
Sneak, The Brown, Nacio Herb
Snowtime Johnson, James P.
Society Coots
Some Fine Day Hammerstein; Mitchell
Some Sunny Day Berlin
Some Sweet Day Buck
Somebody Loves You Hanley
Someday when Love Finds a Way Yellen
Someone Gershwin, Ira
Someone, Tra La La Gershwin, George
Something in Here Coots
Something's Got to Be Done Cohan
Somewhere in Love's Garden Romberg
Song Birds Quartette Johnson, James P.
Song of Persia Egan; Whiting
Songs I Can't Forget Buck
Sophie Silver
South Sea Isles Porter
South Sea Sweethearts Caesar
Southern Hobby, A Turk
Southern Memories Kahn
Southland Turk
Souvenirs Caesar
Sponge, The Porter
Springtime Is the Time for Loving Romberg
Stage Door Johnnies Coots
Starlight Bay Donaldson; Kahn
Starlight of Hope Romberg
Stars of the Stage DeSylva
Steppin' School Ager; Yellen
Stop, Look and Kiss Hammerstein; Mitchell
Stop Your Kiddin' Coslow; McHugh; Mills
Study in Black and White, A Atteridge
Sun Kist Rose Johnson, James P.
Sunny South Buck
Sunny Sunbeam Hanley
Sunshine and Rain Davis
Susie Kalmar; Ruby
Suzanna Davis
Swanee Bluebird Conrad; Friend
Swanee River Johnson, James P.; Turk
Swanee Sway, The Hanley
Sweet As You Can Be Friml; Harbach
Sweet Indiana Home Donaldson
Sweet Little You Parish
Sweet Man o' Mine Turk
Sweetheart Lane Caesar
Sweethearts Gershwin, George
Syncopated Minuet, The Caesar
System Hammerstein; Mitchell
Tact Friml; Harbach
Take a Little Wife Berlin
Tanglefeet Brown, Lew
Tartar Hammerstein
Tell Me Again Schwartz, Arthur

Tell Me Why You and I Should Be Strangers After We Used to Be Such Good Friends? Fisher
Tempting Monaco
Tenement Rose Mitchell
That Little Grey House without Any Key Brennan
That Redhead Gal Fisher
That Spanish Rum Tee Ay Fisher
That's the Way It Goes Romberg
That's What I Call a Pal Donaldson
That's What Keeps Me Broke Clare; Monaco
(When You Do) The Hinky Dee Cohan
Then Comes the Dawning DeSylva; Herbert
There's a Little Bit of Yes in Ev'ry Little Girl's No Lewis; Meyer; Young, Joseph
There's an Old Oaken Bucket in Old Nantucket Bryan
They Call Me Carpenter Motzan
Thief, The Fisher
Think of Me Only With a Smile Egan
This Time It's Love DeSylva; Herbert
Those Blue Eyes Blues Fisher
Those Flippity Floppety Flappers Johnson, Howard
Three Cheers for the Red, White and Blue Berlin
Three Musketeers, The Hart; Rodgers
Three O'Clock in the Morning Baer
Tick, Tick, Tick of the Ticker, The Romberg
Tickle Me Smith, Harry B.; Snyder
Time, Only Time Dear Atteridge; Romberg
Time Will Tell Coots
Ting-A-Ling Atteridge; Romberg
To Make Them Beautiful Ladies Atteridge; Schwartz, Jean
Tomorrow Morning Parish
Tom-Tom Hammerstein; Mitchell
Too Many Girls Berlin
Too Many Kisses Mean Too Many Tears Bryan
Topics of the Day Friend
Tra-La-La Gershwin, Ira
True Blue Sam, the Traveling Man Brown, Lew; Donaldson
Truly Davis
Twelve O'Clock Girl in a Nine O'Clock Town, A Friml; Harbach
Twin Sisters Porter
Two Little Ruby Rings Hammerstein
Two Little Wooden Shoes Hanley
Ukulele Blues Johnson, James P.
Underneath a Pretty Hat Atteridge
Underneath the Palms Atteridge
Until My Luck Comes Rolling Alone Cohan
Until You Say Yes Coots
Up on Your Toes Gilbert
Vaniity Box, The Caesar
Varsity Bug, The Caesar
Venetian Love Rose Coslow
Vision in Vermillion, A Atteridge; Schwartz, Jean
Voice in My Heart, The Cohan
Waikiki, I Hear You Calling Me Kalmar; Ruby
Waltz Is Made for Love, The DeSylva
Waltz It Should Be, A Atteridge; Romberg
Waltz of India McHugh; Mills; Parish
Waltz Song Atteridge; Romberg
Waltz-Duet Atteridge; Romberg
Way Down Home Donaldson
Way Out West in Jersey DeSylva; Herbert
We Are Waiting Coots
We Came, We Saw, We Made 'Em! Hart; Rodgers
We Don't Want Liquor Fisher

Weaker Is the Stronger After All, The   Caesar
Weaving My Dreams   Buck; Herbert
Wedding March, The   Atteridge; Romberg
Wedding Ring   Fisher
Wedding Ring Don't Mean a Thing When You're Married,
    The   Fisher
Wedding Time   Coots
Weeping   Johnson, James P.
We'll Greet Each Tomorrow Together   Caesar
What Can I Do?   Gershwin, Ira
What Does It Matter Who Was Wrong   Gilbert
What I Care!   Youmans
When a Regular Girl Loves a Regular Boy   Coots
When All Your Castles Come Tumbling Down   Gershwin,
    Ira
When Eyes Meet Eyes (When Lips Meet Lips)   Cobb;
    Edwards
When Hearts Are Young (in Springtime)   Romberg
When I Hear an Irishman Sing   Dubin
When I Waltz with You   Friml; Harbach
When Knighthood Was in Flower   Herbert
When My Caravan Comes Home   Porter
When Night Is Near   Egan; Gorney; Whiting
When Songs Were Sung   Caesar
When the Summer Bids the Rose Goodbye   Dubin
When the Wedding Chimes Are Ringing   Atteridge;
    Schwartz, Jean
When Winter Comes   Carroll; Freed, Arthur
When You and I Were Young Maggie Blues   McHugh
When You're Lonesome, You're Lonesome That's
    All   Brown, Lew
When You're Near   Coslow
When You're Only Seventeen   Hammerstein; Hanley;
    Mitchell
Where Have You Been All My Life   Kahn
Where Is the Man of My Dreams?   DeSylva; Goetz
Where the Bamboo Babies Grow   Donaldson
Where the Honeymoon Alone Can See   Friml; Harbach
Wherer Is the Man of My Dreams?   Gershwin, George
While Miami Dreams   Egan; Whiting
While the Years Roll By   Lewis; Young, Joseph
White House in Washington and the White House in the
    Lane, The   Bryan; Howard, Joseph E.
Whose Little Angel Are You   Silver
Why Can't I Agree   Gershwin, George
Why Do They Call Them Show Girls   Fisher
Why Do They Die at the End of Classical Dance?   Atteridge;
    Romberg
Why Do We Love Them?   DeSylva; Herbert
Why Do You Keep Us Guessing?   Hammerstein; Mitchell
Why I Love You   Caesar
Wild Cat   Donaldson
Will She Come from the East (North, West, or
    South)?   Berlin
With Papers Duly Signed   Atteridge; Romberg
Woman's No, A   Romberg
Wonderful You   Cobb; Edwards; Gershwin, George
Wond'ring Night and Day   Porter
Won't You Buy a Flower?   Atteridge; Schwartz, Jean
Won't You Come Back to Me   Cohan
Won't You Take Me to Paris   Romberg
Worried and Lonesome Blues (inst.)   Johnson, James P.
Yankee Doodle Blues   Caesar; DeSylva; Gershwin, George;
    Henderson
You and I   Johnson, Howard

You Are My Rain-Beau   Caesar
You Can Have Every Light on Broadway   Davis
You Can't Hate Me for That   Davis
You Can't Lose Me   Hammerstein
You Don't Love Me As I Do   Goetz
You Gave Me Your Heart   Smith, Harry B.; Snyder
You Haven't Lived If You Haven't Lived Way Down in
    Dixieland   Henderson
You Know You Belong to Somebody Else, So Why Don't You
    Leave Me Alone   Monaco
You Need Someone   Hammerstein; Mitchell
You Remind Me of My Mother   Cohan
You Teach Me   Hanley
You Tell Her I Stutter   Friend; Rose
You, You, You   Friml
You'll Change Your Mind   Stept
You'll Do the Same Thing to Someone Else   Hanley
Your Eyes Shall Speak to Me   Caesar
You're Only a Baby   Kahn
Youth and Spring   Romberg
You've Got to See Mama Ever Night   Conrad
Yvette   Dubin
Zig-Zag   Ager; Yellen

1923

(Nothing Like) A Darn Good Cry   Cohan
Abie's Irish Rose   Hanley
Ach Louis   Fisher
Advertising   Kalmar; Ruby
After Midnight   McHugh
After You Feed the Little Chickens They Want a Little
    Chicken Feed   Atteridge; Schwartz, Jean
Ali Baba   Coots
Alibi Baby   Dietz
All Alone (inst.)   Waller
All for Charity   Hammerstein; Youmans
All My Life   Akst; Davis
All Night Long   Cohan
All Over Town   Gershwin, George
All the Knicker Knockers Wear Knickerbockers Now   Egan;
    Kahn; Whiting
All Wrong   Kahn
Alley-Up   Dixon
American Dancers   Atteridge; Schwartz, Jean
And How   Akst; Kahn
And Now   Akst
Ann and Her Little Sedan   Hanley
Annabelle   Brown, Lew; Henderson
Annabelle Lee   Caesar
Antiques   Harbach
Any Little Girl Will Fall   Atteridge; Caesar; Romberg
Any Little Tune   Gershwin, George
Any Time at All   Friend
Apple Blossoms   Youmans
April Blossoms   Hammerstein; Harbach
Argentine   Smith, Harry B.
Argentine Arango, The   Friml
Arrival of Society, The   Cohan
Arrival of the Plot, The   Cohan
Art of Fascination, The   Edwards; Smith, Robert B.
As Long As He Loves Me   Brown, Lew; Hanley
As Long as the Wife Don't Know   Brown, A. Seymour
At Half Past Seven   DeSylva; Gershwin, George
At Madame Regay's   Cohan

At the Stage Door   Atteridge; Schwartz, Jean
Aux Armes   Atteridge; Romberg; Schwartz, Jean
Babbling Babette   Kern
Baby Buntin'   Blake; Sissle
Baby Me Blues   Gershwin, Ira; Youmans
Back Home   Ager; Yellen
Back to Killarney   Harbach
Bad News Blues   Akst; Davis
Bahama   Woods
Ball Begins, The   Atteridge; Romberg
Baltimore, MD. — That's the Only Doctor for Me   Schwartz, Arthur
Bambalina   Hammerstein; Harbach; Youmans
Band of the Ne'er-Do-Wells, The   Hart; Rodgers
Bang on Your Tambourine   Dixon
Barcarole, The   Caesar; Conrad
Barcarolle Blues   Friend
Barefoot Boy   Kahn
Barney Google   Conrad; Fisher; Rose
Beale Street Mamma   Turk
Beautiful and Damned   Atteridge; Romberg; Schwartz, Jean
Beautiful Girls (You Have the World at Your Feet)   Ager; Yellen
Bebe   Coslow; Silver
Because You Love the Singer   Kern
Bella Donna, Beautiful Lady   Smith, Harry B.; Snyder
Belles of the Bronx, The   Friml
Beneath the Eastern Moon   Gershwin, George
Beside a Babbling Brook   Donaldson; Kahn
Best Dance I've Had Tonight, The   Hammerstein; Harbach; Youmans
Beyond the Moonbeam Trail   Ager; Yellen
Big Blonde Venus   Monaco; Rose
Billy Goat   Young, Victor
Birds of Plumage   Atteridge; Romberg; Schwartz, Jean
Bit By Bit You're Breaking My Heart   Kahn
Bittersweet   Gershwin, Ira
Black and Blue   Akst; Lewis; Meyer
Black Sheep Blues, The   Kahn
Blind Man's Buff   Ellington
Blue Grass Blues   Mills
Blue Hoosier Blues   Baer; Friend
Blue Swanee   Egan; Kahn; Whiting
Blues Never Die (inst.)   Waller
Bob-O-Link   Rodgers
Born and Bred in Brooklyn, Over the Bridge   Cohan
Bowery of Today, The   Atteridge; Caesar; Romberg
Bring on the Girls   Smith, Harry B.; Snyder
Broadway   Dubin
Broadway Caravan   Edwards; Johnson, Howard
Brown, Black and Yellow Blues   Johnson, Howard
Bustle   Caesar; Conrad
Calico Days   Blake; Sissle
California   Bryan
Cane Dance   Buck
Cane Dance (inst.)   Kern
Can't We Be Sweethearts   Coslow
Carmencita   Atteridge; Schwartz, Jean
Casey Is a Wonderful Name   Jerome; Schwartz, Jean
Change Your Step   Ager; Yellen
Changing the Key   Whiting
Chansonette   Buck; Caesar; Friml
Charleston Dance, The   Johnson, James P.
Chase Me Charlie   Von Tilzer
Chattachoochee   Dubin; Fain; Rose

Cheatin' Child   Lewis; Schwartz, Jean; Young, Joseph
Cheer Up   Brown, A. Seymour
Chief Hokum   Von Tilzer
Chinee Lullaby Man, The   Henderson
Chiquette   Coots; Schwartz, Jean
Chocolate Candy Daddies   Blake; Sissle
Chucha-Pacha-Poo-Poo, A   Henderson
Cinderella   Turk
Cinders   Friml
Cleo (inst.)   Brown, Nacio Herb
Climbing Up the Scale   Berlin
Coax Me   Brown, Lew; Hanley
Cock-A-Doodle Doo   Caesar; Conrad; Friend
Come on and Pet Me   Hammerstein; Youmans
Come On Spark Plug   Conrad; Rose
Concentrate   Harbach
Conchita   Caesar
Cottage in Kent, A   Kern
'Course I Will   Hammerstein; Harbach; Youmans
Courtly Etiquette   Rodgers
Cover Me Up with the Sunshine of Virginia   Lewis; Meyer; Young, Joseph
Cows Must Cow and Bull Must Bull   Schwartz, Jean
Cows Must Cow and the Bull Must Bull, The   Lewis; Young, Joseph
Cry Baby   Kalmar; Ruby
Cuddle Me As We Dance   Atteridge; Romberg
Cuddle Up   Atteridge; Caesar; Gershwin, George
Cuddle-Uddle Up   Parish
Daddy Treat Your Baby Right   Razaf
Dance with Me   Brown, A. Seymour
Dancer of the Nile, The   Hanley
Dancin' Dan   Dubin
Dancing   Atteridge; Schwartz, Jean
Dancing Around the Course   Edwards; Smith, Robert B.
Dancing Step Child   Caesar; Conrad
Daughters of Pleasure   Rodgers
Day By Day in Every Way I'm Getting Better Day By Day   Jerome; Schwartz, Jean
Dear Li'l Pal   Blake; Sissle
Dear Little Peter Pan   Kern
Dear Old Lady   Von Tilzer
Dearest, You're the Nearest to My Heart   Davis
Demonstrate   Edwards; Smith, Robert B.
Dickey Birds   Coots
Do You Love As I Love   Caesar
Doing the Apache   Atteridge; Romberg; Schwartz, Jean
Done Gone Mad (inst.)   Waller
Don't Forget to Write a Letter Home   Parish
Don't Give Me the Run Around   Baer; Friend
Don't Kick a Nation when It's Down   Fisher
Don't Love Me Blues   Blake; Sissle
Don't Never Tell Nobody What Your Good Man Can Do   Johnson, James P.
Don't Say You Will When You Know that You Won't   Coslow
Don't Want You No More (inst.)   Waller
Don't We Carry On   Clare; Friend
Down Among the Sleepy Hills of Tennessee   Lewis; Meyer; Young, Joseph
Down at the Hippodrome   Donaldson; Friend
Down Georgia Lane   Gorney
Down in Our Neighborhood   Schwartz, Jean
Down in the Land of Dancing Pickaninnies   Blake; Sissle

Down the Lane that Leads to Home Sweet Home   Brown, Lew; Henderson
Down Through the Ages   Brown, A. Seymour
Down where the Bluebells Grow   Edwards; Smith, Robert B.
Down Where the Mortgages Grow   Hammerstein; Youmans
Dream Lovers, The   Caesar; Conrad
Driftwood   Kahn
Dumber They Come the Better I Like 'Em, The   Ahlert
Egyptian Rose   Smith, Harry B.; Snyder
Elsie   Blake; Sissle
Emblems of Love   Mitchell; Pollack
Eternal City of Dreams   Kahn
Etiquette   Coots
Ever Lovin' Bee   Buck
Every Heart Has a Dream   Smith, Harry B.; Smith, Robert B.
Every Night I Cry Myself to Sleep Over You   Johnson, Howard
Every Step Brings Me Closer to My Lovin' Honey   Lamb   Pollack
Everybody Calls Me Little Red Riding Hood   Kern
Everybody's Struttin' Now   Blake; Sissle
Everything Is All Right   Hammerstein; Harbach; Youmans
Everything Is Jake with Rosie and Everything Is Rosie with Jake   DeSylva; Monaco; Rose
Everything Is K.O. in K.Y.   Egan; Whiting
Everytime   Caesar; Conrad
Evil Eye, The   Ager; Yellen
Ev'ry Day Is Mother's Day   Jerome; Schwartz, Jean
Fabric of Dreams   DeSylva; Gershwin, Ira
Fashion Parade, The   Friml
Feelin' the Way I Do   DeSylva; Donaldson
Fencing   Buck
Fencing Number (inst.)   Herbert
First, Last and Always   Akst; Davis
First Lesson, The   Atteridge; Schwartz, Jean
Flame of Love   Friml
Flannel Petticoat Gal, The   Hammerstein; Youmans
Flannel Petticoat Girl, The   Youmans
Fleeting Honeymoon   Harbach
Flower of the Woodland   Atteridge; Schwartz, Jean
Follow the Midnight Sun   Atteridge; Schwartz, Jean
For Crying Out Loud   Dixon
For the Man I Love   Kern
Friends Who Understand   Hammerstein; Harbach; Youmans
From Morning Till Night   Kahn; Motzan
(The Flowers of Evil) Garden of Evil   Atteridge; Schwartz, Jean
Garden of Love   DeSylva; Gershwin, George
Gathering   Cohan
Georgie   Harbach
Get Together   Friml
Girl from Casimo   Hammerstein; Harbach
Girl from Casino   Youmans
Girl I Love Is Like a Will-O-The-Wisp, The   Ager; Yellen
Girls Grow More Wonderful Day by Day   Harbach
Give a Girl a Chance   Hammerstein; Youmans
Give Me My Mammy   Gershwin, George
Glorifying the Girls   Buck
Glory Shout (inst.)   Johnson, James P.
Go Into Your Dance   Atteridge; Romberg; Schwartz, Jean
God Spare the Emerald Isle   Herbert; Jerome
Gold Digger, The   Hanley
Golden Trail   Caesar
Golfing Blues   Atteridge; Schwartz, Jean
Gondola and the Girl, The   Goetz

Good Bye, Little Rose-Bud   Hammerstein; Harbach
Good Night   Buck
Good Night, My Dear   Gershwin, George
Goodbye Forever   Friml
Goodbye Little Rosebud   Youmans
Good-Night Waltz   Conrad
Grandma's Day   Friml
Grinding Out a Revue   Kalmar; Ruby
Gypsy Rose   Lewis; Meyer; Young, Joseph
Hail U.S.A.   Atteridge; Caesar; Romberg
Happy Blues   Mills
Harlequin's Doll   Buck
Hawaiian Nights in Dixieland   Coots
Hay, Hay, Hazel   Whiting
He Wasn't Born in Araby but He's a Sheikin' Fool   Razaf
Headin' Home   Kahn; Meyer; Rose
Hearts in Tune   Blake; Sissle
Helen of Troy, New York   Kalmar; Ruby
He'll Always Be One of Those Guys   Yellen
Hello! Goodbye   Harbach
Hello, Hello   Smith, Harry B.
Hermits, The   Hart
He's a Wild Man (When It Comes to Playing Jazz)   Friend; Schwartz, Jean
Hey, Hey, Hazel   Egan; Kahn
Hindoo Hop, The   Brown, A. Seymour
His Royal Shyness   Berlin
Hollywood Rose (You're Out of the Picture Now)   Fisher
Home in Pasadena   Clarke; Leslie; Warren
Home Lights I Long to See   Carroll
Hometown Blues   Coots
Honeymoon Isle   Kern
Honorable Moon   Gershwin, Ira
Hoping   Caesar
Hot Diggity Dog   Johnson, James P.
Hot Hindoo   Gershwin, Ira
Hotsy Totsy Town   Kalmar; Ruby
Hottentot, The   Coslow
House of David Blues   Mills
How Can I Be a Sweet Mama to You   Clare; Friend
How Can I Believe You When You've Lied to Me So Many Times   Johnson, Howard
How Did They Know I Was American   Harbach
How My Sweetie Loves Me, She Loves Me All the Time   Mitchell; Pollack
How Proud I'll Be   Akst; Davis
How Ya Gonna Keep Your Mind on Dancing (When You're Dancing with Someone You Love)?   Brown, Lew; Hanley
(On the Beach at) How've-You-Been?   DeSylva; Gershwin, George
Hubby   Gershwin, Ira
Hugo   Silver
Hurdy Gurdy Man, The   Gershwin, George; Gershwin, Ira
I Am Thinking of You   Caesar
I Can Always Find Another Partner   Hammerstein; Harbach; Youmans
I Can't Forget You   Akst; Lewis; Young, Joseph
I Can't Realize You're Gone   Kahn; Meyer
I Don't Want That Kind of Love   Warren
I Dream of a Castle in Spain   Brennan
I Find 'Em, Fool 'Em, Fondle and Forget 'Em   Schwartz, Jean
I Got It the Fidgety Fidge   Pollack
I Left My Heart with You Virginia   Parish

I Like a Big Town, I Like a Small Town   Kalmar; Ruby
I Like to Walk with a Pal Like You   Blake; Sissle
I Love America   Harbach
I Love 'Er   Akst; Davis
I Love Rosie Casey   Jerome; Schwartz, Jean
I Love You, I Love You, I Love You   Hammerstein; Harbach; Youmans
I May Need You Bad but Not As Bad As All That   Friend
I Must Go to Moscow   Dixon
I Never Broke Nobody's Heart when I Said Good-Bye   Bryan
I Never Knew How Much God Gave to Me   Brennan
I Never Met a Girl Like You   Cohan
I Never Miss the Sunshine (I'm So Used to the Rain)   Parish
I Saw the Roses and Remembered You   Kern
I Still Believe in You   Sterling
I Used to Love to Go Dancing (But Now I Go Dancing to Love)   Johnson, Howard
I Want a Pretty Girl   Harbach
I Want 'em Wild, Weak, Warm and Willing   Coslow
I Want to Step   Coots
I Was So Romantic   Freed, Arthur
I Wish I Could Believe You   Smith, Harry B.; Smith, Robert B.
I Wish I Had a Papa Like the Papa who Lives Next Door   Donaldson
I Wish I Had Someone to Cry Over   Parish
I Wonder How They Get that Way   Buck
I Wonder Why the Glow-Worm Winks His Eye   Hammerstein
I Won't Say I Will, but I Won't Say I Won't   DeSylva; Gershwin, George; Gershwin, Ira
I'd Be a Fool to Fool with You   Turk
I'd Be a Wild Man   Brown, A. Seymour
I'd Love to Have You Love Me All the Time   Clare; Kahn
I'd Love to Waltz Through Life with You   Buck; Herbert
I'd Rather Fox Trot than Waltz   Motzan
If I Can't Get the Sweetie I Want I Pity the Sweetie I Get   Lewis; Schwartz, Jean; Young, Joseph
If I Knew You Then As I Know You Now   Brown, Lew; Hanley
If I Told You   Hammerstein; Harbach; Youmans
If I Were in Love with Somebody Else, I Wouldn't Be Here with You   Howard, Joseph E.
If I Were King   Hart
If My Heart Belonged to Somebody Else   Edwards
If She Was What She Was When She Was Sixteen   Lewis; Meyer; Young, Joseph
If You Do What Your Do   Turk
If You Knew Her Side of the Story   Dubin; McHugh
If You Know How to Strut   Berlin
If You Will Marry Us We'll Stroll Beneath the Babbling Brook   Kalmar; Ruby
If You're Single   Hart; Rodgers
I'll Be with You when the Roses Bloom in Spring   Von Tilzer
I'll Collaborate with You   Hammerstein; Harbach
I'll Say Good Morning where the Morning Glories Grow   Schwartz, Jean
I'm a Business Man   Edwards
I'm a Devil with the Ladies   Atteridge; Caesar; Romberg
I'm a One-Man Mama   Coslow; Donaldson
I'm a Prize   Kern
I'm a Society Bud   Kalmar; Ruby
I'm Arranging for Changing the Key   Egan; Whiting
I'm Bugs Over You   Buck

I'm Feeling Blue for Mammy Lou   Pollack
I'm Going to Meet Minnie Tonight   Edwards; Smith, Robert B.
I'm Gonna Steal Somebody Else's Baby Cause Somebody Else Stole Mine   Davis
I'm Jealous   Akst; Davis
I'm Only a Pilgrim   Smith, Harry B.
I'm Simply Mad about the Man   Friml
I'm Simply Wild about You   Brown, A. Seymour
I'm Sitting Pretty in a Pretty Little City   Baer
I'm Somebody Nobody Loves   Akst; Davis
I'm Sorry Now   Clare; Davis
I'm the Answer to a Maiden's Prayer   Monaco; Rose
Immigration Rose   McHugh
In a Tent   Koehler
In Days of Long Ago   Smith, Harry B.; Snyder
In June   Egan; Whiting
In Love with Love   Friml; Kern
In that Southern Harem of Mine   Akst; Lewis; Meyer; Young, Joseph
In the Cottage of My Heart   Atteridge; Schwartz, Jean
In the Evening   Donaldson
In the Land Where the Green Shamrock Grows   Jerome; Von Tilzer
In the Rain   Gershwin, George
In the Slums (Of the Town)   Cohan
Indiana Moon   Davis
Innocent Eyes   Coots; Schwartz, Jean
Innocent Lonesome Blue Baby   Gershwin, George
Insignificant Me   Smith, Harry B.; Smith, Robert B.
It Seems to Me (inst.)   Waller
It Took a Long Time to Make You Care   Brennan
It Was April   Silver
It Was Meant to Be   Kalmar; Ruby
Italian Whirlwind, The   Cohan
It's a Long, Long Day   Kern
It's a Man Every Time, It's a Man   Dubin; McHugh
It's a Thrill   Smith, Harry B.
It's Just that Feeling for Home   Ahlert; Lewis; Young, Joseph
I've Been Waiting for You   Atteridge; Gorney
I've Been Wanting You   Atteridge
I've Got the Yes, We Have No Banana Blues   Brown, Lew; Hanley
I've Got Those Laughin' While My Heart Is Breaking Blues   Meyer
I've Got to Go to Sleep My Baby Blues   Hanley
I've Got You and You've Got Me   Brown, Lew; Henderson
Jack and Jill   Harbach; Hart; Rodgers
Jackie Coogan   Atteridge; Schwartz, Jean
Japanese Willow   Coots
Javanese Flower   Pollack
Jazz Wedding   Atteridge; Schwartz, Jean
Jazzing Thunder Storming Dance (Thunderstorm Jazz)   Blake; Sissle
Jazzmania   Brown, Lew; Hanley
Jewel Song, The   Atteridge; Romberg; Schwartz, Jean
Jingle Step   Blake; Sissle
Joe Is Here   Kalmar; Ruby
Johnnie   Atteridge; Schwartz, Jean
Johnny Stop! Please Don't! Mon-Ma   Fisher
Joy Bells   Kern
Julia   Conrad; Davis
Jungle Land   Coslow
Just a Boy that Girls Remember   Clare; Turk
Just a Little Bit of Dreaming   Egan; Whiting

Just a Little Bit of Love   Smith, Harry B.; Snyder
Just a Little Lie   Hart; Rodgers
Just a Little Love Song (Mais le Son de Ta Voix)   Lewis;
    Young, Joseph
Just a Little Song for You   Smith, Harry B.
Just a Pretty Little Home   Brown, A. Seymour
Just Act Natural   Cohan
Just for Remembrance Bring Me a Red Red Rose   Parish
Just Hot   McHugh
Just Like a Diamond   Atteridge; Schwartz, Jean
Just Look Around   Hammerstein; Youmans
Kaintucky   Kahn
Kama's Garden   Caesar
Katinka   DeSylva; Gershwin, George; Goetz
Kayo Tortoni   Buck
Keep A-Countin' Eight   Cohan
Kerchoo   Dixon; Rose
Keyboard Strut, The   Coslow; Mills
Keys of My Heart, The   Harbach
Kid Is Clever, The   Edwards; Smith, Robert B.
King Solomon   Brown, A. Seymour
Kissable Lips   Atteridge; Schwartz, Jean
Kissing Time   Meyer
La Favorite   Friml
Lace Makers' Song   Harbach
Ladies and Babies a la Mode   Edwards; Smith, Robert B.
Lady   Coots; Friml; Schwartz, Jean
Lady Fair   Buck; Friml
Lady Fan   Buck
Lady of the Lake   Parish
Lady of the Lantern (inst.)   Herbert
Land of Enchantment (Land of Romance)   Smith, Harry B.
Last Kiss of the First Love, The   Fisher
Last Night on the Back Porch (I Loved Her Best of
    All)   Brown, Lew
Laugh It Off   Hammerstein; Youmans
Laugh While You're Dancing Around   Turk
Laugh Your Cares Away   DeSylva; Gershwin, George; Goetz
Laughter and Love and You   Brennan
Lazy Mama, Can't I Get You Up?   Lewis; Young, Joseph
Learn to Do the Strut   Berlin
Left All Alone with the Blues   Kalmar; Ruby
Legend of the Drums   Buck; Herbert
Legend of the Woodland, A   Atteridge; Schwartz, Jean
Lest You Forget   Carroll
Let's Be Lonesome Together   DeSylva; Gershwin, George;
    Goetz
Let's Take a Car Ride   Rose
Let's You and I Just Say Good-Bye   Cohan
Life of a Rose, The   Atteridge; DeSylva; Gershwin, George;
    Romberg; Schwartz, Jean
Life Savin' Jim   Conrad
Lift Every Voice and Sing   Johnson, J. Rosamond
Lilac Lane   Egan
Listen Mr. Verdi   Smith, Harry B.; Smith, Robert B.
Little Angel Cake   Kern
Little Bit of Jazz, A   Kalmar; Ruby
Little Boy Blue Jeans   Edwards; Smith, Robert B.
Little Boy Blues   Turk
Little Butterfly   Berlin
Little Old New York   Buck; Herbert
Little Rhythm, Go 'Way   Gershwin, Ira
Little Rover, Don't Forget to Come Back Home   Donaldson;
    Kahn
Little Scandal Dolls   DeSylva; Gershwin, George; Goetz

Little Wooden Whistle Wouldn't Whistle, The   Von Tilzer
Live While You're Here   Brown, A. Seymour
Lo-La-Lo   DeSylva; Gershwin, George
Lonely for You   Kahn
Lonely Lady   Hammerstein; Youmans
Lonely Little Wallflow'r   Kahn
Lonesome at Twilight   Koehler
Lonesome Cinderella   Brown, Lew; Hanley
Long Ago 'Mid Apple Blossoms   Kahn
Long Lost Mamma (Daddy Misses You)   Woods
Longing   Friml
Look for the Happy Ending   Kalmar; Ruby
Look in the Looking Glass   DeSylva; Gershwin, George;
    Goetz
Looking for a Bully   Howard, Joseph E.
Lost Melody   Kahn
Lotus Flower   Atteridge; Romberg; Schwartz, Jean
Louisville Lou, the Vampin' Lady   Ager; Yellen
Lou'siana   Donaldson; Kahn
Love Dreams   Cohan
Love in a Haystack   Atteridge; Schwartz, Jean
Love Is a Garden of Roses   Edwards; Smith, Robert B.
Love Is All   Brown, A. Seymour
Love Lit Eyes   Atteridge; Romberg
Love, My Heart Is Calling You   Lewis; Young, Joseph
Love Thoughts   Friml
Love through the Ages   Smith, Harry B.; Snyder
Lover   Clare; Conrad
Love's Last Day   Smith, Harry B.
Lovey   Caesar; Conrad
Lovey Came Back   Lewis; Young, Joseph
Lovin' Chile   Blake; Sissle
Lucky in Love   Atteridge; Caesar; Romberg
Lullaby Lane   Caesar
Mad Cause You Treat Me This Way   McHugh
Madame Pompadour   Atteridge; Schwartz, Jean
Magic Eyes   Brown, Lew
Magic Waltz, The   Yellen
Maid of Gold   Buck; Friml
Maid of Mesh   Berlin
Mais le Son de Ta Voix (Just a Little Love Song)   Lewis;
    Young, Joseph
Mama Loves Papa, Papa Loves Mama   Baer; Friend
Mamma Goes Where Papa Goes, or Papa Don't Go Out
    Tonight   Ager; Yellen
Mamma's Baby Boy   Fain
Mammy's Day in Dixie-Land   Akst; Lewis; Meyer; Young,
    Joseph
Mammy's Little Silver Lining   Hanley
Man in the Moon, The   Smith, Harry B.
Man Never Knows when a Woman's Gonna Change Her
    Mind, A   Friend
Man, the Master   Gershwin, Ira
Manita Wanna Eat, Wanna Eat   Coslow
Marathon Step, The   Cohan
March Louis XI (inst.)   Rodgers
Marching Down the Aisle   Monaco; Rose
Married Life Blues   Harbach
(What Do You Do on a Sunday) Mary   Caesar
Mary Jane McKane   Hammerstein; Youmans
Mary Louise   Gershwin, Ira
Mary Rose   Buck
Maxie Jones, King of the Saxie-Phones   Clarke; Leslie
Maybe It's All for the Best   Lewis; Meyer; Young, Joseph
Meadow Scandal, A   Young, Victor

Mean Mean Mean   Parish
Meet Me Down on Main Street   Kern
Melancholy   Friend
Melody Isle   Kahn
Melody of Mine   Coslow
'Member When   Edwards; Smith, Robert B.
Midnight Blues   Gershwin, George
Midnight Rose   Mitchell; Pollack
Mindin' My Business   Donaldson
Minnie the Mermaid   DeSylva
Minuet (inst.)   Rodgers
Minuette, A   Atteridge; Schwartz, Jean
Mirror Mine   Atteridge; Gorney
Miss Whoozis and Mr. Whatchaname   Smith, Harry B.;
    Snyder
(I'm) Missin' Mammy's Kissin'   Pollack
Modern Bride   Friml
Modern Maiden's Prayer, A   Mitchell; Pollack; Silver
Molly O'Mara   Lewis; Young, Joseph
Monkey Business   Dixon
Moon Love   Kern
Moonglow   Motzan
Moonlight and Roses   DeSylva; Donaldson
Moonlight Ballet (inst.)   Herbert
Moonlight in Versailles   Gershwin, George
Moonlight Kisses   Caesar; Conrad
Moonlight on the Waters   Friml
Moonlight Sonata   Caesar
More   Coslow; Mitchell; Pollack; Silver
Mose   Coslow; Mitchell
Mother's Kiss at Praying Time, A   Lewis; Schwartz, Jean;
    Young, Joseph
My All   Gershwin, Ira
My Boy and I   Hammerstein; Youmans
My Brother's Coming with Pineapples   Mitchell; Pollack
My Cavalier   Caesar; Conrad
My Cherokee Rose   Harbach
My Crinoline Girl   Blake; Sissle
My Dutch Lady   Atteridge; Schwartz, Jean
My Gaby Doll   Atteridge; Romberg; Schwartz, Jean
My Gang   Cohan
My Ideal   Kalmar; Ruby
My Isle of Sweethearts   Caesar; Conrad
My Love Bouquet   Atteridge; Caesar; Romberg
My Love Will Outlive It All   Kahn
My Old Ramshackle Shack Where the Rambler Roses
    Ramble 'Round (Where the Rambler Roses Ramble
    'Round My Old Ramshackle Shack)   Ager; Yellen
My Rainbow   Atteridge; Romberg; Schwartz, Jean
My Rose   Coots; Schwartz, Jean
My Studebaker Girl   Leslie
My Sweetie Went Away She Didin't Say Where or When or
    Why   Turk
My Sweetie's Sweeter than That   Koehler
My 'Tucky Home   Lewis; Meyer; Young, Joseph
My Waltz Divine   Razaf
Nashville Nightingale   Caesar; Gershwin, George
'Neath Egyptian Skies   Yellen
Nellie, Take the Whole Darn Farm   Kahn
Nevada, The   Gershwin, Ira
Next Sunday Morning, He'll Get His Where I Got
    Mine   Sterling
Night After Night   Lewis; Meyer; Young, Joseph
Nijigo Novgo   Kalmar; Ruby
Nita, I Need You   Gorney

No, No, Nora   Kahn
No One Can Toddle Like My Cousin Sue   Razaf
No Tickee, No Shirtee   Conrad
Nobody Ever Cried Over Me   Dixon
Nobody Loves You Like I Do   Lewis; Meyer; Young, Joseph
Nobody's Sweetheart   Kahn
Non-Stop Dancing   Kern
Non-Stop Lovin' Man   Ager; Yellen
Not a Chance in the World   Brown, Lew; Clare; Hanley
Not Here, Not There, It's Fifty Miles from Nowhere   Dixon
Not in Business Hours   Hammerstein; Youmans
Not Yet Suzette   Coots; Coslow
Now that I Need You You're Gone   Clarke; Leslie
Nursery Clock (inst.), The   Kern
Nutsey Fagan   Dixon; Rose
Oedipus Rex a la Jazz   Atteridge; Schwartz, Jean
Oh, for the Life of a Bootlegger's Wife   Edwards; Smith,
    Robert B.
Oh, Joe!   Smith, Harry B.; Snyder
Oh! Min   Conrad
Oh! Nina   Gershwin, George
Oh, Those Sunday Drivers   Conrad; Donaldson; Johnson,
    Howard
Old Folks at Home, The   Egan; Kahn; Whiting
Old Kentucky Blues   Kahn
Old King Tut (In King Tutenkhamen's Day)   Jerome; Von
    Tilzer
Old Stuff   Young, Victor
Old Virginia Reel, The   Smith, Harry B.
Old Yeller Dog of Mine   Clarke; Leslie
On a Holiday   Cohan
On Hawaiian Shores   Friml
On Saturday Night   Clare; Conrad
On the Boulevard   Atteridge; Caesar; Romberg
On the Isle of Wicki Wacki Woo   Donaldson; Kahn
On the Screen   Coots
On the Wings of Romance   Gershwin, Ira
Once in a Blue Moon   Kern
One Girl   Berlin
One Good Time   Friml
One Last Waltz (One More Waltz)   Smith, Harry B.; Snyder
Onions Bring Mem'ries of You   Donaldson; Friend
Orange Grove in California, An   Berlin
Oriental Divertissement   Brown, A. Seymour
Oswald, Ah's Wald About You   Clare; Friend
Oui, Oui, Madame   Edwards; Smith, Robert B.
Oui, Oui, Monsieur   Ager; Yellen
Our Little Home   Gilbert
Our Lovely Rose   Kern
Out There in the Sunshine with You   Brennan
Out Where the Blue Begins   McHugh
Overture (inst.)   Herbert
Paisley Shawl   Ager; Yellen
Pal of My Dreams   Friend
Palace Dance (inst.)   Kern
Palula Moon   Schwartz, Arthur
Pango Pango   Atteridge; Caesar; Gershwin, George
Papa Blues   Leslie
Parisienne   Lewis; Young, Joseph
Passers By   Smith, Harry B.; Smith, Robert B.
Passing Fancies   Smith, Harry B.; Snyder
Passionetta   Dixon
Penny for Your Thoughts, A   Hart; Rodgers
Phos-Phos, Phis-Phos, Phos-Phos   Brown, Lew
Pickles   Young, Joseph

Pie   Kern
Piper You Must Pay (Pay the Piper), The   Smith, Harry B.
Plain Jane   Hammerstein; Youmans
Please Come Again, Summer Days   Jerome; Schwartz, Jean
Plot Again, The   Cohan
Polly-olly-o   Dixon; Henderson; Rose
Poor Little Rose   Donaldson; Kahn
Poor Little Wallflower   Johnson, Howard
Poor Old World   Cohan
Portango (inst.)   Motzan
Prelude   Herbert
Prelude (inst.)   Kern
Pretty City Girl   Harbach
Pretty Little Thing   Akst; Davis
Prologue   Atteridge; Romberg; Schwartz, Jean
Queen of the Gas House Gang   Ager; Yellen
Queens of Long Ago   Atteridge; Schwartz, Jean
Radi-adi-o   Johnson, Howard
Radiant Diamonds   Atteridge; Romberg
Raggedy Ann   Kern
Rags Is Royal Raiments   Friml
Rainbow Gold   Smith, Harry B.
Raisin' the Roof   Caesar; Conrad
Ran Tin Tin   Atteridge; Schwartz, Jean
Red Hot   Koehler
Red Light Annie   Buck
Red Light Rosie   Lewis; Meyer; Young, Joseph
Red Moon   Brown, Lew
Red Riding Hood on Broadway   Coots
Red Rose of Spain, Coralito Mine   Caesar
Regret   Friend
Regular Guy, A   Blake; Sissle
Remember the Waltz   Mitchell
Remember You Belong to Me   Monaco
Riga Rose   Dixon
Ring for Rosy   Smith, Harry B.; Smith, Robert B.
Ring to the Name of Rosie, A   Cohan
Ritzi Mitzi   Conrad; Johnson, Howard
Roamin' to Wyomin'   Clare; Donaldson
Rock Me to Sleep with My Virginia Melody   Henderson
Rock-a-Bye Town   Meyer; Sterling
Rocky Mountain Moon   Egan; Whiting
Rocky Mountain Rose   Turk
Roll Along Missouri   Kalmar; Ruby
Romance   Atteridge; Romberg
Romeo   Caesar
Rose, My Heart's Rosary   Donaldson; Jerome
Rose of the Morning   Romberg
Rosie, My Heart's Rosary   Jerome
Royal Wedding   Atteridge; Romberg; Schwartz, Jean
Rumble of the Subway (Subway Chant), The   Hammerstein; Youmans
Russian Art   Buck
Sahara Butterfly   Kahn
Sam Jones' Blues (You Ain't Talkin' to Mrs. Jones)   Turk
Sand Flowers   Blake; Sissle
Sarah from Syracuse   Kalmar; Ruby
Savannah   Donaldson; Kahn
Say It with a Ukelele   Atteridge; Schwartz, Jean
Sayonara   Egan; Whiting
School Days Are Over   Edwards; Smith, Robert B.
School Time   Von Tilzer
Seeing Stars   Caesar; Conrad
See-No-Evil Eye, The   Ager; Yellen
Servants' Frolic Dance, The   Cohan

Sextette   Rodgers
Shake Your Feet   Buck
Shakesperian Blues   Ager; Yellen
Shanghai Lullaby   Kahn
Sheba of Georgia, The   Pollack
She's the Same Old Sunbonnet Sue   Edwards; Smith, Robert B.
Shimmy on Your Own Side   Edwards; Smith, Robert B.
Shoulder Arms   Smith, Harry B.
Shuffle Along   Kahn; Meyer
Sighing Bands   Koehler
Sign of the Rose, The   Brown, Lew
Since You Gave Your Heart to Mother You Took the Heart Out of Me   Coslow
Since You Went Away Dear Old Pal   Egan; Kahn; Whiting
Sing Mammy, Sing, Sweet and Low   Johnson, Howard
Singing in the Rain   Gershwin, Ira
Sing-Sing   Brown, A. Seymour
Sittin' in a Corner   Kahn; Meyer
Skiddad Dad Daddlin' Daddy   Lewis; Meyer; Young, Joseph
Slow Poke   Coslow; Silver
Smile Again, Kathleen Mavoureen   Jerome
Smile Will Go a Long, Long Way, A   Davis
S'Nora, How She Can Snora   Coslow; Fisher
Snug As a Bug in a Rug   Harbach
So This Is Love   Goetz
So This Is Venice   Buck; Clarke; Leslie; Warren
Some Day   Smith, Harry B.
Some Early Morning   Monaco
Some How   Schwartz, Jean
Some Like to Hunt   Hammerstein; Harbach
Some More   Atteridge; Schwartz, Jean
Somebody Else Took You Out of My Arms, but They Can't Take You Out of My Heart   Conrad; Rose
Somebody's Wrong   Egan; Whiting
Someday You'll Realize   Gershwin, Ira
Someone Will Make You Smile (Vienna Dreams)   Caesar
Something's Happened to Rosie   Cohan
Somewhere in Somebody's Arms   Carroll; Kalmar; Ruby
Somewhere, Somehow, Someday   Carroll
Song of a Summer Night   Akst; Kahn
Sorry   Akst; Davis
South Sea Eyes   Akst
South Sea Serenade   Coslow
Spanish Dance   Atteridge; Caesar; Romberg
Spanish Love   Caesar; Gershwin, George
Speed   Hammerstein; Youmans
Springtime   Buck
Stacko Lee   Fisher
Stage Society   Cohan
Star of Stars   Coots
Stay Home, Little Girl, Stay Home   Brown, Lew; Hanley
Steady Eddie   Buck
Stealing to Virginia   Donaldson; Kahn
Steamboat Blues   Donaldson; Kahn
Steamboat Sal   Fisher
Stella   Davis
Step on It   Atteridge; Romberg; Schwartz, Jean
Steppin' Out   Conrad; Johnson, Howard
Stepping   Smith, Harry B.; Snyder
Stepping Stones   Kern
Steve   Snyder
Stick to Your Knitting   Hammerstein
Stingo-Stungo   Brown, Lew; Hanley
Stompin' on the Dime   Friend

What Have You to Declare?   Atteridge; Caesar; Romberg

What Makes a Business Man Tired?   Kalmar; Ruby

What the Girls Will Wear   Kalmar; Ruby

What Will Become of Me?   Lewis; Young, Joseph

What's the Use   Woods

When Do We Eat   Coslow

When I Come Back to You   Woods

When I Get in the Movies   Jerome; Schwartz, Jean

When I Have Become a Social Butterfly   Kalmar; Ruby

When I Look at You   Atteridge; Schwartz, Jean

When I Say It's So, It's So   Smith, Harry B.

When I Wonder   Egan; Whiting

When It's Night Time in Italy, It's Wednesday Over
      Here   Brown, Lew

When June Comes Along with a Song   Cohan

When Lights Are Low   Kahn; Koehler

When Mother Sings Sweet and Low   Johnson, Howard

When the Sandman's on His Way   Atteridge; Romberg

When Those Roly Poly Babies Roll Their Eyes   Kahn; Meyer

When Will the Sun Shine for Me   Davis; Silver

When You Learned How to Cry   Motzan

When You Love   Atteridge

When You Take the Road with Me   Kern

When You Walked Out Someone Else Walked Right
      In   Berlin

When Your Bluebird Flies Away   Von Tilzer

Where Can that Somebody Be   Mills

Where Have You Been All My Life   Schwartz, Jean

Where Is My Boy   Caesar; Conrad

Where Is She?   DeSylva; Gershwin, George

Where Is Your Girl, Where Is My Girl   Howard, Joseph E.

Where the Bamboo Babies Grow   Brown, Lew

Where the Ganges Flow   Brown, A. Seymour

While I'm Swinging   Coots

While You're Gone   Akst; Davis

Whip Dance, The   Cohan

Who Cares for a Name   Smith, Harry B.

Who Will It Be   Johnson, Howard; Pollack

Whoa Pagliacci   Young, Joseph

Who'll Buy My Violets   Goetz

Who-oo Is with You Tonight   Meyer

Who's Sorry Now?   Kalmar; Ruby; Snyder

Whose Girl Is That   Dixon

Whose Izzy Is He, Is He Yours or Is He Mine?   Brown, Lew

Why?   Atteridge; Romberg

Why Am I So Sad?   Atteridge; Caesar; Gershwin, George

Why Did I Buy that Morris Chair for Morris?   Kalmar; Ruby

Why Do I Care for You   Yellen

Why Live a Lie   Koehler

Why Should I Give My Love to You?   Conrad

Why Should I Let You?   Atteridge; Schwartz, Jean

Why Should I Weep about One Sweetie (Two, Three or Four
      Sweeties)?   Hanley

Wild Cat Blues   Waller

Wild-Flower   Hammerstein; Harbach; Youmans

Will You Forgive Me   Hart; Rodgers

Will-o-the-Wisp   Smith, Harry B.

With You   Blake; Sissle

Wonderful Dad   Kern

World's Worst Woman, The   Hammerstein; Harbach

Wrap Me Up and Send Me C.O.D. to Tennessee   Johnson,
      Howard

Yankee Doodle Oo-La-La, The   Atteridge; Schwartz, Jean

Years of Love   Friml

Yes! We Have No Bananas Parody   Berlin

Yesterday   Schwartz, Jean

You and I   Friml

You and I (In Old Versailles)   DeSylva; Gershwin, George;
      Goetz

You Can't (Just) Have No One Man By Yourself   Johnson,
      James P.

You Can't Make Love By Wireless   Kern

You Didn't Care when You Broke My Heart   Johnson,
      Howard

You Didn't Want Me when I Wanted You, I'm Somebody
      Else's Now   Yellen

You Got What Gets 'Em   Friml

You Gotta Toodle-oo on a Saxophone, If You Wanna Keep
      Your Sweet Sweet Mama Home   Lewis; Young, Joseph

You Never Can Blame a Girl for Dreaming   Hammerstein;
      Harbach; Youmans

You Remind Me of Someone   Friml

You Said Something when You Said Dixie   Clare; Friend

You Said You Wouldn't, But You Done It   Johnson, James
      P.

You Wanted Someone to Play with, I Wanted Someone to
      Love   Fisher

You'll Find Me Playing Mah-Jongg   Kern

Your Eyes   Kahn

Your Eyes Have Told Me that You Love Me   Buck

Your Hat and My Hat   Berlin

Your Other Side   Atteridge; Romberg; Schwartz, Jean

You're Near but Yet So Far   Akst; Davis

You're Never too Old   Hammerstein; Youmans

You're Trying to Throw Me Down   Turk

You've Gotta See Mamma Ev'ry Night (Or You Can't See
      Mamma at All)   Rose

Yum Tum Tum   Fisher

Yvonne   Caesar

1924

Africa   Hanley

After the Curfew Rings   Kalmar; Ruby

Ain't Got No One, Never Had   Kalmar; Ruby

Ain't Love Grand   Caesar; Gorney

Alabamy Bound   DeSylva; Henderson

Alaska and a South Sea Island   Young, Victor

All Alone   Berlin

All Alone in a Crowd   Conrad

All Alone with You in a Little Rendezvous   Lewis; Snyder;
      Young, Joseph

All Lanes Must Reach a Turning   Dietz; Kern

All of Them Was Friends of Mine   Gershwin, Ira

All She Did Was This   Youmans

All the Wrongs You Done to Me   Blake; Sissle

All Year 'Round   Romberg

All You Need Is a Girl   Kern

Along the Rio Grande   Caesar; Conrad; Harbach

Aloysius (Al-o-wish-us)   Meyer; Turk

Always Look for a Rainbow   Johnson, Howard

Always the Same   Coslow; Romberg

American Jazz   Atteridge; Romberg; Schwartz, Jean

And the Band Played On   Fisher

Any Day the Sun Don't Shine   Razaf; Waller

Any Time at All   Coots

Any Way the Wind Blows My Sweetie Goes   Hanley

Anything at Any Time   Razaf

Apache Argentine   Caesar; Conrad; Harbach

Apache Dance   Atteridge; Romberg; Schwartz, Jean

Archibald   Dixon; Henderson
Aren't We All?   Conrad
Artists and Models   Coslow; Romberg
As Long As Happiness Is There   Johnson, Howard
As Long As They Keep on Making Them, I'll Keep Taking
   Them All the Time   Johnson, Howard
At 11 P.M.   Gershwin, Ira
At the End of a Winding Lane   Kahn
At the Rainbow's End   Herbert
Athletic Boy   Caesar; Conrad; Harbach
'Atta Girl   Gershwin, Ira
Baby Be Good   Caesar; Conrad; Harbach
Baby Face   Kalmar; Ruby
Back Where the Daffodils Grow   Donaldson
Bad, Bad Men, The   Gershwin, George; Gershwin, Ira
Bagdad   Ager; Yellen
Bal Tabarin, The   Atteridge; Romberg; Schwartz, Jean
Ballet Dance   Atteridge; Romberg; Schwartz, Jean
Ballet Modern   Youmans
Ballet Music   Gershwin, George
Bandana Ball   Berlin
Bang Up Time   Atteridge; Romberg; Schwartz, Jean
Be the Life of the Crowd   DeSylva; Gershwin, George
Beaded Bag, A   Romberg; Schwartz, Jean
Beau Brummel   Gershwin, George
Beau Brummel Joe (The Beau of Memphis Town)   Warren
Beautiful Volga Blues   Donaldson
Because You're You   Caesar
Behind Milady's Fan   Atteridge; Romberg; Schwartz, Jean
Behind My Lady's Fan   Coslow
Believe Me   Kalmar; Ruby
Berkeley Square and Kew   Gershwin, George
Bertie   Romberg
Best in the Trade, The   Kalmar; Ruby
Best of Everything, The   DeSylva
Betty Lee   Caesar; Conrad; Harbach
Between the Dances   Dubin; McHugh
Beware of Me   Herbert
Big Bad Bill Is Sweet William Now   Ager; Yellen
Big Boy!   Ager; Yellen
Big Butter and Egg Man, The   Clare; Friend
Biminy   Buck
Birds Are Winging   Romberg
Bloody Razor Blues   Waller
Blue Nights   Rose
Blue Strain, The   Waller
Blues Have Got Me, The   Clarke; Johnston; Meyer; Silver;
   Turk
Bo Koo   Youmans
Bobbed-Haired Bandit Stole My Heart Away, A   Razaf
Bom-Bom-Beedle-Um-Bo   Caesar; Gorney
Bonga-Boo   Gorney
Bongo on the Congo   Kern
Bonnie   Johnson, Howard
Boost New York   Friend
Bowery Rose   Johnson, Howard
Boxing Bout According to F Sharp, A   Johnson, Howard
Boy Wanted   Gershwin, George; Gershwin, Ira
Breakin' 'Em Down   Blake; Sissle
Bridal Procession   Hammerstein; Harbach
Brindle's Farm   Atteridge
Bring Back Those Rock-a-Bye Baby Days   Silver
Bring Me a Radio   Porter
Brittany   Porter
Broad Highway   Romberg

Broadcast a Jazz   Porter
Broken Butterfly   Brown, Lew
Bubble Song   Herbert
Bubbles   Atteridge; Jerome; Romberg; Schwartz, Jean
Buck   Atteridge; Romberg; Schwartz, Jean
Bullet Wound Blues   Waller
By Our Bearing So Sedate   Romberg
Bye Bye Baby   Motzan
Call of the South, The   Berlin
Call the Plumber In   Razaf; Waller
Cannibal Love   Fisher
Carnival of Springtime   Romberg
Carnival Time   Gershwin, George; Gershwin, Ira
Caterpillar (Winged Dreams), The   Young, Victor
Charleston Charley   Mills
Charley My Boy   Kahn
Charm   Coslow; Romberg
Cheer, Girls, Cheer   Caesar; Conrad; Harbach
Cheer Up the Old Folks at Home   Mitchell; Pollack
Cheerio!   Gershwin, Ira
Chic-Chic Chiquita   Donaldson
Chickie   Mills
Chili Bom Bom   Donaldson; Friend
(Those Beautiful) Chimes   Johnson, Howard
Chiquette   Atteridge; Romberg; Schwartz, Jean
Chocolate Dandies   Blake; Sissle
Cielito Lindo (Beautiful Heaven)   Dubin
Clementine   Brown, Nacio Herb
Cling Cling   Herbert
Cold, Cold Mammas Burn Me Up   Gilbert
Come Along with Alice   Berlin
Come, Answer to Our Call   Romberg
Come Boys   Romberg
Come Down to Argentine   Johnson, Howard
Come On, Let's Go   Youmans
Come on Red, You Red Hot Devil Man   Fisher
Come Sir, Will You Join Our Noble Saxton Corps   Romberg
Come to My Party   Romberg
Cotton Blossom Lullaby   Kahn
Could You Care for Me   Rose
Could You Get Along with Me?   Caesar; Gorney
Countryside (This Is the Life for a Man), The   Gershwin,
   George
Couple of Senseless Censors, A   Berlin
Cowboy Songs   Caesar; Conrad; Harbach
Cross-Word Mamma You Puzzle Me (But Papa's Gonna
   Figure You Out)   Clare; Monaco
Da Da Nellie Goodbye   Fisher
Daffy-Dill, The   Conrad
Daily Dozen, The   Caesar; Conrad; Harbach
Damn Clever, These Chinese   Atteridge; Romberg;
   Schwartz, Jean
Dance Eccentric (inst.)   Romberg
Dance of Beauty   Atteridge; Romberg; Schwartz, Jean
Dance Your Way to Paradise   Gorney
Dancin' on a Dime   Conrad
Dancing   Conrad
Dancing Colors   Coslow
Dancing 'Round   Herbert
Dancing Time   Dietz; Kern
Danse de Volstead   Atteridge; Romberg; Schwartz, Jean
Day Dreams   Atteridge; Kalmar; Romberg; Ruby; Schwartz,
   Jean
Dear Old Correspondence School   Gershwin, Ira

Dear Old Moulin Rouge   Atteridge; Romberg; Schwartz, Jean
Dear One   Coots
Deep in My Heart   Youmans
Deep in My Heart Dear   Romberg
Dipping in the Moonlight   Caesar
Dixie Dreams   Clarke; Johnston; Meyer; Turk
Dixie Moon   Blake; Sissle
Dixie Wildflowers   Clarke; Johnston; Meyer; Turk
Dixie's Favorite Son   Brown, Lew
Do You Love As I Love   Caesar
Does She?   Dixon; Henderson
Does the Spearmint Lose It's Flavor on the Bed Post Overnight   Rose
Doing the Light Fantastic Alley Style   Johnson, Howard
Doing the Town   Kalmar; Ruby
Dollys and Their Collies, The   Porter
Don't Cry for Rover, Fido Is Here   Brown, Lew
Don't Send Me Back to Petrograd   Berlin
Don't You Remember?   Gershwin, Ira
Door of Her Dreams (Bridal Procession)   Friml; Hammerstein; Harbach
Down on the Brandy Wine   Henderson; Rose
Down the Road to Maryland   Coots
Down Where the South Begins   Lewis; Young, Joseph
Dream Maker of Japan   Friml; Lewis; Young, Joseph
Dreamer of Dreams   Kahn
Dreamy Araby   Conrad
Dreamy Delaware   Donaldson
Drinking Song   Romberg
Dublinola   Atteridge; Romberg; Schwartz, Jean
Dumb Dora   Coslow; Silver
Dumb Luck   Blake; Sissle
Easy Goin' Mamma Don't Play Hard to Get with Me   Ahlert; Lewis; Young, Joseph
Eccentric Dance   Hammerstein; Harbach
Egypt, You and I   Kahn
Elegie   Dubin
Eliza   Kahn
Elsie, There Isn't Anybody Else but You   Carroll
En Douce   Atteridge; Romberg; Schwartz, Jean
Enchanted Train, The   Kern
End of a String, The   Gershwin, George; Gershwin, Ira
Evelyn   Conrad
Evening Star   Gershwin, George; Gershwin, Ira
Ever Lovin' Bee   Buck
Every Girl I Get, Somebody Else Takes Her Right Away from Me   Stept
Every Silken Lady   Gorney
Every Time the Clock Ticks   Gorney
Everybody but Me   Meyer; Rose
Everybody Dance   Atteridge; Romberg; Schwartz, Jean
Everybody Yell Meow, Let's See if Kitty's Home   Lewis; Young, Joseph
Ev'ry Time I Pick a Sweetie   Razaf
Faded Rose   Carroll
Fair Weather Friends   Conrad
Fan Number   Atteridge; Romberg; Schwartz, Jean
Farewell Dear   Romberg
Farmer Jacob   Romberg
Fascinating Rhythm   Gershwin, George; Gershwin, Ira
Few Fast Steppers, A   Atteridge; Romberg; Schwartz, Jean
Finale: Can We Do Anything?   Gershwin, George; Gershwin, Ira
First Love   Dubin

First Nighters, The   Johnson, Howard
Flag that Flies, The   Romberg
Flappers   Atteridge; Romberg; Schwartz, Jean
Flat Tire Papa, Mama's Gonna Give You the Air   Waller
Follow Handy Andy   Dietz; Kern
Follow the Swallow   Dixon; Henderson; Rose
Follow Your Star   Coslow
For the Sake of the Baby at Home   Dubin
Forever   Conrad
Forty-Second Street Moon   Caesar; Romberg
Fountain of Youth   Atteridge; Romberg; Schwartz, Jean
Four Little Sirens   Gershwin, George; Gershwin, Ira
Four Little Walls and Me   Akst
Franco-American Step, The   Atteridge; Romberg; Schwartz, Jean
Friendless Blues (inst.)   Waller
Friendship Leads Us to Love   Johnson, Howard
Fun on the Farm   Ahlert; Lewis; Young, Joseph
Garden — The Beauty Contest, A   Herbert
Garden of Love   Schwartz, Jean
Garden of Used to Be, The   Gorney
Garlands Bright   Romberg
Gavotte   Romberg
Get Yourself a Broom and Sweep You Troubles Away   Rose
Giddy-Ap Joe   Lewis; Young, Joseph
Girl Is Like Sunshine, A   Turk
Girl Is Nobody, A   Caesar
Give Him Your Sympathy   Caesar; Conrad; Harbach
Go Away Girls Go Away   Atteridge
Going Rowing   Youmans
Gold Digger's Blues   Coslow
Gold, Silver and Green   Atteridge; Romberg; Schwartz, Jean
Golden Days   Romberg
Goo Googily Goo   Lewis; Young, Joseph
Good Night   Conrad
Good Night, Sleep Tight   Kahn
Good Things and Bad Things   Atteridge; Romberg
Goodbye Dobbin'   Johnson, Howard
Goo-Goo-Good Night Dear   Friend
Gotta Getta Girl   Kahn
Governor's Lady   Caesar
Grab a Girl   Dietz; Kern
Grass Is Always Greener in the Other Fellow's Yard, The   Egan; Whiting
Grass Widows   Coslow
Great Wide Open Spaces, The   Buck
Gypsy Caravan   Dietz; Kern
Gypsy Girl   Herbert
Gypsy Life   Herbert
Gypsy Love Song   Herbert
Gypsy Maid   Wrubel
Half of It, Dearie, Blues, The   Gershwin, George; Gershwin, Ira
Hand in Hand   McHugh
Hand-Me-Down Blues, The   Youmans
Hang on to Me   Gershwin, George; Gershwin, Ira
Hang Up Papa, You're on a Busy Line   Razaf
Happiness   Jerome
Happy Endings   Atteridge
Happy Melody   Caesar
Happy New Year Blues, The   Berlin
Hard Boiled Rose   McHugh; Mills
Hard Hearted Hannah   Ager; Yellen
Hard-Boiled Herman   Hammerstein; Harbach
Hard-Boiled Rose   Dubin

Has Anyone Seen Heine   Rose
Have a Good Time Everybody   Blake; Sissle
Have a Heart   Johnson, Howard
He Looks at Her and Then He Goes
    Ha-Ha-Ha-Ha-Ha   Henderson; Rose
He Only Comes to See Me Once in a While   Clarke;
    Johnston; Meyer; Turk
Heart O'Mine (Merry Wives of Gotham)   Herbert
Hee-Bee Jee-Bees   Gorney
Heebie Jeebie Blues   Clarke; Johnston; Meyer; Turk
Helen Maria   Kahn
Hello Atlanta Town   Waller
Here Comes the Banana Man   Fain
Here It Is Daddy (No Hand Has Touched It but Mine)   Mills
He's the Hottest Man in Town   Gorney
He's the Kind of a Man that You Like (If You Like that Kind
    of a Man)   Lewis; Snyder; Young, Joseph
Hey! Hey! And Hee! Hee! (I'm Charleston Crazy)   Mills
Hey! Hey! Let 'er Go!   DeSylva; Gershwin, George
Hindoo Song of Love   (Inst.)   Henderson
(If I Were of the) Hoi Polloi   Conrad
Holidays   Atteridge; Romberg; Schwartz, Jean
Hollywood   Atteridge; Romberg
Home Alone Blues   Waller
Honduras   Kalmar; Ruby
Honey-Bun   Youmans
Honeymoon Blues   Conrad
Hoodoo Man, The   Brown, Nacio Herb
Hooray for the U.S.A.!   DeSylva; Gershwin, George
Hot Tamale Baby   Razaf
Hot-Hot-Hottentot   Fisher
How Can a Lady Be Certain?   Conrad
How Do I Know He Loves Me?   Conrad
How I Love that Girl   Kahn
How My Sweetie Loves Me, She Loves Me All the
    Time   Coots
Hula Hula Dream Girl   Kahn
Hula, Hula, Sailor Man   Atteridge; Romberg; Schwartz, Jean
Hula Lou   Yellen
Hurry Up   Atteridge; Romberg; Schwartz, Jean
I Ain't Got Nobody to Love   Coslow; Silver
I Am Thinking of You   Caesar; Conrad; Harbach
I Believe You   Buck
I Came Here   Gershwin, Ira
I Can Get More Lovin' from a Dum, Dum, Dummy than I've
    Been Getting from You   Brown, Lew; Henderson; Rose
I Can't Forget Your Eyes   Smith, Harry B.; Snyder
I Can't Get the One I Want   Rose
I Can't Stop Babying You   Kahn
I Cantelope Tonight   Johnson, Howard
I Couldn't Get to It   Woods
I Don't Care What You Used to Be (I Know What You Are
    To-Day)   Dubin; McHugh
I Don't Know Why I Love You, I Only Know I Do   Kahn
I Don't Know Why You Make Me Love You   Dixon;
    Henderson; Rose
I Don't Want a Girlie   Henderson
I Don't Want to Get Married, I'm Having too Much
    Fun   Jerome
I Hear You Calling, Pal of Mine   Dubin; McHugh
I Just Can't Make My Heart Behave   Von Tilzer
I Know that I Love You   Kalmar; Ruby
I Long to Belong   Gorney
I Lost a Wonderful Pal When I Lost You   Dubin
I Lost My Heart in June   Parish

I Love a Lark   Atteridge; Romberg; Schwartz, Jean
I Love a Little Love Now and Then   Donaldson
I Love Him   Friml; Hammerstein; Harbach
I Love Him Just the Same   Rose
I Love the Boys   Atteridge; Romberg; Schwartz, Jean
I Love Them All   Conrad
I Love to Dance When I Hear a March   Coots; Coslow
I Love You, My Darling   DeSylva; Gershwin, George
I Loved Her Best of All   Atteridge; Romberg; Schwartz, Jean
I Make Hay While the Moon Shines   Gershwin, George
I May Be a Little Green, But I Ain't No Fool   Waller
I Must Have Company   Kahn; Meyer
I Need a Garden   DeSylva; Gershwin, George
I Need Some Pettin'   Kahn
I Need Somebody to Lullaby Me   Coslow; Silver
I Never Knew What Love Could Do   Arlen
I Picked the Wrong One to Love   Kahn
I Popped the Question to Her Pop   Johnson, Howard
I Want a Phos Phos   Brown, Lew
I Want to Be a Ballet Dancer   Berlin
I Want to Be Left Alone   Kahn
I Want to Be Loved   Romberg
I Want to Be There   Dietz; Kern
I Want to Go Home   Atteridge; Jerome; Romberg;
    Schwartz, Jean
I Want to See My Tennessee   Ager; Yellen
I Want Twins   Porter
I Wonder What's Become of Sally   Ager; Yellen
I Wonder Who's Dancing with You Tonight   Dixon;
    Henderson; Rose
I Would Rather Dance a Waltz   Kalmar; Ruby
Ice Cold Papa, Mama's Gonna Melt You Down   Razaf;
    Waller
I'd Give Every Rose on Broadway for that Little Rose Back
    Home   Fisher
I'd Like to Believe You   Henderson; Motzan; Rose
I'd Like to Poison Ivy   Hart; Rodgers
I'd Rather Be Blue than Green   Razaf; Waller
If All My Thoughts Were Stars   Conrad
If I Can't Sing About My Mammy, I Don't Want to Sing at
    All   Conrad; Lewis; Young, Joseph
If I Only Had You Back Again How Different Things Would
    Be   Turk
If It's All Right with You, It's All Right with Me   Clare;
    Monaco; Rose
If My Dreams Came True   Johnston
If My Dreams Come True   Clarke; Meyer; Turk
If Somebody Only Would Find Me   Herbert
If We Could Live on Promises   Johnson, Howard
If You Can't Kiss Your Popper Proper, You Can Kiss Your
    Popper Good-Bye   Dixon; Henderson
If You Don't Tell Me How Am I Gonna Know?   Henderson
If You Haven't Got the Things It Takes to Hold Your Man,
    Then You Can't Blame Me   Razaf
If You Think It's Love You're Right   Dietz; Kern
I'll Find My Love in D-I-X-I-E   Blake; Sissle
I'll Make the Pies Like Mother if You'll Make the Dough
    Like Dad   Von Tilzer
I'll See You in My Dreams   Kahn
I'll Take Her Back If She Wants to Come Back   Leslie;
    Monaco
I'm a Little Blackbird Looking for a Bluebird   Clarke;
    Johnston; Meyer; Turk
I'm Blue for My Little Gray Home   Fisher
I'm Coming at Your Call   Romberg

(Oh You Fool) I'm Crazy for You   Silver; Turk
I'm Forever Falling in Love with Someone   Monaco
I'm Goin to Lose Myself when I Find Myself in My Sweetie's
   Arms   Akst
I'm Going Back   DeSylva; Gershwin, George
I'm Going Right Along   Waller
I'm Going to Dance at Your Wedding   Caesar; Conrad;
   Harbach
I'm Gonna Bring a Watermelon to My Girl Tonight   Conrad;
   Rose
I'm Gonna Tie Myself to Dixieland with the Mason-Dixon
   Line   Coots; Mitchell; Pollack
I'm Gonna Tramp, Tramp, Tramp   DeSylva; Woods
I'm Happy Now   Turk
I'm in Love Again   Porter
I'm in Love with the Prince of Wales   Conrad
I'm Only Human, That's All   Johnson, Howard
I'm Satisfied Beside that Sweetie o' Mine   Yellen
I'm Up in Heaven When You're in My Arms   Silver; Turk
I'm Worried Over You   Kahn
Imagine Me Without My You (And You Without Your
   Me)   Gershwin, Ira
Imagine Me without You   Gorney
In a Bungalow   Conrad
In Bamville   Blake; Sissle
In California   Gorney
In Dreams with You   Sterling
In Dutch   Caesar
In Every Dancing Show   Atteridge; Romberg; Schwartz, Jean
In Harlem   Waller
In Harlem's Araby   Waller
In My Baby's Eyes   Waller
In My Own Backyard   Donaldson; Rose
In My Pajamas   Pollack
In Shadowland   Ahlert; Lewis; Young, Joseph
In the Candle-Light   Coots
In the Corner of My Mind   Kalmar; Ruby
In the Middle of the Night   Donaldson; Rose
In the Musical Comedy Shows   Johnson, Howard
In the Night   Motzan
In the Park   Romberg
In the Shade of a Sheltering Palm   Berlin
In the Springtime   Waller
In This Automatical World   Johnson, Howard
Indian Love Call   Friml; Hammerstein; Harbach
Innocent Eyes   Atteridge; Romberg; Schwartz, Jean
Inspiration   Atteridge; Romberg; Schwartz, Jean
Irish Blues   Johnson, Howard
Is It Any Wonder?   Gorney
Isn't It Terrible What They Did to Mary Queen of
   Scots   Gershwin, George
Isn't It Wonderful   Gershwin, George; Gershwin, Ira
It Had to Be You   Kahn
It Is the Fourteenth of July   Gershwin, George
It Might Have Been Me   Coslow
It Must Be Love   Youmans
It Was Only a Dream   Dixon; Henderson; Rose
It's Better to Wait for Someone You Love   Davis; Silver
It's the Dancer You Love Who Makes You Love to
   Dance   Kalmar; Ruby
It's Young and It Doesn't Know   Dubin
I've Got a Feeling for Ophelia   Dixon; Henderson
I've Got a Thousand Plows and Cows and
   Chickens   Donaldson
Jassamine Lane   Blake; Sissle

Jazz Time Came from the South   Clarke; Johnston; Meyer;
   Turk
Jazztime Baby   Blake; Sissle
Je T'aime . . . a Travers les Ages (You Know You Belong to
   Somebody Else, So Why Don't You Leave Me
   Alone)   Monaco
Je Vous Aime   Coslow
Jefferson Davis, The   Donaldson
Jig Walk   Ellington
Jijibo, The   DeSylva; Gershwin, George
Jim Dandy   Ellington
Jockey's Life for Mine   Blake; Sissle
John Held Jr.   Atteridge; Romberg; Schwartz, Jean
Joy and Gloom   Atteridge; Romberg; Schwartz, Jean
Juanita   Dubin; Gershwin, George; Gershwin, Ira
Judgement Day   Young, Victor
Jump Steady   Blake; Sissle
June Night (Just Give Me a June Night, the Moonlight and
   You)   Baer; Friend
Jungle Nights in Dixieland   Clarke; Johnston; Meyer; Turk
Jungle Town Has Moved to Dixieland   Clarke; Johnston;
   Meyer; Turk
Just for Old Time's Sake   Stept
Just Kids   Carroll
Just Lean on Me   Caesar; Conrad; Harbach
Just Missed the Opening Chorus   DeSylva; Gershwin,
   George
Just One More Night in Your Arms   Fisher
Just Supposing   DeSylva; Gershwin, George
Just Think It Over   Davis
Just We Two   Romberg
Just You   Magidson
Keep Coolidge in the White House   Motzan
Keep the Party Going   Kalmar; Ruby
Killarney, the Blarney and You   Leslie
Kiss Me Goodbye with a Smile   Egan
Kiss Me, That's All   Gershwin, Ira
Kiss You Left Behind, The   Dubin
Kongo Kate   DeSylva; Gershwin, George
La Golondrina   Dubin
La Java   Atteridge; Romberg; Schwartz, Jean
Laddie Daddie   Gershwin, George
Laddie Daddy   Gershwin, Ira
Lak Jeem   Friml; Hammerstein; Harbach
(Down in the) Land of Pickaninnies   Blake; Sissle
Land of Rocky Boo   Caesar
Last Sweetheart of Mine, The   Friend; Monaco
(Laff) Laugh It Off!   Kalmar; Ruby
Laughin' at You   Stept
Lazy   Berlin
Lazy Pickaninny   Gilbert
Lazy Waters   Kahn
Leading Man   Atteridge
Leave It to Love   Gershwin, George; Gershwin, Ira
Leaving Town While We May   Gershwin, George
Lena, You're Leaning All Over Me   Lewis; Young, Joseph
Lenore   Sterling
Lesson in Love, A   Atteridge; Romberg; Schwartz, Jean
Let It Rain, Let It Pour, I'll Be in Virginia in the
   Morning   Donaldson
Let Me Linger Longer in Your Arms   Baer; Friend
Let Me Remember   Kahn
Let's Have a Good Time   Romberg; Schwartz, Jean
Let's Have a Good Time Lolita   Atteridge
Let's Kiss Goodbye   Caesar; Conrad; Harbach

Let's Waken the World with a Love Song   Egan; Whiting
Levee Lou   Howard, Joseph E.
Life of a Sailor, The   Porter
Lily Pool, The   Coslow; Romberg
Linger in the Lobby   Gershwin, George; Gershwin, Ira
Linger Longer Love   Donaldson
Listen In, Virginia   Mills
Listening   Berlin
Listening to the Radio   Atteridge; Romberg
Little Black Buddie   Egan; Whiting
Little By Little   Rose; Woods
Little Devil   Johnson, Howard
Little Did I Know   Motzan
Little Dixie Lady   Brown, Lew
Little Jazz Bird   Gershwin, George; Gershwin, Ira
Little Moth Keep Away from the Flame   Von Tilzer
Little Old Clock on the Mantel, The   Kahn
Little Pal (Where Are You Tonight)   Parish
Little Pony of Mine   Caesar; Conrad; Harbach
Little Theatre   Gershwin, George; Gershwin, Ira
Live Wire, The   Gershwin, George
Log Cabin Blues   Mills
Lolita   Romberg; Schwartz, Jean
Lonely Little Melody   Buck
Lonely Me   Stept
Look Out for Us, Broadway   Kalmar; Ruby
Look-A What I Got Now   Lewis; Young, Joseph
Lost World, The   Friml; Smith, Harry B.
Louis XIII Gavotte   Youmans
Louisiana   Romberg
Louwanna   Schwartz, Jean
Love and Leave 'em Joe   Dixon; Henderson
Love C.O.D.   Caesar
Love Comes But Once in a Lifetime   Johnson, Howard
Love in a Cottage   Youmans
Love Is Blind   Dubin
Love Is Just a Gamble (Take Another Chance)   Mills
Love Is Like a Pinwheel   Atteridge; Romberg; Schwartz, Jean
Lovers of Art   DeSylva; Gershwin, George
Lover's Waltz   Yellen
Loving You   Stept
Lucille   Gilbert; Silver
Lucky Boy   Clarke; Leslie; Monaco
Lucky Kentucky   Dixon; Henderson; Rose
Madeline Be Mine   Baer; Friend
Magic of Springtime, The   Romberg
Mah-Jongg   DeSylva; Gershwin, George
Maiden Let Me In   Herbert
Main Street Wasn't Big Enough for Mary   Davis; Silver
Make Every Day a Holiday   Porter
Make Love in the Morning   Herbert
Making a Venus   Herbert
Mama Kiki — Papa Wacki   Fisher
Mama Like You and a Papa Like Me, A   Rose; Woods
Mama Said No   Donaldson
Mamie McGee   Carroll
Man I Love, The   Gershwin, George; Gershwin, Ira
Manda   Blake; Sissle
Mandy, I'm Just Wild about You   Waller
Mandy Make Up Your Mind   Clarke; Johnston; Meyer; Turk
Manners and Motions   Coslow; Romberg
Marjorie   Atteridge
Matrimonial Handicap, The   DeSylva; Gershwin, George
May I Come to See You, Dear, Tonight?   Romberg

Maybe (She'll Write Me) (She'll Phone Me)   Ahlert; Snyder; Turk
Maybe You Will, Maybe You Won't   Dixon
Maybells   Atteridge; Romberg; Schwartz, Jean
Maytime   DeSylva
Me and the Boy Friend   Clare
Me and You   Gorney
Meana Chimes   Motzan
Mediterranean Nights   Coslow
Meet Me in Roseland   McHugh
Memory Lane   Conrad; DeSylva
Millennium, The   Atteridge; Romberg; Schwartz, Jean
Mindin' My Business   Kahn
Minuet of the Minute, The   Hammerstein; Harbach
Mirage, The   Coslow; Romberg
Mistletoe Waltz   Clarke; Leslie
Model Toddle   Coslow
Models, The   Coslow
Molly   Kalmar; Ruby
Monastery   Atteridge
Money Doesn't Mean a Thing   Gershwin, Ira
Monterey   Caesar; Conrad; Harbach
Montmartre   Buck
Mooching Along   Romberg; Schwartz, Jean
Moon of the Orient   Turk
Moonlight Mama   Hart; Rodgers
Mophams, The   Gershwin, George
More You Get It the More You Want It, The   Razaf
Mormon Life, A   Dietz; Kern
Morning Won't You Ever Come 'Round   Silver; Turk
Mounties, The   Friml; Hammerstein; Harbach
Mr. and Mrs. Rover   Kern
Mrs. Murphy's Chowder   Clarke; Leslie
Musical Shoes   Atteridge; Romberg; Schwartz, Jean
Must It Be Good-Bye?   DeSylva
My Baby's Comin' Back Home   Waller
My Beautiful Mexican Rose   Mills
My Best Girl   Donaldson
My Boy   Conrad; Coots
My Daddy's Growin' Old, So I'll Have to Look Aroun'   Razaf
My Dream Girl (I Loved You Long Ago)   Herbert
My Gal Don't Love Me Anymore   Friend
My Gal, Won't You Come Back to Me? (My Gal, My Pal)   Arlen
My Heart Is Yours   Gershwin, Ira
My Heart's Desire   Sterling
My Hero   Herbert
My Houseboat on the Hudson   Dietz; Kern
My Jamaica Love   Razaf; Waller
My Kid   Dubin; McHugh
My Little Dream Boat   Donaldson
(You're Mighty Lucky) My Little Ducky   DeSylva; Gershwin, George
My Long Ago Girl   Porter
My Man Cures the Blues   Waller
My Old Home Town   Freed, Arthur
My Oomday Oombay Down in Boom Boom Bay   Brown, Lew; Dixon; Henderson
My Papa Doesn't Two-Time No Time   Donaldson
My Radio Man (Tell My Mammy to Come Back Home)   Friend
My Rose   Atteridge; Romberg; Schwartz, Jean
My Sweet Baby Irene   Razaf; Waller
My Sweetheart   Kahn

My Twilight Rose   Romberg
Nature   Atteridge
Naughty Baby   Gershwin, George; Gershwin, Ira
Naughty Girl   Dubin
Naughty Kiss   Clare; Conrad
Never Again   Kahn
New Kind of Man (With a New Kind of Love for Me),
    A   Clare
New Moon   Donaldson
New York Ain't New York Anymore   Brown, Lew;
    Henderson; Rose
Nicest Sort of Feeling   Caesar
Night Hawk   Gilbert
Night Time in Araby   DeSylva; Gershwin, George
No One Knows What It's All About   Rose; Woods
No Other Girl   Kalmar; Ruby
No Wonder that I Love You   Davis
Nobody Else Can Do the Things You Do   Bryan
Nobody Loves You Like I Do   Akst; Davis
Nobody Takes Me Bye-Bye   Ahlert; Lewis; Young, Joseph
Not So Long Ago   Gershwin, Ira
'Nother Little Kiss   Fisher
Nothing Naughtie in a Nightie   Atteridge; Romberg;
    Schwartz, Jean
Novelty Dance   Youmans
Number Six   Coslow
O Sole Mio (Just Like the Sunrise)   Dubin
Of All My Wife's Relations, I Love Myself the Best   Sterling
Oh Baby! (Don't Say No Say Maybe)   DeSylva; Donaldson
Oh Eva Ain't You Coming Out Tonight   Clarke; Leslie;
    Warren
Oh! Flo, On a Midnight Choo Choo Honeymoon   Lewis
Oh Flo! On a Midnight Choo-Choo
    Honeymoon   Donaldson; Lewis; Young, Joseph
Oh How I Love My Darling   Leslie; Woods
Oh, How We Enjoy   Dixon; Henderson
Oh Joe   Stept
Oh, Katherina   Gilbert
Oh, Lady, Be Good!   Gershwin, George; Gershwin, Ira
Oh Mabel   Kahn
Oh! Obadiah   Donaldson
Oh, Tell Me If with Your Heart   Romberg
Oh You Can't Fool an Old Hoss Fly   Von Tilzer
Old Brass Rail, The   Dubin; Silver
Old Eva   Clarke; Leslie; Warren
Old Familiar Faces   Edwards; Rose
Old Fashioned Susie's Blues   Razaf; Waller
Old Fashioned Tin Types   Coslow; Romberg
Old Maid Jim   Silver; Turk
Old Pal   Kahn
Old Songs   Herbert
Old Virginia Moon   Kahn
Omar Khyam, Where Did You Hide that Jug of Wine   Bryan
On a Blue Lagoon (With You)   Friml
On a Desert Island with You   Kern
On My Ukelele Tra La La La La   Parish
On Such a Night   Conrad
On the Road Back Home   Meyer; Rose
On the Road to Bal-Na-Pogue   Brennan
On the Shores of Napoli   Brennan
On the Z-R-3   Donaldson; Lewis; Young, Joseph
Once in a While   Conrad
One I Love Belongs to Somebody Else, The   Kahn
One Last Kiss (inst.)   Henderson
One Man Is Like Another   Romberg

One Man Woman   Hammerstein; Harbach
One Million Times a Day   Lewis; Young, Joseph
One Moment of Paradise   Johnson, Howard
One Note   Conrad
Onions, Garlic and Fish   Fisher
Only a Kiss   Hammerstein; Harbach
Only Girl, The   Romberg
Only in Dreams   Caesar
Only, Only One, The   Monaco; Warren
Only Only One for Me, The   Monaco; Warren
Oo La La   Coslow; Romberg
Opening — Crazy Quilt   Gershwin, Ira
Organdie Days   Schwartz, Jean
Oriental Tones (inst.)   Waller
Orphan Is the Girl for Me, An   Youmans
Our Emblem is the Lily   Atteridge; Romberg; Schwartz, Jean
Out of a Million You're the Only One   Clarke; Leslie
Out of the Past   Dubin
Paradise   Johnson, Howard
(Any Old Alley Is) Paradise Alley   Johnson, Howard
Paree   Ahlert
Passing of the Night, The   Conrad
Peacock Strut   Atteridge; Romberg; Schwartz, Jean
Pep! Zip! and Punch!   Gershwin, George
Pepita   DeSylva; Gershwin, George
Percy Have Mercy on Me   Koehler
Perfume Waltz   Atteridge; Romberg; Schwartz, Jean
Peter Pan, I Love You   Henderson
Pianologue   Atteridge; Romberg; Schwartz, Jean
Pickin' 'Em Up and Layin' 'Em Down   Kahn
Pidgy   Dixon; Henderson
Playin' Round   Dubin
Pleasant Greeting, A   Kalmar; Ruby
Please   Lewis; Young, Joseph
Please Be Good to My Old Girl   Dixon; Henderson; Rose
Please, Please Louise   Davis; Silver
Please Take Me   Waller
Please Tell Me Why   Waller
Plot, The   Buck
Popularity   Atteridge
Powder Your Nose   Atteridge; Romberg; Schwartz, Jean
Pretty Ankle   Atteridge; Romberg; Schwartz, Jean
Pretty Soft for You   Ellington
Pretty Things   Friml; Hammerstein; Harbach
Prisoner's Up to Date   Clarke; Johnston; Meyer; Turk
Promises   Johnson, Howard
Pull Your String   Coslow; Romberg
Put Away a Little Ray of Golden Sunshine for a Rainy
    Day   Ahlert; Lewis; Young, Joseph
Put on the Ritz   Johnson, Howard
Put Your Old Bandana On   Clarke; Johnston; Meyer; Turk
Quite a Party   DeSylva; Gershwin, George
Radio Joe   Clare; Conrad; Rose
Radio Lady of Mine   Coslow
Radio Voices   Romberg
Railroad Man's Goodbye Sometimes Ain't Gone, A   Razaf
Rain   Fisher
Rainy Afternoon Girls   Gershwin, George; Gershwin, Ira
Ramblin' Papa Blues   Waller
Reason I Love You, Because I Do, The   Snyder
Red Nose, Where Did You Get that Nose?   Brown, Lew
Ringside Blues   Mills
Rin-Tin-Tin   Atteridge; Romberg; Schwartz, Jean
Riverboat Shuffle (inst.)   Carmichael
Rock Me Just Like a Sweet Daddy Should   Razaf; Waller

Rock-A-Bye Baby   Berlin
Rolland from Holland   Johnson, Howard
Romany Days   Kahn
Romeo, Juliet, Johnny and Jane   Herbert
Rose Marie   Brown, Lew; DeSylva; Henderson
Rose of Madrid   DeSylva; Gershwin, George
Rose of My Heart   Buck
Rose-Marie   Friml; Hammerstein; Harbach
Roses of France   Gershwin, George
Run on the Bank   Blake; Sissle
Runnin' Wild   Johnson, James P.
Safe in Your Heart   Gorney
Same Old Story, The   DeSylva; Gershwin, George
Santa Barbara   Bryan
Santa Claus Blues   Kahn
Sarah Sitting in the Shoe Shine Shop   McHugh
Savannah, That Georgiana Blues   Fisher
Save a Kiss for Rainy Weather   Egan; Whiting
Saxophone Man   Atteridge; Jerome; Romberg; Schwartz,
   Jean
Say It Again   Conrad
Say! Say! Sadie   Conrad; Coslow
School Day Blues   Fisher
Seeing Dickie Home   Gershwin, George; Gershwin, Ira
Serenade   Romberg
Seven Days   Dietz; Kern
(When You and I Were) Seventeen   Kahn
Sextette   Atteridge; Romberg; Schwartz, Jean
Shadow of the Moon   Kern
She Can Be So Nice, But She Don't Wanna   Fisher
She Couldn't Say No   Bryan; Schwartz, Jean
She Fell Down on Her Cadenza   Von Tilzer
She Loves Me   Brown, Lew
She Waits By the Lookout Mountain on the Lookout for
   Me   Brown, Lew
She's Everybody's Sweetheart but Nobody's Gal   Conrad;
   Rose
She's Got To Be Good If She Comes from
   Hollywood   Bryan; Schwartz, Jean
(That's Why They Call Me) S-H-I-N-E   Brown, Lew
Short Trail Became a Long Trail (Since You Left Me to Walk
   Alone), The   Razaf; Waller
Show Me the Way   Davis
Shuffle Your Troubles Away   Hanley
Shufflin' Sam   Kern
Shut Yo' Mouf   Razaf; Waller
Sights of London   Herbert
Since Ma Is Playing Mah Jongg   Conrad; Rose
Sing a Little Song   Romberg
Sing a Song (Croon a Tune)   Pollack
Sing Me 'O Sole Mio'   Kahn
Singin' Pete   Gershwin, George; Gershwin, Ira
Sioux City Sue   Donaldson
Siren of the Sea   Coots
Sirens of the Sea   Coslow; Romberg
Sister Hasn't Got a Chance Since Mother Burned Her
   Hair   Von Tilzer
Sitting Pretty   Kern
Sixteen, Sweet Sixteen   Berlin
Skin-a-Ma-Rink-a-Rink-a-Ree   Dubin; McHugh; Mills
Slave of Love, The   Blake; Sissle
Slaving   Waller
Sneeze   Gershwin, George; Gershwin, Ira
Snowball   Kahn
So Am I   Gershwin, George; Gershwin, Ira

So Far Away, So Long Ago   Smith, Harry B.; Snyder
Society Blues   Atteridge; Romberg; Schwartz, Jean
Some Far-Away Someone   DeSylva; Gershwin, George;
   Gershwin, Ira
Some Golden Day   Kahn
Some Other Girl   Kahn
Somebody Like You   Donaldson; Friend
Somebody Loves Me   DeSylva; Gershwin, George
Someone Believes in You   Gershwin, George
Someone, Someday, Somewhere   Buck; Friml
Someone Who Believes in You   DeSylva; Gershwin, George
Something's Wrong! How Can You Ask Me to
   Smile?   Lewis; Young, Joseph
Sometimes You Will, Sometimes You Won't   Hanley
Somewhere Someone Is Waiting for Me   Razaf
Song of India, A   Dubin
Song of Love   Atteridge; Romberg
Sons of Old Black Joe, The   Blake; Sissle
Souvenir (Fair As a Day in May)   Dubin
Spain   Kahn
Spanish Dance   Atteridge; Romberg; Schwartz, Jean
Spanish Juanita   Coslow
Spoony Croony Tune   Atteridge; Romberg; Schwartz, Jean
Stardust   Gorney
Step Henrietta   DeSylva
Stop, Look and Listen   Herbert
Stop Stutterin', Sam   Warren
Strike, Strike, Strike   DeSylva; Gershwin, George
Striver's Row   Waller
Strollin' Roun' the Town   Waller
Students' Life   Romberg
Study in Porcelain, A   Atteridge; Romberg; Schwartz, Jean
Su L'Boul'vard   Atteridge; Schwartz, Jean
Success   Johnson, Howard
Summer Nights   Johnson, Howard
Super-Shiek   Atteridge; Romberg
Superstitious Blues   Turk
Sur L'Boul'vard   Romberg
Surrounded by the Girls   Atteridge; Romberg; Schwartz,
   Jean
Susie   Kahn
Sweet Arabian Dreams   Caesar; Conrad; Harbach
Sweet as Can Be, The Bamboola   Fisher
Sweet Baby   Waller
Sweet Cactus Rose   Caesar; Conrad; Harbach
Sweet Dreams   Coots
Sweet Little Devil   DeSylva; Gershwin, George
Sweet Mama of Mine   Snyder
Sweet Man   Parish
Sweet Onion Time   Coslow
Sweetest Thing in Life, The   DeSylva; Kern
Sweetie Don't Grow Sour on Me   Waller
Swiss Miss   Gershwin, George; Gershwin, Ira
Syncopated Pipes of Pan   Porter
System   DeSylva; Gershwin, George
Tahiti   Blake; Sissle
Take a Little One Step   Youmans
Take Down Dis Letter   Blake; Sissle
Take Me   Atteridge; Dixon; Henderson; Romberg; Rose;
   Schwartz, Jean
Take Me Back to Your Arms   Henderson; Rose
Take Me Back to Your Heart   Meyer; Rose
Tamara Tango   Dubin
Teapot Dome Blues   Mills
Tell Her in the Springtime   Berlin

Tell Me, Am I Shooting at the Moon   Conrad
Tell Me, Dreamy Eyes   Kahn
Tell Me Radio   Mitchell; Silver
Tell Me Truly   Johnson, Howard
Ten Commandments of Love, The   Fisher
Tenth Interval Rag (inst.)   Ruby
That Charleston Dance   Blake; Sissle
That New-Fangled Mother of Mine   Gershwin, George
That Wonderful Game Called Love   Clare
That's My Man   Waller
That's What I'd Do   Gilbert
(We're Looking for) The Bobbed Hair Bandit   Johnson,
   Howard
Then You Know That You're in Love   Gorney
There Is Music in an Irish Song   Gorney
There Is Somebody for Everybody but Me   Coslow
There's a Million Little Cupids in the Sky   Blake; Sissle
There's Always Room for a Smile   Gorney
There's Lots of Room for You   Dietz; Kern
There's No Place As Grand As Bandanaland   Blake; Sissle
There's Yes, Yes in Your Eyes   Friend
They Always Run a Little Faster   Caesar; Conrad; Harbach
They Don't Make 'Em That Way Any More   Gershwin, Ira
Thief of Bagdad, The   Ager; Yellen
Thinking of Me   Blake; Sissle
Those Panama Mammas   Johnson, Howard
Thoughts Will Come to Me   Romberg
Tie a String Around Your Finger   Youmans
Till I Meet Someone Like You   Gershwin, George
Tiller Girls Dance (inst.)   Herbert
Time and a Half for Overtime   Youmans
Tired of Dreaming   Kalmar; Ruby; Snyder
'Tisn't Easy to Say Goodbye Broadway   Cohan
Titina   Coslow
To the Fair   Dietz; Kern
To the Inn We're Marching   Romberg
Tokyo Blues   Berlin
Tomorrow   Coslow
Tomorrow's Another Day   Coots; Coslow
Top Hole   Gorney
Totem Tom-Tom   Friml; Hammerstein; Harbach
Toy Doll Goodbye   Egan; Whiting
Toy of Destiny   Porter
Trottin' to the Land of Cotton Melodies   Clarke; Johnston;
   Meyer; Turk
Tulip Time in Sing-Sing (Dear Old Fashioned Prison of
   Mine)   Kern
Tune In (To Station J.O.Y)   DeSylva; Gershwin, George
Turn on the Popular Moon   Conrad
Turn to the Dream Ahead   Gershwin, Ira
Twilight Serenade   Caesar
Twilly of Fifth Avenue   Romberg
Twinkle, Little Lucky Star   Dubin
Two Little Babes in the Wood   Porter
Two Time Dan   Turk
Uh-Uh!   Gershwin, Ira
Ukulele Lou   Sterling
Under a One-Man Top   DeSylva; Gershwin, George
Under a Parasol   Coslow; Romberg
Under the Palms   Coots; Rose
Under the Water   Brown, Lew; Henderson
Understudies   Porter
Unlucky in Love   Berlin
Up to Date   Clarke; Johnston; Meyer
Violet Eyes   Bryan

Virginia (Don't Go Too Far)   DeSylva; Gershwin, George
Virginia's Calling Me   Friend
Vive la Canadienne   Hammerstein; Harbach
Voice of Love, The   Gershwin, Ira
Waikiki Is Calling Me   Sterling
Wait a Bit, Susie   Gershwin, George; Gershwin, Ira
Wait for the Moon   Porter
Waitin' Around   Davis; Hanley
Waiting for the Lawn and You   Caesar
Walter Walter Wildflower   Coslow
Waltz Ensemble   Romberg
Wanderer, The   Gorney
Wandering One   Von Tilzer
Wanted Someone to Love   McHugh; Mills
Was It a Dream?   DeSylva
Watchin' the Clock   Kahn
Way Down in Georgia   Mills
We Are Puritans   Atteridge; Romberg; Schwartz, Jean
We Ran Away from School   Gorney
Weather Man   Gershwin, George; Gershwin, Ira
Weeping Willow Tree   Dietz; Kern
Welcome to Prince   Romberg
We'll All Go Voting for Al   Berlin
We'll Link His Name with Lincoln   Jerome
We're Here Because   Gershwin, George; Gershwin, Ira
We're Off to Paris   Romberg
What a Beautiful Face Will Do   Coslow; Romberg
What a Village Girl Should Know   Coslow
What Can Be Wrong with Me   Waller
What Do You Say?   Atteridge
What Has Become of Hinky Dinky Parlay Voo   McHugh;
   Mills
What Has Become of Hinky-Dinky-Parlay Vous   Dubin
What Is the Use   Dubin
What Memories   Romberg
What of It   Gershwin, Ira
What the Future Holds for Me   Johnson, Howard
What Will I Do   Coslow
What You Could Be If You Had Me   Johnson, Howard
What'll I Do   Berlin
What's the Matter with That Girl   Johnson, Howard; Motzan
What's the Use   Dietz; Kern
What's Today Got to Do with Tomorrow?   Donaldson
When Do You Suppose   Dubin
When Evening Shadows Fall   Caesar; Gorney
When Greek Meets Greek   Youmans
When I Dance with You   Coslow
When I Made the Grade with O'Grady   Johnson, Howard
When I'm with You I'm Lonesome   Donaldson
When Knighthood Was in Flower   Atteridge; Romberg;
   Schwartz, Jean
When Lula Does the Hula-Hula Dance   Razaf
When Mother Wields the Shingle   Young, Victor
When My Sugar Walks Down the Street   McHugh; Mills
When Nobody Wants You, and Nobody Cares, Come to
   Me   Stept
When the Funny Paper Folks Were on Parade   Fisher
When the One You Love Loves You   Baer; Friend
When the Weekend Comes Round   Caesar
When They Name You   Stept
When Toby Is Out of Town   Gershwin, George
When We Are Married   Youmans
When You're in Love   Dixon; Gorney; Henderson; Rose
When You're Not at Your Best   Gershwin, George
When You're Tired of Me, Just Let Me Down   Razaf; Waller

Where Are You Tonight?   Caesar; Conrad
Where Have Those Old Timers Gone   Johnson, Howard
Where Is My Little Old New York?   Berlin
Where Is My Love   Turk
Where Is That Old Girl of Mine   Kahn
Where the Dreamy Wabash Flows   Baer; Friend
Where the Lazy Daisies Grow   Friend
Where's the Baby for Me   Baer; Friend
Which Do You Prefer?   Coslow
Whisper to Me   Romberg
Whisper to the Rose   Smith, Harry B.; Snyder
Whistle in the Rain   Coots
Who   Berlin
Who Do You Love, I Hope It's Me   Friend
Who Is the One That You're Fooling Now   Lewis; Young,
    Joseph
Whole World Is Dreaming of Love, The   Kahn
Whole World's Turning Blue   Gershwin, Ira
Who's the Lucky Fellow   Coots; Coslow
Why Can't I Have You   Davis; Woods
Why Couldn't It Be Poor Little Me   Kahn
Why Did I Kiss that Girl?   Brown, Lew; Henderson
Why Did I Let Her Go   Monaco; Motzan
Why Did You Come Into My Life   Johnson, Howard
Why Do They Call Us Johns?   Johnson, Howard
Why Live a Lie   Gilbert
Why Shouldn't We?   Hammerstein; Harbach
Wildcats   Berlin
Will You Remember Me?   Gershwin, George; Gershwin, Ira
With You   Ellington
Wonderful Party, A   Gershwin, George; Gershwin, Ira
Won't You Come Back to My Arms   Dixon; Henderson;
    Rose
Wop Blues   Lewis; Young, Joseph
Words   Dubin
Worries   Kern
Worryin' Blues   Kahn
Wrong Thing at the Right Time, The   Gershwin, Ira
Yankee Strut   Atteridge; Romberg; Schwartz, Jean
———-yanna   Fisher
Year After Year (We're Together)   DeSylva; Gershwin,
    George
Year from Today, A   Kern
Yesterday   Atteridge
You Can't Blame Your Uncle Sammy   Dubin; McHugh
You Flew Away from the Nest   Kalmar; Ruby
You Gave All Your Kisses to Somebody Else (So Why Bring
    Your Tears to Me)   Parish
You Just Can't Have No One Man By Yourself   Johnson,
    James P.
You Know Me, Al   Caesar
You Know Me Al, You Know Me Ed   Dubin; McHugh
You Know Me, Alabam'   Ager; Yellen
You Left Me Out in the Rain   Rose
You Must Come Over Blues   Gershwin, Ira
You Must Come Over Eyes   Gorney
You Ought to Know   Blake; Sissle
You Should Have Told Me You Were Only Fooling   Kahn
You Were Meant for Me   Blake; Sissle
You'll Never Get to Heaven with Those Eyes   Clarke; Leslie;
    Monaco
Your Way or My Way   Johnson, Howard
You're in Heidelberg   Romberg
You're in Love with Every One but the One Who's in Love
    with You   Dixon; Henderson

You're Loveable, So Loveable   Ahlert
You're My Happy Ending   Buck; Hanley
You're the Certain Someone   Kahn
Zulu Lou   Gorney

1925

Across the Bridge of My Dreams   Kahn
Across the Garden Wall   Hart; Rodgers
After a While   Egan; Whiting
After All Is Said and Done   Stept
After Every Quarrel   Rose
Ah-Ha!   Clare; Monaco
Ain't I Got Rosie (Ain't Rosie Got Me)   Dubin; Warren
Ain't Love Wonderful   DeSylva
Ain't My Baby Grand?   Brown, Lew; Henderson
Alabamy Cradle Song   Kahn
Ale, Ale, Ale   Hart; Rodgers
All Aboard for Heaven, All Aboard for Home Sweet
    Home   Rose
All Aboard for Paris   Smith, Harry B.
All for You   Freed, Arthur
All the Girls Think I'm Wonderful   Fisher
All These People I Have Wronged   Hammerstein; Harbach;
    Kern
Alone at Last   Kahn
Alone on Life's Highway   Romberg; Smith, Harry B.
Along Came You   Rose
Always   Berlin
And I Believed in You   Lewis; Young, Joseph
And Thereby Hangs a Tail   Hart; Rodgers
Answer Me   Motzan
Anybody Here Want to Try My Cabbage   Razaf; Waller
Anything   Caesar
Anytime, Anywhere, Anyhow   Hart; Rodgers
April Fool   Hart; Rodgers
Are You Sorry?   Ager; Davis
As Long As I Have You   Stept
As Long As I've Got My Mammy   DeSylva; Hanley
As Long As We're in Love   Brown, Lew; Clare
At the End of the Rainbow of Love   Motzan
At the Hotel   Freed, Arthur
At the Party   DeSylva
Aunt Jemima   Egan; Whiting
Away from You   Ager; Davis
Awful Lot My Gal Ain't Got, An   Waller
Babbitts in Love   Hart; Rodgers
Baby!   DeSylva; Gershwin, George; Gershwin, Ira
Baby Looks Like Me, The   Kalmar; Ruby
B-A-B-Y Spells Baby   Johnson, Howard
Back Home in Illinois   Stept
Ball and Chain Blues   Razaf; Waller
Ballet   Friml
Bam Bam Bammy Shore, The   Dixon; Henderson
Bamboo Babies   Hanley
Bamboola   Conrad
Banana Oil   Dubin; McHugh
Barcarolle   Smith, Harry B.
Be in Style with a Smile   Turk
Be Yourself   Gilbert
Beautiful Baby   Conrad
Beautiful Girls   Coots
Bertie   Romberg
Better Call Preacher Man   Rose

Beware of a Girl With a Fan   Brown, Lew; DeSylva;
    Henderson
Black and White   Hart; Rodgers
Blue Indian   Egan; Whiting
Blushing Rose Where the Volga Flows   Fisher
Bolshevik Love   Caesar; Youmans
Bombay   Clare; Monaco
Born and Bred in Old Kentucky   DeSylva; Hanley
Bounce Away Your Baby Blues   Caesar
Boy Next Door, The   Harbach; Youmans
Brighter Days   Parish
Broadway Butterfly   Carroll
Brother Ben   Waller
Brown Eyes Why Are You Blue   Bryan; Meyer
Bryan Believed in Heaven, That's Why He's in Heaven
    Tonight   Dubin
Burden, The   Brennan
Busy Evening, A   Coots
But I Do — You Know I Do   Donaldson; Kahn
But She's My Girl Now   Brown, Lew; DeSylva; Henderson
But the Wind Blew Through His Whiskers Just the
    Same   Conrad; Rose
Butter and Egg Baby   Warren
Butterflies   Porter
By My Fireside   Johnson, Howard
By the Sign of the Rose   Lerner, Sammy; Rose; Whiting
By this Token   Romberg; Smith, Harry B.
Bye and Bye   Hart; Rodgers
California, Here We Go   Carroll; Freed, Arthur
California Sunshine   Bryan
Call Me Up When You're Lonesome   Warren
Call of the Great White Way, The   Coslow
Call of the Sea, The   Harbach; Youmans
Camp Meetin' Stomp (inst.)   Waller
Candle Light   Kahn
Capering Coopers   Freed, Arthur
Carnival   Caesar; Youmans
Carolina Shout, The   Johnson, James P.
Carolina Stomp   Bloom
Celebration of St. Joan the Good   Romberg
Cellini's Dream   Coots
Charleston   Coots
Charleston Mad   Conrad
Charleston Time   Carroll; Freed, Arthur
Charming Women   Coots
Chase, The   Hammerstein; Harbach; Kern
Chase of the Fox, The   Caesar; Youmans
Cheatin' on Me   Pollack; Yellen
Cheerio   Clare; Hart; Monaco; Rodgers
Cheerio, Old Dear   Clare; Monaco
Cherchez la Femme (Get Your Woman)   Conrad
Chimes of Notre Dame   Bryan
Chimes of the Chapel   Egan; Kahn
Chopsticks   Carroll; Freed, Arthur
Chorus of Soldiers   Romberg; Smith, Harry B.
Church Around the Corner   Freed, Arthur
Cinderella   Gordon
Cinderella Dreams   Whiting
Cinderella's Dreams   Egan; Kahn
Clap Hands Here Comes Charlie   Rose
Clap Hands Till Papa Comes Home   Turk
Co-Ed, The   Conrad
Collegiate   Brown, Lew
Colorado Night   Robison
Colored Soldiers on Parade (inst.)   McHugh

Come on Along   Conrad
Come On and Play   DeSylva; Hanley
Comin' Home   Kalmar; Ruby
Comrade, You Have a Chance Here   Smith, Harry B.
Convent Bells Are Ringing   Romberg; Smith, Harry B.
Cookies and Bookies   DeSylva; Hanley
Coronation Song   Romberg; Smith, Harry B.
Cossack Love Song (Don't Forget Me)   Gershwin, George;
    Hammerstein; Harbach
Couple Upstairs, The   Davis
Cover Me with Kisses   Freed, Arthur
Cross Words, Why Were They Spoken   Dubin
Crossword Puzzle, The   Romberg
Crossword Puzzle Song   Rodgers
Cuckoo Clock, The   Carroll; Freed, Arthur
Cuddles and Kisses   Egan; Whiting
Cup of Coffee, A Sandwich and You, A   Dubin; Rose
Da Da Da Dum Dum Da Dum   Turk
Dan Sing (The China Dancing Man)   Turk
Dance from Down Yonder, The   DeSylva; Hanley
Dance It Again with Me   Freed, Arthur
Dance with Me   Romberg; Smith, Harry B.
Dancing Hour   Gershwin, George; Gershwin, Ira
Dancing in the Dark   Coslow
Danger   Kahn
Darling Will Not Grow Older   Hart; Rodgers
Daughters   Caesar; Youmans
Dawn   Kalmar; Ruby
Day I Rode Half Fare, The   DeSylva; Hanley
Dear Me   Hart; Rodgers
Dearest Enemy   Hart; Rodgers
Deep Elm, You Tell 'Em I'm Blue   Robison
Delaware   Dixon; Henderson; Rose
Dinah   Akst; Lewis; Young, Joseph
Dixie Bungalow   Bryan; Meyer; Rose
Do I Love You when There's Nothing but Yes in Your
    Eyes   Goetz
Do You Love Me?   Hart; Rodgers
Don't Be a Fool You Fool   Conrad; Dixon
Don't Be a Fool You Fool (Don't Be a Foolish Fool)   Rose
Don't Be a Foolish Fool   Conrad; Dixon
Don't Be Afraid to Come Home   Ager; Bryan; Yellen
Don't Be Sorry for Me   Conrad
Don't Blame Me   Stept
Don't Bring Lulu   Brown, Lew; Henderson; Rose
Don't Let Anybody Vamp Your Man   Romberg
Don't Wait Too Long   Berlin
Don't Wake Me Up, Let Me Dream   Baer; Gilbert
Doo-Dab, The   Kalmar; Ruby
Down Deep in an Irishman's Heart   Brennan; McHugh
Dream a Dream   Hammerstein; Harbach; Kern
Dreaming   Conrad
Dreaming of Tomorrow   Davis
Dreamy Argentina   Friend
Drinking Song   Friml
Dummy Song   Brown, Lew; Henderson; Rose
D'Ye Love Me?   Hammerstein; Harbach; Kern
Easy Strain   Arlen
Eddie Be Good   Buck
Edelweiss   Romberg
Egypt's No Place for a Lady   Freed, Arthur
Entrance and Song of Czarina   Smith, Harry B.
Entrance of Czarina   Smith, Harry B.
Entrance of the Emperor and the Empress   Smith, Harry B.
Even As You and I   Brown, Lew; DeSylva; Henderson

Every Day Is Mother's Day for Me   Edwards
Every Girl Must Have a Little Bull   Coots
Everybody Knows what Jazz Is   Buck
Everybody's Does the Charleston Now   Johnson, James P.
Everyone in the World (Is Doing the Charleston)   Berlin
Everything Is Hotsy Totsy Now   McHugh; Mills
Everything's Going to Be All Right   Conrad
Evil Minded Papa Blues   Razaf
Ev'ry Guest Is in the Room   Hammerstein; Harbach; Kern
Ev'ry One Home Is Asking for You   Kahn
Ev'ryone Home Is Asking for You   Donaldson
Eyes that Haunt Me   Smith, Harry B.
Fair Land of Dreaming   Smith, Harry B.
Fairy Tale   Egan; Kahn
Falling for You   Razaf
Family Reputation   Berlin
Far Away   Gershwin, George; Hammerstein; Harbach
Farmer's Life, A   Smith, Harry B.
Fidgety Feet   Freed, Arthur
Fight Over Me   Harbach; Youmans
First Blossom, The   Gershwin, George; Hammerstein;
   Harbach
Five Foot Two, Eyes of Blue (Has Anybody Seen My
   Girl)   Henderson; Lewis; Young, Joseph
Five O'Clock Tea   Berlin
Flapperette (inst.)   Henderson
Flappers   Caesar; Youmans
Flex-a-tone   Coots
Floating Down a Stream   Johnson, Howard
Florida By the Sea   Berlin
Florida Mammy   Atteridge
Fly Butterfly   Brown, Lew; DeSylva; Henderson
Follow the Flag We Love   Smith, Harry B.
Follow the Rajah   Romberg
Follow Your Star   Coots
Fond of You   DeSylva
Forever and Ever with You   Davis
Fox Has Left His Lair, The   Hammerstein; Harbach; Kern
From Now On   Davis
Fu-Ji   Freed, Arthur
Full-Blown Roses   Hart; Rodgers
Gather Ye Rosebuds   Gershwin, George; Gershwin, Ira
Gavotte   Hart; Rodgers
Gee but It's Sweet to Cheat Just a Little   Von Tilzer
Gentlemen Prefer Blondes   Berlin
Ghetto   Brennan
Gigolette   Caesar
Gilding the Guild   Hart; Rodgers
Ginger   Gorney
Girl of Tomorrow, The   Brown, Lew; DeSylva; Henderson
Girl that's Most Chased After, The   Gorney
Girls Do Not Tempt Me   Hart; Rodgers
Girls Dream of One Thing   Coots
Give a Little, Get a Little Kiss   Caesar; Romberg
Give Me Just a Little Bit of What You've Got   Donaldson
Give Me the Corner, Give Me the Girl   Johnson, Howard
Give Us the Charleston   DeSylva; Henderson
Give Your Heart in June-Time   Atteridge; Herbert
Glory of the Morning Sunshine, The   Atteridge
Go Ask Hannah   Brown, Lew; Clare; Friend
Going Home on New Year's Morning   Gershwin, George;
   Hammerstein; Harbach
Golden Memories   Akst; Davis
Goodfellow Days   Egan; Kahn
Got No Time   Kahn; Whiting

Great Big Bear   Hammerstein; Harbach
Greetings to the King   Gorney
G-String Melody   Robison
Gypsy Rose   Gorney
Happy Family, A   Caesar; Youmans
(In a) Happy Home for Two   Freed, Arthur
Happy Prince   Caesar
Harbor of Dreams   Gershwin, George; Gershwin, Ira
Hard to Get Gal   Davis
Harlem River Chanty   Gershwin, George; Gershwin, Ira
Hartman Ballet (inst.)   Kern
Have I Got a Piece of Boiled Beef for You   Brown, Lew;
   Clare; Friend
Have You Heard   Gershwin, George
Hay Foot, Straw Foot   Carroll; Freed, Arthur
Hay Hay Farmer Took Another Load Away (The Farmer
   Took Another Load Away Hay Hay)   Leslie
He Doesn't Know What It's All About   Berlin
He Had to Pay the Piper   Carroll; Freed, Arthur
He Is the Type   Kern
He Writes a Song   Smith, Harry B.
Headin' for Baltimore   Conrad; Coslow
Headin' for Louisville   DeSylva
Heart of the Ghetto   Norworth
Heart that Once Belonged to Me Belongs to Someone Else,
   The   Waller
Heat of a Rose   Coots
Heigh-Ho, Lackaday   Hart; Rodgers
Hello, Hello, Telephone Girlie   Harbach; Youmans
Hello Little Bluebirds Have Flown, The   Atteridge
Hello 'Tucky   DeSylva; Hanley
He-Man, The   DeSylva; Gershwin, George; Gershwin, Ira
Here in My Arms   Hart; Rodgers
Here We Are Together Again (Opening Act
   I)   Hammerstein; Harbach; Kern
Here's a Kiss   Hart; Rodgers
Hermits, The   Rodgers
Hey, Hey, Fever   Gordon
Highway's Call, The   Egan; Kahn
His Master's Voice   Edwards; Johnson, Howard
Hitch Up the Horses   Conrad
Hocus Pocus   Brown, Lew; Hanley
Hold Me in Your Arms Again   Freed, Arthur
Holka-Polka   Egan; Kahn
Hollywood   Carroll; Freed, Arthur
Home Again   Buck
Home from Algeria   Smith, Harry B.
Home of My Heart   Egan; Kahn
Home Pals   Lewis; Young, Joseph
Homeland   Henderson; Romberg
Honey Bunch   Friend
Honey, I'm in Love with You   Conrad
Honey Man Blues   Razaf
Honor and Glory   Smith, Harry B.
Hot Diggety   Donaldson; Kahn
Hot Steps   Carroll; Freed, Arthur
Hotel Never Tell   Caesar; Youmans
Hot-Foot'n, We're Gonna Have Fun   Akst; Lewis; Young,
   Joseph
House Party Stomp (inst.)   Waller
Housekeeping   Freed, Arthur
How Can I Win You Now?   DeSylva; Gershwin, George;
   Gershwin, Ira
How Can We Help but Miss You   Hart; Rodgers
How Do You Doodle Do?   Coots

How I Love Her and She Loves Me Is Nobody's Business   Mills
How'd You Like To   Edwards
How's the King   Gorney
Hugo, I Go Where You Go   Gilbert
Huguette Waltz   Friml
Humpty Dumpty March   Johnson, Howard
Hunt Dance, The (inst.)   Kern
Hunting   Friml
Hurry Up, Matilda   Kalmar; Ruby
I Ain't Gonna Cry No More   Donaldson
I Beg Your Pardon   Hart; Rodgers
I Can't Believe that You're in Love with Me   McHugh
I Can't Realize You Love Me   DeSylva; Donaldson
I Care for Her and She Cares for Me   Stept
I Dare not Love You   Romberg; Smith, Harry B.
I Didn't Want You to Be Sorry for Me   Whiting
I Do   DeSylva
I Do Believe in Fairies, I Do, Don't You   Whiting
I Don't Want a Girlie   DeSylva; Youmans
I Don't Want You to Be Sorry for Me   Kahn; Whiting
I Found Some Body to Love   Stept
I Got My Eyes on You   Brown, Lew; Friend
I Gotta Be Good 'Cause My Baby's in Town   Clare; Monaco
I Hear Love Call Me   Smith, Harry B.
I Know Somebody (Who Loves You)   Gershwin, George; Gershwin, Ira
I Like that Little One   Kahn
I Love My Baby, My Baby Loves Me   Warren
I Love the Moon   Goetz
I Love Them All   Romberg; Smith, Harry B.
I Love You More Than Ever   Davis
I Might Grow Fond of You   Hammerstein; Harbach; Kern
I Need Somebody to Lullaby Me   Coslow
I Never Knew   Kahn
I Think You're Wonderful, Say What Do You Think of Me   Friend
I Wanna Go Where You Go — Do What You Do Then I'll Be Happy   Brown, Lew; Clare; Friend
I Want a Loveable Baby   Brown, Lew; DeSylva; Henderson
I Want a Yes Man   Caesar; Gershwin, Ira; Youmans
I Want Another Chance with You   Baer; DeSylva
I Want My Bib   Von Tilzer
I Want to Be a Bad Little Boy   Egan; Kahn
I Want to Be Free   Brown, Lew
I Want to Be Happy   Caesar; Youmans
I Want to Be Kissed   Fisher
I Want Two Husbands   Hammerstein; Harbach
I Want You   Johnson, Howard
I Want You To Want Me To Want You   Bryan; Fisher
I Want Your Kisses If You Want My Kisses   Arlen
I Was Alone   Harbach
I Was Glad to Let You Go, but I'm So Sorry Now   Donaldson; Friend
I Was Meant for Someone   Hanley
I Wish It Was Me   Brown, Lew; Friend
I Wish that I'd Been Satisfied with Mary   Henderson
I Wish't I Was in Peoria   Dixon; Henderson; Rose; Woods
I Wonder Where My Baby Is Tonight   Donaldson; Kahn
I Wonder Where My Old Girl Is To-Night   Kalmar; Ruby
I Wonder Where My Sweetie Can Be   Blake; Sissle
I Wonder Why   Henderson
I Wouldn't Be One Bit Surprised   Donaldson; Kahn
I Wouldn't Be Where I Am If You Hadn't Gone Away   Brown, Lew; Henderson; Rose

Icky Wicky Woo   Coslow
I'd Like to Be a Gardener in a Garden of Girls   Buck
I'd Like to Corral a Cat   Buck
I'd Like to Hide It   Hart; Rodgers
I'd Like to Take You Home to Meet My Mother   Hart; Rodgers
I'd Love to Love You All the Time   Davis
Ida, I Do   Kahn
If I Had a Girl Like You   Dixon; Henderson; Rose
If I Never See You As Long As I Live That'll Even Be Too Soon   Baer; Turk
If I Were King   Hart; Rodgers
If It Wasn't for My Dear Old Daddy   Parish
If It Wasn't for You   Stept
If It's O.K. with You, It's O.K. with Me   Clare; Monaco
If Rip Van Winkle Had My Gal, He Would Never Have Slept at All   Fisher
If You Could Be as True to Me as I Could Be to You   Hanley
If You Could Uke a Ukelele   Coslow
If You Knew Susie (Like I Know Susie)   DeSylva
If You Love Her (Tell Her So)   Freed, Arthur
If You See that Gal of Mine Send Her Home   Ahlert; Lewis; Young, Joseph
I'll Have the Blues Until I Get to California   Robison
I'll Save All My Evenings for You   Gorney
I'm a Grand Street Boy   Edwards; Johnson, Howard
I'm a Little Bit Fonder of You Than of Myself   Caesar
I'm a Little Jail Bird Looking for a Love Bird Like You   Gordon
I'm a Pickford that Nobody Picked   Carroll; Freed, Arthur
I'm All Upset About You   Gilbert
I'm Always Just a Little Bit Not Just Right   Donaldson; Kahn
I'm Always Thinking of Someone Who's Never Thinking of Me   Donaldson; Kahn
I'm at Home in Any Town but My Home Town   Caesar; Egan; Whiting
I'm Goin' Out If Lizzie Comes In   Brown, Lew; DeSylva; Henderson
I'm Goin' to Wait till the Right One Comes Along   Buck
I'm Gonna Charleston Back to Charleston   Turk
I'm Gonna Pick Myself a Mary Where the Huckleberries Grow   Bryan; Silver
I'm Harold, I'm Harold   Romberg
I'm Head Over Heels in Love   Caesar
I'm in Love with a Certain One, Guess Who   Friend; Turk
I'm Looking for Someone to Look After Me   Parish
I'm Looking for that Man of Mine   Davis
I'm Moving Away   Caesar
I'm on My Way to Dreamland   Leslie
I'm Sittin' on Top of the World (Just Rolling Along, Just Rolling Along)   Lewis; Young, Joseph
I'm So Disappointed in You   Donaldson; Kahn
I'm Somethin' on Avenue A   DeSylva; Gershwin, George; Gershwin, Ira
I'm Still in Love with You   Conrad
I'm Waiting for You   Harbach; Youmans
In a Little While   Egan
In Gingham   Hart; Rodgers
In My Little Blue Bonnet   Freed, Arthur
In Old Chihuahua   Donaldson; Friend
In Our Own Orange Grove   Carroll; Freed, Arthur
In Ruritania   Romberg; Smith, Harry B.
In Sardinia   DeSylva; Gershwin, George; Gershwin, Ira
In the Land of Jack and Jill   Lewis; Young, Joseph
In the Shade of the Alamo   Buck

In the Spring   Donaldson; Kahn
Intermezzo   Atteridge; Romberg; Smith, Harry B.
Is It Love?   Smith, Harry B.
Is Zat So?   DeSylva; Warren
Isn't She the Sweetest Thing   Donaldson; Kahn
It All Depends on You   Brown, Lew; DeSylva; Henderson
It Goes on Like That for Days and Days   Brown, Lew; DeSylva; Henderson
It Happened in 1600   Carroll; Freed, Arthur
It Took Her a Long Time To Learn To Say Yes and Now She Can't Say No   Brown, Lew; Henderson; Rose
It Won't Mean a Thing   Hammerstein; Harbach; Kern
It's a Great Little World   Gershwin, George; Gershwin, Ira
It's a Long Day at Our Hotel   Caesar; Youmans
It's a Walk-In with Walker   Berlin
It's All for You   Turk
It's All in Fun   Stept; Warren
It's All the Same to Me   Turk
It's not the Principle, It's Just the Money   Gorney
It's Quite Enough to Make Me Weep   Hart; Rodgers
It's the Cook Who Saves the Day   Youmans
It's Time to Keep Away from You   Brown, Lew; Friend
It's Tough to Be a Flower Girl in Uric   Gorney
I've Confessed to the Breeze I Love You   Harbach; Youmans
I've Found My Sweetheart Sally   Ager; Pollack; Yellen
I've Got a Day Off Today   Caesar; Youmans
I've Got the Yes Sir, No Sir Blues   Rose; Silver
I've Got to Be a Chaste Woman   Conrad
I've Lost My Head Over You   Razaf
Jew-Boy Blues (inst.)   Carmichael
Journey's End   Kern
Joy Spreader, The   Hart; Rodgers
Joy-Meetin' (inst.)   Johnson, James P.
June of Long Ago   Robison
Just a Cottage Small by a Waterfall   DeSylva; Hanley
Just a Little Bit   Egan; Kahn
Just a Week Ago To-Day   Johnson, Howard
Just Around the Corner   Von Tilzer
Just Around the Corner from Paradise   Stept
Just One Kiss   Johnston
Just to Be with You   Davis
Just Try to Think of Me   Stept
Just You and I and the Baby   Conrad
Katz Is Putting on the Dog   Bryan; Silver
Keep on Croonin' a Tune   Fain; McHugh
Keep Smiling at Trouble (Troubles's a Bubble)   DeSylva
Keep that School Girl Complexion   Freed, Arthur
Keep Your Skirts Down Mary Ann   Henderson; Sterling
Keepin' Out of Trouble   Freed, Arthur
Kenneth Won the Yachting Race   DeSylva; Gershwin, George; Gershwin, Ira
Kentucky's Way of Sayin' Good Mornin'   Kahn
Kermesse Dance   Romberg; Smith, Harry B.
Kickin' the Clouds Away   DeSylva; Gershwin, George; Gershwin, Ira
Kiki   DeSylva
King Isn't King Any More, The   Leslie; Monaco
Kinky Kids Parade, The   Donaldson; Kahn
Kiss from You, A   Mitchell
Kiss Ma Again   Waller
Kissing   Caesar; Youmans
Krazy   Turk
Lackawanna   DeSylva; Hanley
Ladies of the Box Office   Hart; Rodgers
Lady Luck   Gershwin, George; Gershwin, Ira

Lady of the Moon   Blake
Lady of the Nile   Kahn
Lady Who Lives for Love, A   Smith, Harry B.
Lady, You Don't Know Me   Gorney
Last Night on the Radio   Motzan
Lead 'Em On   DeSylva; Hanley
Leave Me Something to Remember   Davis
Let It Rain, Let It Pour, I'll Be in Virginia in the Morning   Friend
Let Me Dance   Coots
Let Me Introduce You to My Rosie   Brown, Lew
Let Nothing Come Between Us   Bryan; Fisher
Let's Say Goodnight 'Til It's Morning   Hammerstein; Harbach; Kern
Letter Song, The   Atteridge
Life's too Short to Be Blue   Gershwin, George; Gershwin, Ira
Like a Bird on the Wing   Caesar; Youmans
Lilies of the Field   Caesar; Youmans
Lillian   Bryan; Snyder
Little Bit Bad, A   Davis
Little Bit Now, A   Caesar
Little Bit of Ev'rything, A   Akst
Little Blue Pig, The   Romberg
Little Bungalow, A   Berlin
Little One I Love Best   Bryan; Schwartz, Jean
Little Peach   Romberg
Little Raindrop   Freed, Arthur
Lo-Man   Stept
Lonesomest Girl in Town, The   Dubin; McHugh; Mills
Longing   Davis
Look Who Is Here   Donaldson; Kahn
Looking for a Boy   Gershwin, George; Gershwin, Ira
Loud Speakin' Papa, You'd Better Speak Easy to Me   Pollack; Yellen
Love for Sale   Friml
Love, I Never Knew   Gershwin, George
Love, I Will Find a Home for You   Caesar
Love Is a Lie   Romberg
Love Is in the Air   DeSylva; Gershwin, George; Gershwin, Ira
Love Is Just a Little Bit of Heaven   Baer; Bryan
Love Is Not for a Day   Smith, Harry B.
Love Me and I'll Live Forever   Bryan; Snyder
Love Me or Leave Me Alone   Johnson, Howard
Love Me Tonight   Friml
Love Sings a Song   Caesar
Love Song, The   Smith, Harry B.
Love Will Find You Some Day   Smith, Harry B.
Lovely Lady   Brown, Lew; DeSylva; Henderson
Low Down Papa Don't You Try to High Hat Me   Kahn
Lucita   Coots
Lucky   Coots; Coslow; Silver
Lucky Boy   Berlin
Lullaby Lady   Donaldson; Kahn
Madeira   Kalmar; Ruby
Mademazelle   Porter
Magic Garden of Love, The   Coots
Mah-Jongg Maid   Hart; Rodgers
Maid of the Milky Way   Coots
Maiden's Prayer, The   Clarke; Monaco
Major Domo, The   Romberg
Make Up Your Mind   Gordon
Make Up Your Mind to Make Up with Someone   Bryan; Schwartz, Jean

Make Your Own Sunshine   Brennan
Mamie   Smith, Harry B.
Manhattan   Hart; Rodgers
March On   Smith, Harry B.
Marian   Silver
Marie, Marie, Marie!   Brown, Nacio Herb
Marionettes   Romberg; Smith, Harry B.
Market Day   Romberg
Martin Luther Drinking Song   Romberg; Smith, Harry B.
Mary to the Market Went   Egan; Kahn
Masculine Women! Feminine Men!   Leslie; Monaco
Maybe You Will Maybe You Won't   Rose; Warren
Mayflower I Love You   Coots
Me and Mamie O'Brien   Woods
Me and Myself   Egan; Kahn; Whiting
Me and the Boy Friend   Monaco
Mediterrania   Brown, Lew; Stept
Melancholy Melody   Donaldson; Kahn
Melody that Made You Mine, The   Friend
Memory Blues   Bryan
Mercenary Mary   Conrad
Merrie Merrie, The   Hart; Rodgers
Merry Widow Waltz   Mitchell
Mia Luna   Goetz
(Lead 'em on) Miami   Conrad; DeSylva
Miami You Own a Lot to Me   Silver
Midnight Bells   Gershwin, George; Hammerstein; Harbach
Midnight Waltz, The   Donaldson; Kahn
Midsummer Night's Dream   Gordon
Mighty Blue   Egan; Whiting
Military Men I Love   Smith, Harry B.
Minstrel Days   Berlin
Mission Bells   Carroll; Freed, Arthur
Mistah Jim   Johnson, James P.
Monkey Doodle Doo   Berlin
Monte Carlo   Rose
Moon Dear   Egan; Whiting
Moon Flower   Romberg
Moonlight, a Waltz and You, The   Koehler
More of the Moonlight   Leslie
Morning Glory Lane   Dixon; Henderson; Rose
Mother Me, Tennessee   DeSylva
Mothers of the World   Romberg
Mr. and Mrs. Sipkin   DeSylva; Gershwin, George; Gershwin, Ira
Mr. Cosy Corner Man   Freed, Arthur
Murderous Monty (And Light-Fingered Jane)   Gershwin, George
Music of a Mountain Stream, The   Robison
Music of Moonlight and Love, The   Smith, Harry B.
My Beautiful Irish Maid   Olcott
My Doctor   Harbach; Youmans
My Fair Lady   DeSylva; Gershwin, George; Gershwin, Ira
My First Love Letter   Caesar; Romberg
My Garret Became a Heaven When You Came Through the Door   Brennan
My Girl Has Halitosis   Brown, Lew
My Home   Coslow; Dubin; Mills
My Honey   Warren
My Kingdom for a Queen Like You   Gorney
My Love for You   Davis
My Million Dollar Man   Clare
My Oriental Symphony   Freed, Arthur
My Puppy Bud   Stept
My Sugar Plum   Hanley

My Violet   Brennan
My Yiddishe Momme   Pollack; Yellen
Mysterious Eyes   Ahlert; Smith, Harry B.
Naughty Little Raindrop   Freed, Arthur
Naughty Little Step   Coots
Never Mind   Stept
New Game, The   DeSylva
New Love   DeSylva
New Revue for Rue de la Paix   Meyer; Turk
Next to You, I Like Me, Next to You   Johnson, Howard
Next Tuesday   Carroll; Freed, Arthur
Nice Baby   Gershwin, George; Gershwin, Ira
Night of Love, A   DeSylva
Nightie-Night   Gershwin, George; Gershwin, Ira
No Man   Fisher
No Man's Mama   Pollack; Yellen
No No Nanette   Caesar; Harbach; Youmans
No One   Yellen
No One Knows (How Much I'm in Love)   Kern
No One Loves Me Like My Wilhemina   Brown, Lew
No One to Love   Ager; Yellen
No Other, No One but You   Davis
Nobody   Egan; Kahn
Nobody but Fanny   Conrad; DeSylva
Nobody But You   Kalmar; Ruby
Nobody Knows What a Red Head Mama Can Do   Dubin; Fain; Mills
Nobody Loves Me and I Wonder Why   Brown, Lew
Nobody Will Know but Me   Ahlert; Lewis; Young, Joseph
Nocturne   Friml
Nothing Else Matters Any More   Koehler
Now that You've Had All the Love that You Want You Don't Want Me Around Any More   Monaco
Of a Mornin'   Brennan
Oh, Comrades   Romberg; Smith, Harry B.
Oh Dear   Hart; Rodgers
Oh Henry   Kahn
Oh! How I Hate Women   DeSylva
Oh, How I Love Fannie   Warren
Oh, How I Miss You Tonight   Davis
Oh How She Can Love   Davis; Woods
Oh Lovey, Be Mine   Donaldson
Oh Mama   Johnston
Oh, Molly   Brown, Lew
Oh, Stop Jollyin' Me   Brown, Lew; Clare
Oh! Those Eyes   Kalmar; Ruby
Oh, Vera   Brown, Nacio Herb
Oh, What Was That Noise?   Gershwin, George; Gershwin, Ira
Oh When I'm Thinking of You Sonya   Fisher
Olcott's Irish Serenade   Olcott
Old Enough to Love   Rodgers
Old Fashioned Rose, An   Kahn
Old Names of Old Flames   Johnson, Howard
(Al-Le-Lu) Old Noah's Ark   Blake; Sissle
Old Shanghai   Brown, Lew; Friend
Old Timer's Rosary, An   Dixon; Henderson
On a Night Like This   Kahn
On Such a Beautiful Night   Caesar
On that Old Beaten Track   Stept
On with the Dance   Hart; Rodgers
Once   DeSylva; Gershwin, George; Gershwin, Ira
Once in a While   Atteridge
One Little Waltz   Coslow
One Smile   Johnson, Howard

One Wonderful Night   Gorney
Only a Dream   Smith, Harry B.
Only a Rose   Friml
Only One   Romberg; Smith, Harry B.
Only One for Me, The   DeSylva
Opera in 1860, The   Atteridge
Opera Star   Porter
Oriental Memories   Coots
Oriental Pearl   Carroll; Freed, Arthur
Original Two-Time Man   Donaldson
Osculation   Freed, Arthur
Our House of Dreams   Brennan
Our Little Captain   Gershwin, George; Gershwin, Ira
Out of a Clear Blue Sky   Edwards
Out of the Night   Brennan
Outdoor Life   DeSylva
Over a Garden Wall   Conrad
Paddlin' Madelin' Home   Woods
Page Mr. Handy   Robison
Pals   DeSylva
Pas D'Equestrienne (inst.)   Kern
Pass the Pickles Henry   Bryan
Pay Day Pauline   Harbach; Youmans
Peaceful Valley   Robison
Peach on the Beach   Harbach; Youmans
Pearl of Hawaii   Parish
Pep   Romberg
Perfect Gentleman, A   Caesar; Youmans
Phoebe Snow the Anthracite Mama   Fisher
Phoney Phil   Fain; Kahal; Mills
Piano Phun (inst.)   Alter
Pipes of Pansy, The   Hart; Rodgers
Play Me a New Tune   Coots
Please, Teacher   Coots
Poetry of Motion, The   DeSylva; Gershwin, George;
     Gershwin, Ira
Police, The   Caesar; Youmans
Polly of Hollywood   DeSylva; Hanley
Portion of Caviar, A   Carroll; Freed, Arthur
Pretty Puppy   Conrad
Prison Glide   Gorney
Professors   Bryan
Promenade Walk, The   Coots
Protest   Gershwin, George; Hammerstein; Harbach
Put Your Troubles in a Candy Box   Coots
Quack, Quack   Freed, Arthur
Queens   Caesar; Youmans
Race Is Over, The   DeSylva; Hanley
Rag Picker's Dance, The   Caesar; Youmans
Rah Rah Cholly   Snyder
Rain or Shine Pal of Mine   Leslie
Rakin' in the Hay   Baer
Read What the Papers Say   Brown, Lew; DeSylva;
     Henderson
Really, Would You Believe It?   Caesar; Youmans
Reason I Love You, Because I Do, The   Smith, Harry B.
Regimental Band   Romberg
Remember I'm Your Pal   Clare; Monaco
Remember Me   Freed, Arthur
Remember Me (Love Song)   Smith, Harry B.
Remembering You   Coots
Reminiscence   Smith, Harry B.
Reveille   Smith, Harry B.
Rhythm Rag   Robison
Rin-Tin-Tin   Romberg

Rio Grande   Caesar
Rising Sun (O! Lead Me to My Love)   Bryan; Motzan
Riverboat Shuffle   Parish
Road of Dreams, The   Coots
Rock-a-Bye Time   Egan; Whiting
Rocky Road to Dublin, Isn't Rocky Any More, The   Lewis;
     Young, Joseph
Room Enough for Me   Brown, Lew; DeSylva; Henderson
Rose of My Heart   Kahn; Whiting
Rose of St. Mary's   Bryan; Snyder
Rose of Yesterday   Gilbert
Rose-Time   Brown, Lew; DeSylva; Henderson
Rosie Posies   Carroll; Freed, Arthur
Rotisserie, The   Coots
Row! Row! Rosie   Bryan; Meyer
Runaway Train, The   Warren
Running After You   Johnson, Howard
Safety in Numbers   Coots
Sally Long   Bryan; Schwartz, Jean
Sally's Got the Blues   Kahn
Sally's Not the Same Old Rally   Stept
Santa Claus   Harbach; Youmans
Save Your Sorrow for Tomorrow   DeSylva
Say, Arabella (What's a Fella to Do)   Kahn
Say It with a Sable   Brown, Lew; DeSylva; Henderson
Say Who Is that Baby Doll   Turk
Schoe Plattler Tanz   Romberg
Schoolday Sweetheart   Bryan; McHugh
Scotch Archer's Song   Friml
Sea Legs   DeSylva
Seminola   Warren
Sentimental Me   Hart; Rodgers
Sentimental Sally   Rose
Sentimental Waltz   Carroll; Freed, Arthur
September in Caroline   Bryan
Serenade   Friml
Settle Down in a Little Town   Buck
Shadows on the Sand   Brennan
Shall I Tell Him?   Smith, Harry B.
She Can't Say No   Bryan; Meyer
She Says No   Rose
She's the Sweetest Gal in Kankakee   Warren
Shop Girls and Mannikins   DeSylva; Gershwin, George;
     Gershwin, Ira
Show Me How to Make Love   Caesar
Signal, The   Gershwin, George; Hammerstein; Harbach
Sing a Song in the Rain   Caesar
Sing Me a Song   Carroll; Freed, Arthur
Sky High   Atteridge
Sleepy Time Gal   Egan; Whiting
Smile All the While   Ager; Davis; Yellen
Smile Comrades   Turk
Snap Your Fingers   Gordon
So Long, I'll See You Again   Brennan; McHugh
So That's the Kind of a Girl You Are   Dixon; Dubin; Rose
So This Is Kissing   Caesar; Youmans
So This Is the States   DeSylva
Soliciting Subscriptions   Hart; Rodgers
Some Ambitious Mama's Hangin' 'Round My Papa   Stept
Some Day   Friml
Some Other Bird Whistled a Tune   Bryan; Fisher
Some Other Time   Davis
Somebody Was a Wonderful Pal when Somebody Won My
     Pal   Gilbert
Somebody's Crazy About You   Gorney

Somebody's Eyes   Kahn
Somebody's Garden   Brennan
Someone to Love   Kahn
Someone's Stolen My Sweet Sweet Baby   Brown, Lew; Clare
Something for Nothing   DeSylva; Hanley
Something Tells Me that One Is You   Turk
Something Wrong with Me   Coots
Sometime   Kahn
Sometimes I'm Happy   Caesar; Youmans
Somewhere in Lovers' Land   Atteridge
Song of the Flame   Gershwin, George; Hammerstein; Harbach
Song of the Vagabonds   Friml
Sonya (Yup Alay Yup)   Fisher
S.O.S. Stay on the Sidewalk   Johnson, Howard
So's Your Old Man   Hammerstein; Harbach; Kern
South Sea Island Baby   Kahn; Whiting
Spanish Eyes   Gilbert
Speech!   Clare; Friend
Spoon Bill from Louisville   Von Tilzer
Spread a Little Sunshine As You Go   Woods
Spring   Caesar
Spring in Autumn   Egan; Kahn
Squeeze Me   Waller
Stage Managers' Chorus (Walk Upon Your Toes)   Hart; Rodgers
Star of Glory, The   Smith, Harry B.
Stay at Home   Freed, Arthur
Steamin' Home   Brown, Lew; DeSylva; Henderson
Steppin' in Society   Akst
Stop, I'm Beginning to Care   Kahn
Stop, Look, Listen   Norworth
(Tell Me Why You and I Should Be) Strangers   Fisher
Strictly Business   DeSylva
Strike   Coots
Strolling, or What Have You?   Hammerstein; Harbach; Kern
Study in Legs, A   Atteridge
(My) Sugar-Plum   DeSylva
Sunny   Hammerstein; Harbach; Kern
Sunshine   Hammerstein; Harbach; Kern
Susan   Egan; Whiting
Suzanne   Donaldson; Kahn
Swanee Butterfly   Donaldson; Rose
Sweet and Low Down   Gershwin, George; Gershwin, Ira
Sweet Child   Whiting
Sweet Hawaiian Dreams   Parish
Sweet Man   Turk
Sweet Peter   Hart; Rodgers
Sweet Pickings   Carroll; Freed, Arthur
Sweet Southern Love   Johnson, Howard
Sweetheart, I Love Only You   Lewis; Young, Joseph
Sweetheart of Mine   Romberg
Sweetheart Rose   Davis
Sympathetic Someone   Kern
Syncopating Sadie   Buck
T'ain't Gold   Mills
Take a Little Baby Home with You   Coots
Take a Little Stroll with Me   Coots
Take a Walk with Me   Smith, Harry B.
Take 'em to the Door Blues   Coots
Take 'em to the Door (That's All There Is, There Ain't No More Blues)   Davis; Henderson; Rose
Take Me Back to Sunshine Land   Baer; Bryan
Take This Rose   Donaldson; Kahn
Taking a Wife   Romberg

Tale of a Shirt, The   Berlin
Tango Melody   Berlin
Tap the Toe   DeSylva; Hanley
Tartar   Gershwin, George; Hammerstein; Harbach
Te Deum Laudamus!   Friml
Tea for Two   Caesar; Youmans
Tell Me Again   Turk
Tell Me Bright Eyes   Motzan
Tell Me How I Can Forget   Brennan
Tell Me More!   DeSylva; Gershwin, George; Gershwin, Ira
Tell Me Not that You Are Forgetting   Smith, Harry B.
Tell Me To-Night   Clare
Telling Eyes   Pollack
Terpsichore and Troubadour   Hart; Rodgers
Thanks   Bryan; Fisher
That Certain Feeling   Gershwin, George; Gershwin, Ira
That Certain Party   Donaldson; Kahn
That Forgotten Melody   Youmans
That South Car'lina Jazz Dance   Blake; Sissle
That's All There Is, There Ain't No More   Woods
That's Her! That's Her! What Did I Tell Ya!   DeSylva; Donaldson
That's When a Fellow Needs a Friend   Conrad
That's Why She Is What She Is Now   Whiting
That's Why You're Mary Mine   Mitchell
(Don't Be Ashamed of) The Name of Abraham   Johnson, Howard
Then I Met You   Coslow; Motzan; Silver
There Is a Garden in Loveland   Smith, Harry B.
There's a Little Bit of Spain in California   Freed, Arthur
There's Life in the Old Dog Yet   Atteridge
These Charming People   Gershwin, George; Gershwin, Ira
They All Remind Me of You   Friend
They Don't Look the Same in the Morning   Freed, Arthur
They Still Look Good to Me   Conrad
They're Blaming the Charleston   Berlin
This Is My Dance   Egan; Kahn
This One Today and That One Tomorrow Means No One at All in the End   Coslow; Silver
Tho' We've No Authentic Reason   Hart; Rodgers
Those Lips Those Eyes Those Nose   Turk
Three Musketeers, The   Hart; Rodgers
Three Times a Day   DeSylva; Gershwin, George; Gershwin, Ira
Three Wise Monkeys, The   Blake; Sissle
Tillie of Longacre Square   Atteridge; Hanley
Ting-A-Ling (The Bell's Ring)   Berlin
Tip-Toes   Gershwin, George; Gershwin, Ira
Titina   Buck
To Be Loved by the One I Love   Alter; Mitchell
Toddle Along   Buck
Toddle Trot   Atteridge
Tomorrow   Conrad; Friml
Tondeleo   Buck
Too Bad, Jim   Razaf
Too Many Kisses in the Summer Bring Too Many Tears in the Fall   Dubin; Rose; Warren
Too Many Parties and Too Many Pals   Henderson; Rose
Too Many Rings Around Rosie   Caesar; Youmans
Too Many Sweethearts   Berlin
Treasure Island   Egan; Whiting
True Hearts   Romberg
True Love   DeSylva; Hanley
Trying   Smith, Harry B.
Tryst of Love (inst.)   Carmichael

Twilight   DeSylva; Gorney
Twilight, the Stars, and You   Brown, Nacio Herb
Twilight Voices   Romberg; Smith, Harry B.
Two Eyes   Johnson, Howard
Two Little Bluebirds   Hammerstein; Harbach; Kern
2:02 Choo Choo Bound for Caroline, The   Brown, Lew; DeSylva; Henderson
Two Together   Kahn; Whiting
Ukelele Baby   Rose
Ukulele Lady   Donaldson; Kahn; Whiting
Ukulele Lorelei   DeSylva; Gershwin, George; Gershwin, Ira
Underneath the Stars with You   Stept
Underneath the Weeping Willow   Brennan; McHugh
Underneath the Yum Yum Tree   Kalmar; Ruby
Ups and Down   Smith, Harry B.
Vagabond King   Friml
Valeska (My Russian Rose)   Mills
Vamp Your Man   Romberg
Veleska (My Russian Rose)   Fain; Kahal
Venetian Isles   Berlin
Venetian Nights   Atteridge
Venetian Wedding Moon   Coots
Victory March, The   Friml
Vintage Chorus   Smith, Harry B.
Violets   Smith, Harry B.
Vision of Hassan, A   Atteridge
Vodka (Don't Give Me Vodka)   Gershwin, George; Hammerstein; Harbach
Voodle-Doodle-Yodel-Indian-Man   Stept
Wait Till the Morning After   Egan; Whiting
Wait Till Tomorrow Night   Leslie; Woods
Wait Till You See My Baby and Me   Bryan
Waiting for Something   Caesar; Youmans
Waiting for the Train   Gershwin, George; Gershwin, Ira
Walking Home with Josie   Kern
Waller-ing Around (inst.)   Waller
Waltz in the Moonlight, A   Parish
Waltz of Love, The   Koehler
Wanda   Egan; Whiting
Wander Away   Hammerstein; Harbach
Wanna Lotta Love   DeSylva
Want a Little Lovin'?   Davis; Warren
War Is War   Hart; Rodgers
Washboard Blues   Mills
Washboard Blues (inst.)   Carmichael
Wasted Years   Dubin
Waters of the Perkiomen   Dubin
'Way Down South in Chicago (By the Old Pacific Shore)   Warren
Wayside Flower   Romberg
We   Gershwin, George; Gershwin, Ira
We Can't Can All the Peaches We Pick, but We Can All the Peaches We Can   Bryan; Schwartz, Jean
We Make the Show   Atteridge
We Should Care   Berlin
We Want the Charleston   Brown, Lew; Henderson
Weaken a Bit   Gershwin, George; Gershwin, Ira
Weary of Waiting for You   Kahn; Whiting
Wedding Bells Were Ringing, The   Carroll; Freed, Arthur
Wedding Knell, The   Hammerstein; Harbach; Kern
Wedding Scene (Finale Act I)   Hammerstein; Harbach; Kern
Wedgewood Maid   Coots
Welcome Home   DeSylva; Hanley
We'll Meet Again in Normandy   Kahn

We're Back Together Again, My Baby and Me   Clare; Monaco
We're Gymnastic   Hammerstein; Harbach; Kern
What a Blue-Eyed Baby You Are   Parish
What a World This Would Be   Brown, Lew; DeSylva; Henderson
What Are We Waiting For   Donaldson; Kahn
What Are You Doing Tonight Blondy?   Dixon; Henderson; Rose
What Are You Gonna Do When You Ain't Got Nothin' to Do   Donaldson; Kahn
What Could Be Sweeter Than You?   Brown, Lew; Friend
What Do I Care   Romberg; Smith, Harry B.
What Do I Care, What Do I Care, My Sweetie Turned Me Down   Donaldson; Kahn
What Does Little Sweetie Want . Von Tilzer
What's a Feller Gonna Do   Woods
What's Become of Josephine   Stept
When a Blond Makes Up Her Mind to Do You Good   Fain
When a Blonde Makes Up Her Mind to Do You Good   Mills
When Autumn Leaves Are Falling   Coslow; Silver
When Do We Dance?   Gershwin, George; Gershwin, Ira
When Eyes of Blue Are Fooling You   Clare; Monaco
When I Dream of the Last Waltz with You   Kahn
When I Fell in Love with You   Kern
When Love Is Near   Egan; Kahn
When My Violin Is Calling   Smith, Harry B.
When Nathan Was Married to Rose of Washington Square   Buck
When She's Getting Cold on You, She's Warming Up to Somebody Else   Bryan; Schwartz, Jean
When Somebody Else Means the World to You   Sterling
When the Day Is Ended   Freed, Arthur
When the Debbies Go By   DeSylva; Gershwin, George; Gershwin, Ira
When the Golden Rod Is Waving Again Dear in the Eternal City   Von Tilzer
When the Right Boy Meets the Right Girl (That's the Right Time to Love)   Gorney
When We Get Our Divorce   Hammerstein; Harbach; Kern
When You Do What You Do   Parish
When You Find Her Remind Her of Me   Johnson, Howard
When You Love More than One You'll Have No One in Love with You   Bryan
When You Roll Your Eyes   Friend
When You See That Aunt of Mine   Johnson, Howard
When Your Door Closed Another Door Opened   Razaf
When You're in the Arms of the One You Love   Edwards; Johnson, Howard
Where Are You Girl of My Dreams   Rose
Where Has My Lima Bean?   Brown, Lew
Where Is My Old Girl Tonight   Dixon; Rose; Woods
Where Is My Old Pal Tonight   Conrad
Where Is My Rose of Waikiki   Egan; Whiting
Where the Four Leaf Clovers Grow   Egan; Whiting
Where the Heck is Mulligan?   Conrad; Rose
Where the Huckleberries Grow   Bryan
Where the Hudson River Flows   Edwards; Hart; Rodgers
Where Would I Be If I Never Met You and You Never Met Me   Gilbert
Whip-Poor-Will   Friml; Smith, Harry B.
Whirled Into Happiness   Atteridge
Whisper Sweet Nothing's to Me   Baer; Kahn
Whisper You Love Me   Friend; Turk
Who?   Hammerstein; Harbach; Kern

Who Calls You Baby Now   Davis
Who Do You Think We Are?   Gorney
Who Told You   Kahn
Who Was Chasing Paul Revere?   DeSylva; Hanley
Who Wouldn't Love You   Davis
Whole World Knows I Love You, The   Kahn
Whoopee   Brown, Lew; Conrad; DeSylva
Who's Lovin' My Sweetie Now   Stept
Who's Loving You Now?   Baer
Who's the Who (Where Has My Hubby Gones
      Blues)   Caesar; Youmans
Who's Who with You   Freed, Arthur
Who's with You Tonight?   Motzan
Whosis Whatsis, The   Brown, Lew; DeSylva; Henderson
Why Am I a Hit with the Ladies?   Berlin
Why Aren't Yez Eatin' More Oranges (From
      Cal-i-for-ni-ay)   Brown, Lew
Why Did I Leave Wisconsin — Kenosha, Wisconsin   Dietz
Why Did You Make Me Care?   Blake; Sissle
Why Do I Love You?   DeSylva; Gershwin, George;
      Gershwin, Ira
Why Don't You Do It Now   Stept
Why Is Love?   Coots
Why Should I Pine for the World to Be Mine   Donaldson;
      Friend
Wide Pants Willie   Atteridge; Hanley
Wind Blew Through His Whiskers   Rose
Window Cleaners, The   Kalmar; Ruby
Without You   Conrad
Woman's Work Is Never Done   Gershwin, George;
      Hammerstein; Harbach
Wonder If You Ever Think of Me   Kahn
Wonderful Girl   Coots
Wondering   Kalmar; Ruby
Won't You Tell Me that You'll Miss Me When You Kiss Me
      Goodnight   Donaldson; Kahn
Workin' Woman Blues   Waller
Would You Come Back to Me?   Brown, Lew; Friend
Ya Ya Alma   Fisher
Ya-Ha-Ha   Fain
Yearning (Just for You)   Davis
Yes or No   Romberg; Smith, Harry B.
Yes Sir! That's My Baby   Donaldson; Kahn
You and You and Me   Hammerstein; Harbach
You Are You   Gershwin, George; Hammerstein; Harbach
You Better Keep the Home Fires Burning Cause Your
      Mama's Getting Cold   Leslie
You Can Dance with Any Girl at All   Caesar; Youmans
You Can't Can Like Girls Can   Johnson, Howard
You Can't Go Wrong with a Love Song   Coslow; Johnson,
      Howard
You Can't Make a Monkey Out of Me   Rose
You for Me — Me for You   Stept
You for Me, Me for You From Now On   Johnson, James P.
You Forgot to Remember   Berlin
You Gotta Know How   Donaldson
You Killed All My Love for You   Lewis; Young, Joseph
You Made Me Give Up Everyone Else and Now You Throw
      Me Down   Gilbert
You Must Come Over Blues   DeSylva; Gershwin, Ira
You Need a Man, Suzanne   DeSylva
You'll Find Me Waiting for You   Stept
You'll Have to Guess   Smith, Harry B.
You'll Love Me Someday, So Why Not Now   Wrubel
Your Country Needs You   Smith, Harry B.

Your Flag and My Flag   Woods
Your Kiss Told Me   Caesar
You're Just a Show-Off   Dubin
You're Just the Kind of a Girl I'd Like to —-   Friend
You've Got to Dance to Win the Prince of Wales   Freed,
      Arthur

1926

Actions Speak Louder than Words   Donaldson
After a While   Akst; Davis
(What Can I Say, Dear) After I Say I'm Sorry   Donaldson
Ain't It Romantic   Gershwin, George; Gershwin, Ira
Alabama Stomp   Johnson, James P.
Alcazar   Smith, Harry B.
Ali Baba Babies, The   Harbach; Kern
Ali-Up   Hammerstein; Harbach; Romberg
All Alone Monday   Kalmar; Ruby
All Hail to the General   Hammerstein; Harbach; Romberg
All I Want to Do (Is Be with You)   Donaldson
All the Boys Keep Looking Down   Von Tilzer
Allez-Up   Hart; Rodgers
(Oh, How We Love Our) Alma Mater   Kalmar; Ruby
Along Came Ruth   Berlin
Along Miami Shore   Warren
Along the Gypsy Trail   Stept
Am I Wasting My Time on You   Johnson, Howard
Amarillo (inst.)   Robison
American Beauty Rose   Hart; Rodgers
American Revue Girls   Conrad
And the Moonlight's Calling You   Schwartz, Jean
And Then I Forgot   Davis
Angel Eyes   Lewis; Young, Joseph
Any Little Tune   Kalmar; Ruby
Arabella's Wedding Day   Meyer
Are You Lonesome Tonight   Turk
Are You Satisfied   Brown, Lew; DeSylva; Henderson
At Peace with the World   Berlin
At Sundown   Razaf
At Ten to Ten in Tennessee   McHugh
At the Foot of the Hill of Dreams   DeSylva; Hanley
At the Party   Kalmar; Ruby
At the Prom   Donaldson
At the Saskatchewan   Hart; Rodgers
Atlantic Blues   Hart; Rodgers
Azuri's Dance of Triumph (inst.)   Romberg
Baby Face   Akst; Davis
Babying You   Kalmar; Ruby
Bachanol   Coots
Back to My Heart   Duke
Back to Nature   Hart; Rodgers
Bad Little Boy with Dancing Legs   Coots
Bambalina Maid   Meyer
Banishment (inst.), The   Romberg
Barcelona   Kahn
Bashful   Kahn
Basket of Oriental Flowers   Johnston; Turk
Be Happy   Meyer
Be Satisfied   Bryan
(You Must Have Been a) Beautiful Baby   DeSylva; Hanley
Beautiful Fan, A   Coots
Beauty Adorned   Coots
Beauty of Another Day, The   Hart; Rodgers
Because I Love You   Berlin
Beethoven's Sangwattni (inst.)   Waller

Behind the Clouds Are Crowds and Crowds of
  Sunbeams   Davis; DeSylva
Beside a Garden Wall   Kahn
Betty   Ahlert
Between You and Me and the Lamp-Post   Bryan
Birds Up High (Birds on High)   Hart; Rodgers
Birth of the Blues, The   Brown, Lew; DeSylva; Henderson
Black Bottom, The   Brown, Lew; DeSylva; Henderson
Black Bottom Betty   Akst
Black Sheep in Our Family Is a Blue Eyed Baby, The   Clare;
  Monaco
Black Sheep of the Family Is a Blue-Eyed Baby Blonde,
  The   Bryan
Blame It on the Waltz   Kahn
Blonde Wimmen   Rose
Blonde Wimmin   Fisher
Blowin' Off Steam   Johnson, Howard
Blowing the Blues Away   Gershwin, Ira
Blue Bonnet (You Make Me Feel Blue)   Bryan
Blue Print Blues   Gorney
Blue Room, The   Hart; Rodgers
Blue Skies   Berlin
Blue Train, The   Gorney
Boarding House Love Call   Schwartz, Jean
Bobbed Haired Baby   Coots
Boneyard Shuffle   Carmichael; Mills
Bounce Me   Conrad; Kahn
Bread and Butter   Harbach; Kern
Breezin' Along with the Breeze   Whiting
Breezing Along   Robin
Bride and Groom   Gershwin, George; Gershwin, Ira
Bridget O'Flynn (Where've You Been)   Sterling
Bring on the Ding Dong Bell   Gershwin, George; Gershwin,
  Ira
Broken Rhythm   Coots
Broken Rhythm (inst.)   Robison
Broken-Hearted   Whiting
Brother of Mine   Smith, Harry B.
Brown Eyes   Friml; Hammerstein; Harbach
Brown-Eyed Girl   Smith, Harry B.
Bugle Blow   Hart; Rodgers
Burn Up   Hart; Rodgers
But Not Today   Conrad
Butcher, the Baker, the Candlestick Maker, The   Meyer
Buy a Little Button from Us   Gershwin, George
By the Sign of the Moon   Rose; Whiting
Bye Bye Blackbird   Dixon; Henderson
Bye Bye Shanghai   Johnston; Turk
Cabarets   Hart; Rodgers
California My Homeland   Brennan
California Skies   Kalmar; Ruby
California Twilight   Turk
(Come at the) Call of Love   Smith, Harry B.
Calling Me Home   Gilbert; Monaco
Camera Shoot   Hart; Rodgers
Camille   Mitchell
Caribbean Sea   Kahn
Carolina   Kahn
Carolina Mine Your Rolling Stone Is Rolling Home   Friend
Caroll-ina, The   Carroll
Castillian Dreams   Johnston; Turk
Charleston Hound   Waller
Charmaine   Pollack
Charming, Charming (Store Opening)   Hart; Rodgers
Chattanooga Choo Choo   Egan; Whiting

Cheri-Beri   Hart; Rodgers
Cherry Blossom Maid   Johnston; Turk
Chick-Keeta   Friend
Chinese Blues   Coslow; McHugh; Mills
Chip-Chip-Chippewa   Hanley
Chiropractic Papa   Conrad
Choo Choo Love   Conrad; Kahn
Chorus Picking Time on Broadway   Hanley
Chuck It   Hart; Rodgers
Cinderella   Hanley
Cinderella Girl   Harbach; Kern
Cinderella's Ride   Harbach; Kern
City Flat, A   Hart; Rodgers
Clap Yo' Hands   Dietz; Gershwin, George; Gershwin, Ira
Cock-a-Doodle, I'm Off My Noodle (My Baby's
  Back)   Johnson, Howard
Cocktail Melody   Donaldson
Colinette   Egan; Whiting
Colleen   Schwartz, Jean
College Days   Coots
Come and Tell Me   Hart; Rodgers
Como Camel Corps, The   Hammerstein; Harbach; Youmans
Congo Lou (inst.)   Waller
Coronation, The   Friml; Hammerstein; Harbach
Cottage I Call Je T'Aime   Schwartz, Jean
Could I? I Certainly Could   Ager; Yellen
Cover Me Up with Sunshine, and Feather My Nest with
  Love   Dixon; Henderson
Cradle of the Deep   Hart; Rodgers
Crazy 'Bout that Man I Love   Waller
Crazy Quilt   Sterling
Creole Crooning Song   Hart; Rodgers
Criss Cross   Harbach; Kern
Cross Your Heart   DeSylva
Crosses Mean Kisses   Bryan
Crystal Ball   Conrad; Kahn
Cup of Tea (Lido Lady, Opening), A   Hart; Rodgers
Curbstone Blues   Whiting
Cute Peekin' Knees   Schwartz, Jean
Damsel Who Done All the Dirt, The   Hart; Rodgers
Dance of the Camel Boys   Harbach; Kern
Dance of the Four Leaf Clovers   Harbach; Kern
Dance of the Golden Sprite   Harbach; Kern
Danse Diversement   Gorney
Dan-Sing   Johnston
David and Lenore   Brown, Lew; DeSylva; Henderson
David Crockett (Davy Crockett) (Who Kept the Wolves Away
  from the Door When Davy Crockett Went to
  War)   Hart; Rodgers
Day Dreams   Duke; Kalmar; Ruby
Day That I Lost You   Fisher
Dear Algerian Land   Harbach; Kern
Dear Home of Mine, Goodbye   Smith, Harry B.
Dear Little Girl (I Hope You've Missed Me)   Gershwin,
  George; Gershwin, Ira
Dear Old Buddy of Mine   Davis; Henderson
Delilah   Fisher
Desert Song, The   Hammerstein; Harbach; Romberg
Desire   Razaf
Devil Is Afraid of Music, The   Robison
Dictation   Gorney
Do a Duet   Schwartz, Jean
Do, Do, Do   Gershwin, George; Gershwin, Ira
Do I Know What I'm Doing   Fisher; Rose
Do that Doo-Da   Brennan

Do You Know Dan McPherson   Fisher
Do You Notice Anything?   Hart; Rodgers
Do You Really Mean to Go?   Hart; Rodgers
Don't Ask!   Gershwin, George; Gershwin, Ira
Don't Be Angry with Me   Donaldson
Don't Believe   Caesar
Don't Call 'em in the Morning   Johnson, Howard
Don't Cry Baby   Silver
Don't Cry When He's Gone   Meyer
Don't Do the Charleston   Buck; Hanley
Don't Fail Me, Dice   Stept
Don't Forget   DeSylva; Hanley
Don't Leave Your Girl Alone   Bryan; Meyer
Don't Take that Black Bottom Away   Coslow
Don't Tempt Me   Smith, Harry B.
Don't You Think She's a Pretty Baby   Silver
Down on the Florida Shore   Carroll
Dream in Your Eyes   Caesar
Dreaming   Conrad; Kahn
(Love's Dear Yearning) Dreaming in Paradise   Hammerstein;
    Harbach; Romberg
Dreaming of Allah   Harbach; Kern
Dreams for Sale   Hanley
Dreams Never Die   Robin
Drifting Apart   Kahn
Early in the Morning   Conrad; Kahn
Eastern and Western Love   Hammerstein; Harbach;
    Romberg
Eat a Piece of Pie   Fisher; Rose
Eccentricity Waltz   Johnson, James P.
Elegy (inst.)   Motzan
(That's My) Elsie Schultz-en-heim   Friend
(That's My) Elsie Shultz-En-Heim   Silver
Even If You Don't Love Me   Dixon; Henderson
Evenin', Caroline   Stept
Every Little Thing You Do   Buck; Hanley
Everybody's Got Somebody But Me   McHugh
Everybody's Sister but Yours and Mine   Lewis; Young,
    Joseph
Everyone Celebrate   Robin
Every-Ready Freddie   Hart; Rodgers
Everything Will Happen for the Best   DeSylva
Everything's Gonna Be All Right   Akst; Davis
(You Know, I Know) Ev'rything's Made for Love   Johnson,
    Howard
Exercise   Hart; Rodgers
Faded Flowers   Brown, Lew; Clare
Fall of the Leaves, The   Coots
Falling In Love with You   Davis
Farewell   Hammerstein; Harbach; Romberg
Fascinating Lady   Coots
Fatal Blonde   Schwartz, Jean
Feeding the Chickens   Gorney
Few Moments at the Piano (inst.), A   Alter
Fiddle-Dee-Dee-Dee   Yellen
Fidgety Feet   Gershwin, George; Gershwin, Ira
Finale Act I: Isn't It Grand?   Gershwin, George; Gershwin,
    Ira
Finaletto act II, Scene I: On Single Life Today   Gershwin,
    George; Gershwin, Ira
Fine Feathers   Coots
Fire   Whiting
Fire Brigades, The   Bryan; Snyder
First We Throw Moe Out (Finaletto, Act II, Scene I)   Hart;
    Rodgers

Flap-a-Doodle   Harbach; Kern
Flirtation Dance   Smith, Harry B.
Floating Along   Youmans
Florida Low Down   Waller
Florida, the Moon and You   Buck; Friml; Hanley
Folks in New York City Ain't Like Folks Down South   Razaf
Follow Me   Smith, Harry B.
Follow On   Hart; Rodgers
Follow the Crowd   Gorney
For Baby and Me   Meyer
For Ching-a-Ling and Me   Johnston; Turk
For Heaven's Sake   Bryan
For My Sweetheart   Donaldson; Kahn
For No Good Reason at All   Baer; Lewis; Young, Joseph
Forever, Forever I Want You   Howard, Joseph E.
Forgive Me   Ager; Yellen
Four Little Song Pluggers   Hart; Rodgers
French Military Marching Song   Hammerstein; Harbach;
    Romberg
Frisco Bay   Fisher; Rose
From Tomorrow Morning On   Dixon; Henderson
Gee, but I'd Like to Be Bad   Hanley
Gee How I Wish I Had You Back Again   Bryan
Gentlemen of the Press   Schwartz, Jean
Gentlemen Prefer Blondes   Caesar; DeSylva; Friml
Georgia Bo-Bo   Waller
Georgianna   Akst; Lewis; Young, Joseph
Georgie and I   Conrad
Get a Load of That   Lewis; Young, Joseph
Gigolo   Hart; Rodgers
Gimme a Little Kiss Will Ya Huh   Turk
Girl Friend, The   Hart; Rodgers
Girl in Your Arms, A   Caesar; Gorney
Girl Is You and the Boy Is Me, The   Brown, Lew
Give Me a Ukulele and a Ukulele Baby and Leave the Rest to
    Me   Brown, Lew
Give Me Your Love Dear   Mills
Give This Little Girl a Hand (Give That Little Girl a
    Hand)   Hart; Rodgers
Golden Dreams   Smith, Harry B.
Golden Gates of Happiness   Coots
Gone   Davis
Gone Again Gal   Kahn
Good Fellow Mine   Hart; Rodgers
Good Old Harry   Hart; Rodgers
Goodbye Lenny   Hart; Rodgers
Goodness Gracious Agnes   Donaldson; Kahn
Great Scott   Waller
Greyhound   Youmans
Guess Who   Gershwin, George; Gershwin, Ira
Guess-Yes   Schwartz, Jean
Gypsy Passion   Smith, Harry B.
Half a Moon Is Better than No Moon   Hanley
Hallowe'en   Hanley
Hands Off, That's My Gal   Razaf
Hard-to-Get Gertie   Ager; Yellen
Harlem Choc'late Babies (inst.)   Johnson, James P.
Harlem Prance, The   Akst; Mitchell
Harmonica Jim   Stept
Harvest Moon Is Shining, Liza (For You and Me), The   Stept
Has Anybody Seen My Bennie   Hammerstein; Harbach;
    Romberg
Havana (Havana Opening)   Hart; Rodgers
Have You Forgotten   Ager; Yellen
He Comes Up to See Me Once in a While   Meyer

He Left Her Behind Before   Bryan; Silver
He May Say 'Yes' Today   Smith, Harry B.
Head Over Heels in Love   Hanley
Heart to Let, A   Razaf
Heaven on Earth   Dietz; Gershwin, George; Gershwin, Ira
Hello!   Hart; Rodgers
Hello, Aloha, How Are You   Baer; Gilbert
Hello Are You There, Hello   Stept
Hello Baby   Whiting
Hello, Bluebird   Friend
Hello, Hello, Sandy   Brown, Nacio Herb; Freed, Arthur
Hello Swanee Hello   Coslow
Her Beaus Are Only Rainbows   Bryan; Meyer
Here Comes Fatima with Her Ta-Ra-Boom Dee-Ay   Brown,
    Lew; Friend
Here Comes Malinda   Akst; Davis
Here Comes the Bride   Gorney
Here I Am   Brown, Lew; DeSylva; Henderson
Here in My Arms   Hart; Rodgers
Here or There As Long As I'm with You   Davis
Here's Hopin'   Davis
He's a Winner (Sporting Life/Reporters' Opening)   Hart;
    Rodgers
Hey! Hey!   Hart; Rodgers
High Hats   Hart; Rodgers
High, High, High Up in the Hills   Lewis
High on a Hill   Hammerstein; Harbach; Romberg
Hi-Ho the Merrio, As Long As She Loves Me   Brown, Lew;
    Conrad; Davis
Ho! (The Riff Song)   Hammerstein; Harbach; Romberg
Hokum-Smokum-Indian-Man   Stept
Hola, Fellow (Song of Greeting)   Smith, Harry B.
Home Again   Meyer
Homely, But Clean   Youmans
Honey, Be Mine   Buck; Hanley
Honeymoon Lane   Hanley
Honky Tonk Toddle   Brown, Nacio Herb; Freed, Arthur
Hoodle Dee Doo Dee Doo Doo   Turk
Hooray for the Irish   Leslie; Monaco
Hop Skip   Caesar
Horses   Whiting
Hot Henry   Carroll
Hotten Trot, The   Meyer
House that Monty's "Jack" Built, The   Robin
How Can I Be Happy with No, No, No-One to Love   Akst;
    Davis
How (Can I Keep from Loving You)   Caesar
How Can You Keep Your Mind on Business?   Friml;
    Hammerstein; Harbach
How Could I Be Blue?   Razaf
How Different Things Would Be   Donaldson
(I'm Tellin' the Birds, Tellin' the Bees) How I Love
    You   Brown, Lew; Friend
How Many Times?   Berlin
How, Where, When, Why, What Made Me Start to Love
    You   Johnson, Howard
How'd Ya Like to Meet Me in the Moonlight   Coslow
Howdy to Broadway   Hart; Rodgers
Hugs and Kisses   Alter
Hum, Hum, Hum, Hum Your Troubles Away   Friend;
    Woods
Hum To   Hart; Rodgers
Hydrophobia Blues   Harbach; Kern
I Adore Eleanor   Coots
I Adore You   Coslow

I Ain't Got No Hard Luck Now   Dixon
I Ain't Got Nobody and I Don't Want Nobody but
    You   Baer; Lewis; Young, Joseph
I Belong to Someone   Silver
I Belong to You, You Belong to Me   Henderson
I Call Upon You Gentlemen   Hart; Rodgers
I Can't Be Happy   Youmans
I Can't Blame the Boys for Lovin' You   Razaf
(I've Got Her Off My Hands, Now That She's Off My
    Hands) I Can't Get Her Off o' My Mind   Lewis; Young,
    Joseph
I Can't Keep You Out of My Dreams   Fain; Kahal
I Can't Make My Husband Behave   Youmans
I Didn't Wanna, But I Wanna Love You Now   Brown, Lew;
    Clare; Monaco
I Don't Believe in Kissing   Johnson, Howard
I Don't Believe It but Say It Again   Silver
I Don't Like Them Too   Donaldson
I Don't Mind Being All Alone, When I'm All Alone with
    You   McHugh; Mills
I Don't Want Him   Conrad; Kahn
I Don't Want the World   Davis
I Found a Million Dollar Baby   Fisher; Rose
I Found a Round-About Way to Heaven   Silver
I Got a Mama Down in New Orleans, Another Mama Up in
    Maine   McHugh; Mills
I Gotta Get Myself Somebody to Love   Lewis; Young,
    Joseph
I Guess I Should Be Satisfied (Finale Act I)   Hart; Rodgers
I Just Made Up with My Darling   Coots
I Just Said Goodbye to My Troubles When I Said Hello to
    You   Davis
I Know that You Know   Youmans
I Know That You Love Me   Kalmar; Ruby
I Long To Belong to Someone Who Longs to Belong to
    Me   Bryan; Silver
I Lost My Heart in Monterey   Egan; Whiting
I Love a Ukelele   Friend; Kahn
I Love My Little Susie   Harbach; Kern
I Love Only You Dear   Friend
I Love the Moonlight   Akst; Davis
I Love to Dance   Conrad; Kahn
I Love You Sincerely   Silver
I May   Smith, Harry B.
I May Be Dancing with Somebody Else (But I Love
    You)   Brown, Lew; Clare; Conrad
I Might Have Known   Stept
I Must Be Going   Hart; Rodgers
I Need Lovin'   Johnson, James P.
I Never Cried Before I Met You   Coslow
I Never Knew what the Moonlight Could Do (Till the Night I
    Met You)   Coslow
I Never Thought That You'd Do That to Me   Kahal
I New Orleans   Hart; Rodgers
I Still Believe in You   Gilbert
I Used to Shower Her with Kisses   Henderson; Lewis;
    Young, Joseph
I Wanna Go Back to Heaven Again   Koehler
I Want a Girl to Call My Own   Buck; Friml
I Want a Kiss   Hammerstein; Harbach; Romberg
I Want a Man   Hart; Rodgers
I Want Somebody to Cheer Me Up   Kahn
I Want to Be a Liberty Belle   Gorney
(Any Time Is Just the Time) I Want to Be with
    You   Donaldson; Kahn

I Wish I Could Stop Remembering   Coslow
I Wish I Had Died in My Cradle Before I Grew Up to Love
    You   Brown, Lew
I Wish I Had My Old Gal Back Again   Ager; Pollack; Yellen
I Wish I Had You Back in My Arms   Davis
I Wish I Was in Prison   Dubin; Fain
I Wonder What's Become of Joe   Turk
I Wonder Where My Buddies Are Tonight   Egan; Rose;
    Whiting
I Won't Go Home Tonight   Conrad; Gilbert
I Would Like to Know Why   Blake; Sissle
I Wouldn't Fool a Little Girl Like You   Conrad; Meyer
I'd Climb the Highest Mountain If I Knew I'd Find
    You   Brown, Lew; Clare
I'd Do It All Over Again   Conrad; Meyer
I'd Give a Lot of Love to Get a Little Love from
    Someone   Woods
I'd Leave Ten Men Like Yours to Love One Man Like
    Mine   Leslie
I'd Love to Meet that Old Sweetheart of Mine   Davis
I'd Rather Be Alone Just Thinking of You   Ager; Yellen
I'd Rather Charleston   Gershwin, George
I'd Steal a Star   Youmans
Idles of the King   Hart; Rodgers
If All the Stars Were Pretty Babies   Fisher; Rose
If I Could Be with You (One Hour Tonight)   Johnson, James
    P.
If I Could Have My Way   Razaf
If I Didn't Know Your Husband and You Didn't Know My
    Wife   Baer; Gilbert
(I'd Climb the Highest Mountain) If I Knew I'd Find
    You   Brown, Lew
If I Only Had You Back Again   Davis
If I Were You   Hart; Rodgers
If I'd Only Believed in You   Akst; Davis
If My Baby Cooks   Kahal
If Tears Could Bring You Back to Me   Johnson, Howard
If You Believed in Me As I Believe in You   Davis
If You Can't Hold the Man You Love (Don't Cry When He's
    Gone)   Fain; Kahal
If You Can't Land 'em on the Old Veranda   Silver
If You Can't Tell the World She's a Good Little Girl (Just Say
    Nothing at All)   Dubin; Fain; Kahal
If You Know What I Mean   Schwartz, Arthur
If You Miss Me As I Miss You   Davis
If Your Name Had Been LaRotta   Hammerstein; Harbach;
    Youmans
I'll Be a Buoyant Girl   Hammerstein; Harbach; Romberg
I'll Get Along As Long As I Have You   Turk
I'll Keep on Dreaming   Smith, Harry B.
I'll Say It with a Pretty Little Song   Stept
I'll See You Some-Moa in Samoa   Johnson, Howard
I'm a Bad Boy Looking for a Good Girl (And Will Make a
    Bad Boy Good)   Stept
I'm a Broken Hearted Blackbird   Fields; McHugh
I'm a Little Blackbird Looking for a Bluebird   Meyer
I'm a Little Movie Queen   Schwartz, Jean
I'm a Little Too Old to Dance   Conrad; Kahn
I'm a One-Man Girl   Robin
I'm a Red Hot Cradle Snatcher   Robin
I'm Arrangin' for Changin' Your Name   Baer; Gilbert
I'm Crazy About the Charleston   Hart; Rodgers
I'm Flirting with You   Friend
I'm Full of Love for Her, She's Full of Love for Me   Rose;
    Woods

I'm Getting Mine   Coots
I'm Going Up the Girl's House Tonight   Baer; Dixon
I'm Gonna Make Haste (To Where the Sun Shines in
    Virginia)   Johnston; Turk
I'm Gonna Pop My Papa   Johnston; Turk
I'm in Love   Conrad; Harbach; Kahn
I'm in Love with You That's Why   Dixon; Henderson
I'm Just Wild About Animal Crackers   Coslow
I'm Lonely (Without You)   Warren
I'm Longing for a Girl Named Mary   Stept
I'm on My Way Home   Berlin
I'm Only Another to You   Johnson, Howard
I'm So Humble (Inferiority Complex)   Hart; Rodgers
I'm Telling the Birds and Bees How I Love You   Brown, Lew
I'm the Extra Man   Friml; Hammerstein; Harbach
I'm Tired of Running After You   Silver
I'm Walking Around in Circles   Lewis; Young, Joseph
In a Little Spanish Town, 'Twas on a Night Like
    This   Lewis; Young, Joseph
In a Taxi Cab   Brown, Nacio Herb; Freed, Arthur
In Araby with You   Hammerstein; Harbach; Kern
In Armenia   Smith, Harry B.
In Darkest Russia   Meyer
In His Arms   Hart; Rodgers
In My Gondola   Warren
In My Indiana Inn   Bryan; Fisher
In Our Parlor on the Third Floor Back   Hart; Rodgers
In Sweetheart Time   Coots
In the Days Gone By   Smith, Harry B.
In the Land of Let's Suppose   Robin
In the Name of Art   Hart; Rodgers
In Variety   Hart; Rodgers
In Your Green Hat   Ager; Yellen
Independance   Gorney
Indignation Meeting   Harbach; Kern
Is It Any Wonder   Rose
Is My Girl Refined?   Hart; Rodgers
Isn't (Ain't) She Beautiful   Razaf
Isn't It Strange   Brown, Nacio Herb; Freed, Arthur
Isn't It Wonderful   Brown, Lew; Friend
It   Hammerstein; Harbach; Romberg
It Made You Happy When You Made Me Cry   Donaldson
It May Rain   Hart; Rodgers
It Pays to Advertise   DeSylva
It Takes a Good Woman to Keep a Good Man at
    Home   Ager; Yellen
It Was Fair   Friml; Hammerstein; Harbach
(How Do You Like My Baby) It Won't Be Long Before She
    Belongs to Me   Friend; Woods
It Won't Be Long Now   Johnson, Howard
It's a Good Thing Cows Don't Cry   Leslie
It's a Struggle   Donaldson; Kahn
It's a Wonderful World After All   Davis
It's All Right with Me Sweetheart   Coslow
It's Alright with Me (If It's Alright with You)   Robin
It's Nicer to Be Naughty   Duke
It's Your Own Fault Annabelle   Whiting
I've Found the Bluebird   Robin
I've Got the Girl   Donaldson
I've Looked for Trouble   Kern
I've Lost All My Love for You   Young, Joseph
I've Waited for This   Egan; Whiting
Iyone, My Own Iyone   Bryan
Jane We'll Start Chasing Rainbows Again   Fisher
Java   Johnston; Turk

Jazz Time Came from the South   Meyer
Jersey Walk (Shake 'em Up Kid)   Hanley
Jingles (inst.)   Johnson, James P.
Journey's End   Schwartz, Jean
Julius You Wonderful Boy   Conrad; Meyer
Jungle Nights in Dixieland   Meyer
Just a Bird's Eye View (Of My Old Kentucky Home)   Donaldson; Kahn
Just a Bunch of Wild Flowers   Schwartz, Jean
Just a Little Extra   Schwartz, Jean
Just a Little Lonely   Kahn
Just a Little Longer   Berlin
Just a Little Rose   Kahn
Just a Smile   Clare; Monaco
Just Another Day Without You   Kahn
Just for a Moment   Meyer
Just One Kiss   Kalmar; Ruby
Just Picture You Lovin' Just Me   Johnston; Turk
Just to Make a Long Story Short   Whiting
Just Wond'ring   Kahn
Kalua Lu   Egan; Whiting
Kandahar Isle   Coots
Keep a Little Sunshine in Your Heart   Von Tilzer
Keepin' Out of Trouble   Brown, Nacio Herb; Freed, Arthur
Ker-Choo (Geshundheit)   Mitchell
Keys to Heaven   Hart; Rodgers
Kickapoo Trail   Egan; Whiting
Kid Next Door, The   Leslie
Kiss a Four Leaf Clover   Harbach; Kern
Kiss Me Good-Night All Night   Bryan
Kiss Your Little Baby Goodnight   Donaldson
Kitty's Kisses   Conrad; Kahn
Kitzel Engagement, The   Hart; Rodgers
Ladies, The   Schwartz, Jean
Lady Fair   Brown, Lew; DeSylva; Henderson
Lady of the Rose   Friml; Hammerstein; Harbach
Lady, You Don't Know Me   Gorney
Laugh at Love   Schwartz, Jean
Laughing Eyes   Sterling
Lay Me Down to Sleep in Carolina   Ager; Yellen
Leaders of the Modern Regime   Harbach; Kern
Learning to Love You   Akst; Davis
Left, Left, My Sweetie Got Mad and She Left   Johnson, Howard
Leonore   Donaldson
Let Love Go   Hammerstein; Harbach; Romberg
Let Me Live and Love You Just for Tonight   Stept
Let's All Henry Ford   Leslie; Monaco
Let's Call It a Day   Friend; Kahn
Let's Forget and Be Sweethearts Again   Whiting
Let's Get Married Right Away   Blake; Sissle
Let's Have a Love Affair   Hammerstein; Harbach; Romberg
Let's Make Believe   Gorney
Let's Talk about My Sweetie   Donaldson; Kahn
Letter from Dixie (inst.), A   Robison
Letter of Farewell, A   Smith, Harry B.
Levee Gang   Meyer
Levee Land (inst.)   Waller
Levee Lovey   Donaldson; Kahn
L'heure d'or (One Golden Hour)   Friml; Hammerstein; Harbach
Liberty March (inst.)   Johnson, James P.
Lido Lady   Hart; Rodgers
Life's One Sweet Song for Me, I'm in Love with You   Alter
Like He Loves Me   Youmans

Like You Do   Kalmar; Ruby
Li'l Brown Baby   Razaf
Lilac Lou   Magidson
Lillie, Lawrence, and Jack   Hart; Rodgers
Lilly   Warren
Lily of the Valley   Youmans
Little Birdie Told Me So, A   Hart; Rodgers
Little Girl, a Little Boy, a Little Moon, A   Warren
Little Igloo for Two   Schwartz, Arthur
Little Marie   Buck; Hanley; Rose
Little Nightie Hanging on the Line, A   Leslie
Little Old New Hampshire   Hanley
Little Siro Told Me So   Davis
Little Smile, a Little Sigh, A   Hanley
Little Song in My Heart, The   Donaldson
Little Souvenir, A   Hart; Rodgers
Little White House at the End of Honeymoon Lane, The   Hanley
Lo-Do De-O   Fain
Lonely Acres   Robison
Lonely Eyes   Akst; Davis
Lonesome and Sorry   Conrad; Davis
Lonesome Boy's Letter Back Home, A   Friend; Woods
Lonesome One   Razaf; Waller
Long Is a Wonderful Thing   Gorney
Look Out Here Comes My Cookie   Donaldson
Looking Around   Robin
Lo-oo De-O   McHugh; Mills
Lopeziana (inst.)   Alter
Louisiana   Coots
Love and Kisses 'n' Everything   Youmans
Love Has Found My Heart   Smith, Harry B.
Love Is a Two-Edged Sword   Hammerstein; Harbach; Romberg
Love Me, Don't You?   Friml; Hammerstein; Harbach
Lovely Lady   Friml; Hammerstein; Harbach
Love's Call   Coots
Love's Dear Yearning (Dreaming in Paradise)   Romberg
Lovin' Joe   Donaldson
Loving You   Schwartz, Jean
Lucky   Duke
(This Is My) Lucky Day   Brown, Lew; DeSylva; Henderson
Lucky Moon   Akst; Davis
Lula Palula   Bryan
Lullaby Blues   Johnston
Lulu Belle   Dixon; Henderson; Robin
Lunatic's Lullaby, The   Leslie
Magic of the Moon, The   Duke
Make Believe You're Mine   Smith, Harry B.
Make Him Feel at Home   Johnson, Howard
Make Me Happy   Johnson, Howard
Make Up Your Mind   Meyer; Smith, Harry B.
Mama Stayed Out the Whole Night Long, but Mama Didn't Do No Wrong   Razaf
Mama's Dancing   Coslow
Mammy's Birthday   Meyer
Margot   Hammerstein; Harbach; Romberg
Marian   Donaldson
Marilyn (inst.)   Alter
Mary Dear, I Miss You Most of All   Hanley
Mary Had a Little Lamb   Dubin
Maybe   Gershwin, George; Gershwin, Ira; Hart; Rodgers
Maybe I Don't   Whiting
Maybe It's Me   Hart; Rodgers
Maybe Yes, Maybe No, Who Can Tell   Dubin; Fain; Kahal

Me   Smith, Harry B.

Me Too   Woods

Meet Me in the Moonlight (With the Lovelight in Your
    Eyes)   Friend; Kahn

Melancholy   Whiting

Melican Man, A   Hart; Rodgers

Melody of Love Coo to Me   Akst; Davis

Messin' Around   Blake; Sissle

Mexico (To Hell with Mexico)   Hart; Rodgers

Midnight Stomp   Waller

Mike   Davis; Hart; Rodgers

Mine   Turk

Minor Gaff (Blues Fantasy) (inst.)   Arlen

Mobile Mud   Robison

Mock the Mocking Bird   Stept

Moments   Youmans

Mona from Bologna   Silver; Turk

Montezuma   Robin

Moon Is on the Sea, The   Gershwin, George; Gershwin, Ira

Moonlight in Normandy   Bryan

Moonlight Trail   Egan

More We Dance, The   Coots

Morning Glory Lane   Friend

Morning Is Midnight   Hart; Rodgers

Morocco Dance of Marriage (inst.)   Romberg

Mountain Greenery   Hart; Rodgers

Movie Ball, The   Kalmar; Ruby

Moving Picture Actors on Parade   Fisher; Rose

Mr. and Mrs.   Conrad; Kahn

Mr. and Mrs. and Company   Gorney

Music Thrills Me, The   Smith, Harry B.

My Baby Knows How   Akst; Davis

My Baby's Come Back to Me   Berlin

My Baby's Gone   Johnston; Turk

My Bundle of Love   Silver

My Caravan   Gorney

My Cutey's Due at Two to Two   Robin

My Darling   Kahn

My Dream of the Big Parade   Dubin; McHugh

My Girl Has Eye Trouble   Kahn

My Heart Is Calling You   Friend

My Heart Is Sheba Bound   Hart; Rodgers

My Heart Will Tell Me So   Kahn

My Jewels   Brown, Lew; DeSylva; Henderson

My Little Bunch of Happiness   Akst; Davis

My Little Castagnette   Hammerstein; Harbach; Romberg

My Man's Done Done Me Dirty   Razaf

My Missus   Hart; Rodgers

My Oriental Home   Johnston; Turk

My Texas Man   Razaf

Nancy   Schwartz, Jean

Natiesha (Bright Eyes)   Razaf

Naughty Riquette   Smith, Harry B.

Naughty with Your Eyes   Dixon; Henderson

Nay Nay Neighbor   Coslow

Needles   Conrad; Kahn

Never Say Never   Schwartz, Jean

Never Without You   Davis

Newport Glide, The   Coots

Nice Small Town Girls   Gorney

Nicodemus   Youmans

Night-Time Is Love-Time (When I'm with You)   Johnson,
    Howard

Nize Baby   Hanley

No   Whiting

No Foolin'   Buck; Hanley

No More Dancing   Coots

No More Worryin'   Donaldson; Kahn

No One Knows but the Red, Red Rose   Mitchell

No Wonder She's a Blushing Bride   Dubin; Mills

Nobody But My Baby Is Getting My Love   Razaf

Nobody Worries 'Bout Me   Lerner, Sammy; Whiting

Nobody's Gonna Keep Me Away from My Girl   Kahn

Nona from Bologna   Silver; Turk

Not for Him   Hammerstein; Harbach; Romberg

Nothing Else Matters but Love   Friend; Kahn

Nothing Seems the Same without You   Davis

O Pretty Maids of France   Hammerstein; Harbach; Romberg

Oh Boy! How It Was Raining   Silver

Oh, Don't You Love It?   Johnson, Howard

Oh, How I Hate Bulgarians   Dixon; Henderson

Oh! How She Could Play a Ukelele   Akst; Davis

Oh, How that Baby Could Baby Me   Gorney

Oh I Love No One But'er My Oleomargerine   Leslie

Oh, Isabella   Gilbert

Oh Kay!   Dietz; Gershwin, George; Gershwin, Ira

Oh, Murphy   Brown, Lew; DeSylva; Henderson

Oh! Oh! Oh! What a Night   Davis

Oh, What a Lovely Day   DeSylva

Oh What a Night for Love   Whiting

Oh What Big Eyes You Have, Oh What Sweet Life You
    Have, Oh If I Only Had You   Friend; Kahn

Old Folks Shuffle   Waller

Old Friend   Lewis; Young, Joseph

Old Ironsides (We're Mighty Proud of You)   Mills

On a Quiet Evening at Home   Baer; Turk

On the Banks of Bango Bay   Dixon; Henderson

On the Riviera   Gilbert; Robin

On to Hollywood   Hanley

One Alone   Hammerstein; Harbach; Romberg

One Finger Lament (inst.)   Robison

One Flower Grows Alone in Your Garden   Hammerstein;
    Harbach; Romberg

One Good Man Gone Wrong   Hammerstein; Harbach;
    Romberg

One I'm Looking For, The   Smith, Harry B.

One of Us Should Be Two   Hart; Rodgers

One Way Street   Donaldson

Only Thing Green about the Girl of Today Is the Green
    Upon Her Hat, The   Buck; Friml

Oo-Long's in Wrong in Hong Kong Now   Stept

Open Your Arms (And Close Your Eyes)   Gorney

Oriental Nights   Coots

Oriental Nights on Broadway   Johnston; Turk

Other Arms   Whiting

Out of the South (inst.)   Robison

Out of the Sun   Brennan

Over the River to Jersey   Bryan; Fisher

Papa Mustn't Do That   Turk

Paris Is a Paradise for Coons   Coots

Paris Is Really Divine   Hart; Rodgers

Parisian Babies   Coots

Parlor, a Sofa and Someone Like You, A   Coslow; Dubin;
    Mills

Party's Getting Rough, The   Rose

Peggy, Peggy (Oh, You Peggy/The Race)   Hart; Rodgers

Pepita (inst.)   Motzan

Petrushka   Fisher; Rose

Petting   Whiting

Pining for You   Kahn

Pipes of Pansy, The   Hart; Rodgers
Plant Roses in Memory's Garden   Smith, Harry B.
Play Gypsies, Dance Gypsies   Smith, Harry B.
Please Come Back to Me and Brighten My Days   Bloom
Poison Ivy   Whiting
Polar Bear Strut, The   Schwartz, Arthur
Poor Little Doll from Japan   Johnston; Turk
Poor Little Marie   Caesar; Hanley
Poor Papa He's Got Nothin' at All   Rose; Woods
Portrait Parade, The   Harbach; Kern
Powder Puff   Coots
Precious   Egan; Whiting
Pretty Lips   Donaldson
Pretty Little Hindoo   Bryan
Promise in Your Eyes, The   DeSylva; Hanley
Promise Your Kisses   Conrad; Kahn
Pump Song, The   Lerner, Sammy; Whiting
Push Around   Hart; Rodgers
Queen Elizabeth   Hart; Rodgers
Rags   Fain; Kahal; Silver
Reaching for the Moon   Davis
Reba   Fisher; Schwartz, Jean
Rio De Janeiro (inst.)   Robison
Riverside Bus   Conrad
Riviera   Friml; Hammerstein; Harbach
Robbers' Dance, The   Whiting
Romance   Hammerstein; Harbach; Romberg
Romany Love-Spell   Caesar
Rosalie, I Don't Want Your Sympathy   Fisher
Rose of Delight   Harbach; Kern
Rose You Gave Back to Me, The   Clare; Friend
Roses for Rememberance   Kahn
Roses Remind Me of You   Davis
Rue de la Paix   Donaldson
Ruffian Ballet, The   Hanley
Rumble, Rumble, Rumble   Friml; Hammerstein; Harbach
Rum-Dum-Dum-Dum   Schwartz, Jean
Sabre Song, The   Hammerstein; Harbach; Romberg
Sad Eyes   Davis
Sad Winds   Robison
Sally McRally   Fain
Sandy McPherson (The Tightest Man in Town)   Fisher
Satisfied with You   Stept
Saturday Night   Schwartz, Jean
Say It with a Kiss   Robin
Say Yes, Sweetheart, Say Yes   Smith, Harry B.
Scalin' the Blues (inst.)   Johnson, James P.
Senorita Mine   Waller
Seven Years Bad Luck   Razaf
Sevilla   Brown, Lew; DeSylva; Henderson; Kahal
Seymour (I Wanna See More of You)   Coots
Shake Me and Wake Me   Robin
Shaking the Blues Away   Coots
She Ain't Your Sweetie   Dixon; Woods
She Belongs to Me   Johnson, Howard; Razaf
(I Met Her in the Moonlight, But) She Keeps Me in the Dark   Bryan
She Knows Her Onions   Ager; Pollack; Yellen
She Was a Wonderful Queen   Youmans
She Was Just a Good Fellow Who Couldn't Say No   Clarke; Monaco
She's on Her Way   Harbach; Kern
She's Still My Baby   Coslow
She's the Hottest Gal in Tennessee   Johnson, James P.
Shootin' at the Moon   Baer; Gilbert

Show Me How to Make Love   Hart; Rodgers
Show Me the Town   Gershwin, George; Gershwin, Ira
Shuffle   Hart; Rodgers
Shufflin' Home   Meyer
Silver Haired Mammy   Leslie
Silver Rose   Meyer
Simple Life, The   Hart; Rodgers
Since Becky Put on a Smock   Johnson, Howard
Since I Found You   Clare; Woods
Sincerest Form of Flattery, The   Brown, Lew; Clare
Sing   Hart; Rodgers
Singing in the Rain   Dubin
Sister Mine   Smith, Harry B.
Sittin' Around   Kahn
Six Little Kitzels   Hart; Rodgers
Six Little Plays (Requiescat in Pace)   Hart; Rodgers
Sleepy Head   Davis
Sleepyhead   Hart; Rodgers
Smilin' Joe   Meyer
Snap Out of the Blues   Robin
Snappy Show in Town   Youmans
Sneeze Song, The   Lerner, Sammy; Whiting
So Does Your Old Mandarin   Henderson; Lewis; Young, Joseph
So Is Your Old Lady   Dubin
So Near Yet So Far   Donaldson
So Will I   Brown, Lew; Friend
Social Work   Hart; Rodgers
Soliloquy (inst.)   Bloom
Some Day You'll Be Sorry Pal o' Mine   Egan; Whiting
Some Sweet Tomorrow   Dubin
Somebody Said   Hart; Rodgers
Somebody's Lonely   Davis
Somehow I'd Rather Be Good   Smith, Harry B.
Someone   Smith, Harry B.
Someone Is Losin' Susan   Meyer; Turk
Someone to Watch Over Me   Gershwin, George; Gershwin, Ira
Something About Love   Gershwin, George
Somewhere Alone with You   Davis
Somewhere Somebody's Waiting for You   Akst; Davis
Song of Shanghai   Egan; Whiting
Song of Sicily   Bryan
Song of the Brass Key   Hammerstein; Harbach; Romberg
Song That Is Locked in My Heart, The   Johnson, Howard
South Wind   DeSylva; Henderson
Sphinx (Just Sits and Thinks and Thinks and Thinks and Thinks), The   Warren
Spring Fever (inst.)   Bloom
Spring Is Here   Hammerstein; Harbach; Youmans
Stares that Lead to Love   Schwartz, Jean
Static Strut   Yellen
Stay Away from My Man   Stept
Step on It   Caesar
Steppin' on the Blues   Conrad; Donaldson; Harbach
Stepping All the Way Home   Robin
Stepping with Baby   Gershwin, George; Gershwin, Ira
Stone Bridge at Eight, The   Hanley
Stonewall Moskowitz March   Caesar; Hart; Rodgers
Studio Stamp   Schwartz, Jean
Sugar   Mitchell
Sun Is on the Sea, The   Gershwin, George; Gershwin, Ira
Sunday   Coots; Styne
Sunny Disposish   Gershwin, Ira
Sunny Hawaii   Stept

Susie   Hart; Rodgers
Susie (Camel Song)   Kern
(I Just Want to Be Known as) Susie's Feller   Brown, Lew
Swanee River Trail (Indian River Trail)   Caesar
Sweet Nothings Always Mean Something to Me   Henderson
Sweet Southern Breeze   Kahn
Sweet Stuff   Von Tilzer
Sweet Virginia Blues   Razaf
Sweet You Know Who   Razaf
Sweeter than You   Kalmar; Ruby
Sweetest Kiss of All, The   Robin
Sweetheart I'm Lonely   Magidson
Sweetheart Memories   Davis
Sweetheart of Long Ago   Kahn
Sweetheart Time   Caesar; Smith, Harry B.
Sweetie Pie   Akst; Davis
Tabloid Papers   Conrad
Tahiti   Sissle
Tahiti Sweetie   Donaldson
Take in the Sun — Hang Out the Moon   Lewis; Woods;
    Young, Joseph
Talent Is what the Public Wants   Brown, Lew; DeSylva;
    Henderson
Tales of Hoffman, The   Caesar
Tell Me that You Love Me   Brown, Nacio Herb; Freed,
    Arthur
Tenderly Think of Me   Whiting
Tennis Champs (Helen! Susanne! and Bill!)   Hart; Rodgers
Tentin' Down in Tennessee   Woods
Thanks Awful   Lewis; Young, Joseph
Thanks to You   Whiting
That Florida Low Down   Coots; Waller
That Little Something   Harbach; Kalmar; Kern; Ruby
That Little World Is Mine   Brennan
That Lost Barbershop Chord   Gershwin, George; Gershwin,
    Ira
That Night in Araby   Rose; Snyder
That Struttin' Eddie of Mine   Waller
That's a Good Girl   Berlin
That's Annabelle   Kahn
That's As Far As It Goes   Buck; Friml
That's Happiness   Gorney
That's My Girl   Davis
That's My Hap-Hap-Happiness   Johnson, Howard
That's What I Call a Pal   Johnson, Howard
That's What I Think of You   Fisher; Rose
That's Where I Meet My Girl   Von Tilzer
That's Why I Love You   Donaldson; Friml; Hammerstein;
    Harbach
(The Girl Is You and) The Boy Is Me   DeSylva; Henderson
Then You Will Know   Hammerstein; Harbach; Romberg
There Ain't No Maybe in My Baby's Eyes   Donaldson; Egan;
    Kahn
There Never Was a Town Like Paree   Coots
There'll Come a Time   Kahn
There's a Boatman on the Volga   Egan; Whiting
There's a Little White House (Where the Red Red Roses
    Grow)   Akst; Rose
There's a Miss I Want To Kiss On the O-Hi-O   Bryan;
    Fisher
There's a New Star in Heaven Tonight   Brennan; McHugh;
    Mills
There's One Lane that Has No Turning   Blake; Sissle
There's Somebody for Ev'rybody (But Me)   Coslow; Silver
There's Something in Sympathy   Coots

There's Something Spanish in Your Eyes   Caesar; Friend
They All Miss You Just Like I Do   Johnson, Howard
Thinkin' of You   Conrad; Kahn
Thinking of You   Donaldson
This Funny World   Hart; Rodgers
Those Knowing Nurses   Brown, Lew; Clare
Thought of You, A   Kahn; Young, Victor
Three Pullman Porters   Meyer
Thumbs Up   Schwartz, Jean
Tiger Baby   Warren
Tiger Eyes   Bryan
Time for Love   Coots
Tinker Tailor   Hanley
Tiny Flat Near Soho, A   Hart; Rodgers
To Be with You   Yellen
Tomboy Sue   Razaf
Tommy Hawk   Johnson, Howard; Warren
Tonight's My Night with Baby   Caesar
Too Many Kisses   Dubin
Town Hall Tonight   Hart; Rodgers
Trampin' Along   Hart; Rodgers
Transformation   Hart; Rodgers
Travelogue   Harbach; Kern
Tree in the Park, A   Hart; Rodgers
Troo-le-oo-le-ay   Stept
True to Two   Robin
Try a Little Kiss   Duke
Try Again Tomorrow   Hart; Rodgers
Tumble in Time   Whiting
Turkey in the Straw   Hart; Rodgers
Turkish Towel   Fain; Mills
Tut-Tut-Tut-Tilly   Carroll
Tweet Tweet   Brown, Lew; DeSylva; Henderson
Twenty Years Ago   Brown, Lew; DeSylva; Henderson
Two Are Company   Smith, Harry B.
Two By Four   Caesar
Two Eyes in Hawaii   Parish
Two Fellows and a Girl   Conrad; Kahn
Two of a Kind   Hart; Rodgers
Two to Eleven   Hart; Rodgers
Two Ton Tessie   Turk
Uncle Tom's Cabin   Schwartz, Arthur
Under a Spanish Moon (inst.)   Young, Victor
Under a Wurzburger Tree   Von Tilzer
Under the Ukelele Tree   Dixon; Henderson
Understudy Dance Specialty, The   Hanley
Up and Down in China (inst.)   Robison
Up and Down the 8 Mile Road   Donaldson; Kahn
Usen't You Used To Be My Sweetie   Bryan
Vi-O-Lets   Baer
(There's a Blue Ridge in My Heart) Virginia   Bryan
Viva Italia   Hart; Rodgers
Voodoo of the Zulu Isle   Coots
Vulgar Boatman, The   Clare; Monaco
Waddya Say We Steal Away   Hanley
Waffles   Fisher
Waika Kiki Blues   Meyer
Wait a Bit   Smith, Harry B.
Wait By the Marne for Me   Bryan
Wait'll We're Married   Clare; Monaco
Wait'll You See Cecilia   Lerner, Sammy; Whiting
Wake Up Every Morning with a Smile   DeSylva
Walkin' the Track   Conrad; Kahn
Walking Dogs Around   Brown, Lew; DeSylva; Henderson
Wasn't It Nice?   Caesar; Friml

Watch Your Hornin' (inst.)   Carmichael
We Always Disagree   Duke
We Can't Be as Good as Last Year   Hart; Rodgers
We Pirates from Weehawken   Hart; Rodgers
We Won't Charleston   Kalmar; Ruby
Weaker Sex, The   DeSylva
Wedding Procession (Finale Act I)   Hart; Rodgers
Week-end in July, A   Youmans
We'll Have a Kingdom   Friml; Hammerstein; Harbach
We'll Never Know   Berlin
We'll Tramp, Tramp Along Together   Brennan
We're Cleaning Up Broadway   Caesar; Friml
We're Mr. and Mrs. Now   Johnson, Howard
We're on the Map   Kalmar; Ruby
We're the Blondes Who Are Preferred   Johnston; Turk
Westward   Whiting
Whadda You Say We Get Together   Turk
What a Man!   Donaldson
What Am I Gettin' Frettin' Over You   Brown, Lew; Clare;
    Friend
What Am I Supposed to Do   Kahn
What Good Is Good-Morning, There's More Good in
    Good-Night   Lewis; Young, Joseph
What Good Is Money?   Robin
What Is It?   Hart; Rodgers
What Will Become of Me   Akst; Lewis; Young, Joseph
Whatcha Gonna Do When I'm Gone   Razaf
What's Good Enough for Washington Is Good Enough for
    Me   Von Tilzer
What's Happened?   Robin
What's the Use?   Gershwin, George; Gershwin, Ira; Hart;
    Rodgers
What's the Use of Talking   Hart; Rodgers
What's Your Name   Turk
When   Coots; Razaf
When a Kid Who Came from the East Side (Found a Sweet
    Society Rose)   Dubin; McHugh
When a Wandering Boy Comes Wandering Back to Home
    Sweet Home   Egan; Whiting
When Banana Skins Are Falling I'll Come Sliding Back to
    You   Mills
When Daddy Goes A-Hunting   Youmans
When Day Is Done   DeSylva
When I Am Queen   Gorney
When I Hear an Old Fashioned Melody   Friml
When I Hear an Old Fashioned Waltz   Buck; Friml
When I'm in Your Arms   Davis
When I'm with You I'm Lonesome   Gilbert
When Knott's Not Tying Knots   Gorney
When Our Ship Comes Sailing In   Gershwin, George;
    Gershwin, Ira
When the Red, Red Robin Comes Bob, Bob, Bobbin'
    Along   Woods
When the Shaker Plays a Cocktail Tune   Buck; Hanley
When the Years Go Drifting By   Kahn
When You Want Someone Who Don't Want You Perhaps
    You'll Think of Me   Leslie
When You're Home   Donaldson; Kahn
When You're in Love   Donaldson
Whenever I Dream   Conrad; Kahn
Whenever You Are Near   Stept
Where Are the Girls   Silver
Where Do You Work-a John? (Push-a Push-a
    Push)   Warren
Where Is That Someone for Me   Davis

Where Is the Sunshine That's Supposed to Follow the
    Rain   Koehler
Where'd You Get Those Eyes   Donaldson
Where's That Rainbow?   Hart; Rodgers
Whispering Trees   Coots
Whispers   Kahal
Whisper-Sh   Bryan
Whistle   Kalmar; Ruby
Who Am I?   Smith, Harry B.
Who Could Be More Wonderful Than You   Davis; Silver
Who Do You Think I'm Doing It For   Silver
Who Does My Sweetie Love   Mills
Who Loves You as I Do   Caesar
Who Wouldn't   Donaldson; Kahn
Who'd Be Blue   Woods
Who'll Mend a Broken Heart   DeSylva
Who's Girl Is That   Henderson
Who's in Your Arms Tonight   Warren
Who's That Little Girl?   Hart; Rodgers
Who's the Who   Caesar
Who's Who's?   Donaldson
Whose Little Sunshine Are You   Parish
Why Did Dr. Jekyll Hyde?   Johnson, Howard
Why Did I Go Wrong?   Razaf
Why Did Minnie Ha-Ha   Johnson, James P.
Why Did We Marry Soldiers?   Hammerstein; Harbach;
    Romberg
Why Do I?   Hart; Rodgers
Why Do You Sit on Your Patio   DeSylva
Why Do You Want to Know Why?'   Berlin
Why Don't You Marry the Girl   DeSylva
Why Is the World So Changed Today?   Smith, Harry B.
Why Should We Be Wasting Time   Coots
Why Should We Marry When We Can Be Good
    Friends   Fisher; Rose
Why Shouldn't I Be Somebody's Baby   Koehler
Why Work and Slave All Day   Smith, Harry B.
Wild Rose   Friml; Hammerstein; Harbach
Wildflower, I Love You   Harbach
Wimmin — Aaah   Warren
Winona   Ahlert
With Pleasure   Clare; Monaco
Without You   Conrad; Davis
Wolf, The   Egan; Rose; Whiting
Woman's Touch, The   Gershwin, George; Gershwin, Ira
Wompum-Pompum   Razaf
(I'm Waiting for a) Wonderful Girl   Youmans
Wondering When   Razaf
Won't You Come Across?   Friml; Hammerstein; Harbach
Ya Gotta Know How to Love   Warren
Yes I Do   Caesar
Yiddisha Charleston   Fisher; Rose
You Are My Star in the Night   Caesar
You Beautiful You   Bryan
You Can't Hang Out with Annie   Rose; Woods
You Can't Shush Katie (The Gabbiest Gal in Town)   Warren
You Killed All My Love for You   Akst
You Smiled at Me   Kalmar; Ruby
You Still Belong to Me   Conrad; Meyer
You Went Away Too Far, and Stayed Away Too
    Long   Bryan; Monaco
You Will, Won't You   Harbach; Kern
You'll Be Sorry in the Morning that You Made Me Cry
    Tonight   Rose
You'll Leave Me Blue   Whiting

You'll Never Know   DeSylva
Your Mother and My Mother   Donaldson
You're on the Lido Now   Hart; Rodgers
You're the Mother Type   Hart; Rodgers
Yours with Love and Kisses   Silver
You've Got Those Wanna Go Back Again Blues   Turk
You've Got to Be an Acrobat   Smith, Harry B.
You've Only Got One Mammy to Love   Fisher; Rose
Yvonne   Duke

1927

Acrobats   Gershwin, George; Gershwin, Ira
Africa   Hammerstein; Harbach
African   Brown, Nacio Herb
After I Gave My Heart to You   Bryan
After I Took You into My Heart, You Took the Heart out of Me   Dubin
After the Shadows Comes the Dawn   Davis
Ain't Love Grand   Robin
Ain't She Sweet   Ager; Yellen
Ain't That a Grand and Glorious Feeling   Ager; Yellen
Alice   Kahal; Snyder
All Aboard for Times Square   Buck
All Alone Monday   Kalmar; Ruby
All By My Ownsome   Dubin
All Decked Out   Brown, Lew; Friend
All I Want Is a Lullaby   Buck
All I Want Is Just Your Love   Von Tilzer
All I Want Is You   Akst; Clare; Davis
(Where Have You Been) All My Life?   Robin
All the Time Is Loving Time   Caesar
All the World Is Lonely for a Little Black-Bird   Razaf
Alligator Crawl (inst.)   Waller
All's Well that Ends Well   Conrad; Coslow
Alomo   Brennan
Alone (My Lover)   Friml
Along the Road to Love   Brennan
America   Brown, Lew; Friend; Smith, Harry B.
America Did It Again   Koehler
Among My Souvenirs   Leslie
And How   Magidson
And the Band Played On   Rose
Any Little Thing   Kalmar; Ruby
Anyone Who Do's That, Can't Be So Dumb   Brown, A. Seymour
Anywhere If You Are There Is a Paradise to Me   Friend
Are You Dreaming Too   Johnson, Howard
Are You Happy   Ager; Yellen
Are You in Love?   Alter
Are You in Love with Me?   Warren
Are You Listening Tonight Mother Dear   Leslie
Are You Thinking of Me Tonight   Akst; Davis; Gilbert
Argentine   Bryan; Schwartz, Jean
Armful of You, An   Robin; Youmans
Ash Can Stomp   Johnson, Howard
Ask Me Another   Brown, Lew; DeSylva; Henderson
At Sundown   Donaldson
At the Ex King's Club   Gershwin, George; Gershwin, Ira
At the Fair   Hammerstein; Kern
At the Round Table (Knight's Opening)   Hart; Rodgers
Au Revoir but not Good-Bye   Alter
Au Revoir (Means We'll Soon Meet Again)   Caesar; Friend
Avalon Town   Brown, Nacio Herb; Clarke
Aviation Ballet   Buck

Aviator   Gershwin, George; Gershwin, Ira
Aw Gee Don't Be that Way Now   Turk
Away Down South in Heaven   Warren
Babbitt and the Bromide, The   Gershwin, George; Gershwin, Ira
Babette's Military Dance   Smith, Harry B.
Babette's Wedding Day   Smith, Harry B.
Baby Feet Go Pitter-Patter   Kahn
Baby Stop-Stop-Stop   Lewis; Young, Joseph
Baby! What?   Brown, Lew; DeSylva; Henderson
Back in Your Own Back Yard   Rose
Bacon and the Egg, The   Duke
Bad Man Number   Friml
Ballet (Pearl of Ceylon) (inst.)   Kern
Baltimore   Kahal; McHugh
Bambazoola   Bryan; Schwartz, Jean
Bangaway Island   Akst; Davis
Banjo Eyes   Kahn; Whiting
Barbara   Rose; Silver
Beautiful Evening   Egan; Whiting
Beautiful Gypsy   Gershwin, George; Gershwin, Ira
Beautiful Show Girls   Coots; Dubin
Because I Love You   Brennan
Beedle Um Bo   Akst; Davis
Beggar, The   Kahal; Snyder
Behind the Mask   Cohan
Bells of San Gabriel's, The   Brennan
Beneath Venetian Skies   Lewis; Young, Joseph
Beside an Indian Wigwam   Dubin
Best Things in Life Are Free, The   Brown, Lew; DeSylva; Henderson
Bill   Hammerstein; Kern
Birthday Party   Gershwin, George; Gershwin, Ira
(I May Feel) Blah! but Not too Blue   Lewis; Young, Joseph
Blondy (With Your Baby Blues Eyes)   Conrad; Meyer
Blow Hot and Heavy   Robin
Blowing the Blues Away   Duke
Blue Eyes   Kahn
Blue Hawaii   Johnson, Howard
Blue Hullaballoo   Gershwin, George; Gershwin, Ira
Blue River   Bryan
Blue Skies, Gray Skies   Cohan
Bluebeard   Gershwin, George; Gershwin, Ira
Bluer Than Blue   Bryan
Blues Stampede   Mills
Bonita   Romberg; Smith, Harry B.
Bonnie Blue Flag, The   Romberg
Boo-Hoo-Hoo   Brown, Lew; DeSylva
Boy, a Girl and the Moon, A   Brennan
Boy in the Blue Uniform   Johnson, Howard
Boys in Gray   Romberg
Bracelets   Brennan
Bravo, Bravo   Smith, Harry B.
Britain's Own Ambassadors   Hart; Rodgers
Broadway (The Heart of the World)   Brown, Lew; DeSylva; Henderson
Buddy Rose   Baer; Lewis; Young, Joseph
Buffalo Rhythm (inst.)   Arlen
Bully Song   Hammerstein; Kern
Busy Little Center, A   Cohan
Byrd, The Bird of the Air   Johnson, Howard
Ca—ing   Silver
Camping on the Campus   Johnson, Howard
Can I Forget (That I Love You)   Caesar
Can't Help Lovin' Dat Man   Hammerstein; Kern

Canzetta   Motzan
Captain Andy's Entrance and Ballyhoo   Hammerstein; Kern
Carlotta   Whiting
Carmela   Buck
Carmen Has Nothing on Me   Buck
Casanasia   Mitchell
Cat, The   Kahn
C'est Bien Paris   Baer; Kahn
Changes   Donaldson
Charming   Cohan
Cheer Up — Keep Smiling   Meyer
Cheerie Beerie Be From Sunny Italy   Lewis; Young, Joseph
Chinchilla   Akst; Davis
Chloe   Kahn
Chop-Stick Blues   Johnston; Turk
Church Bells Are Ringing for Mary, The   Brown, Lew; DeSylva; Henderson
Cingalese Girls   Harbach; Kalmar; Ruby
Cingalese Village   Kalmar; Kern; Ruby
Clementine from New Orleans   Johnson, James P.; Warren
Clowns   Akst; Davis
Coal Black Lady   Hammerstein; Kern
Cobble-Stones   Clare; Pollack
Cohen Is Living the Life O'Reilly   Pollack; Yellen
College Days   Rose
College Humor   Brown, Lew; DeSylva; Henderson
Collette   Baer; Kahn
Come Along, Let's Gamble   Gershwin, George; Gershwin, Ira
Come Back To Little Yo San   Brown, Nacio Herb; Clarke
Come! Come! Come Closer!   Gershwin, George; Gershwin, Ira
Come on and Stomp, Stomp, Stomp   Mills; Waller
Come to Lower Falls   Caesar
Come-Look-At-The-War Choral Society   Gershwin, George; Gershwin, Ira
Conchita   Johnson, Howard
Confirmation   Hanley
Congoland Melody   Johnson, James P.
Consolation   Hammerstein; Harbach
Coo-Coo   Robin
Cottin' Pickin'   Johnson, James P.
Cotton Blossom   Hammerstein; Kern
Couldn't that Baby Baby Me   Gorney
Country Dance   Romberg
Country Mouse   Rodgers
Crazy for You   Kahn
Crazy Words, Crazy Tune, Vo-Do-De-O   Ager; Yellen
Creole Crawl   Johnson, Howard
Creole Love Song, The   Hammerstein; Kern
Cuddle Up   Meyer
Curfew Shall Not Ring Tonight, The   Robin
Curfew Walk, The   Bryan; Schwartz, Jean
Da Da Da   Meyer
Daddy Boy   Motzan
Daisy, Why Won't You Tell   Bryan
Dance Alone with You (Why Does Everybody Have to Cut In)   Gershwin, George; Gershwin, Ira
Dance, Dance, Dance   Friml
Dance Me, John   Johnson, Howard
Dance the Wedding Waltz with Me Before We Steal Away   Conrad; Gilbert
Dancing Hour   Gershwin, George; Gershwin, Ira
Dancing the Devil Away   Harbach; Kalmar; Ruby
Dancing to Grandmother's Waltz   Johnson, Howard

Dandies on Parade (The Sports of Gay Chicago)   Hammerstein; Kern
Darkie's Lament (inst.), A   Waller
Daughter of Sweet Adeline   Dubin; Snyder
Dawn   Brown, Lew; DeSylva; Hammerstein; Harbach; Henderson
Day By Day   Lewis; Young, Joseph
Dear, Dear Departed   Johnson, Howard
Dear Eyes that Haunt Me   Smith, Harry B.
Dear, on a Night Like This   Caesar; Conrad
Deceiving Blue Bird   Coots; Dubin
De-Dum-Dum   Bryan; Schwartz, Jean
Deep Blue   Styne
Delilah   Rose
(What Do We Do on a) Dew, Dew, Dewy Day   Johnson, Howard
Diane   Pollack
Did You Mean It   Bryan; Schwartz, Jean
Didn't I Tell You   Monaco; Rose
Didn't It?   Brown, Lew; Friend
Ding Dong Dell Spells I Love You   Brown, Lew; Friend
Dixie Vagabond, The   Donaldson; Kahn
Do It for Charity   Brown, Lew; Friend
Do that Thing   Akst; Davis
Do the Black Bottom with Me   Meyer
Do You Love As I Love?   Caesar
Does It Make Any Diff'rence to You   Kahn
Does She Love Me — Positively Absolutely   Coslow
Doin' the Gorilla   Robin
Doll Dance (What a Peculiar Tune) (inst.), The   Brown, Nacio Herb
Dolly Dimples (inst.)   Alter
Don't Blame Poor Elaine   Kahal; Snyder
Don't Forget when the Summer Rolls By   Clare; Pollack
Don't Let Your Love Come Down   Razaf
Don't Talk to Me of Spring   Young, Victor
Don't Tell a Blue Bell   Lewis; Young, Joseph
Don't Throw Me Down   Coots; Dubin
Down Alongside the Docks   Johnson, Howard
Down at Dinty Moore's   Johnson, Howard
Down in Old Havana Town   Caesar; Friend
Down with Sauerkraut (It Drives Me to the Dogs)   Johnson, Howard
Draggin' the Dragon Drag   Johnston; Turk
Dream Kisses   Yellen
Dreamy Eyes   Friend; Silver
Dreamy Montmartre   Baer; Lewis; Young, Joseph
Dressed Up for Your Sunday Beau   Robin
Easter Sunday Parade   Cohan
Ebony Dreams (inst.)   Johnson, James P.
Echoes of Dixieland   Johnson, James P.
Eight Ball (inst.)   Robison
El Tango del Perroquet   Dubin
Emigrants' Song   Brown, Lew; Friend
Engagement Ring, The   Johnson, Howard
Enjoy Today   Gershwin, George; Gershwin, Ira
Etiquette Quintette   Romberg
Evelyn, What Do You Say?   Hart; Rodgers
Every Evening (I Miss You)   McHugh; Rose
Every Night I Bring Her Frankfurter Sandwiches   Dubin
Every Rose Must Have a Thorn   Brown, Lew; DeSylva
Everybody's Talking About My Girl   Kahal; Snyder
Everything Is Spanish Now   Dubin
Eviva   Romberg

Ev'rybody Knows I Love Somebody   Gershwin, George;
    Gershwin, Ira
Ev'rybody Loves My Girl   Lewis; Young, Joseph
Eyeful of You   Dubin
Eyeful of You, An   Coots; Dubin
Eyes that Love   Romberg; Smith, Harry B.
Fair Co-Ed, The   Bryan
Falling in Love   Caesar
Fancy Me Just Meeting You   Youmans
Fascination   Mills
Fat Man Blues (inst.)   Waller
Fats Waller Stomp   Waller
Feast of the Lanterns   Romberg; Smith, Harry B.
Feeling in Your Heart, A   Cohan
Fiesta   Romberg; Smith, Harry B.
Fifty Million Frenchmen Can't Be Wrong   Fisher; Rose
Finale Act One (Wedding)   Hammerstein; Kern
Finaletto Act I: He Knows Milk   Gershwin, George;
    Gershwin, Ira
Find a Girl   Mitchell; Motzan
Finest of the Finest, The   Gershwin, George; Gershwin, Ira
Five-Step, The   Brown, Lew; DeSylva; Henderson
Flaming Ruth   Bryan
Flaming Youth   Brown, Lew; DeSylva; Henderson
Fletcher's American Cheese Choral Society   Gershwin,
    George; Gershwin, Ira
Flirtation Waltz   Cohan
Floating Thru the Air   Schwartz, Arthur
Flower of Spain   Meyer
Follow the Drum   Gershwin, George; Gershwin, Ira
Follow the Sun to the South   Romberg
Follow Through   Brown, Lew; Friend
Following in Father's Footsteps   Kalmar; Ruby
Following You Around   Dubin
For a Little While   Egan; Kahn
For Days and Days (I Love You, I Do)   Caesar
For Goodness' Sake   Duke
For Mary and Me   Rose
For My Baby   Kahal; Snyder
For Myself Alone   Robin; Youmans
For No Reason at All   Brown, Lew
For Old Times' Sake   Brown, Lew; DeSylva; Henderson
Forever   Rose
Fortune Teller's Song   Romberg; Smith, Harry B.
Four Walls   Rose
From Now On   Friend; Pollack
From Now On I'm Ready for Love   Johnson, Howard
From Saturday Night Till Monday Morning   Dubin
Funny Face   Gershwin, George; Gershwin, Ira
Gabriel Is Blowing His Horn   Dietz; Gorney
Gates of Love   Brown, Nacio Herb
Gather the Rose   Friml
Gay Cattin' Daddy   Razaf
Gee! I'm Glad I'm Home Again   Monaco; Rose
Georgia Home   Conrad
Geraldine   Akst; Davis
Gid-Ap Garibaldi!   Johnson, Howard; Warren
Gigolo   Hart; Rodgers; Romberg
Gip-Gip   Cohan
Girl I Love, The   Gershwin, George; Gershwin, Ira
Girl of the Pi Beta Phi, A   Brown, Lew; DeSylva; Henderson
Girls, Good Bye   Romberg
Girls, I Am True to All of You (I'm True to
    Everyone)   Smith, Harry B.
Give Me a Day in June   Kahn

Give Me a Night in June   Friend
Give Me a Smile   Sterling
Give Me One Hour   Friml
Give Trouble the Air   Alter; Robin
Glad Tidings in the Air   Gershwin, George; Gershwin, Ira
Glorious Chase, The   Romberg
Go Home and Tell Your Mother that I Love You   Baer
God Is Good to the Irish   Cohan
God Put the Green in the Rainbow to Remind Us of
    Ireland   Johnson, Howard
Goin' Crazy with the Blues   Razaf
Golden Gate   Leslie
Golden Moments of Perfume   Rose
Goldfish Glide   Hanley
Good Bye Lizzie   Baer; Gilbert
Good Morning   Caesar
Good News   Brown, Lew; DeSylva; Henderson
Good Pals   Romberg; Smith, Harry B.
Good-Night Owl   Bryan
Gorgeous   Akst; Davis
Got Everything (Don't Want Anything but You)   McHugh;
    Razaf
Guarded   Smith, Harry B.
Hail Stonewall Jackson   Romberg
Half a Kiss   Duke
Hallelujah   Robin; Youmans
Ham and Eggs in the Morning   Conrad; Dubin; Silver
Happy Days   Brown, Lew; DeSylva; Dietz; Gorney;
    Henderson
Happy Go Lucky   Kalmar
Happy Go Lucky (Bird)   Ruby
Happy Rickshaw Man (Jinrikisha Song)   Romberg; Smith,
    Harry B.
Harbor of My Heart, The   Robin; Youmans
Hard Boiled Mamma   Johnson, J. Rosamond
Hard to Get Along With   Robin
Harlem Choc'late Babies   Johnson, James P.
Havana   Egan
Havana Nights   Razaf
Have You Forgotten?   Johnson, Howard
Hawaiian Harmony Blues   Johnson, Howard
Hawaiian Song of Love   Akst
He Loves and She Loves   Gershwin, George; Gershwin, Ira
He Who Gets Slapped   Schwartz, Arthur
Headin' for Harlem   Hanley
Hear the Trumpet Call   Romberg; Smith, Harry B.
Heart Breaking Sal   Johnson, James P.
Heart Is Free, The   Johnson, Howard
Heart of Kentucky   Johnson, Howard
Heartaches and Dreams   Kahn
Hello Cutie   Friend
Hello Yankee Doodle   Hanley
Help the Drive   Romberg
Henceforth I'll Call on Friday   Stept
Her Waltz   Johnston
Here Am I Broken-Hearted   Brown, Lew; DeSylva;
    Henderson
Here Comes My Baby   McHugh; Mills
Here Comes the Prince of Wales   Schwartz, Arthur
Here I Am   Rose
Here in the Dark   Hammerstein; Harbach
Here's How   Romberg
He's a Ladies Man   Brown, Lew; DeSylva; Henderson
He's the Last Word   Donaldson; Kahn
Hey Feller   Hammerstein; Kern

Hi-A-Le-A-Lou   Baer; Kahn
High Hat   Gershwin, George; Gershwin, Ira
High-High-High Up in the Hills Watching the Clouds Roll
    By   Young, Joseph
Hindoo Moon   Davis; Hanley
Hobohemia   Robin
Hogan's Alley   Dietz; Gorney
Hollywood Relief, A   Freed, Arthur
Hollywood Rose   Kahn
Home Companion, A   Hart; Rodgers
Home for You, A   Friml
Home Town   Caesar
Homeward Bound   Gershwin, George; Gershwin, Ira
Honesuckle Lane   Dixon; Henderson; Rose
Honey   Johnson, James P.
Honey Do   Donaldson
Honeymoon Hop   Brennan
Honolulu Songbird   Leslie
Honor of the Family, The   Cohan
Hoof, Hoof   Robin
Hoping That Some Day You'd Care   Gershwin, George;
    Gershwin, Ira
Hoppin' the Buck   Johnson, Howard; Rose
Hot Heels   Rose
Hot, Hot Honey   Bryan; Schwartz, Jean
Hot-House Rose   Porter
Hours I Spent with You, The   Lewis; Young, Joseph
How About a Man Like Me?   Gershwin, George; Gershwin,
    Ira
How Can You Say No on a Beautiful Night Like
    This   Friend
How D'Ye Do   Brown, Lew; Friend
How Long Has This Been Goin' On   Davis
How Long Has This Been Going On?   Gershwin, George;
    Gershwin, Ira
How They Changed the Day   Akst; Davis
How Ya Gonna Stop Their Petting Parties   Dixon; Monaco
How'd You Like to?   Caesar
Hudson Duster   Brown, Lew; DeSylva; Henderson
Humpty Dumpty   Robin
Hunting Dance, The   Romberg
Hurry Sundown, Let Tomorrow Come   Robison
Hussars' Song, The   Smith, Harry B.
Hymn to the Sun   Friml
I Ain't that Kind of a Baby   Fain; Kahal
I Always Go to Sleep with the Blues   Brown, Lew; DeSylva;
    Henderson
I Am Captured   Romberg; Smith, Harry B.
I Blush   Hart; Rodgers
I Bring, You a Rose   Stept
I Can't Do Without You   Leslie
I Can't Get Into the Quota   Schwartz, Arthur
I Can't Stand It   Ahlert; Kahn
I Dare to Speak of Love to You   Smith, Harry B.
I Don't Wanna Be Loved (By Anyone But You)   Coslow
I Don't Want to Be a Soldier   Smith, Harry B.
I Dream of Your Eyes   Smith, Harry B.
I Feel at Home with You   Hart; Rodgers
I Forget What I Started to Say   Gershwin, George;
    Gershwin, Ira
I Haven't Got You   Rose
I Haven't Told Her, She Hasn't Told Me   Dubin; Fain; Kahal
I Hope I Don't Meet Molly on the Day I Marry Flo   Brown,
    Lew; DeSylva; Woods
I Left My Sugar Standing in the Rain   Fain; Kahal

I Like the Boys   Smith, Harry B.
I Live, I Die for You   Romberg; Smith, Harry B.
I Lost My Heart in Heidelberg   Kalmar; Ruby
I Love a Man in a Uniform   Monaco; Rose
I Love Olive   Baer; Kahn
I Love to Catch Brass Rings on a Merry-Go-Round   Conrad;
    Dubin; Silver
I Love You So   Duke
I Made My Mind Up You're Gonna Wind Up with
    Me   Lewis; Young, Joseph
I May Feel Blah but Not too Blue   Baer; Lewis
I Might Fall Back on You   Hammerstein; Kern
I Must Have an Italian Gal   Yellen
I Need a Little Bit, You Need a Little Bit   DeSylva;
    Henderson
I Need a Little Bit, You Need a Little Bit, It Just Had to
    Happen (A Little Bit of Love)   Brown, Lew; Friend
I Need Some Cooling Off   Hart; Rodgers
I Never Dreamed   Kahn
I Once Was Yours, I'm Somebody Else's Now   Razaf
I Owe It All to You (Mother O' Mine)   McHugh; Mills
I Said Goodbye to My Troubles   Davis
I Scream — You Scream — We All Scream for Ice
    Cream   Johnson, Howard
I Still Believe in You   Duke
I Still Have Your Beautiful Pictures   Leslie; Schwartz, Jean
I Think You're Sweet As Can Be, What Do You Think of
    Me   Brown, Nacio Herb; Friend
I Told Them All About You   Friend
I Wanna Be with You   Stept
I Wanna Go Voom Voom   Brown, Lew; Friend
I Want to Be Glorified   Berlin
I Want to Be There   Romberg; Smith, Harry B.
I Want to Make Up with You   Donaldson; Kahn
I Wish You Were Here Tonight   Hoffman
I Wonder How I Look When I'm Asleep   Brown, Lew;
    DeSylva; Henderson
I Wonder If She Cares   Smith, Harry B.
I Wonder If She Will Remember   Smith, Harry B.
I Wonder Who's With You When I'm Not There   Dixon;
    Monaco
I Wonder Why   Romberg
I Would Like to Play a Lover's Part   Hammerstein; Kern
Ibbidi Bibbidi Sibbidi Sab (Finale, Act I)   Hart; Rodgers
I'd Like You to Love Me   Brown, Lew; DeSylva; Henderson
Idles of the King   Hart; Rodgers
If He'll Come Back to Me   Robin; Youmans
If I Can Take You from Someone   Howard, Joseph E.
If I Cared for Someone Else   Bryan; Monaco
If I Could Get to Paree in 10 Hours   Silver
If I Could Get to Paree in 10 Hours (If I Could Get to Paris
    in 30 Hours)   Dubin
If I Had a Baby (You're the Kind of a Baby I'd Want My
    Baby to Be)   Donaldson; Kahn
If I Had a Lover   Rose
If I Only Had You Now   Kahn
If It Wasn't for Her Tra-La-La-La-La   Lewis; Young, Joseph
If It Wasn't for You   Davis
If Love Should Come to Me   Dietz; Gorney
If That's What You Want   Romberg; Smith, Harry B.
If You Know What I Think   Romberg; Smith, Harry B.
If You See Sally   Donaldson; Egan; Kahn
If You Wanna Be My Sugar Papa (You Gotta Be Sweet to
    Me)   Mills
If You Will Take Our Tip   Gershwin, George; Gershwin, Ira

I'll Be Lonely   Dixon; Woods
I'll Be Your Artist and You Be My Model   Akst; Davis
I'll Fool that Sweet Senorita   Brown, Lew; DeSylva;
   Henderson
I'll Just Go Along   Kahn
I'll Keep on Dreaming of You   Coots; Dubin
I'll Let the World Know I Love You   Brennan
I'll Love You Just the Same   Brown, Lew; Friend
I'll Never Kiss Her Anymore   Johnson, James P.
I'll Peek-a-boo You   Romberg; Smith, Harry B.
I'll Say I Do   Dubin
I'll Take Care of Your Cares   Dixon; Monaco
I'll Take My Baby Back Again   Coslow
I'll Think of You   Coslow; Kahn
I'm a Highway Gentleman   Robin
I'm a Little Bit Fonder of You Than of Myself   Caesar
I'm a Red Hot Hot-House Flower   Dixon; Woods
I'm as Lonesome as the Lonesome Pine   Bryan
I'm Away from the World when I'm Away from You   Clare;
   Pollack
I'm Back in Love Again   Friend
I'm Goin' Huntin'   Waller
I'm Gonna Meet My Sweetie Now   Davis
I'm Happy Now that You're Gone   Von Tilzer
I'm Happy, You're Happy Since We Became
   Sweethearts   Clare
I'm in Love with Someone   Stept
I'm in Love with Two Sweethearts — Mary and
   Mother   Fisher; Rose
I'm Just Drifting Along   Stept
I'm Like a Bird with a Broken Wing   Clare; Pollack
I'm Looking Over a Four Leaf Clover   Dixon; Woods
I'm More than Satisfied   Waller
I'm on My Merry Way   Whiting
I'm One Little Party   Kalmar; Ruby
I'm Pinin' for the Pines of Carolina   Johnson, Howard
I'm Riding to Glory (With a Glorious Girl)   Dixon; Woods
I'm Somebody's Somebody Now   Johnson, Howard; Silver
I'm Stepping Out with Lulu   Johnson, James P.
I'm Still in Love with You   Koehler
I'm Thru' with War   Smith, Harry B.
I'm Wonderful   Duke
I'm Wondering Why   Hoffman
In a Darktown Cabaret   Razaf
In a Little Canoe   Caesar
In Central Park   Caesar
In Dahomey   Hammerstein; Kern
In Love at Last   Dubin
In Mandalay with My Fair Lady   Motzan
In My Castle in Sorrento   Baer; Lewis; Young, Joseph
In My Little Dream House on the Hill   Lewis; Young,
   Joseph
In Our Orange Grove   Freed, Arthur
In the Bathroom Tra La   Dietz; Gorney
In the Evening   Hanley
In the Heart of Spain   Robin
In the Long Run You'll Run After Me   Baer; Lewis; Young,
   Joseph
In the Meantime   Brown, Lew; DeSylva; Henderson
In the Mountains of the Moon   Bryan
In the Swim   Gershwin, George; Gershwin, Ira
In the Woodshed (She Said She Would)   Johnson, Howard
In Those Good Old Bowery Days   Berlin
In Twos   Caesar
In Your Eyes, in Your Arms, in Your Heart   Koehler

Indian Butterfly (Naomi)   Leslie
Indian Ceremonial Music   Friml
Indian Chant   Schwartz, Arthur
Indian Cradle Song   Kahn
Indian Lullaby   Friml
Inspiration Lane   Akst; Clare; Davis
Interlude   Friml
Intermezzo   Romberg
International Vamp   Bryan; Schwartz, Jean
Invalid Entrance   Gershwin, George; Gershwin, Ira
Irresistible You   Monaco; Rose
Is It Ah-Ha or Ugh-Hum Tonight   Rose
Is It Any Wonder   Fisher
Is It Possible (That She Loves Me)   Dixon; Woods
Is She My Girl Friend (How-De-Ow-Dow)   Ager; Yellen
It All Belongs to Me   Berlin
It Just Had to Happen   Brown, Lew; Friend
It Was in the Moonlight   Dubin
It Was Only a Sun Shower   Kahal; Snyder
It Won't Be Long Now   Brown, Lew; DeSylva; Henderson
It's a Million to One You're in Love   Akst; Davis
It's a Wonderful Wonderful World   DeSylva
It's Always the Way   Hammerstein; Harbach
It's Bologny   Rose
It's Easy to Say Hello (But So Hard to Say
   Goodbye)   Brown, Lew; Friend
It's Getting Hotter in the North   Hammerstein; Kern
It's Heaven to Me   Brown, Lew; Friend
It's Just a Tune Without a Name   Brown, Nacio Herb;
   Friend
It's Just Because I'm Falling in Love with You   Turk
It's Not Funny When It Happens to You   Stept
(Hooray, Hooray) It's Ray-Ray-Raining   Johnson, Howard
It's Tough to Be a Hostess   Rose
It's Up to the Band   Berlin
I've Been Longing for a Girl Like You   Johnson, Howard
I've Got a Wonderful Girl   Meyer
I've Got a 'Yes' Girl   Dietz; Gorney
I've Got Nothin', You've Got Nothin', We Ain't Got Nothin'
   to Lose   Davis
I've Got the Man   Smith, Harry B.
I've Lost All My Love for You   Akst; Lewis; Young, Joseph
I've Waited for You   Romberg; Smith, Harry B.
Jack in the Box   Kahal
Japanese Moon   Buck
Japanese Serenade   Romberg; Smith, Harry B.
Japansy   Bryan
Jigaboo Jig, The   Rose
Jiggle Your Feet   Baer; Lewis; Young, Joseph
Jim, How Could You Do Such a Thing?   Gershwin, George;
   Gershwin, Ira
Jimmy   Berlin
Join the Navy   Robin; Youmans
Joy Bells   Friend; Smith, Harry B.
Jubilee (inst.)   Robison
Judy, Who D'ya Love?   Robin
June Night   Romberg
Jungle Jingle   Berlin
Jungle Shadows   Hammerstein; Harbach
Just a Corner of Heaven to Me   Hanley
Just a Cozy Hide-Away   Brown, Lew; DeSylva; Henderson
Just a Little Smile from You   Hanley
Just a Memory   Brown, Lew; DeSylva; Henderson
Just a Song Without a Name   Stept
Just a Year Ago Tonight   Rose

Just Another Day Wasted   Turk
Just As You Are   Kahn
Just Imagine   Brown, Lew; DeSylva; Henderson
Just Like a Butterfly that's Caught in the Rain   Dixon; Woods
Just Like a Wild, Wild Rose   Buck
Just Like the End of a Story   Pollack
Just Love Me   Styne
Just Once Again   Donaldson
(I'll Love You) Just the Same   Brown, Lew; Donaldson; Friend
Kangaroo   Johnson, James P.
Keep Sweeping the Cobwebs Off the Moon   Lewis; Young, Joseph
Keep Your Eye on the Ball   Baer; Lewis; Young, Joseph
Keep Your Eye on the Girl   Brown, Lew; Friend
Keeper, Keeper Take the Boy Away   Brown, Lew; DeSylva; Henderson
Ker-choo!   Romberg
Kiss or Two, A   Robin; Youmans
Kiss the Bride   Romberg
Kiss with a Kick, A   Robin
Kissing Eyes   Hammerstein
Knothole Scene   Brown, Lew; DeSylva; Henderson
Ladies and Gentlemen, We're Here Again (Opening Act II)   Hart; Rodgers
Lady Do   Baer; Lewis; Young, Joseph
Lady of the Lake   Lewis; Young, Joseph
Lady of the Moon   Blake; Sissle
Lamp of Memory   Bryan; Fisher
Lark, The   Romberg; Smith, Harry B.
Laziest Gal in Town, The   Porter
Learn to Sing a Love Song   Berlin
Legend Song   Romberg; Smith, Harry B.
Lenox Avenue Blues (inst.)   Waller
Let a Smile Be Your Umbrella   Fain; Kahal
Let Me Be   Kahn
Let Me Be a Friend to You   Gershwin, George; Gershwin, Ira
Let's All Go to Mary's House   Conrad
Let's Be Happy Now   Dietz; Gorney
Let's Go Over to My House   Caesar; Friend
Let's Go Places and Do Things   Conrad
Let's Kiss and Make Up   Gershwin, George; Gershwin, Ira
Let's Laugh and Be Merry   Smith, Harry B.
Let's Make Whoopee   Rose
Let's Stroll Along and Sing a Song of Love   Brown, Lew; Friend
Levine   Warren
Levine with His Flying Machine   Coslow
Life Upon the Wicked Stage   Hammerstein; Kern
Like a Little Ladylike Lady Like You   Cohan
Like a Wandering Minstrel   Cohan
Like an Angel You Flew into Everyone's Heart   McHugh; Mills
Like You   Smith, Harry B.
Lily   Warren
Lindbergh, the Eagle of the U.S.A.   Johnson, Howard
Little Bit of Love, A   Brown, Lew; Friend
Little Bum   Hanley
Little Change of Atmosphere, A   Brown, Lew; Friend
Little House of Love   Hoffman
Little Log Cabin of Dreams   Hanley
Little Miss Small Town   Baer; Lewis; Young, Joseph
Little Smile, A Little Kiss, A   Davis

Live To-Day   Baer; Lewis; Young, Joseph
Liza   Friend
Liza Jane's Weddin'   Johnson, James P.
Lo Doodle La Da Da   Robison
Lobster Crawl, The   Akst; Davis
Lock and Key   Johnson, James P.
Lolling around with Sally   Turk
Lonely Girl, A   Caesar
Lonely in a Crowd   Rose
Lonely Lights Along the Shore   Dixon; Woods
Lonely Melody   Coslow
Lonesome Ghost Blues   Razaf
Lonesome Romeos   Kalmar; Ruby
Lonesome Waltz   Bryan
Long, Deep and Wide (inst.)   Waller
Longest Way 'Round Is the Sweetest Way Home, The   Brennan
Look at Me Now   Smith, Harry B.
Look in the Mirror and See Just Who I Love   Stept
Look What the Wind Blew Home Today   Kahal; Snyder
Looking for a Thrill   Robin
Looks Like Happy Days   Baer
Looloo   Robin; Youmans
Loose Ankles   Freed, Arthur
(I'm Crying Because I'm) Losing You   Friend
Love Baby   Rose
Love Birds   Caesar
Love Is an Idle Dream   Smith, Harry B.
Love Waltz, The   Brennan
Lovely Little Silhouette   Lewis; Young, Joseph
Lovely Vienna   Smith, Harry B.
Loving You the Way I Do   Davis
Lucious   Lewis; Pollack; Young, Joseph
Lucky   Kalmar; Kern; Ruby
Lucky Bird   Robin; Youmans
Lucky in Love   Brown, Lew; DeSylva; Henderson
Lucky Lindy   Baer; Gilbert
Lucy Is Loose Again Tonight   Dixon; Woods
Lullaby Lady   Hanley
Mademoiselle Mimi   Lewis; Young, Joseph
Magnolia   Brown, Lew; DeSylva; Henderson
Make Believe   Hammerstein; Kern
Make Hey! Make Hay! (While the Moon Shines)   Hart; Rodgers
Mama's Well Has Done Gone Dry   Razaf
Mamma Wants to Go Bye-Bye   Akst; Davis
Man of My Dreams   Johnston; Turk
Manhattan Mary   Brown, Lew; DeSylva; Henderson
March of the Dolls (inst.)   Bloom
Mary   Donaldson
Mary Ann   Davis; Silver
Maybe I Will   Caesar
Maybe I'll Baby You   Buck
Me and Jane in a 'Plane   Leslie
Me and My Shadow   Rose
Meadow Serenade   Gershwin, George; Gershwin, Ira
Meditation (inst.)   Waller
Meet Me in the Moonlight   Conrad; Davis
Melancholy Me   Henderson; Johnson, Howard
Memories   Brown, Lew; DeSylva; Henderson; Robin
Merry-Andrew (inst.)   Gershwin, George
Messin' Around with the Blues   Waller
Mexico   Romberg
Mi Chiquita   Robin

(I Want to Be) Miles Away from Ev'ryone, and Just a Little Closer to You   Brown, Lew; DeSylva; Henderson
Military Dancing Drill   Gershwin, George; Gershwin, Ira
Million Eyes, A   Bryan; Schwartz, Jean
Mine   Brown, Lew; DeSylva; Hanley
Minnetonka Cradle Song   Kahn
Minute I Laid My Eyes on You, The   Stept
Mirror Finale, The   Akst; Davis
Mis'ry's Comin' Aroun'   Hammerstein; Kern
Miss Annabelle Lee   Clare; Pollack
Miss You Just Like I Do   Johnson, Howard
Mississippi Flood Song, The   Ager; Yellen
Mississippi Homeland   Akst; Davis
Missouri Bell   Rose
Mister Aeroplane Man, Take Me Up to Heaven   Conrad
Mister O'Toole   Sterling
Mocking Bird, The   Romberg
Molly Malone   Cohan
Momsy   Yellen
Moonbeam, Kiss Her for Me   Dixon; Woods
Moonlight and Love and All   Brennan
Moonlight Dreams   Sterling
Moonlit Waters   Brown, Nacio Herb; Friend
Morning After the Night Before, The   Pollack; Rose
Moskowitz, Gogeloch, Babblekroit and Svonk   Dietz
Moskowitz, Gogeloch, Babblekroit and Svonk (The Lawyer Song)   Gorney
Mother   Romberg
Mother of Mine, I Still Have You   Clarke
Moulin Rouge Girls, The   Romberg
Move Over   Hanley
Mr. Chamberlin and Mr. Levine   Mills
Mr. Cupid   Romberg
Mulunghu Thabu   Hammerstein; Harbach
Music of a Little Rippling Stream, The   Brown, Lew; Friend
My Angel   Pollack
My Arms Are Waiting   Gorney; Whiting
My Baby Is Driving Me Wild   Coslow
My Blue Heaven   Donaldson
My Blue-Bird's Home Again   Brown, Lew; DeSylva; Henderson
My Bwana   Hammerstein; Harbach
My Connecticut Gal   Donaldson
My Darling Said Yes   Coslow
My Dream Girl of Honolulu   Monaco
My Girl   Hammerstein; Kern
My Hawaiian Song of Love   Akst; Davis
My Heart Is in the Roses   Bryan; Fisher
My Heart Stood Still   Hart; Rodgers
My Heaven with You   Friml
My Honey's Coming Home   Kahn
My Idea of Heaven   Johnson, Howard
My Little Gypsy Sweetheart   Kahal
My Long Lost Man Is Back Again   Brown, Lew; DeSylva; Henderson
My Lucky Star   Hart; Rodgers
My Mimosa   Romberg
My New York   Berlin
My Ohio Home   Donaldson; Kahn
My One and Only (What Am I Gonna Do)   Gershwin, George; Gershwin, Ira
My Own Willow Tree   Romberg; Smith, Harry B.
My Passion Flower   Romberg
My Pipe of Peace   Brennan
My Regular Gal   Warren

My Rose of Spain   Bryan; Schwartz, Jean
My Sighing Siamese   Lewis; Young, Joseph
My Special Friend Is Back in Town   Razaf
My Sunday Girl   Stept
My Sweet Tooth Says I Wanna, but My Wisdom Tooth Says No   Clare; Stept; Young, Joseph
My Sweet Yvette   Akst; Davis
My Tumble-Down Cottage of Dreams   Leslie
My Up to Date Baby   Johnson, Howard
My Wife's in Europe Today   Stept
Naga Saki   Rose
Nagasaki Butterfly   Rose
Naughty Boy   Robin
Naughty Maurette   Fain; Pollack
'Neath the Cherry Blossom Moon   Brennan; Romberg; Smith, Harry B.
Neck Bones and Beans   Johnson, Howard
Nesting Time   Dixon; Monaco
New York Serenade   Gershwin, George; Gershwin, Ira
New York Town (Is Wearing Its Bandannas on Broadway)   Dietz; Gorney
Night After Night   Lewis; Young, Joseph
Night of Masquerade, A   Cohan
Nina   Robin
Nineteen Twenty-Seven   Caesar
99% Pure   Schwartz, Arthur
No Matter How You Slice It It's Bologney   Monaco; Rose
No One Ever Fell in Love at All   Duke
No Wonder I'm Happy, My Baby's in Love with Me   Akst; Davis
No Wonder I'm So Crazy for You   Coots
No Wonder I'm So Crazy Over You   Davis
Nobody Knows   Waller
Nobody Loves Me Now   Davis
Nobody Rings the Telephone   Romberg
Nocturne, The   Bryan; Schwartz, Jean
Normandy   Silver
Nothin'   Ahlert
Nothin' Does-Does Like It Used to Do-Do-Do   Fain; Kahal
Nothing but Love   Brown, Lew; DeSylva; Henderson
Nothing Can Ever Happen in New York   Hanley
Nothing Could Be Sweeter   Robin; Youmans
Nothing's Wrong   Hart; Rodgers
Now That the Dance Is Near   Gershwin, George; Gershwin, Ira
Nursie, Nursie   Gershwin, George; Gershwin, Ira
O Sola Mi Whose Sole Are You   Baer; Lewis; Young, Joseph
Oh Baby, Don't We Get Along   Brown, Lew; DeSylva; Henderson
Oh Baby (I Know that You Wouldn't But Gosh How I Wish That You Would)   Brown, Lew; Friend
Oh Boy! Couldn't You Care for That   Kahal; Snyder
Oh Doris, Where Do You Live   Kahn
Oh, for the Life of a Cowboy   Hanley
Oh Gee Jennie   Donaldson; Kahn
Oh Gee! Oh Joy!   Gershwin, George; Gershwin, Ira
Oh! Georgie Look what You've Done to Me   Johnson, James P.
Oh Golly Ain't She Cute   Turk
Oh, How I Love My Boatman   Gilbert
Oh How I Love to Look at You   Henderson; Johnson, Howard
Oh! How She Loves Me Now   Johnson, Howard
Oh, Lady   Akst; Davis
Oh Malinda   Johnson, James P.; Razaf

Oh, Peggy   Akst; Davis
Oh, This Is Such a Lovely War   Gershwin, George;
   Gershwin, Ira
Oh What a Pal Was Whoozis   Kahn
Oh You Little Indian River   Johnson, Howard
Oh You South   Caesar
Ol' Man River   Hammerstein; Kern
Old Buddy o' Mine   Donaldson; Kahn
Old Guitar and a Old Refrain, An   Kahn
Old John Barleycorn   Romberg
Old New England Lady   Johnson, Howard
Ole Virginny's Lullaby   Mitchell; Pollack
On a Desert Island with Thee   Hart; Rodgers
On a Pony for Two   Buck; Hanley
On Double Fifth Avenue   Baer; Lewis; Young, Joseph
On the Beach at Wai-ki-ki Blues   Meyer
On the Campus   Brown, Lew; DeSylva; Henderson
Once   Gershwin, George; Gershwin, Ira
Once Upon a Time   Brown, Lew
Once Word from You   Johnson, Howard
One Baby   Robin
One Boy's Enough for Me   Caesar
One Dam Thing After Another   Hart; Rodgers
One Golden Hour with You   Pollack
One Love   Caesar
One More Night   Rose
One O'Clock Baby   Brown, Lew; DeSylva
One of Those Things   Kahn
One of Those Windows   Brown, Lew; Friend
One Summer Night   Coslow
One Sweet Letter from You   Brown, Lew; Clare; Warren
One Two Three Four   Akst; Davis
Only a Dream   Pollack
Only Boy, The   Caesar
Only in Dreams   Robin
Only One for Me, The   Akst; Davis
Oo, How I Love You   Caesar
Ooh! Maybe It's You   Berlin
Opened Up Again   Rose
Organ, The   Akst; Davis
Oucha-Ma-Goucha, What Am I Gonna Do
   Withoutcha   Lewis; Young, Joseph
Our American Girl   McHugh; Mills
Our Bridal Night   Romberg
Our Own Way of Going Along   Cohan
Out There in an Orchard   Hammerstein; Kern
Pack of Cards, A   Hammerstein; Kern
Pantry Scene   Hammerstein; Kern
Paree   Robin
Paris Is Really Divine   Hart; Rodgers
Paris Taught Me Zis   Baer; Lewis; Young, Joseph
Park Avenue   Dietz; Gorney
Pearl of Broadway   Kalmar; Kern; Ruby
Pedestrian Song   Brown, Lew; DeSylva; Henderson
Peggy Jean   Whiting
Peggy McCann   Hoffman
Persian Rosebud   Leslie
Persian Rug   Kahn
Phantom Blues   Mills
Pick a Rose in Picardy   Motzan
Pit Solo   Romberg; Smith, Harry B.
Play-Ground in the Sky   Hanley
Playthings of Love   Johnson, Howard
Please Don't Talk About Me when I'm Gone   Clare
Please Tell Me   Styne

Plenty of Sunshine   Brown, Lew; DeSylva; Henderson
Poker Game   Romberg; Smith, Harry B.
Poor Cinderella   Robin
Poor Little Mother of France   Johnson, Howard
Pretty Little Bom Bom from Bombay   Johnson, Howard
Pretty Little Lady   Hart; Rodgers
Pretty Little Stranger   Robin
Pretty Little Thing   Dubin; Rose
Prince Charming   Romberg
Prize Song   Fisher
Promenade the Esplanade   Bryan; Schwartz, Jean
Pull Yourself Together   Robin
Put It in the Bank   Brown, Lew; DeSylva
Put on Your Old Brown Bowler (Take Off Your High, High
   Hat)   Leslie
Queenie's Ballyhoo (C'mon Folks)   Hammerstein; Kern
Quite the Thing   Robin; Youmans
Rainbow of Girls   Berlin
Rainbow Where Have You Been   Leslie; Meyer
Rainy Day Rose   Dixon; Woods
Ranger's Song, The   Romberg; Smith, Harry B.
Red Head Blues   Brown, Lew; Friend
Red Hot Anna   Meyer
Red Lips - Kiss My Blues Away   Bryan
Red Lips, Kiss My Blues Away   Monaco
Regimental Song   Friml
Renita Reinette   Johnson, Howard
Rheims Cathedral, The   Akst; Davis
Rhinestones   Rose
Ribbons and Bows   Berlin
Rippling Waters   Pollack
Roam On, My Gypsy Sweetheart   Kahal; Snyder
Roamin' Into the Sunset, Thinkin' of You, Just You   Hanley
Rolling Around in Roses   Dubin
Romance   Romberg; Smith, Harry B.
Romany   Schwartz, Arthur
Romany Rover   Coots; Dubin
Room for Two   Bryan; Schwartz, Jean
Rosalie   Gershwin, George; Gershwin, Ira
Rose Aria, The   Johnson, Howard
Rose of the Lane   Bryan
Rose of the Studios   Rose
Rose of the Volga   Kahn
Roses (inst.)   Motzan
Roses Understand   Cohan
Rosy Cheeks   Whiting
Russian Doll   Styne
Russian Lullaby   Berlin
Russian Rose   Johnston; Turk
Rusty Pail Blues (inst.)   Waller
'S Wonderful   Gershwin, George; Gershwin, Ira
Sad 'n Blue   Davis
Sad'n' Blue   Akst
Sailin' On   Kahn
Sailor on a Night Like This, A   Dubin
Sally Rose   Friend
Sa-lu-ta   Donaldson; Kahn
Sam the Old Accordian Man   Donaldson
Same Old Love Song   Smith, Harry B.
Same Old Moon, The   Harbach; Kalmar; Ruby
Same Silver Moon, The   Romberg
Sandwich Men, The   Hart; Rodgers
Sapphire (inst.)   Bloom
Savannah Blues   Waller
Save Your Kisses for a Rainy Day   Parish

Say Hello   Bryan
Say It with a Red Red Rose   Rose
Say It with a Solitaire   Monaco; Rose
Say So!   Gershwin, George; Gershwin, Ira
Schottische   Romberg
Scoutin' Around (inst.)   Johnson, James P.
Self-Expression   Schwartz, Arthur
Send for Me, When You Come to the End and Need One
     True Friend   Johnson, Howard
Sentimental Silly   Dietz; Gorney
September Night   Brown, A. Seymour
Seven Veils   Brown, Lew; DeSylva; Henderson
Seventeen and Twenty-One   Gershwin, George; Gershwin,
     Ira
Sex Appeal   Caesar
Shady Tree, A   Donaldson
Shake, Brother!   Robin
Shake Your Feet   Mills; Waller
Shaking the Blues Away   Berlin
Shalimar   Leslie
Shanghai Dream Man   Akst; Davis
She Don't Wanna   Ager; Yellen
She Was It   Silver; Turk
She Won't Charleston   Kalmar; Ruby
Shepherd of the Hills   Leslie
She's Another Sweet Mother Machree   Jerome
She's Crazy Over Me   Dubin
She's Got It   Akst; Davis; Gilbert
She's My Runabout   Gilbert
Shore Leave   Robin; Youmans
Should We Kiss 'Em or Kill 'Em, Yes or No   Johnson,
     Howard
Show Me That Kind of Girl   Dubin
Shuffle   Hart; Rodgers
Side By Side   Woods
Silhouette   Smith, Harry B.
Silhouette (inst.)   Bloom
Silk Stocking Sally   Rose
Silver Song Bird   Bryan
Silver Stars of Hawaii   Parish
Silver Wing   Friml
Simple Spanish Maid   Bryan; Schwartz, Jean
Since Henry Ford Apologized to Me   Rose
Since You Whispered I Love You   Coslow; Mills
Sing a Little Love Song   Meyer
Sing a Little Song   Gershwin, George; Gershwin, Ira
Sing, Dance and Smile   Caesar
Sing Me a Baby Song   Donaldson; Kahn
Sing Me a Song of Araby   Fisher
Singin' in the Rain   Brown, Nacio Herb; Freed, Arthur
Siren Dream, A   Hoffman; Pollack
Sitting in the Sun   Coots; Dubin
Six Little Cinderellas   Robin
Six O'Clock   Caesar
Skeleton Ghost   Johnson, Howard
Sky Girl, The   Bryan; Schwartz, Jean
Sloppy Water Blues (inst.)   Waller
Slow Up, Papa   Razaf
Smile, Darn You, Smile   Friml
Smile Your Blues Away   Davis
Smiling Eyes   Motzan
Smiling Joe   Akst; Davis
Snap Into It   Baer; Lewis; Young, Joseph
Snap Out of It   Akst; Davis
Snowy Morning Blues (inst.)   Johnson, James P.

So Blue   Brown, Lew; DeSylva; Henderson
(So Well, So What) So Maybe I'm Wrong   Kahn
So This Is Venice   Brown, Lew; Friend
Society Ladder   Kalmar; Ruby
Soldier Boy   Smith, Harry B.
Some Day   Romberg; Smith, Harry B.
Some Day You'll Know   Coslow
Some Day You'll Say "O.K."   Donaldson
Some Other Day   Coots; Dubin
Some Sort of Something   Duke
Some Sweet Morning   Hanley
(What Do I Care What) Somebody Said   Clare; Woods
Somebody's Sunday   Duke
Someone Should Tell Them   Hart; Rodgers
Someone's in Love with You   Edwards
Something Old, Something New   Romberg
Something Tells Me   Dietz; Gorney
Sometimes I'm Happy   Robin; Youmans
Son of a Billionaire   Cohan
Song and Dance   Smith, Harry B.
Song Bird of Melody Lane   Bryan
Song of Love, A   Schwartz, Arthur
Song of Safari   Stept
Song of Victory   Romberg
Songs My Mother Used to Sing to Who, The   Brown, Lew
Soothin' Syrup Stomp   Waller
South Wind   Brown, Lew
Southwest Is Calling   Johnson, Howard
Spanish Love   Romberg; Smith, Harry B.
Spanish Shawl, A   Bryan; Schwartz, Jean
Spell o' the Moon, The   Kahn
Spring Is Here   Turk
Spring Is In the Air   Dietz; Gorney
Springtime of Long Ago   Hanley
Springtime on the Avenue   Romberg
St. Louis Shuffle   Waller
Star of Stars   Robin
Start Stompin'   Robin
Start the Band   Akst; Davis
Stella   Akst
Steppe Sisters, The   Romberg
Strawberry Jam   Romberg
Strike Up the Band!   Gershwin, George; Gershwin, Ira
String Along with Texas   Rose
Strolling with the One I Love the Best   Romberg
Sugar   Ager; Yellen
Summertime   Rose
Summertime Sweethearts Shine As They Do in the
     Fall   Kahal; Snyder
Sunday Beau   Robin
Sun-Kissed Isle   Kahn
Sunrise (Will Bring Another Day for You), The   Friend
Sunshine of Your Song   Brennan
Suppose I Came Home at Nine   Brown, Lew
Swamp Blues   Sterling
Swanee Melody   Alter
Swanee River Sandman   Rose
Sweet Dreams   Whiting
Sweet Marie   Rose
Sweet Mistreater   Johnson, James P.
Sweet Stranger   Kahal; Snyder
Sweet Yvette   Davis
Sweetheart's Prayer, A   Motzan
Sweethearts's Parade, The   Johnson, Howard
Table for Two   Hanley

Tait Song   Brown, Lew; DeSylva; Henderson

Take Me in Your Arms Again (Mother Darling)   Sterling

Take the Air   Buck

Talisman (inst.)   Youmans

Talk about a Busy Little Housewife   Cohan

Talk about Girls   Caesar

Tampa   Dietz; Gorney

Tango Espagnol   Buck

Tap Tap, The   Rose

Tappin' the Toe   Coots; Dubin

Tea Time Tap   Kalmar; Ruby

Teddy   Blake

Tell Me, Cigarette (Cigarette Song)   Romberg; Smith, Harry B.

Tell the Doc   Gershwin, George; Gershwin, Ira

Tell the World I'm Through   Kalmar; Ruby

Tell Your Troubles All Goodbye   Dubin; Leslie

Tenderfoot Stomp   Johnston

Texas   Rose

Thanks   Dubin

That and a Nickel Will Get You a Cup of Coffee   Conrad

That Day in June   Mills

That Little Something   Kalmar; Kern; Ruby

That Melody of Love   Adamson; Dietz; Donaldson

That Old Quartette on the Corner   Dietz

That Pretty Kittie So and So of Mine   Friend

That Stupid Melody   Rose

That Volga Boatman Song   Silver

That Was the End of Jack   Johnson, Howard

That's Dolly   Kahn; Styne

That's How I Know I Love You   Kahal; Snyder

That's My Mammy   Baer

That's My Man   Caesar

That's What I Call Love   Dubin; Snyder

That's when My Love Will End   Meyer

There Ain't No Baby (Can Baby Me Like Mine)   Turk

There Ain't No Land Like Dixieland to Me   Donaldson

There Must Be Somebody Else   Clare

There Never Was a Pal Like Aunt Jemima   Motzan

There Ought to Be a Law Against That   Caesar; Friend

There's a Cradle in Caroline   Ahlert; Lewis; Young, Joseph

There's a Quaint Little Country Garden   Norworth

There's a Reason for Me Being in Love with You   Akst; Davis

There's Always a Way to Remember (But I Can't Find a Way to Forget)   Fain; Pollack

There's No One As Sweet As Trilby   Brennan

There's Not a Chance in the World   Kahn

There's Nothing New in Old New York   Akst; Davis

There's One Little Girl Who Loves Me   Kahn; Whiting

There's Something About You   Smith, Harry B.

There's Something Nice About Everyone, but There's Everything Nice About You   Bryan

They Come, They Come   Dietz; Gorney

They're Smiling All Over and All Over Me   Dixon; Woods

Thing to Do, The   Robin; Youmans

Thinking of You   Kalmar; Ruby

This Could Go On for Years   Gershwin, George; Gershwin, Ira

This Is June   Kahn

This Is My Wedding Day   Baer; Lewis; Young, Joseph

This Song Is Not About Lindbergh   Brown, Lew; DeSylva; Henderson

Those Eyes (Your Eyes, Your Smile)   Gershwin, George; Gershwin, Ira

Thou Swell   Hart; Rodgers

Thousand Times, A   Smith, Harry B.

Three Cheers for the Union!   Gershwin, George; Gershwin, Ira

Thunder Dance   Friml

Tickling the Ivories   Berlin

Tie All Your Troubles to the Tail of a Kite   Monaco; Rose

'Til Good Luck Comes My Way   Hammerstein; Kern

Times Have Changed   Mitchell; Motzan

Tin Pan Parade   Whiting

'Tis Love   Romberg; Smith, Harry B.

To Heaven on the Bronx Express   Cohan

Today's the Day   Brown, Lew; DeSylva; Henderson

Toddlin' (inst.)   Johnson, James P.

Together   Brown, Lew; DeSylva; Henderson

Together, We Two   Berlin

Tom-Tom   Rose

Tonight You Belong to Me   Rose

Tony, Tony, Tony   Romberg; Smith, Harry B.

Too Blue   Lewis; Young, Joseph

Tra-La-La-La-La   Lewis; Young, Joseph

Traveling   Johnson, Howard

Tree-Top of Love   Brennan

Trocadero Opening Chorus   Hammerstein; Kern

True to Them All   Gershwin, George; Gershwin, Ira

Try and Get a Kiss from Fifi   Conrad

Try Loving Me   Brown, Lew; DeSylva; Henderson

Tumbleweed   Robison

Twentieth Century Love   Cohan

Two Hearts Blend As One   Gershwin, George; Gershwin, Ira

Two Loving Arms   Robin

Two of Us, The   Caesar

Two Sweethearts of Mine   Fisher; Rose

Typical Self-Made American, A   Gershwin, George; Gershwin, Ira

Ukelele Sweetheart   Mills

Under the Clover Moon   Bryan; Schwartz, Jean

Under the Furlough Moon   Gershwin, George; Gershwin, Ira

Under the Midsummer Moon   Smith, Harry B.

Under the Moon   Snyder

Underneath the Wabash Moon   Rose

Undersea Ballet   Rose

Unknown   McHugh

Unofficial Spokesman, The   Gershwin, George; Gershwin, Ira

Up in the Clouds   Kalmar; Ruby

Varsity Drag, The   Brown, Lew; DeSylva; Henderson

Villain Dance (inst.)   Kern

Vo-de-o-do-do   Rose

Vo-Do-Do-De-O Blues   Ager; Yellen

Voice of the Southland Keeps Calling Me Home, The   Koehler

Voice of the World, The   Akst; Davis

Wait a Little Longer Love Bird   Dixon

Wait and See   Romberg; Smith, Harry B.

Waiters   Smith, Harry B.

Waiting for the Rainbow   Akst; Davis; Rose

War That Ended War, The   Gershwin, George; Gershwin, Ira

Watch the Birdies   Johnson, Howard

Watching the World Go By   Brennan

Way Down in Barbizon   Brennan

'Way Down in Vo-de-o-de-o Town   Warren

Way Down Town   Hanley
Way You Manoeuvre, The   Robin; Youmans
We Americans   Dubin
We Are the Girls in the Chorus   Coots; Dubin
We Don't Know Why — But   Freed, Arthur
We Two   Hammerstein; Harbach
We Two Shall Meet Again   Smith, Harry B.
We Want You   Kalmar; Ruby
Wear Your Sunday Smile   Robin
We'd Rather Dance than Eat   Buck
Wedding Ensemble   Romberg
We'll Go Up in Dose Mountains   Stept
We'll Have a New Home in the Morning   Buck; Robison
We're All A-Worry, All Agog   Gershwin, George; Gershwin, Ira
We're the Girls You Can't Forget   Hanley
We're the Sunday Drivers   Fain; Mills
Weren't We Fools   Porter
We've Got Him   Cohan
We've Had a Grand Old Time   Cohan
What a Baby   Whiting
What a Whale of a Difference a Woman Can Make   Robin
What a Wonderful Wedding that Will Be   Fain; Kahal
What Did William Tell?   Robin
What Do I Care What Somebody Said   Clare
What Does It Matter?   Berlin
What Does It Mean?   Robin
What D'Ya Say   Dietz; Gorney
What Happened to Mammy?   Johnson, Howard
What Have You Done to Make Me Feel This Way   Razaf
What Kind o' Love Is That   Razaf
What Kind of Boy   Caesar
What Makes Me Love You   Berlin
What Will Ya Do When There Ain't No Wimmin   Fisher; Rose
What Women and Men Will Wear   Akst; Davis
What's a Kiss Among Friends?   Robin; Youmans
What's the Big Idea   Davis
When   Brown, Lew; Friend
When All the World Is Fast Asleep   Hoffman
When Cadets Parade   Gershwin, George; Gershwin, Ira
When Erastus Plays His Old Kazoo   Coslow; Fain
When Gentlemen Grew Whiskers and Ladies Grew Old   Robin
When I Crack My Whip   Hammerstein; Harbach
When I Look at You   Friend
When I Love — I Love   Clare; Monaco
When I Play on My Spanish Guitar   Dubin
When I Ring Your Front Door Bell   Snyder
When I Take You All to London   Romberg; Smith, Harry B.
When I Was a Girl Like You   Romberg
When I Was Hikin' with You   Johnson, Howard
When It's Moonlight in Brooklyn   Dubin
When It's Necking Time in Great Neck   Von Tilzer
When Lindy Comes Back   Cohan
When Love Comes Stealing   Pollack
When Morning Glories Wake Up in the Morning   Fisher; Rose
When Spring Comes Peeping Thru   Stept
When the Bo-Tree Blossoms Again   Kalmar; Kern; Ruby
When the Hudson Flows Out to the Sea   Jerome; Schwartz, Jean
When the One You Care For   Robin
When the Right One Comes Along   Gershwin, George; Gershwin, Ira

When Will We Meet Again   Kahn
When You Ain't Got No One to Love   Fisher; Rose
When You Kiss Me   Mitchell; Motzan
When You Played the Organ and I Sang the Rosary   Leslie
When You Smile   Gershwin, George; Gershwin, Ira
When You Were the Blossom of Buttercup Land and I Was Your Little Boy Blue   Baer; Bryan; Gilbert
When You're in Love with More than One   Stept
When You're Single   Gershwin, George; Gershwin, Ira
When You're with Somebody Else   Baer; Gilbert
When You've Been Mothered By a Mother   Jerome
Where Is My Meyer, Where's Himalaya (Was Nacht Der Maler An Himalaya)   Gilbert
Where the Coosa River Flows   Johnson, Howard
Where the Wild, Wild Flowers Grow   Dixon; Woods
Where's the Mate for Me?   Hammerstein; Kern
Wherever You Are   Hanley
Whether It Rains, Whether It Shines   Von Tilzer
Which Is Which and Who Is Who   Brown, Nacio Herb
While We Tell Them About It All (Opening Act II)   Hammerstein; Kern
Whiskers   Johnson, James P.
Whisper Song, The   Friend; Pollack
Whisper Sweet and Whisper Low   Bryan
Whispering Pines of Nevada, The   Leslie
White Lights   Coots; Dubin
White Wings Carry Me Home   Johnson, Howard; Silver; Sterling
(But) Who Cares?   Smith, Harry B.
Who Is the Who   Friend
Who Knows   Dixon; Woods
Who-oo, You-oo, That's Who   Ager; Yellen
Who's Gonna Be Next   Yellen
Who's in Your Arms Tonight?   Stept
Who's Loving You Tonight   Rose
Who's That Knockin' at My Door   Kahn
Why Am I So Wonderful   Kalmar; Ruby
Why Can't We Be Sweethearts   Turk
Why Can't You Find Time for Me   Styne
Why Do I Love You?   Hammerstein; Kern
Why Don't I Hear from You?   Johnson, Howard
Why I Love My Baby   Berlin
Why Oh Why   Robin; Youmans
Why Should He Fly at So Much a Week (When He Could Be the Shiek of Paree)?   Berlin
Wide Open Spaces   Whiting
Wild and Wooly West, The   Buck
(Silver) Wings   Buck
Winona   Friml
With an Angel Like You in My Arms   Leslie
With You in My Arms   Egan; Whiting
Within the Land of Geishas   Romberg; Smith, Harry B.
Without You, Sweetheart   Brown, Lew; DeSylva; Henderson
Woe Is Me   Caesar
Won't You Marry Me?   Romberg
Woolworth of Japan, The   Romberg; Smith, Harry B.
World Is Mine, The   Gershwin, George; Gershwin, Ira
World Owes Nothing to Me, The   Leslie
Wrapped Up in a Blanket   Brennan
Wringin' and Twistin'   Waller
Wy-Lets (Violets)   Johnson, Howard
Ya Gonna Be Home Tonight (Oh Yeh, Then I'll Be Over)   Dubin; Stept
Yamekraw (inst.)   Johnson, James P.
Yankee Father in a Yankee Home, The   Cohan

Yes, Ma'am (You're from the Show Boat)   Hammerstein; Kern
Yes, Yes, Yvette   Caesar
Yesterday   Kahn
Yodelin' Cowboy Joe   Stept
You Appeal to Me   Romberg; Smith, Harry B.
You Are Love   Hammerstein; Kern
You Are Mine Evermore   Smith, Harry B.
You Came Along   Robin
You Can Tell Her Anything Under the Sun (When You Get Her Under the Moon)   Silver
You Can't Eat Peas with a Knife   Von Tilzer
You Can't Eye a Shy Baby   Baer; Lewis; Young, Joseph
You Can't Get to Heaven in an Aeroplane   Bryan; Fisher
You Can't Go Wrong By Going Along with Me   Turk
You Can't Have It Unless I Give It To You   Razaf
You Dear   Akst; Davis
(Who Did) You Did   Kalmar; Ruby
You Do, I Don't   Duke
You Gotta Be Good to Me   Lewis; Young, Joseph
You Gotta Have IT   Berlin
You Know and I Know the Way   Brennan
You Know How It Is   Gershwin, George; Gershwin, Ira
You Never Get Nowhere Holding Hands   Johnson, Howard
You or Nobody   Caesar
You Said Goodnight but You Meant Goodbye   Gorney; Kahn
You Should See Me Tootsie   Ager; Yellen
You Smiled at Me   Kalmar; Ruby
You Took the Heart Out of Me   Lewis; Young, Joseph
You Won't See Me If I See You With Anybody Else at All   Brown, Lew; DeSylva; Henderson
You'll Find the End of the Rainbow in Your Own Back Yard   Rose
You'll Never Be Missed a Hundred Years from Now   Dixon; Rose
Younger Set, The   Hanley
Your Beautiful Eyes   Kahal; Snyder
Your Land and My Land   Romberg
You're a Real Sweetheart   Caesar; Friend
You're a Wonderful Girl   Smith, Harry B.
You're Calling Me, Georgia   Blake
You're Easy to Remember   Dixon
You're Lovely   Clare; Pollack
You're More Like a Pal Than a Sweetheart   Dixon; Rose
You're So Easy to Remember, I'm So Easy to Forget   Dixon; Woods
You're So Nice to Me   Caesar
You're the One for Me   Donaldson
You're What I Need   Hart; Rodgers
You've Lost Your Lovin' Baby Now   Johnson, James P.

1928

(On My Mind and) A New Love   Caesar
Abdication   Romberg
According to Mr. Grimes   Gershwin, George; Gershwin, Ira
Add a Little Wiggle   Ager; Yellen
Adorable Dora   Clare
After My Laughter Came Tears   Turk
Ahoy for a Sailor   Friml
A-Hunting We Will Go   Gershwin, George; Gershwin, Ira
Aimiro   Porter
Alabama Labor Day Parade   Razaf
All Because of You   Stept

All for One and One for All   Friml
All of the Time   Woods
All the World Know's I'm in Love with You   Atteridge
All Thru the Night   Pollack
Aloha Oahu   Mills
Alone on Saturday Night   Davis; Rose
Alone with Only Dreams   Brown, Lew; DeSylva; Henderson
Along Came Sweetness   Dixon; Warren
Alpine Rose   Porter
(A Real) American Tune   Brown, Lew; DeSylva; Henderson
Ameri-can-can, The   Caesar
Americans Are Here, The   Brown, Lew; DeSylva; Henderson
An' Furthermore   Warren
And Then You Came Along   Fain
Angela Mia   Pollack
Anita   Clare; Pollack
Anne Lee   Dubin
Anything You Say   Donaldson
Are We Downhearted? No!   Davis
Are You Going to Be Home   Dixon; Dubin; Stept
As Long As We're in Love   Fields; McHugh
(Some Day) At Sunrise   Parish
At the End of the Trail (I Found You)   Parish
Automobile Horn Song   Donaldson; Kahn
Await Your Love (Concubine's Song)   Hart; Rodgers
Away from You   Koehler
Baby!   Fields; McHugh
Baby, Let's Dance   Porter
Baby's Awake Now   Hart; Rodgers
Baby's Best Friend, A   Hart; Rodgers
Back to the Heather   Kern
Bad Girl   Parish
Ballet Romantique (inst.)   Friml
Bambino   Leslie
Bandanna Babies   Fields; McHugh
Banjo Papa, You'd Better Stop Pickin' on Me   Razaf
Barker, The   Baer; Gilbert
Beautiful Dawn   Brennan
Beautiful Face Have a Heart   Fisher; Monaco; Rose
Beautiful Girl, A   Razaf
Beauty in the Movies   Caesar
Because My Baby Don't Mean Maybe Now   Donaldson
Because You Flew Away (The Younger Generation)   Sterling
Because You're Beautiful   Brown, Lew; DeSylva; Henderson
Before We Say Goodnight   Davis
Before We Were Married   Gershwin, Ira
Beggars of Life   Brennan
Believe in Me   Schwartz, Arthur; Smith, Harry B.
Belle, a Beau and a Boutonniere, A   Schwartz, Jean
Bells of Honolulu   Mills
Beloved   Kahn
Beside a Lazy Stream   Stept
Better Be Good to Me   Hart; Rodgers
Between You and Me and the Floor Lamp   Dubin
Bide-A-Wee   Edwards
Big Hearted Baby   Egan
Billie   Cohan
Bit of Gingham, A   Bryan; Schwartz, Jean
Bless You, Sister   Dubin
Blue Chimes   Hanley; Turk
Blue Eyes   Kern
Blue Grass   Brown, Lew; DeSylva; Henderson
Blue Hour   Coots
Blue Hours   Porter
Blue Land   Johnson, Howard

Blue Little You   Mills
Blue Ocean Blues   Hart; Rodgers
Blue Over You   Davis
Blue Shadows   Alter
Blueberry Lane   Bryan
Bluebird, Sing Me a Song   Davis; Hanley
Bluff   Cohan
Bob White   Friend; Silver
Bobby and Me   Brown, Lew; DeSylva; Henderson
Bobby's Nightmare   Robin
Bon Soir Cherie   Fields; McHugh
Boom Boom By the Sea   Rose
Borneo   Donaldson
Boston Post Road   Caesar
Boulevard Break   Porter
Bow Belles   Kern
Boy Friend, The   Brown, Nacio Herb; Freed, Arthur
Breakfast with You   Ager; Yellen
Bride Bells   Brown, Lew; DeSylva; Henderson
Bride Was Dressed in White, The   Hammerstein; Youmans
Bridge of San Luis Rey, The   Bryan
Broadway Melody, The   Brown, Nacio Herb; Freed, Arthur
Broken Hearted Baby   Stept
Broken Hearted Doll   Sissle
Brown Gal   Razaf
Build Me a Home in the Gloaming   Egan; Whiting
Building a Nest for Mary   Rose
Bums   Brown, Lew; DeSylva; Henderson
Butternut, Neath the Beautiful Butternut Tree   Woods
By Jingo Janette   Dixon; Woods
By the Lotus Pool (inst.)   Robison
Bye and Bye Sweetheart   Yellen
Bye Bye for Baby   Caesar
Call of Home, The   Hammerstein; Romberg
Camera Shoot   Hart; Rodgers
Candied Sweets   Waller
Carmen   Rose
Carolina Moon   Davis
'Cause I'm in Love   Donaldson
Cause of the Situation, The   Cohan
Caveman, The   Leslie
Chanty, A   Hammerstein; Romberg
Charlie, My Back Door Man   Conrad
Charlie (Opening Act I)   Kern
Charming Eyes   Mills
Chee-Chee's Second Entrance   Hart; Rodgers
Cheerio Cheery Lips, Cheerio   Dixon; Warren
Chicago Stomp Down   Johnson, James P.
Chilimar, The   Fisher
Chilly Pom Pom Pee   Bryan
Chinese Dance (inst.)   Rodgers
Chiquita   Gilbert
Chirp-Chirp   Gershwin, Ira
Choc'late Bar   Razaf; Waller
Cingalee   Whiting
Circus Days   Ager; Yellen
Climbing the Rickety Stair   Bryan
Colonel and the Major, The   Friml
Color of Her Eyes, The   Hart; Rodgers
Come On, Baby   Clare
Come on Out and Into My Arms   Dubin
Come to St. Thomas's   Cohan
Come West, Little Girl, Come West   Donaldson; Kahn
Coming Through the Rye   Hammerstein; Youmans
Contented   Mills

Convict's Rosary   Fisher
Cool Off   Kalmar; Ruby
Coquette   Berlin; Kahn
Corn and Bunyon Blues   Razaf
Cosetta   Mitchell; Motzan
Couldn't I   Razaf
Cradle of Love   Gilbert
Crazy Elbows   Hart; Rodgers
Crazy Rhythm   Caesar
Cryin' the Blues   Mills
Curtsey, The   Kern
Dagger and the Rose, The   Eliscu
Daily Dozen   Robin
Dainty Wisp of Thistledown   Hammerstein; Romberg
Dakota   Sissle
Dance Away the Night   Hammerstein; Kern
Dance of the Blue Danube, The   Fisher
Dance of the Two Black Crows (inst.), The   Bloom
Dancing in the Moonlight   Schwartz, Arthur
Dancing on the Levee   Bryan; Schwartz, Jean
Danse Bohemienne (inst.)   Friml
Day After Day   Gershwin, Ira
Day of the Fair   Friml
Dead Men Tell No Tales   Gershwin, George; Gershwin, Ira
Dear, Oh Dear   Hart; Rodgers
Dear to Me   Kahn
Dear, When I Met You   Brown, A. Seymour
Destiny   Pollack
Diamond in the Rough   Hammerstein; Youmans
Did I Say No   Fain; Kahal
Diga Diga Do   Fields; McHugh
Digah's Stomp (inst.)   Waller
Dip Your Brush in the Sunshine and Keep on Painting
    Away   Razaf
Disappointed   Freed, Arthur; Friend
Disappointed Suitors   Kalmar; Ruby
Dismissal Whistle   Caesar
Dixie   Fields; McHugh
Dixieland Echoes   Johnson, James P.
Dizzy Baby   Porter
Do I Do Wrong?   Kern
Do I Hear You Saying "I Love You"?   Hart; Rodgers
Do What You Did Last Night   Razaf
Do You Don't You Love Me   Koehler
Do You Think of Me?   Mills
Do You Wonder that I Love You?   Mills
Doin' the New Low-Down   Fields; McHugh
Dolores   Davis; Silver
Don't Be Like That   Kalmar; Ruby
Don't Be Silly   Brown, A. Seymour
Don't Cry, Baby   Kahn
Don't Go Too Far Girls   Brennan; Smith, Harry B.
Don't Hold Everything, Let Everything Go   Brown, Lew;
    DeSylva; Henderson
Don't Keep Me in the Dark, Bright Eyes   Bryan
Don't Look at Me that Way   Porter
Don't Remind Me (I'm Trying to Forget)   Clare; Pollack
Don't Send My Boy to Prison   Conrad
Don't Turn Your Back on Me   Razaf
Don't Wait Until the Lights Are Low   Johnson, Howard
Down By the Congo   Mills
Down By the Sea (Whoopie)   Hart; Rodgers
Down in Arkansas   Kalmar; Ruby
Down Stream   Whiting
Draggin' the Chain   Bryan; Schwartz, Jean

Dream Days of Auld Lang Syne   Leslie
Dream River   Hoffman
Dreaming in the Gloaming   Whiting
Dreaming of the Day   Turk
Dreamy Eyes   Mills
Dreamy Hawaiian Eyes   Mills
Drifting On   Johnson, Howard
Dusky Stevedore   Razaf
Easin' Right Along   Razaf
Entrance of the Hussars   Romberg
Evangeline   Berlin; Hanley; Rose
Evenin'   Whiting
Evening Star, Help Me Find My Man   Ahlert; Turk
Every Boy in Town's My Sweetheart   Cohan
Every Night in the Week   Lewis
Everybody Does It Now   Johnson, James P.
Everything We Like, We Like Alike   Fain
Ev'ry Little Bit of Me Loves Ev'ry Little Bit of You   Bryan
Ev'ry Little While   Friml
Exhortation   Conrad; Johnson, James P.
Explaining   Razaf
Faded Rose, A   Hammerstein; Youmans
Fair Lady (Opening Act II), A   Kern
Fair Rosita   Hammerstein; Romberg
Falling Leaves   Brennan
Falling Star   Ager; Yellen
Far Away and Long Ago   Brennan; Smith, Harry B.
Far, Far Away   Alter; Mitchell
Farewell, O Life (Finale, Act II)   Hart; Rodgers
Fascinating Eyes   Kahal; Snyder
Fathers of the World   Brown, Lew; DeSylva; Henderson
Feeling I'm Falling   Gershwin, George; Gershwin, Ira
Felix the Cat   Bryan
Figaro   Mitchell; Motzan
Firefly   Leslie
First Kiss, The   Dubin
First Man I Kiss, The   Hammerstein; Romberg
Fish   Porter
Flat in Montmartre, A   Pollack
Fleur de Lis   Bloom
Flo   Bryan
Fly Up to Heaven   Bryan; Schwartz, Jean
Footwork   Brown, Lew; DeSylva; Henderson
For Sweet Charity's Sake   Brown, Lew; DeSylva; Henderson
For You   Romberg
Forever   Ager; Yellen
Forever and Ever   Ager; Yellen
Forget Me Not   Hoffman; Leslie
Forgetting You   Brown, Lew; DeSylva; Henderson
Fortune's Fool   Mills
Forty-Niner and His Clementine   Hammerstein; Youmans
Fountain of Youth   Porter
Funny Little Sailor Men   Hammerstein; Romberg
Futuristic   Razaf
Futuristic Rhythm   Fields; McHugh
Garden of Night   Bryan
Gascony   Friml
Gee But It's Tough to Be Alone on a Saturday Night   Davis; Rose
Gee, It's Great to Be Alive   Brown, Lew; DeSylva; Henderson
Geneology   Brown, Lew; DeSylva; Henderson
George White's Scandals   Brown, Lew; DeSylva; Henderson
Georgia Gut   Razaf
Gershwin Specialty   Porter

Get a Horse, Get a Mule   Hammerstein; Youmans
Get Out and Get Under the Moon   Jerome
Ginette   Schwartz, Jean
Girl Friend of a Boy Friend of Mine, A   Donaldson; Kahn
Girl on the Prow, The   Hammerstein; Romberg
Girl Who Broke My Heart, The   Dubin
Give Me a Chance   Smith, Harry B.
Give Me the Sunshine   Conrad; Johnson, James P.
Glad Tidings   Ager; Yellen
Gloom   Robin
Glorianna   Bryan; Clare; Pollack; Schwartz, Jean
Go Get 'Im   Donaldson; Kahn
(Ev'rybody Ought to Take a Day Back Home) Go Home Ev'ry Once in a While   Cohan
Go Places and Do Things   Kalmar; Ruby
Going Places, Seeing Faces (Looking for Someone to Love)   Woods
Golden Gate   Rose
Good Boy   Kalmar; Ruby
Good Boy Wedding March   Kalmar; Ruby
Good Little Bad Little You   Stept
Good Morning   Egan
Good Times with Hoover, Better Times with Al   Berlin
Good-Bye to the Old Love, Hello to the New   Gershwin, George; Gershwin, Ira
Googilly Goo   Davis
Gorgeous Alexander   Hammerstein; Romberg
Gossips   Friml
Got a Rainbow   Gershwin, George; Gershwin, Ira
Got Myself Another Jockey Now   Razaf; Waller
Grass Grows Greener Way Down Home, The   Yellen
Great Camp Meetin' Day   Sissle
Guatemala Melody   Gilbert
Guess Who's in Town (Nobody but that Gal of Mine)   Razaf
Guiding Me Back Home   Revel; Sissle
Gypsy   Gilbert
Gypsy Joe   Kahn
Gypsy Joe (Gypsy Song)   Donaldson
Gypsy Song, The   Kahn
Halfway to Heaven   Dubin
Hallowe'en Whoopee Ball   Donaldson; Kahn
Hang Your Hat on the Moon   Schwartz, Jean
Hans   Porter
Happy   Cohan
Happy Ending, A   Brown, A. Seymour
Happy Go Lucky Lane   Lewis; Young, Joseph
Happy Go Lucky You and Broken Hearted Me   Friend
Happy Hoboes   Brown, Lew; DeSylva; Henderson
Happy Humming Bird   Dixon; Woods
(Everybody's) Happy in Jimtown   Razaf; Waller
Hard Problems   Robison
Harlem River Quiver   Fields; McHugh
Harlem Rose   Conrad
Have Pity, Sheriff   Schwartz, Arthur
Hay! Straw!   Hammerstein; Youmans
'He' for Me, The   Friml
Hear Me   Eliscu
Heart of Mine   Friml
Heartbroken and Lonely   Conrad; Coslow
Heaven-Hop, The   Porter
Hee-Cup Song   Johnson, Howard
Heel Beat   Brown, Lew; DeSylva; Henderson
Heinie   Ahlert; Turk
Hello Montreal   Dixon; Rose; Warren
Hello, Yourself   Robin

He-Man   Robin
Henry   Kern
Her Hair Is Black as Licorice   Hart; Rodgers
Here Comes Everything   Johnson, Howard
Here Comes My Ball and Chain   Coots
Here Comes My Blackbird   Fields; McHugh
Here She Comes (Musical Entrance — Tilly/All Set! Let's
    Go)   Hart; Rodgers
Here They Are   Romberg
Here's Howe   Caesar
Here's One Who Wouldn't   Brown, Lew; DeSylva;
    Henderson
Here's That Party Now, In Person   Ager; Yellen
Here's to the Girl of My Heart   Donaldson; Kahn
He's Mine   Caesar
He's Worth His Weight in Gold   Bryan
Hey Rube   Ager; Yellen
Hiding in the Corner of Your Smile   Pollack
High Hat (inst.)   Alter
High Life Made a Low Life Out of Me   Stept
High Up on a Hilltop   Gilbert
High Water   Brennan
His Majesty's Dragoons   Kern
Hitch Your Wagon to a Star   Robison
Hog Man Stomp   Waller
Holy of Holies (Prayer)   Hart; Rodgers
Home o' Mine   Smith, Harry B.
Honey   Whiting
Honey, Be My Honey-Bee   Coots
Hooray for Captain Spaulding!   Kalmar; Ruby
Hot and Cold   Hammerstein; Romberg
Hot Choc'late   Bryan; Schwartz, Jean
Hot Pants   Caesar
How About Me?   Berlin
How Could Anything So Good Be So Bad   Whiting
How D'Ya Like to Be Me   Coots
How 'Ja Do   Donaldson; Kahn
How Jazz Was Born   Razaf; Waller
How to Win a Man   Hammerstein; Youmans
How Was I to Know?   Hart; Rodgers
Hula Boola Boo   Gilbert
Humility (inst.)   Robison
Humoreskimo   Bryan
Hungry Women   Ager; Yellen
Hussars March   Romberg
I Ain't Your Hen, Mr. Fly Rooster   Razaf
I Am a Prince   Hart; Rodgers
I Am Yours   Davis
I Bow a Glad Good Day (Tavern Opening)   Hart; Rodgers
I Can't Believe It   Heyman
I Can't Believe You're Alone   Davis
I Can't Do Without You   Berlin
I Can't Give You Anything but Love   Fields; McHugh
I Close My Eyes and Dream   Brennan
I Couldn't If I Wanted To — Wouldn't If I Could   Mills
I Done Caught You Blues   Mills
I Don't Think I'll Fall in Love Today   Gershwin, George;
    Gershwin, Ira
I Found My Sunshine in the Rain   Mills
I Found My Way to You   Brown, Lew; DeSylva; Henderson
I Found Sunshine in Your Smile   Leslie
I Got a Woman Crazy for Me, She's Funny That
    Way   Whiting
I Grovel to Earth (Chee-Chee's First Entrance)   Hart;
    Rodgers

I Grovel to Your Cloth (Chee-Chee's Third Entrance)   Hart;
    Rodgers
I Had to Come Back to You   Rose
I Have My Moments   Kalmar; Ruby
I Have You   Akst; Davis
I Hope You're Satisfied   Waller
I Like You as You Are   Hammerstein; Youmans
I Look for Love   Hammerstein; Youmans
I Lost My Heart   Brennan
I Love Love   Brennan
I Love My Old Fashioned Man   Fain; Kahal
I Love Vanilla   Brown, A. Seymour
I Love You   Hammerstein; Romberg
I Love You and I Adore You   Brennan; Smith, Harry B.
I Love You, Deep River   Robison
I Love You More than Yesterday   Hart; Rodgers
I Must Be Dreaming   Dubin
I Must Have that Man   Fields; McHugh
I Must Love You   Hart; Rodgers
I Need Some Cooling Off   Hart; Rodgers
I Never Kissed a Baby Like You   Johnson, Howard
I Never Saw a Bathing Suit in Russia   Fisher
I Plead, Dear Heart   Smith, Harry B.
I Still Keep Dreaming of You   Davis
I Still Love You   Ager; Yellen
I Still Remember, Do You!   Akst; Davis
I Think I'll Put My Blue Suit on To-Night   Schwartz, Jean
I Think of What You Used to Think of Me   Hanley; Turk
I Think You're Wonderful   Silver
I Treasure You   Leslie; Monaco
I Wake at Morning   Hart; Rodgers
I Wanna Be Loved by You   Kalmar; Ruby
I Want a Good Man and I Want Him Bad   Magidson
I Want a Man   Hammerstein; Youmans
I Want a Yes Girl   Caesar; Friend
I Want Plenty of You   Fields; McHugh
I Want the World to Know   Robin
I Want to Marry a Marionette   Gershwin, George;
    Gershwin, Ira
I Was a Florodora Baby   Carroll
I Wish I Wuz a Kid Again and Knew What I Know
    Now   Edwards
I Wonder   Davis; Silver
I'd Like to Ride Away to a Little Hideaway   Bryan; Hoffman
I'd Rather Be Blue (Over You Than Be Happy with
    Somebody Else)   Fisher; Rose
I'd Rather Cry Over You (Than Smile at Somebody
    Else)   Yellen
I'd Rather Dance Here than Hereafter   Caesar
If I Can't Have You   Donaldson
If I Could Forget (In Dreamland Fancies)   Smith, Harry B.
If I Love Again   Oakland
If I Were You   Hart; Rodgers
If You Don't Love Me   Ager; Yellen
If You Want the Rainbow (You Must Have the Rain)   Dixon;
    Rose
If You're a Friend of Mine   Kern
I'll Always Remember   Schwartz, Arthur
I'll Be a Pal to Your Boy If You'll Be a Pal to Mine   Bryan
I'll Be Smiling   Schwartz, Jean
I'll Get By, As Long As I Have You   Ahlert; Turk
I'll Love Them All to Death   Smith, Harry B.
I'll Never Ask for More   Ahlert; Turk
I'll Never Forget   Kahn
I'll Never Get Along Any Longer Alone   Fain

I'll Never Share You (If You Were My Concubine)   Hart;
   Rodgers
I'll Still Belong To You   Brown, Nacio Herb; Eliscu
I'm a Fool Little One   Hart; Rodgers
I'm a One Girl Man   Cohan
I'm Bringing a Red, Red Rose   Donaldson; Kahn
I'm Flyin' High   Silver
I'm Going Back Again to Old Nebraska   Revel; Sissle
I'm Happy to Know You're Happy with Someone
   Else   Bryan
I'm Just a Sentimental Fool   Hammerstein; Romberg
I'm Ka Razy for You   Rose
I'm Leavin' My Troubles Behind   Mills
I'm Looking for Tulips to Kiss My Troubles Away   Mills
I'm on the Crest of a Wave   Brown, Lew; DeSylva;
   Henderson
I'm Sitting on Top of the World   Brown, Lew; DeSylva;
   Henderson
I'm Sorry   Mills
I'm Sorry Sally   Kahn
I'm Talking About My Wonderful Gal   Mills
I'm the Bluest Man in Town   Bryan
I'm Thirsty for Kisses, Hungry for Love, Lonely with Only
   Just Me   Coots
I'm Walking Between the Raindrops   Fisher; Rose
I'm Waltzing to the Raindrops   Fisher; Rose
I'm Wild About a Baseball Game   Baer; Gilbert
Imagination   Caesar
Impressions (inst.)   Johnson, James P.
In a Bamboo Garden   Donaldson
In a Great Big Way   Fields; Hart; McHugh; Rodgers
In a Little French Cafe   Parish
In a Little Hideaway   Dietz
In a Little Lane in Honoloo   Mills
In a Little Two By Four for Two   Hoffman
In a Moorish Garden   Porter
In a Poinsettia Garden (inst.)   Robison
In Love   Kern
In My Bouquet of Memories   Akst; Lewis; Young, Joseph
In Old Vienna   Leslie
In Poughkeepsie   Coots; Dubin
In Romany   Washington
In the Evening   Hanley
In the Sing Song Sycamore Tree   Dixon; Woods
In the Sweet Bye and Bye   Bryan
Interrupted Love Song, An   Hammerstein; Romberg
Into My Arms in April (Into My Heart in May)   Rose
Iris (inst.)   Revel
Is He My Boy Friend   Edwards
Is It the Uniform?   Hart; Rodgers
Is Something the Matter with Otto Kahn   Rose
Is There Anything Wrong in That   Magidson
It All Depends on You   Brown, Lew; DeSylva; Henderson
It Goes Like This (That Funny Melody)   Caesar; Friend
It Was the Dawn of Love   Coots
It's a Beautiful Day Today   Donaldson; Kahn
It's a Pleasure   Ager; Bryan; Schwartz, Jean; Yellen
It's All Up to You Caroline   Friend; Silver
It's an Old Spanish Custom   Brown, Lew; DeSylva;
   Henderson
It's Awful (I Mean It's Awfully Nice)   Kahal; Snyder
It's Just Because It's You   Young, Victor
I've Got a Crush on You   Gershwin, George; Gershwin, Ira
I've Got Ev'rything (As Long As I've Got You)   Johnson,
   Howard

Ivory Lace (inst.)   Alter
Japanese Mammy   Donaldson; Kahn
Jazz Singer, The   Dubin; Monaco
Je Vous Aime   Silver
Jeannine, I Dream of Lilac Time   Gilbert
Jericho   Robin
Jimmy-Da-Walk, Da Boss-a New York   Johnson, Howard
Jo-Anne   Silver
Jones' Family Friends, The   Cohan
Joy Is Mine   Hart; Rodgers
Joy or Strife   Smith, Harry B.
Judy   Fain; Kahal
Judy (inst.)   Robison
Jumping Jack   Bloom
June   Bryan; Schwartz, Jean
Jungaleena   Arlen; Magidson
Just a Little ———   Conrad
Just a Little Bit o' Driftwood   Davis
Just a Little Faded Rose   Conrad; Silver
Just a Little Kiss at Twilight   Egan
Just a Little Thing   Hart; Rodgers
Just a Little Way Away from Home   Lewis; Young, Joseph
Just a Night for Meditation   Lewis; Pollack; Young, Joseph
Just Another Love Affair   Davis
Just Another Night   Donaldson
Just Give the Southland to Me   Revel; Sissle
Just Keep Singing a Song   Revel; Sissle
Just Kids   Clare; Monaco
Just Like a Melody Out of the Sky   Donaldson
Just Like Darby and Joan   Leslie
Kashmiri Moon   Parish
Keep Moving   Porter
Keep Shufflin'   Razaf; Waller
Key to My Heart, The   Eliscu
Khonghouse Song   Hart; Rodgers
Kiddie Kapers   Hoffman; Pollack
King Can Do No Wrong, The   Romberg
King for a Day   Lewis; Young, Joseph
King of the Sword   Brennan
Kingdom of Dreams   Romberg
Kiss Before I Go, A   Friml
Kiss for Cinderella, A   Hart; Rodgers
Kiss to Remember, A   Bryan
Klown Kapers   Akst; Lewis; Young, Joseph
Know When to Smile   Brennan
Kohala Welcome   Hart; Rodgers
K-r-a-zy for You   Gershwin, George; Gershwin, Ira
Lady Luck   Smith, Harry B.
Lady Luck Is Grinning   Hart; Rodgers
Lady Luck (Smile On Me)   Brown, Lew; DeSylva;
   Henderson
Lady of Love   Bryan
La-La-La-La   Hammerstein; Romberg
Land of Going to Be   Goetz
Land of Provence   Smith, Harry B.
Last Night I Dreamed You Kissed Me   Kahn
Laugh! Clown! Laugh!   Lewis; Young, Joseph
Laughing Water, Stop Your Crying   Bryan
Leave You Cheri, Jamais   Caesar
Leg It   Conrad
Lend Me Your Eyes, Pretty Baby   Bryan
Lenora   Gilbert; Silver
Let Me Give All My Love to Thee   Hammerstein; Youmans
Let Yourself Go!   Gershwin, Ira
Let's All Go to Mary's House   Conrad

Let's Do It, Let's Fall in Love   Porter
Let's Give a Cheer   Kalmar; Ruby
Let's Give Three Cheers (For the Three Volunteers)   Mills
Let's Misbehave   Porter
Let's Sit and Talk about You   Fields; McHugh
Liar   Hammerstein; Romberg
Life as a Twosome   Caesar
Lily Lou   Mitchell
Linger in My Arms   Kahn
Lion's Roar (inst.)   Waller
Little Boy Blue Jeans   Edwards; Kahn
Little Dream Nest   Leslie
Little House in Soho, A   Hart; Rodgers
Little House on a Hill, A   Coots
Little Irish Rose (Abie's Irish Rose)   Bryan
Little Miss Okeechobee, Oh Be Mine   Donaldson
Little Mother   Pollack
Little Orphan Annie   Kahn
Little Town Called Home Sweet Home, A   Donaldson
Little Woman at My Elbow   Eliscu
Live and Love   Bryan; Schwartz, Jean
Living Buddha (Impassive Buddha)   Hart; Rodgers
Living on Love   Kahal; Snyder
Lone Eagle   Turk
Loneliness   Clare; Pollack
Lonely Heart   Brennan
Lonely Little Bluebird   Dixon; Woods
Lonely Vagabond   Snyder
Lonesome Boy's Rosary, A   Johnson, Howard
Lonesome in the Moonlight   Baer
Lonesome Swallow, Gonna Follow You Home   Razaf
Long Island Low Down   Kalmar; Ruby
Long Live Nancy   Kern
Look at the Damn Thing Now   Gershwin, George;
     Gershwin, Ira
Look Pleasant   Brown, Lew; DeSylva; Henderson
Look Up and Smile   Davis
Looking for the Sunshine   McHugh
Lost Liberty Blues, The   Porter
Louisiana   Razaf
Love Affairs   Dubin
Love Boat   Brown, Nacio Herb; Freed, Arthur
Love Is Quite a Simple Thing   Hammerstein; Romberg
Love Is the Sun   Friml
Love Letters   Donaldson; Kahn
Love Me or Leave Me   Donaldson; Kahn
Love Tale of Alsace Lorraine, A   Coots
Love that Lasts, A   Hammerstein; Romberg
Loveable   Whiting
Lovely Lady   Brown, Nacio Herb; Freed, Arthur
Lover, Come Back to Me   Hammerstein; Romberg
Love's a Sunbeam   Smith, Harry B.
Lovie Lee   Razaf; Waller
Low Moon   Friml
Luscious   Pollack; Young, Joseph
Ma Belle   Friml
Magic Violin, The   Leslie
Magnolia's Wedding Day   Fields; McHugh
Makin' Whoopee   Donaldson; Kahn
Mammy Is Gone   Brown, Lew; DeSylva; Henderson
Mammy Sue   Bryan; Schwartz, Jean
Man from the South   Bloom
Manhattan Walk   Kalmar; Ruby
March of the Musketeers   Friml
Marianne   Hammerstein; Romberg

Marie   Berlin
Marion   Pollack
Marionettes (inst.)   Motzan
Mauna Loa   Mills
Maybe It's All for the Best   Rose
Maybe Means Yes   Fields; McHugh
Maybe This Is Love   Brown, Lew; DeSylva; Henderson
Maybe You Will Love Me, Sweetheart, As I Love
     You   Johnson, J. Rosamond
Me an' My Boss   Hammerstein; Kern
Me and the Man in the Moon   Leslie; Monaco
Me 'n' You   Schwartz, Arthur
Melancholy Sally   Monaco
Melodies Within My Heart   Brennan
Memories of France   Dubin
Mi Amado (The Wolf Song)   Lewis; Warren; Young, Joseph
Mia Bella Rosa   Koehler
Midnight Eyes   Bryan
Mid-Summer's Dream   Conrad; Gilbert
Military Maids   Porter
Mine for Aye   Smith, Harry B.
Miranda   Sissle
Mistakes   Leslie
Mister Mississippi   Bryan; Schwartz, Jean
Moments with You   Yellen
Monastery Opening   Hart; Rodgers
Monkey Talk (inst.)   Waller
Monna Vanna Sweetheart Sublime   Dubin
Moon of My Delight   Hart; Rodgers
Moonlight Madness (Then You Were Gone)   Coots
Morning Is Midnight   Hart; Rodgers
Most Majestic Domestic Officials, The   Hart; Rodgers
Mother's Lullaby   Silver
Mr. Hoover & Mr. Smith   Magidson
Music Call, The   Brennan
(We're Three of the Four) Musketeers   Kalmar; Ruby
Must You Wear a Mustache?   Silver
My Arms Are Open   Washington
My Baby Has It   Magidson
My Baby Just Cares for Me   Donaldson; Kahn
My Broadway Racketeer   Leslie; Monaco
My Cavalier   Willson
My Conversational Man   Lerner, Sammy
My Daddy Don't Do Nothin' Bad   Razaf
My Dear Little Home (By the Sea)   Mills
My Dream Comes True   Smith, Harry B.
My Dreams   Friml
My First Love   Lewis; Young, Joseph
My First Sweetheart   Ahlert; Turk
My Flame Is Just a Match for Me   Fain
My Hawaiian Dream Girl   Mills
My Hawaiian Heaven   Parish
My Heart Keeps on Speaking of Love   Kahn
My Hondloo   Parish
My Ideal   Stept
My Inspiration Is You   Leslie
My Kinda Love   Alter
My Life Is in Your Hands   Lewis; Warren; Young, Joseph
My Little Dream Boat   Coots
My Lucky Star   Hart; Rodgers
My Mansion Way Down in the Lane   Bryan; Fisher
My Mexicana Rose (inst.)   Warren
My Mother Told Me Not to Trust a Soldier   Hammerstein;
     Youmans
My Old Girl's My New Girl Now   Caesar; Friend

My Old Man   Dixon
My Pet   Ager; Yellen
My Rock-a-Bye Baby   Leslie
My Sword and I   Friml
My Tonia   Brown, Lew; DeSylva; Henderson
My Troubles Are Over   Leslie; Monaco
My Varsity Girl I'll Cling to You   Bryan
My Window of Dreams   Bryan
My Yankee Doodle Boy   Clare
Nagasaki   Dixon; Warren
'Neath a New Moon   Hammerstein; Romberg
Never for You   Hammerstein; Romberg
New England Bound   Akst; Gilbert
New Hampshire   Sterling
News   Kalmar; Ruby
Night   Parish
Night Life   Schwartz, Arthur
Night of Memories, A   Yellen
Night We Didn't Care, The   Mills
Nina   Kalmar; Ruby
No Monkey Business   Brown, A. Seymour
No One Else but You   Kern
No One's As Lucky As Me   Coots
No Place Like Home   Caesar
Nobody Shows What My Baby Shows   Razaf
Not As Good As Last Year   Brown, Lew; DeSylva;
    Henderson
Not Even You   Schwartz, Arthur
Nothin' on My Mind   Kahn
Nothing Has Changed but You   Sissle
Now That She's Off My Hands I Can't Get Her Off My
    Mind   Lewis; Young, Joseph
Nuts, He Travels with Us Nuts   Hart; Rodgers
Oh, Carmenita   Warren
Oh, Gala Day, Red-Letter Day   Hart; Rodgers
Oh, Gosh   Brown, Lew; DeSylva; Henderson
Oh, How that Man Can Love   Magidson
Oh, How the Girls Adore Me   Smith, Harry B.
Oh Is She Mad at Me   Caesar; Friend
Oh, Look (Finale, Act I)   Hart; Rodgers
Oh, So Nice   Gershwin, George; Gershwin, Ira
Oh, What a Man   Kalmar; Ruby; Schwartz, Arthur
Oh, You Sweet Old Whatcha May Call It   Ahlert; Turk
Old Fashioned Girl, An   Brown, Lew; DeSylva; Henderson
Old Fashioned Locket of Gold   Brennan
Old Fashioned Mother   Brown, Lew; DeSylva; Henderson
Old Man Sunshine, Little Boy Blue Bird   Dixon; Rose;
    Warren
Old Pals Are the Best Pals After All   Rose
Old-Fashioned Girl, An   Porter
Ole Jim Crow   Razaf
Omnibus   Porter
On Candle Light Lane   Lewis; Young, Joseph
On the Golden Trail   Hammerstein; Youmans
On the Levee   Johnson, James P.
On the Night We Did the Boom Boom By the Sea   Monaco;
    Rose
On Top of a Tennessee Hill   Sissle
On Wiener Schnitzel Bay   Fisher; Rose
One Day   Hammerstein; Romberg
One Girl, The   Hammerstein; Youmans
One I'm Looking For, The   Gershwin, Ira
One Kiss   Friml
One Kiss (Is Waiting for One Man)   Hammerstein; Romberg
One Little Kiss in the Moonlight   Dixon; Rose; Warren

One Man Mary   Baer; Bryan
One Night in Havana (inst.)   Carmichael
One Night of Love   Turk
One Sunny Day   Schwartz, Jean
Only a Smile   Smith, Harry B.
Orange Blossoms   Schwartz, Jean
Oriental Dream Eyes   Meyer
Oriental Love Song   Fain; Parish
Oui, Papa . . . (Ev'rybody Loves My Girl)   Lewis; Young,
    Joseph
Our Castle of Love   Brennan
Out o' Town Gal   Donaldson
Out of a Clear Blue Sky   Von Tilzer
Out of the Blue   Kalmar; Ruby
Out of the Dawn   Donaldson
Out of the Heart of the Sunrise   Brennan
Out Where the Blues Begin   Fields; McHugh
Outdoor Man (For My Indoor Sports)   Brown, Lew;
    DeSylva; Henderson
Over the Top of the Hill   Brown, A. Seymour
Owl Song (Song of the Owl)   Hart; Rodgers
Pages   Friml
Pansies   Leslie
Pants Song, The   Hoffman
Papa Got Hot   Kalmar; Ruby
Parade Fantastique (inst.)   Willson
Paree   Hammerstein; Romberg
Paris   Alter; Goetz
Party Line   Fields; McHugh
Passionette   Magidson
Peacock Alley   Kalmar; Ruby
Pep Up, Step Up   Schwartz, Arthur
Personality   Cohan
Pick a Pickaninny   Bryan; Schwartz, Jean
Pickin' Cotton   Brown, Lew; DeSylva; Henderson
Pierotte and Pierette   Ager; Yellen
Pilot Me   Porter
Pining   Conrad
Pipes of Pansy, The   Hart; Rodgers
Place in the Country   Gershwin, George; Gershwin, Ira
Plantation Days   Bryan; Schwartz, Jean
Please, My Nerves   Ager; Yellen
Please Take Me Out of Jail   Waller
Ploddin' Along   Robison
Pompanola   Brown, Lew; DeSylva; Henderson
Poor Lizzie, What'll Become of You Now?   Silver
Porgy (Blues for Porgy)   Fields; McHugh
Pow-Wow Papa   Heyman
Praise the Day   Kern
Precious Little Thing Called Love, A   Coots
Put on the Dog   Donaldson
Puttin' on the Ritz   Brown, Lew; DeSylva; Henderson
Queen of My Heart   Friml
Queen's Aria   Friml
Quelque-Chose   Porter
Rag Doll (inst.)   Brown, Nacio Herb
Rain Drops   Bryan
Rain or Shine   Ager; Yellen
Rainbow's End   Heyman
Ramona   Gilbert
R-a-s-p-b-e-r-r-y — The New Letter Song   Friend
Ready for the River   Kahn
Really and Truly   Schwartz, Jean
Red Hair   Bryan; Snyder
Red Head   Johnson, Howard

Red-Hot Trumpet   Hart; Rodgers
Remember Me to Mary If She Still Remembers Me   Stept
Revenge   Akst; Lewis; Young, Joseph
Reward (For Love)   Clare; Pollack
Rhythmic Moments (inst.)   Arlen
Rich Man! Poor Man!   Hart; Rodgers
Right or Wrong I Love You   Akst; Davis; Rose
River, The   Conrad; Mitchell
Roll of the Drums   Smith, Harry B.
Romeo and Juliet   Kern
Rose of Mandalay   Koehler
Rosemary   Bryan
Roses of Yesterday   Berlin
'Round Evening   Coots
Roustabouts' Song (We Follow the Trail)   Ager; Yellen
Runnin' Around   Fisher
'S All Over but the Shouting   Brown, Lew; DeSylva;
     Henderson
Sabot Dance (inst.)   Friml
Sailing the Sea of Romance   Pollack
Santa Claus Bring My Man Back Home   Mills
Saskatchewan   Leslie
Say that You Love Me   Robin
Say Yes Today   Donaldson
Second Childhood   Brown, Lew; DeSylva; Henderson
Sensational Stomp   Bryan; Schwartz, Jean
Sentimental Swanee   Bryan
Serenata (inst.)   Bloom
Setting Up Exercise   Romberg
She Is So Lovely   Davis
She's a Great, Great Girl   Woods
She's a Home Girl   Brown, Lew; Conrad; DeSylva;
     Henderson
She's Got an Awful Lot of What I Need a Lot of
     Now   Ahlert; Turk
She's the Sweetheart of Six Other Guys   Johnson, Howard
She's Wonderful   Donaldson; Kahn
Shining Shoes   Bryan; Schwartz, Jean
Should I Be Sorry   Johnson, Howard
Show Is Over, The   Coslow; Dubin
Shuffle Your Feet (And Just Roll Along)   Fields; McHugh
Side By Side By the Zuyder Zee   Edwards
Since You Have Left Me   Revel; Sissle
Sincerely I Do   Davis
Sing a Little Love Song   Bryan; Pollack
Sing Me a Song   Davis; Hanley
Sing Me to Sleep with a Twilight Song   Leslie
Sing, Sister, Sing   Johnson, Howard
Singing a Love Song   Hart; Rodgers
Sing-Song Girl of Old Shanghai   Leslie
'Sippi   Conrad; Johnson, James P.
Sittin' on the Curbstone   Whiting
Ska-dut-ee-ut-tut-tut   Gordon
Skull and Bones   Gershwin, George; Gershwin, Ira
Skyline (inst.)   Willson
Sleep, Weary Head   Hart; Rodgers
Sleepy Baby   Kahn
Sleepy Honolulu Town   Warren
Slow and Easy Man   Razaf
Smart People   Hart; Rodgers
'Sno Use Talking I've Got to Be Good   Schwartz, Jean
So Dear   Caesar; Friend
So Do I   Schwartz, Jean
So Far So Good, So Good So Far, but Whatcha Gonna Do
     Do Now   Friend

So Would I   Ager; Yellen
Soda Water Cowboys   Johnson, Howard; Lewis; Pollack
Softly, As in a Morning Sunrise   Hammerstein; Romberg
Soldier of Fortune, A   Smith, Harry B.
Soliloquy   Hammerstein; Youmans
Solita   Mills; Parish
Some Night When You're Lonely   Davis
Some Sweet Someone   Kalmar; Ruby
Somebody Sweet Is Sweet on Me   Donaldson; Kahn
Someday Somewhere   Pollack
Someday You May Change Your Mind   Coots
Someone   Kern
Something to Call Our Own   Kalmar; Ruby
Something to Tell   Coots
Sometime in the Summertime   Donaldson
Song I Love, The   Brown, Lew; Conrad; DeSylva;
     Henderson
Song of Indiana, A   Kahn
Song of the Cowboys   Heyman
Song of the Sap   Brown, Lew; DeSylva; Henderson
Song of the Setting Sun   Donaldson; Kahn
Song of the Sewing Machine   Rose
(Sing Me a) Song of the South   Silver
Sonny Boy   Brown, Lew; DeSylva; Henderson
Sorry for Me   Brown, Lew; DeSylva; Henderson
Sort o' Lonesome, Kind o' Blue   Fain; Kahal
Spanish Dreams   Mills
Speedy   Bryan
Spiritual Melody   Lewis; Young, Joseph
Spirituelle (inst.)   Bloom
Spring Is Here in Person   Hart; Rodgers
Spring Will Come   Bryan
Star in the Twilight   Brennan
Starlight and Tulips   Bryan
Stars, Stars Shining Bright You May See Future Stars
     Tonight   Brown, Lew; DeSylva; Henderson
Stetson   Donaldson; Kahn
Stop! Go!   Coots
Stouthearted Men (Liberty Song)   Hammerstein; Romberg
Struttin' Hound   Bryan; Schwartz, Jean
Summertime   Friml
Sun Is At My Window Throwing Kisses at Me, The   Lewis;
     Meyer; Young, Joseph
Sunbeams (Bring Dreams of You)   Brennan
Sunny Days   Brennan
Sunny Disposish   Caesar
Sunrise   Hammerstein; Youmans
Sunshine   Berlin
Superstition   Alter
Swallows, The   Hart; Rodgers
Swanee Jubilee   Razaf
Sweet and Twenty   Egan; Whiting
Sweet Dreams   Ager; Yellen
Sweet Emmalina   Razaf
Sweet Forget-Me-Not   Kahn; Whiting
Sweet Lorraine   Parish
Sweet So-And-So   Gershwin, Ira
Sweet Somebody of Mine   Koehler
Sweet Sue, Just You   Young, Victor
Sweet Suzanne   Leslie
Sweetheart Days   Clare
Sweetheart of Yesterday   Conrad
Sweetness of Your Song, The   Brennan
Tain't No One but You   Silver
Tain't So, Honey, Tain't So   Robison

Take Your To-Morrow, and Give Me To-Day   Razaf
Talkin' to Myself   Brown, Lew
Tango   Hammerstein; Romberg
(Origin of the) Tap Dance   Brown, Lew; DeSylva;
    Henderson
Taps   Donaldson; Kahn
Tartar Song, The   Hart; Rodgers
Tavern Song (Red Wine)   Hammerstein; Romberg
Tell Her in the Moonlight   Davis; Silver
Tell It to the Marines (A Bunch of Nuts)   Hart; Rodgers
Tell Me that You Care   Johnson, Howard
Tell Me You Love Me   Pollack
Tell Me You're Sorry   Davis
Ten Little Miles from Town   Kahn
Thank You in Advance   Hart; Rodgers
That Brand New Model of Mine   Whiting
That International Melody   Edwards; Rose
That Lovable Baby of Mine   Motzan
That Stolen Melody   Fisher
That's All I Ask of the World   Dubin; Silver
That's How I Feel About You, Sweetheart   Davis
That's My Virginia   Bryan
That's My Weakness Now   Stept
That's What I Call Keen   Kahn
That's What Puts the Sweet in Home Sweet Home   Gordon
Then Came the Dawn   Dubin; Warren
There I'd Settle Down   Gershwin, Ira
There Is a Happy Land Far Far Away   Lewis
There Must Be a Silver Lining   Donaldson
There's a Place in the Sun for You   Fain
There's a Rainbow 'Round My Shoulder   Rose
There's Been Some Changes Made (Since You've Been
    Gone)   Razaf
There's Magic in the Cup (A Cup of Tea)   Hart; Rodgers
There's Somebody Else on Your Mind   Whiting
There's Somebody New   Kahn
There's Something about a Rose   Fain; Kahal
There's Something New 'bout the Old Moon
    Tonight   Hoffman; Mills
They Fall in Love   Cohan
This Is Not Long Island (Opening, Act II)   Hart; Rodgers
This Little Doll   Kalmar; Ruby
This Particular Party   Gershwin, George; Gershwin, Ira
This Rescue Is a Terrible Calamity   Hart; Rodgers
Thomas A. Edison, Miracle Man   Cohan
Those Were the Happy Days Long, Long Ago   Koehler
Those Wonderful Friends   Cohan
Three Bears, The   Kalmar; Ruby
Three Little Maids from School   Fields; McHugh
Thrill of a Kiss, The   Smith, Harry B.
Tip, Tip, Toe Up a Tuck, Tuck, Tucky Lane   Rose; Warren
Tired of It All   Robin
To Be Forgotten   Berlin
To Know You Is to Love You   Brown, Lew; DeSylva;
    Henderson
To the Dance   Robin
Today Tomorrow Forever   Leslie
Together   Conrad; DeSylva
Tomorrow's Violets   Egan
Tonight May Never Come Again   Davis
Too Good to Be True   Brown, Lew; DeSylva; Henderson
Trail of the Tamarind Tree, The   Leslie
Trample Your Troubles   Schwartz, Jean
Treasure Island   Gershwin, George; Gershwin, Ira
Trial (Ladies of the Jury), The   Hammerstein; Romberg

Tripping Along in Tripoli   Johnson, Howard
Trouble About the Drama   Kern
True Blue   Robin
True Love   Davis
Truthful Parson Brown   Robison
Try Again Tomorrow   Hart; Rodgers
Try Her Out at Dances   Hammerstein; Romberg
Turn Yo' Damper Down   Robison
'Twas a Kiss in the Moonlight   Conrad
Twelve O'Clock Waltz   Dixon; Rose; Warren
Twinkle Little Stars   Kalmar; Ruby
Two Black Crows Blues   Dubin; Robison
Two Boys   Brown, Lew; DeSylva; Henderson
Two Lips   Dixon
Two Lips (To Kiss My Cares Away)   Rose; Warren
Two Little Babes in the Wood   Porter
Two of Us, The   Cohan
Two Whippoorwills (inst.)   Robison
Under Starry Skies of Old Hawaii   Mills
Under Your Skies of Blue   Bryan; Snyder
Until Yesterday   Davis
Until You Get Somebody Else   Donaldson; Kahn
Vagabond   Dubin
Vesper Bell   Friml
Virginia   Hammerstein; Youmans
Vive L'Amour (Love Rules Us Ever)   Smith, Harry B.
Vivienne   Porter
Voice in the Dark, A   Hammerstein; Romberg
Voice of the City   Kalmar; Ruby
Wait a Little While Sweetheart   Davis
Wait for Me   Lewis
Wait Till You're Blue Mary   Caesar; Friend
Wait Until You See My Girl's   Sissle
Waitin' for Katie   Kahn; Snyder
Waiting   Kalmar; Ruby
Wake Up Dream Girl   Fain
Waltz I Can't Forget, The   Kahn
Wanting You   Hammerstein; Romberg
Was It Love   Caesar; Conrad
Was Last Night the Last Night with You?   Davis
Wasn't It Great? (It's All Over Now)   Hart; Rodgers
Watching for the Boogie Man   Johnson, Howard
Watching the Clouds Roll By   Kalmar; Ruby
Ways of the World Are Mine, The   Brennan
We All Can Write   Baer
We Are in Society   Rose
We Are the Horrors of Deadliest Woe (Chorus of
    Torments)   Hart; Rodgers
We Drink a Toast to You   Young, Joseph
We Might Play Tiddle De Winks   Robin
We, Oh We Are in Society   Dixon; Warren
Wear a Hat with a Silver Lining   Bryan
Wedding of the Painted Doll, The   Brown, Nacio Herb;
    Freed, Arthur
Wedding Waltz, The   Conrad; Gilbert
Week End   Gershwin, Ira
Weepin' Willow Weep No More   Davis; Warren
Welcome to the Queen   Friml
Well the Irish and the Germans Got Together   Ahlert; Turk
We're Calling on Mr. Brooks   Brown, Lew; DeSylva;
    Henderson
We're Gonna Raise Hell (Finaletto, Scene I)   Hart; Rodgers
We're Looking for the Treasure (Finale Act I)   Gershwin,
    George; Gershwin, Ira
We're Men of Brains   Hart; Rodgers

We're Waiting for the Weather   Brown, Lew; DeSylva; Henderson

West Point Bugle   Romberg

West Point March   Romberg

West Point Song   Romberg

West Wind   Youmans

Westward Bound   Revel; Sissle

What a Girl!   Hart; Rodgers

What a Pretty End to a Pretty Dream   Friend

What Are We Here For?   Gershwin, George; Gershwin, Ira

What Are You Waitin' For, Mary?   Donaldson

What Causes That?   Gershwin, George; Gershwin, Ira

What Do We Care   Revel; Sissle

What Do You Say   Ager; Yellen

What D'Ya Say   Brown, Lew; DeSylva; Henderson

What Makes You So Wonderful?   Kalmar; Ruby

What of It, We Love It   Dixon; Rose; Warren

What Price Love   Hart; Rodgers

What We Do in the Moonlight (We're Not Telling You)   Johnson, Howard

What Would You Do in a Case Like This?   Mills

What's the Reason   Atteridge

What's Your Price   Razaf

When   Razaf

When Birds of a Feather Flock Together, They're Bound to Come Across   Mills; Parish

When Eliza Rolls Her Eyes   Kahn; Warren

When He's Near   Schwartz, Arthur

When I Close My Eyes   Hammerstein; Romberg

When I Go on the Stage   Hart; Rodgers

When I Hit Broadway   Kalmar; Ruby

(I Feel Like a Bee, Stealing Honey from a Rose) When I Kiss You   Mills

When I Look Thru My Book of Dreams   Bryan

When I Love, I Love   Brown, Lew; DeSylva; Henderson

When I Saw Him Last (Finale, Act I)   Hart; Rodgers

When I Smoked My First Cigarette   Gilbert

When I Tip Tip Toe Up a Tuck Tuck Tucky Lane   Dixon; Rose; Warren

When I'm Walking with My Sweetness, Down Among the Sugar Cane   Clare

When Polly Walks Through the Hollyhocks   Woods

When the Banners Lead   Smith, Harry B.

When the Right One Comes Along   Gilbert

When the Roses Bloom Again   Mills

When the World Is at Rest   Fain

When Things Are Bright and Rosy   Kalmar; Ruby

When We Waltzed in the Dark   Bryan

When You Said Goodnight, Did You Really Mean Goodbye   Donaldson

When Your Fair Weather Friends Leave You Out in the Blue   Fisher

When You're in Love   Caesar; Meyer

When You're in Wrong with the Right Little Girl (The World's All Wrong to You)   Johnson, Howard

Where Can the Baby Be?   Hart; Rodgers

Where Is the Song of Songs for Me?   Berlin

Where Love Grows   Smith, Harry B.

Where the Shy Little Violets Grow   Kahn; Warren

Where Were You — Where Was I?   Cohan

Where Will I Be   Coots

(I Love to Be 'Neath the Old Apple Tree) Where Your Name Is Carved with Mine   Brown, Lew; DeSylva; Henderson

Where's the Boy? Here's the Girl!   Gershwin, George; Gershwin, Ira

Which   Porter

While the Others Are Dancing   Fain; Kahal

Whistle and I'll Be There   Whiting

White Lilacs   Brennan

Whiteman Stomp   Waller

Who Am I (That You Should Care for Me)?   Kahn; Youmans

Who Could Help but Fall in Love with You   McHugh

Who Hit You with a Horseshoe   Leslie

Who Put the B on Maloney and Made Baloney Out of Him   Sterling

Who Wants to Love Spanish Ladies?   Hammerstein; Youmans

Who Wouldn't Be Blue   Davis

Whole World Knows I Love You, The   Clare

Whoopee   Gershwin, Ira

Whoopsie   Hart; Rodgers

Who's Been List'ning to My Heart   Kalmar; Ruby

Who's Gonna Get You?   Ager; Yellen

Who's Gonna Love You After I'm Gone   Rose

Why Am I So Romantic   Ruby

Why Be Good?   Gershwin, Ira

Why Can't I?   Hart; Rodgers

Why Can't You Care   Gilbert

Why Did I Ever Kiss You, Tell Me Why   Bryan

Why Must We Always Be Dreaming   Romberg

Why Should We Be Wasting Time   Coots

Wild Oat Joe   Caesar

Will You Be Sorry   Kahn

Willow Tree   Razaf; Waller

Wings of Romance   Smith, Harry B.

Wipin' the Pan   Baer

Witchee Kitchee Koo   Parish

With a Song in My Heart   Hart; Rodgers

With Red Wine   Friml

Wob-a-ly Walk   Warren

Women, Women, Women   Hammerstein; Romberg

Won't You Tell Me Hon, When We're Gonna Be One   Lewis; Warren; Young, Joseph

Wop Song   Brown, Lew; DeSylva; Henderson

Word in Edgeways, A   Hart; Rodgers

Words, Music, Cash   Brennan

Yascha Michaeloffsky's Melody   Berlin

Yep! The 'Zep' Came Over   Mills; Parish

Yes, Sorority   Johnson, Howard

Yo Te Amo Means I Love You   Bryan

You   Brennan

You Alone   Eliscu

You and I Are Passers By   Smith, Harry B.

You and Me   Porter

You Are Both Agreed (Finaletto, Scene 1)   Hart; Rodgers

You Are My Heaven   Magidson

You Bet I Do   Coots

You Can't Have My Sugar for Tea   Kalmar; Ruby

You Never Say Yes   Hart; Rodgers

You Tell Me Your Dream, I'll Tell You Mine   Kahn

You Took Advantage of Me   Hart; Rodgers

You Walked By   Friml

You Were Meant for Me   Brown, Nacio Herb; Freed, Arthur

You Won't Like Margie   Dubin

You'd Rather Forget than Forgive   Johnson, Howard

You'll Come Back to Me   Razaf

You'll Never Know   Rose

Young Black Joe   Caesar

Your Disposition Is Mine   Fields; McHugh

Your Eyes   Friml
Your Worries Ain't Like Mine   Razaf
You're in Love and I'm in Love   Donaldson
You're Just a Little Bit of Everything I Love   Gordon
You're Just the One I've Been Looking For   Silver
You're the Cream in My Coffee   Brown, Lew; DeSylva;
    Henderson
You're the One   Harbach; Schwartz, Arthur
You're the One and Only One   Mills
You're What I Need   Hart; Rodgers
Yours Sincerely   Hart; Rodgers
You've Got a Way with You   Robin
Yvonne   Caesar
Zoup   Silver; Turk

1929

Abadaba Club, The   Caesar
ABC of Traffic (inst.), The   Schwartz, Arthur
Adios   Caesar
Adoration   Brennan
Adored One   Gershwin, George; Gershwin, Ira; Kahn
After All I'm in Love with You   Coots; Davis
After All, I'm Only a Schoolgirl   Porter
After Business Hours (That Certain Business Begins)   Dubin
After the Clouds Roll By   Clare
After Thinking It Over   Davis
Age of Innocence (inst.), The   Schwartz, Arthur
Ain't I Good to You?   Razaf
Ain't Misbehavin'   Razaf; Waller
Ain'tcha   Gordon
Alabamy Snow   Rose
Album of My Dreams, The   Arlen
All Aboard   Eliscu
All I Do Is Follow Butterflies   Dixon; Woods
All I Want to Do-Do-Do Is Dance   Dubin
All Quiet on the Western Front   Mills; Parish
All That I'm Asking Is Sympathy   Davis
Alma Mammy   Whiting
Almanac Covers, The   Eliscu
Am I Blue?   Akst; Clarke
American Express, The   Porter
American in Paris Blues Ballet, An   Gershwin, George; Kahn
Amoeba's Lament (inst.), The   Schwartz, Arthur
And They Still Fall in Love   Dubin
Another Night Within Your Arms   Coots
Anything to Hold Your Baby   Conrad; Mitchell
Anywhere Under the Sun   Hanley
Aqua Sincopada Tango   Porter
Arabian Lover   Fields
Aramis March (inst.)   Willson
Are You Afraid of Me   Oakland
Are You Really Mine   Caesar
Argentina   Razaf
As Long As It's You, Dear, O.K.   Donaldson; Leslie
As Long As You Believe in Me   Davis
As Though You Were There   Hart; Rodgers
At Longchamps Today   Porter
At Mrs. Simpkin's Finishing School   Gershwin, George;
    Gershwin, Ira; Kahn
At the End of the Rainbow of Love   Mills
At the Water's Edge, Just Edging Around   Lewis; Young,
    Joseph
Atlas Is Itless   Brown, Lew; DeSylva; Henderson
Awake, Children, Awake   Gershwin, Ira

Baby — Oh Where Can You Be?   Koehler
Baby, Does Your Maybe Mean Yes   Parish
Baby Follies   Edwards; Johnson, Howard
Baby-Doll Dance   Brennan
Back in My Old Home Town   Edwards
Back in Your Own Back Yard   DeSylva
Banjo that Man Joe Plays, The   Porter
Bashful Baby   Friend; Silver
Battle of Paris   Harburg
Be that Way   Brennan
Be the Secret of My Life   Caesar
Bear Down Pelham   Whiting
Beau Brummel   Edwards; Johnson, Howard
Because I Love Nice Things   Fields; McHugh
Because She's Happy Now   Conrad; Mitchell
Before I Go (Before You Go)   Eliscu; Rose; Youmans
Believe It or Not, It's Always You   Monaco
Believe Me   Bryan
Believe Me, That's Love   Snyder
Belle Baker Wop Song   Lewis; Pollack; Young, Joseph
Best I Ever Get Is the Worst of It, The   Brennan
Big City Blues   Conrad; Mitchell
Bigger and Better than Ever   Friend
Birmingham Bertha   Akst; Clarke
Bismark Is a Herring, Napoleon Is a Cake   Eliscu; Rose;
    Youmans
(What Did I Do to Be So) Black and Blue   Razaf; Waller
Black and White   Gershwin, George; Gershwin, Ira; Kahn
Black Dog Blues   Razaf
Black Man Blues   Razaf
Blondy   Brown, Nacio Herb; Freed, Arthur
Blow the Blues Away   Brennan
Blue Eyes Get Red Red Ready for Love   Hoffman
Blue Hawaii   Baer; Caesar
Blue is the Night   Fisher
Blue Little You and Blue Little Me   Johnson, Howard
Blue Step   Carroll
Blue Waters   Washington
Blue Windows   Egan
Bones and Tambourine   Fisher
Boomerang, The   Rose
Bootlegger's Chantey (We're an English Ship), The   Hart;
    Rodgers
Bottoms Up   Friend
Bounce a Little Ball at Your Baby   Conrad; Mitchell
Boy Friend Back Home, The   Porter
Breakaway, The   Conrad; Mitchell
Breath and Breaches   Razaf
Breathin' Heavy   Von Tilzer
Bring Back My Man   Wrubel
Bring Him Back Here   Arlen
Broadway   Conrad; Mitchell
Broadway Baby Dolls   Bryan; Meyer
Broken Hearted Dolly   Edwards
Broken Up Tune   Clare
Brother, Just Laugh It Off   Harburg
Bug House   Razaf
Button Up Your Overcoat   Brown, Lew; DeSylva; Henderson
By Quiet Firesides (inst.)   Robison
By the Dawn's Early Light   Von Tilzer
By the Way   Lewis; Pollack; Young, Joseph
Call Me to Arms   Alter; Johnson, Howard
Call of Love, The   Parish
Can You Read in My Eyes   Coslow
Can-Canada, The   Davis

Can-Canola, The   Coots
Candlelight   Heyman
Can't Be Bothered Now   Arlen
Can't We Get Together   Razaf; Waller
Can't You See What Troubles Me?   Arlen
Can't You Tell I'm in Love with You   Mills
Can't You Understand   Young, Victor
Casanova, Romeo and Don Juan   Gershwin, George;
    Gershwin, Ira
Catalina Rose   Mills
Catch On   Baer; Gilbert
Caught in the Rain   Schwartz, Arthur
'Cause I'm in Love   Mills
Celia   Robin; Whiting
Chant of the Jungle   Brown, Nacio Herb; Freed, Arthur
Charlie, Ike and Gus   Edwards
Chicken or the Egg, The   Conrad; Mitchell
Chicken Walk, The   Bryan; Meyer
China Girl   Gershwin, George; Gershwin, Ira
Chinese Love Boat, The   Brennan
Chinky Chinee Bogie Man   Whiting
Christina   Conrad; Mitchell
Cinderella's Consolation   Kahal
Circus Days   Johnson, James P.
Climb Those Golden Stairs   Edwards
Close Your Eyes and Make Believe It's Me   Kahal; Monaco
Closer to You   Gilbert
Clowning   Akst; Clarke
Cock-a-Doodle-Doo   Brennan
Collegiana   Fields; McHugh
Collegiate Sam   Coots; Davis
Come on Along with the Bluebird   Fain; Kahal
Come On Baby   Clare
Come On In   Clare
(When Nobody Wants You and Nobody Cares) Come to
    Me   Stept
Comme Ci, Comme Ca   Caesar
Commerce   Lane
Commerce March   Lane
Congratulations   Stept
Consoler of Women   Brennan
Cop Number   Edwards
Cottage for Sale, A   Robison
Cotton   Brown, Nacio Herb; Freed, Arthur
Couldn't You Care for That   Dubin
Crashing the Golden Gate   Gorney; Harburg
Crazy Feet   Conrad; Mitchell
Cross Word Puzzles   Atteridge
Cross Your Fingers   Coots; Davis
Crying for Love   Bryan; Meyer
Crying for Love, Laughing at Love   Alter; Johnson, Howard
Crystal Girl   Bryan
Cuckoo Song, The   Donaldson; Leslie
(I Want to Cuddle Some) Cuddlesome Baby   Coslow; Robin;
    Whiting
Cute Peekin' Knees   Whiting
Daddy Won't You Please Come Home   Coslow
Dance of the Crinoline Ladies   Porter
Dance of the Daffodills   Alter
Dance of the Ragamufins   Porter
Dancing in the Moonlight   Eliscu; Rose; Youmans
Dancing to Heaven   Bryan
Daring Gibson Girl, The   Brown, Lew; DeSylva; Henderson
Dark Eyes   Parish
Daughter of the Latin Quarter   Dubin

Day Dreams   Johnson, James P.
Day You Fall in Love, The   Magidson; Washington
Dear Little Pup   Brennan
Death of Jesse James   Johnson, Howard
Deeper than the Sea   Fain
Defiance (inst.)   Willson
Delphine   Robin
Dixie Cinderella   Razaf; Waller
Dixie Doodle Dandy   Johnson, James P.
Dixie Jamboree   Johnson, Howard
Dizzy Feet   Kalmar; Ruby
Do I Know What I'm Doing   Kalmar; Ruby; Yellen
Do I Know What I'm Doing While I'm in Love   Coslow;
    Robin; Whiting
Do Something   Stept
Do We Understand Each Other   Eliscu; Rose; Youmans
Do What You Do   Gershwin, George; Gershwin, Ira; Kahn
Do What You Like With Me   Baer; Gilbert
Do Ya Wanna Little Iss-kay   Magidson; Washington
Do You Mind If I Fall in Love   Coots
Do You Think I Could Grow on You?   Gordon; Silver;
    Snyder
Do You Think of Me Once in a While   Friend; Silver
Do You Want to See Paris?   Porter
Does an Elephant Love Peanuts   Hanley
(I Ask You) Does It Pay to Be a Lady?   Eliscu; Rose;
    Youmans
Does This Go On Forever?   Arlen; Coots
Doin' the Campus Crawl   Mills
Doin' the Raccoon   Coots; Magidson; Robin; Whiting
Doing the Boom Boom   Conrad; Mitchell
Don't Cry Baby   Johnson, James P.
Don't Do It   Schwartz, Arthur
Don't Ever Leave Me   Hammerstein; Kern
Don't Forget Your Don'ts   Alter; Johnson, Howard
Don't Hang Your Dreams on a Rainbow   Kahal
Don't It Mean a Thing to You?   Akst; Clarke
Don't Wake the Baby Up   Dixon; Woods
Doo, Dah, Deh   Eliscu; Rose; Youmans
Dorothy (inst.)   McHugh
Double Standard, The   Schwartz, Arthur
Down a Daisy Lane (inst.)   Robison
Down Among the Sugar Cane   Clarke
Down Among the Sugar-Cane   Clare
Down By the Old Oak Tree   Leslie
Down in Argentine   Mills
Down on the Bangaway Isle   Brennan
Down South Feeling   Mills
Down with Everybody But Us   Porter
Dream Baby   Caesar; Friend
Dream Man   Kahn
Dream of a Bum, The   Mills; Parish
Drifting Alone   Gordon
Drop Your Kerchief   Caesar; Friend
Drunken Rag   Wrubel
Dry Martini   Mills
(I'm the) Duke of Kak-I-Ak   Donaldson; Leslie
Dusky Dixie Rose   Edwards; Johnson, Howard
Dusty Roads   Pollack
Early Birds   Coslow; Robin
East Is West   Gershwin, Ira
Educate Your Feet   Ager; Yellen
18 Days Ago   Brown, Lew; DeSylva; Henderson
Elenita   Conrad; Mitchell
Embraceable You   Gershwin, George; Gershwin, Ira

Empty Arms   Conrad; Mitchell
Empty House Blues   Razaf
Entrance of Emigrants   Porter
Eve   Mills
Every Day Is Holiday in Kidland   Edwards
Every Once in a While   Stept
Everybody Needs a Buddy   Baer; Gilbert
Everybody Tap   Ager; Yellen
Everything Is Lovely   Johnson, Howard
Ev'ry Month Is May   Brennan
Ev'ry Old Back Porch Is New in the Summertime   Fain;
    Kahal
Ev'rybody Loves You   Warren
Excuse Me Lady   Leslie
Extra Man, The   Porter
Eyeful of You, An   Gilbert
Fading Away   Baer; Gilbert
Fare-Thee-Well   Robin; Whiting
Father Mississippi   Akst; Gilbert
Feeling Sentimental   Gershwin, George; Gershwin, Ira;
    Kahn
Fellow Master   Eliscu
Fin de Siecle   Hammerstein; Kern
Finale of Movietone Follies   Conrad; Mitchell
Find Me a Primitive Man   Porter
Find Out what They Like (And How They Like It)   Razaf;
    Waller
Finding the Long Way Home   Kahn; Warren
Fireworks   Kalmar; Ruby
First Mate Martin   Hammerstein; Kern
Flappers on Parade   Coots; Davis
Fleurette   Fisher; Rose
Flippity Flop, The   Coslow; Robin; Whiting
Flood, The   Eliscu; Rose; Youmans
Flowers of Happiness   Alter; Johnson, Howard
Follow the Minstrel Band   Gershwin, George; Gershwin, Ira;
    Kahn
Follow Thru   Brown, Lew; DeSylva; Henderson
Following Famous Footsteps   Edwards
Football Song   Magidson; Washington
For He's the Prince of Good Fellows   Clare
For One Another   Fields; McHugh
For People Like Us   Kahal
For Someone I Love   Davis; Snyder
For the Likes o' You and Me   Stept
For the Papa   Brennan
For You   Dubin
For You and Me Sweetheart   Silver; Turk
For You Baby   Gordon
Forever with You   Alter
Freeze and Melt   Fields; McHugh
Freshman Hop   Mills
From Now On   Eliscu
Full of Pep   Brennan
Funny What a Little Kiss Can Do   Hoffman; Lerner, Sammy
Gag Song   Baer; Gilbert
Ga-Ga   Eliscu
Gay Love   Clare
Gee Baby, Ain't I Good to You   Razaf
Georgia   Revel
Georgia Gigolo   Johnson, Howard
Get Away from My Window   Johnson, James P.
Get Up Off Your Knees   Razaf
Get Up on a New Routine   Dietz; Schwartz, Arthur

Girl from Noofchateau (Believe Me You Should Know My
    Girl From Noo Chateau), The   Ahlert; Turk
Give It   Magidson; Washington
Give Us a Hitch   Coslow
Glad Rag Doll   Ager; Yellen
Gladly   Arlen; Koehler
Gladyse (inst.)   Waller
Glory of Spring   Atteridge; Brennan
Go Find Somebody to Love   Magidson; Washington
Go to Bed   Dubin
Goddess of Rain   Razaf; Waller
Gone   Razaf; Waller
Good Old Iron Side   Alter; Johnson, Howard
Good Things Come to Those Who Wait   Razaf
Goodness Gracious   Kalmar; Ruby
Got to Keep 'em Struttin'   Revel
Gotta Feelin' for You   Alter
Great Day   Eliscu; Rose; Youmans
Gypsy Charmer   Akst; Clarke
Gypsy Days   Schwartz, Arthur
Hair of the Dog that Bit You, A   Von Tilzer
Hammacher Schlemmer, I Love You   Dietz; Schwartz,
    Arthur
Hands Across the Sea   Eliscu
Hangin' Around with You   Gershwin, George; Gershwin, Ira
Hangin' on the Garden Gate, Sayin' Goodnight   Kahn
Hansom Cab Drivers   Edwards; Johnson, Howard
Happily Ever After   Duke
Happy Because I'm in Love   Eliscu; Rose; Youmans
Happy Birthday   Gershwin, George; Gershwin, Ira; Kahn
Happy Cowboy   Brown, Nacio Herb
Happy Days Are Here Again   Ager; Yellen
Happy Heaven of Harlem, The   Porter
Happy in the Rain   Johnson, Howard
Harlem on the Sand   Hart; Rodgers
Harlem Serenade   Gershwin, George; Gershwin, Ira; Kahn
Harlem Town   Johnson, James P.
Harlemania   McHugh
Harvey   Carmichael; Mills
Haunting My Heart   Rainger; Robin
Have You Been True to Me?   Hart; Rodgers
Have You Forgotten Cherie   Coots; Davis
Having My Own Sweet Way   Eliscu
Hawaiian Love-Bird   Razaf
Hawaiian Romance   Baer; Caesar
He Couldn't Speak a Word of English   Silver
Head Low   Robison
Heart o' Mine   Rose
Heart of Broadway   Edwards
Heavy Sugar   Razaf; Waller
Heel and Toe   Caesar
Heigh-ho, Ev'rybody, Heigh-ho   Woods
Hello Melody, Goodbye Jazz   Edwards
Help Us Tonight   Eliscu; Rose; Youmans
Here Am I   Hammerstein; Kern
Here Am I, Where Are You   Conrad
Here Comes My Ball and Chain   Robin; Whiting
Here Comes the Bandwagon   Porter
Here Comes the Show Boat   Rose
Here Comes the Sunshine, There Goes the Rain   Kahal;
    Snyder
Here We Are   Kahn; Warren
He's a Big, Big Man from the South with a Big Cigar in His
    Mouth   Bloom; Woods
He's a Good Man to Have Around   Ager; Yellen

He's a Man's Man   Brown, Lew; DeSylva; Henderson
He's Just an Old Guy with Whiskers   Johnson, Howard
He's Just My Ideal   Brennan
He's So Unusual   Silver
High and Low   Dietz; Schwartz, Arthur
High, High, High   Brennan
High Silk Hat and Walking Cane   Kahal
High Up on a Hill-Top   Baer
Hinky Dinky   Dubin
Hittin' the Ceiling   Conrad; Mitchell
Hitting the Deck   Johnson, Howard
H'lo Baby   Magidson; Washington
Hokum   Hanley
Hold 'em Cowboy   Brennan
Hold Me Tight and Say How Much You Love Me   Friend
Hollywood Nights   Conrad; Mitchell
Home at the End of My Dreams, The   Monaco
Home Blues   Gershwin, George; Gershwin, Ira; Kahn
Home Is Mine   Leslie
Home Lovin' Gal   Gershwin, George; Gershwin, Ira; Kahn
Home Lovin' Man   Gershwin, George; Gershwin, Ira; Kahn
Home Sweet Home   Conrad; Mitchell
Homestead Must Be Sold, The   Eliscu; Rose; Youmans
Honeysuckle Rose   Razaf; Waller
Hosanna   Conrad; Mitchell
Hot and Bothered   Kalmar; Ruby
Hot Chocolate   Alter; Fields; McHugh
Hot Feet   Fields; McHugh
Hot Footin' It   Conrad; Mitchell
Hot Man   Conrad; Mitchell
Hottentot Trot   Fields; McHugh
(When I Am) Housekeeping for You   Dietz; Gorney
How Can I Show I Love You   Wrubel
How Could I Forget   Gershwin, George; Gershwin, Ira; Kahn
Huddlin'   Magidson; Washington
I Ain't Afraid of Scarecrows (I Ain't Scared of Crows)   Eliscu; Rose; Youmans
I Ain't Never Been Kissed   Leslie
I Came to Life   Harburg
I Came to You   Conrad; Mitchell
I Can Do Wonders with You   Hart; Rodgers
I Can't Forget   Dietz; Schwartz, Arthur
I Can't Go on This Way   Rainger; Robin
I Can't Make My Heart Behave   Eliscu; Rose; Youmans
I Can't Remember the Words   Ager; Yellen
I Can't Wait   Fields; McHugh
I Could Do It for You   Conrad; Mitchell
I Could Give Up Anything But You   Brown, Lew; DeSylva; Henderson
I Didn't Mean It   Davis; Silver
I Don't Love Nobody but You   Johnson, James P.
I Don't Want to Get Thin   Ager; Yellen
I Don't Want Your Kisses If I Can't Have Your Love   Fisher
I Dream of a Girl in a Shawl   Porter
I Dream of Hawaii and You   Mills
I Feel It   Razaf
I Fell in Love with You   Lerner, Sammy
I Found a Friend   Brennan
I Found Happiness Now   Mills
I Found Happiness (When I Found You)   Pollack
I Got a Code in My Doze   Rose
I Gotta Have You   Magidson; Washington
I Guess I'll Have to Change My Plan   Dietz; Schwartz, Arthur

I Had to Fall in Love with You   Coslow
I Have to Have You   Robin; Whiting
I Just Looked at You   Gershwin, George; Gershwin, Ira; Kahn
I Kiss Your Hand Madame   Eliscu; Lewis; Young, Joseph
I Knew that You were Mine   Mills; Parish
I Know   Mills
I Like What You Like, I Wish You'd Never Grow Up at All   Eliscu; Rose; Youmans
I Live to Love and Love to Live   Baer; Gilbert
I Live to Love You Only   Gordon
I Lost My Shirt   Berlin
I Love Anything that Has Anything to Do with You   Fain
I Love to Hit Myself on the Head with a Hammer   Magidson; Washington
I Love You but I Like You Even More   Schwartz, Arthur
I Love You, I Hate You (For Making a Fool Out of Me)   Bryan; Meyer
I Love You More than Yesterday   Rodgers
I Love You More Today Than Yesterday   Hart
I Loved Him But He Didn't Love Me   Porter
I Mean to Say   Gershwin, George; Gershwin, Ira
(I'd Better not Try It) I Might Like It   Magidson; Washington
I Miss a Little Miss Who Kisses Me   Coots
I Must Be Home By Twelve O'Clock   Gershwin, George; Gershwin, Ira; Kahn
I Need Someone Like You (inst.)   Waller
I Need You   Johnson, James P.
I Need You So   Dietz; Schwartz, Arthur
I Never Knew I Could Do Anything Like That   Edwards
I Only Wish I Had You with Me Last Night Honey   Monaco
I Owe You   Lerner, Sammy
I Said Goodbye to the Sunshine When I Said Goodbye to You   Coots; Davis
I Sing All My Love Songs to You   Hoffman
I Speak English Now   Gershwin, Ira
I Still Believe in You   Akst; Clarke; Davis; Robin
I Still Belong to You   Robin; Whiting
I Think You'll Like It   Whiting
I Used to Love Her in the Moonlight, But She's in the Limelight Now   Lewis; Young, Joseph
I Wanna Go Places and Do Things   Robin; Whiting
I Want a Good Time Bad   Coslow
I Want to Be a War Bride   Gershwin, George; Gershwin, Ira
I Want to Be Alone with Mary Brown   Leslie
I Want to Be Bad   Brown, Lew; DeSylva; Henderson
I Want to Be Raided By You   Porter
I Want to Be Your Sweetheart   Revel
I Want to Hear You Say C'est Vous   Lewis; Young, Joseph
I Want To! I Got To! I Have to Be Loved   Fisher
I Want to Meander in the Meadow   Woods
I Want You All to Myself   Eliscu
I Was Not too Particular   Stept
I Will Remember, You Will Forget   Coslow
I Wish I Knew   Young, Victor
I Wish I Were Back in My Cradle   Brennan
I Wish You All the Luck in the World   Washington
I Wonder what Is Really on His Mind   Bryan
I Wonder Where Mary Is Tonight   Parish
I Worship You   Porter
I Wouldn't Care for That   Wrubel
Ich Liebe Dich   Fisher
I'd Do Anything for You   Friend; Pollack
I'd Like to Be Liked   Kalmar; Ruby
I'd Like to Love Them All   Brennan

If I Became the President   Gershwin, George; Gershwin, Ira
If I Came Back to You and Said I'm Sorry   Edwards
If I Can't Have You   Bryan; Meyer
If I Give Up the Saxophone (Will You Come Back to Me)   Fain; Kahal
If I Had a Talking Picture of You   Brown, Lew; DeSylva; Henderson
If I Were You I'd Fall in Love with Me   Fain
If I'm Dreaming, Don't Wake Me Up Too Soon   Dubin
If We Never Should Meet Again   Donaldson; Leslie
If You Believe in Me   Baer; Gilbert
If You Believed in Me   Baer
If You Could Care   Goetz
If You Haven't Somebody to Love   Brown, A. Seymour
If You Like Me Like I Like You   Waller
If You Really Love Your Baby   Razaf
If You Were Mine   Bryan; Meyer
If Your Best Friend Won't Tell You   Dubin
If Your Want to See Paree (Look in My Eyes)   Donaldson; Leslie
Igloo Song   Baer; Gilbert
I'll Always Be in Love with You   Stept
I'll Always Be Mother's Boy   Stept
I'll Be So Happy   Ahlert; Turk
I'll Be There   Coots
I'll Close My Eyes to the Rest of the World and Dream Sweet Dreams of You   Friend
I'll Know and She'll Know   Kalmar; Ruby
I'll Never Ask for More   DeSylva
I'll Tell the World You're All the World to Me   Ahlert; Turk
I'll Wait for You   Revel
Illusion   Coslow
I'm a Dreamer, Aren't We All   Brown, Lew; DeSylva; Henderson
I'm a Gigolo   Porter
I'm a Little Negative Looking for a Positive   Bryan
I'm Afraid that Ev'rything's All Right   Coots
I'm All a Twitter (And All A-Twirl)   Robin; Whiting
I'm All Burned Up   Dubin
I'm Blue for You New Orleans   Akst; Clarke
I'm Choosin' a Tune About June   Coots
I'm Doin' What I'm Doin' for Love   Ager; Yellen
I'm Dreaming of a Bygone Day   Cobb; Edwards
I'm Feathering a Nest (for a Little Bluebird)   Ager; Yellen
I'm for You, You're for Me   Brennan
I'm Glad I'm on the Bum   Mills; Parish
I'm Glad It Was Only a Dream   Mills
I'm Going to Meet Minnie Tonight   Johnson, Howard
I'm Gonna Specialize on You   Johnson, Howard
I'm Happy 'Cause I Was Wrong   Caesar; Woods
I'm Holding My Head Up High   Pollack
I'm in Love   Brennan; Porter
I'm in Love at Last   Coots
I'm in Seventh Heaven   Brown, Lew; DeSylva; Henderson
I'm Just a Bundle of Sunshine   Gershwin, George; Gershwin, Ira; Kahn
I'm Just in the Mood Tonight   Leslie
I'm Just Wild About You   Razaf; Waller
I'm Just Wonderin' Who   Mills
I'm Leaving the Whole Thing to You   Coots
I'm Like a Sailor Home from the Sea   Dietz; Schwartz, Arthur
I'm Looking Into Heaven (When I'm Looking in Your Eyes)   Johnson, Howard
I'm Losing You   Lewis; Young, Joseph

I'm Marching Home to You   Silver
I'm Not Sorry   Ager; Yellen
I'm Not Worrying   Waller
I'm On a Diet of Love   Baer; Gilbert
I'm on the Road to Happiness   Coots; Davis
I'm Only Making Believe   Coots; Davis
I'm Out for No Good Reason Tonight   Gershwin, George; Gershwin, Ira; Kahn
I'm Perfectly Satisfied   Leslie
I'm Referin' Just to Her 'n Me   Coots
I'm Rolling in Love   Mills
I'm Saving All My Kisses for Someone   Woods
I'm So Tired of It All   Hanley
I'm Somebody's Baby Now   Gordon
I'm Spending a Long Day   Donaldson; Leslie
I'm Stuck on Molasses and Molasses Is Stuck on Me   Brown, A. Seymour
I'm that Way Over You   Coots; Davis
I'm the Head Man   Berlin
I'm the Last of the Red Hot Mommas   Ager; Yellen
I'm the Medicine Man for the Blues   Akst; Clarke
I'm the Wealthiest Man in the World   Ahlert; Turk
I'm Thirsty for Your Kisses   Coots; Davis
I'm Too Young To Be Careful (And Too Sweet To Be Good)   Bryan; Meyer
I'm Unlucky at Gambling   Porter
I'm Walking in the Sunshine, Sitting in the Moonlight Now   Friend
I'm Walking Through Clover, I'm Happy in Love   Friend; Pollack
I'm Walking with the Moonbeams, Talking to the Stars   Gordon
I'm Wingin' Home   Baer; Gilbert
I'm Yours   Coots; Davis
Impromptu in Two Keys (inst)   Gershwin, George
In a Big Big Way   Washington
In a Corner of My Heart   Parish
In a Kitchenette   Dubin
In a Little Lane in Honoloo   Parish
In Chicago   Eliscu
In Memory of You   Dubin
In Montmartre   Alter; Johnson, Howard
In Pastures Green (inst.)   Robison
In the Hush of the Night   Hoffman; Lerner, Sammy
In the Land of Jazz   Brennan
In the Land of Let's Pretend   Akst; Clarke
In the Land of Make Believe   Baer; Gilbert
In the Mandarin's Orchid Garden   Gershwin, George; Gershwin, Ira
In the Morning   Berlin
In the Rattle of the Battle   Gershwin, George; Gershwin, Ira
In the Summer   Kalmar; Ruby
In the Valley of My Dreams   Hanley
In You, All My Dreams Come True   Von Tilzer
India   Razaf
Irene   Kahn
Is It Nothing to You   Dubin
Is It Spain?   Lewis; Young, Joseph
Is It True   Baer; Gilbert
Is Izzy Azzy Woz?   Caesar; Friend
Isabella   Lewis; Young, Joseph
It Doesn't Take So Much to Make Me Happy   Brown, A. Seymour
It Don't Mean a Thing Without You   Coots
It Happened in Dreamland   Dixon; Woods

It Isn't Done   Porter
It Looks Like It's Gonna Be You   Dixon; Woods
It Must Be Heaven   Hart; Rodgers
It Must Be Love   Gordon; Snyder
It Took a Lot of Blue   Washington
It's a Great Sport   Brown, Lew; DeSylva; Henderson
It's a Habit of Mine   Robin; Whiting
It's a Man's World   Hart; Rodgers
It's Great to Be Necked   Brown, Lew; DeSylva; Henderson
It's Just Too Bad   Styne
It's Natural   Oakland
It's Unanimous Now   Stept
It's You I Love   Coots; Davis
I've Got a Feeling I'm Falling   Rose; Waller
I've Got a Little Love Song   Ager; Yellen
I've Got a Passport to Heaven Since I Fell in Love with
    You   Coots
I've Got the World Right in the Palm of My Hand   Coots
I've Got the World (With a Fence Around It)   Washington
I've Got Those Old Man River Blues   Sissle
I've Made a Habit of You   Dietz; Schwartz, Arthur
I've Never Been Loved By Anyone Like You   Mills
Jack and Jill   Coslow; Duke
Japanese   Razaf
Japanese Dream, A   Fields; McHugh
Japanese Moon, A   Fields
Japanese Toyland   Carroll
Jazz Heaven   Clare
Jazz Patrol   Caesar
Jazz Reception (Kindly Nullify Your Fears)   Hart; Rodgers
Jennie MacIntyre   Leslie
Jericho   Robin
Jig Jig Jigaloo   Akst; Clarke
Jig-Jig-Jigaloo   Bryan; Meyer
Joanna   Mills
Jolly Troubadour (inst.), The   Schwartz, Arthur
Journey's End (inst.)   Hanley
Joy Street   Conrad; Mitchell
Judgement Day   Brown, A. Seymour
Jumping Jack   Bloom
Jungle Jamboree   Ellington; Razaf
Junio   Donaldson
Junior-Senoir Prom, The   Mills
Just a Big-Hearted Man   Brennan
Just a Little Blue for You   Hanley
Just a Little Daisy for Mary and Me   Von Tilzer
Just a Little Glimpse of Paradise   Kalmar; Ruby; Warren
Just a Melody from a Memory   Fain; Gorney; Kahal
Just an Hour of Love   Bryan
Just an Old Love Affair   Kahn
Just an Out-of-the-Way Little Love Nest   Fain; Lerner,
    Sammy
Just Another Kiss   Coots; Davis
Just As Long As I Have You   Young, Victor
Just As Long As You Belong to Me   Lewis; Pollack; Young,
    Joseph
Just As Long As You're Treatin' Me Right   Mills
Just Be a Builder of Dreams   Lewis; Pollack; Young, Joseph
Just for a Day   Oakland
Just Goofy   Mills
Just Like a Vagabond   Magidson
Just Plain Folk   Leslie
Just Sociable   Razaf
Just Wait and See Sweetheart   Robin; Whiting
Just Whisper I Love You   Gorney; Harburg

K-A-L-A-M-A-ZOO, That's My Home Town   Monaco
Kalua Bay   Parish
Kansas City Kitty   Donaldson; Leslie
Kansas Was Never Like This   Ahlert; Turk
Katie Keep Your Feet on the Ground   Sterling
Keep Your Undershirt On   Kalmar; Ruby
Keeping the Wolf from the Door   Dubin
Kelly Is Living the Life of Reilly   Lewis; Pollack; Young,
    Joseph
Kicking the Blues Away   Hanley
Kind of Man for Me, The   Razaf
Kinda Cute   Gorney; Harburg
King of Jazzmania   Coslow; Robin; Whiting
King of the Air   Bryan
Kitchen Man   Razaf
Knees   Hart; Rodgers
La Hoota-Coota-Boota Mamaseta   Friend
Ladies of the Dance   Coslow; Robin; Whiting
Lady I Love, The   Porter
Lady of the Moon   Gershwin, George; Gershwin, Ira
Lamp, a Chair and a Cigarette, A   Ahlert; Turk
Language of Love, The   Razaf
Lass Who Loved a Sailor, The   Hart; Rodgers
Last Night in Dreamy Dreamland   Leslie
Last Night When We Were All Alone   Mills
Laughing Marionettes   Gilbert
Laughing Water   Razaf; Waller
Lazy Amazon, The   Sissle
Leave Me a Beautiful Melody   Coslow
Leave the Lovin' to Me   Kahal
Legs   Conrad; Mitchell
Legs, Legs, Legs   Gorney; Harburg
Let Him Ramble, Let Him Roam   Ager; Yellen
Let Me Be Alone with You   Mills
Let Me Have My Dreams   Akst; Clarke
Let Me Sing Before Breakfast   Fields; McHugh
Let Me Weep on Your Shoulder   Eliscu
Let Us Drink to the Girl of My Dreams   Baer; Gilbert
Let's Dream   Coots; Davis
Let's Go Walkin'   Wrubel
Let's Make the Best of It   Coots; Davis
Let's Merge   Coots; Davis
Let's Step Out   Porter
Let's Talk It Over   Coots; Davis
Levee Love   Coots
Life Can Be So Lonesome   Dubin
Life Is Like a Checkerboard when You're in Love   Alter;
    Johnson, Howard
Life Is Love   Caesar
Life of a Nurse, The   Eliscu
Lift the Juleps to Your Two Lips   Akst; Clarke
Like a Breath of Springtime   Dubin
Like a Melody   Revel
Like Me Less — Love Me More   Harburg
Like Me Less - Love Me More   Gorney
Li-Po-Li   Bryan
Lips that Laugh at Love   Brennan
Little Baby Curls   Johnson, Howard
Little Black Sheep   Baer; Gilbert
Little Bo-Peep   Caesar
Little Cavalier   Dubin
Little Coat of Tan, A   Coots
Little Dutch Doll, The   Revel
Little Kiss Each Morning, A Little Kiss Each Night,
    A   Woods

Little Old New York   Dietz; Schwartz, Arthur
Little Pal   Brown, Lew; DeSylva; Hanley; Henderson
Liza (All the Clouds'll Roll Away)   Gershwin, George; Gershwin, Ira; Kahn
Load Is Heavy (And I'm Ready to Go), The   Snyder
Lolita, My Love   Gershwin, George; Gershwin, Ira; Kahn
Lon Chaney's Gonna Get You (If You Don't Watch Out)   Edwards
Lonely Lane   Parish
Longing   Schwartz, Jean
Look in My Eyes   Donaldson; Eliscu
Look What You've Done to Me   Conrad; Mitchell
Lookin' Good but Feelin' Bad   Waller
Lookin' Hot and Keepin' Cool   Von Tilzer
Looking at You   Porter
Looking for Love   Fields; McHugh
Lost One   Mills
Lots of Time for Sue   Caesar
Louise   Robin; Whiting
Lovable Rogue   Von Tilzer
Love Birds   Caesar; Friend
Love Come Back to Me   Caesar
Love Is a Dreamer   Stept
Love Is Free to Everyone   Friend
Love Is Heaven, Heaven in Love   Bryan
Love Is in the Air   Coots; Davis
Love Is Like a Rose   Bryan; Meyer
Love Is Like a Watch   Schwartz, Jean
Love Makes the World Go 'Round   Conrad; Mitchell
Love Me, Love My Dog   Von Tilzer
Love Plays a Game   Hoffman; Lerner, Sammy
Love Thrills   Bryan; Meyer
Love to Take a Lesson in Love (Love to Take a Lesson from You)   Clare
Love Will Find a Way   Dubin
Love Will Find You   Baer; Gilbert
Love Will Last Forever If It's Love   Bryan
Loveable and Sweet   Clare
Lovely Night in Spain   Egan
Lovely One   Lerner, Sammy
Lucia   Fisher; Rose
Lucky Boy   Baer; Gilbert
Lucky Little Devil   Dixon; Woods
Lucky Me, Loveable You   Ager; Yellen
Madame Satan (inst.)   Alter
Mademoiselle in New Rochelle   Gershwin, George; Gershwin, Ira
Magic Island   Fain; Mills; Parish
Magnolia Finale   Gershwin, George; Gershwin, Ira
Make Yourself at Home   Gordon
Man About Town   Dietz; Schwartz, Arthur
Man of High Degree, A   Gershwin, George; Gershwin, Ira
Mandel   Lewis; Pollack; Young, Joseph
Mannikin Dolls   Atteridge
Mardi Gras   Eliscu; Rose; Youmans
Marianne   Ahlert; Turk
Married Men and Single Men   Brown, Lew; DeSylva; Henderson
Mary Dugan I Love You   Parish
M-A-R-Y, I Love Y-O-U   Gordon
Maudita   Conrad; Mitchell
May I Do   Oakland
May I Say I Love You?   Coots; Davis
Me and My Buddy   Ager; Yellen
Me for You   Hart; Rodgers

Mean Man   Eliscu; Rose; Youmans
Mean to Me   Ahlert; Turk
Mechanical Man   Dubin
Meditation Brings Me You   Johnson, Howard
Medley   Edwards
Meet My Sister   Brennan
Meet the Boy Friend — Don't Laugh   Eliscu; Rose; Youmans
Melancholy Me   Loesser
Melodrame (inst.)   Henderson
Messin' Around   Johnson, James P.
Messin' Round   Brennan
Mexicali Moon   Mills
Mexicana   Edwards
Midstream   Baer; Gilbert
Mightiest Matador   Coslow; Robin; Whiting
Military Ball   Hoffman
Military March   Bryan
Mind Your P's and Q's   Hart; Rodgers
Minstrel Days   Edwards
Minstrel Memories   Baer; Gilbert
Miss Wonderful   Bryan
Mississippi   Johnson, James P.
Mississippi Day   Johnson, J. Rosamond; Youmans
Mississippi Moan   Johnson, James P.
Missouri Moon   Parish
Moanin' Low   Dietz; Rainger
Mollie O'Donahue   Hammerstein; Kern
Mona   Conrad; Mitchell
Moonlight, a Love Song and You   Koehler
Moonlight Reminds Me of You, The   Kahn
More than You Know   Eliscu; Rose; Youmans
Mother Grows Younger (Daughter Grows Older)   Hart; Rodgers
Mothers of the World   Brennan
Mountains Ain't No Place for Bad Men   Kahal
My Angelina   Gilbert
My Baby Said Yes   Rose
My Baby Sure Knows How to Love   Razaf
My Beauty Shop   Akst; Clarke
My Blackbirds Are Bluebirds Now   Caesar; Friend
My Blue Lagoon   Johnson, J. Rosamond
My Castle in Spain Is a Shack in the Lane   Caesar; Friend
My Darling   Mills; Parish
My Day Dreams Came True Over Night   Hoffman; Silver
My Dear   Kahn
My Dream Memory   Clare
My Dynamo   Schwartz, Arthur
My Fate Is In Your Hands   Razaf; Waller
My Flame of Love   Bryan
My Harlem Wench   Porter
My Hawaiian Sweetheart   Mills; Parish
My Heart Cries Out I Love You   Friend; Silver
My Heart Is Bluer than Your Eyes, Cherie   Bryan
My Heart Wants To Kiss You, Cherie   Bryan
My Heaven of Love   Bryan
My Husband's First Wife   Hammerstein; Kern
My Ideal   Leslie
My Lady Love   Coslow; Robin
My Lahaina Rose   Mills
My Linda   Razaf
My Little Angel   Lewis; Pollack; Young, Joseph
My Little Man   Dixon; Woods
My Louisa   Porter
My Lover, Master of My Heart   Bryan
My Lucky Star   Brown, Lew; DeSylva; Henderson

My Madonna   Fisher; Rose
My Man Is Good for Nothing but Love   Razaf; Waller
My Man Is on the Make   Hart; Rodgers
My Melody Man   Clare
My Mother's Eyes   Baer; Gilbert
My Old Man   Woods
My Paradise   Magidson; Washington
My Rosemarie   Eliscu
My Sin   Brown, Lew; DeSylva; Henderson
My Song of the Nile   Bryan; Meyer
My Strongest Weakness Is You   Akst; Clarke
My Sugar and Me   Koehler
My Sunday Fella   Gershwin, George; Gershwin, Ira; Kahn
My Sunny South   Silver
My Sweet Helene   Bryan; Meyer
My Sweeter than Sweet   Whiting
My Victory (Was Conquering Your Heart)   Styne
My Wedding   Eliscu
My Wild Party Girl   Robin; Whiting
My Window   Conrad; Mitchell
Napoleon Said to Josephine Not Tonight   Revel
Naughty Boy   Hammerstein; Kern
Naughty but Nice   Alter; Johnson, Howard
Navy Blues   Ahlert; Turk
New Yorker, The   Ager; Yellen
Night Club Opening   Porter
Night Club Stomp   Mills
Night of Happiness, A   Conrad; Mitchell
Nightingale Song, The   Ager; Yellen
Nighttime Brings Dreams of You   Davis
Nina   Brennan
1908 Life, The   Brown, Lew; DeSylva; Henderson
No More You   Brown, Lew; DeSylva; Henderson
No, No, Nanette   Bryan
No One but the Right Man Can Do Me Wrong   Rainger
No One Can Take Your Place   Gilbert
No Other Love Was Meant for Me   Brennan
No Wonder   Waller
Nobody but You   Edwards
Nobody Can Change My Mind   Styne
Nobody Cares If I'm Blue   Clarke
Nobody Knows   Burke
Nobody Knows but Rosie, But Oh! What Rosie
      Knows!   Hanley
Nobody Wants Me   Caesar
Nodding Away   Brennan
Nonchalant, The   Von Tilzer
Not Enough Love, Baby   Von Tilzer
Nothing's Right When Your Love's All Wrong   Dietz;
      Gorney; Harburg
Now Go to Your Cabin   Hart; Rodgers
Now I'm in Love   Yellen
October's Melody (inst.)   Robison
Official Resume   Gershwin, George; Gershwin, Ira
Off-Time   Razaf; Waller
Oh Baby what A Night   Brown, A. Seymour
Oh Frenchy   Conrad
Oh How He Plays His Ukulele   Brennan
Oh Listen to the Anvil Chorus   Von Tilzer
Oh, Lord, Pour Down Your Waters and Baptize Me   Baer;
      Gilbert
Oh Ma, What a Man   Bryan
Oh My Stock Is Going Up with Susie   Lewis; Young, Joseph
Oh So Sweet   Silver
Oh, Sweetheart Where Are You Tonight   Coots; Davis

Oh, There's a Mouse   Dixon; Woods
Oh! You Chicago Cubs   Dixon; Woods
Old Man Weaver of Dreams   Washington
Old Soldiers Never Die   Conrad; Mitchell
Old Timer   Rose
On the Border Line   Kalmar; Ruby
On the River   Schwartz, Jean
On the Road to Rainbow Bay   Dixon; Woods
On the Up and Up   Eliscu
On Top   Brennan
On Top of the World Alone   Robin; Whiting
On with the Dance   Caesar; Dubin; Leslie; Monaco
On with the Show   Akst; Clarke
Once in a Blue Moon   Motzan
One for All, All for One   Alter
One I Love Just Can't Be Bothered with Me, The   Kahn
One Love   Eliscu; Rose; Youmans
One Man   Gershwin, George; Gershwin, Ira; Kahn
One Minute of Heaven   Magidson; Washington
One Moment More with You   Egan; Whiting
One Night of Love   Brennan
One Sweet Little Yes   Akst; Clarke
One Sweetheart   Baer; Gilbert
One that I Love Loves Me, The   Ahlert; Turk
Ongsay and Anceday   Hart; Rodgers
Only Song I Know, The   Brennan
Oo-Day Oo-Yay   Magidson; Washington
Oo-La-La-La-La (Joli Fifi)   Ahlert; Turk
Opalisque (inst.)   Willson
Open and Shut Idea   Brennan
Open Book, An   Eliscu
Open Up Your Heart, Play the Game   Eliscu; Rose;
      Youmans
Open Your Eyes   Duke
Open Your Window   Brennan
Operatic Pills   Porter
Ophelia Will Fool You   Bryan; Meyer
Orange Blossom Time   Edwards
Oriental Moon   Hammerstein; Kern
Oui Oui Monsieur   Styne
Our Little Bag of Tricks   Coots
Out in the Cold   Conrad; Mitchell
Out of a Clear Blue Sky   Carroll
Out of the Blue   Hammerstein; Kern
Out Where the Moonbeams Are Born   Coots
Over and Over Again   Kalmar; Ruby
Over Here   Coots; Davis
Pagan Love Song   Brown, Nacio Herb; Freed, Arthur
Page Nine   Yellen
Painting the Clouds with Sunshine   Dubin
Pal of My Sweetheart Days   Coots; Davis
Pals Forever   Yellen
Papa Likes a Hot Papoose   Gorney; Harburg
Papers, The   Kalmar; Ruby
Parade of the Blues   Conrad; Mitchell
Paree, What Did You Do to Me?   Porter
Paris   Bryan
Park Avenue Strut   Atteridge
Pearl of Old Japan   Conrad; Mitchell
Pennington Pep   Dubin
Perhaps   Razaf
Phenomena (inst.)   Willson
Photograph of the Sweeter Half of My Love Affair, A   Kahal
Pick 'em Up and Lay 'em Down   Brennan
Pickaninny's Cryin'   Mills; Parish

Pilly Pom Pom Plee   Bryan; Meyer
Pingo-Pongo   Dubin
Pirate Band, The   Brennan
Pirate Song   Wrubel
Play Us a Polka Dot   Hammerstein; Kern
Playboy   Hart; Rodgers
Please Don't Make Me Be Good   Porter
Poison Kiss of That Spaniard   Dubin
Polly   Caesar
Poor Little Orphans (Sixteen of 'Em)   Eliscu; Rose; Youmans
Poor Punchinello   Lewis; Pollack; Young, Joseph
Poor Unlucky Me   Dixon; Warren
Prep Step, The   Whiting
Pretty Little Maid of Old Madrid   Coots
Prisoner of Love   Razaf; Waller
Prize Fighters' Number   Edwards; Johnson, Howard
Psychological Moment   Brennan
Put on Your Sunday Face   Dixon
Put Your Mind Right on It   Johnson, James P.
Puttin' on the Ritz   Berlin
Queen of Terre Haute, The   Porter
Quiero   Revel
Racket Song, The   Von Tilzer
Rainbow   Conrad; Mitchell
Rainbow Man   Hanley
Rainbow on the Way   Davis
(Shah!) Raise the Dust!   Eliscu
Raisin' the Roof   Fields; McHugh
Reach for a Sweetie   Whiting
Reach Out for a Rainbow   Conrad; Mitchell
Reaching for Someone and Not Finding Anyone There   Donaldson; Leslie
Reaching for the Moon   Kalmar; Ruby
Recollections   Pollack
Red Hair and Freckles   Dietz
Red Hot and Blue Rhythm   Coots; Davis
Redemption   Parish
Redskinland   Razaf; Waller
Reminiscing   Donaldson; Leslie
Revolutionary Rhythm   Coots
Rhythm of Joy   Brennan
Rhythm on the Brain   Revel
Ride 'Em Cowboys   Schwartz, Arthur
Ride On Vaquero   Baer; Gilbert
Right Kind of Man, The   Baer; Gilbert
Right Off the Board   Eliscu; Rose; Youmans
Ring a Ding a Ding Dong Dell   Gershwin, George; Gershwin, Ira
Rising Moon   Arlen
River Song   Eliscu; Rose; Youmans
River, Stay 'Way from My Door   Dixon; Woods
Rose of Algiers   Yellen
Roust-abouts   Johnson, James P.
Rush In Blues   Mills
'S Been a Long Time in Between Time   Monaco
'S Nice Like This   Friend
Sacred Flame, The   Akst; Clarke
Same Old Moon, Same Old June, but Not the Same Old You   Friend
Samoa   Akst; Clarke
Sandman Wrap Me Up in a Silver Cloud   Kahal
Sarah Jane   Leslie
Satisfied   Caesar; Friend
Say a Prayer for Palestine   Johnson, Howard
Say It After Me, I Love You   Parish

Say It with a Big Brass Band   Edwards
Say It with Your Feet   Razaf; Waller
Say Something   Coots
Say That You Have Forgiven Me   Oakland
Say the Word   Baer; Gilbert
Say Young Man of Manhattan   Adamson; Youmans
Scattin' the Cat   Conrad; Mitchell
Schrafft's University   Eliscu
Sentimental Fool   Rose
Sentimental Melody   Coots; Davis
Serenading the Moon   Styne
Shadows   Conrad; Mitchell
Shady Lady   Johnson, Howard
Shake High, Shake Low   Brennan
Share Your Heart   Styne
She Can't Be Bothered with Me   Kahn
She Said 'Uh Huh' to Me   Johnson, Howard
She Was Kicked in the Head by a Butterfly   Magidson; Washington
Shelter of My Baby's Arms, The   Donaldson; Leslie
She's a Good Girl   Fain
She's a New Kind of Old Fashioned Girl   Rose
She's Been a Comfort to Me   Schwartz, Arthur
She's So I Don't Know   Robin; Whiting
She's Such a Comfort to Me   Schwartz, Arthur
Ship of My Dreams   Bryan; Meyer
Ship without a Sail, A   Hart; Rodgers
Shoo Shoo Boogie Boo   Coslow; Robin; Whiting
Should I   Brown, Nacio Herb; Freed, Arthur
Shout On!   Johnson, James P.
Si, Si, Senor   Eliscu; Rose; Youmans
Siege (inst.), The   Willson
Silvery Moonlight (Only a Moonbeam Dream)   Coslow; Robin
Since I Gave My Heart to You   Bryan; Snyder
Since We Became Sweethearts   Clare
Sing a Little Love Song   Conrad; Mitchell
Sing a Song in the Rain   Caesar
Sing a Song of Old Montana   Brown, Nacio Herb
Sing Song Girl   Gershwin, George; Gershwin, Ira
Sing Your Little Folk Song (Sing Me a Little Folk Song)   Donaldson; Leslie
Singin' a Song to My Man   Wrubel
Singin' in the Bathtub   Magidson; Washington
Singin' in the Rain   Brown, Nacio Herb
Sittin' on a Doorstep   Lewis; Pollack; Young, Joseph
Sitting Around Thinking of My Baby   Coslow
Sitting By the Window   Conrad; Mitchell
Sitting in the Sun (Just Wearing a Smile)   Caesar; Friend
Six or Seven Times   Mills; Waller
Skiddle-de-Skow   Johnson, James P.
Sky City   Hart; Rodgers
Sleepy Town   Styne
Sleepy Valley   Hanley; Sterling
Sliding Down a Silver Cloud   Brennan
Slow Caravan   Hoffman; Lerner, Sammy
Slow Down   Eliscu
Slumbertime   Magidson
Snake Hip Dance   Ellington; Razaf; Waller
Snake Hips, Do the Wiggle Waggle Woo   Conrad; Mitchell
Snake in the Grass (inst.), The   Porter
Snowball Man, The   Hanley
So Are You!   Gershwin, George; Gershwin, Ira; Kahn
So Big and Strong   Wrubel
So Dear to Me   Conrad; Mitchell

So Long   Conrad; Mitchell
So Sentimental   Koehler
Soda I, Soda You, Sodas Ev'rybody   Johnson, Howard
Soft Hearted   Lewis; Young, Joseph
Soldier's March   Gershwin, George; Gershwin, Ira
Some Day You'll Realize   Rose
Some Girl Is on Your Mind   Hammerstein; Kern
Some Little Girl   Von Tilzer
Some Sweet Day   Pollack
Somebody Just Like You   Silver
Somebody Mighty Like You   Bryan
Somebody Nobody Loves   Kahn
Somebody Stole My Heart Away   Gershwin, George;
     Gershwin, Ira; Kahn
Somebody's Going to Throw a Big Party   Porter
Someday, Someway, You'll Pay   Howard, Joseph E.
Someone   Bryan; Clare; Meyer
Someone to Love   Hanley
Someone's Always Calling a Rehearsal   Gershwin, George;
     Gershwin, Ira; Kahn
Something Spanish in Your Eyes   Caesar
Something to Live For   Eliscu
Something's Gotta Be Done About That   Johnston
Song of Gold, The   Leslie; Monaco
Song of Margharita, A   Baer; Gilbert
Song of My Heart   Baer; Gilbert
Song of Steel, The   Edwards; Johnson, Howard
Song of the Bayou   Bloom; Johnson, Howard
Song of the Cotton Fields   Razaf; Waller
Song of the Gold Diggers   Dubin
Song of the Great Alone   Hoffman
Song of the Riveter   Schwartz, Arthur
Song of Vienna   Eliscu
Soon   Gershwin, George; Gershwin, Ira
Sorority Stomp, The   Mills
Sorrows   Kahn; Warren
Sorry that I Strayed Away from You   Johnson, James P.
South Sea Rose   Baer; Gilbert
Spanish Eyes   Edwards
Spanish Fado   Atteridge
Speakin' of the Devil Here Comes an Angel   Coots
Spell of the Blues, The   Johnston
S'Posin   Razaf
Spring Is Here   Hammerstein; Kern
Spring Is in the Summer and She'll Fall   Hoffman
Squeaky Shoes   Fields; McHugh
Squire and the Deacon, The   Kahal
Stage Door Scene   Gershwin, George; Gershwin, Ira
Standing on the Corner   Von Tilzer
Star Dust   Carmichael; Parish
Start the Band   Brennan
Still I'd Love You   Brown, Lew; DeSylva; Henderson
Strike Up the Band   Fisher
Strolling on the Lido   Brennan
Such a Funny Feeling   Duke
Sun About to Rise, The   Hammerstein; Kern
Sun Will Shine, The   Schwartz, Arthur
Sunny Side   Johnson, James P.
Sunny Side Up   Brown, Lew; DeSylva; Henderson
Sunny Tennessee   Coots
Swanee Shuffle   Berlin
Sweet As Sugar Cane   Eliscu; Rose; Youmans
Sweet Emmy Lou   Eliscu; Rose; Youmans
Sweet Georgianna and Me   Whiting
Sweet Hawaiian Sweetheart of Mine   Mills

Sweet Liar   Caesar
Sweet Nothings of Love   Donaldson; Leslie
Sweet Savannah Sue   Razaf; Waller
Sweet Seventeen: That's What I Call My Baby   Donaldson;
     Leslie
Sweet Sixteen   Eliscu; Rose; Youmans
Sweeter than You   Kalmar; Ruby
Sweetest Melody   Mills
Sweetheart of Our Student Corps   Brennan
Sweetheart of Yesterday   Johnson, Howard
Sweetheart, You Make Me Laugh   Hart; Rodgers
Sweethearts Holiday   Kahal
Take a Look at Her Now   Clare
Take Everything But You   Brown, Lew; DeSylva; Henderson
Take Me for a Honeymoon Ride   Hammerstein; Kern
Takes You   Davis
Tale of an Oyster, The   Porter
Talk of the Town, The   Kahn
Tambourine Tune   Hanley
Tan Town Rhythm   Razaf
Tanned Legs   Clare
Tell Me There's Hope for Me   Johnson, Howard
Tell Me, What Has Happened?   Gershwin, George;
     Gershwin, Ira
Tell Me You Are Happy   Brennan
Terrible Toreador, The   Edwards
That Is How It's Done on the Stage   Alter
That Jungle Jamboree   Razaf; Waller
That Night Among the Roses   Koehler
That Old-Time Gal of Mine   Lewis; Young, Joseph
That Rhythm Man   Razaf; Waller
That Was My Own Idea   Waller
That Was Yesterday   Razaf
That Where You Come In   Kahal
That Wonderful Something Is Love   Alter
Thata Old-Time Gal of Mine   Lewis
That's Her Now   Ager; Yellen
That's Just My Way of Forgeting You   Brown, Lew; DeSylva;
     Henderson
That's Music to My Ears   Coots
That's My Business   Bryan
That's the Good Old Sunny South   Ager; Yellen
That's the Kind of Man for Me   Razaf
That's What a Child Can Do   Baer; Gilbert
That's What I Call Love   Arlen
That's What I Call Sweet Music   Hoffman
That's What I See in You   Mills
That's Why I Love You   Porter
That's Why I'm Happy   Magidson
That's You Baby   Conrad; Mitchell
(You Can't Take Away) The Things That Were Made for
     Love   Kahal
Theme of Life   Motzan
Theme Song, The   Dietz; Schwartz, Arthur
Then I'll Be Reminded of You   Heyman
Then I'll Have Time for You   Brown, Lew; DeSylva;
     Henderson
Then My Castle Came Tumbling Down   Koehler
Then Someone's in Love   Pollack
Then Things Blow Up Like a Toy Balloon   Robison
Then We Canoe-dle-oodle Along   Woods
Then You've Never Been Blue   Lewis; Young, Joseph
There Is a City   Robison
There Is a Garden in My Dreams   Fisher
There Is a Happy Land Far Far Away   Akst; Young, Joseph

There Must Be Somebody Waiting for Me in Loveland   Donaldson

There Was Never Such a Charming War   Gershwin, George; Gershwin, Ira

There Was Nothing Else to Do   Kalmar; Ruby; Warren

There'll Be You and I   Stept

There's a Rainbow on the Way   Coots; Davis

There's Ain't No Sweet Man That's Worth the Salt of My Tears   Fisher

There's Happiness   Snyder

There's Love in the Heart I Hold   Brennan

There's Love in Your Eyes   Johnson, Howard

There's Something in That   Eliscu

There's Something Spanish in Your Eyes   Caesar; Friend

(I Says to Myself Says I) There's the One for Me   Akst; Yellen

There's Too Many Eyes   Coots; Davis

They All Fall in Love   Porter

They Cut Down the Old Pine Tree   Eliscu

They Sing! They Dance! They Speak!   Hart; Rodgers

Things Look Wonderful Now   Davis

Things We Want the Most Are Hard To Get, The   Bryan; Meyer

Think of You Think of Me in the Moonlight   Fields; McHugh

This Is Heaven   Akst; Yellen

This Is the Day of Days   Dixon; Woods

This Is the Moment   Robin; Whiting

This Thing Called Love   Lewis; Young, Joseph

(Don't You Ever Be 'Fraid to Wade) Those Troubled Waters   Robison

Thousand Miles Away, A   Rose

Three Bears, The   Hart; Rodgers

Three Little Rooms and You   Ager; Yellen

Through! How Can You Say We're Through?   Monaco

Thru the Night (inst.)   Motzan

Thunder in My Dreams   Heyman

Tia Juana   Edwards

Tie a String Around Your Finger   Conrad; Mitchell

Tiller Girls at Home (inst.), The   Schwartz, Arthur

Time Will Tell   Baer; Gilbert

Tin Soldiers on Parade   Edwards

Tinkle! Tinkle!   Ager; Yellen

Tip Toe Through the Tulips (With Me)   Dubin

To Be In Love Espesh'lly with You   Ahlert; Turk

To Be with You   Coots; Davis

To Lola   Robin; Whiting

Toast to Volstead, A   Porter

Today and Tomorrow   Ahlert; Turk

Tommy Atkins on Parade   Brown, Nacio Herb; Freed, Arthur

To-Night I Am Thinking of You   Parish

Tonight's the Night!   Gershwin, George; Gershwin, Ira; Kahn

Too Coo-Coo Birds   Rainger; Robin

Too Much Lovin'   Magidson

Too, Too Divine   Duke

Tornado (inst.), The   Willson

Touch Me Not   Egan

Touchdown (inst.)   Waller

Tree of Love, The   Brennan

Trouble (inst.)   Waller

True Blue You   Coslow; Robin; Whiting

Try Dancing   Kalmar; Revel; Ruby

Turn on the Heat   Brown, Lew; DeSylva; Henderson

Turn to Me   Eliscu

'Twas Not So Long Ago   Hammerstein; Kern

Twilight Melodies   Young, Victor

Twilight Voices   Brennan

Two Little Baby Arms   Baer; Gilbert

Two Pals but Only One Sweetie   Baer; Gilbert

Uh-Uh in the Moonlight   Conrad

Um-Um in the Moonlight   Conrad; Meyer; Mitchell

Under the Cinnamon Tree   Gershwin, George; Gershwin, Ira

Unknown   Fain; Kahal

Until the End   Fisher

Unto My Heart   Brennan

Up the River   Donaldson; Leslie

Used to You   Brown, Lew; DeSylva; Henderson

Valentine Stomp (inst.)   Waller

Vilma   Coots; Davis

Vineyards of Manhattan, The   Schwartz, Arthur

Volga Boat Song   Donaldson; Leslie

Wagon Tracks (inst.)   Robison

Waikiki   Fain; Parish

Wait for Me   Akst; Young, Joseph

Wait for the Happy Ending   Ager; Yellen

Wait Till You See Ma Cherie   Robin; Whiting

Wait Until It's Bedtime   Porter

Waiting   Conrad; Mitchell

Waiting at the End of the Road   Berlin

Wake Up   Edwards

Wake Up and Dream   Porter

Wake Up, Chill'un, Wake Up   Robison

Wake Up Your Feet   Gordon

Walkin' the Streets   Wrubel

Walkin' the Zep   Alter; Johnson, Howard

Walkin' with Susie   Conrad; Mitchell

Walking Off Those Balken Blues   Dubin

Walking with Susie   Conrad; Mitchell

Waltz Divine   Razaf; Waller

Wandering Home   Kahn; Styne

Wasn't It Fate?   Coots; Davis

Wasn't It Fun   Coots; Davis

Wassa Matter with You   Lewis; Young, Joseph

Wasting Away   Razaf

Watching the World Go By   Porter

Way I Feel To-Day, The   Razaf

We Are Visitors   Gershwin, George; Gershwin, Ira

We Have Each Other   Ager; Yellen

We Love to Go to Work   Atteridge

We Toddled Up the Hill   Leslie

We Want You   Kalmar; Ruby

Weary River   Clarke

Wedding Bells Are Breaking Up that Old Gang of Mine   Fain; Kahal

Wedding Bells Ring On   Eliscu; Rose; Youmans

(You'll Always Be) Welcome   Razaf

Welcome Home   Akst; Clarke; Hanley

We'll Be Cutting Paper Dolls Together   Egan

We'll Be There   Coots; Davis

We'll Get Along   Atteridge

We're Going to Make Boom-Boom   Brennan

We're Lonesome for Someone Like You   Burke

What a Day   Woods

What a Girl!   Brennan

What a Whalen of a Difference Just a Few Lights Make   Fields; McHugh

What Can Be Sweeter   Caesar

What Could I Do?   Brennan
What Could I Do with a Man Like That   Johnson, James P.
What Did Della Wear When Georgie Came
      Across   Schwartz, Arthur
What Didja Wanna Make Me Love You For   Dixon; Warren
What Do I Care   Carroll
What Every Little Girl Should Know   Schwartz, Arthur
What Is This Thing Called Love?   Porter
What Kind o' Man Is You   Carmichael
What Makes My Baby Blue   Dietz; Gorney
What Men and Women Will Wear   Brennan
What She Says Goes   Kalmar; Ruby
What Will I Do Without You?   Dubin
What Would I Care?   Kalmar; Ruby
What Wouldn't I Do for that Man   Gorney; Harburg
What'll Become of Me   Dubin
What's Become of Sweet Madelon   Parish
What's the Use of Lovin' (Without Love)   Johnson, James P.
What's the Use of Loving when You Haven't Anyone to
      Love   Johnson, Howard
When a Fellow Meets a Flapper on Broadway   Caesar
When All Hope Was Gone I Found You, Joan   Lewis
When All Hope Was Lost, I Found You Joan   Akst; Young,
      Joseph
When I Dream   Gordon
When I See My Sugar (I Get a Lump in My Throat)   Ahlert;
      Turk
When Little Children Smile   Leslie
When Love Is Dawning   Donaldson; Leslie
When My Dreams Come True   Berlin
When My Toreador Starts to Snore   Baer; Gilbert
When Niccolo Plays the Piccolo   Woods
When Old New York Was Young   Johnson, Howard
When the Harvest Is Over   Conrad; Mitchell
(What Does It Mean) When the Owl Says Whoo   Alter
When They Sing the Wearin' of the Green (In Syncopated
      Time)   Stept
When Two Hearts Are True Hearts   Coots; Davis
When We Got Together in the Moonlight   Rose
When You Carry the Torch   Warren
When You Come to the End of the Day   Kahn
When You Find Me Dreaming, Wake Me Up with a
      Kiss   Fisher
When You Were in Love with No One but Me (And I Was
      in Love with You)   Ahlert; Turk
When You're In Love   Burke
When You're Seeing Sweetie Home   Lewis; Warren; Young,
      Joseph
Where Are You?   Pollack
Where Are You Dream Girl?   Davis; Motzan
Where Have You Been Hiding Dear   Alter
Where Is Your Heart To-Night   Bryan
Where the Sweet Forget-Me-Nots Remember   Dixon;
      Warren
Where the Trade Winds Blow   Mills
Where Were You   Heyman
Where Would You Get Your Coat?   Porter
(With You) Where You Are   Bloom; Dixon
Which   Porter
Whistling in the Dark   Harburg
White Way Blues   Gordon
White Wings   Edwards; Johnson, Howard
Who Cares What You Have Been   Gilbert
Who Could Say No?   Arlen; Koehler
Who Do You Think Is Thinking of You   Dixon; Woods

Who Would Believe   Revel
Who'll Drink Bottoms-Up with Me   Donaldson; Leslie
Who's Blue Now   Caesar
Who's This Girl Named Whoopee, That the Boys All Want to
      Make   Gordon
Why?   Coots; Davis
Why Am I Alone with No One to Love   Razaf; Waller
Why Can't I Be Like You   Conrad; Mitchell
(Birdies Sing in Cages Too) Why Can't You   Brown, Lew;
      DeSylva; Henderson
Why Do You Suppose?   Hart; Rodgers
Why Do You Tease Me?   Atteridge
Why Don't We Try Staying Home   Porter
Why Don't You Believe Me   Revel
Why Shouldn't I Have You?   Porter
Why Was I Born?   Hammerstein; Kern
Wild Party Girl (inst.)   Whiting
Will o' the Wisp   Silver
Wine   Alter; Johnson, Howard
Wine, Woman and Song   Ahlert; Turk
Winter in Central Park   Hammerstein; Kern
Wipin' the Pan   Robison
Wishing and Waiting for Love   Akst; Clarke
With You   Berlin
With You — With Me   Clare
With You Beside Me   Ahlert; Turk
With You in My Arms   Coots
With You Where You Are   Dixon
With Your Looks and My Brain   Leslie; Monaco
Without a Song   Eliscu; Rose; Youmans
Wolf Song, The   Robin; Whiting
Won't You Buy My Dreams   Duke
Won'tcha   Razaf
World Is Yours and Mine, The   Hanley; Stept
World's Greatest Sweetheart Is You, The   Razaf
Would I Love to Love You (I'd Love To)   Clare
Would You Be Happy   Mills
Wouldn't I Like to Have Someone Like You to Like
      Me   Johnson, Howard
Wouldn't It Be Heaven   Coots; Davis
Wouldn't It Be Wonderful?   Akst; Clarke
Wrap Me in a Spanish Shawl   Edwards
Wuzza Matter Baby, Wuzza Matter with You   Gordon
Xylophone   Rainger; Robin
Yankee Doodle   Porter
Yo Te Amo Means I Love You   Whiting
You   Hoffman; Mills
You and I in the Moonlight   Washington
You Are My Day Dream   Caesar; Friend
You Are My Rain Beau, Under a Cry Baby Sky   Lewis;
      Young, Joseph
You Baby Me, I'll Baby You   Bryan; Meyer
You Beautiful So and So   Rose; Snyder
You Can't Believe My Eyes   Bryan; Meyer
You Can't Stop Me from Loving You   Hoffman
You Couldn't Blame Me for That   Kalmar; Ruby
You Darlin'   Woods
You Do Something to Me   Porter
You Don't Know Paree   Porter
You Don't Understand Song   Johnson, James P.
You Find the Time and I'll Find the Place   Brown, Lew;
      DeSylva; Henderson
You Gotta Too Much-a-de Stock   Lewis; Pollack; Young,
      Joseph
You Gotta Wanta Once in a While   Gorney; Harburg

You Want Lovin' but I Want Love   Coslow
You Want Lovin', I Want Love   Coslow
You Went Away Once Too Often   Bryan
You Wouldn't Fool Me, Would You?   Brown, Lew; DeSylva;
   Henderson
You'd Do for Me — I'd Do for You   Duke
You'll Find Your Answer in My Eyes   Baer; Gilbert
You'll Never Be Forgotten   Silver
Younger Set, The   Coots; Davis
Your Eyes   Motzan
Your Love I Crave   Johnson, James P.
Your Love Is All That I Crave   Dubin; Johnson, J.
   Rosamond; Johnson, James P.
Your Mother and Mine   Edwards
You're a Different You   Alter
You're a Pain in the Heart to Me   Hoffman
You're Just Another Memory   Coots
You're Marvelous (To Me She's Marvelous)   Clare
You're My Little Theme Song   Von Tilzer
You're Not Asking Me, I'm Telling You   Lewis; Young,
   Joseph
You're Not the Same Old Sweetheart   Koehler
You're Perfect   Eliscu
You're Responsible   Clare
You're the Jewel in My Heart (Tableaux of Jewels)   Fisher
Yours Is My Heart Alone   Smith, Harry B.
You've Got Me Pickin' Petals Off o' Daisies   Brown, Lew;
   DeSylva; Henderson
You've Got That Thing   Porter
You've Got to Be Modernistic   Johnson, James P.
You've Got to Surrender   Hart; Rodgers
Zonky   Razaf; Waller

1930

Absence Makes the Heart Grow Fonder   Lewis; Warren;
   Young, Joseph
Add Another Line, Sweet Adeline   Gordon
Adieu   Young, Joseph
Admiration (inst.)   Schwartz, Jean
Adorable You   Bloom; Lewis
Adored One   Caesar; Harbach; Romberg
Africa Smiles No More   Akst; Clarke
After a Million Dreams   Donaldson; Leslie
After All, You're All I'm After   Young, Victor
After Your Kiss   Brown, Nacio Herb; Eliscu
Ah! Jus' Like You   Gorney; Harburg
Ain't You Baby   Ager; Yellen
Air Minded   Brown, Lew; DeSylva; Henderson
All Alone Monday   Kalmar; Ruby
All Alone Together   Dubin
All American, The   Meyer; Mitchell
All I Can See Is You   Johnson, Howard
All I Want Is Just One Girl   Robin; Whiting
All My Life   Akst; Clare; Davis
All the King's Horses   Dietz
All the Way from Oklahoma to the Land of La
   Paloma   Leslie
All's Fair in Love and War   Smith, Harry B.
Alma Mater, We're with You   Johnson, Howard
Aloha   Brennan; Friml
Alone with My Dreams   Kahn
Always but All Ways   Robin
Always in All Ways   Whiting
Always in the Dark   Johnson, Howard

Always the Same   Baer; Gilbert
Am I Gonna See You Some More?   Donaldson
Am I You're Once-in-a-While   Hoffman; Silver
Amor Mio (My Love)   Friend; Monaco
And I Have You   Gershwin, George; Gershwin, Ira
Ankle Up the Alter with Me   Eliscu
Annette   Smith, Harry B.
Antoinette (inst.)   Schwartz, Jean
Any One Else   Fields; McHugh
Anything May Happen Any Day   Kern
Anyway We've Had Fun   Youmans
Are You Ashamed of Me?   Hoffman; Lerner, Sammy
Are You Certain that You Care   Parish
Are You Dancing?   Gershwin, George; Gershwin, Ira
Arise (Clock Song)   Robin
Armchair with an Armful of You, An   Gordon; Silver
Around the Corner   Kahn
Arrival of Guests   Caesar; Harbach; Romberg
As Long As I Have You (And You Have Me)   Dubin
As Long As I'm with You   Akst; Clarke
As Long As We're Together   Coslow
As Long As You Love Me   Silver
As Long As You're Near Me   Lane; Lerner, Sammy
As You Come In   Edwards; Johnson, Howard
Ask Me Again   Gershwin, George; Gershwin, Ira
At Last I'm Happy   Conrad; Friend
At Last in Your Arms   Porter
At Least I'm Happy   Clare
Au Revoir, Pleasant Dreams   Schwartz, Jean
Aunt Jemima's Divorce, Minutes of the Case   Blake; Razaf
Aw! C'mon, Whatta Ya Got to Lose?   Robin; Whiting
Aw, What's the Use   Harburg
Babies a la Mode (Frocks and Frills)   Cobb; Edwards
Baby Be Yourself   Duke; Harburg
Baby Fix It for Me   Johnson, Howard; Woods
Baby I Have to Have You   Conrad; Meyer; Mitchell
Baby, It Upsets Me So   Razaf
Baby Lindy   Mills
Baby Mine   Blake; Razaf
Babykins   Caesar
Back Home   Fain; Kahal
Back Where We Started   Razaf
Backsliders   Robison
Bad Baby   Lewis; Warren; Young, Joseph
Bad Boy   Leslie; Monaco
Bagdad   Bryan
Balcony Episode   Johnson, Howard
Bandido Love   Ahlert; Turk
Bang! There Goes My Heart   Schwartz, Arthur
Bantu Baby   Johnson, James P.; Razaf
Barbaric (inst.)   Carmichael
Barbary Coast   Gershwin, George; Gershwin, Ira
Barefoot Girl   Caesar
Bashful   Friend; Monaco
Be Good to Me (Smiles)   Youmans
Be Modern, There's Happiness in Store for You   Waller
Beauty Contest (Miss Hampstead Heath/Opening the Beauty
   Contest/Opening, Act I), The   Hart; Rodgers
Because of You   Edwards
Because We're Young   Hart; Rodgers
Beginner's Luck   Young, Victor
Believe in Me   Hanley
Believe It or Not I Found My Man   Baer; Gilbert
Believe It Or Not I Lost My Man   Baer; Gilbert
Bench in the Park, A   Ager; Yellen

Beneath the Moon of Mexico (Luna Mexicana)   Adamson;
   Gordon; Revel
Beneath the Parisian Moonlight   Young, Joseph
Berries, The   Blake; Razaf
Better Not Try It   Magidson; Washington
Better Things of Life   Fisher
Betty Lou   Johnson, J. Rosamond
Between the Lines   Alter; Johnson, Howard
Beyond the Blue Horizon   Robin; Whiting
Beyond the Horizon   Brown, Nacio Herb; Eliscu
Bidin' My Time   Gershwin, George; Gershwin, Ira
Big Ben Family, The   Alter; Johnson, Howard
Big Bouquet for You, A   Kahn
Big Papoose Is on the Loose   Fields; McHugh
Birds on the Wing (inst.)   Schwartz, Jean
(Who Said) Black Birds Are Blue   Blake; Razaf
Blackbirds on Parade   Blake; Razaf
Blame It on the Blues   David, Mack
Blow Hot — Blow Cold   Alter
Blue Again   Fields; McHugh
Blue Bowery (The Bowery)   Adamson; Youmans
Blue Daughter of Heaven   Egan
Blue Lagoon (inst.)   Schwartz, Jean
Blue Melody   Lerner, Sammy
Blue, Turning Gray Over You   Razaf; Waller
Blue Without You   Parish
Bluebeard's Beard (Inst)   Rodgers
Blushing Rose (inst.)   Schwartz, Jean
Body and Soul   Dietz; Heyman
Boo Hoo Hoo, Ha Ha Ha (I'm Between a Laugh and a
   Cry)   Leslie; Warren
Boop-Boop a Doopa Doo Trot   Burke
Booperadoop   Cobb; Edwards
Born to Be Blue   Hoffman; Silver
Boudoir Dolls   Eliscu
Bouncing the Baby Around   Dubin
Bound for the Bronx   Fain
Bowery, The   Youmans
Bowery After Dark, The   Ahlert; Turk
Boy! What Love Has Done to Me!   Gershwin, George;
   Gershwin, Ira
Brass Band March   Hammerstein; Romberg
Breakfast Dance   Eliscu; Rainger
Brighten the Road   Bryan
Bring Back the Waltz   Fisher
Bring Back Those Southern Skies   Motzan
Broken Dreams   Johnston
Broken Hearted in the Moonlight   Motzan
Broken-Hearted Lover   Bryan; Dubin
Broker's Ensemble   Berlin
Broncho Busters   Gershwin, George; Gershwin, Ira
Brother, Just Laugh It Off   Harburg; Rainger; Schwartz,
   Arthur
Budda   Fisher
Bumpty Bump   Ellington; Mills
Bundle of Old Love Letters, A   Brown, Nacio Herb; Freed,
   Arthur
Burgandy and Wine   Donaldson; Leslie
Business Girl   Whiting
Business Is Business with Me   Friend; Monaco
But Not for Me   Gershwin, George; Gershwin, Ira
Butler's Song   Kalmar; Ruby
Button Up Your Heart   Fields; McHugh
By Welawela   Brennan; Friml
Caballero   Caesar; Harbach; Romberg

Caballeros Number   Kalmar; Ruby
Cabin Door   Razaf
Caddie's Ensemble   Alter; Johnson, Howard
California Skies   Kalmar; Ruby
Call It a Day   Alter; Johnson, Howard
Call of the South, The   Berlin
Call to Arms, The   Brown, Nacio Herb; Freed, Arthur
Can I Help It (If I'm in Love with You)   Friend; Monaco
Can It Be Possible   Conrad; Meyer; Mitchell
Can It Be True   Alter; Johnson, Howard; Razaf
Cane Dance, The   Caesar
Can't Get Along   Harburg
Can't You See I'm Lonely   Kahn
Capitalize That Thing Called It   Duke; Harburg
Carefree and Happy   Alter; Johnson, Howard
Caribbean Sea   Young, Victor
Carry On, Keep Smiling   Adamson; Youmans
Charming Senoritas   Caesar; Harbach; Romberg
Chase the Cat   Arlen; Koehler
Chatter-Box (inst.)   Schwartz, Jean
Cheer Up and Smile   Conrad
Cheerful Little Earful   Gershwin, Ira; Rose; Warren
Cheyenne of the Cherokees   Johnson, James P.
Chicken Pie   Young, Victor
Chico   Baer; Gilbert
Chidlins   Johnson, Howard
Child Is Born, A   Johnson, Howard
Chimes of Spring (Spring Beautiful Spring)   Gilbert
Chinatown   Magidson; Washington
Chinese Party   Youmans
Ching, Ching, Ching   Fisher
Chiropractor Blues   Razaf
Cinderella Brown   Fields; McHugh
Clever, These Chinese   Adamson; Youmans
Closer to Heaven   Brown, Nacio Herb; Freed, Arthur
Clothes Parade   Bryan
College Hymn   Brown, Nacio Herb; Freed, Arthur
Come Back to Me   Akst; Clarke
Come Back to Sorrento (Torna a Sorrento)   Robin
Come Hot It Up with Me   Johnson, Howard
Come On, Men   Hart; Rodgers
Come Out of the Nursery (Come Out of the Nursery and
   Dance)   Hart; Rodgers
Comfy and Cozy in My Baby's Arms   Ahlert; Turk
Conchita   Razaf
Coney Island   Magidson; Washington
Coney Island (Opening, Act I)   Hart; Rodgers
Congratulations   Schwartz, Arthur
Contagious Rhythm   Arlen; Koehler
Cooking Breakfast for the One I Love   Rose
Cook's Song   Bryan; Dubin
Cottage in the Country   Smith, Harry B.
Cottage in the Country, That's the Thing, A   Donaldson
Cotton   Fisher
Could You Use Me?   Gershwin, George; Gershwin, Ira
Counting the Sheep, Counting the Hours   Alter
Couple of Birds (With the Same Thing in Mind),
   A   Johnson, Howard
Cover a Clover with Kisses   Dixon; Warren
Cowboy Dan   Friend
Cowboy Ditty   Johnson, Howard
Crazy 'Bout My Gal   Mills
Cryin' for the Carolines   Lewis; Warren; Young, Joseph
Crystal Lady   Youmans
Crystal Moon   Gilbert

Crystal Waters   Akst; Baer; Clarke; Gilbert
Cuckoo Clock (I Know I'm Cuckoo)   Alter; Johnson, Howard
Cut In   Fields; McHugh
Dames   Coslow
Dance Fool Dance   Fields; McHugh
Dance of Sacrifice (inst.)   Henderson
Dance of the Daffodills   Alter; Johnson, Howard
Dance of the Robots   Alter
Dance of the Wooden Shoes   Magidson; Washington
Dance of Victory (inst.)   Henderson
Dancing on Mars   Magidson
Dancing on the Ceiling   Hart; Rodgers
Dancing the Devil Away   Kalmar; Ruby
Dancing to Save Your Sole   Baer; Gilbert
Dancing Town   Dietz; Schwartz, Arthur
Dancing Wedding   Adamson; Youmans
Dancing with Tears in My Eyes   Dubin
Dancing With Tears in Their Eyes   Dixon; Rose
Dare Me Lovely Lady   Freed, Arthur
Darky Rhythm   Lewis; Young, Joseph
Darn Fool Woman Like Me   Dubin
Daugherty Is My Name   Ager; Yellen
Day of Days   Robin; Whiting
Dear! Dear!   Hart; Rodgers
Dear Sir   Fain; Kahal
Death March   Robin
Death Valley Just Half Way to My Home   Razaf
Deep in Your Heart   Snyder
Department Store Opening   Alter; Johnson, Howard
Dinah (Dianna Lee)   Blake; Razaf
Dip Your Bread in a Bucket of Rum   Bryan
Disappointed Moon   Brown, Nacio Herb; Eliscu
Dissatisfied Blues   Blake; Razaf
Dixiana   Davis
Dixie Twister   Johnson, Howard
Do I Know What I'm Doing?   Ager; Yellen
Do I Really Deserve It from You   Clare
Do what the Bluebirds Do   Caesar
Do You Believe Your Eyes - Or Do You Believe Your Baby?   Berlin
Do You Play, Madame?   Whiting
Do You Think that I Could Grow on You?   Silver
Dodging the Clouds   Ahlert; Turk
Does Baby Want to Be Babied Now   Alter; Johnson, Howard
Does My Baby Love Nobody but Me   Ager; Yellen
Doin' the Crazy Walk   Ellington; Mills
Doin' the Mozambique   Blake; Razaf
Doin' the Sigma Chi   Conrad
Doing a Little Clog Dance (Doing a Little Waltz Clog)   Hart; Rodgers
Doing the Derby   Conrad
Doll Song   Smith, Harry B.
Don't Ask too Much of Love   Mercer
Don't Be a Meanie   Baer; Gilbert
Don't Bring Me Nothing Else but Love   Fisher
Don't End Our Dance of Love Now   David, Mack
Don't Forget Me in Your Dreams   Conrad; Leslie
Don't I Do   Whiting
Don't Tell Her What's Happened To Me   Brown, Lew; Henderson
Don't Tell Your Folks   Hart; Rodgers
Double Check Stomp   Mills
Doughboy's Lullaby   Hanley
Dougherty Is My Name   Yellen

Down at that Ole Cabin Door   Blake; Razaf
Down Back Alleys Up Side Streets Looking for Someone I Love   Burke
Down in Arkansas   Ahlert; Turk
Down in Shenandoah Valley   Gordon; Silver
Down through the Ages   Mercer
Down Where the East River Flows   Adamson; Youmans
Dream a Little Dream of Me   Kahn
Dream Away   Bryan; Dubin
Dream, Dream   Romberg
Dream On   Smith, Harry B.
Dream on a Piece of Wedding Cake   Hanley
Dreamy Waters (inst.)   Schwartz, Jean
Drifting Back to Honolulu   Hoffman
Drifting on to Avalon   Hoffman
(Let Us) Drink to the Girl of My Dreams   Baer; Gilbert
Drinking Song   Brown, Lew; DeSylva; Henderson; Schwartz, Jean
Drugstore Opening   Hart; Rodgers
Drums of Kane   Brennan; Friml
Dull and Gay   Hart; Rodgers
Dust   Fisher
Dust Off Your Knees   Johnson, Howard
Dynamic Personality   Fisher
El Caballero   Magidson; Washington
El Rey Del Jazz   Gorney
Eleanor, the Song that I Sing in My Dreams (Serenade, the Song that I Sing in My Dreams)   Hanley
Elevator Papa, Switchboard Mama   Johnson, James P.; Razaf
Embraceable You   Gershwin, George; Gershwin, Ira
Entrance of Dancers   Caesar; Harbach; Romberg
Evening Star   Akst; Davis
Every Little Girl He Sees   Akst; Clarke
Every Night in the Week   Warren; Young, Joseph
Everybody Tap   Ager; Yellen
Everyday Is a Holiday in Florida   Alter
Ev'ry Second of Ev'ry Minute   Johnson, Howard
Ev'rything Is Even, Even Worse than It Was Before   Young, Joseph
Ev'rything's O.K. with Me Since I'm O.K. with You   Coots
Exactly Like You   Fields; McHugh
Ex-Gigolo   Harburg
Eyes   Young, Victor
Fairyland Parade   Snyder
Fancy Nancy Doing That   Baer; Gilbert
(Once There Was a) Farmer's Daughter   Johnson, Howard
Fascinating Devil (With Those Angel Eyes)   Monaco
Feelin' Blue (inst.)   Johnson, James P.
Fight 'Em   Brown, Nacio Herb; Freed, Arthur
Fire Music (inst.)   Duke
First Sunbeam   Schwartz, Arthur
5-6-7-8 Nine Little Miles from Ten-Tennessee   Conrad
Fleur D'Amour   Conrad; Meyer; Mitchell
Flick Your Troubles Off Your Thumb and Brush Your Blues Away   Ahlert; Turk
Flicker Tail, The   Whiting
Follow a Star   Yellen
Foolish Baby   Harburg; Heyman
Foolish Face   Dietz; Schwartz, Arthur
Fools' Parade, The   Young, Joseph
Football   Brown, Nacio Herb; Freed, Arthur
Football Freddie My Collegiate Man   Conrad; Leslie
For Doin' Things Like This   Freed, Arthur; Woods
For Ev'ry Wave that Leaves the Shore Another Comes Rollin' In   Hanley

For Honor   Robin; Whiting
For I'm a Simple Maid   Clare
For I'm in Love Again   Dixon; Rose
For Mary Jane   Razaf
For One Little Kiss from You   Johnson, Howard
For Sweethearts Only   Lerner, Sammy
Forget All Your Books   Dietz; Lane; Lerner, Sammy
Forward March into My Arms   Smith, Harry B.
Free and Easy, The   Ahlert; Turk
Friends Cause Me to Be Out in the Street   Razaf
Funny Little You   Razaf
Gambler of the West, The   Gershwin, George; Gershwin, Ira
Gaucho Love Song, A   Caesar; Harbach; Romberg
Gaucho March   Caesar; Harbach; Romberg
Gay Love   Clare
Gee It's So Good, It's Too Bad   Arlen; Koehler
Gentlemen of the Press   Caesar
Georgia on My Mind   Carmichael
Get Happy   Arlen; Koehler
Get the Man in the Mood   Whiting
Ghost of Grandfather Clock, The   Alter
Ghosts of Grandfather's Clock   Johnson, Howard
Girl from Oscaloosa, The   Silver
Girl Is Nobody, A   Caesar
Girl Trouble   Fisher
Girls of Long Ago   Caesar
Girls We Remember, The   Dubin
Give a Guy a Kiss   Coslow
Give Me a Kiss Sweetheart   Coslow
Give Me a Moment Please   Robin; Whiting
Give Me the Man (Who Does Things)   Robin
Giving It This and That   Conrad; Meyer; Mitchell
Glad I Have a Boy   Brennan; Friml
Glory   Harburg; Razaf
Glutton for Love, A   Razaf
Go Harlem   Johnson, James P.; Razaf
Go Home and Tell Your Mother   Fields; McHugh
Go Into Your Dance   Porter
Goin' Wild   Ahlert; Turk
Going Up   Gorney; Harburg
Goldfarb, That's I'm!   Gershwin, George; Gershwin, Ira
Good Clean Sport   Dietz; Schwartz, Arthur
Good Evenin'   Hoffman
Good for Nothin'   Johnson, James P.; Razaf
Good for You, Bad for Me   Brown, Lew; DeSylva;
    Henderson
Good Intentions   Friend; Monaco
Good 'n' Plenty   Fain; Kahal
Good Spirits   Robin; Whiting
Goodbye   Kalmar; Ruby
Goodbye, My Love   Hammerstein; Romberg
Goofus   Kahn
Goose Hangs High, The   Akst; Clarke
Got a Man on My Mind (Worryin' Away)   Dietz; Rainger;
    Robin
Gotta Feelin' for You   Alter
Great I Am, Leader of the Band   Schwartz, Jean
Great Indoors, The   Porter
Green Pastures   Blake; Razaf
Gypsy Love   Fields; McHugh
Gypsy Sweetheart   Parish
Ham and Eggs   Blake; Razaf
Hands   Hart; Rodgers
Hang Onto a Rainbow   Stept
Hang Onto Your Happiness   Fisher; Johnson, Howard

Hangin' Round   Donaldson
Happy Cowboy   Freed, Arthur
Happy Days   Hanley
Happy Days and Lonely Nights   Fisher; Rose
Happy Days Are Here Again   Ager; Yellen
Happy Feet   Ager; Yellen
Happy Landing   Brown, Lew; DeSylva; Henderson
(Take a Trip to) Harlem   Razaf
Harlem Fuss (inst.)   Waller
Harlem Heaven   Alter
Harlem Madness   Ager; Yellen
Harlem's Hot As Hades   Arlen; Koehler
Harp with the Broken String, The   Hanley
Has Anybody Seen Our Nellie   Ager; Yellen
Have a Little Faith in Me   Lewis; Warren; Young, Joseph
Hawaiian Moon   Brennan; Friml
Hawaii's Shore   Brennan; Friml
He Got a Poison Ivy Instead of a Clinging Vine   Dubin
He Was Too Good to Me   Hart; Rodgers
Heads Up   Duke; Harburg
Heap o' Misery   Arlen; Koehler
Heart of Heaven   Bryan; Dubin
Heart Strings (inst.)   Schwartz, Jean
Heavy, Heavy, Mah Po'r Heart   Akst; Clarke
Hello Heaven! Hello Love!   Donaldson
Hell's Loose   Freed, Arthur
Help Help   Coslow
Help Yourself to Happiness   Young, Victor
Her Irish Eyes of Blue   Jerome; Schwartz, Jean
Here Comes Emily Brown   Conrad
Here Comes the Sun   Freed, Arthur; Woods
Here Is a Sword   Schwartz, Arthur
Here We Are   Berlin; Hammerstein; Romberg
Here You Are   Akst; Clarke
Here's a Day to Be Happy   Adamson; Youmans
Here's My Hand — You're in My Heart Until We Meet
    Again   Hanley
Here's to Aunt Octavia   Coslow
Here's to Love   Ahlert; Turk
Here's to the Folks Back Home   Hanley
He's a Mean Man   Alter
He's Good Enough for Me   Edwards
He's not Worth Your Tears   Dixon; Rose; Warren
He's That Kind of Pal   Ager; Yellen
High and Dry (inst.)   Carmichael
High Society Blues   Hanley
Highly Respectable You   Adamson; Gordon; Revel
Highway to Heaven   Dubin
Hi-Ho, Good-Bye   Johnson, Howard
Hill Billy Bride, The   Brennan
Hip Hip Hooray for the Rainbows   Johnson, Howard
Hitch Your Wagon to a Star   Alter; Johnson, Howard
Hittin' the Bottle   Arlen; Koehler
Hittin' the Sky   Robin
Hoku Loa   Brennan; Friml
Hold Your Man   Duke; Harburg
Hollywood Nights   Conrad; Meyer; Mitchell
Home Is Heaven, Heaven Is Home   Donaldson; Leslie
Homemade Sunshine   Fain; Kahal
Honeymoon Parade   Edwards; Meyer; Mitchell
Hooray for Baby and Me   Meyer; Mitchell
Hop-Skip and Jump (inst.)   Schwartz, Jean
Horses Number (Opening Bit for Race Track Scene)   Alter;
    Johnson, Howard
Hot   Schwartz, Arthur

Hot Blues (inst)   Rodgers
Hot Curves (inst.)   Johnson, James P.
Hotcha Ma Chotch   Adamson; Youmans
Hottentot Hop   David, Mack
How Are You Tonight in Hawaii   Leslie; Warren
How Do They Do It?   Porter
How I Could Go for You   Alter
How I Wish I Could Sing a Love Song   Harburg
How Long Is That Train Been Gone   Johnson, James P.
How Lovely You Can Be   Conrad; Meyer; Mitchell
How Much I Love You   Berlin
How Shall I Tell?   Lewis; Warren; Young, Joseph
How to Play an Ole Banjo   Blake; Razaf
Howdja Like to Go to Heaven with a Smile   Motzan
Hunting Days   Caesar
Hunting Song   Hart; Rodgers
Hunting the Fox   Hart; Rodgers
I Am Afraid to Waltz with You   Coslow
I Am Headed for Southland   Razaf
I Am Only Human After All   Duke; Gershwin, Ira; Harburg
I Am the Words (You Are the Melody)   Brown, Lew;
    DeSylva; Henderson
I Bring a Love Song   Hammerstein; Romberg
I Came to Life when I Found You   Gorney; Harburg
I Can Do Wonders with You   Hart; Rodgers
I Can Make Most Anything but I Can't Make a Man   Bloom;
    Young, Joseph
I Can't Forget You   Conrad; Mitchell
I Can't Imagine   Fisher
I Can't Make My Feet Behave   Edwards
I Could Go for You   Fields; McHugh
I Could Love a Man Like That   Brown, Lew; DeSylva;
    Henderson
I Do It with My Oo-La-La   Monaco
I Do It with My Oo-La-La-La-La   Friend; Monaco
I Don't Know You Well Enough for That   Hanley
I Don't Mind Walking in the Rain (When I'm Walking in the
    Rain with You)   Hoffman
I Don't Need Atmosphere (to Fall in Love)   Coslow
I Feel that Certain Feeling Coming On   Friend; Monaco
I Feel You Near Me   Hanley
I Give Myself Away   Eliscu
I Got Rhythm   Gershwin, George; Gershwin, Ira
I Got What I Wanted   Friend; Monaco
I Gotta Keep My Eye on You   Smith, Harry B.
I Happen to Like New York   Porter
I Hate Myself (For Falling in Love with You)   Silver
I Hear Your Voice   Freed, Arthur
I Knew Him Before He Was Spanish   Rose
I Know a Lazy Lane   Brennan
I Like a Little Girl Like That   Ager; Yellen
I Like the Looks of You   Revel
I Like to Do Things for You   Ager; Yellen
I Like You   Smith, Harry B.
I Like Your Face   Dietz; Schwartz, Arthur
I Lost My Gal Again   Lewis
I Lost My Heart to the Girl of My Dreams   Mills
I Love Morris, Lovely Morris, but I Don't Like Morris
    Plan   Lane; Lewis
I Love the Girls (In My Own Peculiar Way)   Harburg
I Love the Rain   Bryan
I Love to Do It   Meyer; Mitchell
I Love to Hear You Say I Love You   Edwards
I Love You and I Like You   Schwartz, Arthur
I Love You 'Cause I Love You   Adamson; Gordon; Revel

I Love You So   Kahn
I Love You So Much   Kalmar; Ruby
I Loved that Man   Freed, Arthur
I Loved You Before I Met You (For I Saw You in My
    Dreams)   Hoffman
I May Fall in Love Again   Duke; Harburg
I Might Have Known   Fisher
I Must Be One of Those Roses   Schwartz, Arthur
I Never Can Think of the Words   Yellen
I Only Know that You Are Beautiful   Kahn
I Remember You from Somewhere, Somewhere in My
    Dreams   Leslie; Warren
I See Vienna in Your Eyes (In Deinen Augen Liegt Das Herz
    von Wien)   Young, Joseph
I Started on a Shoestring   Dietz; Schwartz, Arthur
I Still Believe in You   Hart; Rodgers
I Still Call You Sweetheart   Yellen
I Still Get a Thrill Thinking of You   Coots; Davis
I Stumbled Over You and Fell in Love   Adamson; Revel
I Take After Rip   Caesar
I Tried for a Week to Speak to the Sheik   Hanley
I Understand Tonight   Coslow
I Wanna Fall Asleep and Wake Up in Virginia   Young,
    Joseph
I Want That Man   Hart; Rodgers
I Want You   Edwards; Fisher
I Was Alone   Hammerstein; Kern
I Was Born with Blues in My Heart   Arlen; Koehler
I Will Remember, You Will Forget   Coslow
I Wish I Were Back in Your Arms Tonight   Conrad
I Wish We Were Siamese Twins   Magidson; Washington
I Wonder   Burke
I Wonder Who's Keeping Him Now   Alter; Rose
I'd Be So Happy with You   Freed, Arthur
I'd Fall in Love All Over Again (If You Could Just Forgive
    and Forget)   Fain; Kahal
I'd Like to Be a Bee in Your Boudoir   Whiting
I'd Like to Be a Gypsy   Washington
I'd Like To Be a Happy Bride   Bryan; Dubin
I'd Love to Be a Talking Picture Queen   Hanley
I'd Love to Be a Talking-Picture Queen   Hanley
If All the Stars Were Movie Stars   Coslow
If I Ever Find Another Sweetheart   Caesar
If I Give in to You   Hart; Rodgers
If I Were a Traveling Salesman   Dubin
If I Were King   Coslow; Robin
If I Were You   Alter
If I Were You Love, I'd Jump Right in the Lake   Youmans
If My Friends Find You They'll Steal You From Me   Kahn
If She Hums You a Waltz   Whiting
If Someone Should Kiss Me Tonight While I'm
    Dreaming   Hanley
If the Best Things in Life Were Free   Edwards; Johnson,
    Howard
If This Is Love   Coslow
If You Believe   Berlin
If You Can't Have the Girl of Your Dreams   Warren; Young,
    Joseph
If You Haven't Got a Girl   Davis; Hoffman
If You Were a Traveling Salesman   Dubin
If Your Kisses Can't Hold the Man You Love Your Tears
    Won't Bring Him Back   Yellen
If You're Not Kissing Me   Brown, Nacio Herb; Freed, Arthur
If You've Never Been in Love   Conrad; Davis
I'll Always Remember   Schwartz, Arthur

I'll Answer You   Fisher
I'll Be Loving You Forever   David, Mack
I'll Be the Words, You Be the Tune   Coots; Magidson
I'll Be There   Schwartz, Arthur
I'll Bob Up with the Bob-O-Link (In the Morning)   Fain;
  Kahal
I'll Call It Love   Arlen; Koehler
I'll Follow the Trail   Brennan; Friml
I'll Get My Man   Brown, Lew; DeSylva; Henderson
I'll Know Him   Brown, Lew; DeSylva; Henderson
I'll Love You Till the Cows Come Home   Ahlert; Turk
I'll Never Leave You   Schwartz, Arthur
I'll Remember You   Freed, Arthur
I'll Remember Your Eyes   Bryan
I'll Still Belong to You   Egan
I'll Take Care of You   Coslow
I'll Tell You   Smith, Harry B.
I'm a Daughter of Peru   Caesar; Harbach; Romberg
I'm a Gypsy   Kalmar; Ruby
I'm a Simple Hearted Man   Robin; Whiting
I'm a Slave, a Slave to Love   Friend; Monaco
I'm a Stationary Woman Lookin' for a Permanent
  Man   Razaf
I'm Afraid   Caesar
I'm Afraid I Can't Get Out Tonight Marie   Hanley
I'm Afraid of You   Egan; Eliscu; Rainger; Schwartz, Arthur
I'm Afraid to Waltz with You (Vals Ritmo)   Coslow
I'm All Burned Up Over the Firemen   Johnson, Howard
I'm All Wrapped Up in a Bundle of Love   Fisher
I'm Alone Because I Love You   Young, Joseph
I'm an International Sweetheart   Yellen
I'm an Old Fashioned Guy   Ager; Yellen
I'm Blue for You Blonde   Fisher
I'm Crazy for Your Cannibal Love   Bryan
I'm Designed for Love   Schwartz, Arthur
I'm Doin' that Thing   Fields; McHugh
I'm Drunk with Love   Revel
I'm Feelin' Blue 'Cause I've Got Nobody   Fields; McHugh
I'm Feeling My Way Thru' the Fog   Johnson, Howard
I'm Flying High   Brown, Lew; DeSylva; Henderson
I'm Gettin' Tired of My Tired Man   Snyder
I'm Getting Myself Ready for You   Porter
I'm Glad I Waited   Adamson; Youmans
I'm Going Spanish Now   Egan
I'm Gonna March in April with May   Freed, Arthur
I'm Grover   Duke
I'm Hard to Please   Hart; Rodgers
I'm in the Market for You   Hanley
I'm in Training for You   Baer; Gilbert
I'm Just a Fool in Love with You   Conrad
I'm Just a Little Ol' Cowboy   Johnson, Howard
I'm Just Wild about Horses, and Horses Are Wild About
  Me   Silver
I'm Learning a Lot from You   Fields; McHugh
I'm Lonely   Hammerstein; Romberg
I'm Needin' You   Young, Joseph
I'm Not the Same   Oakland
I'm Nuts on You   Brennan; Friml
I'm on My Way to Berlin   Coslow
I'm One of God's Children Who Hasn't Got Wings   Alter;
  Hammerstein
I'm Plenty That Way Too   Harburg
I'm Proud of You   Coots; Magidson
I'm Screwy Over Looey   Dubin
I'm So Afraid of My Shadow Telling on Me   Lewis

I'm So Afraid of You   Kalmar; Ruby
I'm Tellin' the World about You   Friend; Monaco
I'm Telling the World About You   Friend
I'm the Reason   Akst; Clarke
I'm Trailing Arbutus   Alter; Johnson, Howard
I'm Under New Management Now   Conrad; Meyer; Mitchell
I'm Walking Around on Dangerous Ground   Friend
I'm Walking in Between the Raindrops but a Rainbow's
  Shining on Me   Friend; Monaco
I'm Walking on Air   Conrad; Meyer; Mitchell
I'm Yours   Harburg
Imagine   Razaf
Impossible Men   Schwartz, Arthur
Impromptu Song (Talking Song)   Hart; Rodgers
In a Bungalow for You   Hammerstein
In a Canoe (Beneath the Willow on the River)   Styne
In a Jungle Bungalow   Akst; Clarke
In a Window, In a House, In Caroline   Motzan
In Good Old Paree   Freed, Arthur
In My Heart — It's You   Hoffman
In My Heart on My Mind   Smith, Harry B.
In My Little Hope Chest   Coslow
In Old New Hampshire Far Away   Motzan
In Slumberland   Blake; Razaf
In Spanish   Motzan
In the Back of a Hack   Gorney; Harburg
In the Clouds   Brennan; Friml
In the Cool of the Evening   Hart; Rodgers
In the Heart of Old Paree   Robin; Whiting
In the Heart of Sierra Nevada   Parish
In the Meantime   Young, Joseph
In Toddlin' Town   Johnson, Howard
In Your Cradle of Love   Brennan; Friml
In Youth's Fair Springtime   Smith, Harry B.
Indiana Moon   Bloom; Koehler
International Rhythm   Fields; McHugh
Into My Heart   Ahlert; Turk
Is It Love?   Caesar
Is that Religion   Parish
Isn't Nature Wonderful   Fields; McHugh
Isn't This a Cock-Eyed World   Dubin
It Can't Go on Like This   Gorney; Harburg
It Happened in Monterey   Rose
It Looks Like Love   Freed, Arthur; Woods
It Makes Me Happy to Worry Over You   Lane; Leslie
It May Be the Fault of Man   Fain; Kahal
It Must Be Love   Silver
It Must Be You   Ahlert; Eliscu; Turk
It Never Happened Before   Hart; Rodgers
It Seems to Be Spring   Whiting
It Was a Frenchman Who Thought of It First   Rainger
Italian Kisses   Baer; Gilbert
It'll Be the First Time for Me   Henderson
It's a Beautiful Day to Be Glad   Coslow
It's a Funny Little Small World After All   Hanley
It's a Great Life (If You Don't Weaken)   Robin; Whiting
It's a Long Long Road I'm Travelin' on but I Got Good
  Shoes   Young, Joseph
It's All Over but the Memories   Fain; Kahal
It's an Old Spanish Custom in the Moonlight   Leslie; Meyer
It's Only a Song Tonight   Coslow
It's Paradise   Akst; Clarke
It's Ten to One You're Lookin' at Lila   Davis
It's the Doctor's Orders   Brown, Lew; Fain
It's Tough to Be a Prima Donna   Rose

It's Yours   Berlin
I've Been Waiting to Tell You I've Been Wanting
    You   Monaco
I've Been Wanting to Tell You I've Been Wanting You   Kahn
I've Gone Goofy Over Miniature Golf   Parish
I've Got a Bug in My Head   Fields; McHugh
I've Got Ev'rything but You   Burke
I've Got It (But It Don't Do Me No Good)   Fain; Kahal
I've Got My Eye on You   Stept
I've Got the Blues   Fields; McHugh
I've Got to See My Partner   Ager; Yellen
I've Gotta Yen for You   Whiting
Ja, Ja, Ja!   Hammerstein; Romberg
Java   Porter
Jazz Sunday   Johnson, J. Rosamond; Wrubel
Je M'len Fiche du Sex-Appeal   Hart; Rodgers
Je T'Aime   Dietz; Schwartz, Arthur
Jimsy   Brennan; Friml
Jo Jo Josephine   Waller
Job with a Future, A   Robin; Whiting
Joe   Conrad
Joe Jazz   Whiting
Just a Friend of Mine   Schwartz, Arthur
Just a Gigolo   Caesar
Just a Kiss for Now Cherie   Hanley
Just a Kiss in the Moonlight   Coslow; Robin
Just a Little Closer   Johnson, Howard
Just a Little While   Berlin
Just a Melody for a Memory   Harburg
Just a Sentimental Tune   Alter
Just Another Dream Gone Wrong   Harburg
Just Another Love Affair   Lewis
Just Keen about You   Fisher
Just Like in a Story Book   Hanley
Just Like Jimmy and Me   Fain; Kahal
Just One of Those Days   Monaco
Just One of Those Things   Porter
Just to Hear You Say I Love You   Robin
Kangaroo Hop   Lane
Keep a Song in Your Soul   Waller
Keep It Up for Upton   Meyer; Mitchell
Keep Out of the Rain   Fisher
Keep Smiling and Carry On   Donaldson
Keepin' Myself for You   Clare; Youmans
Key to My Heart, The   Blake; Razaf
Keys to Your Heart   Fields; McHugh
Kickin' a Hole in the Sky   Rose
Kindly Remit the Kisses That You Borrowed in Fun   Coots
King Louie   Robin
King of the Pampas, A   Hanley
Kismet   Bryan
Kiss I Must Refuse You, A   Caesar; Harbach; Romberg
Kiss That Made a Fool of Me, The   Coots
Kiss Waltz   Dubin
Kitchen Mechanic's Parade   Johnson, James P.; Razaf
Knee Deep in June   Gorney; Harburg
Knights of the Road   Berlin
Knock Knees   Dubin
Knockin' on Wood   Eliscu
La Reina de Mi Corazon (The Queen of My Heart)   Ahlert
La Rhumba   Arlen; Koehler
Lady Play Your Mandolin   Caesar
Lady without a Name, The   Lewis
Lament   Coslow
Land of Mystery   Ahlert; Turk

Land of the Gay Caballero   Gershwin, George; Gershwin,
    Ira
Latigo   Caesar; Harbach; Romberg
Laugh It Down   Duke; Harburg
Laugh Today and Cry Tomorrow   Kalmar; Ruby
Laughing Eyes (inst.)   Schwartz, Jean
Laughter Opening (inst.)   Duke
Laughter Symphony (inst.)   Duke
Laughter Will Lead You to Love   Johnson, Howard
Lay Off Big Boy You Haven't Got a Chinaman's
    Chance   Leslie; Monaco; Young, Joseph
Lazy Levee Loungers   Robison
Lazy Lou'siana Moon   Donaldson
Leave a Little Smile   Dubin
Leave It that Way   Fisher
Leave It to Love   Smith, Harry B.
Left All Alone with the Blues   Johnson, James P.
Legend of Niagara, The   Harburg
Let Me Sing - And I'm Happy   Berlin
Let Us Have Lettuce To-Night   Fisher
Let's Be Domestic   Coslow
Let's Do Something Different Tonight   Motzan
Let's Drink to the Isle We Love   Bryan
Let's Fly Away   Porter
Let's Go Native   Whiting
Let's Go Places   Friend; Monaco
Let's Suppose   Smith, Robert B.
Letter Song   Smith, Harry B.
Liberty Song   Akst; Clarke
Like Kelly Can   Fields; McHugh
Lily Pond (inst.)   Schwartz, Jean
Linda   Arlen; Koehler
Lindy, Anne 'n' the Baby   Mills
Lion King, The   Hart; Rodgers
Little Bit of Happiness (Will Go a Long Way), A   Coots;
    Davis
Little Bit of Opera, A   Cobb; Edwards
Little Cloud of Sunshine, I Need You   Snyder
Little Did I Know   Duke; Fain; Kahal
Little House to Dream By a Mountain Stream, A   Hanley
Little Privacy, A   Duke; Harburg
Little Sunshine   Meyer; Mitchell
Little Things in Life, The   Berlin
Little White Lies   Donaldson
Little You, a Little Me, a Little Love, A   Johnson, Howard;
    Woods
Liza Lee   Stept
Lock Step   Ahlert; Turk
Locked in Your Arms Makes Me Safe in Your Heart   Fisher
Lo-Lo   Johnson, Howard
Lonely for Love   Livingston, Jerry
Lonely Mothers on Parade   Akst
Lonely Serenade, A   Lawrence
Lonely Stowaway   Burke
Lonesome Cowboy, The   Gershwin, George; Gershwin, Ira
Lonesome Lover   Bryan; Monaco
Lonesome Serenade   Hoffman
Long Day   Donaldson; Leslie
Look Behind the Mask   Hanley
Look for Me on Lookout Mountain   Conrad
Look What a Little Sunshower Can Do   Alter; Johnson,
    Howard
Look What You've Done   Johnson, J. Rosamond
Look What You've Done to Me   Conrad; Mitchell
(Across the Breakfast Table) Looking at You   Berlin

Looking for the Lovelight in the Dark   Dubin
Looking in the Window, Thinking of You   Bryan
Looks Like Pappy   Johnson, Howard
Love Ain't Nothing but the Blues   Alter
Love Among the Millionaires   Baer; Gilbert
Love and Consolation   Alter
Love Boats   Gorney; Harburg
(When) Love Comes in the Moonlight   Dubin
Love Dream River   Friend; Schwartz, Jean
Love Flew in My Window   Hanley
Love for Sale   Porter
Love Has Passed Me By   Friend; Monaco
Love, I Give You My All   Brennan; Friml
Love Is Like a Song   Youmans
Love Rules My Heart   Alter
Love Was in the Air   Brown, Nacio Herb; Freed, Arthur
Loved One   Snyder
Lovely Woman's Ever Young (La Femme a Toujours Vingt
    Ans!)   Hart; Rodgers
Lover's Lane Is a Lonesome Road   Fisher
Love's a Made Humpty Dumpty Out of Me   Razaf
Love's Happy Dream   Smith, Harry B.
Loving You   Yellen
Loving You the Way I Do   Blake
Low Tide   Lane
Luana   Brennan; Friml
Lucky Me, and Loveable You   Ager; Yellen
Lucky Seven   Dietz; Schwartz, Arthur
Lullaby in Blue   Heyman
Lumber-Jack   Razaf
Ma Mere   Caesar; Warren
Mad Daggar   Schwartz, Jean
Madame You've Take My Heart   David, Mack
Madelon   Adamson; Youmans
Magic Music   Hart; Rodgers
Magic Spell of Love, The   Brennan; Friml
Make Believe Ladies Man, A   Bryan
Make Up Your Mind   Fields; McHugh
Makin' Wicky-Wacky Down in Waikiki   Hoffman; Lane
Malibu   Johnson, Howard
Malihini Love Call   Baer; Gilbert
Mama's in the Doghouse Now   Coslow
Mammy Land   Johnson, James P.; Razaf
Mammy's Lullaby, A   Blake; Razaf
Man About Town, A   Magidson; Washington
Man of My Own, A   Ager; Yellen
Man on Earth Is Worth Half a Dozen on the Moon,
    A   Fields; McHugh
Manhattan Moonlight (inst.)   Alter
Manhattan Serenade   Alter; Johnson, Howard
March of Time, The   Arlen; Koehler
Margineers, The   Fields; McHugh
Mars Sequence (inst.)   Henderson
Mary, Queen of Heaven   Robin
Maybe It's Love   Meyer; Mitchell
Maybe It's You   Harbach; Kern
Maybe, Someday   Friend; Monaco
Maybe Yes, Maybe No   Porter
Meaning of the Name of Kelly, The   Alter; Johnson, Howard
Mei Lan-Fong (inst.)   Duke
Memories of You   Blake; Razaf
Mender of Broken Dreams, The   Lewis
Merry-Go-Round, The   Brown, Nacio Herb; Freed, Arthur
Mi Caballero   Magidson; Washington
Mi Triste Adios   Rainger

Mia Cara (My Dear)   Fain; Kahal
Midnight Fancies (inst.)   Schwartz, Jean
Midnight Kiss   Fisher
Mighty Nice and So Particular   Akst; Davis
Miniatures (inst.)   Schwartz, Jean
Minstrel Memories   Baer; Gilbert
Misbehavin' Hips   Arlen; Koehler
Miss Otis Regrets   Porter
Mistaken in Love   Dixon; Pollack
Mister Mammy Man   Razaf
Modern Maidens (inst.)   Brown, Nacio Herb
Moment I Saw You, The   Dietz; Schwartz, Arthur
Moment We Met, The   Freed, Arthur
Mon Amour   Magidson; Washington
Mona and Her Kiddies   Porter
Mona Mia (inst.)   Schwartz, Jean
Monkey Dance (inst.)   Henderson
Mooda's Song   Akst; Clarke
Moon Is Low, The   Brown, Nacio Herb; Freed, Arthur
Moon Shines Down, The   Mercer
More than Ever   Adamson; Youmans
Morenita   Ahlert
Mother's Little Northern Rose   Johnson, Howard
Mothers Ought to Tell Their Daughters   Brown, Lew;
    DeSylva; Henderson
Mountain Song   Brown, Nacio Herb; Eliscu
Movietonia   Hanley
Mrs. Krause's Blue Eyed Baby Boy   Brown, Lew; DeSylva;
    Henderson
Music Hath Charms   Ager; Yellen
Music in the Moonlight   Coslow
Music of the Gypsies (inst.)   Brown, Nacio Herb
Musical Romance of Tom Thumb and Tiny Teena,
    The   Magidson
Must I Say Adios (Amor Querido)   Bryan
My Best Gal   Blake; Razaf
My Bird of Paradise   Brennan; Friml
My Bridal Veil   Ager; Yellen
My Farm in Normandie   Bryan
My Father's Love Is All   Bryan
My First and Only Love   Friend; Schwartz, Jean
My First Love, My Last Love   Caesar; Harbach; Romberg
My Future Just Passed   Whiting
My Handy Man Ain't Handy No More   Blake; Razaf
My Heart's Love Call   Akst; Clarke
My Hero   Ahlert; Turk
My Hills of Home   Brennan; Friml
My Idea of a Wife   Harbach
My Idea of a Wife (My Idea of a Man)   Caesar; Romberg
My Idea of Love   Johnson, James P.
My Ideal   Robin; Whiting
My Impression of You   Magidson; Washington
My Intuition   Dietz; Schwartz, Arthur
My Kalua Rose   Bryan
My Kisses Are Your Kisses, If Your Kisses Are
    Mine   Schwartz, Jean
My Louisa   Porter
My Love Song   Burke
My Lover   Ager; Coslow; Yellen
My Mad Moment   Whiting
My Man from Caroline   Donaldson
My Man Must Dance   Arlen; Koehler
My Man o' War   Razaf
My Marine   Egan; Whiting
My Memories of You   Revel

My Northern Home   Johnson, Howard
My Northern Light (Bride 66)   Brennan; Friml
My One Big Moment   Kahn
My One Big Moment Is You   Johnson, Howard
My One Desire   Alter
My Only One   Razaf
My Only Pal Is My Radio   Leslie; Monaco
My Pals   Coslow; Robin
My Pathway of Love   Razaf
My Photograph of You   Alter
My Private Personal Pal   Kahn
My Real Ideal   Lane; Lerner, Sammy
My Reg'lar Man Is Back in Town   Razaf
My Religion Is You   Webster
My Silent Love Song   Lewis
My Spanish Tambourine   Johnson, Howard
My Story   Lewis; Warren
My Sweetheart Serenade   Revel
My Tennessee   Johnson, Howard
Mystery of Clothes   Dubin
Neapolitan Lullaby (inst.)   Schwartz, Jean
Never Been in Love Before   Caesar
Never Mind   Johnson, James P.
Never Mind How   Schwartz, Arthur
Never Never Wed   Brown, Lew; DeSylva; Henderson
Never Say Die   Robin
Never Swat a Fly   Brown, Lew; DeSylva; Henderson
New Irish Eyes of Blue   Schwartz, Jean
New Love Song, A   Freed, Arthur; Woods
New New York   Dietz; Schwartz, Arthur
Next to Your Mother Who Do You Love   Young, Joseph
Night After Night   Dietz; Schwartz, Arthur
Night Is Darkest Before the Dawn   Fisher
Night Winds   Clare
Nighty Night   Friend; Monaco
Nina Rosa   Caesar; Harbach; Romberg
No One to Blame but You   Schwartz, Arthur
No Place but Home (If We're in China)   Hart; Rodgers
No Use Living with No One to Love   Kahn
No Wonder I'm Blue   Alter; Hammerstein
No Wonder I'm in Love with You   Snyder
Nobody Cares If I'm Blue   Akst
Nobody Home   Burke
Nobody Knows but the Lord   Kalmar; Ruby
Nobody Looks at the Man   Hart; Rodgers
Nothing But Love   Bryan
Nothing's Going to Hold Us Down   Friend; Monaco
Now I Ask You   Hanley
Now that It's All Over   Fisher
Now That You Are Here   Dietz; Rainger
Oh Baby, Do That Little Thing for Me   Parish
Oh Baby! What Do You Do   Friend; Monaco
Oh Have I Got a Way with the Girls   Hanley
Oh How She Can Poo Poo Po Do Po   Fain; Kahal
Oh How We Love Our Alma Mater   Kalmar; Ruby
Oh, King — Oh, Queen!   Ahlert; Turk
Oh, My, What a Wonderful World   Gorney; Harburg
Oh, So Lovely   Hart; Rodgers
Oh, Why   Freed, Arthur; Woods
O.K. Means Old Kentucky   Bryan
Oklahoma Joe   Bryan
Old Black Joe   Gilbert
Old Devil Sea   Duke; Harburg
Old Fashioned   Arlen; Koehler

(There's Something About An) Old Fashioned Girl   Brown, Lew; DeSylva; Henderson
Old Man Blues   Ellington; Mills
Old Man Hard Times Make Way for Kid Prosperity   Coslow
Old Pal, Why Did You Leave Me?   Brown, Nacio Herb; Freed, Arthur
Oli, Oli, Oli   Hammerstein; Romberg
On a Blue and Moonless Night   Hoffman
On Revival Day   Razaf
On the Beat   Arlen; Koehler
On the Boulevard (inst.)   Schwartz, Jean
On the Level with You   Johnson, James P.; Razaf
On the Sunny Side of the Street   Fields; McHugh
On the Winding Santa Fe   Baer; Gilbert
On with the Dance   Rodgers
Once a Gypsy Told Me (You Were Mine)   Fain; Kahal
Once There Was a Farmer's Daughter   Hammerstein; Romberg
One Dream for Two   Livingston, Jerry
One for All   Schwartz, Arthur
One Kiss, Sweetheart, Then Goodbye   Bryan; Dubin
One Life One Love   Bryan; Dubin
One Little Drink   Akst; Clarke
One Little Raindrop   Schwartz, Jean
One Love   Arlen; Koehler
One Loves at Sight   Smith, Harry B.
One Moment Please   Robin; Whiting
One More Waltz   Fields; McHugh
One Night, Madame!   Brown, Nacio Herb; Egan
One Robin Doesn't Make a Spring   Loewe
One Step   Caesar; Romberg
One, Two, Three   Mercer
One Way Street to You   Eliscu
Only a Midnight Adventure   Leslie
Only Love Is Real   Brown, Nacio Herb; Freed, Arthur
Only the Skies Are Blue in Kalua   Bryan
Onward Chicago: World's Fair March   Johnson, Howard
Opera Sequence   Robin; Whiting
Oui-Oui   Meyer; Mitchell
Our Love   Freed, Arthur
Out at the Prairie's End   Schwartz, Jean
Out in the Cold   Conrad; Meyer; Mitchell
Out in the Open Air   Dietz; Lane
Out of a Clear Blue Sky   Arlen; Koehler
Out of Breath and Scared to Death   Mercer
Out of the Nowhere Into the Here   Lane
Outlaw Song, The   Friend
Outside Looking In   Eliscu
Over the Lincoln Trail   Bryan
Over the Plains   Baer; Gilbert
Over the Sea of Dreams   Robin
Overnight   Alter; Rose
Pablo   Caesar; Harbach; Romberg
Painted Rose   Hanley
Palace of Dreams   Schwartz, Arthur
Pampas Rose   Whiting
Panic's On, The   Schwartz, Arthur
Papa Ain't No Santa Claus, Mama Ain't No Christmas Tree   Razaf
Paprika   Schwartz, Jean
Parade of the Blues   Conrad; Meyer; Mitchell
Paradise   Coslow
Parisian Moonlight, Many the Night   Young, Joseph
Parsons   Meyer; Mitchell
Parting   Schwartz, Jean

Passing Fancy   Akst; Clarke
Pay Day   Caesar; Harbach; Romberg
Pay Some Attention to Me   Gershwin, George; Gershwin, Ira
Payador   Caesar; Harbach; Romberg
Peach of a Pair, A   Whiting
Pearl Ballet   Fisher
Pearls (inst.)   Schwartz, Jean
Pepola   Whiting
Perfectly in Love   Snyder
Perusing in Peru   Caesar; Harbach; Romberg
Peter Pan   Hart; Rodgers
Petrograd   Akst; Clarke
Pharaoh Had a Daughter and Her Name Was Cleopatra   Coslow
Physically Fit   Dubin
Pick Up, The   Whiting
Pick Yourself Up, Brush Yourself Off   Hanley
Picture No Artist Can Paint, A   Friend; Monaco
Pirate Song   Johnson, Howard
Pirates of Love   Edwards
Pitter Patter   Gordon
Pizarro Was a Very Narrow Man   Caesar; Harbach; Romberg
Planting Flowers of Happiness   Alter; Johnson, Howard
Play It Slow and Easy — I'll Dance All Night   Akst; Clarke; Robin; Whiting
Play Me a Blue Song   Johnston
Playin' Around   Stept
Please Be Good to Me   Silver
Please Don't Talk About Me when I'm Gone   Stept
Poem of Mine   Parish
Polish Up Your Funny Bone   Hanley
Poor Blind Men   Akst; Clarke
Poor but Honest   Edwards
Poor Little G String   Ahlert; Turk
Poor Little Mary Dugan   Bryan; Edwards
Poor Rich, The   Porter
Por Que   Freed, Arthur; Woods
Porter's Love Song to a Chambermaid, A   Johnson, James P.; Razaf
Practising Up on You   Dietz
Prayers of Tears and Laughter   Hart; Rodgers
Pretending   Lawrence
Pretty Gypsy   Hammerstein; Romberg
Prince Charming   Smith, Harry B.
Push the Clouds Out of Heaven   Snyder
Put a Little Salt on the Bluebird's Tail Before It Flies Away   Hanley
Puttin' It On for Baby   Bloom; Koehler
Race Track Finale   Alter; Johnson, Howard
Rags and Tatters   Hart; Rodgers
Rag-Tag Musketeers   Motzan
Rain or Shine   Ager
Rainbow Rhapsody   Magidson; Washington
Rain-Flower   Robin
Raisin' the Racket   Adamson; Gordon; Revel
Rally 'Round Me   Youmans
Rarin' to Go   Baer; Edwards; Gilbert
Rattling Along   Freed, Arthur
Reach Out for a Rainbow   Conrad; Meyer; Mitchell
Reaching for the Moon   Freed, Arthur
Reception of the Court   Schwartz, Arthur
Red Hot Chicago   Brown, Lew; DeSylva; Henderson
Red Roses and Pale White Moonlight   Akst; Clarke

Reflections (inst.)   Schwartz, Jean
Regards   Myrow
Regimental March   Hammerstein; Romberg
Reminiscing   Warren
Reno Blues   Hanley
Reno, the Land of the Free   Gordon; Silver
Riders of the Night   Schwartz, Jean
Riding on a Moonbeam   Burke
Riffs (inst.)   Johnson, James P.
Right at the Start of It   Dietz; Schwartz, Arthur
Right Beside You   Johnson, Howard; Woods
Right Way to Love, The   Freed, Arthur
Ring Dem Bells   Ellington; Mills
Ring Out the Blues   Gorney; Harburg
Rippling Brook (inst.)   Schwartz, Jean
River and Me, The   Dubin; Warren
Road of Romance   Lerner, Sammy
Rockin' Chair   Carmichael
Roll, Jordan, Roll   Blake; Razaf
Rollin' Down the River   Waller
Rolling Stone   Fisher
Romance of Elmer Stremingway, The   Brown, Lew; DeSylva; Henderson
Romancing Around   Kahn
Romany Romance, A   Johnson, Howard
Rosa Dolores   Hanley
Rosalie   Fields; McHugh
Rose in Your Hair (A Rose in My Hair)   Schwartz, Arthur
Rose Petals (inst.)   Schwartz, Jean
Roses Are Forget-Me-Nots Reminding Me Of You   Hoffman
Rubberneckin' Around   Akst; Clarke; Magidson; Washington
Rumba Rhythm   Johnson, James P.
Rusty's Up in the Air   Brown, Lew; DeSylva; Henderson
Sailor Song   Clare
Sailor's Hornpipe   Akst; Davis
Sam and Delilah   Gershwin, George; Gershwin, Ira
Sambo's Syncopated Russian Dance   Johnson, James P.; Razaf
Sandy   Edwards
Sasha (The Passion of the Pascha)   Rose
Sas-Katch-A Widja-Go-Way-Go-On!   Hanley
Sassy (inst.)   Schwartz, Jean
Satan's Holiday   Duke; Fain; Kahal
Say It in a Nutshell   Hanley
Say It with Gin   Porter
Say It with Your Feet   Coslow
Say Oui Cherie   Youmans
Say When — Stand Up — Drink Down   Hart; Rodgers
Say You Love Me   Parish
Scotch Song   Edwards; Johnson, Howard
Secret of My Life, The   Caesar; Harbach; Romberg
(It) Seems to Me   Dietz; Rainger
Send for Me   Hart; Rodgers
Serenade of Love   Romberg
Serenade of Love Tango   Caesar; Harbach
Shake It Off and Smile   Clare
Shake Your Duster   Johnson, James P.; Razaf
Shakin' Like a Leaf   Johnson, Howard
Shakin' the African   Arlen; Koehler
Sharing   Coots; Davis
Shavian Shivers   Duke; Harburg
She'll Love Me and Like It   Robin; Whiting
She's a Gorgeous Thing   Coots; Davis
She's Got to Be Some Woman to Steal My Man Away   Akst; Clarke

She's the Reason   Akst; Clarke
Shoestring (inst.)   Schwartz, Jean
Shoo the Hoodoo Away   Silver; Snyder
Shore Leave   Brennan; Friml
Should I   Brown, Nacio Herb; Freed, Arthur
Show Me the Way to Love   Donaldson
Shufflin' on Saturday Night   Johnson, Howard
Side By Side   Meyer; Mitchell
Silent Love   Johnson, Howard
Simple Simon Instep, The   Hart; Rodgers
Since Hannah from Savannah Came to Harlem   Blake;
      Razaf
Since It Started to Rain in Lover's Lane   Hoffman
Since I've Been Knowin' You   Brown, Nacio Herb; Egan
Since Maggie Became Marguerite   Leslie
Since My Wife Took Up Miniature Golf   Schwartz, Jean
Sing (a Happy Little Thing)   Johnson, Howard
Sing a Little Song   Friend; Schwartz, Jean
Sing a Little Song Every Morning   Edwards
Sing a Little Theme Song   Dubin
Sing a Song of Old Montana   Brown, Nacio Herb; Freed,
      Arthur
Sing Glory Hallelujah   Hart; Rodgers
Sing Sing for Sing-Sing   Porter
Sing Song Girl (Little Yella Cinderella)   Hanley
Sing You Sinners   Coslow
Sing Your Way Home   Leslie; Monaco; Young, Joseph
Singing a Song to the Stars   Johnson, Howard
Sittin' on a Rainbow   Yellen
(We Are) Six Poor Mortals   Freed, Arthur
Skippy   Conrad; Davis
Slave to Love, A   Friend; Monaco
Sleep Baby Sleep   Kalmar; Ruby
Slippery Hips   Johnson, James P.; Razaf
Slumber Valley   Motzan
Smile   Adamson; Youmans
Smile, Comrades (Smile While We May)   Ahlert; Turk
Smiling Skies   Robin; Whiting
Snake Hips   Mitchell
Snap Your Fingers at the Blues   Ahlert; Turk
Snowball Man, The   Monaco
So I Picks Up My Ukelele (And I Sings Her a Little
      Song)   Burke; Parish
So Long Cowboys   Coslow
So Near, So Dear, So Sweet   Freed, Arthur; Woods
So Sorry   Johnson, James P.
So Sympathetic   Kahn
Softer Than a Kitten (That's My Feeling for You)   Hart;
      Rodgers
Soldara Song   Bryan
Some Sunday   Edwards; Johnson, Howard
Some Time in Springtime   Coslow
Somebody   Ahlert; Turk
Someone   Clare
(I'm Unhappy 'Cause) Someone Else Is on Your
      Mind   Parish
Someone Must Be Getting Married Somewhere   Hart;
      Rodgers
Something to Remember You By   Dietz; Schwartz, Arthur
Something to Sing About   Adamson; Youmans
Somewhere in Dreamland   Bryan
Son of the Sun, A   Brennan; Friml
Song o' My Heart   Hanley
Song of a Fool, The   Lewis
Song of Love Is Singing in My Heart, A   Friend; Monaco

Song of Sorrow   Lawrence
Song of The Big Trail (Old Fashioned Song of Love)   Hanley
Song of the Blue Lagoon   Kahn
Song of the Congo   Magidson; Washington
Song of the Dawn, The   Ager; Yellen
Song of the Gigolo   Arlen; Koehler
Song of the Lark   Schwartz, Jean
Song of the South   Johnson, Howard
Song of the Waters   Coslow
Song of Troy   Freed, Ralph
Song of Vienna (In Wien, Wo der Wein und der Walzer
      Bluht), The   Young, Joseph
Sonya (inst.)   Schwartz, Jean
Sound of the Gourd, The   Akst; Baer; Clarke; Gilbert
South Breeze   Carmichael
Spain   Fields; McHugh
Sparkling and Refreshing (inst.)   Schwartz, Jean
Speed   Magidson; Washington
Spring Fever   Fields; McHugh
Star Showers (inst.)   Schwartz, Jean
Steeplejack   Schwartz, Arthur
Steps   Arlen; Koehler
Stop, Put That Stick Down (Entr'acte)   Gershwin, George;
      Gershwin, Ira
Strumming on an Old Guitar   Hanley
Subway (inst.)   Schwartz, Jean
Summer Breeze (inst.)   Schwartz, Jean
Sunday Afternoon   Schwartz, Arthur
Sunday Girl   Livingston, Jerry
Sunrise Dance, The   Caesar
Surely   Snyder
Swanee Fashion Plate   Johnson, James P.; Razaf
Swanee River Rhapsody   Ellington; Mills
Swedish Pastorale   Johnson, Howard
Sweeping the Clouds Away   Coslow
Sweet Forget-Me-Not   Robison
Sweet Jennie Lee   Donaldson
Sweet Romance   Donaldson; Leslie
Sweet So-and-So   Gershwin, Ira
Sweet Solitude   Robison
Sweetenheart   Hart; Rodgers
Sweetheart   Brown, Nacio Herb; Freed, Arthur
Sweetheart of My Student Days   Kahn
Swing Me in a Hammock of Dreams   Parish
Swing Your Tails   Dietz; Schwartz, Arthur
Swinging Along the Blue Ridge Trail   Motzan
Ta Ta Old Bean   Eliscu
Tain't No Sin   Brown, Lew; DeSylva; Henderson
'Tain't No Sin to Dance Around in Your Bones   Donaldson;
      Leslie
Take a Letter to the King   Schwartz, Arthur
Take a Trip to Harlem   Blake
Take Along a Little Love   Whiting
Take It on the Chin   Dubin
Take Me Back to Manhattan   Porter
Taking It Easy   Fisher
Talk with My Heel and Your Toes   Caesar
Talkative Toes   Dietz; Duke
Tell Us Which One Do You Love   Dubin
Tellin' It to the Daisies (But It Never Gets Back to
      You)   Young, Joseph
Telling It to the Daisies (But It Never Gets Back to
      You)   Warren
Ten Cents a Dance   Hart; Rodgers
Ten Sweet Mamas   Ager; Yellen

Thank You So Much Mrs. Lowsborough—Goodby Porter
Thank Your Father (Thank Your Mother) Brown, Lew;
    DeSylva; Henderson
That Lindy Hop Blake; Razaf
That Little Photograph of You Koehler
That Tired Feeling Friml; Hammerstein; Harbach
That Was Destiny Kahn
That Well-Known Smile Gershwin, George; Gershwin, Ira
That's Enough for Tonight! Whiting
That's My Sweetheart Motzan
That's the Low-Down on the Low-Down Stept
That's What I Like About You Friend; Monaco
That's Where the South Begins Yellen
That's Why We're Dancing Fields; McHugh
That's Worth While Waiting For Baer; Gilbert
(We're) The Berries Razaf
There Are No Tomorrows Brennan; Friml
There Can Only Be One for Me Harbach
There Can Only Be Only One for Me Caesar; Romberg
There'll Never Be Another Girl Like Mary This Side of
    Paradise Rose
There'll Never Be Another Mary Ager; Yellen
There's a Kick in the Old Girl Yet Fields; McHugh
There's a Little Bit of Irish in the Rainbow Hanley
There's a Tear for Every Smile in Hollywood Stept
There's a Wah Wah Gal in Agua Caliente Donaldson
There's Gold in the Sky Snyder
There's Happiness Over the Hill Silver
There's Not a Rock on the Road to California Johnson,
    Howard
There's Nothin' That Love Won't Cure Hoffman
There's Nothing Wrong in a Kiss Caesar
There's Only One (Who Matters to Me) Baer; Gilbert
There's Religion in Rhythm Robison
There's Something Missing in Your Eyes Gilbert
They Satisfy Kahn
They'll Still Keep Dancing (Der Tanz Geht Waiter) Ahlert;
    Turk
Things that Money Can't Buy Caesar
This Is the Moment Robin; Whiting
This Must Be Illegal (It's So Nice) Rainger
(It'll) This Will Be the First Time for Me Brown, Lew;
    DeSylva; Henderson
Three Cheers for the Red, White and Blue Alter; Edwards
Three Guesses Mercer
Three Little Maids Edwards; Johnson, Howard
Three Little Words Kalmar; Ruby
Through the Eyes of Love Lerner, Sammy
Through the Miracle of Love Bryan; Dubin
Throw It Out the Window Alter
Ticker Tape Talk Loesser
Tickle Toe (inst.) Schwartz, Jean
Tie a Knot in the Rainbow Lewis
Till I Met You Burke
Time on My Hands, You in My Arms Adamson; Gordon;
    Youmans
Tip Top (inst.) Schwartz, Jean
To a Tango Melody Berlin
To Fall in Love in Venice Coslow
To Have, to Hold, to Love Smith, Harry B.
To Hold You Baer; Gilbert
To My Mammy Berlin
To the Only One Youmans
To Whom It May Concern Meyer; Mitchell
Toast, A Conrad; Meyer; Mitchell

Toast to Prohibition Berlin
Toast to the Girl I Love, A Hanley
To-Day Is the Day (inst.) Schwartz, Jean
Toddlin' Along Gershwin, George; Gershwin, Ira
Tokens of Love Coslow
Tomorrow Is Another Day Stept
Too Bad I Can't Be Good Dubin
Too Bad I'm Good! Whiting
Too Late Akst; Clarke
Too, Too Divine Duke; Harburg
Toothache Blues Arlen; Koehler
Topsy and Eva Fields; McHugh
Trailing a Shooting Star Schwartz, Arthur
Treat Me Rough Gershwin, George; Gershwin, Ira
Trimmin' the Women Robin; Whiting
Triumphant (inst.) Schwartz, Jean
Tropical Moon Blake
Troubadour Gorney; Harburg
Try This for That Tired Feeling Alter
Twenty Swedes Ran Through the Weeds, Chasing One
    Norwgeian Bryan
Two Hearts Swing in Three-Quarter Time (Zwei Herzen Im
    Dreivierteltakt) Young, Joseph
Two Perfect Lovers Lane; Lerner, Sammy
Two Strangers Razaf
Ukulele Moon Conrad; Davis
Unaccustomed As I Am Duke; Harburg
Unaccustomed As I Am to Falling in Love Magidson;
    Washington
Under Persian Skies Edwards
Under the Jungle Moon Blake; Razaf
Under the Monkey Moon Johnson, Howard; Woods
Under the Sweetheart Tree Fisher; Stept
Under Vesuvian Skies Lane; Leslie
Until Love Comes Along Clare
Until Today I Had No Tomorrow Duke; Harburg
Until We Kiss Mercer
Up an' at 'Em Magidson; Washington
Upper Park Avenue, The Porter
Us and Company Burke
Vagabond Dreams Coslow
Vagabond King Opening Chorus Robin
Valse Brilliant (inst.) Schwartz, Jean
Valse Duet Caesar; Harbach; Romberg
Valse Futuristique (inst.) Revel
Valse Imogene (inst.) Schwartz, Jean
Valse Marie (inst.) Schwartz, Jean
Varsity Walk (inst.) Hanley
Venice Porter
Verdict Is, Life with You Razaf
Vienna Morning (inst.) Schwartz, Jean
Village Choir! Baer; Bryan
Violet (inst.) Schwartz, Jean
Wail of the Congo Trail, The Johnson, Howard; Woods
Wait Until We Get Alone Johnson, James P.
Waiting Hammerstein; Romberg
Waiting for the Leaves to Fall (She Was Poor) Hart;
    Rodgers
Wake Up Hammerstein; Romberg
Wake Up! Little Rip Van Winkle Bryan
Wakin' Up the Folks Down Stairs Blake; Razaf
Walkin' My Baby Back Home Ahlert; Turk
Wall Street Magidson; Washington
Waltz with Me Smith, Harry B.
Waltz You Saved for Me, The Kahn

Wanapoo Bay   Brennan; Friml
Want a Good Time Bad   Coslow
Was I Just Another Love Affair to You   Conrad
Was I to Blame (For Falling in Love with You)   Kahn;
    Young, Victor
Washin' the Blues from My Soul   Robison
Wasn't It Beautiful While It Lasted   Brown, Lew; DeSylva;
    Henderson
Wasn't It Nice?   Young, Joseph
Wasting My Love on You   Leslie; Warren
Watching My Dreams Go By   Dubin
We Need Affection   Kahn
We Never Sleep   Caesar
Wedding of the Valley and the Hills, The   Eliscu
Welcome Home   Hanley
We'll Always Be Sweethearts   Friend
We'll Build a Little World of Our Own   Hanley
We're Friends Again   Ahlert; Turk
We're on the Verge of a Murder   Robin
We're the Berries   Blake
We've Been Spending the Summer with Our
    Families   Porter
Whaler's Song, The   Bryan
What a Case I've Got on You   Dietz; Schwartz, Arthur
What a Dream to Dream About   Alter; Johnson, Howard
What a Lot of Loving   Brennan; Friml
What a Lucky Break for Me   Berlin
What Am I Bid for My Apple   Robin
What Can I Say?   Youmans
What Do You Want from Somebody Else that You Didn't
    Get from Me   Conrad; Leslie
What D'Ya Say, Let's Get Married (What D'Ya
    Say)   Gordon; Silver
What France Needs   Robin
What Good Am I Without You?   Ager
What Good Is the Lane, If You Can't Have the Girl of Your
    Dreams?   Dixon; Warren; Young, Joseph
What Has Become of Marie   Edwards
What Have We Lost (We Found Each Other)   Schwartz,
    Jean
What If We Do   Johnson, James P.
What Is a Heart For   Johnson, Howard
What Is this Power I Have?   Coslow
What Is Your Price, Madam?   Johnson, Howard
What Kind of People Are You?   Hoffman
What Will Become of Me   Freed, Arthur; Woods
Whatever It Is It's Grand   Robin; Whiting
What's My Man Gonna Be Like   Porter
What's the Big Idea?   Lewis; Warren; Young, Joseph
What's the Good of Good Morning, When You Have No
    One to Love and to Kiss You Goodnight   Fisher
What's the Use of Living when You've Got Nobody to Love
    (What's the Use of Living without Love)   Hanley
When a Black Sheep Is Blue for Home   Razaf
When a Pansy Was a Flower   Rose
When a Woman Loves a Man   Rainger; Robin; Rose
When Beau Brummel Meets Fluffy Ruffles   Edwards;
    Johnson, Howard
When I Dream of the Sweethearts I've Had   Parish
When I Met You   Brown, Nacio Herb; Freed, Arthur
When I Think of the Sweethearts   Fisher
When I Write a Song   Styne
When I'm Dreaming of Your Spanish Eyes   Bryan
When I'm with You   Edwards

When It's Cactus Time in Arizona   Gershwin, George;
    Gershwin, Ira
When It's Daylight Saving Time in Oshkosh   Robin; Whiting
When Kentucky Bids the World Good Morning   Leslie
When Little Red Roses Get the Blues for You   Dubin
When Love Awakens   Coslow
When Love Comes Stealing into My Heart   Snyder
When My Prince Charming Comes Along   Akst; Clarke
When the Frost Is on the Daisy   Bryan
When the Moon Comes Over the Mountain   Johnson,
    Howard; Woods
When the Robin Sings After the Rain   Hanley
When the World Was Young (Quand Notre Vieux Monde
    Etait Tout Neuf)   Hart; Rodgers
When Vagabond Dreams Come True   Parish
When You Don't Know What to Do with It   Hanley
When You Have No Man to Love   Hammerstein; Romberg
When You Press Your Lips to Mine   Razaf
When Your Hand First Touched Me   Freed, Arthur
Where Have You Been?   Porter
Where the Little Bridge Crosses the Stream   Hanley
Where You Lead   Brennan; Friml
Wherever You Are   Kalmar; Ruby
While We Waltz   Schwartz, Jean
Whisper to the Whisp'ring Pines   Hanley
Whisper You Love Me and Make My Dreams Come
    True   Friend; Monaco
Whispering Through the Pines   Freed, Arthur
Whistle While You Work, Boys   Smith, Harry B.
Who Wants a Girl Like Me   Robin
Whole Darned Thing's For You, The   Ahlert; Turk
Who's Little Baby Is Oo   Hanley
Why Ain't I Home   Youmans
Why Am I So Romantic   Kalmar
Why Am I So Sensitive to You   Robin; Whiting
Why Did You Make Me Cry   Magidson
Why Have You Forgotten Waikiki   Kahn
Why Must I Always Be Without You   Mitchell; Pollack
Why Not Have a Little Party?   Schwartz, Arthur
Why Talk About Sex?   Porter
Wild and Woolly (inst.)   Schwartz, Jean
Wings in the Morning   Schwartz, Arthur
Winter and Spring   Eliscu; Friml
Wipe 'Em Off   Johnson, James P.
With All My Heart   Adamson; Gordon; Revel
With My Guitar and You   Heyman; Silver; Snyder
With the Dawn   Caesar; Harbach; Romberg
Without Love   Brown, Lew; DeSylva; Henderson
Woman in the Shoe, The   Brown, Nacio Herb; Freed, Arthur
Women   Hammerstein; Romberg
Wonder   Razaf
Won't You Get Off It, Please (inst.)   Waller
Won't You Please Help Me Find My Little Heinie   Coots;
    Davis
Words Can't Express   Razaf
World of Dreams   Eliscu; Herbert
World of Melody, A   Brennan; Friml
World Was in My Heart, The   Donaldson; Leslie
Would He Do the Same for Me   Parish
Would You Like to Take a Walk (Sump'n Good'll Come from
    That)   Dixon; Rose; Warren
Wrapped Up in Red, Red Rose   Hanley
Ya Gotta Be Versatile   Johnson, James P.; Razaf
Yankyula   Brennan; Friml
You   Schwartz, Arthur

You Appeal to Me   Whiting
You Are a Song   Robin
You Are the Jewel of My Heart   Fisher
You Brought a New Kind of Love to Me   Fain; Kahal
You Can Have It — I Don't Want It, Daylight Savings
    Time   Friend; Monaco
You Can Only Wear One Pair of Pants at a Time   Friend;
    Monaco
You Can't Get to Heaven that Way   Caesar
You Can't Stop Me from Falling in Love with You   Coots;
    Davis
You Can't Unscramble Scrambled Eggs   Gershwin, George;
    Gershwin, Ira
You Do, Don't You   Hanley
You Gotta Be Modernistic   Friend; Monaco
You Learn About Love Every Day   Stept
You Left Me So Blue   Young, Victor
You Made Up My Mind   Parish
You Never Can Tell about Love   Coots; Davis
You Never Did That Before   Ahlert; Turk
You Only Want Me, When No One Else Wants You   Fisher
You Ought to See the Horse   Dubin
You Oughta Know   Coots; Davis
You Still Retain Your Girlish Figure   Bryan; Dubin
You Too (Auch du Wirst Mich Einmal Betrugen)   Young,
    Joseph
You Wanted Me, I Wanted You   Arlen; Koehler
You Will Never Know   Youmans
You Will Remember Vienna   Hammerstein; Romberg
You'll Be Sorry in the Morning   Fisher
You'll Give In   Hanley
Your Heart Just Can't Go Wrong   Robin; Whiting
Your Rose   Caesar; Harbach; Romberg
Your Smiles, Your Tears   Caesar; Harbach; Romberg
Your Song Was a Long Song (That You Never
    Meant)   Myrow
You're Always Sure of My Love for You   Kahn
You're an Angel   Brennan; Friml
You're Driving Me Crazy   Donaldson
You're in a Class By Yourself   Brown, Nacio Herb; Freed,
    Arthur
You're Just a Lover   Brown, Nacio Herb; Egan
You're Lucky to Me   Blake; Razaf
You're My Captain Kidd   Stept
You're Simply Delish   Freed, Arthur
You're the Better Half of Me   Fields; McHugh
You're the Bride and I'm the Groom   Brown, Nacio Herb;
    Freed, Arthur
You're the Cure for what Ails Me, Baby You're Doin' Me
    Good   Gorney; Harburg
You're the One   Youmans
You're the Sunrise   Dietz; Schwartz, Arthur
You're the Sweetest Girl This Side of Heaven   Kahn
You're Too Far Away   Porter
Yours and Mine   Burke
Yours and Yours Alone   Brown, Nacio Herb; Eliscu
You've Got to Be Hard-Boiled   Porter
Yubla   Brennan; Friml
Yvonne's Song   Robin; Whiting

1931

Affection   Bryan; Monaco
Africa Shrieks   Eliscu
African Lament   Gilbert

African Ripples (inst.)   Waller
After Every Wedding There's Always Someone Blue   Caesar;
    Motzan
After the Dance (The Bells Ding-Dong) (Der Tanz Is
    Aus)   Caesar; Motzan
After Tonight   Yellen
Ain't Everything Grand!   Hammerstein; Whiting
Ain't That the Way It Goes   Ahlert; Turk
All I Need Is Your Love   Coslow
All's Well with the World   Harbach; Kern
Alma Mater   Arlen; Yellen
Alone in a Corner   Yellen
Along the Way that Leads to Yesterday   Bloom; Clare
Always Goodbye (Toujours Adieu)   Hanley
Always Keep Me in Your Heart   Egan
Americans Are Coming, The   Hammerstein; Romberg
And Then You Happened Along   Lerner, Sammy
And They Lived Happily Ever After   David, Mack
Anvil Chorus, The   Brown, Lew; Henderson
Any Love Today   Berlin
Anybody but You   Brown, Nacio Herb; Eliscu
Anyone Else   McHugh
Are You Love?   Hammerstein; Romberg
Aren't We All   Brown, Lew; DeSylva; Henderson
Aria from Antonia   Hammerstein; Romberg
A-Rovin' I'll Go   Woods
As Long As You're There   Leslie; Monaco
At the Canton Tea Garden with You   Burke
Auf Widersehn   Porter
Aunt Jemima's Birthday (inst.)   Bloom
Autumn Leaves Are Falling   Kalmar; Ruby
Baby Racketeers   Bryan
Baby Save Your Tears (Baby Weine Nicht)   Gilbert
Back from Hollywood   Brown, Lew; Henderson
Back Yard Follies   Oakland
Bad Temptation Like You, A   Leslie; Meyer
Ballet Music (inst.)   Schwartz, Arthur
Barnyard Romeo   Alter; Freed, Arthur
Be Sweet to Me Cherie   Bryan
Beatin' Around the Bush   Akst; Kahn; Whiting
Beatin' the Blues   Arlen; Yellen
Beautiful Love   Young, Victor
Because, Because   Gershwin, George; Gershwin, Ira
Because I Worship You   Freed, Arthur
Because of You   Dubin
Before You Say Good-Bye   Akst; Clarke; Whiting
Beggar Waltz, The   Dietz; Schwartz, Arthur
Beginning of Love, The   Brown, Lew; Henderson
Bend Down Sister   Conrad
Beside the Side of a Stream   Lerner, Sammy
Best Part College Days   Arlen; Yellen
Bet You a Little Kiss I'll Kiss Ya   Hoffman
Better Think It Over   Eliscu
Better Wait Till You're Eighteen   Hanley
Between the Devil and the Deep Blue Sea   Arlen; Koehler
Between You and Me   Freed, Arthur
Beyond the Moon   Mercer
Big Temptation Like You, A   Leslie; Meyer
Birthday of a Kiss, The   Webster
Black Rhythm   Mills
Blah, Blah, Blah   Gershwin, George; Gershwin, Ira
Blame It on the Moonlight   Ager; Yellen
Blame It on the Wine (Zu Jeder Liebe Gehort ein Glaschen
    Wein)   Young, Joseph
Bless Ya, Honey Babe, I Love You   Magidson; Wrubel

Blow My Black Bird Home   Egan
Blue Blazes   Robin; Whiting
Blue Danube Ballet   Fain; Kahal
Blue Flame   Mills
Blue Kentucky Moon   Donaldson
Blue Nevada Moon   Egan
Blue Rhythm   Mills
Blue Ridge Moon   Kahn
Blues in My Heart   Mills
Blues (inst.)   Bloom
Boom-Boom-Boomerang   Johnson, J. Rosamond
Boston   Johnson, James P.
Boy Oh Boy Oh Boy I've Got It Bad   Leslie; Monaco
Breakfast Dance   Arlen; Koehler
Breeze Kissed Your Hair, The   Harbach; Kern
Bright and Early   Arlen; Yellen
Bring on the Follies Girls   Buck
Broadway Reverie   Buck
Broke Down Papa   Razaf
Bubbling Over with Love   Ager
Building a Home for You   Kahn
But He Never Says He Loves Me   Porter
But How Soon We Forget   Gilbert
By a Lazy Country Lane   Stept
By the River Sainte Marie   Leslie; Warren
Cafe Scene   Harbach; Kern
Call Me Whate'er You Will   Gershwin, George; Gershwin, Ira
Calling Me Over the Hill   Hanley
Can't We Talk It Over   Washington; Young, Victor
Can't You Read Between the Lines   Dubin; Meyer
Can't You See   Ahlert; Turk
Canzonetta (I'll Share them All with You)   Harbach; Kern
Carefree Miner, The   Hammerstein; Whiting
Caroline My Caroline   Coots
Cat Can Look at a Queen, A   Hart; Rodgers
Catch'm   Gordon; Revel
C'est Pas Comme Ca (It's Not Like That)   Washington
Chamber Music and Boy's March   Harbach; Kern
Chances Are   Freed, Ralph
Changing of the Guards   Oakland
Chase All Your Cares (And Got to Sleep, Baby)   Berlin
Cheerio   Fields; McHugh
Children of Dreams   Hammerstein; Romberg
Children, Walk with Me   Razaf
Choir   Harbach; Kern
Cigarettes, Cigars!   Gordon; Revel
Cigars! Cigarettes! Nuts!   Brown, Lew; Henderson
Cinderella Sue   Fain; Kahal
Cinema Lorelei   Eliscu
Clinching the Sale   Oakland
Come Easy Go Easy Love   Carmichael
Come on Slowpoke   Ahlert; Turk
Come Take Me   Heyman
Come to Me   Brown, Lew; DeSylva; Henderson
Concentratin' on You   Razaf; Waller
Confession   Dietz; Schwartz, Arthur
Congai   Hammerstein; Romberg
Congo   Kahn
Consolation   Robin; Whiting
Constantly   Stept
Contented   Hanley
Cottage of Content   Harbach; Kern
Couldn't Help It If I Tried   Burke
Cover a Clover with Kisses   Dixon; Warren

Cowboy Serenade, A   Freed, Arthur
Cowboy's Serenade, A   Whiting
Crazy Quilt   Dixon; Warren
Crazy Quilt Sextette, The   Harburg; Rose; Warren
Crazy Street   Adamson; Lane
Crosby, Columbo and Vallee   Dubin
Crumbs of Your Love, The   Razaf; Waller
Crying in My Coffee (Since Someone Else Is Taking You to Tea)   Parish
Crystal Candalabra   Harbach; Kern
Cubalero, The   Young, Joseph
Cuban Holiday   Parish
Cuban Love Song   Fields; McHugh
Cuckoo in the Clock   Freed, Ralph
Cute Little Things You Do, The   Hanley
Cute Peekin' Knees   Adamson; Lane
Cutest Kid in Town, The   Hoffman; Magidson
Daily Bread   Dubin; Hanley
Dance   Egan; Gordon; Revel
Dance Hall Doll   Yellen
Dance of the Mirrors   Fain; Kahal
Dance We All Do for Al, The   Caesar
Dancing Debutantes   Wrubel
Dancing in the Dark   Dietz; Schwartz, Arthur
Dancing with the Daffodils, Down at the Garden Ball   Young, Joseph
Day In, Day Out   Ahlert; Turk
Deep in Your Eyes   Parish
Deep Water   Bryan; Schwartz, Jean
Delishious   Gershwin, George; Gershwin, Ira
Die Glocke Toent Bim-Bam   Caesar
Dimple on My Knee, The   Gershwin, George; Gershwin, Ira
Discord in "A" Flat   Oakland
Do I Know Why   Fields; McHugh
Do I Really Deserve It from You   Williams
Do Something Different   Gordon; Revel
Do What You Like!   Robin
Do You Believe in Love at First Sight   Kahn
Doin' the New York   Oakland
Doin' the Rhumbatamba   Wrubel
Doin' the Rumba   Mills
Doin' what I Please   Johnson, James P.; Razaf
Doing the Dumbbell   Gordon; Revel
Donaldson's New Moon Song   Donaldson
Don't Ask Me Not to Sing   Harbach; Kern
Don't Ask Me Why   Young, Joseph
Don't Be Mad at Me   Donaldson
Don't Do Anything 'Till You Hear from Me   Clare; Leslie; Stept
Don't Ever Be Blue   Dubin
Don't Tell Her What's Happened to Me   DeSylva
Dorine   Gorney; Harburg
Down Among the Sleepy Pines   Clare
Down Around These Old New Hampshire Hills   Davis
Dream of All My Dreams   Coslow
Dream Sequence (We're from the Journal, The Wahrheit, the Telegram, The Times. . .)   Gershwin, George; Gershwin, Ira
(Let's Drift Away On) Dreamers Bay   Spina
Dreaming   Fields; McHugh
Dreaming Dreams that Won't Come True   Friend
Drums in My Heart   Heyman; Youmans
Duet   Gorney; Harburg
Dunk, Dunk, Dunk   Conrad
Dying Flamingo, The   Caesar

East Wind   Hammerstein; Romberg
Eight Little Letters   Donaldson
Electrician Blues   Razaf
Elizabeth   Caesar
Embrace Me   Hammerstein; Romberg
Empire State Opening   Brown, Lew; Henderson
Empty Arms   Howard, Joseph E.
Entrance of Mary and Wintergreen   Gershwin, George; Gershwin, Ira
Entrance of Supreme Court Judges   Gershwin, George; Gershwin, Ira
Entrance of the French Ambassador   Gershwin, George; Gershwin, Ira
Episode in Victor's Play The Passionate Pilgrim   Harbach; Kern
Even As You and I   Fain; Kahal
Everybody's Crazy Over Winnie   Edwards
Everyone in Town Loves Little Mary Brown   Davis
Everything That's Nice Belongs to You   Stept
Ev'ning in Caroline   Donaldson
Ev'ry Little While   Harbach; Kern
Examination Number   Fields; McHugh
Excuse for a Song and Dance   Dixon; Warren; Young, Joseph
Exotic Melody   Freed, Arthur
Face It with a Smile   Baer; Gilbert
Faithfully Yours   Snyder
Fast and Furious   Gordon; Revel
Fate Is Late Again   Rainger
Fate Misunderstood You   Johnson, James P.
Father of the Land We Love   Cohan
Feather in a Breeze   Fain; Kahal
Feed Me with Love   Schwartz, Jean; Young, Joseph
Five Minutes of Spring   Gorney; Harburg
Flag (inst.), The   Schwartz, Arthur
Flowers to Remember You (Me) By   Friml
Flying Field   Harbach; Kern
Foolin' Around with Love   Johnson, James P.
For Honor   Robin; Whiting
For You For Me   Coslow
Forever   Myrow
Forgotten Melody   Kahn
Freddy the Freshman, the Freshest Kid in Town   Friend
(I Don't Wanna Be) Free   Clare
Free for All   Hammerstein; Whiting
From Niagara Falls to Reno Is Only a Step Away   Akst; Clarke; Whiting
From One Pair of Arms to Another   Dubin; Fain; Kahal
Frowns   Gordon; Revel
Fruit Pickers' Song   Hammerstein; Romberg
Garcon, S'il Vous Plait   Gershwin, George; Gershwin, Ira
Garden By the Sea in Old Hawaii, A   Parish
Get Up, Get Out, Get Under the Sun   Arlen; Koehler
Gettin' Sentimental   Kahn
Gigolo Joe   Mills
Gigoloes   Brown, Lew; Henderson
Girl Next Door, The   Hammerstein; Whiting
Give Me Your Affection, Honey   Bryan
Glory! Glory! I'm a Sap   Razaf
God Gave Me Eyes   Hart; Rodgers
Goin' to Town with Me   Adamson; Lane
Going, Going, Gone!   Eliscu
Golden West and You, The   Coslow
Good Evening, Friends   Caesar
Good Spirits   Robin; Whiting

Good Times Are Here, When My Baby Is Near   Ahlert; Turk
Goodbye Little Captain of My Heart (Adieu, Mein Kleiner Gardeoffizier)   Young, Joseph
Goodnight Moon   Donaldson
Goodnight Serenade   Brown, Nacio Herb; Eliscu
Goose Pimples   Conrad
Got to Go to Town   Dixon; Warren; Young, Joseph
Gotta Go Now   Dixon; Warren; Young, Joseph
Gotta Settle This Tonight or Never   Robin
Green Eyes (Aquallos Ojos Verdes)   Gilbert
Green Fields   Bryan; Schwartz, Jean
Guilty   Ahlert; Akst; Kahn; Turk; Whiting
Gypsy (inst.)   Bloom
Ha! Cha! Cha!   Harbach; Kern
Ha-Ha-Ha (Gang Song)   Arlen; Koehler
Hand in Hand   Leslie; Monaco; Washington
Hang Out the Stars in Indiana   Woods
Hangin' Around Your Door   Johnson, James P.
Happy Little Worries   Hoffman
Happy New Year   Hoffman
Harlemania   Fields
Have a Heart   Adamson; Lane
Have a Heart, Have Mine   Baer
Have a Little Drinkee   Eliscu
Have You Forgotten   Robin
Having a Good Time Wish You Were Here   Dubin; Fain; Kahal
Hawaiian Memory   Caesar
He and I   Heyman; Youmans
He Doesn't Love Me Anymore   Oakland
He Looks So Good To Me   Hart; Rodgers
He Say Go I Say No   Rainger
Hear O Israel   Gilbert
Heart of Stone   Waller
Heartache   Hoffman
Heaven on Earth   Hoffman
Heavenly Night   Brown, Nacio Herb; Eliscu
Heigh Ho, the Gang's All Here   Adamson; Lane
Hello Beautiful!   Donaldson
Hello, Good Morning   Gershwin, George; Gershwin, Ira
Hello, My Lover, Goodbye   Heyman
Help Yourself to Happiness   Gordon; Revel
Here Come the Waiters   Hanley
Here It Is   Brown, Lew; Henderson
Here We Are in Love   Oakland
Here's a Kiss for Cinderella   Gershwin, George; Gershwin, Ira
High and Low   Dietz; Schwartz, Arthur
Hikin' Down the Highway   Kahal
Hilltop Heaven   Coots; Eliscu
Hittin' the Trail for Hallelujah Land   Bloom; Young, Joseph
Ho-Hum   Heyman
Honest, Really, Truly   Ahlert; Turk
Honestly   Bryan
Hoops   Dietz; Schwartz, Arthur
Hosanna   Robin
Hot Dog, A Blanket and You, A   Coots
Hot Feet   Gordon; Revel
Hot Harlem   Johnson, James P.
Hot Moonlight   Gorney; Harburg
Hot Rhythm   Johnson, James P.
Hour of Parting, The   Kahn
How About It   Hart; Rodgers
How About Me Calling You My Sweetheart   Snyder
How Beautiful   Gershwin, George; Gershwin, Ira

How Can a Girl Say No   Heyman

How Can I Change My Luck   Berlin

How Can You Say You Love Me   Ahlert; Turk

How Do You Like My Eyes   Wrubel

How Happy Is the Bride   Heyman; Youmans

How I React to You   Hammerstein; Whiting

How the Time Can Fly whenever I'm with You   Donaldson

How's Your Uncle?   Fields; McHugh

Hula Love Tune   Freed, Arthur

Huntsman's Song of Love, The   Robin

I Apologize   Hoffman

I Belong to Everybody   Brown, Nacio Herb; Eliscu

I Can Sympathize with You   Davis

I Can't Get Along Without My Baby   Mills

I Can't Get Mississippi Off My Mind   Akst; Young, Joseph

I Can't Get Used to Being Your Used to Be   Burke

I Can't Go on This Way   Robin; Whiting

I Don't Know Why, I Just Do   Ahlert; Turk

I Don't Suppose   Kahn

(If This Is Love) I Don't Want Love   Heyman

I Found a Million Dollar Baby in a Five and Ten Cent Store   Dixon; Rose; Warren

I Get a Kick Out of You   Porter

I Hate You Because I Love You   Gilbert

I Have You   Yellen

I Hope You'll Like It   Kahn

I Keep on Believing in You   Kahn

I Like You   Gordon; Revel

I Look at You and a Song Is Born   Rainger

I Love a Parade   Arlen; Koehler

I Love Him, the Rat   Hammerstein; Whiting

I Love Louisa   Dietz; Schwartz, Arthur

I Love You As Much As I Love Myself   Baer; Gilbert

I Love You More Each Day   Parish

I Only Love One   Lerner, Sammy

I Qual Que Tu   Gorney

I Saw Your Eyes   Hammerstein; Romberg

I See My Mother in You   Fisher

I Should Have Known Better   Coots; Davis

I Still Love the Red, White and Blue   Porter

I Stumbled Over You and Fell in Love   Gordon; Revel

I Thank You, Mr. Moon   Baer

I Understand Tonight   Coslow

I Wanna Be Around My Baby All the Time   Meyer; Young, Joseph

I Wanna Be Kissed   Brown, Nacio Herb

I Wanna Be Loved   Heyman; Rose

I Wanna Count Sheep Till the Cows Come Home   Young, Joseph

I Wanna Sing about You   Friend

I Want a Man   Hart; Rodgers

I Want to Dream By the Old Mill Stream   Bryan

I Want Your for Myself   Berlin

I Was Born to Be Loved   Clare

I Was the Most Beautiful Blossom   Gershwin, George; Gershwin, Ira

I Watch the Love Parade (Crystal Candalabra)   Harbach; Kern

I Will Love You Tomorrow and Tomorrow   Parish

I Wish I Could Laugh at Love   Dixon; Warren; Young, Joseph

I Wish Someone Was Waiting for Me   Bryan

I Wish There Were a Television to Heaven   Parish; Silver

I Wonder Where Sweet Genevieve Can Be   Parish

I Wonder Who's Under the Moon with You Tonight   Coots; Davis

I Won't Give Up Till You Give In   Robin; Whiting

I Worship You   Porter

Ice Man Live in an Ice House, The   Waller

Ich Denk' Oft an Meine Jugendzeit   Lerner, Sammy

I'd Be a Fool   Hammerstein; Romberg

I'd Like to Tie You to My Heart Strings   Burke

I'd Like You to Like Me to Like You   Lane

Ida, I Don't Wanna Be Blue   Leslie; Meyer; Young, Joseph

If He Really Loves Me   Arlen; Yellen

If I Could Live My Life All Over Again   Gordon; Revel

If I Could Only Have My Way   Razaf

If I Didn't Have You   Ager; Harburg

If I Had a Girl   Hammerstein

If I Had a Girl Like You   Romberg

If I Had Been So Sure of You   Clare; Stept

If I Have to Go On Without You   Dubin; Woods

If I Thought I Could Live Without You I'd Die   Brown, Lew; Henderson

If It's Good Enough for the Birds and Bees, It's Good Enough for You and Me   Friend

If Little If Were Not a Word (Ja, Wenn Das Wortchen Wenn Nicht War)   Young, Joseph

If Mother Has a Radio in Heaven   Bryan

If Someone Should Kiss Me Tonight While I'm Dreaming   Hanley

If They Ever Had an Income Tax on Love   Monaco; Washington

If You Can't Be Good in Hollywood, Be as Good as You Can   Hanley

If You Haven't Got Love   Brown, Lew; DeSylva; Henderson

If You Knew You'd Hurt Somebody, Why Did It Have to Be Me   Stept

If You Should Ever Need Me   Dubin

If You Want to Be Successful in the Cinema   Gordon; Revel

If You Were Mine   Lerner, Sammy

If You're Happy, I'll Be Glad   Johnson, Howard

Igual Que Tu   Gorney; Harburg

I'll Always Remember September   Hoffman

I'll Be a Star   Hart; Rodgers

I'll Come Back to You   Heyman; Youmans

I'll Give All My Tomorrows for Just One Yesterday   Kahn

I'll Love You in My Dreams   Baer

I'll Make a Happy Landing (The Lucky Day I Land You)   Fields; McHugh

I'll Make a Home for You in This Heart of Mine   Harburg

I'll Miss You in the Evening   Berlin

I'll Never Stand in Your Way   Silver

I'll Smile Away Your Sorrows, and Kiss Away Your Tears   Conrad

I'll Take You To Paradise   Brown, Nacio Herb

Illegitimate Daughter, The   Gershwin, George; Gershwin, Ira

I'm a Beggar of Love   Lewis

I'm About to Be a Mother (Who Could Ask for Anything More?)   Gershwin, George; Gershwin, Ira

I'm Afraid to Waltz with You   Coslow

I'm All Dressed Up With a Broken Heart   Fisher

I'm All Wrapped Up in You   Adamson; Gordon; Revel

I'm Always on the Wrong Side of the Right Girl   Lewis

I'm an Unemployed Sweetheart Looking for Somebody to Love   Leslie; Monaco; Washington

I'm Bidding My Buddy Good-Bye   Dixon; Woods

I'm Counting on You   Monaco; Washington

I'm Crazy About My Baby, and My Baby's Crazy 'Bout Me   Waller
I'm Falling in Love   Caesar
I'm Feelin' Blue   Fields; McHugh
I'm for You One Hundred Percent   Rose
I'm Getting Superstitious About Delicious You   Spina
I'm Glad I Said I'm Sorry   Coots
I'm Glad I'm Here   Heyman
I'm Happy When You're Happy   Baer; Davis
I'm in Love with a Voice on the Radio   Kahal
I'm in that Mood   Brown, Lew; Henderson
I'm Just a Fool in Love with You   Meyer; Mitchell
I'm Lonesome in Your Arms   Bryan
I'm Mad at Me   Heyman
I'm Makin' Hay While the Sun Shines, By Makin' Hey Hey Under the Moon   Burke
I'm More than Satisfied   Lawrence
I'm on My Own   Adamson
I'm on the Right Side of the Right Girl Now   Coots; Davis
I'm Only Guessin'   Brown, Nacio Herb; Egan
I'm Painting Pictures   Leslie; Monaco
I'm Saying Goodbye to You While the Music Plays   Carroll
I'm So Backward and She's So Forward   Fields; McHugh
I'm So in Love with You   Ellington; Mills
I'm Spending too Much Time By Myself   Fain; Kahal
I'm Still in Love with You   Snyder
I'm Thankful   Johnston
I'm Through with Love   Kahn
I'm Treatin' Myself to a Birds-Eye View of Heaven   Lane
I'm Walkin' on Air   Lewis
I'm Wide Awake when I Dream   Gilbert
I'm with You   Donaldson
In a Cabaret in Old Paree   Fain; Kahal
In a Garret in Old Paree   Fain; Young, Joseph
In a Little Bamboo Bungaloo   Robin
In a Little Patio Down in Mexico   Coots
In a Silly Little Hilly Billy Town   Dubin
In Californ-i-a   Hart; Rodgers
In Love with a Memory of You   Loesser
In My Looking Glass of Dreams   Wrubel
In My Ohio Home To-Night   Schwartz, Jean
In Old Nantucket By the Sea   Bryan; Schwartz, Jean
In Perfect Harmony   Hoffman
In the Candle Light   Young, Joseph
In the Heart of Old Paree   Robin; Whiting
In the Merry Month of Maybe   Gershwin, Ira; Rose; Warren
In the Shanty Where Santy Claus Lives   Woods
In the Twee Twee Twilight   Parish
In the Valley of the Moon   Hanley
In Winter Dear I Love You   Snyder
Innocent Chorus Girls of Yesterday   Hart; Rodgers
Inside Story, The   Heyman
Instead of You   Robin
Invitation, An   Heyman; Youmans
Is It All a Dream   Dietz; Schwartz, Arthur
Is Rhythm Necessary   Fain; Kahal
Is This the Music of Love?   Coslow; Rainger
Islands of Love   Freed, Arthur
It Better Be Good   Dietz; Schwartz, Arthur
It Costs Nothing to Dream   Fields; McHugh
It Doesn't Pay to Fall in Love   Young, Joseph
It Looks Like Susie   Friend
It Means So Little to You   Heyman
It's a Beautiful Day to Be Glad   Coslow
It's a Girl Like You   Magidson

It's a Happy World   Harburg
It's a Long Time Between Kisses   Akst; Kahn; Whiting
It's a Wonderful World   Hammerstein; Romberg
It's Different with Me   Arlen; Yellen
It's Easy as A.B.C.   Lewis
It's Every Girl's Ambition   Heyman; Youmans
It's Great to Be in Love   Friend
It's in the Air   Alter; Harburg; Rose
It's Moonlight on the Prairie, Mary   Conrad
It's My Nature   Heyman
It's No Use Trying to Leave that Man   Coslow
It's Probably Just as Well   Porter
It's Raining Tonight in Jersey   Hanley
It's the Darndest Thing   Fields; McHugh
It's the Girl!   Baer
It's the Same Old Play with a New Leading Man   Burke
It's the Yacka Hula in Me   Stept
It's Up to You   Conrad; Friend
I've a Feeling You'll Say Yes To-Day   Young, Joseph
I've Fallen Out of Love   Gordon; Revel
I've Got a Communistic Feeling for You   Wrubel
I've Got a New Sweetheart Now   Friend
I've Got Ants in My Pants (Bugology)   Friend
I've Got Five Dollars   Hart; Rodgers
I've Got the Blues for You   Kahn
I've Got You on My Mind   Porter
I've Just Got Eyes for Susie   Lewis; Woods
Jacob's Ladder   Johnson, J. Rosamond; Wrubel
Je T'Aime   Hoffman
Jealousy   Gordon; Revel
Jilted   Gershwin, George; Gershwin, Ira
June Time Is the Love Time for Everyone but Me   Clare
Just a Blue-Eyed Blonde   Kahn
Just a Little Bit of Lovin' When You're Feeling Lonesome   Fisher
Just a Little Sweeter than the Rest   Lerner, Sammy
Just a Minute More to Say Good-Bye   Lewis
Just Another Dream of You   Burke
Just Another Love Affair   Yellen
Just Another Night   Conrad
Just Another Rendezvous   Lewis
Just Another Romance, Now I Know It's Love   Conrad
Just Because You Used to Be an Old Sweetheart of Mine   Lewis
Just Begging for Love   Berlin
Just Eighteen   Hammerstein; Whiting
Just Friends   Lewis
Just Like Frankie and Johnnie   Kahal
Just One More Chance   Coslow; Johnston
Kathleen, Mine   Heyman; Youmans
Katinkitschka   Gershwin, George; Gershwin, Ira
Keep Doing It   Hanley
Kept in Suspense   Rose
Key to My Heart, The   Alter; Gershwin, Ira
Kickin' the Gong Around   Arlen; Koehler
Kinda Like You   Heyman; Youmans
Kismet   Edwards
Kiss an Make Up with Baby   Egan
Kiss Me Back to Heaven   Fain; Kahal
Kiss Me Goodnight, Not Goodbye   Hanley
La Bella Fiorentina   Caesar
Ladies and Gentlemen that's Love   Brown, Lew; Henderson
Ladies of the Evening   Harburg; Rose
Lady Must Live, A   Hart; Rodgers
Lady Tambourine   Koehler

Laugh Parade, The   Dixon; Warren; Young, Joseph

Laughing While My Heart Is Breaking   Baer; Lewis; Young, Joseph

Lazy River   Carmichael

Learn to Croon   Arlen; Yellen

Lease in My Heart   Fain; Kahal

Lenox Avenue   Caesar

Lesson in Love (Business Rhythm), A   Oakland

Let Me Hum a Hymn to Her Tonight   Young, Joseph

Let's Get Friendly   Yellen

Let's K'nock K'nees   Gordon; Revel

Life Is a Dream   Freed, Arthur

Life Is a Song Let's Sing It Together   Stept

Life Is Just a Bowl of Cherries   Brown, Lew; Henderson

Like a Falling Star   Mercer

Like Ordinary People Do   Hart; Rodgers

Listen to the German Band   Gordon; Revel

Little Brown Betty   Waller

Little Homestead   Davis

Little Hunka Love   Donaldson

Little Joe   Styne

Little Less of Moonlight (A Little More of You), A   Kahal

Little Mascot (Du Bist Mein Mascottchen)   Young, Joseph

Little Old Church in the Valley, The   Kahn

Little Too Late, A   Kahn

Live and Love Tonight   Coslow

Living in Sin   Hammerstein; Whiting

Lo and Behold   Heyman

Lolita   Fields; McHugh

Lonely Little Extras   Gordon; Revel

Longer that You Linger in Virginia, the More You Long to Stay, The   Donaldson

Look in the Looking Glass   Heyman

Looking Thru My Dreams   Burke

Lost without You   Coots; Davis

Love Alone Lives On   Bloom; Koehler

Love Came Into My Heart   Adamson; Lane

Love Cannot Die   Heyman; Youmans

Love Goes on Just the Same   Baer; Kahal

Love Is Sweeping the Country   Gershwin, George; Gershwin, Ira

Love Letters in the Sand   Coots

Love Magician   Fields; McHugh

Love Me Forever   Dixon; Warren; Young, Joseph

Love Songs   Leslie; Meyer

Lovely Lady of My Dreams   Brown, Lew; Henderson

Lover Where Are You   Leslie

Lover's Luck   Fain; Kahal

Lucille   Donaldson

Ma Mere   Caesar; Warren

Mahatma Gandhi   Lewis

Mahoneyphone, The   Adamson; Lane

Mailu   Gorney; Harburg

Make Up Your Mind   Burke

Make Your Life a Ballgame   Wrubel

Make Yourself at Home   Clare

Makin' Faces at the Man in the Moon   Hoffman; Washington

Making the Best of Each Day   Clare

Mama Don't Want No Peas an' Rice an' Cocoanut Oil   Gilbert; Johnson, J. Rosamond

Mama Inez   Gilbert

Man in the Sky   Harbach; Kern

Man with the Lantern of Love, The   Dixon; Leslie; Meyer

Many Happy Returns of the Day   Dubin

Mardi Gras (While We Danced at the Mardi Gras)   Mercer

Maria My Own (Intermedia, Maria La O)   Gilbert

Marta, Rambling Rose of the Wildwood   Gilbert

Mary I'm in Love with You   Coots

Mary Jane   Razaf

Masquerade   Webster

May I Have the Next Dance with You?   Burke

Maybe It's the Moon   Whiting

Me!   Berlin

Me Minus You   Baer

Men and Women Are Awful   Hammerstein; Whiting

Metropolitan (inst.)   Bloom

Millie   Brown, Nacio Herb

Mine Completely   Clare

Minnie   Hammerstein; Romberg

Minnie the Moocher (The Ho Do Ho Song)   Mills

Minstrel Dance   Edwards

Miserable with You   Dietz; Schwartz, Arthur

Misery   Johnson, James P.; Razaf

Mister and Missus Fitch   Porter

Moanin'   Mills; Parish

Moment I Think of You, The   Hoffman

Monkey on a String   Hanley

Monongaheela   Fisher

Montmartre   Revel

Mood Indigo   Ellington; Mills; Parish

Moon Music   Magidson

Moonlight Memory, A   Kahn

Moonlight Nights in Nassau   Gilbert

(There Ought to Be a) Moonlight Saving Time   Kahal

Moonlight Sweetheart   Coots; Davis

More You Hurt Me, the More You Make Me Care, The   Dixon; Warren; Young, Joseph

Mother Indiana   Bryan; Schwartz, Jean

Mother's Prayer, A   Gilbert

Movin' Day   Johnson, James P.

Mr. Doland Is Passing Through   Hart; Rodgers

Muchacha   Duke; Gorney; Harburg

Mush   Hanley

Music Hath Charms   Oakland

Music in My Fingers   Heyman

Must It Be the End   Kalmar; Ruby

My Baby Said Yes, Yes   Friend

My Bathing Suit   Heyman

My Bluebird's Back Again   Friend

My Canary Has Circles Under His Eyes   Koehler

My Cymbalum   Brown, Nacio Herb

My Feelin's Are Hurt (inst.)   Waller

My Fortune Is Love   Harburg

My Goodbye to You   Kahn

My Heart Is Young   Heyman; Youmans

My Heart's a Banjo   Gorney; Harburg

My Lips Tell the World It's All Over but My Heart Says 'I Love You'   Friend

My Little Prayer   Gorney; Harburg

My Love Will Never Grow Old   Razaf

My Moonlight Rosary   Stept; Young, Joseph

My Name's Marie, Who Wants to Be My Peanut Vendor   Brown, Lew; Henderson

My Racket Is You   Hanley

My Secret Love   Coots

My Song   Brown, Lew; Henderson

My Sweet   Hart; Rodgers

My Sweetheart 'Tis of Thee   Heyman

My Temptation   Dubin

My Who! My What! My Why!   Fisher
Mysteriously   Porter
Nanette   Dietz; Schwartz, Arthur
'Neath the Pale Cuban Moon   Arlen; Koehler
Nevada Moonlight   Hammerstein; Whiting
Never Was There a Girl So Fair   Gershwin, George;
     Gershwin, Ira
Nevertheless I'm in Love with You   Kalmar; Ruby
New Love Is Old, A   Harbach; Kern
New Sun in the Sky   Dietz; Schwartz, Arthur
New York Rhapsody   Gershwin, George; Gershwin, Ira
New York Town   Wrubel
Nichevo Means Yes   Robin
Night Our Love Song Was Born, The   Freed, Arthur;
     Woods
Night Was Made for Love, The   Harbach; Kern
Nighty Night Until Tomorrow   Magidson
Nina   Razaf
No Me Creas   Gorney; Harburg
Nobody Knows (Just What It Is But Me)   Burke
Nobody Loves a Riveter   Hart; Rodgers
Nobody Loves No Baby Like My Baby Loves
     Me   Donaldson
Nobody's Baby Is Somebody's Baby Now   Kahn
Nobody's Fool   Fields; McHugh
Nod, Nod, Nod, Little Golden Rod   Fain; Kahal
Noisy Neighbors   Johnson, James P.
Not that I Care   Hammerstein; Whiting
Notre Dame Marie   Bryan
Now I Ask You What Would You Do   Robin; Whiting
Now I Believe   Hart; Rodgers
Now That You're Gone   Kahn
Now You're in My Arms   Wrubel
Nudist Colony   Berlin
O Baby, I Go for You   Snyder
O! Mister Carpenter   Akst; Eliscu
Of Thee I Sing (Baby)   Gershwin, George; Gershwin, Ira
Oh, Couldn't I Love that Girl   Hammerstein; Romberg
Oh Donna Clara   Caesar
Oh! I'd Love to Be a Sailor (When a Sailor's Making
     Love)   Clare
Oh, It Looks Like Rain   Ager; Harburg
Oh, My Yes   Adamson; Lane
Oh Tell, Oh Tell Me Honey   Caesar; Motzan
Oh! What a Thrill to Hear It from You   Hoffman
Ohhh! Ahhh!   Heyman
Old Fashioned Home in New Hampshire, An   Lewis
Old Man Blues   Oakland
On a Certain Sunday   Gordon; Revel
On a Little Journey in Springtime with You   Robin
On My Word of Honor   Hoffman
On the Other Side of the Moon   Monaco; Washington
Once in May   Kahn
One Day of Love   Willson
One Finger Joe   Bloom; Koehler
One in a Million   Gordon; Revel
One Little Hour with You   Buck
One Little Kiss from You   Young, Joseph
One Little Quarrel   Hoffman
One Little Word from You   Kalmar; Ruby
One Love   Freed, Arthur
One Moment Alone   Harbach; Kern
One More Kiss   Magidson
One More Time   Brown, Lew; DeSylva; Henderson
One of Us Was Wrong   Kahn

One Second of Sex   Heyman
Only a Voice on the Air   Dubin
Only, Only, Only in My Dreams   Brown, Lew; Henderson
Only Your Heart Can Tell   Gilbert
Ooh Hoo, You-hoo, Don't Cha Know the Moon Is
     New-hoo   Woods
Ooh that Kiss   Dixon; Warren; Young, Joseph
Open Up Those Eyes   Heyman
Open Your Eyes   Hammerstein; Whiting
Opening Act One (Street Vendors)   Kern
Opportunity Has Beckoned   Gershwin, George; Gershwin,
     Ira
(You Came Along From) Out of Nowhere   Heyman
Out Where the North Begins   Gilbert
Pagan Moon   Bryan; Dubin
Parisian Lover   Coslow; Johnston
Peanut Vendor   Gilbert
Pell Street Blues   Fisher
Peter Pan   Rose
Pick Me Up and Lay Me Down   Porter
Pie Eyed Piper   Fain; Kahal
Police of New York   Berlin
Poor Kid   Gilbert
Poor Marionette   Kahn
Poor Pierrot   Harbach; Kern
Posterity Is Just Around the Corner   Gershwin, George;
     Gershwin, Ira
Presents from Home   Bryan; Hoffman
Primitive (inst.)   Bloom
Prison College Song   Hanley
Prisoner of Love   Robin
Promise You'll Remember Me (For I'll Remember
     You)   Brown, Nacio Herb
Psychoanalyst Me   Hammerstein; Whiting
Punch and Judy Man   Dixon; Warren; Young, Joseph
Quando te Digo te Amo No Me Creas   Gorney; Harburg
Queen Was in the Parlor, The   Freed, Arthur
Queen's Mules, The   Friend; Monaco
Racketeer Rose   Fisher
Reaching for the Moon   Berlin
Red Devil   Mills
Red, Red Roses and Pale White Moonlight   Coslow
Redheaded Baby   Coots; Davis
Reflections of You   Gilbert; Pollack
Regardez-moi   Hammerstein; Romberg
Rest of My Life Is Yours, The   Hoffman
Rest Room Rose   Hart; Rodgers
Rhumbatism   Gordon
Rhyming Song, The   Lerner, Sammy
Rhythm for Sale   Razaf
Rhythm of the Day   Oakland
Ridin' but Walkin' (inst.)   Waller
Right Across the Way   Ahlert; Turk
Rip the Blues from the Blue Skies   Fisher
Road to Home, The   Heyman; Youmans
Rock Me in a Cradle of Kalua   Bryan
Rock Me in a Rocky Mountain Cradle   Bryan
Rockin' in Rhythm   Ellington
Rosalinda   Gilbert
Rose of the Rancho   Coslow
'Round My Kingdom's Door   Hanley
Rumba Made a Hot Number of Me, The   Meyer; Mitchell
Rumbatism   Revel
Rumbola   Johnson, James P.
Russian Song   Hammerstein; Whiting

Salem Town   Bryan
Satan   Loesser
Satan Leads the Band   Arlen; Koehler
Say Hello to the Folks Back Home   Davis
Say It!   Harburg
Say the Word   Adamson; Lane
Scene on the Dock   Fields; McHugh
Senatorial Roll Call, The   Gershwin, George; Gershwin, Ira
Send Me Your Love (Er und Seine Schwester)   Robin
(There I Go Again) Sentimental Me   Lawrence
Sevilla   Eliscu
Shadows on the Wall   Fisher; Gordon; Revel
Shake Well Before Using   Heyman
She Didn't Say Yes   Harbach; Kern
She's So Nice   Coots; Davis
She's Somebody's Baby   Burke
She's the Sister of Annabelle Lee   Clare; Pollack
Shoes   Hanley
Sholom Aleichem   Gilbert
Shop of Santa Claus   Egan
Silver Nights in Honolulu   Hanley
Since an Angel Like Mary Loves a Devil Like Me   Leslie;
    Meyer; Young, Joseph
Sing a Little Jingle   Dixon; Warren
Sing Me a Hill-Billy Song   Heyman
Sing Sing Again of an Old Shady Lane   Fain; Kahal
Singin' the Blues   Fields; McHugh
Sittin' on a Rubbish Can   Burke
Sleeping Beauty   Hammerstein; Romberg
Slumber Song (Goodnight)   Hammerstein; Whiting
Snake Hips (inst.)   McHugh
Snuggled on Your Shoulder, Cuddled in Your Arms   Young,
    Joseph
So Lonesome   Johnson, J. Rosamond
So Long   Young, Joseph
(If I Hadn't Been) So Sure of You   Stept
Some Girls Can Bake a Pie   Gershwin, George; Gershwin,
    Ira
Somebody from Somewhere   Gershwin, George; Gershwin,
    Ira
Someone Loves You   Parish
Something Seems to Tell Me   Caesar
Something's Gonna to Happen to Me and You   Johnson,
    James P.
Song for Reri   Gorney
Song of a Lonesome Guitar, The   Parish
Song of the Foreign Legion (Foreign Legion
    Number)   Brown, Lew; Henderson
Southern Charms   Bloom; Koehler
Spanita, a Gigolo Here, a Gigolo There   Fisher
Spring Holiday   Bloom; Koehler
Starlight, Help Me Find the One I Love   Young, Joseph
Stasha   Lerner, Sammy
Stolen Dreams (Who Steals All My Dreams?)   Harbach;
    Kern
Story of My Love for You, The   Johnson, Howard
Strange As It Seems   Duke; Harburg
Strangers   Coots
Strike the Loud-Resounding Zither   Gershwin, George;
    Gershwin, Ira
Strike Up the Band   Brown, Nacio Herb; Freed, Arthur
Suavacito (Sweet and Tender)   Gilbert
Such Is Life, Such Is Love   Gordon; Revel
Sugar   Meyer; Young, Joseph
Sugar Beat   Rainger

Suzette   Harbach; Kern
Sweet and Hot   Arlen; Yellen
Sweet Geraldine   Hart; Rodgers
Sweet Music   Dietz; Schwartz, Arthur
Sweet Nellie Brown   Caesar; Motzan
Sweetheart of the Moon   Egan
Sweetheart on the Rhine (Du Blonde Lindenwirtin Vom
    Rhein)   Young, Joseph
Tabu   Coslow
Take It from Me, I'm Takin' to You   Waller
Talking to My Shadow on the Wall   Coots; Davis
Tango D'Amour   Hammerstein; Romberg
Tee Total   Egan
Tell Me with a Love Song   Arlen; Koehler
Temporarily Blue   Fain; Kahal
Tennessee Dan   Hart; Rodgers
Thanks to You   Clarke; Gershwin, George; Gershwin, Ira
That Night in Montmartre   Heyman
That Rare Romance   Hammerstein; Romberg
That's All (inst.)   Waller
That's Good, That's Bad   Fain; Kahal
That's My Opinion of You   Bryan; Schwartz, Jean
That's the Time a Fellow Needs a Girl   Clare; Stept; Young,
    Joseph
That's What I Like about You   Donaldson
That's Where You'll Find Me   Coslow
That's Why Darkies Were Born   Brown, Lew; Henderson
That's Why I'm Jealous of You   Fain; Kahal
There Are No Bad Times for Wifey, and My Good Times Are
    Here   Young, Joseph
There Goes the Girl for Me   Kahn
There Is No One Like You   Clare
There Will Be a Girl (There Will Be a Boy)   Gordon; Revel
There's a New Moon Shining Through the Old Apple
    Tree   Egan; Kahn; Whiting
There's a Ring Around the Moon   Lewis
There's a Time and Place for Everything   Ahlert; Turk
There's Love in the Air   Fields; McHugh
There's No Depression in Love   Yellen
There's No Other Girl, After Loving You   Davis
There's Nothing Too Good for My Baby   Akst; Davis
There's Rhythm in the River   Webster
There's So Much More   Hart; Rodgers
These Tropics   Hammerstein; Romberg
They Learn About Woman from Me   Arlen; Yellen
They'll All Be There but Me   Fain; Kahal
Think a Little Kindly of Me   Johnson, Howard; Woods
Think of Me, I'll Be Thinking of You   Kahn
This Is the Missus   Brown, Lew; Henderson
Those Lonesome Nights   Akst; Kahn; Whiting
Those Were the Good Old Days   Brown, Lew; Henderson
Though You're not the First One   Dubin
Three Dames Ziegfeld Failed to Glorify, The   Johnson, J.
    Rosamond
Three Little Girls in Blue   Johnston
Thrill Is Gone, The   Brown, Lew; Henderson
Through the Years   Heyman; Youmans
Thumpin' 'n' Bumpin'   Johnson, James P.; Razaf
Tiddle de Winka and Blinken and Kinky Koo   Schwartz,
    Jean
Tiddle de Winks and Blinken and Kinky Koo   Bryan
Tillie the Toiler   Coots
Tinkle Song, The   Woods
To Be Worthy of You   Coots; Davis
To Have and Hold You in My Arms   Dubin

To Remind Me of You   Kahn
To Think that Once We Were Sweethearts (And Now We're Not Even Friends)   Leslie; Monaco; Rose
Today, Tomorrow, Forever   Ager
Tom-Boy   Young, Joseph
Tonight   Hammerstein; Whiting
Tonight or Never   Hart; Rodgers
Too Late   Lewis; Young, Victor
Torch Song, The   Dixon; Warren; Young, Joseph
Trail Through Lonesome Valley Is the Trail of Long Lost Dreams, The   Burke
Tramps at Sea   Fields; McHugh
Treat Me Like a Baby   Razaf
Trickeration   Arlen; Koehler
True and Sincere Love   Gilbert
True to You   Parish
Trumpeter and the Lover, The   Heyman; Youmans
Trumpeter, Blow Your Horn   Gershwin, George; Gershwin, Ira
Try to Forget   Harbach; Kern
Trying to Forget (Where the Sweet Forget-Me-Nots Grow)   Coots; Davis
Turn that Frown Upside Down, Smile at the Cockeyed World   Stept; Young, Joseph
Two Blue Eyes, One Little Green Isle   Bryan
Two Cheers Instead of Three   Berlin
Two Heads in the Moonlight Are Better than One   Freed, Arthur
Two Little Blue Little Eyes   Webster
Two Little Eyes, Two Little Lips, One Little Nose (Deux Jolis Yeux, Une Nez Charmant, Deux Levres Roses)   Motzan
Two Little Eyes, Two Little Lips, One Little Rose   Caesar
Two Unfortunate Orphans   Hart; Rodgers
U.C.L.A. Rally Song   Coslow
Un Sueno   Coslow
Under a Roof in Paree (Sous les Toits de Paris)   Caesar
Under Your Window Tonight   Clare
Unemployed Papa, Charity Workin' Mama, You Can't Take Advantage of Me   Razaf
Until the End   Young, Victor
Valse Petite (inst.)   Bloom
Victim of the Talkies   Oakland
Vienna, Home of Songs (Wien, Du Stadt der Lieder)   Young, Joseph
Vision of the Future, A   Gilbert
Walkin' on Air   Gordon; Revel
Waltz Me Again with Your Heart   Fisher
Waltz Me to Sleep in Your Arms   Monaco
Waltz of the Dreamers   Myrow
Was That the Human Thing to Do   Fain; Young, Joseph
Was Your Heart in Your Song   Egan
We Know Reno   Heyman
We Salute You Admiral Byrd   Baer; Gilbert
Wearin' Off the Green   Fields; McHugh
Wedding Day in Flowerland   Bryan
We'll Be the Same   Hart; Rodgers
We'll Dance Until the Dawn   Fields; McHugh
Well, You See, I, Oh, You Know   Heyman
We're a Couple of Soldiers, My Baby and Me   Woods
We're Goin' Together Once More   Ahlert; Turk
We're Gonna Have a Happy New Year All Year Round   Hoffman
We've Got to Put that Sun Back in the Sky   Kahal
Wha'd Ja Do to Me?   Ager
What a Little Bit of Love Will Do   Fisher

What Am I Gonna Do for Lovin'   Hoffman; Magidson
What Can I Do, I Love that Man   Freed, Arthur
What Did I Get for Loving You   Conrad
What Did You Do with It?   Kalmar; Ruby
What Do I Have to Do (To Make You Do What I Want You To)?   Ahlert; Turk
What Do the Dickey-Birds Say   Akst; Kahn; Whiting
What Do We Care?   Arlen; Yellen
What Good Would Be Tomorrow Without You Dear?   Freed, Ralph
What Happened to the Couple Next Door   Fain; Kahal
What Have I Done?   Johnson, James P.
What Have We Got to Do Tonight but Dance   Kahn
What Price Love!   Akst; Davis
What'd We Come to College For?   Arlen; Yellen
What's Become of Spring   Harbach; Kern
What's the Difference   Heyman
What's the Matter with Harry   Heyman
When He Waltzed in the Dark   Meyer
When I Can't Be with You   Johnson, James P.; Razaf
When I Discovered Sweet You   Hoffman
When I Look in the Book of My Memory   Lerner, Sammy
When I Sat on Your Doorstep and You Sat on My Knee   Conrad
When I Take My Sugar to Tea   Fain; Kahal
When Our Hearts Go Waltzing Along (Mein Herz Hat Leise Dein Herz Gegrusst)   Young, Joseph
When Our Love Was New   Parish
When Spring Breaks Through   Bloom; Koehler
When the Autumn Leaves of Life Begin to Fall   Brown, Lew; DeSylva; Henderson
When the Clock Is Striking Twelve   Eliscu
When the Folks High-Up Do that Mean Low-Down   Berlin
When the Lord Created Adam   Blake; Razaf
When the Old Oaken Bucket Was New   Meyer; Young, Joseph
When the Rain Goes Pitter Patter (inst.)   Schwartz, Arthur
When the Rest of the Crowd Goes Home I Always Go Home Alone   Dubin
When the Roses Bloom Again in Normandy   Bryan
When the Shepherd Leads His Flock Back Home   Warren
When the Shepherd Leads His Flock (The Sheep) Back Home   Leslie
When We Put Two and Two Together We Found Ourselves in Love   Burke; Monaco
When We Waltzed in the Dark   Bryan; Lewis; Meyer; Young, Joseph
When You Are Young   Hammerstein; Romberg
When You Find the One You Love   Friend
When You Were the Blossom of Butter Cup Lane and I Was Your Little Boy Blue   Bryan; Dubin; Meyer
When Your Boy Becomes a Man   Hammerstein; Whiting
Where Can He Be?   Dietz; Schwartz, Arthur
Where in the World Is the Moon To-Night   Fain; Young, Joseph
Where the Blue of the Night Meets the Gold of the Day   Ahlert; Turk
Where the Four Leaf Clovers Grow   Parish
Where the Lilies of the Valley Grow   Kahn
Where Were You Last Night   Dubin; Woods
Where's My Happy Ending?   Adamson; Gordon; Revel
While Canoeing Along with You   Lawrence
While We're Waiting for the Baby   Gershwin, George; Gershwin, Ira
While You Are Young   Arlen; Yellen

While You're Crying in My Face, You Laugh Behind My Back   Fisher
Whisper to the Whisp'ring Pines   Hanley
Whisper Waltz, The   Webster
White Heat   Dietz; Schwartz, Arthur
Who Are You (To Say Adieu)?   Bryan; Pollack
Who Cares   Gershwin, George; Gershwin, Ira
Who Is the Lucky Girl to Be?   Gershwin, George; Gershwin, Ira
Who Killed Who   Oakland
Who Will Want Me   Baer
Who'd Believe   Baer; Davis
Who's Babying My Baby Tonight   Fisher
Who's in Your Arms Tonight?   Warren
Why Dance?   Ahlert; Turk
Why Did I Fall in Love with You   Magidson; Wrubel
Why Shouldn't I   Freed, Arthur
Will You Wait in the Valley for Me   Burke
Wintergreen for President   Gershwin, George; Gershwin, Ira
Wipe that Frown Right Off Your Face   Gordon; Revel
Without Rhythm   Arlen; Koehler
Without that Gal   Donaldson
Without Warning You Kissed Me Goodbye   Hoffman
Woe Is Me   Willson
Worryin' All Night Long   Kahn
Wrap Your Troubles in Dreams (And Dream Your Troubles Away)   Koehler
(I'm) Wrapped Up in You   Oakland
Wrong Number   Parish; Silver
Ya' Got Love   Hoffman
Yankee Doodle Doll   Hoffman
Yes, I Love You, Honey   Johnson, James P.
Yes, Sir   Hammerstein; Romberg
Yonkele and Rifkelel   Gilbert
You Ain't Got No Savoir-Fair   Hart; Rodgers
You Are Mine 'Til the End of the Waltz   Razaf
You Are My Sweetheart (Du Bist Mein Liebchen)   Motzan
You Are My Woman   Hammerstein; Romberg
You Call It Madness, but I Call It Love   Conrad
You Called It Love   Hanley
You Can Bet Your Life It's Love   Coots
You Can't Fool a Hula Hula Girl   Meyer; Mitchell
You Can't Mean Maybe with Those Eyes   Donaldson
You Could Have Been the One, Baby   Brown, Lew; DeSylva; Henderson
You Did   Ahlert; Turk
You Didn't Have to Tell Me, I Knew It All the Time   Donaldson
You Didn't Know the Music, I Didn't Know the Words   Coslow
You Didn't Live to Love   Brown, Lew; Henderson
You Don't Have to Be a Sherlock Holmes   Ahlert; Turk
You Don't Know What You're Doin'   Meyer; Young, Joseph
You for Me and Me for You   Edwards
You Forgot Your Gloves   Eliscu
You Gave Me Ev'rything but Love   Kahn
You Gotta Live Today   Gorney; Harburg
You Know That It's All Worth While, The   Kahn
You Leave Me Limp   Brown, Lew; DeSylva; Henderson
You Made Up My Mind for Me   Fisher
You Might As Well Pretend   Eliscu
You Misunderstood   Snyder
You Only Want Me when Nobody Else Is Around   Burke; Monaco
You Really Started Something   Freed, Ralph

You Said It   Arlen; Yellen
You Started It   Gershwin, George; Gershwin, Ira
You Started Something   Gorney; Harburg
You Told Me with Your Eyes, Now Prove It with Your Kisses   Burke
You Try Somebody Else, and I'll Try Somebody Else   Brown, Lew; DeSylva; Henderson
You'll Do   Arlen; Yellen
You'll Fall in Love with Venice   Coslow
You'll Give In   Hanley
You'll Pardon Me If I Reveal   Gershwin, George; Gershwin, Ira
Young Man in Love   Hammerstein; Romberg
Your Sunny Southern Smile (I'm All Wrapped Up in You)   Gordon; Revel
You're Baby Minded Now   Dubin
You're Everywhere   Heyman; Youmans
You're Famous   Hoffman
You're in Every One's Arms (But in Nobody's Heart)   Hoffman
You're in Love   Heyman; Youmans
You're Just About Right for Me   Ahlert; Turk
You're Mine   Fisher
You're My Everything   Dixon; Warren; Young, Joseph
You're not the Same   Kalmar; Ruby
You're the Cats   Hart; Rodgers
You're the First Thing I Pray for Each Morning (Du Bist Mein Morgen - Und Mein Nachtgebetchen)   Young, Joseph
You're the Surest Cure for the Blues   Lerner, Sammy
Yours for the Asking   Friend
You've Got a Lease on My Heart   Fain; Kahal
You've Got to Meet Marguerite   Harbach; Kern
Yvonne's Song   Robin; Whiting
Zwei Hertzen   Gershwin, George; Gershwin, Ira

1932

A la Lenox Avenue   Arlen; Koehler
After Awhile   Ahlert; Leslie
After Tonight   Friend
After Twelve O'Clock   Carmichael; Mercer
After You, Who?   Porter
Ah, But I've Learned   Coots; Turk
Ain't It the Truth   Fields; McHugh
Aintcha Got Music?   Johnson, James P.; Razaf
Ain'tcha Kinda Sorry Now?   Ager
All Aboard   Arlen; Koehler
All Aboard for Dreamland, Baby Kiss Mama and Papa Goodnight   Baer; Young, Joseph
All I Want Is Just One   Robin; Whiting
All of a Sudden   Woods
All that I Ever Get Is Sympathy, All that I Want Is Love   Fisher
All the World Will Smile Again After Tomorrow   Hanley
All's Fair in Love and War   Smith, Harry B.
All's Well   Dietz; Schwartz, Arthur
Alone Together   Dietz; Schwartz, Arthur
Alphabet of Love Begins and Ends with You, The   Mercer
Always in My Heart, Forever on My Mind   Coots; Turk
Am I Awake or Am I Dreaming   Razaf
Am I too Fresh?   Hanley
And Love Was Born   Hammerstein; Kern
And So To Bed   Gordon; Revel
And Still I Came   Heyman
Angeline   Waller

Another Dream Gone Wrong   Hoffman; Lerner, Sammy
Another Night Alone   Arlen; Koehler
Any Time at All   Hoffman
Apple of My Eye, The   Waller; Young, Joseph
April in Paris   Duke; Harburg
Arabian Moon   Blake; Sissle
Are You a Dream   Parish
Are You Listenin'   Young, Victor
Arm in Arm   Washington; Young, Victor
Around the Rainbow (There Is No Color Line)   Caesar
Around You   Robin; Whiting
As Long As I Live   Gordon; Revel
As Long As Love Lives On   Young, Joseph
As Long as We Have   Bromo Seltzer in Our Love
    Nest   Harburg
As the Years Roll By   Hanley; Mitchell
As You Desire Me   Wrubel
Ask Yourself Who Loves You, Tell Yourself It's Me   Davis
At Stony Brook   Hammerstein; Kern
Auditions   Rainger; Robin
Auf Wiedersehen, My Dear   Ager; Hoffman
Baby, We're Through   Harburg
Back Home Among the Carolina Pines   Parish; Snyder
Bahama Mama (That Tropical Charmer) (That Goombay
    Tune)   Gilbert
Ballyhooey Lassies (Opening Act II)   Harburg
Ballyhujah   Harburg
Bandana Ways   Blake; Sissle
Banking on the Weather   Fain; Young, Joseph
Bauer's House   Gershwin, George; Gershwin, Ira
Bed of Roses   Brown, Lew; Henderson
Beggars of Love   Fain; Kahal
Belfry Bells   Young, Joseph
Beside a Wayside   Gordon; Revel
Beside the Coral Sea   Gilbert; Hanley
Beside the Sunset Trail   Hoffman
Best Sweetheart of All, The   Friend
Best Wishes   Ellington; Koehler
Betty Boop   Heyman
Birds of a Feather   Caesar
Bit of Green, a Blade of Grass, A   Wrubel
Blessed Event   Conrad; DeSylva; Silver; Whiting
Blow Gabriel   Eliscu
Blowing of the Breeze Blew You into My Arms   Waller
Blue Drag   Myrow
Blue Dreams   Davis
Blue Moon (I'm As Blue As You)   Friend; Monaco
Blue Music   Parish
Blue Over Two Brown Eyes   Ager
Bootblack Blues   Gordon; Revel
Boswell Weeps, The   Rainger; Robin
Boy and a Girl Were Dancing, A   Gordon; Revel
Bread and Kisses   Gordon; Revel
Breakin' 'Em In   Blake; Sissle
Breakin' My Heart   Waller
Brother Can You Spare a Dime?   Gorney; Harburg
Bubble Dance (Pas Seul) (inst.)   Kern
Buddie   Razaf; Waller
Burmese Babies   Razaf
But Tom-Tom Tommy   Washington
By the Dawn's Early Light   Heyman; Hoffman
Cabin in the Cotton   Arlen; Caesar; Parish
Can It Be Me   Dixon
Candles in the Sky   Kahn
Cane Dance   Gordon; Revel

Can't Get Rid of Me   Gordon; Revel
Can't Take It Papa   Johnson, James P.; Razaf
Can't We Ever Be Alone   Hoffman
Can't We Get Together   Akst; Yellen
Careless Kisses   Brown, Lew; Clare; Stept
Carnival (inst.)   Revel
Carolina Pines   Parish
'Cause You Won't Do Right by Me   Harburg
Celebration   Dietz; Schwartz, Arthur
Charity   Brown, Nacio Herb; DeSylva; Whiting
Charlie Two-Step   Carmichael
Cher Ami (inst.)   Coslow
Cherie, Paree Is Mine (Paris, C'est Toi)   Hanley
Chickens Come Home to Roost   Blake; Sissle
Chip o' the Old Block   Wrubel
Church Bells   Coots; Young, Joseph
Cleaning Up the Floor with Lulu   Hart; Rodgers
Clouds Will Soon Roll By   Woods
Colet and Company   Robin
College Love   Dubin
Come Home   Koehler; Warren
Come Home Prosperity, All Is Forgiven   Caesar
Come on and Sit Beside the Sea   Ahlert; Turk
Come on Baby and Beg for It   Hanley
Conchita   Brown, Lew; Henderson
Confession   Heyman
Congorilla   Bryan
Convention, The   Hart; Rodgers
Cop on the Boat, the Man in the Moon and Me,
    The   Hoffman
Corrine Corrina   Parish
Cottage in the Hills, A   Gilbert; Silver
Country Needs a Man, The   Hart; Rodgers
Crazy People   Leslie; Monaco
Cuckoo Clock, The   Young, Victor
Dancing Butterfly   Young, Joseph
Dancing in the Streets   Gershwin, George; Gershwin, Ira
Danger I Love You   Eliscu
Dat Ol' Devil Sea   Wrubel
Day After Day   Dietz; Schwartz, Arthur
Daybreak   Carmichael
Dear Old Crinoline Days   Berlin
Dear Old Mother Dixie   Kahn
Deep in My Dreams — Deep in the Night   Young, Joseph
Deep in the Heart of the Rockies, Just Across the Great
    Divide   Freed, Ralph
Deep in Your Eyes   Dixon; Warren
Deep Sea Divin' Papa   Arlen; Koehler
Deep South in My Heart   Mercer
Did You Mean What You Said Last Night   Lewis; Young,
    Joseph
Dish Ran Away with the Spoon, The   Robin
Dixie Doorway   Parish
Do Me a Favor, Lend Me a Kiss   Razaf; Waller
Do Say You Do   Adamson; Gordon; Revel
Don't Be Afraid of Love   Dubin
Don't Be Mad at Me   Young, Joseph
Don't Go to Sleep   Freed, Arthur
Don't Let the Parade Pass You By   Young, Joseph
Don't Tell Me, Let Me Guess   De Lange
Dou Dou   Eliscu
Down Around Those Indiana Hills   Davis
Down on the Delta   Stept; Waller
Down the End of the Road   Lewis
Down Thru Melody Lane   Wrubel

Down Where the South Begins   Donaldson; Kahn
Dream of All My Dreams   Coslow; Rainger
Dresden Northwest Mounted, The   Gershwin, George;
    Gershwin, Ira
Drifting Down the Shalimar   Monaco
Dusting Around   Blake; Sissle
Eadie Was a Lady   Brown, Nacio Herb; DeSylva; Whiting
Eat, Drink and Be Merry   Friend; Stept
Elegant Swelegant You   Hoffman; Lerner, Sammy
Enclosed Please Find   Robin; Whiting
End of a Perfect Night   Duke; Harburg
Episode of the Swing   Hammerstein; Kern
Evening   Kahn
Everyone Knows It but You   Coslow; Johnston
Everything is Buttercups and Daisies   Woods
Everything's the Same   Koehler; Myrow; Young, Victor
Ev'ry Little Bit of Me Loves Ev'ry Little Bit of You   Bryan;
    Meyer; Young, Joseph
Ev'ry Time My Heart Beats   Davis
Ev'ryone Says, I Love You   Kalmar; Ruby
Ev'rything's the Same   Koehler
Falling in Love   Blake; Sissle
Falling Off the Wagon   Harburg
Falling Out of Love   Gordon; Revel
Falling Star   Heyman
Fancy Nancy Clancy   Coots; Turk
Fatal Fascination   Dietz; Schwartz, Arthur
Fate   Porter
Fatherland, Mother of the Band   Gershwin, George;
    Gershwin, Ira
Feet in the Gutter, Looking Up at the Stars   Gilbert; Hanley
Feminine Rhythm   Gordon; Revel
Fiddle Just a Little   Spina
Fiesta   Brown, Lew; Henderson
Finery   Gordon; Revel
First Mrs. Frazer, The   Woods
Five Minutes of Spring   Gorney; Harburg
For All You Care   Davis
For Old Times' Sake   Kahn
For You   Brown, Lew; Gordon; Henderson; Revel
Forbidden Love   Lewis
Forever in Your Arms   Parish
Forgetting a Love Affair   Kahal
Forsaken Again   Heyman
Forward March Into My Arms   Gordon; Revel
Freud and Jung and Adler   Gershwin, George; Gershwin, Ira
Funiculi Funicula   Johnson, Howard
Gee! But It Was Hot in Chile   Young, Joseph
Get a Little Fun Out of Life   Kalmar; Ruby
Get Off   Johnson, James P.; Razaf
Get that Sun into You   Harburg
Get Yourself a Girl and Fall in Love   Gordon; Revel
Get Yourself a Little Cup of Sunshine   Gordon; Revel
(I Don't Stand a) Ghost of a Chance with You   Washington;
    Young, Victor
Girl Who Gets Her Man, The   Razaf
Give Her a Kiss   Hart; Rodgers
Give Me a Chance at Heaven   Magidson
Give Me Just a Moment   Hart; Rodgers
Give Me Those Good Old Circus Days   Gordon; Revel
Give Your Heart a Holiday   Gilbert; Hanley
Glories Good Mornin' (inst.)   Waller
Glory   Blake; Sissle
Go Home to Your Next Pal, Go Home   Stept
Going Back to the One I Love   Friend

Good Night My Lady Love   Young, Joseph
Good People All   Dietz; Schwartz, Arthur
Good Time's Comin'   Kahn
Good-Bye Blues   Johnston
Gosh Darn   Coots; Young, Joseph
Got the South in My Soul   Washington; Young, Victor
Got You where I Want You Right in My Arms   Yellen
Gotta Be, Gonna Be Mine   Razaf; Waller
Gotta Lotta Love for You   Baer; Lewis
Grand   Ahlert; Turk
Grand Opera Sequence   Robin
Great Big Bunch of You, A   Dixon; Warren
Gretchen   Egan
Gypsy Hearts   Bryan
Hail, The Happy Couple   Gershwin, George; Gershwin, Ira
Hangin' at the End of a Rope   Hanley
Happy Little Butterfly   Dixon; Fain
Happy Times   Fields; McHugh
Happy-Go-Lucky You and Broken Hearted Me   Hoffman
Harlem Holiday   Arlen; Koehler
Harlem Hot-Cha   Johnson, James P.; Razaf
Harlem Moon   Blake; Sissle
Hats Off — Here Comes a Lady   Young, Joseph
Haunted Organ, The   Young, Joseph; Young, Victor
Have a Little Faith in Uncle Sam   Adamson; Coots
Have You Forgotten What I Can't Forget   Young, Joseph
He Has Such Charm (Il est Charmant)   Harburg
Heaven Only Knows   Adamson; Coots; Wrubel
Hello Gorgeous   Donaldson
Hello, Sweetheart, Hello (I Just Called to Say Goodnight)
    Sissle
Here Again, Gone Again Love Affair   Magidson;
    Washington; Wrubel
Here Comes the Cheer Parade   Parish
Here Is My Heart   Spina
Here Lies Love   Rainger; Robin
Here 'Tis   Blake; Sissle
Here's Hoping   Adamson; Coots
Here's to Night   Eliscu
Here's Your Chance   Young, Joseph
He's a Son of the South   Razaf
He's Not Himself   Gershwin, George; Gershwin, Ira
He's Oversexed   Gershwin, George; Gershwin, Ira
Hey Young Fella!   Fields; McHugh
High Speed   Fain; Kahal
Hokum March (inst.)   Hanley
Hold 'Em   De Lange
Hold Your Head Up High (Opening Hymn)   Hammerstein;
    Kern
Hold Your Horses   Bryan; Monaco
Home Folks   Hanley
Home Made Heaven   Rainger; Robin
Homesick and Lonesome   Hoffman; Magidson
Honey Do   Razaf
Hot Voo-Doo   Coslow; Rainger; Robin
How About a Little Date for Breakfast?   Harburg
How About You and Me   Yellen
How Are You My Honey   Young, Joseph
How Can You Cry with Those Beautiful Eyes   Ager; Fisher
How Can You Face Me   Razaf; Waller
How Can You Say No When All the World Is Saying
    Yes   Dubin; Kahal
How Deep Is the Ocean? (How High Is the Sky?)   Berlin
How Do You Do, Beautiful You   Magidson
How Do You Do It?   Harburg

How Long Has This Been Going On?   Mercer
How Nice of Love   Heyman
How's Your Romance?   Porter
Hula Holiday   Rainger; Robin
Hum a Tune   Gordon; Revel
Humoresque   Johnson, Howard
Humpty-Dumpty   Brown, Nacio Herb; DeSylva; Whiting
Hungry   Razaf; Waller; Young, Joseph
I Always Wear My Derby When It Rains   Fain; Young, Joseph
I Am So Eager   Hammerstein; Kern
I Beg Your Pardon Mademoiselle   Magidson; Stept
I Called to Say Good-Night   Conrad; Young, Joseph
I Came, I Saw, You Conquered   Heyman
I Cannot Tell You Why All I Know Is I'm in Love with You   Coots; Turk
I Can't Believe that It's You   Gilbert; Silver
I Can't Forget that You Forgot About Me   Kahn
I Can't Forget the Minuet   Burke; Hoffman; Spina
I Could Expect It from Anyone but You   Hoffman
I Couldn't Be Annoyed   Robin; Whiting
I Didn't Dream It Was Love   Conrad; Waller
I Didn't Mean to Hurt Your Feelings, I Didn't Mean to Make You Cry   Coots; Kahn
I Don't Know How I Can Do Without You   Egan
I Don't Wanna Be Married (I Just Wanna Be Friends)   Berlin
I Forgive You   Arlen; Yellen
I Found My Romance for Ten Cents a Dance   Dubin; Kahal; Stept
I Got Myself in Bad Being too Good to You   Fain; Lewis
I Got Religion   DeSylva; Youmans
I Gotta Right to Sing the Blues   Arlen; Koehler
I Guess It Wasn't Meant to Be   Donaldson; Kahn
I Had You and Then I Lost You   Fisher
I Have a Run in My Stocking   Eliscu
I Hear the Voice of an Angel   Burke
I Know You're Lying but I Love It   Stept
I Lerve You   Harburg
I Love to Go to School 'Cause I Love My Teacher   Hoffman; Young, Joseph
I Love You Because I Love You   Hoffman
I Love You Dear!   Ahlert; Turk
I Love You, Mary Darling   Eliscu
I Loved Ya   Heyman
I Loved You Wednesday   Silver
I Make Up for That in Other Ways   Brown, Lew; Henderson
I May Never Pass Your Way Again   Kahal; Warren
I Never Liked, Like I Like You   Young, Joseph
I Only Know that I Love You, That's All that Matters to Me   Magidson; Stept
I Played a Fiddle for the Czar   Gordon
I Played Fiddle for the Czar   Revel
I Said Goodbye to Happiness, When I Said Goodbye to You   Ahlert; Turk
I Saw My Future in Your Eyes   Hanley
I Say It's Spinach - And the Hell with It   Berlin
I See By the Papers   Hoffman; Washington
I Send My Love with These Roses   Davis; Dubin
I Shouldn't Care   Ahlert; Turk
I Still Love the Red, White and Blue   Porter
I Stumbled Into Heaven (Falling for You)   Koehler; Mitchell; Pollack
I Tank I Go Home   Edwards
I Think Too Much of You   Donaldson; Kahn
I Think You're Swell   Johnson, James P.; Razaf

I Told You So   Clare; Stept
I Want Another Portion of That   Brown, Lew; Henderson
I Want to Be with You   DeSylva; Youmans
I Was Left Behind   Lawrence
I Was So Weak, Love Was So Strong   Johnson, James P.; Razaf
I Wish I Could Leave You Alone   Young, Joseph
I Wish I Had Wings   Woods
I Wish I Hadn't Said Hello   Young, Joseph
I Wish We Could Dance Forever   Hoffman
I Wonder How the Old Folks Are Tonight   Yellen
I Wonder (If You're Lonesome)   Koehler
I Wouldn't Care   Robin
I Wouldn't Trade the Silver in My Mother's Hair for All the Gold in the World   Coots
Ich Liebe Dich (I Love You)   Lewis
I'd Like to Get Together with You   Friend; Monaco
If I Had a Girl Like My Mother, I'd Be a Feller Like Dad   Young, Joseph
If I Only Had a Five Cent Piece   Caesar
If I Were Adam and You Were Eve   Hanley
If I'm Blue to You   DeSylva; Whiting
If I'm Nice to You   Brown, Nacio Herb; Whiting
If It Ain't Love   Razaf; Waller
If It's Any News to You   Blake; Sissle
If Love Were King   Fain; Kahal
If She Hadn't Dropped Her Love   Hoffman; Washington
If We Never Meet Again   Lerner, Sammy
I'll Always Speak Well of You   Clare
I'll Ballyhoo You   Eliscu
I'll Be Among Those Present   Dixon
I'll Be Seeing You   Brown, Nacio Herb; Egan; Whiting
I'll Be the Meanest Man in Town (Till You're Nice to Me)   Stept
I'll Follow You   Ahlert; Turk
I'll Never Be the Same   Kahn
I'll Never Grow Tired of You   Leslie
I'll See You in the Morning   Loesser
I'll Take You Back If You Want to Come Back   Young, Joseph
I'm a Good Girl, Dammit   Gordon; Revel
I'm Afraid of the World Without You   Kahal
I'm Afraid to Waltz with You   Coslow
I'm Against It   Kalmar; Ruby
I'm Alone   Hammerstein; Kern
I'm Burning for You   Coslow; Johnston
I'm Coming Home   Hammerstein; Kern
I'm Crooning a Love Song to Heaven   Hoffman
I'm Forever Falling in Love with Someone   Leslie
I'm Forgetting Myself for You   Caesar
I'm Getting Sentimental Over You   Washington
I'm Getting What I Want   Robin; Whiting
I'm Glad You Met Me   Heyman
I'm Gonna Take Possession of You   Coslow
I'm Happy when You're Jealous   Kalmar; Ruby
I'm in Love with a Tune   Rainger
I'm in the Mood for You   Parish
I'm Just a Fool, in Love with You   Kahn
I'm Just a Little Olive   Gordon; Revel
I'm Just a Sentimental Soul   Leslie
I'm Left Out in the Cold   Gilbert; Hanley; Silver
I'm Living My Life for You   Washington
I'm Lost without You, Sally   Ager; Lewis
I'm Never Blue Where the Grass Is Green   Coots; Young, Joseph

I'm Not Complaining   Ahlert; Turk

I'm Now Prepared to Tell the World It's You!   Razaf; Waller

I'm Off of You   Harburg

I'm on Pins and Needles, 'Cause I'm Dead Stuck on You   Young, Joseph

I'm One of God's Children   Harburg

I'm Playing with Fire   Berlin

I'm Positively in Love, and Absolutely with You   Ahlert; Turk

I'm Simply Crazy 'Bout You Now   Monaco

I'm So Alone with the Crowd   Young, Joseph

I'm So in Love   Donaldson

I'm Sorry My Dreams Came True   Gordon; Revel

I'm Still without a Sweetheart with Summer Coming On   Ahlert; Turk

I'm Sure of Everything but You   Meyer

I'm Thankful for the Love You Showed Me   Young, Joseph

I'm Tired of Love   Harburg

I'm Watching the World Thru My Grandmother's Glasses   Egan

I'm Way Ahead of the Game   Brown, Nacio Herb; DeSylva; Whiting

I'm Wearing My Heart on My Sleeve   Parish

I'm Yours for Tonight   Leslie; Monaco

In a Little German Garden Underneath the Pretzel Vine   Coots; Kahn

In a Little Stucco in the Sticks   Gordon; Revel

In a Park in Paree   Robin

In a Shanty in Old Shanty Town   Young, Joseph

In an Old Arm Chair   Johnson, Howard

In Egern on the Tegern See   Hammerstein; Kern

In Havana   Gordon; Revel

In Indiana   Caesar; Friend

In the Dim Dim Dawning   Hoffman

In the Hills of Tennessee   Lewis

In the Land of Sunny Sunflowers   Blake; Sissle

In the Middle of a Kiss   Freed, Ralph

In the Old Kentucky Hills of Tennessee   Magidson; Wrubel

In the Silence of the Night   Arlen; Koehler

In the Still of the Night   Carmichael

In Three Quarter Time   Gershwin, George; Gershwin, Ira

In Your Forgettery   Brown, Nacio Herb; Egan

Inside Looking Out   Eliscu

Instead of a Million Dollars   Akst; Freed, Arthur

Interlude   Hammerstein; Kern

Is It Just Another Thrill   Monaco

Island of Dreams   Freed, Arthur

Isn't It a Pity?   Gershwin, George; Gershwin, Ira

Isn't Is Heavenly   Harburg

Isn't It Romantic   Hart; Rodgers

It Costs Just a Nickel   Kahal

It Costs Me Just a Nickel   Fain

It Don't Mean a Thing (If It Ain't Got that Swing)   Ellington; Mills

It Seems Like Yesterday   Hoffman

It Was Never Like This   Dietz; Schwartz, Arthur

It Was Only a Dream Kiss   Robin

It Was So Beautiful   Freed, Arthur

It Won't Be Long Now   Hoffman; Washington

It'll Take a Little Time   Hoffman

It's About Time   Mercer

It's All My Fault   Meyer

It's Gonna Be You   Young, Joseph

It's Great to Be Alive   Brown, Lew; Henderson

It's Just an Old Spanish Custom   Gordon; Revel

It's Mighty Sweet of You, to Be So Nice to Me   Young, Joseph

It's Not a Secret Anymore   Freed, Ralph; Hoffman

It's Only a Paper Moon (If You Believed in Me)   Arlen; Harburg; Rose

It's Terrific   Rainger

It's Winter Again   Freed, Arthur; Hoffman

It's Within Your Power   Gordon; Revel

I've Been Expecting You   Parish

I've Got a Date with Hate   Fields; McHugh

I've Got My Old Love on My Mind Tonight   Ahlert; Turk

I've Got Nothin', You've Got Nothin', We've Got Nothin' to Lose   DeSylva; Whiting

I've Got the Words, I've Got the Tune, Hummin' to Myself   Fain; Magidson

I've Got the World on a String   Arlen; Koehler

I've Got to Be There   Gershwin, George; Gershwin, Ira

I've Got You on My Mind   Porter

I've Gotta Keep My Eye on You   Gordon; Revel

I've Told Ev'ry Little Star   Hammerstein; Kern

Jose, Can't You See   Brown, Lew; Henderson

Joshua Fit de Battle   Blake; Sissle

Journey's End   Fields; McHugh

Just a Child of Manhattan   Bryan; Edwards

Just a Corporal   Egan

Just a Little Home for the Old Folks   Ahlert; Leslie

Just an Echo in the Valley   Woods

Just Another Dream of You   Davis

Just Another Waltz that Goes with the Night   Young, Joseph

Just Around the Corner   Dietz; Schwartz, Arthur

Just Because You're You   Friend

Just Like Your Shadow   Davis; Stept

Keep a Little Song Handy   Lerner, Sammy

Keep Away   Ahlert; Turk

Keep Your Chin Up   Blake; Sissle

Keep Your Last Goodnight for Me   Ahlert; Turk

Keep Your Nose Out of Mama's Business   Razaf

Keepin' Out of Mischief Now   Razaf; Waller

Kissing in the Rain   Bryan; Clare

(You've Got to Have) Koo Wah   Blake; Sissle

La Spagnola   Johnson, Howard

Labor Day Parade   Blake; Sissle

Lady — I Love, The   Young, Joseph

Lady, Don't Look at Me Like That   Magidson; Stept

Landler (inst.)   Kern

Landlord at My Door!   Gordon; Revel

Landlord, Stay 'Way from My Door   Woods

Language of Love, The   Friend

Last Mile Is the Longest When You're on the Way Home   Davis; Silver

Laughing on the Outside Crying on the Inside   Coslow

Lawd, You Made the Night too Long   Lewis; Young, Victor

Lazy Day   Kahn

Leave a Little Love Dream   Robin

Leave a Little Love for Me   David, Mack

Leave It to Love   Gordon; Revel

Leopard Cannot Change His Spots, A   Hanley

Let Fate Decide   Smith, Harry B.

Let Me Match My Private Life with Yours   Duke; Harburg

Let Them Fight It Out in Their Own Back Yard   Hoffman; Washington

Let's Be Dreamers in Love   Egan

Let's Have a Party   Friend

Let's Have Another Cop O' Coffee   Berlin

Let's Make Hay While the Moon Shines   David, Mack

Let's Put on the Ritz   Arlen; Koehler
Let's Put the Sun to Bed and Wake Up the Moon   Baer
Letters from an Old Sweetheart   Conrad; Young, Joseph
Lieberstraum   Johnson, Howard
Life of the Party, The   Brown, Nacio Herb; DeSylva; Whiting
Light Up   Gordon; Revel
Like an Old Forgotten Refrain   Dubin; Friend
Linger a Little Longer in the Twilight   Woods
Little Man   Gilbert; Hanley
Little Moments of Love   Coots
Little Old Cross-Road Store   Mercer
Little Old New York   Brown, Lew; Henderson
Little Spanish Villa By the Sea   Conrad; Young, Joseph
Little Street Where Old Friends Meet, A   Kahn; Woods
Living Old Memories Over Again   Dubin; Friend
Load Is Heavy (And I'm Ready to Go), The   Snyder
Lonely Park   David, Mack
Lonesome Man   Blake; Sissle
Lonesome Me   Conrad; Razaf; Waller
Lonesome Melody   Young, Joseph
(Oh, How I) Long to Belong to You   DeSylva; Youmans
Look Here Comes a Rainbow   Hanley
Look What I've Got   Rainger; Robin
Look Who's Here   Adamson; Lane
Lookin' for a Sweetheart   Wrubel
Looking for a Sweetheart   Magidson
Lorelei, The   Gershwin, George; Gershwin, Ira
Lorraine   Young, Joseph
Lost in the Crowd   Conrad; Dietz; Schwartz, Arthur
Lost in Your Arms   Lewis
Louisiana Hayride   Dietz; Schwartz, Arthur
Lovable   Kahn; Woods
Love at Dusk   Hanley
Love I'm Calling   Razaf
Love Is Calling Me   Hanley
Love Me Tonight   Hart; Rodgers; Washington; Wrubel; Young, Victor
Love, Nuts and Noodles (Bring 'Em Back Alive)   Harburg
Love Was Gone   Adamson; Lane
Love Will Say Goodbye to Tears   Young, Joseph
Love Words from You   Akst; Davis
Love You Are My Inspiration   Koehler
Love, You Funny Thing   Ahlert; Turk
Lovely Little Fraulein   Gordon; Revel
Lover   Hart; Rodgers
Luckiest Boy in the World, The   Gershwin, George; Gershwin, Ira
Luckiest Man in the World   Gershwin, George; Gershwin, Ira
Lucky Little Accident   Lane; Young, Joseph
Lullaby Lady   Young, Joseph
Lullaby of the Leaves   Young, Joseph
Lunching at the Automat   Berlin
Mad Moments   Gordon; Revel
Madame Has Lost Her Dress   Rainger
Madame T.N.T.   Johnson, James P.; Razaf
Make Love the King (Long Live the King)   Conrad; Young, Joseph
Make Me Yours   Freed, Arthur
Man About Yonkers   Harburg
Man for Me (The Letter Song), The   Hart; Rodgers
Manhattan Madness   Berlin
Manhattan Masquerade (inst.)   Alter
Manhattan's the Loneliest Isle   Duke; Harburg
Mannikin   Young, Joseph

March for Queen Kelly   Fain; Kahal
Marching By   Edwards
Matador Song   Brown, Lew; Henderson
Maybe in a Dream   Rainger; Robin
Me Minus You   Webster
Medicine Show, The   Hart; Rodgers
Meet Me Tonight in the Cowshed   Conrad
Mein Kleine Akrobat   Dietz; Schwartz, Arthur
Melodies of May   Hammerstein; Kern
Mighty Sweet   Akst; Davis
Million Dreams, A   Kahn
Mimi   Hart; Rodgers
Mine Completely   Johnston
Mine, Once Upon a Time   Gordon; Revel
Mine Until the End of Time   Friend; Stept
Minnie the Moocher's Wedding Day   Arlen; Koehler
Miserable Me   Rainger; Robin
Miss Liza Jane   Coots
Mississippi River, Keep on Croonin'   Johnson, J. Rosamond
Modern Little Red Riding Hood   Gordon; Revel
Molly and Me   Lerner, Sammy
Moment in the Dark, A   Freed, Arthur
Mona   Johnston
Monsieur Baby   Rainger; Robin
Moon Mad   Rainger; Robin
Moon Over Dixie   Ellington; Koehler
Moonlight Brought Me the Sunshine   Ahlert; Turk
Moonlight for Two   Kahal
Moonlight Melody   Lawrence
Moonlight Millionaires   Hanley; Kahal; Meyer; Rose
More and More I'm Caring for You   Monaco
More Beautiful than Ever   Washington; Young, Victor
Most Beautiful Girls in the World, The   Arlen; Koehler
Mother Mississippi, There's No Rest for the Weary No Time   Bryan; Fisher
Mother Told Me So   Dietz; Schwartz, Arthur
Mother's Little Man   Razaf; Sissle
Mouthful of Jam   Mercer
Mrs. Winchell's Boy   Gilbert; Silver
Music and Moonlight   Freed, Arthur; Meyer
Music, Music, Everywhere   Arlen; Koehler
My Beautiful Rhinestone Girl   Berlin
My Blue Danube   Johnson, Howard
My Cousin in Milwaukee   Gershwin, George; Gershwin, Ira
My Darling   Heyman
My Flower of Japan   Rainger
My Gift of Dreams   Razaf; Waller
My Girl Is Named Yvonne   Rainger
My Happiness Is You   De Lange
My Headache   Johnson, James P.; Razaf
My Heart Is Home   Dixon
My Heart Is Part of You   Dietz; Schwartz, Arthur
My Heart's at Ease   Waller; Young, Joseph
My Heaven on Earth   Gilbert
My Hour Has Come   Rainger
My Isle of Hilo Bay   Gilbert
My Liebchen and Me (Mein Liebchen und Mich)   Young, Joseph
My Lips Want Kisses, My Heart Wants Love   Baer; Fisher
My Little Swanee Sue   Coots
My Loved One   Fain; Kahal
My Lover   DeSylva; Youmans
My Mom   Donaldson
My Palace Where Love Is King   Johnson, J. Rosamond
My River Home   Young, Joseph

My Romance   Washington; Young, Victor
My Sacrifice   David, Mack; Heyman
My Silent Love   Heyman
My Silver Rose   Leslie; Monaco
My Wishing Song   Kahal
My World Begins and Ends with You   Hanley
Mystery Song, The   Ellington; Mills
'Neath the Silv'ry Moon   Friend
New Kind of Rhythm   Arlen; Koehler
New Orleans   Carmichael
Night   Ager; Harburg
Night Again   Koehler
Night and Day   Porter
Night Club Nights   Eliscu
Night Flies By   Hammerstein; Kern
Night, Hold Back the Dawn   Brown, Nacio Herb; DeSylva; Whiting
Night when Love Was Born, The   Baer; Young, Joseph
Night You Stole My Kisses, The   Lewis; Schwartz, Jean; Young, Joseph
Nightfall   Lewis
No More Love 'Cause There's No More You   Friend
No One Could Love You, As Much As I Do   Young, Joseph
No One Else Can Love Me Like You, Baby   Carroll
No Tickee, No Washee   Gershwin, George; Gershwin, Ira
Nobody Else but Elsie   Kahal; Monaco
Nobody Ever Brings Me Violets   Hanley
Not a Penny in My Pocket, But I'm a Millionaire   Wrubel
Now I Lay Me Down to Sleep   Hanley
Now You've Got Me Worryin' for You   Fain; Young, Joseph
Off Again — On Again   Hoffman
Off Again, On Again   Duke; Harburg
Oh Baby, Obey   Rainger; Robin
Oh, Lady   Magidson; Stept
Oh Maria   Johnson, Howard
Oh! That Mitzi   Robin
Oh! You Sweet Thing   Razaf; Waller
O.K. California   Gilbert; Silver
Ol' King Cotton   Fain; Kahal
Old Fashioned Wedding   Harburg
Old Forgotten Waltz, An   Myrow
Old Friend Is Sweet in September, An   Egan; Whiting
Old Kitchen Kettle   Woods
Old Ladies Home (One Friend), The   Caesar
Old Love Letters   Davis; Silver
Old Man of the Mountain, The   Young, Victor
Old Soldiers Never Die   Conrad
Old Yazoo (inst.)   Waller
Ole Aunt Mariar   Hanley
On a Chill-Chill-Chilly Night   Coots
On a Roof in Manhattan   Berlin
On the Fence Together   Brown, Nacio Herb; Egan
On Through the Night   Gordon; Revel
One Day in May   Lewis
One Evening in September   Washington
One Hour with You   Robin; Whiting
One Little Keepsake   Lewis
One More Dance   Hammerstein; Kern
One Step Ahead of My Shadow   Fain; Kahal
Only Sometimes   Waller; Young, Joseph
Organ Grinder, The   Magidson; Stept
Our Jim   Carmichael
Our Little Love Affair Is Ended   Parish
Out of the Blue   Eliscu

Out of the Darkness (You Have Come to Me)   Turk; Young, Victor
Over the Weekend I Fell in Love   Monaco; Washington
Pagan Paradise   Koehler
Panther Woman, The   Coslow
Paradise Bound   Young, Joseph
Pardon My English   Gershwin, George; Gershwin, Ira
Par-ee, You're Mine, All Mine   Hanley
Parisian Tango (inst.)   Revel
Parkin' in the Park with You   Conrad
Penny for Your Thoughts, A   Duke; Harburg
Personality   Dixon; Stept
Picnic for Two, A   Hoffman
Pink Elephants   Dixon; Woods
Play, Fiddle, Play (Sumna Violino)   Lawrence
Pleasant Dreams   Coslow
Please   Rainger; Robin
Po' Tired Chillun   Robison
Police Number   Robin
Poor Apache, The   Hart; Rodgers
Poor Little, Shy Little, Demure Little Me   Gordon; Revel
Poor Michael! Poor Golo!   Gershwin, George; Gershwin, Ira
Poor Old Joe   Carmichael
Prayer (Our Journey May Be Long)   Hammerstein; Kern
Pretty Little Words   Harburg
Private Confidential Secretaries   Gordon; Revel
Puce and the Green, The   Gilbert; Hanley
Put a Tax on Love   Silver
Quick Henry, the Flit!   Gordon; Revel
Rackety Rax   Gilbert; Hanley
Radio City Overture   Caesar
Radio Papa, Broadcastin' Mama   Razaf; Waller
Rah, Rah, Rah   Caesar; Magidson; Stept
Rain Rain Go Away   David, Mack; Heyman
Rainy Day, A   Dietz; Schwartz, Arthur
Red Head (With Those Mean Green Eyes)   Hanley
Red Headed Woman, The   Egan; Whiting
Reefer Man (Have You Ever Met That Funny Reefer Man)   Razaf
Remember Me   Kahn
Remember Our Romance   Woods
Reminiscing   Blake; Sissle
Rhythm of Love, Stop Playing with My Heart   Young, Joseph
Riddle Me This   Harburg
Riding Habit   Dietz; Schwartz, Arthur
Riding High   Gordon; Revel
Rio De Janeiro   Eliscu
Rise 'N' Shine   DeSylva; Youmans
Robinson Crusoe   Johnston
Rock-a-Bye Moon   Johnson, Howard
Rockin' in Rhythm   Arlen; Koehler
Rosa Mia   Fisher
Rose of the Snowlands   Young, Joseph
Roses Are Red, the Violets Are Blue, The   Clare
Roses at Dawning   Kahn
'Round My Heart   Young, Joseph
'Round the Bend of the Road   Lewis
Row, Row, Row with Roosevelt on the Good Ship U.S.A.   Coots
Sad Horns, Don't Blow Your Horns at Me   Robison
Salt Air   Porter
Sandman   Adamson; Lane
Santa   Lewis
Santa Lucia   Johnson, Howard

Satan's Li'l Lamb   Arlen; Harburg; Mercer
Saturday Afternoon   Blake; Sissle
Say! Can't You See, What You're Doin' to Me   Young, Joseph
Say It Isn't So   Berlin
Say That You Were Teasing Me   Ahlert; Turk
Say the Word   Friend
Say (What I Wanna Hear You Say)   Brown, Lew; Henderson
Say You'll Be Good to Me   Hanley
Say, Young Lady   Gordon; Revel
Scat Song, The   Parish
Scena (Tingle Tangle)   Hammerstein; Kern
Schnozzola   Hart; Johnston
Sentimental Gentleman from Georgia   Parish
Seven Little Steps to Heaven   Mercer
Shadows on the Window   Washington; Young, Victor
Shakin' the Shakespeare   Gordon; Revel
Shaking Hands with the South   Young, Joseph
Sharing My Love with You   Stept; Young, Joseph
She Went to Old St. Mary's and I Went to Notre Dame   Bryan; Meyer
She'll Be Coming 'Round the Catskill Mountains   Harburg
Sheltered By the Stars, Cradled By the Moon   Waller; Young, Joseph
She's Nuts About Me   Brown, Nacio Herb; DeSylva; Whiting
Shine on Your Shoes, A   Dietz; Schwartz, Arthur
Shotgun Papa   Razaf
Should I Be Sweet   DeSylva; Youmans
Shoutin' in that Amen Corner   Razaf
Sick   Hart
Since I Gave Up the Old Gang for a Little Gang of My Own   Hoffman; Washington
Since Won Long Hop Took One Long Hop to China   Waller
Sing a New Song   Ager
Sing a Song of Romance and You'll Wake Up the Love in My Soul   Young, Joseph
Sing and Dance Your Troubles Away   Blake; Sissle
Sing It Way Down Low   Carmichael
Sing Me a Song of the Sun   Johnson, Howard
Sing No More   Friend
Singing Myself to Sleep   Fisher
Sittin' By the Fire with You   Meyer
Sittin' in a Swing   Livingston, Jerry
Sittin' in the Dark   Adamson
Sittin' on the Fence   Gilbert; Hanley
Sleep Come On and Take Me   Young, Joseph
Sleep, My Sweet   Brown, Nacio Herb
Sleeping on the Benches   Woods
Smart Set   Gordon; Revel
Smokin' Reefers   Dietz; Schwartz, Arthur
So Ashamed!   Ager; Davis
So Do I   DeSylva; Youmans
So Does Mahatma Ghandi   Hanley
So Grateful   Kalmar; Ruby
(And) So I Married the Girl   Magidson; Stept
So Nonchalant   Duke; Harburg
So Tender   Coots; Young, Joseph
So This Is Mexico   Brown, Lew; Henderson
So What?   Gershwin, George; Gershwin, Ira
Sob Song   Rainger; Robin
Soft Lights and Sweet Music   Berlin
Soliloquy   Rainger; Robin
Some Don't Believe in Miracles, I Do — Don't You   Hanley

Some Happy Day   Yellen
Somebody Ought to Wave a Flag   Hart; Rodgers
Someday We'll Meet Again   Ager; Hoffman
Someone Stole Gabriel's Horn   Mills
Someone to Care For   Kahn; Warren
Someone's Stole Gabriel's Horn   Washington
Something in the Night   Young, Joseph
Something to Think About   Gordon; Revel
Something's Gotta Be Done   Koehler
Sometime in Summertime   Donaldson
Somewhere East of Sunrise   Coots
Somewhere in the West   Freed, Arthur
Son of a Gun Is Nothing but a Tailor, The   Hart; Rodgers
Song Is You, The   Hammerstein; Kern
Song of the Red Headed Woman   Egan; Whiting
Song that Makes Me Blue, The   Arlen; Yellen
Songs for Sale   Young, Joseph
Sore Foot Blues   Blake; Sissle
Souvenir of Love   Hanley
Sparrows in the Rain   Egan
Speaking of Love   Duke; Harburg
Sport a Sport   Gordon; Revel
Spring Is in My Heart Again   Mercer
Starry Sky   Eliscu
Stars   Koehler
Stay Away from San Antone   Coots; Turk
Stealin' Apples   Razaf; Waller
Stepping Into Love   Arlen; Koehler
Stop Cryin'   Gordon; Revel
Stop that Dog   Johnson, James P.; Razaf
Stories Morning Glories Tell, The   Coots; Kahn
Strange As It Seems   Razaf; Waller
Strange Interlude   Bryan
Strangers May Kiss   De Lange; Wrubel
Street of Dreams   Lewis; Young, Victor
String Bean Anne from San Antone   Coots; Turk
Stupid Melody   Rose
Sugar Babe   Blake; Sissle
Suicide Song   Rainger; Robin
Summer Was Made for Lovers (Why Let It Go Rolling By)   Johnson, James P.; Razaf
Sun's in My Heart, The   Baer; Freed, Arthur
Suzanne   Heyman; Hoffman
Sweet Chariot   Ellington; Mills
Sweet Liar   Caesar
Sweet Little Girl Next Door   Mercer
Sweet Little Stranger   Gordon; Revel
Sweet Muchacha   Ager; Hoffman
Sweet Thing   Coots
Sweetheart Hour   Monaco; Washington
Sweethearts Forever   Caesar; Friend
Sweetheart's Lullaby   David, Mack
Sweetness   Freed, Arthur
Swingin' Along   Arlen; Koehler
Syncopate Your Sins Away   Magidson
Take Me Away   Clare
Take Me in Your Arms   Parish
Take My Song   Harburg
Take the Moonlight Express, Find Two New Lips to Press, You Don't Belong in My Dreams   Young, Joseph
Taking My Lessons in Rhythm   Johnson, James P.
Te Traigo Flores   Coslow; Rainger
Tell Me Why You Smile, Mona Lisa   Egan
Tell Me with a Kiss You're Mine   Adamson; Coots
Tell Me with Tulips that You'll Forget Me Not   Coots

Temporarily Blue   Arlen; Koehler
Tender Child   Young, Joseph
Terzetto   Hammerstein; Kern
Thank My Stars   Harburg
Thank You for a Lovely Time   Conrad; Young, Joseph
Thank You for the Use of Heaven   Kahal
Thank You, You're Welcome, Don't Mention It   Gordon;
   Revel
Thanksgivin'   Carmichael; Mercer
That Daddy and Mother of Mine   Bryan
That Night   Magidson
That'll Be All   Hoffman
That's All I Want to Know   Coots; Kahn
That's Life   Duke; Harburg
That's Living   Ahlert; Turk
That's the Song of Paree   Hart; Rodgers
That's What Heaven Means to Me   Akst; Yellen
That's What I Hate about Love   Arlen; Koehler
That's Where the South Begins   Waller
That's You, That's Me, That's All   Coots; Turk
Then You Went and Changed Your Mind   Fields; McHugh
There He Is — Theodore K. Blair   Hart; Rodgers
There I Go Dreaming Again   Brown, Lew; Henderson
There Never Was a Girl Like You   Friend; Magidson
There You Go, Doing It Over Again   Adamson; Lane
There's a Cozy Little Cottage Down the Lane   Spina
There's a Good Time Comin'   Yellen
There's a Hill Beyond a Hill   Hammerstein; Kern
There's a Little Bit of Devil in Your Angel Eyes   Coots
There's a Little Side Door to Heaven   Lewis
There's a Million Ways to Say I Love You   Ager; Lewis
There's a New Gang on the Corner Where the Old Gang
   Used to Be   Motzan
There's a Rainbow on the River   Stept; Young, Joseph
There's Always Somebody Else   Davis
There's No Light in the Window of the House on the
   Hill   Young, Victor
There's No One Livin' Gonna Break My Heart   Young,
   Joseph
There's Nothing the Matter With Me   Brown, Lew;
   Henderson
There's Oceans of Love By the Beautiful Sea   Coots
There's Romance in the Air   Meyer; Young, Joseph
There's Something to Be Thankful For   Young, Joseph
They All Need a Little Hot-Cha   Brown, Lew; Henderson
Think of My Reputation   Gordon; Revel
This Is My Love Song   Dubin
This Is Romance   Duke; Heyman
This Is the Night   Coslow; Rainger
This Is the Real Thing Now   Young, Joseph
This Time It's Love   Koehler
Three Guesses — Who Do I Love?   Akst; Davis
Three on a Match   Egan
Three Times a Day   Robin; Whiting
Three's a Crowd   Dubin; Kahal; Warren
Thrill Me   Harburg
Thrill that Comes Once in a Lifetime, The   Stept
Throw a Little Salt on the Bluebird's Tail   Robin; Whiting
Throwing a Party   Eliscu
Tickled Pink   Brown, Nacio Herb; DeSylva; Whiting
'Till the Real Thing Comes My Way   Akst; Egan; Eliscu
Till We Meet Again   Whiting
Time and Tide   Duke; Harburg
To Arms   Magidson

To the Rhythm of the River Rhine in Tulip Time   Bryan;
   Fisher
To the Sweetest Girl in the World   Davis
To the Victor Belongs the Spoils   Gordon; Revel
Together Again   Freed, Ralph; Hanley
Together at Last   Gershwin, George; Gershwin, Ira
Tom, Dick or Harry   Adamson; Youmans
Tonight   Gershwin, George; Gershwin, Ira; Johnston
Tonight Is All a Dream   Coslow; Rainger
Tonight Is Opening Night   Brown, Nacio Herb; DeSylva;
   Whiting
Tonight's the Night   Egan; Whiting
Tony Spagoni   Parish
Too Many on Your Mind, Nobody in Your Heart   Kahn
Too Many Tears   Dubin; Warren
Torch Song   Berlin
Trail of Glory, The   Kalmar; Ruby
Trouble in Paradise   Robin
True Love Never Runs Smooth   Conrad
Try a Little Tenderness   Woods
Turn Out the Light   Brown, Nacio Herb; DeSylva; Whiting
'Twas Only a Summer Night's Dream   Kahn
Two Empty Arms, One Little Empty Heart   Young, Joseph
Two Feet in Two Four Time   Arlen; Caesar
Two Guitars   Johnson, Howard
Two-Faced Woman   Dietz; Schwartz, Arthur
Unaccustomed As I Am   Duke; Harburg
Uncle Sam Needs a "Man Who Can Take It"   Harburg
Under a Shady Tree with You   Coots
Under the Moon Talking to You About Me   Snyder
Underneath the Harlem Moon   Gordon; Revel
Vals Song (The Lady of the Amazon)   Gilbert
Vas Villst Du Haben?   Bryan; Monaco
Vass You There, Sharlie   Monaco
Voice in the Old Village Choir, The   Kahn; Woods
Wah-Dee-Dah   Mills; Washington
Wail of the Reefer Man, The   Arlen; Koehler
Waiting for the Whistle to Blow   Blake; Sissle
Waiting for You to Begin   Waller; Young, Joseph
Waiting in a Dream   Washington
Wake Up the Gypsy in Me   Pollack
Walkin' the Floor   Razaf; Waller
Waltz that Brought You Back to Me, The   Caesar
Waltzing in a Dream   Washington; Young, Victor
Was That All I Meant to You?   Davis
Wassa Matter, No Ice Today, Marie   Gordon; Revel
Waste a Little Time with Me   Coots
Watch Your Head   Gershwin, George; Gershwin, Ira
Way Down South   Johnson, James P.; Razaf
Way I Feel Tonight, The   Parish
We Belong Together   Hammerstein; Kern
We Better Get Together Again   Conrad; Friend
We Just Couldn't Say Goodbye   Woods
We Need a Man   Cohan
We Were Only Walking in the Moonlight   Burke; Spina
We Will Always Be Sweethearts   Robin
Weary of Me   Parish
Weekend Affair, A   Porter
Well Done My Lad, Well Done   Burke; Monaco
We'll Find a Way   Kahn
We'll Go Out and Find Another Rainbow   Ager
We'll See It Through   Friend
Well, Well, Well   Donaldson
We're a Couple of Salesmen   Blake; Sissle
We're Alone   Freed, Arthur

We're Gonna Make Love Tonight   Magidson; Stept
We're on Our Way to Hell   Gordon; Revel
We've Been So Long Together, Why Leave Each Other
    Now   Bryan; Clare
Whadda Ya Say to Saying We Do   Baer; Egan
What a Life! Trying to Live Without You!   Alter
What a Little Thing Like a Wedding Can Do   Robin
What an Existence   Young, Joseph
What Are Little Girls Made Of   De Lange
What Did I Get in Return   Young, Joseph
What Do I Care about Anything If You Don't Care about
    Me   Akst; Yellen
What Great Big Eyes You Have   Eliscu
What Have You Got to Have?   Harburg
What, No Mickey Mouse, What Kind of a Party Is
    This   Caesar
What Sort of Wedding Is This?   Gershwin, George;
    Gershwin, Ira
What Will Become of Our England?   Porter
What Will Tomorrow Bring   Kahn
What Would Happen to Me If Something Happened to
    You   Woods
What Would You Do?   Robin; Whiting
What Would You Say   De Lange
What'll You Do   Parish
When a Pal Bids a Pal Goodbye   Leslie; Stept
When Gabriel Blows His Horn   Razaf; Waller
When Grimble Hits the Cymbal   Gordon
When I Come Home   Caesar
When I Knelt at the Alter and You Sang in the Choir   Coots
When I See Roses   Donaldson; Kahn
When I Was a Guy from the Mountains (And You Were a
    Girl from the Hills)   Young, Victor
When I'm Sippin' a Soda with Susie   Gordon; Revel
When It Rains You Are My Rainbow   Bryan
When It's Darkness on the Delta   Livingston, Jerry
When Love Is Near You   Fain; Kahal
When Old Vienna Was New   Egan
When That Band Plays   Eliscu
When the Lights Are Soft and Low   Freed, Arthur
When the Morning Rolls Around   Woods
When the Right One Comes Along   Davis
When the Spring Is in the Air   Hammerstein; Kern
When the Sun Goes Down on a Little Prairie Town   Kahn
When the World Was New   Kahn
When Times Get Better   Fain; Kahal
When We Ride on the Merry-Go-Round   Mercer
When You Hear this Song, Remember Me   Freed, Ralph;
    Hanley
When You're Gettin' Along with Your Gal   Fain; Kahal
Where Are You   Gorney; Harburg
Where Did You Get that Pair of Big Bright Eyes   Motzan
Where Have We Met Before?   Duke; Harburg
Where Oh Where Were You   Coots; Young, Joseph
Where the Dew Drops Kiss the Morning   Waller
Where You Go I Go   Gershwin, George; Gershwin, Ira
Wherever You Are I'll Come to You   Kahn
While We're Sitting in the Dark   Stept
Whiling My Time Away   Eliscu
Whisper in the Moonlight   Fields; McHugh
Whistle and Blow Your Blues Away   Young, Joseph
Whistling for a Kiss   Harburg; Mercer
White House of Our Own, A   Freed, Arthur
Who, Besides Me, Sits Beside You   Burke
Who Do You Love, Baby   Davis

Who Said I Was a Bum?   Johnson, Howard
Who Was Made for Who   Coslow
Who'd Believe You're in Love with Me   Davis
Who's Gettin' Your Goodnight Kisses Now   Davis
Why Can't I Find Somebody to Love?   Ahlert; Turk
Why Can't This Go on Forever   Ahlert; Turk
Why Do You Roll Those Eyes?   Harburg
Why Marry Them   Porter
Why Must I Say Goodbye to My Summer Love   Young,
    Joseph
Wiegenlied   Johnson, Howard
Winter Is in My Heart   Lewis
Wish I Only Knew Which Way the Wind Was Gonna
    Blow   Young, Joseph; Young, Victor
With a Feather in Your Cap   Fields; McHugh
With My Sweetie in the Moonlight (Under Dreamy Southern
    Skies)   Clare; Freed, Arthur
With You or Without You, I Will Get Along   Razaf
With Your Looks and My Disposition   Clare
Without a Sweetheart   Fain
Woman Needs Something Like That, A   Hart; Rodgers
Won't You Stay for Tea   Gordon; Revel
World Owes Me a Loving, The   Conrad; Young, Joseph
Wouldja for a Big Red Apple   Mercer
Y' Got Me, Baby   Arlen; Yellen
Yeah Man   Sissle
Year Ago Today   Parish
Yes Sir There's People Like That   Young, Joseph
Yes-Suh   Razaf
Yesterday's Kisses   Ager; Bryan; Fisher
Yi-I-Add-I-Ay Get in Good Humor Today   Young, Joseph
You and I Could Be Just Like That   Eliscu
You Are My Ideal   Freed, Arthur
You Are the First Love   Harburg
You Are the One for Me   Pollack
You Are the Song in My Heart   Livingston, Jerry
You Burn Me Up when You Turn Me Down   Smith, Harry
    B.
You Can Make My Life a Bed of Roses   Brown, Lew;
    Henderson
You Can't Tell Love What to Do   Friend; Monaco
You Don't Belong in My Dreams   Young, Joseph
You Don't Look for Love   Blake; Sissle
You Fascinate Me   Clare
You Gave Me a Rose but I Gave You My Heart   Parish
You Gave Me Ev'rything but Love   Arlen; Koehler
You Little So-and-So   Coslow; Robin
You Must Be Born with It   Berlin
You Opened My Eyes   Heyman
You Satisfy   Harburg
You Threw Me Overboard   Coslow
You Wonderful Thing   Parish
You'll Do   DeSylva; Whiting
You'll Fall in Love with Venice   Coslow
You'll Get By with a Twinkle in Your Eye   Coots; Turk
You'll Never Lose Me   Harburg
You're a Symphony of Love   Gordon; Revel
You're All that I'm Living For   Donaldson
You're All There Is   Freed, Arthur
You're an Old Smoothie   Brown, Nacio Herb; DeSylva;
    Whiting
You're Charming   Turk
You're Dancing on My Heart   Bryan; Meyer
You're Foolin' Yourself When You Try to Fool Me   Ager;
    Hoffman

You're in Love   Porter
You're Never More than Sweet Sixteen   Bryan; Fisher
You're Not Pretty but You're Mine   Harburg; Lane
You're Still in My Heart   Yellen
You're Telling Me   Donaldson; Kahn
You're the World's Sweetest Girl   Kahn
You're Too Careless with Your Kisses   Dixon; Woods
You're Worth While Waiting For   Gilbert; Hanley
Yours, All Yours   Johnson, James P.; Razaf
You've Been So Nice and Sweet to Me   Fain; Young, Joseph
You've Got Me in the Palm of Your Hand   Friend; Leslie;
    Monaco
You've Got Me Worrying for You   Kahal
You've Got to Sell Yourself   Eliscu
You've Got What Gets Me   Gershwin, George; Gershwin,
    Ira
Ziguyner Melody   Lawrence

1933

Absent Minded Flo   Clare; Coots
Adantino (Starlight & Sunshine)   Johnson, Howard
Adorable   Whiting
After All, You're All I'm After   Heyman; Schwartz, Arthur
After Sundown   Brown, Nacio Herb; Freed, Arthur
Ah, but Is It Love   Gorney; Harburg
Ah, Go On   Coots; Young, Joseph
Ah! Surprise   Akst; Eliscu
Ah the Moon Is Here   Fain; Kahal
Ain't She the Dainty   Woods
Ain't We Like Two Millionaires — Ain't We   Livingston,
    Jerry
Ain't-Cha Glad   Razaf; Waller
Alabama Man   Gordon; Revel
Alice in Wonderland   Robin
All I Want Is a Home   Hammerstein
All Night (Long)   Johnson, James P.
All That Is Mine Is Yours   Yellen
Alone Beside the Lonesome River   Johnson, Howard
Alone in the Dark   Dixon
Alone with My Tears   Parish
Alpha, Beta, Pi   Harbach; Kern
Among the Missing   Webster
And I Thought I Was Through with Love   Davis; Oakland
And So Goodbye   Wrubel
And Still I Love You   Caesar; Friml
And Then   Young, Joseph
And There You Are Again   Burke; Spina; Young, Joseph
And This Is Life   Razaf; Waller
Animated Objects   Hart; Rodgers
Annie Doesn't Live Here Anymore   Burke; Spina; Young,
    Joseph
Another Case of the Blues   Mercer
Another Language   Silver
Another Night in Your Arms   Hanley
Any Place Is Paradise As Long As You Are There   Coslow
Any Time, Any Day, Anywhere   Washington
Any Way the Wind Blows   Friend; Stept
Anyt Time, Any Day, Anywhere   Young, Victor
Anything You Say   Parish
Arlene   Pollack
Armful of Trouble   Harbach; Kern
At Sea   Fields; McHugh
At the Bottom of the Hill   Coots; Young, Joseph
At the Bow-Wow Ball   Heyman

Autumn's Elegy   Motzan
Away, Way Out in the Sticks   Fain
Baby   Monaco
Baby, Exceptional Baby   Bryan; Monaco
Baby, Wait Till It Happens to You   Hammerstein
Back to Nature   Porter
Ballad of the Easy Life   Weill
Ballad of the South (Lazy, Lazy Liza)   Gordon; Revel
Barn Dance (inst.)   Bloom
Baron de Ragotin   Romberg
Bath and Dressmaking Sequence   Hart; Rodgers
Bath Scene (inst.)   Brown, Nacio Herb
Be Optimistic   Rainger; Robin
Be Ready   Razaf
Beautiful Girl   Brown, Nacio Herb; Freed, Arthur
Because of Once Upon a Time   Young, Joseph
Before that Last Goodnight   Turk
Beneath the Spell of a Yellow Delta Moon   Robison
Better Think Twice   Coots
Between You and Me   Burke; Spina
Birthday Party   Brown, Nacio Herb; Freed, Arthur; Kahn
Black Eyed Susan Brown   Hoffman; Magidson
Black Moonlight   Coslow; Johnston
Blame It on My Youth   Heyman
Bless You   Heyman
Blonde, Blase and Beautiful   Gordon; Revel
Blue, Blue, Blue   Gershwin, George; Gershwin, Ira
Blue River   Washington; Young, Victor
Blue Roses   Ahlert; Leslie
Bluer than Blue   Pollack
Bonnie Jean of Aberdeen   Bryan
Boo, Boo, Boo   Coslow; Johnston
Boots and Saddles   Kahn
Breakfast Ball   Arlen; Koehler
Broadway Lady   Stept
Bubbling Over   Burke; Spina
Buckin' the Wind   Coslow; Johnston
Buggy Song, The   Young, Joseph
Build a Little Home   Dubin; Warren
Bulls and Bears   Parish
Bumper Found a Grand   Hart; Rodgers
Bumper's Going to Work (Kangaroo Court)   Hart; Rodgers
Bumper's Home Again (My Pal Bumper)   Hart; Rodgers
Bus Ride Sequence   Fields; McHugh
But Think of the Fun We Had   Ager
By a Waterfall   Fain; Kahal
Cafe Terrace (inst.)   Brown, Nacio Herb
Calico Days   Arlen; Koehler
Camp, Camp, Campin' on Your Doorstep   Coots; Johnson,
    Howard
Cancion de Carnaval (Carnival Song)   Gilbert
Cancion de las Buenaventura (Fortune Telling Song)   Gilbert
Carioca   Eliscu; Kahn; Youmans
Casanova   Porter
C'est Paree   Caesar; Romberg
Chant des Galleriens   Romberg
Charlie's Home   Coots; Young, Joseph
Chatanooga Playboy   Parish
Cher Ami   Coslow
Chimes in the Chapel, The   Livingston, Jerry
Choir Boy Days   Wrubel
Cinderella's Fella   Brown, Nacio Herb; Freed, Arthur
Ciribiribin   Johnson, Howard
Class Room Number   Coslow; Johnston; Robin
Clean As a Whistle   Fields; McHugh

Clementina   Harbach; Kern
Climb Up the Social Ladder   Gershwin, George; Gershwin, Ira
Clowns in Clover   Fields; McHugh
Cocotte, The   Porter
Colleen O'Killarney   Johnston; Robin
College Song, The   Kalmar; Ruby
Come On, You Moon   Wrubel
Come Out — Come Out — Wherever You Are   Freed, Arthur
Come Out, Come Out, Wherever You Are   Hoffman
Come Up and See Me Sometime   Alter
Comes the Revolution   Gershwin, George; Gershwin, Ira
Company's Comin'   Burke; Spina
Corn Beef Hash   Rainger
Cosmics (inst.)   Carmichael
Country's Going to War, The   Kalmar; Ruby
Cradle Me with a Ha Cha Lullaby   Coslow; Johnston
Cradle Song   Rainger; Robin
Crazy Walk   Stept
Cry from the Dungeon   Weill
Crying in the Moonlight   Gordon
Cuando el Amor Llama (Love Calls)   Gilbert
Cuban Cabaret   Heyman
Cupid in the Moonlight (Trip to Nowhere)   Gilbert
Dancing Lady   Hart; Rodgers
Dancing the Devil Away   Johnson, Howard
Dancing with the One You Love   Hoffman
Dark Is the Night   Mercer
Darkies Never Dream   Burke; Spina
Dawn Patrol   Lawrence
Day Without You, A   Coslow
Day You Came Along, The   Coslow; Johnston
Dear June   Hart; Rodgers
Debts   Berlin
Deep Forest (A Hymn to Darkness)   Razaf
Deep in the Dark of the Night   Livingston, Jerry
Did My Heart Beat, Did I Fall in Love   Meyer
Did You Ever See a Dream Walking?   Gordon; Revel
Dinner at Eight   Fields; McHugh
Disillusioned   Webster
Do I Know What I'm Doing While I'm in Love   Robin
Doin' What I Please   Razaf; Waller
Doin' What You're Doin'   Kalmar; Ruby
Doing the Uptown Lowdown   Gordon; Revel
Don't Ask Me Not to Sing   Harbach; Kern
Don't Be a Cry Baby   Rainger; Robin
Don't Believe a Word They Say   Parish
Don't Blame Me   Fields; McHugh
Don't Change, Be As You Are   Turk
Don't Do Anything I Wouldn't Do   Donaldson
Don't You Remember Me   Magidson; Stept
Double Dummy Drill   Gershwin, George; Gershwin, Ira
Down a Carolina Lane   Parish
Down a Long Long Road   Mercer
Down at the Old Barn Dance   Johnson, Howard
Down the Fairway   Warren
Down the Old Ox Road   Coslow; Johnston
('Cause I'm Just a) Downstream Drifter   Egan; Kahn
Dream Lady   Schwartz, Jean; Young, Joseph
Dream On   Clare
Dreamy Street   Webster
Drop Me Off in Harlem   Ellington
Drumming Out   Fields; McHugh
Dusty Shoes   Gorney; Harburg

Early Birds   Robin
East of the Sun — West of the Moon, Where Can You Be   Livingston, Jerry
Easter Parade   Berlin
Easy Going Woman   Lawrence
Eat Marlowe's Meat   Clare; Gorney
Eighteenth Amendment Repealed   Berlin
Emperor Jones   Wrubel
Ever Since the Day I Found You   Heyman
Everybody Likes Music   Burke; Spina
Everyone Remembers But You   Oakland
Everything I Have Is Yours   Adamson; Lane
Everything's As It Should Be   Schwartz, Jean; Young, Joseph
Ev'rybody Loves My Marguerite   Woods
Ev'ryone Remembers but You   Davis
(Musical Scene #2) Examination of Loo Loo   Whiting
Experiment   Porter
Face the Facts   Hart; Rodgers
Fare-Thee-Well to Harlem   Mercer
Farewell   Razaf
Farewell Tango   Weill
Farewell to Arms   Silver; Wrubel
Farmer's Daughter's Wedding Day, The   Magidson; Washington; Wrubel
Fashion Show (inst.)   Kern
Father, Mother, Sister and Brother   Bryan
Fear   Fain; Young, Joseph
Feeling's Mutual, My Dear, The   Hoffman
First Finale   Weill
First Lady and First Gent   Gershwin, George; Gershwin, Ira
First Spring Day, The   Eliscu
First Thing I Knew, The   Conrad; Kahn
Fit As a Fiddle (And Ready for Love)   Freed, Arthur; Hoffman
Five Love Songs   Friml
Flying Down to Rio   Eliscu; Kahn; Youmans
Fond Recollections, Mem'ries of Old   Young, Joseph
For Laughing Out Loud   Rainger; Robin
Forget the Past   Akst; Mitchell
Forgive Me for Loving You   Dubin; Warren
Forty-Second Street   Dubin
Forward March   Brown, Lew; Henderson
Four Moon Skits (I Can't Find a Mountain for My Moon)   Gordon; Revel
Franklin D. Roosevelt   Caesar
Free   Heyman
Freedonia Hymn   Kalmar; Ruby
Frivolette Valse   Romberg
Funnies, The   Berlin
Gather Lip Rouge While You May   DeSylva; Robin; Whiting
Georgia Sand   Porter
Get Hot Foot   Stept
Get Yourself a New Broom   Arlen; Koehler
Ghost of Love   Mercer; Spina
Girl Like Nina, A   Hammerstein
Give Me a Roll on a Drum   Caesar; Romberg
Give Me Liberty or Give Me Love   Rainger; Robin
Give Me Tonight   Carmichael
Goin' to Town Figurin' Out the Long Way Home   Meyer
Going Hollywood   Brown, Nacio Herb; Freed, Arthur
Goitie   Rainger
Good Evenin', Mister Nightingale   Pollack
Good Friends Surround Me   Caesar; Romberg
Good Luck Sweetheart   Coots
Good Morning Glory   Gordon; Revel

Goodbye Again   Adamson; Coots; Lewis
Good-Bye Love   Conrad; Mitchell
Good-Bye Prohibition, Good-Bye Blue Nose   Johnson, J.
 Rosamond
Goody Goody Girl   Young, Joseph
Goona Goona   Parish
Got the Jitters   Webster
Grand Central Episode   Brown, Nacio Herb; Freed, Arthur
Grapefruit Acres   Dubin; Warren
Grass Is Gettin' Greener All the Time, The   Burke; Spina
Guy What Takes His Time, A   Rainger
Gypsy Fiddles   Wrubel
Gypsy of Song, A   Friml
Hail to the Baron Maunchausen   Fields; McHugh
Hallelujah, I'm a Bum   Hart; Rodgers
Handful of Keys   Razaf; Waller
Handwriting's on the Wall, The   Fain; Young, Joseph
Hanging Throttlebottom in the Morning   Gershwin, George;
 Gershwin, Ira
Happy as the Day Is Long   Arlen; Koehler
Harbor of Home Sweet Home, The   Ahlert; Leslie
Harlem Flat   Burke; Spina
Harlem Hospitality   Van Heusen
Harlem Lullaby   Robison
Harlem on My Mind   Berlin
Harlem Rhythm Dance   Razaf
Haven't Got No Peace of Mind   Rainger
He Always Gets His Man   Burke; Spina
He Passed Me By   Rainger
He Thinks, He Thinks   Burke; Spina
Headin' for a Weddin'   Adamson; Lane
Headin' for Heaven   Parish; Pollack
Heat Wave   Berlin
Heigh Ho the Gang's All Here   Lane
Hell and High Water   Coslow; Johnston
Hell of a Hole, A   Gershwin, George; Gershwin, Ira
Her Bodyguard   Coslow; Johnston
Here Lies Love   Rainger; Robin
Here's to You   Turk
He's a Cute Brute (A Gentleman and a Scholar)   Revel
He's a Cute Little Brute (A Gentleman and a
 Scholar)   Gordon; Revel
He's Mine   Johnson, Howard
Hey Young Fella   Adamson; Lane
Hey Young Fella Close Your Old Umbrella   Fields; McHugh
Hiawatha's Lullaby   Donaldson; Young, Joseph
Hi-Ho, Lack-a-Day, What Have We Got to Lose   Alter;
 Kahn
His Excellency Is Due   Kalmar; Ruby
His Honor, the Mayor   Burke; Spina
Hi'Ya Duchess   Burke; Spina
Hold Your Man   Brown, Nacio Herb; Freed, Arthur
Holding Up the Parade   Hoffman
Hollywood Be Thy Name   Loesser
Hollywood, Park Avenue and Broadway   Brown, Lew;
 Henderson
Home to Harlem   Brown, Lew; Henderson
Honey What a Pleasure Meetin' Up with You   Coots; Turk
Honeymoon Hotel   Dubin; Warren
Hot Choc'late Soldiers   Brown, Nacio Herb
Hot Spot   Harbach; Kern
Hot-Cha Joe the Georgia Gigolo   Yellen
How Could a Girl Like You Do a Thing Like That To a Boy
 Like Me on a Night Like This — Well, I Like
  That   Gordon; Revel

How Could We Be Wrong   Porter
How Could You Forget   Razaf
How Do I Look   DeSylva; Robin; Whiting
How Much Longer   Akst; Mitchell
How's Chances?   Berlin
Hundred Years Ago, A   Friend; Magidson
Hundred Years from Today, A   Washington; Young, Joseph;
 Young, Victor
Hush My Mouth If I Ain't Goin' South   Hoffman
Hustlin' and Bustlin' for Baby   Woods
I Always Keep My Girl Out Late   Hammerstein
I Am the Singer, You Are the Song   Caesar; Romberg
I Belong in Alabam'   Ager; Young, Joseph
I Bring a Song   Kahn; Young, Victor
I Can Sew a Button   Lerner, Sammy
I Can't Remember   Berlin
I Couldn't Tell Them What to Do   Turk
I Cover the Waterfront   Heyman
I Didn't Mean It   Magidson; Monaco
I Do   Webster
I Don't Wanna Lose You   Alter
I Dream of Indiana   Parish
I Envy the Moon   Ager; Young, Joseph
I Found You, I Lost You, I Found You Again   Gilbert
I Give You the Ladies   Egan
I Gotcha Where I Wantcha   Heyman
I Gotta Back to New York   Hart; Rodgers
I Hate to Think That You'd Grow Old Baby   Brown, Lew;
 Henderson
I Have to Laugh   Rainger; Robin
I Hear My Heart Saying You're Mine (I Hear My Heart
 Saying Mm-Mm)   Coots; Lewis
I Knew I'd Find You   Burke; Spina
I Knew You When   Coots
I Knew You'd Pass Me By   Lawrence
I Know a Foul Ball   Gershwin, George; Gershwin, Ira
I Know the Kind of Girl (A Girl Like You)   Schwartz, Arthur
I Lay Me Down to Sleep   Wrubel
I Learned About Love from Her   Parish
I Live for Love   Hammerstein
I Lost Another Sweetheart   Dixon
I Lost My Heart in the Subway   Gordon; Revel
I Love Only You   Porter
I Love You (Prince) Pizzicato   Gordon; Revel
I Married an Angel   Rodgers
I Never Make Love   Johnson, Howard
I Oughta Hate Ya — But I Don't   Ager; Young, Joseph
I Sing for You Alone   Washington
I Think I'm in Love with My Wife   Hammerstein
I Thought I Heard a Voice   Burke; Spina
I Wake Up Smiling   Ahlert; Leslie
I Wanna Meander with Miranda   Gordon; Revel
I Want a Fair and Square Man   Woods
I Want to Ring Bells   Coots
I Will Be a Soldier Bride   Kahn
I Wonder Who's Waltzing with the One I Love   Parish
I Won't Think about Tomorrow (As Long As You Love
 Me)   Gorney; Lerner, Sammy
I Would If I Could But I Can't   Parish
I'd Be Crazy If I Wasn't Crazy Over You   Bryan; Meyer
I'd Be Telling a Lie   Washington; Young, Victor
I'd Do It Again   Hart; Kahn; Rodgers
I'd Like to Take a Flying Leap Over the Moon   Lawrence
I'd Write a Song   Caesar; Romberg
If I Can Count on You   Ager

If I Ever Get a Job Again   Baer; Lewis
If I Feel This Way Tomorrow, Then It's Love   Brown, Lew;
   Henderson
If I Forgive You   Caesar
If I Had Napoleon's Hat   Woods
If I Had Waited for You   Razaf; Waller
If It's Good Enough for Gentlemen   Hammerstein
If Love Should Die   Wrubel
If that Dog o' Mine Could Talk   Magidson; Monaco
If You Don't Want to Be Sweehearts (I Don't Want to Be
   Friends)   Fain; Kahal
If You Ever Came Back   Conrad; Coslow
If You Lived in the Mountains   Burke; Spina
Il Est de Beaux Reves   Romberg
I'll Be Faithful   Washington; Wrubel
I'll Be Hard to Handle   Kern
I'll Pin Another Petal on the Daisy (So It'll Tell Me You
   Care)   Fain; Kahal
I'll Remember Only You   Brown, Nacio Herb; Freed, Arthur
I'll See You in Church   Hoffman
I'll Show You Off   Hammerstein
I'll Take an Option on You   Rainger; Robin
I'm a Bachelor in the Art of Ha-Cha-Cha   Coslow; Johnston
I'm a Lover of Paree   Rainger; Robin
I'm a Seeker of Beauty   Coslow
I'm a Singer   Cahn
I'm Dancin' on a Rainbow   Brown, Nacio Herb; Freed,
   Arthur
I'm Full of the Devil   Fields; McHugh
I'm Gettin' a New Deal from that Old Gal of Mine   Turk
I'm Gonna Go Go Go — To Chicago in 1933   Caesar;
   Friend
I'm Gonna Love You More in 1933   Washington
I'm Living on Love   Young, Joseph
I'm Lookin' for Another Handy Man   Arlen; Koehler
I'm Nuts About Mutts   Dixon; Woods
I'm Pally with Sally Again   Coots
I'm Sorry I Can't See My Old Gal Tonight   Fain; Young,
   Joseph
I'm Spending Tonight with Mother   Washington; Wrubel
I'm Taking a Chance on You   Stept
I'm That Way About Broadway   Magidson
I'm the Little Peanut Vendor's Little Missus   Carroll
I'm Thru (with) Saying I'm Thru   Kahn; Kalmar; Ruby
I'm Twisting Loops in Pretzels to Pass the Time
   Away   Johnson, Howard
In a Beer Garden Waltzing with You   Heyman
In a Cafe in Montmartre   Mercer
In a Midnight Club   Rainger; Robin
In a One Room Flat (And a Two Pants Suit)   Rainger; Robin
In Every Nook and Corner You Are Missing   Fain; Kahal
In My Garden   Caesar; Romberg
In the Little White Church on the Hill   Fields; McHugh
In the Moonlight   Kalmar; Ruby
In the Park in Paree   Rainger; Robin
In the Red   Akst; Eliscu
In the Silence of the Night   Washington; Young, Victor
In the Still of the Night   Gordon; Revel
Indian Summer   Mercer
Irish Serenade   Brown, Nacio Herb; Freed, Arthur
Isn't It Swell to Dream   Stept
(I Guess) It Had to Be that Way   Coslow; Johnston
It Isn't So Much That I Wouldn't   Adamson; Lane
It Looks Like Old Times Again   Johnson, Howard
It Might Have Been a Diff'rent Story   Monaco

It Must Be June   Dubin; Warren
It Was a Night in June   Clare; Gordon; Revel
It's a Long Dark Night   Rainger; Robin
It's All for the Best (I Loved You Yesterday)   Whiting
It's Bad for Me   Porter
It's Easy to Say Hello! It's Hard to Say Good Bye   Akst;
   Eliscu
It's from Hunger   Fain; Young, Joseph
It's Great to Be Alive   Brown, Lew; Henderson
It's Just a Song and Dance   Washington; Young, Joseph;
   Young, Victor
It's Midnight My Love   De Lange
It's Never Too Late   David, Mack; Heyman
It's Oh, It's Ah! (It's Wonderful)   Rainger; Robin
It's Paddy Again   Robin; Whiting
It's Sunday Down in Caroline   Livingston, Jerry
It's the Irish in Me   Clare; Gorney
It's the Music — Not the Words   Styne
It's the Talk of the Town   Livingston, Jerry
It's Time to Go Home   Johnson, Howard
It's Time to Sing Sweet Adeline Again   Davis; Fain
I've a Rendezvous with Spring   Duke; Harburg
I've Fallen for Love   Johnson, James P.; Razaf
I've Got a Little Confession to Make   Davis
I've Got a Roof Over My Head   Fields; McHugh
I've Got a Warm Spot in My Heart   Burke; Spina
I've Got a Warm Spot in My Heart for You   Young, Joseph
I've Got My Fingers Crossed till You Come Home   Turk
I've Got My Man Where I Want Him   Parish
I've Got the Funniest Feeling   Meyer
I've Got to Pass Your House to Get to My House   Brown,
   Lew
I've Got to Sing a Torch Song   Dubin; Warren
I've Got You Where I Want You   Waller
Je Vous Aimerai dans L'Ombre   Romberg
Jealousy Duet   Weill
Jimmy Had a Nickel   Hoffman
Josephine   Ahlert; Leslie
Juggling a Jig-Saw   Ahlert; Leslie
Just a Little Flower Shop Around the Corner   Woods
Just a Rose Covered Doorway   Hanley
Just Born to Be Lonesome   Kahn; Pollack
Just Follow the Sun   Donaldson; Kahn
Just Give Me the Girl   Donaldson
Just Like a Corner of Heaven to Me   Hanley
Kalua Lullaby   Kahn
Keep Young and Beautiful   Dubin; Warren
King Can Do No Wrong, The   Kalmar; Ruby
Kiss Her for Me   Hoffman
Kiss in the Moonlight and the World Began, A   Fain; Kahal
Knee Deep in Rhythm   Kahn
La Cancion Del Paris (Derelict Song)   Akst; Gilbert
Lady for a Day, A   Conrad; Mitchell
Lady of the Night   Kahn
Laugh, You Son of a Gun   Rainger; Robin
Lay Your Head on My Shoulder   Conrad; Coslow
Laying the Cornerstone   Hart; Rodgers
Lazy, Lousy Liza   Gordon; Revel
Lazybones   Carmichael; Mercer
Le Marquis de Faublas   Hammerstein
Learn to Croon   Coslow; Johnston
Legend of Mackie Messer   Weill
Lehua (Crimson Flower-Tree)   Friml
Let 'Em Eat Cake   Gershwin, George; Gershwin, Ira
Let 'Em Eat Caviar   Gershwin, George; Gershwin, Ira

Let Me Be Born Again   Washington; Young, Joseph; Young, Victor
Let Me Look Deep into Your Eyes   Egan
Let There Be Love, and There Was Love   Gorney
Let Your Way Home Be My Way Home   Monaco
Let's All Go Places   Donaldson
Let's Begin   Harbach; Kern
Let's Call It a Day   Brown, Lew; Henderson
Let's Confess   Freed, Arthur; Hoffman
Let's Fall in Love   Arlen; Koehler
Let's Give Love Another Chance   Magidson; Stept
Let's Go Bavarian   Adamson; Lane
Let's Go Down to the Beer Garden   Meyer
Let's Make Love Like the Crocodiles   Gorney; Harburg
Let's Sit This One Out   Fields; McHugh
Let's Whistle a Waltz   Fields; McHugh
Life Is a Merry-Go-Round   Brown, Nacio Herb; Freed, Arthur
Life's So Complete   Mercer
Life-Saver's Song, The   Schwartz, Arthur
Lifetime of Love   Wrubel
Lights, Camera, Action, Love   Gordon; Revel
Little Alibis   Baer
Little Beer, a Pretzel and You, A   Johnson, Howard
Little Bit of Love, A   Brennan
Little Hug, a Little Kiss, then You Fall in Love Again, A   Meyer
Little Locket of Long Ago, A   Woods
Little White Cross on a Little Green Hill, A   Parish
Little Women Like You (Little Women and Little Men)   Ahlert; Leslie
Little You Know   Ager; Schwartz, Jean; Young, Joseph
Live, Laugh and Love   Stept
Lonely Heart   Berlin
Lonely Lane   Fain; Kahal
Lonely Little Senorita   Rainger; Robin
Lonesome River   Magidson
Longing   Monaco
Look What You've Done   Kalmar; Ruby
Looking Forward   Davis; Oakland
Losing You   Harburg
Lou'siana Lullaby   Burke; Spina
Love and Kisses   David, Mack; Hoffman
Love and Rhythm   Brown, Lew; Henderson
Love Duet   Weill
Love Is Life   Gilbert
Love Is Love Anywhere   Arlen; Koehler
Love Is Queen, Love Is King   Hart; Rodgers
Love Is the Thing   Washington; Young, Victor
Love Lost   Dietz; Schwartz, Arthur
Love Songs of the Nile   Brown, Nacio Herb; Freed, Arthur
Love Tales   Ager; Davis; Stept
Love Theme Reel 4 No. 1   Warren
Love, You Are the Sunrise   Adamson; Lane
Lovely   Ahlert; Leslie
Lovely Lady   Brown, Nacio Herb; Freed, Arthur
Lovey   Freed, Arthur; Hoffman
Low Down Upon the Harlem River   Gordon; Revel
Lucky Fella   Fields; McHugh
Lucky Star, A   Whiting
Lucy's Song   Weill
Lullaby Lady   Johnson, Howard
Lullaby Moon   David, Mack; Hoffman; Silver
Ma Belle Petronille   Romberg
Madrigal   Harbach; Kern

Maedchen in Uniform   Fisher; Parish
Make a Note of It   Burke; Spina
Make Up Your Mind   Fields; McHugh
Making History   Washington; Young, Joseph; Young, Victor
Malibu   Ahlert; Leslie
Mamma Mockingbird (inst)   Carmichael
Mansion Sin Amor (Without Love in a Palace of Dreams)   Gilbert
Many Moons Ago   Gordon; Revel
March of Time, The   Alter
Marching Along Together   Dixon
Marching Song, The   Gilbert
Margineers   Fields; McHugh
Marlen (You Are My Song of Songs)   Heyman
Masquerading Is the Name of Love   Hoffman
May I?   Gordon; Revel
Maybe I Love You Too Much   Berlin
Mazie   Rainger
Me and Mine Are Doin' Fine   Woods
Me for You Forever   Heyman
Me Lord and Me Lady   Egan
Meet Me in the Gloaming   Freed, Arthur; Hoffman
Meet the Man About Town   Parish
Melody   Caesar; Romberg
Memory Waltz, The   Davis
Men of Calvert (Football Song)   Fain; Kahal
Metropolitan Opening   Berlin
Milkman's Blues   Lawrence
Mine   Gershwin, George; Gershwin, Ira
Minnie's Divorce   Young, Joseph
Mississippi Basin   Razaf
Mister Interlude   Hoffman; Parish
Modernistic   Johnson, James P.
Moody and Blue   Lerner, Sammy
Moon of Asia Land   Livingston, Jerry
Moon Song (That Wasn't Meant for Me)   Coslow; Johnston
Moon Will Ride Away, The   Hammerstein
Moonlight and Melody   Kahn
Moonlight and Pretzels   Gorney; Harburg
Moonlight in Your Eyes   Parish
Moonlight Memory   Heyman
Moon's on the Nile, The   Brown, Nacio Herb; Whiting
Moonstruck   Coslow; Johnston
Morning Glory   Young, Joseph
Morning, Noon and Night   Alter
Mother Mississippi   Meyer; Young, Joseph
Muggin' Lightly   Arlen; Koehler
Music from Across the Sea   Mercer
Music Makes Me   Eliscu; Kahn; Youmans
Music to My Ears   Coslow; Johnston
Musical Opening   Fields; McHugh
Musical Scene No. 1: Opening   DeSylva; Robin; Whiting
Musical Scene No. 2: Examination of Loo Loo   DeSylva; Robin
My Baby Made a Cry Baby of Me   Coots; Johnson, Howard
My Blue Bird's Singing the Blues   Rainger; Robin
My Castle in Maine   Heyman
My Dancing Lady   Fields; McHugh
My Design for Living   Gordon; Revel
My Favorite Person   Fields; McHugh
My Fiddle and Me   Young, Joseph
My First Love to Last   Whiting
My Future Wife   Rainger; Robin
My Girl Don't Love Me   Caesar; Motzan
My Great Desire   Von Tilzer

My Gypsy Rhapsody   Lawrence
My Hat's on the Side of My Head   Woods
My Heart's Desire   Whiting
My Imaginary Sweetheart   Akst; Eliscu
My International Girl   Lerner, Sammy
My Louisa   Porter
My Love   Washington; Young, Victor
My Moonlight Madonna   Webster
My Mother in the Fatherland   Young, Joseph
My Mother's Garden   Hanley
My! Oh, My!   Gordon; Revel
My Old Man   Mercer
My Picture Puzzle of You   Washington; Wrubel
My Queen of Lullaby Land   Coslow; Johnston
My Rose Town   Lawrence
My Soul Mate   Washington; Wrubel
My Sunday Gal   Parish
My Wild Oat   Woods
Mysterious Mr. Zilch, The   Parish
42nd Street   Dubin; Warren
Neauville Sur Mer   Porter
Never Before   Davis
Never Had an Education   Caesar; Romberg
Never Say No   Porter
New Deal Rhythm   Harburg; Rose
Niagara Moon   Heyman
Nice Goings On   Schwartz, Arthur
Night   Gilbert
Night Time on the Danube   Fisher
No Comprenez, No Capish, No Versteh!   Gershwin, George; Gershwin, Ira
No More Love   Dubin; Warren
No No War   Akst; Eliscu
Normandy Eyes   Bryan
Not for All the Rice in China   Berlin
Nothing Less than Beautiful   Wrubel
Nova Scotia Moonlight   Coslow; Johnston
N.R.A. March   Woods
N.R.A. Song   Cohan
Nursery Rhymes   Kahn
Nymph Errant   Porter
Odds and Ends of an Old Love Affair   Livingston, Jerry
Oh How I Adore You   Turk
(I Won't Be There to Hear) Oh Promise Me   Myrow; Parish
Okay G-A!   Ager; Schwartz, Jean; Young, Joseph
Ol' Debbil Microphone   Robison
Ol' Pappy   Livingston, Jerry
Old Aunt Kate   Mercer
Old Friends, Old Wines, Old Love Songs   Webster
Old Man Harlem   Carmichael
Old Mother Nature   Brown, Lew; Henderson
Old Neighborhood   Coots
Old, Old Man, with an Old, Old Pipe and an Old, Old Lady Beside Him, An   Gordon; Revel
Ole Mammy Ain't Gonna Sing No More   Magidson; Monaco
Ole-O the Gigilo   Hanley
On and On and On   Gershwin, George; Gershwin, Ira
On Any Street   Brown, Lew; Henderson
On My Calendar of Love   Gilbert; Hanley
On Sunday, When We Gathered 'Round the Organ   Razaf; Waller
On Sweetheart Bay   Johnson, Howard
On the Bosphorus   Hammerstein
On to Africa   Caesar; Romberg

Once in a While   Lerner, Sammy
One Heart   Stept
One Minute to One   Coots; Lewis
One Morning in May   Carmichael; Parish
One Note Trumpet Player, The   Hoffman
One of These Days the Two of Us Are Gonna Be Blue   Coots; Lewis
One Sunday Afternoon   Coslow; Johnston
One Tiny Tear   Woods
Only Yesterday   Donaldson; Lawrence
Ooh, Gee, What You Do to Me   Burke; Spina
Ooh, I'm Thinking   Brown, Lew; Henderson
Ooh! What I Could Do to You!   Friend; Magidson; Stept
Oo-oo-ooh! Honey! What You Do to Me   Friend
Orchid to You, An   Gordon; Revel
Orchids in the Moonlight   Eliscu; Kahn; Youmans
Our Big Love Scene   Brown, Nacio Herb; Freed, Arthur
Our Little Lady Upstairs   Caesar; Romberg
Our Secret   Egan
Our Wedding Day   Berlin
Out in the Apple Orchard (With the Apple of My Eye)   Burke; Spina; Young, Joseph
Out in the Great Open Spaces   Coslow; Johnston
Out of the Deep   Kahn
Pais Ideal (The Islands Are Calling Me)   Akst; Gilbert
Palooka (It's a Grand Old American Name)   Burke
Panhandler   Carroll
Paradise Waltz   Stept
Paris   Akst; Eliscu
Part Two Opening   Kalmar; Ruby
Passe   Egan
Patter 42nd Street   Dubin; Warren
Peanuts and Kisses   Alter
Peter, Peter   Woods
Pettin' in the Park   Dubin; Warren
Physician, The   Porter
Pickaninnies' Heaven   Coslow; Johnston
Pirate Jenny   Weill
Place in the Sun   Schwartz, Arthur
Play Ball   Coslow; Johnston
Play Half a Chorus   Fields; McHugh
Playin' with the Devil (And Raisin' Cain)   Myrow
Please Don't Talk about My Man   Razaf
Please Mr. President   Wrubel
Plumbing   Porter
Polly Wants a Cracker   Burke; Spina
Pompadour   Caesar; Romberg
Poor Mrs. Peachum   Weill
Positively Love You   Fields; McHugh
Pour Faire le Tournedos   Romberg
Pour se Faire Adorer   Romberg
Pour Vivre Aupres de Vous   Romberg
Practising the Piano   Silver; Wrubel
Presidents on Parade   Fisher
Pretty Lady   Dubin; Warren
Pretzels   Turk
Pride of the Mountainside   Fields; McHugh
Prologue   Fields; McHugh
Puddin' Head Jones   Bryan
Put a Tax on Love   Gilbert; Warren
Quand les Soldats Vont au Pas   Romberg
Queenie   Conrad
Quiche (inst.)   Youmans
Ragamuffin Jane   Burke; Spina
Raisin' the Rent   Arlen; Koehler

Rasputin (That Highfalutin' Lovin' Man)   Wrubel
Reflections in the Water   Webster
Remember My Forgotten Man   Dubin; Warren
Rendezvous   Caesar; Egan; Romberg
Renunion in Vienna   Turk
Rest Is History, The   Stept
Restless   Brown, Lew; Henderson
Revolt in Cuba   Berlin
Rhythm   Hart; Rodgers
Rhythm of the Raindrops   Hanley; Kahn
Road Is Open Again, The   Fain; Kahal
Rock-a-Bye River   Parish
Roll Out of Bed with a Smile   Ager; Young, Joseph
Roll Up the Carpets, Push Back the Chairs   Hoffman
Roll Your Bones   Akst; Mitchell
Rollin' on Our Roller Skates   Washington; Wrubel
Romance (inst.)   Bloom
Romance of Our People, The   Hoffman; Silver
Rome Wasn't Built in a Day   Dubin; Warren
Rose de France   Romberg
Rubadub Dub   Egan
Ruins   Porter
Rumpus on the Campus   Hoffman
Runaway Blues   Eliscu
Same Time, The Same Place, Tomorrow Night, The   David, Mack; Davis
Save Me from Being Lonesome   Baer
Say It's Not the Last Time   Johnson, Howard
Say What You Mean, and Mean What You're Saying   Young, Joseph
Say Yes to Me   Meyer
Scene and Pas de Seul   Harbach; Kern
Second Finale   Weill
Send a Melody Around the World   Donaldson
Send My Mail to Tennessee   Wrubel
Serenade   Johnson, Howard
Serenata Bufa (Serenade)   Gilbert
Sewing Department Dance   Harbach; Kern
Shadow Waltz   Dubin; Warren
Shadows on the Swanee   Burke; Spina; Young, Joseph
Shake Your Head from Side to Side   Cahn
Shall We Love   Sigman
Shame on You   Arlen; Heyman
Shanghai Lil   Dubin; Warren
She Changed Her Hi-De-Hi-De for His Yodal-O-De-Ay   Schwartz, Jean
She Loves Me Not   Heyman; Schwartz, Arthur
(She Walks Like You, She Talks Like You) She Reminds Me of You   Gordon; Revel
She Was a China Tea Cup   Rainger; Robin
Sherman   Wrubel
She's Not the Type   Arlen; Koehler
Shim Sham Shimmy Dance, The   Razaf
Shirts By the Millions   Gershwin, George; Gershwin, Ira
Shoo Shoo Boogie Boo   Robin
Show Us the Way, Blue Eagle   Willson
Shuffle Off to Buffalo   Dubin; Warren
Si Petite   Parish
Si Vous Aimez les Poitrines   Porter
Sidewalk Waltz, The   Coots; Young, Joseph
Siempre (Till the End of Time)   Akst; Gilbert
Silvery Moonlight (Only a Moonbeam Dream)   Robin
Since You Have Chosen Me   Young, Joseph
Sing American Tunes   Akst; Eliscu
Sing High, Sing Low   Adamson; Lane

Sing to Me   Akst; Eliscu
Singing to You   Oakland
Sit Down and Tell Me How I Stand   Gordon; Revel
Sittin' on a Backyard Fence   Fain; Kahal
Sittin' Up Waitin' for You   Razaf; Waller
Skate with Me   Berlin
Sleep Me Darling Sleep Within My Arms   Lawrence
Sleeping Beauty   Hart; Rodgers
Slower than Molasses   Razaf; Waller
Smile On Dearie   Bryan
(When Your Heart's on Fire) Smoke Gets in Your Eyes   Harbach; Kern
Smoke Rings   Washington
Snap Out of It   Rainger; Robin
Snowball   Carmichael
Snowflakes   David, Mack
So It's Bridge Again Tonight   Ahlert; Leslie
So This Is Susie   Coots; Lewis
Society Wedding   Berlin
Soldier's Song, The   Weill
Soliloquy   Hammerstein
Solomon   Porter
Someday, Sometime, Somewhere   Hanley
Something Came and Got Me in the Spring   Schwartz, Jean
Something Had to Happen   Harbach
Something's Got to Happen   Harbach; Kern
Something's in the Air   David, Mack
Somewhere in Sonora   Parish
Song of the Aimlessness of Life   Weill
Song Without a Mountain, A   Washington; Wrubel
Sophisticated Lady   Ellington; Mills; Parish
Southern Memories (inst.)   Bloom
Spaghetti   Loesser; Motzan
Spanish in My Eyes, The   Johnson, James P.
Spanish Love Song: Chiquita Senorita   Young, Joseph
Spanish Sweetheart   Caesar
Speakin' of the Devil Here She Is   David, Mack
Spending My Time, Saving My Love   Adamson; Coots
Spring Fever   Silver; Wrubel
Springtime in Old Granada   Hanley
Stately Mansion (inst.), A   Bloom
Stay on the Right Side of the Road   Bloom; Koehler
Stay Out of My Dreams   Washington
Steins   Brown, Lew; Henderson
Steins on the Table   Kahn
Stormy Weather   Arlen; Koehler
Strange Case of Hennessy, The   Burke; Spina
Street Scene   Eliscu; Kahn; Youmans
Strike Me Pink (If I Don't Think I'm Falling in Love)   Brown, Lew; Henderson
Stringin' Along on a Shoestring   Adamson; Lane
Strolling Thru the Park One Day   Motzan
Summer Is Over and So Is My Dream of Love   Friend
Summertime Pal Have You Forgotten Me   Coots; Johnson, Howard
Sunshine Ahead   Conrad; Coslow
Supper Time   Berlin
Sur la Mer Immense   Romberg
Sure of Me   Hoffman
Surprise!   Hoffman
Sweet Betty   Lerner, Sammy
Sweet Dreams, Pretty Lady   Hanley
Sweet Little Sweetheart   Wrubel
Sweet Madness   Washington; Young, Victor
Sweet Nudity   Porter

Sweet One   Schwartz, Arthur
Sweet Things in Life, The   Lawrence
Sweetheart Darlin'   Kahn
Sweetheart of Sweet Sixteen   Coots; Kahn
Sweetheart Song, The   Magidson; Wrubel
Sweets   Clare; Magidson; Stept
Swingy Little Thingy   Stept
Sympathizin' with Me   Coslow; Johnston
Take Your Time   Burke; Spina
Talking in My Sleep   Mercer
Tall Timber   Razaf; Waller
Tango Ballad   Weill
Tappin' the Barrel   Washington; Young, Joseph; Young, Victor
Tell Me I Know How to Love   Hart; Rodgers
Tell Me Oriole   Ahlert; Leslie
Temptation   Brown, Nacio Herb; Freed, Arthur
Testament   Weill
Thank Heaven for You   Rainger; Robin
Thanks   Coslow; Johnston
That Dame from Rio   Rainger
That Great American Home   Wrubel
That's Me without You   Coots; Johnson, Howard
That's the Rhythm of the Day (Go, Go, Go)   Hart; Rodgers
That's What He Did   Gershwin, George; Gershwin, Ira
That's What I Like 'Bout the South   Razaf
Theatre Marquis   Brown, Lew; Henderson
There Is a Ball at the Savoy   Hammerstein
There Must Be a First Time   Egan
There'll Never Be Another Girl Like You   Friend; Magidson
There's a Bluebird at My Window (And a Landlord at My Door)   Gordon; Revel
There's a Little Bit of You (In Every Love Song)   Fain; Harburg
There's a Lucky Guy   Rainger; Robin
There's a New Day Comin'   Ager; Young, Joseph
There's a New Moon Over My Shoulder   Dubin; Fain
There's a Ring Around My Rainbow   Dixon
There's a Ring Around the Moon   Mercer
There's Always Tomorrow   Hoffman; Silver
There's No Harm in Hoping   Woods
There's Nothing New in I Love You   Davis; Oakland
They Can't Repeal My Love for You   Johnson, Howard
They're All Congratulatin' Me   Meyer
They're Always Entertaining   Porter
Things Look Brighter Again   Coots; Lewis
Third Finale   Weill
This Is Only the Beginning   Arlen; Koehler
This Is the Night   Coslow
This Little Piggie Went to Market   Coslow
This Lovely Night   Hammerstein
This Program Comes to You from My Heart   Hoffman
This Time It's Love   Coots; Lewis
Those Eddie Cantor Eyes   Akst; Gilbert
Three Cornered Moon   David, Mack; Hoffman; Silver
Three Greeks, The   Eliscu; Kahn; Youmans
Throttle Throttlebottom   Gershwin, George; Gershwin, Ira
Tick-Tock   Hart; Rodgers
Till Doomsday   Lerner, Sammy
Till Then   Gershwin, George; Gershwin, Ira
To Be or Not to Be   Berlin
To Think That You Should Care for Me   Parish
Tomorrow My Honey's Comin' Home   Turk
Tonight May Never Come Again   Caesar; Romberg
Tony's Wife   Adamson; Lane

Torch Singer, The   Rainger; Robin
Torch Songs   Brown, Lew; Henderson
Touch of Your Hand, The   Harbach; Kern
Tramp Tramp Tramp the Boys Are Marching   Kahal
Tree Was a Tree, A   Gordon; Revel
Trouble in Paradise   Ager; Schwartz, Jean
True Love   Robin; Whiting
Tumble in a Rumble Seat   Coots
Turn Back the Clock   Parish
Turn That Frown Upside Down   Rainger; Robin
'Twas a Balmy Summer's Evening   Friend; Magidson; Stept
'Twas Awfully Nice of You   Caesar; Friend
Tweedledee for President   Gershwin, George; Gershwin, Ira
Twenty Four Hours a Day   Ager; Young, Joseph
Twenty Million People   Coslow; Johnston
Twixt the Devil and the Deep Blue Sea   Schwartz, Arthur
Two Aristocrats   Coslow; Johnston
Two Buck Tim from Timbuctoo   Heyman; Hoffman
Two Lips Like Cherries   Kahn
Two Little Windows and One Little Door   Lewis
Two Tickets to Georgia   Coots; Young, Joseph
Under a Blanket of Blue   Livingston, Jerry
Under My Umbrella   Meyer
Under the Lamp of Love   Fain; Kahal
Union Square   Gershwin, George; Gershwin, Ira
Up and at 'Em   Gershwin, George; Gershwin, Ira
Up and Down   Hammerstein
Up in a Tree   Akst; Gilbert
Victims of the Voodoo Drums   Washington; Young, Joseph; Young, Victor
Vienna in May   Kahn
Viennese Refrain   Johnson, Howard
Vilia   Johnson, Howard
Virgins Wrapped in Cellophane   Webster
Voice of the City   Lawrence
Voo Doo Pageant (inst.)   Washington; Young, Victor
Waiter's Song   Eliscu; Kahn; Youmans
Waiters v. Waitresses   Porter
Wait'll My Ship Comes In   Parish
Waltz Away the Night   Egan
Waltz Is On, The   Bloom; Koehler
Waltz with Me   Gordon; Revel
Waltzing in the Carolines   Young, Joseph
Was My Face Red   Akst; Freed, Ralph
Waterfall Melody   Donaldson
Way to Love, The   Coslow; Johnston; Rainger; Robin
We Couldn't Do Better than That   Akst; Eliscu
We Reached a Perfect Understanding   Parish
We Were the Best of Friends   Lewis; Meyer; Young, Joseph
We Won't Have to See the Place   Bryan; Wrubel
We Won't Have to Sell the Farm   Bryan; Wrubel
Wedding Song   Weill
Wee Willie Winkle   Coots
Weep No More, My Baby   Heyman
We'll All Be in Heaven When the Dollar Goes to Hell   Berlin
We'll Have a Honeymoon Someday   Woods
We'll Make Hay While the Sun Shines   Brown, Nacio Herb; Freed, Arthur
We'll Make Love When It Rains   Brown, Nacio Herb
We're Going to Be Dramatic   Heyman
(Gold Diggers Song) We're in the Money   Dubin; Warren
We're Not Too Poor for That   Caesar; Motzan
We're Only Little Extras Looking for an Opportunity   Gordon; Revel

We're Together Again   Brown, Nacio Herb; Freed, Arthur
West Wind Blow in the Windmill's Face   Egan; Hoffman
We've Got to Get On   Schwartz, Arthur
What — No Dixie?   Washington; Young, Joseph; Young,
    Victor
What a Man   Coots
What a Perfect Combination   Akst; Caesar; Kalmar; Ruby
What a Pleasant Surprise   Heyman
What a Young Girl Ought to Know   Schwartz, Arthur
What Are We Waiting For   David, Mack
What Do I Care It's Home   Turk
What Do You Want with Money   Hart; Rodgers
What Is There About You   Fields; McHugh
What Will I Do Without You   Mercer
Whatever It Is, I'm Against It   Kalmar
Whatever You Do   Schwartz, Arthur
What'll Become of Me   Stept
What's Good for the Goose Is Good for the Gander   Friend
When I Dance with You   Clare; Monaco
When I Kiss You Goodnight in the Morning   Lawrence
When I Played Peek-a-Boo with Daddy and He Played
    Peek-a-Boo with Me   Bryan
When Old Friends Are Drifting Apart   Woods
When the Chapel Bells Tolled on the Hill   Johnson, Howard
When the Judges Doff the Ermine   Gershwin, George;
    Gershwin, Ira
When the Last Rose of Summer Whispers
    Goodbye   Livingston, Jerry
When the Moon Swings Low Along the Ohio   Johnson,
    Howard
When the One You Love Is Gone   Pollack
When the Robins Return in the Spring   Livingston, Jerry
When the Sweet Magnolias Bloom Again   Young, Joseph
When Tomorrow Comes   Fain; Kahal
When You Kissed Me   Clare
When You Tell Me that You Dare   Lawrence
When You Were the Girl on a Scooter and I Was a Boy on
    the Bike   Gordon; Revel
When Your Love Comes Your Way   Porter
When You're Falling in Love with the Irish   Hart; Rodgers
Where Have I Heard that Melody   Coslow; Johnston
Where the Mountains Touch the Sky   Cahn
Whippoorwill Warble Away   Coots; Dixon
Whistlin' Cowboy, The   Webster
Who Cares About Tomorrow?   Dubin; Warren
Who Committed the Murder?   Heyman
Who Do You Think You Are   Heyman
Who Walks in When I Walk Out   Freed, Ralph; Hoffman
Whole World Loves, The   Caesar; Romberg
Whoops-A-Daisy There I Go! Fallin' in Love
    Again   Monaco; Parish
Who's in Love   Baer; Young, Joseph
Who's the Greatest —?   Gershwin, George; Gershwin, Ira
Why Do We Hurt the Ones We Love?   Razaf; Waller
Why Have You Eyes?   Hart; Rodgers
Why Is It Night in My Heart?   Lewis
Will It Always Be Me   David, Mack
Will You Love Me Tomorrow, As You Love Me
    Today   Davis; Hanley; Oakland
Wind's in the West, The   Woods
Winter Interlude   Hoffman; Parish
With All My Heart   Burke; Spina
With You Beside Me   Kahn; Young, Victor
With You Here and Me Here   Schwartz, Arthur
Won't You Say Hello   Bryan; Meyer

Would You Believe Me Sweetheart   Conrad; Coslow
Wrong   Schwartz, Jean; Young, Joseph
Yes Me   Hart; Rodgers
Yes, My Dear   Gordon; Revel
Yesterdays   Harbach; Kern
You   Mercer
You and the Moon and Me   Baer
You Are My Destiny   Johnson, Howard; Silver
You Are Too Beautiful   Hart; Rodgers
You Can Be Had (Be Careful)   DeSylva; Robin; Whiting
You Can't Play My Ukelele   Hoffman
You Done Me Dirty   Johnson, James P.; Mills
You Excite Me   Parish
You Have Taken My Heart   Mercer
You Inspire a Mad Desire   Harbach; Kern
You Made a Jig-Saw Puzzle Out of My Heart   Coots; Young,
    Joseph
You Never Need Latin or Greek   Caesar; Romberg
You Ought to See Sally on Sunday   Woods
You Took the Words Right Out of My Mouth   Lane
You'll Never Get Up to Heaven that Way   Baer; Lerner,
    Sammy
Young and Healthy   Dubin; Warren
Your Type Is Coming Back   Stept
You're Beautiful Tonight, My Dear   Young, Joseph
You're Devastating   Harbach; Kern
You're Easy on the Eyes   Coots; Johnson, Howard
You're Getting to Be a Habit with Me   Dubin; Warren
You're Gonna Be Surprised Tonight   Dixon
You're Gonna Lose Your Gal   Monaco; Young, Joseph
You're in My Power Ha! Ha! Ha! Ha! Ha!   Hoffman
You're Mine You   Heyman
You're My Past, Present and Future   Gordon; Revel
You're My Thrill   Clare; Gorney
You're OK   Parish
You're Such a Comfort to Me   Gordon; Revel
You're Too Far Away   Porter
You've Got a Right to Be Wrong   Fain; Kahal
You've Got Everything   Donaldson; Kahn
You've Gotta Eat Your Spinach, Baby   Gordon; Revel
Yow Sah   Waller; Young, Joseph
Zingara Vagabundo (Song of the Romany Band)   Gilbert

1934

Absentminded   Dietz; Schwartz, Arthur
Ace in the Hole   Waller
Adam Never Had Any Mammy, Got Along, Got Along, Got
    Along   Young, Joseph
After My Blues Came a Bluebird   Gordon
Afternoon in Amsterdam, An   Heyman
Ain't It Nice?   Mills
Ain't That Sumpin'   Donaldson; Kahn
Album Song   Arlen; Gershwin, Ira; Harburg
All I Do Is Dream of You   Brown, Nacio Herb; Freed, Arthur
All Is Forgiven Baby Come Home   Coots; Parish
All on Account of a Strawberry Sundae   Dixon; Wrubel
All the Elks and Masons   Arlen; Gershwin, Ira; Harburg
All Through the Night   Porter
All Washed Up   Dubin; Warren
Alone on the Range   David, Mack
Alphabet Song   Johnson, Howard
Am I to Blame?   Baer; Lewis
Amigo Mio   Burke; Spina
And I Still Do   Ahlert; Leslie

Annina   Friml
Anything Goes   Porter
Anything That's Part of You   Dixon; Wrubel
Apassionette   Heyman
Arabian Number   McHugh
As Far As I'm Concerned   Livingston, Jerry
As Long As I Live   Arlen; Koehler
Autograph Your Photograph for Me   Hoffman
Autumn in New York   Duke
Baby Duck   Young, Victor
Baby Stars   Hart; Rodgers
Baby, Take a Bow   Brown, Lew; Gorney
Baby's Bottle   Woods
Bachelor of the Art   Coslow; Johnston
Bad in Every Man, The   Hart; Rodgers
Barcarolle   Johnson, Howard
Bathtub Ran Over Again   Mercer
Be Like the Bluebird   Porter
Beat of My Heart, The   Burke; Spina
Beautiful Face — Have a Heart   Rose
Beautiful Lady   Friend
Beautiful Land of My Dreams   Razaf
Beautiful Night   Hanley
Beautiful You   Carroll
Beautifying the City (Life Begins at City Hall)   Arlen;
     Gershwin, Ira; Harburg
Beauty and the Beast   Kalmar; Ruby
Beauty Must Be Loved   Fain; Kahal
Beginning of a Beautiful Love, The   Stept; Washington
Behold a Prima Donna   Smith, Harry B.
Belle of the Nineties   Coslow; Johnston
Beneath the Curtain of Night   Mercer
Best of Things Are Free, The   Young, Victor
Better for Both of Us   Ager; Coots; Young, Joseph
Better to Love You My Dear, The   David, Mack; Hoffman
Billy Symphony   Pollack
Black Diamond   Hart; Rodgers
Blankety Blank, I'm a Son-of-a-Gun (If I'm Not in
     Love)   De Lange
Blow, Gabriel Blow   Porter
Blue Bird of Happiness   Heyman
Blue in Love   Young, Joseph
Blue Moon   Hart; Rodgers
Blue Sky Avenue   Conrad; Magidson; Mitchell
Blue White Moonlight   Donaldson; Kahn
Bluebird Come Back and Feather Your Nest   Gilbert
Bon Voyage   Porter
Bonita   Lewis
Boogie Man, The   Coslow
Born to Be Kissed   Dietz; Schwartz, Arthur
Bottoms Up   Adamson; Lane
Boulevard of Broken Dreams, The   Dubin; Warren
Bowl of Chop Suey and You-ey, A   Bullock
Brazilian Baby   Edwards
Breakfast Ball   Arlen; Koehler
Bridesmaids Ballet   Henderson; Koehler
Broadway's Gone Hill-Billy   Brown, Lew; Gorney
Buddie Beware   Porter
Burning!   Hart; Rodgers
Butterfingers   Berlin
Butterfly   Webster
Buy My Violets   Johnson, Howard
By the Great Horn Spoon (You Can Bet You're in Love)   De
     Lange; Mills
By the Taj Mahal   Brown, Nacio Herb; Freed, Arthur

Cabin Dance   Henderson
Cabin in the Cotton & Cotton in the Cabin   Caesar
Call It Anything, It Wasn't Love   Fisher
Call of Love   Kahn
Call of the Road, The   Young, Joseph
Call to Arms   Heyman
Calling All Cars   Monaco
Calling All Stars   Akst; Brown, Lew
Candle in the Window, A   Parish
Can't Find My Way   Heyman
Captain's Daughter, The   Bryan
Carefree   Heyman
Careful with My Heart   Harburg
Careless-Like   Ager
Carlo, The   Brown, Nacio Herb; Freed, Arthur
Carnival Ballet   Friml
Carnival Song (Czardas)   Gilbert
Carolina   Brown, Lew; Gorney
Carolina Cabin Days   Johnson, Howard
'Cause You Won't Play House   Harburg
Cavachok   Heyman
Cavaliers   Friml
C'est la Vie   Arlen; Gershwin, Ira; Harburg
Christmas Night in Harlem   Parish
Circus Queen   Hammerstein; Kern
Clothes Line Ballet (inst.)   Waller
Clouds   Donaldson; Kahn
Cocktails for Two   Coslow; Johnston
Coffee in the Morning and Kisses at Night   Dubin; Warren
College Hymn   Brown, Nacio Herb; Freed, Arthur
College Rhythm   Gordon; Revel
Collegiate Wedding   Fain; Kahal
Colonel, Major and Captain   Donaldson; Kahn
Color Music   Smith, Harry B.
Come on a Dip, Dip, Dip in the Deep Deep
     Water   Livingston, Jerry
Comedy Dance   Friml
Congo Kate   Johnson, James P.
Congress of the U.S.A.   Motzan
Continental Honeymoon   Hanley
Continental (You Kiss While You're Dancing), The   Conrad;
     Magidson
Corn Beef and Cabbage I Love You   Rainger; Robin
Cosmetics By Dupree   Dixon; Wrubel
Count Your Blessings   Caesar
Countess Dubinsky   Rose
Court Dance   Friml
Cowboy, Where Are Your Riding To   Dietz; Schwartz,
     Arthur
Crazy Dream, A   Ahlert; Leslie
Creole   Caesar; Meyer
Creole Man   Gordon; Revel
Cuban Serenade   Burke; Spina
Cubanola Rumbanette   Lerner, Sammy
Cuh-Razy for Love   Coots
Cupid   Coslow
Cute Little Rumba (Rum-Ti-Di-Um-Ba Bay)   Clare; Gorney
Dames   Dubin; Warren
Dance Charactuertique   Friml
Dance of Times   Friml
Dancing and Dreaming   Ager; Coots; Davis
Dancing in the Moonlight   Donaldson; Kahn
Dancing with My Darling   Parish
Dancing with My Shadow   Woods
Danse Modern   Friml

Dawn (My Dawn of Love)   Pollack; Webster
Day Without You, A   Coslow
Debutante   Fields; McHugh
Debutante Waltz, The   Meyer
Declaration Day   Henderson; Koehler
Devil in Disguise   Heyman; Romberg
Did You Ever Have the Feeling You're Flying   Hoffman
Dinah's Daughter   Fields; McHugh
Ding Dong   Smith, Harry B.
Disappointed in Love   Razaf
Dixie After Dark   Mills; Oakland; Parish
Do I Love You?   Rainger; Robin
Do Me a Favor   Lawrence
Doesn't that Mean Anything to You   Loesser
Doin' the Dumb-Bell   Gordon; Revel
Doll Dance (inst.), The   Gorney
Dolores   Hart; Kahn; Rodgers
Don't Ever Do That to Me   Fisher
Don't Kiss Me Again   De Lange; Mills
Don't Let It Bother You   Gordon; Revel
Don't Let It Happen Again   Livingston, Jerry
Don't Never Do-o-o That, You Nasty Man   Conrad;
     Oakland
Don't Say Good-Bye to Your Summer Love   Fisher
Don't Say Goodnight   Dubin; Warren
Don't Stay Away too Long, Baby   Johnson, Howard
Don't Stop Me If You've Heard It Before   Hoffman
Don't Take My Boop-oop-a-doop Away   Lerner, Sammy
Don't Tell Me It's Bad   Henderson; Koehler
Doo-ah Doo-ah Know What I'm Doing   Akst; Turk
(While the Sun Is Going Down) Down Home   Rainger;
     Robin
Down on the Old-Time Farm   Schwartz, Arthur
Down T'Uncle Bill's   Carmichael; Mercer
Down Where Banjoes Were Born   Robison
Dr. Watson and Mr. Holmes   Mercer
Dream Kingdom   Heyman
Dream Man, Make Me Dream Some More   Ager; Young,
     Joseph
Dream of Me Darling Tonight   Johnson, Howard
Dream Stars   Friend
Dream Was So Beautiful, The   Brown, Nacio Herb; Freed,
     Arthur
Dreaming Out Loud   Rainger; Robin
Earful of Music, An   Donaldson; Kahn
East River   Yellen
Easy Come, Easy Go   Heyman
Easy Goin' Gal   Rainger; Whiting
Easy on the Eyes   David, Mack; Hoffman
Easy to Love   Fain; Kahal
Ebony Rhapsody   Coslow; Johnston
Effervescent (inst.)   Waller
Eight Girls in a Boat   Coslow
Eight Little Darkies on a Fence   Kahn
El Choclo   Fields; McHugh
Elegie   Johnson, Howard
Emaline   Parish
Endless Nights   Kalmar; Ruby
European Importation, A   Young, Joseph
Evenin'   Parish
Ever Since the Night You Left Me   Ager; Young, Joseph
Every Day Is Father's Day with Baby   Caesar; Henderson;
     Yellen
Everybody   Burke; Spina
Everything Changes but Love   Friml

Everything Is Coming Back Again (Won't You Come Back to
     Me)   Parish
Ev'rybody Get Hot   Razaf
Ev'rybody Loves a Sailor   Parish
Ev'rything Is Peaches 'neath the Old Apple Tree   Meyer
Ev'rything You Said Came True   Friend; Monaco
Excuse Me   Young, Joseph
Exquisite Moment   Caesar; Friml
Eyes of the Night   Dixon; Wrubel
Fair and Warmer   Dubin; Warren
Fairer on the Riviera   Warren
Fare Thee Well   Coslow; Johnston
Farewell Covina   Fain; Kahal
Farmer Takes a Wife, The   Freed, Ralph
Father Wanted to Two-Step, Mother Wanted to
     Waltz   Ager; Schwartz, Jean; Young, Joseph
Father's Day March (inst.)   Henderson
Feathers in the Wind   David, Mack; Silver
Feelin' High   Dietz; Donaldson
Fences   Young, Victor
Few of the Things I'd Like to Do for You, A   Friend;
     Monaco
Fiddlesticks   Henderson
Fifth Avenue — A Sidewalk in Paris   Harburg
Fight 'Em   Brown, Nacio Herb; Freed, Arthur
First Kiss of Spring, The   Webster
Flamenco   Dietz; Schwartz, Arthur
Flirtation Walk   Dixon; Wrubel
Fly Away to Ioway   Hart; Rodgers
Follies Chorale Ensemble, The   Harburg
Following in Mother's Footsteps   Caesar; Henderson; Yellen
Fool that I Am   Mercer
Fool There Was, A   Fisher
Foolin' with the Other Woman's Man   Akst; Brown, Lew
For All We Know   Coots; Lewis
For Ev'ry Little Girl Who's Lonely, There's a Boy Who's
     Blue   Monaco; Parish
For the Thrill of a Hill Billy Waltz   Schwartz, Jean; Young,
     Joseph
For Your Convenience   Young, Joseph
Forbidden Lips   Gorney
Forever   Donaldson; Kahn
Forsaking All Others   Donaldson; Kahn
Four Frightened People   Rainger; Robin
F'r Instance   Gorney
'Fraidy Cat   Magidson; Monaco
Freckle Face, You're Beautiful   Friend
Friendly Moon, The   Young, Victor
From Now On   Brown, Nacio Herb; Freed, Arthur
Frosted Chocolate   Rose; Webster
Fruitti Di Mare   Friml
Full of the Devil   Fields; McHugh
Fun to Be Fooled   Arlen; Gershwin, Ira; Harburg
Funny Old House   Hammerstein; Kern
Gaiety Chorus Girls, The   Hammerstein; Kern
Gallant Lady   Ahlert; Leslie
Garret in the Gay Montmartre, A   Meyer; Young, Joseph
Gavotte   Friml
General Hiram Johnson Jefferson Brown   Donaldson; Kahn
George White's Scandals   Caesar; Yellen
Georgia May   Razaf
Georgia's Gorgeous Gal   Parish
Get Goin'   Conrad; Oakland
Get Thee Behind Me Satan   Berlin
Gift from Heaven, A   Young, Joseph

Gift of Gab   Conrad; Magidson
Gimme Some More, More   Meyer; Young, Joseph
Girl at the Ironing Board, The   Dubin; Warren
Girl By the Tree, A   Coslow
Girls, Girls, Girls!   Hart; Kahn
Girls of All Nations   Akst
Give a Man a Job   Hart; Rodgers
Give Me a Heart to Sing To   Washington; Young, Victor
Give Us this Day   Coots
Go 'Long Sundown   Akst; Turk
Go South Young Man   Heyman; Romberg
Goin' to Heaven on a Mule   Dubin; Warren
Goin' to Town   Conrad; Mitchell
Golden Harvest Days   Lewis
Goldfish Song   Fain; Kahal
Gondolier Song   Friml
Goo Goo   Gordon; Revel
Good Advice   Young, Victor
Good Morning   Clare; Whiting
Good Night, Lovely Little Lady   Gordon; Revel
Good Old Days   Conrad; Mitchell
Goodbye Blues   Fields; McHugh
Goodnight Kiss   Gorney
Goo-Goo Da Da (Goo Goo G'Da)   Loesser
Got the Jitters   Rose
Gotta See a Man About His Daughter   Hanley
Grandfather's Clock   David, Mack; Silver
Green Eyes   Harburg
Guess Again   Gordon; Revel
Guess We're Gonna Get Along   Razaf
Gypsy   Heyman; Kahn
Gypsy in Me, The   Porter
Gypsy Serenade   Coslow
Haberdashers Department   Gordon; Revel
Ha-Cha-Cha   Kahn
Hand in Hand   Hammerstein; Kern
Hand Me Down My Walking Cane   Parish
Hands Across the Table   Parish
(There Must Be) Happiness Ahead   Dixon; Wrubel
Happy   Livingston, Jerry
Happy, I Am Happy   Kahn
Happy Week (Operetta), A   Young, Victor
Harlem Madness   Mills
Harlem Vs. Jungle (Ain't Ya Givin' in to Harlem)   Akst;
    Brown, Lew
Harmony Hill   Smith, Harry B.
Haunting Me   De Lange
Have a Little Dream on Me   Rose
Have You Ever Been in Love   Lerner, Sammy
Having You Is Heaven   Johnson, Howard
Haywire   Heyman
He Didn't Even Say Goodbye   Hoffman
He Isn't My Style At All   Smith, Harry B.
He Just Beats a Tom-Tom   Akst; Brown, Lew
Heaven on Earth   Akst; Turk
Hello!   Hart; Rodgers
Hello Dynamite   Stept
Her Easter Bonnet   Young, Victor
Here Come the British   Mercer
Here Comes Company   Lawrence; Young, Joseph
Here Goes   Arlen; Koehler
Here Is My Heart   Rainger; Robin
Here It Comes   Hammerstein; Kern
Here Today, Gone Tomorrow   Lewis; Meyer
Here You Are   Rainger; Robin

Here's Looking at You   Davis; Hanley; Heyman
Here's the Key to My Heart   Clare; Whiting
Here's to Love   Magidson; Wrubel
Here's to You   Heyman
He's a Colonel from Kentucky   Baer
He's a Humdinger   Hoffman
Hey Sailor   Fain; Kahal
Hi Nellie   Dixon; Wrubel
Hi-De-Home Sweet Home   Dietz; Schwartz, Arthur
High Brown (inst.)   Johnson, James P.
Hold My Hand   Caesar; Henderson; Yellen
Holding Hands with Myself   Hoffman; Washington
Holiday   Dixon
Hollywood Party   Hart; Rodgers
Home Is Everything   Styne
Home Ties   Loesser
Honest to Goodness   Conrad; Oakland
Honey Dear   Conrad; Heyman
Hope   Ager; Schwartz, Jean; Young, Joseph
Hot Choc'late Soldiers   Freed, Arthur
Hotcha Chornia Brown   Stept
Hotcha Razz-Ma-Tazz   Mills; Razaf
House Is Haunted (By the Echo of Your Last Goodbye),
    The   Rose
House Where I Was Born, The   Caesar; Carroll
Housewear Department   Gordon; Revel
How Can I Resist You   Gordon; Revel
How Can It Be a Beautiful Day   Kahn
How Do I Know It's Sunday   Fain; Kahal
How High Can a Little Bird Fly   Dietz; Schwartz, Arthur
How Was I to Know   De Lange
How's About Tomorrow Night?   Bloom; Koehler
Hurdy Gurdy Man, The   Dietz; Schwartz, Arthur
Hurryin' Home   Ager; Schwartz, Jean; Young, Joseph
Hush Your Fuss   Brennan; Snyder
I Ain't Gonna Carry No Torch   Coslow
I Ain't Gonna Sin No More   Conrad; Magidson
I Believe in Miracles   Lewis; Meyer
I Cannot Be Faithful   Friml
I Can't Go on Like This   Johnson, Howard
I Couldn't Hold My Man   Arlen; Gershwin, Ira; Harburg
I Didn't Wanna Love You   Ager; David, Mack; Schwartz,
    Jean
I Didn't Want to Love You (I Don't Want to Love
    You)   Conrad; Washington
I Don't Wanna Play   Coslow; Johnston
I Don't Want to Be President (If It Means Losing
    You)   Akst; Brown, Lew
I Feel Like a Million Dollars   Davis; Hanley
I Feel Sorta—   Heyman
I Found Out Where Annie Lives   Hoffman; Washington
I Found the Fountain of Youth   Coslow
I Get a Kick Out of You   Porter
I Got an Aunt in Bridgeport   De Lange
I Gotta See a Man about a Girl   Oakland
I Hate Myself for Being So Mean to You   Ager; Davis;
    Young, Joseph
I Knew   Robin
I Knew Him When   Arlen; Gershwin, Ira; Harburg
I Knew You When   Magidson
I Like It that Way   Conrad; Mitchell
I Like Myself for Liking You   Gorney
I Like the Likes of You   Duke; Harburg
I Looked in Your Eyes   Freed, Arthur
I Looked Into Your Eyes   Brown, Nacio Herb

I Lost My Job on Account of You   Hoffman
I Love Gardenias   Fields; McHugh
I Love the Horses and the Hounds   Woods
I Love to Dance with You   Friend
I Met My Waterloo   Coslow; Johnston
I Need New Words   Harburg
I Never Had a Chance   Berlin
I Never Slept a Wink Last Night   Razaf
I Only Have Eyes for You   Dubin; Warren
I Positively Refuse to Sing   Gordon; Revel
I Saw Stars   Hoffman
I Saw You Looking in My Dreams   Mercer
I See Two Lovers   Dixon; Wrubel
I Talked with a Tree   Burke; Spina
I Think You're Wonderful   Adamson; Lane
I Want a Wife that Can Cook   Smith, Harry B.
I Want to Be a Minstrel Man   Adamson; Lane
I Was Waiting for You   Smith, Harry B.
I Wish I Were a Fisherman   Egan
I Wish I Were Twins   De Lange; Loesser
I Wonder What's Become of Yaaka Hickey Doola
      Lou   Donaldson; Kahn
I Won't Dance   Hammerstein; Kern
I Won't Say Good-Bye Until My Heart Says
      Good-Bye   Bryan
Ice Cream Fantasy   Donaldson; Kahn
I'd Give Anything Under the Sun to Get You Under the
      Moon   Friend; Mitchell
I'd Like to Dunk You in My Coffee   Akst; Brown, Lew
I'd Rather Write a Song   Cohan
If I Could Have My Way   Mercer
If I Could Only Read Your Mind   Mercer
If I Didn't Care   Ager; Schwartz, Jean; Young, Joseph
If I Had a Million Dollars   Mercer
If It Wasn't for an Early Bird — I'd Still Be Dreaming of
      You   Hoffman
If It's Love   Akst; Brown, Lew
If Love Makes You Give Up Steak and Potatoes, Then I
      Don't Want Love   Alter; Brown, Lew
If There Is Someone Lovelier than You   Dietz; Schwartz,
      Arthur
If Widows Are Rich   Kahn
If Widows Are Rich (Widows Are Gay)   Hart
If You Can't Get Five Take Two   Razaf
If You Ever See Anything of Flora   Ager; Schwartz, Jean;
      Young, Joseph
If You Love Me Like I Love You   Edwards
I'll Bet on You   Clare; Whiting
I'll Blame the Waltz (Not You)   Gordon; Revel
I'll Go to Flannigan   Yellen
I'll Make You Happy   Dietz; Schwartz, Arthur
I'll Remember Everything that You'll Forget   Bryan
I'll Save My Heart   Heyman; Romberg
I'll String Along with You   Dubin; Warren
I'll Take You Home in My Old Wheel-Barrow   Burke; Spina
Ill Wind   Arlen; Koehler
I'm a Black Sheep Who's Blue   Rainger; Robin
I'm a Collector of Moonbeams   Arlen; Gershwin, Ira;
      Harburg
I'm a Hundred Percent for You   Mills; Oakland; Parish
I'm a Part of You   Dietz; Schwartz, Arthur
I'm a Queen in My Own Domain   Hart; Rodgers
I'm a Seeker of Beauty   Coslow; Johnston
I'm All In   Alter
I'm Between Two Fires   Stept; Washington

I'm Counting on You   Oakland
I'm Facing the Music   Pollack; Webster
I'm Feelin' High   Dietz; Donaldson
I'm Glad It's Raining   Dietz; Schwartz, Arthur
I'm Growing Fonder of You   Meyer; Young, Joseph
I'm Holding the World in My Arms   Sterling
I'm Hummin' — I'm Whistlin' — I'm Singin'   Gordon;
      Revel
I'm in Love with a Tattooed Man   Coslow; Johnston
I'm Just a Little Boy Blue   Washington; Young, Victor
I'm Just that Way   Akst; Turk
I'm Laughin'   Brown, Lew; Gorney
I'm Lookin' Forward to Goin' Back Home   Baer; Lewis
I'm Not Lettin' On   Monaco; Young, Joseph
I'm Not Myself   Arlen; Gershwin, Ira; Harburg
I'm One of the Boys   Hart; Rodgers
I'm Out of My Mind   Fisher
I'm Popeye the Sailor Man   Lerner, Sammy
I'm Putty in Your Hands   Adamson
I'm Satisfied   Freed, Ralph
I'm Singing Your Praises   Gordon; Revel
I'm Throwin' My Love Away   Adamson; Lane
I'm Whistlin' for My Honey   Monaco; Young, Joseph
I'm Willing to Be Your Good Man Friday   Monaco
In a Blue and Pensive Mood   Livingston, Jerry
In a Cosy Corner   Livingston, Jerry
In a Hut in Old Havana   Myrow
In a Little Red Barn on a Farm Down in Indiana   Ager;
      Schwartz, Jean; Young, Joseph
In a Town in Old New England   Bryan
In Louisiana   Adamson; Lane
In My Country That Means Love   Burke; Spina
In My Lonely Little Room   Parish
In Old Vienna   Fisher
In Other Words — We're Through   Livingston, Jerry
In the Bottom of My Glass   Meyer; Young, Joseph
In the Churchyard   Carmichael
In the Garden   Brown, Lew; Gorney
In the Good Old Winter Time   Adamson; Gordon; Revel
In the Hash in the Stew   Adamson; Lane
In the Middle of a Kiss   Coslow; Pollack; Webster
In the Middle of the Night   Dietz; Schwartz, Arthur
In the Noonday Sun   Dietz; Schwartz, Arthur
In the Valley of Yesterday   Johnson, Howard
Indians and Trees   Cohan
Irresistible   Burke; Spina
Isn't It June?   Henderson; Koehler
Isn't This the Night, Isn't That the Moon   Caesar; Carroll
It Happened   Friml
It Happened One Night   Burke; Spina
It Happens to the Best of Friends   Bloom; Parish
It Must Be Love   Hart; Kahn; Rodgers
It Must Have Been the Night   Henderson; Koehler
It Was Long Ago   Arlen; Gershwin, Ira; Harburg
It Was Never Like This   Arlen; Gershwin, Ira; Harburg
It's All for the Best (I Loved You Yesterday)   Whiting
It's an Old Fashioned World After All   Bryan; Meyer
It's an Old-Fashioned World After All   Meyer
It's Dark on Observatory Hill   Burke; Spina
It's High Time I Got the Low Down on You   Heyman
It's Home   Gorney; Yellen
It's Just a New Spanish Custom   Gordon; Revel
It's Mating Time   Baer; Coots
It's Swell Even Tho' It's Just a Dream   Livingston, Jerry
It's the Animal in Me   Gordon; Revel

It's the Irish in Me   Yellen
It's Three O'Clock   Friml
It's Thrilling   Heyman
It's True   Woods
It's You I Want to Love Tonight   Friml
I've Been Fooling Around   Smith, Harry B.
I've Got a Watch   Coots
I've Got an Invitation to a Dance   Livingston, Jerry
I've Got Rhumbatism   David, Mack; Hoffman
I've Got Sand in My Shoes   Alter
I've Got You on the Top of My List   Clare; Gorney
I've Had My Moments   Donaldson; Kahn
I've Loved the Same Girl for Fifty Years   Alter; Brown, Lew
I've Nothing to Offer   Akst; Brown, Lew
Je T'Adore   Akst
Jingle of the Jungle   Mills; Oakland; Parish
Jitterbug   Mills
Jogging Along through the Park   Hanley
Jonny   Heyman
Judy   Carmichael; Lerner, Sammy
Juliet   Kalmar; Ruby
June Bug, The   Young, Victor
June in January   Rainger; Robin
Jungle Fever   Dietz; Donaldson
Jungle Nights in Harlem   Ellington; Mills
Junk Man   Loesser
Just a Barefoot Boy Awhistlin' to His Dog   Hanley
Just a Fair Weather Friend   Mercer
Just a Little Lane Off Main Street   Coots; Magidson
Just Across the River on the Hill   Von Tilzer
Just an Old Banjo Without Any Strings   Johnson, J. Rosamond
Just Mention Joe   Akst; Brown, Lew
Just Once Too Often   Stept; Young, Joseph
Kaintucky Colonel   Donaldson
Kate the Great   Porter
Keep Away from the Moonlight   Hart; Rodgers
Keep in Tune with the Times   Henderson; Koehler
Keep Me in Your Dreams   Freed, Ralph
Keep on Doin' what You're Doin'   Kalmar; Ruby
Keep Romance Alive   Kalmar; Ruby
Keep Smiling   Hammerstein; Kern
Keeper of the Ivory Keys, The   Heyman; Romberg
King Has Had a Change of Heart, The   Burke; Spina
Kiss and Make-Up   Rainger; Robin
Kiss Me Goodbye   Parish
Kiss Me Like You Kissed Me Last Night   Magidson; Stept
Kiss the Bride Now   Carroll
Kissing Games   Hoffman
Knife, the Fork and the Spoon, The   Young, Joseph
La Cucaracha   Bullock; Burke; Parish; Spina; Washington
La Rhumba   Burke; Spina
Ladies, Beware   Friml
Last Waltz with You   Heyman; Romberg
Laugh, You Son of a Gun   Robin
Laughing the Clouds Away   Coslow; Robin
Lawd, I Give You My Children   Mercer
Lazy Day in the Sun Just Readin', Fishin', and Dreamin', A   Hoffman
Lazy Rhapsody   Washington
Learning   Livingston, Jerry
Let Me Be Free   Friml
Let Me Be Your Lover   Conrad
Let Me Call You Mine   Johnson, Howard

Let Me Go to Sleep in Dreamland (and Wake Up Dreaming of You)   Johnson, Howard
Let Us Be Gay   Stept; Washington
Letitia's Song   Warren
Let's Be Thankful   Oakland
Let's Call It All a Dream   Pollack; Webster
Let's Double Up   Gordon; Revel
Let's Dress for Dinner Tonight   David, Mack; Silver
Let's Forget To-Morrow Tonight   Harburg
Let's Gather 'round the Old Piano   David, Mack
Let's Give Three Cheers for Love   Gordon; Revel
Let's Have a Jubilee   Mills
Let's Have Another   Gorney; Yellen
Let's Have Breakfast in Bed   Stept; Washington
Let's Kiss and Tell   Wrubel
Let's Knock Knees   Revel
Let's Play House   David, Mack
Let's Pretend We're Kids Again   Edwards
Let's Put Two and Two Together   Conrad; Mitchell
Let's Spend an Evening at Home   Freed, Ralph
Let's Take a Walk Around the Block   Arlen; Gershwin, Ira; Harburg
Let's Take Advantage of Now   Henderson; Koehler
Life Begins   Gershwin, Ira
Life Begins at 8:40 (or Thereabouts)   Arlen; Gershwin, Ira; Harburg
Light a Bolt from the Blue   Oakland
Lights Are Low, the Music Is Sweet, The   Friend
Like a Bolt from the Blue   Mills; Parish
Like a Star in the Night   Heyman; Romberg
Like a Story in a Magazine   Livingston, Jerry
Like Me a Little Bit Less (Love Me a Little Bit More)   Adamson; Lane
Like Taking Candy from a Baby   Hoffman
Lily the Contortionist   Lane
Limehouse Nights   Coslow
Limerick Song   Gordon
Listen to the Raindrops Fall   Young, Joseph
Little Angel Told Me So, A   Coslow
Little Artists   Young, Victor
Little Bit of Heaven Known As Mother, A   Gordon; Revel
Little Did I Dream   Adamson; Lane
Little Housekeeper, The   Young, Victor
Little Liza Lee   Donaldson; Kahn
Little Man — You've Had a Busy Day   Hoffman
Little Mother o' Mine in the Mountains   Johnson, Howard
Little Ray of Sunshine   Brown, Nacio Herb; Freed, Arthur
Live and Love Tonight   Conrad; Coslow; Dubin; Johnston
Liza Lou   Dietz; Schwartz, Arthur
Local Boy Makes Good (inst.)   Willson
London on a Rainy Night   Stept; Washington
Lone Cowboy   Rainger; Robin
Lonely Feet   Hammerstein; Kern
Lonesome in a Crowd   Dietz; Schwartz, Arthur
Long about Midnight   Mills
Long Live Love   Donaldson
Long May We Love   Freed, Ralph
Longing   Friml
Looking for a Little Bit of Blue   Woods
Looks Like a Beautiful Day   Meyer
Looks Like Old Times   Donaldson; Kahn
Lost in a Fog   Fields; McHugh
Lot of You, A   Henderson; Koehler
Lotus Blossom (Marahuana)   Coslow; Johnston
Love and Kisses Finnegan   Gordon; Revel

Love and Let Love   Gordon; Revel
Love at Last   Gorney
Love Came to Me but It Didn't Stay Long   Johnson, J.
    Rosamond
Love, Can't You Hear Me Calling?   Freed, Ralph
Love Divided By Two   Rainger; Robin
Love in Bloom   Rainger; Robin
Love Is in Command   Pollack; Young, Joseph
Love Is Just Around the Corner   Robin
Love Is Only What You Make It   Friml
Love Me   Washington; Young, Victor
Love Me for a While   Webster
Love Takes a Holiday   Young, Joseph
Love Thy Neighbor   Gordon; Revel
Love Time, Calling All Hearts   Pollack; Young, Joseph
Lovely One   Coslow; Johnston
Lovey-Dovey   Friml
Low Down Lullaby   Rainger; Robin
Isn't It June   Koehler
Lucky Beggar   Razaf
Lucky Duck   Fields; McHugh
Lucky Waltz, The   Coots
Lullaby   Johnson, Howard
Lullaby in Blue   Magidson; Wrubel
Lulu (You're Nobody's Fool)   Parish
Mad about You   Koehler; Stept
Mad at the World   Oakland
Mad Manhattan   Johnson, James P.
Mahster's Coming, The   Hart; Rodgers
Malibu   Caesar
Man, a Maid, a Moon, A   Burke; Spina
Manhattan Melodrama   Hart; Rodgers
Many Thanks for the Dance   David, Mack
Marahuana   Coslow; Johnston
Marcelina   Stept
Marchin' Towards Ya', Georgia   Friend
Marching Thru Mexico   David, Mack
Maria   Dietz; Schwartz, Arthur
Maria (Annina)   Friml
Maria Mia   Motzan
Maxim's   Hart; Kahn
May I?   Gordon; Revel
Me and Anthony Adverse in the Morning   Egan
(I Can't Imagine) Me Without You   Robin
Meanest Gal in Town, The   De Lange
Meet Mister Hines that Piano Man   Razaf
Meet the King   Johnston
Melancholy Nights Who's Afraid of You Now   Young,
    Joseph
Melody (inst.)   Carmichael
Melody of Laughter   Hart; Kahn
Melody of the Mill   Lewis
Memphis Blues   Coslow
Merry Widow Waltz   Hart; Kahn
Merry-O Cheerio Drinking Song, A   Clare
Midnight Flirtation   Friml
Midnight on Main Street   Heyman
Midnight with the Stars and You   Woods
Mighty Thankful   Bloom; Koehler
Milady   Burke; Spina
Minuet   Friml
Mirror Song, The   Rainger
Mirror Song (scene), The   Robin
Miser's Dream, The   Conrad; Magidson
Miss 1934   Conrad; Mitchell

Miss Killarney   Jerome; Schwartz, Jean
Mississippi Honeymoon   Donaldson; Kahn
Mississippi Marbles   Parish
Missouri Misery   Harburg
Moment He Turned His Back, The   Burke; Spina
Money in My Clothes   Fain; Kahal
Monte Christo   Clare; Whiting
Moods (inst.)   Bloom
Moon About Town   Harburg
Moon Country Is Home to Me   Carmichael; Mercer
Moon of Desire   Webster
Moon Over Monte Carlo   Clare; Whiting
Moon Over Napoli   Berlin
Moon Was Yellow (And the Night Was Blue), The   Ahlert;
    Leslie
Moonglow   De Lange; Mills
Moonlight on the River Danube   Freed, Ralph; Pollack
Moonlight on the Riviera   Fields; McHugh
Moonlight Parade, The   Baer; Coots
Moonlight Waltz, The   Washington
Moontime   Hoffman
More Music   Van Heusen
Morning After, The   Coslow; Johnston
Mother's Crazy Quilt   Conrad; Oakland
Mother's Quilting Party   Robison
Mr. and Mrs. Is the Name   Dixon; Wrubel
Muchacha (Little Dolores)   Hart; Kahn; Rodgers
Mumbo Jumbo King of the Congo   Freed, Ralph
Murder at the Vanities (Opening)   Coslow; Johnston
Music Hath Charms (My Heart Is Yours)   Friml
Musical Culture   Smith, Harry B.
Must It Be Platonic Forever?   Ahlert; Leslie
Mutton Song   Fisher
My American Beauty   Coslow; Johnston
My Arab Complex   Hanley
My Baby's on Strike   Hoffman
My Beautiful Circus Girl   Hammerstein; Kern
My Carolina Hide-Away   Coots
My Dog Loves Your Dog   Caesar; Henderson; Yellen
My Father Said   Dietz; Schwartz, Arthur
My Friend the Night   Hart; Rodgers
My Future Star   Clare; Whiting
My Gigolo   Coslow; Johnston
My Heart Does a Rumba   Rainger; Robin
My Heart Is an Open Book   Gordon; Revel
My Heart Will Sing   Donaldson; Kahn
My Heart's an Open Book   Heyman
My Heart's in the Right Place   Monaco
My Journey's End   Fain; Kahal
My Last Year's Girl   Alter
My Little Girl   Cohan
My Middle Name Is Love   Coots
My Mother in the Fatherland   Conrad
My Old Flame   Coslow; Johnston
My Old Hoss   Akst; Brown, Lew
My Palace of Dreams   Friml
My Paramount-Publix-Roxy Rose   Arlen; Gershwin, Ira;
    Harburg
My Personal Rainbow   Hanley
My Used to Be Is Like She Used to Be   Monaco; Young,
    Joseph
My Whole Day Is Spoiled   Monaco; Young, Joseph
Nasty Man   Caesar; Henderson; Yellen
Nearer My Heart to Thee   Heyman
Needle in a Haystack, A   Conrad; Magidson

Never Felt Better, Never Had Less   Hoffman
Never Let the Blues Go to Your Feet   Razaf
Never Marry a Dancer   Dietz; Schwartz, Arthur
New England in the Rain   Webster
New Moon Is Over My Shoulder, A   Brown, Nacio Herb;
    Freed, Arthur
New Mown Hay   Kahn
Night After Night   Rainger; Whiting
Night Remembers, The   Lawrence
Night Shall Be Filled with Love, The   Rainger; Robin
Night that She Cried in Her Beer, The   Stept; Washington
Night Was Made for Dancing, The   Hart; Rodgers
Night Wind   Heyman
No Horse, No Wife, No Mustache   Dixon; Wrubel
No Lovers Allowed   De Lange
No More Thrills   Razaf
No More Women   Gordon; Revel
Not in a Month of Sundays   De Lange; Myrow
Not One   Young, Victor
Nothing More or Nothing Less   Stept
Nothing Was Ever Like This   Heyman
Now and Forever   Pollack; Young, Joseph
Now I Lay Me Down to Sin   Loesser
Now I Understand   Coslow
Now that I Have Springtime   Hammerstein; Kern
Now that We're Sweethearts Again (Tell Me What You Told
    Me)   Fisher
Now the Wedding Day Is Here   Smith, Harry B.
Ocean Will Never Run Dry, The   Heyman
Oh Henry   Burke; Spina
Oh How Weary   Kahn
Oh, I Heard, Yes I Heard   Dubin; Warren
Oh, Leo, It's Love   Clare; Whiting
Oh Me! Oh My! Oh You!   Adamson; Lane
Oh Susanna, Dust Off that Old Pianna   Caesar; Lerner,
    Sammy
Oh! The Pity of It All   Burke; Spina
Oh What a Beautiful Baby You Turned Out to Be   Coots;
    Loesser
Okay Toots   Donaldson; Kahn
Old Fashioned Waltz and the Old Fashioned Girl,
    The   Stept; Washington
Old Man Jingle   Stept
Old Mother Oak   Young, Victor
Old Oak Tree, The   Loesser
Old Red Rooster, The   Johnson, Howard
Old Skipper   Carmichael; Mercer
Old Village Doctor, The   Schwartz, Jean; Young, Joseph
On a Honolulu Honeymoon   Johnson, Howard
On a Little Side Street   Akst
On a Pretty Picture Postal Card   Burke; Spina
On Accounta I Love You   Stept
On Blue Hawaiian Waters   Livingston, Jerry
On that Carpet of Cotton   Livingston, Jerry
On the Good Ship Lollipop   Clare; Whiting
On the Green (inst.)   Bloom
On the Wrong Side of the Fence   Wrubel
Once in a Blue Moon   Gordon; Kahn; Revel
Once in a Lifetime   Kahn
Once in a Lifetime (Once in a Blue Moon)   Donaldson
Once You're Mine   Egan
Once-in-a-While   Dietz; Schwartz, Arthur
One in Love   Heyman
One Little Drink-o I Go Boom   Coots
One Little Kiss   Kalmar; Ruby

One Little Thing at a Time   Schwartz, Jean; Young, Joseph
One Night of Love   Kahn
One Tender Smile   Friml
Only Love Can Lead the Way   Woods
Ooh! You Miser You!   Lewis
Oompa, Oompa   Smith, Harry B.
Orticinas   David, Mack
Our Honeymoon   Smith, Harry B.
Out for No Good   Dubin; Warren
Out in the Cold Again   Bloom; Koehler
Out of a Dream   Mills; Washington
Over on the Jersey Side   Fields; McHugh
Pacing the Wailing Wall   Gilbert
Paid in Full   Turk
Pal-Sie-Walsie   Stept
Pancho   Rainger; Robin
Papa, At Last I Met You   Smith, Harry B.
Pardon My Southern Accent   Mercer
Party Waltz (inst.), The   Rodgers
Party's Over, The   Conrad; Oakland
Pass the Word Around   Hoffman
Paying for It Now   Caesar; Friend
Penthouse Romance (inst.)   Bloom
Phi Phi Phi   Clare
Phi-Phi-Phi   Whiting
Picture of Mary, A   Bryan
Piquant Love Song   Gorney
Place in Your Heart, A   Coslow
Please Make Me Care   Brown, Nacio Herb; Freed, Arthur
Pleasure Was Mine, The   Van Heusen
Polka   Friml
Polka Dot Stomp   Sissle
Pom Tiddley Om Pom   Coslow
Poor Fellow   Oakland
Poor Girl   Young, Joseph
Poor People   Livingston, Jerry
Pop Goes Your Heart   Dixon; Wrubel
Poppin' the Cork   Davis; Hanley
Pots, The   Hart; Rodgers
Powder, Lipstick and Rouge   Gordon; Revel
Prayer   Hart; Rodgers
Prelude to We're Out of the Red   Brown, Lew; Gorney
Press Your Lips to Mine   Freed, Ralph; Styne
Primitive Prima Donna   Arlen; Koehler
Prince Charming   Heyman
Prize Waltz, The   Hoffman
Processional   Friml
Prunes, Prisms, Potatoes   Smith, Harry B.
P.S. I Love You   Mercer
Public Enemy Number One   Porter
Puppchen   Kalmar; Ruby
Puppet Love Song   Whiting
Pussy Cat Love   Bryan
Put a Little Rhythm in Every Little Thing You Do   Gordon;
    Revel
Put on Your Glasses   Ahlert; Leslie
Put Your Heart in a Song   Henderson; Koehler
Quartet Erotica (We're Not What We Used to Be)   Arlen;
    Gershwin, Ira; Harburg
Rack and Ruin   Young, Victor
Rain in My Heart   Alter
Rain Song   Fisher
Rainbow in the Flame of an Old Log Fire   Monaco; Young,
    Joseph
Rainy Day   Young, Victor

Reaching for the Cotton Moon   Stept
Reincarnation   Hart; Rodgers
Remember When   De Lange; Mills
Reno   Silver
Restless   Coslow
Rhythm Lullaby, A   Razaf
Rhythm of Romance, The   Heyman; Romberg
Rhythm of the Moon, The   Rainger; Robin
Riptide   Donaldson; Kahn
Rock and Roll   Clare; Whiting
Roll on Rolling Road   Hammerstein; Kern
Roll Up the Score   Adamson; Lane
Romance   Friml
Rose of the Stingaree   Kahn
Roses in the Rain   Whiting
Roses Make Me Cry   Parish
'Round the Christmas Tree   Young, Victor
Royal Wedding, The   Johnston
Rumba Fan Dance (inst.)   Henderson
Rumbalero   Fisher
Russian Folk Song   Dubin; Parish
Sailor's Chanty (It's a Lie)   Gordon; Revel
Sandman   Freed, Ralph
Santa Claus Is Comin' to Town   Coots
Sarah, the Sunshine Girl   Rose
Savage in My Soul   Bloom; Parish
Say How D'Ye Do-a to Kalua   Fields; McHugh
Say Something Sweet Sweetheart   David, Mack
Say When   Henderson; Koehler
Scandal Number   Friml
Search for Beauty   Rainger; Robin
Sequoia   Brown, Nacio Herb; Freed, Arthur; Kahn
Serenade   Johnson, Howard
Serenade for a Wealthy Widow   Fields; McHugh
Serves Me Right for Treating Him Wrong   Hoffman
Shadows of Yesterday's Stars, The   Dubin; Warren
Shadows on the Wall   Carroll
Shall We Dance   Burke; Spina
She Didn't Hear the Curfew Bell   Burke; Spina
She Didn't Say   Burke; Spina
She Learned About Sailors   Clare; Whiting
She Wore a Little Jacket of Blue   Bryan; Fisher
She's a Good Dame   Rainger; Robin
She's an Old Fashioned Girl from an Old Fashioned
   Town   Johnson, Howard
She's Way Up Thar (I'm Way Down 'Yar)   Brown, Lew
Shim Sham   Alter
Shine Boy   Hoffman
Shirley   Johnson, Howard
Shoein' the Mare   Arlen; Gershwin, Ira; Harburg
Show Is Over   Conrad; Coslow; Dubin
Show Me Your Qualifications   Razaf
Sidewalks of Cuba   Mills; Oakland; Parish
Sidioso   Adamson; Lane
Silver Sails   Heyman
Simple and Sweet   Fain; Kahal
Simple Simon and Simple Sue   Bryan
Sing, College Boy   Young, Joseph
Sing You a Couple of Choruses   Fields; McHugh
Singing Between Kisses   Caesar; Friend
Singing Heart   Friend
Sittin' on the Bridge at Midnight   Kalmar; Ruby
Six of a Kind   Rainger; Robin
Six Women (Me and Henry the Eighth)   Caesar; Henderson;
   Yellen

Skip It, Baby, Skip It   Gordon; Revel
Sleepy Head   Donaldson; Kahn
Sleepy Time in Sleepy Hollow   Hoffman
(It's) Smart to Be Smart   Duke; Harburg
Smile, a Kiss, Sweet Fool, A   Friml
Smile a Little Bit   Davis; Hanley
Smoking in the Dark   Dixon; Wrubel
Snake Dance, The   Brown, Nacio Herb; Freed, Arthur
Snake in the Grass, A   Razaf
Snuggle Song, The   Young, Victor
So Close to the Forest   Young, Joseph
So Help Me   Berlin
So Long for Ever So Long   Henderson; Koehler
So Nice   Caesar; Henderson; Yellen
So This Is Heaven   Magidson
So, You're Not Gonna Kiss Me   Oakland
Soft Green Seas   Dixon; Wrubel
Solitude   De Lange; Ellington; Mills
Some Time   Parish
Somebody Wants to Go to Sleep   Hammerstein; Kern
Something About Romance   Coslow; Johnston
Song of a Dreamer   Gorney
Song of Steel, The   Willson
Song of Surrender   Dubin; Warren
Song of the Evening   Henderson; Koehler
Song of the Hoofer   Henderson; Koehler
Soul Mate   Razaf
Soul Saving Sadie   Rose
South American Joe   Caesar; Friend
Souvenir   Johnson, Howard
Sparklets in the Sky   Livingston, Jerry
Speak to Me with Your Eyes   Parish
Spin a Little Web of Dreams   Fain; Kahal
Spiritual   Coslow; Johnston
Spring Fever   Arlen; Gershwin, Ira; Harburg
Spring Is At My Window, The   Parish
Square Dance   Dietz; Schwartz, Arthur
Stacey Cheer   Gordon; Revel
Stacey Closets   Gordon; Revel
Stand Up and Cheer!   Akst; Brown, Lew
Starlight on the Trail   Coslow
Stars Fells on Alabama   Parish
Stay As Sweet As You Are   Gordon; Revel
Stay Out of the Moonlight   Alter
Step In   Fields; McHugh
Stepping Out of the Picture   Akst; Brown, Lew
Stop that Clock   Duke; Harburg
Stork Song   Hanley
Straight from the Shoulder (Right from the Heart)   Gordon;
   Revel
Strangers in the Street   Parish; Wrubel
Straw Hat in the Rain   Akst; Brown, Lew
Suddenly   Duke; Harburg; Rose
Suddenly You   Freed, Arthur
Summer Wind, The   Young, Victor
Summertime   Young, Victor
Sunday Morning   Henderson; Koehler
Sunshine   Young, Joseph
Sunshine and Poinsiettas   Burke; Spina
Suntan Charlie   Monaco
Supper Song   Kalmar; Ruby
Swanee Melody Man   Mills
Swanee River Dream Man   Friend
Sweet and Simple   Caesar; Henderson; Yellen
Sweet As a Song from Heaven   Bryan

Sweet Music Dubin; Warren
(It Was) Sweet of You Clare; Whiting
Sweetest Music this Side of Heaven, The Friend
Sweetheart Moon Conrad; Magidson
Sweetheart of Auld Lang Syne Johnson, Howard
Sweetheart of Red River Valley Johnson, Howard
Swing It Sister Adamson; Lane
Swing on Mississippi Waller; Washington
Sympathizin' with Me Coslow; Johnston
Ta Rah Ta Rah Smith, Harry B.
Table, a Tavern and You, A Gordon; Revel
Taboo De Lange; Mills
Take a Lesson from the Lark Rainger; Robin
Take a Number from One to Ten Gordon; Revel
Take My Word Mills
Talkin' to Myself Conrad; Magidson
Tall Buildings Johnson, Howard
Tarentella Friml
Tarts and Flowers Heyman
Tea Cup (inst.) Rainger
Telephone Your Mother Parish
Tell Me Fields; McHugh
Tell Me an Old Fashioned Story Caesar; Friend
Tell Me I'm Wrong Bryan
Tell Me Why Smith, Harry B.
Ten Days of Romance on a Ten-Day Cruise Wrubel
Thank You for a Lovely Evening Fields; McHugh
That Fellow Manuelo Dietz; Schwartz, Arthur
That Grand Terrace Trot Razaf
That Way Over You Donaldson; Kahn
That's All There Is Burke; Spina
That's Love Hart; Rodgers
That's the Way I Like to Hear You Talk Hoffman
That's What Love Did to Me Cahn
That's What Makes the World Go 'Round Stept
That's Where We Come In Harburg
Then I'll Be Tired of You Harburg; Schwartz, Arthur
There Are No Words Burke; Spina
There Goes My Heart Davis; Silver
There Never Was a Night Like This Rainger; Robin
There Was a Goose Young, Victor
There'll Always Be a Lady Fair Porter
There's a Bit of Paree in You Gorney
There's a Cottage in Killarney Dixon; Wrubel
There's a Cross in the Argonne Pollack; Webster
There's a House in Harlem for Sale Van Heusen
There's a Joy that Steals Upon You Hammerstein; Kern
There's a Method to My Madness (And My Madness Is
    You) Pollack; Webster
There's No Cure Like Travel Porter
There's Nothing Else to Do in
    Ma-La-Ka-Mo-Ka-Lu Friend; Mitchell
There's Nothing Like an Old Fashioned Waltz Stept;
    Washington
There's Someone Dreaming Tonight Donaldson; Kahn
There's Someone in Your Family I'm Crazy About Fain;
    Kahal
There's Something About the Climate Akst
They Follow Me Around Smith, Harry B.
Thief of Bagdad, The Freed, Ralph
Thingamabobs (inst.) Willson
Things! Arlen; Gershwin, Ira; Harburg
Think It Over Dietz; Schwartz, Arthur
Thinking of You All Night Long Bryan
Thinking Out Loud Akst; Brown, Lew

This Is an Unexpected Pleasure Johnson, J. Rosamond
This Is not a Song Duke; Harburg
This Is Our Last Night Together Brown, Lew; Gorney
This Is the Kiss of Romance Parish
This Is the Night Brown, Nacio Herb; Freed, Arthur
This Night Rainger; Robin
Those Who Dance Arlen; Koehler
Thoughts While Strolling (inst.) Willson
Thousand Good Nights, A Donaldson
Three Little Pigs Are Pork Chops Now, The Davis; Hanley
Three Musketeers Kahn
Three Sisters Opening (Act Two) Hammerstein; Kern
Thrill of a Hill Billy Waltz, The Schwartz, Jean; Young,
    Joseph
Throw Out Your Chest, Keep Up Your Chin Razaf
Tiger Roar Gordon; Revel
Time Is a Gypsy Harburg
Ting-A-Ling-A-Ling Gorney
Tired of It All Kalmar; Ruby
To Be or Not to Be in Love Dixon; Wrubel
To the Beat of My Heart Harburg
Tonight Schwartz, Arthur
Tonight Is Mine Kahn
Torch Parade Henderson; Koehler
Trav'lling the Road Lerner, Sammy
Trivers Livers Conrad; Magidson
Trocadero, The Lane
Troubled Waters Coslow; Johnston
Trust in Me Schwartz, Jean
Try to See It My Way (Baby) Dixon; Wrubel
Tulips and Apple Strudel Bryan
Turn on the Moon Adamson; Lane
Twenty-four Hours in Georgia Livingston, Jerry
Twice a Year Arlen; Koehler
Twilight Razaf
Two Alone Burke; Spina
Two Chairs and a Table Lewis; Meyer
Two Cigarettes in the Dark Pollack; Webster
Two Little Flies on a Lump of Sugar Fain; Kahal
Two Little Peas in a Pod Gordon; Revel
Uncle Don's Song Young, Victor
Under the Dreamy Creole Moon Sissle
Under the Snookyookum Moon Johnson, J. Rosamond
Under Your Spell Dietz; Schwartz, Arthur
Unsophisticated Sue Razaf
Vampires in the Dusk Johnson, James P.
Vanessa Fisher
Vilia Hart; Kahn
Vipers Drag (inst.) Waller
Viva La France Warren
Vive la France Dubin
Waitin' at the Gate for Katy Kahn; Whiting
Walk the Plank Carroll
Walkin' with My Shadow Mercer
Walter Walter Wall-Flower Coots; Lewis
Waltz Down the Aisle Porter
Wand'ring Heart Dietz; Schwartz, Arthur
Wanna Buy a Duke? Akst; Brown, Lew
Wanted — Someone Akst; Clare
Was It Love or Wine Whiting
Washington Square Carroll
Watching the Moon Through the Trees Cahn
Watching the Stars Hoffman; Lerner, Sammy
Water Under the Bridge Duke; Harburg; Pollack; Webster
Way Down South in North Carolina Freed, Ralph; Styne

We Are the Roman Soldiers   Brown, Lew
We Can't Make a Monkey of the Moon   Rainger; Robin
Weakness   Mills
Wedding Chorus   Smith, Harry B.
Wedding Waltz   Carroll
Weekend Cruise (Will You Love Me Monday Morning as You Did on Friday Night?)   Arlen
Welcome Home   Motzan
Welcome to the Bride   Hammerstein; Kern
We'll Stay Over Here   Monaco; Young, Joseph
We're Here to State   Gordon; Revel
We're Just Poor Folks Rolling in Love   Gordon; Revel
We're Just Simple Folk   Woods
We're Out of the Red   Brown, Lew; Gorney
Were You Foolin'?   Ahlert; Leslie
Were Your Ears Burning   Coslow; Gordon; Johnston; Revel
What a Joy to Be Young   Porter
What a Little Moonlight Can Do   Woods
What a Man   Cohan
What a Night   Friend
What About Me   Dietz; Schwartz, Arthur
What Are Your Intentions?   Dubin; Warren
What Can You Say in a Love Song?   Gershwin, Ira
What Can You Say in a Love Song? (That Hasn't Been Said Before?)   Arlen; Harburg
What Do I Have to Do to Make You Love Me   Coots
What Good Are Words?   Hammerstein; Kern
What Good Is the Good in Goodbye   David, Mack; Hoffman
What Is There to Say?   Duke; Harburg
What's Gonna Be with You and Me   Coots
What's in the Air Tonight?   Hammerstein; Kern
When a St. Louis Woman Comes Down to New Orleans   Coslow; Johnston
When a Woman Loves a Man   Mercer
When Do We Eat   Dixon; Wrubel
When Ezra Plays the Fiddle (In the Old Town Hall)   Gordon; Revel
When He Comes Home to Me   Coslow; Robin
When I Hear Your Voice   Schwartz, Arthur
When I Look at Myself in the Mirror   Woods
When I Look at You   Kalmar; Ruby
When I Told the Village Belle   Gilbert
When Love Comes Swingin' Along   Henderson; Koehler
When Madame Reaches Her High C   Heyman
When My Dixie Dreams Go Drifting Along   Johnson, J. Rosamond
When My Ship Comes In   Donaldson; Kahn
When Spring Comes 'Round   Washington
When the Dance Is Over (Let Me Linger in Your Arms)   De Lange
When the Golden Gate Was Silver   Rainger; Robin
When the Last Year Rolls Around   Clare; Whiting
When the New Moon Shines on the New Moon Bay   Woods
When the Roll Is Called Alma Mater   Fain; Kahal
When You Are Mine   Conrad; Mitchell
When You First Ate an Olive   Coots
When You Love Only One   Dietz; Schwartz, Arthur
When You Were a Freshie (And I Was a Sophomore)   Parish
When You Were a Smile on Your Mother's Lips and a Twinkle in Your Daddy's Eye   Fain; Kahal
Whenever Bing Begins to Sing   Dubin; Warren
Where Are the Men?   Porter

Where Can I Find a Cherry   Razaf
Where Do They Come From (And Where Do They Go)   Coslow; Johnston
Where Have You Been, You Beautiful Thing?   Gorney
Where There's Smoke — There's Fire   Livingston, Jerry
Where Your Ears Burning?   Revel
While the Night Is Young   Rainger; Whiting
Whisper Sweet   Johnson, James P.
Whistle   Young, Victor
Whistle While You Work   Burke; Spina
Whittlin' My Wood   Dubin; Warren
Who but You?   Akst; Turk
Who Do You Say Good Evening to when You Say Good Night to Me   Caesar
Who Is It?   Davis; Hanley
Who Made Bluebeard Blue?   Razaf
Who Made Little Boy Blue? (inst.)   Kern
Who Said that Dreams Don't Come True   Fields; McHugh
Why Am I in Love?   Burke; Spina
Why Do I Dream Those Dreams?   Dubin; Warren
Why Don't You Practice What You Preach   Hoffman
Why Not?   Conrad; Heyman
Widow Is a Lady, A   Hart; Kahn; Rodgers
Wild About You   Berlin
Will You Love Me Monday Morning As You Did on Friday Night? (A Weekend Cruise)   Harburg
Will You Love Me Monday Morning As You Did on Friday Night? (Weekend Cruise)   Gershwin, Ira
Wine Song   Kahn
Wine, Women and Song   Conrad; Mitchell
Wise Resolution, A   Young, Victor
Wish Me Good Luck — Kiss Me Good-Bye   Ager; Davis
With All My Heart and Soul   De Lange; Mills
With Every Breath I Take   Rainger; Robin
With My Eyes Wide Open I'm Dreaming   Gordon; Revel
With the Curls Hanging Down Your Back   Young, Joseph
Without a Shirt   Young, Joseph
Wonder Bar   Dubin; Warren
World Is Mine, The   Harburg
Wrap Your Arms Around Me, I'll Never Be Cold   Bryan
Wynken, and Blynken and Nod   David, Mack
Yes Sir, I Love Your Daughter   Conrad; Magidson
Yes to You   Clare; Whiting
You and the Night and the Music   Dietz; Schwartz, Arthur
You and Who Else!   Hoffman; Washington
You Are   Hart; Rodgers
You Are Doing Very Well   Hammerstein; Kern
You Bring Out the Savage in Me   Coslow
You Can Always Come Back to Me   Johnson, James P.; Razaf
You Can Have It Baby   Johnston
You Can Put It in the Papers   Stept; Washington
You Can't Buy Everything   Freed, Ralph
You Don't Know What You're Doin' to Me   Gordon; Revel
You Gotta Give Credit to Love   Hoffman
You Hit a New High   Gordon; Revel
You Love Me   Smith, Harry B.
You Must Have Known   Parish
You Ought to Be Arrested for Breaking My Heart   Alter
You Oughta Be in Pictures   Heyman
You Say That to All the Girls   Gordon; Revel
You Sure Don't Know How to Shake that Thing   Arlen; Koehler
You Went Over with a Bang   Gordon; Revel
You'll Grow Sweeter As the Years Roll By   Coots

You'll Never Get Rid of Me Now   Davis; Oakland
You'll Never Know   Donaldson
Your Eyes   Rainger; Whiting
Your Guess Is Just As Good As Mine   Hoffman
Your Head on My Shoulder   Adamson; Lane
Your Love   Washington
Your Mother   Turk
Your Prince Was Not So Charming   Heyman
You're a Blessing to Me   Rainger; Robin
You're a Builder-Upper   Arlen; Gershwin, Ira; Harburg
You're an Angel Playing Hookey from Heaven   Hoffman
You're Everywhere   Caesar
You're Gorgeous, But Dangerous, You're Much too Much for
     Me   Koehler; Stept
You're My Fourth of July   Coots
You're Not the Only Oyster in the Stew   Burke; Spina
You're One in a Million   Heyman
You're Responsible   Monaco
You're Sensational   Webster
You're So Divine   Dubin; Warren
You're So Happy   Donaldson; Kahn
You're That Girl   Young, Joseph
You're the Top   Porter
You've Got a Future with Me   Coots; Magidson
You've Got Me on a Merry-Go-Round   Pollack
You've Got That   Hart; Rodgers
Ziegfeld Walk, The   Conrad
Zing! Went the Strings of My Heart   Hanley

1935

About a Quarter to Nine   Dubin; Warren
According to the Moonlight   Magidson; Yellen
Adieu   Washington
Adios Argentina   Porter
Admiration   Mills
African Lullaby   Mills
After Dark   Brown, Nacio Herb; Freed, Arthur
Afterglow, An   Young, Joseph
Alabamy Beauty Shop   Ahlert; Young, Joseph
Alimony Club   Conrad; Mitchell
All Aboard the Navy   Dubin; Warren
All for the Love of a Girl   Gorney
All for You   Washington
All I Do Is Dream of You   Brown, Nacio Herb
All's Well (In Coronado By the Sea)   Coslow; Whiting
Alone   Brown, Nacio Herb; Freed, Arthur
Alone Again   Woods
Alt Wein   Dietz; Schwartz, Arthur
Always Be a Gentleman   Hammerstein; Romberg
American Bolero (inst.)   Brown, Nacio Herb
And I'm So Glad   Schwartz, Jean
And It Happened Last Night   Clare; Johnston
Animal Crackers in My Soup   Caesar; Henderson; Koehler
Annapolis Farewell   Coslow
Anorita   Heyman
Another Night Together   Adamson; Donaldson
Anything Can Happen   Henderson; Yellen
Appasionato   Heyman
Army Band (Here Comes the Band), The   Adamson; Lane
As I Live and Breathe (I Live and Breathe for You)   Pollack;
     Webster
As Long As I Love   Weill
As Long As There's Love   Schwartz, Jean
Asi Se Besa   Kern

At Last   Lewis
At the Reefer Smoker's Ball   Razaf
At Your Service Madame   Dubin; Warren
Awake or Dreaming   Coots; Parish
Babs   Ahlert; Young, Joseph
Baby, Ain'tcha Satisfied?   Mills
Back Beats   Mills
Back Seat Drivers   Loesser
Bad Man   Rainger; Robin; Whiting
Balcony Waltz, The   Johnson, Howard
Ballad in Blue   Carmichael; Kahal
Barnum and Beery and Me   Johnson, Howard
Barrel-House Music   Robison
Be Careful Young Lady   Coslow
Be Still My Sorrow   Pollack; Webster
Beach Scene   Porter
Beautiful Isle of Oomph (Down on the Island of
     Oomph)   Whiting
Beautiful Isle of Oomph (Down on the Isle of Oomph),
     The   Coslow
Beautiful Lady in Blue, A   Coots; Lewis
Before You Go   Burke; Spina
Begin the Beguine   Porter
Bells of Monterey   Stept; Washington
Bess, You Is My Woman Now   Gershwin, George;
     Gershwin, Ira
Beyond the Shadow of a Doubt   Adamson; Lane
Beyond You   Whiting
Birth of Rumba   Rainger
Bless Our Happy Home   Davis; Silver
Blossoms on Broadway   Rainger; Robin; Whiting
Blue Interlude   Mills
Blue Jeans   Conrad; Magidson
Blue Lou   Mills
Blue Midnight   Davis
Blue Nile   Friend
Blue Notes   Cahn
Blue Serenade   Adamson; Lane
Blues in B-Flat   Mills
Blues Serenade, A   Parish
Bonjour Mam'selle   Gordon; Revel
Born to Be Bored   Livingston, Jerry
Born to Dance   Brown, Nacio Herb; Freed, Arthur
Bouncin' in Rhythm   Mills
Boys Will Be Boys — Girls Will Be Girls   Mercer
Bradley's Dance   Gordon; Revel
Bread and Gravy   Carmichael
Bright Lights   Dixon; Wrubel
Broadway Cinderella   Dubin; Warren
Broadway Rhythm   Brown, Nacio Herb; Freed, Arthur
Broken Record, The   Friend
Broken Serenade   Kalmar; Ruby
Brokenhearted Troubadour   David, Mack
Brown Sugar Mine   Mills
Brownstone Baby (I've Got the Blues for You)   Dubin;
     Warren
Buffo Terzetto   Kern
Bug House   Mills
Busy Body   Brown, Nacio Herb; Freed, Arthur
Busy Keepin' Happy   Henderson; Koehler
Buxom Mrs. Bascom, The   Henderson; Yellen
Buzzard Song, The   Gershwin, George
By a Silvery Stream   Loesser
By All That's Beautiful   Brown, Nacio Herb; Freed, Arthur
By Yonder Moon   Dubin; Warren

Byrd (You're the Bird of Them All)   Johnson, Howard
Cabinet Music   Porter
Cabinet Number   Coslow
Call of the Delta   Mills
Campus Moon   Coots
Can't We Dream a Midsummer Night's Dream (Though
      There's Frost on the Moon)   Ahlert; Young, Joseph
Can't We Fall in Love   Donaldson
Careful with My Heart   Harburg
Carlo's Song   Coslow
Casino de Paree   Dubin; Warren
Castles in the Clouds   Livingston, Jerry
Celebratin'   Woods
Central Park   Mercer
Champagne and Orchids   Hammerstein; Kern
Chanson on the Prater, A   Hammerstein; Romberg
Charm   Schwartz, Jean
Chasing Shadows   Davis; Silver
Cheek to Cheek   Berlin
China Seas   Brown, Nacio Herb; Freed, Arthur
Chiripah, The   Porter
Church Bells Told, The   Schwartz, Jean; Young, Joseph
Cigarette   Henderson; Yellen
Circulatin' 'Round   Coots
Circus   Adamson; Lane
Circus Is on Parade, The   Hart; Rodgers
Clara, Don't You Be Downhearted   Gershwin, George
Cling to Me   Leslie
Close Your Eyes and See   Gorney
Come On Home   Hanley
Comes the Revolution Baby   Mercer
Comrades, Try Out My Song   Smith, Harry B.
Coney Island   Dubin; Warren
Connecticut March   Dixon; Wrubel
Cosi Cosa   Washington
Cottage By the Moon, A   Freed, Ralph
Cotton   Bloom; Koehler
Crap Game Fugue   Gershwin, George
Crooner's Lullaby   Coslow; Johnston
Curly Top   Henderson; Koehler
Cyclone   Adamson; Donaldson; Kahn; Lane
Dagger Dance (inst.)   Warren
Dance Like a Fool   Hammerstein; Kern
Dance, My Darlings   Hammerstein; Romberg
Dance of the Marionettes   Herbert; Kahn
Dance with Me   Coslow
Dancing the Viennese   Coslow
Darkies Have Music in Their Souls   Cahn
Darling of My Dreams   Parish
Darn Clever, These Chinese   Robin
Day You Were Born, The   Heyman
Death in the Afternoon   Dietz; Schwartz, Arthur
Delta Serenade   Ellington; Mills
Devil in the Moon   Mills
Devil's Holiday   Mills
Diavolo   Hart; Rodgers
Dinah Lou   Bloom; Koehler
Dixieland Band, The   Mercer
Do a Little Rumba with Me   Rainger; Robin
Do I Love My Teacher   Dubin; Warren
Do the Truck   Cahn
Do You Intend to Put an End to a Sweet Beginning Like
      This   Ahlert; Young, Joseph
Do Your Stuff   Rainger; Robin
Doll Fantasy, A   Hammerstein; Romberg

Don't Believe Me (No Me Creas)   Gorney
Don't Fence Me In   Porter
Don't Forget Me in Your Dreams Tonight   Friend; Stept
Don't Give Up the Ship   Dubin; Warren
Don't Go on a Diet Baby   Fain; Kahal
Don't Grow Any Older (My Little Boy Blue)   Loesser
Don't Look Now   Kahal
Don't Mention Love to Me   Fields
Don't Say a Word — Just Dance   Burke; Spina
Double Trouble   Rainger; Robin; Whiting
Down at the Old Church Bazaar   Ager
Down at the Old Minstrel Show   Von Tilzer
Down by the River   Hart; Rodgers
Down South Camp Meetin'   Mills
Down the Lane to Yesterday   Loesser
Dream Lullaby   Mills
Dream of a Ladies Cloakroom Attendant (inst.)   Kern
Dream Shadows   Coots; Parish
Drifting Alone on Dreamy River   Johnson, Howard
Drum Brigade, The   Cahn
Duchess Has a Twinkle in Her Eye, The   Washington
Dusty Road   Parish
Each Morning After an Evening with You   Lerner, Sammy
Easter Bunnies   Heyman
Easy Goin' Gal   Rainger; Robin; Whiting
Easy on the Eyes   Coslow
Echoes   Mills
Eenie Meenie Minee Chinee   Edwards
Eenie Meenie Minie Chinee   Bryan
Eeny Meeny Miney Mo   Mercer
El Cubanito   Fain; Kahal
El Tenorio de Broadway (The Tenor of Broadway)   Gorney
Entrance of Eric   Porter
Everglades   Leslie
Every Little Doggie Has His Day   Livingston, Jerry
Every Little Moment   Fields; McHugh
Every Night at Eight   Fields; McHugh
Everybody's Ship Comes In (Not Mine)   Loesser
Everybody's Whispering   Coots; Davis
Everything's Been Done Before   Adamson
Everything's in Rhythm in My Heart   Hoffman
Ev'ry Day   Fain; Kahal
Ev'rybod-ee Who's Anybod-ee   Porter
Face Lifting   Smith, Harry B.
Fagin You'se Is a Viper   Gordon; Revel
Fare Thee Well Annabelle   Dixon; Wrubel
Farewell, My Lovely   Dietz; Schwartz, Arthur
Farewell, Sweet Senorita   Woods
Fascination   Young, Victor
Fashion Show   Fields
Fickle Flo   Yellen
Fiddle 'em Up Again   Johnson, J. Rosamond
Fiddlin' Joe   Mills
Finale — First Act Naughty Marietta   Herbert; Kahn
Finders Are Keepers   Mercer; Sigman
Flagenheim's Odorless Cheese   Dubin; Warren
Flame Within (inst.), The   Kern
Flower on My Lapel   Conrad; Magidson
Flowers for Madame   Dixon; Wrubel
Following in Your Footsteps   Stept; Washington
Following the Stars   Stept
Footloose and Fancy Free   Kahn
For Lovers Only   Dubin; Mercer; Warren
Four-Score and Seven Years Ago   Cahn
Free with Love   Mitchell; Stept

Fresh from the Country   Clare; Stept
From the Top of Your Head to the Tip of Your
   Toes   Gordon; Revel
Functionizin'   Mills; Waller
Functionizin' (inst.)   Waller
Gaby Can Can (inst.)   Gorney
Garden in Old Kentucky   Bryan
Gather Ye Autographs While Ye May   Porter
Gaucho, The   DeSylva
Gay Little Wives (Six Little Wives)   Porter
Georgia Rockin' Chair   Fisher
Get Acquainted with Yourself   Cahn
Get Away from It All   Dietz; Schwartz, Arthur
Get That Ho Do Ho in Your Soul   Mills
Get Under the Sun   Loesser
Get Yourself a Geisha   Dietz; Schwartz, Arthur
Ghost of Dinah, The   Young, Joseph
Ginger   Freed, Ralph; Stept
Girl Friend   Johnston; Kahn
Girl I Left Behind Me, The   Leslie; Meyer; Rose
Girl on the Little Blue Plate, The   Alter
Give Me Sincerity   Woods
Give Us This Night   Lawrence
Go Into Your Dance   Dubin; Warren
Goblin Market   Mills
Goil on the Flying Trapeze, The   Johnson, Howard
Golden Wedding Waltz, The   Oakland
Gone, Gone, Gone!   Gershwin, George
Good for Nothin' Joe   Bloom; Koehler
Good Green Acres of Home, The   Fain; Kahal
Good Morning, Miss Standing   Porter
Good Old Fashioned Cocktail (With at Good Old Fashioned
   Girl), A   Dubin; Warren
Good Old Noah   Sterling
Good Sauce From the Gravy Bowl   Mills
Goodbye Forever   Coslow
Got a Bran' New Suit   Dietz; Schwartz, Arthur
Got a Gal in Californ-i-a   Rainger; Robin
Got a New Kind-a Rhythm   Clare; Stept
Got a New Lease on Life   Fields
Got a Tickle in My Toes   Woods
Got a Way of Doin' Things   Rainger; Robin; Whiting
Got Me Doin' Things   Gordon
Graduation Waltz, The   Livingston, Jerry
Greek Scene   Porter
Gypsy Madness   Coslow
Gypsy Moon   Young, Victor
Hail and Reign   Smith, Harry B.
Hail! Hail! Hail to Ellum Dale   DeSylva
Hail the Groom   Gordon; Revel
Half of Me Wants to Be Good   Lewis
Harlem at Its Best   Fields; McHugh
Hate to Talk About Myself   Rainger; Robin; Whiting
Haunting Chopin Strain   Johnson, Howard
Havana Heaven (Cielo de la Habana)   Johnson, Howard
Have a Little Sympathy Cherie   Fisher
Have You Written Home to Mother   Davis
He Was a Gentleman   Gorney
He Was Her Man   Dixon; Wrubel
Headin' Home   Washington
Hear What My Heart Is Saying   Adamson; Lane
Heart Like the Ocean, A   Mills
Heat It Up   Rainger; Robin
Hell and High Water   Coslow
Her Bodyguard   Coslow

(Lookie-Lookie-Lookie) Here Comes Cookie   Gordon
Here's to Romance   Conrad; Magidson
Here's to the Builder   Loesser
He's a Bad Man   Fain; Kahal
He's a Fox Hunting Polo Playing Son of a British
   Nobleman   Fain; Kahal
Hi-Diddle-Dee-Dem   Conrad; Magidson
Hiking   Adamson; Lane
Hollywood Holiday   Coots; Parish
Homer, the Old Trombone   Parish
Homeward Bound on the Old Greyhound   Bryan
Honestly   Parish
Honey Chile   Clare
Hooray for Love   Fields; McHugh
Hot Bolero   Conrad; Magidson
Hottentot Potentate   Dietz; Schwartz, Arthur
House Rent Party Day   Mills
How Can I Hold You Close Enough   Harburg; Heyman
How Can There Be So Many Moons   Caesar; Henderson;
   Koehler
How Do I Rate with You   Coslow; Whiting
Humble Side of the Town, The   Fain; Kahal
Hunkadola   Friend
I Ain't Gonna Love No More   Von Tilzer
I Built a Dream One Day   Hammerstein; Romberg
I Can Wiggle My Ears   Hoffman
I Can't Escape from You   Coslow
I Can't Get to First Base with You   Fisher
I Can't Waltz Alone   Fields
I Do It All By Proxy   Smith, Harry B.
I Don't Know Your Name (But You're Beautiful)   Caesar;
   Lerner, Sammy
I Don't Love You — Not Much   Akst; Brown, Lew
I Don't Want to Make History (I Just Want to Make
   Love)   Rainger; Robin
I Dream too Much   Fields; Kern; McHugh
I Feel a Song Coming On   Fields; McHugh
I Feel So Spanish Tonight   Friend; Stept
I Found a Dream   Gorney
I Got Love   Fields; Kern; McHugh
I Got Plenty o' Nuthin'   Gershwin, George; Gershwin, Ira
I Got Shoes You Got Shoesies   Friend; Yellen
I Had a Dream Last Night   Alter
I Hate to Be Alone   Adamson; Lane
I Hate to Love You So   Smith, Harry B.
I Have a Rendezvous with Love   Parish
I Just Came Back to Haunt You, Bogey, Bogey, Bogey
   Boo   Loesser
I Keep on Singing   Hart; Rodgers
I Killed Him 'Cause I Loved Him   Hanley
I Knew   Robin
I Like It with Music   Henderson; Yellen
I Live for Love   Dixon; Wrubel
I Lost My Heart   Robin
I Lost My Heart in the Subway (When I Gave My Seat to
   You)   Fisher
I Love to Dream   Akst
I Love to Ride the Horses on a Merry-Go-Round   Pollack;
   Yellen
I Loves You, Porgy   Gershwin, George; Gershwin, Ira
I Met My Waterloo   Johnston
I Must Obey My Heart   Davis; Silver
I Never Had a Man to Cry Over   Gordon; Revel
I Never Saw a Better Night   Mercer
I Saw Her at Eight O'Clock   Mercer

I See Two Lovers   Dixon; Wrubel
I Still Want You   Mills
I Threw a Bean Bag at the Moon   Ager
I Threw a Pebble in the Pond   Hanley; Leslie
I Wanna Make Love   Friend
I Wanna Play House with You   Dixon; Wrubel
I Want a Red Blooded Papa to Chase My Blues
      Away   Coslow
I Want to Dance a Little, Romance a Little   Coslow
I Want to Report a Fire   Heyman
I Was Born too Late   Friend; Yellen
I Was So Happy I Cried   Burke; Spina
I Was Taken By Storm   Alter; Heyman
I Went Merrily Merrily on My Way   Fain; Kahal
I Wish I Were Aladdin   Gordon; Revel
I Wished on the Moon   Rainger
I Wonder what They're Doin' Down in Ding Dong
      Dell   Woods
I Won't Dance   Fields; Hammerstein; Kern
I'd Hate to Tell You   Adamson; Donaldson
I'd Like to Dance the Whole Night Thru   David, Mack
I'd Love to Take Orders from You   Dubin; Warren
I'd Rather Be with You   Akst; Brown, Lew
I'd Rather Listen to Your Eyes   Dubin; Warren
If   Razaf
If I Can't Sell It I'll Keep Sittin' on It   Razaf
If I Can't Sing, I've Got to Dance   Woods
If I Had My Way   Kahal
If I Knew   Rainger
If I Should Lose You   Rainger; Robin
If I Were Anybody Else but Me   Herbert; Kahn
If Love Came Wrapped in Cellophane   Heyman
If There's Love in Your Heart   Johnston; Kahn
If They Feel Like a War Let Them Keep It Over
      There   Johnson, Howard
If You Could Love Me   Porter
If You Were As Lonely (As You Are Lovely)   Burke; Spina
If You Were I and I Were You   Coslow
If You Were Mine   Mercer
I'll Be There with Bells On   Rainger; Robin; Whiting
I'll Do What My Heart Tells Me To   Stept
I'll Do What My Heart Tells Me to Do   Friend
I'll Never Say "Never Again" Again   Woods
I'll Take a Little of You on Toast   Hart; Rodgers
I'll Tell the World That's News   Mills; Razaf
I'm a Fugitive from a Chain Letter Gang   Caesar; Lerner,
      Sammy
I'm a Gambler   Leslie; Monaco
I'm a Little Big Shot Now   Dixon; Wrubel
I'm a Seeker of Beauty   Johnston
I'm Betting on You   Akst; Brown, Lew
I'm Bound for Heaven   Adamson; Lane
I'm Building Up to an Awful Let Down   Mercer
I'm Goin' Shoppin' with You   Dubin; Warren
I'm Gonna Fall in Love, I Feel It in My Bones   Akst; Brown,
      Lew; Henderson
I'm Gonna Sit Right Down and Write Myself a
      Letter   Ahlert; Young, Joseph
I'm Gonna Take Possession of You   Eliscu
I'm Gonna Take You Home Tonight to Meet the
      Family   Gilbert
I'm in Another World when I'm with You   Stept;
      Washington
I'm in Love All Over Again   Fields; McHugh
I'm in the Mood for Love   Fields; McHugh

I'm Just a Slave to Your Crave   Cahn
I'm Keeping those Keepsakes You Gave Me   Ahlert
I'm King Again   Friend
I'm Livin' in a Great Big Way   Fields; McHugh
I'm Lost for Words   De Lange
I'm on My Way   Gershwin, George
I'm Painting the Town Red to Hide a Heart that's
      Blue   Stept
I'm Shootin' High   Koehler; McHugh
I'm Sittin' on Top of a Hill Top (I'm Sittin' High on a Hill
      Top)   Johnston; Kahn
I'm So Happy I Could Cry   Heyman
I'm the Echo (You're the Song I Sing)   Fields; Kern;
      McHugh
I'm the Fellow Who Loves You   Henderson; Yellen
I'm with the Right Girl Now   Bloom
I'm Yours for Tonight   Rainger
Image of You, The   Burke; Spina
Imitations of You   Blake; Mills
In a Little English Inn   Coslow
In a Little Gypsy Tea Room   Leslie
In a Little Street Cafe   Conrad
In a Sentimental Mood   Ellington; Mills
In a Soda Fountain Mirror   Ahlert
In Caliente   Dixon; Wrubel
In Monticello's Kingdom Grand   Smith, Harry B.
In My Wildest Dreams   Carmichael; Heyman
In Other Words I'm in Love   Clare
In that Vine Covered Chapel in the Valley   Fisher
In the Hash Lane
In the Magic of Maytime   Livingston, Jerry
In the Middle of a Kiss   Coslow
In the Sweet Long Ago   Leslie
In Your Memory   Gilbert
Indian Moon   Loesser
Interlude in a Barber Ship   Hammerstein; Romberg
International, The   Livingston, Jerry
Is Love a Moon Flower?   Rainger; Robin
Isn't Love the Grandest Thing?   Alter
Isn't Love the Sweetest Thing?   Alter
Isn't This a Lovely Day (To Be Caught in the Rain)   Berlin
It Ain't Being Done No More   Blake
It Ain't Necessarily So   Gershwin, George; Gershwin, Ira
It Looks Like an Early Fall   Coots
It Must Be Love or Something   Coslow; Rainger
It Never Dawned on Me   Coots; Lewis
It Take a Long Pull to Get There   Gershwin, George
It Was a Dark and Stormy Night   Fain; Kahal
It's a Lot of Idle Gossip   Livingston, Jerry
It's a Night in a Million   Mercer; Warren
It's About Time   Livingston, Jerry
It's All So New to Me   Henderson; Heyman
It's an Old Southern Custom   Friend; Yellen
It's Easy to Remember   Hart; Rodgers
It's Grand to Be So Beautiful   Blake
It's Great to Be in Love Again   Fields; McHugh
It's No Fun   Ager
It's Only a Hole-in-the-Wall   Young, Joseph
It's Only Human   Adamson; Lane
It's the Rhythm in Me   Mills
It's Time to Say Goodnight   Friend; Yellen
Ivan's Song   Adamson; Lane
I've Been Waiting All Winter (For a Summer Night Like
      This)   Mills; Oakland; Parish
I've Found My Place in the Sun   Adamson; Lane

I've Gone Off the Deep End   Robin
I've Got a Feelin' You're Foolin'   Brown, Nacio Herb; Freed, Arthur
I've Got a Lazy Way of Living   Freed, Arthur
I've Got a Pocket Full of Sunshine   Johnston; Kahn
I've Got My Fingers Crossed   Koehler; McHugh
I've Got Some New Shoes   Bullock; Coslow; Whiting
I've Got to Get Hot   Henderson; Yellen
I've Got Your Future All Planned   Gorney
I've Spent Half a Moon   Burke; Spina
Jamboree   Mills
Jane (From a Little Town in Maine)   Gilbert
Jealousy   Gordon; Revel
Joan of Arkansaw   Heyman
Jockey on the Carousel, The   Fields; Kern; McHugh
Johnnie Get Your Hair Cut Short Like Mine   Johnson, J. Rosamond
Jubilee Presentation   Porter
Judgement of Paris, The   Porter
Just a Moment   Donaldson
Just As Long As the World Goes 'Round and Around, and I Go Around with You   Woods
Just By Your Example   Woods
Just Once Around the Clock   Hammerstein; Romberg
Just One of Those Things   Porter
Keep that Twinkle in Your Eye   Clare; Eliscu
Keep the Rhythm Going   Mills
Keep Your Fingers Crossed   Coslow; Whiting
Keeper of My Heart, The   Mercer
King Can Do No Wrong, A   Coslow
King of Swing Is Havin' a Dream, The   Cahn
Kiss and Make Up Waltz, The   Freed, Ralph
Kiss from Angelina   Heyman
Kiss to Build a Dream On, A   Hammerstein; Kalmar; Ruby
Kisses in My Dreams   Bryan
Kling-Kling Bird on the Divi-Divi Tree, The   Porter
La Locumba   Clare
Lady in Red, The   Dixon; Wrubel
Lady with the Tap, The   Dietz; Schwartz, Arthur
Last Night When We Were Young   Arlen; Harburg
Laugh   Hart; Rodgers
Laughin' at the Weather Man   Rainger; Robin
Lazy Bones Gotta Job Now   Robin
Lazy but Free (inst.)   Kern
Lazy Little Stream Ripple Along   Rose
Least Little Thing You Do, The   De Lange
Leavin' fo' de Promis' Lan'   Gershwin, George
Lena, I Love You   Hammerstein; Romberg
Let It Be Me   Dixon; Wrubel
Let Me Present You With My Heart   Johnson, Howard
Let Me Sing You to Sleep with a Love Song   Gordon; Revel
Let the Man Who Makes the Gun   Egan
Let Your Heart Make Up Your Mind   Caesar; Lerner, Sammy
Let's Leave It to Love   Parish
Let's Make a Night of It   Rainger; Robin
Let's Play House   David, Mack
Let's Spill the Beans   Gordon; Revel
Let's Stop Saying Goodbye   Bryan; Leslie; Meyer
Life Begins at Sweet Sixteen   Henderson; Yellen
Life Begins when You're in Love   Brown, Lew
Life Is a Song, Let's Sing It Together   Ahlert; Young, Joseph
Lift Your Glass   Romberg
Like a Bird in the Night   Johnson, Howard
Lilly the Contortionist   Adamson

Little and Lovely   Bryan
Little Angel Told Me So, A   Coslow
Little Bit Independent, A   Leslie
Little Blue Gown (Blue Jeans)   Conrad; Magidson
Little Colonel   Pollack; Webster
Little Door, A Little Lock, A Little Key, A   Woods
Little Girl Blue   Hart; Rodgers
Little Girl from Who Knows Where   Johnson, Howard
Little Kisses   Ager
Little Man with the Hammer, The   Mercer
Little Miss Mischief   Loesser
Little of Rhythm (In the Best of Us)   Cahn
Little Rendezvous in Honolulu, A   Leslie
Little Rose of the Rancho   Rainger; Robin
Little Silkworm, The   Hoffman
Little Things You Used to Do, The   Dubin; Warren
Little White Gardenia, A   Coslow
Little White House a Little White Lady, A   Johnson, Howard
Living on Velvet (Helping Each Other Along)   Dubin; Warren
Loadin' Time   Dietz; Schwartz, Arthur
Loafin' Time   Ager
Lonely Boy   Gershwin, George
Lonely Feet   Hammerstein; Kern
Lonely Gondolier   Dubin; Warren
Look What the Wind Blew In   Adamson; Donaldson
Looka Him   Oakland; Parish
Looking Forward to Looking After You   Woods
Lost My Rhythm, Lost My Music, Lost My Man   Akst; Brown, Lew
Louisiana Fairy Tale   Coots; Parish
Love Among the Roses   Parish
Love and Learn   Yellen
Love Can Be Fun   Coslow
Love Clouds   Gilbert
Love Dropped in for Tea   Burke; Spina
Love Has Passed Me By   Cahn
Love Is a Dancing Thing   Dietz; Schwartz, Arthur
Love Is a Flame   Lewis
Love Is Just Around the Corner   Robin
Love Is Love (In Any Woman's Heart)   Fain; Kahal
Love Makes the World Go 'Round   Heyman
Love Me Forever   Kahn
Love Me in Viennese   Johnson, Howard
Love Song of Tahiti   Kahn
Love Takes a Holiday   Lawrence
Love Tiptoed through My Heart   Loewe
Love, You're Just a Laugh   Cahn
Lovely Lady   Koehler; McHugh
Lovely Liza Lee   Razaf
Lovely to Look At   Fields; Kern
Love's Dream After the Ball   Johnson, Howard
Loves of New Orleans   Herbert; Kahn
Love's Serenade   Mills
Lullaby of Broadway   Dubin; Warren
Lulu's Back in Town   Dubin; Warren
Machinery   Razaf
Magic of You, The   Rainger
Magnin Fashion Show   Lane; Washington
Making Merry in the Month of May   Johnson, Howard
Mama Don't Allow It   Cahn
Mammy, I'll Sing about You   Dubin; Warren
Man, a Maid, a Moon, A   Rainger; Robin
Manana   Rainger; Robin; Whiting

Marching Along   Brown, Nacio Herb
Marriage Is a Game of Blind Man's Bluff   Smith, Harry B.
Martinique, The   Alter
Mashed Potatoes   Coslow; Whiting
May I Have My Gloves?   Henderson; Yellen
May I Have the Next Dream with You?   Coslow
Maybe You Know What I Mean   Carmichael; Mercer
Me and Marie   Porter
Meet Miss America   Mercer
Meet the President   Cahn
Mellow Music and Moonlight   Johnson, Howard
Melody Lingers On, The   Silver
Memories of Madison Square Garden   Hart; Rodgers
Metropolitan Nocturne (inst.)   Alter
Mexicana   Dixon; Wrubel
Midnight in Paris   Conrad; Magidson
Midsummer Madness   Coslow; Whiting
Mine Alone   Dixon; Wrubel
Miss Brown to You   Rainger; Robin; Whiting
Mist on the Mirror   Heyman; Romberg
Mister Deep Blue Sea   Johnson, James P.
Moaning in the Moonlight   Conrad; Magidson
Model Happy Fair, A   Smith, Harry B.
Models   Henderson; Yellen
Moon Crazy   Alter
Moon Hangs High, The   Stept
Moon Is in the Sky, The   Kalmar; Ruby
Moon Mad   Rainger; Robin
Moon Over Miami   Leslie
Moon Over Monte Cristo   Whiting
Moon Over Mulberry Street   Egan
Moonlight and You (inst.)   Warren
Moonlight in Heaven   Alter
Moonlight Maneuvers   Berlin
Moonlight on the Meadow   Ruby
More I See of Other Girls (Elephant Song), The   Hart;
   Rodgers
Morning After, The   Coslow
Most Beautiful Girl in the World, The   Hart; Rodgers
Motherless Child (Recitative)   Gershwin, George; Gershwin,
   Ira
Mr. and Mrs. Smith   Porter
Mr. Bluebird   Carmichael
Muchacha   Dubin; Warren
Muggin' the Pillow   Cahn
Murder in the Moonlight (It's Love in the First
   Degree)   Lewis
Mush You Haulers   Coslow; Whiting
Music Hall Rag   Mills
Music in My Heart   Fields; McHugh
Music Is Magic   Clare; Johnston
My Angel Mother's Serenade   Johnson, Howard
My Foolish Heart   Bullock; Whiting
My Gink   Schwartz, Jean
My Great Waltz   Johnson, Howard
My Heart Is a Violin   Pollack; Webster
My Heart Is an Open Book   Gordon
My Heart Is Still Among the Hills of Ireland   Johnson,
   Howard
My Heart Jumped Over the Moon   Kahal
My Home Town   Oakland
My Introduction to Love   Caesar; Carmichael
My Kid's a Crooner   Dixon; Wrubel
My Kingdom for a Kiss   Rainger; Robin; Whiting
My Loulou   Porter

My Man's Gone Now   Gershwin, George
My Medicine Man   Coslow
My Most Intimate Friend   Porter
My Old Mare   Hammerstein; Romberg
My One Big Moment   Pollack; Webster
My Other Me   Harburg
My Right Hand Man   Razaf
My Romance   Hart; Rodgers
My Sweet   Friend
My Unfinished Symphony of Love   Coslow
My Very Good Friend the Milkman   Burke; Spina
My Weeping Willow's Smiling Just for Me   Pollack; Webster
Napoleon's Exile   Johnston; Kahn
Nature and I   Cahn
'Neath the Southern Moon   Herbert; Kahn
New O'leans   Johnston; Kahn
New Pan-Ameri-Can-Can   Rainger; Robin; Whiting
Nickel in the Slot   Mills
Night Is Blue   Mills
Night Is Young, The   Hammerstein; Romberg
Night of Nights   Adamson; Donaldson
Night, the Wind, and Me, The   Razaf
Nighty Night   Adamson; Donaldson
Ninon   Adamson
No Bottom (Mississippi Opening/The Leadsman's
   Song)   Hart; Rodgers
No Callin' Card   Mills
No Can Do   Rainger; Robin; Whiting
No Doggone Business   Carmichael
No Letter in the Morning Mail   Leslie
No More Ladies   Washington
No Strings (I'm Fancy Free)   Berlin
Noble Duchess, The   Hammerstein; Romberg
Nothing Lives Longer than Love   Lewis
Notorious Colonel Blake, The   Hart; Rodgers
Now I'm a Lady   Coslow; Fain; Kahal
Now You've Got Me Doing It   Burke; Spina
Numb Fumblin'   Waller
O Leo!   Dietz; Schwartz, Arthur
O What a Wonderful World   Dietz; Schwartz, Arthur
Octoroon   Warren
Oh Baby, Obey   Rainger; Robin
Oh Bess, Where's My Bess   Gershwin, George; Gershwin,
   Ira
Oh de Lawd Shake de Heaven   Gershwin, George
Oh, Doctor Jesus   Gershwin, George; Gershwin, Ira
Oh! Frenchy (Come to Yankee Land)   Conrad
Oh, I Can't Sit Down   Gershwin, George; Gershwin, Ira
Oh I Didn't Know (You'd Get that Way)   Friend; Yellen
Old Fireplace   Coots; Davis
Old Man Rhythm   Mercer
Old Man with the Whiskers, The   Coots; Parish
Old New York   Dubin; Warren
Old Village Square, The   Robison
Olga   Johnson, Howard
On a Sunday Afternoon   Brown, Nacio Herb; Freed, Arthur
On Account Of   Coslow
On the Nodaway Road   Mercer
On the Other Side of the Jordan   David, Mack
On the Trail   Kahn
On the Wings of a Waltz   Rainger; Robin
On to Victory   Smith, Harry B.
On Treasure Island   Leslie
Once to Ev'ry Heart   Mills
Once Upon a Midnight   Burke; Spina

One in a Million   Alter
One Way Street   Caesar; Henderson; Koehler
Only Time You're Out of Luck, The   Razaf
Opening — First Act Naughty Marietta   Herbert; Kahn
Our Crown   Porter
Our First Rendezvous   Coslow
Our Little Girl   Pollack; Webster
Out of Sight, Out of My Mind   Fields
Out of the Frying Pan, Into the Fire   Monaco
Out on the Broad Prairie (Broad Western
    Prairie)   Hammerstein; Kern
Outside of You   Dubin; Warren
Over a Chocolate Sundae on Saturday Night   Fisher
Over and Over Again   Hart; Rodgers
Over My Shoulder   Woods
Over the Waves to the Port of Your Heart   Johnson,
    Howard
Overflow   Gershwin, George
Pablo, You Are My Heart   Hart; Rodgers
Pagan Star   Carmichael
Page Miss Glory   Dubin; Warren
Pair of Dimples and a Picture Hat, A   Ager
Palsie Walsie   Fields; McHugh
Pampas Moon   Whiting
Panic Is On, The   Mills; Waller
Pardon My Dust   Rainger; Robin; Whiting
Paree   Dietz; Schwartz, Arthur
Paris in Spring   Schwartz, Jean
Paris in the Spring   Gordon; Revel
Paris Police   Schwartz, Jean
Penguin Parade   Whiting
Penny in My Pocket, A   Rainger; Robin
Penthouse in the Moon   Bryan
Piccolino, The   Berlin
Picture of Me Without You, A   Porter
Pied Piper of Harlem   Henderson; Yellen
Pig and the Cow and the Dog and the Cat, The   Dubin;
    Warren
Pimento   Dubin; Warren
Play Mates — School Mates — Soul Mates   Schwartz, Jean;
    Young, Joseph
Playboy of Paree   Dixon; Wrubel
Please Make Me Be Good   Hart; Rodgers
Please Take My Heart   Razaf
Pleasure Was All Mine, The   Mills
Plow Boy   Brennan; Snyder
Polly-Wolly-Doodle   Clare; DeSylva
Powder My Back   Dixon; Wrubel
Prayin' in Rhythm   Stept; Washington
Prelude to Champagne and Orchids (inst.)   Kern
Printemps   Gordon; Revel
Punchinello   Herbert; Kahn
Puppets on the Strings of Love   Cahn
Querida Mia (My Sweetheart)   Pollack; Webster
Quicker than You Can Say Jack Robinson   David, Mack;
    Meyer
Rain on the Range   Mills
Rainbow Filled with Music, A   Mills
Real True Pal, A   Loesser
Reckless   Hammerstein; Kern
Reckless Dormitory Sequence (inst.)   Kern
Red Headed Woman, A   Gershwin, George; Gershwin, Ira
Redheads on Parade   Gorney
Rehearsal Number   Hammerstein; Kern
Remember Cherie   Coslow

Remember Last Night   Coslow
Rhythm Holiday   Cahn
(If I Had) Rhythm in My Nursery Rhymes   Cahn; Raye
Rhythm Is Our Business   Cahn
Rhythm Makes the World Go Round   Cahn
Rhythm of the Rain   Gordon; Revel
Rhythm of the Rumba, The   Rainger
Rhythm River   Bloom; Koehler
Ride, Red, Ride   Mills
Ridin' Up the River Road   Woods
Roll, Mississippi   Hart; Rodgers
Rolling Along   Akst; Brown, Lew
Rolling in the Snow   Fain
Rose in Her Hair, The   Dubin; Warren
'Round My Old Deserted Farm   Robison
Russian Fantasy (inst.)   Waller
Russian Lullaby   Fields; Kern
Sabers   Gorney
Saddest Tale   Ellington; Mills
Sailing on the Night Boat where the Hudson Flows   Caesar;
    Lerner, Sammy
Sailor Beware   Robin; Whiting
Same of You (Igual Que Tu), The   Gorney
Sandy and Me   Clare; Stept
Santa Claus Came in the Spring   Mercer
Say Goodnight but Not Goodbye   Johnson, Howard
Say the Word and It's Yours   Hoffman
See If I Care   Stept; Washington
Seein' Is Believin'   Ager
Selzer Theme Song   Fain; Kahal
Send Me   Mills
September in the Rain   Dubin; Warren
Shadows   Mills
Shadows of Yesterday's Stars   Dubin
Shattuck on Parade   Davis; Silver
Shaving Song (A Man Must Shave)   Dixon; Wrubel
She Was an Acrobat's Daughter   Kalmar; Ruby
She's a Latin from Manhattan   Dubin; Warren
Shoe Shine Boy   Cahn
Shoot the Works   Mills
Short and Sweet   Fain
Should I Be Sweet   Brown, Lew; Youmans
Side Car, The   Porter
Silver Wings   Dixon; Wrubel
Simple Things in Life, The   Henderson; Koehler
Simply Grand   Koehler
Since O'Keefe Is on Relief   Johnson, Howard
Since We Fell Out of Love   De Lange
Sing an Old Fashioned Song to a Young, Sophisticated
    Lady   Ahlert; Young, Joseph
Sing Before Breakfast   Brown, Nacio Herb; Freed, Arthur
Sing Jubilee   Porter
Sing of Spring   Clare
Singing a Song in Your Arms   Hammerstein; Kern
Singing in the Saddle   Porter
Sittin' Around on Sunday   Ahlert; Young, Joseph
Skating Our Way Into Love   Johnson, Howard
Sleep and Dream   Gordon; Revel
Sleep, Baby, Sleep   Coslow
Sleepy Time in Topsy-Turvy Town   Ager
Slipping Thru My Fingers   Mills
Slowly but Surely   Heyman
Snow Flakes, The   Loesser
So Nice Seeing You Again   Dixon; Wrubel
So Red the Rose   Lawrence

So This Is Heaven   Burke; Spina
So What?   Akst
Soldier of Love   Caesar; Lerner, Sammy
Some Other Time   Coslow
Somebody Ought to Be Told   Hammerstein; Romberg
Someone Else Was There   Sigman
Someone I Love   Herbert
Something in My Heart   Harburg
Something in the Air of May   Hammerstein; Romberg
Something New Is in My Heart   Hammerstein; Romberg
Something's Gotta Happen Soon   Brown, Nacio Herb;
    Freed, Arthur
Son of God's Country, A   Coots
Song of Spring   Carmichael
Song of the Autumn and You   Johnson, Howard
Song of the Crusades   Robin; Whiting
Song of the Flea   Johnson, Howard
Song of the Gigolo   Dubin; Warren
Song of the Roustabouts   Hart; Rodgers
Soon   Hart; Rodgers
Spain   Dubin; Warren
Spanish Blonde, A   Burke; Spina
Spanish Butterfly   Bryan
Speaking Confidentially   Fields; McHugh
Spirit of the Tom Tom, The   Cahn
Spreadin' Rhythm Around   Koehler; McHugh
Spreading Love Around   Henderson; Heyman
Star and the Rose, The   Schwartz, Jean; Young, Joseph
Star Gazing   Livingston, Jerry
Starlight Waltz   Adamson; Lane
Stars Over Broadway   Dubin; Warren
Start My Heart Again   Coslow
Stay As Sweet As You Are   Gordon
Steamboat Round the Bend   Clare
Steamboat Whistle, The   Dietz; Schwartz, Arthur
Steely Glint in My Eye, The   Hart; Rodgers
Stingaree   Mills
Stolen Harmony   Lawrence; Young, Joseph
Stop, Look, and Listen   Freed, Ralph
Strange Blues   Mills
Street Cries (Strawberry Woman, Crab Man)   Gershwin,
    George
Sugar Cookie Mountain   Rose
Sugar Is Sweet and So Are You   Mills
Sugar Plum   Johnston; Kahn
Suicide Part II   Gordon; Revel
Summer Night   Dubin; Warren
Summertime   Gershwin, George
Sump'n 'bout Rhythm   Ellington; Mills
Sunbonnet Blue and a Yellow Straw Hat, A   Fain; Kahal
Sunday at Sundown   Loesser; Motzan
Sunday Morning, Breakfast Time   Porter
Surprise, Surprise, I'm Giving Me to You   Von Tilzer
Surrender   Donaldson
Suzannah   Akst; Brown, Lew
Swank, The   Conrad; Magidson
Sweet and Slow   Dubin; Warren
Sweet Flossie Farmer   Dixon; Wrubel
Sweet Hoodoo   Heyman
Sweet Surrender   Heyman
Sweet Thing   Ahlert; Baer; Young, Joseph
Sweet Virginia Lee   Adamson; Donaldson
Sweetheart of the Flowers   Johnson, Howard
Swing Me with Rhythm   Mills
Swing that Swing   Porter

Swingin' on the Moon   Carmichael; Young, Joseph
Swingin' on the Strings Like Nobody's Business   Fisher
Symphony in Brown (inst.)   Johnson, James P.
Symphony in Green, A   Loesser
Symphony in Riffs   Mills
Synthetic Love   Mills; Washington
Taggin' Along with You   Mills
Take It Easy   Fields; McHugh
Take Love While You May   Schwartz, Jean
Take Me Home to the Mountains   Loesser
Take My Kiss to Dreamland with You   Coots; Parish
Take the Ache from My Heart   Johnson, Howard
Take This Little Rose   Mills
Take This Ring   Heyman
Takes Two to Make a Bargain (What's the Answer — What's
    the Verdict — How's About It Baby)   Gordon; Revel
Taking Care of You   Akst; Brown, Lew
Tallahassee   Mills
Tap Happy   Rainger; Robin
Tell Me   Bryan; Meyer
Tell Me Again (inst.)   Warren
Tell Me That You Care (inst.)   Warren
Tell the Truth   Henderson; Yellen
Ten Little Miles from Town   Stept
Tender Is the Night   Adamson; Donaldson
Thank Your Stars We're Under the Moon Tonight   Bryan;
    Meyer; Young, Joseph
Thanks a Million   Johnston; Kahn
That Goes for You   Adamson; Donaldson
That Rhythm Parade   Razaf
That's How Little Dreams Are Born   Parish
That's Not Cricket   Dietz; Schwartz, Arthur
That's the Hollywood Low-Down   Fields; McHugh
That's What I Get for Wearing My Heart on My
    Sleeve   Stept; Washington
(If It Isn't Pain) Then It Isn't Love   Rainger; Robin
Then You Walked in the Room   Akst; Brown, Lew
There Is My Love   Rainger; Robin
There'll Be a Great Day in the Mornin'   Mills
There'll Be No South   Brown, Lew
There's a Bit of Paree in You   Gorney
There's a Boat dat's Leavin' Soon for New York   Gershwin,
    George; Gershwin, Ira
There's a Chill in the Air   Lane; Washington
There's a Diff'rent You in Your Heart   Fain; Kahal
There's a Four Star Moon Tonight   Coots; Parish
There's a Little Picture Playhouse in My Heart   Leslie
There's a Method in My Madness   Adamson; Donaldson
There's a Riot in Havana   Hammerstein; Romberg
There's a Shadow in the Sunshine of Your Smile   Ahlert;
    Young, Joseph
There's a Smile on My Face   Berlin
There's a Spot 'Neath the Sun for Everyone   Edwards;
    Johnson, Howard
There's a Vacant Chair for Will Rogers in Every Home
    Tonight   Parish
There's a Whistle in the Thistle   Freed, Ralph; Washington
There's Another Little Wrinkle on Her Brow   Ahlert; Young,
    Joseph
There's Champagne in Your Eyes   Stept; Washington
There's Music in a Kiss   Silver
There's Nothing Like a College Education   Mercer
There's Nothing Like Swimming   Porter
There's Something in a Big Parade   Washington
They Pass By Singing   Gershwin, George

Thief in the Night   Dietz; Schwartz, Arthur
Things Might Have Been So Diff'rent   Coots; Lewis
This is Love   Akst; Brown, Lew
This Is My Story   Sigman
This Is My Year   Fisher
This Is the Night   Brown, Nacio Herb; Freed, Arthur
This Is Wonderful, Just As It Is   Livingston, Jerry
Three Feet Two of Rhythm   Cahn
Three Sweethearts Have I   Rainger; Robin
Through the Doorway of Dreams (I Saw You)   Rainger;
     Robin; Whiting
Thunder   Lewis
Thunder Over Paradise   Rainger; Robin
Tia Juana (inst.)   Gorney
Tie Your Troubles to a Toy Baloon   Adamson; Donaldson
Tillie the Tight Rope Walker   Washington
Time and Time Again   Gershwin, George
Time Out for Love   Coots; Lewis; Parish
Times May Change   Schwartz, Jean
Ting a Ling a Ling   Gorney
Tinkle, Tinkle, Tinkle   Woods
Tiny Little Fingerprints   Stept
To Call You My Own   Dixon; Wrubel
To Get Away   Porter
To Think that You're Mine Again   Davis; Silver
Today Is Saturday   Mills
Toddlin' Along with You   Dixon; Wrubel
Tonight There's a Spell on the Moon   Gorney
Too Much Imagination   Burke; Spina
Top Hat, White Tie, and Tails   Berlin
Topic of the Tropics, The   Livingston, Jerry
Traffic Was Terrific, The   Loesser; Motzan
Tramp, Tramp, Tramp   Herbert; Kahn
Truckin'   Bloom; Koehler
Truckin' in My Tails   Henderson; Yellen
Truckin' on Down   Blake
Twenty-Four Hours a Day   Hanley
Twilight at Noon   Kahal
Twilight Caresses (inst.)   Gorney
Twilight in Sweetheart Lane   Johnson, Howard
Twilight Rhythms   Schwartz, Jean
Two for Tonight   Coslow; Gordon; Revel
Two Heads Against the Moon   Ager
Two Heads in the Moonlight   Adamson; Donaldson
Two Hearts   Weill
Two Hearts Carved on a Lonesome Pine   Ahlert; Young,
     Joseph
Two Little Candles on One Little Cake   Stept
Two Together   Johnston; Kahn
Two-Cent Stamp (Brought Me Back a Million Dollar Love),
     A   Ager
Two-Gun Cowboy   Fisher
Ubangi Man   Mills
Ufty - Mufty and Gufty   Leslie; Monaco
Under Your Thumb and Close to Your Heart   Bryan;
     Schwartz, Jean
Up the Creek   Dietz; Schwartz, Arthur
Valse Moderne (inst.)   Oakland
Vamp of the Pampas, The   Robin; Whiting
Varsity Dance (inst.)   Coslow
Venezuela, The   Washington
Venezuela, The (Ven-ez-wee-la)   Lane
Vesuvius   Razaf
Vienna Will Sing   Hammerstein; Romberg
Vigilante Song   Rainger; Robin

Waiting for the Tide to Turn   Von Tilzer
Waiting in the Garden   Bloom; Koehler
Walking the Floor   Rainger; Robin
Walking the Streets   Mills
Waltz Down the Aisle   Porter
Waltz I Love, The   Washington
We Agree Perfectly   Coots; David, Mack
We Made Up Again   Stept
We Were Meant to Meet Again   Woods
We Were So Young   Hammerstein; Kern
We Work Away   Smith, Harry B.
We Wouldn't Take a Million for Our Baby   Fisher
Wealthy, Shmelthy As Long As You're Healthy   Fain; Parish
Weary   Dixon; Wrubel
Weather Man   Caesar
Wedding Song   Carmichael
Welcome to Napoleon   Johnston; Kahn
We're All in the Bread Line Together   Smith, Harry B.
We're Gonna Have Smooth Sailing   Ager
We're Jolly Good Fellows All   Johnson, Howard
We're Off to a Wonderful Start   Oakland
We're Off to Feathermore   Porter
We're Pirates Bold   Adamson; Lane
We're the Statesmen Great   Smith, Harry B.
Weren't We a Couple of Fools?   Ahlert; Young, Joseph
What a Beautiful Night   Kalmar; Ruby
What a Nice Municipal Park   Porter
What Are We Waiting For?   Revel
What Are You Doing in Here?   Hart; Rodgers
What Harlem Is to Me   Razaf
What Is This Power   Johnston; Kahn
What Will I Do when It's Spring?   Burke; Spina
What Would You Do Mr. Moon   Oakland
What You Want with Bess?   Gershwin, George
What's Gonna Be the Outcome If the Income Don't Come
     In   Von Tilzer
What's On Your Mind   Cahn
What's the Use   Smith, Harry B.
When a Great Love Comes Along   Leslie
When April Comes Again   Livingston, Jerry
When Dad and Mother Danced to the Scarf
     Dance   Johnson, Howard
When I Come Back   Stept
When I Grow Too Old to Dream   Hammerstein; Romberg
When I Grow Up   Henderson; Heyman
When I've Got the Moon (Banjo Song)   Hammerstein; Kern
When Little Bo-Peep Saw Her Little Beau Peep   Bryan
When Love Comes Your Way   Porter
When Me, Mowgli, Love   Porter
When Morning Comes   Heyman
When My Prince Charming Comes Along   Coslow
When Night Comes On   Coots; Lewis
When Somebody Thinks You're Wonderful   Woods
When the Rain Comes Rollin' Down   Fisher
When the Robin Sings His Song Again   Coots; Parish
When You Are in My Arms   Mercer
When You're Away   Dietz; Schwartz, Arthur
When You've Got a Little Springtime in Your Heart   Woods
Whenever I Think of You   Woods
Where Am I?   Dubin; Warren
Where Is My Love   Rainger; Robin
Where the Sweet, Sweet Cactus Grows   Dubin; Warren
Where Were You on the Night of June the Third   Stept
Which Is Which   Clare
While the Night Is Young   Rainger; Robin; Whiting

While We Dance the Waltz of Spain   Johnson, Howard
Whisper That You Love Me Only   Parish
Whistling Waltz, The   Woods
White Shadowland   Johnson, Howard
Whittlin' My Wood   Dubin; Warren
Who but You   Dixon; Wrubel
Whoops My Dear   Schwartz, Jean
Whose Big Baby Are You   Koehler; McHugh
Why Did Bluebeard's Beard Turn Blue   Von Tilzer
Why Do the Bees Hum   Heyman
Why Do They Call It Gay Paree?   Gordon; Revel
Why Dream   Rainger; Robin; Whiting
Why Have a Falling Out Just When We're Falling in Love   Johnson, Howard
Why Shouldn't I?   Porter
Wiener Schnitzel   Hammerstein; Romberg
Will Wonders Never Cease   Freed, Ralph; Oakland
Winding the Trail   Stept
Winter Waltz, The   Ager
With Louise on Lake Louise   Bryan
With My Eyes Wide Open I'm Dreaming   Gordon
With the Whole World Listening In   Coslow
Without a Word of Warning   Gordon; Revel
Without Rhythm   Yellen
Woman Is a Sometime Thing, A   Gershwin, George
Woman to Lady   Gershwin, George
Women   Hart; Rodgers
Words Are in My Heart, The   Dubin; Warren
World of Dreamland, The   Smith, Harry B.
Would There Be Love?   Gordon; Revel
Wouldn't I Be a Wonder   Woods
Wrap Yourself in Cellophane   Carmichael; Mercer
Yankee Doodle Never Went to Town   Freed, Ralph
Yascha and Sascha   Adamson; Lane
Yesterthoughts   Herbert; Kahn
You Always Can Come Back to Me   Razaf
You Are My Lucky Star   Brown, Nacio Herb; Freed, Arthur
You Are So Lovely and I'm So Lonely   Hart; Rodgers
You Belong to Me   Friend; Yellen
You Bother Me an Awful Lot   Fain; Kahal
You Broke It Up (When You Said Dixie)   Razaf
You Can Be Kissed   Dubin; Warren
You Can't Keep Me Away from You   Smith, Harry B.
You Don't Even Know that I'm Alive   Burke; Spina
You Get a Lot of Help when You're in Love   Akst; Brown, Lew; Henderson
You, I Adore You   Burke; Spina
You Let Me Down   Dubin; Warren
You Little Mischief Maker   Freed, Ralph; Young, Victor
You Make Heaven So Beautiful   Johnson, Howard
You May Be Far Away from Me   Dietz; Schwartz, Arthur
You, Me and Company   Coslow
You Opened My Eyes   Gilbert
You Saved My Life   Freed, Ralph; Young, Victor
You Stepped Out of a Dream   Lane; Washington
You Took My Breath Away   Coslow; Whiting
You Took the Words Right Out of My Mouth   Adamson
You Wait and Wait and Wait   Hammerstein; Romberg
You Wrote Your Name in My Heart   Parish
You'll Never Be Sorry   Rainger; Robin; Whiting
Your Eyes   Rainger; Robin; Whiting
Your Eyes Have Said   Rainger
You're a Blessing   Freed, Ralph
You're a Blessing to Me   Rainger; Robin
You're a Heavenly Thing   Young, Joseph
You're a Vision to Behold   Young, Joseph
You're All I Need   Adamson; Kahn
You're an Angel   Fields; McHugh
You're an Eyeful of Heaven   Dixon; Wrubel
You're Married Under False Pretenses   Smith, Harry B.
You're My Poem of Love   Johnson, Howard
You're My Thrill   Lane; Washington
You're So Darn Charming   Burke; Spina
You're So Indifferent   Fain; Parish
You're So Lovely   Magidson
You're Too Good for Me   Adamson; Lane
You're Walking in My Sleep   Oakland
You're Waltzing on My Heart   Akst; Brown, Lew
Yours   Porter
Yours and Mine   Brown, Nacio Herb; Freed, Arthur
You've Got a Sweetness All Your Own   Adamson; Lane
You've Got That   Hart; Rodgers

1936

Adios Muchachos   Johnson, Howard
Aggie's Sewing Machine Song   Weill
Ah Still Suits Me   Hammerstein; Kern
Ah Woo Ah Woo to You   Friend
Alabama Barbecue   Coots; Davis
All Dressed Up and No Place to Go   Heyman
All I Do Is Think of You   Brown, Nacio Herb
All My Life   Magidson; Mitchell; Stept
Allied High Command, The   Weill
All's Fair in Love and War   Dubin; Warren
Along Came Pete   Stept
Along Came Pete (If It Wasn't for Pete)   Washington
Am I Dreaming?   Baer
Am I Gonna Have Trouble with You   Fain
Am I On?   Razaf
Am I the Only One Who Cares for Me?   Bryan
American Lullaby (inst.)   Romberg
Americana   Conrad; Magidson
Amigo   Dietz; Schwartz, Arthur
Ancestors   Akst; Clare
And That Woman Made a Monkey Out of Me   Clare
And Then   Mitchell; Stept
Animal Ballet   Adamson; Conrad; Magidson
Another Dream Gone Wrong   Wrubel
Another Mile   Kahal; Rose
Another Perfect Night Is Ending   Coots; Davis
Answer to the Maple on the Hill   Fisher
Are You Havin' Any Fun   Fain; Yellen
Are You My Love?   Hart; Rodgers
Arrival of Steamboat   Caesar
Arrival of Tourists   Caesar
Asylum Chorus   Weill
At the Beach at Malibu (Hullabaloo at Malibu)   Akst; Clare
At the Codfish Ball   Mitchell; Pollack
At Ye Olde Coffee Shoppe in Cheyenne   Porter
Autumn in Argentina   Leslie
Avalon By Moonlight   Lawrence
Avenue of Trees   Oakland
Awake in a Dream   Robin
B Flat Stride, The   Mills
Bal Masque   Coslow; Young, Victor
Balboa, The   Mitchell; Pollack; Razaf
Ballad of Baby Face McGinty, The   Duke; Gershwin, Ira
Bang — The Bell Rang   Loesser
Battle (inst.), The   Weill

Battle of San Juan Hill, The   Weill
Be Good Baby   Fisher
Be Mine   Washington
Beat of the Feet in the Street, The   Carroll; Parish
Bellport Will Shine Tonight   Robin
Bells of Honolulu   Mercer
Beneath the Stars   Gordon; Revel
Benny Sent Me   Waller
Bermuda Buggyride   David, Mack
Bertie and Gertie   Porter
Beside the Sea Beside You   Coots; Davis
Better Get Off Your High Horse   Friend
Bevans, Dear Bevans   Gordon; Revel
Biddle-e-um-de-dum   Fisher
Big Chief de Sota   Razaf
Blame It All on the Night   Romberg
Blame It on the Night   Harbach
Bless You, Darlin' Mother   Stept
Blow that Horn   Donaldson
Blue English (inst.)   McHugh
Blue Eyes   Caesar
Blue Mood   Mills
Blue Night   Webster
Blue Thoughts (inst.)   Blake
Bojangles of Harlem   Fields; Kern
Boulevardier from the Bronx   Dubin; Warren
Boy, a Girl and a Moon Means Love, A   Friend
Boy Meets Girl   Fain
Brazilian Love Song   Coslow; Young, Victor
Breakfast in Harlem   Caesar; Lerner, Sammy
Breakin' in a Pair of Shoes   Stept; Washington
Breathes There a Man   Lane; Magidson
Broken Dreams of You   Mills
Brown Eyes Looking into Eyes of Blue   Bryan; Edwards
Bucharest   Harbach; Romberg
Bury Me Under the Willow   Rainger; Robin
But Definitely   Gordon; Revel
But Where Are You?   Berlin
Buy a Bar of Barry's   Gordon; Revel
By Strauss   Gershwin, George; Gershwin, Ira
Cabin in the Sky   Leslie
Cabin on the Hilltop   Kalmar; Ruby
Cachucha   Brennan
Calabash Pipe   Arlen; Brown, Lew
Call of the Siren   Akst; Clare
Call to Arms, The   Heyman; Schwartz, Arthur
Calypso   Koehler
Can't We Fall in Love   Adamson
Captain Valentine's Tango   Weill
Carriage Duet   Rainger; Robin
Carry On   Porter
Casa Loma Meeting, The   Cahn
Casanova   Duke; Fisher; Rainger; Robin
Champagne Safari   Robin
Chance of a Life Time, The   Coslow
Chile Moonlight   Loesser; Motzan
Chimes at the Meetin'   Fisher
(Here Comes) Chiquita   Dubin; Warren
Christopher Columbus   Razaf
Cielito Lindo   Robin
Circus   Adamson; Lane
Close to Me   Lewis
Close to You   Young, Joseph
Cocktail Time   Hoffman
Come and See Me Tomorrow   Rainger

Comme un Oiseau   Heyman
Completely   Robin
Conchita   Coslow
Coney Island   Dubin; Warren
Congress and the Senate, The   Bryan
Construction Song   Stept
Copper Colored Gal   Coots; Davis
Cotton Mill Blues   Fisher
Cowboy Song (Oh, the Rio Grande)   Weill
Cowshed Rhapsody   Caesar
Crazy Language   Fisher
Crazy with Love   Hoffman
Curfew Shall Not Ring Tonight, The   Heyman
Dancing Conversation   Caesar; Schwartz, Arthur
Dancing Feet   Mitchell; Stept
Dancing in the Open   Clare
(I'm in a) Dancing Mood   Hoffman
Dancing to Our Score   Duke; Gershwin, Ira
Dangerous You   Schwartz, Arthur
Darling, Not Without You   Heyman; Silver
Day at the Races, A   Kalmar; Ruby
Dedicated to You   Cahn
Democracy's Call   Weill
Desdamona   Brown, Nacio Herb; Freed, Arthur
Desire   Robin
Devoted to You   Washington; Wrubel
Did I Get Stinkin' at the Club Savoy   Harburg
Did I Remember (To Tell You I Adore You)?   Adamson;
     Donaldson
Did You Mean It   Dixon
Dixie Anna   McHugh
Dixie Isn't Dixie Any More   Bloom
Dixie Isn't Dixie Anymore   Mercer
Dixie-Anna   Koehler
Doctor Quackenbush   Kalmar; Ruby
Doctor Song   Clare
Does a Duck Love Water?   Duke; Gershwin, Ira
Does You Wanna Go to Hebben   Akst; Clare
Does Your Heart Beat for Me   Parish
Doin' All Right   Rainger; Robin
Doin' the Cut-In   Gilbert
Doin' the Suzi-Q   Coots; Davis
Don Carlos Is Riding Tonight   Rainger; Robin
Donald Duck   Bryan
Don't Come Crying to Me   Adamson; Donaldson
Don't Count Your Kisses (Before You're Kissed)   Freed,
     Ralph
Don't Give a Good Gosh Darn   Gordon; Revel
Don't Kiss Me Goodnight   David, Mack; Meyer
Don't Laugh When I Cry   Cahn
Don't Let Me Love You   Loesser
Don't Look Now   Cahn
Don't Save Your Smiles   Coots; Davis
Don't Say It If You Don't Mean It   Coots; Davis
Don't Sing — Everybody Swing   Akst; Clare
Doubting Thomas   Gershwin, George
Doughboy's in the Dough Again, The   Ahlert; Turk; Young,
     Joseph
Down Aroun' Malibu Way   Akst; Clare
Down in the Depths   Porter
Dream Awhile   Mercer
Dream Boat   Adamson
Dream House Number   Adamson; Donaldson
Dream Kisses   Adamson; Donaldson
Dream Time   Coots; Davis

Dreaming By the Fireside   Livingston, Jerry
Dreaming of You   Mitchell; Stept
Dreaming Out Loud   Rainger; Robin
Dreamland Choo-Choo to Lullaby Town, A   Gordon; Revel
Drifting   Dixon; Henderson
Drink It Down   Rainger; Robin
Early Bird   Mitchell; Pollack
Easy to Love   Porter
Economic Situation (Aren't You Wonderful), The   Duke;
    Gershwin, Ira
El Relicario (Rendezvous of Love)   Johnson, Howard
El Tango de Reve   Johnson, Howard
Empty Saddles   Brennan
End Title   Loesser
Entrance of Lucy James   Porter
Epilogue   Duke
Epitaph   Weill
Evening in Manhattan   Snyder
Evening with You, An   Dubin; Warren
Every Day's a Holiday   Coslow
Every Once in a While   Dixon; Henderson
Everybody Dance   Gordon; Revel
Everybody's Swingin' It Now   Coots; Davis
Everything's Talent Today   Cahn
Ev'ntide   Carmichael
Evolution   Stept; Washington
Ev'rytime I Look at You   Mitchell; Stept
Fancy, Fancy   Duke; Gershwin, Ira
Fancy Meeting You   Arlen; Harburg
Fanny Frankenstein   Fisher
Farewell, Goodbye   Weill
Farewell Malihini (Hawaiian Farewell)   Gilbert
Farewell My Country (Adios Mi Tiera)   Mitchell
Fashion Show   Gordon; Revel
Feelin' Low   Parish
Fellow with the Yellow Carnation, The   Parish
Fifty Million Sweethearts   Rainger; Robin
Fight, The   Magidson; Oakland
Finding You — Losing You   Caesar; Henderson
Fine Romance, A   Fields; Kern
Firefly   Blake
First Rose of Summer (The Last Rose of My Heart),
    The   Caesar; Lerner, Sammy
First You Have Me High (Then You Have Me Low)   Arlen;
    Brown, Lew
Five A.M.   Duke; Gershwin, Ira
Five Hundred Million   Porter
Floating on a Bubble   Friend
Flying Off the Handle   Fisher
Follow Your Heart   Bullock; Mitchell
For a Buck and a Quarter a Day   Dubin; Warren
For Sentimental Reasons   Heyman; Silver
For You Alone   Snyder
Forbidden Melody   Harbach
Four Fugitives from a Bolero Cabin Gang   Arlen; Harburg
Franklin's Foods   Pollack; Yellen
Friendly Moon   Coots; Davis
Frisco Flo   Coots; Davis
Frisky   Norworth
From the Circle to the Square   Oakland
Funnies Aren't Funny When I'm Blue   Hoffman
Funnies on Parade   Razaf
Funny Paper Capers (In a Dream)   Gilbert
Gallavantin' Around   Hammerstein; Kern
Garbo Green   Fisher

Gazooka, The   Duke; Gershwin, Ira
Gee, but You're Swell   Baer
Get in Step   Mitchell; Stept
Gettin' Nowhere Road   Koehler
Getting Away with Murder   Kalmar; Ruby
Give Her a Pint and She'll Tell It All   Cahn
Give Us This Night   Hammerstein
Glad to Be Unhappy   Hart; Rodgers
Gloomy Sunday   Lewis
Glory   Koehler
Go West, Young Man   Burke; Johnston
Goin' Down to the River Jordan   Fisher
Gone   Kahn
Gone with the Dawn   Rose
Gong Song, The   Bullock
Gonna Hitch My Wagon to a Star   Lewis
Good Luck, Best Wishes   Davis; Hanley
Good-Bye, Au Revoir, Auf Wiedersehen   Caesar
Good-Bye, Little Dream, Good-Bye   Porter
Goodnight, My Love   Gordon; Revel
Goody-Goody   Mercer
Goona Goo, The   Ahlert; Young, Joseph
Goose Hangs High, The   Friend
Got My Eye on You   Hammerstein; Kern
Got to Dance My Way to Heaven   Coslow
Gotta See a Man About a Dog   Fisher
Green Fields and Bluebirds   Bryan
Greenback Dollar   Fisher
Guess Who   Freed, Ralph; Lane
Guitars of Love   Brennan
Hail Alma Mater   Stept; Washington
Hail to Chester   Rainger; Robin
Half-Past Lovin' O'Clock   Bryan
Hand in Hand   Razaf
Hand in Hand in Heaven   Oakland
Hang Up My Saddle   Bullock; Whiting
Happy Birthday   Kahn
Happy Time Again   Koehler
Harlem to Hollywood   Bloom; Mercer
Hate to Talk About Myself   Robin; Whiting
Hats Off   Magidson; Oakland
Have You Forgotten So Soon   Von Tilzer
Havin' a Ball   Johnson, James P.; Razaf
Having a Wonderful Time (Wish You Were Here)   Dubin
He Hasn't a Thing Except Me   Duke; Gershwin, Ira
He Met Her on the Prairie   Rainger; Robin
He Played on His Old Bazooka   Conrad; Kahn
He Was a Dandy   Koehler; McHugh
Head Over Heels in Love   Gordon; Revel
Hear the Gypsies Playing   Harbach; Romberg
Heart Is Quicker than the Eye, The   Hart; Rodgers
Hearts in Harmony   Rainger; Robin
Heigh-Ho the Radio   Rainger; Robin
Her Master's Voice   Robin
Here Comes Love   Stept
Here I Am Again   Stept
Here's Looking at You   Arlen; Harburg
Here's Love in Your Eye   Rainger; Robin
Hey Babe Hey   Porter
Hey! Hey! Hey! Hey! Your Cares Away   Johnson, James P.
Hey, What Did the Bluejay Say   Koehler; McHugh
Hidden Valley   Mitchell; Stept
Hide and Seek   David, Mack; Monaco
Hi-De-Ho Miracle Man   Coots; Davis
High Hat, a Piccolo, and a Cane, A   Akst; Brown, Lew; Fain

High Hat Hop, The   Rainger; Robin
High Up in the Hills   Caesar
Hills of Old Wyoming, The   Rainger; Robin
Hippopotamus   Fisher
Hold that Bulldog   Mitchell; Pollack
Holiday Sweetheart   Caesar; Henderson
Holy Lie Production Routine   Akst; Clare
Home-Cookin'   Raye
Honey Chile   Rainger; Robin
Honey, Please Don't Turn Your Back on Me   Clare; Stept
Honey, You're a Honey   Parish
Honolulu Lulu   Robin
Honolulu Stars and Hawaiian Guitars   Lawrence
Hopelessly in Love   Robin
Hot Honey   Bryan
Hot Number   Duke; Gershwin, Ira
Hot Spell   Mills; Myrow
Hot Towel   Loesser
House Jack Built for Jill, The   Robin
How Can I Keep My Mind on Driving   Fisher
How Can We Part   Rainger; Robin
How Could a Fellow Want More   Harbach; Romberg
How Sweetly Friendship Binds   Weill
How'm I Doin' with You   Mitchell; Stept
How's By You   Arlen; Harburg
Humpty Dumpty's Holiday   Coots
Hurdy-Gurdy Man   Cahn
Hush Ma Mouth   Arlen; Harburg
Hymn to Hymen   Porter
Hymn to Peace   Weill
I Adore You   Rainger; Robin
I Believe Ev'ry Word I've Heard about You   Bryan
I Can Pull a Rabbit Out of My Hat   David, Mack
I Can See You All Over the Place   Waller
I Cannot Live Without Your Love   Caesar
I Can't Believe It's True   Whiting
I Can't Escape from You   Robin; Whiting
I Can't Get Started   Duke; Gershwin, Ira
I Can't Lose that Longing for You   Dixon
I Could Be in Heaven If You'd Come Down to
   Earth   Hoffman
I Don't Give a Continental   Hoffman
I Don't Have to Dream Again   Dubin; Warren
I Don't Know Myself Since I Know You   Akst; Clare
I Don't Mean a Thing to You I Knew   Robin
I Don't Sleep at Night, but Oh How I Dream All
   Day   Caesar
I Feel Like a Feather in the Breeze   Gordon; Revel
I Got Time and I Got No Place to Go   Coslow
I Have the Room Above Her   Hammerstein; Kern
I Heard a Song in a Taxi   Caesar; Henderson
I Knew   Bloom; Mercer; Robin
I Know a Road   Brennan
I Know I'm in Harlem   Loesser
I Let My Heart Command Me   Coslow
I Like to Go Strange Places   Loesser
I Lost My Heart (And Found My Heart's Desire)   Robin
I Love Only One Girl, at a Time   Edwards; Johnson,
   Howard
I Love to Be in Love   Robin
I Love to Sing-a   Arlen; Harburg
I Make a Motion   Hoffman
I Mean to Say I Love You   Hammerstein
I Nearly Let Love Go Slipping Through My Fingers   Woods
I Nominate You (To Be My Sweetheart)   David, Mack

I Nominate You (To Me My Sweetheart)   Schwartz, Jean
I Remember a Dream   Caesar; Schwartz, Arthur
I Sing of Spring   Clare
I Still Believe in Love   Whiting
I Thought I Knew   Harbach
I Used to Be Above Love   Duke; Gershwin, Ira
I Wanna Go to the Zoo   Gordon; Revel
I Want the Whole World To Love You   Bryan
I Was Saying to the Moon   Burke; Johnston
I Welcome You   Robin
I Wish I Were a Clown Like Pagliacci   Leslie; Monaco
I Wonder   Robin
I Won't Give Up Till You Give in to Me   Gershwin, George;
   Gershwin, Ira
I Would Love to Have You Love Me   Caesar; Lerner,
   Sammy
I'd Be a Fool Again   Livingston, Jerry
I'd Be Lost Without You   Donaldson
I'd Like to Be in Your Shoes   Fisher
I'd Rather Lead a Band   Berlin
If I Feel This Way Tomorrow Then It's Love   Arlen; Brown,
   Lew
If I Were You   Blake
If You Can't Sing It You'll Have to Swing It (Mr.
   Paganini)   Coslow
If You Didn't Love Me, Who Else Would   Loesser
I'll Bet You Tell that to All the Girls   Stept
I'll Miss You   Parish
I'll Sing You a Thousand Love Songs   Dubin; Warren
I'll Stand By   Coots; Davis
I'll Thank You to Stay Out of My Dreams   Arlen; Harburg
I'm a Fool for Loving You   Lewis
I'm a Little Moon Mad   Dixon
I'm a Little Moon-Mad   Henderson
I'm an Old Cowhand   Mercer
I'm Askin' Ye (Ain't It the Truth)   Fisher
I'm at the Mercy of Love   Coots; Davis
I'm Dancing To Be Near You   Bryan
I'm Glad It's Me (inst.)   Stept
I'm Grateful to You   Coots; Davis
I'm in Love   Mills; Myrow
I'm Mad About You   Koehler; Stept
I'm Never too Busy for You   Hoffman
I'm on a Wild Goose Chase   Lawrence
I'm One Ahead of My Shadow   Cahn
I'm Pixilated Over You   Heyman; Spina
I'm Putting All My Eggs in One Basket   Berlin
I'm Setting a Trap to Catch You   Blake
I'm Sharing My Wealth   Duke; Gershwin, Ira
I'm You   Loesser
In a Little Hole in the Wall   Fisher
In a Little Wayside Inn   Bryan; Meyer
In a Village (Where the Lazy Daisies Grow)   Fisher
In and Out (inst.)   Stept
In My Estimation of You   Coots; Davis
In My Lonely Reverie   Parish
(On a Holiday) In My Playroom   Clare
In Our Cocktail of Love   Von Tilzer
In Rockabye Baby Land   Razaf
In the Arms of an Army Man   Dubin; Warren
In the Garden of Allah   Donaldson
In the Timberland of Old Wyoming   Mills
In Times of War and Tumult   Weill
In Your Own Quiet Way   Arlen; Harburg
Introducing   Fisher

Introduction to Betty Jane Cooper   Gordon; Revel
Is a Daffydill As Crazy As a Crazy Quilt   David, Mack
Is It True What They Say About Dixie   Caesar; Lerner,
    Sammy
Is Love a Beautiful Illusion   Rainger; Robin
Is Your Face Red   Dixon
Island in the West Indies   Duke; Gershwin, Ira
Isn't Love the Strangest Thing   Coots; Davis
It Can Happen to You   Ahlert; Turk; Young, Joseph
It Don't Make Sense   Rainger; Robin
It Happened in Chicago   Kahal; Rose
It Happened When Your Eyes Met Mine   Akst; Turk
It Happens in the Best of Families   Coots; Davis
It Will Have to Do Until the Real Thing Comes Along   Cahn
It's a Different World   Duke; Gershwin, Ira
It's a Great Life   Porter
It's a Long, Long Way to Broadway   Arlen; Harburg
It's a Small World   Adamson; Donaldson
It's Been So Long   Adamson; Donaldson
It's De-lovely   Porter
It's Easy to Love   Carmichael
It's Got to Be Love   Hart; Rodgers
It's Great to Be in Love Again   Koehler; McHugh
It's Julep Time in Dixie Land   Akst; Clare
It's Love Again   Coslow
It's Love I'm After   Mitchell; Pollack
It's Not in the Cards   Fields; Kern
It's Vacation Time Again   Livingston, Jerry
It's You I'm Talking About   Gordon; Revel
I've Got a Heavy Date   Kahn
I've Got Something in My Eye   Monaco
I've Got to Be a Rug Cutter   Ellington
I've Got You Under My Skin   Porter
Jamboree Jones   Mercer
Je Vous Adore   Coslow; Young, Victor
Johnny's Arrest and Homecoming   Weill
Johnny's Melody   Weill
Johnny's Song (Listen to My Song)   Weill
Johnny's Speech   Weill
Join the Party   Clare
Jo-Jo the Cannibal Kid   Bloom; Mercer
Josephine Waters   Dietz; Schwartz, Arthur
Jungle Jigolo   Fisher
Just as Easy as Rolling Off a Log   Bryan; Schwartz, Jean
Just for You   Friml; Kahn
Just Hello   Harbach; Romberg
Just In Case You Change Your Mind   Freed, Ralph
Just One More Dance Madame   Webster
Just Remember   Mercer; Sigman
Keep a Twinkle in Your Eye   Bloom; Mercer
Keep Your Eye in the Sky   Hoffman
King of Swing   Gershwin, George
Kiss a Lonely Wife   Fisher
Kiss Me Goodnight (Not Goodbye)   Clare; Hanley
Kiss Me Like This   Edwards
Kiss Me While We're Dancing   Bryan
Kisses from My Violin to You   Bryan
Kissin' My Baby Good-Night   David, Mack; Meyer
Knife-Thrower's Wife, The   Duke; Gershwin, Ira
Knock Wood   Cahn
La Bomba   Rainger; Robin
La Cumparsita   Johnson, Howard
La-De-De La-De-Da Says I'm in Love with You   Lewis
Lady Dances, The   Arlen; Brown, Lew
Lady from Hollywood   Conrad; Magidson

Lady in the Moon   Arlen; Harburg
Lady in the Window   Harbach; Romberg
Lady Known as Lulu, The   Stept; Washington
Lady Twinklepuss   Fisher
Land of Dreams (inst.)   Stept
Last of the Cabbies, The   Duke; Gershwin, Ira
Laughing Generals (inst.)   Weill
Laughing Irish Eyes   Magidson; Mitchell; Stept
Lazy Bones Gotta Job Now   Robin
Lazy Weather   Kahal
Learn How to Lose   Fields
Learn to Be Lovely   Gordon; Revel
Leave It to Katarina   Caesar
Let Me Be Your Sweetheart Once Again   Fisher
Let Yourself Go   Berlin
Let's Be a Little More Friendly   Woods
Let's Be Gay   Koehler; McHugh
Let's Call a Heart a Heart   Burke; Johnston
Let's Compromise   Wrubel
Let's Dance and Dream   Koehler; Stept
Let's Face the Music and Dance   Berlin
Let's Get Going Baby   Clare
Let's Have Another   Magidson; Oakland
Let's Have Blue Birds   Loesser
Let's Make a Wish   Kalmar; Ruby
Let's Put Our Heads Together   Arlen; Harburg
Let's Sing Again   Kahn; McHugh
Lieberstraume   Robin
Life Insurance Song   Arlen; Harburg
Light Up Your Face   Rainger; Robin
Lilly the Contortionist   Lane
Lita   Mitchell; Pollack; Yellen
Little Bit Later On, A   Livingston, Jerry
Little Boys Had a Band, The   Johnson, Howard
Little Chin-Chin (Keep Your Chin Up)   Fain
Little Lady of the Lamp Light   Robin; Whiting
Little Odd Rhythm   Magidson; Oakland
Little Old Lady   Carmichael
Little Robin Told Me So, A   Coots; Davis
Little Skipper from Heaven Above, A   Porter
Little White Gardenia, A   Coslow
Little Words of Kindness   Friend
Living from Day to Day   Livingston, Jerry
Loafin' on the Levee   David, Mack; Meyer
Lolita   Caesar; Schwartz, Arthur
Londonderry Air   Mitchell
Lone Cowboy   Rainger; Robin
Lone Star   Kahal; Rose
Lone Wolf on the Indian Trail, A   Bryan
Lonely Heart   Alter; Webster
Lonely Mannequin   Bloom; Lerner, Sammy
Lonely Road   Berlin
Lonely Star   Porter
Lonesome Lullaby   Ahlert; Young, Joseph
Long Ago and Far Away   Rainger; Robin
Long As You've Got Your Health   Harburg
Longtime with a Short Girl   Fisher
Lookie Lookie Lookie Here Comes Cookie   Gordon; Revel
Lookin' Around Corners for You   Gordon; Revel
Looking Down at the Stars   Parish
Lost   Mercer
Lost Again   De Lange
Lost in My Dreams   Mitchell; Stept
Lotus Lou   Robin
Love and Learn   Heyman; Schwartz, Arthur

Love Commands   Robin
Love Is a Pow'rful Thing   Cahn
Love Is a Ripple on the Water   Carroll; Parish
Love Is Good for Anything that Ails You   Friend
Love Is Just Around the Corner   Robin
Love Marches On!   Dubin; Warren
Love Me, Love My Pekinese   Porter
Love or Infatuation   Coslow
Love Scene in Pasadena   Coots; Davis
Love, What Are You Doing to My Heart?   Lewis
Love Will Tell   Pollack; Yellen
Lovely Lady in White   Mitchell; Pollack
Love's Hour   Brennan
Loving for a Living   Bryan
Low   Rainger; Robin
Low Tide Down in My Heart   Razaf
Lucky Starlets   Coslow
Luigi   Hammerstein; Whiting
Lyin' to Myself   Carmichael
Madly in Love   Fields
Magnolias in the Moonlight   Bullock
Maharanee   Duke; Gershwin, Ira
Make Believe Ball Room   Razaf
Marching to the Music of the Stars   Brennan
Market Day in the Village   Caesar
May I Have the Next Romance with You?   Gordon; Revel
May in Monterey   Rainger; Robin
Maybe We'd Still Be Sweethearts (If We Hadn't Listened to Friends)   Davis
Mayfair (inst.)   Stept
(I Can't Imagine) Me Without You   Robin
Media Luz, A   Johnson, Howard
Meetin's Called to Order, The   Razaf
Melody from the Sky (Love Is Everywhere), A   Alter; Mitchell
Men, Awake   Rome
Midnight Blue   Leslie
Military Man   Gordon; Revel
Milkman's Matinee, The   Razaf
Miller's Daughter (And the Shepherd on the Hill), The   Bryan
Minerva   Robin
Minny Belle's Song   Weill
Minstrel Show Opening   Freed, Ralph; Lane
Modernistic Moe   Duke; Gershwin, Ira; Rose
Moment   Burke; Johnston
Mon Ami, My Friend   Weill
Moon and Music, A   Rainger; Robin
Moon Face   Heyman; Schwartz, Arthur
Moon Is Grinning at Me, The   Mills
Moon Mist   Dubin; Warren
Moon Rose   Fisher
Moonburn   Carmichael; Heyman
Moonlight and Shadows   Robin
Moonlight and Violins   Harbach; Romberg
Moonlight in Rio   Friend
Moonlit Waltz, The   Mitchell; Pollack
Moonrise on the Lowlands   Livingston, Jerry
Moon's Our Home, The   Coslow
More I Know You the More I Love You, The   Coots; Davis
More Than a Sweet Romance   Rainger; Robin
More We See of People, the Better We Like Horses, The   Arlen; Harburg
Mr. Ghost Goes to Town   Mills; Parish
Mr. Swing for President   Razaf

Mr. T. from Tennessee   Mercer
Much Too Much   Cahn
Music in the Night   Hammerstein
Music of the Stricken Redeemer   Weill
Mutiny in the Parlor   Heyman
Mutiny on the Bandstand   Cahn
My Caravan of Love   Bryan
My Day Begins and Ends with You   Coots; Davis
My Favorite Girl   David, Mack; Meyer
My Grandfather's Clock in the Hallway   Gordon; Revel
My Heart and I   Rainger; Robin
My Heart Is a Violin   De Lange
My Heart Is Back Again   Ager
My Heart Is Singing   Kahn
My Heart Sings   Rainger; Robin
My Heart Wants to Dance   Kalmar; Ruby
My Heart Was in My Mouth   Bryan
My Heart's in the Heart of the West   Coslow; Young, Victor
My, How This Country Has Changed   Arlen; Harburg
My Kingdom for a Kiss   Dubin; Warren
My Little Garden of Dreams   Woods
My Little Mule Wagon   Dietz; Schwartz, Arthur
My Long Gone Baby Came Home   Dixon; Wrubel
My Love and I   Hammerstein
My Mistake   Coslow
My Nephew from Nice   Heyman; Schwartz, Arthur
My Newest Excitement   Mills
My Red Letter Day   Duke; Gershwin, Ira
My Rose of the Rancho   Coslow
My Saddle Is My Throne   Caesar; Schwartz, Arthur
My Topic of Conversation Is You   Coots; Parish
My True Lover   Rainger; Robin
My Voice Is Like a Flute of Gold   Brennan
My, What a Diff'rent Night   Gordon; Revel
My Wife Sleeps with One Eye Open   Bryan
Nero   Razaf
Never Give Up (inst.)   Stept
Never Gonna Dance   Fields; Kern
Never Should Have Told You   Friend
New Parade, The   Arlen; Harburg
New York   Rainger; Robin
Nicotina   Schwartz, Arthur
Night Has Lost the Moon, The   Caesar; Schwartz, Arthur
Night in Manhattan   Rainger; Robin
Night Is Beginning, The   Kahn
Night Is Young and You're So Beautiful, The   Kahal; Rose
Nighttime in Rio   Friend
No Account Noah   Robin
No Use Pretending   Harbach; Romberg
Nobody Knows but the Posies   Livingston, Jerry
Nothing's Blue but the Sky   Spina
Now   Duke
Now I've Got Some Dreaming to Do   Burke; Johnston
Now or Never   Lewis
O, Heart of Love   Weill
Oh, Babe, Maybe Someday   Ellington
Oh for a Singer (inst.)   Kern
Oh God, Give Us Rain   Atteridge; Hanley
Oh Mister Man Up in the Moon   Koehler; McHugh
Oh, My Goodness   Gordon; Revel
Oh So Lovely   Donaldson
Old Country Doctor, The   Schwartz, Jean; Young, Joseph
Old Dan Tucker   Coslow
Old Forgotten Lullaby, An   Meyer
Old Homestead   Loesser

Old New England March Fisher
Omaha-Ha and Idaho-Ho Bryan
On a Cold Winter Night Fisher
On a Pearly Pebble Beach in Catalina Ahlert; Young, Joseph
On a Typical Tropical Night Burke; Johnston
On the Beach at Malibu Clare
On the Sunset Trail Mitchell; Stept
On Your Toes Hart; Rodgers
One in a Million Mitchell; Pollack
One Kiss in a Million Lewis
One Never Knows, Does One? Gordon; Revel
One, Two, Button Your Shoe Burke; Johnston
One-Two-Three-Four Hey Mitchell; Pollack
Only Because I Love You Ahlert; Young, Joseph
Oo-ooh I Wanna Have a Little Dance with You Ahlert; Young, Joseph
Organ Grinder's Swing Mills; Parish
Our Little Home on Wheels (Rolling Along) Coslow
Ours Porter
Out of the Goodness of Your Great Big Heart Brennan
Out of the Night Johnson, Howard
(Trouble Ends) Out Where the Blue Begins Friend
Over a Cup of Coffee Akst; Clare
Over in Europe Weill
Ozarks Are Callin' Me Home, The Porter
Padre and the Bride, The Rainger; Robin
(In Old) Palm Springs Rainger; Robin
Panamericana Robin; Whiting
Papa Tree-Top Tall Carmichael
Paradise in Waltz Time Coslow
Pardon Me for Dreaming Conrad; Magidson
Pardon Me, Madame Kahn
Peck's Theme Song (Where There's Life There's Soap) Gordon; Revel
Pennies From Heaven Burke; Johnston
Perennial Debutantes Porter
Peter Piper Mercer; Whiting
Pick, Pick, Pickaninny (Pick Dat Cotton) Akst; Clare
Pick Yourself Up Fields; Kern
Picture Me Without You Koehler; McHugh
Plant a Little Smile in the Garden in Your Heart Coots; Davis
Please Send My Daddy Back Home Duke; Gershwin, Ira
Poor Little Me Gordon; Revel
Poorest Man in Town, The Alter; Mitchell
Poppy Coslow
Poverty Row or Luxury Lane Edwards; Johnson, Howard
Prayer for Mother and Dad, A Razaf
Printemps A la Rumba Gordon; Revel
Prologue Dietz; Schwartz, Arthur; Weill
Prom Waltz, The Rainger; Robin
Promise with a Kiss Robin
Proposal Waltz, The Livingston, Jerry
Proud Coots; Davis
Psychiatry Song, The Weill
Put Down an Empty Blues Parish
Put on a Uniform Dubin; Warren
Put Your Heart in a Song Coots; Lewis
Queen of the Jungle Adamson; Donaldson
Quiet Night Hart; Rodgers
Rain Finale Caesar
Rainbow on the River Alter; Webster
Rampart Street Blues Razaf
Rap Tap on Wood Porter
Readin' Rittin' and Rhythm Blake

Reason I Call You Sweetheart David, Mack
Red, Hot and Blue Porter
(My) Red Letter Day Hoffman
Rendezvous with a Dream, A Rainger; Robin
Restful Adamson; McHugh
Rhyme for Love, A Rainger; Robin
Rhythm on the Range Bullock; Whiting
Rhythm Saved the World Cahn
Rhythmatic Gordon; Revel
Ridin' High Porter
Ridin' the Rails Heyman; Spina
(I'm with You) Right or Wrong Koehler; Stept
Right Somebody to Love, The Pollack; Yellen
Robins and Roses Leslie
Rock Church Rock Blake
Rolling Along Akst; Brown, Lew
Rolling Home Porter
Rooster's Crowin' Caesar
Russian Rhumba Fisher
Sailor Beware Rainger; Robin; Whiting
Salt of the Earth, Salt of the Sea Brennan
San Anton' Razaf
San Francisco Adamson; Donaldson; Kahn
Sandman's Serenade, The Woods
Saskatchewan Caesar; Lerner, Sammy
Save Me Sister Arlen; Harburg
Save Your Yesses Duke; Gershwin, Ira
Say Ah! Brown, Nacio Herb
Scared Friend
Seal It with a Kiss Heyman; Schwartz, Arthur
Seems I've Done Something Wrong Again De Lange
Sentimental Weather Duke; Gershwin, Ira
Serenade Robin
Serenade to the Emperor Caesar
Sergeant's Chant Weill
Serpentin Caesar; Schwartz, Arthur
Shadows that Walk in the Night Harbach; Romberg
Shake It Off (with Rhythm) Arlen; Brown, Lew
Shakin' It All Night Long Waller
Shanghai Dee Ho Robin; Whiting
She Looks Like Helen Brown Fisher; Rose
She's a Follies Girl Adamson; Donaldson
She's a Wonderful Cook Fisher
She's the Darling of the Boys (Darling of the Guards) Parish
Shirley and the Black Dots (inst.) McHugh
Show Is On, The Carmichael
Show Me a Rose (Or Leave Me Alone) Kalmar; Ruby
Sing, Baby, Sing Pollack; Yellen
Sing Me a Song of Nonsense (Pocketful of Love) Carmichael
Sing Me a Swing Song and Let Me Dance Carmichael
Singapore Sal Stept
Singin' Your Praises Coots; Davis
'Sippy Adamson; McHugh
Sittin' in the Sand A-Sunnin' Lerner, Sammy
Sitting on the Moon Mitchell; Stept
Skeleton in the Closet, The Burke; Johnston
Sleigh Bells Caesar; Dietz; Schwartz, Arthur
Small Town Girl Kahn
Smashing Thirds (inst.) Waller
Smile Will Do the Trick, A Gordon; Revel
Smile with Me Willson
Smoke Dreams Brown, Nacio Herb; Freed, Arthur
So Do I Burke; Johnston

So What? Rainger; Robin
Soliloquy Rainger; Robin
Solomon Fisher
Sombrero Dance Rainger; Robin
Some Day We'll Meet Again Conrad; Magidson
Someone to Care for Me Kahn
Something's Gotta Happen Soon Brown, Nacio Herb
Somethin's Gotta Happen Soon Freed, Arthur
Sometime in Spring Donaldson
Song Bird Brennan
Song of the Coyotes Akst; Clare
Song of the Goddess Weill
Song of the Guns Weill
Song of the Tule Brennan
Song of the Woodman Arlen; Harburg
Song of the Wounded Frenchman Weill
Sons of Sierra Robin
Sooner or Later (Mark My Words) Livingston, Jerry
Sound of Your Voice, The Parish; Silver
South Boy Wants to Go Home, A Livingston, Jerry
South Wind Bloom; Mercer
Spade Ballet Caesar
Spanish Jake Caesar; Lerner, Sammy
Speaking of the Weather Arlen; Harburg
"Special Material" Arlen; Harburg
Spending Your Vacation in Maine Livingston, Jerry
Sport a Sport Gordon; Revel
Spring Is in the Air Edwards
Spring Prelude Kalmar; Ruby
Star Fell Out of Heaven, A Gordon; Revel
Stars in My Eyes Fields
State of My Heart, The Heyman; Spina
Statues Brown, Nacio Herb; Freed, Arthur
Stay Razaf
Stella, the Belle o' the Town Coots; Davis
Stolen Holiday Dubin; Warren
Stompin' at the Savoy Razaf
Strike Up the Band for U.C.L.A. Gershwin, George; Gershwin, Ira
Sue Me Fisher
Sugar Rose Waller
Summer Night Dubin; Warren
Sunday Tan Duke; Gershwin, Ira
Sunshine at Midnight Heyman
Sunshine for Sale Styne
Sway Brittania Duke
Sweet Heartache Stept; Washington
Sweet Melody of Night Hammerstein
Sweetheart, Sweetheart, Pronounced Darling Lawrence
Sweetheart Waltz, The Freed, Ralph; Lane
Sweetly and Tenderly Coots; Davis
Swing for Sale Cahn
Swing Gate Swing Fisher
Swing Is the Thing, The Bloom; Mercer
Swing Low, Swing High Fields; Kern
Swing Me a Lullaby Raye
Swing Tap, The Rainger; Robin
Swing-a-roo Koehler; McHugh
Swingin' the Jinx Away Porter
Table Under a Tree Lawrence
'Tain't a Fit Night Out for Man or Beast Cahn
Tain't No Use Lane; Magidson
Take My Heart and Do with It what You Please Ahlert; Young, Joseph
Take Your Time Young, Joseph

Talking Through My Heart Rainger; Robin
Tambourine Jamboree Oakland
Tap Your Feet Rainger; Robin
Tea on the Terrace Coslow
Tea Song, The Weill
Tell Me Little Dream Girl Coots; Davis
Tell Me with Your Kisses David, Mack; Meyer
Tell Me Your Troubles Dixon; Henderson
Tell the Truth Ager
Terrific Bryan; Schwartz, Jean
Texas Ranger Song Coslow
Texas Tornado, The Mitchell; Pollack
That Certain Woman Warren
That Little Spanish Hacienda Edwards
That Lovely Night in Budapest Lewis
That Moment of Moments Duke; Gershwin, Ira
That Never to Be Forgotten Night Fain
That's How Virginia Began Kahal
That's Life, I Guess Lewis
That's the News I'm Waiting to Hear Porter
That's What I Want for Christmas Caesar
That's What I'm Talking About Friend
That's What You Mean to Me Coots; Davis
Then I Could Forget You Friend
There Goes that Feeling Again Stept; Washington
There I Go Again Akst; Clare
There Isn't Any Limit to My Love Hoffman
There Must Be a Heaven for that Little Dog of Mine Bryan; Caesar
There's a Friendly House Davis; Hanley
There's a Home in the Mountain Adamson
There's a Small Hotel Hart; Rodgers
There's a Twinkle in Your Eye, Madame Stept; Washington
There's Always a Happy Ending Hoffman
There's Frost on the Moon, Spring in My Heart Ahlert; Young, Joseph
There's Gold in Monterey Rainger; Robin
There's Life in Your Eyes Tonight Friend
There's Love in My Heart for You Coots; Davis
There's No Two Ways About It Conrad
There's Something in the Air Adamson; McHugh
There's that Look in Your Eyes Again Gordon; Revel
There's Two Sides to Ev'ry Story Ahlert; Young, Joseph
There's "Yoo Hoo" in Your Eyes Baer
Things Are Coming My Way McHugh
This'll Make You Whistle Hoffman
Those Bootblack Blues Rainger
Thousand Dreams of You, A Alter; Webster
Three B's (Questions and Answers), The Hart; Rodgers
Three Cheers for Love Rainger; Robin
Through a Window in Japan Bryan
Through My Venetian Blind Heyman
Through the Courtesy of Love Gordon; Revel
Tie Your Troubles to a Toy Balloon Adamson; Donaldson
Time Marches On! Duke; Gershwin, Ira
To Be Near Him Coslow
To Know You Is to Want You Lewis
To Love You and To Lose You Heyman; Weill
To Mary — With Love Gordon; Revel
Tonight We Ride Rainger; Robin
Tony's in Town Woods
Too Good for the Average Man Hart; Rodgers
Top Gallants (Legionaires) Akst; Clare
Tragedian Ballet (inst.) Duke

Trailer Song (Roamin' in a Home on Wheels), The   Ahlert; Young, Joseph

Transatlantic Rhythm   Caesar; Henderson

Tree in Tipperary, A   Loesser

Trouble Doesn't Like Music — Everybody Sing   Cahn

True Confession   Coslow

Trust in Me   Ager

T.S.U. (Alma Mater)   Mitchell; Pollack

Tulip Told a Tale, A   Kalmar; Ruby

Tweet, Tweet, Tweedle in the Trees, The   Dixon; Henderson

Twiddlin' My Thumbs   Livingston, Jerry

Twilight on the Trail   Alter; Mitchell

Twinkle Twinkle Little Star   Magidson; Oakland

Two a Day for Keith (Twice a Night)   Hart; Rodgers

2/4 Girl Number (inst.)   Arlen

Two Hearts Divided   Dubin; Warren

Two in Love   Myrow

Two Ladies and a Man   Harbach; Romberg

Uncle Dan the Hockshop Man   Fisher

Uncle Tom's Cabin Is a Cabaret   Akst; Clare

Uncle Tom's Cabin Is a Roadhouse Now   Fisher

Under Your Spell   Brown, Nacio Herb; Dietz; Freed, Arthur; Schwartz, Arthur

Unforgettable   Van Heusen

Until Today   Coots; Davis

Up Chickamauga Hill   Weill

Vaquero, The   Livingston, Jerry

Veterans of Future Wars   Cahn

Voom Voom   Coslow

Vote for Mr. Rhythm   Rainger; Robin

Wah Hoo   Friend

Wait and See   Razaf; Waller

Wake Up and Sing   Friend

Waltz Fantasies   Harbach; Romberg

Waltz in Swing Time (inst.), The   Kern

Waltz of Love, The   Caesar

Waltz of the Flowers   Dubin; Warren

Waltz Was Born in Vienna, A   Loewe

Waltzing with an Angel   Bryan

Wanderers (My Lop-Eared Mule, My Broken Down Horse 'n Me)   Webster

Was There Ever a Voice?   Hammerstein

Way You Look Tonight, The   Fields; Kern

We Have Met Before   Coslow

We Need a Man   Weill

We Prize Most the Things We Miss   Caesar

We Saw the Sea   Berlin

We Walked Right in Turned Around and Walked Right Out Again   Fisher

We Wrote Our Love Song Together   Fisher

Weddin' of Mister and Missus Swing, The   Coots; Davis

Wedding of the Chocolate Soldier and the Coffee Colored Doll, The   Razaf

Welcome Stranger   Mercer

Welcome to the Landing Stage   Caesar

We'll Have a Bushel of Fun   Schwartz, Jean

We're About to Start Big-Rehearsin'   Porter

We're Back in Circulation Again   Mitchell; Pollack

We're Healthy Like Anything   Fain

We're Nuts About Midget Auto Races   Cahn

We're Off to a Wonderful Start   Freed, Ralph

West Pointers, The   Weill

West Wind   Ager

We've Got a Style of Our Own   Cahn

What a Great Pair We'll Be   Porter

What a Pleasure to Work with You   Freed, Ralph; Lane; Robin

What Could Be Sweeter   Motzan

What D'ya Think of That, Boys   Woods

What Has He Got?   Duke

What Shall Remain   Fields

What Shall We Do for an Encore Baby   Leslie

What This Country Needs   Burke; Johnston

What Will Become of Me?   Kalmar; Ruby

What Would You Be Doing Today   Fisher

Whatcha Gonna Do When There Ain't No Swing   Livingston, Jerry

What'll I Do with My Nights the Rest of My Days   Leslie; Meyer

What's Happened to Me   Van Heusen

What's the Use of Washing Your Face   Fisher

What's This?   Monaco

When a Girl Forgets to Scream   Harbach; Romberg

When and Where Will I Find Someone to Care   Coots; Davis

When Business Interferes with Pleasure   Parish

When Did You Leave Heaven?   Bullock; Whiting

When Grimble Hits the Cymbal   Gordon; Revel

When I March in April with May   David, Mack

When I Turned Over That Apple Turnover   Bryan; Fisher

When I'm with You   Gordon; Revel

When Louis from St. Louis Plays the St. Louis Blues   Fisher

When Love Comes Marching Along   Kahn; Romberg

When My Dream Boat Comes Home   Friend

When the Campfire Is Low on the Prairie   Stept

When the Moon Hangs High (And the Prairie Stars Hang Low)   Bullock

When the Shadows Grow Longer   Parish

When You Call the Roll Alma Mater   Fain; Kahal

When Your Troubles Have Started   Porter

When You're Dancing the Waltz   Hart; Rodgers

Where?   Porter

Where Have You Been All My Life?   Magidson; Oakland

Where Is My Heart   Rainger; Robin

Where Is My Rainbow   Edwards

Where the Lazy River Goes By   Adamson; McHugh

Where the Mountains Reach the Moon   Bryan

Which Little Boy Wants to Play with Me   Edwards

Whipoorwill in the Weeping Willow Tree, The   Arlen; Harburg

Whispers in the Dark   Robin

White Horse Inn, The   Caesar

White Sails   Caesar

Who Am I   Gordon; Mitchell; Revel; Stept

Who, but You   Porter

Who Loves You   Coots; Davis

Who Loves You Now   Johnson, James P.

Who Minds 'bout Me   Bullock

Who Wouldn't Be Thrilled   Coots; Davis

Whoa! Ya Got Me   Friend

Who'll Buy My Song of Love   Caesar; Henderson

Who's Afraid of Love!   Mitchell; Pollack

Who's Afraid of the Bogey Man?   Razaf

Who's That Knockin' at My Heart   Freed, Ralph; Lane

Why Can't I Remember Your Name?   Arlen; Harburg

Why Can't It Be Me?   Bloom; Mercer

Why Do I Lie to Myself About You   Coots; Davis

Why Pretend   Meyer

Why Save for that Rainy Day?   Duke; Gershwin, Ira

Widow's Daughter, The   Hanley

Wild and Wooly West, The   Koehler; Stept
Wild Trumpets and Crazy Piano (Got a Gal to Forget)
    Loesser
Will I Ever Know   Gordon; Revel
Will To-Morrow Ever Come   Friml
William Tell   Razaf
William Tell Overture   Robin
Wings of the Morning   Koehler; McHugh
Wintertime Dreams   Bryan
Wishing Tree of Harlem   Duke; Gershwin, Ira
With a Banjo on My Knee   Adamson; McHugh
With All My Heart   Kahn; McHugh
With Plenty of Money and You   Dubin; Warren
Without Rhythm   Hoffman
Wo! Ho! That's Love!   Rainger; Robin
Woman Hasn't Got Enough Eyes for a Man that
    Flies   Ahlert; Young, Joseph
Women in White   Kalmar; Ruby
Words and Music   Brown, Nacio Herb; Freed, Arthur
Words Fail Me   Coots; Davis
Words Without Music   Duke; Gershwin, Ira
Wotcha-Ma-Callit, The   Carroll; Parish
Would You?   Brown, Nacio Herb; Freed, Arthur
Would'ja Have a Cup o' Java with Me   Caesar; Lerner,
    Sammy
Yearning for Love   Ellington; Mills; Parish
Yes, Yes, My, My   Cahn
Yes! Yes! Yes! Yes! I'm Falling in Love with You   Mills
You   Adamson; Donaldson
You Angel   Schwartz, Jean; Young, Joseph
You Are All I've Wanted   Harbach; Romberg
You Came to My Rescue   Rainger; Robin
You Can Call It Swing   Cahn
You Can Tell She Comes from Dixie   Ager
You Can't Pull the Wool Over My Eyes   Ager
You Can't Tee Off My Fairway   Fisher
You Do the Darndest Things, Baby   Mitchell; Pollack
You Dropped Me Like a Red Hot Penny   Ahlert; Young,
    Joseph
You Gotta Eat Your Spinach, Baby   Gordon; Revel
You Gotta Know How to Dance   Dubin; Warren
You Gotta Pull Strings   Adamson; Donaldson
You Hit the Spot   Gordon; Revel
You Know I Know what Makes the Grass Grow   Fisher
You Never Looked So Beautiful   Adamson; Donaldson
You on My Mind   Sigman
You Put that Bug in My Ear   Fisher
You Started Me Dreaming   Coots; Davis
You Took Me from the Gutter   Clare
You Took My Heart Walking   David, Mack; Meyer
You Turned the Tables on Me   Alter; Mitchell
Young Forever   Kahn
Your Feet's Too Big   Fisher
Your Heart and Mine   Bloom; Mercer
Your Minstrel Man   Rainger; Robin
Your Need Is Greater than Mine   Ahlert; Young, Joseph
You're a Bad Influence on Me   Porter
You're a Breeze in the Desert   Rainger; Robin
You're a Four Star Picture to Me   Rainger; Robin
You're a Knockout   Akst; Clare
You're a Part of Me   Gilbert
You're Everything Beautiful   Coots; Davis
You're Ev'rything Sweet   Razaf
You're Giving Me a Song and a Dance   Ager
You're Guilty   Robin

You're Kinda Grandish   Arlen; Harburg
You're Like a Toy Balloon   Kahal; Rose
You're My Favorite One   Clare; Pollack
You're Not the Kind   Mills
You're Number One on My Hit Parade   Robison
You're Pretty As a Picture   Brown, Nacio Herb; Freed,
    Arthur
You're Slightly Terrific   Mitchell; Pollack
You're Still Mine in My Dreams   Leslie
You're the Cure for What Ails Me   Arlen; Harburg
You're the Last of My Past   Oakland
You're Too Sure of Me   David, Mack; Meyer
Yours Truly Is Truly Yours   Coots; Davis
You've Got Me Guessin' Again   Livingston, Jerry
You've Got Something   Porter
You've Got the Wrong Rhumba   Hoffman
You've Gotta S-M-I-L-E to be H-A-Double-P-Y   Gordon;
    Revel

1937

Action   Loesser
Afraid to Dream   Gordon; Revel
After That I Don't Remember   Parish
After You   Coslow
A-Hunting We Will Go   Loesser
Ain't We Got Love   Blake
Alabamy Home   Ellington
Alibi Baby   Heyman
All Day   Heyman
All Dressed Up in Rhythm   Bullock
All God's Chillun' Got Rhythm   Kahn
All of a Sudden   Pollack; Yellen
All Over Nothing At All   Lawrence
All the Things I've Missed   Howard, Joseph E.
All You Want to Do Is Dance   Burke; Johnston
Allegheny Al   Hammerstein; Kern
Alligator Crawl   Razaf; Waller
Along the Broadway Trail   Coslow
Am I in Love?   Dubin; Warren
American Couple (inst)   Rodgers
Angel   Robin
Angel in a Furnished Room   Dubin
Another Lovely April Day   Loewe
Another New Year   Rose
April in My Heart   Carmichael
Arabiana   Gordon; Revel
Are You in Trouble   Loesser
Argentine Nights   Akst; Clare
Argentine Swing   Akst; Clare
Artist and Model   Schwartz, Jean
At a Carnival in Venice   Livingston, Jerry
At the Old Barn Dance   Lawrence
Automobile Has Two Big Eyes, An   Caesar
Azure   Ellington; Mills
Babes in Arms   Hart; Rodgers
Baby Bond for Baby, A   Hart; Rodgers
Baby, Whatcha Gonna Do Tonight?   Hoffman; Lerner,
    Sammy
Back in Your Arms   De Lange; Mills
Back to Work   Rome
Ball Dance   Loesser
Ballet Moderne (inst.)   McHugh

All at Once   Hart; Rodgers
All Dark People   Hart; Rodgers

Balloon Ballet (Inst.)   Gershwin, George
Bane of Man, The   Eliscu
Be a Good Sport   Gordon; Revel
Beethoven, Mendelssohn and Lizst   Coslow
(I've Got) Beginner's Luck   Gershwin, George; Gershwin, Ira
Bernie's Love Song   Gordon; Revel
Beside a Moonlit Stream   Coslow
Better Luck Next Time   Lawrence
Between a Kiss and a Sigh   Burke; Johnston
Beware of Those Who Gossip   Razaf
Beyond My Fondest Dreams   Kahn
Big Boy Blues   Lawrence
Big Chief "Swing It"   Mitchell; Pollack
Bill Robinson Walk, The   Coots; Davis
Birchlake Forever   Alter; Webster
Birdie Out of a Cage   Hoffman; Lerner, Sammy
Black and Tan Fantasy   Ellington
Black Butterfly   Ellington; Mills
Blame It on the Rhumba   Adamson; McHugh
Blossoms on Broadway   Rainger; Robin
Blue Classique (inst.)   Blake
Blue Hawaii   Rainger; Robin
Blue Venetian Waters   Kahn
Bluer than Blue   Donaldson
Blues — Why Don't You Let Me Alone   Blake
Blush and Sing   Kahn
Bob White Whatcha Gonna Swing Tonight   Mercer
Boo-Hoo   Heyman
Booloo   Coslow
Bored   Martin
Born to Be Loved   Heyman
Born to Swing   Mills
Brand New Song in Town   Romberg
Broadway's Gone Hawaii   Gordon; Revel
Buds Won't Bud   Arlen; Harburg
Bulldogs of Gonzaga   Burke; Monaco
Burn a Candle at St. Mary's for Me   Egan
But Me No Buts   Hoffman; Lerner, Sammy
But We Say No "Buts"   Hoffman; Lerner, Sammy
Buzzin' Round with the Bees   Fisher
By Myself   Dietz; Schwartz, Arthur
By the Sweat of Your Brow   Blake
Bye-Bye Butterfly Lover   Dietz; Schwartz, Arthur
Call It Un-American!   Rome
Call on the Marines   Stept; Washington
Call to Colors   Kahn
Camera Doesn't Lie, Neither Do I, The   Leslie
Can I Forget You?   Hammerstein; Kern
Can You Imagine   Loesser
Can't You Hear that Mountain Music   Coslow
Canzonetta   Hammerstein; Kern
Captain, Mate and Crew   Blake
Caravan   Ellington; Mills
Carolina Sandman   Fain
'Cause My Baby Says It's So   Dubin; Warren
Celina Couldn't Say 'No'   Dietz; Schwartz, Arthur
Chain Store Daisy   Rome
Champagne Waltz, The   Conrad; Oakland
Change of Guard   Kahn; Romberg
Charlie McCarthy   Kalmar; Ruby
Chasing   Loesser
Chile   Ellington; Mills; Razaf
Chimes of Indiana   Carmichael
China Stomp (inst.)   Fisher
Chinese Rhythm   Mills

Chinese Serenade   Loesser
Chinkee Chinee Charlie Chan   Coots
Chirp a Little Ditty   Magidson; Wrubel
Close   Porter
Clouds in My Heart   Ellington; Mills
Cocktail, The   Dietz; Schwartz, Arthur
Coronation Waltz   Parish
Cotton Club Express   Ellington; Mills
Could I Be in Love   Robin
Cowboy's Gal, A   Brown, Lew; Fain
Crazy Dreams   Magidson; Oakland
Cream of Mush Song   Rome
Cross-Eyed Cowboy on the Cross-Eyed Horse, The   Stept
Cryin' Mood   Razaf
Cuba-Duba-Doo   Bryan; Caesar
Curly Top's Birthday   Mitchell; Pollack
Dance of the Golden Calf, The   Weill
Dance of the Waves (Inst.)   Gershwin, George
Dancing Into My Heart   Freed, Ralph; Lane
Dancing Partners   Baer; Lewis
Dancing to the Music in Our Hearts   Bullock
Danger — Love at Work   Gordon; Revel
David's Psalm   Weill
Decoy, The   Loesser
Deep in the Heart of the South   Lawrence
Delighted to Meet You   Coslow
Delusion   Bryan
Devil Dance, The   Rose
Did Anyone Ever Tell You?   Adamson; McHugh
Do You Like Me?   Loesser
Doin' the Reactionary   Rome
Donkey Serenade, The   Friml
Don't Cry Little Fish   Kahn
Don't Dally with the Devil too Long   Robison
Don't Go Away Monsieur   Dietz; Schwartz, Arthur
Don't Look at Me that Way   Coslow
Don't Save Your Love for a Rainy Day   Bullock; Spina
Don't Take Me Home   Von Tilzer
Don't Talk to the Driver (Talking to the Driver)   Caesar
Don't Throw Kisses   Akst; Clare
Don't Wait   Burke; Johnston
Don't You Care What Anyone Says — You Fall in Love with
    Me   Cahn
Don't You Know or Don't You Care   Fain; Kahal
Door Is Open Again, The   Caesar; Lerner, Sammy
Double or Nothing   Burke; Young, Victor
Double Trouble   Dietz; Rainger; Robin; Schwartz, Arthur
Down in Arkansas   Coslow
Down the Colorado Trail   Bryan
Down with Love   Arlen; Harburg
Dream Boat   McHugh
Dream for You, a Dream for Me, A   Woods
Dream Moon Valley   Bryan
Dream of Love   Kahn
Dream Tonight   Loesser
Duck Antics   Loesser
Duck Fights, The   Loesser
Duck Hunt Finale   Loesser
Easy Living   Rainger; Robin
Easy on the Eyes   Coslow
Ebb Tide   Rainger; Robin
Echo of a Love Song, An   Friend
Economics   Rome
Educated Rhythm   Kalmar; Ruby
El Gaucho   Fain; Kahal

English March   Friml
Entrance of Prince Paul   Porter
Every Day's a Holiday   Coslow
Everybody Sing   Akst; Brown, Nacio Herb; Freed, Arthur
Everybody Sings   Loesser
Everybody Swing   Akst; Clare
Everyone's Wrong but Me   Cahn
Everything You Said Came True   Friend
Ev'rybody Loves   Hart; Rodgers
Ev'ryone's Out, So Let's Stay in Tonight   Caesar
Experience   Dietz; Schwartz, Arthur
Extraordinary High Pressure   Loewe
Eyes of the World Are on You, The   Hoffman; Lerner,
    Sammy
Fade Out   Mills
Fair Lady (inst.)   Whiting
Fair Lombardy   Mitchell; Pollack
Farewell to Dreams   Kahn; Romberg
Fashion Girl, A   Arlen; Harburg
Fee-Fie-Fo-Fum   Schwartz, Arthur
Fellow Who's Singing This Love Song Loves You   Brown,
    Lew; Henderson
Fields, The   Hammerstein; Kern
Fifi   Coslow
Fifty-Second Street   Bullock; Spina
Fill It Up   Gordon; Revel
Fireman, Save My Child   Adamson; McHugh
First Impressions   Rome
First Time I Saw You, The   Wrubel
Five O'Clock   Dietz; Schwartz, Arthur
Flight of the Birds   Loesser
Flutter By, Little Butterfly   Coslow
Fly by Night   Dietz; Schwartz, Arthur
Foggy Day (In London Town), A   Gershwin, George;
    Gershwin, Ira
Folk Song   Loesser
Folks Who Live on the Hill, The   Hammerstein; Kern
Follow in My Footsteps   Brown, Nacio Herb; Freed, Arthur
Fond of You   Gordon; Revel
Fool There Was, A   Porter
Foolin' Myself   Lawrence
(That) Foolish Feeling   McHugh
For Every Lonely Heart   Kahn
For One!   Rome
For You   Koehler
Found When I Found You   Davis
Four Little Angels of Peace   Rome
French Ballet Class (Inst.)   Gershwin, George
Front Page News   Dietz; Schwartz, Arthur
Fun and Things and Stuff   Fisher
Gangway   Hoffman; Lerner, Sammy
Gasoline Gypsies   Mercer; Whiting
Gendarme, The   Dietz; Schwartz, Arthur
General Unveiled (inst.)   Rome
Get It Southern Style   Mills
Getting Some Fun Out of Life   Leslie
Ginger's Rhumba (Inst.)   Gershwin, George
Girl on the Police Gazette, The   Berlin
Girl You Used to Be, The   Dubin; Warren
Give Him a Roll on the Drum   David, Mack
Give Me a Cigarette, Please   Livingston, Jerry
Glow-Worm Ball   Howard, Joseph E.
Go Choose Your East   Kern
Go South Young Man   Coots; Davis
God's Country   Arlen; Harburg

Golf Song   Loesser
Golfers (Intermezzo), The   Loesser
Gone with the Wind   Ahlert; Magidson; Wrubel; Young,
    Joseph
Gong Song   Bullock
Good and Lucky   Schwartz, Arthur
Good Mornin'   Coslow
Good Night My Lucky Day   Koehler; Mitchell; Stept
Goodbye Again   Eliscu
Goodbye Jonah   Schwartz, Arthur
Good-Night Kisses   Kalmar; Ruby
Goof Plays on the Roof, A   Caesar
Got a Pair of New Shoes   Brown, Nacio Herb; Freed, Arthur
Governor's Ball Solo   Hammerstein; Kern
Graceful and Elegant (Inst.)   Gershwin, George
Grandma's Song   Hammerstein; Kern
Greatest Enemy of Love, The   Gilbert
Green and Blue   Blake
Hail Alma Mater   Stept
Handy with Your Feet   Mercer; Whiting
Happy Birthday to Love   Rose
Happy Daddy   Gilbert
Happy Go Lucky   Stept; Washington
Harlem Bolero   Coots; Davis
Harmony Boys, The   Rome
Have You Ever Been in Heaven   Lawrence
Have You Forgotten the You and Me that Used to
    Be   Bullock; Wrubel
Have You Got Any Castles, Baby?   Mercer; Whiting
Have You Met Miss Jones?   Hart; Rodgers
He Ain't Got Rhythm   Berlin
He Who Loves and Runs Away   Friml; Kahn
Heart and Soul   Parish
Heart of Harlem   Loesser
Heart of the Ukraine   Gilbert
Heaven Help a Sailor on a Night Like This   Coslow
Heaven Sent Wonderful You   Blake
Heilige Sekele   Motzan
Here Comes the Sandman   Dubin; Warren
Here Comes Tomorrow (Gimme Another Kiss Goodnight)
    (Actman, Irving)   Loesser
Here He Is   Hart; Rodgers
Hero Ballet (inst.)   Arlen
Heroes of Peace   Caesar
Hi, Ho, the Merrio (Inst.)   Gershwin, George
Hi-De-Higher Education   Yellen
Hi-De-Ho Romeo   Coots; Davis
High, Wide and Handsome   Hammerstein; Kern
Hi-Ho!   Gershwin, George; Gershwin, Ira
His Chances Are Not Worth a Penny   Hart; Rodgers
Hoctor's Ballet (Inst.)   Gershwin, George
Hold Your Hats, Here We Go Again   Loesser
Home Road   Hanley
Homogeneous Cabinet, A   Hart; Rodgers
Hooray for What?   Arlen; Harburg
Horse with the Dreamy Eyes, The   Donaldson
Hot and Cold Water   Caesar
Hot Bread   Loesser
Hot Towel   Loesser
Hot Turkey   Loesser
Hottest Gal in Town, The   Fisher
House of Melody   Willson
How Can I Sleep at Night when My Wife Eats Crackers in
    Bed   Rose; Silver
How Could You?   Dubin; Warren

How Do Yo Do?   Dietz; Schwartz, Arthur
How Many Rhymes Can You Get   Friend
How'd You Happen to Fall for Me?   Ager
Huggin' and Muggin'   Blake
Hula Baloo   Rainger; Robin
Hurdy-Gurdy   Loewe
Hustle, Bustle, Rustle of Spring   Hoffman; Lerner, Sammy
Hymn   Rainger; Robin
I Asked My Heart   Eliscu
I Believe in You   Dietz; Schwartz, Arthur
I Can Take It on the Chin but not on the Heart   Fisher
I Can't Be Bothered Now   Gershwin, George; Gershwin, Ira
I Can't Break the Habit of You   Razaf
I Click ze Heel and I Kees ze Hand   Arlen; Harburg
I Don't Like Music   Oakland
I Forgot to Get the Lady's Name   Carroll
I Got a Gal Back Home   Pollack; Yellen
I Have Eyes   Rainger; Robin
I Hear a Call to Arms   Coslow
I Heard a Forest Praying   Lewis
I Hum a Waltz   Gordon; Revel
I Know It's Not Meant for Me   Porter
I Know Now   Coots; Dubin; Warren
I Know What Aloha Means   Rainger; Robin
I Live a Little While   Van Heusen
I Love You Much Too Much Muchacha   Gordon; Revel
I Met Him in Paris   Carmichael
I Must Be Lucky   Donaldson
I Owe You   Lawrence
I Remember   Cahn
I See Your Face Before Me   Dietz; Schwartz, Arthur
I Still Love to Kiss You Good Night   Bullock; Spina
I Think You Have Got Something There   Loesser
I Think You're Ducky   Clare
I Wanna Be in Winchell's Column   Gordon; Revel
I Wanna Hum Sumpin' Pretty to a Sweet Pretty
    Thing   Ahlert
I Want a New Romance   Lane
I Want the World to Know   Friml; Kahn
I Want to Look Nice for You   Mills
I Want You for Christmas   Stept; Washington
I Was Anything but Sentimental   Hoffman; Lerner, Sammy
I Was in Kalua   Baer
I Wasn't Born Yesterday   Burke; Johnston
I Wish I Were in Love Again   Hart; Rodgers
I Won't Lose My Faith in Them All   Fisher
I Won't Take No for an Answer   Baer
I Wouldn't Change You for the World   David, Mack; Meyer
Ice Skating Is Nice Skating   Caesar
I'd Like to Do Things for You   Coslow
I'd Like to See Some Mo' of Samoa   Spina
I'd Like to See Somoa of Samoa   Bullock
I'd Love To Have a Million Eyes   Bryan
I'd Rather Be Right   Hart; Rodgers
If I Didn't Have You   Brown, Lew; Fain
If I Look Like I Feel   Van Heusen
If I Loved You More   Coots
If I Put My Heart in My Song   Coslow
If I Were a Little Pond Lily   Dubin; Warren
If It Isn't Pain (Then It Isn't Love)   Rainger; Robin
If It's the Last Thing I Do   Cahn
If Mothers Could Live on Forever   Johnson, Howard
If They Gave Me a Million   Oakland
If This Isn't Dreaming   Dubin
If You Ever Should Leave   Cahn

If You Were Someone Else   Schwartz, Arthur
If You're Ever in My Arms Again   Van Heusen
I'll Be Sittin' in de Lap o' de Lord   Schwartz, Arthur
I'll Follow My Baby   Coslow
I'll Never Lose You   Duke
I'll Never Tell You I Love You   Mills
I'll Settle for Love   Akst; Clare
I'll Take Romance   Hammerstein; Oakland
I'm a Musical Magical Man   Cahn
I'm a Swingin' Dingin' Daddy   Mills
I'm Against Rhythm   Dietz; Schwartz, Arthur
I'm Always in the Mood for You   Coots; Davis
I'm Bubbling Over   Gordon; Revel
I'm Dependable   Raye
I'm Feelin' High   Freed, Ralph; Lane
I'm Feelin' Like a Million   Brown, Nacio Herb; Freed, Arthur
I'm Happy Darling, Dancing with You   Ahlert; Lewis;
    Young, Joseph
I'm Happy when You're Happy   Hoffman; Lerner, Sammy
I'm Hittin' the Hot Spots   Adamson; McHugh
I'm in Heaven, Campin' in Caroline   Livingston, Jerry
I'm in Love with a Lover   Cahn
I'm Just Nuts About You   Rome
I'm Laughing Up My Sleeve Ha-Ha-Ha-Ha-Ha   Lawrence
I'm Olga from the Volga   Gordon; Revel
I'm Tellin' You in Front, So You Won't Feel Hurt
    Behind   Razaf
I'm Yours for the Asking   Kalmar; Ruby
Image of You, The   Ahlert; Lewis; Young, Joseph
Imagine   Hart; Rodgers
Improvisation   Akst; Clare
In a Little Hula Heaven   Rainger; Robin
In a Little Roadside Rendezvous   Coots; Davis
In an Old Cathedral Town   Baer
In More Ways than One   Van Heusen
In Our Little Wooden Shoes   Mitchell; Pollack
In Sunny Isles   Monaco
In the Boat   Loesser
In the Shade of the New Apple Tree   Arlen; Harburg
In the Still of the Night   Porter
In Your Eyes, When I Met You   Burke
In Your Own Little Way   Coots
Indian Serenade (inst.)   Motzan
Interlude   Stept; Washington
Intermezzo   Loesser
Introduction   Caesar
Is It Love or Infatuation   Coslow
Is It Possible You're Possessable?   Dubin; Warren
Is There Anyone More Wonderful than You   Hoffman;
    Lerner, Sammy
Is This Gonna Be My Lonely Summer?   Bloom; Davis
It Goes to Your Feet   Brown, Lew; Fain
It Looks Like Rain in Cherry Blossom Lane   Leslie
It Must Be Love   Koehler; Mitchell; Stept
It Was All in Fun   Freed, Ralph; Lane
It's All Over but the Shouting   Porter
It's Always Summer in the Winter, in the South   Monaco
(Bertha the Sewing Machine Girl) It's Better with a Union
    Man   Rome
It's Love   Kahn
It's On, It's Off   Coslow
It's Our Duty to the King   Schwartz, Arthur
It's Raining Sunbeams   Coslow
It's Round Up Time in Reno   Lawrence
It's Swell of You   Gordon; Revel

It's the Natural Thing to Do   Burke; Johnston
It's the Smile that Gets 'Em   Ahlert; Lewis; Young, Joseph
It's the Youth in Me   Blake
I've a Strange New Rhythm in My Heart   Porter
I've Dreamed About This   Bullock
I've Found You at Last   Howard, Joseph E.
I've Gone Romantic on You   Arlen; Harburg
I've Got a New Lease on Love   Ahlert; Young, Joseph
I've Got Manhattan on My Mind   Coslow
I've Got My Heart Set on You   Gordon; Revel
I've Got My Love to Keep Me Warm   Berlin
I've Got Rain in My Eyes   Livingston, Jerry
I've Got the Nerve to Be in Love   Rome
I've Made Up My Mind   Dietz; Schwartz, Arthur
Jamboree   Adamson; McHugh
Jammin'   Coslow
Jazz a la Carte   Ellington; Mills
Jealousy Begins at Home   Eliscu
Jingle Bells, I'm in Love   Friend
Jingle Jag   Howard, Joseph E.
Jingle of the Jungle   Hoffman; Lerner, Sammy
Joe the Bomber   Mills
John Henry, That Superman   Razaf; Waller
Johnny One-Note   Hart; Rodgers
Johnny Q. Public of the U.S.A.   Cohan
Jolly Tar and the Milkmaid, The   Gershwin, George;
    Gershwin, Ira
Josephine   Kahn
Jubilee   Carmichael
Just a Quiet Evening   Mercer; Whiting
Just a Simple Melody   Cahn
Just a Sweet Old Gent and a Quaint Old Lady   Brown, Lew;
    DeSylva; Henderson
Just for a Change   Loesser
Just Joggin' Along   Loesser
Just Like That   Loesser
Just Whisper I Love You   Silver
Keeno, Screeno and You   Coslow
Keep the Magic of Maytime   Kahn
Keep to the Right   Caesar
King of Jam (inst.)   Alter
Kiss for Consolation, A   Leslie
Kiss for You, A   Livingston, Jerry
Kiss to Remind You, A   Eliscu
Labor Is the Thing   Hart; Rodgers
Lady Is a Tramp, The   Hart; Rodgers
Lady of the Evening   Alter; Webster
Lady on the Second Floor, The   Dixon; Woods
Lady Who Couldn't Be Kissed, The   Dubin; Warren
Lady Who Swings the Band, The   Cahn
Lament for Lost Love   Ellington; Mills
Language of Love, The   Lawrence
Lani's Song   Rainger
Last Night I Missed You in My Dreams   Gilbert
Latin Rhythm (inst.)   Young, Victor
Laugh Your Way Through Life   Gordon; Revel
Laughing Song   Koehler
Law Is Law   Loewe
Lazy Rhythm   Magidson; Oakland
Least You Can Do for a Lady, The   Dubin
Lena from Palestreena   Conrad
Let Down Your Hair   Coslow
Let Down Your Hair and Sing   Bullock; Spina
Let Me Day Dream   Donaldson
Let Me Have a Rainy Sunday   Coots

Let the Ball Roll   Caesar
Let's Call the Whole Thing Off   Gershwin, George;
    Gershwin, Ira
Let's Finish the Dream   Stept; Washington
Let's Grow Old Waltzing Together   Howard, Joseph E.
Let's Have Another Cigarette   Magidson; Wrubel
Let's Keep It a Dream   Razaf
Let's Make the Most of Our Dream   Berlin
Let's Raise an Army of Sweethearts   Bryan; Fisher
Let's Stop the Clock   Coots
Let's Waltz for Old Time's Sake   Koehler; Stept
Life Is Peaches and Cream   Loesser
Life Is Tough   Loewe
Life of the Party   Magidson; Wrubel
Life's a Dance   Arlen; Harburg
Line of Least Resistance Is to Fall in Love with You   Fain
Listen My Children and You Shall Hear   Freed, Ralph; Lane
Little Cooperation from You, A   Hoffman; Lerner, Sammy
Little Dancing Boy   Monaco
Little House on the Hill, The   Mercer; Whiting
Little House that Love Built, The   Dubin; Warren
Little Old Lady of Poverty Street   Hoffman; Lerner, Sammy
Little Old-Fashioned Music Box   David, Mack; Meyer
Little White Lighthouse   Leslie
Little Wooden Soldier and the Walking, Talking Doll,
    The   Coslow
Live a Love-Dream   Rainger; Robin
Live and Learn   Mitchell; Pollack
Living in Seclusion   Mills
Living on the Town   Akst; Clare
Lobelia's Wedding Day   Alter; Webster
Locker Room Sequence   Adamson; Lane
Lonely Little Lighthouse   Bryan
Lonesome River   Stept; Washington
Lord and Lady Whoozis   Hoffman; Lerner, Sammy
Losin' Your Love   Livingston, Jerry
Lost Horizon   Kahn
Lost in Your Eyes   Gordon; Revel
Lost Love   Razaf; Waller
Love Came and Swept Me Off My Feet   Hoffman; Lerner,
    Sammy
Love Didn't Know Any Better   Burke; Johnston
Love for a Day   Loesser
Love from a Stranger   Hoffman; Lerner, Sammy
Love Hasn't Time   Burke; Spina
Love in the Air   Van Heusen
Love Is a Merry-Go-Round   Bloom; Mercer
Love Is Like a Firefly   Friml; Harbach
Love Is Love   Loewe
Love Is Never Out of Season   Brown, Lew; Fain
Love Is News   Mitchell; Pollack
Love Is on the Air Tonight   Mercer; Whiting
Love Letters of a Lady   Burke; Johnston
Love Song of Long Ago, A   Kahn; Romberg
Love Was in the Air   Brown, Nacio Herb; Freed, Arthur
Loveliness of You, The   Gordon; Revel
Lullaby for a Debutante   Spina
Magic of Maytime   Kahn
Maile Dance   Rainger; Robin
Make a Wish   Alter; Webster
Make Me a Christmas Present of You   Egan
Make Way for Tomorrow   Coslow; Robin; Schwartz, Jean
Making Up a Song As I Go Along   Hoffman; Lerner,
    Sammy
Mammy Don't Let Pappy Go   Conrad; Magidson; Oakland

March of the Cardinals   Cohan
March Song   Loesser
March to Zion, The   Weill
Marinella   Parish
May Day   Rome
May I Have the Next Dream with You?   Coslow
Maybe   Spina
Maybe It's the Moon   Donaldson
Meany Miny Moe   Loesser
Meet Me at the Fair   Schwartz, Arthur
Meet Me at the New York World's Fair   Howard, Joseph E.
Melody for Two   Dubin; Warren
Memories of Southern Seas   Razaf
Mene, Mene, Tekel   Rome
Merry-Go-Round Broke Down, The   Friend
Message from the Man in the Moon, A   Kahn
Midnight at the Onyx   Parish
Million Miles from Your Heart, A   Pollack; Yellen
Ming Toy Mischa   Oakland
Moanin' in the Mornin'   Arlen; Harburg
Momi Pele   Rainger
Montreal, The   Silver
Moods of Harlem (inst.)   Blake
Moon Got In My Eyes, The   Burke; Johnston
Moon of Mannakoora   Loesser
Moon or No Moon   Hoffman; Lerner, Sammy
Moon Sails   Donaldson
Moondust   Parish
Moonlight and Music   Lewis
Moonlight Fiesta   Mills
Moonlight on the Campus   Mercer; Whiting
Moonlight on the Highway   Leslie
Moonlight on the Sunset Trail   Freed, Ralph; Lane
Morning Serenade   Loesser
Mr. and Mrs. Doakes   Dubin; Warren
Mr. Esquire   Koehler; Young, Victor
Mr. Rhythm for President   Cahn
Music for Madame   Magidson; Wrubel
Music in My Dreams   Coslow
Music in My Heart   Alter; Webster
Music Makin' Man, The   Coots
Music to My Ears   Fisher
My Bridal Gown   Schwartz, Arthur
My Campfire Dreams   Alter; Webster
My Dreams Have Gone with the Wind   Oakland
My Friends, the Stars   Hoffman
My Funny Valentine   Hart; Rodgers
My Heart Is Dancing   Schwartz, Arthur
My Heart Skips a Beat   Donaldson
My Heart Still Belongs to You   Cahn
(In) My Home Town   Oakland
My Kid Sister   Oakland
My Mistake   Coslow
My Old Time Swing Rhythm Is a Racket   Blake
My Only Friend   Howard, Joseph E.
My Only Romance   Mitchell; Pollack
My Room   Heyman
My Rosary of Broken Dreams   Friend
My Secret Love Affair   Mitchell; Pollack
My Secret Song   Coslow
My Silver Dollar Man   Dubin; Warren
My Spies Tell Me (You Love Nobody but Me)   Caesar;
   Lerner, Sammy
My Sweet Bambina   Friml; Kahn
My Swiss Hill Billy   Mitchell; Pollack

My Topic of Conversation   Myrow
My Window Faces the South   Livingston, Jerry; Parish;
   Silver
Nani Oni Pua   Rainger
Napoleon's a Pastry   Arlen; Harburg
Naughty, Naughty, I'm Surprised at You   Oakland
52nd Street   Cahn
Near You   Coots; Davis
Nearness of You, The   Carmichael; Washington
'Neath the Moon at Saskatoon   Akst; Gilbert
Never Be Afraid of Anything   Caesar
Never Climb Fences, Never Climb Walls (Johnny Climbs
   Fences, Johnny Climbs Walls)   Caesar
Never in a Million Years   Gordon; Revel
Never Strike Anything (Striking Things)   Caesar
New Love   Schwartz, Jean
New Universal Signature (inst.)   McHugh
New York After Dark   Duke
Nice Work If You Can Get It   Gershwin, George; Gershwin,
   Ira
Night Before the Morning After, The   Dietz; Schwartz,
   Arthur
Night Over Shanghai   Mercer; Warren
Nightfall in Louisiana   Coots; Davis
Nile   Howard, Joseph E.
No More Tears   Freed, Ralph; Lane
No One Can Like the Drummer Man   Hoffman; Lerner,
   Sammy
No Ring on Her Finger   Loesser
Nobody but You   Loesser
Nobody Makes a Pass at Me   Rome
Nobody's Baby   Bullock
North Pole Sketch   Gordon; Revel
Not Cricket to Picket   Rome
Not So Innocent Fun (Nine Young Girls and Nine Old
   Men)   Hart; Rodgers
Nothing   Loesser
Nothing Can Stop Me Now   Bullock; Spina
Now You're Talking My Language   Koehler; Mitchell; Stept
Off the Record   Hart; Rodgers
Oh, Give Me the Good Old Days   Rome
Oh Say, Can You See Me?   Burke; Johnston
Oh What a Man   Mitchell; Pollack
Okolehao   Rainger; Robin
Ol Man Rip   Webster
Old Flame Never Dies, An   Schwartz, Arthur
Old King Cole   Mercer; Whiting
Old Man Moon   Carmichael
Old Man Rip   Alter
Ole South   Bryan
Omar Khayam, Come On   Howard, Joseph E.
On a Certain Saturday Night   Stept; Washington
On or About the First of June   Kalmar; Ruby
On Oublie Tout   Gilbert
On the Avenue   Berlin
On the Mediterranean Sea   Silver
On the Steps of Grant's Tomb   Berlin
On with the Dance   Mercer; Whiting
Once You're in Love   Adamson; McHugh
One Big Union for Two   Rome
One Rising Star   Eliscu
One Robin Doesn't Make a Spring   Loewe
Ooh, But I'm Happy   Gordon; Revel
Ooh! La! La!   Wrubel
Ooh!, What a Terrible Man   Kahn

Opening for Fifi Number   Coslow
Operatum (Greek Opera Sequence)   Freed, Ralph
Ordinary Guy   Rome
Our Little Home on the Highway   Coslow
Our Love Was Meant to Be   Waller
Our Penthouse on Third Avenue   Brown, Lew; Fain
Our Song   Fields; Kern
Our Team Is on the Warpath   Mitchell; Pollack
Out in the Cow Country   Stept; Washington
Out in the Sun   Eliscu
Over Night   Mitchell; Pollack
Overheard in a Cocktail Lounge (inst.)   Myrow
Panamania   Coslow
Pancho's Widow   Stept; Washington
Papa Don't Love Mama Any More   Rome
Papa Lewis, Mama Green   Rome
Parade of the Chocolate Dolls   Coots; Davis
Paraphrase   Loesser
Paris in Swing   Coslow
Paris in the Evening   Snyder
Pay Some Attention to Me   Gershwin, George; Gershwin,
     Ira
Pearls on Velvet (inst.)   Young, Victor
Peckin'   Ellington; Mills
Penny for Your Dreams, A   Freed, Ralph
Peter Pan of Tin Pan Alley, The   Arlen; Harburg
Pickles   Akst; Clare
Pin a Bluebonnet on Your New Bonnet   Fain; Kahal
Pineapple Swing   Fisher
Pins and Needles, Needles and Pins   Caesar
Pity Sakes   Mills
Plain Old Blues, The   Burke; Johnston
Play My Request   Coslow
Please Pardon Us — We're in Love   Gordon; Revel
Police Line Up (Grand Finale in Police Station)   Loesser
Polka Tina   Rainger; Robin
Pomponette   Gilbert
Pop Goes the Bottle   Oakland
Pop Goes the Bubble (And Soap Gets in My Eyes)   Koehler;
     Lane
Pop-Guns and Rifles   Caesar
Poppy Dreams   Howard, Joseph E.
Posin'   Cahn
Post-Office (I've Got to Be Kissed)   Adamson; McHugh
Prairie Rose   Mitchell; Stept
Preacher's Sermon, The   Loesser
Promise   Weill
Public Enemy No. 1   Rome
Public Melody Number One   Arlen; Koehler
Put Down Your Glass (Pick Up Your Girl and
     Dance)   Gordon; Revel
Put Me to the Test   Gershwin, George; Gershwin, Ira
Put the Swanee Up in Bottles, and Send It Up To
     Me   Bryan; Caesar
Quien Sabe   Bullock; Spina
Radio in Heaven so Mother Can Listen In   Fisher
Railroad that Ran through Our Land, The   Loesser
Ray Bolger Specialty Number   Kahn; Romberg
Red and White of Santa Clara, The   Adamson; McHugh
(Turn On That) Red Hot Heat (Burn Your Blues
     Away)   Alter; Webster
Red Mikado   Rome
Red Seal Malt (Drink Red Seal Malt When You Are
     Blue)   Gordon; Revel
Remember Me?   Dubin; Warren

Remember Your Name and Address   Caesar
Rhumba   Loewe
Rhumba Goes Collegiate, The   Mitchell; Pollack
Rhythm of the Moon, The   Rainger; Robin
Rhythm Racketeers   Hoffman; Lerner, Sammy
Rhythm, Rhythm   Fisher
Rhythmania   Conrad; Coslow
Riding Hobby Horses in the Park   Fisher
Rid'n   Young, Victor
Ring Around a Romance   Dubin; Warren
Riviera Moon   Davis
Robbers Song   Loesser
Rockin' in Rhythm   Ellington; Mills
Room for One   Rome
Rosalie   Porter
Rose in the Heather   Eliscu
Roses in December   Magidson; Oakland
Rue de la Paix   Koehler
Run for It, A   Loesser
Run for Your Lives   Loesser
Safety Patrol   Caesar
Salute to Spring   Loewe
Saratoga   Donaldson
Sasha Pasha Sasha   Koehler
Savage Rhythm   Coots; Davis
Save That Last Grave for Me   Brown, Nacio Herb
Say Ah   Freed, Arthur
Scareecrow, The   Loesser
Scattin' at the Kit Kat   Ellington; Mills
Scotch Air   Loesser
Secret Love Affair, The   Mitchell; Pollack
See Your Dentist Once a Day   Adamson; Lane
Send One Angel Down   Schwartz, Arthur
Sentimental and Melancholy   Mercer; Whiting
September in the Rain   Warren
Seven Different Sweeties a Week   Hoffman; Lerner, Sammy
Seventh Heaven   Mitchell; Pollack
Shag, The   Ager; Livingston, Jerry
Shall We Dance   Gershwin, George; Gershwin, Ira
Sheep Were in the Meadow, The   Hoffman; Lerner, Sammy
She's a Girl Scout at Heart (Park Number)   Coslow
She's Tall, She's Tan, She's Terrific   Coots; Davis
Shooting   Loesser
Should I   Loesser
Shy Violet   Akst; Clare
Since When   Loesser
Sing and Be Happy   Akst; Clare
Sing Me a Song with Social Significance   Rome
Sing of Spring   Gershwin, George; Gershwin, Ira
Sittin' in the Jail-House   Kahn; Romberg
Sitting on Your Status Quo   Rome
23-Skidoo   Bullock; Spina
Skies Are Blue   Cahn
Slap That Bass   Gershwin, George; Gershwin, Ira
Sleepy   Loesser
Slumbertime   Friend
Slumming on Park Avenue   Berlin
(You Know It All) Smarty   Freed, Ralph; Lane
Snug As a Bug in a Rug   Loesser
So I'll Never Be a Millionaire   Coots; Davis
So Many Memories   Woods
So You Won't Sing   Magidson; Wrubel
Some Sweet Day   Howard, Joseph E.
Somehow   Loewe
Something Has Happened   Myrow

Song of Ruth   Weill
Song of the Humming Birds   Loesser
Song of the Marines, The   Dubin; Warren
Song of the Rabbit   Gilbert
Song of the Samovar   Myrow
Song of the Sparrow   Loesser
Song of Virtue   Weill
Sons and Daughters of the Sea   Blake
Sophisticated Swing   Parish
Southland Serenade   Coots
Spades Is Trumps   Coots; Davis
Speaking of Love   Freed, Ralph; Lane
Speaking of the Weather   Harburg
Spelling Bee, The   Fain
Spring in Vienna (Spring in Milwaukee)   Hart; Rodgers
Spring Is in the Air   Freed, Ralph
Spring Love Is in the Air   Porter
Stay Away from the Railroad Tracks   Caesar
Stay Out, Sammy   Rome
Sticks and Stones Will Break My Bones   Razaf
Stiff Upper Lip   Gershwin, George; Gershwin, Ira
Stolen Holiday   Dubin; Warren
Stop! You're Breakin' My Heart   Koehler; Lane
Stormy Love   Eliscu
Strike While the Iron Is Hot   Stept; Washington
Stumbling Over Words   Dubin; Warren
Sun Showers   Brown, Nacio Herb; Freed, Arthur
Sunday in the Park   Rome
Sunset in Vienna   Hoffman; Lerner, Sammy
Sunset on the Moon   Fisher
Surrealism (inst.)   Myrow
Susan Belle, The   Blake
(Dear) Susie Sapple   Rainger; Robin
Sweet Is the Word for You   Rainger; Robin
Sweet Sixty-Five   Hart; Rodgers
Sweet Someone   Gordon; Revel
Sweetheart Time   Coslow
Swing High, Swing Low   Freed, Ralph; Lane
Swing Is Here to Sway   Gordon; Revel
Swing Is in the Air   Hoffman; Lerner, Sammy
Swing It Mr. Wu   David, Mack
Swing Sister   Berlin
Swingin' Hound   Waller
Sympathy   Friml; Kahn
Symphony Under the Stars   Donaldson
Tahitian Lullaby   Gilbert
Take and Take and Take   Hart; Rodgers
Take the World Off Your Shoulders   Brown, Lew; Fain
Tale of the Samovar (inst.)   Bloom
Tall, Dark, Lonesome Gentleman, A   Coslow
Taps Is Tops   Razaf
Teasin' Tessie Brown   Razaf
Tempest   Loesser
Temptation Waltz   Gilbert
Ten Little Miles   Lawrence
Terrific (Just a Bum)   Cahn
Texatina   Fain; Kahal
20th Century Rhapsody (inst.)   Revel
Thar She Comes (Hill Billy Wedding Song)   Coslow
That Certain Woman   Dubin; Warren
That Foolish Feeling   Adamson; McHugh
That Gal Salome   Coslow
That Night of the Embassy Ball   Arlen; Harburg
That's Southern Hospitality   Coslow
(That's) The Least You Can Do for the Lady   Warren

There Must Be Paint in the Sky   Fisher
There'll Be the Devil to Pay   Hoffman; Lerner, Sammy
There's a Little Bit of Heaven in Hawaii   Edwards
There's a Lull in My Life   Gordon; Revel
There's April in My Heart   Carmichael
There's Dust on the Trail   Cahn
There's Music in My Heart, Cherie   Hanley
There's No Two Ways About It   Adamson; McHugh
There's Nothing Like a Good Old Song   Howard, Joseph E.
There's Rhythm in Them Thar Hills   Freed, Ralph
They All Laughed   Gershwin, George; Gershwin, Ira
They Blew Themselves Out of Breath   Clare
They Can't Take That Away from Me   Gershwin, George; Gershwin, Ira
They Don't Grow Them Anymore Like You   Edwards
Things Are Looking Up   Gershwin, George; Gershwin, Ira
Things I Want, The   Hammerstein; Kern
This Must Be Heaven   Kalmar; Ruby
This Night   Rainger; Robin
This Way Please   Coslow
This Year's Kisses   Berlin
Three Black Crows   Loesser
Thrill Me Again   Parish
Thrill of a Lifetime   Coslow
Time Off for Love   Loewe
Tippety Witchet   Rainger; Robin
Titusville Square and Shanty Boat (Jenny Dear)   Hammerstein; Kern
(I Wanna Hum Sumpin' Pretty) To a Sweet Pretty Thing   Young, Joseph
To Love or Not to Love   Porter
To the Hum of My Heart   Carmichael
To Think You Could Care for Me   Kahn; Romberg
To You, Mio Rio de Janeiro   Gorney
To You Mio Rio de Jeneiro   Gilbert
Tomorrow Is Another Day   Kahn
Tonight We Love   Rainger; Robin
Tonight Will Never Come Again   Kahn
Too Marvelous for Words   Mercer; Whiting
Too Much Time Between Kisses   Kalmar; Ruby
Top of the Town   Adamson; McHugh
Travelin' Light   Akst; Clare
Treat for the Eyes, A   Friend; Stept
Treaty, My Sweetie, With You, A   Hart; Rodgers
Triplets   Dietz; Schwartz, Arthur
Tropical, The   Coslow
Truthfully   Livingston, Jerry
Tune in on My Heart   Gilbert
Turkey Dinner   Loesser
Turkey Giblets   Loesser
Turkey Trot   Loesser
Turn Off the Moon   Coslow
Turn on the Tap   Oakland
Turning the Town Upside Down (O.H.M.S.)   Hoffman
Two Birdies Up a Tree   Freed, Ralph; Lane
Two Chairs and a Table   Parish
Two of You   Carmichael
Under a Banana Tree   Silver
Uniform, The   Dietz; Schwartz, Arthur
Very Charming Spot, A   Loewe
Virginia   Schwartz, Arthur
Viva for Geneva   Arlen
Vive for Geneva   Harburg
Voice of Romance, The   Coslow
Voom Voom   Coslow

Vote for Honest Abe   Gordon; Revel
Wake Up and Live   Gordon; Revel
Wake Up, Brother, and Dance   Gershwin, George;
    Gershwin, Ira
Walking on the Ceiling   Adamson; Lane
Walking the Dog (Promenade) (inst.)   Gershwin, George
Waltz Was Born in Vienna, A   Loewe
Wand'ring Lover   Dietz; Schwartz, Arthur
Wanted   Lawrence
Wanted: A Wonderful Dancer   Howard, Joseph E.
Water Pitcher Episode   Kern
Way Out West   Hart; Rodgers
We Had to Rehearse   Schwartz, Arthur
We Happen to Be in the Army   Koehler; Mitchell; Stept
We Haven't a Moment to Lose   Burke; Johnston
We Just Sing and Dance   Hart; Rodgers
We Love Dear Old Appleton   Kalmar; Ruby
We Love the South   Bullock; Spina
We Only Love Once   Coots; Parish
We Sing America   Rome
We'd Rather Be Right   Rome
We'll Never Run Short of Love   Hoffman; Lerner, Sammy
We're Going to Balance the Budget (Tune Up,
    Bluebird)   Hart; Rodgers
We're Working Our Way through College   Mercer; Whiting
West Ain't Wild and Wooly Anymore, The   Bullock
We've Just Begun   Rome
Whale Song, The   Carmichael
What a Beautiful Beginning   Akst; Clare
What a Heavenly Night   Kalmar; Ruby
What Aloha Means   Rainger; Robin
What Do I Want with Love?   Blake
What Good Is Love?   Rome
What Is Love   Rainger; Robin; Young, Victor
What Makes You So Sweet   Oakland
What the Well-Dressed Man Will Wear   Berlin
What This Party Needs   Rome
What Will I Tell My Heart   Lawrence
What Would You Give in Exchange for Your Soul   Fisher
What's All the Shouting For?   Kalmar; Ruby
What's the Good Word   Oakland
What's with Me   Cahn
When a Gal from Alabama Meets a Boy from
    Tennessee   Akst; Clare
When a Maid Comes Knocking at Your Heart   Friml;
    Harbach
When Did I Hear You Tell Me You Love Me   Akst; Clare
When I Grow Up (The G-Man Song)   Rome
When I Hear You Tell Me You Love Me   Akst; Clare
When is a Kiss Not a Kiss   Freed, Ralph; Lane
When Love Is Young   Adamson; McHugh
When Morning Comes   Washington
When New York Was New York, New York Was a
    Wonderful Town   Cohan
When Summer Days Are Come   Silver
When the Campfire Is Low on the Prairie   Mitchell; Stept
When the Wind Blows South   Arlen; Harburg
When You Dream About Hawaii   Kalmar; Ruby
When You Gotta Sing You Gotta Sing   Hoffman; Lerner,
    Sammy
When You Ride a Bicycle   Caesar
When You Swim   Caesar
When Your College Days Are Gone   Mercer; Whiting
When You're Watching the Parade   Caesar
Where Are You?   Adamson; McHugh

Where I Ain't Been Before   Brown, Nacio Herb; Freed,
    Arthur; Freed, Ralph; Lane
Where or When   Hart; Rodgers
Whippoorwill in a Willow Tree, A   Ahlert; Lewis; Young,
    Joseph
Whistling Boy, The   Fields; Kern
Who Knows   Lawrence; Porter
Who Put that Moon in the Sky?   Kalmar; Ruby
Who Wants Love?   Kahn
Whoa Whoopee — Whoa Whippee (Yippy-I-O-I-Ay)   Akst;
    Clare
Who'll Be the One this Summer   Heyman
Who's in Love with Who   Howard, Joseph E.
Why Did You Do It?   Dietz; Schwartz, Arthur
Why Did You Kiss My Heart Awake   Eliscu
Why Do Hawaiians Sing Aloha   Stept
Why Must We Say Goodbye   Howard, Joseph E.
Why Should I Care?   Porter
Why Talk About Love?   Mitchell; Pollack
Widow in Lace, The   Bullock; Spina
Will You Marry Me Tomorrow, Maria?   Hammerstein; Kern
Woman I Love, The   Heyman; Spina
Woman in Love Ain't Got No Sense, A   Razaf
Woman's Kiss, A   Friml
Woods Are Full of Cuckoos and My Heart Is Full of Love,
    The   Coots
Word to Remind You, A   Eliscu
Words and Music   Brown, Nacio Herb; Freed, Arthur
Workmen's Chorus   Hammerstein; Kern
World Is My Apple, The   Mercer; Whiting
World Is My Oyster, The   Hart; Rodgers
Would You Like to Buy a Dream   Cahn
Yankee Doodle Band   Magidson; Wrubel
Yonkle Doodle Goes Steppin'   Mills
You and I Know   Schwartz, Arthur
You Are So Fair   Hart; Rodgers
You Can't Have Everything   Gordon; Revel
You Can't Run Away from Love Tonight   Dubin; Warren
You Can't Stop Me from Dreaming   Friend
You Can't Tell a Man By His Hat   Loesser
You Gambled with Love   Freed, Ralph; Lane
You Grow Sweeter Every Day   Stept; Washington
You Have Everything   Dietz; Schwartz, Arthur
You Hit the Nail on the Head   Ager
You Struck the Right Note   Hoffman; Lerner, Sammy
You Were Only Romancing   Coslow
You'll Get a Cold in Your Toes   Ahlert; Lewis; Young,
    Joseph
You'll Get Over It, She'll Get Over It   Parish; Silver
You'll Never Go To Heaven (If You Break My Heart)   Bryan
Your Broadway and My Broadway   Brown, Nacio Herb;
    Freed, Arthur
You're a Blessing to Me   Rainger; Robin
You're an Education   Dubin
You're Gonna Wake Up Some Day   Ager
You're Here, You're There, You're Everywhere   Kahal
You're in My Heart Again   Adamson; McHugh
You're Laughing at Me   Berlin
You're Looking for Romance, I'm Looking for
    Love   Livingston, Jerry
You're My Desire   Mills
You're My Heart   Loesser
You're Out of This World to Me   De Lange
You're Setting Me on Fire   Donaldson
You've Got a Certain Something   Donaldson

You've Got Something There   Mercer; Whiting

1938

Abe Lincoln Had Just One Country   Hammerstein; Harbach; Kern
Adios Panama   Parish
After Looking at You   Hoffman
Ain't He Good Lookin'   Clare
Ain't You Comin' Back from California   Fisher
Alexander's Back in Town   Razaf
All American Swing, The   Gordon; Revel
All Dressed Up with No One to Love   Gordon; Revel
All for One and One for All   Lawrence
All Hail the Political Honeymoon   Weill
All Mixed Up   Clare
All My Life I've Been a Slave   Kalmar; Ruby
All Right for You   Rainger; Robin
Allow Me to Present Myself to You   Lawrence
Alma Mater   Oakland
Alone with You   Mitchell; Pollack
Along Fraternity Row   Lawrence
Am I in Another World?   Koehler
Am I the Lucky One   Lane; Loesser
And So Will You   Loewe
And You Forgot About Me   Hanley
Angel Child   Johnston
Angel Without Wings   Hart; Rodgers
Angels with Dirty Faces   Fisher
Annabelle   Parish
Another Law   Weill
Any Old Lane Is Lovers' Lane (As Long As I'm with You)   Johnson, Howard
Any Time at All   Van Heusen
Are Your a Dreamer   Lawrence
Argentina Skies   Van Heusen
Army Blue   Hammerstein; Harbach; Kern
As I Was Say'n to the Duchess   Washington
As Long As I Love   Oakland
As Long As It's Not About Love   Porter
As Long As We're Together   Friend
As Long As You Live You'll Be Dead If You Die   Mercer
At a Perfume Counter on the Rue de la Paix   Leslie
At Last   Howard, Bart
At Long Last Love   Porter
At the End of the Sunset Trail   Edwards
At the Roxy Music Hall   Hart; Rodgers
At Your Beck and Call   De Lange
Au Revoir, Cher Baron   Porter
Bach Up to Me (inst.)   Waller
Bachelor Song, The   Weill
Back to the Backwoods   Lawrence
Backstage Music (Opening Scene) (inst.)   Kern
Ballad of the Robbers   Weill
Band Played Out of Tune, The   Stept
Be a Good Scout   Adamson; McHugh
Be Optimistic   Bullock; Spina
Beans   Loesser
Beautiful Isle of Love   Bryan
Bei Mir Bist du Schon (Means that You're Grand)   Cahn
Bells Are Ringing   Freed, Ralph
Bells of Treasure Isle, The   Webster
Beneath the Winter Snows   Kahn; Romberg
Benny Sent Me   Rome
Bewitched By the Night   Gorney

Big Brother   Hart; Rodgers
Big Mouth Minnie   Razaf
Birdie Song, The   Hoffman
Black Maria   Razaf
Black Raspberry Jam (inst.)   Waller
Blame It on the Danube   Akst; Loesser
Blossoms in the Moonlight   Washington
Blossoms on Broadway   Rainger; Robin
Blow a Balloon Up to the Moon   Fain
Blue and Sentimental   David, Mack; Livingston, Jerry
Blue Dawn   Washington
Blue Grass   Razaf
Blue Is the Evening   Akst; Clare
Bluer than the Ocean Blues   Waller
Bonnie Blue Flag   Hammerstein; Harbach; Kern
Boogie-Woogie   Coots; Davis
Boom   Goetz
Boomps-a-Daisy   Fain
Born to Swing   Freed, Ralph; Lane
Boy Meets Girl   Mercer; Warren
Boy with a Drum   Harbach; Kern
Boys in the Band   Loesser
Braggin' in Brass   Ellington; Mills
Brand New Song in Town   Kahn
Brass Buttons and Epaulets   Bullock; Spina
Bravo New Song in Town   Romberg
Bright Square (inst.)   Kern
Broadcasting Medley   Gordon; Revel
Broadway Beauty Doctor Ain't Done Right By Our Nell   Leslie
Broadway Jamboree   Adamson; McHugh
Brom's Complaint   Weill
Bublitchka   Fain; Parish; Silver
Bus Sequence   Kahn
Butterfly Love   Leslie
By a Wishing Well   Gordon; Revel
By An Old Sun Dial   Norworth
By Candlelight   Porter
Can This Be the End of the Rainbow   Cahn
Can't Teach My Heart New Tricks   Mercer
Can't Teach My Old Heart New Tricks   Whiting
Cantabile (A Song Without Words) (inst.)   Kern
Care-Free   Berlin
Carefree Camp   Stept
Carnival in Caroline   Ellington; Mills
Carnival Song (Czardas) (What a Gay Occasion)   Akst; Clare
Center of Attraction   Brooks
Change Partners   Berlin
Chapel Bells   Adamson; McHugh
Chasing You Around   Loesser
Chatterbox   Ellington; Mills
Cherry and White Wins the Day   Davis
Chimes in the Steeple   David, Mack; Meyer
Chimes of Notre Dame, The   McHugh
Cigarette and a Silhouette, A   De Lange; Van Heusen
Cinderella Goes to Town   Hanley
City Kept Gal   Blake
Classy Clothes Chris   Gordon; Revel
Clickety-clack   Weill
Clump! Clump! Swish!   Weill
Coffee and Kisses   Freed, Ralph
College Swing   Carmichael; Loesser
College Widow   Mills
Colorado Sunset   Conrad; Gilbert
Come and Get Your Happiness   Yellen

Come on Leathernecks   Stept; Washington
Come to the Fair   Robison
Come with Me   Hart; Rodgers
Comrade Alonzo   Porter
Confidentially   Dubin; Mercer; Warren
Confidentially Yours   Lawrence
Congo Conga   Coots; Davis
Consequence Is Awful, The   Weill
Coronation of King Neptune (inst.)   Myrow
Corrigan Bop   Mills
Cottage in the Rain   Waller
Cotton Club   Ellington; Mills
Could Be   Donaldson; Mercer
Could She — Could She Kiss   Hoffman
Could You Pass in Love   Gordon; Revel
Court House Scene   Johnson, James P.
Cowboy from Brooklyn   Mercer; Warren
Crackly Grain Flakes   Mitchell; Pollack
Crimson Street   Brooks
Crystal Temple, The   Rose
Cure Me with Love   Fisher
Dance Must Go On (inst.), The   Kern
Dance of the Aborigines   Weill
Dancing My Heart Away   Conrad; Gilbert
Danger Ahead   Lawrence
Darling the Answer Is in this Song   Fisher
Daughter of Mademoiselle   Akst; Clare
Day Dreaming (All Night Long)   Dubin; Mercer; Warren
De Chain Gang   Johnson, J. Rosamond
De Land o' Good Times   Hammerstein; Harbach; Kern
De Ye Ken John Peel   De Lange
Dear Old Syracuse   Hart; Rodgers
Deed I Do Do Blues   Johnson, James P.
Deep in a Dream   De Lange; Van Heusen
Dewey Blues   Johnson, James P.
Diamonds on the Moon   Kahn; Romberg
Did an Angel Kiss You (The Day You Were Born)   Freed, Ralph
Did You Ever Get Stung?   Hart; Rodgers
Dirge for a Soldier   Weill
Disappointed and Disgusted   Ahlert; Young, Joseph
Dixie Dreams   Clarke; Johnston
Do the Buckaroo   Rainger; Robin
Do You Tell Her the Things You Told Me   David, Mack; Meyer
Do You Wanna Jump, Children?   Van Heusen
Doctor Rhythm   Burke; Monaco
Don't Be That Way   Parish
Don't Let It Get Your Down   Porter
Don't Let that Moon Get Away   Burke; Monaco
Don't Let the Rhythm Go to Your Head   Cahn
Don't Tell a Secret to a Rose   Rainger; Robin
Don't Wait Till the Night Before Christmas   Baer; Lewis
Don't Wake Up My Heart   Lewis; Meyer
Doughnuts and Coffee   Fain; Kahal
Down Beat   Blake
Dream Boat   Kahn; Romberg
Dream Caravan   Razaf
Dream Dust   Coots
Dreamy Isle of Dreams   Bryan
Drifting Down a Little Dutch Canal   Coots
Drop a Nickel in the Slot   Ahlert; Young, Joseph
Dry Bones   Johnson, J. Rosamond
Dusk on the Desert   Ellington; Mills
Dust Over the West   Lawrence

Early Morning Sequence   Kahn
Echo Waltz   Howard, Bart
Eight Little Notes   Fain
Ensenada Nights   Washington
Entre-Nous   Rome
Entry of the Council   Weill
Ever Since Adam   Stept; Washington
Every Blossom I See Reminds Me of You   Buck
Everybody's Laughing   Lerner, Sammy; Oakland
Everything to Make Us Happy   Norworth
Fair and Square   Razaf
Falling in Love with Love   Hart; Rodgers
Fantasie   Hammerstein; Harbach; Kern
Far Away   Porter
Fare Thee Well Annie Laurie   Parish
Fashion Show   McHugh
Faster, Faster My Heart Is Breaking   Caesar
Feelin' High and Happy   Bloom; Koehler
Five Years Ain't So Long   Coslow; Weill
Flower of Dawn   De Lange
Food for Scandal   Hart; Rodgers
For No Rhyme or Reason   Porter
For the First Time   Adamson; McHugh
For the First Time in My Life   Mills
Fractious Fingering (inst.)   Waller
Franklin D. Roosevelt Jones   Rome
From Alpha to Omega   Porter
From Now On   Porter
From the First Good-Morning to the Last Good-Night   Schwartz, Jean
From the U.S.A. to the U.S.S.R   Porter
Fuddle-Dee-Duddle (Funny Little Tune)   Fain
Fun on the Beach   Parish; Silver
Funny Little Song   Friend
Funny Old Hills, The   Rainger; Robin
Funny Things Happen in Dreams   Friend
Gang Song   Koehler
Garden in Granada, A   Baer; Lewis
Garden of the Moon   Dubin; Mercer; Warren
Garden Scene   Hammerstein; Harbach; Kern
Gay Desperado, The   Freed, Ralph; Lane
Gay Nineties, The   Fain
Geneva (A Satrical Ballet) (inst.)   Rome
Gentlemen Unafraid   Hammerstein; Harbach; Kern
Get Along Without Me (inst.)   Kern
Get Out of Town   Porter
Girl Friend of the Whirling Dervish, The   Dubin; Mercer; Warren
Girl of the Golden West   Kahn; Romberg
Give Me a Sailor   Carmichael; Coslow; Loesser
Give Them Girls   Rose
Go Back Over There   Fisher
God's Morning   Brennan
Gone-Again Corrigan   Mills; Myrow
Good Evening, Princess   Porter
Good for Nothin' (But Love)   De Lange; Van Heusen
Good Night Angel   Magidson; Wrubel
Goodbye, My Dream, Goodbye (inst.)   Young, Victor
Good-bye, My Dreams, Good-bye   Webster
Goodbye My Heart   Akst; Clare
Goodnight — Molly O'Day   Bryan
Got My Mind on Music   Gordon; Revel
Grazioso in D Major (inst.)   Kern
Greatest Attraction in the World, The   Oakland
Greek to You   Porter

Gypsy of Love   Lawrence
Gypsy Told Me, A   Yellen
Gypsy Without a Song   Ellington
Ha, Ha, Ha   Porter
Hail Sigma Psi   Koehler
Half Moon on the Hudson   Bullock; Spina
Handlebar Moustache, The   Rose
Happy As a Lark   Webster
Happy Ending   Mitchell; Pollack
Happy-Go-Lucky Guy   Howard, Bart
Hard to Replace   Gershwin, Ira; Kern
Harlem Number Man   Johnson, James P.
Harlem Woogie   Johnson, James P.
Harmony in Harlem   Ellington; Mills
Has Anyone Ever Told You, You're As Pretty As a
   Picture   Adamson; McHugh
Have a Dream on Me   Mercer; Warren
Have It Your Way Foolish Heart   Kahal; Warren
Have You Forgotten So Soon   Coslow
Havin' a Ball   Johnson, James P.
Havin' Myself a Time   Rainger; Robin
He and She   Hart; Rodgers
He Can Dance   Fain; Kahal
Heads High   Brown, Lew; Pollack
Hear My Shout Bubilchka   Mills
Heart and Soul   Carmichael; Loesser
Heart of Mine   Heyman
Hearts Are Never Blue in Blue Kalua   Bryan
Heaven O'Clock   Magidson; Wrubel
Heavenly Party   Fields; Kern
Heel and Toe Polka   Rainger; Robin
Heigh-Ho the Merry-O   Adamson; McHugh
Hellzapoppin   Fain
Help Wanted — Male   Bullock; Spina
Here Am I Doing It   Gordon; Revel
Here I Am Doing It   Gordon; Revel
Here We Are - In Heaven Alone   Ahlert; Young, Joseph
Here's that Heart Again   Bullock; Pollack
Highland Swing   Coots; Davis; Johnston
History of New York, A   Weill
Hi-Yum Hi-Yum Hi-Yum   Mills
Hold My Hand   Waller
Hold on to Your Heart Here We Go Again   Mitchell; Stept
Hold That Co-Ed   Gordon; Revel
Hole in the Wall, A   Young, Joseph
Home in Your Arms   Hammerstein; Oakland
Honey Where You Been So Long   Fisher
Honeymooning in Hawaii   Hanley
Hooray for Hollywood   Mercer; Whiting
Hop, Skip and Jump   Bullock; Spina
Hopeless Love Affair, A   Razaf; Waller
Hot and Happy   Yellen
Hot Tamale Man, The   Washington
Hot Water Bottle   Fisher
House on Chapel Row, The   David, Mack; Livingston, Jerry
How Can I Thank You   Bullock; Spina
How Can I, With You in My Heart   Waller
How Can We Be Wrong   Dietz; Schwartz, Arthur
How Can You Forget?   Hart; Rodgers
How Can You Tell an American?   Weill
How Do You Spell Ambassador   Porter
How Far Will You Go with Me   Weill
How Long Can Love Keep Laughing?   Rome
How Long Has This Been Going On   Magidson; Wrubel
How to Win Friends and Influence People   Hart; Rodgers

How Would I Know? (I Wish Dat Dere Wasn't No
   War)   Hammerstein; Kern
How Would You Feel   Rainger; Robin
How Ya Baby   Waller
How'dja Like to Love Me   Lane; Loesser
Howdy Stranger   Mercer; Whiting
Humming   Caesar; Henderson
Hungarian Rhapsody   Washington
Hush Hush   Weill
Hush My Heart   Yellen
I Ain't Comin' on that Tab (If You Go Barrel House)   Mills
I Am Gaston   Porter
I Am Praying Humble   Lawrence
I Can Dream, Can't I   Fain; Kahal
I Can Tell By Looking in Your Eyes   Howard, Joseph E.
I Can't Face the Music (Without Singin' the Blues)   Bloom;
   Koehler
I Can't Forgive You   Waller
I Can't Make Up My Mind   Kahn; Romberg
I Could Kick Myself (For Getting a Kick Out of
   You)   Hoffman
I Could Use a Dream   Bullock; Spina
I Do Business in My Hat   Weill
I Fall in Love with You Every Day   Loesser
I Fell Up to Heaven   Rainger; Robin
I Get Along Without You Very Well (Except
   Sometimes)   Carmichael
I Got Love   Waller
I Had to Do It   Razaf; Waller
I Had Twins (He Had Twins)   Hart; Rodgers
I Hate to Say Goodnight   Mills
I Have Eyes   Rainger; Robin
I Have Room in My Heart   Loewe
I Haven't Changed a Thing   Mills
I Hit a New High   Adamson; McHugh
I Keep Coming Back for More   Ager
I Let a Song Go Out of My Heart   Ellington; Mills
I Like Humped-Backed Salmon   Lane; Loesser
I Love Elephants (Cause Elephants Don't Forget)   Bryan
I Love the Way We Fell in Love   Fain; Kahal
I Love to Rhyme   Gershwin, George; Gershwin, Ira
I Love to Sing the Words While We're Dancing   Caesar;
   Lerner, Sammy
I Love to Walk in the Rain   Bullock; Spina
I Love to Whistle   Adamson; McHugh
I Love You in Technicolor   Van Heusen
I Married an Angel   Hart; Rodgers
I Miss You in the Morning   Leslie
I Never Dreamed   Howard, Bart
I Never Had Waltzes Before   Howard, Bart
I Never Saw a King Before   Loewe
I Ought to Dance   Cahn
I Passed Up a Wonderful Thing   Fisher
I Pledge Allegiance to Your Heart   Fain
I Promise You   Lerner, Sammy; Oakland
I Saw the Light of Day Last Night   Van Heusen
I Ups to Her and She Ups to Me   Hoffman
I Used to Be Color Blind   Berlin
I Used to Laugh at Love   Hanley
I Wanna Go Back to Bali   Dubin; Warren
I Want a New Romance   Coslow
I Want to Go Home   Porter
I Was Doing All Right   Gershwin, George; Gershwin, Ira
I Was Naive   Gershwin, Ira; Kern
I Was the Power Behind the Throne   Lawrence

I Was Young in Budapest (inst.)   Kern
I Wish I Was the Willow   Lane; Loesser
I Wonder Where My Hula Girl Has Gone   Donaldson
I Won't Go Home   Friend
I'd Love to Play a Love Scene (Opposite You)   Coslow
I'd Rather Look at You   Coslow
If All the World Were Paper   Bullock; Spina
If Anything Happened to You   Van Heusen
If Dreams Come True   Mills
If I Had Someone to Love Me the Way I Love You   Friend
If I Hadn't Met You   Baer; Lewis
If I Meant Something to You   Waller
If It Rains Who Cares   Leslie
If This Isn't Dreaming   Warren
If You Can Take It   Mercer; Warren
If You Leave Paris   Howard, Bart
If You Were in My Place   Ellington; Mills
I'll Always Be Lucky with You   Bullock; Spina
I'll Be Glad   Johnson, J. Rosamond
I'll Be Seeing You   Fain; Kahal
I'll Black His Eyes   Porter
I'll Build a Broadway for You   Bullock; Spina
I'll Come to the Wedding   Loesser
I'll Do the Strutaway (In My Cutaway)   Caesar
I'll Dream Tonight   Mercer; Whiting
I'll Never Change   Clare; Johnston
I'll Never Fail You   Mills
I'll Never Let You Cry   Clare; Mitchell; Pollack
I'll Sing of a Golden Age   Weill
I'll Tell the Man in the Street   Hart; Rodgers
I'm a Gypsy   Bullock; Spina
I'm a Stranger in My Own Home Town   Oakland
I'm a Yank Full of Thankfulness   Fain
I'm Afraid It's Love   Fisher
I'm Afraid the Masquerade Is Over   Magidson; Wrubel
I'm Back in Circulation   Porter
I'm Glad for Your Sake but I'm Sorry for Mine   Lawrence
I'm Going in for Love   Porter
I'm Gonna Fall in Love   Waller
I'm Gonna Hit the Number Today   Johnson, James P.
I'm in a Fog About You   Dixon
I'm in a Happy Frame of Mind   Bloom; Parish
I'm in Dreamland   Lane; Loesser
I'm in Love with Vienna   Hammerstein
I'm in My Glory   Adamson; McHugh
I'm in the Pink   Lane; Loesser
I'm Just a Jitterbug   David, Mack; Livingston, Jerry
I'm Like a Fish Out of Water   Mercer; Whiting
I'm Madly in Love with You   Coots; Davis
I'm Marching Along with Time   Berlin
I'm Not Complaining   Gershwin, Ira; Weill
I'm Not Myself Today   Bullock; Spina
I'm Ruined   Hart; Rodgers
I'm Savin' Up My Pennies (inst.)   Waller
I'm Slappin' Seventh Avenue (With the Sole of My
   Shoe)   Ellington; Mills
I'm Still Yours Tho' You're No Longer Mine   Coots; Davis
I'm Taking a Shine to You   Magidson; Wrubel
I'm Taking the Steps to Russia   Porter
I'm Yours   Porter
In a Heart As Brave As Your Own   Kahn; Romberg
In a Little Dutch Kindergarten (Down By the Zuider
   Zee)   Bryan
In a Moment of Madness We Found a Lifetime of
   Love   Coslow; Silver

In and Out the Window   Hoffman
In Any Language   Gordon; Revel
In Bad with Sinbad   Fisher
In Blue Samoa   Bryan
In Old Chicago   Gordon; Revel
In Old Wyoming   Fisher
In the Carefree Realm of Fancy   Loewe
In the Merry Month of May   Fisher
Information Please   Porter
Inside This Heart of Mine   Waller
Interlude in the Dark (We Are a Band of
   Brothers)   Hammerstein; Harbach; Kern
International Cowboys   Styne
Invitation to Love   Gordon; Revel
Irish Lullaby (inst.)   Kern
Isn't It Wonderful, Isn't It Swell   Mitchell; Pollack
It All Belongs to You   Porter
It Don't Make Sense   Rainger; Robin
It Never Entered My Head   Porter
It Never Rains — But What It Pours   Gordon; Revel
It Never Was You   Weill
It's a Hundred to One You're from Washington   Hoffman
It's a Law   Weill
It's Blue on the Blue Danube   Fisher
It's Gayer Whistling As You Go (Gaily I Whistle a
   Song)   Harbach; Kern
It's Great to Be Home Again   Fain; Kahal
It's Hard to Sing the Old Songs All Alone   Hanley
It's No Laughing Matter   Porter
It's Raining Sunshine   Bryan; David, Mack; Meyer
It's the Dreamer in Me   Van Heusen
It's the Happiest Time of Their Lives   Norworth
It's the Strangest Thing   Akst; Clare
It's Time to Say 'Aloha'   Fain
It's Unbelievable   Bullock; Spina
It's Wonderful   Parish
I've Got a Date with a Dream   Gordon; Hanley; Revel
I've Got a Heartful of Music   Mercer; Whiting
I've Got a Moonlight Date (At the Golden Gate)   Webster
I've Got A Pocketful of Dreams   Burke; Monaco
I've Got Everything   Ager
I've Got to Stop Dreaming of You   Kalmar; Ruby
I've Hitched My Wagon to a Star   Mercer; Whiting
I've Taken a Fancy to You   Clare; Mitchell; Pollack
I've Turned the Corner   Gershwin, Ira; Kern
Jealous of Me   Razaf; Waller
Jeepers Creepers   Mercer; Warren
Jezebel   Mercer; Warren
Jitterbug Tree, The   Razaf; Waller
Jitterbug's Lullaby   Mills
Jitterbug's Lullaby (Jitterbug's Holiday)   Ellington
Joint Is Jumpin', The   Razaf; Waller
Joobalai   Rainger; Robin
Joseph, Joseph   Cahn
Jubilesta   Ellington; Mills
Julianne   Egan
Jungle Love   Freed, Ralph; Rainger; Robin
Junior   Lane; Loesser
Just a Kid Named Joe   David, Mack; Livingston, Jerry
Just a Kiss   Parish
Just a Love Song at Sundown   David, Mack; Livingston,
   Jerry
Just a Simple Melody   Cahn
Just an Error in the News   Mills
Just Another Page in Your Diary   Porter

Just Another Rhumba   Gershwin, George; Gershwin, Ira
Just Let Me Look at You   Fields; Kern
Just My Luck   Bullock; Pollack
Just Plain Folks   Fisher
Keep Away from Those Swinging Doors   Mercer; Warren
Keep Your Hand on My Heart   Loewe
Kentucky in the Moonlight   Styne
Kentucky Opera   Styne
Killy-Ka-Lee   Dixon
Kiss a Miss from Tennessee   Fisher
Ladies of the Evening   Hart; Rodgers
Lady on the Two-Cent Stamp, The   Dubin; Mercer; Warren
Lamp on the Corner (Farolito)   Washington
Land of Make Believe   Friend
Last Dance (Our Last Dance), The   Hammerstein; Harbach; Kern
Last Love Song, The   Olcott
Latch On (inst.)   Waller
Latin Quarter, The   Dubin; Warren
Laugh and Call It Love   Burke; Monaco
Laughing Boy Blues   Cahn
Legend of Niagara, The   Gorney
Legend of Robin Hood, The   Cahn
Lesson in C, A   Ellington; Mills
Let Antipholus In   Hart; Rodgers
Let Me Sleep Tonight My Aching Heart   Ahlert; Young, Joseph
Let Me Whisper (Murmullo)   Heyman
Let That Be a Lesson to You   Mercer; Whiting
Let This Be a Warning to You   Davis
Let's Dream Again   Hanley; Rose
Let's Dream in the Moonlight   Loesser
Let's Drink to a Dream   Dubin; Warren
Let's Give Love Another Chance   Adamson; McHugh
Let's Sail Away to Sweetheart Bay   Bryan
Let's Sing a Song about Nothing   Hart; Rodgers
Let's Tie the Old Forget-Me-Not   Gorney; Webster
Limpy Dimpy   Clare; Styne
Little Bit of Everything, A   Lawrence
Little Corporal, The   Loewe
Little Ham   Johnson, James P.
Little Kiss at Twilight, A   Rainger; Robin
Little Miss Broadway   Bullock; Spina
Little Old Rhythm   Magidson; Oakland
Little Robber (inst.)   Kern
Little Zouave   Hammerstein; Harbach; Kern
Living Like a Millionaire, in Jungle Land   Johnson, J. Rosamond
Living on the Town   Akst; Clare
London Bridge Is Falling Down   Baer
Lost in a Dream   Parish
Lost in Meditation   Ellington; Mills
Lost on an Island of Dreams   Parish
Lounging at the Waldorf (inst.)   Waller
Love Call (Halloo of My Heart)   Johnson, Howard
Love Doesn't Grow on Trees   Freed, Ralph; Lane
(I Promise To) Love, Honor and Oh Baby   Magidson; Wrubel
Love in Springtime   Mills
Love Is Here to Stay   Gershwin, George; Gershwin, Ira
Love Is Love in Any Language   Edwards
Love Is Where You Find It   Dubin; Mercer
Love Is Where You Find It Something Tells Me   Warren
Love Knows Best   Hart; Rodgers
Love Like Ours, A   Mitchell; Stept

Love Makes You Do Crazy Things   Livingston, Jerry; Parish; Silver
Love Opened My Eyes   Freed, Ralph; McHugh
Love Takes a Holiday   Koehler
Love Walked In   Gershwin, George; Gershwin, Ira
Love with a Capital "U"   Hoffman
Love with a Capital "You"   Rainger; Robin
Loveland in the Wintertime   Friend
Lovelight in the Starlight   Freed, Ralph
Loveliness of You, The   Gordon
Lovely One   Loesser
Love-Nest in Kalua   Bryan
Love's a Necessary Thing   Arlen; Koehler
Lullaby Ostinato (inst.)   Kern
Ma (He's Making Eyes at Me)   Clare; Conrad
Madame Is at Home   Loewe
Maiden By the Brook   Rainger; Robin
Mama, that Moon Is Here Again   Rainger; Robin
Man from Music Mountain   Lawrence
Many a Lofty Mountain   Hammerstein; Kern
Marching Along (Plymouth Welcome Song)   Gordon; Revel
Maria   Porter
(Fiesta) Mariachie   Kahn; Romberg
Marianina   Donaldson
Mary, Mary, Quite Contrary   Lane; Loesser
Mary, the Milkman's Daughter   Bryan
Masher Is a Bad, Bad Boy, A   Adamson; McHugh
May and January   Weill
May I Drop a Petal in Your Glass of Wine   Gordon; Revel
May I Suggest Romance   Loewe
Me 'n' You 'n' Him   Egan
Meet the Beat of My Heart   Gordon; Revel
Melody Farm   Kahn
Melos, That Lovely Smiling Isle   Porter
Men from Milwaukee   Hart; Rodgers
Men with Wings   Carmichael; Loesser
Merci Beaucoup   Gordon; Revel
Midnight on the Stormy Deep   Fisher
Millions of Dreams Ago   Mercer; Warren
Miss Hallelujah Brown   Coots; Davis
Mist Is Over the Moon, A   Hammerstein; Oakland
Mister Man   Hammerstein; Harbach; Kern
Mister McCue, How Do You Do (inst.)   Kern
Mitzi   Dietz; Schwartz, Arthur
Modiste, The   Hart; Rodgers
Moments Like This   Lane; Loesser
Monday Morning on Saturday Night   Evans; Livingston, Jay
Monte Carlo   Fisher
Moon Looks Down and Laughs, The   Kalmar; Ruby
Moonlight in Waikiki   Friend
Moonlight Mood   Waller
Moonshine Over Kentucky   Mitchell; Pollack
More Power to You   Adamson; McHugh
More than I Can Tell You   Donaldson
Morning Glories in the Moonlight   Magidson; Wrubel
Morocco   De Lange
Mosquito   Fain
Most Gentlemen Don't Like Love   Porter
Mr. Roosevelt Won't You Please Run Again   Gorney
Mr. Sweeney's Learned to Swing   Mills
Music, Maestro, Please   Magidson; Wrubel
Must Have a Chorus   Johnston
Mutiny in the Nursery   Mercer
My Adventure   Mercer; Warren
My Best Wishes   Koehler

My Billboard Girl   Johnston
My Fine Feathered Friend   Adamson; McHugh
My First Impression of You   Stept
My First Love (Mujer)   Washington
My Golden West   Kahn; Romberg
My Heart Belongs to Daddy   Porter
My Heart Is a Gypsy   Kahn
My Heart Is My Master   Heyman
My Heart Is Taking Lessons   Burke; Monaco
My Heart Is Unemployed   Rome
My Heaven in the Pines   Conrad
My Imaginary Love   Coslow
My Land and Your Land   Friend
My Little Road   Woods
My Love Affair Is Falling Down (London Bridge)   Mills
My New Homeland   Caesar
My Own   Adamson; McHugh
My Palm Tree Rendezvous   Bryan
My Pillow   Gilbert
My River   Johnston
My South Sea Heart's Desire   Bryan
My Walking Stick   Berlin
My Warm Heart, Your Cold Shoulder   Gorney
My Yakahula Lady Love   Bryan
Nami-Nami-Nam Inamorata (Sweetheart)   Mills; Myrow
Naughty Naughty   Oakland
Never Felt Better, Never Had Less   Baer
Never Was There Such a Perfect Day   Kahn
Never You Mind (inst.)   Kern
New Love, New Lips   Dixon; Woods
New Trail   Freed, Ralph
New York on Parade   Rose
Night Is Filled With Music, The   Berlin
Night You Name the Day, The   Heyman; Romberg
Night You Said Goodbye, The   Stept
Nights of Memory   Bryan
Nighty Night   Stept
No Question in My Mind (You're in My Heart)   Gershwin,
    Ira; Kern
No Tax on Love!   Rome
Nobody's Gonna Take You From Me   Kalmar; Ruby
Not So Warm (inst.)   Kern
Not There, Right Here   Waller
Now It Can Be Told   Berlin
Now That We Are One   Gershwin, Ira; Kern
Nutty Nursery Rhymes   Cahn; Raye
Off Again-On Again   Mills
Oh Baby, Obey   Rainger; Robin
Oh, Diogenes   Hart; Rodgers
Oh Dream of Love   Kahn
Oh! Ma-Ma! The Butcher Boy   Brown, Lew
Oh! Oh! Oklahoma   Adamson; McHugh
Oh, Oh, What Do You Know about Love   David, Mack;
    Livingston, Jerry
Oh What A Day that Will Be   Caesar
Oh, What a Horse Was Charlie   Dubin; Mercer; Warren
Old Curiosity Shop   Coslow; Silver
Old Fashioned Song, An   Kahn; Romberg
Old Folks   Robison
Old Pete Is in the City   Weill
Old School Bell, The   Loesser
Old Soldiers Never Die   Conrad
Old Straw Hat, An   Gordon; Revel
On a South Sea Isle   Von Tilzer
On a Tropic Night (Noche de Vera Cruz)   Washington

On Rainy Days   Razaf; Waller
On the Bumpy Road to Love   Hoffman
On the Sentimental Side   Burke; Monaco
On the Wings of a Breeze   Washington
Once I Was Young   Hart; Rodgers
Once There Were Two of Us   Gershwin, Ira; Kern
Once to Every Heart   Kahn; Romberg
One Day When We Were Young   Hammerstein
One I Love, The   Kahn
One Indispensable Man, The   Weill
One More Dream   Coots
One of These Fine Days   Rome
One Step Ahead of Love   Porter
One Touch of Alchemy   Weill
Only a Gypsy Knows   Burke; Monaco
Only You   Hammerstein
Opening (Greet Your Candidate)   Hammerstein; Harbach;
    Kern
(Just an) Ordinary Guy   Rome
Oriental Yogi   Rose
Othello (inst)   Rodgers
Our Ancient Liberties   Weill
Our Golden Wedding Day   Edwards
Our Hearts Will Never Grow Old   Mercer; Warren
Our Last Dance   Kern
Our Navy Second to None   Cobb; Edwards
Outside of Paradise   Lawrence
Pagliacci — Prologue   Styne
Pange Rosebud   Bryan
Papa's Rocking Baby on the Dance Floor   Fisher
Paswonky (inst.)   Waller
Patty Cake, Patty Cake (Baker Man)   Razaf; Waller
Peck-A-Doodle-Doo   Mills
Penny for Your Dreams, A   Freed, Ralph
People from Missouri   Gershwin, Ira; Kern
Perhaps   Young, Joseph
Piano Tuner Man   Duke
Piccadilly, The   Johnston
Pickaninny Paradise   Oakland
Picketing the Old Plantation   Coots; Davis
Picture Me in a Picture Hat   Bullock; Spina
Pied Piper of Hamlin Town, The   David, Mack; Livingston,
    Jerry
Plastered in Paris   Mills
Playing Bingo   Blake
PLaza 6-9423   Rome
Please Be Kind   Cahn
Please Come Out of Your Dreams   Sigman
Please Forgive Me   Ellington; Mills
Plymouth Farewell Song (Alma Mater)   Gordon; Revel
Plymouth Rock   Gordon; Revel
Poor Butterfings   Howard, Bart
Poor Loulie Jean   Robison
Prelude to a Kiss   Ellington; Mills
Prologue   Johnson, James P.
Prom Waltz   Rainger; Robin
Promenade, A   Loewe
Pross-Tchai   Cahn
P.S. Forty-Three   Burke; Monaco
Puff-A-Puff   Gordon; Revel
Put That Down in Writing   Dubin; Warren
Put Your Heart Into a Song   Webster
Pyramid   Ellington; Mills
Quainty, Dainty Me   Kalmar; Ruby
Rain on the Pane   Woods

Rainbow Round the Moon   Donaldson; Rose
Recall Goodhue   Porter
Regimental Song   Kahn; Romberg
Rendezvous in Rio   Kahn
Rest   Razaf
Reuben, Reuben I've Been Swingin'   Mitchell; Pollack
Revolutionary March   Hammerstein
Rhumba on the Right   Rome
Rhythmettes   Akst
Ribbons and Roses   Lewis; Meyer
Ride Tenderfoot Ride   Mercer; Whiting
Ridin' on a Blue Note   Ellington
Riding on a Blue Note   Mills
Riff Van Winkle   Raye
Right Guy for Me, The   Coslow; Weill
River God   Porter
River Is Blue, The   Weill
Rockin' the Town   Koehler
Romance and Musketeer   Weill
Romance in the Dark   Coslow; Washington; Young, Joseph; Young, Victor
Romance of Love Is a Waltz, The   Hanley
Rose of St. Martin's Lane   Johnston
Sailing Along   Johnston
Sailing at Midnight   Leslie
Sam the College Leader Man   Donaldson
Saturday Night at the Old Barn Dance   Gilbert
(I've Been) Saving Myself for You   Cahn
Say It with a Kiss   Dubin; Mercer; Warren
Say Something Sentimental   Van Heusen
Says My Heart   Lane; Loesser
Scarlett O'Hara   Coots; Davis
Scars (2), The   Weill
Scrubbing Song   Weill
Send My Mail to the County Jail   Lawrence
Senorita   Kahn; Romberg
September Song   Weill
Serenade for Two   Washington
Serenade to the Stars, A   Adamson; McHugh
Shack in the Back of the Hills, A   Ahlert; Young, Joseph
Shadow Sweetheart   Parish; Van Heusen
Shadows on the Moon   Kahn; Romberg
Shaganola   Fain
Shake Down the Stars   De Lange; Van Heusen
Sha-Sha   Van Heusen
Shenanigans   Lawrence
She's the Sweetheart of the Navy and He's True to the Red, White and Blue   Fisher
Shoot the Rhythm to the One that Wants It   Mills
Shortest Day of the Year, The   Hart; Rodgers
Show Must Go On, The   Kahn
Shrug, The   Akst; Clare
Silence   Howard, Bart
Silhouetted in the Moonlight   Mercer; Whiting
Silly Little Sally   Freed, Ralph
Silver on the Sage   Rainger; Robin
Simple and Sweet   Baer
Since They Turned Loch Lomond into Swing   Berlin
Since You Said Goodbye   Norworth
Sing a Song of Harvest   Mitchell; Pollack
Sing for Your Supper   Hart; Rodgers
Sing You Son-of-a-Gun   Mercer; Whiting
Sissy   Kahal
Sisters Under the Skin   Loewe
Sitting in the Gaol   Weill

Six of One and Half a Dozen of the Other   Adamson; McHugh
Sixty Seconds Got Together   David, Mack; Livingston, Jerry
Skrontch   Ellington; Mills
Sky High   Oakland
Sloe Gin Fizz   Mills
Small Fry   Carmichael; Loesser
Snooky-Cookie   Gilbert
So Big   Donaldson
So Does an Automobile   Heyman
So Help Me If I Don't Love You   De Lange; Van Heusen
Soldier of the Czar   Kahn; Romberg
Soldiers of Fortune (Are We)   Kahn; Romberg
Soldiers Song   Weill
Solid Eclipse   Waller
Something Tells Me   Mercer
Something's Wrong   Gershwin, Ira; Kern
Somewhere There's a Silver Lining   Norworth
Somewhere with Somebody Else   Leslie
Song of Rockwell   Akst; Clare
Song of the Cash Register   Coslow; Weill
Song of the Fisherman (Ay Ay Ay), The   Washington
Song of the Gypsy Band   Akst; Clare
Song of the Lie (What Are You Doing), The   Burke; Weill
Song Without You   Howard, Bart
Sons of the Legion   Freed, Ralph
South Sea Sweetheart   Bryan
Souvenir of Love   Johnston
Speak Your Heart   Magidson; Wrubel
Spider and the Fly (Poor Fly, Bye-Bye), The   Razaf; Waller
Spring Again   Duke; Gershwin, Ira; Weill
Spring Is Here   Hart; Rodgers
Start Cheering   Oakland
Steppin' Into Swing Society   Ellington; Mills
Stolen Heaven   Freed, Ralph
Stop Being So Beautiful   Bullock; Spina
Stranger in Paree, A   Dubin; Warren
Strictly Formal   Mills
Strolling Thru the Park   Fain
Style   Coots; Davis
Summer Souvenirs   Coots
Sun Will Shine Tonight, The   Rose
Sunny Side of Things, The   Webster
Sun-Up to Sundown   Kahn; Romberg
Swami Song (Use Swami Salts)   Lane
Sweet and Tender   Razaf
Sweet as a Rose   Hammerstein; Harbach; Kern
Sweet As a Song   Gordon; Revel
Sweet Dreams   Freed, Ralph; Lane
Sweet Irish Sweetheart of Mine   Lawrence
Sweet Stranger   Ager; Livingston, Jerry
Sweet William   Loewe
Sweeter Than Ever   Freed, Ralph
Sweethearts Again   Magidson; Wrubel
Swing Me an Old Fashioned Song   Bullock; Spina
Swing, Mister Mendelssohn   Kahn
Swingin' in the Corn   Magidson; Wrubel
Swingtime in Honolulu   Ellington; Mills
Take a Dip in the Sea   Clare; Mitchell; Pollack
Take a Tip from a Gypsy   Akst; Clare
Take a Tip from the Tulip   Magidson; Wrubel
Tales from the Vienna Woods   Hammerstein
Tarzan   Fisher
Tea Time   Parish
Tee-Um-Tee-Um Tee-I Tahiti   Johnson, Howard

Tell Me that Story Again   Monaco
Tell Me with Your Kisses   Friend
Tellin' My Troubles to a Mule   Webster; Young, Victor
Ten Easy Lessons   Lane; Loesser
Ten Little Bridesmaids   Norworth
Ten Pins in the Sky   Ager
Thanks for Ev'rything   Gordon; Revel
Thanks for the Memory   Rainger; Robin
Thanks to You Mr. Handy   Coots; Davis
That Certain Age   Adamson; McHugh
That Night in Avalon   Kalmar; Ruby
That Old Feeling   Brown, Lew; Fain
That Week in Paris   Hammerstein; Oakland
That's for Me   Rainger; Robin
That's What I Call Heaven   Howard, Joseph E.
There Had to Be the Waltz   Loewe
There Is No Breeze (Bea Lillie Ballad)   Kern
There is Something About a Kitchen (inst.)   Kern
There'll Come a Time   Hammerstein
There's a Boy in Harlem   Hart; Rodgers
There's a Brand New Picture in My Picture Frame   Friend
There's a Building Boom   Rainger; Robin
There's a Fan   Porter
There's a Happy Hunting Ground   Coslow
There's a Mist on the Mountains This Morning   Dixon;
    Woods
There's a New Moon (Over the Old Mill)   Magidson;
    Wrubel
There's a Sunny Side to Every Situation   Mercer; Warren
There's a Sunny Side to Everything   Coots; Davis
There's a Village in a Valley   Parish; Silver
There's Honey on the Moon Tonight   Coots; David, Mack
There's Nowhere to Go but Up   Weill
There's Rain in My Eyes   Ager; Schwartz, Jean
There's Something about an Old Love   Mills
These Precious Moments   Ager
They Say I Oughta Dance   Cahn
Things Are Coming My Way   Adamson
Think Twice   Bullock; Spina
This Can't Be Love   Hart; Rodgers
This Is a Happy Little Ditty   Bullock; Spina
This Is Madness to Love Like This   De Lange; Van Heusen
This Is My Night to Dream   Burke; Monaco
This Is My Song   Howard, Bart; Kahn
This Is the Night   Lawrence
This Is Where I Came In   Bullock; Spina
This Little Ripple Had Rhythm (Mr. Ripple's
    Animation)   Rainger; Robin
This May Be the Night   Gordon; Revel
This Never Happened Before   Adamson; McHugh
This Time of the Year   Washington
Those Eyes You're Wearing   Lane; Loesser
Though Tongues May Wag   Loewe
Three Cheers for Henry Smith   Gordon; Revel
Throw a Little Party   Rose
To Do What We Like   Johnson, James P.
To Make It Short and Sweet, I Love You   Ager; Davis; Silver
To Swing or Not to Swing   Davis
To War!   Weill
To Whom It May Concern   Loewe
Tomorrow   Porter
Tonight We Love   Rainger; Robin
Tonight Will Live (Oracion Caribe)   Washington
Toscanini, Stokowski and Me   Bullock; Spina
Toy Trumpet   Brown, Lew; Mitchell; Pollack

Travellin' Down the Trail Back Home   Mills
Tribute (inst.)   Alter
Trumpet Player's Lament, The   Burke; Monaco
Trusting My Luck   Johnston
Try an Experiment (inst.)   Kern
Tuli-Tulip Time   Lawrence
Twelve Little Cuties   Kalmar; Ruby
Twelve O'Clock and All's Not Well   Oakland
Twinkle in Your Eye, A   Hart; Rodgers
Two Dreams Got Together   Friend
Two Silhouettes (In the Setting Sun)   Coslow
Two Sleepy People   Carmichael; Loesser
Under the Midnight Sun   Coslow; Lane
Under the Moon of Waikiki   Bryan
Undercurrent (inst.)   Waller
Unknown   David, Mack
U.S.A. and You, The   Rainger; Robin
Ve Vouldn't Gonto Do It   Weill
Victory Song   Oakland
Vigoroso in D Flat (inst.)   Kern
Virginia Hoe Down   Hammerstein; Harbach; Kern
Vite, Vite, Vite   Porter
Wait Until My Heart Finds Out   Cahn
Walking My Baby Back Home   Johnson, James P.
Walking on the Sea (inst.)   Kern
Waltz Lives On, The   Rainger; Robin
Waltz of the Flowers   Mercer; Warren
Washington Irving's Song   Weill
Watching   Mills
Watching the Ships Go By   David, Mack
We Are Cut in Twain   Weill
We Drink to You, J.H. Brody   Porter
We Should Be Together   Bullock; Spina
We, the People   Razaf
We Want Sweetheart Security   Baer; Lewis
We Want to Make the Laws   Weill
Wedding Song   Weill
Week End of a Private Secretary, The   Mercer
Weep and You Dance Alone   Johnston
We're the Kind of People Who Sing Lullabies   Burke; Weill
We're Two Together   Coots
West Ain't Wild Any More, The   Kahn; Romberg
West Point Hop, The   Myrow
We've Got the Song   Rome
What a Pretty Miss   Waller
What a Priceless Pleasure   Porter
What a Rumba Does to Romance   Loesser
What Can I Do for You   Heyman
What Can You Do with a Man?   Hart; Rodgers
What Did Romeo Say to Juliet   Lane; Loesser
What Do You Hear from the Mob in Scotland   Cahn
What Do You Know about Love?   Gordon; Revel
What Goes on Here (In My Heart)   Rainger; Robin
What Have You Got That Gets Me   Rainger; Robin
What Is That Tune?   Porter
What Kind of Soldier Are You?   Hammerstein; Harbach;
    Kern
What Shall I Do?   Porter
What This Country Needs Is a Song   Cohan
What Will I Do in the Morning   Waller
What's Good about Good-Night?   Fields; Kern
What's Your Name   Waller
When a Cowboy Sings a Song   Lawrence
When a Glow Worm Gets a Gleam in His Eye   Hanley
When a Prince of a Fella Meets a Cinderella   Van Heusen

When Father Was a Boy   Fisher
When I Catch Con Carney   Fisher
When I Truck on Down   Oakland
When It's All Said and Done   Porter
When It's Blossom Time in Yakima Valley   Lawrence
When It's Hog Callin' Time in the Valley   Magidson; Wrubel
When McGregor Sings Off Key   Fain
When My Baby Talks that Double-Talk to Me   Coots
When the Bells of St. Mary's Answer the Bells of St. James   Mills
When the Cat's Away   Hanley
When the Hen Stops Laying   Porter
When the Stars Go to Sleep   Adamson; McHugh
When the Sun Sets Down South   Sissle
When You Got Love   Hanley
When You Hear that Humming   Harbach; Kern
When You Look in Your Looking Glass   Lewis
When You're Away (inst.)   Warren
When You're in the Room   Hammerstein; Oakland
When Za-za Does the Can-Can   Freed, Ralph
Where Are You Little Boy Blue   Edwards
Where Have We Met Before   Parish
Where in the World?   Gordon; Revel
Where Is Central Park?   Burke; Monaco
Where the Dog Sits on the Tucker Box Five Miles from Gundagei   Gilbert
Where's the Girl?   Kahn; Romberg
White Clouds   Blake
Who Are We to Say (Obey Your Heart)   Kahn; Romberg
Who Are We Today   Romberg
Who Blew Out the Flame   Fain; Parish
Who Did It — You Did It   Magidson; Wrubel
Who Do You Think I Saw Last Night   Friend
Who Done It   Lawrence
Who Killed Maggie?   Adamson; McHugh
Who Stole the Jam?   Bullock; Spina
Who'll Tie the Bell on the Old Cat's Tail   Coots
Why? Because!   Kalmar; Ruby
Why Can't This Night Last Forever?   Loewe
Why Do the Boys Love the Married Women   Fisher
Why Do You Make Me Love You   Donaldson
Why Must I Love You   Magidson; Wrubel
Why Not String Along with Me   Brown, Lew; Pollack
Why'dya Make Me Fall in Love   Donaldson
Wigwammin'   Mills
Wild Wedding Bells   Porter
Will You Remember Me?   Weill
Will You Remember Tonight Tomorrow   Friend
Wind in the Trees, The   Kahn; Romberg
Wings on High   Willson
Winter Wedding Bells   Bryan
With You on My Mind   Brown, Lew; Pollack
Women Are Women   Hart; Rodgers
Work While You May (Bulgarian Rose Song)   Rainger
World Began with You, The   Washington; Young, Joseph; Young, Victor
World Is Ours Tonight, The   Kahn; Romberg
Wrap Your Cares in Rhythm   Cahn
Y' Had It Comin' to You   Lerner, Sammy
Yam, The   Berlin
Yancey Special   Razaf
Yes, Yes, Yes   Porter
Yip! Ahoy! (Adrift on the Lo-one Prairie!)   Rome
Yonny and His Oompah   Yellen
You Ain't Got Time for Love   Johnston

You and Me   Coslow; Freed, Ralph; Weill
You Appeal to Me   Bullock; Spina
You Are My Melody   Johnston
You Are the Music to the Words in My Heart   Yellen
You Better Keep Babying Baby   Dubin
You Can Be My Cave Man   Berlin
You Can Read Me Like a Book   Van Heusen
You Can't Get Something for Nothing   Coslow; Weill
You Couldn't Be Cuter   Fields; Kern
You Go to My Head   Coots
You Have Cast Your Shadow on the Sea   Hart; Rodgers
You Hold My Heart in the Hollow of Your Hand   Brennan
You Leave Me Breathless   Freed, Ralph
You Little Rascal (inst.)   Warren
You Look Good to Me   Donaldson; Rose
You Make Me That Way   Akst; Clare
You Must Have Been a Beautiful Baby   Mercer; Warren
You Never Know   Porter
You Ought to See Suzy Now   Fisher
You Took the Words Right Out of My Heart   Rainger; Robin
You Will Lose Your Heart in Honolulu   Brown, Nacio Herb; Freed, Arthur
You, You, You   Johnson, James P.
Young People Think about Love   Weill
Your Dream (Is the Same as My Dream)   Hammerstein; Harbach; Kern
Your Heart Skips a Beat   Johnston
You're a Blessing to Me   Rainger; Robin
You're a Natural   Loesser
You're a Sweet Little Headache   Rainger; Robin
You're a Sweetheart   Adamson; McHugh
You're an Education   Dubin; Warren
You're Gonna See a Lot of Ma   Hoffman
You're Like a Song   Adamson; McHugh
You're Lovely, Madame   Rainger; Robin
You're My Dish   Adamson; McHugh
You're My Ideal   Waller
You're Something New Under the Sun   Raye
You're Stepping on My Toes   Hoffman
You're the Apple of My Eye (You Little Peach)   Magidson; Wrubel
You're the Very Last Word in Love   Leslie
You're the World's Fairest   Gordon; Revel
Yours, All Yours   Mitchell; Stept
Zing, Zing Go the Tambourines   Burke; Monaco

1939

A Francesa   Johnson, Howard
Adeste Fidelis   Johnson, Howard
After the Rain   Freed, Ralph
After We Say Goodnight   Davis
Afterwards   Johnson, Howard
Ain't Cha Comin' Out?   Kalmar; Ruby
Alice Where Art Thou   Johnson, Howard
All Aboard for Georgia   Razaf
All I Remember Is You   De Lange; Van Heusen
All in Favor Say 'Aye'   Friend
All in Fun   Hammerstein; Kern
All the Things You Are   Hammerstein; Kern
All the Time   Fields; Schwartz, Arthur
All Those in Favor of Swing Say Aye   Davis
All's Well   Rainger; Robin
Almost   Lerner, Sammy; Oakland
Aloha Oe   Johnson, Howard

Always Take Mother's Advice   Johnson, Howard
Amber Threads Tied in Blue   Johnson, Howard
American Humoresque (inst.)   Romberg
Among the Lillies   Johnson, Howard
And the Angels Sing   Mercer
Andantino   Johnson, Howard
Angelina Baker   Johnson, Howard
Anita (inst.)   Waller
Annie Laurie   Johnson, Howard
Answer Is Love, The   Stept
Any Old Dream in a Storm   Blane
Apple Blossoms and Chapel Bells   Hoffman
Apple for the Teacher, An   Burke; Monaco
Arbor Day   Clare
Are You Angry with Me Darling   Johnson, Howard
Are You in the Mood for Mischief   Gordon; Revel
Arioso   Johnson, Howard
As of Today   Fields; Schwartz, Arthur
Ask Your Heart   Davis
Asleep or Awake   Lawrence
At a Little Hot Dog Stand   Coslow
Audition   Hammerstein; Kern
Auld Lang Syne   Johnson, Howard
Aura Lee   Johnson, Howard
Ave Maria   Johnson, Howard
Baa, Baa Black Sheep   Johnson, Howard
'Baby Wampus' Stars, The   Brown, Lew; Stept
Baby's Asleep   Heyman; Romberg
Back to Back   Berlin
Bambuco   Mills
Band Played On, The   Johnson, Howard
Basket Weaver Man   Donaldson
Bavarian Yodel   Johnson, Howard
Beautiful Buxom Barmaid   Coslow
Beautiful Dreamer   Johnson, Howard
Beautiful Isle of the Sea   Johnson, Howard
Beautiful Romance   Ellington
Beautiful Ulalee   Bryan
Beer Barrel Polka, The   Brown, Lew
Begin the Beguine   Porter
Believe Me If All those Endearing Young Charms   Johnson, Howard
Ben Bolt   Johnson, Howard
Bend Your Knee and Tie My Shoe   Duke
Best Years of My Life, The   Bullock; Spina
Between Two Fires   Adamson; Johnston
Between You and Me   Porter
Beyond the Moon   Rainger; Robin
Bill Bailey Won't You Please Come Home   Johnson, Howard
Billy Boy   Johnson, Howard
Billy Boy — Billy Boy   Lawrence
Bird in the Hand Is Worth Two in the Bush, A   Razaf
Birth of a Snowbird   Webster; Young, Victor
Blame It on Chichita   Lerner, Alan Jay
Blame It on My Last Affair   Mills
Blow Me Down   Rainger; Robin
Blue Algerian Skies   Razaf
Blue and Disillusioned   Coots; Davis
Blue Bouquet   Mills
Blue Danube   Johnson, Howard
Blue Dawn   Adamson
Blue Italian Waters   Webster
Blue Nightfall   Lane; Loesser
Blue Orchids   Carmichael
Blue Rain   Mercer; Van Heusen

Blue September   Friend
Bluebirds in the Moonlight   Rainger; Robin
Bobotchka   Rainger; Robin
Bonjour Goodbye   Duke
Bonnie Eloise   Johnson, Howard
Bowery, The   Johnson, Howard
Boy Meets Horn   Ellington; Mills
Boy Named Lem (and a Girl Named Sue)   Brown, Lew; Stept
Boys in the Backroom, The   Loesser
Bridal Chorus   Johnson, Howard
Broadway Serenade   Kahn
Broken Guitar, A   Gorney; Harburg
Bubbles in the Wine   Loesser
Buffalo Gals   Johnson, Howard
Burlesque (inst.)   Rome
Bury Me Beneath the Willow   Johnson, Howard
Busy As a Bee, I'm Buzz, Buzz, Buzzin'   Sigman
But in the Morning, No   Porter
But It Didn't Mean a Thing   David, Mack; Livingston, Jerry
By Killarney's Lakes and Falls   Johnson, Howard
By the Blue Alsatian Mountains   Johnson, Howard
California   Eliscu
Call Me Thine Own   Johnson, Howard
Calling All Lovers   Kahn
Calvary   Johnson, Howard
Can I Help It?   De Lange; Van Heusen
Cancion de Cuba (Starland)   Freed, Ralph
Carry Me Back to Old Virginny   Johnson, Howard
Catherine the Great   Brown, Lew; Stept
'Cause We Got Cake   Hart; Rodgers
Celesete Aida   Johnson, Howard
Cheerio   Rainger; Robin
Choo Choo   Razaf; Waller
Chopsticks   Lawrence
Ciribiribin   Lawrence
Class Will Tell   Leslie
Colorado Sunset   Conrad; Gilbert
Come Back to Erin   Johnson, Howard
Come Back to Sorrento   Johnson, Howard
Come on In   Porter
Come to the Sea   Johnson, Howard
Come Where My Love Lies Dreaming   Johnson, Howard
Come Where the Lillies Bloom   Johnson, Howard
Comes Love   Brown, Lew; Stept
Comin' Thru the Rye   Johnson, Howard
Comrades Fill No Glass for Me   Johnson, Howard
Concert in the Park   Friend
Confucius Say   Friend
Corn Pickin'   Mercer; Warren
Crying in My Dreams for You   Robison
Cuckoo in the Clock   Donaldson; Mercer
Curtains of Night, The   Johnson, Howard
Cynthia   Donaldson
Daisy Bell   Johnson, Howard
Dance of the Waitresses   Duke
Dancing on the Stars   Ellington; Mills
Danger in the Dark   Dubin; McHugh
Danger Men Blasting   Raye
Danse Erotique   Porter
Danse Tzigane   Porter
Danse Victoire   Porter
Darling Nellie Gray   Johnson, Howard
Darn that Dream   De Lange; Van Heusen
Daughter of Mademoiselle, The   Akst; Clare

Dawn of a New Day   Gershwin, George; Gershwin, Ira
Day In — Day Out   Bloom; Mercer
De Camp Town Races   Johnson, Howard
Deanna   Adamson; McHugh
Deep in the Shadows   Adamson; Duke
Deep Purple   Parish
Der Deitcher's Dog (Where, O Where Has My Little Dog
      Gone)   Johnson, Howard
Ding-Dong! The Witch Is Dead   Arlen; Harburg
Do I Know what I'm Doing   Lawrence
Do I Love You?   Porter
Do You Remember?   Kalmar; Ruby
Doin' the 1940   Lerner, Sammy; Oakland
Doin' the Chamberlain   Dubin; McHugh
Doin' the Socialite   Akst; Clare
Doing the Saboo   De Lange; Van Heusen
Dolly Doolittle   Bryan
Donald Duck   Washington
Don't Change Your Heart in the Middle of a
      Dream   Lawrence
Don't Cry Little Cloud   Lane; Loesser
Don't Forget the Sailor Lad   Fisher
Don't Worry 'Bout Me   Bloom; Koehler
Down de Curtains of Night   Johnson, Howard
Down de Road   Johnson, Howard
Down Home Rag (Deeten Datten Dooten)   Brown, Lew
Down in a Coal Mine   Johnson, Howard
Down Moonlight Lane   Bullock; Spina
Dr. Hackenbush   Kalmar; Ruby
Dream Clouds   Egan
Dream Faces   Johnson, Howard
Dream Sequence   Bullock
Dream Serenade   Bryan
Dream Shadows   Adamson
Dream Song   Porter
Dreamy Kalua   Parish
Drifting Down the River of Dreams   Lawrence
Drink from the Cup of Tomorrow   Bullock
Drink to Me Only with Thine Eyes   Johnson, Howard; Mills
Drinking Song   Johnson, Howard
Du Barry Was a Lady   Porter
Dunes of Doorma, The   Rainger; Robin
Dusty Trails   Heyman
Early Mornin' Blues   Razaf
East Side of Heaven   Burke; Monaco
Echoes of Hawaii   Mitchell; Pollack
El Choclo   Johnson, Howard
El Huapango   Loesser
Ellen Bayne   Johnson, Howard
Emmett's Lullaby   Johnson, Howard
Eternally Yours   Gilbert
Evening Star   Johnson, Howard
Everyone Knows It but You   Coslow; Johnston
Ev'ry Day a Holiday   Porter
Eyes of Thee I'm Fondly Dreaming   Johnson, Howard
Face in the Crowd, A   Alter; Webster
Faithful   Rainger; Robin
Faithful Forever   Rainger; Robin
Farmer in the Dell, The   Johnson, Howard
Father Mountain   Razaf
Fidgety Joe   Loesser
Fifteen Kisses on a Gallon of Gas   David, Mack; Livingston,
      Jerry
Fight on for Madison   Loesser; Young, Victor
Fisherman's Chanty   Young, Victor

Fit to Be Tied   Donaldson
Flea Flew in My Flute, A   Loesser
Floogie Walk   Bloom; Koehler
Florida Flo   Johnson, Howard
Flow, Flow White Wine   Kahn
Flow Gently Sweet Afton   Johnson, Howard
Flower to Me Thou Seemest, A   Johnson, Howard
Flowers That Bloom in the Spring, The   Johnson, Howard
Flying Home   De Lange; Van Heusen
Follow My Footsteps   Woods
Follow the Yellow Brick Road   Arlen; Harburg
Fool and His Money Are Soon Parted, A   Lawrence
For Dancers Only   Raye
For He's a Jolly Good Fellow   Johnson, Howard
For the Sake of Lexington   Brown, Lew; Stept
Forever   Rainger; Robin
Forget Me   Loesser
Forsaken   Johnson, Howard
413   Blane
Fragrant Night   Alter; Loesser
French Have a Word for It, The   Rome
Friendship   Porter
From Me to You   Lerner, Alan Jay
Gabby's Exploits   Rainger; Robin
Gal from Joe's   Ellington; Mills
Gal that Used to Do the Hootchy Kootchy   Baer; Lewis
Gates of Emerald City   Arlen; Harburg
Gavotte   Porter
Georgia   Razaf
Ghost of Smokey Joe, The   Bloom; Koehler
Girl Behind the Venetian Blind, The   Friend
Girl I Left Behind Me, The   Johnson, Howard
Girl with the Pigtails in Her Hair   Cahn
Give Him the Oo-La-La   Porter
Give It Back to the Indians   Hart; Rodgers
Glad to See You Again   Johnson, James P.
Go Fly a Kite   Burke; Monaco
Go In and Out the Window   Bullock; Pollack
(He's) Goin' Home   Fields; Schwartz, Arthur
Golden Wedding Song   Burke; Monaco
Gonna Have Lassies in the Mornin'   Johnson, Howard
Goo   Hoffman
Good Morning   Brown, Nacio Herb; Freed, Arthur
Good Night Ladies   Johnson, Howard
Good Night, My Beautiful   Ager; Fain; Yellen
Good Night Sweetheart   Johnson, Howard
Goodbye Sweetheart Goodbye   Johnson, Howard
Got No Time   Bloom; Cahn; Koehler
Gotta Get Home (The Train Song)   Hanley
Gotta Get Some Shut-Eye   Donaldson; Mercer
Grandfather's Clock   Johnson, Howard
Grandma Said   Magidson; Wrubel
Greatest Show on Earth, The   Rose
Grievin'   Ellington
Guess I'll Go Back Home This Summer   Robison
Habanera   Johnson, Howard
Hail to Colby   Snyder
Hail Yale '29   Rome
Hang Your Heart on a Hickory Limb   Burke; Monaco
Hark Hark the Lark   Johnson, Howard
Harp That Once Thro' Tara's Halls, The   Johnson, Howard
Hat Like That, A   Ager; Fain; Yellen
Have You Forgotten So Soon   Coslow; Heyman; Silver
Hawaii Sang Me to Sleep   Loesser
He Died of Love   Loesser

Heart Bowed Down, The   Johnson, Howard
Heart of Mine   Freed, Ralph
Heaven Can Wait   De Lange; Van Heusen
Heaven in My Arms (Music in My Heart)   Hammerstein;
    Kern
Heav'n Heav'n   Johnson, Howard
Hedge Rose   Johnson, Howard
Hello, My Darling   Loesser
Here Comes the Night   Loesser
Here's a Heart   Loesser; Young, Victor
Here's to Love   Freed, Ralph; Lane
Heroes in the Fall   Rodgers
Hey, Good Lookin'   Loesser
High School Cadets   Freed, Ralph
High Up in Harlem   Hammerstein; Kern
Hinky Dinky Parlee Voo   Johnson, Howard
History Is Made at Night   Rome
Hitler und Goering und Goebbels und Schacht   Gorney;
    Harburg
Hoiriger Schottische   Coslow
Hollywood and Vine   Brown, Lew; Stept
Holy Smoke, Can't You Take a Joke   Mercer
Home Again   Lerner, Alan Jay
Home Bound   Razaf
Home Made Heaven   Lerner, Alan Jay
Home on the Range   Johnson, Howard
Home Sweet Home   Johnson, Howard
Honey Hush   Waller
Hong Kong Blues   Carmichael
Honolulu   Kahn; Warren
Hooray for Spinach   Mercer; Warren
Horse and Buggy Ride   Kalmar; Ruby
Hot Tamale Man   Mills
Hot Tamales   Kalmar; Ruby
How Can I Leave Thee   Johnson, Howard
How Lovely You Are   Washington
How Strange   Kahn
How Warm It Is the Weather (How Cold It Is Your
    Heart)   Blane
Howdy Cloudy Morning   Dixon; Woods
Hoy, Hoy, Hoy   Cahn
Humpty Dumpty   Johnson, Howard
Hungry Blues   Johnson, James P.
Hunted Stag, The   Hart; Rodgers
I Be Gwine Back to Dixie   Johnson, Howard
I Cannot Sing the Old Songs   Johnson, Howard
I Can't Afford to Dream   Brown, Lew; Stept
I Can't Imagine   Freed, Ralph; Lane
I Can't Throw the Old Dreams Away   Hanley
I Cling to You   Duke
I Concentrate on You   Porter
I Cried for You (Now It's Your Turn to Cry Over
    Me)   Freed, Arthur
I Did It for the Red, White and Blue   Bloom; Mercer
I Didn't Know what Time It Was   Hart; Rodgers
I Don't Believe in Signs   Mercer; Warren
I Don't Want to Play in Your Yard   Johnson, Howard
I Dream of You   Lerner, Alan Jay
I Found My Love   Loesser
I Gave My Heart Away   Adamson; McHugh
I Get that Cold Shoulder from You   Lerner, Sammy;
    Mitchell; Pollack
I Go for That   Loesser
I Happen to Be in Love   Porter
I Have My Arms Around the World   Burke; Warren

I Hear a Dream (Come Home Again)   Rainger; Robin
I Kinda Dream   Loesser
I Know I'm Nobody   Brown, Lew; Stept
I Know Something I Won't Tell   Adamson; Donaldson
I Know What Aloha Means   Rainger; Robin
I Like to Recognize the Tune   Hart; Rodgers
I Love Thee   Johnson, Howard
I Love to Ride on a Choo Choo Train   Baer
I Must Have One More Kiss Kiss Kiss   Hoffman
I Must Love Someone   David, Mack; Livingston, Jerry
I Must See Annie Tonight   Friend
I Never Knew Heaven Could Speak   Gordon; Revel
I Never Thought I'd Fall in Love Again   Freed, Ralph; Lane
I Paid for the Lie I Told You   Hoffman
I Poured My Heart Into a Song   Berlin
I Should've Stood in Bed   Rainger; Robin
I Thought About You   Mercer; Van Heusen
I Want My Share of Love   Cahn
I Want to Be a Hill-billy Bride   Hanley
I Was Afraid of That   Rainger; Robin
I'd Give a Million Tomorrows (For Just One
    Yesterday)   Livingston, Jerry
If Ever a Heart Was in the Right Place, It's Yours   Woods
If I Didn't Dare   Lawrence
If I Feel This Way Tomorrow   Brown, Lew; Henderson
If I Only Had a Brain   Arlen; Harburg
If I Only Had a Heart   Arlen; Harburg
If I Only Had the Nerve   Arlen; Harburg
If I Were King of the Forest   Arlen; Harburg
If I Were Sure of You   Bloom; Koehler
If Love Were What the Rose Is   Johnson, Howard
If What You Say Is True   Gordon
I'll Pay the Check   Fields; Schwartz, Arthur
I'll Put the Blue Back in Your Eyes   Bryan; Meyer
I'll Remember   Freed, Ralph; Lane
I'll Sing Thee Songs of Araby   Johnson, Howard
I'll Supply the Title, You Supply the Tune   Arlen; Gershwin,
    Ira
I'll Swing for This   Cahn
I'll Take You Home Again Kathleen   Johnson, Howard
I'm Afraid of You   Freed, Ralph
I'm All A-Tremble Over You   Loesser
I'm Always Chasing Rainbows   Johnson, Howard
I'm Building a Sailboat of Dreams   Friend
I'm Checking Out — Goom Bye   Ellington
I'm Going Down to Dance at Clancey's   Conrad; Magidson
I'm Happy about the Whole Thing   Mercer; Warren
I'm in Another World   Ellington; Mills
I'm in Love with a Jitterbug   Burke; Monaco
I'm in Love with the Honorable Mr. So and So   Coslow
I'm Like a Bird (French Gergerette)   Adamson
I'm Longing for My Carolina Home   Fisher
I'm Never in Tune with You   Woods
I'm So in Love with You   Porter
I'm Sorry for Myself   Berlin
I'm Takin' My Time with You   Ahlert
I'm the Captain of the Pinafore   Johnson, Howard
I'm the Stupidest Girl in the Class   Loesser
I'm Thrilled   DePaul
I'm Throwing Good Love After Bad   Caesar
Imagination   Burke; Van Heusen
In a Moment of Weakness   Mercer; Warren
In an Eighteenth Century Drawing Room   Lawrence
In an Old Dutch Garden (By an Old Dutch Mill)   Gordon
In My Memoirs   Dubin; McHugh

In Old Madrid   Johnson, Howard
In Other Words, Seventeen   Hammerstein; Kern
In Our Little Part of Town   Hanley
In the Big Money   Porter
In the Evening By the Moonlight, Dear Louise   Johnson, Howard
In the Gloaming   Johnson, Howard
In the Heart of the Dark   Hammerstein; Kern
In the Land of Happy People   Hanley
In the Mood   Razaf
In Waikiki   Ager; Fain; Yellen
Indian Summer   Dubin; Herbert
Invitation to Happiness   Loesser
Is It Possible?   Dubin; McHugh
It Ain't Etiquette   Porter
It Ain't Gonna Rain No Mo'   Johnson, Howard
It Can't Be Done   Fisher
It Happened at the Fair   Mills; Myrow
It Happened in Miami   Rose
It Must Have Been Two Other People   Lawrence
It Seems Like Old Times   Stept
It Twas Not So To Be   Johnson, Howard
It Was Written in the Stars   Porter
Italian Village (inst.)   Ruby
It's a Dog's Life   Adamson; McHugh
It's a Me O Lord   Johnson, Howard
It's a Whole New Thing   Monaco
It's a Wonderful World   Adamson
It's All Yours   Fields; Schwartz, Arthur
It's Easy to Blame the Weather   Cahn
It's Funny to Everyone but Me   Lawrence
It's Grand   Lane; Loesser
It's Me Again   Brown, Lew; Stept
It's My Turn Now   Cahn
It's the Tune that Counts   Raye
It's You Who Taught It to Me   Razaf
I've Gone Off the Deep End   Rainger; Robin
I've Got a Sneaky Feelin'   Baer
I've Got My Eyes on You   Porter
I've Got the Beer Barrel Polka Blues   Brown, Lew
I've Taken a Fancy to You   Clare; Pollack
Jack and Jill   Johnson, Howard
Jean the Campus Queen   Coots
Jersey Bull Blues   Fisher
Jingle Bells   Johnson, Howard
Jitterbug, The   Arlen; Harburg
Jitterbug Jamboree   Bloom; Koehler
Juanita   Johnson, Howard
Jumpin' at the Woodside   De Lange; Van Heusen
Junior   Lane; Loesser
Just a Little Bit More   Fields; Schwartz, Arthur
Just an Old Lady   Fisher
Just for a Thrill   Raye
Just for Awhile   Cahn
Just Tell Them That You Saw Me   Johnson, Howard
Katie Went to Haiti   Porter
Kentucky Colonel Song   Mills
Kicking Over the Traces   Woods
Kinda Lonesome   Carmichael; Coslow; Robin
Kiss and Remember   Bryan
Kiss Me with Your Eyes   Lane; Loesser
La Cucaracha   Johnson, Howard
La Paloma   Johnson, Howard
Lady Needs a Change, The   Fields; Schwartz, Arthur
Lady of Tomorrow   Rose

Lady on the Cameo   Hoffman
Lady's in Love with You, The   Lane; Loesser
Lamp Is Low, The   Parish
L'Apres Midi d'Un Boeuf   Porter
Last Night a Miracle Happened   Lawrence
Last Rose of Summer, The   Johnson, Howard
Last Two Weeks in July, The   Baer; Lewis
Laugh It Off   Lerner, Sammy; Oakland
Leader Doesn't Like Music, The   Kahn; Warren
Leaders Digest   Cahn
Legionnaire's Song, The   Loesser
Let a Man who Knows How Show You How   Adamson; Donaldson
Let It Rain Let It Pour!   Gershwin, Ira
Let Me Fool Myself   Brown, Lew; Pollack
Let's All Go Dancing in Our Stocking Feet   Robison
Let's Disappear   Cahn
Let's Hit the Nail on the Head   Arlen; Koehler
Let's Make Memories Tonight   Brown, Lew; Stept
Let's Say Good Night to the Ladies and We'll Come Right Back Again   Brown, Lew
Let's Start Where We Left Off   Clare; Styne
Let's Stay Over Here   Howard, Joseph E.
L'Histoire de Madame de la Tour   Hammerstein; Kern
Lieber Augustin   Johnson, Howard
Lilacs in the Rain   Parish
Lisette   Duke
Listen to My Heart   Silver
Listen to the Mocking Bird   Johnson, Howard
Little Annie Rooney   Johnson, Howard
Little Bits and Pieces of an Old Romance   Adamson; Johnston
Little Bo-Peep   Johnson, Howard
Little Boy Blue   Johnson, Howard
Little Brown Jug   Johnson, Howard
Little Jack Horner   Johnson, Howard
Little Jitterbug   Cahn
Little Joe, the Wrangler   Loesser
Little Things that Mean So Much, The   Adamson
Loch Lomond   Johnson, Howard
Lola's Song   Johnson, Howard
Lonely Co-Ed   Ellington; Leslie
Lonesome Walls   Kern
Look at Things the Way I Do   Mills
Look Out   Hart; Rodgers
Lorelei, The   Johnson, Howard
Lost — A Man's Best Pal   Gilbert
Lost Chord, The   Johnson, Howard
Lottery Blues   Lerner, Alan Jay
Love Fell In   Blane
Love Is Ridin' the Range Tonight   DeSylva
Love Is Such a Cheat   Caesar
Love Letter, A   Loesser
Love Makes Up for Everything   Hoffman
Love Never Went to College   Hart; Rodgers
Love Told a Terrible Lie   Burke; Warren
Love with a Capital "You"   Loesser
Lovely Flowers   Johnson, Howard
Love's a Riddle   De Lange; Van Heusen
Love's Got Me Down Again   Cahn
Lucille   Razaf
Lullaby   Johnson, Howard
Lullaby to a Landlord (inst.)   Rome
Lulu Is Our Darling Pride   Johnson, Howard
Lydia, the Tattooed Lady   Arlen; Harburg

Magic of Your Love, The   Kahn
Maid of the Mist   Carmichael
Make with the Kisses   Mercer; Van Heusen
Man About Town   Loesser
Man and His Dream, A   Burke; Monaco
Many Dreams Ago   Ahlert
March of the Owls   Heyman; Romberg
Mary Had a Little Lamb   Johnson, Howard
Massa's in de Cold Ground   Johnson, Howard
May Tells All   Hammerstein; Kern
Mayor of Harlem, The   Bloom; Koehler
Me and the Role and You   Hammerstein; Kern
Melancholy Lullaby   Heyman
Merry Minstrel Men   Bullock
Merry Old Land of Oz (Renovation Sequence), The   Arlen;
   Harburg
Merry Widow Waltz   Johnson, Howard
Mesdames and Messieurs   Porter
Methus'lah   Mills
Mexiconga, The   Ager; Fain; Magidson; Yellen
Miami, the Moonlight and You   Friend
Midnight   Freed, Ralph
Mile After Mile   Weill
Minuet for Milady, A   Burke; Monaco
Miracle at Midnight   Mills
Moment with You, A   Duke; Gordon
Monkeys Have No Tails in Pago Pago   Raye
Moon Is a Silver Dollar, The   Fain; Parish
Moon Love   David, Mack
Moonland   De Lange; Van Heusen
Moonlight Serenade   Parish
Moonrise   Adamson
More I See You the More I Love You, The   Hoffman;
   Lerner, Sammy
Mother   Johnson, Howard
Mr. and Mrs. America   Henderson; Webster
Mule Walk (inst.)   Johnson, James P.
Munchkinland   Arlen; Harburg
Music on the Shore   Loesser
My Dream and I   Oakland
My Dreams and I   Lerner, Sammy
My Hands Are Tied   Stept
My Heart at Thy Sweet Voice   Johnson, Howard
My Heart Is a Gypsy   Kahn
My Lady   Bullock; Johnson, Howard
My Love for You   Heyman
My Nelly's Blue Eyes   Johnson, Howard
My Old Dutch   Johnson, Howard
My Own True Love   David, Mack
My Prince (What a Prince!)   Hart; Rodgers
My Son, My Son   Gilbert; Pollack
Name It and It's Yours   Fain; Parish; Silver
Nearness of You, The   Carmichael
Nelly Was a Lady   Johnson, Howard
Never a Dull Moment   Fields; Schwartz, Arthur
New Moon and an Old Serenade   Coslow; Silver
Nice Goin'   Rainger; Robin
Nicknames   Hoffman
No Go   Donaldson
No One to Blame but Myself   Donaldson; Parish
No Star Is Lost   Fisher
No Time to Argue   Kahn; Romberg
Nobody Knows the Trouble I've Had   Johnson, Howard
None but the Lonely Heart   Johnson, Howard
North and South Dakota Moon   Conrad; Magidson

Now the Day Is Over   Johnson, Howard
O Charlie Is My Darling   Johnson, Howard
Oft in the Stilly Night   Johnson, Howard
Oh Bury Me Not on the Lone Prairie   Johnson, Howard
Oh Susanna   Johnson, Howard
Oh! You Crazy Moon   Burke; Van Heusen
Oh, You Mississippi   Lane; Loesser
Okay for Sound   Fields; Schwartz, Arthur
Old Black Joe   Johnson, Howard
Old Fashioned Love   Loesser
Old Fashioned Tune Always Is New, An   Berlin
Old Gray Mare, The   Johnson, Howard
Old Hundred   Johnson, Howard
Old Man Mose Ain't Dead   Cahn
Old Mill Wheel   Ager; Davis; Yellen
Old Oaken Bucket, The   Johnson, Howard
Old Old Castle in Scotland, An   Magidson; Oakland
Old Tin Can, The   Baer; Lewis
On a Night Like This   Koehler
On Bubbling-Well Road, in Old Shanghai   Hanley
(Love for Two) On the Isle of Taboo   Mills
On the Rancho with My Pancho   Akst; Clare
Once More   Brennan
One Brief Moment   Fields; Schwartz, Arthur
One Little Drink to You   Kahn
Only Once   Woods
Only When You're in My Arms   Conrad; Kalmar; Ruby
Opera, Pyramus and Thisbe, The   De Lange; Van Heusen
Optimistic Voices   Arlen; Harburg
Our First Kiss   Ager; Fain; Yellen
Over the Rainbow   Arlen; Harburg
Pagan Love Song   Johnson, Howard
Palms, The   Johnson, Howard
Pancho Gonzales Etcetra the Gaucho   Freed, Ralph
Pandemonium   Sigman
Papa's Got a Job   Rome
Pappy's Little Jug   Kahal
Parade of the Little White Mice   Lawrence
Park Avenue Gimp   Loesser
Passing By   Johnson, Howard
Peace, Brother!   De Lange; Van Heusen
Peach Tree Street   Razaf
Penthouse Promenade (inst.)   Rome
Petty Girl Routine   Loesser
Pick a Rib   De Lange; Van Heusen
Piggy Wiggy Woo   Baer
Places, Everybody   Fields; Schwartz, Arthur
Please Don't Monkey with Broadway   Porter
Polka Dots and Moonbeams   Burke; Van Heusen
Polly Wolly Doodle   Johnson, Howard
Pottawatomie   Hart; Rodgers
Pretzel Man, The   Myrow
Promise   Hanley
Purple Hills of Hawaii   Kahn
Pussy-Footin' Around   Rainger; Robin
Quick! Cupid Shoot that Arrow   Mills
Radio Ball Room, The   Razaf
Rainbow Valley   Leslie
Raindrops   Brown, Lew
Rains Came, The   Gordon
Reading, Writing and a Little Bit of Rhythm   Dubin;
   McHugh
Red River Valley   Johnson, Howard
Remember Dad   Mercer
Rendezvous in Rose Time, A   Rainger; Robin

Rendezvous Time in Paree   Dubin; McHugh
Rhythm of Romany   Bryan
Ridin' Home   Adamson; McHugh
Ring de Banjo   Johnson, Howard
Ring the Door Bell, and Ask for Alice   Hanley
Riverboat Shuffle   Carmichael; Mills
Robert the Roue (From Reading, Pa.)   Dubin; McHugh
Rock-a-bye Town   Hanley
Roll Jordan Roll   Johnson, Howard
Roller Skating on a Rainbow   Kahal; Rose; Warren
Romance Runs in the Family   Hoffman
Rose of Tralee, The   Johnson, Howard
Ruble a Rhumba, A   Bryan
Sally in Our Alley   Johnson, Howard
Say Ah!   Fisher
Say Au Revoir but Not Goodbye   Johnson, Howard
Say It All Over Again   Hoffman
Say Yes   Razaf; Waller
See Saw Margery Daw   Johnson, Howard
Self-Made Man   Fields; Schwartz, Arthur
Sell Your Cares for a Song   Young, Victor
Serenade   Johnson, Howard
Serenade to a Traffic Light (inst.)   Rome
720 in the Books   Adamson
Sextette   Johnson, Howard
Shadow of Love   Duke
Shadows of Midnight Blue   Evans; Livingston, Jay
Shanty Boat on the Mississippi   Carroll
She Could Shake the Maracas   Hart; Rodgers
She Had to Go and Lose It at the Astor   Raye
She May Have Seen Better Days   Johnson, Howard
She Was Happy Till She Met You   Johnson, Howard
She Was Wearing a Big Sombrero   Lane; Loesser
She'll Be Coming Round the Mountain   Johnson, Howard
Shepherd, The   Freed, Ralph
Shepherd Lullaby   Freed, Ralph
Ship Has Sailed, The   Brown, Lew; Stept
Shirley   Mills
Shoemaker's Holiday   Raye
Show Your Linen Miss Richardson   Mercer
Siciliana   Johnson, Howard
Silver on the Sage   Rainger; Robin
Silver Threads Among the Gold   Johnson, Howard
Simon Legree   Robison
Simple Simon   Razaf
Sing a Song of Sunbeams   Burke; Monaco
Sing My Heart   Arlen; Koehler
Sleep Baby Sleep   Johnson, Howard
Sleepy House, The   Young, Victor
Sleepytime Soldier Boy   Coots
Smart Little Girls   Ager; Fain; Yellen
Smarty Pants   Donaldson; Mercer
Smother Me with Your Love (inst.)   Waller
Snug As a Bug in a Rug   Loesser
So Tired of It All   Rainger; Robin
So You Wanna Fall in Love   Mills
Softly Now the Light of Day   Johnson, Howard
Some Like It Hot   Loesser
Somebody Nobody Knows   Warren
Somebody Told Me   Gordon
Something I Dreamed Last Night   Ager; Fain; Magidson; Yellen
Something to Live For   Ellington
Sometime   Parish
Somewhere in Paradise   Henderson

Song in My Heart Is a Rhumba, The   Lane; Loesser
Song of India, A   Johnson, Howard
Song of Italy   Webster
Song of the Metronome, The   Berlin
Song of the Musketeers   Bullock
Song of the Newlyweds   Burke; Monaco
Song's for Free, The   Ager; Fain; Yellen
Songs That Mother Taught   Johnson, Howard
South American Way   Dubin; McHugh
Speaking of Heaven   Gordon; Van Heusen
Spic and Spanish   Hart; Rodgers
Sport of Kings, The   Duke
Spring in My Heart   Freed, Ralph
Spring Song   De Lange; Van Heusen
Stairway to the Stars   Parish
Stand By for Further Announcements   Brown, Lew; Stept
Starlight and Music   Hoffman
Starry Eyes   Loesser
Stars of the Summer Night   Johnson, Howard
Stay Up Stan, the All Right Record Man   Robison
Step Up and Shake My Hand   David, Mack; Livingston, Jerry
Step Up and Take a Bow   Arlen; Harburg
Stevedore Stomp   Ellington; Mills
Stevedore's Serenade   Ellington
Stick to Your Arithmetic   Rainger; Robin
Sticks and Stones   Hoffman
Still As the Night   Johnson, Howard
Still the Bluebird Sings   Burke; Monaco
Story of the One Man Band   Cahn
Strange Case of Adam Standish, The   Hammerstein; Kern
Strange Enchantment   Loesser
Stranger than Fiction   Parish
Stranger Things Have Happened   Davis
Street Song   Loesser
Streets of Paris, The   Dubin; McHugh
Stuttering in the Starlight   Hoffman
Sunbeams in the Moonlight   Rainger; Robin
Sunrise Serenade   Lawrence
Sunshine of Paradise Alley, The   Johnson, Howard
Suzi of the Islands   Lawrence
Swallow, The   Johnson, Howard
Sweet and Low   Johnson, Howard
Sweet Dreams, Sweetheart   Ager; Davis
Sweet Land of Liberty   Razaf
Sweet Marie   Johnson, Howard
Sweetest Sight that I Have Seen, The   Hammerstein; Kern
Sweethearts of the Team, The   Hart; Rodgers
Swing Left, Sweet Chariot   Fields; Henderson
Swing Low, Sweet Chariot   Johnson, Howard
Swingali   Arlen; Harburg
Swingin' a Dream   De Lange; Van Heusen
Swingin' at the Golden Gate   Razaf
Table in a Corner   Coslow
Take It Like a Soldier   Heyman; Pollack
Take the World Off Your Shoulders   Brown, Lew; Fain
Tears from My Inkwell   Dixon; Warren
Tempt Me Not   Hart; Rodgers
Terribly Attractive   Fields; Schwartz, Arthur
Thank the Man Upstairs   Robison
Thanks for the Franc   Dubin; McHugh
That Lucky Fellow   Hammerstein; Kern
That Lucky Lady   Kern
That Sentimental Sandwich   Loesser

That Sly Old Gentleman from Featherbed Lane   Burke;
	Monaco
That's All, Brother   David, Mack; Livingston, Jerry
That's Right — I'm Wrong   Carmichael
Then I Wrote the Minuet in G   Loesser
Then You'll Remember Me   Johnson, Howard
There'll Be Other Nights   Brown, Lew; Pollack
There's a Girl in the World for Every Boy   Edwards
There's a Green Pasture in the Blue Heaven   Hoffman
There's a Robin 'Round the Corner Singin'
	La-Da-Da-Da-Dee Coots
There's Gotta Be a Wedding   De Lange; Van Heusen
There's Something Magic Saying "Nitchevo"   Freed, Ralph
They Ought to Write a Book about You   Burke; Van Heusen
They Say   Heyman
They Would Wind Him Up and He Would Whistle   Kalmar;
	Ruby
Thine Eyes So Blue and Tender   Johnson, Howard
This Changing World   Adamson
This Heart of Mine   Kalmar; Ruby
This Is It   Fields; Schwartz, Arthur
This Is No Dream   Davis
This Night (Will Be My Souvenir)   Kahn; Warren
Thoughtless   Livingston, Jerry
Three Little Maids   Dubin; McHugh
Thrill of a New Romance   Adamson
Time After Time   Adamson; Duke
Time Changes Everything but Love   Donaldson; Kahn
Time for Jookin'   Brown, Lew; Stept
Tit Willow   Johnson, Howard
To You   Davis
Today's Your Anniversary   Mills
Tomorrow Night   Coslow
Tonight Is the Night   Adamson; McHugh
Too Many Girls   Hart; Rodgers
Toreodor Song   Johnson, Howard
Tra La La and the Oom Pah Pah, The   Rainger; Robin
Trail of Dreams   Johnson, Howard
Turkey in the Straw   Johnson, Howard
Twickenham Ferry   Johnson, Howard
Twinkle Twinkle Little Star   Johnson, Howard
Two Against One   Gilbert; Pollack
Two Blind Loves   Arlen; Harburg
Two Roses, The   Johnson, Howard
Uncle Sam's Lullaby   Brown, Lew; Stept
Under the Dream Tree   Hanley
Unforgettable   Sigman
Until We Kiss Again   Duke; Parish
Up the Chimney Go My Dreams   Henderson; Webster
Utt Day Zay   Mills
Vagabond Dreams   Carmichael; Lawrence
Valse des Fleurs   Loesser
Voila   Bullock
Volga Boat Song   Johnson, Howard
Wail of the Winds (inst.)   Warren
Wait for the Wagon   Johnson, Howard
Wait Till the Clouds Roll By   Johnson, Howard
Waiter's Melody, The   Conrad; Gilbert
Waltz in Blue (inst.)   Revel
War Song   Hanley
Watching the Clock   Russell; Sigman
Watermelon Man   Ellington
We Can Live on Love (We Haven't a Pot to Cook
	In) Dubin; McHugh
Wedding of the Wooden Soldier and the Painted Doll   Raye

Welcome Yule   Johnson, Howard
Well All Right, Tonight's the Night   Raye
Well, Did You Evah!   Porter
Wer Hat Die Schonsten Schafchen   Freed, Ralph
We're All Together Now   Rainger; Robin
We're Back Again   Raye
We're Breaking Up a Lovely Affair   Mills
We're Off to See the Wizard   Arlen; Harburg
We're Trimmin' the Old Grey Bonnet   Egan
What a Night   Sissle
What Am I to Do   Porter
What Are the Wild Waves Saying?   Adamson
What Do You Use for a Heart   Fain
What Ev'ry Young Girl Should Know   Burke
What Goes Up Must Come Down (And Baby, You've Been
	Flyin' Too High) Bloom; Koehler
What Have I?   Porter
What Makes the World Go 'Round   Kahn; Warren
What More Can I Give You   David, Mack
What Used to Was Used to Was Now It Ain't   Cahn
Whatever You Say, Will Be Held Against You   Adamson;
	Coots
What's the Use of Loving   Mills
Wheels Through the Night   Weill
When I Gave My Love to You   Kahn
When Love Beckoned   Porter
When Love Is Kind   Johnson, Howard
When Roses Bloom No More   Webster
When the Berry Blossoms Bloom   Brown, Lew; Stept
When the Corn Is Waving, Annie Dear   Johnson, Howard
When the Dark Becomes Dawn   Myrow
When the Lights Are Low   Johnson, Howard
When the Moon Bids the Night Good-Bye   Ahlert; Young,
	Joseph
When the Robins Nest Again   Johnson, Howard
When the Swallows Homeward Fly   Johnson, Howard
When We Heard the Music Play 'Home Sweet
	Home' Gilbert
When Winter Comes   Berlin
When You and I Were Young Maggie   Johnson, Howard
When You Go   Blane
Where Else but Here?   Heyman; Romberg
Where the Turf Meets the Surf   Burke; Monaco
Where Was I?   Dubin
Where Were You Last Night   Akst; Davis
Where's Louie?   Porter
While Strolling Thru the Park One Day   Johnson, Howard
While the Music Plays On   Mills
While We're in the Mood   Adamson
Whispering Hope   Johnson, Howard
White Lies and Red Roses   Magidson; Wrubel
Who Is Sylvia   Johnson, Howard
Who Misses Who?   Ager
Who Would Ever Dream?   Adamson; Duke
Who Writes the Plot for Your Dreams?   Hanley
Whodunit?   Carmichael; Loesser
Who'll Buy My Flowers?   Clare; Styne
Who's Gonna Keep Your Wigwam Warm   Lerner, Sammy;
	Oakland
Who's That Calling   Johnson, Howard
Why Begin Again   Raye
Why Don't You Answer My Letter   Heyman
Will You Love Me Then As Now   Johnson, Howard
Wind at My Window, The   Rainger; Robin
Wings Over the Navy   Mercer; Warren

Winter Blossoms   Gilbert
Wishing (Will Make It So)   DeSylva
Woman Is Fickle   Johnson, Howard
Woodman Spare that Tree   Johnson, Howard
Work While You May (Bulgarian Rose Song)   Robin
Wren (La Capinera), The   Johnson, Howard
Ya Gotta Lot to Learn   Ager
Yankee Doodle's Gonna Go to Town Again   Rose
Yes, My Darling Daughter   Warren
Yodelin' Jive   Raye
You   Cahn
You and Your Love   Mercer
You Asked for It, You Got It   Baer
You Brought Me to My Senses   Davis
You Can Buy the Sun for a Song   Rainger; Robin
You Can Count on Me   Myrow
You Don't Know How Much You Can Suffer Until You Fall
      in Love   Friend
You Fascinate Me   Livingston, Jerry
You Gave Me the Gate and I'm Swinging   Ellington
You Grow Sweeter As the Years Go By   Mercer
You Meet the Nicest People in Your Dreams   Hoffman
You Out-Smarted Yourself   Razaf
Young Man of Manhattan   Livingston, Jerry
Young Man Sings, A   Raye
Your Love Has Faded   Ellington
You're a Dream Set to Music   Sissle
You're a Lucky Guy   Cahn
You're Just a No Account   Cahn
You're Lettin' the Grass Grow Under Your Feet   Ager;
      Livingston, Jerry
(T' Me Baby) You're News   Gershwin, Ira; Harburg
You're Sensational   Stept
You're the Greatest Discovery   David, Mack
You're Too Good to Be True   Rose
Yours for a Song   Rose
You've Got Me Sittin' on the Fence   Arlen; Koehler
You've Got that Look (That Leaves Me Weak)   Loesser
Zaza   Loesser

1940

(It Seems There Was) A Fellow and a Girl   Eliscu; Gorney
Abbul Babble Gabble   Mills
Adagio Dan   Duke
Adios Americano   Coslow
Adored One   Gordon
A-Flat Blues (A-flat Dream) (inst.)   Johnson, James P.
After Ev'ry Rainstorm   Lerner, Sammy
After I've Spent My Best Years on You   Razaf
Agua Agua   David, Mack
Ain't It a Shame About Mame   Burke; Monaco
Air-Minded Executive   Mercer
All American   Brennan; Snyder
All I've Got to Get Now Is My Man   Porter
All or Nothing at All   Lawrence
All This and Heaven Too   De Lange; Van Heusen
All This Thunder and Lightnin'   Robison
All Through the Night   Mercer
All Too Soon   Ellington; Sigman
Along the Santa Fe Trail   Dubin
Alpha Ro Song   Loesser
Always Comb Your Hair   Styne
Always Help Your Mommy   Styne
Always Say Please   Styne

Always Say Thank You   Styne
Amazing   Razaf
Amazing what Love Can Do   Carmichael; Mercer
America Marches On   Adamson
American Barcarolle (inst.)   Warren
American Plan   Gorney
American Waltz, The   Parish
Americans All Drink Coffee   Porter
Americonga   Adamson
Amigo We Go Riding Tonight   Cahn
And So Do I   De Lange
And You Forgot About Me   Hanley
Angel   Parish
Another New Day   Hammerstein; Schwartz, Arthur
Any Minute Now   Loesser
April Birthday Song   Caesar
April Played the Fiddle   Burke; Monaco
Arise My Love   Washington
As If I Didn't Know   Kahn
Ask Your Heart   Lawrence
At a Dixie Roadside Diner   Leslie
At the Fancy Dress Ball   Sigman
At the Psychological Moment   Burke; Van Heusen
August Birthday Song   Caesar
Back in My Shell   Fields; Kern
Bagpipe Rhumba, The   Bullock; Wrubel
Bagpipes on Parade   Von Tilzer
Ballad of Magna Carta   Weill
Barking Baby Never Bites, A   Hart; Rodgers
Bats About You   Gershwin, Ira; Weill
Bayou Trouble Tree   Hammerstein
Be Neat, Be Tidy   Styne
Be Quiet When People Talk   Styne
Be Sure   De Lange
Beard in a Gilded Frame   Silver
Beat Me Daddy Eight to the Bar   Raye
Bedtime on the Prairie   Harburg; Lane
Before You Throw the Match Away   Caesar
Bells of Monterey, The   Freed, Ralph; Stept
Best Years of His Life, The   Gershwin, Ira; Weill
Better Get Away from Here   Russell
Between Romances   Dubin; Fain
Between You and Me and the Lamppost   Duke
Beware, I'm Beginning to Care   Burke; Monaco
Beware the Dragon   Rome
Bewitched, Bothered and Bewildered   Hart; Rodgers
Big Chief Suzique   Kalmar; Ruby
Bill of Rights (Congress Shall Make No Law), The   Gorney
Blitzkreig Baby, You Can't Bomb Me   Fisher
Blue Danube Dream   Kahn
Blue Dream   Razaf
Blue Lovebird   Kahn
Blue Monday   Hart; Rodgers
Blue Rendezvous   Razaf
Blue September   Parish
Blueberry Rhyme (inst.)   Johnson, James P.
Bond Street (inst.)   Waller
Boogy-Woogy   Duke
Born to the Bayou   Robison
Boss Is Bringing Home a Bride, The   Gershwin, Ira; Weill
Bounce   Evans; Livingston, Jay
Bow, Wow, Wow, Wow, Wow   Caesar
Boy Climbed Up the Ladder, The   Caesar
Break It to Me Gently   Sigman
Break It Up Cinderella   Carmichael; Mercer

Broadway's Still Broadway   Revel
Buck Up!   Buck
Bunch of Cows, A   Rome
Bunker Hill   Razaf
Busy As a Bee, I'm Buzz, Buzz, Buzzin'   Russell
Buzz-Buzz-Buzz Lookin' for My Honey   Lawrence
By the By   Loesser
By the People   Hammerstein; Schwartz, Arthur
Cabby's Serenade, The   Dubin; McHugh
Cabin in the Sky   Duke
Calliope Jane   Carmichael
Can't Get Indiana Off My Mind   Carmichael
Captain Custard   Burke
Carmenita McCoy   Lerner, Sammy
Carolina Moon   Davis
Casbah Blues   Raye
Central Park (inst.)   Ruby
Chance of a Lifetime   Lerner, Sammy
Charm Against Trouble   Blane
Charming Little Faker   Burke
Chicago (A Great Big Town)   Hart; Rodgers
Chile Con Conga   Mills
Chula Chihuahua   Clare; Styne
Clear Out of This World   Dubin; McHugh
Coffee Bean Conga   Raye
Colonna and Vague Specialty   Styne
Color of Your Eyes, The   Freed, Ralph
Concerto in E-Flat Major   Dubin; Fain
Congo Cohen   Duke
Corn Silk   Kahal
Corny Talk   Revel
Court Dance   Rome
Cowboy's Gal, A   Brown, Lew; Fain
Crazy As a Loon   Dubin; McHugh
Crazy Dreams   Magidson; Oakland
Crispy, Crunchy Crackers   Harburg; Lane
Crossover   Johnson, James P.
Cupid's After Me   Styne
Customer's Always Right, The   Dubin; Fain
Cut Off My Heels and Call Me Shorty   Raye
Daddy's on the Phone   Styne
Dance and Dream   Schwartz, Jean
Dance of the Tumblers, The (inst.)   Weill
Dance with Me (At the Mardi Gras)   Berlin
Dancing for Nickels and Dimes   Loesser
Dark Eyes   Johnson, Howard
Darn Clever These Chinese   Carmichael; Mercer
Dawn of Love, The   Freed, Ralph
Day Dream   Ellington
Day Dreams Come True at Night   Freed, Ralph
Day Is Here   Herbert
Dear Little Cafe   Kahn
Dearest, Darest I   Burke; Van Heusen
December Birthday Song   Caesar
Deep in the Blues   Parish
Den of Iniquity   Hart; Rodgers
Dentist Song (Easy, Mister, Easy), The   Razaf
Devil Can't Hurt Me   Razaf
Devil May Care   Burke; Warren
Diamond Jubilee Song   Ellington
Disgustingly Rich   Hart; Rodgers
Dixie Ann in Afghanistan   Blake; Razaf
Do It the Hard Way   Hart; Rodgers
Do What You Wanna Do   Duke
Do You Hear What I Hear   Hoffman

Do You Know Why?   Burke; Van Heusen
Does the Moon Shine Through the Tall Pine   Loesser;
    Young, Victor
Dollar for a Dime   Blake; Razaf
Dolly Doolittle   Fisher
Don't Be Greedy   Styne
Don't Eat too Much Candy   Styne
Don't Let It Get You Down   Gordon; Harburg; Lane
Don't Let It Get Your Goat   Mills
Don't Say I Didn't Tell You   Mitchell; Pollack
Don't Think This Ain't Been Charming   McHugh; Mercer
Don't You Think We Better Dance   Burke
Double or Nothing   Duke
Down Argentina Way   Gordon; Warren
Down By the Railroad Track   Blake; Razaf
Down on the Dude Ranch   Harburg; Lane
Dowry Song, The   Cahn
Drago and the Colonel   Carmichael
Dragon Dance   Rome
Dream Blues   Mills
Dreaming Out Loud   Coslow
Driving on Monday or Tuesday or Sunday   Caesar
Drums in the Night   Loesser; McHugh
Early to Bed, Early to Rise   Styne
Easy Does It   Rome
Eating Is Such Fun!   Rome
Egyptian Ballet   Duke
El Botecito (Ferry-boat Serenade)   Adamson
El Pajaro Carpintero   Adamson
Eleanor, I Adore You   Rose; Van Heusen
Escapade   Burke; Van Heusen
Even If I Say It Myself   Carmichael; Mercer
Everybody Knew but Me   Berlin
Everything Happens to Me   Carmichael; Mercer
Ev'ry Sunday Afternoon   Hart; Rodgers
Ev'rybody Goes when the Wagon Comes   Razaf
Ev'ryone's a Fighting Son of that Old Gang of Mine   Caesar
Exile   Caesar
Exile's Haven   Herbert
Fable of the Rose, The   Myrow
Fabulous Mister Crow   Sigman
Fairy Tales Are All Untrue, The   Rome
Falling Leaves   David, Mack
Farandola   Fields; Kern
February Birthday Song   Caesar
Fifth Avenue   Gordon; Warren
Figaro and Cleo   Washington
Finis   Razaf
First Lady of the Land, The   Brown, Lew; DeSylva;
    Henderson
Five O'Clock Whistle   Myrow
Flags of Freedom (Banderas de Libertad)   Mills
Flatfoot's Theme (inst.)   Duke
Flower Garden of My Heart, The   Hart; Rodgers
Fool that I Am   Mills
Fools Fall in Love   Berlin
Fools Rush In (Where Angels Fear to Tread)   Bloom; Mercer
For a Good Game of Marbles   Caesar
For Forty-Eight Reasons We Love You   Caesar
For the People   Hammerstein; Schwartz, Arthur
Formula for Love   Monaco
Four A.M.   Lawrence
Frenesi   Russell
Fresh As a Daisy   Porter
Friend of Mine, A   Rome

Friend of the Family   Carmichael; Mercer
From Another World   Hart; Rodgers
Fugitive from Esquire, A   Dietz; McHugh
Fugue   Duke
Funny Old Phonograph, The   Hoffman
Garden in Encino, A   Carroll
General's Song, The   Duke
Georgia Gal   Razaf
Georgia Trail   Razaf
Ghost Routine   Styne
Giovanni   Monaco
Girl from Havana, The   Styne
Girl of the Moment   Gershwin, Ira; Weill
Girl Who Works in the Laundry, The   Dubin; Fain
Git Away!   Razaf
Give a Little Whistle   Washington
Give Her My Love   Cahn
Give Out when You're Blue   Washington; Young, Victor
Glide, Glider, Glide   Porter
Go 'Way Blues Ya Bother Me   Adamson
Go West   Kahn
God Bless the Women   Porter
Gold Dusters Song   Porter
Goodnight Again   Magidson
Goodnight, Mother   Bryan; David, Mack
Gospel   Duke
Grandmother's Clock (inst.)   Romberg
Great Big Baby, A   Blake; Razaf
Great Day   Duke
Greatest General of Them All, The   Brown, Lew;
   Henderson
Greatest Show on Earth, The   Gershwin, Ira; Weill
Greeks Have No Word for It, The   Hart; Rodgers
Greetings, Gates   Carmichael; Mercer
Gut Stomp (inst.)   Johnson, James P.
Gypsy Lullaby (Scak Egy Szep Lany Van E Vilagon)   Freed,
   Ralph
Ha Ya, Bud   Hoffman
Hail Number One   Rome
Half and Half   Rose
Handful of Stars   Lawrence
Handy Andy   Razaf
Happily Ever After   Rome
Happy Birthday to Love   Rose
Happy Days   Herbert; Loesser
Happy Feeling (inst.)   Waller
Happy Hunting Horn   Hart; Rodgers
Happy New Year for You   Carmichael; Mercer
Harem Days   Rainger
Havana   Lerner, Sammy
Havana for a Night   Hammerstein
Have You Met My Oucho Ma Gaucho   Gordon; Warren
Hawaiian War Chant (Ta-hu-wa-hu-wai)   Freed, Ralph
Head Man   Buck
Heaven   Caesar
Heaven on a Hilltop   Lawrence
Hep Cat, The   Blake; Razaf
Hep Cat's Ball   Robison
Here Come the Clowns   Coots; Egan
Here's to Panama Hattie   Porter
Hero, A   Rome
Hero of Yesterday   Freed, Ralph; Styne
He's My Uncle   Pollack
Hey Junior   Styne
Hi-Diddle-Dee-Dee (An Actor's Life for Me)   Washington

High As a Georgia Pine   Razaf
High School Cadets   Freed, Ralph
Hilo Hattie   Adamson
Hissing Song, The   Brown, Lew; Henderson
Hit Parade Finale   Bullock; Styne
Hit the Road   Raye
Hold on to Your Hats   Harburg; Lane
Holding Hands in the Moonlight   Akst; Davis
Honchi Chonch   Ellington
Honest John   Washington
Honey in the Honeycomb   Duke
Hooray, Hooray for Nancy Mix   Caesar
Hot Catfish and Corn Dodgers   Alter; Loesser
How Can I Ever Be Alone?   Hammerstein; Schwartz, Arthur
How Is Your Technique?   Dubin; Fain
How Nice for Me   Carmichael; Mercer
How's Your Health?   Hart; Rodgers
Huckleberry Duck   Lawrence
Huckleberry Man, The   Koehler; Warren
Huxley   Gershwin, Ira; Weill
I Can't Get Along with Horses   Kahn
I Can't Love You Any More (Any More than I
   Do)   Magidson; Wrubel
I Close My Eyes   Styne
I Could Make You Care   Cahn
I Could Write a Book   Hart; Rodgers
I Don't Want to Be Gay!   Rome
I Fell Overboard (I Fall Overboard)   Loesser
I Found a Rose   Revel
I Get a Kick Outa Corn   Adamson
I Got the Bird on the Canary Islands   Heyman
I Hate to Tell a Lie   Livingston, Jerry
I Have a Song   Rome
I Have Everything to Live For   David, Mack
I Haven't Time to Be a Millionaire   Burke; Monaco
I Hear Bluebirds   Woods
I Heard You Were Lovely (I Heard You Were
   Lonely)   Adamson
I Just Wanna Play with You   David, Mack
I Like Everything About You   Brown, Lew; Henderson
I Like Love   Martin
I Live Again (Because I'm in Love Again)   Washington;
   Young, Victor
I Love to Watch the Moonlight   Myrow
I Love You Much Too Much   Raye
I Must Be Out of Your Mind   Raye
I Never Felt This Way Before   Dubin; Ellington
I Saw You First   David, Mack
I Should Have Known You Years Ago   Carmichael
I Think a Lot of You   Coslow
I Walk with Music   Carmichael; Mercer
I Wanna Make with the Happy Times   Loesser
I Want Romance   Rome
I Want to Be a Good Lamb   Herbert
I Want to Live (As Long As You Love Me)   Fain; Yellen
I Was a Fool to Let You Go   Razaf
I Wonder How She Is Tonight   Heyman
I Wouldn't Take a Million   Gordon; Warren
I'd Be Lost in Someone Else's Arms   Raye
I'd Know You Anywhere   McHugh; Mercer
I'd Love to Be Shot from a Cannon with You   Berlin
If I Ever Lost You   Kalmar; Ruby
If Tears Would Bring You Back   Freed, Ralph
If They Gave Me a Million   Magidson; Oakland
If You Can't Control Your Man   Razaf

I'll Applaud You with My Feet   Dubin; McHugh
I'll Be a Hero Too!   Rome
I'll Be Close to You   Coslow
I'll Keep It Turned to the Wall   Razaf
I'll Settle for You   Rainger; Robin
I'll Take the High Note   Adamson
I'll Wait for You Forever   Coots
I'm a Happy-Go-Lucky Fellow   Washington
I'm a King   Rome
I'm Afraid   Hart; Rodgers
I'm Cynical   Rome
I'm Gonna Salt Away Some Sugar (For My Sugar and
    Me)   Coots
I'm Home Again   Wrubel
I'm in a Loveable Mood Tonight   Coots; De Lange
I'm Just a Weakie   Styne
I'm Making a Play for You   Rainger; Robin
I'm Not Hep to that Step (But I'll Dig It)   Mercer
I'm Off the Wagon   Carmichael; Mercer
I'm Stepping Out with a Memory Tonight   Magidson;
    Wrubel
I'm Talking to My Pal   Hart; Rodgers
I'm the Guy Who Loves You   Kahn
I'm Through   Lawrence
I'm Throwing a Ball Tonight   Porter
I'm Toein' the Line   Blake; Razaf
Impromptu in E Flat (inst.)   Romberg
In a Mellow Tone (Baby, You and Me)   Ellington
In a Persian Palace   Harbach
In a Spring Parade   Kahn
In Chi-chi-castinango   Gorney
In My Moonlight Memories   Johnson, Howard
In Our Little San Fernando Valley Home   Gershwin, Ira;
    Weill
In the Cool of the Evening   Bullock; Styne
In the Doorway   Coots; Dixon
In This Our Last Night Together   Coslow
Inconvenience   Razaf
Island Serenade   Adamson
Isn't That Just Like Love   Burke; Van Heusen
It Can't Happen Here   Rose
It Happened in Kaloha   Freed, Ralph
It Happened, It's Over, Let's Forget It   Rainger; Robin
It Looks Like Liza   Gershwin, Ira; Weill
It Must Have Been the Wine   De Lange
It Never Entered My Mind   Hart; Rodgers
It Started with a Kiss   Bullock
It Won't Be Fun (But It's Gotta Be Done)   Rainger
It'll Come to You   Berlin
It's a Good Thing I Don't Care   Burke; Monaco
It's a Lovely Day Tomorrow   Berlin
It's Foolish — But It's Fun   Kahn
It's Hot in Chile   David, Mack; Heyman; Livingston, Jerry
It's Never Too Late to Mendelssohn   Gershwin, Ira; Weill
It's Not So Bad to Be Good   Duke
It's Pretty in the City   Hart; Rodgers
It's Raining Dreams   Spina
It's the Last Time I Fall in Love   Stept
It's the Principle of the Thing!   Rome
It's the Same Old South   Eliscu; Gorney
I've Been in Love Before   Loesser
I've Got a One Track Mind   McHugh; Mercer
I've Got No Strings   Washington
I've Still Got My Health   Porter
I've Walked Through Wonderland   Loesser

January Birthday Song   Caesar
Jazz Fugue (inst.)   Duke
(The Saga of) Jenny   Gershwin, Ira; Weill
Jenny Lind   Hammerstein; Schwartz, Arthur
Jim Corny Well Dressed Man   Styne
Jiminy Cricket Is the Name   Washington
Jitterbugging with the Young Folks   Fain
Johnny Peddler (I Got)   Brown, Lew
Johnson Rag   Lawrence
Join It Right Away   Porter
July Birthday Song   Caesar
Jungle Jingle   Loesser
Just a Few Thrills Ago   Coslow
Just a Little Affection   Livingston, Jerry
Just Across the Way   Lewis
Just One of Those Nights   Myrow
Just Suppose   De Lange
Just the Girl   Razaf
Kaigoon   Burke
Keep the Songs of Safety Ever in Your Mind   Caesar
Kingdom of the Future   Bullock
Kiss Me Yes, Kiss Me No   Fisher
Kissy Face   Oakland
K-K-K-Katy   Gordon
Ladies of the Town   Kahn
Lady in Blue   Ellington; Mills
Lady's in Distress, The   Brooks
Lafayette We're Here   Brown, Lew; Henderson
Last Kiss You Gave Me, The   Ruby
Last Night's Gardenias   Coslow
Last Time I Saw Paris, The   Hammerstein; Kern
Latin in Me, The   Fain; Yellen
Latin Tune, A Manhattan Moon and You, A   Dubin;
    McHugh
Latins Know How   Berlin
Lay-De-O   Bullock
Lazy Step   Duke
Lazy-Lack-a-Daisy Melody   Lawrence
Le Can Can   Rose; Van Heusen
Leading Girl, The   Fain; Yellen
Legend of Old California, The   Mercer; Warren
Lend Me Your Heart   Johnson, J. Rosamond
Let Me In Out of the Rain   Bullock; Wrubel
Let Me Live Today (inst.)   Romberg
Let's Be Buddies   Porter
Let's Have Another One Before We Say Good Night   Raye
Let's Pretend   Bryan; Silver
Let's Steal a Tune from Offenbach   Gorney
Liable to Catch on   Fain
Liberty Bell, The   Willson
Life! Liberty!   Hart; Rodgers
Life Was Pie for the Pioneer   Harburg; Lane
Like the Fella Once Said   McHugh; Mercer
Li'l Abner   Oakland
Li'l Boy Love   Loesser
Little Bronze Lady in the Harbor   Gilbert; Ruby
Little Brown Jug   Lawrence
Little Cowboy Blue   Donaldson; Mercer
Little Man Who Wasn't There, The   Adamson
Little Papa Satan   Duke
Little Pops Is Tops with Me   Razaf
Little White Pill on the Little Green Hill, The   Burke;
    Monaco
Little Wooden Head   Washington
Living It Up   Duke

Liza   Johnston
Loca Illusion   Mercer
London Love Song   Johnston
Lonesome Reverie (inst.)   Johnson, James P.
Long Horn   Donaldson
Long Time No See   Donaldson; Mercer
Look Out for My Heart   Dubin; McHugh
Looking for Yesterday   De Lange; Van Heusen
Looks Like I'm Off o' Ya   Harburg; Lane
Looks Like Winter   Fisher
Lord Done Fixed Up My Soul, The   Berlin
Louisiana Purchase   Berlin
Love in Any Language   Kahn
Love Is My Friend   Hart; Rodgers
Love Lies   Freed, Ralph; Sigman
Love Life   Freed, Ralph
Love Me Tomorrow (But Leave Me Alone To-Day)   Duke
(Would You Like to Be the) Love of My Life   Mercer
Love Song   Carmichael; Mercer
Love Song of Renaldo   Fain; Kahal
Love Turned the Light Out   Duke
Lovely Day for a Murder, A   Hart; Rodgers
Lover's Lullaby, A   Razaf
Love's in My Heart   Ellington; Mills
Loving You to Music   Howard, Joseph E.
Lyrics by Johnny Burke: Kaigoon   Monaco
Magic Mountain   Stept
Maharajah, The   Hoffman
Make Believe Danceland   Razaf
Make Believe Island   Coslow
Make It Another Old Fashioned, Please   Porter
Make Way   Duke
Make Yourself at Home   Bullock; Styne
Man Upstairs, The   Duke
Man Who Came to Win 'Er, The   Dubin; Fain
Manhattan Holiday   Styne
Manhattan in the Spring   Carmichael
Man's in the Navy, The   Loesser
Mapleton High Chorale   Gershwin, Ira; Weill
March Birthday Song   Caesar
March, March, March the Boys Are Tramping   Kahn
Marianne   De Lange; Myrow
Martinique   Adamson
Mason Dixon Line   Gordon; Warren
May Birthday Song   Caesar
Maybe It's the Moon   Donaldson
Me and the Evening   Monaco
Me and the Ghost Upstairs   Mercer
Me and You   Ellington
Meet the Elite   Dubin; Fain
Meet the People   Gorney
Meet the Sun Halfway   Burke; Monaco
(I Must Have) Melody and Moonlight   Styne
(Stake Your Dreams on) Melody Ranch   Styne
Meow   Cahn
Merrily on My Way   Dubin; Fain
Mexican Jumping Bean   Russell
Mexican Magic   Loesser; Revel
Mighty Fine   Razaf; Waller
Minnie Hotcha   Styne
Minstrel Dream   Gershwin, Ira; Weill
Miss Johnson Phoned Again Today   Mills
Mister Meadowlark   Donaldson; Mercer
Molasses   Russell
Monstro the Whale   Washington

Moon and the Willow Tree, The   Burke
Moon Over America   Hoffman
Moon Over Burma   Loesser
Moonrise and Violins   Webster
Morning's at Seven   Hart; Rodgers
Movies Gonna Get Ya (If Ya Don't Watch Out),
    The   Harburg; Lane
Music from Paradise   Loesser; McHugh
Music in the Barn   Carmichael; Mercer
My Baby Knows How   David, Mack; Stept
My Beautiful   Loesser; Young, Victor
My Bicycle Girl   Hammerstein; Schwartz, Arthur
My Colleen from Killarney   Mills
My Country   Brennan; Snyder
My DeeTees   Dubin; Fain
My Heart Is a Hobo   Burke; Monaco
My Heart Is At Your Command   Johnson, Howard
My Heart's Popping   Evans; Livingston, Jay
My Kind of Country   Loesser; McHugh
My Lonely Wood   Mills
My Most Embarrassing Moment   Dubin; Fain
My Mother Would Love You   Porter
My! My!   Loesser; McHugh
My Next Romance   Freed, Ralph
My Old Man Was an Army Man   Rainger; Robin
My Old Virginia Home (On the River Nile)   Duke
My Piggy Bank Is Jing-a-Ling Again   Livingston, Jerry
My Rainbow from Little Green Isle   Johnson, Howard
My Ship   Gershwin, Ira; Weill
My White Haired Boy   Brown, Lew; Henderson
My Wonderful One, Let's Dance   Brown, Nacio Herb; Freed,
    Arthur
Name Song, The   Caesar
Naughty Hula Eyes   Adamson
Nenita   Gordon; Warren
Never a Dull Moment   Adamson
Never Brag About Your Man   Razaf
Never Play Hookey   Styne
Never Point at People   Styne
Never Say Love   Freed, Ralph
Never Take No for an Answer   Dubin; Fain
Never Tell a Lie   Styne
Never Took a Lesson in My Life   Lawrence
Newsy Bluesies   Carmichael; Mercer
Nice Going   Donaldson
Nickel for a Dime, A   Blake; Razaf
Nickel Man, The   Adamson
Nightcap Song, The   Donaldson; Mercer
No Lookin' Back   Eliscu; Gorney
No Love Blues   De Lange
No Matter Under What Star You're Born   Gershwin, Ira;
    Weill
No Wonder the Danube Is Blue   Brown, A. Seymour
Not a Care in the World   Duke
Not Yet   Warren
Nothing but You   Hart; Rodgers
Nothing Ever Happens to Me   David, Mack
Nothing to Do (And All Day to Do It)   Hoffman
November Birthday Song   Caesar
Now Kiss Me   Carmichael; Mercer
Now That I Know You   Hart; Rodgers
October Birthday Song   Caesar
Ode to Joy (Siwash Spring Song)   Loesser
Of Maestro and Men   Raye
Of the People   Hammerstein; Schwartz, Arthur

Of the People Stomp   Rome
Oh, Fabulous One in Your Ivory Tower   Gershwin, Ira; Weill
Old Folks at Home   Gordon
Old Grand Dad (inst.)   Waller
Old Jitterbug   Dubin; McHugh
Old Man's Darling, Young Man's Slave   Berlin
Old Park Bench, The   Dietz; McHugh
Old Pigeon-Toed Joad   Robison
Old Timer   Harburg; Lane
On a Side Street in Gotham (inst.)   Alter
On Behalf of the Visiting Fireman   Donaldson; Mercer
On Lookout Mountain   Lewis
On Repentin' Day   Razaf
On the Isle of May   David, Mack
Once in a Lovetime   Akst; Davis
Once Upon a Dream   Cahn
One in a Million   Hammerstein; Schwartz, Arthur
One Life to Live   Gershwin, Ira; Weill
One Look at You   Washington; Young, Victor
Only Forever   Burke; Monaco
Ooh! What You Said   Carmichael; Mercer
Oo-oo-oo a Jula Hula Moonlight   Snyder
Or Have I   Stept
Orchids for Remembrance   Parish
Our Love Affair   Freed, Arthur
Our Memoirs   Dubin; Fain
Out with Your Chest and Up with Your Chin   Loesser
Outside of that I Love You   Berlin
Over the Hills (And Through the Woods)   David, Hal
Pal Joey (What Do I Care for a Dame?)   Hart; Rodgers
Palms of Paradise   Loesser
Parade of the Teddy-Bears   Cahn
Party Parlando   Gershwin, Ira; Weill
Pay Heed   Duke
Pele   David, Mack; Livingston, Jerry
Pennsylvania 6-5000   Sigman
Pessimistic Character (With the Crab Apple Face),
    The   Burke; Monaco
Plant You Now, Dig You Later   Hart; Rodgers
Plymouth Rock   David, Mack
Poor Ballerina   Coots; Egan
Poor Mister Chisholm   Mercer
Poppin' the Corn   Styne
Porky the Porcupine   Cahn
Prairie Fairy Tale, A   Stept
Prairie Mary   Baer
Prayer (Child of All Nations, Mother to All)   Caesar
Pretty Little Petticoat   Lawrence
Pretty Please   Donaldson; Mercer
Princess of Pure Delight, The   Gershwin, Ira; Weill
Public Jitterbug No. 1   Cahn
Puddin' Head   Styne
Put Music in the Barn   Carmichael; Mercer
Querido   Styne
Raffles   Dubin; Duke
Rancho Santa Fe   Donaldson; Kahn
Red Heads   Rome
Red Rosey Bush (inst.)   Young, Victor
Remind Me   Fields; Kern
Rhett, Scarlet, Ashley   Dubin; McHugh
Rhumboogie   Raye
Rhythm on the River   Burke; Monaco
Ribbon, a Ring and a Rose, A   David, Mack
Ring Around the Bathtub   Styne
River Song, The   Herbert

Rock Was in the Snowball, A   Caesar
Rock-a-bye Baby   Loesser
Rondolet   Hammerstein; Romberg
Rooftop Serenade   Styne
Rose of the Rockies   Wrubel
Roses 'Round My Room   Loesser; McHugh
Rumba Jumps!, The   Carmichael; Mercer
Sadie Hawkins Day   Raye
Safety for You and for Me   Caesar
Sailor Beware   Hammerstein; Kern
Sailor Who Never Came Home, The   Bryan
Sailor with the Navy Blue Eyes, The   Hoffman
Sailors of the Sky   Porter
Sam, You Made the Pants Too Long   Lewis; Young, Joseph;
    Young, Victor
Samoa   Bullock; Spina
Savannah   Duke
Savoy (Home of Happy Feet)   Razaf
Say Hello to the Folks Back Home   Blake; Razaf
Say It (Over and Over Again)   Loesser; McHugh
Say Your Prayers   Styne
Scatterbrain   Burke
Scatterbrain Finale   Styne
Scrub Me Mama with a Boogie Beat   Raye
Secrets in the Moonlight   Gordon
Senate in Session   Gorney
Send Me Jackson   Friend
September Birthday Song   Caesar
Serenade to a Chambermaid   Dubin; Fain
Seventeen   Loesser
Sex Marches On   Berlin
Shake Hands with Your Neighbor   Loesser; Young, Victor
Shakin' Up the Folks Below   Blake; Razaf
She Believed a Gypsy   Brown, Lew; Henderson
She Came, She Saw, She Can Canned   Harburg; Lane
She's a Good Neighbor   Rainger; Robin
Shoe Shine Song   Hammerstein; Romberg
Show You What Love Can Do   Cahn
Side Street Troubadour   Ager; Akst; Davis
Silver Threads and Golden Dreams   David, Mack; Stept
Sing a Song of Sixpence (Four and Twenty Hot
    Blackbirds)   Rome
Sing High, Sing Low   Gordon; Revel
Sing Out when You're Blue   Washington; Young, Victor
Sing to Your Senorita   Gordon; Warren
Siwash Alma Mater   Loesser
Sky Fell Down, The   Alter; Heyman
Slav Annie   Carmichael
Sleepy Lagoon   Lawrence
Slow Freight   Mills
Smile for the Press   Carmichael; Mercer
Snow Drift's in My Heart   Carmichael
So Far So Good   Lawrence
So Long but Not for Long, Aloha   Bryan
So Long, Samoa   Porter
Sombrero   Brown, Lew; Henderson
Some Things a Man Must Have   Rome
Someday You'll Find Your Bluebird   Gordon
Something I Dreamed No Doubt   Burke
Something Seems to Call Me Back to You   Carmichael
Somewhere (Always Somewhere Just Beyond)   Raye
Song of Mojave   Donaldson; Gilbert
Song of the Ads (The Pluto Boys) (The Pluto Boys, We're the
    Ads)   Rome
Song of the Zodiac   Gershwin, Ira; Weill

Sour Serenade, The   Hoffman; Stept
South American Way   McHugh
South of Pago Pago   Pollack
Spend Your Vacation on Broadway   Dubin; Fain
Starlit Hour, The   Parish
Stars Remain, The   Gorney
Stayin' at Home (Happy to Be By Myself)   Razaf; Waller
Stranger in the Mirror   Dubin; Fain
Strangers in the Dark   Rose
Stroll on the Plaza Sant'Ana, A   Porter
Such Stuff as Dreams Are Made Of   Fain; Kahal
Sun'll Be Up in the Morning, The   Fain; Yellen
Swap Shop   Bullock; Styne
Sweet Angeline   Lawrence
Sweet Little Sweetheart   Brown, Lew
Sweet Magnolia Rose   Blake; Razaf
Sweet Potato Piper, The   Burke; Monaco
Swing Low Sweet Rhythm   Bullock; Styne
Swing Your Calico   Harburg; Lane
Swinga-Dilla Street   Johnson, James P.; Razaf; Silver
Swingin' at the Lido (inst.)   Johnson, James P.
Swiss Bellringer, The   Freed, Ralph
Sympathy   De Lange; Van Heusen
Taboo   Russell
Tahiti Honey   Styne
Take a Little Care   Caesar
Take Him   Hart; Rodgers
Take It From Me   Lawrence
Taking a Chance on Love   Duke
Tan Manhattan   Blake; Razaf
Tarzan of Harlem   Mills
Tchaikowsky   Fain
Tennessee Fish Fry   Hammerstein; Schwartz, Arthur
Tentacion de Amor   Adamson
Tequila   Styne
That Friendly Feeling   Loesser; McHugh
That Old Ghost Train   Revel
That Terrific Rainbow   Hart; Rodgers
That's for Me   Burke; Monaco
That's My Boy   Brennan
That's When Your Heartaches Begin   Fisher
That's Why We Make Him Leader   David, Mack
That's Your Umbrella When It Rains   Brown, Lew;
    Henderson
(Ting a Ling) The Bad Humor Man   McHugh; Mercer
There Goes My Dream   Loesser
There Must Be an Easier Way to Make a Living   Stept;
    Woods
There's a Great Day Coming Manana   Harburg; Lane
There's a New Gang on the Way   Rose; Van Heusen
There's a New Moon Over the Old Corral   Kahn
They Ain't Done Right By Our Nell   Porter
Things I Should Have Said, The   Alter; Lawrence
Think of Me   Sigman
This Angel of Old Devil's Inn   Bryan
This Is My Country   Raye
This Is New   Gershwin, Ira; Weill
This Is Our Side of the Ocean   Cohan
This Is Spring, This Is Winter   Dubin; McHugh
This Is the Beginning of the End   Gordon
This Woman at the Altar   Gershwin, Ira; Weill
Three at a Table for Two   Johnston
Three Cheers for Anything   Washington
Three Little Topical Debutantes   Dubin; McHugh
Times Square Dance   Fain; Yellen

Tiny Blue Shoe   Fisher
To Fly a Kite Is Lots of Fun   Caesar
Today I Am a Glamor Girl   Carmichael; Mercer
Tomboy   Van Heusen
Tonight at the Mardi Gras   Berlin
Tonight Will Live   Gordon
Too Much Love   Stept
Too Romantic   Burke; Monaco
Too Toy   Styne
Top of the Mornin'   Styne
Torpedo Joe   Styne
Toscanini, Stokowski and Me   Dubin; McHugh
Trade Winds   Friend
Trading Post of the Air   Bullock; Styne
Trail's End   Brooks
Tra-la-la   Gordon; Warren
True Love   Donaldson; Kahn
Tschaikowsky (And Other Russians)   Gershwin, Ira; Weill
Turn on the Old Music Box   Washington
Twilight Troubadour   David, Mack; Silver
Two Dreams Met   Gordon; Warren
Two in a Taxi   Dietz; McHugh
Two Little Doodle Bugs   Friend
Uncle Sam Gets Around   Rainger; Robin
Unfair to Love   Lerner, Sammy
(You Are) Unforgettable   Weill
Union Label   Eliscu; Gorney
Up in the Ozark Mountains   Fisher
Use a Handkerchief   Styne
Use Me, Lawd   Robison
Vision Ballet (inst.)   Duke
Visit Panama   Porter
Voulez Vous, May I Have the Next Waltz, Mrs.
    Yiffnif   Gorney
Wade in the Water   Duke
Wait Till I Catch You in My Dream   Brown, Lew; Coots
Wait Till She Sees You in Your Uniform   Leslie
Wait Till You See Me in the Morning   Carmichael; Mercer
Wake Up Little Rip Van Winkle   Bryan
Walkin' Along Mindin' My Business   Harburg; Lane
Waltz Is King   Gordon
Waltzing in the Clouds   Kahn
Wash Behind Your Ears   Styne
Way Back in 1939 A.D.   Carmichael; Mercer
Way Out West in Idaho   Fisher
Way Out West Where the East Begins   Harburg; Lane
We Are Americans Too   Blake; Razaf
We Detest a Fiesta   Porter
We Have Sandwiches   Gorney
We Know Where You're Goin'   Baer
We Like It Over Here   Hammerstein; Schwartz, Arthur
We Rule the Waves   Rose
We Want Wilkie   Kalmar
Wear a Straw Hat in the Rain   Johnston
Wear Your Rubbers When It Rains   Styne
Weaver Specialty   Styne
Welcome to Jerry   Porter
We'll Live All Over Again   Duke
We're All Here at Siwash   Loesser
We're Off the Wagon   Carmichael; Mercer
We've Come a Long Way Together   Koehler; Stept
What a Lovely Day for a Wedding   Gershwin, Ira; Weill
What a Man   Razaf
What Are Cowboys Made Of   Styne
What Chance Have I with Love   Berlin

What Fools These Mortals Be   Styne
What Good Is the Moon Without You   Johnson, Howard
What Is a Man?   Hart; Rodgers
What Would Shakespeare Have Said   Burke; Monaco
Whatcha Gonna Do (When There Ain't No Swing)   Styne
Whatever Happened to You?   De Lange
What'll I Do If I Marry a Soldier
    Tush-Doo-Woggle-Oh-Toog-In-Da-Shin   Lawrence
What'll They Think of Next?   Carmichael; Mercer
What's Cookin'   Razaf
What's Cookin' Cookie   Wrubel
What's the Matter with Me?   Lewis
What's What   Burke
What's Your Story, Morning Glory   Lawrence; Webster
When a Fella's Got a Girl   Styne
When April Sings   Kahn
When Banana Blossoms Bloom   Lerner, Sammy
When Spring Comes Springin' Along   Johnson, Howard
When the Congressman from Tennessee Meets the Senator
    from Maine   Fisher
When the Moon Comes Over Madison Square (The Love
    Lament of a Western Gent)   Burke; Monaco
When the Sails Are Set for Home   Mills
When the Spirit Moves Me   Rose; Van Heusen
When They Went Driving   Caesar
When You Hear the Sirens Blow   Caesar
When You Tend Baby   Caesar
When You Wish Upon a Star   Washington
Whenever You Walk Along the Road at Night   Caesar
Where Do I Go from You?   Bullock; Wrubel
Where Do You Keep Your Heart?   Ahlert
Whisper Confidentially   Heyman
Whispering Grass (Don't Tell the Trees)   Fisher
Whistler's Ditties (inst.)   Loesser
White Shadows of the Moon   Loesser
Who Am I   Bullock; Styne
Who Are You?   Hart; Rodgers
Who Dreamed You Up?   Bullock; Wrubel
Who Is the Beau of the Belle of New York   Gordon
Who Would Have Dreamed   Porter
Who'll Buy My Dream?   Van Heusen
Who's Beatin' My Time with You?   Ahlert; David, Mack
Why Didn't I Sleep Last Night   Oakland
Will You Love Me on Monday Morning   Arlen; Harburg
Willie of the Valley   Oakland
Window Wiper Song   Evans; Livingston, Jay
With a Banjo on My Knee   Alter; Loesser
With a Dream   Blake; Razaf
With the Wind and the Rain in Your Hair   Lawrence
With You with Me   Mercer
Wonderful Dreams   Herbert; Loesser
Woodpecker Song, The   Adamson
World Is in My Arms, The   Harburg; Lane
Worry   Blake; Razaf
Would You Be So Kindly   Harburg; Lane
Wrap Your Dreams in the Red, White and Blue   Coots
Yanks Aren't Coming!, The   Rome
Yesterday   Ruby
You and Who Else   Coslow
You and Your Kiss   Fields; Kern
You Are Beautiful   Herbert; Loesser
You Are Unforgettable   Gershwin, Ira
You Broke It Up when You Said "Georgia!"   Razaf
You Can't Argue with Love   Kahn
You Can't Brush Me Off   Berlin

You Can't Put Catsup on the Moon   Fain; Kahal
You Catch on Quick   Stept
You Danced with Dynamite   Burke; Van Heusen
You for Me   Dubin; Fain
You Got No Time for Me   Wrubel
You Had It Comin' to You   Oakland
You Little Heartbreaker You   Hoffman
You Mustn't Kick It Around   Hart; Rodgers
You Said It   Porter
You Say the Sweetest Things Baby   Gordon; Warren
You Started Something   Rainger; Robin
You Think of Everything   Rose; Van Heusen
You Wouldn't Give a Pal/Gal a Break   Monaco
Young People   Gordon; Warren
Your Eyes Are Like a Million Stars   Monaco
Your Flag and Mine   Akst; Davis
Your Homeland and My Homeland   Coots; Lewis
Your Kiss   Loesser
You're a Glamour Girl   Silver
You're Lonely and I'm Lonely   Berlin
You're Nearer   Hart; Rodgers
You're Such an Angel   Razaf
You're Tellin' I   Styne
You're Through   Mills
You're You   Rome
You're Your Highness to Me   Rome
Youth Will Be Served   Alter; Loesser
You've Got Me This Way   McHugh; Mercer
Yum! Yum!   Carmichael
Zip   Hart; Rodgers

1941

Absent Minded Moon   Burke; Van Heusen
Ace in the Hole   Porter
Ad Ripae Mildewensis Fluminis   Eliscu; Gorney
Adios Amigos   David, Mack
African Etude   Burke; Van Heusen
After the Rain   Drake
Afterglow, The   Fain
Ah Loo Loo   Cahn
All for One?   DePaul; Raye
All I Want To Do Is Love You   Brown, Nacio Herb; Freed,
    Ralph
All Out Moon Man   Donaldson
All that Meat and No Potatoes   Waller
Alma Mater   Styne
Aloha Lowdown   DePaul; Raye
Aloma of the South Seas   Loesser
Along the Winding Road   Hammerstein; Romberg
Am I on a Wild Goose Chase?   Ahlert
Am I Wasting My Dreams on You   Dixon
Amarillo   Hart; Rodgers
America Calling   Willson
Angel Puss   Donaldson; Parish
Angels Came Thru, The   Dubin
Anniversary Waltz, The   Dubin
Another Little Dream Won't Do Us Any Harm   Rainger;
    Robin
Any Bonds Today   Berlin
Anything Can Happen in New York   Harburg; Lane
Arabella, I Wuv Awa-Bewwa   Friend
Army Air Force, The   Gorney
As If You Didn't Know   Cahn
ASCAP Song, The   Duke

Ask Her While You're Dancing   Freed, Ralph; Lane
A-Stairable Rag   Porter
At a Masquerade in Rio   Revel
At Last   Gordon; Warren
At the Cinderella Ball   Baer
At the Crossroads   Russell
Aurora   Adamson
Autumn Nocturne   Myrow
Ay Ay Ay   Russell
Babalu   Russell
Babes on Broadway   Freed, Ralph; Lane
Baby Games   Porter
Baby Mine   Washington
Baby, When You Ain't There   Ellington; Parish
Banbury Lane   David, Mack
Banjo Eyes   Duke
Baron Is in Conference, The   Gordon; Warren
Be Pan-American   Ager; David, Mack
Beau Night in Hotchkiss Corners   Magidson; Oakland
Beer Barrel Polka   Styne
Belle of the Baltimore Ball   Lawrence
Below the Equator   Friend
Beside the Big Tonto   DePaul; Raye
Bessie-Whoa Babe   Ellington; Webster
Between You and Me and the Lamp Post   Ahlert
B-I-Bi   Russell
Big Chief No-Pain   De Lange
Big Time Comin'   Arlen; Koehler
Birds of a Feather   Burke; Van Heusen
Blackout Over Broadway   Freed, Ralph; Lane
Bli-Blip   Ellington
Blossoms in the Dust (inst.)   Brown, Nacio Herb
Blue Dreams   Burke
Blue Moon on the Silver Sage   Freed, Ralph; Stept
Blue Moon Over the Redwoods   David, Mack; Meyer
Blue Moonlight   Ager
Blue Raindrops   Leslie; Meyer
Blue Rhumba   Brown, Nacio Herb; Freed, Ralph
Blue Tahitian Moon   Gordon
Blue Velvet   Waller
Blues in the Night   Arlen; Mercer
Boa Noite (Good Night)   Gordon; Warren
Bonita   Styne
Boogie Barcarolle   Porter
Boogie Woogie Bugle Boy   Raye
Boogie Woogie Conga   Revel
Boogie-Woogie Man   Cahn
Boogly Woogly Piggy   Cahn
Born to Love   Washington; Young, Victor
Bounce Me Brother with a Solid Four   Raye
Bow-Legged Sal   Hammerstein; Romberg
Boy, Oh Boy   Loesser
Boy with the Wistful Eyes, The   DePaul; Raye
Brazil   Russell
Brown-Skin Gal in the Calico Gown, The   Ellington;
    Webster
Buckle Down Winsocki   Blane
Bug, The (inst.)   Arlen
Bugle Is Calling Goodnight, A   Coots; Harbach
Bundling   Hammerstein; Romberg
(What Would You Rather Have Boys?) Bunds or
    Bonds!   Brown, Lew; Henderson
Butterflies and the Bees, The   Hammerstein
By Lo Baby   Styne
Call It a Dream   Hammerstein; Romberg

Call It Anything but Love   Lawrence
Call Me a Taxi   Sigman
Call of Love   Styne
Calypso, The   Magidson; Oakland
Calypso Kitty   Harburg; Sigman
Can You Sing?   Hammerstein; Romberg
Candles in the Wind   David, Hal
Captain Brown   Raye
Carefree Careterro   Hart; Rodgers
Caribbean Love Song   Freed, Ralph
Casey Jones   Styne
Casey Junior   Washington
Celery Stalks at Midnight   Sigman
Centerville Alma Mater   Young, Victor
Central Two-Two-Oh-Oh   Rainger; Robin
Chapman's Cheerful Cheese   Warren
Chapman's Cheerful Cheese   Gordon
Chattanooga Choo Choo   Gordon; Warren
Cherry   Russell
Cherry Blossoms on Capitol Hill   Sigman
Chica Chica Boom Chic   Gordon; Warren
Chimes of Big Ben   Parish
Chin Up! Cheerio! Carry On!   Harburg; Lane
China Jumps (inst.)   Waller
Ching   Hanley
Chiquita   Stept
Chocolate Shake   Ellington; Webster
Cigarette (inst.)   Kern
Cigarettes   Kalmar; Ruby
Cleopatra   Loesser; Styne
Compared to You   David, Mack
Concerto for Two   Lawrence
Coney Island Ballet   Duke
Conference, The   Gordon; Warren
Confidentially Yours   Gilbert; McHugh
Conga Beso   DePaul; Raye
Congeroo   DePaul; Raye
Consider Yourself in Love   Bullock; Spina
Contrapunto   Hart; Rodgers
Coppin' a Plea   Cahn
Cracker Barrel County   Loesser; Styne
Cutting the Cane   Hart; Rodgers
Dancing on a Dime   Lane; Loesser
Day Dreaming   Kahn; Kern
Daybreak   Duke
Debutante Number One   Loesser; Young, Victor
Did Anyone Ever Tell You?   Cahn
Din't Cha Mother Tell You Nothin'?   Kalmar; Ruby
Do You Believe in Fairy Tales?   David, Mack
Do You Call That a Buddy   Raye
Doggie, Take Your Time   Cahn
Dolores   Alter; Loesser
Don Pedro Pistachio   Styne
Donna Maria   Wrubel
Don't Blow That Horn, Gabriel   Duke
Don't Cry, Cherie   Brown, Lew; Henderson
Don't Cry Little Cloud   Loesser
Don't Ever Break a Promise   David, Mack
Don't Forget to Say "No" Baby   Carmichael
Don't Let It Happen Again   Duke
Don't Sell the Night Short   Blane; Martin
Down in the Carolines   Young, Joseph
Down Mexico Way   Styne
Down the Glacier Trail   Stept
Dream Dancing   Porter

Drinking Song   Styne
Duello, The   Hammerstein; Romberg
Eenie, Meenie, Minee, Mo   Duke
Elevator Man, The   Caesar
Eleven Levee Street   Hammerstein; Romberg
Emancipation   Livingston, Jerry
Emperor's Bones, The   Webster
Empty Interlude   Razaf
Encanto   Hart; Rodgers
Enchanted April   Egan
Evening Star   Parish
Ev'ry Time   Martin
Ev'rything I Love   Porter
Falling Castle (inst.)   Waller
Falling Star   De Lange; Willson
Faraway Islands, The   Loesser
Farming   Porter
(I'm) Feeling Lucky Today   Duke
Felicia   Russell
Find Yourself a Melody   Loesser
Flame Indigo   Ellington; Webster
Fooled   Russell
For You   Dubin
Forever and a Day   Hammerstein; Kern
Forever and Ever   Styne
Forgive Me   Ager; Yellen
Frere Jacque   Styne
From You   Styne
Full Moon   Russell
Fussin' with the Budget   Robison
Gaucho with the Black Mustache, The   Davis; Stept
Gay White Way   Magidson; Oakland
Gee, I Wish I Listened to My Mother   McHugh; Mercer
General's Lookin'   David, Mack
Get Rhythm in Your Feet   Razaf
Get Thee Behind Me, Clayton   Rainger; Robin
Get Yourself a Girl   Porter
Ghost of an Old Romance, The   Brown, A. Seymour
Giddy-Bug Galop (inst.), The   Ellington
Gimme Some Skin   DePaul
Gimme Some Skin (My Friend)   Raye
Girl with the Sugar Brown Hair, The   Bullock
Girls, The   Kalmar; Ruby
Give a Viva!   Rome
Give My Best to Bessie   Wrubel
Go Easy on the Money   Robison
Go West Young Lady   Cahn
Gold and Silver   Johnson, Howard
Goodbye Mama I'm Off to Yokahama   Coots
Grand Vacation with Pay, A   Gilbert; McHugh
Great American Broadcast, The   Gordon; Warren
Greeting Cards, The   Duke
Guy Who Brought Me, The   Martin
Guy with the Polka Dotted Tie, The   Styne
Hail to Bolenciecwcz   Rainger; Robin
Hang On to Your Lids, Kids   Arlen; Mercer
Happiest Birthday Routine   Styne
Happy Cowboy   Styne
Happy in Love   Fain
Happy in Love, Hi, Ho the Hoe-Down Way   Yellen
Harlem   Blake
Has Anybody Seen My Man   Styne
Has to Be   Styne
Hawaiian Party   Mercer; Schwartz, Arthur
He Lied and I Listened   Loesser

He Plays Gin Rummy   David, Mack; Silver
Heaven for Two   DePaul; Raye
Hello Ma! I Done It Again   Rainger; Robin
Hello Red, You're Lookin' Blue   Sigman
Hellzapoppin'   DePaul; Raye
Here I Am in the Army and I Don't Look Good in
      Brown   Coots; Egan
Here We Are Studying History   Loesser; Styne
Here's to the I.B.M.   Kalmar; Ruby
Hi, Ho the Hoe-Down Way   Fain
Hickory Stick   Webster
Hit the Ramp   Duke
Hi-Ya Love   Rainger; Robin
Hoe Down   Freed, Ralph
Hollywood Cinderella   Pollack
Home Town Paper   DePaul
Hometown Paper   Raye
Honolulu Lu   Cahn
Honor Bright   McHugh; Mercer
Hooray for Today   Rainger; Robin
Hop on Your Pogo Stick   Washington
How About You   Freed, Ralph; Lane
How Do You Say It   Cahn
How Green Was My Valley   Davis; Silver; Webster
How Long Did I Dream   Burke; Van Heusen
How Would You Feel   Kahn
Hula Ba Luau   DePaul; Raye
Humpty Dumpty Heart   Burke; Van Heusen
Hunky Dunky Dory   Styne
Hush-A-Bye Land   Duke
I Always Think of Sally   Duke
I Beg Your Pardon   Coots; Gordon
I Boogied when I Should Have Woogied   Mercer
I Caught a Ball at the Ball Game   Hoffman; Livingston, Jerry
I Close My Eyes   Styne
I Congratulate You, Mr. Cowboy   Hart; Rodgers
I Could Do This All Night Long   Brown, Lew; Henderson
I Could Get Along Without You   Burke; Van Heusen
I Could Kiss You for That   McHugh; Mercer
I Fell in Love with the Leader of the Band   Magidson; Styne
I Got Dat Feelin'   Arlen; Koehler
I Got It Bad and That Ain't Good   Ellington; Webster
I Got Tookin By a Good Good Lookin Man   Spina
I Gotta Ride   Lane; Loesser
I Guess We're Gonna Get Along   Razaf
I Hate You, Darling   Porter
I Haven't a Thing to Wear   Revel
I Hear America Singing   Parish
I Know Why (And So-Do-You)   Gordon; Warren
I Know You By Heart   Martin
I L-L-Love You So   Heyman
I Love You More   Cahn
I Repent (inst.)   Waller
I Struck a Match in the Dark   Hoffman; Livingston, Jerry
I Take to You   Gordon; Warren
I Turned White Overnight Over You   Revel
I Wanna Ride with the Man Who Blows the
      Whistle   Webster
I Want to Be the Guy   Rainger; Robin
I Want to Follow You   Freed, Ralph
I Wish I Had a Dime for Ever Time I Missed You   Hoffman;
      Livingston, Jerry
I Wish That I Could Be a Singing Cowboy   Cahn
I Wish You Were Here   Raye
I Yi Yi Yi Yi (I Like You Very Much)   Gordon; Warren

I'd Gladly Trade   Martin
I'd Like to Talk About the Weather   Duke
I'd Rather Dance   Brown, Nacio Herb; Freed, Ralph
If I Was Only Twenty-One   Fisher
If It's You   Oakland
If Life Were All Peaches and Cream   Webster
If That's Propaganda   Arlen; Gershwin, Ira; Harburg
If You're in Love   Loesser; Styne
I'll Be a Good Soldier Too   Razaf
I'll Dance at Your Wedding (Honey Dear)   Carmichael;
   Loesser
I'll Get You — In the End   McHugh; Mercer
I'll Meet You at Sundown   Mills
I'll Never Ever Pass Your House Again   Johnson, Howard
I'll Never Let a Day Pass By   Loesser
I'll Take the City   Duke
I'm a Little Wabbit in Da Sunshine   David, Mack
I'm Afraid of Myself   Lawrence; Silver
I'm Alive and Kickin'   Rainger; Robin
I'm Dancing with the Mamas with the Moolah   Fain; Kahal;
   Yellen
I'm Here Lawd!   Arlen; Koehler
I'm in Glory   Adamson; McHugh
I'm in Good Shape (For the Shape I'm In)   Revel
I'm in No Mood for Music   Loesser
I'm Making a Play for You   Rainger; Robin
I'm Missin' Mississippi   Donaldson
I'm Satisfied   Ellington; Parish
I'm the One Who's Lonely   Styne
In a Moment of Surrender   McHugh; Mercer
In Buenos Aires   Styne
In Copacabana   Revel
In Old Champlain   Friend
In the Middle of a Dance   Yellen
In Waikiki   Mercer; Schwartz, Arthur
Is It Taboo to Fall in Love with You   Leslie
Is that Good?   Rainger; Robin
It Ain't Right to Say Ain't   De Lange
It Can Happen to Anyone   Hammerstein; Romberg
It Could Only Happen in the Movies   Adamson; Duke
It Happened in Hawaii   Dubin
It Happened in Sun Valley   Gordon; Warren
It Just Happened   Freed, Ralph; McHugh
It Won't Be Fun (But It's Gotta Be Done)   Robin
It's a Mighty Fine Country We Have Here   Fain; Kahal;
   Yellen
It's a New Kind of Thing   Fain; Kahal; Yellen
It's All in a Lifetime   Gordon; Warren
It's Always You   Burke; Van Heusen
It's Circus Day Again   Washington
It's in the Cards   Coslow; Rainger; Robin
It's New to Us   Berlin
It's No Fun Eating Alone   Eliscu; Gorney
It's One of Those Days   Donaldson
It's People Like You   DePaul; Raye
It's Spring Again   Washington
I've Got a Bone to Pick with You   Gordon; Warren
I've Got a Passport from Georgia (And I'm Going to the
   U.S.A.)   Webster
I've Got Some Unfinished Business with You   Porter
I've Got Somethin'   Kalmar; Ruby
I've Got to Hand It to You   Duke
I've Got You All to Myself   Rainger; Robin
Jack of All Trades   Magidson; Oakland
Jerry, My Soldier Boy   Porter

Joe O'Grady   Styne
Johnny Jones   Loesser
Julie   De Lange
Jump for Joy   Ellington; Webster
Just a Little Joint with a Juke Box   Martin
Just a-Settin' and a Rockin'   Ellington
Just Squeeze Me   Ellington
Karinina   Revel
Katy-Did, Katy-Didn't   Carmichael; Loesser
Keep Your Thumbs Up   Brooks
Kickin' the Conga Around   Stept
Kid with the Drum, The   Cahn
Kindergarten Conga (Ring Around the Rosie), The   Rainger;
   Robin
Kiss Me Tonight for Tomorrow   Washington
Kiss Polka, The   Gordon; Warren
Kiss the Boys Goodbye   Loesser
Ladies from Paree   Lerner, Sammy
Lady   Duke
Lady Needs a Rest, A   Porter
Lailu   Mercer; Warren
Land of the Loon   De Lange
Last Call for Love   Monaco
Last Time I Saw Paris, The   Hammerstein
Leave My Women Alone   Adamson; Duke
Lesson in Latin, A   Freed, Ralph
Let Me Live Today   Hammerstein; Romberg
Let Me Love You Tonight   Parish
Let Us All Take Care of Tillie, While the Government Is
   Taking Care of Willie   Brown, Lew
Let's Face It   Porter
Let's Go Home   Evans; Livingston, Jay
Let's Keep 'Em Flying   DePaul; Raye
Let's Not Talk About Love   Porter
Let's Play Cowboys and Indians   David, Mack
Let's Play We're Having Fun   Romberg
Let's Say Goodnight with a Dance   Fain; Kahal; Yellen
Letter Song, The   Freed, Ralph
Like a Straw in the Wind   Arlen; Koehler
Lilly and Billy   Styne
Little Ace o' Spades   Arlen; Koehler
Little Boy in Corduroy   Russell
Little Old Church in England, A   Berlin
Little Red Caboose   David, Mack
Little Rhumba Numba, A   Porter
Lolita   Hart; Rodgers
Lo-Lo-Lita   Russell
Lonely Hills   Styne
Lonesome and Low   Arlen; Koehler
Long Ago   Duke
Long Ago Last Night   Gordon; Warren
Look at You, Look at Me   Loesser; Styne
Look Out for Mister Stork   Washington
Lordy   Hammerstein; Romberg
Love Can Settle Everything   Eliscu; Gorney
Love in a Changing World   Eliscu; Gorney
Love Is Such an Old Fashioned Thing   Loesser
Love Me As I Am   Alter; Loesser
Loveable Lady of the Night   Mills
Loveable Sort of Person   Loesser; Young, Victor
Loved One   Russell
Loveliness and Love   Rainger; Robin
Lovely   Dietz; Schwartz, Arthur
Luna de Cuba   Ellington
Magic of Magnolias   Loesser

Make a Date with a Great Psychoanalyst   Porter
Make with the Feet   Adamson; Duke
Making Conversation   Hammerstein; Romberg
Man with the Lollypop Song, The   Gordon; Warren
Manana   Lane; Loesser
Manuelo   Fain; Kahal; Yellen
Maria Elena   Russell
Maria Inez   Gilbert
Memories   Kalmar; Ruby
Memphis Blues   Loesser
Men of Clayton   Rainger; Robin
Message from the U.S.A., A   Baer
Mexican Jumping Beat   DePaul; Raye
Miami   Rainger; Robin
Military Love Song, The   Brown, Nacio Herb; Freed, Ralph
Milk, Milk, Milk   Porter
Miserlou   Russell
Mister Dodd   DePaul; Raye
Mittel-Europa   Eliscu; Gorney
Modern Design for Love   Friend
Modes Made in Manhattan   Duke
Moments to Remember   Egan
Monkey on a String, The   David, Mack
Moon Fell in the River, The   Parish
Moonlight in Hawaii   DePaul; Raye
Moonlight Masquerade   Lawrence
Moon-tide   Robison
More Mittel-Europa   Eliscu; Gorney
Most Gentlemen Don't Prefer a Lady   Cahn
Mother Never Told Me Why   Cahn
Mr. Dodd   DePaul; Raye
Music Makers   Raye
Musical Chairs   Eliscu; Gorney
My Boy, My Boy   Loesser
My Dream Feathered Nest   Stept
My Dream of My Paree   Donaldson
My First Promise   Blane
My Girl and I   Hammerstein; Romberg
My Heart Jumped Over the Moon   Mills
My Kind of Country   Loesser; McHugh
My Kinda Love   Cahn
My Kinda Music   Cahn
My Love Is Yours Forever   Adamson
My Own America   Wrubel; Young, Victor
My Rainbow Song   Parish
My Song Without Words   Duke
(That's How I Got) My Start   Loesser
My Sweetheart Mamie   Kalmar; Ruby
Nango, The   Gordon; Warren
Navy Blues   Mercer; Schwartz, Arthur
Never Feel Too Weary to Pray   Willson
Never Go to Argentina   Hart; Rodgers
Never Never Never   Styne
New World, The   Donaldson; Kahn
Nickel to My Name, A   Duke
Night Song   Mills
Night You Name the Day (inst.), The   Brown, Nacio Herb
Nip Ups to McCarthy   Donaldson
No! No! No!   Lewis
North America Meets South America   Hart; Rodgers
Nostalgia   Ellington; Webster
Not too Lovely to Love (inst.)   Kern
Obviously the Gentleman Prefers to Dance   Cahn
Off to See the World   DePaul; Raye
Oh Auntie   Fain; Kahal; Yellen

Oh He Loves Me   Cahn
Oh How He Can Salute   Hanley
Oh, Joyful Day   Lerner, Sammy
Old Honolulu (inst.)   Schwartz, Arthur
Old Pardner   Brown, Lew; Stept
(Give Me an) Old-Fashioned Waltz   Ellington
On Lake Louise   Adamson
On Miami Shore   Loesser; Young, Victor
On the Banks of the Mildew River   Eliscu; Gorney
On Wings of Song   Loesser
Once Upon a Summertime   Brooks
One Love   Robin
Opening Chorus (George M. Krause's High
      Kickers)   Kalmar; Ruby
Operatic Prelude to Show   Loesser; Styne
Orange Blossom Lane   Parish
Palm Garden (inst.)   Waller
Panic in Panama   Kalmar; Ruby
Paul Lawrence Dunbar   Razaf
Peaceful Valley   Robison
Peekaboo to You   Mercer; Sigman
Pen of Stephen Foster, The   Johnston; Robison
Pets   Porter
Petunia   Brown, Lew; Brown, Nacio Herb
Phi Beta Conga   Freed, Ralph
Pig Foot Pete   DePaul; Raye
Pink Cocktail for a Blue Lady, A   Magidson; Oakland
Pink Elephants on Parade   Washington
Play Fiddle Play   Lawrence
Poi   DePaul; Raye
Pot, Pan and Skillet   Ellington; Webster
Pound Your Table Polka   Drake
Prairie Belle   Duke
Prairie Serenade   Styne
Prairieland Lullaby   Loesser; Young, Victor
Printer's Lament   Styne
P.S. I Got the Job   McHugh; Mercer
Purple Sage in the Twilight   Styne
Pussy Cat Agony Five   Russell
Puttin' on the Dog   DePaul; Raye
Que Chica   Burke; Van Heusen
Queen of the Opera, The   Duke
Rainbow Bridge   Russell
Reap the Wild Wind   Pollack; Washington
Red Moon of the Caribees (Cancion Del Mar)   Drake
Remember Pearl Harbor   Howard, Joseph E.
Return to Dora Flora   Eliscu; Gorney
Revenge   Porter
Reverend Johnson's Dream   Arlen; Koehler
Ride 'Em Cowboy   DePaul; Raye
Ridin' on a Rocky Road   Styne
Ridin' the Range   Styne
Ring Those Bells   David, Mack; Silver
Rio Cristal   Duke
Rio De Janeiro, The   Cahn
Rockabye Bay   Revel
Rock-a-bye the Boogie   Raye
Rockin' and Reelin'   DePaul
Rocks in My Bed   Ellington
Romance and Rhumba   Gordon; Monaco
Romeo Smith and Juliet Jones   Burke; Van Heusen
Rookies on Parade   Styne
Rub Your Lamp   Porter
Run, Little Raindrop, Run   Gordon; Warren
Sailor Boy   Cahn

Sailor Routine   Loesser; Styne
Sailor's Life for Me, A   DePaul; Raye
Salt o' the Sea   Lerner, Sammy
Saludos Amigos   Washington
Sand in My Shoes   Loesser
Says Who, Says You, Says I!   Arlen; Mercer
Scandinavian Polka (Polka Scandinavieene) (inst.)   Kern
Secluded   Donaldson
Sentimental Folks   Loesser; Styne
Serenade to a Pullman Porter   Hammerstein; Ruby
Shady Lady Bird   Blane
Share a Little   Harburg; Lane
Sharp Easter   Ellington
She Gave Her Heart to a Soldier Boy   Bryan
She Got Him   Hammerstein; Romberg
Shhhhh! He's on the Beat!   Ellington
Ship o' Dreams   Davis; Stept
Shootin' the Works for Uncle Sam   Porter
Shows How Wrong a Gal Can Be   Cahn
Sign Up for Happy Days   Styne
Simpatica   Hart; Rodgers
Since I Kissed My Baby Goodbye   Porter
Since You   Loesser; Styne
Sing a Song of Laughter   Styne
Sing de Lawd's Music   Freed, Ralph
Sing Out the Answer (Join the C.I.O.)   Eliscu; Gorney
Sing-Time Boogie-Boo Man   Sterling; Von Tilzer
Sinner Kissed an Angel, A   David, Mack
Sir Pumphrey Mildew   Eliscu; Gorney
Six Lessons from Madame La Zonga   Monaco
Skylark   Carmichael; Mercer
Sneakin' Home (inst.)   Waller
So Near and Yet So Far   Porter
So Shy   Magidson
So What Goes?   Ahlert
Solitary Seminole (Seminole Legend)   Rainger; Robin
Somewhere Along the Trail   Cahn
Song of the Roustabouts   Washington
Song of the Valley, The   David, Hal
Spread Your Wings   Washington
Starlight, Starbright   DePaul; Raye
Stealing the Star of Asia (inst.)   Brown, Nacio Herb
Story of a Starry Night, The   Hoffman; Livingston, Jerry
Strawberry Lane   McHugh; Mercer
Street Was Crowded, The   Fisher
String of Pearls, A   De Lange
Subtle Slough   Ellington
Summer Is A-Comin' In   Duke
Sun Will Soon Be Setting, The   Lerner, Sammy
Sunny River   Hammerstein; Romberg
Sweet Is the Blush of May   Lerner, Sammy
Sweet Patootie Kitty   Styne
Sweet Talk   Razaf
Swingin' Sam the Cowboy Man   Styne
Take Her My Boy   Eliscu; Gorney
Take My Heart   Styne
Tale of Two Cities, A   Lewis
Tales from the Vienna Woods   Johnson, Howard
Tan Town Divorce   Blake; Razaf
Tango   Duke
Tap It Out   Freed, Ralph; Lane
Tattletale   Lawrence
Tears in Tennessee   Robison
Texas Trail   Styne
Thank You, South America   Fain; Kahal; Yellen

Thank Your Lucky Stars and Stripes   Burke; Van Heusen
Thanks for the Boogie Ride   Mitchell
That Ain't Hay (That's the U.S.A.)   Loesser; Styne
That's How I Love the Blues   Martin
That's Southern Hospitality   Coslow
That's the Kind of Work I Do   Cahn
(The Flow'rs, the Trees) The Butterflies and Bees   Romberg
There Ain't Any Chorus to This Song   Livingston, Jerry
There Are Such Things   Baer; Meyer
There's a Happy Hunting Ground   Coslow
There's a Little Bit of Scotch in Me   Razaf
There's No Forgetting You   Loesser
There's Nothing Like a Hoedown   Styne
They Can't Get You Down   Eliscu; Gorney
They Met in Rio (A Midnight Serenade)   Gordon; Warren
Think Well of Me   Robison
This Is the House that Love Built   De Lange
This Is the Night of My Dreams   McHugh; Mercer
This Is Where I Came In   Duke
This Night Will Seem Long Ago   Romberg
This Time the Dream's on Me   Arlen; Mercer
Those Good Old Fluffy Ruffle Days   Baer
Three B's, The   Martin
Three Little Wishes   Styne
Three Men on a Date   Blane; Martin
Three Rousing Cheers   Duke
Time Is Standing Still   Hammerstein; Romberg
Time Out for Rhythm   Cahn
Time to Sing, The   Kalmar; Ruby
Time Was   Russell
To Your Hearts Content   Russell
Toast of the Boys at the Post, The   Duke
Together   DePaul; Raye
Tojo, Benito and Adolph   Stept
Tonight at Sundown   Duke
Toodles Imitation   Loesser
Toy Meets Girl   Heyman
Tres Bien   Styne
Tropical Magic   Gordon; Warren
Trout, The   Freed, Ralph
Try Love   Davis
Try Not to Forget   Drake
Tumble Down Shack in Havana   Styne
Twenty-Five Bucks a Week   Gorney
Twenty-One Bucks a Week   Eliscu; Gorney
Twiddlin' My Thumbs   Cahn
Two in Love   Willson
(Cindy with the) Two Left Feet   Webster
Two Little Squirrels, The   David, Mack
Two of a Kind   Ahlert
Two Tickets to Heaven   Silver
Uncle Luke Had a Beard   Styne
Uncle Sammy Here I Am   Johnson, James P.
Uncle Tom's Cabin Is a Drive-In Now   Webster
Under Your Window   Coots; Harbach
Until the Stars Fall Down   Donaldson
Unzer Amerika   Eliscu; Gorney
Up Jumped the Devil with the Jive   Silver
Up to His Old Tricks Again   Porter
Upsala   Duke
Wa Wa Watermelon   Styne
Wait Till It Happens to You   Arlen; Mercer
Waiter and the Porter and the Upstairs Maid, The   Mercer
Waltzing in the Moonlight   Kalmar; Ruby
Waltzing on the Kalamazoo   Drake

Wan'rin Aroun' (inst.)   Waller
Warm Valley   Ellington; Russell
Watch the Birdie   DePaul; Raye
Water   DePaul; Raye
Water Melon Moon   Sterling
Waterloo Bridge   Lawrence; Silver
We Did It Before (We'll Do It Again)   Friend
We Must Have Music   Brown, Nacio Herb; Kahn
We Walked in the Garden   Lawrence
We Watch the Skyways   Kahn
Wedding Cake Walk, The   Porter
Weekend in Havana, A   Gordon; Warren
We'll Have A Lot of Fun   DePaul; Raye
We'll Knock the Japs Right in the Laps of the
     Nazis   Pollack; Washington
Well, Well   Loesser; Styne
We're Having a Baby, My Baby and Me   Adamson; Duke
We're in the Navy   DePaul; Raye
We're Living in a Wonderful County, I Wouldn't Worry
     about a Thing If I Were You   Koehler; Monaco
We're on the Track   Hart; Rodgers
We're the Couple in the Castle   Carmichael; Loesser
We're the Sun Tan Tenth of the Nation   Webster
We've Got to Do a Job on the Japs, Baby   Baer; Leslie;
     Meyer
We've Met Somewhere Before   Loesser
Wham   Martin
What Are Little Husbands Made Of   Porter
What Do You Think I Am   Martin
What Every Young Man Should Know   Duke
What Is This Magic That's Yours   Washington
What Kind of Love Is This?   DePaul; Raye
What More Do You Want   Cahn
What's All the Shoutin' For   Pollack
What's Happened   Stept
What's New   Burke
What's on the Penny   Ahlert
What's Your Favorite Holiday   Styne
When   Davis; Stept
When a Lark Learns to Fly   Romberg
When a Sailor Goes Ashore   Loesser; Styne
When Are We Going to Land Abroad   Mercer; Schwartz,
     Arthur
When I Love, I Love   Gordon; Warren
When I See an Elephant Fly   Washington
When I Sing   Lerner, Sammy
When Private Brown Becomes a Captain   Raye
When the Sun Comes Out   Arlen; Koehler
When You Sign Off My Heart   Fisher
Where Are You?   Warren
Where Do We Dream from Here   Styne
Where Do You Travel?   Blane
Where Is Dis Road A-Leadin' Me To?   Arlen; Koehler
Where the River Meets the Range   Styne
Where You Are   Gordon; Warren
Wherever You Are   Revel
White Blossoms of Tah-ni   Loesser
Who Killed Vaudeville   Fain; Yellen
Who Should Come Along but You   Parish
Who Started the Rhumba? (Who Made the Rhumba)   Duke
Who Threw the Whiskey in the Well   De Lange
Who's to Blame   Duke
Why Don't We Do This More Often   Wrubel
Why Is It So   Cahn
Wings of England, The   Adamson; Revel

Wishful Thinking   Rainger; Robin
Won't You Come Over to Dover, Jerry   Fisher
Woodland Symphony   David, Hal
World Is Waiting to Waltz Again, The   Gordon; Warren
Ya Should a Seen Pete   Styne
Yankee Doodle Polka, The   Duke; Parish
Yanks Are on the March Again, The   Adamson
Year Isn't Such a Long, Long Time, A   Brown, A. Seymour
Yes My Darling Daughter   Lawrence
Yogi (Who Lost His Will Power), The   McHugh; Mercer
You and I   Willson
You Can Kiss These Goodnight Kisses Goodbye   Freed,
     Ralph; Hoffman
You Can't Beat My Bill   Porter
You Can't Blackout Romance   Bryan; Schwartz, Jean
You Don't Know What Love Is   DePaul; Raye
You Go Your Way (And I'll Go Crazy)   Revel
You Gotta Pull Strings   Donaldson
You Irritate Me So   Porter
You Lucky People, You   Burke; Van Heusen
You Never Saw a Bigger Little Man   Livingston, Jerry
You Started Something   Rainger
You Stepped Out of a Dream   Brown, Nacio Herb; Kahn
You Tell Her I Stutter Introduction   Loesser
You Took Me by Surprise   Duke
You Were There   DePaul; Raye
You'll Never Get Rich   Cahn
Your Eyes   Blane; Martin
Your Words and My Music   Freed, Arthur
You're a Lucky Fellow Mr. Smith   Raye
You're a Natural   Mercer; Schwartz, Arthur
You're Dangerous   Burke; Van Heusen
(T' Me Baby) You're News   Harburg
You're on My Mind   Kalmar; Ruby
You're Only a Barefoot Boy   Eliscu; Gorney
You're the One for Me   McHugh; Mercer
You've Got the Best of Me   Hart; Rodgers
You've Got What It Takes   DePaul; Raye
Zoompa Polka, The   Brown, Lew

1942

Abraham   Berlin
Abraham Lincoln (The White House in the Boy)   Davis;
     Parish
Adieu, Madame   Egan
Ai Paisano   Loesser
Ain't Got a Dime to My Name (Ho Ho Hum)   Burke; Van
     Heusen
Aladdin's Daughter   Burke; Van Heusen
All Done All Through   Cahn; Styne
All I Need Is You   Davis; Parish
All My Life   Mitchell; Stept
All Through the Night   Schwartz, Arthur
Alone in a Crowd   Loewe
American Serenade (inst.), An   Alter
And Still the Volga Flows   Willson
And then Came Love   Razaf
Angels of Mercy   Berlin
Annabella's Bustle   Pollack
Any Place Down South   Razaf
Any Way the Wind Blows   Burke; Van Heusen
Anywhere on Earth Is Heaven   Washington; Young, Victor
Apple Blossoms in the Rain   Pollack
Are You Kiddin'?   Rainger; Robin

Are You Kiddin' Bud?   Davis
Are You Living Old Man   Silver
Arms for the Love of America   Berlin
Army of Hippocrates, The   Carmichael
Army's Made a Man Out of Me, The   Berlin
Arthur Murray Taught Me Dancing in a Hurray   Mercer
At Last   Gordon; Warren
At Sonya's Cafe   Hoffman; Livingston, Jerry
(Did I Get Stinking) At the Club Savoy   Donaldson
Atlas Did It (But He Won't Admit It)   DePaul; Raye
Au Revoir, Paree   Dietz; Schwartz, Arthur
Azalea   Ellington
Baby   Loesser; McHugh
Baby That's for Me   Donaldson
Baby's a Big Girl Now   Cahn; Styne
Back the Red, White and Blue with Gold   Hoffman;
     Livingston, Jerry
Backwoods Barbecue   Revel
Bad Little Three Blind Mice, The   Lerner, Sammy
Baltimore Oriole   Carmichael; Webster
Bandage on Your Knee   Caesar
Barrel House Bessie from Basin Street   Magidson; Styne
Barrelhouse Beguine   Kern; Mercer
Be a Good Soldier While Your Daddy's Away   Caesar
Be Calm   Rome
Be Careful It's My Heart   Berlin
Beat Beat Drums   Weill
Before You Know It I'll Be Home Mary   Silver
Beware   Revel
Bim Bam Boom   Adamson
Blue Is My Heart   Davis; Silver
Blue Shadows and White Gardenias   Gordon
Blue Sweetheart   Friend
Blues   De Lange
Bombardier Song   Hart; Rodgers
Boogie Woogie Bunga Boo   Razaf
Booker T. Washington Brigade, The   Loesser; Styne
Bottoms Up   Hart; Rodgers
Bowery Serenade (Sweet Pippy)   De Lange
Boy I Left Behind Me, The   Hart; Rodgers
Boy in Khaki, a Girl in Lace, A   Wrubel
Boys with the Wistful Eyes, The   DePaul; Raye
Bravest of the Brave   DePaul; Raye
Brazilian Boogie Woogie   Davis
Brazilian Samba   Schwartz, Jean
Buckle Down Buck Private   Blane
Bunny, Bunny, Bunny (The Bunny Song)   Rome
Burning Sands   Myrow
But Are We Worried Yes!   Revel
Bye, Bye, Benito   Brown, Lew
Bye Bye Bonnie   Warren
Cairo   Harburg; Schwartz, Arthur
Call Out the Marines   Revel
Can't Get Out of This Mood   Loesser; McHugh
Canzonetta   David, Mack
Captains of the Clouds   Arlen; Mercer
Careless Rhapsody   Hart; Rodgers
Cash for Your Trash   Waller
Changeable Heart   Brooks
Cherokee Charlie   Brooks
Cindy Lou McWilliams   Revel
Close to You   Livingston, Jerry
Coast to Coast on a Bus   Baer
Come Back Again Ya Hear   DePaul; Raye
Comin' In on a Wing and a Prayer   Adamson; McHugh

Conchita Marquita Lolita Pepita Rosita Juanita
     Lopez   Magidson; Styne
Conga Beso   DePaul; Raye
Conga Tap, The   Razaf
Congalero   Mills
Constantly   Burke; Van Heusen
Cooperate with Your Air Raid Warden   Magidson; Styne
Cotcha Too-ta Mee (Alma Mater)   Cahn; Styne
Count Me In   Stept
Couple of Caballeros, A   Arlen; Harburg
Cradle of Rhythm   Razaf
Cradle Song   Freed, Ralph
Cranky Old Yank (In a Clanky Old Tank), The   Carmichael
Crispus Attucks   Razaf
Dance Me Again Till I'm Dreamy   Howard, Joseph E.
Dark Eyes   Razaf
Dearly Beloved   Kern; Mercer
Delicious Delirium   Revel
Did You Happen to Find a Heart   Pollack
Did You Happen to Find a Heart (This Morning)   Magidson
Dig Dig Dig for Victory   Styne
Dirge for Two Veterans   Weill
Dixie   Revel
Do I Need You   Cahn
Do It Now   Lawrence
Do You Still Love Me   Wrubel
Don't Disappear   Burke; Van Heusen
Don't Ever Say Goodnight   Sigman
Don't Get Around Much Anymore   Ellington; Russell
Don't Let a Blackout Give You a Knockout   Caesar
Don't Sit Under the Apple Tree with Anyone Else but
     Me   Brown, Lew; Stept
Don't Steal the Sweetheart of a Soldier   Brown, Lew; Coots
Don't You Know   Burke; Van Heusen
Down Louisiana Way (Cane Grinding) (inst.)   Kern
Down on Ami Ami Oni Oni Island   Gordon
(That Place) Down the Road a Piece   Raye
Dream Dance   Schwartz, Jean
Dreamer's Lullaby   Freed, Ralph
Dreamy   Johnson, James P.
East of the West Wind   Davis; Parish
El Rancho   Loewe
Ever So Often   Silver
Every Night About This Time   Monaco
Every Time a Moment Goes By   Brooks
Everybody Dance   Coslow
Ev'ry Night About this Time   Koehler
Ev'rything I've Got   Hart; Rodgers
Except with You   Rainger; Robin
Fare Thee Well to Eldorado   Webster
Fats Waller et le Swing (inst.)   Waller
Feller Who Plays in a Band   Coslow
Fireside Chat, A   Hoffman; Livingston, Jerry
Five O'Clock Drag   Adamson; Ellington
Flag of Freedom, The   Freed, Ralph
Fleet's In, The   Mercer
Flotsom and Jetsam   DePaul; Raye
Fool Meets Fool   Hart; Rodgers
For Jupiter and Greece   Hart; Rodgers
For the Flag, For the Home, For the Family (For the Future
     of All Mankind)   Cohan
Forgive Me Again   Donaldson
Franklin D. — Winston C. — Joseph V. — Victory
     Jones   Rome
Friendly Little Farm   Hammerstein

From the Coast of Maine to the Rockies   Davis
Full Moon and an Empty Heart, A   Revel
Fun to Be Free   Alter; Heyman
Funny Money Man, The   Hoffman; Livingston, Jerry
Gateway of the Temple of Minerva, The   Hart; Rodgers
General MacArthur's Army   Eliscu; Gorney
Get on Board Little Children   DePaul; Raye
Gibbs and Finney   Baer
Give Me a Saddle   DePaul
Give Me My Saddle   Raye
Give the Kids a Chance   Cahn; Styne
Glory Day   Rainger; Robin
Go Get 'Em Soldier Boys   Howard, Joseph E.
Golden Wedding Day   DePaul; Raye
Gonna Be a Judgement Day   Wrubel
Goodnight Captain Curlyhead   Ahlert; Lewis
Gorgeous to Gaze At   Schwartz, Jean
Got a New Boy Friend   Schwartz, Jean
Got the Moon in My Pocket   Burke; Van Heusen
Got to Have a Man of My Own   Razaf
Got Wings on My Broncho in the Sky   Baer; Meyer
Greeks Have Got the Girdle, The   Hart; Rodgers
Guardian Angel   Monaco
Guerillas' Song, The   Webster
Hail and Farewell   Pollack
Hand Me Down, The   Loewe
Hands Across the Border   Revel
Happiness Calling   Schwartz, Jean
Happy Journey   Koehler; Monaco
Harbor of My Heart, The   Heyman
Harlem's a Garden   Razaf
Harvey, the Humble Bumble Bee   Burke; Van Heusen
Have a Heart Josephine   Davis
Hawaiian Prelude   Gordon; Warren
Hayfoot, Strawfoot   Drake
He Didn't Ask Me   Cahn
He Loved Me Till the All Clear Came   Arlen; Mercer
Heavenly, Isn't It   Revel
Here Comes Katrinka   Loesser; Styne
Here Comes that Moon Again   Caesar
Here You Are   Rainger; Robin
Here's a Hand   Hart; Rodgers
Here's a Toast to the Coast Guard   Lawrence
Here's to the Flag! Keep It Flying Over Her, Over There,
    Everywhere   Coots
He's My Guy   DePaul; Raye
Hey Zeke! Your Country's Callin'   Hoffman; Livingston,
    Jerry
Hip Hip Hooray   Loesser; Styne
His Word Is As Good As His Bond   Coots
History Eight to the Bar   Rome
Hit the Road to Dreamland   Arlen; Mercer
Homecoming   Donaldson; Mercer
Horse and Buggy and Freedom   Kahal; Stept
Hot Dog (Ain't that Wiener Good)   Raye
Hot Gavotte   Loewe
Hot Meat Blue Plate Special   David, Mack
How About a Cheer for the Navy?   Berlin
How Did It Happen   Kahal; Warren
How to Write a Popular Song   Donaldson
Humming-Bird   Adamson
I Came Here to Talk for Joe   Brown, Lew; Stept
I Can See You Now   Magidson; Pollack
I Can't Tell a Lie   Berlin

I Can't Wait Until Tomorrow 'Cause Tomorrow I Go Home
    on Leave   Drake
I Dare You   Freed, Ralph; Lane
I Did It for Defense   Rome
I Don't Know What Kind of Blues I've Got   Ellington
I Don't Mind   Ellington
I Don't Repent   Schwartz, Jean
I Don't Want Anybody At All (If I Can't Have
    You)   Magidson; Styne
I Don't Want to Be Loved by Anyone Else but
    You   Livingston, Jerry
I Don't Want to Walk Without You   Loesser; Styne
I Follow Shadows   Raye
I Found a Peach in Orange, New Jersey   Heyman; Spina
I Get the Neck of the Chicken   Loesser; McHugh
I Got Sugar, Plenty Sugar   Razaf
I Had the Craziest Dream   Gordon; Warren
I Haven't a Thing to Wear   Revel
I Heard It on the Hit Parade   Ruby
I Heard the Birdies Sing   Rainger; Robin
I Just Kissed Your Picture Goodnight   David, Mack
I Knew It Would Be This Way   Coslow
I Know what You Do   Mills
I Laughed at Love (Now Love Has the Laugh on
    Me)   Gilbert
I Learned to Cry   Baer; De Lange
I Left My Heart at the Stage Door Canteen   Berlin
I Like a Man Who Makes Music   Magidson; Pollack
I Like a Military Tune   Gordon; Warren
I Like to Be Loved by You   Gordon; Revel; Warren
I Loved Him So   DePaul; Raye
I Met Her on Monday   Wrubel
I Met You in a Dream   Donaldson
I Must Have Priorities on Your Love   Clare; Pollack
I Never Had a Dream to My Name   Webster
I Paid My Income Tax Today   Berlin
I Put a Four Leaf Clover in Your Pocket   Davis
I Remember You   Mercer
I Said "No"   Loesser; Styne
I Threw a Kiss in the Ocean   Berlin
I Wanna Marry a Bombardier   David, Mack
I Wonder Who's Kissing the Girl I Left Behind   Howard,
    Joseph E.
I'd Like to Do What I'd Like to Do   Friend
I'd Love to Know You Better   Magidson; Styne
I'd Rather Stay Home and Be Lonely (Than Go Out with
    Somebody Else)   Davis
If   DePaul; Raye
If I Do, I Ded a Whippin', I Dood It   Baer
If I Ever Get Back to Hannah   Henderson
If I Were Santa Claus for a Day   Clare; Pollack
If I'm Not Back in Five Minutes (Start Without
    Me)   Hoffman; Livingston, Jerry
If It's a Dream   Brooks
If It's Love   Cahn; Styne
If Mother Could Only See Us Now   Pollack
If You Build a Better Mouse Trap   Mercer
If You Can't Enlist, Buy a Victory Bond   Razaf
If You're Spanish   Cahn
I'll Be Back   Razaf
I'll Be Marching to a Love Song   Rainger; Robin
I'll Capture Your Heart   Berlin
I'll Have to Make a Safety   Caesar
I'll Leave My Heart with You   Davis
I'll Never Forgive Myself   David, Mack; Davis

I'll Never Make the Same Mistake Again   Coots
I'll Remember April   DePaul; Raye
I'll Take Manila   Arlen; Harburg
I'll Take Tallulah   Arlen; Harburg; Lane
I'll Tell the World   Loewe
I'm a Sailor   Schwartz, Jean
I'm Afraid of You Tonight   Dubin; Friend
I'm Amazed at You   Loesser; Spina
I'm Buying a Bond for My Baby   Gilbert; McHugh
I'm Cookin' with Gas   Mercer
I'm Doin' It for Defense   Arlen
I'm Doing It for Defense   Mercer
I'm Getting Tired So I Can Sleep   Berlin
I'm Gonna Move to the Outskirts of Town   Razaf
I'm Gonna Take You Dancin' (on Saturday Night)   Baer
I'm Mighty Proud of That Old Gang of Mine   Koehler; Stept
I'm Not Good Enough for You   David, Mack
I'm Not Just Anybody's Baby   Russell
I'm Old Fashioned   Kern; Mercer
I'm on My Way to College   Cahn; Styne
I'm Percy Pinchill of Harlem   Razaf
I'm Red, White and Blue Over You   De Lange; Stept
I'm Rhythm Crazy Now   Mills
I'm So Glad   Schwartz, Jean
I'm Still Crazy for You   Rainger; Robin
I'm Threading My Needle with Twilight   Coots
In an Old Cathedral Garden   Clare; Pollack
In My Wildest Dreams   Cahn
In the Army   Loesser; Spina
In the Spell of the Night   Brennan; Friml
In Times Like These   Dietz; Schwartz, Arthur
In Trinidad   Schwartz, Jean
Infantry Song, The   Wrubel
Isabella Kissed a Fella   Hoffman; Livingston, Jerry
Island of the Moon, The   DePaul; Raye
It Doesn't Make Sense   Brooks
(How Do You Fall in Love) It Just Happens to
      Happen   Revel
It Just Isn't There   Cahn
It Pays to Advertise (inst.)   Waller
It Takes a Guy Like I   Cahn; Styne
It's a Long Long Way to Yesterday   Adamson
It's Fun to Be Free   Rome
It's Gettin' the Best of Me   Coots; De Lange
It's People Like You   DePaul; Raye
It's the Lover's Knot   Gordon; Warren
It's the New Generation   Donaldson
I've Got a Gal in Kalamazoo   Gordon; Warren
I've Got Plenty to Be Thankful For   Berlin
I've Got You   Loesser
I've Heard that Song Before   Cahn; Styne
Java Jive   Oakland
Jingle Jangle Jingle   Loesser
Jitterbug, The (inst)   Styne
Jitterbug Waltz (inst.), The   Waller
Jitterbug's Lullaby (Jitterbug's Death)   Loesser; Spina
Jive Samba   Pollack
Johnny Get Your Gun Again   DePaul; Raye
Johnny Is a Hoarder   Rome
Johnny's Patter   Loesser
Journey to Your Lips, A   Webster
Juke Box Jump   Mills
Jungle Rhythm Roundup   Razaf
Jupiter Forbid   Hart; Rodgers
Just As Though You Were Here   De Lange

Just Over the Hill   Razaf
Just Plain Lonesome   Burke; Van Heusen
Just to Be Near You   DePaul
Keep 'Em Laughing   DePaul; Raye
Keep 'Em Rolling   Hart; Rodgers
Keep 'Em Smiling   Ager; Rose
Keep Mum Chum   Howard, Joseph E.
Keep the Light Burning Bright (In the Harbor)   Dietz;
      Harburg; Schwartz, Arthur
Keepin' Out of Trouble   Razaf
Kissing Rock, The   Hammerstein; Harbach; Kern
Knock Me a Kiss   Razaf
Ladies of St. James, The   Duke
Ladies of the Chorus   Berlin
Lady from Lockheed   Revel
Lady Is a WAAC, The   Rome
Lady with the Light in the Harbor   David, Hal; David, Mack
Lalapaluza Lu   Hoffman; Livingston, Jerry
Lamplighter's Serenade, The   Carmichael; Webster
Land of Dreams   De Lange
Land on Your Feet   Rainger; Robin
Last Call for Love, The   Arlen; Harburg; Lane
Laugh, Laugh, Laugh with Hey, Abbott/Hey, Costello   Mills
Lazy Mary (Johnny Darling Can't You Get Up)   Caesar
Let It Be Gay   Davis
Let Me Ride By Your Side in the Saddle   Howard, Joseph E.
Let's All Meet at My House   Burke; Van Heusen
Let's Bring New Glory to Old Glory   Gordon; Warren
Let's Dance to Victory   Baer
Let's Do It All Over   Howard, Joseph E.
Let's Get Over and Get It Over   Razaf
Let's Go Sailor (Shore Leave)   Mercer
Let's Go to Caliacabu   Brooks
Let's Hitch a Horsie to the Automobile   Hoffman;
      Livingston, Jay; Livingston, Jerry
Let's Make Murgatroyd Mayor   DePaul; Raye
Let's Start the New Year Right   Berlin
Let's Waltz and Whistle   Loewe
Let's Wander Down thru Mem'ry Lane   Baer
Let's Wander Down to a One Horse Town   Baer
Letter to General MacArthur   Rome
Life Could Be a Cakewalk with You   Arlen
Life of the Party   Loewe
Life Was Monotonous   Hart; Rodgers
Life with Father   Hart; Rodgers
Life Would Be a Cake-Walk with You   Koehler
Light of My Life, The   Revel
Lily of Laguna   Webster
Little Green Pocket of Green   Hanley
Little Miss Victory Jones   Rome
Little Pal (At the End of the Trail)   Pollack
Little Tingle Tangle Toes (In Her Wooden Shoes)   Webster
Little Wily Miss   Hammerstein; Harbach; Kern
Little Woman   Leslie
Liver Lipped Louie   Revel
Living High (On a Western Hill)   Rainger; Robin
Long Before You Came Along   Arlen; Harburg
Long Long Miles Between Us   Egan
Lord and Lady Gate   DePaul; Raye
Lose the Blackout Blues   Russell
Love Fell In   Blane
Love Is Such an Old Fashioned Thing   Loesser; Styne
Love Laughs at Anything   DePaul; Raye
Love Made a Mess Out of Me   De Lange
Love Me   DePaul; Raye

Lovely Luana   DePaul; Raye
Lovin' Man   Razaf
Loyal Sons of Leighton   Cahn
Mad   Cahn; Styne
Malay Love Song   Loesser; Styne
Maluna, Malalo, Mawaena (Hawaiian Drinking
      Song)   Gordon
Mama Come Home   Myrow
Man Without a Woman, A   Schwartz, Arthur
Mandy Is Two   Mercer
Manhattan Serenade   Adamson; Alter
Marines Have Landed, The   Monaco
Mark Twain Suite (inst.)   Kern
Massachusetts   Razaf
May I Have the Next Trance with You   Coslow
Me and My Fella and a Big Umbrella   Rainger; Robin
Me and My Melinda   Berlin
Men Behind the Man Behind the Gun, The   Rome
Midnight at the Masquerade   Rainger; Robin
Million Miles from Manhattan, A   Revel
Miss Gabriella Brown   Magidson; Wrubel
Mister Five By Five   DePaul; Raye
Mister Kelly (He Velly Nice Man)   Wrubel
Mittel-Europa   Gorney
Moment I Laid Eyes on You, The   Arlen; Koehler
Mommy Dear, I Want My Daddy   Howard, Joseph E.
Moonlight Becomes You   Burke; Van Heusen
Moonlight Mood   Adamson
Morning Glory   Carmichael; Webster
Most Unusual Weather (It's Such Unusual Weather)   Arlen;
      Harburg
Mother Nature, Father Time   Ahlert; Russell
Motor Boat Song (Put-Put-Put Your Arms Around Me),
      The   Hoffman; Livingston, Jerry
Mound Bayou   Razaf
Move Over, Jehovah (I'm Moverin' In)   Robison
Mr. Chucklehead   Rome
My Gal Alice   Revel
My Heart and I Decided   Donaldson
My Heart Belongs to America   Stept
My Heart Isn't In It   Lawrence
My Little Prayer   Gorney; Harburg
My Poor Heart Is Full of Scars   Revel
My Sentimental Heart   Parish
My Sergeant and I   Berlin
My Silent Symphony   Egan
My Song of Hate   Razaf; Waller
My Sugar's Plenty Sweet Enough for Me   Davis
My Ten Ton Baby and Me   Willson
Native Son, A   Razaf
Need I Speak?   Loesser; Spina
News Is Good, the News Is Bad, The   Caesar
Night Has a Thousand Eyes, The   Duke
Nighty-Night, Little Sailor Boy   Hoffman; Livingston, Jerry
No and Yes   Duke
No Hard Feelings   Davis
No, Mother, No   Hart; Rodgers
No Olive in My Martini, Please   Loewe
No One but You   De Lange
Nobody Knows   Styne
Nobody's Heart   Hart; Rodgers
(Somebody Else's Moon —) Not Mine   Mercer
Not Now   Russell
Not So Deep As a Well   De Lange
Nothing Can Change My Mind   Revel

Nothing on My Mind but You   Koehler
Now and Then   Pollack
Now That I've Got My Strength   Hart; Rodgers
Now What Do We Do?   Brooks
Now You See It, Now You Don't   Loesser
O Captain, My Captain   Weill
O Spirit of the Summertime   Duke
O'Brien Has Gone Hawaiian   Gordon
Of the People Stomp   Rome
Oh, Baby!   Blake; Razaf
Oh, How I Hate to Go Home By Myself   Lawrence
Oh, How I Love a Wedding   Loesser
Oh, Miss Flanagan (Heh, Heh, Heh, Heh, Miss
      Flanagan)   Brown, Lew; Stept
Oh, Miss Jaxson   Ellington
Oh the Pity of It All   Rainger; Robin
Old Glory   Arlen; Mercer
On the Beam   Kern; Mercer
On the Friendly Side   Mercer
On the Gay White Way   Rainger; Robin
On the Swing Shift   Arlen; Mercer
Once Upon a Time   Mills
One Kiss (Il Bacio)   Raye
One More Hill to Climb   Woods
One Night in Acapulco (Mexico)   Magidson; Pollack
Only a Moment Ago   Ager; Rose
Ophelia   Loesser; Spina
Over Here   Akst
Overture to Love, An   Ahlert; Lewis
Pagan Lullaby   Loesser; Styne
Pan American Jubilee   Gordon; Warren
Panama   Gordon; Warren
Paoli Local   De Lange
Passe   De Lange; Sigman
Passion   De Lange
Patriotic Rhythm   Baer
Pay Day   Loesser; Styne
Peaceful Ends the Day   Brooks
Pedro Mio (inst.)   Kern
Penny for Your Thoughts, Junior Miss   Howard, Joseph E.
People Like You and Me   Gordon; Warren
Perdido   Drake
Pic, Click, Look and Life   Gordon; Warren
Pickle Puss   Coslow
Pinto   Egan
Please Think of Me   Davis
Please Won't You Leave My Girl Alone   Loesser; McHugh
Poem Set to Music, A   Gordon; Warren
Poor Little Fly on the Wall   Fisher
Poor Whippoorwill   Arlen; Harburg
Poor You   Arlen; Harburg; Lane
Pouring Out My Heart   Razaf
Praise the Lord and Pass the Ammunition   Loesser
President's Birthday Ball, The   Berlin
Private Buckaroo   Wrubel
Puerto Rico   Loesser; McHugh
Pull the Trigger   Revel
Put Your Shoulder to the Wheel (inst.)   Young, Victor
Rainbow in the Night   Styne
Rainbow Land   Razaf
Rainbow Valley   Pollack
Ranch Up in Heaven   Fisher
Rancho Pillow   Wrubel
Ready-Aim-Kiss   Pollack
Red, A   Razaf

Reincarnation   Mills
Remember Hawaii   Willson
Remember or Forget   Duke
(We'll Always) Remember Pearl Harbor   Bryan; Wrubel
Rendezvous with Spring   Duke; Harburg
Rhapsody in Red, White and Blue   Duke
Ring Up the Curtain   Rome
Riverboat Jamboree   DePaul; Raye
Road to Morocco, The   Burke; Van Heusen
Rockin' and Reelin'   Raye
Romp in the Hay   Schwartz, Jean
Ruisenor   Schwartz, Jean
Run, Little Raindrop, Run   Gordon; Warren
Sally, My Dear Old Sally   Revel
Saskatchewan   Freed, Ralph
Say It with Dancing   DePaul; Raye
Say It with Firecrackers (inst.)   Berlin
Say When   Carroll
Scherzetto (inst.)   Young, Victor
Sea Chanty   Loesser; Young, Victor
Sentimental Rhapsody   Adamson
Serenade in Blue   Gordon; Warren
Serenade to the Sun, The   Friend
Shake Hands with Your Air Raid Warden   Caesar
Sharp as a Tack   Arlen; Mercer
She Can't Make Coffee   Schwartz, Jean
She Couldn't Say No to a Sailor Named Joe   Johnson, J. Rosamond
Sheik of Araby, The   Robin; Snyder
Shore Leave   Freed, Ralph; Lane
Shore Leave (Let's Go Sailor)   Arlen
Shorter Than Me Routine   DePaul; Raye
Shorty George, The   Kern; Mercer
Shout Hooray!   Baer
Sign of the "V", The   DePaul; Raye
Simply Because You're Away   Egan
Since the Farmer in the Dell Learned to Swing   Brooks
Sing Me a Song of the Islands   Gordon
Sing Out   Waller
Sing, Sing, Sing, Singapore   Donaldson
Sing Your Worries Away!   Revel
Sioux City Sue   Pollack
Snooty, The   Razaf
Soft Hearted   Loesser; McHugh
Soldier Dreams of You Tonight   Dubin; Friend
Soldier of the Home Defense   Caesar
Soldier's Dream, A   Berlin
Soldier's Safety Song   Caesar
Some Day   Baer
Some Fine Day   Ager; Rose
Somehow   Loewe
Son of a Gun Who Picks on Uncle Sam, The   Harburg; Lane
Song Is Born, A   Donaldson
Song of Freedom   Berlin
Song of the Free   Weill
Song of the Refugee   Harbach
Song the Angels Sing, The   Webster
Spangles on My Tights   Loesser; Spina
Spirit of Yankee Doodle, The   Baer; Lewis
Star Eyes   DePaul; Raye
Strip Polka   Mercer
Sun Will Be Shinin' for You   Johnson, James P.
Sunny Day   Loewe
Suspicion   Revel
Susquehanna Transfer   Silver

Sweater, a Sarong, and a Peek-a-boo Bang, A   Arlen; Mercer
Sweater Girl   Loesser; Styne
Sweep No More My Lady   Razaf
Sweet Eloise   David, Mack
Sweetheart of the A.E.F.   Hoffman; Livingston, Jerry
Sweethearts of America (Women of the Army Corps)   Freed, Ralph
Sweethearts of the U.S.A., The   Pollack
Swing in Line   Loesser
Swing-A-Bye My Baby   Brooks
Symphony of Love   Lawrence
Taffy   DePaul; Raye
Tahiti Honey   Styne
Take It from There   Russell
Take Me   Bloom; David, Mack
Taking My Mind Off You   Monaco
Tale of Manhattan, A   Webster
Tall Grows the Timber   Loesser
Tangerine   Mercer
12th Street Rag   Razaf
Thank You Columbus   Harburg; Lane
That Good for Nothin' Man of Mine   Freed, Ralph
That Good-for-Nothin' Man o' Mine   Freed, Ralph
That Mysterious Lady Called Love   Harburg; Lane
That Old Black Magic   Arlen; Mercer
That Russian Winter   Berlin
That's Sabotage   Gordon; Warren
(I Fell in Love with) The Leader of the Band   Magidson; Styne
There Are Rivers to Cross (Before We Meet Again)   Henderson
There Will Be No Blackout of Democracy   Pollack
There Will Never Be Another You   Gordon; Warren
There's a Girl in the World for Ev'ry Boy   Cobb
There's Something in My Eye and I Can't Get It Out   Howard, Joseph E.
These Orchids   Kern; Mercer
They Laughed at Him in His Home Town   Brown, Lew; Stept
This Is It   DePaul; Raye
This Is New York   Davis
This Is Our War!   Rome
This Is the Army, Mister Jones   Berlin
This Is Worth Fighting For   De Lange; Stept
This Is Your Chance   Gilbert
This Time (Is the Last Time)   Berlin
Three Cheers for Our President   Razaf
Three Cheers for the Yanks (We've Done It Before, We Can Do It Again)   Martin
Thumbs Up and "V" for Victory   Webster
'Til You Return   Dietz; Schwartz, Arthur
Till I Return to You   Baer
Till We Dream Together Again   Henderson
Time After Time   Egan
Tin Horn (inst.)   Spina
To Arms (Dear One, Divine)   Razaf
Tomorrow You Belong to Uncle Sammy   Mercer
Tomorrow's Sunrise   Leslie
Tondelayo   Dietz; Duke
Tonight In Dreamtime   Coslow
Touch of Texas, A   Loesser; McHugh
Traffic that Roars in the Spring, The   Caesar
Train Whistles   Razaf
Trains in the Night   Russell

Trinidad   Cahn
Tropicana   DePaul; Raye; Schwartz, Jean
Tulip Time   Freed, Ralph; Lane
Tulips Are Talking Tonight, The   Magidson; McHugh
Tuscarora, The   Willson
Twine for Mayor   Brooks
Two Hearts in Wintertime   Bryan
Two Sparkling Eyes   Duke
Unknown Soldier Lives Again, The   Sissle
Until I Live Again   Revel
Velvet Moon   De Lange; Myrow
Victory Caravan   Cahn; Styne
Victory Garden   Leslie
Villa in the Valley, A   Adamson
Vingo   Raye
Vingo Jingo   DePaul; Raye
Wacki for Khaki   Loesser; Spina
Wait 'Til You See My Twist and Twirl   Ager
Wait Till You See Her   Hart; Rodgers
Waiting for You   DePaul; Raye
Wake Island   Young, Victor
Wake Up! America   Johnson, J. Rosamond
Wake Up, Jacob   DePaul; Raye
Walk with Uncle Sam (Walk to Work)   Caesar
(When I'm) Walking Arm in Arm with Jim   Pollack
Waltz Is Over, The   Harburg; Schwartz, Arthur
Wandering   Johnson, James P.
Wasn't It Wonderful   DePaul; Raye
Watching Little Alice (inst.)   Kern
We — All Together   Alter; Cahn
We Must Be Vigilant — American Patrol   Leslie
We Ought to Dance Don't You Think?   DePaul; Raye
Wearin' the Grin   Loewe
Wedding in the Spring   Kern; Mercer
We'll March to Hell and Back Again   Razaf
We're All Friends Together   Adamson
We're All in the Same Boat Now   Hoffman; Livingston, Jerry
We're Building Men   Loesser; Spina
We're Coming Over   Howard, Joseph E.
We're Happy Again   Revel
We're in the Navy   DePaul
West Is Best, The   Loewe
Westchester Limited   Myrow
We've Got a Wonder Down Under   Hoffman; Livingston, Jerry
Whad'dya Gonna Do Now   Baer
What Am I Doing Here in Your Arms?   Revel
What Am I Here For?   Ellington
What D'ja Do Sunday Junior   Caesar
What Do You Hear from Your Dreams   Wrubel
What Gives Out Now   Loesser; Styne
What Kind of Love Is This   DePaul; Raye
What the Country Needs   Coslow
What the Well-Dressed Man in Harlem Will Wear   Berlin
What's Become of the Night   Hammerstein; Harbach; Kern
What's Buzzin' Cousin?   Gordon
When a New Star   Harbach; Kern
When It's Celery Time in Kalamazoo   Sterling
When It's Chilly Down in Chile   Styne
When It's Moonlight on the Blue Pacific   Davis
(In that Moment) When Love Was There   Robison
When Romance Comes Along   Magidson; Pollack
When that Man Is Dead and Gone   Berlin
When the Cat's Away   Magidson; Styne
When the Crimson Snow of Russia Is White Again   Robison

When There's a Breeze on Lake Louise   Revel
When This Crazy World Is Sane Again   Berlin
When You Hear the Time Signal   Mercer
When You're Alone   Revel
Where a Water Wheel Keeps Turning On   Stept
Whisper   David, Mack
White Christmas   Berlin
Who Knows   Revel
Who'll Buy a Rose from Margareeta   Brown, Lew; Henderson
Why You No Knock   Davis
William Tell Routine   Styne
Windmill Under the Stars   Kern; Mercer
With a Forty Dollar Buggy and a Twenty Dollar Horse   Bryan
With Your Looks and My Brains   Freed, Ralph; Lane
Woman Without a Man, A (A Man Without a Woman)   Harburg; Schwartz, Arthur
Women of America   Gershwin, Ira
Wonderful   Blake
World We Love Will Live Again (Things We Love Will Live Again), The   Gilbert
Ya Darn Tootin' Gabriel   Webster
Yankee Doodle Tan (The "Double V" Song), A   Razaf
Yanks Are Coming, The   Pollack
You and the Waltz and I   Webster
You Can't Say No to a Soldier   Gordon; Warren
You Do My Eyes a Favor   Cahn; Styne
You Get on the Fence   Egan
You Got to Study Buddy   Cahn; Styne
You Gotta Swing It (inst.)   Waller
You Just Can't Copa with a Copacabana Baby   Davis
You Left Me Everything but You   David, Mack
You Speak My Language   Loesser; McHugh
You Were Never Lovelier   Kern; Mercer
Your Blind Date   Pollack
Your Dad and My Dad Were Buddies, Buddy   Kalmar; Ruby
Your Face Looks Familiar   Revel
You're a Shot in the Arm   Coslow
You're Bad for Me   Revel
You're Easy to Dance With   Berlin
You're In Love with Someone Else (But I'm in Love with You)   Loesser; Styne
You're So Good to Me   Cahn; Styne
You've Got to Be Fast   Schwartz, Jean
You've Got to Pay   Schwartz, Jean
Zana Zaranda   Revel
Zip Your Lip!   Pollack

1943

Adolfo and Benito   Caesar
Ain't It de Truth   Arlen; Harburg
Ain't That Just Like a Man   DePaul; Raye
Air Transport Command   Washington
Alexander's Blitztime Band   Hart
All Dressed Up to Go Dreamin'   Webster
All Dressed Up to Go Dreaming   Revel
All er Nothin   Hammerstein; Rodgers
All Is Well   Gilbert
All the Way   Styne
Allegiance to the Flag   Wrubel
Alligator and the Crocodile, The   Dubin; Monaco
Along Came Georgia Lee   Parish
Always Hold Your Umbrella High   Caesar

American Boy   Dubin; Monaco
Announcement of Inheritance   Porter
Any Friend of Yours Is a Friend of Mine   Hoffman
Any Old Port in a Storm   Pollack
Army Air Patrol, The   Adamson; McHugh
Army Service Forces, The   Rome
At the World's Fair   Caesar
Baby Don't You Cry   Washington
Baby Knows Best   Brown, Lew
Baby Please Stop and Think about Me   Ellington
Baby You're Zoot   Fain; Harburg
Bacchanale (inst.)   Weill
Back Bay Beat   David, Mack; Livingston, Jerry
Bad Little Apple and the Wise Old Tree, The   Hart
Bagpipes of Buckingham, The   Gordon; Warren
Ballad of Sloppy Joe, The   Rome
Barbecue Song   Johnson, James P.
Baroness Bazooka   Comden and Green
Bay of Botany   Dietz; Duke
Beale Street Trolley   Brown, Lew; Fain; Freed, Ralph
Beat Out Dat Rhythm on a Drum   Hammerstein
Beautiful Coney Island   Rainger; Robin
Best Is None Too Good for Me, The   Stept
Best Tunes of All Come from Carnegie Hall, The   Strouse
Beware the Safety Pirate   Caesar
Blackout Boogie   Young, Joseph
Blue Ramble   Ellington
Blue Ridge Mountain Blues   DePaul; Raye
Boll Weevil   Gilbert
Boogie Dreams (inst.)   Johnson, James P.
Boogie Woogie Runway (inst.)   Johnson, James P.
Bouncing on the Bayou   Gilbert
Boys and Girls Like You and Me   Hammerstein; Rodgers
Boys, Boys, Boys   Dietz; Duke
(Got a) Bran' New Daddy   Dietz; Duke
Brazilian Boogie   Blane
Breakfast with Hazel   Caesar
Breezy Young Fellow and a Gay Young Thing,
   A   Henderson; Kahal
Bring Your Rubber Around   Caesar
Broken Dreams to Mend   Gilbert
By the Light of Your Eyes I Read Your Heart   Drake
By the Mississinewah   Porter
Cadence Count   Lawrence
Can Can   Dietz; Duke
Can I Help It?   Gershwin, Ira
Candlelight and Wine   McHugh
Can't Get Stuff in Your Cuff   Cahn
Can't You Do a Friend a Favor?   Hart; Rodgers
Careful Kate   Caesar
Careless Joe   Caesar
Carless Carrie   Caesar
Carmen Jones Is Goin' to Jail   Hammerstein
Carmen Was (The Saga of Carmen)   Henderson; Yellen
Carnival   Russell; Warren
Catch Hatch   Weill
Cathedral 'Neath the Sky   Friend
Censored Letter   Hoffman; Livingston, Jerry
Censored Mail   Hoffman; Livingston, Jerry
Change of Heart, A   Adamson; Styne
Charcoal Man   Drake
Cherry   Drake
Chicken Feed   Ellington; Russell
Children at Play   Caesar
Cleanin' My Rifle (And Dreamin' of You)   Wrubel

Close to You   Hoffman
Closer and Closer   Parish; Woods
Collective Loading-Time Song   Gershwin, Ira
Come to Loveland   Blane; Martin
Come Up and Have a Cup of Coffee   Henderson; Yellen
Comforts of Home, The   Dietz; Duke
Completely   Silver
Connecticut   Blane
Cook of Company B, The   Baer; Lewis
Cotton Club Stomp   Ellington
Could It Be You   Brown, Nacio Herb; Caesar; Porter
Couldn't Be   Porter
Cow Cow Boogie   DePaul; Raye
Crispus Attucks   Eliscu; Gorney
Damn the Torpedoes (Full Speed Ahead)   Eliscu; Gorney
Dancing in the Dawn   Brown, Nacio Herb; Robin
Dancing in the Streets   Dietz; Duke
Dat Ol' Boy   Hammerstein
Dat's Love   Hammerstein
Dat's Our Man   Hammerstein
Daybreak   Adamson
Daydreams in the Moonlight   Drake
De Cards Don't Lie   Hammerstein
Dear Friends and Gentle Hearts   Carmichael
Dear Joe   Rome
Dear Mister Sinatra   Hoffman; Livingston, Jerry
Dear Son of Mine, My Little Lad   Caesar
Dere's a Cafe on de Corner   Hammerstein
Devil Dogs in the Air   Martin
Ding Dong, Sing a Song   Styne
Dis Flower   Hammerstein
Do I Know what I'm Doing   Pollack
Do I Love You?   Hart
Do Nothin' Till You Hear from Me   Ellington; Russell
Do These Old Eyes Deceive Me   Adamson; Styne
Do You   Dubin
Do You Hear Music?   DePaul; Raye
Do You Remember Jimmy Jones   Hoffman
Don't Be a Furniture Climber   Caesar
Don't Believe Everything You Dream   McHugh
Don't Break the Spell   Dubin
Don't Cry When We Say Goodbye   Woods
Don't Follow the Fellow Ahead   Caesar
Don't Forget the Girl from Punxsutawney   David, Mack;
   Livingston, Jerry
Don't Get Your Education in the Middle of the
   Street   Caesar
Don't Leave Banana Peels on the Street   Caesar
Don't Let's Be Beastly to the Germans   Gershwin, Ira
Don't Take a Fast Ride, It May Be Your Last Ride   Caesar
Don't Wish Your Life Away   Strouse
Don't Worry   Styne
Don't Worry Island   Dubin; Monaco
Doo Dat, The   Raye
Down By the Ocean   Fain; Freed, Ralph
Dr. Crippen   Weill
Dream Girl   Johnson, Howard
Dreamer, The   Loesser; Schwartz, Arthur
Dreaming of Louise   Bryan
Dreaming to Music   Washington
Drip Drop!   Carmichael
Drive Under Thirty-Five   Caesar
Driver's Prayer, A   Caesar
Drums and Dreams   Robin; Warren
DuBarry Was a Lady   Freed, Ralph; Lane

Duke the Spook   Burke; Van Heusen
Early Monday Morning   Eliscu; Gorney
Easy Does It   Russell
Egypt   Silver
Ella the Elephant   Dietz; Duke
Eskimo Named Moe   Donaldson
Etiquette in the Zoo   Caesar
Evening at Ciro's, An   Pollack
Everything Is Talent Today   Cahn
Ev'rything Goes when the Whistle Blows   Robison
Factory Whistles Are Bugles Too   Caesar
Faithful to the Homeland   Leslie
Faithfully Yours   Romberg
Farewell for a While   Dietz; Duke
Farmer and the Cowman, The   Hammerstein; Rodgers
Fascination   Heyman
Father in That Factory   Caesar
Father's Day   Ruby
Feet on the Sidewalk (Head in the Sky)   Lerner, Sammy
Fight on for Tannenbaum   Ruby
Fire Up   Willson
Flag's Still There Mr. Key, The   Oakland
Flight of the Bomber B-17   Hoffman; Livingston, Jerry
Flyers' Safety Song   Caesar
Flying Marines, The   Fain; Freed, Ralph
Foolish Heart   Weill
For the Want of You   Styne
Forty and One for All   Brennan
Forty Minutes for Lunch (inst.)   Weill
Forty-Eight Hour Leave   Coots
Forward (Song of the Red Army Tank Brigade)   Rome
Four Freedoms, The   Eliscu; Gorney
Four Rivers, The   Eliscu; Gorney
France Is Free   Hart
Fresh Air and Exercise   Weill
Friendly Bar, A   Dietz; Duke
From Here on In   Cahn; Styne
From the Chimney to the Cellar   Lerner, Alan Jay; Loewe
Fuddy Duddy Watchmaker, The   Loesser; McHugh
Gallagher and Shean Parodies   Caesar
Gas-Rubber Hog, The   Caesar
George Washington Carver   Razaf
Get Aboard the Bondwagon   Russell
Get Away Young Man   Waller
Get Off the Pot   Ruby
Get the Money   Rainger; Robin
Get Your Man   Hart; Rainger; Robin
Get Your Police Gazette   Gordon; Warren
Get Your Program for de Big Fight   Hammerstein
Ghost of Love   Lawrence
G.I. Jive   Mercer
Girl I Love to Leave Behind, The   Hart; Rodgers
Girl Is Like a Book, A   Lerner, Alan Jay; Loewe
Girl Should Never Ripple When She Bends, A   Waller
Girl That Waits for Me, The   Rome
Girl with the High Button Shoes, The   Washington
Git It, I'd Like to See You Wid It   Russell
Glory Be (A New York Spiritual)   Revel; Webster
God Bless Every State in the U.S.A.   Ruby
God Is My Co-Pilot   Russell
Goin' My Way   Woods
Goin' to the County Fair   Gordon; Warren
Good Luck, Mr. Flyin' Man   Hammerstein
Good News, Bad News   Caesar
Good Night, Good Neighbor   Loesser; Schwartz, Arthur

Great Guns, How the Money Rolls In   Fain; Harburg
Great News Is in the Making   Adamson; McHugh
Grizzly Bear   Gordon
Guess My Heart Is Haunted   Parish; Woods
Guy from Albuquerque, The   Akst
Guy in the Next Bunk to Me, The   Brown, Lew; Stept
Hands Across the Border   Carmichael; Washington
Hang Your Troubles on a Rainbow   Revel; Webster
Hangin' On to You   Arlen; Mercer
Hanging Out a Rainbow Over the U.S.A.   Fain; Freed, Ralph; Harburg
Happiness Ahead   Revel
Happiness Ahead (Happiness Bound)   Webster
Happiness Bound   Revel
Happiness Is a Thing Called Joe   Arlen; Harburg
Happy Anniversary to You   Wrubel
Happy Go Lucky   Loesser
Happy-Go-Lucky   Loesser; McHugh
Harlem Sandman   Adamson; Styne
Harvey, the Victory Garden Man   Arlen; Mercer
Hasta Luego   Porter
Have I Ever Told You   DePaul; Raye
Have I Stayed Away too Long   Loesser
Have You Love to Go with That   De Lange
Haven't We Met Before?   David, Mack; Livingston, Jerry
He Looks Like an Angel, but Fights Like the Devil   Hoffman; Livingston, Jerry
He Was All Right Here (He'll Be All Right There)   Eliscu; Gorney
Heavenly Music   Coslow
Hello Darlin'   De Lange
Hello, Mi Amigo   Eliscu; Gorney
Hello, Mom   Loesser
Hep, Hot and Solid Sweet   Henderson; Yellen
Here Comes the Coast Guard   Brown, Lew
Here Comes the Navy   Brown, Lew
Here's Martin the Groom   Hart; Rodgers
Here's to Tomorrow   Pollack
He's a Right Guy   Porter
He's Got a Secret Weapon   Adamson; McHugh
He's My Guy   DePaul; Raye
He's Not an Aristocrat   Ruby
Hey, Good Lookin'   Porter
Hi De Hi Ho in Harlem   Waller
Hidden Valley   Bullock; Wrubel
Higher and Higher   Adamson; McHugh
Hill-Billy-Hop, Zu-Zu-Zu-Zu   Drake
Hindoo Serenade   Henderson; Yellen
Hindustan Maid   Silver
Hip   Dietz; Duke
Hit the Leather (Cavalry Song)   Willson
Hitch Your Wagon to Forty-Eight Stars   Caesar
Hitler's Funeral March   Silver
Hold Ev'rything 'Til I Get Back to You   Stept
Hold Me Thusly   Ruby
Hold That Smile   Henderson; Yellen
Holiday Forever   De Lange
Holiday Parade   Parish
Homespun   Davis
Honey Gal o' Mine   Hammerstein
Honeymoon of Pancho Pincus, The   Caesar
Honeypie's Dance (inst.)   Duke
Honk Honk (Rumble Seat Song)   DePaul
Honorable Moon   Gershwin, Ira; Harburg; Schwartz, Arthur
Honya   Baer

Horse that Knows the Way Back Home, A   Burke; Van Heusen

Hostess in the U.S.O., The   Baer

How Can I Forget We're not Together?   Razaf

How Fly Times   Lerner, Alan Jay; Loewe

How Much I Love You   Weill

How Sweet You Are   Loesser; Schwartz, Arthur

Hul A Bal Loo Ba Lay   Russell

Humpty Dumpty   Caesar

Hup! Tup! Thrup! Four! (Joe, the Sleepy Jeep)   Rome

Hurry Up and Find Some Scrap   Caesar

Hut! 2-3-4 (I Love the Marching Song)   Friend

I Almost Forgot   Clare

I Always Knew   Porter

I Always Wanted to Waltz in Berlin Under the Linden Tree   Caesar

I Cain't Say No   Hammerstein; Rodgers

I Can Do Without Tea in My Teapot   Porter

I Can Make You Love Me   Russell

I Can't Stand Losing You   Myrow

I Care for You — You Care for Me   Caesar

I Could Do This All Night Long   Brown, Lew; Freed, Ralph; Henderson

I Couldn't Sleep a Wink Last Night   Adamson; McHugh

I Didn't Know About You   Russell

I Dug a Ditch   Brown, Lew; Freed, Ralph; Lane

I Gave You All I Could Give   Dubin

I Got a Song   Arlen; Harburg

I Got Ten Bucks and 24 Hours' Leave   Livingston, Jerry

I Have Faith, So Have You   Brown, Lew; Stept

I Have Grown to Love New York   Dietz; Duke

I Knew You When   Drake

I Like It Here   Brown, Nacio Herb; Robin

I Lost You (The Moment I Found You)   Martin

I Love an Esquire Girl   Brown, Lew; Freed, Ralph

I Love to Sing the Words   Caesar

I Meant to Tell You   Cahn

I Ought to Dance   Cahn

I Planted a Rose (In the Garden of Your Heart)   Brown, Lew; Brown, Nacio Herb; Freed, Ralph

I Run to You   Stept

I Saw My Sweetie in the Newsreel   De Lange

I Saw You First   Adamson; McHugh

I Sing a Hymn to Men   Pollack

Ice Cold Katy   Loesser; Schwartz, Arthur

I'd Like to Set You to Music   Revel; Webster

I'd Love to Take Orders from You   Warren

If I Had Only Known   Livingston, Jerry

If the Shoe Fits You, Wear It   Pollack

If You Are There   Washington

If You Can't Swim or Float, Don't Change Places on a Boat   Caesar

If You Like Bananas   Caesar

If You Please   Burke; Van Heusen

If You Want to Be an Edison   Caesar

If You Want to Make a Deal with Russia   Caesar

If You Would Only Come Away   Hammerstein

I'll Always Practice Safety   Caesar

I'll Do It For You   Styne

I'll Never Change Again   Brown, Lew

I'll Never Love Again   Gilbert

Ill-Tempered Clavichord, The   Lerner, Alan Jay; Loewe

I'm a Cossack   Pollack

I'm a Fool about My Mama   Robison

I'm a Stranger Here Myself   Weill

I'm Afraid of You   Freed, Ralph

I'm All A-Twitter Over You   Brown, Nacio Herb; Robin

I'm Going North   Loesser; Schwartz, Arthur

I'm Hitting a High Spot   Raye

I'm in a Lazy Mood   Leslie

I'm in Love with a Dame   Dietz; Duke

I'm in Love with a Soldier Boy   Porter

I'm Just a Stranger in Town   Eliscu; Gorney

I'm Like a Fish Out of Water   Revel; Webster

I'm Living from Kiss to Kiss   Drake

I'm Not Myself Anymore   Washington

I'm Only Happy, That's All   Carmichael

I'm the Secretary to the Sultan   Robin

In a Penny Arcade   DePaul; Raye

In a Ten Gallon Hat   Pollack

In Grandpa's Beard   Pollack

In Hitler's Hat   Sterling

In My Dreams   Dietz; Duke

In the Great Smokies (inst.)   Young, Victor

In the Parlor   Hoffman; Livingston, Jerry

Inamorata   Caesar

Indefinable Charm   Dietz; Duke

Indelible You   Ruby

Injun Gal — Heap Hep   Rainger; Robin

Irresistible You   Dietz; Duke

Is It Really Love (Or Just the Gypsy in Me)   Webster

Is It True What They Say About Safety   Caesar

Isn't Love a Rainbow   Heyman

It Happened in the Dark   Hart

It Might Have Been   Porter

It Must Be Ernie   Weill

It Was Written in the Stars   Coots

It's a Most Important Affair   Adamson; McHugh

It's a Scandal! It's an Outrage!   Hammerstein; Rodgers

It's Love Love Love   David, Mack

It's Patriotic and Sporty Not to Drive Over Forty   Caesar

It's the Love that I Feel for You   Parish

I've Been in the Country So Long   Johnson, J. Rosamond

I've Forgotten You   Brown, Lew; Fain; Freed, Ralph

I've Got a Gal in Ev'ry Port   Gordon

I've Got a Pal in Guadalcanal   Magidson; McHugh

I've Gotta Have You   Gordon; Warren

I've Gotta See for Myself   Pollack

I've Had This Feeling Before, But Never Like This   Stept

Jane and Jim, the Safety Twins   Caesar

Jaywalker, The   Caesar

Jean's Magic Song   Hart

Jerry or Joe   Loesser; McHugh

Jersey Plunk, The   Weill

Jersey Sweet (inst.)   Johnson, James P.

Jervis Bay (inst.)   Willson

Jezebel Jones   Arlen; Harburg

Johnnie's Comin' Home Tonight   Wrubel

Johnny Zero   David, Mack

Joshua   Lerner, Alan Jay; Loewe

Journey to a Star, A   Robin; Warren

J.P. Boogie (inst.)   Johnson, James P.

Juarez and Lincoln   Eliscu; Gorney

Judaline   DePaul; Raye

Jumping to the Jukebox   Rome

Just an Old Manuscript   Razaf

Just an Ordinary Guy   Johnson, James P.

Just As Long As I Know Katie's Waitin'   Brown, Lew; Freed, Ralph

Just Dreaming Till You Come Home   Dubin; Friend

Just for You Alone   Baer
Just Loving You   Brown, Lew; Freed, Ralph
Just to Make a Long Story Short, I Love You   Coots
Kansas City   Hammerstein; Rodgers
Keep Your Amateur Standing   Dietz; Duke
Ke-tonky-i-o   Willson
Kick in the Pants, The   Berlin
Kinda Peculiar Brown   Burke; Van Heusen
Kiss Your Baby Goodbye   Dietz; Duke
Koni Plenty Hu-Hu   Pollack
Kulebiaka   Webster
Ladies Who Sing with a Band, The   Waller
Lady in the Tutti-Frutti Hat, The   Robin; Warren
Lady Who Didn't Believe in Love, The   Styne
Lady's on the Job (on Time), The   Rome
Last Will and Testament   Caesar
Later Tonight   Brown, Nacio Herb; Robin
Laugh It Off   Caesar
Laughing Tony   Burke; Van Heusen
Lazy Rhapsody   Parish; Washington
Leader of a Big-Time Band, The   Porter
Leave Us Root for the Dodgers, Rodgers   Fisher
Left — Right   Styne
Let Doctor Schmet Vet Your Pet   Porter
Let Safety Have Priority   Caesar
Let There Be Music   Harburg
Let's Drive Out to a Drive-In   Akst; Davis
Let's Get Lost   Loesser; McHugh
Let's Go Out and Ring Doorbells   Eliscu; Gorney
Let's Keep It That Way   Drake
Let's Kiss and Tell   Leslie; Stept
Let's Pay the Two Dollars   Brown, Lew; Stept
Let's Show 'em How This Country Goes to Town (no music)   Gershwin, Ira
Let's Sing a Song about Susie   Gordon
Life's Full of Consequence (Dat Old Debbil Consequence)   Arlen; Harburg
Lift 'Em Up and Put 'Em Down   Hammerstein
Light on a Flame, A   Coots
Li'l Black Sheep   Arlen; Harburg
Lili Marlene   David, Mack
Listen to My Song of Love   Gilbert
Little Brown Suit My Uncle Brought Me, The   Rome
Little Gamins   Caesar
Little High Chairman   Robison
Little Miss Jesse James   Brooks
Loading Time at Last Is Over (From the Baltic to the Pacific)   Gershwin, Ira
London Lullaby   De Lange
Lonely Room   Hammerstein; Rodgers
Long Ago and Far Away   Lawrence
Long Time No Song   Waller
Look in the Mirror   Mercer; Wrubel
Loose Lady   Ruby
Lot in Common with You, A   Arlen; Mercer
Lotus Bloom   Porter
Louisiana   Gilbert
Love in a Changing World   Eliscu; Gorney
Love in a Mist   Weill
Love Is a Balmy Thing   Cahn; Styne
Love Is a Corny Thing   Cahn; Styne
Love Is Such a Cheat   Caesar
Love Isn't Born (It's Made)   Loesser; Schwartz, Arthur
Love Like This, A   Washington; Young, Victor
Love Sometimes Has to Wait   Rome

Love Songs Are Made in the Night   Henderson; Yellen
Loved One   Heyman
Lovely Way to Spend an Evening, A   Adamson; McHugh
Lucio's Victorian Family   Hart
Lucky Cowboy   Rainger; Robin
Lulu   Caesar
Lummir Alla Zingen (Let's All Sing)   Lawrence
Machine Gun Song, The   Dubin; Hoffman; Livingston, Jerry; Monaco
Madame, I Love Your Crepes Suzettes   Brown, Lew; Freed, Ralph; Lane
Main Title   Harburg
Mairzy Doats   Hoffman; Livingston, Jerry
Mama, It's Saturday Night   Eliscu; Gorney
Many a New Day   Hammerstein; Rodgers
Marching with Johnny   Eliscu; Gorney
May All Our Children Have Rhythm   Caesar
May in Mexico   Wrubel
Me and My Old World Charm   Waller
Me for You, Forever!   Revel; Webster
Meadowland   Rome
Meet Miss Victory   Caesar
Melinda the Mousie   Myrow
Mess Call, The   Rome
Messieurs, Mesdames   Hart
Mexico City   Donaldson
Micromaniac, The   Rome
Midnight Jump   David, Mack; Hoffman; Livingston, Jerry
Midnight Music   Coslow
Mind If I Tell You I Love You   Willson
Minnie's in the Money   Robin; Warren
Minuet for Milady, A   Dubin
Minuet in Boogie   Adamson; McHugh
Miss Jemima Walks By   Burke; Van Heusen
Miss Langley's School for Girls   Lerner, Alan Jay; Loewe
Miss Lulu from Louisville   Rainger; Robin
Mississippi Dream Boat   Brown, Lew; Fain; Freed, Ralph
Mister Pollyanna   Carmichael; Mercer
Moke from Shamokin, The   Adamson; McHugh
Moon Dreams   Mercer
Moon Kissed the Mississippi, The   Pollack
Moonlight Over Molokai   Lawrence
More Now than Ever   Koehler; Monaco
More than Ever   Fain; Freed, Ralph
Mother, Look, I'm an Acrobat   Hart
Movie Ads, The   Comden and Green
Mr. Five By Five   DePaul; Raye
Mr. Roosevelt and Mr. Churchill   Eliscu; Gorney
"Murder" He Says   Loesser; McHugh
Music from Paradise   Loesser; McHugh
Music Stopped, The   Adamson; McHugh
Music, Wind, an Old Bouquet   Gilbert
Must You Be an Elite Driver   Caesar
My Absent Lover   Gilbert
My British Buddy   Berlin
My Dear Public   Caesar
My First Love   David, Mack
My Heart Tells Me (Should I Believe My Heart?)   Gordon; Warren
My Joe   Hammerstein
My Last Love   Lerner, Alan Jay; Loewe
My Pin-Up Girl   Rome
My Sam   Gordon; Warren
My Secret Love   Parish
My Shining Hour   Arlen; Mercer

My Spies Tell Me (You Love Nobody but Me)   Caesar; Lerner, Sammy
My Wife's a W.A.A.C.   Styne
Nevada   Donaldson
Never a Day Goes By   Donaldson; Parish
Never Before   Brown, Nacio Herb; Robin
New Art Is True Art   Weill
(There Are) New Roses Every Summer   Yellen
New World Will Soon Be Here, A   Leslie
New York Number   Hart
Nita   Raye
No Love, No Nothin'   Robin; Warren
No Surrender   Coslow
No Village Like Mine   Gershwin, Ira
No You No Me   Loesser; Schwartz, Arthur
Nobody Loves a Bugler   Lawrence
Now that I'm Free   Caesar; Lerner, Sammy
Now We Know   Robison
Ode to a Marine (What Makes a Marine)   Myrow
Ode to Victory   Johnston
Off the Shores of Somewhere   Romberg
Oh, How I Could Go for You   Porter
Oh, Please Tell Me, Darling   Hoffman; Livingston, Jerry
Oh, What a Beautiful Mornin'   Hammerstein; Rodgers
Oklahoma   Hammerstein; Rodgers
Old Demon Rum   Rainger; Robin
Old Music Master   Carmichael; Mercer
Old Sad Eyes   Fain; Kahal
Old Timer   Revel; Webster
On that Old Production Line   Rome
On the Corner of Sunshine and Main   Styne
On the Old Assembly Line   Henderson
On Time   Rome
On Your Mark   Waller
One Down and Two More to Go, Boys   Brown, Lew; Henderson
One for My Baby (And One More for the Road)   Arlen; Mercer
One Girl and Two Boys   Brown, Lew; Brown, Nacio Herb; Freed, Ralph
One Little Lie Too Many   Hoffman; Livingston, Jerry
One Pair of Pants for You   Caesar
One Touch of Venus   Weill
One Who Yells the Loudest Is the Captain, The   Hart
Only in Dreams   Lerner, Sammy
Ooh, What You Can Do!   Rainger; Robin
Opening — 2nd Minstrel Show   Burke; Van Heusen
Opening of the 40 Man Minstrel Show, The   Burke; Van Heusen
Otto and the Elephants   Hart
Otto's German/English Song   Hart
Otto's Patter Song   Hart
Our Boy   Rome
Our Generals!   Rome
Our Private Love Song   Lerner, Sammy
Out of My Dreams   Hammerstein; Rodgers
(I Was) Out of My Mind   De Lange
Out of Reach   Myrow
Out of This World   Styne
Paducah   Robin; Warren
Paging Mr. Greenback   Brown, Lew; Fain; Harburg
Palsy Walsy   Arlen; Mercer
Pan American Conference   Russell
Papeechee La Maar   Brown, Lew; Fain
Partners   Styne

Passing the Buck   Rome
Patriotic Family Are We, A   Caesar
Patter   Koehler
Penny-Ante Polka   Brown, Lew; Stept
People Will Say We're in Love   Hammerstein; Rodgers
Petunia's Prayer   Arlen; Harburg
Philadelphia, Pa.   Brown, A. Seymour
Pickin' on Your Mama   Robin; Warren
Pipes of Pan Americana   Caesar
Plain Jane Doe   Cahn; Styne
Please Louise   DePaul; Raye
Political Satire   Washington
Polka Dot Polka, The   Robin; Warren
Poncho de Panther from Brazil   Hammerstein
Pore Jud Is Daid   Hammerstein; Rodgers
Pretty Mary Ann McCann   Bryan
Prince Charming   Dubin
Private Jones of the U.S.A.   Revel; Webster
Private Miss Jones   Harburg
Production Lines Are Battle Lines   Caesar
Propaganda   Mercer
P.T. Boat Song (Steady As You Go), The   Hammerstein; Rodgers
Put It in Reverse   Akst; Davis
Quick Sands   Dubin; Monaco
Rain on the Sea   Caesar; Lerner, Sammy
Reader's Digest, The   Comden and Green
Remember Thomas Jefferson   Rome
Rhumba Jake   Caesar
Rhythm in the Rockies   Rainger; Robin
Ribbon, a Ring and a Rose, A   Oakland
Rickety Rickshaw Man   Drake
Riddle Diddle Me This   Porter
(I'm) Ridin' for a Fall   Loesser; Schwartz, Arthur
Right Down the Middle of the Road   Woods
Ring Around the Moon   Ellington; Russell
Rinso White Song   Rome
Roads   Rome
Robot Ballet (inst.)   Young, Victor
Roll 'Em   Styne
Roll Up Your Sleeves   Brown, Lew; Stept
Roodle-Ee-Doo   Adamson; McHugh
Rookie and His Rhythm, A   Dubin; Monaco
Rose of Santa Rosa   Hoffman; Livingston, Jerry
Rubber Around and Find It   Caesar
Rubbin' Elbows with an Angel   Russell
Russian Rhapsody   Webster
Sad Parisienne   Warren
Saddle Song   Gilbert
Safe-T-Party   Caesar
Safety Alphabet Song   Caesar
Safety Begins in Your Home   Caesar
Safety Symphony   Caesar
Safety Waltz   Caesar
Saga of Carmen (Carmen Was), The   Yellen
Sailor Safety Song, The   Caesar
Salome   Harburg
Same Time Same Place   Weill
Santa, Bring My Daddy (Mommy) Back to Me   Lewis
Say a Prayer for the Boys Over There   Magidson; McHugh
School's Out, Watch Out   Caesar
Scram Scoundrel Scram   Waller; Washington
Seasick Sailor, The   Adamson; McHugh
Seattle   Fain; Freed, Ralph
See that You're Born in Texas   Porter

Shadow Lane   De Lange
Share Croppin' Blues   Robison
She Was in Last Night   Coots
She's a Bombshell from Brooklyn (And Not from
      Brazil)   Dubin; Monaco
She's From Missouri   Burke; Van Heusen
Short, Fat and 4F   DePaul; Raye
Should I Reveal   Brown, Nacio Herb; Freed, Arthur
Shout 'em Aunt Tillie   Ellington; Mills
Shy Sweetheart, The   Rome
Sierra   Russell
Sighted Dame — Loved Same   De Lange
Silent Senorita   Robin; Warren
Simpatica   DePaul; Raye
Sing a Tropical Song   Loesser; McHugh
Sing the Song of the Hammer   Baer; Lewis
Singing the News   Caesar
Slap Polka, The   Revel; Webster
Sleep Baby Sleep (In Your Jeep)   Dubin; Monaco
Sleepy Moon   Robin; Warren
Slidin' Down a Rainbow   Fain; Freed, Ralph
Slightly Less than Wonderful   Waller
Smile, Sonya Smile   Hoffman; Livingston, Jerry
So Long, San Antonio   Porter
So Long Sarah Jane   Brown, Lew; Fain; Freed, Ralph
So This Is You   Akst; Cahn
Some Folks Work (Is You Man or Mule?)   Arlen; Harburg
Someone Else's Sweetheart (Is the Girl of My
      Dreams)   Hoffman; Livingston, Jerry
Something to Shout About   Porter
Song of Farewell   Rome
Song of Freedom   Hanley
Song of Reverie   Rome
Song of Stalingrad   Rome
Song of the Baltic Fleet   Rome
Song of the Cannon   Brown, Lew
Song of the Casbah   Freed, Ralph
Song of the Fatherland   Gershwin, Ira
Song of the Guerrillas   Gershwin, Ira
Song of the Sea   Rome
Speak Low   Weill
Spirit of the A.B.C.   Heyman
Stan' Up and Fight   Hammerstein
Stone Is Rolled Away, The   Brennan; Friml
Story of an Inventory   Weill
Sudsy Suds Theme Song   Carmichael; Mercer
Sunbeam Serenade, The   Revel; Webster
Sunday in Sorrento   Lewis; Meyer
Sunday, Monday or Always   Burke; Van Heusen
Sunkissed Days and Moonkissed Nights   Hoffman;
      Livingston, Jerry
Supple Couple   Waller
Sure An' It's the Luck of the Irish   David, Mack
Surrey with the Fringe on Top, The   Hammerstein; Rodgers
Susie on the Sewing Machine   Drake
Swattin' the Fly   Dietz; Duke
Sweet Evening Breeze   Donaldson
Sweetheart Waltz, The   Parish
Sweethearts of America (Women of the Army Corps)   Lane
Swing Your Lady, Mrs. Hemingway   Henderson; Yellen
Ta Ra Ra Boom Der E   Willson
Tahiti Honey   Styne
Tahm Boom Bah   Adamson; Styne
Take Everything, But Leave Me You   Romberg
Take It Easy   Porter

Take It from There   Rainger; Robin
Take It Off the E String (Put It on the G String)   Akst; Cahn
Take Me Home in Your Heart Tonight   David, Mack; Meyer
Tallahassee   Dietz; Duke
Tempus Do Fugit   DePaul; Raye
Ten Little Men with Feathers   Stept
Ten Little Motorists   Caesar
Tete a Tete at Tea Time   DePaul; Raye
Texas Will Make You a Man   Porter
Thank Your Lucky Stars   Loesser; Schwartz, Arthur
That Ain't Right   Mills
That Mittel-Europa Europe Man   Eliscu; Gorney
That Wonderful Worrisome Feeling   Hoffman; Livingston,
      Jerry
That's Him   Weill
That's How I Love the Blues   Martin
That's How to Write a Song   Adamson; Styne
That's Living   DePaul; Raye
That's My Pop   Rome
That's What Love Did for Me   Brennan
That's What You Jolly Well Get   Loesser; Schwartz, Arthur
There Ain't No Color Line Around the Rainbow   Caesar;
      Lerner, Sammy
There Are New Roses Every Summer   Henderson; Yellen
There Goes My Dream   Loesser
There Goes that Guitar   Eliscu; Gorney
There Goes That Song Again   Wrubel
There She Was   Carmichael
There You Were   Revel; Webster
There'll Always Be a Lindy's   Ruby
There's a Big Blue Cloud Next to Heaven   Drake
There's a Fly on My Music   Brown, Lew; Fain; Freed, Ralph
There's a Happy Land in the Sky   Porter
There's a Man in My Life   Waller
There's Danger in a Dance   Rainger; Robin
There's No Two Ways About Love   Johnson, James P.;
      Koehler; Mills
There's Something in My Heart   Hoffman; Livingston, Jerry
There's Yes in the Air   Waller
These Are the Times   Eliscu; Gorney
They Died with Their Boots Laced   DePaul; Raye
They Just Chopped Down the Old Apple Tree   Adamson;
      McHugh
They Looked So Pretty on the Envelope   Eliscu; Gorney
They're Countin' in the Mountains   Pollack
They're Either Too Young or Too Old   Loesser; Schwartz,
      Arthur
Thinkin' About the Wabash   Bullock; Cahn; Styne
Thinkin' 'Bout Home (inst.)   Johnson, James P.
Thirty-Five Summers Ago   Henderson; Yellen
This Dreaming   Harbach
This Gets Better Ev'ry Minute   Pollack
This Is It   Henderson; Yellen
This Is My Night to Howl   Hart; Rodgers
This Is Our Private Love Song   Caesar; Lerner, Sammy
This Is So Nice   Waller
This Particular Party   Dietz; Duke
Thoughtless   David, Mack; Livingston, Jerry
Three Dreams   Styne
Three Girls in a Boat   Lerner, Alan Jay; Loewe
Three Letters in the Mail Box   Webster
Three Little Mosquitos   Pollack
Through the Moonlit Fog   Wrubel
Through Thick and Thin   Porter
Tico-Tico   Drake

Titina's Tavern   Brown, Lew
To Keep My Love Alive   Hart; Rodgers
Today I'm a Debutante   Adamson; McHugh
Tom Tom the Piper's Son   Harburg; Lane
Tongue-Tied   Bloom; Woods
Tonight I Shall Sleep (With a Smile on My Face)   Ellington
Tonight Is Ours (Estrana Vida)   Drake
Too Soon   Weill
Trav'lin' Light   Mercer
Trembling of a Leaf   Lawrence
Trouble with Women, The   Weill
Try Not to Be Lonely   Robison
Trylon Song   Mills
Turandot — 3rd Act   Lerner, Sammy
Twelfth Avenue (inst.)   Johnson, James P.
Two Friends, The   Rome
Two on a Bike   Raye
Under My Umbrella   Dietz; Duke
Under the Coconut Tree   Razaf
United Nations (On the March)   Harburg; Rome
United States Submariners, The   Wrubel
Upa-Upa   Drake
Variety   Caesar
Ve Don't Like It   Berlin
Vendor's Song   Hart
Venus in Ozone Heights (inst.)   Weill
Venus Was a Modest Goddess   Weill
Very, Very   Weill
Victory Pie   Caesar
Victory Polka   Cahn
Victory Symphony, Eight to the Bar   Rome
Village Scene Jingles   Gershwin, Ira
Vive la Difference   Weill
Voice of a Rose   Leslie
Wagon Song   Gershwin, Ira
Wait for the Bus to Stop   Caesar
Walk to the Exit Near You   Caesar
Walkin' the Bass (inst.)   Johnson, James P.
Waltz of the South   Gilbert
Warm Valley   Russell
Washington, D.C.   Porter
Way Down Yonder By Myself, Can't Hear Nobody
     Pray   Brennan
Way Out West in Jersey   Weill
Way Up North   Loesser; Schwartz, Arthur
We Always Get Our Girl   Brown, Nacio Herb; Robin
We Belong Together   Fain; Freed, Ralph
We Had a Show   Comden and Green
We Meet in the Funniest Places   Dubin; Monaco
We Musn't Say Goodbye   Dubin; Monaco
We Never, Never Lost a War, and Never Never
     Will   Howard, Joseph E.
Welcome to Victory Ranch   Akst
Well, I Just Wouldn't Know   Porter
We're Having Our Fling   David, Mack; Livingston, Jerry
We're in the Navy   DePaul; Raye
We're Looking for the Big Bad Wolf   Styne
We're Staying Home Tonight (My Baby and Me)   Loesser;
     Schwartz, Arthur
We're the Guys Who Shoot Supplies   Buck
West Wind   Weill
We've Been Through the Mill Together   Dietz; Duke
We've Got the Lord on Our Side   Magidson; McHugh
Wha' D'Ya Do When It Rains?   Styne
What Do You Do in the Infantry   Loesser

What Do You Think Those Ruby Lips Were Made For (If
     They Weren't Made To Kiss?)   Bryan
What Does It Take   DePaul
What Have You Got to Lose but Your Heart   Drake
What's the Good Word, Mr. Bluebird   Hoffman; Livingston,
     Jerry
When a New Star   Hammerstein
When Banana Blossoms Bloom   Lerner, Sammy
When I Look at You   Webster
When Love Walks By   Carmichael; Mercer
When Magnolias Bloom Again in Old Virginia   DePaul;
     Raye
When My Baby Goes to Town   Porter
When Noses Are Red and Eyelids Are Blue   Caesar
When the Nylons Bloom Again   Waller
When They Ask About You   Stept
When We're Home on the Range   Porter
When You Climb the Stairs in School   Caesar
When Your Heart's on Easy Street   Washington
When Your Man Is Coming Home   DePaul; Raye
When You're on My Mind   Blane
Where Am I Without You (Baby)   DePaul; Raye
Where, Oh Where (Is the Groom?)   Gordon; Warren
Whistling in the Light   Rainger; Robin
White Keys and the Black Keys, The   Eliscu; Gorney
Whizzin' Away Along de Track   Hammerstein
Who Am I   Weill
Who Are the British   Cahn; Styne
Who Dealt?   Weill
Who Did? I Did — Yes, I Did   Cahn; Styne
Who Took Me Home Last Night   Adamson; Styne
Who's My Baby's Baby Tonight   Donaldson
Who's Who   DePaul; Raye
Why Can't I Sing a Love Song   Akst
Why Didn't You Tell Me   Lawrence
Willie the Wolf of the West   Robin
Wintertime   Brown, Nacio Herb; Robin
Wise Guy   De Lange
Wishing Waltz, The   Gordon; Warren
Woe Is Me   Lawrence
Women in Uniform, The   Rome
Wooden Wedding   Weill
Workers of All Nations   Gershwin, Ira
Wouldn't It Be Crazy   Porter
Wrong Neighborhood   Merrill
Yankee Doodle Girl   Willson
Ye Lunchtime Follies   Hart; Rodgers
Yes, I Love You Honey   David, Mack; Johnson, James P.
You Always Love the Same Girl   Hart; Rodgers
You and Your Broken Heart   Eliscu; Gorney
You Are Like a Song By Victor Herbert (That Is My
     Impression of You)   Bryan
You Can't Spell Victory with an Absent "T"   Carroll
You Could Have Knocked Me Over with a Feather   Davis
You Could Hear a Pin Drop   Pollack
You Could'a Knocked Me Down with a Feather   Akst
You Crazy Little Things (Fall in Love)   Hart
You Discover You're in New York   Robin; Warren
You Must Go Down Again   De Lange
You Talk Just Like My Maw   Hammerstein
You Tempt Me   Drake
You the Fondest Thing I Am Of   Washington
You Wash and I'll Dry   Lerner, Alan Jay; Loewe
You Who Go Driving for Pleasure   Caesar
You'd Be So Nice to Come Home To   Porter

You'd Better Dance   David, Mack; Livingston, Jerry
You'd Make a Wonderful Dream   Brown, Lew; Freed, Ralph
You'll Be Sorry   Friend
You'll Find It on the Bill   Weill
You'll Never Know   Gordon; Warren
Younger Generation   Gershwin, Ira
Your Face Is Your Fortune   David, Mack; Livingston, Jerry
Your Father Must Have Loved Your Mother   Brown, Lew
Your Mother Must Have Loved Your Father   Fain; Freed, Ralph
You're a Myst'ry to Me   Coots
You're Dreamlike   Dietz; Duke
You're Good for My Morale   Eliscu; Gorney
You're Merely Wonderful   DePaul; Raye
You're Mine in My Memories   Coots
You're My Dream Girl   Baer
You're My Extra Cup of Coffee in the Morning   Bryan
You're on Your Own   Adamson; McHugh
You're Pretty Terrific Yourself   Dubin; Monaco
You're So Nice to Remember   Robin
You're the Keeper of My Heart   Stept
You're the Rainbow   Rainger; Robin
You've Got a Hold on Me   Lerner, Alan Jay; Loewe
You've Got Your Daddy's Fighting Heart   Bryan
You've Gotta Have Personality   Raye

1944

(There'll Be) A Yankee Christmas   Alter; Webster
Abracadabra   Porter
Ac-cent-tchu-ate the Positive   Arlen; Mercer
Aches, Pains and Strains   Spina
Adolescence   Duke
After the Tryst   Duke
Ain't Got No Tears Left   Comden and Green
All I Want Is You   Leslie
All of My Life   Berlin
All Out for Freedom   Arlen; Koehler
All Quiet on the Old Back Porch   Wrubel
All the Latin I Know Is "Si Si"   Pollack
Along the Santa Fe Trail   Dubin
Always Remember   Adamson
Amo Amas   Porter
And Now Tomorrow   Heyman; Young, Victor
And Russia Is Her Name   Harburg; Kern
And Then You Kissed Me   Cahn; Styne
Angel May Care   Drake
Angels Are with You Tonight   Bryan
Anima Anceps (Or the Negro's Heart)   Johnson, James P.;
   Razaf
Annabella's Bustle   Pollack
Another Love   Comden and Green
Anthem of the Union of Soviet Socialist Republics   Rome
Any Fool Can Fall in Love   Cahn; Styne
Any Moment Now   Gershwin, Ira; Kern
Any Woman Who Is Willing Will Do   Dietz; Duke
Apprentice Seaman   Dietz; Duke
April Can't Do This to Me   De Lange
April in Harlem (inst.)   Johnson, James P.
April Wants to Dance Again   Burke; Van Heusen
Are You Bucking Up Your Commander-In-Chief   Eliscu;
   Gorney
Are You Happy in Your Work   Evans; Livingston, Jay
Arm in Arm   Dietz; Duke
As If You Didn't Know   Stept

As Long As There's Music   Cahn; Styne
Ask the Madame   Cahn; Styne
At Twilight   Razaf; Waller
Aunt Molly   Johnson, J. Rosamond
Autumn Lullaby, An   Razaf
Aw Come On Now   Mercer
B Apostrophe K Apostrophe L-Y-N   Styne
B Aprostrophe K Apostrophe L-Y-N   Cahn
Baby, I'm Holding Out for You   Raye
Back in Circulation   Dietz; Duke
Bahia   De Lange; Stept
Ballad of Millicent De Vere, The   Burke; Van Heusen
Band Started Swinging a Song, The   Porter
Barrel of Beads   Dietz; Duke
Battle Was Over, It Was Quiet Now, The   Spina
Because of You   Freed, Ralph
Belle of the Yukon, The   Burke; Van Heusen
Beloved (Aloha - Nui - Ia)   Koehler; Lane
Below the Equator   Dietz; Duke
Bessie, Bessie, Bessie   Waller
Bessie in a Bustle   Gordon; Monaco
Best of All!   Wrubel
Better Day Is Comin', A   Cahn; Styne
Big Bad Moon, The   Freed, Ralph; Hoffman
Big Boy   Razaf
Big Parade, The   Porter
Big Town   Porter
Bigger the Army and Navy, The   Yellen
Blind Date   Dietz; Duke
Blue Candlelight and Red, Red Roses   Revel; Webster
Blue Island   Washington
Blue Moods, 1, 2, and Sex (inst.)   Johnson, James P.
Bluebirds in My Belfry   Burke; Van Heusen
Boogie Woogie Boogie Man   Koehler; Lane
Boogie Woogie Stride (inst.)   Johnson, James P.
Book at My Bedside   Robison
Boom! Boom! 's' Great to Be Crazy   Friend
(You'll Be) Born All Over Again   Dietz; Duke
Boy Next Door, The   Martin
Brazilian Boogie   Martin
Brazilian Can-Can   Davis
Burnin' Up   De Lange
Cafe Society Still Carries On   Porter
Candlelight   Revel
Candy Sweets (inst.)   Johnson, James P.
Can't You Read Between the Lines   Cahn; Styne
Carlotta   Porter
Carnegie Hall Pavanne   Comden and Green
Carr Saltines   Baer
Carried Away   Comden and Green
Chestermeyer's Chewing Gum   Ruby
Chinese Love Song   Friml
Chug Chug, Choo-Choo, Chug   Gordon; Monaco
Cinderella Story   Russell
Cindy   Revel; Webster
Civil War Ballet (inst.)   Arlen
Civilian   Dietz; Duke
Classification Blues   Loesser
Climbin' Up Dem Golden Stairs   Adamson; McHugh
Close to Me   Porter
Colonel Corn   Fisher
Come and Get It   Waller
Come On! Come On!   Cahn; Styne
Come Out, Come Out Wherever You Are   Cahn; Styne
Come Up to My Place   Comden and Green

Come with Me My Honey   David, Mack
Comin' Home When the Last Bugle Blows   Coots
Connecticut   Martin
Contrary Mary   Hammerstein; Kern
Corny Horn Harry   Baer
Count Your Blessings   Porter
Cover Girl (That Girl on the Cover)   Gershwin, Ira; Kern
Cradle Song   Duke
Crazy Me   Adamson; McHugh
Creole Rhapsody   Ellington
Crucible's Toast, The   Herbert
Dainty, Quainty Me   Porter
Dance to the Sun God   Dietz; Duke
Dancin' to a Jungle Drum (Let's End the Beguine)   Porter
Dancing Daffodils (Inst.)   Warren
Dancing Lesson   Dietz; Duke
Dancing Politely   Dietz; Duke
Dancing to the Rhythm of Love   Davis
Dark Haired Girl, The   Duke
Daughters of Mademoiselle from Armentiers, The   Pollack
Day After Forever, The   Burke; Van Heusen
Dear Friend   Hammerstein; Rodgers
Dear Little Cottage   Dietz; Duke
Dear Little Mountain Sweetheart   Waller
Decca Blues   Rome
Deep Down Inside You   Dietz; Duke
Deep River (inst.)   Johnson, James P.
Deep Summer Music   Robison
Destination Unknown   Razaf
Destiny   DePaul
Devil in You Is Strong, The   Dietz; Duke
Did You Happen to Find a Heart (This Morning)   Pollack
Do You Have to Go   Waller
Do You Remember Jimmy Jones   Livingston, Jerry
Do-Do-Re-Do   Comden and Green
Dog Face   Loesser
Don't Be Subtle, Don't Be Coy   Cahn; Styne
Don't Break Up That Team   Caesar
Don't Carry Tales Out of School   Gordon; Monaco
Don't Change Horses   Hoffman; Livingston, Jerry
Don't Give Me that Jive, Come on with the Come
    On   Waller
Don't Let Me Down   Robison
Don't Look Now Mr. Dewey (But Your Record's
    Showing)   Harburg; Schwartz, Arthur
Don't Sweetheart Me   Friend
Don't Take Your Meaness Out on Me   Robison
Don't Tell a Man about His Woman   Robison
Don't You Know I Care (Or Don't You Care to
    Know)   David, Mack; Ellington
Down Time   De Lange
Dream   Mercer
Dream with Me   Comden and Green
Drink   Porter
Duration Blues   Mercer
Eagle and Me, The   Arlen; Harburg
Eighty Miles Outside of Atlanta   Adamson; McHugh
Enchilada Man, The   Washington
Entrance of Montana   Porter
Evelina   Arlen; Harburg
Eventually Comes Love   Brown, Lew
Ev'ry Girl Is Diff'rent   Burke; Van Heusen
Ev'rytime We Say Goodbye   Porter
Exhibition Dance (inst.)   Duke
Fa Deedle Dee, Fa Deedle Doo, Fa Deedle Da   Davis

Far from Love   Johnson, James P.; Razaf
Farewell for a While   Dietz; Duke
Farmer's Daughter   Arlen; Harburg
Feeling Zero   Revel
Fifth Army's Where My Heart Is, The   Berlin
First Class Private Mary Brown   Loesser
First Hundred Years, The   Burke; Van Heusen
First Night   Dietz; Duke
Fisherman's Wharf   Dietz; Duke
Flamingo and the Rose, The   Burke; Van Heusen
Fleur-de-lis Will Bloom Again, The   Wrubel
Florida Garden   Robison
Fool That I Was   Dietz; Duke
Footprints in the Sands of Time   Russell
For the Flag He Loved So Well   Herbert
For the Life of Me   Gershwin, Ira; Warren
Forget-Me-Nots in Your Eyes   Leslie; Warren
Frahngee-Pahnee   Porter
Free and Equal Blues   Harburg
From the Cradle to the Grave   Dietz; Duke
Fuzzy Wuzzy   Hoffman; Livingston, Jerry
Gabey's Comin'   Comden and Green
Garden in the Sky   Dietz; Duke
General Orders   Loesser
Get on Board Little Children   DePaul; Raye
Girls   Porter
Give Me a Band and a Bandana   Brown, Nacio Herb; Robin
Give Me that Rose   Herbert
Give Us Dames   Cahn; Styne
Give Yourself a Pat on the Back   Davis
Gloria from Peoria   Baer
Glorifying the American Girl   Fain; Freed, Ralph
Go Home, Little Girlie, Go Home!   Razaf
God Shall Abade Us (inst.)   Herbert
Goin' on an Errand for Uncle Sam   Razaf
Going My Way   Burke; Van Heusen
Good Girl   Hammerstein; Kern
Goodbye, World   Fain; Freed, Ralph
Good-Lookin', It's Good Lookin' at You   Caesar
Goodnight Wherever You Are   Hoffman
Good-Will Movement, The   Porter
Got an Invitation   Evans; Livingston, Jay
Got to Be Bad to Be Good   Comden and Green
Got to Wear You Off My Weary Mind   Arlen; Mercer
Gotta Get Joy   Dubin; Lane
Great Man Says, The   Heyman; Spina
Grown-ups Are the Stupidest People   Cahn; Styne
Hail, Alma Mater   Burke; Van Heusen
Hail, Hail, America   Wrubel
Hail the Home of Freedom   Freed, Ralph
Half Moon in Three Quarter Time, A   Revel; Webster
Happy Again   Dietz; Duke
Hasten Jason!   Freed, Ralph; Stept
Have You Written Him Today   De Lange
Have Yourself a Merry Little Christmas   Martin
He Certainly Kills the Women   Porter
He Lost   Spina
He Walks Across the Sky   Heyman; Spina
He Went to Work in the Morning, She Went to Work in the
    Night   Gilbert; Oakland
Heart to Heart Talk with My Heart   Howard, Joseph E.
Heathen   Dietz; Duke
Heave-Ho, Let the Wind Blow   Arlen; Harburg
Heavens Declare!, The   Johnson, J. Rosamond
Hence It Don't Make Sense   Porter

Here Come the Waves   Arlen; Mercer
Hereafter   Porter
Here's a Cheer for Dera Old Ciro's   Porter
He's Good for Nothing but Me   Dietz; Duke
Hey Bub! Let's Have a Ball   Gordon; Monaco
Hey Rookie   Eliscu; Gorney
Hi, Good Lookin'   Raye
Highway Polka, The   Evans; Livingston, Jay
Hip, Hip Hooray for Andy Jackson   Porter
His Rocking Horse Ran Away   Burke; Van Heusen
Hit Me with a Hot Note and Watch Me Bounce   Ellington
Hits and Misses   Baer
Hold on to Your Hats   Pollack
Holiday in Heaven   Woods
Hollywood Canteen   Koehler
Honest Abe   Spina
Hosanna   David, Mack
Hour Ago, An   Dietz; Duke
How Blue the Night   Adamson; McHugh
How Can I Hold You Close Enough   Harburg; Heyman
How Could You Put Me Down   Johnson, James P.; Parish
How Do I Grow a Rose?   Spina
How Does Your Garden Grow?   Burke; Van Heusen
How Many Times Do I Have to Tell You   Adamson;
   McHugh
How Would I Know   Fain; Kahal
How Ya Doin' in the Love Department   Russell; Spina
Humble Hollywood Executive, A   Porter
Hurdy Gurdy   Dietz; Duke
I Ain't Got Nothin' but the Blues   Ellington
I Betcha (She Won't Let-cha Get Out of Her Arms)   Wrubel
I Can Cook Too   Comden and Green
I Can Still Remember   De Lange; Stept
I Can't Help It If I Love You   Stept
I Can't Put My Arms Around a Memory   Ellington
I Dearly Adore a Saloon   Dietz; Duke
I Didn't Know About You   Ellington
I Don't Care If the World Knows It   Revel; Webster
I Don't Love You No More, No More   Cahn; Styne
I Don't Want a Million Dollars   Gordon; Monaco
I Feel Like I'm Not Out of Bed Yet   Comden and Green
I Found Out This Morning, that I Fell in Love Last
   Night   Freed, Ralph; McHugh
I Guess I'll Hang My Tears Out to Dry   Cahn; Styne
I Hear Your Voice in the Wind   Heyman
I Killed Myself Because of You   Wrubel
I Know a Man   Spina
I Know It's Wrong   DePaul
I Know the Name of Every Flower Now   Hoffman;
   Livingston, Jerry
I Laughed When I Should Have Cried   Lawrence
I Like Pretty Things   Porter
I Like to Make Music for You   Pollack
I Lived in a House with a Piano   Dietz; Duke
I Lost My Beat   Cahn; Styne
I Love Corny Music   DePaul; Raye
I Love Olive   Baer
I Love You   Porter
I Murdered Them in Chicago   Cahn; Styne
I Never Was Born   Arlen; Harburg
I Own a Piece of a Girl   Dietz; Duke
I Promise You   Arlen; Mercer
I See a Morning Star   Arlen; Harburg
I Told You So   DePaul; Raye

I Understand   Comden and Green
I Walked with the Angels   David, Mack
I Wanna Go Back   Dietz; Duke
I Want Everyone to Know   Davis
I Was Waltzing to a Rhumba Last Night   Revel
I Wish We Didn't Have to Say Goodnight   Adamson;
   McHugh
I Won't Be a Nun   Duke
I Won't Forget the Dawn   DePaul; Raye
I Wrote a Play   Porter
I Wuv a Wabbit   Drake
I'd Like To Write a Song To Win the War   Bryan; Caesar
If I Hadn't a Husband   Porter
If Washington Needs Me I'll Answer the Call but They Better
   Not Call Me Collect   Caesar
If You Can't Get the Love You Want   Dietz; Duke
If You Leave London   Ahlert; Howard, Bart
If You Would Listen   Robison
Ikky Tikky Tanbo   Hoffman; Livingston, Jerry
I'll Always Be Beside You   Hoffman
I'll Be There   Stept
I'll Eat My Hat   Evans; Livingston, Jay
I'll Hate Myself in the Morning   Cahn; Styne
I'll Remember April   DePaul; Raye
I'll Walk Alone   Cahn; Styne
Illinois Republican, An   Spina
I'm Afraid I Love You   Porter
I'm Afraid It's Love   Comden and Green
I'm Beginning to See the Light   Ellington
I'm Blue (I Wish I Was Dead)   Comden and Green
I'm in a Jam with Baby   Koehler
I'm in Love with My Top Sergeant   Dietz; Duke
I'm Just a Lucky So and So   David, Mack; Ellington
I'm Laying Away a Buck   Cahn; Styne
I'm Making Believe   Gordon; Monaco
I'm Not Myself at All   Porter
I'm on a Green Branch Now   Coots
I'm on the Gravy Train   Robison
I'm Only Teasin'   Heyman
I'm So Glahd to Meet You   Porter
I'm Thinking of My Darling   David, Mack
I'm Tired of My Tired Man   Snyder
In a Little Cafe in Calais   Coots; Lewis
In a Magic Garden   De Lange
In a Moment of Madness   Freed, Ralph; McHugh
In a Persian Market   David, Mack
In a Shower of Stars   Heyman
In Kansas   Robison
In My Arms   Loesser
In Paris and Brussels and Prague   Stept
In Sweet Cherry Time   Lerner, Sammy
In the Green Hills of County Mayo   Porter
In the Middle of Nowhere   Adamson; McHugh
In Times Like These   Fain; Harburg
Infantry, the Infantry (The Bunion Brigadiers), The   Caesar
Innocent Stander-By, The   Cahn; Styne
Intermission's Great, The   Comden and Green
Iowa   Willson
Irresistible You   DePaul; Raye
Is It Me or My Uniform   Coots
Is It the Girl? (Or Is It the Gown?)   Porter
It Could Happen to You   Burke; Van Heusen
It Goes to Your Toes   Brown, Nacio Herb; Robin
It Is Written   DePaul; Raye
It Looks Like More People Were Agin' Him   Spina

It Must Be Fun to Be You   Porter
It Was Good Enough for Grandma   Arlen; Harburg
It Was Nice Knowing You   Dietz; Duke
It Would Be No Holiday   Spina
It's a Big Night   Porter
It's a Crying Shame   Russell; Stept
It's a Small World   Revel; Webster
It's a Swelluva Life in the Army   Eliscu; Gorney
It's All for Art's Sake   Brown, Nacio Herb; Robin
It's Easy to Say You're Sorry   Hoffman; Livingston, Jerry
It's Great to Be Alive   Eliscu; Gorney
It's Great to Be in Uniform   Eliscu
It's Just Like the Good Old Days   Porter
It's Just Yours   Porter
It's Smart to Be People   Harburg; Lane
It's the Old Army Game   Adamson; McHugh
I've Always Loved   DePaul; Raye
I've Been in a Daze for Days   Martin
I've Got a One Track Mind   Dietz; Duke
I've Got My Heart Set on You   Freed, Ralph; McHugh
I've Got the Blues for Maryland   Parish
I've Turned the Corner   Gershwin, Ira; Kern
Jackpot   Dietz; Duke
Jail Song   Weill
Jamboree   Fisher
January Through December   Stept
Japan (An American Battle Song)   Razaf
Java Junction (inst.)   Warren
Jenny   Burke; Gershwin, Ira; Weill
Jesusita en Chihuahua (The Cactus Polka)   Drake
Jivey Jones   Baer
Joe Carioca   Heyman
John Saw the Number   Blake
Join the Marines   Dietz; Duke
Join the Navy (The Navy Song)   Arlen; Mercer
Juke Box Millionaires   David, Mack
Just Because I'm French   Razaf
Just for You   Cahn; Styne
Ka-choo! (The Sneezing Song)   Razaf
Kathleen   Porter
Kath'rine the Great!   Razaf
Keep Your Powder Dry   Cahn; Styne
Keeping It Private (Me and Private Joe)   Donaldson
Key to the Gates, The   Dietz; Duke
Kid that I've Never Seen, The   Akst; Kalmar
(How Would You Like to) Kiss Me in the
     Moonlight   Adamson; McHugh
Knocking on Your Own Front Door   Burke; Van Heusen
Know Where You're Goin' and You'll Get There   Martin
La Orchidea (Orchid Lady)   De Lange
La Pintada   De Lange
Ladies Don't Have Fun   Cahn; Styne
Lady Lovely   Heyman; Spina
Largo (inst.)   Johnson, J. Rosamond
Last Long Mile, The   Dietz; Duke
Last Night   Adamson
Last Night I Kissed a Dream   Razaf
Laura   Mercer
Leave Me Just a Little Bit of You   Stept
Leave Us Face It, We're in Love   Loesser
Let There Be Peace   Lerner, Sammy
Let's Capture This Moment   Evans; Livingston, Jay
Let's End the Beguine   Eliscu; Gorney
Let's Help the Red Cross Save a White Cross   Adamson;
     McHugh

Let's Take the Long Way Home   Arlen; Mercer
Let's Walk Home the Long Way 'Round   Heyman; Spina
Life's a Funny Present from Someone   Dietz; Duke
Like Someone in Love   Burke; Van Heusen
Lincoln Soliloquy   Spina
Little Big Shot   Akst; Davis
Little Marriage Is a Dangerous Thing, A   Dietz; Duke
Little Mousie Brown   Carmichael
Little Paris Breeze   Whiting
Little Red Roof Tops   Loesser
Little Soft Music Professor, A   Hoffman; Livingston, Jerry
Little Streptococcus, The   Dietz; Duke
Little Thing Called Love, A   Johnson, J. Rosamond
Livin' in My Own Sweet Way   Revel; Webster
Liza Crossing the Ice   Arlen; Harburg
Loading Song   Porter
Loco Over You   Razaf
Lonely Me   Comden and Green
Lonely Town   Comden and Green
Long Ago (And Far Away)   Gershwin, Ira; Kern
Loo-Low   Spina
Love and I Went Waltzing   Cahn; Styne
Love Came Between Us   Evans; Livingston, Jay
Love Has Made This Such a Lovely Day   Cahn; Styne
Love I Long For, The   Dietz; Duke
Love that Never Happened, The   Parish; Woods
Love Was Young as an April Leaf   Spina
Loveliness of You, The   De Lange
Lucky to Be Me   Comden and Green
Lullaby (Satin Gown and Silver Shoe)   Arlen; Harburg
Lumberjack Joe   Baer
Mail Call March   Willson
Make No Mistake about Love   Robison
Make Way for Tomorrow   Gershwin, Ira; Harburg; Kern
Mamalu (Boojee Bee — Boojee Boo)   Brown, Lew
Mamie Magdalin   Porter
Man for Sale   Arlen; Harburg
Man with the Curly Mustache, The   David, Mack
Matthew A. Henson   Razaf
Memory Song   Mercer
Men's Dance   Dietz; Duke
Merry Go Round   Fisher
Merry-Go-Round   Carmichael
Mexico Canta   Lawrence
Midnight Madness   Gershwin, Ira; Kern
Midnight Music   Gershwin, Ira; Kern
Milkman Keep Those Bottles Quiet   DePaul; Raye
Miss Turnstiles   Comden and Green
Mississippi Belle   Porter
Mister Beebe   Cahn
Mister Jive Has Gone to War   Gilbert; Oakland
Mooning   Hoffman
Moonlight Fiesta   Washington
Moonlight Masquerade   Drake
Moonlight Mississippi   Robison
Most Important Job   Loesser
Most Unusual Weather (For This Time of Year)   Cahn; Styne
Mother's Prayer, A   Heyman; Spina
Moulin-Rouge   Duke
Mountain Whippoorwill   Kahn
Mountains of Nebraska Ballet, The   Dietz; Duke
Mousie   Coots
Mr. and Mrs. Wright   Bryan
Mr. Beebe   Styne
Mulberry Tree, The   Duke

Music to My Ears   Evans; Livingston, Jay
My American Creed   Revel; Webster
My Bamboo Cane   Revel; Webster
My Broth of a Boy   Porter
My Christmas Song for You   Carmichael; Webster
My Favorite Song   Magidson
My Follies Girl   Akst
My Friend Franklin   Rome
My Gal and I   Loesser
My Gal's Working at Lockheed   Loesser
My Handsome   Dietz; Duke
My Heart's Wrapped Up in Gingham   Burke; Van Heusen
My Imaginary Love   Lawrence
My Journey's End   Fain; Kahal
My Love You Haven't Gone Away   Brown, Lew
My Lovin' Baby and Me   Ellington
My Mama Thinks I'm a Star   Arlen; Mercer
My Moonlight Madonna   Webster
My Mother Told Me   Freed, Ralph; McHugh
My Neck of the Woods   Robison
My Rosanna   Parish
My Song   Brown, Lew; Henderson
Mynah Bird, The   Heyman
Na-Mi   Gilbert
Nancy with the Laughing Face   Van Heusen
National Emblem   Freed, Ralph
Navy Song, The   Arlen; Mercer
New Moon   Koehler; Lane
New York, New York   Comden and Green
Nicest Time of the Year   Comden and Green
Nickel's Worth of Sunshine, A   Burke; Van Heusen
No More   Russell
No Smoking   Ellington
Nobody Ever Pins Me Up   Dietz; Duke
Now I Know   Arlen; Koehler
Now, Right Now   Johnson, James P.
Octet   Porter
Oh, My Dear   Hammerstein; Kern
Ohio   Adamson; McHugh
Old Family Reunion   Robison
Old Heads Upon Young Shoulders   Bryan
Old Mother Earth   Robison
Old New Hampshire Valley   Robison
Old Rob Roy   Mercer
On the Corner of Dream Street and Main   Dixon;
    Henderson
On the Roadway to the Moon   Johnson, J. Rosamond
Once to Every Heart   Lane
Once Too Often   Gordon; Monaco
Once Upon a Song   Heyman
One Chord in Two Flats   Gordon; Monaco
One Little W.A.C.   Loesser
One More Mile and We're There   Russell
One More Smile   Cahn; Styne
One Pip Wonder   Loesser
Only Another Boy and Girl   Porter
Open Up that Door and Let Me In   Stept
Opening Title   Freed, Ralph
Orchid Lady (La Orchidea)   Myrow
Palm Beach   Dietz; Duke
Panhandle Pete   Fain; Freed, Ralph
Paris   Coots
Parrot from San Domingo, The   Drake
Parting Song   Mercer
People from Missouri   Kern

Pevullia   Hoffman; Livingston, Jerry
Piece of a Girl, A   Dietz; Duke
Please Won't You Leave My Girl Alone   Loesser; McHugh
Poco Loco   De Lange; Stept
Poor As a Church Mouse   Dietz; Duke
Poor Little Rhode Island   Cahn; Styne
Prayer of a Nation, The   Davis
Pretty As a Picture   Arlen; Harburg
Pretty Little Missus Bell   Porter
Purple Sage in the Twilight   Styne
Put a Sack Over Their Heads   Porter
Put a Three Cent Stamp on Me and Send Me Back to
    Tennessee   David, Mack
Put Me to the Test   Gershwin, Ira; Kern
Quoth the Raven   Revel; Webster
Rainbow Island   Coots
Rakish Young Man with the Whiskers, The   Arlen; Harburg
Red Hot Mama Is a Hep Cat Jitterbug Now   Yellen
Red Robins, Bob Whites and Bluebirds   Gordon; Monaco
Remember Me to Carolina   Revel; Webster
Right As the Rain   Arlen; Harburg
Rio De Janeiro   Washington
Rip Van Winkle Junior Never Slept a Wink for Twenty
    Years   Bryan
Road to Victory, The   Loesser
Rump Steak Serenade   Waller
Sad Bombadier, The   Loesser
Sad Sapsucker   Waller
Sailing at Midnight   Dietz; Duke
Salute to the Army Service Forces   Loesser
Samba-Boogie   Adamson; McHugh
Saturday Night Is the Loneliest Night in the Week   Cahn;
    Styne
Say 'Bye-Bye' to the Things you Buy, Buy!   Caesar
Say It with Love   Evans; Livingston, Jay
Say When   Comden and Green
School, School, Heaven-Blessed School   Porter
Schottische with Me   Clare; Lerner, Sammy
Send Me a Picture of the Baby   Brown, Lew
Serenading You   Leslie
Seven Miles   Spina
Seventh Air Force, The   Burke; Van Heusen
Shake Hands with Your Neighbor   Loesser; Young, Victor
Shake His Hand and Call Him Brother   Gilbert
Shakin' Hands with the Sun   Revel; Webster
Shame in Two Voices (inst.)   Johnson, James P.
Shame on Me   Donaldson
She Broke My Heart In Three Places   Hoffman; Livingston,
    Jerry
She Didn't Have the Heart to Say "No"   Freed, Ralph
She Parted with Her Lover   Duke
Shepherd's Holiday, The   Duke
Shicklegruber   Fain; Harburg
Show Must Go On, The   Gershwin, Ira; Kern
Sight-Seeing Tour, A   Porter
Silver Shadows and Golden Dreams   Pollack
Silver Shield   Dietz; Duke
Simon Legree   Arlen; Harburg
Simple Little Things, The   Brown, Lew
Since the Ballet Came to Shubert Alley   Dietz; Duke
Since You Went Away   Hoffman
Sing to Me Guitar   Porter
Singing Hills, The   David, Mack
Sippin' Cider with My Ida (Down Beside the Zuyder
    Zee)   Coots

Siren of the Tropics   Dietz; Duke
Skip to My Lou   Martin
Skirts   Loesser
Sky Ran Out of Stars, The   De Lange
Slap Happy   Davis
Sleep in Your Baby's Arms   Comden and Green
Sleigh Ride in July   Burke; Van Heusen
Smile Will Go a Long, Long Way, A   Akst
Smiles for Sale   Baer
S.N.A.F.U.   Adamson; McHugh
So Long   Porter
So Long Baby   Comden and Green
So This Is Italy   Cahn; Styne
Softly My Heart Is Singing   Heyman; Spina
Soldier's Wife   Weill
Solid Potato Salad   DePaul; Raye
Some Day Sweetheart   Coots
Some Other Time   Cahn; Comden and Green; Styne
Someday I'll Meet You Again   Washington
Somewhere a Boy Lies Dreaming   Revel; Webster
Song of the Seabees, The   Lewis
Song of the Ski-Troops   Coslow
Sons of the Desert   Fain; Freed, Ralph
Southland   Adamson; McHugh
Spiked Fist of War, The   Spina
Spring Will Be a Little Late This Year   Loesser
Stayin'-in Woman   Dietz; Duke
Stella By Starlight   Washington; Young, Victor
Stop the Hubbub Bub   Evans; Livingston, Jay
Story of the Very Merry Widow, The   Gordon; Monaco
Straighten Up and Fly Right   Mills
Strange As It Seems   Wrubel
Streamlined Sheik   Eliscu
Stremlined Sheik   Gorney
Style Show Ballet (inst.)   Arlen
Suddenly It's Spring   Burke; Van Heusen
Sugarfoot   Dietz; Duke
Sunday in Cicero Falls   Arlen; Harburg
Sure Thing   Gershwin, Ira; Kern
Sweet and Low-Down   Gordon; Monaco
Sweet Dreams, Sweetheart   Koehler
Sweet Get-Together, A   Stept
Sweet Melody Brown   Hoffman; Livingston, Jerry
Sweetheart of Baby Talk Days   Clare; Lerner, Sammy
Sweetheart's Cotillion, The   Spina
Swing Out to Victory   Waller
Swinging on a Star (Would You Like to Swing on a
    Star?)   Burke; Van Heusen
Tailgate Ramble, The   Mercer
Take a Bow   Davis
Take Care of You for Me   DePaul; Raye
Take My Heart   Parish
Teakettle's Song, The   Young, Victor
Teen Age, The   Henderson
Tell Me, Tell Me Evening Star   Arlen; Harburg
Tell Us More   Gordon; Monaco
Ten Days with Baby   Gordon; Monaco
Tequila   Porter
Tess's Torch Song   Arlen; Koehler
Texas Panhandle   Robison
496th Marching Song, The   Freed, Ralph
Thaddeus Stevens   Razaf
Thank Dixie for Me   Burke; Van Heusen
Thank You for the Bitter Truth I'm Learning   Razaf
Thanks A Lot   Cahn; Styne

That Reminds Me   Pollack
That Was Then   Johnson, James P.
That's Just for Kids   David, Mack
That's My Middle Name   Burke; Van Heusen
That's the Best of All   Gershwin, Ira; Kern
That's the Way It Goes   Friend
That's What You Mean to Me   Porter
That's Why I Buy Bonds   Johnson, J. Rosamond; Razaf
Theme in Two Voices (inst.)   Johnson, James P.
There Are No Wings on a Foxhole   Berlin
There Are Yanks (From the Banks of the Wabash)   Dietz;
    Duke
There Goes Taps   Eliscu; Gorney
There Goes that Song Again   Cahn; Styne
There Must Be Someone for Me   Porter
There Were a Lot o' People for 'Im   Spina
There's a Bluebird in the Weeping Willow   Wrubel
There's a Fella Waitin' in Poughkeepsie   Arlen; Mercer
There's Trouble Brewin'   Spina
They Can't Keep You Down   DePaul; Raye
They're Coming Home   Carroll
This Christmas   Cahn; Styne
This I Love Above All   Ager
This Is It   Gordon; Monaco
This Is Love   Freed, Ralph
This Is Our Lucky Day   Brown, Nacio Herb
This Little Song Went to Battle   Fain; Freed, Ralph
Thought of Losing You, The   Johnson, J. Rosamond
Three Cheers for the Customer   Revel; Webster
Three Day Pass   Hammerstein; Meyer
Thru Your Eyes to Your Heart   Heyman
Time Alone Will Tell   Gordon; Monaco
Time: The Present   Gershwin, Ira; Kern
Time Waits for No One   Friend
T'morra', T'morra'   Arlen; Harburg
Tomorrow   Koehler; Lane
Tonight   Donaldson
Tonight You're Mine   Washington
Too Bad, Too Sad   Donaldson
Toscanini, Stokowski and Me   Spina
Touch of You, A   De Lange; Myrow
Toussaint L'Overture   Blake; Johnson, James P.; Razaf
Tra La La   Gershwin, Ira
Trinity Blue   Herbert
Trio   Dietz; Duke
Trolley Song, The   Martin
Tropical Night   Gershwin, Ira; Kern
Tsk, Tsk, That's Love (The Click Click Song)   Gordon;
    Monaco
Turn Off the Rain (Turn on a Rainbow)   Brown, Lew;
    Henderson
Two Tone Poems (Suite)   Johnson, James P.
Umbriago   Caesar
Until Eternity   Spina
Up Jumped You with Love   Waller
Vaquero Song   Washington
Victory Stride   Johnson, James P.
Vict'ry Polka   Cahn; Styne
Vingo Jingo   Raye
Violate Me in Violet Time   Wrubel
Violins Are Saying "Wanting You", The   Bryan
Viva Amigos   Davis
WAC Hymn, The   Loesser
Waiting for the Evening Whistle   Parish
(Adios Mi Amor) Wake Up, Wake Up Your Heart   Lewis

Waller's Original E Flat Blues Waller
War Bond Man, The Razaf
Washboard Blues Carmichael
Way That I Want You, The De Lange; Myrow
We Have So Little Time Koehler; Lane
We Love the Place, O God Bullock
We Need a Little Love, That's All Waller
Weeping Sky, The Dietz; Duke
Welcome Hinges Arlen; Harburg
Welcome Love Razaf
We'll Be Dancing on the Sidewalk Silver
We're Here Because We're Here Hoffman; Livingston, Jerry
We're Off for a Hayride in Mexico Porter
We're Off to the Races De Lange; Stept
We're on Our Way Hammerstein; Rodgers
We're the Ones Pollack
What a Crazy Way to Spend Sunday Porter
What a Day Koehler; Lane
What Are We Going to Do with All the Jeeps? Berlin
What Are You Doin' the Rest of Your Life Koehler; Lane
What Are You Gonna Do with All Your Money Coots
What Did I Do Cahn; Styne
What Does It Take? DePaul; Raye
What Happened? Dietz; Duke
What I Love to Hear Gershwin, Ira; Kern
What'll I Use for Money Washington
What's Mine is Yours Dietz; Duke
When a Man Is Free Freed, Ralph
When a Woman's in Love Porter
When Eden Was a Garden Lewis
When He Comes Home Loesser
When I Get Time Burke; Van Heusen
When I Was a Little Cuckoo Porter
When I'm With You Brown, Lew
When Love Walks By Arlen
When McKinley Marches On Porter
When My Boy Comes Home Brennan
When Stanislaus Got Married Burke; Van Heusen
When the Bells Ting-a-ling (For Ching-a-ling) Bryan
When the Boys Come Home Arlen; Harburg
When the Chimes on Chapel Hill Ring Ave Maria Coots
When the Jailbirds Come to Town Eliscu; Gorney
When the Logs Come Rolling Down the River Coots; Davis
When the River Don Runs Dry Razaf
When You and I Were Strangers Porter
When You Live on an Island Dietz; Duke
Where Can You Be Evans; Livingston, Jay
Where Do We Go From Here? Porter
Where Does Love Begin (And Where Does Friendship End) Cahn; Styne
Where the Hudson Meets the Sea Silver
Where the Sun God Walks Dietz; Duke
Where'd dat Money Go Robison
Whisper in the Night Caesar
Whispering Pine Lawrence
Whistling in Wyoming Davis
Who Knows DePaul; Raye
Who Said Dreams Don't Come True Akst; Davis
Who'll Bid Porter
Who's Complaining? Gershwin, Ira; Kern
Who's Got a Match? De Lange
Who's Kidding Who? Burke; Van Heusen
Who's Who DePaul; Raye
Why Do They Call a Private a Private? Loesser
Why Don't They Let Me Sing a Love Song Akst; Davis

Why Don'tcha Kiss Me Like You Kissed Me Last Night Wrubel
Why Must There Be an Op'ning Song Cahn; Styne
Why Not? Razaf
Willow in the Wind Arlen; Harburg
(We're Gonna) Win This War in 44 Friend
Winter Holiday Davis
Winter in My Heart Mercer
Wish You Were Waiting for Me Russell
Wishing Star David, Mack
With My Old Sweetheart in a New World Brown, Lew; Henderson
Wolf Song, The David, Mack
Woman's Work Is Never Done, A Arlen; Mercer
Wond'ring Friend
Won't Be Long Now Blake; Sissle
Working Girl Razaf
World Keeps Turning 'Round To Look at You, The Bryan
World of No Goodbyes, A Carmichael
Would You for a Big Red Apple? Lerner, Sammy; Myrow
Wouldn't It Be Nice Adamson; McHugh
Wow-Ooh-Wolf Porter
Ya Got Me Comden and Green
Yank, Yank, Yank Loesser
Yankee Doodle Hayride Gordon; Monaco
Yes I Know It Was Long Ago Spina
You and I Brown, Nacio Herb; Freed, Arthur
You Bring the Scotch and I'll Bring the Soda Davis
You Can Always Tell a Yank Harburg; Lane
You Can Say that Again Mercer; Sigman
You Can't Brush Off a Russian Pollack
You Can't Change My Dream Caesar
You Can't Lose a Broken Heart Johnson, James P.
You Dear Fain; Freed, Ralph
You Gotta Get Out and Vote Harburg
You Gotta Go East to Go West De Lange; Stept
You Gotta Talk Me Into It, Baby Brown, Nacio Herb
You Left Me Everything but You Ellington
You Make Me Dream Too Much Cahn; Styne
You May Not Remember Oakland
You Must Be Losin' Your Mind Waller
You Never Say Yes, You Never Say No Caesar
You Send Me Adamson; McHugh
You Slipped Right thru My Fingers Freed, Ralph; McHugh
You U.S.A. Dietz; Duke
You Wouldn't, Would You Russell
You'd Be So Nice to Have Around Robison
Young Man with a Horn, The Freed, Ralph
Your Father Must Have Loved Your Mother Brown, Lew; Fain; Freed, Ralph
You're an Angel DePaul; Raye
You're Good for My Morale Eliscu
You're Haunting Me Again Drake
You're My Little Pin-Up Girl Gordon; Monaco
You're Such a Character Stept
You're the Dream, I'm the Dreamer Davis
Yours for a Song Porter
You've Got Me Where You Want Me Mercer; Warren
You've Gotta Have "Oomph" in the Infantry Baer
Zuyder Zee Alter; Cahn; Styne

1945

(I'm) A Square in the Social Circle Evans; Livingston, Jay
Absolutely, Posilutely, Most Emphatic'lly, Yes! Razaf

Afternoon Moon   De Lange
Ah' Bin Rich (an' Ah'm Gwynme t'be Rich Agin')   Blane
Alessandro the Wise   Gershwin, Ira; Weill
All at Once   Gershwin, Ira; Weill
All I Do Is Beat This Gol-Durn Drum   Coslow
All I Owe Ioway   Hammerstein; Rodgers
All I Want to Do Is Sing   Brooks
All of a Sudden My Heart Sings   Rome
Along the Navajo Trail   De Lange
Always True to the Navy   Adamson; McHugh
Amy's Apology   Russell
And There You Are   Fain; Koehler
Angel   Freed, Arthur; Warren
Another Kiss   DeSylva
Answer to Lilly the Werewolf   Caesar
Any Moment Now   Harburg; Kern
Anywhere   Cahn; Styne
April Face   Blane
April Snow   Fields; Romberg
Are You with It?   Revel
Aren't You Glad You're You   Burke; Van Heusen
As I Recall   Cahn; Styne
As I Remember You   Blane
As Long As He's a Regular Guy   Blake; Sissle
As You Are   Stept
As You Were   Cahn; Styne
Asbestos (inst.)   Waller
Ashby de la Zooch   Hoffman; Livingston, Jerry
At the Yankee Doodle Ball   Adamson; McHugh
Ave Regina   Brown, Nacio Herb
Back Home for Keeps   Russell
Back in Circulation Now   Razaf
Back the Bringin' 'Em Back   Cahn; Styne
Bad Timing   Comden and Green
Bal Masque   Coslow; Young, Victor
Balalaika Boogie Woogie   Coots
Ballet of the Book According to Gerald   Lerner, Alan Jay;
     Loewe
Bananas   Freed, Arthur; Warren
Barber of Seville   Brooks
Beautiful Madness   Wrubel
Beauty for Sale   De Lange
Behold How Beautiful   Carmichael
Bicycle Song, The   Blane
Big Back Yard, The   Fields; Romberg
Billy-A-Dik   Carmichael; Webster
Birds and the Bees, The   Fields; Romberg
Blond Sailor, The   Parish
Blondie   Cahn; Styne
Blow High, Blow Low   Hammerstein; Rodgers
Blue Mizz (inst.)   Johnson, James P.
Blues Ain't Got No Religion   Russell
Blues for Jimmy (inst.)   Johnson, James P.
Blues Idiom (inst.)   Waller
Bon Bon Steppers Parade (inst.)   Johnson, James P.
Boogie Woogie   Freed, Arthur; Warren
Boogie Woogie Beguine   Blake; Sissle
Boogie Woogie Blues (inst.)   Waller
Boogie Woogie Jump (inst.)   Waller
Boogie Woogie Rag (inst.)   Waller
Boogie Woogie Stomp (inst.)   Waller
Book I've Read, The   Pollack
Boss Tweed   Fields; Romberg
'Bout Eighty Miles Outside of Atlanta   Adamson; McHugh
Bowler's Song, The   Strouse

Boy I Left Behind, The   Cahn; Styne
Brazilian Bolero (inst.)   Coots
Breath of Air, A   Blane
Bride's Wedding Day Song, A   Mercer
Bring on the Girls   Adamson; McHugh
British Subjec' Blues   Razaf
Broadway Blossom   Comden and Green
Brothers   Johnson, James P.
Buy a Bond   Adamson; McHugh
Buy a Piece of the Peace   Cahn; Styne
Buy Your Bonds in Brooklyn   Baer
By Candlelight   Freed, Arthur; Warren
Bye Bye Butterfly   Coots
California Sunbeam   Stept
Californ-i-ay   Harburg; Kern
Calling All Cars   Raye
Camptown Races   Mercer
Candlelight and Wine   Adamson; McHugh
Can't Find a Furnished Room   Carroll
Can't Help Singing   Harburg; Kern
Carousel in the Park   Fields; Romberg
Cat and Canary   Evans; Livingston, Jay
C'est Vous (The Madonna's Secret)   Washington
Charleston   Comden and Green
Charm of You, The   Cahn; Styne
Chester Must Have His Siesta   Baer
Chico Chico (From Porto Rico)   Adamson; McHugh
Children's Music Box, The   Pollack; Webster
Children's Song   Washington
Clara the Crumb of the Chorus   Raye
Close as Pages in a Book   Fields; Romberg
Close Those Eyes   Washington
Cocabola Tree, The   Blane
Cockebur Song, The   Blane
Coffee Time   Freed, Arthur; Warren
Come Forward   Robison
Come Let's Have a Good Cry   David, Mack
Come Out, Come Out   Cahn; Styne
Come to Florence   Gershwin, Ira; Weill
Come to Paris   Gershwin, Ira; Weill
Connecticut   Silver
Conversation While Dancing   Mercer
Cooking Up a Show   Gordon; Warren
Co-op-hooray-shun   De Lange; Myrow
Country Boy Blues   Robison
Crescendo (inst.)   Romberg
Cry and You Cry Alone   Cahn; Styne
Curfew Song   Caesar
Currier and Ives   Fields; Romberg
Dance with Me   Brooks
Dancing with Lucilla   Gershwin, Ira; Weill
Darktown Interlude   Gordon
Day Before Spring, The   Lerner, Alan Jay; Loewe
Day By Day   Cahn
Day Dream   Rome
De Corazon a Corazon (Heart to Heart)   Washington
Deacon Is Speakin', The   Hoffman; Livingston, Jerry
Deevil, Devil, Divil, The   Russell; Sigman
Dessert Finale   Gordon; Warren
Dig You Later (A-Hubba-Hubba-Hubba)   Adamson;
     McHugh
Dizzily, Busily   Gershwin, Ira; Weill
Do You Do, Do You Do, Do You Do, Do You Don't, Do You
     Don't, Do You Don't   Drake
Doctor, Lawyer, Indian Chief   Carmichael; Webster

Don't Be Subtle, Don't Be Coy   Cahn; Styne
Don't Be Too Old Fashioned (Old Fashioned Girl)   Gordon
Don't Believe Everything You Dream   Adamson; McHugh
Don't Let Me Dream   Washington
Don't You Believe It   De Lange; Myrow
Don't You Ever Let Me Go   Parish
Doolittle Hop, The   Lane
Dream Concerto, A   David, Mack
Dreamer, Dreamer   Caesar
Dreams Are Just a Dime a Dozen   Parish
Dreams Come True   Comden and Green
Duchess's Entrance   Gershwin, Ira; Weill
Dusky Rose (inst.)   Johnson, James P.
Effie Klinker   Henderson
Elbow Room   Harburg; Kern
Enlloro (Voodoo Moon)   Rome
Evening Star   Brooks
Every Day Is Lovely   Hoffman; Livingston, Jerry
Every So Often   Cahn; Parish; Styne; Woods
Everyone (Everybody) Wants to Get in the Act   De Lange; Myrow
Ev'ry Hour on the Hour I Fall in Love with You   Ellington
Faithless   Comden and Green
Fame of a Name Cannot Die   Caesar
Feeling No Pain   Leslie
Felicia No Capicia   Hoffman; Livingston, Jerry
Feminine Fashions   Freed, Arthur; Warren
Festive Overture   Raye
Feudin' and Fightin'   Lane; Loesser
Few Conversations Ago, A   Meyer
Fiesta (Inst.)   Warren
Fifi's Song   Romberg
Fireman's Bride, The   Fields; Romberg
Five a Four Blues   Myrow
Five A.M. Ballet   De Lange; Myrow
Five More Minutes in Bed   Revel
Florida   Coots
Flourish (inst.)   Romberg
For the Life of Me   Gershwin, Ira; Warren
Friend of Yours, A   Burke; Van Heusen
Friends to the End   Lerner, Alan Jay; Loewe
Fussin' Around (inst.)   Waller
General Ike   Caesar
Geraniums in the Winder   Hammerstein; Rodgers
Girl in Nottingham Lace, The   Cahn; Styne
Girls! Girls! Girls!   Brown, Lew; Henderson
Go Down to Boston Harbor   Lane
God's Green World   Lerner, Alan Jay; Loewe
Gold Diggers Are Back Again, The   Adamson; McHugh
Golden Eagle March (inst.), The   Coots
Gonna Build a Big Fence Around Texas   Friend
Good Little, Bad Little Lady   Brooks
Good Time Charlie   Burke; Van Heusen
Good Time Polka   Friend
Goodnight My Sweet   David, Mack
Gossip   Young, Victor
Got a Million Dollars Worth of Dreams   Brooks
Got that Good Time Feelin'   Lane
Gotta See a Girl about Love   Hoffman
Greatest Mistake of My Life, The   Lawrence
Half a Dream to Go   De Lange; Myrow
Halfway Down on Jackson Street   Mills
Happy, Happy, Happy, Happy, Happy, Happy, Happy, Happy, Happy, Happy, Happy Wedding Day   Willson
Happy Medium Song   Caesar

Happy-Go-Lucky Lady   Brooks
Hard Way, The   Burke; Van Heusen
Hasta Manana (Toda Una Vida)   De Lange
Have You Been to Gay Paree   Gordon
Have You Got Old Clothes   Caesar
Have You Heard About the Meeting?   Harburg
Havin' a Time   Comden and Green
Hayride   Mercer; Warren
He Only Had 84 Points   Cahn; Styne
He Was a Perfect Gentleman   Burke; Van Heusen
Hear Ye! Hear Ye!   Weill
Heart of Harlem   Ellington
Heartless   Washington
Heaven Is a Place Called Home   Magidson; Wrubel
Heaven Watch the Philipines   Berlin
He'll Have to Cross the Atlantic to Get to the Pacific   Cahn; Styne
Hellzapoppin Polka, The   Lane
Here Comes Heaven Again   Adamson; McHugh
Here I Go Again   Revel
Here Ye! Hear Ye!   Gershwin, Ira
Hey Pop, Buy Me Another Bond!   Rome
Hey, What's Your Name   Cahn; Styne
Highest Judge of All, The   Hammerstein; Rodgers
Holding Hands (J'ai ta Main)   Rome
Holiday Greetings   Stept
Home in Oklahoma (Way Down Thar on the Farm)   Carroll
Honey Won't You Call Me   Evans; Livingston, Jay
Hong Kong Blues   Carmichael
Honky-Tonk (inst.)   Kern
Hooray for Anywhere   Lane
Hooray for Our Side   Brooks
Horizontal   David, Hal
Hot Tamale Man, The   David, Mack
How Can I Forget You   Washington
How Little We Know   Carmichael; Mercer
How Much I Care   Friml
How Wonderfully Fortunate   Gershwin, Ira; Weill
How Would You Like to Take My Picture   Adamson; McHugh
How'd You Get Out of My Dreams   Fain; Yellen
I Am Happy Here   Gershwin, Ira; Weill
I Begged Her   Cahn; Styne
I Believe in Santa Claus   Coots; Egan
I Can Make You Love Me   Russell
I Can't Begin to Tell You   Gordon; Monaco
I Can't Believe My Eyes   De Lange
I Can't Get You Out of My Mind   Brooks
I Could Be Wrong   Gilbert
I Don't Care If I Never Dream Again   Brooks
I Don't Care If I Never Go to Bed   Hoffman; Livingston, Jerry
I Don't Care Who Knows It   Adamson; McHugh
I Don't Want to Change the Subject (But Did You Buy a Bond Today?)   Brown, Lew; Henderson
I Fall in Love Too Easily   Cahn; Styne
I Fall in Love with You Ev'ry Day   Stept
I Gotta Gal I Love (In North and South Dakota)   Cahn; Styne
I Had Just Been Pardoned   Gershwin, Ira; Weill
I Hear a Song in My Heart   Mercer
I Hope the Band Keeps Playing   Blane
I Just Got In   Brooks
I Know   Russell
I Know Where There's a Cozy Nook   Gershwin, Ira; Weill

I Left a Good Deal in Mobile   Mills
I Like Love   Blane
I Like This Loving You   Cahn
(Oh Mom, Dear Mom) I Lost My Job Again   Coots; Lewis
I Love an Old Fashioned Song   Cahn; Styne
I Love You but Good   De Lange; Myrow
I Love You For That   Stept
I Love You This Morning   Lerner, Alan Jay; Loewe
I Owe It All to You   Arlen; Mercer
I Passed this Way Before   Robison
I See You Everywhere   Brown, Nacio Herb
I Shall Return   Parish
I Should Care   Cahn
I Wake Up in the Morning   Fain; Yellen
I Walked In (With My Eyes Wide Open)   Adamson;
     McHugh
I Want to Be a Drummer (In the Band)   Fain; Yellen
I Want You to Love Me   Blane
I Was Here When You Left Me, I'll Be There When You Get
     Back   Stept
I Wish I Knew   Gordon; Warren
I'd Like To Write a Song To End All War   Bryan
I'd Rather Be Me   Coslow
I'd Rather Do Without You Baby   Gilbert
Idle Dollars — Busy War Bonds   Johnson, J. Rosamond;
     Razaf
If He Wears a Little Golden Eagle   Coots
If I Had a Dozen Hearts   Revel; Webster
If I Had a Wishing Ring   Alter
If I Loved You   Hammerstein; Rodgers
If It Could Happen   Adamson; McHugh
If It's for Me, I'm not Home   David, Hal
If Love Remains   Gershwin, Ira; Weill
If Promises Were Made of Gold   David, Mack
If You Care for the Boys   Cahn; Styne
I'll Buy that Dream   Magidson; Wrubel
I'll Dance Rings Around You   Berlin
I'll Follow Your Smile   Harburg; Kern
I'll Remember April   DePaul; Raye
I'll Sing a Hymn to You at Twilight   David, Mack
I'm a Big Girl Now   Hoffman; Livingston, Jerry
I'm Down to My Last Dream   Coots
I'm Going to Adopt a Little Boy   Norworth
I'm Gonna Hate Myself in the Morning   Adamson; McHugh
I'm Guilty   Evans; Livingston, Jay
I'm Holding Heaven in My Arms   Drake
I'm in the Mood for Solitude   Livingston, Jerry
I'm Lonesome Virginia   David, Mack
I'm Looking for a Rainbow (inst.)   Waller
I'm Not Having Any (This Year)   Raye
I'm Sure of Your Love   Comden and Green
I'm the First Man   Blane
I'm the Guy Who Can Do It   Russell
In a Wistful Vista   Gilbert
In Acapulco   Gordon; Warren
In Our Cozy Little Cottage of Tomorrow   Revel
In the Land   Cahn; Styne
In the Mood for Solitude   Hoffman; Livingston, Jerry
In the Valley (Where the Evening Sun Goes Down)   Mercer;
     Warren
Indians in the Evening   Hoffman; Livingston, Jerry
Invitation, The   Lerner, Alan Jay; Loewe
Island of the Moon, The   DePaul; Raye
Isn't It Kinda Fun?   Hammerstein; Rodgers
Isn't It Love   Mills

It Can't Be a Sin to Love You   Coots
It Could Only Happen in Brooklyn   Cahn; Styne
It Doesn't Cost You Anything to Dream   Fields; Romberg
(It Could Have Happened to Anyone) It Happened to
     Happen to Me   Gershwin, Ira; Weill
It Might as Well Be Spring   Hammerstein; Rodgers
It Must Be Spring   Blane
It Seems Like Yesterday   Stept
It Takes a Little Bit More   Coslow
It'll Always Be You   Stept
It's a Grand Night for Singing   Hammerstein; Rodgers
It's a Great Big World   Mercer; Warren
It's a Great Life If You Weaken   De Lange; Myrow
It's Anybody's Spring   Burke; Van Heusen
It's Been a Long, Long Time   Cahn; Styne
It's Me Oh Lord   Raye
It's Smart to Be People   Lane
I've Always Loved You   Rome
I've Got a Date with Judy   Pollack
I've Got a Locket in My Pocket   David, Mack
Javanese Temple Dance (inst.)   Coots
Jeep (inst.)   Young, Victor
Jim   Raye
Jitterbug   Cahn; Styne
Jolly Friars March (inst.), The   Coots
Josie   Cahn; Styne
Joyride   De Lange; Myrow
Jug of Wine, A   Lerner, Alan Jay; Loewe
Julie O'Dooley   Leslie
Jumpin' on Saturday Night   Brooks
June Comes Around Every Year   Arlen; Mercer
June Is Bustin' Out All Over   Hammerstein; Rodgers
Just a Blue Serge Suit   Berlin
Just Beyond the Rainbow   Revel
Just in Case   Gershwin, Ira; Weill
Just the Way You Are   Revel
Katherine Receives Advice   Lerner, Alan Jay; Loewe
Keep Movin'   Johnson, James P.
Kid with the Whiskers   David, Mack; Meyer
Kiss at Midnight   Loesser
Kiss at Twilight   Loesser
Kitty   Evans; Livingston, Jay
Ladies Don't Have Fun   Cahn; Styne
Ladies, Ladies   Caesar
Lady Has a Right (March of the Suffragettes), A   Blane
Lady on Bedloe's Island   Coots; Lewis
Lady Who Walks Alone   Lawrence
Lady with a Parasol, A   Wrubel
Lament   Brown, Nacio Herb
Last Dance with You, The   Hoffman
Let Ev'ry Day Be Mother's Day   Stept
Let It Snow, Let It Snow, Let It Snow   Cahn; Styne
Let Us All Sing Auld Lang Syne   Brown, Lew; Henderson
Let's Go Americana   Brooks
Let's Have An Old-Fashioned Christmas (And Pray for a
     Happy New Year)   Adamson; Fields; McHugh
Let's Have Fun Tonight   Friend
Let's Play House   Brooks
Let's Take the Long Way Home   Arlen; Mercer
Life of the Party, The   Brooks
Life with Rocky, A   Comden and Green
Linda   Lawrence
Linda Mujer (You Never Say Yes)   Caesar
Little Naked Boy, The   Gershwin, Ira; Weill
Little Pink Clouds in the Little Blue Sky, The   Coots

Loafin'   Drake
Local to Cheyenne   Merrill
Lonely Wolf Blues (The Lonesomest Wolf in the
    Town)   Rome
Long Live the Night   Romberg
Long, Strong and Consecutive   David, Mack; Ellington
Look-a-Here (inst.)   Waller
Lord's Been Good to Me, The   Stept
Lost (A Wonderful Girl)   Davis; Hanley
Love and I Went Waltzing   Cahn; Styne
Love Flies Out the Window   Hoffman; Livingston, Jerry
Love Is a Bluebird on the Wing   Brooks
Love Is My Enemy   Gershwin, Ira; Weill
Love Letters   Heyman; Young, Victor
Love Me   Cahn; Styne
Loveliness of You, The   Stept
Lovely Girl, A   Comden and Green
Lovely Luana   DePaul; Raye
Lovely You (Only You, Only Me)   Friml
Love's What You Make It   Drake
Lucky Legs   Cahn
Lupita   Washington
Mad   Cahn; Styne
Madame Butterball   DePaul; Raye
Made in the U.S.A.   Freed, Arthur; Warren
Man with the Cigarette, The   Gorney
Man with the Weird Beard, The   Hoffman; Livingston, Jerry
Many Happy Returns   Dietz
March (inst.)   Kern
March of the Dogies, The   Mercer; Warren
March of the Spades (inst.)   Waller
Master Is Free Again   Gershwin, Ira; Weill
Maypole Dance (inst.)   Romberg
Melody in G (inst.)   Warren
Memphis in June   Carmichael; Webster
Mexican Sombrero Dance (inst.)   Coots
Mexicana   Washington
Michael the Bicycle Rider   Cahn
Mike's Took Bad   Young, Victor
Million Dollar Hat   Coots
Million Dollar Smile   Comden and Green
Mink Lament, The   Gordon; Warren
Mister Snow   Hammerstein; Rodgers
Moody   Gordon; Warren
Morale   Gershwin, Ira; Weill
More and More   Harburg; Kern
More I See You, The   Gordon; Warren
Mother Mississippi   Lane
Mound Bayou   Johnson, James P.
Mucho Gusto (Oye Needa)   Caesar
Music Box Fantasy (inst.), A   Coots
Musical Wedding   Brooks
My Christmas Wish   Parish
My Dear Benvenuto   Gershwin, Ira; Weill
My Desert Rose   David, Mack
My First, My Last, My Only   Caesar
My Head Upon Your Shoulder   Washington
My Heart Is Filled with You   Coots
My Heart Tells Me It's You   Johnson, Howard
My Intuition   Mercer; Warren
My Lord and Ladies   Gershwin, Ira; Weill
My Love Is a Married Man   Lerner, Alan Jay; Loewe
My Old Home Town   Blane
Never Too Late to Pray   Robison
New Day, A   Brooks

Nickel's Worth of Jive, A   Gordon; Warren
Nighttime Is No Time for Thinking, The   Gershwin, Ira;
    Weill
Nina, the Pinta, the Santa Maria (Columbus),
    The   Gershwin, Ira; Weill
No Matter Where You Are   Brooks
No More Toujours L'Amour (Hoya, Hoya)   Carmichael;
    Webster
No More Women   De Lange
Nostalgia (inst.)   Myrow
Novelette   Kern
Now the Madame Swings   Raye
Now We're Getting Somewhere   Burke; Van Heusen
Nutcracker Suite   Brooks
Nutmeg Insurance   Revel
Ode to Dorie Miller   Johnson, James P.; Razaf
Oh How I Love that Man   Coots; Magidson
Oh, To Be Home Again   Berlin
Oh What a Lovin' the Girls Will Get (When the Boys Come
    Home)   Johnson, Howard
Oh, What I Know About You   Wrubel
Oh, You Kid   Mercer; Warren
Old and the New Prelude, The   Gordon; Warren
Old Love for New   Caesar
Old Time Get-Together, An   Stept
On the Atchison Topeka and the Santa Fe   Blane; Mercer;
    Warren
Once in a Million Moons   Harburg; Kern
Once to Every Heart   Koehler
Once Upon a Dream   Brooks
Once-T Around the Park   Lawrence
One Little Dream   David, Mack
One Man's Death Is Another Man's Living   Gershwin, Ira;
    Weill
One More Tear Over You   Coots
(I Got a) One Track Mind   Comden and Green
Onion Time (inst.)   Waller
Only in Dreams   Lerner, Sammy
Ooh! What You Do to Me   Brooks
Opaltine   Raye
Orchids for Madame   David, Mack
Orchids or Roses   Carroll
Oriental Suite (inst.)   Buck
Our Master Is Free Again   Gershwin, Ira; Weill
Our Music Box   Hoffman
Our State Fair   Hammerstein; Rodgers
Out of My Mind   De Lange; Myrow
Out of Sight   De Lange
Out of This World   Arlen; Mercer
Paraphernalia (inst.)   Waller
Parrot on the Fortune Teller's Hat, The   Drake
Pass Me the Nutcracker, Sweet   Wrubel
Pass That Peace Pipe   Blane; Martin
Passe Qui   Robison
Pastel for Piano (inst.)   Coots
Patricia Donahue   Davis
Peekin' in Seek (inst.)   Waller
Personality   Burke; Van Heusen
Peter Had a Wife and Couldn't Keep Her   Brooks
Pied Pipers from Swingtown U.S.A.   Brooks
Play Me an Old Fashioned Melody   Gordon; Warren
Playing Around (inst.)   Kern
Please Don't Say No   Fain; Freed, Ralph
Poor Lenore   Drake
Poor Little Me   Revel

Prairie Mary   Baer
Promises   Hoffman; Livingston, Jerry
Publicity   De Lange; Myrow
Put - Put - Put (Your Arms Around Me)   Hoffman;
    Livingston, Jerry
Put It There, Pal   Burke; Van Heusen
Puttin' on Airs   Blane; Warren
Race Horse and the Flea, The   Berlin
Real Nice Clambake, A   Hammerstein; Rodgers
Red, Hot and Beautiful   Adamson; McHugh
Rednow Lipstick   Coslow
Reporter Scene   Gordon
Rhyme for Angela, A   Gershwin, Ira; Weill
Ridin' on the Crest of a Cloud   Brooks
Rip Van Winkle   Fields; Romberg
Road to Utopia   Burke; Van Heusen
Rodger Young   Loesser
Rollin' Down the River   Brooks
Romeo and Juliet   Brooks
Rose, My Rose   Blane
Running Around with Rosie   Bryan
Sailor Routine   Gordon
Sailor Takes a Wife, The   Blane
Saint and Sinner   Coots
Same Boat Brother, The   Harburg
Same Little Chapel, The   Willson
Santa Marta   Drake
Say It with Love   Evans; Livingston, Jay
See Mexico   Washington
Send Us Back to the Kitchen   Revel
Serenade to a Sponsor's Ugly Daughter (inst.)   Strouse
Sergeant Housewife   Fields
Seven O'Clock in the Morning   Magidson; Wrubel
Sextette from Lucia   Brooks
Shake Your Salt on the Bluebird's Tail   Blane
She of the Black Coffee Eyes   Spina
She's a Gypsy from Brooklyn   Gilbert; Oakland
Short and Sweet   De Lange; Myrow
Should I Believe My Heart   Hoffman
Silly Boy   Ruby
Sing Me Not a Ballad   Gershwin, Ira; Weill
Situation's Well in Hand, The   Merrill
Sleepy Baby (Dream of Me)   Spina
Slightly Perfect   Revel
Slightly Slightly   Revel
So Soon   Razaf
Soft and New   Myrow
Soft and Warm   De Lange; Myrow
Soliloquy   Hammerstein; Rodgers
Some Sunday Morning   Koehler
Somebody's Walkin' in My Dreams   Adamson; McHugh
Someday, We Will Remember   Brooks
Something in My Heart   Harburg
Somewhere on Via Roma   Carmichael
Somewhere There's a Rainbow   Washington
Son of a Gun Who Picks on Uncle Sam, The   Harburg; Lane
Song for American Union   Rome
Song of Old Mexico, A   Coots
Song of the Hangman   Gershwin, Ira; Weill
Song of the Rhineland (Trenton Bieretuse)   Gershwin, Ira;
    Weill
Song to Remember, A   Cahn
So-o-o in Love   Robin
Soup Wouldn't Be Soup   Parish
Souvenirs   Gershwin, Ira; Weill

Speaking of Pals   Comden and Green
Spellbound   David, Mack
Spooky Wooky Polka   Hoffman; Livingston, Jerry
Spreadin' the Jam   Blane
Starry Summer Night   Blane
Steps of the Capitol, The   Lane
Stop and Make Love   Brooks
Stop that Dancing   Lane
Stuff Like That There   Evans; Livingston, Jay
Suddenly It's Spring   Lawrence
Sunday, Monday or Always   Burke
Sunday Night Supper   Blane
Sunflower   Cahn
Sunflower Song   Styne
Sunny California   Lane
Sweet I've Gotten on You   Robison
Swing It, Mister Chumbly   Brooks
Swing Your Partner Round and Round   Mercer; Warren
Swing Your Sweetheart   Harburg; Kern
Symphony   Lawrence
Taliami Moon   David, Mack
Talking to Myself About You   Friend
Taps Miller   Russell
Tattle Tale   Coots
Telephone Passage   Gershwin, Ira; Weill
Tell Me Why   Parish
Texas Is Tops with Me   Blane
Thank the Lawd for Small Favors   DePaul; Raye
Thank You Columbus   Harburg; Lane
Thank You, Joe   Dubin
Thanks for the Loan of Your Heart   Revel; Webster
That Day   Kalmar; Ruby
That Does It   De Lange; Myrow
That's for Me   Hammerstein; Rodgers
That's How It Is   Gershwin, Ira; Weill
That's The Kind of Work I Do   Raye
That's the Stuff You Got to Watch   Johnson, James P.
That's the Stuff You Gotta Watch   Sissle
(I Fell in Love with) The Leader of the Band   Magidson;
    Styne
There Ain't a Better Buy in the Land   Styne
There Ain't No Better Buy in the Land   Cahn
There I'd Be   Comden and Green
There Isn't Any Harm in That   Brooks
There Were Others Passing By   Blane
There'll Be a Yankee Christmas   Webster
There'll Be Life, Love, and Laughter   Gershwin, Ira; Weill
There'll Come a Day   Harburg; Kern
There's a Hundred Million Stars in the Star Spangled
    Banner   Davis
There's a New Flag on Iwo Jima   Adamson; McHugh
There's an Old Corral in Heaven   Coots
There's Nothin' So Bad for a Woman   Hammerstein;
    Rodgers
(They May Change the Name of Ireland, But) They Can't
    Change Those Irish Eyes   Bryan
They Went to Get Married   Brooks
This Changes Everything   Wrubel
This Is As Far As I Go   Lane
This Is My Beloved   Revel
This Is My Holiday   Lerner, Alan Jay; Loewe
This Is the Day for Love   Freed, Arthur; Warren
This Night in Florence   Gershwin, Ira; Weill
Three Little Ships   Carmichael
Three Quarter Blues (inst.)   Myrow

Throw It Out of Your Mind   Razaf
Thursday Night   Blane
Till the Last Beat of the Drum (I'll Be There)   Ahlert; Bryan
Time Out for Dreaming   Washington
To Be Young   De Lange; Myrow
To Have You To Hold You   Gordon; Revel
Tonight and Every Night   Cahn; Styne
Touring San Francisco   Adamson; McHugh
Toy Piper (inst.), The   Johnson, James P.
Train Must Be Fed, The   Mercer; Warren
Train Wheels Sang a Song, The   Friend
True to the Navy   Adamson; McHugh
Trumpet in Stringtime   Drake
Two on an Island   Lane
Twould Take a Gypsy Rose Lee to Find Out   Blake; Sissle
Uncle Sammy Hit Miami   Adamson; McHugh
Uncle Tom's Cabin   Brooks
Under an April Moon   Coots
Up Comes Love   Brooks
Up from the Gutter   Fields; Romberg
Upbeat   Freed, Arthur; Warren
Victory Parade, The   Pollack
Victory Polka   Johnson, James P.
Village Ballroom Polka, The   Clare
Viva America   Rome
Vive L'Amour   Blane
Vivian's Reverie   Revel
Voice in the Wind   De Lange; Henderson
Wait and See   Mercer; Warren
Walkin' and a Talkin' Doll, A   Gilbert
Waltz Time in Vienna   Caesar
Watch Out, Angel!   De Lange; Myrow
Wave to Me, My Lady   Loesser
We Hate to Leave   Cahn; Styne
We Have Been Around   Gordon
We Will Meet Again in Honolulu   Brown, Nacio Herb;
    Freed, Arthur
We'd Better Stop Kiss-Kiss-Kissin'   Bryan
Weekend at the Waldorf   Blane; Koehler
Welcome Burleigh   Cahn; Styne
Welcome to My Dream   Burke; Van Heusen
Welcome to the Diamond Horseshoe   Gordon; Warren
Well, Natch   David, Hal
We've Got Another Bond to Buy   Adamson; McHugh
What a Deal   Evans; Livingston, Jay
What a Fool I Was   Freed, Arthur
What Am I Saying   Evans; Livingston, Jay
What Did I Do   Cahn; Styne
What Do You Think My Heart Is Made Of   Parish
What Does an English Girl Think of a Yank   Cahn; Styne
What Makes the Sunset   Cahn; Styne
Whatcha Say   Koehler; Lane
What's Going On Over My Shoulder   Brown, Lew;
    Henderson
What's He Got?   Cahn; Styne
What's New in New York   De Lange; Myrow
What's the Use of Wond'rin'   Hammerstein; Rodgers
When a Good Man Takes to Drink   Revel
When Danny Brought Annie Home from Ireland   David,
    Mack; Hoffman; Livingston, Jerry
When I Dream, I Dream About Hawaii   Hoffman
When I Get to Town   Cahn; Styne
When I Think of Heaven   Brooks
When It's Love   De Lange
When She Walks in the Room   Fields; Romberg

When the Children Are Asleep   Hammerstein; Rodgers
When the Duchess Is Away   Gershwin, Ira; Weill
When the Old Gang's Back on the Corner   Hoffman
When the Party Gives a Party   Fields; Romberg
When We Were Both in Kindergarten   Cahn; Styne
Where Do We Go from Here?   Gershwin, Ira; Weill
Where Is the Boss   De Lange; Myrow
Where's My Wife?   Lerner, Alan Jay; Loewe
Whippoorwill Bill   Hoffman; Livingston, Jerry
Who Dat Up Dere?   Russell
Who Killed Vaudeville   Fain; Yellen
Who Knows Why April Dances   Webster
Who Was the First to Make Love?   Brown, Lew; Henderson
Who's Gonna Be the Winner?   Comden and Green
Who's Helping Who?   Van Heusen
Whose Dream Are You   Willson
Wild Rose of Old Cheyenne   Friend
Wild, Wild West, The   Mercer; Warren
Wilhelmina   Berlin
Will Rogers American   Robison
Will the Next Kiss Always Be Mine   Bryan
Will You Love Me Tomorrow (Will You Always
    Remember)   Caesar
Will You Marry Me?   Freed, Arthur; Warren
Wis-s-s-con-sin   Brown, Lew; Henderson
Woman's Work Is Never Done, A   Blane
Wonder of You, The   Ellington
Woo, Woo, Woo, Woo, Manhattan   Gershwin, Ira; Weill
Woodland Reverie   Baer
World Is Full of Villains, The   Gershwin, Ira; Weill
Worry Song, The   Fain; Freed, Ralph
Worryin' the Life Out of Me   Russell
Would You   Burke; Van Heusen
Xanadu   Rome
Yacht Club Swing   Waller
Yah-ta-ta, Yah-ta-ta (Talk, Talk, Talk)   Burke; Van Heusen
Yolanda   Freed, Arthur; Warren
You Are Springtime   Caesar
You Came Along   Cahn
You Can See with Your Heart   David, Mack
You Can't Be Here and Can't Be There   Harbach
You Can't Get Over the Wall   Fields; Romberg
You Can't Have Your Cake and Eat It   Waller
You Can't Stop Now   Brown, Lew
You Could Sell Me the Brooklyn Bridge   David, Hal
You Excite Me   Cahn; Lane; Styne
You Forgotcha Guitar   Monaco
You Gotta Keep Saying 'No'   Revel
You Have to Do What You Do Do   Gershwin, Ira; Weill
You Haven't Changed at All   Lerner, Alan Jay; Loewe
You Love Me Only in My Dreams   Brown, Lew
You Moved Right In   Adamson; McHugh
You, So It's You!   Brown, Nacio Herb
You'll Be There   Coots
You'll Never Walk Alone   Hammerstein; Rodgers
Young Girls Are a Problem   Blane
Your Top's Too Tall   Evans; Livingston, Jay
You're a Queer One, Julie Jordan   Hammerstein; Rodgers
You're Far Too Near Me   Gershwin, Ira; Weill
You're Not Giving — You're Lending   Cahn; Styne
You're So Worth the Waiting For   Drake
You're the Cause of It All   Cahn; Styne
You've Got a Lot to Learn about Love   Kalmar

1946

After the Show   Fain; Freed, Ralph
After Tonight   Brooks
Afterglow, The   David, Mack
Ain't God Good to Indiana   Carmichael
Aladdin's Daughter   Van Heusen
All Around the World   Burke; Van Heusen
All Suit, No Man   Coots
All the Time   Fain; Freed, Ralph
All Things Are Passing   Clare
All Through the Day   Hammerstein; Kern
All-American Man   Fain
(If We Could Be) A-l-o-n-e   Hoffman; Livingston, Jerry
Alone with You   Dietz
Along about Evenin'   Pollack
Along with Me   Rome
Always the Lady   Gordon; Myrow
American Soldier   Sigman
'Ampstead Way, The   Burke; Van Heusen
And Dreams Remain   Freed, Ralph
And So to Bed   Mercer
(Yo Te Amo Mucho) And That's That   Drake; Stept
Andalusia Bolero   Herbert
Another Day Goes By   Brooks
Any Place I Hang My Hat Is Home   Arlen; Mercer
Anyone Can Dream   David, Mack
Anything You Can Do   Berlin
April Made a Fool of Me   Parish
Archie's Little Love Song   Carmichael
Arizona Sundown   Alter; De Lange
Army Brat, The   Fain; Freed, Ralph
As Long As I've Got My Art   Martin
As the Wind Bloweth (There I Goeth)   Webster
At the Fireman's Ball   Adamson; McHugh
Autumn Twilight   Fain; Freed, Ralph
Avalon   Evans; Livingston, Jay
Ave Maria and Finale   Freed, Ralph
Ayes Have It   David, Hal
Baby, Don't Be Mad at Me   David, Mack
Baby Let's Face It   Fain
Bad Man's Life, A   Revel
Ballet Divertissement (dance)   Herbert
Ballyhoo   Berlin
Be Brave Men   Brooks
Behind the Eight Ball   Bryan
Bet Your Bottom Dollar   De Lange; Myrow
Big City Blues   Russell
Billy's Fight with Chuck   Russell
Bing, Bang   Loesser
Bluebird Is Singing to Me, A   Adamson; McHugh
Blues for Pete   Johnson, James P.
Blues Nocturne (inst.)   Revel
Bolero (inst.)   Blake
Boogie on the Prairie (inst.)   Ruby
Boy Takes a Girl In His Arms, A   Revel
Broken Hearted Troubadour   David, Mack
Brown Penny   Ellington
But Me No Buts   David, Mack
Cakewalk Your Lady   Arlen; Mercer
Calendar Girl   Adamson; McHugh
California (Opening Title)   Harburg
California or Bust   Harburg
California Scene Dance   Porter
Call Me Mister   Rome
Can Can   Burke; Van Heusen

Can You Guess   Drake
Candle Is Burning Low, The   Robison
Candlelight and Roses   Robison
Catalina   Evans; Livingston, Jay
Celestial Nocturne   Revel
Centennial   Kern; Robin
Chase, The   Ellington
Chick with the Band   Merrill
Child of All Nations   Caesar
Chin-Cha   Russell
Chinquapin Bush   Arlen; Mercer
Chisholm Trail   Revel
Choral Russe   Burke; Van Heusen
Chorus of Citizens   Ellington
Christmas Came in May   De Lange
Cinderella Jones   Cahn; Styne
Cinderella Sue   Harburg; Kern
Cindy   Mercer
Clock (inst.), The   Kern
Coach and Four, A   Evans; Livingston, Jay
Cocabola Tree, The   Blane
(It's a) Cold, Cruel World   Russell
Colonel Buffalo Bill   Berlin
Come Along to the County Fair   Johnson, J. Rosamond
Come In Out of the Rain   Russell; Sigman
Come Lonely Lover   Brooks
Come On, Li'l Augie   Arlen; Mercer
Come Rain or Come Shine   Arlen; Mercer
Common Sense   Fain
Confusion   Razaf
Conscience   Johnson, J. Rosamond
Continental Can-Can, The   Blane
Continental Polka, The   Blane
Conversation (inst.)   Blake
Corn Is Green, The   Coots
Corn Shuckin' Time   Johnson, J. Rosamond
Couple of Song and Dance Men, A   Berlin
Cowboy and the Senorita, The   Washington
Cradle of Democracy (inst.)   Kern
Creole Caprice (inst.)   Coots
Creole Lullaby   Johnson, James P.
Crispy and Crunchy   Duke
Curse of the Blues   Blake
Daffodils and Red Red Robins   De Lange
Dance of the Little Dutch Doll (inst.)   Coots
Dancing with You   Coots; Lewis
Dangerous (Peligrosa)   Blane
Dark Is the Night   David, Hal
De Lawd Looks After All His Chillun'   Washington
Dear Boy (Shall We Dance)   Stept
Dew Was on the Rose, The   Gershwin, Ira; Schwartz, Arthur
Diana   Duke
Did the Moon Tap on Your Window   Parish
Did-Ja   Waller
Dingbat, the Singing Cat   Hoffman
Dinner Song   Gershwin, Ira; Schwartz, Arthur
Divertissement   Burke; Van Heusen
Do the New Fangled Spelling Bee   Fain
Do You Know What It Means to Be Lonely   Hoffman; Livingston, Jerry
Do You Love Me   Ruby
Do You Think It's Fair   Howard, Joseph E.
Does Baby Feel All Right?   Burke; Van Heusen
Doin' What Comes Natur'lly   Berlin
Dom Pedro of Brazil (inst.)   Kern

Don't Be a Woman If You Can   Gershwin, Ira; Schwartz, Arthur

Don't Call on Me   Cahn; Styne

Don't Change Sweethearts in the Middle of a Dream   Evans; Livingston, Jay

Don't Come Back Until You Say You're Sorry   Stept

Don't Ever Run Away from Love   Webster

Don't Marry that Girl   Stept

Don't Talk Back to Baby   Baer

Dos Almas (My Lady of the Roses)   David, Hal

Down By the Ocean   Fain; Freed, Ralph

Down Where the Bluebells Grow   Coots; Friend

Dream Street   David, Hal

Dreamboat   Evans; Livingston, Jay

(I'm) Dreamin' Out Loud   Pollack

Dreaming Is Fine for Passing the Time   Razaf

Dreamland Rendezvous   Gilbert; Oakland

Drifting Along the Delaware (inst.)   Kern

Drowsy Lullaby (inst.)   Kern

Drug Store Song, The   Rome

Easter Nocturne (inst.)   Coots

Eat Mush, Mush, Mush, Mush, Mushroom Soup   Styne

Echo (inst.)   Schwartz, Arthur

El Morocco (inst.)   Coots

Election Day   Caesar

Encore, Cherie   Coots

Eskimo Bacchante   Duke

Everybody Has a Laughing Place   Wrubel

Face on the Dime, The   Rome

Facts of Life Backstage, The   Herbert

Far-Away Island   Davis

Farewell My Lovely   Coots

Farmer's Life Is a Very Merry Life, A   Gordon; Myrow

Fifth Avenue   De Lange

Fifth Avenue Bus (inst.)   Bloom

Fifth Maxixe, The   Burke; Van Heusen

Fifty Friendly Nations   Caesar

Figaro   Washington

Fire Chief's Daughter, The   Fain; Freed, Ralph

Firstest with the Mostest, The   David, Mack

Five Minutes More   Cahn; Styne

Flame In My Heart   Lawrence

Flight Eight   Mills

Flow Gently, Sweet Rhythm (inst.)   Bloom

Flower Song, The   Adamson; McHugh

Fogarty and Mandolin Girls   Burke; Van Heusen

Fogarty and Nelly Bly Parade   Burke; Van Heusen

Fogarty the Great   Burke; Van Heusen

Fol-de-rol-rol   Ellington

Follow the Band   De Lange; Myrow

Fooled By the Fickle Fingers of Fate   David, Hal

Footloose   Russell

For the Life of Me   Gershwin, Ira; Schwartz, Arthur

For Those in Love   Davis

Forever Yours   Silver

Fragment (inst.), A   Young, Victor

Free!   Russell

Friendly Country   Russell

Future Mrs. Coleman, The   Gershwin, Ira; Schwartz, Arthur

Gal in Calico, A   Robin; Schwartz, Arthur

Gambler's Lullaby   Webster

Games a la Francaise (inst.)   Coots

Garden in Versailles (inst.)   Coots

Gay Little Melody, A   Hoffman; Livingston, Jerry

Gee, I'm Glad to Be the One That I Am   Lerner, Sammy

Gentleman of the Old School   Webster

German Town (inst.)   Kern

Get Me Some Acres of Land   Revel

(Running Around in Circles) Getting Nowhere   Berlin

G.I. Song   Koehler

Ginger and Spice   Carmichael

Girl in the Front Porch Swing, The   Coots

Girl That I Marry, The   Berlin

Girls Want a Hero   Ellington

Give Me Something to Dream About   David, Mack; Hoffman; Livingston, Jerry

Give Me the Simple Life   Bloom; Ruby

Give to the March of Dimes   Caesar

Give Us Peace   Robison

Goin' Home Train   Rome

Gold Rush (Gold Discovery Montage), The   Harburg

Gonna Fall in Love with You   Blane

Good Deed for Today   Duke

Good for Nothing but Love   Pollack

Good Morning, Heartache   Drake

Good-Bye to All That   Gershwin, Ira; Schwartz, Arthur

Goodnight, Goodnight (Sweet Dreams to You)   Spina

Gotta Get Me Somebody to Love   Wrubel

Grandma's Flowers   Robison

Great Adventure   Revel

G'wan Home, Your Mudder's Callin'   Fain; Freed, Ralph

Gypsy Wedding Waltz (inst.)   Coots

Hallelujah, Bless the Peace   Caesar

Ham That I Am   Duke

Happiness   Parish

Happy Anniversary   Kern; Robin

Harmony   Burke; Van Heusen

Harriet   Baer

Harry Is Only Physical   Webster

Hat that I Kissed You Under, The   Howard, Joseph E.

Havana Moon   Russell

Have I Told You Lately   Adamson; McHugh

Have the Last Kiss on Me   Evans; Livingston, Jay

Heart Full of Love, A   Hoffman; Livingston, Jerry

Heartbreak   Brooks

Heave Ho! My Lads, Heave Ho!   Lawrence

Heavenly Day   Gershwin, Ira; Schwartz, Arthur

He'll Make Some Girl a Wonderful Husband   Russell

Here's to the Girls   Freed, Arthur

Here's to the Ladies   Freed, Ralph

He's a Hero   Cahn; Styne

He's Mine! All Mine!   Johnson, J. Rosamond

Hey Joe   Revel

Hey, Jose (Que Sera)   Evans; Livingston, Jay

Hey Wollyo (inst.)   Revel

High, Low, Jack and the Game   Arlen; Mercer

Hip-Di-Dee-O-Tee   Russell

His Old Man   Rome

Holiday in Mexico   Fain; Freed, Ralph

Home of My Own, A   Woods

Home of Our Own, A   Rome

Hong Kong to Hoboken   Burke; Van Heusen

Hop, Skip and Jump   Hoffman; Livingston, Jerry

Hope for the Best   Gershwin, Ira; Schwartz, Arthur

Hospital, Scene Commercial (Eat Mush, Mush, Mush, Mush, Mushroom Soup)   Cahn

Hour Before the Dawn, The   Parish

House, a House (My Life for a House), A   Raye

House of Blue Lights, The   Raye

How About a Date?   Burke; Van Heusen

How Do I Know   De Lange
How Do You Do It?   Burke; Van Heusen
How Thoughtful of You   Sigman
How to Spell Friendship   Caesar
How Would You Feel   Brooks
Howdy Stranger   Revel
Hunted, The   Ellington
Hyde Park on a Sunday   Burke; Van Heusen
Hymn   Duke
I Ain't Nobody's Fool   Washington
I Always Meant to Tell You   Cahn; Styne
I Can't Get You Out of My Mind   Brooks
I Couldn't Love You Anymore   Brooks
I Did It for the Missus   Burke; Van Heusen
(I'm Sorry) I Didn't Mean a Word I Said   Adamson;
   McHugh
I Didn't Think I'd Like To   Johnston
I Do You — Do You Me?   Friend
I Don't Care If I Never Dream Again   Brooks
I Don't Need Any Dreams   Burke
I Feel My Luck Comin' Down   Arlen; Mercer
I Got Lost in His Arms   Berlin
I Got the Sun in the Morning   Berlin
I Had Myself a True Love   Arlen; Mercer
I Had too Much to Dream Last Night   Hoffman; Livingston,
   Jerry
I Happen to Love You   Woods
I Happened to Walk Down First Street   Robin; Schwartz,
   Arthur
I Hate Myself Ev'ry Morning   Razaf
I Have a Love in Every Port   Cahn; Styne
I Haven't Got a Worry in the World   Hammerstein; Rodgers
I Just Wanna Be Like You   Revel
I Knew I'd Love You   Adamson
I Know   DePaul; Raye
I Know a Friendly City   Caesar
I Know What It Means to Be Lonesome   David, Mack
I Like Mike   Gordon; Myrow
I Love Eggs   Cahn; Styne
I Love to Dance   Freed, Ralph; Lane
I Love to Sing a Duet   Friend
I Love You Darling   Revel
I Love You, I Adore You   Herbert
I Love You More in Technicolor   Blane; Martin
I Love You Truly   Evans; Livingston, Jay
I Never Had a Chance   De Lange
I Never Knew What Love Was (Till I Met You)   Howard,
   Joseph E.
I Never Say Oui, Oui!   Brooks
I Says to Him   Duke
I Should'a Stood in Pennsylvania   Harburg
I Wanna Be Bad   Ellington
I Wanna Go to City College   Fain
I Want a Beautiful Doll for Christmas   Hoffman; Livingston,
   Jerry
I Want to Be Talked About   Brooks
I Was Silly, I Was Headstrong, I Was Impetuous   Cahn;
   Styne
I Wish I Could Tell You   Bloom; Ruby
I Wish that I Could Love You   Revel
I Wonder What Became of Me?   Arlen; Mercer
Ibbedy Bibbedy Sibbedy Sab   Loesser
I'd Love to Go on Dreaming   Fain; Freed, Ralph
If I Had to Do It All Over Again   Spina
If I Only Had a Match   Johnston

If I'm Lucky   De Lange; Myrow
If Spring Were Only Here to Stay   Burke; Van Heusen
If You Are There   Washington
If You Could See Me Now   Sigman
If You Smile at Me   Porter
If You're Waiting I'm Waiting Too   Cahn; Styne
I'll Share It All with You   Berlin
I'll Take Mah Troubles Down to the River   Washington
Illusion   Russell
I'm a Bad, Bad Man   Berlin
I'm an Indian Too   Berlin
I'm Easy to Get Along With   Baer
I'm Getting Married in the Morning (I'm Gonna Get Married
   in the Morning)   Carmichael
I'm Glad I Waited for You   Cahn; Styne
I'm Gonna Lasso a Dream   David, Mack; Hoffman;
   Livingston, Jerry
I'm Gonna Take What's Coming   Revel
I'm Payin' You (Pay Day)   Russell
I'm Right   Revel
I'm Takin' the Dream Train (Hug-A-Chug)   Friend
I'm Telling You Now   Adamson; McHugh
Impatient Years   Fain; Freed, Ralph
(I've Got Me) In Between   Ellington
In Love in Vain   Kern; Robin
In the Courtroom (inst.)   Schwartz, Arthur
In the Evening By the Moonlight   Waller
In the Middle of May   Ahlert
In the Moonmist   Lawrence
In the Shadows of Dreamland Isle   Young, Joseph
Indian Holiday   Fain; Freed, Ralph
Indiana County Fair (inst.)   Coots
Ingle-Go-Jang-Go-Jay   Washington
Interlude   Herbert
Into the Sun   Bloom; Ruby
Is It Worth It   De Lange
Isn't It Strange How the Weather Can Change Over
   Night   Coots; Lewis
Isn't This a Cockeyed World   De Lange
It Hasn't Been Chilly in Chile (Since Lilly O'Reilly's
   Around)   Burke; Van Heusen
It Is Always Music to His Ear   Caesar
It Shouldn't Happen to a Dream   Ellington
It'll Be Great to Get Back Home   Freed, Ralph
It's a Big Country   Revel
It's a Fake   David, Mack
It's a Gentleman's World   Burke; Van Heusen
It's a Lie (It's a Lie, It's a Lie)   Hoffman; Livingston, Jerry
It's a Lonely Life without a Wife   Livingston, Jerry
It's All Up to You (To Make North Carolina No. 1 in Good
   Health)   Cahn; Styne
It's Fun to Take a Bubble Bath   Fain; Freed, Ralph
It's Getting Hot in Tahiti   Blane
It's Good   Duke
It's Lonely, Life without a Wife   David, Mack; Hoffman
It's the Better Me   Webster
It's Time for the Love Scene   Loesser
It's Time I Had a Break   Webster
It's Way Past My Bedtime   Heyman; Spina
It's Your Life   Burke; Van Heusen
I've a Lover in My Heart   Johnson, J. Rosamond
I've Been there Before   Russell
I've Got to Get Somewhere with You   Burke; Van Heusen
I've Never Forgotten   Cahn; Styne
Jam Session in Brazil (The Batacada)   De Lange; Myrow

January, February (The Calendar Song)   Stept
Johnny Fedora and Alice Blue Bonnet   Wrubel
Just Before Daybreak (inst.)   Johnson, James P.
Just Like a Man   Duke
Just My Luck   Burke; Van Heusen
Keepsakes   Herbert
Kid Stuff   Russell
King Cocoa   Evans; Livingston, Jay
Kiss Me Hello (After the War Baby)   Cahn; Styne
La Brea Tar Pits   Cahn; Styne
Lady with the Mop, The   Cahn; Styne
Land of Opportunitee, The   Gershwin, Ira; Schwartz, Arthur
Lanterns in the Sky   Fain; Freed, Ralph
Least That's My Opinion   Arlen; Mercer
Leavin' Time   Arlen; Mercer
Legalize My Name   Arlen; Mercer
Less than Eighty Days   Burke; Van Heusen
Let Us Gather at the Goal Line   Fain
Let's Be Young   Duke
Let's Get This War Over With   Blane
Let's Go Back and Kiss the Girls Goodnight Again   David,
    Mack; Stept
Let's Go for a Spin on Our Bicycle   Johnson, J. Rosamond
Let's Go South   Coots
Let's Go West Again   Berlin
Let's Have Some Pretzels and Beer   Adamson; McHugh
Let's Make the World of Tomorrow Today   Caesar
Let's Spend a Quiet Evening at Home   Spina
Let's Take a Ride on a Rocket   Howard, Joseph E.
L'Exposition Universalle   Burke; Van Heusen
Life Is a Dirty Business   Herbert
Li'l Augie Is a Natural Man   Arlen; Mercer
Lily-I-Lay-De-O   Harburg
Lim'ricks   Arlen; Mercer
Linger in My Arms a Little Longer   Magidson
Listen to the German Band   Johnson, J. Rosamond
Little Bluebird Told Me, A   Hoffman; Livingston, Jerry
Little Jim   Fain; Freed, Ralph
Little Patch o' Land   Young, Victor
Little Quaker (inst.), A   Kern
Little Surplus Me (Surplus Blues)   Rome
Little Washerwoman (Down in Rio), The   Coots
Long Live Our Free America   Kern; Robin
Long Long Ago   Evans; Livingston, Jay
Look and Listen   Sigman
Look What I Found   Porter
Loretta   Davis; Silver
Louella   Mills
Louisiana Landscape (inst.)   Coots
Love   Martin
Love and Learn   De Lange
Love Is a Funny Little Fellow   Revel
Love Is a Merry-Go-Round   Cahn; Styne
Love Is a Penny Postcard   Fain; Freed, Ralph
Love Is a Random Thing   Fain
Love Is a Wonderous Thing   Freed, Ralph
Love Is the Darndest Thing   Burke; Van Heusen
Love on a Greyhound Bus   Blane
Love Remains the Same   Rome
Love Will Have to Do   Stept
Lovely Night to Go Dancing   Adamson; McHugh
Low and Lazy   Duke
Lucky Duck   Webster
Lullaby   Arlen; Mercer
Lullaby for a Grown Up Baby   Pollack

Lullaby for Junior   Ellington
Lullaby to Love   Drake
Lunar Rhapsody (inst.)   Revel
Lunette   Revel
Mabel, Mabel   Drake
Madame Butterfly Jones   Russell; Stept
Magic Moon   Gordon
Main Street U.S.A.   Revel
Main Title   Freed, Ralph
Make Mine Latin   Davis
Mama Mia   Revel
Mama Never Told Me   Lawrence
Man and a Maid, A   Caesar
Man with a Horn   De Lange
Man with the Initials, The   Harburg
Man's Gotta Fight, A   Arlen; Mercer
March of the Sengalese (inst.)   Blake
Marguerita   Revel
Maria Mia   Sigman
Mariachi Serenade, The   Drake
May the Best Man Win   Burke; Van Heusen
Maybe I Should Change My Ways   Ellington
McInerney's Farm   Fain
Me and the Blues   Koehler; Warren
Me Go Where You Go, Amigo   Razaf
Meerahlah   Porter
Merry Ha Ha, The   Russell
Midnight Mood (inst.)   Ruby
Mighty Big Dream Footloose   Russell
Military Life   Rome
Minneapolis Ain't Talkin' to St. Paul   Merrill
Minuet Modernistique (inst.)   Coots
Minute Maid   Burke; Van Heusen
Mission of the Rose, The   Drake
Missus Aouda   Porter
Mist o' the Moon (inst.)   Revel
Monastery Processional (inst.)   Coots
Money in the Pocket   Russell; Sigman
Moon Moods   Revel
Moon, Moon   Willson
Moon Over Nowhere   Lawrence
Moon Trail, The   Robin
Moonlight Over the Islands   Pollack
Moonlight Propaganda   Magidson
Moonlight, Starlight, Lovelight and You   Johnson, J.
    Rosamond
Moonshine Lullaby   Berlin
Moppin' and Boppin'   Waller
More I Know of Love, The   Brooks
More than Ever   Fain; Freed, Ralph
Most Emphatically Yes   Razaf
Mr. Bach and Mr. Boogie #2   Brooks
(Hey) Mr. Postman   Raye
Music to a Dancing Bird   Russell
My Beautiful Senorita   Revel
My Broker Told Me So   Duke
My Crystal Ball   Johnson, J. Rosamond
My Defenses Are Down   Berlin
My Dream Concerto   David, Mack
My Dream Song   Coots
My First Waltz   Herbert
My Heart Goes Crazy   Burke; Van Heusen
My Love Gets Hungry Too   Waller
My Number One Dream Came True   Brown, Lew
My Right Hand Doesn't Know   Gorney

My Sentimental Nature   Loesser
My Son-In-Law   Gershwin, Ira; Schwartz, Arthur
My Story of Love   Lawrence
My Treasure   Herbert
Nancy Clancy   Drake
Near to You   Sigman
Nellie Bly   Burke; Van Heusen
Nellie Martin   Fain; Freed, Ralph
Nevertheless I Can Dream   Johnston
New Dawn — A New Day, A   Robin
New Day, A   Brooks
New Day Prayer, A   Razaf
New York Is a Nice Place to Visit   McHugh
New York's a Nice Place to Visit   Adamson
Night in Paradise   Brooks
Nightingale's Dream (inst.)   Bloom
No News Today   Burke; Van Heusen
No One Seems to Care   De Lange
No Restricted Signs Up in Heaven   Drake
No Ross Dixon Lincoln Plaza Saloon   Russell
Nobody Else but Me   Hammerstein; Kern
Nora   Coots
Not Now   Razaf
Nothin'   Russell
Novelette   Robin
Numb, Dumb and Glum   Evans; Livingston, Jay
Oh Brother   Wrubel
Oh, But I Do   Robin; Schwartz, Arthur
Oh Henry   Cahn; Styne
Oh! My Love   Monaco
Oh, No, John   Lawrence
Oh What a Lovely Dream   Oakland
Oka Saka Circus   Porter
Old Fashioned Tune   Duke
Old Rainmaker, The   Drake
Ole Buttermilk Sky   Brooks; Carmichael
On a Slow Boat to China   Fain; Freed, Ralph
On a Wonderful Day Like Today   Herbert
(Plough, Plough Tra Tra La) On Chante Dans Mon
    Quartier   Heyman
On the Boardwalk (In Atlantic City)   Gordon; Myrow
On the Other End of a Kiss   Evans; Livingston, Jay
On the Roadway to the Moon   Johnson, J. Rosamond
On the Trail   Adamson
Once in a Dream   Revel
Once Upon a Dream   Brooks
Once Upon a Moonlight Night   Clare
One More Kiss   De Lange; Myrow
One More Tomorrow   De Lange; Myrow
One More Vote   De Lange; Myrow
Only for Me   De Lange
Only for Men   Burke; Van Heusen
Opening (Concerted Piece)   Kern; Robin
Opening The Statue Song   Loesser
Opera Sequence   Freed, Ralph
Opus #1   Mills
Ore for a Gold Mine   Ellington
Our Football Team   Caesar
Our Theme   Cahn; Styne
Out of My Way   Sigman
Out on a Limb   Webster
Overture to Love   Davis
Pancho   Davis; Silver
Pantomime   Herbert
Party Dance   Russell

Pass That Peace Pipe   Blane; Martin
Pay Attention to the Girls   Davis
Pay Day   Russell
Pepper Pot   Kern; Robin
Petty Girl Is Like a Melody, A   Martin
Philadelphia Feeling   Fain
Pi Phi Sweetheart   Willson
Pick Up the Phone   Revel
Pickle in the Middle (And the Mustard on Top)   Sigman
Piff Paff   Herbert
Pigeon Talk   Lawrence; Mancini
Pipe Dreaming   Porter
Plane Balle   Burke; Van Heusen
Plantation Portrait (inst.)   Coots
Plymouth Rock, The   Drake
Poco a Poco   Fain; Freed, Ralph
Pola Espagnole (inst.)   Coots
Political Satire March   Washington
Politics   Johnson, J. Rosamond
Poochinella's Band   Coots
Poor Lonesome Maiden   Brooks
Poor Miriam   Mercer
Poor Mrs. Tracy (The Mother of Dick)   Coots
Premiere Danseuse (inst.)   Coots
Pretty Woman   Ellington
Promenade   Burke; Van Heusen
Publicity   De Lange; Myrow
Purple Moonlight   De Lange
Put that Kiss Back Where You Found It   Sigman
Quarrel for Three   Ellington
Racin' Form   Arlen; Mercer
Radar Blues   Revel
Railroad Song   Kern; Robin
Rainbow's End   Drake
Raindrops (inst.)   Blake
Rainy Night in Rio, A   Robin; Schwartz, Arthur
Ranch House Saturday Night (inst.)   Bloom
Rascal with the Twinkle in His Eye, The   Stept
Reality   Herbert
Really O'Reilly   Robison
Red Ball Express   Rome
Ridin' on the Moon   Arlen; Mercer
Right Romance, The   Kern; Robin
Rio   David, Mack
Rogue River Valley   Carmichael
Rooster Man   Ellington
Rose and the Star, The   David, Mack
Roses Are Blooming, The   Spina
Roundabout   Duke
Saga of Billy the Kid   Russell
Said I to My Heart, Said I   Harburg
Salvo   Cahn; Styne
Same Old Blues   Bloom
Same Old Routine, The   Brooks
Sands of San Jose, The   David, Hal; David, Mack
Santa Catalina (Island of Romance)   Spina
Santa Fe Sketches   Spina
Say What You Mean and Mean What You Say   David,
    Mack; Hoffman; Livingston, Jerry
Scarecrow in the Cornfield (inst.)   Coots
Scherzo (inst.)   Blake
Scotch Bagpipe Dance (inst.)   Coots
Scratchin' Up a Batch   De Lange
Scrimmage of Life, The   Ellington
Sea Chantey   Porter

Searching Wind, The   Heyman; Young, Victor
Seattle   Fain; Freed, Ralph
Secrets   Lawrence
Senators' Song   Rome
Sepulveda   Evans; Livingston, Jay
Serenade (inst.)   Blake
Serenade to an Old-Fashioned Girl, A   Berlin
Serenade to Love   David, Mack; Stept
Set 'Em Up Joe   Brooks
Seven Days a Week   David, Hal
Seven Pounds of Heaven   David, Mack
Shadow of the Moon   Revel
Shauny O'Shea   Martin
She Went Out to Mail a Letter   Hoffman; Livingston, Jerry
Should I Tell You I Love You   Porter
(There's No Business Like) Show Business   Berlin
Silver in Your Hair   Howard, Joseph E.
Silver Saddle   Carmichael
Sing Me a Song of Texas   Revel
Singing Commercial   Duke
Sit Tight   Mills
Sittin' on the Inside   Brooks
Six Little Squirrels   Revel
Six Shades of Blue (inst.)   Blake
Sky Blue Pink   De Lange
Sky High   Burke; Van Heusen
Slave Auction   Porter
Sleep Peaceful, Mr. Used-to-Be   Arlen; Mercer
Slight Case of Ecstasy, A   Fain
Snagtooth Gertie   Porter
So Far So Wonderful   Revel
So Goes My Love   Brooks
So Would I   Burke; Van Heusen
Solid Citizen of the Solid South, A   Robin; Schwartz, Arthur
Someone to Love   Freed, Ralph
Somethin' You Gotta Find Out for Yourself   Arlen; Mercer
Something I Never Told You   Howard, Joseph E.
Something Tells Me   Razaf
Something to Say (No One to Say It To)   Johnston
Sometime Tomorrow   Russell
Somewhere in the Night   Gordon; Myrow
Sonata   Drake
Song of the Good Neighbor   Caesar
Song of the South   Coslow; Johnston
Song that Was Born in My Heart, The   Howard, Joseph E.
South America, Take It Away   Rome
Souvenir of Suzanne (inst.)   Coots
Sow the Seed and Reap the Harvest   Arlen; Mercer
Spring Will Miss You and So Will I   Fain; Freed, Ralph
Springtide   Herbert
Square Dance (inst.)   Kern
Starlight Enchantment (inst.)   Coots
Start Dancing   Burke; Van Heusen
Stay As We Are   Gershwin, Ira; Schwartz, Arthur
Stingy   Razaf
Stingy Blues   Merrill
Strange Love   Heyman
Straws in the Wind   Baer; Herbert
Streamline the Gordon Place   Johnson, J. Rosamond
Street Scene in Budapest (inst.)   Coots
Street Scene in Dublin (inst.)   Coots
Street Scene in London (inst.)   Coots
Street Scene in Paris (inst.)   Coots
Street Song   Styne
Strolling and Patrolling (inst.)   Kern

Suez Dance   Porter
Sugar Cane   Coots
Suttee Procession   Porter
Sweet Bye and Bye   Duke
Sweet Nevada   Gershwin, Ira; Schwartz, Arthur
Swiss Yodeler Waltz (inst.)   Coots
Take Five   David, Mack
Take It in Your Stride   Berlin
Take Love Easy   Ellington
Take Your Brother's Hand   Robison
Talkin' Glory   Arlen; Mercer
Talking Is a Woman   Russell; Sigman
Tell Me, Tell Me, Dream Face   Ellington
Tell Ya What I'm Gonna Do   Blane
Tenderly   David, Hal
Texas, Brooklyn and Love   Duke
Texas Moon   Sigman
10th Avenue Waltz   Davis
That American Look   De Lange; Myrow
That Little Dream Got Nowhere   Burke; Van Heusen
That Mexican Look   De Lange; Myrow
That's Class   Burke; Van Heusen
That's What Every Young Girl Should Know   David, Mack
(On) The Red Ball Line   Sissle
Them Who Has, Gets   DePaul; Raye
There Are Two Sides to Ev'ry Girl   Fain; Freed, Ralph
There He Goes, Mr. Phileas Fogg   Porter
There Must Be Little Cupids in the Briny   Willson
There's a New World A-Comin'   Coots
There's a Smile in Your Eyes (Va Sonrie el Amor)   Sigman
There's Beauty Everywhere   Freed, Arthur; Warren
There's Danger in Dancing   Robin
There's Laughter After Tears (There's Laughter After the Blues)   Evans; Livingston, Jay
There's No Holding Me   Gershwin, Ira; Schwartz, Arthur
There's Nothin' Papa's Doin' that Mama Ain't Did   Razaf
There's Nothing Like Marriage for People   Gershwin, Ira; Schwartz, Arthur
There's Nothing Like Travel   Burke; Van Heusen
There's Something about America   Caesar
These Patient Years   Fain; Freed, Ralph
They Say It's Wonderful   Berlin
Things Have Changed   Carmichael; Webster
Things That Most Appeal to Me (inst.), The   Kern
Things We Did Last Summer, The   Cahn; Styne
This Heart of Mine   Freed, Arthur; Warren
This Is Always   Gordon; Myrow; Warren
This Is Miami   Davis
This Is Our Last Chance for Peace   Caesar
Thomas Jefferski   Caesar
Three Little Girls in Blue   Myrow
Three Little Girls in Blue — Prayer Sequence   Gordon; Myrow
Through a Thousand Dreams   Robin; Schwartz, Arthur
Time Will Tell   Brooks
Tinge of the West (inst.), A   Bloom
TNT   Ellington
To Each His Own   Evans; Livingston, Jay
To Me   Wrubel
To the Banquet We Go   Brooks
Toast the Pirate King   Brooks
Tommy Tax   Caesar
Tomorrow Is the Time   Gershwin, Ira; Schwartz, Arthur
Tomorrow Mountain   Ellington
Too Late for Conversation   Merrill

Tooth and Claw   Ellington
Torch of Victory   Johnson, Howard
Twilight Song   Lawrence
Two Dachshunds (inst.)   Kern
Two Hearts Are Better than One (Duettino)   Kern; Mercer
Two Hearts Together   Freed, Ralph
Under My Umbrella   Dietz; Schwartz, Arthur
Undertow   Spina
United Nations   Caesar
Up with the Lark   Kern; Robin
Very Silly Story, A   Burke; Van Heusen
Viva . . .Vem-Vem (The Cuban Kissing Song)   Drake
(We Met Over a Bottle of) Vivo   Cahn; Styne
Wait 'Til I Get You in My Dreams Tonight   Spina
Wake Up Song   Burke; Van Heusen
Walter Winchell Rhumba   Sigman
Waltzing Around the Maypole (inst.)   Kern
Wandering   Dietz
Warm As Wine   Evans; Livingston, Jay
Washington   Carmichael
Waterfall Serenade (inst.)   Bloom
We Address Him as Mister President   Caesar
We Have a Law   Caesar
We Love Us   Duke
We Met Over a Bottle of Vivo   Styne
We Shall Meet to Part, No Never   Arlen; Mercer
Wedding Ballet   Ellington
Wedding Bells Polka   Drake
Wedding Song   Revel
We'll Drink Every Drop in the Shop   Evans; Livingston, Jay
We'll Meet Again in Honolulu   Freed, Arthur
We'll Soon Be One World   Caesar
We're All a Happy Lot   Brooks
What Could Be Sweeter   Wrubel
What Do I Have to Do?   Russell
What Is Love?   Brooks
What Makes You Beautiful, Beautiful   Cahn; Styne
When a Fellow Gets to Thinking   Burke; Van Heusen
When a Girl Needs a Friend   Johnson, J. Rosamond
When Are You Coming Home, My Baby   Robison
When I Fall in Love   Brooks
When I Get to Town   Cahn; Styne
When I Walk with You   Ellington
When the Moon Is Gone   Hoffman
When the One You Love Simply Won't Love Back   Cahn; Styne
When We Meet Again   Rome
When You Broke the Seventh Commandment   David, Mack; Hoffman; Livingston, Jerry
When You Go Down by Miss Jenny's   Ellington
Where Did You Learn to Love   Cahn; Styne
Where Do We Go from Here   Webster
Where Is Bundy?   Duke
Wherever they Fly the Flag of Old England   Porter
Whiddle-Dee Wee and Whaddle-Dee Woo   Johnson, J. Rosamond
White Camelias   Washington
Who Could Forget You   Loesser
Who Do You Love, I Hope?   Berlin
Who Said I Said I Don't Love You   Coots; Lewis
Who? Where? When?   Evans; Livingston, Jay
Whose Who Are You   Lerner, Sammy
Why Do I Like You   Burke; Van Heusen
Why Do We Say Good Morning   Robin
Why Does It Get So Late So Early   Wrubel

Why Must I Live Alone   Johnson, J. Rosamond
Why Not   Sigman
Wife of the Life of the Party, The   Evans; Livingston, Jay
Wind Me Up and Run Me Down   Johnson, J. Rosamond
Winter Blossoms   Woods
Winter in California   Davis
Winter Scene   Johnson, J. Rosamond
With Music   Berlin
Wolf Time   Fain
Woman Is a Tangle, A   Johnson, J. Rosamond
Woman's Perogative, A   Arlen; Mercer
Women, Women, Women   Ellington
Wonderful Husband, A   Russell
Work in the Morning   Robin
World and I, The   Herbert
Worm Song, The   Heyman; Spina
Wouldn't You Know I'd Fall   Revel
Wrong Side of the Railroad Tracks, The   Ellington
Ya Gotta Have Music   David, Mack
Ye Shall Be Free   Robison
Yes, Yes   Duke
You Are Everything to Me   David, Mack
You Are My Downfall   Fain
You Can't Get a Man with a Gun   Berlin
You Can't Keep a Good Dreamer Down   Burke; Van Heusen
You Can't Make Me Believe that It Was All Make Believe   Coots; Lewis
You Dare Not Meet Her Eyes   Johnson, J. Rosamond
You Did Your Best to Break My Heart   Carmichael
You Didn't Come Back (When You Said You'd Come Back)   Sigman
You Don't Have to Come from Ireland (To Love an Irish Song)   Coots
You Don't Love Me No More   Ellington
You Gotta Crawl Before You Walk   Ellington
You Heart Just Can't Go Wrong   Robin; Whiting
You I Love   Revel
You Keep Coming Back Like a Song   Berlin
You Make Me Feel So Young   Gordon; Myrow
You May Not Love Me   Burke; Van Heusen
You Never Know Where You're Going Till You Get There   Cahn; Styne
You Never Saw That Before   Burke; Van Heusen
You Put a Song in My Heart   Friend
You Twisted My Arm   Martin
You Were Somebody Else's Sweetheart   Spina
You'll Be Regimented   Johnson, J. Rosamond
Young Lady a la Mode   Herbert
Your Conscience Tells You   Raye
Your Eyes   Parish
Your Kiss   Loesser
You're Dreamlike   Dietz; Schwartz, Arthur
You're Gonna Make a Wonderful Sweetheart (For Somebody Else)   Drake
You're So Good to Me   Cahn; Styne
You're So Reliable   Loesser
You're the One for Me   Merrill
You're the Reason   De Lange
Yuletide, Park Avenue   Rome
Zip-a-dee Doo-dah   Wrubel

1947

Acapulco Polka   Wrubel

Accusation Johnson, James P.
Advertising for a Baby Lawrence
Advertising Song (I Believe), The Rome
After All Arlen; Koehler
Ain't It Awful, the Heat? Weill
All My Love Akst; Caesar
All the Love in the World Parish
All Wet McHugh
Allegro Hammerstein; Rodgers
Almost Like Being in Love Lerner, Alan Jay; Loewe
Always You Alone Young, Joseph
And That Is You Blake
Angel Face (You've Got the Devil in Your Big Blue
     Eyes) Spina
Anna Rosa David, Mack; Hoffman; Livingston, Jerry
Another Night Like This Ruby
Anywhere Cahn
Apalachicola, F.L.A. Burke; Van Heusen
Aren't You Kind of Glad We Did? Gershwin, George;
     Gershwin, Ira
Arkansas Coots
As Long As I'm Dreaming Burke; Van Heusen
Ask Me No Questions, I'll Tell You No Lies Russell;
     Sigman
At Home with My Range Johnson, James P.
At the Carnival Evans; Livingston, Jay
Au Revoir Drake
Away Out West Cahn; Styne
Azuza, Cucamonga and Anaheim Stept
Baby, Do I Make Myself Clear Mills
Baby, Have You Got a Little Love to Spare Koehler; Warren
Bach Invention #1 Cahn; Styne
Back Bay Polka, The Gershwin, George; Gershwin, Ira
Balboa Bay Blane; Brown, Nacio Herb
Ballerina Sigman
Balloon Song, The Clare
Bally Cottin Robison
Banquet at Buckingham (inst.) Coots
Basket of Buttercups (inst.) Coots
Bathing Beauty Ballet (inst.) Styne
Begat, The Harburg; Lane
Beside You Evans; Livingston, Jay
Beware My Heart Coslow
Beyond the Sea (Le Mer) Lawrence
Big Banana Man from Yucatan, The Silver
Big Brass Band from Brazil Sigman
Bird Watcher's Song (We're the Ladies' Walking
     Society) Cahn; Styne
Birmingham Boogie (inst.) Revel
Black Cat Rag (inst.) Waller
Bless Our Home Cahn; Styne
Bloop Bleep Loesser
Blue Rhythm Be-Bop Mills
Blue Rhythm Blues Mills
Blue Rhythm Jam Mills
Blue Rhythm Swing Mills
Bluebirds on a Blackboard Burke; Van Heusen
Blues Are Brewin', The Alter; De Lange
Boin-n-n-ng Stept
Bonanza Comden and Green
Bootblack Man from Gramercy Square, The Meyer
Born in April Harbach; Kern
Boy in the Celluloid Collar, The Blane; Warren
Boy Like You, A Weill
Breezy Sigman

Brigadoon Lerner, Alan Jay; Loewe
Broadway Prologue to Kokomo, Indiana Gordon; Myrow
Brooklyn Bridge, The Cahn; Styne
Brooklyn Bridge Is Falling Down Strouse
Buenos Noches, Buenos Aires Heyman
Bug-a-Boo David, Hal
Bumble Boogie Samba, The David, Hal; David, Mack
Buon Giorno, Signore Weill
But Beautiful Burke; Van Heusen
Butler and the Cook Desire Johnson, James P.
Butler and the Handy Man Johnson, James P.
Bye Bye, Alibi Baby Drake
Cafe de Janeiro Drake
California Is Wonderful (If You're a Grapefruit) David,
     Mack; Hoffman; Livingston, Jerry
Canada Dry and I Willson
Can't You Just See Yourself Cahn; Styne
Capriccio Espanol Brooks
Caravan of Dreams Ahlert; Leslie
Caress Me David, Mack; Hoffman; Livingston, Jerry
Casanova Cricket Carmichael
Castle Walk (inst.), The Styne
Catana (Cah-Tah-Na) De Lange
Catch Me If You Can Weill
Cats Are Goin' to the Dogs, The Adamson; McHugh
Ce Soir, Cherie David, Mack
Changing My Tune Gershwin, George; Gershwin, Ira
Chase, The Lerner, Alan Jay; Loewe
Chauffeur Johnson, James P.
Chaug-Buma-Guma-Maug Lake Russell
Chi-Baba, Chi-Baba (My Bambino, Go to Sleep) David,
     Mack; Hoffman; Livingston, Jerry
Children's Game Weill
Children's Song Freed, Ralph
Chillicothe, Ohio Drake
Chiquita From Santa Anita Adamson; McHugh
Chocolate Sundae on a Saturday Night, A David, Hal
Christmas Comes But Once a Year Razaf
Christmas Spell, The Robison
Church Bells on Sunday Morning Fain; Yellen
Circus Is Coming to Town, The Mercer
Cissy & Bob Blake
Civilization (Bongo Bongo Bongo) Sigman
Cling a Little Closer Parish
Cling to Me David, Mack; Hoffman; Livingston, Jerry
Cobbleskill School Song Brooks
Coldest Gal in Town, The Fain; Yellen
Colombo Weill
Come Home Hammerstein; Rodgers
Come to Me, Bend to Me Lerner, Alan Jay; Loewe
Come to the Circus Lawrence
Come to the Mardi Gras Drake
Company She Keeps, The Burke; Van Heusen
Competition Silver
Concerto Jazz-a-Mine (inst.) Johnson, James P.
Costa Rica Ruby
Couldn't Be More in Love Adamson; McHugh
Couldn't Get In Johnson, James P.
Couldn't If I Tried De Lange
Count Me Out Alter; De Lange
Country Style Burke; Van Heusen
Cow Parade, The Caesar
Cowboy's Never Lonesome, A Brooks
Coz D'Or Brooks
Cruikshank March Comden and Green

Cumana   Spina
Customer Is Always Wrong, The   Adamson; McHugh
Dance Ballerina Dance   Russell
Dance in the Snow   Comden and Green
Dance of the Tumblers   Brooks
Darn Nice Campus, A   Hammerstein; Rodgers
Dear Old Pal   David, Mack
Deduco Commercial   Robin
Deedle-Dee-Dum Teasy Easy Tune   Razaf
Deep Down 'n Your Heart   Friend
Demon Rum   Gershwin, George; Gershwin, Ira
Dickey Bird Song, The   Dietz; Fain
Dixie Down Beat   Mills
Do Unto Others   Drake
Do We Have to Say Goodnight   David, Mack; Hoffman;
   Livingston, Jerry
Do You Know Any Chicks in Chicago   Silver
Do You Know What It Means to Miss New Orleans?   Alter;
   De Lange
Dodger's Song, The   Caesar
Dog Song, The   Heyman
Donna   Spina
Don't Bother to Cry   Merrill
Don't Call It Love   Washington; Wrubel
Don't Forget the Lilac Bush   Weill
Don't Kill the Goose (That Lays the Golden Egg)   Fain;
   Magidson
Don't Lose Your Head (And Lose Your Gal)   Johnson,
   James P.
Don't Pass Me By   Harburg; Lane
Don't Wait Up for Me, Mom   Sigman
Don't You Love Me Anymore   David, Mack; Hoffman;
   Livingston, Jerry
(Ev'ryone Is Singing) Down at My House   Sigman
Down on MacConnachy Square   Lerner, Alan Jay; Loewe
Down the Milky Way   David, Hal
Dream After Dream   Parish
Dream Sonata   Bullock
Dreamer's Hill   Mills
Dreamer's Holiday   Friend
Dreams Do Come True   Robin
Easier Way, An   Comden and Green
Easiest Thing in the World, The   David, Hal
Easy Come Easy Go   Evans; Livingston, Jay
Edison March (inst.)   Young, Victor
Egg and I, The   Akst; Kalmar; Ruby
Eleanor   Mills
Endie   Alter; De Lange
Every So Often   Mercer; Warren
Everybody Loves Somebody   Coslow
Experience   Burke; Van Heusen
Fandango   Brooks
Far Into the Night   David, Mack; Hoffman; Livingston, Jerry
Fare-Thee-Well, Dear Alma Mater   Gordon; Myrow
Farewell Duet   Weill
Fat, Fat the Water Rat   Weill
Feathery Feelin', The   Loesser
Fellow Needs a Girl, A   Hammerstein; Rodgers
Fido and Me   Alter; Heyman
Fill 'Er Up   Comden and Green
Finale Love   Johnson, James P.
Fine and Dandy, Andy   Mills
Fine Thing!   Mercer
Fireman's Ball, The   Loesser
First Time I Kissed You, The   Blane; Warren

Foolin' Nobody But Me   Russell
For What   Burke; Van Heusen
For You, For Me, For Evermore   Gershwin, George;
   Gershwin, Ira
Forever Amber   Mercer
Forsaking All Others   Wrubel
French, The   Loesser
French Lesson   Comden and Green
Friendly Doctor (I Am the Friendly Doctor), The   Caesar
Friendship Song, The   Caesar
From This Day On   Lerner, Alan Jay; Loewe
Front Porch Talk (And Rocking Chair Music)   Robison
Frustration   Mills
Funniest People Fall in Love, The   David, Hal
Funny Little Money Man   David, Hal
Funny Papers   Sigman
Gentleman Is a Dope, The   Hammerstein; Rodgers
Get a Job for Purple Heart Joe   Coots
Get a Load of That   Weill
Get Away for a Day in the Country   Cahn; Styne
Girl with the Spanish Drawl, The   David, Mack
Give Me a Rod, a Reel (a Boat and a Creel)   Johnson, J.
   Rosamond
Glory of the Corps   Harbach; Kern
Glub-iddy-glub-iddy-glub   Stept
Go West, Young Man   Kalmar; Ruby
Going Back to Old Cheyenne   Koehler
Golden Earrings   Evans; Livingston, Jay; Young, Victor
Goldie Goes with the Mine   Loesser
Gone Are the Days   Cahn; Styne
Gonna Go Along with Lincoln   Harbach; Kern
Goodbye, Good Luck, Get Lost   Baer
Gossip Trio   Weill
Grauman's Chinese Sequence   Loesser
Great Big Sky, The   Weill
Great Feelin'   Evans; Livingston, Jay
Green Love for Walter, A   Burke; Van Heusen
Guess I'll Be on My Way   Russell
Gui-Pi-Pia   Ruby
Gypsy Song   Brooks
Hail to the School   Weill
Hand in Hand   Lawrence
Handy Man   Johnson, James P.
Have a Heart, Taft-Hartley, Have a Heart   Lawrence
Have a Little Lunch with Maggi McNellis and Herb
   Sheldon   Sigman
Have I Told You   DePaul; Raye
He Can Waltz   Loesser
He Makes Me Believe He's Mine   Ellington
He Tried to Make a Dollar   Cahn; Styne
He Wants to Get Into My Pantry   Mills
Headin' for a Weddin' in the Sky   Harbach; Kern
Heard a Mocking Bird Singing (In California)   Robison
Heather on the Hill, The   Lerner, Alan Jay; Loewe
Hector the Humble Bumble Bee   Burke; Van Heusen
Hello Again   Spina
Hello, New Year, Hello   Razaf
Help Me to Help My Neighbor   Berlin
(Oh How I Love My) Hildegarde   Coots
Ho! Ho! Jose   Evans; Livingston, Jay
Holler Blue Murder   Sigman
Home, Home, Home   Spina
Hot Tempered Fugue (inst.), The   Rome
Hot-Dog Waltz   Weill
How Are Things in Glocca Morra?   Harburg; Lane

How Can I Stop Loving You   De Lange
Hurry Up! (Alberto's Lullaby)   Robin
Hush-a-Bye Island   Adamson; McHugh
Hush-a-bye Wee Rose of Killarney   Koehler
Hymn to the Sun   Brooks
I Believe   Cahn; Styne
I Can Count the Times on My Fingers   Wrubel
I Can't Believe It Was All Make Believe (Last Night)   Coots; Lewis
I Didn't Know Where My Next Dream was Comin' From   Russell; Sigman
I Do, Do, Do Like You   Wrubel
I Don't Know Why I Love You So   Ellington; Mills
I Got a Marble and a Star   Weill
I Guess I'll Have that Dream Right Now   Adamson; McHugh
I Guess the Cards Were Stacked Against Me   Blake
I Had a Feeling (There Was Somebody Else)   Ager
I Had Your Number   Mills
I Haven't Got a Thing to Sell   Coslow
I Heard a Bugle Blowing   Harbach; Kern
I Know It Can Happen Again   Hammerstein; Rodgers
I Like This Loving You   Cahn
I Like to Get Up Early in the Morning   Lawrence
I Live for that Day   Weill
I Love a Mystery   Robin
I Loved Her, Too   Weill
I Miss that Feeling   Adamson; McHugh
I Must Have Been Madly in Love   Loesser
I Owe You a Kiss   Cahn; Styne
I Saw Flying Saucers   Silver
I Still Get Jealous   Cahn; Styne
I Still Have My Dream   Koehler; Stept
I Theenk   David, Mack; Hoffman; Livingston, Jerry
I Theenk You Weenk   Fain
I Used to Be   Oakland
I Wanna   David, Mack
I Want My Money Back   Loesser
I Want to Talk with You   Howard, Joseph E.
I Went Merrily Merrily on My Way   Kahal
I Wish I Didn't Love You So   Loesser
I Wish I were a Goldfish   Alter; De Lange
I Woke Up with a Cold   Caesar
Ice Cream Sextet   Weill
I'd Like a Memory   Willson
I'd Rather Look at You   Revel
I'd Rather Stay Home with a Memory   Drake
Idle Cloud Drifts By (inst.), An   Coots
If a Man Answers, Hang Up   Drake
If I Had a Penny   Russell; Sigman
If I Only Had a Match   Meyer
If I Were You   Heyman
If It Wasn't for the Irish   Blane; Warren
If It Were Easy to Do   Sigman
If It's All the Same to You   Sigman
If Someone Should Ask You   Cahn; Styne
If This Isn't Love   Harburg; Lane
If You See Sally Kiss Her for Me   David, Mack
If You Want to Make a Hit with Fifi   Coslow
Il Trovatore   Robin
I'll Dance at Your Wedding   Magidson; Oakland
I'll Give You One Guess   Cahn; Styne
I'll Go Home with Bonnie Jean   Lerner, Alan Jay; Loewe
I'll Hate Myself in the Morning   Lawrence
I'll Know It's Love   Ruby

I'll Never Belong to Anyone Else If I Can't Belong to You   Drake
I'll Never Go to Heaven   Brooks
I'll Never Make the Same Mistake Again   Magidson; Oakland
Illinois   Harbach; Kern
I'm A-Comin' A-Courtin', Corabelle   Wrubel
I'm As Ready As I'll Ever Be   Cahn; Styne
I'm Betwixt and Between   Cahn; Styne
I'm Going to Hang My Hat on Broadway   Howard, Joseph E.
I'm Happy-Go-Lucky and Free   Robin
I'm Healthy Cause I'm Happy   Caesar
I'm on My Way to Rio   David, Mack
I'm So in Love (I Don't Know What I'm Doin')   Koehler
I'm Still Sitting Under the Apple Tree   Cahn; Styne
Impossible Things   Loesser
In a Little Soda Shop   Meyer
In Every Way   Revel
In Good Old San Jose   Revel
In Love at Last   Wrubel
In the Blue Velvet Night   David, Mack; Hoffman; Livingston, Jerry
In the Shadows   Harbach; Kern
Indigo Echoes   Ellington; Mills
Innocent Stander-By, The   Cahn; Styne
Inspiration   Comden and Green
Intrigue   Akst; Lerner, Sammy
Investigator's Song, The   Rome
Is There Anyone Here from Texas?   Adamson; McHugh
It Always Rains But Always   David, Hal
It Could Happen to Me   Adamson; McHugh
It May Be a Good Idea   Hammerstein; Rodgers
Italy in Technicolor   Weill
It's a Wonderful Day for a Ball Game   Cahn; Styne
It's a Wonderful, Wonderful Feeling   Revel
It's Always a Beautiful Day   Robin
It's Dreamtime   Brooks
It's Just Like Taking Candy from a Baby   Russell
It's Kind of Lonesome Out Tonight   Ellington
It's Not the Mountain Air (It's the Mountaineer)   David, Hal
It's Off Again — On Again   De Lange; Warren
It's Only Love   Robin
It's the Irish   Weill
It's the Same Old Dream   Cahn; Styne
It's the Truth   Drake
It's Wonderful to Be Married   Mills
I've Been to Hollywood   Merrill
I've Got a Funny Feeling   Blane; Warren
I've Got to Be Lovely to Harry   Johnson, James P.
Ivy   Carmichael
Je Vous Aime   Coslow
Jeannie's Packin' Up   Lerner, Alan Jay; Loewe
Jester's Song (Jester and Me), The   Robin
Jews Have Got Their Irish Up, The   Fain; Yellen
John and Mary Upright   Caesar
Johnny's Got a To-To   Mills
Jose   Mills
Joseph Taylor, Jr.   Hammerstein; Rodgers
Just Hold Her Hand (She'll Understand)   Howard, Joseph E.
Kate (Have I Come Too Early, Too Late)   Berlin
Keep Your Eye on the Boy   Loesser
Keepin' a Prayer in Your Heart   Burke; Van Heusen
Kids in School, The   Weill
Kokomo, Indiana   Gordon; Myrow

Lady from Twenty-Nine Palms, The   Wrubel
L'Amour Toujours   Mills
Last Thing I Want Is Your Pity, The   Loesser
(Love's Got Me in a) Lazy Mood   Mercer
Legendary Tale   Brooks
Let Me Dream Some More   Koehler
Let Things Be Like They Always Was   Weill
Let Your Heart Lead the Way   David, Mack; Hoffman;
      Livingston, Jerry
Let's Dance Till the Dawn   Harbach; Kern
Let's Do the Copacabana   Coslow
Let's Dream Together   Harbach; Kern
Let's Get Up and Do Some Dancing   Robison
Life Can Be Beautiful   Adamson; McHugh
Lindy Lou   Johnson, James P.
Little Bit of Love Goes a Long Way, A   Johnson, J.
      Rosamond
Little Boy in the Barber Shop Chair, The   Robison; Woods
Little Fish   Comden and Green
Little Further Down the Road a Piece, A   DePaul; Raye
Little Pitchers Have Big Ears   Cahn; Styne
Little Romero (Chic-a-lu-cheet)   Sigman
Little Sleepy Head   Lawrence
Little Swing for Swinging, A   Weill
Livin' the Life of Love   Adamson
Lone Star Moon   Friend
Lonely House   Weill
Lonely Little Ranch-House   Brooks
Long After Tonight   Drake
Long Green Blues   Sigman
Long Night, The   Washington
Longing I Have for You, The   Robison
Look to the Rainbow   Harburg; Lane
Lost April   De Lange
Love   Johnson, James P.
Love and the Weather   Berlin
Love for Love   Koehler
Love Is the Time   Friml; Heyman
Love Just Isn't My Game   Mills
(I'm Gonna Be a) Love Me Not   Merrill
Love of My Life, The   Lerner, Alan Jay; Loewe
Love Will Keep Us Young   Leslie
Luana (Flower of Love)   Spina
Lullaby (Sleep, Baby, Sleep)   Weill
Made for Each Other (Tu Felicidad)   Drake
Ma-ha-lani Papa-Doo (Hey, Hey)   Hoffman; Livingston,
      Jerry
Mandy's Blessing   Johnson, James P.
Maracas   Ruby
Marcho Poco (inst.)   Coots
Marsa's Come Home to Stay   Evans; Livingston, Jay;
      Young, Victor
Martinique   Brooks
Matinee   Russell; Sigman
May I Still Hold You   Russell
Maybe You'll Be There   Bloom
Me-ha-lani Papa-doo (Hoy Hoy)   David, Mack; Livingston,
      Jerry
Melody Has to Be Right, The   Robin
Melody of Spring   Freed, Ralph
Men Are Not Gods   Blake
Me-O-My   Blane; Warren
Mi Vida   Ruby
Midnight Man   Mercer
Million Dollar Pier   Cahn; Styne

Minor Drag (inst.)   Waller
Miracle of the Bells   Brooks
Miss Lindy Lou   Koehler
Mister Miracle Man   Drake
Misty Eyed   Loesser
Misunderstood   Comden and Green
Molly Come Out of the Kitchen   Mills
Molly O'Malley   Donaldson
Money Isn't Ev'rything   Hammerstein; Rodgers
Moon of Jade (inst.)   Myrow
Moon Was Yellow (El Amor Llamo), The   Ahlert; Leslie
Moon-Faced, Starry-Eyed   Weill
Moonflower Lane   Heyman
Moonlight Music   Robison
Moonrise   Alter
Morning   Weill
Most Beautiful Time of the Year, The   Freed, Ralph
Music Box You Gave Me, The   Spina
Music from Beyond the Moon   Lawrence
Music Grew Softer and Softer, The   David, Mack; Hoffman;
      Livingston, Jerry
My Bel Ami   Lawrence
My Castle on Riverside Drive   Evans; Livingston, Jay
My Concerto to You   Mills
My Fair Lady   Sigman
My Favorite Brunette   Evans; Livingston, Jay
My Feet Takes Me Away   Russell
My Heart Is a Hobo   Burke; Van Heusen
My Heart Was Doing a Bolero   Coslow
My Heart Whispers Beware   Mills
My How the Time Goes By   Adamson
My Mother's Wedding Day   Lerner, Alan Jay; Loewe
My Own True Love   Evans; Livingston, Jay
My Peaceful Valley Home   Young, Joseph
My Private World   Lawrence
My Promise to You   Drake
My Secret Love   Friml
My Sweet Patoot with the Bumbershoot   Mills
My Wife   Hammerstein; Rodgers
Natchez and the Robert E. Lee   Koehler
Nation of Nations, A   Weill
Nearer and Dearer   Friml; Heyman
Necessity   Harburg; Lane
Needles and Pins   Lawrence
Never Make Eyes (at the Gals with the Guys Who Are Bigger
      than You)   Fain; Yellen
New Orleans Masquerade   Mills
Next to Texas, I Love You   Cahn; Styne
Night Blooming Jasmine   Loesser
No Mind of Your Own   Comden and Green
No More, No Less   David, Mack; Hoffman; Livingston, Jerry
No One Woman Can Satisfy Any One Man All the
      Time   Yellen
No Rest for the Weary   Russell
Nobody Ever Died for Dear Old Rutgers   Cahn; Styne
Nobody in Particular   Lawrence
Nobody Loves You Like I Do   Cahn
Nobody Thought It Would Last   Gilbert
None but the Lonely Heart   David, Mack; Hoffman;
      Livingston, Jerry
O Israel, Do Not Despair   Gorney
O Pedro (Song of the Jealous Caballero)   Spina
Oh, Gee   Ellington
Oh, I Wanna Go   Willson
Old Devil Moon   Harburg; Lane

Old Sombrero (And an Old Spanish Shawl), An   Brown, Lew; Henderson

Old Toymaker, The   David, Mack; Hoffman; Livingston, Jerry

Older They Get the Younger They Want 'Em, The   Yellen

(Rolling Down Bowling Green) On a Little Two Seat Tandem   Myrow

On a Slow Boat to China   Loesser

On a Sunday by the Sea   Cahn; Styne

On an Island with You   Heyman

On Green Dolphin Street   Washington

On the Avenue   Rome

On the Banks of the Old Raritan   Cahn; Styne

Once Around the Moon   Sigman

Once in the Highlands   Lerner, Alan Jay; Loewe

One Foot, Other Foot   Hammerstein; Rodgers

One Little Tear Is an Ocean   Merrill; Spina

One Love for Two   David, Hal

One Man Woman   Brooks

One More Kiss   Silver

One More Mile to Go   Friml; Heyman

One, Two, Three   Gershwin, George; Gershwin, Ira

Ooh! What I'll Do (To that Wild Hungarian)   Robin

Our Hour (The Puppy Love Song)   David, Mack; Hoffman; Livingston, Jerry

Out of My Mind   Fain

Out of the Dark   Howard, Joseph E.

Papa, Won't You Dance with Me?   Cahn; Styne

Passing By   Lawrence

Peanut Butter Sandwiches and Hard Boiled Eggs   Cahn; Styne

Piccadilly Tilly   Evans; Livingston, Jay

Pico and Sepulveda   Styne

Please Don't Play that Old Song   Lawrence

Please Don't Save a Place at Supper (For I'm not Coming Home)   Spina

Polly Pigtails   David, Mack; Hoffman; Livingston, Jerry

Poor Joe   Hammerstein; Rodgers

Poppa, Don't Preach To Me   Loesser

Prologue to Vaudeville Act   Gordon; Myrow

Psychology   Harbach; Kern

Put Yourself in My Place, Baby   Carmichael

Puttin' on Airs   Blane; Warren

Queen of the Hollywood Islands, The   Loesser

Rainbow Over Chicago   Howard, Joseph E.

Rainbow Trail, The   Coots

Raindrops on a Drum   Friml; Heyman

Red Leaves and Blue Skies   Sigman

Refugee's Lullaby   Fain; Yellen

Remember that I Care   Weill

Remember the Girl You Left Behind   Revel

Remind Me to Tell You   David, Mack; Hoffman; Livingston, Jerry

Reprise Love   Johnson, James P.

Ride-Ride-Ride   Blane; Warren

Ridin' Home (When the Round-Up Is Over)   Coots

Rocky Mountain Lullaby, A   Meyer

Rolling Along   Revel

Rolling Down Bowling Green on a Little Two-Seat Tandem   Gordon

Rose of Killarney   Young, Joseph

Rose of Santa Rosa   Hoffman

Rose's Goodbye to Easter   Weill

Round-Up Is Over, The   Spina

Rub-A-Dub-Dub (I've Had a Good Rub)   Caesar

Rumba Maria (inst.)   Young, Victor

Rumba-bomba   Ruby

Rumble, Rumble, Rumble   Loesser

Sacramento   Russell

San Antone Story   Russell

Sandman's House on Hush-A-Bye Hill, The   Burke; Van Heusen

Saturday Date   Brooks

Save a Dime Out of Ev'ry Dollar   Spina

Say No More   Akst; Davis

Say Something Nice About Me   Stept

Scherazade   Brooks

Secretary Song (Bidibi Bot Bot), The   Fain

See If I Care (Eso Eres Tu)   David, Mack

Senor Sam   Blake

Sewing Machine, The   Loesser

Shake that Tree   David, Mack; Livingston, Jerry

She Who Walks in Beauty   Oakland

She's a Good Kid   Cahn; Styne

She's Right (Security)   Cahn; Styne

Show Me the Way to the Kerry Fair   Koehler

Siguiendote   David, Mack

Sleep My Love   Coslow

Slow and Easy Melody   Bullock

Smack in the Middle of Maine   Burke; Van Heusen

Small World   Rome

Smile Right Back at the Sun   Burke; Van Heusen

S'No Wonder They Fell in Love   Fain; Freed, Ralph

So Far   Hammerstein; Rodgers

(You're) So Well Remembered   Stept

So You Fell for Him Too   Mills

Soda Jerk at Walgreens   Mills

Soft and Low   Parish

Soldier Like You, A   Harbach; Kern

Soldier's Dream   Johnson, Howard

Solution   Johnson, James P.

Somehow I Never Could Believe   Weill

Someone Cares   Drake

Someone Like You   Blane; Warren

Something for Nothing   Robison

Something in the Wind   Robin

Something Sort of Grandish   Harburg; Lane

Something to Remember Him By   Mills

Song of India, A   Brooks

Song of the Ladies Man   Brooks

Song of the Napkin Rings   Harbach; Kern

Song's Gotta Come from the Heart, The   Cahn; Styne

Speak My Heart!   Revel

Spring   Comden and Green

Spring Cleaning   Johnson, James P.

Spring in My Room   Blane; Warren

Stand Up and Fight   Gershwin, Ira

(If You Don't Like Living in a Land That's Free) Stay Away from the U.S.A.   Mills; Styne

Story of Sorrento, The   Russell

Strange What a Song Can Do   Alter; De Lange

Stranger Things Have Happened   Coslow

Street Light Is My Moonlight   Weill

Summer in the Snow   Comden and Green

Summer Incident   Cahn; Styne

Sweet Elizabeth   Blake

Sweet Memories   Revel

Sweet Packard   Gershwin, George; Gershwin, Ira

Sweet Talk   Blake

Take Me Back to Old New Hampshire   Young, Joseph

Takin' Miss Mary to the Ball   Heyman
Tallahassee   Loesser
Tambourine   Sigman
Tango (inst.)   Styne
Tears, I Shed a Million Tears   Blake
Tell Me Why   Comden and Green
Tell Me with Your Eyes   Friml; Heyman
Ten Percent Off   Fain; Freed, Ralph
Tenderly   Lawrence
That Five O'Clock Feeling   Meyer
That Great Come and Get It Day   Harburg; Lane
That's Not the Knot   Evans; Livingston, Jay
That's What Christmas Means to Me   Revel
That's Where Our Horoscopes Lie (She's a Gemini
     Girl)   Weill
(I've Got) The Cutest Little Red-Headed Doll   Sigman
There Ain't No Guy   Mills
There but for You Go I   Lerner, Alan Jay; Loewe
There Goes My Runaway Heart (Running After You)   Coots
There Was a Time   Revel
There Was Moonlight in Her Hair   Hoffman; Livingston,
     Jerry
There'll Be Trouble   Weill
There's a Barber in the Harbor of Palermo   David, Mack;
     Hoffman; Livingston, Jerry
There's a Mist Upon the Meadow   David, Mack
There's Nothing Like a Model T   Cahn; Styne
There's Nothing Like a Song   Gordon; Myrow
There's Nothing Lovelier than You   Spina
There's Room in My Heart for Them All   Koehler
There's Something About Midnight   Robin
This Is My Favorite City   Gordon; Myrow
This Is the Moment   Robin
This Time for Keeps   Fain; Freed, Ralph
This Time of the Year   Harburg; Lane
This Was Meant to Be   Comden and Green
Thousand Islands Song, The   Sigman
Time After Time   Cahn; Styne
Time Drags On   Blake
Time of Your Life, The   Brooks
To Have and to Hold   Hammerstein; Rodgers
To Make a Mistake Is Human   Drake
Tonight   Evans; Livingston, Jay
Tonight Is the Last Night   Howard, Joseph E.
Too Soon   Cahn; Styne
Totem Dance   Comden and Green
Tough Truckin'   Ellington; Mills
Tour of the Town   Gershwin, George; Gershwin, Ira
Tra-La-La-La   Gordon; Warren
Travelin' Light (inst.)   Young, Victor
T.T. on Toast   Ellington; Mills
Tune on the Tip of My Heart, The   Drake
Tunnel of Love, The   Loesser
Turntable Song (Round an' Round an' Round), The   Robin
Two Times a Day   Caesar
Un Poquito de Amor   Freed, Ralph
Undercurrent   Freed, Ralph
Up in Smoke   Comden and Green
Up the River   Merrill
Valley of Dreams-Come-True   Lawrence
Vein of Gold, The   Comden and Green
Vendors' Calls   Lerner, Alan Jay; Loewe
Versatile DaVincis, The   Comden and Green
Victor Vitamin Brown   Burke; Van Heusen
Viddle-de Vop   David, Mack; Livingston, Jerry

Waitin' for My Dearie   Lerner, Alan Jay; Loewe
Walking Alone in the Dark   De Lange
Waltzing Is Better Sitting Down   Gershwin, George;
     Gershwin, Ira
Wanderlust   Sigman
We French Get So Excited   Loesser
We Knew It All the Time   Styne
Weary   Blake; Friml; Heyman; Razaf
Welcome Song   Gershwin, George; Gershwin, Ira
We'll Go Away Together   Weill
We're Goin' Home   Brooks
We're Keeping It Private   Donaldson
We've Come to the Copa   Coslow
What a Crisis   Robin
What a Fool I Have Been   Monaco; Washington
What a Lovely Day for a Wedding   Hammerstein; Rodgers
What Am I Gonna Do About You?   Cahn; Styne
What Are You Doing New Year's Eve   Loesser
What Did I Do   Gordon; Myrow
What Do I Want with Money   Adamson
What Do You See   Robin
What D'Ya Say U.C.L.A.   Adamson; McHugh
What Good Would the Moon Be?   Weill
What Kind of Fool   Loesser
When a Woman Has a Baby   Weill
When Am I Gonna Kiss You Good Morning   De Lange
When I Open the Gate   Parish
When I Speak of You   Ruby
When I'm Not Near the Girl I Love   Harburg; Lane
When Tallulah Does the Hula Out of Brooklyn   Mills
When the Idle Poor Become the Idle Rich   Harburg; Lane
When the Nightingale Sings   David, Mack; Hoffman;
     Livingston, Jerry
When the White Roses Bloom (Down in Red River
     Valley)   Wrubel
When They Call the Roll at West Point   Harbach; Kern
When You Play with Fire   Hoffman; Robin
Where Is the Handy Man   Johnson, James P.
Whippoorwill's a Singin'   Evans; Livingston, Jay; Young,
     Victor
Who But You   Brown, Nacio Herb; Heyman
Who Killed 'Er? Who Killed the Black Widder?   Carmichael
Who Wants them Tall, Dark and Handsome   Yellen
Whoops My Dear   Brooks
Whose Baby Are You   Cahn; Styne
Why Did I Leave My Home   Young, Victor
Why Do Men Bring Out the Mother in Me   Ruby
Why Does It Have to Rain on Sunday   Merrill
Why Go to Havana   Yellen
Why Try   Brooks
Wildcats   Hammerstein; Rodgers
Wildest Gal in Town, The   Fain; Yellen
Winter in Havana   Fisher
Winters Go By   Hammerstein; Rodgers
Wish Them Well   Hammerstein; Rodgers
With My Rub-Rub-Rubbers   Caesar
With the Roses in Her Hair   Spina
With Your Permission   Silver
Without Magic   De Lange
Without Music   Alter; De Lange
Woman Alone with the Blues, A   Robison
Woman Who Lived Up There, The   Weill
World Is Longing for the Sunshine, The   David, Mack
Wouldn't You Like to Be on Broadway?   Weill
Wrapped Up in a Ribbon (And Tied in a Bow)   Weill

Yatata, Yatata, Yatata   Hammerstein; Rodgers
Yiddle-de Vop   David, Mack; Livingston, Jerry
You Are My Heart   Blane
You Are Never Away   Hammerstein; Rodgers
You Can't Sew a Button on a Heart   Yellen
You Do   Gordon; Myrow
You Don't Have to Know the Language   Burke; Van Heusen
You Drive Me to Dream   Coots
You Said a Baddy   Adamson; McHugh
You Wanna Keep Your Baby Lookin' Right   Robin
You Were Born to Be Loved   Blake
You, Wonderful You   Revel
You'll Always Be the Girl in My Heart   Howard, Joseph E.
Your Heart Calling Mine   Loesser
Your Heart Will Tell You So (Cinderella Waltz)   Mercer
Your Red Wagon   DePaul
You're a Sweet Patootie   Cahn; Styne
You're Breaking in a New Heart (While You're Breaking Mine)   Drake
You're Everywhere   Revel; Webster
You're Gonna Get My Letter (In the Morning)   Merrill
You're in My Heart   Revel
You're Just an Old Antidisestablishmentarianismist   Ellington
You're My Boy   Cahn
You're My Boy (Girl)   Styne
You're My Girl   Cahn
You're My Rose   Johnson, James P.
You're Not So Easy to Forget   Magidson; Oakland
You're Over the Hill   Leslie
You've Got to Be Loved to Be Healthy   Yellen

1948

About Face   Lerner, Sammy
Adios-Adieu   Brooks
Afraid to Fall in Love   Blane; Warren
After All These Years   Koehler
Ahleff Baze Gimmell Dollid   Schwartz, Jean
Albert the Great   Gordon
All Full of Empty   Schwartz, Jean
All Hail to Danville High (Dan-Dan-Danville High)   Blane; Warren
All Is Well   Razaf
Always True to You in My Fashion   Porter
Always You   Lerner, Sammy
American Cannes   Adamson; McHugh
Angels Cried, The   Mercer
(You'll Be Just) Another Notch on Father's Shotgun Effen You Don't Marry Me   Wrubel
Another Op'nin', Another Show   Porter
Anticipation Without Realization   Friend
Anything Can Happen   Gorney
Apple Jack   Gorney; Johnson, James P.
Argument, The   Loesser
Aria   Romberg
Arizona   Spina
As the Girls Go   Adamson; McHugh
At the Candlelight Cafe   David, Mack
At the End of an Evening (With You)   Howard, Joseph E.
At the Flying "W"   Wrubel
At the Mardi Gras   Dietz; Schwartz, Arthur
At the Nickleodeon   Evans; Livingston, Jay
At the Opera   Caesar
At the Red Rose Cotillion   Loesser

At the Rodeo   Cahn; Styne
Atlanta   Dietz; Schwartz, Arthur
Baby   Lerner, Alan Jay; Weill
Baby, Don't Start Cheating on Me (Not After All These Years)   Mills
Baby, It's Cold Outside   Loesser
Bad Bill Jones   Johnson, James P.
Bah, Bah Black Sheep   Johnston
Ballad of Marcia LaRue, The   Rome
Ballet Mignon   Razaf
Bamboula   Evans; Livingston, Jay
Barons   Sigman
Batten Down Her Hatches   Loesser
Be a Clown   Porter
Bee, The   Loesser
Before Long   Sigman
Behold My Love   Russell
Believe in Love   Brooks
Bella Donna   Romberg
Belles of Gay Madrid, The   Gordon; Myrow
Belles of Gay Paree, The   Gordon; Myrow
Bench in the Park   Gorney
Best Days of Our Lives, The   Howard, Joseph E.
Best of Friends, The   Drake
Better Get Out of Here   Loesser
Better Luck Next Time   Berlin; Dietz; Schwartz, Arthur
Betty (inst.)   Revel
Beyond Glory   Evans; Livingston, Jay
Bianca   Porter
Big Clock, The   Evans; Livingston, Jay
Big High Mountain with Nothing on the Top, The   Sigman
Big Show   Brown, Nacio Herb
Birthday Polka, The   De Lange; Revel
Blue Bay of Old San Jose, The   Spina
Blue Grass   Dietz; Schwartz, Arthur
Blue Skirt Waltz, The   Parish
Blues Are Mighty Pretty Music   Robison
Blues for Fats (inst.)   Johnson, James P.
Borscht   Brooks
Bounce the Berry   Merrill
Brave Heart, A   Blane; Warren
Brighten Up and Be a Little Sunbeam   Adamson; McHugh
Brush Up Your Shakespeare   Porter
Bubble-Loo, Bubble-Loo   Carmichael; Webster
Buck in the Bank   Lerner, Sammy
Busy Body   Johnson, James P.
Button, Button, Who's Got the Button?   Mills
Button Up with Esmond   Robin; Styne
Buttons and Bows   Livingston, Jay
By the Way   Gordon; Myrow
Bye Bye Baby   Robin; Styne
Candle in the Wind (inst.)   Alter
Can't Get You Out of My Mind   Howard, Joseph E.
Can't Stop Talking   Loesser
Can't We Have a Rally?   Lerner, Alan Jay; Weill
Careless Hands   Sigman
Caribees, The   Mercer
Caught   Johnson, James P.
Changes   Yellen
Cheap Cigars   Fain
Chivalry Reel   Rome
Chivaree   Johnson, James P.
Cincinnati   Evans; Livingston, Jay
Come Farballe   Romberg
Come O Come (Pittsburgh)   Dietz; Schwartz, Arthur

Come to the Beach Tonight   Blane; Warren
Control Yourself   Coots
Cop's Lament   Lerner, Alan Jay; Weill
Cop's Serenade   Lerner, Alan Jay; Weill
Coquette   Robin; Styne
Could You Love a Dreamer   Robin; Styne
Count Your Blessings   Brooks
Couple of Swells, A   Berlin
Courage   Lerner, Sammy
Cow Ponies Always Weep Just a Little   Willson
Cry, Baby   Rome
Crying for Joy   Monaco; Rose
Csardas   Lerner, Alan Jay; Weill
Daddy-O (I'm Gonna Teach You Some Blues)   DePaul; Raye
Dagger Dance (inst.)   Brown, Nacio Herb
Dance of Fury (inst.)   Brown, Nacio Herb
Day   Blane
Debutante   Romberg
Deep Blue Water   Robison
Delivery 'Mon', What Is in That Bag You Got   Brown, Lew
Desire   Romberg
Determined Woman, A   Rome
Diamonds Are a Girl's Best Friend   Robin; Styne
Dismal Mood, A   Razaf
Divertissement Parisien (inst.)   Razaf
Doc   Yellen
Don't Forget to Dream   Gorney
Don't Introduce Me to that Angel   Loesser
Don't Leave Me Now   Russell
Don't Smoke in Bed   Robison
Dorothy Anne (inst.)   Revel
Dost Thou   Rome
Down in the Indies   Mills
Down in the Valley   Weill
Down the Stairs and Out the Door (Went My
     Baby)   Loesser
Down the Well   Lerner, Sammy
Down Through the Valley   Young, Victor
Dream Girl   Evans; Livingston, Jay
Dreamy Day   De Lange
Dreamy Eyes   Koehler; Stept
Drum Crazy   Berlin
Drunk with Love   Evans; Livingston, Jay
Economics   Lerner, Alan Jay; Weill
1898   Romberg
Emperor Waltz   Burke
Enjoy Yourself (It's Later than You Think)   Magidson;
     Sigman
Ensemble Song   Romberg
Entre Nous   Romberg
Evening Star   Brown, Nacio Herb
Ever Homeward   Cahn; Styne
Every Time I Meet You   Gordon; Myrow
Everybody Wants My Business   Fain; Yellen
Everytime I Dance the Polka   Romberg
Ev'ry Day I Love You (Just a Little Bit More)   Cahn; Styne
Ev'ry Second, Ev'ry Minute, Ev'ry Hour, Ev'ry Day   Razaf
Eye-Catcher   Robison
Fair Sex, The   Rome
Far-Away Love   Johnson, James P.
Father's Day   Adamson; McHugh
Fella with an Umbrella, A   Berlin
Feller from Indiana, A   Dietz; Schwartz, Arthur
Fifty   Yellen
First Baseball Game, The   DePaul; Raye

First Bouquet   Romberg
First Prize at the Fair   Dietz; Schwartz, Arthur
First Time I Kissed You, The   Blane; Warren
Fishing Song, The   Mills
Follow Me to My Grave (If You Love Me)   Friend
Food for Thought   Romberg
For Every Man There's a Woman   Arlen; Robin
Forty Golden Nuggets   Drake
Forty Winks   Dietz; Schwartz, Arthur
1400 Dream Street   Wrubel
Freedom Train, The   Berlin
Friendly Enemy   Lerner, Sammy
Friendly Henry Wallace   Ager; Harburg
Friendly Mountains   Burke
Friendly Polka   Brooks
From Now Onward   Romberg
Fundamental Character   Lerner, Sammy
Gal in Malibu, The   Drake
Gentlemen Prefer Blondes   Robin; Styne
Get Yourself a Phonograph   Burke; Van Heusen; Young,
     Victor
Gift Number   Gorney
Gigolette   Sigman
Gimme the Casbah   Silver
Gin Rummy Rhapsody   Rome
Gingerbread House   David, Hal
Girls Were Made to Take Care of Boys   Blane
Good Corn Liquor and Bad Champagne   Lawrence
Gossips, The   Loesser
Gotta Dance   Martin
Granny's Rocking Chair   Johnston
Greatest Man in the World, The   Russell
Green-Up Time   Lerner, Alan Jay; Weill
Guatemala   Davis
Guest in the Nest   Russell
Hands Off   Harbach
Hankerin'   Cahn; Styne
Happiness   Brooks
Happy Easter   Berlin
Harlem Band (inst.)   Johnson, James P.
Harlem Butterfly   Mercer
Haunted Heart   Dietz; Schwartz, Arthur
Hawaiian Melody   Friml
Heaven on Earth   Gorney
Heaven Sent   Lerner, Sammy
Heavens to Betsy   Johnston
Hebrew Chant (inst.)   Young, Victor
Hee-Hoo Song (Hip de Minnega Honnega Rock de Bumpty
     la Hee-Hoo), The   Revel
Her Lover   Russell
Her Name Was Nina   Davis; Silver
Here Comes Baby Now   Russell
Here I'll Stay   Lerner, Alan Jay; Weill
Here's to Love   Livingston, Jay
Hey Paisan   Davis; Silver
Ho, Billy, O!   Lerner, Alan Jay; Weill
Hold It!   Lerner, Sammy
Holiday in the Country   Adamson; McHugh
Home Is Where the Heart Is   Gorney
Home of Our Own, A   Lerner, Alan Jay; Weill
Homesick Blues   Robin; Styne
Hooray for Love   Arlen; Robin
Hop Up   Weill
Horrible, Horrible Love!   Martin
Hotel Oasis   Arlen; Robin

House on Rittenhouse Square, A   Robin; Styne
How Can I Hold Somebody Else in My Arms   Koehler
How Peaceful Is the Evening   Rome
How Sad My Love (Je Vous Attends)   Gorney
How So Dear to My Heart   Coslow; Johnston
How'd You Like an Apple   Meyer
Hyacinth, The   Loesser
I Am Ashamed that Women Are So Simple   Porter
I Come from Delaware   Blane
I Don't Care If It Rains All Night   Cahn; Styne
I Don't Feel at Home on the Range   Evans; Livingston, Jay
I Don't Know Where My Next Kiss Is Coming From   Fain; Yellen
I Don't Want Any Labor in My Job   Johnson, James P.
I Feel So Jazzy   Robin; Styne
I Gave Her My Heart in Acapulco   Berlin
I Give You a Jewel   Russell
I Hain't Tain't Ain't   Evans; Livingston, Jay
I Hate Husbands   Russell
I Hate Men   Porter
I Have Plenty of Men in My Life but No Life in My Men   Mills
I Haven't Got a Thing to Lose   Sigman
I Hope You Settle for Me   Brown, Nacio Herb
I Just Can't Remember the Words   Spina
I Kissed Her in My Dreams   Drake
I Like You   Brown, Nacio Herb
I Love an Elephant (Cause an Elephant Don't Forget)   Bryan
I Love Those Men   Loesser
I Love What I'm Doing   Robin; Styne
I Love You - You Love Him   Berlin
I Love You to Little Pieces   Sigman
I Need You Like I Need a Hole in the Head   Wrubel
I Never Go Anywhere (That I Can't Come Back From)   Johnston
I Never Met a Texan   Cahn; Styne
I Owe It All to You   Friend
I Remember It Well   Lerner, Alan Jay; Weill
I Saw You on Television   Sigman
I Shoulda Quit When I Was Ahead   Evans; Livingston, Jay
I Shouldn't Love You   Rome
I Sing of Love   Porter
I Wanna Be a Cowboy in the Movies   Cahn; Styne
I Wish Somebody Cared Enough to Cry   Merrill
I Wish You'd Have Happened to Me   Robison
I'd Rather Be Wrong than Be Sorry   David, Hal
If Ever Married I'm   Porter
If I Steal a Kiss (Dear)   Brown, Nacio Herb; Heyman
If I Steal Your Heart   Brown, Nacio Herb; Heyman
If Only   Romberg
If We Had a Little More Time   Dietz; Schwartz, Arthur
If You'll Be Mine   Martin
If You'll Believe in Me   David, Mack
I'll Always Love You   Loesser
I'll Get Him Back   Russell
Illinois   Evans; Livingston, Jay
I'm a Slave to You   David, Mack
I'm Afraid, Sweetheart, I Love You   Porter
I'm Afraid to Like You too Much   Mills
I'm Afraid to Remember   Caesar
I'm A'Tingle, I'm A'Glow   Robin; Styne
I'm Headin' for a Shotgun Weddin'   Friend
I'm in Love   Cahn; Styne
I'm Looking Down at the Moon   Schwartz, Arthur
I'm Not So Bright   Martin

I'm the First Girl in the Second Row in the Third Scene of the Fourth Number   Martin
I'm Tired of Texas   Martin
I'm Your Man   Lerner, Alan Jay; Weill
In Love with Romance   Romberg
In the Back of a Hack   Gorney
In the Champs de Mars   Robin; Styne
In Trinidad   Cahn; Styne
Independence Day   Blane; Warren
Indiana Dinner   Evans; Livingston, Jay
Inside U.S.A.   Dietz; Schwartz, Arthur
Iowa Indian Song (I-o-wun), The   Willson
Irish Recruiting Song   Brooks
Is I Gotta Ma   Raye
Is It Him or Is It Me?   Lerner, Alan Jay; Weill
Is It Yes, or Is It No   Brooks
Isn't It a Crazy World   Silver
It Ain't Far to the Bar   Merrill
It Only Happens when I Dance with You   Berlin
It Takes a Woman to Get a Man   Adamson; McHugh
It Was Great Fun the First Time   Porter
It Was So Nice Having You   Lerner, Sammy
It Was Sweet While It Lasted   Freed, Ralph
It Was Written in the Stars   Arlen; Robin
It's a Dirty Shame   Livingston, Jay
It's a Most Unusual Day   Adamson; McHugh
It's a Quiet Town (Crossbone County)   Russell; Spina
It's a Scream How Levene Does the Rhumba   Mills
It's Delightful Down in Chile   Robin; Styne
It's Fair Time   Johnston
It's High Time   Robin; Styne
It's Magic   Cahn; Styne
It's More Fun than a Picnic   Adamson; McHugh
It's Not a Secret Anymore   Koehler
It's So Easy to Sing (About Things in the Southland)   Harbach
It's the Little Things You Do that Count   Merrill
It's Whatcha Do with Watcha Got   DePaul; Raye
It's You or No One   Cahn; Styne
It's Yours at the Statler Hotel   Coots
Itsa-Bitsa Cooka-Ritsa (Nuts, Nuts, Nuts)   Hoffman
I've Come to Wive It Wealthily in Padua   Porter
I've Got the President's Ear   Adamson; McHugh
I've Got to Be Lovely to Harry   Johnson, James P.
Jack and the Beanstalk   Loesser
Jazz   Martin
Johnny and Lucille   Blane
Joy   Russell
Judaline   DePaul; Raye
July and I   De Lange
June Is Living the Life of Reilly   Mills
Just a Couple of Kids (Who Never Grew Up)   Schwartz, Jean
Just a Kiss Apart   Robin; Styne
Just a Record on the Phonograph   Coots
Just a Shade on the Blue Side   Adamson; Carmichael
Just Across the Street   Rome
Just Becuz   Willson
Just for a While   Brooks
Just Reminiscing, Still in Love with You   Drake
Karen Lynn   Drake
Keep 'em Guessing   Johnson, James P.
Keeping Cool with Coolidge   Robin; Styne
Kiss in Your Eyes, The   Burke
Kiss Me Kate   Porter

Kobblerrumba   Fain; Yellen
Laramie   Evans; Livingston, Jay
Laugh at Life   Romberg
Leadin' Up the Stairs   Russell
Leave My Pulse Alone   Dietz; Schwartz, Arthur
Let Us Dance Till the Dawn   Harbach
Let's Do a Ballet   Martin
Let's Get Together and Sing   Wrubel
Let's Have Breakfast in Hollywood   Johnston
Letter, The   Gorney
Little Black Train   Weill
Little Boy Blues, The   Martin
Little Emmaline   Romberg
Little Girl from Little Rock, A   Robin; Styne
Little Old Man with the Big Red Coat, The   Spina
Little Toot   Wrubel
Livin' the Life of Love   McHugh
Living Alone   Yellen
Locker Room, The   Lerner, Alan Jay; Weill
Loneliness   Washington; Young, Victor
Lonely Ballerina (inst.)   Alter
Lonesome Dove, The   Weill
Look at Me   Robin; Styne
Look Out Below   Carmichael; De Lange
Looking for a Candidate   Rome
Looks Like You'd Like Some Love   Martin
Lost In this Town   Martin
Lost Moment, The   Brooks
Louie Sands and Jim McGee   Brooks
Love and Laughter   Romberg
Love Don't Need a Referee   Johnson, James P.
Love Is New   Romberg
Love Is Where You Find It   Brown, Nacio Herb
Love Me Once More   Parish
Love of My Life   Porter
Love Song   Lerner, Alan Jay; Weill
Love Street   Howard, Joseph E.
Love That Boy   DePaul; Raye
Lovelier than Ever   Loesser
Loveliest Thing in Life, The   Razaf
Lover Boy   Davis; Silver
Lovin' Ain't My Aim   Johnson, James P.
(I Got) Lucky in the Rain   Adamson; McHugh
Lucy   Fain; Yellen
Lullaby   Martin
Lulu Belle   De Lange
Mack the Black   Porter
Madame Zuzu   Lerner, Alan Jay; Weill
Mademoiselle de Paris   Parish
Magic Moment   Romberg
Make a Miracle   Loesser
Make Your Vote Count   Rome
Mamie Is Mimi   Robin; Styne
Mam'selle   Gordon
Manuela   Porter
Marriage of Convenience, A   Russell
Martinique   Porter
Massachusetts Mermaid   Dietz; Schwartz, Arthur
Matador, The   Russell
May Night   Brown, Nacio Herb
Me and Your Cigarette   David, Hal
Meetcha 'Round the Corner   Livingston, Jay
Men Move Mountains   Russell
Merry Go Round Polka   Friend
Mexican Moon Dance (inst.)   Brown, Nacio Herb

Millefleurs   Romberg
Ming Toy Noodle Company, The   Loesser
Minstrel Parade   Lerner, Alan Jay; Weill
Mirage   Russell
Miss Julie July   Evans; Livingston, Jay
Mississippi Siren   Evans; Livingston, Jay
Mister Answer Man   Razaf
Mister, You've Gone and Got the Blues   Russell
Mmm-mm Good   Wrubel
Money Song, The   Rome
Monkey Sat in the Cocoanut Tree, The   Arlen; Robin
Moon-Mad Mama from Memphis   Wrubel
Moonrise   Alter; De Lange
(The Birth of the Copa) More Coffee   Davis; Silver
Mother's Getting Nervous   Lerner, Alan Jay; Weill
Mr. Dumbell and Mr. Tough   Johnson, James P.
Mr. Monotony   Berlin
Mr. President, Please Admit Me to the U.S.A.   Sigman
Mr. Right   Lerner, Alan Jay; Weill
Mr. Right and Mrs. Dream   Lerner, Alan Jay; Weill
Mulligatawney   Brown, Nacio Herb
Musical Tour of the City   Gorney
My Book of Memory   Heyman
My Darling, My Darling   Loesser
My Fair Lady   Johnston
My Feet Takes Me Away   Russell
My Friend Irma   Livingston, Jay
My Gal Is Mine Once More   Dietz; Schwartz, Arthur
My Heart Beats Faster   Loesser
(Don't Look Now but) My Heart Is Showing   Weill
My Heart Left Me   Brown, Nacio Herb
My How the Time Goes By   McHugh
My Kind of Night   Lerner, Alan Jay; Weill
My Lady   Weill
My Lady of the Lake   Brown, Nacio Herb
My Love Loves Me   Evans; Livingston, Jay
My Name Is Samuel Cooper   Lerner, Alan Jay; Weill
My One, My Only, My All   Livingston, Jay
My Sweet Hunk o' Trash   Johnson, James P.
My Week   Weill
Nacio Herb Brown's Dance of Fury (inst.)   Brown, Nacio Herb
Nacio Herb Brown's New Mexico March (inst.)   Brown, Nacio Herb
Neptune's Daughter   Loesser
Never Again   Blane; Warren
Never Let the Same Dog Bite You Twice   Fain; Yellen
Nevermore   Lerner, Sammy
New Ashmolean Marching Society and Students Conservatory Band, The   Loesser
New Look, The   Martin
New Mexico (inst.)   Brown, Nacio Herb
Newsreel   Rome
Next Time I Fall in Love   Stept
Night Song   Brooks
Nina   Porter
No, No and Moi   Spina
No, No, No, Not That   David, Hal
No One Knows, No One Cares   Brooks
No One's Heart   Romberg
No Used Actin' Coy with a Boy from Illinois   Harbach
Nobody's Heart but Mine   Adamson; McHugh
Nora   Ruby
Oh! I'm So Busy Dreaming   Lewis
Oh! Say Can You See   Fields; Romberg

Oh, Them Dudes   Loesser
Oh You Merry Widow   Clare; Pollack
Old Gal's Got that New Look, The   Fain; Yellen
Old Village Barn, The   Silver
Olivia from Olvera Street   Evans; Livingston, Jay
Omar and the Princess   Blane; Warren
On the Level It's You   Schwartz, Jean
Once in Love with Amy   Loesser
One Man that I Loved Said Goodbye, The   Myrow
One Man Woman   Brooks
One More River   Razaf
One Sunday Afternoon   Blane
Ooh, What You Just Said   Clare; Stept
Open Your Heart   Drake
Our Home Town   Blane; Warren
Out of the Corner of My Eye   Parish
Pajama Dance   Martin
Paradise Stolen   Romberg
Paris Aller et Retour   Duke
Peace, Sister, Peace   Johnson, James P.
Peek-a-boo   David, Hal
Pernambuco   Loesser
Perpetual Motion (inst.)   Young, Victor
Pick Up and Go   Russell
Pindy-Fendy   Loesser
Pine Top Boogie   Mercer
Play the Playera   Drake
Please Don't Paint a Mustache on the Girl in the Cigarette
    Ad   Sigman
Please Put Out the Light   Evans; Livingston, Jay
Poem of Love (inst.)   Johnson, James P.
Political Lady   Rome
Polka   Romberg
Popolena   Friend
Practice, The   Robin; Styne
Prayer   Romberg
Prelude to the Dawn (inst.)   Myrow
Pretty Mathilda   Johnston
Progress   Lerner, Alan Jay; Weill
Protect Me   Dietz; Schwartz, Arthur
Push a Button in a Hutton   Gorney
Put 'Em in a Box, Tie 'Em with a Ribbon and Throw 'Em in
    the Deep Blue Sea   Cahn; Styne
Quality   David, Hal
Rachel (inst.)   Revel
Read All About It   Rome
Reality!   Lerner, Alan Jay; Weill
Red Light   Ahlert; Leslie
Remember Mother's Day   Akst
Revel No. 5 (inst.)   Revel
Revel No. 6 (inst.)   Revel
Revel No. 7 (inst.)   Revel
Revel No. 8 (inst.)   Revel
Rhode Island Is Famous for You   Dietz; Schwartz, Arthur
Rhumba Cristobal   Cahn
Ridin' on the Ninety-Nine   Johnston
Rock, Rock, Rock   Adamson; McHugh
Roll 'Em   Lerner, Sammy
Romance   Romberg
Romance with Music   Romberg
Run Run Run   Cahn; Styne
Sad Cowboy, The   Carmichael
Samba Lady   Drake
Same Ol' Cry   Russell
San Gabriel   Willson

Sarong   De Lange
Saunter Away   Loesser
Save It for Me   De Lange
Scherzo (inst.)   Styne
Schoene Maedel (Pretty Girl)   David, Hal
School for Waiters   Dietz; Schwartz, Arthur
Sender   Johnson, James P.
(I Offer You the Moon) Senorita   Brown, Nacio Herb;
    Heyman
Senorita What's Her Name   Mills
Senorita's Bouquet, A   Sigman
Sepia Fashion Show   Johnson, James P.
Serenade to a Presidential Candidate   Lawrence
Serenade with Asides   Loesser
Shauny O'Shae   Martin
She Picked It Up in Mexico   Yellen
Shine Yo' Shoes   Gordon; Myrow
Shmoo Song, The   Styne
Short and Sweet   Lewis
Siesta   Brown, Nacio Herb
Sing About Something   DePaul; Raye
Slacks from Coma   Pollack
Smilin' Through My Tears   Johnson, James P.
Snowman   Sigman
So Belongs My Heart to You   Friend
So Happy I Could Cry   Alter; De Lange
So in Love   Porter
Someday   Blane
Someday You'll Be Sorry   Howard, Joseph E.
Song to Forget, A   Dietz; Schwartz, Arthur
Song Was Born, A   DePaul; Raye
Sourwood Mountain   Weill
Souvenir   Romberg
Spring in December, Winter in May (Passano Gli
    Anni)   Rome
Spring Isn't Everything   Blane; Warren
Square Dance   Blane
St. Joe, Mo.   Webster
Stanley Steamer, The   Blane; Warren
Stay Out of the Kitchen   Johnson, James P.
Steppin' Out with My Baby   Berlin
Story of My Life, The   Russell
Sugar Me Sweet   Russell
Summer Starlight   De Lange
Sunday People   Sigman
Sunflower   David, Mack
Sunshine   Robin; Styne
Susan's Dream   Lerner, Alan Jay; Weill
Suzanne Marie (inst.)   Revel
Swag Man, The   Brooks
Sweet Corner Girl   Blane
Sweet Summer Sweetheart of Mine   Coots
Sweetest Kid I Ever Met, The   Blane; Warren
Swinging Heart   Friend
Swing-Time at the Savoy   Blake; Sissle
Take Me to Your Heart Again   Carmichael
Take Off the Coat   Rome
Taking No Chances   Lerner, Alan Jay; Weill
Tale of Nevada   Brooks
Talk to Me Tomorrow   Robin; Styne
Tangier   Spina
Tell You What I'm Gonna Do   Stept
Ten Commandments   Leslie
Texas, Brooklyn and Heaven   Drake
Thank You   Drake

Thanks for Thanksgiving   Rome
That Element of Doubt   Dietz; Fain
That Was Then   Johnson, James P.
That's the Way It Goes   Parish
That's What the Man Said   Robison
Then I'll Be Closer to You   Brown, Nacio Herb
There Are Other Things a Girl Can Do   Adamson; McHugh
There Was Moonlight in Her Hair   David, Mack
There's a Barber in the Harbor of Palermo   Livingston, Jay
There's a Rising Moon (For Every Falling Star)   Webster
There's Music in the Land   Cahn; Styne
There's No Getting Away from You   Adamson; McHugh
There's No Song Like an Old Song   Akst; Gilbert
There's Nobody Else but Elsie   Wrubel
There's Nothing Left for Daddy (But the Rhumba)   Lerner,
    Alan Jay; Weill
Thin   Yellen
This Is the Life   Lerner, Alan Jay; Weill
This Is Your Life   Gilbert
This Time of the Year   Koehler; Stept
This Time Tomorrow   Stept
Tiger Lily (inst.)   Schwartz, Arthur
Time Stood Still   Pollack; Styne
Tiny Room   Martin
To Each His Own   Evans; Livingston, Jay
Toast, The   Martin
Today Didn't Pay to Get Up   Merrill
Tom, Dick or Harry   Porter
Tomorrow Means Romance   Brown, Nacio Herb
Tonight Is a Night for Romance   Brown, Nacio Herb
Too Darn Hot   Porter
Too Heavenly for This World   Drake
Too Much-a Manana   Carmichael
Tourist Trade, The   Cahn; Styne
Toy Ballerina (inst.)   Alter
Train that Brought You to Town, The   Loesser
Trio in Rio (Saudade)   Heyman
Tunnel of Love, The   Loesser
Twenty Third Psalm   Johnston
Two Lovers Met in the Night   Cahn; Styne
Two of Us, The   Martin
Two Roses of Tapolorambo   Stept
Two-Time, Hot-Time, Ragtime Daddy   Evans; Livingston,
    Jay
Umbrella Weather   David, Hal
Until You Are Caught   Johnson, James P.
Vision, The   Romberg
Viva the Women!   Lerner, Alan Jay; Weill
Voodoo   Porter
Waltz Interlude   Romberg
Way It Might Have Been, The   Martin
We Got to Put Shoes on Willie   Fain; Yellen
We Open in Venice   Porter
We Shall Never Be Younger   Porter
We Watch the Skyways   Kahn
We Won't Take It Back   Dietz; Schwartz, Arthur
Weary Blues   Blane; Warren
Wedding in the Park   Gorney
We're Goin' to Blitz the Ritzes   Johnson, James P.
We're Going Back   Rome
We're Not Getting Any Younger Baby   Magidson; Oakland
We're On Our Way   Brown, Nacio Herb
We're Selling Sunshine   Lerner, Alan Jay; Weill
We're Spending Our Honeymoon in Escrow   Willson
We're Taking Over Now   Lerner, Alan Jay; Weill

Were Thine That Special Face   Porter
West Virginia   Blane
What Can You Do with a General   Berlin
What Did I Do?   Gordon; Myrow
What Do I Want with Money   McHugh
What Does Your Servant Dream About   Porter
What Kind o' Tune Did Old Nero Play   Johnson, James P.
What More Do I Want   Lerner, Alan Jay; Weill
What's Good about Goodbye   Arlen; Robin
What's the Matter with Our City?   Gorney
What's Under Your Mask, Madame?   Evans; Livingston, Jay
What's Wrong with Me?   Brown, Nacio Herb; Heyman
When His Lips Met Mine   Brown, Nacio Herb
When I Get Out of School   Brown, Nacio Herb
When You Find the Right Baby   Mills
When Your Sweetheart Comes Home   Wrubel
Where Am I Without You   DePaul; Raye
Where Do I Belong?   Lerner, Alan Jay; Weill
Where Is the Life That Late I Led?   Porter
Where's Charley   Loesser
While the Men Are All Drinking   Blane; Warren
Whisper a Word of Love (Meditation de Thais)   Rome
Whispering Waters   Hoffman; Livingston, Jay; Livingston,
    Jerry
Who Believes in Santa Claus?   Brooks
Who but You   De Lange
Who Can Tell (Not I)   Brooks
Who Is Samuel Cooper?   Lerner, Alan Jay; Weill
Who Says Crime Doesn't Pay?   Lawrence
Who Told You?   Lewis
Who Walked Out when I Walked In?   Lewis
Why   Romberg
Why Are the Wheels of My Bicycle Round?   Schwartz, Jean
Why Can't You Behave   Porter
Why Fight the Feeling   Loesser
Wind in My Sails   Drake
Wish I Had a Braver Heart   Blane; Warren
With a Bing Bang Banjo on Your Knee   Sigman
Without a Friend   De Lange
Woman in His Room, A   Loesser
Woman's Career, A   Porter
Women's Club Blues   Lerner, Alan Jay; Weill
Wondrin' When   Evans; Livingston, Jay
Wooden Shoe Polka, The   Revel
Wove Me, Willian (Love Me, Lillian)   Robison
Written in Your Hand   Romberg
Wunderbar   Porter
'Ya Never Know Just 'Oo Yer Gonna Meet   Brooks
Years Before Us, The   Loesser
You Are Not My First Love   Howard, Bart
You Are So Near (So Near and Yet So Far)   Gorney
You Came a Long Way from St. Louis   Russell
You Can Call Me Peter   Schwartz, Arthur
You Can Do No Wrong   Porter
You Can in Yucatan   Drake
You Can Take the Boy Out of the Country   Russell
You Can't Lose a Broken Heart   Johnson, James P.
You Can't Run Away from Love   Gordon
You Gotta Stay Happy   Brooks
You Kissed the Words Right Out of My Mouth   Mills
You Never Know What Hit You — When It's Love   Rome
You Never Leave Me   Parish
You Say the Nicest Things, Baby   Adamson; McHugh
You Say You Care   Robin; Styne
You Took Possession of Me   Lerner, Sammy

You Understand Me So   Lerner, Alan Jay; Weill
You Was   Webster
You Were Made for Love   Russell
Your Daddy Was a Soldier, Your Mommy Was a
   WAC   Mills
Your Own College Band   Loesser
You're My Rose   Johnson, James P.
You're Near and Yet So Far   Romberg
You're Next   Blane; Warren
You're Sailing Away with My Heart   David, Mack; Hoffman;
   Livingston, Jerry
You're the First Cup of Coffee   Gorney
You're too Dangerous, Cherie (La Vie en Rose)   David,
   Mack
Yours for a Song   Carroll
Yum-Yum-Kiss-Kiss   David, Hal

1949

Affable Balding Me   Mercer
Ain't It Crazy to Be Nuts   Hoffman
Ain't Love the Darndest Thing   Friend
All Ears   Razaf
All for You   Johnston
All on Account of a Schmoo   Robison
Always Leave Them Laughing   Cahn
American Primitive   Gorney
And It Still Goes   Stept
And So on Down the Line   Eliscu
Another Day, Another Darling   Sigman
Ardent Night (inst.)   Revel
Arizona Weddin', An   Stept
At the Cafe Rendezvous   Cahn; Styne
At the Psychological Moment   Burke; Van Heusen
Baby I'd Know It Was You   Coots
Baby Sitter (I'm Goin' to Sit with Baby)   Burke
Bagdad   Brooks
Bali Hai   Hammerstein; Rodgers
Be a Mess   Gorney
Be Faithful   Coots
Be Sure   David, Mack
Be-Bop La Rumba   Coslow
Before You Can Say Jackie Robinson   Blake
Begger and the Rose, The   Webster
Big Mole   Weill
Big Movie Show in the Sky, The   Mercer
Bird of Passage, A   Weill
Black Coffee   Webster
Blame My Absent-Minded Heart   Cahn; Styne
Bloody Mary   Hammerstein; Rodgers
Blossoms on the Bough   Sigman
Blue for a Boy, Pink for a Girl   David, Hal
Blue Jean Polka, The   Warren
Blue Rhythm Bounce   Mills
Blue Rhythm Chant   Mills
Blue Rhythm Ramble   Mills
Blue Rhythm Serenade   Mills
Blue Sails Upon a Silver Sea   Egan; Kahn; Whiting
Blue (With You or Without You)   Kalmar
Bop! Goes My Heart   Styne
Bouncin' the Blues (inst.)   Warren
Breath of Scandal   Robison
Breeze Is My Sweetheart, The Brook Is My Song,
   The   Sigman
Bride and Groom Waltz, The   Hoffman

Broadway Love Song   Gorney
Buenos Noches, Buenos Aires   Brown, Nacio Herb
Burro Flats   Webster
Business for a Good Girl Is Bad   Berlin
Busy Doing Nothing   Burke; Van Heusen
Bye Bye My Baby   Parish
Califo'nia   Razaf
Call on Us Again   Gershwin, Ira; Warren
Camp Meetin'   Coots
Can't We Talk It Over   Washington; Young, Victor
Carousel of Love   Parish
Charisse   Brown, Nacio Herb
Chicken Soup (I Ain't Gonna Take It Sittin' Down)   Merrill
Christmas Valley   Razaf
Church Music   Russell
Cigolette   David, Mack; Sigman
Circus   Alter; Russell
Clink Your Glasses   Cahn
Clowning at the N.V.A.   McHugh
Cockeyed Optimist, A   Hammerstein; Rodgers
Colleen Fair with the Raven Hair   Merrill
Count on Me   Comden and Green
Couple of Sweethearts, A   Sigman
Courtin' of Elma and Ella, The   Gershwin, Ira; Warren
Cowbells at Eventide   Robison
Crazy He Calls Me   Russell; Sigman
Cry, the Beloved Country   Weill
Cuckoo and the Canary, The   Wrubel
Darling, It's Been Fun, Hasn't It   Duke
(Lonesome Little) Daylight Moon   Robison
Dear Wife   Evans; Livingston, Jay
Desert of Dreams   Brennan
Ditto (inst.)   Strouse
Do Me a Favor Please   Lewis; Meyer
Do Something   Wrubel
Doctor Jim   Robison
Dog Song, The   Brown, Nacio Herb
Don't Hate Me 'Cause Yo Own Me Money   Robison
Don't Promise Me the Moon   Fain
Don't Send Me to Bed   Sigman
Don't Try to Explain   Drake
Down in the Valley   Mercer
Dream Baby   Friend
Dreamy Indiana Moonlight   Parish
Driftin' Down the Dreamy Ol' Ohio   Spina
Easy Does It   Gorney
Edward My Son   Davis; Silver
Eight Piece Band on a Nine Day Cruise, An   David, Hal
Empty Promises   Robison
Enchantment   DePaul; Raye
Evening in 32 Bars, An   Russell
Every Day   Willson
Evolution   Mills
Ev'ry Night's Like New Year's Eve   Stept
Exquisite   Brennan
Extra! Extra!   Berlin
Falling Out of Love Can Be Fun   Berlin
Fame (inst.)   Revel
Farewell, Amanda   Porter
Farewell Waltz   Wrubel
Fat Philistine Merchant, The   Young, Victor
Father William   Eliscu
Fear!   Weill
Fiddle Dee Dee   Cahn; Styne
First Song of Christmas, The   Coots

Flowers that Never Die   Sigman
Follow the Leader Jig   Berlin
Follow the Swallow to Hide-a-Way Hollow   Carmichael;
    Webster
Follow the Swallow to Old Sleepy Hollow   Carmichael;
    Webster
Fool There Was, A   Davis; Silver
Fool's Paradise   Merrill
For to Win a Bride   Young, Victor
Forbidden Love   Spina
Forty-Eight Kisses   Coots
Four O'Clock   Weill
Four Winds and the Seven Seas, The   David, Hal
Frankie and Johnny   Brooks
Freddie, Get Ready   Blane; Warren
Friend of Mine, A   Wrubel
Funny Little Old World   Gorney
Galloping Comedians, The   Rome
Give Me a Song with a Beautiful Melody   Cahn; Styne
Give Me a Tam Tam Tambourine   Cahn
Give Me Your Tired, Your Poor   Berlin
Give Thy Love   Evans; Livingston, Jay
Gold!   Weill
Gone to Chicago   Willson
Good in Me, The   Robison
Good News for You, Brother   Robison
Grandma Teeter Totter   Carmichael
Great Guns   Mercer; Warren
Guadalajara Hop   Coslow
Hamlet   Loesser
Hang Your Teardrops in the Sunshine   Yellen
Happiness, Happiness   Magidson; Oakland
Happy Talk   Hammerstein; Rodgers
Happy Valley   Friend
Haunting Eyes   Razaf
Havin' a Wonderful Wish (Time You Were Here)   Evans;
    Livingston, Jay
He Rides the Range   Webster
He Went That-a-Way She Went This-a-Way   Hoffman
Headless Horseman, The   DePaul; Raye
Health, Harmony and Happiness   Robison
Here Comes the Spring   Duke
Here's to Love   Evans
Hermit in the Heart of Town   Coots
Highbrow, Lowbrow   Gorney
Hills of Ixopo, The   Weill
Hobble-de-hoy and a Gallop a Trot, A   David, Hal
Hoe Cake, Hominy and Sassafras Tea   Hoffman
Homework   Berlin
Honey Bun   Hammerstein; Rodgers
Hon'rable Profession of the Fourth Estate, The   Berlin
Hooray for the United States   Yellen
Hootin' Owl Trail   Mercer
Hop-Scotch Polka (Scotch Hot)   Sigman
Horse and Buggy Doctor, A   Razaf
Horseshoes Are Lucky   Mercer
Hot Dog, Mustard and You   Brennan
How It Lies, How It Lies, How It Lies   Webster
I Can't Wed Ya (But My Sister She Might)   Mills
I Could Get Along with You   Burke; Van Heusen
I Don't Know Whether to Laugh or to Cry Over You (The
    Hysteria Song)   Coslow
I Hate to Leave You Now   Waller
I Hope You're Not in Love with Anyone   Stept
I Know, I Know, I Know   Russell

I Lost a Day   Lewis; Meyer
(Just One Way to Say) I Love You   Berlin
I Promise   Freed, Ralph
I Should Hate You   Friend
I Wake Up in the Morning Feeling Fine   Loesser
I Want to Be Teacher's Pet   Gordon; Myrow
I Was Born Happy   Sigman
I Wish I Had a Record (Of the Promises You Made)   David,
    Hal
Ichabod   DePaul; Raye
I'd Give them All Up for You   Sigman
I'd Like My Picture Took   Berlin
I'd Like to Find You in My Stocking when I Wake Up
    Christmas Morn   Coots
I'd Like to Wrap You Up and Put You in My Pocket   David,
    Hal
I'd Love to Put My Arms Around You   Friend
If I Could Make You Cry I'd Be Happy   Davis; Silver
If I Could Only Borrow Something on My Dream   Koehler;
    Stept
If I Knew You Were Comin' I'd've Baked a Cake   Hoffman;
    Merrill
If I Were You   Brown, Nacio Herb
If the Wealth of This World Belonged to Me   Sissle
If You Don't Love Me   Carmichael
If You Stub Your Toe on the Moon   Burke; Van Heusen
I-Itty-Love-Itty-You-Itty   Hoffman
I'll Take You Home in My Heart Tonight   David, Mack;
    Livingston, Jerry
I'm an Old Spanish Customer   Russell
I'm Beginning to Miss You   Berlin
I'm Gonna Tie a String Around My Finger   Wrubel
I'm Gonna Wash That Man Right Outa My
    Hair   Hammerstein; Rodgers
I'm Headin' Home   Rome
I'm Living a Day at a Time   Davis; Silver
I'm Not too Sure of My L'Amour   Hoffman
I'm Oh So Lonesome Tonight   Merrill
I'm Skipping Rope with a Rainbow   Drake
I'm Upside Down   Eliscu
In My Hour of Need   Sigman
In the Shadows of the Alamo   Stept
Irish Is in My Heart, The   Davis; Silver
It Happened on a Train   Hoffman
It Happens Every Spring   Gordon; Myrow
It Looked So Good in the Window   Merrill
It'll Be All Right in a Hundred Years   Gorney
It's a Cruel, Cruel World   Davis; Silver
It's a Great Feeling   Cahn; Styne
It's Fate Baby, It's Fate   Comden and Green
It's Great to Be Alive   Mercer
It's Only a Man   Webster
It's Too Late Now   Coots
It's Your Birthday   Sigman
I've Got a Sunday Feeling in My Heart   David, Mack;
    Livingston, Jerry
I've Got to Thank You for That   Davis; Silver
Jamaica Rumba   DePaul; Raye
Jello Family Round   Willson
Jello Pudding Sounds   Willson
Jello Shimmer   Willson
Jet   Revel
June   Johnson, J. Rosamond
Just for Fun   Evans; Livingston, Jay
Just Over the Mountain   Razaf

Kansas City Blues   Robison
Kappa Sigma Girl, The   Carmichael
Kathy   Washington
Katrina   DePaul; Raye
Killarney   Brooks
Lament, A   Johnson, Howard
Land of Might Have Been   Rome
Lenox Avenue Waltz   Blake
Let's Take an Old-Fashioned Walk   Berlin
Life Is Fine   Blake
Lingering Down the Lane (Ah Le Petit Vin
      Blanc)   Lawrence
Lips that Touch Another's Life (Shall Never Touch
      Mine)   Sigman
Little Bit of Country   Mercer
Little Fish in a Big Pond   Berlin
Little Gray House, The   Weill
Little Love, a Little Money, A   Duke
Little Miss Grown-Up   Sigman
Little Scrap of Paper, A   DePaul; Raye
Little Tin God, The   Weill
Little Yellow Ribbon in Her Hair, A   Davis; Silver
Lollipop Interlude   Gordon
Lollypop Prelude   Gordon
Loneliness of Evening   Hammerstein; Rodgers
Look at Me   Brooks
Look in Your Eyes, The   Kalmar
Lost in a Dream   Bloom; Leslie
Lost in the Stars   Weill
Love Birds   Merrill
Love Finds a Way   Blane; Warren
Love Is Strange   Brooks
Love Me, Love My Dog   Mercer
Love Woke Me Up this Morning   Mercer; Warren
Lovers' Gold   Merrill
Lovesick Blues   Friend; Mills
Lucky Us!   Evans; Livingston, Jay
Mad About You   Washington; Young, Victor
Main Street   Comden and Green
Main Title   Coslow
Majarajah   Coslow
Make Believe Ballroom   Mercer
Make Morris Mayor   Lawrence
Mama, What's Love   De Lange
Man Chases a Girl (Until She Catches Him), A   Berlin
Manhattan Downbeat   Gershwin, Ira; Warren
Manuelo Tarantel, The   Sigman
Marionette   Drake
Marshmallow World, A   Sigman
May I Still Hold You (When the Dance Is Over)   Russell
Maybe It's Because   Ruby
McHugh's Melody (inst.)   McHugh
Me an' My Bundle   Berlin
Melody   Evans; Livingston, Jay
Melody of Paree   Friend
Memories I'll Never Forget   Willson
Memory Train, The   David, Mack; Livingston, Jerry
Men Are Little Children   Brooks
Men of the Watermark   Gorney
Merry Christmas Polka, The   Webster
Merry Christmas Waltz, The   David, Hal
Milton Berle Polka, The   Brown, Lew
Minstrels on Parade   Gershwin, Ira; Warren
Miss Liberty   Berlin
Miss Ma-Goof   Friend

Miss Platt Selects Mate   Gorney
Missouri Walking Preacher (With a Little Book in His
      Hand)   Robison
Mister Brown, Miss Drupree   Gorney
Mister He Kissed Her   Carmichael
Momma's Cooking   Rome
Month of Sundays, A   Mercer
Moon Kissed Maid   Russell
Moonflower Lane   Brown, Nacio Herb
Moonlight Silhouette   Coslow
More than Anything in the World   Drake
More We Are Together (The Less We Are Apart),
      The   Hoffman
Most Expensive Statue in the World, The   Berlin
Mother, Mother, Mother, Pin a Rose on Me   David, Hal
Mr. Broadway   Coslow
Mr. Disk Jockey (Play Our Love Song Again)   Robison
Murder in Parkwold   Weill
My Blue Eyed Madonna   Davis; Silver
My Child   Livingston, Jerry
My Dream Is Yours   Blane; Warren
My Foolish Heart   Washington; Young, Victor
My Friend Irma   Evans
My Girl Back Home   Hammerstein; Rodgers
My One and Only Highland Fling   Gershwin, Ira; Warren
My One, My Only, My All   Evans
My Schoolday Sweetheart   Yellen
Natchez on the Mississip'   Gershwin, Ira; Warren
New Sun Ridin' in the Sky, A   Stept
Next Time I Care (I'll Be Careful), The   Gilbert; Oakland
Night After Night   Cahn
Nightingale and the Rose, The   Young, Victor
No One's Loved No One So Much   Merrill
No Range to Ride Anymore   Sigman
Nobody Knows   Razaf
Nobody's Lost on the Lonesome Trail   Gilbert
Nothing Ever Happens   Duke
Now and Forever   Evans; Livingston, Jay; Young, Victor
(Where Are You) Now that I Need You   Loesser
Nuggets   Brennan
O Tixo, Tixo, Help Me   Weill
Oatmeal and Farina   Leslie
O'Brien to Ryan to Goldberg   Comden and Green
Ol' Man Spider Fingers   DePaul; Raye
Old Fashined Christmas   Merrill
Old Jello Theme   Willson
Old Story Teller, The   Hoffman
Oley's Melody   Fain; Yellen
On an Island with You   Brown, Nacio Herb
On Guard   Rome
On the Town   Comden and Green
Once Again   Rome
Once and for Always   Burke; Van Heusen
One More Time   David, Mack; Livingston, Jerry
One, Two, Three O'Leary   David, Hal
Only for Americans   Berlin
Opening for Everybody, An   Gorney
Our Family Tree   Mercer
Out of a Blue Sky   Conrad
Out of Love   Fain
Over a Bottle of Wine   Stept
Paris Wakes Up and Smiles   Berlin
Parting Is Such Sweet Sorrow   Mercer
Patsy's Pizza Beat   DePaul; Raye
Peaceful Waters   Robison

Pearl of the Persian Sea   Comden and Green
Penguins   Brennan
Penny   Drake
Peony Bush, The   Willson
Pin Striped Pants   Russell
Play the Game   Eliscu
Playin' Hookey with Cookie   De Lange
Poetry of Motion, The   Gershwin, Ira; Warren
Pole Cat Polka   Friend
Policeman's Ball, The   Berlin
Politics   Mercer
Possession (inst.)   Revel
Prehistoric Man   Comden and Green
Reckon I'm in Love   David, Mack; Hoffman
Revolvin' Jones   Robison
Ride 'Em Cowboy   Mercer
Right Girl for Me, The   Comden and Green
Ringin' the New Year In (Ringin' the Old Year Out)   Gilbert
Rock-a-bye Bangtail   Evans; Livingston, Jay
Rockabye Ranch   Sigman
Roll Pony, Roll   Brennan
Rolling in Rainbows   Burke; Van Heusen
Rosa   Brown, Lew
Rosary of the Rose, The   David, Mack; Livingston, Jerry
Rosita and Joe   Brooks
Run for the Roundhouse, Nelly   Robison
Saddle Up the Palomino   Drake
Sailor's Hornpipe   Gordon
Sand Man   Comden and Green
Sarah, My Sarah   Robison
Say Farewell   Cahn
Scotch Plaid   Turk
Search, The   Weill
Second Fiddle to a Harp   Gershwin, Ira; Warren
See You Around   Coslow
Seeing Red and Singing Blue (The Color Song)   Bloom; Leslie
Selfish Love   Friend
Shade Went Up, The   David, Hal
Shadowy Glass, The   Weill
Shennigans (Two of Irish)   Sigman
She's a Home Girl   Davis; Silver
Shoes with Wings On   Gershwin, Ira; Warren
Silver Dollars Tinkling Down   DePaul; Raye
Sing an Old Fashioned Song   Adamson; McHugh
Single Saddle   David, Hal
Situation Wanted   Brown, Nacio Herb
Skeets Song, The   Robison
Sleeping on a Sealy   Razaf
Sleepy Hollow   DePaul; Raye
Slum and Gravy   Friml
Small Town Gossip   Robison
Smooth Sailing   Russell
So Long-No Longer   Brennan
Soliloquy   Weill
Some Day   Ruby
Some Enchanted Evening   Hammerstein; Rodgers
Someone Called Manon   Russell
Someone Like You   Blane; Warren
Something in Common   Burke; Van Heusen
(Lost My Baby) Somewhere Along the Line   Stept
Song of Delilah, The   Evans; Livingston, Jay
Song of Surrender   Evans; Livingston, Jay; Young, Victor
Song of the Desert   Brooks
Sorry   Whiting

Spring Made a Fool of Me   Stept
Square Dance   Mercer
Star of Bethlehem   David, Mack
Stay Well   Weill
Story of Annie Laurie, The   Lewis; Meyer
Story of My Life, The   Russell; Sigman
Story of the Lovebird   Sigman
Streets of Laredo   Evans; Livingston, Jay
Strong Silent Type   Sigman
Strummin' on the Old Banjo   David, Hal
Suitcase on the Railroad Track   Coots
Summer Met September   Russell
Sunset   Razaf
Sweet Rice Cake   Merrill
Sweetest Word of All Is Sweetheart, The   Hoffman
Swing Trot   Gershwin, Ira; Warren
Take a Crank Letter   Mercer
Take Back Your Paper Heart   Schwartz, Jean
Takin' Miss Mary to the Ball   Brown, Nacio Herb
Taking No Chances on You   Gershwin, Ira; Warren
Tapioca Polka   Willson
Tell Me in Your Own Sweet Way   Arlen
Texas Born   David, Hal
Texas Li'l Darlin'   Mercer
13th Street Rag   Mercer
That Was a Big Fat Lie   Cahn; Styne
That's All There Is Folks   Comden and Green
That's How Dreams Are Made   Gilbert
That's Loyalty   Loesser
There Is No Music   Gershwin, Ira; Warren
There Is Nothin' Like a Dame   Hammerstein; Rodgers
There's a Mile Between the Ess-Es in Smiles   Sigman
There's an Empty Stool at the End of the Bar   Robison
There's Nothin' Rougher than Love   Cahn; Styne
There's Something About Paree   Davis; Silver
These Days   Gershwin, Ira; Warren
They Talk a Different Language (The Yodel Blues)   Mercer
They're Doin' the Square Dance in the Finest Circles   Stept
They're Playing Our Song   Drake
They've Never Figured Out a Woman   Brooks
This and No More   Bullock
This Had Better Be Love   Gorney
This Is It   Razaf
This Is My Night with Trixie   Gilbert
This Is Not Goodbye   Cahn
This Love   Russell
This Nearly Was Mine   Hammerstein; Rodgers
Those Were the Days   Webster
Thousand Violins, A   Evans; Livingston, Jay
Thousands of Miles   Weill
Three Rivers (The Allegheny, Susquehanna and the Monongahela), The   Carmichael; Webster
Through a Long and Sleepless Night   Gordon
Thursday Would Have Been a Year   Webster
Tick, Tick, Tick   Blane; Warren
Time   Friend
To Know You Is to Like You   Brennan
To You and Yours, Merry Christmas   Koehler
Tomorrow's My Lucky Day   Burke; Van Heusen
Too Much Love   Blane
Top o' the Morning   Burke; Van Heusen
Toujours Moi (Always Me) (inst.)   Revel
Train, The   Berlin
Train to Johannesburg   Weill
Traveling Men Are Traveling Again, The   Fain; Yellen

Trouble Man   Weill
Truly   Mercer
T.S.U. Alma Mater   Pollack
Tulsa   Wrubel
Tweet Tweet Tweet   Washington
Twin Soliloquies   Hammerstein; Rodgers
'Twixt Myself and Me   Burke; Van Heusen
Two Little — New Little — Blue Little Eyes   Friend
Tzigane (Gypsy) (inst.)   Revel
Under the Sleeping Volcano   Gorney
Uno, Dos, Tres, Quattro, Cinco, Seis! (The Mexican Dancing
    Teacher)   Brown, Nacio Herb
Upside Down Parade   Fain
Vera Do Minho   Yellen
Waltz of the Mission Bells, The   Webster
Way Back When   David, Hal
Way Up the Hudson   Stept
Weekend in the Country   Gershwin, Ira; Warren
Welcome to My Heart   Duke
Well Known Skies of Blue, The   Gershwin, Ira; Warren
What Can I Do? (Qu'est-ce Que J'ai?)   Rome
What Do I Have to Do   DePaul; Raye
What Have You Got in Those Eyes   DePaul; Raye
What Will We Name the Baby   De Lange
Whatever Happened to Ol' Jack   Russell; Sigman
When April Climbs the Hill   Coots
When Is Sometime   Burke; Van Heusen
When It's Christmas Time in Toyland   Baer
When Sally Walks Along Peacock Alley   Mercer; Warren
When the Lights of the Chapter Are Low, The   Carmichael
When the Moon Comes Up on County Down   David, Hal
When the Organ Played Ave Maria   Davis; Silver
When You Break an Irishman's Heart   Brown, Lew; Stept
When You March Back in My Arms   De Lange
Where Are You, Blue Eyes   Drake
Where Ya Goin', What's Your Hurry, Where's the
    Fire   Hoffman
Whichway'd They Go   Mercer
Whispering Waters   David, Mack
Whistles 'n' Trestles 'n' Trains   Merrill
Who Cares — Who Cares   Heyman
Who Misses Who   David, Mack; Livingston, Jerry
Who'll Buy?   Weill
Whoopin' and A-Hollerin'   Mercer
Wild Justice, The   Weill
William the Conqueror   Eliscu
Willson Tag   Willson
Wine of Old Giuseppe, The   Evans; Livingston, Jay
Wish Me Luck   Gorney
With All My Broken Heart   Merrill
With Love   Razaf
Woman and the Bottle, The   Duke
Wonder of It All, The   Cahn
Wonderful Guy, A   Hammerstein; Rodgers
World Goes Spinning Around, The   Sigman
Would I Love You (Love You Love You)   Russell; Spina
Yes, Indeedy   Comden and Green
You Are All the World to Me   Gilbert
You Belong to the Night   Duke
You Bring Out the Worst in Me   Duke
You Can Do It, Kid   Sigman
You Can Have Him   Berlin
You Can't Knock It to Me   Fain; Yellen
You Could   Stept
You Really Do Get Around   Magidson; Oakland

You Told Me to Tell You   Ruby
You'd Be Hard to Replace   Gershwin, Ira; Warren
Younger than Springtime   Hammerstein; Rodgers
Your Eyes   DePaul; Raye
Your Mom's Like Mine   Merrill
Your Red Wagon   DePaul; Raye
You're a Joy to the World (But a Tear in My Heart)   Fain
You're Awful   Comden and Green
You're Building a Wall Between Us   Fain
You're Cuter than the Devil (Maria Belen Chacon)   Drake
You're in Love with Someone   Burke; Van Heusen
You're Only Saying It Because It's True   Stept
You're Too Intense   Cahn
You've Got a Wonderful Sense of Humor   Fain
You've Got the Indian Sign on Me   Hoffman; Stept
You've Got to Be Carefully Taught   Hammerstein; Rodgers
Yum, Yummy, Yummy, Yum-Yum (The Jelly Apple Song)
    David, Mack; Livingston, Jerry
Zinzinnati Polka   Brown, Lew

1950

Accidents Will Happen   Burke; Van Heusen
Across the Meadow and Over the Hill   Drake
Across the River (And Into the Trees)   Silver
Across the Wide Missouri (A-Roll, A-Roll, A-Ree)   Drake
Action   Loesser
Adelaide's Lament   Loesser
Affair with a Stranger (Kiss and Run)   Coslow
After Midnight   Evans; Livingston, Jay
After the Rain Is Over   Coots
Ah Loves Ya!   Arlen; Mercer
All I Need Is a Little More Sleep   Coots
All My Love   Parish
All Tied Up   Carmichael; Mercer
Alone (The Whaling Widows)   Duke; Rome
American Beauty Rose   David, Hal
And There I Stood with My Piccolo   Willson
And You'll Be Home   Burke; Van Heusen
Anthem of the Atomic Age   Willson
Any Similarity Is Just Coincidental   Carmichael; Mercer
Anything Can Happen in the Moonlight   Adamson;
    McHugh
Apple Jack   Weill
Apple Pie Guy   Coots
Are We Picking Up Where We Left Off   Baer; Leslie
Arithmatic   Merrill
Arizona   Stept
Arm with a Bow in It's Hand (Yipaloo), An   Sigman
Around the Old Saskatchewan   Bryan
Ask Anybody (Who Loves You)   Coots
Assignment   Johnson, J. Rosamond
At the Jazz Band Ball   Mercer
Autumn   Koehler; Stept
Autumn Leaves   Mercer
Away from It All   Porter
Baby, Baby, Baby   David, Mack; Livingston, Jerry
Baby Blue Eyes   Leslie
Baby, Obey Me!   Evans; Livingston, Jay
Baby, Won't You Say You Love Me   Gordon; Myrow
Bad Bill Jones   Johnson, James P.
Bambino   Coots
Bayou Lullaby, The   Cahn
Be a Folk Singer   Rome
Be My Love   Cahn

Be Yourself   Blake
Because You're in Love   Brooks
Beer That I Left on the Bar, The   Brown, Lew; Cobb
Bella Bella Mia   Hoffman
Bella Signora   Heyman; Young, Victor
Beloved, Be Faithful   Drake
Benny the Bow Legged Bowler   Gilbert; Oakland
Bessie Guessie   Caesar
Best Thing for You, The   Berlin
Bibbidi-Bobbidi-Boo (The Magic Song)   David, Mack;
        Hoffman; Livingston, Jerry
Big Lie, The   Robison
Birthday Song, The   Styne
Bitter and the Sweet, The   Russell
Blame It on Yourself   Koehler
Bless You All   Rome
Blue Day   Bullock
Blue Jean Polka, The   Gordon; Revel; Warren
Bon Nuit   Evans; Livingston, Jay
Boom Biddy Boom Boom   Cahn
Bouncy Bouncy Bally   Hoffman
Bowling Alley   David, Mack; Livingston, Jerry
Boy! That's Love   Johnson, J. Rosamond
Brand New Rainbow in the Sky, A   Stept
Buddha Man   Sigman
Bushel and a Peck, A   Loesser
Busybody   DePaul; Raye
But They Better Not Wait Too Long!   Carmichael; Mercer
Butch, the Rocking Horse Cowboy   Coots
Button, Button, Who's Got the Button   Drake
By the Kissing Rock   Cahn; Styne
By Your Side   Hoffman
Call It Love   Bullock
Calling Romance   Blake
Calypso Song   Arlen; Mercer
Can I Come in for a Second   Cahn
Can I Help It (If I'm Helpless in Your Arms)   Parish
Can You Use Any Money Today?   Berlin
Candy and Cake   Merrill
Cane Bottom Chair   Robison
Captain and the Nancy Lee, The   Meyer
Captain Kidd   Strouse
Carlotta   Cahn
Casper the Friendly Ghost   David, Mack; Livingston, Jerry
Catfish Song, The   Weill
Champagne and Music   Silver
Chase Me, Catch Me Polka   Sigman
Chee Chee Mood   Razaf
Cheeky-Cheeky Hoopla   Hoffman; Merrill
Cherry Pies Ought to Be You   Porter
Chi-Chi Club   Gordon
Children Belong in the Country   Robison
Children's Day, A   Razaf
Christmas Chimes   Clare
Cinderella   David, Mack; Hoffman; Livingston, Jerry
Cinderella Work Song (The Work Song)   Hoffman
Clap Hands, Clap Hands till Daddy Comes Home   Merrill
Clean Up Chicago   Gordon; Myrow
Climb Up the Mountain   Porter
Coal-Black Eyes and Lily-White Hands   Sigman
Come In Mornin'   Weill
Copenhagen Polka, The   Coots
Copper Canyon   Evans; Livingston, Jay
Corky the Camel (With the Knock Knock Knees)   Coots
Corn Keeps A-Growin', The   Lerner, Sammy; Oakland

Cosmo Cosmetics   Arlen; Blane
Cow and a Plough and a Frau, A   Fields
Crazy Things You Do When You're in Love, The   Hoffman
Crime Will Never Pay   Robison
Cry, Baby, Cry   Rome
Daddy's Not My Daddy Anymore   Razaf
Dancing with You (Dance Avec Moi)   Rome
Darkness Gives Me You Again (inst.), The   Revel
Das Glueck Kommt Auch Zu Dir   Woods
Dear! Dear! Dear!   Russell
Dear Diary   Washington
Dear Hearts and Gentle People   Fain
Dear to Me   Razaf
Deep End   Blake
Delectable Dream   Evans; Livingston, Jay
Derry-Up, Derry-Down Dey   Willson
Desert Flame, The   Rome
Did You Ever Have One of Those Days   Cahn
Diddle-daddle   Duke; Rome
Did-ee Did-ee Do Right By You?   Clare
Dig, Dig, Dig, Dig for Your Supper   Gordon; Revel; Warren
Disordered Dream, A   Johnson, James P.
Dixieland Daddy   Merrill
Do You Know a Better Way to Make a Living   Rome
Don't Be Far Away   Silver
Don't Be too Big for Your Britches   Robison
Don't Bring Your Heartaches to Me   David, Mack;
        Livingston, Jerry
Don't Care — For the Heck of It   Carmichael; Mercer
Don't Misunderstand   Sigman
Don't Rock the Boat, Dear   Arlen; Blane
Don't Run Mirandy   Harburg; Lane
Don't Say You Care Unless You Really Do   Hoffman
Don't Stay Away Too Long   Stept
Don't Take Away My Jesus   Friml
Don't Talk   Fields
Don't Wanna Write About the South   Rome
Doughnut Song, The   Merrill
Down on Wabash Avenue   Gordon; Myrow
Dream By Dream   Hoffman
Dream Is a Wish Your Heart Makes, A   David, Mack;
        Hoffman; Livingston, Jerry
Dream Peddler's Serenade, The   Mercer
Dream Weaver   Fain
Dreamer Who Gets Things Done, The   Burke; Van Heusen
Dreamin' Is My Business   David, Mack; Livingston, Jerry
Dreams Ago   Bullock
Drop Another Bean in the Bucket Joe   DePaul; Raye
Duet   Sigman
Early American   Burke; Van Heusen
Early Morning Song, The   Fain
East River Drive   Styne
Eeny Meany Miney But What Became of Mo   Kalmar
Enchanted April   DePaul; Raye
Ephraham the Bunny   Coots; Egan
Etiquette   Freed, Arthur; Warren
(The) Everlasting Arms   Webster
Everybody Knows You By Your First Name Baby   Russell
Everything Isn't Sunshine and Roses   Davis
Ev'rybody Clap Hands   Hoffman
Face in the Crowd, A   Heyman; Young, Victor
Fall in Love   Gordon; Revel; Warren
Fancy Free   Arlen; Mercer
Fancy Pants   Evans; Livingston, Jay
Feel of the Land, The   Bullock; Spina

Fiddle and Gittar Band, The   Evans; Livingston, Jay
Fiddle-Faddle   Parish
Fifth Avenue   Gordon; Warren
Fight, Fight for Southern   Bullock; Spina
Fighter Waltz, The   David, Mack; Livingston, Jerry
Five Little Miles from San Berdoo   Coslow
Flower Song, The   Heyman; Young, Victor
Flying Dutchman, Ahoy, Ahoy, Ahoy, The   Drake
Follow the Fold   Loesser
For Alma Mater   Bullock; Spina
For Instance   Woods
For the Want of a Nail   Webster
Francie   Styne
Francis (The Talking Mule)   Mills
Frank the Bank   Caesar
Free   Berlin
French with Tears   Rome
Friendly Islands, The   Arlen; Blane
Friendly Night   Razaf
Friendly Star   Gordon; Revel; Warren
From This Day On   Bullock
From This Moment On   Porter
Frosty Mornin'   Caesar; Lerner, Sammy
Fugue for Tinhorns   Loesser
Gee, It's Gonna Be Wonderful   Evans; Livingston, Jay
Genieve   Hoffman
Get a Model   Johnson, J. Rosamond
Get Me One of Those   David, Hal
Getting Dressed   Loesser
Ghost at Gettysburg   Loesser; Spina
Gimme the Shimmy   Rome
Girl of My Heart (Is You Mother Dear), The   Coots
Girl with a Flame, A   Fields
Girl with the Maracas, The   Adamson; McHugh
Girl with the Yellow Hair, The   Dietz
Give It All You've Got   Evans; Livingston, Jay
Give Me One of Those Old Hellos   Caesar
Give the Little Girl a Great Big Hand   Evans; Livingston, Jay
Gloria, Get Busy   Johnson, J. Rosamond
Go to Sleep, Go to Sleep, Go to Sleep   Cahn
God Has His Hands on My Shoulders   Coots
God Is My Friend   Coots
Good and Welfare Polka   Russell
Good Morning, Morning Glory   Adamson; McHugh
Good Night, Good Morning   Burke; Van Heusen
Got a Hula Hula Honey   Baer
Got What It Takes   Stept
Gravy Train   Carroll
Group Voice   Young, Victor
Guys and Dolls   Loesser
Guys and Dolls Preamble   Loesser
Hail, Hail, Hail   Porter
Hallelujah Round-Up   Razaf
Hallowe'en   Arlen; Blane
Hammock on the Porch   Dietz; Schwartz, Arthur
Hand-Shakin' Day   Robison
Happy Little Verse and Chorus   Arlen; Blane
Happy Train, The   Koehler; Stept
Harbor of Home Sweet Home   Webster
Hark to the Song of the Night   Porter
Have of Me   Heyman; Young, Victor
Have You Written Any Good Books Lately   Mercer
Have Yourself Some Fun   Stept
He Didn't Have the Know How No-How   Mercer
He Walks with Me   Romberg

He Was My Partner   Oakland
He Will Tonight   Fields
Heaven Is Where You Are   Hoffman
Here Comes Talullah   Akst; Davis
Here in Tahiti We Make Love   Freed, Arthur; Warren
Here's to the Ladies   Brooks
Here's to Us   Koehler; Stept
He's a Demon, He's a Devil, He's a Doll   Raye; Spina
He's Dead but He Won't Lie Down   Carmichael; Mercer
Hey You in the Looking Glass   Silver
High on the List   Burke; Van Heusen
Hokey Pokey Polka, The   Adamson; McHugh
Hold Me Just a Little Longer, Daddy   Baer
Hold My Hand   Lawrence
Hold Out Your Hand to an Old Friend (Who Holds Out a Heart to You)   Coots
Holiday Cruise   Evans; Livingston, Jay
Home Cooking   Evans; Livingston, Jay
Home Is a Little Bit of Heaven   Stept
Homing Pigeon, Fly Away, Fly Away Back Home   Drake
Honest Abe   Bullock
Honey Babe   Blake
Honey, Won't You Honeymoon with Me   Hoffman
Hoop-de-doo   Loesser
Hop Hop Hop Along to Bed   Silver
Hopalong Cassidy March   Gilbert
Hoppy, Topper and Me   Brown, Nacio Herb; Gilbert
Horse Sense   David, Mack
Horse Told Me, The   Burke; Van Heusen
Horse-Sense   Hoffman; Livingston, Jerry
Hostess with the Mostes' on the Ball, The   Berlin
House of Singing Bamboo   Freed, Arthur; Warren
Howdy Neighbor, Happy Harvest   Gordon; Revel; Warren
Huckleberry Pie   Adamson; McHugh
Hush, Hush, Hush   Porter
I Am Loved   Porter
I Believe in Santa Claus   David, Hal
I Came All the Way from Texas   Adamson; McHugh
I Can Hear It Now   Rome
I Can't Sleep   Adams; Strouse
I Challenge You   Cahn
I Didn't Expect It from You   Clare
I Do Better Up in the Mountains than I Do Down By the Sea   Stept
I Do, I Do, I Do   Razaf
I Don't Know Where My Next Kiss Is Coming From   McHugh
I Don't Need a Psychiatrist   Johnson, J. Rosamond
I Dream of a Past Love (inst.)   Revel
I Feel Sorry for You   David, Hal
I Got Beauty   Porter
I Got No Talent   Spina
I Got Tookin By a Good Good Lookin Man   Spina
I Guess It Was You All the Time   Carmichael; Mercer
I Hate a Parade   Rome
I Jupiter, I Rex   Porter
I Kissed My Heart Goodbye   Adamson; McHugh
I Kissed My Heart Goodnight   Washington
I Knew You Well   Duke; Rome
I Know What You're Thinkin' (But You're Wrong)   Hoffman
I Like It Here   Fields
I Lost My Heart At the Ball   David, Mack; Hoffman; Livingston, Jerry
I Love a Genius   Myrow
I Love a New Yorker   Arlen; Blane

I Love Lydia   Evans; Livingston, Jay

I Love You Dear and What's More Who Wouldn't   Meyer

I Met My Waterloo (When I Met Lulu)   Coots; Lewis

I Never Had It So Good   Oakland

I Never Knew I Loved You   Yellen

I Only Want to Love You   Spina

I Ought to Know More About You   Young, Victor

I Oughta Know More About You   Heyman

I Saw You Smile   Harbach

I Should Have Quit When I Was Ahead   Evans; Livingston, Jay

I Sleep Easier Now   Porter

I Think You've Got Something There   Raye

I Told My Heart   Cahn

I Want You As You Are   Johnson, J. Rosamond

I Was Waiting for You   Evans; Livingston, Jay

I Wish, I Wish I Had a Picture of You   Merrill

I Wish that Kisses Grew on Trees   Merrill

I'd Like to Hitch a Ride with Santa Claus   Burke; Van Heusen

If He's Good Enough to Fight For His Country   Yellen

If I Can't Have You All for Myself (Then I Don't Want You At All)   Davis

If I Could Say to You in English (What I Think of You in French)   Cahn

If I Could Write a Love Song   Friend

(What Would I Do) If I Didn't Have You   Spina

If I Were a Bell   Loesser

If My Prayers Are Answered   Coots

If You but Knew   Silver

If You Can't Get a Drum with a Boom-Boom-Boom (Get a Tuba with an Oom-Pah-Pah)   David, Hal

If You Can't Get a Girl in the Summertime   Davis; Silver

If You Don't Love   Webster

If You Feel Like Singing, Sing   Gordon; Revel; Warren

If You Had Only Remembered   Friend

If You Never Get the One You Want   Bryan

If You Saw What I Saw in Nassau   Hoffman

If You Should Leave Me   Stept

If You Smile at the Sun (The Sun Will Smile at You)   Hoffman

I'll Always Love You (Querida Mia)   Evans; Livingston, Jay

I'll Be There with Bells On   Hoffman

I'll Forgive Anything but a Lie   Merrill

I'll Know   Loesser

I'll Never Learn   Fields

I'll Never Let My Heart Get Out of Hand   Burke; Van Heusen

I'll Never Love You   Cahn

I'll Never See You Again   Fields

I'll See You After Church on Sunday Mornin'   Wrubel

I'll Tell a Policeman on You   David, Mack; Livingston, Jerry

Illinois Republican, An   Bullock

I'm Bashful   Merrill

I'm Breakin' My Back (Puttin' Up a Front for You)   Wrubel

I'm Cuckoo-Crazy 'Bout You   Baer

I'm from Dalius, Texas   Carmichael

I'm Goin' 'Round in Circles   Spina

I'm Gonna Ask the Moon a Little Favor   Parish

I'm Gonna Live Till I Die   Hoffman

I'm Gonna Make a Fool Out of April   Heyman; Young, Victor

I'm Happy to Know You're Happy   Hoffman

I'm in Love with You   DePaul

I'm in the Middle of a Muddle   David, Mack; Hoffman; Livingston, Jerry

I'm Jealous of Your Time   Johnson, J. Rosamond

I'm Left with an Old Love Song   Meyer

I'm Rolling in Rainbows   Burke; Van Heusen

I'm Scared   Fields

I'm Takin' a Shine to You   Merrill

In Idyllwild (An American Anthem)   Willson

In One Little Lifetime   Brown, Lew; Lewis

In the City of the Angels   Adamson; McHugh

In the Cool, Cool, Cool of the Evening   Carmichael; Mercer

Indian Country   Spina

Indian on the Nickel, The   Ruby

Indian Talk   Baer; Leslie

International Melody, The   McHugh

It Feels Like Forever   Loesser

It's a Big, Big, Big, Big Day   Spina

It's a Long Time Till Tomorrow   Bullock

It's a Lovely Day Today   Berlin

It's a Real Real Purty   David, Hal

It's Bigger than Both of Us   Fain

It's Catching   Burke; Van Heusen

It's Deductible   Arlen; Blane

It's Raining Sundrops   Cahn; Styne

It's So Nice to Have a Man Around the House   Spina

It's Takes a Lot of Raindrops (To Grow a Little Rose)   Drake

It's Tough to Be Tattooed with Tillie (When You Want to Get Married to May)   Woods

I've Got that Old Christmas Feeling (In My Heart Tonight)   Coots

I've Got to Get Out of the Habit   Burke; Van Heusen

I've Never Been in Love Before   Loesser

I've Shed a Hundred Tears   Brooks

Jazz Legato   Parish

Jazz Pizzicato   Parish

Je T'Aime — I Love You   Duke; Rome

Jing-a-ling Jing-a-ling   Raye

Joe, Jack, Moe and Mack   Gordon; Myrow

Johannesburg   Magidson; Oakland

Johnny Cake   Fields

Jug of Jive, a Loaf of Bread and Thou, A   Razaf

Jumpin' Jubilee   Harburg; Lane

Just a Little White House   Rome

Just in Case We Have to Say Goodbye Again   Cahn; Fain; Kahal

Just One of the Boys   Styne

Just the Way You Are (I Like My Eggs Over Easy)   Freed, Ralph

Keep Off the Grass   DePaul; Raye

King Cotton   Robison

Kiss in a Cab, A   Blake

Kiss Me Tonight, and Forever   Caesar

Kiss Me with Your Eyes   Silver

Kisses and Tears   Styne

K-K-K-Kiss Me A-Ga-Ga-Gain   DePaul; Raye

La Lee, La Loo, La Laa   David, Hal

Land of Make Believe, The   Razaf

Laughing at Love   Evans; Livingston, Jay

Le Dimanche Est a Nous   Brooks

Leaving Town   Merrill

Lecon le Danse   Evans; Livingston, Jay

Let Me Down Easy   Brown, Lew; Henderson

Let Me Put It This Way   Evans; Livingston, Jay

Let Me Tell You 'Bout Louisa   Hoffman

Let's Fly Away   Adams; Strouse

Let's Go Shopping   Friend
Let's Have a Party   Bullock
Let's Live, Think, Talk America   Washington; Young, Victor
Let's Not Have Another Party   Cahn
Let's Play Post Office   Merrill
Let's Play (What's My Name)   Coots
Let's Stay Home Tonight   Stept
Lie, The   Evans; Livingston, Jay
Life Begins at Fourteen   Evans; Livingston, Jay
Life Is So Peculiar   Burke; Van Heusen
Life of Her Own, A   Webster
Lighthouse Keeper, The   Coots
Like a Lonely Raindrop   Fisher
Little Boy with the Big Horn   Friend
Little Indians (Happy-In-the-Heart)   Merrill
Little Johnny Chickadee   Coots
Little More Love in Our Heart, A   Hoffman
Little More Love in Our Hearts, A   Merrill
Little Old Cabin Door Mister Washington! Uncle
    George   Fields
Little Pete the Pirate   Coots
Little Sally One Shoe   Coots
Little Things Meant So Much to Me   Rome
Little Toy Town Parade   Friend
Live Hard, Work Hard, Love Hard   Arlen; Blane
Livingston and Evans' Melody   Evans
Lock, Stock and Barrel   Fain; Webster
Lonesome in the Saddle   Brooks
Long Ago Last Night   David, Hal
Long Before I Knew You   Cahn; Styne
Longing   Drake
Look in Your Eyes, The   Ruby
Look Me Over Once (Laughing Song)   Dietz
Lord Is a Trav'lin' Man, The   Webster
Love Is a Gambling Thing   Davis; Silver
Love Is a Masquerade   McHugh
Love Is Like an Elephant   Duke; Rome
Love Is What You Give to Loving   Johnson, J. Rosamond
Love, It Hurts So Good   Rome
Love Letter to Manhattan   Rome
Love Me, Love Me, Love Me   Coslow
Love Means Love   Sigman
Love that Man   Rome
Love You, Love You, Love You Till the Cows Come
    Home   Stept
Loveliest Night of the Year, The   Webster
Luck Be a Lady   Loesser
Lucky Level, The   Carmichael
Lucky People   Merrill
Made in Nantucket   Duke; Rome
Maggi   Coots
Magic Words of Honolulu Kana-Nuka-Wahyn-Iahn,
    The   Hoffman
Maiden Fair   Porter
Make Believe Land   Davis; Silver
Mam'selle   Friml
Man of the Hour   Koehler; Stept
(I've Got a) Manager in Heaven   Robison
Mandy Come Along   Howard, Joseph E.
Maple Leaf Rag   Russell; Styne
Marriage Waltz, The   Razaf
Marry the Man Today   Loesser
Marrying for Love   Berlin
Mary Ann   Carroll
May I Take Two Giant Steps   Drake

May I Tempt You with a Big Red Rosy Apple   Gordon;
    Myrow
May the Good Lord Bless You and Keep You   Willson
Me and My Imagination   Hoffman; Merrill
Me and My Teddy Bear   Coots
Me Myself and I   Webster
Meet Me at the Copa   Cahn
Melancholy Rhapsody   Cahn
Memories of Santa Lucia   Hoffman
Mem'ry Island   Gordon; Revel; Warren
Mercer's Melody   Mercer
Merry Little Christmas Elf, The   Sigman
Michael McInerny   Stept
Midsummer Night   Porter
(If I Linger with) Milady   Burke; Van Heusen
Military Polka, The   Cahn; Styne
Miss Annabell   Blake
Missus O'Malley and Mister Malone   Webster
Model Hasn't Changed, The   Rome
Mommy, Daddy   Razaf
Mona Lisa   Evans; Livingston, Jay
Monsieur   Brooks
Moon in the Mulberry Tree   Mercer
Moonlight Troubadour, The   David, Hal
Moonlight Valse (inst.), The   Romberg
More I Cannot Wish You   Loesser
Mound City Blue Boys from Ol' St. Lou   Robison
Mr. Moon Man   Monaco
Mr. Music   Burke; Van Heusen
Mrs. Sally Adams   Berlin
Music in My Heart   Mills
Music on the Water   Freed, Arthur; Warren
My Baby's Baby Blue Eyes   Akst; Davis
My Cadill-liddle-ol-lac   Carmichael; Mercer
My Christmas Song for You   Carmichael; Webster
My Dad's Violin   Howard, Joseph E.
My Destiny   David, Mack; Livingston, Jerry
My Faith   Razaf
My Fence Around Your Heart   Johnson, J. Rosamond
My First Love Letter   Davis; Silver
My Gypsy Heart   DePaul; Raye
My Heart Cries for You   Sigman
My Heart Decided   Duke; Rome
My Heart Follows My Eyes   Carroll
My Little Racket   Koehler; Stept
My Lost Melody   Rome
My Love   Brooks
My Most Delectable Dream   Evans; Livingston, Jay
My Mother's Sabbath Candles   Yellen
My, My, My   Carroll
My Navajo (An Indian Lament)   Bryan
My Scandinavian Baby   Merrill
My Silent Merry Xmas to You   Wrubel
My Silhouette Sweetheart   Coots
My Time of Day   Loesser
My Town   Hoffman
My Troubles Float Away Like Falling Leaves (inst.)   Revel
My Wag-a-long, Tag-a-long Too   Woods
Narrative for Orchestra (inst.)   Strouse
Nation of the People (By the People, For the People),
    The   Bryan
National Love Song (Sweethearts Are We), A   Blake; Sissle
Navy Gets the Gravy, but the Army Gets the Beans,
    The   David, Mack; Livingston, Jerry
Never in My Wildest Dreams   Gordon; Warren

New Casanova, A   Koehler; Stept
New York Sketches (inst.)   Coleman
Night, the Stars, the Wind, the Sea, The   Merrill
Nightfall   Brooks; Washington; Young, Victor
Nineteen Hundred and Fifty   Coots
No Lover   Porter
No One but You   Sigman
No Other Love   Russell
No Sad Songs for Me   Akst
Nobody Ever Said No to Nora   Ruby
Nobody's Chasing Me   Porter
Nonchalant   Cahn
Nothin' for Nothin'   Fields
Nothing Is Too Good   Duke; Rome
Now I Know   Brooks
Now that You Know (Our Song, Mi Cancion)   Caesar
O Queen of Victory   Spina
Oh, It Must Be Fun   Porter
Oh, My Darlin' — Keep Rememberin'   Brown, Lew; Lewis
Oh Sing Sweet Nightingale   David, Mack; Hoffman;
     Livingston, Jerry
Ol' Kris Kringle   McHugh
Old Overcoat   Carroll
Oldest Established, The   Loesser
On a Day Like This   Merrill
On a Three Party Line   David, Hal
On the Outgoing Tide   Brown, Lew
On the Rue de la Paix in Paree   Stept
Once More the Blue and White   Burke; Van Heusen
Once Upon a Time Today   Berlin
One Finger Melody, The   Hoffman
One Last Fling   Evans; Livingston, Jay
One Man Woman   Brooks
One! Two! Three!   Webster
One-Sided Love   Parish
Only a Mother Could Love You   Sigman
Oop Sah-sah   Brown, Lew; Lewis
Open the Window in Your Heart (And Let the Lovelight
     Come In)   Coots
Or   Robison
Order of the Garter, The   Evans; Livingston, Jay
Our Happy Home   Sigman
Our Lady of Fatima   Lewis
Our Very Own   Young, Victor
Over the Garden Wall   Hoffman
Padre of San Jose   Silver
Paint Yourself a Rainbow   Sigman
Pals of the Pentagon   Rome
Paramount Don't Want Me Blues, The   Evans; Livingston,
     Jay
Party Is Over, The   Webster
Patricia   Davis
Penguins on Parade   Razaf
Peter Please   Caesar
Petty Girl, The   Arlen; Mercer
Pianola   Monaco
Pin a Rose on the Christmas Tree   Baer; Leslie
Pincus et Cie   Duke; Rome
Plantation in Philadelphia   Fields
Please Believe Me   Merrill
Plowboy Wants to Go Home, A   David, Mack; Livingston,
     Jerry
(I've Got a) Pocketful of Dreams   Rome
Poco Loco in the Coco   Hoffman
Poison Ivories   Akst

Poker-Polka, The   Heyman; Young, Victor
Pokey Little Puppy   Friend
Polly Polite   Caesar
Port of Missing Men   Oakland; Russell
Portland Fancy   Gordon; Warren
Practical Pete   Razaf
Prayer of Saint Francis of Assisi, A   Stept
Prologue   Porter
Promenade   Parish
Propinquity   Webster
P's and Q's   Dietz
Pudgy the Whistling Piggy   Drake
Pullman Porter and the Travelin' Man, The   Stept
Pumpernickel   Coslow
Queenie, the Quick Change Artist   Carmichael; Mercer
Quit While You're Ahead   Merrill
R and H Robin Hood Jingle (Robin Hood Beer Song)   Baer
Raga-Daga-Day   David, Mack; Hoffman; Livingston, Jerry
Readin' for a Weddin'   Bullock
Reckon I'm in Love   Livingston, Jerry
Red Cheeks and White Whiskers   Hoffman; Merrill
Redecorate   Bullock
Remember Me in Your Dreams   David, Hal
Remembering Time   Yellen
Remembering Your Lips (inst.)   Revel
Riddle, The   Bullock
Right About Now   Myrow
River Chanty   Weill
River of Smoke   Sigman
River, River   Oakland; Russell
Riviera   Evans; Livingston, Jay
Roaring Twenties Strike Up, The   Rome
Roly Poly Platypus   Friend
Rose Is a Rose, A   Rome
Roseanna   Loesser
Sailor Sails the Sea, A   Brooks
Sam the Slam   Caesar
Same Old Story, The   Brooks
Sandy and Suzie Squirrel   Coots
Santa Has His Eye on You   Razaf
Saturday Night Excursion Boat   Friend
Say It Soft, Say It Low   Parish
Says So Here   Gordon; Myrow
Scandal in Toyland   Bryan
Scat Mr. Crow!   Razaf
Sea of the Moon, The   Freed, Arthur; Warren
Second Hand Romance   Spina
Second Sunday in June, The   Friend
Seems Like Yesterday   Stept
Sense of Humor   Hoffman
Serenata   Parish
Shadow Time   Webster
Shango   Loesser
She Does a Little Business on the Side   Silver
She's Exciting   Fields
Shirley Early, Early Shirley   Caesar
Shivk-a-ree   Robison
Show Must Go On, The   Ager; Davis
Silent Movie Rag, The   Sigman
Sinatra Theme (inst.)   Young, Victor
Sing Me an Old Fashioned Song   Spina
Singing in the Sun   Freed, Arthur; Warren
Sit Down, You're Rockin' the Boat   Loesser
Six Foot of Hickory   Spina
Sleigh Ride   Parish

Small Town Boy with Big Town Dreams, A   David, Hal
Snow Flower   Merrill
Snowman, The   Burke; Van Heusen
So Deep My Love   Drake
So Long Sally   Merrill
So This Is Love   David, Mack; Hoffman; Livingston, Jerry
Some Days You Are Lonely (Czardas)   Dietz
Some Says There Just Ain't No Fish   Russell; Sigman
Someone's Gonna Get Kissed   Friend
Someplace on Anywhere Road   Burke; Van Heusen
Something to Dance About   Berlin
Somewhere In a Corner of Your Heart   Burke; Van Heusen
Somewhere on the Island of Somewhere   Silver
Song for an Autumn Afternoon   Wrubel
Song of Delilah, The   Young, Victor
Song of Our Love   Duke; Rome
Song of the Owl and the Duck, The   Friend
Sparkling Drink   Johnson, James P.
Sparrow in the Tree Top   Merrill
'Spesh'lly You   DePaul; Raye
Spider and the Fly   Koehler; Stept
Sta Di Va   Cahn
Stars and Stripes Forever   Russell
Stay with the Happy People   Styne
Stop Your Gamlin'   Robison
Story in Variety, The   Burke; Van Heusen
Story of Kitty, The   Bullock
Stowaway   Sigman
Straddlin' the Fence   Friend
Stranger in the City   Alter
Stranger in the Mirror, The   Kahal
Stranger in the Night   Gordon
Strike a Happy Medium   David, Hal
Struttin' with Some Barbecue   Raye
Sue Me   Loesser
Sugar Throat Burns   Ruby
Summer Dresses   Rome
Sunday in the Valley   Davis; Silver
Sunny Sue   Silver
Sunset Boulevard   Davis; Evans; Livingston, Jay; Silver
Sunshine Cake   Burke; Van Heusen
Sure I Are, Ev'rybody Do   Hoffman; Merrill
(We've Got a) Sure Thing   Burke; Van Heusen
Susie 'Scuse Me   Caesar
Suzanne   Ruby
Sweetest Day, The   Gilbert
Sweetheart Semicolon   Heyman; Young, Victor
Tahiti   Coots; Freed, Arthur; Warren
Take Back Your Mink   Loesser
Take Off the Coat   Rome
Take Teena Too   Sigman
Talk Fast My Heart Talk Fast   DePaul; Raye
Talkin' to the River   David, Hal
Talking Tree, The   Drake
Tall in the Saddle   Adamson; McHugh
Tall Pines of Oregon   Carroll
Tall Slender Weaver   Brooks
Tame Me   Adams; Strouse
Tapatina, The   Hoffman
T.C. Roundup Time   Evans; Livingston, Jay
Tee Hee Hee, You Can't Scare Me   David, Mack; Hoffman; Livingston, Jerry
Tee-ka Tee-ka Tah   David, Hal
Tell Me   Oakland
10,400 and 32 Sheep   Cahn; Styne

Teresa   David, Mack; Livingston, Jerry
Texaco Opening   Cahn; Styne
Thank You, Mrs. Butterfield   Bullock
Thanks for Your Kisses but Where Is Your Heart   Merrill
That Christmas Feeling   Burke; Van Heusen
That Great Rodeo in the Sky   Stept
That Honky Tonk Melody   Spina
That Real Sunday Feeling   Harburg; Lane
(Be Hap-Hap-Happy My Love) That We Is Me and You   Merrill
That's a Man Everytime   Bullock
That's A-Plenty   Pollack
That's My Boy   Fain
That's My Fella   Fields
That's What I Told Him Last Night   Fields
(Which Came First) The Egg or the Chicken   Davis; Silver
(Dance to the Music of) The Ocarina   Berlin
Theme, The   Koehler; Stept
There   Silver
There Is No Christmas Like a Home Christmas   Sigman
There Must Be Somebody for Me   Coots
There Must Be Somethin' Better than Love   Fields
There You Are Again   Duke; Rome
There's a Brighter Day on the Way   Davis; Silver
There's a Building Going Up   Fain; Webster
There's a City on a Hill By the Sea   Merrill
There's Mutiny in Baby's Eyes Tonight   Stept
There's No Man Like a Snowman   Heyman; Young, Victor
There's Nothing Like It   Bullock
They Couldn't Compare to You   Porter
They Like Ike   Berlin
They Never Told Me   Duke; Rome
This Could Be Forever   Ruby
This Is a Tree   Burke; Van Heusen
This Is It   Willson
This Is the Finale   Cahn; Styne
This Is the Time (To Fall in Love)   Washington; Young, Victor
This Little Dream Was a Good Little Dream   David, Hal
This Room Is My Castle of Quiet (inst.)   Revel
This They Call Love   Cahn
This Time Next Year   Weill
Three Cornered Tune   Loesser
Three Dollars and Ninety-Eight Cents   Drake
Three Little Models from an Agency   Johnson, J. Rosamond
Thunder in My Heart   Drake
Ticket to Tomahawk (On the Colorado Trail), A   Gordon; Warren
Tick-Tock   Razaf
Tiddley Winks   Coots
Time Alone (Can Heal a Broken Heart)   Robison
Tin Horn   Bullock
Tin Pan Alley Rag, The   Rome
Tina-Lina, The   Cahn
To Get Us All Together   Adams; Strouse
To Hell with Everyone but Us   Porter
To Me You're a Song   Merrill
Toast of New Orleans, The   Cahn
Tommy Thank You   Caesar
Tonda Wanda Hoy   David, Mack; Livingston, Jerry
Tonight   Coots
Tonight I Love You More   Porter
Too Many Hearts   Webster
Toscanini, Tschaikowsky and Me   Spina

Toys Gave a Party for Poppa Santa Claus, The   Burke; Van Heusen
Travelin' Light   Loesser
Trolleys of Old Broadway, The   Howard, Joseph E.
Trousers   Johnson, J. Rosamond
Trumpet Man   DePaul; Raye
Try Love   Davis
Try Your Luck   Arlen; Mercer
Tune for Humming, A   Loesser
Twiddle-Dee the Clown   Coots
Two Brothers   Washington
Two Little Ex-WACS   Johnson, J. Rosamond
Tzena, Tzena, Tzena, Tzena   Parish
Tzin-Tzun-Tzan   Lawrence; Sigman
Under the Pinewood Trees   Razaf
(Let Me Walk) Under Your Umbrella   Adams; Strouse
Unknown   Young, Victor
Unlucky Pierre   Duke; Rome
Until My Heart Says Goodbye   Bryan
Until Tonight   Heyman; Young, Victor
Use Your Imagination   Porter
Utterly Lovely   Blake
Venezia and Her Three Lovers   Heyman; Young, Victor
Violet of N.Y.U.   Parish
Violets and Violins (Mon Coeur Et unm Violon)   Lawrence
Violins from Nowhere   Fain; Magidson
Vision of Bernadette, The   Hoffman
Viva la Buck   Evans; Livingston, Jay
Viva la Duel   Evans; Livingston, Jay
Voting Blues   Rome
Waitin' at the Station   Spina
Waitin' for the Day   Razaf
Walter Walter Wallflower   Coots
Waltz   Bullock
Waltz Song, The   Friml
Washington Square Dance   Berlin
Wasn't I There?   Burke; Van Heusen
We Said Our Goodbyes Too Soon   Coots; Egan
Welcome to Lichtenburg   Berlin
We'll Only Be Lonely Apart   Merrill
We're On the Road to Athens   Porter
Whaler's Life, A   Duke; Rome
Whaler's Return, The   Duke; Rome
What a Day!   Bullock
What a Delightful   Fain; Webster
What a Man!   Arlen; Blane
What a Wonderful Way to Go Crazy   Adamson; McHugh
What Do You Think About Men?   Porter
What Is Wrong with Me   Blake
What Will Be Will Be   Hoffman
When   Rome
When I Grow Up   Friend
When It's Love   Duke; Rome
(The Angels Cry) When Sweethearts Tell a Lie   Merrill
When the Devil Played the Fiddle   Duke; Rome
When the Sheets Come Back from the Laundry   Bullock
When You're Crying on My Shoulder   Oakland
Whenever Night Falls   Friml; Harbach
Where, Oh Where?   Porter
Where Rainbows End   Ahlert
Where's the Little Darlin'   Brooks
Whistlin' Wind, The   Merrill
Whistling Song, The   Leslie; Schwartz, Jean
Who Done It?   Bullock
Who Stole the Jam   Bullock; Spina

Why Did I Send You Roses   DePaul; Raye
Why Do You Want to Hurt Me So?   Porter
Why Is Love So Crazy?   Freed, Arthur; Warren
Wilhelmina   Gordon; Myrow
Wind that Shakes the Barley, The   Webster
Winter Scene, A   Carroll
Wise Old Owl (Caw-Caw-Caw), The   Robison
With These Hands   Davis; Silver
Woman in the Shoe   Koehler; Stept
Woman Likes to Be Told, A   Adamson; Carmichael
Woman Needs So Little, A   Spina
Wondering Who   Evans; Livingston, Jay
Work Song (Cinderella Work Song), The   David, Mack; Livingston, Jerry
World of Strangers, A   Fain; Webster
Wouldn't It Be Funny?   Burke; Van Heusen
Ye'sm Lord   Evans; Livingston, Jay
You Above All   Webster
You After All These Years   Duke; Rome
You and I   Dietz
You and Your Beautiful Eyes   David, Mack; Livingston, Jerry
You Appeal to Me   Bullock
You Are My Love   Friend
You Bother Me   Heyman; Spina
You Don't Have to Be a Baby to Cry   Merrill
You Don't Have to Drop a Heart to Break It   Coots
You Don't Know How Big Your Heart Is Till It Starts Breaking   David, Mack; Meyer
You Don't Remind Me   Porter
You Fool You   Hoffman
You Get Me All A-Dither With Your Zither   Baer
You Kissed Me   Fields
You Look Like Someone I Used to Know   Spina
You Love Me   Cahn; Styne
You Missed the Boat   Friend
You Said No Yesterday, Won't You Say Yes Today?   Akst
You Spoke, I Never Heard a Word   Blake
You Waited Too Long   Coots
You, Wonderful You   Brooks; Warren
You'll Never Get Anyone to Love You (The Way that I'm Loving You Tonight)   Coots
You'll Never Know What Hit You (When It's Love)   Rome
Your Honor   Spina
Your Soft Hand on My Brow (inst.)   Revel
You're Getting a Good Girl   Friend
(I Wonder Why) You're Just in Love   Berlin
You're My Silvery Symphony   Blake
You're Not in My Arms Tonight   Washington; Young, Victor
You're Nowhere Until You're Home   Raye
You're Wonderful   Evans; Livingston, Jay; Young, Victor
You've Got Me Wrapped Around Your Little Finger   Coslow
You've Gotta Make Up Your Mind   Monaco
You've Never Been Loved   Stept
Zing Zing-Zoom Zoom   Romberg

1951

(Ev'ry Day Is Like) A Day in Maytime   Robin; Styne
(It's Gonna Be) A Long, Long Winter   Styne
Across the River from Sing Sing   Martin
Ah Ah Ah Ah Baby   Fain
Alice in Wonderland   Fain
All for Him   Lerner, Alan Jay; Loewe
All in the Golden Afternoon   Fain
All Together   Davis

All-Army Team, The   Stept
Allegheny Fiddler (Fiddle-Didle-Do)   Drake
Ambiguous Means I Love You   Mercer
America, Here's Looking at You   Caesar
And I Was Kissing You   Spina; Webster
And There You Are   Gordon
Andiamo   Arlen; Fields
Anne of the Indies   Lerner, Sammy
Another Autumn   Lerner, Alan Jay; Loewe
Another Human Being of the Opposite Sex   Burke; Van
     Heusen
Aphrodesia   Myrow
Arabian for 'Get Happy'   Fain; Harburg
Araminta to Herself   Lawrence
Are You Just a Beautiful Dream   Robin; Styne
Ask Me! Because I'm So in Love   Rome
Asparagus Is Served   Lane; Lerner, Alan Jay
Attitude of Doin' Right, The   Carmichael
Avenida De La Rosa   Russell
Babbit the Rabbit   Coots
Baby Doll   Mercer; Warren
Baby, You'll Never Be Sorry   Robin; Styne
Bachelor Dinner Song   Mercer; Warren
Baltimore and Ohio   Magidson; Sigman
Barley 'n' Beans   David, Hal
Be My Guest   Mercer
Be Sure, My Heart, Be Sure   Drake
Beautiful Madness   David, Mack
Beautiful Senorita   Revel
Beautiful Soup   DePaul; Raye
Beccha, Reecha La-ree-a-la   Hoffman; Merrill
Beg, Steal or Borrow   Lawrence
Beggar in Love, A   Merrill
Belle, Belle, My Liberty Belle   Merrill
Betting on a Man   Robin; Styne
Beware the Jabberwock   DePaul; Raye
Beyond the Laughing Sky   Fain
B.G. Bigelow, Inc.   Fain; Harburg
Big Chief Hole in the Ground   Robin; Styne
Big Sister Blues   Russell
Bit Player Polka   Fain; Webster
Bless All the Beautiful Girls   Davis
Bless Your Heart   Mercer
Blue Plate Special   Burke
Bohemian Lullaby   Revel
Bon Soir (Gigi)   Adamson
Bonne Nuit (Good Night)   Evans; Livingston, Jay
Bride Wore Something Old, The   Fields; Schwartz, Arthur
Bride's Wedding Day Song (Thank You Mr. Currier, Thank
     You Mr. Ives), A   Mercer; Warren
Brownstone Front   Young, Victor
Business in Missouri   Sigman
But I Love You, My Darlin'   David, Hal
Buzz, Buzz, Buzz   Cahn
By the Light of the Campfire Glow   Brown, Nacio Herb;
     Gilbert
California Moon   Lerner, Sammy
Call on Your Neighbor   Fields; Schwartz, Arthur
Camel with the Wrinkled Knees, The   Coots
Carino Mio   Lerner, Alan Jay; Loewe
Carnation Time   Washington; Young, Victor
Castle Rock   Drake
Catch Our Act at the Met (Vaudeville Ain't Dead)   Comden
     and Green; Styne
Caucus Race, The   Fain

Caught in the Rain   De Lange
Chances Are   David, Hal
Chante Moi   David, Mack
Chapel of the Roses   Baer
Cherie   Revel
Cherry Pink and Apple Blossom White   David, Mack
Chesapeake and Ohio, The   Magidson; Sigman
Chimney Corner Dream   Mercer
Choo Choo Song   David, Hal
Choose Your Partner   Lawrence
Choy-Choy-Hoy-Toy (Ch-Boom, Ch-Bah)   Drake
Christine the Christmas Tree   Drake
Christmas Song   Fain; Harburg
Ciribiribin on the Mandolin   Hoffman
Civic Improvement   Fain; Webster
Closer You Are, The   Robin; Styne
Cloudy   Sigman
Clown, The   Comden and Green; Styne
Coffee Cocoa Tea   Hoffman
Cold Hearted Woman   Hoffman; Merrill
Come Back Little Genie   Fain; Harburg
Connie's Pitch   Fields
Consternation   Fain; Harburg
Cool Off   Sigman
Cornie's Pitch   Warren
Country Boogie   Raye; Spina
(Where Did He Get Those) Crazy Red Shoes   DePaul; Raye
Cross of God, The   Coots
Crosswinds   Evans; Livingston, Jay
Curiosity   David, Mack; Hoffman; Livingston, Jerry
Dark Is the Night (C'est Fini)   Cahn
Darling, How Could You   David, Mack; Livingston, Jerry
Dear Daddy Long-Legs   Martin
Devotion   Brooks
Dimples and Cherry Cheeks   Oakland; Raye
Ding-Dong Blues   Koehler
Dingle-Dee   Coots
Dirty Pitchers, Dirty Books   Martin
Do I Love You   DePaul; Raye
Do My Mother a Favor   Davis
Do Your Moonlight Shopping Early   Oakland; Webster
Does It Belong to Me?   Ruby
Dog Is a Man's Best Friend, A   Mercer
Dolly Show Your Dimple   David, Hal
Domino   Raye
Don't Be Afraid   Fields; Schwartz, Arthur
Don't Call Me Darlin' My Darlin'   David, Mack; Hoffman
Don't Play that Song   Oakland; Raye
Don't Put Bananas on Bananas   Willson
Don't Stop   David, Mack; Livingston, Jerry
Dream Caravan   Fain
Dream Express   Rome
Drumstick Parade, The   Coots; Egan
Easter Sunday Morning   Drake
Echoing Mountains and Whisperin' Trees   Silver
Echoing Mountains and Whispering Trees   Davis
Ecstacy (inst.)   Young, Victor
Eh   Cahn
Elevator Song   Mercer
Enchanted Land   Cahn
Enchantment   Fain; Harburg
Esta Noche (Tonight)   Young, Victor
Evenings We Spent at Joe's, The   Stept
Everlasting   Comden and Green; Styne
Every Moment of My Life   Davis; Silver

Everybody's Falling in Love   Coots

Everything Has a Useness   David, Mack; Hoffman; Livingston, Jerry

Ev'ry Night at Seven   Lane; Lerner, Alan Jay

Ev'rybody Else   Brown, Lew; Lewis

Ev'rybody's Crazy But I'm All Right   DePaul; Raye

Fa La Nana Bambin   Evans; Livingston, Jay

False Opinion   Robison

Far Above Cayuga's Waters   Cahn

Farewell My Love   Wrubel

Farmers Market Hoe Down   Fain; Webster

Fickle-Hearted Fair Weather Gal   Hoffman

(I Wish We Were Sweethearts) Fifty Years Ago   Freed, Ralph; Hoffman

Fixin' for a Long Cold Winter   Lawrence

Flaggin' the Train to Tuscaloosa   David, Mack

Flahooley   Fain; Harburg

Foolish Little Rumors   Mills

For Practical Reasons   Cahn

Friendly Finance Company   Evans; Livingston, Jay

Fryin' that One Lonely Egg   Wrubel

Funny (Not Much)   Merrill

Gay Waltz, The   Davis

Gentle Carpenter of Bethlehem, The   Drake

Get a Horse   Fields; Schwartz, Arthur

Getting to Know You   Hammerstein; Rodgers

Ghost Town   Coots

Giddy-Ap! (Buggy Ride Song) (Chic a Chiquito)   Rome

Girl Named Mary and a Boy Named Bill, A   David, Mack; Livingston, Jerry

Girl of All Nations   Mercer

Girls We Never Did Wed, The   David, Hal

Give a Little Get a Little   Comden and Green; Styne

Gloria's Got a Glow   Merrill

Go, Go, Go, Go   David, Mack; Livingston, Jerry

Goin' Steady   Fields; Schwartz, Arthur

Gold Can Buy Anything (But Love)   Sherman

Golden Moment   Lawrence

Gonzaga Men   Burke; Van Heusen

Good Morning (Irish Theme) (inst.)   Young, Victor

Good Morning, Morning Glory   David, Hal

Good Neighbor Doctor, The   Robison

Good Night Now (My Dove)   Robison

Goodbye   Lawrence

Goodbye Darling, Hello Friend (C'est Fini)   Rome

Goodbye, Dear Friend   Lawrence

Goodbye for Just a While   Hoffman

Goodbye G.I. Al   Akst

Got Her Off My Hands but Can't Get Her Off My Mind   Lewis; Young, Joseph

Greatest Story Ever Told   (inst.), The   Young, Victor

Growing Pains   Fields; Schwartz, Arthur

Hail to MacCracken's   Mercer

Half a Photograph   Russell

Halloween Ballet (inst.)   Schwartz, Arthur

Hand Me Down that Can o' Beans   Lerner, Alan Jay; Loewe

Happiest Day of My Life, The   Lane; Lerner, Alan Jay

Happiness Is Where You Find It   Russell

Happy Birthday America   Cahn; Duke

Happy Days   Davis

Happy Hunting   Fain; Harburg

Happy Little Verse and Chorus   Fain; Gordon

Haul Away, My Lou   Evans; Livingston, Jay

Havin' a Ball   Mercer

He Had Refinement   Fields; Schwartz, Arthur

Heart in Hand   Lawrence

Heaven Help You (When You Fall in Love)   Fain; Webster

Heavenly Harvest   David, Hal

Heavy Bomber Song, The   Washington; Young, Victor

Helen of Troy   Hoffman

Hello, Hello, Hello   Martin

Hello, Young Lovers   Hammerstein; Rodgers

Here Come the Springtime (Ho-Dalee, Hi-Dalee, Hay)   Willson

Here Comes Love Again   Ruby

Here Ends the Rainbow (I Found My Love)   Burke

Here Pidgie Pidgie   Hoffman

Here She Comes Now (East River Hoedown)   Comden and Green; Styne

Here We Are Again   Drake

Here's to J. Spencer Gray   Coots

Here's to My Lady   Bloom; Mercer

Here's to Your Illusions   Fain; Harburg

He's Only Wonderful   Fain; Harburg

Hitsitty Hotsitty   Hoffman

Ho-Ho (Deedle-ee-di-di)   Merrill

Hold Me Sweetheart   Coots

Hold Me-Hold Me-Hold Me   Comden and Green; Styne

Holdin' Up the Parade   Merrill

Home Is Where the Heart Is   Coots

Honeychile   Spina

Hopalong Cassidy March   Brown, Nacio Herb

Hoppy and the Hopi Indians   Brown, Nacio Herb; Gilbert

Hoppy Wishes You a Happy Birthday   Brown, Nacio Herb; Gilbert

House and the Old Wisteria Tree, The   Silver

House Is a Home, A   David, Hal

How Can I Wait?   Lerner, Alan Jay; Loewe

How Could You Believe Me When I Said I Love You When You Know I've Been a Liar All My Life   Lane; Lerner, Alan Jay

How D'Ya Like Your Eggs in the Morning   Cahn

How Much More Can You Hurt Me   Davis; Silver

How Strange   Young, Victor

How Will He Know?   Comden and Green; Styne

Huckleberry Finn   Lane; Lerner, Alan Jay

Hundred Hills, A   Merrill

I Ain't Never Felt So Good Before   Lane; Lerner, Alan Jay

I Am Music   Revel

I Belong to You   Hoffman

I Can See You   Cahn

I Do! He Doesn't!   Lawrence

I Feel Like Dancing   Robin; Styne

I Fought Every Step of the Way   Mercer

I Get a Warm Feeling   Cahn

I Got Me a Baby   Lane; Lerner, Alan Jay

I Have Dreamed   Hammerstein; Rodgers

I Heard a Song   Freed, Ralph

I Just Can't Do Enough for You Baby   Fain; Gordon

I Just Telephone Upstairs   Lewis

I Left My Hat in Haiti   Lane; Lerner, Alan Jay

I Lie Awake and Dream   Parish

I Like It, I Like It   David, Mack; Livingston, Jerry

I Lost You   Martin

I Love Lucy   Adamson

I Love the Way You're Breaking My Heart   Alter

I Love to Beat the Big Bass Drum   Mercer; Warren

I Miss My Darling   Davis; Silver

I Only Meant   Martin

I Only Wanted to See If You Loved Me   Hoffman

I Promise   Wrubel
I Put My Money in Dreams (And Bet Them All on
   You)   Robison
I Refuse to Answer on the Ground That It May Intend to
   Incriminate Me (Do You Love Me)   Robison
I Remember You Love   Drake
I Said My Prayers Last Night   Coots
I See the Moon   Willson
I Should Have Told You Before   Cahn
I Still See Elisa   Lerner, Alan Jay; Loewe
I Talk to the Trees   Lerner, Alan Jay; Loewe
I Tried not to Love You (O Cara Diletta Del Cuore)   Mills
I Wanna Be a Dancin' Man   Mercer; Warren
I Wanna Be Good 'n' Bad   Martin
I Wanna Sing, I Wanna Laugh, I Wanna Love   Alter; Eliscu
I Want to Thank You   Baer
I Whistle a Happy Tune   Hammerstein; Rodgers
I Wind Up Taking a Fall   Mercer
I Wish I Were Somebody Else   Burke; Van Heusen
Ice Cream Baby   Russell
I'd Like to Take You Out Dreaming   Fields; Schwartz,
   Arthur
If I Were You   Coots
If Only There Were Something I Could Do   Sigman
If That Doesn't Do It!   Burke; Van Heusen
If You Hadn't But You Did   Comden and Green; Styne
If You Haven't Got a Sweetheart   Fields; Schwartz, Arthur
If You Turn Me Down   Sigman
If You'll Believe in Me   Hoffman; Livingston, Jerry
I'll Be There with Bells On   Freed, Ralph; Hoffman
I'll Buy You a Star   Fields; Schwartz, Arthur
I'll Meet You Down by the River   Lane; Lerner, Alan Jay
I'll Never Make a Frenchman Out of You   Martin
I'll Take Love   Friend
I'll Tell a Policeman on You   Evans; Livingston, Jay
I'll Wait for You by the River   Lane; Lerner, Alan Jay
I'm from Missouri   Lane; Lerner, Alan Jay
I'm Gonna Spread My Wings (And Fly a Little)   Coots
I'm Happy 'Cause I'm Lucky   Parish
I'm Late   Fain
I'm Like a New Broom   Fields; Schwartz, Arthur
I'm Not Giving You Up   Wrubel
I'm Odd   Fain
I'm on My Way   Lerner, Alan Jay; Loewe
I'm Saving Up To Buy a Saddle   Brown, Nacio Herb; Gilbert
I'm Sending You Roses   Merrill
I'm Waiting Just for You   Leigh
In a World of My Own   Fain
In Between   Lerner, Alan Jay; Loewe
In the Evening By the Fire   David, Hal
In the Eyes of Your Mother   Hoffman
In the Meantime   David, Mack
In the Red   Fain
In Times Like These   Fain; Harburg
Inner Office Scene   Fain; Harburg
Introduction to a Scotch Medley   Merrill
Iowa Fight Song   Willson
Is That My Prince?   Fields; Schwartz, Arthur
It Began in Yucatan   Robin; Styne
It Couldn't Happen to a Nicer Guy   Coots
It Couldn't Happen to Two Nicer People   Fields; Schwartz,
   Arthur
It Doesn't Cost a Dime to Dream   Evans; Livingston, Jay
It Isn't Any Trouble Just to S-M-I-L-E   Hoffman
It Isn't Easy   Cahn

It Will Always Be You   Oakland
It's a Hot Night in Alaska   Robin; Styne
It's a Man's World   Gordon; Myrow
It's a Priv'lege to Live in Brooklyn   Evans; Livingston, Jay
It's All in the Game   Sigman
It's Beginning to Look Like Christmas   Willson
It's Catching   Van Heusen
It's Dynamite   Fields; Warren
It's Easter Time   Willson
It's Raining (Why Must It Keep Raining)   Mills
It's You I Love   Wrubel
I've Been Kissed Before   Russell
I've Got that Lonesome Feeling   Hoffman
I've Got to Fall in Love Again   Burke; Van Heusen
Janette   Martin
January, February, March   Sigman
Japanese Girl Like 'Merican Boy (Too Much — Too
   Much)   Fain; Gordon
Johnny and the Puckwudgies   Lawrence
Johnny Ride the Sky   Lawrence
Joop Joop   Freed, Ralph; Hoffman
Jourdain the Would — Be Gentleman (Epilogue)   Drake
Jump, Little Chillun   Fain; Harburg
June, Why Did July to Me   Rome
Just a Little Bit More   Ruby
Just a Moment More   Evans; Livingston, Jay
Just Like Clingin' Roses on a Clingin' Vine   Davis; Silver
Just Once Around the Moon (And then Home)   Merrill
Just One Kiss   Washington; Young, Victor
Just When We're Falling in Love   Russell
Kip   Martin
Kiss and a Promise, A   Davis
Kissing Song, The   Oakland
Kit's Last Fight, The   Merrill
Lady Bug   Webster
Lady Love   Russell
Lament   Fain; Harburg
L'Amour Toujours (Tonight for Sure)   Cahn
Laugh   David, Hal
Laura Lee   Willson
Laurie Ann   Revel
Let Freedom Ring (The Freedom Song)   Willson
Let Go of My Heart   Robin; Styne
Let Me In   Merrill
Let Me Kiss Your Tears Away   Spina
Let Me Look at You   Arlen; Fields
Let the Worry Bird Worry for You   Robin; Styne
Let's Do Something New   Robin; Styne
Let's Gather 'Round the Parlor Piano   Adamson; McHugh
Let's Make Comparisons   Cahn
Letter (Dear John), The   Webster
Li'l Ol' You and Li'l Ol' Me   Robin; Styne
Lilac Tree, The   Revel
Lilacs in the Spring   Kalmar
Listen to Sheldon   Sigman
Little Boats of Barclona, The   Mercer
Little Child   Sigman
Little Dead-Eye Dick   Stept
Little Half Pint in a Ten Gallon Hat   Coots
Little Hiawatha   Silver
Little Hours Music, The   Willson
Little Montague the Mouse   Coots
Little Ol' State of Texas, The   Cahn
Little Rock Getaway   Sigman
Little Soda Fountain Luncheonette, A   Baer; Leslie

Littlest Angel's Christmas, The   Young, Victor
Lock the Barn Door   Mercer
London in July   Cahn; Duke
Lonesome Cup of Coffee (inst.), A   Spina
Lonesome Gal   Brooks
Long Ago in Mexico   Merrill
Long Live Tonight   Henderson; Kahal
Look in the Mirror   Silver
Look Who's Dancing   Fields; Schwartz, Arthur
Lorelei Brown   Fields; Schwartz, Arthur
Losing You   Yellen
Lotus Flower   Oakland; Raye
Louisville Lodge Meeting   Drake
Love   Coots
Love Is a Lovely Word   Fields; Warren
Love Is a Wonderful Thing   Ruby
Love Is Back in Business   Fain; Gordon
Love Is the Reason   Fields; Schwartz, Arthur
Love Laughs at King   Evans; Livingston, Jay
Love Made a Dreamer of Me   Coots; Egan
Love Me Now (Pou de Vous)   Adamson
Love Song to Ruth, A   Van Heusen
Love Story   Adams; Strouse
Love Waltz, The   Cahn
Love Will Come Tomorrow   Coots
Lovely Is the Evening   Webster
Lovely Weather for Ducks   Evans; Livingston, Jay
Lover's Waltz, The   Revel
Love's a Lovely Thing   Koehler
Lucky Little Penny   Davis
Lygia   Webster
Mademoiselle   Russell
Maine Will Remember the Maine   Lawrence
Make a Wish   Martin
Make the Man Love Me   Fields; Schwartz, Arthur
Man Never Marries a Wife, A   Lawrence
Man of the Year This Week, The   Mercer
March of Cards, The   Fain
Marines' Hymn, The   Adamson; McHugh
Masculinity   Lawrence
Mating Season, The   Evans; Livingston, Jay
Meany, Meany   Sigman
Meet Me After the Show   Robin; Styne
Meet Me at the College Bowl   Loesser
Meet Miss Blendo   Mercer
Merci Beaucoup   David, Mack; Livingston, Jerry
Mess Call March   (inst.)   Young, Victor
Military Life — The Jerk Song   Rome
Mill on the Floss, The   David, Mack; Livingston, Jerry
Mine   Romberg
Mine and Mine Alone   Russell; Spina
Mine 'til Monday   Fields; Schwartz, Arthur
Miracle of the Wheat, The   Drake
Miracle on Main Street   Alter
Mississippi Miss   Sigman
Mister Pessimist   DePaul; Raye
Misto Christofo Columbo   Evans; Livingston, Jay
Monkey Song   Carmichael
Monotonous Ain't It   Brooks
Moon June Spoon   Hoffman
More Love   Merrill
Motoraa Rahi   David, Mack
Movin'   Lerner, Alan Jay; Loewe
Mr. and Mrs. Nobody   Burke; Van Heusen
My Buick, My Love and I   Brooks

My Castle in the Sand   Blane
My Darlin' Man   Merrill
My Downfall   Russell; Spina
My Dream Affair   Cahn
My Egotism Is Hurtin' Me   Robison
My Home Is in My Shoes   Mercer
My Humble Heart   Drake
My Lord and Master   Hammerstein; Rodgers
My Love an' My Mule   Arlen; Fields
My Man Friday   Lawrence
My Mother's Wedding Dress   Bryan
(You Are) My One Love   Washington
My Resistance Is Low   Adamson; Carmichael
My Rosa   Hoffman
My Second Love   Heyman
My Truly, Truly Fair   Merrill
Native Son   Fain; Webster
Naughty but Nice   Mercer; Warren
Navy Blue (Make Way for Navy Blue), The   David, Mack;
    Livingston, Jerry
Never Before   David, Mack; Livingston, Jerry
New York (Let Me Sing)   Robin; Styne
Next Voice You Hear, The   Webster
Niccolina   Harbach; Kern
Night Was Designed for Music, The   Drake
No More Flahooleys!   Fain; Harburg
No Talent Joe   Robin; Styne
Nobody Understands Me   Mercer
Nocturne (inst.)   Young, Victor
Now and Forever   Hoffman
Now You Leave   Hammerstein; Rodgers
Oh, He Looked Like He Might Buy Wine   Cahn
Oh, What a Silly Little Song (C'est Chouette la
    Musique)   Rome
Oh Why Did I   Cahn
(You're) O.K. for TV   Mercer
Old Bar 20 Quartet, The   Brown, Nacio Herb; Gilbert
Old Calliope, The   David, Mack; Livingston, Jerry
Old Family Bible, The   Webster
Old Piano Copy, An   Robison
Old Soldiers Never Die   Spina
Old-Fashioned Glimmer in Your Eye, An   Lawrence
Oldies   Sigman
On the First Warm Day   Howard, Bart
On the Seventh Day He Rested   Fain; Webster
Once   Russell
One Desire   Hoffman
One I Need, The   Martin
One Is a Wanderer   Martin
One More You   Fields; Schwartz, Arthur
One, Two, Three, Make a Box   David, Mack
Only If You're in Love   Mercer
Ooh, What You Did (Eterno Ritornello)   Rome
Oops!   Mercer; Warren
Open Your Eyes   Lane; Lerner, Alan Jay
Operetta   Washington; Young, Victor
Our Little Gray Home (In the Red)   Fain; Webster
Over and Over   Martin
Oysters in July   Fields; Schwartz, Arthur
Painting the Roses Red   Fain
Pank Upstairs, The   Robison
Paris   Cahn
Paris, France   Martin
Pa's Not Home, He's Upstairs   Wrubel
Patisserie, The   Martin

Patter of the Raindrops   Sigman

Payday   Fields; Schwartz, Arthur

Pelican Falls High   Robin; Styne

Penny   Ahlert; David, Mack

People Are Funny   DePaul; Raye

Picture You in Your Little White Apron and Me in My Blue
    Overalls   Coots

Pittsburgh Blue   Lane; Lerner, Alan Jay

Place in the Sun, A   Evans; Livingston, Jay

Please God   Coots

Prayer of a Nation, A   Davis; Silver

Pretty Your Face   Merrill

Prince of Peace, The   Russell

Put the Old Man Away   Robison

Puzzlement, A   Hammerstein; Rodgers

Quizas, Quizas, Quizas   Burke

Rainbow's End   Martin

Ram's Song   Cahn; Styne

Rendezvous   Evans; Livingston, Jay

Repello Wine   Young, Victor

Ridgeville Fight Song   Evans; Livingston, Jay

Ring Fell Under the Sofa   Fain

Rio (A Tribute to the World's Most Beautiful City)   Wrubel

Rockin' Chair Doctor, The   Robison

Rocky Mountain Moon   Mercer

Rollin' Stone, A   Russell

Roses and Champagne   Duke

Royal Bangkok Academy, The   Hammerstein; Rodgers

Rumson   Lerner, Alan Jay; Loewe

Sad Little Rain of China   Mercer

Sailor's Polka, The   David, Mack; Livingston, Jerry

Sale (inst.), The   Martin

Salt Water Tears   David, Hal

Same Ol' Me   Russell

Sans Souci   Mercer

Saturday Night in Davenport, Ioway   Merrill

Save the World   Hoffman

Say Nice Things About People   Hoffman; Merrill

Scene at Slave Market   Lane

Scheherazade's Interlude   Fain; Harburg

Schnapps   Fields; Warren

Screen Writer's Guild Song   Ruby

Seeing's Believing   Mercer; Warren

Send Her Some Flowers   Coots

Senorita Diaz   Mercer

Sensible Thing to Do, The   Lawrence

Shall I Tell You What I Think of You?   Hammerstein;
    Rodgers

Shall We Dance?   Hammerstein; Rodgers

She's Not in a Class with You   Martin

Show Train   Comden and Green; Styne

Sidewalk Shufflers, The   DePaul; Raye

Silver Bells   Evans; Livingston, Jay

Sing the Merry   Fain; Harburg

Slogan Song   Mercer

Smile Awhile   Lawrence

Snow in Central Park   Spina

So Far, So Good   Comden and Green; Styne

So Long for Now   David, Hal

So This Is the Copa   Cahn

Something for the Books   Fain; Webster

Something Wonderful   Hammerstein; Rodgers

Son of a Sailor, The   David, Hal

Song of the Enchanted Rope   Fain; Harburg

Song of the King   Hammerstein; Rodgers

Sorry 'Bout the Whole Darned Thing   Robison

Speak My Heart   Cahn

Speak Your Love   Raye; Spina

Spirit of Capsulanti   Fain; Harburg

Spring Came Early This Year   Russell

Spring Has Sprung   Fields; Schwartz, Arthur

Springtime Cometh, The   Fain; Harburg

Star-Gazing   Stept

Star-Spangled Hill of Home   Robison

Stay Awhile   David, Hal

Step to the Rear of the Car Please   Mercer

Stop the Flahooleys   Fain; Harburg

Stop the Music   Coslow

Strawberry Tears   Spina

Strike!   Lerner, Alan Jay; Loewe

Stringin' Along (inst.)   Young, Victor

(Rachael) Struttin' with Clayton (inst.)   Revel

Student's Ball (We're Havin' a Ball)   Martin

Suits Me Fine   Martin

Sunday Jumps (inst.)   Lane

Sunny   Sigman

Sunshowers   Hoffman

Surrounded By Roses   Davis

Susquehanna Transfer   Russell

Sweetheart of Yesterday   Sigman

Sympathetic Little Star   Razaf

Syncopated Clock, The   Parish

Tahiti, My Island   David, Mack; Young, Victor

Take Care of My Little Girl   Ruby

Take Me Back to Texas with You   Martin

Take Me Home   Sigman

Tango of Love   David, Mack

Telephone Song   Sigman

Telephone Switchboard Scene   Fain; Harburg

That Face!   Martin

That Saturday Night Feelin'   Russell

That's a Fine, Fine, Fine Howdy Ya Do   David, Hal

That's for Children   Fields; Schwartz, Arthur

That's for Sure   Mercer

That's Good, That's Bad   Drake

That's How It Goes   Fields; Schwartz, Arthur

That's How Love Should Be (La-le-lu)   David, Mack

That's How Our Love Will Grow   Sigman

That's My L.A.   Fain; Webster

That's the Tune   Robin; Styne

Theme for Love (inst.)   Young, Victor

There Never Was a Baby Like My Baby   Comden and
    Green; Styne

There She Goes   David, Hal

There She Was   Sherman

There'll Be Mournin' in the Mornin'   Spina

There's a Coach Comin' In   Lerner, Alan Jay; Loewe

There's Always a Rain Check for a Lovely Day   Brown, Lew;
    Henderson

There's Always My Heart   Sigman

There's Always Room at Our House   Merrill

There's Music in the Metro   Martin

There's No Tomorrow   Hoffman

They All Kissed the Bride   David, Hal

They Call the Wind Maria   Lerner, Alan Jay; Loewe

They Obviously Want Me to Sing   Evans; Livingston, Jay

This Could Be Love   Coots; Egan

This Is Magic   De Lange

This Is the Kiss   Bloom

This Life   Sigman
This, That, and the Other Thing   Burke
Three Chimes of Silver   Willson
Three Little Hollywood Wolves   Coslow
Till All the Stars Fall in the Ocean   Spina
Time Step, The   Martin
Ting-a-ling-a-ling   Howard, Joseph E.
To Be or Not to Be in Love   Coslow
Toast, The   Martin
Today at Your House, Tomorrow at Mine   Lawrence
Today, Tomorrow, Forever   David, Mack; Livingston, Jerry
Tonight My Love   Evans; Livingston, Jay
Tonight You Are in Paree   Martin
Too Late Now   Lane; Lerner, Alan Jay
Too Much Trouble   Lawrence
Top Banana   Mercer
Torchy   Sigman
Tour Must Go On, The   Martin
Trav'lin' Free   Evans; Livingston, Jay
Triangle (inst.)   Styne
Trick or Treat   Coots
Trick or Treat (For Halloween)   Hoffman
Trinidad Lady   Russell
Trio   Lerner, Alan Jay; Loewe
Trouble with Women Is Men, The   Fain; Webster
True Love   David, Hal
Turtle Dove River   Robison
Tuscaloosa   Fields; Schwartz, Arthur
'Twas Brillig   DePaul; Raye
Twelve O'Clock Kiss   Friend
Twilight Nocturne (Beverly Hills, Blue Nocturne)
    (inst.)   Young, Victor
Twilight Song   Evans; Livingston, Jay
Twist My Arm   Fain; Webster
Two Lonely Hearts   Sigman
Two Tickets to Broadway   Robin; Styne
Unbirthday Song   David, Mack; Hoffman; Livingston, Jerry
Underneath the Southern Cross   Meyer
Up the Delaware Down the Delaware Bay   Johnson,
    Howard
Up Your Bustle   Sherman
Valentino Tango   Lawrence
Valley of Beautiful Dreams (The Shannon, the Shamrocks
    and You), The   David, Mack
Very Good Advice   Fain
Vienna Dreams   Caesar
Village in Peru, A   Russell
Vive Le Jourdain (Prologue)   Drake
Vive the U.S.A.   Martin
Wait Till the Sun Shines Nellie Blues   Sterling; Von Tilzer
Waiting   Hammerstein; Rodgers
Walking in the Sunshine   Merrill
Walking Music   Sigman
Wall Between Us, The   David, Hal
Walrus and the Carpenter, The   Fain
Waltzing Cat, The   Parish
Wand'rin Star   Lerner, Alan Jay; Loewe
Water Lily   David, Mack; Livingston, Jerry
Wax Works, The   David, Mack; Livingston, Jerry
Way Down South of Dixie   Robin; Styne
We Have Never Met As Yet   Gordon; Myrow
We Have with Us Tonight   David, Hal
We Kiss in a Shadow   Hammerstein; Rodgers
We Never Talk Too Much   Cahn

We Were Married in Nevada Many, Many Years
    Ago   Woods
We Won't Live in a Castle   Merrill
Weather's in Your Eyes, The   Martin
Weaver of Dreams   Young, Victor
Wedding of Dan McCann to Molly McGee, The   Baer
Welch's Grape Juice   Baer
We're Coming, Leo   Evans; Livingston, Jay
We're Through   Raye; Spina
Were Your Ears Burning Last Night   Baer; Leslie
Western People Funny   Hammerstein; Rodgers
Wham   Blane
What a Lovely Day for a Wedding   Lane; Lerner, Alan Jay
What Does It Take?   Burke; Van Heusen
What Good?   Razaf
What I Was Warned About   Martin
What More Can I Do   David, Mack
What Shall We Do with the Drunken Sailor   Evans;
    Livingston, Jay
What's Goin' on Here?   Lerner, Alan Jay; Loewe
What's Gonna Become of Me (Now that I'm in
    Love)   Kalmar; Ruby
What's the Use of Lovin' You when the Whole World Loves
    You Too   Caesar; Howard, Joseph E.
When   Silver
When Does This Feeling Go Away?   Martin
When I'm Out with the Belle of New York   Mercer; Warren
When My Darling Calls Me Darling   David, Mack
When My Ship Turns Around and Come In Again   Ruby
When the Frost Is on the Punkin   Carmichael
When the World Was Young (Ah the Apple Tree)   Mercer
When Worlds Collide   Evans; Livingston, Jay
When You Come Home   Parish
When You Come to the End of the Day   Sigman
When You Grown Up You'll Know   Lane; Lerner, Alan Jay
Where Can I Run from You   Fields; Schwartz, Arthur
Where To, My Love   David, Hal
Whisper Waltz, The   Adamson; McHugh
Whistle and Walk Away   Fain; Gordon
Who Am I   Martin
Who Gives a Sou   Martin
Who Said There Ain't No Santa Claus?   Fain; Harburg
Who Would Refuse?   Hammerstein; Rodgers
Whoa, Emma   Fields; Warren
Whoo-ee Loo-ee-Siana   Bergman
Whoop-Ti-Ay   Lerner, Alan Jay; Loewe
Why Do I Fall in Love   DePaul; Raye
Why Should We Say Goodbye and Cry Tomorrow?   Lewis
Windmill Song, The   Brown, Nacio Herb; Gilbert; Parish
(If I Had) Wings on My Wishes   Webster
Wishbone Song, The   Lawrence
With All My Heart   Carroll
With God's Hand in Mine   Coots
Woman's Intuition, A   Washington; Young, Victor
Wonder Why   Cahn
Word a Day, A   Mercer
World Is Your Balloon, The   Fain; Harburg
World's Full o' Suckers, The   Lane; Lerner, Alan Jay
Would I Say I Love You If I Didn't?   Lewis
Yankee Doodle Bunny   Friend
Yes You Are   Merrill
You   Koehler
You Belong to Me   David, Hal
You Blew Out the Flame in My Heart   Drake
You Can't Get Far Without a Guitar in Texas   Woods

You Can't Have a Show Without Durante   Cahn; Willson
You Can't Hurt Me Any More   Freed, Ralph; Hoffman
You Can't Pick Berries in Wintertime   Henderson; Yellen
You Don't Have a Leg to Stand On   Robison
You Gotta Have a Slogan   Mercer
You Haven't Lived   Fain
You Haven't Lived Until You've Died in L.A.   Webster
You Need a Little Magic   Fain; Harburg
You Never Fall in Love Again   Oakland; Webster
You Too Can Be a Puppet   Fain; Harburg
You'll Know   Adamson; McHugh
Young Folks Should Get Married   Fields; Warren
Your Home Is in My Arms (Swedish Rhapsody)   Raye
Your Own Little House   Evans; Livingston, Jay
You're All the World to Me   Lane; Lerner, Alan Jay
You're Lovely Love   Martin
You're Right I'm Wrong   Davis; Silver
You're So Beautiful — That   Mercer
You're the One   Washington; Young, Victor
You're Trapped   Cahn
You've Got a Face Full of Wonderful Things   Fields; Warren
You've Got Me Singin'   Davis
You've Got the Indian Sign on Me   Fain
Zum Galli Galli   Freed, Ralph

1952

(A Mother Tonight Is Rocking) A Cradle in
      Bethelehem   Bryan
(I'm on the Wrong Side of) A One-Sided Love
      Affiar   Lawrence
According to the Stars   Friend
Afraid   Brooks
After All   Drake
Ain't Nature Grand   Mercer; Rome; Schwartz, Arthur
All About Love   Evans; Livingston, Jay
All Day Singin' and Dinner on the Ground   Hoffman
All Hail to Midwest State   Cahn; Duke
All I Want Is You   Silver
All My Life   Evans; Livingston, Jay
All Over the World   Brown, Lew; Henderson
All the Time and Ev'rywhere   Merrill
All the Way for Jesus   Razaf
Al-lee-o Al-lee-ay   David, Hal
Alone at Last   Young, Victor
Alone on the Lonesome   Lawrence; Young, Victor
Alone with Love   Blake; Sissle
Am I in Love   Brooks
Am I My Brother's Keeper   Razaf
Ambolyn   Lane; Robin
Americana, U.S.A.   Goetz
And They Said It Wouldn't Last   David, Mack
And You Know Why   Friml
Angeline   Freed, Ralph
Anna Mary   Martin
Answer the Call   Willson
Anthem for Presentation Theme   Berlin
Any Old Time (Mu Quarto e Luna)   Rome
Anything for a Laugh   Russell
Anywhere   Young, Victor
Anywhere I Wander   Loesser
April Face   Blane
April Sings   Washington
April Special   Oakland
Army Mule Song, The   Blane

Army's Always There, The   Stept
Arriverderci   Coots
As Long as I Live   Merrill
At the Garden Gate   Carmichael
At the Teddy Bear's Birthday Party   Coots
Aupres de Ma Blonde   Cahn; Duke
Aye Aye Aye Aye O   Russell
Baby Couldn't Dance   Duke
Bachelor's Life, A   Russell
Baminay (The New Orleans Chimney Sweep)   Fain;
      Lawrence
Banners and Bonnets   Willson
Barber Shop Boogie, The   Drake
Barnum and Bailey Ball, The   Burke; Van Heusen
Barrels 'n' Barrels of Roses   Merrill
Be a Jumping Jack   Washington; Young, Victor
Be My Baby   Drake
Beans   Gordon
(Beautiful Faces Need) Beautiful Clothes   Pollack
Beautiful Mucho Chito (Muchachita)   Revel
Beautiful Music to Love By   Sigman
Because You're Mine   Cahn
Believe You Me   Oakland
Belle of the Ball   Parish
Beloved   Webster
Beloved Philippines   Razaf
Benny the Magic Bunny   Hoffman
Best Part of a Letter, The   Drake
Big Blue Sky (Is the Place for Me), The   David, Mack;
      Livingston, Jerry
Blonde in the Green Coupe, The   Russell
Blue Tango   Parish
Bongo-Boola   Blake; Sissle
Bonne Nuit   Mercer
Boom Boom Song, The   Spina
Boss (For You I Shout Hooray)   Drake
Boys Are Better than Girls   Fields; Schwartz, Arthur
Boys Up on the Hill, The   Caesar
Bright College Days   Rome
Bright Stars and Soft Guitars   Coslow
Bugle Blues   Russell
Bumble Bee Bumble By   Woods
Burning Bush of Israel, The   Razaf
Butterfly Lament   Goetz
Buy Her a Hat   Brooks
Bye   DePaul; Raye
Bye-Bye, Be Seein' You-All   Drake
Bzzzzzz (The Whisper Song)   Drake
California Rose   Evans; Livingston, Jay
Call Me Tonight   Robin; Warren
Cambridge Valley   Martin
Camp Karefree   Rome
Can Love Come Back Again   Brooks
Can You Better Your Condition   Caesar
Casablanca   Bullock
'Cause I Love Ya, That's A-Why   Merrill
Certain Individuals   Rome
C'est La Guerre   Mercer; Schwartz, Arthur
Checkin' My Heart   Robin; Warren
Chicago Style   Burke; Van Heusen
Children's Children's Children   Martin
Ching Ching-a-ling (Zing-Zing-a-Ling)   Merrill
Chords   Willson
Chores   Evans; Livingston, Jay
Chose Your Partner for the Last Dance   Drake

Christmas Day   Davis
Cigarette   Robison
Circus Day   Coots
City Called Heaven   Blake; Sissle
Cling to Me   David, Hal
Clip-Clop Song (Le Fiacre), The   Rome
Close to My Heart   Sigman
Come Along to the Circus   Coots
Come Here, You   Leigh
Come on Home   Ellington
Come Out of the Rain   Leigh
Come to Life   Sigman
Come-Tooly-Um-Tooly-Ay-O   Drake
Consideration   Robison
Coronation Polka, The   Coots
Could Be   Rome
Crazy Red Lips   DePaul; Raye
Daddy Long-Legs   Martin
Dance Me Around   Fields; Schwartz, Arthur
Dangling in the Air   Hoffman
Danny's Hideaway   Stept
Darlene   Russell
Darling Je Vous Adore   Friml
Del Icado   Lawrence
Derby Day Honeymoon   Goetz
Derry Down Dilly   Mercer
Devil Me, Angel You   Bryan
Did Anyone Call   Sigman
Did You Have Fun   McHugh
Dim Cafe, A   David, Mack; Livingston, Jerry
Do You Think I Came Here for My Health   Sigman
Don Jose of Far Rockaway   Rome
Don't Cry, Darling   Gorney
Don't Ever Be Afraid to Go Home   Sigman
Don't Give Your Kisses to Somebody Else (Save All Your
     Kisses for Me)   Adamson; McHugh
Don't Make Faces   Sigman
Don't Rush Me   Wrubel
Don't Say You Love Me If You Don't Mean It   Stept
Don't Send Me Home   David, Hal
Don't Stop Loving Me   Drake
Don't Tempt Me (For When I Love, I Love)   Spina
Don't You Care   Stept
Doodle-Bug Rag, The   Carmichael
Door Opened, The   Howard, Bart
Door Senor, The   Hoffman
Down at the Farm   Martin
Dream Dream Dream   Hoffman
Dream Dream, Dream (Long, Long, Long)   Parish
Dream Fantasy   Loesser
Dream Was Born, A   Young, Victor
Dreamer's Cloth   Russell
Dreams   Carmichael
Dumb-Dumb-Dumb   Martin
Early Autumn   Mercer
Echoes of the Jungle   Mills
Eighteenth Century Blues   Oakland; Raye
Eisenhower Song   Brown, Lew
Elegant Captain Hook, The   Cahn; Fain
Enbothered   Carmichael
Esther   Cahn; Duke
Everybody Loves Everybody   Rome
Everybody's Sweetheart   David, Hal
Everyone Is Wanted in Wyoming   Revel
Ev'ry Little Stone   Howard, Joseph E.

Exotica (inst.)   Myrow
Fabulous   Harburg
Fall Into Somebody's Arms   Lawrence
Far Away   Van Heusen
Farewell   Brooks
Farewell with Love   Blake; Sissle
Fedelia   Willson
Feet Up (Pat Him on the Po-po)   Merrill
Fellow I'd Follow, The   Robin
Fifi   Mercer; Schwartz, Arthur
Fine! Fine! Fine!   Robin
Fisherman's Bride, The   Coots
Five Wives   Magidson
Flattery   Rome
Flight of Fancy, A   Robin; Warren
Flirt, The   Brooks
Flirting with Danger   Sigman
Foolish   Davis
For the Life of Me   David, Hal
For the Very First Time   Berlin
For Want of a Kiss   David, Hal
Four Legged Friend   Brooks
Four O'Clock Groove (inst.)   Johnson, James P.
Free to Be Free   Webster
From Island to Island   Arlen
Gal Named Cinderella, A   Fain; Harburg
Gelt   Gilbert
Gentlemen   Drake
Get a Horse (For Your Horseless Carriage)   Martin
Girl Hunt Ballet (inst.)   Schwartz, Arthur
Girl that I Court in My Mind, The   Blane
Girl with the Stardust in Her Eyes   Russell
Girls Are Marching, The   Comden and Green; Styne
Girls! Girls! Girls!   Webster
Girls School Alma Mater   Loesser
(I Would) Give Heaven Back to the Angels   Drake
Give Me Your Lips   Cahn; Duke
Give This Little Girl a Great Big Hand   Coslow
Glad to Have You Aboard   Blane; Warren
Glimpse of Love   Rome
Glorious Day   Revel
Glory Alley   David, Mack; Livingston, Jerry
Glow Worm   Mercer
Go and Get Your Old Banjo   Martin
Go Back to Your Doll, Little Girl   Bryan
Goin' Back to School   Martin
Goin' on a Hayride   Blane
Goin' with the Birds   Fields; Schwartz, Arthur
Gold Dollar Moon   Goetz
Golden Hair   Hoffman
Gone Are the Days   Goetz
Good Little Girls   Cahn; Duke
Good Luck, Good Health, Happiness   Magidson
Goodbye Little Girl   Oakland; Webster
Goodbye Love   Rome
Good-Bye, My Hello Baby   Bryan
Goodbye My Love   Young, Victor
Goodbye to Love that Overtakes Us   Dietz
Goodnight Good Friends (Wherever You Are)   Coots
Goofy Newsreel   Coslow
Great Musician, The   Razaf
Greatest Man on Earth, The   Coots
Greatest Papa in the World, The   Robin
Greatest Show on Earth (Come to the Circus),
     The   Washington; Young, Victor

Green Pine Tree, The   Merrill
Guy Sat at a Piano, A   Hoffman
Gypsy   Webster
Ham and Candy   Revel
Hang Out the Stars   Lawrence
(Here Comes) Hank the Whip   Coots
Happy Christmas, Little Friend   Hammerstein; Rodgers
Happy Time, The   Washington
Happy Tree   Young, Victor
Hats   Akst; Davis
Haunted Hot Spot   Duke
Have a Heart, Gigolette (Gigolette)   Rome
He Is My Friend   Silver
He Never Looked Better in His Life   Russell
Hear My Plea   Stept
Heartbreak Avenue   Merrill
Heart-Breaker   Sigman
Hello Out There, Hello   Mercer
Her Innocent Pretension Is a Veil of Invention   Dietz
Here We Are   Martin
He's Just Crazy for Me   Robin; Warren
Herman the Mouse   David, Hal
Hi Wyoming   Revel
High Noon   Washington
Hilda Matilda   Blane; Warren
Hillbilly Grand Opera   Coslow
Hit the Dirt   Stept
Hoby Tyler Campaign Song   Lane; Robin
Hocus Pocus   Brooks
Hokey Pokey Polka   Coslow
Hold Me Close to You   Blane; Warren
Hold Me in Your Heart   Hoffman
Honey, Oh, My Honey   Evans; Livingston, Jay
Honeymoon Cake   Stept
Hooray for Ghio   Lane; Robin
Hoot Mon   Burke; Van Heusen
Horn in a Fiddle Shop (inst.), A   Romberg
(Blue Eyes) How Could You!   Brooks
How Lucky Can You Get?   Fain; Harburg
How Many People Can Say   Hoffman
How Much Is that Doggie in the Window   Merrill
How Wonderful   Razaf
Howdy Doody Polka, The   Coots
Howdy-Do Valley   Freed, Ralph; Hoffman
Hurry, Hurry, Hurry (Darling, Come Home)   Robison
I Ain't Gonna Marry   Martin
I Am Only Mimi   Dietz
I Ask You   Cahn; Duke
I Believe   Drake
I Believe in God   Bryan
I Can't Get Enough of You   Adamson; McHugh
I Can't Resist a Boy in a Uniform   David, Mack; Livingston, Jerry
I Count My Blessings   Ruby
I Cried Enough Tears (To Float a Boat)   Drake
I Did It and I'm Glad   Fields; Schwartz, Arthur
I Do, I Don't Know Why   Friml
I Don't Know What I've Got   Cahn; Duke
I Don't Need to Know   Robison
I Fear Nothing   Russell
I Feel a Polka Coming On   Stept
I Get a Funny Feeling   Blane; Warren
I Go My Way   Dietz
I Got a Big Surprise for You   Friend
I Got News   Willson

I Got Out of Bed on the Right Side   Mercer; Schwartz, Arthur
I Gotta Hear that Beat   Robin
I Have Love   Friml
I Hope She'll Be Happy   Coots
I Keep Coming Back for More   David, Hal
I Know   Martin
I Know a Dream When I See One   David, Mack; Livingston, Jerry
I Know a Place (The Place You Hold My Heart)   Cahn; Duke
I Laughed at Love   Davis; Silver
I Like Ike   Berlin
I Like Men   Mercer; Schwartz, Arthur
I Love to Hear a Choo Choo Train   DePaul; Raye
I Need You   Stept
I Never Dream When I'm Asleep   Martin
I Never Should Have Let You Go   Von Tilzer
I Passed Your House Tonight   Raye
I Remember the Darkness   Dietz
I Shall Return   Drake
I Shoulda Said   Hoffman
I Take a Dim View   Willson
I Think You're Pretty Too   Duke
I Thought of You Last Night   Freed, Ralph
I Told You (He Wasn't for You)   Mills
I Want You   Davis
I Was Born to Sing   Oakland; Raye
I Wish I Was Back in St. Louis   Revel
I Wonder What They're Doin' Back in Punxsatawney   Drake
I Wonder Why (inst.)   Young, Victor
I Won't Cry   Lawrence; Young, Victor
I Write My Buddies   Drake
I'd Like to Baby You   Evans; Livingston, Jay
If God Can Forgive Me, Why Can't You   Bryan; Caesar
If I Should Love Again   Coots
If It Were Up to Me   Stept
If My Heart Could Only Talk   Drake
If You Would Love Me   Baer
If You're Gettin' Bad Breaks Pull Up Your Stakes and Move On   Brown, Lew; Henderson
If You're in Love   Washington
I'll Be Hard to Handle   Fields; Kern
I'll Be Loving You   Cahn; Duke
I'll Hold Your Hand in Mine   Dietz
I'll Never Love Another Gal   Coslow
I'll Si, Si Ya in Bahia   Robin; Warren
I'll Sing You a Song   Blane
I'll Take Chicago   Cahn
I'll Walk with God   Webster
I'm a Ruler of a South Sea Island   Arlen
I'm Always Romantic (But You're Always Hungry)   Webster
I'm Getting Used to a Broken Heart   Bryan
I'm Gonna Be Busy Dating You, Darling, Monday thru Sunday   Baer
I'm Gonna Ring the Bell Tonight   Cahn; Duke
I'm Gonna Stay Awake All Night   Drake
I'm Gonna Vote for Santa Claus   Hoffman
I'm Hans Christian Andersen   Loesser
I'm in Love with a Song   Coslow
I'm Lookin' for the Guy that Stole My Gal   Freed, Ralph; Hoffman
I'm Looking at Tomorrow   Revel
I'm Not Blaming You   Davis
I'm on My Way Special   Oakland

I'm Proud of You   Fields; Schwartz, Arthur
I'm Saving Up for Lost Time   Sigman
I'm the Greatest Papa in the World   Lane
I'm the Worryin' Kind   Mercer
In My Wildest Dreams   Mercer; Schwartz, Arthur
In the Lanes of the Seven Seas   Harbach
In the Old Rope Swing   Coots
In the Sweet Long Ago   David, Mack; Livingston, Jerry
In Zinzinnati   Brown, Lew
Inch Worm, The   Loesser
Indians Never Say Why   Revel
Inspection   Arlen
Investigation   Rome
Invitation   Webster
Iron Horse   Drake
Isn't That a Pretty Picture   Drake
It Just Happened One Day (At a Sidewalk Cafe)   Revel
It Just Occurred to Me   Cahn; Duke
It Must Be Good   Cahn; Duke
It Must Be Spring   Blane
It Takes Two (To Make a Dream Come True)   Lerner, Sammy
It Used to Be   DePaul; Raye
It's a Boy   Drake
It's a Wishing World   Blane
It's a Wonderful Day Today   Coots
It's a World of Color   Cahn; Duke
It's Better Rich   Martin
It's Better to Dream than to Cry   Robin
It's Christmas Time   Young, Victor
It's Great to Be an Orphan   Martin
It's Half Past Kissin' Time and Time to Kiss Again   Willson
It's Love - Love - Lovely You   Lane; Robin
It's Not the Same Without You   Ruby
It's Only Money   Cahn; Styne
It's Shadow Time Again   Webster
It's that Time of the Evening   Coots
It's the Beast in Me   Russell
It's the End of My Life   Dietz
It's Time to Go   Oakland
I've Always Meant to Tell You   Cahn; Styne
I've Been Alone too Long (Flavia)   Sigman
I've Just Had a Good Cry   Silver
I've Lost Enough Sleep Over You   Bullock
Jack and the Beanstalk   Russell
Jack of Diamonds   Oakland; Webster
Jamie's Responsibilities   Blane
Jersey City   Robison
Jive Drill   Blake; Sissle
Johnny Has Gone for a Soldier   Lawrence
Jollyanna   Harburg
Jungelitis (The Monkey Song)   Carmichael
Jungle Honeymoon   Burke; Van Heusen
Jungle Wedding March, The   Burke; Van Heusen
Just Because You're You   Leigh
Just for You   Robin; Warren
Just Give Me Time   Leigh
Just Like a Man   Duke
Keep a Little Dream Handy   David, Mack; Livingston, Jerry
Keep A-Lookin' Straight Ahead   Cahn
Keep That Great Wheel Turning   Woods
Kevin   Blane
Ki Yi Yippee Yi Yo What a Night!   Lane; Robin
Kiddie Polka   Friend
Kind to Animals   Martin

King's New Clothes, The   Loesser
Kiss, A   Brooks
Kisses and Tears   Cahn
Kitchen Music   Carmichael
Lady Out on a Late Evening (inst.)   Bloom
Lafayette   Fields; Kern
L'Affaire (inst.)   Myrow
Last Chance   Raye
Laughing Polka, The   Heyman
Leave a Message   Harburg
Lesson of the Lord, The   Coots
Let Me Love You   Howard, Bart
Let's Go Over to Charlie's   Coots
Let's Have a Party   Drake
Let's Keep on Falling in Love Again   Mills
Let's Say It Never Happened   Robison
Letter, The   Drake
Letter Reaches Santa   Drake
Life Is a Beautiful Thing   Evans; Livingston, Jay
Life Is Such a Pleasure   Cahn; Duke
Lights of Rome, The   Mercer
Like Ya — Honey, I Love Ya   Woods
Lilly the Blue Loon   Robison
Liquapep   Mercer; Schwartz, Arthur
Little Bit of Magic, A   Harburg; Lane
Little Did I Know   David, Mack
Little Kiss Goodnight, A   Merrill
Little Train A-Chuggin' in My Heart   Sigman
Little Wendy Why-Why   Hoffman
Live Oak Tree, The   Robin; Warren
Loch Lomond Swing   Coslow
Londonderry Air (inst.)   Romberg
Lonesome Coyote, The   David, Mack; Livingston, Jerry
Look Up and Know I'm Loving You (Ben Je in Rotterdam Geboren)   Rome
Look Younger, Live Longer   Coslow
Louisiana Lullaby   Meyer
Love and Hate   Spina
Love and Kisses   Webster
Love from Judy   Martin
Love Has Nothing to Do with Looks   Blane
Love Him   Evans; Livingston, Jay
Love Is a Lady in Blue   David, Hal
Love Is Still for Free   Cahn; Duke
Love Laughs at Kings   Young, Victor
Love to Be with You   Webster
Lovely Luawana Lady   Goetz
Low in the Lehigh Valley   Lawrence
Lucky Horseshoe, The   Coots
Lullaby   Martin
Lullaby of the Lord, The   Robin
Luncheon with Buster Crabbe   Coots
M M M M M M Boy   Davis
Ma Petite Folie   Merrill
Magic Carpet, The   Coslow
Magic Touch, The   Stept
Magic Tree   Blane
Maiden of Guadalupe, The   Robin; Warren
Make 'Em Laugh   Brown, Nacio Herb; Freed, Arthur
Making a Play for Love   Sigman
Male Call (The Leap Year Song)   Raye
Mama, Mama, Mama   Merrill
Ma-Ma, Ma-Ma, Put the Kettle On   Drake
Mambo on My Mind   Russell
Mamma Ain't Cookin' Today   Robison

Mardi Gras   Martin
Marguerite's Waltz   Willson
Marilyn   Drake
Marines Have Landed, The   Drake
Marshmallow Moon   Evans; Livingston, Jay
Maxims   Webster
Maybe It's a Woman's World   Blane
Mayor's Entrance   Young, Victor
Me and My Piano   Caesar
Meant to Tell Yuh   Mercer
Meet Captain Kidd   Russell
Meet Mister Callaghan   Drake
Melancholy Trumpet (Ooh-wah), The   David, Hal
Merry Widow Waltz   Webster
Merry-Go-Runaround, The   Burke; Van Heusen
Metronome Fantasy   Loesser
Mexican Maidens   Merrill
Mexico Blues   Brooks
Mighty Pretty Waltz, A   Hoffman
Military Policeman, The   Evans; Livingston, Jay
Mind If I Come Aboard Ship, Sailor   Drake
Minnehaha   Goetz
Miss Nellie Machree   Coots
Mister Banjo Man   Evans; Livingston, Jay
Mister Midnight   Lewis
Mix and Mingle   Rome
Mon Amour   Adamson; McHugh
Monarch of All I Survey   Young, Victor
Montmartre   Adamson; McHugh
Moon Came Up with a Great Idea, The   Burke; Van Heusen
Moonflowers   Burke; Van Heusen
More or Less   David, Hal
Moses   Comden and Green
Most Exciting Night, The   Fields; Harbach; Kern
Most Important Man in the U.S.A., The   Drake
Mountain Dew   Coslow
Mountain High, Valley Low   David, Hal
Moving Away   Sigman
Mulberry Street   Davis; Silver
Mumbles Blues   Gilbert
Musgrove Military Prep   Evans; Livingston, Jay
Music Box   Martin
Music Box (inst.), The   Young, Victor
Musical Prince, A   Oakland
My Beloved   Evans; Livingston, Jay
My Darling, My Sweetheart, My Love   Hoffman
My Dog and Me   Merrill
My Ever-Lovin'   Sigman
My Flaming Heart   Robin
My Gaucho   Robin
My Girls   Drake
My Guardian Angel   Stept
My Heart Skips a Beat   Drake
My Heart's Darlin'   Blane
My Heart's Desire   Heyman; Young, Victor
My Home's a Highway   Blane
My Imaginary Love   David, Hal
My Lady Love   Russell
My Love   Warren
My Love My Life   Evans; Livingston, Jay
My True Love   Martin
Navy Blue Blues   Lawrence
Navy Waltz, The   Blane; Warren
Never Say Goodbye   Friml; Webster
Never Smile at a Crocodile   Lawrence

New Orleans, the Mardi Gras and You   Goetz
Nice Doggy-Nice Kitty   Carmichael
Nickle and Dime Man   Merrill
Night   Webster
Night After Night   Hoffman
Night that We Remember, A   Robin
Nina Never Knew   Alter
No Two People   Loesser
None but the Brave   Robison
North of Nowhere   Russell
Now Is Wonderful   Fields; Schwartz, Arthur
Now that I've Told You My Story   Revel
Now, Vote Republican   Razaf
O Prehistoric Raiment   Dietz
Ocean Breeze   Robin; Styne
Off Again, On Again Blues   David, Hal
Off to Wonderland   Lane; Robin
Oh Christmas Tree   Brooks
Oh, How I Wish It were More   Woods
Oh Me Oh My Oh Me-O   Cahn; Duke
Ol' Shank's Mare   DePaul; Raye
Old Fashioned Song for an Old Fashioned Girl, An   David, Mack; Livingston, Jerry
Old Love   Davis
Ole   Robin
Ole Spring Fever, The   Warren
On Stage Interlude   Evans; Livingston, Jay
On the Pillow Next to Mine   Howard, Joseph E.
On the Ten-Ten from Ten-Ten-Tennessee   Robin; Warren
Once Upon a Dream   Lawrence
One Diamond Morning   Wrubel
One Girl   Davis
One Last Cigarette   Sigman
One Love too Many   Sigman
One Wonderful Night   Friml
Only Once   Cahn; Duke
Opening Night   Kern
Opposite Sex, The   Arlen
Original Introduction and Tag   Brooks
Our Day of Independence   Berlin
Our Future Has Just Begun   Leigh
Out of the Clear Blue Sky   Duke
Out of the Shadow (And Into the Light)   Koehler
Outline of Jitterbug History   Coslow
Owen Roe   Blane
Pa Don't 'Low No Strangers Here   Razaf
Paminay   Lawrence
Papaya Man, The   Bullock
Parachute Jump, The   David, Mack; Livingston, Jerry
Passionata   Brooks
Pastoral   Martin
Peculiar   David, Hal
Pee Wee the Bunny with the Big Blue Eyes   Coots
People Talk Too Much   Blane
Peter Pan   Lawrence; Young, Victor
Pie-Wock-A-Jilly-Wook   Drake
Pioneer Stock   Martin
(There's a Pawn Shop on a Corner In) Pittsburgh, Pennsylvania   Merrill
Please Be My Sweetheart, Sweetheart   Spina
Poor Willie   Mills
Portrait, A   Young, Victor
Pot Luck   Hoffman
Praise Ye   Robison
Precious Rosary   Razaf

President Is Going to Be a Daddy, The   Gershwin, George;
   Gershwin, Ira
Professor, Play Those Blues   Magidson
Professor, The   Fields; Schwartz, Arthur
Puppy Love   Oakland; Raye
Purple Rose   Duke
Purt' Nigh' but Not Plumb   Evans; Livingston, Jay
Quiet Hill, The   Raye; Spina
Quilting Song   Revel
Ramshackle Shack, The   Drake
Razzle Dazzle   Merrill
Ready for Action   Drake
Red Is for Roses   Fain; Lawrence
Relatives of the Bride, The   Drake
Relax   Rome; Silver
Remember the Girl You Left Behind   Revel
Remember Your Promise (Say the Bells of St.
   Thomas)   David, Hal
Rendezvous, The   Coots
Reveille in Harlem   Raye
Reveille on Vine Street   Raye
Rhythm of America   Blake; Sissle
Right or Wrong   Evans; Livingston, Jay
Right Place for a Girl, The   Friml; Webster
Road to Bali, The   Burke; Van Heusen
Roaring Twenties   Merrill
Robin in the Redwood Tree, The   Adamson; McHugh
Rodeo Rose (Giddyap Gal)   Wrubel
Roll Along, Sadie   Duke
Roll Out the Crimson Carpet   Sherman
Royal Danish   Loesser
Saint Patrick's Prayer   Blane
Saturday Night in Punkin Crick   Evans; Livingston, Jay
Say It Over   Spina
Search, The   Blane
Second Star to the Right, The   Cahn; Fain
Senorita   Revel
Serenade for a Tin Horn (inst.)   Stept
Sewing   Martin
She Had the Face of an Angel   Revel
She Wears Red Feathers (And a Huly-Huly Skirt)   Merrill
Shoe Song, The   Loesser
Shopping Around   Rome
Shrine of Saint Anne De-Beaupre, The   Spina
Shrine of St. Anne the Beaupre, The   Webster
Silent Partner   Robison
Silent Serenade   Rome
Since I Met You   Oakland
Since You Went Away   Merrill
Sing a Song of Santa Claus   Coots
Singing Lesson, The   Coslow
Skiddle Diddle Dee-Skiddle Diddle Dey   David, Hal
Skipping Rope Hornpipe   Martin
Skirts Ahoy!   Blane; Warren
Sleep It Off   Drake
Sleigh Bell Serenade   Webster
Small Towns Are Smile Towns   Robin
Smoke Ascending, The   Dietz
Snows of Yesteryear   Robison
Social Director   Rome
Soda Shop   Evans; Livingston, Jay
Someday Today Will Be the Good Old Times   Goetz
Song of the Robin   Russell
Song of the Women's Army Corps   Spina
Spark of Your Love Lit the Torch in My Heart, A   Bryan

Speak to Me of the Tall Pine   Russell
Spider and the Fly, The   Evans; Livingston, Jay
Springtime in Avalon   Friend
States Song (I Love the Panorama of Alabama), The   Drake
Step Right Up   Evans; Livingston, Jay
Stevenson the Man Who Takes Orders from None   Caesar
Still Water   Evans; Livingston, Jay
Stop, You're Killing Me   Sigman
Strange Faces   Coots
Strawberry Roan, A   Merrill
Street Voices   Loesser
Stubborn Mule   Davis; Silver
Stuff that Dreams Are Made Of, The   Cahn; Duke
Sugaring Off   Martin
Summer Afternoon   Rome
Summertime in Heidelberg   Webster
Swanee Moon   Blake; Sissle
Sweet Evening Breeze   Egan; Webster
Swifty the Thrifty Squirrel   Coots
Sympathetic Eyes   Drake
Take Care of Yourself   Howard, Bart
Take Comfort   Blane
Take Me to Broadway   Robin
Takes Two to Tango   Hoffman
Talk to Me Tomorrow   Robin; Styne
Tap on the Shoulder and a Guilty Conscience, A   Sigman
Tattle Tale   Oakland
Tattle Tale Heart   Bullock
Tears   Spina
Tears in Your Eyes   Silver
Tell Me You Love Me   Coots
Temperance Blues   Brooks
16th Century Blues   Oakland; Raye
Thank You for the Lovely Summer   Howard, Bart
Thanks for the Kind Words, Lady   Drake
Thanks to You   Evans; Livingston, Jay
That Ticklish Feeling   Mills
That's Entertainment   Dietz; Schwartz, Arthur
That's Him Over There   Bergman
That's What I'd Like to Be   Mills
That's What Makes Paris, Paree   Cahn; Duke
(At) The General Store   Evans; Livingston, Jay
Theatre Is a Lady, The   Duke
Then I Had to Go and Fall in Love   Mills
There Are Not Enough People in Love   Gordon; Revel
There Is a Way   Davis
There's a New Bird this Year in Last Year's Nest   Stept
There's a Place Called Omaha, Nebraska   Ruby
There's Nothing Nicer than People   Rome
They Couldn't Have Picked a Better Night   Drake
They Won't Know Me   Rome
Things I Might Have Been   Sherman
Think Twice   Hoffman
This Is My Show   Coots
This Is the Day   Howard, Bart
Thistles and Thumbs   Burke; Van Heusen
Though Your Love Is Gone   Dietz
Three Little Puppies   Hoffman
Three Things a Man Should Do   Drake
Thumbelina   Loesser
'Til Now   Hoffman
Time to Be Happy Is Now, The   Oakland
Tirolian Woodchoppers March (inst.)   Romberg
'Tis a Wonderful Thing in Nature   Blane
To See You   Burke; Van Heusen

To the Ladies   Oakland; Webster
Tommy Tom Tom   Stept
Tomorrow You Go to the Dentist   Eliscu; Gorney
Tonight Is Opening Night   Fields; Kern
Tonight or Never   Oakland; Webster
Too Late to Be Sorry (Too Early to Cry)   David, Hal
Touch of Voodoo, A   Martin
Trick or Treat (For Halloween)   David, Mack; Livingston,
   Jerry
Tripping the Light Fantastic   Rome
Trottin' to the Fair   Blane
Turkish Folk Song   Evans; Livingston, Jay; Young, Victor
Turkish Jerk, The   Coslow
Turn Me Loose on Broadway   Duke
27 Elm Street   Arlen
Two Guitars in Jive   Coslow
Two Who Love As One   Alter
Two Wrongs Never Make a Right   Cahn
Ugly Duckling, The   Loesser
Under the Lamp Post   Merrill
Under the Sweetheart Moon   Friend
U.S.A. Canteen   Drake
Vilia   Webster
Violin Solo   Martin
Violins in Virginia   Robison
Vote for Adlai   Caesar
Wake, The   Blane
Walk Away with a Smile   David, Hal
Walkin' to Missouri   Merrill
Waltz of the Bells   David, Mack
Want Me   Razaf
Watermelon Weather   Carmichael; Webster
Way We Are, The   Lane; Robin
We Can Live on Love   Coslow
We Know   Merrill
We Sail Tonight   Russell
We Will Fight   Blane; Warren
Wedding March, The   Blane
Wedding Waltz   Robison
We're for Love   Blane
We're Gonna Be Photographed   Drake
Western Style   Baer; Leslie
What a Dirty Shame   Evans; Livingston, Jay
What Do I Know?   Blane
What Do I See in You?   Martin
What Do Yo Do with a Broken Heart   McHugh
What Do You Do with a Broken Heart   Adamson
What Good Is a Gal (Without a Guy?)   Blane; Warren
What Happened to the Music   Leigh
What Have You Done for Me Lately   David, Mack;
   Livingston, Jerry
What Made the Red Man Red?   Cahn; Fain
What Make de Difference?   Arlen
What Makes a WAVE?   Blane; Warren
What's Gonna Happen?   Harburg; Lane
What's the Matter with Him   Drake
Whatsoever   Robison
When All the World Is Old   Lawrence
When Desire Dances for Me   Merrill
When I Fall in Love   Heyman; Young, Victor
When My Love Comes Back to Me   Stept
When Taft Says Yes, Then Ike Says Yes   Caesar
When the Great Even-Upper Comes to Supper   Robison
When the Teddy Bears Go Marching on Parade   Coots
When We Were Very Young (Terzettino)   Fields; Kern

When You're in Love   Arlen
Where Did the Night Go?   Rome
Where Do I Go from You   Fields; Schwartz, Arthur
Where in the World Could I Ever Find Another You   Freed,
   Ralph
Where There's Smoke There's Fire   Spina
Where You Are   Cahn
Which   Leigh
Whistle Stop   Martin
Whistling Kettle and a Dancing Cat, A   Merrill
Whistling Train, The   Eliscu
Who Can Tell?   Cahn; Duke
Who Could Eat Now   Rome
Who Did It   Wrubel
Who Did It — You Did It   Magidson
Who Do You Have to Know   Washington
Who Needs It   Cahn; Duke
Who Needs What Moonlight   Willson
Who Will It Be When the Time Comes?   Arlen
Who's Excited   Mercer
Why?   Razaf
Why Do I Cry in My Sleep?   Sherman
Why Don't You Let Me Be   Ruby
Why Oh Why   Snyder
Why Should I Believe in Love?   Evans; Livingston, Jay
Why Should I Go Home   Merrill
Why Try to Change Me Now   Coleman
Will o' the Wisp   Spina
Will You Be at Home in Heaven?   Evans; Livingston, Jay
Willie the Whipperwill   Robin
Wing-Ding Tonight   Evans; Livingston, Jay
Wings   Merrill
Winter in Hoosick Falls   Martin
Wintertime of Love (After You)   Heyman
Wise Man or a Fool, A   Merrill
Wish You Were Here   Rome
Wish You Were Special   Oakland
Witch of Salem, The   Bryan; Caesar
With a Nimble Little Thimble on Her Finger   Bryan
Woman Is a Fickle Thing, A   Webster
Woman's Work, A   Blane
Wonder Boy from Peru   Brooks
Wonderful Copenhagen   Loesser
Wonderful Wasn't It   David, Hal
Word of Kindness   Robison
Would You Believe It   Howard, Bart
Wouldn't You Rather Make Love   David, Hal
Ya Gotta Get Up Early in the Morning   Gordon; Revel
Yes, Lord   Robison
Yes Mister Cosgrove   Lane; Robin
Yo Ho and Off We Go   David, Hal
You and Me Together (The Marine's Drill)   Evans;
   Livingston, Jay
You Are So Dear to Me   Davis
You Are the Light of My Life   Leigh
You Can Do It   Sigman
You Can Fly! You Can Fly! You Can Fly!   Cahn; Fain
You Can Just Tell Christmas Is in the Air   Stept
You Can't Turn Back the Clock   Young, Victor
You Couldn't Do Enough for Me (He Couldn't Do Enough
   for Me)   Revel
You Didn't Have the Heart To Tell Me   Brown, Nacio Herb
You Gave Me Your Word   Adamson; McHugh
You Get Me So Excited   Stept
You Gotta Sing   Revel

You Haven't Lived Until You've Died in L.A.   Fain
You Haven't Missed a Thing   David, Hal
You Kill Me   Robin; Styne
You Look So Much Better When You Smile   Davis; Silver
You Made a Woman, You Made a Man   Revel
You Set Me Free   Kahn
You Still Do Those Things to My Heart   Merrill
You Too Can Be a Puppet   Harburg
You Won't Be Sorry   Davis
You'll Be Sorry   Leigh
You'll Get Your Picture in the Paper   Drake
You'll Never Go Panhandling with a Banjo on Your
    Knee   Caesar
Your Love Is Like a Sweetheart Rose   Baer
Your Mother and Mine   Cahn; Fain
You're Asking for It   Robin
You're Bound to Meet a Party   Drake
You're Devastating   Fields; Harbach; Kern
You're Gonna Break Somebody's Heart When You Grow
    Older   Davis
You're More Like Your Mommy Ev'ry Day   Drake
You're Only Fooling You   Mills
You're So Right   Drake
You're Unfair to Me   Coslow
You've Been Looking Through My Dreams   Burke; Van
    Heusen
You've Changed   Heyman; Young, Victor
You've Got to Give Them What They Want   Cahn; Duke
Zing a Little Zong   Robin; Warren

1953

(Ho Hum — Ho Hum) A Quiet Little Place in the
    Country   Gordon; Myrow
Abe an' Anna   Clare; Snyder
Ach, Du Lieber Oom-Pah-Pah   Gershwin, Ira; Lane
Afraid   Willson
Afternoon Dream   Lawrence
Ain't There Anyone Here for Love   Adamson; Carmichael
Ain't Ya Kinda Sorry   Davis
Ali Baba (Be My Baby)   Evans; Livingston, Jay
All in God's Good Time   Silver
All Is Forgiven (And All Is Forgotten)   Loesser
Allez-Vous-En (Go Away)   Porter
Always, Always in My Dreams   Merrill
Am I in Love?   Porter
Anaconda Copper   Willson
Analyse My Baby Back to Me   Ahlert
And There You Are   Gordon; Myrow
Anema E Core   Akst
Another Season   Davis
Answer Me   Sigman
Any Questions?   Russell
Anyone but You   Washington
Apaches, The   Porter
Applause! Applause!   Gershwin, Ira; Lane
Apple on a Stick   Coots
Apple Seed Love   Carmichael
April Springs   Adamson; Carmichael
Are You This Wonderful Every Day   Revel
Arfie the Doggie in the Window   Merrill
Argentine Fire Brigade   Spina
A-Rhythm-a-Tic   DePaul; Raye
Arkansas   Willson
Armed Forces on Parade, The   Stept

Around the Bend   Mercer
Arsenic and Old Waffles   Oakland; Raye
Ask Me   Spina
At Least It Was Good for a Laugh   Burke
At the Junction of the Chenango and the Susquehana
    Rivers   Willson
Autograph Chant (An Autograph of Hazel Flagg)   Styne
Autumn Twilight   Mercer
Baby You Haunt Me   Friend
Baby You Love, The   Hammerstein; Rodgers
Back Where I Come From   Blane
Ballerina   Revel
Ballin' the Blues   Ellington
Baloombala   Adamson
Battle Song   Burke; Van Heusen
Be Careful Song, The   Brooks
Be Patient, My Darling   Sigman
Be Smart My Heart   Dixon; Henderson; Rose
Beata Beata Drum   Merrill
Beautiful Tunes   Drake
Beautiful Way to Go Crazy   Brown, Lew; Henderson
Beautiful Woman   Spina
Because We Love Each Other   Silver
Behind the Mask   Sigman
Bell Bottom Blues   David, Hal
Bellissima   Oakland; Raye
Benny to Helen to Chance   Loesser
Big Big Lie, The   Lawrence
Big Black Giant, The   Hammerstein; Rodgers
Biggest Bloomin' Bumbershoot in the World   Hoffman
(When the Wild Wild Women Go in Swimmin' Down in)
    Bimini Bay   Adamson; Carmichael
Bing Bang Boom   David, Hal
Bird and the Cricket and the Willow Tree, The   Webster
Black Hills of Dakota, The   Fain; Webster
Blind Date Opened My Eyes, A   Clare; Snyder
Bloomington, Indiana   Drake
Blowing Wild   Webster
Blue Baby   Razaf
Blue Gardenia   Russell
Blue Love   Davis
Blue Reverie   Merrill
Blue Ridge Mountains of North Carolina   Willson
Blue Ridge Mountains of South Carolina   Willson
Blue Ridge Mountains (Tennessee Style)   Willson
Bluebirds, Robins and Meadowlarks   Hoffman
Blues-Reel   Carmichael
Bluesten Bowl   Willson
Bon Soir   Heyman; Young, Victor
Bongo Bingo, The   David, Mack; Livingston, Jerry
Boomerang Kisses   Friend
Botany Bay   Evans; Livingston, Jay
Bottle Me Up and Send Me Sailing   Stept
Bottom of the Barrel   Robison
Bowbells, North Dakota   Willson
Boy Meets Girl   Willson
Boy's Theme (inst.)   Young, Victor
Breakfast in Bed   Sigman
Bright Eyes and Bushy Tailed   Merrill
Bringin' Up a Boy (To Be a Man)   Leigh
(We Are) Brothers in Arms   Washington
(I Have Loved Before) But Never Like This   Silver
But Never My Love for You   Hoffman; Silver
But You're Wrong   Drake
Butterflies   Merrill

Cadenza   Willson
Calico Square Dance   Willson
California   Heyman; Young, Victor
Call Me Oop-a-Sometime   Merrill
Call of the Far-Away Hills (Alone on a Lonesome Trail),
    The   David, Mack; Young, Victor
Call of the Wild, The   Washington
Can You Spell Schenectady?   Arlen; Fields
Can-Can   Porter
Can't Get to Tucson too Soon   Robison
Caravelas   Young, Victor
Carlotta, Ya Gotta Be Mine   Robin
Carnival Ballet (inst.)   Van Heusen
Cash Register Heart   Silver
Cat with Nine Tails   Coots
Celebrity   Oakland; Raye
Centennial   Willson
Centennial Song   Merrill
Certain As the Sea Is Blue   Revel
C'est Magnifique   Porter
C'est Merveilliux   Van Heusen
Chameleon   Raye
Change of Heart   Heyman; Young, Victor
Chased to Be Married   Leigh
Cheerio, but Not Goodbye   Razaf
Cherokee Kid   Willson
Chestnut Street   Willson
Chick-a-Boom   Merrill
Child's Letter, A   Willson
Child's Play (inst.)   Strouse
Choo Choo Train (Le Petit Train)   Lawrence
Choro   Washington
Chorus Girl's Dream, The   Oakland; Raye
Christmas Blues, The   Cahn
Christopher Street   Comden and Green
Chuck Wagon Gang   Willson
Chuckle a Day, A   Willson
Clap Your Hands   Clare; Young, Victor
Cleo and Me-O   Merrill
Collage November   Mercer
Come Along with Me   Porter
Come Back, Little Sheba   Freed, Ralph
Come to Me   Heyman; Stept; Young, Victor
Come to My Arms   Robin
Complexities of Radio   Willson
Concrete and Steel   Ruby
Conga!   Comden and Green
Contentment   Ruby
Conversation Piece (Nice People, Nice Talk)   Comden and
    Green
Cook's Cookin' Boogie   Razaf
Count Your Calories   Gordon; Myrow
Crazy Blues   Carmichael
Creep, The   Sigman
Crusade for Freedom   McHugh
Crying Polka   Loesser
Crypto-Vestimenta-Cyclo-Furo-Mania   Willson
Crystal Chandelier (inst.)   Spina
Cuff of My Shirt, The   Merrill
Daddy's Report Card   Drake
Daffy Doodle   Coots
Darling They're Playing Our Song   Coslow
De Lawd's Plan   Mancini
Deadwood Stage (Whip-Crack-Away!), The   Fain; Webster
Deep River   Robison

Dennis the Menace   Hoffman
Desiree   Oakland; Raye
Devil's Serenade, The   Friend
Did You Notice   Drake
Did You See a Couple of WAVES (Of G.I. Guys)   Drake
Did You Try the Pasta   Drake
Dig You Most   Mercer
Dining Car   Willson
Do Something   Drake
Do What Your Heart Tells You   Parish
Does Anybody Want My Fido   Von Tilzer
Donna Marie   Coots
Don't Fool Around (With My Poor Heart)   Spina
Don't Forget to Write   Lawrence
Don't Go Now (Soldier Girl)   Drake
Don't Hurt this Heart   Silver
Don't Let 'em Catch You with Your Sunshine Down   Merrill
Don't Listen to Gossip   Stept
Don't Run Away from the Rain   Mercer
Don't Take My Heart   Evans; Livingston, Jay
Doors of the World Swing on New Britain Hinges,
    The   Willson
Down Boy   Carmichael
Dream World   Gershwin, Ira; Lane
Dreaming of You   Martin
Dynamite Blasting   Willson
Easy, Brother, Easy   Brooks; Warren
Ebb Tide   Sigman
Eeny Meeny Miney Pow   Evans; Livingston, Jay
Empty Ballroom   Spina
Empty House Blues   Razaf
Enchilada Man, The   David, Mack; Livingston, Jerry
Enclosed Are My Tears   Coots
End of a Beautiful Friendship, The   Adamson; Duke
Endless   Davis
Every Man Is a Stupid Man   Porter
Every Night   Drake
Every Street's a Boulevard in Old New York   Styne
Everybody Has a Favorite Song   Drake
Everybody Knows Everybody   Willson
Everybody Loves Money   Spina
Everybody Loves to Take a Bow   Styne
Everybody's Happy   Drake
Everyone Baby   Cahn; Livingston, Jerry
Everyone Wants Something   Van Heusen
Everything Is Still the Same   Stept
Everything Was Wonderful   Drake
Everything's Bigger Down in Texas   Oakland; Raye
Everything's Rosey   Revel
Everytime You Pray   Davis
Evils of Drink!, The   Arlen; DePaul; Fields
Ev'ry Show Must Have a Finale   Razaf
Eyes of Blue (Shane)   Young, Victor
Face to Face   Cahn; Fain
False Love   Davis
Fanmail   Willson
Fellow I'd Follow, The   Cahn
Figaro and Cleo   Washington
Fillmargo   Willson
Finagle   Willson
Fine, Fine, Fine   Cahn
First Christmas, The   Washington
Five Senses, The   Cahn; Fain
Florida Oranges   Willson
Foolin' Around with Love   Bloom; Leslie

Foolish Waltz   Lawrence
For a Moment of Your Love   Burke; Van Heusen
For Me   Hoffman
For the Longest Time   Baer
Foremost Dairy   Mercer
Forever June   Heyman; Young, Victor
Forget Me   David, Hal
Forth and Back   Willson
Four Walls (And One Dirty Window Blues)   Robison
Frenchman Thought of It First, A   Revel
Friend of Mine, A   Merrill
From Island to Island   Blane
Gadabout   Evans; Livingston, Jay
Garden of Eden, The   Porter
Gave of Give and Take, The   Lawrence
Gay Continental Am I, A   Brooks; Warren
Gee, But It's Great to Be Falling in Love   McHugh
Gee Willikens! (inst.)   Warren
Gene's Gem   DePaul
Gentlemen of the Press   Gordon; Myrow
Geraldine   Clare; Young, Victor
Get a Load of that Crazy Walk   DePaul; Raye
Gibbledy Gob   Hoffman; Silver
Gimme a Man Who Makes Music   Washington
Girls   Evans; Livingston, Jay
Girls Want Everything They See   Drake
Git Along   Drake
Give a Girl a Break   Gershwin, Ira; Lane
Give Every Child a Chance   Adamson; McHugh
Give Her Perfume   Revel
Give Me a Look   Hoffman
Give Your Back a Pat (When You Tuck Yourself in
      Bed)   Woods
Gleason Glide, The   Davis
God Is Everywhere   Coots
Gold Rush Towns   Willson
Golden Years, The   Evans; Livingston, Jay
Good Evening, Madamoiselle   Adamson; Duke
Good Friends Are Few (And Far Between)   Robison
Good Old Days, The   Drake
Got a Feelin'   David, Mack; Livingston, Jerry
Grab Him!   Razaf
Grand Old Acquaintance (Of Mine)   Robison
Granny   Razaf
Great White Way, The   Gordon; Myrow
Green Bay, Wisconsin   Willson
Greenwich Village   Drake
Guess Who's Boffo   Drake
Gypsy Romance (inst.)   Young, Victor
Half a Photograph   Russell
Happy Go Lucky   Mitchell
Happy the Bride the Sun Shines Upon   Arlen; Fields
Haven't Got a Worry   Evans; Livingston, Jay
Havin' a Birthday   Merrill
He Who Has Love   Hoffman
Hear No Evil, See No Evil, Speak No Evil   Washington
Heartless Heart   David, Hal
Heat Is On, The   Washington
Heavenly Days   Evans; Livingston, Jay
Hello, Hazel   Styne
Hello Summer, Where You Been All Winter   Caesar
Hello Timmie Rogers   Carmichael
Her Heart Was in Her Work   Porter
Here Comes the Navy   Cahn; Fain
Here's That Rainy Day   Burke; Van Heusen

Here's to Ninety-Nine (Birthday Toast)   Leslie
Hi There   Drake
Higher than a Hawk (Deeper than a Well)   Fain; Webster
Hive Full of Honey   Fain; Webster
Hold Me in Your Arms for 30 Days   Russell
Home Is Where the Heart Is   Cahn; Fain
Homecoming   Brooks
Honestly (Amore Baciami)   Adamson
Honey Darlin'   Merrill
Honeycomb   Merrill
Hooray for Looey   Drake
Horse on the Carousel, The   Stept
Horse Sense   Willson
Hot Dog that Made Him (Her) Mad   Raye
How Do You Speak to an Angel?   Styne
How Far Can a Lady Go?   Burke; Van Heusen
How Long Does It Take to Get Lonesome   Woods
Hug Me a Hug, Kiss Me a Kiss   David, Hal
Huggable and Kissable   Stept
Husband   Willson
Hush-a-Bye   Fain
I Always Shake the Tree   Drake
I Am in Love   Porter
I Can Do Without You   Fain; Webster
I Can't Help Loving You   Magidson
I Confess   Lawrence
I Could Cook   Arlen; Fields
I Couldn't Be True to an Angel   Brown, Lew; Henderson
I Couldn't Take My Eyes Off You   Merrill
I Do   Porter
I Do! I Do! I Do!   Evans; Livingston, Jay
I Don't Care If the Sun Don't Shine   David, Mack
I Don't See You Anymore   Warren
I Don't Want Your Sympathy   Sigman
I Feel Like I'm Gonna Live Forever   Styne
I Feel Like They Feel in Castile   Burke; Van Heusen
I Got Butterflies   Cahn; Fain
I Got Happy Too Soon   Dixon; Henderson; Rose
I Gotta Have Love — I've Gotta Have Music   Ruby
I Guess I'll Dress Up for the Blues   David, Mack
I Guess It Was You All the Time   Carmichael; Mercer
I Guess I've Made a Mess of Things   Merrill
I Had to Kiss You   Robin
I Have One Gift   Russell
I Hear the Music Now   Fain
I Know I'm not Your Mother   Merrill
I Know It and You Know It   Willson
I Love Dixie   Brooks
I Love Halloween   Davis
I Love Paris   Porter
I Love You   Willson
I Made Myself a Promise   Cahn; Fain
I Never Felt Better in My Life   Stept
I Never Felt this Way Before   Gordon; Myrow
I Never Left Home   Hoffman; Silver
I Passed By Your Window   Lawrence
I Pray   Mercer
I Shall Positively Pay You Next Monday   Porter
I Take Just as Much Pride in My Dear Little Bride   Willson
I Wanna Be a Buccaneer   Leigh
I Wanna Wander   Gordon; Myrow
I Want You for a Sunbeam   Merrill
I Was Wearin' Horseshoes   Arlen; Fields
I Wish I Could Be a Singing Cowboy   Cahn
I Wish I Were a Fish   Brooks; Young, Victor

I Wonder What He Said to Her   Drake
I'd Give a Dollar for a Dime   Blake; Razaf
I'd Like to Find the Guy Who Stole My Gal (And Thank Him from the Bottom of My Heart)   Freed, Ralph; Hoffman
I'd Rather Forgive You than Forget You   Bryan
I'd Rather Have a Pal than a Gal Anytime   Gordon; Myrow
If I   Friend
If I Could Love You   Baer
If I Had a Golden Umbrella   Merrill
If I Love You a Mountain   Gordon; Myrow
If It's All the Same to You (Cela M'est Egal)   Burke; Van Heusen
If Only You Could Love Me   Porter
If Santa Claus Would Fill My Stocking with a Brother Just for Me   Von Tilzer
If There Were No Men in the World   Willson
If There Were No Women at All   Willson
If There's Anybody Here from Out of Town   Robison
If You Can't Be Good, Be Careful   Razaf; Waller
If You Don't Like the Jokes Watch the Girl   Davis
If You Haven't Lost Your Sense of Honor (You Haven't Lost a Gosh Darn Thing)   Davis
If You Loved Me Truly   Porter
If You Should Say Goodbye   Hoffman
If You Want My Love   Hoffman
If You Were Mine   Merrill
If Your Heart Should Skip a Beat   Caesar
If You're Nice to Me   Mitchell; Stept
Ignore Dior   Willson
Ike's Golf Game   Willson
I'll Come to You   Coots
I'll Go   Sigman
I'll Go on Loving You   Merrill
I'll Miss You   Merrill
I'll Never Say Goodbye to You Again   Willson
I'll Sing No Duet with You   Willson
I'll Take You As You Are   Sigman
I'm a Ruler of a South Sea Island   Blane
I'm Afraid to Love You   Coots
I'm Glad I'm Leaving   Styne
I'm Glad You're Sorry, Ain't You Sorry I'm Glad   Stept
I'm Gonna Hang Up Mommy's Stocking Instead of Mine on Christmas Night   Coots
I'm in Love with My Best Friend's Sweetheart   Raye; Spina
I'm Invited to a Wedding   Coots
I'm Lost, in Dreams of You   Johnson, J. Rosamond
I'm Mad About the Girl Next Door   Gordon; Myrow
I'm Not So Very Sure   Stept
I'm One of Your Admirers   Burke; Van Heusen
I'm Thru with You   Howard, Bart
I'm Your Girl   Hammerstein; Rodgers
I'm-a Love You   Hoffman
In a Very Special Way (Pour la Toute Premiere Fois)   Razaf
In My Neck o' the Woods   Hoffman
In Our United State   Gershwin, Ira; Lane
In San Domingo   Stept
In the Clear Light of Dawn   Burke; Van Heusen
In the Night (inst.)   Young, Victor
In Walked Luck   Revel
In Your Eyes   Coots
Inchin' Up   Sherman
Indian Music   Willson
Inspection   Blane
Intermission Talk   Hammerstein; Rodgers
Invitation   Drake

Invitation to the Mardi Gras   Drake
Irvington   Revel
Is It True What They Say about Worry   Caesar
Is It Worth It   Drake
Isn't It Strange   Drake
It Feels Good   Hammerstein; Rodgers
It Feels Like Saturday Night   Lawrence
It Happened to Me   Brooks; Young, Victor
It Happens Ev'ry Time   Gershwin, Ira; Lane
It Looks Like Arabia   Drake
It Was Great While It Lasted   Washington
It Was Worth It (That's What I'll Say)   Howard, Bart
It's a Fine Old Institution   Burke; Van Heusen
It's a Good Night for Stayin' at Home   Drake
It's a Long Way from Broadway (To Leicester Square)   Davis
It's a Matter of Military Tactics   Burke; Van Heusen
It's a Miracle   Hoffman
It's a Whistle-in Kinda Morning   Brooks; Warren
It's All in Your Heart   Drake
It's All Right with Me   Porter
It's an Old Spanish Custom   Burke; Van Heusen
It's Gonna Be a Big Hit   Cahn; Fain
It's Good for You   Willson
It's Lonesome Out Tonight   Clare
It's Love   Comden and Green
It's Me   Hammerstein; Rodgers
It's Nice in Nice   Revel
It's That Time Again   Cahn
It's the Army Everytime   Davis
It's the End of the World   Adams; Strouse
It's Tomorrow   Evans; Livingston, Jay
It's Torment   Evans; Livingston, Jay
I've Been Writing My Heart Out to You   Stept
I've Got a Problem   Drake
I've Got My Arms Wrapped Around a Rainbow   Coots
I've Gotta Hear that Beat   Cahn
J'ai Vu Dans Ter Yeux   McHugh
Johnny Crewcut   David, Mack
Johnny Guitar   Hoffman; Silver
Jolson Tribute, The   Oakland
Jubilee Trail   Clare; Young, Victor
Junkman's Jingle, The   Gordon; Myrow
Just Across the River on a Hill   Carmichael
Just Another Chance   Mancini
Just Another Polka   Loesser
Just As Long As You're With Me   Stept
Just Blew in from the Windy City   Fain; Webster
Just Married   Drake
Just One Kiss   Washington; Young, Victor
Katchen-Polka   Parish
Keep It Gay   Hammerstein; Rodgers
Keep It Under Your Hat   Fain; Webster
Keep Your Eye on My Darlin'   Leigh
Keys to the City, The   Drake
Kind of Moody   Ellington; Sigman
King of New Orleans   Brooks
King Size Kisses   David, Hal
Kiss Me or I'll Scream   Cahn; Fain
Kiss Special   Oakland; Raye
Kissin' Cake Polka   Drake
Kitty in a Basket   Merrill
Knockin' Song (True Love Is Knockin' at My Door), The   Freed, Ralph; Hoffman
La Baie Verte   Willson
La Conchita   Coots

La Petite Trianon (inst.)   Warren
La Volta   Spina
Lady Loves, A   Gordon; Myrow
Lady of Guadalupe   Drake
Lady of the Lake   Drake
La-La-Lalapalooza   Evans; Livingston, Jay
Lallapalooza   Comden and Green
Land of Lemonade and Lollipops, The   Coots
Land of the Setting Sun   Johnson, Howard
Las Vegas   Adams
Last Word, The   Willson
Lately Song, The   Cahn; Fain
Latin Lovers   Robin
Laughs   Evans; Livingston, Jay
Laundry Scene   Porter
Laura De Maupassant   Styne
Law, The   Porter
Lawn Mower Waltz   Willson
Leaping Music   Raye
Lemon Drop Moon   Webster
Les Trois Etroit Trottoirs   Revel
Let It Come Down   Comden and Green
Let Me Tell You a Tale   Drake
Let's Do It Again   Washington
Let's Dream Together   Harbach
Let's Drink to Happiness   Hoffman
Let's Give Every Child a Chance   McHugh
Let's Have a Meeting of the Lips   David, Hal
Let's Love Tonight   Baer
Let's Make Memories Tonight   Coots
Life Can Be Oh So Sweet   Baer
Life Has Its Funny Little Ups and Downs   Gordon; Myrow
Lift Up Your Voice   Willson
Little Bit in Love, A   Comden and Green
Little Choo Choo, The   Coots
Little Goldie Goldfish   Coots
Little More Heart, A   Styne
Little More of Your Amor, A   Robin
Little Tin Soldier (And the Little Toy Drum) (C/L Coots, J. Fred), The   Coots
Little White Stone   Robison
Live and Let Live   Porter
Living the Life I Love   Fain
London After Dark   Caesar
Lonely   Davis
Long Live Love   Spina
Look at that Girl   Merrill
Look Who's Been Dreaming   Arlen; Fields
Lord Above Is My Partner, The   Spina
Louella   McHugh
L-O-V-E   Merrill
Love and Hate   Raye
Love Is a Sacred Thing   Ager; Akst; Davis
Love Is Somethin' Money Can't Buy   Hoffman; Silver
Love Is the Same   Brooks
Love Lingers On   Baer
Love, Look what You've Done to Me   Washington
Love Me Now   David, Hal; Hoffman
Love of My Life (inst.)   Young, Victor
Love Will Soon Be Here   Adamson; Carmichael
Lovely Weather for Ducks   Evans; Livingston, Jay
Lullaby of the Lord, The   Cahn
Luna (Crazy Light)   Robison
Mad-Man Moon   Leigh
Madonna of Donwoolie Hill   Robison

Magic Horseshoe, The   Coots
Magic Lamp   Coots
Magic Strings (inst.)   Young, Victor
Magic Valley   Willson
Magic Window, The   Burke; Van Heusen
Maidens Typical of France   Porter
Make Me Make You Mine   Adamson; Carmichael
Make the People Cry   Styne
Mama Nicolini   Coots
Man Is a Man, A   Clare; Young, Victor
Man Must His Honor Defend, A   Porter
Man with the Whiskers (And the Apple Cheeks), The   Stept
Marriage Type Love   Hammerstein; Rodgers
(There Never Was a Girl Named) Mary   Bryan
Matador's Prayer, The   David, Mack
May I Sing to You   Akst
May Your Blessings Be Many   Young, Victor
Maybe It's the Mood I'm In   David, Hal
Mazurka (inst.)   Styne
Me You See, The   Dixon
Meanwhile   Alter
Melody   Webster
Mem'ries of the Past   Baer
Merrie Mending   Ellington
Mine to Love   Young, Victor
Miracle of Prayer, The   Davis
Miracle of the Rose, The   David, Mack
Missouri Mazurka   Styne
Mister Fidgety Feet   Drake
Money Burns a Hole in My Pocket   Styne
Montmart'   Porter
Moon Is Blue, The   Baer
Moonlighter Song, The   Sigman
Mother Darling   Willson
Motherhood   Webster
(Sometimes I Feel Like a) Motherless Child   Robison
Mr. Banjo Man   Evans; Livingston, Jay
Mule   Willson
Music Across the Waters   Willson
Musical Chairs   Mercer
My Blue Print of Dreams   DeSylva
My Book of Animal Songs   Coots
My Conversation   Adamson; Carmichael
My Darlin' Eileen   Comden and Green
My Darlin' Has a Cordial Eye   David, Hal
My Dolly and Me   Coots
My English Into French Dictionary   Burke; Van Heusen
My Flaming Heart   Cahn
My Friend   Drake
My Gaucho   Cahn
My God Is So High   Robison
My Grandmother's Grandfather's Clock   Willson
My Guy and I   Brooks; Young, Victor
My Heart Has Many Dreams   Sigman
My Heart Is a Singing Heart   Cahn; Fain
My Heart Is Home   Evans; Livingston, Jay
My Heart's Desire   David, Mack
My Jealous Eyes (That Turn from Blue to Green)   David, Mack
My Kind o' Day   Evans; Livingston, Jay
My Little Bird   Willson
My Love for You   Gordon
My Love Is a Wanderer   Howard, Bart
My Signature   Willson
My Weeping Heart   Coots

My Wild Imagination   Styne
N.A.G., The   Razaf
Native Dancer   Hoffman; Silver
Never Again   Sigman
Never Give Anything Away   Porter
Never, Never Be an Artist   Porter
Never So Beautiful   Evans; Livingston, Jay
New Orleans Street Crime   Lawrence
New Year's Eve 1953   Drake
New York City Ghost   Young, Victor
Newspaperman's Blues, The   Razaf
Nice to See You   Caesar; Yellen
Nicest Thing about Saying Goodbye (Is Sayin' Hello Again),
    The   Davis
Night and You   Robin
No More Goodbyes   Hoffman
No One   Adams; Strouse
No Other Love   Hammerstein; Rodgers
No Swallerin' Place   Loesser
Nobody Asked Me to Dance   Merrill
Not Until Now   Razaf
Nothin', Nothin', Baby (Without You)   Ellington
Nothing Is Impossible   Gershwin, Ira; Lane
Nothing to Do But Work   Porter
Now I've Heard Everything   Drake
Now, Now, Now   David, Hal
Now that I'm in Love   Burke
Nowhere   Hoffman
Nowhere Guy   Gordon; Myrow
Nylons   Willson
Occupancy of This Building is Limited to 382 Persons By
    Order of the New York Fire Department   Willson
Ode to a Southern Woman   Drake
Oh Ma Ma   McHugh
Ohio   Comden and Green; Mercer
Old Actor's Dream, The   Oakland; Raye
Old Fashioned Waltz   Willson
Old Hoagy   Carmichael
Old Iron Horse, The   Webster
Old Love, The   Van Heusen
On the Erie Canal   Arlen; Fields
On the Rue de la Paix   Heyman; Young, Victor
On the Ten o' Ten for Ten-Ten-Tennessee   Coots
On Top of Old Dumkopf   Drake
On Very Slowly with the Dance   Revel
Once a Teacher   Revel
(It Takes a Lot of Little Likes to Make) One Big
    Love   Brooks; Warren
One Day   Spina
One Hot Dog to a Customer   Blake
One Hundred Easy Ways   Comden and Green
One Misty Moisty Morning   Hoffman
One Moment More   David, Mack
One More Love   Heyman
One Sided Love Affair   Davis
One Step Ahead of Everybody   Sigman
Only Love Me   Sigman
Only One Revival   Robison
Opposite Sex, The   Blane
Orchid for the Lady, An   Ager
Our World   Razaf
Out of the Frying Pan Into the Fire   Lawrence
'Ow Are You Feelin', 'Arry Boy   Mancini
Ozzie the Ostrich   Coots

Pachenza Pachenza (Patience Patience)   Hoffman
Pagan In Paris, A   DePaul
Pagnnin Paris, A   Raye
Paid in Full   Sigman
Pain in the Heart   Caesar; Yellen
Palmy Pinellas Peninsula   Willson
Pals   Baer
Parade of Clowns   Robison
Pardon My Head   Drake
Paris Gown (inst.)   Styne
Pass the Football   Comden and Green
Passengers Will Kindly Step Back in the Sub   Willson
(Cookie's Song) Peaches an' Cream   Spina
Peggy's in the Pantry   David, Hal
Peruvian Fire Brigade   Spina
Phantom Violin, A   Snyder
Physician Heal Thyself   Robison
Piccolo Polka   Willson
Pinones   Bergman
Plundering of the Town (inst.), The   Van Heusen
Po Ling Ming Toy Chinese Love Story   Friml
Politely   Willson
Pony on the Merry-Go-Round, The   Coots
Pool Hall Blues   Brooks
Pot and Pan Parade, The   Mercer
Practice Makes Perfect   Willson
Prayer   Bryan
Prologue and Interlude   Oakland
Propos De Rien, A   Burke; Van Heusen
Purple Cow, A   Webster
Quadrille   Porter
Queen of New Orleans, The   Washington
Quiet Girl, A   Comden and Green
Rag, a Bone and a Hank of Hair, A   Razaf
Rain in My Heart   Caesar; Yellen
Ranch House Square Dance   Drake
Rather   Hoffman
Reach for the Stars   Evans; Livingston, Jay
Restless Heart   Bergman
Return to Paradise   Washington
Ridin' Up to Heaven   Clare
Ring the Bell   Burke; Van Heusen
Rio at Your Feet   Drake
Rita, Rio   David, Hal
River of Silver (And a Meadow of Gold), A   Robison
Riviera, The   Coleman
Rosalie   Willson
Rruff (Ruv) Song   Evans
Rruff Song   Livingston, Jay
Ruby   Parish
Run Away   David, Hal
Running Water   Willson
Rutland Bounce (inst.), The   Styne
Ruv Song No. 1   Livingston, Jay
Ruv Song No. 2   Evans; Livingston, Jay
Sad Parisianne   Gordon; Revel
Salomee (With Her Seven Veils)   Styne
San Domingo   David, Mack; Livingston, Jerry
Sangaree   Evans; Livingston, Jay
Satin Doll   Ellington; Mercer
Saturday Afternoon Before the Game   Gordon; Myrow
Say What You Will   Heyman; Young, Victor
Saying No   Clare; Young, Victor
Sayonara, Sayonara   Berlin
Scene Is Spain, The   Drake

Scratch My Back   Freed, Ralph; Livingston, Jerry
Secret Love   Fain; Webster
Secretly Mine   Alter; Eliscu
See the Circus   Evans; Livingston, Jay
Seeds of Brotherhood   Razaf
Self-Expression   Comden and Green
(Kalu) Senor   Adamson
Sentimental Things You Do, The   Merrill
Serenade to a Tony   Gorney
Serenade to Whom It May Concern, A   Revel
Seventeen Gun Salute, A   Burke; Van Heusen
Shades of Old Blarney   Stept
Shall We Sing   Drake
She Still Loves You   Fain; Webster
Shelter in the Time of Storm   Robison
She's Something Spanish   David, Hal
Shimmy Special   Oakland; Raye
Shoot the Moon (Patio Song)   Gordon; Myrow
Show Me a Happy Woman (And I'll Show You a Miserable
    Man)   Cahn; Fain
Show Starts Right Away, The   Evans; Livingston, Jay
Signs   Mercer
Silver Cobwebs   Ellington
Silver Horseshoe   Coots
Simonetta   Caesar
Since I Kissed the Blarney Stone   Young, Joseph
Sincerely   Hoffman
Sing a Song of Friendship   Caesar
Sing for Your Special   Oakland; Raye
Sing Me a Song of the Islands   Stept
Sittin' in the Sun (Countin' My Money)   Berlin
Sleepy Hollow Home   Carmichael
Slow & Funny   Carmichael
Slowly but Surely   Heyman; Young, Victor
Small Things, The   Burke; Van Heusen
Small Towns Are Smile Towns   Cahn
Snerling Through the Flowers   Hoffman
Snow, Snow, Beautiful Snow   Sigman
So Big   Washington
Soft Music Professor   Parish
Somebody Else's Sweetie   Lerner, Sammy
Somebody Laid a Hand on My Shoulder   Robison
Someone Turned the Moon Up Side Down   Burke
Someone's Been Readin' My Mail   Sigman
Somethin' Real Special   Arlen; Fields
Something Better than Being in Love   Burke; Van Heusen
Something for the Browns   Revel
Something in the Wind   Styne
Somewhere Over the Moon (Gitarren-Serenade)   Rome
Song of India   Mercer
Song of the Comb, The   Hoffman
Spanish Of Course   David, Mack; Livingston, Jerry
Spindletop   Willson
Spring Never Came Around This Year   David, Mack
Squee Jee (The Happy Little Clown)   Coots
St. Anthony's Alma Mater Hymn   Cahn
Star Sapphire (inst.)   Alter
Star Was Born, A   Ager; Rose
Steamboat Song   Leigh
Stop, Sit Down, Relax, Think   Magidson
Story of My Life, The   Comden and Green
Strike a Match   Spina
String of Broken Hearts, A   Hoffman; Silver
Stringbean Boy   DePaul; Raye
Stronger Sex, The   Burke; Van Heusen

Sudden Thrill, The   Burke; Van Heusen
Summer Green — Autumn Gold   Webster
Summer Vacation   Oakland
Summertime U.S.A.   Drake
Sunday, Monday, Tuesday   Hoffman
Sunshine Followed By Sunshine   Drake
Sunshine Hurts My Eyes, The   Sigman
Sweet as a Bunch of Roses   Burke
Sweet Dreams of You   Baer
Sweetheart   Raye; Spina
Swing!   Comden and Green
Take It Easy   Blake; Razaf
Take Me to Broadway   Cahn
Take Me Where I Can Be Happy   Merrill
Take Me With You   Freed, Ralph
Take the High Ground   Washington
Take the Note the Bluebird Wrote   David, Hal
Take the Word of a Gentleman   Burke; Van Heusen
Takin' a Slow Burn   Washington
Talk to Me   Leigh
Talking Chorus, The   Drake
Talking to Your Picture on the Wall   Coots
Tattle-Tale Duck   Merrill
Tegucigalpa   David, Mack
Tell Me, Tain't True   Sigman
Tell Us Where the Good Times Are   Merrill
Tenderly Special   Oakland; Raye
That Great Getting Up Morning   Carmichael
That Man Is Doing His Worst to Make Good   Burke; Van
    Heusen
That's All   Drake
That's Amore   Brooks; Warren
That's the Very Spot   Drake
That's the Way It Happens   Hammerstein; Rodgers
That's What a Woman Can Do   Sherman
That's What They Like About Autumn   Drake
That's Where I'm So Different   Adamson; Carmichael
(Sadie Thompson's Song) The Blue Pacific
    Blues   Washington
(On) The Erie Canal   Arlen; Fields
There Must Be a Reason   Cahn; Fain
There You Are   Van Heusen
There'll Come a Time When You'll Need Me   Mills; Waller
There's a Bell that Rings in My Heart, Ding, Ding   Adams;
    Strouse
There's a Corny Little Corner in the Corner of My
    Heart   Dixon; Rose
There's Music in You   Hammerstein; Rodgers
There's No Place Like the Lambs   Stept
There's Nobody Richer than Me   Davis
There's Plenty of Fish in the Ocean   Brooks
These Are the Things I Remember   Washington
They've Got the Loopiest Loop in Chicago   Drake
They've Got to Be Dreams to Start   Merrill
Think How Many People Never Find Love   Styne
Thirty Two Bars of I Love You   Willson
This and No More   Spina
This Christmas   Stept
This Is Greece   Drake
This Time   Coots
This Too Shall Pass Away   Drake
Three Ways   Willson
Throw a Curve   Revel
Ties that Bind, The   Sigman
Time Ain't Long   Robison

Timpanogos Glacier   Willson
Tin Pan Alley   Coleman
'Tis Harry I'm Plannin' to Marry   Fain; Webster
To Comfort Me   Leigh
To Think that This Could Happen to Me   Porter
Today I Love Ev'rybody   Arlen; Fields
Too Little Time   Mancini; Raye
Toot-a-Loor   Willson
Toys   Merrill
Triskaidekaphobia   Drake
Trousseau for Trudy   Alter
True or False   Sigman
(Don't Let Temptation) Turn You 'Round   Friend
Turquoise Blue (inst.)   Alter
Twenty-seven Elm Street   Blane
Unaccustomed As I Am   Burke; Van Heusen
(I Never Missed Your Sweet Hello) Until We Said
     Goodbye   Ager; Akst; Davis
Vagabonds   Burke
Vanessa   Revel
Velvet Glove, The   Spina
Velvo Suds Commercial   Fain
Very Necessary You, The   Burke; Van Heusen
Very Special Day, A   Hammerstein; Rodgers
Vignette   Oakland; Raye
Voice of P.O.W. (inst.), The   Young, Victor
Voila   Drake
Vola, Columba   Sigman
Wait'll You Meet My Darlin'   Hoffman
Walk with a Wiggle   David, Hal
Walkin' and Wond'rin' (My Heart Cried Out in
     Vain)   Merrill
Walking Tune, A   David, Hal
Waltz that Broke My Heart, The   David, Mack
Watch Over Daddy   Silver
Waukegan Was a Thriving and Prosperous City Before Jack
     Benny Came Along   Willson
We Deserve Each Other   Hammerstein; Rodgers
We Girls of the Chorus   Gordon; Myrow
We Have Never Met As Yet   Gordon; Myrow
Wedding Dance   Rome
Welcome to Hollywood   Drake
We're Doin' It for the Natives in Jamaica   Arlen; Fields
We're in Business   Arlen; Fields
What a Fair Thing Is a Woman   Porter
What a Night, What a Night, What a Night   David, Hal
What a Waste   Comden and Green
What Am I Gonna Give My Girl for Xmas   Drake
What Are New Yorkers Made Of   Fain
What Are You Gonna See   Drake
What Does a Soldier Want for Christmas   Berlin
What Have You Done for Me Lately?   David, Mack;
     Livingston, Jerry
What Have You Got for Tonight   Drake
What Make de Difference?   Blane
What More Is There   Davis
What Wouldcha Do Without Me?   Brooks; Warren
When I Close My Door   Arlen; Fields
When I Was Young (Yes, Very Young)   Merrill
When I'm with You   Davis
When It's Love   Cahn
When Love Comes to Call   Porter
When Love Goes Wrong (Nothin' Goes Right)   Adamson;
     Carmichael
When Mama Calls   Merrill

When Someone Wonderful Thinks You're
     Wonderful   David, Mack; Livingston, Jerry
When You Love Someone   Evans; Livingston, Jay
When You're in Love   Blane
Where Did He Go   Washington
Where Did You Learn to Dance   Gordon; Myrow
Where Do Lonely People Go   Leigh
Where the Honeysuckle Grows   Waller
Whisper   David, Mack; Donaldson
Whistle'n Jim   Coots
Whistles of the Hills, The   Merrill
Who Is the Bravest?   Styne
Who Said Gay Paree?   Porter
Who Sir, Me Sir?   Evans; Livingston, Jay
Who Wants to Fall in Love   Howard, Bart
Who Will It Be When the Time Comes?   Blane
Who's the Gal   Drake
Why Am I Happy?   Arlen; Fields
Why Come Crying to Me   Sigman
Why Does It Have to Be Me   Sigman
Why Don't You Join the Air Force Reserve   David, Hal
Why Don't You Speak for Yourself, John   Brooks
Why Don't You Tell Me   Burke; Van Heusen
Why Let a Lie Break Your Heart   Coots
Why Say Goodbye   Bryan
Why Tell a Lie (A Song of Alabama)   Caesar
Wild Horses   Burke
Will You Remember Tomorrow Night (All That You Told Me
     Tonight)   Hoffman
Winding Road   Ager
Wish Me Good Luck (As You Wish Me Goodbye)   David,
     Hal
With the Sun Warm Upon Me   Arlen; Fields
Woman, There Is No Living with You   Gershwin, Ira; Lane
Woman's Touch, A   Fain; Webster
Wonder Why   Cahn
World Famous Horseshoe Curve, The   Willson
World Is Beautiful Today, The   Styne
World's Your Oyster, The   Willson
Wrong Note Rag   Comden and Green
Ya Got Class   Evans; Livingston, Jay
Yes!   Arlen; Fields
You   Gordon; Myrow
You and Your Flourescent Eyes   Gorney
You Are My Love   Webster
You Are There   Drake
You Can Depend on Us   Drake
You Can't Get Away from the Lawd   Razaf
You Fooled Me   Davis
You Had a Wonderful Time   Drake
You Never Know   Razaf
You Opened My Eyes   Brooks
You Rang the Bell with Me, Ting-A-Ling, Ting-A-Ling   Baer
You Will Hear It Soon   Willson
Young at Heart   Leigh
Your Face Is My Fortune   Caesar
Your Spell   Styne
You're a Friend, You're a Pal, You're a Sweetheart   Hoffman
You're but Oh So Right   Cahn; Fain
You're Dead!   Burke; Van Heusen
You're Doin' All Right   Gordon; Myrow
You're Gonna Dance with Me, Willie   Styne
You're So Simpatico   Coots
You're the Greatest   Davis
You're the Right One   Brooks; Warren

Yours Alone   Drake

1954

Acre of Heaven   Alter
Addio   Hoffman
Adventuring   Leigh
Ahoy There   Drake
Alabama Christmas   Willson
All for You   Sondheim
All I Have Is You   Mills
All Over the Country   Drake
Allan Owen Theme   Oakland
Alone Too Long   Fields; Schwartz, Arthur
Alright Already   Parish
Alter of the Angels, The   Livingston, Jerry; Webster
And Away We Go (Aw-a-a-a-y)   Davis
And I Love You   Evans; Livingston, Jay
And So I Sorrow   Blake
And So I Walked Home   Merrill
Angel Bells   Ruby
Angel in the Christmas Play, The   Merrill
Angel Kissed Me Last Night, An   Washington; Young, Victor
Angel's Tears   David, Mack
Another Princely Scheme (Tarantella)   Leigh
Antonia   Mercer
Any Gal from Texas   Blane; Myrow
Anyone Can Fall in Love   Cahn
Anyone for Tennis   Drake
Anything Can Happen in Brooklyn   Baer; Leslie
Apple on a Pear Tree   Hoffman
Applejack, The   Livingston, Jerry; Sigman
Armful of You (inst.), An   Waller
Army Song   Weill
Art Pallen Theme   Oakland
At Our House   Oakland
At the Copa   Drake
(A la Fin de la Se-Mane) At the End of the Week   Robison
Athena   Blane; Martin
Autumn in Rome   Cahn
Average American Guy, An   Oakland
Awake My Love   Parish
Away Up There   Drake
Baby Be Smart   Blake
Bachelor Party (And the Linen Shower), The   Drake
Back Home   Evans; Livingston, Jay
Bad News   Evans; Livingston, Jay
Ballad of Dependency   Weill
Ballad of the Easy Life   Weill
Banana Boat   Evans; Livingston, Jay
Barbara   Weill
Barney Brontosaur   Sherman
Baton Rouge   Merrill
Battle, The   Leigh
Be a Little Darlin'   David, Hal
Be Kind to Your Parents   Rome
Be My Guest   Heyman; Young, Victor
Be Our Mother   Leigh
Be Our Parents   Leigh
Beachcomber, Beachcomber   Robison
Because I'm Still in Love with You   Coots
Beer Here (Bier Her)   Webster
Beetle Dance Theme (inst.)   Youmans
Before We Start   Drake

Best Things Happen While You're Dancing, The   Berlin
Best Yet, The   Clare
Beware of the Boy with His Mind Made Up   Leigh
Biddy Deane Theme   Oakland
Bide-a-Wee in Soho, The   Weill
Big Battle, The   Leigh
Big Doin's   Evans; Livingston, Jay
Big Name Dropper, The   Robison
Big Pet Peeve Society   Robison
Big Polka (inst.), The   Young, Victor
Big Sunday School   Robison
Bill Randle Theme   Oakland
Birthday Kid, The   Drake
Birthday Song   Rome
Bitter Beguine, The   Oakland
Bless the Land I Love   Silver
Bless Your Beautiful Hide   DePaul; Mercer
Bless Your Little Heart, My Dear   Gilbert; Oakland
Blind Man Stood on the Road (And Cried)   Robison
Blossom   Ellington; Mercer
Blue Bells of Broadway (Are Ringing Tonight), The   Fain; Webster
Blue Interlude   Razaf
Blue Jeans and Pink Lemonade   Fain; Webster
Blue Mirage (Don't Go)   Coslow
Bob Kaye Theme   Oakland
Bob Maxwell Theme   Oakland
Bob Murphy Theme   Oakland
Bob Richmond Theme   Oakland
Bonnie Old Earth, The   Drake
Boo Kangaroo   Hoffman
Booth Hotel, The   Drake
Boulevard of Nightingales   Hoffman
Boy Millionaire   Drake
Boy Wanted   Merrill
Brave Man   Evans; Livingston, Jay
Breezin' (inst.)   Waller
Broadway   Drake
Bundle of Sweetness, A   Sigman
Burbank Bounce   Fain; Webster
But I Ain't Got a Man   Berlin
Butterscotch Man, The   Merrill
By Candlelight   Lawrence
By Madame Firelle   Blane; Myrow
Call from the Grave   Weill
Can I Leave Off Wearin' My Shoes?   Arlen
Can You Explain?   Arlen
Canada Dry Water   Willson
Can't Sleep for Dreaming   Spina
Captain Hook's Waltz   Comden and Green; Styne
Capturing the Boys and Wendy   Leigh
Cardinal's Guard Are We, The   Robin; Romberg
C'est la Guerre   Evans; Livingston, Jay
Chain Reaction   David, Hal
Champagne and Wedding Cake   Styne
Change of Heart   Stept
Change of Scene   Drake
Charity Bazaar   Drake
Chihuahua Choo-Choo   Evans; Livingston, Jay
Choreography   Berlin
Christmas Carol, A   Young, Victor
Christmas Is a Little Doll   Sigman
Christmas Waltz   Cahn; Styne
City of Hope   Freed, Ralph
Class   Sondheim

Clean Break   Sigman
Clink Clank Clunk   Evans; Livingston, Jay
Close Your Eyes and Make Believe   Cahn
Club Time   Spina
Cocoanut Oil Shampoo (TV Commercial)   Arlen; Gershwin, Ira
Code of the West, The   Evans; Livingston, Jay
Cold Cream Jar Song   Rome
Come Across for the Red Cross   Lerner, Sammy; Oakland
Come Back   Drake; Oakland
Come Back to My Arms   Freed, Ralph
Come Boys, Let's All Be Gay Boys   Romberg; Webster
Come Out, Come Out   Drake
Come with Me and Be Beloved   Coots
Comment Allez Vous (How Are Things with You)   Blane; Myrow
Commercial   Arlen; Gershwin, Ira
Coney Island Boat   Fields; Schwartz, Arthur
Continental Waltz, The   Hoffman
Conversation   Adams; Strouse
Could I   Drake
Couldn't Care More   Coslow
Count Your Blessings Instead of Sheep   Berlin
Country Music   Drake
Couple of Kids in Love, A   Oakland
Cover My Face with Shame   Merrill
Crambambuli   Webster
Crooner - A Comic, A   Berlin
Cuacamonga   Freed, Ralph
Cut Yourself a Tiny Slice of Dream Cake   Coslow
Dance   Russell
Dancing Partner   Arlen; Gershwin, Ira
Daniel the Cocker Spaniel   Hoffman; Silver
Dark Glasses   Coots
Dave Waldman Theme   Oakland
Dawn   David, Mack; Livingston, Jerry
Day By Day   Young, Victor
Day that the Circus Left Town, The   Leigh; Spina
Death Message   Weill
Death of Tinker Bell   Leigh
Dedication   Drake
Deep in My Heart Dear   Romberg; Webster
Delighted, I'm Sure   Sondheim
Dick Gilbert Theme   Oakland
Dick Smith Theme   Oakland
Did You Know   Drake
Dime and a Dollar, A   Evans; Livingston, Jay
Dissertation on the State of Bliss (Love and Learn)   Arlen; Gershwin, Ira
Distant Melody   Comden and Green; Styne
Dodo Bird in the Banyan Tree, The   David, Mack
Does He Know   Rome
Doesn't Anybody Love Me   Davis
Don't Believe Me   Bryan
Don't Do Anything that I Wouldn't Do   David, Hal
Don't Let Our Love Die on the Vine   Freed, Ralph; Livingston, Jerry
Don't Lie to Me   Mills
Don't Like Goodbyes   Arlen
Don't Make Me Cry   David, Hal
Don't Say It   Coslow
Don't Stay Away too Long   David, Hal
Don't Take Your Lips Away   Hoffman
Down on the Farm   Drake
Downtown   Adams

Dream Dream, Dream (Long, Long, Long)   McHugh
Dream Harbor   Lawrence
Dreaming of You   Ruby
Dreamland   Goetz
Dreams Are Made for Children   David, Mack; Livingston, Jerry
Dressing Up   Leigh
Drinking Song   Romberg; Webster
Drum Beat   Washington; Young, Victor
Duo   Drake
Earl Pudney Theme   Oakland
East of Siam   Lawrence
Easter in Napoli   Gilbert; Oakland
Easter in Your Heart   Young, Victor
Easy to Have Around   Robison
Easy to Kiss   Merrill
Eat a Big Breakfast   Robison
Eat, Drink and Be Healthy   Willson
Echo Song   Leigh
Edward   Merrill
Ergo Bibamus   Webster
Every New Tomorrow   Ager; Akst; Davis
Every Night   Rome
Everything I Do   Heyman; Young, Victor
Exhibit "A"   Sondheim
Faith Has Many Voices   Robison
Faith that You Have in Me, The   Silver
Fall   Drake
Fall in Line with Joe McCarthy   Leslie
Falling in Love Waltz, The   Burke
Fanny   Rome
Fast Talk   Blake
Faster Than Sound   Blane; Martin
Fellow Citizens   Drake
Fiesta   Goetz
Figi Islands   Webster
Fingerprints of Heaven   Bryan
First Impressions   Leigh
Fishin' from the Bridges (On the Florida Keys)   Robison
$500 Reward   Leigh
Florida Fresh Frozen Concentrate   Willson
Flowers on the Water   Mancini
Fly Me to the Moon (In Other Words)   Howard, Bart
Football Special   Drake
For 1 for 6 Forever   Willson
For Better, For Worse   Coslow
For Ever   David, Mack
For Lovers   Lawrence
(This Night Was Made) For Lovers Only   Livingston, Jerry
Fords Out Front   Willson
Forgotten Dreams   Parish
Fortune's Darling   Leigh
Free to Be Free   Friml
French Line (1), The   Blane
French Line, The   Myrow
Frou, Frou   Sigman
Fum Fiddle Dee Dum   Sherman
Funny Face   Coslow
Funny Little Ole Bluebird   Young, Victor
Funny Thing   Sigman; Van Heusen
Funny-Paper Capers in a Dream   Oakland
Gamblin' Man, The   David, Hal
Garden of Eden   Adams; Strouse
Gary, Indiana   Willson

Gay Monte Carlo   Drake
Gee, I Wish I Was Back in the Army   Berlin
Gentleman in the Next Apartment, The   Van Heusen
Gilly Gilly Osenfeffer Katzenellen Bogen By the
    Sea   Hoffman
Girl Can't Say, A   David, Hal
Girl Next Door, The   Blane; Martin
Glow Worm (inst.)   Young, Victor
God Bless the One I Love   Willson
Goin' Co'tin'   DePaul; Mercer
Going Away Party   Drake
Going to the Devil with Me   Robin; Romberg
Golden Bands of Nassau   Stept
Golden Bells   Adamson; Warren
Golden Days   Romberg; Webster
Gondolier's Serenade, The   David, Mack
Good Intentions   Evans; Livingston, Jay
Good Time Charlie   Fields; Schwartz, Arthur
Goodbye My Love   Coots
Got a Cold in the Nose for Christmas   Merrill
Gotta Have Me Go with You   Arlen; Gershwin, Ira
Great, Great Choir in the Sky, The   Woods
Great Leader, Krantz, The   Bryan
Green Fire   Brooks
Green Light Ahead   Arlen; Gershwin, Ira
Guadeamus (Finale)   Webster
Hail to Thee, Peppelbrink   Drake
(The Adventures of) Hajji Baba   Washington
Hal Murray Theme   Oakland
Hallelujah Train Routine   Styne
Hang Up!   Fields; Schwartz, Arthur
Hansel and Gretel Theme   Coots
Happily Ever After   Styne
Happiness Is Where You Find It   Russell
Happy Day (inst.)   Youmans
Happy Habit   Fields; Schwartz, Arthur
Happy Hollywood   Adams; Strouse
Happy Is the Boy   Leigh
Harmonize   Blane; Martin
Harry Nigocia Theme   Oakland
Harvey Hudson Theme   Oakland
Has Anybody Seen My Kitty   Hoffman
Has I Let You Down?   Arlen
Have a Drink on Me   Warren
Have a Hope, Have a Wish, Have a Prayer   David, Hal
He Knocked at the Door of Heaven   Bryan
He Put the "Uh" in the Mambo   Blane; Martin
Hear Those Drums   Drake
Heart of a Fool, The   David, Hal
Heart of a Girl, The   Adams; Strouse
Heaven Be Praised   Magidson; Oakland
Heaven Was Never Like This   David, Mack
Heel, The   Robison
Here Comes a Blackbird   Burke
Here It Is, Come and Get It   Mills
Here She Comes   Drake
Here We Come   Drake
Here You Are   Evans; Livingston, Jay
Here's Charlie   Davis
Here's to the Bridegroom   Drake
Here's What I'm Here For   Arlen; Gershwin, Ira
Hey, Punchinello   Evans; Livingston, Jay
Hi Lee, Hi Low   Willson
Hidden in My Heart   Young, Victor
High and the Mighty, The   Washington

High Heels   Adams; Strouse
High Hopes   Fain; Webster
His Songs Will Never Grow Old   Drake
Hold On   Robison
Home Again   Razaf
Honey, Ain't It Thrillin'   Drake
Honorable Ladies   Drake
Hook's Entrance Song   Leigh
Hook's Hook   Styne
Hooray for George the Third   Fields; Schwartz, Arthur
Hoping   Mercer
Hour After Hour   Friend
House of Flowers   Arlen
House of Flowers Waltz (inst.)   Arlen
House on Easy Street, The   Heyman; Young, Victor
How Long Will You Take to Get Lonely   Brown, Lew;
    Woods
How Much Do You Love Me   Drake
How to Survive   Weill
How's About an Orchid (For Walter Winchell)   Robison
Human Race, The   Robison
Hundred Miles from Nowhere, A   Styne
Hurst & Grady Theme   Oakland
Husband Cage   Arlen
I Am Inkas   Sherman
I Can Make You Laugh (But I Wish I Could Make You
    Cry)   Berlin
I Can't Feel Too Bad   Drake
I Can't Tell a Waltz from a Tang   Hoffman
I Could Have Told You   Sigman; Van Heusen
I Cried Like a Baby   Drake
I Don't Care If She's Not Good Lookin'   Leslie
I Don't Know How It Happened   Parish
I Don't Know If I Want You   Oakland
I Don't Wanna Be Alone Again   Mercer
I Feel Like I'm Falling in Love with You   Coots
I Forgot to Forget   Lewis; Meyer
I Guaran-Tootin'-Tee Ya   Hoffman
I Have the Love   Friml; Webster
I Have to Tell You   Rome
I Just Can't Resist You   Baer
I Just Wanna Cuddle Up, Cuddle Up   Baer
I Just Want to Be with You   Bergman
I Know a Girl   Drake
I Know You'll Be Very Happy   Hoffman
I Learned to Pray   Leigh
I Like You   Rome
I Live for You   Sigman
I Love New York   Revel
I Love You Do   Young, Victor
I Love You Madly   Baer
I Never Dreamed   Akst
I Never Felt Better   Blane; Martin
I Never Felt More Like Falling in Love   Freed, Ralph
I Never Has Seen Snow   Arlen
I Offer You My Heart   Davis
I Promised Their Mothers   Robin; Romberg
I Remember That   Sondheim
I See Wheatfields in the Moonlight   Robison
I Speak to the Stars   Fain; Webster
I Still Like Ike   Berlin
I Think of You   Mancini
I Took a Walk   Livingston, Jerry
I Wanna Love You, Cara Mia (Te Voglio, Bene, Tanto,
    Tanto)   Bullock

I Wanna Sing Like an Angel (Dance Like a Devil) Fain; Webster
I Want My Mommy and Daddy Together for Christmas Burke
I Want to Go to Chicago Willson
I Want to Sing, Sing, Sing for You Sigman
(If I Love Ya, then I Need Ya, If I Need Ya) I Wantcha Around Merrill
I Wish We Were Sweethearts Again Hoffman
I Wonder Lewis; Meyer
I Wonder If a Certain Girl Is Listening Drake
I Won't Grow Up Leigh
I Won't Let You Out of My Heart Mancini
I Wouldn't Know Lawrence
I'd Rather Wake Up By Myself Fields; Schwartz, Arthur
If He Phones Silver
If I Ever Lose My Heart Davis
If It Don't Belong to You Robison
If It's Love Cahn; Styne
If You Believe in Me Heyman; Young, Victor
If You Follow the Bluebird Coots
If You Love Me, Why Don't You Tell Me Woods
If You're List'ning to This Record Carmichael
I'll Never Need the Moon ('Nu Quarto 'e Luna) Rome
I'm a Strange Little Girl Today Evans; Livingston, Jay
I'm a Traveling Salesman (For the U.S.A.) Robison
I'm Allergic to You Drake
I'm Alone but Never Lonely Hoffman
I'm Dancing with Empty Arms Drake
I'm Flying Leigh
I'm Getting Nowhere Fast Blake
I'm Gonna Sleep with One Eye Open (So I Can See You in My Dreams) Parish
I'm Grateful Drake
I'm His Mother Bryan
I'm Home Adams; Strouse
I'm Not Afraid (I Believe in America) Berlin
I'm Off the Downbeat Arlen; Gershwin, Ira
I'm Out of this World when I'm in Your Arms Baer
I'm So Glad (I'm a Little Boy and You're a Little Girl) Merrill
Imagine Blane; Martin
In a House of Gingerbread and Sugar Candy Coots
In Paris and In Love Robin; Romberg
In the Eyes of the Girl You Love Silver
In the Movies Sondheim
In the Spring Drake
In the Wee Small Hours David, Mack
Indians Leigh
Indians Are About Leigh
Indiscretion Cahn
Indoor Girl Arlen
Instead Of Song Weill
Interlude (inst.) Young, Victor
Introduction to Neverland Leigh
Irene (Old Gypsy) (inst.) Young, Victor
Is She the Only Girl in the World Berlin
Is That Asking too Much Fain; Gilbert
Isn't It Sondheim
Isn't It a Wonderful Night Drake
It Goes without Saying Clare
It Happened Burke
It Just Isn't Home without You David, Mack
It Not Where You Start Fields
It Seems Like Only Yesterday Livingston, Jerry; Webster

It Worries Me Sigman
It's a New World Arlen; Gershwin, Ira
It's a Woman's World Cahn; Evans; Livingston, Jay
It's All Mine Fields; Schwartz, Arthur
It's Been Fun Cahn
It's Mine, It's Yours (The Pitchman) Arlen; Gershwin, Ira
It's Never too Late to Have a Little Fun Yellen
It's Not Easy to Forget (I Love You) Mancini
It's Not Where You Start Fields; Schwartz, Arthur
It's that Kind of Neighborhood Sondheim
It's Time to Say Goodnight Again Davis; Silver
It's Up to You Fields; Schwartz, Arthur
It's What You Believe In Leigh
I've Been Looking Drake
I've Got a Date Drake
I've Got Nothing to Lose but the Blues Bergman
I've Gotta Crow Leigh
I've Had Enough Evans; Livingston, Jay
I've Heard Lawrence
I've Never Known a Night Like Tonight Warren
I've Only Just Started to Care Freed, Ralph; Livingston, Jerry
Jack Thayer Theme Oakland
Jamboree Willson
Jay McMaster Theme Oakland
Jazzadadadoo Atteridge
Je T'Aime Commercial Mercer
Jealousy Weill
Jerry Nebler Theme Oakland
Jerry Strom Theme Oakland
Jesse James Freed, Ralph; Livingston, Jerry
Jimmy Lowe Theme Oakland
Joe Deane Theme Oakland
John Wrigley Theme Oakland
Johnny Fedora and Alice Blue Bonnet Wrubel
Johnny Guitar Young, Victor
Joker (In the Card Game of Life), The Parish
Josie Spina
Joy of Easter Young, Victor
Jubilee Trail Clare; Young, Victor
Jug of Wine, A Spina
Jules Theme Styne
June Bride DePaul; Mercer
Kadey Song, The Oakland
Kala Kala Polee Kala Oakland
King Has Everything, The Heyman; Young, Victor
Kiss Across the Continent, A Parish
Kiss By Kiss Brooks
Kiss Intended for Linda, The Robison
Kiss Me Now David, Hal
Kiss the Girls Good Morning Willson
Kisses I'll Never Forget Merrill
Knowing You Are Going Home Robison
Kow Tow Adamson; Warren
Kublai Kahn's Song Adamson; Warren
Ladies and Gentlemen Drake
Lady and the Fan, The Livingston, Jerry; Webster
Lady and the Tramp Wrubel
Lady Killer Evans; Livingston, Jay
Lady Mary's Song to Taberie Friml
Lament DePaul; Mercer
Land Around Us, The Arlen; Gershwin, Ira
Language of Hawaii, The Drake
Language of Romance, The Parish
Languida Lawrence

Larry Brownell Theme   Oakland
Larry Wilson Theme   Oakland
Las Vegas   Norworth
Last Time We'll Say Goodnight, The   Razaf
Lazy Little Donkey   Stept
Leg of Mutton   Romberg
Let Me Hear You Whisper   Evans; Livingston, Jay
Let Me Love You (Que Te Amo!)   Evans; Livingston, Jay
Let Me Walk on the Water, Oh Lord   David, Mack
Let the World Be Full of Sunshine   Parish
Let's Dance   Baer
Let's Fly Away   Adams; Strouse
Let's Go Back   Drake
Let's Mambo   Raye
Let's Talk about a Woman   Rome
Light's Diamond Jubilee (inst.)   Young, Victor
Lisa (Rear Window Theme)   Rome
Little Bit More, A   Oakland
Little Crazy Quilt   David, Hal
Little Doggie with the Big Woof-Woof, The   Hoffman
Little House   Lawrence
Little Man in the Big Sombrero, The   Coots
Little Miss Tippy Toes   Adamson; Warren
Little Rock Roll, The   Evans; Livingston, Jay
Livin' Lovin' Doll   Evans; Livingston, Jay
Lonely Holiday   Sigman
Lonesome Polecat   DePaul; Mercer
Long Long Long   McHugh
Look at What the Wind Blew In   Russell
Lookin' for Trouble   Blane; Myrow
Looking at You   Heyman; Young, Victor
Looking for a Bachelor   Drake
Lord Knows the Way Back Home, The   Koehler
Lose that Long Face   Arlen; Gershwin, Ira
Losing You   Coots
Lost in Loveliness   Robin; Romberg
Lost Love   Parish
Lottie Gibson Specialty (Please Don't Send Me Down a Baby
   Brother)   Fields; Schwartz, Arthur
Lou Barile Theme   Oakland
Lou German Theme   Oakland
Love and Kisses   Friml
Love Can Change the Stars   Blane; Martin
Love Finds a Way   Leigh
Love I Have for You, The   Hoffman
Love Is a Very Light Thing   Rome
Love Is Eternal   Myrow
Love Is the Funniest Thing   Robin; Romberg
Love Like Ours   Blake
Love Me If You Love Me   Livingston, Jerry; Russell
Love Song   Mercer; Weill
Love Song of a Thief, The   Friml
Love That Cannot Be   Friml
Love Ya Like Crazy   Silver
Love You Dearly   Fain; Webster
Love, You Didn't Do Right By Me   Berlin
Love's a Bond   Sondheim
Love's No Stranger to Me   Arlen
Luck Am I (inst.)   Youmans
Lucky in Romance   Drake
Lucky Me   Fain; Webster
Lucky Town   Drake
Mack the Knife   Weill
Madame Tango's Tango   Arlen
Madonna, Madonna   Merrill

Make Faith   Coots
Make Yourself Comfortable   Merrill
Mama Mama Mama Where Did You Get de Cigar   Evans;
   Livingston, Jay
Mambo Italiano   Merrill
Man and Woman   Evans; Livingston, Jay
Man that Got Away, The   Arlen; Gershwin, Ira
Many Dreams Ago   David, Mack
Marco's Rebuttal   Adamson; Warren
Mardi Gras   Arlen
Maria Maria Maria   Raye
Marie of the High Sea   Coots
Marry a Rich Woman   Adamson
Marty Hogan Theme   Oakland
Mason City, Iowa   Willson
Me and Pollyanna   Fields; Schwartz, Arthur
Mean and Melancholy   Robison
Medicine Show Is Coming to Town   Bergman
Meet a Happy Guy   Evans; Livingston, Jay
Men   Fain; Webster
Merle Edwards Theme   Oakland
Merry Gallows, The   Friml
Mighty Mikado, The   Drake
Mister and Missus Coconut   Merrill
Mister Philosophy   Drake
Misty   Burke
Misty Valley   Parish
(Me and My) Mixed Up Guy   Robison
Mom-e-le (Mother Dear)   Parish
Moment with You, A   Sondheim
Moments from Shakespeare   Fields; Schwartz, Arthur
Mona From Arizona   Fields; Schwartz, Arthur
Monday through Sunday   Arlen
Moon Is on Fire, The   Merrill
More Love than Your Love   Fields; Schwartz, Arthur
More More More   Oakland
More Powerful Than Voodoo   Drake
More Than Anyone   DePaul; Raye
Morning Anthem   Weill
Mother's Lullaby   Gilbert; Oakland
Mounted Messenger, The   Weill
Mounties, The   Friml; Hammerstein; Harbach; Webster
Mr. Good-for-Nothing Heart   Burke
Mr. Publisher (Have I Got a Song for You)   Gilbert; Oakland
Muriel   Freed, Ralph; Hoffman
My Bambino   Hoffman
My Favorite Memory   Lawrence
My Fellow Guests   Drake
My Fifty Golden Years   Yellen
My Heart Is Yours   Silver
My Heart Is Yours (Mi Amor e Tuo)   Johnson, James P.
My Heart Will Belong to You   Baer
My Heart Will Miss You   Baer
My Heart Won't Say Goodbye   Robin; Romberg
My Heaven and Earth   Merrill
My Little Dream Toy Shop   Blake
My Lonesome Heart Is Crying for You   Johnson, J.
   Rosamond
My Name Is Love   Parish
My Osh-Kosh Gal   Coots
My Own Academy Awards   Drake
My Pretty Shoo-Gah   Drake
My Very Own   Davis
Mysterious Lady   Comden and Green; Styne
Nearer My Love to Me   Drake

Neath the Eucalyptus Tree   Silver
Never Land   Leigh
Never Never Land   Comden and Green; Styne
Never Too Late for Love   Rome
New Kind of Show Business, A   Drake
New Year's Eve 1954   Drake
Niagara Falls   Baer; Drake; Leslie
Nickel Machine Samba   David, Mack
Night of Stars, A   Hoffman
Night Time   Ellington
No Matter Where You Go (Sole Lucenta)   Hoffman
No One but You   David, Mack; Lawrence
No One Else   Hoffman; Silver
Nobody Cares   Evans; Livingston, Jay
Nobody Wants to Go Home   Spina
Nostalgia   Evans; Livingston, Jay
Now   Burke
Now It's Hook or Me   Leigh
Nowhere   Silver
Octopus Song   Rome
Of Course It's Crazy   David, Mack
Oh How We Danced   Coots
Oh, the Big Red Letter   Willson
Old Enough to Love   Fields; Schwartz, Arthur
Old Holler Family, The   Robison
Old Man, The   Berlin
O-lee-ay-ee-o   Drake
On an Empty Stage   Oakland
On and On   Spina
Once   Russell; Spina
Once Upon a Time   Adams
One God   Drake
One Man Ain't Quite Enough   Arlen
One More River to Cross   Styne
One of These Days Pow   Davis
One of Those Days   Leigh
One that Got Away, The   DePaul; Raye
One Wonderful Day   Sondheim
Open the Window of Your Heart (And Let the Sunshine
   In)   Hoffman
Open Your Arms   Evans
Open Your Arms (Let Me Walk Right In)   Livingston, Jay
Opening Night   Drake
Orange Suspenders   Robison
Oscar Song, The   Drake
Other Hands, Other Hearts   Rome
Otto the Auto   Robison
Out of the Way   Robin; Romberg
Over and Over Again   Hoffman
Oysters, Cockles and Mussels (Fish Market)   Rome
Pack Home   Evans; Livingston, Jay
Pakistan   Burke; Van Heusen
Panama   Styne
Panisse and Son   Rome
Pantomime (inst.)   Youmans
Papa Loves Mambo   Hoffman
Parade, The   Leigh
Parisian Pretties   Fain; Webster
Party Polka (inst.)   Young, Victor
Pas de Deux (inst.)   Romberg; Styne
Pass It Along   Woods
Pasta Cheech   Warren
Pat Chamers Theme   Oakland
Paul Bartell Theme   Oakland
Paul Flanagan Theme   Oakland

Peasant King, The   Adams
Peddler Man (Then I Loved)   Lawrence
Penny By Penny   Oakland
Pink and Blue   Adamson; Warren
Pirate Song   Leigh
Please Help Us Find Our Way Home   Coots
Please Tell Me Now   Ruby
Please Tell Me When   Brown, Nacio Herb
Poisoning Peter's Medicine   Leigh
Polly's Song   Weill
Pom Pidi Pom   Hoffman
Poor Andre   Blane; Myrow
Poor Little Side Street Girl   Robison
Poor Mouth Papa   Robison
Poor Soul, The   Davis
Pop Pom Pom-a-Diddle   Livingston, Jerry
Portugee Fisherman (Ho Ho Bim Bahle Bahm), The   Merrill
Positively No Dancing   Leigh
Pour the Corn John   Mills
Pow Wow, The   Leigh
Power of Love, The   Heyman; Young, Victor
Pow-Wow Polka (inst.), The   Styne
Pretty Mandolin (Tic a Tic a Tic)   Evans; Livingston, Jay
Pretty Moon   Adamson; Warren
Prince of Peace, The   Russell
Princely Scheme (Hook's Tango), A   Leigh
Prisoner of the Stocks, The   Drake
Prize of Gold   Washington
Promise Me You'll Be Lonely   David, Hal
Punch and Judy Love   Merrill
Put a Four-Cent Stamp on My Heart   Drake
Putty in Your Hands   Spina
Quick Like a Bunny   Silver
Quierme Y Veras   Mercer
Red Ball, The   Drake
Red Dale Theme   Oakland
Red Garters   Evans; Livingston, Jay
Reggie Van Gleason the Third   Davis
Remember Me   Leigh
Restless Heart   Rome
Reverie in the Rain   Lawrence
Rich in Love   Lewis; Meyer
Right Kind of Love (From the Wrong Kind of Guy), The
   Adams; Strouse
Roaving and Dreaming   Willson
Robin Randall Song, The   Evans; Livingston, Jay
Rocket to the Moon   Goetz
Roger Clark Theme   Oakland
Roll Out the Hose, Boys   Robin; Romberg
Romantic Night   Adams; Strouse
Rose Marie   Friml; Hammerstein; Harbach; Webster
Ross Miller Theme   Oakland
Round and Round and Round   Webster
Run! Run! Run! Run!   Sherman
Russ Coglin Theme   Oakland
Rusty Old Halo, A   Merrill
Sackbut, the Psaltar and the Dulcimer, The   Hoffman
Said My Right Eye to My Left Eye   Hoffman
Sailor's Not a Sailor ('Til a Sailor's Been Tattooed), A   Berlin
Santa Claus Blues, The   Merrill
Santo Natale   Hoffman
Satins and Spurs   Evans; Livingston, Jay
Saturday Night   Sondheim
Saturday Night Polka   Leigh
Say Hey, Willie Mays   Robison

Scharline   Blake
Sea Song (By the Beautiful Sea), The   Fields; Schwartz,
   Arthur
Search Is Through, The   Arlen; Gershwin, Ira
Second Fiddle   Friend
Second to None   Heyman; Young, Victor
Self-Pity Tears   Robison
Senorita   Stept
Sentimental   Hoffman
Serenade   Romberg; Webster
Seven Long Years   Robison
Sexy Saddle   Evans; Livingston, Jay
Shangri-La   Sigman
She Made Me Promise   Freed, Ralph; Livingston, Jerry
Shika, Shika   Rome
Shining World   Drake
Shipwrecked (On a Desert Island)   Spina
Side By Side By the Beautiful Seaside   Coots
Siesta, Fiesta and Amor   David, Hal
Singer - A Dancer, A   Berlin
Singing in the Moonlight   Mercer
Sister of Tokio Rose   Styne
Sisters   Berlin
Six Bridges to Cross   Mancini
Sleepin' Bee, A   Arlen
Sleepy Babe   Webster
Slide, Boy, Slide   Arlen
Slow   Willson
Slowly but Surely (Quanto te Voglio)   Parish
Smellin' of Vanilla (Bamboo Cage)   Arlen
Smile, a Tear, a Kiss Dear, A   Howard, Joseph E.
Smile on Her Lips, The   Drake
Smile, Smile, Smile   Coots
Snow   Berlin
Snow Dreams   Webster
So Few Words   Bryan
So Many People   Sondheim
Sobbin' Women   DePaul; Mercer
Social Season, The   Drake
Soft Shoulders and Dangerous Curves   David, Hal; Hoffman
Solfeggio (The Do-Re-Mi Song)   Sigman
Soliloquy and Song   Leigh
Solomon Song   Weill
Some Day (inst.)   Youmans
Somebody Goofed   Hoffman
Somebody Loves Me   Cahn; Styne
Someone at Last   Arlen; Gershwin, Ira
Something in the Air   Drake
Somewhere Across the Sea   Baer
Son of the Emperor, The   Drake
Song Allegretto (inst.)   Youmans
Song for Sweethearts (Come Close)   Sigman
Song of a Lost Love   Young, Victor
Song of the Barefoot Contessa   Lawrence
Song of the Gondolier   Adamson; Warren
Sounds Exciting to Me   Burke
Souvenir of Madeira   Drake
Spanish Allegretto (inst.)   Youmans
Spanish Allegro (inst.)   Youmans
Spanish Love   Hoffman
Spanish Moderato (Lotta's Song) (inst.)   Youmans
Speaker of the House   Robison
Sphinx Won't Tell, The   Adams; Strouse
Spring Came Early This Year   McHugh; Russell
Spring Spring Spring   DePaul; Mercer

Spy Menace   Styne
Square Dance on the Mall   Drake
Star (inst.)   Youmans
Stick with Me, Baby   Drake
Still You'd Break My Heart   Friend
Storm, The   Leigh
Stow-a-way   Livingston, Jerry
Stranger at the Waterfall   Robison
Straw Hat   Evans; Livingston, Jay
Summer Holiday   Drake
Summer Is Here   Oakland
Summer Rain   Livingston, Jerry; Webster
Sunday in the City (inst.)   Warren
Superstition Song, The   Fain; Webster
Susan Slept Here   Lawrence
Susquehanna Transfer   Russell
Su-Tan-Tan   Stept
Swedish Rhapsody   Sigman
Symphony Special   Gilbert; Oakland
Table for Two   Lawrence
Tag   Comden and Green; Styne
Take a Memo to the Moon   Fain; Webster
Tal Hood Theme   Oakland
Talk Talk Talk   Oakland
Tame Me   Adams; Strouse
Tango — Ballad   Weill
Tango (inst.)   Youmans
Teach Me Tonight   Cahn; DePaul
Teardrop Avenue   Leigh
Teardrops in the Rain   Coots
Teen-age Rag   Razaf
Tell Me, Tell Me   Merrill
Temple of an Understanding Heart   Evans; Livingston, Jay
Tender Shepherd   Leigh
Texas Boys, The   Raye
Thank You Mr. Judge   Drake
That Don't Do Me No Good   Mills
That Lingering Longing   David, Hal
That Naughty Show from Gay Paree   Robin; Romberg
That Ol' Judge   Drake
That's Falling in Love   Leigh
That's Life   Evans; Livingston, Jay
That's What a Woman Is For   Bloom; Cahn
That's What I Like   Styne
That's What It's Like   Drake
Them   Hoffman
(When Coffee Goes Back to a Nickel a Cup) Then I'll Go
   Back to You   Bryan
There Is No Affair Like a Country Fair   Drake
There Must Be a Reason   Davis
There's Just One Thing to Say   Drake
There's No Substitute for a Man   Arlen; Dietz
There's Nothing Like Staying Alive   Caesar
They Don't Play the Piano Anymore   Hoffman
They Say You're Laughing at Me (While I'm Crying for
   You)   Livingston, Jerry
They Were Doin' the Mambo   Raye
Think of Me Kindly   Cahn; Robison
Thirty Weeks of Heaven   Fields; Schwartz, Arthur
This I Promise You   David, Hal
This Is Greater than I Thought   Evans; Livingston, Jay
This Is the Moment (Russian Gypsy Song)   Robin; Whiting
This Lovely Lassie   Drake
This Time It's Hook or Me   Leigh
This Wonderful Land of Ours   Drake

Those Who Believe in Forever   Adamson; Warren
Thought of You, The   Rome
Thoughts   Robison
Three Coins in the Fountain   Cahn; Styne
Three Little Bunnies   Hoffman
Throw the Anchor Away   Fields; Schwartz, Arthur
'Til You're Back   Drake
Time   Snyder
Tina Marie   Merrill
To Be in Love   Burke
To Get Us All Together   Adams; Strouse
To My Wife   Rome
To the Ends of the Earth   Adamson; Warren
To the Inn We're Marching   Romberg; Webster
To You   Myrow
Today I Went Adventuring   Leigh
Today, Tonight and Tomorrow   Coots
Tommy Edwards Theme   Oakland
Tondra   Mills
Tonight's the Night   Silver
Too Bad We Couldn't Fall in Love   Adams
Too Happy to Fall in Love   Evans; Livingston, Jay
Toodle-oodle-oo   Coots
Toy March (inst.)   Young, Victor
(Come on Back to) Trinidad   McHugh
Trouble Seems to Follow Me Around   Blake
Tularosa   Livingston, Jerry
Tune #6 Sept. 14 (inst.)   Youmans
Turtle Song   Arlen
Turtle Theme (inst.), The   Young, Victor
Tuscaloosa   Fields; Schwartz, Arthur
Two Ladies in de Shade of de Banana Tree   Arlen
Two Little Magic Words   Hoffman
Two Little Shnooks, Still in Love   Rome
Ugg-a-Wugg   Comden and Green; Styne
U.N.   Goetz
Under the Big Top   Drake
Unique Eunuch, The   Adamson; Warren
Unrequited Love   Adamson; Warren
Until You Fall in Love   Cahn
Up in the Elevated Railway   Robin; Romberg
Useless Song   Weill
Va Va Va Voom (Song of the Bassoon and the
      Piccolo)   David, Hal
Vaquero!   Evans; Livingston, Jay
Ve Grow Too Old Und Too Late Shmart   Drake
Venezia   Blane; Martin
Veni, Vidi, Vici   Livingston, Jerry; Webster
Very Bad   Young, Victor
Virginia and Truckee Line, The   Brooks
Visit Panama (inst.)   Styne
Vocalize   Blane; Martin
Wait Til' You See Paris   Blane; Myrow
Waitin'   Arlen
Wake the Town and Tell the People   Livingston, Jerry
Wally Nelskog Theme   Oakland
Waltzing and Waiting   David, Mack
(She/He Keeps Me) Warm in the Winter   David, Hal
Warmed Over Kisses (Left Over Love)   Livingston, Jerry
Watch Your Language   David, Hal
Wayne Cody Theme   Oakland
We Are Free   Coots
We Sail Tonight   Russell
Web of Lies   Lawrence
Webson's Meat Jingle   Blane; Martin

Wedding Dance   Rome
Wedding Song   Weill
Welcome Home   Drake; Rome
Well! I'll Be Switched   Blane; Myrow
Wendy   Comden and Green; Styne
We're All in the Same Boat   Robin; Romberg
We're Dancers on Parade   Razaf
We're Going to Schnectady   Willson
We're the Gentlemen of the Press   Davis
What a Man Won't Do for a Woman   Arlen
What Am I Doin' in Kansas City (When You're in New
      Orleans)   Merrill
What Do You See in Him/Her   David, Hal
What Do You Use for a Heart   Coslow
What Do You Want for Christmas Dear Santa   Hoffman
What Happens Now   Sigman
What Is a Friend For?   Arlen
What Is This That I Feel (Is This Really Love)   Blane; Myrow
What More Do I Need?   Sondheim
What 'Tis, What 'Tis — 'Tis Spring   Woods
What's in the Pocketbook   Howard, Bart
What's the Rush   Adams; Strouse
What's the Weather Like in Paris   Parish
When I Am Free to Love   Robin; Romberg
When I Get Back to Caroline   Coots
When I Was a Little Girl   Drake
When I Went Home   Leigh
When It's Peach Blossom Time in Lichtenburg   Berlin
When We See One   Drake
When You Grow Up   Adams; Strouse
When You Kiss Me Va-Room   Hoffman
When You Look at Me   Bergman
When You're In Love   DePaul; Mercer
Where Are You   Kahn
Where Can I Go Without You   Young, Victor
Where Do They Go   Drake
Where Do You Think You're Going   Howard, Bart
Which One   Washington
Who Are You   Leigh
Who Done It   Hoffman
Who Else Can I Tell It but You   Clare
Whole Long Year from Today, A   Leigh
Whoops-A-Daisy Day   Burke
Whop-Diddy-Ay   Evans; Livingston, Jay
Who's Afraid (Not I, Not I, Not I)   Lawrence
Whose Little Heart Are You Tearin' Apart   Stept
Why Am I in Love   Evans; Livingston, Jay
Why Be Afraid to Dance?   Rome
Why Do You Look So Happy   Drake
Why Should I Be Sorry   Sigman
Wild Indians   Leigh
Wildcat Smathers   Evans; Livingston, Jay
Williamsburg, Virgin-ee-ya   Drake
Winko   Drake
Wisconsin Cheese   Willson
(The Frenchman Always Says It) With a Kiss   Blane; Myrow
With My Song   Coots
With My Strings   Coots
Without Him   Evans; Livingston, Jay
Wonderful Plan   Willson
Wonderful Show, A   Drake
Wonderful Wonderful Day   DePaul; Mercer
World Is Mean, The   Weill
Worlds Apart   Russell
Yellow Rose of Texas   Leslie

Yes, He Is   Drake
You Ain't Livin' If You Ain't Lovin'   Caesar
You Are the Bravest   Styne
You Can't Be Too Choosy   Hoffman
You Can't Get Away from Love   Razaf
You Can't Take It with You When You Go   Gilbert; Oakland
You Fascinate Me   Mills
You Stand Accused   Parish
You Too Can Be a Dreamer   Livingston, Jerry; Parish
You Won't Be Happy   Baer
You Won't Have to Cry Over Me   David, Hal
You'll Be Dancing with Someone Tonight (The Fortune Teller
    Song)   Warren
You'll Come Running Back to Me   Baer
Your Heart, My Heart   Sigman
Your Last Adios   Young, Victor
Your Name Is Love   DePaul
You're a Dan-Dan-Dandy   Davis
You're a Nice Man   Davis
You're Acting Strange   Caesar
You're Deeper in My Heart   Livingston, Jerry
You're Gonna Dance with Me, Baby   Styne
You're Not Living in Vain   Hoffman; Silver
You're So Right   Evans; Livingston, Jay
You're So Right for Me   Evans; Livingston, Jay
You're the Best Thing That's Happened to Me   Adamson;
    McHugh
You're the Heart that Loves Me   Merrill
Yours for the Dreaming   Magidson
Youth, Joy and Freedom   Styne
You've Got to Be a Little Crazy   Robin; Romberg
You've Got to Let Me Love You   Spina
You've Gotta Make Up Your Mind   Ruby
You've Ruined Me for Anybody's Love but Yours   Merrill
Yu-Hy-Day Yu-Hy-Dee   Webster
Ze Repartee   Robison

1955

(Build Yourself) A Sky House with a Prayer   Lewis; Meyer
Addio   Willson
Adelaide   Loesser
Aesop, That Able Fable Man   Berlin
Ah How I Love Thee   Spina
Ain't Ya Gonna Swim   Gordon
Air Force Takes Command, The   Washington; Young, Victor
All Around the Christmas Tree   Coots
All at Once You Love Her   Hammerstein; Rodgers
All Day   Robin; Styne
All I Want Is a Lolli-Lollipop   Razaf
All Kinds of People   Hammerstein; Rodgers
All of You   Porter
Alley Oop   Evans; Livingston, Jay
Alone on a Lonesome Trail   Lawrence
Alone with Me   Howard, Bart
Am I in Love   Baer
American Flag (inst.), The   Young, Victor
Amontillado (A Case of Amontillado) (inst.)   Young, Victor
Amukirki (The Lord Willing)   Livingston, Jerry; Russell
Anna Maria   McHugh; Sigman
Annabelle   Duke
Anniversary Rose   Evans; Livingston, Jay
Another Day, Another Buck   Duke
Anything, Everything for Love   Livingston, Jerry
Are You Now   Eliscu; Gorney

Art   Porter
Art of Conversation Has Declined, The   Bergman; Mercer
Artists and Models   Brooks; Warren
As I Love You   Evans; Livingston, Jay
As on Through the Seasons We Sail   Porter
As Soon As They See Eileen   Robin; Styne
As Young As We Are Tonight   Merrill
Astroidiana (inst.)   Revel
At Last We're Alone   Blane; Martin
At Maxims   Leigh
At Such a Tender Age   Leigh
Atmosphere (For Love)   Robin; Styne
Autumn Rhapsody   Leigh
Baby You Knock Me Out   Comden and Green
Bachelorhood   Duke
Backlot Blues, The   Duke
Baffi Bajon   Sigman; Spina
Ballads, Boogie and Blues   Leslie; Schwartz, Jean
Ballo Felicidad Amor   Brooks
Barbara Fritchie (inst.)   Young, Victor
Bartered Bride As She Might Have Been (I Wanna Go),
    The   Willson
Bass Fiddle Boogie Woogie Blues, The   Sissle
Bat Lady, The   Brooks; Warren
Be Like Me   Cahn; Styne
Be My Guest   Coslow
Be Sure Beloved   Sigman
Bebe of Gay Paree   Porter
Bee Bop on the Range   Revel
Believe in Me   Sigman
Bella Bella Napoli   Revel
Belonging   Sigman
Beloved When I Adore   Spina
Beware   David, Mack
Beyond Tomorrow   DePaul
Birmin'ham   Blane; Martin
Birthdays   Caesar
Black Pearl of Tahiti (inst.)   Alter
Black (Sorrow) (inst.)   Young, Victor
Bless You, My Sweet   Revel
Blessings   Young, Victor
Blow Those Trumpets   Gordon
Blue Danube   Comden and Green
Blue Sleep   Webster
Blue Star   Heyman; Young, Victor
Blue Violin   Razaf
Blues Theme   Mercer
Board of Directors of Continental Steel, The   Coslow
Bongo the Camel   Coots
Bonjour Finis   Coslow
Booga-Da-Woog   Mancini; Raye
Boom Song, The   Hoffman
Bottle Up the Moonlight   Alter; Sigman
Boy in Buckskin and a Gal in Calico, A   Coots
Brazilian Rose   Razaf
Bride and Groom   Russell
Bring Your Smile Along   Davis
Br-rrr-rr-m (Kiss)   Leigh
Bubbles   Merrill
Bums' Opera   Hammerstein; Rodgers
Calendar Song, The   Drake
Camille, Colette, Fifi   Young, Victor
Can't Do Without You   Hoffman
Can't Stop   Silver
Cantata   Leigh; Spina

Careless Lips (Tango Roulette) Raye
Cargo Watch Oakland; Webster
Cat 'n' Mouse Razaf
C-A-T Spells Cat Mercer
Catch a Star! Fain; Webster
C'est la Vie Young, Victor
Champagne Blane; Martin
Chance at Love, A Sigman
Change of Scenery, A Coots
Chico's Reverie Young, Victor
Chocolate Soldier Leigh
Chow Mein Merrill
Christmas Chimes Baer
Christmas in America Cahn
Christmas in Rio Oakland; Webster
Christmas Is A-Comin DePaul; Raye
Christmas (Where's the Family) Mills
Cinerama Holiday (Souvenirs of Paris) Lawrence
City of Enchantment Drake
Clarabelle's Clarabus Coots
Close Beside You Carmichael
Code, The Fain
Columbus (inst.) Young, Victor
Come to the Pavilion Leigh
Conqueror, The Heyman; Young, Victor
Conqueror (inst.), The Young, Victor
Cosmic Capers (inst.) Revel
Could Be I Love You (Balad de Copacabana) Hoffman
Cposo Dance (inst.) Young, Victor
Crazy Kind-a-Love Davis
Crazy Otto Polka Brown, Lew
Crocodile Crawl, The Coslow
Cryin' for Your Kisses Livingston, Jerry
Cuckoo in the Cuckoo Clock Coots
Daddy Long Legs Mercer
Dan Dailey's Solo Comden and Green
Dance Finale Fain
Dancing and Dreaming Hoffman
Dancing Mountains Spina
Dancing through Life Mercer
Dangerous David, Hal
Daybreak Blues, The Mercer
Dead Fall Silver
Dear, Dear School Drake
(Devil that You Are) Delilah Leigh
Desert Sands Heyman
Desperate Hours, The Bacharach
Diamond Earrings (inst.) Alter
Dilly Duke
Dip Your Pen in Sunshine and Write a Letter to the One
    You Love Coots
Distance to the Moon, The Spina
Do As You Would Be Did By Hoffman
Do Do Do What Your Heart Says Lawrence
Do You Remember Brown, Nacio Herb
Doctor Sunshine's Almanac Merrill
Doin' the French Can-Can Merrill
Don't Be a Snork DePaul; Raye
Don't Forget to Mention Drake
Don't Just Sit There Freed, Ralph; Livingston, Jerry
Don't Let This Night Get Away Adamson; Lane
Don't Let Your Baby Go to Miami Hoffman; Silver
Don't Say Goodbye to Love Oakland
Don't Stampede Me Hoffman
Don't Stay Away too Long Hoffman

Don't Take the Bums from Brooklyn Robison
Don't Tell a Soul Howard, Bart
Don't Throw My Love Away David, Hal
Don'tcha Hate It Duke
Down Boy! Down Boy! Adamson
Dream Along with Me, I'm on My Way to a Star Sigman
Dream World Leigh
Dreams Were Made for Lovers Coots
Dress Is Cool, The Gordon
Drums and Drill Robin; Youmans
Dude Ranch Boogie Drake
Dull Dance Mancini
Eleven O'Clock Song Fain
Emerald Eyes (inst.) Alter
Enchanted Ballroom Spina
Endless Love Myrow
Enough of This David, Hal
Entire History of the World in Two Minutes and Thirty-Two
    Seconds Strouse
Epitomy of Femininity, The Gordon
Era of Jazz Evans; Livingston, Jay
Every Day's a Happy Day Cahn; Schwartz, Arthur
Everybody Be Happy Hoffman
Everytime I Look at You Stept
Ev'rybody's Got a Home but Me Hammerstein; Rodgers
Experience Mills
Extraordinary Is the Ordinary, The Drake
Face the Fact Mills
Face the Music Cahn; Schwartz, Arthur
Facts of Life, The Fain; Leigh
Faggot Dance Mancini
Farewell to New York Duke
Fascination Waltz, The Hoffman
Fault of the Nightingale, The Spina
Feelin' Mighty Perky Drake
Fidelity Leigh
Fidgety Feet Sigman
Finally Fain
Fireflies Shall Light You, The Spina
First Auto Theme Mercer
First Chinese Theme Mercer
First Love Coslow
First Snowfall, The Webster
Flaggin' the Train to Tuscaloosa David, Mack
Follow that Man Sigman
Foolin' Myself Razaf; Waller
For Better or Worse Razaf
For Now and Always Stept
For Only You Merrill
For the First Time Adamson; McHugh
Forget My Name and Address Davis
Forgive Leigh
Fountain of Youth, The Livingston, Jerry; Webster
Foxfire Mancini
Frankie Laine Time Drake
From Now On Stept
From the First Cigarette in the Morning to the Last Cigarette
    at Night Robison
Fromage Coslow
Fun with Music David, Mack; Hoffman; Livingston, Jerry
G'Bye Now, New York Robin; Styne
Get a Load o' Me Bergman
Get Along Home, Cindy Drake
Get Rid of Monday Burke; Van Heusen
Ginny Silver

Girl Behind the Man Behind the Ball, The   Drake
Girl Rush, The   Blane; Martin
Girl Upstairs, The   Cahn
Girls, Girls, Girls   Leigh
Give Me   Merrill
Give Me a Band and My Baby   Robin; Styne
Give Me a Shoulder to Cry On   David, Mack
Give Me Something I Can Dream About   David, Hal
Give Me the Land   Porter
Give Me Your Hands   Lawrence
Give My Lonely Heart a Break, Cherie   Baer
Give the Kids a Break   Gilbert; Oakland
Glove Dance   Young, Victor
Go for Broke   Drake
Go Go Go You Bruins   Freed, Ralph; Livingston, Jerry
Go Home, Little Girl   Robison
God Be with You Tonight My Love   Coots
Golden Song, A   Oakland; Webster
Good Night, Joe   Bryan
Good Night People   Howard, Joseph E.
Goodbye My Coney Island Baby   Coots
Goodbye to Rome (Arrivederci Roma)   Sigman
Goodnight, My Darling   Willson
Goo-Goo Doll Song   David, Hal
Got No Room for Mr. Gloom   Robin; Styne
Gotta Sing, Gotta Dance   Davis
Greener Pastures   Leigh
Grovers Corner   Cahn; Van Heusen
Guardian Angel   Mercer
Hail Bibinski   Porter
Hall of Fame   Drake
Hand Me Down Love   Ellington; Sigman
Handful of Dreams, A   Webster
Handful of Scales and a Ching-Boom, A   Willson
Hannibal's Victory March   Adamson; Lane
Happiest House on the Block, The   Hammerstein; Rodgers
Happy Harvest   David, Hal
Happy Little Crook   Young, Victor
Happy Little Mill   Adamson; McHugh
Happy New Year from Howdy Doody, A   Coots
Hare Pieces   Mercer
Harp in the Wind   Woods
Headin' for the Bottom   Fain
Heart of Paris (I Left My Heart in the Heart of
   Montmartre)   Parish
Heidi   Leigh
Heidi Doody   Coots
Hello New York   Robin; Styne
Here Come the Blues   DePaul; Raye
Here's to Dear Old Us   Fain
He's Back in Town   Duke
Hey, Marty   Warren
His and Hers   Fain
His Eye Is On the Sparrow   Webster
His Name Was Judas   Oakland
History of the Beat (That'll Get It), The   Mercer
Hoe-Polli   Evans; Livingston, Jay
Hold Me Close (Love Beat)   Parish
Hold Me Tight   Bergman
Holiday in Hollywood   Duke
Homesick Hillbilly   Blane; Martin
Honey in the Rock   Hoffman
Honey Trust Me   Eliscu; Gorney
Honey-Babe (The Marching Song)   Webster
Honeymoon   Fain

Horatio's Narration   Adamson
Hottentot, The   Cahn; Styne
House of Bamboo   Brooks
How About   Bacharach
How Can I Replace You?   Van Heusen
How Can I Tell Her   Evans; Livingston, Jay
How Can I Tell You (How Much I Love You)   Coots
How Could I Ever Be Untrue to You   Hoffman
How I Loved You in Your Sleep   Spina
How Long?   Hammerstein; Rodgers
How to Be Very, Very Popular   Cahn; Styne
Howdy Doody's Birthday   Coots
Hullabaloo and Hoopahlah   Drake
Hush, Little Heartache   Livingston, Jerry; Parish
Hustle Bustle   Drake
I Accuse You   Davis; Silver
I Adore New York   Cahn; Styne
I Ain't Gonna Give Nobody None of My Love   Blake
I Ain't Mad at Nobody   Robison
I Am a Witch   Hammerstein; Rodgers
I Am Waiting in the Desert   Spina
I Belong to You   Brooks
I Can Spell Banana but I Never Know when to Stop   Mercer
I Can't Forget (N'Oublie Jamain)   Lawrence
I Can't Say Manana   Gilbert
I Couldn't Get Along (Without You)   Mills
I Do Not Choose to Swim   Gordon
I Found Myself a Guy   McHugh
I Go for You   David, Hal
I Go My Way   Leigh
I Have a Dream   Adamson; Lane
I Have Loved You   Spina
I Just Dropped in to Say Goodbye   Coslow
I Know Your Mother Loves You   Cahn; Schwartz, Arthur
I Like Myself   Comden and Green
I Like to Hike   Cahn; Schwartz, Arthur
I Live for Only You (India)   Hoffman
I Live for You (Just You)   Gilbert
I Love a Stranger   Heyman
I Love Her That's Why   Hoffman
I Love My Mommy Best of All   Coots
I Love that Rickey Tickey Tickey   Cahn
I Love to Dance with You   Raye
I Love to Ramble   Leigh
I Married for Money   Oakland; Webster
I Might Drop Around in Your Dreams   Merrill
I Never Trust a Woman   Adamson; Lane
I Never Wanna Look into Those Eyes Again   Mercer
I Raised My Boy to Be a Soldier in the Army of the
   Lord   Bryan
I Saw You Dancing   Oakland
I Said Good Morning   Comden and Green
I Sure Have Been in Love   Duke
I Take a Dim View of the West   Blane; Martin
I Thought They'd Never Leave   Comden and Green
I Wanna Woman   Robin; Styne
I Wish I Had an Elephant   Coots
I Wish You All the Best   Stept
I Would Do Most Anything for You   David, Mack
I'd Give a Lot to Know Just What Is on His Mind   Cahn;
   Styne
I'd Love to Make Love to You   Bergman
If Ever We Get Out of Jail   Porter
If I Ever Fall in Love   DePaul; Raye
If I Had Married Rip Van Winkle   Howard, Joseph E.

If I Were King   Merrill
If I'm Lucky   Myrow
If It's a Dream   Young, Victor
If It's Love   Cahn; Styne
If Only I Listened to You   Sigman
If This Be Slav'ry   Adamson; Lane
If You Only Had a Heart (To Go with That Beautiful
      Face)   Livingston, Jerry; Webster
If You Want Love   Mills
If You'll Only Take a Chance   Blane; Martin
Il Mio Muletto (My Little Mule)   Merrill
I'll Forgive You   Cahn; Duke
I'll Never Stop Loving You   Cahn
I'll Take the Blame   David, Mack; Van Heusen
I'm a Little Tired Baby   Coots
I'm a Sinner   Lewis; Meyer
I'm About to Become a Lover   Duke
I'm Great   Robin; Styne
I'm Hurtin'   Fain
I'm Just a Simple Girl   Blake
I'm Starting All Over Again   Yellen
I'm the Greatest Father of Them All   Jerome
I'm the Queen Thamar   Porter
I'm Thrilled   Baer
I'm with You   Mercer
Impatient Years, The   Cahn; Van Heusen
Impossible   Caesar
In Our Chateau in Brooklyn   Duke
In the Air   Russell
In the Back of a Hack   Gorney
In the Winter   David, Mack
Innamorata (Sweetheart)   Brooks; Warren
Is It Asking too Much   Sigman
Is It Really Me   Blane; Martin
Is There Something I Should Know   Silver
It Could Have Been Me   Russell
Italy   Fain
It's a Chemical Reaction, That's All   Porter
It's a Great Country   Adamson; Warren
It's a Great Day in Brooklyn Tonight   Coots
It's Been Done   Duke
It's Bigger Than You and Me   Robin; Styne
It's Great to Be Young   Bacharach
It's June   Blane; Martin
It's Never too Warm to Wear Mink   Coots
It's Rumor   Ellington
It's That Time of Day   Coots
It's True, It's True   Cahn
I've Got Nothing to Lose but the Blues   Bergman
I've Got Rhythm   Styne
I've Got the Best Shoulder in Town   Cahn; Styne
Jim Bowie   Clare
Jobo (The Funny Little Clown)   Coots
John Barleycorn   Schwartz, Arthur
Johnny Christmas   David, Mack
Josephine   Porter
Julie's Dream (inst.)   Mercer
June in Genoa   Russell
Jupiter Jumps (inst.)   Revel
Just a Scamp   Razaf
Just Lucky, I Guess   Duke
Keep a Song in Your Heart   Coots
Keep Me in Mind   Bacharach
Keep Your Chin Up   Porter
Kentucky   Koehler

Key to My Heart, The   Merrill
King of a Slave, A   David, Hal
Kiss, The   Brown, Nacio Herb
Kiss Me and Kill Me with Love   Fain
Kissing Song, The   Duke
Know   Robison
La Festa   Fain
La Grenouille (Mister Froggy) (Ticky, Ticky, Tick)   Merrill
Lad for Ev'ry Lass, A   Duke
Ladies and Gents and Pals   Gordon
Lady, a Lad and a Lantern, A   Drake
Lady from the Bayou, The   Robin; Youmans
Lady in Lace   Bryan
Lady Isn't Interested, The   Drake
Lady of Jade (inst.)   Alter
Lady Was Made to Be Loved, The   Coslow
Land of the Pharoahs   Washington
Landing of the Pilgrims (Landing of the Pilgrim Fathers)
      (inst.)   Young, Victor
Las Vegas   Drake
Last Frontier, The   Washington
(I Don't Know Whether To) Laugh or Cry   Coslow
Leaving Me   Razaf; Waller
Legend of Vilia, The   Leigh
Legend of Wyatt Earp, The   Adamson; Warren
Let Me Cry   Davis
Let Your Intuition Be Your Guide   Schwartz, Jean
Let's Bring Back the Old Fashioned Parlor   Caesar
Let's Get Busy Too   Oakland
Let's Get to the Main Event   Leigh
Let's Go On with the Show   Evans; Livingston, Jay
Let's Make It a Night   Porter
Let's Pretend that We're in Love   Baer
Let's Wreck the Joint   Blake
Letter Song   Leigh
Lie Still, Beloved   Spina
Life of an Elephant, The   Adamson; Lane
Like a Train   Ellington
Listen to the Music Box   Drake
Little Fish that Never Saw the Sea, The   Coots
Little Girl at Heart, A   Merrill
Little Johnny Jelly Beans   Coots
Little Love, a Little While, A   Schwartz, Arthur
Little Love Can Go a Long, Long Way, A   Fain; Webster
Little Peter Potter   Coots
Little Polly Parakeet   Coots
Little Traveling Music, A   Webster
Littlest Angel, The   David, Mack
Live a Little, Love a Little   Coslow
Living One Day at a Time   Schwartz, Arthur
Liza's Eyes   Coslow
Lizzie the Busy Squirrel   Coots
Lonely Star   Davis
Lonely Street   Davis
Lonesome Old Hoot Owl, The   DePaul; Raye
Look at Me   Duke
Look to Your Heart   Cahn; Van Heusen
Looking Glass Waltz, The   Alter
Looz-iana   Brooks
Lopsided Bus, A   Hammerstein; Rodgers
Love Affair, The   Howard, Bart
Love and Marriage   Cahn; Van Heusen
Love Can Happen Anytime   Myrow
Love Has Come to Our House   DePaul
Love Is a Many Splendored Thing   Fain; Webster

Love Is All that Matters   Cahn; Schwartz, Arthur
Love Is Nothing but a Racket   Comden and Green
Love, Love, Love   Young, Victor
Love Me Now   Duke
Love Sneaks Up on You   Young, Victor
Love Songs Are Not for Me   Evans; Livingston, Jay
Love's Little Island   Merrill
Lucky Song, The   Brooks; Warren
Lucre, Love or Liquor   Duke
Madeline's Commercial   Comden and Green
Magic Touch (I Promise), The   Livingston, Jay
Magic Waltz, The   Drake; Leigh
Make Each Day a Holiday   Mills
Make Friends   Howard, Bart
Make Me a Child Again   Washington
Mama Mia (Italian Mother Song)   Washington
Mama's in the Park   Caesar
Mambo (inst.)   Mercer
Man and Wife   DePaul
Man Behind the Badge, The   Gilbert
Man from Laramie, The   Washington
Man I Used to Be, The   Hammerstein; Rodgers
Man in the Next Apartment, The   Van Heusen
Man with a Dream, A   Young, Victor
Man with the Golden Arm   Cahn; Van Heusen
Man's Got a Right, A   Leigh; Spina
Man's Inhumanity to Man   Strouse
March, March   Comden and Green
Marching to the Fight   Leigh
Maria Marimba   Evans; Livingston, Jay
Marry the Man   David, Hal
Mars Meditates (inst.)   Revel
Me and My Puppy Dog   Coots
Me You See, The   Henderson; Rose
Melancholy Melody   Davis
Men Don't Cry   Leigh
Mercury Muses (inst.)   Revel
Merman Mambo, The   Styne
Merry-Go-Round (Complainte de la Butte)   Lawrence
Merrymakers, The   Drake
Methinks   Russell; Styne
Midnight Madness   Coslow
Midway Polka, The   Drake
Milky Way (inst.)   Revel
Minor Nursery   Mercer
'Miss You' Kiss, A   Young, Victor
Mississippi Honeymoon   Blake
Mocambo Mambo   Duke
Montage Theme   Mercer
Moon, The   Gilbert
More the Less, The   Leigh
Morning Dew   David, Mack
Most, The   Berlin
Most Respectable Married Woman, A   Cahn; Styne
Mr. Berle Theme (inst.)   Young, Victor
Mule, You Lazy Mule   Livingston, Jerry
Music Is Better Than Words   Comden and Green
Musical Station Breaks   Bergman
Mustang   Washington
My Baby's Got Such Lovin' Ways   David, Hal
My Crazy Little Mixed Up Heart   Coslow
My Dearest, My Darling, My Sweetheart   Livingston, Jerry
My Dream Sonata   David, Mack; Van Heusen
My Girl Friend's Boy Friend   Hoffman; Merrill
My Heart Doesn't Know   Friend

My Heart Says Yes   Coslow
My Heart Song   Sigman
My Social Hot Dog (from the Ivy League)   Livingston, Jerry
My Son John   Fain; Leigh; Webster
My Song   Blane; Martin
My Tzatskele (Little Darling)   Ager; Davis
My Wayward Heart   Leigh
Naked Sea   Brooks
Nancy Hanks (inst.)   Young, Victor
Never Come Sunday   Washington; Young, Victor
Never, Never Again   Comden and Green
New Hollywood Plots   Fain; Webster
Next Time It Happens, The   Hammerstein; Rodgers
Night After Night   Sigman
Night Camp   Young, Victor
Night Flight   Leigh; Spina
Night Flight (inst.)   Young, Victor
Nina the Ballerina   Coots
Nine Thorny Thickets   Mercer
Nineteenth Hole   Drake
No Love Daboodle, The   Merrill
No One Thanks the Go-Between   Leigh
Not As a Stranger   Van Heusen
Nothing at All   Fain
Nothing Can Replace a Man   Fain
Now Is the Time for All Good Men   Duke
Occasional Man, An   Blane; Martin
Officer O'Mahoney   Merrill
Oh! It Looked Like He Might Buy Wine   Cahn
Old Fashioned Mothers   Fain
Old Left Hander, The   Robison
Ole Man River Is Lonely Now   Blake
Olympian Gods (Tale of the Olympian Gods) (inst.)   Young, Victor
On Honolulu Bay   Caesar
On the Lonely Mission Trail   Baer
Once   Coots
Once Upon a Garden   Mills
Once Upon a Long Ago   Schwartz, Arthur
Once Upon a Time   Comden and Green
One   Silver
One-Two-Three   Drake
Only Forever   Stept
Oo   Ellington
Ooh Bang Jiggilly Jang (But My Guy)   Merrill
Ooh La La Boom Boom   Coslow
Oooh! I Like You!!!   Cahn; Styne
Optimism   Mills
(Otto Drives Me Crazy) Otto's Gotta Go   David, Hal
Our Dream Waltz   Coslow
Our Town   Cahn; Van Heusen
Out Comes Oom-Pa-Pa   Leigh
Out of Doors   Blane; Martin
Out of This World Into My Arms   Berlin
Overnight   Lawrence
Panama   Sigman
Parade of Broken Hearts   Merrill
Paris Loves Lovers   Porter
Party Gets Going, The   Hammerstein; Rodgers
Party That We're Gonna Have Tomorrow Night, The   Hammerstein; Rodgers
Paul Revere's Ride (inst.)   Young, Victor
Pearl of the Orient (inst.)   Alter
Pendulum Song, The   Hoffman
Perfect Married Life, A   Cahn; Van Heusen

Perfume, Candy and Flowers   Merrill
Perfume of Love, The   Porter
Pet Me, Poppa   Loesser
Pete Kelly's Blues   Cahn
Phoenix City Blues   Spina
Pick Your Hero   Leigh
Pick Yourself a Star   Leigh
Pickle Packer Polka   Oakland
Picnic May Not Be a Picnic, A   Drake
Pied Piper (Pied Piper of Hamlin) (inst.)   Young, Victor
Pink Tights   Cahn; Styne
Please Don't Go So Soon   Sigman
Please Don't Touch   Merrill
Please Let Me Come Back to You   Berlin
Please Wait for Me   Sigman
Pledge of Allegiance to the Flag   Caesar
Polaris (North Star) (inst.)   Revel
Polite Rhumba from Havana   Loesser
Poppa Pappadopolis   Silver
Possibility's There, The   Burke; Van Heusen
Prayer, A   Blane
Problem Child   Leigh
Punch and Judy   Livingston, Jerry
Quarrelling Song (You're a Cad, You're a Bounder),
   The   Coslow
Quiet Little Rendezvous   Coslow
Quiet Voice, A   Leigh
Rag Me that Mendlessohn March   Sondheim
Rainbow Round the World   Caesar
Rainy Day (inst.), The   Young, Victor
Ready Cash   Fain
Red Blues, The   Porter
Red Confetti, Pink Balloons and Tambourines   David, Mack;
   Livingston, Jerry
Relax-ay-voo   Cahn; Schwartz, Arthur
Remarkable Fellow   Young, Victor
Remembering   Sigman
Rice   David, Mack
Ride of Fury   Brown, Nacio Herb
Rising Hour, The   Robison
Robin Hood   Sigman
Rockin' and Yodelin'   Sigman
Rolling Stone Gathers No Love, A   Livingston, Jerry
Romance in Candlelight   Coslow
Romantically Inclined   Drake
Rosa   Russell
Rose Tattoo, The   Brooks; Warren
Roses and Revolvers   Raye; Webster
Roses in the Rain   Duke
Ruby and the Rose, The   Alter
Ruby Red (inst.)   Alter
Run Away   Leigh
Run for Cover   Brooks
Run for Your Life   Cahn; Styne
Sad is the Life of a Sailor's Wife   Schwartz, Arthur
Saint of Broadway, The   Silver
Same Old Saturday Night   Cahn
Santa Claus Parade   Coots
Satin and Silk   Porter
Saturn Soliloquizes (inst.)   Revel
Say the Word   Stept
Sayonara G.I.   Revel
S-chut-ya Ding   Merrill
Second Auto Theme   Mercer
Second Greatest Sex, The   Evans; Livingston, Jay

See You Tomorrow — So Long for Now   Wrubel
Seek the Spy   Leigh
Sell It   Howard, Bart
Send Me a Piece of Your Wedding Cake   Bryan
Senor Jose Durante   Evans; Livingston, Jay
Senor Turista   Drake
Sensation   Sigman
Sentimental Moments   Freed, Ralph
Seven Pretty Dreams   David, Hal
Seven Year Itch, The   Cahn; Styne
Seventeen Summers   Leigh; Spina
She   Ellington
She'll Say Bye Bye to You   Blake
Sheridan's Ride (inst.)   Young, Victor
Show Me that You Love Me   Hoffman
Show Stoppers   Styne
Siberia   Porter
Sidewalk Cafe, A   Drake
Sidi-El-Abbes   Lawrence
Silk Stockings   Porter
Silly Song, The   David, Mack
Silvana Mangano Mambo, The   David, Mack
Silver Wings in the Moonlight Over the China Sea   Blake
Simpatico   Cahn; Schwartz, Arthur
Simplicity   Carmichael
Since Yesterday   Duke
Sincerely Yours   Webster
Sing Me a Riddle   Carmichael
Sister Anne   Stept
Sitting on the Back Porch   Hammerstein; Rodgers
Situation Wise   Comden and Green
Sixty Seconds Apart   DePaul
Skip the Build-Up   Fain
Slave of Love, A   Spina
Sluefoot   Mercer
Small One (inst.), The   Young, Victor
Small Talk   Duke
Small World   Duke
So I Said Si, Si   Russell
So Right for Me   Blane; Martin
So That's What Love Is   Leigh; Spina
Solar Siesta (inst.)   Revel
Solo   Russell
Something So Delightful   Leigh
Something's Gotta Give   Mercer
Song I Heard Last Night, The   Parish
Song of Omar Khyyam, The   Evans; Livingston, Jay
Song of Provincetown   Drake
Song of the Future (inst.)   Young, Victor
Souvenir D'Italie   Sigman
Space   Gilbert
Spin Around   Drake
Spring Is Getting On   Drake
Stage, The   Drake
Star You Wished Upon Last Night, The   McHugh
Stars Remain, The   Leigh; Livingston, Jerry
Stay on the Right Side Sister   Bloom
Staying Away   Sigman
Step Down Off the Minus (Climb Aboard the Plus)   Drake
Sterophonic Sound   Porter
Stillman's Gym   Comden and Green
Storm Fear   Brooks
Story Conference, The   Duke
Stowaway, The   Leigh
Stradivarius   David, Mack; Warren

Straight from the Shoulder   Silver
Strange Lady in Town   Washington
Strange Melody   Russell
Strange What Love Will Do   Blake
Such a Noble Lover   Leigh
Summer Interlude   Koehler
Summer Storm   Burke; Van Heusen
Summertime in Venice   Sigman
Summery Winter Cruise   Drake
Sun at My Window, Love at My Door   Young, Victor
Sunset Strip   Brooks
Suzy Is a Good Thing   Hammerstein; Rodgers
Sweet Thursday   Hammerstein; Rodgers
Swim, Swim, Swim   Gordon
Swingin' Uptown   Parish
Sympathy   Leigh
Symphony of the Clocks   Stept
Table Manners   Leigh
Take Back Your Kisses (And Give Me Back My
    Heart)   Coots
Take Me Back   Hoffman
Take Me with You   David, Hal
Take Mine   David, Hal
Take the Money   Duke
Talk to Me Tomorrow   Robin; Styne
Tambourine Waltz, The   Carmichael; Webster
Tango (inst.)   Mercer
Tears Come Easy, The   David, Hal
Tell Me More   Coslow
Tell My Love   Livingston, Jay
Texas Romp and Square Dance   Mercer
Texas Waltz   Mercer
86th! the 86th! The Fighting Men of the 86th!, The   Cahn;
    Van Heusen
Thank You All   Livingston, Jay
Thanks a Lot but No Thanks   Comden and Green
That Mittel-Europa Mine   Eliscu; Gorney
That Shufflin' Tune   Razaf
That's the Kind of Dame I Am   Styne
That's What's Wrong with Jimmy   David, Hal
(I Couldn't Get the Hang of) The Merengue   Livingston,
    Jerry
(Love Is) The Tender Trap   Cahn; Van Heusen
Then and Now   Merrill
There Must Be a Million Ways (To Say I Love You)   Cahn;
    Styne
There's a Corny Little Corner in the Corner of My
    Heart   Henderson
There's a Hollywood that's Good   Porter
There's a Kiss in Your Eyes   Howard, Joseph E.
There's a Rising Moon (For Every Falling Star)   Fain;
    Webster
There's a Shadow Between Us   Livingston, Jerry; Parish
There's Nothin' Like Love   Robin; Styne
There's Nothing Like This Old Fashioned   Duke
These Things Are Mine   Coots
They All Took a Lesson from Me   Evans; Livingston, Jay
Think It Over   David, Mack
Think, Think, Think   Robison
Thinkin'   Hammerstein; Rodgers
Third Day Rag   Mercer
This Is Forever (Theme for Love)   Young, Victor
This Is the Dance   Drake
This Is What I Love   Adamson; Lane
This Old Love (inst.)   Young, Victor

This Too Shall Pass   Washington
Though I Said No to You Yesterday   Duke
Thousand Burning Bridges, A   Fain
Three Cheers for Holidays   Caesar
Three Loves   Strouse
Thrill in Spain   Blake
Tide Pool, The   Hammerstein; Rodgers
Tightwad   Caesar
Till My Love Comes to Me   Webster
Timberjack   Washington; Young, Victor
Time for Parting   Comden and Green
Time Out for Thinking   Razaf
Tira, La La   Leigh
To Dance with You   Razaf
(I Only Live) To Love You   Gordon; Young, Victor
To My Love (Je Ne Sais Pas)   Lawrence
To the Music of Windchimes   Spina
To Those Who Wait   Leigh
Tomorrow Song, The   Howard, Bart
Tonight   Robin; Styne
Too Bad   Porter
Too Many Chiefs and Not Enough Injuns   David, Hal
Too Many Nights   Howard, Joseph E.
Too Much, Baby, Baby   Sigman
Topaz Tango (inst.)   Alter
Touch of Love, The   Silver
Toujours L'Amour on the Cote D'Azur   Coslow
Towers to the Sky Town   Drake
Toy Tiger   Mancini
Toy Town Tune Parade   Coots
Trick in Arithmetic, A   Drake
Trinidad Rhumba   Cahn
Trouble with Harry, The   David, Hal; Loesser
T.V. Magic   Drake
Twenty-Six Toots   Willson
Twilight Time   Ellington
Twist My Arm   Fain; Webster
Two Castanets   Hoffman; Merrill
Two Characters   Drake
Two Lovers and Two Lives   Russell
Under the Dress   Porter
Underwater   Brooks
Unexpectedly   Heyman
Uninvited Love   Leigh; Livingston, Jerry
Uranus Unmasked (inst.)   Revel
Vibrations from Venus (inst.)   Revel
Village Called Hollywood, A   Duke
Villain Always Gets It, The   Fain
Vino, Vino   David, Hal
Visit with Me, Lord   Robison
Voulez Vous   Duke
Walk Along with Kings   Merrill
Walk Like a Sailor   Fain
Walking Papers   Merrill
Waltzing Down the Aisle   Hoffman
Waltzing Into Love   Koehler
War Is Over, The   Leigh
Wasn't It a Wonderful Wedding   Cahn; Van Heusen
We Are Here to Sing a Chorus   Leigh
We Can Make It   Robin; Styne
We Had a Little Rain Today   Drake
We Laughed at Love   Kahn
Weatherman   Ellington
Weepin' and a Wailin' Song (I'm Happy When I'm Singin'),
    A   Gilbert

Welcome   Sigman
Welcome Egghead   Mercer
We've Come a Long, Long Way   Leigh
Whale of a Tale   Hoffman
What a Ball   Porter
What a Face, What a Beauty   Gordon
What a Wonderful Way to Die   Merrill
What a Wonderful Way to Spend a Summer Sunday   Drake
What Did I Do   Myrow
What Ev'ry Young Girl Should Know   Carmichael; Webster
What Happened to the Conga   Robin; Styne
What If You're Not   Duke
What the Country Needs   Coslow
Whatever Goes Swoop Lilting Lofting   Eliscu; Gorney
What's Good for You (Is Bad for Me)   Lawrence
What's So Great About Beethoven   Willson
When a Carnation Meets a Red Red Rose   Blake
When All the Streets Are Dark   Merrill
When Am I Getting the Mink, Mister Fink   Yellen
When Eden Was a Garden (A Sermon in Music)   Meyer
When Eden Was a Rock (A Sermon in Music)   Lewis
When Ella Bops   Mills
When My Love Smiles   Webster
When We're Alone (Rita) (inst.)   Young, Victor
When When When   Hoffman; Silver
When You Dance (For the Love of the Dance)   Leigh
When You Pretend   Brooks; Warren
When Your Birthday Rolls Around   Baer
When You're in Love   Schwartz, Arthur
Where   McHugh
Where Is that Someone for Me?   Young, Victor
Where Is the Rooster (Meow-Wa, Ba Ba Ko-Goo-Ta)   Mills
Where Will the Dimple Be   Hoffman; Merrill
Whist-a-lin' Dixie   Merrill
White and Gold Ballet   Young, Victor
White Buffalo, The   Bergman
Who Are We   Livingston, Jerry; Webster
Who Loves You Like I Do   Merrill
Who Needs an Opening Song   Oakland
Who Says I Wronged Thee   Spina
Who's Excited   Duke
Why Did You Have to Kiss Me   Russell
Why Do I   Sigman
Why Do I Miss Mississippi   Caesar
Why Do They Call It Greenland   Brooks
Why Don't They Leave Us Alone   Mills
Why Should I Trust You?   Porter
Wichita   Washington
Wild Bill   Leigh
Will You Marry Me?   Hammerstein; Rodgers
Window of Dreams   Friend
With All My Heart   Evans; Livingston, Jay
With All My Love   Heyman
With No One Playing the Organ   Merrill
With You or Without You   Livingston, Jerry; Parish
Without Love   Porter
Woman in Love, A   Loesser
Wonder of You (The Lincoln Theme), The   Heyman; Young, Victor
Wonderful Thing Happened Today, A   Adamson; McHugh
World Is Mine, The   Young, Victor
Wouldn't Hurt You for the World   Russell
Ye Olde Antique Sale   Drake
Year After Year   Howard, Bart
Yodalo   Evans; Livingston, Jay

Yodel Song   Leigh
You Could Hear a Pin Drop   Russell
You Go to Your Church and I'll Go to Mine   Drake
You Gotta Be Different   Evans; Livingston, Jay
You Have a Way with You   Coslow
You Look So Familiar   Brooks; Warren
You My Love   Gordon; Van Heusen
You Send Me   Caesar
You Started Something   Coslow
You'll Always Be My Lifetime Sweetheart   Burke
You'll Get Yours   Van Heusen
You'll Love Me in Paris   Leigh
Your Ever Lovin' Arms   Spina
Your Understanding Heart   Robison
You're Here My Love   Burke
You're Mine Forever   Baer
You're Never Too Young (Face the Music)   Cahn; Schwartz, Arthur
You're not the One and Only (Lonely One)   Woods
Zap-a-zoo   David, Mack

1956

Abbondanza   Loesser
Acey Deucey   Cahn; Van Heusen
After Midnight (inst.)   Revel
After You   Drake
Ah, Ah, Ah (The Song that Haunts My Heart) (Je N'en Connais Pas La Fin)   Rome
All About Love   Gordon; Myrow
All Day   Burke
All Is Well   Akst
All the Colors of the Rainbow   Blane; Martin
All This is Home   David, Mack; Livingston, Jerry
Alla Breve Song (inst.)   Kern
Allegheny Moon   Hoffman
Allegretto Grazioso (inst.)   Kern
Alma Mater   Styne
Always (Death of a Ballad)   Leigh
Amore Mio   Stept
Anastasia   Webster
And That Is That   Willson
And Then I Met Yvette   Hoffman
Another Love   Stept
Answer Me   Willson
Anybody Can Write   Berlin
April Fooled Me   Fields; Kern
Are You a Flop   Drake
Are You for Real   Friend
Are You Mine   Cahn
Aren't You Glad   Loesser
Around the Corner from the Blues   Sigman
Around the World in 80 Days   Adamson; Young, Victor
Arts, The   Adams; Strouse
Ascot Gavotte   Lerner, Alan Jay; Loewe
At the Beaux Arts Ball   Drake
At the Cross of God   Coots
At the Drive-In Movie   Silver
Away Out West   Adamson; Young, Victor
Baby, Let Me Take You Dreaming   Cahn
Baby that Should Have Been Mine, The   Baer
Balboa   Blane; Martin
Ballad of Jack and the Beanstalk, The   Livingston, Jerry
Ballad of Wes Tancred   Myrow
Ballet (inst.)   Kern

Bangin' the Bongo   Hoffman
Bargain Counter Doll   Merrill
Bass Fiddle Boogie Woogie, The   Blake; Sissle
Be Close to Paradise   Merrill
Be Good to Me   Brooks
Be My All (Or Be My Nothing)   Howard, Bart
Be Yourself   Drake
Beautiful Face (With a Figure to Match), A   David, Hal
Beautiful Girls of Vienna (The Beautiful Girls of Berlin),
      The   Coots
Beautiful Women   Howard, Bart
Beauty in a Song   Willson
Beauty Isn't Everything   Bacharach; Heyman
Beetle Race, The   Warren
Behind These Prison Walls   Silver
Believe in Love   Webster
Bell for Adano, A   Dietz; Schwartz, Arthur
Belle of Madrid   Gordon; Revel
Bells Are Ringing   Comden and Green; Styne
Bells Contretemps (inst.)   Kern
Benvenuta   Loesser
Better Than a Dream   Comden and Green; Styne
Big D   Loesser
Big Dreams   Hoffman
Big Record, The   Drake
Big Town   Kalmar
Bigger than Both of Us   Howard, Bart
Black, the Bottomless (inst.)   Young, Victor
Bless You, Gentle Woman   Robison
Blue Bluebird (inst.), The   McHugh
Blue Fandango   Coslow
Blue Harmonica   Hoffman
Boarding House Blues (inst.)   Warren
Bonjour   Burke; Friml
Bonjour Madame   Raye
Boom Cheela Bim Bahm   Merrill
Born Too Late   Duke
Boy!   Hoffman
Boy Do We Look to the Monkeys   Hoffman
Boy on Page 35   David, Hal
Brass Band on Float   Merrill
Breathtaking   Robison
Bubble Ballet (inst.)   Kern
Buckskin Beauty   Cahn; Van Heusen
Bundle of Joy   Gordon; Myrow
By the Rippling Waters   Willson
California Story, The   Willson
Call Me Irresponsible   Cahn; Van Heusen
Call of the Wild   Leigh
Cap with the Strap in the Back, The   Silver
Caroline   Porter
Carry Me Back to Laramie   Cahn; Van Heusen
Cha-Cha-Cha for Gia   Mancini
Chaps from Annapolis   Adamson; McHugh
Chicago Bears   Johnson, Howard
China Gate   Adamson
Chinese Lantern Love (inst.)   Kern
Chosen Few, The   Leigh; Livingston, Jerry
Christmas in Birdland   Mancini
Christmas Presents   Willson
Christmas Waltz, The   Webster
Climbing Some Other High Hill   Von Tilzer
Closing Love Duet   Merrill
Clouds   Carmichael
Coax Me a Little   Webster

Cold and Dead   Loesser
Colorado   Styne
Comme Ca   Parish
Comparisons   Burke; Friml
Comrades   Carmichael
Cool Tango (inst.)   Oakland
Country Tunes   Willson
Country's in the Very Best of Hands, The   DePaul; Mercer
Cowboy Hoedown   Loesser
Cozy Corner   Russell
Crazy Horse   Blane; Martin
Cry in the Night, A   Washington
Crystal   Caesar
Dame Crazy   Adamson; McHugh
Dance of Moderate Chastity (inst.)   Warren
Dance of Time (inst.)   Warren
Dance of Welcome (inst.)   Warren
Day Dreams   Hoffman
Day in the Country, A   Fain; Webster
Decorating Eliza   Lerner, Alan Jay; Loewe
Dell, The (inst.)   Warren
Dere's Yellow Gold on de Trees   Cahn
Diamond, a Pearl and an Ermine Wrap, A   Fain
Do You Wonder   Raye
Dodie   Freed, Ralph
Do-It-Yourself Cha Cha, The   Evans; Livingston, Jay
Don't Count the Stars   Washington
Don't Cry   Loesser
Don't Forget to Say Your Prayers   Sigman
Don't Join the Navy to See the World   Adamson; McHugh
Don't Thank Me   Comden and Green; Styne
Don't Wait Too Long   Coots
Doo-Hickey Thing-Ma-Jiggy, The   Merrill
Dorioso   Howard, Joseph E.
Dos I Dos   Willson
Do-Sol-Do   Willson
Down Town Blues (inst.)   Warren
Downtown   Adams; Strouse
Dream Fantasy   Oakland
Dream Girl   Hoffman
Dream Street   Robison
Dream Waltz (Inst.)   Warren
Dreamy River   Egan; Whiting
Drop that Name   Comden and Green; Styne
Drummer Boy   Strouse
Each Time I Dream   David, Mack; Warren
Echo of Love   Sigman
Egghead   Hoffman
Eight P.M.   Drake
Embassy Waltz (inst.)   Loewe
End, The   Strouse
Every Man Should Marry   Davis; Silver
Every Night   Warren
Every Time You Danced with Me   Warren
Everybody's Buddy   Adams
Everyday's an Opening Night on Wall Street   Stept
Everytime We Meet   Cahn
Eyes Like a Stranger   Loesser
Fall in Love with Me   Friend
Far from Wonderful   Duke
Farewell, Alma Mater   Drake
Farmer's Life, A   Silver
Fee Fi Fo Fum   Livingston, Jerry
(When Your Heart Is) Feeling Foolish in Brazil   Sigman
Fiddle-Foot Fanny (On Shoo-Shoo Street)   Friend

Fiddle-iddle-up   Willson
Finishing School   Adamson; McHugh
First One, The   Willson
First Time, The   Strouse
Fish   Dietz; Schwartz, Arthur
Flaming Rose, The   David, Mack
Flash of Lightning, A   Silver
Flirting (inst.)   Kern
Flower of San Antone, The   David, Mack
Fly Now, Pay Later   Duke
Fly the Magic Carpet   Yellen
Folk Song (inst.)   Kern
Follow Your Dreams   Ahlert
For a New America   Lawrence
For a Song   Willson
For Your Applause   Evans; Livingston, Jay
Forbidden Fruit   Silver
Forever, Darling   Cahn
Forget Her (Forget Him)   Hoffman
Fort Knox   Silver
48 Letters from 48 States   David, Hal
Four Leading Ladies   Cahn
Four Seasons, The   Russell
Fourth, The   Willson
Frangipani Blossom   Evans; Livingston, Jay
Frank Merriwell Opening   Styne
Frankie and Johnny   Cahn
Fraulein   Lawrence
Fresno Beauties   Loesser
Friendly Persuasion (Thee I Love)   Webster
From the First Hello to the Last Goodbye   Burke
G Minor Is My Favorite Key   Willson
Gaby   Parish
Gall with the Yaller Shoes, The   Cahn
Gay and Joyous (inst.)   Kern
Gay Friends Are Essential   Willson
Gentle and Sentimental   Willson
Get Me to the Church on Time   Lerner, Alan Jay; Loewe
Giant   Webster
Girl at the End of Our Street Back Home (inst.)   Kern
Girl Has Got to Do the Best She Can, A   Yellen
Girl Named Mary, A   Bryan
Girl with the Bells, The   David, Mack; Van Heusen
Girls of Summer, The   Sondheim
Give a Thought   Baer
Give Me You   David, Hal
Go Away My Love   Evans; Livingston, Jay
God Has His Arms Around Me   Adamson; Young, Victor
Good Old Days of Burlesque, The   Adamson; McHugh
Goodbye Darlin'   Loesser
Goodbye Lolipops, Hello Lipstick   Hoffman
Goodbye My Friend   Merrill
Got a Little Brush (inst.)   Kern
Gotta Have a Man, Sometime   Adamson; McHugh
Grace Kelly Wedding Waltz, The   Washington
Grapevine   Silver
Green Grow the Grass   Hoffman
Guard Watch   Oakland; Webster
Guy with the Polka Dotted Tie, The   Styne
Haffner   Willson
Half of My Heart   Washington
Happy Face Baby   Brooks
Happy Falling Said I to My Heart   Burke
Happy to Make Your Acquaintance   Loesser
Harp and a Fiddle and a Flute, A   Burke; Friml

Hawaiian Band on Float   Merrill
He Never Looks My Way   Livingston, Jerry
Heads Up, America   Cahn
Hell Hath No Fury   Cahn
Hello   Russell
Hello, Hello There   Comden and Green; Styne
Hello to the Blues   Lawrence
Here Come the Stars of Tomorrow   Coots
Here Comes the Queen   Willson
Here's a Song Everyone Can Sing   Willson
He's Got Time   Merrill
Hey, Gang   Drake
Hey, Jealous Lover   Cahn
Hey Sexy   Porter
High Society   DePaul; Mercer
High Society, Calypso   Porter
Hoedown   Loesser
Hold Back the Dawn   David, Mack
Hollywood or Bust   Fain; Webster
Holy Cow   Evans; Livingston, Jay
Holy Smoke   Merrill
Hometown Rag, The   Livingston, Jerry
Honking Bird in the Willow Tree, The   Webster
Honolulu Rock-A Roll-A   Hoffman
Hot and Cold   Comden and Green; Styne
Hot Diggity   Hoffman
House and Garden   Loesser
How Beautiful the Days   Loesser
(Home) How Dear Can It Be   Robison
How Little It Matters, How Little We Know   Leigh
How Sweet Is the Summer (inst.)   Kern
How Well I Remember (The Things You Forgot)   David, Hal
Howdy Friends and Neighbors   DePaul; Mercer
Human of the Year, The   Drake
Humming (inst.)   Kern
Hurray Hurray   Myrow
Hymn to Him, A   Lerner, Alan Jay; Loewe
I Ain't Gonna Love No More   Warren
I Am   Merrill
I Ay Ay   Russell
I Belong, Belong, Belong   Drake
I Came Back to Say I'm Sorry   David, Hal
I Can't Forget   Cahn
I Can't Spell Hippopotamus   Coots
I Could Have Danced All Night   Lerner, Alan Jay; Loewe
I Cry More   Bacharach; David, Hal
I Didn't Want to Love You   Russell
I Don't Know What I Want   Blane; Martin
I Don't Like this Dame   Loesser
I Don't Want to Know   Hoffman
I Dreamed of Foster   Silver
I Feel Like a Mountain   Silver
I Happy New Year to You   Friml
I Hear You, Master   Drake
I Just Found Out About Love   Adamson; McHugh
I Just Want to Be a Song and Dance Man   Adamson; McHugh
I Know How It Is   Loesser
I Lead a Charmed Life   Russell
I Left the Door Wide Open   Cahn; Van Heusen
I Like, but You I Love   David, Hal
I Like Ev'rybody   Loesser
I Like the Feeling   Blane; Martin
I Live to Love   Cahn
I Lost the Rhythm   Strouse

I Love Gina   Stept
I Love Him   Loesser
I Love You, Samantha   Porter
I Love You, That's Why   Ahlert
I Love Your Sunny Teeth   Comden and Green; Styne
I Made a Fist   Loesser
I Met a Girl   Comden and Green; Styne
I Never Felt This Way Before   Gordon; Myrow
I Never Got Out of Paris   Silver
I Never Knew   Mercer
I Never Thought I'd Be Along Here   Willson
I Never Wanna Hear that Song Again   Davis
I Never Want to See You Again   Berlin
I Offer You   Oakland
I Once Had a Heart   Young, Victor
I Refuse to Rock 'n Roll   Cahn
I Seen Her at the Station   Loesser
I Used to Hate Ya   Hoffman
I Waited So Long   Evans; Livingston, Jay
I Wanna Know   David, Hal
I Was a Little Too Lonely   Evans; Livingston, Jay
I Was Once in Love When (inst.)   Kern
I Wish I Was a Bunny   Coots
I'd Like to Say a Few Words about Texas   Hoffman
I'd Rather Have a Maybe (From You Baby)   Hoffman
If a Vagabond Were King   Burke; Friml
If All Who Pray Would Pray for All   Robison
If I Can't Take It with Me When I Go   David, Mack
If I Had My Druthers   DePaul; Mercer
If the Good Lord's Willin'   Hoffman
If They Could See You through My Eyes   Merrill
If You Become Bored   Hammerstein; Kern
If You Can Dream   Cahn
If You Come Through   Bloom; Mercer
If You Have Ever Loved   David, Hal
If You Really Want to Know   Hoffman
If You Wanna See Mamie Tonight   Fain; Webster
If You've Never Been to Vegas   Cahn
Ike for Four More Years   Berlin
Il Torrente (You Can't Keep Running)   Sigman
I'll Be Worthy of You   De Lange
I'll Buy Everybody a Beer   Loesser
I'll Cry Tomorrow   Mercer
I'll Go Along with You   Livingston, Jerry
I'll Take You Dreaming   Cahn
I'm a Happy Guy   Bergman
(Doctor) I'm Allergic to Love   Howard, Bart
I'm an Ordinary Man   Lerner, Alan Jay; Loewe
I'm Glad I'm Not a Man   Duke
I'm Going Back   Comden and Green; Styne
I'm Gonna Get Him   Berlin
I'm Innocent   Silver
I'm Just a Little Bit Confused   Warren
I'm Nothin' but a Dreamer   Merrill
I'm Part of You   Dietz; Schwartz, Arthur
I'm Past My Prime   DePaul; Mercer
I'm Simply Starved   Drake
I'm Tellin' You   Merrill
In Love with Paree   McHugh
In My Dreams   Hoffman
In Society   DePaul; Mercer
In the Back of a Hack   Harburg
In the Dark of an Arkansas Moon   Leigh
In the Hollow of His Hand   Warren
Indecision   Blane; Martin

Independent   Comden and Green; Styne
Indiana Holiday   Webster
Inferiority of Your Sex (And the Superiority of Mine),
   The   Drake
Inspector Barnes   Comden and Green; Styne
Intrigue   Drake
Introduce Me   Fields; Kern
Intuition   Comden and Green; Styne
Is It a Crime?   Comden and Green; Styne
Island in the Sun   Fain; Webster
It Happened One Night   DePaul; Mercer
It Is G, It Is Minor, It's Mozart   Willson
It Looks Like Love   Fain; Webster
It Only Hurts for a Little While   David, Mack
It Takes More Than Love to Keep a Lady Warm   Berlin
It's a Nuisance Having You Around   DePaul; Mercer
It's a Perfect Relationship   Comden and Green; Styne
It's a Simple Little System   Comden and Green; Styne
It's a Typical Day   DePaul; Mercer
It's Better in the Dark   Cahn; Van Heusen
It's Better than a Dream   Styne
It's Fun to Be in London   Warren
It's Fun to Be in Love   Cahn
It's Fun to Do a Show   Cahn
I've Grown Accustomed to Her Face   Lerner, Alan Jay;
   Loewe
Jack and the Giant   Livingston, Jerry
Jack O'Rourke's Party Line   Razaf
January (inst.)   Young, Victor
Jett Rink Ballad   Webster
Joey   Loesser
Johnny's on a Journey   Lane; Lawrence
Join in the Dances (inst.)   Kern
Josephine   Willson
Joyous and Thankful   Willson
Jubilation T. Cornpone   DePaul; Mercer
Jungle Red   Cahn
Just a Little Word (inst.)   Kern
Just in Time   Comden and Green; Styne
Just Like a Song   Willson
Just Like a Woman   Willson
Just You Wait   Lerner, Alan Jay; Loewe
Kewtee Bear Song, The   Freed, Ralph; Livingston, Jerry
Kickin' Up a Storm   Adamson; McHugh
Kiss is Forever, A   Cahn
Klondike Kate   Berlin
La Parisienne   David, Mack; Warren
Lady Is Indisposed, The   Coleman
Lake Tahoe   Washington; Young, Victor
Language of Love   Spina
Lauderdale By the Sea   Howard, Joseph E.
Lazy Hour   Revel
Leap Year   Brooks
Let's Be Friendly   Fain; Webster
Let's Get the Show on the Road   Cahn
Let's Vocalize   Porter
Letter Theme, The   Loesser
Life Could Not Better Be   Cahn
Life of the Party, The   Drake
Like a Woman Loves a Man   Loesser
Listen to the Sound of My Love   Warren
Little Church Around the Corner, The   David, Hal
Little Love, a Little Money, A   Duke
Little Mistakes   Kahn
Little Old Woman Who Lived in a Shoe, The   Coots

Little One   Porter
Lively Melody (inst.)   Kern
Living End, The   Mancini
Living Idol, The   Heyman
Liza's Eyes   Coslow
Lonely City   Oakland
Lonely Man, The   Brooks
Lonely Ones (Solitary Street), The   Lawrence
Lonesome Cup of Coffee, A   Russell
Long Ago   Warren
Long Before I Knew You   Comden and Green; Styne
Long Time Ago, A   Loesser
Looka Me   Livingston, Jerry
Lord, I'm Glad That I Know Thee   Burke; Young, Victor
Lord's Got His Arms Around Us, The   Stept
Lost Horizon   Warren
Lost in a Crowded Place   Caesar
Lotus Land   Parish
Loud and Soft   Willson
Love and Kindness   Loesser
(You Can Tell When There's) Love in a Home   DePaul;
     Mercer
Love Is Still in Town   Duke
Love Is What I Never Knew   Warren
Love Leads to Marriage   Berlin
Love Me As Though There Were No Tomorrow   Adamson;
     McHugh
Love Sick   Merrill
Love Theme from The Mole People   Evans; Livingston, Jay
Love Won't Wait Until Tomorrow   Raye
Love You More Than   Styne
Lullaby in Blue   Gordon; Myrow
Madame (Ma-dahm)   Evans; Livingston, Jay
Madly in Love   Duke
Magic Garden   Bergman
'Magine   Stept
Maim Frank   Styne
Make Love to Me   Blake
Make Me Yours   David, Hal
Make-Believe Stranger   Drake
Maladjusted Jester, The   Cahn
Mama, Mama   Loesser
Mama, Teach Me to Dance   Hoffman
Man from Galilee   David, Mack
Man I Never Met, The   Warren
Man in the Dark   Warren
Man Who Owns the Sunshine, The   Van Heusen
Manhattan Rag (inst.)   Carmichael
March of the Hoodlums (inst.)   Carmichael
March of the Ill-Assorted Guards, The   Livingston, Jerry
Marcha Del Toros   Fields; Kern
Marlon Mood, The   Comden and Green; Styne
Marry Me, Marry Me   Webster
Martitia   Bacharach; David, Hal
Matador   Mercer
Matrimonial Stomp, The   DePaul; Mercer
Maverick Queen, The   Washington; Young, Victor
May Is the Month That I May   Russell
Maybe He's Some Kinda Crazy   Loesser
Maybe, Maybe, Maybe   David, Mack
Me 'n' You 'n' the Moon   Cahn; Van Heusen
Meet Me in Las Vegas   Cahn
Meeting Time   Evans; Livingston, Jay
Melody for Cello (inst.)   Kern
Melody in F (inst.)   Kern

Melody Man, The   Willson
Melted Rainbow   Sigman
Men Are Only Boys Grown Tall   Warren
Merengue of Love   Sigman
Mi Mujer (inst.)   Warren
Midas Touch, The   Comden and Green; Styne
Mind If I Make Love to You   Porter
Miracle in the Rain (I'll Always Believe in You)   Washington
Miracle of Love   Merrill
Miss Dynamite   Evans; Livingston, Jay
Mississippi Steamboat   Comden and Green; Styne
Missouri Mule (inst.)   Kern
Mockingbird in the Willow   Webster
Moderation   Magidson; Oakland; Warren
Mom   Comden and Green; Styne
Moment We Met, The   Hoffman
Moondrift   Cahn
Moonlight Love   Parish
More, More and More (Un Grand Amour)   Cahn
Morning Mail, The   Bacharach; David, Hal
Most Happy Fella, The   Loesser
Mother Nature's Cabaret   Razaf
Mother Sir   Brooks
Motherhood   Strouse
Mountain, The   David, Mack
Mrs. Santa Claus   Livingston, Jerry
Mu-Cha-Cha   Comden and Green; Styne
Music for Lovers   Howard, Bart
Music Lessons (C'est Chouette La)   Rome
My Anna   Merrill
My Broken Dream   Sigman
My Crazy Little Mixed-Up Heart   Coslow
My Destiny   Cahn
My Dreamboat Is Drifting (Down the River of
     Doubt)   Bacharach
My Guiding Star   Comden and Green; Styne
My Heart Is a Chapel   David, Mack
My Heart Is So Full of You   Loesser
My Heart Knows a Love Song   Cahn
My Hearts Desire   Young, Victor
My Home Town   Cahn
My Last Night in Rome   Freed, Ralph; Livingston, Jerry
My Love Is a Little Kitten   Hoffman
My Lucky Charm   Cahn
My Papa from Panama   Adamson; McHugh
My Runaway Heart   Coots
My Song   Blane; Martin
Nacio Herb Brown's Blue Train (inst.)   Brown, Nacio Herb
Nacio Herb Brown's Hymn to the Moon (inst.)   Brown,
     Nacio Herb
Nacio Herb Brown's Mexican Moon Dance (inst.)   Brown,
     Nacio Herb
Namely You   DePaul; Mercer
Natives Are Restless Tonight, The   Drake
Nature of Things, The   Leigh
Navy's in Town, The   Silver
Never a Day Goes By   Coslow
Never Bite Off More than Your Mate Can Chew   Drake
Never Kiss   Howard, Bart
Never Let Me Go (Ceux Qui M'ont Quitte)   Livingston, Jay
New Sensation in Sound   David, Mack
Next Time, The   Strouse
Nice to Be Near   Fields; Kern
Night Song   Mercer
No Home, No Job   Loesser

No Night to Fear   Warren
No Waiting Time   Robison
Nobody's Ever Gonna Love You   Loesser
Not As Much As I Need You   David, Mack
Not Love   Woods
Not that I Care   David, Mack
Nothing Much to Do   Warren
Nouveau Favori (inst.)   Kern
November Twilight   Webster
Now! Baby! Now!   Cahn
Now We Sing   Willson
Now You Has Jazz   Porter
Now You Say You Care   Lawrence
Number Four   Willson
Oakaloosa   Hoffman
Octopus Song, The   Freed, Ralph; Livingston, Jerry
Oh Come to the Ball   Lerner, Alan Jay; Loewe
Oh, Happy Day   DePaul; Mercer
Oh How It Hurts   Comden and Green; Styne
Oh, My Maria (Pia Maria)   Cahn
Oh, What a Diff'rence You Made   DePaul; Raye
Oh What a Memory We Made   Mercer
Oh, What a Wonderful Song   Willson
Oh, Where Can There Be   Willson
Oh Where, Oh Where   Willson
Okay, Mister Major   Dietz; Schwartz, Arthur
Old Cathay (China) (inst.)   Kern
Old Lamb and New Lamb, An   Stept
Old Man Winter   Bergman
Old People   Loesser
Old Reporters Never Die   DePaul; Mercer
Old World Folk Song (inst.)   Kern
Om Mani Padme Hum   Warren
On a Gettysburg Farm   Robison
On Earth As It Is   Robison
On My Own   Comden and Green; Styne
On the Outside Looking In   Merrill
On the Promenade (inst.)   Kern
On the Street Where You Live   Lerner, Alan Jay; Loewe
Once in a Blue Moon   Bacharach; David, Hal
Once Upon a Time   Adams; Strouse
One Day   Coleman; Leigh
One Kiss Away from Heaven (Malatia)   Coslow
One Look at You   Howard, Bart
One Potater, Two Potater   Silver
One, Two, Three, Pause (The Dancing Lesson)   Burke; Friml
Oogie-Woogie-Shoogie   Comden and Green; Styne
Ooh He's a Tiger   Raye
Ooh, My Feet   Loesser
Oom-Pah Papa   Evans; Livingston, Jay
Opening the Mizner Story   Berlin
Opposite Sex, The   Cahn
Otherwise   DePaul; Mercer
Our First Kiss   Merrill
Our Home Town   Willson
Out-Fox the Fox   Cahn
Papa-Mama-Cha-Cha   Hoffman
Pardners   Cahn; Van Heusen
Party's Over, The   Comden and Green; Styne
Pas de Quarto (inst.)   Kern
Pass the Basket   Cahn
Peacock Today — Tomorrow a Feather Duster, A   Drake
Peasant King, The   Strouse
Peggy's in the Pantry   Bacharach
People Should Listen to Me   Livingston, Jerry

Perfect Love, A   Cahn
Pigalle Saint Germain de Pres   Rome
Pink, the Powder Puff (inst.)   Young, Victor
Pizza Song, The   Friend
Pizzicato (inst.)   Kern
Plant a Little Love in Your Heart   Adams; Strouse
Playful Melody (inst.)   Kern
Please Let Me Tell You   Loesser
Please Take Back Your Introduction   Caesar
Plenty Bambini   Loesser
Polly's Entrance   Gordon; Myrow
Poodle Walk, The   Silver
Poor Little Doll   Pollack
Poor People of Paris, The   Lawrence
Postmark Vienna   David, Mack
Precipevolissimevolmentge (That's Me Falling for
    You)   Willson
Pregunta   Cahn
Pretty Night (The Humming Waltz)   Hoffman
Primavera   Russell
Prince and the Princess Waltz, The   Washington
Principle of Love, The   Robison
Progress Is the Root of All Evil   DePaul; Mercer
Put 'Em Back   DePaul; Mercer
Queen   Willson
Quick Like a Bunny   Silver
Quiet Song (inst.), A   Kern
Quincannon, Frontier Scout   Cahn
Rag Offen the Bush   DePaul; Mercer
Rain in Spain, The   Lerner, Alan Jay; Loewe
Rainmaker, The   David, Hal
R.C.A. Theme   Young, Victor
Red, White and Blue Can't Live on Your IOU, The   Caesar
Regatta   Styne
Religion of Love, The   Robison
Remember Dad on Mother's Day   Mercer; Warren
Remember Him   Warren
Remember Me to You   Woods
Remembering When   Webster
Requiem   Warren
Reverie in Blue   Leigh
Rhythmical Song (inst.)   Kern
Rififi   Lawrence
Right Way Wins the Right of Way, The   Robison
Ritual of Knighthood   Cahn
Robert Schuman   Willson
Rock and Roll Boogie   Silver
Rock and Roll Bump   Adamson; McHugh
Rock and Roll Tumbleweed, The   Cahn
Rocket Ship   Carmichael
Rocky Mountain Rose   Hoffman
Romance Is a Silken Affair   Sigman
Rosabella   Loesser
Roses, Roses, Roses   David, Mack
Rural Melody (inst.)   Kern
Saddled Bridled Harnessed and Tamed   Hoffman
Sadie Hawkins Ballet   DePaul
Saint She Ain't, A   Merrill
Salzburg   Comden and Green; Styne
Santa's Lullaby   Comden and Green; Styne
Saroyan   Harburg
Say a Prayer for Me Tonight   Lerner, Alan Jay; Loewe
Scherzo, The   Willson
School Room (inst.)   Kern
Second Avenue and 12th Street Rag   Duke

Second Time in Love   Warren
Second-Hand Turban and a Crystal Ball, A   Cahn; Van
    Heusen
Security   Cahn
Sentimental Song (inst.)   Kern
Sequence   Willson
Serenade   Cahn
Serenade (inst.)   Kern
Serenade (Napoli) (inst.)   Warren
Serenata (inst.)   Kern
Seven Million Crumbs   Loesser
Shangri-La   Warren
Share the Luck   Willson
Sharing   Blake; Sissle
She's Gonna Come Home with Me   Loesser
Should I Believe You   Silver
Show Me   Lerner, Alan Jay; Loewe
Shut-Eye   Eliscu
Silly Signs Song, The   Drake
Silver Spoon   Alter
Silver Waltz, The   Young, Victor
Sing Fiddle Sing   Willson
Sing It Lightly and Tenderly (inst.)   Kern
Singing in a Garden (inst.)   Kern
Singing to the Stars (inst.)   Kern
Sixth Finger Theme (Sixth Finger Tune) (inst.)   Strouse
Sky Fell Down, The   Ellington
Slave Girl   Drake
Sleep Well, Little Children (A Christmas Lullaby)   Bergman
Slow Down, Slow Down, Slow Down   Silver
Smiling Geisha   Berlin
So Beautiful Is the Glow   Merrill
So Little Time   Evans; Livingston, Jay
So What?   Porter
Soft Shoe (inst.)   Kern
Solo   Hoffman
Some Day Soon   Myrow
Some Sweet Day   Cahn; Van Heusen
Somebody Has to Help Somebody (All the Time)   Robison
Somebody Stole My Muchacha   Hoffman
Somebody Up There Likes Me   Cahn
Someday Soon   Gordon
Someone in Love   Bergman
Something Inside of Me Singing   Russell
Something on My Mind (inst.)   Kern
Somewhere   Warren
Song in C (inst.)   Kern
Song of a Summer Night   Loesser
Song of Song   Robison
Song of the Harp   Livingston, Jerry
Song That's Got a Beat, A   Blake; Sissle
Soon You Gonna Leave Me, Joe   Loesser
Sorry   DePaul; Mercer
Sounds in the Night   Dietz
Speak for Yourself   Styne
Special Delivery   Loesser
Spinning, Spinning, Spinning   Hoffman
Spozalizio   Loesser
Spread the Word   Russell
Spring Doth Let Her Colors Fly   Adams; Strouse
Spring in Maine   Leigh
Staccato Theme (inst.)   Kern
Standard Oil Theme   Young, Victor
Standin' on the Corner   Loesser
Star Bright (Mara)   Coslow

Stay Out of My Dreams   Arlen; Harburg
Steal Away   Dietz; Schwartz, Arthur
Step Montage, A   Porter
Stephanie   Sigman
Stop the World (I Wanna Get Off)   Oakland
Story You're About to Hear Is True, The   Hoffman
Strange Melody   Russell
Stranger in a Dream (Stranger in the Night)   Caesar
Strip for Action   Adamson; McHugh
Stumble (inst.), A   Kern
Stumbling Blocks (inst.)   Warren
Sue! Sue!   Comden and Green; Styne
Summer Breeze Song   Willson
Summer Love   Young, Victor
Surrender to Me   Sigman
Sweet Old-Fashioned Girl Skoob-el-ee Doo-bee-dum,
    A   Merrill
Sweet World   Livingston, Jerry
Sweetie Bear   Coots
Swing High   Carmichael
Take My Heart   David, Mack
Talkin' with Your Feet   Warren
Technique   Merrill
Teeter Totter Love   Hoffman
Tell Me More   Lawrence
Tell the Truth and Shame the Devil   Bacharach; David, Hal
Tell Tony and Rosabella Goodbye for Me   Loesser
Tempo Fugit   Gordon; Myrow
Temporarily   DePaul; Mercer
Test of Time, The   Cahn; Van Heusen
Texas Kindness   Robison
Texas Oil Man's Ball   Gilbert; Oakland
11th Hour Melody   Sigman
That Fortunate Feeling   Fain; Webster
That's How It Is   Evans; Livingston, Jay
That's What You Mean to Me   Evans; Livingston, Jay
(The Same Thing Happens with) The Birds and the
    Bees   David, Mack; Warren
(I Wish You) The Very Best Luck in the World   Livingston,
    Jerry
There Is No Cure for L'Amour   Hoffman
There Isn't Anybody Like You   Russell
There's a Rainbow on the Moon   Washington
There's Always One Day More   Leigh
There's Never Been Anyone Else but You   Webster
There's Room Enough for Us   DePaul; Mercer
There's Somethin' Mighty Peculiar Goin' On   DePaul;
    Mercer
These Things I Know Are True   Strouse
Thirteen Dola' on Fourteen   Hoffman
This Concerto Has It   Willson
This Is Home   David, Mack; Livingston, Jerry
This Is Laurie (inst.)   Young, Victor
This Is the Haffner   Willson
This Is the One   Livingston, Jerry
This Is the Song   Willson
This May Be the Place   Hoffman
This Same Heart   Burke; Friml
Thorny, Thorny Rose   Leigh
Those Evenings Spent at Joe's   Stept
Three Roads   Lawrence
Thumbin' a Ride   DePaul; Mercer
Tiger By the Tail   Leigh
Till the Ocean Freezes Over   Hoffman
To Love Again   Washington

To Love You   Young, Victor
To the Lilt of a Gay Mandolin   Kahal; Stept
Tony's Thoughts   Loesser
Too Bad We Couldn't Fall in Love   Strouse
Too Little Time   Evans; Livingston, Jay
Too Many Teardrops   Silver
Too Much   David, Hal
Too Young to Go Steady   Adamson; McHugh
Toodeloo   Willson
Touche (You Have Hit the Target at Last)   Parish
Trapeze   Burke
Traveling Down a Lonely Road   Raye
Travelogue   Blane; Martin
Tried and True   Raye
True Blue   Styne
True Love   Porter
Try a Little Prayer   Magidson
Tune to Tap My Toe To, A   Hoffman
Twelfth of Never, The   Livingston, Jerry; Webster
Twelve Feet Tall   Livingston, Jerry
Two of You, The   Sondheim
Una Momento   David, Mack
Uninvited Dream   Bacharach
Unnecessary Town   DePaul; Mercer
Valse Lente (inst.)   Kern
Value of Love, The   Sigman
Vanishing American, The   Silver
Ven Papa Vould Cut a Figure Eight   Bergman
Ver Giacoso   Willson
Vibrations   Sherman
Vive La You!   Burke; Friml
Wait for Love   Washington
Wake Up to Music   Hoffman
Walk in the Country   Howard, Bart
Walk Sweet   Warren
Walk Up   Howard, Bart
Walkin' Home with the Blues   Washington
Walking Happy   Cahn; Van Heusen
Warm   Russell
Warm All Over   Loesser
Warm and Tender   Bacharach; David, Hal
Warm in December   Russell
Warm Sun Cold Moon   Evans; Livingston, Jay
Watch Out for the Devil   Burke; Friml
Watching the Door   Robison
Way That Lovers Use, The   Kern
Way to a Man's Heart, The   DePaul; Mercer
We All Need Love   Sigman
We Gotta Keep Up with the Joneses   Blane; Martin
We Like Working Together (We Like Working with Each
    Other)   Cahn; Van Heusen
We Like Working with Each Other   Van Heusen
Wedding Song   DePaul; Mercer
Wedding Waltz, The   Young, Victor
Weepin' and a Wailin' Song (I'm Happy When I'm Singin'),
    A   Myrow
Welcome to Union City   Adamson; McHugh
We'll Be Comin' Down the Chimney   Silver
Well, Did You Evah!   Porter
We'll Love Again   Evans; Livingston, Jay
We're Still Holding Hands   Hoffman
Western Theme   Bergman
We've Decided to Stay   Warren
What Do You Do   Warren
What Do You Feel in Your Heart   Howard, Bart

What Every Old Girl Should Know   Warren
What Is a Girl   Merrill
What Should a Teen Heart Do   David, Hal
What Would People Say   Lawrence
Whatcha-Ma-Call-It   DePaul; Mercer
Whatever Will Be, Will Be (Que, Sera, Sera)   Evans;
    Livingston, Jay
What's Good for General Bullmoose (Is Good for the
    U.S.A.)   DePaul; Mercer
What's It Gonna Be   Mancini
What's It Like in Paree   Sigman
What's So Good about Good Morning   Gordon; Myrow
What's Wrong with the Song   Hoffman
When a One Star General's Daughter Meets a Four Star
    General's Son   Berlin
When I Go, I Go All the Way   Russell
When I'm Loving You   Snyder
When the Circus Wagon Came to Town   Willson
When We Are Born Again   Warren
When, When   Merrill
When Will I Know   Silver
When You Add Religion to Love   Bryan
When You Are Seventeen   Bergman
Where Are the White Birds Flying   Livingston, Jerry
Where Jesus Is   Robison
Where Walks My True Love   Cahn
Where's the Third One   Willson
Whispering Campaign   Bacharach; Heyman
Whistle the Blues (Pretty! Pretty! Blues!)   Spina
White, the Young at Heart (inst.)   Young, Victor
Who Are We   David, Hal
Who Can Explain   Silver
Who Wants to Be a Millionaire?   Porter
Who, Who, Who Do You Think Of   Cahn; Van Heusen
Why Can't the English   Lerner, Alan Jay; Loewe
Why Do I Always Have to Be a Dame   Stept
Why Do I Care   Young, Victor
Why Not Surrender   Dietz; Schwartz, Arthur
Wide Wide World   Lawrence
Wild and Woolly West, The   Fain; Webster
Will o' the Wisp   Freed, Ralph; Livingston, Jerry
Wind, the Wind, The   Cahn; Van Heusen
Wisdom of a Fool, The   Silver
With a Little Bit of Luck   Lerner, Alan Jay; Loewe
With All My Heart   Bergman
Without You   Lerner, Alan Jay; Loewe
World in My Corner, The   Mancini
World Outside, The   Warren
Worry About Tomorrow, Tomorrow   Gordon; Myrow
Would I   Stept
Wouldn't It Be Loverly?   Lerner, Alan Jay; Loewe
Wouldn't It Be Nice?   Cahn; Van Heusen
Written on the Wind   Cahn; Young, Victor
Ya Gotta Give the People Hoke   Cahn; Van Heusen
Yes, My Love   Kern; Robin
You Bring Out the Lover in Me   Leigh
You Brought Me Love   Blake; Sissle
You Can Bounce Right Back   Cahn; Van Heusen
You Can't Be True to Two   Hoffman
You Can't Run Away from It   DePaul; Mercer
You Couldn't Help but Be Wonderful   Woods
You Did It   Lerner, Alan Jay; Loewe
You Don't Have to Tickle Me with a Feather   Woods
You Got Looks   Cahn
You Happened to Me   Coots

1930

You Know It (inst.)   Kern
You Make Nice   Hoffman
You Mustn't Believe a Word She Says   Cahn; Duke
You Were There   Oakland
You'll Love the Singing   Willson
Your Lips Are Warmer   Bacharach; David, Hal
Your Prayers Are Always Answered   Drake
You're a Sentimental Guy   Berlin
You're a Sucker for a Dame   Berlin
You're Sensational   Porter
You're Young, But You Believe   Livingston, Jerry; Raye
You've Got to Do It   Comden and Green; Styne
You've Never Been in Love   Brooks
Yuka and Fun   Willson

1957

Adult Delinquency   Razaf
Adventure   Russell
Affair   Russell
Affair to Remember, An   Adamson; Warren
Ages Ago   Duke
Ain't It the Truth   Arlen; Harburg
All I Have Is a Love Song   Yellen
All I Want in This World (Is You)   Robison
All I Want Is You for Christmas   Coots
All the Way   Cahn; Van Heusen
Along the Way   Sigman
Amarillys at the Piano   Willson
America   Sondheim
And So Am I   Drake
And So To Sleep (inst.)   Revel
(Sweet) Angeline   Willson
Anna Lilla   Merrill
Another Birthday, Another Year (Voice in the Night)   Revel
Anyone for Love   Washington
April Love   Fain; Webster
Are You Gettin' On   Robison
Arguements   Merrill
Ariane   Mercer
Arkansaw Rip-Saw   Robison
Art of Conversation, The   Russell
Art of Love, The   Robison
As If You Didn't Know   Spina
As Long As You Live (You Gonna Be My Baby)   Blake
At the Check Apron Ball   Merrill
Atom Bomb Baby (Mambo)   Sondheim
Au Revoir Cherie   Spina
Aurora   Razaf
Automobiles   Fain; Webster
Autumn in Azusa   Spina
Baby It Isn't in the Cards   Russell
Baby Y'Know   Russell
Ball Was Had By All, A   Coots
Bamboo Tamboo   Bergman
Band of Angels   Sigman
Barbara   Carmichael
Baseball Hoedown   Drake
Bay of Naples   Spina
Bazazz   Blane
Be Graceful (Something's Wrong with Me)   Kern
Be My Guest   Adams; Strouse
Beatin' on the Bongos   Mancini
Beauty Is Only Skin Deep   Raye
Because Him Is a Baby   Merrill

Beginnin' of Sinnin', The   Davis
Belonging To Someone   Hoffman
Bentonville Fair, The   Fain; Webster
Bernadine   Mercer; Rome
Best Ain't Good Enough, The   Adams; Strouse
Better Loved You'll Never Be   David, Mack
Better than Ever   Lawrence
Big City Blues   Mancini
Big Hand, Little Hand   David, Hal
Big Sister Blues   DePaul; Russell
Big Town Blues   Davis
Blame It on Paree   Stept
Blessing in Disguise, A   Fain
Blessings   Willson
Blue Light Waltz, The   Hoffman
Blue Mood   Razaf
Bold Journey   Livingston, Jerry; Russell
Bon Bon   Hoffman; Merrill
Bon Jour La Vie   Russell
Bon Voyage, Mon Ami   Spina
Bonjour Tristesse (inst.)   McHugh
Born to Be Happy   Davis
Boy Like That, A   Sondheim
Boy on a Dolphin, The   Webster
Boy-ee-yoing   Johnson, James P.
Bread and Butter Love   Hoffman
Breezy and Easy   Martin
Bright Lights (inst.)   Young, Victor
Bring on the Girls   Lawrence
Broken Arrow   Washington
Brushoff, The   Hoffman
Bulfightin' Baby   Sherman
Buster   Young, Victor
Bustin' Out of Doors   Carmichael
Busy Night   David, Hal
Buy Why   Merrill
By Love Possessed   Sigman
Ca C'est L'Amour   Porter
Calypso Rock   Strouse
Can You Blame Me   Sigman
Can't We Be Enemies   DePaul
Care a Little Bit More for Me   Coots
Cha-Lypso, The   Hoffman
Champagne Cocktail (inst.)   Stept
Change for a Penny   Merrill
Chasin' After Him   Strouse
Chess and Checkers   Merrill
Chicago   Willson
China Gate   Young, Victor
Cholla Gardens (inst.)   Young, Victor
Christina   Adamson
Christmas Is Coming   Blake
Christmas Toyland Wedding   Drake
Cinderelvis   Drake
Cleo Steps Out   Blake
Clover in the Meadow   Fain; Webster
Cocoanut Sweet   Arlen; Harburg
Cocoanut Water   Raye
Cocoanuts   DePaul; Russell
(You Can't Lose the Blues with) Colors   Berlin
Come Out of the Clouds   Friend
Comic Land   Brooks
Comin' Home to You   Bergman
Continue   Adamson; Warren
Convict Song, The   Spina

Cooking   Carmichael
Cool   Sondheim
Cool New World   Magidson; Oakland
Corner in Paradise, A   Bryan
Counting Sheep (inst.)   Revel
Crazy Love   Cahn
Cuba Libra (inst.)   Stept
Daiquiri (inst.)   Stept
Dance at the Gym, The   Sondheim
Dance de Limbo Lower the Stick   Bergman
Danser Calenda   Bergman
De Best I Like   Bergman
Dear Miss Lonely Hearts   Raye
Designing Woman   Brooks
Devil's Child   Adams; Strouse
Did You Close Your Eyes?   Merrill
Ding-A-Ling   Mancini
Do I Love You Because You're Beautiful?   Hammerstein;
    Rodgers
Do I Need You   Sigman
Do It Yourself   Fain; Webster
Do You Recall?   Parish
Doin' the Town   Davis
Donkey Small   Bergman
Don't Go Near the Water   Cahn
Don't Shut Me Out   Sigman
Don't Take a Rose from the Devil   Silver
Don't Touch Me   Freed, Ralph
Double Cross   Spina
Down on the Desert   Friend
Dream Dust   Leigh
Dream Men   Friend
Dreamsville   Hoffman
Dreamy   Spina
Drinking Song   Porter
Dry Martini (inst.)   Stept
Duet   Adams; Strouse
Duettino   Kern; Mercer
Duke's Place   Ellington
Easter   Carmichael
Echoes   Mercer
Echoes in the Night (Lassame Sunna)   Raye
Eileen Christy Polka (inst.)   McHugh
Escapade   Russell
Ethics Waltz, The   Adams; Strouse
Even though You're Not Beside Me   Brooks
Everybody Said   Spina
Everybody Want to Live a Long, Long Time (But Nobody
    Want to Grow Old)   Gilbert
Everytime You Smile   Parish
Eyes of the Night   David, Mack
Face of an Angel, The   Silver
Fairy Tale Stomp   Brooks
Farewell to Arms, A   Webster
Far-Off Land   Friend
Fast Goodnight, A   Friend
Fated to Be Mated   Porter
Ferryboat Called Minerva, A   Hoffman
Few Small Tasks, A   Adams; Strouse
Fiesta in Brazil   Mills
Fightin' Mad 'Cause I'm a Bad Loser   Raye
Fighting Kid from Cripple Creek, The   Raye
Fine Vignettes, The   Brooks
Fire Down Below   Washington
Fireworks   Willson

Fit for a King   Bergman
Flame and the Rose, The   David, Mack
Flings   Merrill
Follow the River   Washington
Fool's Errand   Sigman
For Every Fish (There's a Little Bigger Fish)   Arlen; Harburg
Forever Faithful   Bacharach; David, Mack
Fortissimo (I'm Yours to Love)   Coots
Fountains of Versailles   Russell
Fran and Bill's Tune   Merrill
Free and Easy   Mancini
French Heels   Evans; Livingston, Jay
From a Logical Point of View   Raye
From the Sidewalks to the Stand   Drake
Full of Love   Bergman
Funny, What a Kiss Can Do   Hoffman
Gallop   Parish
Gary, Indiana   Willson
Gates of Happiness, The   Parish
Gee, Officer Krupke   Sondheim
Gent from Georgia, The   Spina
Get Along, Little Dream   Howard, Bart
Gift of Love, The   Fain; Webster
Gin and Tonic (inst.)   Stept
Gina Mia (I Love You)   Spina
Girl Most Likely, The   Russell
Girl on My Mind (inst.)   Revel
Girl with the Storybook Dream, The   Oakland
Give a Look (Looky Look)   Hoffman
Give Me a Gentle Girl   Fain; Webster
Glockenspiel Song, The   Drake
Go Home, Ulysses   Spina
Gobel Dreaming   Brooks
God Has His Arms Around Me   Adamson; Young, Victor
Gold   Freed, Ralph
Golden Anniversary   Lawrence
Golden Guitars (inst.)   Livingston, Jerry
Golfer's Glide, The   Webster
Golly   Hoffman
Gone for the Day   Russell
Gonna Hand in My Guitar   Sigman
Good for Him — Good for Me   Spina
Good Intentions   Coleman; Leigh
Good Lord Never Made a Bad Day, The   Caesar; Robison
Goodbye, My Love   Cahn
Goodnight My Someone   Willson
Goombay Drum   Bergman
Gossip (inst.)   Burke
Grandfather Clock   Carmichael
Grasshopper (inst.)   Stept
Greatest, The   Hoffman
Greatest Little Sign in the World, The   Cahn; Van Heusen
Gunfight at the O.K. Corral, The   Washington
Ha Ha Ha (Chella Lla)   Hoffman
Half a Dozen Dreams Ago   Adamson; McHugh
Hand that Swept the Stars Across the Sky, The   Livingston,
    Jerry
Happiness Theme   Fain
Happy, Happy Day   Parish
Happy Heart, The   Fields; Lane
Happy Land of Hunzac, The   Washington
Happy New Year, A Wonderful New Year   Brown, Nacio
    Herb
Have Feet Will Dance   Fields; Lane
Hawaiian Wedding Song, The   Hoffman

He Knows By the Way I Live Each Day   Spina
He, She and Me   Egan; Whiting
He Will Forgive You   Robison
Heart Is a Lonely Hunter, The   Fain; Webster
Heart of a Sailor, The   David, Mack; Livingston, Jerry
Heart You Break May Be Your Own, The   Hoffman
Here We Are Again   Merrill
Here's an Invitation   Brooks
High Flyin' Wings on My Shoes   Porter
High Hopes and Empty Pockets (The Gambler's
    Lament)   Fain; Webster
High Ridin' Woman   Adamson
Hills Are Free, The   Drake
His Honor, the Mayor of New York   Cahn
His Rock Will Never Roll   Caesar; Robison
Hold It Down   Friend
Hold on To Love   Webster
Home Should Be Your Heaven, The   Robison
Honest Love   Sigman
Honeymoon Train, The   Drake
Honorable Congratulations   Evans; Livingston, Jay
Hoopla   Hoffman
Hoppy   Coots
Hot Summer Night   Russell
House with Stained Glass Windows, The   Silver
How Do You Know We're in Love   Evans; Livingston, Jay
How Long Can You Play Around   Merrill
(My) How the Time Goes By   Coleman; Leigh
Humble Pie   Bacharach; David, Hal
Hungry for Love   Spina
Hypnosis (inst.)   Revel
I Ain't Been Right Since You Left   Hoffman
I Always Say   Sigman
I Could Kick Myself   Porter
I Dance when I Walk   Hoffman
I Don't Care What They Say About Me   Davis
I Don't Think I'll End It All Today   Arlen; Harburg
I Don't Want Sympathy I Want Love   Lawrence
I Don't Want to Be a Gentleman   Robin; Styne
I Feel Pretty   Sondheim
I Found a Horseshoe   Willson
I Found Contentment   Ruby
I Get a Hankerin' for You   Russell
I Got a Lot of Love in My Heart   Hoffman
I Got No Talent   Spina
I Have a Love   Sondheim
I Have a Single Track Mind   Parish
I Have You to Thank   Robin; Styne
I Just Ain't Lucky with Men   Merrill
I Just Don't Believe in Being Lonely   Robison
I Just Want You to Want Me   Washington
I Keep Running Away from You   Berlin
I Knew a Girl in Barcelona   Parish
I Learn a Merengue Mama   Raye
I Like You Like   Spina
I Loved Her (A Little Bit More than He Did)   Dietz
I May Have Left Paree (But Paree Has Never Left
    Me)   Hoffman
I May Never Go Home Anymore   Brooks
I Miss You   Russell
I Need You   Bacharach
I Never Had a Dream Like This Before   Coslow
I Only Saw You for a Moment   Bergman
I Only Want to Love You   Spina
I Surrender, My Darling   Coots

I Think of You Every Hour of the Day   Spina
I Told the Daisies   Spina
I Tried!   Evans; Livingston, Jay
I Waited for You   Russell
I Wanna Walk in the Rain   Spina
I Want It to Be Right   Adams; Strouse
Iaydor   Johnson, Howard
If I Could Hold You in My Arms   David, Hal
If I Don't Love You   Burke
If I Ever Saw a Dream It's You   Spina
If I Weren't King   Hammerstein; Rodgers
If that Was Love   Merrill
If You Don't Love Me (O'Jin-Ja)   Brooks
If You Don't Mind My Saying So   Willson
If You Said No   Cahn
If You Walk Out that Door   Fain
If Your Heart Doesn't Dance, It Isn't Love   Hoffman
If You're Askin' Me   Bergman
I'll Be Thinking of You   Hoffman
I'll Buy It   Fields; Lane
I'll Kiss You Goodnight in the Morning   Bacharach; David,
    Hal
I'll Know Better the Next Time   Berlin
I'm Away from It All   Lawrence
I'm Going to Scotland   Webster
I'm Havin' a Party   Carmichael
I'm in Pursuit of Happiness   Robin; Styne
I'm Never Gonna Tell   Hoffman
I'm Not Afraid Anymore   Sigman
I'm Not Supposed to Be Blue, Blues   Russell
I'm Only Human   Lawrence
I'm Rich   Bergman
I'm So in Love with You   Gordon; Spina
I'm Sorry I Made You Cry   Spina
Impossible   Hammerstein; Rodgers
In a Cup of Tea Leaves   Coots
In My Own Little Corner   Hammerstein; Rodgers
In Pursuit of Happiness   Coleman; Leigh
In the Middle of a Dark, Dark Night   Merrill
In Tune   McHugh
Incompatibility   Arlen; Harburg
Independence   Russell
Individuality   Robison
Interlude   Russell; Webster
Iowa Stubborn   Willson
Irving Berlin Barrett   Berlin
Is Better When You Ain't Got on the Shoes   Yellen
Is He Nisnardi?   Parish
Is It Joy?   Porter
Isabella   David, Hal
Islola Bella   Spina
It Cannot Be   Bergman
It Could Be You   Davis
It Is the Most Unusual Weather for This Time of the
    Year   Cahn; Styne
It Must Add Up   Drake
It's a Big Big Day for Love   Spina
It's a Glorious Fourth   Robin; Styne
It's a Good Thing I Don't Care   Burke; Cahn; Van Heusen
It's a Topsy Turvy World   Adams; Strouse
It's All Over Town   Livingston, Jerry
It's Gettin' too Hot for Me   Spina
It's Good to Be Alive   Merrill
It's Just About that Time Again   Bergman
It's Just What I Wanted   Fields; Lane

It's Like Gettin' a Donkey to Gallop   Burke
It's Matrimonial Weather   Parish
It's Possible   Hammerstein; Rodgers
It's Something New to Me   Parish
It's Terribly, Horribly, Frightfully Nice   Robin; Styne
It's You   Willson
I've Been All Over the World   Spina
I've Come to California   Adamson; Warren
I've Tried   David, Mack; Livingston, Jerry
Ivy Rose   Hoffman
Janis (inst.)   Brooks
Janis' Philosophy (inst.)   Brooks
Jawohl, Mein Liebchen, Jawohl   Ruby
Jazz Band Jamboree   Raye
Je Vous Adore (I Love You)   Hoffman
Jean and Dinah (Yankee Gone)   Raye
Jet Song   Sondheim
Jewels in the Sky (inst.)   Livingston, Jerry
Jim Ameche Time   Spina
Joanie the Genie   Brooks
Joe Martin Calling   Lawrence
Jump Up Carnival   Raye
Jungle of Love, The   Howard, Bart
Junior Fire Marshal Song (Junior Fire Marshals Are We),
    The   Caesar
Junior Miss   Fields; Lane
Junior Miss with a Senior Kiss, The   Hoffman
Junkman's Song   Carmichael
Just an Echo of Aloha   Ahlert; Young, Joseph
Kashmir   Washington
Kickapoo Kick, The   Robin; Styne
Kids Ain't (Like Everybody Else)   Sondheim
Kitty   Sigman
Know How   Drake
Krasilofsky for Justice of the Peace   Dietz; Schwartz, Arthur
La-de-da Song, The   David, Mack
Ladies in Waiting   Porter
Last Dance, The   Sigman
Last Song and Dance, The   Leslie
Lazy in Love   Bergman
Learning to Love   Webster
Leave the Atom Alone   Arlen; Harburg
Leila   David, Mack
Lemon Drops and Gum Drops   David, Hal
Les Girls   Porter
Let Me Be Loved   Evans; Livingston, Jay
Let Us Give Thanks   Spina
Let's Be Happy   Webster
Let's Fall in Love Again   Brown, Nacio Herb
Let's Get Some Pizza Pie   Hoffman
Let's Go to de Market Place   Bergman
Let's Kiss and Make Up   McHugh
Let's Make It Christmas All Year Long   Fields; Lane
Let's Rock Tonight in a Satellite   Robison
Let's Start with a Kiss   Egan; Whiting
Let's Try Love Again   Adams
Letter Gets Better (As It Goes Along), The   Hoffman
Lida Rose   Willson
Like Wow   Livingston, Jerry
Limbo   Washington
Listen to Buddy, Stay in Bed   Bergman
Little Biscuit   Arlen; Harburg
Little Bit More, A   Brooks
Little Cafe in Calais, A   Coots; Lewis
Loma Linda   Livingston, Jerry

Lonely Winter   Mancini
Lonesome Road   Brooks
Look at 'er   Merrill
Lord Made a Peanut, The   Merrill
Lost Love   Friend
Lost Watch (Tick Tick Tick), The   Raye
Louella   Adamson
Lou'sianna Moonlight   Spina
Lovable   Spina
Love and Affection   Hoffman
Love Bank   Bacharach; David, Hal
Love Birds   Oakland; Russell
Love in the Afternoon   Mercer
Love Is a Pain in the Heart   Brooks
Love Is Like a Candle in the Wind   Spina
Love Me Ever (Leave Me Never)   Webster
Love (My Everything)   Ellington
Love, Wonderful Love   Cahn
Lovely Night, A   Hammerstein; Rodgers
Lovely Party   Adams; Strouse
Lover's Waltz   Mancini
Loves of Omar Khayyam, The   Evans; Livingston, Jay
Lullaby   Rome
Make Me an Miracle   Hoffman
Male Is an Animal, A   Fields; Lane
Malora   Webster
Mama Rosa   Revel
Mama Talks Calypso Now   Cahn
Man, A   Bergman
Man from Idaho, The   Webster
Man of Music   Robison
Man on Fire   Fain; Webster
March Goes in Like a Lion   Spina
Marching Polka, The   Blane
Maria   Sondheim
Marian the Librarian   Willson
Me and My Piano   Woods
Mexicano   Young, Victor
Mi Casa, Su Casa (My House Is Your House)   Hoffman
Milkman Cometh (inst.), The   Revel
Millionaire, The   Spina
Minute of Prayer   Robison
Miracle of the Rose   David, Mack
Mission Bell By the Wishin' Well, The   Bacharach; David,
    Hal
Mix!   Sondheim
Moment of Madness, A   Coleman; Leigh
Moment We Met, The   Hoffman
Monday, Wednesday, Friday   Evans; Livingston, Jay
Money Hungry Mama   Robison
Money Is a Problem   Cahn
Monkey in the Mango Tree   Arlen; Harburg
Monkey See, Monkey Do   Coots
Moonbeams, Soft Lights and Music   Stept
Moonlight Souvenirs   Cahn
More than Ever   Mancini
Mountains Beyond the Moon, The   Sigman
Music, Always Music   Carmichael
Music for Madame   Lawrence
Music for the Feet   Yellen
Music of My Lord   Robison
My All   Russell
My Apple Pie Guy   Coots
My Budapest   Cahn
My Darling Is Never Late   Porter

My Greatest Day!   Sondheim
My How the Time Goes By   Brooks
My Last Frontier   Coleman; Leigh
My Little Piece o' Pie   Porter
My Man Pete   Hoffman
My Prayer for Today   Carmichael
My Reputation   Merrill
My Town   Robison
My White Knight   Willson
Napoleon   Arlen; Harburg
Never Be Afraid   Bergman
Never Had It So Good   Davis
Never Let Me Go (Ceux Qui M'ont Quitte)   Evans
Never Never Knew   Friend
New Clothes   Bergman
New Fangled Moon   Howard, Bart
New Year Song, The   Brown, Nacio Herb
Next Time Around, The   Livingston, Jerry
No Letter Today   Raye
Noche de Amor (Night of Love)   David, Mack
Not Me   Raye
October Mist   Webster
Of All the People   Cahn
Oh What a Beautiful World   Burke
Old Fashioned (inst.)   Stept
Old Prospector, The   Carmichael
Old Timer's Tune   Raye
On Broadway and Off Broadway   Drake
On the Farm   Merrill
On the Mercury   Drake
Once Around the Park (inst.)   Strouse
Once in a Lifetime   Russell
Once in a Million Years   Russell
Once in Your Life   Sondheim
One Hand, One Heart   Sondheim
One Is a Lonely Number   Webster
One Love, The   Cahn
One More Kiss   Sigman
One Small Voice   Strouse
One Starry Night   Spina
Only Trust Your Heart   Cahn
Oooh, My Love   Bacharach; David, Hal
Oo-Wah-Oh   Evans; Livingston, Jay
Other City (inst.), The   Strouse
Our Escapade (inst.)   Coots
Padre   Webster
Parade   Parish
Pay As You Go   Merrill
Peacock Rock   Brooks
Per Favore   Porter
Perfect Stranger   Howard, Bart
Perserverance   Spina
Philadelphia   Bergman
Piano Lesson   Willson
Piazza San Marco (inst.)   Livingston, Jerry
Pick-a-Little Talk-a-Little   Willson
Piney Woods (Biarn's Song), The   Mercer
Pink Lady (inst.)   Stept
Pity de Sunset   Arlen; Harburg
Plain Old Alice   Brooks
Pomegranate   Ellington
Pound in Your Pocket, A   Adams; Strouse
Presents from the Past   Bacharach; David, Hal
Pretty to Walk With   Arlen; Harburg
Primavera   Russell

Prince Is Giving a Ball, The   Hammerstein; Rodgers
Princess Procession   Spina
Private Property   Silver
Producer's Office   Lawrence
Promises   Freed, Ralph
Proposal, The   Bergman
Puh-leeze Mister Brown   DePaul
Pure White Robe   Robison
Purple Hills, The   Washington
Purple Hills (2), The   Young, Victor
Push de Button   Arlen; Harburg
Raffles   Carmichael
Ragamuffin Rag (inst.)   Drake
Rainy Night   Mercer
Ramblin' Ever, Ramblin' Heart   Coots
Rasmussin's Law   Willson
Record Room, The   Parish
Red Dust   McHugh
Red Letter Day   Bergman
Red Light Ballet   Merrill
Red Lips and Green Eyes   Freed, Ralph
Relaxation (Je T'Aime) (inst.)   Revel
Religion Is Like a River   Robison
Revel's Nocturne (inst.)   Revel
Revenge   Bergman
Rich Old Woman, Poor Young Man   Razaf
Ride on a Rainbow, A   Robin; Styne
Ridin' Into Tulsa   Blane
Right or Wrong   Spina
Ritz Roll and Rock, The   Porter
Rock City Rock   Ellington
Rock Island Rock   Willson
Rock 'n Roll Lover (Come Back to Me)   Cahn
Rockabilly Party   Hoffman
Rock-a-Bye Bluebird   Adamson; McHugh
Rockalypso   Mills
Roll Yer Socks Up   Merrill
Roma Rocka-Bolla   Stept
Romance on the Cerebellum   Drake
Rose and the Heather, The   Webster
Roses in the Snow   Spina
Rub Pub Rub   Brooks
Rumble, The   Sondheim
Runaway Heart   Woods
Sad Sack   Bacharach; David, Hal
Sadder-but-Wiser Girl, The   Willson
Sailing with My Dreamboat   Hoffman
Sailor's Life, A   Merrill
Salesmanship   Leigh
Saturday Night Satellite   Robison
Saturday's Kiss   David, Hal
Savannah   Arlen; Harburg
Savannah's Wedding Day   Arlen; Harburg
Say It with Your Eyes   Russell
Scotch Mist (inst.)   Stept
Screw Driver (inst.)   Stept
Scusami   Sigman
Sea Breeze   Hoffman
Sea Symphony (inst.)   Young, Victor
Search for Paradise   Washington
Segue   Brooks
Sell Me   Howard, Bart
Seven Hills of Rome, The   Young, Victor
Seven Nights a Week   Cahn; Van Heusen
Seven Wonders of the World, The   Spina

Seventy Six Trombones   Willson
Seymour   Bergman
Shake Hands with a Fool   Livingston, Jerry
Shalimar   Washington
Shenandoah Rose   Livingston, Jerry; Webster
Ship in the Bottle, The   DePaul; Raye
Shipoopi   Willson
Shooting Stars   Carmichael
Shower of Stars   Spina
Showstopper Theme   Styne
Side Car (inst.)   Stept
Silhouettes (In the Snow) (Mojave Dusk in the Desert)
     (inst.)   Warren
Silver Platter   Berlin
Simple Girl, A   Adams; Strouse
Sincere   Willson
Sinful   Davis
Sing a Kris Kringle Jingle   Coots
Sing Me Another Riddle   Carmichael
Sleeping Beauty Song   Young, Victor
Sleeping Dreams, Waking Dreams   Adams; Strouse
Slow Me Down, Lord   Robison
Slow Song   Kern; Robin
Small Potatoes   Robison
Smoke Another Cigarette (inst.)   Revel
Smokey the Bear Is a Wise Bear   Willson
Snowballs   Bacharach; David, Hal
So?   Russell
So Long, My Love   Cahn
So This Is Bagdad   Brooks
Sold to the Man with the Broken Heart   Cahn; Van Heusen
Somebody's Keeping Score   Fain; Webster
Someone Who Cares   Adams; Strouse
Something's Coming   Sondheim
Somewhere   Sondheim
Song for Elizabeth Esther Barrett   Berlin
Sounds Like October's Here   Spina
Spare Me   Sigman
Sparkling Burgandy   Spina
Sport Car   Bergman
Spring Reunion   Mercer; Warren
Stars, the Sea and I, The   Drake
Stay Out of My Dreams   Razaf
Stepsisters' Lament   Hammerstein; Rodgers
Stinger (inst.)   Stept
Story of Jazz   Bergman
Story of My Life, The   Bacharach; David, Hal
Stranger Said, The   Webster
Strangers When We Meet   Bergman
Strip Calypso   Evans; Livingston, Jay
Stuff Like that There   Lawrence
Summer Love   Mancini
Sunset on the Bayou   Spina
Sunshine Girl   Merrill
Sure I Could   Livingston, Jerry
Susan   Mancini
Sway Me   Hoffman
Sweet Someone to Love, A   Sigman
Sweet Wind Blowin' My Way   Arlen; Harburg
Sweeter than Sweet   Davis
Sweetheart of the Ivy League   Silver
Swinging Sweethearts   Leigh
Take It Slow, Joe   Arlen; Harburg
Take Me Down to Lover's Row   DePaul
Take My Heart   Young, Victor

Talking Tango (inst.)   Warren
Tammy   Evans; Livingston, Jay
Tango in the Rain   Parish
Technique   Mercer; Rome
Teen-Age Favorite   Drake
Teen-Age Special, The   Drake
Tel Aviv   Evans; Livingston, Jay
Tell Me More, Tell Me More   Spina
Tell My Love   Evans; Young, Victor
Ten Commandments of Love, The   Cahn
Ten Minutes Ago   Hammerstein; Rodgers
Ten Thousand Bedrooms   Cahn
Tender and True   Adamson
That Element of Doubt   Dietz
That Face   Bergman
That Happy Feeling   Russell
That Hate-to-Face-the-Night Feeling   Evans; Livingston, Jay
That Kinda Night   Merrill
That Sounds Exciting   Burke
That's Jazz   Bergman
That's What I Like about the North   Razaf
That's What Makes the World Go Round   Spina
There Ain't No Flies on Me   Merrill
There Are Two Eyes in Hawaii   Hoffman
There Comes a Time   Drake
There Isn't Anybody Like You   Russell
There's a Sweet Wind Blowin' My Way   Arlen
They Begged Me   Drake
They Dance All Night (Sleep All Day)   Raye
They're Off and Runnin'   Spina
They're Playing Our Song   Spina
Think of All the Nice Things He's Done   Hoffman
Thirty Days Hath September   Carmichael
This Could Be the Night   Cahn
This Is It   Coslow
This Is Love   Coots
This Is the Year   Drake
This Love   Brown, Lew
This Turf Is Ours   Sondheim
Tho' I Had Never Meant to Tell You   Parish
Three Little Witches   Carmichael
Three Sheets to the Wind   David, Mack; Livingston, Jerry
Three Strange Men   Adams
3:10 to Yuma, The   Washington
Till   Sigman
Till There Was You   Willson
Time Flies   Livingston, Jerry
Time Remembered   Duke
Tin Star, The   Brooks
Tiny Scout, The   Adamson; Warren
Tiny Toys   Evans; Livingston, Jay
To Be in Love   Howard, Bart
To Be in Paree   Merrill
To Know You Is to Love You   Mancini
To My Love   Webster
To Pass the Time Away   Brooks
Tomorrow   Willson
Tomorrow Land   Adamson; Warren
Tonight   Sondheim
Tonight I'll Dream of You   Coots
Tonight I'll Kiss Hello Again (The One I Kissed
     Goodbye)   Coots
Tonight, My Darling, Tonight (Kinderoogjes)   Coslow
Tonight Quintet   Sondheim
Too Good To Talk About   Coleman; Leigh

Tournament of Roses Parade, The   Russell
Toys for Tots   Fain; Webster
Traveling   Carmichael
Trav'lin' Man   Robison
Trinidad Daddee   Adams
Tropic Mood (inst.)   Myrow
Trust in Him   Davis
(I've Already Started In to) Try to Figure Out a Way to Go to
    Work to Try to Get You   Willson
Turn Around and Go Back Home   Hoffman
Twelve O'Clock Rock   Raye
Twilight in Tennessee   Hoffman
Two Against the World   Bacharach; David, Hal
Two Loves and Two Lives   Russell
Underneath the Overpass   Bacharach; David, Hal
Unforgivable   Evans; Livingston, Jay
United States Moon   Heyman; Spina
Until a Moment Ago   Hoffman
Until They Sail   Cahn
Up Above the World So High   Hoffman
Up to the Moon   Sondheim
Upstairs at the Downstairs Waltz, The   Howard, Bart
Va De Dum   Spina
Valley of Roses   Robison
Vampire, The   Bergman
Variations (The Carnival of Venice) (inst.)   Magidson; Stept
Veil of Years   Sigman
Velvet Moon   De Lange; Myrow
Ven I Valse   Merrill
Voice in the Night (inst.)   Revel
Wagon Train   Russell
Wandering Minstrel   Spina
Warm Lips and Cold Kisses   Coots
Warmed Over Kisses, Leftover Love   David, Mack
Watch Sputnik when She Crosses the Sky   Burke
Water   Bergman
'Way Down in Arkansas   Fain
Way to a Family's Heart, The   Robin; Styne
Wear This Ring   Russell
Weaver's Song   Bergman
Wedding Waltz, The   Spina
Welcome Home   Robin; Styne
Wells Fargo Wagon, The   Willson
We're for You, Ed Wynn!   Rome
We're Happy   Brooks
We're Old Enough to Cry   David, Mack
Westport!   Leigh
What Did I Do that Was Wrong   Hoffman
What Did Noah Do (When the Big Wind Came)?   Arlen;
    Harburg
What Fun   Porter
What Good Does It Do?   Arlen; Harburg
What Is It   Spina
What Is My Destiny   Sigman
What Is This Generation Coming To   Raye
What the Day Brings Forth   Robison
What's That   Hoffman
When I Plot a Plan   Adams; Strouse
When Love Was All   Berlin
When Lovers Meet   Coots
When the Band Comes Marching In (When the Band Comes
    Swingin' In)   Russell
When You Dance in Paris, France   Robin; Styne
When You Kiss Me   Hoffman

When You're Driving Through the
    Moonlight   Hammerstein; Rodgers
Where Do We Go from Here   Russell
Where Is Cinderella?   Hammerstein; Rodgers
Where There's Love There's a Way   David, Hal
While I Lie Here Dreaming   Brooks
While the City Sleeps (inst.)   Revel
Whimsically (inst.)   Kern
Whippoorwill   Arlen; Harburg
Whistlin' Kind of Tune, A   Adamson
Whistling at Dawn (inst.)   Revel
Who Else   Davis
Who Else but God   Warren
Who Knows   Bergman
Who Will It Be After Me?   Hoffman
Why Am I So Gone About that Gal   Porter
Why Are Your Eyes So Red   Cahn
Why Don't You Give In   Spina
Why Wake Up the Echoes (Of Yesterday)   Robison
Wild Honey   Bacharach; David, Hal
Wild Is the Wind   Washington
Will I Ever Tell You   Willson
Will You Be My Valentine   Spina
Wings of Eagles, The   Brooks
Winter Interlude   Russell
Winter Moon   Adamson; Carmichael
Winter Warm   Bacharach; David, Hal
Wishful Thinking   Robison
Witchcraft   Coleman; Leigh
With Me   Robison
Wonderful Season of Love, The   Webster
Wonderful Things   Rome
Wooden Shoes   Razaf
Workin' for the Yankee Dollar (Hooray for de Yankee
    Dollar)   Harburg
World Is Mine, The   Cahn
Worry Is a Rockin' Chair   Hoffman
Ya Got Trouble   Willson
(Workin' for the) Yankee Dollar   Arlen
Yankee Doodle Doo   Spina
Yellow Bird   Bergman
You Can't Get Far Without a Railroad   Washington
You Don't Have to Kiss Me Goodnight   Willson
You Gave Me Wings to Fly (Then Took Away My
    Sky)   Livingston, Jerry
You I Love   Cahn
You Look Like Someone I Used to Know   Spina
You Make It Easy to Be True   Adamson; Warren
You Name It   Livingston, Jerry
You Were Made Just for Me (To Make Love to You)   Spina
You'll Never Lose Me   Spina
Your Book of Life   Drake
Your Family   Russell
You're Cheatin' Yourself If You're Cheatin' Me   Hoffman
You're Gettin' Warm   Hoffman
You're in the Army Now (inst.)   Stept
You're Just Too, Too   Porter
You're Looking for Romance, I'm Looking for
    Love   Lawrence
You're My Friend Ain'tcha   Merrill
You're the Love of My Life   Spina
You're the Prize Guy of Guys   Porter
Youth Must Have It's Fling   Cahn

1958

(Doop Doo-De-Doop) A Doodlin' Song   Coleman; Leigh
Absent Minded Me   Merrill
Abu Ali the Mouse and Boomalakia Wee   David, Mack;
    Livingston, Jerry
After a Parade (Manhattan Beach)   Bergman
After You   DePaul; Raye
Aladdin   Porter
All   Robison
All a Dream   Styne
All Across the Nation   Brooks
All Around the Clock   Hoffman
All the Time   Evans; Livingston, Jay; Magidson
All Work No Play   Brooks
All You Have to Do Is Knock on Wood   Brooks
Alma Mater, Hail to Thee (Glaudemus Igitur)   Bergman
Almost in Your Arms   Evans; Livingston, Jay
American Rhapsody, The   Hoffman
And a Host of Others Too Numerous to Mention   Comden
    and Green; Styne
And I Love You   Burke; Van Heusen
Angry Young Men, The   Raye
Another Time Another Place   Evans; Livingston, Jay; Russell;
    Warren
Any Fool Would Have Known   David, Mack
Any Ol' Woes   DePaul; Raye
Any Old Thing   Drake
Any Thing Can Happen in the Moonlight   McHugh
Anything That's Near to Where You Are   Styne
Anytime You Need Some Love   Sigman
Anywhere but Here   Evans; Livingston, Jay
April Song   Coleman; Leigh
Are You Really Mine (Really)   Hoffman
Area, The   Robison
As I Love You   Evans; Livingston, Jay
As Long As I Have You   Silver
As the Parade Goes Marching By   Bergman
At the Cafe de la Paix (Fredo)   Raye
At the End of a Kiss   Coots
At the Sugar Shoppe   Drake
Aupres de Ma Blonde   Bergman
Baby Face the Elephant   Martin
Back to the Woodwork!   Styne
Ballad of Thunder Road   Raye
Batter Up (inst.)   Drake
Beautiful, Beautiful   David, Mack; Livingston, Jerry
Beautiful Princess, The   David, Mack; Livingston, Jerry
Beauty and the Beat   Drake
Beedle Booper's Song, The   Warren
Before I Get Over   Gordon
Beggar's March   David, Mack; Livingston, Jerry
Beginning of Love, The   Russell
Belong to Me   Blake; Sigman
Beyond the Mountains   Bergman
Biarritz   Coots
Big Dig, The   DePaul; Raye
Big Reign, The   Robison
Big Turntable   Robison
Big White Mountain   Ellington
Bigger than Texas   Fain; Webster
Bimbombey   David, Mack
Bing Bang Bong   Evans; Livingston, Jay
Biography   DePaul; Raye
Bioscope Song, The   Ellington
Blessing of Love, The   Drake

Blob, The   Bacharach; David, Hal; David, Mack
Blow Blow Blow   Brooks
Blow, Northwind, Blow   Brooks
Blue Boy (inst.)   Oakland
Bluebell   Livingston, Jerry; Webster
Bluest, The   Raye
Boombah!   Rome
Born too Late   Strouse
Bottomless Cup, A   Bacharach; David, Hal
Bourbon Street Blues   Fain; Webster
Bowser   Spina
Boys and Girls   Brooks
Brazilly Willy   Evans; Livingston, Jay
Break the Wall   Robison
Brief and Breezy   Cahn; Mancini
Bring Out the Cryin' Towel   David, Hal
Brothers (inst.)   Drake
Bubbling Over with Love   DePaul; Raye
Buona Fortuna   Mercer
By All That's Beautiful (Sole Lucente)   Hoffman
Bye Bye Boogie   Brooks
Cajun Dance, The   Blake
Calcutta   Evans; Livingston, Jay
California   Cahn; Van Heusen
Call the Tribe   Robison
Call of the Brands   Styne
Call of the Clans   Styne
Canada, You're Tops!   Johnson, Howard
Captain Henry St. James   Evans; Livingston, Jay
Carefree Years, The   Silver
Carmen, Carmela   Bergman
Carnival Song, The   Comden and Green; Styne
Carribean Dream   Russell
Casetta in Canada (El Rancho de Maria)   Sigman
Cat's Eye in the Night (inst.)   Alter
Celebration Song, The   David, Mack; Livingston, Jerry
Certain Smile, A   Fain; Webster
Cha Cha Cha Romance   Coots
Chapel in Apple Valley, A   Adamson; McHugh
Cherry Blossom   Bergman
Chief of Love   Comden and Green; Styne
Chin Up, Stout Fellow   Mercer
Chinese Nightingale   David, Mack; Livingston, Jerry
Chop Suey   Hammerstein; Rodgers
Christmas Dinner Country Style   Freed, Ralph
Christmas Hop   Freed, Ralph
Cinderella Waltz, The   Mercer
Civil Defense March   Cahn
Clop, Clop, Clop   Martin
Closer than a Kiss   Cahn; Van Heusen
Cobra   Sherman
Coconut and Banana   Bergman
Come Along Children   Blake; Sissle
Come Back to Me   DePaul; Raye
Come Dance with Me   Cahn; Van Heusen
Come Fly with Me   Cahn; Van Heusen
Come Love Me   Lawrence
Come to the Supermarket in Old Peking   Porter
Composers Corner   Drake
Congo Ivory   Gorney
Cool Alaska Rock and Roll, The   Brown, Nacio Herb
Couldn't You (inst.)   Drake
Country Music Holiday   Bacharach; David, Hal
Creation   David, Mack; Livingston, Jerry
Creole Gal   DePaul; Raye

Cuckoo Clock   Gorney
Cuddled in Your Arms   DePaul; Raye
Cushion Dance   David, Mack; Livingston, Jerry
Dad's Lullaby (inst.)   Oakland
Dance Only with Me   Comden and Green; Styne
Dance with Me (Moisson)   Yellen
Dancing on Daisies   Yellen
Dawning of Love, The   Lawrence
Day the Rains Came, The   Sigman
Dear Fatherland Farewell   Bergman
Dear Little Shadow   David, Mack
Dear Tommy   Russell
Destiny   DePaul; Raye
Discouraged Over You   Burke; Van Heusen
Do You Believe (I Do)   Davis
Does It Show   Strouse
Does She or Doesn't She Love Me and Only Me   Caesar
Don't Be a Geografoof   Gorney
Don't Believe Everything You Read   Evans; Livingston, Jay
Don't Cheat on the Meat   Blake
Don't Do Anything Half Way   Merrill
Don't Ever Say Goodbye   Ellington
Don't Forget I Love You   Merrill
Don't Get Married   Hoffman
Don't Give Me a Ring on the Telephone Until You Give Me a Ring on My Hand   Burke; Van Heusen
Don't Make a Plaything Out of My Heart   Blake; Sissle
Don't Marry Me   Hammerstein; Rodgers
Don't Nobody Move   Sigman
Don't Stop Now   Friend
Don't Wake Me Up (Un Ange Comme Ca C'est du Tonnerre)   Raye
Doodle Do'd It   Friend
Dormi, Dormi, Dormi (Sleep, Sleep, Sleep)   Cahn; Warren
Double Standard   Evans; Livingston, Jay
Dream Big   Bacharach
Dream for a Lovely Night, A   David, Mack; Warren
Dream House   Bryan
Dream of a Girl, A   Hoffman
Dream Waltz   DePaul; Raye
Dreaming of Love   Coots
Dreams Are Made for Children   David, Mack; Livingston, Jerry
Dutch Treat   David, Mack; Evans; Livingston, Jay; Livingston, Jerry
Each Spring   DePaul; Raye
Eltibadabo Pooka-Pooka   Livingston, Jerry
Elvis   Adams
Emperor's Guards, The   David, Mack; Livingston, Jerry
(Why Do I Feel So) Enchanted   David, Mack; Livingston, Jerry
Eubie's Boogie Woogie Rag (inst.)   Blake
Every Night When You Say a Prayer   McHugh
Everything Is Tickety-Boo   Mercer
Evig Evol   Lawrence
Ev'ry Night at Nine O'Clock They Pull in the Sidewalks   Hoffman
Ev'rybody Needs a Helping Hand   Robison
Fan Tan Fannie   Hammerstein; Rodgers
Fancy Meeting You Here   Cahn; Van Heusen
Farewell, Old Friends   DePaul; Raye
Farewell to Juanita   Webster
Fascination   Coslow
Femininity   Evans; Livingston, Jay
Fez, He Says, A   Russell

Fiddle, a Rifle an Axe and a Bible, A   Fain; Webster
Fifty Gals for Every Guy in Argentina   Hoffman
Fire in the Night (Feuer der Nacht)   Raye
Firefly   Coleman; Leigh
Five Minutes After Forever   Washington
Flag's Flying High, The   Bergman
Fly in Ireland (inst.)   Oakland
Fly in Israel (inst.)   Oakland
Foof to Old Geography   Gorney
For You, for Me, for Love   Johnson, Howard
Forty Thieves Forty   Cahn
Fountain, The   Bergman
Frenchman's Paree, The   Evans; Livingston, Jay
Full of Shadows   Ellington
Funshine   Friend
Gal from Baton Rouge, The   Blake
Garden of Love   Bergman
Gaston's Soliloquy   Lerner, Alan Jay; Loewe
Geisha Boy, The   Brooks
Genie's Theme   Porter
Georgy Porgy Comes to the Fair   David, Mack; Livingston, Jerry
Gettin' It All for Free   Adamson; McHugh
Ghost Goes West, The   Styne
Gift of Love   Fain; Webster
Gigi   Lerner, Alan Jay; Loewe
Gimme a Clue   Drake
Girl Is Out to Get a Man   Brooks
Girls Are Different   Lawrence
Give Me the Right to Be Wrong   David, Hal
Gliding Through My Memoree   Hammerstein; Rodgers
Go Man Go   Brooks
Gobble-De-Gook   Hoffman; Silver
God Is Good to Me   Hoffman
Good Fairy, The   David, Mack; Livingston, Jerry
Goodbye Boogie   Brooks
Gossip   Lerner, Alan Jay; Loewe
Got My Workin' Papers   Drake
Gotta Lotta Tunes in My Guitar   Hoffman
Grace   Burke; Van Heusen
Grand Street Boys   Blake; Sissle
Grandpa's Very Old   Brooks
Grant Avenue   Hammerstein; Rodgers
Great Vino, The   Martin
Grind Me a Pound   Sherman
Ground You Walk Upon, The   David, Hal
Guilty Heart   Sigman
Gulf Crest Gasoline   Coleman; Leigh
Haggis, Baggis   Drake
Hail to the King   David, Mack; Livingston, Jerry
Ha-Ja-La-Ka   Hoffman
Handsome Prince, The   David, Mack; Livingston, Jerry
Happy Song (Eine Zwei), The   Livingston, Jerry
Harbor Bells of Normandy, The   Livingston, Jerry; Webster
Hasta La Vista, Goodbye   Merrill
Hatcheck Girl   Merrill
Have a Cup of Tea   Gorney
Have a Heart (Be My Valentine)   Brooks
Have Guitar Will Travel   Silver
Have You No Pity on Me   Coots
Havin' a Hoedown   Drake
H.C. Potter's Ball   DePaul; Raye
He Cha Cha'd In   Burke
He Knows   Robison
He Outfoxed the Fox   Ellington

It's 1200 Miles from Palm Springs to Texas   Cahn; Van Heusen
It's a Bore   Lerner, Alan Jay; Loewe
It's Doom   Comden and Green; Styne
It's Easy to Say You're Sorry   David, Hal
It's Great Not to Be Nominated   Cahn; Van Heusen
It's Hard to Love Somebody (When that Somebody Don't Love You)   Blake
It's Never Quite the Same   Evans; Livingston, Jay
It's Nice to Go Trav'ling   Cahn; Van Heusen
It's Nice to Reminisce   Brooks
It's Not Wrong to Have Fun   Blake
It's Raining Again   Evans; Livingston, Jay
It's Saturday   Ellington
It's So Easy   Drake
It's the Second Time You Meet that Matters   Comden and Green; Styne
It's Time to Say Goodbye   Fain
I've Been There   David, Mack
I've Been There and I'm Back   Evans; Livingston, Jay
I've Got Your Picture Over the Telephone   McHugh
I've Gotta Be On My Way (You'll Have the Blues I Know)   Mercer
I've Never Left Your Arms   Bergman
Jamaica (Tahiti)   Yellen
Jamboree Opening   Brooks
Jazz Chase   Washington
Job for Me, A   Martin
Joe Hill   Robison
Johnston for Governor   McHugh
Jolly Hunters, The   David, Mack; Livingston, Jerry
Journey into Love, A   Coots
Joy Ride   Webster
J.P. Williamson   Ellington
Jubi-lie, Jubi-lo   Evans; Livingston, Jay
Jump when I Say Frog   Merrill
Jumpin' on the Moon   Friend
Jungle Mess Around   Johnson, James P.
Just a Good Joe   Leigh
Just One Olay and a Day from the Border   Bergman
Just to Be Near You   Raye
Keep It Simple   Evans; Livingston, Jay
Keep Our Love on an Even Keel   Styne
Kickin' the Can   Raye
Killers, The   Raye
Kiss   DePaul; Raye
Kiss and Run Lover   DePaul; Raye
Kiss for Consolation, A   Parish
Kiss Me Like You Kissed Me Last Night   McHugh
Knock Knock   Brooks
Ladies in Waiting, The   David, Mack; Livingston, Jerry
Land of Green Ginger, The   David, Mack; Livingston, Jerry
Land of La La La, The   Cahn; Warren
Last Dance, The   Cahn; Van Heusen
Last Time I Saw My Heart, The   Bacharach; David, Hal
Lately   Sigman
Lazy Summer Night   Spina
Lazy Train   Hoffman
(I'm) Left with Memories   Brooks
Legend of the Violin, The   Blane
Let the Lower Lights Be Burning   Comden and Green; Styne
Let the Notes Sing Loud and Clear   Brooks
L'Etang (Live for Love)   Sigman
Let's Change   DePaul; Raye

Let's Get the Show on the Road   Brooks
Let's Go Romancin' in the Rain   Clare
Let's Go to the Movies   Rome
Life Ain't What It Used to Was   Coleman; Leigh
Life Does a Man a Favor (When It Gives Him Simple Joys)   Evans; Livingston, Jay
Life Is for Livin'   Cahn; Van Heusen
Lift a Glass to Friendship   Bergman
Lift Up   Robison
Like a God   Hammerstein; Rodgers
Like Young   Webster
Lilac Tree   Bryan
Little Boy Lost   DePaul; Raye
Little Guy   DePaul; Raye
Little More Time, A   Styne
Little People, The   David, Mack; Livingston, Jerry
Little Tin Man, The   Friend
Live Dangerously   Washington
Livin' with the Blues   Bergman
Lonely Birch Tree, The   Bergman
Lonely Heart and a Friendly Face, A   David, Mack; Livingston, Jerry
Lonely Rider   Bergman
Lonesome Freight Train   Robison
Long Black Nylons   Raye
Long Hot Summer, The   Cahn
Longing   Bryan; Mercer
Look Forward   Hoffman
Loudenhammer Bird, The   Hoffman
Love Is a Four Letter Word   Cahn; DePaul; Raye; Van Heusen
Love Is a Lonely Thing   Cahn; Warren
Love is a Season   Howard, Bart
Love Is Hell   Evans; Livingston, Jay
Love Is Unpredictable   Drake
Love Look Away   Hammerstein; Rodgers
Love Me for Myself   Lawrence
Love of God (Is with You Where Ever You Are), The   Robison
Love Song from Beauty and the Beast   David, Mack; Livingston, Jerry
Love Theme   Webster
Love Won't Let You Get Away   Cahn; Van Heusen
Lover Doll   Silver
Lover's Gold   David, Mack
Lovesville   Freed, Ralph
Loyalty   Fain; Webster
Lucky Me   Burke
Lullaby of the Shepherd   Bergman
Lullaby to Love   Webster
Magic In the Moonlight   Mercer
Magic Island, The   Mercer
Magic Moments   Bacharach; David, Hal
Magic Touch (I Promise), The   Evans
Majorca   Merrill
Make a Wish   Merrill
Make Way for the Emperor   Porter
Make Way for the Fife and Drum Corps   Bergman
Make Way for the Rangers (The Northwest Passage Song)   Dietz; Schwartz, Arthur
Makin' Love   Hoffman
Making Believe You're Here   Cahn; Van Heusen
Mama Don't A-Wanna Hear Her Baby Cry, A   Burke
Mama They Wanna Mambo   DePaul; Raye
Man in Love, A   Styne

Man Once Said, A   Livingston, Jerry
Marching Along   Bergman
Mardi Gras March, The   Fain; Webster
Marianni   Bergman
Marion   Robison
Marry a Woman Uglier Than You   DePaul; Raye
Mary, the Mother of Eternity   Young, Joseph
Mary's Favorite Poem   Robison
Mass in Honor of Saint Anthony   Warren
Matches Burn   Merrill
Maverick   Merrill; Webster
May in Monte Carlo   Livingston, Jerry
Me and My Baby   Cahn; Warren
Mediterranean Love   Carmichael
Meet Me Out on the Golf Course   DePaul; Raye
Melancholy Moon   Coleman; Leigh
Men Are All the Same   DePaul; Raye
Merry Christmas One and All   Bergman
Mice Wanna Play (Mazeltov) (Tu Frappes Mon Coeur),
    The   Hoffman
Midnight Blue   DePaul; Raye
Midnight Oil   Sherman
Mine, Mine, Mine   Sigman
Mirage (Follow Your Heart)   Fain; Lawrence
Mississippi Moon   Burke; Van Heusen
Monique   Cahn
Monte Carlo Calling   Coots
Moon Is Low, The   Merrill
Moon Is Shining   David, Mack; Livingston, Jerry
Moon Mist (inst.)   Warren
Moon Talk   Hoffman
More the Merrier (The More We Are the Merrier We Be),
    The   Martin
Morning Music of Montmartre, The   Evans; Livingston, Jay
Morning Star   David, Mack
Mother Goose Has Come to the Fair   David, Mack;
    Livingston, Jerry
Movie Star   Russell
Murdoch, My Son (Start Haunting Around)   Styne
Music Box, The   Oakland
Music, Romance and 'Specially Love   Stept
My Arms   Ellington
My Best Love   Hammerstein; Rodgers
My Creed   Robison
My Favorite Chair   Evans; Livingston, Jay
My Fellow Entertainers   Drake
My First Alphabet Song   Bergman
My First Counting Song   Bergman
My Fraulein   Evans; Livingston, Jay
My Heart Is an Open Book   David, Hal
My Heart Is Like a Little Canoe   Bryan
My Heart Is Like Missouri   Drake
My Heart, My Mind, My Everything   Ellington
My Heart Still Remembers   Webster
My Home   Cahn; Van Heusen
My Home Lies Quiet   Ellington
My Last Romance   DePaul; Raye
My Little Yellow Dress   Comden and Green; Styne
My Love Is Forever   Freed, Ralph
My Love Song   Stept
My Mistake   DePaul; Raye
My Own Individual Star   Cahn
My Piano Won't Play   Mercer
My Rebel Heart   Washington
Mysterious Scene   Gorney

Nairobi   Merrill
Naked City   Washington
Nancy Lee   Davis
Natives Are Restless Tonight, The   Hoffman
Navy Swings, The   McHugh
Never the Twain Shall Meet   Freed, Ralph
Never Till Now   Webster
New Love   McHugh
New Shoes   Ellington
(Manhattan) News Beat (inst.)   Oakland
Night that Heaven Fell, The   Bacharach; David, Hal
Night They Invented Champagne, The   Lerner, Alan Jay;
    Loewe
Nine Out of Ten   Merrill
No Good Man (Will Make a Good Good Woman Bad),
    A   Blake
No Talent Joe   DePaul; Raye
No Wonder Taxes Are High   Porter
Nobody but the Lord (Ever Heard Him Pray)   Robison
North Wind   Brooks
Nothing in Common   Cahn; Van Heusen
Now I Know   Stept
Now I Lay Me Down to Sleep   Coleman; Leigh
Now I Won't Be Lonely Anymore   David, Hal
Now You See It (Now You Don't) (inst.)   Drake
Now's the Time (When They're Young)   Friend
'Nuff Said   Sherman
Octavians   Spina
Oh Oh, I'm Falling in Love Again   Hoffman
Oh to Be in Paris (inst.)   Oakland
Oh Wendy, Wendy   Bacharach; David, Hal
Old Bachelor Bill   Robison
Old Fashioned Christmas, An   Freed, Ralph
Old Friends (inst.)   Oakland
Old Pizza Maker, The   Adams; Strouse
On the Bridge of Avignon   Mercer
On This Show   Evans; Livingston, Jay
Once More   Sigman
Once More, My Love, Once More   Coslow
Once Upon a Dream   Fain
Once Upon a Horse   Evans; Livingston, Jay
One Chocolate Soda with Two Straws   David, Mack
One Glourie   Styne
One of Us Is a Thief   Cahn
One Rich Brother   Cahn
Only the Lonely   Cahn; Van Heusen
Only Those in Love   Hoffman
Only with You (Io Sono Te)   Raye
Only Yesterday   Ellington
Open Sesame   Cahn
Opportunity Knocks but Once   Porter
Oshkosh   Hoffman
Other Generation, The   Hammerstein; Rodgers
Other Voices, Other Rooms   Russell
Out of Step March (Picadore March)   Bergman
Outa My Mind   Bergman
Paradise Island   Bacharach; David, Hal
Pardon My Sarong   DePaul; Raye
Paris Holiday   Cahn; Van Heusen
Parisians, The   Lerner, Alan Jay; Loewe
Party Girl   Cahn
Pat Boone Blues, The   Evans; Livingston, Jay
Pearl Harbor   DePaul; Raye
Pepita   Bergman
Perfect Symphony, The   Harbach

Perfume   Russell
Periwinkle Blue   Livingston, Jerry; Webster
Piano Talk   Gorney
Picture Dance   Brooks
Piddle 'n' a Now   Hoffman
Piel's Beer   Loesser
Pipes of Pan, The   Mercer
Pitter Patter Serenade (Lazzarella), The   David, Mack
Plant a Packet of Seeds   Brooks
Polka Me   Leigh
Poodle Cut   DePaul; Raye
Poodle Walk, The   Silver
Prayer for Elaine, A   Russell
Prettiest Girl in Town, The   David, Hal
Prove It   Styne
Puddle Duck, The   Merrill
Purple Reef, The   Mancini
Rain Falls on Ev'rybody, The   Alter
Raintree Country   Webster
Rawhide   Washington
Real Love   Raye
Real McCoys, The   Ruby
Record Shop, The   Stept
Remember December   DePaul; Raye
Reunion   Bergman
Reverie (inst.)   Oakland
Rhythmitis   Burke; Van Heusen
Right to the End   Coots
Ring a Dang Ding   Sherman
Ring and the Ding Dong   Friend
Ring Ting Tong   Merrill
Rio De Janeiro   Spina
Rock and Ree-Ah-Zole (The Teen-Age Talk)   Sigman
Rock and Roll Funeral   DePaul; Raye
Rock Baby Rock (inst.)   Oakland
Rock Gently   Raye
Rock 'n' Roll Kisses   David, Mack
Rock-a-Bye Baby   Cahn; Warren
Rock's Song for Victory   Blake; Sissle
Rooftop Rendezvous   DePaul; Raye
Room Full of People, A   Strouse
Roots of Heaven, The   Washington
Roses of Rio   Sigman
Royal Procession, The   David, Mack; Livingston, Jerry
Rumplestiltskin   David, Mack; Livingston, Jerry
Saddle the Wind   Evans; Livingston, Jay
Saga of Goldie Or, The   Brooks
Salud   Mercer
Same Old Song and Dance   Cahn; Van Heusen
San Diego Waltz   Willson
Sands Hotel Song   Cahn; Van Heusen
Saturday Night in Tia Juana   Bacharach; David, Hal
Saturday's Children   Russell
Say, Darling   Comden and Green; Styne
Seaman's Home   Merrill
Secretly   Hoffman
See You Around   Sigman
Separate Tables   Adamson; Warren
Seven Hills of Rome, The   Adamson
Shack Town   Blake
Shadow Dance   Brooks
Shaky Little Baby   David, Hal
Shark in the Bathtub   Drake
She Is Not Thinking of Me   Lerner, Alan Jay; Loewe
Sheriff Honest John Baile   David, Mack

She's Just a Junior   Adams
Shirley Take a Chance   Brooks
Show Is Over, The   Friend
Show Me that You Love Me   Hoffman
Silver Skates   Martin
Sing One Song Mrs. Brown   DePaul; Raye
Sittin' in a Tree House   Bacharach; David, Hal
Sitting on the Fence   Ruby
Sleep Warm   Bergman
Sleeping Beauty Song   Lawrence
Sleepy Hollow   David, Mack; Livingston, Jerry
Sleepyhead   Mercer
Slow Down and Live   Caesar
Smoky Valley   Ruby
So Many Things to Remember   Sigman
Soft Sounds   Cahn; Mancini
Sogni D'Oro   Bergman
Sold Food Solitude and You   Washington
Soldier's Love Song, A   Young, Joseph
Something to Dream About   Sigman
Something's Always Happening on the River   Comden and
    Green; Styne
Somewhere   Bryan
Somewhere Wisconsin   Washington
Song My Mother Loved, The   Hoffman
Song of the Spirits, The   David, Mack; Livingston, Jerry
Song of the Subway   Oakland
Song of the Wheel   Evans; Livingston, Jay
Sorry, Sorry, Sorry   Hoffman
Sorta Blue   Cahn; Mancini
Sounds in the Night   Cahn; Russell
Spanish Dancer, The (inst.)   Warren
Spell Me a Riddle   Styne
Spin the Records   Raye
Square of the Hypotenuse, The   Mercer
Stars and Shadows   Bergman
Stars and Stripes, The   Bergman
Steady   Hoffman
Steppin' Out with My Baby   Brooks
Still, Still, Still   Bergman
Stonewall Jackson   Fain; Webster
Story of Christmas, The   Freed, Ralph
Story of Sinbad, The   Brooks
Story of the Blues   Burke
Straight Down the Middle   Cahn; Van Heusen
Strange Are the Ways of Love   Washington
Strange What Love Will Do   Blake
Street in the Rain (Strada 'Nfosa)   Raye
Sugar Lips   DePaul; Raye
Sugarfoot   Webster
Sunbeams (Bestowal of Gifts)   Fain; Lawrence
Sunbeams in Your Pocket   Fain; Lawrence
Sunday   Hammerstein; Rodgers
Sunset and Moonrise   Bergman
Sunset Bay   Johnson, Howard
Sunshine Companions   Merrill
Surprise   Evans; Livingston, Jay
Sweet Engagement   Bryan
Sweet Tooth   Russell
Swimmin' Suit   Merrill
Take It Easy   DePaul; Raye
Take Your Time (inst.)   Oakland
Tall Paul   Sherman
Teach Me the Dance of Love   Sigman
Tears in My Eyes   Burke; Van Heusen

Tell It on Your Piano   Bryan
Tell the World   Bryan
Tender and True   Adamson; Warren
10th Anniversary of Israel   Oakland
Thank Heaven for Little Girls   Lerner, Alan Jay; Loewe
Thank My Stars   Harburg
Thanks, Professor   Drake
That Ain't Right   Evans; Livingston, Jay
That Man Could Sell Me the Brooklyn Bridge   Fain; Webster
That Mysterious Lady Called Love   Coots; Harburg
That's Anna   Cahn
That's How   DePaul; Raye
That's What Elvis Means to Me   Adams; Strouse
The Four Seasons   Russell
(Like) The Love Birds in a Tree   Merrill
There Ain't Nothin' Love Can't Do   Strouse
There Are Some Things (You Just Can't Tell About)   Blake
There Will Never Be Another Night Like This   Stept
There's a Country   Gorney
There's a Flaw in My Flue   Burke; Van Heusen
There's Always the Blues   Burke
There's Nothing Like a Marching Band   Bergman
These Lush Moments   Burke; Van Heusen
They All Lived Happily Ever After   Cahn
They Can See Your Name in My Eyes   Carmichael
They Had to Get the Rhythm Out of Their Souls   Blake;
      Sissle
They Say   Ellington
They Went That-a-Way   Cahn; Van Heusen
Things Money Cannot Buy (Things That Money Cannot Buy),
      The   Cahn; Van Heusen
Things They Don't Teach You in School   Freed, Ralph
Third from the Left   Bacharach; David, Hal
This Happy Feeling   Evans; Livingston, Jay
This Is the Naked City   Washington
This Is the Night   Coots
This Is the Same Cafe   Wrubel
This Man   Ellington
This Night of Stars   Sigman
This Was My Sin   Sherman
Three B's, The   Bergman
Three Paradises   Evans; Livingston, Jay
Time   Strouse
Time Never Erases   Drake
To Be a Performer   Coleman; Leigh
To Love and Be Loved   Cahn; Van Heusen
Toasts, The   Brooks
Today Is Your Birthday   Martin
Tonight Is the Night   DePaul; Raye
Tony the Monkey   Martin
Too Early for the Blues   David, Hal
Too Young to Bop   Sherman
Top Hat and Cane Dance   Brooks
Top of the Tower   Washington
Torere   Hoffman
Tortured   Burke; Van Heusen
Toujours, A   Lerner, Alan Jay; Loewe
Traveling Salesman and the Farmer's Daughter, The   David,
      Mack; Livingston, Jerry
Trinidad   DePaul; Raye
Trinka Brinker   Martin
Trust Your Destiny to Your Star   Porter
Try to Love Me Just As I Am   Comden and Green; Styne
Tune In   Robison
Twilight Waltz, The   Ruby

Two Arms   Russell
Two Days Out of Delaware   Russell
Two of Us, The   David, Hal
U-Gotta-Soda   Spina
Under Fourteen   Merrill
Under the Sycamore Tree   Von Tilzer
Unkw-in-it   Spina
Until He Gets a Girl   Merrill
Utilize   Robison
Valencinita   Bergman
Verboten   David, Mack
Vertigo   Evans; Livingston, Jay
Very Precious Love, A   Fain; Webster
Very Proper Town, A   Evans; Livingston, Jay
Very, Very Young, The   Drake
Vigolin   Bergman
Viva Italia   Gorney
Volare   Parish
(Roll Along) Wagon Train   Brooks; Fain
(Fifi's) Walking the Poodle   David, Hal
Warm and Willing   Loesser
Way I Love You, The   Lawrence
Ways of Love, The   Mancini; Raye
We All Gotta Live in His House   Merrill
We Gotta Get Hitched Baby   Blake
We Mustn't Part   Sigman
We Took a Chance   McHugh
We Won't Forget   DePaul; Raye
Weather Medley   Brooks
Welcome to the Royal American   DePaul; Raye
Welcoming Song   Styne
We're Not Children   Evans; Livingston, Jay
We're Off to a Wonderful Start   Woods
What a Way to Go   Drake
What Did We Do Last Night   Evans; Livingston, Jay
What Have You Got to Have   Harburg
What Is It Going to Be Boys   DePaul; Raye
What Would You Call It   DePaul; Raye
Whatever May Be Tide   Evans; Livingston, Jay
Whatever May Betide   David, Mack; Livingston, Jerry
What's 'a Matter Baby   Merrill
What's a Parade Without a Drum and Bugle
      Corps   Bergman
Wheel Has Been Spun, The   Evans; Livingston, Jay
Wheels   Evans; Livingston, Jay
When Father Carves the Bird (Turkey Day)   DePaul; Raye
When I Dream of You   Livingston, Jerry
When I Marry You   Bryan
When I Walk My Baby   DePaul; Raye
When the Boys Talk About the Girls   Merrill
When the Good Lord Troubles the Waters (Be
      Ready)   Robison
When the Storm Clouds Form   Brooks
When They Handed Out Hearts   Strouse
When You Fall   Freed, Ralph
When You Know Your Man Is Comin' Home   DePaul; Raye
When You Look at Me (Nostalgia di Mandolini)   Brooks;
      Raye
When's Your Birthday Baby   Merrill
Where   Livingston, Jerry
Where in the World   Fain; Lawrence
Whippoorwill, The   Raye
Whispers in the Wind   Lawrence
White Virgin of the Nile, The   Cahn; Warren
Who Are They to Say   Cahn

Who Wants Love   Caesar
Who Was That Lady I Saw You With?   Bergman
Whoops-A-Daisy   Hoffman
Who's to Say?   Freed, Ralph
Whose Hat Is That in the Hall   DePaul
Why Ain'tcha   David, Hal
Why Am I Crying   David, Hal
Why Can't He Care for Me   Cahn; Warren
Why Do I Feel So Enchanted   David, Mack; Livingston, Jerry
Why Should I Worry   Cahn
Why Wonder Why   David, Mack
Wicked Witch, The   David, Mack; Livingston, Jerry
Willingly   Sigman
Window of Dreams, The   Evans; Livingston, Jay
Window Shade Dance   Brooks
Window Where God Looks In, A   Bryan
Winter Interlude   Russell
With Love   Davis
With One Side of Your Heart (The Other Side of Your Heart)   Merrill
Witness, The   Cahn
Wizard, The   David, Mack
Woman Sweet   Bergman
Wonderful As Love   Bryan
Wonderful Years, The   Fain; Leigh
Words Have So Many Meanings   David, Mack; Meyer
World of Strangers   Fain; Webster
World of Your Arms, The   David, Hal; Livingston, Jerry
World Outside, The   Sigman
Wouldn't It Be Fun   Porter
Woulds't   David, Mack; Livingston, Jerry
Year In, Year Out   Cahn
Ye'll Be Returnin' Again   Styne
You Are Beautiful   Hammerstein; Rodgers
You Are Lonely   Ellington
You Are So Sweet to Me   Johnson, James P.
You Are So Tempting   De Lange
You Can Always Judge a Gal (By the Songs She Keeps)   Cahn; Van Heusen
You Can Say That Again   DePaul; Raye
You Can Take the Boy Out of the Country   Russell
You Can Walk Under Ladders   Brooks
You Can't Always Have what You Want   Mercer
You Can't Cash in on an Alibi   Blake
You Don't Have to Tell Me   Stept
You Don't Know Him   Evans; Livingston, Jay
You Fascinate Me So   Coleman; Leigh
You Good Boy, You Get Cookie   David, Mack
You Got to Git the Gittin' (While the Gittin' Is Good)   Blake
You Gotta Get Lucky Sometime   Burke
You Know You Love It   Russell
You Rocked When You Should-a Rolled   Raye
You Said You Wouldn't Do It (But You Did)   Gordon; Monaco
You Understand Me   Hoffman
You Walkin' My Dreams   Ellington
You Were Made for Love   Freed, Ralph
You Will Find Your Love in Paris   Gordon
You, You Darlin'   David, Hal
Young Lions, The   DePaul; Raye
Your Dream Is a Flying Carpet   Cahn
Your Family   Russell
Your Kiss   Bergman
Your Majesty   Burke
You're Bringing Out the Dreamer in Me   Burke

You're Growing On Me   Robison
You're Merely Wonderful   DePaul; Raye
You're My Kissin' Girl   DePaul; Raye
You're Part of Me   Sigman
You're So Danceable With   Hoffman
You've Got the Indian Sign on Me   Burke
Yuletide Tango   Sherman

1959

(You're) A Handy Thing to Have Around the House   Rome
(Love Is) A Private Affair   Livingston, Jay; McHugh
Advice to the Lovelorn   Drake
After Dark   Revel
Afterbeat, The   Mercer
Al Fresco   Arlen; Mercer
Alaskans (Gold Fever), The   David, Mack; Livingston, Jerry
All for the Love of Gold   Robison; Woods
All I Need Is the Girl   Sondheim; Styne
All My Tomorrows   Cahn; Van Heusen
All Night Long in Paris   Coleman; Leigh
All the Love in the World   Adams; Strouse
All the Luck in the World   Duke
Always Keep on Smiling (inst.)   Revel
Amigos   Fain; Webster
Amour! Amour! I Have Love   Spina
And I'll Be There   Burke
Angeltown   Evans; Livingston, Jay
(As One Door Closes) Another Door Opens   David, Hal
Anybody for the Blues   McHugh
Anyone Would Love You   Rome
Anything Can Happen   Burke
Are You Ready, Gyp Watson?   Rome
Ashandai Aschandai   Spina
Assignment Hollywood   Hoffman
At the Carnival in Rio   Revel
At the Eleventh Hour   Drake
Automobile Ballet   Brooks
Autumn Night   Alter
Autumn Reverie (inst.)   Warren
Baby, Be Nice to Me   Revel
Baby June and Her Newsboys   Sondheim; Styne
Baby that's Me   Martin
Back at the Grind   Brooks
Back Part of the Paper, The   Brooks
Backyard Cook Out (Stereo Patio Party)   Robison
Bad Boys and Girls   Robison
Bad for My Complexion   Dietz; Schwartz, Arthur
Baker's Keyboard Blues   Drake
Ballad of a Gun   Rome
Ballad of Sam Older, The   Carmichael
Band, The   Willson
Barbary Coast Saloon   Adamson; Young, Victor
Barrel of Monkeys, A   Burke; Van Heusen
Beach Time   Sherman
Beardley Ballet (inst.)   Merrill
Beat of the Blues, The   Evans; Livingston, Jay
Beat the Band   Spina
Beautiful Mohongahela   David, Mack; Oakland
Bees 'n' Flowers   Arlen; Mercer
Before and After   Hoffman
Behave Yourself   Fields
Bells of Heidelberg, The   David, Mack
Beloved Bandit   Dietz; Schwartz, Arthur
Beloved Infidel   Webster

Best Is Yet to Come, The   Coleman; Leigh
Best of All   Freed, Ralph
Best of Everything, The   Cahn
Best Style Show   Brooks
Bettin' Calls   Arlen; Mercer
Big Circus, The   Fain; Webster
Big Tree Tall   David, Hal
Birth of Love, The   Howard, Bart
Black Roses   Spina
Blessed Are They   Davis
Blind Man   Arlen; Mercer
Blow de Whistle   Arlen; Mercer
Blow the Man Down   Duke
Blue Afternoon   Adamson; McHugh
Blue Am I   Martin
Blue Bobby Socks   David, Hal
Blue Midnight (inst.)   Warren
Blue Vignette   Coots
Blues Boogie   Arlen; Mercer
Blues, Country Style, The   David, Mack; Livingston, Jerry
Blues Is a Tale of Trouble, The   Bergman
Blues Is a Travelin' Thing, The   Bergman
Blues Is an Old Old Story, The   Bergman
Bon Appetit (Menu Song)   Arlen; Mercer
Bon Vivant (Bone Vi-vawn)   Livingston, Jerry
Bon Voyage   Adamson; Young, Victor
Bonanza   Evans; Livingston, Jay
Boom-a-ladda Boom-Boom   Livingston, Jerry
Born to Be Loved   Bullock
Boss' Love Call, The   Brooks
Bottleneck   Rome
Bouncin'   Hoffman
Bourbon Street Beat   David, Mack; Livingston, Jerry
Brazilian Love Song (Andorinha Prata)   Hoffman
Brian   Duke
Broken Hearted Melody   David, Hal
Bronco   David, Mack; Livingston, Jerry
Buddy Boy   Merrill
But   Ellington
But Yours   Merrill
By the Bay of Napoli   Warren
Bye-Bye   Evans; Livingston, Jay; Mancini
Cackling Chickens   Friml
Cake Song   Arlen; Mercer
Cakewalk Turns   Arlen; Mercer
Call Me   Bacharach
Camp Meetin' Friends   Robison
Candidates, The   Brooks
Candle in the Wind, A   Adamson; McHugh
Candle Light (inst.)   Revel
Can't Get Used to These Clothes   Martin
Cap Is on the Go (The Civil Air Patrol March), The   Myrow
(Love Is a) Career   Cahn; Van Heusen
Carioca Capers (inst.)   Warren
Catalog Day   Burke; Van Heusen
C'est la Vie, C'est l'Amour   Coslow
Champagne fo' de Lady   Arlen; Mercer
Chevy Moon   Brooks
Cheyenne   David, Mack; Livingston, Jerry
Cheyyanos   Brooks
Chic Talk   Duke
Chicago Fair Waltz   Gordon; Revel
Chico's Choo-Choo (The Choo-Choo Cha-Cha)   Cahn; Van Heusen
Christmas Is for Children   Cahn; Van Heusen

Ciao Ciao Bambino   Parish
City Street   Brooks
City Within a City   Washington
Ciu-e, A   David, Hal
Clementine   Martin
Climb Ev'ry Mountain   Hammerstein; Rodgers
Close Quarters   Bacharach; David, Hal
(It Must Be Getting) Close to Christmas   Cahn; Van Heusen
Cloud Nine   Johnson, James P.
Coke! The Cat! The Cook!, The   Cahn; Van Heusen
Color Green, The   Brooks
Colors of Autumn   Brooks
Come Completely to Me   Bacharach
Come On Let's Go   Brooks
Come Over Here   Sondheim; Styne
Come Sing with Me   Cahn; Van Heusen
Come Spring   Cahn; Van Heusen
Come to Order, Men   Wrubel
Comic Strips   Brooks
Comin' 'Round the Bend   Brooks
Company of Men, The   Merrill
Conjure Man   Arlen; Mercer
Cops and Robbers   Spina
Could I Love You More   Raye
Countin' Our Chickens   Arlen; Mercer
Court of Last Resort   Raye
Cow Song   Sondheim; Styne
Cowboy's Time of Day   Brooks
Crazy   Bergman
"Cues"   Martin
Cure, The   Arlen; Mercer
Curse   Arlen; Mercer
Cute Little Wiggle   Hoffman
Dainty June and Her Farmboys   Sondheim; Styne
Dandilova   Evans; Livingston, Jay
Darling, He's Playing Our Song   Lawrence
Days of the Week   Brooks
De Oily Boid   Dietz; Schwartz, Arthur
De Right Answer   Arlen; Mercer
Deefeecult for You — Easy to Me   Hoffman
Della's Entrance (Whatcha Sayin' Della?)   Arlen; Mercer
Deming, New Mexico, High School Wildcats' Song   Brown, Nacio Herb
Diamond for Carla, A   Fain; Webster
Dis Is de Day   Arlen; Mercer
Dis Little While   Arlen; Mercer
Dissolves   Arlen; Mercer
Dixieland   Mercer
Does Santa Claus Believe in You   Cahn; Van Heusen
Dog Eat Dog   Arlen; Mercer
Dolly Dimple   Merrill
Don't Dream of Anybody but Me   Howard, Bart
Don't Leave Me   Freed, Ralph
Don't Need a Horseshoe   Brooks
Don't Unless You Love Me   Bacharach; David, Hal
Don't Wish Your Life Away   Heyman
Don't You Ever Cross Me Path   Duke
Do-Re-Mi   Hammerstein; Rodgers
Down By the Shore   Johnson, James P.
Dragon Rag   Brooks
Dream Rag (inst.)   Blake
Dreaming About You   Johnson, Howard
Dreams Patter   Brooks
Dreamsville   Evans; Livingston, Jay; Mancini
Drinking Song   Brooks

Drums Are the Heartbeat Passin' with the Dragon   Brooks
Du Bist Mein Liebe   David, Mack
Ducky Christmas   Sherman
Easy Street   Arlen; Mercer
Echo of a Dream   Mercer
Echoes of Aloha   Stept
Eddie's Song   Merrill
Edelweiss   Hammerstein; Rodgers
Elegy   Arlen; Mercer
Endless River   Robison
Erbie Fitch's Twitch   Fields
Eternal Love   Revel
Ever Near, Never Far   Bacharach; David, Hal
Ever So Lightly   Cahn; Van Heusen
(What) Every Girl Should Know   Revel
Every Once in a While   Brooks; Rome
Every Week We Get a Stack of Mail   Brooks
Everything's Comin' Up Roses   Sondheim; Styne
Everything's the Same   Brooks
Ev'rybody Wants to Be Loved   Howard, Bart
Ev'rything Is Shapin' Up Fine   Hoffman
Excitingly Diff'rent   Johnson, James P.
Facts of Life, The   Coleman; Leigh
Fair Warning   Rome
Fair Weather Friend   Heyman
Faithful Heart, The   Cahn; Van Heusen
Faithfully   Bacharach; Cahn; Van Heusen
Faker, Faker   Bacharach; David, Hal
Family Lovin' Folks   Caesar; Robison
Far, Far Away from Home   Dietz; Schwartz, Arthur
Farewell My Lassie   Bergman
Father of the Bride   Ruby
Fiesta in Spain   Young, Victor
Firebird Two   Brooks
First March   Arlen; Mercer
First Year of Love, The   Livingston, Jerry
Fix Yo'self Up   Arlen; Mercer
Flang Dang Saturday Night   Hoffman
Floatin' Like a Feather   Cahn
Flower Vendor   Arlen; Mercer
Fogg's in Yokohama   Adamson; Young, Victor
Folks   Arlen; Mercer
Folks Are Walkin' 'Round   Brooks
For Sweet Charity   Merrill
For the Love of You   Fain; Webster
Forget Me   Drake
Fountain of Dreams   Fain; Webster
Four Star Napoleon (Grenadier's March)   Spina
Free As the Air   Duke
Frere Jacques   Brooks
Fudge   Dietz; Schwartz, Arthur
Funeral Music (inst.)   Duke
Future Is Here to Stay   Brooks
Gamble in the Wind, A   McHugh
Game of Poker, A   Arlen; Mercer
Game of Romance   Brooks
Genteel Bastard   Arlen; Mercer
Gentle Love   Washington
Gentlemen, Why Don't You Mingle   Brooks
Gettin' a Man   Mercer
Gettysburg Address   Livingston, Jerry
Ghost Music (inst.)   Duke
Girl Like You, A   Bacharach
Girl Most Likely to Succeed, The   Cahn; Van Heusen
Girls Are at It Again, The   David, Hal

Give Me a Song to Sing   Davis
Go 'Way Mister Moon   Bacharach
Goin' to the Door   Merrill
Good Good Thing, A   Rome
Good Old Songs, The   Cahn; Van Heusen
Goose Never Be a Peacock   Arlen; Mercer
Gossip Theme (Have You Heard About Phileas
      Fogg?)   Adamson; Young, Victor
Got a Locket in My Pocket   David, Hal
Got the Feeling   Sherman
Grandpa's Old But Very Happy   Brooks
Hadacol   Burke; Van Heusen
Haga-Daga-Day   David, Mack
Half-sies   Mercer
Half-sies (Hav-Zies)   Bloom
Handle My Heart with Care   Revel
Hanging Tree, The   David, Mack; Livingston, Jerry
Hangman, The   Bacharach; David, Hal
Happy and His One Man Band   Bacharach
Happy Bachelor (Or the Courtship of Miles Standish),
      The   DePaul; Mercer
Happy Birthday Dear Country   Spina
Happy People   Davis
Happy Polka, The   Mills
Harvey's Theme (inst.)   Duke
Hasta La Vista, Senora   Livingston, Jerry
Have You Heard? (Gossip Song)   Arlen; Mercer
Hawaii Swings   Hoffman
Hawaiian Eye   David, Mack; Livingston, Jerry
Heaven Only Knows   Revel
Heavenly   Bacharach
Heavenly Lover   David, Hal
Heaven's Just a Kiss Away   Revel
Heir to the Throne   Spina
Helping Our Friends   Wrubel
Here We Go   Brooks
Here's Where I Came In   Coleman; Leigh
He's Starting to Get to Me   Cahn; Van Heusen
Hey, Fifi!   Sherman
Hey, Sport   Raye
Hide Me in Your Arms   Sigman
High Hopes   Cahn; Van Heusen
Higher den de Moon   Arlen; Mercer
His Majesty the Clock   Revel
Hold On to Your Heart   Revel
Holiday for Cars   Brooks
Holiday for Lovers   Cahn; Van Heusen
Hollywood Jubilee (inst.)   Brown, Nacio Herb
Home from the Hill   David, Mack
Home Is My Lover   David, Mack
Home Is the Place   Sondheim; Styne
Home on the Range Cha Cha   Brooks
Hong Kong, Take a Little Rickshaw Ride   Adamson; Young,
      Victor
Honolulu Lu   Hoffman
Hoop-de-Dingle   Rome
Horoscope   Brooks
How Can I Be Alone   Evans
How Can I Be Alone Again   Livingston, Jay
How Can Love Survive?   Hammerstein; Rodgers
How Long Will You Remember (How Soon Will You
      Forget)   Leslie
How Should You Feel   Brooks; Revel
Hundred Women in One, A   Duke
Hurt They Write About, The   Merrill

Hurtin' (For the Love of You)   Sherman
Hypnotique   David, Mack
I Ain't Afraid   Arlen; Mercer
I Ain't Gonna Lead This Life No More   Drake
I Couldn't Care Less   Cahn; Van Heusen
I Don't Dig You, Kookie (Whatcha Tryin' to Say)   Drake
I Don't Have to Look in the Papers   Brooks
I Don't Know Where My Next Kiss Is Coming
        From   Adamson
I Don't Wanna Lose Ya   David, Hal
I Don't Wanna Say Goodnight   David, Hal
I Dropped By to Say Hello   David, Hal
I Get Embarrassed   Merrill
I Get So All Fired Tired   Robison
I Hate Him   Rome
I Have Double-Checked   Brooks
I Haven't Got a Thing to Wear   Wrubel
I Heard   Evans; Livingston, Jay
I Know what God Is   Raye
I Know Your Kind   Rome
I Like My Love This Way   Burke; Revel
I Long to Be Loved   Sigman
I Look Across the Table   Wrubel
I Looked for You   Bacharach; David, Hal
I Only Know One Way to Love   Revel
I Say Hello   Rome
I Think It's Here to Stay   Myrow
I Wanna Be Around   Mercer
I Want the South to Win the War for Christmas   Cahn; Van
        Heusen
I Wish It Could Be Otherwise   DePaul; Mercer; Raye
I Wish that I Could Try   David, Hal
I Would Die   Merrill
I'd Climb to Heaven   Revel
I'd Rather Be Me   David, Hal; Livingston, Jerry
Ida from Idaho   Adamson; McHugh
If He Brings You Flowers   Brooks
If I Choose (I Can Go Home)   Brooks
If I Had Three Wishes for Christmas   Styne
If Jesus Don't Love You   Merrill
If Momma Was Married   Sondheim; Styne
If There Are Stars in My Eyes   Hoffman
If We Hadn't Taken in Boarders   Dietz; Schwartz, Arthur
If You Like to Get Around   Brooks
I'll Be Respectable   Arlen; Mercer
I'll Bet My First Dream and Last Dream on You   Woods
I'll Have to Ask My Mother (inst.)   Revel
I'll Try   Fields
I'm Back in Circulation   Fields
I'm Calling You from Las Vegas   Brown, Nacio Herb
I'm Glad I Took that Second Look at You (inst.)   Gordon;
        Revel
I'm Gonna Getcha   Revel
I'm Gonna Go Fishin'   Ellington
I'm Headed for Big Things   Arlen; Mercer
I'm in Another World with You   Revel
I'm Looking for an Honest Face   Wrubel
I'm Never Alone   Cahn; Van Heusen
I'm Not Too Young to Dream   Davis
I'm Sorry, I Want a Ferrari   Wrubel
Imitation of Life   Fain; Webster
In a Little Waterfront Cafe   Robison
In the Cradle of My Arms (inst.)   Revel
In Times Like These   Bacharach; David, Hal
India Countryside   Adamson; Young, Victor

Innocent Appearance   Wrubel
Israel   Berlin
It Doesn't Take a Minute   Fields
It Takes Love to Build a Home   Wrubel
It Took Dreams   Sherman
It Was Love   Adamson
It Won't Cool Off   Cahn
It's All a Part of Love   Davis
It's All There in the Papers   Brooks
It's Cruel to Take a Sweetheart   Merrill
It's Tough to Be a Man   Duke
It's Tough to Be a Working Girl   Duke
It's Twelve O'Clock   Coots
I've a Fever   Brooks
I've Seen All Sides   Washington
Japanese Evening (Japanese Hello)   Brooks
Japanese Goodnight   Brooks
Japanese Thank You   Brooks
Jenny on a Horse   Livingston, Jerry
J.J. Jones   Evans; Livingston, Jay
Joanna   Mancini; Mercer
Jo-Jo the Dog-Faced Boy   Sherman
Jolly Jingle Bells   Sherman
Judge, Don't Send Me to Jail!   Lawrence
June Is Warm   Brooks
Just an Old Pressed Rose in the Old Family Album   Revel
Just Come Home   Sigman
Just for Once   Fields
Just Like Children   Duke
Just Like That   Brooks
Just What I Wanted for Christmas   Cahn; Van Heusen
Kansas City Blues   Bergman
Kelly Green (inst.)   Warren
Key to the Kingdom, The   Sigman
Kick It Around   Spina
Killing Sequence   Arlen; Mercer
Kiss and a Promise, A   Cahn
Kiss Can Tell a Lie, A   David, Hal
Kiss Me and Kiss Me and Kiss Me   Hoffman
Kissin' on the Red Light   David, Hal
Knights on White Horses   Merrill
Kris Kringle Rides Again   Gorney
La Plume de Ma Tante   Hoffman
(We're) Ladies   Rome
Ladies 'n' Gentlemen   Arlen; Mercer
Lana, Lovely Lana   Martin
Large As Life   Russell
Last Star of Evening, The   Sigman; Young, Victor
Last Train from Gun Hill, The   Webster
Lawman, The   David, Mack; Livingston, Jerry
Le Son d'Amour (I Hear)   Drake
Least That's My Opinion   Arlen
Leit Motif   Drake
Lessons in Love   Arlen; Mercer
Let 'Em Dig Way Down   Brooks
Let Go the Rope   Freed, Ralph
Let Me Drift on the Pillow of a Cloud   Revel
Let Me Entertain You   Sondheim; Styne
Let's Go Shopping   Brooks
Let's Go to Press   Brooks
Let's Go to the Movies   Sondheim; Styne
Let's Make This Christmas the Greatest Xmas of All   Coots
Let's Pow-Wow, Not Mau Mau   Caesar
Let's Talk about a Woman   Rome
Lightnin' Bug   David, Hal

Like Clouds Up in the Sky   Arlen; Mercer
Lilly-lu (Lily Lou)   Hoffman
Listen My Love   Bacharach; David, Hal
Little Green Snake   Merrill
Little Lamb   Sondheim; Styne
Little Sailboat in the Harbor   Hoffman
Live Hard, Work Hard, Love Hard   Arlen; Mercer
Lloyds of London   Adamson
Lola-Lola   Evans; Livingston, Jay
London Waltz, The   Bergman
Lonely Christmas   Freed, Ralph
Lonely Goatherd, The   Hammerstein; Rodgers
Lonely Lonely Winter   Johnson, James P.
Lonely Lover   Cahn
Lonesome Thoughts (Lonesome Heart)   Brooks
Long Ago Last Summer   Bacharach; David, Hal
Long and I Waited (inst.)   Revel
Long Live the English Scene   Adamson; Young, Victor
Look at the Sun   Brooks
Look What a Hole You're In   Arlen; Mercer
Look Who's in Love   Fields
Lookin' fo' Somebody   Arlen; Mercer
Lookin' Out the Window   Raye
Lord Looked Down, The   Brooks
Lorna Doone   Bacharach; David, Hal
Losing End   Friend
Love Ain't Nothin' but the Blues   Revel
Love Among the Young   Styne
Love Does That   Friend
Love for Sure   Duke
Love Held Lightly   Arlen; Mercer
Love Is Just a Dream   Coots
Love Is Like Champagne   Sigman
Love Machine   Sherman
Love Me Forever   Adamson
Loveliest Night of the Year   Friml
Lovers in the Dark   Mercer
Lovey Dove   Friend
Loving Is a Way of Living   Bacharach; David, Hal
Lu Lu Lu, My Darlin' (Sleep, My Little One, Sleep)   Revel
Lulu Had a Baby   Hoffman
Lumpin'   Arlen; Mercer
M-10   Duke
Madame Rose's Toreadorables   Sondheim; Styne
Magoo's Blues   Washington
Main Street   Brooks
Make Mine Love   Adamson; Warren
Make Room for the Joy   Bacharach; David, Hal
Mama, May I   Hoffman
Mama Used to Say   Spina
Man in My Life, The   Arlen; Mercer
Manhunt   Brooks
Many Kinds of Love   Arlen; Mercer
March to Freedom (inst.)   Willson
Mardi Gras Parade   Spina
Maria   Hammerstein; Rodgers
Market Looks Great, The   Brooks
Marry Me in Laramie   Carmichael
Marry Young   Coleman; Leigh
Marvelous Fire Machine   Merrill
Mary Lou Wilson and Johnny Brown   Livingston, Jerry
Mating Game, The   Adams; Strouse
May We Entertain You   Sondheim; Styne
Meanwhile Back at the Ranch   Brooks
Men   Brooks

Men Who Run the Country, The   Mercer
Men with Whips   Lawrence
Merely Marvelous   Fields
Middle of a Madhouse   Freed, Ralph
Minuet   Arlen; Mercer
Miranda   Howard, Bart
Momma's Talkin' Soft   Sondheim; Styne
Mon Petit   Washington
Money Mad Men   Sherman
Moods (inst.)   Warren
Moon Man   Bacharach; David, Hal
More I Think About You, The   Heyman
More People   Cahn; Van Heusen
Mother of Mine   Bergman
Mr. Goldstone, I Love You   Sondheim; Styne
Mr. Masterson, Mr. Gun   Brooks
Music from Another World   Lawrence
Mustafa (The Sheik of Chicago)   Merrill
My Baby Walked Out on Me   Revel
My Destiny Is You (inst.)   Revel
My Dream   Hoffman
My Favorite Things   Hammerstein; Rodgers
My Gal's a Mule   Fields
My Girl Is Just Enough Woman for Me   Fields
My Heart Became of Age   Sherman
My Heart Belongs to You   Washington
My Heart of Hearts   David, Hal
My Love for You   David, Hal
My Love Is Like a Red, Red Rose   Van Heusen
My Main Title and Yours   Brooks
My Prayer of Love   Davis
My Problem   Livingston, Jerry
My Rifle, My Pony and Me   Webster
My Sky Without a Star   Duke
My Sweetheart Is Connecticut   Merrill
My Very Fav'rite Christmas Card   Cahn; Van Heusen
My Very First Kiss   David, Hal
Name It and It's Yours (inst.)   Revel
Natchul Man   Arlen; Mercer
Nearer to Heaven (Song of the Trapeze)   Fain; Webster
Ne'er Do Well   Revel
Net, The   Bacharach; David, Hal
Never Got to the Dance   Freed, Ralph
Never Steal Anything Small   Wrubel
New Orleans Cha-Cha   Spina
New Orleans the Cradle of Love   Revel
New Stars and Stripes Forever, The   Parish
News Chant   Arlen; Mercer
News Is Always Happening   Brooks
Nice Pizza Pie   Leslie
Nice She Ain't   Sondheim; Styne
Night of Stars   Brooks
Night of the Quarter Moon   Cahn; Van Heusen
Night Rock and Roll Died (Almost), The   Cahn; Van Heusen
Nine O'Clock   Merrill
Nine to Five   Brooks
No Way to Stop It   Hammerstein; Rodgers
Nobody but Tess   Duke
Nobody Knows How Much I Love You   Howard, Bart
Not Enough Faith in the Lord   Robison
Not Guilty   Rome
Not Quite a Waltz   Evans; Livingston, Jay
Nothing to Do but Pass the Time of Day   Ruby
Nothing Will Keep Me Away   Evans; Livingston, Jay
Now Is the Only Time Ever   Wrubel

Now You Know   Freed, Ralph
O Oio Mio   Hoffman
Off Again, On Again   Bergman
Off We Go   Brooks
Oh Baby I'm on the Moon   Leslie
Oh, Oh, Rosie   Merrill
Oh, Please   Merrill
Ol' Kris Kringle   Adamson
Old Fashioned Love   Lawrence
Old Fashioned Political Rally (Invitation)   Wrubel
Old Neighbor   Robison
Old Old Tunes, The   Adams; Strouse
Old-Fashioned Christmas, An   Cahn; Van Heusen
On the Second Floor   Brooks
On the Way   Robison
Once Around the Rainbow   Brooks
Once in a Lifetime   Dietz; Schwartz, Arthur
Once Knew a Fella   Rome
One Hand Tied Behind My Back   Evans; Livingston, Jay
One Hundred Women in One   Duke
One Man's Love Song Is Another Man's Blues   Van Heusen
One Step, Two Step   Arlen; Mercer
One Two Three Waltz   Spina
Only Pair I've Got, The   Merrill
Only Time Will Tell   Rome
Only You — Only Me   Davis
Open Your Heart to Me   Parish
Opening A, B, C, D   Arlen; Mercer
Ordinary Couple, An   Hammerstein; Rodgers
Oscar   Blane; Martin
Other-Women Blues, The   Robison
Our Wedding Song   Webster
Out with Somebody Else   Van Heusen
Over   Brooks
Pandemonium   Arlen; Mercer
Panorama   Brooks
Parade, The   Merrill
Paris in New York   Duke
Paris Valentine, A   Webster
Parisian Heiress (inst.)   Drake
Parks of Paris, The   Arlen; Mercer
Patience of a Saint, The   Merrill
Peace on Earth   Freed, Ralph
Penetone   Revel
Persian Room-Ba   Duke
Petticoat High   Arlen; Mercer
Piccadilly Schleppers   Dietz; Schwartz, Arthur
Picnic Song II and Girls Walk By   Merrill
Pigeon Song, The   Spina
Pink Jungle, The   Duke
Pink Polemoniums   Hoffman
Pixie from Paree, The   Livingston, Jerry
Plaza Music   Duke
Plea for Understanding, A   Martin
Please Don't Go   Sigman
Please Love Me Too   Johnson, James P.
Plum Pudding   Cahn; Van Heusen
Pork Chop Charlie   Merrill
Portraits (inst.)   Warren
Possibly, Possibly   Livingston, Jerry
Postman's March (Hurray for the Postman)   Gorney
Power of Prayer, The   Livingston, Jerry
Prelude   Duke
Preludium   Hammerstein; Rodgers
Prisoner's Barcarolle, The   Spina

(Love Is a) Private Affair, A   Evans
Private Jones of the U.S.A.   Gordon
Professor, Professor   Cahn; DePaul
Promenade   Evans; Livingston, Jay
Promenade (Street Cries)   Arlen; Mercer
Promise Me a Rose (A Slight Detail)   Merrill
Punch and Judy   Evans; Livingston, Jay; Mancini
Puppets on Parade   Friml
Put Me in Your Heart   Friend
Put Your Rocks in a Box   Hoffman
Race   Arlen; Mercer
Ragtime Rag (inst.)   Blake
Reading the News   Arlen; Mercer
Real Thing, The   Hoffman
Reap the Harvest   Arlen; Mercer
Reflections   Burke
Reflections (inst.)   Warren
Remington Rollamatic March (inst.)   Willson
Respectability   Rome
Ride the Carousel   Revel
Right Finger of My Left Hand, The   Fields
Ring on the Finger   Rome
Rio Bravo   Webster
Rollin' Stone, A   Russell
Rosalyn   Hoffman
Rose Lovejoy of Paradise Alley   Rome
Rose's Turn   Sondheim; Styne
Sailing Home to England   Adamson; Young, Victor
'S-All Right   Hoffman
Same Old Army, The   Evans; Livingston, Jay; McHugh
Same Old Love   Duke
San Diego   Raye
Santa Claus Valley   Revel
Saratoga   Arlen; Mercer
Save Me   Drake
Save Your Love for Me   Warren
Saving My Kisses   Sherman
Say One for Me   Cahn; Van Heusen
Scent of the Orient   Merrill
Second March   Arlen; Mercer
Second Wind   Arlen; Mercer
Secret of Christmas, The   Cahn; Van Heusen
Seeing You Again (Did Me No Good)   David, Hal
Seeing You Tell a Lie   David, Hal
Seems Like When It Comes in the Morning   Bergman
Send Me Letters Filled with Kisses   Bacharach
Senorita Pepita   Parish
September Morning   Howard, Bart
Session at Pete's Pad   Evans; Livingston, Jay; Mancini
Seven Best Years   Davis
77 Sunset Strip (Swingin' on the Strip) (Blue Nite on the Strip)   David, Mack; Livingston, Jerry
Shamrock Waltz   Revel
She Sells Seashells By the Seashore   Alter; Heyman
She's Not Enough Woman for Me   Fields
She's Sick   Brooks
Ship (inst.), The   Revel
Ship Sailed, The   David, Mack
Shirl's Theme   Cahn
Show 'Em You Got Class   Ellington
Show Must Go On, The   Spina
Sid, Ol' Kid   Merrill
Side Saddle   Parish
Sidewalks of Paris   Young, Victor
Silent Movies   Brooks

Silent Stranger, The   Johnson, James P.; Russell
Silver Wings   David, Mack; Livingston, Jerry
Simpson Sisters, The   Fields
Sin   Evans; Livingston, Jay
Six Boys and Seven Boys   Sigman
Sixteen Going on Seventeen   Hammerstein; Rodgers
Sky Symphony   Adamson; Young, Victor
Small Town Boy   Washington
Small World   Sondheim; Styne
Smile Girls   Sondheim; Styne
Snake Eyes   Arlen; Mercer
So Apart   Brooks
So Long, Farewell   Hammerstein; Rodgers
So Near and Yet So Far   Strouse
Social, The   Rome
Soft-Shoe, Sword Dance   Arlen; Mercer
Sole to Sole   David, Mack; Livingston, Jerry
Some People   Sondheim; Styne
Some People Take a Walk   Brooks
Somebody's Silver Jubilee   Burke
Somethin' Ya Gotta Find Out Yo'self   Mercer
Something in the Air   David, Hal
Something Is Going On   Myrow
Sometime Promises   Cahn; Van Heusen
Song of Green Mansions   Webster
Song of Unity   Revel
Sound and the Fury, The   Cahn
Sound of Music, The   Hammerstein; Rodgers
Souvenir de Montmartre   Drake
Spain   Adamson
Spring Is the Season for Remembering   Oakland
St. Peter's Square   Adamson; Warren
Stars Over the Pacific   Webster
Starting Out to Live Alone Again   Wrubel
Stay in Accord (With the Lord)   Robison
Staying Young   Merrill
Step Lightly Lady   Harburg
Step Right Up   Brooks
Step Up Closer   Brooks
Storm, The   Mercer
Straight to Baby   Evans; Livingston, Jay; Mancini
Straight to the Heart   Evans; Livingston, Jay; Mancini
Streak o' Lightnin'   Arlen; Mercer
Strum Strum Boogie   Brooks
Style   Martin
Summer in Your Eyes   Webster
Sunshine Song, The   Rome
Sunshine Song (inst.), The   Revel
Supplication   Revel
Swap Her for a Mule   Rome
Swing into Spring   Mercer
Swing Low, Sweet Chariot   Brooks
Swinging Along the Highway   Revel
Take a Giant Step   Evans; Livingston, Jay
Take Me Along   Merrill
Take Over   Robison
Talk It Out   Robison
Tambourine   Arlen; Mercer
Tangissimo   Arlen; Mercer
Taurus and Virgo   Spina
Te Guiero   Sigman
Teenie Weenie Bikini   Hoffman
Telephone Song   Brooks
Television U.S.A.   Cahn; Van Heusen
Tender Are the Ties   Sherman

Tess Mambo   Duke
Thank the Lord for This Thanksgiving Day   McHugh
That Kind of Woman   Bacharach; David, Hal
That Man's Wife   Merrill
That Old Enchanted Feeling   Burke
That's All I Need to Know   David, Hal
That's All (inst.)   Revel
That's How It Starts   Merrill
That's My Doll   Revel
That's What I Want for Christmas   Cahn; Van Heusen
That's What Love Is For   Revel
(I Love) The Way You Say It   Hoffman
(New In) The Ways of Love   David, Hal
Them Contrapuntal Eyes of Blue   Drake
Then Suddenly   Arlen; Mercer
There I Was   Duke
There Must Be a U.N. of Love   Spina
There'll Be a Hot Time in the Old Town Tonight   Brooks
There's a Rising Moon for Every Falling Star   Revel; Webster
There's Nothing Left to Do   Cahn; Van Heusen
These Thousand Hills   Warren; Washington
They Came to Cordura   Cahn; Van Heusen
Thin Man, The   Cahn
Thing-A-Ma-Jig, The   Hoffman
Things   Merrill
Think Love   Livingston, Jerry
Thinkin' Things   Merrill
Thinking It Over   Merrill
Third March   Arlen; Mercer
36-24-36   Evans; Livingston, Jay; McHugh
This Earth Is Mine   Cahn; Van Heusen
This Is My Town   Brooks
This Time of Year   Livingston, Jerry
Thou Shalt Not Love   Drake
Though   Drake
Though Half My Life (Is Spent)   Brooks
Though She Can't Add Up   Brooks
Three Hundred and Sixty-Five Days   Sherman
Three Little Maids from Damascus   Washington
Three Loves   Bacharach; David, Hal
(If I Had) Three Wishes for Christmas   Sondheim; Styne
Thunder in the Sun   Washington
Tick Tock — I'm a Cuckoo Clock (inst.)   Revel
Timeless Tide, The   Bacharach; David, Hal
Times Change   Bergman
To Dad with Love   Sherman
To Me   Davis
To Mother with Love   Sherman
To My Love   Evans; Livingston, Jay; Mancini
Toastin' Sequence   Arlen; Mercer
Together in Central Park   Duke
Together, Wherever We Go   Sondheim; Styne
Tomorrow Morning   Rome
Tomorrow's Mother's Day   Sondheim; Styne
Too Late (inst.)   Revel
Too Neat to Be a Beatnik, Too Proud to Be a Square   Cahn;
    Van Heusen
Toom Balalaika (Play Balalaika)   Hoffman
Torture   Freed, Ralph
Touch, The   David, Hal
Traffic Jam   Brooks
Tricky Fingers (inst.)   Blake
Trousseau Song   Fain; Webster
Twang, Twang, Twang   Cahn; Van Heusen
Twice as Tall   Cahn; Van Heusen

1960

Another Big Strike   Willson
Another Miracle of Love   Johnson, James P.
Anthem of the Clams   Van Heusen
Apache Dance (Inst.)   Brooks
Apple on a Cherry Tree   David, Hal
Arabian Market Place, The   Brooks
Arabian Mwaaah   Brooks
Are You Sure?   Willson
Arm of the Law (inst.), The   Revel
As Big As My Love for You   David, Hal
As I Was Walkin'   David, Hal
Asking for You   Comden and Green; Styne
At the Fair   Brooks
At the Quilting Party (inst.)   Revel
A-Tangle, A-Dangle   Loesser
Autumn Courting (inst.), The   Loesser
Baby, Talk to Me   Adams; Strouse
Back to Normal   Livingston, Jerry
Ballad of Caryl Chessman (Let Him Live, Let Him Live, Let
    Him Live), The   Hoffman
Ballad of Scatter Gun Hill, The   Livingston, Jerry
Ballad of the Alamo   Webster
Banks of the Danube   Revel
Bay of Angels   Fain; Parish
Be Anything but a Girl   Blane; Martin
Be Sure   Sigman
Be Yourself   Bergman
Bear Likes Honey, A   Brooks
Beatnik Do   Robison
Beautiful People of Denver   Willson
Before I Gaze at You Again   Lerner, Alan Jay; Loewe
Before We Leave the Air   Brooks
Belly Up to the Bar, Boys   Willson
Bet Steal or Borrow (Why Oh Why)   Lawrence
Between the River and the Railroad Track   Robison
Beware   Brooks
Beware of the Flaterer   Bergman
Bharatha Natyan   Fain; Webster
Big Brown Eyes, Red Cherry Lips   Friend
Bigger and Better Things   David, Hal
Birthdays Are Fun   Brooks
Blue for Blues   Bergman
Blue Note, A   Russell
Blues, Blues, Blues (If the Blues Was Money)   Bergman
Bon Jour (The Language Song)   Willson
Bookends   Brooks
(We Keep) Bouncing Back for More   Coleman; Leigh
Bowl of Boullabaisse, A   Revel
Break the Ice   Robison
Bring Back the Old Fashioned Waltz   Revel
Brother Against Brother   Livingston, Jerry
Buffalo Fight Song   Willson
Bunker Hill to Yorktown   Livingston, Jerry
By Golly, By Jingo   Hoffman
Cafe Badna Waltz   Revel
Call, The   Loesser
Call Me a Fool   Warren
Call to Wander, The   Loesser
Camelot   Lerner, Alan Jay; Loewe
Captain Buffalo   David, Mack; Livingston, Jerry
Catch Me If You Can   Livingston, Jerry
Celluloid Soliloquy   Oakland
Certain As the Sea Is Blue   Revel
C'est Moi   Lerner, Alan Jay; Loewe
Chicago Fire, The   Styne

Chick-a-pen   Willson
Child Is Born, A   Livingston, Jerry
Ching, Ching (Ding, Ding, Ding)   Sherman
Chisholm Trail   Brooks
Christ Has Come, The   Livingston, Jerry
Christ Is Alive   Livingston, Jerry
Christine   Fain; Webster
Cincinnati Tomorrow Night   Freed, Ralph
Circus Theme   Brooks
Clang Dang the Bell   Loesser
Class   Davis
Clean Livin'   David, Hal
Close   Bacharach
Cobra Ritual Dance (inst.)   Fain
Colonna Opening   Oakland
Colorado, My Home   Willson
Come Light the Lovelight   Sherman
Come on Down to Venezuala   Comden and Green; Styne
Como Esta Usted?   Sherman
Corduroy Road   Coleman; Leigh
Cottleston Pie   Brooks
Could've Been a Ring   Loesser
Courting, The   Loesser
Cradle in Bethlehem, A   Bryan
Crazy Times   Bacharach
Cremes   Bacharach
Cricket Song, The   Brooks
Crossroads   David, Mack
Crosstown Bus   Bacharach; David, Hal
Crucifixion, The   Livingston, Jerry
Cry for the Man   David, Hal
Cry Like the Wind   Comden and Green; Styne
Cry Wolf   Bergman
Cryin', Sobbin', Wailin'   Bacharach
Danny the Dragon   Styne
Date Night in Hawaii   Sherman
Dawn of Love, The   Sigman
Day Borrowed from Heaven, A   Loesser
Day I Do, The   Coleman; Leigh
Dear Liar   Eliscu
Denver Police, The   Willson
Devil with the Devil (The Devil Don't Frighten Me),
    The   Ruby
Diamonds in the Starlight   Blane; Martin
Divali Festival, The   Fain; Webster
Do It Yourself   Comden and Green; Styne
Doctor's Soliloquy, A   Fain; Webster
Dodie Ann   Sherman
Dolce Far Niente   Willson
Don't Be Ashamed of a Teardrop   Comden and Green;
    Styne
Don't Be Mean, Geraldine!   Sherman
Don't Oversell Me, Baby   Robison
Don't Run Upstairs   Robison
Don't Try to Figure It Out   Comden and Green; Styne
Dorrie's Wish   Loesser
Dragon's Last Ballad   Brooks
Dream Boy   Sherman
Dream with Me   David, Mack
Dreams for Sale   Friend
Dwight D. Eisenhower   Livingston, Jerry
Early Spring   McHugh; Washington
Eddie Jordan Story, The   Oakland
Eee-o Eleven   Cahn; Van Heusen
Eight Note Symphony, The   Oakland

I Gotta Go Home   Freed, Ralph
I Grew Up Last Night   Sigman
I Hear (Oil)   Coleman; Leigh
I Know about Love   Comden and Green; Styne
I Like the Ladies   Coleman; Leigh
I Love Him   Fain; Webster
I Loved You Once in Silence   Lerner, Alan Jay; Loewe
I May Never Fall in Love with You   Willson
I Need a Girl   Johnson, James P.
I Never Meant to Fall in Love   Fain; Webster
I Sang a Thousand Songs   Drake
I Was Yours   Russell
I Wish It Were Now   David, Hal
I Wisht I Wuz a Woman with a Past   Oakland
I Wonder What the King Is Doing Tonight   Lerner, Alan
      Jay; Loewe
If Ever I Would Leave You   Lerner, Alan Jay; Loewe
If I Had an Igloo   Blane; Martin
If I Knew   Willson
If I Should Love You Now   Robison
I'll Be Waiting for You   Brooks
I'll Bring the Ring   David, Hal
I'll Butter Him Up   Bergman
I'll Forsake You Not My Darling (inst.)   Revel
I'll Haunt You   Sigman
I'll Love You Always   David, Hal
I'll Never, Never Forget What's Her Name   Bacharach;
      David, Hal
I'll Never Say No   Willson
I'm a Cheese Man Myself   Bergman
I'm a Star of the Cinema   Oakland
I'm Building Castles Again   Coots
I'm from Hollywood   Oakland
I'm Going to the Ball (We're Going to the Ball)   Brooks
I'm in Love with You   Oakland; Raye
I'm Just a Little Sparrow   Fain; Webster
I'm Part of a Family   Brooks
I'm Ready   Friend
In My Own Irresistible Way   Coleman; Leigh
Incurably Romantic   Cahn; Van Heusen
Indoor Sport   Bacharach
Ireland Was Never Like This   Fain; Webster
Irvington   Revel
Is It Better?   Freed, Ralph; Livingston, Jerry
It Ain't Right   David, Hal
It Never Was You   Brooks
Italiannette   Sherman
It's Legitimate   Comden and Green; Styne
It's Lonely   Bergman
It's Only Or-ee-vwor (Au Revoir)   Livingston, Jerry
I've A'ready Started In   Willson
I've Got a Dream on My Hands   McHugh
I've Got Charm   Cahn; Van Heusen
I've Got Everything   Howard, Bart
I've Got Something to Sing About   Oakland
I've Had about As Much As I Can Take   Bergman
Jack the Ripper Song   McHugh
Jalopy Song, The   Styne
Jamie   David, Hal
Jazz in a Harem   Brooks
Jesus Died that Man Might Live   Livingston, Jerry
Joanie's Forever   Bacharach
Joe Dynamite's Dentistry Song   Coleman; Leigh
Johnny Fiddle   Livingston, Jerry
Johnny Freedom   Styne

Joseph   Livingston, Jerry
Jousts (inst.), The   Lerner, Alan Jay; Loewe
Joy of Loving You, The   Howard, Bart
Jubilee Tonight   Blake; Sissle
Juke Box Hop, The   Comden and Green; Styne
Just One Girl   Razaf
Just the Way You Are   Oakland
Kathakali   Fain; Webster
Keep-a-Hoppin'   Willson
Kelly Green (A Bit o' the Auld Sod) (inst.)   Warren
Kids   Adams; Strouse
King Midas Birthday Song   Brooks
Kiss Me Quick and Go   David, Hal
Korea, a Long Way from Home   Oakland
Lady of the Roses, The   Livingston, Jerry
Last Year's Love   Bacharach
Late, Late Show, The   Comden and Green; Styne
Leadville Johnny Brown   Willson
Let Me Be a People (Plain Old Me)   Brooks; Warren
Let's All Rally   Warren
Let's Make an Old Fashioned Christmas   Adamson;
      McHugh
Let's Make Love   Cahn; Van Heusen
Lie to Me   Russell
Liebelei   David, Hal
Life   Davis
Life's Not that Simple   Comden and Green; Styne
Light of My Life, The   David, Hal
Light Up!   Warren
Like Love   Ellington; Russell
Lipstick on Your Lips   David, Hal
Little Old New York   Styne
Little What-If, Little Could-Be   Coleman; Leigh
Living for Tonight   Sigman
Lone Wolf   Bergman
Lonely Blues   Friend
Lonesome Sailor Boy   Livingston, Jerry
Looking for Your Heart   Sherman
Lot of Livin' to Do, A   Adams; Strouse
Lovable Lips   David, Hal
Love in Outer Space   Comden and Green; Styne
Love Song   Adams; Strouse
Lovelight   David, Hal
Lovely Girls of Akbarabad, The   Fain; Webster
Luau Cha Cha Cha (Surfin' Luau)   Sherman
Lusty Month of May, The   Lerner, Alan Jay; Loewe
Magic Opera   Oakland
Magic Rabbit   Bergman
Mainly That (My Honey)   Robison
Make Someone Happy   Comden and Green; Styne
Man Is Nothing   Oakland
Man of the Hour   Brooks
Manhattan News Beat   Oakland
Many a Wonderful Moment   David, Hal
Many's the Time   Freed, Ralph
Manzinata (inst.)   Revel
Marcelle Wahine Special   Oakland; Raye
Marigold, Marry Me   Brooks
Mary's Prayer   Livingston, Jerry
Maybe, Baby, Maybe   Livingston, Jerry
Melancholy Madonna   Livingston, Jerry
Member of the Family   Robison
Men Are All Alike   Brooks
Mia Cara (Mia Amore)   Sherman
Mind Your Own Business   Robison

Mine Is but to Love You   Livingston, Jerry
Miracle of Love, The   Livingston, Jerry
Miscellaneous   Oakland
Moment of Madness, A   Russell
Mon Ami   Eliscu
Moonlight Madness   David, Hal
More and More   Bacharach
Movie Star   Russell
Mr. Ed   Evans; Livingston, Jay
Mr. Lucky Goes Latin   Evans; Livingston, Jay
Mr. Prairie (inst.)   Revel
Music of Home, The   Loesser
My Beauty   Loesser
My Confession of Love   Strouse
My Consolation   Washington
My Heart Goes Out to You   David, Hal
My Heart Will Tell You So   Lawrence
My Indian Family   Fain; Webster
My Little Lost Girl   Fain; Webster
My Little Room   Robison
My One and Only Girl   Webster
My Own Brass Bed   Willson
My Prairie Home   Robison
My Room   David, Mack
My Son   Livingston, Jerry
Mysterious   Friend
Naked Truth, The   Robison
Need for Love, The   Washington
Nellie Bly Song   Brooks
Never Will I Marry   Loesser
New Frontiers   Lawrence
New York, My New York!   Alter
Nice 'n' Easy   Bergman
Nicest Thing (That Ever Happened to Me), The   Hoffman
Nixon and Lodge (inst.)   Blake
No Hard Times   Robison
No More than Always   David, Hal
No More Women   Brooks
No Substitute for Love   Lawrence
No Trespassing   Johnson, Howard
No Wings on My Angel   David, Hal
Noah Was His Name   Livingston, Jerry
Noah's Ark   Livingston, Jerry
Nobody's Perfect   Cahn; Van Heusen
Nothing, Nothing, Nothing (inst.)   Revel
Nothing Personal   Bergman
Nothing Stays the Same   Friend
Oh, What a Difference You Made   DePaul
Ol' Circuit Rider, The   Robison
Ol MacDonald   Bergman
Old Country Doctor, The   Robison
Old Oaken Bucket, The   Drake
Older and Wiser   Adams; Strouse
On the Showboat   Styne
Once   David, Hal
Once a Teacher   Revel
One Boy (One Girl)   Adams; Strouse
One Day at a Time   Willson
One Day We Dance   Coleman; Leigh
One Last Kiss   Adams; Strouse
One Man Is Not Enough (inst.)   Revel
One Really Big Chance   Bacharach
One Way to Love   Oakland
Other Fella, The   Brooks; Warren
Our Concerto   David, Hal

Out of My Sentimental Mind   Bacharach
Outside My Window   David, Hal
(I Still Love You All) Padam . . . Padam   Raye
Paint Me a Picture   Howard, Bart
Parade (inst.)   Loewe
Path of Pride, The   Bacharach
Payday Today (Ole! It's Payday Today)   Sherman
People's Choice, The   Livingston, Jerry
Persuasion, The   Lerner, Alan Jay; Loewe
Philosophy   Oakland
Phoenix   Drake
Picture Medley 1 & 2   Oakland; Raye
Pine Country   Styne
Pineapple Princess   Sherman
Pink Pussy Cat, The   Livingston, Jerry
Pippi's Lullaby   Brooks
Playing Politics   Cahn; Van Heusen
Please, Please Signore   Sherman
Po Po Pocohantas   Brooks
Poor Archie (inst.)   Blake
Poor Katie Red (inst.)   Blake
Poor Little Tigger   Brooks
Popcorn Machine Broke Down, The   Sherman
Pray for Me   Cahn
President, The   Livingston, Jerry
Primitive Island   Davis
Princess Waltz (Once Upon a Time), The (inst.)   Warren
Private Eye   Oakland
Promised Land, The   Livingston, Jerry
Public Is Always Right, The   Cahn; Van Heusen
Put on a Happy Face   Adams; Strouse
Ragtime Polish Dance (inst.)   Blake
Railroad Soliloquy (inst.)   Revel
Raving Beauty, A   Blane; Martin
Reach for Tomorrow   McHugh; Washington
Read the Label on the Bottle (Don't Take My Word for It
    Neighbor) (Get Away Boys You Bother Me)   Willson
Recipe for Falling in Love (Quando Vien Labera)   Raye
Red, White and Blue of Hawaii, The   Adamson; Fain
Remember the Alamo   Livingston, Jerry
Reminiscing   Sigman
Ricksha   Brooks
Riddleweed   Loesser
Right Approach, The   Bergman
Right Girl on the Left Hand, The   David, Hal
Rise Up to Heaven   Livingston, Jerry
River and I, The   Myrow
River of His Pleasure, The   Robison
River, River   David, Hal
River Road   David, Hal
Road to God Knows Where (inst.)   Revel
Roaring Twenties, The   David, Mack; Livingston, Jerry
Rockin' and Rollin' in Loch Lomond   Davis
Rollin' On (inst.)   Revel
Romance   Donaldson; Leslie
Room in My Heart   Fain; Webster
Rosie   Adams; Strouse
Rough Riders, The   Livingston, Jerry
Rules of the Road, The   Coleman; Leigh
Runnin' Scared   Friend
Saddle and Go (inst.)   Revel
Safe in Your Arms   Russell
Saga of the Presidents, The   Livingston, Jerry
Sam, Sam (The Man What Am)   Berlin
Sam Spug Routine   Oakland

San Francisco Fran   Styne
Satellite City   Styne
Save a Place for Me   Brooks
Schmaltzy Waltz, The   Howard, Bart
Schonbrun Waltz   Revel
Sea of Heartbreak   David, Hal
Second Time Around, The   Cahn; Van Heusen
Sentimental Sailor   David, Hal
Sermon, The   Loesser
Seven Deadly Virtues, The   Lerner, Alan Jay; Loewe
Sewing Ballet (Inst.)   Brooks
Shall I Go, Shall I Tarry (inst.)   Revel
She Doesn't Understand Me   Comden and Green; Styne
She's Got the Biggest Parakeets in Town   Oakland
Ship's Concert   Brooks
Shortnin' Bread Special   Oakland
Showmanship   Cahn; Van Heusen
Shriner's Ballet   Strouse
Si, Si, Si   Baer
Sick Song, The   Sherman
Silver Dollar Boys   Robison
Simple Joys of Maidenhood, The   Lerner, Alan Jay; Loewe
Sing Ho for the Life of a Bear   Brooks
Sleepless Nights   Livingston, Jerry
Slow but Sure   Bergman
So Long   Friend
So Long Ma (Headin' for New Orleans)   Styne
So What's New   Oakland
Somebody   Brooks; Warren
Someone to Tell It To   Cahn; Van Heusen
Somewhere in My Heart   Friml
Song from Meantown   Brooks
Song Magician, The   Oakland
Song of Ruth, The   Webster
Song of the Camels   Blane
Song Without End   Washington
Sooner or Later   David, Hal
Spanish Rose   Adams; Strouse
Spare Me Your Kindess   Coleman; Leigh
Specialization   Cahn; Van Heusen
Spend the Afternoon with Me   Cahn; Van Heusen
Spring in Central Park   Gorney
Spring in Vienna   Revel
Spring Is Spring   Brooks
Square Jungle, The   Bergman
St. George Is Comin'   Brooks
Stagecoach to Mars   David, Hal
Star in the East, A   Livingston, Jerry
Stay in Love   Oakland
Stop Criticizin'   Robison
Street Songs   Adams; Strouse
Success   Comden and Green; Styne
Summer in Tyrol   Revel
Summer School   Brooks
Summertime Love   Loesser
Super Type o' Hypochondriac   Oakland
Surfside 6   David, Mack; Livingston, Jerry
Surprise Package   Cahn; Van Heusen
Suzie Wong (The Cloud Song)   Cahn; Van Heusen
Swiss Family Calypso   Sherman
Swiss Family Limbo   Sherman
Switch, The   Johnson, Howard
Sympatica   Oakland
'Tain't What Money Itself Can Do   Robison
Take a Job   Comden and Green; Styne

Take Me to You Ladder   Bacharach
Take My Love   Oakland
Takin' Time Out for Dreamin'   Woods
Talking Piano   Oakland
Tall, Dark and Handsome   Livingston, Jerry
Tall Hope   Coleman; Leigh
Telephone Hour, The   Adams; Strouse
Tell Me, Who's the Girl?   Sherman
Tell Us a Story   Bergman
Tempo of the Times, The   Coleman; Leigh
Ten Commandments, The   Livingston, Jerry
10,000 Years Ago   Bacharach
Ten Years Old   Sondheim
Tennessee Babe   Webster
Thanks to You I'm a Brand New Woman   Howard, Bart
That Man!   Cahn; Van Heusen
That's What I Want for Jamie   Coleman; Leigh
Theme from The Courtship of Eddie's Father   Young, Victor
Then It All Came True (inst.)   Revel
Then You May Take Me to the Fair   Lerner, Alan Jay; Loewe
There Comes a Time   Adams; Strouse
There's a Right Time   Robison
There's a Time   Warren
There's Someone Missing in the Picture   Woods
These Things I Know Are True   Adams; Strouse
They Really Don't You Know   McHugh
They've All Got Tails but Me   Brooks
Thieves Song, The   Brooks
Thieving Stranger   Drake
Thing Operetta   Oakland
Things I Thought I'd Hate About You (Turned Out to Be the Things I Love), The   Robison
Things with Strings   Friend
Thinkability   Coleman; Leigh
Thirty-three Years   Livingston, Jerry
This Is America   Davis
Tick-Dee   Brooks
Tiddley Pom   Brooks
Tim and Jim   Oakland
Time and Again   Sigman
Time to Love Is Now, The   Davis
Tippecanoe and Tyler Too   Livingston, Jerry
(Dancin' on My) Tippy Tippy Toes   Coleman; Leigh
To Love and to Lose   Comden and Green; Styne
To the Resuce   Bergman
Tomorrow   Willson
Tonight We Dance (inst.)   Revel
Touch of the Blues, A   Livingston, Jerry
Toy Carousel, The   Myrow
Trav'lin'   Robison
Tribute   Oakland
Tribute to Ted   Oakland
Trick, The   David, Hal
Troubles Are Bubbles   Brooks
Truck Driver's Lament   Brooks
Turf Routine   Oakland
Turn It On   Brooks; Warren
"Tweets" Says: I've Got Nine Lives — Do You?   Sissle
Tweets Says, I've Got Nine Lives, Do You?   Blake
Twenty Four Little Hours Ago   Von Tilzer
Two Arms   Russell
Two Figures on a Wedding Cake   Bacharach
Two Hour Honeymoon   Bacharach
Two Hugs (With a Kiss in the Middle)   Hoffman
Two of a Kind   Mercer

Unforgettable   Evans; Livingston, Jay
UNICEF Marching Song, The   Fain; Webster
Unloved   David, Hal
Up Where the Joke's Goin' Up   Willson
Up Where the People Are (inst.)   Willson
U.S. Grant   Livingston, Jerry
Vespers   Brooks
(He's a) V.I.P.   Styne
Visiting Firemen Opening   Oakland; Raye
Voodoo Man   Blake
Voulez-Vous Cha Cha Ma'm'selle?   Hoffman
Waiting, Waiting   Comden and Green; Styne
Wake Me When It's Over   Cahn; Van Heusen
Walkin' to Paradise   Friend
Walking Away Whistling   Loesser
War of 1812, The   Livingston, Jerry
Watch Out, New York!   Warren
Watch Out, Wake Up   Warren
Way Back West   Oakland; Raye
We Have Nothing to Fear   Livingston, Jerry
We Have So Much in Common   Coleman; Leigh
We Love You, Conrad!   Adams; Strouse
We Traveled Around   Brooks
Welcome Mat   Russell
Welcome Song (Your Indian Family), The   Fain; Webster
Well Thank You   Bergman
We're the Two Greatest Lovers in the World   Magidson;
   Oakland
What a Blessing   Loesser
What Did I Ever See in Him?   Adams; Strouse
What Do the Simple Folk Do?   Lerner, Alan Jay; Loewe
What Takes My Fancy   Coleman; Leigh
What's New at the Zoo?   Comden and Green; Styne
What's She Really Like   Silver
What's-His-Name   Blane; Martin
When a Woman Loves a Man   Young, Victor
When I Was One and Twenty   Bergman
When the Green Leaves Come Again   David, Hal
When You Come to the End of a Lollipop   Hoffman
When You Least Expect It   Stept
When You Walked By   Burke
When Your Lips Are Close to Mine   Livingston, Jerry
Where Does a Dream Go to Die   Livingston, Jerry
Where Else but the U.S.A.   Cahn; Van Heusen
Where in the World   Comden and Green; Styne
Where the Hot Wind Blows   McHugh
Whip of the Wind, The   Livingston, Jerry
Who Do We Thank   Adams; Strouse
Who Is Mr. Big?   Comden and Green; Styne
Who Needs It   Brooks
Who Was that Lady   Cahn; Van Heusen
Why Don't They Play the Old Songs on a New
   Piano   Oakland
Why Me?   Bergman
Wildcat   Coleman; Leigh
Windy City Special   Sherman
Wine, Women, Song, Women and Women, Women   Brooks
Woman I Was Before, The   Fain; Webster
Woman's Rights   Brooks
Word Portrait   Oakland
World at Large, The   Adams; Strouse
World I Live In, The   Lawrence
World of Miracles, A   Livingston, Jerry
Would You Let Me   Blane; Martin
Would You Mind   Revel

Ya Getta Get Up Early in the Morning (inst.)   Revel
Yamo Yamo   Oakland
Yes   Loesser
You Are for Loving   Blane; Martin
You Belong in Someone Else's Arms   Bacharach
You Go Into Your Dance   Bergman
You Make Me Feel at Home   Russell
You Meet the Strangest People   Oakland
You Nasty Clarinet   Gilbert; Oakland
You Take a Girl Like Me (inst.)   Revel
You'll Answer to Me   David, Hal
Young Emotions   David, Mack; Livingston, Jerry
Your Kisses Are Still on My Lips   David, Hal
You're a Liar   Coleman; Leigh
You're Everything I Love   Friend
You're Far Away from Home   Coleman; Leigh
You're My May Day   Warren
You're Sixteen   Sherman
You're the One Who Knows   Young, Victor
You've Come Home   Coleman; Leigh
Zazu Zazu Tree, The   Merrill

1961

Ada   David, Mack
Adrift on a Star   Harburg
All Aboard the Mine Train   Sherman
All Hands on Deck   Evans; Livingston, Jay
All' Italiana   Lawrence
Along Came Joe   Bacharach; David, Hal
Along the Prado   Coots
Am an Is, A   David, Mack
Amorita   Bergman
And I'll Be There (inst.)   Revel
And This Is Mine   Bacharach; David, Hal
Angel Baby   Parish
Angels Are Crying, The   Livingston, Jerry
Answer to Everything, The   Bacharach
Ants, The   Adams; Strouse
Apacionada   Russell
Astronaut of Space (Alan Shepard), The   Gilbert; Oakland
Audience, The   Adams; Strouse
Baby It's You   Bacharach; David, Mack
Baby's First Christmas   Davis
Bachelor in Paradise   David, Mack; Mancini
Bachelor's Ball, The   Fain; Raye
Backward Child   Davis
Barracuda   Bacharach
Be a Santa   Comden and Green; Styne
Be Prepared   Brooks
Beaucoup D'Amour   Howard, Bart
Beautiful Candy   Merrill
Been a Long Day   Loesser
Belinda's Rainy Day   Livingston, Jerry
Best Undressed Girl in Town   Evans; Livingston, Jay
Bloom Is Off the Rose, The   Dietz; Schwartz, Arthur
Blues in New Orleans (inst.)   Blake
Boom-Ti, Boom-Ti, Boom   Howard, Bart
Boy and His Dreams, A   David, Mack
Bozo's Hobby Song   Livingston, Jerry
Bozo's Magic Whistle   Livingston, Jerry
Brasilia (Sernata Negra)   Mercer
Breaking Point, The   Bacharach; David, Hal
Bright and Shiny   Sherman
Bring Your Darling Daughter   Dietz; Schwartz, Arthur

Broads Ain't People   Evans; Livingston, Jay
Brotherhood of Man   Loesser
By Love Possessed   Cahn
Carnival Ballet   Merrill
Carnival Samba   Sherman
Catalina Moon   Adamson
C'est La Vie   Coleman; Leigh
Cheatin' Billy   Bergman
Cheers for the Hero   Harburg
Chic, Chic, Chic Are We   Harburg
Chicken Fat   Willson
Chimneys Are Black, The   Blane
Christmas Wish, A   Blake
Cimarron   Webster
Cinderella, Darling   Loesser
Cobbler Cobbler   Sherman
Cockney Rhyming Slang   Bergman
Coffee Break   Loesser
Come A-Wandering with Me   Dietz; Schwartz, Arthur
Come Away   Dietz; Schwartz, Arthur
Come, Sweet Love   Howard, Bart
Come Waltz with Me   Cahn; Van Heusen
Comes Once in a Lifetime   Comden and Green; Styne
Company Way, The   Loesser
Danceannette   Sherman
Day By Day   Blake
Day the Snow Is Meltin', The   Burke
Dear Lord   Drake
Dee-lightful Is the Word   Burke
Deeply   Bacharach
Devil Does a Jig, The   Oakland
Dicty's on 7th Avenue (inst.)   Blake
Ding Dong Daddy Time   Livingston, Jerry
Direct from Vienna   Merrill
Disneyland '61   Sherman
Dog's Life, A   David, Hal
Donnybrook   Burke
Don't   Livingston, Jerry
Don't Break the Heart that Loves You   Davis
Don't Do Anything Dangerous   Bacharach; David, Hal
Don't Envy Me   Bacharach; David, Hal
Don't Go to Paris   Brooks; Warren
Don't Make Me Love You   David, Hal
Dowdling   Burke
Drink the Waters   Dietz; Schwartz, Arthur
Drinking Again   Mercer
Ellen Roe   Burke
Entrance of the Courtesans   Harburg
Esmeralda   David, Hal
Esmerelda   David, Mack
Eureka   Harburg
Evergreen Tree, The   Robison
Everybody's Lookin' (Around for an Angel)   Howard, Bart
Everything Beautiful   Evans; Livingston, Jay
Everything's Ducky   Spina
Ev'rybody Likes You   Merrill
Excuse My Laughter   Harburg
Explosive Generation, The   Webster
Fairyland   Merrill
Falcon and the Dove (Love Theme from El Cid),
    The   Webster
Far Off Village   Blane
Father, Brother, Uncle, Nephew   David, Mack; Livingston,
    Jerry
First Lady Waltz, The   McHugh; Washington

Five Minutes of Spring   Harburg
Flapper Flip, The   Sherman
Flubbber Theme (Flubber Song)   Sherman
Follow the Footprints   Howard, Bart
For My Own   Burke
For the First Time   Dietz; Schwartz, Arthur
Forever My Love   Bacharach; David, Hal
Frame without a Picture, A   David, Hal
Friendly Crickets, The   Robison
Full Moon Street   Blane
Gay Life, The   Dietz; Schwartz, Arthur
Gentle Love   Washington
Getting Married   Comden and Green; Styne
Girl Like That, A   Dietz; Schwartz, Arthur
Girl Like You, A   Blane
Girl Named Gigolette, A   Oakland; Webster
Girls Like Me   Comden and Green; Styne
Giuggiola   Cahn
Glide, The   Sherman
Glory That Is Greece, The   Harburg
God Is in the Plan   Robison
Golden, Delicious Fish   Merrill
Good Guy Always Wins, The   Livingston, Jerry
Goodbye   Bergman
Gotta Get a Girl   Bacharach; David, Hal
Grand Imperial Cirque de Paris   Merrill
Grand Old Ivy   Loesser
Great Expectations   Fain
Greek Marine Hymn, The   Harburg
Greeks Had a Word for It (The Olympics), The   Harburg
Green with Envy Blues   Sherman
Guns of Navarone, The   Webster
Happiest Girl in the World, The   Harburg
Happy Birthday Erwin   Evans; Livingston, Jay
Happy to Keep His Dinner Warm   Loesser
Happy with the Blues   Arlen
Hardest Thing in the World to Do, The   Blane
Hate   Howard, Bart
Have You Tried a Prayer   Fain; Raye
He Doesn't Know   Brooks; Warren
He Makes Me Feel I'm Lovely   Burke
He Needs You   Evans; Livingston, Jay
Heartless Human   Robison
Heigh Ho — Howdy Do   Bergman
Her Face   Merrill
Here She Is   Burke
Hey Fellas Let's Talk   Comden and Green; Styne
Hey Jimmy, Joe, John, Jack   Evans; Livingston, Jay
Hideaway Heart   Bacharach; David, Hal
His Own Little Island   Evans; Livingston, Jay
Honest Work   Evans; Livingston, Jay
Honestly   Harburg
Honey Bear   Evans; Livingston, Jay
How Can You Describe a Face   Comden and Green; Styne
How Many Stars Are There in the Sky?   Blane
How Soon, Oh Moon?   Harburg
How to Succeed in Business without Really Trying   Loesser
How Will I Remember You   Sigman
Howdy Friends (Salud Amigo)   Coots
Humming   Merrill
Hunder Runs Off to the Sea (inst.)   Blane
Hup-Two-Three   Harburg
I Am a Fact (I Am an Is)   David, Mack; Livingston, Jerry
I Am An Is   Livingston, Jerry
I Am Only Me   Lawrence

I Believe in Me   Blane
I Believe in You   Loesser
I Belong to Something   David, Mack; Livingston, Jerry
I Belong to the Majority   David, Mack; Livingston, Jerry
I Bought It   Lawrence
I Don't Think You Know How Much It Hurts Me   David, Hal
I Got It Made   Evans; Livingston, Jay
I Hate Him   Merrill
I Have My Own Way   Burke
I Hunder   Blane
I Just Can't Wait   Comden and Green; Styne
I Lost the Love of Anatol   Dietz; Schwartz, Arthur
I Love a Wedding   Dietz; Schwartz, Arthur
I Never Had a Chance   Dietz; Schwartz, Arthur
I Never Heard of a Singer that Didn't Want to Be   Cahn
I Remember   David, Hal
I Said It and I'm Glad   Comden and Green; Styne
I Wake Up Crying   Bacharach; David, Hal
I Walk a Little Dog   Comden and Green; Styne
I Want to Love You   Ellington
I Was a Shoo-In   Comden and Green; Styne
I Wish that I Could Say the Same   David, Hal
I Won't Twist   Cahn; Van Heusen
I Worry About You   Loesser
I Wouldn't Bet One Penny   Burke
I Wouldn't Have Had To   Evans; Livingston, Jay
I Wouldn't Marry You   Dietz; Schwartz, Arthur
Identify   David, Mack; Livingston, Jerry
If Flutterby Wins   Evans; Livingston, Jay
If It Hadn't Been for You   Dietz; Schwartz, Arthur
If It Isn't Everything   Burke
If Santa Claus Fell Asleep   Akst
If You Can Take Her from Someone (Someone Else Can Take Her from You)   Caesar
If You Don't Think I'm Leaving (Just Count the Days I'm Gone)   Cahn
If You Don't Want Me Now   David, Hal
I'll Be Forgetting You   Oakland; Raye
I'll Bring Along My Banjo   Bacharach
I'll Learn Ya   Evans; Livingston, Jay
I'll Meet You in Las Vegas   Oakland; Raye
I'll Never Waltz Again Without You   Cahn; Van Heusen
I'm Falling in Love with You Tonight   Davis
I'm Glad I'm Single   Dietz; Schwartz, Arthur
I'm Just Taking My Time   Comden and Green; Styne
I'm Kissing Her Now   Bryan
I'm Ludwig Von Drake   Sherman
I'm Not Lonely   Bergman
I'm with You   Friend
In a Fanciful Mood   Lerner, Sammy
In the Night (inst.)   Strouse
In the Privacy of My Dreams   David, Mack
Incidental Music   Gorney
International Twist, The   Oakland
Introduction to Foreign Carols   Freed, Ralph
Is It Just for Tonight   Coots
Is This a Private Song (Or Can Anyone Sing Along)   Hoffman
Island Lullaby   Howard, Bart
It Does My Heart Good   Baer
It Gets You   Sherman
It Hurts too Much to Laugh   David, Hal
It Moves   David, Hal
It Only Took a Minute   David, Hal

It Was a Very Good Year   Drake
It Was Always You (Always, Always You)   Merrill
It's a Great Time of the Year   Howard, Bart
It's a Great World After All   Razaf
It's a Serious Situation!   Blane
It's Funny (When You Fall in Love)   Warren
It's Goodnight Time (It's Time to Say Goodnight Again)   Davis
It's Spring, It's Spring   Raye
It's You and Me   Johnson, James P.
I've Cried a Million Years   Davis
I've Got the Place for You, Baby   Howard, Bart
I've Got to Find a Reason   Merrill
James Van Heusen's Melody (inst.)   Van Heusen
Judy Says   David, Hal
Just an Honest Mistake   Evans; Livingston, Jay
Just As You were in My Dreams   Johnson, James P.
Just Right for Saturday Night   David, Hal
Just What I Wanted   Dietz; Schwartz, Arthur
Knit Pretty   Loesser
La Caranga   David, Hal
Label on the Bottle, The   Dietz; Schwartz, Arthur
Ladies' Man   Brooks; Warren
Lady Luna   Howard, Bart
Last Bus Left at Midnight, The   David, Hal
Laurie, My Love   Livingston, Jerry; Oakland; Webster
Lemon Twist   Mills
Let It Ride   Evans; Livingston, Jay
Let Me Be with You   David, Mack
Let Me Get Away   Howard, Bart
Let Your Lips Tell Me Once   Caesar
Let's Back Jack!   Coots
Let's Get Together   Sherman
Let's Go Bowling   Coots
Let's Sing Like a Dixieland Band   Bergman
Little Friend (Lullaby to a Turkey)   Evans; Livingston, Jay
Little Jazz Cantata   Rome
Little Old Gehenna   Harburg
Little White Diamonds   David, Hal
Live It Up   Bergman
Loneliness or Happiness   Bacharach; David, Hal
Lonesomest Girl in the World, The   Harburg
Look at All I Belong To   David, Mack; Livingston, Jerry
Look in Your Eyes, The   Bergman
Look of Love, The   Bergman
Looking for Myself   Merrill
Love from a Heart of Gold   Loesser
Love in a Goldfish Bowl   Bacharach; David, Hal
Love Is Crazy   Brooks
Love Is the Greatest   Evans; Livingston, Jay
Love Lessons   Bacharach; David, Hal
Love Let Me Know   Evans; Livingston, Jay
Love Looks So Well on You   Bergman
Love Makes the World Go 'Round (Theme from Carnival)   Merrill
Love Songs Are Born in Paris (Tout le Sonheur du Monde)   Parish
Loveable Irish, The   Burke
Lovers in New York   Evans; Livingston, Jay; Mancini
Love-Sick Serenade   Harburg
Lysistrata's Serenade   Harburg
Maggie's Theme (For Now, For Always)   Sherman
Magic Age Is Seventeen, The   Styne
Magic Falute, The   Harburg
Magic, Magic   Merrill

Magic Moment   Dietz; Schwartz, Arthur
Magical Island, The   Howard, Bart
Make Believe Lover   David, Hal
Make Me Look Good Tonight   Robison
Make-Believe Lover   Drake
Man Must Be Something, A   David, Mack; Livingston, Jerry
Man of Vision, A   Comden and Green; Styne
Man Who Shot Liberty Valance, The   Bacharach; David, Hal
Man with a Plan, A   Comden and Green; Styne
Manpower   Bacharach
Many Tears on Many Pillows   David, Hal
Marianna   Webster
Marriage-Go-Round   Bergman
Maybe Tomorrow but Not Today   David, Hal
Medfield Fight Song (Absent-Minded Professor
      March)   Sherman
Memphis Kindness   Robison
Men in Meninak, The   Coots
Mighty Smith Is She, The   Fain
Million and Fifty Things, A   David, Mack; Livingston, Jerry
(Can You Imagine That) Mira   Merrill
Miracle of St. Marie, The   Bacharach
Miss Satan   Lawrence
Miss Universe   Davis
Miss U.S.A.   Davis
Mocking Bird Song   Drake
Money Doesn't Care Who Has It   Hoffman
Moods (inst.)   Warren
Moon Guitar   Bacharach; David, Hal
Moon River   Mancini; Mercer
Moonlight Music   Spina
More, More, More   Raye; Sigman
Morgan the Pirate   McHugh
Move Me on the Back Beat   Bacharach; David, Mack
Mr. Flynn   Burke
My Heart Is a Ball of String   Bacharach; David, Hal
(Within the Bound'ries of) My Little Bitty Ever Lovin'
      Heart   David, Hal
My Love   Bergman
My Mind Says Don't   Harburg
My State, My Kansas, My Home   Willson
Name It and It's Yours   Cahn; Van Heusen
Never Be-Devil the Devil   Harburg
Never Trust a Virgin   Harburg
New Mexico Alma Mater Hymn, The   Brown, Nacio Herb;
      Freed, Arthur
Nicest Thing, The   Evans; Livingston, Jay
Night Time in New York   Davis
N.M.S.U. Aggie Alma Mater   Brown, Nacio Herb
No News Blues   Clare
No Regrets   David, Hal
Nobody But Nobody   Lawrence
Now I Have Someone   Comden and Green; Styne
Now I'm Ready for a Frau   Dietz; Schwartz, Arthur
Oasis   Mercer
Oath, The   Harburg
Oceans of Love   Sigman
Offering Ballet (inst.), The   Blane
Oh — What a Crazy Song   Webster
Oh, Mein Liebchen   Dietz; Schwartz, Arthur
Oh What a Wonderful Night   Stept
Old Doc Flirtingrinder   Oakland
Old Man Time   Friend
Old Pied Piper, The   Harburg
On Second Thought   Coleman; Leigh

Once in a Dream   Gordon
One Happy Family   Ruby
One Hundred and One Dalmatians   Sherman
One Part Dog, Nine Parts Cat   Bacharach
Organization Man   Loesser
Our Church Is So Active   Gorney
Overture to the Blues   Howard, Bart
Papa Loves Twistin'   Hoffman
Paradise Harbour Coconut Beach Hotel   Howard, Bart
Parent Trap, The   Sherman
Paris Original   Loesser
Pause in the Day's Recreation (Wassail and Skoll),
      The   Gorney
Persian Women   Harburg
Pick Up the Pieces   David, Hal
Pillow Magic   Eliscu
Pipe and Slippers   David, Mack; Livingston, Jerry
Playhouse Rock   Adams; Strouse
(Don't Go) Please Stay   Bacharach
Pleasure of His Company, The   Cahn
Pocketful of Miracles   Cahn; Van Heusen
Politics   Harburg
Portofino   Sigman
Prelude to Love   Friend
Prettier Than a Picture   Revel
Pretty Little Girl in the Yellow Dress   Washington
Profit and the Loss, The   Gorney
Puffed Up Proud   Eliscu
Quiet Life, A   Burke
Quillow Plants the Blue Men   Blane
Ragtime Piano Tricks (inst.)   Blake
Restless Love   Adamson
Return to Peyton Place Theme   Webster
Rhodopa's Tavern   Harburg
Rich, The   Merrill
Ride Through the Night   Comden and Green; Styne
Ring-a-Ding Ding   Cahn; Van Heusen
Rising Moon (inst.), A   Revel
Rock and Rollin' on a Saturday Night   Blake
Rock Me, Lord   Robison
Rock-a-Cha   Sherman
Rock-a-Polka   Sherman
Roll Call   Blane
Romany Eyes of Love   Bryan
Rosa Linda   Sigman
Rosemary   Loesser
Rosita   Johnson, James P.
Run, Run, Run   Evans; Livingston, Jay
Sabre Song   Harburg
Sad Was the Day   Burke
Sanctuary (Don't Know Where I'm Goin')   Bergman
Saturday Sweethearts   David, Hal
Schlissel's Retort   Merrill
Scratch a Wife and Find a Doll   Harburg
Scuttlebutt Walk (inst.), The   Spina
Seasons of Youth   Drake
Secretary Is Not a Toy, A   Loesser
Seeing You with Somebody Else   Coots
Sentimental Baby   Bergman
Serendipity   Sherman
Seven Kinds of Lonesome   David, Mack
Sez I   Burke
Shadows in My Heart   Coots
Shall We Say Farewell?   Harburg
She's My Love   Merrill

She's So Beautiful   Howard, Bart
Sick, Sick, Sick   Harburg
Simple Serenade   Harburg
Slowly   Harbach
Snow Man   Oakland
So Do I   Davis
So Long As He Loves You   Howard, Bart
Somebody Else's Sweetheart   Bacharach; David, Hal
Something You Never Had Before   Dietz; Schwartz, Arthur
Somewhere There's a Home   Evans; Livingston, Jay
Song of the Rain   Parish
Song of the Teamsters Union   Caesar
Spectrum Song   Sherman
Spin I'm In, The   Sherman
St. Tropez   Warren
Starting with You (I'm Through)   Ellington
Station Dance (inst.)   Styne
Station Rush (inst.)   Styne
Status   Loesser
Stickum   David, Hal
Story Behind My Tears, The   Bacharach; David, Hal
Strange Duet (When You Help a Friend Out)   Comden and
    Green; Styne
Strategy   Harburg
Strollin' thru the Park   Bergman
Strummin' Song   Sherman
Subway Directions   Comden and Green; Styne
Subway Incident (inst.)   Styne
Subways Are for Sleeping   Comden and Green; Styne
Suddenly You Were Mine   Sigman
Summer Night (Cielito Lindo)   Bergman
Sunday Morning   Burke
Sweet Man   Evans; Livingston, Jay
Sweet Thursday   Livingston, Jerry; Webster
Sweet Violets   Sigman
Swing Your Projects   Comden and Green; Styne
Swingin' thru the Park   Bergman
Sword, the Rose and the Cape, The   Merrill
Take Apart My Broken Heart (inst.)   Revel
Tall the Sky   Styne
Tanz Mit Mir (Blue Bird Girls)   Merrill
Tender Is the Night   Fain; Webster
Test of Time, The   David, Mack
Thank You, Thomas Cook   Lawrence
(With) That Sophisticated Twist   Coleman; Leigh
That'll Be the Day   Harburg
That's My Kind of Christmas   Livingston, Jerry; Webster
That's The Way with Love   Sigman
There Ain't Nothin' Bigger than My Love for You   Oakland;
    Webster
There's a Friendly Feeling in the Air   Davis
There's No One Like You   Evans; Livingston, Jay
There's No Such Word as "Can't"   Blane
There's Something About a Horse   Evans; Livingston, Jay
Third Window from the Right, The   Bacharach; David, Mack
Thirty Miles of Railroad Track   Bacharach
This Is It   David, Mack; Livingston, Jerry
This Kind of a Girl   Dietz; Schwartz, Arthur
This Much I Understand   Lawrence
This World We Love In (Il Cielo in una Stanza)   Raye
Thousand Blue Bubbles, A   Howard, Bart
Three Friends (Two Lovers)   Bacharach; David, Hal
Three Wheels on My Wagon   Bacharach
Thunder and Lightning   Russell
Tiger By the Tail, The   Gorney

Time and Time and Time Again   Oakland
Tina   Cahn; Van Heusen
To Be Continued   Oakland
Toast to the Bride, A   Burke
Too Late to Worry   Bacharach
Torch Burns at Midnight, The   Parish
Touchstone   Oakland
Tower of Strength   Bacharach
Town Without Pity   Washington
Train's Gonna Be Dere Tonight, The   Robison
Traveling Around the World   Brooks
Trust Me   Evans; Livingston, Jay
Turn Back the Clock   David, Hal
26 Miles of Barbed Wire   Freed, Ralph
Under the Yum Yum Tree Cha Cha   Sterling; Von Tilzer
Unknown   David, Hal; Russell
Until I Get You in My Arms   David, Hal
Valerie   David, Hal
Very Nice Man, A   Merrill
Vignettes   Dietz; Schwartz, Arthur
Vive la Virture   Harburg
Wastin' Away for You   Bacharach; David, Hal
Ways of Love, The   Bergman
We Meet Again   Bergman
We Rich, Rich, Rich   Howard, Bart
We're Off to the Races   Harburg
What a Charming Couple   Dietz; Schwartz, Arthur
What a Wonderful Life   Livingston, Jerry
What Is This Feeling in the Air   Comden and Green; Styne
Whatever That May Be   Harburg
What's an Isn't   David, Mack; Livingston, Jerry
What's in Your Heart   Friend
When a Girl Is Beautiful   Cahn
When Does It Get to Be My Time   Lawrence
When I'm Dancing   Eliscu
When It's Summer   Burke
When Knighthood Was in Flower   Bergman
When You Look at the World   Howard, Bart
When Your Heart Is Too Young   Harburg
Where Have I Heard that Song Before?   Harburg
Where the Four Winds Blow   Webster
Whistling at the Boys   Sherman
Who Can Say   Russell
Who Can? You Can!   Dietz; Schwartz, Arthur
Who Knows What Might Have Been   Comden and Green;
    Styne
Who Needs a Woman?   Harburg
Who's Doing What to Erwin?   Evans; Livingston, Jay
Who's in Your Arms Tonight (inst.)   Revel
Whose Hat Is That (In the Hall)   Raye
Why Go Anywhere at All?   Dietz; Schwartz, Arthur
Wind Quillow Up (inst.)   Blane
Wind Song   Howard, Bart
Winning Combination   David, Hal
Wisha Wurra   Burke
Without a Word of Complaint   Ellington
Wonder of Moods   Bacharach; David, Hal
Wonderful Wonderful   Washington
Wonderful World of Color, The   Sherman
Word of Praise   Robison
Words of Uncle Jim, The   Robison
World of No Goodbyes, A   Fain; Webster
World of Tomorrow, The   Heyman
Would You Let Me   Blane
Wowee   Livingston, Jerry

1962

Yassu (Wedding Song)   Washington
Yes, My Heart   Merrill
You Can Have Paris   Russell
You Don't Have to Be a Tower of Strength   Bacharach
You Live in a House   David, Mack; Livingston, Jerry
You Make Me Feel So Loved   David, Hal
You Mean Everything to Me   Evans; Livingston, Jay
You Only See What You Want to See   David, Hal
You Will Never Be Lonely   Dietz; Schwartz, Arthur
You Wish I'll Wash   Russell
You Won't Be Sorry   David, Hal
Your Favorite Fool   David, Hal
Your Hand in Mine   Eliscu
You're Following Me   Bacharach
You're Not the Type   Dietz; Schwartz, Arthur
You're Someone Special   Evans; Livingston, Jay
You're Telling Our Secrets   Bacharach; David, Hal
You're the Acme of Perfection (inst.)   Revel
You're Tired of Me (Mi Vudi Lasciar)   Raye
Yum, Tiki, Tiki, Tum, Tum   Merrill

1962

Above the Stars   Merrill
Adios Amigo   Freed, Ralph; Livingston, Jerry
After One Kiss   Heyman; Mancini
Ah-oom   Merrill
Al-Di-La   Drake
All My Hopes, All My Dreams, All My Prayers   David, Hal
All That I Do   Livingston, Jerry
All the Love in the World   Adams; Strouse
All the Sad Young Man   Livingston, Jerry; Webster
Allo, Allo, Allo   Cahn
Alone in the World   Merrill; Styne
Although I Dropped $100,000   Sherman
And Still I Love Her   Bergman
And then Some   Ellington
Animal Attraction   Adams; Strouse
Anonymous Phone Call   Bacharach; David, Hal
Another Tear Falls   Bacharach; David, Hal
Any Day Now   Bacharach
Argentine   Ellington; Mills; Parish
As Big As Texas   David, Mack
As Young as You Feel   Martin
Baby Elephant Walk   David, Hal; Mancini
Baby-o   Mercer
Back to School Again   Adams; Strouse
Ballad of the Garment Trade   Rome
Ballad of the Mooncussers   Sherman
Baltimore Todalo (inst.), The   Blake
Be a Mother   Coleman; Leigh
Be a Performer!   Coleman; Leigh
Be Careful   Livingston, Jerry
Be My Host   Rodgers
Being in Love   Willson
Bell that Couldn't Jingle, The   Bacharach
Bella Bella Florence   Sherman
Big Red Theme   Sherman
Big Town Blues, The   Carmichael
Biggest Sin of All, The   Davis
Bird Man, The   David, Mack
Birthday Child   Baer; Leslie
Birthday Party (Rich Kid's Rag)   Coleman; Leigh
Blanket on the Beach   David, Hal
Blue Butterfly   Drake

Blue Mood   Ellington
Blues Don't Care Who Gets Them, The   Bacharach; David, Hal
Blues Is What I Got   Hoffman
Bon Voyage   Sherman
Bon Voyage Waltz   Sherman
Boogie Woogie Bakery Man   Sherman
Boom-Boom (Le Grand Boom-Boom)   Coleman; Leigh
Both Ends Against the Middle   Eliscu
Bottom of the Middle Class   Lawrence
Bozo's Holiday   Livingston, Jerry
Bozo's Marching Song   Livingston, Jerry
Bozo's Pocket Rocket   Livingston, Jerry
Brand New Boy   David, Hal
Bride, The   Fain; Webster
Bride of the Sea   David, Hal
Bring Me My Bride   Sondheim
Brittwood Rag (inst.)   Blake
Broken-Hearted Boy   David, Hal
Bubbles   Arlen; Harburg
Bumper to Bumper   Baer; Leslie
Butterfly (De Jour La)   Parish
Bye Bye Birdie   Adams; Strouse
Call Off the Wedding (Without a Groom there Can't Be a Bride)   Bacharach; David, Hal
Can't You Believe It   Bacharach
Canzone D'Amore   Sherman
Cara Mia   Freed, Ralph
Carriage for Alida, A   Eliscu
Castaway   Sherman
Celebration #1   David, Mack
Changeable   Parish
Charleston Charlie   Sherman
Christmas Land   Merrill
Christmas Song   Warren
Cissy, I Love You   Johnson, James P.
Clock without Hands, A   Livingston, Jerry; Webster
Cloud By Day, A   Livingston, Jerry
Come on Strong   Cahn; Van Heusen
Comedy Tonight   Sondheim
Coming Down the Stairs   Johnson, James P.
Cornflower Blue   David, Mack
Corporation Is Our Soul, The   Gorney
Cream Puff   Mancini; Mercer
Creole   Johnson, James P.
Cripple Creek   Bergman
Dancing Princess   Merrill
Danny   Raye
Darktown Huskin' Bee, The   Johnson, James P.
(We Had a) Date with Destiny   Revel
Daughter of Silence   Sigman
Deep Down Inside   Coleman; Leigh
Diamond Head   David, Mack
Did I Just Fall in Love?   Martin
Dimples   Coleman; Leigh
Dirty Face   Martin
Do I Have to Say More   Bacharach; David, Hal
Do I Need You?   Harburg
Doing Time   Coleman; Leigh
Donna Means Heartbreak   David, Hal
Don't Be Afraid of Romance   Berlin
Don't Do It Darlin'   Adamson; McHugh
Don't Let It Get Away   David, Hal
Don't Make Me Over   Bacharach; David, Hal
Don't Rush Me   Livingston, Jerry

Down Home Stomp   Ellington
Downtown Saturday Night   David, Hal
D-R-A-G-O-N (Dee-Are-A-Gee-O-En)   Merrill
Dream Along with Bozo   Livingston, Jerry
Dreamin' All the Time   Bacharach
Dreaming   Bloom; Koehler
Eager Beaver   Rodgers
Eat a Little Something   Rome
Echo Song, The   Sondheim
Emile's Reel   Sherman
Empty Pockets Filled with Love   Berlin
Enjoy It   Sherman
Enthusiasm   Brooks
Errand of Mercy, An   Bacharach; David, Hal
Eubie's Slow Drag (inst.)   Blake
Everybody Ought to Have a Maid   Sondheim
Everybody's Twisting   Bloom; Koehler
Everyone Who's Been in Love with You (Has Cried and
    Cried and Cried)   Bacharach; David, Hal
Everything They Say About Love Is True   Blake; Sissle
Evil Eye   Russell
Face, The   Martin
Family Way, The   Rome
Fanfare and Drums   David, Mack
Fate Said Only You   Young, Joseph
Father's Daughter   Eliscu
Feeling No Pain   Bacharach
Feeling of Jazz, The   Ellington
Few Tender Words, A   David, Mack
Fight Song, The   Adams; Strouse
Find a Star of Your Own   Livingston, Jerry
First Lady, The   Berlin
First Sip of Love   Young, Joseph
Flamenco Guitar   Parish
For Adults Only   Drake
For Every Young Heart   Davis
For Want of Your Love   David, Hal
Forgetting You   Raye
Forgive Me (for Giving You Such a Bad Time)   Bacharach;
    David, Hal
Fortune Teller (inst.)   Johnson, James P.
Forty Long Years   Livingston, Jerry
Framed   Ellington; Razaf
Free   Sondheim
Free at Last   Arlen; Harburg
Funeral Dirge   Sondheim
Funny Thing Happened (On My Way to Love), A   Rome
Gaggle of Geese, The   Sondheim
Game of Chance, A   Drake
Genteel   Eliscu
Gentlemen's Understanding   Eliscu
Get Off the Grass Liza Jane   Johnson, James P.
Gift of a Second Chance, The   Coleman; Leigh
Gift (Recado Bossa Nova), The   Webster
Gift Today (The Bar Mitzvah Song), A   Rome
Gigot   Cahn
Glad to Be Home   Berlin
Glamorous   Ellington; Mills
Go Ahead, Break My Heart   Freed, Ralph
Goin' to the Zoo   Livingston, Jerry
Golden Calf, The   Livingston, Jerry
Gone But Not Forgotten   Bergman
Goodbye Is a Lonesome Sound   Bergman
Grab Them While You Can   Rome
Greyfriar's Bobby   Sherman

Gypsy Camp   David, Mack
Gypsy Fire   Merrill
Hail Alma Mater   Willson
Hands   Russell
Hang a Lantern in Your Window   Sherman
Happy Lot, A   Martin
Harlem Bon-Bon Babies   Johnson, James P.
Have a Dream   Adams; Strouse
Have I Told You Lately?   Rome
Hav-Zies   Mercer
Hazel   Cahn; Van Heusen
He Had a Little Gun   Russell
He Pulled the Temple Down   Johnson, James P.
Head in the Stars   Eliscu
Hear o' Israel   Livingston, Jerry
Heart of Mine   Washington
Hello Dere   Davis
Her Name Is Joanna   David, Hal
Here Come the Dreamers   Martin
Here's to Us   Coleman; Leigh
Hey, Little Girl   Young, Joseph
Hold On to Your Heart   Revel
Home in the Meadow   Cahn
Home Is the Shepherd   Livingston, Jerry
Home Is Where the Heart Is   David, Hal
Honorable Bozo   Livingston, Jerry
Horse Won't Talk, The   Arlen; Harburg
House of Marcus Lycus, The   Sondheim
How   Livingston, Jerry
How Dad   Rodgers
How Happy We'll Be If You'll Just Care Again   Burke
How Small We Are   Van Heusen
I Can Teach Them   Adams; Strouse
I Can't Reach Your Heart   Davis
I Couldn't Have Done It Alone   Adams; Strouse
I Didn't Ask to Be Born   Ruby
I Didn't Believe   Young, Joseph
I Do Like You   Sondheim
I Find I'm Lost without You   Lewis
I Just Don't Know what to Do with Myself   Bacharach;
    David, Hal
I Know Someone   Brooks
I Let a Tear Fall in the River   David, Mack; Livingston, Jerry
I Love to Sing   Davis
I Love You (As Much As I Am Able)   Coleman; Leigh
I Love You Too Much   Washington
I Lulee, Lulee   David, Mack
I Met Lincoln   Leslie; Schwartz, Jean
I, Miles Gloriousus   Sondheim
I Miss You and You're Not Even Gone   David, Hal
I Sailed Yesterday   Bacharach
I Smiled Yesterday   Bacharach; David, Hal
I Used to Be Everybody's Baby   Davis
I Wonder What It's Like to Be in Paris   Warren
If and When   Cahn; Myrow
If I Can't Have All   Johnson, James P.
If I Ever Catch the Guy Who Taught My Wife the
    Twist   Fain
If I Never Get to Love You   Bacharach; David, Hal
If I Were You   Adams; Strouse
If You Haven't Got an Ear for Music   Berlin
I'll See You at the "Mets"   Baer
I'm a Stranger to Myself   Bergman
I'm Blue for You   Sherman
I'm Calm   Sondheim

I'm Fascinating   Adams; Strouse
I'm Not a Well Man   Rome
I'm Not in Philadelphia   Adams; Strouse
I'm Not the Marryin' Kind   David, Mack
I'm Setting a Trap   Blake; Sissle
Impossible   Sondheim
In Our Hide-Away   Berlin
In the Land of Elephants   Sigman
In the Stores (Quartermaster Stories)   Russell
In the Wilderness   Livingston, Jerry
In Time In a Brownstone Mansion   Eliscu
In Your Arms   Davis
Inspiration   Martin
Instant Love   Bergman
Invocation   Sondheim
Irish Twist   Mills
Is He the Only Man in the World   Berlin
Island Called Love, An   Oakland
It Get's Lonely in the White House   Berlin
It Happens Every Spring   Raye
It's a Darn Good Thing   Cahn; Van Heusen
It's Fun to Think   Adams; Strouse
It's Funny When You Fall in Love   Warren
It's Great to Be Back on Broadway   Merrill; Styne
It's Heartbreak Time   David, Hal
It's Love that Really Counts (in the Long Run)   Bacharach;
   David, Hal
It's Me Remember   McHugh
It's So Heartwarming   Eliscu
It's the Little Things in Texas   Rodgers
It's Up to Me   Adams; Strouse
I've Got Class   Brooks
I've Got to Be Around   Berlin
I've Got Troubles   Young, Joseph
I've Got Your Number   Coleman; Leigh
I've Just Seen Her   Adams; Strouse
I've Never Seen Anything Like It in My Life   Adams;
   Strouse
Jeanne with the Light Brown Rug   Brooks
Joanie's Shadow   David, Hal
Joey   Cahn; Van Heusen
Johnny Get Angry   David, Hal
Judy, You'll Never Know   Freed, Ralph
Just for Tonight   Carmichael; Mancini; Mercer
Keep on Treating Me Sweet   Ellington
Keep Passing the Buck   Gorney
Keep Your Eyes Open   Livingston, Jerry
Kitchen Tom (inst.)   Blake
Knights of the Headless Horse   Sherman
La, La, La   Rodgers
Lafayette   Coleman; Leigh
Land of No Love, The   David, Hal
Latin Quarter Twist   Mills
Laugh It Up   Berlin
Lazy Rhapsody   Ellington; Parish
Legend of Echo Mountain, The   Livingston, Jerry
Legend of Lobo, The   Sherman
Let's Climb (Grimpons)   Sherman
Let's Go Back to the Waltz   Berlin
Let's Make History Tonight   David, Hal
Let's Not Be Sensible   Cahn; Van Heusen
Let's Sit this One Out   Cahn; Van Heusen
Life   Revel
Light Goes On, the Light Goes Off, The   David, Hal
Light in the Piazza   Freed, Arthur

Like the Fellow and the Girl on the Late, Late Show   David,
   Hal
Little Betty Falling Star   Bacharach
Little Cutey   Johnson, Howard
Little Drops of Rain   Arlen; Harburg
Little Me   Coleman; Leigh
Little Night Music, A   Martin
Livin' Doll   David, Hal
Living Alone   Adams; Strouse
Loads of Love   Rodgers
Long After Tonight   Bacharach; David, Hal
Look No Further   Rodgers
Look of Love, The   Drake
Lord Provideth, The   Livingston, Jerry
Lord's Bright Blessing, The   Merrill; Styne
Love, I Hear   Sondheim
Love in Loveliness, The   David, Hal
Love Is a Lovely Word   Webster
Love Is in the Air   Sondheim
Love Makes the World Go   Rodgers
Love of a Boy, The   Bacharach; David, Hal
Love Story   Webster
Lovely   Sondheim
Lucinda Lee   Blake; Sissle
Lucy Brown   Johnson, James P.
Ma Belle Paree   Mercer
Mad   Livingston, Jerry
Magic Little Words   Blake
Main Street USA   Sherman
Maine   Rodgers
Make It Easy on Yourself   Bacharach; David, Hal
Mama Mia   McHugh
Mama's Little Girl   Coleman; Leigh
Man Named Moses, A   Livingston, Jerry
Man Who Has Everything, The   Rodgers
Mardi Gras Waltz, The   McHugh; Washington
Massachusetts   McHugh
Matter of Who, A   Russell
Me   David, Hal
Meat and Potatoes   Berlin
Melody for Two Sonnets, A   Raye
Melt Us!   Adams; Strouse
Merci Beaucoups   Sherman
Mets Are on the Move, The   Coots
Mewsette   Arlen; Harburg
Mexican Divorce   Bacharach
Midian   Livingston, Jerry
Miles Gloriosus   Sondheim
Minor Melody for Mavis, A   David, Mack
Minor Poet, The   Raye
Miss Marmelstein   Rome
Mister Piano Man   Sherman
Momma, Momma   Rome
Mon Amour Perdu   Sherman
Money Cat, The   Arlen; Harburg
More Hearts Are Broken that Way   Davis
More than Just a Friend   Rodgers
More than Likely   Cahn; Van Heusen
More than One More Day   Eliscu
Morning After, The   Arlen
Morning Star   Martin
Move Over and Make Room for Me   Bacharach; David, Hal
Mr. President   Berlin
Music Box Twist   Sigman
My Baby Loves to Swing   Cahn; Van Heusen

My Dearest One   David, Mack
My Geisha (You Are Sympathy to Me)   David, Hal
My Six Loves   Cahn; Van Heusen
My Sons My Sons   Evans; Livingston, Jay
My Window Faces the Street   David, Hal
Name of the Game Is Love, The   David, Hal
Needy, The   Fain
Nero, Caesar, Napoleon   Eliscu
Never Once Did I Cry   David, Hal
Never Say No to a Man   Rodgers
Nightlife   Adams; Strouse
Nighty Night   Parish
No One Ever Sends Me Roses   Davis
No Strings   Rodgers
Nobody Knows de Trouble I've Seen   Johnson, James P.
Nobody Told Me   Rodgers
Not Enough Faith (In the Word)   Robison
Notorious Landlady, The   David, Mack; Fain
Now that I've Lost You   Johnson, James P.
Old Immigration and Naturalization Rag, The   Adams;
   Strouse
On a Little Street in Venice   Davis
On Such a Night as This   Martin
Once Ev'ry Four Years   Berlin
One More Day   Eliscu
Only Dance I Know (Song for Belly Dancer), The   Berlin
Only in America   Gilbert
Only Love Can Break a Heart   Bacharach; David, Hal
Only Way to Travel, The   Cahn
Original Pianistic Trick (inst.)   Blake
Orthodox Fool, An   Rodgers
Other Side of the Tracks, The   Coleman; Leigh
Our Children   Adams; Strouse
Paper Heart   Russell
Paradise Bound   Livingston, Jerry
Paris Is a Lonely Town   Arlen; Harburg
Particular Funicular   Russell
Pastoral   David, Mack
Physical Fitness   Adams; Strouse
Pick Up the Pieces   Bacharach
Pigtails and Freckles   Berlin
Playboy Girl   Friend
Plink Plank Plunk   Evans; Livingston, Jay
Poor Joe   Berlin
Poor Little Hollywood Star   Coleman; Leigh
Popular Song, The   Berlin
Pretty Little Picture   Sondheim
Prince's Farewell (Goodbye), The   Coleman; Leigh
Pripoz Diva Se   Adams; Strouse
Psychology   Johnson, James P.
Punxatawney Rose   David, Hal
Puppy Love Is Here to Stay   Sherman
Rain from the Skies   Bacharach; David, Hal
Raise a Rukus Tonight   Mercer
Real Live Girl   Coleman; Leigh
Real Me, The   Adams; Strouse
Right Now   Sigman
Ringle, Ringle   Merrill; Styne
Rise Ye Shepherds   David, Mack
Rites of Love, The   Caesar
Road to Hong Kong, The   Cahn; Van Heusen
Rock, Rumble and Roar   Sherman
Roses Always Remember   David, Hal
Roses Red, Violets Blue   Arlen; Harburg
Rutabaga Rag   Sherman

Saints and Sinners Theme   David, Mack
Satan Never Sleeps   Adamson; Warren
Say No More   Eliscu
Say That You Love Me Once More   Heyman
Scherzo (inst.)   Strouse
Scruples! Scruples!   Gorney
Secret of Staying Young, The   Bacharach; David, Hal
Secret Service, The   Berlin
Sentimental Dreamer   David, Hal
Sentimental Sunday   Sherman
Serenade in F (inst.)   Blake
Seven Moons (Moon Pilot Melody)   Sherman
Seven Plagues   Livingston, Jerry
Shadows   Heyman
"Sing Another Song" (And Then We'll All Go
   Home)   Burke
Singing Bone   Merrill
Sinner's Devotion, A   Bacharach
Sleep, O Sleep   Eliscu
Sleepyland   Davis
Smart People Stay Single   Coleman; Leigh
Society Twist   Mills
Somebody Else   Rome
Someday Soon   Carmichael
Someday Soon (In a Mist)   Webster
Someone to Talk To   Martin
Something About a War   Sondheim
Something Special   Cahn; Van Heusen
Somewhere in the Used to Be   David, Mack
Somewhere Near Someplace   Davis
Sonata (inst.)   Strouse
Sound of Money, The   Rome
Sounds of the Night, The   Mercer
Space Man   Heyman
Spring Appears   Raye
Springtime   Livingston, Jerry
Stand By Blues   Ellington
Step Through a Moon Gate   Blane
Such a Beautiful World   Eliscu
Sun Rises, The   Eliscu
Swanee Lullaby   Ellington; Mills; Parish
Sweet Dreams of Love   Ellington; Mills
Sweetest Sounds, The   Rodgers
Taffetas   David, Mack
Tahlequah   David, Hal
Take My Hand Paree   Arlen; Harburg
Team Work   Cahn; Van Heusen
Technique   Martin
Telegram, The   Freed, Ralph
Ten Girls Ago   Fain
Thanks! Don't Mention It   Coleman; Leigh
That Dirty Old Man   Sondheim
That Feeling of Belonging   Baer
That Old Song and Dance   Bergman
That'll Show Him   Sondheim
That's Jelly Roll (inst.)   Blake
That's Not the Answer   Bacharach; David, Hal
(There Goes) The Forgotten Man   Bacharach; David, Hal
Theme from The Wonderful World of the Brothers Grimm
   (inst.)   Merrill
There Goes the Bride   Bloom; Burke
There Was a Little Frog   Johnson, James P.
There's Lots More Where This Came From   David, Hal
There's Only a Few of Us Left   Davis
They   Russell

They Love Me   Berlin
They Say   David, Mack
This Is a Great Country   Berlin
This Is My Pray'r for Christmas   Cahn
This Isn't Heaven   Rodgers
This Time of Year   David, Mack; Van Heusen
3 Pieces (For Jazz Violin) (inst.)   Strouse
Three Songs on Poems of William Blake   Strouse
Through   Revel
Time to Laugh, a Time to Cry, A   David, Hal
Tina's Opening   Brooks
To Kill a Mockingbird   David, Mack
Too Many Times   Friend
Too Soon   Rome
True Love Is an Apricot   Sherman
True Love Never Runs Smooth   Bacharach; David, Hal
Truly Content   Sondheim
Truth, The   Coleman; Leigh
Truth About Youth, The   Sherman
Twistin' in the Old Town   David, Mack
Twistin' Time   Ellington
Twizzle, The   David, Mack; Livingston, Jerry
Unexpectedly   Eliscu
Unknown   Ruby
Unusual Weather   Arlen; Harburg
"Up" Number, The   Martin
Variety Reel   Oakland
Violins in My Heart   Davis
Vitabelle   Coleman; Leigh
Void, The   Sherman
Von Drake Quake, The   Sherman
Wait for the Wagon   Mercer
Waitin' for Charlie to Come Home   Bacharach
Walk on the Wild Side   David, Mack
Waltz Martinique   Johnson, James P.
Warm   Bergman
Warmer than a Whisper   Cahn; Van Heusen
Washington Twist, The   Berlin
Wasn't It Romantic?   Martin
Way Over in Jordan   Johnson, James P.
Way Things Are, The   Rome
Way with a Woman, A   Livingston, Jerry; Webster
We Speak the Same Language   Adams; Strouse
Wedding Cake   Davis
We're Americans   Livingston, Jerry
We're Despicable (Plunderers' March)   Merrill; Styne
What a Country!   Adams; Strouse
What Are They Doing to Us Now?   Rome
What Do I Do with My New Tattoo of You   Livingston, Jerry
What Now My Love (Et Maintenant)   Sigman
What Was Your Name in the States   Mercer
What Would It Mean Without You   Ellington; Mills
What's in It for Me   Rome
When Gemini Meets Capricorn   Rome
When Stella Did the Rhumba   Johnson, James P.
When the Boys Get Together   David, Hal
When the Fiddlers Fiddled on Fiddler's Green   Yellen
When Was the Last Time   Oakland
When You Fall in the Fall of the Year   David, Hal
Which Way?   Adams; Strouse
Whistlin' Tune, A   David, Hal
Who Ever Heard of an Angel?   Freed, Ralph
Who Forgot Who   Cahn
Who Is She?   Ellington; Mills

Who Knows?   Rome
Who Would Have Thought   Berlin
Who'll Be the Boy This Summer   David, Mack; Livingston, Jerry
Who's Got the Action   Brooks
Who's in Your Arms Tonight?   Revel
Why Do You Push Me Around!   Adams; Strouse
Why Won't He Answer Me   David, Mack
Wide Open Spaces, The   Webster
Wild and Wooly West, The   Livingston, Jerry
Willing and Eager   Rodgers
Window Across the Way   Sondheim
Winter Was Warm   Merrill; Styne
Wishing Star, The   David, Mack
Wonderful to Be Young   Bacharach; David, Hal
World of Dreams   David, Hal
Write About What You Know   Martin
Yankee, Go Home   Rodgers
Yellow Sailboat from Hawaii   Hoffman
You and Me   Raye
You Are   Stept
You Don't Tell Me   Rodgers
You Have a Way with You   Drake
You Know — I Know   Johnson, James P.
You Need a Hobby   Berlin
Young, Alive and in Love   Cahn; Van Heusen
Young Willie Wilkins   David, Hal
Your Eyes Are Blue (Once Upon a Time) (Love Story)   Sondheim
You're About to Be Beautiful   Martin
You're Everything to Me   Parish
You're the Only One Can Hurt Us   Davis
Youth   Raye
You've Got the Love I Love   Ellington
Zaparozhti   David, Mack

1963

Above and Beyond   Coleman; Leigh
Adobe   Bergman
After You   David, Mack
Alive and Kicking   Blane; Martin
Alive at Last   Duke
All that a Girl Should Be   Livingston, Jerry
All the Way Home   Styne
All Yours   Heyman
Alone at Night   Duke
(It's) Always the Same   Berlin
Amor, Mon Amour, My Love   Sigman
And So Goodbye, My Love   Bacharach; David, Hal
Angelus Bells   Bergman
Announcement/Rehearsal (inst.)   Duke
Anyone Who Had a Heart   Bacharach; David, Hal
Are We Talking About the Same Thing?   Adamson; Fain
Arm in Arm   Willson
Artists   Duke
Ask a Foolish Question   David, Mack
Athena   Duke
Athena's Dance (inst).   Duke
Baby, the Ball Is Over   Bergman
Bad for Each Other   Arlen; Leigh
Ballad of Johnny Cool, The   Cahn; Van Heusen
Balloon Underplay (inst.)   Fain
Barbary Coast   Adamson
Barbie Goodnight   Livingston, Jerry

Barbie Look, The   Livingston, Jerry
Barbie's Fashion Parade   Livingston, Jerry
Be True to Yourself   Bacharach; David, Hal
Beautiful Beulah (Railroad Rag)   Sherman
Before I Kiss the World Goodbye   Dietz; Schwartz, Arthur
Bells of Santa Ynez   Bergman
Big Ca-lown Balloons, The   Willson
Big Cat   David, Mack
Big Game, The   Livingston, Jerry
Bird That Never Learned to Fly, A   Duke
Birdman of Alcatraz   Webster
Bless the Land   Strouse
Blue Guitar   Bacharach; David, Hal
Blue Oak Tree, The   Sherman
Blue on Blue   Bacharach; David, Hal
Blue Piano   Ellington
Blues for a Four String Guitar   David, Mack
Born Again   Dietz; Schwartz, Arthur
Born at Last   Duke
Bounce   Duke
Bouquet   Mercer
Boys' Night Out, The   Cahn; Van Heusen
Bozo's Teach-a-rena   Livingston, Jerry
B-R-A-N-E Spells Brain!   Cahn; Van Heusen
Breakfast for Two   Duke
Bugle, The   Willson
Burning of the Henrietta (inst.)   Fain
Business or Pleasure   Duke
Butcher Song, The   Livingston, Jerry
Campus Queen   Livingston, Jerry
Canodlin'   Livingston, Jerry
Can't You See the Signs (That I No Longer Care)   Robison
Capricious Harlem (inst.)   Blake
Cardinal, The   Leigh
Carry On   Adamson; Fain
Castle of Love   Blake; Sissle
Cat from Carolina   Monaco
Cathy   Cahn; Van Heusen
Chapman Report Marching Song, The   Webster
Charming Waltz (inst.)   Duke
Christmas Is the Season of the Bells   Bergman
Christmas Star   Webster
Christmas Time Is Coming   Robison
Christmas Vacation   Livingston, Jerry
Cleopatra   Webster
Close Your Eyes   Dietz; Schwartz, Arthur
Come Back to Me   Lerner, Alan Jay
Come Blow Your Horn   Cahn; Van Heusen
Come Fly with Me   Cahn; Van Heusen
Come to Me   Duke
Comes Another Spring   Gordon; Myrow
Command Performance   Duke
Concerto for Piano and Orchestra (inst.)   Strouse
Count the Stars   Duke
Country Bumpkin   Bergman
Dance of Sacrifice (inst.)   Fain
Day with Barbie, A   Livingston, Jerry
Days of Wine and Roses, The   Mancini; Mercer
Dear Mr. Santa Claus (If Santa Claus Were Crazy)   Willson
Dinner Is Served   Dietz; Schwartz, Arthur
D.J. Ghost   Coots
Dodgers, The   Cahn; Van Heusen
Don't Call Me, I'll Call You   David, Mack; Van Heusen
Don't Laugh   Sondheim
Don't Stop the World for Me   Yellen

(I Love You and) Don't You Forget It   Mancini
Dream Big (Work Hard, Aim High)   Robison
Duty, Honor, Country   Blane
Elephant Never Forgets, An   Cahn; Van Heusen
Elusive Mr. Rassendyl, The   Duke
Enchanted Mountain   Bergman
Enchanting Girls   Duke
Ever-Lovin' Lover   Ellington
Every Stand Up Act Is Sitting Down Today   Cahn; Van Heusen
Everything's Already Alright   Robison
Expect Things to Happen   Willson
Eyes of Fire   Bergman
Fa La La, Fa, Fa La La   Willson
Fallen Woman   Leigh
False Friends   David, Hal
Faraway Land, A   Cahn; Van Heusen
Father of Girls, The   Drake
Femininity   Sherman
Femme Fatale   Dietz; Schwartz, Arthur
Festive March (inst.)   Duke
Fiesta in Spain   Adamson
55 Days at Peking   Webster
Fight On, Men of Westwood   Livingston, Jerry
First Night of the Full Moon, The   David, Hal
Flavia (inst.)   Duke
Flitterin'   Sherman
Follow Me (Love Song)   Webster
Fool Killer, The   Bacharach; David, Hal
For Better or Worse   Dietz; Schwartz, Arthur
For the Common Good of Mankind   Duke
Four for Texas   Cahn; Van Heusen
Frankenstein   Webster
Free Am I   Adams; Strouse
Freud   Webster
Fun Is More Fun   Livingston, Jerry
Gather Your Dreams   Howard, Bart
Get Off the Cotty, Potty (The Tide Is Coming In)   Robison
Gift for Every Day of the Week, A   Duke
Gift of Love, A   Duke
Gift of Time, A   Duke
Girl Named Tamiko, A   David, Mack
Girls   Duke
Girls and Rassendyl   Duke
God-Given Goodness   Robison
Good Neighbor Song, The   Livingston, Jerry
Goody, Goody Gum Drops   Livingston, Jerry
Guitar Country   Mercer; Robison
Guy on Monday, A   Berlin
Half a Love   David, Hal
Happy Barbie Birthday, A   Livingston, Jerry
Happy Horns and Merry Bells   Duke
Have Reindeer, Will Travel   Livingston, Jerry; Webster
Have You Heard about Philias Fogg?   Young, Victor
He Who   Adams; Strouse
He Wouldn't Dare   Duke
Hello, Must Do a Show, Goodbye!   Duke
Helpless   Warren
Here and There   Duke
Here Pretty Kitty   Livingston, Jerry
Here's Hoping   Coleman; Leigh
Here's Love   Willson
Hide Your Sister   Adamson; Fain
Higgitus-Figgitus   Sherman
High Is Better Than Low   Dietz; Schwartz, Arthur

Hindu Dance Tag (inst.) Fain
His and His Cahn; Van Heusen
His Delay Is Not His Denial Caesar; Robison
His Hand Is on Your Shoulder Coots
His Little World Adamson; Fain
Ho-Hum Livingston, Jerry
Hollywood Story, The Martin
Horse on the Carousel, The Cahn; Van Heusen
How Lovely to Love a Woman Adams; Strouse
How Much Will I Love You Evans; Livingston, Jay
How Sweet It Is Caesar
Hud David, Mack
I Believe in Takin' a Chance Dietz; Schwartz, Arthur
I Can't Make Up My Mind Cahn; Van Heusen
I Could Go on Singing (Till the Cows Come Home) Arlen; Harburg
I Forgot What It Was Like Bacharach; David, Hal
I Go Off in All Directions Cahn; Van Heusen
I Go to Sicily Burke
I Hate to Travel Adamson; Fain
I Heard from a Mem'ry Last Night Livingston, Jerry
I Laughed at Love Adams; Strouse
I Like Being Alone Cahn; Van Heusen
I Love to Dance a Waltz Adams; Strouse
I Picked a Daisy Lerner, Alan Jay
I See It All Now David, Hal
I Still Look at You That Way Dietz; Schwartz, Arthur
I Think I'm Going to Like It Over Here Dietz; Schwartz, Arthur
I Used to Play It by Ear Berlin
I Was Talking to Myself, I Was Revel
I Wish I Were Strouse
I Wish You Needed Me Burke
I Wonder What He Meant By That Duke
I Won't Stand in Your Way Duke
If Love Ain't There (It Ain't There) Burke
If She Were Mine Sigman
If You Can't Say Something Nice Sherman
If You're Gonna Be a Witch — Be a Witch! Cahn; Van Heusen
Ignatz Evans; Livingston, Jay
I'll Call Him "Bambi" Sherman
I'll Marry a Soldier Duke
I'm a Sleuth Adamson; Fain
I'm Going Steady with a Memory Ruby
In San Jose Baer
In the Land of Make Believe Bacharach; David, Hal
In the Shade of the Shally-Go-Shee Livingston, Jerry; Webster
Indian Raid (inst.) Fain
Indian Scene (inst.) Fain
Introducing Mr. Rassendyl (inst.) Duke
It Does Not Duke
It Had Better Be Tonight (Meglio Stasera) Mercer
It Hurts Me to See You So Happy Freed, Ralph
It Isn't What You Have Dietz; Schwartz, Arthur
It Might As Well Be Me David, Hal
It Only Happens Once Cahn
It Was So Good Once David, Hal
It's a Quaint Little Custom Duke
It's a Small World Pollack; Webster
It's Enough to Make a Country Boy Cry Robison
It's Murder Cahn
It's Time for Love Adamson
I've Been Had Cahn; Van Heusen

Jail Blues Ellington
Jail of Jealousy Robison
Jealous Blues Friend
Jennie Dietz; Schwartz, Arthur
Johnny Shiloh Sherman
Judgement at Nuremberg Webster
Just Say, 'Auf Weidersehen' Sherman
Just the Letter "Q" Mercer
Kate the Great Cahn; Van Heusen
Keep a Happy Thought Cahn; Van Heusen
Keep You Spirits High Robison
King Fit the Battle of Alabam Ellington
Kings and Cabbages Duke
Kolin Kelly Evans; Livingston, Jay
La La La La Bergman
Lady Chatterly's Lover Webster
Lawrence of Arabia Webster
Legend of the Sword in the Stone Sherman
Legion of the Lost Freed, Ralph; Livingston, Jerry
Legs Cahn; Van Heusen
Let Her Not Be Beautiful Duke
Let Me Sing Berlin
Let's Dance Mam'selle Friml
Let's Get with It Stept
Let's Suppose I Never Knew Raye
Let's Tell the Truth Robison
Life's a Dance Freed, Ralph
Lifetime of Loneliness, A Bacharach; David, Hal
Little Christmas Tree, The Adamson; Warren
Little Ole Lovemaker, Me Freed, Ralph
Lloyd's of London Young, Victor
Lonely Nights Dietz; Schwartz, Arthur
Long As I Can Take You Home Berlin
Long Live Love Coleman; Leigh
Look Ahead, Little Girl Fain
Look in My Eyes, Maria Bacharach; David, Hal
Look, Little Girl Willson
Look of Love, The Cahn; Van Heusen
Look Out Koehler; Stept
Losing You Sigman
Lost Little Girl Bacharach; David, Hal
Love, Come Take Me Again Willson
Love Is Oh So Easy Cahn; Van Heusen
Love Is Such a Little Word (Precious and Absurd) Monaco
Love Letter Kisses Robison
Loveless You and Hateful Me Duke
Macy's Parade Willson
Mad Madam Mim Sherman
Magic Is the Night Fain
Magic Music (inst.) Duke
Magic Potion Bacharach; David, Hal
Make a Wish Livingston, Jerry
Make the Music Play Bacharach; David, Hal
Mama, What Is in the Pot Today Bergman
Man Loves Me, The Duke
Man to Cook For, A Berlin
Manchurian Candidate, The Webster
Manhattan (What a Town) Cahn
Man's Favorite Sport Mancini; Mercer
March of the Grenadiers (inst.) Fain
Mass Retaliation Oakland
Mazurka (inst.) Duke
Meet Me at Meetin' Time Robison
Merry Christmas Bergman
Merry Christmas Eve Livingston, Jerry

Message to Michael   Bacharach; David, Hal
Mi Amor   Bergman
Montage Poster (inst.)   Duke
Monte Carlo   Sigman
Morning You Were Born, The   Duke
Most Befuddling Thing, A   Sherman
Mother Who's Really a Mother, A   Dietz; Schwartz, Arthur
Mr. Yesterday   Robison
Mrs. Kwakk-Kwakk   Evans; Livingston, Jay
My Best Beau   Gordon; Myrow
My Heart Has Come a Tumbling Down   Duke
My Love for You   Mercer
My Masterpiece   Magidson; McHugh
My Motto Is You   Sigman
My Royal Majesty   Duke
My Son in Law the King   Duke
My Wish   Willson
Natasha   Webster
National Anthem   Duke
Never Let Them Know What's Going On   Duke
Nicest Gift of Them All, The   Livingston, Jerry
Night Has Eyes, The   Coots
Night Is Filled with Wonderful Sounds, The   Duke
Night May Be Dark, The   Dietz; Schwartz, Arthur
Nile, The   Mercer
No Hope for the Human Race   Dietz; Schwartz, Arthur
No Ifs! No Ands! No Buts!   Duke
No More Love   Duke
No One Owns Tomorrow   Duke
No Two Ways About Love   Duke
Nothing in Common   Willson
Nothing in the World   Bergman
Nothing to Do   Livingston, Jerry
Now (Is the Moment)   Comden and Green; Styne
Now the World Begins Again   Duke
O'Conner   Dietz; Schwartz, Arthur
Offissa Pup   Evans; Livingston, Jay
Old Brownstone in Brooklyn   Robison
Old Friend   Duke
Old Songs, The   Davis
On a Little Street in Napoli   Coots
On My Own   Duke
On the Front Porch   Sherman
On the Other Hand   Dietz; Schwartz, Arthur
On the Thomas J. Muldoon   Dietz; Schwartz, Arthur
Once I Wondered   Adamson; Fain
One Man Woman   Berlin
One Night Ago   Duke
One Woman Man   Fain
One-Woman Man   Adamson
Organization   Duke
Our Usual Place   Duke
Outside of Loving You, I Like You   Berlin
Palermo in the Moonlight   Parish
Parade (inst.)   Willson
Patroness of Art   Duke
Penny Polka   Revel
Perfect Fool, A   Monaco
Perfect Paris Night, A   Carmichael
Philbert   Fain
Pine Cones and Holly Berries   Willson
Pink Lemonade   Livingston, Jerry
Pink of Perfection, The   Sherman
Pink, Purple and Plaid   Livingston, Jerry
Plastic Alligator, The   Willson

Please Make Him Love Me   Bacharach; David, Hal
Pleasure Him   Friend
Poem, The   Livingston, Jerry
Pull a Rabbit Out of the Hat   Duke
P.X., The   Berlin
Queen Mother's Crossover (inst.)   Duke
Rampage   David, Mack
Raving Beauty, A   Martin
Reach Out for Me   Bacharach; David, Hal
Red River Blues   Blake
Red Slippers   Friend
Remember I Still Love You   Sigman
Return to the Land of Oz March   Cahn; Van Heusen
Rich Livin' Woman   Freed, Ralph; Livingston, Jerry
Room for One More   David, Mack; Livingston, Jerry
Rose and the Butterfly, The   Young, Victor
Royal Confession, A   Duke
Run and Games   Livingston, Jerry
Sad-Eyed Baby   Van Heusen
Sailor's Song   Adamson; Fain
Saturday Sunshine   Bacharach; David, Hal
Scarlet Bird in a Yellow Tree   Livingston, Jerry; Webster
Season for Love, The   Adams; Strouse
See Seattle   Dietz; Schwartz, Arthur
Segue to Palace (inst.)   Duke
She Hadda Go Back   Willson
Short Time to Get There   Robison
Sidewalks of Paris   Adamson; Fain
Sign on the Dotted Line   Duke
Silent Spring, The   Arlen; Harburg
Sing Along with God   Webster
Skipper   Livingston, Jerry
Skipper, Skooter and Ricky   Livingston, Jerry
So Little Time (The Peking Theme)   Webster
So Long, Big Time!   Arlen
Sodom and Gomorrah   Webster
Something for Somebody Else   Livingston, Jerry
Something New   Duke
Something Warm for Christmas   Coleman; Leigh
Song About Love   Mancini
Songs I Love, The   Cahn; Van Heusen
Sons of Westwood   Livingston, Jerry
Sounds of Christmas, The   Livingston, Jerry; Webster
Spanish Villa (inst.)   Fain
Speak Not a Word   Adamson; Fain
Spin-Drift   Robison
Splendor in the Grass   Webster
Spring Will Never Come Again   Adams; Strouse
Star and the Rose, The   Bergman
Stay with Me   Leigh
Step in the Right Direction, A   Robison
Step That'll Stop the Show, A   Cahn; Van Heusen
Stolen Hours, The   Bergman
Street Car Conductor Song, The   Livingston, Jerry
Street Cleaner Song (Nobody Litters Anymore)   Livingston, Jerry
Summer Magic   Sherman
Summertime Promises   Cahn; Van Heusen
Sunrise Bells and Alabado   Bergman
Surfin' Santa   Robison
Sweetheart Roses   Heyman
Take It from One Who Knows   Heyman
Take Me Home for New Years   Livingston, Jerry
Tango   Leigh
Ten Best Undressed Women in the World, The   Berlin

Thanks to Love   Duke
Thanks to You   Webster
Thanksgiving Day   Livingston, Jerry
That Feeling for Home   Cahn; Van Heusen
That Man Loves Me   Duke
That Man Over There   Willson
That Was Then, Mr. Rassendyl   Duke
That's Good, That's Bad   Sondheim
That's My Style   Coleman
That's the Way I'll Come to You   Bacharach; David, Hal
That's the Way It Goes   Duke
That's What Makes the World Go 'Round   Sherman
There Are Girls   Duke
There Goes Another Pal of Mine   Carmichael
There Is No Land of Oz   Cahn; Van Heusen
There Is Nothing Like a Wedding   Duke
There's an Awful Lot of Yes in the Way You Say
    No   Adams; Strouse
There's Nothing Wrong with Marriage   Duke
There's Room for Her   Duke
These Are My United States   Livingston, Jerry
These Little Mem'ries   Livingston, Jerry
They Long to Be Close to You   Bacharach; David, Hal
They'll Soon Be Gone   Livingston, Jerry
Things Look So Diff'rent in the Moonlight   Heyman
Things to Remember   Livingston, Jerry
This Empty Place   Bacharach; David, Hal
This Is a Musical   Cahn; Van Heusen
This Is a Song   Cahn; Van Heusen
Three Little Angels   Livingston, Jerry
Through the Forest   Sherman
Tiki Tiki Room, The   Sherman
To Wait for Love (Is to Waste Your Life Away)   Bacharach;
    David, Hal
Too Beautiful Tonight   Duke
Too Late, My Love (inst.)   McHugh
Tour de Force   Duke
Tradewinds Aloha   Drake
Train Music (inst.)   Duke
Trust in Me   Duke
Turlututu   Duke
Turn It into a Musical   Cahn; Van Heusen
Twenty Four Hours from Tulsa   Bacharach; David, Hal
Ty Cobb (The Georgia Peach)   Coots
U.C.L.A.   Livingston, Jerry
Ugly American, The   Webster
Ugly Bug Ball, The   Sherman
Under the Yum-Yum Tree   Cahn; Van Heusen
Underneath the Kiss'l-Toe   Coots
Valley Song   Bergman
Verdi Duo (inst.)   Duke
Vernon Duccini (inst.)   Duke
Very Bozo Birthday, A   Livingston, Jerry
V-Room   Livingston, Jerry
Wait a Minute   Livingston, Jerry
Wait until You're Married   Berlin
Waitin' for the Evening Train   Dietz; Schwartz, Arthur
Waltz Fantasy (inst.)   Duke
Want Me   Sigman
We   Duke
We Just Might   Duke
We Live on Park   Willson
Wedding March (inst.)   Duke
Welcome   Dietz; Schwartz, Arthur
Wendy   Drake

We're Getting Too Old for This Jazz   Cahn; Van Heusen
What Can I Give Him   Webster
What Color Is Virtue?   Ellington
What Does One Do?   Duke
Whatever Happened to Baby Jane   Webster
What'll We Buy   Livingston, Jerry
What's This World A-Comin' To   Robison
What's Your Hurry, Beatrice   Oakland
Wheeler Dealers, The   Cahn; Van Heusen
When Athena Dances (inst.)   Duke
When in Rome   Coleman; Leigh
When Paris Smiles   Webster
When You Stop and Think   Duke
When You're Far Away from New York Town   Dietz;
    Schwartz, Arthur
Where Did Ev'ryone Go?   David, Mack; Van Heusen
Where You Are   Dietz; Schwartz, Arthur
Whisper It   Berlin
Who Is there Among Us Who Knows?   Lerner, Alan Jay
Whole Lot of Happy, A   Duke
Who's Been Sleeping in My Bed   Bacharach; David, Hal
Who's Gonna Teach Me (To Forget)   David, Hal
Who's Got the Action   Bacharach
Whose Heart Are You Breaking Tonight   Davis
Why   Adams; Strouse
Why Did She Have to Cry   David, Hal
Why Not?   Duke
Will, The   Sigman
Willow, The   David, Mack
Willow, Will Me   Webster
Wind in the Willows, The   Livingston, Jerry
Wine Is Mine, The   Duke
Winter Sun   Oakland; Webster
Wishin' and Hopin'   Bacharach; David, Hal
Wives and Lovers   Bacharach; David, Hal
Wonderful World of Love   Brooks
Words, Words, Words   Duke
World Beauty Fair, The   Livingston, Jerry
World of Barbie, The   Livingston, Jerry
World of Make-Believe, The   Livingston, Jerry; Webster
Writing on the Wall, The   Drake
Yesterday's Forgotten   Duke
You Are All That's Beautiful   Duke
You Don't Have to Prove It If You Sing It   Willson
You Don't Know   Willson
You Have Only You   Cahn; Van Heusen
You Know You Don't Want Me (So Why Don't You Leave
    Me Alone)   Mercer
You Never Lose what You Never Had   Lerner, Sammy
You Shouldn't Have Said What You Said   Hoffman;
    Livingston, Jerry
You Took My Breath Away   Duke
You're Impossible   Arlen
You're It   Cahn; Van Heusen
You're Not At All Like You   Duke
You're Not Old Enough   Duke
You're So Good to Me (And I'm So Tired of It All)   Robison
Zamar Moded   Hoffman
Zarape (Antoinette's Dance) (inst.)   Duke
Zenda   Duke

1964

A-1 March   Sondheim
Absent Minded Me   Merrill; Styne

Farewell My Lady Love   Howard, Joseph E.
Fear   Comden and Green; Styne
Febbre Siciliana   Warren
Feed the Birds   Sherman
Few Days   Robison
F.F. (Forbidden Fruit)   Comden and Green; Styne
Fickle Finger of Fate, The   Lawrence
Fiddler and the Fighter, The   Comden and Green; Styne
Fidelity Fiduciary Bank   Sherman
Fight, The   Adams; Strouse
Find Yourself a Man   Merrill; Styne
Fish Don't Fly   Styne
Flowers   Martin
Flute Segue (inst.)   Willson
For the Sake of the Children   Cahn; Van Heusen
For Those Who Think Love   David, Mack; Livingston, Jerry
Forever and a Day   Martin
Forever Nearer to Me   Martin
Forever Yours I Remain   Bacharach; David, Hal
Foxy   Mercer
Freedom Is the Word   Harburg; Lane
Friendliest Thing, The   Drake
From Rocking Horse to Rocking Chair   Bacharach; David, Hal
Funny Girl   Merrill; Styne
Funny Little Girl   McHugh
Garside the Great   Lawrence
Get on Ted   Robison
Gimme Some   Adams
Gimme Some (Beer and Whiskey)   Strouse
Girl Friday Blues   Robison
Girl of the Year   Drake
Girl to Remember, A   Comden and Green; Styne
Girl Who Knows It All, The   McHugh
Give Praise! Give Praise! Give Praise!   Cahn; Van Heusen
Go Home Train   Comden and Green; Styne
Go Into Your Trance   Martin
Golden Boy   Adams; Strouse
Goldwater Fairyland   Rome
Gone with the Beat   Gorney
Good Morning Mrs. Benson   Comden and Green; Styne
Good Old Fashioned Get Together   Styne
Gossip   Blane; Martin
Grazie Per Niente   Bergman; Fain
Great American Dream, The   Carmichael; Parish
Green, White and Red in Italy   Warren
Greta the Misfit Greyhound   Sherman
Ha   Styne
Half-Forgotten Teddy Bear   Rome
Happy Dogs   Styne
Have an Umbrella   Martin
Have You Found Heaven   Howard, Joseph E.
He   Merrill; Styne
Heart Must Learn to Cry, A   Webster
Heartache High School, U.S.A.   Freed, Ralph
Hector, the Stowaway Pup   Sherman
Helluva Group, A   Merrill; Styne
Henry Street   Merrill; Styne
Her Lover   Russell
Here Comes the Sun   Comden and Green
Here Is My Heart for Christmas   Baer
Hero Is Coming, A   Sondheim
He's Got Larceny in His Heart   Merrill; Styne
He's My Friend   Willson
His Love Makes Me Beautiful   Merrill; Styne

Home   Merrill; Styne
Home, Sweet Heaven   Martin
Honey   Adams; Strouse
Honeymoon Hotel   Cahn; Van Heusen
House Is Not a Home, A   Bacharach; David, Hal
How Can Anyone Keep from Singin'   Fain
How Could You Do It to Me   Howard, Joseph E.
How Many Days of Sadness   Bacharach; David, Hal
How Now Dow Jones   Leigh
Hurt but Happy   Arlen
Hush, Hush, Sweet Charlotte   David, Mack
I Am Mrs. Stanhope Van Hepworth And   Cahn; Van Heusen
I Can See It All Now   Bergman; Fain
I Can't Get You Out of My Mind   Blake; Sissle
I Can't Go Back   Comden and Green; Styne
I Can't Stop Crying   McHugh
I Can't Wait to Take You Home to Mother   Cahn; Van Heusen
I Could Be Good for You   Arlen
I Did It on Roller Skates   Merrill; Styne
I Don't Hurt Anymore   McHugh
I Feel Humble   Drake
I Fell in Love with Your Picture   Bacharach; David, Hal
I Had a Ball   Lawrence
I Know Your Heart   Martin
I Like to Lead when I Dance   Cahn; Van Heusen
I Live My Love (inst.)   Coleman
I Lost My Heart in a Drive-In Movie   Brooks
I Love Louisa   Comden and Green; Styne
I Love to Hear a Banjo   Baer
I Love to Laugh   Sherman
I Love You Miss Annabelle   Blake; Sissle
I See Something   Drake
I Think That You and I Should Get Acquainted   Comden and Green; Styne
I Tried   Merrill; Styne
I Wanna Hurt You   Freed, Ralph
I Want to Be Seen with You   Strouse
I Want to Be Seen with You Tonight   Merrill; Styne
I Want to Be with You   Adams; Strouse
I Wish I Were a Fish   Adamson; Fain
I'd Love to Hate You, But If I Love You, How Can I Hate You   Yellen
If a Girl Isn't Pretty   Merrill; Styne
If I Gave You   Martin
If You Ever Need Me   Warren
Il Mio Mondo (You're My World)   Sigman
I'll Get Even   Mercer
I'll Hold You in My Heart (Until You Hold Me in Your Arms)   Robison
I'll Never Make the Same Mistake Twice   Heyman
I'll Remember This Night   Baer; Lewis
I'm a Poached Egg   Gershwin, George; Gershwin, Ira
I'm Gonna Take My Love Where I Find It   Coots
I'm Gonna Write a Letter to Jesus   Robison
I'm in Love Again   Coleman
I'm Just a Fool with a Fantasy   Robin
I'm Kooky Over You   Blane; Martin
I'm Like the Bluebird   Sondheim
I'm the Greatest Star   Merrill; Styne
I'm Way Ahead of the Game   Mercer
I'm with You   Comden and Green; Styne
Immaturity   Cahn; Van Heusen
In Loving Memory   Mercer

Ode to a Key   Bergman; Fain
Oh Those Thirties   Comden and Green; Styne
Oky Doky Tokyo   Leslie
Old Friend   Robison
Old Guitaron   Mercer
On My Way   Evans; Livingston, Jay
On Our Houseboat in the Hudson (Happy
    Houseboat)   Comden and Green; Styne
On the Wings of Romance   Cahn; Van Heusen
Once You Say Hello to Miami Beach You Never Want to Say
    Goodbye   Davis
One Long Last Look   Bergman; Fain
One Night Stand   Heyman
One Who's Always There, The   Burke
Opening to Kelly-Mac Laine Musical Extravaganza   Comden
    and Green
Opening to MacLaine and Kelly Musical   Styne
Other Half of Me, The   Lawrence
Out in All that Rain   Evans; Livingston, Jay
Paint a Rainbow   Drake
Painting Pictures   Fisher
Parade in Town, A   Sondheim
Pardon Me, I've Got Some Crying to Do   McHugh
Party Talk   Bergman; Fain
Peace   Bergman
People   Merrill; Styne
Perfect Nanny, The   Sherman
Perfect Paris Night, A   Mercer
Playground Songs   Adams; Strouse
Pleasure Seekers, The   Van Heusen
Pleasure Seekers Bossa Nova, The   Cahn; Van Heusen
Poppa   Adams; Strouse
Portofino   Bergman; Fain
Power of Love, The   Mercer
Private Schwartz   Merrill; Styne
Prologue   Mercer
Pussy Cat   Coleman
Put on Your Rubbers   Howard, Joseph E.
"R" Is for Ringo   Freed, Ralph
Rabbit's Foot   Mercer
Racing Form Lullaby   Merrill; Styne
Rat-Tat-Tat-Tat   Merrill; Styne
Razzle Dazzle   Cahn; Van Heusen
Red-Blooded American Boy   Lawrence
Refugee Song   Fisher
Respectability   Mercer
Road Tour, The   Adams
Road Tour (The Road Town), The   Strouse
Rollin' in Gold   Mercer
Rome Will Never Leave You   Bacharach; David, Hal
Room Without Windows, A   Drake
Run, Run, Run Cinderella   Mercer
Sad and Sorry   Coots
Sadie Fats   Cahn; Van Heusen
Sadie, Sadie (Married Lady)   Merrill; Styne
Saga of Sadie Thompson   Evans; Livingston, Jay
Sandwich Man, The   Martin
Santa's Little Helper   Coots
Saving Up for Sunday   Parish
Say No More   Leigh
Scandalize My Name   Robison
Scherzo No. 1 (inst.)   Blake
Scrambled Egg-Head, The   Sherman
Searchin'   Ellington
Season, The   Martin

See What It Gets You   Sondheim
Send Me No Flowers   Bacharach; David, Hal
Seventh Dawn   Webster
Shadows of Paris, The   Mancini
Shake Hands, Dear Mrs. Cow   Rome
Share and Share Alike   Mercer
She's My Kind of People   Silver
Shivaree   Mercer
Shot in the Dark, A   Mancini
Shy   Rome
Simple   Sondheim
Sing a Song of Hollywood   Warren
Single-o   Mercer
Sinner, The   Parish
Sister Suffragette   Sherman
Sky's the Limit   Coleman
Sleep Now, Baby Bunting   Merrill; Styne
Sleepy Baby   Webster
Slow Hot Wind   Mancini
Smile Looks Good on Any Face, A   Fain
Society, The   Martin
Some Crummy Season   Lawrence
Some Days Everything Goes Wrong   Drake
Some of the Blues   Coleman
Something About Me   Merrill; Styne
Something Borrowed — Something Blue   Sherman
Something Is Coming to Tea   Martin
Something More   Bergman; Fain
Something Tells Me   Martin
Something to Live For   Drake
Something to Think About   Cahn; Van Heusen
Somewhere Down the Line   Robison
Song for the World to Sing, A   McHugh
Sophia   Gershwin, George; Gershwin, Ira
Spoonful of Sugar, A   Sherman
Spring Will Come Again   Comden and Green
S.S. Commodore Ebenezer McAffee the Third   Mercer
Station Wagon Polka   Coleman
Stay Awake   Sherman
Step in Time   Sherman
Stick Around   Adams; Strouse
Stop Waltzing Around in My Mind   Rome
Stormy   Robison
Story of My Life, The   Comden and Green; Styne
Strange What Love Will Do   Blake; Sissle
Stranger or Lover (Quat Tro Chitarre)   Sigman
Straw That Broke the Camel's Back, The   Bergman; Fain
Style   Cahn; Van Heusen
Sundown Deacon   Robison
Super Doodle Dandy (Mr. Limpet March)   Adamson; Fain
Supercalifragilisticexpialidocious   Sherman
Sweet Talk   Coleman
Sweetie!   Drake
Sylvia   Webster
Sympatico   McHugh
Take a Little Walk   Coleman
Take It from a Lady   Mercer
Take the Time to Fall in Love   Comden and Green; Styne
Talk to Me, Baby   Mercer
Talking to You   Martin
Tallulah — Tallulah   Freed, Ralph
Tandy   Adamson
Tango Diablo   Rome
Tapeteers (inst.), The   Coleman
Tea Time in Timbuctoo   Comden and Green; Styne

Temporary Arrangement, A   Styne
Tender Spot, A   Drake
Thanksgiving   Blane; Martin
That Faraway Look   Bergman; Fain
That Was the Love that Was   Arlen
That's Pollyanna   Sherman
That's What a Sweetheart Was Made For   Coots
The Color of Love   Russell
Then I'll Know   Johnson, James P.
There Comes a Time   Adams; Strouse
There Won't Be Trumpets   Sondheim
There'll Be Some Blues Tomorrow   Bergman
There's a Change in Me   Coleman
There's a Great Big Beautiful Tomorrow   Sherman
There's a Party Going On Somewhere   Adams; Strouse
There's Always a Woman   Sondheim
There's Gold in Them Thar Hills   Cahn; Van Heusen
There's Music in that Boy   Adams; Strouse
They Can't Ration Love   Howard, Joseph E.
They Don't Make 'em Like That Anymore   Martin
They're at the Post   Comden and Green; Styne
Think Beautiful   Lawrence
Thirty One Flavors   David, Mack
This Book   Robison
This Is My Happiest Moment   Davis
This Is the Life   Adams; Strouse
This Strange Affair   Young, Victor
Till It Goes Outta Style   Mercer
'Tis Summer   Coots
Tjilerham   Russell
Tobacco, The Red Man's Revenge   Rome
Tonight May Have to Last All My Life   Mercer
Too Little Time   Mancini; Raye
Took Me a Little Time   Merrill; Styne
Trains and Boats and Planes   Bacharach; David, Hal
True Blue Pals   Lawrence
Tutti for Cootie   Ellington
Two Cent Encyclopedia, A   Drake
Undercover Story, The   Coleman
Underneath the Marquee   Adams; Strouse
Up and Down   Heyman
Usher from the Mezzanine, The   Comden and Green; Styne
Valentino   Johnson, James P.
Valley of Tears, The   Freed, Ralph
Variety   Coleman
(He Is) Very Close to Wonderful   Cahn; Van Heusen
Very Warm for Christmas   Coleman; Leigh
Wait Until You Meet Her   McHugh
Walk on By   Bacharach; David, Hal
Wanna Trade   Bergman; Fain
War for Justice   Warren
Warm Spot in My Heart, A   Drake
Warm Summer Kisses for a Cold Winter's Night   McHugh
Warm Summer Love   McHugh; Washington
Was She Prettier than I?   Martin
Way of Life, A   Fain
We Love You, Beatles   Adams; Strouse
We Who Are About to Die   David, Mack
Wedding of the Year   Drake
Welcome   Comden and Green; Styne
Welcome Home, Angelina   Howard, Bart
We're L-Losing Our L-Little Girl   Cahn; Van Heusen
What a Ball We Had   Oakland
What a Day   David, Mack
What a Way to Go   Comden and Green; Styne

What Do I Do for an Encore   McHugh
What Do You Want from Me   Brooks
What I Don't Know Will Never Hurt Me   McHugh
What in the World Did You Want   Martin
What in the World Do They Want?   Blane; Martin
What Is This Thing I've Got   Comden and Green; Styne
What Would Happen?   Bergman; Fain
What's Yours   Evans; Livingston, Jay
When a Hound Dog Man Has a Good Hound
    Dog   Sherman
When I Talk about You   Merrill; Styne
Where Is the Man I Married?   Martin
Where Love Has Gone   Cahn; Van Heusen
Which Way Is Home   Rome
While the City Sleeps   Adams; Strouse
White Bird and the Sycamore, The   Robison
Who Are You Now?   Merrill; Styne
Who Is Sylvia?   Blane; Martin
Who Taught Her Everything   Merrill; Styne
Whole Lotta Woman, A   McHugh
Why Is My Heart Such a Fool   Fain
Wintertime and Christmastime   Fain
With So Little to Be Sure Of   Sondheim
Wolf that Swallowed Red Riding Hood, The   Rome
Woman Alone, A   Coots
Woman's Place   Styne
Wonderful World of Beverly Hills, The   McHugh;
    Washington
(The Wonder of It All) Wonderworld   Styne
Work Song, The   Drake
Workout   Adams; Strouse
World's Not Ready, The   Washington
Wrong Number, A   Robison
Yellow and Green Make Blue   Freed, Ralph
Yes, I Can   Adams; Strouse
Yet I Know   Raye
You Are Woman   Merrill; Styne
You Can Trust Me   Drake
You Can't Make It Anywhere   Cahn; Van Heusen
You Deserve Me   Lawrence
You Go Your Way   Russell
You Gotta Taste All the Fruit   Bergman; Fain
You Help Me   Drake
You Meet the Nicest People at the Race Track   Coots
You Mustn't Be Discouraged   Comden and Green; Styne
You Never Had It So Good!   Cahn; Van Heusen
You Satisfy My Soul   David, Mack
You'd Better Love Me   Martin
You'll Never Get to Heaven (If You Break My
    Heart)   Bacharach; David, Hal
Young Lovers   Russell
Your Isle   Styne
You're a Boy After My Heart   Robison
You're It   Cahn; Van Heusen
You're No Go   Drake
You're the Girl for Me   Blane; Martin; Warren
Yours Could Be the Love   Coots
Zol Zein Mit Mazel   Yellen

1965

Adios Senorita   Evans; Livingston, Jay
Afterthoughts   DePaul; Leigh
Ah to Be Home Again Barabanchik   Loesser
Along Came Henry   Styne

Along the Way   Merrill; Styne
Amen to That   Friend
And Then I Wrote   Oakland; Spina
And Your Mother Said   Cahn; Van Heusen
Andy's Mystery Tune   Evans; Livingston, Jay
Are You Asking Me to Forget   Cahn; Van Heusen
Are You There (with Another Girl)   Bacharach; David, Hal
Art of Love, The   Coleman; Raye
Autograph Your Photograph   David, Mack
Autumn's in the Air   Styne
Ballad of Cat Ballou, The   David, Mack; Livingston, Jerry
Bargaining   Rodgers; Sondheim
Be a Man   Ellington
(I Feel) Beautiful Inside   Howard, Bart
Bells, The   Webster
Big One, A   Rome
Biggest Men Stumble, The   Rome
Bill the Buffalo   Caesar
Bittersweet   Mercer
Bless You, Darling   Baer; Leslie
Blue Print   Parish
Blue Was My Favorite Color (I Am)   Heyman
Bookworm (inst.)   Bacharach
Boot Camp A-Go-Go   Mills
Boss Is Not Here (All at Once It's Sunday), The   Bacharach; David, Hal
Boy Ten Feet Tall, A   Washington
Breakaway   Bergman
But Call Me   Freed, Ralph
Cabin Raising Song   Sherman
Can I Rely on You   Davis
Catch As Catch Can (inst.)   Bacharach
Cathedral   Parish
C'est Defendu   Rome
Chateau Chantal (inst.)   Bacharach
Cheat on Me   Mercer
Child, The   Webster
Chita (Chee-Tah)   Myrow
Christmas Surprise   Ellington
Circle of Your Arms, The   Leigh
Close Beside You   Adamson; Carmichael
Close Your Eyes, Mr. Moon   Sherman
Cold, Cold, Room   Rome
Colloque Sentimental   Parish
Come Back to Me   Lane; Lerner, Alan Jay
Come Love   Bergman
Compensation   Parish
Cousin Victor's Elixer   Sherman
Crocodile Wife   Rome
Dance Mamma, Dance Pappa, Dance (Marriage French Style)   Bacharach; David, Hal
Dancing Lesson   Lane
Dandy Sandy   Fain
Daphne   Coleman
Darlin' Girl   Bergman
Daughter of Molly Malone, The   Evans; Livingston, Jay
Dear Heart   Evans; Livingston, Jay; Mancini
Declaration   Parish
Delicatessen (A Way of Life) (Gaiety)   Cahn; Van Heusen
Delilah Done Me Wrong (The No Haircut Song)   Rome
Destination Is Love   Leigh
Dingle Ling, Dingle Ling   Merrill; Styne
Disenchanted Castle   Leigh
Disneyland Anniversary March   Sherman
Do I Hear a Waltz?   Rodgers; Sondheim

Dolly's Seduction   Lane; Lerner, Alan Jay
Domestic Champagne Waltz, The   Lane; Lerner, Alan Jay
Don't Go Breaking My Heart   Bacharach; David, Hal
Don't Say I Didn't Love You   Bacharach; David, Hal
Don't Take My Heart   Davis
Don't Tamper with My Sister   Lane; Lerner, Alan Jay
Don't Worry, Don't Worry (I Don't Worry)   Cahn; Van Heusen
Down, Down, Down, Down   David, Mack
Downhill and Shady   Bacharach; David, Hal
Dream, The   Webster
Eagle Soliloquy   Rome
Early Morning Blues   Coleman
Emily   Mercer
Epitaph for a Poet   Parish
E.S.P.   Lane
Every Child Is So Happy   Burke
Everybody Loves Leona   Rodgers; Sondheim
Ev'rybody Has the Right to Be Wrong   Cahn; Van Heusen
Expectation   Parish
Eye of a Needle, The   Bacharach; David, Hal
Far Far Far Away   Loesser
Flugel Street Rag   Ellington
Follow the Boys   Davis
Foolish Ones, The   Parish
Footsore Blues   McHugh; Razaf
For You   Rome
Forget It, Baby   Freed, Ralph
Fountain in the Rain   Mercer
Fountain of Teardrops   Sherman
Gallagher   Sherman
Gentle Is My Love   Raye
Get a Horse   Mancini; Mercer
Getting Myself Annoyed with Floyd   Robison
Ghost Town Music   Spina
Gina   Myrow
Girl, The   Webster
Girl's Best Friend, A   Ellington
Girls, Glorious Girls   Sherman
Give a Man a Tree   Freed, Ralph
Glad Days   Webster
Go to Sleep   Lane; Lerner, Alan Jay
Golden Broom and the Green Apple, The   Ellington
Gout (The Spasm) (inst.), The   Lane
Granny   Merrill; Styne
Granny's Gulch   Merrill; Styne
Hail Majesty   Loesser
Hamburg Waltz   Rome
Happy Song   Rome
Happy Time, The   Leigh
Harlow   Bacharach; David, Hal
Haute Couture   Cahn; Van Heusen
Have a Heart   Mercer
Have the Time of Your Life (With NBC)   Cahn
Hawaii   Rome
He Came Along   Adamson; Youmans
He Knew What He Wanted   Webster
He Shouldn't-a, Hadn't-a, Oughtn't-a Swang on Me   Mancini; Mercer
He Will Always Carry You Through   Blane; Martin
Hear that Band   Evans; Livingston, Jay
Hellraker's Dance (inst.), The   Lane
Here I Am   Bacharach; David, Hal
Here We Are Again   Rodgers; Sondheim
Here Where There Is Love   Bacharach; David, Hal

My Lover Is a Scoundrel   Loesser
My North Dakota Home   David, Mack
My Red Riding Hood   Merrill; Styne
Neither the Time Nor the Place   Loesser
Never Too Late   Evans; Livingston, Jay
New Vienna Woods, The   Evans; Livingston, Jay
Next Day Hill   Bacharach
Next Train Out, The   Russell
Nikki   Coleman
Nineteenth Hole, The   Styne
No Understand   Rodgers; Sondheim
Normal Thing to Do, The   Lane; Lerner, Alan Jay
Nostalgia   Parish
Nothing Has Changed   Freed, Ralph
Occasional Flight of Fancy, An   Cahn; Van Heusen
Oisgetzaichnet (Out of This World)   Rome
Old Milano   Coleman
Ole Friend   Freed, Ralph
Oliphant the Elephant   Caesar
On a Clear Day You Can See Forever   Lane; Lerner, Alan Jay
On a Snowy, Blowy Day   Baer
On the S.S. Bernard Cohn   Lane; Lerner, Alan Jay
One of the Best Dressed Women   Russell
Only the Strong, Only the Brave   Bacharach; David, Hal
Only Trust Your Heart   Cahn
Opposites   Cahn; Van Heusen
Orang-Utang   Caesar
Out of the Mist   Webster
Out of the Sound   Webster
Ouzo   Leigh
Pass Me By   Coleman; Leigh
Perfectly Lovely Couple   Rodgers; Sondheim
Perhaps   Rodgers; Sondheim
Philadelphia   Rodgers; Sondheim
Pianissimo   Parish
Picture, The   Heyman
Pleasure's About to Be Mine, The   Leigh
Pleasures and Palaces   Loesser
Poor Mouse (inst.)   Styne
Post-Mortem   Parish
Pray, And He Will Answer You   Washington
Pray Jezebel   David, Mack; Livingston, Jerry
Profile in Courage, A   Webster
Prologue   David, Mack; Livingston, Jerry
Promise Her Anything   David, Hal
Propaganda   Loesser
Pussy Cats on Parade (inst.)   Bacharach
Question of Love, A   Bacharach
Rawhide   Russell
Restless River   Spina
Reverie   Parish
Rhyme-Around   Sherman
Right to Love, The   Drake
Ring Out the Bells   Lane; Lerner, Alan Jay
Rivers of Tears   Rome
Roodle Doodle   David, Mack; Livingston, Jerry
Round and Round the Romance Tree   Evans; Livingston, Jay
Run for Your Life   Cahn; Van Heusen
Running Patter   David, Mack; Livingston, Jerry
Sadie the Seal   Caesar
Salute   Loesser
Salvage   Parish
Salvation   Ellington
Sandwich for Two   Rome

Say Goodbye   Bacharach; David, Hal
School for Anatomy (inst.)   Bacharach
Sea Gulls   Webster
Second Best Secret Agent in the Whole Wide World, The   Cahn; Van Heusen
See You Around   Evans; Livingston, Jay
Seed, The   Webster
September of My Years, The   Cahn; Van Heusen
She Wasn't You   Lane; Lerner, Alan Jay
Ship of Fools   Washington
Shoulda Stood in Bed   Arlen
Sings of Love, The   Sigman
Sins of Sura, The   Loesser
Sit Yourself Down   Freed, Ralph
Slender Thread, The   David, Mack
Slippy Sloppy Shoes   Rome
Snows of Yesteryear   Webster
Snubbed   Merrill; Styne
So Long Baby   Coleman
So Warm, My Love   Webster
Solicitor's Song   Lane; Lerner, Alan Jay
Soliloquy   Parish
Some Smart, Some Smart   Cahn; Van Heusen
Some Things   Rome
Someday You'll Be Sorry   Evans; Livingston, Jay
Someone in April   Lane; Lerner, Alan Jay
Someone Like You   Rodgers; Sondheim
Someone Woke Up   Rodgers; Sondheim
Something Big   Bacharach; David, Hal
Something Good   Rodgers
Sometime When You're Lonely (inst.)   Coleman
Somewhere, Someday   Baer
Song for a Merry-Go-Round   Parish
Song for an Anniversay   Parish
Song for Muted Strings   Parish
Song in Four Languages   Lane
Songwriter   Parish
Spanish Dance   Rome
Spare that Building   Cahn; Van Heusen
Spring Cleaning   Parish
Star Sounds   Mercer
Stay   Rodgers; Sondheim
Step to the Rear   Leigh
Stranger, The   Parish
Stripping Really Isn't Sexy, Is It (inst.)   Bacharach
Stuck for an Answer   Cahn; Van Heusen
Student's Demonstration Song   Lane
Such a Good Time   Freed, Ralph
Summer in Brooklyn   Arlen
Summer Wind   Mercer
Sweet Pussycat   Coleman
Sweetheart Tree, The   Mancini; Mercer
Sweetly and Completely   David, Mack
Take the Moment   Rodgers; Sondheim
Talkin' a Blue Streak   Russell
Tarnished Virtue   David, Mack; Livingston, Jerry
Teach Me to Pray   Webster
Teardrops from the Sky   Gorney
Tears   Sigman
Tears of Joy   Loesser
Temple Houston   Washington
Tenderfoot, The   Sherman
Terminus   Parish
Thank You So Much   Rodgers; Sondheim
That Ain't Love, Baby   David, Mack

That Darn Cat   Sherman
That Does It   Baer
That Travelin' Two-Beat   Evans; Livingston, Jay
That Was Then and Now Is Now   Coleman
That's a Fine Kind of Freedom   Arlen
That's the Way the Ball Bounces   Fain
That's What It Takes   Coleman
There's Love and There's Love and There's Love   Cahn; Van Heusen
There's More to Life   Cahn; Van Heusen
They Can't Make Her Cry   David, Mack; Livingston, Jerry
They Don't Make Them Like That Any More   Leigh
Think Ginger Rogers   Leigh
Thinkin' Chair   Robison
Thinking   Rodgers; Sondheim
This Is Our Secret Star   Webster
This Ol' World   Arlen
This Week Americans   Rodgers; Sondheim
Thrill of a Lifetime   Styne
Thunder and Bells   Loesser
Thunder and Lightning   Loesser
Time for Glory   Webster
Time o' Day, The   Bergman
Time of Decision, A   Webster
Tkambuza (Zulu Hunting Song)   Rome
To Be Continued   Brooks
To Marry   Loesser
To Your Health   Loesser
Tonight's My Night   Davis
Tosy and Cosh   Lane; Lerner, Alan Jay
Tracey   Styne
Trip to the Hole in the Wall   David, Mack; Livingston, Jerry
Truly Loved   Loesser
Truth, The   Ellington
Try a Little Forgiveness   Baer
Turkish Delight (inst.)   Loesser
Twinkle Twinkle   Howard, Bart
Twist-o-Flex   Carmichael
Two by Two   Rodgers; Sondheim
Tying Up the Loose Ends   Robison
Ugly Dachshund, The   Sherman
Underneath the Swanee Moon   Blake; Sissle
Unity Is Diversity   Washington
Up Your Ante   Ellington
Voice in the Wind, A   Webster
Voice Inside Me, A   Baer
Wait 'Til We're Sixty-Five   Lane; Lerner, Alan Jay
Waiting for Billy   Davis
Walk on the Wild Wharf, A (inst.)   Bacharach
Wallpaper Roses   Spina
Warm Summer Kisses for a Cold Winter's Night   Washington
Water Wears Down the Stone, The   Rome
We Wish the World a Happy Yule   Merrill; Styne
We're Gonna Be All Right   Rodgers; Sondheim
We're Gonna Howl Tonight   Merrill; Styne
What Did Dottie Do?   Baer; Gilbert
What Did I Have that I Don't Have   Lane; Lerner, Alan Jay
What Do We Do? We Fly!   Rodgers; Sondheim
What Is Life?   Loesser
What the World Needs Now Is Love   Bacharach; David, Hal
What's New Pussycat   Bacharach; David, Hal
What's the Use of Crying   Evans; Livingston, Jay
When I Come Around Again   Lane; Lerner, Alan Jay
When I Join the Circus   Blane

When I'm Being Born Again   Lane; Lerner, Alan Jay
When You Come Back to Me   Myrow
Whenever I Dream of You   Sherman
Where Is the Dear Man   Robison
Where You Are   Leigh
White World of Winter, The   Carmichael; Parish
Who Am I to Say No   Howard, Bart
Win the Big "E" with John V. Lindsay   Robison
Window Wishing   Bacharach; David, Hal
Winter Song   Parish
Wisdom   Parish
With Feeling   Howard, Bart
With Open Arms   Bergman
Wolf City   David, Mack; Livingston, Jerry
Wonderful World of Las Vegas   Styne
Woodman's Serenade   Merrill; Styne
Word of the Heart, The   Mercer
World of the Heart, The   Mercer
Wrong!   Cahn; Van Heusen
Xanadu (Les Elephants Roses) (La Marijuana)   Rome
Yankee Doodle   Lane; Lerner, Alan Jay
Year of the Tear, The   Russell
Yi, Yi, Yi (Aye, Aye, Aye)   Rome
Yo-Ho! Heave Ho! Yo-Ho!   Baer
You Bug Me Ann-Arlene   Sherman
You Gotta Pay the Freight   Bergman
You'll Get Over It   Leigh
You'll Walk in the Sun   Sherman
Young Americans, The   Webster
Your Smile   Parish
You're a Little Bit of Ev'rything (That I Like)   Baer
You're No Brother, No Brother of Mine   Adams; Strouse
Zulu Love Song (Wait for Me)   Rome

1966

Academy Award Song   Sherman
After the Fox   Bacharach; David, Hal
Ages Ago   Webster
Alfie   Bacharach; David, Hal
All of the Time   David, Mack
All the Love in the World   Sigman
Amazing   Ellington
Angela   Evans; Livingston, Jay
Another Night   Bacharach; David, Hal
Answer My Heart   Comden and Green; Styne
Any Wednesday   Bergman
Anywhere You Go   Drake
Around the Corner (Come Petred Dimenticarti)   Sigman
Baby, Dream Your Dream   Coleman; Fields
Baby San   Arlen
Baby, You're Right for Me   Mills
Bachelor, The   Merrill
Bad Is for Other People   Coleman
Ballad of Alvarez Kelly, The   Mercer
Ballad of Will Kane, The   Adamson
Be Joyful   Cahn; Van Heusen
Beatnik Bull Fighter (Beatnik Matador), The   Brooks
Been a Hell of an Evening   Arlen
Beg, Borrow or Steal   Freed, Ralph; Livingston, Jerry
Beginning of Loneliness, The   Bacharach; David, Hal
Bessie's Blues   Merrill
Better Together   Merrill
Big Spender   Coleman; Fields
Bird Bath (inst.)   Bacharach

I'm Serving Out a Heavy Sentence (Loving You) (Huddleston, Floyd)   Coleman
I'm the Bravest Individual   Coleman; Fields
I'm the Greatest Individual   Fields
I'm too Young to Die   Adams
I'm Too Young to Die It's a Long, Slow Climb Going Up but a Short, Fast Slide Coming Down   Strouse
I'm Way Ahead   Coleman; Fields
Imagine My Frustration   Ellington
Impossible   Freed, Ralph
In the Arms of Love   Evans; Livingston, Jay; Mancini
It Doesn't Matter Anymore   Bacharach; David, Hal
It Might As Well Be You   Cahn; Van Heusen
It Must Be Her (Him)   David, Mack
Italian Fuzz (inst.)   Bacharach
It's a Happening (The Happening)   Strouse
It's a Long, Slow Climb Going Up but a Short, Fast Slide Coming Down   Adams
It's Been Nice   Cahn; Van Heusen
It's Super Nice   Adams; Strouse
It's Superman   Adams; Strouse
I've Got a Penny   Merrill
I've Tried Everything   Coleman; Fields
Jack Go Back to Jill   Heyman
Jazzabeaux   Mills
Je N'Ai Rien   Ellington
Jive Stomp   Ellington
Joyful Thing, A   Cahn; Van Heusen
Juanita's Place Montage   Bacharach; David, Hal
Keep It in the Family   Coleman; Fields
Kip's Tune   Warren
Lament of Ten Men   Merrill
Lazy Sunday   Mills
Let Him Live (Dejalo Vivir)   Brooks
Let's   Ellington
Life's a Game   Adams; Strouse
Little Black Rain Cloud   Sherman
Little Travel Bug   Arlen
Love Theme from Torn Curtain   Evans; Livingston, Jay
Love Will Find a Way — They Say   Cahn; Van Heusen
Love X Two (inst.)   Bacharach
Lulamae   Merrill
Make a Movie in Sevalio   Bacharach; David, Hal
Man Has Got to Wear the Pants, The   Cahn; Van Heusen
Mardi Gras   Coleman
Maybe September   Evans; Livingston, Jay
Meanwhile   Adams; Strouse
Merry Go Round (inst.)   McHugh
Mind Over Matter   Sherman
Moment of Weakness, A   Heyman
Momma Knows Best   Arlen
Moonlight Matador   Brooks
More Time to Be with You   Bacharach
More You See of It, The   Arlen
Most Girls   Cahn; Van Heusen
Mount Harissa   Ellington
Must You Go   Cahn; Van Heusen
My Dream of the South of France   Kalmar; Ruby
My Garden of Prayer   Webster
My Lady Fair   Arlen
My Nice Ways   Merrill
My Red Roses Are Blue (inst.)   McHugh
My Wishing Doll   David, Mack
Natchez Trace   Ellington
NBC Jingle (inst.)   Willson

Nevada Smith   David, Hal
New York Is Go Go Going for the Mets, The Mets Are Go Go Going for New York   Davis
No More Mr. Nice (People Who Are Nice)   Cahn
Nobody Loves an Old Carousel   David, Mack
Nothing Is New in New York   Merrill
Now   Livingston, Jerry
Now I Know what Love Is   Howard, Bart
Old Fashioned Fourth, An   Willson
Old Fashioned Wedding, An   Berlin
Old World Charm   Ellington
Once I Wore Ribbons Here   Arlen
One Never Knows   Cahn
One of Those Goldarn UFO's   Robison
One Starry Moment   Cahn; Van Heusen
Only in the Movies   Bergman
Ooh, Do You Love You   Adams; Strouse
Pacific   Arlen
Parade   Russell
Paris Lullaby   Fain; Webster
Paris Smiles   Evans; Livingston, Jay
Pathfinder   Sigman
People Who Are Nice (No More Mr. Nice)   Van Heusen
Picture of You, A   Warren
Pink Taffeta Sample Size 10   Coleman; Fields
Policeman's Whistle, A   Cahn; Van Heusen
Poor Everybody Else   Coleman; Fields
Pow! Bam! Zonk!   Adams; Strouse
Prelude to America (inst.)   Willson
Promise Her Anything   Bacharach
Puzzle, The   Spina
Renco   Brooks
Revenge   Adams; Strouse
Rhythm of Life, The   Coleman; Fields
Rich Man's Frug   Coleman
Rose, The   Merrill
Rules and Regulations   Ellington
Rumbly in My Tumbly   Sherman
Run Girl Run (inst.)   Coleman
Same Mistakes   Merrill
Sand and Sea   David, Mack
Santa, Bring My Daddy Home for Xmas   Freed, Ralph
Santiago   David, Mack
Scum-Dee-Dum   Merrill
Second Portrait of the Lion, The   Ellington
Settle for Less   Ellington
Shadow of Your Smile, The   Webster
Shooby-Dooia   Mercer
Signora   Mercer
Silencers, The   David, Mack
(Remember) Smoke Tree Mountain   Spina
So Here We Are Again   Merrill
So Long, Big Guy   Adams; Strouse
Someone to Care For   Ellington
Somewhere My Love   Webster
Song for Christmas, A   Ellington
Song of the Bible   Webster
Sonnet   Blane
Sorry 'Bout That   Livingston, Jay
Space Race   Coleman
Spacious and Gracious   Ellington
Spanking Brand New Doll   Ellington
Speaking of Dreams   Adamson; Oakland
Spider and Fly, The   Ellington
Spring Has Me Out on a Limb   Arlen

Stay with Me   Merrill
Stiffen Up that Upper Lip   Cahn; Van Heusen
Stop Close to Me   Webster
Strongest Man in the World, The   Adams; Strouse
Such a Sociable Sort   Cahn; Van Heusen
Suddenly the Sunrise   Arlen
Sugar City   Ellington
Superman March (inst.), The   Strouse
Supernote, The   Adams; Strouse
Sure As You're Born   Bergman
Sweet Charity   Coleman; Fields
Sweet Love   Sigman
Swivel   Ellington
Take a Broken Heart   Bacharach; David, Hal
Take Me to the World   Sondheim
Tango d'Amor, The   Mills
Tell Me It's the Truth   Ellington
Tell Me Now   Russell
Temples   Arlen
Tender and Loving Care   Mercer
Texas Across the River   Cahn; Van Heusen
Thank You Ma'am   Ellington
Thank Your Stars   Adamson; Silver
(She Has) That Certain Something   Cahn
That Is the Moment of Truth (Esa es la Hora de la
   Verdad)   Brooks
That's How I Am (Asi es Que Soy Yo)   Brooks
(Who Needs) The Birds and Bees   Berlin
There Are They   Webster
There's a Girl in the Heart of Wheeling, West Virginia (With
   a Watch that Belongs to Me)   Ruby
There's Gotta Be Something Better than This   Coleman;
   Fields
There's No Love Like   Cahn; Van Heusen
These Are the Good Old Days   Ellington
They Don't Give Medals (To Yesterday's
   Heroes)   Bacharach; David, Hal
They'll Never Split Us Apart   Adams; Strouse
They're Gonna Love It   Bacharach; David, Hal
Think of Something Else   Cahn; Van Heusen
This Is the Place (inst.)   Myrow
Three Little Fishes   Kalmar; Ruby
Time for Love, A   Webster
Time to Smile   Mercer
Tiny Bit of Faith, A   Cahn; Van Heusen
Tired of Explaining   Razaf
To Keep the Chill Off the Bones   Cahn; Van Heusen
Today's a Wonderful Day   Adams; Strouse
Too Many Tomorrows   Coleman; Fields
Touch a Hair of His Head   Cahn; Van Heusen
Tourist Trap (inst.)   Bacharach
Toys in the Closet   Spina
Travellin'   Merrill
Trial By Jury   Bacharach; David, Hal
Try to See It My Way   Bacharach; David, Hal
Ukeatalia (inst.)   Bacharach
Ukelele Talk   Drake
Up, Down, and Touch the Ground   Sherman
Use Your Noggin   Cahn; Van Heusen
(Is He) Very Close to Wonderful   Cahn; Van Heusen
Via Veneto (inst.), The   Bacharach
Vincennes   Spina
Visiting Day   Bacharach; David, Hal
Walking Happy   Cahn
Was It Worth It   David, Mack

We Don't Matter at All   Adams; Strouse
We Need Him   Adams; Strouse
We Were Always to be Married   Arlen
Wedding, The   Ellington
Wedding Gown, Bridal Veil (For Sale)   Spina
Wednesday's Child   David, Mack
We've Loved Before   Evans; Livingston, Jay; Mancini
What Do You Think About Me?   Evans; Livingston, Jay
What Have I Done?   Brown, Lew; DeSylva; Henderson
What I've Always Wanted   Adams; Strouse
What Makes It Happen   Cahn; Van Heusen
Whatever Happened to Love (inst.)   McHugh
What's a Nice Kid Like You Doing in a Place Like
   This   Adams; Strouse
Wheeler Dealer (inst.)   Bacharach
When Daddy Came Home   Merrill
When Did You Know?   Coleman; Fields
When Willie Waltzes with Me   Cahn; Van Heusen
Where?   Sondheim
Where Am I Going?   Coleman; Fields
Where Was I   Cahn; Van Heusen
Who Could Love Me   David, Hal
Who Needs Her?   Merrill
Who Needs Who?   Cahn
Who's Afraid   Webster
Why Do You Make Me Like You?   Arlen
Wild, Wild River   Davis
Wintertime   Coleman
Wish Me a Rainbow   Evans; Livingston, Jay
Woggle Bird Song, The   Cahn; Van Heusen
Woman Alone, A   Adams; Strouse
Woman for the Man (Who Has Everything), The   Adams;
   Strouse
World of Make Believe   Bacharach; David, Hal
Wouldn't It Break Your Heart   Cahn; Van Heusen
Yellow Rain   Arlen
You Are Tomorrow   Arlen
You Can't Lose 'em All   Coleman; Fields
You Should See Yourself   Coleman; Fields
You Wanna Bet   Coleman; Fields
You're Not Fully Dressed Without a Smile   Arlen
You're Right, You're Right   Cahn; Van Heusen
You've Got Possibilities   Adams; Strouse
You've Got What I Need   Adams; Strouse
You've Never Kissed Her   Merrill
Zimba, Limba, Lay   Gorney

1967

A-B-C   Leigh
Academic Fugue   Merrill
After Everything I Doodle, Doodle, Doodle Do   Caesar
Agreer, The   Merrill
Alma Mater   Bacharach
Along About Now   Sigman
Another Day   Comden and Green; Styne
Answer My Heart   Comden and Green; Styne
Anticipation   Cahn
Are We Dancing?   Sherman
Baby, Don't You Quit Now   Mercer
Baby, You're Too Much   Ellington
Bach & Me   Oakland
Back in Mothers Day   Davis
Back in the Kitchen   Comden and Green; Styne
Barefoot in the Park   Mercer

Being Good Isn't Good Enough   Comden and Green; Styne
Bell for Adano   Styne
Best Performance, The   Cahn
Best Wishes   Cahn; Van Heusen
Big Beautiful Ball, A   Mercer
Big Cowboys and Indians Fight at Casino Royale (inst.),
   The   Bacharach
Big Talk   Comden and Green; Styne
Big Trouble   Leigh
Blue Matador   Cahn
Blushing Bride, A   Harburg; Styne
Bobo, The   Cahn
Bond Street (inst.)   Bacharach
Bonnie and Clyde (inst.)   Strouse
Bowlegged Polly   Bergman
Bramble Bush, The   David, Mack
Breadfruit Tree, The   Drake
Butler in the Abbey   Harburg; Styne
Bye-Yum Pum Pum   Sherman
Californee Gold   Sherman
Casino Royale   Bacharach; David, Hal
CFD and G Seventh Blues   Robison
Charlie's Number   Leigh
Clem's Drill (Dance Drill) (inst.)   Styne
Coliseum March, The   Drake
Colonel Hathi's March (The Elephant Song)   Sherman
Come Back to God/Me   Harburg; Styne
Crazy Night Ballet   Leigh
Credo (Rich Is Better)   Leigh
Darling of the Day, The   Harburg; Styne
Day I Say I Love You, The   Spina
Dearest Darling   Merrill
Delilah   Evans; Livingston, Jay
Detroit   Sherman
Do You Ever Go to Boston?   Merrill
Don't Be Afraid of an Animal   Rodgers
Don't Let a Good Thing Get Away   Leigh
Don't Pour the Thames Into the Rhine   Harburg; Styne
Don't Turn Me Off Baby   Brooks
Double Soliloquy   Harburg; Styne
Drawing of a Gardener's Hat (with Flowers)   Loesser
Dream On, James   David, Hal
Dream On, James, You're Winning (inst.)   Bacharach
Dream, Sweet Dreamer   Bacharach; David, Hal
Emperor's Thumb, The   Rodgers
Encore, Encore, Encore   Parish
Enter Laughing   David, Mack
Everybody Misses You   Spina
Eyes of Love, The   Russell
Face of My Love, The   Cahn
Far From the Madding Crowd   Webster
Far Out   Lawrence
Farewell, Farewell   Comden and Green; Styne
Feet Do Yo' Stuff   Comden and Green; Styne
F.F. (Forbidden Fruit)   Styne
Fine Young Man, A   Rodgers
Finisterre (inst.)   Johnson, James P.
Flying Saucer — First Stop Berlin (inst.)   Bacharach
Follow in Our Footsteps   Rodgers
For Squares Only   Oakland
Forever   Merrill
Fortuosity   Sherman
Foul Owl   Bergman
Frantically Romantic   Merrill
Freedom March (inst.)   Styne

Fun City   Cahn
Gentleman's Gentleman, A   Harburg; Styne
Getting Married (Living As One)   Styne
Girls of San Francisco, The   Sherman
Gnome-Mobile Song (In Me Jaunting Car), The   Sherman
Go Yankee Go   Davis
God Is Love   Strouse
Golden Voyage   Warren
Goodbye, Failure, Goodbye (Gawk, Tousle and
   Shucks)   Leigh
Greek Goddess   Spina
Guess What   Merrill
Guess What Charlie   Leigh
Hallelujah Baby!   Comden and Green; Styne
Hands of Time   Webster
Happy New Year to You   Coleman
Harry the Hat   Robison
Henry Leek   Harburg; Styne
Henry Sweet Henry   Merrill
Her Petticoat Was Showing   Ruby
Here I Am   Merrill
Here's a Salute to the Army   Cahn
He's a Genius   Harburg; Styne
He's Here   Leigh
Hey   Comden and Green; Styne
Hi There, Miss Goodthighs (inst.)   Bacharach
Home, James, Don't Spare the Horses (inst.)   Bacharach
How Can I Tell Her   Coots
How Do You Say Auf Wiedersehn   Mercer
How Long Is Forever?   Evans; Livingston, Jay
How Now Down Jones   Leigh
I Ain't Got It for the Guy That's Got It for Me   Leigh
I Believe in This Country   Sherman
I Depend on You   Evans; Livingston, Jay
I Don't Know Where She Got It   Comden and Green; Styne
I Just Stood and Stared   Warren
I Like the Look   Mancini
I Love You and You Love Me   Spina
I Say a Little Prayer   Bacharach; David, Hal
I Wanna Be Like You (The Monkey Song)   Sherman
I Want a Man for All Seasons   Fain
I Want to Get Arrested   Comden and Green; Styne
I Wanted to Change Him   Comden and Green; Styne
I Wonder How It Is (To Dance with a Boy)   Merrill
I'll Always Be Irish   Sherman
I'll Never Be Alone Again   Alter; Kahal
I'm Blue Too   Merrill
I'm Gonna Make You Love Me   Spina
I'm in Love with an Older Man   Fain
I'm in Love with You   Spina
I'm Not in Love Anymore (Acre Mentuer)   Webster
I'm Simply Mad for Bones   Harburg; Styne
Imagine   Cahn
In the Garden, Under the Tree   Webster
In the Heat of the Night   Bergman
Isn't This a Day   Harburg; Styne
It Only Happens Once   Webster
It Sure Is Groovy   Bergman
It's Always Linda   Heyman
It's Crazy   Sigman
It's Enough to Make a Lady Fall in Love   Harburg; Styne
It's Gonna Be You   Leigh
I've Been Here Before   Cahn; Van Heusen
I've Got a Rainbow Working for Me   Harburg; Styne
Jersey Americans, The   Alter; Davis

Joie De Vivre   Sherman
Just How Much Do I Love You   Spina
Knickerbocker Grey's March   Merrill
Knock-Knock-Knock (Let Me In)   Gorney
Lady Alice   Harburg; Styne
Las Vegas   Spina
Le Chiffre's Torture of the Mind (inst.)   Bacharach
Lesson, The   David, Mack
Let It Happen   Adams; Strouse
Let Your Love Come Through   Bacharach; David, Hal
Let's Have a Drink on It   Sherman
Let's See What Happens   Harburg; Styne
Life Oh Life   Merrill
Like Heaven   David, Hal
Limbo Dance (inst.)   Styne
Lisa   Bacharach; David, Hal
Little Action, A   Merrill; Styne
Little Button, A   Merrill; Styne
Little French Boy (inst.)   Bacharach
Little Investigation, A   Leigh
Little Red Apple   Evans; Livingston, Jay
Live a Little   Leigh
Lonely Is the Name   Sigman
Long Ago Last Night   Webster
Long Ride Home, The   Washington
Look of Love, The   Bacharach; David, Hal
Los Angeles, Los Angeles   Oakland
Love Casts Its Shadow   Bacharach
Love, Happiness and Peace of Mind   Spina
Love Is Our Umbrella   Comden and Green; Styne
Love of My Life   Merrill
Loves of July (Les Amours de Julliet), The   Webster
"Luv" Is a Three Letter Word   Ruby
Lying in State   Harburg; Styne
Mad for Art   Harburg; Styne
Make Me Rainbows   Bergman
Marguerita's Getting Mad   Oakland
Marilyn   David, Mack
Maybe God Is Black   Oakland
Meaning of Spring, The   Livingston, Jerry
Mercy McBee   David, Mack
Mommy Cat   Merrill
Mon Amour, Mon Amour   Sigman
Money, Money, Money   Harburg; Styne
Money Penny Goes for Broke (inst.)   Bacharach
More and More Amore   Webster
Mr. Thrumm's Chase   Webster
Music to Their Ears   Leigh
My Inamorata   Mercer
My Kind of Person   Merrill
My New York   Cahn; Van Heusen
My Own Home (Jungle Book Theme)   Sherman
My Own Morning   Comden and Green; Styne
Nan   Webster
Need of You, The   Cahn
Nervous   Merrill
Night the Rabbi Didn't Show, The   Drake
Nikki   Bacharach; David, Hal
No Going Back   Sigman
No More Waiting   Rodgers
Nobody Steps on Kafritz   Merrill
Not Mine   Comden and Green; Styne
Not on Your Nellie   Harburg; Styne
Not with My Wife, You Don't   Mercer
Now's the Time   Comden and Green; Styne

Oh Dad, Poor Dad, Mamma's Hung You in the Closet and
     I'm Feelin' So Sad   David, Hal
Oh, Where Are You?   Blake
On the Downtown Side of an Uptown Street   Livingston,
     Jerry
One Little Girl at a Time   David, Hal
One More Day of Sunshine   Merrill
One of Those Moments (Just for the Moment)   Leigh
Our Little Mid Manhattan Pied a Terre   Leigh
Panache   Harburg; Styne
Panic   Leigh
Papa Good Time   Mercer
People Watchers, The   Merrill
Phantom of Pigalle, The   Oakland
Pillar to Post   Merrill
Please Be an Angel, Angel   Spina
Poor Little Person   Merrill
Pretty Thing   Merrill
Priam Faril   Harburg; Styne
Private Line to Heaven   Robison
Psychadelic Sally   Livingston, Jerry
Putney on the Thames   Harburg; Styne
Reckless Rooster March   Merrill
Rich Kid, The   Cahn
Rio de Janeiro (In Copacabana)   Sigman
Roots   Comden and Green; Styne
Rose Loved Roses   Cahn; Van Heusen
Rosie!   Mercer; Warren
Sands of Time   Sherman
Say Goodbye (Turn Around Walk Away)   Sigman
Sea Chanty   Leigh
Serpent, The   Webster
Shakespeare Lied (You'll Get Over It)   Leigh
She Needs Me   Sondheim
She's Too Hip to Be Happy   Coleman
Shy Old Billionaire, The   Robison
Silent Treatment   Hoffman
Silently   Coots
Sir James' Trip to Find Mata (inst.)   Bacharach
Slice, The   Comden and Green; Styne
Smile, Smile, Smile   Comden and Green; Styne
Soap and Water Are My Friends   Caesar
Some Little World   Merrill
Somebody Some Place   Merrill
Someday I'll Grow Up   Caesar
Something Extra   Adams; Strouse
Sometimes (I Just Can't Stand You)   Spina
Sorry About That   Drake
Soul Savin' Sara   Robison
Spider Man   Webster
Spongecake and Wine   Davis
Status Quo   Leigh
Step to the Rear   Leigh
Strangers   Rodgers
Strength Is My Weakness   Rodgers
Strengthen the Dwelling   Sherman
Summer Love   Myrow
Swahili Serenade   David, Mack
Sweet Mouth   Cahn
Swindle, The   Webster
Take a Bow   Livingston, Jerry
Take Me There   Leigh
Talking to Yourself   Comden and Green; Styne
Tangiers   Leigh
(Tap-Tap-) Tapioca, The   Cahn; Van Heusen

Tears of Joy   Webster
Temple of the Tall Trees, The   Russell
Tennessee Rose   Spina
That Something Extra Special   Harburg; Styne
That Stranger in Your Eyes   Harburg; Styne
That's a Miracle   Heyman
That's Good Enough for Me   Leigh
That's Music   Leigh
That's What Friends Are For (Vulture Song)   Sherman
There Are Those   Sherman
There Is a Place for Lovers   Spina
There Was a Time   Sigman
There's Magic in the Name of the Palace   Davis
This Could Have Been Mine   Evans; Livingston, Jay
Thoroughly Modern Millie   Cahn; Van Heusen
Times Will Change, The   Sigman
To Be Artistic   Merrill
To Get Out of this World Alive   Harburg; Styne
Tomorrow Never Comes   Mercer
Too Late for Tears   Cahn
Touch and Go   Leigh
Trust in Me (Python's Song)   Sherman
Two Clean Hands   Caesar
Two for the Road   Mancini
Ugly, Ugly Gal   Comden and Green; Styne
Under the Ropes (inst.)   Styne
Under the Sunset Tree   Harburg; Styne
Up in Smoke   Leigh
Valentine Candy   Sherman
Velvet Paws   Rodgers
Venerable Mr. James Bond (inst.), The   Bacharach
Venetia   Comden and Green; Styne
Vino D'Amore   Cahn
Voice of Love (The Sound of Love), The   Heyman
Wait Until Dark   Evans; Livingston, Jay; Mancini
Walk Away   Leigh
Walk, Little Dolly   Bacharach; David, Hal
Wall Street Hoedown   Leigh
War Wagon Theme Song   Washington
Watch My Dust   Comden and Green; Styne
Watch Your Footwork   Sherman
Way West, The   David, Mack
We Will Find a Way   Adams; Strouse
Weary Near to Dyin'   Merrill
W.E.E.P.   Bacharach; David, Hal
Welcome to My Love   Cahn
We'll Stand and Cheer   Leigh
Westminster Funeral   Harburg; Styne
What Do We Do with the World   Mancini; Russell
What Makes a Marriage Merry   Harburg; Styne
What's Wrong with That?   Sherman
When a Man Has a Daughter   Sherman
When I Marry Alice   Harburg; Styne
When the Weather's Better   Comden and Green; Styne
When You Care a Lot for Someone Who Cares So Little for
     You   Davis
Where You Are   Leigh
Whereas   Merrill
Whoever You Are   Sherman
Why Do We Have to Fight to Fly Old Glory   Robison
Wide Place in the Road   Mercer
Wind Song   Webster
Windows of the World, The   Bacharach; David, Hal
Witches' Brew   Comden and Green; Styne
(You Look Like a) Woman in Love (To Me)   Merrill

World of Your Embrace, The   Drake
World that Never Was, A   Fain; Webster
You Ain't Gonna Shake Them Feathers No More   Comden
     and Green; Styne
You and Me   Comden and Green; Styne
You Are There   Webster
You Might Get to Like Me   Merrill
Your Kind of Man   Comden and Green; Styne
You're the Apple of My Eye (And I Love Apples)   Ruby
You're the Greatest (The Complimentary Song)   Baer
You're Welcome   Comden and Green; Styne
You've Got to Be Way Out to Be In   Berlin

1968

Afternoon Delight   Duke
Age of Innocence   Lawrence
Ain't It the Truth Babe   David, Mack
Albertina's Beautiful Hair   Arlen
All in God's Good Time   Robison
All of My Life   Oakland
Amanda   Rome
Anthony for President   Brooks
Arouse, Arouse   Rome
As Long As There's an Apple Tree   Bacharach; David, Hal
Autumn Sings a Sad, Sad Song   Cahn
Ban the Book!   Duke
Be Cool and Groovy for Me   Ellington
Boozers and Losers   Coleman
Bossa Nova Roma   Cahn
'Bout Time   Sherman
Candles in the Wind   Webster
Can't Make It with the Same Man Twice   Fain
Carousel, The   Cahn
Cats at the Va-dee-gan   Johnson, James P.
Censorship   Duke
Chi-Chi Face   Sherman
Chihuahua Choo Choo Train   Carmichael
Chitty Chitty Bang Bang   Sherman
Christmas Day   Bacharach; David, Hal
Christmas Is for Children   Van Heusen
Coolie's Prayer   Sondheim
Cowpoke Song, The   Sherman
Dakota   Sherman
Dangerous Age, The   Drake
Dark Song   Arlen
Deborah   Sigman
Diamond in the Rough   Duke
Didn't The Angels Sing? (Martin Luther King)   Blake; Sissle
Do Not Be Afraid of Love   Arlen
Do You Know the Way to San Jose   Bacharach; David, Hal
Doll on a Music Box   Sherman
Don't Fool Around with the Moon   Ager
Don't Get Down on Your Knees to Pray Until You Have
     Forgiven Everyone   Ellington
Don't Trust Anyone   Blane; Martin
Door Will Be Open (A Light Will Be Burning), The   Sigman
Dream of My Dream   Sigman
Drummin' Drummin' Drummin'   Sherman
East of Java   David, Mack
Even When You Cry   Bergman
Everytime I Think of You   Bergman
Ev'ry One of Us   Duke
Facade   Russell
Face in the Mirror, The   Russell

Fact Can Be a Beautiful Thing, A   Bacharach; David, Hal
Far Away Rooms and Long Ago Moments   Bergman
Father Forgive   Ellington
Finesse   Ellington
Fini for Now   Russell
Five Card Stud   Washington
Five Pounds Overweight   Fain
Flame Water   Blane; Martin
Flea in Her Ear, A   Cahn
Folk Dance   Sondheim
For Losers Only   Oakland
For Love of Ivy   Russell
Fred   Cahn
Freedom (Parts 1-7)   Ellington
Freedom (Sweet Fat and That)   Ellington
Freedom (Word You Heard)   Ellington
Fun Fair   Sherman
Funny Girl   Merrill; Styne
Gamblin' Fool, A   Oakland
Give Me the Open Air   Sondheim
God Has Those Angels   Ellington
Going Great   Cahn
Good Guys, The   Evans; Livingston, Jay
Grand Manner, The   Duke
Grapes of Roth (inst.)   Bacharach
Great Chord Sequence, Man   Russell
Greek Dance   Sondheim
Guess Who's Coming to Dinner   David, Mack
Hail to the Sphinx   Drake
Half As Big As Life   Bacharach; David, Hal
Hang In There   Sondheim
Happiest Girl Alive, The   Sherman
He Who Loves   Bacharach; David, Hal
Heaven   Ellington
Heffalumps and Woozles   Sherman
Heigh Ho for Mother (Heigh Ho for a Husband)   Blane; Martin
Her First Roman   Drake
Here Comes the Summertime   Coots
Here's Looking at You   Fain; Kahal
He's a Fallen Angel   Blane; Martin
Hip Hip Pooh-Ray!   Sherman
His Eyes — Her Eyes   Bergman
Hot Food   Bacharach; David, Hal
House of 7 Joys   David, Mack
How Can Anything So Wrong Be So Right   Evans; Livingston, Jay
How Can the Radio Know   Sigman
How Do I Feel   Blane; Martin
How Do You Get to Doodletown   Bergman
How I Loved Her   Adams; Strouse
How Lucky Can a Guy Get   Oakland
How Shall We Begin   Evans; Livingston, Jay
How to Save Your Marriage and Ruin Your Life   David, Mack
How You Played the Game   Cahn
Hushabye Mountain   Sherman
I Cannot Make Him Jealous   Drake
I Don't Know Where I'm Going   Drake
I Fell and Broke My Heart   Ellington
I Fell in with Evil Companions   Drake
I Had a Dream   Alter; Davis
I Have Given My Love   Ellington
I Love Your Vibrato   Blane; Martin
I May Never Get Well Again   Duke

I Taught Her Everything She Knows   Leigh
I Turn to You   Evans; Livingston, Jay
I Wrote a Song for You (Canzonne Per Te)   Sigman
I'd Be So Happy   Coots
I'll Never Fall in Love Again   Bacharach; David, Hal
I'll Never Forgive Myself   Mercer
I'm Not His Sister Anymore   Duke
In Rome Do As the Romans Do   David, Mack; Oakland
In the Days of Splendor   Webster
In the Right Kind of Light   Bacharach; David, Hal
In Vino Veritas   Drake
It Isn't Quite the Same   Cahn
It's a Nice Face   Coleman; Fields
It's Always Four A.M.   Cahn
It's Turkey Lurkey Time   Bacharach; David, Hal
I've Been Loved   Cahn
Jets March Song   Caesar
Jump de Broom   Arlen
Jumpin' Frog   Duke
Just Across the Mountains   Mercer
Just for Today   Drake
Kind of a Girl I'd Like to Be, The   Blane; Martin
Kiss of Long Ago, The   Webster
Laughter and Tears   Evans; Livingston, Jay
Let Me Be Lonely   Bacharach; David, Hal
Let Me Lead the Way   Drake
Let's Make America What It Used to Be   Webster
Let's Pretend We're Grownup   Bacharach; David, Hal
Let's Put It Over with Grover   Sherman
Life and Times of Lady Milicant Widdicomb James   Russell
Like a Lover   Bergman
Live and Love A Lot   Duke
Lizzette   Cahn; Van Heusen
Lonely Creatures   Merrill
Look Around   Bergman
Look No Further, Angel   Merrill
Losers, The   Cahn; Van Heusen
Lovely, Lonely Man   Sherman
Low   Duke; Oakland
Loyal, Resourceful and Cooperative   Bacharach; David, Hal
Lylah   David, Mack
Madam Tango's Particular Tango   Arlen
Magic Carpet   Drake
Man Called Gannon, A   Bergman
Man Has to Love, A   Fain
Man You Are, The   Duke
Man's Delight, A   Oakland
Many Young Men from Now   Drake
Me Old Bamboo   Sherman
Meet Me Halfway   Drake
Melting Pot   Blane; Martin
Merchant's March   Sondheim
Merry Came By   Russell
Miracles from Molecules   Sherman
Moondust   Sigman
Movie Theme (inst.)   Henderson
My Child Wants to Know   Leigh
My Lonely Love   Ellington
My Love Has Two Faces   Lawrence
My Personal Property   Coleman; Fields
My World   Drake
Nearly   Cahn
New Pilgrims' Prayer, The   Duke
New Year Filled with Love, A   Duke
New York   Blane

New York When I Join the Circus   Martin
New York's Good Morning Song   Blane; Martin
Nice Old Fashioned Girl, A   David, Mack
Night They Raided Minsky's, The   Adams; Strouse
Night Train to Memphis   Ellington
Nine Out of Ten Girls   Alter; Davis
No One   Oakland
Nothin'   Sherman
Nothing to Lose   Mancini
Now I Lay Me Down to Sleep   Heyman
Nowhere   David, Mack
Odd Couple, The   Cahn
Ol' Benjamin Harrison   Sherman
Old Friends   Bergman
Once Upon a Yesterday   Cahn
One and Only, Genuine, Original Family Band,
    The   Sherman
One Day   Bergman
One Day at a Time   Russell
One Good Friend's Enough   Blane; Martin
One Less Bell to Answer   Bacharach; David, Hal
One Man   Alter; Davis
Our Little Secret   Bacharach; David, Hal
Our Own Living Love Song   Oakland
Parable of the Monkey, The   Drake
Party, The   Mancini
Pendulum Swings Both Ways, The   David, Mack
Penny Arcade (inst.)   Strouse
Perfect Chaperone, The   Duke
Perfect Gentleman   Adams; Strouse
Petulia   Leigh
Phone Calls   Bacharach; David, Hal
(Locked in a) Pink Velvet Jail   Merrill; Styne
P.J.'s Theme   Cahn
Please Be Patient with Me   Duke
Pleasure Him   Drake
Pompeii Club (inst.), The   Coleman
Posh!   Sherman
Powder My Back   Adams; Strouse
Prologue March   Sondheim
Promises, Promises   Bacharach; David, Hal
Quadrille, The   Duke
Race Through the Desert (I Have Got to Get There in Seven
    Days Flat)   Sondheim
Raggedy Ann and Raggedy Andy   Bergman
Rainbow People   Heyman
Rather Blustery Day, A   Sherman
Reserved for Lovers   Livingston, Jerry; Webster
Rita   Johnson, James P.
Roller Skate Rag   Merrill; Styne
Rome   Drake
Roses of Success, The   Sherman
Safe Little World   Duke
Samantha   Oakland
Sanka Commercial #1   Rome
Save Me from Caesar   Drake
Seven Deadly Virtues, The   Drake
She Has to Be the Right Girl   Duke
She Likes Basketball   Bacharach; David, Hal
She'll Be There   David, Mack
Smile, A Mem'ry and an Extra Shirt, A   Bergman
So Many Stars   Bergman
So Pretty   Comden and Green
Soft of a Hand, The   Rome
Somehow   Cahn

Somethin' Cold to Drink   Arlen
Something 'Bout Believing   Ellington
Song of Long Ago, The   Carmichael; Mercer
Song of the Land I Love   Cahn
Song Without a Name   Webster
Spell You Spin, the Web You Weave, The   Russell
Stanley Jones, Meet Amelia Furst   David, Mack
Star!   Cahn; Van Heusen
Stay Til Morning   Russell
Step Into My Parlor   Oakland
Stranger Don't Go   Lawrence
Suspicion Song   Sondheim
Swan, The   Merrill; Styne
Sweet Charity   Coleman; Fields
Take 10 Terrific Girls (But Only 9 Costumes)   Adams;
    Strouse
Take Break Blues   Sondheim
Target for Tonight   Oakland
Tattered Tom   Blane; Martin
Ten Feet Off the Ground   Sherman
T.G.T.T.   Ellington
Thankful   Cahn
There Was No Room at the Inn   Fain
There's a World Out There   Sigman
There's No Place Like Home   Cahn
They Got This Little Secret   Sondheim
Things I Should Have Said, The   Lawrence
Things We Think We Are, The   Drake
This Guy's in Love with You   Bacharach; David, Hal
Tick Tock Goes the Clock   Bacharach; David, Hal
To America — With Love   Webster
Tokyo   Ellington
Tomatoes   Cahn
Tomorrow Valley   Sherman
Tony Pastor's   Blane; Martin
Toot Sweets   Sherman
Trial, The   Sondheim
Truly Scrumptious   Sherman
Two Friends   Strouse
2 Is Company   Blane; Martin
Two's Company   Martin
Up to My Elbows   Blane; Martin
Upstairs   Bacharach; David, Hal
Urga   Sondheim
Valse Erda (inst.)   Blake
Velvet Night   Mercer
Viva el Amor   Sigman
Vulgarian March   Sherman
Wait for Me   Adams; Strouse
Wait 'Till Tomorrow   DePaul
Walk to de Grave   Arlen
Walkin' Backwards Down the Road   Bacharach; David, Hal
Wanting Things   Bacharach; David, Hal
We're All Going on a Honeymoon   Duke
West of the Wide Missouri   Sherman
What Am I Doing Here   Bacharach; David, Hal
What Are We Doing in Egypt?   Drake
What Became of Me?   Adams; Strouse
What Do You Wanna Get Married For?   Duke
Whatagot   Oakland
What's in It for Harry   Merrill
When I Join the Circus   Blane; Martin
When I Was a Little Boy   Duke
When My Back Is to the Wall   Drake
When Summer Comes   Webster

When Summer Turns to Snow   Bergman
When the Rain Rain Rain Came Down   Sherman
When You've Had It All   Ellington
Whenever I'm with You   Blane; Martin
Where Can You Take a Girl   Bacharach; David, Hal
Where There Is Love   Fields
Where Would I Go   Bacharach; David, Hal
Who Is Gonna Love Me   Bacharach; David, Hal
Whoever You Are, I Love You   Bacharach; David, Hal
Wife Never Understand   Arlen
Windmills of Your Mind, The   Bergman
Winds of Change, The   David, Mack
With Love   Evans; Livingston, Jay
Woman   Ellington
Woman Are Here to Stay   Blane; Martin
Women Are Here to Stay   Blane; Martin
Wonderful Thing About Tiggers, The   Sherman
Wonders of a Barrel, The   Arlen
World Goes On, The   Bergman
Wouldn't that Be a Stroke of Luck   Bacharach; David, Hal
Wrong Man, The   Drake
You Are Youth   Duke
You Make That Hat Look Pretty   Ellington
You Rat, You   Adams; Strouse
You Two   Sherman
You'll Think of Someone   Bacharach; David, Hal
Young, Pretty Girl Like You, A   Bacharach; David, Hal
You're a Little Black Sheep   Ellington
You're Laughin', I'm Cryin'   Alter; Davis
(I'm the Singer) You're the Song   Sigman
You've Set Your Watch   Cahn

1969

All at Once   Cahn
Alone in My Own Little House   Blane
Alone Too Long   Russell
Always Mademoiselle   Lerner, Alan Jay
Anticipation and Hesitation   Ellington
Anyone and Everyone   Sigman
April Fools, The   Bacharach; David, Hal
Are You Smiling?   Gorney
As I Was Remarking   Rome
Ask   Spina
Ballad of Marshall Flagg, The   Washington
Ballad of Smith and Gabriel Jimmy Boy, The   Russell
Baloo's Blues   Sherman
Beast's Song, The   Martin
Bells of Christmas, The   Cahn; Van Heusen
Best Score of a Musical   Bergman; Mancini
Best Things   Lerner, Alan Jay
Better Way, A   Blane
Birthday. . .   Willson
Blissful Christmas   Rome
Blue Rag in Twelve Keys (inst.)   Blake
Blue Seas   Bacharach; David, Hal
Blueberry Eyes (Kokemomo No Hitomi)   Rome
Bobtail   Blane
Bonnie Blue Flag, The   Rome
Bonnie Gone (Boni No Shi)   Rome
Born in a Briar Patch   Blane
Brand New Dress, A   Lerner, Alan Jay
Bunny Song   Harburg
But I Will Never Say   Willson
But That's the Way You Are   Lerner, Alan Jay

Charro!   Bergman
(It Must Be Getting) Close to Christmas   Van Heusen
Coco   Lerner, Alan Jay
Companeros   Loesser
Corner Chestnut and Low in Baltimore (inst.)   Blake
Could Be   Gorney
Cumberland County Jail   Drake
Daisy and Rainbows   Harburg
Darling, I Am Growing Young   Gorney
Delfy's Song   Martin
Etta in Bolivia (inst.)   Bacharach
Every Woman Is a Queen   Willson
Faith Is a Song   Cahn; Van Heusen
(If You) Fall in Love in Rome   Spina
Falling Leaves   Cahn
Father's Song, The   Martin
Fiasco   Lerner, Alan Jay
Fine Art of Treachery, The   Gorney
First Six Days, The   Drake
First Thing You Know, The   Lerner, Alan Jay
Five O'Clock Sky   Fields
For Me Alone   Sigman
Forever Waltz, The   Cahn
Forgive and Forget   Blane
Gabrielle   Lerner, Alan Jay
Gaily, Gaily   Bergman; Mancini
Gambling Man   Rome
General Douglas MacArthur's "Duty, Honor, and
     Country"   Blane
Genius   Willson
Get a Map   Willson
Girl that I Know   Duke; Kern
Girl that Was, The   Harburg
Glory-Land Intro   Willson
God Is Alive   Cahn; Van Heusen
Gold Fever   Lerner, Alan Jay
Gospel of No Name City, The   Lerner, Alan Jay
Green Years of Love, The   Webster
Guardin' the Garden   Blane
Happy Anniversary Baby   Bergman
He Ain't Heavy. . . He's My Brother   Russell
Heaven Helps Him, Who Helps Himself   Cahn; Van Heusen
Heaven Smiles on Tepancingo   Loesser
Henry   Rome
Hey-O   Blane
Hit the Road (You Bumble Bee)   Blake; Razaf
How Close He Came   Cahn
How Come?   Oakland
How Does a Man Become a Puppet   Bacharach; David, Hal
Hurry Up 'n Hurry Down   Bergman
I Am Never Alone   Cahn; Van Heusen
I Cannot Let You Go   Loesser
I For My Glory Land   Willson
I Got to Have a Somebody   Loesser
I Love Him   Loesser
I Love My Machine Gun   Gorney
I Would Trade Christmas (And All that Jolly Jazz)   Cahn;
     Van Heusen
I Wouldn't Want Her Any Other Way   Spina
If I Should Ever Get You (I'll Never Let You Go)   Woods
If Santa Gets Stuck in the Chimney!   Styne
I'll Never Say I Love You   Willson
I'm a Better Man (for Having Loved You)   Bacharach; David,
     Hal
In My Own Way   Spina

In the Front o' the Bottom of Me Middle   Blane
Ingratitude   Blane
Isabella Catholica   Willson
It Won't Be Long Till Christmas   Sherman
It's a Kick   Sherman
It's Afro-American Day   Blake; Sissle
Just a Gentle Word from You Will Do   Ellington
Just Strike a Match   Spina
Lady   Willson
Lady Lizzie of Milan   Gorney
Lantern Lights   Spina
Lash the Wheel   Willson
Last Leaf on the Apple Tree, The   Spina
Let Me Go to Rio   Bacharach; David, Hal
Let's Go Home   Lerner, Alan Jay
Little Bit Older (A Little Bit Wiser), A   Parish
Little Wonders (Kawaii Odoroki)   Rome
Lonely Place, A   Webster
Lonely Stranger   Rome
Lonely Stranger (Passing Through) (Sabishii Tabibito)   Rome
Look Around (You'll Find Me)   Sigman
Love Doesn't Grow Like Apples on a Tree   Cahn
Love Is a Headache   Spina
Love Is a Two-Way Street   Baer
Love Letter   Drake
Love Like Yours   Mercer
Love Story   Sigman
Love That Game   Rome
Love You   Rome
Mademoiselle Cliche de Paris   Lerner, Alan Jay
Madrigal   Gorney
Mary Pistologlione   Rome
May I Present   Blane
Maybe Tomorrow   Bergman
Me   Cahn
Mexicali Brass   Ellington
Mexico City   Loesser
Million Miles Away Behind the Door, A   Lerner, Alan Jay
Mine and Mine Alone   Russell
Miracle of Christmas   Mercer
Miracle of Spring, The   Warren
Mirror of Morning, The   Russell
Money Rings Out Like Freedom, The   Lerner, Alan Jay
Moon Maiden   Ellington
Moon Suite, The   Ellington
My Heart Is Like the Willow   Harburg
My Soldier (Watashi No Heishi)   Rome
Natalie   Mancini
Near but Never Too Near   Willson
Newlyweds' Song, The   Rome
Night in Las Vegas, A   Blane
Not Goin' Home Anymore (inst.)   Bacharach
Now that I've Known Your Love   Cahn
Odds and Ends (Of a Beautiful Love Affair)   Bacharach; David, Hal
Oh, I Want to Go Home   Strouse
O'Hara   Rome
Ohrbach's, Bloomingdale's, Best and Saks   Lerner, Alan Jay
Old Fun City (inst.), The   Bacharach
On a Bicycle Built for Joy   Bacharach
On a Bicycle Built for Two (inst.)   Bacharach
On Her Majesty's Secret Service   David, Hal
On the Corner of the Rue Cambon   Lerner, Alan Jay
One Does Not Smile   Willson
One Sweet Day   Harburg

Pacific Coast Highway   Bacharach; David, Hal
Padre, I Have Sinned   Loesser
Pan Pan Pan   Loesser
Pancito, She Would Call Me   Loesser
Papa, Come Home   Loesser
Paper Mache   Bacharach; David, Hal
Paseo, The   Loesser
Phone Call to the Past   Mancini; Mercer
Poor Jimmy Green (inst.)   Blake
Poor Man's Polka   Brown, Lew; Henderson
Preparation, The   Lerner, Alan Jay
Pretty Girl   Willson
Pretty World   Bergman
Queen and the Sailor, The   Willson
Rag Modern (inst.)   Blake
Rainbow Rider, The   Cahn; Van Heusen
Raindrops Keep Falling on My Head   Bacharach; David, Hal
Rebirth (inst.)   Coleman
Rise and Shine   Martin
River Song, The   Willson
Rose Duet, The   Martin
Rosie   Rome
Russian Roulette (inst.)   Coleman
Sail On   Willson
Santa, Please Repair My Toys for Xmas   Freed, Ralph
Scarlett (Skarettu)   Rome
Second Love Gets By, The   Ahlert; Cahn; Turk; Van Heusen
September's Comin' (inst.)   Coleman
She's Gone Away   Bacharach; David, Hal
She's Something Else   Cahn
Siege at Loha   Willson
Silken Song, The   Willson
Sing, Sorrow, Tomorrow or Joy   Gorney
Singing Wind   Webster
Sister, Brother   Rome
Small Petrushka   Alter; Mercer
Some Hearts   Cahn
Someone on Your Side   Lerner, Alan Jay
Something for Everybody   Bergman
Somewhere Beyond the Shadow of Today   McHugh
Song and Dance Man   Rome
Song of the Molly Maguires, The   Strouse
South American Way (inst.)   Bacharach
Spongecake and Wine   Alter
Stay with Me   Martin
Strange and Wonderful (Fushigisa to Subarashisa de Ippai)   Rome
Sugar in the Rain   Bergman
Summer Me, Winter Me   Bergman
Sundance Kid (inst.), The   Bacharach
Tale Ain't a Tale, A   Blane
That's How It Looks from Here   Oakland
There's Enough to Go Around   Bergman; Mancini
There's No Greater Fan than a Met Fan   Davis
Things Go Bump in the Night   Harburg
Tickle the Ivories (inst.)   Blake
Time for Love (Imakoso Koi No Toki), A   Rome
Tio Paco   Willson
To See Her   Loesser
Tomorrow Is My Friend   Bergman; Mancini
Trastamara Rose, The   Willson
Turn on the Lights   Lerner, Alan Jay
Twelve Days of Christmas, The   Cahn; Van Heusen
Two of a Kind (Nitamono Doshi)   Rome
Unknown River   Eliscu

Up to Maggie Jones   Russell
Very Good Sense   Blane
Walk with Love   Russell
Was It Really Love?   Webster
We   Mancini
We Belong to You (Watashi Mo Kokoro Mo Anatano Monoyo)   Rome
Wedding Day Song, The   Martin
Welcome to Milan   Gorney
What Are You Doing the Rest of Your Life?   Bergman
What Does a Queen Have?   Willson
What Is Love?   Rome
When I Enter Paree   Gorney
When Love's in Your Heart   Martin
When There's a Heartache (There Must Be a Heart)   Bacharach
When Your Lover Says Goodbye   Lerner, Alan Jay
Where There Is Love There Is Hope   Fields
Where There's a Heartache there Must Be a Heart   Bacharach; David, Hal
Which Way Is Home? (Ie Wa Doko)   Rome
Whistler's Holiday, The (inst.)   Warren
Who Can Forget a First Love   Spina
Why Not   Willson
Wilderness Man, The   Harburg
Wine Is Young (Our Dreams Are Old), The   Bacharach; David, Hal
Wisdom of the Heart, The   Loesser
With Love   Willson
Woman   Willson
Woman Is How She Loves, A   Lerner, Alan Jay
Wonderful Plan, The   Willson
World Belongs to the Young, The   Lerner, Alan Jay
World of Whispers, A   Webster
World Peace   Loesser
Worth Remembering   Cahn
Yiddishkeit   Oakland
You Get in My Way   Rome
You Understand Me   Loesser
Young and Foolish (And in Love)   Spina
Young and Wild and Free   Sigman

1970

Aces and Deuces   Brooks
Across the River, 'Round the Bend   Bacharach; David, Hal
All Mine   Evans; Livingston, Jay
Among My Memories   Evans; Livingston, Jay
Angel Que   Merrill
Another Hundred People   Sondheim
A.O.K.   Evans; Livingston, Jay
Applause   Adams; Strouse
April Child   Evans; Livingston, Jay
Aristocats, The   Sherman
As Far as I'm Concerned   Rodgers
As Long As You Live   Sissle
As the Case May Be   Rome
Ask Yourself Why   Bergman
Babbler's Exit   Adams; Strouse
Backstage Babble   Adams; Strouse
Barcelona   Sondheim
Beautiful Life, The   Evans; Livingston, Jay
Because I Love Him   David, Mack
Being Alive   Sondheim
Belinda's Love Song   Rome

Best Night of My Life, The   Adams; Strouse
Blue World   Oakland
Brother Department, The   Rodgers
But Alive   Adams; Strouse
But Where Young Man   Merrill
Cancelling   Livingston, Jerry
Casamagordo, New Mexico   Cahn; Styne
Cat Don't Like, A   Sherman
Chant   Cahn; Styne
Children and Mothers   Styne
Company   Sondheim
Covenant, The   Rodgers
Cross Each "T" with Your Kisses   David, Mack
Darling Lili   Mancini; Mercer
Death of Me, The   Rodgers
Dirty Dingus Magee   David, Mack
Dirty Dozens   Brooks
Disco for Margo   Adams; Strouse
Does It Really Matter?   Cahn; Styne
Dolphin Fan Song, The   Davis
Don't Send Out My Laundry, Baby   David, Mack
Don't Settle for Less (Than the Best)   Sherman
Don't Talk About God   Cahn; Styne
Dream a Golden Day Dream   Oakland
Engaged   Rome
Escapade   Mercer
Ever Since Leavin' Wichita   Warren
Everybody's Out of Town   Bacharach; David, Hal
Everything That's Gonna Be Has Been   Rodgers
Fairfield County   Adams; Strouse
Farewell, My Life's True Love   Rome
Fasten Your Seat Belts   Adams; Strouse
First Act Finale   Oakland
First Class Number One Bum   Cahn; Styne
Follow the Lamb   Cahn; Styne
For Twenty Dollars Plain   Oakland
Forty Nights   Rodgers
Get Her Away from Me   Adams; Strouse
Getting Married to a Person   Rodgers
Getting Married Today   Sondheim
Girl in No Man's Land, The   Mancini; Mercer
Gitka's Song, The   Rodgers
Go Easy with Mama   Styne
Go Easy with Rosa   Styne
Go Get Em Yankees   Davis
God Bless!   Adams; Strouse
Golden Day Dream   Oakland
Golden Ram, The   Rodgers
Good Evening Once Again   Oakland
Good Friends   Adams; Strouse
Good Morning, God   David, Mack
Good Place to Be, A   David, Mack
Good Times Are Comin'   David, Hal
Gott Iss Gut   Cahn; Styne
Green Apple One Step, The   Spina
Green Grass Starts to Grow   Bacharach; David, Hal
Happily Ever After   Sondheim
Happiness Now   Cahn
Happy Hindu Waltz   Rome
Happy Time   Warren
Hasbrook Heights   Bacharach; David, Hal
Have I Got a Girl for You?   Sondheim
Here's Cheers!   Warren
Hey Girlie   Rodgers
Hills of Yesterday, The   Mancini; Webster

Himmlisher Vater   Cahn; Styne
Homer's Pitch   Cahn; Styne
Human Race, The   Sherman
Hurry Back   Adams; Strouse
I Admire You Very Much, Mr. Schmidt   Cahn; Styne
I Am Losing My Little Wren   Rome
I Am What I Am   Cahn; Styne
I Can't Complain   Rodgers
I Can't Fool My Heart   Davis
I Do Not Know a Day I Did Not Love Her   Rodgers
I Got the Message   Warren
I Hate Her   Rome
I Intend to End It All   Rome
I Look at You with Love   Styne
I Shall Be Happy   Rome
I Shall Not Let Money Get in My Way   Rome
I Wonder Where I'll Be Next Christmas   Warren
I Yes, Me! That's Who   Cahn; Styne
I'd Sure Like to Give It a Shot   Cahn; Styne
I'll Fly the Skyway   Sherman
I'll Give You Three Guesses   Mancini; Mercer
I'll Go On Caring   Davis
I'm Still Me   Adams; Strouse
Inner Thoughts   Adams; Strouse
Iowa — A Place to Grow   Willson
It Was a Good Time (Rosie's Theme)   David, Mack
It Was Always You   Adams; Strouse
It'll Be Good for Me   Adams; Strouse
It's a Hit, It's a Flop   Adams; Strouse
It's Delightful!   Kern
Jamie Boy   Freed, Ralph
Jethro and Jezebelle   Warren
Jig   Dietz; Schwartz, Arthur
Jungle of Your Heart, The   Drake
Kathy   Evans; Livingston, Jay
Kick the Door   Cahn; Styne
Ladies Who Lunch, The   Sondheim
Lady of the Year   Styne
Let's Talk About the Weather   Warren
Little Birds (Les P'tits Oiseaux), The   Mancini; Mercer
Little Things You Do Together, The   Sondheim
Loneliest Man in Town, The   Adams; Strouse
Long Time Dead, A   Styne
Look at Me with Love   Styne
Look to the Lilies   Cahn; Styne
Love Comes First   Adams; Strouse
Love with All the Trimmings   Lane; Lerner, Alan Jay
Luanne   Evans; Livingston, Jay
Magic's Missing, The   Warren
Man Who Had Power Over Women, The   David, Hal
Margo's Theme   Adams; Strouse
Marriage   Rome
Me and You   Styne
Meet My Seester   Cahn; Styne
Moondreams (You, Love and Me)   Evans; Livingston, Jay
Mountie Gets His Man, The   Dietz; Schwartz, Arthur
Move   Bergman
Multitudes of Amys   Sondheim
Musica de Roma   Mercer
My Guiding Star   David, Mack
My Heart Is Always in Waltz Time (Until I Meet
    You)   Brown, Lew; Henderson
Name the Lady   Rome
Never Again   Kern; Webster
New Orleans   Styne

Nicest Time to Say Goodnight, The   Cahn; Styne
Ninety Again!   Rodgers
Nobody Knows   Bergman
Not Me   Livingston, Jerry
Nothing Can Get to Me Now   Adams; Strouse
Now that You Mention It   Livingston, Jerry
Oh, I Want to Go Home   Adams
Old Man, An   Rodgers
On Cleveland On   Willson
On that Day of Days   Cahn; Styne
One at a Time   Bergman
One Hallowe'en   Strouse
One Hallowe'en (Remember That Hallowe'en)   Adams
One Little Brick at a Time   Cahn; Styne
One of a Kind   Adams; Strouse
Only One Man   Styne
Open Your Arms (Let Me Walk Right In)   Evans
Orange Bird Song   Sherman
Orange Tree   Sherman
Perfect Picnic, The   Sherman
Piccadilly Circus   Mancini; Mercer
Pieces of Dreams (Little Boy Lost)   Bergman
Poor Baby   Sondheim
Poppa Is Home   Styne
Poppa Knows Best   Rodgers
Prayer   Cahn; Styne
Put Him Away   Rodgers
Rebecca   Oakland
Rosario   Styne
Rose of Araby (inst.)   Blake
Run, Brother Rabbit, Run   Bergman
Sarafina   Styne
Scales and Arpeggios   Sherman
Send My Picture to Scranton, Pa.   Bacharach; David, Hal
She Never Felt Alone   Sherman
She Walks in Beauty   Oakland
She's No Longer a Gypsy   Adams; Strouse
Side by Side by Side   Sondheim
Sing All Day   Sherman
Skal (Let's Have Another on Me)   Mancini; Mercer
Slow and Easy   Spina
Smashing, New York Times   Adams; Strouse
Smile Away Each Rainy Day   Mancini; Mercer
So You Did It Your Way   Oakland
Some Kind of Man   Cahn; Styne
Someone Is Waiting   Sondheim
Something Bad   Bacharach; David, Hal
Something Doesn't Happen   Rodgers
Something Greater   Adams; Strouse
Something, Somewhere   Rodgers
Sometimes   Mancini
Song of the Molly Maguires, The   Adams
Sorry-Grateful   Sondheim
Steal Two Eggs   Mancini; Mercer
Sweet Gingerbread Man   Bergman
Sweet Sweet Ma-Ma   Evans; Livingston, Jay
Take a Longer Look   Sherman
Tell Your Friends   Adams; Strouse
Tete-a-Tete (Kraemer, Richard O.)   Warren
Thank God for People Like Me   Lane; Lerner, Alan Jay
That's the Time   Livingston, Jerry
Them and They   Cahn; Styne
There Comes a Time   Cahn; Styne
There Goes a Time to Do a Little Good   Cahn
There Was a Crooked Man   Adams; Strouse

Things a Girl Should Be, The   Styne
Think How It's Gonna Be   Adams; Strouse
Three Important Things   Bacharach; David, Hal
Threshold   Webster
Tick, Tock   Sondheim
Time Goes By   Styne
Time of Roses, The   Styne
To Do a Little Good   Styne
To Rome with Love   Evans; Livingston, Jay; Livingston, Jerry
Too Many!   Kern; Webster
Two By Two   Rodgers
Two Little Kittens   Rome
Una a Dieci   Styne
Very First Person I Met (in California), The   Bacharach; David, Hal
Wake Up and Smile   Evans; Livingston, Jay
Walk the Way You Talk   Bacharach; David, Hal
Wanted   Brooks
Way It Was, The   Warren
We Are Yankee Doodle Winners   Cohan
We Have All the Time in the World   David, Hal
Wedding Is Off!, The   Sondheim
Wee Bit o' Scotch, A   Rome
Welcome to the Theater   Adams; Strouse
Well Wishers, The   Adams; Strouse
What Am I?   Rome
What Would We Do Without You?   Sondheim
What's My Name?   Evans; Livingston, Jay
When I Was Young   Cahn; Styne
When It Dries   Rodgers
Where Did To-Day Go   Oakland
Whistling Away the Dark   Mancini; Mercer
White Flags   Styne
Who Gets the Girl (Who Gets the Guy)   Bacharach; David, Hal
Who Is There Among Us Who Knows?   Lane; Lerner, Alan Jay
Who Needs You   Styne
Who's that Girl?   Adams; Strouse
Why Can't He See?   Cahn; Styne
Why Me?   Rodgers
Winds of Chance   Webster
Without My Money   Rodgers
World Doesn't Want My Song, the   Warren
World Is Such a Beautiful Place, The   Cahn
Worlds   Bergman
You   Rodgers
You Are the Tree   Rome
You Could Drive a Person Crazy   Sondheim
You Have Got to Have a Rudder on the Ark   Rodgers
You Look Like Someone I Used to Know   Oakland
You Never Spoke a Word   Kern; Webster
Your Good-Will Ambassador   Mancini; Mercer
You're a Rock   Cahn; Styne

1971

Adirondacks   Merrill; Styne
Age of Not Believing, The   Sherman
Ah, Paris!   Sondheim
All His Children   Bergman; Mancini
All the Way Home   Leigh
All Things Bright and Beautiful   Sondheim
All You Can Do Is Tell Me You Love Me   Lerner, Alan Jay
And Still I Love Her   Cahn

And the People were with Her   Bacharach; David, Hal
At the Bed-D-Bye Motel   Lerner, Alan Jay
At the Hockey Game   Leigh
Average   Cahn; Van Heusen
Axe the Axis Polka   Sherman
Back from the Great Beyond   Merrill; Styne
Barry   Strouse
Basket of Dreams   Webster
Basketball   Leigh
Be Aware   Bacharach; David, Hal
Beardsley School for Girls   Lerner, Alan Jay
Beautiful Briny, The   Sherman
Beautiful Girls   Sondheim
Beginning, The   Strouse
Blue, Green, Grey and Gone   Bergman
Blues Ain't, The   Ellington
Bolero d'Amour   Sondheim
Boy in Love, a Girl in Love, A   Burke
Brave and the Free, The   Leigh
Bring on the Girls   Sondheim
Broadway Baby   Sondheim
Buckin' for Beardsley   Lerner, Alan Jay
Cafe   Ellington
California 500, The   Livingston, Jerry
California Christmas   Lawrence
Can that Boy Fox Trot!   Sondheim
Charge   Leigh
Charlotte's Letter   Lerner, Alan Jay
Children's Play Song   Harburg
Come Into My Arms or Get Out of My Life   Sigman
Come Summer   Leigh
Coming Attractions   Strouse
Congratulations   Oakland
Could I Leave You?   Sondheim
Critic, The   Strouse
Dante, Petrach and Poe   Lerner, Alan Jay
Day Late and a Dollar Short, A   David, Mack
Defense   Leigh
Demon in the Compass   Harburg
Don't Let Me Down   Sherman
Don't Look at Me   Sondheim
Doughnuts   Sherman
Dream, The   Strouse
Dump the Ump   Leigh
Eglatine!   Sherman
Ever So Gently   Cahn; Van Heusen
Everything I Dreamed   Burke
Ev'rytime You Make the Ends Meet   Cahn; Van Heusen
Face in the Crowd, A   Bergman
Farewell, Little Dream, Goodbye   Lerner, Alan Jay
Father of the Man   Rodgers
Feathers   Coleman; Leigh
First Family of Christmas, The   Webster
Free Fall   Bacharach; David, Hal
Funeral Exit (inst.)   Merrill; Styne
Garden, The   Strouse
Girl on My Mind, The   Burke
Give Me a Share in America (I Want a Share in America)   Styne
Give Me (I Want) a Share in America   Merrill
God's Garden   Merrill; Styne
God-Why-Don't-You-Love-Me Blues, The   Sondheim
Going, Going, Gone   Lerner, Alan Jay
Good King Phillip   Harburg
Goodbye Chickasaw County   Merrill; Styne

Gossip   Fain; Webster
Greatest Miracle of All, The   Cahn; Styne
Grown Ups   Harburg
Half Time   Leigh
Hallelujah Pray for Peace   Caesar
Happy Happenstance, A   Cahn; Van Heusen
Happy Night   Evans; Livingston, Jay
Happy Tomorrows   Sherman
Have a Nice Day   Mercer
Have You Got What You Came With?   Lerner, Alan Jay
Hawks!   Sherman
He Will Walk with Thee   Harburg
Hold My Hand   David, Mack
Hollywood and Vine   Sondheim
How Could I Know What Was Goin' On?   Merrill; Styne
How Far is It to the Next Town?   Lerner, Alan Jay
How Lovely You Are   Heyman; Silver
Hymn to Thanksgiving   Lawrence
I Always Believe Me   Lerner, Alan Jay
I Belong to You   Mercer
I Dearly Do Love to Eat   Cahn; Van Heusen
I Found You at Last   Lerner, Alan Jay
I Gave You a River   Evans; Livingston, Jay
I Just Need a Lover   Cahn
I Met a Man   Merrill; Styne
I Never Did Imagine   Merrill; Styne
I Prithee Please   Cahn; Van Heusen
I Will Say Goodbye   Bergman
I Wouldn't Dream of It   Cahn; Van Heusen
I'd Like to Poison the Cook   Baer; Lewis
Identification   Lawrence
If It Ain't Fun   Lerner, Alan Jay
If They Could Talk (Amour, Amour)   Bergman
If We Had Met Before   Burke
I'll Be with You Again   Burke
I'll Run Out of Time (Before I Run Out of Love for You)   Warren
I'm a Fan   Leigh
I'm Doin' Okay in My Own Way   Merrill; Styne
I'm in a Tree   Merrill; Styne
I'm Still Here   Sondheim
In Accordance with the Customs   Lawrence
In Buddy's Eyes   Sondheim
In Someone's Eyes   Sondheim
In the Arms of Love   Revel
In the Broken Promise Land of Fifteen   Lerner, Alan Jay
In the Japanese Gardens   Merrill; Styne
Individual Thing, An   Merrill; Styne
Invisible Man, The   Strouse
It Never Ends   Cahn
It Wasn't Meant to Happen   Sondheim
It's a Bad, Bad World   Lerner, Alan Jay
It's Delightful!   Webster
It's Great to Be a Yankee   Davis
It's Great to Communicate   Cahn; Styne
Japanese Procession (inst.)   Styne
Jerusalem   Bergman; Harburg
John Sweet Ballet (inst.), The   Styne
Jubilation!   Blane
Just Don't Take It Away   Merrill; Styne
La Tra Ma La (Latramalay)   Harburg
Lafayette, We're Here!   Sherman
Legend of Robin Hood, The   Van Heusen
Let's Go Native   Sherman
Let's Not Behave Like People   Cahn; Styne

Life Is What You Make It   Mercer
Lifelong Love Affair, A   Kern; Webster
Listen to Me   Lawrence
Little Bird   Lawrence
Little Ships   Harburg
Little White House   Sondheim
Little World, Good Morning   Harburg
Live, Laugh, Love   Sondheim
Lolita   Lerner, Alan Jay
Long Ago Tomorrow   Bacharach; David, Hal
Look Who's Mine (Dia de Victoria)   Bergman
Looking Back   Burke
Loose Lips (Sink Ships)   Sherman
Losing My Mind   Sondheim
Lost Sheep The Sermon, the Sword and the Song   Harburg
(They Just Can't Ration) L-O-V-E   Sherman
Love Song   Strouse
Love Will See Us Through   Sondheim
Loveland   Sondheim
Lovin' Lover   Ellington
Man Is not a Man — Until!, A   Cahn; Van Heusen
Manic Depressives (Don't Do Rewrites)   Merrill; Styne
March Out of My Life   Lerner, Alan Jay
Mexican Erection! (inst.)   Styne
Mother Needs a Boyfriend   Lerner, Alan Jay
Mother's Blues   Merrill; Styne
Music from Across the Bay   Sigman
My Cousin Beauregard   Leigh
My Heart   Burke
My Little Guy   Coslow
My Window Full of Stars   Sherman
New Orleans Poon   Merrill; Styne
99 Percent   Ellington
No-Tell Motel, The   Merrill; Styne
Nottingham Fair, The   Cahn; Van Heusen
October Night (inst.)   Myrow
Old Gypsy Man   Evans; Livingston, Jay
Old Home Guard, The   Sherman
One More Kiss   Sondheim
One of the Beautiful People   Lawrence
One Sweet Morning   Harburg
Only Memories of You   Burke
Only You Will Do   Burke
Out in the Open Air   Cahn; Van Heusen
Parable, A   Cahn; Styne
Perdido Cha Cha Cha   Ellington
Picyumi Gazette   Merrill; Styne
Place Like This, A   Cahn; Styne
Plastic Dreams   Sigman
Pleasant Little Kingdom   Sondheim
Plymouth Rock Rock!   Lawrence
Policemen's Hymn   Merrill; Styne
Portobello Road   Sherman
Portobello Street Dance   Sherman
Prettybelle   Merrill; Styne
Putting Our Lives Together   Lawrence
Quans, The   Raye
Rain Falls Anywhere It Wants To   Bergman
Rain on the Roof   Sondheim
Rape and Resurrection   Merrill; Styne
Right Girl, The   Sondheim
Road of the Phoebe Snow   Ellington
Road You Didn't Take, The   Sondheim
Sad Am I   Cahn
Same Old Song, The   Lerner, Alan Jay

Saturday   Lerner, Alan Jay
Season in the Sun   David, Mack
Sha-Sha-Nay (Walk in Peace)   David, Mack
Shine Your Lantern   Merrill; Styne
Sissiphus   Strouse
Six   Strouse
Smoke 'Em Up, Smoke 'Em Up, Smoke 'Em Up!   Sherman
So Old So Young   Drake
Some Beer, Some Bowlin'   Merrill; Styne
Song of Assisi, The   Harburg
South Sea Island Rhapsody   Sherman
Sport Star of T.V. Today, The   Leigh
Star Beyond the Star, The   Cahn; Van Heusen
Step in the Right Direction, A   Sherman
Story of Lucy and Jessie, The   Sondheim
Substitiary Locomotion   Sherman
Summer Knows, The   Bergman
Sur les Quais   Lerner, Alan Jay
Tasty Freeze   Merrill; Styne
Tell Me, Tell Me   Lerner, Alan Jay
Ten Strokes Under Par   Leigh
That Old Piano Roll   Sondheim
Those Were the Days   Adams; Strouse
Time Out   Leigh
To a Small Degree   Merrill; Styne
Too Beautiful to Last   Webster
Too Many Faces   Kern; Webster
Too Many Mornings   Sondheim
Touching   Lawrence
Trip   Strouse
Troublesome Ivories (inst.)   Blake
United Way Song, The   Sherman
Uptown, Downtown   Sondheim
Va-Va-Va-Vee (For Victory)   Sherman
Venezuela   Cahn
Victory Canteen   Sherman
Waiting for the Girls Upstairs   Sondheim
Waiting for You   Harbach; Youmans
Wake Up   Harburg
Walk Among the Leaves, A   Warren
We Two (Someday)   Sherman
What a Day for a Miracle   Harburg
What If   Strouse
What Is There to Sing About?   Strouse
What's Come Over Me?   Burke
When I'm Drunk I'm Beautiful   Merrill; Styne
When You Have Forgotten My Kisses (And I Have Forgotten
     Your Name)   Harburg
Where Were You   Sigman
Who Could Be Blue?   Sondheim
Who Will Walk with Me?   Harburg
Who's That Woman?   Sondheim
Will, The   Coleman
With a Flair   Sherman
Wolf of Gubbio, The   Harburg
Word Is Love, The   Harburg
Words   Lawrence
World's Full of Girls (Boys), The   Sondheim
Wouldn't that Be Something Now (Je Ne Me Souviens de
     Rien)   Sigman
You Ain't Hurtin' Your Ole Lady None   Merrill; Styne
You Blew It   Coslow
You Mean Something Special to Me   Burke
You Never Looked Better   Merrill; Styne
You're Gonna Love Tomorrow   Sondheim

You're Wasting Your Time   Burke

1972

Act of Love (L'Amour de Sarah)   Lawrence
After Forty It's Patch, Patch, Patch   Coleman; Fields
All Glass   Adams; Strouse
All that Love Went to Waste   Cahn
All the Irish   Cohan
All You Gotta Do Is Tell Me   Merrill; Styne
Almighty God   Ellington
Amor Mio   Cahn
Answer Man, The   Oakland
Architect, The   Martin
Area Code 213   David, Mack
At the Beach   Sherman
Balance of Nature   Bacharach; David, Hal
Beautiful People   Coleman
Beautiful Through and Through   Merrill; Styne
Beauty That Drives Men Mad, The   Merrill; Styne
Best of Buddies, The   Sherman
Big Trouble   Cahn; Van Heusen
Blessed Event   Evans; Livingston, Jay
Buon Giorno, Colombo   Cahn
Butterfly (inst.)   Blake
Care Enough   Oakland
Charge   Coleman; Fields
Charlie Brown's Calliope (inst.)   Sherman
Color Your Life   Oakland
Columbus' Blues   Comden and Green
Come Dream with Me   Cahn; Van Heusen
Come Summer   Cahn; Coleman; Van Heusen
Come to Me   Coleman
Daphne   Merrill
Deck the Halls   Cahn; Van Heusen
Disraeli   Martin
Don't Be Afraid   Merrill; Styne
Don't Touch Him   Comden and Green
Drama Quartet   Martin
Draw the Blinds   Adams; Strouse
Dulcima   Cahn
El Casino   Mercer
Enough   Adams; Strouse
Eubie Duebie   Blake
Eubie's Classical Rag (inst.)   Blake
Everyone   Ellington
Farewell   Sondheim
Fifer, The   Cohan
First Day of My Life, The   Cahn
Flirtations Frascita   Comden and Green
Fool   Sigman
For Fun   Rome
Frank and Johnnies   Martin
Frazier (The Sensuous Lion)   Mercer
Fundamental-Friend-Dependability   Sherman
Genius of Me, The   Adams; Strouse
Get Me Out of Here   Martin
Gettin' It Together   Sherman
Girls in the Band, The   Merrill; Styne
Givers and Takers   Merrill; Styne
Go to It, Old Girl!   Adams; Strouse
Good Impression, A   Coleman; Fields
Goodnight, Mrs. Calabash   Fain; Harburg
Harvey, I Lost You   Martin
Hey, Why Not!   Merrill; Styne

High Muck di Muck (inst.)   Blake
His Royal Highness   Adams; Strouse
How Can I Face Tomorrow?   Coleman
I Ain't Gonna Love No More   Warren
I and Albert   Adams; Strouse
I Can Still Smile   Warren
I Can't Let You Go   Coleman; Fields
I Just Have to Breathe   Bacharach; David, Hal
I Love You Florida   Davis
(That's How) I Remember Rome   Cahn; Van Heusen
I Struck Out   Coleman; Fields
I Was Only Pretending   Adamson
If You Never Say Goodbye   Bacharach; David, Hal
If You Were Mine   Adamson
I'm Gonna Try   Oakland
I'm Only Human   Young, Joseph
I'm Tall   Coleman
I'm There   Bergman
In the Springtime of Life   Adamson
Infinity   Sigman
Invisible Man   Martin
It Changes   Sherman
It Has All Begun   Adams; Strouse
It Was You   Coleman
It's Always Love   Merrill; Styne
I've 'Eard the Bloody 'Indoos 'As It Worse   Adams; Strouse
Jerry's Ectasy   Merrill; Styne
Judy   Martin
Just You and Me   Adams; Strouse
Keep It in the Family   Coleman; Fields
Kooka Rooki Bongo   Merrill; Styne
Last of the Red Hot Lovers   David, Mack
Leave It Alone   Adams; Strouse
Life Time, A   Cahn
Lila's Theme (Do You Remember Me?)   Sherman
Love and Logic   Coleman; Fields
Love Cycle (inst.)   Oakland
Love I Never Met, The   Webster
Love Is the Answer   Webster
Love Song (inst.)   Warren
Magic Moments   Coleman
Magic Nights   Merrill; Styne
Make Way for the Law   Comden and Green
Margie, Who's Watching the Baby   David, Mack
Marmalade, Molasses and Honey   Bergman
Massacre, The   Merrill; Styne
Maybe There's More   Coleman
Meat and Potatoes   Coleman; Fields
Melodic Rag (inst.)   Blake
Mighty Joe   Young, Joseph
Minha Vos Vira de Sul Da America   Sigman
Moment of Your Love   Cahn
My Friend   Comden and Green
My Nice Ways   Merrill; Styne
My Twilight Reflections   Mercer
New York, New York   Ellington
Nicole, You Is My Woman Now   Comden and Green
Night Has Many Eyes, The   Cahn
No Dogs Allowed   Sherman
No One to Call Me Victoria   Adams; Strouse
Novelty Rag (inst.)   Blake
November Song   Merrill; Styne
Nudge Me Every Morning   Cahn
October Twilight (Those Days Before the War)   Mercer; Myrow

Ode to a List   Oakland
Oh, Lady   Coleman
Old Fashioned Xmas, An   Webster
Old Kitchen Sink, The   Coleman; Fields
On the Sleepy Shores   Sigman
Paradise Lost   Martin
Party's Over Now, The   Martin
Peace for Our Children (inst.)   Oakland
Penniless Bums   Merrill; Styne
People in My Life, The   Merrill; Styne
Pray for Me I'm in Love   Cahn
Red Hot Tomatoes   Coleman; Fields
Reflection   David, Hal
Rook in a Weary Land, A   Mercer
Roses in the Rain   Cahn
Sacred Bodies   Coleman
Search Your Soul   Sigman
See You Around   Merrill; Styne
She's the Greatest   Cohan
Show Girl   Martin
Silence Is Golden   Martin
Sixty Percent of the Accidents   Coleman; Fields
So What Now?   Coleman; Fields
Someone   Cahn
Sorry Wrong Valley   Martin
Spats-s-s Palazzo   Merrill; Styne
Speakeasy, The   Merrill; Styne
Successame Street   Comden and Green
Sugar   Merrill; Styne
Sun on My Face   Merrill; Styne
Sunset Boulevard   Martin
Swanislavsky   Martin
Tear the Town Apart (inst.)   Styne
Ten O'Clock Friday Night   Oakland
These Eyes Have Seen Too Much   Merrill; Styne
They Don't Make 'Em Like That Anymore   Martin
They Handed Me You   Comden and Green
Think Love   Coleman
This Gentle Land   Adams; Strouse
This Is What I Want   Coleman
This Noble Land   Adams; Strouse
Three Hot Tamales, The   Merrill; Styne
Tina   Ellington
Tomorrow I'll Be Gone   Oakland
Too Many People   Coleman
Touch of Class, A   Cahn
Travelin' on My Thumb   Coleman
Valse Amelia (inst.)   Blake
Valse Eileen (inst.)   Blake
Valse Eth-el (inst.)   Blake
Valse Marion (inst.)   Blake
Valse Vera (inst.)   Blake
Victoria   Adams; Martin; Strouse
Victoria and Albert Waltz, The   Adams; Strouse
Vivat Regina   Adams; Strouse
We are the Royal Canadian Mounties   Comden and Green
We Could Be Close   Merrill; Styne
We Wish We Could Turn Back the Clock   Merrill; Styne
We Wish You a Merry Christmas   Cahn; Van Heusen
Wealthiest Girl in the Country   Comden and Green
What Are Heavy (inst.)   Coleman
What Do I Do?   Coleman; Fields
What Do You Give to a Man Who's Had Everything?   Merrill; Styne
What's His Name   Martin

When You Meet a Man in Chicago   Merrill; Styne
When You Speak with a Lady   Adams; Strouse
Where Did I Go Wrong   Webster
Where in the World   Webster
Whisper on the Wind   Coleman; Fields
Who Am I to Love You?   Adamson
Widow of Windsor, The   Adams; Strouse
Wild Geese   Oakland
Windy City Marmalade   Merrill; Styne
Women's Emancipation Proclamation   Coleman; Fields
Woodstock's Samba (Inst.)   Sherman
Would You Believe   Coleman

1973

Afternoon of Your Years, The   Livingston, Jerry
All Woman   Leigh
Am I in Love Again?   Leigh
Appointments   Livingston, Jerry
Ashley's Departure   Rome
Atlanta Burning   Rome
Aunt Polly's Soliloquy   Sherman
Baby Let Me Hear from You   Sigman
Bang   Sondheim
Bazaar Hymn   Rome
Because There's You   Rome
Before Your Very Eyes   Livingston, Jerry
Big Fat Heart   Coleman; Fields
Brand New Friends   Rome
Breezy's Song   Bergman
Bronx, The   Livingston, Jerry
Caesar Comes   Leigh
Cahoots   David, Mack; Livingston, Jerry
Cakewalk   Rome
Capricious (inst.)   Blake
Cat's Away, The   Leigh
Cedar Point Parade   Mercer
Celebration   Ellington
Chapter 54, Number 1909   Coleman; Fields
Charlotte's Web   Sherman
Chin Up   Sherman
Class of Summer '32, The   Livingston, Jerry
Clippity Clop and Clementine   Arlen
Contract, The   Lerner, Alan Jay; Loewe
Cross-Country   Spina
Dancing Machine   David, Hal
Day Late and a Dollar Short, A   Fain; Harburg
Deep in the Dark   Sherman
D-E-N-V-E-R   Spina
Did You Ever Look at You   Coleman; Fields
Did You Know It Was Me   Bergman
Dreamin' Suits Me Just Fine   Arlen
Earth and Other Minor Things, The   Lerner, Alan Jay; Loewe
Every Day a Little Death   Sondheim
Feelin'   Schwartz, Jean
Fifty Years of Disneyland   Sherman
Fraternal Order of the Eagles, The   Fain
Freebootin'   Sherman
Glamorous Life, The   Sondheim
Go in the Best of Health   Livingston, Jerry
Gone with the Wind   Rome
Good Evening — Good Morning   Oakland
Goodbye My Honey   Rome
Gratification   Sherman

Half of Life   Strouse
Hannibal, Mo (Zour-ee)   Sherman
Happy Ending (inst.)   Strouse
Happy Recipe, A   Arlen
Haunted Ballroom   Spina
Have You Heard?   Livingston, Jerry
Heebie Jeebie River, The   Evans; Livingston, Jay
He's Good for Me   Coleman; Fields
High Class Ladies and Elegant Gentlemen   David, Mack; Livingston, Jerry
Hitchhikers (On that Highway Called Life)   Harburg
Hospitality   Coleman; Fields
How Come?   Sherman
How Lucky   Rome
How Often   Rome
Hurry on Home   Leigh
I Believed It All   Mancini
I Can Talk!   Sherman
I Come to You   Bacharach; David, Hal
I Had a Love Once   Arlen
I Had a Night   Livingston, Jerry
I Might Frighten Her Away   Bacharach; David, Hal
I Need a Change of Sky   Ellington; Harburg
I Never Want to Go Home Again   Lerner, Alan Jay; Loewe
I See a Man   Livingston, Jerry
I Want to Share It with You   David, Mack; Livingston, Jerry
I Was There   David, Mack; Livingston, Jerry
I Whoever I Am   Fain; Harburg
If Everyone Got What They Wanted   David, Mack; Livingston, Jerry
If I Could Be Back   Bacharach; David, Hal
If Only   Rome
If There Were More People Like You   Coleman; Fields
If You Love a Man   Livingston, Jerry
If'n I Was God   Sherman
I'm in a Highly Emotional State   Coleman; Fields
I'm in Love with You   Livingston, Jerry
I'm Shadowing You   Mercer
In Our Time   Sigman
In Praise of Women   Sondheim
In the Afternoon of Our Years   Livingston, Jerry
In this Wide, Wide World   Lerner, Alan Jay; Loewe
In Tune   Coleman; Fields
In Your Eyes   David, Mack; Livingston, Jerry
Is What's It's All About   Arlen
It Doesn't Matter Now   Rome
It Pays to Have Friends   Livingston, Jerry
It Would Have Been Wonderful   Sondheim
It's Not Where You Start   Coleman; Fields
I've Got a Molly   Livingston, Jerry
Jailbreak   David, Mack
Johnny Is My Darling   Rome
Jumping Room Only   Ellington
Kinder, The   Livingston, Jerry
Later   Sondheim
Let Me Try Again   Cahn
Let's Celebrate   Cahn
Liasons   Sondheim
Like a Main Theme   David, Mack
Living Together, Growing Together   Bacharach; David, Hal
Lobby of the Roxy, The   Livingston, Jerry
Long Goodbye, The   Mercer
Lost Horizon   Bacharach; David, Hal
Love Is Forever   Evans; Livingston, Jay
Man and a Train, A   David, Hal

Man Called Noon, The   Cahn
Mandarin Palace on the Grand Concourse, The   David,
    Mack; Livingston, Jerry
Man's Gotta Be (What He's Born to Be), A   Sherman
Marrying for Fun   Rome
Maybe I Ought to Stay   Livingston, Jerry
Me that I Want to Be, The   Martin
Miller's Son, The   Sondheim
Miss Fiddle-Dee-Dee   Rome
Mister Misbehave   Evans; Livingston, Jay
Molly   Livingston, Jerry
More People Like You   Coleman; Fields
Mother Earth and Father Time   Sherman
Mothers   Livingston, Jerry
My City   Coleman; Fields
My Compliments to the Chef   Evans; Livingston, Jay
My Husband the Pig   Sondheim
Neighbor's Song, The   David, Mack; Livingston, Jerry
Night Waltz   Sondheim
Nobody Does It Like Me   Coleman; Fields
Not Quite Night (Crickets)   Sondheim
Nothing's All Good and Nothing's All Bad   Livingston, Jerry
Now   Sondheim
Oak Leaf Memorial Park, The   Livingston, Jerry
Oh, There You Are   Livingston, Jerry
Organic Food   Arlen
Paris Is Paris Again   Lerner, Alan Jay; Loewe
Party's on Me, The   Coleman; Fields
Perpetual Anticipation   Sondheim
Peter Rabbit   Livingston, Jerry
Phony King of England, The   Mercer
Pick Up the Pieces   Coleman; Fields
Piece of the Rainbow, A   David, Mack; Livingston, Jerry
Pity the Fond Endeavor   Willson
Progress Report   Leigh
Quadrille   Rome
Question Me an Answer   Bacharach; David, Hal
Rainy Nights   Ellington
Reflections   Bacharach; David, Hal
Remember?   Sondheim
Rhapsody in Ragtime (inst.)   Blake
Ride Out the Storm   Coleman; Fields
Ridin' Through the Park in a Hansom Cab   Arlen
River Song   Sherman
Salt   Coleman; Fields
Seen One, You've Seen 'Em All   Leigh
Seesaw   Coleman; Fields
Send a Little Love My Way   David, Hal; Mancini
Send in the Clowns   Sondheim
Share the Joy   Bacharach; David, Hal
Silly People   Sondheim
Simon's Song   Livingston, Jerry
Slue Foot Nelson (inst.)   Blake
So I'll Tell Him   David, Mack; Livingston, Jerry
Soldier's Goodbye, A   Rome
Something Happens   Cahn
Sometimes There's a Moment   Evans; Livingston, Jay
Soon   Sondheim
Southern Lady, A   Rome
Spanglish   Coleman; Fields
Strange Are the Ways of Love   Fain; Webster
Sullivan's Got a Job   Livingston, Jerry
Sun Won't Set, The   Sondheim
Sunshiny California   Livingston, Jerry
Syncopated Lady (inst.)   Strouse

Take My Place   Leigh
Tara   Rome
That's Her (That's Him)   Leigh
That's the Way to Go   Evans; Livingston, Jay
(I Love) The Old Tunes   Adams
There Must Be Something More   Sherman
There's a New Deal on the Way   David, Mack; Livingston,
    Jerry
There's Gold on the Trees   David, Mack; Livingston, Jerry
Things I Will Not Miss, The   Bacharach; David, Hal
Thirteen Is a Lucky Number   Rome
This Is Home   Evans; Livingston, Jay
This Land Is a Big Land   David, Hal
This Way or No Way at All   Arlen
Time Is On Our Side (Mary Kaye's Theme)   Evans;
    Livingston, Jay
To Give Myself to You (Is More than Giving)   David, Hal;
    Mancini
Today's the Day (He Loves Me)   Rome
Tom Sawyer!   Sherman
Tomorrow Is Another Day   Rome
Tomorrow Is Only a Moment   Livingston, Jerry
Tootsie   Bergman
Tremont Avenue Cruisewear Fashion Show,
    The   Livingston, Jerry
Tutu and Tights   Coleman; Fields
Two Fairy Tales   Sondheim
Veritable Smorgasbord, A   Sherman
Virginia Reel   Rome
Visitors   Coleman; Fields
Vocal Overture   Sondheim
Walk on Air   Leigh
Way We Were, The   Bergman
Way We Weren't, The   Bergman
We Talk, We Speak   Cahn
Wedding, The   Rome
Weekend in the Country, A   Sondheim
Welcome to Holiday Inn   Coleman; Fields
We've Got It   Coleman; Fields
We've Got Lots in Common   Sherman
What Am I Doing Wrong?   Leigh
What Else Is There to Do   Livingston, Jerry
When You Have a Son   Livingston, Jerry
Where Do I Go from Here (Sandy's Theme)   Evans;
    Livingston, Jay
Where Is My Soldier Boy?   Rome
Where Knowledge Ends (Trust Me)   Bacharach; David, Hal
Why Did They Die?   Rome
Winning the West   Livingston, Jay
World Is a Circle, The   Bacharach; David, Hal
Yoohoo   Livingston, Jerry
You Must Meet My Wife   Sondheim
You Remember   Livingston, Jerry
You're a Lovable Lunatic   Coleman; Fields
You're All I Know of Love   Webster
You've Married a Man (Who's Been Married Before)   Leigh
Zuckerman's Famous Pig   Sherman

1974

After Commencement (inst.)   Blane; Martin
All in a Lifetime   Russell
All Mucked Up   Mercer
America, Spirit of 76 (oral only)   Adams; Strouse
American Dollars   Comden and Green; Styne

And Points Beyond   Mercer
And then She Walked Right Through the Door   Bacharach
And Then You Know What He Did   Bacharach
Asking for Trouble   Loesser
Auto Da Fe (What a Day)   Sondheim
Aye, Lad   Mercer
Be Happy   Lerner, Alan Jay; Loewe
Best Time of Your Life, The   Sherman
Big Beat, The   Sherman
Big Talk   Lewis; Young, Joseph
Bluebird in the Rain   Russell
Boy, Do We Need It Now   Strouse
Brother Can You Spare a Buck? (Anthem for a New
     Depression)   Gorney; Harburg
Bruin Song, The   Livingston, Jerry
But Who   Heyman
But You Do It   David, Hal
Buy a Victory Bond   Sherman
Cairo, Illinois   Sherman
California   Willson
California Rag, The   Livingston, Jerry
Camaraderie   Mercer
Carlotta and the Bandit (inst.)   Spina
Charlie's Place   Sherman
Christmas Is in Your Heart   Adams
Closer and Closer and Closer   Lerner, Alan Jay; Loewe
Dance of Life   Mercer
Darkest Before the Dawn   Mercer
Diet Song   Comden and Green; Styne
Don't Go Lookin' for Trouble   Spina
Don't Pull Up the Flowers   David, Hal
Don't Shoot the Hooey to Me Louie   Sherman
Don't Talk, Don't Think   David, Hal
Down to Steamboat, Tennessee   Robison
Dream Drummin'   Sherman
Easy Baby   Bergman; Mancini
Easy Does It   David, Hal
Empty Tables   Mercer; Van Heusen
Everything I Need   Bacharach
Everything that Happens to You   David, Hal
Evoe for the Dead   Sondheim
Evoe! (Hymn to Dionysos)   Sondheim
Extravaganza   Mercer
Face, Not the Image, The   David, Hal
Filomena   Adamson
First Time I Heard a Bluebird, The   David, Hal
Flowerpot Blues   Lewis; Young, Joseph
Footloose   Mercer
Freedom   Sherman
French Way, The   Strouse
Frogs, The   Sondheim
Generation Gap   Young, Joseph
Girl Like I, A   Comden and Green; Styne
Good Companions   Mercer
Good Time Girl (V.D. Polka), The   Sherman
Goodbye   Mercer
Got a Bad Case of Loving You   Lewis; Young, Joseph
Grandpeople   Davis
Grass Grows Green (In No Man's Land), The   Sherman
Great North Road, The   Mercer
Heart of a Woman, The   Adams; Strouse
Hey, Yvette!   Sherman
How Many Times Have I Told You   Warren
Huckleberry Finn   Sherman
I Came Home to an Empty Heart   Webster

I Know You Are There   David, Hal
I Need Air   Lerner, Alan Jay; Loewe
I Never Met a Rose   Lerner, Alan Jay; Loewe
I Never Met a Russian I Didn't Like   David, Hal
I Won't Let You Get Away   Comden and Green; Styne
I'll Tell the World   Mercer
I'm a Person Too   Coleman
I'm on Your Side   Lerner, Alan Jay; Loewe
I'm Tired of Me   David, Hal
In the Mornin'   Oakland
In the Morning of My Life   David, Mack
Into His Hands   Sherman
Invocation to the Gods and Instructions to the
     Audience   Sondheim
It's a Short, Short Walk to a Long Sleep   Harburg
It's Bad for My Complexion   Schwartz, Arthur
It's My Turn Now   Alter; Davis
It's Only a Play   Sondheim
I've Been Starting Tomorrow   David, Hal
Jenny Kissed Me   Loesser
Jesus Loves Me   Oakland
Job Is a Home to a Homeless Man, A   David, Hal
Just a Little Space Can Be a Growing Place   David, Hal
Just a Minute (inst.)   Young, Joseph
Keep on Believin'   Oakland
Lay the Music Down   David, Hal
Let Me Be Your Mirror   David, Hal
Let Me Into Your World   Sigman
Let Me Think for You   David, Hal
Let's Live in Sin   Comden and Green; Styne
Life Is for the Living   David, Hal
Life Is Happiness Indeed   Sondheim
Little Lost Dream   Mercer
Little Prince   Lerner, Alan Jay; Loewe
Little Traveling Music, A   Mercer
Lookin' for You (Lookin' for Someone)   Lewis; Young,
     Joseph
Looking Back   Comden and Green; Styne
Lorelei   Comden and Green; Styne
Love Game, The (inst.)   Spina
Love Is Just for Lovers   Warren
Love Isn't Love Till You Give It Away   David, Hal
Low Bottom Woman   David, Hal
Many People Live Inside My Mind   David, Hal
Matter of Consequence   Lerner, Alan Jay; Loewe
Mean Tight Woman   Razaf
Melange (inst.)   Warren
Memories of You   Oakland
Men   Comden and Green; Styne
Mighty Man   Lewis; Young, Joseph
Miss Lorelei Lee   Comden and Green; Styne
Monterey Peninsula (inst.)   Bacharach
Mother Nature and Me   Livingston, Jay
Move on Higher   Lewis; Young, Joseph
My Dream for Tomorrow   Sherman
99 Miles from L.A.   David, Hal
No Faceless People   David, Hal
No Goodbyes   Sherman
On My Way   Mercer
One Good Boy Gone Wrong   Hammerstein; Harbach
One Life   David, Hal
One of Us Has Got to Go   Leigh
Other Woman, The   David, Mack
Our Town   Strouse
Over Here!   Sherman

Paris   Comden and Green; Styne
Peaches Don't Grow on a Cherry Tree   Bacharach
Pickin' Moss   Livingston, Jay
Place with No Name   Bacharach
Plastic City   Bacharach
Pleasure of Your Company   Mercer
Pools, The   Mercer
Put Your Trust in Me   Oakland
Rams Are Rollin', The   Evans; Livingston, Jay; Mancini
Randi's Rag (inst.)   Blake
Rivers Are for Boats   David, Hal
Rose in a Bible, A   Sherman
Rotten Luck   Sherman
Royal Nonesuch, The   Sherman
Royalty!   Sherman
Sally Ensalada   David, Hal
(Hey! I'm on My Way to) San Diego Bay   Spina
Seconds   Bacharach
Serve My Time   Lewis; Young, Joseph
Sheep's Song   Sondheim
Since You're Not Around   Sherman
Slippin' Around the Corner   Mercer
Snake in the Grass   Lerner, Alan Jay; Loewe
Soft Music   Sherman
Somebody's Happiness   David, Hal
Someday, Honey Darlin'   Sherman
Something on Your Mind   Lewis; Young, Joseph
Sound of Poets, The   Sondheim
St. Paul   Bacharach
Stage Door John   Mercer
Stage Struck   Mercer
Sunny Days   Oakland
Susie for Everybody   Mercer
Sweet Brotherly Love   Oakland
Ta, Luv   Mercer
Take Courage   Oakland
Take Over Chicago   Lewis; Young, Joseph
Teach Me Dear Lord   Oakland
Temporary Jones   Russell
That Was My Love I Gave You   Loesser
That's What Friends Are For   Comden and Green; Styne
That's You   Evans; Livingston, Jay
This Life Alone   Oakland
This Old World   Sigman
This World   Sondheim
Time Goes By   Webster
To All the Girls I've Loved Before   David, Hal
Us   Bacharach
Wait for Me Marlena   Sherman
Waiting   Comden and Green; Styne
Wartime Wedding   Sherman
We Are the Dreamers   Webster
We Got It!   Sherman
What Happened to Muffin   Spina
What Is It?   David, Hal
What's Right? What's Wrong?   Sherman
When Jeremiah Can Be with Me   Leigh
Where Did the Good Times Go?   Sherman
Whispers in the Night   Sigman
Why Did It Have to Be You   Cahn
Why Is the Desert?   Lerner, Alan Jay; Loewe
Win   Willson
You Don't Want Me Then   David, Mack
You're a Child   Lerner, Alan Jay; Loewe

1975

Alderberan   Coleman
(It's Time to Sing) Another Song   Mancini
Any Day's a Perfect Day for a Wedding   Strouse
At Any Age at All   Strouse
At the Palace   Strouse
Atlantic City   Coleman
Axion Theme (inst.)   Strouse
Bertram's Nonny   Strouse
Big Night of the Year, The   Strouse
Blue Fantasy (inst.)   Blake
Bring Back Those Good Old Days (inst.)   Coleman
Cat's Got Your Number, The   Strouse
Ciao Always Ciao   Sigman
Cinderella Stay a While   David, Mack
Clumsy Waltz, The   Strouse
Cold in the Morning   Coleman
Come Let in Love   Webster
Cote D'Azur (inst.)   Coleman
Country Gal Blues   Robison
Damn You, Sheriff Black   David, Mack
Dark Side of Love, The   Fain; Webster
Day You Leave Me, The   Coleman
Easy to Be With   Coleman
Eureka   Strouse
Evening Sun, Morning Moon   Bergman
Every Moment of My Life   Adamson
Find the Foot   Strouse
Free Indeed   Carroll
Glorious Fourth, The   Sherman
Glory to the Great I Am   Carroll
Goin' Home   Coleman; Comden and Green
Greatest Gift, The   David, Hal; Mancini
Guilt   Strouse
Help Stamp Out Dirt   Strouse
Hip Trip   David, Mack
Hollywood Boulevard   Cahn
I Remember   Webster
If You Do It Without the Army   Cahn
I'll Be Waiting Down in Rio   Warren
In Old Tijuana Town   Warren
I've Got What It Takes   Warren
Kaleidescope   David, Hal
Light Up a Muriel   Strouse
Long Lonely Season, The   Cahn
Lost Word   Coleman; Comden and Green
Mahogany   David, Mack
Movie Magic   David, Hal
My Little Friend   Cahn
New Kind of Girl   Strouse
Nobody Listens — Nobody Cares   Evans; Livingston, Jay
Now It's Her and Him   Adams
Now That We're in Love   Cahn
Once Is Not Enough   Mancini
Once to Each Man   Webster
Playboy-Pussycat   Coleman; Leigh
Princess for the Prince, A   Strouse
Questions and Answers   Cahn
Ready for You   Strouse
Save Me   David, Mack
Silver Bells   Loesser
Simplified Language   Coleman; Comden and Green
Some Kind of Music   Coleman; Leigh
Song of the Dove   Drake
Specialist, The   Fain; Webster

Sylvia   Blake; Sissle
There's a Feeling in the Air   Mancini
True Love at Last   Stept
Truth About Cinderella, The   Strouse
When Things Were Rotten   Adams; Strouse
Who Knows the Answers   Cahn
Wonder What Became of You   Coleman
World Is Sick and Weary, The   Warren
World that Never Was, A   Fain; Webster
You Remind Me   Warren
You're Never Too Old to Be Kissed   Schwartz, Jean
You've Got What It Takes   Warren

1976

'A' Is for Aardvark   Spina
Advantages of Floating in the Middle of the Sea,
   The   Sondheim
Against a Crooked Sky   David, Mack
All I Know Is What I Feel   David, Hal
All the Way to Paradise (And Back Again)   Bacharach;
   David, Hal
Alphabet Song, The   Cahn; Lane
America, This Wonderland   Leigh
American Dreaming   Lerner, Alan Jay
And This I Find Is Beautiful   David, Mack
And We Were in Love   Webster
Angelina   Harburg; Lane
Anna   Loesser
Armful of Sunshine, An   Cahn; Lane
As Once I Loved You   Rodgers
At the Alter   Spina
Auctions   Lerner, Alan Jay
Away from You   Rodgers
Before the Show   Cahn
Before You Leave Me   Bacharach; David, Hal
Betty Washboard's Rag (inst.)   Blake
Blimey   Cahn
Bowler Hat, A   Sondheim
Bride Finding a Ball, A   Sherman
Bright and Black   Lerner, Alan Jay
Buddy, Can You Spare a Buck   Gorney
But I Love Her (Just the Way She Is)   Spina
By the Pond Again   Bergman
Can You Imagine   Cahn; Lane
Chase, The   Rodgers
Chiffon   Russell
Christmas at Hampton Court   Rodgers
Christmas-y Day, A   Cahn; Lane
Chrysanthemum Tea   Sondheim
Come to Me   Mancini
Creation of the World, The   Spina
Curad (inst.)   Strouse
Desiree (inst.)   Warren
Disenchanted (inst.)   Alter
Drag Race for Cockroaches   Spina
Duet for One (The First Lady of the Land)   Lerner, Alan Jay
Early Morning Strangers   David, Hal
Eighth Avenue   Leigh; Styne
Elizabeth   Rodgers
Empty Place, The   Bacharach; David, Hal
Escape   Spina
Eubie's E-flat Blues (inst.)   Blake
Everybody's Got to Be Somebody   David, Hal
Everyone Kiss the Bride   David, Mack

Field of Cloth of Gold, The   Rodgers
Follow a Dream   Webster
Fools Gold   Cahn
Forgive Me   Spina
Forty Acres and a Mule   Lerner, Alan Jay
Four Black Dragons   Sondheim
From Afar   Rodgers
Garage Sale   Spina
God Is Never too Busy   Spina
Good at Making Friends   Cahn; Lane
Grand Old Party, The   Lerner, Alan Jay
Great Entertainer, The   Strouse
Green Light   Lewis; Young, Joseph
Happiness Is Just the Other Side of Loneliness   David, Hal
He Danced with Me (The Slipper and the Rose
   Waltz)   Sherman
Heidi   Cahn; Lane
Hello and Goodbye   Bergman
Hello, Mom   Leigh; Styne
Hellzapoppin   Leigh; Styne
Here Come Those Lies Again   David, Mack
Here Comes the Rain   David, Hal
Honor of Your Presence, The   Lerner, Alan Jay
I Am Over 25 but You Can Trust Me   David, Mack
I Believe in Love   Bergman
I Brought You a Gift   Rodgers
I Can't Forget the Melody   Sherman
I Give   Lewis; Young, Joseph
I Got the Message   Warren
I Just Can't Wait to See You with Your Clothes On   Strouse
I Love My Wife   Lerner, Alan Jay
I Love this Land   Lerner, Alan Jay
I Never Do Anything Twice   Sondheim
I Never Said I Love You   David, Hal
I See Things Differently Now   Bacharach; David, Hal
I See You for the First Time   Bacharach; David, Hal
I Took My Strength from You   Bacharach; David, Hal
I'd Still Be a Fool   Bacharach; David, Hal
If I Was a Dove   Lerner, Alan Jay
If Someday Ever Comes Again   Mercer
If Someone Ever Breaks My Heart   David, Mack
If You Can Learn How to Cry   Bacharach; David, Hal
I'll Come Back As Many Times As You Need Me   David,
   Hal
I'll Miss You   Rodgers
I'm a Genius Too   Leigh
I'm All Yours   Leigh; Styne
I'm Alone, That's Where I Am   David, Hal
I'm Harry   Bergman
I'm Walter   Bergman
In Time   Rodgers
It Got to Be a Habit   Leigh
It's a Living   Leigh
It's All in the Hands of the Lord   Spina
It's the Least I Can Do for You   David, Hal
(Gimme Jimmy) Jimmy Carter   Leigh
Joke's on Me, The   Evans; Livingston, Jay; Mancini
Kingdom of Love   Bergman
Kit Carson   Evans; Livingston, Jay
Lady Beautiful (inst.)   Blake
Lemon Drops, Lollipops and Sunbeams   Cahn
Let's Celebrate   Cahn
Lion Dance   Sondheim
Little Big Man   Arlen; Harburg
Little White Lie, The   Lerner, Alan Jay

Living on Plastic   Bacharach; David, Hal
Looks Like the End of a Beautiful Friendship   Arlen;
    Harburg
Love Life of a Dangling Participle   Spina
Love'll Work It Out   Cahn
Lud's Wedding   Lerner, Alan Jay
Make Way for a Star   Leigh; Styne
Mama-in-Law Blues   Lewis; Young, Joseph
Man, Man, Man   Spina
Mark of a Man, The   Lerner, Alan Jay
Masque, The   Rodgers
Men in My Life, The   Leigh
Middle C   Lerner, Alan Jay
Miss Wallflower of '46   Spina
More and More   Freed, Ralph
Nation that Wasn't There, The   Lerner, Alan Jay
Need a Friend   Lewis; Young, Joseph
New Orleans Woman   Lewis; Young, Joseph
Next   Sondheim
Night   Bacharach
Night the Kissing Booth Burned Down, The   Spina
Nightmare Ballet (inst.), The   Lane
No One Remembers My Name   Bacharach; David, Hal
No Song More Pleasing   Rodgers
Nobody's Perfect   Bergman
Nothing Lasts Forever (Not Even Forever)   David, Hal
Ode to a Rat   Cahn; Lane
Old Family Bible, The   Spina
On Ten Square Miles by the Potomac River   Lerner, Alan
    Jay
Once I Was Loved   Sherman
One Two Three Four Five   Schwartz, Arthur
Only One to a Customer   Leigh; Styne
Overnight in a Warehouse of Naked Mannequines   Spina
Papa's Advice   Spina
Peaceful Warriors   Leigh
Pears of Anjou, The   Rodgers
Philadelphia   Lerner, Alan Jay
Pity the Poor   Lerner, Alan Jay
Please Don't Touch My Plums   Cahn
Please Hello   Sondheim
Please Let Go   Bacharach; David, Hal
Poems   Sondheim
Position and Positioning   Sherman
Prayers   Sondheim
Prelude   Lerner, Alan Jay
President Jefferson Sunday Luncheon Party March,
    The   Lerner, Alan Jay
Pretty Lady   Sondheim
Promise Me Not to Love Me   Arlen; Harburg
Protocoligorically Correct   Sherman
Proud   Lerner, Alan Jay
Rainy Afternoon   Spina
Red Tape Blues   Leigh
Red, White and Blues, The   Lerner, Alan Jay
Rehearse!   Lerner, Alan Jay
Rex   Rodgers
Robber-Baron Minstrel Parade, The   Lerner, Alan Jay
Rock, Little Children   Fain; Harburg
Say a Prayer   Spina
Secret Kingdom   Sherman
Secretary Bird   Leigh
Seena   Lerner, Alan Jay
Serenade to a Veal Cutlet   Spina
She's a Nothing   Cahn; Lane

Slow, The   Spina
So Long Lily   Leigh
So Much You Loved Me   Rodgers
Someone in a Tree   Sondheim
Something to Do   Leigh
Sonatina   Lerner, Alan Jay
Sounds around the House, The   Mercer
String Save in a Spaghetti Factory   Spina
Suddenly, It Happens   Sherman
Suitor Scene   Bergman
Take Care of This House   Lerner, Alan Jay
Take Me Up with You Lord   Spina
Take My Advice (She Likes the Blues and Barbecue)   Lewis;
    Young, Joseph
Takes Money   Lewis; Young, Joseph
Talk to Me 'Bout the Hard Times   Lawrence
Te Deum   Rodgers
Teacher, The   Fain; Webster
Tears in Her Letter Where the Perfume Used to Be   Fain
Tell Him Anything (But Not That I Love Him)   Sherman
Tell Me, Dear Jane   Rodgers
That Chaplin Man   Leigh; Styne
That House/This Time   Lerner, Alan Jay
That's What Friends Are For   Cahn; Lane
There Is No Other Way   Sondheim
There'll Be Time   Bergman
There's Always Tomorrow   Cahn
These Hands   Spina
Thieves   Cahn
Throckmorton's Permanent Pleasure   Leigh
'Till We All Belong   Arlen; Harburg
Time and Tenderness   Bacharach
Time to Ride   David, Mack
To Catch a Thief   Heyman
Tobacco's but an Indian Weed   Spina
Top That If You Can   Leigh; Styne
Touch   Spina
Touch of Love, The   Cahn
Two Can Go to Helen   Caesar
Twobly's Thingamajig   Leigh
Uncle Tom   Lerner, Alan Jay
Unkind Word, An   Cahn; Lane
Until You Love Me   Mancini
Valse Delma (inst.)   Blake
Way I Feel About You, The   Bacharach; David, Hal
We Float   Sondheim
We Must Have a Ball   Lerner, Alan Jay
Wee Golden Warrior, The   Rodgers
Welcome Home Miz Adams   Lerner, Alan Jay
Welcome to Kanagawa   Sondheim
We've Got Forever   David, Mack
What a Comforting Thing to Know   Sherman
What Did You Do?   Leigh; Styne
What Has Love Got to Do With Getting Married?   Sherman
Where Is My Son?   Rodgers
Who Can Tell Us Why   Cahn
Why?   Rodgers
Why Can't I Be Two People?   Sherman
With Benjamin   Bergman
With These Hands   Leigh
Woman Without Feelings, A   David, Hal
Write a Letter to Me at the Old Folks Home   Caesar
Wunderhorn   Cahn; Lane
You Were Talking in Your Sleep Last Night   David, Mack
You'll Never Be Poor New York   Styne

Young Grow Every Day, The   Bacharach

1977

Adios for Now   Spina
All I Bring to You Is Love   Berlin
All My Love   Spina
Alone at a Table for Twelve   Spina
Always Tomorrow   Russell
Annie   Strouse
Anniversary Song (Remembrance)   Leigh
Another Spring Will Rise (inst.)   Bacharach
Anybody's Gal   Spina
Apples   Strouse
Azalia (inst.)   Warren
Bab's Melody   Spina
Ballad of the Lily of Hell   Weill
Ballet for a Dinosaur   Spina
Barbara   David, Mack; Van Heusen
Barney's Beanery   Spina
Basket Weaver, The (inst.)   Spina
Bilbao Song, The   Weill
Black Orchid, The   Spina
Blair Rose   Cahn
Bremen Town Musician, The   Cahn
Brother, Give Yourself a Shove   Weill
By Threes   Coleman
Camellia (inst.)   Warren
Candlelight Concerto (Until Eternity)   Spina
Cassandra (inst.)   Warren
Charlie   Bacharach
Children at Play (inst.)   Blake
Chimes of Avalon   Spina
Cocoanut Tree, The   Russell
Constantly (L'Eriera)   Sigman
Convict's Song (I've Got a Number for a Name), The   Spina
Day of Day   Cahn
Don Quixote de la Mancha (inst.)   Spina
Don't Be Afraid   Weill
Don't Be Such a Wolf, Mr. Fox   Yellen
Don't Ever Let Me Be Yours   Livingston, Jerry; Russell
Don't Tell Me   Russell
Don't Tell Me I'm Flying   Cahn
Dream Theme   Spina
Dude and a Doll, A   Evans; Livingston, Jay
Easy Street   Strouse
Enter Juliet   Leigh
Everybody Today Is Turning On   Coleman
Everyone Needs Someone (to Love)   Bacharach; David, Hal
Ev'ry Minute of the Day   Spina
Fiesta of the Bulls, The   Sigman
Flowers Never Die   Sherman
Fool's Advice, A   Young, Joseph
Four Seasons of Love, The   Spina
Francophile   Adams; Strouse
Friday Afternoon Bus   Yellen
Fun 'n' Games   Spina
Futures (inst.)   Bacharach
God Bless Rockefeller   Weill
Good Times   Coleman
Goodbye Today! Hello Tonight   Martin
Got Love   Russell
Graffitti   Spina
Great Chord Sequence Man   Russell
Hannah   Spina

Happily Married Wolf, A   Cahn
Happy End, The   Weill
Has Anybody Got a Place for Me in California   Leigh
Hattie's Place   Spina
Ha-Ya Soph   Yellen
He Doesn't Know   Strouse
He Had a Little Gun   Russell
He Would Never Leave Me   Russell
Hell's Kitchen   Spina
Here Comes Stanley   Styne
He's Gay   Leigh
Hey There   Coleman
History of the World   Spina
Home Wrecker   Evans; Livingston, Jay
Hong Kong Ferry   Spina
How to Be a Successful Failure   Spina
How to Make Love to an Heiress   Spina
How Will I Know   Russell
I Didn't Know She Loved Me   Spina
I Don't Need Anything but You   Strouse
I Get Married   Leigh
I Keep Looking for You   Cahn
I Love a Fat Man   Cahn
I Love My Wife   Coleman
I Love New York   Spina
I Made a Deal   Cahn
I Think I'm Gonna Like It Here   Strouse
If the Shoe Fits   Cahn
I'll Be There   Russell
I'll Be Waiting Down in Rio   Warren
I'm a Lover   Spina
I'm Jealous   Spina
I'm Laughin' at Love   Spina
I'm Rotten I'm Rotten   Cahn
In Our Childhood's Bright Endeavor   Weill
In the Barrio   Leigh
In the Middle of the Night   Russell
Inhibition Papa   Yellen
It Was Almost Like a Song   David, Hal
It's Christmas   Strouse
It's Christmas on the Islands (inst.)   Spina
It's the Hard-Knock Life   Strouse
I've Never Been So Happy   Strouse
Jamie   Bullock; Spina
Jing Jang   Spina
Just Wait   Strouse
Kaminsky Rag, The (Inst.)   Styne
(It's a) Keystone Comic World   Spina
Kumquat   Russell
La Franchesa (inst.)   Warren
Last Night (You Promised Me the Moon)   Spina
Late Showdown   Russell
Legend of the Lovers   Spina
Let Me Be Your Little Love   Russell
Liebchen   Spina
Lieutenants of the Lord   Weill
Life Can Be a Fairy Tale   Cahn
Life Is not a Fairy Tale   Cahn
Life (Just What in Hell's It All About??)   Spina
Liquor Dealer's Dream, The   Weill
Little Bottles (Sittin' on a Shelf), The   Spina
Little Girls   Strouse
Loozeyana   Leigh
Lord Come and Live with Us   Martin
Love Bandit, The   Spina

Love Is a Traveler   Spina
Love Is for Lovers   Spina
Love Is What I Got a Heartful Of   Spina
Love Revolution   Coleman
Love Takes Time (Night Waltz)   Sondheim
Love Theme for Scene #82   Spina
Loveliest of Feelings, The   Sherman
Lovers on Christmas Eve   Coleman
Lovers' Waltz (You I Adore You)   Spina
Major Is a Minor, The   Spina
Make Him Say Please   Yellen
Man Bites Dog (inst.)   Spina
Man Must Belong to a Woman, A   David, Hal
Mandalay Song, The   Weill
March Ahead   Weill
Married Couple Seeks Married Couple   Coleman
Maybe   Strouse
Me and Him   Cahn
Meadow, The   Russell
Mister Siegal   Yellen
Misty Music (Do I Hear Music)   Spina
Monica   Coleman
Mover's Life, A   Coleman
My Dream   Yellen
My Name Is Rumpelstiltskin   Cahn
My New Celebrity Is You   Mercer
Name Song, The   Cahn
Nashville (Music City USA)   Spina
Need to Be Loved, The   Fain; Webster
Never Underestimate the Power of a Woman   Spina
New Deal for Christmas, A   Strouse
No, Dammit, I Don't Hafta!!!!   Spina
No, He Can't Be the One for Me   Spina
No Walls, No Ceilings, No Floors   David, Hal
No (You Can't Have Him)   Russell
Notes on an Instrumental Theme   Spina
Nothing Is Forever   Leigh
N.Y.C.   Strouse
Oh Boy!   Russell
Once Upon a Time Is Always   Cahn
Only Way to Go Is Up, The   Cahn
Painting Myself Into a Corner   David, Hal
Palma de Majora (inst.)   Spina
Person to Person   Coleman; Comden and Green
Pompous Circumstance   Spina
Prima Vera (inst.)   Warren
Prologue   Strouse
Relationship, The   Russell
Rescue Aid Society, The   Fain
Rest of Your Life, The   Bergman
Rose Is a Song   Cahn
Runaway Lovers (Of Cathay), The (inst.)   Spina
Rusted Strings   Spina
Sailor's Tango, The   Weill
Saturday Night   Cahn; Styne
Saturday Night CBS T.V. Special   Cahn
Schlaf Mein Kind   Cahn
Scream   Coleman
Secret Word Is 'Escargots', The   Spina
Seeing Things the Way They Really Are   David, Hal
Serenade to Santa Fe   Spina
Sexually Free   Coleman
Shama (inst.)   Warren
She Wants a Man   Yellen
Sixth Sense, The   Spina

Some Body Else   Blake; Razaf
Somehow (Somehow I Remember)   Spina
Someone Wonderful I Missed   Coleman
Someone's Been Opening My Mail   Spina
Someone's Waiting for You   Fain
Something Was Missing   Strouse
Song of the Big Shot   Weill
Song of the Moose   Snyder
Sophie Tucker School for Red Hot Mamas   Yellen
Spin-Off, The   Cahn
Spin-Off Blues, The   Cahn; Styne
Squirrel Cage, The   Spina
Sunset Harbor   Spina
Surabaya Johnny   Weill
Suzzetta (inst.)   Warren
Swamp Volunteers March (inst.)   Fain
Sweets for Sweet   Cahn
Swords and Roses (inst.)   Spina
Teasing the Blues   Lewis; Young, Joseph
Thank Zeus!!!!   Spina
Thanks for the Use of Your Heart   Harburg
That Face (Like a Jig-Saw Puzzle)   Spina
That Man!!!!   Spina
That's Our Annie   Strouse
That's the Way It Goes   Spina; Strouse
That's What Love Is All About   David, Mack
Theme for Gina (inst.)   Spina
Today's the Day   Leigh
Tomorrow   Strouse
Tourist in Mexico   Spina
Toy Balloon (Edie's Library)   Spina
Truth in a Concrete Nutshell, The   Spina
Twilight   Spina
Tze Tze (inst.)   Spina
Unknown   Martin
Using Things and Loving People   David, Hal
Utopia   Spina
Vitamins Hormones and Pills   Yellen
We Got Annie   Strouse
We'd Like to Thank You   Strouse
We're Gonna Do It 'Till We Get It Right   Leigh
We're Still Friends   Coleman
West Indies on a Banana Boat, The   Spina
What Beautiful Is   Leigh
What Have You Got to Lose????   Spina
What'sa Matter with Angelo (inst.)   Spina
Where Are You   Bacharach
Where's the Mustard   Spina
Who Needed You   Leigh
Wind in the Night, The   Leigh
Windchimes   Spina
Wine of Marie Dellamore, The   Russell
Without Him   Leigh
Yankee Enterprise, The   Spina
You   Cahn
You Ask Me Why   David, Hal
You Won't Be an Orphan for Long   Strouse
You're All the Women in the World to Me   Spina
You're Never Fully Dressed without a Smile   Strouse

1978

Above the Tears Beyond the Pain   David, Hal
And So On   Cahn
Babette   Coleman; Comden and Green

Banjo King   Sherman
Bar Mitzvah, The   Styne
Bar Mitzvah of Eliot Green   Styne
Be Like a Basketball and Bounce Right Back   Adams;
    Strouse
Beverly (Take Care of Your Baby)   David, Mack
Blessings Before Reading Torah   Styne
Brass Rings and Daydreams   Sherman
Broadway, Broadway   Adams; Strouse
Broadway Musical, A   Adams; Strouse
Bus To Tuscaloosa   David, Hal
Carriages at Midnight   Styne
Child in a Man's World (A Woman in a Man's World),
    A   David, Hal
Dance Montage, The   Bergman
Dancing   Adams; Strouse
Did He Write That?   Warren
Do I Make You Happy?   Merrill
Don't Tell Me   Adams; Strouse
Dream of Love   Bergman
Dreams   Bergman
Ella Vino Al Valle   David, Mack
Entertaining Papa   Yellen
Fifty Cents   Merrill
Fifty Percent   Bergman
Five Zeros   Coleman; Comden and Green
Goin' to Broadway (Disco)   Adams; Strouse
Goodnight Is Not Goodbye   Bergman
Grand Central Station   Coleman; Comden and Green
Grand Street Presentation, A   Merrill
Grand Street Tivoli Presentation, A   Merrill
Great News, The   Styne
Harolds of This World, The   Styne
Here in the Playbill   Adams; Strouse
How Can I Tell Her   Bergman
How Y' Doin' in the Love Department   Yellen
I Am a Living Thing   David, Hal
I Can't Say Goodbye Nobody's Property   Sherman
I Have Written a Play   Coleman; Comden and Green
I Hurry Home to You   Adams; Strouse
I Know the Way to Timbuktu   David, Hal
I Know What It Is to Be Alone   Merrill
I Love to Dance   Bergman
I Rise Again   Coleman; Comden and Green
I Saw Myself in Your Eyes   David, Hal
I Wish You a Waltz   Bergman
I Won't Ever Let You Go   David, Hal
I Would Have Bet Against It   Cahn; Schwartz, Arthur
If Anyone Had Told Me   Bergman
If Ever Day Were Valentine's Day   Fain; Harburg
If Only a Little Bit Sticks   Styne
I'll Never Say Goodbye   Bergman
I'm a Girl with Too Much Heart   Merrill
I'm a Star   Merrill
I'm Glad I'm Your Woman   David, Hal
I'm Having More Fun Since I'm Sixty   Yellen
Indian Maiden's Lament, The   Coleman; Comden and
    Green
It's All in the Mind   Mancini
It's Gonna Take a Red Hot Mama   Yellen
It's Nothing   Styne
It's Time for a Cheer-Up Song   Adams; Strouse
I've Been in Those Shoes   Adams; Strouse
I've Been Waiting All My Life   Bergman
I've Got It All   Coleman; Comden and Green

I've Just Begun   Styne
Job Application, The   Bergman
Jokes   Adams; Strouse
Just Tell Me What You Want   Strouse
Kill Him   Styne
Lawyers   Adams; Strouse
Legacy, The   Coleman; Comden and Green
Let Me Sing My Song   Adams; Strouse
Let Me Spend the Night with You   Spina
Life Begins at Forty   Yellen
Life Is a Carousel   Evans; Livingston, Jay
Life Is Like a Train   Coleman; Comden and Green
Like Her   Bergman
Lily Garland   Coleman; Comden and Green
Lily, Oscar   Coleman; Comden and Green
Living the Life of a Lover   David, Hal
Look at Me   Merrill
Love Being What It Is   Harburg; Van Heusen
Love Life in My Dream Life, The   David, Hal
Love Song   Adams; Strouse
Lucky Lily   Coleman; Comden and Green
Man Who Looks Like a Fool, A   David, Hal
Max Jacobs   Coleman; Comden and Green
Mine   Coleman; Comden and Green
Moonraker   David, Hal
More of the Same   Bergman
Morris Kaplan of Hampstead Gardens   Styne
Move 'Em Out   Mancini
My Potential   Merrill
Never   Coleman; Comden and Green
Never's Here   Cahn
1934 Hot Chocolate Jazz Babies Revue, The   Adams; Strouse
No One Man Is Ever Goin' to Marry Me   Yellen
Not Again   Cahn
Now Is Forever   Cahn
Oh Yeah! Oh Yeah! Oh Yeah!   Cahn
Older and Wiser   Adams; Strouse
On the Old East Side   Yellen
On the 20th Century   Coleman; Comden and Green
One and Only, The   Bergman
One By One   Bergman
Opening Night   Adams; Strouse
Orange & Moon (VPI & SU), The   Willson
Our Private World   Coleman; Comden and Green
Out-A-Town   Adams; Strouse
Pavanne   Bergman
Place in the World, A   Merrill
Play the Magic Carpet   Yellen
Prince of Grand Street, The   Merrill
Red Eye Back to L.A.   David, Hal
Repent   Coleman; Comden and Green
Rita's Request   Styne
Road I Didn't Take, The   Webster
Rose Is not a Rose (Without the Thorns), A   Sherman
Saddle Up the Horse   Coleman; Comden and Green
Sakura   Bergman
Selling Blue Skies   David, Hal
Sew a Button   Merrill
Sextet   Coleman
She Came to the Valley   David, Mack
Shema Lo-ed (What Does It Mean?)   Styne
She's a Nut   Coleman; Comden and Green
Sign, Lily, Sign   Coleman; Comden and Green
Simchas (Joyous Occasions)   Styne
Smoke and Fire   Adams; Strouse

Somebody Did All Right for Herself   Bergman
Song for Dancing, A   Bergman
Stardust Waltz, The   Bergman
Stars and Shadows (Beau Soir)   Bergman
Stay with Me   Merrill
Stranded Again   Coleman; Comden and Green
Sun Shines Out of Your Eyes, The   Styne
Tango Contest, The   Bergman
Terrific Band and a Real Nice Crowd, A   Bergman
Thanksgiving Prayer   Sherman
That Hometown Feeling   Sherman
There'll Be Other Friday Nights   Sherman
There's a Lot of Little Boy in Every Grown Up Man   Yellen
This Is Caplan's   Styne
This Is the Day   Coleman; Comden and Green
This Time Tomorrow   Styne
Thou Shalt Not   Styne
Together   Adams; Coleman; Comden and Green; Strouse
Travellin' Music   Sherman
Trust Me   Styne
Unapproachable   Drake
Vergeblichen Standchen (Come and Dance with
    Me)   Bergman
Veronique   Coleman; Comden and Green
Victor's Request   Styne
Was It Loneliness or Love   David, Hal
We Still Have Us   David, Hal
We've Done All Right   Styne
What Do I Do Now?   Merrill
What Harm Can It Do   Styne
What Would You Want to Be   Friend
What You Go Through   Adams; Strouse
When All My Wishes Were Your Dreams   Mancini
When You're Loved   Sherman
Where Does Love Go?   Merrill
Where Has the Rainbow Gone?   Fain; Harburg
Where's the Music Coming From?   Styne
Who Am I?   Adams; Strouse
Who Forgets   Heyman
Who Gave You Permission   Bergman
Who Says You Always Have to Be Happy?   Adams; Strouse
Why   Styne
Why Can't He Like Me?   Styne
Why Does It Have to Be Funny?   Adams; Strouse
Wild About Jazz (inst.)   Blake
Wild Rover, The   David, Mack
Will You Remember Me?   Webster
Wrong Song, A   Adams; Strouse
Yenta Power   Adams; Strouse
You Can't Deep Freeze a Red Hot Mama   Yellen
You Gotta Have Dancing   Adams; Strouse
You Know How to Hurt a Guy   David, Hal
You Only Get One Chance   Adams; Strouse
You, Too, Can Be a Red Hot Mama   Yellen
You Wouldn't Be You   Styne
Youngest Person I Know, The   Merrill
You're Only As Good As Your Last Kiss   Yellen

1979

Ah, Miss   Sondheim
All for Love   Coleman
All that He'd Want Me to Be   Lane; Lerner, Alan Jay
America Don't Know How Any More   Coleman
America Is Bathed in Sunlight   Coleman

Amnesia (The Inderal Song)   Bacharach
Baby My Baby   David, Mack
Ballad of Sweeney Todd, The   Sondheim
Barber and His Wife, The   Sondheim
Bat Song   Mancini
Belle of Buttercup Lane, The   David, Mack
Big People   Coleman
Blues Improvisation   Mercer
By the Sea   Sondheim
Carmelina   Lane; Lerner, Alan Jay
Change of Seasons (Where Do You Catch the Bus for
    Tomorrow), A   Mancini
Change of Sky   Harburg
Chicago Farewell   Bacharach
Church   Lane; Lerner, Alan Jay
City on Fire!   Sondheim
Come with Me to San Torino   Lane; Lerner, Alan Jay
Contest, The   Sondheim
Crazy Old World   Harburg
Dancing Fool, The   Bacharach
Dear Mom and Dad   Bergman; Mancini
Deedle, Deedle Dumpling (The Beggar Woman's
    Lullaby)   Sondheim
Don't Call It Love   Mancini
Dreamer, The   Livingston, Jay
Drivin' and Dreamin'   Harburg
Easy Come, Easy Go   Rodgers
Edelaine   Harburg
Enchanted Clock, The   Harburg
Epiphany   Sondheim
Eternal Summer   Warren
Ev'ry Day (Comes Something Beautiful)   Rodgers
Fair Trade   Rodgers
Fam'ly We Will Be, A   Rodgers
Find Love   Bacharach
French   Coleman
Gefrunk   Mercer
God, That's Good   Sondheim
Good Old Burlesque Show, A   McHugh
Green Finch and Linnet Bird   Sondheim
Happily Ever After   Comden and Green
He Pleases Me   Mancini
Headlines   Cahn
He's Lyin'   David, Mack
Home Again   Coleman
How Can You Say You Feel Rich Anymore   Coleman
I Ain't Gonna Love Any More   Warren
I Can Still Smile   Warren
I Can't Hold On   David, Hal
I Don't Know How   Rodgers
I Don't Need You Anymore   Bacharach
I Gotta   Coleman
I Have an Ear for Love   Mancini
I Live in the Woods   Bacharach
I Must Have Her   Lane; Lerner, Alan Jay
I Remember Mama   Rodgers
If It Wasn't for Love   Razaf
I'm a Great Big Baby   Blake; Razaf
I'm a Woman   Lane; Lerner, Alan Jay
I'm Keeping Myself Available for You   McHugh
I'm Tying the Leaves Back on the Trees   David, Mack
I'm Your Guy   Coleman
Image of Me, The   Lane; Lerner, Alan Jay
In Louisiana   McHugh
It Is Not the End of the World   Rodgers

It's Easy to Say   Mancini
It's Going to Be Good to Be Gone   Rodgers
It's Time for a Love Song   Lane; Lerner, Alan Jay
I've Got My Mind Made Up   Bacharach
Johanna   Sondheim
Just Tell Me What You Want   Adams; Strouse
Katie   Fain
Kiss Me   Sondheim
Ladies in Their Sensitivities   Sondheim
Lars, Lars   Rodgers
Last Ride (Another Spring Will Rise) (inst.)   Bacharach
Last Time I Felt Like This, The   Bergman
Leave It All to Me   Bergman
Little Bit More, A   Rodgers
Little Priest, A   Sondheim
Love Before Breakfast   Lane; Lerner, Alan Jay
Love Comes in Different Colors   Harburg
Love Has Found a Way   Warren
Love Me Good   David, Hal
Lover Knows, A   Sigman
Lullaby   Rodgers
Magdelena (inst.)   Bacharach
Magician of Lublin, The   Webster
Mama Always Makes It Better   Rodgers
Man on the Merry-Go-Round, The   Harburg
Marriage (Wedding) Song   Coleman
Maybe, Maybe, Maybe   Rodgers
Medium Couldn't Get Through, The   Mercer
Men in My Life, The   David, Hal
Midsummer Night   Rodgers
Most Disagreeable Man, A   Rodgers
Move Over Juanita   David, Mack
Music of Love, The   Leigh
My Friends   Sondheim
My Greatest Sin   David, Mack
New York Lady (211) (inst.)   Bacharach
No Place Like London   Sondheim
Not While I'm Around   Sondheim
Now While I Still Remember How   David, Hal
Old City Boy at Heart, An   Rodgers
One More Walk Around the Garden   Lane; Lerner, Alan Jay
Parlor Songs   Sondheim
Philadelphia (America's Home Town)   Harburg
Pirelli's Miracle Elixer   Sondheim
Poor Thing   Sondheim
Pretty Women   Sondheim
Quartet   Sondheim
River Boat (Comes In) (inst.)   Bacharach
Sally   McHugh
Same Time Next Year   Bergman
Shuffle Song, The   David, Mack
Signora Campbell   Lane; Lerner, Alan Jay
Sing a Little Song of Christmas   Leigh
Single Girl   Bacharach
Such Good Fun   Rodgers
Suddenly It's You   Cahn
Sugar Baby Bounce, The   Evans; Livingston, Jay
Summer '77 (inst.)   Bacharach
Superland   Coleman
Tell It to Me Dad   Coleman
Tell Me, Gypsy   Cahn
Tennessee Sandman   David, Mack
Thank You Lord   David, Hal
That Happy American Dream   Coleman
There Is Time   Bacharach

There's Something Funny Going On   Bergman
Thomas Jefferson Witherspoon   Coleman
Time   Rodgers
Time You Old Gypsy Man   Harburg
Traveling Together   Coleman
Uncle Chris   Rodgers
Wait   Sondheim
Walk Among the Leaves, A   Warren
Water Wonderland   Sherman
Way I See It, The   Coleman
We've Got a Lot of Catching Up to Do   Harburg
What Am I Supposed to Do   David, Hal
What'll It Take   Coleman
When   Rodgers
When It Comes to Loving   Coleman
When the Going Gets Tough   Coleman
Where Was I When the Parade Went By   David, Mack
Where We Came From   Rodgers
Why Him?   Lane; Lerner, Alan Jay
Wild Red Cherry River   Harburg
Winter Rain   Coleman
Worst Pies in London, The   Sondheim
Wouldn't You Like to Taste My Pear?   McHugh
Writer Writes at Night, A   Rodgers
Yankee Doodles Are Coming to Town   Lane; Lerner, Alan Jay
You Can't Go Home Again   Cahn
You Can't Say You Feel Rich Anymore   Coleman
You Could Not Please Me More   Rodgers
Your Life, My Life (Woman) (inst.)   Bacharach
You're the Song   David, Mack

1980

Alike, Alike   Cahn
All I Need Is a Handshake   Cahn; Strouse
Almost   Cahn
And Suddenly It's Christmas   Drake; Lane
Another Song About a Woman That a Man Done Wrong   Cahn; Strouse
April Song, An   Cahn
As Good As a Man   Coleman
At Least I Tried   Coleman
Because We Care   Bergman
Being Good for My Baby   Cahn
Bigger Isn't Better   Coleman
Black and White   Coleman
Bojangles   Cahn; Strouse
Call Me a Fool   Warren
Change of Seasons (Where Do You Catch the Bus for Tomorrow), A   Bergman
Charlie   Strouse
Charlie and Algernon   Strouse
Christmas in Los Angeles   Sherman
Colors of My Life, The   Coleman
Come Follow the Band   Coleman
Coral Sea   Parish
Don't It Break Your Heart   David, Mack
Don't Kick My Dreams Around   Styne
Dream, Safe with Me   Strouse
Dreamer, The   Evans
Everybody Loves Me   Styne
Everything Was Perfect   Strouse
Fantasy   Warren
Follow the Way of the Lord   Cahn; Strouse

For You   Styne
Gettin' Some   Styne
Go Out Big   Styne
Half of Me   David, Hal
Harry Who?   Warren
Have I the Right   Strouse
Hawaiian Love Call   Parish
Hello   Cahn; DePaul
Here Comes Never   Styne
Hey, Boy!   Cahn; Strouse
Hey, Granny   Cahn; Strouse
Hey Look at Me   Strouse
His Name Is Charlie Gordon   Strouse
Hot Feet   Blake; Sissle
I Always Wanted to Be a Dancin' Man   Cahn; Strouse
I Am Writing a Love Song for You   Styne
I Can Hardly Wait   Bergman; Lane
I Can't Tell You   Strouse
I Care   Cahn; DePaul
I Got a Friend   Strouse
I Like Your Style   Coleman
I Lost My Cat Today!   Cahn; DePaul
I Need Music   Cahn; Strouse
I Really Loved You   Strouse
I Think I'm Gonna Fall in Love   Bacharach
I Worship at Your Shrine (Madame)   Parish
If We Ever Get Out of Here (inst.)   Bacharach
If You Like to Learn   Cahn; DePaul
Imagined Death Sequence (inst.)   Bacharach
Imaginings   Cahn; DePaul
In that Sunny Honey Comb of Mine   Parish
In Tune   Bacharach
Island, The (Linz, Ivan)   Bergman
It Hasn't Got a Chance   Cahn; Strouse
It Isn't Easy Being a Star   Cahn; Strouse
It Was Worth the Price   Cahn; Strouse
It's Good   Cahn
It's Nobody Else but You   Cahn; Strouse
It's Spring   Cahn
Jacques and Jill   Bergman
Jelly Donuts and Chocolate Cake   Strouse
Join the Circus   Coleman
June   Parish
Just Friends   Bacharach
Let Me Hear You Love Me   Styne
Life Is Like an Old La-soo Makin' It   Cahn; Strouse
Little Piece of Chalk, A   Cahn; DePaul
Little Rose Covered Shack   Parish
Little Travelin' Music Please, A   Styne
Long Way from Home   Styne
Love Is a Private Affair   Warren
Love Is Hate   Cahn
Love Is Just for Lovers   Warren
Love Makes Such Fools of Us All   Coleman
Love Song   Warren
Love Without Words   Cahn
Luisa (inst.)   Bacharach
Man Who Invented Ice Cream, The   Cahn; Strouse
Manhattan Showboat   Cahn
Maze, The   Strouse
Meanwhile   Sigman
Midnight Riding   Strouse
Miss Peach of the Kelly School   Cahn
Moonlight on the Lagoon   Parish
Most Difficult Man, A   Cahn; Strouse

Museum Song   Coleman
My Big Moment   Cahn
Never in My Wildest Dreams   Warren
New York Women   Cahn; Strouse
No More Shadows   Heyman
No Surprises   Strouse
Not Another Day Like This   Strouse
Now   Strouse
'Now' Dance (inst.), The   Styne
Now You See It Now You Don't   Coleman
Oh Mother, Mother (Please Speak to Willie)   Parish
On Rainy Afternoons   Bergman
On the Beach (inst.)   Bacharach
On the Boulevard   Cahn
One Brick at a Time   Coleman
One Step at a Time   Strouse
Our Boy Charlie   Strouse
Out There   Coleman
Perfect Example, The   Bergman
Praise Him with Joyful Song   Willson
Prince of Humbug, The   Coleman
Reading   Strouse
Save Me the Dance (Where the Lights Go Down
    Low)   Drake
Say Goodbye to Sally for Me   Parish
Shake It, but Don't Break It   Mercer
She   Cahn
Sing Me No April Songs   Cahn
Singy Kind of Song, A   Cahn; DePaul
Siren of the Nile   Parish
Some Bright Morning   Strouse
Some Day Soon   Styne
Somebody New   Strouse
Somebody Stole My Kazoo   Styne
Soon You'll See Me in the Movies   Cahn; Strouse
Spread It Around   Cahn; Strouse
Star of Love, The   Webster
Sweetheart of the Nation   Cahn; Strouse
Tell Me, What Does He See in Me?   Cahn; Strouse
Thank God I'm Old   Coleman
That's What the Poor Woman Is   Coleman
There Are No Girls Quite Like Showgirls   Cahn
There Was a Time   Styne
There's a Sucker Born Every Minute   Coleman
There's No Greater Sound than Da, Da, Da, Da, Da,
    Da   Cahn; Strouse
Too Old to Be So Young   Styne
Try to Forget Me   Cahn
Unusual Weather   Harburg
We Used to Talk Once   Styne
Welcome   Warren
What Does He See in Me?   Strouse
What Matters Most   Bergman
Whatever Time There Is   Strouse
When Do You Walk Away?   Cahn; Strouse
When Two Lips Call   Parish
Where Did the Time Go   Bacharach
Where Have I Seen Your Face Before   Harburg; Lane
Why Can't I?   Cahn; Strouse
World Weary (Gotta Get Back to You)   Parish
You Are Your Own Best Friend   Cahn; DePaul
You Smoke too Much (inst.)   Bacharach
You're at the Music Hall   Cahn
(Eyes of Blue) You're My Waterloo   Parish
You're Probably in Love   Cahn

1981

American Way, The   Schwartz, Arthur
Arthur's Theme (The Best That You Can Do)   Bacharach
Ask Me No Questions (I'll Tell You No Lies)   Bergman;
    Mancini
Baby, You Can Count on Me   Adams; Strouse
Back in Show Biz Again   Adams; Strouse
Ballad of Mary Jane   Cahn
Bells Bells Bells   Cahn
Bittersweet   Mancini
Blob, The   Sondheim
Bobby and Jackie and Jack   Sondheim
Bring Back Birdie   Adams; Strouse
Brunswick Yodel (That's All I Did)   David, Mack
Darling!   Sondheim
Don't Say F-A-T in Front of Conrad   Adams; Strouse
Easy to Love Again   Bacharach
Every Day Is Sunday   Davis
Fam'ly Trouble   Schwartz, Arthur
Filth   Adams; Strouse
Fool Me Again   Bacharach
Franklin Shepard, Inc.   Sondheim
Get Used to Me   Davis
God Bless You All the Day   Burke
Good Thing Going   Sondheim
Goodbye for Now   Sondheim
Half of a Couple   Adams; Strouse
Here Comes My Bride   Oakland; Webster
Hills of Tomorrow, The   Sondheim
Honey   Sondheim
How Old Do You Have to Be to Fall in Love   Davis
Howdy Christmas   Lawrence
I Hate Little Boys   Burke
I Like what I Do   Adams; Strouse
I Love 'Em All   Adams; Strouse
I Wish You Needed Me   Burke
I Wonder   Lawrence
I Won't Break   Bacharach
If the Girl Has Charm   Burke
I'm Myself   Burke
Inner Peace   Adams; Strouse
It's a Crying Shame   Drake
It's a Hit!   Sondheim
It's All for the Best   Lerner, Alan Jay
It's the Company   Burke
Jennifer   Evans; Livingston, Jay
Let's Go to the Movies   Strouse
Like It Was   Sondheim
Love's a Pretty Thing   Davis
Man Worth Fightin' For, A   Adams; Strouse
Merrily We Roll Along   Sondheim
Middle Age Blues   Adams; Strouse
Moody's Mood   McHugh
Movin' Out   Adams; Strouse
Moving Pictures   Bacharach
Ne Monus You   Fain
No One's Here   Lawrence
Not a Day Goes By   Sondheim
Now You Know   Sondheim
Old Friends   Sondheim
Opening Doors   Sondheim
Our Time   Sondheim
Papa's Got a Brand New Pig Bag   Leigh
Planet Claire   Mancini
Refer Them to Me   Burke

Rich and Happy   Sondheim
Sandy (Dumb Dog)   Strouse
Say Hello   Cahn
Serenade for Savan   Bergman
Shape Up   Adams; Strouse
Show Girls   Adams; Strouse
Sign   Strouse
Small Town Kind of Love, A   Davis
So Near, So Far   Evans; Livingston, Jay
Sometimes Late at Night   Bacharach
Spanish Dreams   Fisher
Stronger than Before   Bacharach
Take It from the Top   Coleman; Leigh
Takes Time   Davis
4th of July Parade   Burke
Thank You for Coming   Sondheim
There's a Brand New Beat in Heaven   Adams; Strouse
They Told Me   Cahn
Tomorrow World   Merrill
Touch (inst.)   Bacharach
Twenty Happy Years   Adams; Strouse
Ungrateful Heart   Warren
Waiting in the Wings   Evans; Livingston, Jay
Well, I'm Not!   Adams; Strouse
Well Minnie   Lawrence
When Will Grown-Ups Grow Up?   Adams; Strouse
Where Do You Catch the Bus for Tomorrow   Mancini
Who Was the Fool   Davis
Worry Not a Whit Not   Burke
You Can Never Go Back (I'll Never Go Back)   Adams;
    Strouse
You Can Take Music Away   Lawrence
You Don't Bring Me Flowers   Bergman
Young   Adams; Strouse

1982

(Someone They Call) A Senior Citizen   Livingston, Jerry
Arrival   Comden and Green
Arroz   Mercer
At Last   Comden and Green
Canadian Way, The   Schwartz, Arthur
Charming   Strouse
Chicago, Illinois   Mancini
Comin' Home to You   Bergman
Computer Song, The   Sherman
Crazy World   Mancini
Death Duet   Strouse
Departure   Comden and Green
Di Quando In Quando   Drake
Don't Ask a Lady   Coleman; Leigh
Emperor Is a Man, The   Strouse
Every Day Is New Year's Eve   Cahn
Finale (Can You Hear Me Now?)   Comden and Green
Front Page Story   Bacharach
Gay Paree   Mancini
Girls Know How   Bacharach
Grand Cafe, The   Comden and Green
Hate the Lies, Love the Liar   David, Mack
Hey Look, No Crying   Styne
How Do You Keep the Music Playing?   Bergman
I Wanna Be Yours   Coleman; Leigh
I Was Lost   Strouse
If We Were in Love   Bergman
I'm a Cinch to Fall in Love   Clare

In a Jocular Vein   Fain; Harburg
In Ensenada   Bacharach
It Might Be You   Bergman
Jailer, Jailer   Comden and Green
Jason   David, Mack
Kid Next Door, The   Cahn
Le Jazz Hot   Mancini
Learn to Be Lonely   Comden and Green
Letter from Klemnacht   Comden and Green
Letter to the Children   Comden and Green
Loki and Baldur   Comden and Green
Lost Among the Stars   Bacharach
Love Being What It Is   Fain; Harburg
Love Too Good to Last, The   Bacharach
Magic Journeys   Sherman
Makin' Memories   Sherman
Making Love   Bacharach
Mechanical Bird, The   Strouse
Munch Theme   Comden and Green
Never Speak Directly to an Emperor   Strouse
New Year's Eve   Comden and Green
Night Shift   Bacharach
Nightingale   Strouse
No More Mornings   Comden and Green
Now That I Have Everything   Drake
N.Y. City Opera Jingle   Comden and Green
One Little Spark   Sherman
Perfect Harmony   Strouse
Please Don't Make Me Hear that Song Again   Strouse
Please Don't Turn My Picture to the Wall   Clare
Power   Comden and Green
Prologue   Comden and Green
Rare Wines   Comden and Green
Rats and Mice and Fish   Comden and Green
Rivers Cannot Flow Upwards   Strouse
Shady Dame from Seville, The   Mancini
Singer Must Be Free, A   Strouse
Someone in the Dark   Bergman
Stay with Me, Nora   Comden and Green
Take Us to the Forest   Strouse
That's What Friends Are For   Bacharach
There She Is   Comden and Green
Think About Love   Bergman
To Love a Child   David, Hal
Tootsie   Bergman
Toy Store   Comden and Green
Two People Who Love   Comden and Green
We Are China   Strouse
We Can Never Light that Old Flame Again   David, Mack
Where Can I Go (To Find that Gallop Man)   Clare
Who Are These People?   Strouse
Why Am I So Happy?   Strouse
Woman Alone, A   Comden and Green
World Is Turning Fast, The   Schwartz, Arthur
World Showcase March   Sherman
You and Me   Mancini
You Don't Know Me   Bacharach
You Interest Me   Comden and Green
You're Good for Me   Clare

1983

Alter of Love   Webster
Amaryllis   Bergman
Another Life   Lerner, Alan Jay; Strouse

Anyone Who Loves   Lerner, Alan Jay; Strouse
Auf Wiedersehen   Lerner, Alan Jay; Strouse
Big Day   Adams
Calypso Fever   Bergman
Child of the Sixties (inst.)   Coleman
Class of Fifty-Nine, The   Sherman
Colony Motel, The   Sherman
Dance a Little Closer   Lerner, Alan Jay; Strouse
Daughter of the Devil   Adams
Don't Ask a Lady   Coleman
Don't Give Up on Me   Webster
Down on the Farm   Adams
Ellenville   Coleman; Leigh
Flim Flam   Adams
For You, My Love, On Christmas   Bergman
Garden of Love, A   Adams
Gonna Join the Navy   Webster
Happy, Happy New Year   Lerner, Alan Jay; Strouse
He Always Comes Home to Me   Lerner, Alan Jay; Strouse
Holy Smoke   Mercer
Homesick   Lerner, Alan Jay; Strouse
I Don't Know   Lerner, Alan Jay; Strouse
I Got a New Girl   Lerner, Alan Jay; Strouse
I Hope I Don't Love Him   Adams
I Hum to Myself   Sherman
I Never Want to See You Again   Lerner, Alan Jay; Strouse
I See. . .   Adams
I Wanna Be Yours   Coleman
I Wish I Could Forget Your Kisses (Like You Forgot My Tears)   Parish
Image of His Papa, The   Adams
Is It a Dream or Do These Things Really Happen   Webster
It Never Would Have Worked   Lerner, Alan Jay; Strouse
Just Say, "Yes I Can"   Sherman
Just What My Heart Had in Mind   Robison
Killing Time   Leigh; Styne
La Cabeza. . .   Adams
L.A. Is My Lady   Bergman
Little Boys   Bergman; Mancini
Lonely   Robison
Love Makes Us Whatever We Want to Be   Cahn; Styne
Mad   Lerner, Alan Jay; Strouse
Married Ten Weeks   Webster
Maybe   Bacharach
Meet the World   Sherman
Mein Shana Hadass   Bergman
Men!   Adams
Money Means Nothing to Me   Adams
My Only Love (Ich Liebe Dich)   Bergman
My Serenade   Bergman
Naztrov'eych   Bergman
Never Say Never Again   Bergman
Night Is Filled with Music (Auf Flugeln des Gesanges), The   Bergman
No Man Is Worth It   Lerner, Alan Jay; Strouse
No Matter What Happens   Bergman
No Wonder   Bergman
None but the Lonely Heart (Nur Wer Die Sensucht Kennt)   Bergman
On Top of the World   Lerner, Alan Jay; Strouse
Once Every Year   Webster
One World   Webster
Papa, Can You Hear Me   Bergman
Piece of Sky, A   Bergman
Progress   Adams

Rabbit's Racing Song   Bergman
Right Side, The   Sherman
Searching   Cahn; Styne
Somebody   Coleman
Street Talk (inst.)   Bacharach
Strictly Business   Adams
That's Me   Adams
There's Always One You Can't Forget   Lerner, Alan Jay; Strouse
There's Never Been Anything Like Us   Lerner, Alan Jay; Strouse
This Goodbye   Webster
This Is One of Those Moments   Bergman
To a Painting (Auf Ein Altee Bild)   Bergman
Tomorrow Night   Bergman
Train of Sin   Webster
Try a Little Something New   Sherman
Turtle's Racing Song   Bergman
Way He Makes Me Feel, The   Bergman
Way Things Are, The   Sherman
Wedding Night Waltz   Bergman
What a Woman   Adams
What Are Ya' Going to Do About It?   Lerner, Alan Jay; Strouse
What Is a Street Man   Adams
Where Is It Written   Bergman
Why Can't the World Go and Leave Us Alone?   Lerner, Alan Jay; Strouse
Will Someone Ever Look at Me that Way   Bergman
Without Me   Adams
Woman Who Thinks I'm Wonderful, A   Lerner, Alan Jay; Strouse
Yosheke, Yosheke   Bergman
You Go Your Way   Adams
You There in the Back Row   Coleman
You're the Only You   Sherman

1984

All One Large Family (At Christmas)   Sherman
Baby, I Don't Like You!   Howard, Bart
Beautiful   Sondheim
Beware of the Woman   Howard, Bart
Blame It on Rio   Coleman
Bow Wow Ball, The   Sherman
Brand New Woman   Howard, Bart
Bunny Bee Song, The   Sherman
Cabbage Patch Dreams   Sherman
Cabbage Patch Parade   Sherman
C'est L'Amour   Sherman
Children and Art   Sondheim
Christmas Hoop-De-Do   Sherman
Chromolume #7   Sondheim
Color and Light   Sondheim
Cuddle Me   Sherman
Dawgs (Are Man's Best Friends)   Sherman
Day After Day After Day   Mercer
Day Off, The   Sondheim
Did You Know?   Cahn
Everybody Loves Louis   Sondheim
Everything's Lovely in the Morning   Strouse
Finishing the Hat   Sondheim
First, Last and Always   Mercer
Fool Number One   Sigman
G'bye Now   Evans; Livingston, Jay

Gimme-Gimme Take-Take   Sherman
Good Ol' Otis Lee   Sherman
Gossip   Sondheim
Gotta Keep 'Em Humming   Sondheim
Hail, Cape Cod   Howard, Bart
Happy Birthday Dear Heartache   David, Mack
Happy Birthday Hoe Down   Sherman
Hey, Did You Know?   Coleman
Hey, Joe   Adams; Strouse
I Must Be Doing Something Right   Coleman
I Never Knew Why   Coleman
I Start Sneezing   Coleman
I'll Sing You Home   Sigman
I'm Gonna Worry   Howard, Bart
It's Gonna Take Time   Howard, Bart
It's Hot Up Here   Sondheim
It's My Body   Coleman
I've Been in Love with You   Howard, Bart
Kisses   Bergman
Kissin' Kitty   Howard, Bart
Lesson #8   Sondheim
Love Is Why They Invented the Blues   Cahn; Coleman
Miracles   Howard, Bart
Move On   Sondheim
Mrs. Santa Claus   Sherman
No Life   Sondheim
Old Tunes   Adams
One More Dream 'Til Christmas   Sherman
One on the Left, The   Sondheim
Plain Ev'ry-Day Blues, The   Howard, Bart
Putting It Together   Sondheim
Reach for Me   Howard, Bart
She Was My First Love   Coleman
Sincerely I'm Yours   David, Mack
Sleep with Me Tonight   Bacharach
Soldiers and Girls   Sondheim
Something New in My Life   Bergman
Something Special   Cahn; Coleman
Southwind   Mercer
Still Doing the Same Thing   Styne
Sunday   Sondheim
Sunday in the Park with George   Sondheim
Take My Baby   Howard, Bart
There's a Change in Me   Leigh
To All the Girls I've Loved Before   David, Hal
To Me   David, Mack
Too Good to Be Meant for Me   Howard, Bart
Townsend Harris March, The   Drake
Turn Around   Bacharach
Wake Me Up   Howard, Bart
We Do Not Belong Together   Sondheim
Welcome Welcome   Coleman
What Can I Do for You, Baby   Howard, Bart
When October Goes   Mercer
When Somebody Cares   Howard, Bart
Who Are We   Howard, Bart
Who Believes You   Howard, Bart
Windy City   Coleman
Winners   Adams; Strouse
Yoo-Hoo!   Sondheim

1985

After High School   Leigh
All That I Dreamed He Would Be   Lane

America Is   David, Hal
Any Moment Now   Leigh
Apples   Styne
Awards   Leigh
Benn Gunn Dance Music (inst.)   Styne
Beyond My Wildest Dreams   Styne
Bit of Home, A   Styne
Blind Pew's Lament   Styne
Blue Willow Wind   Styne
Bullfights in Madrid, The   Sherman
Buy Bonds for Bob   Evans; Livingston, Jay
Classical Music   Leigh
Dancin' My Blues Away   Lerner, Alan Jay
Doctor and Squire's Lament   Styne
Drum in My Heart — Gun in My Hand   Styne
Fightingest Bull in Spain, The   Sherman
Find Me   Styne
Find the Map   Styne
Finder of Lost Loves   Bacharach
Fraternal Fiesta   Leigh
Garbage   Lerner, Alan Jay
Gentlemen of Fortune   Styne
God Bless the Glory of Rum   Styne
Good Times   Strouse
Greatest City, The   Mancini
Growing Up   Sondheim
Happy Thanksgiving   Lerner, Alan Jay
He Died Like Every Pirate Should from Rum   Styne
Heat Is On, The   Leigh
Here's Looking at You   Leigh
Hootspa   Strouse
How'm I Doin'   Strouse
I Belong   David, Hal
I Have a Secret   Styne
I Wanna Be Real (Slowly Surely)   Sherman
I Will Kill Her   Lane
I'd Do It All Again   Styne
I'd Do It All Over Again   Styne
If I Were She   Lane
If I Were Your Son   Styne
If You Believe in Make-Believe   Sherman
I'll Never Leave You   Strouse
Interviews   Leigh
Isn't It Time for the People   Strouse
It Goes Like This   Leigh
It Was You Again   Lerner, Alan Jay
I've Been Married   Lerner, Alan Jay
John and Jim   Styne
Just a Big Ego   Caesar
Keep Me Close to You   Styne
Last I Love New York Song, The   Strouse
Lie a Little   Leigh
Love Me Tomorrow   Lane
Luxury Lane   Styne
Made in Nashville, Tennessee   Strouse
Made in the U.S.A.   Leigh
Man, A   Styne
Man Who Was My Boy, The   Styne
March of the Yuppies   Strouse
Marine's Gun Drill   Styne
Mayor   Strouse
Me & Thee   Styne
Miss Hilary Bacon of Beacon Hill   Lerner, Alan Jay
Mountains of Gold   Styne
My City   Strouse

My Last Strike   Styne
My Part of Somewhere   Styne
My Treasure Island   Styne
New York   Strouse
Next Year   Leigh
Night Life in Santa Rosa   Leigh
Nothing but the Best   Leigh
Oh, I Want to Be the Mayor   Strouse
Oh You Could Set Up for a Gentleman   Styne
One Leg Is Better Than Two   Styne
Rainbows End   Styne
Rehearsal   Leigh
Relax! Enjoy a Cigar   Drake
Ribbity Rabbity Run   Sherman
Rig My Gallant Ship   Styne
Rum   Styne
Sailor Beware   Evans; Livingston, Jay
Sailor Talk   Styne
Sea, The (1)   Styne
Sea, The (2)   Styne
Sea Shell, The   Styne
Search, The   Styne
Secret, A   Styne
Secret Place   Lerner, Alan Jay
Seven Thousand Islands   Styne
Sing Every Song   Mercer
Six Bells   Styne
Six O'Clock News   Leigh
Smart as Pint   Styne
Smile   Leigh
So This Is the World   Styne
Solomon Gundy   Styne
Some People   Lerner, Alan Jay
Something Turns Up to Make It Right!   Styne
Sorry As I Am   Lane
Still It Might Be Nice   Styne
Talent   Leigh
That Frank   Sondheim
That's Dancing   Mancini
That's Hollywood (If You Ever Need Me)   Warren
That's the Time to Go   Styne
There Are No Heroes   Styne
There's Still a Boy in Every Man   Styne
Those Royal Princesses   Leigh
To Become a Man   Styne
To Smell the Flowers   Sherman
Treasure Island   Styne
Vets   Leigh
Walking in the Sunshine   Leigh
What You See Is What You Get   Strouse
Whatever Became of Jenny?   Styne
Where First?   Styne
Where Would You Be?   Styne
Who Stole My Leg   Styne
Who'll Be the First!   Styne
Why Must We Fight?   Sherman
Wizard of Magic Town, The   Leigh
Y.A.M. Survival Manual, The   Leigh
You and Me   Styne
You Can Be a New Yorker Too   Strouse
You'll Never Forget Me   Styne
Your Captain   Styne
You're a Woman   Lane
You're Not the Mayor   Strouse

1986

Are You the One Who Loves Me   Mancini
Best Seat in the House, The   Bergman
Blame It on the Summer Night   Strouse
Brand New World   Strouse
Bread and Freedom   Strouse
Cheer Up Hamlet   Strouse
Cherry Street Cafe   Strouse
Children of the Wind   Strouse
Dancing with the Fools   Strouse
Democratic Club Dance   Strouse
Easy for You   Strouse
Extravagant Gestures   Bacharach
Fine Mess, A   Mancini
For My Mary   Strouse
Fourth of July, The   Strouse
Goodbye, So Soon   Mancini
Greenhorns   Strouse
How Long   Bacharach
I'll See You on the Radio (Laura)   Bacharach
It's Gonna Belong to Me   Strouse
Kaddish   Strouse
Keeps Gettin' Better All the Time   Coleman
Life in a Looking Glass   Mancini
Music of Goodbye, The   Bergman
My Own Drum   Sherman
Mystic Magic Mastermind   Sherman
Nashville Sings   Sigman
Nothing Will Hurt Us Again   Strouse
Now that Papa's Back   Strouse
On My Own   Bacharach
Open Your Eyes   Strouse
Penny a Tune   Strouse
Questions   Sherman
Rags   Strouse
Santa's Theme   Mancini
Sound of Love, The   Strouse
Stay Devoted   Bacharach
They Don't Make 'Em Like They Used To   Bacharach
Three Sunny Rooms   Strouse
To Deride You   Bacharach
Try   Bergman
Tunes (inst.)   Strouse
Uptown   Strouse
Wanting   Strouse
Why Haven't I Found Love?   Sherman
World's Greatest Criminal Mind, The   Mancini
Yankee Boy   Strouse

1987

Agony   Sondheim
Any Moment   Sondheim
Anything Can Happen on Halloween   Strouse
Back to the Palace   Sondheim
Boom Crunch   Sondheim
Break My Heart Again   Lane
Call Your Police   Strouse
Canvas, Sawdust and Dreams   Sherman
Children Will Listen   Sondheim
Cinderella at the Grave   Sondheim
Country House   Sondheim
Crocodile, A Crocodile, A   Strouse
Don't Leave Me Now   Strouse
Eileen Aroon   Bergman

Ever After   Sondheim
Everchanging Times   Bacharach
First Midnight   Sondheim
Giants in the Sky   Sondheim
Growing Up Isn't Easy   Strouse
Has Anyone Seen My Crocodile   Strouse
Heartbreak of Love   Bacharach
Hello, Little Girl   Sondheim
Homeless   Strouse
How Much I Care   Cahn
I Guess This Is Goodbye   Sondheim
I Have Never Danced Before   Lane
I Know   Strouse
I Know Things Now   Sondheim
I Never Danced Before   Drake
I Never Thought You'd Say Goodbye   Bacharach
I Won't Believe My Eyes   Bergman
In a World Such as This   Bacharach
In My Reality   Bacharach
Interesting Questions   Sondheim
Into the Woods   Sondheim
It Takes Two   Sondheim
I've Got to Keep Busy   Strouse
Just Like Last Night   Sondheim
Lament   Sondheim
Last Midnight   Sondheim
Let Them See A Star   Strouse
Look on the Bright Side   Strouse
Love Like Ours   Bergman
Love Power   Strouse
Loveland   Sondheim
Lyle and Valenti   Strouse
Mailman's Song   Strouse
Make the Most of Your Music   Sondheim
Maybe They're Magic   Sondheim
Me Oh My Oh Man Do I Miss Milwaukee   Strouse
Meadow Serenade — Verse   Lane
Moments in the Woods   Sondheim
Moving Into a New House   Strouse
My Heart Will Still Be Young   Bacharach
No More   Sondheim
No One Is Alone   Sondheim
Nobody Loves You Like I Do   Strouse
On the Steps of the Palace   Sondheim
Over You   Bacharach
Ready for the Woods   Sondheim
Sea of Heartbreak   David, Hal
Second Midnight   Sondheim
Secret of Love, The   Bacharach
Simply Meant to Be   Mancini
So Happy   Sondheim
Social Dancing (inst.)   Sondheim
Split Decision   Bacharach
Stay with Me   Sondheim
There's No Hotel Like the Algonquin   Strouse
Very Nice Prince, A   Sondheim
Your Fault   Sondheim

1988

Alimony Jail   Coleman
Alimony Rap   Coleman
Anatomy of a Love Song   Howard, Bart
At My Side   Coleman
Bachelors   Coleman

Best of Times (inst.), The   Bacharach
Boom Chicka Boom   Coleman
By Dawn's Early Light   Coleman
Chickabees   Coleman
Combat Pay   Coleman
Comedy Ain't No Joke   Coleman
Doin' the Bob Hope Show   Coleman
Guilty   Coleman
Holidays   Coleman
Honeymoon Is Over, The   Coleman
I Get Tired   Coleman
I Know the Feeling   Bergman
In the Name of Love   Coleman
It Wouldn't Be You   Coleman
It's Love   Coleman
King of the Mound   Coleman
Late Bloomer   Coleman
Let 'Em Rot   Coleman
Love Behind Bars   Coleman
Love Is Fire (Love Is Ice)   Bacharach
Love is My Decision   Bacharach
Love Light   Bacharach
Love Makes the Changes   Bergman
Love Theme (inst.)   Bacharach
Man of the People, A   Coleman
Miami Beach   Coleman
Mother-in-Laws   Coleman
Mrs. Meltzer Wants the Money Now   Coleman
No Croissants   Coleman
No Walls Are High Enough   Bergman
One More Time Around   Bacharach
Oscar and Me   Coleman
Overnight Success   Bacharach
Pal Is a Pal, A   Coleman
Pay the Lawyer   Coleman
Peace of Mind   Coleman
Piece of Cake, A   Coleman
Rap-Up, The   Coleman
Single   Coleman
Southern Comfort   Coleman
That Meyer Chickerman!   Coleman
That's a Woman   Coleman
To Live Again   Coleman
Travelin' Man   Coleman
Trouble with You, The   Coleman
Two of Us, The   Coleman
Two People   Bergman
Vaudeville   Coleman
Welcome to the Club   Coleman
Where Do You Start?   Bergman
Why Let It Go?   Bergman
You and Me for Always   Bacharach
Young Just Once   Howard, Bart
You're Invited to a Party   Coleman

1989

All Dolled Up   Strouse
All I've Got Is Me   Strouse
All You Have to Do Is Wait   Coleman
Ball Is in Your Court, The   Coleman
Beautiful   Strouse
Beverly Hills (Anthem)   Mancini
Buddy System, The   Coleman
But You Go On   Strouse

Christmas Love Song, A   Bergman
City of Angels Theme   Coleman
Coney Island   Strouse
Cortez   Strouse
Double Talk   Coleman
Etiquette   Sherman
Everybody's Gotta Be Somewhere   Coleman
Flip's Theme   Sherman
Fun and Laughter   Sherman
Funny   Coleman
Girl Who Used to Be Me, The   Bergman
He Doesn't Know I'm Alive   Strouse
How Could I Ever Say No   Strouse
I Could Get Used to This   Strouse
I Don't Wanna Die   Strouse
I Won't Believe My Eyes   Bergman
It Needs Work   Coleman
Just Let Me Get Away with This One   Strouse
Killer Love   Mancini
Lady of the House, The   Strouse
Let Me Be Surprised   Strouse
Let's Go to Tokyo   Strouse
Let's Make Music Together   Strouse
Lost and Found   Coleman
Most of All You   Bergman
1934   Strouse
Not My Baby   David, Mack
Of Course It's Crazy   David, Mack
Slumberland   Sherman
Song of the Boomps   Sherman
Tenement Lullaby, The   Strouse
Welcome to Being Dead   Strouse
What You Don't Know About Women   Coleman
What's Mine Is Yours (The Sharing Song)   Strouse
When You Smile   Strouse
Why Can't We Be Together   Bacharach
With Ev'ry Breath I Take   Coleman
You Ain't Seen the Last of Me   Strouse
You Can Always Count on Me   Coleman
You Can't Keep a Good Dog Down   Strouse
You! You! You!   Strouse
Younger Man, A   Strouse
You're Nothin' Without Me   Coleman

1990

Ah, Our Germans   Merrill
Another National Anthem   Sondheim
Back in Business   Sondheim
Ballad of Booth, The   Sondheim
Ballad of Czolgosz, The   Sondheim
Ballad of Guiteau, The   Sondheim
Between Yesterday and Tomorrow   Bergman
Born to Be Blue   David, Mack
Can You Tell the Moment   Bergman
Empress of Crime, The   Strouse
Everybody's Got the Right   Sondheim
Gentle Afternoon   Merrill
Get the Feel of the Wheel of a Ford   Sherman
Gun Song   Sondheim
Hannah Will Take Care of You   Merrill
Hotsy Totsy Nazi   Merrill
How I Saved Roosevelt   Sondheim
I Don't Do Duets   Bergman
I'll Get Away with It   Strouse

Kissed On the Eyes   Merrill
Learn About Life   Merrill
Martina   Merrill
More   Sondheim
Mother and Child   Bergman
Music of Being Free, The   Bergman
No Give, No Take   Merrill
November 22, 1963   Sondheim
On This Merry Christmas Eve   Strouse
One Song   Bergman
Opening   Merrill
Our Little World   Sondheim
Pearl We Called Prague, The   Merrill
Perfect World, A   Strouse
Pretty Thing   Merrill
Radio Dance   Merrill
Right Kind of Man (The Wrong Kind of Man), The   Strouse
Security   Strouse
Sew a Button   Merrill
So Good to See You   Merrill
Someday   Merrill
Sooner or Later   Sondheim
Ugly Identical Twins   Drake
Unworthy of Your Love   Sondheim
Wall of Fire   David, Hal
We Dance   Merrill
Wear a Little Grin   Merrill
What Can You Lose   Sondheim
What Kind of Crime   Strouse
When We're Dancing   Drake
Who Is Hannah?   Merrill
You Can Close the New York Stock Exchange   Sondheim

1991

As Long As You're Happy   Strouse
Attwater Prairie Chickens   Sherman
Beyond Words   Strouse
Big Time, The   Coleman; Comden and Green
Biggest Little Scam in Old New York   David, Hal; Strouse
Boom Chicka Boom   Strouse
Busy Night at Lorraine's, A   Strouse
Class   Strouse
Detectiveland   Strouse
Elegant Elephant, The   Sherman
English Hedgehogs   Sherman
Everybody Wants to Do a Musical   Strouse
Everyone Who Is Anyone (Is Going to Be There)   David, Hal; Strouse
Florida Panthers   Sherman
Giant Step, A   Adams; Strouse
Give a Man Enough Rope   Coleman; Comden and Green
Good Lookin'   David, Hal; Strouse
Good Times   David, Hal; Strouse
Hot Water   David, Hal; Strouse
I Got You   Coleman; Comden and Green
I Was Something   David, Hal; Strouse
I'm Proud to Be a Platypus   Sherman
Is There Anything Better Than Dancing?   Strouse
It's a Boy   Coleman; Comden and Green
I've Been There Before   David, Hal; Strouse
Let Me Tell You I Won't   David, Hal; Strouse
Let's Go Flying   Coleman; Comden and Green
Let's Go Home   Strouse
Living Doll   David, Hal; Strouse

Look Around   Coleman; Comden and Green
Look Who's Alone Now   Strouse
Looking Back   David, Hal; Strouse
Mamushka, The   Comden and Green
Married Life   Strouse
Marry Me Now   Coleman; Comden and Green
May the Best Man Win   Strouse
Men   Strouse
Mother Doesn't Matter Anymore, A   Adams; Strouse
My Big Mistake   Coleman; Comden and Green
My Unknown Someone   Coleman; Comden and Green
Never Met a Man I Didn't Like   Coleman; Comden and Green
No Man Left for Me   Coleman; Comden and Green
Not Me   Strouse
Our Favorite Son   Coleman; Comden and Green
People Get Hurt   Strouse
Presents for Mrs. Rogers   Coleman; Comden and Green
Snow Leopards   Sherman
So Long Pa   Coleman; Comden and Green
Swell   Strouse
Take My Breath Away   David, Hal; Strouse
(Gorillas Are) The Gentlest Creatures   Sherman
(Better Beware of) The Grizzly Bear   Sherman
Timberland Brown   Sherman
Times Square   David, Hal; Strouse
Too Young to Be Old   David, Hal; Strouse
We Speak the Same Language   David, Hal; Strouse
We're Heading for a Wedding   Coleman; Comden and Green
Where Were You   David, Hal; Strouse
Willamania   Coleman; Comden and Green
Without You   Coleman; Comden and Green
You Shouldn't Never Have Lied   David, Hal; Strouse
You Take My Breath Away   David, Hal; Strouse
You're Fired   David, Hal; Strouse

1992

All We Need Is Love   Cahn; Lane
Bloom Is Still on the Rose, The   Lane
Karabitz!   Adams; Strouse
Later   Adams; Strouse
Nuts to You   Adams; Strouse
Something Just Broke   Sondheim
Thanks to You   Adams; Strouse

1993

Above the Law   Strouse
Ain't Broadway Grand   Adams
Alone in the Light   Merrill; Styne
Am I to Wish Her Love   Merrill; Styne
Annie Ain't Annie Anymore   Strouse
Audition, The   Merrill; Styne
Be Somewhere   Merrill; Styne
Beautiful Word, A   Mancini
Beginning   Strouse
Big Job, A   Adams
Changes   Strouse
Charity Party   Strouse
Christmas in New York   Drake
Class   Adams
Clean Sweep   Strouse
Come Home   Merrill; Styne

Corps de Ballet   Merrill; Styne
Do Svedanya   Merrill; Styne
Friends to the End   Mancini
Girls Ahoy!   Adams
God's Little Creatures   Mancini
Hans the Man   Adams; Strouse
He's My Guy   Adams
Home Again   Styne
I Always Knew   Strouse
I Don't Want Anyone to Love You but Me   Strouse
I Don't Want to Grow Old   Strouse
I Got Me   Strouse
I Miss You   Mancini
I'll Never Know   Styne
I'm Back in Love   Strouse
Impresario   Merrill; Styne
It Would Have Been Wonderful   Strouse
It's a Fairy Tale   Merrill; Styne
It's Always Like the First Time   Styne
It's Time to Go   Adams
I've Done It All   Mancini
Jerusalem   Strouse
Joke's on Me, The   Strouse
Lady   Strouse
Leave It to the Girls   Strouse
Lindy's   Adams
Love   Strouse
Love Can Sometimes Make You Cry   Strouse
Man I Married, The   Adams
Maybe, Maybe Not   Adams
Miss Page   Merrill; Styne
My Star   Adams; Strouse
On the Street   Adams
One and One Are Two   Styne
Other Woman, The   Strouse
Pills and Booze   Strouse
Plam Beach   Strouse
Quintet   Strouse
Rag, The   Merrill; Styne
Red Shoes (inst.), The   Styne
She   Strouse
She's Gonna Love Me   Strouse
She's Not Made for You   Strouse
Shloop, The   Strouse
Somebody's Gotta Do Somethin'   Strouse
Start of an Affair, The   Strouse
Tall Dames and Low Comedy   Adams
Tete A Tete   Warren
That's the Kind of Woman   Strouse
Theater, the Theater, The   Adams
They'll Never Take Us Alive   Adams
Top of the Sky   Merrill; Styne
Vot Makes Zanta Run?   Drake
Waiting in the Wings   Adams
Wedding, Wedding   Strouse
Welcome to Washington   Strouse
What Do We Care   Mancini
When It Happens to You   Merrill; Styne
When You Dance for a King   Merrill; Styne
You're My Star   Adams

1994

All My Saturday Nights   Cahn; Coleman
Break My Heart Again   Drake

City with a Caring Heart   Drake
Everyone but You   Drake
Farewell Letter   Sondheim
First Letter   Sondheim
Flashback   Sondheim
Forty Days   Sondheim
Fosca's Entrance   Sondheim
Fourth Letter   Sondheim
Garden Sequence   Sondheim
Happiness   Sondheim
He's Younger Than I Am   Drake
I Can't Stop Dancing   Strouse
I Read   Sondheim
I Wish I Could Forget You   Sondheim
In the Afternoon   Drake
Love Like Ours   Sondheim
Loving You   Sondheim
Man Who Has It All, The   Drake
No One Has Ever Loved Me   Sondheim
Painted Mem'ries   Drake
Second Letter   Sondheim
Soldiers' Gossip   Sondheim
Sunrise Letter   Sondheim
They Hear Drums   Sondheim
Third Letter   Sondheim
Washington Square   Drake
We Arrested the Moon   Drake
What If?   Drake
Who Needs Another Song about New York?   Drake
You Turn on My Music   Drake

1995

All Around the Town   Sherman
Almost a Love Song   Mancini
Attitude   Mancini
Baby Me   Sherman
Blow Us a Kiss   Sherman
Brighton   Sherman
Busker Alley   Sherman
Cat and Mouse   Mancini
Charley the Busker   Sherman
Crazy 'Appy Tears   Sherman
Doomed, Damned and Delighted   Drake
East River Drive   Drake
Funnybone   Sherman
God Bless the Buskers   Sherman
He Has a Way   Sherman
How Long Have I Loved Libby?   Sherman
Hula Love Song   Sherman
I Guess It's Time   Mancini
I Know Where I'm Going   Mancini
If I Were a Man   Mancini
I'm on the Inside   Sherman
I've No Idea Where I'm Going   Mancini
King's Dilemma   Mancini
Libby   Sherman
Mates   Sherman
Memory Ballet (inst.)   Sherman
Million Miles from You, A   Sherman
Ordinary Couples   Sherman
Paris by Night   Mancini
Paris Makes Me Horny   Mancini
Plain Jane   Sherman
She Has a Way   Sherman

So Long Sadness   Drake
Someone Else   Mancini
Strays   Sherman
Tap 'Appy Feet   Sherman
This Is Not Going to Change My Life   Mancini
Tin Whistle Tune   Sherman
Victor/Victoria   Mancini
Waitin' for Ann   Sherman
What to Do With 'Er   Sherman
When Do I Get Mine?   Sherman
When the Moonlight's Bright in Brighton   Sherman
Where Are the Faces?   Sherman
Where the 'Ell Is 'Ome?   Sherman
World of Beautiful Girls, The   Sherman

1996

Argument   Adams; Strouse
Charley Express, The   Adams; Strouse
Check It Out!   Coleman
Counting All the Days   Adams; Strouse
Don't Leave Me Now   Adams; Strouse
Don't Take Much   Coleman
Easy Money   Coleman
End, The   Adams; Strouse
Everybody Loves Me   Lane
Family   Adams; Strouse
Fanfare for If the King Stops Here   Lane
Getting Over You   Drake
God Give Me Strength   Bacharach
Golden Oldies   Drake
Hats   Adams; Strouse
He's No Good   Coleman
Hey, Daddy - Go Home   Coleman
Hooker's Ball, The   Coleman
I Still Have That Other Girl   Bacharach
I Was Wrong   Sondheim
If the King Stops Here   Lane
I'm Leaving You   Coleman
I'm Not in Philadelphia   Adams; Strouse
In the Darkest Place   Bacharach
Invitation, The   Adams; Strouse
Is This What You Call Love?   Sondheim
It Takes All Kinds   Sondheim
Little Dream   Sondheim
Long Division, The   Bacharach
Lovely Day to Be Out of Jail, A   Coleman
Margo   Adams; Strouse
Millionaire Blues   Adams; Strouse
Mr. Greed   Coleman
My Body   Coleman
My Friend   Coleman
My Thief   Bacharach
My Way or the Highway   Coleman
No Pretty Rich Girl   Adams; Strouse
Oh Daddy   Coleman
Oh, Those Eyes   Lane
Oldest Profession, The   Coleman
Painted from Memory   Bacharach
People Magazine   Coleman
Piece of the Action   Coleman
Pine Point   Adams; Strouse
Remember Me   Adams; Strouse
She Killed Them   Adams; Strouse
Such Unlikely Lovers   Bacharach

Sweetest Punch, The   Bacharach
Tears at the Birthday Party   Bacharach
They Look to Us   Adams; Strouse
This House is Empty Now   Bacharach
Toledo   Bacharach
Train in the Night, A   Adams; Strouse
Use What You Got   Coleman
Vamp Dolce   Bacharach
We Gotta Go   Coleman
We Hate Paree!   Drake
What Do You Do?   Adams; Strouse
What Does He Mean I Can't Love?   Adams; Strouse
What's Her Name Today?   Bacharach
What's Right   Adams; Strouse
Who's to Say?   Adams; Strouse
Why Don't They Leave Us Alone   Coleman
With Hearts Ablaze   Lane
Without You   Adams; Strouse
You Can't Get to Heaven   Coleman

1997

Chanukah Time in Dublin   Drake
Draw Up the Pre-Nup   Drake
Seulement Toi   Drake

1998

Giving   Drake
Nobody but You   Drake

1999

Ain't He Cute   Coleman
Burlesque at the Deli   Strouse
Clara the Turtle   Strouse
Cockney (Piccadilly Lil)   Strouse
Cottage By the Sea   Coleman
Could'a Been Worse   Strouse
Courtroom Cantata   Coleman
Doctor, A   Strouse
Don't Mess Around With Your Mother-In-Law   Coleman
Dracula   Strouse
Every Minute of the Day   Strouse
Every Number Needs a Button   Strouse
Eyes Like That   Strouse
Fraction of an Inch   Strouse
Gay Paree   Strouse
Good Day   Coleman
Happy Birthday   Strouse
Home   Strouse
How Did You Know?   Drake
I Could Get Used to This   Strouse
I Gotta Get Outta Here   Strouse
I Love You So   Strouse
I Must Have Been Crazy   Strouse
I Want the Best for Him   Coleman
It Isn't Easy   Strouse
It's Happening Here   Strouse
Joan of Arc   Strouse
Just What I Need   Strouse
Let's Kiss   Strouse
Life in Venetia, Life in Vienna   Sondheim
Life Is Sweet   Strouse

Marty   Strouse
Montana Chem   Sondheim
My Mother-in-Law   Strouse
My Star   Strouse
New Kind of Broadway, A   Strouse
Niente da Fare   Strouse
Night They Raided Minsky's, The   Strouse
No Further Questions Please   Coleman
No Way to Treat a Lady   Strouse
Opening Night   Strouse
Our Almost Perfect Love   Drake
Perfect Lady, A   Strouse
Phoning Mary Feeney   Strouse
Poor Cleopatra   Strouse
Rio   Coleman
Saturday Night Girl   Strouse
Shake 'em but Don't Break 'em!   Strouse
She Makes Me Laugh   Coleman
She Sees Who I Am   Strouse
Smile for the Camera   Strouse
Sweet Revenge   Strouse
Thanks to Mom   Coleman
That Damn Blue Suit   Strouse
That's Burlesque   Strouse
Think Lunch   Strouse
Two Great Minds   Strouse
Whatd'ya Feel Like Doing?   Strouse
What's Right for Me?   Strouse
While I'm Here   Drake
Why Did You Have to Be a Lawyer   Coleman
Why Not   Strouse
Words   Strouse
Work of Art, A   Strouse
Workin' Hot   Strouse
Wrong Girl, The   Strouse
You're Good for Me   Coleman
2X a Loser   Strouse

2000

Butterfly   Strouse
Every Living Thing   Drake
Everybody's Got a Price   Strouse
Everything Can Be Lovely in the Morning   Strouse
He's a Jolly Good Fellow   Strouse
Mother of All the Blues   Drake
Natural African Man   Strouse
No Big Deal   Strouse
Non Vedo L'Ora   Drake
Playing the Game   Strouse
Road Tour, The   Strouse
What Am I Gonna Do Without You?   Strouse
Why Should I Change a Thing?   Strouse
Winners   Strouse
Workout Song   Strouse

Date Unknown

Ad   Sondheim
After Tonight   Johnson, James P.; Razaf
Ain't Nothin' but Trouble Trouble   Russell
All I Want Is Not to Want   Strouse
All My Life, I'll Make You Happy, Dear   Brown, Lew; DeSylva; Henderson
All My Sweeties Rolled into One   Carroll

All My Tomorrows (For One Yesterday)   Razaf
All My Victories Are Losses   Razaf
All the Grey Haired Men   Russell
All Year Long   Sondheim
Alone in Your Class, Little Girl   Loesser
Always Leave Them Asking for More   Loesser
Amazons, The   Razaf
(A Sky of Blue, with You) And So Forth   Johnson, Howard
And Yet the World Rolls On   Harburg
Angel in the Night   Evans; Livingston, Jay
Angelique   Atteridge
Annette   Sterling
Another Night Together   Adamson; Donaldson
Another World   Sondheim
Any Questions?   Oakland; Russell
Anything Is Nice If It Comes from Dixieland   Yellen
Art of Self-Defense, The   Razaf
As Long As the Band Will Play   Atteridge
As the Day Went On   Strouse
Ashley   Strouse
Ask Me Again   Gershwin, George; Gershwin, Ira
Atomic Lace   Razaf
Auf Japan   Friml
Ave Maria   Warren
Baby Please Hurry to Me   Razaf
Bachelor's Dream, The   Buck
Back Home for Keeps   Russell
Bad News   Leigh
Ballad of Surfer Bill   Russell
Ballett (inst.)   Warren
Band, Band, Band   Brown, A. Seymour
Band from Dixie-Land   Atteridge
Baseball Papa — Race Track Mama   Razaf; Waller
Be Sweet to Me   Warren
Beautiful Legs   Razaf; Waller
(I Hear) Bells   Warren
Best Time of the Day, The   Sondheim
Better Way, A   Lane
Beverly Hillbillies   Russell
Big Apple   Warren
Big Chief Burke   Atteridge
Big City Blues   Russell
Big Towns and the Small Towns, The   Cahn; Duke
Big-Hearted Joe   Razaf
Bitter Sweet Memories (inst.)   Warren
Black Man, Black Woman   Strouse
Blarney Kate   Atteridge
Blue Monday   Razaf; Waller
Blue on My Way to Reno   Fisher
Blue Pillow   Carmichael
Blue Serenade   Adamson
Blues in the Morning (Inst.)   Warren
Bobbin' Up and Down   Carroll
Boogie Woogie Bunga Boo   Blake
Born to Swing   Razaf
Brazilian Baion   Russell
Breakfast at Arable's   Strouse
Bright Star   Sondheim
Broke but Happy   Razaf; Waller
Broken Wing, The   Carroll
Brook, The (inst.)   Warren
Bumble Bee   Coslow
Buy a Bond for Baby   Razaf
Bye-Bye Sorrow   Razaf
Cabaret Song   Warren

Call Me a Taxi   DePaul; Russell
Camp Wigwam Hiking Song   Hart
Can-Can   Warren
Candy College Boys   Atteridge
Candy Opening   Hart; Rodgers
Carolina Balmoral (inst.)   Johnson, James P.
Celle Qui Refusait   Dubin; Warren
Cellophane   Razaf
Chance to Dream   Lerner, Alan Jay
Chanson Des Chercheuses D—-   Hoffman; Warren
Charleston Waterfront   Razaf
Charlotte's Spinning Song   Strouse
Chicago   Clare
China (Temple Bells) (inst.)   Warren
Christmas Is a Day of Joy   Warren
Christmas Island at Christmas Time   Sondheim
Christobel   Sondheim
City Kept Gal   Sissle
Civilian Mary   Yellen
Clarinet and the Coronet   Atteridge
Clarinet's Love, The   Atteridge
Climb High   Sondheim
Cocktail Party   Sondheim
Colossal, Tremendous, Terrific   Rose
Come On In, the Water's Fine   Styne
Come Up and See Me Sometime   Razaf
Conga Tap, The   Blake
Cops   Warren
Coster's Glide, The   Johnson, J. Rosamond
Country Fair   Strouse
Crime Doesn't Pay   Sondheim
Cupid's Lane   Atteridge
Curtain Calls   Strouse
Cutest Kid in Town, The   Turk
Daddy's Away   Hart; Rodgers
Dancing Devil   Caesar
Daniel the Great Social Lion   Arlen; Harburg
Dark Rosaleen   Bryan; Fisher
Daughters of the Evolution   Hart; Rodgers
Dawn   Sondheim
Deep Are the Roots (Of My Love)   Razaf
Deep in My Soul   Razaf
Deep Silence   Razaf
Delta Iota Mu   Sondheim
Desert Lullaby, The   Hart; Rodgers
Destiny   Bryan; Fisher
Dinah   Turk
Don't   Strouse
Doucement   Warren
Down in Papeetee Tahiti   Warren
Down Stream   Loesser
Dr. Bernstein   Russell
Dream Waltz (inst.)   Warren
Dreamer, The   Razaf
Dreamer (inst.)   Warren
Drop a Penny in the Wishing Well   Webster
Drop the Old Folks a Line   Razaf; Waller
Duck, The   Loesser
Dynamite Joe   Henderson; Razaf
Earnin' a Living'   Styne
Eating   Strouse
Elephant Skid   Freed, Arthur
Ellie   Styne
Everlasting Mountain, The   David, Mack; Warren
Every Night Dear   Caesar

Every Night (inst.)   Warren
Everybody Loves Everybody   Duke
Everyone's Wrong but Me   Fain
Everything Is Lovely   Adams
Ev'rybody's Gal   Razaf
Exclusive Love   Razaf
Extenuatin' Circumstances   Cahn; Duke
Eyes of Love (inst.)   Warren
Fair Lady   Sondheim
Fallen Idols   Fisher
Fanfare and Arena Sequence   Sondheim
Fantasy   Warren
Farewell My Darling Farewell   Loesser
Festive Days   Atteridge; Romberg
Fight Duet, The   Strouse
Fight Over Me   Cahn; Duke
Fish, The   Loesser
Flow On River   Hart; Rodgers
Flow on Silvery Hudson   Bryan; Fisher
For Johnny and Me   Brown, Lew; Henderson
Forgive Me   Robin; Warren
Freedom Now   Strouse
French Waltz   Sondheim
Gal that Used to Do the Hootchy Kootchy, The   Gilbert
Game of Love, The   Warren
Ghost of a Love   Russell
Gimme the Shimmie   Clare
Gipsy Song (inst.)   Warren
Girl with the Prettiest Legs in Town, The   Cahn; Duke
Girls   Fisher
Give My Regards to Broadway   Bryan; Fisher
Glamour Girl   Rose
Glen, The (inst.)   Warren
Go Easy with My Dreams   Warren
God Gives Us One Mother That's All   Brown, Lew;
   Henderson
Good Bad Woman!   Hart; Rodgers
Good Provider   Hart; Rodgers
Goodbye, Shanghai   Fisher
Goodbye Still Means Goodbye   Russell
Good-bye Wild Women, Good-Bye   Yellen
Gotta Get Myself a Brand New Gal   Turk
Green Fields   Warren
Half of Life   Adams
Hard to Get (inst.)   Warren
Harlem's a Garden   Blake
Harry Warren O Melody (Inst.)   Warren
Haunting Me   Myrow
Havana Anna Ann   Atteridge
Have It Your Way, Foolish Heart   Kahal; Warren
Have You Been Waiting Long   Sondheim
He Said   Cahn; Duke
He Was the Last Rose of Summer   Hart; Rodgers
Heartease   Bryan; Fisher
Helfried   Friml
He's Mine and I Love Him   Adamson; Warren
Hey for the Tartan   Warren
High Tor   Sondheim
Hippity Hop   Ahlert; Turk
His Majesty the American   Brown, Lew; Henderson
Honey Sal   Atteridge
Honeymooning in the Sky with You   Ager; Yellen
Honor Me with This Dance   Cahn; Duke
Hot Jello   Razaf
How About a Hand for the Comic   Lane

How Can I Make the One That I Love Love Me   Lane
How Did It Happen?   Kahal; Warren
How Easy We Forget   Russell
Hunky Dory   Strouse
I Can Take It or Leave It   Cahn; Duke
I Can't Afford to Dream   Henderson
I Can't Stop Loving   Gordon; Warren
I Come A-Runnin'   Loesser
I Could Have Told You   Loesser
I Could Say Goodnight to a Thousand Girls (But Only
    Dream of One)   Cobb
I Didn't Know How Much I'd Miss ——   Russell
I Didn't Think You Cared   Warren
I Don't Love You Anymore   Strouse
I Don't Trust . . .   Styne
I Don't Want to Fall in Love with You   Sondheim
I Don't Want to Grow Old   Strouse
I Don't Want to Love No One but You   Brown, Lew;
    Henderson
I Found Your Purse Madam   Bryan; Fisher
I Give My Love to You This Christmas   Warren
I Happen to Love You   Russell
I Have My Arms Around the World   Warren
I Have the Funniest Feeling   Sondheim
I Haven't a Bean in My Jeans   Duke
I Haven't Heard a Word from You   Gordon; Revel
I Just Don't Deserve It (Long, Long, Lashes)   Loesser
I Keep Coming Back for More   Yellen
I Like London   Lane
I Love Him   Brown, Lew; Henderson
I Love My Babe   Johnson, J. Rosamond
I Love to Lie Awake in Bed   Hart; Schwartz, Arthur
I Love to Raise the Dickens   Buck
I May Say Maybe   Cahn; Duke
I Never Danced Before   Lane
I Never Knew I Had a Wonderful Wife   Brown, Lew;
    Henderson
I Picked a Pansy in the Garden of Love   Yellen
I Saw the Light of Day Last Night   Burke
I See a Rainbow   Arlen
I Sing Tra-La   Atteridge
I Thought I Meant Something to You   DePaul; Russell
I Told You So   Brown, Lew; Henderson
I Want to Make Sure You Love Me   Henderson
I Want to Sleep with You Now   Strouse
I Will Show You the Way   Atteridge
I Wonder What They're Doing Tonight, Your Girl and
    Mine   Henderson
I Wonder Why (Once I Had a Friend)   Sondheim
I Won't Come Back   Atteridge
I Wouldn't Change a Thing   Sondheim
I Wrestled with the Devil   Dubin; Warren
I'd Like to Be Rip Van Winkle, in Rip Van Winkle
    Town   Ahlert; Turk
I'd Like to Say I Love You   Warren
Idle Hours   Ahlert; Turk
If I Could Be the Only Child   Strouse
If They Ever Put a Tax on Love   Yellen
If This Is a Dream   Lane
If You Don't Do Your Homework   Dubin; Warren
If You Don't Want to Love Me   Brown, Lew; Henderson
If You Lived Here, You'd Be Dead By Now   Lane
If You Should Ever Leave   Fain
I'll Always Need You   Loesser
I'll Do No Turkey Trotting   Atteridge

I'm Above All That   Sondheim
I'm Called the King   Duke
I'm Clean   Styne
I'm Getting Better!   Hart; Rodgers
I'm Glad to See You Back   Warren
I'm Goin' Places   Cahn; Duke
I'm Going Back to Old Virginia   Buck
I'm Here   Strouse
I'm in Love With a Beautiful Baby   Brown, Lew; Henderson
I'm in Love with a Boy   Sondheim
I'm Missin' Mammy's Kissin'   Clare
I'm Not That Kind of Girl   Brown, Lew; Henderson
I'm Over Here and You're Over There   Atteridge
I'm Over Here, You're Over There   Brown, Lew; Henderson
I'm Percy Pinchill of Harlem   Blake
I'm Seein' the World at Home   Dubin; Warren
In a Little Italian Garden   Lane
In a Year from Now   Sondheim
In Loveyland   Conrad
In Secret Service I Won Her Heart   Bryan; Fisher
In the Absence of Monsieur   David, Mack; Warren
In the Glow and Sighs of Texas   Sterling
In the Sweet Dry and Dry   Yellen
In Your Arms I'll Always Feel at Home   Dubin; Warren
Invocation to Venus   Duke
I.O.U., An   Blake; Razaf
Is the Curtain Up?   Arlen
Isabelle   Mercer; Warren
Isle of Romance   Clarke; Coslow
Isle of Zanzibar   Razaf
It Ain't Like It Used to Was   Clare
It Comes Up Love   Loesser
It Cost Me Just a Nickel   Fain; Kahal
It Never Can Happen Again   Atteridge
It Never Ends   Cahn; Warren
Italian Serenade (inst.)   Warren
Italy   Hart; Rodgers
It's Been Pleasant, Pleasant   Duke
It's Me Again   Henderson
It's the Goods   Loesser
It's Worth Imagining   Adamson; Warren
I've Got Everything   Yellen
I've Had a Terrible, Horrible, No Good, Very Bad
    Day   Strouse
I've Known You All of My Life   Sondheim
I've Lived, I've Loved, I'm Satisfied   Brown, Lew;
    Henderson
I've Made Up My Mind to Sail Away   Sterling
I've Said It a Thousand Times   Russell
Jake the Baker   Hart; Rodgers
Jake the Sheik   Yellen
Jenny, Jenny (Save Your Dreams)   Duke
Jophe's Waltz   Warren
Josephine (inst.)   Warren
Judgement of Paris, The   Duke
June My Honeymoon Girl   Fisher
Jungle Chant   Carmichael
Just a Little Brook   Coslow
Just a Moment Please   Warren
Just Call Me Sunny   Warren
Just for You   Brown, Nacio Herb; Freed, Arthur
Just Two Sweethearts — Mother and Dad   Bryan; Fisher
Keep Paramount Friendly   Lane
Keep Your Eye on the Sky   Loesser
King and Queen Sequence   Sondheim

Kiss Her for Me (Be Sure and Say Hello)   Adamson; Warren
Kiss Me to Sleep   Warren
Kisses in the Moonlight   Dubin
Kisses in the Night   Warren
Knocking at Your Door   Dixon; Warren
Ladies and Gentlemen, Good Evening   Hart; Rodgers
Ladies Like Us   Cahn; Duke
Lady Butterfly   Caesar
Laffs and Lies   Gilbert; Warren
Lalita   Mercer; Warren
Lamplight Is Moonlight   Loesser
Language of Love, The   Duke
Last Two Weeks in July, The   Gilbert
Lay of a Gay Young Man, The   Sondheim
Lazy Yellow Moon   Brown, A. Seymour
Let Me Fool Myself   Henderson
Let Me Walk   Hart; Rodgers
Let's Drink to a Dream   Dubin; Warren
Let's Incorporate   Loesser
Let's Knock the Bull Out of the Bolsheviki   Johnson, Howard
Let's Sing the Chorus Again   Howard, Joseph E.
Libere Sur Parole   Russell
Lion Sort Ses Griffes   Russell
List a While, Lady   Sondheim
Little Chatterbox   Leigh
Little Drop of Irish and a Wee Bit of Scotch, A   Fisher
Little Lady on the Cameo   Arlen; Koehler
Little Tender Things   Dubin; Warren
Living Alone   Strouse
Lollypop Ball, The   Russell
Lonely in Paris   Duke
Lonely Traveling Man, A   Hart; Rodgers
Longed to Be Loved by the Girls   Carroll
Look Me Over and Tell Me, If I Am Worth Your Liking   Johnson, J. Rosamond
Looking for Daddy   Strouse
Looks   Sondheim
Love Alone Lives On   Arlen
Love Can Get You Crazy   Strouse
Love Is Like a Mushroom   Carroll
Love Race   Carroll
Love that Will Never Die, A   Conrad
Lovely Ladies   Sondheim
Lover's Rendezvous (inst.)   Warren
Love's a Riddle   Burke
Lunch   Sondheim
Madame Esther, Queen of Hester Street   Hart; Rodgers
Makes Me Feel Good All Over   Loesser
Makin' Love Mountain Style   Warren
Mama You Don't Understand Me   Strouse
Mammy's Melody   Brown, Lew
Man My Mother Married, The   Cahn; Duke
Manhattan Melody   Warren
Marching Along   Freed, Arthur
Marjorie Morningstar   Adams; Strouse
Martinique   Carmichael
Mary Beaty's Birthday   Sondheim
Mary's Lamb   Howard, Joseph E.
Meet My Mother   Hart; Rodgers
Memories of Long Ago   Arlen; Koehler
Metropolitan Handicap   Carroll
Mi Ti Ya, A   Brown, Nacio Herb; Freed, Arthur
Milano   Adamson; Warren
Mine to Kiss   Caesar

Minnie the Queen of the Schuetzenfest   Atteridge
Miss Andrew   Sondheim
Miss O'Brien   Rome
Mister Harvey Pruitt   Cahn; Duke
Mistletoe Waltz (inst.)   Warren
Mrs. Chisolm   Cahn; Styne
Moment with You, A   Revel
Moody's Mood   Fields
Moonlight on Broadway   Dubin; Warren
Moonlight on the Ocean   Loesser
Mouse, The   Loesser
Music and the Emotions   Hart; Rodgers
My Angel   Adamson; Warren
My Country Cousin   Bryan; Youmans
My Daddies   Hart; Rodgers
My Home Among the Hills   Sterling
My Honey of My Heart   Atteridge
My I.B.M. and I   Rome
My Joe Louis of Love   Razaf
My Laddie   Akst
My Little Sunshine   Conrad
My Melody of Memory   Johnson, Howard
Myrtle's March   Leigh
Naomi   Howard, Joseph E.
Native Son, A   Blake
New York Follies, The   Sondheim
Nice to See You   Strouse
Nice Town   Sondheim
Nicol in the Picolo   Razaf
Nineteen Sixty Five   Warren
Ninetta   Warren
No, Mary Ann   Sondheim
No One Is Perfect   Duke
No Sad Songs for Me   Sondheim
No Star of Night   Sondheim
Nobody Reads Books   Sondheim
Not for Children   Sondheim
Not Yet   Warren
O Southland   Johnson, J. Rosamond
Oh Mother, I'm Wild   Johnson, Howard
Oh! Tennessee, You've Won the Heart of Me   Brown, Lew; Henderson
Oh! That Hindu Skindu Dance   Conrad
Oh! You La La   Brown, Lew; Henderson
Old Army Game, The   Fain; Rose
Old Biological Urge, the   Dubin; Warren
On Robinson Crusoe Isle   Razaf
On the Bahamas   Hart; Rodgers
On the Levee Before the War   Atteridge
On the River   Sondheim
On the Road to Romance   Loesser
Once I Fall   Cahn; Duke
One Romance   Loesser
Only Me   Brown, Lew; Henderson
Onward, America   Johnson, Howard
Opera Song   Warren
Orient   Fisher
Orientala (inst.)   Warren
Ouijie of the Keys   Carroll
Out of My Dreams Into My Heart   Arlen; Koehler
Over the Hill (inst.)   Warren
Palm Beach   Strouse
Pardon Me for Dreaming   Conrad; Magidson
Paris After Dark   Duke
Parties   Cahn; Duke

Party, Party   Sondheim
Pep Step, The   Brown, Nacio Herb; Freed, Arthur
Perfect Lover, A   Bryan; Fisher
Phantom Penthouse, The   Gordon; Revel
Pharaoh's Daughter   Buck
Piccadilly Band, The   Atteridge
Pietro   Atteridge
Playin' the Game   Strouse
Poo-Poo   Clare; Coslow
Pour Le Sport   Sondheim
Queen Is Always on Display, A   Duke
Ragtime Geography   Conrad
Ragtime Love   Atteridge
Railroad Woman, A   Cahn; Duke
Rainbow of My Dreams   Brown, Nacio Herb; Freed, Arthur
Rainbows   Sondheim
Rainy Afternoon, A   Lane
Rector Rhythm   Razaf
Red, A   Blake
Red Pepper   Atteridge
Refrain (inst.)   Arlen
Regular Girl, A   Kalmar; Ruby
Remi Ram Jam   Conrad
Right to Happiness, The   Bryan; Fisher
Robin Hood   Hart; Rodgers
Rodgers and Hammerstein   Sondheim
Rumbalero, The   Lane
Run for the Hills, Cowboy   Warren
Running Around the Raindrops   Styne
Saga of Lenny   Sondheim
Same As a Man   Cahn; Duke
Same As You Did to Me, The   Brown, A. Seymour
Sand   Sondheim
Sarah, Come Over Here   Conrad
Say a Little Prayer for Home Sweet Home   Johnson,
    Howard
Saying My Say   Gershwin, George; Gershwin, Ira
School of Hard Knocks   Sondheim
Send Me a Man   Razaf
Serenade (inst.)   Warren
She!   Strouse
She's Gonna Love Me!   Strouse
She's Not Made for You   Strouse
Shim Sham Rhumba   Loesser
Shorty the Gunner   Hart; Rodgers
Shoulder Shakin' Blues, The   Brown, Lew; Henderson
Side Street Serenade   Loesser
Sights and Sounds of the Monterrey Peninsula
    (inst.)   Warren
Simple and Sweet   Gilbert
Since You Went Away   Caesar; Gershwin, George
Sing Me an Irish Come-All-Ye   Atteridge
Singing Out Loud   Sondheim
Small Mama — Big Mama   Razaf
Snooty, The   Blake
So Far, So Good   David, Mack; Warren
So Long Sing Song   Atteridge
So Much to Do, So Little Time in the Morning   Strouse
Some Day You'll Be Sorry that You're Glad   Conrad
Some Pig   Strouse
Someday You'll Find Your Bluebird   Revel
Someone   Ager; Yellen
Something Sort of Silly   Kalmar; Ruby
Sometimes Is Forever   Warren
Song a Child Could Sing, A   Lane

Song for Humming, A   Sondheim
Song of the Windshield Wiper   Loesser
Sooner or Later   Leigh
Spanish Dancer, The   Hart
Speaking of Heaven   Revel
Springtime in Milano (inst.)   Warren
Stand Up and Fight like H—-   Bryan; Fisher
Star Spangled Night, A   Gordon; Revel
Star Spangled Susan Brown   Razaf
Starlight Waltz   Adamson
Stars Give Light   Sondheim
Stars on the Highway   Loesser
Start of an Affair   Strouse
Stealin' My Thunder   Razaf
Step Up and Shake   Cahn; Duke
Steps   Hart; Rodgers
Stone Walls   Loesser
Strivers' Row to Sugar Hill   Loesser
Struggles   Razaf
Summer   Strouse
Sun Is Blue, The   Sondheim
Sunday Dress   Razaf
Sunflower Sue   Razaf
Swank, The   Conrad; Magidson
Sweep No More My Lady   Blake
Sweet Cherie   Johnson, J. Rosamond
Sweet Kisses   Henderson
Sweet Rain   Johnson, J. Rosamond
Sweetness   Akst
Swing That Dear Old Alma Mater   Warren
Switch It Miss Mitchell   Razaf
Tag, You're It   Loesser
Take Me   Lane
Take Your Girlie to the Movies If You Can't Make Love at
    Home   Ahlert; Turk
Tea   Sondheim
Tell It on Your Piano   Schwartz, Jean
Tell Me No Tall, Tall Tale   Loesser
Tell Me with Your Eyes   Yellen
Telltale Eyes   Hart; Rodgers
Ten Years Old   Sondheim
Texas Blues   Strouse
Thank God You're Here, Mother Mine   Ager; Johnson,
    Howard; Yellen
That Goes for You   Adamson; Donaldson
That Mysterious Lady Called Love   Lane
That Night in Paris   Loesser
That Possum Rag   Atteridge
That Promise in Your Eyes   Loesser
That's My Boy   Sterling
That's the Law   Rome
There Comes a Time   Cahn; Duke
There Is One Born Every Minute   Atteridge
There Must Be a Better Way   Lane
There's a Happy Heart in Maryland and a Broken Heart in
    Brittany   Fisher
There's a Little Lost Dream   Warren
There's a Reason (inst.)   Warren
There's More to Dreams Then Just Dreaming   Lane
There's Rain in My Eyes   Yellen
These Precious Moments   Yellen
They Ask Me Why I Believe in You   Sondheim
Things Are Changing   Cahn; Styne
This is One of Those Moments   Dubin
This Is Show Biz   Sondheim

Three Faces East   Johnson, Howard
Three-a Poppa, Don't Your Four-Five   Yellen
Tillie   Brown, Lew; Henderson
Tiny Chinee Little Girl   Gershwin, George
Tippin' Out Tonight   Razaf
To Make It Short and Sweet, I Love You   Yellen
Tomorrow   Turk
Tonight Is Ours (inst.)   Warren
Topaz Waltz (inst.)   Warren
Twenty-four Hours of Love   Brown, Lew; Henderson
Two Behind the Eight-Ball!   Bryan; Fisher
Uncertain   Warren
Unknown   Schwartz, Arthur; Strouse
Vienna Garden — Waltz No. 10 (inst.)   Warren
Voice of Love, A   Gershwin, George
Wail of the Winds (Inst.)   Warren
Wait Till You See New York   Cahn; Duke
Waltz   Sondheim
Waltz Moderne (inst.)   Warren
Waltz No. 3 (inst.)   Warren
Waltz No. 4 (inst.)   Warren
Waltz No. 5 (inst.)   Warren
Waltz No. 6 (inst.)   Warren
Waltz No. 8 (inst.)   Warren
Waltz No. 9 (inst.)   Warren
Waltz No. 16 (inst.)   Warren
Waltz No. I (inst.)   Warren
Waltz No. II (inst.)   Warren
Waltz with Me (inst.)   Warren
Wandering Minstrel, The   Hart; Rodgers
War Song   Harburg
War Song (Title Unknown)   Gershwin, George
Wastin' Our Talents   Razaf
Water Babies   Styne
Water Under the Bridge   Sondheim
Wear a Bouquet of Smiles   Blake; Sissle
Wedding Trip, A   Hart; Rodgers
Welcome   Warren
Welcome to the Party   Warren
Welcome to Washington   Strouse
Wells Fargo Theme (Inst.)   Warren
We're Alone in the World   Cahn; Duke
What a Mornin'   Strouse
What Are You Gonna Do? (inst.)   Coleman
What I Want to Be   Cahn; Styne
What Is Love?   Leigh
What Is Love If It's Not Magic   Lewis; Young, Joseph

What Was   Warren
What's the Good of Just a Song at Twilight   Johnson,
   Howard
When I Get Famous   Sondheim
When That Dixie Sun Goes Down   Razaf
When the Snow Is on the Ground   Sterling
When the Sun Sets Down South   Blake
When You Wore a Crown of Shamrocks   Sterling
When You're Dressed in Blue   Loesser
Where Do I Belong   Sondheim
Where Ever You Go   Warren
Where Is the Right Prayer for Me?   Lane
Where You Are   Lane
Whispering Grass (inst.)   Warren
White Way Blues   Coslow
Who Says We Can't Be Friends?   Strouse
Who Was the Kiddo that Captain Kidd Was Saving His
   Treasure For?   Johnson, Howard
Who's Afraid of Who?   Cahn; Styne
Why So Gloomy, Why So Sad   Freed, Ralph
Wilbur   Strouse
Winning the West   Evans
With a Man on First   Cahn; Duke
Yea Boys, Let's Have a Time   Atteridge
Yes   Sondheim
Yesterday's Love   Loesser
Yoo Hoo, Hi, There!   Sondheim
You Can Tell that He's an American   Johnson, Howard
You Can't Cook Hugs and Kisses   Yellen
You Can't Put the Petals Back on a Rose   Freed, Ralph
You Carry My Heart   Hart; Rodgers
You Don't Have to Tell Me   Gordon; Revel
You Had That Everlasting Appeal   Loesser
You Let Me Go for Somebody Else   Clare
You Oughta Go an' See the Wimmin Swimmin'   Conrad
You Say You're Sorry   Lane
You Should Have Told Me   Ager
You Tickle Me   Clare
You'll Be Sorry   Ager; Yellen
You'll Come Back Someday   Dubin; Warren
You'll Know It   Lane
You're Meant for Me to Love   Baer; Gilbert
You're Old Enough to Know   Dubin; Warren
You're Working for Me Now   Strouse
You're You   Strouse
Yours the Power   Warren

ISBN 0-02-865477-3

90000